P9-DDF-144

The American Horticultural Society

Encyclopedia of Gardening

THE AMERICAN HORTICULTURAL SOCIETY

ENCYCLOPEDIA OF GARDENING

Editor-in-Chief —
CHRISTOPHER BRICKELL

— *Editor-in-Chief, American Horticultural Society* —
ELVIN McDONALD

— *Consulting Editor* —
TREVOR COLE

DORLING KINDERSLEY
LONDON • NEW YORK • STUTTGART

A Dorling Kindersley Book

Managing Editor Jane Aspden
Managing Art Editor Ina Stradins

Senior Editor Kate Swainson
Senior Art Editor Lynne Brown

Supervising Editor Ray Rogers

Editors Claire Calman, Alison Copland, Annelise Evans, Jill Hamilton, Helen Partington, Jane Simmonds

Editorial assistants Judith Chambers, Katie John, Teresa Pritlove, Melanie Tham

Additional editorial assistance from Jackie Bennett, Carolyn Burch, Joanna Chisholm, Allen Coombes, Heather Dewhurst, Angela Gair, Lin Hawthorne, Jonathan Hilton, Laaren Brown Hort, Jeanette Mall, Jane Mason, Ferdie McDonald, Andrew Mikolajski, Christine Murdock, Lesley Riley

Editorial Director Jackie Douglas

Art Editor Gillian Shaw
Designers Gillian Andrews, Johnny Pau, Vicky Short, Chris Walker

Additional design assistance from Rhonda Fisher, Bob Gordon, Sally Powell, Steve Wooster

Photography Peter Anderson (with Steve Gorton, Dave King, and Matthew Ward)

Demonstrators Anne-Marie Dorenbos (with Peter Bainbridge, Mark Lamey, Dorling Kindersley staff, and RHS Wisley staff)

Location assistants Diana Mitchell, Reg Perryman

Illustrations Karen Cochrane, Simone End, Will Giles, Vanessa Luff, Sandra Pond, John Woodcock (with Andrew Farmer, Aziz Khan, Liz Peperall, Barbara Walker, and Ann Winterbotham)

Picture research Sue Mennell, assisted by Ginny Fitzgerald (with Alexandra Truitt)

Page makeup and typesetting Cooling Brown Partnership, Icon Associates, Johnny Pau, Debbie Rhodes

Production Hilary Stephens

Index Dorothy Frame

Special thanks to the staff of the Royal Horticultural Society at Wisley Garden, Surrey, and Vincent Square, London; Frank Robinson

First American Edition, 1993
8 10 9 7

Reprinted 1993, 1994
Published in the United States by Dorling Kindersley, Inc.,
95 Madison Avenue, New York, New York 10016

Library of Congress Cataloging-in-Publication Data

The American Horticultural Society encyclopedia of gardening/
editor-in-chief, Christopher Brickell;
editor-in-chief, American Horticultural Society, Elvin McDonald;
consulting editor for Canada, Trevor Cole –1st American ed.
p. cm.
Includes index.
ISBN 1-56458-291-4
1. Gardening--Encyclopedias. 2. Gardening--Pictorial works.
I. Brickell, Christopher. II. McDonald, Elvin. III. Cole, Trevor
J. (Trevor Jack). IV. American Horticultural Society. V. Title:
Encyclopedia of gardening.SB450.95.A45 1993
635--dc20 93-3042
CIP

Reproduced by Colourscan, Singapore
Printed and bound in the United States by R. R. Donnelley & Son Company

PREFACE

NEVER BEFORE have so many Americans seriously engaged in gardening as a leisure activity. These vast numbers of gardeners are constantly searching for new, practical information about how to make their gardens more lush, more beautiful, more productive, more rewarding. To end the search, we present *The American Horticultural Society Encyclopedia of Gardening*. Through the pages of this book, the myriad techniques that fill gardening with success and pleasure can be learned by amateurs and professionals alike.

An illustrated guide to gardening techniques is an essential reference source for every gardener, whatever his or her level of expertise, because many skills applied in the course of cultivating a garden are practiced only once each season or sometimes even less frequently. There is a constant need to brush up, even on once-familiar techniques. *The American Horticultural Society Encyclopedia of Gardening* is the one-volume reference book that answers that need, serving as both an introduction and a refresher course. The main aim of the book is to present in a clear, practical, and authoritative style all the information that gardeners need on how to design their gardens and cultivate, maintain, and increase plants of all types, whether they are ornamentals, fruits, or vegetables. Each chapter is clearly structured to make the material easily accessible.

The American Horticultural Society is one of the leading gardening societies in the United States. Founded early in the twentieth century to promote an understanding and appreciation of horticulture, the AHS serves as a clearinghouse for the dissemination of news, knowledge, and wisdom for individuals and organizations devoted to plants, gardens, and gardeners. The publication of *The American Horticultural Society Encyclopedia of Gardening* is a triumph of the AHS's mission.

Christopher Brickell, the book's Editor-in-Chief, is Director General of the Royal Horticultural Society in Great Britain and one of the foremost authorities on practical gardening matters. Working with a team of distinguished experts from around the world, and with editors, designers, and photographers from Dorling Kindersley in London, he guided the development of every aspect of the book for its first publication in Great Britain in 1992.

Unlike some gardening books brought to the United States from Great Britain with only minor changes, *The American Horticultural Society Encyclopedia of Gardening* has undergone a rigorous Americanization process. It comes as a truly all American book, packed with fully revised plant information, additional step-by-step techniques, and new photographs. This book presents techniques that are commonly practiced by American gardeners in every part of the country, across all climate zones. The American Horticultural Society has worked in tandem with Trevor Cole, Consulting Editor, a horticulturist who has spent much of his professional life caring for respected public gardens as well as for his own private garden. A dedicated staff of editors and designers at Dorling Kindersley in New York and London has helped us to realize our ambitions for a completely North American encyclopedia.

As readers gain in skill and expertise, *The American Horticultural Society Encyclopedia of Gardening* will provide a continuing source of reference on how to garden creatively and successfully. We believe that this all-inclusive single work will become not only a necessity, but a gardener's best tool.

George Ball
President
American Horticultural Society

Elvin McDonald
Editor-in-Chief
American Horticultural Society

Contents

Preface 5 How to Use this Book 8

Part I: Creating the garden

— 1 —

Garden Planning and Design 12

— 2 —

Ornamental Trees 32
Dwarf Conifers 38
Hedges and Screens 58

— 3 —

Ornamental Shrubs 61
Topiary 90

— 4 —

Climbing Plants 92
Clematis 106

— 5 —

The Rose Garden 114
Roses for Display and Exhibition 134

— 6 —

Perennials 135
Grasses, Bamboos, Sedges, and Rushes 142
Irises 144
Peonies 148
Daylilies 149
Ground Covers 150
Hostas 152
Chrysanthemums 154
Ferns 158
Wildflower and Meadow Gardening 167
Pelargoniums 168

— 7 —

Annuals and Biennials 170

— 8 —

The Rock Garden 185
Alpine Houses and Frames 210

— 9 —

Bulbous Plants 213
Tulips and Daffodils 220
Dahlias 222
Lilies 239

— 10 —

The Water Garden 240
Water Lilies 244
Aquariums 245

— 11 —

Cacti and other Succulents 258

— 12 —

The Lawn 272

— 13 —

The Herb Garden 287

— 14 —

The Vegetable Garden 299

— 15 —

The Fruit Garden 355

— 16 —

The Indoor Garden 426
Bromeliads 432
Bonsai 434
Orchids 440
Hydroculture 447
Fuchsias 448

Part II: Maintaining the garden

1

Tools and Equipment 458

2

Greenhouses and Frames 474

3

Structures and Surfaces 492

4

Climate and the Garden 514

Cold and Wind Protection 520

Gardening in Different Regions 522

5

Soils and Fertilizers 524

6

Principles of Propagation 537

7

Plant Problems 547

8

Basic Botany 580

Seasonal Reminders 583

Glossary of Terms 585

Index 591

Acknowledgments 648

Contributors and Consultants

Tom Wright *Garden Planning and Design*
Jim Gardiner *Ornamental Trees, Dwarf Conifers, Hedges and Screens, Ornamental Shrubs, Topiary*
Caroline Boisset *Climbing Plants*
Raymond Evison *Clematis*
Michael Gibson *The Rose Garden* **(with Steve Scanniello)**
Roy Cheek *Perennials* **(with Graham Rice)**, *Ground Covers*
Mervyn Feesey *Grasses, Bamboos, Sedges, and Rushes*
Jack Elliott *Irises, Bulbous Plants, Tulips and Daffodils*
Elvin McDonald *Peonies, Gardening in Different Regions*
Trevor Cole *Daylilies, Hostas, Cold and Wind Protection*
Larry Barlow *Chrysanthemums*
Hazel Key *Ferns, Pelargoniums*
Christopher Brickell *Wildflower and Meadow Gardening*
Arthur Hellyer *Annuals and Biennials*
Kath Dryden and Christopher Grey-Wilson *The Rock Garden* **(with John Warwick)**, *Alpine Houses and Frames*
Roger Aylett *Dahlias*
Bill Baker *Lilies*
Peter Robinson *The Water Garden, Water Lilies, Aquariums*
Clive Innes *Cacti and other Succulents, Bromeliads*
John Hacker *The Lawn*
Deni Bown *The Herb Garden*
Joy Larkcom *The Vegetable Garden*
George Gilbert *The Fruit Garden*
Don Tindall *Tender vegetables and fruits*
Deenagh Goold-Adams *The Indoor Garden*
Susan M. Bachenheimer Resnick *Bonsai*
Alec Bristow *Orchids*
Arthur Haywood-Costa *Hydroculture*
John Wright *Fuchsias*
Peter McHoy *Tools and Equipment, Greenhouses and Frames, Structures and Surfaces*
Michael Pollock *Climate and the Garden*
Tony Kendle *Soils and Fertilizers*
Keith Loach *Principles of Propagation, Basic Botany*
Pippa Greenwood and Andrew Halstead *Plant Problems* **(with Trevor Cole, William E. Ferguson, R. Kenneth Horst, and Donald Schuder)**; **David Pycraft** *Weeds*

How to Use this Book

Clear, concise, and easy to use, *The American Horticultural Society Encyclopedia of Gardening* is the perfect horticultural reference library. It gives detailed information on how to create and design an attractive garden, and demonstrates a vast range of horticultural techniques that apply to both ornamental and productive plants.

Written to appeal to the novice and the experienced gardener alike, the text is lavishly illustrated with full-color photographs and artworks showing design ideas, planting plans, and practical techniques. Illustrated lists of plants help the reader to choose the right plants and act as a quick reference source on how to care for them.

Part I: Creating the Garden is a complete guide to garden design and all aspects of plant cultivation and care, including pruning and propagation. **Part II: Maintaining the Garden** helps you to choose garden equipment and materials, provides a practical guide to building a framework for the plants, and sets the plants in the context of their physical environment.

A glossary and a comprehensive index make this book easy to use and understand.

Plant names

In general, plants are referred to by their botanical name. Some plants, however, including vegetables, fruits, and herbs, are referred to by their common name in preference to their botanical name. To find out the botanical names of these plants, consult the index.

The index includes common and botanical names for all plants mentioned in the book.

Part I: Creating the Garden

The chapters in Part I cover everything you need to know to choose and grow plants successfully. Each chapter is dedicated to either a different plant group – for example Ornamental Trees or Climbing Plants – or an area of the garden, such as The Herb Garden or The Water Garden.

The chapters are all structured in a similar way, so readers can become familiar with where to find the information they need quickly and easily. Each chapter has sections on design (using the particular plant group), as well as soil preparation and planting, routine care, propagation, and, where appropriate, pruning and training. Some chapters have other sections that are appropriate to the subject matter: for example, The Herb Garden has a directory of common herbs, and The Lawn has a section on establishing a lawn.

The chapters on vegetables and fruits each have a general section at the beginning describing techniques that are common to growing all vegetables or fruits; this has the same structure as the other chapters. Entries on individual vegetables and fruits follow, grouped according to their type (for example, podded vegetables, leafy and salad vegetables, tree fruits, or soft fruits). Within these groupings entries are ordered by botanical name.

Chapter Structure

Section Headings
All chapters are split into sections covering "Design," "Soil preparation and planting," "Routine care," "Pruning and training," and "Propagation." The headings are clearly displayed at the beginning of each section and in the running head.

Running Heads
Clear running heads help you find the section of the book that you want. The running head on the left-hand page has the name of the chapter; the running head on the right has the title of the section.

Chapter Heading
This indicates which plant group or area of the garden is discussed in this chapter. It has a short introduction giving general information about the plant group.

Feature boxes

Part I of the encyclopedia includes a number of short features that focus on a specific plant group or area of interest, for example Pelargoniums, Topiary, and Alpine Houses and Frames. Because of their importance to the gardener, each of these subjects is given separate coverage in a feature box containing more detailed information than would be possible within a chapter. The boxes include explanations of techniques that are specific to that group of plants: for example, the Ferns feature shows you how to raise new plants from spores, and the Orchids feature tells you how to cultivate and propagate this specialized group of plants.

The feature boxes accompany the most closely related chapter: the feature on Clematis appears in the chapter on Climbing Plants, and that on Tulips and Daffodils is found in the Bulbous Plants chapter. All the feature boxes are listed on the Contents pages.

Box Rule
A rule around a feature box sets it apart from the chapter and makes it easy to find.

Plant Portraits
These indicate the range and types of plant covered in the feature box.

Planting Suggestion
Text and photographs suggest ways of creating a display.

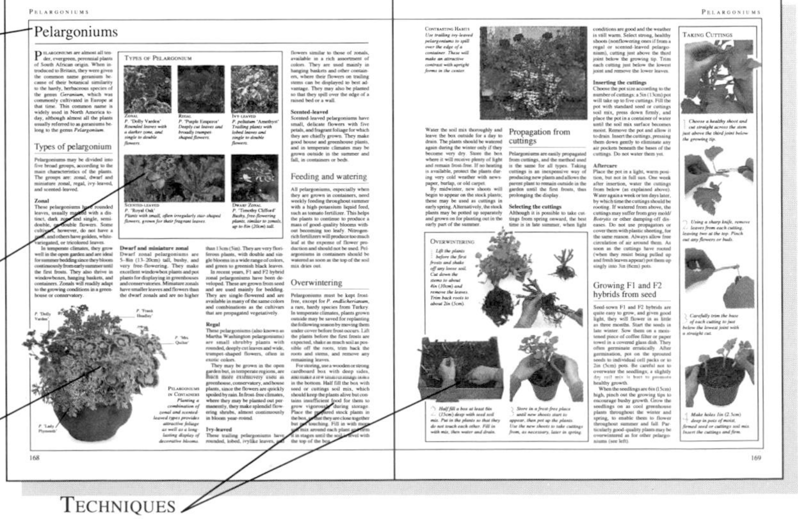

Techniques
Techniques that are specific to the subject of the feature box are explained fully both in the text and in the step-by-step picture sequences.

The Elements on a Page

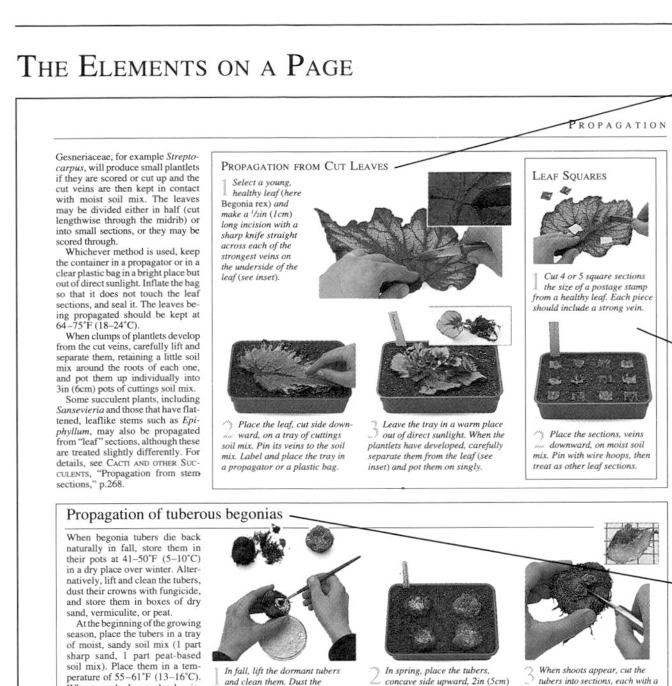

Gesneriaceae, for example *Streptocarpus*, will produce small plantlets if they are scored or cut up and the cut veins are then kept in contact with moist soil mix. The leaves may be divided either in half (cut lengthwise through the midrib) or into small sections, or they may be scored through.

Whichever method is used, keep the container in a propagator or in a clear plastic bag in a bright place but out of direct sunlight. Inflate the bag so that it does not touch the leaf sections, and seal it. The leaves being propagated should be kept at 64–75°F (18–24°C).

When clumps of plantlets develop from the cut veins, carefully lift and separate them, retaining a little soil mix around the roots of each one, and pot them up individually into 3in (6cm) pots of cuttings soil mix.

Some succulent plants, including *Sansevieria* and those that have flattened, leaflike stems such as *Epiphyllum*, may also be propagated from "leaf" sections, although these are treated slightly differently. For details, see Cacti and other Succulents, "Propagation from stem sections," p.268.

Propagation from Cut Leaves

1 *Select a young, healthy leaf (here* Begonia rex) *and make a* ½*in (1cm) long incision with a sharp knife straight across each of the strongest veins on the underside of the leaf (see inset).*

2 *Place the leaf, cut side downward, on a tray of cuttings soil mix. Pin its veins to the soil mix. Label and place the tray in a propagator or a plastic bag.*

3 *Leave the tray in a warm place out of direct sunlight. When the plantlets have developed, carefully separate them from the leaf (see inset) and pot them on singly.*

Leaf Squares

1 *Cut 4 or 5 square sections the size of a postage stamp from a healthy leaf. Each piece should include a strong vein.*

2 *Place the sections, veins downward, on moist soil mix. Pin with wire hoops, then treat as other leaf sections.*

Propagation of tuberous begonias

When begonia tubers die back naturally in fall, store them in their pots at 41–50°F (5–10°C) in a dry place over winter. Alternatively, lift and clean the tubers, dust their crowns with fungicide, and store them in boxes of dry sand, vermiculite, or peat.

At the beginning of the growing season, place the tubers in a tray of moist, sandy soil mix (1 part sharp sand, 1 part peat-based soil mix). Place them in a temperature of 55–61°F (13–16°C). When new buds are clearly visible, cut the tubers into sections, making sure that each has at least one bud and some roots. Dust the sections with fungicide and allow them to dry for a few hours in a warm place. When the cut surfaces have formed calluses, pot up the sections in soil-based potting mix. Do not firm the mix heavily or water it, since this encourages fungal attack.

Alternatively, allow new shoots to develop on the tubers, and use these as basal cuttings. Take the cuttings so that each retains an eye. Dip the base of each cutting in hormone rooting powder and insert them, ¾in (2cm) deep, around the edge of a pot or pan of soil-based potting mix.

1 *In fall, lift the dormant tubers and clean them. Dust the crowns with fungicide and overwinter them in a dry place.*

2 *In spring, place the tubers, concave side upward, 2in (5cm) apart and 1in (2.5cm) deep, in a tray of moist, sandy soil mix.*

3 *When shoots appear, cut the tubers into sections, each with a bud and some roots. Dust cut surfaces with fungicide and allow to dry.*

4 *Pot up the sections singly in 5in (13cm) pots, with the top of each level with the soil mix surface. Water a little, and label.*

5 *Keep the pots in a propagator in a warm, frost-free place until the sections are established, then pot them on singly.*

Basal Cuttings

Remove 2in (5cm) shoots from the tuber, each with an eye of tuber at the base. Pot them up and treat as divided tubers.

455

Step-by-step Sequences
Photographic sequences show you how to carry out a technique in easy-to-follow stages. Each has a clear heading, and captions for each step that explain what to do.

Alternative Method
One or more photographs in a tinted box within a sequence explain an alternative method to the main one shown.

Text Box
A text box consists of text and pictures that relate to a specific plant or to a technique that is not explained in the running text.

Insets
Inset photographs provide a close-up view for more detail or to show a "before" or "after" step.

Pruning and Training Artworks

Caption
The caption gives general information on what to do.

Artwork
The artwork shows the extent of pruning in relation to the whole plant. The gray tone indicates the parts of the plant that should be cut out. The green and brown areas delineate the appearance of the plant after pruning and training.

Cut Marks and Arrows
The red marks show where to cut. The light green areas show the shoots before they have been trained in and the red arrows show where to tie them.

Insets
The insets are photographic representations of parts of the artwork, showing a symptom or a pruning cut. Leader lines point to the appropriate place on the artwork. The captions explain in detail what to do.

Plant Lists
These list plants to which certain techniques apply. They are annotated and have a key.

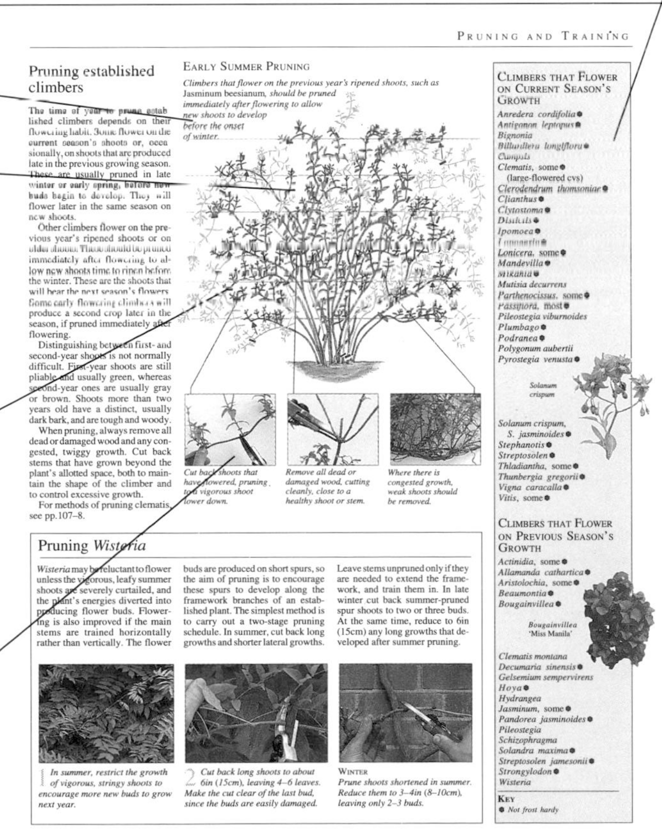

Pruning established climbers

The time of year to prune established climbers depends on their flowering habit. Some flower on the current season's shoots or, occasionally, on shoots that are produced late in the previous growing season. These are usually pruned in late winter or early spring, before new buds begin to develop. They will flower later in the same season on new shoots.

Other climbers flower on the previous year's ripened shoots or on older shoots. These should be pruned immediately after flowering to allow new shoots time to ripen before the winter. These are the shoots that will bear the next season's flowers. Some early flowering climbers will produce a second crop later in the season, if pruned immediately after flowering.

Distinguishing between first- and second-year shoots is not normally difficult. First-year shoots are still pliable and usually green, whereas second-year ones are usually gray or brown. Shoots more than two years old have a distinct, usually dark bark, and are tough and woody.

When pruning, always remove all dead or damaged wood and any congested, twiggy growth. Cut back stems that have grown beyond the plant's allotted space, both to maintain the shape of the climber and to control excessive growth.

For methods of pruning clematis, see pp.107–8.

Early Summer Pruning

Climbers that flower on the previous year's ripened shoots, such as Jasminum beesianum, *should be pruned immediately after flowering to allow new shoots to develop before the onset of winter.*

Cut back shoots that have flowered, pruning to a vigorous shoot lower down.

Remove all dead or damaged wood, cutting cleanly, close to a healthy shoot or stem.

Where there is congested growth, weak shoots should be removed.

Climbers that Flower on Current Season's Growth

Anredera cordifolia ●
Antigonon leptopus ●
Bignonia
Billardiera longiflora ●
Campsis
Clematis, some ● (large-flowered cvs)
Clerodendrum thomsoniae ●
Clianthus ●
Clytostoma ●
Distictis ●
Ipomoea ●
Lapageria ●
Lonicera, some ●
Mandevilla ●
Mikania ●
Mutisia decurrens
Parthenocissus, some ●
Passiflora, most ●
Pileostegia viburnoides
Plumbago ●
Podranea ●
Polygonum aubertii
Pyrostegia venusta ●

Solanum crispum

Solanum crispum, S. jasminoides ●
Stephanotis ●
Streptosolen ●
Thladiantha, some ●
Thunbergia gregorii ●
Vigna caracalla ●
Vitis, some ●

Climbers that Flower on Previous Season's Growth

Actinidia, some ●
Allamanda cathartica ●
Aristolochia, some ●
Beaumontia ●
Bougainvillea ●

Bougainvillea 'Miss Manila'

Clematis montana
Decumaria sinensis ●
Gelsemium sempervirens
Hoya ●
Hydrangea
Jasminum, some ●
Pandorea jasminoides ●
Pileostegia
Schizophragma
Solandra maxima ●
Streptosolen jamesonii ●
Strongylodon ●
Wisteria

Key
● *Not frost hardy*

Pruning *Wisteria*

Wisteria may be reluctant to flower unless the vigorous, leafy summer shoots are severely curtailed, and the plant's energies diverted into producing flower buds. Flowering is also improved if the main stems are trained horizontally rather than vertically. The flower buds are produced on short spurs, so the aim of pruning is to encourage these spurs to develop along the framework branches of an established plant. The simplest method is to carry out a two-stage pruning schedule. In summer, cut back long growths and shorter lateral growths. Leave stems unpruned only if they are needed to extend the framework, and train them in. In late winter cut back summer-pruned spur shoots to two or three buds. At the same time, reduce to 6in (15cm) any long growths that developed after summer pruning.

1 *In summer, restrict the growth of vigorous, stringy shoots to encourage more new buds to grow next year.*

2 *Cut back long shoots to about 6in (15cm), leaving 4–6 leaves. Make the cut clear of the last bud, since the buds are easily damaged.*

Winter
Prune shoots shortened in summer. Reduce them to 3–4in (8–10cm), leaving only 2–3 buds.

103

How to plan your garden

For inspiration and practical advice on how to design your garden, turn to the first chapter in Part I, Garden Planning and Design, which leads you through the process in simple stages. This chapter is also full of ideas and guidelines on planting associations and garden styles.

For information on how to incorporate a particular kind of plant into your garden, look at the design section at the beginning of each chapter. This gives specific suggestions with plans for planting designs and shows you how to combine different plants effectively. Every garden is unique, however, and many have problematic areas such as exposed sites and dry, shady areas. For these there are numerous plant suggestions in the "Planter's guides" at the end of the design section in each chapter. The plant lists in the "Soil preparation and planting" sections give examples of plants to suit particular soil types.

How to cultivate and care for your garden

This book includes information on how to cultivate and maintain the plants in your garden, from simple, routine tasks such as weeding and watering to more specialized techniques.

How to find information on a technique

To find general information about techniques that apply to a particular plant group, look in the appropriate section of each chapter; for example, to find out how to prune roses, look in the "Pruning and training" section of The Rose Garden.

Sometimes plants demand different treatment from others in the same plant group. In such cases, information about a specific technique is given within the relevant section. For example, special techniques for dividing hostas and peonies are covered in Perennials, "Propagation." If you are unsure about where to look, consult the index.

How to find information about a plant or group of plants

At the beginning of each chapter there is an overview of the kinds of plant that it covers; for example, Bulbous Plants includes not only bulbs but corms, tubers, and rhizomes as well.

For general information on a major plant group, consult the relevant chapter or feature box. For more specific advice on a particular plant, consult the index.

Cross-references

Cross-references direct you to further information about a subject. They are made to both text and pictures. A cross-reference to a whole chapter is printed in capital letters, for example: see The Water Garden, pp.240–57; one to a section or subsection within a chapter is in quotation marks, for example: see "Routine care," pp.70–72. Cross-references to illustrations or plant lists are in italics, for example: see *Planting a Fruit Tree*, p.361.

Part II: Maintaining the Garden

The second part of the encyclopedia consists of chapters on equipping the garden and on the garden environment – all the background information you need to supplement Part I.

Equipping the garden

Guidelines on choosing and using garden equipment are given in the chapter on TOOLS AND EQUIPMENT. The chapter on GREENHOUSES AND FRAMES gives information on how to choose a greenhouse and maximize the space. There is also advice on how to ensure that the greenhouse will provide the environment you need. The chapter on STRUCTURES AND SURFACES shows you how to build walls, pergolas, and raised beds, for example, to create a framework for the garden, and explores the variety of materials that are available.

The garden environment

The environment of the garden has a direct impact on the health and vigor of the plants that grow there. The chapter on CLIMATE AND THE GARDEN explains what effect the climate has upon plants and how to make the most of the microclimate in your garden, and that on SOILS AND FERTILIZERS explains how to cultivate and improve your soil.

Principles of propagation

This chapter sets out the basics of propagation and explains why certain plants are best propagated by a particular method so that the gardener can better understand the processes involved.

Plant problems

The chapter on PLANT PROBLEMS helps you to identify the causes of problems in the garden, such as pests, diseases, and weeds, and tells you how to control or prevent them. It takes a symptomatic approach and is divided into sections, each on a part of the plant that may be affected.

Quick reference

The chapter on BASIC BOTANY provides a brief explanation of a plant's makeup to help the gardener understand the principles behind the practical techniques demonstrated elsewhere in the book.

The glossary provides concise definitions of horticultural terms used in the encyclopedia. The two-page section on Seasonal Reminders tells you what needs to be done in the garden and when. It follows the same structure as the chapters in Part I so that you can turn to the appropriate chapter and section for full details.

The comprehensive index will help the reader to find plants or techniques in the book. It includes both the botanical and the common name of plants. Page numbers in italics indicate that a picture of the subject appears on that page.

GARDEN EQUIPMENT AND STRUCTURES

SECTION HEADING
As in Part I, the chapters in Part II are divided into major sections, each with a section heading.

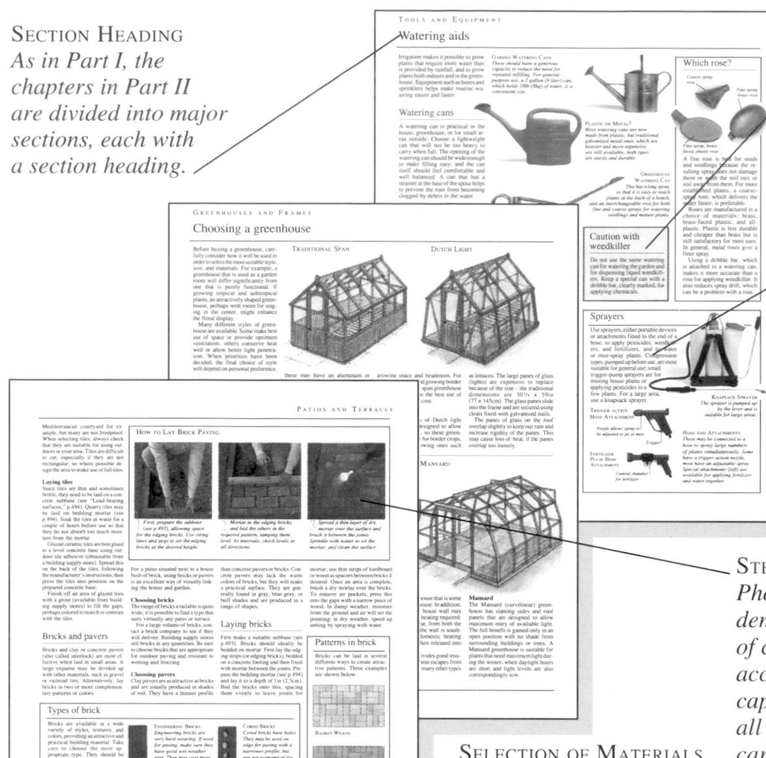

SAFETY BOX
Boxes with a gray tint give advice on safety precautions needed when using tools or chemicals.

SELECTION OF EQUIPMENT
Relevant chapters include illustrations of garden equipment to show the range that is available.

STEP-BY-STEP SEQUENCES
Photographic sequences demonstrate each stage of construction and are accompanied by clear captions that tell you all you need to know to carry out the technique successfully.

SELECTION OF MATERIALS
Where appropriate, photographs illustrate the range of materials available for a particular project.

PLANT PROBLEMS

MAIN HEADING
This indicates the area of the plant on which symptoms are most visible. A problem that affects a plant's roots may have an entry in the "Leaf problems" section if the symptoms are most commonly seen in the leaves.

SUBHEADING
This gives the main visible symptom. Problems with similar symptoms under this are grouped together.

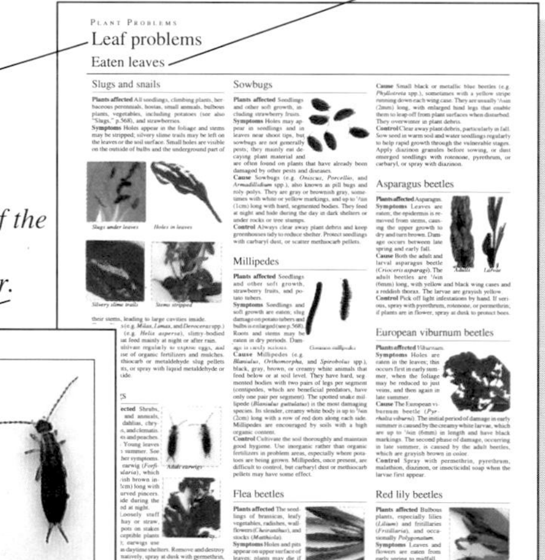

ENTRY HEADING
This gives the name of the pest, disease, or physiological disorder.

TEXT
The text for each entry lists the plants that are most commonly affected, the most visible symptoms, the cause of the problem, and information on how to control it. Controls include organic and chemical treatments as well as preventive measures.

Earwigs

Plants affected Shrubs, perennials, and annuals, commonly dahlias, chrysanthemums, and clematis. Also apricots and peaches.
Symptoms Young leaves are eaten in summer. See p.563 for other symptoms.
Cause The earwig (*Forficula auricularia*), which is a yellowish brown insect ¾in (2cm) long with a pair of curved pincers. Earwigs hide during the day and feed at night.
Control Loosely stuff pots with hay or straw, and invert pots on stakes among susceptible plants (see p.548); earwigs use these traps as daytime shelters. Remove and destroy pests. Alternatively, spray at dusk with permethrin, diazinon, carbaryl, or rotenone.

Adult earwigs

Leaves eaten away

SYMPTOM
Photographs show the pest and the damage it causes to the plant.

CROSS-REFERENCES
If you cannot find the apparent cause of the symptoms of your plant, see the entries listed in the gray tint box at the end of a page.

PART ONE

CREATING THE GARDEN

How to design your garden; select, cultivate, and propagate plants; and display them to their best advantage

1

Garden Planning and Design

Some of the *finest gardens may look as though they have not been designed at all, but have simply sprung up – rich tapestries of colors, textures, and shapes in apparently natural harmony. This may be an illusion, however, for the casual cascade of a rambling rose or the lazy sprawl of a lavender bush onto a path often owes almost as much to the gardener's forethought as to nature. Whether informal and cheerfully chaotic or elegant and formal, a successful design is usually the result of careful planning. There is a great difference between a garden where the plants and features are haphazardly arranged and one that, although seemingly naturalistic, is actually well controlled so that all the elements work together to form a cohesive and attractive design. A thoughtfully conceived garden, a beautiful garden – one with an aura of unity and style, balance and proportion, in harmony with its surroundings – provides a relaxing place, a joy to the senses, and a comfort to the soul.*

Planning the garden

Creating or redesigning a garden is, in many ways, like decorating the interior of a house. Your main objective in each case is to end up with practical, pleasurable living space that suits both you and your family. Three major factors govern your choices: the site, its proposed functions, and your own personal taste – in other words, what you have, what you need, and what you like. Both garden and interior design are also influenced by other variables such as the size, character, and period of the garden or house.

Unlike a house, however, a garden does not remain static, even from one week to the next; indeed, this element of change and surprise is the essence of gardening. Certain plants may be spectacular in one season yet quite unobtrusive in the next. Even after the garden has been created, a continuous design process will be required to accommodate and enhance it as it develops.

The importance of planning
Although much of the pleasure in gardening derives from serendipitous effects, thorough planning is essential to ensure a cohesive design. Determining at least the basic framework of the garden on paper before making any actual changes helps prevent costly mistakes. Minor alterations may be made later,

Informal Abundance
The charm of this informal garden owes more to sound design than to serendipity. A simple path leads the eye to the fields beyond, which act as a foil for the jewel-like planting. The predominantly pink and mauve color scheme is enlivened by the inclusion of boldly placed splashes of red, yellow, and white.

BALANCING FORMAL DESIGN ELEMENTS
The upright geometric shapes of the clipped hedge and the classic elegance of the statue complement the large circular pool with its restrained planting of irises and water lilies.

of course, but the position of long-term features such as patios, walls, and trees should be worked out in advance. Plan the garden as a whole rather than tackling different parts piecemeal; this makes it easier to create a sense of continuity, so that the separate elements are not merely interesting in their own right but cohesive when viewed as a whole.

Planning should be a logical process to create a design that combines the functional and desirable with the realistic. The budget and the design may determine how much, if any, of the work you want to undertake yourself. If it is simply a matter of cultivation, seeding or laying sod, and planting, then you may well feel able to tackle it. However, leveling and construction work such as building retaining walls, terraces, ponds, and patios involves costly materials and requires knowledge and skill. Because these elements are permanent and mistakes are expensive to rectify, it is wise to hire professional help if you do not possess building skills (see also STRUCTURES AND SURFACES, pp.492–513). Decide also whether help will be needed for routine maintenance once the garden is established. It is possible to plan a garden so that relatively little upkeep is required.

Changing an existing garden

In most cases, planning involves modifying an existing garden rather than creating a completely new one, and there are various reasons for wishing to redesign.

After moving into a house, you may wish to change part of the existing garden design to suit your preferences. The layout or character of a garden may need to be adapted to accommodate a different use such as providing play areas, space for vegetables, or greater privacy.

If the garden requires a high level of maintenance, it may be necessary to adapt its style in order to reduce the amount of work needed. More rarely, an overgrown or neglected garden may require restoration or, for some elements, renewal, to reestablish its original design (see also "Restoring old and historic gardens," p.31).

Initial assessment

Resist the temptation to be hasty: if faced with junglelike tangles of neglected shrubs, overhanging trees, and weeds, it may seem simplest to dig up the entire garden and start again, but it is better to proceed with caution. The disarray may conceal some interesting or useful plants that should be retained. The presence of one or two more mature specimens in a new garden provides a framework around which to create the planting design and also helps to counteract a raw appearance.

Let ideas for redesigning the garden develop gradually so that they incorporate the best of the inherited features, rather than impose a preconceived image on the site. If possible, live with the garden as it is for a calendar year. Keep notes on any features that may be worth saving, such as an overgrown hedge that provides valuable shelter from prevailing winds, or a shrub that brightens a dull corner with a display of attractive berries in winter.

During this initial period, additional color and interest may be provided by containers, bedding plants, and fast-growing annual climbers

DESIGNING A GARDEN TO SUIT YOUR NEEDS

LOW-MAINTENANCE DESIGN
Hard paving facilitates care of the lawn and borders, which are closely planted with low-maintenance shrubs, small trees, and ground cover plants.

HIGH-MAINTENANCE GARDEN
There is a more varied range of plants here, including fruit, vegetables, container-grown plants, and climbers trained on a pergola, all requiring detailed attention and regular maintenance throughout the year.

trained on a trellis. Routine maintenance work such as pruning dead and damaged wood from trees and shrubs, cutting grass, removing perennial weeds, and clipping hedges should be carried out as usual to keep the garden in good condition.

Formal Open-plan Garden
A framework of tall hedges surrounds this garden, making it a peaceful and secluded haven. An ornamental bench provides a strong focal point as well as a place to enjoy the pink and white borders densely planted with heavily scented Nicotiana, *white* Buddleia, *and stately* Cleome.

Creating a new garden

Making a garden on a new site that has not previously been cultivated as a garden may be daunting, but it should also prove to be an exciting and rewarding challenge. Because there are fewer constraints imposed by existing garden features, there is more freedom to follow the dictates of your imagination. It is important, however, to design the garden in relation to its setting and to take account of such factors as soil type and climate.

Types of garden

There is a style of garden to suit every personality. For some, a productive kitchen garden is a priority; for others, an area for entertaining or a secluded place to relax is more important. The following are examples of some common garden types, but it is, of course, possible to combine elements of two or three different types or, indeed, to create something entirely different.

Family garden Usually fairly formal in design, this type of garden provides a safe space where children may play, as well as areas for flower borders, fruit and vegetables, and a patio or terrace.

Cottage garden This is usually informal in layout and contains many unusual and interesting plants; it may also include some wild or conservation areas and a water feature. The maintenance of this type of garden may require a high degree of horticultural expertise.

Formal outdoor living room With such constructions as a patio, low walls, steps, and perhaps a raised pool, this style of garden may have plenty of plants in containers but little other planting and probably no lawn. It usually requires only minimal maintenance. This formal style is often especially suitable for small urban gardens.

Open-plan garden Possibly on ground sloping away from the house, this type of garden is generally low-maintenance and ideal for passive recreation, with good views of the surrounding landscape. It may be terraced and have space for growing some fruit and vegetables.

Screened, secluded sanctuary Where privacy is a priority or where the garden can be seen from above or has ugly views, this type of design usually incorporates a pergola or arbor and plenty of climbing plants.

Making a rough plan

At the preliminary design stage, sketch a rough outline of the garden site to note down the main elements to be included. Mark in the position of the house and any other fixed features, such as the boundaries. Then allocate approximate areas for beds, borders, a lawn, pool, patio, or whatever else is required. Allow space, where necessary, for purely functional fixtures such as a compost heap or a toolshed; these are best sited away from the house, or hidden from view.

Urban Patio Garden
Wide wooden decking creates an unusual stepped patio with a dynamic diagonal pattern. Plants have been chosen for their low-maintenance requirements and attractive architectural foliage.

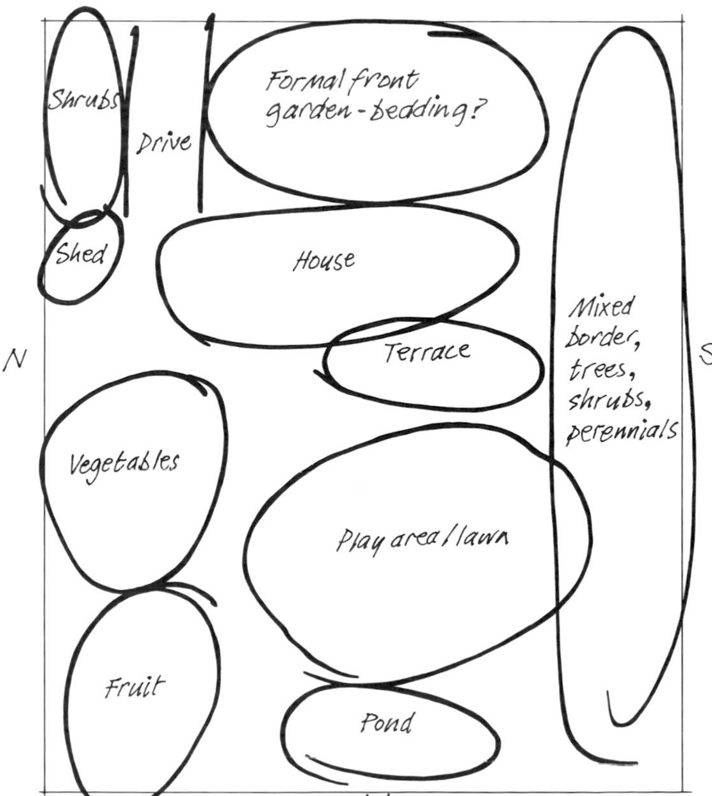

Planning the Garden's Components
Make a simple, graphic note of all the features you intend to have in the garden, roughly sketching their position in relation to the house and any other fixed features as well as external boundaries.

Appraising the site

Before drawing up the next stage of the plan, assess the site thoroughly: good initial preparation pays rich dividends later. The survey should detail factors such as climate and soil type, since this sort of information is invaluable when making decisions about which plants to grow and where to site them.

Planning to Suit Local Conditions
In this waterfront garden, tall trees help to reduce the force of the wind without spoiling outward views. Sturdy plants such as dusty pink Eupatorium *and golden* Rudbeckia fulgida *are untroubled by the wind, and the flexible stems of* Miscanthus *grasses sway in the breeze without being damaged.*

Climate considerations

It is helpful to find out the local figures for annual rainfall, temperatures, and sunshine hours, as well as details of any special climatic influences such as frost pockets. The geographical setting may also make a difference: for example, open hilltop sites are generally several degrees colder than protected low-lying places, so the growing season may start later and end earlier. City gardens are usually warmer and more sheltered throughout the year than those in rural areas. Coastal gardens are vulnerable to salt-laden winds but, owing to the moderating influence of the sea, temperatures are less extreme on the coast than inland.

In addition, the microclimate should be assessed: note which way the garden faces and which parts receive the most sun and shade from one season to the next and at different times of day. For example, the shade cast by a deciduous tree is more dense in late spring and summer than during the rest of the year.

Some corners of the garden may be sheltered, while others may be exposed and need screening if they are to be used fully, depending on the direction and force of the wind. There may also be damp and dry patches and hot and cold spots; none of these is necessarily bad, but they all directly influence which plants will thrive. Make the most of the microclimates that occur within the garden itself by growing plants that enjoy the given conditions, rather than trying to nurture species that are inappropriate. For further details, see "Microclimate," p.519.

Soil

Unless planning to create a "hard" garden with mostly gravel or paving, it is essential to find out the type, texture, and acidity level (pH) of the soil; it may be heavy clay, light and sandy, alkaline (limy), or peaty and acidic. The soil type determines drainage, the type of plants that may be grown, and the ease of tasks such as digging and planting.

Commercial soil-testing kits are widely available from nurseries for determining the pH level of a soil, although the presence of certain plants may also give a rough indication: for example, rhododendrons, blue hydrangeas, heathers, and blueberries normally thrive on acid soil. For further details, see "Acidity and alkalinity," p.525.

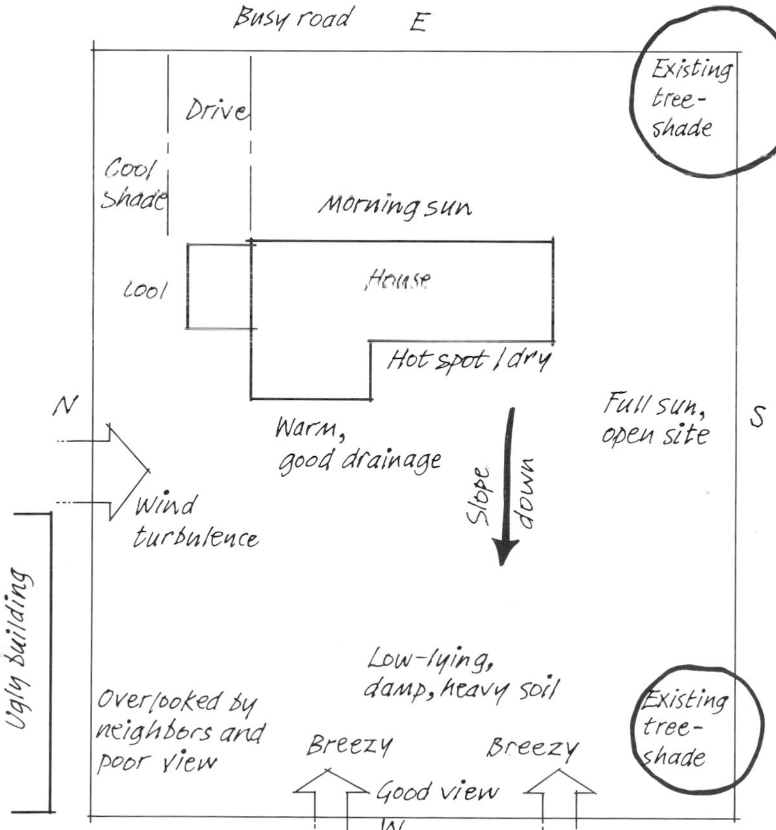

Garden Microclimate Plan
Assess the conditions and site features, and plan appropriately – a pond in the dampest spot, for instance, and sun-loving species in the warmest place.

Planting for Moist Shade
Check the garden's soil type, drainage, and exposure before selecting plants. Here, a damp, shady site provides a perfect environment for these blue-green and variegated hostas and intense blue Iris sibirica.

The garden setting

When designing a garden, consider it in the context of its immediate surroundings rather than in isolation. It may be in a terrace or suburban setting with both good and bad views, for example, or in an elevated position that has fine vistas but needs shelter from strong winds.

A more detailed plan can now be drawn, showing good and bad views, the direction of prevailing winds, and an indication of where additional shelter or screening may be required. Another factor that may be a concern is noise; if it is minor, a dense evergreen planting or solid banks of soil may help. A simpler and sometimes equally effective approach is to create a competing distraction with, for example, a tinkling fountain or splashing waterfall.

Borrowed Landscape
This slightly raised garden takes advantage of uninterrupted views over open countryside. A low fence allows a clear outlook, while the winding path and upright conifer echo the twisting river and tall tree beyond.

Low-maintenance Garden
A balanced framework of hard materials and trees and shrubs forms an effective, low-maintenance design.

Maintenance considerations

All gardens, even if informal or wild, need some care and attention to keep them in good condition. Before deciding on a design, be realistic about the amount of work and energy that you are prepared to expend. If you want upkeep to be minimal, opt for a garden style that does not demand a constant round of mowing, clipping, staking, weeding, and tidying to be attractive. Assess how much time and help will be available or affordable to keep it looking good, and match this to the maintenance schedules most gardens need. Some periods are particularly busy – spring and early summer, for example – so extra assistance may be necessary at these times of the year.

Long- and short-term expectations

Plants grow, mature, and decline at different rates, so certain parts of a garden look well established while others are still some way from their prime. Trees are usually the largest and most long-lived plants, but some species may live many times longer than others; oaks (*Quercus*) may last for more than 200 years whereas some flowering cherries (*Prunus*) and birches (*Betula*) may decline after only 20 or 30. This also applies to shrubs. In general, the faster the growth of a tree or shrub, the shorter its effective life may be.

Although the life expectancy of herbaceous perennials is less variable, certain plants, for example peonies (*Paeonia*) and *Baptisia*, live for many years; others, such as delphiniums and phlox, are short-lived.

When planning a garden, take into account the rates at which the components will look well established. Structures such as paving, pergolas, or walls have an immediate impact; a lawn soon looks presentable if sodded but will take longer if grown from seed; and some herbaceous plants, shrubs, and hedges mature within five years. More patient gardeners may plan to a ten-year time scale, including slow-growing plants with those that are faster maturing but more ephemeral.

Short- and Long-term Planting Results
An abundant, full look can be created quickly using fast-growing perennials interspersed with annuals to fill gaps and provide plenty of color, but such a design may require more maintenance in the long term (right). A more structured design with a sculptural framework of trees, shrubs, and clipped hedges will take much longer to reach maturity (far right).

Creating a design

Once the soil type and climatic conditions have been checked, a more detailed site study should be carried out. Assess the condition of any existing constructions and plants in the garden to decide whether they should be included in the new garden design and measure the site to provide a base plan.

Exploiting natural characteristics

Always work with the given conditions initially, using natural site features as part of the design where possible. Slopes, banks, and changes in level may offer scope for constructing terraces, retaining walls, stepped beds, a watercourse, or a rock garden, as well as providing good views out over the garden. Woodland ground cover plants and bulbs can be used to colonize shaded banks and provide color.

Poorly drained and damp problem areas make a good home for many bog and moisture-loving plants. These areas are often difficult (and expensive) to drain; use plants that have adapted naturally to the conditions. If there is a large piece of damp ground, there may be space for ornamental willows (*Salix*) and alders (*Alnus*), with candelabra primroses (*Primula*), some *Caltha*, and other moisture-loving plants around them (see also THE WATER GARDEN, "Bog gardens," p.241).

If large areas of rubble or subsoil have been left from building and construction, they may be used successfully to form the base of an alpine scree or gravel garden, rather than spending time and effort on digging them out and replacing them with good soil. This type of site provides ideal conditions for plants that prefer sharply drained soil. An advantage with gravel and scree gardens is that they often require minimal maintenance once they are established (see also THE ROCK GARDEN, "The scree bed," p.188).

Assessing existing features

Make a list of the long-lived plants in the garden, identifying them where possible. Note the condition of the trees, shrubs, hedges, and perennial plants, as well as the lawn, and work out how much pruning or renovation is required. Then make an estimate of the current and eventual sizes of the trees and shrubs.

Make a separate list of all the hard elements of the garden, such as patios, walls, paths, greenhouse, pools, and pergolas. Indicate the materials these structures are made from, their condition, and their orientation. When preparing your garden plan, this information will help you to decide which plants to reposition or remove, and which hard elements to retain or modify.

MAKING THE MOST OF NATURAL SITE FEATURES
The informal planting on these steep, rocky banks integrates the natural features of the site to create a richly planted woodland garden.

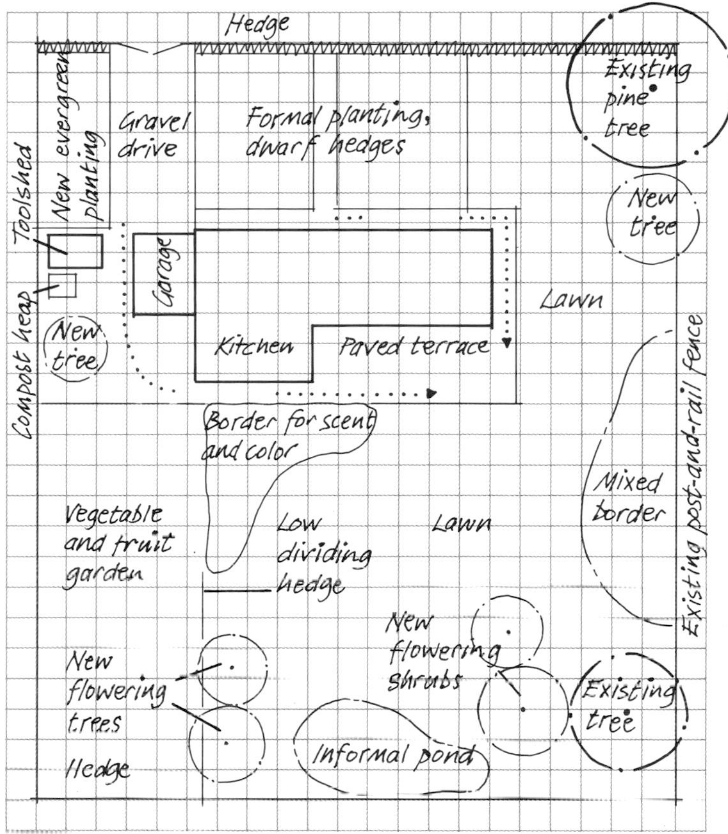

DRAWING THE DESIGN TO SCALE
Make a scale plan of the garden, marking in boundaries, existing structures, and other features you plan to keep; then add the proposed new elements.

Making a scale plan

Unless the proposed alterations are very minor, draw a scale diagram of the site as a basic plan on which various designs may be drawn. These may differ greatly in the style, the space allocated for each feature, and the sense of proportion, but make each one on a scale plan so that it has a realistic basis.

Measuring the site

First, measure the boundaries of the plot, using an extra-long measuring tape. If the site is irregularly shaped, divide it into small sections with clear, fixed points and measure each section individually. Alternatively, a surveyor can be employed to prepare a scale plan.

It may be possible to use an existing plan – perhaps one that is part of the house deeds – although these are often inaccurate and may only include the boundaries of the garden and the position of the house.

Changes of level

If there are marked changes of level on the site, indicate this at the survey stage since the new design may need to incorporate features to accommodate the gradient. A steeply sloping garden may require the building of terraces or retaining walls. A gentle downward slope away from the house is usually worth keeping because it facilitates drainage for a lawn or patio next to the house.

Preparing the first plan

Transfer the site measurements onto paper to create a scale base plan of the garden. Include all the boundaries as well as any elements that you want to retain from the existing garden, such as trees, shrubs, paths, and walls. If you make several different designs for comparison purposes, draw each one on tracing paper stuck over this scale plan so that the details can be altered easily without redrawing the original outline.

Sketch in the design elements that you consider essential, but be realistic about what you can fit in the garden, otherwise the design may lack cohesion and appear muddled. Do not include too many garden structures or potentially large trees in a relatively small plot because they will overpower the garden and make the design look unbalanced.

Choosing the design style

There are many variations of style that provide potential for creating a unique design; personal taste may be the main deciding factor. Some people prefer plenty of open space, others a more divided and secret garden. There may be symmetrical formal areas or irregular and flowing shapes. It is possible to create strikingly different effects depending on whether straight-sided shapes or curves are used while maintaining a well-proportioned design.

There are a few basic principles of design that are best observed whatever the style. Balance and harmony are very important: try to include features that complement each other and the overall setting to create a cohesive whole. Scale and proportion should also be considered; this can be quite difficult with a living composition like a garden because plants change in size and shape over a number of seasons. Always take into account the eventual height, spread, habit, and growth rate of plants before including them in the design. Relate the plants to each other and to adjacent features such as walls and paths (see also "Height and scale relationships," p.22).

Vistas or focal points may also help to give more substance and definition; they are best worked out on site initially before incorporating them into the design. As with all features, some adjustment may be needed when finally marking out the design on the ground.

DETERMINING SHAPE AND STYLE
Within the same framework, gardens of radically different tone and style have been created. The first garden (right) is based on rectilinear design principles of straight lines and blocks that give it regularity and formality and draw attention to each distinct element within the framework. In contrast, the garden on the far right uses a softly sweeping curvilinear design for a much more flowing, informal style.

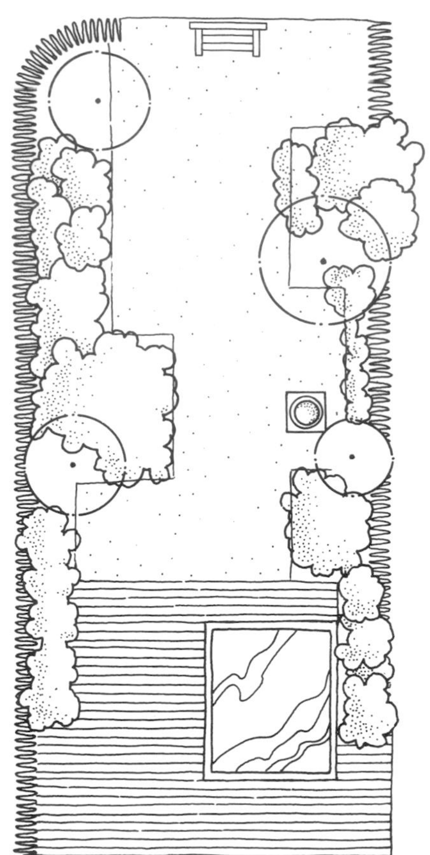

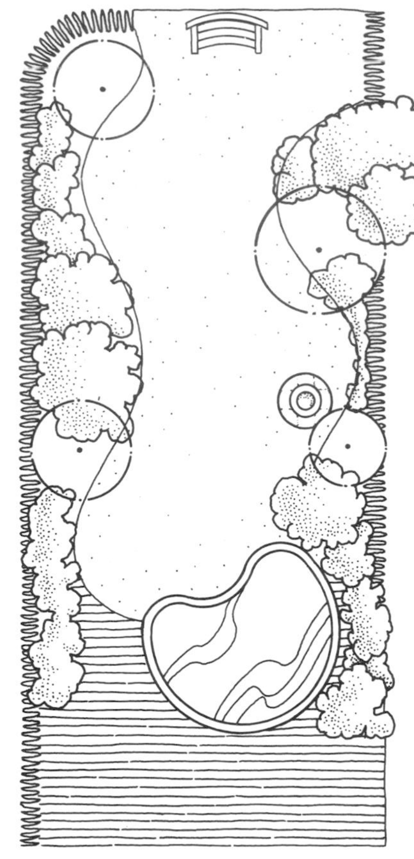

Perspective and proportion

It is possible to make a garden appear shorter and wider or longer and narrower by manipulating the apparent perspective and proportion.

Make a garden seem longer by establishing a long axis and then accentuating it. Site tall plants in the foreground, grading down to shorter ones along the axis, perhaps with a focal point such as a specimen tree at the end. This must not be too tall or the perspective will be altered. Alternatively, consider exaggerating the perspective (see below).

In a long, narrow garden, breaking up the length may often improve the apparent proportions as well as making it more mysterious, inviting exploration. The choice of divisions will depend on the garden: a trellis with an off-center archway provides a pronounced division, whereas a border that intrudes across the long axis creates a gentler break.

Colors can also alter the sense of distance: strong, hot colors have a shortening effect because they seem to come forward in a planting; cooler, misty colors appear to recede.

Deceiving the eye

A garden may be designed so that its shape is altered visually and its apparent proportions made more appealing. In the first design on the right, the urn at the back is the same size as the one in the foreground, whereas in the garden in the center, a smaller urn of the same shape is placed at the far end, suggesting that the garden is longer than is really the case. This imitation of natural perspective creates an impression of length, which is reinforced by the rest of the design: the path narrows at the rear of the garden, successively smaller trees recede into the distance, and even the hedge has been cut lower at the back to strengthen the illusion. The garden on the far right is made to seem shorter and wider by partitions placed at intervals along its length.

ORDINARY PERSPECTIVE
This design does not alter the garden's apparent size or perspective.

EXAGGERATED PERSPECTIVE
A tapering path and trees decreasing in size visually lengthen a garden.

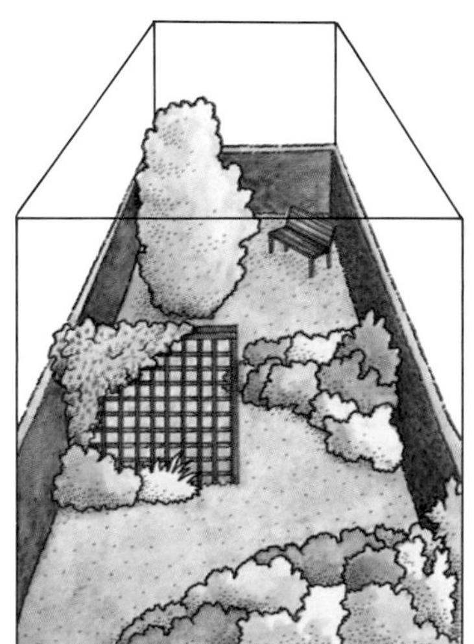

BREAKING UP THE LENGTH
Partial divisions foreshorten the perspective in a long, narrow garden.

Drawing up the final design plan

All the elements may now be brought together in the completed jigsaw puzzle that will provide the final design. Draw this working plan accurately to scale on graph paper, using numbers or symbols for the various features. Indicate the spread of trees and shrubs precisely to make sure that sufficient space is allowed for them in relation to other plants and elements.

Plans on paper may sometimes appear unsatisfactory when they are transferred to the ground so, before preparing the final design on site, mark out the different areas using string and pegs to indicate the proportions and size of the features. It will almost certainly be necessary to make adjustments on site at this stage, so try out some variations. Once you are satisfied that the sizes and proportions of the features and areas work well together, incorporate them into the design.

When designing beds and borders, mark their outlines on the main plan but work out the detailed planting plan separately, preferably to a larger scale (see p.20). It is only necessary to draw in framework and specimen plants accurately.

THE FINISHED GARDEN

The final design plan (right) is drawn to scale, with each element clearly indicated; the mature garden (below) makes good use of the natural features of the site and incorporates practical considerations as well.

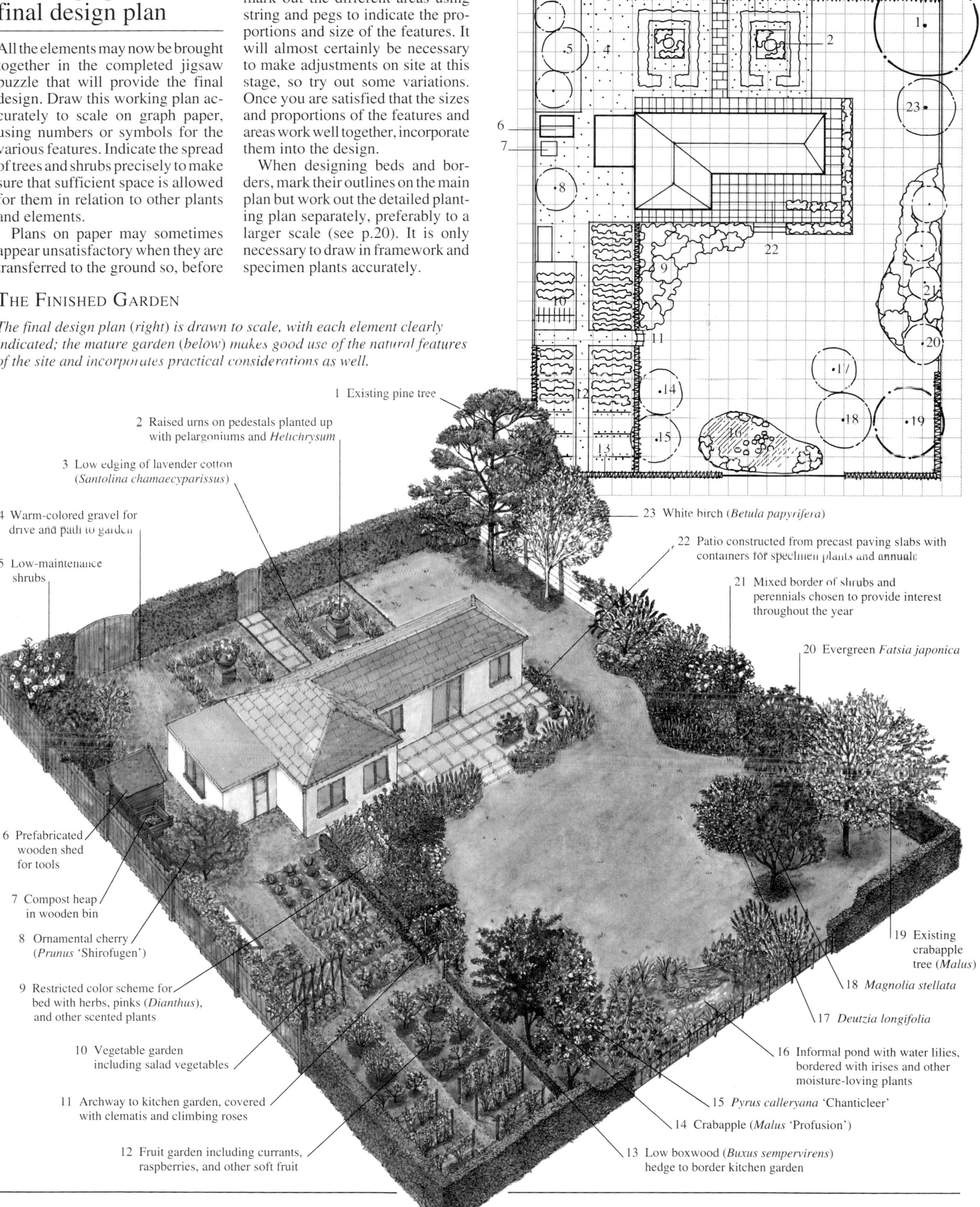

Planting plans

Once the basic design of the garden has been determined, more detailed planning can follow, including deciding exactly which plants to grow and where to site them. Your site survey will have noted any existing plants that may be worth incorporating in the new design. If there are useful trees, shrubs, and hedges that are to be retained but are in poor condition, they should be pruned and fed to renovate them.

Planting plans are best drawn separately to a larger scale. They do not need to be works of art – aim to sketch a planting plan that is simple and realistic. Include other features immediately adjacent or that relate to the planting – for example, a shed that will have climbing plants trained against the sides.

When siting plants, allow sufficient space for each to develop fully to the ultimate height and spread that it is likely to achieve. This is particularly important for trees and shrubs because they usually form the major, permanent "skeleton" in the design (see also "Principles of planting," pp.21–6).

Mixed Border

A detail of the mixed border from the main planting plan shows how a limited color scheme creates a harmonious whole. Shrubs give height and structure, while perennials flesh out the design, forming a balanced display.

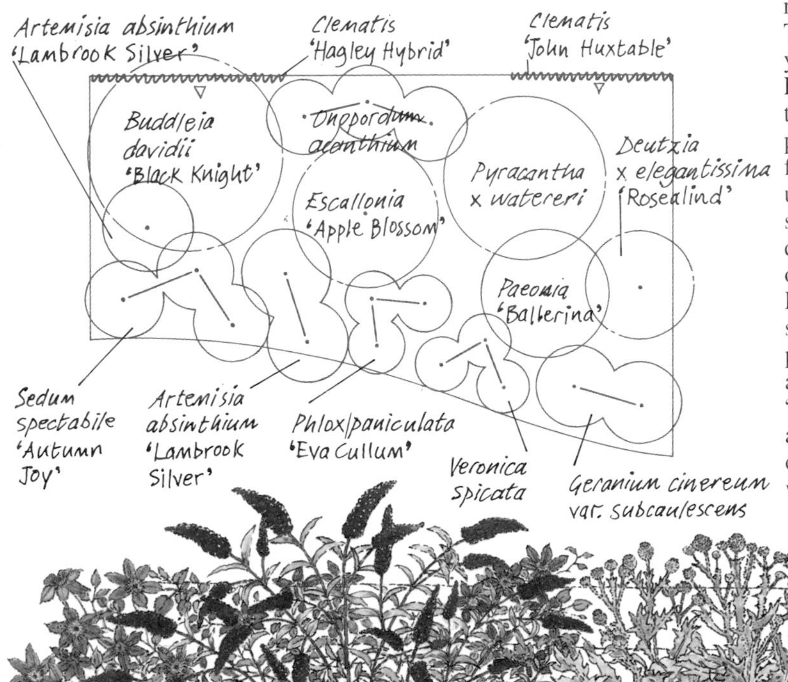

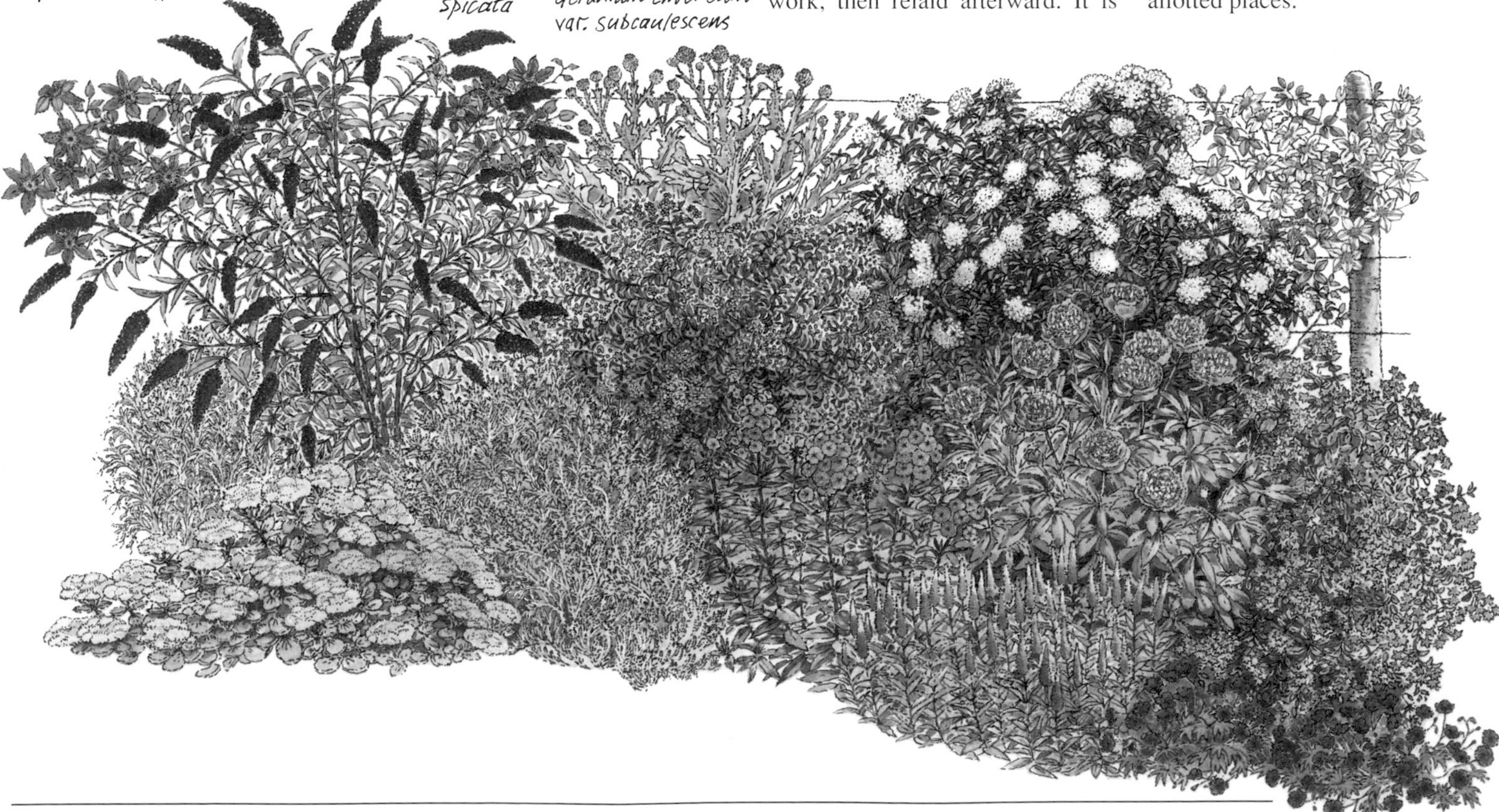

Planning the work

Before embarking on construction and cultivation, prepare a schedule to minimize disruption on the site. Tackle the work in a logical order so that the messiest and most elaborate operations, such as constructing a patio or wall, are carried out first.

Operations such as sowing, planting, transplanting, or sodding should be undertaken at an appropriate time; otherwise, the plants may not survive – fall or early spring is usually best. Construction work may be better in summer or fall when bad weather conditions are less likely to hinder operations. Plan these stages first, then structure the rest of the timetable around them.

Schedule of operations

Existing hard elements Repair or renovate existing garden structures. This may be done at any time of year, weather conditions permitting.

Existing planting If necessary, protect any plants to be retained in their present positions, to avoid damage from construction work. Remove unwanted plants. In the dormant season, lift any plants that are required elsewhere, transplant them, or heel them in temporarily.

Existing lawns If the lawn is in reasonable condition and its shape or position is to be changed, lift the sod and relay it as soon as possible (see "Moving sod," p.279). Sod should also be lifted if it is likely to be damaged by heavy construction work, then relaid afterward. It is best to move sod in early spring or early fall, but if moved during a mild winter it may be kept stacked for three or four weeks before relaying (see "Storing sod," p.278). Do not lift sod in summer unless essential.

New construction work If possible, complete this before beginning any cultivation or planting. Before major site works are started, check the location of all buried utility pipes and cables to ensure that they are not damaged.

Soil cultivation Get rid of any debris, rubble, or scrub. If the soil has been compacted by machinery or trampling, cultivate it deeply (see "Simple digging," p.527, and "Double digging," p.528). Spring or early summer are the best times, since the ground may be left fallow for a while and any weeds removed (see "Weeds," pp.575–9). Also remove any stumps and roots because they can be the source of *Armillaria* root rots (p.567). Preparing the soil before planting may involve incorporating well-rotted organic matter, removing stones, fertilizing, and raking the soil to a fine tilth. This should be done just before planting or a few weeks beforehand.

New planting and lawns This is best carried out in fall, although it is also satisfactory in spring. Plant beds, borders, and containers in accordance with the detailed plans. Lay sod or sow grass seed as required. Plants that have been kept in temporary positions should be transplanted now into their final, allotted places.

Principles of planting

PLANTS are the most important features of a garden, determining the style, character, scents and the changing pictures from season to season and year to year. They are the living essence of gardening and give tremendous potential for creating a pleasurable, individual design.

Some modern garden designers favor the concept of the outdoor living room, using a large number of hard elements such as walls, paths, paving, patios, and gravel. In these gardens there is still plenty of opportunity to use plants in interesting ways, and they are essential to balance and soften the hard features. The plants should be included as an integral part of the design rather than added as a final cosmetic touch.

Most gardens either are designed with a balance between planting and hard landscape or are dependent upon plants as the dominant features. Limited hard elements provide focal points or fulfill practical functions integrated into the garden.

Planting design

There are an infinite number of ways of growing and combining ornamental plants, and there are many thousands of readily available plants with which to plan a design. In a small garden, it is particularly difficult to decide which plants to include. The fewer plants that can be used, the more value each should provide for maximum interest, whether from shape, flowers, foliage, or attractive fruit or bark. Plants with a showy but very brief display may be tempting to grow but are unlikely to merit inclusion.

Deciding on a theme or planting design concept is helpful as a basis for selecting and siting plants. The following broad categories of planting styles provide a few examples.

Formal planting

This type of planting is suitable to provide a simple, symmetrical, and architectural theme, with precisely clipped boundary or dividing hedges. Formal beds, knots, or parterres may be included, allowing finely balanced and controlled planting within the beds using limited colors, shapes, and textures (see also "Formal gardens," p.29; "Knot gardens" and "Parterres," p.31). Considerable discipline is necessary in both the design and maintenance of this style. If dividing up a large garden, it may be appropriate to treat only one section in this way.

Framed planting

Sometimes used in large gardens, this style is also quite easily modified to suit smaller sites. The principle is to create a clearly defined framework using hedges, fences, or walls; the area between them is usually divided by a simple, often formal network of paths that form a frame for planting. The design is structured and ordered but has plenty of scope for very different planting designs within the frame.

Usually a theme is used to link the planting: perhaps aromatic plants and herbs, or old roses underplanted with pinks or violas. It may also be pleasing to have a restricted color scheme or to create a seasonal garden that contains plants chiefly for spring or winter interest.

The term "framed planting" also describes the use of a background or living frame to enhance a special feature, plant group, specimen tree or shrub, or a distant view. For example, a flight of steps or the start of a pathway could be framed by formal, clipped shrubs or upright conifers to form living gateposts. A charming, tantalizing view into another part of the garden or the world outside may be highlighted by the creation of "windows" in a hedge or screen to offer a surprise in an otherwise enclosed space.

Free and mingled planting

This style allows planting to be free-flowing and more natural than formal or framed designs. Charming and unstructured, sometimes even a little chaotic, free planting may combine a wide range of plants in an attractive, informal way. While considerations of balance and uniformity are not as important as in formal gardens, there should be a feeling of rich profusion, and the overall composition should be harmonious in both color and form. These gardens are rarely easy to manage and are usually the creations of avid gardeners who have the time and the inclination to cultivate comprehensive collections of plants.

FRAMED PLANTING
A geometric design delineated by paths and evergreen boxwood (Buxus sempervirens) *hedges forms a permanent framework for a mixed and quite unstructured planting of low-growing shrubs and perennials. The use of limited color gives a sense of continuity, while the bright touches of white and yellow stand out well against a predominantly green backdrop, adding highlights to the planting, yet preserving the tranquility of the garden.*

FREE PLANTING
A joyous array of plants thrives in this informal garden, creating a feeling of spontaneity and abundance. The cool blues of Eryngium *and* Campanula *contrast well with the orange and yellow* Helenium *and* Hemerocallis.

Garden backgrounds

Although the boundaries and internal divisions of a garden are often not fully exploited in the design, their materials, size, and character should figure into the overall picture. Hedges, screens, walls, or fences all serve well as backgrounds and may act as a foil for a planting or ornamental statuary. Remember to use compatible textures, colors, and styles: for example, while a clipped yew hedge may set off a classical stone figure to perfection, a picket fence would be inappropriate.

Hedges and screens

As well as having a practical value for bordering or dividing the garden, hedges and plant screens form ornamental living barriers and provide attractive backgrounds. White or pale flowers or foliage, for example, stand out particularly well against the dark green of a dense cypress (*Cupressus*) or yew (*Taxus*) hedge. Seats, urns, and statues look dramatic set in an alcove in a well-clipped hedge.

Evergreen hedges make excellent backgrounds for shrub and herbaceous borders and for showing off specimen plants. However, some hedging plants have very fibrous, spreading roots and may compete for moisture and nutrients with nearby plants. Density of growth is particularly important if the hedge is intended primarily as a background foil for an ornamental feature.

Flowering or berrying shrubs, for example roses or pyracanthas, may also be used, especially in informal gardens, to provide a visual boundary or division. Growth is usually less dense than in a traditional hedge.

Hedges may take several years to become established and need more maintenance than walls or fences, but the interest they provide in texture, color, and shape is invaluable. Most are also long-lived and so are often more permanent features than fences (see also Hedges and Screens, pp.58–60).

Walls

Although expensive to build, walls of stone or brick provide excellent boundaries for gardens and offer considerable scope for vertical gardening. The height and orientation of a wall usually determines what may be grown on or against it. Plants that grow well on a south-facing wall, for example, are usually unsuitable for one facing north.

When choosing climbers, make sure that the color of the flowers or foliage harmonizes well with that of the walls. Red or yellow brick walls show off greens, dark reds, blues, purples, and whites well, while pale or gray walls accentuate pinks, yellows, reds, and blues.

Background Planting
A high brick wall supports the magnificent purple swath of a clematis, which forms a living canopy above the ornamental garden seat.

Golden- or silver-variegated forms of ivy (*Hedera*) can lighten up dark or gloomy walls and are ideal for such sites. Although they normally do not damage walls in good condition, they are not recommended for walls in poor repair because their aerial roots frequently loosen the mortar. For more information, see Climbing Plants, pp.92–113.

Even when unadorned with plants, some walls, especially old, mellow ones, make attractive backgrounds, so it may be desirable to leave a quarter or a half uncovered.

Fences

Where an instant physical boundary is required, fencing may be the best solution. Usually relatively inexpensive and easy to install, fences are available in a wide range of heights and styles and may be used to set or emphasize the tone of the garden. Woven wattle fences are attractive in an informal, rural setting, while white picket fencing is pretty around a cottage garden, and wrought iron railings are in keeping with the formality of an elegant town garden. Fences that are purely utilitarian are often better covered with climbing or scrambling plants.

Trellises

Trellises, both square- and diamond-patterned designs, may be used against a fence or wall to provide support for plants; if sufficiently sturdy, they may be used on their own provided that they are attached to strong supports. This is a good option where a screen is required that does not block out light or an attractive view. Trellises may be stained or painted for decorative accent.

Height and scale relationships

When deciding on a planting design, take the height and shape of a plant into account, both in relation to other plants and to the scale and size of the area. For example, a small garden would look overcrowded if it contained a large tree such as a horse chestnut (*Aesculus*), while a smaller-growing species such as mountain ash (*Sorbus aucuparia*) would be more in proportion.

Successful plant associations often depend on harmony of scale; a grouping that combines many different plants, all of greatly differing heights, may simply look unplanned and uncoordinated. On the other hand, there should be some variation so the planting does not look regimented. Even on a small scale, such as in a rock garden, consider combining dwarf shrubs and conifers with cushion- and carpet-forming rock plants to create variety and interest. They will contrast in height, yet relate in scale, appearing in balanced proportion with each other. If grouped with larger species, these plants often appear insignificant and are easily overlooked.

Perennial and shrub borders are often arranged by height, with the tallest plants at the back and the lowest in the front, so that they may all be clearly seen. Such a design seems less formal, however, if the regularity is broken in one or two places, perhaps by including a tall plant midway. In this case, plants that allow a view beyond them should be chosen, for example a rather narrow tree such as a columnar yew (*Taxus* x *media* 'Hicksii') or a plant with airy, filigree foliage such as fennel (*Foeniculum vulgare*).

Structural planting

A number of plants have a striking architectural or sculptural impact – some from their natural growth habit, others from their foliage, stems, or flowers. The variety of forms and silhouettes ranges from the spreading mass of a prostrate juniper

Structure and Mass
This planting design adopts a sculptural approach using a variety of shrubs and conifers to make a tableau of shapes and textured masses.

(*Juniperus communis* 'Prostrata') to the stately, upright flower spikes and arching, thistlelike leaves of *Acanthus spinosus*.

Structural plants are often used singly as a focal point, but they are also useful as part of the design framework. A structural plant at the end of a border provides a distinctive conclusion, while a pair, one on either side of a path or doorway, acts as an enhancing frame. Architectural plants are excellent for visually linking the house (or other hard feature) with the garden – the sculptural, but living, forms span the transition from hard elements to soft planting. Including a few strongly shaped plants in an otherwise unstructured and informal plan helps to give the design a focus and contrasts well with the soft lines of the free planting.

With deciduous or herbaceous plants, plan the design so that other features or plants provide a similar function during winter months. For example, a group of redtwig dogwoods (*Cornus alba*) could be planted next to a clump of *Heracleum mantegazzianum* so that the dogwoods become a spectacular feature once the *Heracleum* dies back.

IMITATING NATURE
Moisture-loving plants such as candelabra primroses (Primula) *and the white-flowered* Anthericum liliago *look natural on this waterside bank.*

Specimen plants

Plants that have a particularly fine shape or those with very attractive flowers, foliage, fruit, or stems are best grown with enough space around them for them to be seen and appreciated individually. Site them so that they form focal points from the house, terrace, or lawn. In large gardens, such plants may be grouped in threes or fours for bolder impact. Some plants may also be enhanced if grown in ornamental containers.

SINGLE SPECIMEN
The sculptural form, foliage, and flower clusters of many Yucca *make them ideal specimen plants.*

Planting in groups

Although single specimens may be used on their own or as part of a design, a much bolder and more harmonious effect is often achieved by planting in groups or drifts, particularly with small plants. This avoids the cluttered effect that may result from "dot" planting of many different single plants. Growing a group of the same plants together provides a stronger impact, especially when viewed from a distance, and makes any planned color scheme more emphatic. Usually groups look best if planted in odd numbers of three, five, or seven plants since this avoids a regimented look.

Groups of plants with bold foliage or other striking characteristics may also be used, informally, to divide or screen areas in a less formal manner than hedges.

Naturalistic plant associations

Pondering ways in which plants can be combined is a major part of garden design. Familiar groupings abound and work well, but with so many plants available, countless other combinations of color, texture, and form remain to be tried.

When deciding which plants to place together, bear in mind how they would grow naturally so that the grouping as well as the selection of plants is appropriate. Imitating plant associations from nature has two important advantages. In every natural or seminatural habitat, associations of plants have developed that blend well together in different layers and groupings. These plant communities are adapted to the soil and microclimate of their natural locale. Give them the same growing conditions in your garden and they will thrive. The range of plants that thrive may be influenced by other factors. For example, a pasture, if left ungrazed, will be invaded by shrubs and trees and the grassland plants will quickly decline and disappear.

Monocultures of one species seldom occur in nature and, with some soils and habitats, the variety is very rich indeed. Any bare soil is rapidly colonized by local flora. Different

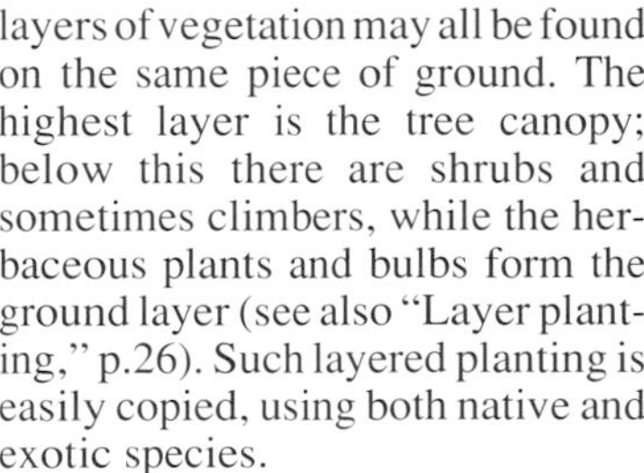

layers of vegetation may all be found on the same piece of ground. The highest layer is the tree canopy; below this there are shrubs and sometimes climbers, while the herbaceous plants and bulbs form the ground layer (see also "Layer planting," p.26). Such layered planting is easily copied, using both native and exotic species.

Wildlife gardens contain mostly indigenous plants that attract birds, insects, and other wildlife. The use of some appropriate exotics and selected cultivars of suitable species will often add to the interest and quality of the planting, particularly in fall and winter.

Shape and form

When designing, always look at the contours of a plant in addition to its foliage, flowers, and other features. The wide assortment of plant shapes affords almost endless possibilities to create lively, well-balanced groupings. Keep in mind, however, that each plant has a natural growth pattern, and as the plant matures, its silhouette may change. Such changes, if unanticipated, could produce some jarring juxtapositions in your garden.

Of course, you can prune some plants to correct a problem or to achieve a particular result in a design. Coppicing, for example (see p.49), will produce young, colored shoots on willows (*Salix*) for winter display.

Since you may not be able to predict what the adult form of a

CONTRASTING FORMS
Foliage plants of different shapes and forms have been combined to create an interesting and balanced design. The upright spears of Iris laevigata 'Variegata' *are superbly offset by the giant rounded leaves of* Hosta 'Buckshaw Blue' *and the open form and horizontal, divided foliage of* Heracleum mantegazzianum.

plant will be from the shapes and sizes of young ones in a nursery or garden center, try to see more mature specimens in gardens or parks where possible.

Many shrubs and perennials have a rounded, hummocky shape, which may be contrasted with different forms – such as a columnar tree or prostrate ground cover plants – for extra interest. Shrubs with bare basal stems can be used with low, bushy plants in front to hide the base. Those with rounded contours and dense habits are better suited to undulating ground cover plantings.

Many herbaceous and bulbous plants provide striking shapes and forms with bold foliage and flower spikes when in growth, but are of little interest in winter after they have died down. The problem may be solved by placing an evergreen plant or suitable feature nearby to provide continuing interest (see also "Successional interest," opposite).

Breaking the Color Rules
This clashing scheme of red rhododendrons and pink lupines (Lupinus) *and giant poppies* (Papaver) *shows how the rules may be broken successfully.*

Color

The most striking but sometimes rather transient color in plants generally comes from the flowers, with a dazzling range of shades and tints. Flowers are not the only source of color, however, since foliage is often ornamental. Also, many plants have attractive stems, bark, berries, or seedheads that provide interest during fall and winter.

Color preferences are often a question of personal taste, but there are general guidelines that can be followed. The color spectrum may be divided into two ranges – the blues and the yellows. The blue range includes the bluish whites, bluish pinks, magenta, fuchsia, crimson-reds, blues, and purples. The yellow range includes the creamy whites, ivories, salmon-pinks, scarlet-reds, oranges, and yellows.

Associations between the two ranges generally harmonize well, but mixing colors within a range may be less successful. In the blue range, for example, pinks and reds may not always be restful together, whereas taking a color from each range and mixing them, such as blue and yellow, can be pleasing. There are exceptions, however: blues and mauves usually combine well, for example. Restricting the colors often helps to create a harmonious and attractive design; if a wide range of colors is used, the effect may be disjointed and fussy.

With all color planting, light is a major factor. In areas where the light is soft and on the blue side, prominence should be given to pastel colors such as pale pinks, lilacs, and blue-grays. In the stronger light and the more brilliant sunshine of Mediterranean or Californian landscapes, hotter colors may have more impact than pale colors, which often appear bleached in strong sunlight. On the other hand, a shaded, rather sunless court or terrace may be enlivened with salmon-pinks, oranges, reds, and yellows, while a hot, sunbaked courtyard may seem cooler if grays, blues, and whites are used.

Strong color may also be used to lead the eye to a particular feature, while soft blues and grays are less distinct and therefore seem to recede. This principle may be used to create an illusion of distance – for example, planting red roses in the foreground with blue-green grasses at the rear of the garden could make it seem longer (see also "Perspective and proportion," p.18).

Texture

This is mainly provided by foliage, but other features, such as fruit and bark, and the outline of a plant's silhouette, may also have interesting

Restricted Color
Here, colors have been limited to create a coordinated, calm feeling, while the relaxed plant groupings underline the informality of the design.

The Effect of Light
For a dazzling impact in strong sunlight, group plants with intense colors, such as lavender (Lavandula) *and oleander* (Nerium oleander).

TEXTURAL CONTRASTS
The feathery branchlets of Chamaecyparis pisifera 'Filifera Aurea' *and the dense foliage of* Euphorbia characias *subsp.* wulfenii *form a striking contrast.*

textures. When combining different plants, consider how their varying textures will work together, and aim to set up contrasting groupings so that they complement each other. For example, the lacy fronds of a clump of ferns would attractively offset the ridged leaves of a hosta.

Successional interest

Many gardens are at their peak in summer, with colorful plantings that rely largely on herbaceous plants. These usually provide little interest for the rest of the year, and a planting plan that creates a succession of color and vitality is likely to give more pleasure. Trees, shrubs, and hedges are invaluable for establishing a lasting framework, while including a variety of bulbs and herbaceous plants provides changing color and texture in successive seasons.

Spring

Bulbs are unrivaled for bringing color to the garden early in the year, from the white snowdrops (*Galanthus*) of late winter to the bright crocuses and daffodils of spring; many, such as tulips, flower almost into summer. Bulbs can be grown with ground cover plants to provide interest once the bulbs' foliage dies down. Spring-flowering climbers, such as *Clematis montana*, can be grown up a light-foliaged, deciduous tree to add color while the tree is coming into leaf.

Summer

In summer, many herbaceous plants are at their best, with an enormous range of species from which to create a rich tapestry of color. These include perennials, which contribute interest year after year, and annuals and biennials, such as poppies (*Papaver*) and sweet peas (*Lathyrus odoratus*), which add variety and fill in between established plants. The foliage of some bulbous plants such as *Eremurus* and ornamental onions (*Allium*) begins to die back before they flower. Plant these so that the leaves are hidden among the foliage of a late-flowering herbaceous plant.

Fall

Shrubs with berries, fall-flowering bulbs, and dwarf conifers all provide interest in fall. Many trees and shrubs that have attractive foliage, such as the fiery hues of Japanese maples (*Acer palmatum* and *A. japonicum*), are particularly spectacular at this time.

WINTER IMPACT
The bright colors of redtwig and yellowtwig dogwoods (Cornus alba 'Sibirica' *and* C. stolonifera 'Flaviramea') *are seen at their best in winter.*

SPRING
The proud heads of colorful and striped tulips bring a wealth of color to the border in spring, while the airy blue flowers of forget-me-nots (Myosotis) *add extra interest at ground level.*

SUMMER
An old garden rose is at its prime in summer, its deep magenta blooms complementing the pink, mauve, and blue color scheme. Perennials such as ornamental onions (Allium), *hardy* Geranium, *and irises fill out the design of the shrub framework.*

FALL
Ornamental cabbages with attractive pink and green leaves add soft color, while the golden yellow foliage of the rose brightens up the border. The structural elements of the painted trellis and the Euphorbia *now start to become more prominent.*

WINTER
As the perennials die down, the skeleton of the design comes to the fore – the bare stems of the rose, the bold cone shape of the gold-variegated holly (Ilex), *the frost-tinged heads of the* Euphorbia, *and the distinctive arch of the trellis.*

Winter

Although often regarded as a dull period in the garden, winter is a time when many plants have attractive foliage, flowers, fruits, bark, or stems. If space permits, an area of the garden can be devoted to plants of winter interest, perhaps where they can be seen from the house. Trees and shrubs with ornamental bark, for example the glossy mahogany trunk of *Prunus serrula*, provide structural features as well as color and texture. Evergreen ground cover plants or winter-flowering heathers can be grown at the front of a border for extra winter color.

Layer planting

The aim of layer planting is to achieve continuity and balance of color, form, and texture in the same area. This mirrors natural habitats where plants grow in close proximity but often have distinct life cycles; this minimizes competition for moisture, food, and light. A good natural example is an English bluebell wood, where the bluebells bloom in late spring and die down before bracken, brambles, and foxgloves have developed fully. This interplanting or tiered planting can be copied; for example, white birches (*Betula*) could form the tree layer, in whose light shade could be planted Japanese maples (*Acer*) or dogwoods (*Cornus*) as the shrub layer. These could be underplanted with hostas or ferns and, since these do not come into leaf until late spring, they might be interplanted with spring bulbs.

On a smaller scale, the same principles can be followed using specimen shrubs surrounded by carpets of ground cover plants and bulbs. Trees that have dense canopies, however, including beech (*Fagus*) and evergreens such as hollies (*Ilex*), may cast deep shade or have branches right to the ground, making it difficult for plants beneath to grow well.

Plant spacing

When creating a planting design, allow enough space between plants so that they have room to develop to their full size; if planted too closely, they may soon need to be thinned to avoid becoming overcrowded. There may be occasions, however, when close planting can be employed to provide a particular design feature, such as a knot garden.

Planting distances and spacings also depend upon the soil, climatic conditions, and the time that the species or cultivar takes to mature while the flowerbed is developing. Young plants are less costly than more mature specimens, but their impact is less immediate, and there may be a delay of several years before the planting begins to look mature. The decision on whether to use young or mature plants will depend on your budget.

As a general rule, close planting and the use of fast-maturing plants creates a good short-term impact, but more thinning, maintenance, and renewal is required in the longer term. A balance between fast- and slow-growing plants yields the most satisfactory results. Using temporary fillers such as colorful annuals and bulbs in the gaps is a way of providing plenty of interest initially while the other plants are becoming well established.

GROUPING CONTAINERS
Siting containers together creates bold compositions. Here, a group ranged by height – from a huge Nerium oleander *at the rear to sweet alyssum* (Lobularia maritima) *in front – forms a transition between house and garden.*

LAYER PLANTING
The small canopy and light foliage of a Robinia pseudoacacia 'Frisia' *allow many plants to grow underneath it; similarly, the foxgloves* (Digitalis) *and* Crambe cordifolia *do not restrict the growth of low perennials beneath.*

Gardening in containers

There is ample scope for including planted containers in a garden, especially on terraces, patios, and steps, where they create attractive changes of level and soften the rigid appearance. Containers form structural points of interest and may be used in various ways – singly to enhance specimen plants, in pairs to frame a view or flight of steps, or in small groups to link the house with the terrace and garden, for example.

Most plants may be grown in containers, including bedding plants and bulbs. A more permanent planting of shrubs and trees provides long-term interest. Bonsai, or miniaturized trees in shallow containers, may be used as an attractive accent (see pp.434–5). Even climbers may be planted in containers next to a wall.

Containers are available in a wide range of sizes, shapes, and styles; select those that complement both the house and planting. For example, a clipped boxwood (*Buxus sempervirens*) would be enhanced by an elegant stone trough, but diminished by a wooden half barrel.

Garden styles

WHILE there are almost no limits to the potential range of garden designs, several classical and natural styles have provided inspiration for gardeners for centuries. These may assist you in planning and combining all the various elements of your garden to create a well-focused and consistent design.

Combining two or more styles may also be appropriate, perhaps by dividing the garden into smaller rooms with ornamental hedges or trellises. Even in a small area, stylistic contrasts may provide an interesting change of key: the strong, clean lines of a contemporary, formal pond can be attractively offset by a background border overflowing with old-fashioned rambling roses and complementary annuals. Plan the linking of areas or the juxtaposition of different styles with great care, however, to avoid a discordant jumble. Mixing formal and informal styles is best achieved by framed planting (see p.21).

COTTAGE GARDEN
A productive screen of scarlet runner beans creatively combines the functional with the ornamental, while wigwams support scented sweet peas (Lathyrus odoratus), *which can be cut for indoor decoration.*

Informal and naturalistic gardens

These garden styles, as their names imply, tend generally to have no strong, symmetrical, rigid, or ordered lines. Gracefully flowing shapes, less regulated and controlled planting, and soft, curved patterns are typical. Informal groups of plants in overflowing beds and borders, such as those in cottage gardens, are often included. If a more naturalistic look is wanted, the planting design can be even simpler.

The concept of a wild garden is to grow native species in natural associations and groups, imitating the best of nature while exerting some selection and control. Simply letting a garden run wild does not achieve the same result; it tends to be messy rather than pleasantly relaxed and flowing. A degree of maintenance is necessary in a naturalistic garden, but the effect of this should be unobtrusive. Use the natural characteristics of the site as much as possible, whether developing a woodland garden, a wildflower meadow, or a sanctuary tó attract birds and other wildlife.

Cottage gardens

In the past, cottage gardens were primarily utilitarian, with fruit, vegetables, herbs, flowers, and shrubs crowded into a very small area. Lawns were rare because any spare ground was thought better used for growing more plants. The garden was typically divided by paths of compacted soil edged with stones, tiles, shells, or clumps of flowers such as pansies (*Viola x wittrockiana*). A great variety of plants, often highly fragrant, was grown – old roses billowing over cabbages, and Madonna lilies (*Lilium candidum*) next to pot marigolds (*Calendula*), while towering hollyhocks (*Alcea rosea*) and sunflowers (*Helianthus annuus*) framed the doorway.

While it is possible to re-create a traditional cottage garden accurately, the maintenance demands are high and the characteristic plants usually do not provide much interest in fall and winter. Many of the principles are valuable ideas for modern gardens, however, and can be borrowed or adapted to suit individual sites. Certain typical plants and features are often used today to create a relaxed and rural feeling in a planting design.

Paths made from bricks, wood chips, or gravel are practical as well as appropriate in style, while an edging of lavender (*Lavandula*) provides scented flowers outdoors and for drying as well as attractive evergreen foliage. A rustic wooden arch is an ideal feature for supporting scented climbing plants such as roses or honeysuckle (*Lonicera*), and borders overflowing with peonies (*Paeonia*), lupines (*Lupinus*), wallflowers (*Cheiranthus*), and pinks (*Dianthus*) re-create the feeling of unchecked abundance.

Woodland gardens

A woodland garden is often a peaceful, sheltered retreat, based on a natural grouping of trees, possibly with an appropriate underplanting of shrubs, herbaceous plants, and bulbs. Trees such as some oak (*Quercus*), white birch (*Betula papyrifera*), and wild cherry (*Prunus serotina*) cast only light or dappled shade. They allow a greater range of plants to grow beneath them than do conifers and other trees that have a dense canopy (see also "Layer planting," opposite).

Growing other plants as well as trees makes it easier to create a succession of interest and provides a display at different levels of height. Hardy cyclamen and English bluebells (*Hyacinthoides non-scripta*) can be planted in drifts to form swaths of color, while ornamental members of the mint family (such as *Lamium maculatum*) are attractive as ground cover. In moist sites, for example near a woodland stream, primroses (*Primula*) and many ferns thrive, while foxgloves (*Digitalis*) tolerate the dry, shady conditions found at a woodland edge. There are a number of shrubs such as rhododendrons and Japanese maples (*Acer*) that grow well in shady woodland sites and, since they also form a transition between low bulbs and perennials and tall trees, they help to create an interesting and well-balanced planting.

Fast-growing species such as alders (*Alnus*) and willows (*Salix*) will provide a tree canopy fairly quickly, but may then soon form shade that is

WILD GARDEN
Species such as pink willow herb (Epilobium) *and yellow loosestrife* (Lysimachia punctata) *thrive in this naturalistic corner. The pond and dense cover of the reeds and other plants make it an alluring haven for wildlife.*

too heavy for many woodland plants to thrive. Slower-growing species such as Scots pine (*Pinus sylvestris*), red oak (*Quercus rubra*), and sugar maple (*Acer saccharum*) will provide a more satisfactory canopy.

If the site is partially wooded already, it may be necessary to clear areas for glades and underplanting by removing unwanted scrub and saplings or thinning the tree canopy. Denser planting at the edges of the site is best left because it provides valuable shelter from the wind and refuge for wildlife.

Given plenty of space, it is possible to create a new woodland garden, but patience is essential; even if large sites are planted, a true woodland takes some years to establish. A minimum area of about 1/4 acre (1,000sq m) is needed, but on a smaller scale a few groups of birches (*Betula*), Japanese maples (*Acer* spp.), or other trees with light foliage will provide sufficient shade in which to grow a succession of woodlanders such as *Anemone nemorosa*, *Trillium*, and snowdrops (*Galanthus*).

When establishing a woodland on an open site, it is best to keep the area around the trees clear so that for the first year or two they develop with little or no competition from other plants.

Access to the garden is best provided by paths made from loose materials such as bark chips, pine needles, or, if the site tends to be wet, gravel. For an informal garden environment, naturally meandering paths that are neither very wide (except for maintenance purposes) nor conspicuous are most suitable. Straight paths look out of place in a woodland garden.

SHADY WOODLAND
The canopy created by deciduous trees provides the right conditions for many shade-loving plants and a cool refuge in which to sit in summer.

Wildlife and conservation gardens

In many areas, the natural habitat of much of the flora and fauna is being eroded, and therefore the idea of providing a refuge for wildlife in the garden is appealing. Any garden with a wide range of plants will attract some animals and birds, but growing a wider variety of plant communities will provide better conditions for a greater diversity of wildlife.

The main aim of this style of garden should be to provide both habitats and food; if preferred, these can be selected to attract particular creatures. For example, hawthorn (*Crataegus*) hedges are suitable nesting sites for birds, while berrying trees and shrubs are a source of food in winter. Including a pond should attract a great many different forms of wildlife such as birds, frogs, newts, and dragonflies and other insects.

Meadows

Prairie meadows with a rich wildflower population once covered a large part of North America, but are now becoming increasingly rare, and the interest in meadow gardens has risen accordingly. It is important to select plants that are suitable for the site and conditions and to establish and maintain them well if they are to look natural. It is possible to develop a meadow garden easily and satisfactorily on even relatively poor soil because some of the most attractive meadow and grassland species prefer these conditions rather than richer, heavily fertilized garden soils.

Many meadow wildflowers are perennials that persist well once they are established in an appropriate, correctly managed habitat. Seed mixtures of annuals and perennials are sometimes recommended for meadow gardening. They are not always suitable, since they require regularly cultivated soil to thrive, and would soon die out in grassland. For more information, see WILDFLOWER AND MEADOW GARDENING, p.167.

Water gardens

The allure of water brings a special fascination to any garden: a pool has an inherent tranquility, while a stream offers the extra pleasures of restful sound and movement. If incorporating a water feature into the garden, ensure that its design is in harmony with the rest of the garden and the house.

In a formal garden, a symmetrical pool with a distinct edge is usually appropriate. A waterspout, fountain, or evenly stepped waterfall could also be included to add an interesting change of level as well as movement. A more naturalistic pond with a curving, irregular shape is desirable in an informal setting; the edge is best partially softened or hidden by moisture-loving plants and attractive stones.

If there is space, a stream or watercourse leading into the pond and channeled over stones or cobblestones creates appealing sights and sounds in the garden. It is best to use local stone or slate if constructing a

WATER IN THE GARDEN
This delightful pool forms the centerpiece of an informal area set apart from the formality glimpsed beyond and framed by a clipped hedge. The water's calm, reflective surface is attractive in its own right, while the pond margin also provides an ideal spot to grow moisture-loving plants such as hostas and Rodgersia.

water feature that is to blend in well with the natural landscape. For more information on design, construction, and planting, see THE WATER GARDEN, pp.240–57.

Patios and courtyards

These hard-surfaced and usually enclosed gardens are often ideal in towns and cities, where garden space is typically very restricted and lawns are difficult to establish and maintain well. Even in a small area, an enchanting garden can be created. To create the best effect, the design should be simple; the temptation to pack in many different features or plants should be resisted.

In addition to providing an area for sitting out and an informal eating place in fine weather, a patio can be used as a setting for displaying a wide range of plants in containers, including bulbs, alpines, herbs, small trees, shrubs, roses, and fruit. Raised beds around a patio or courtyard area can also be planted with climbers and trailing plants to spill over the edge and soften the rigid aspect of the hard elements. Ensure that the materials selected for use are appropriate to the style and character of the house and to the climate.

When designing a patio, bear in mind which parts of the site are sunny or shaded at different times of day, and plan areas for sitting out in the morning or evening accordingly. Shade cast by trees and adjacent buildings will vary during the year, depending on the density of foliage present and the differences in the angle of the sun.

An enclosing screen or trellis clothed in decorative climbers, vines, or annual runner beans in summer provides seclusion as well as some protection from wind. Trees in pots can be used as movable shelters for the same purpose. Privacy and shade can be increased by including a pergola or arbor, which also provides an ornamental framework to support fragrant and colorful honeysuckles (*Lonicera*), roses, and clematis.

Changes of level are often useful in developing a compact space attractively; steps may be enhanced by pots or by growing climbers up a handrail or railings. If the patio can be seen from an upstairs window, make sure that the overall design will also be pleasing from above, since small gardens often have a mosaic-like quality that is particularly attractive from this viewpoint.

Electric lighting can be both practical and attractive in a courtyard or patio garden. It can be used in various ways, for example to cast the shadow of a tree or statue against a brick wall, or to backlight a striking architectural plant. In a pool, illuminate the fine spray of a fountain from underneath or shed light across the water surface to enjoy its reflections after dark.

BALCONY GARDEN
Raised wooden beds and large terracotta pots are planted with standard shrubs, ground cover plants, and bright annuals such as fibrous-rooted begonias to enliven this rooftop terrace. The square-patterned trellis picks up the design of the windows, linking the inside with the outside.

ENCLOSED PATIO
A table and seat, framed by clipped Cupressus glabra *standards and foliage plants, form an elegant focal point in this patio garden.*

Roof gardens and balconies

Many of the same considerations apply to roof gardens and balconies as to patios, although they are more exposed to both sun and wind. Low-maintenance design and planting are usually priorities, and the weight of containers is also important. If there are weight restrictions, plastic or fiberglass containers are preferable to those made from terracotta or stone. Similarly, if additional flooring is required, choose lightweight materials rather than heavy paving slabs.

If the garden is subject to strong winds, sturdy trellis screens or other windbreak filters provide shelter for both plants and people, although they may also obstruct views. Any screens used must be very securely fixed to permanent roof structures for safety reasons.

Balconies are usually more sheltered than roof gardens and may also be shaded from above. Use all of the available space, adding sturdy brackets and shelves to the house wall to support pots and troughs of trailing plants, or grow climbers up an ornamental trellis (see "Gardening in containers," p.26).

Formal gardens

From the simplicity of a lawn punctuated by a single island bed to the complexity of an intricate parterre, many types of formal garden can be designed. However simple they may be, formal designs are characteristically elegant and ordered, balanced and well proportioned, and often strongly patterned or symmetrical. Features typically include closely mown lawns, straight paths, neatly clipped hedges or topiary, borders defined by edging plants or low hedges, framed vistas and focal points, formal bedding in blocks of strong color, and, on occasion, parterres and knot gardens.

Formal gardens require very precise and regular maintenance and are usually labor intensive. The more regular the design, the more any minor flaws will stand out.

Classical and Italianate gardens

The formal gardens that existed in ancient Greece and Rome were the inspiration for the splendid palatial and villa gardens of Italy and France in the 17th and 18th centuries. The essential characteristics of these gardens are their strong architectural and symmetrical designs, which follow closely the proportion and scale of the building that they surround or enhance.

Italianate gardens are often set on elevated or imposing sites, with terraced gardens and flights of steps leading to long, shaded walks, fountains, cascades, and canals. In a hot Mediterranean climate, the cooling benefits of water and avenues or canopies of evergreen trees are all part of the pleasures of these gardens. On the terraces there might be parterre designs with boxwood-lined scrolls of flowerbeds and symmetrically sited topiary obelisks or pyramids. Color is generally limited, however, to the dark green of the plants, the pale colors of the stone and gravel, and the waters. Other typical components include statuary, balustrades, and classically proportioned urns for citrus and ornamental plants.

Many of these features can be incorporated into contemporary garden designs to create a sense of elegance, formality, and ordered calm. Even in a small area, the careful attention to scale, proportion, balance, and harmony noticeable in classical gardens can be copied to create a simple, effective design.

Formal Design
Notable for both its simplicity and symmetry, this formal garden has a pleasing restfulness and is a splendid example of nature tamed by art.

Oriental influences

Garden design in China is an ancient art, going back over 3,000 years. Gardens were created by scholars and philosophers as essentially quiet, sublimely peaceful places for contemplation and meditation. Traditionally, the elements are simple and symbolic, mirroring China's vast and superb landscape of mountains, rocks, falling water, green valleys, and lakes. The inclusion of a few small, scaled-down features (especially rocks) in a walled enclosure is sufficient to suggest these distant scenes. Paths wind or zigzag to reveal gradually a wide variety of views while steeply arched bridges over water offer glimpses of fish or reflections. Views out from these secret gardens are often through cutouts in the walls, encouraging the imagination to fly out of the garden into the landscape beyond.

Planting is restrained and limited, and each tree or shrub in the garden has a meaning or symbolic place in the overall composition. Although China has one of the richest natural floras in the world, only a relatively small range of plants is found in traditional Chinese gardens; this is primarily because the gardens were conceived by artists, poets, or scholars rather than botanists.

Japanese garden styles were borrowed from the Chinese 1,200 years ago and have their sources of inspiration in the hills, lakes, and islands of Japan. They differ from the Chinese in that they have richer, denser plantings of carefully shaped and dwarfed trees and shrubs, symbolic groups of shaped stones, raked gravels or sands around mounded "islands," and stone lanterns. Over the centuries three types of oriental garden have evolved. The first is the flat garden containing the simplest elements of raked sand or gravel, a vertical or flat stone, and a bamboo. The second is the dry garden, which consists of hills and stones in dry watercourses and channels, and is more like a Chinese composition. The third oriental garden is the hill-and-water, or tea, garden, which comprises a complete landscape of hills, a watercourse, and pines and other trees among rocks and a lake.

Simple buildings are an essential feature of Chinese and Japanese gardens, with teahouses, pavilions, or temples all intended for resting, viewing, and contemplation.

While it is difficult to reproduce these oriental gardens accurately in a modern garden, some of the design principles can be copied: balance, simplicity, symbolism, and calm are the elements that are suitable for various garden designs. The imaginative use of hard materials and water can provide inspiration for designing even the smallest garden, while on a larger scale the idea of sculpting the landscape can be helpful in planning garden views.

Formal bedding

With their ordered groups of colorful plants, formal beds have declined in popularity in favor of informal styles, but their bold blocks of color make an immediate and vivid impact. Flowers with strong, even clashing, colors are often included side by side, but the color combinations should be carefully selected so that the use of too many different shades does not detract from the overall design. Try limiting the range of plants used, perhaps with only two or three cultivars or colors, using a formal frame to create a striking display that is also relatively easy to plant and maintain (see also Annuals and Biennials, "Formal bedding designs," p.172).

Many of the plants used traditionally are annuals or half-hardy plants. It may be expensive to buy a large number of these, but most can easily be raised from seed or cuttings. Perennials, bulbs, and some shrubs provide a background structure in planting designs and also help to extend the period of interest.

Topiary

For over 2,000 years, the art and craft of topiary has been practiced in gardens. With time, patience, and

Classical Elegance
The framed steps, controlled use of color, and carefully sited clipped evergreen topiary and hedges show how a classical approach can be adapted to suit a modern garden. Offsetting the steps to one side of the path and mixing different hard materials have helped to soften the formality of the design.

Japanese Style
The calming water, winding paths, strictly limited color, and half-hidden views and features in this garden are characteristic of the mood and style of many oriental gardens.

suitable plants, "living sculptures" can be produced without too much skill being required.

Topiary is often used in formal gardens to add height, shape, and sculptural interest. Well-clipped columns, pyramids, or spirals are used to provide vertical punctuation marks and accentuate the symmetry and proportion of a design. A single piece of topiary forms a strong focal point, while several clipped shrubs or trees grown together can become cornerstones for the garden or a sharply defined framework for looser, more unstructured plantings.

Simple, geometric shapes such as spheres or cones are best used if topiary is desired in a classical or formal garden. More fanciful forms such as birds, animals, or objects – even chesspieces – add a lively and amusing touch; they may be suitable in both formal and informal gardens, depending on the style, but would be inappropriate in a naturalistic or wild garden setting.

The best plants to use are generally those that are evergreen, dense, and slow-growing: yew (*Taxus*) and boxwood (*Buxus sempervirens*) are ideal and provide interest throughout the year. Ivies (*Hedera*) can also be clipped and trained over frames into appropriate shapes. For further details, see Topiary, pp.90–91.

A Topiary Garden

Shrubs shaped into tall spirals, rectangles, and globes add sculptural interest to this formal garden and emphasize the symmetry of its design.

Knot gardens

These were particularly popular in the 16th century, taking the form of interlacing bands and abstract patterns, combining colored sands, gravel, or plants, marked out and framed by low hedges. They often reflected the knots and strapwork patterns of English Elizabethan and Tudor needlework and plaster ceiling decorations. To appreciate the detail, knot gardens are best viewed from above and should be designed so that they can be seen easily from a raised terrace or house window.

Given an appropriate setting and a level, well-drained site, knot gardens are not difficult to create and are fairly easy to maintain. The patterns should be kept simple or the design may be obscured, as well as becoming very difficult to maintain. Some suitable plants are dwarf boxwood, germander (*Teucrium chamaedrys*), and lavender cotton (*Santolina chamaecyparissus*). If using plants rather than gravel to fill in the areas between the hedges, select those that are in keeping with the scale and character of the knot, most low-growing plants are usually suitable. Consider more unusual plantings, perhaps using succulents such as houseleeks (*Sempervivum*) and *Sedum*. Weeds that appear in the gravel should be removed by hand since weedkillers could damage the shallow-rooting hedges.

A Parterre

The intricate and decorative design of low boxwood hedges enclosing masses of pink and red dahlias re-creates the deliberately neat and tailored quality of a classical parterre.

Parterres

Often confused with knot gardens, parterres are larger in scale, and consist of more or less flat, regular flowerbeds that form decorative patterns within a particular design. These designs are often very ambitious and complicated, with flowering, scroll-like patterns or symbolic themes formed initially from low hedges of boxwood. The areas between the hedges are then filled in with gravel of different hues, compact and colorful bedding plants, or plants that have subdued pastel shades. Evergreen shrubs trimmed into neat pyramids or globes, and other clipped formal shapes in yew or boxwood can also be included. Parterres became very popular in the Victorian and Edwardian periods, especially in English parks and gardens, where they were transformed into elaborate floral displays and extravagant bedding patterns.

If designing a parterre in a modern garden, make sure that it is in scale with the size of the house or adjacent terrace.

Sunken gardens

Changes of level, even comparatively small ones, provide interesting features in a garden. A sunken garden that is well devised can add a feeling of space and adventure as well as bring another dimension to the design.

Traditional sunken gardens were usually square or rectangular, enclosed by walls, and surrounded by raised grass or paved paths so that they could be viewed from above. The layout was typically simple and geometrical, with flowerbeds divided by a symmetrical framework of paths and walkways, perhaps with a central sculptural feature such as a fountain or sundial.

Because they are lower than the rest of the garden, sunken gardens are often sheltered and very secluded, with a secret, sanctuary-like quality that is particularly restful and appealing. Herbs, roses, and formal bedding lend themselves particularly well for use in sunken gardens.

Restoring old and historic gardens

If re-creating or restoring an old garden, the degree and nature of the work will vary widely, depending on its size, condition, and character. As well as surveying the site and assessing the condition of the existing features (see "Appraising the site," p.15), try to research the history and development of the garden.

A cautious approach is advisable: seeing the garden throughout a year helps to establish an idea of the original planting design, as well as making it easier to determine which plants must be pruned or renovated and which should be replaced. Clearing overgrown paths, steps, and other hard elements may also be helpful in revealing the original framework of the design. Work on the site should respect any elements of the original garden that remain. Unusual plants may also have survived, such as rare old rose or rhododendron cultivars. There may be old trees that could be preserved with prudent surgery but, if they are diseased or dangerous, they should be removed (see "Cutting down a tree," p.45) and, if appropriate, replaced.

Overgrown hedges may sometimes be cut back hard to renovate them (see Hedges and Screens, pp.58–60). If neglected boxwood hedges remain from an old knot garden or parterre, they may also be renovated if not too old or overgrown, but they do not respond well to severe pruning. If there is any doubt concerning their survival, it is better to replant.

Lawns and other turf areas, if part of the original design, may not be beyond restoration. Often high-quality sod was used in lawnmaking a century or more ago and, if this is still in place, it may respond well to the necessary leveling, feeding, and proper mowing schedules (see "Renovating a neglected lawn," p.285).

2

Ornamental Trees

More than any *other plants, trees give a sense of permanence and maturity to a garden and link it with the broader, external landscape. They add height, structure, and sculptural focal points to a design, while their large scale and distinctive silhouettes form an attractive contrast with the softer lines of other plantings. There is an enormous variety of trees, differing in shape and form as well as in the color and texture of foliage, flowers, and bark. Each has a particular appeal, from the dark, pointing column of a cypress to the blazing fall color of a Japanese maple or the patterned cinnamon trunk of a eucalyptus. Trees may be grown in many ways: in an informal setting, a woodland grouping of redbuds and white birches, surrounded by bulbs, is highly evocative, while in a formal garden, an avenue of copper beeches or pleached lindens is suitably elegant. Some trees, such as magnolias with their exquisite gobletlike blooms, are best sited on their own as a garden feature.*

Designing with trees

Ornamental trees are grown for the beauty of their flowers, bark, or decorative fruits, rather than for edible or timber crops. Many fruit trees, however, are graced by beautiful flowers, and a few ornamental trees such as crabapples (*Malus*) bear rich crops of fruits for preserving. The distinction between trees and shrubs is similarly blurred: trees usually (but not always) have a single trunk; shrubs, for example lilac (*Syringa*), are usually multistemmed, although they sometimes reach treelike proportions.

Choosing trees

Trees are generally the largest, most expensive, and longest-lived garden plants, and selecting and siting them are major design decisions. The fewer trees a garden can accommodate, the more important careful choice and siting become; in a one-tree garden these points are crucial to the success of the design. A tree's general appearance and special features obviously matter, but its suitability for a garden's soil, climate, and exposure, and its ultimate height, spread, and growth rate are equally important. Once a tree is chosen, the design process continues by deciding where to plant it (see "Choosing a planting site," p.39). Garden centers carry a limited range of the most popular ornamental trees. Specialist nurseries, some with a mail-order service, offer a wider choice.

Heights range from around just 3ft (1m) for some dwarf conifers to the massive 300ft (90m) of a redwood (*Sequoia*). Growth rates vary from 1in (2.5cm) or less a year for dwarf conifers to 3ft (1m) or more for some poplars (*Populus*). A young tree in a garden center gives little or no indication of its potential size; some species, particularly conifers, include both miniature and giant cultivars. Select cultivars with care and, if offered substitutes, make sure that they will be equally appropriate for your specific needs.

Trees in the Garden
The architectural outlines of trees add structure to a garden and form a long-term part of the design framework. In a large garden, several trees may be grouped together to create a strong impact of color and form, as with this informal arrangement of maples (Acer) *and other deciduous trees.*

Trees as design elements

Trees create a strong visual impact in the same way as hard landscape features. They also help to form a garden's permanent framework, around which the more temporary elements come and go.

Trees may be used as living sculptures (see "Specimen trees as focal points," p.33): a simple, contrasting setting is most likely to enhance a tree used in this way. A tree with pale foliage looks striking against a

ENCLOSING SPACE
The arching fronds of palms are used as structural features to enclose and delineate a seating area. They create a lush, cool screen that forms a less rigid division than a wall or fence.

hedge of dark green yew (*Taxus*), for example, while the bold winter tracery of bare branches stands out dramatically in front of a white-painted wall.

Used structurally, trees can also define or enclose space. A row or informal clump of trees can mark the boundary of a property, separate one part of the garden from another, or emphasize a path. A pair of trees might act as a verdant frame for a distant view or form a living arch through which the garden is entered.

Shape and form

A tree's shape and form are as important as its size – in setting the mood and style as well as in practical considerations of space. Some trees, such as many ornamental cherries (*Prunus*), are small and charming, while others, such as cedars (*Cedrus*), are grand and monumental. Most can be formal or informal, according to the setting and treatment. Staghorn sumac (*Rhus typhina*) has a striking architectural form, ideal for a modern garden, while the arching fronds of many palms bring lushness to a courtyard or conservatory. Mountain ash (*Sorbus*) and hollies (*Ilex*) are typical English cottage garden trees; Japanese maples (*Acer palmatum*) and the large *Salix matsudana* 'Tortuosa' are suitable for oriental gardens. Native species are ideal for wild gardens.

Narrow, upright trees such as *Malus tschonoskii* are suitable for small gardens but have a formal, sometimes artificial appearance. Round-headed, widely spreading trees seem more informal but cast much more shade and rain shadow, making underplanting difficult, while those with an irregular, open-branch framework have a naturalistic appeal. Conical and pyramidal trees have a sculptural quality, while weeping trees have a softer silhouette.

Consider how long the tree takes to develop its characteristic shape – in some cases, it can be decades. *Prunus* 'Kanzan', for example, has a stiff growth habit when young, with awkwardly angled branches. After ten years the branches begin to arch, and by 30 years the tree has a graceful, rounded crown.

Where space allows, combining contrasting tree shapes can create a dynamic effect, but planting many differently shaped trees may simply appear fussy and uncoordinated.

SPECIMEN TREE
Trees that are particularly attractive or well shaped look good sited on their own so that they stand out in a planting. This double pink hawthorn (Crataegus laevigata) *has a fine show of blossoms that may be enjoyed from all viewpoints as well as forming a cornerstone in the design.*

Specimen trees as focal points

A specimen tree is grown on its own and so can develop and display its full natural beauty without competition from other trees. Depending on the climate, weeping willow (*Salix* x *sepulcralis* 'Chrysocoma'), flowering dogwood (*Cornus florida*), various ornamental cherries (*Prunus*), and palms such as *Howea* and *Phoenix* are popular specimen trees. Select a tree that is the right size for its setting; tiny specimen trees look lost in vast gardens, and outsized ones overbearing in confined spaces.

TREE SHAPES

SPREADING
Prunus americana
(American plum)

PYRAMIDAL
Carpinus betulus
'Fastigiata'
(European hornbeam)

CONICAL
Pseudotsuga menziesii var. *glauca*
(Blue Douglas fir)

WEEPING
Salix caprea 'Kilmarnock'
(Kilmarnock willow)

ROUND-HEADED
Malus
'Magdeburgensis'
(Crabapple)

ARCHING
Archontophoenix alexandrae
(King palm)

COLUMNAR
Acer rubrum
'Columnare'
(Red maple)

FOLIAGE COLOR AND TEXTURE
Here, the fall foliage of a deciduous tree is offset by the blue-green mass of a conifer, creating a contrasting tableau of color, texture, and shape.

Specimen trees, particularly in formal gardens, are traditionally placed in the center of a lawn. Siting a specimen tree to one side, however, can add a sense of liveliness and informality to a design as well as allowing a view down the garden. Other options include planting a specimen tree next to a gate or garden entrance, or at the bottom or top of a flight of steps, to mark the transition from one space in the garden to another.

Planting in a swath of gravel or ground cover plants such as ivy (*Hedera*) or periwinkle (*Vinca*) provides a complementary foil for a specimen tree. In a mixed border, use a tree as the keystone around which to build the color and form of the surrounding groups of plants. A specimen tree may be reflected in a garden pond or offset by a statue or white-painted bench beneath it, so that each element enhances the other to make a complete picture.

COLOR FROM FLOWERS
The large blooms of Magnolia campbellii *var.* mollicomata *stand out against the bare branches.*

Grouping trees

If space allows, consider planting three or more trees together in an informal clump of the same or different species. A group of trees also creates a more substantial, curtain-like frame than a single tree for one or both sides of a view. Clumps of large trees such as oaks (*Quercus*) or beeches (*Fagus*) make focal points on a grand scale, as exemplified in the landscapes designed by the great 18th-century English landscape gardener Capability Brown. In warmer climates, stands of tall, bare-trunked palms can be equally impressive on their own in grass or interplanted with lower-growing or multistemmed species.

On a smaller scale, a modest group of deciduous trees with light foliage, such as poplars (*Populus*) or maples (*Acer*), can form the backbone of an appealing miniature woodland. The dappled shade and leafy soil are perfect for English bluebells (*Hyacinthoides non-scripta*), daffodils, and primroses (*Primula*).

Trees in informal groups can be planted closer than the combined potential spread of their crowns. Relatively tall, narrow, or asymmetrical growth may result but the effect can be pleasantly informal, with intermingled branches forming attractive tracery against the sky.

Features of interest

Although trees are most often valued for their architectural qualities, they also provide interest through particular features such as flowers, foliage, berries, and bark. Site a tree so that its attractive characteristics are shown off to advantage (see also "Successional interest," p.35).

Leaves

For sheer mass and duration of display, leaves are by far the most important feature. Their shape, size, and color offer infinite variation, from the delicate, golden, ferny foliage of *Gleditsia triacanthos* 'Sunburst' to the huge, architectural leaves of palms such as *Phoenix*. Surface texture determines how light is reflected, with glossy leaves adding a bright touch. The density of the canopy ranges from opaque to airy, an important factor if considering underplanting around a tree.

Trees with colored or variegated foliage, such as the reddish purple of *Cercis canadensis* 'Forest Pansy' or the white-edged leaves of *Acer negundo* 'Variegatum', provide a mass of color that contrasts especially well with green-leaved trees.

Some leaves, such as those of eucalyptus, are pleasantly aromatic, while others, such as those of a poplar, quiver in the slightest breeze, adding the extra pleasure of sound.

Flowers

Flowers have a fleeting but memorable presence and range from modest to opulent. Fall, winter, and early spring flowers are especially valuable to provide a display when there may be little interest from other, still-dormant plants.

Flower color should complement the larger design. Pale flowers stand out against dark leaves, while dark flowers show up best in a pale setting. By training climbers such as clematis or roses up mature trees, you can extend the floral display.

Fragrance is a bonus, ranging from the subtle winter perfume of *Acacia dealbata* to the heady summer scent of frangipani (*Plumeria rubra* var. *acutifolia*). For flowers and fragrance a sheltered spot is best, while growing a tree next to a path or patio makes it easy to enjoy its scent.

Fruits, berries, and pods

These can rival or exceed flowers in beauty, ranging from the bright red, strawberry-like fruits of *Arbutus* and

INTEREST FROM BARK AND STEMS
The striking skeleton of a white birch (Betula utilis *var.* jacquemontii) *brings bright relief to the garden in the gloom of winter, while its bold silhouette forms a strong focal point in the planting design throughout the year.*

the yellow crabapples of *Malus* 'Golden Hornet', to the sculptural seedpods of magnolias. In warm climates, trees such as lemons and figs may be laden with eye-catching fruits.

Certain trees such as hollies (*Ilex*) need cross-pollination to fruit; others fruit only when mature or when particular climatic conditions are met. Birds find some berries such as those of mountain ashes (*Sorbus*) tempting and may strip them when barely ripe, but you can choose trees with less appealing berries. Ask garden center staff for advice.

Bark and branches

Bark can provide color and textural interest, especially in winter. Options include the mahogany-red, silky sheen of *Prunus serrula*, the ghostly white bark of *Betula utilis* var. *jacquemontii*, and the exotic patterning of *Eucalyptus dalrympleana* with its green, gray, and creamy white pythonlike bark.

The young branches of the scarlet willow (*Salix alba* 'Britzensis') are scarlet-orange, brilliant when lit from behind, and the golden willow (*S. a.* var. *vitellina*) has rich yellow shoots. These fast-growing trees are best pruned regularly to produce new shoots since these have the strongest color. Some trees produce showy bark only when mature, while others color well when young.

TREES WITH ORNAMENTAL BARK

Acer capillipes

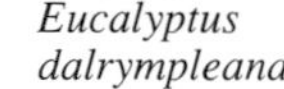

Eucalyptus dalrympleana

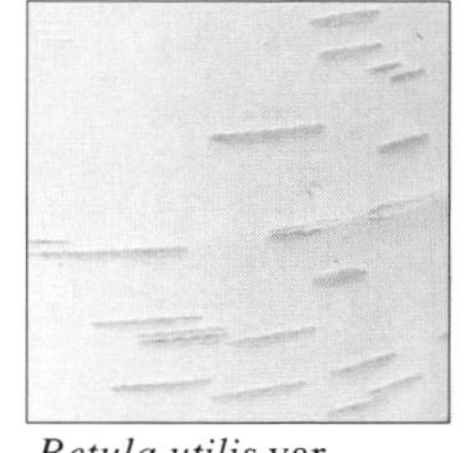

Betula utilis var. *jacquemontii*

Acer griseum

Acer pensylvanicum

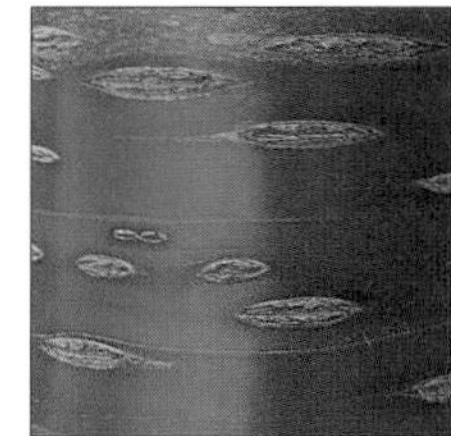

Prunus serrula

Successional interest

Plants that change character with the seasons give a garden a lively tempo. Orchestrate their display with careful choice and planning so that foliage, flowers, fruits, berries, and pods come and go against a permanent framework of branches and bark. By planting trees that flower successively, such as a Judas tree (*Cercis siliquastrum*) for spring, *Catalpa bignonioides* for summer, *Eucryphia* x *nymansensis* for early fall, and *Prunus subhirtella* 'Autumnalis' for winter, ongoing interest is maintained, with the focal point altering as the seasons change. Some trees provide interest all year, either from their evergreen foliage or from their fine shape.

Deciduous trees offer the greatest scope to exploit seasonal changes, especially in spring when many ornamental cherries (*Prunus*) are covered with beautiful blossoms, and in fall when many maples (*Acer*) have brilliantly colored foliage. Evergreen trees, on the other hand, provide a sense of continuity rather than change. Selecting and planting a mixture of deciduous and evergreen trees provides lasting interest in the garden that changes with the seasons to create a dynamic, rather than a static, composition.

Spring and summer

In spring, emerging leaves and flower buds bring fresh life to the bare branches of deciduous trees. Some – such as the silver-leaved *Sorbus aria* 'Lutescens' – have particularly fine young foliage. As the trees come fully into leaf, they take on their characteristic outlines while the canopies provide striking blocks of color and texture as well as shade.

In late spring and summer, flowers ranging in color and form from the trailing yellow chains of goldenchain tree (*Laburnum*) to the dramatic gold-filled white cups of *Stewartias* add extra color and interest, lightening the dense quality of the massed leaves.

Fall and winter

When most herbaceous plants die down in fall, the color provided by deciduous trees is particularly welcome, whether from leaves turning from green through shades of yellow, orange, and red to brown, or from the bright flecks of color from fruits or berries. Ornamental members of the Rosaceae, especially those from the genera *Cotoneaster*, *Crataegus*, *Malus*, and *Sorbus*, include many species, cultivars, and hybrids that have a handsome display in fall. In some cases, the fruits will remain on the tree right through the winter months.

Winter is often regarded as a bleak time, but this is when many trees stand out most effectively with little else in the garden to compete with them. It is in winter that a tree's skeleton or silhouette becomes most noticeable and creates the greatest sculptural impact. The color and texture provided by coniferous and broad-leaved evergreens may be used to complement and soften the architectural, "hard" look of nearby deciduous trees, while patterned, textured, or peeling bark adds an extra point of interest. A few conifers such as forms of Japanese cedar (*Cryptomeria japonica*) have foliage that takes on attractive russet overtones in winter.

Trees for small gardens

For small gardens, trees that do not reach more than about 20ft (6m) in height are the most suitable. There may be space for only one tree (see "Specimen trees as focal points," p.33), so those that provide more than one season of interest are especially appreciated. A Japanese crabapple (*Malus floribunda*), for example, produces masses of crimson buds, then pale pink or white flowers, and finally small red or yellow fruits on arching branches.

A deciduous tree's appearance when leafless is very important in a small garden, since the tree may be bare for six months each year and visible from every window facing the garden. Good choices include staghorn sumac (*Rhus typhina*) and *Pyrus salicifolia* 'Pendula'. Neither has showy flowers but both have handsome foliage and winter silhouettes with character.

Heavily thorned or prickly trees such as hawthorns (*Crataegus*) or hollies (*Ilex*) may be unsuitable in a very small garden because they may restrict access on either side. Those such as lindens (*Tilia*) that drip sticky

SMALL-GARDEN TREE
The modest stature of this Robinia pseudoacacia 'Frisia' *makes it a suitable choice for a small garden. Its airy foliage brightens up the gray stone wall behind and casts only light shade, allowing other plants to grow beneath it.*

honeydew should not be sited where they will overhang an area for sitting outside. If planning to underplant, choose a light-foliaged, deep-rooted tree, since it is hard for small plants to compete with the shallow, greedy roots of ornamental cherries (*Prunus*), for example.

Trees for avenues

Primarily used in formal settings, avenues rely on the uniformity of trees and spacing for their grand presence. The longer and straighter the avenue, the more impact the rhythm of the trees and their shadows have on the landscape. Trees should be sited so that they lead the eye to an impressive focal point; large trees are frequently used on both sides of a driveway to line it. Long-lived forest trees such as beeches (*Fagus*) and horse chestnuts (*Aesculus*) are traditionally used for avenues, while the strong shapes of conifers may be more striking in a contemporary design.

Informal avenues may also be created, perhaps with the trees trained to form an arch over a walkway. The spacing may be less rigid than for a formal avenue to avoid a regimented appearance. Trees such as whitebeam (*Sorbus aria*) or the evergreen Chinese privet (*Ligustrum lucidum*) are particularly suitable for smaller gardens.

FORMAL PLEACHED AVENUE
In this large formal garden, rows of pleached lindens lead the eye to the two arches framing the view beyond, linking the garden with the landscape.

Training for effect

Trees may be pleached to create an elegant formality. The side branches are trained to meet in horizontal, parallel lines and other growth is cut back or interwoven to form a vertical screen. Beeches, lindens (*Tilia*), hornbeams (*Carpinus*), and sycamores (*Platanus*) are traditional trees for pleaching and, in the fruit garden, espaliered apples and pears are a variation of this technique.

Pollarding involves regularly lopping back the entire crown to short stumps that produce dense, thin branches and a single, tight ball of foliage. It achieves a formal, if artificial, result and is useful in urban areas where a natural crown would cast too much shade or impede traffic. Some willows (*Salix*) are often pollarded or coppiced (cut back to ground level) for their colorful young shoots. Coppiced trees look appropriate in a naturalistic or informal setting such as a woodland garden or on the banks of a pond.

INFORMAL WALKWAY
Flowering cherries, arching over a path, bring height and structure to a garden with free, informal planting while complementing the character of the setting. The spring display of the arch draws attention up and away from the borders, which will in turn fill out and become the center of interest as the blossoms fade.

Trees for screens and shelterbelts

Large-scale tree planting can screen buildings and roads, deaden noise, and give shelter from wind and frost. A row of fast-growing Lombardy poplars (*Populus nigra* 'Italica') may be used, but their great height and fingerlike shape tend to highlight

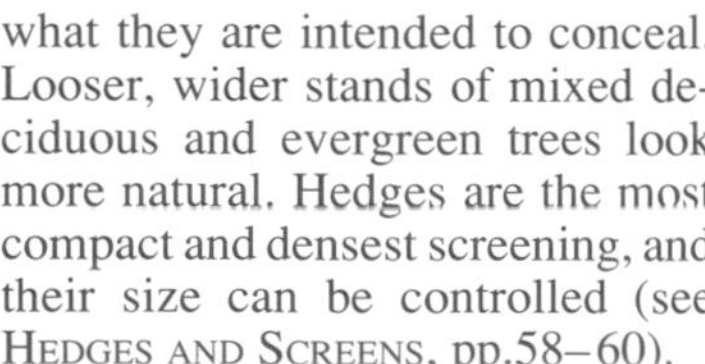

what they are intended to conceal. Looser, wider stands of mixed deciduous and evergreen trees look more natural. Hedges are the most compact and densest screening, and their size can be controlled (see HEDGES AND SCREENS, pp.58–60).

Trees *en masse* can filter wind, reducing potential damage more efficiently than solid barriers, which often create wind swirl on the leeward side. A shelterbelt or group of trees can protect vulnerable plants from frost, especially in spring.

Trees in containers

Growing trees in large pots or tubs greatly extends their design potential. In roof, patio, or courtyard gardens, a collection of containerized trees is the quickest way to create a well-established appearance, adding height and structure to the design.

Use trees in large pots to frame a doorway surrounded by hard paving or to flank steps; these positions are usually appropriate for topiary (see pp.90–91). A group of bonsai, or miniaturized trees in shallow containers, also makes an interesting outdoor feature (see pp.434–5).

Trees too tender to overwinter outside may be grown in containers, displayed outdoors in summer, and moved to a frost-free place as cold weather approaches. Annuals and tender plants such as petunias, fuchsias, or trailing nasturtiums (*Tropaeolum*) may be included in the container for seasonal color and interest, or ivy (*Hedera*) for permanent ground cover.

Containerized trees are long-term features, so use attractive containers. A wide range of styles and materials is available, such as stone or reconstituted-stone, plain or decorated terracotta pots, wooden half barrels, or wooden Versailles planters. Make sure that the containers are frostproof if they are to be used in an area subject to frost.

CONTAINER-PLANTED TREES
Small trees grown in containers are valuable for bringing color, vitality, and sculptural interest to a patio, terrace, or balcony. Here, plain paving acts as a stage on which to display a striking Japanese maple (Acer palmatum 'Dissectum Atropurpureum') *in an ornamental trough.*

Planter's guide to trees

EXPOSED SITES

Trees that tolerate exposed or windy sites; those marked ❧ are not suitable for coastal sites

Acer pseudoplatanus
Betula pendula ❧, *B. pubescens* ❧
Crataegus x *lavallei*, *C. monogyna*
Fraxinus excelsior
Laburnum (spp. and cvs)
Picea abies ❧, *P. sitchensis* ❧
Pinus contorta, *P. nigra*, *P. sylvestris*
Quercus robur
Salix alba
Sorbus aria, *S. aucuparia* (and cvs)

AIR POLLUTION

Trees that tolerate polluted air

Acer platanoides (and cvs), *A. pseudoplatanus* (and cvs), *A. saccharinum* (and cvs)
Aesculus hippocastanum
Alnus cordata, *A. glutinosa*
Betula pendula
Carpinus betulus (and cvs)
Catalpa bignonioides
Corylus colurna
Crataegus
Fraxinus
Ginkgo biloba
Ilex x *altaclerensis*
Magnolia grandiflora
Malus
Populus
Pyrus
Robinia

Pyrus calleryana 'Chanticleer'

Salix
Sophora japonica
Sorbus aria, *S. aucuparia*, *S. intermedia*
Taxus baccata, *T.* x *media*

SALT TOLERATION

Trees that tolerate salt

Acer platanoides (and cvs) *A. pseudoplatanus*
Aesculus
Ailanthus altissima
Carya ovata
Celtis spp.
Elaeagnus angustifolius
Eucalyptus
Fraxinus americana
Gleditsia triacanthos var. *inermis*
Nyssa sylvatica
Picea pungens var. *glauca*
Pinus nigra, *P. sylvestris*
Populus nigra 'Italica'
Quercus rubra, *Q. virginiana*
Taxodium distichum

WINTER INTEREST

Decorative flowers

Magnolia campbellii (and forms)
Prunus mume, *P. subhirtella* 'Autumnalis'

Golden foliage

Chamaecyparis lawsoniana 'Lanei', *C. l.* 'Stewartii', x *Cupressocyparis leylandii* 'Castlewellan Gold'
Cupressus macrocarpa 'Goldcrest'
Juniperus chinensis 'Aurea'

Gray foliage

Cedrus atlantica f. *glauca*
Cupressus glabra 'Pyramidalis'
Eucalyptus pauciflora
Tsuga mertensiana f. *argentea*

Decorative bark

Acer capillipes, *A. davidii*, *A. griseum*, *A. grosseri* var. *hersii*, *A. palmatum* 'Senkaki', *A. pensylvanicum* (and forms)
Arbutus menziesii
Betula albo-sinensis var. *septentrionalis*, *B.* 'Jermyns', *B. pendula*, *B. utilis* var. *jacquemontii*
Eucalyptus dalrympleana
Myrtus luma
Pinus bungeana
Prunus maackii 'Amber Beauty', *P. serrula*
Salix acutifolia 'Blue Streak', *S. alba* 'Britzensis', *S. daphnoides*, *S.* x *sepulcralis*
Stewartia pseudocamellia

TWO OR MORE SEASONS OF INTEREST

All year

Acacia dealbata ✽
Arbutus x *andrachnoides*, *A. menziesii*
Betula albo-sinensis var. *septentrionalis*, *B. ermanii*, *B.* 'Jermyns', *B. utilis* var. *jacquemontii*
Ilex x *altaclerensis* 'Golden King'
Magnolia grandiflora

Winter/Spring

Acer negundo

Spring/Fall

Amelanchier lamarckii
Crataegus x *lavallei* 'Carrierei'
Malus, *M.* 'Golden Hornet'
Prunus 'Okame', *P. sargentii*

Summer/Fall

Catalpa bignonioides
Cladrastis lutea
Cornus kousa, *C. k.* var. *chinensis*
Eucryphia glutinosa
Fagus sylvatica 'Dawyck Gold'
Liriodendron tulipifera
Stewartia pseudocamellia

Fall/Winter

Acer capillipes, *A. davidii*, *A. griseum*, *A. palmatum* 'Senkaki', *A. pensylvanicum*
Stewartia pseudocamellia

TREES FOR CONTAINERS

Acacia dealbata ✽
Acer palmatum cvs
Chamaedorea ✽
Cupressus macrocarpa 'Goldcrest', *C. sempervirens*

Ficus benjamina 'Variegata'

Ficus benjamina ✽
Howea ✽
Jacaranda mimosifolia ✽
Juniperus scopulorum 'Skyrocket'
Lagerstroemia indica ✽
Laurus nobilis
Olea europaea
Phoenix ✽
Prunus 'Amanogawa', *P.* 'Kiku-shidare'
Rhapis ✽
Sabal ✽
Taxus baccata 'Standishii'
Washingtonia ✽

TREES FOR SMALL GARDENS

Those marked ♠ may grow to 20ft (6m) or more

Acer capillipes, *A. griseum* ♠, *A. palmatum*, *A. p.* 'Senkaki', *A.* 'Silver Vein'
Amelanchier lamarckii
Arbutus x *andrachnoides*
Betula albo-sinensis var. *septentrionalis* ♠, *B. ermanii* ♠, *B. pendula* ♠, *B. p.* 'Dalecarlica' ♠, *B. utilis* var. *jacquemontii* ♠
Catalpa bignonioides 'Aurea'
Cercidiphyllum japonicum ♠
Cercis siliquastrum
Cinnamomum ✽
Cornus kousa
Crataegus laevigata 'Paul's Scarlet', *C.* x *lavallei* 'Carrierei'
Eucalyptus niphophila ♠
Eucryphia x *nymansensis* 'Nymansay' ♠
Fagus sylvatica 'Dawyck Gold' ♠
Gleditsia triacanthos 'Sunburst' ♠
Grevillea robusta ✽ ♠
Laburnum x *watereri* 'Vossii'
Magnolia 'Elizabeth', *M.* x *loebneri* 'Merrill', *M. salicifolia*
Malus 'Dartmouth', *M. floribunda*, *M.* 'Golden Hornet', *M. tschonoskii* ♠
Melia azedarach
Phoenix dactylifera ✽ ♠
Pinus halepensis ♠
Prunus – many including *P.* 'Okame', *P.* 'Pandora', *P.* 'Spire', *P. subhirtella*, *P.* x *yedoensis*
Pyrus calleryana 'Chanticleer', *P. salicifolia* 'Pendula'
Robinia pseudoacacia 'Frisia' ♠
Sorbus aria (some forms), *S. aucuparia* (some forms), *S. cashmiriana*, *S. commixta* 'Embley', *S. vilmorinii*
Stewartia pseudocamellia
Vitex agnus-castus

SPECIMEN TREES

Abies magnifica, *A. procera*
Acer pseudoplatanus, *A. rubrum*
Aesculus hippocastanum
Alnus cordata
Betula pendula 'Dalecarlica'
Cedrus
Cercidiphyllum japonicum
Eucalyptus coccifera ✽, *E. dalrympleana*
Fraxinus oxycarpa 'Raywood'
Liquidambar styraciflua

Liriodendron tulipifera

Liriodendron tulipifera
Livistona ✽
Magnolia campbellii, *M. c.* 'Charles Raffill'
Metasequoia glyptostroboides
Nothofagus procera
Nyssa sylvatica
Phoenix ✽
Picea breweriana, *P. omorika*
Pinus nigra, *P. radiata*, *P. sylvestris*, *P. wallichiana*
Platanus x *hispanica*
Roystonea ✽
Salix x *sepulcralis* 'Chrysocoma'
Sequoiadendron giganteum
Tilia 'Petiolaris', *T. platyphyllos*
Tsuga heterophylla
Zelkova carpinifolia

KEY
✽ *Not frost hardy*

Dwarf conifers

Dwarf conifers are particularly suited to the small, modern garden, because they can be grown in compact beds or containers and are easy to maintain. Colors range from rich gold, through brilliant greens to pale blues and silvers, and shapes include globose, pyramidal, and slender, spire-shaped forms. Habits are diverse, with prostrate, mound-forming, erect, and weeping types; the variation in their foliage texture ranges from soft and feathery to dense and spiky. With careful planning, this rich variety of color, form, and texture can provide interest throughout the year. For details on cultivation, routine care, and propagation, see Ornamental Trees, pp.39–46 and 52–7.

Selecting the plants

When selecting conifers for a small space, it is important to recognize the true dwarf and slow-growing species and cultivars; sometimes so-called dwarf conifers are simply slower-growing variants of large trees. Conifers can be very difficult to identify when young, since their juvenile foliage often differs widely from that when adult. Check that the plants are correctly named when buying, to avoid introducing plants that will rapidly outgrow their allotted space. If in any doubt, seek advice from a specialist supplier.

Designing with dwarf conifers

Dwarf conifers are suitable for a wide range of garden situations. They may be planted individually to form a feature or collectively to create a band of colors, and they may be used either to complement other plants or to provide ground cover. Rock gardens, mixed borders, and ornamental containers are also excellent locations for growing many types of dwarf conifer.

Enhancing Conifers
To display dwarf conifers to their best advantage, add other evergreens such as heathers, boxwood, and Vinca *for flower and foliage contrasts.*

A Range of Dwarf Conifers

***Thuja orientalis* 'Aurea Nana'**

***Pinus sylvestris* 'Gold Coin'**

***Juniperus squamata* 'Blue Star'**

***Thuja occidentalis* 'Caespitosa'**

***Picea glauca* var. *albertiana* 'Conica'**

***Picea pungens* 'Montgomery'**

***Chamaecyparis obtusa* 'Nana Aurea'**

***Picea mariana* 'Nana'**

Specimen plants

Some of the slow-growing conifers are suitable for use as specimen plants. Spreading forms, for example, may be used to soften the edges of paths and patios, while columnar specimens create a focal point.

Group planting

If space allows, a collection of dwarf conifers can make a very attractive feature. The color spectrum in conifers may also be used to highlight areas at different times of year; blues and silvers, for example, are at their most beautiful in the cool light of winter, while golds and greens appear at their most fresh in spring.

Steep slopes and banks, which are often difficult to plant successfully, can make striking landscape features when planted with bold drifts of prostrate conifers. Once the plants are established, these often problematic areas are easy to maintain and are more or less weed-free.

Associating with other plants

Dwarf conifers associate well with other plants that are similar in character. They are often used in heather gardens to extend the season of interest and provide contrast in color and form with the foliage and color variants of *Calluna*, *Daboecia*, and *Erica* cultivars. Other complementary plants include dwarf azaleas (*Rhododendron*), boxwood (*Buxus sempervirens*), and the smaller cotoneaster species and cultivars.

Rock gardens

In the rock garden, dwarf conifers provide an air of permanence and create the framework for other plants. The complete repertoire of colors, textures, and shapes can be used, but take care to select plants that will not become too large or dominant. The smaller species and cultivars, such as *Juniperus communis* 'Compressa', are ideal for the miniature landscapes of compact, raised beds as well as for troughs, sink gardens, and other ornamental containers.

Ground cover

Many dwarf conifers make an excellent weed-smothering ground cover, either by forming dense mats, as with *Juniperus horizontalis* cultivars, or by growing taller and spreading to exclude light beneath them. Some Pfitzer junipers are particularly useful for screening utility meters or for softening paving (see Ground Covers, pp.150–51).

Specimen Planting
Ideal for a focal point, the golden yew, Taxus baccata 'Aurea', *has golden foliage all year.*

Soil preparation and planting

ONCE planted, a tree may remain in place for decades or even centuries, so it is essential to provide it with the best possible growing conditions. Climate, soil type, and the amount of light and shelter available all affect a tree's growth, so take these factors into account when deciding on a planting position. Careful preparation and planting as well as aftercare are vital in helping a tree to establish quickly and grow well.

Climate considerations

Before selecting a tree, check that it will flourish in the temperature range, rainfall, and humidity levels of the site. Special local factors, such as strong winds on exposed hilltop sites, will also influence your choice. Even within a species, different cultivars may be more suited to certain conditions, so one plant may thrive while another may not: various cultivars of *Magnolia grandiflora*, for example, tolerate minimum temperatures ranging from 10°F to 43°F (-12°–6°C).

In areas subject to spring frosts, choose trees that come into leaf late because frost frequently damages young growth. In cold areas, trees that are not fully hardy may be grown outdoors, but they will need protection from cold during winter (see COLD AND WIND PROTECTION, pp.520–21) and should be planted in a sheltered site. If growing tender or tropical species in temperate areas, keep them under cover or grow them in containers so that they may be brought indoors for the winter.

Trees rarely grow well in regions where the annual rainfall is less than 10in (250mm) and most need at least four times this amount. Most trees do not require irrigation, however, except when newly planted, since they obtain enough water from rain and, in some areas, from heavy mists condensing on their foliage.

Choosing a planting site

When planting a tree, choose the best position for it within the garden because the microclimate may vary considerably from one part to another. Make sure that the selected site will provide an appropriate amount of light and shelter: many

CHOOSING TREES

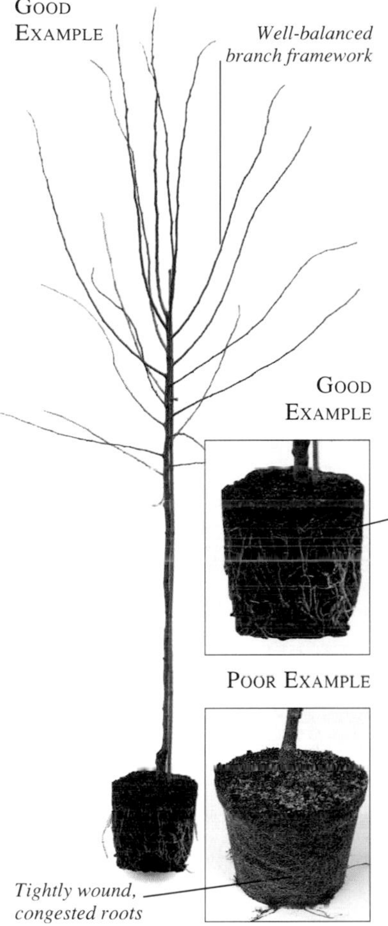

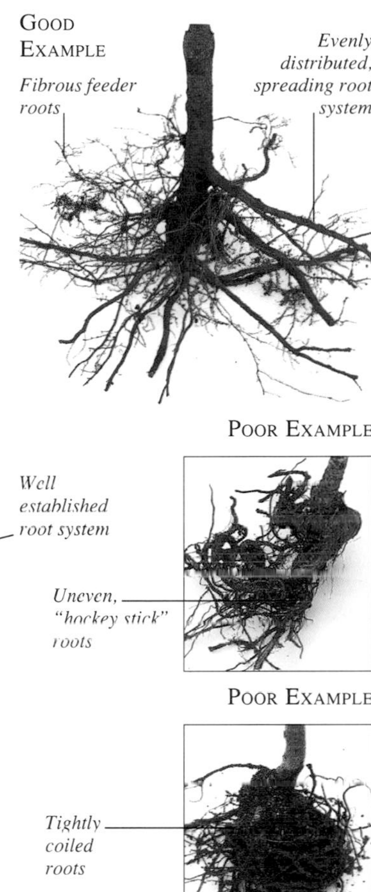

x CUPRESSOCYPARIS LEYLANDII

large-leaved trees, for example, will thrive in a sheltered, partially shaded position but may not grow well in an exposed site where the foliage would be subjected to strong winds and high light levels.

In coastal areas, choose a planting site that is sheltered since sea spray and salt-laden winds (even a few miles inland) may scorch foliage and cause damage to the growth buds. Some trees, however, tolerate coastal conditions (see "Planter's guide to trees," p.37) and may be planted as windbreaks to help screen other, more vulnerable, plants from strong winds.

Similarly, if trees are being planted on a slope, bear in mind that tender trees are more likely to succeed in a position halfway down where it is usually warmer and more sheltered than at either the top or the bottom (see also "Frost pockets and frost damage," p.515).

It is best not to plant trees very close to walls or buildings; otherwise, when young, the trees may suffer from reduced light and moisture as a result of the "rain shadow" effect. In addition, the strong, fibrous roots of some trees, for example poplars (*Populus*) and willows (*Salix*), may damage drains and the foundations of buildings as they develop. Tender species may be planted near a warm wall, however; there they will benefit from the wall's retained heat and so may be grown in a region where they would fail to survive in more open conditions.

When choosing a site, ensure that the trees will not interfere with overhead wires and underground cables and pipes, which may obstruct trees or be damaged by them.

Selecting a tree

Trees may be bought container-grown, bare-root, or balled-and-burlapped, although conifers and palms are rarely available bare-root. They may be purchased in a variety of sizes and stages of maturity, from seedlings to semimature trees. Young trees tend to become established more quickly than older trees, while the latter create a strong and immediate impact in the garden but are more expensive. Whichever type you choose, check that the tree has healthy, vigorous top growth and roots with no sign of pests, disease, or damage. Look for branch and root systems that are well developed and evenly balanced around the stem.

Container-grown trees

These are widely available and may be planted throughout the growing season. Container-grown trees are usually more expensive than bare-root or balled-and-burlapped specimens of comparable size. This is the best method of buying trees that do not establish easily when transplanted, such as magnolias and *Eucalyptus*, since there is less root disturbance. Exotic and nonnative trees are usually sold this way.

Before buying a tree, remove it from its container, if possible, so that you can see the roots clearly. Do not buy a potbound tree with a mass of congested roots or one with thick roots protruding through the drainage holes. Such trees may not establish well and, because the resulting root system is unstable and not well anchored, the mature tree will be liable to wind-rock. Equally, if the soil mix does not cling to the root ball when the tree is removed from its container, do not buy it since its root system is not sufficiently established. Make sure that the container is large enough in relation to the tree: as a guide, the container's diameter should be at least one-sixth of the tree's height. A tall tree growing in a small container will almost certainly be potbound.

The potting medium is also important: trees that are containerized in soil-based mixes establish more quickly in open ground than those grown in other mixes, since they have less of an adjustment to make to the surrounding soil.

Bare-root trees

Trees sold bare-root, which are almost always deciduous, are grown in open ground, then lifted with virtually no soil around the roots. It is essential to buy them when they are dormant, preferably in fall or early spring; they are unlikely to survive transplanting if bought and planted when in leaf. Ash (*Fraxinus*), poplars (*Populus*), and many rosaceous trees such as crabapples (*Malus*) are often sold bare-root.

Make sure that the tree you choose has well-developed roots spreading evenly in all directions. A number of small roots about $^{1}/_{16}$–$^{1}/_{4}$in (2–5mm) in diameter is a good sign because it indicates that they have been undercut every year or so, a technique that encourages sturdy growth and vigorous root systems. Examine the roots to check that they are not damaged or diseased and that there is no sign of dryness that may have been caused by exposure to wind. Do not buy trees with "hockey stick" roots, where all the growth is on one side; these will not establish well.

Balled-and-burlapped trees

These trees are also grown in open ground, but, when the trees are lifted, the roots and surrounding soil are wrapped in burlap or netting to hold the root ball together and to stop the roots from drying out. Deciduous trees of more than 12ft (4m), and many evergreens, especially conifers and palms of more than 5ft (1.5m), are often sold this way.

Buy and plant a balled-and-burlapped tree when dormant in fall or early spring, following the same criteria as for both container-grown and bare-root trees. Check that the

Staking

Because the root system of a newly planted tree will need one or more growing seasons to anchor it firmly in the soil, staking against strong winds may be necessary initially. Drive the stake in about 24in (60cm) below soil level so that it is completely stable. After two or three years, the tree should be sufficiently established for the stake to be removed. The method of support chosen depends on the tree, the proposed planting site, and personal preference.

Traditionally, a high, vertical stake has been used, placed on the side of the prevailing wind and long enough to reach to just below the crown. A low stake is now often preferred, since it allows the tree to move naturally in the wind.

With flexible-stemmed trees such as crabapples, use a high stake in the first year after planting, cut it down to the lower level in the second year, and remove the stake in the third year.

For container-grown and balled-and-burlapped trees, a low stake angled into the prevailing wind is preferable since it can be driven in clear of the root ball even after the tree has been planted. Alternatively, space two or three vertical low stakes evenly around the tree outside the area of the ball.

In windy sites or for trees more than 12ft (4m) tall, insert two vertical stakes when planting, one on either side of the root ball, to provide support. Large trees are often secured by guy ropes attached to low stakes. Covering the guys with hose lengths or white tape makes them more visible and helps prevent the likelihood of people tripping over them.

High Stake
Drive in a single, high stake before planting. Secure the tree to the stake using two padded or buckle-and-spacer ties.

Low Stake
A low stake allows the tree's stem some movement; insert it so that only about 20in (50cm) protrudes above ground level.

Angled Stake
A low, angled stake may be added after planting. Drive it into the ground at a 45° angle, leaning into the prevailing wind.

Two Stakes
Insert two stakes so that they are on opposite sides of the tree, and secure them to the tree with heavy-duty rubber ties.

Guy Ropes
For strong support, attach guy ropes to low stakes angled at 45° away from the tree. Space the guys evenly around the tree and secure them to the stakes with long eye bolts or U bolts which you can adjust when necessary (see inset, far right). Cushion the guys with hose lengths where they touch the tree to prevent damage (see inset, right).

Tree ties

Tree ties need to be secure, long-lasting, and able to accommodate the tree's girth as it grows without cutting into the bark. Various commercial ties are available, or you can make them from nylon webbing or rubber tubing. To prevent the stake from chafing the bark, use a spacer or form a padded tie into a figure eight and nail it to the stake. When using two or three stakes, secure the tree to the stakes with heavy-duty rubber or plastic strips. If supporting a large tree with guys, use multistrand wire or nylon rope.

Buckle-and-spacer Tie
Thread the tie through the spacer, around the tree, and back through the spacer; buckle it so that it is taut but will not damage the bark.

Rubber Tie
If using a rubber or plastic tie without a buckle, nail it to the stake to prevent bark damage caused by friction.

root ball is firm and its wrapping is intact before purchase: if there is any sign of drying out or root damage, the tree is less likely to establish quickly or well.

Seedlings, transplants, and whips

Seedlings up to one year old are usually available only from specialist nurseries. Transplants are seedlings or cuttings that have been transplanted in the nursery and are up to four years old. They make sturdy, bushy plants and are usually 2–4ft (60cm–1.2m) tall. The age and treatment may be given by the nursery in shorthand: "1 + 1" denotes a seedling left for one year in the seedbed and then transplanted for a further season; "1 u 1" means that it was undercut (see "Bare-root trees," p.40) after the first year and remained *in situ* for a further year.

Whips are single, whiplike shoots sold by height; they are generally 3–6ft (1–2m) tall and will have been transplanted at least once.

Feathered trees

These trees have a single main leader with a spread of lateral branches, or "feathers," down to ground level. They will have been transplanted at least once and are usually 6–8ft (2–2.5m) tall.

Standards and large trees

Standard trees are approximately 10ft (3m) high and have been pruned to create a single main stem without any lateral branches for about 6ft (2m) above ground level. Central-leader standards are similar to feathered trees but have a clear length of stem at the base, while branched-head standards have been pruned so that they have an open center. Trees of 6½ft (2.1m) in height with a clear stem of 4–5ft (1.2–1.5m) are half-standards, while trees 11ft (3.5m) tall are selected standards. Larger trees, available from specialist nurseries, include extraheavy standards which are 15ft (5m) tall and semimature trees which are 15–40ft (5–12m).

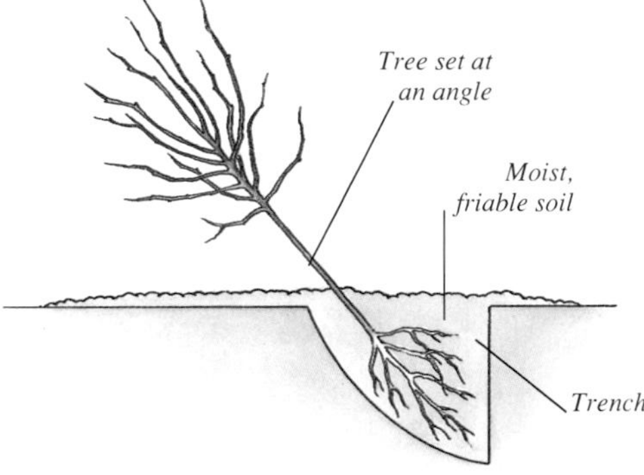

Heeling in
If planting is delayed, heel in the tree: first prepare a trench, then set the tree in it. Angle the tree so that the trunk is supported. Cover the roots and base of the trunk with moist, friable soil and do not allow the roots to dry out.

When to plant

Container-grown trees may be planted at any time of year, except during drought or cold. Deciduous bare-root trees should be planted between midfall and midspring (avoiding periods of severe cold). Hardy evergreens and hardy deciduous trees with fleshy roots should be planted in midfall or mid- to late spring, and half-hardy trees in midspring. Balled-and-burlapped trees are best planted in early to midfall or mid- to late spring; if deciduous, they may be planted out in winter in mild conditions.

Fall planting allows a tree's roots to become established before the onset of winter. This helps the tree to withstand any hot, dry spells the following summer. In cold regions, however, planting in spring may allow trees to establish more successfully. If planting in winter, the ground may be lifted by subsequent cold spells and if so should be refirmed once it has thawed.

Heeling in

It is best to plant trees as soon as possible after purchase, although container-grown and balled-and-burlapped trees may be stored in frost-free conditions for a few weeks if kept moist. If a further delay is unavoidable, heel in the trees in a sheltered place, and keep moist.

Soil preparation

Preparing the site in advance allows the soil to settle and minimizes delay between buying and planting a tree. Choose a well-drained site; one that is poorly drained may need to be improved before planting (see "Improving drainage," p.531). Remove all plant growth in the immediate area to eliminate competition for nutrients and water in the soil, then double dig the soil, incorporating organic matter in the lower trench (see "Double digging," p.528).

Most trees require a soil depth of 20in–3ft (50cm–1m) to grow well. Some may grow on soils only 6in (15cm) deep, although they are then less stable and less drought-tolerant.

Trees that Prefer Acid Soil

Abies
Arbutus menziesii
Cercidiphyllum japonicum
Cornus nuttallii
Cryptomeria
Embothrium coccineum
Fagus grandifolia
Magnolia acuminata, *M. campbellii* (and cvs)

Magnolia campbellii

Michelia ❄
Oxydendrum arboreum
Picea (most spp.)
Pseudolarix amabilis
Pseudotsuga
Rhodoleia championii ❄
Sciadopitys verticillata
Stewartia
Styrax japonica
Tsuga heterophylla

Trees that Tolerate very Alkaline Soil

Acer campestre, *A. lobelii*, *A. negundo* (and cvs), *A. platanoides* (and cvs)
Aesculus
Carpinus betulus
Cedrus libani
Cercis siliquastrum
Chamaecyparis lawsoniana (and cvs)
Crataegus
x *Cupressocyparis leylandii* (and cvs)
Cupressus glabra
Fagus sylvatica (and cvs)
Fraxinus excelsior, *F. ornus*
Juniperus
Malus
Morus nigra
Ostrya carpinifolia
Phillyrea latifolia
Pinus nigra
Populus alba
Prunus avium 'Plena', *P. sargentii*

Prunus sargentii

Pyrus (spp. and cvs)
Robinia (spp. and cvs)
Sorbus aria (and cvs)
Taxus baccata (and cvs)
Thuja
Tilia tomentosa

Key
❄ *Not frost hardy*

Planting trees

Once the site has been prepared, dig the planting hole between two and four times the width of the tree's root ball, depending on whether the tree is container-grown, bare-root, or balled-and-burlapped. If doing this in advance, backfill it loosely until ready to plant the tree so that the soil remains warm. Do not improve the soil that has been removed since this inhibits the tree roots from growing beyond the planting hole, especially on poor soils. Fork over the sides and base of the hole to break up the soil and allow the tree roots to spread into it more easily; this is particularly important in heavy, sticky soils. If you are using a single stake, drive it into the hole just off-center before planting the tree to ensure that the root ball is not damaged later (see also "Staking," p.40).

Container-grown trees

First thoroughly moisten the soil mix in the container – if it is very dry, stand the container in water for half an hour or until the soil mix is moist throughout. Then remove the container, cutting it away if necessary, taking care not to damage the roots. Gently tease out the roots with your fingers or a hand fork to encourage them to grow into the surrounding soil; this is essential with a potbound plant. If there are any broken or damaged roots, trim them back at this stage with pruners. It is important to check that the planting depth is correct. If a tree is planted too deeply, its roots may not receive enough oxygen and may slow down in growth or even die; if planted too shallowly, the roots may dry out. Place the tree in the hole and locate the soil mark – a dark mark near the base of the stem indicating the soil

TREES THAT PREFER SANDY SOIL

Abies grandis
Acacia dealbata ❄
Acer negundo (and cvs)
Agonis flexuosa ❄
Banksia serrata ❄
Betula pendula (and cvs)
Castanea sativa
Celtis australis
Cercis siliquastrum
Cupressus glabra
Eucalyptus ficifolia ❄
Gleditsia triacanthos
Juniperus
Larix decidua
Melia azedarach
Nothofagus obliqua
Phoenix canariensis ❄
Pinus pinaster, *P. radiata*
Quercus ilex
Schinus molle ❄
Tabebuia chrysotricha ❄
Thuja occidentalis (and cvs)

Tabebuia chrysotricha

TREES THAT TOLERATE CLAY SOIL

Acer platanoides (and cvs)
Castanospermum australe ❄
Crataegus laevigata (and cvs)
Fraxinus
Juglans nigra
Malus

Malus 'Cowichan'

Metasequoia glyptostroboides
Populus
Pterocarya fraxinifolia
Pyrus calleryana 'Chanticleer'
Quercus palustris, *Q. robur*
Salix
Taxodium distichum

KEY
❄ *Not frost hardy*

PLANTING A CONTAINER-GROWN TREE

1 *Mark out the area of the hole to be dug – about 3 or 4 times the diameter of the tree's root ball. Lift any turf or weeds, then dig out the hole to about $1^1/_2$ times the depth of the root ball.*

2 *Scarify the sides and bottom of the hole with a fork. There is no need to improve the soil.*

3 *If using one stake, hammer it into the hole, just off-center and on the windward side.*

4 *Lay the tree on its side and slide it out of the pot. Gently tease out the roots without breaking up the root ball and remove any weeds from the soil mix.*

5 *Hold the tree next to the stake and spread out the roots. Lay a stake across the hole to check the planting depth. Adjust this by adding or removing some soil.*

6 *Backfill around the tree with more topsoil, working it down the root ball, then build a ring of soil around the hole to form a water-catching moat.*

7 *Cut back damaged stems, long side shoots, and lower feathers. Mulch 2–3in (5–7cm) deep around the tree.*

level when the tree was growing in the nursery. Place a stake across the hole alongside the stem and add or remove soil from beneath the root ball, if necessary, so that the soil mark is level with the stake.

Backfill the hole, firming the soil in stages to remove any air pockets; take care not to firm too heavily on clay soils since this may compact the ground and impede drainage. On sandy soils, a shallow moat around the tree helps to channel water to the roots. Conversely, on clay soils, a slight mound around the stem drains water away from the root ball.

Lightly prune the top-growth to balance it with the root system (see "Formative pruning," p.48), then secure the tree to the stake with one or more ties (see "Tree ties," p.41). Water well and apply a thick mulch to conserve moisture in the area where the roots will be developing.

Bare-root trees

Prepare the site in the same way as for container-grown trees, ensuring that the planting hole is wide enough for the tree's roots to be spread out fully. Trim back any damaged roots to healthy growth. If using a single stake, drive it in just off-center of the planting hole, and spread out the tree's roots around it in the hole. Adjust the planting depth if necessary, then partly backfill the hole and gently shake the stem up and down to settle the soil around the roots. Firm the backfilled soil in stages, taking care not to damage the roots. Finally, water the tree well and mulch the area around it.

Balled-and-burlapped trees

The method of planting balled-and-burlapped trees is very similar to that used for container-grown trees. However, the planting hole should be twice the width of the ball, or, in heavy clay soils, three times the width. Place the tree in the hole at the correct depth, then loosen the burlap or netting surrounding the root ball. If using an angled stake or two stakes, one on either side of the root ball, drive them in at this stage; they should rest firmly against the ball without piercing it.

In heavy clay soils, it is possible to improve drainage by planting so that the top of the root ball is slightly above soil level, and covering the exposed part with 2–3in (5–7cm) of friable soil, leaving a gap of 1–2in (2.5–5cm) around the stem. Water thoroughly and mulch.

Aftercare

For the first two or three years after planting, it is important to provide trees with plenty of water, particularly in dry spells. Failure to do this may impede establishment, or the tree may even die. Keep the surrounding area clear of grass and weeds, and feed and mulch regularly (see "Routine care," pp.44–6).

Some trees need extra protection from cold and wind; evergreens in an exposed site should be protected initially from drying winds with windbreaks, for example (see COLD AND WIND PROTECTION, pp.520–21).

PLANTING A BALLED-AND-BURLAPPED TREE

1 Dig a planting hole 2–3 times the diameter of the tree's root ball. Mix the removed soil with well-rotted organic matter, then place the tree in the hole and untie the wrapping.

2 Tilt the tree to one side and roll the material up under the root ball, then tilt the tree the other way and carefully pull out the material. Backfill the hole, firm, and water well.

Protecting the stem

In many regions, it is necessary to protect young trees from damage caused by rabbits or other animals that strip bark. Either surround the tree with a barrier of chicken wire or wire netting secured in place with several stakes, or place a commercial tree guard around the tree trunk. There are many types of guard available from garden centers and nurseries, including spiral wraparound guards made of flexible plastic, as well as those made from wire mesh or heavy-duty plastic. Degradable plastic-net tree guards are also available in a range of heights from 2ft (60cm) up to 6ft (2m).

In exposed sites, such as on hillsides, tree shelters may be used to assist young transplants and whips to become well established; these degradable plastic structures are up to 4ft (1.2m) long, and between 3in (8cm) and 6in (15cm) across.

A

B

C

D

Protect the bark of newly planted trees from animal damage with a barrier of wire mesh or netting secured to the ground with stakes (A), *a rigid plastic tree shelter* (B), *a heavy-duty rubber or plastic stem guard* (C), *or a spiral, wraparound plastic guard* (D).

Planting trees in containers

Containers are excellent for displaying trees on a patio, for tender trees that need to be brought under cover in winter, and for species that prefer a different soil type from that in the open garden.

Use a container that has a diameter of between one-sixth and one-quarter of the tree's height and a depth of at least one and a half times the tree's root ball. This provides a fairly even soil temperature and a good reserve of moisture, and also allows space for the roots to develop. Make sure that there are drainage holes to prevent waterlogging.

Preparing the container

If reusing an old container, scrub the inside with water to remove any disease-causing organisms. Cover all holes with broken crocks and add a layer at least 1in (2.5cm) deep of broken crocks or coarse gravel. Then add a soil-based potting mix enriched with a slow-release fertilizer. If planting a standard, insert a stake into the soil mix before planting.

Planting

Prepare the tree and check the planting depth as for container-grown trees (see opposite). After planting, firm the tree in well and top-dress with an organic or grit mulch 1–1½in (2.5–4cm) deep to help retain moisture and prevent compaction of the soil mix. Then water well, using soft water or rainwater for lime-hating species. Stand the container on bricks or blocks to aid free drainage.

Insert the stake into the soil mix and then plant the tree so that the soil mark is about 1½–2in (4–5cm) below the rim.

Routine care

THE amount of maintenance that a tree needs largely depends on the species, microclimate, soil type, and site. Most trees require watering, feeding, and a clear, weed-free area during the first few years if they are to establish well. Container-planted trees should also be regularly top-dressed and occasionally repotted. In addition, other procedures such as removing suckers or controlling pests or diseases are sometimes necessary, while in certain circumstances – for example, if a tree is not thriving – the best solution may be either to cut down the tree or to transplant it.

Watering

Most trees need plenty of water to grow well, especially on light, sandy soil or if they have been planted recently. As a general guide, apply 10–15 gallons (50–75 liters) of water for every square yard (square meter) of area beneath the canopy each week in dry weather during the growing season. Once they have become well established, most trees need to be irrigated only during drought.

Fertilizing

All trees benefit from feeding, particularly on soils low in nutrients and during the first few years after planting. Older trees usually require feeding only occasionally. Trees grown for their flowers and fruit require more potassium and phosphorus than do trees grown for their foliage, which need more nitrogen.

Organic fertilizers such as well-rotted manure or compost are usually applied as a mulch: in fall, or during any frost-free period in the dormant season, spread the material in a layer 2–3in (5–8cm) deep around the tree, keeping a clear area immediately around the trunk. When feeding a young tree, extend the mulch to the drip line, the ground beneath the outer edge of the canopy. An area 10–12ft (3–4m) in diameter is appropriate for a larger tree.

ROOT FEEDING
The root feeder's long nozzle (inset) injects fertilizer deep into the soil.

Inorganic fertilizers are usually applied in spring. Broadcast the fertilizer around the base of the tree, at a rate of 2oz/sq yd (50g/sq m), or mix it with compost and insert it into small holes dug 6ft (2m) apart around the drip line.

Trees planted in grassed areas may need to be fed every year if they are not thriving. Grass between the trunk and the drip line may be removed by hand or sprayed with herbicide, and a mulch applied. Alternatively, use a root feeder (see left) to inject the fertilizer deep into the soil. Push the feeder vertically into the soil at the recommended depth, distributing the total amount of fertilizer among several holes outside the drip line.

Mulching

Mulching around a tree keeps down weeds, reduces harmful temperature extremes around the roots, and cuts down moisture loss from the soil surface. In general, organic materials such as bark chips are used because they are also attractive. Black plastic is also useful, but do not use

Maintaining trees planted in containers

Container-planted trees generally require watering and feeding more frequently than those planted in open ground since the small amount of soil mix in which they are growing can store only limited reserves of water and nutrients. During hot, dry weather, they may need to be watered at least twice a day. Apply an annual mulch of bark chips or similar material on top of the soil mix to help retain moisture. In addition, top-dress the tree each spring before it starts into growth. This involves replacing some of the old soil mix with fresh soil mix enriched with fertilizer. At the same time, prune back any dead, damaged, weak, or straggly stems to rejuvenate the tree and ensure that it produces healthy, vigorous growth.

Every three to five years, repot the tree completely, either into the same container or, preferably, into a larger one. To do this, first remove the tree carefully from the container, then tease out the roots, cutting back by up to one-third any that are long, large, or coarse. Soak the root system well, if dry, then repot the tree into fresh soil mix (see "Planting trees in containers," p.43). If using the same container, wash it out before adding fresh soil mix and repotting.

TOP-DRESSING

1 *Using a trowel or your hands, remove any mulch and the top 2in (5cm) of soil mix.*

2 *Replenish the container with fresh soil mix combined with a slow-release fertilizer. Water the soil mix well, and mulch.*

REPOTTING

1 *Carefully lay the tree on its side and, with one hand supporting the stem and root ball, knock it out of its pot by sharply tapping the base. Remove any top-dressing or mulch material.*

2 *Using a hand fork, gently tease out the roots, removing some of the old soil mix. Trim any long, large or coarse roots.*

3 *Repot the tree so that the fresh soil mix reaches the soil mark. Firm with your fingers, water well, and mulch.*

REMOVING SUCKERS

Using pruners, cut off the suckers as close to the trunk as possible, then pare over the cut surface with a knife. Rub off any regrowth as it appears.

clear plastic since heat is rapidly transferred to the soil and may damage surface roots. Mulches that are rich in nutrients are usually used only if a tree needs feeding.

Mulches are best applied in spring but, provided that the soil is moist, they may be spread at any time except during cold or drought. Apply mulch over an area about 12–18in (30–45cm) larger than the tree's root system. Add some fresh mulch every year or two under young trees.

Weeding

The area beneath a tree's canopy should be kept clear of weeds and grass because this ensures that the tree's feeding roots do not need to compete for water and nutrients. If a tree's growth is too rapid, retaining or establishing grass around it will help to reduce its vigor by competing for food and water.

Some weedkillers may be used around trees because they do not harm tree roots. Mulching, however, should make weeding largely unnecessary. For treatment of weeds, see "Weeds," pp.575–9.

Suckers and water shoots

Suckers and water shoots will divert nutrients from the main shoots of the tree if they are left to develop unchecked. Remove them as soon as they appear.

Stem and root suckers

A tree may produce both stem and root suckers: a stem sucker is a shoot that appears just beneath the graft union on the rootstock of a grafted tree; a root sucker is one that develops directly from the roots. Suckers of a grafted plant may quickly grow larger than the top-growth or even replace it within a few years so that the rootstock species predominates rather than the grafted cultivar.

Trees that are particularly vigorous or that have roots near the soil surface, such as poplars (*Populus*) and ornamental cherries (*Prunus*), may form root suckers if the root system is damaged. They may be used for propagation, but are a nuisance if they come up in lawns and paths.

Cut or pull off the suckers as close to the base as possible, digging down to where the sucker joins the root, if necessary. For some genera such as *Prunus*, painting the cuts on the roots with ammonium sulphamate usually prevents regrowth and, in small amounts, does not harm the tree.

Water shoots

Epicormic, or water, shoots may grow directly out of the trunk, often around pruning wounds. Rub them out with your fingers or thumb as soon as they appear, or cut them back to the base and rub them out as they regrow.

Frost and wind

Trees may be broken up by strong winds, and severe frosts may harm young growth, so provide protection such as windbreaks, particularly in exposed sites. Windbreaks may be natural, such as hedges, or constructed, such as fencing (see also "How a windbreak works," p.519).

The soil around newly planted trees may be lifted by frost heaving; if this occurs, refirm it after thawing so that the roots do not dry out. For further information, see COLD AND WIND PROTECTION, pp.520–21.

Tree problems

Lack of vigor is a reliable indicator that there is a problem with a tree. As well as checking for pests and diseases, make sure that the tree has not been planted too deeply or that the roots and stems have not been damaged, since these are possible causes of poor growth and dieback.

The most common pests are aphids (p.552) and spider mites (p.552). A wide range of diseases attacks trees; most are specific to a few species. Some, including fire blight (p.555), may be lethal. To minimize risk, keep trees properly fed and maintained and the surrounding area clear of weeds and debris.

Cutting down a tree

Tree felling, which may be undertaken at any time of year, is a skilled and potentially dangerous operation; if the tree is taller than 15ft (5m), it should be tackled by a tree surgeon. Ensure that the tree, if on a boundary, legally belongs to you; if not, you should get written permission from your neighbor to remove it.

Make sure that there is space for the tree to fall safely and that there is an escape route at right angles to the proposed fall line, so that you can move out of the way.

A tree is usually taken down in stages. First remove any large branches in sections (see "Removing a branch," p.47), then cut down the rest of the trunk by taking out a wedge of wood on the side where you want the tree to fall and making another cut on the opposite side of the trunk. The tree can then be pushed over in the required direction. If felling a large tree, tie ropes around the trunk to guide its fall.

It is best to remove the stump, but if this is impractical it may be treated with chemicals. If left to rot it may take many years to disappear. Dig out the stump and any large roots; tough roots should be severed with an ax. If the stump is large, you may need to employ a contractor to grind it up or winch it out with special tools.

Alternatively, cut the stump flush with the ground and treat the cut surface with a commercial solution of ammonium sulphamate. Allow at least 12 weeks before planting in the vicinity.

1 *On the side where you want the tree to fall, make an angled cut. It should be just over one-third of the trunk diameter and about 3ft (1m) from the ground.*

2 *Cut out a wedge by sawing horizontally to meet the base of the angled cut. Remove the wedge; this ensures that the tree will fall in the right direction.*

3 *On the opposite side of the trunk, make the final cut just above the base of the wedge cut. As the tree starts to fall, push it in the right direction if necessary.*

4 *Remove the remaining stump by digging a wide trench around it, loosening the roots with a fork or spade, and then winching or digging it out.*

Transplanting a tree

It is best to prepare the tree a year before transplanting because this will greatly increase its chances of reestablishing. Unless the tree is quite young, it may be difficult to transplant and may not adjust well; if taller than 8ft (2.5m), it may be difficult to establish in its new position. Large trees may need to be transplanted by a specialist.

Preparation

In early fall the year before the planned move, while the soil is still warm and the tree roots are in active growth, mark out the optimum rootball diameter for the tree – about one-third of its height. Dig a trench about 12in (30cm) wide and 24in (60cm) deep just outside the marked area, and mix the removed soil with large quantities of well-rotted organic matter.

Using a sharp spade, undercut the root ball as far as possible to sever any large, coarse roots. This has the benefit of stimulating the growth of fibrous feeder roots, which will help the tree to develop and grow successfully after transplanting. Then replace the mixture of soil and organic matter in the trench.

Lifting the tree

Transplant the tree the following fall (see "When to plant," p.41), first carefully tying in the branches to the central stem to protect them and to increase the amount of working space around the tree.

Dig a trench just outside the one made the previous year and of similar dimensions, and gradually fork away the excess soil until the root ball is of a manageable size and weight; take care not to damage the fibrous roots. Then cut through any roots underneath the root ball to separate it completely from the surrounding soil. Wrap the root ball securely in some burlap or plastic; this will hold it together and stop the roots from drying out while the tree is removed from the hole and transported to its new position.

Replanting

The tree may then be replanted in its new site (see *Planting a Balled-and-burlapped Tree*, p.43). Until it is well established, support the tree with guy ropes (see "Staking," p.40), and keep it mulched and well watered. If it is impossible to replant the tree immediately, give it the same care as you would a newly purchased tree (see *Heeling In*, p.41).

How to Transplant a Young Tree

1 *After digging a trench around the tree, carefully fork away the soil from around the root ball.*

2 *Undercut the root ball with a spade, and cut back any awkward roots protruding from the root ball (see inset).*

3 *Tilt the tree to slide a roll of burlap underneath; tilt the other way and pull the burlap through. The root ball should rest on the center of the burlap.*

4 *Pull the burlap up around the root ball so that it is completely covered. Tie it securely with rope to keep the root ball intact while the tree is being moved.*

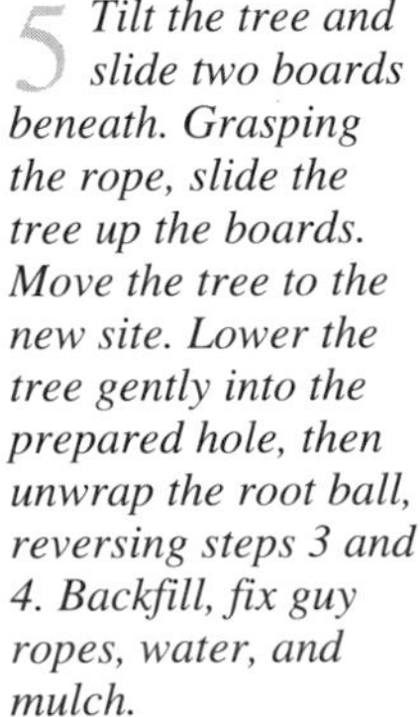

5 *Tilt the tree and slide two boards beneath. Grasping the rope, slide the tree up the boards. Move the tree to the new site. Lower the tree gently into the prepared hole, then unwrap the root ball, reversing steps 3 and 4. Backfill, fix guy ropes, water, and mulch.*

Changing the grade

If it is necessary to change the grade (soil level) around a large tree, for example to level a slope, precautions must be taken or the tree may die.

If the grade must be raised, build a dry-stone wall (see "Dry-stone walls," p.506) around the trunk (leaving room for future growth) and into this set drainage pipes radiating out to the drip line. Cover these with crushed stone and on top a layer of gravel. Add a top layer of sandy soil to enable grass to grow. Do not simply cover a tree's entire root area with soil: roots need oxygen to grow, and even a thin layer of additional soil could kill them.

When lowering the grade of the surrounding soil, excavate just outside the tree's drip line (farther out, if possible, where winters are severe) to the depth needed, and build a retaining wall of stone, brick, or wood (see "Retaining walls," p.506) to hold the soil in place.

Raising the Grade

Build a dry-stone retaining wall to protect the trunk. Lay drainage pipes in a cartwheel configuration around the tree (see inset) and build up the level of the soil using layers of crushed stone, gravel, and sandy soil.

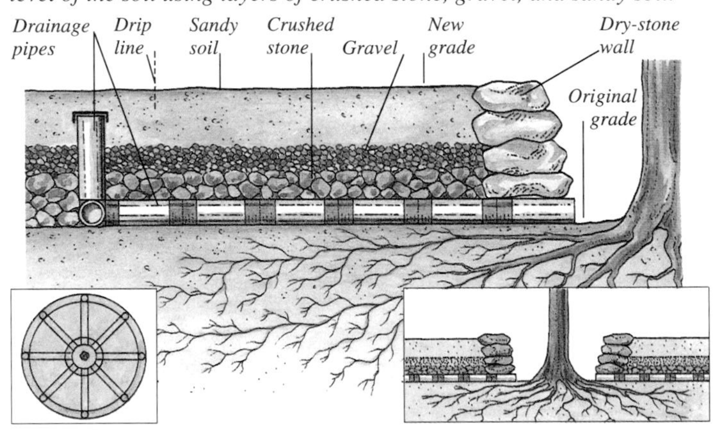

Lowering the Grade

To retain the original grade and prevent erosion, construct a dry-stone retaining wall just outside the drip line of the tree.

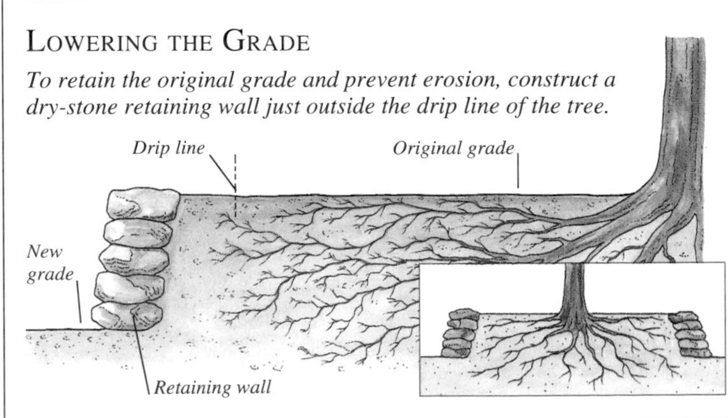

Pruning and training

CORRECT pruning and training help to maintain a tree's health and vigor, regulate its shape and size, and, in some instances, improve ornamental qualities. It is important to prune young trees correctly to develop a strong framework of evenly spaced branches; thereafter most trees need minimal pruning.

The degree of pruning and training depends on the type of tree and the desired result. Relatively little is required to produce a well-balanced tree, whereas creating a pleached avenue with interwoven branches demands considerably more work and expertise.

When to prune

Most deciduous trees are best pruned when dormant in fall or winter. They may also be pruned at other times, except in late winter or early spring when many trees bleed (exude sap) if cut. Maples (*Acer*), horse chestnuts (*Aesculus*), birches (*Betula*), walnuts (*Juglans*), and cherries (*Prunus*) all bleed extensively, even toward the end of their dormant season; prune these in midsummer after new growth has matured. Evergreens require little or no pruning except the removal of dead or diseased branches in late summer.

The principles of pruning

The first stage of pruning a tree is to remove any dead, diseased, or damaged wood, and to cut out weak or straggly shoots. Then assess the remaining framework and decide which branches should be pruned back or removed for well-balanced growth. Take care not to impair the natural growth habit of a tree by pruning, unless aiming to produce a certain shape or form, such as an espalier. Hard pruning stimulates vigorous growth; light pruning produces only limited growth.

It is important to make pruning cuts accurately to minimize damage to the tree. If cutting back a stem, cut just above a healthy bud, pair of buds, or side shoot pointing in the required direction of growth. For example, if thinning out congested stems, cut back to a bud or shoot that is growing outwards so it will not rub against another stem as it grows. Cut neither too far from the bud, which leaves a stub that provides an entry point for disease, nor too close, which could damage the bud itself.

When pruning trees with opposite buds, make a straight cut with sharp pruners directly above a pair of buds. For trees with alternate buds, make a sloping cut $^{1}/_{8}$–$^{1}/_{4}$in (3–5mm) above a bud so that the base of the cut is just level with the top of the bud, on the opposite side of the stem.

If pruning back a branch completely, cut just outside the branch collar – the slight swelling on the branch where it joins the trunk. This is where the callus is formed that will eventually cover the wound. Never cut flush with the main stem since this damages the tree's natural protective zone, making it more vulnerable to disease. The branch collar on dead branches may extend some way along the branch, but it is still important to make any cut outside it.

WHERE TO CUT

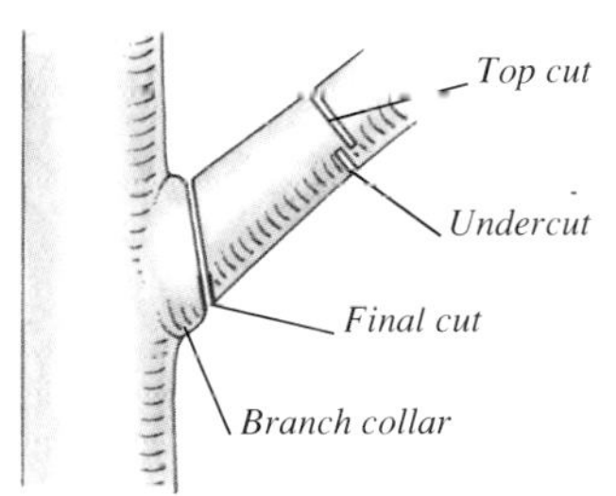

When removing a branch, take care not to damage the branch collar: first remove the bulk of the branch with two cuts, then cut off the stub just outside the collar.

CUTTING BACK A STEM

ALTERNATE BUDS
For trees with alternate buds, make a clean, angled cut just above a healthy, outward-facing bud.

OPPOSITE BUDS
For trees with opposite buds, make a clean, straight cut directly above a strong pair of buds.

Removing a branch

If removing whole branches of less than 1in (2.5cm) diameter, make a single cut with a pruning saw or pruners. For branches that are thicker than this, first remove the bulk of the weight; partially undercut the branch at least 12in (30cm) from the trunk, then, a little farther out, saw through the branch from above. If no undercut is made, the branch may break off in midcut, ripping the bark back to the trunk and leaving it open to infection.

To remove the remaining stub, undercut it just outside the branch collar, then cut through from above. If you find it difficult to locate the collar, cut through the stub at a short distance from the trunk, making a downward-sloping cut. If the angle between the branch and the trunk is very acute, it may be easier to cut through the stub from beneath.

Do not apply a wound paint or dressing: there is no clear evidence that they speed up the healing process or prevent disease.

CUTTING OFF A BRANCH

1 *Using a pruning saw, undercut the branch by one-quarter of its diameter, 12in (30cm) from the trunk to keep the bark from tearing back if the branch breaks.*

2 *Make the second cut about 1in (2.5cm) farther away from the trunk, sawing through the branch from above. The undercut will close up, making sawing easier.*

3 *Remove the remaining stub by making 2 further cuts. First make a small undercut just outside the branch collar.*

4 *Make the final cut just outside the branch collar, angling the saw slightly away from the trunk. Saw through cleanly until the top cut meets the undercut.*

Formative pruning

Young trees benefit from formative pruning to ensure that they develop a strong, well-balanced framework of evenly spaced branches. At its simplest, this involves the removal of dead, damaged, and diseased wood, as well as any weak or crossing branches.

Formative pruning may also be used to determine the tree's shape as it grows: for example, a young feathered tree may be pruned over several years to form a standard, or trained against a wall as an espalier. The extent of the pruning depends on both the type of tree selected and the required shape when mature. As with all types of pruning, care should be taken not to spoil the tree's natural growth characteristics.

It is especially important to prune young tropical trees since the growth rate is very rapid and the girth of both main stems and branches develops very quickly. Provided that they have been pruned correctly during the first few years after planting, they may then be left to grow naturally. Most other evergreens, on the other hand, will develop naturally into well-shaped specimens with little or no attention; pruning is usually restricted to the removal of dead, damaged, or crossing stems, and badly placed laterals.

The formative pruning of ornamental garden trees depends on the type of tree bought or required. Feathered trees have a single, central leader and laterals along the whole length of the stem. Central-leader standards have a clear length of stem at the base, while branched-head standards also have a clear stem but have their central leader removed to encourage the formation of vigorous lateral branches – as commonly seen in many Japanese cherries (*Prunus*).

PRUNING AND TRAINING YOUNG TREES

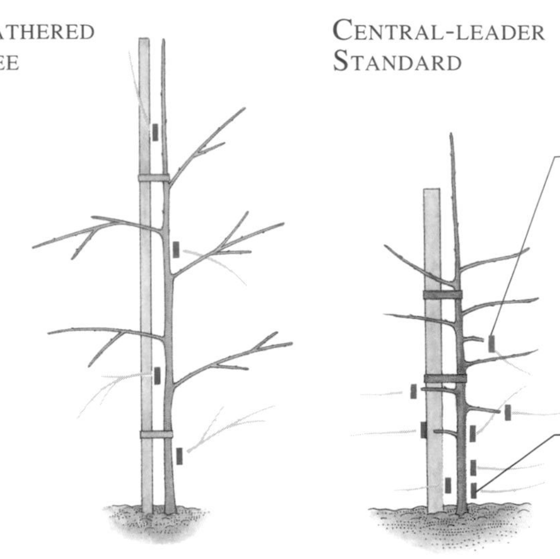

Cut back laterals by half.

Cut back laterals flush with stem.

Remove congested and crossing shoots, then cut out any laterals that are small, spindly, or badly positioned, to achieve a well-balanced framework of branches.

YEAR 1
On the lowest third of the tree, cut back laterals to the main stem; on the middle third, cut back laterals by half. Remove any weak or competing leaders.

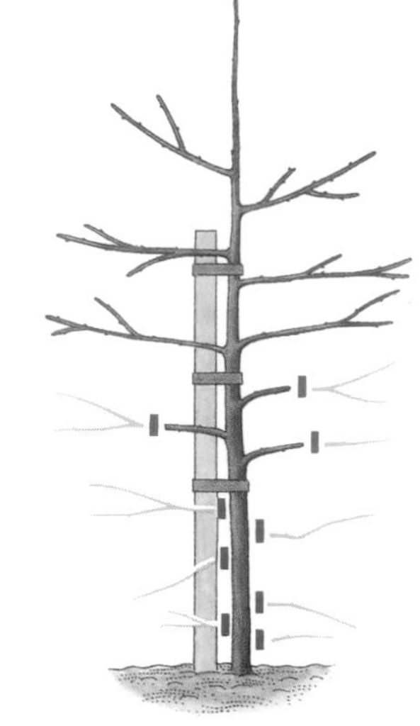

YEARS 2 AND 3
Continue the pruning process, removing the lowest laterals completely and cutting back by about half those laterals that are on the middle third of the tree.

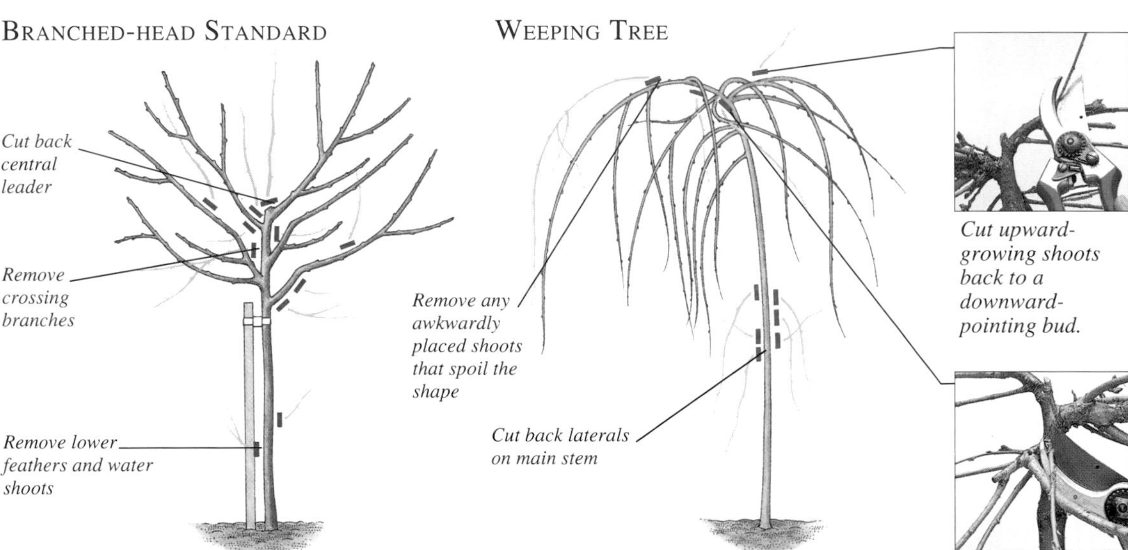

Remove crossing laterals and any growths on the lower third of the tree. Cut back the leader to a healthy bud or shoot.

Cut back crossing or vertical branches that spoil the symmetry of the tree. Remove any growths on the main stem.

Feathered trees

Feathered trees may be simply pruned to enhance their natural shape or more extensively pruned to train them into standards. This process also sometimes occurs naturally. Although many feathered trees retain their lower branches, these die back in some species and the tree becomes a central-leader standard. Other trees also lose their central-leader dominance and therefore become branched-head standards.

Early training is straightforward, however, regardless of the eventual habit of the tree. First remove any competing shoots to leave a single main leader. Then take out any small, weak, or poorly placed laterals, so that the framework of branches around the main stem is evenly spaced and well balanced.

Central-leader standard trees

Feathered whips may be pruned over two to three years to form a standard. A technique called feathering is often used since it also channels food to the main stem, which thickens and becomes sturdier. Initially, prune a feathered whip to remove any competing leaders or weak laterals. Then, on the lowest third of the tree, cut back all the feathers to the main stem; on the middle third, reduce the feathers by about half; leave the top third unpruned, but remove any upright shoots that might form a competing leader.

In late fall or early winter, cut back the pruned laterals to the main stem. Repeat the procedure over the next two or three years to form a tree with approximately 6ft (1.8m) of clear stem.

Branched-head standard trees

To form a branched-head standard, train the tree initially as a central-leader standard to achieve the desired length of clear stem. Then, in mid- to late fall, cut back the leader to a strong, healthy bud or shoot to leave a framework of four or five strong, well-placed lateral branches. At this stage, also remove any crossing or congested laterals and any that spoil the balance of the branch framework.

In subsequent years, prune the tree as much as necessary to keep the crown well balanced and with an open center. Remove any vigorous vertical shoots that may grow into a new leader, and cut back any feathers to the main stem as soon as possible. Some branched-head standards can be formed by top-working (or top-grafting) as for weeping standards (see opposite).

Weeping standards

A weeping standard is formed by grafting one or two scions of a weeping cultivar onto a stock plant with a clear stem of about 6ft (1.8m). This is known as top-working or top-grafting, a technique that is most commonly used for fruit trees (see "Top-working," p.379) but also for weeping ash (*Fraxinus excelsior* 'Pendula'), the Kilmarnock willow (*Salix caprea* 'Kilmarnock'), and a large number of other weeping ornamentals. Young, pendulous branches start to develop once the grafts have taken.

Pruning is best restricted to the removal of crossing and vertical branches and any that spoil the overall symmetry of the framework. Although upward-growing branches are usually removed, leave some semiupright stems to develop naturally since they often grow downward later and produce tiers of weeping branches. If growths appear on the main stem, rub or pinch them out as soon as they appear.

Espalier and fan-trained trees

The aim of both espalier and fan-training is to form a symmetrical, attractive network of branches in a single plane by pruning and training a young tree over several years. These techniques are occasionally used for growing ornamental trees against fences or walls, but they are more commonly associated with growing fruit trees.

Pruning times vary according to the selected species. For example, *Magnolia grandiflora*, which flowers in summer, should be pruned at the start of growth in spring, while the spring-flowering *Acacia dealbata* should be pruned directly after flowering. For further instructions on the pruning techniques, see THE FRUIT GARDEN, "Espalier," p.378, and "Fan," p.389.

Pruning established deciduous trees

Once a deciduous tree is well established, there is little need for further pruning. Major pruning of a mature tree is best carried out by a tree surgeon or arborist, since the work is both skilled and dangerous and, if poorly executed, may ruin the tree.

Many branched-head trees become overcrowded in the center as they mature, restricting the amounts of air and light that reach the central branches. Cut out inward-growing shoots and any branches that spoil the balance of the framework.

REMOVING A COMPETING LEADER

Prune out a competing leader by making a clean cut at the base with pruners or loppers, taking care not to damage the remaining leader.

TRAINING IN A NEW LEADER

Replace a damaged leader by training in a strong shoot vertically. Attach a stake to the top of the main stem and tie the shoot to the stake. Prune out the old, damaged leader. Remove the stake once the new leader is dominant and growing strongly.

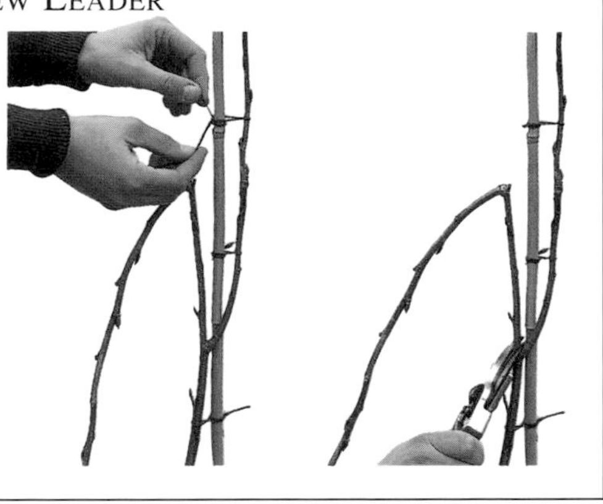

If a tree is too large for its situation, do not attempt to restrict its size by heading back all new growth each year. This "haircut" pruning produces an unsightly, congested cluster of shoots each season which spoils the tree's natural appearance and reduces flower and fruit production. The correct treatment is as for the renovation of old trees (see p.50).

As a result of hard pruning or the removal of large branches, a tree may produce a mass of epicormic or water shoots; rub or cut these out immediately (see p.45).

If the central leader is damaged, select a strong shoot close to the top of the main stem and train it vertically as a replacement leader. Tie the selected shoot to a stake secured high on the main stem, and prune out any potential competing shoots. Once the shoot has developed into a strong, dominant growth, the stake may be removed.

If a tree develops two or more competing leaders, remove all but the strongest shoot. The very narrow crotch angle between rival leaders is a source of structural weakness, and the tree could split open at this point in a high wind.

Vigorous, upright shoots may develop on young, branched-head trees. If left, these will quickly grow into competing leaders and so it is important to remove them entirely as soon as possible.

Pruning established evergreen trees

Broad-leaved evergreens need minimal pruning. Provided that the trees have an established leader and that any badly placed laterals have been cut out when young, it is only necessary to remove any dead, damaged, or diseased wood.

Conifers require only basic pruning once established, except when they are grown as a hedge (see HEDGES AND SCREENS, pp.58–60). On some pines (*Pinus*), firs (*Abies*), and spruces (*Picea*), the terminal bud on the leader may die; if this occurs, train in the best placed lateral as a replacement leader (see above) and cut out any competing, upright shoots. Established palms require no pruning apart from the removal of dead leaves, which should be cut back to the main stem.

Root pruning

If an established tree is growing vigorously, but producing very few flowers or fruit, pruning the roots will help slow down growth and stimulate better flowering or fruiting performance.

In early spring, dig a trench just outside the extent of the tree canopy. Then prune back any thick roots to the inner edge of the trench, using a pruning saw, pruners, or loppers. Retain any fibrous roots at the inner edge of the trench, backfill the soil, and firm. For further details, see THE FRUIT GARDEN, "Root pruning," p.366. In some instances, it may be necessary to support the tree with stakes or guy ropes if it seems unstable afterward (see "Staking," p.40).

For root pruning of trees in containers, see "Maintaining trees planted in containers," p.44.

Pruning container-planted trees

Container-planted trees should be pruned annually, following the same principles as for other trees, to regulate their shape and size and maintain a strong, balanced framework of evenly spaced branches.

Coppicing and pollarding

Coppicing is the regular pruning of a tree close to the ground to encourage strong basal shoots to grow. Pollarding is the pruning of a tree back to the main stem or branch framework, stimulating new shoots at this level. Traditionally, both techniques were used to give a supply of firewood or pliable stems for basketwork and fencing. Now they are used in gardens to enhance leaf color and size or the color of ornamental stems, or to restrict tree size.

HOW TO COPPICE A TREE

Coppicing may be used to restrict a tree's size, to enlarge leaves, or to enhance stem color.

Use loppers to cut back all stems to 3in (7cm); do not cut into the swollen, woody base of the tree.

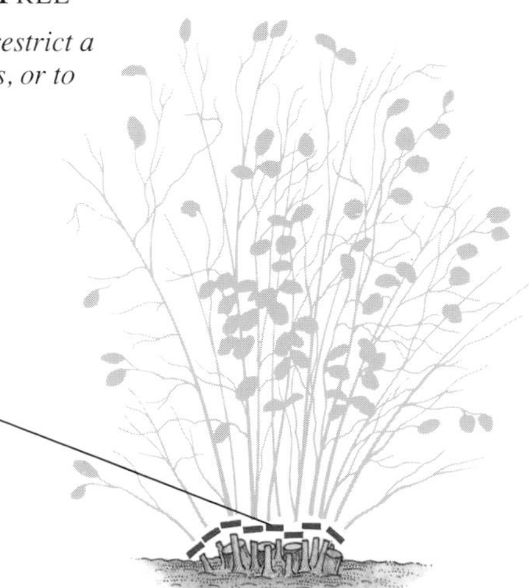

Coppicing

Trees should be coppiced in late winter or early spring; some willows,when grown for their colored stems, may be left until midspring, however, and pruned just before or very shortly after the buds break into new growth. Cut back all stems to the base, leaving the swollen basal wood unpruned because all new growth forms from here.

Pollarding

To form a pollard, plant a young branched-head standard (see p.48). When its trunk has reached 6ft (2m) or the desired height, prune back the branches to 1–2in (2.5–5cm) from the main stem in late winter or early spring. This results in a mass of shoots developing from the top of the cut stem. Prune back these shoots annually (or every second year) to stimulate growth of further young shoots from the enlarged head of the stem. Thin them if they become congested. Remove shoots that grow on the trunk as soon as they appear.

To produce a pollard with a main branch framework, allow the tree to develop a well-balanced branch system at the desired height. In late winter or early spring, prune back the branches to about 6ft (2m). Cut back the resulting secondary shoots every two to five years, depending on the species, until the pollard is established. Thereafter, prune every year or two, and thin the shoots as required. If too many enlarged heads develop close together, cut out some of them entirely.

PRUNING AN ESTABLISHED POLLARDED TREE

Prune back the shoots every 1–2 years in late winter or early spring to 1/2–3/4in (1–2cm) from the pollarded head of the main stem. This will stimulate new shoot production the following spring. The new wood of trees such as this Salix alba *var.* vitellina, *grown for its ornamental stems, is particularly highly colored.*

Using pruners or loppers, cut back the old stems to the base, taking care not to damage the enlarged head.

TREES FOR COPPICING AND POLLARDING

Acer pensylvanicum 'Erythrocladum'
Corylus avellana 'Contorta' ⩛
Eucalyptus dalrympleana, *E. globulus* ✽ ⩛, *E. gunnii* ⩛, *E. pauciflora*

Populus candicans 'Aurora'

Populus x *canadensis* 'Serotina Aurea', *P. candicans* 'Aurora'
Salix acutifolia 'Blue Streak', *S. alba* 'Britzensis', *S. a.* var. *sericea*, *S. a.* var. *vitellina*, *S. daphnoides* 'Aglaia', *S. irrorata* ⩛, *S.* x *sepulcralis* 'Erythroflexuosa'
Tilia platyphyllos (cvs)
Toona sinensis 'Flamingo'

KEY
✽ *Not frost hardy*
⩛ *Coppice only*

Renovating old trees

Trees that have outgrown their situation, or that have been neglected, should be either removed and replaced, or renovated to return them to full health and vigor. Renovation requires considerable care and expertise, and it is advisable to consult an experienced tree surgeon. In some cases, a tree may be too old and potentially dangerous to renovate, so it may be better to replace it.

Renovation may be undertaken at any time except the start of growth in spring. For most trees, however, and particularly those that produce a lot of sap, such as horse chestnuts (*Aesculus*) and birches (*Betula*), late fall or early winter is the best time. Prune flowering cherries in early summer to reduce the production of overvigorous new growth which might favor leaf diseases.

The first stage is to remove all dead, diseased, and damaged wood. Then prune out any crossing or congested branches and those that spoil the balance of the framework. It is best to carry out extensive renovation over two or three years to allow gradual recovery because drastic pruning may severely weaken or even kill a tree in poor health. If you need to remove any large branches, cut them off in sections (see "Removing a branch," p.47).

After renovating the tree, feed it by mulching with well-rotted manure and apply fertilizer to the ground beneath the tree canopy in spring for two to three years. Hard pruning may stimulate the growth of a mass of side shoots; if congested, thin some of them out to leave a well-balanced framework. Any suckers and water shoots should be removed as soon as they are noticed (see p.45).

Renovating "haircut" pruned trees

Trees that have had all their new growth trimmed back annually produce a congested cluster of shoots every season on knobby branches, but without the balanced framework of a true pollard. Such "haircut" pruning is unsightly and reduces flowers and fruit. To correct it, first thin out the knobby stumps at the ends of the main branches. Cut out most of the young shoots on the remaining stumps to leave just one or two and cut these back by about one-third; repeat this procedure in the following three or four seasons to develop a more natural growth habit.

Tree surgeons

For pruning, renovation, or removal of large trees, it is advisable to consult a qualified tree surgeon. The International Society of Arboriculture, P.O. Box 908, 303 West University Avenue, Urbana, IL 61801, has branches across the US and Canada. They can advise you of registered arborists in your area. Also check the yellow pages under Tree Service. Before inviting contractors to give estimates, decide exactly what work is required, including the disposal of any debris. Get several estimates: they are normally provided free, but a fee may be charged if advisory work is involved.

RENOVATING A TREE

YEAR 1
Cut out any dead, diseased, and damaged wood, and remove any branches that cross or rub against others and that spoil the balance of the framework.

YEARS 2 AND 3
The following year, thin out the new growth that results from the initial pruning and remove any water shoots. Repeat the next year if necessary.

Pleached trees

Pleached trees are clear-stemmed trees planted in one or more rows with their branches trained horizontally to intertwine, creating a formal, raised wall of foliage when in leaf (see "Trees for avenues," p.36). Hornbeams (*Carpinus*) and lindens such as *Tilia platyphyllos* and *T.* 'Euchlora' make excellent pleached avenues, since they can be clipped precisely and, within four or five years, develop an attractive, boxed appearance. It is best to use young trees with pliable stems; attempts to pleach mature trees are generally unsatisfactory.

Constructing the framework

Until the trees are established, they should be trained in to a framework. First, using one stake for each tree to be planted, set up a row of stout, 8–10ft (2.5–3m) high stakes an equal distance apart. Once driven into the ground to a depth of approximately 2–3ft (60cm–1m), they should be at the required height of the lowest branches – about 6ft (2m) or more for people to be able to walk comfortably underneath. Attach a secondary framework of thinner posts to these stakes to create the desired overall height.

Initial training

Plant a young tree next to each stake in late fall or early winter. Choose trees that are sufficiently tall so that their laterals may be trained in to the framework. Cut back any lower feathers below the lowest horizontal rail, and prune out any sublaterals that cannot be tied in easily. The leader may either be bent horizontally and tied in, if tall enough, or left to grow for another season before being trained.

Further training

Late the next summer, intertwine any untrained branches into the framework and cut back any long laterals to stimulate new growth. Sublaterals growing at right angles to the branches may be tied in along the stakes. Continue to develop a boxed appearance in subsequent seasons by tying in branches and cutting back the laterals to stimulate new shoots and dense growth.

Once the pleached trees are fully established and the branches have intertwined, the framework may be dismantled. Maintain healthy, dense growth by removing any dead, damaged, or diseased wood, and strongly outward-growing laterals; rub out young shoots on main stems as soon as you notice them.

Establishing the Framework

YEAR 1

Drive a row of stakes into the ground about 7–9ft (2.2–2.7m) apart. Secure strong, vertical posts to the stakes, then fix horizontal rails about 24in (60cm) apart to these to form the framework. Plant a young standard or feathered tree next to each stake.

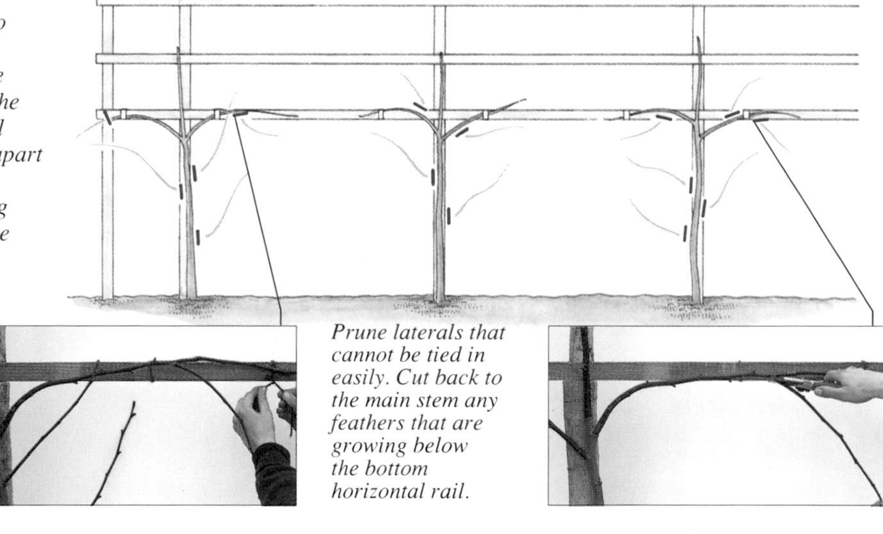

Bend over any laterals adjacent to the horizontal rails and tie them in without straining them excessively.

Prune laterals that cannot be tied in easily. Cut back to the main stem any feathers that are growing below the bottom horizontal rail.

YEAR 2

Late in the following summer, tie in any untrained branches to the framework to fill in spaces, and prune back long laterals to two or three buds to encourage the growth of new side shoots.

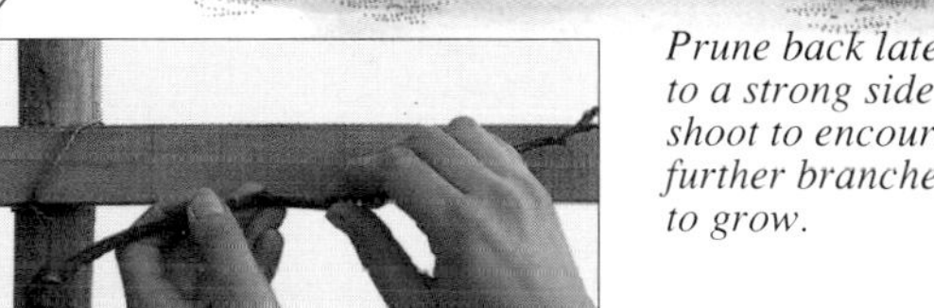

Once the leader is tall enough, bend it over onto the top horizontal of the framework, and tie it in.

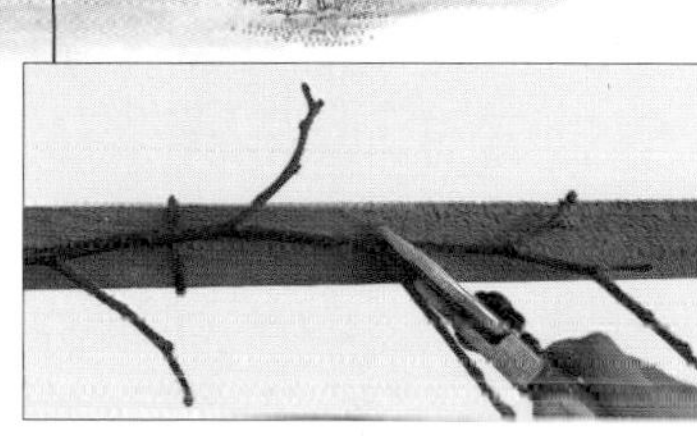

Prune back laterals to a strong side shoot to encourage further branches to grow.

Annual Maintenance

Tie in all untidy and awkward branches to maintain the pleached effect, and prune back laterals to encourage new growth and a dense branch framework.

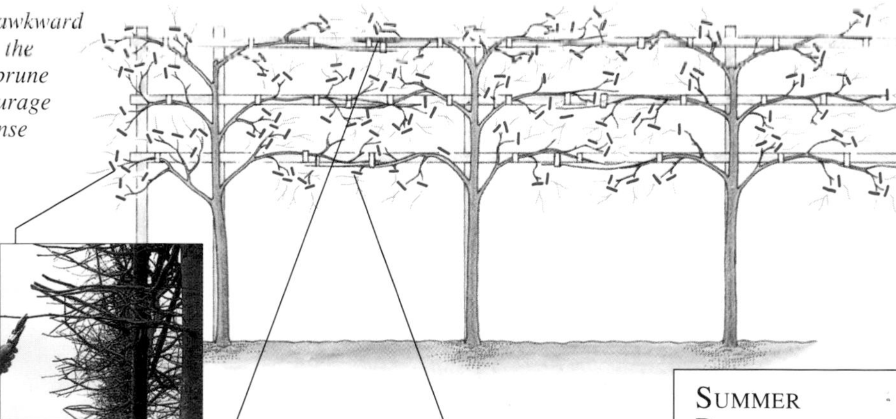

Cut back awkward stems growing away from the framework to maintain a neat, well-trained shape.

Continue to tie in new stems to the framework; check old ties and replace them where necessary.

Prune any long laterals pointing away from the desired shape to encourage further side shoots to grow along the framework.

SUMMER PRUNING

Tie in untrained stems and cut back long laterals to 2 or 3 buds. Prune stems growing strongly from the framework to a well-placed bud or shoot.

Propagation

Trees may be propagated from cuttings, seed, layering, or grafting. Taking cuttings is probably the most common method of propagation since it is fairly simple and provides new plants fairly quickly, while raising trees from seed or layering is easy but very slow. Grafting is rarely used by amateur gardeners because it requires considerable expertise to grow new plants successfully this way.

Tree species may be propagated from seed, but seeds from hybrids and cultivars rarely produce plants that are true to type. Vegetative methods of propagation, such as taking cuttings, layering, and grafting, may be used for hybrids and cultivars as well as species. However, some care in the selection of plant material is required for success.

Hardwood cuttings

Many deciduous trees may be propagated from hardwood, or dormant, cuttings. In early fall, prepare the ground for the cuttings while it is still warm. Where winters are long and harsh, the cuttings usually die if left outside: they can be rooted in deep boxes in a basement or frost-free root cellar.

Cuttings of trees that root easily, such as willows (*Salix*), may be inserted directly into a trench, while those that are more difficult to root, such as *Metasequoia*, should be inserted in a sand bed, and then transplanted into a trench early the next spring. In either case, make the trench narrow and with one side vertical so that the cuttings are held upright while they root. The depth of the trench will depend on the type of plant to be rooted. For multistemmed trees, it should be 1in (2.5cm) shallower than the length of the cuttings; for single-stemmed trees, it should be the same depth as the cuttings so that the top bud is barely covered and the lack of light inhibits the growth of all other buds.

For best results, dig the trench in friable, well-drained soil; in heavy clay soil, add some coarse sand to the base. If preparing a few trenches, space them 12–15in (30–38cm) apart in open ground, or about 4in (10cm) apart in a cold frame.

Slow-rooting Hardwood Cuttings

1 *For species that do not root easily (here* Metasequoia*), tie cuttings into bundles. Dip the ends in hormone rooting powder.*

2 *Insert the bundles of cuttings in a sand bed and leave in a cold frame over winter. In spring, insert them individually in a trench in a prepared site outside.*

Preparing and inserting the cuttings

Select the cuttings just after leaf fall. Choose strong, vigorous shoots of the current season's growth and remove them by cutting just above a bud or pair of buds at the junction between the current and the previous season's growth. Trim down the cuttings as shown and dip the basal cuts in hormone rooting powder to encourage them to root. Place the cuttings against the vertical side of the trench at the correct depth, and backfill with soil. Then firm in gently and water well.

For species that do not root easily, tie cuttings into small bundles and then plunge them into a sand bed (see p.546) in a cold frame for the winter, where they should callus or root before being transplanted.

Fast-rooting Hardwood Cuttings

1 *To prepare the trench, push the spade vertically into the soil, then press it forward slightly to form a flat-backed trench about 7in (19cm) deep.*

2 *Select strong, straight stems with healthy buds (right); avoid old, soft, spindly, or damaged stems (left). Remove about 12in (30cm) of the stem, cutting just above a bud.*

3 *Remove any leaves. Trim the cuttings to about 8in (20cm): make an angled cut just above the proposed top bud and a horizontal cut below the bottom one.*

4 *Insert the cuttings in the trench 4–6in (10–15cm) apart, and at the correct depth depending on whether a multi- or single-stemmed tree is required.*

Planting Depths

Multistemmed Trees

For multistemmed trees, insert cuttings with the top 1–1½in (2.5–3cm) above the soil surface.

Single-stemmed Trees

The top bud of each cutting should be just below the soil surface.

5 *Firm the soil around the cuttings, rake the surface, and label. Space any additional rows 12–15in (30–38cm) apart.*

6 *Lift the rooted cuttings the following fall. Then pot them up individually or transplant them into open ground in their final positions.*

Aftercare

Label the cuttings and leave them until the following fall. During the winter, the ground may be lifted by frost; refirm the soil around the cuttings if this occurs. By fall, they should be well rooted and may then be transplanted individually into open ground or into containers, as required. If they have been kept in a cold frame, harden them off the first spring, then transplant outside; the following spring, pot them up or move them to their final positions in open ground.

Semiripe cuttings

Many conifers, as well as certain broad-leaved evergreens such as *Magnolia grandiflora* and *Prunus lusitanica*, may be propagated readily from semiripe cuttings. These cuttings are taken in late summer or fall from stems that have virtually ripened; that is, when they have thickened and become harder (see also ORNAMENTAL SHRUBS, "Semiripe cuttings," p.82).

Selecting the cuttings

In a closed case, at 70°F (21°C), or in a cold frame, prepare a suitable rooting medium for the cuttings. This should consist of equal parts of grit and compost or peat (see also "Standard cuttings soil mix," p.536). Using a sharp knife, take heel cuttings from healthy side shoots, including a sliver of hardened wood from the main stem. Alternatively, take 4–6in (10–15cm) long cuttings from leaders or side shoots and trim immediately below a node with pruners or with a sharp knife.

For cuttings from conifers, choose leaders or side shoots that are characteristic of the parent, since conifer shoots vary considerably in their growth patterns. It is particularly important to select cutting material carefully from slow-growing and dwarf conifers: since some may produce reverted or uncharacteristic growth, use only shoots that typify what you want to propagate.

Preparing and inserting the cuttings

For all semiripe cuttings, cut off the lower pair of leaves with a sharp knife and reduce the remaining leaves by one-third or a half to minimize the loss of moisture; if the cutting tips are soft, pinch them out. To encourage the cuttings to root, use the tip of the knife to make two shallow, vertical wounds, about 1in (2.5cm) long, on opposite sides of each cutting down to the base. Alternatively, make a longer wound along the side of each cutting with a knife, and remove a sliver of bark as well. In either case, dip the basal cut, including the wound, in hormone rooting powder.

Use a dibber to make a hole in the rooting medium, and insert the bottom third of each cutting, taking care to leave enough space between the cuttings so that they do not overlap; this allows air to circulate freely around them. Then firm the soil mix, water thoroughly with a solution containing fungicide, and label.

Aftercare

Check the cuttings periodically, watering them only to keep them from drying out. Remove any fallen leaves as soon as they appear since these may rot and spread disease to the cuttings. During cold spells, cold frames should be insulated with burlap or a similar covering.

If the cuttings are being kept in a closed case with bottom heat, they should root by early spring. Cuttings in a cold frame are usually left until the following fall, although it is preferable to leave them in the frame for a second winter and pot them up the following spring.

During the summer, mist-spray the cuttings often to stop them from drying out and control any pest or disease infestations that might develop. If the cuttings are in strong, direct sunlight they risk being scorched, so it may be necessary to shade them. Apply a greenhouse shading paint or place shading material over the frame (see p.484). Once the cuttings root, lift them out carefully with a hand fork and transplant them into individual pots, then harden them off (see p.545) before potting them on further or planting them out in open ground. Rooted cuttings in a cold frame may be hardened off while still in the frame by raising the frame cover for short then longer periods. Give the cuttings a liquid feed and pot them up or transplant them outside.

PREPARING A SEMIRIPE CUTTING

Cut a shoot 4–6in (10–15cm) long from a leader or side shoot and trim immediately below a node. Strip off the lower leaves (here of Chamaecyparis obtusa 'Nana Aurea'*) and pinch out the tip if it is soft. Make a shallow wound, about 1in (2.5cm) long, down the cutting and dip it in rooting hormone.*

Softwood cuttings

This method of propagation is suitable for some ornamental cherries (*Prunus*) and a few other tree species, although it is more commonly used for shrubs. Softwood cuttings are taken in spring from the fast-growing tips of new shoots and usually root very easily. They wilt rapidly, however, so it is vital to prepare and insert them as quickly as possible after removing them from the parent plant.

Preparing and inserting the cuttings

In spring, before taking the cuttings, prepare containers by filling them with an appropriate soil mix and then firming to just below the rim. Take the cuttings by removing the new growth from stem tips, cutting just above a bud or leaf joint with pruners or a sharp knife. To reduce any moisture loss, immerse the cuttings in water immediately or place them in an opaque plastic bag and seal it. Even a small loss of water will hinder the development of new roots.

Prepare the cuttings by trimming them with a sharp knife to about 2½in (6cm), cutting just below a leaf joint. Remove the lower leaves and dip the base of each cutting in hormone rooting powder to encourage rooting. Insert the cuttings into the prepared pots of soil mix, label them, and water them with a dilute solution of fungicide.

To encourage rapid rooting, place the containers in a mist unit or closed case at 70–75°F (21–4°C), preferably with bottom heat, and water with a fungicide once a week to protect against rotting and disease. Once they are rooted, the cuttings may be hardened off gradually before they are transplanted carefully into individual pots.

TREES THAT MAY BE PROPAGATED BY CUTTINGS

Hardwood

Cordyline ❁
Ficus ❁
Metasequoia glyptostroboides
Morus
Platanus
Populus
Salix

Morus alba 'Laciniata'

Semiripe

Austrocedrus ▽
Calocedrus ▽
Chamaecyparis ▽
Cinnamomum ❁ ▽
x *Cupressocyparis* ▽
Cupressus ▽
Distylium racemosum ▽
Drimys winteri
Eucryphia

Eucryphia x *nymansensis* 'Nymansay'

Grevillea ❁
Ilex
Juniperus ▽
Ligustrum lucidum
Magnolia grandiflora ▽
Metrosideros excelsa ❁,
M. robusta ❁,
M. umbellata ❁
Michelia ❁ ▽
Nothofagus dombeyi
Podocarpus, some ❁, ▽
Prunus lusitanica
Quercus ilex ▽,
Q. myrsinifolia ▽,
Q. semecarpifolia ▽
Thuja ▽
Thujopsis ▽
Trochodendron aralioides ▽
Tsuga ▽
Weinmannia ❁

Softwood

Acer cappadocicum
Betula
Catalpa
Celtis occidentalis
Cotinus coggygria
Eucryphia lucida
Ginkgo biloba
Halesia
Koelreuteria paniculata
Lagerstroemia, some ❁
Liquidambar styraciflua
Metasequoia glyptostroboides
Prunus
Ulmus

KEY
❁ *Not frost hardy*
▽ *Take cuttings with a heel*

Raising trees from seed

Tree species may be propagated from seed since their seedlings usually retain the characteristics of the parent plant. Hybrids and cultivars rarely come true to type. Raising a tree from seed is a relatively simple process; it is, however, a slow method if a tree is being grown mainly for its flowers, because it will take a number of years to reach flowering size.

Extracting seed

The protective covering of some seeds should be removed first. The method for this varies, depending on the type of seed coat. The coating on winged seed may be removed by rubbing it between finger and thumb. Some cones disintegrate naturally and the scales may then be separated. Place pine and spruce cones in a paper bag and keep them in a warm, dry place until the cone scales open and shed the seed into the bag. Immerse cedar cones in hot water and allow them to soak until the scales open.

The method of extracting seed from fruits or berries depends on the seed size and type of flesh. Large fruits, such as those of crabapples (*Malus*), may be cut open and the seeds extracted. Soak smaller fruits, such as those of *Sorbus*, in warm water for several days; viable seed will sink. Discard the pulp and soak again until the seed can be removed and any remaining flesh picked off.

Storing

Once the seed has been extracted, dry it if necessary and place it in a sealed and labeled plastic bag. If planning to sow the seed within a few days, store it at room temperature; for longer-term storage, keep it on the top shelf of a refrigerator so that it is cool but not frozen.

CLEANING FLESHY SEED

1 *Remove the fleshy seed with your fingers. Immerse it in warm water, and soak for 1–2 days. Once the fleshy coating has softened and split, drain off the water.*

2 *Pick off the remaining coating and dry the seed with tissue. Sow the seed fresh or store it in a plastic bag in a refrigerator for no more than a few weeks.*

Breaking seed dormancy

Some seeds have a natural period of dormancy to prevent germination in adverse climatic conditions that would threaten the survival of the seedlings; this has to be overcome before the seed will germinate. Several kinds of dormancy occur, sometimes combined, which vary according to the species. Most commonly, dormancy is achieved either by a hard, thick seed coat, which prevents water being taken up, or by a chemical inhibitor, which delays germination until there is a significant temperature change. In most cases, dormancy can be broken artificially by wearing away the seed coat or by chilling the seed.

Scarification

Before sowing seeds with an impermeable coating, scarify them to allow germination to occur. Large seeds with a particularly hard covering, such as oaks (*Quercus*), may be nicked with a sharp knife, or a section of the seed coat filed away to let in moisture. Smaller seeds that are not easily nicked, such as those of pines, may be shaken in a jar that has been lined with sandpaper or partly filled with sharp grit, or they may be filed individually with an emery board. Seed from legumes (for example *Acacia* and *Robinia*) should simply be left to soak in a container of hot water for approximately 24 hours in a ratio of 3 parts hot water to 1 part seed.

Stratification

Dormancy in seed of trees from temperate climates is commonly overcome by chilling (stratification). Seed may either be sown outside so that it is chilled naturally during winter or, more reliably, stratified artificially by being stored in a refrigerator.

If refrigerating seed, first mix it with moistened vermiculite, or peat and sand. Place it in a clear plastic bag, then seal the bag and put it in a refrigerator. Check the seed regularly through the unopened bag – it should be sown as soon as there are signs of germination.

The length of chilling time required varies considerably: as a guideline, many deciduous species require about six to eight weeks of chilling at below 41°F (5°C), while conifers need only about three weeks. Some seeds germinate only after they have been sown and once chilling has ceased. Sow batches of such seed at intervals – for example after four, eight, and twelve weeks of chilling – since this should ensure that at least some seeds germinate.

Sowing seed in containers

This is a simple way of raising a small number of seedlings. Thoroughly clean any work surfaces and containers to be used before sowing the seed to avoid contamination from soilborne pests and diseases. First fill the pots, pans, or seed trays up to the rimwith seed soil mix.

Large seeds or those that produce seedlings with long taproots, such as oaks (*Quercus*), should be sown about 3in (8cm) apart in deep seed trays or packs, or in individual pots that are about 4in (10cm) deep. Using a presser board, press the seeds into unfirmed soil mix, then cover them to their own depth with soil mix and firm to about 1/4in (5mm) below the rim (see opposite).

Sow very large seeds, for example those of horse chestnut (*Aesculus*), singly in 4–6in (10–15cm) pots. Insert the seed in firmed soil mix, so that just the top of the seed is exposed above the surface.

Small seeds, for example those of *Sorbus*, may be either scattered evenly or, if sufficiently large, individually pressed into prepared pots or trays of firmed soil mix. They should then be barely covered with sieved soil mix followed by a layer of fine grit 1/4in (5mm) deep.

After sowing, thoroughly water all seeds from above and label. Place the containers in a cold frame or,

SOWING IN CONTAINERS

1 *Sow fine seed (here* Sorbus*) onto firmed seed soil mix, making sure it is scattered evenly; keep your hand low to stop the seeds from bouncing.*

2 *Hold a sieve containing seed soil mix over the tray, then tap the side of the sieve until the seeds are just covered to their own depth with sieved soil mix.*

3 *Cover the sown seeds with a 1/4in (5mm) deep layer of horticultural grit. Label the seeds and water with a fine spray.*

4 *Once the seedlings are large enough to handle, gently prick them out into individual pots, taking care not to crush the delicate stems or roots.*

SOWING LARGE SEED

1 *Press large seeds and those of trees with long taproots into unfirmed soil mix in individual pots. Cover with soil mix.*

2 *Sowing in deep pots allows the taproot (see inset) of each seedling (here* Quercus*) to develop without any restriction to root growth.*

within a greenhouse, in a closed propagation case or under a pane of glass. Temperate species are best kept at 54–9°F (12–15°C), and warm-temperate and tropical species at 70°F (21°C) to stimulate germination. Once the seeds have successfully germinated, spray them periodically with a fungicide to discourage damping off (see p.566).

Pricking out

When the seedlings are large enough to be handled by their seed leaves, prick them out so that they have more space to grow. This may be done by knocking the container sides to loosen the soil mix, and then lifting and transplanting the seedlings into individual pots. Alternatively, remove all the seedlings and soil mix together from the container so that the seedlings may be separated with minimal root disturbance. After transplanting, firm the soil mix gently around the seedlings, then level it by gently tapping the pot on the work surface.

Aftercare

Water and label the seedlings, and keep them out of direct sunlight in a temperature similar to that needed for germination until established. Gradually harden them off over a few weeks, feeding them regularly, and spraying them with fungicide. Do not overwater, but make sure that the soil mix does not dry out. Once hardened off, they may be planted out if there is no danger of frost.

Sowing seed outdoors

If raising a large number of seedlings, seed may be sown in an outdoor seedbed. With this method, the seedlings require less regular attention and their growth is less restricted than if sown in containers, but a special bed must be prepared. If possible, do this a few months before sowing by thoroughly digging the area to a spit deep (see "Single digging," p.527), incorporating organic matter and some coarse grit. Keep the ground clear of weeds.

When ready to sow, rake the soil down to a fine tilth, then broadcast small seeds or sow larger ones singly. (For depth of sowing, see "Sowing seed in containers," opposite.) Lightly rake over the seeds, cover the bed with a 1/4–1/2in (0.5–1cm) layer of grit, and firm with a presser. If the soil is at all dry, water thoroughly; then label with the plant name and sowing date.

In exposed sites, young seedlings may need to be protected with windbreak netting (see p.521) or with a floating row cover (see p.490). If the seeds are well spaced, disease should not be a problem and the seedlings may be grown on *in situ* for 12 months before being pricked out. Water the seedlings as necessary and check them regularly in case treatment is needed for pests such as aphids (p.552) and spider mites (p.552).

Layering

Layering may be used to propagate hybrids and cultivars as well as species. This method of propagation occurs naturally in some plants, when a low-growing stem roots itself in the ground; once this happens, the stem may be removed from the parent plant and grown on. Air layering, where the shoot remains above ground, may be used for trees without low-growing stems.

The advantage of layering is that the layered stem needs very little attention while the roots become established. It is a slow method, however, because in order to obtain suitable material the plant must be prepared a year in advance and the layered stem may take a year or more to root.

SIMPLE LAYERING

Cut a 2in (5cm) tongue 12–18in (30–45cm) behind the tip of a vigorous shoot, or remove a narrow ring of bark at this point. Brush the wound with hormone rooting powder and peg the shoot into a shallow hole. Tie the shoot to a supporting stake and backfill the hole.

Vigorous shoot
Friable soil
Peg
Tongue

Simple layering

In this method, a shoot is pegged down into the ground until it has rooted and is then cut off from the parent plant (see also *Propagating a Shrub by Simple Layering*, p.86).

Prepare the parent plant a year before layering is to take place. In late winter or early spring, prune a low branch to stimulate new, young shoots that will root easily. In early spring the following year, select a vigorous shoot and make a small wound 12–18in (30–45cm) from the tip. Brush this with hormone rooting powder to encourage rooting. Add plenty of leaf mold or similar organic matter and sharp grit to the soil where the shoot touches it and peg the shoot down into a shallow hole, tying it to a vertical stake.

Backfill the hole and firm the soil well, leaving the shoot tip exposed, then water thoroughly and, if necessary, protect the shoot from rabbits and other animals with wire netting. About 12 months later, check to see whether the shoot has rooted. If it has, sever it from the parent and either plant it in open ground or pot it up; if it has not rooted, leave it in place and check a month later.

Air layering

The principle of air layering is the same as simple layering, except that the layered shoot roots above the ground rather than in it (see also *Air Layering a Shrub*, p.87). In spring, select a strong stem that has ripened in the previous year, and remove any leaves 12–18in (30–45cm) behind the growing tip. Prepare the stem either by cutting a tongue 2in (5cm) long in the bark, 9–12in (22–30cm) behind its tip, or by removing a 1/4–3/8in (6–8mm) wide ring of bark from the stem at this point. In either case, brush the wound with hormone rooting powder.

Surround the cut stem with a moist rooting medium and seal it in. To do this, first make a plastic sleeve by cutting off the sealed end of a plastic bag, then slide it along the stem until it surrounds the cut, and secure the lower end with string. Moisten some well-aerated rooting medium (such as sphagnum moss or a mix of equal parts of peat and perlite), then use it to wedge open the tongue. Add more medium around the stem inside the sleeve and seal the top.

If the layer has rooted by the next spring, carefully sever the stem from the parent plant, remove the sleeve, and pot on; if the layer has not rooted, however, it should be left in place for another year.

TREE SEED REQUIRING STRATIFICATION

Acer (some)
Betula
Carya
Fagus
Sorbus

TREES THAT MAY BE LAYERED

Simple layering
Cercidiphyllum
Chionanthus retusus
Corylus
Davidia
Dipteronia
Eucryphia
Halesia
Hoheria lyallii
Laurus
Magnolia campbellii,
M. grandiflora,
M. hypoleuca

Magnolia hypoleuca

Air layering
Ficus ❁
Magnolia campbellii,
M. grandiflora

KEY
❁ *Not frost hardy*

Grafting

Grafted plants, unlike cuttings, have the benefit of a developed root system so they establish relatively quickly. Part of a stem (the scion), taken from the plant to be propagated, is joined to a compatible rootstock of another plant, usually of the same genus. In some cases, the rootstock may confer a desirable characteristic, such as a particular growth habit or high resistance to disease, on the resulting plant.

Grafting methods include side-veneer, chip-budding, apical-wedge, whip-and-tongue, and basal-whip (or splice). For details of basal-whip and whip-and-tongue grafting, see Principles of Propagation, p.544. Check that the rootstocks and scions are compatible; if necessary, seek advice from a specialist nursery.

Side-veneer grafting

This is the most common grafting technique for ornamental trees; a one-year-old stem is used for the scion and is grafted onto the side of the prepared rootstock. It is usually carried out just before leaf break, in mid- to late winter, although for maples (*Acer*) summer grafting is sometimes more successful.

Prepare the rootstocks a year in advance by potting up one- or two-year-old seedlings in the fall and establishing them in an open frame. About three weeks before grafting, bring them into a cool greenhouse to force them gently into growth. Keep the rootstocks dry, particularly those from trees that bleed sap, such as birches (*Betula*) and conifers, since excessive sap may prevent successful union with the scions.

For the scions, collect strong, one-year-old stems from the tree to be propagated; the diameter should be similar to that of the rootstock stems, if possible. Trim scions down to 6–10in (15–25cm), cutting just above a bud or pair of buds, and place them in a plastic bag in a refrigerator until ready to graft. Either cut back the top-growth of the rootstocks to about 2–3in (5–7cm) or leave some top-growth above the graft and cut this back in stages later (see "Aftercare," opposite).

Prepare the rootstocks and scions, one pair at a time, with compatible cuts. It is important to unite the rootstock and scion immediately; even slight drying out is likely to impede successful union. If the scion is narrower than the rootstock, align one edge to ensure that at

Trees that may be Grafted

Chip-budding
Crataegus
Laburnum
Magnolia
Malus
Prunus
Pyrus
Sorbus

Aesculus indica 'Sydney Pearce'

Apical-wedge
Aesculus
Catalpa
Cercis
Fagus

Side-veneer
Abies
Acer
Betula
Carpinus
Cedrus
Cupressus
Fagus
Fraxinus
Ginkgo
Gleditsia
Larix
Magnolia
Picea
Pinus
Prunus
Robinia
Sorbus

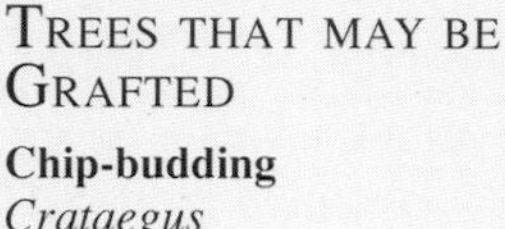

Robinia pseudoacacia 'Frisia'

Whip-and-tongue
Fraxinus
Gleditsia
Robinia

Propagating Trees by Side-veneer Grafting

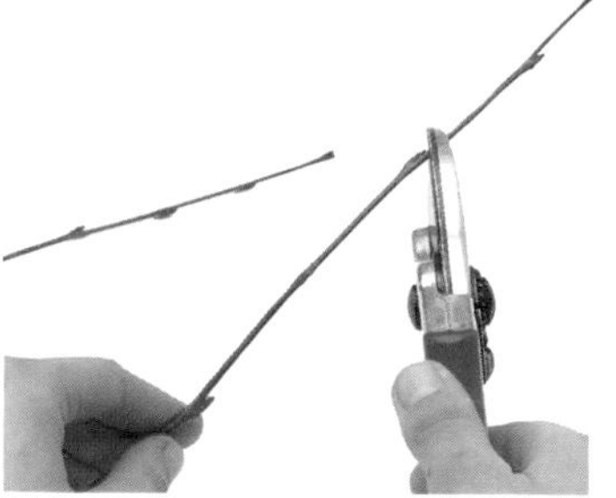

1 *Trim the scion to a length of 6–10in (15–25cm), cutting just above a bud or pair of buds. Place it in a plastic bag and refrigerate until ready to graft.*

2 *Using a sharp knife, make a short, downward, inward nick about 1in (2.5cm) from the top of the rootstock.*

3 *Starting near the top of the rootstock, make a sloping, slightly inward cut down to the inner point of the first cut. Remove the sliver of wood.*

4 *Make the final cut on the rootstock by slicing straight up from the first cut below. This leaves a flat cut on one side of the rootstock (see inset).*

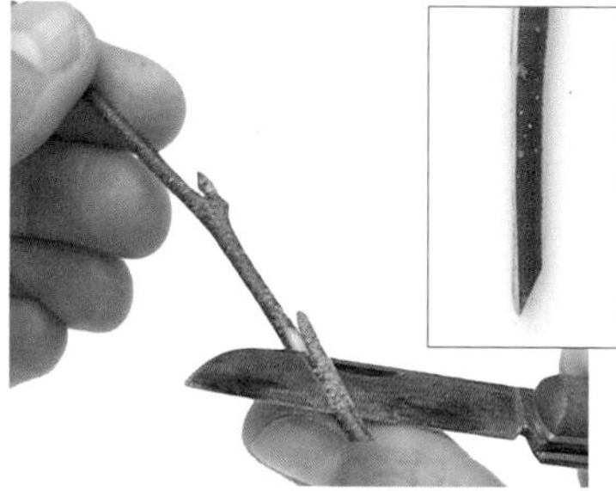

5 *Now prepare the scion: make a shallow, sloping cut about 1in (2.5cm) long down to the base; then make a short, angled cut at the base, on the opposite side (see inset).*

6 *Fit the base of the scion into the cut in the rootstock (see inset). Starting at the top, wrap a length of grafting tape around the union to secure it.*

7 *Brush grafting wax over the external cut surfaces on both the rootstock and the scion. In addition, wax the top of the scion if it has been trimmed back.*

8 *A few weeks later, if the graft has taken, the buds of the scion will show signs of growth. Remove any suckers that may have appeared on the rootstock or they will divert growth away from the scion.*

least one side of the cambium layer unites. Tie the scion in position with clear plastic, grafting tape, raffia, or a rubberized strip, then wax over all external cut surfaces to reduce moisture loss. For aftercare, see right.

Chip-budding

Mainly used for fruit trees, this is also a good way to propagate plants of the Rosaceae family, for example crabapples (*Malus*). In this method, the scion includes a single bud from which the new growth develops, and the grafted plant remains outdoors rather than being potted up.

During fall, establish one- or two-year-old seedlings or hardwood cuttings in open ground for the rootstocks. In midsummer, remove any lateral branches from the bottom 18in (45cm) of the stem. For the scions (or budsticks), select vegetative (nonflowering) shoots that are of similar diameters to those of the rootstocks from well-ripened, current season's growth.

The rootstocks and budsticks are then prepared and united (see below). If successful, the graft should take within a few weeks; the tape or tie may then be removed and the bud should start to swell. For aftercare, see right.

Apical-wedge grafting

This grafting method is similar to side-veneer grafting, except that the scion is placed directly on top of the rootstock. In late winter, collect some stems of the previous season's growth from the plant to be propagated, and heel them into the ground. In late winter or early spring, lift and wash one-year-old seedlings or vigorous plants for the rootstocks, then cut them back to 2in (5cm) above the roots. Make a vertical cut 1–1¼in (2.5–3cm) down the center of each rootstock. Cut the base of each scion into a wedge, and insert them into the tops of the rootstocks; leave the top of the cut on the scion exposed. Bind and pot up the grafted plants, then follow the aftercare guidance given below (see also ORNAMENTAL SHRUBS, "Apical-wedge grafting," p.89).

Aftercare

Deciduous trees should be kept in the greenhouse at 50°F (10°C), while conifers, broad-leaved evergreens, and summer-grafted trees should be kept in an enclosed, humid environment at 59°F (15°C). The graft should take in a few weeks and new growth will be seen on the scion. Pinch off any suckers appearing below the union, since these are growing from the rootstock. After six to ten weeks, harden off the grafted plants. If not cut back at grafting, reduce top-growth of the rootstock to within 4in (10cm) of the union.

Tie the growing bud to the remaining top of the rootstock to ensure that the new shoot grows straight. In midsummer, cut back the rootstock to just above the union and tie in the new shoot to a supporting stake. Alternatively, the rootstock may be cut back to just above the union in late spring. Once they are beginning to grow vigorously, pot on the grafted trees or transplant them into open ground.

PROPAGATING TREES BY CHIP-BUDDING

1 *Select and cut the budstick (here* Malus*), choosing a long, vigorous shoot of the current season's ripened wood. It should have well-developed buds and be roughly the thickness of a pencil.*

2 *Cut off the soft wood and strip away any leaves at the tip of the shoot.*

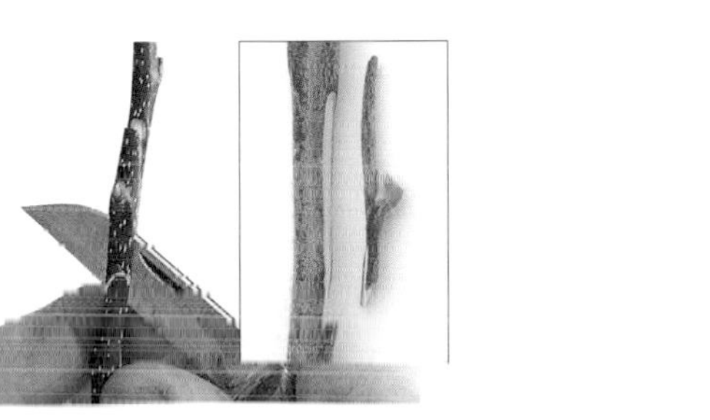

3 *Using a sharp knife, make the first cut ¾in (2cm) below a healthy bud, inserting the blade about ¼in (5mm) deep at an angle of approximately 45°.*

4 *Start making a second cut about 1½in (4cm) above the first. Cut down through the wood to meet the first cut, taking care not to damage the bud.*

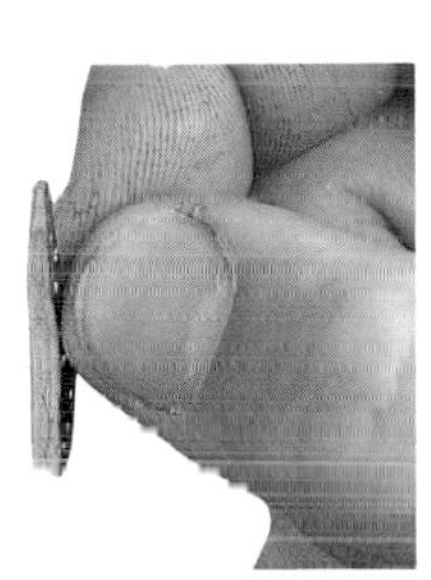

5 *Remove the budchip, holding it by the bud between finger and thumb to keep the cambium layer clean. Place it in a clean plastic bag to prevent it from drying out.*

6 *To prepare the rootstock, cut off all the shoots and leaves from the bottom 12in (30cm) of the stem; it is easiest to do this while standing astride the stock.*

7 *Make two cuts in the rootstock to correspond with those on the budchip so that the stock can be united with the chip. Remove the resulting sliver of wood, taking care not to touch the stem's cut surface (see inset).*

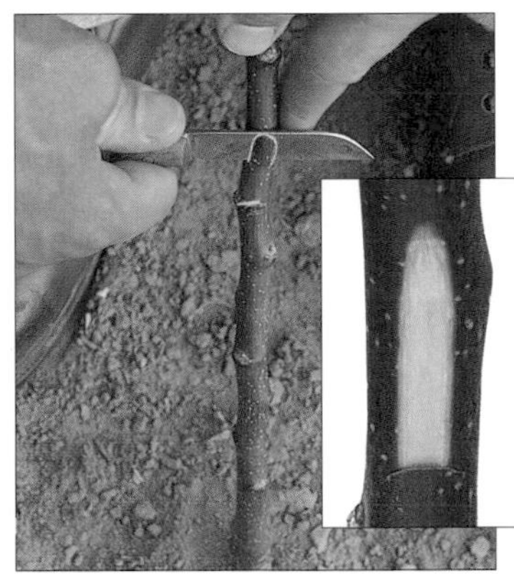

8 *Place the budchip into the lip of the cut rootstock, so that the cambium layers of the chip and stock match as closely as possible (see inset). Bind the join tightly with grafting tape. If the graft takes, the bud will start to swell and develop; the tape can then be removed.*

9 *Next spring, cut back the stock just above the union; the bud will develop as the leader.*

Hedges and screens

Hedges and screens, both formal and informal, can play an important role in the structure and character of a garden as well as having a variety of practical uses.

Practical uses

Most hedges, whether informal, open hedges or formal, solid, clipped ones, are planted for utilitarian purposes, to delineate boundaries, to provide shelter and shade, and to screen the garden. It is possible, however, to combine use with beauty.

Living barriers

As living barriers, hedges may take some years to establish but, if properly maintained, they are often preferable to fences because they provide changing textures, colors, and shapes. Most plants used for hedging are long-lived; if correctly maintained, they will provide dense and sometimes virtually impenetrable barriers for many years.

Shelter

Hedges make excellent windbreaks, filtering fast-moving air and reducing the impact caused by turbulence when wind hits a solid object such as a wall or fence. The porosity of a hedge varies between species and times of year; a close-clipped, evergreen yew hedge (*Taxus*) will be considerably less porous than a deciduous beech hedge (*Fagus sylvatica*) during winter. At the ideal of 50 percent porosity, it has been calculated that with a 5ft (1.5m) hedge, wind speed is reduced by 50 percent at a distance of 24ft (7.5m) from the hedge; by 25 percent at a distance of 50ft (15m); and by 10 percent at a distance of 100ft (30m). The shelter provided by hedges is invaluable, particularly in windswept gardens, where even hardy plants may suffer damage as a result of heavy storms and strong winds.

Year-round Color
x Cupressocyparis leylandii *cultivars produce contrasting shades of foliage in a mixed conifer hedge.*

Noise barriers

Hedges may contribute to noise reduction by screening out unwelcome sounds. One of the most efficient types is a green "environmental barrier." A horizontal weave of pussy willow (*Salix caprea*) is threaded through two rows of vertical stakes and the core is packed with soil to form a solid wall. The willow roots into the soil core, and the top and side growth are pruned back to the woven wall at regular intervals.

Ornamental hedges

A wealth of plants of diverse shape, size, texture, and color can be used for hedges, deciduous or evergreen, formal or informal, or with flowers and fruit. Mixing two or more species selected for flower and foliage creates a living mosaic.

Plants for Informal Hedges

***Pyracantha* 'Golden Charmer'**

***Hibiscus syriacus* 'Red Heart'**

***Escallonia* 'Langleyensis'**

***Ilex aquifolium* 'Madame Briot'**

***Rosa* 'Roseraie de l'Haÿ'**

***Forsythia* x *intermedia* 'Spectabilis'**

Formal

Arborvitae (*Thuja*) makes an excellent hedge, provided that four to six years are allowed for establishment. A hedge of x *Cupressocyparis leylandii* grows extremely rapidly and has to be clipped at least twice a year to keep it neat and within bounds. Low formal hedges are frequently seen in parterres as well as knot gardens. Various forms of boxwood (*Buxus sempervirens*), especially 'Suffruticosa', are commonly used, as are *Santolina* and

Formal, Clipped Hedges

Hedging Plants	Planting Distance	Appropriate Height	Clipping Times	Responds to Renovation
Evergreen				
Buxus sempervirens (boxwood)	12in (30cm)	1–2ft (30–60cm)	Twice/3 times, in growing season	Yes
Chamaecyparis lawsoniana (Lawson cypress) – most cultivars except dwarf types	24in (60cm)	4–8ft (1.2–2.5m), but may be larger	Twice, in spring and early fall	No
x *Cupressocyparis leylandii* (Leyland cypress)	30in (75cm)	6–12ft (2–4m), but up to 20ft (6m)	Twice/3 times, in growing season	No
Ilex aquifolium (holly) and cultivars	18in (45cm)	6–12ft (2–4m)	In late summer	Yes
Lavandula (lavender)	12in (30cm)	18–36in (45–90cm)	In spring and after flowering	No
Ligustrum (privet)	12in (30cm)	5–10ft (1.5–3m)	Twice/3 times, in growing season	Yes
Lonicera nitida	12in (30cm)	3–4ft (1–1.2m)	Twice/3 times, in growing season	Yes
Pinus strobus (white pine)	30in (75cm)	6–12ft (2–4m), but up to 20ft (6m)	Once as candles extend	No
Taxus x *media* (yew)	24in (60cm)	4–12ft (1.2–4m), but up to 20ft (6m)	Twice/3 times in summer and fall	Yes
Thuja (arborvitae)	24in (60cm)	5–10ft (1.5–3m)	In spring and early fall	No
Deciduous				
Caragana aurantiaca	18in (45cm)	2–4ft (60cm–1.2m)	Once, in summer	Yes
Carpinus betulus (hornbeam)	18–24in (45–60cm)	5–20ft (1.5–6m)	Once, in mid- to late summer	Yes
Crataegus monogyna (hawthorn)	12–18in (30–45cm)	5–10ft (1.5–3m)	Twice, in summer and fall	Yes
Fagus sylvatica (beech)	12–24in (30–60cm)	4–20ft (1.2–6m)	Once, in late summer	Yes

Lonicera nitida. Tapestry or mosaic hedges combine a number of compatible plants within the same hedge line to provide changing visual impact throughout the year. Useful species include *Taxus* x *media*, *Ilex aquifolium*, *Carpinus betulus*, and *Fagus sylvatica*.

Mixing evergreen and deciduous species provides an interesting and colorful background throughout the year. Species used must have similar rates of growth if overvigorous species are not to dominate.

Informal

Informal hedges combine practical and ornamental qualities. Although not suitable for strictly formal designs, they can be very decorative and still provide useful screening and shelter. Many of the plants used in these informal boundaries produce flowers and fruit, or both, contributing form and color to the garden.

Integrate the different color backgrounds carefully into the overall design. *Berberis julianae*, *Chaenomeles speciosa*, or forsythia are often used; hybrid shrub roses and species also make fine informal hedges. Most strong-growing bamboos are suitable for areas where soil moisture is high and a wind filter is needed.

FORMAL ELEGANCE
The symmetrical use of dwarf hedges in shades of green frames the brick path and draws attention to the ornamental sculpture.

Choosing plants

Before selecting species for hedging, consider their eventual height, spread, and speed of development, and ensure that species chosen are hardy within the climatic zone and are suited to the soil type of the garden. Plants for formal hedges must have a dense habit of growth and be tolerant of close clipping. For informal hedges grown for their flowers or berries, choose plants that need pruning only once a year. The timing of pruning is critical, otherwise the next season's display of flowers or fruit may be spoiled.

The choice of evergreens or deciduous species is partly a matter of taste, but bear in mind that evergreens and conifers provide a dense, windproof screen throughout the year, offering protection that may be critical in severe winters.

Soil preparation and planting

Hedges are a permanent feature of the garden. It is therefore important to prepare the site thoroughly before planting, and to top-dress each spring with a well-balanced fertilizer and mulch. Soil preparation and planting techniques are the same as for trees and shrubs (see pp.39–43 and pp.67–9). The width of ground preparation required will be between 24–36in (60–90cm).

Spacing for most hedging plants is 12–24in (30–60cm) – see the charts below. If a hedge 36in (90cm) thick or more is required, plant a double, staggered row with spacing of 36in (90cm) between plants, and 18in (45cm) between rows. Plants for all dwarf hedges, parterres, and knot gardens should be spaced about 4–6in (10–15cm) apart.

Pruning and training

The initial training of a formal hedge is crucial to promote even growth from the base of the hedge to the top. Careful attention to pruning in the first two to three years is essential.

Early pruning and shaping

Most deciduous plants, especially those with a naturally bushy, low-branching habit, need to be cut back by one-third on planting, with strong laterals also cut back by one-third of their length. In the second winter, cut back again by about one-third.

INFORMAL AND FLOWERING HEDGES

HEDGING PLANT	ORNAMENTAL QUALITIES	PLANTING DISTANCE	APPROPRIATE HEIGHT	WHEN TO PRUNE
EVERGREEN				
Berberis julianae	Yellow flowers, blue-black fruits	24in (60cm)	5–7ft (1.5–2.2m)	In summer
Berberis verruculosa	Yellow flowers, blue-black fruits	18in (45cm)	2–3ft (0.6–1m)	In summer
Escallonia	White, red, or pink flowers	18in (45cm)	4–8ft (1.2–2.5m)	Immediately after flowering
Garrya elliptica	Gray, green, red, or yellow catkins	18in (45cm)	5–7ft (1.5–2.2m)	Immediately after flowering
Ilex aquifolium	White flowers, berries	18–24in (45–60cm)	6–20ft (2–6m)	In late summer
Lavandula	Purple flowers, gray foliage	12in (30cm)	2–3ft (0.6–1m)	After flowering
Pyracantha	White flowers, red berries	24in (60cm)	6–10ft (2–3m)	For pruning, see p.79
DECIDUOUS				
Berberis thunbergii	Pale yellow flowers, red fruits, red fall foliage	12–15in (30–38cm)	3–4ft (1–1.2m)	After flowering, if required, to keep in check
Chaenomeles speciosa	White, pink, red flowers	24in (60cm)	8ft (2.5m)	Immediately after flowering
Crataegus monogyna	Fragrant white flowers, red berries	18–24in (45–60cm)	10ft+ (3m+)	In winter, remove selected vigorous shoots
Forsythia x *intermedia* 'Spectabilis'	Yellow flowers	18in (45cm)	5–7ft (1.5–2.2m)	After flowering, remove old stems
Hibiscus syriacus	White, pink, blue flowers	18in (45cm)	5–7ft (1.5–2.2m)	In spring
Potentilla fruticosa	Bright yellow flowers	12–18in (30–45cm)	2–4ft (0.6–1.2m)	In spring
Prunus tomentosa	White flowers, edible red fruit	18in (45cm)	5ft (1.5m)	In winter, remove selected vigorous shoots
Rosa 'Nevada'	Fragrant cream flowers	24in (60cm)	5–6ft (1.5–2m)	In spring, remove thin twigs
Rosa 'Roseraie de l'Haÿ'	Fragrant crimson flowers	18in (45cm)	5ft (1.5m)	In spring, remove thin twigs
Ribes odoratum	Fragrant yellow flowers	12–15in (30–38cm)	3–4ft (1–1.2m)	After flowering

PLANTING IN SINGLE AND DOUBLE ROWS

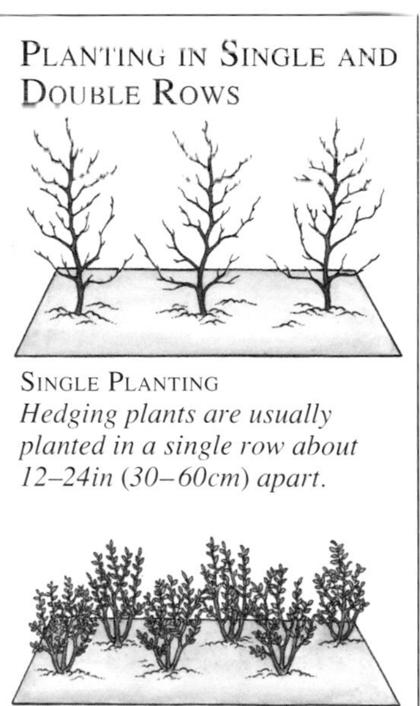

SINGLE PLANTING
Hedging plants are usually planted in a single row about 12–24in (30–60cm) apart.

DOUBLE PLANTING
For a denser, wider hedge space the plants 36in (90cm) apart in a double, staggered row.

FORMATIVE PRUNING

BEFORE PRUNING
Leaders and laterals have grown unrestricted; the hedge (Lonicera nitida) *needs formative pruning.*

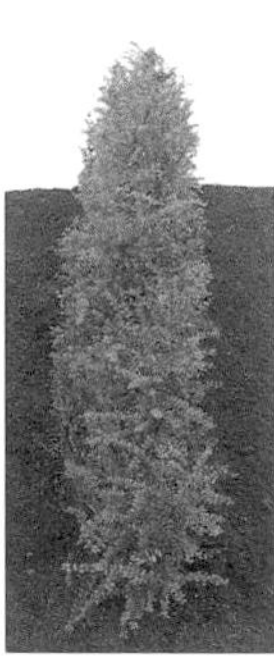

AFTER PRUNING
Cut back the laterals by half and prune the leaders to the required height to encourage bushy growth. Water, feed, and mulch if needed.

HOW TO SHAPE A HEDGE

1 *Stretch a taut, level string between two upright posts to act as a guideline for the highest point of the hedge, then cut the top of the hedge along this line.*

2 *Cut a template of the shape required. Place the template on the hedge and cut following the line of the template, moving it along as you proceed, then cut the sides.*

3 *Once you reach the end of the hedge, remove the template, posts, and lines of string. Clip the end of the hedge neatly.*

To shape strong-growing plants and those with an upright habit of growth, such as privet (*Ligustrum*) and hawthorn (*Crataegus*), cut them back to within 6–12in (15–30cm) above ground level in late spring, followed by a further clipping back of laterals in late summer. During the second winter or early spring, cut back hard, removing at least half of the previous season's growth.

Even from this early stage the hedge sides should be cut at a more or less oblique angle (referred to as the slope), with the base as the widest point. Hedges with a flat-topped A shape or a gently curved, pointed top are less vulnerable to snow and strong winds. Snow will quickly fall away down the sides of a tapered hedge; high winds or storms will be deflected by its sloping sides, causing minimal plant damage.

A level top is achieved by cutting to a straightedge or to a garden line stretched between stakes. It is important to use a guide when clipping low hedges too, since discrepancies are just as likely to occur when looking down as when viewing the hedge from eye level. Once the size and slope have been achieved, clipping to keep the hedge in shape is all that is required in subsequent seasons.

Conifers and many evergreens are used extensively as hedges. In most cases, laterals only are pruned during the early years, particularly in the formative second year, allowing the apical shoot to grow to the desired height before trimming back.

Maintaining a hedge

A formal hedge needs to be clipped regularly to maintain its shape: in most cases the hedge should be trimmed twice annually, in spring and late summer (see *Formal, Clipped Hedges*, p.58). Most formal hedges are cut with shears or an electric trimmer. Use a straightedge or a garden line as a guide when trimming the hedge to shape.

Informal hedges also need regular pruning to shape. Remove misplaced growths, and cut back within the required bounds. Flowering or fruiting hedges must be pruned only at the appropriate season (see *Informal and Flowering Hedges*, p.59). Informal hedges and those with large evergreen leaves should, where practical, be trimmed with pruners to avoid unsightly damage to the leaves.

SHAPING HEDGES

Make hedges narrower at the top to deflect strong winds and snow. In heavy snowfall areas, hedges should have pointed tops to prevent snow from settling and causing damage.

HORNBEAM

YEW

Renovation

A number of hedging species, notably hornbeam (*Carpinus*), honeysuckle (*Lonicera*), and yew (*Taxus*), respond well to renovation even where hedges have been neglected and have become overgrown. For best results, deciduous hedges should be renovated in winter, and evergreen ones in midspring.

If drastic pruning is required, alternate sides should be cut back in subsequent seasons. If the renovation is to be successful, it is most important to feed and mulch the plants in the season before pruning, and then again after cutting back to encourage healthy new growth.

TRIMMING HEDGES

TRIMMING WITH SHEARS
To ensure that the top of the hedge is cut level and flat, keep the blades of the shears parallel to the line of the hedge at all times.

CUTTING WITH HEDGE TRIMMERS
When using an electric trimmer, keep the blade parallel to the hedge and use a wide, sweeping action.

HOW TO RENOVATE AN OVERGROWN HEDGE

Cut back growth to the main stems on only one side of a neglected, deciduous hedge, trimming the other side as usual (right). A year later, if growth has been vigorous, cut back growth on the other side to the main stems (far right).

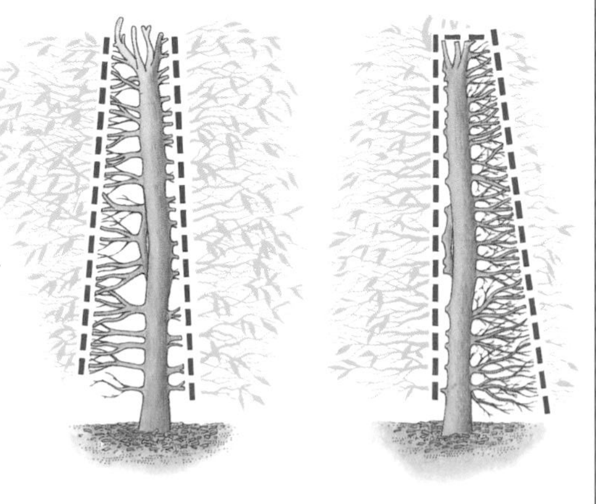

3

ORNAMENTAL SHRUBS

VALUED BY GARDENERS *for their architectural quality and long-term interest, shrubs are unequaled for forming the skeleton of a planting design. In a mixed border, they provide welcome solidity and substance, balancing the more transitory pleasures of herbaceous plants. Grouping evergreen and deciduous shrubs together allows you to create an attractive year-round display which is also relatively low in maintenance. As well as a diversity of shapes and forms, shrubs possess a magnificent variety of features: from the glossy, maplelike leaves of* Fatsia japonica *or the heavily perfumed plumes of lilac to the beadlike berries of pyracanthas or the spectral white stems of* Rubus biflorus, *there is a shrub to fit every size of garden in every location and climate.*

Designing with shrubs

SHRUBS are woody-stemmed plants that typically produce a framework of branches from the base, unlike the single trunk characteristic of most trees. The division between shrubs and trees is not a rigid one, however, because some shrubs (such as fuchsias) can be trained as standards with a single trunk, and a number of trees are multistemmed. Similarly, the difference in scale is not a clear one, since some shrubs grow larger than some trees.

Whether the term "shrub" is used very strictly or rather more loosely, it covers an enormous choice of plants suitable for gardens of any size and style. Species have been collected from many parts of the world, and these have given rise to numerous cultivars and hybrids of ornamental value.

Choosing shrubs

Shrubs are invaluable in the garden for many reasons. Perhaps most important of all, they impart shape, structure, and substance to a design and provide a framework. They are far from being purely functional keystones, however. They are also endowed with a variety of ornamental qualities, including fragrant and colorful flowers, evergreen or variegated foliage, attractive fruits, and colored or shapely stems.

These decorative attributes exert great influence on your choice of plants. There are, however, important practical considerations to take into account when deciding which shrubs to grow.

INFORMAL PLANTING
In this garden, an informal grouping of shrubs, including a variegated holly (Ilex aquifolium), *the fiery* Euonymus alatus, *and a tall* Aesculus parviflora, *provide an ever-changing display of contrasting colors and shapes.*

Compatibility with the given or adapted growing conditions is essential (see "Suiting plants to site conditions," p.62), while a shrub's growth rate, habit, and eventual height and spread also determine whether it is suitable for a garden or not and where it is best sited.

Form and size
Shrubs range in size from dwarfs, such as the mat-forming *Penstemon newberryi* at only 6–8in (15–20cm) high, that are suitable for the rock garden, to much more substantial plants that are 15–20ft (5–6m) in height, such as some of the handsome evergreen rhododendrons.

Shrubs have many different forms and habits, including rounded, arching, and vertical. Some – for example *Yucca glauca*, with its explosive spray of swordlike leaves and erect panicles of flowers – are worth growing for their form alone. Others, such as *Chaenomeles japonica*, have a sprawling habit that often looks better if wall-trained.

Shrubs as design features

When selecting shrubs, consider how they will associate with the other planting as well as any structural elements nearby, such as the house or patio. If they are to form part of the design framework, shrubs with distinctive, sculptural silhouettes are usually most suitable – for example the spreading, wavelike form of *Juniperus squamata* 'Blue Carpet' or the bold, upright mass of *Mahonia bealei*. Think of them as abstract shapes that may be used singly or in combination to create a balanced planting of contrasting and complementary forms.

Foundation planting
Shrubs are often used as foundation planting to link the house with the garden, forming a transition between the rigid lines of the building and the softer shapes and textures of border plants and lawn.

This type of planting is effective when used to mark the entrance to the house. For example, symmetrical groups or rows of shrubs could flank the drive or the doorway, or an informal curved bed might border a winding path to the door.

Design the planting so that it complements the style, color, and scale of the building. Evergreen shrubs are often chosen because of their continuous display but, especially in an informal setting, including deciduous plants as well creates a greater variety of interest while still providing mass and structure.

Suiting plants to site conditions

To ensure that shrubs flourish and give pleasure for a long time, it is essential to invest in plants that are suited to the particular conditions of your garden. Even within a small garden, these growing conditions often vary considerably. Since there are so many shrubs from which to make a selection, there is no need to grow plants that are unsuited to the chosen site.

Soil types

The character of the soil should be the first consideration; in many cases, it can be improved to widen the range of plants that can be grown satisfactorily. It is particularly important to make heavy soils more open and free-draining and light soils more moisture-retentive, as well as to moderate any excessive acidity or alkalinity that may be a problem.

Successful planting must take into account the soil's underlying character, however. Even for relatively extreme conditions, there are a number of plants from which to choose: dogwoods (*Cornus*) and willows (*Salix*) like moist soils, while broom (*Cytisus/Genista*), lavender (*Lavandula*), and *Phlomis* thrive on well-drained soils. Rhododendrons and other ericaceous plants generally require acidic conditions, but many shrubs do well on alkaline soils, including *Deutzia*, *Hypericum*, and *Philadelphus*.

Exposure and microclimate

A plant's preference for sun or shade should also be borne in mind. Sun-lovers such as *Cistus* will become drawn and straggly if not planted in full sun, but many shrubs tolerate or even prefer some shade. Shade-loving shrubs are often ideal for town gardens, where instead of dappled light filtering through the tree canopy there tend to be sharp contrasts between full sun and deep shade cast by surrounding buildings.

The hardiness of shrubs is another factor to consider. The temperature range, altitude, degree of shelter, exposure, and length of growing season all affect the range that may be grown. The sea has a moderating influence on temperature, but salt-laden winds can damage many plants in gardens near the coast. There are, however, shrubs (such as most *Escallonia* and *Genista*) that benefit from the mild conditions and tolerate salt spray. Plants of borderline hardiness for the area that might well succumb if grown in the open garden are more likely to thrive as wall-trained specimens in a sheltered position.

GROWING PLANTS IN THE RIGHT CONDITIONS
Light shade from the tree canopy and acid soil are ideal for these impressive banks of rhododendrons lining an informal grass path. Contrasting shades have been boldly mixed to create a spectacular avenue of color.

RECOMMENDED SHRUBS FOR ACID SOIL

***Rhododendron* 'Homebush'**

***Camellia* x *williamsii* 'Donation'**

***Erica* x *williamsii* 'P.D. Williams'**

Eucryphia milliganii

Gaultheria shallon

Vaccinium parvifolium

Rhododendron wardii

***Pernettya mucronata* 'Wintertime'**

Zenobia pulverulenta

Successional interest

When selecting shrubs, take account of the seasonal interest that they provide and whether it is continuous, as from evergreen foliage, or transitory, as from a burst of summer blooms. A shrub with a brief period of splendor is often best sited near one that reaches its peak shortly afterward to create a changing but unbroken display.

Spring

Shrubs bearing spring flowers in addition to their newly emerging leaves are valued for the color and vitality that they bring early in the year. Combine them to provide interest throughout the season – from the early *Salix melanostachys*, with its black catkins borne on dark red twigs, to the fragrant, white and pink flower clusters of *Daphne* x *burkwoodii* 'Somerset' in late spring.

Summer

The choice of summer-flowering shrubs is immense and, again, they are best combined to form a continuous display. Invaluable shrubs such as *Potentilla* 'Elizabeth' and *Syringa microphylla* 'Superba' deserve to be widely grown, since their flowering period extends from spring until early fall.

Fall

This is the season when many deciduous shrubs really come to the fore, with colorful foliage providing an eye-catching spectacle. Shrubs for fall interest include *Euonymus alatus*, with its intense red leaves, and the various cultivars of *Cotinus coggygria*, with yellow, red, or purple foliage. Color from berries, such as the orange clusters of *Pyracantha* 'Mohave' or the shiny red fruits of *Cotoneaster divaricatus*, is also valuable, often lasting into winter.

Winter

Shrubs are vital elements in the winter garden, with a rich variety of features. Evergreen foliage probably makes the greatest contribution, providing bold masses of color and texture. Flowers also play their part, with a choice ranging from the sculptural *Mahonia japonica*, with its spreading yellow sprays, to the spiderlike red flowers of *Hamamelis* x *intermedia* 'Diane'. Other fragrant shrubs such as *Viburnum* x *bodnantense* are equally welcome. Less common are shrubs with ornamental stems, such as *Cornus stolonifera* 'Flaviramea' which has vivid lime-green shoots.

Shrub borders

One of the most satisfactory ways of using shrubs in the garden is to grow them in a border on their own. From the large range available that will suit the soil, climate, and site, a selection may be made that will give a succession of color and interest throughout the year. The aim is to create a balanced design, taking into

Design for a Shrub Border
This plan includes a number of plants that provide interest in fall and winter from foliage, form, flowers, and berries. Plants of different growth habit are combined to create a balanced design enlivened by contrasts.

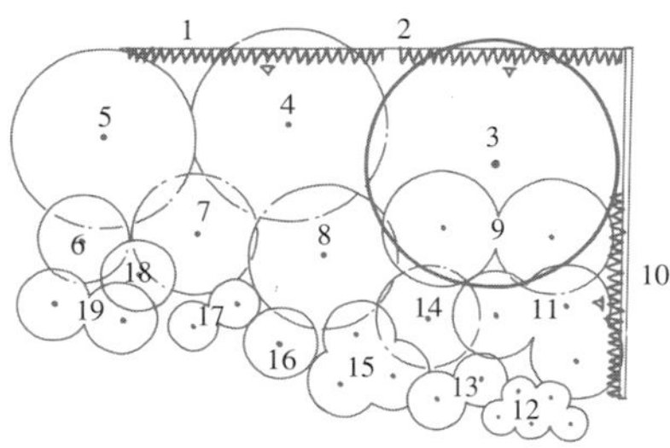

1 *Pyracantha coccinea*
2 *Pyracantha* 'Mohave'
3 *Hamamelis mollis*
4 *Garrya elliptica* 'James Roof'
5 *Viburnum* x *bodnantense*
6 *Perovskia atriplicifolia* 'Blue Spire'
7 *Daphne bholua*
8 *Viburnum tinus* 'Eve Price'
9 *Euonymus fortunei* 'Silver Queen'
10 *Jasminum nudiflorum*
11 *Daphne mezereum*
12 *Erica carnea* 'Vivellii'
13 *Ceratostigma willmottianum*
14 *Lonicera fragrantissima*
15 *Sarcococca confusa*
16 *Cotoneaster* 'Autumn Fire'
17 *Caryopteris* x *clandonensis* 'Arthur Simmonds'
18 *Skimmia japonica* 'Fragrans'
19 *Skimmia japonica* subsp. *reevesiana*

account the shape, form, height, and spread of each shrub, as well as its ornamental qualities and any seasonal changes in its appearance.

The planting may rely almost entirely on a blend of foliage textures and colors, but other features may also play their part. Include shrubs with interesting shapes, for example, and others with colorful berries or stems to maintain interest throughout the year. Resist the temptation to rely on flowers, since their display may be impressive but transitory. By careful selection, however, it is possible to sustain a long succession of flowers in the shrub border.

Some shrubs may be regarded as long-term plants, while others tend to mature and fade quickly. When planning a border, space out the long-term shrubs so that they will not need thinning or drastic pruning to keep them in check once mature. Fast-growing shrubs can also be included, but they should be thinned as soon as they threaten to crowd out the core planting of shrubs.

Restricted Color Border
Here, a restricted color scheme with a predominance of yellow, gold, and bright green creates a sunny, cheerful feeling with evergreen and deciduous shrubs including elders (Sambucus), *golden conifers, and* Euphorbia.

Herbaceous perennials, annuals, and other plants may be interplanted initially, so that in the short term the shrub border might have the same components as a mixed border. Dense planting, including ground cover, may help to keep down weeds, although mulching is advisable to reduce weeds and water loss while the plants are becoming established.

Mixed borders

The idea of a mixed border is to combine a framework planting of shrubs with a variety of herbaceous plants to reap the benefits of both. Its main advantage is that the shrubs provide long-term, sometimes year-round, interest and a background to a succession of other plants. As the shrubs provide height and structure, there is less need to grow tall perennials that require staking than in a traditional herbaceous border.

The mixed border can be designed to suit various settings. If it is situated next to a wall, the planting may include a combination of wall-trained and other shrubs at the back as well as climbers. Other plants may be introduced in loosely shaped niches between shrubs in the foreground. In an island bed, shrubs are normally used to form an irregular core at the center, surrounded by other plants in clumps or drifts.

Managing a mixed border is sometimes more complex than managing a shrub border, because the various plants have different requirements. It is, however, one of the most attractive ways of bringing together the wide-ranging qualities of many different groups of plants.

Specimen shrubs

Shrubs that are particularly beautiful – perhaps because of their fine shape or a characteristic such as exquisite flowers or striking foliage – may be best planted as individual specimens, sited so that they can be seen from a number of viewpoints.

Suitable shrubs

Since a shrub grown in this way clearly stands out in the garden, it is important that its appearance warrants its prominent position. Shrubs with very shapely silhouettes are especially suitable, such as the dense, symmetrical cone of *Picea glauca* var. *albertiana* 'Conica'. A flowering shrub such as *Camellia japonica* 'Mathotiana' would also be an impressive focal point.

When selecting a plant to be grown as a specimen, its long-term interest is an important consideration. In a large garden, a relatively short but magnificent display may be sufficient. A shrub occupying a prime spot in a small garden, however, needs to justify itself by contributing color and form throughout the year or by having more than one season of interest – spring flowers and good fall foliage, for example.

Siting a specimen shrub

When deciding where to site a specimen shrub, ensure that its size will be in keeping with its position in the garden and that it relates well to the overall design. Often the best location is as the focal point of a view from a main window of the house or at the meeting point of two vistas. The background is as important as the shrub itself; usually, a uniform texture and color, as provided by a dense, evergreen hedge or the green carpet of a lawn, forms the most complementary foil. There is, however, scope for experimenting with the positioning of specimen shrubs, particularly in combination with other garden features, such as a pool that creates appealing reflections. Before planting, roughly assess the effect of the shrub's scale and position in the design by substituting stakes of the same height and width.

Specimen Shrub
In late spring and early summer, the spreading tiers of Viburnum plicatum 'Mariesii' *are richly clothed with blooms, but its unusual shape ensures its value as a strong feature throughout the year.*

Wall shrubs

A border at the foot of a warm, sheltered wall is a prime site, although it often tends to be rather dry. If the plants are adequately watered, the conditions suit many shrubs that might otherwise be too tender.

Training shrubs against a wall is often the best option for lax types such as *Forsythia suspensa* that make tangled growth unless supported. For a number of shrubs, it is the best way of displaying their ornamental features, such as the orange or red berries of pyracanthas. Some hardy shrubs that can also be grown free-standing, such as *Chaenomeles*, look attractive when trained against a wall.

Wall-trained Shrubs
Growing a shrub such as this pyracantha against a wall enhances its display of ornamental red berries.

Sometimes no training is needed: shrubs such as myrtle (*Myrtus*) may simply be planted close to the foot of a wall for them to benefit from the warmth and shelter. Other shrubs such as *Buddleia crispa* do need training to flower well.

Dwarf and ground cover shrubs

Planting low shrubs (such as many *Hebe* or *Daphne blagayana*) in raised beds or containers makes it easy to enjoy them at close quarters, as well as providing structure and long-term interest in the overall planting. On a large scale, use low-growing shrubs to balance contrasting rounded or upright forms in beds and borders.

These shrubs are also excellent where interest is needed at ground level; *Helianthemum* cultivars and a vast array of colorful heathers (*Calluna*, *Daboecia*, and *Erica*) brighten up the front of a mixed border or soften the hard edges of a path.

Some spread into an attractive carpet that forms a fine foil for other planting. Those that are relatively fast-growing can be used as ground cover (see pp.150–51). Ground cover shrubs present one of the best solutions for sites such as steep banks that are difficult to cultivate. Even in the unpromising, shady areas directly beneath trees, shrubs such as *Mahonia repens* and cultivars of *Euonymus fortunei* grow well.

Foliage

The substance and seasonal continuity of a garden depend to a large extent on foliage. Evergreen shrubs, in particular, hold the garden together all through the year. The leaves of deciduous shrubs – from spring growth to fall leaf – also give a much longer period of interest than most flowers.

Color

Much may be made of foliage color, which includes not only every shade of green but also silvers and grays, reds, and purples, as well as yellow, gold, and variegated forms.

The boldest leaf colors, such as the gold and red of *Spiraea japonica* 'Goldflame', the red of the young growth of some *Pieris*, or the white-splashed green of *Euonymus fortunei* 'Silver Queen', may be used in much the same way as flower color.

Shape and texture

There are many other attributes of shrub foliage that are worth exploiting in an ornamental display. Large or distinctively shaped leaves such as those of Japanese aralia (*Fatsia japonica*) are particularly striking, and changes of texture, from smooth and glossy to matte and felted, also provide satisfying contrasts.

Colorful Ground Cover
To create a colorful patchwork pattern, use harmonizing and contrasting low-growing shrubs. Here, massed heathers make an exciting display.

Flowers

There is an impressive diversity of shrub flowers, ranging from the tiny, pealike flowers of many brooms (*Cytisus/Genista*) to the large, heavy panicles of lilacs (*Syringa*).

Color and form

Shrubs have flowers in every color, with endless variations of each: for example, shades of pink range from the pale pinkish white of *Syringa yunnanensis* to the crimson of *Rhododendron* 'Hinodegiri'.

Sometimes it is the sheer mass of flowers that appeals, as with the dense blue clusters of *Ceanothus* or the sprays of starlike yellow flowers of forsythias, while other shrubs – such as the exquisite but short-lived flowers of *Paeonia suffruticosa* – seduce by the sumptuous beauty of their individual blooms.

In a large garden it does not much matter that a plant's star turn is only brief, but in a small garden, this can be a serious drawback. Consider a plant's form and foliage if its floral display is very short.

Scent

While the appeal of some flowers lies largely in their color and form, scented ones give the garden another dimension. The flowers may be showy and also deliciously fragrant, as are many mock oranges (*Philadelphus*), or, like the minute flowers of *Sarcococca*, more muted in appearance but casting their fragrance through the garden in early spring.

FLOWERS FOR SCENT
Fragrant shrubs are often best grown next to a path or patio so that their scent may be easily enjoyed. This sweetly perfumed Carpenteria californica *(with white flowers) also benefits from the warmth and shelter of the wall behind it.*

Berries

Berrying shrubs are valuable for continuing color from late summer into winter, and also for attracting birds into the garden. On evergreens such as pyracanthas, bright berries framed by green foliage make an attractive contrast, while those on deciduous shrubs such as *Viburnum opulus* are seen against a changing backdrop of fall foliage followed by bare winter stems.

Orange and red berries are common, but there are other colors – from the yellow of *Viburnum dilatatum* 'Xanthocarpum' to the pink of *Pernettya mucronata* 'Seashell'.

Bear in mind that with some species of shrubs, male and female flowers are borne on separate plants. Satisfactory fruiting is possible only when male and female plants are grown near each other.

ORNAMENTAL STEMS
An informal group of redtwig dogwoods (Cornus alba) *forms a striking blaze of color rising from a spreading mass of variegated* Euonymus fortunei.

Bark and stems

In winter, the silhouettes of bare stems can be very striking. Some, in their sculptural simplicity, are strongly colored, such as dogwoods (*Cornus*), while others, for example *Salix irrorata*, are overlaid with an attractive glaucous bloom.

Group a few shrubs of the same type together to reap the benefit of their massed stems, or site a single fine specimen against a simple background. Imagine the brilliant red stems of *Cornus alba* 'Sibirica' offset by a plain white wall, or the chalk white skeleton of *Rubus biflorus* by a dark one.

The delicate tracery of fine stems is often overlooked unless it is highlighted by vivid coloring, but unusual shapes and heavily thorned or contorted shoots provide added interest. The bizarrely twisted stems of *Corylus avellana* 'Contorta' and *Salix* x *erythroflexuosa* make them interesting curiosities to set against a plain wall or plants of more familiar growth pattern.

Many shrubs grown for their stems require regular pruning, because it is the new wood that is most eye-catching (see "Coppicing and pollarding shrubs," p.77).

Shrubs in containers

Provided that they are watered regularly, many shrubs adapt happily to life in containers. Grown in this way, they make versatile as well as ornamental features. Use them as living sculptures to provide strong shapes and a framework to offset other planting. An evergreen shrub or dwarf conifer forms a year-round centerpiece in a tub or planter, which may be complemented by bulbs in spring and colorful, trailing annuals in summer.

A container-grown shrub is particularly valuable in a small paved garden. It can be used alone as an isolated specimen or combined with a changing display of other plants in containers. In a larger garden, a single, handsomely potted shrub can make a more striking focal point than a piece of statuary. Container-grown shrubs may introduce a formal note simply, such as a pair flanking a flight of steps or an archway, or, more elaborately, making a symmetrical framework or an avenue in grander designs.

Selecting plants

The most suitable shrubs are those with a long season of interest. Good examples for containers include evergreen camellias and rhododendrons, which remain attractive even after their flowers have faded. For a striking foliage display, consider the tender *Chamaerops humilis*, which has huge, palmlike, glossy fans, and conifers with their wide range of colors and textures.

Deciduous foliage can change from spring to fall and, in the case of Japanese maples (*Acer palmatum*), an intricate pattern of delicate stems remains when all the leaves have fallen. Shrubs such as *Spiraea japonica* 'Goldflame', with its strikingly colored leaves and heads of rose-pink flowers, often look particularly attractive growing in an ornamental container.

Practical advantages

An advantage of growing shrubs in containers is that tender plants, such as *Nerium oleander* and palms, may be used to give the garden a Mediterranean or subtropical look in the summer, and then be moved to a protected site for winter. It is also an excellent way of including shrubs that would not otherwise tolerate the soil of the open garden. For example, given lime-free water and ericaceous soil mix, camellias and rhododendrons can be grown in pots or other containers even in limestone areas.

GROWING IN CONTAINERS
A bright oleander (Nerium) *brings color to a cobbled area.*

Planter's guide to shrubs

EXPOSED SITES

Shrubs that tolerate exposed or windy sites; those marked ✎ are not suitable for coastal sites

Arctostaphylos uva-ursi
Bupleurum fruticosum
Calluna vulgaris (and cvs)
Cassinia fulvida
Cistus, some ❄
Cordyline ❄
Cotoneaster (dwarf spp.), *C. horizontalis*
Elaeagnus commutata
Erica carnea (and cvs) ✎
Escallonia
Euonymus fortunei (and cvs)
Fuchsia magellanica (and cvs)
Gaultheria shallon ✎

Fuchsia magellanica

Genista, some ❄
Griselinia, some ❄
Halimodendron halodendron
Hebe, some ❄
Hippophäe rhamnoides
Ilex aquifolium
Lavatera
Myrica, some ❄
Olearia, some ❄
Phormium
Prunus spinosa ✎
Pyracantha
Rhamnus alaternus
Rhododendron ponticum ✎
Salix
Senecio, some ❄
Spartium
Spiraea
Tamarix
Ulex
Yucca, some ❄

SHELTERED SITES

Shrubs that prefer sheltered sites

Abelia floribunda ❄
Abutilon, some ❄
Acer palmatum (cvs)
Ardisia ❄
Banksia ❄
Beschorneria ❄
Bouvardia ❄
Brachyglottis ❄
Citrus ❄
Coprosma ❄
Datura ❄
Dendromecon rigida ❄
Euryops pectinatus ❄
Musa basjoo ❄
Nerium ❄
Rhododendron maddenii (and subsection), *R. vireya* (sections) ❄

WALL SHRUBS

Abelia, some ❄
Abutilon, some ❄
Acacia dealbata ❄
Azara, some ❄
Buddleia crispa
Callistemon, some ❄
Camellia, some ❄
Ceanothus, some ❄
Cestrum, some ❄
Chaenomeles
Daphne bholua
Euonymus fortunei (and cvs)
Fremontodendron
Itea ilicifolia
Pyracantha
Solanum crispum 'Glasnevin', *S. jasminoides* ❄

AIR POLLUTION

Shrubs that tolerate polluted air

Aucuba
Berberis, some ❄
Buddleia davidii
Camellia japonica (and cvs)
Cornus stolonifera
Cotoneaster
Elaeagnus
Euonymus japonicus
Fatsia japonica
Fuchsia magellanica (and cvs)
Garrya
Ilex x *altaclerensis*, *I. aquifolium*
Leycesteria, some ❄
Ligustrum
Lonicera pileata
Magnolia grandiflora
Mahonia aquifolium
Philadelphus
Phillyrea
Salix
Spiraea
Viburnum

DRY SHADE

Shrubs that tolerate dry shade

Aucuba
Cornus canadensis
Daphne laureola
Euonymus fortunei, *E. japonicus*
Fatsia japonica
Hedera, some ❄
Ilex aquifolium
Pachysandra

MOIST SHADE

Shrubs that prefer moist shade

Aucuba
Buxus sempervirens
Camellia japonica
Cornus canadensis
Daphne laureola
Euonymus fortunei, *E. japonicus*
Fatsia japonica

Sarcococca hookeriana var. *digyna*

Ilex aquifolium
Lonicera pileata
Mahonia aquifolium
Osmanthus, some ❄
Sarcococca
Skimmia
Vinca
Xanthorhiza simplicissima

TWO OR MORE SEASONS OF INTEREST

All year

Acacia baileyana ❄
Ardisia japonica ❄
Convolvulus cneorum ❄
Elaeagnus x *ebbingei* 'Gilt Edge'
Euryops acraeus
Lavandula stoechas
Ozothamnus ledifolius

Winter/Spring

Berberis temolaica
Corylus avellana 'Contorta'
Salix irrorata

Spring/Summer

Calycanthus occidentalis
Pieris 'Forest Flame'

Spring/Fall

Cornus 'Eddie's White Wonder'

Summer/Fall

Aesculus parviflora
Citrus 'Meyer's Lemon' ❄
Cornus mas 'Variegata'
Cotinus coggygria 'Flame'
Cotoneaster conspicuus
Dipelta yunnanensis
Hydrangea quercifolia 'Snowflake'
Lonicera korolkowii
Myrtus communis var. *tarentina*

Myrtus communis

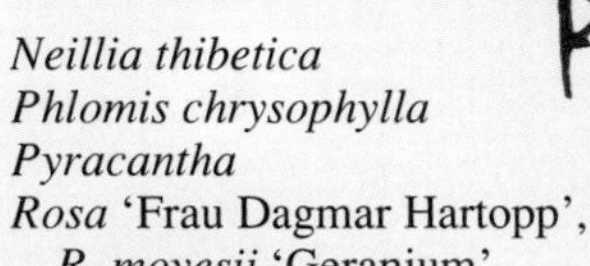

Neillia thibetica
Phlomis chrysophylla
Pyracantha
Rosa 'Frau Dagmar Hartopp', *R. moyesii* 'Geranium'

Fall/Winter

Arbutus unedo
Berberis temolaica
Cornus mas 'Variegata'

FRAGRANT FLOWERS

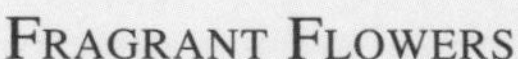

Abeliophyllum distichum
Buddleia alternifolia
Camellia sasanqua
Choisya 'Aztec Pearl', *C. ternata*
Clethra alnifolia 'Paniculata'
Colletia armata 'Rosea'
Cytisus battandieri
Daphne (many)
Elaeagnus
Erica lusitanica
Hamamelis mollis 'Pallida', *H. vernalis*, *H. virginiana*
Lonicera x *purpusii* 'Winter Beauty', *L. standishii*
Magnolia sieboldii, *M.* x *thompsoniana*
Mahonia japonica
Osmanthus fragrans ❄
Philadelphus (many)
Pittosporum tobira
Rhododendron auriculatum, *R. edgeworthii* ❄, *R.* 'Fragrantissima' ❄, *R.*, Ghent Hybrids, *R.*, Loderi Group, *R. luteum*, *R. occidentale* (and Hybrids), *R.* 'Polar Bear', *R.*, Rustica Hybrids, *R. viscosum*
Rosa (many)
Sarcococca
Syringa (many)
Viburnum (many)

Rhododendron luteum

AROMATIC FOLIAGE

Calycanthus
Caryopteris
Perovskia
Prostanthera ❄
Santolina

ARCHITECTURAL SHRUBS

Agave ❄
Aralia elata 'Aureo-variegata'
Chamaerops ❄
Cocos ❄
Cordyline ❄
Cycas revoluta ❄
Dracaena ❄
Eriobotrya japonica
Howea ❄
Jubaea ❄
Pandanus ❄
Phoenix ❄
Phormium
Sabal ❄
Yucca, some ❄

KEY

❄ *Not frost hardy*

Soil preparation and planting

Most gardens allow you to grow a wide range of shrubs even though the soil falls short of ideal – a fertile loam that is well drained but moisture-retentive. Improving the drainage of wet soils and, by the addition of humus, the structure and moisture-holding properties of dry soils will greatly increase the range of shrubs that may be grown satisfactorily. The level of acidity or alkalinity, another factor limiting the range of plants that can be grown, can also be modified.

Important though these improvements may be, garden soil will still naturally tend toward being moist or dry, heavy or light, and acidic or alkaline. The best shrubs for your garden are those suited to the growing conditions available.

Selecting shrubs

Shrubs may be bought from garden centers, nurseries, and from non-specialist outlets such as supermarkets. They are sold in containers, balled-and-burlapped, or bare-root. Shrubs for sale should be accurately labeled, healthy, undamaged, and free of pests and diseases. Inspect the plants thoroughly and select a specimen with evenly distributed branches close to ground level or, with standard shrubs, at the head of a clear stem of the desired height.

Shrubs sold in the warm, dry atmosphere of a supermarket have a short shelf life. Reliable suppliers will give a year's guarantee to replace the shrub if it is not true to name or if it dies within its first year, provided that it has been given reasonable care. Some nurseries also sell shrubs by mail order; plants are normally shipped during their dormant period.

Shrubs in containers

Shrubs are most commonly sold as container-grown specimens, the containers ranging from rigid pots to heavy paper. Most shrubs sold in this way have been container-grown throughout their lives. Others are field-grown and potted up (containerized) in the season before sale to prolong their sale life. Look through the drainage holes to see whether there is a well-developed root system. If so, the shrub is most probably container-grown and not containerized. If possible, slide the shrub out of its container; the roots should show healthy, white tips. Reject plants with poorly developed root systems, and those that are potbound (with roots protruding from the container), since these rarely grow well.

A major advantage of container-grown shrubs is that they can be bought and planted out at any time, except when there are extremes of temperature or drought. Containerized shrubs can be safely planted out in winter, but before buying and planting in the growing season check that they have a well-developed root system (if so, they will retain all or most of the soil mix around the roots when removed from the pot).

Bare-root shrubs

Deciduous shrubs that are easily propagated are sometimes lifted from the open ground during their dormant season and sold with their roots bare of soil. The buying season for these bare-root shrubs is from fall to spring. To prevent them from drying out, the roots are normally wrapped in plastic. Before purchasing, check that bare-root shrubs have an evenly developed fibrous root system.

Balled-and-burlapped shrubs

Some shrubs, especially conifers, are sold with their roots and soil wrapped in burlap or netting. The buying season for these balled-and-burlapped shrubs is fall or early spring. Always check that the wrapping is intact, so that the roots have not been exposed to drying wind, and that the root ball is firm.

Shrubs that Prefer Sandy Soil

Berberis empetrifolia
Calluna vulgaris (and cvs)
Ceanothus thyrsiflorus (and forms)
Cistus x *cyprius*

Cistus x *cyprius*

Cytisus scoparius (and forms)
Erica arborea var. *alpina*, *E. cinerea* (and cvs)
Fuchsia magellanica (and cvs)
Genista tinctoria
Hakea lissosperma
Halimodendron halodendron
Helianthemum
Helichrysum, some ❄
Lavandula, some ❄
Olearia, some ❄
Ozothamnus, some ❄
Phlomis
Phormium
Rosa pimpinellifolia
Spartium junceum
Tamarix
Ulex europaeus

Shrubs that Tolerate Clay Soil

Amelanchier
Aralia 💧
Aronia arbutifolia 💧
Aucuba
Berberis 💧

Chaenomeles x *superba* 'Nicoline'

Chaenomeles x *superba* 💧
Citrus ❄
Clethra alnifolia 💧
Cornus alba 'Sibirica' 💧
Cotoneaster 💧
Forsythia
Garrya
Hippophäe
Kalmia latifolia
Lonicera, some ❄
Mahonia x *media* group 💧
Philadelphus
Pyracantha
Rosa
Salix caprea 💧
Taxus
Tetrapanax papyriferus ❄
Viburnum opulus 💧

Key
❄ *Not frost hardy*
💧 *Tolerates waterlogged soil*

When to plant

Fall to spring is the planting season for balled-and-burlapped and bare-root shrubs, and the optimum time for container-grown and containerized shrubs. Planting in fall allows the roots to establish while the ground is still warm, so the shrub should be growing vigorously before dry weather the next summer.

In some areas, planting can be carried out during mild weather in winter, but not when the ground is frozen. Roots will not commence growth in very cold soil, and there is a risk that they may freeze.

The major disadvantage of spring planting is that top-growth is likely to develop before the roots establish and, if there is an early spell of dry weather, watering may be required to help the plants to survive.

Soil preparation

Many shrubs are potentially long-lived, so the ground needs to be thoroughly prepared before planting. The aim should be to cultivate an area well beyond the planting site for an individual shrub and, preferably, the entire bed.

The best seasons for cultivation are late summer and fall. Remove or kill all weeds first, taking particular care to eradicate perennials (see "Weeds," pp.575–9). Double dig (see p.528), incorporating a 3–4in (8–10cm) layer of well-rotted organic matter into the lower trench. If this is impractical, work large quantities of organic matter into the top 12–18in (30–45cm) of soil. Add fertilizer if appropriate (see "Soil nutrients and fertilizers," pp.532–3).

How to plant

The planting hole for a shrub must be wide enough to accommodate the root ball. For container-grown or balled-and-burlapped plants, make the hole twice the width of the contained root mass, or as much as three times the width if planting in clay soils. For bare-root shrubs, the hole must be large enough to allow the roots to be spread out fully, as well as sufficiently deep to allow the shrub to be planted at the same level as it was in its container or in the open ground. This is indicated by the soil mark – a dark mark near the base of the stem. A stake laid across the top of the planting hole provides a useful guide to the depth of planting. Treatment of a containerized shrub depends on how developed the root system is when removed from the pot. If the soil mix falls away, plant as for a bare-root shrub; if it does not, treat as if container-grown. Remove or untie and spread out the burlap or netting surrounding a balled-and-burlapped shrub after it is in the hole. When backfilling the hole, shake a bare-root plant gently to settle the soil. Gently firm the soil in stages.

To improve drainage around a shrub planted in clay soil, plant the

PLANTING A WALL SHRUB

1 *Dig a hole at least 9in (22cm) away from the wall. Plant the shrub (here a pyracantha) and tie in the supporting stake to a wire.*

2 *Replace the soil. Secure lateral stakes to the central stake and both wires, so that the side shoots can be supported and tied in (see inset).*

PLANTING A CONTAINER-GROWN SHRUB

1 *Dig a hole about twice the width of the shrub's root ball (here a* Viburnum). *Fork over the base and sides of the hole.*

2 *Placing one hand on top of the soil mix and around the shrub to support it, carefully ease the plant out of its container. Place the shrub in the prepared hole.*

3 *Lay a stake alongside to check that the soil level is the same as before. Adjust the planting depth, if necessary, by adding or removing topsoil beneath the shrub.*

4 *Backfill around the shrub with the removed soil, firming in stages to prevent air pockets from forming.*

5 *Once the hole has been filled with soil, carefully firm around the shrub with your heel or hands.*

6 *Prune any diseased, damaged, or weak wood and cut back any inward-growing or crossing stems to an outward-growing shoot or bud.*

USING A WATERING RING

To help retain water, leave a shallow depression with a low wall of soil around the shrub. After several waterings, push the wall into the depression and mulch.

shrub slightly above soil level and mound soil around the exposed section of the root ball up to the level of the soil mark. On sandy soil, plant the shrub in a slight dip to channel water around the plant's roots. Water the shrub and mulch.

Planting wall shrubs
Some shrubs may be trained on wires fixed to a wall or fence. Plant these as for free-standing shrubs, at least 9in (22cm) from the wall so that the roots are not in its rain shadow, and lean the plant in toward the wall. Support the main stem and laterals of the shrub with stakes, which are then tied into the wires (see also "Wall shrubs," p.78).

Staking

Shrubs do not normally need staking, except for large, rootbound specimens and standards. The former, which ideally should not be selected, will almost certainly need some support in their first year or two at least, until their roots begin to spread out and they become stable.

The best method for any shrub that branches from near ground level is to brace the shrub with guys fixed to three stakes spaced evenly around a circle with a radius of about 3ft (1m) centered on the shrub. To prevent bark damage, cover the guys where they touch the branches with rubber or similar material (see also ORNAMENTAL TREES, "Staking," p.40).

For a standard, insert the stake in the planting hole before planting to avoid damaging the root system. The top of the stake should be just below the first branches. Secure the stem to the stake, using a commercial tie with a spacer or a homemade figure-eight tie to prevent chafing.

STAKING A STANDARD SHRUB

1 *Drive a stake into the hole just off-center. The stake should reach to just below the head of the shrub after planting. Plant the shrub next to the stake.*

2 *If the depth is correct, backfill and firm in. On free-draining soil, form a well around the shrub to retain moisture. Secure the stem with a suitable tie (see inset).*

Protecting newly planted shrubs

Newly planted shrubs may suffer from drying out or cold if not protected. Broad-leaved evergreens and conifers in exposed positions are particularly vulnerable.

A screen of burlap or mesh significantly reduces the drying force of cold winds. Erect a strong, wooden framework 12in (30cm) away from the windward side of the shrub needing protection. Tack the burlap or the mesh to the frame, which should extend at least 12in (30cm) above and to either side of the shrub. More complete protection is given by surrounding individual plants with a four-sided framework to which burlap or mesh is tacked.

Another measure, which may be used either alone or in addition to screening, is to spray the plants with an antidesiccant to reduce drying out. Apply a thin film of spray to both sides of the leaves.

A mulch spread around the base of the shrub will help to protect the roots from ground frost. It is best to spread the mulch during mild weather, preferably when the ground is reasonably warm and damp.

In areas of heavy snow, particularly vulnerable evergreen shrubs may need additional protection. This is best provided by placing a wooden A-frame over them. Dislodge any heavy accumulations of snow promptly. More extreme measures may be needed to protect half-hardy and tender shrubs (see COLD AND WIND PROTECTION, pp. 520–21).

When removing the insulation in spring, check for pests and diseases that may have benefited from the winter protection.

SHRUBS THAT REQUIRE ACID SOIL

Andromeda
Arbutus (most spp.)
Arctostaphylos, some ❄ (some spp.)
Calluna
Camellia, some ❄

Camellia x *williamsii* 'Wilber Foss'

Clethra, some ❄
Cornus canadensis
Corylopsis (most spp.)
Desfontainia spinosa
Enkianthus
Erica (most spp.)
Fothergilla
Hakea, some ❄
Hamamelis
Kalmia
Leucothöe
Magnolia (some spp.)
Menziesia
Pernettya
Philesia magellanica ❄
Pieris
Rhododendron, some ❄ (most spp.)
Styrax officinalis
Telopea speciosissima ❄
Vaccinium
Zenobia pulverulenta

SHRUBS THAT TOLERATE VERY ALKALINE SOIL

Aucuba japonica (and cvs)
Berberis darwinii
Buddleia davidii (and cvs)
Buxus
Ceanothus impressus
Chamaerops ❄
Choisya ternata
Cistus, some ❄
Cotoneaster (all)
Cytisus, some ❄
Deutzia
Euonymus
Forsythia
Hebe, some ❄
Hibiscus, some ❄
Hypericum, some ❄
Ligustrum
Lonicera, some ❄
Nerium oleander ❄

Philadelphus 'Dame Blanche'

Philadelphus
Phlomis fruticosa
Potentilla (all shrubby spp.)
Rosa rugosa
Rosmarinus
Syringa
Viburnum tinus
Vitex agnus-castus
Yucca aloifolia ❄

KEY
❄ *Not frost hardy*

Planting shrubs in containers

Late summer to fall is the main period for planting shrubs in containers, although container-grown shrubs can be planted in an ornamental pot at most times.

Select a container that is the right size for the shrub. When transplanting a shrub, the new container should be about 2in (5cm) larger in depth and diameter than the previous one. If it has already been used, scrub its inside surface thoroughly.

Heavy containers should be placed in position before planting. Stand the container on bricks or blocks to allow free drainage. Place broken crocks over the drainage holes and then add a 1in (2.5cm) layer of drainage material, such as coarse gravel.

A soil-based potting mix, which is rich in nutrients, is preferable to a peat-based mix, which contains only limited added nutrients. Shrubs are likely to remain in their containers for years, and any grown in peat-based soil mixes will require frequent feeding. Additionally, peat-based soil mixes dry out more rapidly than soil-based ones. Use an ericaceous soil mix for rhododendrons and other lime-haters, or to obtain blue flowers on hydrangeas. Ensure that the soil mark is level with the soil mix surface.

With container planting, ensure that the soil mix is at least 1½in (4cm) below the rim to allow room for mulching and watering.

Routine care

The following guidelines for maintenance are generally applicable, although not all shrubs have the same requirements. Newly planted shrubs usually need watering, while those planted in containers should also be periodically top-dressed or repotted. In addition, fertilizing, deadheading, removing suckers, weeding, and controlling pests and diseases may all be necessary.

Watering

Established shrubs need watering only in periods of prolonged drought, but young specimens may need regular watering. Apply the water to the ground around the shrub, soaking the soil. Do not water often and lightly, since this encourages root growth close to the surface. Shallow roots make shrubs vulnerable in drought conditions. The best time to water is in the early evening, when evaporation is minimal.

Fertilizing and mulching

Most shrubs benefit from regular applications of organic or inorganic fertilizers. These are available in a variety of forms.

Mulching with well-rotted, bulky manures helps soil conserve moisture and, if nutrient-rich, improves soil fertility. It also moderates extremes of temperature around the roots and inhibits weeds.

Fertilizers

Shrubs, especially if pruned regularly, are usually fed with slow-release fertilizers, which are best applied in early spring. Some of these fertilizers release their nutrients only when temperatures are high enough for plants to use them. A standard rate of application is 2oz/sq yd (60g/sq m).

Quick-release powder fertilizers are useful to boost growth as it commences in spring. Liquid fertilizers work even faster than powders, and these should be applied once the shrub is growing.

Fertilizers in granular or powder form should be worked into the soil over an area slightly wider than the spread of the top-growth of the shrub. With surface-rooting shrubs, allow the fertilizer to leach in naturally or water it in to avoid the risk of the roots being injured by forking. The application of fertilizers may alter the soil's pH level; most inorganic, nitrogenous fertilizers, for example, make the soil more acidic (see also "Soil nutrients and fertilizers," pp.532–3).

Mulches

Apply the mulch around newly planted shrubs over an area about 18in (45cm) wider in diameter than the plant's root system. The mulch around established shrubs should extend beyond the area of top-growth by 6–12in (15–30cm). A mulch of bark chips, wood chips, or manure should be 2–4in (5–10cm) deep but kept clear of the stems of the shrub. Do not apply any mulch in cold weather or when the soil is dry.

Weeding

Weeds compete for nutrients and moisture, so it is essential to clear the ground of all weeds before planting. The area around newly planted ground cover shrubs needs weeding until the plants form dense growth that suppresses competition. For treatment, see "Weeds," pp.575–9.

Removing suckers

Some grafted shrubs, including rhododendrons, are prone to producing growths, or suckers, beneath the graft union, from either stems or roots. Rub out suckers between finger and thumb as soon as they are noticed; if too large to treat in this way, cut them off as close as possible to the stems or roots from which they are growing. Pulling them off helps to remove any dormant growth buds, but take care not to damage the stem or root. Watch for further growth.

Reversion and mutation

Many variegated shrubs are propagated from green-leaved plants that have produced mutated branches, known as sports. From time to time, branches of variegated shrubs revert to the original foliage of the parent plant or mutate to plain cream or yellow leaves. Since these branches are usually more vigorous, they eventually crowd out those showing variegation, and should be cut out.

Deadheading a Rhododendron

Before new buds have fully developed, snap each dead flowerhead off at the base of its stem. Take care not to damage any young growth.

Deadheading

Some shrubs, including rhododendrons, lilacs (*Syringa*), and *Kalmia*, benefit if their faded flowerheads are promptly removed, where possible, before seed sets. Removing old flowers diverts energy into growth, improving the flowering potential for the following season, but it is not essential to the health of a shrub.

To avoid damage to new growth buds, deadhead as soon as the flowers fade, using fingers and thumb to pick off each one where it joins the stem. Most flowerheads come away cleanly, but any snags should be trimmed with pruners.

How to Remove Suckers

Sucker Removal
Pull or cut off the sucker (here on a Hamamelis*) at the base. If it is pulled off, pare over the wound to leave a clean cut (see inset).*

Recognizing Suckers
A sucker can usually be distinguished by its leaves: a normal stem from the top-growth, left; a sucker from the root, right.

Removing Nonvariegated and Reverted Shoots

Nonvariegated Shoot
With variegated shrubs (here Euonymus fortunei 'Emerald 'n' Gold'*), cut any plain shoots back to the variegated growth.*

Reverted Shoot
Cut back reverted shoots (here on E. f. 'Emerald Gaiety'*) to the main stem. If necessary, remove the entire stem.*

Maintaining shrubs in containers

Container-grown shrubs need more care and attention than those grown in open ground, since they have less access to any available moisture and nutrients.

Watering

Even in rainy weather conditions, check the soil mix at least once or twice a week, since the canopy formed by the leaves often prevents rain from reaching the soil mix beneath. In windy weather, plants are likely to need additional watering, since wind can cause rapid moisture loss.

The container itself also affects the rate at which the soil mix dries out – more quickly in terracotta pots than in wooden or plastic ones. When watering, soak the soil mix thoroughly until water starts to drain through the holes in the base of the container.

Feeding

Use a quick-release, balanced liquid fertilizer two or three times between the start of growth in early spring and midsummer, at the rate recommended by the manufacturer.

Repotting and top-dressing

Until shrubs reach maturity, repot them every year or two in spring. When mature, instead of repotting just remove the top 2–4in (5–10cm) of soil mix in spring and replace it with a top-dressing of fresh soil mix and a slow-release fertilizer. Surface-rooting shrubs might be damaged by this, so ease the plant out of its container, take soil mix from the bottom, and replace it with a smaller quantity of enriched soil mix. The shrub will sit lower than before, leaving room for a top-dressing. Root pruning may be necessary when repotting a shrub if the roots are congested.

TOP-DRESSING

1 *If not repotting, top-dress shrubs in pots (here a rhododendron) annually. First, remove the top 2–4in (5–10cm) of the old soil mix, taking care not to damage the roots.*

2 *Replace with fresh soil mix to the same level as before. Water well and apply a mulch of bark chips or grit if required.*

REPOTTING A CONTAINER-PLANTED SHRUB

1 *If a shrub (here* Cestrum elegans*) is lacking in vigor and appears either unbalanced or too large for its present container, it will almost certainly benefit from being repotted.*

2 *Carefully lay the shrub on its side. Then, supporting the main stems with one hand, ease it out of its container. If necessary, slide a long-bladed knife between soil mix and pot to loosen the root ball.*

3 *If the roots have become very congested, gently tease them out. Remove the surface soil mix and any moss or weeds. Prune back about a quarter of the non-fibrous roots by up to two-thirds.*

4 *Place crocks over the drainage holes of the pot and cover these with soil mix. Position the plant in the pot, spreading its roots out evenly.*

5 *Add more soil mix around the roots, gently firming it in stages, until the soil mix is at the same level on the plant as in its previous pot.*

6 *Leave 1–2in (2.5–5cm) of space below the rim of the container to allow for watering and top-dressing. Prune out any dead, twiggy, or damaged growth, and remove any snags that may have been left by broken stems (see inset). Carry out additional pruning as necessary to create a well-balanced framework of stems.*

Moving an established shrub

Careful selection and siting of a shrub should make transplanting unnecessary, although sometimes it may be desirable or unavoidable. In general, the younger the shrub, the more likely it is to reestablish after being moved.

When to transplant

Most young shrubs may be lifted bare-root when dormant. Established shrubs that have large root systems should be lifted with a ball of soil around the roots before being moved. Fall is the best time to do this.

Balling-and-burlapping a shrub

Most often, it is best to ball-and-burlap a shrub so that root damage is kept to a minimum. Prepare the new position before lifting the shrub.

Dig a trench around the shrub just beyond the spread of its branches. Cut through woody roots but leave fibrous ones intact. Use a fork to loosen the soil around the root ball and reduce its size. Then undercut it with a spade and use pruners to sever any woody taproots.

Once the root ball is free, work a sheet of burlap or similar material underneath it, tipping the shrub from side to side carefully so that the soil is not disturbed. Tie the burlap firmly around the ball, lift the shrub from the hole, and transplant it. Untie the burlap before replanting.

The shrub needs the same treatment as one that has been planted for the first time, but it may take longer to reestablish (see p.69).

Shrub problems

Plants are less likely to succumb to pest attack or disease if they are given good growing conditions and care. Many problems originate from poor drainage, lack of moisture, planting too deeply, compaction of the soil, or exposure to temperature extremes in an unsuitable site.

Physical damage

Wounds caused by a jagged pruning cut, a badly placed cut, or pruning at the wrong time may allow disease organisms to establish. This may also cause dieback. Mechanical wounding of bark, stems, or roots, for example by lawn mowers, also provides an entry point for disease.

Pests and diseases

As shrubs age, they lose vigor and become more prone to pests and diseases. Old or diseased shrubs that have lost their vigor are rarely worth saving and should be replaced.

Pests and diseases most likely to affect shrubs are aphids (p.552), spider mites (p.552), black vine weevils (p.551), *Phytophthora* stem rots (see "*Phytophthora* root rots," p.560), and powdery mildew (p.552). Be alert to the signs of a problem, which include streaking and changes in the color of foliage, drooping leaves, loss of leaves, distorted growth, and the development of mushrooms.

Maintaining good garden hygiene minimizes the chance of pests and diseases establishing a foothold. Dispose of dead and diseased wood, and keep the ground around a shrub free of debris such as old fruit.

Cold and wind

When selecting and siting shrubs, it is vital to take account of the general weather pattern of the area as well as the garden's own individual microclimate. It is almost impossible, however, to take precautions against freak extremes of temperature or exceptional winds.

There is a wide range of hardy shrubs available, and many gardeners choose to rely on these rather than risk the loss of more tender specimens. If growing shrubs that are of borderline hardiness for the area, then it is worth using the appropriate cold and wind protection methods (see pp.520–21).

Container-grown shrubs are more vulnerable to extremes of weather than those grown in the open garden. In areas where temperatures only occasionally fall below freezing, most container-grown hardy shrubs can be overwintered outdoors (except those that are root-tender such as camellias). In colder areas, however, move shrubs indoors to where the ambient daytime temperature is about 45–55°F (7–13°C) or higher, according to the species.

TRANSPLANTING A SHRUB

1 Using a spade, mark out a circle around the extent of the shrub's branches (here Ilex aquifolium 'Golden Milkboy'). *If necessary, tie in any trailing stems or wrap the shrub in burlap to prevent the stems from being damaged.*

2 Dig a trench around the circle, then use a fork to loosen the soil around the root ball. Take care not to damage too many fibrous roots.

3 Continue carefully to fork away soil from around the shrub's root ball to reduce its size and weight.

4 Undercut the root ball with a spade, cutting through woody roots if necessary to separate them from the surrounding soil.

5 Roll up a length of burlap. Tilt the shrub to one side and unroll the burlap beneath the root ball. Tilt the root ball the other way, and unroll the rest of the burlap.

6 Pull the burlap up around the root ball and tie it securely. Remove the shrub from its hole and transport it to its new position.

7 Remove or untie the burlap when replanting in the newly prepared hole. Plant with the soil mark at the same level as before. Firm, water well, and mulch.

Pruning and training

SOME shrubs, particularly evergreens of naturally compact habit such as *Sarcococca*, make attractive plants with little or no pruning or training. They may require no more than the removal of dead, damaged, and diseased wood. If left untreated, this will be unsightly and, more seriously, may put the health of the whole shrub in jeopardy. Many shrubs, however, need pruning or a combination of pruning and training in order to realize their full ornamental potential.

Aims and results of pruning and training

The most common requirement is for formative pruning that creates a vigorous and well-shaped shrub. Many shrubs also require a regular schedule of pruning to maintain or enhance the ornamental quality of their flowers, fruit, foliage, or stems. The timing of this pruning, which may often be critical, varies depending on the growth pattern of the shrub and the result desired.

Pruning can also be a way of bringing neglected and overgrown plants back to healthy, manageable growth. It is a matter of judgment whether a shrub warrants being rescued. Replacement is often the best course when a shrub requires regular cutting back because it is too large for the space available.

Shrubs grown as topiary or hedges require specialized pruning from their formative stage. For further information see TOPIARY, pp.90–91, and HEDGES AND SCREENS, pp.58–60.

In training, the gardener plays an active role in directing the growth of plants. Most shrubs grown in the open require no training at all. Shrubs grown against supports, however, normally need a combination of pruning and training to form a well-spaced framework of branches.

Principles of pruning and training

Pruning normally stimulates growth. The terminal shoot or growth bud of a stem is often dominant, inhibiting by chemical means the growth of buds or shoots below it. Pruning that removes the ends of stems affects the control mechanism, resulting in more vigorous development of lower shoots or growth buds.

WHERE TO CUT

OPPOSITE SHOOTS *Prune stems with opposite buds to just above a strong pair of buds or shoots, using a clean, straight cut.*

ALTERNATE SHOOTS *For shrubs with alternate buds, prune to just above a bud or shoot, using a clean, angled cut.*

MAKING AN ANGLED CUT *Angle the cut so that its lowest point is opposite the base of the bud and the top just clears the bud.*

Hard or light pruning

Hard pruning promotes more vigorous growth than light pruning. This needs to be borne in mind when correcting the shape of an unbalanced shrub. Hard cutting back of vigorous growth often encourages even stronger growth. Prune weak growth hard but strong growth only lightly.

How to prune

Pruning wounds, like other injuries that a shrub might suffer, are possible entry points for disease. The risk is reduced by making well-placed, clean cuts with sharp tools.

Stems with alternate or whorled arrangements of growth buds should be cut just above a bud pointing in the desired direction of growth – for example, an outward-facing bud that will not cross another shoot as its growth develops. Use an angled cut, starting opposite a healthy growth bud, and slant the cut so that it finishes slightly above the bud. If the cut is too close, the bud may die; if too far, the stem itself may die back.

With shrubs that have buds in opposite pairs, cut straight across the shoot just above a pair of healthy buds. Both buds will develop, resulting in a forked branch system.

In the past, gardeners have often been advised to use a wound paint on pruning cuts, but research now suggests that wound paints are not generally an effective way of controlling diseases and in some cases may even encourage them.

Pruning alone will not promote vigorous new growth. Shrubs that are renovated or regularly cut back benefit from feeding and mulching. Apply a general-purpose fertilizer at the beginning of the growing season at a rate of 4oz/sq yd (120g/sq m) and mulch to a depth of 2–4in (5–10cm) with well-rotted organic material in spring, when the ground has warmed up a little.

Training

The growth of lower buds or shoots on a stem may also be modified by training. When a stem is allowed to grow upright, the lower shoots on the stem usually grow weakly. With stems that are trained more horizontally, however, the lower shoots and buds grow more vigorously. Training branches near the horizontal can substantially increase the amount of flower and fruit that a shrub is able to carry. Wall-trained shrubs should be tied in to supports as growth develops. As stems ripen and turn woody they become far less flexible and are therefore more difficult to train successfully.

Formative pruning

The aim of formative pruning is to ensure that a shrub has a framework of well-spaced branches so that it will develop according to its natural habit. The amount of formative pruning required depends very much on the type of shrub and on the quality of the plants available. When

FORMATIVE PRUNING

After planting a young shrub (here a Philadelphus*), cut out any dead, damaged, and weak stems, and remove crossing and congested stems to form a well balanced framework with an open center.*

Prune back crossing or congested shoots to an outward-facing bud or, if necessary, cut right back to the base.

Prune out any very weak and spindly, or long and straggly stems, cutting them right back to the base.

Also remove any very awkward stems that spoil the shape of the shrub to leave an evenly branching framework.

Deciduous Shrubs that Need Minimal Pruning

Amelanchier
Aronia
Buddleia globosa
Caragana
Chimonanthus
Clethra ❁ (deciduous spp.)
Cornus alternifolia 'Argentea'
Corokia, some ❁
Corylopsis

Daphne mezereum

Daphne (deciduous spp.)
Decaisnea
Disanthus
Enkianthus
Eucryphia (deciduous spp.)
Fothergilla
Hamamelis
Hoheria (deciduous spp.)
Lindera, some ❁
Poncirus
Ptelea
Pterostyrax
Rhamnus (deciduous spp.)
Viburnum (deciduous spp.)

Deciduous Shrubs that should be Pruned in Spring

Abelia x *grandiflora*
Abutilon, some ❁
Aloysia, some ❁
Buddleia davidii
Caryopteris x *clandonensis*
Ceanothus 'Autumnal Blue', *C.* 'Gloire de Versailles'
Ceratostigma willmottianum
Colquhounia
Cotinus
Datura ❁
Fuchsia (hardy cvs)
Hibiscus syriacus
Hydrangea
Hypericum, some ❁
Indigofera
Lavatera

Lavatera assurgentiflora

Leycesteria, some ❁
Perovskia
Prunus triloba
Salvia, some ❁
Sorbaria
Spiraea douglasii, *S. japonica*
Tamarix ramosissima
Zauschneria

Key
❁ *Not frost hardy*

buying shrubs, look for sturdy specimens with a well-balanced branch formation.

Evergreen shrubs generally need little formative pruning. Excessive growth resulting in a lopsided, unbalanced shape should be lightly pruned in midspring, after the shrub has been planted.

Deciduous shrubs are much more likely to require formative pruning than evergreen shrubs. This should be carried out in the dormant season, between midfall and midspring, at or after planting.

The following guidelines apply to most deciduous shrubs. If a particularly vigorous shoot distorts the framework, cut it back lightly rather than severely. If the shrub does not have a well-spaced branch framework, cut it back hard to promote strong growth.

In the case of most shrubs, remove completely any spindly and crossing branches that clutter the framework. An exception is made for a handful of slow-growing deciduous shrubs, in particular Japanese maples (*Acer japonicum* and *A. palmatum*). The numerous maple cultivars have a complex growth pattern that can be easily spoiled by this type of pruning.

Sometimes an apparently good specimen will make too much top-growth in relation to the size of its roots. Reducing the number of stems by up to one-third, and then shortening those stems that remain, also by one-third, will help to create a more stable plant.

Minimal Pruning of Deciduous Shrubs

Immediately after flowering, prune out any dead wood, weak stems, and congested growth to maintain a balanced, open-centered framework on shrubs such as Hamamelis.

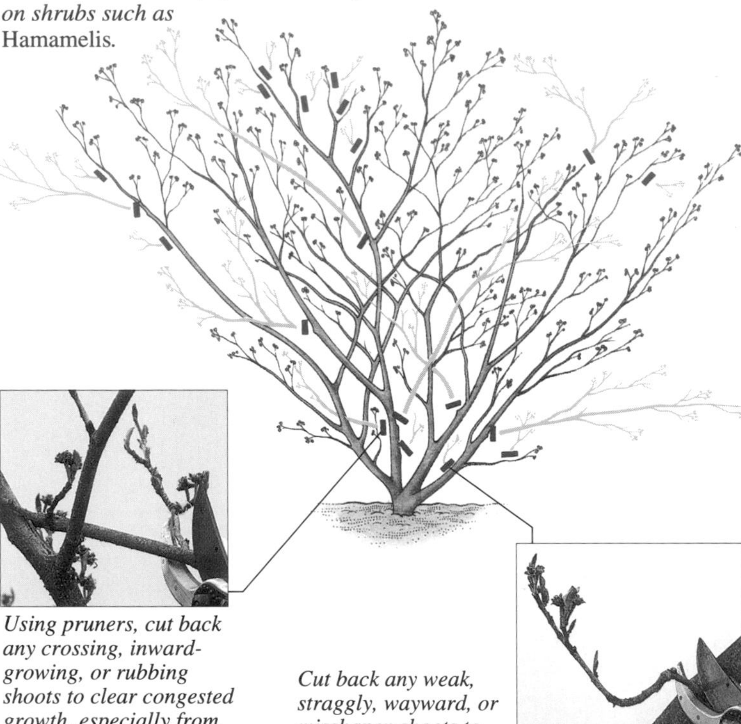

Using pruners, cut back any crossing, inward-growing, or rubbing shoots to clear congested growth, especially from the center of the shrub.

Cut back any weak, straggly, wayward, or misshapen shoots to the main stems.

Deciduous shrubs

These can be divided into four groups: those that require minimal pruning; those that are pruned in spring and usually flower on the current season's growth; those that are pruned after flowering in summer, and usually flower on the previous season's wood; and those of suckering habit. Two important factors are the degree to which shrubs produce replacement growths and the age of the flower-bearing wood.

Shrubs that are Pruned in Spring

Shrubs (here Spiraea) *that flower on wood produced during the current growing season should be pruned in spring in order to encourage the growth of new flowering stems.*

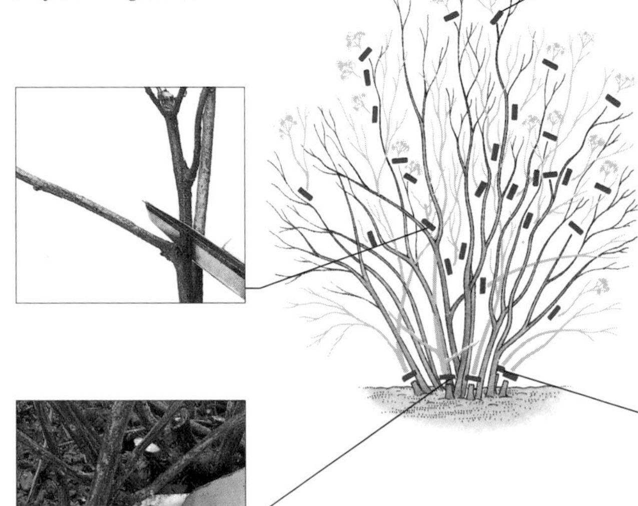

Prune out any dead or damaged stems back to healthy growth or, if necessary, cut them right back to the base of the shrub.

Using loppers, cut back some of the main stems to the base to retain an open framework.

Prune out stems of the previous year's growth to within 2–4 buds of the older wood to stimulate new flowering shoots.

Using pruners, cut back any weak, twiggy, or spindly growth right to the shrub's base.

Minimal pruning

Shrubs that do not regularly produce vigorous growths from the base or lower branches need little pruning. The chief need is to remove dead, diseased, and damaged wood and to cut out crossing or weak growth just after flowering. Many may require formative pruning. Feed and mulch in spring. Japanese maples (*Acer* spp.) and other shrubs prone to heavy bleeding if pruned in spring should be pruned in mid- to late summer, when their sap is least active.

Pruning in spring

Left unpruned, deciduous shrubs that bear flowers on the current season's growth tend to become congested and flower quality deteriorates. When pruned in spring, these shrubs generally produce vigorous shoots that carry flowers in summer or early fall. To minimize the risk of wind-rock, shorten flowered stems in fall as well.

Some large shrubs, such as deciduous *Ceanothus*, develop a woody framework. In their first spring, lightly prune the main stems of less vigorous shrubs and, in the second spring, reduce the previous season's growth by half. In late winter or early spring of subsequent years, prune hard to leave only one to three pairs of buds of the previous season's growth. Prune framework branches to different heights to encourage flower production at all levels. On mature specimens, cut out some of the oldest wood as part of the annual pruning operation to prevent congestion. For pruning *Buddleia davidii*, see above.

Some subshrubs, for example *Perovskia*, may form a woody base that allows them to be pruned back hard to a 6–12in (15–30cm) high framework. Cut back the previous season's growth annually in spring, leaving one or two buds.

A few shrubs (such as *Prunus triloba*) that flower in late winter or early spring on wood produced in the previous season are best pruned hard in spring after flowering, and so may be treated as other shrubs in this group. In the first spring after planting, shorten the main stems by about half to form a basal framework. After flowering in subsequent years, cut back all growth to two or three buds of the framework stems. Where annual growth is limited by cool summers, cut back only one-third of shoots near to ground level, and the others to 6–12in (15–30cm).

For all shrubs in this group, apply fertilizer just after pruning. In midspring, mulch the area matching the spread of the shrub before pruning.

Pruning *Buddleia davidii*

Because it is very vigorous, *Buddleia davidii* needs more drastic formative pruning than most shrubs that flower on new wood. At the back of a border, where a tall plant is required, prune to leave a woody framework 3–4ft (90–120cm) high. In another position, however, this may be no more than 2ft (60cm) high.

In the first spring after planting, shorten main stems by a half to three-quarters, pruning to pairs of shoots or buds. Cut out growths other than main stems. In early to midspring of subsequent years, cut back the previous season's growth and shorten new growth from the base. To stop congestion, cut out one or two of the oldest branches each year.

Using loppers, cut back some of the woody spurs to clear congested growth and produce an open, balanced framework.

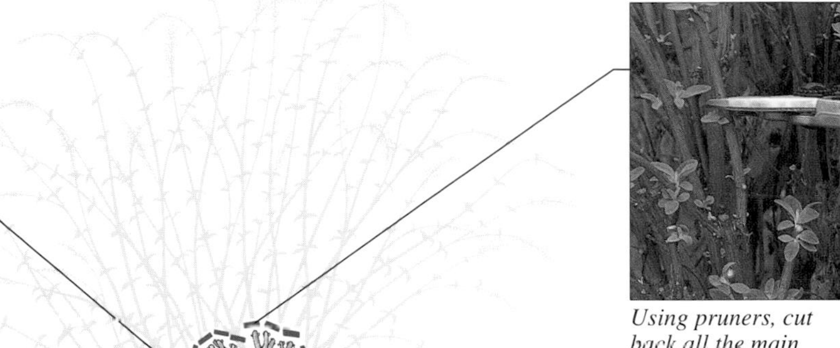

Using pruners, cut back all the main shoots that flowered the previous year to within 1–3 buds of the old wood.

Hydrangeas

For pruning purposes, hydrangeas (excluding climbing species such as *Hydrangea anomala* subsp. *petiolaris*) fall into three groups.

The first group (for example *H. paniculata*) flowers from midsummer onward on the current season's growth, and these plants should be treated in the same way as other shrubs that require hard pruning in spring (see opposite).

In early spring of the first year after planting, cut out all but two or three strong stems, pruning these back to a healthy pair of buds about 18in (45cm) from ground level. If the shrub is planted in an exposed position, and where summer temperatures will not ripen the stems sufficiently to withstand very cold winters, prune to just above ground level. Apply a quick-release fertilizer at a rate of about 4oz/sq yd (120g/sq m) and a 4in (10cm) deep mulch in a 24in (60cm) circle around the shrub. In early spring of subsequent years, cut back the previous year's growth to leave one or two strong pairs of growth buds. Then feed and mulch.

The second group, consisting of mophead and lacecap hydrangeas (*H. macrophylla*), also flowers from midsummer but on shoots made during the previous growing season. Lightly prune young plants in early spring, cutting out thin, twiggy growth and any old flowerheads. Once the plant is established and about three or four years old, remove some of the oldest wood annually in early spring. Cut out stems that are more than three years old and shorten the other stems that flowered in the previous season, cutting back to a strong pair of buds 6–12in (15–30cm) from the base. Then feed and mulch.

Other species such as *H. aspera* and related forms constitute a third group and need only minimal pruning in spring.

In spring, prune back all flowered stems and all damaged and weak growth, and cut back some older wood to the base.

Cut back any dead wood to healthy growth or right back to the base, if necessary.

Prune out all flowered stems, making a straight cut above a strong pair of growth buds.

Shrubs pruned in summer after flowering

Many deciduous shrubs that flower in spring or early summer carry their flowers on wood produced in the previous growing season. Sometimes the flowers are formed on last year's wood, as with *Chaenomeles* and forsythias, for example. Other shrubs bear their flowers on short lateral growths produced from last year's wood – for example *Deutzia*, *Philadelphus*, and *Weigela*.

Without regular pruning to encourage development of vigorous, young growth from close to ground level, many shrubs in this group tend to become densely twiggy, often top-heavy, and the quantity and quality of flower deteriorate. The removal of spent flowerheads also prevents shrubs from expending energy in seed production.

When planting any shrub in this group, cut out all weak or damaged growth and trim back the main shoots to a healthy bud or pair of buds, to encourage the development of a strong framework. If any flowers are produced in the first year, prune again immediately after flowering. Cut back flowered shoots to a strong bud or pair of buds and remove any spindly growth. After pruning, lightly work in fertilizer and apply a mulch around the shrub.

Carry out the same procedure immediately after flowering in subsequent years. Although it is desirable to cut back flowered wood to the strongest buds, do not adhere to this rigidly since it is also important to maintain a well-balanced shape. Feed and mulch as a matter of course after pruning.

As plants mature, more drastic pruning may be required to encourage growth. After the third year, up to one-fifth of the oldest stems may be cut back annually to within 2–3in (5–8cm) of the ground.

Use your discretion when following these guidelines, since harsh pruning of young specimens of some shrubs in this group, for example forsythias, can result in an awkward and unnatural shape.

Other shrubs in this group, especially when grown as free-standing rather than as wall shrubs, require very little pruning. *Chaenomeles*, for example, has a naturally twiggy habit, with numerous crossing branches, and mature specimens need little pruning. Spur pruning will, however, encourage heavier flowering (see THE FRUIT GARDEN, "Spur pruning," p.374); shorten spurs and side shoots to three to five leaves in midsummer.

Particular care must be taken in pruning shrubs, such as lilacs (*Syringa*), that come into growth during flowering. The new shoots that form below the flowers can be easily damaged when the old flowerheads are cut, and this reduces flowering in the next year.

Flowering shrubs of suckering habit

A few shrubs that are grown for their flowers produce them on wood of the previous year. Most of the new growth is made from ground level. These shrubs spread by suckers and need to be pruned in a different way from those that form a permanent woody framework.

After planting, prune suckering shrubs by cutting out weak growth but retain vigorous stems and their side shoots. The following year, immediately after flowering, remove any weak, dead, or damaged stems, then cut back flowered stems hard to a strong bud or pair of buds.

From the third year, annually cut back one-quarter to a half of all flowered stems to 2–3in (5–8cm) above ground level. Prune back others by about half to vigorous replacement shoots. After pruning the shrubs, feed and mulch.

SHRUBS THAT SHOULD BE PRUNED IN SUMMER AFTER FLOWERING

Buddleia alternifolia
Calycanthus
Chaenomeles
Corylopsis
Cotoneaster (deciduous spp.)
Deutzia
Exochorda
Forsythia
Jasminum humile
Kolkwitzia
Magnolia x soulangiana, M. stellata

Neillia thibetica

Neillia
Philadelphus
Photinia villosa
Rhododendron (deciduous spp.)
Ribes sanguineum
Rubus deliciosus, R.'Tridel'
Spiraea x arguta, S. prunifolia, S. thunbergii
Stephanandra
Syringa
Weigela

PRUNING SHRUBS IN SUMMER

After shrubs such as Weigela *have flowered, cut back flowered shoots and remove dead and spindly stems. Also prune out some old main stems.*

Using pruners, cut any dead wood back to healthy growth.

Cut out up to one-fifth of the oldest wood to within 2–3in (5–8 cm) of the ground.

BEFORE

Cut out any very weak, twiggy, or straggly stems back to the base just above soil level.

AFTER

Continue cutting out weak or crossing stems to form a well-balanced, open-centered shrub.

PRUNING A DECIDUOUS SUCKERING SHRUB

After flowering, prune back all flowered stems on deciduous suckering shrubs (here Kerria*), most by about half, the remainder almost to the ground. Cut out any weak, dead, or damaged growth.*

Prune the flowered stems by about half their length, cutting back to strongly growing new shoots.

Cut back up to half of the flowered stems to within 2–3in (5–8cm) of the ground. Also cut to the ground any dead or damaged shoots.

Coppicing and pollarding shrubs

A number of deciduous shrubs grown for the ornamental value of their stems or leaves require severe pruning in spring. Most of them flower on shoots formed the previous season but, when grown for their stems or leaves, their flowers are sacrificed. The method of hard pruning used on these shrubs is essentially an adaptation of traditional methods of managing trees and shrubs to give a constant and renewable supply of wood for stakes, firewood, and fencing materials. In coppicing, shrubs and trees are cut back regularly to near ground level. In pollarding, growth is cut back each year to a permanent framework of a single stem or several stems.

Coppicing shrubs such as *Cornus alba* ensures a regular supply of young growths, which are more strikingly colored than older wood and showier in winter. On shrubs such as *Sambucus racemosa* 'Plumosa Aurea' that are grown for their foliage, hard pruning generally results in larger leaves. Just before growth commences in early to midspring, coppice vigorous shrubs such as *Salix alba* 'Britzensis' (syn. *S. a.* 'Chermesina') by pruning all shoots to within about 2–3in (5–8cm) of ground level. It may be preferable to vary the height to which stems are cut back to avoid a rigid, uniform outline. Weaker shrubs such as *Cornus alba* 'Sibirica' may be cut back less severely by coppicing only about one-third to one-half of the stems. Then apply a quick-release fertilizer and mulch liberally, covering a circle of 24in (60cm) radius around the shrub.

Shrubs that have been trained so that they have one or more clean, main stems are pruned back – or pollarded – to this stem framework each season. The aim of pruning in the first year is to establish the framework. After planting, before growth commences in spring, cut back a young plant to form a standard with a single stem of 1–3ft (30–90cm). Alternatively, leave three, five, or seven stems, depending on the size of plant required and the space available in the garden. Apply a quick-release fertilizer and mulch around the stem (or stems), as for shrubs that are coppiced.

During the plant's first growing season, restrict the number of shoots growing from below the cut to only four or five, rubbing out all others that are superfluous and any that develop low down on the main stem. Continue this process for the next year or two; this will allow the main stem to thicken so that it will be able to support heavier top-growth. In spring of the second and subsequent years, reduce the previous season's growths to above a bud within 2–3in (5–8cm) of the framework (see also *Pollarding a Eucalyptus*, above). If a larger specimen is needed, prune only a half or one-third of the stems. Feed and mulch.

POLLARDING A EUCALYPTUS

Establish a framework by cutting back a young shrub to one or more main stems (below). Each subsequent spring, cut the previous year's growth back hard, either to within 2–3in (5–8cm) of the framework or to the base, since eucalyptus can regenerate from ground level (right).

COPPICING A SHRUB FOR WINTER STEM COLOR

With shrubs that have colored stems (here a Cornus stolonifera *cultivar), cut back hard all the shrub's stems to about 2–3in (5–8cm) from the base before growth begins in spring (see inset). Apply fertilizer around the shrub to promote new growth, and then mulch. Coppicing stimulates the growth of new, vigorous stems whose color is especially strong.*

SHRUBS FOR COPPICING AND POLLARDING

Coppicing
Cornus alba 'Aurea',
C. a. 'Elegantissima',
C. a. 'Flaviramea',
C. a. 'Kesselringii',
C. a. 'Sibirica',
C. a. 'Spaethii',
C. a. 'Variegata'

Corylus maxima 'Purpurea'

Corylus maxima 'Purpurea'
Cotinus coggygria,
C. 'Grace'
Hydrangea paniculata 'Floribunda',
H. p. 'Grandiflora',
H. p. 'Unique'
Rubus biflorus,
R. cockburnianus,
R. thibetanus
Salix alba 'Britzensis',
S. daphnoides,
S. irrorata
Sambucus racemosa 'Plumosa Aurea'

Pollarding
Cornus stolonifera
Eucalyptus, some ❄
Salix acutifolia

KEY
❄ *Not frost hardy*

Evergreen shrubs

The appropriate method for pruning and training most evergreen shrubs depends on the size they are expected to reach when mature. All evergreens that show signs of dieback after a particularly hard winter, however, should be treated in the same way, regardless of size.

In midspring, prune out all dead wood to where the shrub has started to regenerate, and thin out the new shoots if they are overcrowded or crossing. If a shrub shows no sign of life by midspring, nick the bark to see if there is any live green wood beneath. Some shrubs may remain dormant for a whole growing season.

Small shrubs up to 3ft (90cm)
Low-growing evergreen shrubs can be divided into two main groups, each requiring a different pruning technique. The first group includes a number of relatively short-lived shrubs that flower profusely, provided that they are trimmed each year and are not overmature. Examples of these shrubs include lavender (*Lavandula*), lavender cotton (*Santolina chamaecyparissus*), and most heathers (*Calluna*, *Daboecia*, and *Erica*, but not tree heaths). These shrubs are generally best replaced about every ten years or so. Also replace plants that have been left unpruned for several years since they become weak and leggy and seldom flower or regenerate successfully.

In midspring, use pruners or garden shears to cut out any weak growth or flowering shoots on newly planted shrubs. This ensures that new growth is generated from basal shoots in the center of the plant. Each subsequent year in midspring, remove the old flowerheads, as well as any dead, diseased, or damaged shoots. Some heathers have attractive winter foliage and these, as well as other evergreens, are sometimes deadheaded in fall. In very cold areas, however, there is a risk of dieback after fall deadheading, and for this reason pruning is normally delayed until midspring. After pruning, apply slow-release fertilizer at a rate of 2oz/sq yd (60g/sq m) and apply a mulch to a depth of 2in (5cm).

The second group consists of slow-growing shrubs such as dwarf cotoneasters and *Hebe*. These require less pruning than those in the first group, the main purpose in pruning being to remove dead, diseased, damaged, or severely congested shoots in midspring. Deadheading, however, is not necessary.

Medium-sized evergreen shrubs up to 10ft (3m) tall

Most medium-sized evergreen shrubs require little pruning once a well-balanced framework has been established. This principle applies to *Berberis darwinii*, camellias, *Escallonia*, *Hibiscus rosa-sinensis*, and many rhododendrons.

In midspring, just before growth is about to commence, remove any weak or crossing shoots as well as any that may upset the overall symmetry and balance of the shrub. Feed and mulch. Subsequent pruning is normally limited to cutting out straggly growth, restricting size, and shaping the plant to suit its position in the garden. Use pruners or long-handled loppers to remove all or part of selected branches.

Winter- or spring-flowering shrubs, such as *Berberis darwinii* and *Viburnum tinus*, should be pruned immediately after flowering. Prune *Escallonia* and others that flower from midsummer onward by removing older wood at the start of growth in midspring or by cutting out flowered stems in late summer. *Hibiscus rosa-sinensis*, with a flowering season from spring to fall, is best pruned in midspring. Feed and mulch spring-pruned shrubs after pruning. Shrubs pruned in late summer should not be fed or mulched until the following spring, since any new, soft growth produced would be highly vulnerable to damage from winter cold.

Large, evergreen shrubs more than 10ft (3m) tall

Large rhododendrons and other tall evergreens require little pruning but may need shaping as young plants to create a well-balanced framework. Prune young plants in midspring or wait until the flowers have faded.

The aim of pruning here is to encourage an open-centered bush with well-spaced branches. Cut out all weak and crossing branches, and feed and mulch after pruning. Regular pruning is generally limited to the removal of dead, damaged, and diseased wood. Some large evergreens such as cherry laurels (*Prunus laurocerasus*) may also be used for hedging (see pp.58–60).

Palms

These require little or no pruning apart from the removal of dead leaves. Certain rhizomatous palms, for example *Chamaedorea*, can be invasive, however, in which case unwanted stems should be removed at ground level in spring.

The palmlike *Cordyline* needs pruning only if it has suffered frost damage or if a bushy, multistemmed specimen is required. Once new growth has started to appear, cut damaged branches back to just above newly formed shoots. Feed and apply a mulch. To create a multibranched specimen, remove the growing point before growth commences in spring, then feed and mulch.

Wall shrubs

There are three reasons for growing shrubs against walls. First, some are too tender for the open garden in frost-prone areas, but will thrive if sheltered against a warm wall. Second, training shrubs against a wall (including hardy shrubs such as pyracanthas) makes it possible to accommodate plants for which there might not otherwise be space. Third, some shrubs are natural scramblers (for example *Cestrum elegans*) and therefore need to have support of some kind.

It is important to train and prune all wall shrubs from an early stage so that they present a compact and well-tailored appearance and produce plenty of flowering shoots. When training wall shrubs, provide a framework to which growth can be tied. A trellis, netting, or regularly spaced horizontal wires as used for wall-trained fruit trees (see p.356) may be used. Plant hardy shrubs in fall, half-hardy or tender ones in spring.

Recommendations for pruning free-standing shrubs also apply to wall-trained specimens, but more care is needed for formative training and pruning. It is vital to tie in shoots as they grow and cut back sublaterals growing strongly away from the wall.

Formative training and pruning

During the first growing season, train in the leader and main laterals to form a framework. Prune back any outward-growing laterals to encourage short side shoots to develop close to the framework. Remove completely any laterals growing toward the wall or fence, and any shoots that are growing outward in the wrong direction. The aim should be to create a neat, vertical carpet of foliage to cover the allotted space.

Routine pruning

In the second and subsequent seasons, flowering laterals should be formed. After flowering, cut back the flowered shoots to within 3–4in (7–10cm) of the main framework. This encourages new flowering laterals to develop, which will provide next season's display. Continue tying in framework shoots; trim outward-pointing laterals and remove inward-growing and other wrongly aligned shoots. Do not trim wall shrubs after midsummer since this may reduce the next year's flowering shoots. It may also induce *Ceanothus* and many half-hardy evergreen shrubs to produce soft growth liable to frost damage. Feed and mulch wall-trained shrubs annually in spring to maintain healthy growth.

Shrubs such as pyracanthas that are grown both for flowers and fruits or berries need slightly modified pruning. The shoots that have flowered

EVERGREEN SHRUBS THAT TOLERATE SEVERE PRUNING

Aucuba
Berberis darwinii
Buxus
Choisya ternata
Citrus ❅
Escallonia 'Donard Seedling'
Euonymus fortunei, *E. japonicus*
Hibiscus rosa-sinensis ❅
Ilex x *altaclerensis*, *I. aquifolium*
Ligustrum japonicum
Lonicera nitida, *L. pileata*
Nerium oleander ❅
Phillyrea
Prunus laurocerasus, *P. lusitanica*
Rhododendron ponticum, *R.* Subsection Triflora (incl. *R. augustinii*)
Santolina
Sarcococca humilis
Taxus
Viburnum tinus

KEY
❅ *Not frost hardy*

PRUNING EVERGREEN SHRUBS

After flowering, prune evergreen shrubs (here Prunus lusitanica*) by removing damaged or dead wood and cutting back flowered stems and any awkward or straggly stems that mar the shape.*

Cut back flowered stems to a main stem. Cut out thickly congested and crossing stems.

Cut back awkwardly growing stems to well-placed, healthy, outward-growing shoots.

Cut out any dead or damaged wood back to healthy growth or, if necessary, to the base.

PRUNING AND TRAINING A YOUNG WALL SHRUB

In the first year, prune the shrub (here a pyracantha) to build up a balanced framework, tying in main stems. In subsequent years, tie in new growth in spring; in midsummer, cut back inward- and outward-growing shoots to form a vertical "carpet"; and remove dead, damaged, or spindly growth entirely.

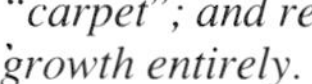

Using pruners, cut back any weak, spindly stems as well as any dead or damaged wood.

Check and replace any broken ties, using garden twine tied in a figure eight to resecure the stem to the wire.

Trim back any outward-growing stems to 3–4in (7–10cm) from the framework in midsummer.

PRUNING AN ESTABLISHED WALL SHRUB

Prune mature plants to maintain a well-balanced framework of stems and, on berrying shrubs, to expose the berries. In late summer, remove outward-growing shoots and, with the exception of shrubs grown for their fruits or berries, cut back flowered shoots to promote dense growth. The shrub shown here is a pyracantha.

Cut back young shoots to 2–3 leaves from their base to expose the ripening berries.

In late summer, check and replace ties where necessary; in spring, tie in new shoots.

Using pruners, cut back any damaged or dead wood to healthy growth.

are not cut back but are left to develop fruits. Trim back any laterals to two to three leaves from their base as the fruits swell, so that they are exposed to more light and ripen well. Old fruit clusters may be cut out in spring as young growths develop.

Summer- and fall-flowering wall shrubs, including some *Ceanothus*, should be trained as described earlier but pruned according to whether they flower on the previous season's wood (see "Shrubs pruned in summer after flowering," p.76) or that of the current season (see "Pruning in spring," p.75). Some half-hardy or tender shrubs, particularly *Ceanothus*, do not grow readily from old wood and are difficult to renovate once neglected.

Scrambling shrubs

These also require careful training to contain their flexuous shoots. On some (such as the half-hardy *Cestrum elegans*) that produce flowers in late summer on terminal shoots or short laterals, the flowered shoots may be cut out entirely or cut back to strong, low, lateral growths in spring. Others flower in summer mainly on lateral growths, which should be cut back after flowering to 3–4in (7–10cm) and will often produce further sublaterals that flower the same season. In spring, these laterals are pruned back again to 3–4in (7–10cm) and will flower in summer.

Fan-training ornamental shrubs

A few shrubs, such as ornamental peaches (for example *Prunus persica* 'Klara Meyer'), are suitable for fan-training like fruit trees. In the first spring after planting, cut back the plant 15–18in (38–45cm) above the graft union, retaining three or four strong shoots. Train the shoots on stakes tied to horizontal wires. Toward the end of the growing season, remove the central shoot if three strong shoots were retained; if four shoots were kept, space these out to form a fan. In winter, reduce all shoots by half their length.

The following growing season, select two or four new shoots on each stem. Attach each of these to a stake tied to the wires. Then, in midsummer, remove all other shoots. In the third year, immediately after flowering, cut back all framework shoots by a quarter to one-third. Tie in two or three new shoots on each framework stem. Remove unwanted shoots in midsummer. If there are gaps in the fan, prune back adjacent shoots by one-third after flowering has finished to encourage new growth. Cut back all other extension growths to 2–3in (5–7cm) to encourage flowering on one-year-old spurs. For full details, see THE FRUIT GARDEN, "Fan," p.389.

PRUNING CEANOTHUS

Immediately after flowering, cut back new shoots of spring-flowering Ceanothus to 2–3 leaves. Tie in new shoots and trim back outward-growing shoots to keep growth trained close to the wall or fence.

FAN-TRAINING A SHRUB

This fan (Prunus mume 'Beni-shi-dare') *has been trained to develop an evenly spaced branch framework, in the same way as pruning fan-trained fruit trees.*

Training and pruning standard shrubs

Some shrubs, for example fuchsias and *Buddleia alternifolia*, can be grown as standards. The height of the stem varies according to the vigor of the plant and the result wanted. For details on training a standard fuchsia, see p.449; for pruning a standard rose, see p.126.

To train a shrub such as *Buddleia alternifolia* as a standard, tie a strong stem to a stake in the first growing season. Pinch all side shoots back to two or three leaves, leaving a few growing near the stem tip. As the stem grows, continue to pinch back. When the clear stem is at the desired height, pinch the terminal shoot to encourage shoots to form the head. In early spring of the following year, shorten the branches of the head to about 6in (15cm). Retain two or three of the shoots that each produces. Feed and mulch. Prune subsequently as for other shrubs pruned in summer after flowering (see p.76).

Some pendulous cultivars are grafted onto the clear stem of a rootstock. Remove any suckers (see p.70) from the stock and treat as for roses (see "Suckers and how to deal with them," p.123).

Root pruning

Root pruning is sometimes used to control the top-growth of vigorous shrubs and to make them flower more freely. Grafted specimens that are making prolific leaf growth but producing few flowers or fruits usually benefit from root pruning.

In early spring, dig a trench around the shrub to a depth of 12–24in (30–60cm) with a circumference just beyond the spread of the top-growth. Use loppers or a saw to cut back the thick, woody roots; as a guideline, shorten them to about half the radius of the trench. Leave fibrous roots unpruned. Control further spreading of the roots by inserting a barrier of rigid plastic or heavy-gauge plastic sheeting around the circumference of the trench (see *Restricting Wide-spreading Grasses*, p.143). After backfilling, mulch the area within the trench.

Root pruning is often used to control container-grown shrubs. This is best carried out when repotting the shrub. Shorten up to one-fifth of woody roots by a quarter and cut back others so that they fit comfortably in the container. Repot, using fresh soil mix with a slow-release fertilizer added, and water thoroughly.

Renovation

Old, tangled, or overgrown shrubs can sometimes be renovated by extensive pruning. Shrubs that respond well usually produce young growth from the base. It is not worth trying to salvage a shrub that is badly diseased. Some shrubs do not tolerate drastic pruning; if in any doubt about a particular shrub, stagger a program of heavy pruning over a period of two or three years.

Renovate deciduous shrubs such as lilacs after flowering or when dormant; for evergreens such as *Viburnum tinus*, delay renovation until midspring.

Renovating old or overgrown shrubs

Cut out all weak and crossing stems and shorten main stems to 12–18in (30–45cm) above ground level, ensuring that a balanced framework is left. Apply a slow-release fertilizer at 4oz/sq yd (120g/sq m), and mulch the area around the shrub to a depth of 2–4in (5–10cm). Keep the shrub well watered throughout summer.

During the following growing season, a mass of shoots should grow from below the cuts on the main stems. Retain only two to four of the strongest on each stem to provide the new branch framework. On deciduous shrubs, cut out superfluous shoots during the dormant season. On evergreen shrubs, do this in midspring.

In the following growing season, some secondary growth may occur where shoots have been cut. Rub out these growths.

Staggered renovation

An alternative, less drastic method is to spread the pruning over two or three years. Prune deciduous shrubs after flowering, evergreens in midspring. Prune half of the oldest stems to 2–3in (5–8cm) from the ground. Where possible cut back the remaining stems by about half to new, vigorous shoots. Apply a slow-release fertilizer, water well, and mulch. At the same time the following year, repeat the process on the remaining old stems. Thereafter, prune the shrub according to its growth and flowering characteristics.

DRASTIC RENOVATION

A shrub that produces new growth from the base (here lilac) can be renovated when dormant if it is deciduous or in midspring if evergreen. Cut back all main stems to within 12–18in (30–45cm) of the ground. Remove suckers by cutting them off at the base.

GRADUAL RENOVATION

Renovate deciduous shrubs after flowering and evergreens in midspring. Cut back a third to a half of the oldest main stems (here on a Philadelphus*) almost to the ground and remove dead, twiggy stems. Over the next year or two cut back remaining old main stems.*

Cut back about half of the stems to within 2–3in (5–8cm) of the base. Remove the oldest stems and any that spoil the shrub's shape.

Cut back older stems by half to new, vigorous shoots, and remove any weak, twiggy growth or dead wood.

Prune back any crossing, rubbing, or congested stems to a bud or stem that will not cause another crossing shoot to develop.

Propagation

THERE are many ways to propagate shrubs to raise new plants, including taking cuttings, sowing seed, layering, division, and grafting.

Taking cuttings is a simple way of propagating many shrubs and, unlike seed, which may produce variable offspring, it may be used for cultivars, hybrids, and sports.

Sowing seed is simple and inexpensive but it is relatively slow to produce plants of flowering size. Some shrubs can be divided, while others can be layered – a method of stimulating stems to root while still attached to the parent plant.

Grafting involves uniting a stem from the plant to be propagated with the rootstock of a compatible plant. It is not commonly used since it requires more expertise and skill than other methods, but it is the most suitable method for some shrubs.

Softwood cuttings

This technique is suitable for raising several (mainly deciduous) shrubs, for example *Fuchsia* and *Perovskia*. Softwood cuttings are taken in spring from fast-growing stem tips. They have a soft base and a higher capacity to root than cuttings of maturer wood.

Preparing the cuttings

Take the cuttings early in the morning. Select healthy, pliable, single-stemmed shoots and seal them in an opaque plastic bag. Prepare the cuttings as soon as possible after collection. Trim the cuttings to 3–4in (8–10cm), just below a node, and remove the lower leaves. Use a cuttings soil mix of equal parts peat and either perlite or sharp sand. Insert the cuttings into the soil mix. Water them in, applying a fungicide to minimize rot, and label.

Aftercare

Softwood cuttings wilt quickly if not kept in a humid atmosphere, so aftercare is very important.

Cover the pots with a clear plastic bag or, alternatively, place them in a mist box. A mist box, or fogging chamber, is a simple way to control humidity for softwood cuttings. Construct mist boxes by covering a homemade wood frame with sturdy clear plastic. Use pieces of film long enough to be tucked underneath the edges of the frame. A cool-mist humidifier designed for household use is ideal for maintaining the humidity inside the box, but it should not be used constantly or moisture levels will get too high. A humidistat can be a useful addition. Air the box every few days to ensure good air circulation, or leave one side open. Remove fallen leaves daily and apply a fungicidal spray weekly. Harden off the rooted cuttings and transplant into individual pots. Water, label, and keep them in a shaded position. Alternatively, grow on the rooted cuttings in the original container, giving a supplementary feed every two weeks and planting out individually in the next spring.

USING A MIST BOX

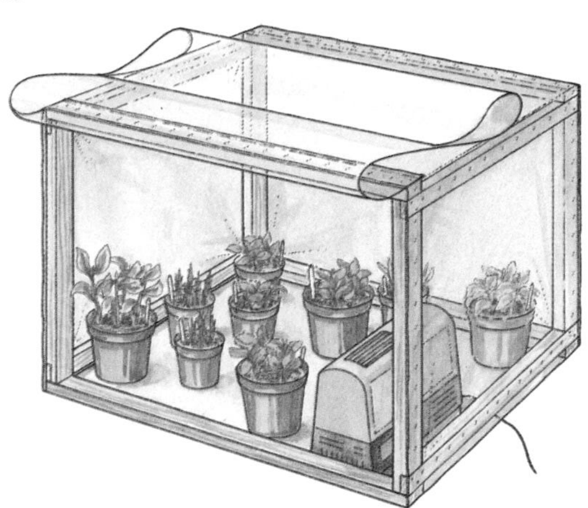

A mist box may be used to maintain the high humidity needed for softwood cuttings. Attach plastic sheets to a homemade frame and place a cool-mist humidifier inside. Do not run the humidifier constantly, or moisture levels will rise too high.

PROPAGATING SHRUBS BY SOFTWOOD CUTTINGS

1 *In spring, cut off young, non-flowering shoots (here from* Hydrangea paniculata) *with 3–5 pairs of leaves. Seal them in an opaque plastic bag and keep shaded until they can be prepared.*

2 *Reduce each cutting to 3–4in (8–10cm) in length, making a straight cut just below a node (see inset). Trim off the lower leaves.*

3 *Insert the cuttings into prepared pots of cuttings soil mix, ensuring that the leaves do not touch each other.*

4 *Water the cuttings with a fungicidal solution, then label and place them in a propagator. Maintain a temperature of 64–70°F (18–21°C).*

5 *Once the cuttings have rooted, harden them off, then remove them from the pot and carefully tease them apart.*

6 *Transplant the separated cuttings into individual pots and firm in. Water, label, and keep the cuttings in a shaded position until well established.*

SHRUBS THAT MAY BE PROPAGATED BY SOFTWOOD CUTTINGS

Abelia, some ❁
Abutilon, some ❁
Aloysia, some ❁
Boronia ❁
Buddleia, some ❁
Calluna
Caryopteris
Ceanothus, some ❁ (deciduous spp.)
Ceratostigma, some ❁
Cestrum, some ❁
Cotoneaster (deciduous spp.)
Cytisus, some ❁
Daboecia
Daphne x *burkwoodii*
Enkianthus
Erica
Forsythia
Fuchsia, some ❁
Genista, some ❁
Halesia
Hydrangea
Kolkwitzia
Lagerstroemia ❁
Lantana ❁
Lavatera
Nandina
Perovskia
Philadelphus
Potentilla
Viburnum (deciduous spp.)

KEY
❁ *Not frost hardy*

PROPAGATING BY SEMIRIPE CUTTINGS

1 *In mid- to late summer, select healthy shoots of the current season's growth for the cuttings. Sever them from the parent plant (here* Ilex x altaclerensis 'Golden King'*) just above a node. They should be semiripe – still soft at the top but firm at the base.*

2 *Remove the side shoots from the main stem. Trim each side shoot to 4–6in (10–15cm) long, cutting just below a node.*

3 *Trim off the soft tip of each cutting and then remove the lowest pair of leaves, cutting flush with the stem.*

4 *Stimulate rooting by wounding the cutting: carefully cut away a piece of bark about 1–1½in (2.5–4cm) long from one side of the base.*

5 *Dip the base of each cutting in hormone rooting powder, then insert it into cuttings soil mix in a propagator or in pots in a cold frame.*

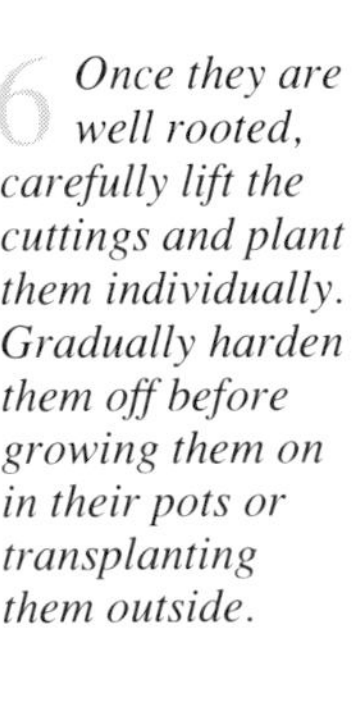

6 *Once they are well rooted, carefully lift the cuttings and plant them individually. Gradually harden them off before growing them on in their pots or transplanting them outside.*

Semiripe cuttings

Many evergreen as well as some deciduous shrubs may be propagated from semiripe cuttings, including some that are difficult to propagate from hardwood cuttings such as *Aucuba* and *Choisya*.

Suitable cuttings

The cuttings are normally taken from mid- to late summer and sometimes into the early fall. Select shoots from the current season's growth that are firm and woody near the base but still soft at the tip. Unlike softwood cuttings, they should offer some resistance when bent. Some shrubs are propagated by variations of this semiripe cuttings technique, such as mallet cuttings (see opposite) or leaf-bud cuttings (see opposite).

Preparing the rooting medium

Before collecting the cutting material from the parent shrub, fill sufficient containers of appropriate size or a propagator (equipped with basal heating) with a suitable rooting medium: use fine-grade pine bark or a mixture of equal parts of peat and either grit, sharp sand, vermiculite, or perlite.

Preparing the cuttings

Cuttings may be taken with a heel (see opposite) or as nodal cuttings. Heel cuttings should be 2–3in (5–7cm) long, trimmed to a short heel at the base. Nodal cuttings should be 4–6in (10–15cm) long, taken from leaders or side shoots, and cut with a sharp knife just below a node.

Remove the soft tips of nodal and heel cuttings. In both cases, remove the lowest pair of leaves, and with large-leaved plants reduce the size of the remaining leaves by about a half to minimize moisture loss.

An optional step is to prepare the base of the cuttings by making a shallow wound at one side. On plants that are difficult to root, such as *Daphne sericea*, this cut should be made deeper so that a sliver of bark is also removed.

Potting up

Dip the bases of the cuttings, including the entire wound on wounded cuttings, in a rooting hormone before using a dibber to insert them in the prepared soil mix, either directly in a propagator or in containers.

Space the cuttings approximately 3–4in (8–10cm) apart, and make certain that their leaves do not overlap, since this may create stagnant conditions in which rot fungi thrive. Gently firm the soil mix around the cuttings. Label each container and water the cuttings thoroughly with a fungicidal solution to protect them against damping-off diseases (see p.570).

Correct temperature

Overwinter cuttings in containers in a cold frame or greenhouse. Those that have been inserted directly in a propagator should have basal heat maintained at 70°F (21°C).

Aftercare

Inspect the cuttings periodically during the winter, removing any fallen leaves promptly. Water the containers if the soil mix shows any signs of drying out, such as slight shrinking toward the edges of the container. If the cuttings are being overwintered in a cold frame, it may need some form of insulation, such as a burlap cover or a piece of old carpet, to protect the cuttings from damage by cold.

Cuttings kept in a cold frame or unheated greenhouse will almost certainly need a further growing season in their containers before rooting satisfactorily. Keep the frame closed, except on very mild days. The glass should be kept clean and free of any condensation, since the high moisture content of the air inside the frame provides ideal conditions for fungal infection to occur. In late spring and early summer, gradually open the cover for longer and longer periods to harden off the rooted cuttings. If necessary, protect the cuttings from strong, direct sunlight by covering the glass with suitable shading material.

Throughout the growing season, apply a liquid feed every two weeks to all semiripe cuttings. Check them regularly, and remove any that are weak or showing signs of disease.

Transplanting

Cuttings overwintered in a propagator should have rooted by early spring, since the basal heat helps to speed up root development. Check that there is strong root growth before transplanting the cuttings. Ease them from their containers, separate each cutting carefully, and either pot up individually or plant, clearly labeled, in the open ground. If some cuttings have not rooted but have formed a callus, scrape off some of the callus to stimulate rooting and reinsert the cuttings in the soil mix until roots have formed.

Cuttings grown in a cold frame may be planted out in fall, if well developed, or kept in a sheltered position outside or in the cold frame until spring. They are then potted up individually or planted out.

Heel cuttings

Heel cuttings, which may be taken from greenwood, semiripe, or hardwood stems, are vigorous side shoots of the current season's growth. Each cutting is taken with a "heel" of old wood at its base, in which the growth hormones that assist the rooting process are concentrated.

Heel cuttings are particularly suitable for a number of evergreen shrubs such as *Pieris* and some azaleas (*Rhododendron*), deciduous shrubs that have pithy or hollow stems such as barberry (*Berberis*) and elder (*Sambucus*), and those shrubs that have greenwood stems such as broom (*Cytisus* and *Genista*).

Select as cuttings healthy side shoots that are characteristic of the parent. Carefully pull the shoot from the main stem so that a small strip of bark from the parent comes away with it. Avoid excessively tearing the bark of the main shoot since this may expose it to infection. Trim the heel and follow the technique for greenwood (see p.540), semiripe (opposite), or hardwood cuttings (see right), according to the stem's maturity.

1 *Pull away healthy side shoots of the current season's growth (here on* Prunus laurocerasus 'Schipkaensis') *with a heel of bark.*

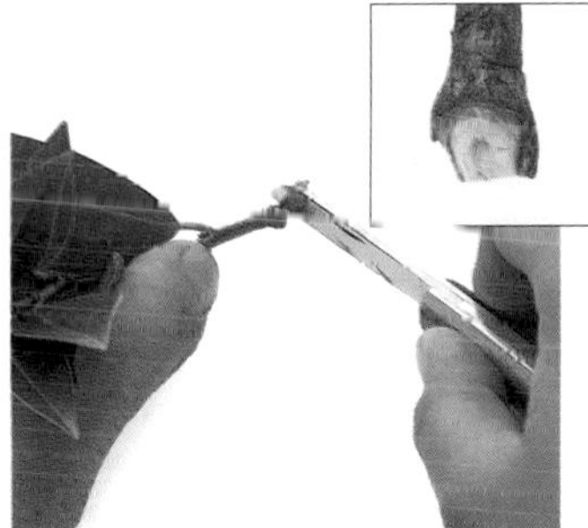

2 *Using a sharp knife, trim off the tail at the base of the cutting before inserting it in cuttings soil mix.*

Mallet cuttings

A mallet cutting, which is taken from semiripe stems, is a ripened shoot of the current season's growth attached to a piece of wood from the previous season, forming a mallet-shaped plug at its base. These cuttings are often used to propagate shrubs with pithy or hollow stems, because rot fungi are less likely to affect older wood. It is particularly suitable for many *Spiraea* and deciduous *Berberis*, which produce short side shoots on main branches.

In late summer, remove a stem of the last season's growth from the parent and cut it into sections, each containing a vigorous side shoot of new growth. If the mallet is more than 1/4in (5mm) in diameter, slit it lengthwise. Then treat as for semiripe cuttings (see opposite).

MALLET CUTTINGS

Remove a stem produced the previous year, and cut it above each side shoot and about 1in (2.5cm) below. Reduce it to 4–5in (10–13cm), and trim off lower leaves.

Leaf-bud cuttings

A leaf-bud cutting is taken from a semiripe stem and consists of a short piece of stem bearing a leaf and a leaf bud. In comparison with stem cuttings, leaf-bud cuttings make much more economical use of the material that is taken from the parent plant. This method of propagation is most commonly used for camellias.

In late summer or early fall, select a vigorous shoot of the current season's growth bearing healthy leaves and well-developed buds. Using a sharp knife or pruners, cut the stem just above each leaf, then make a cut about 3/4in (2cm) below the petiole so that the shoot is divided into several sections.

Leaf-bud cuttings do not need to be treated with hormone rooting powder before potting up, but may be wounded at the base to hasten rooting. Insert them in containers of cuttings soil mix and treat as for semiripe cuttings (see opposite).

To save space, roll up any large leaves and secure them with rubber bands. A stake inserted down the middle of a rolled-up leaf will give extra support by helping to anchor it firmly in the soil mix. Trim compound leaves on shrubs such as *Mahonia* by a half.

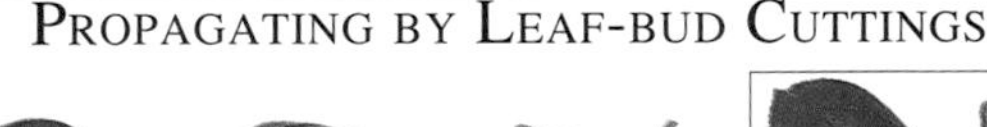

PROPAGATING BY LEAF-BUD CUTTINGS

1 *Select semiripe shoots (here of* Camellia japonica). *Make a straight cut 3/4in (2cm) below each leaf and a further cut just above.*

2 *Remove a 1/4in (5mm) sliver of bark at the base of each cutting (see inset). Insert the cuttings in the soil mix so that the leaf axils are just visible above the surface.*

Hardwood cuttings

Where the soil does not freeze deeply, an easy way to raise many shrubs is from hardwood cuttings. Use ripe, vigorous growths of the current season, taken from midfall to early winter. Take cuttings of deciduous shrubs just after leaf fall.

Preparing the ground

Cuttings are best rooted in a prepared bed or containers kept in a

SHRUBS THAT MAY BE PROPAGATED BY SEMIRIPE CUTTINGS

Andromeda
Arctostaphylos, some ❁
Aucuba▽
Azara, some ❁,▽
Berberis, some ❁,▽
Boronia ❁ ▽
Brachyglottis ❁
Bruckenthalia
Bupleurum▽
Callistemon, some ❁,▽
Camellia, some ❁
Cantua ❁ ▽
Carmichaelia, some ❁,▽
Carpenteria▽
Cassinia▽
Cassiope▽
Ceanothus, some ❁,▽
Colletia▽
Coprosma ❁ ▽
Corokia, some ❁,▽

Cotoneaster 'Firebird'

Cotoneaster▽
Cytisus, some ❁,▽
Daphne
Deutzia
Drimys
Elaeagnus▽
Escallonia▽
Garrya▽
Gordonia ❁ ▽
Grevillea ❁ ▽
Hibiscus rosa-sinensis ❁
Ilex, some ❁
Itea ilicifolia▽
Lavandula, some ❁
Leptospermum, some ❁,▽
Leucothöe▽
Magnolia grandiflora▽
Mahonia
Nerium ❁ ▽
Olearia, some ❁,▽

Olearia phlogopappa

Philadelphus
Photinia▽
Pieris▽
Pittosporum, some ❁
Prunus (evergreen spp.)▽
Pyracantha
Rhododendron▽
Skimmia▽
Spiraea
Viburnum
Weigela

KEY
❁ *Not frost hardy*
▽ *With a heel*

SHRUBS THAT MAY BE PROPAGATED BY HARDWOOD CUTTINGS

Atriplex halimus
Aucuba japonica
Buddleia
Buxus
Cornus alba, C. stolonifera
Cotoneaster x *watereri*
Deutzia x *elegantissima* 'Rosealind', *D. longifolia, D.* x *rosea, D. scabra*
Forsythia
Hypericum x *moserianum*
Ligustrum ovalifolium
Philadelphus

Deutzia longifolia 'Veitchii'

Ribes
Rosa rugosa
Rubus
Ruta graveolens
Salix
Sambucus
Spiraea
Symphoricarpos
Tamarix
Viburnum (deciduous spp.)
Weigela

cold frame, but they may also be inserted in a bed in open ground.

Prepare the bed in late summer or early fall, first working the soil until it is friable, and then digging out a flat-backed trench 5–6in (12–15cm) deep. To encourage rooting, put a 1–2in (2.5–5cm) layer of coarse sand in the base of the trench; this is essential on heavy soils. Space the trenches 15in (38cm) apart.

Preparing the cuttings

Take cuttings that are about pencil thickness, cutting at the junction of the current and the previous season's growth.

Trim the cuttings into 6in (15cm) lengths, cutting at the top just above a bud or pair of buds and, at the bottom, below a bud or pair of buds; on evergreens, make the cuts above and below leaves. Take heel cuttings of pithy stems (see p.83). Remove all leaves on the bottom two-thirds of evergreen cuttings, and cut large leaves in half. Treat the basal cut with a rooting hormone. Removing a sliver of bark near the base may encourage difficult cuttings to root.

Insert the cuttings in containers of cuttings soil mix. Alternatively, place them against the vertical side of the prepared trench, 6in (15cm) apart in open ground or, in a cold frame, 4in (10cm) apart. Leave 1–2in (2.5–5cm) of the cuttings above ground. Backfill the trench and firm in the cuttings.

Aftercare

If the ground is lifted by frost, firm it down around the cuttings. Keep the bed weed-free and well watered during the growing season. Cuttings in a cold frame will normally root by the following spring. Harden them off before potting up or planting out. Those in the open ground should be left in place until the following fall and then transplanted to their permanent position.

Root cuttings

Shrubs that may be propagated from root cuttings include *Aesculus parviflora*, *Aralia*, *Clerodendrum*, *Myrica*, *Rhus*, and *Xanthorhiza simplicissima.* Lift a young plant when dormant and tease the soil from its roots. If this is not practical, expose part of the shrub's root system. Cut off young roots – 1/4in (5mm) in diameter or more – close to the main stem. Keep them in moist burlap or a plastic bag until they can be prepared.

Preparing the cuttings

First remove and discard fibrous lateral roots. Then make a straight cut on an undamaged root at the end where it was severed from the plant. At the opposite end of the root, make a slanting cut. Cuttings should be 2–6in (5–15cm) long, so several cuttings may be prepared from the same root. The colder the rooting environment and the thinner the root, the longer the cutting needs to be; cuttings to be rooted outdoors need to be at least 4in (10cm) long. Dust each cutting with fungicide but do not treat with a rooting powder, since this will tend to discourage the production of shoots.

Inserting the cuttings

Aralia and other shrubs that reproduce readily from root cuttings may be inserted in open ground. For shrubs that root less readily, a controlled environment is preferable. Prepare containers of cuttings soil mix large enough for several cuttings. Firm the soil mix lightly and insert each cutting vertically 2in (5cm) apart with the slanted end down. Firm the soil mix so that the flat end of each cutting is just visible. Cover with 1/8in (3mm) of grit, and water. This watering may be sufficient to last until the shoots develop; excessive moisture may lead to rotting.

Aftercare

Cuttings will root in ten weeks outdoors, eight weeks in a cold frame or cool greenhouse. Under glass, cuttings will produce shoots in four to six weeks if they are kept at 64–75°F (18–24°C). Cuttings from shrubs that make rapid growth should be repotted as soon as they have rooted. Other root cuttings may be left in their containers for a further 12 months; apply a liquid feed once or twice a month. Then pot up singly or plant out in nursery beds.

Raising shrubs from seed

Growing shrubs from seed is simple and economical. In genera whose species hybridize readily, only use seed produced by controlled pollination.

Collecting and cleaning seed

Gather the seed capsules or fruits when ripe. Extract the seed, then clean and dry it before sowing or storing. Soak fleshy fruits in warm water or squash them so that the

EXTRACTING SEED FROM BERRIES

1 *Mash the berries (here pyracantha) between finger and thumb, removing most of the outer flesh. Wash the seeds by rubbing in warm water.*

2 *Dry the seeds and place them in a clear plastic bag with a little sphagnum moss or coarse sand, then refrigerate them until ready to sow.*

PROPAGATING SHRUBS BY HARDWOOD CUTTINGS

1 *Select strong, healthy, ripened shoots from this year's growth for the cuttings (see inset, left); avoid weak, thin stems (center) and older wood (right).*

2 *Remove any deciduous leaves and trim off the soft wood at the tip. Cut the stem into 6in (15cm) lengths. Then dip the bases into hormone rooting powder.*

3 *Insert the cuttings into prepared pots of cuttings soil mix so that approximately 1–2in (2.5–5cm) of each is visible. Label the pots and place in a cold frame.*

seed may be picked out more easily. Collect fine seed by gathering whole capsules, preferably when they have already turned brown. Place the capsules in a paper bag and keep at room temperature until they split open.

Storing seed

The length of time seed is viable depends on the species and the storage conditions. Oily seeds do not store well and should be sown soon after collection. The viability of seed may be prolonged if it is stored at a temperature of 37–41°F (3–5°C) in low humidity.

Breaking seed dormancy

The seeds of some shrubs have a form of dormancy to prevent germination in adverse conditions. This dormancy may be broken artificially by scarification or stratification (see also PRINCIPLES OF PROPAGATION, "How to overcome dormancy," p.537).

To allow air and moisture to penetrate large seeds with hard coats, such as peonies (*Paeonia*), scarify them by nicking the seed coat with a knife or filing away a small section before sowing. Hard-coated seeds that are too small to be nicked may be rubbed with sandpaper. Germination of some seeds may be aided by soaking the seed in either cold water (for example *Camellia* and *Pittosporum*) or hot but not boiling water (for example *Caragana* and *Coronilla*) for a few hours. This softens the hard seed coat, allowing water to enter and the germination process to begin.

Some seeds need a period of chilling, or stratification. As soon as the seed is gathered, put it in a plastic zip-locking bag and add a mix of equal parts of barely moist peat and sand. Store in the refrigerator below 41°F (5°C), plunge the container in the open garden, or place it in a cold frame. After about 90 days (or in spring for seeds kept outside during winter), the mix should be spread on the surface of a pot of seed soil mix and placed in a warm location to germinate.

Some seeds may not require 90 days' stratification, so inspect the bags from time to time and, if germination is occurring, remove and sow. Other seeds may need more than the 90-day period; if in doubt, sow portions of the seed at two-week intervals thereafter.

Sowing seed in containers

Most seed should be sown in fall; however, seeds of tender shrubs that in temperate regions are germinated under glass should be sown in spring. Clean all containers, implements, and surfaces. Use a standard seed soil mix, but for lime-haters use an ericaceous soil mix.

Station sow large seeds. Overfill a pot or tray with soil mix and gently firm before scraping off the surplus. Firm again with a presser board so that the level is $^{1}/_{2}$in (1cm) below the rim of the pot or tray. Sow the seeds 2in (5cm) apart, then firm them evenly into the soil mix. Cover with a $^{1}/_{4}$in (5mm) layer of sieved soil mix and a $^{1}/_{4}$in (5mm) layer of clean grit. Label and date each container and water the seeds. Many medium-sized seeds may also be sown in this way, but the gap between the rim and soil mix should be $^{1}/_{4}$–$^{3}/_{8}$in (5–8mm). Cover seeds with sieved soil mix and then $^{1}/_{4}$in (5mm) of clean grit. Place wire netting over the container to protect the seedlings from small animals. When sowing fine seed, firm the soil mix to within $^{1}/_{4}$in (5mm) of the container rim. Water and allow the soil mix to drain before sowing, carefully shaking the seed out over the surface. Do not cover the seed or water it from above.

Aftercare for seedlings in containers

After sowing, place the containers in a propagator, greenhouse, or cold frame. Temperate species need a temperature of 54–9°F (12–15°C); warm-temperate and tropical species prefer 70°F (21°C). For seed sown in spring under glass, a temperature of 54–9°F (12–15°C) should be maintained. Inspect containers of seed regularly and water as necessary. Never water fine seed from above; place the container in a shallow water tank for a short time so that water is taken up by capillary action. When the seeds have germinated, spray occasionally with fungicide.

Pricking out

Once large enough to handle, prick out the seedlings. Either knock the sides of the container to loosen the soil mix, or remove the seedlings and soil mix together and separate the seedlings, disturbing their roots as little as possible.

Transfer the seedlings into clean pots or seed trays of cuttings soil mix, leveled but not firmed. Make a hole in the soil mix and insert the seedling. Level the soil mix by tapping the top of the container and firm in, then label and water. Until the seedlings are established, the pots should be placed out of direct sunlight in a temperature similar to that needed for germination.

Sowing seed outdoors

Open-ground seedbeds are useful for sowing large batches of seed that do not require daily attention. Prepare the bed between six months and a year before sowing the seeds, and get rid of weed seedlings as they appear.

In fall, rake the soil to a fine tilth. Sow the seed in rows 18in (45cm) apart, station sowing medium or large seeds 4–6in (10–15cm) apart and sowing fine seed thinly.

Cover large and medium seeds to a depth of $^{1}/_{4}$–$^{1}/_{2}$in (0.5–1cm) but leave fine seed uncovered. Then place a $^{1}/_{4}$–$^{1}/_{2}$in (0.5–1cm) layer of grit over the seedbed. Firm the grit with a presser board, and label the rows.

Aftercare for seedlings outdoors

Protect seedlings from wind with a burlap screen. If the seeds are well spaced, they should not be troubled by disease, but spider mites (p.552), aphids (p.552), and mice, rats, and voles (p.568) may be a problem.

If the spacing is adequate, the seedlings may be left in the seedbed until the following fall, at which time they should then be either potted up or transplanted into a separate nursery bed.

SOWING SEED IN CONTAINERS

1 *Sow seeds evenly onto a prepared tray of sieved seed soil mix by tapping them from a folded piece of paper.*

2 *Cover the seeds with a fine layer of soil mix, then add a $^{1}/_{4}$in (5mm) layer of grit. Label and place in a cold frame until the seeds have germinated.*

3 *When the seedlings are large enough to handle, prick them out, lifting them carefully with a widger and holding them gently by their leaves.*

4 *Transfer the seedlings into individual pots or insert 3 into a 5in (13cm) pot. After the second pair of leaves has formed, pot them up individually.*

SHRUB SEED THAT REQUIRES SPECIAL TREATMENT

Stratification
Amelanchier
Cotoneaster
Euonymus
Hippophäe
Viburnum (some spp.)

Scarification
Camellia, some ❁
Paeonia

Soaking
Arbutus
Camellia, some ❁
Caragana
Coronilla, some ❁
Cytisus, some ❁
Pittosporum, some ❁

Sown when fresh
Acer palmatum
Daphne
Kalmia
Rhododendron, some ❁

KEY
❁ *Not frost hardy*

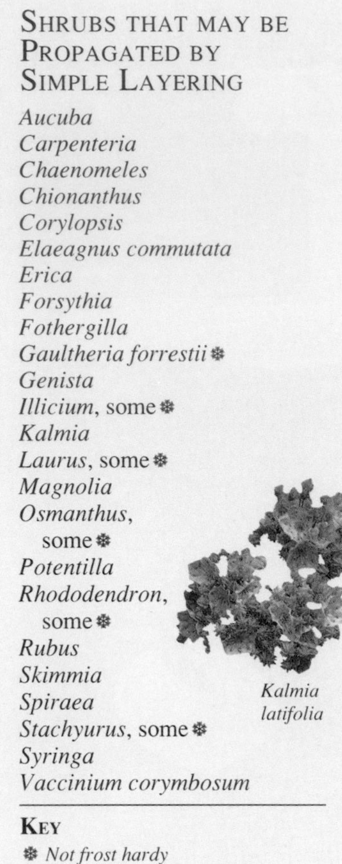

SHRUBS THAT MAY BE PROPAGATED BY SIMPLE LAYERING

Aucuba
Carpenteria
Chaenomeles
Chionanthus
Corylopsis
Elaeagnus commutata
Erica
Forsythia
Fothergilla
Gaultheria forrestii ❄
Genista
Illicium, some ❄
Kalmia
Laurus, some ❄
Magnolia
Osmanthus, some ❄
Potentilla
Rhododendron, some ❄
Rubus
Skimmia
Spiraea
Stachyurus, some ❄
Syringa
Vaccinium corymbosum

Kalmia latifolia

KEY
❄ *Not frost hardy*

Propagation by layering

Layering is a method of propagating shrubs whereby a stem is encouraged to develop roots before being removed from the parent plant. Dropping and stooling, techniques often used commercially, are variations of layering.

Simple layering

Many deciduous and evergreen shrubs may be propagated by this method. In fall or spring, about 12 months before layering is to take place, prune a low branch on the parent plant to encourage vigorous shoots, which have a greater capacity to root. Between the following late fall and early spring, prepare the soil around the stem to be layered so that it is friable. Add grit and compost if the ground is heavy.

Retain any leaves at the tip of the selected shoot, but strip off others and any side shoots. Bring the stem down to ground level and mark the ground about 9–12in (22–30cm) behind its tip. Dig a shallow hole or trench at this point for the stem. Wound the stem at the point where it will be pegged into the hole, that is about 12in (30cm) behind its tip, either with an angled cut or by removing a ring of bark. Dust the cut with rooting hormone, then peg the stem in the hole with bent wire, turning up the tip and securing it to a stake. Fill in the trench and firm the soil, leaving the tip exposed.

Throughout the growing season keep the area around the layer moist. The layer should have rooted by fall. In the following spring, check that there is a good root system before severing the layer from the parent plant and potting it up or planting it out in the open garden. If it has not rooted or there are only a few roots, keep it attached and in place for another growing season.

Air layering

This technique is particularly suitable for shrubs with branches that are difficult to lower to ground level.

In spring, choose a strong, healthy one-year-old stem that has ripened. Trim the side shoots or leaves to leave a clear length of stem behind the tip. Wound the stem with an angled cut, and dust the cut surface with a rooting hormone.

Cut off the sealed end of a black or opaque plastic bag, about 7 x 9in (18 x 22cm). Slip it over the stem like a sleeve and secure the end farthest from the growing tip by tying the bag tightly around the stem using insulating tape, raffia, or string.

Moisten a well-aerated rooting medium of sphagnum moss or equal parts of perlite and peat so that it is wet but not sodden. Pack the moist medium into the bag around the stem's cut surface and seal the top end. Keep the bag in position for a complete season.

The following spring, check that the layer has rooted. If so, sever it immediately below the point of layering. Remove the bag and tease out the roots. Prune back any new growth on the layered stem to a leaf or bud close to the old wood. Pot up using a standard or ericaceous potting soil mix, as appropriate. Label and place the layer in a cool greenhouse or cold frame until the young plant is well established. If only a few (or no) roots have developed when the bag is removed, reseal it and leave it in place for several months more. Then carry out the process described above.

Tip layering

A few shrubs, mainly species and hybrids of the genus *Rubus*, root readily from the tips of stems and may be propagated in this way. In spring, select a vigorous one-year-old shoot and pinch out the growing point to promote side shoots. In late spring, cultivate the soil around the shoot. Work in organic matter and grit if the soil is heavy.

In midsummer, when the tip growth has firmed slightly, bring the stem down to ground level and mark the position of the tip. At that point, dig a trench about 3–4in (7–10cm) deep, with one side vertical and the other sloping toward the parent plant. Using inverted U-shaped wire staples, peg the growing tip at the bottom of the trench close to the vertical side. Fill in the trench, firm lightly, and water.

By late fall, well-rooted plants should have developed. Sever these at the point where the arched stem enters the trench. Lift the rooted layers and pot on or replant outdoors. (See also *Tip Layering*, p.407.)

Dropping

With this technique a plant is almost buried. It is used to raise dwarf shrubs such as low-growing rhododendrons and heathers (*Erica*, *Daboecia*, *Calluna*) from parent plants that have become straggly.

In the dormant season, thin out branches of plants that have a mass of congested stems, to allow the remaining stems sufficient contact

PROPAGATING A SHRUB BY SIMPLE LAYERING

1 *Select a young, pliable, low-growing stem. Bring it down to the soil and mark its position with a stake about 9–12in (22–30cm) behind the tip.*

2 *At the marked point, dig a hole in the prepared soil about 3in (8cm) deep, with a shallow slope on the side where the stem joins the parent plant.*

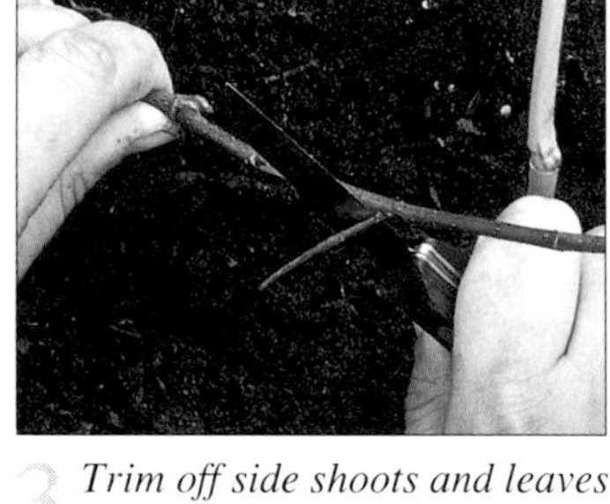

3 *Trim off side shoots and leaves on the selected stem. On the underside of the stem, at a point where it touches the ground, cut a tongue of bark.*

4 *Apply a rooting hormone to the wound on the stem. Peg down the stem with bent wire so that the stem's cut surface is held in contact with the soil.*

5 *Gently bend up the stem's tip vertically and secure it to the stake with a tie. Fill in the hole with more soil. Lightly firm with your fingers and water in.*

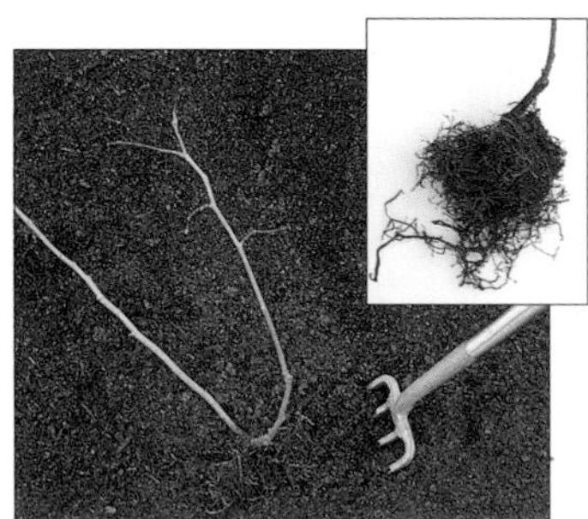

6 *Once rooted (see inset), lift the layered stem and cut it off the parent plant, severing it close to the new roots. Pot up the layer or plant it out.*

Air Layering a Shrub

1 Select a healthy, horizontal stem from the previous year's growth. Trim off any leaves and side shoots to provide a 9–12in (22–30cm) section of clear stem.

2 Slide a plastic sleeve over and along the stem; seal and secure the lower end of the sleeve to the stem with adhesive tape.

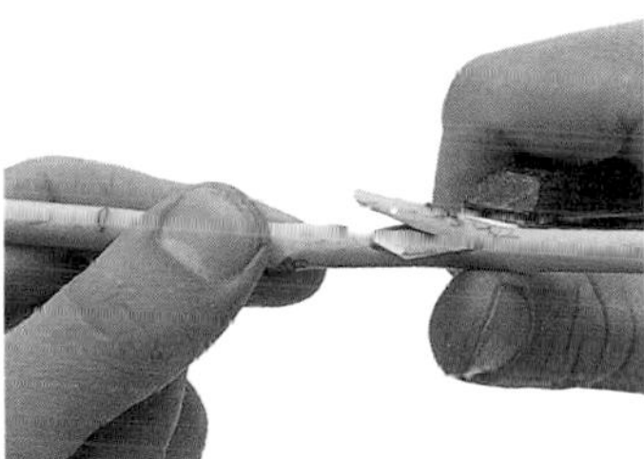

3 Fold back the plastic. Make a 1½in (4cm) diagonal cut ¼in (5mm) into the stem in the direction of growth, away from the shrub. Apply rooting hormone.

4 Soak about 2 handfuls of sphagnum moss in water, then gently squeeze it out. With the back of the knife, pack the cut with moss, wedging it open.

5 Pull back the plastic sleeve over the cut. Carefully pack the sleeve with more moistened moss so that the moss is all around the stem.

6 Continue to pack the sleeve until the moss is about 2in (5cm) from the open end. Close the end and secure it firmly in place with adhesive tape.

7 The sealed sleeve encourages rooting by retaining moisture. Leave it in place for at least a growing season to allow new roots to develop.

8 Once the layer has rooted, remove the sleeve and cut off the layer below the roots. Pot up or plant out the new shrub (here a rhododendron) in the open ground.

Stooling

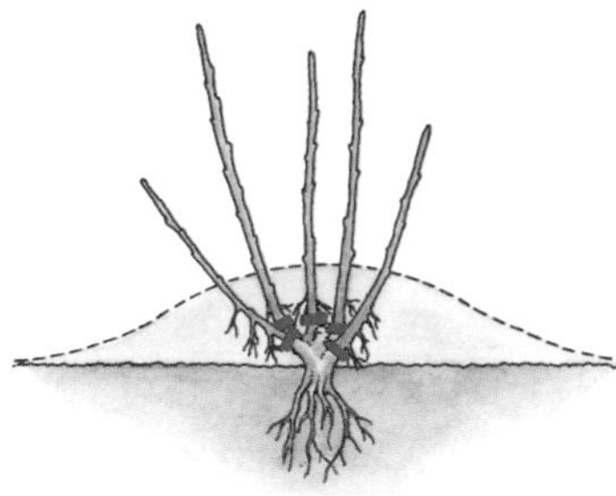

Cover shoots with free-draining soil, adding more as they grow. The shoots will root down and can be separated in fall and potted on.

with the soil to develop roots once buried. Before growth starts, but after the risk of penetrating frosts has passed, dig a pit large enough to bury the plant with only the branch tips visible. If the soil is heavy, add grit and organic material.

Lift the parent plant with the root ball as complete as possible and "drop" it into the prepared hole. Work the soil around each stem, leaving 1–2in (2.5–5cm) of each tip exposed. Firm the soil and label the plant. In summer, keep the soil moist and, in fall, carefully tease away the soil around the plant to check for rooting. Sever any rooted shoots from the parent plant, and pot up or plant out, clearly labeled. If rooting has not occurred, replace the soil and leave for a further 12 months.

Stooling

Although primarily used to raise fruit tree rootstocks, stooling may also be used to propagate deciduous ornamental shrubs such as dogwoods (*Cornus*) and lilacs (*Syringa*) from ungrafted plants.

Plant a rooted layer or other young plant in spring, label, and grow on for a season. The next spring, cut back the stem to within 3in (8cm) of the ground and apply a balanced fertilizer at 4oz/sq yd (110g/sq m). When the resulting shoots from this stem (or stool) are 6in (15cm) long, work friable soil enriched with organic matter between the shoots and bury them. Add grit if the ground is heavy. As the shoots grow, continue mounding up soil until about 9in (22cm) of each shoot is buried. Keep the soil moist in dry weather.

In fall, gently fork away the soil to ground level straight after leaf fall, leaving the rooted shoots exposed. Cut them off and pot them up or plant them out. Provided that the stools are kept fertilized, the process may be repeated annually and the same stool used for propagation in subsequent years.

Shrubs that may be Propagated by Air Layering

Citrus ❄
Ficus, some ❄
Hamamelis
Kalmia latifolia
Magnolia
Rhododendron, some ❄

Shrubs that may be Propagated by Stooling

Amelanchier
Cotinus coggygria (and cvs)
Hydrangea arborescens, *H. paniculata*
Prunus glandulosa
Ribes
Salix
Stephanandra

Ribes sanguineum

Key
❄ *Not frost hardy*

French layering

This method of propagating shrubs is a form of stooling and is suitable for increasing the stock of deciduous shrubs such as dogwoods (*Cornus alba*, *C. stolonifera*) and *Cotinus coggygria*.

In spring, plant a rooted layer or young plant, label it, and grow it on for a season. Then, in the dormant season, cut back the stool to within 3in (8cm) of the ground. In the following spring, apply a balanced fertilizer at the rate of 2–4oz/sq yd (60–110g/sq m).

The following fall, cut out all but about the ten best stems; shorten the tips of these so that they are all about the same length. With U-shaped wire staples, pin each stem to the ground, spreading the stems evenly around the parent stool. Each bud along the length of the stem should break evenly in spring.

When the new shoots on the pegged-down stems are approximately 2–3in (5–8cm) long, take out the pegs and cultivate the ground around the parent stool, incorporating a balanced fertilizer at a rate of 2–4oz/sq yd (60–110g/sq m). Space the stems evenly again, dropping each into a 2in (5cm) deep trench. Peg down each stem and cover with soil, leaving the shoot tips exposed. Hill up all but 2–3in (5–8cm) of the new shoots as they develop, until the mound is 15cm (6in) high. Water in hot, dry weather.

After leaf fall, carefully fork away the soil from around the new shoots until the stems that were laid horizontally are exposed. Cut these flush with the central stool. Then cut the stems to separate the rooted sections. Pot these up or plant them out in the open garden, and label them. The same stool may be used to produce further layers.

Division

Division is an easy way of increasing shrubs that produce suckers. Suitable shrubs include *Ruscus*, *Kerria*, *Gaultheria*, and *Sarcococca*. Shrubs must be grown on their own roots, not grafted onto another rootstock.

Before growth starts in spring, lift the plant. Break the clump into sections, retaining those with vigorous shoots and well-developed roots. Prune any damaged roots, and cut back the top-growth by one-third to a half to reduce water loss. Replant the divisions in the open, and water in dry weather. Alternatively, simply lift a suckering root, severing it from the parent plant, and then replant it in the open.

With a few shrubs, including *Rhus*, suckering may be encouraged by digging deeply around the parent plant in summer or fall. This damages the roots and stimulates adventitious buds to develop suckers in spring. These rooted suckers may then be lifted and potted up or planted out.

Grafting

This technique is used to unite two plants so that they grow together as one. One part, known as the scion, is taken from the plant to be propagated and provides the top-growth of the new plant, while the other part, known as the rootstock or stock, provides the root system. The rootstock and scion must be compatible, so they are normally of the same or closely related species.

Grafting is an important way of propagating shrubs that are difficult to root or that are unlikely to come true from seed. By using selected rootstocks, it is possible to improve a plant's vigor, disease resistance, or tolerance to specific growing conditions, or sometimes to control its basic growth pattern.

Among the many variations of this technique, three that are widely used are saddle, side-veneer, and apical-wedge grafting. In all cases, the stocks and scions should be joined immediately after they have been cut, and the cut surfaces of each should be kept clean.

Saddle grafting

This grafting technique is predominantly used to propagate evergreen rhododendron species and hybrids, with *Rhododendron ponticum* generally serving as the rootstock. About one month before grafting is to commence, in late winter or early spring, bring the rootstock into a greenhouse maintained at a temperature of 50–54°F (10–12°C).

In late winter or very early spring, select the scion material so that it is ready for grafting. The scions selected should be about 2–5in (5–13cm) long, and taken from vigorous, nonflowering, one-year-old shoots on the plant to be propagated. If only shoots with flower buds are available, pinch these out. The scions should be labeled and stored in a plastic bag in a refrigerator.

Select a straight-stemmed rootstock of about pencil thickness and cut it back to within 2in (5cm) of the base, making a straight cut across the stem with pruners. Then, using a knife, make two slanting cuts to make an upside-down V wound on the top of the stock. Prepare the scion by making two corresponding angled cuts so that its base – the saddle – will fit snugly onto the apex of the rootstock.

Ensure that the two sections of the graft fit well together, and then bind the stock and scion together with a length of clear grafting tape. Cut back any very large leaves by half to reduce moisture loss. Label clearly, and then place the grafted plant in a propagator and shade it from direct sunlight. Check the plant daily for watering and hygiene, and spray it once a week with a fungicide solution. Union normally takes place within four to five weeks.

Once the scion starts to grow, remove the tape and gradually harden off the grafted plant – opening the propagator for longer periods each day. If the grafted plant is kept in the original pot for a season, give it a liquid feed once a month.

Side-veneer grafting

This grafting technique is used to propagate a variety of both evergreen and deciduous shrubs. Most side-veneer grafting is carried out in midwinter, but deciduous shrubs such as *Hamamelis* may also be grafted during the summer.

For the appropriate rootstocks, choose one- to three-year-old seedlings that are compatible with the plant to be propagated. The stems should be of pencil thickness. About three weeks before grafting, bring the rootstock into the greenhouse. Water it sparingly so that the rootstock does not break dormancy too quickly, since vigorous sap movement may prevent successful grafting. If grafting in summer, use two-year-old seedlings for the rootstocks and keep them fairly dry for a month in advance.

For both summer and winter grafting, prepare and unite the stocks and scions in the same way.

Just before grafting takes place, collect vigorous one-year-old shoots that have some mature wood to be used as scions. They should be of a similar thickness to the rootstocks onto which they will be grafted. If there will be any delay, label the scions and place them in a plastic bag in a refrigerator.

When grafting, first trim the scion to a length of 5–8in (12–20cm), or 4–5in (10–12cm) for magnolias. Make a sloping cut at the base of the scion 1–1½in (2.5–4cm) long, turn it over, and make a small wedge-shaped cut on the other side.

Reduce the rootstock stem to about 12in (30cm). Make two cuts in the

SUCKERING SHRUBS THAT MAY BE DIVIDED

Amelanchier canadensis
Andromeda
Aronia
Aster albescens
Berberis buxifolia
Buxus sempervirens
Cassiope hypnoides
Ceratostigma plumbaginoides
Clerodendrum bungei
Cornus alba,
C. canadensis,
C. stolonifera

Cornus canadensis

Danäe racemosa
Diervilla lonicera
Erica
Euonymus fortunei
Gaultheria, some ❄
Itea virginica
Kerria
Mahonia repens
Menziesia ciliicalyx
Paxistima
Pernettya
Polygala, some ❄
Rhus, some ❄
Ruscus aculeatus
Sarcococca
Spiraea japonica (cvs)

KEY
❄ *Not frost hardy*

PROPAGATING SUCKERING SHRUBS BY DIVISION

1 *Lift a root with suckers on it, without disturbing the parent plant. Check that there are fibrous roots at the base of the suckers.*

2 *Remove the suckering root by cutting it off close to the parent plant. Firm back the soil around the parent plant.*

3 *Cut the main root back to the fibrous roots, then divide the suckers so that each has its own roots. Cut back the top-growth by about half.*

4 *Replant the suckers in open ground in prepared planting holes. Firm the soil around the suckers and water in. (The plant used here is* Gaultheria shallon.)

SADDLE GRAFTING

1 *Select vigorous, nonflowering shoots of the previous year's growth from the plant to be propagated (here a rhododendron) as scions.*

2 *Prepare a selected rootstock of about the same diameter as the scion by cutting it back to within about 2in (5cm) of the base.*

3 *Using a sharp knife, cut the stock with 2 upward angled cuts so that its apex is shaped like a slightly rounded, upside-down V.*

4 *Make compatible, angled cuts on the scion (see inset), trimming its length to about 2–5in (5–13cm).*

5 *Place the cut scion (see inset) on top of the stock so that they fit together. If the scion is too narrow, place it so that one side of the cambium layer meets that of the stock.*

6 *Bind the scion in place with plastic grafting tape or raffia. Cut back very large leaves by half. Leave the grafted plant in a propagator until union occurs.*

SHRUBS THAT MAY BE GRAFTED

Saddle
Rhododendron, some ❄ (many hybrids and species)

Side-veneer
Acer palmatum (cvs)
Aralia elata 'Aureovariegata'
Arbutus unedo (cvs)
Camellia reticulata, *C. sasanqua*
Caragana arborescens
Cotoneaster 'Hybridus Pendulus'
Daphne bholua, *D. petraea*
Hamamelis
Magnolia
Pittosporum eugenioides 'Variegatum' ❄
Prunus glandulosa
Rhaphiolepis

Hibiscus sinosyriacus 'Lilac Queen'

Apical-wedge
Caragana arborescens 'Walker'
Daphne arbuscula
Hibiscus, some ❄
Syringa

KEY
❄ *Not frost hardy*

stock, starting 3in (8cm) above soil level, to take out a sliver of wood, leaving a cut that roughly matches that on the scion.

Place the rootstock and scion together so that the cambium layers match as closely as possible, and if necessary on one side only for stocks and scions of differing widths; tie them securely in position with grafting tape. Label the grafted plant and place it in a propagator at an even temperature of 50–59°F (10–15°C). Water the plant regularly and spray with a fungicide once a week.

Union should occur in four to five weeks. Harden off the grafted plant over the next four weeks, then remove it from the propagator and grow it on in a cool greenhouse.

As the scion starts to grow, gradually cut back the stem of the stock; by the end of the first growing season, all the stock above the graft union should have been cut back. During the first season, remove the initial tie and, if growth is rapid, replace it with a single raffia tie.

On plants that have been grafted in the summer, cut back the stock just above the union before growth starts in spring. Replace the original tie with a small one around the union, since there is a tendency for the scion to be pushed off the stock. Support the leader with a stake after repotting. For further details, see *Propagating Trees by Side-veneer Grafting*, p.56.

Apical-wedge grafting

Apical-wedge grafting, or cleft grafting, is a comparatively straightforward technique and is suitable for the propagation of a number of shrubs, including *Caragana*, *Hibiscus*, and lilac (*Syringa*).

During midwinter, collect vigorous one-year-old stems for use as scions. Place these in a clearly labeled plastic bag and store them in a refrigerator in order to retard their development.

Also in midwinter, select one-year-old seedlings of compatible shrubs as rootstocks. Stock and scion should both be about the thickness of a pencil. Immediately prior to grafting, lift the rootstock and wash it. Cut its stem horizontally, about 1in (2.5cm) above the roots. With a sharp knife, make a 1in (2.5cm) vertical cut down the center of the rootstock stem.

Remove the scions from the refrigerator and select one with healthy buds that is of similar diameter to the rootstock. Trim it down by making a horizontal cut just above a healthy bud or buds and a similar cut 6in (15cm) below. To form the wedge, make a 1–1½in (2.5–4cm) long, sloping cut down toward the middle of the scion base, and a similar cut on the other side.

Push the scion into the prepared cut on the stock. If the scion is narrower than the stock, align one edge of the scion so that it is flush with one edge of the stock. Bind them with grafting tape or moist raffia. If raffia is used, coat the union edges with grafting wax to stop moisture loss and to seal the top of the scion.

Either pot up the grafted plants or insert them in potting mix in a seed tray. Label and then place them in a propagator at 50–59°F (10–15°C), the higher temperature inducing a faster union.

The union of the stock and scion should take place within about five to six weeks. Remove the tape or raffia when there is a firm union. Pot up the plants that are in seed trays and harden them off gradually. Grow the plants on for a further year in a cold frame before planting them out.

APICAL-WEDGE GRAFTING

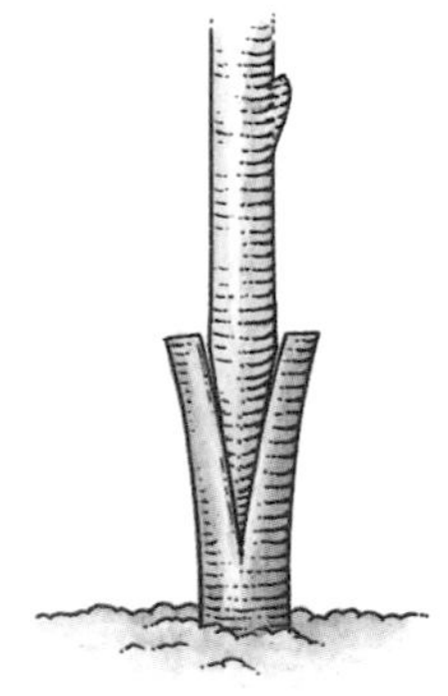

Make a simple vertical cut down into the stock. Cut the base of the scion with 2 downward cuts into a V and push the base into the stock. Bind them together, pot up, and place in a propagator.

Topiary

A FORM of training and pruning trees and shrubs to create attractive, boldly artificial shapes, topiary is a garden art that has been popular since Roman times. Traditionally used to produce strongly architectural and geometric shapes in formal gardens, it has been developed to include birds, animals, and unusual features such as furniture, giant chesspieces, and full-size trains.

Designing with topiary

Different styles of topiary may be used to create a variety of effects. Imaginative, living sculptures express personal style and add a humorous or bizarre touch. Using topiary in geometric shapes such as cones, obelisks, and columns provides a strong, structural element in a design. This type of topiary may be valuable both in formal gardens, perhaps to frame a vista or form an avenue, and in informal gardens, as a contrasting foil for less structured planting.

In some gardens, it may be appropriate to treat part of the hedge top as topiary, clipping it into one or more birds, spheres, or cubes, for example. Topiary may also be pleasing in containers; use a single container plant as a centerpiece, a pair to flank a doorway, or several to line a path.

ELEGANT SIMPLICITY
This formal, spiral topiary perfectly complements the classical statue nearby, and its square pot mirrors the statue's pedestal.

SUITABLE PLANTS FOR TOPIARY

Taxus* x *media (yew)

Buxus sempervirens (boxwood)

***Ilex aquifolium* 'Crispa Aurea Picta'** (holly)

Laurus nobilis (bay)

Ligustrum ovalifolium (privet)

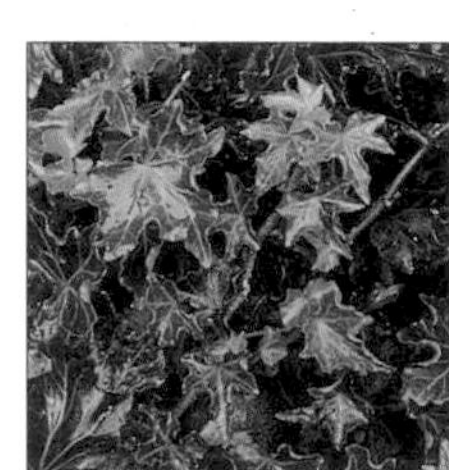

***Hedera helix* 'Ivalace'** (ivy)

TRAINING IVY ON A FRAME

Stuff a 1/2in (1cm) layer of moss between 2 pieces of chicken wire, secure it, and form it into the desired shape. Place it in position and train ivies up around the frame.

Plants for topiary

Plants to be used for topiary need dense, pliable growth, small leaves, and the ability to recover quickly from clipping. Evergreens such as yew (*Taxus* spp.), boxwood (*Buxus sempervirens*), and *Lonicera nitida* are ideal in a temperate climate. *Cupressus sempervirens* can be trained into geometric shapes, but it is suitable only in warmer climates. Many deciduous shrubs such as *Euonymus*, cotoneaster, and *Ligustrum* are good choices for colder areas.

Ivies (*Hedera*) are very adaptable and may easily be trained to grow over an open frame; alternatively, several cuttings can be taken from an existing plant to grow up a moss-stuffed structure.

Creating a shape

Most topiary designs are best formed with the aid of a guiding framework, although some simple shapes may also be cut free-hand.

Simple designs
Using young plants, select the stem or stems that will form the core of the design; this can be either a single shoot or several shoots that are then spread out. The simplest shape to produce is a cone: for this, only guiding stakes are needed. For other shapes, attach a framework made from chicken wire or single wires attached to stakes placed in the ground next to the main group of shoots. Tie the stems to the wire framework and then pinch back the shoots to encourage them to branch and cover the form.

Train new shoots into the framework to fill in gaps, until they meet around its perimeter. Growth will vary around the plant, depending on the exposure to light. Shoots trained downward always grow slowly.

Complex designs
To form complex topiary designs, make a basic framework from sturdy materials such as heavy-duty fencing wire. Chicken wire or thin-gauge wire may then be intertwined to form a more precise shape. Garden stakes are also useful as a temporary aid in developing and shaping a framework. Green garden twine is good for tying shoots onto a framework, since it eventually decays.

HOW TO CREATE A SIMPLE DESIGN

1 *If using a young plant (here a boxwood) to form a geometric shape, first cut to shape by eye.*

2 *The following year, make a cutting guide from stakes and wire, place over the plant, and cut the plant to shape.*

3 *When the plant is the desired shape, clip each year with pruners to retain a crisp outline.*

Clipped Bird
Traditional shapes are still the most popular for topiary. This delightful bird sits on top of its nest surveying the surrounding gardens.

Training stems

Young stems being trained onto a frame grow quickly, and considerable work is thus required to tie in new shoots throughout the growing season. Tie in the shoots while they are young and pliable, and check previous ties to make sure that they are not broken, rubbing, or in any way restricting the shoots.

If stakes have been used in the framework, make sure that they are still firm and have not cracked, snapped, or bent. If they are defective, replace them with new ones.

Clipping

Topiary involves much more precise clipping than is required for normal hedge cutting. Take time, particularly when initially forming topiary pieces, to cut the branchlets carefully to the required shape. Do not cut too much in one place, since it may spoil the symmetry of a topiary design for a whole season until new replacement growth appears.

Even if you have a good eye for shaping plants, use levels, plumb lines, and any other aids available to check the accuracy of a cut. Always work from the top of the plant downward and from the center outward, cutting both sides together in order to retain a balanced symmetry.

Rounded topiary pieces are easier to produce and maintain than angular, geometric shapes and may often be cut free-hand. To produce a spherical shape, first trim the top of the plant and then cut a channel downward around the circumference to leave a ring. A further ring at 90° should then be cut, leaving four distinct quarters to be trimmed.

Geometric topiary that has precise, flat surfaces and angled or squared edges is difficult to form and maintain, and needs to be tackled with confident, accurate clipping for a well-defined shape. Such geometric designs are best cut using guidelines attached to stakes.

When to clip

Once a topiary feature is established, it will need frequent routine clipping during the growing season. The time between cuts will depend on the rate of growth. An intricate, geometric design in boxwood may need to be cut at four- to six-week intervals. Trim when any new growth begins to appear uneven.

If a perfect finish is not required throughout the year, two cuts during the growing season are usually sufficient for a reasonably clean-cut look, depending on the plant used. Yew, however, can be cut from one to three times a year, depending on the length of the growing season. Boxwood (*Buxus sempervirens*) usually needs to be cut once or twice (depending on the cultivar), and *Lonicera nitida* three times.

Clip plants at the appropriate time of year. Do not clip after early fall because young shoots need to ripen sufficiently to withstand low winter temperatures. In warm climates where growth is almost continuous, regular trimming will be required throughout the year.

Architectural Designs
These complex, abstract shapes need frequent clipping but they form an impressive centerpiece, their forms echoing the cascade of the fountain.

Routine care

Weeding, watering, and mulching are essential in the same way as for free-growing shrubs (see p.70). It is important, however, to apply two or three feeds of a balanced fertilizer at a rate of 2oz/sq yd (60g/sq m) during the growing season.

Winter care

In regions where regular snowfalls occur, netting topiary pieces will help prevent the branches from breaking under the weight of snow. Knock snow off any flat surfaces since it may damage the framework.

Repairs and renovation

If a leader, a section, or a branch of topiary has been damaged or broken, cut it back cleanly with pruners. Manipulate nearby shoots by tying them in to fill the gap.

If topiary plants have been left unclipped for one or two years, regular clipping should restore the original form within the season. If the topiary has been neglected for years, and the shape has been lost, severe pruning to restore the outline should be carried out the first spring, followed by two or three seasons of more precise clipping.

Scorch and dieback

The foliage of some evergreens may be scorched in severe winters and can die. The damaged foliage will soon be covered by new growth in spring, but cut it back where it is unsightly, taking care to follow the shape of the topiary piece. If shoots do not fill the gap, there may be a root problem, which will need to be treated.

How to Create a Complex Design

1 *Make frameworks for large topiary from strong materials because they will be in place for several years. Clip the plant (here yew) as necessary to keep it within the framework.*

2 *As the plant fills the frame, clip it regularly, following the outline of the framework (see inset) and pinching out shoots to encourage bushy growth.*

3 *When mature, the plant will form a dense bush and cover the framework. It needs regular clipping to maintain the precise outline of the design.*

4

Climbing Plants

Woody and herbaceous climbers make up one of the most versatile of plant groups, providing enormous scope for imaginative design in the garden. Climbing plants introduce a strong vertical element to planting designs when grown with support, whether against the house wall or on free-standing pergolas. If unsupported, some climbers sprawl luxuriantly, adding a horizontal line as well as color and texture to plantings; others perform a lowly task as weed-smothering ground cover. When allowed to scramble upward through other tall plants, climbers can prolong the season of interest. They can also be used to weave together different color and textural elements of the garden design. Perhaps one of their greatest assets is their potential for clothing unsightly garden features – fences, walls, tree stumps, toolsheds, or other garden buildings. Many of the most popular climbers have heavily scented flowers on their high and far-reaching stems which cast their perfume over the garden.

Designing with climbers

Gardens of every size and situation can be enhanced by climbing plants. Some, such as clematis and *Passiflora* species, are grown primarily for the exquisite beauty of their flowers. Others – *Lonicera periclymenum*, for example – are equally valued for their fragrance. Many are appreciated for their handsome evergreen foliage, or their rich and spectacular fall color, as with *Parthenocissus* species and *Vitis coignetiae*. Even when leafless, their elegant habit and often strong architectural form enhance the stark winter outlines of fences, archways, and other hard landscape features. Some climbers produce fruits or berries that are attractive both to gardeners and to wildlife.

In their natural habitats, climbers use various techniques to climb through host plants to gain access to the light. Plants, walls, and other features can be used to provide support for the wide range of growth habits among climbers.

A Floral Entrance
Bougainvillea *gracefully links a series of archways in this elegant courtyard setting. The brilliant spectacle of its showy magenta bracts harmonizes well with the sun-baked supporting wall. In frost-free gardens, it is one of the most vigorous and luxuriant of all climbers.*

Climbing methods and supports

Some climbers are self-clinging, attaching themselves to their supports either by aerial roots (adventitious rootlets), as do ivies (*Hedera* spp.), or by adhesive tendril tips, as does Virginia creeper (*Parthenocissus quinquefolia*). These cling to any surface offering sufficient foothold, including walls and tree trunks. They need no additional support except during the early stages, when they require the guidance of a stake, string, or wire until they are able to establish secure contact. Climbers with aerial roots are also particularly well suited for use as ground cover.

Twining species coil their stems in a spiral habit around their support, clockwise or counterclockwise, depending on their anatomical and morphological characteristics. Both *Lonicera periclymenum* and *Humulus lupulus*, for example, twine clockwise, whereas *Ceropegia sandersonii* and *Wisteria sinensis* twine counterclockwise. All twining species need some form of permanent support, usually provided by a trellis or wire, attached to an overhead support. The plants may also be grown up the stems of a sturdy host plant (see also "Growing climbers through other plants," p.94).

A few climbers like clematis and some nasturtiums (*Tropaeolum*) attach themselves to supports by means of curling leaf stalks. Many others are tendril climbers that twine around their supports by means of contact-sensitive tendrils. These tendrils are often modified leaves

Garden Design
Framing a formal piece of statuary, the fresh lime-green leaves of Humulus lupulus 'Aureus' *help to reinforce a striking focal point in this garden.*

or leaflets, as in *Bignonia capreolata* and sweet peas (*Lathyrus odoratus*); terminal shoots, as in grapes; or axillary shoots, as in *Passiflora*. In *Parthenocissus*, the tendrils develop adhesive disks at the tips once they come into contact with a support.

Scandent, scrambling, and trailing climbers, such as *Bougainvillea* species, *Quisqualis indica*, and winter jasmine (*Jasminum nudiflorum*), produce long, arching stems that attach themselves only loosely, if at all, to their supports. These plants need to be tied in to a wire framework or trellis with plastic twist-ties or vine ties. Alternatively, they may be left to sprawl over walls and banks for a less formal look. Plants in this group are also sometimes used as ground cover.

Some species, including climbing roses and certain *Rubus* species, are equipped with hooked thorns that help them to scramble naturally through host plants. If not grown through other plants, these need to be tied in to sturdy supports.

Site and exposure

To achieve their full potential, a number of climbers prefer a sunny position with their roots in shade, although some need a cooler spot. Many others, including *Parthenocissus* and *Schizophragma*, are less demanding and, while preferring a sunny exposure, tolerate shade.

Tender climbers may require the protection of a south-facing wall in cool climates. There are numerous hardy climbers, however, that will perform perfectly well without any protection at all.

Sunny or sheltered sites

In temperate areas, a sheltered wall provides a suitable microclimate for growing tender or exotic flowering climbers. *Lapageria rosea* and blue passionflower (*Passiflora caerulea*) both thrive with winter protection in such a position; the heat reflected by the wall helps to ripen the wood so that the plants are better able to withstand cold winter temperatures.

The wall also gives protection against temperatures slightly below freezing. If frost is likely at flowering time, avoid planting climbers in positions where the flower buds are exposed to early-morning sun, because the buds often will be damaged as a result of rapid thawing. Sun-loving herbaceous plants and bulbs may be planted at the base of the climbers to help keep their roots cool.

Cool or exposed sites

For shady, north-facing walls and those exposed to cold winds, vigorous, hardy climbers – Virginia creeper (*Parthenocissus quinquefolia*) and some honeysuckles, in particular – are the most suitable plants. In very cold climates, using annuals will extend the range of suitable climbers; scarlet runner beans (*Phaseolus coccineus*) and canary creeper (*Tropaeolum peregrinum*) are good choices.

Climbers on walls, buildings, and fences

Whether complementing or camouflaging their support, climbing plants make an immediate visual impact. Most buildings can be enhanced by the softening appearance of a climber, and garden walls and fences become decorative features when clothed with plants bearing blossoms and foliage.

Enhancing a building

Before planting, assess the architectural merits of a building, using the plants to emphasize its good points. A well-designed building may be complemented by climbers that have a strong visual impact, with, for example, distinctively shaped or colored foliage or outstanding flowers. *Actinidia kolomikta*, with its pink- or white-tipped leaves and cup-shaped white flowers in summer, is one of the most spectacular climbers for this purpose.

A less visually pleasing building can also be made more attractive by using climbers. Regular panels of plants may be used to break up long stretches of blank wall, and may also serve to exaggerate or lessen strong vertical or horizontal lines. Narrow panels of foliage that extend upward can make a building seem taller than it actually is. On the other hand, wider panels of plants allowed to grow only as high as the second floor will make a tall, narrow building appear broader. The most suitable plants for this purpose include most species of ivy (*Hedera*) and other self-clinging root climbers, such as *Schizophragma hydrangeoides* and *Hydrangea anomala* subsp. *petiolaris*. Their rich panels of foliage may be pruned into the desired shape.

In a more relaxed, informal setting, vigorous climbing plants can be combined for a profusion of flowers and fragrance. The dark green foliage and white flowers of *Clematis paniculata*, together with the strongly fragrant red and yellow flowers of *Lonicera* x *americana*, combine well with many species of climbing rose, perhaps with annual sweet peas (*Lathyrus odoratus*) grown through them. This combination can be particularly attractive around a window or doorway, where the flowers and scents of the plants are best appreciated.

Screening with climbers

The more vigorous climbing plants can be relied upon to camouflage an unattractive toolshed, wall, or fence

An Informal Screen
These clematis and yellow climbing roses weave through wires to provide an attractive mix of color and a long season of interest.

remarkably quickly. Use plants such as *Clematis montana*, for its profusion of creamy white flowers in late spring, or the silver lace vines (*Polygonum aubertii* and *P. baldschuanicum*), which soon produce dense cover combined with clusters of tiny flowers in late summer. Both *P. aubertii* and *P. baldschuanicum* are also known as mile-a-minute vine for a good reason – they are extremely rampant and must therefore be sited with great care, since they will swamp even reasonably vigorous neighbors. They also need regular and severe pruning to keep them within bounds.

Where year-round cover is required, ivies may be more appropriate. Alternatively, use a combination of evergreen and deciduous plants; the bluish green, evergreen leaves of *Lonicera sempervirens*, for instance, provide the perfect foil in summer for the soft pink blooms of the climbing rose 'New Dawn'.

Climbers on pergolas and pillars

Pergolas, pillars, and other man-made structures enable climbers to be viewed from all sides and, in addition, contribute strong stylistic elements to the garden design. They can be used to add height to an otherwise flat garden. Depending on materials used, they may be formal and elegant, or informal and rustic. If designed well, they can be at their most attractive when only partially covered with plants. They must, however, be strong enough to carry the often considerable weight of stems and foliage and should also be durable, since the plants will need their support for many years.

Pergolas

Pergolas or arbors festooned with climbers provide a cool, shady sitting area in the garden and bring a sense of seclusion and privacy to an otherwise open site. The most suitable plants are those that put on their best display at the time of day or during the particular season when the structure is most often used.

If an arbor is to be used often on summer evenings, suitable plants might include common white jasmine (*Jasminum officinale*), *Lonicera periclymenum* 'Graham Thomas', or the climbing rose 'Mme. Alfred Carrière', all with beautifully fragrant blooms in pale colors that show up well in the fading light. For summer shade, use large-leaved climbers such as *Vitis coignetiae* (which also gives splendid fall color) or *V. vinifera* 'Purpurea', whose claret-colored young leaves turn dusky purple as they mature. Alternatively, use the massed floral display of *Wisteria sinensis* 'Alba' as a spring canopy. The flowers of this plant look beautiful if grown up pergolas flanking walkways. Ensure that the crossbeams are high enough, however, so there is no need to stoop to avoid the flowers.

For winter interest, plant evergreens such as ivy or, in mild areas, tender *Lardizabala biternata*. Alternatively, use deciduous plants such as *Celastrus* or *Wisteria* species, whose bare stems take on beautiful sculptural qualities in winter.

GROWING ON PERGOLAS
Wisteria sinensis 'Alba' *is an ideal choice for a pergola over a walkway. It produces a mass of fragrant white blooms in spring that hang down in garlands, releasing their welcome scent at just the right height to be appreciated.*

Pillars

To add a strong vertical element to a mixed or herbaceous border, climbers such as clematis or *Passiflora* species may be grown up and around pillars. Also consider using pillars to mark an axis or focal point, perhaps at the corner of a border or at a point where the garden level changes. A series of pillars at the back of a flowerbed or along a path can also be linked by rope or chain swags, and climbers trained along them.

For an evergreen climber, or as a temporary feature, a stout post with mesh panels wrapped around it will provide adequate support. If growing a deciduous plant, which means that the pillar will be visible in winter, buy a ready-made trellis obelisk or column, which will be attractive when it is bare.

Growing climbers through other plants

In the wild, many climbers grow naturally through other plants, which is a habit that may be copied successfully in the garden – although

NATURAL SUPPORT
The scarlet flowers of Tropaeolum speciosum *are made yet more intense by the deep green backdrop of a hedge of yew* (Taxus baccata).

PLANT ASSOCIATION
The heart-shaped leaves of Vitis coignetiae *make a striking contrast of shape and texture with those of* Euonymus fortunei 'Silver Queen'.

the climbers should not be too vigorous for the hosts. Always plan color combinations before planting, taking flowers, foliage, and fruit into consideration. The climber may either complement or contrast with its host when the latter is putting on its best display, or it may extend the season of interest.

Climbers that are suitable for growing through shrubs include *Clematis viticella* hybrids and those large-flowered clematis that are cut back each year. It is also a useful method for growing most annual climbing plants and *Tropaeolum speciosum*, whose stems and fiery red flowers are best supported by another plant.

For growing through trees, vigorous species such as *Ampelopsis brevipedunculata* var. *maximowiczii* or *Schizophragma hydrangeoides* produce beautiful combinations of foliage, fruit, and flower. Alternatively, try mingling the cascading blooms of *Rosa filipes* 'Kiftsgate' with the white or pink sprays of *Clematis montana*. Both produce strong, twining stems that quickly scramble into the branches of a tree.

GROUND COVER
Clematis viticella *cultivars* 'Etoile Violette' *and* 'Abundance' *make a carpet of color, using winter-flowering heathers* (Erica) *as host plants.*

Climbers as ground cover

Some climbers, particularly those with aerial roots or those with a scandent, trailing, or scrambling habit, may be grown without support to produce swaths of ground cover. They are particularly useful when allowed to sprawl over a sloping bank or when trailing over a wall, where they will often root in the soil beneath.

Climbers that attach themselves by means of adhesive tendrils, such as *Parthenocissus* species, and root climbers are extremely effective at suppressing weeds when grown as ground cover. Take care when siting these plants, however, because if there is any other plant nearby that could serve as a support, it may be swamped. To reduce the risk of this, choose less vigorous climbing species or relocate other plants so that the climber has a free run.

Twining climbers may also be used as ground cover, provided that their shoots are spread evenly across the ground; if needed, wire hooks can be used to keep the shoots in place. The large, deeply colored flowers of *Clematis* 'Ernest Markham' and *C.* 'Jackmanii' are very eye-catching at ground level, as are the blue-green leaves and scarlet flowers of *Tropaeolum speciosum*.

Colorful climbers

Color impact varies according to light levels in different parts of the garden. In a sunny spot, bright or deep colors, which absorb light, show up more strongly than paler ones, which reflect light. The latter, on the other hand, may look washed out in bright light but may successfully illuminate a dull, dark space. They can be used to great advantage in gardens that are most often viewed in the fading light of evening.

Before planting climbing plants, consider the color of the garden's permanent features. If the wall or support is already bright, use plants with more subtle coloring, unless you wish to create a particularly vibrant combination.

Color combinations

Growing different climbers together or in combination with other plants adds another dimension to color schemes. Climbers can be particularly useful for interweaving the different color components of a planting design, creating brilliant combinations with complementary colors or more subtle harmonies with closely related tones.

Flowers for color

The flowers of climbers occur in colors across the spectrum, from the deep violet of *Clematis viticella* 'Etoile Violette' through the brilliant scarlet of *Campsis radicans* to the soft, creamy white of *Araujia sericofera*. A large number of the most vividly colored climbers are tropical in origin and are not hardy in temperate zones, however.

Climbers with strongly colored flowers have a bold and exuberant appearance, but these usually need thoughtful placement if they are not to be overwhelming. Those that offer softer colors, such as the pink of *Clematis montana* 'Tetrarose' or the pale violet-blue of *Codonopsis convolvulacea*, are more suitable for subtle-hued plantings.

Foliage and fruits for color

Make use of the leaves of climbers as well as their flowers in a planting design. Leaf tone can provide soothing contrasts and balance vivid flower color. *Humulus lupulus* 'Aureus' has yellow leaves that appear almost gold if placed against a dark background. Even more striking is *Actinidia kolomikta*, which has leaves tipped with creamy white and pink. The variegated ivies are almost as showy and, being evergreen, give a year-round display.

Other climbers bear fruits that are at least as colorful as their flowers: outstanding among these are the fruits of *Akebia quinata* (purplish), the slightly frost-tender *Billardiera longiflora* (purple-blue or white), and *Celastrus orbiculatus* (green, then tan, splitting to show yellow insides with red seeds).

Interest through the seasons

For continuity of interest throughout the year, devise a planting plan in which different climbers succeed each other as the seasons progress.

COMPLEMENTARY COLORS
An old stone wall provides a natural setting for climbing plants. This one has an unobtrusive wire framework supporting clematis and the golden-leaved Humulus lupulus 'Aureus' *twining around it.*

FOLIAGE PATTERNS
Actinidia kolomikta *is a deciduous climber with highly unusual and decorative foliage; many of the leaves are tipped with bold splashes of pink or white. Small, cup-shaped, scented white flowers appear in the summer.*

CLIMBING ANNUALS
Hyacinth bean (Lablab purpureus) *is a deciduous plant often grown as an annual for quick cover in summer. This huge and gnarled old tree trunk lends its support to the twining stems and pealike, pink and purple flowers.*

This technique may be applied to climbers that are being grown together or in separate parts of the garden, so that there is always something to catch the eye.

Spring and summer

Numerous climbers put on their best show in spring and summer. The early-flowering *Clematis macropetala* and *Lonicera periclymenum* 'Serotina', which reaches its peak in midsummer, make an extremely attractive combination. The flowers of the clematis also leave behind fluffy seedheads to augment the beauty of the honeysuckle's scented tubular blooms, and often continue the display throughout fall and sometimes even into winter.

Fall color

Some climbers produce glorious fall leaf color. The deeply cut, sometimes crinkled, leaves of *Parthenocissus tricuspidata* may be the most spectacular of all, turning scarlet, crimson, and burgundy before they fall.

Winter interest

Climbers that flower in winter are few and are not generally hardy, but winter jasmine (*Jasminum nudiflorum*), hardy to 0°F (-18°C), produces delicate yellow blooms even on a north-facing wall. The tender *J. polyanthum* produces a profusion of flowers in warmer areas, and *Clematis cirrhosa* blooms during frost-free weather.

Evergreens with unusual foliage provide interest in winter, too. Ivies are the most versatile, since most are hardy to 0°F (-18°C) and are widely adaptable. The bold variegation of some ivies, such as *Hedera helix* 'Buttercup' and 'Goldheart', is especially attractive. Other ivies are grown for their leaf shape – good examples include the bird's-foot ivy (*H. h.* 'Pedata'), with leaves shaped like a bird's foot, and 'Parsley Crested', with crinkly-edged leaves.

FALL FOLIAGE
This striking display combines the crimson leaves of Parthenocissus tricuspidata *with the reddening foliage of* Vitis coignetiae.

Scented climbers

Perfumed climbers, such as the tropical *Beaumontia grandiflora* and the sweet pea (*Lathyrus odoratus*), have special appeal. To appreciate the fragrance to the full, plant sweet peas near doorways or windows. If planted in a border, place them close to the outer edge.

Some release their fragrance at a particular time of day. Jasmine species (*Jasminum*) are more heavily scented at night, so are well placed over an arbor or near a terrace or patio that is used in the evening.

Annual climbers

Annual climbers and those that are treated as annuals in cool-temperate climates, such as *Eccremocarpus scaber* and kudzu (*Pueraria lobata*), are particularly useful for short-term enjoyment. Annuals provide an excellent way of introducing variety into planting designs, since they can be changed every year, if desired. They may also be used to fill gaps in the border until more permanent plants become well established.

Climbers in containers

Climbers grown in containers may be trained over walls and pillars in the same way as those in open ground; if the support is fixed to the container, the plant can be moved around as desired. Some lower-growing climbers, such as *Clematis macropetala*, may also be grown without support. Plant them in tall containers, so that their stems trail gracefully to the ground. Ivies are well suited to being grown in this way but need regular pruning once established.

In gardens where space is limited, it is still possible to grow more rampant climbers, such as *Bougainvillea* and *Wisteria* species, in containers. Their growth will be checked, and winter protection may be required. Regular repotting will also be needed to keep them healthy.

Containers are especially suitable for less hardy climbing species that may need winter protection, such as *Hardenbergia comptoniana* and *Senecio macroglossus* 'Variegatus'. Simply take the containers indoors or into a heated greenhouse at the onset of fall frosts, putting them outside again the following spring.

Planter's guide to climbers

North-facing Walls

Climbers that may be grown against north-facing walls

Agapetes ❄ (some spp.)
Akebia quinata
Allamanda cathartica ❄
Aristolochia elegans ❄
Berberidopsis corallina
Cissus ❄
Clematis, some ❄
Clerodendrum thomsoniae ❄
Clytostoma callistegioides ❄
Codonopsis convolvulacea
Dioscorea discolor ❄
Epipremnum ❄
Hardenbergia ❄
Hedera, some ❄
Hoya ❄
Humulus lupulus
Hydrangea anomala subsp. *petiolaris*
Kadsura japonica
Lapageria rosea ❄
Lathyrus latifolius
Lonicera x *americana*, *L.* x *brownii*, *L.* x *heckrottii*, *L. sempervirens*, *L.* x *tellmanniana*
Mitraria coccinea ❄
Monstera deliciosa ❄
Parthenocissus, some ❄
Philodendron ❄
Pileostegia viburnoides
Schizophragma hydrangeoides
Stigmaphyllon ciliatum ❄
Syngonium podophyllum ❄
Tropaeolum speciosum
Vitis coignetiae

Air Pollution

Climbers that tolerate polluted air

Campsis radicans
Clematis, some ❄
Hedera, some ❄

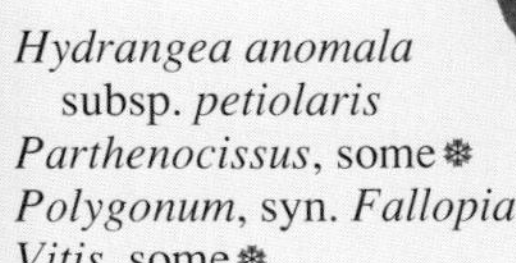

Clematis 'Elsa Spath'

Hydrangea anomala subsp. *petiolaris*
Parthenocissus, some ❄
Polygonum, syn. *Fallopia*
Vitis, some ❄

Shade

Climbers that tolerate shade

Actinidia
Asteranthera ovata ❄
Euonymus fortunei and variants
Humulus lupulus
Parthenocissus tricuspidata
Polygonum, syn. *Fallopia*

Fragrant Flowers

Anredera cordifolia ❄
Beaumontia grandiflora ❄
Clematis armandii, *C. montana*
Hoya australis ❄, *H. carnosa* ❄
Jasminum, some ❄
Lathyrus odoratus
Lonicera spp. (not *L. sempervirens* or *L.* x *tellmanniana*), some ❄
Quisqualis indica ❄
Schisandra, some ❄
Solandra maxima ❄

Stephanotis floribunda

Stephanotis floribunda ❄
Trachelospermum
Wisteria

Climbers for Containers

Asarina erubescens ❄
Bougainvillea ❄ (prune very hard)
Cissus ❄ (some spp.)
Clematis alpina, *C. macropetala*
Dioscorea discolor ❄
Epipremnum ❄
Gynura aurantiaca ❄
Hardenbergia ❄
Hedera helix
Jasminum officinale, *J. polyanthum* ❄
Lapageria rosea ❄
Monstera deliciosa ❄
Philodendron ❄ (some spp.)
Senecio macroglossus 'Variegatus' ❄
Stephanotis floribunda ❄
Streptosolen jamesonii ❄
Syngonium ❄ (some spp.)
Tetrastigma voinierianum ❄
Thunbergia alata ❄
Wisteria (prune very hard)

Evergreen Climbers

Allamanda ❄
Anemopaegma ❄
Anredera ❄
Araujia ❄
Argyreia ❄
Asteranthera ovata ❄
Beaumontia ❄
Berberidopsis
Calceolaria pavonii ❄
Calochone ❄
Cissus ❄
Clerodendrum splendens ❄, *C. thomsoniae* ❄
Clytostoma ❄
Combretum grandiflorum ❄
Decumaria sinensis ❄
Dioscorea discolor ❄
Distictis ❄
Epipremnum ❄
Gelsemium sempervirens
Hardenbergia ❄
Hibbertia scandens ❄
Holboellia ❄
Hoya ❄
Jacquemontia ❄
Kennedia ❄
Lapageria ❄
Lardizabala ❄
Macfadyena ❄
Mandevilla ❄
Merremia ❄
Monstera ❄
Mucuna ❄
Mussaenda ❄
Mutisia, some ❄
Pandorea ❄
Pileostegia
Podranea ❄
Pyrostegia ❄
Rhoicissus ❄
Semele ❄
Senecio confusus ❄, *S. macroglossus* ❄, *S. mikanioides* ❄, *S. tamoides* ❄
Solandra ❄
Stauntonia
Stephanotis ❄
Stigmaphyllon ❄
Strongylodon ❄
Syngonium ❄
Tecomanthe ❄
Tecomaria ❄
Tetrastigma ❄
Trachelospermum
Wattakaka

Climbers that may be Grown through or over Other Plants

Bomarea caldasii ❄
Bougainvillea ❄

Bomarea caldasii

Celastrus
Clematis, some ❄
Codonopsis convolvulacea
Humulus lupulus
Lonicera, some ❄
Mutisia, some ❄
Tropaeolum peregrinum ❄, *T. speciosum*
Vitis coignetiae
Wisteria sinensis

Fast-growing Climbers

Allamanda cathartica ❄
Ampelopsis
Anredera cordifolia ❄
Antigonon leptopus ❄
Aristolochia elegans ❄
Clematis, some ❄
Clitoria ternatea
Clytostoma callistegioides ❄

Cobaea scandens f. *alba*

Cobaea scandens ❄
Epipremnum aureum ❄
Humulus lupulus
Kennedia rubicunda ❄
Parthenocissus, some ❄
Passiflora, most ❄
Phaseolus coccineus
Philodendron scandens ❄
Plumbago auriculata ❄
Polygonum, syn. *Fallopia*
Pyrostegia venusta ❄
Solanum, some ❄
Stigmaphyllon ciliatum ❄
Strongylodon macrobotrys ❄
Vitis vinifera

Annual Climbers

Asarina erubescens ❄
Convolvulus tricolor
Eccremocarpus scaber ❄
Ipomoea ❄ (some spp.)
Lablab purpureus ❄
Lathyrus odoratus
Mikania scandens ❄
Phaseolus coccineus
Quisqualis indica ❄
Thunbergia alata ❄
Tropaeolum peregrinum ❄

Herbaceous Climbers

Bomarea caldasii ❄
Codonopsis convolvulacea
Humulus lupulus
Lathyrus grandiflorus, *L. latifolius*
Pueraria lobata
Tropaeolum speciosum, *T. tricolorum* ❄, *T. tuberosum* ❄

Climbers for Ground Cover

Clematis, some ❄
Hedera, some ❄
Mitraria ❄
Parthenocissus, some ❄
Pileostegia
Plumbago auriculata ❄
Senecio, some ❄
Tecomaria ❄
Trachelospermum
Tropaeolum, some ❄

Key
❄ *Not frost hardy*

Soil preparation and planting

GIVEN ideal growing conditions, climbing plants bring enduring rewards, so always ensure that they are well suited to the type of soil in which they are planted. Climbers seldom thrive in excessively damp or dry conditions. A few, such as *Agapetes* and *Mitraria*, do not tolerate alkaline conditions; others, such as clematis, thrive on alkaline soils but also grow well on all but the most acid soils. Many climbers are vigorous and require ample nutrients, so dig and fertilize the soil well before planting (see also "Soil nutrients and fertilizers," pp.532–3).

When planting climbers, it is important to use the correct support. Choose one that will easily accommodate the eventual height, spread, and vigor of the plant.

Types of support

The three main types of support used for climbers are wooden or plastic trellis panels, wire or plastic mesh, and wires (usually plastic-covered) stretched between vine eyes or rustproof nails. Horticultural string or reinforcing wire may be adequate for annuals or for herbaceous climbers if the supports are replaced each year. Make sure that the supports are fixed securely in the correct position before planting. Do not use U-shaped metal staples to attach stems to a support. Plants rapidly outgrow these staples and the stems may become constricted and die back.

Choose a support that will match the size and strength of the climber. One that is not sufficiently sturdy for a vigorous climber may quickly become engulfed and will eventually collapse. A trellis is the most reliable support for all twining climbers, and may also be used for scramblers if they are tied in. Wires or mesh are appropriate supports for tendril climbers.

If the support is not to be a permanent structure, use climbers that are either herbaceous (*Lathyrus grandiflorus* and *L. latifolius*, for example) or cut to ground level each year (late-flowering *Clematis viticella* hybrids and cultivars), or annual climbers such as *Ipomoea hederacea*. When growing plants against a flat, free-standing trellis or over a pillar, bear in mind that climbers grow toward the light, and flower on one side of the support only, so plants should always be positioned to provide their display where it will be most prominent.

Trellises and mesh

To allow air to circulate freely, fix a trellis panel or mesh so that it is held slightly away from the wall or fence and make sure that the base of the framework is approximately 12in (30cm) above soil level.

Walls are likely to need maintenance (repointing, painting, or repairing) at some time, so wherever possible, attach a trellis or mesh with hooks at the top and hinges at the base, or hooks at the top and bottom. The whole plant and its support can then be lowered from the wall or, if hooks only are used, taken down and laid flat on the ground while the wall is repaired.

Wires

Wires can be stretched horizontally or vertically between vine eyes or rustproof nails. As with trellis panels, the wires should be held 2in (5cm) from the surface of the wall or fence, and must be kept taut to prevent sagging. Either tighten the vine eyes with pliers or attach tensioners at approximately 6ft (2m) intervals. Space the wires 12–18in (30–45cm) apart, with the lowest horizontal wire (or the base of vertical wires) 12in (30cm) above soil level.

VIGOROUS CLIMBERS

Actinidia chinensis
Akebia quinata
Beaumontia grandiflora ❋
Bougainvillea ❋
Cissus ❋
Clematis montana
Distictis buccinatoria ❋
Ipomoea horsfalliae ❋

Mandevilla ❋
Parthenocissus quinquefolia, P. tricuspidata
Passiflora, most ❋
Petrea volubilis ❋
Polygonum aubertii
Pueraria lobata
Solandra maxima ❋
Solanum wendlandii ❋
Tetrastigma voinierianum ❋
Vitis coignetiae
Wisteria sinensis

KEY
❋ *Not frost hardy*

Climbing methods

Climbers attach themselves to supports by various means. Many climbers have aerial roots that readily attach to vertical surfaces without support. Other methods, all of which require some support, include twining stems and leaf stalks, and coiling tendrils. Scandent and scrambling climbers, such as *Bougainvillea*, produce long stems that need to be tied in at regular intervals.

AERIAL ROOTS
Ivy (Hedera) *is a self-clinging plant.*

LEAF STALKS
Clematis climbs using its leaf stalks.

COILING TENDRILS
Passiflora *attaches itself with tendrils.*

TWINING STEMS
Akebia *weaves its stems in a spiral around the support.*

Fixing a trellis panel to a wall

To mount a trellis support, first securely attach vertical wooden laths at least 2in (5cm) thick to the wall and trellis. This allows the trellis to be suspended away from the wall and enables air to circulate freely. The trellis can then be permanently fixed to the laths with screws (right); however, this restricts access to the wall. Using hooks and hinges (below) enables the plant and support to be lowered, if required. Hooking the trellis to the laths at both top and bottom allows it to be removed from the wall altogether.

USING LATHS
Screw the trellis to thick wooden laths.

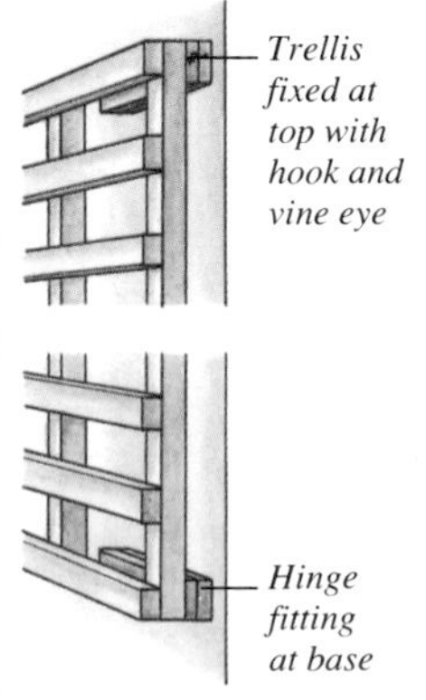

USING HOOKS AND HINGES
To allow access to the wall for maintenance, attach laths to both the wall and the trellis. Fix hinges along the bottom of the panel with hooks at the top to hold it in place.

How to Select Climbers

Good Example

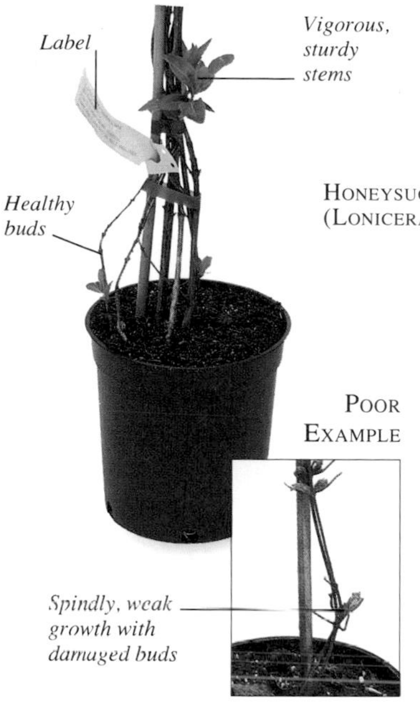

Label

Vigorous, sturdy stems

Healthy buds

Honeysuckle (Lonicera)

Poor Example

Spindly, weak growth with damaged buds

Good Example

Roots are visible and healthy but not coiled

Poor Example

Roots coiled tightly around the root ball

Buying climbers

Climbing plants are usually sold container-grown, although a few (including climbing roses) may be sold with bare roots. Choose a healthy plant with a well-balanced framework of strong shoots, and reject any that show signs of pest infestation or disease. Bare-root plants should have plenty of healthy, well-developed fibrous roots that are in proportion to the amount of top-growth. For potgrown plants, turn the pot over and check that the tips of the young roots are just showing; if so, the plant is well rooted. Reject potbound plants – those that have tightly coiled roots around the root ball or a mass of roots protruding through the drainage holes in the pot – since they seldom grow satisfactorily.

Planting outdoors

In cooler areas, certain climbers may be of borderline hardiness. Plant these in spring, so that they are well established before their first winter. Evergreen and herbaceous climbers are more quickly established if planted in spring when the soil is warming up, but they may also be planted in fall in a protected situation or if the weather is mild. All other container-grown climbers can be planted in spring, fall, or any other time of year as long as the ground is not frozen or waterlogged. Planting during dry spells in summer is not recommended, but if this is unavoidable, make sure that the plant is watered daily while dry conditions persist.

Positioning the plant

Walls and solid fences create their own rain shadow, so plants that are to be trained against them should be planted at least 18in (45cm) from

Planting a climber in a container

Select a container large enough to accommodate the climber for at least two seasons. Concrete, stone, or terracotta pots are more stable than plastic ones. Shallow pots are not suitable. Choose a frost-proof pot if the climber is to remain outdoors in winter.

The potting medium should be moisture-retentive but also free-draining. Use a mixture of two parts of regular soilless potting mix and one part of sharp sand. Supplement this with a slow-release fertilizer, and combine it with the soil mix according to the manufacturer's instructions.

Trellis panels specially made for containers are available, with two legs at the base. Anchor these into the soil mix before planting rather than after, to avoid damaging the plant's roots. Tie the top of the trellis to a wall or fence to keep it steady.

1 Put crocks at the base of the pot to assist drainage and bed the support into the base of the container with soil mix.

2 Plant the climber at the same level as in the original pot. Fill in with soil mix, leaving 2in (5cm) below the rim to allow for watering.

3 Tie the main shoots to the support, and water the plant thoroughly to settle the roots.

Climbers that Tolerate Sandy Soil

Adlumia fungosa
Anredera cordifolia ❁
Asarina ❁
Bomarea andimarcana ❁
Ceropegia ❁ (spp. only)
Clianthus puniceus ❁
Ercilla volubilis
Gloriosa superba ❁
Ipomoea ❁

Kennedia rubicunda

Kennedia rubicunda ❁
Merremia tuberosa ❁
Mutisia oligodon
Parthenocissus, some ❁
Passiflora, most ❁ (some spp.)
Petrea volubilis ❁
Solanum wendlandii ❁
Streptosolen jamesonii ❁
Thunbergia alata ❁

Climbers that Tolerate Clay Soil

Aristolochia durior
Campsis
Celastrus scandens
Clematis, some ❁ (most)
Distictis ❁
Euonymus fortunei 'Silver Queen'
Hedera, some ❁
Humulus lupulus 'Aureus'
Hydrangea anomala subsp. *petiolaris*
Lathyrus latifolius
Lonicera, some ❁ (some spp.)

Parthenocissus tricuspidata 'Lowii'

Parthenocissus, some ❁
Passiflora, most ❁
Vitis coignetiae
Wisteria

Climbers that Require Acid Soil

Agapetes ❁ (several spp.)
Asteranthera ovata ❁
Beaumontia grandiflora ❁
Berberidopsis corallina
Billardiera ❁ (spp. only)
Lapageria rosea ❁
Lardizabala biternata ❁
Mitraria coccinea ❁
Mutisia, some ❁ (some spp.)

Key
❁ *Not frost hardy*

the foot of the support. In this way, once established, they normally receive sufficient rain to grow without additional water. A pillar or free-standing trellis does not produce the same density of rain shadow and so the planting distance need be only 8–12in (20–30cm).

When grown through another plant, the climber will compete with the host plant for food and moisture. To minimize this, plant the climber so that its roots stay as far away as possible from those of its host. If the host plant has deep roots, and a sufficient depth of soil is available, plant the climber fairly close to the host's main stem. If the host has a mass of rhizomatous or shallow roots, however, plant the climber about 18in (45cm) from the root spread. A stake tied to the host, inserted just behind the climber's main stems, can be used to train the climber toward it at an angle.

Preparing the soil

Remove all weeds from the planting area, using a systemic weedkiller to kill perennial weeds, if necessary. Then dig in coarse organic matter; this will improve the water retentiveness and fertility of sandy soils, and lighten the texture of heavy clay soils. Carefully fork in a dressing of slow-release fertilizer, at a rate of 2–3oz/sq yd (50–85g/sq m).

The planting hole should be at least twice the diameter of the container in which the climber was grown in order to allow the roots ample room to spread in the prepared soil. This may not be possible, however, if the climber is to be encouraged to grow through a tree or shrub. In these cases, dig a hole large enough to accommodate the root ball, and leave plenty of room for the roots to spread.

How to plant

Before removing the plant from its pot, make sure that the soil mix is moist. Water the plant well so that the root ball is thoroughly wet and then allow it to drain for at least an hour. Remove the surface layer of soil mix to eliminate weed seeds, and then invert the pot, taking care to support the plant as it slides out. If the roots have begun to curl around inside the pot, gently tease them out. Any dead, damaged, or protruding roots should be cut back to the perimeter of the root ball.

Position the plant so that the top of the root ball is just level with the surrounding soil. It is advisable to plant clematis more deeply, however (see *Planting a Clematis*, p.107). Climbers that have been grafted (as is the case with most wisterias) should be planted with the graft union 2½in (6cm) below soil level. This encourages the scion itself to root, and reduces the incidence of sucker growths from the stock. For information on planting bare-root climbers, see "Planting a bush rose," p.121.

Fill the planting hole with soil, then firm the plant in and water well. Insert stakes at the base of the plant and secure them to the support. Fan out the main shoots and tie them individually to the stakes and to the support itself (if they will reach) to train them in. Do not damage the stems by attaching them too tightly. Remove dead or damaged growth and cut back wayward shoots.

Tendril climbers readily attach themselves to a support, but the shoots may require gentle guidance and some tying in until they become firmly established. Twining climbers soon fasten their shoots to a support in their natural direction of growth (clockwise or counter-clockwise) but may also need tying in initially. Scramblers that do not support themselves should have their shoots carefully fastened to the support at regular intervals with appropriate ties. For further information, see "Training established climbers," p.104.

Watering and mulching

Water the newly planted climber thoroughly, then cover the surface of the soil surrounding the plant with a 2–3in (5–7cm) layer of mulch to a radius of about 2ft (60cm). This is beneficial to the roots because it retains moisture throughout the area, giving the roots a chance to establish themselves. In addition, the mulch discourages the germination of weeds that would otherwise compete with the newly planted climber for nutrients and moisture.

CLIMBERS THAT TOLERATE VERY ALKALINE SOIL

Actinidia kolomikta
Akebia quinata
Ampelopsis brevipedunculata
Asarina antirrhiniflora ❄
Campsis x *tagliabuana* 'Mme. Galen'
Celastrus scandens
Clematis, some ❄ (cvs)
Eccremocarpus scaber ❄
Hedera, some ❄
Hydrangea anomala subsp. *petiolaris*
Jasminum officinale, *J. polyanthum* ❄

Lathyrus grandiflorus

Lathyrus grandiflorus, *L. latifolius*
Lonicera, some ❄ (some spp.)
Parthenocissus tricuspidata
Passiflora caerulea ❄
Polygonum aubertii, *P. baldschuanicum*
Schizophragma integrifolium
Solanum crispum
Trachelospermum jasminoides
Vitis, some ❄
Wisteria sinensis

KEY
❄ *Not frost hardy*

PLANTING A CLIMBER AGAINST A WALL

1 *Fix a support 12in (30cm) above the soil and 2in (5cm) from the wall. Dig a hole 18in (45cm) from the wall. Loosen the soil at the base and add soil mix.*

2 *Soak the climber's root ball well. Position it in the hole at a 45° angle, placing a stake across to check the planting level. Spread the roots away from the wall.*

3 *Fill in around the plant and firm and level the soil, ensuring that no air pockets remain between the roots and that the plant is fully supported.*

4 *Untie the stems from the central stake and select 4 or 5 strong shoots. Insert a stake for each shoot and attach it to the lowest wire. Tie in the shoots.*

5 *Using pruners, trim back any weak, damaged, or wayward shoots to the central stem. This establishes the initial framework for the climber.*

6 *Water the plant thoroughly (here* Jasminum mesnyi*). Cover the surrounding soil with a deep mulch to retain moisture and discourage weeds.*

Routine care

CLIMBERS need feeding annually to maintain healthy growth, and the soil around their base should be kept moist. Climbers grown in containers need top-dressing or re-potting regularly, and adequate watering is essential. Regular dead-heading helps to prolong flowering. Plants also need protection from pests, diseases, and (if tender) cold.

Feeding

Feed climbers in spring during their first two seasons with a dressing of 2–3oz (50–85g) of a balanced fertilizer. Thereafter, apply a slow-release fertilizer annually at the manufacturer's recommended rate.

Watering

During dry periods, water climbers weekly. Soak thoroughly around the base of the plant. Apply a 2–3in (5–7cm) mulch over the root area to prevent the soil from drying out.

Deadheading and tying in

Where practical, deadhead climbers as the flowers fade. This enables the plant to concentrate its energies on producing more flowers, rather than fruits or seedheads. However, if fruits or seedheads are desired for ornamental purposes, deadhead only a quarter to one-third of the flowered shoots. This will be enough to encourage a continuing display.

Tie in new shoots as they develop, while still flexible, and cut back overgrown plants as needed (see "Pruning and training," pp.102–5).

Pests and diseases

Check carefully for signs of pests and diseases and treat any affected plants as recommended in PLANT PROBLEMS, pp.547–79.

Protecting tender climbers

In winter, and particularly in cold periods or when frost is likely, wrap up, in protective covering, the top-growth and base of tender climbers that are grown outside (see COLD AND WIND PROTECTION, pp.520–21).

CUTTING BACK CLIMBERS

Where a climber (here Hedera colchica 'Sulphur Heart') *has outgrown its allotted space, cut it back with pruners. Trim the stems irregularly for a natural look.*

Maintaining container-grown climbers

Container-grown climbers may need to be watered once or twice a day in dry weather. When cold is likely, they may be moved indoors or plunged in the ground in a sheltered part of the garden. During the year, a climber grown in a container uses up most of the nutrients in the potting medium. The top-dressing (the top layer of the soil mix and any mulch) should therefore be renewed annually. When the plant is watered, the fresh nutrients will gradually permeate and replenish the soil mix below. All but the most slow-growing climbers need to be moved into a larger container, using fresh soil mix, every three to four years. Spring-flowering plants should be repotted in fall, others in fall or spring.

RENEWING THE TOP-DRESSING OF A CONTAINER-GROWN CLIMBER

1 In spring or early summer, scrape away and discard the top 1–2in (2.5–5cm) of soil mix in the container. Take care not to disturb any surface roots of the climber and the companion planting.

2 Replace the discarded soil mix with a layer of fresh soil mix mixed with a little slow-release fertilizer. Firm gently to eliminate air pockets. Make sure that the level of the soil mix is the same as before. Water well.

3 To aid moisture retention during the summer months, cover the soil mix in the container with a light, decorative mulch such as cocoa shells or bark chips.

REPOTTING A CONTAINER-GROWN CLIMBER

1 Every 3 or 4 years repot container-grown climbers (such as this variegated ivy) to prevent them from becoming pot-bound (see inset). Soak the soil mix well, then carefully slide the root ball out of the container.

2 Tease out the roots and trim back the thicker roots by about one-third. Leave fibrous roots intact and retain as much soil mix as possible around them.

3 Prune the top-growth by a third and remove dead or damaged stems. Repot the plant in fresh, moist soil mix, adding slow-release fertilizer to the top 1–2in (2.5–5cm).

4 Ensure that the final planting level is the same as before. Insert a triangle of stakes, and tie in the main shoots securely but not too tightly.

Pruning and training

During the early years, pruning is carried out to build a strong framework for a plant; to promote vigorous growth of healthy, productive wood; and to facilitate training over the support. Training should be aimed at guiding a selected number of strong, major stems over and across a support while they are flexible, to create a pleasing shape.

Some climbers, for example silver lace vines (*Polygonum aubertii* and *P. baldschuanicum*), send out a mass of small shoots in addition to main stems, and these need to be regularly tied in during initial training to retain the required shape. Frequently, however, vigorous climbers are difficult to train after the first year and are best left to grow freely. Restrict them only when they grow beyond their allotted space.

Basic principles

Routine pruning is essential to the successful cultivation of almost all established climbers. Without this control, the plants may fail to flower well, and, equally importantly, some of the more vigorous climbers may swamp nearby plants or damage roofs, gutters, and masonry. Training can be combined with pruning to achieve the most desirable structure and appearance for the plant.

Where to cut

The stems should be cut $^1/_{16}$ – $^1/_8$in (2–3mm) above a plump bud. Select an appropriately placed bud that faces the direction in which a new shoot is required. Then, as the shoot develops, it can be tied in either to fill the framework or to replace an old shoot.

Make each pruning cut cleanly with sharp pruners, at an angle slanting slightly away from the bud. This ensures that rainwater does not gather around the bud and encourage possible disease infection. The position of the cut is important: a cut that is made too close to the bud may damage it, while one made too far away from the bud will leave a stub that dies back and may provide an entry point for disease.

Using the correct tools

A pair of sharp pruners is the best tool for most types of pruning. Long-handled loppers may also be useful, especially for thicker stems, and shears can be used where a great deal of dead or weak growth needs to be removed (see "How to prune honeysuckle," p.105).

Formative pruning and training

At planting time, and as the plant starts to grow, training consists of tying in the strongest shoots to the support to achieve a balanced framework. During the growing season, a little guidance will be needed to ensure that the soft, twining stems or tendrils attach themselves to their support while they are still pliable and before the wood becomes too mature. Hardened stems cannot be bent into the required position without damaging them.

In late winter or early spring following initial planting, once all danger of severe frost has passed, cut back each side shoot to an appropriately placed bud that is near the central or main stem, tying the pruned shoots to the support. Several strong stems will grow from these pruned shoots during the following season, from which the framework of the plant develops. These should be trained in as they develop, as before.

The following year, cut back each stem, and possibly the leader, to a bud that is pointing in the direction in which the stem is to be trained. This results in the growth of vigorous shoots with which to extend the main framework. Carefully tie in all the stems, and cut back any other shoots to within two buds of the nearest stem.

Formative Pruning and Training

In order to establish a healthy, strong framework for a climbing plant, begin pruning and training as soon as possible after planting, in late winter or early spring. The plant here is Jasminum nudiflorum.

Remove any crossing shoots. Use sharp pruners to cut just above a healthy bud.

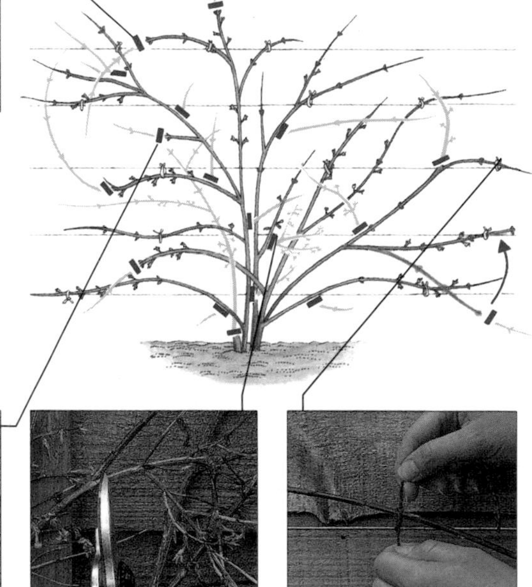

To encourage new, strong growth, prune back side shoots to an appropriately placed bud.

Cut out any congested growth from the center of the plant.

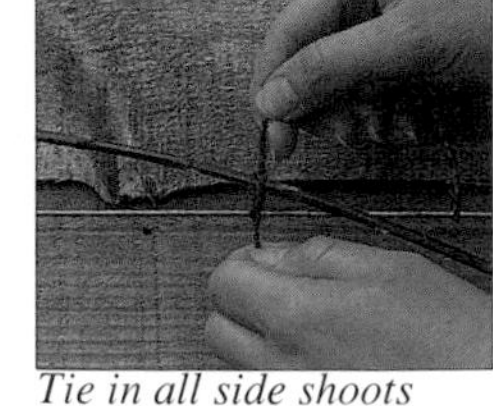

Tie in all side shoots securely to the support with twine or string.

Spring Pruning

Climbers that flower on the current season's shoots, such as Solanum crispum *shown here, should be pruned in late winter or early spring.*

Cut out all congested growth, removing crossing shoots and the weaker of any shoots that are competing.

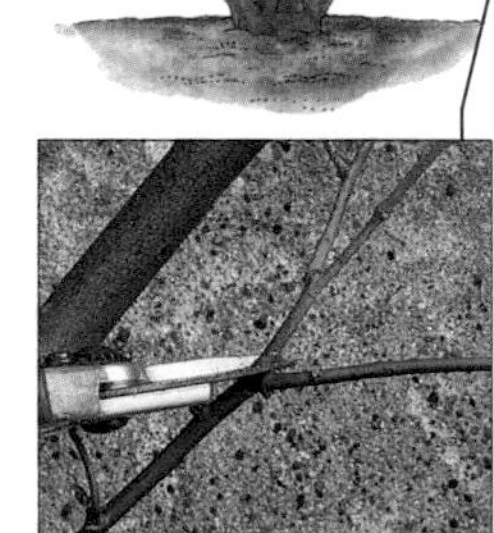

Remove dead or cold-damaged shoots and stems, cutting back to live, healthy wood.

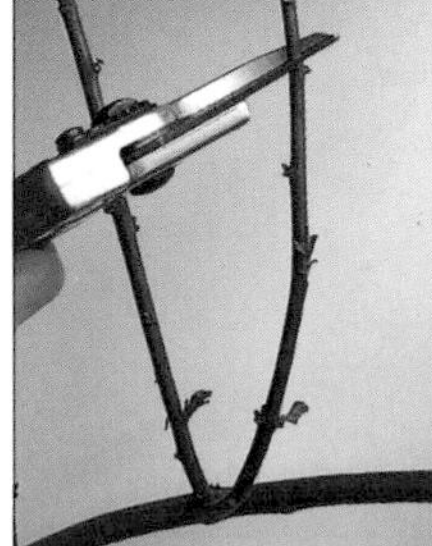

To encourage flowering, cut back side shoots to 5 or 6 strong, healthy buds, making an angled cut just above a bud.

Pruning established climbers

The time of year to prune established climbers depends on their flowering habit. Some flower on the current season's shoots or, occasionally, on shoots that are produced late in the previous growing season. These are usually pruned in late winter or early spring, before new buds begin to develop. They will flower later in the same season on new shoots.

Other climbers flower on the previous year's ripened shoots or on older shoots. These should be pruned immediately after flowering to allow new shoots time to ripen before the winter. These are the shoots that will bear the next season's flowers. Some early-flowering climbers will produce a second crop later in the season, if pruned immediately after flowering.

Distinguishing between first- and second-year shoots is not normally difficult. First-year shoots are still pliable and usually green, whereas second-year ones are usually gray or brown. Shoots more than two years old have a distinct, usually dark bark, and are tough and woody.

When pruning, always remove all dead or damaged wood and any congested, twiggy growth. Cut back stems that have grown beyond the plant's allotted space, both to maintain the shape of the climber and to control excessive growth.

For methods of pruning clematis, see pp.107–8.

EARLY SUMMER PRUNING

Climbers that flower on the previous year's ripened shoots, such as Jasminum beesianum, *should be pruned immediately after flowering to allow new shoots to develop before the onset of winter.*

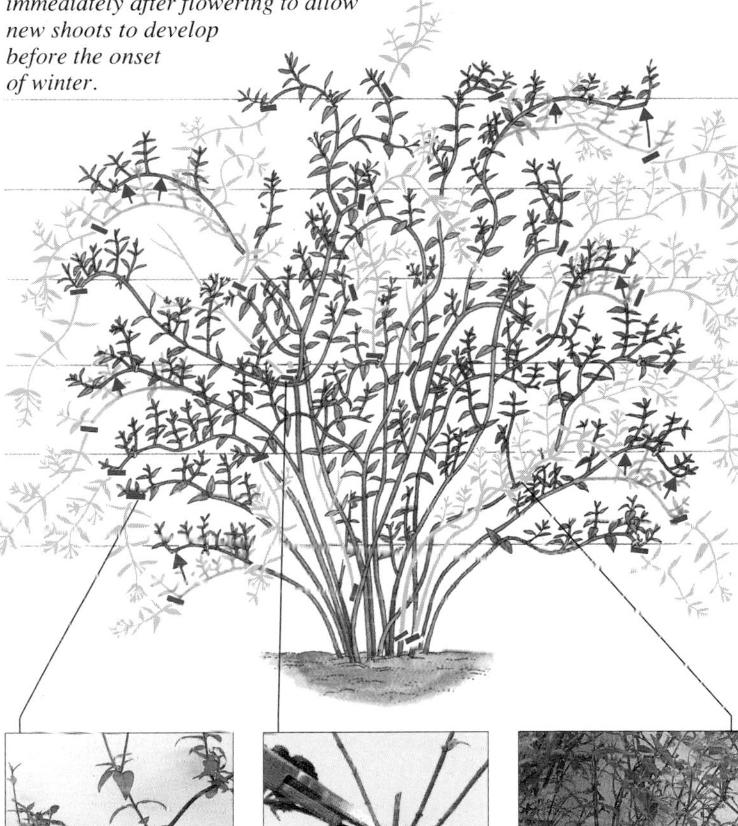

Cut back shoots that have flowered, pruning to a vigorous shoot lower down.

Remove all dead or damaged wood, cutting cleanly, close to a healthy shoot or stem.

Where there is congested growth, weak shoots should be removed.

Pruning *Wisteria*

Wisteria may be reluctant to flower unless the vigorous, leafy summer shoots are severely curtailed, and the plant's energies diverted into producing flower buds. Flowering is also improved if the main stems are trained horizontally rather than vertically. The flower buds are produced on short spurs, so the aim of pruning is to encourage these spurs to develop along the framework branches of an established plant. The simplest method is to carry out a two-stage pruning schedule. In summer, cut back long growths and shorter lateral growths. Leave stems unpruned only if they are needed to extend the framework, and train them in. In late winter cut back summer-pruned spur shoots to two or three buds. At the same time, reduce to 6in (15cm) any long growths that developed after summer pruning.

1 *In summer, restrict the growth of vigorous, stringy shoots to encourage more new buds to grow next year.*

2 *Cut back long shoots to about 6in (15cm), leaving 4–6 leaves. Make the cut clear of the last bud, since the buds are easily damaged.*

WINTER
Prune shoots shortened in summer. Reduce them to 3–4in (8–10cm), leaving only 2–3 buds.

CLIMBERS THAT FLOWER ON CURRENT SEASON'S GROWTH

Anredera cordifolia ❄
Antigonon leptopus ❄
Bignonia
Billardiera longiflora ❄
Campsis
Clematis, some ❄ (large-flowered cvs)
Clerodendrum thomsoniae ❄
Clianthus ❄
Clytostoma ❄
Distictis ❄
Ipomoea ❄
Lapageria ❄
Lonicera, some ❄
Mandevilla ❄
Mikania ❄
Mutisia decurrens
Parthenocissus, some ❄
Passiflora, most ❄
Pileostegia viburnoides
Plumbago ❄
Podranea ❄
Polygonum aubertii
Pyrostegia venusta ❄

Solanum crispum

Solanum crispum, *S. jasminoides* ❄
Stephanotis ❄
Streptosolen ❄
Thladiantha, some ❄
Thunbergia gregorii ❄
Vigna caracalla ❄
Vitis, some ❄

CLIMBERS THAT FLOWER ON PREVIOUS SEASON'S GROWTH

Actinidia, some ❄
Allamanda cathartica ❄
Aristolochia, some ❄
Beaumontia ❄
Bougainvillea ❄

Bougainvillea 'Miss Manila'

Clematis montana
Decumaria sinensis ❄
Gelsemium sempervirens
Hoya ❄
Hydrangea
Jasminum, some ❄
Pandorea jasminoides ❄
Pileostegia
Schizophragma
Solandra maxima ❄
Streptosolen jamesonii ❄
Strongylodon ❄
Wisteria

KEY
❄ *Not frost hardy*

WINTER PRUNING

When pruning climbers in winter, it is easy to assess the framework of the plant and train in any new growth. The climber shown here is Schisandra glaucescens.

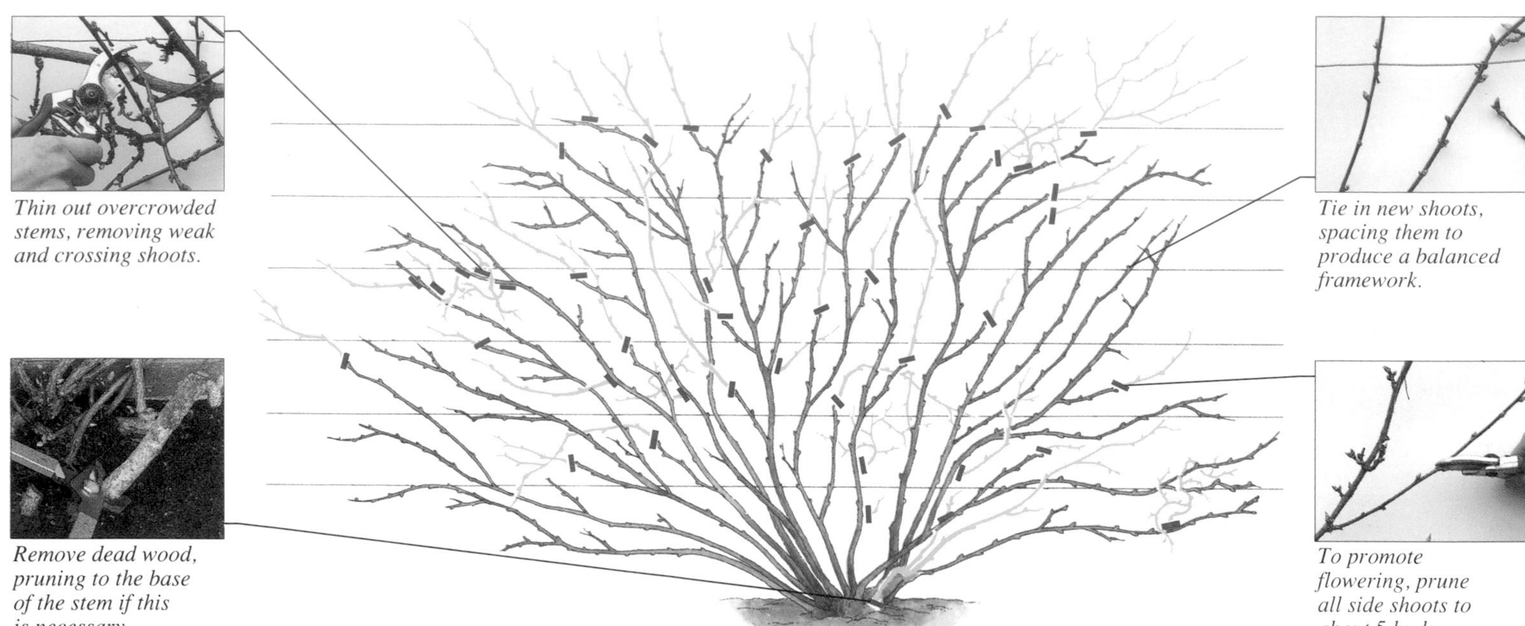

Thin out overcrowded stems, removing weak and crossing shoots.

Remove dead wood, pruning to the base of the stem if this is necessary.

Tie in new shoots, spacing them to produce a balanced framework.

To promote flowering, prune all side shoots to about 5 buds.

Evergreen climbers
Prune evergreen climbers in spring, after all danger of frost has passed and as the plants are about to begin fresh growth. Evergreen climbers that are grown for their flowers as well as their foliage produce flowers on the previous season's wood, so delay pruning these until after flowering. In both cases, simply remove dead or damaged wood and trim stray shoots to shape.

Winter pruning
Climbers that have already had at least one pruning during the previous growing season may be pruned again in winter to tidy up their appearance (see illustrations above). This is particularly useful for deciduous plants, whose frameworks can be assessed more easily when the branches are bare. Do not remove ripened wood, which will carry the next season's flowers. If in mild spells winter-pruned plants are stimulated into new growth, the new young shoots may later be damaged by frost. Prune these back in spring.

Ornamental grape vines (*Vitis*) should be pruned in early winter, when the plants are dormant and pruning cuts may be made without the risk of bleeding, or loss of sap, occurring. If the stems are cut in spring when the sap is rising, they bleed profusely; this is difficult to stop and weakens the plants. (For information on how to prune grapevines, see pp.398–402.)

Training established climbers

Climbers that attach themselves by means of aerial roots need very little training, except in the first few years until enough aerial roots have formed to support the plant. All other climbing plants need their new shoots trained in each year to maintain the desired shape.

Each year during the growing season, select the strongest new stems, before they become hard and woody, and train them in to continue the basic framework. Follow the shape of the allocated space, and allow the leading stem to extend in a straight line until it has reached the required height. Tie all stems securely to the

Pruning *Bougainvillea*

Bougainvillea is rampant and flowers reliably whether pruned or not. Prune between midwinter and early spring to keep the plant in check. Shorten side shoots to within a few inches of the main stems, but leave any needed to extend the main framework.

1 *Trim wayward side shoots to within 1–2in (2.5–5cm) of the main framework stems.*

2 *Cut cleanly, close to a healthy bud. The buds will soon produce new growth.*

Training climbers on pergolas and pillars

To produce an even distribution of growth over a pergola or pillar, tie in the main stems throughout the growing season, spreading them out as required to fill any gaps. To promote flowering lower down a plant's stem, regularly train side shoots of twining species around their support, making sure that the shoots are following their natural direction of growth: clockwise or counterclockwise.

After the flowering season, remove any dead or diseased shoots and prune the main stem and any leaders. This will encourage the plant to produce strong lateral growth in the following year.

1 *Guide stray side shoots onto the support in their natural direction of growth and tie in.*

2 *After flowering, cut back all the leading stems by one-third to promote lateral growth.*

support at regular intervals using plastic twist-ties or vine ties. Make sure that the ties are tight enough to prevent the stems from being blown about in strong winds and rubbing against the support; however, they should not restrict the stem's development. The ties will need to be loosened periodically as the stems thicken with age.

How to prune honeysuckle

Climbing honeysuckles (*Lonicera*) require little pruning to flower profusely but tend, if neglected, to develop into a mass of thin, tangled stems that bear foliage and flowers only at the top of the shoots. To renovate a honeysuckle in this condition, prune it severely in early to midspring, at the beginning of the growing season. New shoots will soon begin to develop, and these should be trained in to provide an evenly balanced framework.

If such severe pruning is not required, it is still possible to renovate the plant by removing dead or damaged shoots and stems from beneath new, young growth. Use a pair of shears, rather than pruners, for speed.

RENOVATION PRUNING
If the plant is badly overgrown, cut back all the stems with long-handled loppers to within 1–2ft (30–60cm) of ground level.

ALTERNATIVE METHOD
If it is undesirable or unnecessary to prune so severely, cut away all dead material from underneath the new, fresh growth.

Renovating an old or neglected climber

Unpruned climbers – or those that have not been trained – often become a mass of tangled, woody stems, and produce a poor display of flowers. Such plants can be pruned hard to rejuvenate them. Most climbers withstand pruning close to the base or to main framework stems, but an unhealthy plant may not survive this treatment. In this case, it is preferable to reduce the size of the plant gradually over a period of two or three years, in conjunction with annual feeding.

For a plant that is to be pruned to the base, cut back all growth in early spring to within 1–2ft (30–60cm) of the ground. To promote rapid new growth, apply a dressing of quick-acting, balanced fertilizer at a rate of 2–3oz/sq yd (50–85g/sq m). Soak the root area with water, and mulch. Train in all new growth as for newly planted climbers.

Renovation over a two- to three-year period (see below) is more difficult, since the stems frequently become entangled. In spring, remove as much congested growth as possible, then cut to the base one in every two (or three) main stems. Gently unravel the top-growth of the severed stems. If any shoots are damaged, cut them out after the pruned main stems and their top-growth have been removed. Cut out the weak, spindly shoots, which will not flower satisfactorily, and any dead wood. Feed, water, and mulch, as when pruning to the base, to encourage healthy new growth. Train in fresh basal shoots to fill gaps, making sure they do not become entangled with old shoots. The following spring, repeat the process and feed, water, and mulch the plant.

RENOVATING A NEGLECTED CLIMBER
A neglected climber (here Celastrus orbiculatus*) can be renovated gradually over 2 or 3 seasons by pruning hard each spring.*

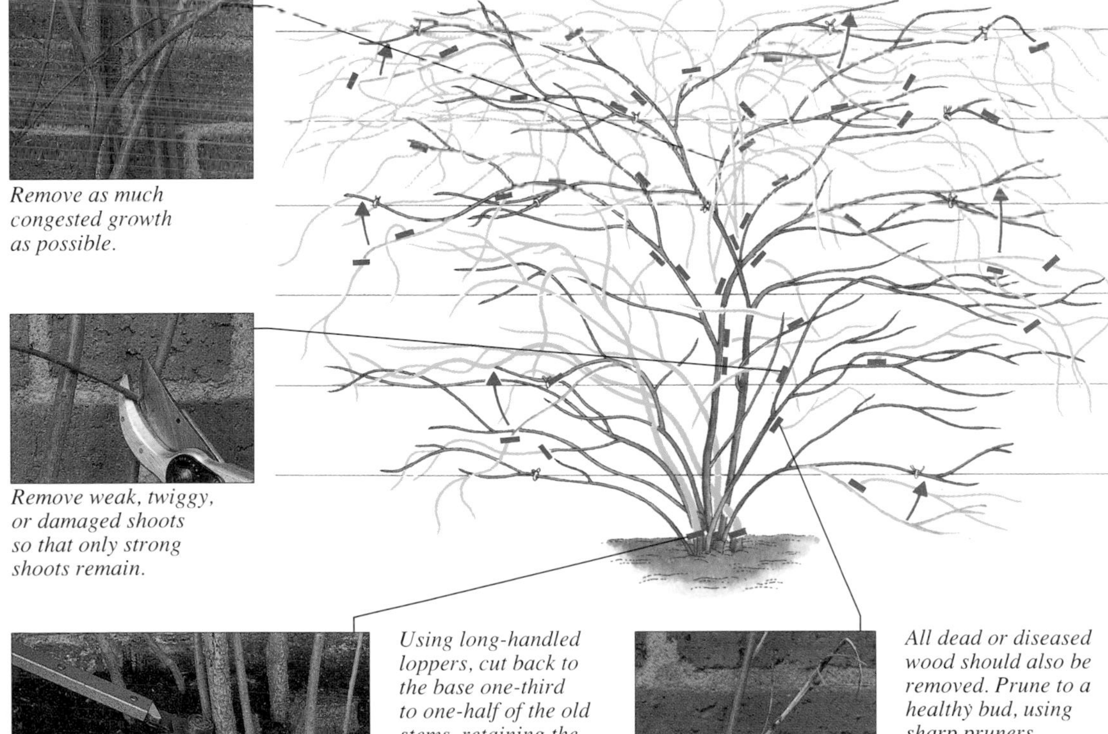

Remove as much congested growth as possible.

Remove weak, twiggy, or damaged shoots so that only strong shoots remain.

Using long-handled loppers, cut back to the base one-third to one-half of the old stems, retaining the more vigorous ones.

All dead or diseased wood should also be removed. Prune to a healthy bud, using sharp pruners.

CLIMBERS THAT MAY BE CUT TO THE GROUND

Allamanda cathartica ❄
Anredera cordifolia ❄
Antigonon leptopus ❄
Aristolochia, some ❄
Campsis x *tagliabuana*
Clematis, some ❄ (most spp.)
Clerodendrum thomsoniae ❄
Clytostoma callistegioides ❄
Distictis buccinatoria ❄
Lonicera, some ❄ (most spp.)
Macfadyena unguis-cati ❄
Manettia cordifolia ❄,
M. inflata ❄

Passiflora x *caponii* 'John Innes'

Passiflora, most ❄
Petrea volubilis ❄
Polygonum aubertii
Pyrostegia venusta ❄
Quisqualis indica ❄
Solandra maxima ❄
Solanum, some ❄
Stigmaphyllon ciliatum ❄
Strongylodon macrobotrys ❄
Thunbergia ❄

KEY
❄ *Not frost hardy*

Clematis

CLEMATIS are suited to almost any situation and climate. Of all the climbers, they offer the longest flowering period, with species or hybrids that bloom in almost every month of the year, many with the additional interest of silvery clustered seedheads appearing after flowering. Their diverse habits range from herbaceous plants, for example *C. integrifolia* and the clump-forming *C. recta*, to sprawling subshrubs such as *C.* x *jouiniana*, as well as the better-known climbers.

Clematis also present a huge range of flower color and flower forms, ranging from the attractive sprays of delicate, ivory-colored bells of *C. rehderiana*, and exotic-looking, fleshy, golden lanterns in *C. tangutica*, to the simple but richly colored blooms of *C. viticella* and its many hybrids, or the more complex forms of large-flowered double clematis such as *C.* 'Proteus' and *C.* 'Vyvyan Pennell'.

Where to grow clematis

Clematis can be chosen to suit almost any garden setting. The vigorous spring-flowering species and cultivars are ideal for clothing and camouflaging unsightly buildings, fences, and walls, or for scrambling over old trees, tree stumps, and arbors, adding color and interest to otherwise dull features.

Less rampant types may be wall-trained on trellises and pergolas or allowed to cascade over terraces; at ground level, more delicate species will sprawl where their blooms can be best appreciated.

Some clematis are suitable for container cultivation, on patios, or, for tender species, under glass. Others have great potential for being grown through host plants – trees, climbers, and sturdy shrubs, for example – to provide an extended season of interest, a splash of color, or to create unusual and unexpected plant associations.

CLEMATIS

GROUP 1

C. montana var. *rubens*

C. alpina 'Frances Rivis'

C. macropetala 'Markham's Pink'

GROUP 2

C. 'The President'

C. 'Henryi'

C. 'Nelly Moser'

GROUP 3

C. 'Ernest Markham'

C. 'Jackmanii'

C. viticella 'Mme. Julia Correvon'

Clematis groups

Clematis may be divided into three main groups, based on their flowering time and habit.

Group 1 is made up of the early-flowering species and their cultivars, and the Alpina, Macropetala, and Montana groups, which flower directly from the previous season's ripened stems. In Group 2 are the early, large-flowered cultivars, blooming on the current season's short stems, which arise from the previous season's ripe wood. Groups 1 and 2 are sometimes known as old-wood-flowering clematis. Group 3 includes the late-flowering species, late, large-flowered cultivars, and herbaceous types, which flower on the current season's growth.

Early-flowering species and cultivars

The early-flowering evergreen species and their forms are mostly from warm climates and must be grown, therefore, with protection in areas with severe cold. Among the hardiest evergreens are the vigorous *C. armandii* and smaller *C. cirrhosa*. Both grow best in a south- or southwest-facing site and are lovely when growing through other wall-trained plants.

The Alpina and Macropetala groups withstand low winter temperatures and are ideal for growing through shrubs and wall-trained trees in any exposure. Do not grow them through climbing roses or other shrubs that need annual pruning, since these clematis need little or no cutting back. They are suitable in exposed sites such as northeast corners of buildings, but also make superb container plants for the patio and can be trained to any support.

The members of the Montana group are hardy and vigorous, climbing 22–40ft (7–12m). These plants will cover walls and arbors and are dramatic growing through conifers or old fruit trees that are past their productive best, but may damage the foliage of evergreens with their rampant, dense growth.

Early, large-flowered cultivars

These are generally hardy, growing to 8–12ft (2.5–4m). The more compact cultivars such as *C.* 'Edith', which are normally the first to flower, are ideal for containers. The double and semidouble cultivars and the midsummer-flowering types with very large flowers are best grown through the branches of other wall-trained trees or shrubs, where their flowers are protected from severe wind or heavy rain. Paler-flowered cultivars with pink or mauve-striped flowers are best planted in the shade where their flowers may be used to lighten a dark wall and they will not be bleached. The deep reds and purples are more suited to sunny situations because they develop better color in warmth.

Late-flowering species and cultivars

This group of clematis includes the late, large-flowered cultivars such as *C.* 'Jackmanii', small-flowered *C. viticella* and its hybrids, and a whole range of species and their forms, including the herbaceous clematis. The Jackmanii types are superb when grown through climbing roses, shrub roses, or most medium-sized shrubs, both evergreen and deciduous, whether free-standing or wall-trained. The *C. viticella* hybrids in particular are excellent for growing through ground cover plants, especially the summer- or winter-flowering heathers (*Calluna*, *Daboecia*, and *Erica*).

Of other members in this group, *C.* x *jouiniana* makes ideal ground cover, and the miniature, tuliplike flowers of *C. texensis* and its hybrids look well on a background of low-growing evergreens. The vigorous *C. orientalis* and *C. tangutica* need a large wall or tree where they can grow unconfined and display their many flowers and their fluffy seedheads. *C. heracleifolia* var. *davidiana* and other herbaceous species do not climb and should be grown in mixed or herbaceous borders; *C. integrifolia*, for example, associates very well with cluster-flowered bush roses.

Soil preparation and planting

When using vigorous clematis to clothe trellises or pergolas, ensure that the support structure is strong and sound before planting. Similarly, when growing clematis through old trees, the branches must be robust enough to bear the often considerable weight. For clematis grown through other host plants, it is essential to match the vigor of the clematis with that of its host, if the host is not to be swamped. Also ensure that the pruning requirements of host and clematis are compatible.

Most climbing species can be sited in part shade or in sun, provided that the roots are cool and shaded. Either underplant them with low shrubs or plant on the shaded side of the host tree or wall. The herbaceous species thrive in a sunny situation. To grow clematis on a patio, use a container with dimensions of 18in diameter x 18in deep (45 x 45cm).

Most clematis will thrive in any rich, fertile, and well-drained soil, especially if it is neutral or slightly alkaline. Evergreens and species such as *C. tangutica* and *C. orientalis* should not be grown in soil that remains wet during the winter months because they have fine, fibrous root systems that quickly rot. Planting details are the same as for other climbers (see "Soil preparation and planting," pp.98–100), except that clematis should be planted about 2in (5cm) deeper than normal to encourage basal buds to develop below soil level. If the stems are damaged, the plant may then grow again from below soil level.

Routine care

Keep newly planted specimens well watered until established, and mulch climbing and herbaceous species annually in spring with compost or well-rotted manure.

Fresh young growth is very susceptible to slug damage (p.550) in early spring. Clematis may be prone to attack from aphids (p.552), and the later-flowering, large-flowered

PLANTING A CLEMATIS

Plant clematis 2in (5cm) deeper than the nursery planting level. This helps buds to develop below soil level and overcome clematis wilt.

cultivars may be afflicted by powdery mildew (p.552). Clematis wilt, a condition that is caused by a fungus, can attack newly planted, large-flowered clematis (see p.571).

Pruning and training

Pruning requirements vary for each group, so always check before cutting back. If pruned incorrectly, the flowering wood may be cut out.

Initial pruning and training for all groups

Clematis climb by means of leaf-stalk tendrils that attach themselves to their support. They need to be trained to reach their support, and new growth will need tying in during spring and summer. Tie just below a node (or leaf axil buds), and space stems evenly on the support, leaving enough room for further growth to develop.

Clematis require special care in initial training and pruning. If they are left untrained, plants frequently produce one or two stems that are 50–60ft (15–18m) long and then a top-heavy tangle of growth, leaving a bare base. To avoid this, all newly planted clematis should be pruned hard the first spring after planting.

Unless the plant already has three or four stems growing from the base, cut back all the stems just above a strong, healthy pair of leaf buds about 12in (30cm) above soil level. If this hard pruning does not produce three or four extra stems in early spring, any new stems should be pruned to about 6in (15cm), just above a strong pair of leaf buds.

Group 1

Many of these vigorous clematis require little, if any, regular pruning, especially if cut back hard when first planted. If restricting the size or tidying tangled growth is necessary, pruning should be done after flowering. Any dead, weak, or damaged stems can also be removed at this time. New growth will ripen during late summer and fall and provide flowers the following spring. Any excess growth may be reduced during the fall, and tied into its support, but bear in mind that this will reduce the flowering display. *C. armandii*, which produces a mass of flowers on trailing stems, may be thinned annually to avoid congestion; cut back to well-placed young shoots immediately after flowering.

GROUP 1 – EARLY-FLOWERING SPECIES

C. alpina and cvs
C. armandii and cvs
C. cirrhosa

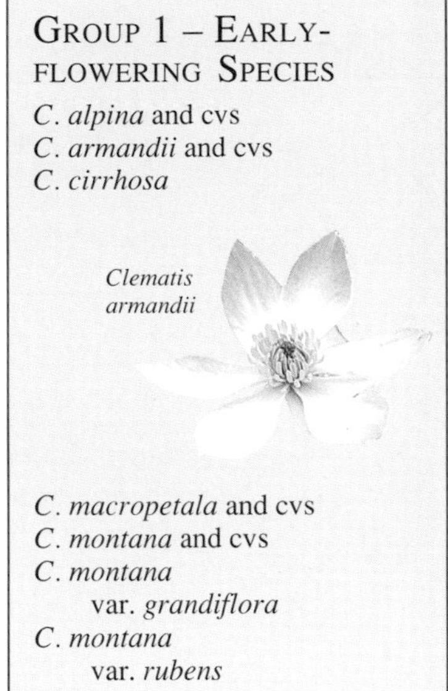

Clematis armandii

C. macropetala and cvs
C. montana and cvs
C. montana var. *grandiflora*
C. montana var. *rubens*

Flower stem growing directly from last season's ripened stem

PRUNING GROUP 1 CLEMATIS

Ripened stems of Group 1 clematis produce flower stems for the next season, so prune after flowering only if the plant has become overgrown.

Thin or remove stems that are growing densely or that have outgrown the available space, cutting them back to their point of origin.

Cut back any damaged shoots to a healthy pair of buds or to the main stem.

COLOR CONTRAST
Clematis are excellent as companion plants and can be grown through a variety of host plants to create an unusual display. Here, the bright petals of C. viticella 'Venosa Violacea' *present an attractive contrast to the green of* Juniperus sabina *var.* tamariscifolia *over which it is scrambling.*

Group 2

The solitary, large flowers are produced on stems of lengths varying from 6in to 24in (15–60cm) which arise from the previous season's ripened stems. Prune these plants in early spring, just before the new growth commences.

Remove any dead, weak, or damaged stems, and cut back healthy stems to just above a strong pair of leaf buds. These buds will produce the first crop of flowers. This group may also produce a second, but smaller, flush of blooms on new shoots in late summer.

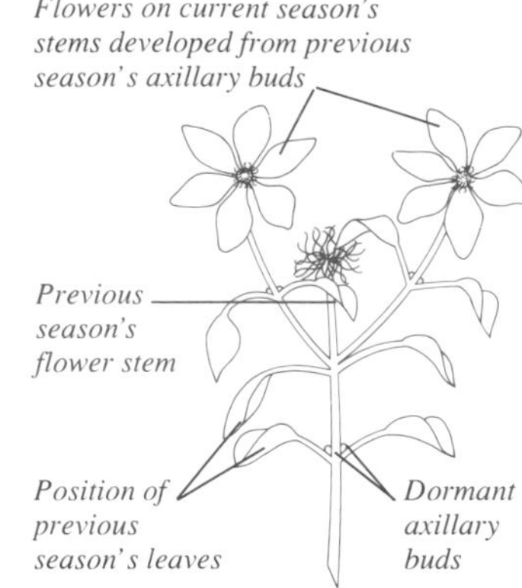

PRUNING GROUP 2 CLEMATIS

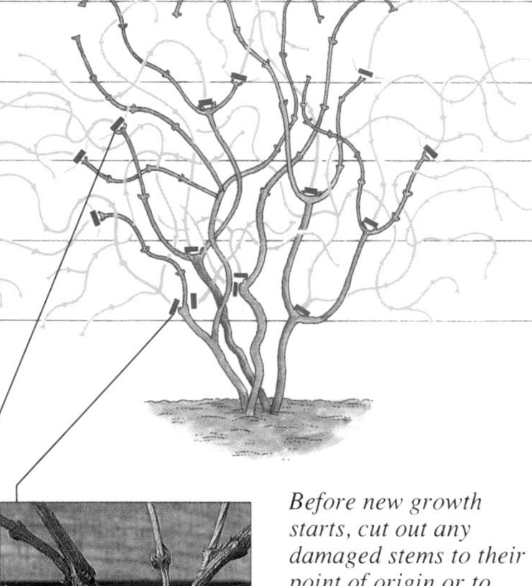

Group 2 clematis flower on the current season's stems, so prune in early spring before growth starts.

Cut back old stems to a strong pair of buds. Growth from these will produce this season's flowers.

Before new growth starts, cut out any damaged stems to their point of origin or to ground level.

Take care with the soft, and often brittle, new stems. Space them evenly and tie in at regular intervals.

Clematis growing over host or ground cover plants, such as heathers, should also be pruned. In late fall remove excessive growth to keep the plant and host tidy and less prone to wind damage. When clematis are grown over winter-flowering heathers, all clematis top-growth should be removed down to 12in (30cm) in late fall, before the heathers come into flower.

Group 3

Flowers produced by this group are on stems of the current season's growth. Prune in early spring before new growth commences. Remove all the previous season's stems down to a strong pair of leaf buds just above the base of the previous season's growth, 6–12in (15–30cm) above soil level. As new growth appears, tie it to its support or host.

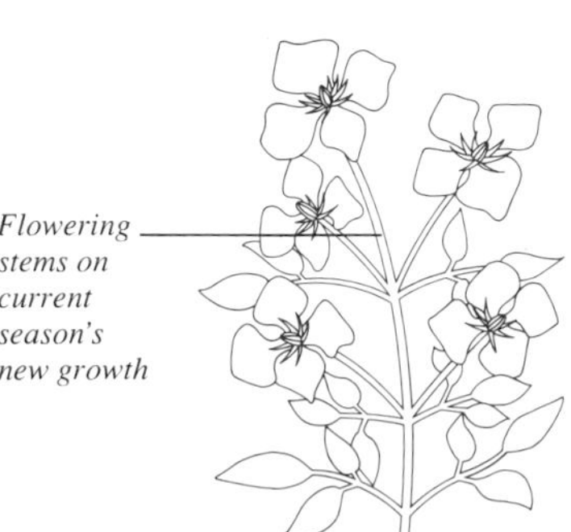

PRUNING GROUP 3 CLEMATIS

Group 3 clematis produce flowers on the current season's growth, so prune in early spring before new growth begins.

Cut just above the lowest pair of strong buds on each stem – this will be 6–12in (15–30cm) above soil level. Make a straight cut with sharp pruners, ensuring that the buds are not damaged.

Propagation

Clematis species can be propagated by seed sown in fall and overwintered in a cold greenhouse or frame (cultivars do not come true from seed). Cultivars are usually increased by softwood or semiripe cuttings (see pp.540–41) or layering (see p.539); division (see p.451) or basal stem cuttings (see p.164) are used for herbaceous types.

Internodal cuttings of softwood and semiripe wood are preferred to nodal cuttings. Take them in spring just above a node, and trim the stem to 1–2in (2.5–5cm) below the node. Remove one of the pair of leaves 1/4in (1cm) away from the node. Reduce the remaining leaf area by half, and cut the stem above the node back to approximately 1/4in (1cm). Treat the base with hormone rooting powder. Root in a closed propagating case with bottom heat. Harden off the new plants gradually (see p.545) before planting out the young clematis in spring.

INTERNODAL CUTTINGS

Make cuttings 2in (5cm) long by trimming just above a node and 1 1/2in (3.5cm) below the node. Remove one leaf from each cutting.

GROUP 2 – EARLY, LARGE-FLOWERED CULTIVARS

C. 'Barbara Jackman'
C. 'Carnaby'
C. 'Daniel Deronda'

Clematis 'Vyvyan Pennell'

C. 'Duchess of Edinburgh'
C. 'Elsa Spath'
C. 'General Sikorski'
C. 'Henryi'
C. 'Lasurstern'
C. 'Marie Boisselot', syn. *C.* 'Mme. Le Coultre'
C. 'Mrs. N. Thompson'
C. 'Nelly Moser'
C. 'Niobe'
C. 'The President'
C. 'Vyvyan Pennell'

GROUP 3 – LATE-FLOWERING SPECIES AND CULTIVARS

C. 'Comtesse de Bouchaud'
C. 'Duchess of Albany'
C. 'Ernest Markham'

Clematis 'Perle d'Azure'

C. florida and cvs
C. 'Hagley Hybrid'
C. 'Jackmanii'
C. 'Lady Betty Balfour'
C. paniculata
C. 'Perle d'Azure'
C. tangutica and cvs
C. 'Ville de Lyon'
C. viticella and cvs

Propagation

CLIMBING plants may be propagated from seed, from stem or root cuttings, or by layering. *Wisteria* is also often propagated by grafting (for further information on this technique, see ORNAMENTAL TREES, "Grafting," p.56).

Propagation from seed is the most cost-effective way of producing large quantities of plants. It is also the only practical method for increasing annuals and the easiest method for propagating herbaceous climbers. Hybrids and cultivars, however, seldom reproduce true from seed, so it is therefore advisable to propagate these by vegetative methods, such as cuttings. Also, woody plants may take several years to reach flowering size if they are raised from seed.

Propagation from stem cuttings that are taken from soft or semiripe wood can be carried out successfully for almost all climbers and is the best method for selected cultivars. Propagation from hardwood cuttings is normally used only for grapevines (*Vitis*). Root cuttings can be used for a small number of plants, such as *Celastrus*. Some climbers produce new plants naturally by self-layering. If only a few plants are required, simple and serpentine layering are both straightforward methods of propagating climbers that are difficult to raise successfully from cuttings.

Propagating climbers from seed

Many species produce viable seed without any difficulty. In the case of plants that are not fully hardy, however, a long, hot summer is necessary for the seed to ripen fully. To obtain seed from unisexual plants, such as *Actinidia deliciosa* and *Celastrus* species, plants of both sexes must be grown reasonably close together to ensure that they pollinate each other.

The sex of any seedling is unknown until the time that it reaches flowering size. Named, vegetatively propagated male and female clones are available for some plants, such as *Actinidia deliciosa*. For sowing and planting annual climbers, see ANNUALS AND BIENNIALS, pp.176–82.

Preparing the seed

For certain climbers it may be necessary to soak the seeds in water before sowing them: *Hardenbergia* seeds should be left in the water for 24 hours, and *Lapageria* for 48 hours. Seeds with a hard outer coating may need to have their dormancy broken by a period of cold, which is best achieved by putting them in a refrigerator for at least six to eight weeks (for further information, see PRINCIPLES OF PROPAGATION, "Cold stratification," p.538.)

Sowing

If sowing seed in a clay pot, first cover the drainage holes with crocks (this is not necessary when plastic pots, seed trays, or pans are used). Then fill the pot, pan, or tray with seed soil mix. Firm with a presser board to ensure that there are no air spaces or hollows. Large seeds should be evenly spaced; press them gently into the soil mix and then cover them to their own depth with a layer of sifted soil mix that has been mixed with a small amount of fine grit. Combine tiny seeds with a little fine, dry sand so that they may be sown evenly and thinly; no extra covering of soil mix is needed.

Label the pot and water the soil mix with a fine spray. Add a thin layer of fine grit or place clear plastic film or glass over the container to stop the soil mix from drying out.

The seeds of certain climbers such as *Eccremocarpus* and *Tropaeolum peregrinum* require artificial heat to germinate when grown in a cool climate and so should be placed in a propagator at 55–60°F (13–16°C). Sow *Cobaea*, if grown as an annual, in late winter with heat so that young plants are well developed by the time they are planted out. Most other seeds should be kept in a warm place out of direct sunlight. Hardy climbers such as most clematis, however, germinate best in cold conditions: plunge the containers into a protected place such as a cold frame.

SOWING SEED

1 *Harvest seed (here clematis) from the plant when ripe – it should pull away from the seedhead easily. There is no need to remove the fluffy "tails".*

2 *Sow thinly in a prepared pan or other container of firmed, moist, gritty seed soil mix.*

3 *Cover the seeds with a thin layer of gritty soil mix, add a shallow layer of fine grit, and label. Plunge in a sand bed or cold frame outdoors.*

4 *After germination, prick out the seedlings. Loosen a clump with a widger, then lift and replant the seedlings singly, holding each gently by the leaves.*

5 *When the seedlings have developed their first pair of true leaves, pot them on individually in moist potting mix. Label and place in a cold frame.*

6 *Grow on the seedlings until well established. They are then ready for planting out in their permanent positions.*

Pricking out

As soon as the seedlings emerge, remove the glass or plastic film, if used. When the first pair of true leaves has formed (the seedling's first leaves may differ significantly from the leaves of the adult plant), prick out the seedlings singly into small pots. If they are very small, however, it is best to use a tray, pricking out into rows separated by the space of about one leaf's width.

Inspect the base of the pots or tray at frequent intervals. As soon as the roots are visible through the drainage holes, pot on the seedlings. Seedlings that were germinated in a cold environment should be grown on in warmer conditions under cover.

Planting out

Plant out the seedlings when they are well established. Fast-growing climbers, both annual and perennial, can be planted where they are to flower. If frosts are likely and the climbers are not fully hardy, either plant them under a cloche for protection or delay planting out until all danger of frost has passed.

Slow-growing climbers should be potted on each time the roots begin to appear through the base of the pot. In their first season, grow them on in a sheltered position or in a nursery bed. Provide stakes to support the plants in all cases, and keep the soil mix of potgrown plants moist.

CLIMBERS THAT MAY BE PROPAGATED BY SOFTWOOD CUTTINGS

Allamanda ❄
Anemopaegma ❄
Anredera cordifolia ❄
Antigonon ❄
Asarina ❄
Bignonia
Ceropegia ❄
Clematis, some ❄

Allamanda cathartica 'Hendersonii'

Clerodendrum, some ❄
Clitoria ❄
Codonopsis
Convolvulus, some ❄
Cryptostegia ❄
Distictis ❄
Hedera, some ❄
Hibbertia ❄
Hydrangea
Ipomoea ❄
Lonicera, some ❄
Manettia ❄
Mikania ❄
Parthenocissus, some ❄
Philodendron ❄
Schisandra, some ❄
Schizophragma

Senecio macroglossus 'Variegatus'

Senecio, some ❄
Solanum, some ❄
Sollya ❄
Streptosolen ❄
Thladiantha, some ❄
Thunbergia ❄
Tropaeolum, some ❄
Wisteria

CLIMBERS THAT MAY BE PROPAGATED BY SEMIRIPE CUTTINGS

Actinidia, some ❄
Agapetes ❄
Akebia
Ampelopsis
Anemopaegma ❄
Araujia ❄
Aristolochia, some ❄
Asteranthera ❄
Beaumontia ❄
Berberidopsis
Berchemia
Billardiera ❄
Bougainvillea ❄
Campsis
Celastrus
Cissus ❄

KEY
❄ *Not frost hardy*

Propagation from softwood cuttings

Softwood is the youngest and greenest part of a stem resulting from the spring flush of growth. Take the cuttings in late spring or early summer, after new growth has started but before the stems have begun to harden. Prepare a pot, pan, or tray by filling it almost to the brim with moist cuttings soil mix, and firm.

Taking the cuttings

Cut lengths of stem approximately 6in (15cm) long, making cuts above leaf joints or nodes on the parent plant. Then trim the base of each cutting immediately below a node. (Clematis is an exception to this rule: cuttings should be internodal, with a small piece of stem below the node – see "Propagation," p.108.)

Softwood cuttings are particularly vulnerable to water loss, so place them immediately in a clear plastic bag to retain moisture.

Preparing and inserting the cuttings

Remove the leaves from the bottom third of the softwood stems with a clean, sharp knife. Dip the bottom ¼in (½cm) of each cutting in a softwood-strength hormone rooting powder that contains fungicide, and tap off the excess. Insert each cutting into the soil mix so that the lowest leaf or pair of leaves is just above the surface.

Label the cuttings, then moisten them with a fine spray. Place them in a propagator, cover trays with sheets of glass, or affix clear plastic bags over pots with a rubber band. Keep the cuttings in good light, checking them daily to make sure that they do not dry out.

Potting up

The cuttings generally take four to eight weeks to root, although honeysuckles (*Lonicera*) may take longer. Pot them up in standard, soil-based mix. Alternatively, use a mixture of two parts soilless mix to one part sand; since this contains no nutrients, apply a liquid or foliar feed every two weeks.

Cuttings taken in early spring should be ready to plant out in fall. Any taken later should be overwintered under cover and planted out the following spring once there is no danger of frost. In cold areas, all tender cuttings should be overwintered in a frost-free place, gradually hardened off the following spring, and then planted out when all danger of frost has passed.

Propagation from semiripe cuttings

From midsummer to early fall, take semiripe cuttings from healthy shoots. Prepare a pot or pan of moist cuttings soil mix, as for softwood cuttings. Select lengths of about 4–6in (10–15cm) from wood that has not fully hardened, making the cuts above leaf joints or nodes.

PROPAGATION FROM SOFTWOOD CUTTINGS

1 *Fill a 5in (13cm) pot with moist, standard cuttings soil mix. Remove any surplus with a straightedge to level the surface, and firm lightly.*

2 *Select 6in (15cm) lengths from the soft growing tips of healthy shoots (here* Solanum crispum*). Place the cutting material in a clear plastic bag to prevent drying out.*

3 *Trim the stem of each cutting to approximately 4in (10cm), straight across just below a leaf joint. Remove the lower leaves, cutting flush with the stems.*

4 *Dip each cutting in hormone powder. Insert two or three to a pot, with the lowest leaves just above the soil mix. The cuttings must not touch each other.*

5 *Water the cuttings with a fine mist-spray, label, and place the pot or pots in a propagator or in clear plastic bags filled with air so that they do not touch the cuttings.*

6 *After they have rooted, pot on the cuttings into individual pots. Keep the cuttings moist by spraying lightly with a mist-spray.*

PROPAGATION FROM SEMIRIPE CUTTINGS

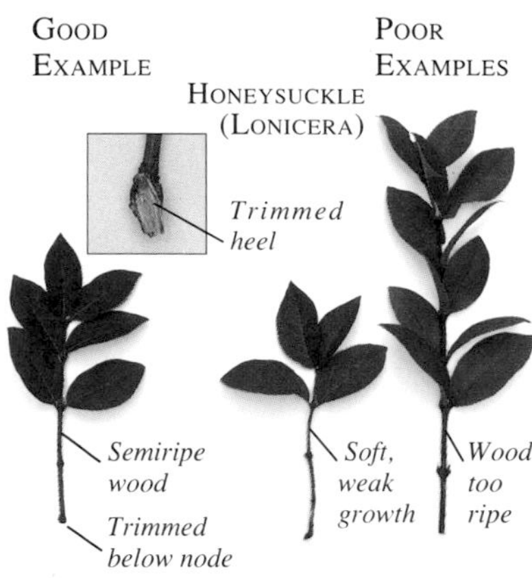

Select 4–6in (10–15cm) lengths from healthy new wood and trim just below a node. Some cuttings are taken with a small heel of bark at the base (see inset). These should be trimmed before use.

Then trim the bases to just below a node, as for softwood cuttings.

Alternatively, make a clean cut through the base of the selected shoot where it is attached to the parent plant. Some cuttings root more readily if taken with a heel, by gently tugging a shoot away from the parent plant; the shoot peels away with a small triangular section of bark, or heel, at its base. Trim the heel of each cutting and treat with hormone rooting powder, then insert it into the soil mix and label. The pot or pan should then be placed in a propagator. Semiripe cuttings generally take eight to twelve weeks, sometimes longer, to root.

When the cuttings have rooted, pot them on using a standard potting soil mix and grow on in a cold frame once reestablished. The rooted cuttings should be ready for planting out into their permanent positions the following spring, after they have been hardened off.

Propagation from hardwood cuttings

Take hardwood cuttings in fall and early winter from healthy shoots that have become woody during the growing season. Using pruners, remove a length of stem, cutting just above a bud. Trim off any side shoots, then divide the stem into pieces 2–3in (5–8cm) long, using a sloping cut above a bud at the top and a straight cut at the bottom. Longer cuttings, with two or more buds, may also be taken. To encourage rooting, wound each cutting at the base by removing a thin sliver of bark with a sharp knife. An application of hormone rooting powder to the wounded section may speed up rooting for climbers that are difficult to root, but is not always needed if suitable stems are taken at the appropriate season.

Inserting the cuttings

Prepare a pot or pan of free-draining cuttings soil mix (add a little extra sand or grit to the soil mix), filling the pot almost to the brim, and moisten the soil mix well. Insert the cuttings around the edge of the pot, approximately 2in (5cm) apart. Gently insert the cuttings by up to two-thirds of their length, so that just the top buds are visible. Firm the soil mix, then water the cuttings, label the pot, and place it in a cold frame to overwinter. Alternatively, insert the cuttings directly into a cold frame or in a trench in a sheltered part of the garden (see ORNAMENTAL TREES, "Hardwood cuttings," p.52). Hardwood cuttings of plants that are not fully hardy should be overwintered in a frost-free place.

Hardwood cuttings may take several months to root, but most should be ready for potting up or transplanting by midspring of the following year. Either pot them into a standard soil mix, or grow them on in a sheltered place before planting them out in their permanent positions the following fall.

PROPAGATION FROM HARDWOOD CUTTINGS

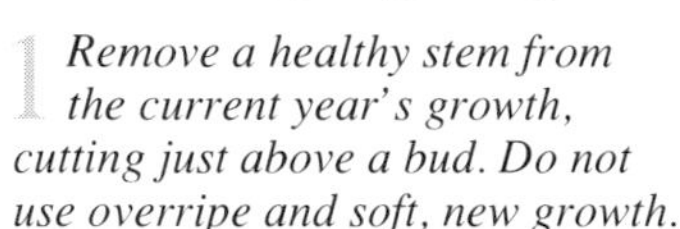

1 *Remove a healthy stem from the current year's growth, cutting just above a bud. Do not use overripe and soft, new growth.*

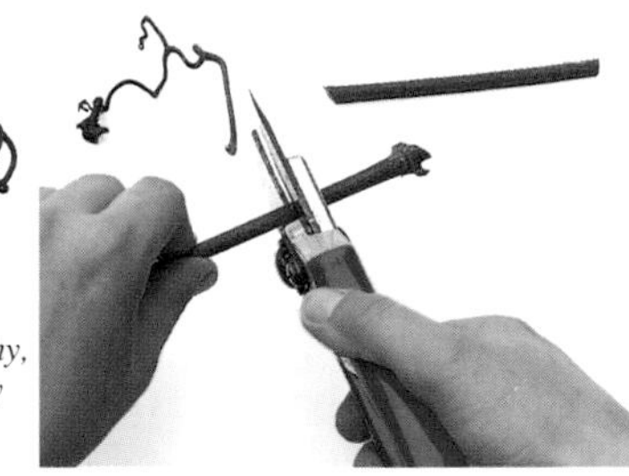

2 *Trim off tendrils and side shoots. Cut the stem into pieces, with an angled cut above a bud and a straight cut at the base.*

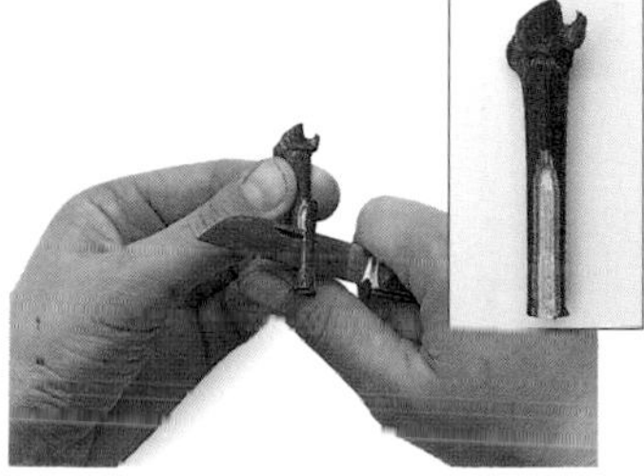

3 *Pare away the outer bark of each cutting, making a clean, downward cut, to reveal the cambium layer (see inset).*

4 *Insert the cuttings into gritty soil mix so that the top buds just show above the surface. Label, water, and place in a cold frame.*

5 *When the cuttings are well rooted, pot on into a larger pot. Stake, as required, and grow on before planting out.*

CLIMBERS THAT MAY BE PROPAGATED BY SEMIRIPE CUTTINGS (CONT.)

Clematis, some ❄
Clianthus ❄
Clytostoma ❄
Decumaria ❄
Dioscorea ❄
Distictis ❄
Ercilla
Euonymus
Gelsemium sempervirens
Hardenbergia ❄
Hedera, some ❄
Hoya ❄
Jacquemontia ❄
Jasminum, some ❄
Kennedia ❄
Lonicera, some ❄
Macfadyena ❄

Mandevilla x amabilis

Mandevilla ❄
Manettia ❄
Mitraria ❄
Mutisia, some ❄
Paederia
Pandorea ❄
Passiflora, most ❄
Petrea ❄
Pileostegia
Plumbago ❄
Podranea ❄
Polygonum, syn. *Fallopia*
Pyrostegia ❄
Quisqualis ❄
Sarmienta ❄
Schisandra, some ❄
Schizophragma
Senecio, some ❄
Solandra ❄
Solanum, some ❄
Stauntonia
Stephanotis ❄
Stigmaphyllon ❄
Strongylodon ❄
Tecoma ❄
Tecomanthe ❄
Tecomaria ❄
Thunbergia ❄
Trachelospermum
Wattakaka

CLIMBERS THAT MAY BE PROPAGATED BY HARDWOOD CUTTINGS

Actinidia kolomikta
Bougainvillea ❄
Lonicera, some ❄
Parthenocissus, some ❄
Vitis, some ❄

Actinidia kolomikta

KEY
❄ *Not frost hardy*

Root cuttings

A few climbers, notably *Celastrus* and *Solanum*, may be propagated from root cuttings, taken from late winter to early spring.

Taking the cuttings

Dig a hole 18–24in (45–60cm) away from the base of the plant to expose roots that are about 1/2in (1cm) thick; these provide the best cutting material. Remove sections of root up to 8–12in (20–30cm) long, depending on how many cuttings are required. Cut straight across the top of the root (nearest the plant) and cut the base of the root at an angle. Place the cutting material in a clear plastic bag to prevent it from drying out.

Preparing and inserting the cuttings

Wash the sections of root to remove any soil, then cut them into smaller pieces and remove the fibrous laterals. Make a horizontal cut at the top and a slanted cut at the base. Insert the cuttings, with the slanted cut downward, in a pot filled with a rooting medium of equal parts peat and sand. Space them approximately 3in (7cm) apart, with the tips protruding slightly. Cover them with a 1/2in (1cm) layer of sand. Moisten the soil mix thoroughly, label the pot, and place it in a cold frame or propagator, or plunge it in a trench. Keep the soil mix moist.

Hardening off and potting on

Buds will appear near the top of the cuttings in spring. Pot up the cuttings individually during early summer, and harden them off gradually, occasionally applying a liquid or foliar feed. Stake the cuttings as they develop. The new plants can be planted in their permanent positions the following fall.

PROPAGATION FROM ROOT CUTTINGS

1 *Dig a hole well away from the base of the plant to expose some of the roots.*

2 *Cut off sections of root with pruners. The pieces should be about 1/2in (1cm) thick and at least 4in (10cm) long.*

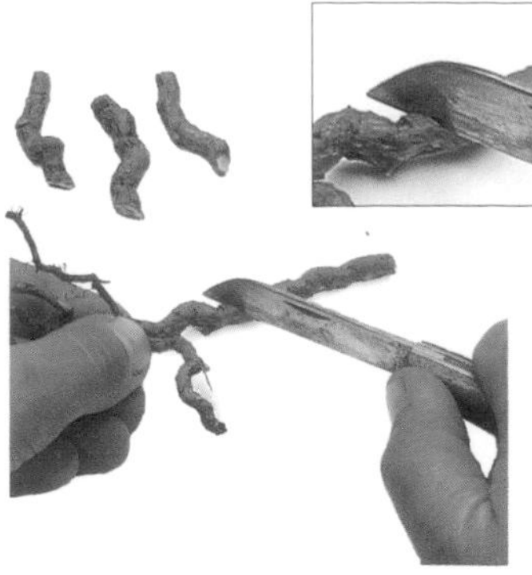

3 *Wash the roots and divide into pieces 1 1/2–2in (4–5cm) long, cutting horizontally at the top and obliquely at the base (see inset).*

4 *Insert each cutting vertically into a pot of soil mix, so that the tips are just protruding above the surface of the soil mix.*

5 *Cover with a 1/2in (1cm) layer of sand. Water, label, and place in a cold frame or protected spot.*

6 *Pot on into individual pots once the cuttings are well rooted and young shoots are 1–2in (2.5–5cm) high.*

Self-layering climbers

Many climbers have trailing shoots that root naturally where they come into contact with the surrounding soil. A shoot that has self-layered can be lifted and severed from the parent plant in fall or early spring. Choose a healthy-looking, well-rooted layer that has fresh new growth. Lift it carefully and cut it off. Trim back the layered shoot, retaining only the piece or pieces of stem that have produced new roots and that have healthy new buds forming. Strip off any leaves growing near the roots. Pot up the rooted layers individually into standard cuttings soil mix consisting of half peat and half sand, and water them in well. Alternatively, if the layer is well developed with strong, vigorous roots and shoots, it can be planted immediately in its permanent position.

PROPAGATION OF SELF-LAYERING PLANTS

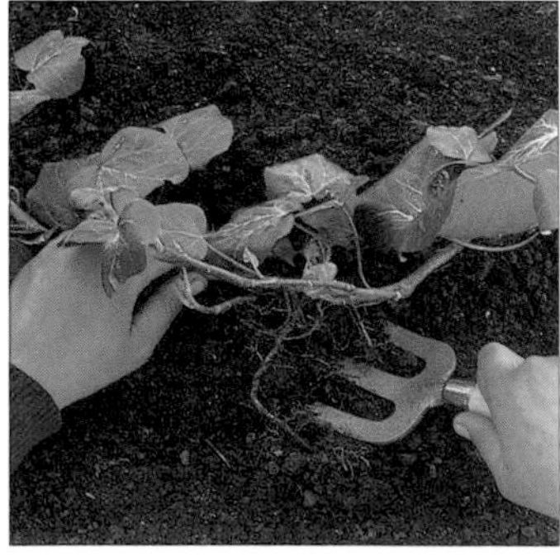

1 *Select a low-growing shoot that has rooted into the ground and lift the rooted section with a hand fork.*

2 *Sever the shoot from the parent plant (here an ivy,* Hedera helix*), cutting between two nodes with pruners.*

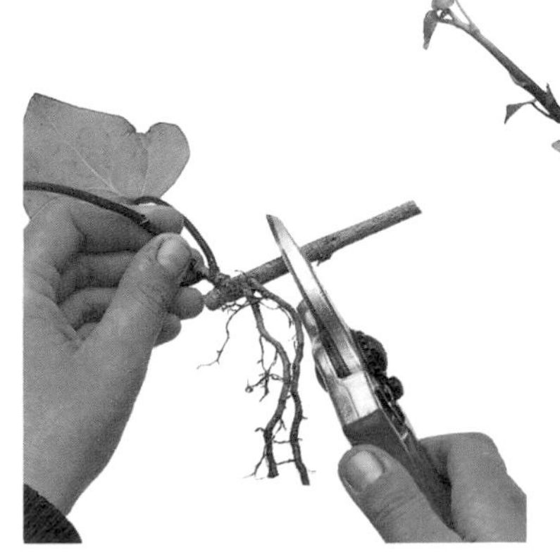

3 *Cut the shoot into sections, each with a healthy root system and vigorous new growth. Remove the lower leaves.*

4 *Replant each section of rooted shoot either into a pot of cuttings soil mix or in its permanent position.*

Simple layering

The long, trailing shoots of climbers may often be propagated by simple layering if they do not root naturally. A shoot is wounded and pegged down into the surrounding soil. This induces it to root at a node to provide a young plant that is later separated from the parent.

Layers of many climbers that have been pegged down in spring will develop strong root systems by fall, at which time they can be separated from the parent plant. *Akebia*, *Campsis*, and *Vitis* should be layered in late fall or winter, however, because if the stems are wounded in spring, the layers bleed sap and are less likely to root.

Soil preparation

If the surrounding soil is poor, fork in some organic matter at least a month before layering takes place. Alternatively, fill a pot with soil mix and plunge it into the ground at the place where the layer is to be pegged down.

Making the layer

Choose a healthy, vigorous, non-flowering shoot or stem that is long enough to trail along the ground. Trim the leaves and any side shoots from the section of stem to be layered to provide a clear length of stem for about 12in (30cm) behind the tip of the shoot.

Gently bend the stem down to the ground and, to encourage root formation, wound the underside of the stem close to a node, making an angled cut halfway through with a sharp knife. For most climbers, apply hormone rooting powder to the wound and shake off any surplus powder. Vigorous climbers such as *Wisteria*, however, do not require it.

Peg the stem firmly to the ground with one or more U-shaped pieces of wire, and cover with not more than 3in (8cm) of soil. Attach the tip of the layered stem to a stake so that it is kept upright.

Separating the rooted layer

In fall, when new shoots and roots have grown from the buried part of the stem, sever the rooted layer from the parent plant and pot it up or plant it out. Trim back the old stem before replanting and stake the new plant. If the layer is planted in a pot, it should be overwintered in a cold frame or plunged into a protected spot, and mulched lightly. Pot on, as necessary, before gradually hardening off and planting out into its permanent position the following year.

PROPAGATION BY SIMPLE LAYERING

1 *Select a young, low-growing shoot (here* Akebia quinata*). Trim off the leaves to provide a clear length of stem behind the tip.*

2 *Make an angled cut on the underside of the shoot to form a tongue in the center of the trimmed length of stem.*

3 *Using a clean brush, dust the incision with fresh hormone rooting powder (see inset) and gently shake off any surplus.*

4 *Peg down the shoot firmly in the prepared area, using wire pegs. Cover with up to 3in (8cm) of soil.*

5 *The following fall, sever the layered shoot close to the parent plant. Lift with a hand fork and trim back the old stem.*

6 *Plant the layer in a 5in (13cm) pot of standard potting mix or into its permanent position. Then water and label.*

Propagation by serpentine layering

Carefully bend a trailing shoot down to the prepared soil and trim off leaves and side shoots. Make several wounds close to nodes, leaving at least one bud between each incision. Apply hormone rooting powder and peg down the wounded sections, as for simple layering. Separate plantlets in fall, when roots will have formed from each of the wounds. Trim the old stem from the new plants before replanting and staking.

Several new plants may be produced by serpentine layering. Peg down layers with wire pegs (see inset).

CLIMBERS THAT MAY BE LAYERED

Self-layering
Asteranthera ❄
Celastrus
Euonymus
Ficus pumila ❄

Hedera helix 'Atropurpurea'

Hedera, some ❄
Hoya ❄
Hydrangea
Mitraria ❄
Monstera deliciosa ❄
Parthenocissus, some ❄
Philodendron ❄
Scindapsus ❄
Tecomaria ❄
Trachelospermum
Tripterygium
Vigna ❄

Simple layering
Actinidia, some ❄
Akebia
Beaumontia ❄
Campsis
Cissus ❄
Humulus
Lapageria ❄

Lonicera x *americana*

Lonicera, some ❄
Mandevilla ❄
Monstera ❄
Mucuna ❄
Mutisia, some ❄
Passiflora, most ❄
Pileostegia
Podranea ❄
Schizophragma
Solanum, some ❄
Strongylodon ❄
Tecomanthe ❄
Thunbergia ❄
Vitis amurensis, *V. coignetiae*
Wisteria

Serpentine layering
Ampelopsis
Campsis
Celastrus
Clematis, some ❄
Holboellia ❄
Kennedia ❄
Parthenocissus, some ❄

Parthenocissus tricuspidata

Polygonum, syn. *Fallopia*
Sarmienta ❄
Schisandra, some ❄

KEY
❄ *Not frost hardy*

5

The Rose Garden

Gardeners and poets since before Roman times have revered the rose as the queen of flowering plants for the extraordinary beauty of its blooms. Roses offer an enormous range of flower color, shape, and scent, whether it be the simple purity of the wild rose, the soft, pastel charm of the old garden rose, or the jewel-like brilliance of the modern hybrids. Few plants are so varied or versatile as the rose in its growth habit, height, foliage, and form. It is possible to clothe the whole summer garden in rose blooms, from the delicacy of a tiny pot rose to the foaming mass of a huge rambler. Whether grown alone in the splendor of a formal garden, or bringing a touch of class to the profusion of a mixed planting, roses epitomize the glory of the garden on a summer's day.

Designing with roses

Whether you choose to grow old garden roses for their grace of habit, foliage, and scent, or modern roses for their long flowering season and showy blooms, the diversity among roses makes it possible to find a plant for almost every part of the garden. Use them to create many styles and moods of planting, from restrained classicism to luxuriant informality.

Roses are adaptable plants that grow well in almost all parts of the world. They are most vigorous in warm-temperate regions, although some adapt well to subtropical or cold regions. In hot climates, some may flower most of the year.

Choosing roses

The number of rose cultivars available is bewildering, with many new ones added to the lists each year. Before making a final choice, it is well worth making a visit to some established gardens to observe as many different roses as possible growing in garden conditions. Do this over a period of time to assess the plants' habits, eventual heights, health, vigor, fragrance, fastness of flower color in strong sun, continuity of flowering, and all the other desirable features of a good rose.

Most national rose associations publish listings that give details of where species roses and cultivars stocked by member nurseries may be purchased; these listings are often invaluable in locating suppliers of more unusual roses.

Old World Charm
The open blooms and sprawling habit of shrub roses, including 'Constance Spry', 'Céleste', *and* 'Cerise Bouquet', *blend with perennials in a subtle color theme to create a mood of informal and restful abundance. The proximity of the beds and the grass walk provide a secluded setting in which to enjoy the heady rose scents.*

Fragrance

Roses have long been prized for their scent. Most old garden cultivars and species, and many modern roses possess enchanting and diverse perfumes with hints of clove, musk, honey, lemon, spice, and even tea, as well as the "true" rose fragrance. It is not easy to be specific about rose scent since its character and intensity may vary greatly with the time of day, the humidity, the age of the bloom, and the nose of individual gardeners; some will find a particular cultivar fragrant, while others will not.

With some roses one must be quite close to smell them; they are best enjoyed by planting them near a door or a window where their scent may drift into the house on summer evenings, around the patio or along a path, or in a sheltered position in the garden. Other roses, particularly many vigorous old garden roses, are so freely scented that they can perfume the whole garden.

Flower color

Modern roses embrace virtually every color of the spectrum, from pale pastels to bold, bright reds and yellows. The blue rose remains the stuff of legend, despite the use of the word "blue" in such cultivars as 'Blue Moon', which is actually pale lilac. Old garden roses range in hue from white, through the palest of blush pinks, deep pink, crimson, and violet, to purple; many are striped pink and white or purple and white. Many roses coordinate beautifully together and with other plants, but combining too many brilliant colors, for instance bright vermilion with cerise pink and golden yellow, may create a discordant clash. Plant white roses or those with softer, pastel hues between groups of strongly toned roses to cool them down and to prevent them from clashing.

Flower shapes

Roses offer a great variety of forms of flower, from the simple, single flowers of the species rose to the elegantly furled blooms of the modern rose and the cabbagelike complexity of many old rose flowers.

The main flower shapes illustrated on this page give a general indication of the shape of the flower when in its perfect state (which in some cases may be before it has fully opened). The flowers may be single (4–7 petals), semidouble (8–14 petals), double (15–20 petals), or fully double (over 30 petals).

Foliage color

As well as producing a fine flowering display, some groups of roses provide color in other ways to extend the season of interest. The Alba roses and many of the species (see below) have pleasing foliage, from a soft gray-green to a deep, glossy blue-green, making them attractive even when the bush is not in flower. The rich green foliage of Rugosa roses has an interesting wrinkled (rugose) texture and, if the roses are planted as a hedge, it makes a good background for other plantings. The leaves of some species are a dusky plum-purple, as in *R. glauca*, while the foliage of some, such as *R. virginiana* and *R. nitida*, turns to vivid sunset tints in fall.

Ornamental rose hips or thorns

Rugosa roses with single or semidouble flowers also develop bright red, decorative hips at the end of the flowering season. Some of the species, such as *R. moyesii* and its hybrids, display ornamental hips in

FLOWER SHAPES

Flat *Open, usually single or semidouble, with petals that are almost flat.*

Cupped *Open, single to fully double, with petals curving outward from the center.*

Pointed *Semi-double to fully double Hybrid Tea type, with high, tight centers.*

Urn-shaped *Classic, curved, and flat-topped, semi- to fully double Hybrid Tea type.*

Rounded *Double or fully double, with overlapping, even sized petals forming a bowl-shaped outline.*

Rosette *Flattish, double or fully double, with many confused, slightly overlapping petals of uneven size.*

Quartered-rosette *Flattish, double or fully double, with confused, uneven petals in a quartered pattern.*

Pompon *Small, rounded, double or fully double, with masses of small petals; blooms are usually borne in clusters.*

Rose classification

There are about 250 naturally occurring species roses, as well as many natural hybrids, growing in the wild. After 2,000 years of being grown as ornamentals, rose cultivars now number in the thousands. The ancestry of almost all of them is so mixed, after many centuries of casual and indiscriminate breeding before cross-pollination was understood and proper records of parentage kept, that it is impossible to classify them precisely.

The borderlines between established groups have become blurred; for example, the flower size of the Floribundas has been increased by crosses with Hybrid Tea roses. Similarly, the hybridizing of miniature roses with Floribundas has led to recently developed Patio roses, intermediate in stature between the parents.

Naming rose categories

In 1979, the World Federation of Rose Societies decided that long-established terms such as "Hybrid Tea" and "Floribunda" had lost their original meaning because of the results of hybridization, and agreed to adopt a new rose classification to clarify the groups so that they could be understood readily.

The new classification keeps most of the traditional rose group names; two differences most likely to affect gardeners are the changes of the names "Large-flowered bush" to "Hybrid Tea," and "Cluster-flowered bush" to "Floribunda." In 1987, the World Federation adopted the category "Dwarf cluster-flowered bush" for "Patio" roses.

However, although this system is regarded as the official classification by most rose-growing bodies, the American Rose Society (ARS) has not chosen to adopt it.

The World Federation terminology is included here for reference. The ARS groupings are as follows, with synonymous classification names in parentheses.

Modern garden roses

Hybrid Tea and Grandiflora (Large-flowered bush) Upright, remontant (repeat-flowering) shrubs with large flowers carried one to a stem, or in small clusters.

Floribunda (Cluster-flowered bush) Upright, remontant shrubs with better continuity of bloom than Hybrid Teas; the smaller flowers are borne on large sprays.

Patio (Dwarf cluster-flowered bush) Similar to Floribundas, but with a smaller, neat habit.

Miniature Tiny counterparts of Hybrid Teas and Floribundas.

Ground cover Low-growing, trailing or spreading roses. Some flower once a year; others are remontant.

Climbing Climbing roses with long, strong shoots and large flowers borne singly or in small clusters. Some flower once a year; most are remontant. Climbing roses include a small group of roses, such as 'Albertine', which in habit are between a climber and a rambler. They used to be classed as ramblers, but culturally they should be treated as climbers.

Rambler Vigorous, climbing roses with long, flexible shoots that bear small blooms in large clusters, flowering once a year.

Shrub A widely varying group impossible to classify further, ranging from low, mound forming cultivars to wide spreading shrubs and giant cluster-flowered bushes. Some bloom once a year; many are remontant.

Old garden roses

Alba Large, freely branching roses with flower clusters borne once among abundant, gray-green foliage.

Bourbon Very vigorous, open, fully or partly remontant roses that bear double, fragrant flowers, often three to a cluster. Many grow tall and open.

Centifolia (Provence) Rather lax, thorny shrubs bearing fragrant flowers once a year. Commonly called cabbage roses.

China Small to medium remontant shrubs of twiggy, airy growth, bearing small, mainly double flowers singly or in clusters.

Damask Open shrubs bearing loose clusters of very fragrant flowers, mainly once a year.

Gallica Fairly dense shrubs that produce richly colored flowers, often three to a cluster, once a year.

Hybrid Musk Vigorous, remontant shrubs with abundant foliage and fragrant, primarily double blooms borne in trusses.

Hybrid Perpetual Vigorous, sometimes remontant, shrubs with flowers borne singly or in threes.

Moss Often lax shrubs with a furry, mosslike growth on stems and calyx; blooms once a year.

Noisette Remontant climbing roses that bear large clusters of flowers with a slightly spicy fragrance.

Portland Upright, dense, and less vigorous (but more remontant) version of the Bourbon rose.

Tea Remontant shrubs and climbers bearing loose, usually double flowers that have a spicy fragrance.

Species roses

Wild, or species, roses and species hybrids (which share most characteristics of both parent species) are mainly large, arching shrubs bearing one flush of single, five-petaled flowers in spring or summer and decorative hips in fall.

Notable among the species is *Rosa rugosa*, the parent of a diverse group of dense, very hardy and disease-resistant, vigorous shrubs bearing extremely fragrant, single to semidouble blooms. A few are more open in habit, less hardy, and not as fragrant as some.

Consult local rose experts for further information suited to specific regional and garden conditions.

DESIGN FOR A FORMAL ROSE GARDEN

Here, all is symmetry and order, with clean lines and color laid out in patterns of geometric simplicity. This design creates a restrained setting in which to enjoy the classic beauty of roses. Formal yew hedges enclose beds of massed bush roses in pale and deep golds and white, which in turn focus on a graceful, trailing rose in the center. Red standard roses lift the planting with a bold contrast of color and form.

1 Yew (*Taxus*)
2 *Rosa* 'Golden Showers'
3 *R.* 'Europeana'
4 *R.* 'Summer Fashion'
5 *R.* 'Amber Queen'
6 *R.* 'Sunsprite'
7 *R.* 'Margaret Merril'
8 *R.* 'Swany'

fall that range from yellow and orange, through all the shades of red, to a blackish purple.

R. sericea subsp. *omeiensis* (syn. *R. omeiensis pteracantha*) has huge, flat thorns which, when young, glow ruby-red if the sun is behind them.

The garden setting

One of the best settings for the beds of a rose garden is a smooth, green lawn, but the subtle gray and honey tones of stone paving can be just as attractive. A mellow brick path may complement a rose planting alongside it, especially one of soft, pale tones. Whatever the material, avoid multicolored patterns that may compete with the roses. Gravel, although pleasant in appearance and texture, can be troublesome to look after because weeds soon appear, and the stones may gradually spread or disappear into the soil.

Edging plants may be used to frame a rosebed. A traditional boxwood hedge makes a formal boundary, but many other plants may be used more informally, particularly those that provide gray-green or silver-gray foliage. Pearly everlasting (*Anaphalis*) and pussytoes (*Antennaria*), with their woolly leaves, or the more dwarf forms of lavender are suitable, as is catmint (*Nepeta*) if there is room for it to sprawl over the path.

Many of the more restrained species and hybrids of *Geranium*, in particular those with blue flowers, are similarly appealing. Even miniature roses, in contrasting or complementary colors, may be grown on the sunny side of a bed.

Formal rose gardens

A popular way to grow roses is in a formal rose garden, devoted to displaying the glories of the rose in beds shaped to reflect the plant's classic elegance. Generally, modern cultivars grown as bushes and standards are used as permanent bedding plants, grouped in blocks of color. The rather stiff and upright growth of many such bushes lends itself to the formality of bedding and tends not to blend so well with other plants, although roses may be attractively underplanted (see opposite).

Rosebeds may be designed in any shape or size – square, oblong, triangular, or round; at the edges of paths or drives they may be narrow and ribbonlike. Before creating new rosebeds, draw a plan on paper and experiment with different shapes and layouts of beds in order to decide which is the best design for the site that has been chosen. Do not make the beds so wide that access to the roses for spraying, mulching, and pruning becomes difficult.

Not all cultivars reach their peak of flowering at exactly the same time. If mixing cultivars in the same bed, plant no less than five or six plants of the same cultivar together in a regular formation for substantial clumps of color. A garden planted with variations on a color theme, for instance pale and deep pinks with a touch of apricot-blush or white, creates a harmonious picture that is more pleasing than a busy crowd of color.

When planting, bear in mind the variations in eventual height of different cultivars. For a bed in an open area, choose cultivars of a more or less uniform height. A rosebed that is backed by a wall or hedge is more attractive if the roses at the front are shorter than those behind.

Standard roses may be used to give height to any bedding design. Placing a single standard in the center of a round bed that echoes the shape of the rose creates a graceful symmetry, while several standards placed at intervals of about 5ft (1.5m) along the middle of a long bed help to break up its uniformity.

Informal plantings

The charm of roses may be enjoyed in a wide range of informal planting designs, particularly with herbaceous plants or many shrubs. Roses suitable for virtually any garden site may be chosen from the multitude of shrub, miniature, climbing, and ground cover roses of varied stature and habit now available.

Roses combine well with other plantings. For instance, miniature roses give both summer color and height to a planting of rock plants that are mainly spring-flowering, and a ground cover rose may clothe a bank with fragrant flowers.

The belief that roses do not mix with other plants probably dates from the days when many commonly used cultivars were large and ungainly and did not suit the Edwardian and Victorian bedding designs. They were grown in separate walled gardens simply to provide cut blooms for the house. It has, however, long been recognized that roses need not be grown in isolation.

Roses with herbaceous plants

Growing roses in beds or borders with herbaceous plants both highlights the beauties of the rose in flower and provides interest when the rose itself is dormant. The growth habit of many shrub roses, such as the light and airy China roses or the lax and open Damasks, perfectly suits the casual profusion of an informal planting while bringing it height and structure.

Muted drifts of flower or foliage, for example the haze of tiny white *Crambe cordifolia* flowers, best complement the showy flowers of roses in the summer. At other times of the year, use more flamboyant flowering plants or some with evergreen foliage to extend the season and to conceal the bare rose stems.

Many plants may enhance an area dominated by roses. For example, the tall spikes of purple foxgloves (*Digitalis purpurea*), white *Lilium regale*, or other white and pink lilies pushing up through a planting of lush, old garden roses make for a striking contrast, both in growth habit and flower form.

Roses with other shrubs

Both shrub and species roses combine well with other shrubs, as long as they receive enough sunlight. They provide abundant, beautiful, often fragrant flowers to set against the foliage of other spring-flowering shrubs, sometimes right through the summer. Many such roses have almost evergreen foliage and colored hips in the fall (see "Ornamental rose hips or thorns," p.115). Smaller shrub roses as well as the Gallicas, most of the Damasks, the Portland roses, and many modern cultivars of similar stature make an excellent ornamental foreground to any planting of shrubs.

Roses that have long, questing branches, such as the freely flowering 'Sea Foam' or 'Complicata' with its deep pink blooms, may scramble through and enliven a dull, evergreen shrub. Ramblers may adorn a tree's foliage with their blooms or transform a dead tree into a spectacular feature.

The soft colors of old roses are particularly attractive when planted with subshrubs that combine gray-green leaves with blue flowers, such as the free flowering *Caryopteris* x *clandonensis*, the ethereal *Perovskia atriplicifolia*, certain *Hebe* cultivars, and most lavenders.

INFORMAL STYLE
Large roses, including 'Penelope' *in the foreground, clothe the background walls with a fragrant mass of summer color. They provide a magnificent foil for the tall spikes of plants such as* Campanula *and delphiniums and the low mounds of the other perennial plants in an informal mixed border of cool blues and whites.*

Underplanting a rosebed

The display in a rosebed may be enhanced and extended beyond the rose flowering season by growing low, shallow-rooted plants between the roses. A wide range of plants may cover the ground and provide the roses with a background of contrasting color, texture, and form. Violets (*Viola*) are a favorite choice: the white, soft blue, and mauve cultivars complement roses well. All such ground cover plants make mulching difficult, however. Take care not to step on the ground cover planting when spraying the roses in a particularly wide bed.

When planting between roses, take account of the eventual heights of the various companion plants, and place them so that they will not obscure each other or the roses when they are mature.

The yellow green of *Alchemilla mollis*, pink and white heads of *Armeria maritima*, and spreading, hardy *Geranium* species also make a fine display under roses.

Use spring bulbs to brighten up bare rosebeds early in the year: try planting blue or white *Chionodoxa*, daffodils, snowdrops (*Galanthus*), and white, starry *Tulipa turkestanica* to create a bright patchwork of color. Their only drawback is their dying foliage, which looks messy until it is removed and may make it difficult to maintain the bed.

A number of fragrant herbs are good companion plants for roses: use lavender cotton (*Santolina chamaecyparissus*), various thymes (*Thymus*), or sages (*Salvia*) – either the culinary kind or any that have attractive, variegated leaves. Roses always look well when they are contrasted with the silver foliage of perennial plants such as the fern-leaved *Artemisia* 'Powis Castle' and *A. frigida*, or the gray, woolly-leaved, mat-forming *Stachys byzantina* (syn. *S. lanata*).

FLOWERS AND FOLIAGE
Richly colored rose blooms are set like jewels against the elegant gray-green foliage of underplanted herbs and the golden tones of gravel.

Terraces

On a steep hillside, terraces may be used to transform a difficult site into a striking showcase for roses. They provide areas sufficiently level for planting and retain moisture, which the roses need, while creating eye-catching gradations of height and perspective. The terrace walls look best if made of weathered brick or mellow stone. Bush roses may be grown in the terrace beds, and ramblers or ground cover roses may be planted to tumble over the retaining walls, creating curtains of bloom.

Smaller terraced beds are ideal for growing miniature roses. It is much easier to savor the beauty and scent of their tiny, individual flowers if they are raised some way above ground level. Each bed for miniature roses should be approximately 1½–2ft (45–60cm) wide. Place miniature standards along the top bed of the terrace to draw the eye, and use some of the smaller and more dainty ground cover roses to tumble over the walls.

Terraced beds are not a good idea in areas where winter temperatures may drop to -20°F (-30°C). This would kill many roses.

Specimen planting

A rose planted on its own makes a handsome specimen plant, perhaps in a lawn or to mark a focal point in a garden, as long as it is an outstanding rose of its type; any defects in a specimen are immediately obvious.

SINGULAR SPLENDOR
A standard rose, 'Little White Pet', *provides a handsome focal point.*

Used in this way, weeping standard roses can be especially striking. These are formed by grafting rambler cultivars onto a 5ft or 6ft (1.5m or 2m) stem, so that their long, flexible shoots, laden with blossoms in summer, hang down all around, right to the ground. They usually flower for a limited period, unless a standard grafted from a remontant ground cover rose is chosen.

Climbing roses grown as standards may provide a profusion of blooms throughout the entire summer, but their stiff growth does not produce the same dramatic waterfall effect as weeping standards.

Many of the larger shrub roses are natural choices for planting as specimens in larger gardens. 'Nevada', for example, which can reach 6 x 6ft (2 x 2m) or even more, is smothered with large, cream blooms in early summer, and again in late summer. Other roses, particularly most species roses and many of their hybrids, such as 'Frühlingsgold', have no second blooming.

For a small garden where space for flowering plants is limited, use remontant roses such as the strongly scented 'Frau Dagmar Hartopp'. Smaller shrub roses, such as 'Sally Holmes' with large, white flowers clustered above the foliage, and 'Chinatown' which has masses of gold blooms tinged with pink, are not quite large enough to justify being planted on their own, but are very handsome if planted in specimen groups of three.

SUMMER RETREAT
A mature rambler rose in full, glorious bloom transforms this trelliswork arbor into an eye-catching feature that is at once intimate and airy. The floral canopy fills the air within the arbor with its delicious perfume and provides a cool, leafy shelter from which to enjoy the views of the surrounding garden.

Walls, arbors, and pergolas

Most ramblers and climbing roses are very vigorous and produce exuberant bloom from summer until the first frosts. They may drape structures such as arbors, walls, and fences; disguise unsightly features; or give height to the summer display in the garden. Be sure to choose a rose with an eventual height that will cover the intended area well without outgrowing it.

Ramblers and climbing roses may be trained on a range of plastic-coated metal bowers, tunnels, arches, and tripod pillars now on the market. Although metal supports may not look so attractive initially as ones made from rustic poles, they have a much longer life and are soon concealed once the roses trained on them become well established. Rustic arches, even if treated, eventually rot at soil level.

Other climbing plants, such as clematis or honeysuckle, may be planted to grow through the rose, to complement the rose blooms as well as to extend the flowering season; climbers with blue flowers are particularly suitable. Some of the more vigorous shrub roses, particularly Bourbons, also make excellent short climbers for a pillar or small wall.

AN ORNAMENTAL ARCH
The old-fashioned, rich pink flowers of Rosa 'Bantry Bay' *festoon this rustic arch to form an enticing and decorative frame to the view beyond.*

Ramblers

Ramblers have more flexible shoots than climbers and are easier to train along complex structures such as pergolas, arches, and trellises to form a great mass of flowering shoots. When grown against walls, however, they may become mildewed as a result of the poor air circulation.

To cover a long pergola, use one of the vigorous, small-flowered, white ramblers such as 'Trier' or 'Seagull', but remember that they can grow to 30ft (10m) or more and will, therefore, overwhelm a small structure.

For a picturesque effect, try training roses along chains or ropes that are suspended between uprights to create great swags of bloom.

Climbers

The stiffer shoots of climbing roses are less easy to prune than those of ramblers but still may grace walls and fences. Many of the less robust modern climbers may be grown on pillars or as free-standing shrubs with great results. 'Dr. J.H. Nicolas' is pleasantly scented but is too stiff and upright in habit for an arch, although it would suit the pillar supports of a tall pergola.

The Bourbon rose 'Zéphirine Drouhin', which has medium pink flowers, is an old favorite for growing on arches, trellises, and pergolas because it is one of the few climbers that is both thornless and fragrant. It is, however, prone to mildew.

Rose hedges and screens

Roses may, if carefully chosen, provide some of the most colorful and attractive plants for an informal hedge or screen. A few, such as *R. rugosa* and its hybrids, may be shaped to some extent by gentle clipping in winter to make dense hedges while maintaining the natural outline of the shrub. No rose is fully evergreen – few provide a screen that gives privacy all year, although the thorns make the hedge virtually impenetrable. For further details, see HEDGES AND SCREENS, pp.58–60.

The Hybrid Musk roses, such as the apricot 'Buff Beauty', grow into a thick, thorny screen up to 6ft (2m) in height covered in fragrant flowers all summer long – if their natural unpredictability of growth is curbed by training on horizontal wires or

FALL TINTS
The brilliant scarlet hips of this species rose contrast vividly with its yellowing foliage.

Decorative Hedging
Rosa gallica 'Versicolor' *(often more commonly known as* 'Rosa Mundi'*) is one of the oldest roses available and has unusually striped petals. It forms an attractive informal hedge that bursts into a riot of bloom to create an enchanting ribbon of color. Here, the line of the rose hedge provides a pleasing contrast of height and perspective with the tall spikes of mulleins* (Verbascum). *The deep pink flowers in the rose hedge show reversion to its parent,* R. gallica *var.* officinalis.

chain link fencing. If a rose hedge is intended to line a path, use upright cultivars for this purpose, since those of unpredictable growth may impede the pathway.

For a small garden, a hedge of taller Floribunda roses is preferable. These are generally upright plants with little spread and, if planted in two staggered rows (see *Planting Distances for a Rose Hedge*, p.121), cultivars such as the apricot-yellow 'Apricot Nectar' rapidly form a pretty screen about 4ft (1.2m) tall. Some shorter-growing old garden roses, such as *Rosa gallica* 'Versicolor' ('Rosa Mundi'), have attractive foliage and form hedges of similar height, but they flower only once. Their natural vulnerability to mildew is, however, increased by close planting.

A delightful way of dividing one part of a garden from another is to train climbing roses or ramblers on decorative screens formed by constructing open, wooden frameworks of the desired height. Ready-made wooden trellises are available, but make sure that they are sturdy, since they must support a considerable weight and last for years.

Ground cover roses

Some low-growing roses readily spread along the ground to form a dense and floriferous carpet. These may be used to continue the theme of a rosebed, or as a prettily sprawling edging to a cottage border. They may also disguise an unsightly feature such as a utility meter, or scramble down a steep bank that would otherwise be difficult to plant.

Some more recently introduced cultivars, such as 'Red Bells', cover the soil very well although, at 3–4ft (1–1.2m), they grow too tall for true ground cover and are not remontant. Others suitable for a small space are 'Rosy Cushion', 'Ralph's Creeper', or 'Red Cascade'.

Ramblers such as 'Grouse' and 'Pheasant', which both have small, pink flowers and glossy foliage, make marvelous ground cover roses, but their vigor makes them unsuitable for a small garden. They grow naturally along the ground, rooting as they go and covering the soil very closely, but need strict control to stop them from spreading too far.

If you have a sunken rose garden with fairly low walls, roses such as 'Nozomi' or 'Raubritter' are suitable for planting along the top, since they have the right kind of low, spreading growth to form waterfalls of flowers over the walls.

Some cultivars sold as ground covers are simply low-growing but fairly wide-spreading bushes. They are seldom dense enough in growth to be very efficient weed-smotherers, and in winter they shed their leaves, thus allowing in air and light, which enable weeds to germinate.

A Carpet of Bloom
This ground cover rose, 'Max Graf', *attractively masks an expanse of bare soil with a delightful profusion of dainty flowers.*

A Movable Feast
The exquisite, pale pink flowers of the miniature rose 'Judy Fischer' *are elegantly offset by the simple shape of the terracotta container, here placed on a low wall at the edge of a terrace.*

Roses in containers

Roses are invaluable for their summer color and fragrance in patio gardens where the surface is mostly paved and there are few or no beds. Containers of many sorts are suitable as long as they are in a position that receives sun for at least half a day. Choose modern cultivars that are bushy and compact, since leggy roses with bare basal stems look unsightly. If grouping a number of roses in a container, make sure it is large enough for the roses to be spaced out to allow for future growth.

Even quite vigorous climbers may, given the support of a wall, be grown in tubs or half barrels. They should be planted and trained as other climbing roses but since the nutrients in the containers will be quickly exhausted (and the roses difficult to repot), they will require regular feeding.

Miniature roses are ideal plants to use in containers, whether on their own or with other plants. Try cultivars such as 'Baby Masquerade' (whose abundant blooms change from yellow to pink and finally to rose-red), the brilliant orange 'New Beginning', or Patio roses such as the pointed, white 'Stardance'. They look especially good in a planting trough built into a low wall bordering one or two sides of a patio or terrace. Even an old washtub may be used to display miniature roses as long as it is at least 8–10in (20–25cm) deep to allow sufficient space for the root growth of the roses.

Roses grown in containers do not have to be confined to a patio garden. They may bring color to other paved areas, such as the center of an herb garden, the area around a pool, or along a broad walkway.

Soil preparation and planting

GROWING roses in the garden is not difficult if their basic needs are satisfied. They are relatively long-lived flowering plants, so it is worth investing time and effort in choosing a suitable site, properly preparing the soil, selecting cultivars appropriate to the conditions, and planting the roses correctly.

Site and exposure

All roses need a site that is open to the sun and sheltered from strong winds, with good air circulation and a fertile soil. They do not thrive in deep shade, under trees, if crowded by deep-rooted plants, or in "rose-sick" (see below) or waterlogged soil. Most sites may be improved to meet these needs, for example by erecting windbreaks or by draining heavy, wet soils (see SOILS AND FERTILIZERS, "Improving drainage," p.531). Planting roses in an appropriate soil mix in raised beds or containers may solve the problem of unsuitable soil.

Evaluate the planting site carefully before choosing a cultivar: the enormous variety among roses provides plants that tolerate a range of conditions. Most modern roses do not flourish in alkaline soil, but almost all the old garden roses grow well in it if given large quantities of organic material when being planted and mulched. *Rosa rugosa* and *R. pimpinellifolia* groups do well on sandy soil. These are generalizations since even among modern roses there may be great differences between cultivars: for example, on poor soils 'Gold Medal' and 'Maid of Honor' suffer, but 'Elina', 'Crimson Glory', and others thrive if given extra food and moisture. Certain rootstocks may help in some circumstances: for example, *R. multiflora* tolerates and often grows well in heavy, cold soils.

Soil quality

Roses grow in most types of soil but prefer slightly acid conditions, about pH 6.5. If in doubt, use a commercial soil-testing kit to gauge the acidity of the soil. A water-retentive yet well-drained soil is ideal. Always clear weeds when preparing the soil so the young roses will not have to compete with them for light, moisture, and nutrients.

Improving the soil

The drainage of clay soils, the water-retentiveness of light, sandy soils, and the pH level of alkaline soils may be improved by incorporating plenty of organic matter. Excavate very shallow topsoil to about 24in (60cm) when planting, and replace some of the subsoil with extra organic matter. For further information on how to influence the acidity of the soil, and on general soil preparation, see "Soil cultivation," pp.526–9. If possible, prepare the soil approximately three months before planting to allow it to settle.

Rose-sick soil

New roses do not thrive if planted in a rosebed where roses have been grown for several years, because they will almost always succumb to "rose sickness," indicated by reduced vigor. It seems that the fine feeding roots of new roses are more prone to attack than are the older, tougher roots of roses that are already growing in the bed.

If replacing only one or two roses in an established bed, dig a hole at least 18in (45cm) deep by 24in (60cm) across and exchange the soil with some from a part of the garden where roses have not grown for several years. Since this is a daunting task for an entire rosebed, either locate the bed on a different site, or have the soil chemically sterilized by a qualified contractor.

Choosing roses

Where and how you buy roses will depend to some extent on the particular cultivars that you wish to buy. Many old roses are obtainable only from specialist nurseries by mail order if they are not situated locally. Bear in mind that catalog photographs may not always accurately represent the flower color, nor is it possible to assess the quality of the plant before it arrives, although with a reputable nursery this should not be a problem. Beware of special "bargains," often advertised in the press, that offer bedding or shrub roses cheaply, since the plants may be of poor quality.

Nurseries in North America use a variety of rose species as rootstocks, depending on the climate of the region where the mature plants will be grown. Rootstocks may be purchased by gardeners wishing to bud their own roses (see also "Hybridizing," p.132).

Bare-root roses

Mail-order suppliers, stores, and supermarkets sell roses bare-root; local retailers usually sell them in sleeves or boxes filled with peat. The roses are in a semidormant or dormant state and their roots are essentially clean of soil. Provided that they have not dried out in transit and are planted as soon as possible after arrival, they should establish quite satisfactorily.

When buying a bare-root rose in a store, examine it carefully. If the environment in which the rose has been kept is too warm, the rose either dries out or starts growing prematurely, producing blanched, thin shoots that usually die after planting. Do not purchase any roses that display such symptoms.

Container-grown roses

Roses grown in containers may be planted at any time, except during periods of prolonged drought or when the ground is frozen. Many garden centers and suppliers trim the roots of unsold bare-root roses and pot them into containers for convenience of sale, so before buying a rose in a container, check that it has not been recently potted up – hold the plant by its main shoot and gently shake it. If the rose is not firmly rooted and moves about in the soil mix, it probably has not been grown in its container.

Suppliers whose priority is quick, convenient production tend to select roses that fit into standard-sized containers rather than picking the largest and best plants. These roses may be acceptable provided that they are in general good health and

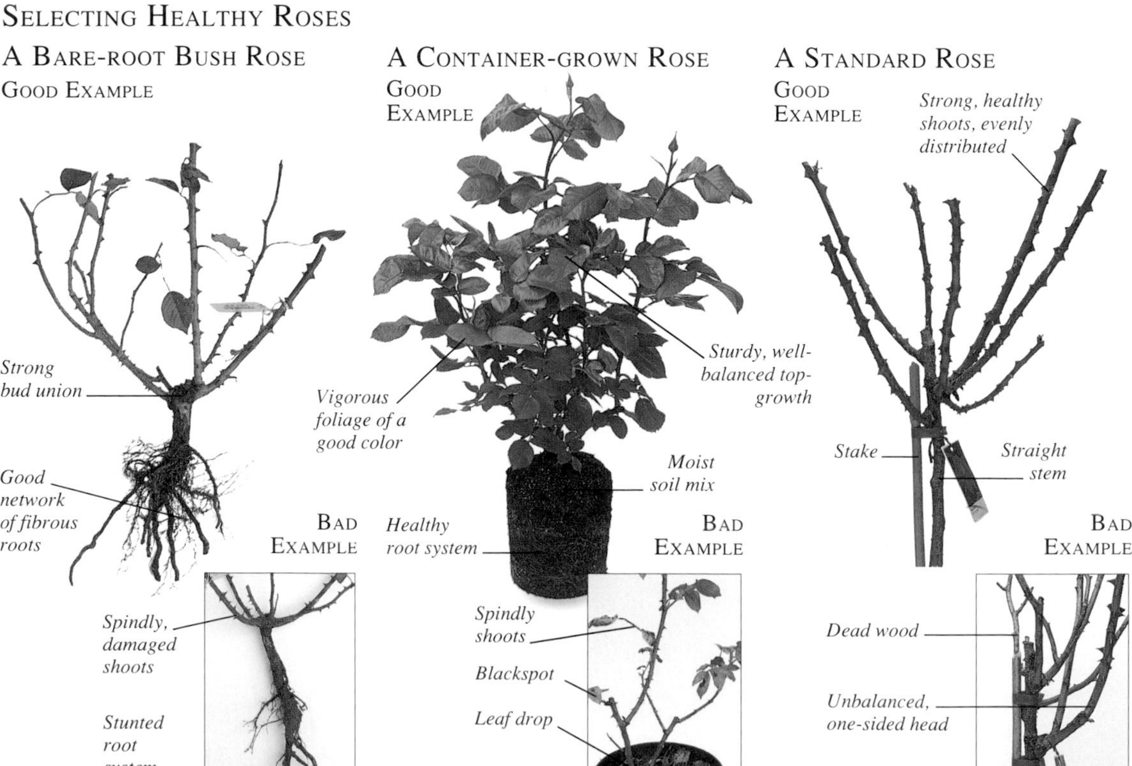

PLANTING DISTANCES FOR A ROSE HEDGE

TALL SHRUB ROSES
Plant the roses in a line 3–4ft (1–1.2m) apart, so that when mature, the branches intermingle to form an effective screen.

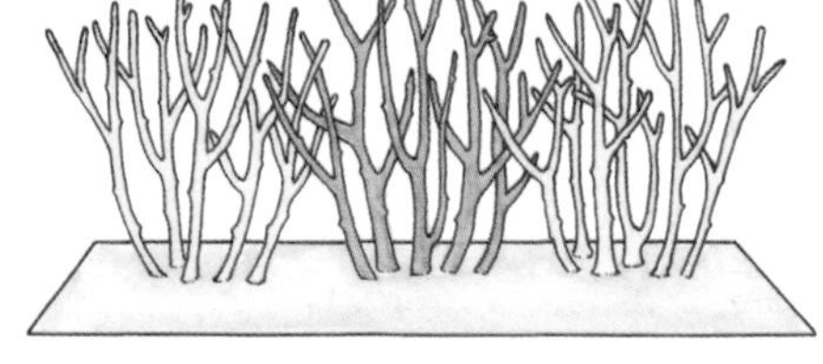

MODERN BUSH ROSES
For a denser hedge, plant roses in a staggered formation in 2 rows that are 18–24in (45–60cm) apart.

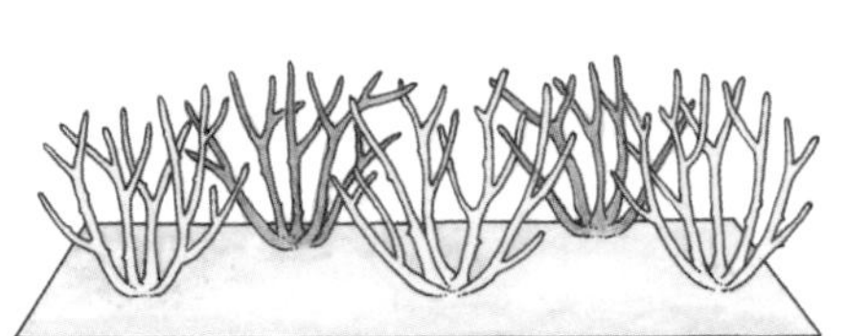

do not have spindly, weak growth. Treat them as bare-root roses where storage and planting are concerned. If any roots are growing through the drainage holes in the container, knock the plant out of its pot and check that its roots are not thickly coiled around the root ball – a sign that the rose is potbound and has been in the container for too long.

Selecting a healthy rose
Whether bare-root or container-grown, the plant should have at least two or three strong, firm shoots and a healthy network of roots in good proportion to the top-growth. Any foliage on container-grown roses should be vigorous. If buying a climbing rose, check that the shoots are healthy and at least 12in (30cm) long. Choose a standard rose with a balanced head since it is likely to be viewed from all sides; a straight stem is best, although a slightly crooked stem is acceptable.

Preparing to plant

Following a few simple principles at the planting stage, such as observing correct planting distances and depths, handling the roots carefully, and providing proper support where necessary, avoids problems with routine care later on. Delay planting for a few days if the ground is frozen, too wet, or too dry for roots to adjust easily to the soil.

When to plant bare-root roses
Bare-root roses are best planted just before or at the beginning of their dormant period, in fall or early winter, to lessen the shock of transplanting. Early spring may be better in areas that have bad winters. Plant the roses as soon as possible after purchase. If there is any delay, perhaps because of unsuitable weather, it is best to heel them into a spare piece of ground, with the roots buried in a shallow trench (see ORNAMENTAL TREES, *Heeling In*, p.41). Alternatively, store the roses in a cool and frost-free place, and keep the roots moist.

When to plant container-grown roses
These may be planted at any time of the year in suitable weather conditions. Container-grown roses, unlike bare-root roses, may be left outdoors in their containers for three weeks or more while awaiting planting, as long as they are kept properly watered. Even though they are frost hardy, do not risk exposing them to prolonged cold since the roots in the containers may suffer some damage in very cold conditions.

Spacing bedding roses
The growth habit determines the planting distances between bedding roses. Close planting makes mulching, spraying, and pruning more difficult and may create stagnant air conditions, which allow rapid spread of mildew and blackspot. A narrow, upright cultivar needs less space for healthy growth than a lax, sprawling one and so tolerates closer planting. Plant the bushes 18–24in (45–60cm) apart and about 12in (30cm) from the edge of the rosebed.

If underplanting modern roses or very large species roses, allow more space, about 2½–4ft (75–120cm), depending on their ultimate size and growth habit. Space miniature roses roughly 12in (30cm) apart.

Spacing roses for a hedge
The size and growth habit of the chosen cultivar govern the position of roses in forming a hedge. To gain uniformly dense growth, plant tall shrub roses such as 'Penelope' and 'Golden Wings', which reach 4ft (1.2m) or more across, in a single line, and modern bush roses such as 'Tropicana' in two rows in a staggered formation.

Planting a bush rose

The first stage in planting a rose is to prepare the plant. If the roots of a bare-root rose look dry, soak the plant in a bucket of water for an hour or two until thoroughly moist. Place a container-grown rose in a bucket of water until the soil mix surface appears moist. If the root ball is wrapped in plastic or burlap, cut away the wrapping carefully. Remove any loose soil mix, gently tease out the roots, and prune any damaged or diseased parts.

Make a planting hole that is wide enough to accommodate the roots or root ball, and deep enough so that, when planted, the bud union is about 1in (2.5cm) below ground level or ½in (1cm) for budded miniatures. Position the bud union just above the soil surface in Zones 8–10. The bud union is easily recognizable as a bulge at the base of the shoots.

Position the rose in the center of the hole and check that the planting depth is correct. If the roots of a bare-root rose all point in one direction, place the rose close to one side of the hole and fan the roots out. Water and backfill the hole in stages, shaking the rose a little to allow the soil to settle around the roots. Do not compact the wet soil around the rose, especially if the soil is heavy.

Carefully mound soil over the crown of a newly planted bare-root bush to protect the new shoots while the roots become established. The mound should then be removed in stages over the course of two to three weeks; use a gentle stream from a hose for a few minutes each day. Retain the mound to protect fall-planted roses during winter.

To lessen stress on a newly planted container-grown rose, remove flowers and larger buds or spray with an antidesiccant.

HOW TO PLANT A BARE-ROOT BUSH ROSE

1 *Remove diseased or damaged growth, crossing shoots, and thin or straggly stems; trim thick roots by one-third. Dig a hole and fork in compost mixed with bone meal or balanced fertilizer.*

2 *Center the rose in the hole and spread out the roots evenly. Lay a stake across the hole to check that the bud union will be at the correct depth for the type of rose and your climate zone.*

3 *In 2 or 3 stages, water the hole and backfill with soil after the water has drained out. Do not tread on the backfilled soil to avoid compacting the soil and breaking the roots.*

4 *Loosely mound the rose with soil to protect it from the sun, cold, and wind. If spring-planted, gradually remove the soil mound; retain the mound if planted in fall.*

How to Plant a Climbing Rose

1 Place the rose in the planting hole, leaning it toward the wall at an angle of about 45° so that the shoots reach the lowest support wire. Place a stake across the hole to check the planting depth.

2 Use stakes to guide the shorter shoots toward the wires. Tie all the shoots to the stakes or wires with plastic straps (see inset).

Planting a climbing rose or a rambler

Train climbers grown against a wall or fence along horizontal wires that are about 18in (45cm) apart and held in place by tapered vine eyes or strong nails driven into the surface. If the brickwork or masonry of a wall is very hard, drill holes for the vine eyes with a 3/16in (4.7mm) bit. Keep the wires 3in (7cm) away from the wall to allow air circulation and discourage diseases. A rambler has more flexible stems than a climber and may be trained on a hinged trellis that folds away from the wall so that the wall may be maintained without harming the rose.

The ground next to a wall is likely to be dry, since it is in a rain shadow and the masonry absorbs moisture from the soil. Plant about 18in (45cm) from the wall where the soil is less dry and water from any eaves will not constantly drip on the rose.

Prepare the soil and planting hole, and trim the rose as for bush roses. Position the plant, leaning it toward the wall at 45°, and fan out its roots toward moist ground. If necessary, train the shoots along stakes pushed into the ground, but keep each stake far enough from the roots to avoid damaging them.

After planting as for a bush rose, attach the shoots to the support wires with plastic, string, or burlap ties or with plastic straps designed for tying in roses. Take care not to tighten the straps too much around the rose's stems since room must be left for the shoots to grow. Check the ties frequently and loosen and retie them when necessary.

Prune the main shoots of a climber or a rambler at this stage. For further pruning instructions, see "Climbing roses and ramblers," p. 128. Keep the roots thoroughly watered and uncrowded by other plants to help them establish.

Planting a rambler by a tree
Choose a rose that will not overwhelm the host tree while scrambling up it. Plant it on the windward side of the tree so that the rose's young, flexible shoots blow toward and around it, rather than away from it. Dig a planting hole at least 3ft (1m) away from the trunk to increase the amount of rain that reaches the roots of the rose. Train all the new shoots toward the tree along sloping stakes, tied at their upper ends to the trunk and inserted just behind the rose. If planting in this way on a boundary, bear in mind that the blooms grow toward, and are visible from, the direction of the strongest sunlight.

Planting a standard rose

Some nurseries bud their standard roses onto stocks which have a tendency to sucker, although a few are experimenting with better rootstocks. To keep suckering to a minimum, plant the rose no deeper than the recommended depth for your area (see "Planting a bush rose," p.121). Deeper planting will encourage increased sucker growth.

A standard rose needs a stake, placed on the side of the prevailing wind, to support it. Paint the whole stake with a preservative that is not toxic to plants and allow it to dry. Insert the stake very firmly near the center of the planting hole before positioning the rose to avoid damaging the roots and, as a result, encouraging suckers. Position the rose next to the stake and check that it just reaches the base of the lowest branches; if necessary, adjust the height of the stake. Use a stake or rake handle to make sure that the bud union is at the correct level.

Fill in the soil and water as for a bush rose. Secure the stem to the stake with two ties. These need to incorporate a buffer (such as in a figure-eight tie) to prevent the stake from rubbing the stem. Do not tighten the ties fully until the rose has settled in the soil. They will need to be loosened at least once during the growing season as the diameter of the stem increases.

Planting roses in containers

The container should be at least 12–18in (30–45cm) deep for bush roses or 9–14in (23–35cm) deep for miniatures to allow for root growth. Place a layer of crocks over the drainage holes in the base of the container and fill it with a standard soil-based potting mix. Plant the roses in the same way, and at the correct depth, as bush roses (see p.121). Take care to space them correctly.

How to Plant a Standard Rose

1 Position the stake in the hole so that the rose stem will be in the center. Drive the stake into the ground and check that the top is just below the head of the rose.

2 Place a stake across the hole to check the planting depth. Use the old soil mark on the stem as a guide and plant at the correct depth. Fill in the hole and water.

3 Use a tie (see inset) just below the head of the rose, and another halfway up the stem, to attach the rose to the stake. Cut out weak or crossing shoots.

Routine care

ROSES need regular care to produce healthy, vigorous plants that are resistant to pests and diseases. Attention paid to fertilizing, watering, mulching, and general maintenance will be rewarded with a fine display throughout the season.

Fertilizing

Roses are gross feeders and quickly exhaust even a well-prepared rosebed that is rich in nutrients. Many essential mineral salts rapidly leach out in the rain, especially from light soils. If the roses are to flourish, they require regular feeds in a balanced formulation of essential nutrients (nitrogen, phosphorus, and potassium) and trace elements. Many suitable commercial rose fertilizers are available, mostly in powder or granular form. For information on how to deal with particular nutrient deficiencies, see PLANT PROBLEMS, pp.547–79.

After pruning in the spring, and when the soil is moist, sprinkle a small handful, 1–2oz (25 50g), of fertilizer around each rose. Hoe or rake it in lightly and evenly, keeping it clear of the stems. Repeat this application about a month after the first bloom flush, before a second crop of bloom develops. Do not apply a general fertilizer later in the year, because this encourages soft growth in fall that may suffer frost damage. A dressing of potassium sulfate, however, applied at a rate of 2oz/sq yd (75g/sq m) in early fall, protects late shoots by helping them to ripen before the first frosts.

Foliar feeding (spraying a liquid feed on the leaves and bypassing the roots) is recommended for producing larger blooms and leaves, especially on exhibition roses. It may also help in a prolonged drought or on alkaline soils: in both instances, roses may have difficulty in taking in nourishment through the roots.

Fertilizing roses in containers
Roses in containers soon use up the soil mix nutrients. Compensate for this loss by top-dressing annually with a balanced fertilizer and foliar feeding every week or two in the growing season to maintain vigor.

Suckers and how to deal with them

Suckers are shoots that grow below the bud union, directly from the rootstock onto which a cultivar has been grafted. They are usually narrower and a much lighter green than those of the cultivar, often with thorns of a different shape or color, and the leaves may have seven or more leaflets.

Remove any suckering shoots as soon as they appear. This prevents the rootstock from wasting energy on the sucker's growth at the expense of the cultivar. Some rootstocks produce suckers more readily than others, especially if they have been planted at the wrong depth. Damage to the roots, caused by severe cold or any accidental nicks from hoes, other implements, or a stake, may also stimulate the production of suckers.

Pull the sucker to detach it from the rootstock: this removes any dormant buds that may be present at the point where it joins the roots. Do not cut it since this is the equivalent of pruning it and only encourages more vigorous growth. It may, however, sometimes be necessary to cut a sucker if it originates from beneath the rose and if pulling it off would mean damaging or lifting the rose.

Shoots on the stem of a standard rose are also suckers, since the stem is part of the rootstock. As with other grafted roses, any suckers will look different from the cultivar. Snap them off or pare them cleanly from the stem with a sharp knife.

REMOVING A SUCKER FROM A STANDARD ROSE
Pull away any suckers growing from the rose stem (see inset), taking care not to rip the bark.

REMOVING A SUCKER FROM A BUSH ROSE

1 *With a trowel, carefully scrape away the soil to expose the top of the rootstock. Check that the suspect shoot arises from below the bud union.*

2 *Using a glove to protect your hand, pull the sucker away from the rootstock. Refill the hole and gently firm the soil.*

HOW A SUCKER GROWS

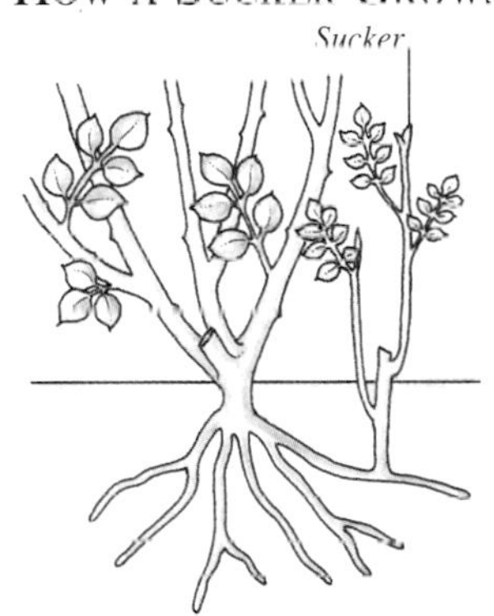

The sucker (right) grows directly from the rootstock. If cut back only at ground level it will shoot again and divert further energy from the rose.

Watering

Roses need plenty of water for healthy growth, especially if they are newly planted. Watering too little and too often can be counterproductive because it encourages the roots to grow toward the surface. Give the roses enough water to soak the soil thoroughly around their roots instead. Try not to wet the foliage because this spreads some diseases.

Roses are deep-rooted plants and can flourish even in long, dry summers and near-drought conditions, particularly if they are well established. In such conditions, the flowers may be smaller than usual and may open very quickly. The petals may also be vulnerable to scorching by the sun. In hot, dry climates, do not water roses in strong light because the blooms may spoil. Water roses in containers every other day, or even daily if the weather is exceptionally hot and dry.

Eradicating weeds

To avoid damaging the roots of roses when weeding around them, do not disturb the soil too deeply. Control annual weeds by hand or with light use of a hoe. Use weedkillers carefully because they may severely damage roses. Mulching roses (see right) or underplanting them with shallow-rooted ground covers also suppresses weeds.

Hygiene

The uncollected fallen leaves, prunings, and any other debris from infected plants can spread diseases among roses. Gather up and destroy such material regularly, if possible by burning it; never put it on a compost heap because any disease organisms present may survive to infect other roses in your garden.

Mulching roses

A 3in (8cm) layer of mulch, if applied in early spring after pruning and feeding, helps to smother any weed seeds and to maintain high moisture levels and even temperatures in the soil. Well-rotted stable manure is an ideal mulch, providing many of the nutrients that roses need, but if this proves difficult to obtain, bark chips or shredded leaves are both satisfactory. For further details, see also SOILS AND FERTILIZERS, "Top-dressings and mulches," p.534.

Deadheading

The purpose of deadheading, that is, removing faded flowers, is to stimulate the earliest possible development of new, young shoots and further blooms throughout the flowering season. Once a rose flower has been pollinated, it starts to fade. If left on the plant, it may delay the production of new shoots below the old flower cluster.

In some roses, a seedpod (hip) forms, and this diverts energy from further flower production; remove the dead flowers regularly unless you desire the hips for ornamental purposes. In late summer, even if some roses continue to bloom, stop deadheading to avoid encouraging new, soft growth which would be damaged by the first frosts.

HOW TO DEADHEAD ROSES

1 *The central bloom of a spray fades first and should be cut out to maintain the display.*

2 *When all the flowers have faded, remove the whole spray by cutting back to an emerging bud or a fully formed shoot.*

HYBRID TEA ROSES
Cut back stems bearing faded flowers to an outward-facing bud (see inset) or fully formed shoot.

Moving roses

A rose may be moved at almost any age, but the older it is the greater is the risk that it may resettle badly. It is not difficult to move roses that are up to three or four years old, but do not risk planting in old rosebeds (see "Rose-sick soil," p.120). The roots of older roses are thick and spread deeply, and also have fewer of the fine feeding roots that are essential for reestablishing the plant.

If circumstances allow, move a rose only when it is dormant and always into a well-prepared bed. First loosen the soil by cutting down on all sides with a spade at least 10in (25cm) out from the root ball. Insert a fork well away from the center of the plant and lift it, taking some soil with it and disturbing the roots as little as possible; on light soils, use a spade since the soil is likely to fall away from the roots. Trim off any coarse roots and wrap the root ball in plastic or burlap to prevent the roots from drying out before transferring the plant to its new position. Water immediately after replanting and regularly until the rose is established.

Blind shoots

These are shoots that develop without a terminal flower bud. They divert the plant's energy in the same way as a sucker (see "Suckers and how to deal with them," p.123) so prune out any as soon as they appear.

Cut the blind shoot by about a half to an outward-facing bud to encourage it to grow away and flower. If no bud is visible, cut back to the main stem.

Fall cutback

Strong winter winds may rock taller roses and loosen their roots, making them vulnerable to cold damage. To help prevent this, shorten any overlong shoots in fall.

Winter protection

In temperate climates, roses need protection in a cold winter. In heavy and poorly drained soils, any accumulated water will later freeze. The expansion of the water as it freezes lifts and breaks the roots, and it may damage the bud union – the most vulnerable part of the rose. Mound soil, brought from another part of the garden, 6–8in (15–20cm) above the bud union. Loosely packed leaves or straw, held in place by a staked ring of chicken wire, gives an added measure of protection.

Roses that are hardy between -4°F and -10°F (-20°C to -23°C) include Centifolias, *Rosa californica*, and *R. wichuraiana*. At colder temperatures, provide protection or choose roses that tolerate extreme cold. Hybrid Teas, Grandifloras, and Floribundas may tolerate temperatures as low as -20°F (-29°C) for a week or so if soil is mounded over the crown. Pack the crowns of standard roses with straw or leaves, loosely tied in place with twine. Grow Alba, Damask, and Gallica roses, and some of the species roses, such as *R. multiflora* and *R. palustris*, in areas where the temperature falls to -22°F (-30°C). A few roses, such as *R. virginiana*, *R. blanda*, *R. canina*, *R. glauca*, and *R. rugosa*, survive cold as severe as -35°F (-37°C). For full instructions on protecting roses during the winter, see COLD AND WIND PROTECTION, pp.520–21.

Pests and diseases

Aphids (p.552), blackspot (see "Fungal leaf spots and blotches," p.554), rose dieback (p.571), powdery mildew (p.552), and rusts (p.554) are common problems. Inspect regularly and control diseases or pests at once. As a general rule, modern roses are more prone to pests and diseases than are species and most old garden roses.

CUTTING BACK IN THE FALL

BEFORE
In mid- to late fall, cut back overly tall Hybrid Tea, Grandiflora, and Floribunda roses (left) to avoid damage from wind-rock.

AFTER
Reduce the entire bush by one-third to a half of its height, cutting all shoots above a bud.

Pruning and training

THE purpose of pruning is to speed up the natural process of new, vigorous, disease-free shoots developing to replace the old, weakened ones, and so produce an attractive shape and the optimum display of blooms. Training a plant on supports stimulates the production of flowering side shoots and directs new growth into the given space. The severity of pruning depends on the rose type; certain principles of pruning, however, apply to all roses.

Basic principles of pruning roses

A pair of sharp, high-quality pruners is essential; loppers and a fine-toothed pruning saw are also useful for removing gnarled, woody stumps and thicker shoots. Wear strong, protective, comfortable gloves for all pruning tasks.

How to prune
Always make a clean, angled cut above a bud that faces in the direction in which the resultant new shoot should develop. This is usually an outward-facing bud, but it may face inward on a lax, sprawling rose if the center of the bush needs filling out. Cut to the appropriate height if a dormant bud is not visible, and cut out any stubs that develop later.

Always remove dead and dying shoots, cutting back to disease-free, usually white pith, even if this means pruning almost to ground level. Remove any crossing growth that might impede the main shoots, or twiggy growth, such as the matchstick-thin twigs that bear only a leaf or two. This concentrates energy in the more vigorous and productive shoots, and allows good air circulation, which helps prevent disease.

Applying wound paint to large cuts after pruning is often recommended for modern hybrids to prevent entry of disease spores or pith-boring insects. However, there is no guarantee that such treatment works. If pruning is properly carried out, the cut develops a natural seal, making wound paint unnecessary.

When to prune
Prune roses when they are dormant or semidormant, between leaf drop in the fall and when the buds are just beginning to break in the spring. Heavily pruning a rose in active growth is sometimes necessary but severely checks growth. Do not prune in cold conditions because the growth bud below the cut may be damaged and the shoot may die back. Following a very severe winter, cut back cold-damaged shoots in spring to a healthy bud; if the winters are always severe, prune roses in spring, immediately after removing any winter protection material. Conversely, in a climate so warm that the roses flower almost continuously, prune them in the cooler months to induce dormancy and give them an artificial period of rest.

MAKING A PRUNING CUT

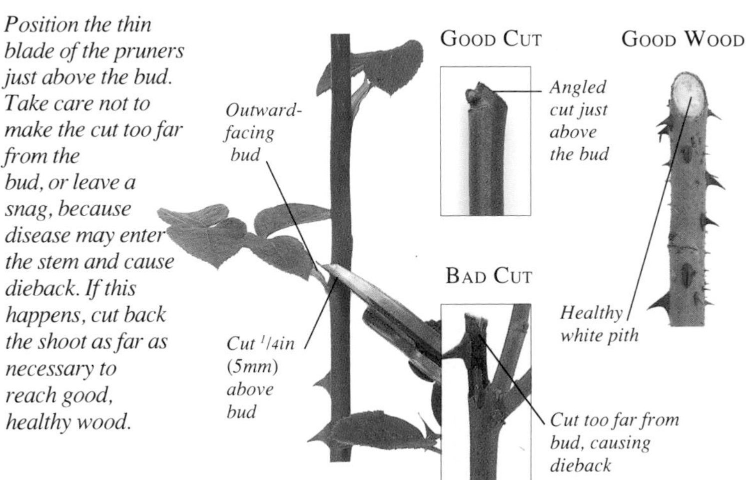

Pruning roses after planting

Almost all newly planted roses should be pruned hard to encourage the development of vigorous shoot and root systems. Fully leafed-out, containerized roses are an exception to this rule – give them only a light pruning to remove any weak, dead, or damaged shoots. Remove any weak, dead, or crossing growth from standard roses. Less severe pruning and regular fertilizing are preferable for roses grown in soils that are deficient in nutrients.

PRUNING A NEWLY PLANTED BUSH ROSE

Prune a newly planted bush rose to about 3in (8cm) above ground level. Cut back to outward-facing buds and remove any cold-damaged growth.

HOW TO PRUNE A HYBRID TEA OR GRANDIFLORA ROSE

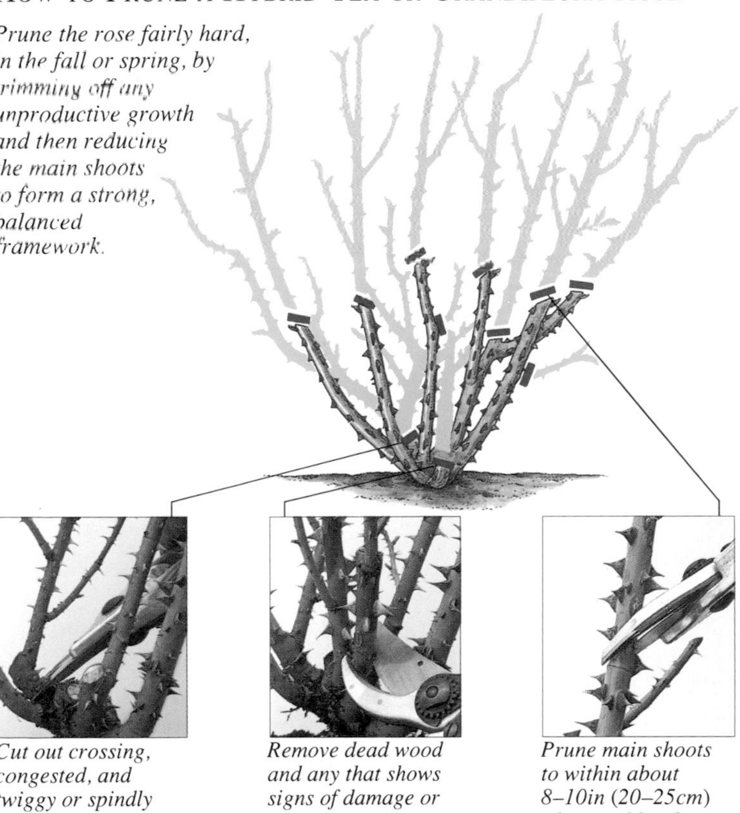

Cut out crossing, congested, and twiggy or spindly growth.

Remove dead wood and any that shows signs of damage or disease.

Prune main shoots to within about 8–10in (20–25cm) of ground level.

Pruning modern garden bush roses

Modern roses flower best on new or the current season's growth, so they are pruned fairly severely to stimulate vigorous new shoots and to produce a good display of blooms.

Hybrid Teas and Grandifloras (Large-flowered bush roses)
Remove completely any dead, diseased, thin, or twiggy shoots. Using long-handled pruners or loppers, cut out stumps from previous years which, although healthy, have not produced any worthwhile new growth in recent years.

Thin out any weak or crossing shoots from the center of the bush to leave a well-balanced framework and allow free air circulation around the plant. It is not as important to produce a balanced framework for closely planted bedding roses as for one that is grown as a specimen which will be seen from all sides.

Depending on the extent of winter kill and on the differences among cultivars, in temperate climates the main shoots should then be pruned back to between 8–10in (20–25cm). In extremely mild areas, the shoots may be cut down less severely, to about 18–24in (45–60cm). To achieve blooms that are of exhibition quality, cut the main shoots back hard to leave only two or three buds.

Floribundas (Cluster-flowered bush roses)

When pruning this type of rose, cut out any unproductive wood as for Hybrid Teas (see p.125). Reduce any side shoots by about one-third on smaller cultivars and by two-thirds on taller-growing cultivars such as 'Fred Loads'. Cut back the main shoots to 12–15in (30–38cm), but reduce the shoots of taller cultivars by about one-third of their length. Do not prune them any harder, unless growing the roses for exhibition, because this reduces the number of blooms that will be produced in the following season.

Patio roses (Dwarf cluster-flowered bush roses)

These are smaller versions of Floribunda roses, and should be pruned in fall or spring following the same principles as above.

Miniature roses

There are two distinct methods of pruning miniature roses. The simpler of the two is to give them only the minimum of attention: remove shoots that have died back, thin out occasionally the shoots of those cultivars that produce a dense tangle of twiggy growth, and shorten any overvigorous shoots that may throw the whole plant out of balance.

The second method is to treat them as if they were miniature Hybrid Teas or Floribundas. Remove all growth except the strongest shoots, and then cut them back by about one-third. This method is used satisfactorily for cultivars introduced from distant areas that do not adapt easily to their new conditions. Such plants benefit from the extra stimulus of a severe pruning and produce strong new growth.

How to Prune a Floribunda Rose

In fall or spring, cut out unproductive growth and prune the side shoots. Reduce the main shoots by a proportion suitable to the eventual height of the cultivar.

Remove crossing or congested wood and twiggy, spindly growth.

Prune out all dead, damaged, or diseased wood to a healthy bud.

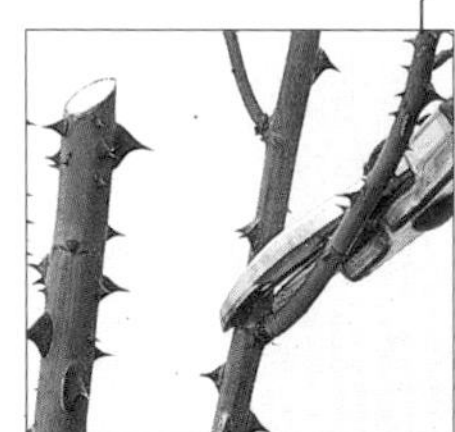

Prune main shoots to 12–15in (30–38cm) from ground level.

Reduce side shoots by one- to two-thirds, cutting to a bud.

Pruning standard roses

The majority of standards are formed from Hybrid Teas or Floribundas or from small shrub roses budded onto a straight, unbranched stem, usually $3^{1}/_{2}$–4ft (1.1–1.2m) high. Prune as for bush or shrub rose equivalents, but cut back the main shoots by about one-third, so that they are all roughly equal in length. It is especially important to achieve a balanced head that will look pleasing from all sides. If the head is unbalanced, prune the shoots on the denser side less hard so that they do not produce as much new growth as those on the thinner side.

Weeping standards

These roses are usually formed from cultivars of small-flowered ramblers grafted onto especially tall standard stems of about 5ft (1.5m). The flexible shoots are pendent and require only limited pruning: remove the old, flowered wood when the blooms have faded, leaving growth from the current season intact.

Pruning shrub and old garden roses

Although these vary enormously in their growth habit, most modern and old garden shrub roses, and all the species roses, flower on wood that is two or more years old. They should be pruned fairly lightly to leave the flowering wood intact. Many flower freely for years without any formal pruning if allowed to develop naturally. It is necessary to cut out only any dead, damaged, diseased, or weak wood to keep the roses really healthy. Despite this, some pruning may help to increase the number and quality of the blooms.

Give a mature remontant shrub rose a light renewal pruning each winter by cutting down some of the older main stems to the base. This encourages the production of vigorous new basal shoots that will flower the following summer. Over a four-year period of renewal pruning, all the shoots are replaced and, with regular fertilizing, the bushes will remain free-flowering and healthy for many years. Treat nonremontant roses similarly, but prune them immediately after flowering.

Rugosa, China, and Hybrid Musk roses may be given a similar annual renewal pruning.

How to Prune a Miniature Rose

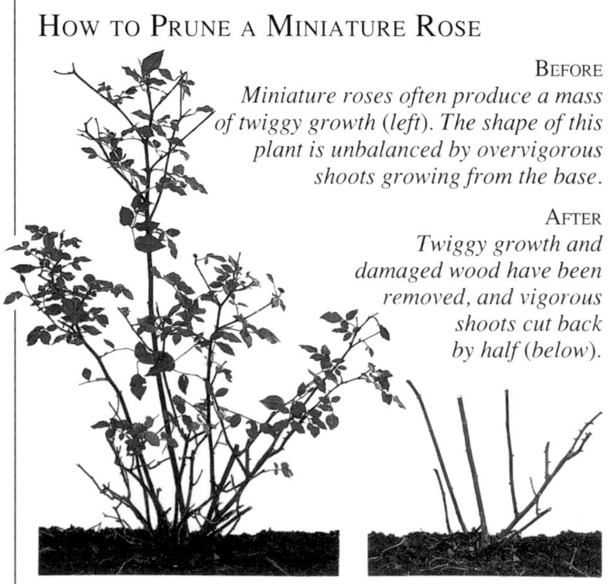

BEFORE
Miniature roses often produce a mass of twiggy growth (left). The shape of this plant is unbalanced by overvigorous shoots growing from the base.

AFTER
Twiggy growth and damaged wood have been removed, and vigorous shoots cut back by half (below).

How to Prune a Standard Rose

BEFORE
In the spring, prune a standard rose to prevent the plant from becoming too top-heavy and to retain an evenly shaped, floriferous head.

AFTER
All dead and damaged wood and any crossing stems have been removed to leave healthy shoots. The main shoots have been reduced to 8–10in (20–25cm) and the side shoots by about one-third.

PRUNING A GALLICA ROSE

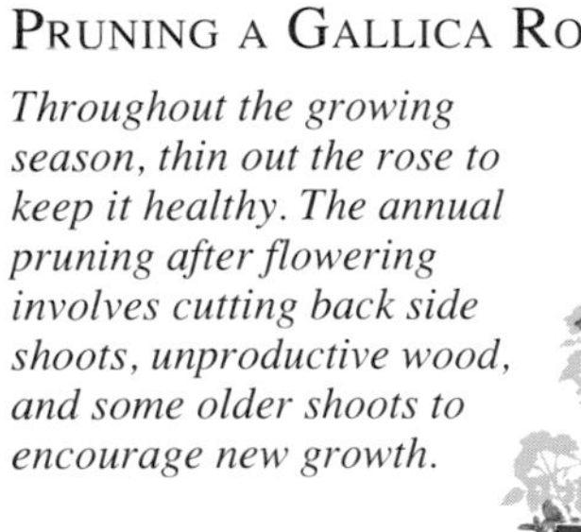

Throughout the growing season, thin out the rose to keep it healthy. The annual pruning after flowering involves cutting back side shoots, unproductive wood, and some older shoots to encourage new growth.

Thin out twiggy growth regularly, and remove spent blooms by cutting back to the main shoot.

On mature roses, cut out up to one-quarter of old main shoots at the base.

Shorten side shoots, but not the main shoots, by about two-thirds. Cut out any dead, diseased, or weak wood.

PRUNING ALBA, CENTIFOLIA, DAMASK, AND MOSS ROSES

Prune after flowering, cutting back both main shoots and side shoots. If necessary, prune again in late summer to remove any overlong shoots that have developed.

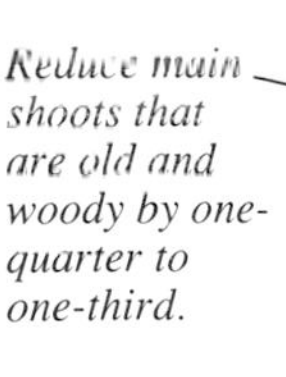

Reduce main shoots that are old and woody by one-quarter to one-third.

LATE SUMMER

Cut back any overlong, whippy shoots by about one-third.

Prune side shoots to about two-thirds of their length.

Gallica roses

Many of these produce a twiggy tangle of shoots that should be regularly thinned out to improve air circulation. After flowering, shorten the side shoots only and remove any dead or diseased wood. Gently clip over Gallica roses used for hedging to maintain a neat shape. Follow their natural outline and do not attempt to shape them into a formal hedge since this would remove many of the side shoots on which flowers are produced in the following year.

Species roses

Much of the charm of these roses lies in their arching shoots which, in the second and subsequent years, carry flowers all along their length, often on short side shoots. Formative pruning is needed to establish a balanced framework of strong, new growth. Thereafter these roses need no further pruning other than the removal of dead and diseased wood, unless they become too dense or produce few flowers, in which case renewal prune them in the same way as nonremontant shrub roses.

Severe pruning encourages strong vegetative growth but produces few, if any, flowers until the second year. If the bush becomes lopsided, reshape it after flowering and trim back all the overlong shoots.

Alba, Centifolia, Damask, and Moss roses

After flowering, reduce both main shoots and side shoots. At the end of the summer, cut back any vigorous, overlong shoots that might whip about in the wind and cause wind-rock damage to the roots.

Bourbon and Hybrid Perpetual roses

These are usually remontant, so prune them, and all hybrids partly derived from *Rosa rugosa*, in early spring as you would Hybrid Teas (see p.125), but much more lightly.

Pruning ground cover roses

The majority are low-growing, spreading, modern shrub roses, so renewal prune them as for shrub roses. Some, mostly related to *Rosa wichuraiana*, creep over the ground, rooting as they go. Prune these only to stop them from spreading beyond the available space.

Prune shoots to well within the intended area of spread, cutting to an upward-facing bud.

Pegging down roses

This technique is an effective, although time-consuming, way of increasing flower production on Bourbon and Hybrid Perpetual roses that tend to send up long, ungainly shoots with flowers only at the tips. Instead of pruning the shoots in late summer or fall, bend them over gently, taking great care not to snap them. Peg the shoots firmly into the ground. Alternatively, tie the tips to pegs in the ground, to wires strung between pegs, or to a low wire frame placed around the plant. Shorten side shoots on the pegged shoots to 4–6in (10–15cm).

This has much the same result as horizontally training the shoots of climbing and rambler roses (see p.128) and produces an arching mound covered with a large number of flowering side shoots in the following season.

Select long, nonflowering shoots and prune the soft tips. Gently bend each shoot over and fasten it to the soil with sturdy wire hoops (see inset).

Climbing roses and ramblers

These roses require minor pruning but regular annual training. Neither climbing roses nor ramblers are self-supporting; if trained incorrectly, they may not flower freely and may become bare at their base. Some bush roses that send out large shoots at awkward angles, such as a few of the Hybrid Musks, may also be trained against walls, fences, or other supports for an attractive display.

HOW TO PRUNE AND TRAIN A CLIMBING ROSE

In the first two years after planting, restrict pruning to cutting out unproductive growth. From the third year, prune in fall after flowering.

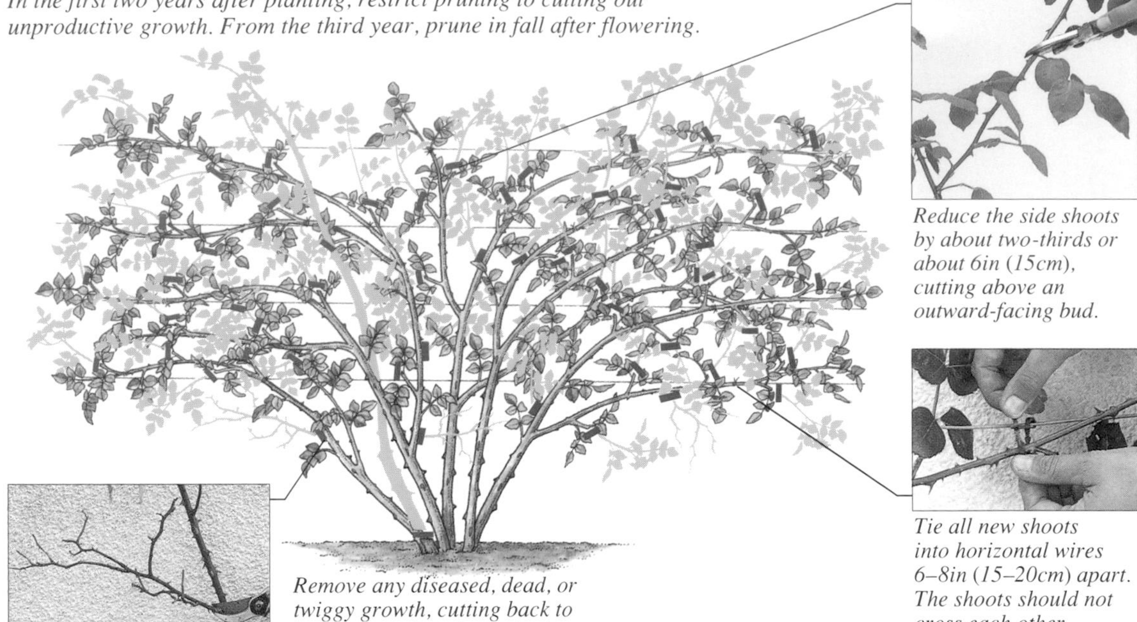

Reduce the side shoots by about two-thirds or about 6in (15cm), cutting above an outward-facing bud.

Tie all new shoots into horizontal wires 6–8in (15–20cm) apart. The shoots should not cross each other.

Remove any diseased, dead, or twiggy growth, cutting back to healthy wood or the main shoot.

Climbing roses

In their first year, and in their second unless they have made exceptional growth, do not prune climbing roses except to remove any dead, diseased, or weak, twiggy growth. Never prune climbing sports of bush roses (roses with the word "climbing" before the cultivar name, for example 'Climbing Shot Silk') in the first two years, since they may revert to the bush form if cut back hard too soon.

Begin training as soon as the new shoots are long enough to reach the supports; train them sideways along horizontal supports to encourage flowering. Where this is not possible, such as on a narrow area between a door and a window, choose a cultivar that is halfway between a tall shrub and a climbing rose. Many of these flower well from the plant base without special training: examples are 'Golden Showers', 'Joseph's Coat', and some of the more vigorous Bourbon roses.

Many climbing roses flower well for years with little pruning, except the removal of dead, diseased, or twiggy growth. Prune them in the fall, after flowering. Leave the strong main shoots unpruned unless they are exceeding their allotted space, in which case shorten them as appropriate. Otherwise simply shorten the side shoots. Train in all the new season's growth to the supports while it is still flexible.

Occasional renewal pruning may be necessary if the base of a climbing rose becomes very bare. Cut back one or two of the older main shoots to within 12in (30cm) or so above ground level to encourage vigorous new shoots to develop and replace the older growths. Repeat this as required in subsequent years.

Rambler roses

Like climbing roses, ramblers flower satisfactorily for a good many years without any routine pruning. However, they produce much more growth from the base than most climbers and, if not carefully trained, grow into a tangle of unmanageable shoots. This results in poor air circulation, which encourages disease, and makes it extremely difficult to spray the plants thoroughly.

Prune ramblers in summer, after they flower. In the first two years, restrict pruning to cutting back all the side shoots by about 3in (7.5cm) to a vigorous shoot; also remove dead or diseased wood. In later years, prune more heavily to maintain the framework. Untie all the shoots from their supports and, if possible, lay them on the ground. Cut no more than one-third of the oldest, spent shoots to ground level, leaving the new shoots and some older, but still vigorous, shoots for tying in to form a well-balanced framework.

Remove any unripe wood from the tips of the main shoots and cut back any side shoots. Cut back any wayward shoots that are outgrowing the available space or spoiling the overall shape of the rose. Train in the shoots, as close to the horizontal as possible, to encourage flowering on new, short side shoots that will develop all along the main shoots.

HOW TO PRUNE AND TRAIN A MATURE RAMBLER ROSE

After the first two years, prune as soon as flowering is over, cutting out any dead, diseased, or weak wood. Then train in the new shoots.

Cut side shoots back to leave between 2 to 4 healthy buds or shoots.

Cut back any old, spent shoots to ground level, using loppers.

Tie all shoots into the wires as close to the horizontal as possible. Secure any loose wires.

Training on arches, pergolas, pillars, and trees

Climbing roses or ramblers may be trained up pillars, arches, or pergolas. Twist the main shoots around the uprights to encourage flowering shoots to form low down. Carefully train the shoots in the direction of their natural growth before they have matured and hardened. This is vital for climbers that have stiff, semirigid shoots. Tie them in using twine or other rose ties; these are easy to undo when pruning or to loosen as the shoots develop. Once the main shoots reach the top of the support, regularly prune them to keep the rose within bounds.

An excess of overlong side shoots may spoil the appearance of a pillar rose, but a little additional pruning soon remedies this. Cut side shoots back to three or four buds or by about 6in (15cm) in the spring.

Propagation

ROSES may be propagated in three main ways: by taking cuttings, budding onto a rootstock, or from seed. Taking cuttings is the easiest method but it involves the longest wait: it takes about three years for the new plant to become established, except for miniature roses. Budding requires rootstocks that have grown on in advance, but usually produces stronger and more vigorous plants. Many species roses (*Rosa glauca*, for example) readily breed true from seed. Cross hybrid roses with other hybrids, or sometimes with species, to produce new cultivars.

Hardwood cuttings

Most roses may be propagated from hardwood cuttings, particularly some cultivars that are related quite closely to wild species, such as rambler roses. Cuttings taken from miniature roses root so easily and develop so quickly that they are propagated this way commercially. Hybrid Teas and others of complex parentage do not root so readily and, consequently, may not be of sufficient size to sell commercially for two or three years, so they are seldom available on their own roots.

One advantage of roses grown from cuttings is that they do not have a different rootstock and so do not produce suckers. The disadvantages include a loss of vigor with some cultivars (although this may be useful with miniatures), and a tendency toward vigorous but nonflowering growth in the first few years, particularly with species.

In many climates, roses from hardwood cuttings are the most reliable, but success in rooting them is variable; it is therefore sensible to take a good number of cuttings to allow for possible failures.

Preparing the cuttings

In early fall, select the material for cuttings from the current season's healthy growth. Trim any old flowerheads from the chosen shoots and put the cuttings into a transparent plastic bag to stop them from drying out. Cut them into 9in (23cm) lengths and remove their leaves. Carefully breaking off the thorns will make the cuttings easier to handle. Moisten the base of each cutting, dip it into hormone rooting powder, and shake off the surplus.

Take shorter lengths of stem for miniature rose cuttings, which need be only 2–4in (5–10cm) long.

Preparing the cutting bed

Choose an open site for the cutting bed, preferably one that is sheltered from the midday sun. Single dig the area required, firm, and rake it to produce an even surface.

Inserting the cuttings

Make a series of deep planting holes with a stake or dibber, and trickle a little coarse sand into the bottom of each one to improve the drainage. Alternatively, dig a narrow, slitlike trench to the same depth and trickle sand along the base. On light, sandy soil, it is sufficient to push a spade vertically into the soil along a center line, working it backward and forward to widen the slit.

Insert the cuttings vertically into the holes or trench, leaving about one-third of their length above ground. They should be inserted far enough apart so that, once rooted, they may be lifted individually without disturbing adjacent cuttings. Firm and water the soil around the cuttings. In any dry spells that follow, water them again; after frost, which may loosen the roots in the ground, refirm the soil.

Another option is to root hardwood cuttings in deep pots of light, sandy soil. Plunge the pots in soil or sand in a shady outdoor site, and water them as needed. Growing miniature rose cuttings in bags or pots in a cold frame or cool greenhouse may be more convenient.

Development of the cuttings

During the fall a callus should develop at the base of each cutting, from which the roots will be produced in spring. Once rooted, the young plants should develop strongly, but if flower buds form during the summer, remove them so that the plants can concentrate their energy on the production of new, strong, vegetative growth. The following fall, provided they are large enough, that is, about 9–12in (23–30cm), transplant the young roses to their permanent positions; if they are not yet large enough, allow them to grow on for another year.

Semiripe cuttings

Semiripe cuttings may be more successful than hardwood cuttings in areas that experience severe winters. In the late summer after flowering, select mature side shoots that are still green. Take 6in (15cm) lengths, cutting above a bud where the shoot is beginning to turn woody, and trim off the soft tips. Prepare cuttings about 4in (10cm) long, following the same procedure as for hardwood cuttings.

Insert them into deep pots of sandy soil mix (equal parts peat and sand). Cover the pots with plastic bags or put them in a propagator to prevent the cuttings from losing moisture. Keep in a cool, frost-free place. In spring, plant out the rooted cuttings in a nursery bed.

HOW TO PROPAGATE ROSES FROM HARDWOOD CUTTINGS

1 *Select a healthy, well-ripened shoot of roughly pencil thickness that has flowered in the summer and is about 12–24in (30–60cm) long. Remove it, cutting at an angle, just above an outward-facing bud. Prepare the cuttings by removing the leaves and soft tips.*

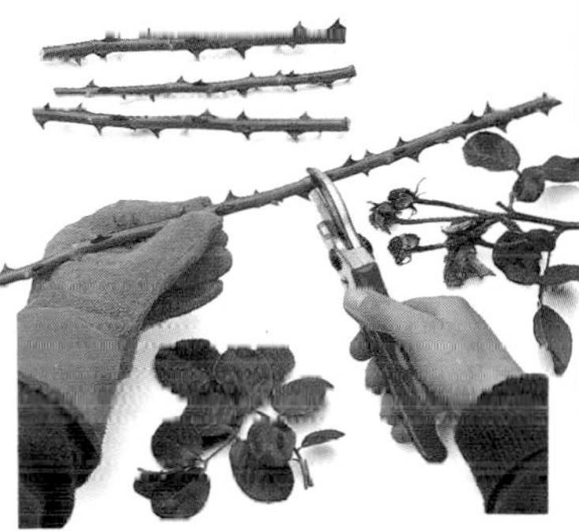

2 *Cut into 9in (23cm) lengths, making an angled cut above each top bud and a straight cut below the bottom bud. Dust the base with hormone rooting powder.*

3 *Make a row of planting holes 6in (15cm) deep and the same distance apart. In heavy soil, put a little coarse sand to a depth of about 1in (2.5cm) in each hole.*

4 *Insert a cutting into each hole: make sure that it reaches the bottom and that about 6in (15cm) of the cutting is buried. Firm the soil, water, and label the cuttings.*

5 *A year later, lift each rooted cutting with a hand fork, taking care not to damage the roots. Plant them in a bed or put them in a cold frame to grow on.*

How to Bud-graft a Rose

1 Select a flowered shoot about 12in (30cm) long, with 3–4 growth buds. Remove it, making an angled cut above an outward-facing bud on the parent plant.

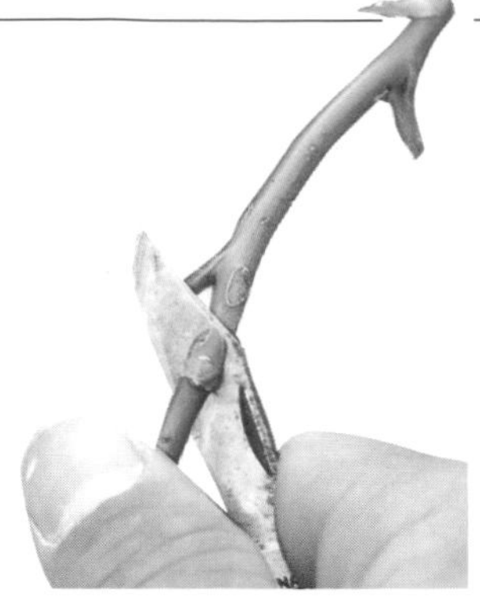

2 Hold the budwood so that the buds point downward. Insert the knife 1/4in (5mm) from a bud. With a scooping action, remove the bud with a 1in (2.5cm) long tail.

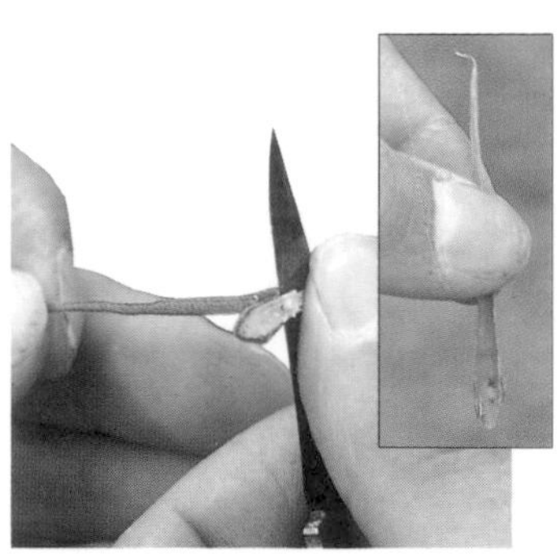

3 Holding the scion by the tail between thumb and forefinger (see inset), carefully remove the coarse, woody material from behind the bud by pulling it away.

4 Use the blunt side of the knife to remove the thorns from the stem of the rootstock, cleaning a section about 1 1/2in (4cm) long.

5 Cutting just deeply enough to pierce the bark, make a T-shaped incision, with the horizontal cut about 1/4in (5mm) long and the vertical cut 3/4in (2cm) long.

6 Insert the tapered end of the budding knife under the flaps of the T, and ease them outward to reveal the inner, white cambium layer.

7 Hold the scion by its tail and insert it behind the bark flaps of the rootstock, sliding it well down so that the bud is held firmly in place, just below the cross-stroke of the T.

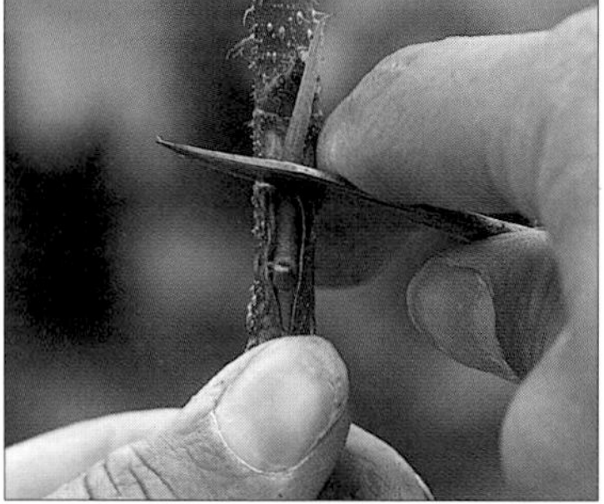

8 Using the knife, carefully trim away the surplus tail protruding above the T, following the line of the horizontal cut. Try to do this without damaging the wood beneath the bark. Discard the tail.

9 Secure a rubber binding tie tightly around the grafted area, pinning it on the side opposite the bud. This binds the stock and scion tightly together.

STANDARD ROSES
Graft 3 buds around the stem (left). Cut back the stock in spring just above the new shoots (right).

BUSH ROSES
If grafting a bush rose, insert only 1 bud (or 2, equally spaced on the stem) onto the rootstock (see inset). In the spring, cut back the rootstock just above the new shoots.

Bud-grafting

The budding process involves uniting plant material taken from two different roses in order to combine the virtues of both. A dormant bud (the scion) from the top-growth of one plant, usually chosen for its display, is inserted under the bark and just above the roots of a rootstock, normally a rose species or a specific clone that is selected for its vigor and hardiness. Different rootstocks may be used to suit the soil conditions or climate or to promote the vigorous growth of the scion.

Choosing a suitable rootstock

Many stocks are used to suit varying conditions: the hardy and vigorous *Rosa multiflora* is widely used as a rootstock, particularly where the winters are cold; it is also suitable for use on poor soils although plants budded onto this stock are not long-lived. *Rosa canina* produces hardy plants and is popular on heavy soils or where winters are severe, but it suckers freely; the crimson climber 'Dr. Huey' (at one time known as 'Shafter' when used as a stock) is more frequently used where the dormancy period is shorter. The selected clone 'Laxa' has now largely replaced most other commercial stocks, since it performs reliably in most soils and climatic conditions, is almost thornless, is easy to use for budding, and rarely produces suckers. Any commercial supplier of rootstocks, or a local nursery, should be able to advise on the best stock to use for local growing conditions.

Stocks may be obtained from roses growing in fields and on roadsides, but their quality is unreliable. It is better to use stocks with more uniform growth characteristics.

Planting the rootstocks

Plant the rootstocks in fall in a nursery bed, about 12in (30cm) apart and with 30in (75cm) between the rows. For bush roses, the scions are inserted at the point where the shoots and roots join (the "neck"), so for ease of budding, plant the rootstocks at an angle of 45°, with the top of the root just at soil level. Mound soil up to the base of the shoots to keep the bark moist and supple at the point where the scion is to be inserted. Standard rootstocks must be grown on to about 6–7ft (2–2.2m), and any buds rubbed off before they develop to create a straight, bare stem.

When to bud-graft

Budding should be carried out from mid- to late summer, preferably in cool, showery weather, when the air is not too dry. If the weather is very dry in the months that precede budding, water the rootstocks regularly and thoroughly. This ensures a free flow of sap that prevents the wood from drying out, so that it is possible to lift the bark from the wood without bruising the wood underneath. Speed is also important to prevent the wood of both bud and rootstock from drying out before they have been grafted together.

A budding knife, with a single, specially formed blade and a sharp, tapered end (see "Garden knives," p.463), may be used, but an ordinary horticultural knife is also suitable. Any knife used for budding must be kept scrupulously clean and sharp.

Selecting the budwood

Prepare scions from well ripened shoots that have well-formed, dormant growth buds in their leaf axils. These shoots are known as the budwood. Cut off the leaves and leaf stalks; alternatively, leave the stalks as handles for inserting the buds later. Place the budwood in a plastic bag to prevent it from drying out before it is used.

Preparing the scion

Hold a piece of budwood upside down and, from just above the base of a bud, use the budding knife to scoop out the bud together with a thin tail. This shieldlike piece of bark, about 1in (2.5cm) long, within which the growth bud is contained, is known as the scion. Remove the small sliver of pith behind the bud; if retained, it will prevent the bud from uniting with the rootstock ("taking"). It is difficult to do this without damaging the bud if the shield has been cut too deeply from the shoot. The base of the bud should then be visible as a small, circular growth.

Preparing the rootstock

For a bush rose, clear the soil from the rootstock neck, take off the thorns, and wipe the neck clean. With the budding knife blade, make a T-shaped cut in the neck, penetrating the bark without cutting into the wood, since this causes damage.

Grafting the bud onto the rootstock

Carefully peel back the cut bark of the rootstock with the blunt side of the knife blade, taking care not to tear the bark or the wood beneath. Gently push the scion into position in the T so that the bud faces upward. Trim off any of the tail that may still be visible and, if necessary, the leaf stalk. Use damp raffia, knotted well clear of the bud, or a special rubber binding tie to hold the bud securely in place and keep the flaps of bark tightly closed to avoid moisture loss. The rubber tie is easily pinned in place and does not inhibit the growth of the bud because it soon rots away. Inserting two scions opposite one another on the rootstock is sometimes recommended to produce balanced shoot growth more rapidly. This is seldom practiced commercially, except on standard roses.

Cutting back the rootstock

If the scion takes successfully, the bud will quickly swell and will then produce a shoot, generally by the following spring. Once the shoot develops, cut off the growth of the rootstock above the scion. If the shoot needs support, stake it; this is not usually necessary, however.

Bud-grafting a standard rose

Budding onto a standard rootstock is performed near the top of the stem at the desired height, usually about $3^1/_2$–4ft (1.1–1.2m); weeping standards are usually budded a little higher, at about 5ft (1.5m). Insert two or three buds around the stem to achieve an evenly balanced head. If using *Rosa canina* rootstocks, insert the buds into equally spaced lateral growths, close to the main stem. It is more usual to place three buds around the main stem of *R. rugosa* stock, staggered vertically.

Layering roses

Any rose which possesses shoots that are long and flexible enough to be bent over and pegged into the ground may be successfully propagated by simple layering.

In late summer after flowering, choose a shoot of healthy, mature wood and trim some of the leaves to create a clear length of stem. Work some compost or peat into the soil where the shoot is to be layered and peg the shoot down into the prepared ground to encourage it to root. The next spring, separate the rooted layer from the parent by cutting the shoot just behind the roots, and plant it out into its destined position to grow on.

Ramblers and climbing roses are ideal for layering, although if they are planted in narrow beds along the base of a wall there may not be a large enough area of exposed soil to peg down the shoots, particularly if other plants are growing around the base of the rose. Many shrub roses, such as Damask, Centifolia, Bourbon, and most Alba and species roses, are suitable for layering because they have a lax growth habit and are likely to have more exposed soil around the base into which the selected shoots may be inserted.

Modern shrub roses such as 'Chinatown', which are in fact very tall growing Floribunda roses, have fairly stiff shoots, so train these shoots horizontally while still young and flexible to prepare for layering. Cultivars of ground cover roses lend themselves to this method of propagation. The shoots of some, such as 'Pheasant' or 'Grouse', root naturally into the soil; simply separate them from the parent and plant them out.

The modern Hybrid Tea and other roses found in the majority of gardens are almost without exception too stiff and upright in their habit of growth for successful layering; they should be increased by grafting or taking cuttings. Only a few cultivars which are lax, wide-spreading growers, such as 'Europeana', are easily increased by layering.

How to Layer Roses

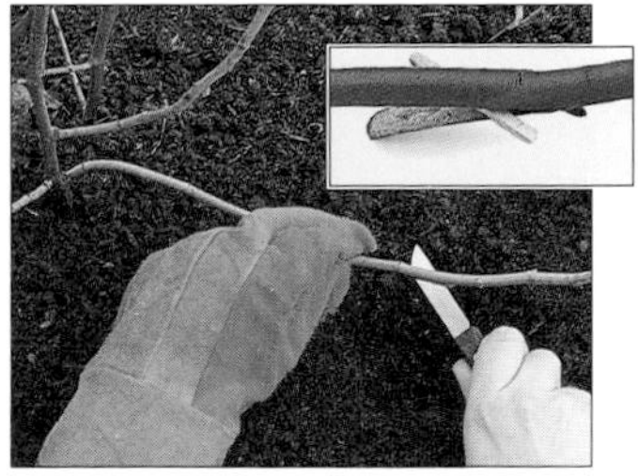

1 *Make a 1in (2.5cm) slit on the lower side of a long, ripe, but flexible shoot. Dust the cut with hormone rooting powder and then wedge it open with a twig or matchstick (see inset).*

2 *Position the shoot in a small depression in prepared soil and peg it down firmly with a wire hoop. Cover it with soil, firm, and tie in the tip of the layered shoot to a short stake.*

Propagation by division

If a rose is growing on its own roots, taking rooted suckers and planting them out is an easy method of propagation. Most roses from nurseries are grafted onto rootstocks, so suckers will be from the stock and not the cultivar budded onto it.

Some species grown from seed, and some roses grown from cuttings, sucker naturally. In the dormant period, detach the rooted suckers or shoots from the parent and plant them out, either in a nursery bed or into permanent positions. Deep planting of budded shrub roses sometimes stimulates the cultivar shoots to produce roots (in effect, a form of layering). Treat such rooted shoots as rooted suckers.

Roses that sucker freely, such as the cultivars of *Rosa pimpinellifolia*, *R. rugosa*, and some Gallica roses, are readily propagated in this way.

Propagating Roses by Division

1 *In late fall or early spring, select a well-developed sucker. Scrape away the soil to expose its base. Sever it from the rootstock, with as many roots as possible.*

2 *Prepare a hole, wide and deep enough for the roots. Plant the sucker immediately and water and firm the soil (see inset). Trim shoots to 9–12in (23–30cm).*

Raising Roses from Seed

1 *Slit open a ripe hip (see inset), taken from the parent plant, with a clean, sharp knife. Take out individual seeds carefully with the back of the knife blade.*

2 *Place the seeds in a plastic bag of moist soil mix or peat and keep it for 2–3 days at room temperature. Then put it in a refrigerator for 3–4 weeks.*

3 *Sow the seeds singly onto the surface of a sandy soil mix (1 part sand:1 part peat). Cover with grit, label, and put in a cold frame or other protected spot.*

4 *When the seedlings have their first pairs of true leaves, prick them out singly into 2in (5cm) pots filled with soil-based potting mix.*

Propagating roses from seed

Species roses, unlike cultivars, are self-fertile and may be raised from seed in the same way as other shrubs. Although seeds are not generally available from commercial sources, it is easy to extract them from mature roses in the garden. Hybrid roses do not breed true to type from seed so they are usually propagated by bud-grafting (see p.130).

Extracting and sowing seed

In the fall, when the rose hips are swollen and ripe, extract the seeds and stratify them before sowing. Stratification, which is the simulation of natural temperature changes to induce the seeds to germinate evenly, is considered necessary for all seed of species roses.

Sow the rose seeds into seed trays, packs, or individual pots, which should be at least 3in (8cm) deep. If using a seed tray, place the seeds on the soil mix about 2in (5cm) apart, and cover them to their own depth with sand or grit. Then leave the tray or pack in a cold frame to protect it from mice and other animals. The seeds may take up to a year to germinate. Prick out the seedlings into individual containers as soon as the first true rose leaves have formed; the first pair, the seed leaves, are oval, unlike typical rose leaves. Care is needed in handling the seedlings since they are very fragile at this stage in their development.

Grow on the young seedlings in the cold frame until they have become established in their pots. Then harden them off by moving them out of the cold frame during the day. Once acclimatized, the seedlings may be kept in the open. Pot them on as necessary until they are large enough to be planted out.

Hybridizing

New rose cultivars are created by hybridizing, a process by which one cultivar or species is cross-pollinated with another and the new seed sown and grown on. The aim is to create a new rose that inherits the best characteristics of both parents.

Selecting the parents

Most roses are of mixed ancestry, so it is impossible to predict the results of hybridization, and the chances of producing a quality cultivar with distinct characteristics are small. Knowledge of the parent roses' genetic characteristics, in particular their chromosomal number and structure, is important in breeding.

The chromosomes are the parts of plant cells that control the inheritance of characteristics through the genes. Roses may have different chromosome numbers, although the total number per cell in each case is always a multiple of seven. Most of the species roses have 14 (diploid), 28 (tetraploid), 42 (hexaploid), or 56 (octoploid) chromosome numbers. When two roses have been cross-pollinated, equivalent chromosomes from the parents arrange themselves in pairs, which then join and count as one in the chromosome number of the new cultivar. Most garden roses are tetraploids, and two tetraploids brought together in this

How to Hybridize Roses

Preparing the Seed Parent

1 *Select an unblemished bloom (here* 'Sun Flare'*) that has not fully unfolded its petals and should therefore not yet have been pollinated.*

2 *Remove the petals, taking off the outer ones first. Work gradually toward the center, taking care not to damage the stigmas as they become exposed.*

3 *Using tweezers or a small pair of scissors, remove the stamens around the stigmas and all fragments of stamens or petals.*

4 *Use a magnifying glass to inspect the rose and make sure that no fragments remain. If left they may decay and allow rot fungi to enter the rose hip.*

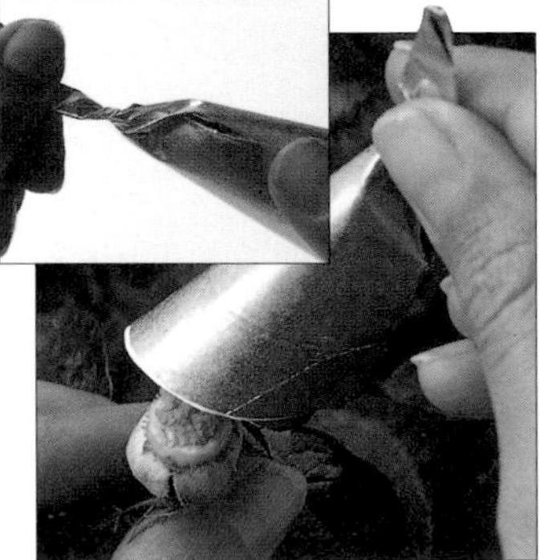

5 *Make a paper cone, twisting its point firmly closed (see inset). Holding back the sepals, cover the flower with the cone, and tie securely around the stem.*

Alternative Step
Place a clean, dry plastic bag over the flower and secure it with a firm tie. The flower is thus protected from pollinating insects.

fusion produce another tetraploid rose. A diploid (14) crossed with a tetraploid (28), however, results in 7 + 14 chromosomes, or a total of 21 (triploid) in the new rose. Since this is not an even number, there are seven chromosomes left without comparable chromosomes with which to pair. Triploids are often sterile and of little or no use in breeding.

Where the chromosome count is known, it is given in the most recent edition of *Modern Roses* (published by the American Rose Society on behalf of the International Registration Authority for Roses). This also details the pedigree of many roses.

Heredity is not the only factor influencing the selection of parent plants. Some hybrid roses make good pollen (male) parents, but poor seed (female) parents, and vice versa. Some are completely infertile and others almost so. In a rose with a very large number of petals, such as a Centifolia, a proportion of these may have taken the place of the stamens, so that little pollen is available for hybridizing. Crossing a nonremontant rose with a remontant one may be a problem if remontancy is one of the desired characteristics, since the first generation from such a cross is always nonremontant. At least one more cross is needed before remontancy reappears in the offspring.

This is a simplification of a very complex subject, and there is a good deal of chance involved in rose breeding. However scientific an approach is taken, the result is still largely unpredictable. As a general principle, choose the healthiest cultivars available as parents, and start with what is perhaps the easiest cross of all, that between two different cultivars of Floribunda roses.

PREPARING THE POLLEN PARENT

6 *Select an unblemished bloom that is not yet fully open (here* 'Elina'*). Cut the stem of the flower at an angle just above a bud.*

7 *Place the chosen flower in water and keep it indoors, free from insects, until it opens fully (usually overnight).*

8 *When the flower is open and the anthers split, revealing the pollen, gently remove all the petals.*

9 *The exposed anthers are now ready to release their tiny pollen grains.*

POLLINATING THE SEED PARENT

10 *Uncover the seed parent and brush the anthers of the pollinator across its stigmas. The pollen grains will adhere to the sticky stigmas of the seed parent.*

11 *Replace the protective cone over the seed parent and tie securely. Label the rose with the names of the seed parent and pollen parent, and allow it to ripen.*

Controlling the growing environment

Except in a frost free climate, use potgrown roses in a greenhouse, since this allows greater control of temperature, humidity, insect pests, and diseases, and gives the hips a better chance of ripening properly. Precise record-keeping is essential: after crosses have been made, carefully identify all the flower stems with a dated label on which is written the names of both parent plants, giving the seed parent first, for example 'Europeana' x 'Showbiz'.

Preparing the seed parent

First select a bloom of the rose you have chosen for the seed parent, at the stage when it is starting to unfold but before insects could have reached the stamens in the center and contaminated them with alien pollen. Carefully remove the petals and the stamens (a process called emasculation), and make sure that no tissue is left that could later lead to rot in the hip. Tie a paper cone or plastic bag over the emasculated flower and leave it for one or two days to allow the stigmas to mature.

Preparing the pollen parent

Cut the flower that is to be the pollen parent, which should be at about the same stage as the seed parent. Stand the pollen parent in a vase of water and protect it from insects until the anthers release tiny orange pollen grains, usually on the day after being cut. The stigmas of the seed parent should begin to exude a sticky secretion, indicating that they are ready to receive the pollen. Pull off the petals from the pollen parent, leaving the anthers intact.

Pollinating the seed parent

Remove the protective covers and brush the stamens of the pollen parent against the stigmas of the seed parent; their sticky secretion helps the pollen adhere to the stigmas. Replace the cover on the pollinated flower and label the stem.

An alternative method is to cut off the pollen parent's anthers, place them in a small, clean container (such as a plastic pillbox labeled with the name of the rose), and store it in cool, dry conditions until the released pollen grains are visible in the box. Using a fine brush, dust pollen from the box onto the stigmas of the seed parent. If carrying out more than one cross with different roses, make sure that the brush has been thoroughly cleaned between each operation, preferably with rubbing (isopropyl) alcohol.

If the cross has not taken successfully, the newly forming hip will shrivel quickly. If it has been successful, the sepals will begin to lift and the hip to swell; once this is evident, remove the protective cone or bag to allow the hip to grow.

The hip will continue to swell; it normally takes about two and a half months to ripen, depending on the climate. As it ripens, the hip changes color from green to red, to yellow, or possibly maroon, depending on the individual rose.

Harvesting and sowing

Remove the ripened hip from the plant and carefully extract the seeds. Sow and raise the seed (see "Extracting and sowing seed," p.132). Seed resulting from hybridization, however, may be sown fresh without a stratification period.

Selection

The seedlings are likely to flower in the first year – often within a few weeks of germination in a greenhouse – but it is only in the second year that the blooms will be more or less typical of the new hybrid and it is possible to judge whether it should be kept and developed or discarded.

Promising new seedlings can be budded onto rootstocks (see "Bud-grafting," p.130) when they have stems of sufficient thickness, that is about 1/4in (5mm). Even experienced hybridizers, however, find this stage challenging, because it is often not easy to detect faults until a selection has been grown in trials for several years.

Roses for exhibition

Entering roses in a local rose society show and, with time, in a regional or national rose society show can be very rewarding. Higher levels of competition, however, do require more dedication and time than the average gardener can give.

Rules for exhibiting roses vary from country to country, depending on the requirements of local and national rose associations. It is as important for serious exhibitors as it is for judges to be familiar with the details of such rules, so always check with your local association before entering a show.

Cultivating roses for exhibition

Grow several bushes of the same cultivar to ensure a wide choice of blooms. Some cultivars are as good in the garden as on the show table, provided that they are well looked after and the foliage is kept free from pests and disease. Prune severely to produce a limited number of strong shoots per season from which to choose exhibition blooms. Maintain vigorous growth with extra water and fertilizer. Roses are often disbudded to produce exhibition quality blooms: remove the newly formed side buds from Hybrid Tea roses so that the main bud develops strongly. Removing the central bud of Floribunda roses ensures that all the other buds develop at roughly the same time.

Some blooms are easily damaged by rain, so show rules usually permit the use of individual bloom protectors, or "Chinese hats," in the form of plastic cones fixed to stakes. They are by no means essential, however. Aluminum pie plates are easier to use over the sprays of Floribundas.

DISBUDDING ROSES

HYBRID TEA ROSES
As soon as they are large enough to handle easily, pinch out all the side buds, leaving the central bud to grow on.

FLORIBUNDA ROSES
Pinch out the young central bud of each spray for uniform development.

CHINESE HATS

To protect a show bloom from rain damage, insert a stake with a "Chinese hat" by the rose stem and tie the stem in to the stake.

Selecting blooms

Timing is crucial in exhibiting. A Hybrid Tea bloom should, at the moment of judging, be only two-thirds open. A Floribunda spray should have the maximum number of flowers open in various stages from bud to fully open bloom. Blooms should be of typical size for the cultivar. Good, healthy foliage is also important.

Preparing for a show

The novice exhibitor should restrict entries in any one show to a manageable number at first. Cut more than the number of roses to be entered, with stems at least 12in (30cm) long, on the day before the show, and label them. Remove the lowest leaves and plunge the stems into buckets of tepid water, right up to the necks of the flowers. Recut them underwater, and keep them overnight in a cool place.

Do not be put off if some of your blooms suffer weather damage. Other people may be in the same position, so bring in your blooms and take your chances. If the roses must be transported any distance, keep each bloom or spray separated, so that they are not damaged.

Staging the blooms

Once at the show, obtain some entry cards from the show secretary and carry your roses to the staging table. The show committee usually supplies containers for roses. Staging the blooms always takes longer than expected, but greater speed will come with experience.

Recut the stem of every rose before putting it into the container. To keep the roses as straight as possible, you may stuff foil or plastic wrap into the neck of the container around the stem, but be neat. Cut out faded blooms, but do not leave obvious cut stems or gaps. Use a watercolor brush to remove insects or dust specks, and sponge off any insecticide residues with a cotton ball. If needed, "dress" blooms by gently teasing into the correct position any petals that are slightly out of place. Do not reposition the petals too much, because overdressed blooms may lose points. Carefully remove any outer petals that are damaged.

EXHIBITION-QUALITY BLOOMS

A HYBRID TEA ROSE 'VALERIE MARGARET'

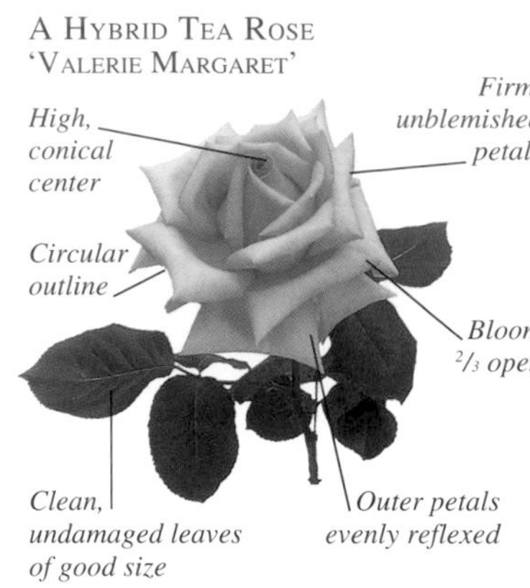

A FLORIBUNDA ROSE 'HANNAH GORDON'

When arranging the blooms, check that they conform to the schedule, for example "medium pink Hybrid Tea, one bloom per stem without side buds." If there is any deviation, the entry may be disqualified and removed from competition. Place the entry card with the exhibit, and carry it to the correct class.

EQUIPMENT FOR EXHIBITING ROSES

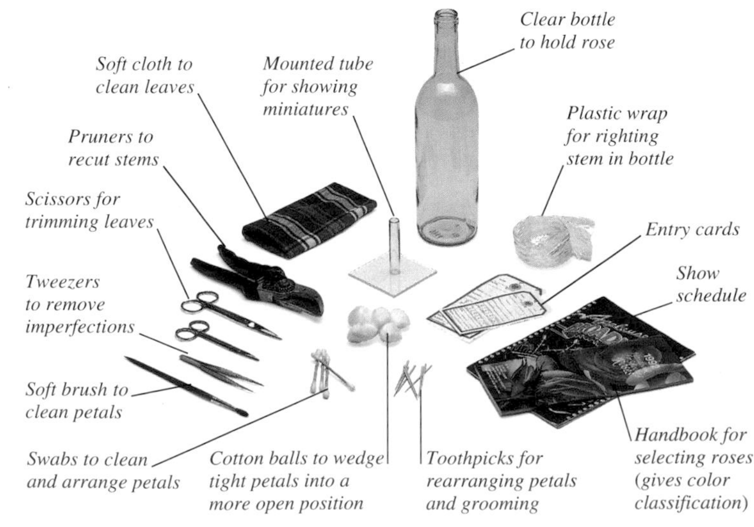

6

Perennials

THE FAVORITES OF *gardeners just about everywhere, perennials richly deserve their popularity. They include plants that have flowers in every color of the rainbow, an enormous array of shapes and textures, and scents that are often heavenly. Their diversity makes them suitable for many different sizes and types of garden, while their reliability makes them a lasting source of pleasure. For many people, a traditional herbaceous border in full bloom is the epitome of garden beauty, but perennials can be equally attractive in mixed borders, interplanted with shrubs, annuals, bulbs, or even fruits and vegetables. Alternatively, they can be grown in containers or as ground cover. There are flowers to suit all tastes, from delicate* Gypsophila *to sumptuous peonies and spiky delphiniums, and some are followed by attractive seedheads. Perennials can introduce variety to even a tiny garden or bring greater detail to a large one, providing a virtually unlimited palette for a garden that is an original masterpiece.*

Designing with perennials

PERENNIALS are nonwoody plants that live for two or more years. Most are herbaceous, dying back in fall to ground level, or to a woody base, and sending up new growth in spring. A few, such as the Christmas rose (*Helleborus niger*), are evergreen, and so have a valuable winter presence. Most perennials flower in summer. But some, such as *Liriope muscari* and *Iris unguicularis*, bloom in fall and winter, and others, such as the Lenten rose (*Helleborus orientalis*) and *Pulmonaria*, flower in the spring.

Choosing perennials

More than any other group of plants, perennials have an immense variety of shape, form, color, texture, and scent. Often valued most for their flowers, many also have attractive foliage, ranging from the ribbed, furling leaves of hostas, or the swordlike straps of iris, to the fine tracery of fennel (*Foeniculum vulgare*). In general, the foliage outlasts the floral display, so selecting perennials that have ornamental leaves helps to extend the season of interest, a factor that is particularly important in a small garden.

Perennials range in height from creeping deadnettle (*Lamium maculatum*), at just 4–6in (10–15cm) tall, to statuesque pampas grass (*Cortaderia selloana*), which is 8ft (2.5m) tall or more. Low-growing, ground cover perennials are ideal for the front of borders or for containers. On the other hand, tall, stately plants may be better grown on their own as specimen plants, or at the back of a border to give height and structure to the planting design.

Some perennials, such as many carnations and pinks (*Dianthus*) and sweetly scented phlox (*Phlox paniculata*), are worth growing for their fragrance alone, making them ideal for raised beds. Other perennials, especially *Sedum spectabile*, some wallflowers (*Cheiranthus*), and many herbs, have flowers that attract bees and butterflies.

As with all plants, when choosing perennials, make sure that they are appropriate for the given growing conditions such as the garden soil, microclimate, and exposure. In the right situation, the plants are much more likely to flourish, and usually need less maintenance, than those struggling in an unsuitable position (see also "Site and exposure," p.145).

Herbaceous borders

The most common form of planting with perennials is the herbaceous border, which dates back to late Victorian times. Traditionally, herbaceous borders consisted of long, rectangular plots, usually framed by an expanse of green lawn. They were filled exclusively with summer- and early fall-flowering perennials, banked according to height, with the shortest at the front and the tallest at the back. Plants characteristic of the border ranged from Shasta daisies

PERENNIAL BORDER
Hot-colored flowers such as the poker-headed Kniphofia, *yellow* Achillea, *and pink* Echinacea purpurea *are offset by the cool, silver-gray foliage of two* Senecio *cultivars. Low, rounded plants contrast with tall, upright forms.*

FORMAL BORDERS
In this formal garden, a traditional grass path divides a pair of wide, straight borders. The plants are arranged by height, with low plants such as Sedum spectabile *at the front so that all can be clearly seen. While the planting in each border is not a rigid mirror image of the other, a number of plants are used in both to provide balance and harmony.*

(*Leucanthemum* x *superbum*), *Scabiosa*, iris, and phlox, traditionally grown in cottage gardens for their charm and pretty colors, to the stately and splendid forms of daylily (*Hemerocallis*) and *Agapanthus*, which make elegant additions to a formal border.

In the past, depending on the size and style of the garden, a single border might be backed by a wall, fence, or hedge, while a pair of borders might flank a path, allowing the banks of color and scent to be easily appreciated.

Modern herbaceous borders are usually on a more modest scale than their Victorian counterparts, but they may still exploit some of the same ideas effectively. For a traditional, formal approach, arrange the plants in large, distinct groups of a single type of plant. If a more informal, fluid effect is desired, form drifts of each plant that flow into each other. This allows you to create impressive swaths of color and texture with less clearly defined edges.

If a long season of interest is particularly important, perhaps where planting space is very limited, it may be preferable to include shrubs and bulbs in the border as well as perennials (see "Mixed borders," right). In a large garden, however, there may be space to include some traditional, purely herbaceous borders and to feature substantial winter and spring planting elsewhere, providing continuing seasonal interest.

Herbaceous borders do certainly provide a dazzling display in summer, when the garden is probably used and enjoyed most, but they often prove to be less attractive at other times of the year. They can, however, always be justified if the pleasure gained from their relatively short-lived beauty outweighs the drabness of the dormant period between one yearly display and the next (see also "Designing beds and borders," opposite).

Island beds

Unlike borders, island beds, which are surrounded by lawn or paving, may be seen from all sides, so the planting design should be effective from a number of viewpoints. Island bed designs often include a majority of plants selected for their sturdy, dwarf, or compact habit, since these do not require staking. As with borders, beds that are dedicated solely to herbaceous plants are at their most impressive in summer; for a more enduring display, interplant the perennials with a variety of bulbs and perhaps one or two shrubs.

Geometrical round, square, or rectangular island beds suit a formal setting; loosely curved island beds are more appropriate in an informal garden or one with gently undulating ground. Generally avoid intricate shapes and tight curves because they are awkward to maintain and may detract from the planting.

Raised island beds are attractive in paved gardens, and they can provide improved conditions for growing a greater range of perennials in those gardens where the soil is poor or waterlogged. Their height enables plants to be cared for with minimal stooping, an important factor for impaired or elderly gardeners.

Mixed borders

As their name suggests, mixed borders may contain a combination of small trees, shrubs, climbers, bulbs, annuals, and biennials, as well as perennials. They provide the greatest opportunity for creating year-round interest and imaginative plant

MIXED ISLAND BED FOR COLOR THROUGH THE SEASONS

This island bed, shown here in spring, includes perennials and bulbs to provide color from early spring through to fall. Tall, sculptural plants are included to add height at the center and give the bed a strong impact.

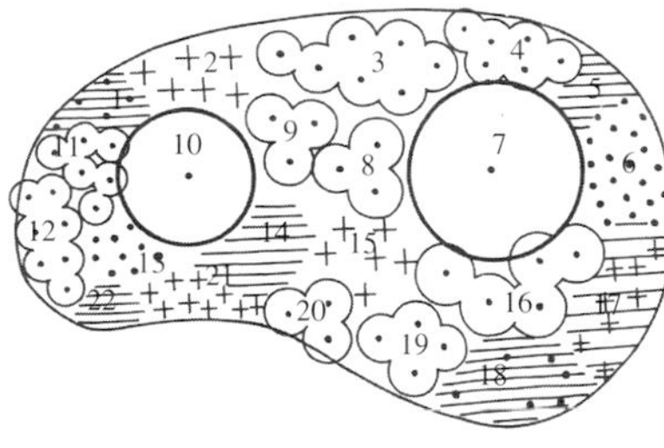

1 *Lamium maculatum* 'White Nancy', interplanted with *Scilla siberica* 'Atrocoerulea'
2 *Iris foetidissima* 'Variegata'
3 *Pulmonaria saccharata*
4 *Heuchera cylindrica* 'Greenfinch'
5 *Galanthus* 'Atkinsii'
6 *Festuca glauca*
7 *Phormium tenax* 'Sundowner'
8 *Anaphalis margaritacea*, syn. *A. yedoensis*
9 *Limonium latifolium* 'Blue Cloud'
10 *Acanthus mollis*
11 *Heuchera* 'Palace Purple'
12 *Euphorbia amygdaloides* subsp. *robbiae*
13 *Oenothera tetragona* 'Fireworks'
14 *Narcissus* 'February Gold'
15 *Libertia grandiflora*
16 *Bergenia* 'Ballawley'
17 *Ophiopogon planiscapus* 'Nigrescens', interplanted with *Galanthus* 'Magnet'
18 *Sedum spectabile* 'Brilliant', interplanted with *Crocus tommasinianus*
19 *Lamium maculatum* 'Roseum'
20 *Achillea* 'Moonshine'
21 *Iberis sempervirens* 'Snowflake'
22 *Chionodoxa forbesii*, syn. *C. luciliae* of gardens

Mixed Borders
Colorful tulips provide spring interest, while shrubs such as a golden-leaved Spiraea *and the sculptural mass of* Euphorbia characias *subsp.* wulfenii *add color and form from spring through to fall, extending the period of interest beyond the summer burst of color offered by the hardy* Geranium *species and other perennials.*

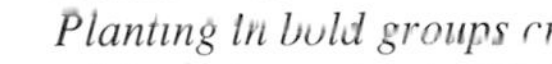

Massed Form and Color
Planting in bold groups creates a strong impact. Here, the rounded leaves of a Ligularia *contrast with the pointed swords of red* Crocosmia

associations. Unlike exclusively herbaceous borders, well-planned mixed plantings can form an attractive display in all seasons.

The amount of space given to each type of plant can vary according to taste. A mixed border with a predominance of perennials and only a few nonherbaceous plants usually needs more maintenance than one with a high proportion of shrubs and a small number of perennials. A varied design that provides year-round interest may be achieved using shrubs for one-third to a half of the planting, including a good selection of evergreens.

A newly planted mixed border may require large groups of bulbs, annuals, and biennials to fill in the gaps between the shrubs and perennials, but these may gradually be decreased as the latter become established and reach their mature size.

Designing beds and borders

When creating a planting design, the principles are broadly similar whether planning a herbaceous or mixed border or an island bed. Considerations of height, mass, texture, sequential interest, form, and color are all variable factors that may be widely exploited to achieve particular results. Imagination and personal taste will influence your planting designs, but there are a few basic guidelines to follow.

General principles

Herbaceous borders may be designed in various styles so that they set or strengthen the character and tone of the garden. In a formal setting, straight borders with a restricted color scheme look elegant and well ordered. In an informal garden, irregular or curved shapes with a more relaxed and free approach to planting would complement the overall design.

The size of a border or bed can vary but, as a rough guide, the larger the garden setting, the bigger the border or bed should be. The size and shape should be proportionate to and compatible with the house and any other nearby features such as a patio. Generally, 5ft (1.5m) is the minimum width for a bed or border to have any impact in a planting design, and to create a layered, well-balanced grouping of plants.

When deciding which plants to include in the border and how best to position them, remember to allow sufficient room for the plants to spread as they mature, taking account of the different rates at which they grow. If using plants grown in containers, it is helpful to set them out still in their pots according to your planting plan and make any adjustments at this stage, before planting them.

Height

In general, site tall plants at the back of a front-facing border, graduating towards the shortest ones in the front, to create a tiered effect in which no plant is hidden behind another. In an island bed, place the tallest plants in the center, with the smallest along the outer edge.

This formal regularity may be inappropriate or undesirable in many gardens, however, and the occasional anarchic touch may add greatly to the freshness and individuality of a design. Provided that they are not too dense or spreading, a few tall plants sited toward the front of the border breaks the monotony. Vary the position of the tallest and the shortest plants to create a softly undulating outline when the design is viewed from the side.

Generally, the wider the bed or border, the taller the plants may be; very tall plants in narrow borders may look awkward and may make the angle from the tallest to the shortest look uncomfortably steep.

Planting in groups

For the greatest impact, mass small and medium-sized plants in groups of one type, rather than planting isolated specimens. Planting in odd-numbered groups, with the plants placed at random rather than in lines, establishes a fluid, natural-looking picture. The smaller the plant, the larger the group should be: *Bergenia* species and hybrids may be planted in threes, for example, while London pride (*Saxifraga* x *urbium*) is best in groups of seven or more. The huge *Gunnera manicata*, however, is striking enough to be planted singly,

Planting in Drifts
Crimson Rosa moyesii *and yellow* Thalictrum flavum *form counterpoints with purple drifts of* Salvia nemorosa *and catmint* (Nepeta).

HARMONIZING TEXTURES
This mixture of plants with airy and feathery flowers, including Astilbe, Lythrum virgatum, Filipendula palmata, *and tall, yellow* Ligularia stenocephala, *forms a satisfying pattern of textures.*

CONTRASTING FORMS
Foliage plants can be grouped so that differences in form and texture are emphasised. The impressive, jagged foliage of Rheum palmatum *at the rear contrasts with the heart-shaped leaves of* Ligularia dentata *and the softly arching straps of an ornamental grass.*

as may medium-sized and large shrubs in a mixed border (see "Specimen planting," p.140).

Plants that have strong outlines, such as *Kniphofia caulescens* with its upright pokerhead flowers, are striking when planted in smaller groups than those plants with less distinct forms such as the feathery *Aster ericoides*. Also try to plant groups in a range of sizes.

Form

Perennials have a variety of forms and silhouettes, including upright, rounded, arching, and horizontally spreading. Juxtapose groups of plants with contrasting forms to create a series of vignettes which build up within a bed or border. The slim spikes of delphiniums or *Eremurus*, for example, act like giant, colorful exclamation points when seen against the foaming, cloudlike cushions of *Gypsophila paniculata* or *Crambe cordifolia*.

Some plants are two-tiered, and have their own contrasting form: a fine example is *Rheum palmatum* 'Atrosanguineum' which makes a horizontal layer of reddish purple leaves that grows 3ft (1m) tall, above which are held smoky pink plumes of tiny flowers.

Texture

While flowers and stems contribute to the texture of a planting, foliage provides the strongest impact. Even when seen from a distance, it has the greatest potential for creating striking contrasts and subtle harmonies. The dainty leaves of *Artemisia* 'Powis Castle' or the needlelike foliage of *Coreopsis verticillata* 'Moonbeam' are very delicate. Large individual leaves such as those of *Hosta sieboldiana* var. *elegans* create a bold textural statement in shady spots.

Texture is also determined by the leaf surface, whether it is the matte, waxy foliage of *Sedum spectabile*, the glossy, leathery leaves of *Bergenia purpurascens*, or the woolly texture of *Lychnis coronaria*.

As with form, juxtaposing groups of plants that have contrasting textures creates interest; for example, the downy, pleated leaves of *Alchemilla mollis* would contrast well with the spiny stems and jagged foliage of *Eryngium*. Ground cover perennials such as hardy *Geranium* species and cultivars and *Ajuga reptans* are especially useful for growing as a low foil for other plants, and for filling in gaps in a planting to complete the textural tapestry (see GROUND COVERS, pp.150–51).

COOL BORDER

Restful blues, greens, and white combine to form a calm scheme that is ideal for the cool conditions of a semishaded, moist site.

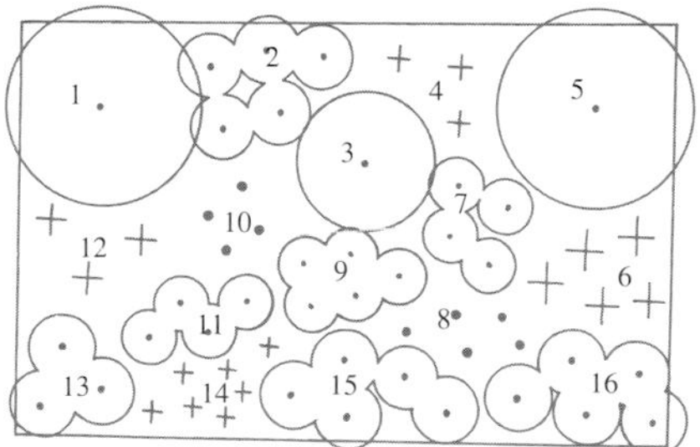

1 *Yucca flaccida* 'Ivory'
2 *Aster turbinellus*
3 *Ferula communis*
4 *Veronica virginica* f. *alba*
5 *Cynara cardunculus*
6 *Iris sibirica*
7 *Amsonia tabernaemontana*, syn. *A. salicifolia*
8 *Aster thomsonii* 'Nanus'
9 *Dicentra spectabilis* f. *alba*
10 *Tradescantia* 'Osprey'
11 *Astrantia major* var. *involucrata*
12 *Eryngium* x *oliverianum*
13 *Tiarella cordifolia*
14 *Veronica* 'Crater Lake Blue'
15 *Alchemilla mollis*
16 *Platycodon grandiflorus*

HOT BORDER

A bright color scheme including vivid reds and yellows looks spectacular in a hot, sunny position.

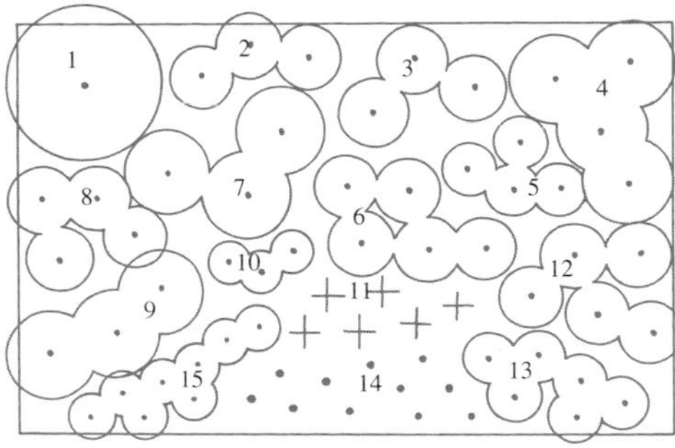

1 *Kniphofia caulescens*
2 *Salvia fulgens*
3 *Euryops pectinatus*
4 *Canna indica*
5 *Mimulus aurantiacus*
6 *Penstemon* 'Garnet'
7 *Hedychium gardnerianum*
8 *Cosmos atrosanguineus*
9 x *Venidio-arctotis* 'Apricot'
10 Yellow form of *Calceolaria*, Bikini Series
11 *Iris* 'Early Light'
12 *Osteospermum* 'Buttermilk'
13 *Hemerocallis* 'Stella de Oro'
14 *Gazania uniflora*
15 *Verbena peruviana*

Color

The use of color in perennial beds and borders may be as daring and experimental or as subtle and restrained as you like. Schemes may be based on a single color, such as the famous white garden at Sissinghurst, Kent, in England, or on limited bands of color, for example various shades of pink and red, cream and yellow, or blue and mauve. For a bolder and contrasting scheme, mix striking combinations of reds and blues or yellows and purples. Multicolored designs offer scope for creating very different moods and pictures, depending on whether they are limited to pastel shades, intense hues, or a glorious mixture of the two.

White is a relatively easy monochromatic scheme to plan, since many plants have white-flowered forms or complementary silver or gray foliage. Consider softening the effect by including other pale colors as well. White, pale pink, cream, and gray are invaluable for enlivening a shady border or one in a dark setting, such as a border backed by a yew hedge. These colors may also be used to provide a restful area between strong or clashing colors. By contrast, hot colors usually show up best in bright sunlight. Golden or yellow schemes are warming, and particularly welcome in spring and fall. Adding one or two sparks of contrasting color can give vitality to a limited scheme.

When you plan a bed or border, bear in mind that foliage color is as important as that of flowers. The white- or cream-variegated leaves of plants such as *Hosta crispula* can enhance a white scheme, or the golden foliage of *Filipendula ulmaria* 'Aurea' a yellow one. Generally, golden foliage colors best in sun, and white in light shade, but very hot, dry conditions may scorch yellow leaves. Plants with silver and gray foliage tend to grow well in hot, sunny beds and counterbalance the hot colors of perennials such as Michaelmas daisies (*Aster*), *Gaillardia*, and *Cosmos*.

LONG-LASTING DISPLAY
The rich brown seedheads of Sedum spectabile *may be left uncut to provide interest in late fall and winter long after the succulent leaves have died back.*

Seasonal interest

In a mixed border, it is possible to plan a succession of color schemes that change with the course of the seasons. For example, a bright and cheerful springtime planting could include a predominance of yellow, from primroses (*Primula*) and *Doronicum*, and pale blue, from irises and *Pulmonaria*, interspersed with grape hyacinths (*Muscari*) and daffodils. Summer brings with it the freedom to choose from a more varied palette. You can create a joyful fiesta of color, with vividly hued, exotic subtropical plants, combining them with more subtle shades and the rich, warm pinks and reds of roses. The perennials' season ends with the fiery, intense, autumnal colors of asters, chrysanthemums, dahlias, sunflowers (*Helianthus*), *Rudbeckia*, and *Kniphofia*.

Planning any bed or border involves coordinating the timing of each plant's display, so that one feature smoothly follows another and fading flowers pass unnoticed, eclipsed by nearby plants coming into bloom. A planting that manages to maintain a succession of interest requires forethought, but most mistakes are easily corrected if any offending plants are re-sited when they are still young.

It is sometimes possible to extend the effect of a particular plant or group by growing a plant next to it that gives a similar impression. The deep blue flower spikes of *Delphinium* 'Black Knight', for example, could be followed by those of *Aconitum carmichaelii* var. *wilsonii*, and if the latter is planted in front, the yellowing delphinium foliage will be hidden. Try to position perennials such as lupines (*Lupinus*), which die back early, behind plants such as *Physostegia* that develop later in the season, to hide awkward gaps or fading leaves.

In mixed borders, bulbs are particularly useful for providing color in late winter and spring when perennials are starting into growth. Similarly, the new growth of the latter masks the fading foliage of the bulbs once their flowers have finished. For example, the black-purple leaves of the evergreen *Ophiopogon planiscapus* 'Nigrescens' or the soft purple-green foliage of *Viola labradorica* 'Purpurea' make excellent foils for snowdrops (*Galanthus*) and continue to provide interest after the snowdrops are past their best.

In summer, perennials are at their peak, creating a rich, full display, but as they start to die down in fall, the display created by shrubs is invaluable, maintaining the shape and structure of the design as well as contributing both color and texture.

INFORMAL STYLE *Sprawling plants such as pink* Helianthemum *soften the edges of stone steps in an informal cottage garden, while more sculptural plants such as the variegated* Hosta 'Thomas Hogg' *and the arching, golden* Carex elata 'Bowles' Golden' *add structural interest.*

The inclusion of deciduous shrubs with attractive fall foliage (such as *Cotinus*) and those with bright berries (such as many pyracanthas) will help to draw attention away from the perennials as their foliage dies back.

Few perennials are renowned for their winter appeal but some, such as *Bergenia* and many hellebores (*Helleborus*), soften the sturdy effect created by a shrub framework, contrasting with the mass of an evergreen shrub or with the architectural form of a deciduous one.

Cottage gardens

Traditional cottage gardens are an abundant mixture of plants – herbs, roses, climbers, annuals, fruits, and vegetables, as well as perennials. In the past, cottagers bred plants themselves and produced treasured perennials such as pansies (*Viola* x *wittrockiana*), auricula primroses (*Primula auricula*), and scented pinks (*Dianthus*).

Typical perennial plants include peonies (*Paeonia*), delphiniums, and lupines (*Lupinus*). Wildflowers with fragrant, double, extra-large, or unusually colored blooms are also especially appropriate here. Old-fashioned plants dating back to Victorian times and earlier are often favored, but they may be combined with modern forms and cultivars for a varied design.

Perennials in woodland gardens

Deciduous woodland provides conditions of shelter, light shade, and humus-rich soil suitable for many perennials. A small grove of birches (*Betula*) and other light-foliaged, deciduous trees can create an ideal setting for a number of shade-loving plants; site the perennials where they will not face too much competition from the tree roots.

Group plants of one type in drifts and intermingling at the edges, or in substantial clumps, to match the scale of the setting. Ferns, in particular, thrive in a woodland setting and add architectural interest when planted in bold swaths.

Some of the most enchanting perennials are the small woodland plants that usher in the spring. Snowdrops (*Galanthus*), primroses (*Primula*), wood anemones (*Anemone nemorosa*), and *Ranunculus ficaria* provide color and interest while the overhead canopy is still leafless. Combine them with woodland bulbs and shade-loving shrubs.

In cool, dry woodland shade, grow ground cover perennials such as the superbly scented lily-of-the-valley (*Convallaria majalis*); Solomon's seal (*Polygonatum*), with its pendent, pearly white flowers; and *Pulmonaria*, which has attractively marked foliage.

Specimen planting

In large areas of lawn or gravel, stately perennials with an architectural form or sculptural foliage, such as *Acanthus spinosus*, may be sited on their own as specimen plants to create a striking accent. In smaller gardens, a specimen perennial, surrounded by low ground cover, could be used to provide a focal point where a border projects into a lawn or hard paving, or in a corner of a garden where two borders meet. The jutting, sword-shaped leaves and arching, fiery red flower stems of *Crocosmia* 'Lucifer', for example, look spectacular rising from the silvery sea of an ornamental deadnettle (*Lamium maculatum* 'White Nancy' or 'Beacon Silver').

For year-round interest, evergreen perennials such as *Phormium tenax* are excellent, while the tall, airy plumes of pampas grass (*Cortaderia selloana*) may be left uncut for an impressive feature through fall and winter. Other perennials that provide a briefer display may also make spectacular specimens because of their form, flowers, or foliage. They include the towering, felty stems of *Verbascum olympicum* to the massive leaves of *Gunnera manicata*, or the glorious, medium pink blooms of *Paeonia* 'Sarah Bernhardt'. As they die down in fall, it may be desirable to place another feature (such as a container-planted shrub) nearby to give interest during their dormant period.

Specimen plants are best offset by a neutral backdrop such as a hedge, wall, or stretch of lawn, so that nothing detracts from their impact (see also GARDEN PLANNING AND DESIGN, "Specimen plants," p.23).

Growing perennials in containers

Perennials are as welcome in containers on a paved patio, courtyard, balcony, or roof garden as they are in open beds and borders. Growing them in this way also makes it possible to include tender plants that must be brought under cover for winter and plants that require a different soil type from the garden soil.

Containers generally look better grouped rather than scattered around the garden, and the plants benefit from the favorable microclimate created by each other's company.

Evergreen perennials such as *Bergenia purpurascens* and *Liriope muscari* can be on display in pots throughout the year. Herbaceous perennials may be better planted with an evergreen shrub to extend the season of interest.

Specimen plants

A clump of one type of perennial in a large container can perform the role of a specimen plant in a paved area. Those with sculptural foliage or flowers, for example *Agapanthus* and *Hosta sieboldiana*, are particularly attractive in appropriate containers. They may be left for years to increase in size.

Mixed planting

In large planters, experiment with mixed planting, combining different types of perennial, such as ground-hugging *Stachys byzantina* 'Silver Carpet'; shiny, round-leaved species and cultivars of *Bergenia*; and burgundy *Euphorbia amygdaloides* 'Purpurea'. Combining one each of many different types of perennial, however, is liable to appear cluttered and dull as well as being difficult to maintain.

POTTED PERENNIALS *A simple, weathered, terracotta pot is the perfect foil for the golden* Hakonechloa macra 'Aureola'.

Planter's guide to perennials

Exposed Sites

Perennials that tolerate exposed or windy sites; the plant marked ☘ is not suitable for coastal sites

Agapanthus, some ❄
Anaphalis
Anemone hupehensis ☘
Artemisia absinthium
Centaurea dealbata, *C. hypoleuca*
Centranthus ruber
Eryngium variifolium
Euphorbia characias
Festuca glauca
Kniphofia caulescens
Lavatera maritima, *L. thuringiaca*
Limonium latifolium
Phlomis russeliana
Phormium cookianum, *P. tenax* ❄
Sedum spectabile, *S. telephium*
Stachys byzantina
Yucca filamentosa, *Y. flaccida*

Air Pollution

Perennials that tolerate polluted air

Aconitum napellus
Aquilegia vulgaris
Bergenia cordifolia
Dicentra eximia, *D. formosa*
Euphorbia amygdaloides
Geranium endressii
Helleborus niger, *H. orientalis*
Hemerocallis
Heuchera
Hosta
Iris
Lamium
Leucanthemum x *superbum*
Libertia grandiflora
Polemonium
Polygonatum, some ❄
Pulmonaria

Rudbeckia laciniata 'Goldquelle'

Rudbeckia
Sedum spectabile, *S. telephium*
Sisyrinchium striatum
Smilacina racemosa
Symphytum
Thalictrum
Tiarella
Veronica gentianoides, *V. spicata*

Dry Shade

Perennials that tolerate dry shade

Acanthus mollis
Aconitum carmichaelii, *A. napellus*
Anemone hupehensis, *A.* x *hybrida*
Aquilegia vulgaris
Dicentra
Digitalis grandiflora, *D. lutea*
Epimedium
Euphorbia amygdaloides
Geranium, some ❄
Helleborus foetidus, *H. orientalis*
Iris foetidissima
Luzula sylvatica 'Marginata'
Ophiopogon, some ❄
Saxifraga umbrosa, *S.* x *urbium*
Symphytum grandiflorum
Tellima grandiflora 'Purpurea'
Vinca minor
Viola labradorica, *V. odorata*

Moist Shade

Perennials that prefer moist shade

Astilbe simplicifolia
Astrantia major
Bergenia
Brunnera macrophylla
Convallaria majalis
Gentiana asclepiadea

Hemerocallis 'Marion Vaughn'

Hemerocallis
Hosta
Kirengeshoma palmata
Ligularia przewalskii
Peltiphyllum peltatum
Phlox stolonifera
Polygonum bistorta 'Superba'
Primula bulleyana, *P. florindae*, *P. japonica*, *P. pulverulenta*
Rodgersia aesculifolia, *R. pinnata*
Thalictrum
Trillium grandiflorum, *T. sessile*

Winter Interest

Decorative flowers

Bergenia 'Ballawley', *B. cordifolia*
Doronicum
Euphorbia amygdaloides subsp. *robbiae*, *E. characias*
Helleborus argutifolius, *H. niger*
Iris unguicularis
Pulmonaria
Ranunculus ficaria

Decorative leaves

Arum italicum 'Marmoratum'
Bergenia 'Ballawley', *B. cordifolia*
Euphorbia amygdaloides subsp. *robbiae*, *E. characias*
Festuca glauca
Helleborus argutifolius
Heuchera 'Palace Purple'
Iris foetidissima 'Variegata'
Lamium maculatum 'Chequers'
Liriope muscari 'Variegata'
Ophiopogon planiscapus 'Nigrescens'
Phormium (cvs)
Stachys byzantina 'Silver Carpet'
Tiarella polyphylla
Vinca (variegated cvs)

Fragrant Flowers

Centranthus ruber
Convallaria majalis
Cosmos atrosanguineus ❄
Dianthus 'Brympton Red', *D.* 'Old Clove Red'
Dictamnus albus
Dracocephalum moldavicum
Filipendula ulmaria
Galium odoratum
Hosta plantaginea var. *grandiflora*
Iris graminea
Oenothera odorata
Paeonia lactiflora
Petasites fragrans
Phlox paniculata
Viola odorata 'Czar'

Flowers for Cutting

Alstroemeria
Aquilegia
Aster, some ❄
Astrantia
Centaurea
Cephalaria
Delphinium, some ❄
Dicentra
Doronicum
Erigeron
Gypsophila
Helenium
Helleborus, some ❄
Kniphofia, some ❄
Monarda
Paeonia
Phlox, some ❄
Primula, some ❄
Rudbeckia
Scabiosa
Solidago
Stokesia
Veronica

Flowers for Drying

Acanthus spinosus
Achillea
Alchemilla mollis
Anaphalis
Aruncus dioicus
Astilbe
Catananche
Cynara
Echinops bannaticus, *E. ritro*
Limonium, some ❄
Phlomis russeliana
Rodgersia
Sedum spectabile, *S. telephium*
Solidago

Decorative Seedheads

Acanthus
Eryngium
Festuca glauca
Iris foetidissima
Lunaria rediviva
Papaver orientale
Physalis alkekengi
Typha

Architectural Plants

Acanthus hungaricus, *A. mollis*
Angelica archangelica
Arundo donax 'Variegata' ❄
Bergenia 'Ballawley'
Cortaderia selloana
Crambe cordifolia
Cynara cardunculus, *C. scolymus*
Foeniculum vulgare
Gunnera manicata
Helleborus argutifolius
Heracleum (can be invasive)
Hosta sieboldiana var. *elegans*
Ligularia dentata 'Othello'
Lysichiton americanus
Melianthus major ❄
Miscanthus sinensis
Phormium tenax ❄
Rheum palmatum 'Atrosanguineum'
Rodgersia

Fast-growing Perennials

Artemisia lactiflora
Aruncus sylvester
Arundo donax 'Macrophylla' ❄
Campanula lactiflora
Centaurea macrocephala
Cephalaria gigantea
Crambe cordifolia

Cynara cardunculus

Cynara cardunculus, *C. scolymus*
Euphorbia characias
Ferula communis
Filipendula rubra
Galega x *hartlandii*
Gunnera manicata
Helianthus
Kniphofia caulescens, *K. uvaria*
Lavatera cachemiriana, *L. maritima*
Ligularia stenocephala
Macleaya cordata
Malva alcea var. *fastigiata*, *M. moschata*, *M. sylvestris*
Miscanthus
Phormium tenax ❄
Rheum palmatum 'Atrosanguineum'
Romneya coulteri
Rudbeckia laciniata 'Goldquelle'
Salvia confertiflora ❄, *S. sclarea* var. *turkestanica*, *S. uliginosa* ❄
Silphium perfoliatum
Solidago canadensis
Thalictrum flavum

Key

❄ *Not frost hardy*

Grasses, bamboos, sedges, and rushes

THESE plants have a variety of elegant and architectural forms which, combined with arching or upright stems, feathery inflorescences, and subtly colored seedheads, make an outstanding display. Grow them grouped together, as specimen plants, or in borders.

Grasses are often confused with other grasslike plants, particularly sedges and rushes, but each of them belongs to a separate family.

The grass family

True grasses (those of the Gramineae family) almost always have hollow, round stems, with solid nodes at regular intervals. The woody-stemmed, perennial bamboos (subfamily Bambusoideae) are good examples with the obvious hollowness of their canes. Grass blades extend in two ranks from a sheath that can be split or peeled back. Grass flowers are borne in panicles, racemes, or spikes.

Grasses

These vary widely in color and habit. The architectural qualities of the taller grasses make them a striking feature in the herbaceous border, while low-growing grasses provide a contrast at the front of the bed. Do not choose vigorous, creeping grasses such as *Phalaris arundinacea* var. *picta* for this purpose, however, because they are likely to engulf adjacent weaker plants. More easily managed are the tufted grasses, which slowly build up and out from a central crown.

Some are suitable for paved areas, such as *Molinia caerulea* subsp. *caerulea* 'Variegata'; for a warm, sunny pocket on the patio, use the taller *Helictotrichon sempervirens*, with slender blue leaves that are upright and stiffly radiating. For a lawn specimen, good choices include pampas grass (*Cortaderia*), with tall, nodding plumes in late summer, or *Miscanthus*, with more delicate inflorescences. For the water's edge, species such as *Glyceria maxima* 'Variegata', display attractive form and variegation, and provide interesting reflections.

Most grasses prefer full sun to very light shade, an open position, and well-drained but moisture-retentive soil. Very fertile soil encourages lush, often floppy foliage at the expense of flowers. A few species, mainly tall ones such as *Phragmites australis*, need moist soil, growing well alongside stream banks.

ORNAMENTAL GRASSES
The subtle colors and feathery heads of many grasses (here mostly forms of Cortaderia selloana *and* Miscanthus) *make an animated, informal display.*

Bamboos

Evergreen and woody-stemmed with delicately handsome foliage and architectural outlines, bamboos make ideal specimen plants. A few species flower regularly, but most do not bloom for many years.

Bamboos need ample space since they grow up to 12ft (4m) tall with an arching spread of 20ft (6m), and they often spread quickly. The canes take about three years to mature, although *Phyllostachys nigra* will develop the full beauty of its polished ebony-black stems in its second year. Bamboos grow strongly in most soils once established, and they form excellent screens, hedges, or windbreaks in milder, windswept zones. Many are tropical, but a considerable number are hardy in temperate regions.

Sedges and rushes

Sedges (Cyperaceae family) have three-sided stems that are solid and pithy throughout. The leaf blades tightly encase the stem, arising from each side in threes: in cross section they are concertina-like and cannot readily be split or rolled back.

The family Juncaceae contains two cultivated genera, *Juncus* and *Luzula*, both known commonly as rushes. In *Juncus*, the leaves are cylindrical in cross section and have a solid pith; in *Luzula*, the leaves are flat and usually edged with hairs.

Woodrushes (*Luzula* spp.) are most appealing when used to provide spreading ground cover in areas of shady woodland. A number of sedges, such as *Carex elata* 'Aurea' and *C. oshimensis* 'Evergold', with their attractive golden or variegated foliage, also offer fine color contrasts in the border.

The woodrushes thrive in semishade, but they will also tolerate open conditions. The sedges, although most often found in damp habitats, are usually very tolerant of drier sites, with the exception of moisture-loving species such as *Carex acuta* and *C. riparia*.

LAWN SPECIMEN
The strong shape and tall, graceful plumes of pampas grass (Cortaderia selloana) *are most suited to specimen planting.*

Drying grasses for ornamental use

Dried grasses are ideal for indoor decoration. Their bold shapes and neutral colors are appealing whether displayed alone or arranged with more colorful dried flowers. To ensure that they are at their best for ornamental use, cut the grasses when the inflorescence is well developed but not open, then stand them in a vase, not too tightly packed together, in a cool, airy place to dry.

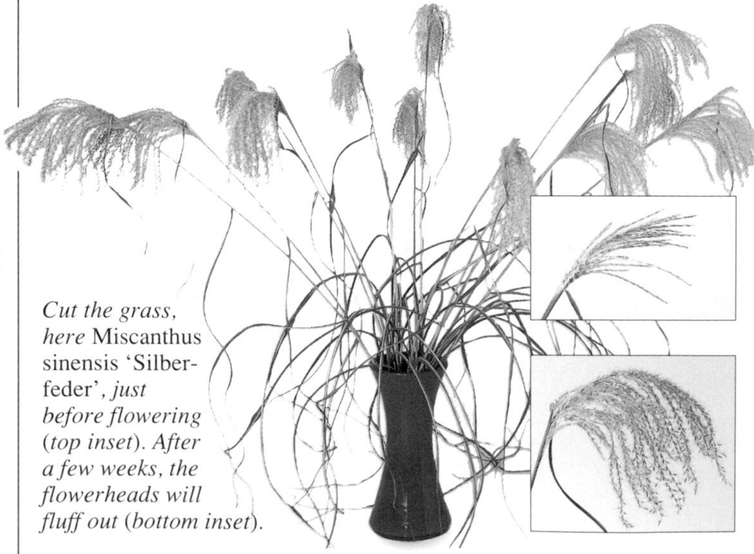

Cut the grass, here Miscanthus sinensis 'Silberfeder', *just before flowering (top inset). After a few weeks, the flowerheads will fluff out (bottom inset).*

Restricting Wide-spreading Grasses

1 *Dig a trench about 8in (20cm) wide, 12in (30cm) from the base of the clump. Make it deeper than the roots of the plant.*

2 *Insert a barrier made of nonperishable material such as rigid plastic, then fill in the trench and firm the ground well.*

Routine cultivation

In general, most ornamental grasses require little care, as long as they are grown in an appropriate, correctly prepared site. Sedges and rushes are generally treated as grasses.

Preparing the soil

On dry soils, incorporate plenty of organic or fibrous matter to ensure adequate moisture retention, this should not be rich in nutrients, however. In mild areas with high rainfall, grasses from the subtropics and very dry regions need a deep, gritty soil with excellent drainage. A top-dressing of stone chips around the crown in winter helps to disperse surface moisture which, in combination with cold, can kill many plants from warm zones and high altitudes; this is not necessary in regions with cold winters where the ground remains frozen.

Cutting Back Pampas Grass

In early spring, cut back the dead foliage and flower stems as far as possible without damaging the new growth (see inset). Wear thick, protective gloves and use shears.

Cutting back

Deadhead annual grasses after flowering to prevent self-seeding, but do not deadhead perennials, since the parchment colors of the fading inflorescences are often an essential part of their winter appeal.

As grasses begin to wither and become unsightly, trim off the old, untidy growth. In early spring, cut back the plant to ground level to encourage vigorous foliage to develop. Grasses from warm climates should be cut back in spring, because the old foliage helps to protect the crown from winter cold.

Pampas grass (*Cortaderia selloana*) and *Miscanthus* species may be cut back using a scythe or shears. Do this in fall in mild areas, or in spring in colder zones. When handling pampas grass, wear thick gloves because the sawlike leaf edges are razor sharp and may cause injury.

Bamboos may be damaged by cold even in regions where they are hardy, but they usually recover quickly in spring provided there is ample rainfall. One or two species, such as *Sinarundinaria nitida*, survive temperatures as low as -35°F (-37°C). They grow only about 3ft (1m) tall since frost kills the above-ground growth; the roots, however, survive to produce new growth.

Restricting the growth of grasses and bamboos

Most wide-spreading grasses with invasive root systems may be contained by digging a large trench and lining it with rigid plastic (see above). The root systems of most bamboos are extremely invasive, so containerize them to prevent spreading. Choose a container that is at least 2ft (60cm) deep and large enough for the clump to grow for several years without division. The container must be very strong – concrete sewer pipes are ideal.

Propagation

Perennial grasses may be propagated from seed (see PERENNIALS, "Seed," p.160) or by division. Annuals are increased by seed sown in spring or fall, depending on the desired time of flowering.

Seed

Collect the seeds when they are fully ripe, that is, when the inflorescence is dry and fluffy and the seeds can be easily pulled away from the spike. Sowing seeds in small pots or cell packs allows you to pot on without disturbing the young plants. If sown as soon as the seeds are ripe, germination is quick, but the young seedlings need some protection from winter cold.

Division

Clump-forming grasses are easily increased by simple division in spring or fall. Many gardeners prefer division in spring, when new growth is visible, since the plants establish more successfully.

To increase rhizomatous species, lift the clump and cut it into sections, ensuring that each has at least one growing point. Do not damage the fine roots. Insert the sections into individual pots of a free-draining soil mix and cover them to their original depth. Keep them cool and moist, and in good light, but shaded from strong sun until the young plants are established. For further information, see "Dividing perennials," p.162.

Transplanting bamboos

The best time for dividing and transplanting bamboos is spring, just as the shoots are emerging. Water liberally after transplanting, since if the foliage is allowed to wither, which it does quickly, the transplant is unlikely to survive. Spray water on divided plants regularly and liberally until they are established.

Collecting Seeds

Collect the seeds of annual grasses when the inflorescence has fluffed up fully. Pull away the ripe seeds from each spike.

Propagating Bamboos by Dividing Rhizomes

1 *Dig around the clump to expose the outer rhizomes with new shoots. Separate these from the parent plant.*

2 *Cut the rhizomes into pieces, each with at least one shoot. Dust the cut surfaces with fungicidal powder (see inset).*

3 *Pot up each piece with the rhizome just below the surface of the soil mix and the shoots exposed. Firm in and water.*

Propagating Grasses by Division

Cut down the foliage to 6–8in (15–20cm). Lift the clump and divide it by hand or with two hand forks. Pot up each division in sandy soil mix in 6in (15cm) pots.

Irises

THE genus *Iris* includes some of the loveliest of flowering plants. Their intricate blooms offer a rich spectrum of colors as well as satin or velvet textures. Species can be selected for diverse situations, ranging from woodland and rock garden, waterside and bog, to herbaceous border. Botanically, *Iris* is divided into subgenera, sections, and series; these divisions vary in their cultural needs and form a convenient horticultural classification.

Routine care and propagation
Species may be propagated in the fall or spring by division of offsets or rhizomes, or by seed in fall (named cultivars by division only). For further information, see PERENNIALS, "Routine care," pp.155–7; BULBOUS PLANTS, "Routine care," pp.230–2, and also "Propagation," pp.233–8.

Rhizomatous irises

Irises in this group have rhizomes as rootstocks, and their sword-shaped leaves are arranged in a basal fan. Botanically, they are divided into several subgenera and series, but for horticultural purposes the main groups are bearded, crested, and beardless irises.

Bearded irises
Characterized by a "beard" along the center of the falls – the hanging or horizontal petals – this group includes common irises and thousands of their cultivars and hybrids, most flowering in spring and early summer. Suitable for herbaceous and mixed borders, they are easy to grow in rich, well-drained soil in sun; many also tolerate partial shade and poorer soils.

Based on bloom height, bearded irises are divided into six groups: miniature dwarf bearded (MDB), standard dwarf bearded (SDB), intermediate bearded (IB), miniature tall bearded (MTB), border bearded (BB), and tall bearded (TB). Within these groups are some that rebloom in summer or fall. Rebloomers generally benefit from extra fertilizer and water in summer.

Oncocyclus irises are natives of areas with little summer rainfall and need the protection of an alpine house or frame in climates that are subject to summer rains. They have large, beautiful, and arguably bizarre blooms but are exacting in their requirements and are not easy to grow. They need a fertile, sharply drained soil and full sun, with a dry, dormant period after flowering. If they are grown in pots, the soil mix must be nutrient-rich, well drained, and preferably alkaline.

Regelia irises are related to the Oncocyclus irises and have similar cultural requirements, although they are easier to grow. Some species may be grown outside if they are given good drainage and a hot, dry site in the summer.

Crested irises
These have ridges, or cockscomb-like crests, instead of beards.

Evansia irises are usually found in damp woodland. Larger species, such as *I. confusa* and *I. japonica*, are not fully hardy and need a sheltered position in humus-rich soils, with some shade provided in warm climates. Smaller species such as *I. cristata* and *I. gracilipes* are ideal for planting in peaty pockets in a shaded rock garden.

INFORMAL ELEGANCE
The colorful blooms of Siberian irises (blue and white) and I. pseudacorus *(yellow) provide a focal point by a garden pond.*

RHIZOMATOUS AND BULBOUS IRISES

***I.* 'Bold Print'**
(bearded)

***I.* 'Carnaby'**
(bearded)

I. innominata
(Pacific Coast)

***I.* 'Geisha Gown'**
(Japanese)

I. bucharica
(Juno)

***I.* 'Joyce'**
(Reticulata)

Beardless irises
Irises in this group do not have bearded falls, but usually have marks called signals. Most have similar cultural requirements to bearded irises, but some prefer heavier soil.

Siberian irises have slender leaves and beautifully formed, delicately marked flowers. This group includes *I. chrysographes* and *I. sibirica*, plus many cultivars. They are easily grown in borders in rich soil that does not dry out, and are particularly suited to moist, waterside soil. The flowers last well when cut.

Spuria irises have narrow, reed-like foliage and elegant blooms. Spurias – *I. orientalis*, *I. graminea*, and *I. spuria* – are suited to sunny herbaceous borders, in well-drained soil; they tolerate drier conditions than the Siberian irises.

Pacific Coast irises, a group that includes *I. innominata* and *I. tenax*, are useful for cutting. Many good, free-flowering hybrids have been produced that are excellent for humus-rich, acid soils, in sun in cool regions or in shade in warmer climates. Others from groups that need similar conditions include *I. missouriensis*, which is more tolerant of alkaline soils; *I. verna* and *I. prismatica*; and *I. setosa*, which is more tolerant of sun.

Water irises are a group of elegant, moisture-loving plants that thrive in pond margins, bog gardens, or rich, permanently damp soils. They include *I. laevigata*, *I. pseudacorus*, *I. ensata* (syn. *I. kaempferi*), *I. versicolor*, and the Japanese and Louisiana irises. They may be difficult to establish.

Bulbous irises

The storage organs of these irises are bulbs, sometimes with thick, fleshy roots. Subgenera include Reticulata, Juno, and Xiphium irises.

Reticulata irises
These are dwarf, hardy bulbs that flower early. They prefer a sunny position in well-drained, acid or alkaline soil, or may be grown in pots in the bulb frame.

Juno irises
Junos need similar conditions to the Oncocyclus irises and are often difficult to grow. Vigorous species such as *I. bucharica* and *I. magnifica* grow well in warm, outdoor sites.

Xiphium irises
These include the brightly colored Dutch, English, and Spanish irises, often grown for cut flowers. Any well-drained soil in full sun is suitable. In cold areas, lift the bulbs in fall to overwinter in a frost-free place. Replant in spring.

Soil preparation and planting

HERBACEOUS perennials originate from many regions that have widely varying climatic and soil conditions, so whether the proposed site is sheltered or exposed, fertile or stony, there is always a number of plants that will thrive. It is better to select plants that will flourish in the given growing conditions rather than struggle against nature.

Site and exposure

When deciding which plants to grow, take into account climate, exposure, and soil, as well as the amount of sun, shade, and shelter the site receives at different times of day and from season to season. For example, shade cast by deciduous trees is densest in late spring and summer when the trees are in full leaf.

Different areas of the garden may provide varying growing conditions: for example, a south-facing border would be ideal for plants that thrive in sun, such as sedums, while a north-facing site or a position beneath a tree would be better for shade-loving species such as hostas, if they can be kept moist.

The ground next to a wall, fence, or hedge is usually fairly dry due to the effect of rain shadow, but since it also tends to be warm and sheltered, it may be a good position for plants that are not fully hardy.

Altering conditions

Especially in small gardens, it may be necessary to adapt some elements to create growing conditions that suit a wide range of plants. Heavy, waterlogged soils may be drained or the plants grown in raised beds or containers, while lighter soils may benefit from the addition of organic matter. Shade from trees may be reduced by judicious pruning, and shelter provided by shrubs, hedges, or windbreaks (see also COLD AND WIND PROTECTION, pp.520–21, and HEDGES AND SCREENS, pp.58–60).

Soil preparation

The ideal soil for the majority of perennial plants is a fertile loam that is well drained but retains adequate moisture. Use a commercial soil-testing kit to find out the degree of acidity or alkalinity of the soil because this partly determines which plants will thrive there.

It is also important to check soil drainage; if much of the ground remains waterlogged in wet weather, then tile or French drains must be installed (see SOILS AND FERTILIZERS, "Installing drains," p.531).

Clearing the site

All weeds should be cleared from the site prior to planting since once other plants are established, perennial weeds, in particular, are difficult to eradicate. If the ground is infested with weeds, treat the whole area with an appropriate weedkiller during the season before planting. If there are only a few perennial weeds, however, fork them out when you prepare the soil before planting.

During the first growing season, any remaining perennial weeds should be carefully removed with a hand fork as soon as they are noticed, or treated with a systemic weedkiller, taking care not to harm the newly planted perennials. Annual weeds can be either sprayed or forked out before the site is planted.

Improving the soil structure and fertility

All soils may be improved by the addition of humus or well-rotted organic matter such as manure or compost; this increases the water retention of light, free-draining soils and helps to open up the texture of heavy clay soils. It also improves the soil's fertility. Before planting (preferably a few weeks in advance), apply a 2–4in (5–10cm) layer of well-rotted organic matter over the site, then fork or rototill it into the top spit of the soil. Allow the soil to settle before planting. Provided that the soil is fertile and rich in humus, it is usually unnecessary to use fertilizer when planting perennials, although they may require feeding in subsequent seasons (see "Fertilizing," p.155).

CHOOSING PERENNIALS

GOOD EXAMPLE

LUPINE

Strong, healthy top-growth

Moist soil mix

Established, vigorous roots

POOR EXAMPLES

Weak, woody top-growth

Underdeveloped root system

Dry soil mix

Moss and weeds growing on the soil mix

Potbound roots

Selecting plants

Most perennials are sold container-grown, but bare-root plants are also sometimes available from fall to early spring, when they are dormant. When selecting plants, look for healthy, vigorous specimens with no sign of dieback or abnormally colored leaves that may indicate a lack of nutrients. If buying herbaceous plants at the beginning of the growing season, check that there are strong, emerging shoots. Plants that have a few fat, healthy looking buds are better than those that have a large number of weaker ones.

One or two annual weeds growing in the soil mix may be removed easily enough, but do not buy any container-grown plants that have perennial weeds, moss, or liverworts. These often indicate that the plant has been in its container for too long and may be starved of nutrients or that the soil mix is poorly drained, in which case the plant's roots may have rotted or died back.

When possible, remove the plant from its container and inspect the roots. Do not choose a plant with a mass of tightly coiling roots or one that has large roots pushing through the drainage holes. The roots should, however, be sufficiently established to retain most of the soil when the plant is removed from its container. Look for withered tips on the shoots: this can indicate a plant that has been allowed to dry excessively.

If buying bare-root plants, ensure that the root systems are strong and have not dried out, and that the young shoots are not wilting. Plant them as soon as possible after purchase, or protect them against moisture loss by wrapping them in plastic or wet newspaper until ready to plant.

DIVIDING LARGE PLANTS

1 *When buying easily divided perennials, look for a large plant with several strong shoots (here* Aster tongolensis*).*

2 *Gently pull the plant apart to make several small sections, each with its own roots. Keep plenty of soil around the roots.*

Dividing large plants

When buying fibrous-rooted plants, choose large examples with a number of healthy shoots that may be divided before planting, rather than a few smaller, cheaper specimens. Divide the plant by pulling it apart with your hands or two hand forks used back-to-back, taking care that each division has its own root system and retains as much soil around the roots as possible (see also "Dividing perennials," p.162).

PERENNIALS THAT PREFER SANDY SOIL

Acanthus spinosus
Achillea
Alchemilla
Armeria
Asphodeline lutea
Centranthus ruber
Dianthus, some ❄

Echinops ritro 'Veitch's Blue'

Echinops
Eryngium tripartitum
Gaillardia x *grandiflora* (cvs)
Globularia
Limonium latifolium
Nepeta x *faassenii*
Origanum vulgare 'Aureum'
Papaver orientale
Romneya coulteri
Sedum, some ❄
Sempervivum
Sisyrinchium, some ❄

PERENNIALS THAT TOLERATE CLAY SOIL

Aruncus dioicus
Astilbe
Butomus 💧
Caltha 💧
Cardamine pratensis
Dodecatheon
Eomecon
Filipendula ulmaria 'Aurea'
Gunnera manicata 💧
Hemerocallis
Hosta
Houttuynia
Lobelia cardinalis, *L. fulgens* ❄
Lysichiton 💧
Lysimachia, some ❄
Lythrum
Mimulus guttatus 💧
Myosotis scorpioides 💧
Peltiphyllum peltatum
Phormium
Polygonum
Pontederia 💧

Primula bulleyana

Primula bulleyana, *P. florindae*, *P. rosea*
Ranunculus ficaria, *R. flammula* 💧
Rheum
Rodgersia
Sagittaria, some ❄
Scrophularia auriculata
Trollius

KEY
❄ *Not frost hardy*
💧 *Tolerates waterlogged soil*

When to plant

Perennials grown in containers may be planted out at any time of year when the soil is workable, but the best seasons are spring and fall. Planting in fall helps the plants to establish quickly before the onset of winter because the soil is still warm enough to promote root growth, yet it is unlikely to dry out.

In cold areas, however, spring planting is better for perennials that are not entirely hardy or that dislike wet conditions, such as *Kniphofia*, *Schizostylis*, *Lobelia cardinalis*, and *Scabiosa caucasica*. This ensures that they are fully established before their first winter.

Bare-root specimens should generally be planted in spring or fall, although a few, such as hostas, may be transplanted successfully during the growing season.

Planting perennials

Plant perennials in prepared ground, taking care to position them at the right depth (see below): for example, those prone to basal rot are best planted slightly above ground level so that excess water may drain away.

Container-grown plants
First dig a planting hole, then water the plant thoroughly and remove it from its container, taking care not to

HOW TO PLANT A CONTAINER-GROWN PERENNIAL

1 *In a prepared bed, dig a hole 1½ times wider and deeper than the plant's root ball.*

2 *Soak the soil mix in the pot before sliding out the plant (here an* Aster).

3 *Gently scrape off the top 1½in (3cm) of soil to remove weeds and weed seeds. Carefully tease out the roots around the sides and base of the root ball.*

4 *Check that the plant crown is at the correct depth when planted and fill in around the root ball. Firm in around the plant and water thoroughly.*

Planting depths

While most perennials are best planted out at the same soil level as they were in their pots, a number grow better if planted higher or deeper, depending on their individual requirements. Some prefer a raised, well-drained site while others thrive in deeper, moist conditions.

ASTER

GROUND-LEVEL PLANTING
The majority of perennials should be planted so that the crown of the plant is level with the surrounding soil.

SISYRINCHIUM STRIATUM 'AUNT MAY'

RAISED PLANTING
Set plants that are prone to rot at the base, and variegated plants that tend to revert, with their crowns slightly above the ground.

HOSTA

SHALLOW PLANTING
Plant perennials that require a moist environment with their crowns about 1in (2cm) below ground level.

POLYGONATUM

DEEP PLANTING
Plant perennials with tuberous root systems so that their crowns are about 4in (10cm) below the soil surface.

damage the roots. To help the plant establish quickly, carefully loosen the sides and base of the root ball, particularly if rootbound, by teasing out the roots with your fingers or a hand fork. Place the plant at the appropriate depth in the prepared hole, backfill with soil, and firm. Loosen the surface of the soil with a hand fork and water in thoroughly.

Bare-root plants

To prevent dehydration, plant bare-root perennials as soon as possible after purchase. Prepare a hole as for container-grown plants, spread out the roots evenly, check the planting depth, and work in soil between the roots as you firm. Water well.

Transplanting self-sown seedlings

A number of perennials, for example *Aquilegia* and foxgloves (*Digitalis*), regularly produce self-sown seedlings that can be transplanted to a nursery bed or moved to another position in the garden.

Before lifting the seedlings, prepare suitable planting holes, spacing them to allow room for the plants to develop. Then gently lift each seedling with a trowel, taking care to retain as much soil around the roots as possible, and replant it immediately. Firm it in well and water it thoroughly. Shade the plants in sunny weather, and water them regularly until they are established.

Raised and peat beds

These beds are often used for growing acid-loving plants in a garden with alkaline soil or for providing a free-draining bed on heavy, clay soil. Plants that thrive in acid soil alone are best planted in a raised bed filled with an ericaceous soil mix (see also THE ROCK GARDEN, "Raised beds," p.189, and "Peat beds," p.188).

Raised beds may be constructed from a variety of materials including wood, bricks, stone, and logs (see also STRUCTURES AND SURFACES, "Raised beds," p.507). Include a deep layer of coarse drainage material (such as broken bricks) in the base – about one-third of the depth of the bed is ideal. Cover this with a layer of fibrous material and fill in with good topsoil.

Containers

As well as being a highly attractive way of displaying a number of plants, growing perennials in containers provides an opportunity to include plants that would not flourish in the open garden, either because they are too tender, or because the soil type is not suitable. If growing different plants together in one container, take care to choose those that thrive in similar conditions.

When choosing a container, make sure that it is sufficiently deep and wide to allow room for the plants' roots to develop properly. Consider how the selected plants will look when in full growth in relation to the container to achieve a pleasing balance between them. Tall plants in deep, narrow containers and small plants in large, wide ones may seem out of proportion.

TRANSPLANTING SEEDLINGS

Lift seedlings with soil around their roots to avoid breaking up the root ball. Plant out and water well.

Planting in containers

If using a heavy container such as a stone urn, lead trough, wooden half barrel, or large terracotta pot, place it in position before filling and planting since it will be very cumbersome to move afterwards. Plastic containers are, of course, considerably lighter, but they are less stable and may be blown over in strong winds. Set the container on a support of blocks or bricks to allow free drainage.

Make sure that the container has drainage holes in the base or low on the sides to prevent waterlogging. Cover the holes with 2–3in (5–8cm) of broken crocks or stones and add a layer of fibrous material, for example sphagnum moss or peat chunks; this allows water to filter through freely yet prevents soil mix from being washed out or blocking the drainage holes.

Most potting mixes are suitable, although acid loving plants must be planted in an ericaceous soil mix. A prepared general soil mix containing a slow-release fertilizer suits most plants; those that need extra drainage (such as *Sedum* or *Achillea*), prefer a soil mix containing additional grit or sharp sand.

Before planting, arrange the plants on the soil mix to ensure that they have enough room to develop freely. Plant as for perennials in open ground and keep well watered until established.

1 *When planting in a container, group the plants while still in their pots to determine the spacing and arrangement. Then plant, firm in, and water well.*

2 *A few months later, the plants will have grown and developed to form a well-balanced, attractive display.*

PERENNIALS THAT REQUIRE ACID SOIL

Anigozanthos manglesii ❄
Cypripedium reginae
Darlingtonia

Anigozanthos manglesii

Drosera, some ❄
Nepenthes ❄
Pinguicula, some ❄
Sarracenia flava ❄
Trillium
Uvularia

PERENNIALS THAT TOLERATE VERY ALKALINE SOIL

Acanthus spinosus
Achillea filipendulina 'Gold Plate'
Aconitum
Anchusa
Anemone hupehensis, *A.* x *hybrida*
Anthyllis
Bergenia
Berkheya, some ❄
Brunnera
Campanula lactiflora
Catananche
Centranthus
Clematis heracleifolia, *C. recta*
Coronilla varia
Corydalis lutea
Dianthus
Doronicum
Eremurus
Eryngium, some ❄
Galega
Geranium pratense
Gypsophila paniculata
Helenium
Helleborus, some ❄
Heuchera
Kniphofia, some ❄
Linaria purpurea
Linum narbonense
Lychnis chalcedonica
Paeonia
Salvia nemorosa
Saponaria
Scabiosa

Scabiosa caucasica 'Clive Greaves'

Sidalcea
Stachys, some ❄
Verbascum
Veronica spicata

KEY
❄ *Not frost hardy*

Peonies

THE exotic, often fragrant blooms of peonies are one of the delights of the garden in spring. After flowering, they maintain their attractive, deeply divided leaves into the fall, and some species, such as *Paeonia mlokosewitschii*, bear colorful seedpods.

The genus includes herbaceous perennials (common garden peonies), which often reach a height of 3ft (1m), and deciduous shrubs (tree peonies) up to 6ft (2m). Their cup-shaped or globular flowers are classified as single, double, semidouble, or anemone-form. Colors range from pure white through pink to crimson and purple, plus shades of yellow and salmon. Peonies combine easily with other perennials and woody plants. They prefer sun but tolerate light shade.

Herbaceous peonies

The spectacular blooms of some herbaceous peonies have traditionally mingled well in cottage gardens (see p.140). They may be planted as a hedge, lasting from the bronze-red shoots in spring until the foliage is cut down by fall frosts. Once established, herbaceous peonies can also be cut freely for indoor decoration.

Herbaceous peonies need 30–60 days with night temperatures around freezing in order to flower.

Planting

Herbaceous peonies should be planted bare-root in early fall (see p.147); if planted in spring, they may not bloom for a year or two. Space them at least 18in (45cm) apart with 2in (5cm) of soil over the buds or "eyes"; if planted too deeply, the peony may not flower, and if too shallowly, the buds may dry out. Maintain a loose, 1in (2.5cm) mulch throughout the year.

Routine care and propagation

Apply a high-phosphorus fertilizer in early spring. Support herbaceous peonies when the new shoots are ankle-high (see "Staking," p.156). For extra-large or exhibition blooms, disbud in spring when the lateral buds are pea sized.

PRUNING A TREE PEONY

In spring, prune tree peonies to remove any dead or frost-damaged wood and crossing branches.

Remove any branches that overlap or cross each other.

Cut out dead wood at the base, using loppers if necessary.

Cut back frost-damaged shoots to where new growth starts.

TYPES OF PEONY

Paeonia mlokosewitschii (single; herbaceous)

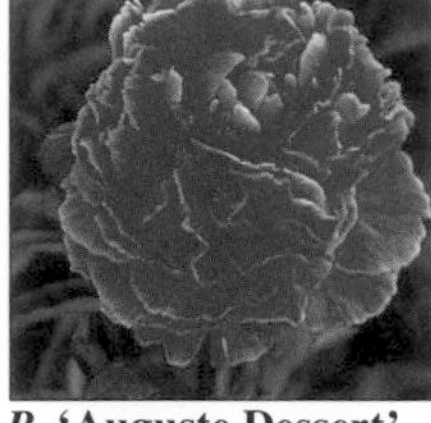

***P.* 'Auguste Dessert'** (semidouble; herbaceous)

***P.* 'Souvenir de Maxime Cornu'** (double; tree)

***P.* 'Bowl of Beauty'** (anemone; herbaceous)

***P.* 'Krinkled White'** (single; herbaceous)

***P.* 'Coral Supreme'** (double; herbaceous)

After a severe frost in fall, cut the stems to the ground. Peony wilt (p.571) and gray mold/*Botrytis* (p.559) may be troublesome.

Propagate by division in late summer or fall (see "Dividing peonies," p.163); peonies are slow to reestablish. Alternatively, sow seed in fall after cold stratification (see p.160); it may take three years to germinate.

Tree peonies

Tree peonies are often planted in front of evergreens, such as yew (*Taxus*), *Euonymus*, or holly (*Ilex*), which show off the peony blooms. They may also be used as accent shrubs in herbaceous borders and mixed borders where their flowering time coincides with *Dicentra*, candytuft (*Iberis*), irises, tulips, crabapples (*Malus*), azaleas (*Rhododendron*), and *Wisteria*. Tree peonies make perfect cut flowers if the blooms are cut as the flower buds show color and start to open.

Tree peonies are usually bought container-grown and grafted onto a readily available rootstock so that the cultivar comes into flower more quickly. Tree peonies prefer a slightly alkaline pH; prepare the soil for and plant as for other shrubs in fall (see "Soil preparation" and "How to plant," p.68). Space them at least 4ft (1.2m) from nearby plants. Bury the rootstock 4in (10cm) below soil level so that the grafted cultivar develops its own roots.

DISBUDDING

When the lateral buds below the top bud of each shoot are about 1/2in (1cm) in diameter, pinch them out to concentrate growth into the central bloom.

Routine care and pruning

Feed with a high-phosphorus fertilizer in spring. Protect from small animals (p.551) in the first few years, and from spring frosts.

Prune tree peonies to improve their shape and, occasionally, to maintain or reduce size. In spring, cut out dead and crossing branches, and any frost-damaged shoots. After flowering, cut back new growth that is straggly or unbalanced to a shoot or bud facing in the required direction.

Propagation

Propagate by semiripe cuttings in late summer (see p.82) or by apical-wedge grafting in winter (see p.89). Species may also be propagated by seed in fall (see p.84).

Daylilies

ALTHOUGH they belong to the lily family (Liliaceae), daylilies (*Hemerocallis*) are not true lilies; their common name comes from the lily-shaped flowers that, in the older varieties, open in the morning and fade before sunset. Many modern cultivars stay open into the evening, whereas others, such as 'Stella de Oro', open in the evening and last through the following day.

Types of daylily

There are two main types of daylily: evergreen and herbaceous. Current breeding programs are developing crosses between them to produce semievergreen cultivars. Daylilies range in size from compact plants that grow to only 12–15in (30–38cm) tall, to large plants that may reach 5ft (1.5m). Tetraploid daylilies, available from nurseries, have four sets of chromosomes, in contrast to diploids, with two sets. Tetraploids are larger than diploids and produce sturdier growth. However, they tend to be less graceful than diploids and too large for small gardens.

Modern hybrids are available in a wide range of colors, from near white, through shades of yellow, orange, red, pink, and purple to almost black. Some flowers have differently colored eye-zones or bands of varied colors on the petals. The flowers may be from 1½in (4cm) to more than 9in (22cm) in diameter, and they come in a variety of shapes, usually classified as single, double, or spider.

Daylilies bloom throughout late spring to early fall. Most flower for four to six weeks. Extended-flowering cultivars continue for up to eight weeks, and there are some repeat-flowering varieties. A few cultivars, such as *H.* 'Frozen Jade', are strongly fragrant.

Using daylilies

With their long period of flowering, daylilies are suited to a wide variety of situations. In the mixed border, for example, daylilies make good accent plants; choose tall cultivars with showy flowers, such as 'Susie Wong' or 'Look'. Their abundant leaves may be used to hide the foliage of sprawling plants such as *Papaver orientale*. Repeat-flowering cultivars such as 'Stella de Oro' and 'Happy Returns' are colorful additions to the cottage garden.

Shorter-growing daylilies make ideal ground covers since they need little maintenance; choose cultivars such as 'Bitsy' and 'Elf Cap'. These also make attractive edging. For containers, use fast-growing, upright cultivars such as 'Country Club'.

Cultivation

Evergreen daylilies are generally best suited to warm climates and herbaceous ones to cold, whereas semievergreen types are suitable for both. Local nurseries will sell appropriate cultivars for your climate. All have the same cultural needs.

DAYLILY FLOWERS

***Hemerocallis* 'Ice Carnival'** (single; herbaceous)

***H.* 'Cream Drop'** (single; semievergreen)

***H.* 'Circle Round'** (single; herbaceous)

***H.* 'Leebea Orange Crush'** (single; evergreen)

***H.* 'Milk Chocolate'** (single; herbaceous)

***H.* 'Louise Mercer'** (double; herbaceous)

Site and planting

Daylilies will survive in almost any soil, except solid clay. They thrive in sun or shade, but bloom best if they are in sunlight for at least half the day. When grown in shade, the blooms will be fewer and the plants taller. For details of how to plant, see "Planting perennials," p.146.

Routine care

For the greatest number of flowers, feed daylilies in early spring and again in summer, using a balanced fertilizer at a rate of 2oz (50g) per established plant. Water daylilies well, especially during bloom. In cold climates, keep the foliage over winter to protect the crowns.

An established clump needs dividing to maintain vigor once its flower size becomes smaller and the clump becomes congested. Division is usually necessary every three to five years in rich soil, especially for repeat-flowering cultivars, but less often poorer soil. Divide when the plant is dormant.

Pests and diseases

Thrips (p.562) may feed on flower buds, causing pale streaks on the petals, most noticeable on dark cultivars. Japanese beetles (p.563) and spotted cucumber beetles (p.563) eat the buds, flowers, and leaves. Crown rot (p.571) can cause problems in wet soils during hot, humid weather.

Propagation

The easiest method is by division when the plant is dormant (see "Fibrous-rooted plants," p.162). To make the clump easier to handle, cut the foliage down to about 8in (20cm) and trim and wash the roots before dividing the plant. Aim for new plants with at least four shoots (ramets) each.

Daylilies are also easy to raise from seed (see p.160); they should come into flower from one to three years after sowing.

DAYLILIES IN A MIXED BORDER
Daylilies blend with other herbaceous perennials, including hostas, hardy asters, and delphiniums. Here, the foliage hides maturing Papaver orientale.

REPEAT-FLOWERING DAYLILIES
Cultivars such as 'Stella de Oro' *offer an extended flowering season.*

Ground covers

COVERING the ground with a dense carpet of flowering or foliage plants is a fairly recent planting technique designed primarily to reduce the labor of weeding among ornamental plants. Many ground cover plants are also decorative in their own right, however, adding both attractive pools of color and contrasting textures, while unifying areas between larger plants and between other garden features.

Once established, ground cover plants will smother most weed seedlings that attempt to grow beneath their canopy by depriving them of light, as well as by competing with them for water and nutrients. In the wild, this is frequently a natural process; nature may be imitated in the garden to create attractive, integrated plant associations requiring very little aftercare.

Selecting ground cover plants

Choose attractive, vigorous plants that will quickly cover their allotted space with close, dense growth, without becoming unduly invasive. They should be perennial, either remaining above ground throughout the year, or reemerging and developing rapidly in spring. Annuals and biennials are normally unsuitable except as seasonal fillers while the ground cover is establishing. Similarly, tender plants, which can form good cover in frost-free conditions, are of only temporary value in cold climates.

A ground cover should be selected to suit its location, for example wet and shady, or dry, hot, and sunny situations. It should be easy to care for, routinely requiring only an annual clipping and feeding. Choose long-term plants that should remain healthy for five to ten years or more. Finally, look for species, cultivars, and forms that will provide interesting and attractive foliage and habit as well as flowers and fruit.

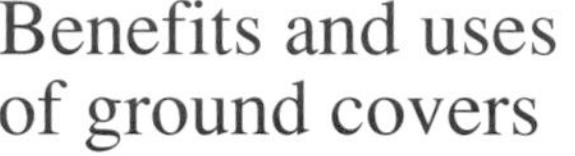

Benefits and uses of ground covers

Apart from reducing the need for weeding, ground covers can reduce evaporation from exposed, freely draining soils. A dense planting of drought-resistant ground covers such as *Juniperus horizontalis* 'Wiltonii', *Cotoneaster horizontalis*, *Ajuga reptans*, *Thymus serpyllum*, and lavender (*Lavandula*) will shade the soil and keep it cool, while their slowly decomposing leaf litter also acts as a mulch.

Steep banks, highly subject to erosion by rain and wind, may be planted with ground cover plants such as *Juniperus squamata* 'Blue Carpet', *Cotoneaster dammeri*, or *Hypericum calycinum*. Their low, spreading habit, evergreen foliage, and vigorous suckers and rooted layers combine to form a stable cover that prevents erosion.

In open gardens, shrubby evergreen ground cover plants can act as low boundary markers. Unfortunately, they also trap windblown rubbish beneath their branches, which should be raked out occasionally.

In a wildlife garden, ground covers can be used to attract bees and butterflies. Several species of fritillary butterfly feed on the foliage of violets (*Viola* spp.), which makes a dense, informal ground cover. The creeping thymes, such as *Thymus praecox* and its cultivars, are very attractive to bees.

Combining plants

Ground cover plants with various colors, textures, and forms may be combined to make garden features in their own right, or may provide an attractive linking element in a design.

Backgrounds for bulbs

A low carpet of plants can make an excellent, low-maintenance background for naturalized bulbs and, unlike grass, will not need mowing as the bulb foliage fades. *Vinca minor* 'Atropurpurea', with dark-green leaves and purple flowers, looks superb as a foil for white daffodils such as *Narcissus* 'Silver Chimes' or 'Thalia'. Similarly, *Lysimachia nummularia* 'Aurea' is a good foil for crocuses such as the white 'Snow Bunting' or the copper and yellow 'Zwanenburg Bronze'.

Ground cover tapestry

A patchwork effect can be created by combining low ground cover plants of different color and leaf size. For example, the long, glossy leaves and blue flowers of *Ajuga reptans* 'Atropurpurea' are offset by the matte, heart-shaped leaves of *Tiarella cordifolia*. Both contrast beautifully with the red-flushed *Epimedium* x *rubrum* in spring. Take care not to plant slow growers with small leaves next to large-leaved, vigorous species, which can swamp them.

Color in corners

Ground cover plants that thrive in permanent shade are useful for brightening dark corners: contrast

ORNAMENTAL GROUND COVER PLANTS

***Hosta fortunei* 'Aurea Marginata'**
Plant 12–18in (30–45cm) apart.

***Houttuynia cordata* 'Chameleon'**
Plant 12–18in (30–45cm) apart.

***Lamium maculatum* 'Beacon Silver'**
Plant 8–12in (20–30cm) apart.

Tanacetum densum
Plant 6–8in (15–20cm) apart.

Tiarella cordifolia
Plant 12in (30cm) apart.

***Epimedium* x *youngianum* 'Niveum'**
Plant 12in (30cm) apart.

***Erica carnea* 'December Red'**
Plant 12in (30cm) apart.

***Vinca major* 'Variegata'**
Plant 24in (60cm) apart.

Cotoneaster horizontalis
Plant 3ft (1m) apart.

TEXTURAL CARPET
A vigorous dwarf juniper, Juniperus squamata 'Blue Carpet', *provides a spreading mat of color and texture up to 10ft (3m) wide.*

PLANTING THROUGH LANDSCAPE FABRIC

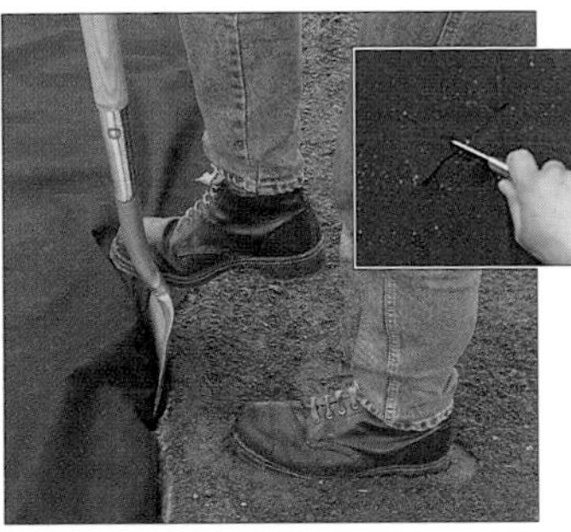

1 *Push the edges of the fabric into the ground with a spade, and make X-shaped slits with a knife (see inset) for the plants.*

2 *Plants with a number of shoots (here* Bergenia) *may be divided into smaller clumps, each with healthy buds and a root system.*

3 *Insert a plant through each slit, using a trowel. Firm the soil around the roots of the plants and water them in.*

4 *Apply a decorative mulch on top of the fabric to a depth of at least 2in (5cm).*

the bold, shining deep red winter leaves of *Bergenia* 'Ballawley' with the rough-textured and cream-edged leaves of *Symphytum* x *uplandicum* 'Variegatum'. Further contrast can be provided by the small, golden-variegated, dark green leaves of *Euonymus fortunei* 'Gold Spot'.

An undercanopy

Ground cover plants are not always low growing; many of the taller shrubs completely suppress weeds beneath them. Shrubs are particularly useful for providing medium-height cover, or as an undercanopy below trees. *Cotoneaster conspicuus*, with bright, scarlet berries, *Prunus laurocerasus* 'Otto Luyken', with glossy, dark green leaves, and *Fatsia japonica* 'Variegata', with deeply lobed leaves edged in white, cover the ground well and provide interest, even in winter.

Planting

It is essential to prepare the soil thoroughly before planting: the ground must be free of weeds, especially creeping, perennial weeds that will be difficult to eradicate from established dense cover. This can be achieved by chemicals or hand-weeding, or by using a sheet mulch.

There are several ways of planting ground cover plants to ensure quick cover: plant them at spacings recommended for the species or cultivar concerned and cover the soil with a loose mulch, plant them at recommended spacings through weed-resistant landscape fabric or black plastic; or plant them more densely than would be usual to provide cover more quickly.

The recommended spacing for most plants is just a little less than the approximate spread of a mature specimen. To calculate the number of plants required, measure out the area and then divide this by the total spread of the chosen plant. For example, an area of 80sq ft (8sq m) that is planted with bergenias spaced apart at about 24in (60cm) would require about 30 plants.

The choice of method will depend on the type and cost of plants used, the climate and soil conditions, and how long you are willing to wait for the final result. Fast-growing plants in favorable conditions and at recommended spacings will generally fill in within two to three years.

Growth is determined by many variable factors, but in general, if plants are spaced at two-thirds of the normal distances, they should join up in 18 months to two years. More plants are needed, of course, but some can be increased by inserting cuttings at close spacing into their final planting positions (see below).

Propagation by cuttings

Some ground cover plants, such as *Euonymus fortunei*, *Hypericum calycinum*, and ivies (*Hedera*), may be propagated from hardwood cuttings that are inserted directly into their final growing position through holes in landscape fabric.

In fall, when the soil is still warm and moist, take cuttings about 6–8in (15–20cm) long and remove the leaves along the lower two-thirds of the stem. Make holes through the fabric and then insert the cuttings so that about two-thirds of their length is in the ground. Space them at about half the normal planting distance for faster cover. The cuttings normally root very quickly and the young plants develop rapidly during the spring, without heavy competition from weeds.

Mulching ground covers

When ground cover plants have been newly planted at the correct distance, the ground between them will still be bare. Until the plants have begun to spread over the surrounding area, it is advisable to apply a mulch in the gaps around them. This will help to retain moisture in the soil, and will also discourage the growth of weeds. A loose mulch such as bark chips or pine needles is ideal for the purpose, and should be applied to a depth of about 2in (5cm).

To preserve moisture between new plants (here Erica carnea), *apply a loose mulch about 2in (5cm) deep.*

Pruning

Most ground cover plants need very little or no regular pruning, although many shrubby plants benefit from an occasional trim to keep them compact. Remove any dead foliage from herbaceous plants.

A few plants need more regular attention. *Vinca* species and cultivars often produce long, straggling, wiry shoots. In late winter or very early spring, cut them back to near the base with pruners. Fresh shoots, which produce more compact growth and denser cover, will soon appear and fill the gaps.

Santolina, when a few years old, tends to open out, revealing its center. Pruning the plants back hard in the spring encourages rapid new growth, but can leave them looking bare for a period of time. A good way of avoiding this problem is to prune back about one-third of the number of plants each year.

Hypericum calycinum may, after a few years, become rather straggly with thin, weak stems. Trim plants annually with shears, a nylon-line trimmer, or a mower set on high, in early spring before growth begins.

PRUNING GROUND COVERS

SANTOLINA
Some bushy plants need hard pruning. Cut back to the main woody stems, just above where new growth is breaking.

HYPERICUM CALYCINUM
In spring, cut the previous season's shoots back hard.

Hostas

Grown primarily for their bold, sculptural foliage, many hosta species and cultivars also produce attractive white, lilac, or purple flowers. Easy to maintain and long-lived, hostas make a valuable addition to any garden.

Although there are over 800 registered cultivars, there is no formal classification system for hostas. Many nurseries classify hostas by their size when mature: miniatures are under 10in (25cm) tall and up to 12in (30cm) wide; small are 10–15 x 12–15in (25–38 x 30–38cm); medium 15–18 x 15–24in (38–45 x 38–60cm); large 18–24 x 24–30in (45–60 x 60–75cm); and extra-large taller than 24in (60cm) and wider than 30in (75cm).

Using hostas in the garden

Hostas are highly sought after as foliage plants for shaded areas, and make eye-catching displays in pots or beside ponds. The range of colors, textures, and shapes of their foliage is stunning: modern hybrids may have leaves patterned in shades of green, white, and gold, or edged in a different, contrasting color. Their texture may be rich and glossy or soft and velvety. Leaves may be narrow and ribbonlike, heart-shaped, or almost circular. There are hostas suitable for any degree of shade, from light or dappled, to deep. In general, the blue-leaved hostas flourish in deep shade, while yellow-leaved cultivars prefer some sun.

Hostas for shady places

Hostas make excellent companion plants for other shade-loving perennials. They act as a foil for bright flowers such as those of *Astilbe*, while their large leaves make a counterpoint to the finer foliage of other plants including Japanese painted fern (*Athyrium niponicum* 'Pictum') and sedges (*Carex*). For shady locations in the rock garden, choose miniature hostas such as *H. venusta* and *H.* 'Tot Tot'.

Consider planting a hosta to enliven a shady entrance. Choose a variety with striking foliage such as the platelike *H.* 'Blue Angel' or yellow-leaved *H.* 'Zounds', both of which have showy flowers in midsummer. Fragrant hostas ideal for planting close to the house include *H.* 'Sugar and Cream', *H.* 'So Sweet', and *H. plantaginea*, which is one of the last to flower.

On a shaded patio, grow hostas in containers to contrast with more flamboyant annuals. The bright green *H.* 'Sum and Substance' or delicately mottled *H. tokudama* 'Aureo-nebulosa' are excellent plants for containers.

Mixed Border
Hostas blend well with other shade plants, acting as a foil for summer flowers, and providing interest after the flowers have finished.

Ground cover

Hostas make a particularly striking ground cover when planted as a mass. Choose cultivars carefully for continuous interest from both foliage and flowers. For example, a combination of *H.* 'Green Piecrust', *H.* 'Krossa Regal', *H.* 'Honeybells', and *H. plantaginea* makes an exotic planting that will flower for several months in succession. A more subtle effect is achieved by restricting the design to a few hostas within a limited spectrum of leaf colors. For a fast-growing, low ground cover, choose cultivars such as *H.* 'Blue Cadet' and *H.* 'Ground Master'.

Hostas in other locations

Several hostas planted together may be used as a low summer hedge that needs no clipping. The lance-leaved hosta (*H. lancifolia*) is ideal for this and will take full sun in all but the hottest regions; it gives a display of slender purple bells in midsummer.

Hostas for Different Situations

***H. tokudama* 'Aureo-nebulosa'**
Medium-size, for moderate to deep shade

H. decorata* f. *decorata
Medium-size, for light to deep shade

***H.* 'Gold Standard'**
Medium-size, prefers light shade

***H.* 'Halcyon'**
Medium-size, for quite heavy shade

H. plantaginea
Extra-large, likes morning or evening sun or light shade

***H. ventricosa* 'Aureo-maculata'**
Extra-large, prefers light to moderate shade

***H. montana* 'Aurea Marginata'**
Extra-large hosta, for light to medium shade

H. lancifolia
Small to medium, tolerating full sun

***H.* 'August Moon'**
Large hosta, for dappled shade

H. sieboldiana* var. *elegans
Medium, for light shade

H. ventricosa
Medium to large, for medium to dark shade

Most hostas grow well in sites that are close to water; *H.* 'Midas Touch', *H. undulata* var. *erromena*, and *H. u.* 'Albomarginata' are especially good in moist soils.

Cultivation

Hostas tolerate a wide range of soils, except for heavy clay or pure sand. They grow best in a good, moist loam, rich in organic matter, with a pH from 6.5 to 7.3. Prepare the soil well before planting, particularly if it is lacking in nutrients (see "Soil preparation," p.145).

Planting hostas

Bare-root hostas can be planted in spring or fall. Container-grown hostas can be planted at any time, but do not disturb the roots if planting while they are in active growth (see "Planting perennials," p.146). In spring or fall, however, unless the container is full of roots, it is better to shake off much of the soil and treat as a bare-root hosta.

Plant with the crown slightly buried so that it remains moist (see "Planting depths," p.146), but on heavy soils, plant with the crown at ground level. Do not allow any manure to come into contact with the roots at planting since it may cause discolored foliage in the first year. Leave a slight depression around the plant at first so that when you water, the moisture soaks directly down into the roots.

Routine care

Hostas take about five years to reach maturity and can then be left undisturbed for many years. Water only in prolonged periods of drought.

To produce lush foliage of a good color, feed hostas with well-rotted manure or compost since these increase the soil humus content. In spring, apply an all-purpose inorganic fertilizer to hostas in poor soil.

Mulching

Apply a spring mulch while the soil is moist. Use only well-rotted materials in order to discourage slugs. In regions with very cold winters, apply a mulch of straw or leaves around each hosta after the ground is frozen; take care not to cover the crown of the plant. On new, shallow-rooted plants the mulch prevents them from lifting after a severe frost, while on established plants it often reduces crown rot. If very coarse material is used as a mulch, it should be removed in the spring.

Pests and diseases

Slugs may devastate hostas, sometimes reducing leaves to tatters by the end of the season (p.550); snails (p.550) and earwigs (p.550) also chew holes in leaves. Crown rot (p.571) may cause problems, especially on heavy soils.

GROUND COVER
In a border with dappled shade, hostas make an ideal ground cover. Select leaf colors to go with the varying degrees of shade.

Propagation

Hostas are easily increased by division (see "Dividing hostas," p.162); it is also possible simply to cut a slice out of a crown with a sharp spade. Hostas may be raised from seed collected when the pods turn brown. Sow the seeds outside in fall or inside in the winter (see p.160).

The Ross method

A practical method of propagating hostas is the Ross method in which small cuts are made in the rootstock in spring to stimulate new buds and roots to form.

By fall, the cuts will have callused and developed new roots and dormant buds. The entire plant can then be lifted either in fall or the following spring and divided into pieces (as for division), each with its own bud. After transplanting, the new plants should each be allowed to grow on for at least a year before this process is repeated.

PROPAGATING HOSTAS BY THE ROSS METHOD

1 *In spring when the buds have started to grow, carefully scrape away the soil from around the base of a young plant to expose the crown.*

2 *Carefully wipe the surface of the rootstock clean with a soft, moistened cloth, taking care not to disturb the roots.*

3 *With a sharp knife, make a vertical cut through the crown. Unless the plant is very small, make a second cut at right angles to the first.*

4 *Dust each cut with hormone rooting powder and insert a toothpick to hold the cut open.*

5 *Pack soil back around the crown of the plant, firm, and water well. Give routine care throughout the growing season. By fall, dormant buds will develop.*

6 *Lift and divide the clump the following spring when new shoots emerge. Alternatively, divide the previous fall.*

Chrysanthemums

THE rich colors and luxuriant shapes of their long-lasting flowerheads make chrysanthemums (*C. morifolium* hybrids) ideal for garden displays and cutting. The flower types are classified by the type and arrangement of the florets, and by the flowering season.

Chrysanthemums naturally form a number of flowerheads on side shoots; these are known as sprays. Disbuds are produced by removing the side buds of sprays to leave one terminal bud that forms a larger flowerhead. Early-flowering chrysanthemums flower from late summer to early fall. Late-flowering types bloom from mid- to late fall.

Early-flowering chrysanthemums

These need a sunny site with well-drained, slightly acid soil. Set out small plants in spring (see "Soil preparation and planting," p.145–7).

TYPES OF CHRYSANTHEMUM FLOWERHEAD

INCURVED
C. 'Alison Kirk'
Fully double flowerheads with incurved florets closing tightly over the crown.

REFLEXED
C. 'Rose Yvonne Arnaud'
Fully double flowerheads with partly reflexed florets and a spiky outline.

INTERMEDIATE (FORMAL)
C. 'Skater's Waltz'
Fully double flowerheads with loosely incurving florets and a regular shape.

POMPON
C. 'Maria'
Fully double, dense flowerheads bearing tubular florets with flat, rounded petals.

SINGLE
C. 'Rytorch'
Flowerheads with prominent central discs and 5 rows of flat-petaled florets.

SPOON
C. 'Pennine Jewel'
Single flowerheads with tubular florets. Florets open at the tips to form a spoon shape.

C. 'Morning Star'
Dwarf plant, bearing a mass of single flowers, each with a diameter of 1in (2.5cm). The blooms densely cover the plant to form a rounded head.

Pinching and disbudding
Soon after planting, pinch central growing tips of chrysanthemums grown as sprays or disbuds to encourage lateral displays.

For sprays, when laterals are 3in (8cm) long, reduce to four per stem and pinch again. Another pinch may be made in long growing seasons, but allow six weeks from the last pinch to flowering. For small, even-sized flowerheads, pinch the terminal bud to encourage side shoots.

For disbuds, reduce laterals to four to six well-spaced shoots. To produce one flower per lateral, snap off all the side shoots and remove the side buds.

DISBUDDING

For disbuds, once the side buds around each terminal bud have tiny stalks, pinch them out so that only the central bud develops.

Routine care
A month after the final pinch, apply a balanced fertilizer at a rate of 2oz/sq yd (70g/sq m). Repeat this one month later. Give a weekly liquid feed until the buds show color.

In frost-free climates, overwinter early-flowering types in the ground, cutting down stems in spring. In temperate climates, lift plants and trim to 9in (22cm). Shake off surplus soil and store the rootstocks in a shallow box of slightly moist soil-based potting mix. Do not bury too deeply. Keep them almost dry and store in a frost-free place. In early spring give light and heat, then water to encourage new shoots.

Taking cuttings
Take cuttings four to six weeks after new shoots appear (see *How to Propagate by Basal Stem Cuttings*, p.164). Pot up the rooted cuttings and grow on. Harden them off and plant out when danger of frost is past.

Late-flowering chrysanthemums

Usually grown in pots so that they may be easily moved, these are unsuitable for planting out in the North.

Pot up young plants in late spring into soil-based potting mix with a slow-release fertilizer. In summer, stand the pots outside in a sunny, sheltered place and water well. Pinch and disbud in midsummer as above.

In temperate areas, move the pots to a cool greenhouse in early fall; keep them at 50°F (10°C). Cut back the plants after flowering to about 9in (22cm). Overwinter at 40°F (5°C), in a cool greenhouse if necessary. Bring them into growth at about 45°F (7°C). Take cuttings as above.

PINCHING AND REMOVING LATERALS

PINCHING
When the cutting is 6–8in (15–20cm) high, pinch out 1/2in (1cm) at the tip to encourage new laterals.

REMOVING EXCESS LATERALS
About 2 months later, select 3 or 4 healthy, evenly spaced laterals and remove any others.

Routine care

ALTHOUGH most perennials will thrive with only little maintenance, certain routine tasks help to keep them looking attractive and in the peak of health through the growing season. Occasional watering and feeding is necessary, and the surrounding ground should be kept clear of competing weeds. In addition to this, many perennials produce further growth and flowers if deadheaded or cut back, while dividing the plants from time to time renews vigor. Tall, fragile perennials, or those with top-heavy flowerheads, may also require staking, particularly in exposed gardens.

Watering

The amount of water that plants require depends on the site, climate, and the individual species. Provided that they are grown in appropriate conditions, established perennials generally need little or no additional irrigation. If there are prolonged dry spells during the growing season, give extra water to the plants to keep them turgid. If they wilt or die back from lack of water, they will normally recover fully after heavy rainfall or will become dormant until the following season.

Young plants need to have sufficient water to become established, but they should not be watered once they are growing satisfactorily, except in very dry weather. In regions where summer drought is normal, such as the Southwest, installing irrigation tubing around the plants, with individual emitters for each plant, may be required.

Fertilizing

In soil that has been thoroughly prepared before planting, few perennials require more than an annual top-dressing of a balanced slow-release fertilizer, preferably applied in early spring after rain.

If conditions are dry, first water the soil thoroughly, then work the fertilizer into the soil surface with a hand fork. Do not let the fertilizer touch the leaves since it may scorch them. Plants that are grown primarily for their ornamental foliage, for example *Rheum* and hostas, benefit from an occasional liquid feed during the growing season.

If a plant is not growing well, in spite of being in a suitable site, look carefully to see if it has been attacked by pests or disease, and treat accordingly. Foliage that is yellowing prematurely may indicate problems with soil drainage or a lack of certain nutrients. If appropriate drainage or feeding does not seem to improve the condition of the plant, send a soil sample for analysis by a laboratory to determine which elements are lacking (see also "Soil nutrients and fertilizers," pp.532–3).

Mulching

An annual mulch of organic matter such as spent mushroom compost or bark chips helps to suppress weed growth, reduce soil moisture loss, and improve the soil structure. Apply when the ground is moist during spring or fall by spreading a 1–2in (2.5–5cm) layer around the crowns of the plants (see also SOILS AND FERTILIZERS, "Mulches," p.534).

Weeding

Keep beds and borders free from weeds at all times, if practical, because they compete with the ornamental plants for moisture and nutrients in the soil. Underplanting with suitable ground cover plants (see GROUND COVERS, pp.150–51) or mulching in spring helps to reduce problems with annual weeds. Any weed seedlings that do appear from windblown seed or seeds that have been dormant in the soil should be removed by hand before they become established.

If perennial weeds appear in the ground after initial cultivation, carefully dig them out with a hand fork. It is usually impractical to apply systemic weedkillers at this time because, to be effective, they must be applied when the weeds are in full growth, usually as they reach the flowering stage. At this point it is virtually impossible to avoid accidentally spraying the ornamental plants at the same time.

If the roots of a perennial weed have grown into those of a border plant, dig up the plant in early spring, wash the roots, and carefully pull out the weed. Then replant the border plant, ensuring that no part of the weed is left in the original site. Do not hoe around perennials since this may cause damage to any surface roots and emerging shoots. For further information on controlling weed growth, see PLANT PROBLEMS, "Weeds," pp.575–9.

APPLYING MULCH

Clear any weeds, and apply a 1–2in (2.5–5cm) layer of mulch to moist soil; do not damage the young shoots of the plant (here a peony).

Improving flowering

Certain perennial plants may be cut back during growth in one of three ways to improve the number or size of their flowers or to extend the flowering season.

Thinning

Although most herbaceous plants produce numerous vigorous shoots in spring, some of these may be spindly and thin. If these weak shoots are removed at an early stage of growth, the plant then goes on to develop fewer, sturdier shoots that usually produce larger flowers. When the plant is about a quarter to one-third of its eventual height, pinch out or cut back the weakest shoots. This thinning technique may be used successfully with, for example, delphiniums, phlox, and Michaelmas daisies (*Aster*).

Pinching

It is possible to increase the number of flowers on perennial plants that readily produce side shoots, such as *Helenium* and *Rudbeckia* species and cultivars, by removing (pinching) the growing tip of each stem. This technique also produces sturdier growth and prevents plants from becoming too tall and straggly. Pinching should be carried out when the plant is about one-third of its ultimate height. Pinch off 1–2in (2.5–5cm) of each shoot using your fingers or cut back with pruners just above a node. This encourages the buds in the uppermost leaf axils of the shoot to develop.

Individual plants in a group may be pinched a few days apart; this has the added benefit of producing a longer flowering season overall. For further information on how to produce fewer but larger blooms, see DAHLIAS, "Pinching and disbudding," p.222.

Deadheading

Unless decorative seedheads are desired or the seed is to be collected to raise further plants, remove the

HOW TO THIN AND PINCH PERENNIALS

THINNING
Thin young shoots (here of a phlox) when no more than one-third of their final height. Remove about 1 shoot in 3 by pinching or cutting weaker shoots at the base.

PINCHING
When the shoots (here of an Aster*) have reached one-third of their final height, pinch out the top 1–2in (2.5–5cm) to promote bushier growth.*

CUTTING BACK TO EXTEND FLOWERING

DELPHINIUM
After flowering, cut back old stems to ground level. In colder climates, remove only partway.

PHLOX
Cut back the central part of the flowerhead as the blooms fade to encourage the side shoots to flower.

flowers as they begin to fade. Additional flowering side shoots may then develop on the plant and extend the flowering season.

With a number of perennials, for example delphiniums and lupines (*Lupinus*), cutting back the old flowering stems partway when the first flowers have faded may encourage new shoots to develop that will produce a second display of flowers later in the season.

Cutting back

Shrubby perennials, for example the Nippon daisy (*Nipponanthemum nipponicum*, syn. *Chrysanthemum nipponicum*), should be pruned annually in early spring. Cut back the main stems with pruners to reduce the plant to less than half its former size. Also remove all twiggy, unproductive shoots. This encourages the growth of more compact plants that will better support the blooms throughout the flowering season.

Fall cleanup
Once perennial plants have finished flowering in fall, cut down the shoots to the base and remove them. In cold climates, leave about 6in (15cm) of stem to trap insulating snow, and cut this back later in spring. For plants that are not fully hardy, the entire top-growth should be left to protect the crown from frost; the dead top-growth is then removed in spring. Some perennial plants, such as *Sedum spectabile* and many grasses, have foliage or flowerheads that remain attractive even when brown, and these may be left on the plant to provide winter decoration if desired until early spring.

Transplanting established perennials

Most perennials may be transplanted easily if you wish to change the planting design. If possible, move them when dormant in fall, or when just coming into growth in spring. Plants that dislike cold, wet conditions, such as *Kniphofia*, and those that are not fully hardy, should be moved in spring once the soil has warmed to encourage rapid growth. A few long-lived plants, notably peonies (*Paeonia*) and hellebores

CUTTING DOWN IN THE FALL

In fall or early winter, cut dead stems (here of Rudbeckia) *to ground level, or to just above new growth.*

Staking

Tall and fragile perennials may need stakes to support them, particularly in windy situations. Insert stakes early in the season, since staking is harder to do and more likely to cause damage when growth is more developed. Push the stakes deeply into the ground so that they can be raised in stages as the plant grows.

For delphiniums and other tall, single-stemmed perennials, use sturdy stakes that are two-thirds of the stem's eventual height. Push a stake firmly into the ground near the base of each shoot, taking care not to damage the roots. Secure the stem to the stake with figure-eight twine ties as it grows.

To support plants with many stems, it may be easier to use a number of stakes placed at intervals in a circle around the plant. Loop twine around the stakes at about one-third and two-thirds of the plant's height. Clump-forming plants, such as peonies (*Paeonia*), may also be supported with commercial devices such as ring stakes and link stakes, or similar homemade supports constructed from large-gauge wire mesh fixed to stakes. Stems grow through the support and eventually hide it.

There are two other fairly unobtrusive methods of staking. Push several twiggy stems, or peasticks, into the soil next to the young shoots and bend them toward the center of the clump to form a sturdy cage that will soon be covered by the plant as it grows. Alternatively, insert one stout stake in the center of a small group of plants or stems and radiate ties out to each stem.

RING STAKE
Stake low, clump-forming plants (here peony) early in the season. Raise the stake as the plant grows.

LINK STAKES
For taller plants such as this Aster, *push link stakes deep into the soil, then raise them as the plant grows.*

SINGLE STAKE
Stake single-stemmed plants (here delphinium) when 8–10in (20–25cm) high. Tie in the stem loosely.

RING OF STAKES
Encircle weak-stemmed plants (here Centaurea) *with twine, looped around thin stakes.*

(*Helleborus*), resent disturbance and may take two or more years to establish after transplanting. Normally they should be lifted only if it is necessary to propagate them.

Prepare the new site as for planting, and dig a hole of suitable size. Lift the plant, keeping as much soil around the root ball as possible. It is best to divide the plant at this stage (see "Lifting and dividing," right). Remove any weeds from the clump by hand, then replant the divisions as for container-grown perennials (p.146), firming the plant in and watering it well.

Moving plants during the growing season

Occasionally, it may be necessary to move a plant while in full growth; however, mature plants may not transplant successfully and should be treated carefully if transplanting is essential at this time. To minimize the stress caused to the plant, soak it in a bucket of water for several hours after lifting it. Then cut back the top-growth to 3–5in (8–12cm) above the base and pot up the plant into a good potting mix. Keep the plant in a cool, shaded position, spraying daily but lightly until there are signs of healthy, fresh growth, then replant it in its new, prepared position, and keep it watered.

Storing plants

Perennials may be lifted and stored over winter or if replanting is to be delayed, such as when transplanting them to a new garden during a house move. The plants should be lifted when they are dormant and carefully packed in boxes or crates of moist bark or peat so that they do not dry out; they should then be stored in a cool place.

Lifting and dividing

Where practical, perennials in a bed or border should be lifted, divided, and replanted every three to five years. Fast-growing, vigorous species, particularly those with a mat-forming habit such as *Ajuga* and *Stachys*, may need to be divided every other year. Plants that become woody, with signs of dieback at the center, or that look congested and flower less freely than in previous years, need to be divided. Some plants, such as peonies, must be divided with particular care (see p.163).

Lifting plants makes it possible to clear the site of any weeds and to dig over and incorporate well-rotted organic matter or fertilizer as required. Dividing a plant rejuvenates it, keeps it healthy, and checks over-vigorous growth.

In late fall or early spring, lift the plant, taking care not to damage its roots, and divide it into several portions by gently pulling them away from the main plant. Discard the old, woody center. Each division should contain a number of healthy, young shoots and its own root system (see also "Dividing perennials," p.162). Then dig over and lightly fertilize the original site as necessary and replant the divisions, leaving enough space between each for the plants to develop. Alternatively, replant the divisions in prepared ground in a new position as required.

Pests and diseases

Perennial plants, if grown in fertile soil, are not usually seriously troubled by fungal diseases, insects, or other pests. Slugs, snails (p.550), aphids (p.552), thrips (p.553), mildews (p.552), and viruses (p.555) may attack a wide range of perennials but seldom give cause for concern. Check plants regularly during the growing season and treat them with an appropriate control if necessary. To help prevent problems, use clean tools and keep the garden tidy.

Preparing Plants for Temporary Storage

Lift the plants when dormant and place them in a box half-filled with moist bark or peat. Cover the roots with more bark or peat to keep them from drying out.

Maintaining perennials in containers

Perennials planted in containers require more care than those in open ground since they have limited reserves of food and water. Ensure that the soil mix does not dry out during the growing season: daily watering may be necessary in hot, dry weather. Plant roots should always remain moist but not wet. Ensure that water can drain through the container.

Mulching helps to reduce soil water evaporation and suppresses weeds; if using an organic mulch, replace it periodically when dividing or repotting the plants.

Every year or two in spring or fall, divide the plants and replant the most vigorous portions using fresh soil mix; otherwise, they soon exhaust the available nutrients and become too large for the container. If using the same container, wash the inside well before replanting, or pot up into a larger container (see "Planting in containers," p.147). Cut back the roots of shrubby perennials by about one-quarter before repotting.

In cold areas, bring in half-hardy and tender plants in the fall, keeping them protected until all danger of frost has passed (see Cold and Wind Protection, pp.520–21).

1 *In early spring or fall, rejuvenate perennials in containers by thinning out plants and renewing the soil mix.*

2 *Lift out the plants, separating them carefully, and shake the old soil mix from their roots. Discard half of the old soil mix.*

3 *Refill the container with fresh soil mix to within 4in (10cm) of its rim. Divide overgrown plants and arrange as required.*

4 *Plant up the container, fill in with more fresh soil mix around the plants, and firm them in with your fingers.*

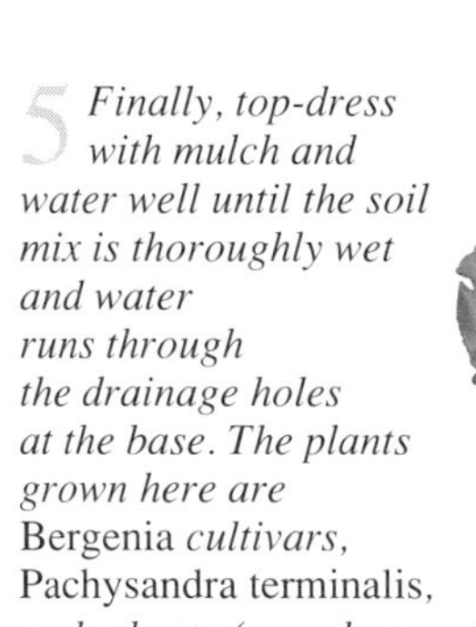

5 *Finally, top-dress with mulch and water well until the soil mix is thoroughly wet and water runs through the drainage holes at the base. The plants grown here are* Bergenia *cultivars,* Pachysandra terminalis, *and a hosta (now dormant).*

Ferns

AMONG the most popular of the foliage plants, ferns add texture and atmosphere to the house or garden, where they are particularly appropriate in settings by streams or in damp, shady corners.

Cultivation

Hardy ferns are suitable for growing in the open garden, whereas tender tropical ferns are best cultivated indoors in a greenhouse or conservatory, or as house plants.

Hardy ferns

Most hardy ferns are easily grown and are suitable for shaded, moist conditions. Being very tough, they require the minimum of cultivation and upkeep once they have become established. With the exception of *Thelypteris oreopteris* and all the *Blechnum* and *Cryptogramma* species, which require very acid soil, ferns grow best in neutral soils (pH of 6.5 to 7.5). Garden soil with added humus suits most species.

Planting may be carried out at any time if container-grown plants are used. Water them regularly in dry weather until established. Always plant in full or dappled shade. Some genera, such as *Dryopteris*, will tolerate dry conditions if they are well shaded, but almost all require damp conditions to thrive.

Many ferns, such as *Athyrium*, *Cryptogramma*, and *Osmunda*, die down at the first touch of frost, but some *Dryopteris* retain their fronds well into winter. Leaving the old fronds on the plant until early spring protects the crowns, but these should be removed as the young ones start to uncurl. Many species and cultivars of *Asplenium*, *Cyrtomium*, *Polystichum*, and *Polypodium* make good plants for the cool greenhouse, flourishing in a minimum daytime temperature of 41°F (5°C), and a nighttime temperature of no less than 35°F (2°C).

ROCK CREVICE
The lance-shaped fronds of the semi-evergreen Ceterach officinarum *contrast well with the rock behind that provides shade and shelter.*

Tender tropical ferns

Ferns that will not withstand frost make excellent greenhouse or conservatory foliage plants, grown in pots or hanging baskets. Some also make good house plants. Most require a winter minimum temperature of 50°F (10°C) but do not like hot, dry conditions and should be shaded from direct sunlight. A north-facing position on a bed of gravel that can be damped down in hot weather is ideal.

Tender ferns are usually sold in small pots and should then be potted up into 5in (13cm) or 6in (15cm) pots using a soilless potting mix. For this, use 3 parts peat-based potting mixture to 2 parts coarse sand or medium-grade perlite or vermiculite. Add a cupful of charcoal granules to every 1¾ pints (1 liter) of mixture and, following the package instructions, a balanced granular or powdered fertilizer.

The root ball should not dry out completely; keep the plant in its pot inside a watertight outer container with about 1in (2.5cm) of sand or gravel permanently kept damp at its base. Ferns, particularly *Adiantum* species, should not be sprayed or overwatered, and *Nephrolepis*, probably the easiest to keep as house plants, should be almost dry before watering. Feed the ferns occasionally with a liquid house plant fertilizer.

WATER SETTING
Matteuccia *thrives in damp conditions by a stream and provides a striking contrast of form and texture with the* Rodgersia *in the foreground.*

Propagation

Ferns are mainly raised from spores, but may be propagated by division or, in some species, by bulbils.

PROPAGATION BY BULBILS

1 *Select a frond that is drooping under the weight of bulbils. The bulbils may have tiny green fronds emerging from them. Cut off the parent frond close to the base. The plant shown here is* Asplenium bulbiferum.

2 *Peg down the frond onto prepared soil mix. Make sure the frond's ribs are flat.*

3 *Water thoroughly, label the tray, and put it in a plastic bag. Seal the bag and leave the tray in a warm, light place until the bulbils have rooted.*

4 *Remove the wire pegs and lift each rooted bulbil with a widger or knife; if necessary, cut it away from the parent frond.*

5 *Put each rooted bulbil into a 3in (6cm) pot of moist, soilless potting mix. Keep moist in a warm, light place until the plants are large enough to transplant.*

Bulbils

Asplenium bulbiferum and some of the hardy *Polystichum* species produce bulbils or small plantlets along the fronds. These can be used for propagation by pegging down that part of the frond with bulbils onto a tray of seed or cuttings soil mix. The bulbils soon produce rooted plantlets, which can then be separated and potted up. The bulbils root fastest when the parent plant is actively growing during the dormant season; rooting may take six months.

Spores

Ferns produce neither flowers nor seeds and have a unique way of reproducing. Fronds carry on their undersurfaces very small capsules (sporangia) that release large numbers of powdery spores which, when sown on damp soil mix, produce small growths (prothalli). Each prothallus carries both the male and female organs: the male organ (antheridium) produces spermatozoids which swim across the surface moisture of the prothallus to fertilize the egg cell lying within the female organ (archegonium). After fertilization, a zygote is formed, which eventually develops into a tiny new fern. In this way the normal cycle of growth is continued.

Growing ferns from spores may take 18 to 24 months from sowing the spores to planting out the new ferns. Collect the spores by removing mature fronds that are almost ready to shed their spores. Ripe sporangia are plump and vary in color between species; many are dark brown, some blue-gray, others orange. Immature sporangia are flat and green or pale yellow. If the sporangia are dark brown and rough, they will probably already have shed their spores. Lay the fronds on a sheet of clean paper and leave them in a warm room. In a day or so the spores will be shed onto the paper, looking like brown dust. Transfer them to a labeled seed envelope.

Fill a 3in (6cm) pot with standard seed soil mix; firm and smooth the surface. Sterilize the soil mix by carefully pouring boiling water through a piece of paper towel laid on the surface until water comes through the drainage holes. When the soil mix has cooled, remove the paper towel and sow spores very thinly over the surface. Cover the pot, or put it in a propagator, and leave it in a warm, light place out of direct sunlight. To keep the surface constantly moist, mist-spray it regularly with previously boiled, lukewarm water. Remove the cover when the top of the pot is covered with a green, velvetlike "moss"; if the soil mix seems dry, moisten it by standing the pot in a saucer of boiled water for a short time.

Depending on the species, it takes from six to 12 weeks for the young prothalli to cover the soil mix surface. Prick them out by lifting small pieces of the "moss." Space them evenly, green side up, on the surface of other pots of sterilized seed soil mix, press them down, and spray with lukewarm water that has been boiled. Cover the pots with plastic wrap or return them to the propagator. As the prothalli develop, spray them daily with lukewarm water until tiny plantlets appear. When they are large enough to handle, transplant them separately into pots of soilless mix and grow them on, potting up as necessary, until they are large enough to plant out.

FORMAL PLANTINGS
The clean, horizontal line of the golden boxwood (foreground) provides a perfect foundation for the shuttlecock shapes of Matteuccia struthiopteris.

PROPAGATION BY SPORES

1 *Examine the undersides of the fronds to find one with sporangia that are ready to release their spores. Cut off the selected frond with a clean, sharp knife and place it carefully on clean, white paper to collect the spores. The plant shown here is* Adiantum fritzluthii.

NOT READY

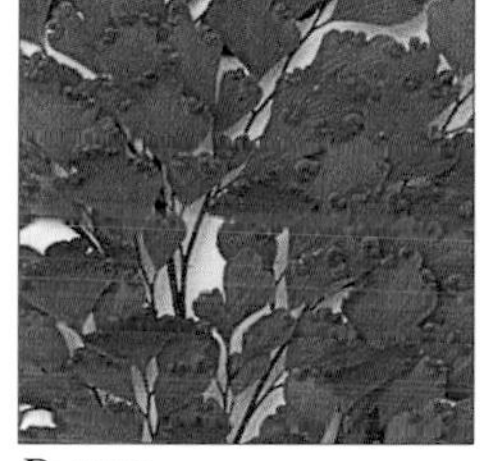

READY

TOO LATE

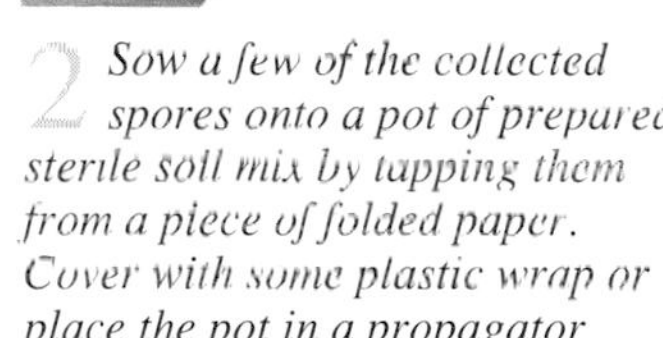

2 *Sow a few of the collected spores onto a pot of prepared sterile soil mix by tapping them from a piece of folded paper. Cover with some plastic wrap or place the pot in a propagator.*

3 *Mist-spray twice a week until the surface is covered with a bumpy green "moss." Lift small clumps with a widger or a knife.*

4 *Divide the clumps into small pieces and gently firm them down onto sterile soil mix. Spray with water and then return them to the propagator.*

5 *When leaflike plantlets appear, lift them carefully. Firm into packs or small pots of moist soil mix. Pot on when they have developed small fronds.*

Propagation

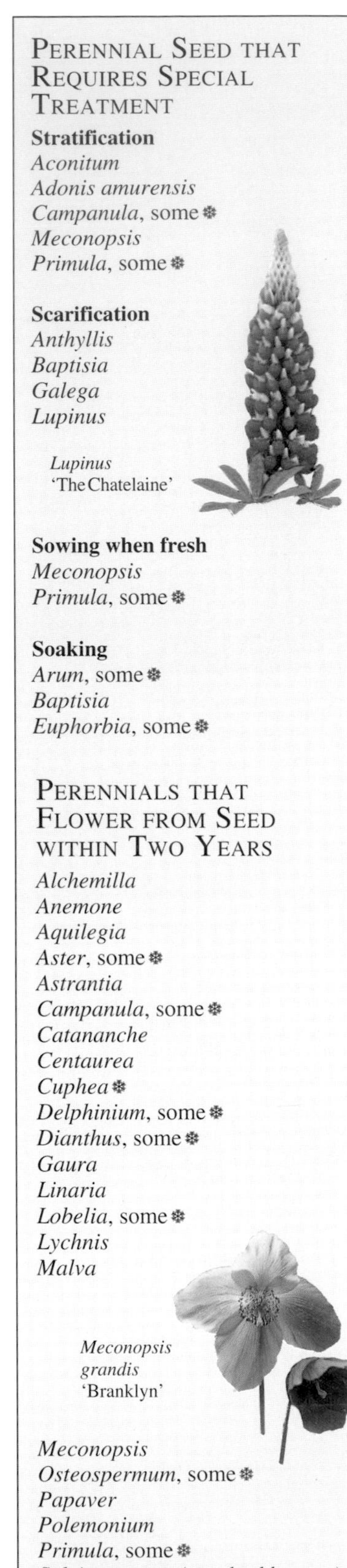

PERENNIAL SEED THAT REQUIRES SPECIAL TREATMENT

Stratification
Aconitum
Adonis amurensis
Campanula, some ❄
Meconopsis
Primula, some ❄

Scarification
Anthyllis
Baptisia
Galega
Lupinus

Lupinus 'The Chatelaine'

Sowing when fresh
Meconopsis
Primula, some ❄

Soaking
Arum, some ❄
Baptisia
Euphorbia, some ❄

PERENNIALS THAT FLOWER FROM SEED WITHIN TWO YEARS

Alchemilla
Anemone
Aquilegia
Aster, some ❄
Astrantia
Campanula, some ❄
Catananche
Centaurea
Cuphea ❄
Delphinium, some ❄
Dianthus, some ❄
Gaura
Linaria
Lobelia, some ❄
Lychnis
Malva

Meconopsis grandis 'Branklyn'

Meconopsis
Osteospermum, some ❄
Papaver
Polemonium
Primula, some ❄
Salvia, some ❄ (not shrubby spp.)
Scabiosa
Sidalcea
Silene, some ❄
Verbascum

KEY
❄ *Not frost hardy*

THERE are several ways of propagating herbaceous perennials. Growing them from seed is ideal where a large number of new plants is desired. Little experience or expertise is needed to raise the seedlings successfully, but this method is generally suitable for propagating species rather than cultivars.

For many perennials, the simplest and most common method of propagation is to lift them and divide clumps into separate plants. Others are better raised from seed or by vegetative means such as cuttings or, more rarely, grafting. Vegetative methods should be used for propagating almost all named cultivars.

Seed

Raising plants from seed is a simple and inexpensive way to propagate many perennials but, apart from a few named cultivars (for example, *Aquilegia* 'Crimson Star'), most cultivars do not come true from seed. Most species also show some variation in habit and flower color so, if collecting seed yourself, always gather it from plants with the best flower and growth characteristics.

Seed of early-flowering perennials, which ripens on the plant in early to midsummer, usually germinates quickly if sown as soon as it is ripe, producing young plants that may be overwintered successfully in open ground or in a cold frame. For most perennials, however, sow the seed immediately after it has been gathered in fall so that it germinates early the following spring. If stored in cool, dry conditions, most seed also germinates well when sown in spring.

Seed of herbaceous plants such as peonies (*Paeonia*) and hellebores (*Helleborus*) usually remains dormant for a considerable period unless suitable conditions are provided or occur naturally to break dormancy and induce germination. Some require a period of exposure to cold or light, while others have hard seed coats that should be weakened by scarification or softened by soaking before sowing (see also PRINCIPLES OF PROPAGATION, "How to overcome dormancy," p.537).

Pregermination treatment of seeds

Seeds that need to be subjected to a cold period to break dormancy may be either sown outside in fall or winter (see also *Sowing Seed that Requires Chilling*, opposite) or chilled in a refrigerator for a few months before sowing in spring. This method of breaking dormancy is suitable for many genera, including *Aconitum*, *Adonis*, *Campanula*, and *Primula*. Seeds of a few plants, such as those of *Gentiana asclepiadea*, require a period of exposure to light for successful germination.

Scarifying and soaking

A number of perennials, particularly those of the pea family Leguminosae, have seeds with hard coats that impede rapid and uniform germination. Just before sowing the seeds, scarify them either by rubbing with sandpaper or by chipping each one slightly with a sharp blade to allow water to be taken up and then germination to occur.

Alternatively, many seeds may have their hard coats softened by being soaked in initially hot, but not boiling, water for 12–24 hours; this allows the seed to absorb water and germination to take place. Soaking is suitable for a number of perennials, for example *Baptisia* and *Euphorbia*. Once soaked, the seed should be sown immediately.

Double dormancy

Peony and *Trillium* seeds usually require two periods of cold to trigger germination of both roots and shoots. Root development from the germinating seed occurs during the first season, but the shoots do not normally start to appear until the seeds have received a second period of cold, usually during the following winter. Sow the seeds in containers in fall in the normal way.

Sowing seed in containers

Unless a very large number of plants is desired, it is easiest to sow seed in containers. A plastic half tray accommodates as many as two or three hundred seeds, while even a large square pot is adequate for sowing up to 50 seeds, depending on their size. Square pots fit closely in rows and provide a greater area of soil mix than round pots of the same width.

Whether using trays or pots, place a layer of broken crocks or grit in the base to provide drainage, and fill them with an appropriate seed soil mix. Soil-based mixes are often preferred to peat-based ones if the young seedlings are to be kept in them for more than a short period after germination. Gently press the soil mix around the edges of the container, then roughly level the surface and firm it with a presser so that it is about 1/2in (1cm) below the container rim.

Sowing

The seeds should always be sown thinly – about 1/4in (0.5cm) apart; sowing too densely may result in thin, spindly plants that are prone to damping off (see p.566). Fine seeds, and those that require light to germinate, for example some gentians

Collecting seed

Collect the seed as it ripens: shake it from the pods or tie the seedheads into small bunches, enclosed in paper bags, and hang them upside down so that the seeds fall into the bags. Make sure that the seed is completely dry before storing it in clean paper bags or envelopes labeled with the plant name and harvesting date.

Collect ripened seedpods (here of Meconopsis*) when they have turned brown. Shake the seeds out of each pod onto a piece of paper and store in a cool, dry place until ready to sow.*

RAISING PLANTS FROM SEED

1 *Fill a 5in (13cm) pot with moist seed soil mix. Firm the soil mix to about 1cm (1/2in) below the rim, using a presser.*

2 *Using a clean, folded piece of paper, scatter the seeds (here* Leucanthemum x superbum) *sparingly over the soil mix.*

3 *Cover the seeds with a shallow layer of fine, sieved soil mix. Label and then water without displacing the seeds.*

4 *Cover with glass or a clear plastic sheet to retain moisture. Place the pot in a cold frame until the seedlings develop 2 to 4 true leaves.*

5 *Prick out the seedlings into pots; peat pots (inset) allow planting out direct. Handle the seedlings by the leaves because the stems are easily damaged.*

6 *When the seedlings have developed into small plants with a good root system, plant them out or pot them up, as appropriate.*

SOWING SEED THAT REQUIRES CHILLING

1 *In fall, sow the seed thinly in pots of soil mix, then cover with a thin layer of fine soil mix and top-dress with fine grit.*

2 *Label the pots with the seed name and date of sowing, and water thoroughly. Then plunge the pots in an open sand bed outside to encourage the seeds to germinate.*

(*Gentiana*), may be left uncovered or sprinkled with a shallow layer of fine, sieved soil mix and then gently firmed with a presser. Larger seeds, such as those of peonies, should be covered with a 1/4in (0.5cm) layer of sieved soil mix.

Aftercare

Label the containers with the seed name and sowing date, then water them with a fine spray, taking care not to dislodge the seeds. Alternatively, if small seeds are being sown, stand the containers in a bowl or tray of water for a short time until they have absorbed enough to moisten the soil mix throughout; this method prevents the seeds from being washed away. Minimize evaporation by covering the containers with glass, a plastic sheet, or plastic film, and place them in a cold frame, greenhouse, or windowsill. In sunny weather, provide some shade with newspaper or netting. Once the seeds have started to germinate, remove the cover and reduce any shading.

Plunging the containers in an outdoor bed

If the containers are to be placed outside, unprotected from the weather during fall and winter to break seed dormancy, add a covering of grit over the sown seeds. This prevents them from being washed out of the containers by heavy rain and, to some extent, deters mosses and liverworts from growing on the soil mix surface. Cover the containers with fine-mesh chicken wire to protect the seed if rodents or birds are likely to be a problem.

Plunge the pots in an open sand bed since this provides stable, even conditions for germination. Once the seed has germinated and the seedlings are visible, place the containers in a cold frame or other protected spot and care for the seedlings as for those raised under cover.

Pricking out

Once the seedlings are large enough to handle, that is when the first or second pair of true leaves has formed, they may be pricked out. Either space them evenly in seed trays with about 30–40 in each tray or prick them out into individual containers. The latter is advisable for seedlings that do not tolerate much root disturbance. Alternatively, prick out the seedlings into cell packs (compartmentalized trays). In all cases, use a good, soil-based potting mix.

Water the seedlings thoroughly, label them, and then place them in a cold frame or cool greenhouse until they are established. They may then be potted on individually or planted out in their permanent site in open ground when they are large enough.

Sowing outside in open ground

If large numbers of plants are needed, it may be more convenient to sow seed outside. Prepare an area in fertile, well-drained soil by clearing any weeds and cultivating the soil to a fine tilth. Using a line or a straight-edged board as a guide, make a seed drill using a draw hoe, onion hoe, or the point of a large label.

The depth of the drill depends on the size of the seed to be sown: about 1/4in (0.5cm) deep is adequate for small seeds, while large seeds require a drill at least 1/2in (1cm) deep. If the seedlings are to be transplanted when young, set the drills 4–6in (10–15cm) apart; if, however, they are to be grown on in rows, allow about 6–9in (15–22cm) between them. Sow small seeds thinly so that they are about 1/4in (0.5cm) apart, large seeds such as peonies at intervals of 1in (2.5cm) or more.

After sowing, cover the drills by raking soil lightly over them, then label each drill with the name of the seed and the date. Water carefully, without washing away the soil. For further details, see ANNUALS AND BIENNIALS, *Sowing in Drills*, p.177.

Dividing perennials

This method is suitable for propagating many perennials that have a spreading rootstock and produce plenty of shoots from the base. As well as being a way of increasing stocks, in many cases division rejuvenates the plants and keeps them vigorous, since old or unproductive parts may be discarded (see also "Lifting and dividing," p.157).

Some perennial plants can be divided simply by pulling sections apart by hand, or by using two forks back-to-back; other plants that have fleshy roots are best split apart by using a spade or knife.

When to divide

Most plants should be divided when they are dormant, from late fall to early spring, but not in extremely cold, wet, or dry weather because these conditions may make it difficult for the divided plants to re-establish successfully.

Fleshy-rooted perennials are usually best moved in late summer in order to give them time to make new roots before winter sets in. Irises, peonies (*Paeonia*), and poppies (*Papaver*) are the most common fleshy-rooted perennials. Potted plants may be planted in spring.

Preparation

First lift the plant to be divided by loosening the surrounding soil, taking care not to damage the roots, then levering it up gently with a fork. Shake off as much loose soil from the roots as possible and remove any dead leaves and stems to make it easier to see the best points for division. This also enables you to see which are the healthy parts of the plant to be retained and which are the old, unproductive parts that can be discarded.

Wash most of the soil off the roots and crowns of fleshy-rooted plants, so that all the buds are clearly visible and therefore do not become damaged inadvertently when you are dividing the plant.

Fibrous-rooted plants

Insert two hand forks back-to-back near the center of each plant so that the tines are close together and the handles apart. Push the handles gently backward and forward so that the prongs gradually tease the plant apart, then separate the clumps into two smaller portions. Repeat this process with each portion to divide the plant into more sections, each with some new shoots.

Plants that tend to form woody clumps or that have thick, solid roots should be cut into portions with a spade or sharp knife. Make sure that there are at least two growth buds or shoots on each piece. The sections containing vigorous young shoots and healthy roots tend to grow at the perimeter of the plant. Discard the old, weak, and often woody growth from the center of the plant.

Perennial plants that have loose, spreading crowns and numerous shoots, for example Michaelmas daisies (*Aster*), are easy to pull apart by hand or with two hand forks. Simply separate off single stems growing at the edges of the crown so that each has its own root system.

Fleshy-rooted plants

Plants that have bulky, almost solid, fleshy roots, such as *Rheum*, may need to be divided with a spade since it would be difficult to separate the crowns using back-to-back forks. After cleaning the plant so that the developing buds are clearly visible, slice through between them with a spade, taking care to leave two or more buds on each piece. Then trim each division neatly with a knife, discarding any old, woody material and any damaged or rotting roots.

Plants with numerous, intertwined crowns, such as *Kniphofia* and tufted ornamental grasses, may also be divided with two forks.

Replanting and aftercare

After dividing a plant, dust any cut surfaces with an appropriate fungicide (see PRINCIPLES OF PROPAGATION, "How roots form," p.540). Replant the divisions as soon as possible. It

Dividing hostas

Large hostas with tough rootstocks should be divided using a spade. Include several buds on each division and trim any damaged parts with a knife. Hostas that have looser, fleshy rootstocks may be separated by hand or with back-to-back forks; each division should have at least one eye (shoot).

TOUGH, FIBROUS ROOTS
Divide the crown with a spade; each section should include several developing buds.

LOOSE, FLESHY ROOTS
Divide small plants and those with a loose rootstock by pulling the clump apart by hand.

HOW TO PROPAGATE PERENNIALS BY DIVISION

1 *Lift the plant to be divided, taking care to insert the fork far enough away from the plant so that the roots are not damaged. Shake off surplus soil. The plant shown here is a* Helianthus.

2 *Separate plants with a woody center by chopping through the crown with a spade.*

3 *Divide the plant into smaller pieces by hand, retaining only healthy, vigorous sections, each with several new shoots.*

4 *Cut back the old top-growth and replant the divided sections to the same depth as before. Firm in and water thoroughly.*

ALTERNATIVE METHOD

Divide fibrous-rooted, herbaceous plants (here Hemerocallis*) using 2 forks back-to-back.*

is important that they do not dry out, so if replanting is unavoidably delayed for a couple of hours, dip the plants briefly in water and keep them in a sealed plastic bag in a cool, shady place until you are ready to replant them.

Large divisions, if replanted immediately in spring, may still provide a good show of flowers in the same season although the stems are often slightly shorter than those of more established plants. Very small divisions, however, are best grown on for a season in a nursery bed or in pots in order to become established. In general, the divisions should be replanted at the same depth as the original plant, but those plants that are prone to rotting at the base are best set slightly above the surrounding soil level to keep their crowns free of excess water (see also "Planting depths," p.146).

When replanting, ensure that the roots are well spread out in the planting hole and the plant firmed in. Water newly planted divisions thoroughly; take care not to expose the roots by washing away any soil.

Division of rhizomatous plants

Divide plants with thick rhizomes, such as *Bergenia* and rhizomatous irises, by splitting the clump into pieces by hand, then cutting the rhizomes into sections, each with one or more buds (see right). Bamboos have tough rootstocks that either form dense clumps with short rhizomes or have long, spreading rhizomes. Divide the former with a spade or two back-to-back forks; cut the latter into sections with pruners, each of which should have three nodes or joints (see also GRASSES, BAMBOOS, SEDGES, AND RUSHES, p.142).

1 Lift the plant to be divided (here an iris), inserting the fork well away from the rhizomes to avoid damaging them.

2 Shake the clump to remove any loose soil. Using your hands or a hand fork, split the clump into manageable pieces.

3 Discard any old rhizomes, then detach the new, young rhizomes from the clump and neatly trim off their ends.

4 Dust the cut areas with fungicide. Trim long roots by one-third. For irises, cut the leaves to a miter about 6in (15cm) long to prevent wind-rock.

5 Plant the rhizomes about 5in (12cm) apart. The rhizomes should be half buried, with their leaves and buds upright. Firm in well and water.

Dividing peonies

Peonies should be divided with particular care because they tend to reestablish slowly after being transplanted. For best results, lift and divide the plants toward the end of summer, when the swelling red growth buds are clearly visible. The crown should be cut into sections, each with a few buds. Take care not to damage the thick, fleshy roots. See also PEONIES, p.148.

1 Lift the plant in late summer, when healthy growth buds are visible. Remove old stems, then cut the plant into sections, each one with several buds.

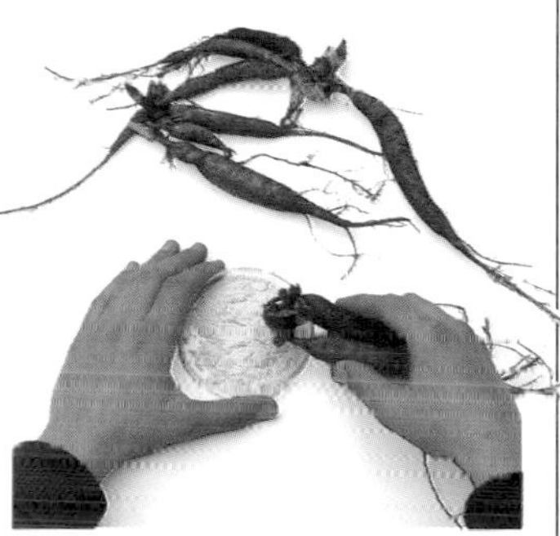

2 Dust all the cut surfaces of the divided sections with fungicide to discourage infection and rot.

3 Plant the divided sections approximately 8in (20cm) apart. The buds should be 1 to 3in (2.5–8cm) deep. Firm the soil well and water.

PERENNIALS THAT MAY BE DIVIDED

Achillea
Aconitum
Adenophora
Anemone hupehensis
Arum, some ✽
Aster, some ✽
Astilbe
Astrantia
Bergenia

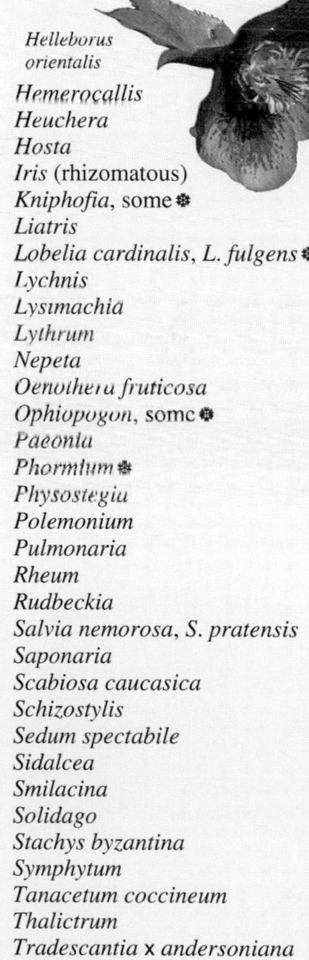

Aster novae-angliae 'Harrington's Pink'

Buphthalmum
Campanula, some ✽
Centaurea dealbata
Clematis (herbaceous)
Coreopsis verticillata
Crambe cordifolia
Doronicum
Epilobium
Galega
Geranium, some ✽
Helenium
Helianthus
Helleborus orientalis

Helleborus orientalis

Hemerocallis
Heuchera
Hosta
Iris (rhizomatous)
Kniphofia, some ✽
Liatris
Lobelia cardinalis, *L. fulgens* ✽
Lychnis
Lysimachia
Lythrum
Nepeta
Oenothera fruticosa
Ophiopogon, some ✽
Paeonia
Phormium ✽
Physostegia
Polemonium
Pulmonaria
Rheum
Rudbeckia
Salvia nemorosa, *S. pratensis*
Saponaria
Scabiosa caucasica
Schizostylis
Sedum spectabile
Sidalcea
Smilacina
Solidago
Stachys byzantina
Symphytum
Tanacetum coccineum
Thalictrum
Tradescantia x *andersoniana*
Trollius
Veronica

KEY
✽ *Not frost hardy*

PROPAGATING PERENNIALS BY STEM TIP CUTTINGS

1 *Select short lengths of soft wood about 3–5in (7–12cm) long from the tips of strong, healthy shoots. The plant shown here is a* Penstemon *cultivar.*

2 *Trim the lower end of each cutting just below a node, with a straight cut, reducing the length to 2–3in (5–7cm). Carefully remove the lower leaves.*

3 *Insert the cuttings around the edge of a 6in (15cm) pot of cuttings soil mix and water in. Cover with a plastic bag, held away from the cuttings by stakes.*

4 *When the cuttings have rooted, gently lift them and pot them up individually into 4in (10cm) pots.*

PERENNIALS THAT MAY BE PROPAGATED BY STEM CUTTINGS

Tip
Anisodontea ❋
Arctotis ❋
Argyranthemum ❋
Calceolaria integrifolia ❋
Cuphea ❋
Dianthus, some ❋
Diascia
Epilobium canum
Erysimum
Euryops, some ❋
Felicia, some ❋
Gazania ❋
Helichrysum petiolare ❋
Lavatera
Lotus berthelotii ❋
Malvastrum ❋
Mimulus aurantiacus ❋
Oenothera missouriensis
Osteospermum, some ❋

Osteospermum 'Buttermilk'

Parahebe
Pelargonium ❋
Penstemon, some ❋
Phygelius
Salvia, some ❋
Scrophularia auriculata
Sphaeralcea ❋
Trifolium pratense
Verbena ❋
Viola, some ❋

Basal
Anthemis tinctoria
Chrysanthemum, some ❋
Delphinium, some ❋
Lupinus
Monarda

Anthemis tinctoria 'E.C. Buxton'

KEY
❋ *Not frost hardy*

Stem tip cuttings

This method of propagation is used most commonly for herbaceous perennials that are difficult to divide successfully and for cultivars that do not come true from seed. Cuttings may be taken at any time during the growing season provided that suitable shoots are available.

Select strong growing tips without flower buds, rejecting any that are thin, weak and leggy, or damaged. If there is likely to be any delay before inserting the cuttings, place them in a sealed plastic bag to protect them from dehydration.

Preparing and inserting the cuttings

Take cuttings with pruners or a sharp knife, cutting across the stem immediately above a node. Trim the cuttings to just below a node, then remove the leaves from the lowest third of each cutting. Insert the cuttings into prepared pots or trays of an appropriate cuttings soil mix and firm in with your fingers. Leave sufficient space between the cuttings so that the leaves do not touch each other and air can circulate freely. This inhibits the spread of damping-off diseases (see p.566).

Aftercare

Water the cuttings carefully with a fine spray and treat them with a fungicide to reduce the risk of infection and rot. It is important that the cuttings are maintained at a high humidity level; otherwise, they will wilt. If possible, keep them in a mist unit or propagator. Alternatively, cover the cuttings with a plastic tent or bag. This should be supported on stakes or hooped wires to prevent the plastic from touching the leaves, since any condensation forming on the foliage could encourage fungal infection and rot.

In hot weather, shade the cuttings with newspaper, commercial shade netting, or other semitranslucent material to prevent the leaves from scorching or wilting. Take off the shading as soon as possible after the hot weather to allow the cuttings plenty of light. Inspect them daily, removing any fallen and dead leaves and any material that is infected. Water the soil mix as necessary so that it remains moist but not wet.

After about two to three weeks, the cuttings should produce roots and may be potted on into individual pots. Any healthy cuttings that have not developed roots by this stage should be reinserted and cared for as before until they have rooted.

Basal stem cuttings

This type of cutting is suitable for taking from a wide range of herbaceous plants that produce clusters of new shoots at the base in spring. Short, basal cuttings may also be taken in midspring from sturdy shoots of plants, such as lupines

HOW TO PROPAGATE BY BASAL STEM CUTTINGS

1 *Take cuttings when the shoots (here of* Chrysanthemum*) are* $1^1/_2$*–2in (3.5–5cm) high, each with a small piece of basal wood.*

2 *Remove the basal leaves from each cutting and trim the lower end, making a straight cut.*

3 *Insert the cuttings into a prepared pot of moist cuttings soil mix. Place the pots in a propagator or plastic bag to encourage rooting.*

4 *When the cuttings have rooted, separate them, retaining as much soil mix as possible around the roots. Pot up the cuttings individually.*

(*Lupinus*) and delphiniums, that later develop hollow or pithy stems, as well as those that have soft tissue.

If required, the plants to be propagated may be lifted and grown in pots or trays in a warm greenhouse to encourage the production of basal shoots earlier than if the plants were growing in the open ground. The cuttings may then be rooted and young plants established earlier in the season. The plants from which cuttings have been taken may then be replanted in the garden.

Preparing and inserting the cuttings

Select strong, sturdy shoots whose first leaves have just unfolded and, using a sharp knife, remove them as close to the base as possible. Include part of the woody basal tissue in the cutting. Do not use any shoots that are damaged or hollow.

Trim off the lower leaves of the cuttings, dip them in hormone rooting powder, and insert them in cuttings soil mix, either individually or several to a pot, or in trays. Firm in the cuttings, water thoroughly, and allow the containers to drain before placing them in a cold frame or propagator. Alternatively, cover each of the containers with a clear plastic bag supported on wire hoops firmly inserted into the soil mix. Shade the cuttings from direct sunlight to prevent the leaves from scorching or wilting.

Aftercare

Check the cuttings every few days, removing any dead or decaying foliage as soon as possible to prevent the spread of rot. Ensure that the soil mix is moist, but not wet, at all times, and wipe or shake away excess water and condensation from the glass or plastic covers. The cuttings should be well rooted within a month; they may then be potted on into individual pots filled with equal parts of soil, sand, and peat, or a commercial soil mix.

Root cuttings

This is a useful method of propagating perennials that have fairly thick, fleshy roots, such as *Verbascum* and *Papaver orientale* cultivars. It is also the only way of raising new, healthy plants from border phlox cultivars that are affected by nematodes. Because the nematodes occur in the top-growth of affected phlox, but not in the roots, taking root cuttings makes it possible to produce healthy, nematode-free plants. This method is not used for those phlox cultivars with variegated foliage, however, because the resulting plants produce only plain green leaves.

Take care to minimize damage to the parent plant when cutting its roots, and replant it immediately after taking the cuttings. Root cuttings are most successful when they are taken during the plant's dormant period, usually in winter.

Preparation

Lift a strong, healthy plant and wash off the soil so that all the roots can be clearly seen. Select roots that are young, vigorous, and fairly thick, since these are more likely to produce successful new plants than those that are weak and thin or old, gnarled, and woody. Cut off the young roots close to the crown and replant the parent plant.

When propagating plants with thick roots, for example *Acanthus*, *Anchusa*, *Romneya*, and *Verbascum*, choose roots that are about the thickness of a pencil and cut them into sections 2–4in (5–10cm) long. With thin-rooted perennials, cut the roots into 3–5in (7–12cm) lengths so there is sufficient food storage for the developing cuttings.

Trim each section so that the top end (that nearest the plant's stem) is cut straight across and the bottom end (nearest the root tip) is cut at an angle; this makes it easy to insert the cuttings the correct way up. Shoots will develop from the top end of the cutting and roots from the lower end. Trim off any fibrous roots before inserting the cuttings.

Inserting the cuttings

After preparing the cuttings, dust them with fungicide to protect against rot. Then insert them vertically, straight ends at the top, in prepared pots or trays of cuttings soil mix about one and a half times their depth. The tops of the cuttings should be level with the surface. Cover the pots with a thin layer of fine sand or grit; label, and place them in a propagator or cold frame. Do not water the cuttings until they begin to root. Once young shoots have developed, pot them up singly into an appropriate soil mix.

Plants with thinner roots, such as *Anemone hupehensis*, *A.* x *hybrida*, *Campanula*, phlox, and *Primula denticulata*, are often treated slightly differently because their roots may be too fine to insert vertically. Lay the root cuttings flat on the surface of pots or trays of firmed soil mix, then cover with more soil mix. Then treat as for standard root cuttings.

How to Propagate Perennials by Root Cuttings

1 *Lift the plant (here* Acanthus*) when dormant and wash the roots. Select roots of pencil thickness and cut them off with a knife, cutting close to the crown.*

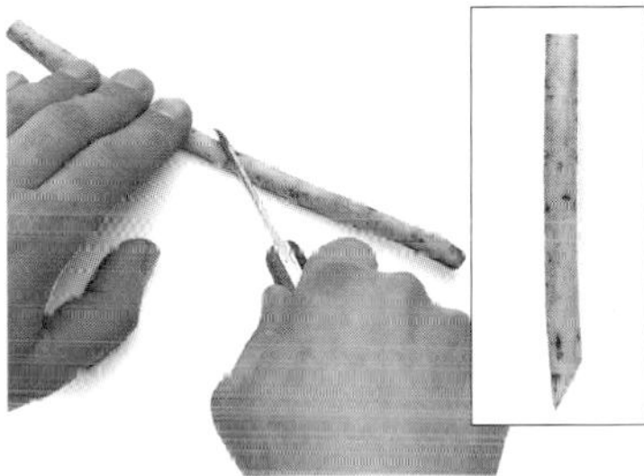

2 *Trim the roots and cut each into lengths of 2–4in (5–10cm). Make a straight cut at the upper end of each cutting and an angled cut at the lower end (see inset).*

3 *Insert the cuttings into holes made in pots of moist cuttings soil mix, and firm. The top end of each cutting should be flush with the soil mix surface.*

4 *Top-dress the pots of cuttings with coarse grit, label them, and place them in a cold frame until the cuttings root.*

5 *When the cuttings have developed young shoots, pot them up into individual pots filled with soil-based potting mix. Water and label the pots (see inset).*

Alternative Method for Thin Roots

Place the trimmed cuttings horizontally on moist, firmed soil mix. Cover with soil mix and firm lightly.

Perennials that may be Propagated by Root Cuttings

Acanthus
Anchusa azurea
Anemone hupehensis, *A.* x *hybrida*
Arnebia
Campanula, some ❄
Catananche caerulea
Echinops

Catananche caerulea 'Major'

Erodium, some ❄
Eryngium, some ❄
Gaillardia
Geranium, some ❄
Gypsophila
Limonium latifolium
Mertensia
Morisia
Papaver orientale
Phlox decussata, *P. subulata*
Primula denticulata
Pulsatilla vulgaris
Romneya
Trollius
Verbascum

Key
❄ *Not frost hardy*

Grafting

The majority of perennial cultivars do not come true from seed, so new plants must therefore be raised by vegetative methods such as cuttings. Cultivars of *Gypsophila paniculata* do not root readily from cuttings, however, so grafting (more commonly associated with trees and shrubs) is the only reliable way of increasing stocks of 'Flamingo', 'Rosy Veil', and 'Bristol Fairy'. This method of propagation should produce vigorous plants.

Preparing the scion plant

Lift the plants of the cultivar to be propagated in fall, pot them up, and grow them on in a cool greenhouse. These conditions encourage them to produce vigorous young shoots earlier than usual, in mid- to late winter, the optimum time for grafting.

Preparing the rootstocks

For the rootstocks, use one- to two-year-old seed-grown *Gypsophila paniculata*; these should be lifted and put in cold storage until needed. Choose roots at least the thickness of a pencil and 3–4in (7–10cm) long, cutting them off straight at the top and trimming them with an angled cut at the base. Any small lateral roots should be cut back and any fibrous roots growing on the stock discarded. Then make a small, vertical cut in the top about 1/2in (1cm) deep.

Place the prepared roots in a sealed plastic bag to keep them moist while the scions are being prepared. It is important that the cut surfaces do not dry out because this can prevent a successful union between the stock and scion.

Selecting and preparing the scion material

For the scions, select strong, young shoots 1 1/2–3in (3–7cm) long and detach them from the base of the plant. The lower ends should then be trimmed into a wedge shape.

Uniting the stocks and scions

Pot up the rootstock into an individual pot of cuttings soil mix. Then insert the scion, trimming it if required, so that its lower end fits neatly into the cut in the prepared stock. Bind the grafted area with plastic tape or raffia to hold it firmly in place.

Alternatively, the plants may be potted up after grafting. In either case, water thoroughly and allow the pots to drain. Place the grafted plants in a propagator or mist unit, preferably with bottom heat, or cover each one with a clear plastic bag supported by stakes or wires. Ensure that the plastic does not touch the foliage, because condensation on the inside of the bag could lead to rotting. Secure the bag in place with an elastic band around the pot.

Aftercare

Check the grafted plants regularly to make sure that the soil mix does not dry out. Water them from beneath, when necessary, by standing the pots in a tray of water; alternatively, remove the plastic bags and mist-spray the plants with water.

The grafts should knit fairly quickly, and new roots form in about four to six weeks. The grafted plants can then be removed from the propagator or plastic bags and kept in cool, but frost-free, conditions until new shoots start to develop. Once new growth is visible on each grafted plant and the union seems firm, the tape or raffia binding may be removed. When the plants are well established, repot them using a standard soil-based potting mix, and grow them on in a cool greenhouse or cold frame. Then plant them out in early summer, either in a nursery bed or in their final positions in the open garden.

PROPAGATION BY GRAFTING

1 First select and prepare the rootstock. Cut a piece of straight, healthy root about 1/2in (1cm) thick and 3 1/2in (9cm) long from the parent plant (here Gypsophila paniculata*).*

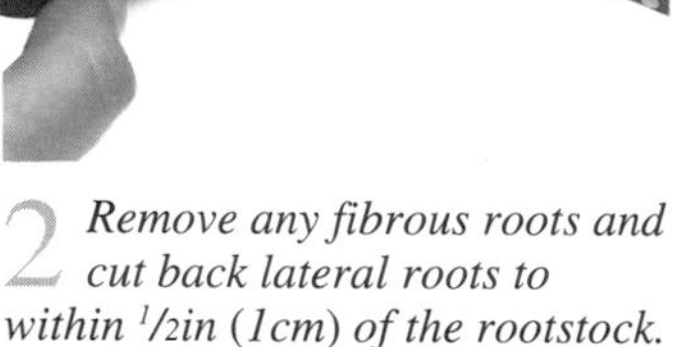

2 Remove any fibrous roots and cut back lateral roots to within 1/2in (1cm) of the rootstock. Make a straight cut across the top of the stock and an angled cut at the lower end.

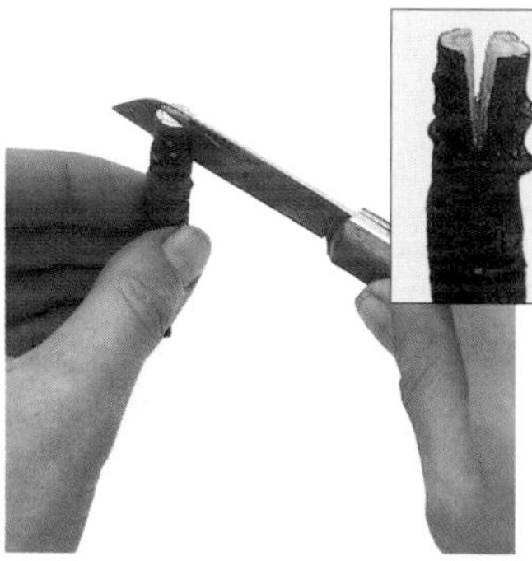

3 Using a sharp knife, make a clean, vertical incision, about 1/2in (1cm) deep, in the top of the rootstock.

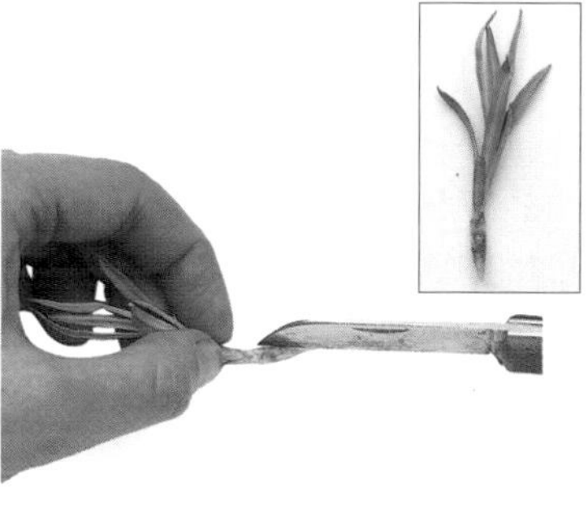

4 For the scion, select a vigorous shoot about 1/8in (3–4mm) thick and 1 1/2–3in (3–7cm) long. Trim the lower end to make a wedge that will fit into the cut in the rootstock.

5 Insert the rootstock into a 3in (6cm) pot of cuttings soil mix and firm in. Carefully insert the lower end of the scion into the vertical incision in the rootstock, so that it fits closely.

6 To hold the scion firmly in position, bind the grafted area with plastic tape or raffia. Label the grafted plant, and water thoroughly.

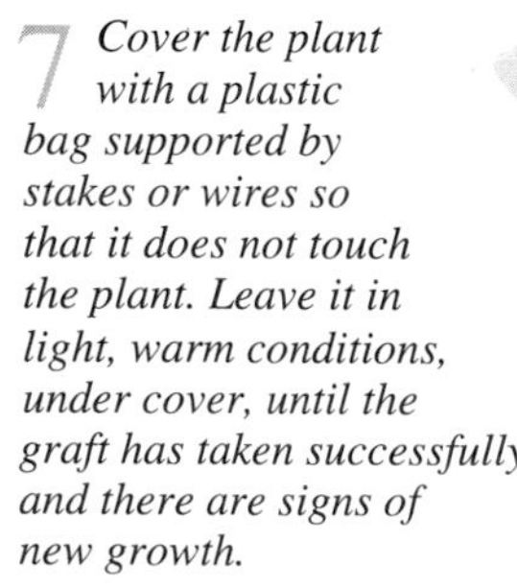

7 Cover the plant with a plastic bag supported by stakes or wires so that it does not touch the plant. Leave it in light, warm conditions, under cover, until the graft has taken successfully and there are signs of new growth.

Wildflower and meadow gardening

WILDFLOWER gardening stems in part from a wish to conserve native species that are threatened by the erosion of their natural habitats. While it is not possible to re-create such habitats exactly, growing even a small area of wildflowers contributes to their conservation and attracts a variety of insects (often beneficial) and other wildlife into the garden.

Creating a wildflower area is often the best way of using part of the garden that does not lend itself to more conventional cultivation, perhaps because it is too exposed, sloping, or dry, or has poor soil.

Wildflower gardens

Wildflower habitats are extremely diverse and include meadows or flower-rich grasslands (see p.275), alpine meadows, cornfields, wetlands, and woodlands (see p.27).

When planning a wildflower area, assess the site, taking into account climate, soil type, and drainage, and the degree of sun, shade, and shelter. The growing conditions will determine the plants that will thrive and look natural in the setting.

An open, sunny site with well-drained soil is ideal for a meadow with purple coneflower (*Echinacea purpurea*), Indian blanket (*Gaillardia aristata*), and butterfly weed (*Asclepias tuberosa*). A more exposed site may suit an alpine meadow, with short grass and low growing plants such as little red elephant (*Pedicularis groenlandica*) and blue-eyed grass (*Sisyrinchium bellum*) that will not be damaged by wind. Damp or waterlogged ground may be used for a bog garden (see p.241) with plants such as turtlehead (*Chelone glabra*).

Observe the local wild flora since this will indicate which species to grow, but never take plants from the wild without gaining permission from the landowner. You can also include some nonnative plants that require the same conditions and are in keeping with the planting style.

Seasonal variation

Depending on the site and the selected plants, the main display may be planned for a particular season or to extend over a longer period. A woodland habitat favors spring-flowering plants, for example, because the tree canopy lets through more light than it does later on. Meadows are at their peak in summer but have a long span of interest, from the spring-flowering bluets (*Houstonia caerulea*) through fall-flowering New England asters (*Aster novae-angliae*).

THE WILDFLOWER BORDER
Many species bloom profusely in this garden, providing an attractive display and a rich source of nectar for a diversity of bees and butterflies.

Establishing a meadow garden

A meadow garden should preferably be established on soil that is low in fertility, using a mixture of fine grasses such as bents (*Agrostis*) and fescues (*Festuca*) that will not outgrow and suppress the flowering plants. Typical meadow flowers include perennials such as bottle gentian (*Gentiana andrewsii*) and annuals such as California poppy (*Eschscholzia californica*).

Sowing and planting

Eliminate vigorous, perennial weeds such as docks (*Rumex*) and dandelions (*Taraxacum officinale*) with a systemic weedkiller. Then strip off any sod and remove the upper layer of fertile topsoil for use elsewhere. Cultivate the soil to a fine tilth, firm by treading or rolling, and rake lightly. The stale seedbed technique may be used (see SOILS AND FERTILIZERS, p.528) to reduce weed competition. In early fall or spring, sow the wildflower seed mixture (with fine sand for even distribution) at a rate of 1/8oz/sq yd (4g/sq m) or as advised by the supplier.

If establishing wildflowers in existing grassland or in an orchard, reduce the soil fertility over one or two years by mowing regularly and removing the clippings. Then introduce potgrown plants, using a small bulb planter to remove cores of sod.

Maintenance

During the first summer after seeding, spot-treat any invasive weeds such as thistles or plantains as they appear. If annuals were included in the seed mix, they will come into flower, but the perennials will not bloom until the second summer. Mow the meadow in the fall, after plants have seeded, cutting to 3–4in (7–10cm). Rake up and remove the clippings so that soil fertility remains low. In areas where open fires are permitted, you may adopt a burnoff program to remove plant debris, but do this with great care.

STREAMSIDE PLANTINGS
A food plant for the caterpillars of the orange-tip butterfly, the sweetly fragrant Hesperis matronalis *happily colonizes damp soils.*

FLOWERING PLANTS FOR DIFFERENT HABITATS

Rudbeckia hirta (meadow)

Monarda fistulosa (meadow)

Caltha palustris (bog)

Sanguinaria canadensis (woodland)

Arisaema triphyllum (woodland)

Erythronium americanum (woodland)

Pelargoniums

PELARGONIUMS are almost all tender, evergreen, perennial plants of South African origin. When introduced to Britain, they were given the common name geranium because of their botanical similarity to the hardy, herbaceous species of the genus *Geranium*, which was commonly cultivated in Europe at that time. This common name is widely used in North America today, although almost all the plants usually referred to as geraniums belong to the genus *Pelargonium*.

Types of pelargonium

Pelargoniums may be divided into five broad groups, according to the main characteristics of the plants. The groups are: zonal, dwarf and miniature zonal, regal, ivy-leaved, and scented-leaved.

Zonal

These pelargoniums have rounded leaves, usually marked with a distinct, dark zone and single, semidouble, or double flowers. Some cultivars, however, do not have a zone, and others have golden, white-variegated, or tricolored leaves.

In temperate climates, they grow well in the open garden and are ideal for summer bedding since they bloom continuously from early summer until the first frosts. They also thrive in windowboxes, hanging baskets, and containers. Zonals will readily adapt to the growing conditions in a greenhouse or conservatory.

TYPES OF PELARGONIUM

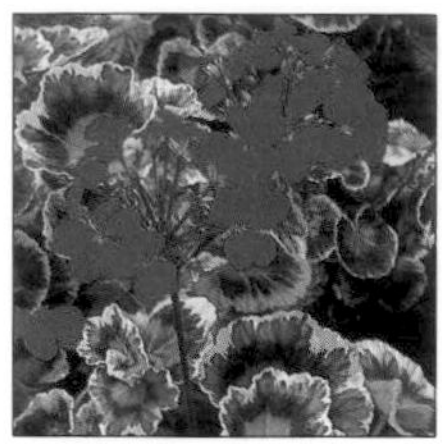

ZONAL
P. 'Dolly Varden'
Rounded leaves with a darker zone, and single to double flowers.

REGAL
P. 'Purple Emperor'
Deeply cut leaves and broadly trumpet-shaped flowers.

IVY-LEAVED
P. peltatum 'Amethyst'
Trailing plants with lobed leaves and single to double flowers.

SCENTED-LEAVED
P. 'Royal Oak'
Plants with small, often irregularly star-shaped flowers, grown for their fragrant leaves.

DWARF ZONAL
P. 'Timothy Clifford'
Bushy, free-flowering plants, similar to zonals, up to 8in (20cm) tall.

Dwarf and miniature zonal

Dwarf zonal pelargoniums are 5–8in (13–20cm) tall, bushy, and very free-flowering. They make excellent windowbox plants and pot plants for displaying in greenhouses and conservatories. Miniature zonals have smaller leaves and flowers than the dwarf zonals and are no higher than 13cm (5in). They are very floriferous plants, with double and single blooms in a wide range of colors, and green to greenish black leaves.

In recent years, F1 and F2 hybrid zonal pelargoniums have been developed. These are grown from seed and are used mainly for bedding. They are single-flowered and are available in many of the same colors and combinations as the cultivars that are propagated vegetatively.

PELARGONIUMS IN CONTAINERS
Planting a combination of zonal and scented-leaved types provides attractive foliage as well as a long-lasting display of decorative blooms.

Regal

These pelargoniums (also known as Martha Washington pelargoniums) are small shrubby plants with rounded, deeply cut leaves and wide, trumpet-shaped flowers, often in exotic colors.

They may be grown in the open garden but, in temperate regions, are much more extensively used as greenhouse, conservatory, and house plants, since the flowers are quickly spoiled by rain. In frost-free climates, where they may be planted out permanently, they make splendid flowering shrubs, almost continuously in bloom year-round.

Ivy-leaved

These trailing pelargoniums have rounded, lobed, ivylike leaves, and flowers similar to those of zonals, available in a rich assortment of colors. They are used mainly in hanging baskets and other containers, where their flowers on trailing stems can be displayed to best advantage. They may also be planted so that they spill over the edge of a raised bed or a wall.

Scented-leaved

Scented-leaved pelargoniums have small, delicate flowers with five petals, and fragrant foliage for which they are chiefly grown. They make good house and greenhouse plants, and in temperate climates may be grown outside in the summer and fall, in containers or beds.

Feeding and watering

All pelargoniums, especially when they are grown in containers, need weekly feeding throughout summer with a high-potassium liquid feed, such as tomato fertilizer. This helps the plants to continue to produce a mass of good-quality blooms without becoming too leafy. Nitrogen-rich fertilizers will produce too much leaf at the expense of flower production and should not be used. Pelargoniums in containers should be watered as soon as the top of the soil mix dries out.

Overwintering

Pelargoniums must be kept frost-free, except for *P. endlicherianum*, a rare, hardy species from Turkey. In temperate climates, plants grown outside may be saved for replanting the following season by moving them under cover before frost occurs. Lift the plants before the first frosts are expected, shake as much soil as possible off the roots, trim back the roots and stems, and remove any remaining leaves.

For storing, use a wooden or strong cardboard box with deep sides, and make a few small drainage holes in the bottom. Half fill the box with seed or cuttings soil mix, which should keep the plants alive but contains insufficient food for them to grow vigorously during storage. Place the prepared stock plants in the box, so that they are close together but not touching. Fill in with more soil mix around each plant and firm it in stages until the soil is level with the top of the box.

CONTRASTING HABITS
Use trailing ivy-leaved pelargoniums to spill over the edge of a container. These will make an attractive contrast with upright forms in the center.

Water the soil mix thoroughly and leave the box outside for a day to drain. The plants should be watered again during the winter only if they become very dry. Store the box where it will receive plenty of light and remain frost-free. If no heating is available, protect the plants during very cold weather with newspaper, burlap, or old carpet.

By midwinter, new shoots will begin to appear on the stock plants; these may be used as cuttings in early spring. Alternatively, the stock plants may be potted up separately and grown on for planting out in the early part of the summer.

Propagation from cuttings

Pelargoniums are easily propagated from cuttings, and the method used is the same for all types. Taking cuttings is an inexpensive way of producing new plants and allows the parent plant to remain outside in the garden until the first frosts, thus prolonging the display.

Selecting the cuttings

Although it is possible to take cuttings from spring onward, the best time is in late summer, when light conditions are good and the weather is still warm. Select strong, healthy shoots (nonflowering ones if from a regal or scented-leaved pelargonium), cutting just above the third joint below the growing tip. Trim each cutting just below the lowest joint and remove the lower leaves.

Inserting the cuttings

Choose the pot size according to the number of cuttings: a 5in (13cm) pot will take up to five cuttings. Fill the pot with standard seed or cuttings soil mix, press down firmly, and place the pot in a container of water until the soil mix surface becomes moist. Remove the pot and allow it to drain. Insert the cuttings, pressing them down gently to eliminate any air pockets beneath the bases of the cuttings. Do not water them yet.

Aftercare

Place the pot in a light, warm position, but not in full sun. One week after insertion, water the cuttings from below (as explained above). Water again a week or ten days later, by which time the cuttings should be rooting. If watered from above, the cuttings may suffer from gray mold/*Botrytis* or other damping off diseases. Do not use propagators or cover them with plastic sheeting, for the same reason. Always allow free circulation of air around them. As soon as the cuttings have rooted (when they resist being pulled up and fresh leaves appear) pot them up singly into 3in (6cm) pots.

Growing F1 and F2 hybrids from seed

Seed-sown F1 and F2 hybrids are quite easy to grow, and given good light, they will flower in as little as three months. Start the seeds in late winter. Sow them on a moistened piece of coffee filter or paper towel in a covered glass dish. They often germinate erratically. After germination, pot on the sprouted seeds to individual cell packs or to 2in (5cm) pots. Be careful not to overwater the seedlings; a slightly dry soil mix is best to promote healthy growth.

When the seedlings are 6in (15cm) high, pinch out the growing tips to encourage bushy growth. Grow the seedlings on as cool greenhouse plants throughout the winter and spring, to enable them to flower throughout summer and fall. Particularly good-quality plants may be overwintered as for other pelargoniums (see left).

OVERWINTERING

1 *Lift the plants before the first frosts and shake off any loose soil. Cut down the stems to about 4in (10cm) and remove the leaves. Trim back roots to about 2in (5cm).*

2 *Half fill a box at least 6in (15cm) deep with seed soil mix. Put in the plants so that they do not touch each other. Fill in with mix, then water and drain.*

3 *Store in a frost-free place until new shoots start to appear, then pot up the plants. Use the new shoots to take cuttings from, as necessary, later in spring.*

TAKING CUTTINGS

1 *Choose a healthy shoot and cut straight across the stem just above the third joint below the growing tip.*

2 *Using a sharp knife, remove leaves from each cutting, leaving two at the top. Pinch out any flowers or buds.*

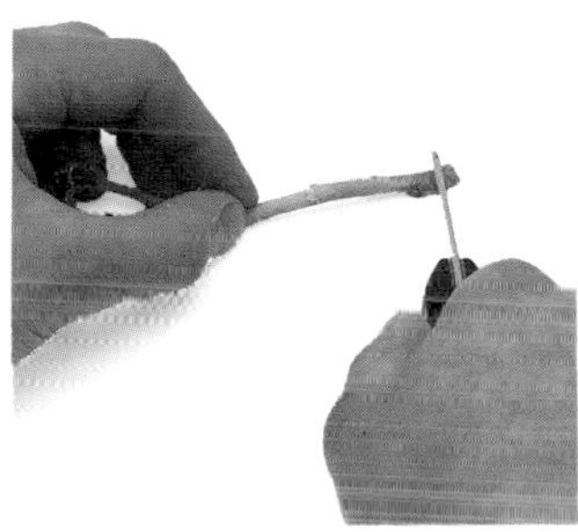

3 *Carefully trim the base of each cutting to just below the lowest joint with a straight cut.*

4 *Make holes 1in (2.5cm) deep in pots of moist, firmed seed or cuttings soil mix. Insert the cuttings and firm.*

7

Annuals and Biennials

Annuals and biennials are traditionally regarded as a quick and inexpensive means of adding color to the garden. To restrict their use in this way, however, is to overlook the vast range of foliage, fragrance, texture, and stature they have to offer. Their uses are as varied as their attributes. They can bring to life any garden within just a few months or, as cut or dried flowers, transform the home inside. Annuals and biennials also provide opportunities to experiment in the garden by altering color schemes from one year to the next. Although short-lived, a large number of these plants flower freely over many weeks and even months. The gardener can use this profusion of color to create infinite patterns of bedding with plants that are planned to flower in succession. While annuals and biennials are most often used to adorn beds and containers, some varieties with a trailing or climbing habit are particularly striking grown up a support or allowed to sprawl luxuriantly over a bank.

Designing with annuals and biennials

The term "annual" describes a plant whose entire life cycle, from germination to seed production through to death, takes place within one year. Those that can withstand some frost are known as hardy annuals; those that are not are known as half hardy and must be raised under glass and planted out after all danger of frost has passed.

Biennials, however, require two growing seasons. During their first season after sowing they produce leaf growth; they then overwinter and flower in the following year.

Many plants grown as annuals are actually tender perennials and will survive where frosts do not occur.

Summer-flowering Annuals
An exuberant display in a small area is created by the vivid colors of Impatiens *cultivars, shapely clusters of* Schizanthus, *loose masses of* Lobelia, *and petunias. Pelargoniums and fuchsias add to the richness.*

Annual borders

Whole borders or beds devoted to annuals produce colorful displays. Ideal in a new garden where they quickly provide a vibrant show, annuals may also be used as features in established gardens. The plants can be changed several times in a season to create different displays.

Color

The most attractive annual borders are often those that rely on a limited range of colors – dazzling oranges and reds, muted pinks and purples, soft blues and mauves. Plan the planting with a broad sweep of color, selecting tones that blend together harmoniously. Grays, greens, and whites are particularly useful for providing a respite from some of the more vibrant reds and blues. Many annuals, such as snapdragons (*Antirrhinum*), pansies (*Viola* x *wittrockiana*), and petunias, are available in a range of colors, making it possible to select a plant whatever the color range. A bed devoted to pure white flowers looks fresh and crisp, but green-foliaged plants prevent the planting from looking cold. Creams should not be substituted for cleaner whites here.

Form and texture

Border compositions are often enhanced by the leaf texture or the overall plant shape as much as by color alone. Place plants with contrasting leaf or flower textures in adjacent groupings. Their differing characteristics will then be better

A Tapestry of Summer Color
This beautiful display of half-hardy and hardy annuals is attractively offset by the mellow tones of the vine-clad wall in the background.

appreciated. Form and texture of annuals are often overlooked, but they add greatly to the character of a planting, whether it be with the wispy flowers of *Nigella*, the bold spikes of *Salvia*, or the sprawling informality of the poached-egg flower (*Limnanthes douglasii*). A particularly valuable plant is the ornamental corn (*Zea mays* 'Japonica Multicolor'), with its variegated leaves, plumelike flower tassels, and ears of variously colored kernels.

Including a variety of shapes and sizes also adds interest to the planting. For example, select the daisy-like shapes of *Gaillardia*, the golden discs of sunflowers (*Helianthus annuus*), the large bells of petunias, the feathery plumes of *Celosia cristata*, or the tiny pompons of English daisies (*Bellis perennis*) or double-flowered feverfew (*Tanacetum parthenium*, double white).

Grouping the plants

Many annuals look their best when planted in large groups of one cultivar to give a bold block of color. Single plants can otherwise easily become isolated and weaken the structure of the planting. Sow in irregular patches so that the impact as the plants mature is similar to the interlocking drifts of flowers made by perennials in a traditional herbaceous border. The shapes and sizes of the groups should be varied to create a natural, free-flowing look.

When a border is to be viewed mainly from one direction, perhaps from a path or lawn, or is backed by a fence or hedge, graduate plants according to height. Plant the tallest plants, such as hollyhocks (*Alcea*), *Amaranthus*, and sunflowers, at the back. Place naturally low-growing species such as *Ageratum*, sweet alyssum (*Lobularia maritima*), and annual phlox at the front of the border. Between them, juxtapose groups of intermediate, but slightly different, heights to achieve variation. This produces a billowing, undulating informality.

Combine plants that flourish in similar conditions. For instance, species or cultivars of *Nicotiana*, which have loose clusters of tubular flowers on short to tall stems, combine well with the low-growing, flower-covered, compact shapes of *Impatiens* cultivars, since both generally prefer cool and shady sites.

Foliage plants

There are several annuals grown chiefly for their foliage to harmonize or contrast with bright flower color, and to add to the range of textures in a bed or border.

The silver-gray *Senecio maritima* is easily grown from seed. Although often treated as a half-hardy annual, it is in fact a perennial, and may be kept for years if protected from frost. A clump of castor bean plants (*Ricinus communis*), another perennial that flourishes in cooler climates when treated as a half-hardy annual, provides a striking accent with its green or purplish bronze leaves.

The curious, bright green, cup-like flowers of the annual bells-of-Ireland (*Moluccella laevis*) contrast well with colorful planting designs. Selected cultivars of *Coleus* have a range of foliage color in reds, purples, yellows, and greens.

Other colorful foliage plants include 'Ruby' chard (a cultivar of *Beta vulgaris*), with its vivid red, upright stalks, and ornamental cabbages (*Brassica oleracea* forms), which have low-growing, muted foliage in pinks, greens, and white.

Seasonal display

Plan the planting so that the flowering periods of the annuals coincide as much as possible to avoid gaps appearing in the design. To provide interest over a long period, use annuals that bloom in succession; for specific color combinations, make sure that the chosen plants bloom at the same time.

For a spring display choose wallflowers (*Cheiranthus*), forget-me-nots (*Myosotis*), pansies (*Viola* x *wittrockiana*), and primroses (*Primula vulgaris* and *P.* x *polyanthus*). For summer and early fall, the range of plants coming into flower is much greater, and the scope for creating pleasing combinations is limitless.

Petunias have been diversified so greatly that elaborate color schemes may be created using them alone. Choose from the boldly contrasting, striped blooms, the bright, single colors, or the subtly shaded ones, using them either singly or in combinations. Both the multiflora and grandiflora types are excellent.

Marigolds also offer a wide range of colors, from cream to deep orange to mahogany-red, and the flower heads vary from the single daisies of

An Annual Border

A complete border may be devoted to annuals, biennials, and other short-lived plants. In this design, good use has been made of the different growth habits of, for example, the climbing Cobaea scandens *and the spreading sweet alyssum* (Lobularia maritima)*, which softens the front of the border. The architectural foliage of the castor bean plant* (Ricinus communis) *makes a strong focal point in contrast to the more informal flower shapes.*

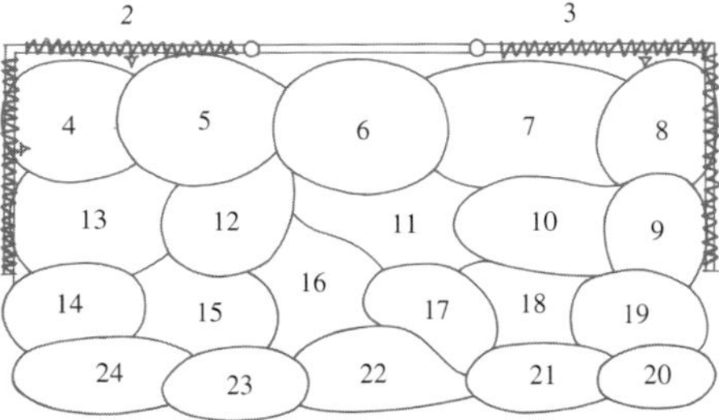

1 *Tropaeolum majus*
2 *Eccremocarpus scaber*
3 *Cobaea scandens*
4 *Chrysanthemum* 'Primrose Gem'
5 *Digitalis purpurea* f. *alba*
6 *Ricinus communis*
7 *Lavatera trimestris* 'Mont Blanc'
8 *Centaurea cyanus*
9 *Tagetes patula* 'Naughty Marietta'
10 *Salvia farinacea*
11 *Nicotiana alata* 'Lime Green'
12 *Nigella damascena* 'Miss Jekyll'
13 *Calendula* 'Orange King'
14 *Arctotis stoechadifolia* var. *grandis*
15 *Gypsophila* 'Covent Garden White'
16 *Rudbeckia* 'Marmalade'
17 *Echium* 'Blue Bedder'
18 *Eschscholzia* 'Monarch Art Shades'
19 *Dimorphotheca*, Sunshine Hybrids
20 *Lobularia maritima* 'Snow Crystal'
21 *Lobelia* 'Crystal Palace'
22 *Convolvulus* 'Royal Ensign'
23 *Tagetes* 'Golden Gem'
24 *Ageratum* 'Blue Danube'

FORMAL BEDDING
Perfect for coloring in a preexisting pattern, scarlet pelargoniums and orange pot marigolds (Calendula) *make vivid monochromatic panels.*

A MIXED BORDER
Annuals and biennials create a rich tapestry when planted among perennials. Tall yellow spires of biennial Verbascum, *golden sunflowers, and pot marigolds are interwoven with blue cornflowers and pink* Cosmos.

Tagetes signata to the great globes of the African cultivars. French marigolds (*Tagetes patula*), with single and double flowerheads, display rich crimson or mahogany-red coloring. Many other marigolds, intermediate between the African and French types, are also available.

Formal bedding designs

The wide variation of color, shape, and size, as well as the uniformity of growth obtainable in many modern cultivars of annuals, provides opportunities to create long-lasting displays from spring to fall. One of the glories of annuals is the intensity of color achieved when a single cultivar of one of the low-growing, floriferous kinds is massed in a bed so that individual plants merge together. A scarlet carpet of pelargoniums or of *Salvia splendens*, for example, makes a vivid display when set into a fresh, green lawn. Patterned designs, using annuals of different colors, can produce similarly eye-catching effects.

The dense growth habit and continuous flowering of many annuals make them ideal candidates for these complex, formal patterns. There is a wide range of dwarf and intermediate cultivars available. Plants may be used to add color to designs that have been delineated with bricks, gravel, or other architectural materials.

Annuals are excellent for knot gardens and parterres where small evergreen plants such as boxwood (*Buxus*), thyme (*Thymus*), or lavender (*Lavandula*) are clipped to create permanent outlines. Vary color schemes with the seasons: a spring planting of pansies can be followed by a summer one of dwarf zinnias, for example.

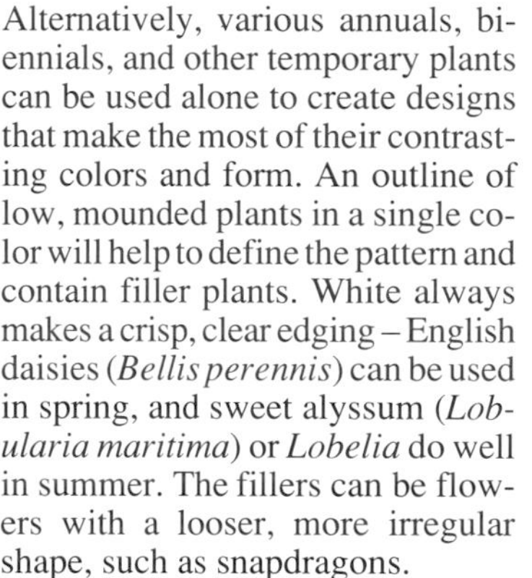

Alternatively, various annuals, biennials, and other temporary plants can be used alone to create designs that make the most of their contrasting colors and form. An outline of low, mounded plants in a single color will help to define the pattern and contain filler plants. White always makes a crisp, clear edging – English daisies (*Bellis perennis*) can be used in spring, and sweet alyssum (*Lobularia maritima*) or *Lobelia* do well in summer. The fillers can be flowers with a looser, more irregular shape, such as snapdragons.

Mixed borders

A mixed border, containing shrubs, perennials, bulbs, and annuals, is one of the delights of the garden. With such a diversity of plants, it offers the greatest possible variety of color, contour, texture, season of interest, and design. Annuals and biennials warrant a place in any permanent planting plan, in which they can be sown each year or left to self-seed. If allowed to self-sow they will produce a random profusion of flowers reminiscent of the traditional English cottage garden, where all manner of plants, including fruit, salad vegetables, and crops, jostle for space in the same informal plot.

ANNUALS IN MIXED BORDERS

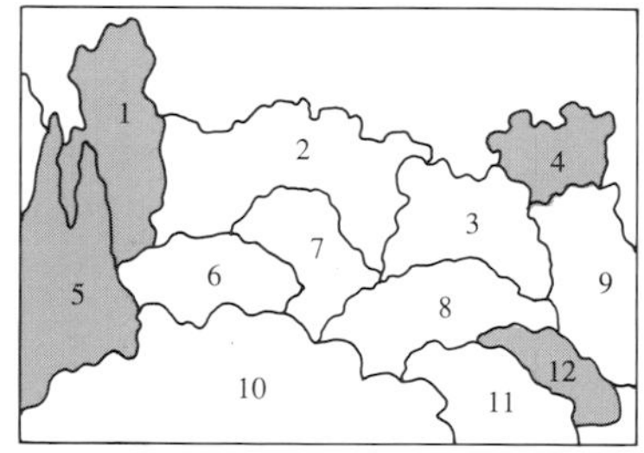

1 *Onopordum acanthium*
2 *Papaver orientale*
3 *Paeonia* 'Sarah Bernhardt'
4 *Papaver somniferum*
5 *Digitalis purpurea* cvs
6 *Bergenia cordifolia* 'Purpurea'
7 *Thalictrum aquilegiifolium*
8 *Ornithogalum narbonense*
9 *Dianthus* 'Mrs. Sinkins'
10 *Allium giganteum*
11 *Dicentra formosa*
12 *Viola tricolor*

In this bed, annuals (represented by gray areas on the diagram) have been planted between the perennials and bulbs to fill the gaps and to provide extra interest as well as wonderful splashes of bright color throughout the summer months. The sculptural, silvery gray Scotch thistle and the tall, purple and white spikes of foxgloves appear majestically above the interlocking clumps of perennials. Bright red opium poppies punctuate the planting and, at the front of the border, the delicate Viola tricolor *sprawls out over the path. The pinkish purple of the* Viola *complements the pink of the peony* 'Sarah Bernhardt'. *The rich purple foxgloves and the profuse blooms of* Thalictrum aquilegiifolium *help create an integrated and attractive planting design.*

Used as color highlights among perennials and shrubs, both annuals and biennials bring life to established borders. Possibilities range from cheerful mixtures of *Clarkia* (syn. *Godetia*), *Cosmos*, and California poppies (*Eschscholzia californica*), to carefully coordinated one-color schemes. For instance, flowering annuals such as crimson *Amaranthus caudatus* and *Nicotiana alata*, or scarlet begonias, pelargoniums, and *Verbena* cultivars, will add highlights to a red border with a framework of purplish foliage.

Self-sown annuals and biennials may soon become a permanent feature in a mixed border, helping to unify the planting and introducing a pleasing unpredictability. In early summer, love-in-a-mist (*Nigella damascena*) makes a hazy web of color, filling any gaps and weaving together neighboring blooms and the young leaves of later-flowering plants. The spirelike stems of certain biennials such as *Verbascum* and foxgloves (*Digitalis*) add an air of cottage garden informality to an otherwise structured border.

Architectural plants

Handsome leaves, eye-catching flower shapes, and striking habits of growth make certain plants stand out from their companions. Annuals or biennials with such architectural qualities can be key features in a mixed border, enhancing the composition. These plants have the greatest impact when they complement – rather than dominate – the other plants in the vicinity. The large, spiny gray leaves and tall, widely branched flower stems of the Scotch thistle (*Onopordum acanthium*), for instance, make a statuesque centerpiece in a border that features other types of silver-foliaged plants. The flower spikes of the Excelsior Series foxgloves and larkspur (*Consolida*) rise gracefully above all the neighboring plants. Shapely blooms, such as those of *Cleome*, will also command attention.

Plants grown primarily for their foliage also play an architectural role. In large borders the green or purple palmate leaves of castor bean plants (*Ricinus communis*) add a strong textural quality, as do the bold leaves of the ornamental cabbages (*Brassica oleracea* forms).

ANNUALS TO TRAIL
With its tumbling form, shapely leaves, and long-lasting, attractive double flowers, this annual nasturtium, Tropaeolum 'Hermine Grasshof', *needs no companion plants to make a vivid and striking focal point in a decorative terracotta pot.*

Annuals and biennials as fillers

Since they grow rapidly and are relatively cheap to raise, use annuals and biennials to fill gaps. Place them where a plant has failed, or between immature perennials or recently planted shrubs in a new border. Select species that contrast in form or texture, choosing cultivars in a height and color range to suit the permanent plantings.

In warmer areas, at the end of the season, plant wallflowers (*Cheiranthus*) for their winter foliage and spring flowers. Multicolored carpets of winter-flowering pansies (*Viola* x *wittrockiana*) and primroses (*Primula vulgaris*) may be interplanted with spring-flowering bulbs, such as daffodils, hyacinths, or late-flowering tulips.

Until alpines become established, gaps in the rock garden may be filled by sun-loving annuals that enjoy the same conditions. To avoid overwhelming the delicate colors and modest stature of the alpines, however, choose annuals that are on a similar scale, such as *Viola tricolor*, *Lobelia erinus*, *Thymophylla tenuiloba*, and *Portulaca*.

GROUND COVER ANNUALS
Low-growing Impatiens *cultivars form a carpet of intense color in the cool shade under trees or shrubs.*

Annuals and biennials for ground cover

Some annuals and biennials may be used as temporary ground cover, creating pools of color in an otherwise bare space. There are annuals to suit shade as well as sun, poor soil as well as rich. Single-color cultivars of sweet alyssum (*Lobularia maritima*) or annual candytufts (*Iberis*) may be used to provide dense cover in a sunny spot. Use *Impatiens* cultivars in shade, where their spreading growth and colorful, continuous blooms will quickly cover bare ground. For a more textured quality as well as lively color, sow corn poppies (*Papaver rhoeas*) or California poppies; both spread quickly. Attractive ground cover is also swiftly created by using cultivars of *Catharanthus roseus* in white or rose, or nasturtiums (*Tropaeolum*) in red, orange, and yellow.

Climbers and trailers

Vigorous annuals and biennials that climb and trail may quickly transform an expanse of wall or fence with a colorful curtain of foliage and flower, weaving a screen to provide privacy, or embellishing an existing structure. Many annuals have attractive leaves as well as beautiful flowers, and a few, such as sweet peas (*Lathyrus odoratus*), offer the added pleasure of scent.

Plants with a climbing or trailing habit are particularly valuable in restricted spaces such as patios and balconies, where they make use of the vertical space as well as the ground area. Moreover, many annual climbers can be grown in pots. They are ideal for furnishing new gardens, softening bleak surfaces, and disguising or distracting from an unsightly view.

Exuberant annuals that twine around and clothe architectural features may be used to provide an abundance of summer flowers in company with more permanent perennial climbers. Try morning glories (*Ipomoea*), twining cultivars of nasturtium (*Tropaeolum*), or cup-and-saucer vine (*Cobaea scandens*) with its large bell-shaped flowers in purple or greenish white. For quick results, grow *Thunbergia alata* or *Rhodochiton atrosanguineum*, which is a fascinating plant with curious, deep purple, tubular flowers in dusky maroon calyces.

Climbing annuals are intriguing when grown through host plants such as ivy (*Hedera*) or conifers. Use the twining canary creeper (*Tropaeolum peregrinum*), which has broadly lobed leaves and bright yellow, fringed flowers. Another choice is the half-hardy *Eccremocarpus scaber*, which climbs by means of tendrils and has a long flowering season, with clusters of tubular flowers that glow yellow, orange, or red among its small, tooth-shaped, pinnate leaves. For a dense, leafy screen, plant scarlet runner beans (*Phaseolus coccineus*), which bear delicate, scarlet flowers and a bonus of edible pods.

Annuals in containers

Whether it is a pot, tub, or windowbox, any container is a potential focal point in the garden, and the plants grown in it can make an eye-catching feature. F1 hybrid annuals, with their uniform growth habit and consistent flower colors, are specifically bred to provide reliable, long-lasting displays. However, most annuals may be used in containers, either on their own or to complement other plants.

The shape, style, and material of the container may be chosen to play a major part in the display, or it may be completely subordinate to the planting. A shapely urn or a handsome stone trough can be veiled by wisps of foliage, while a more functional container can be disguised with trailing leaves and flowers.

Increasing the range

The range of annuals suitable for containers or patio beds close to the house may be greater than that for the open garden, since the protection of adjacent buildings often enables plants to be grown that are normally too tender for more exposed sites in the same area. Consider how sunny, shady, or windy the site is before deciding which plants to grow.

Annuals are available for an all-season display. In late spring and early summer, some cultivars of pansies and primroses continue to provide color when growing in sheltered spots. Protected but sunny sites on patios are also ideal for gazanias, *Coleus*, and New Guinea *Impatiens* cultivars, which maintain their color throughout the summer and into fall.

WINDOWBOX COMPOSITIONS
This restrained cream, blue, and green combination mixes begonias and pansies with trailing Lobelia, *ivy,* Helichrysum, *and* Lysimachia.

PLANTING IN THE VERTICAL PLANE
Hanging baskets and windowboxes transform a bare wall. Trailing plants such as ivy-leaved pelargoniums contrast with bright yellow and rust marigolds, creating a continuous curtain of color.

Selecting cultivars

Compact cultivars are particularly useful since they will better withstand windy sites and will not need support. Choose dwarf and intermediate snapdragon cultivars rather than tall ones, and dwarf bedding pelargoniums. Ivy-leaved pelargoniums, which have a long flowering season, can be raised from seed and grown as half-hardy annuals. New hybrid pelargoniums, intermediate in habit between the trailing and the bushy types, include the Sensation, Breakaway, and Multibloom Series. They have been specially bred for production from seed and are ideal for growing in containers. For further details see PELARGONIUMS, pp.168–9.

Gazanias grow well in hanging baskets and containers positioned in sunny spots, where they open their brightly colored flowerheads. Heliotrope is valuable around the house in containers near a window or doorway, where its perfume can be appreciated. Stocks (*Matthiola*) have similar qualities of beauty and scent, particularly the Ten-week Series in summer and the East Lothian and Brompton Series in both fall and spring.

Hanging baskets and windowboxes

Plants with a trailing habit are ideal for growing in windowboxes and hanging baskets, and appealing displays can be created by a mass of foliage and flower. Reliable performers include trailing petunias, *Lobelia erinus* such as the Cascade Series, and *Verbena* x *hybrida* cultivars, available in a wide range of colors, including pure reds and scarlets, deep purples, crimsons, and whites. Trailing and spreading F1 pelargoniums, renewed annually from seed, are also good value (see PELARGONIUMS, pp.168–9).

Annuals for cutting and drying

Many annuals provide excellent cut flowers. If space is available in your garden, it is worth growing a number of flowers especially for cutting. They may be either integrated into borders or sown in a separate area. Taller cultivars may be particularly suitable; choose cornflowers (*Centaurea cyanus*), snapdragons (*Antirrhinum*), stocks, and *Gypsophila*. Sweet peas (*Lathyrus odoratus*) are particularly good as cut flowers and fill the house with their heady fragrance; if the flowers are cut regularly the plants will bloom for many weeks. Larkspur (*Consolida*) is also useful for cutting and is equally attractive whether fresh or dried.

Many annuals may be grown to dry as everlasting flowers for indoor display throughout the year, including *Helichrysum*, *Limonium*, and *Amaranthus caudatus*. Others such as honesty (*Lunaria*) and *Nigella* are grown for their decorative seedheads. Annual grasses, such as *Panicum capillare*, are also worth growing because their feathery seedheads make a fine display.

Planter's guide to annuals and biennials

EXPOSED SITES

Annuals and biennials that tolerate exposed or windy sites

Borago officinalis
Calendula
Catharanthus roseus
Centaurea cyanus
Cheiranthus
Chrysanthemum carinatum, *C. coronarium*, *C. segetum*
Clarkia
Dianthus barbatus, *D. chinensis*
Echium vulgare
Eschscholzia
Glaucium flavum
Iberis amara, *I. umbellata*
Lavatera trimestris
Limnanthes
Linum grandiflorum
Lobularia maritima
Lunaria
Malcolmia
Oenothera biennis
Papaver rhoeas, *P. somniferum*
Petunia ❄
Rudbeckia hirta (hybrids)

Rudbeckia hirta

Salvia horminum
Tagetes signata ❄
Vaccaria hispanica

DRY SHADE

Annuals and biennials that tolerate dry shade

Digitalis purpurea
Matthiola bicornis

MOIST SHADE

Annuals and biennials that prefer moist shade

Impatiens walleriana ❄
Matthiola bicornis
Mimulus – seed selections including: *M.*, Calypso Series ❄ *M.*, Malibu Series ❄
Oenothera biennis
Primula vulgaris
Viola x *wittrockiana*

FRAGRANT FLOWERS

Centaurea moschata
Dianthus, Chabaud Series ❄, *D. chinensis*
Exacum affine ❄
Heliotropium, some ❄
Humea elegans ❄
Lathyrus odoratus
Lobularia maritima
Matthiola, Brompton Series, *M.*, East Lothian Series, *M.*, Ten-week Series
Nicotiana alata ❄, *N.* x *sanderae* ❄ (some cvs)
Primula, some ❄
Reseda odorata
Viola x *wittrockiana*

FLOWERS FOR CUTTING

Agrostemma githago 'Milas'
Antirrhinum, some ❄ (tall cvs)
Calendula
Callistephus ❄ (tall cvs)
Centaurea cyanus
Cheiranthus cheiri
Chrysanthemum carinatum ❄, *C. coronarium*, *C. segetum*
Consolida ambigua
Coreopsis Series
Cosmos ❄
Dianthus barbatus, *D.*, Giant Chabaud Series, *D.*, Knight Series
Gaillardia pulchella
Gilia capitata
Gomphrena globosa ❄
Gypsophila elegans
Helianthus annuus, *H.*, Color Fashion Series
Helipterum ❄
Lathyrus odoratus
Limonium sinuatum ❄
Lunaria annua
Matthiola, Brompton Series, *M.*, East Lothian Series, *M. incana*, *M.*, Ten-week Series
Moluccella laevis ❄
Nigella damascena
Papaver nudicaule, *P.*, Summer Breeze Series
Psylliostachys suworowii ❄
Rudbeckia hirta (hybrids)
Salvia horminum
Xeranthemum annuum ❄
Zinnia ❄

FLOWERS FOR DRYING

Ageratum ❄
Amaranthus ❄
Avena sterilis
Briza maxima, *B. minor*
Calendula
Celosia ❄
Centaurea cyanus
Clarkia
Consolida ambigua
Gomphrena globosa ❄
Helipterum ❄
Hordeum jubatum
Lagurus ovatus
Limonium sinuatum ❄
Lonas ❄
Moluccella laevis ❄
Nigella
Panicum violaceum
Pennisetum villosum
Salvia horminum
Setaria glauca ❄
Stipa pennata

ARCHITECTURAL PLANTS

Alcea rosea, syn. *Althaea rosea*
Amaranthus caudatus ❄, *A. tricolor* ❄
Brassica oleracea 'Cabbage Cherry Sundae' (F1), *B. o.* 'Kale Red and White Peacock' (F1)
Cleome hassleriana ❄
Digitalis purpurea
Helianthus annuus

Helianthus annuus

Kochia scoparia f. *trichophylla* ❄
Onopordum acanthium
Ricinus communis ❄
Salvia sclarea var. *turkestanica*
Silybum marianum
Verbascum bombyciferum, *V. densiflorum*
Zea mays 'Gracillima Variegata' ❄, *Z. m.* 'Japonica Multicolor' ❄

TRAILING PLANTS FOR CONTAINERS

Ageratum ❄
Arctotis stoechadifolia ❄
Begonia semperflorens ❄, *B.* 'Non stop' ❄
Brachycome iberidifolia
Convolvulus tricolor
Gazania ❄
Heliotropium, some ❄
Impatiens walleriana ❄
Lobelia erinus ❄
Osteospermum 'Starshine' (and other seed selections) ❄
Pelargonium 'Breakaway' ❄, *P.* 'Multibloom' ❄, *P.* 'Sensation' ❄, *P.* 'Summer Showers' ❄ (and other F1 and F2 Series)
Petunia ❄
Senecio ❄
Thymophylla tenuiloba ❄
Tropaeolum majus (semitrailing cvs), *T. m.* 'Empress of India', *T. m.*, Gleam Series, *T. m.*, Whirlybird Series
Verbena x *hybrida* ❄
Viola x *wittrockiana*

ANNUAL CLIMBERS

See list on p.97.

POT PLANTS

Annuals suitable for growing from seed as (greenhouse) pot plants

Antirrhinum, some ❄
Begonia semperflorens ❄
Campanula pyramidalis ❄
Capsicum ❄ (ornamental fruit cvs)
Centaurea moschata
Coleus ❄
Exacum affine ❄
Humea elegans ❄
Impatiens walleriana ❄ (tall cvs)
Osteospermum ❄
Pelargonium ❄ (F1 and F2 hybrids)
Petunia ❄
Primula malacoides ❄, *P. obconica* ❄, *P. sinensis* ❄
Psylliostachys suworowii ❄
Salpiglossis ❄
Schizanthus ❄
Senecio x *hybridus* ❄ (cvs)
Thunbergia alata ❄
Torenia fournieri ❄
Trachelium caeruleum ❄
Trachymene coerulea, syn. *Didiscus coeruleus* ❄

PERENNIALS THAT MAY BE GROWN AS ANNUALS

Alternanthera ❄
Antirrhinum, some ❄

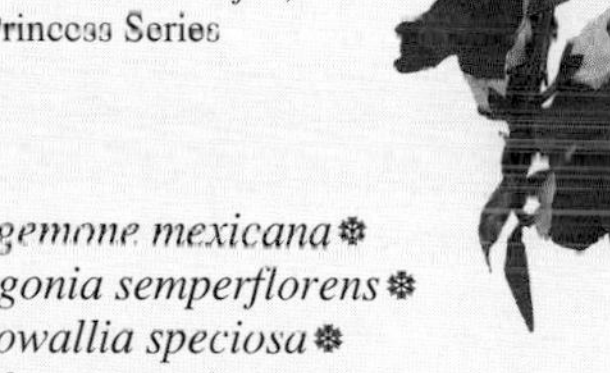

Antirrhinum majus, Princess Series

Argemone mexicana ❄
Begonia semperflorens ❄
Browallia speciosa ❄
Cobaea scandens ❄
Coleus ❄
Coreopsis, Early Sunrise Series
Eccremocarpus scaber ❄
Gazania ❄
Gomphrena globosa ❄
Heliotropium arborescens ❄
Impatiens walleriana ❄
Mimulus, Malibu Series ❄ (and other seed selections)
Nierembergia rivularis ❄
Pelargonium ❄ (all F1 and F2 seed selections)
Ricinus communis ❄
Salvia farinacea ❄, *S. splendens* ❄
Senecio cineraria ❄
Verbena x *hybrida* ❄

KEY

❄ *Not frost hardy*

Sowing and planting

ANNUALS AND BIENNIALS THAT PREFER SANDY SOIL

Anchusa capensis
Argemone mexicana ❁
Brachycome iberidifolia
Calendula officinalis
Centaurea cyanus
Chrysanthemum segetum
Clarkia amoena
Coreopsis tinctoria
Eschscholzia californica
Glaucium flavum
Helichrysum bracteatum ❁
Impatiens ❁
Lavatera trimestris
Limnanthes douglasii
Limonium sinuatum ❁
Linaria maroccana
Lobularia maritima
Mentzelia lindleyi
Oenothera biennis

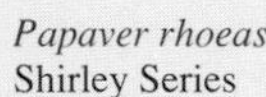

Papaver rhoeas, Shirley Series

Papaver rhoeas, Shirley Series, *P. somniferum*
Portulaca grandiflora ❁
Rudbeckia hirta
Schizanthus ❁
Tagetes ❁
Tropaeolum majus
Verbascum bombyciferum
Verbena x *hybrida* ❁

ANNUALS AND BIENNIALS THAT TOLERATE VERY ALKALINE SOIL

Ageratum houstonianum ❁
Antirrhinum majus ❁
Calendula officinalis
Callistephus chinensis ❁
Cheiranthus cheiri
Cosmos
Dianthus, some ❁
Gomphrena globosa ❁
Humea elegans ❁
Lavatera trimestris

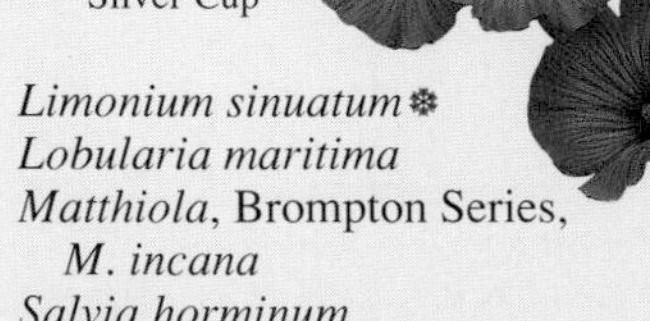

Lavatera trimestris 'Silver Cup'

Limonium sinuatum ❁
Lobularia maritima
Matthiola, Brompton Series, *M. incana*
Salvia horminum
Tagetes ❁
Tropaeolum, some ❁
Ursinia anthemoides ❁
Xeranthemum annuum ❁
Zinnia ❁

KEY
❁ *Not frost hardy*

ANNUALS and biennials are among the easiest of plants to raise from seed. They can also be obtained as seedlings or young plants from nurseries or garden centers, and will provide an instant display of color in a garden border or container placed indoors or outside.

Hardy and half-hardy annuals and biennials

Annuals complete their life cycle in a year, while biennials require two years. Horticulturally, annuals and biennials are termed hardy or half hardy. Hardy annuals are resistant to frosts and so may be sown early in open ground and will be established before more frost-prone annuals. Half-hardy annuals withstand only a limited amount of cold and are killed or badly damaged at freezing temperatures; they need to be maintained in frost-free conditions of 55–70°F (13–21°C) to germinate and become established.

Hardy biennials should be sown by midsummer to allow the plants to become well established by the winter. Overwinter half-hardy biennials in a cool greenhouse or insulated cold frame.

Buying seeds

Always buy fresh seeds that have been stored in cool conditions. Their viability varies greatly; some, such as members of the family Leguminosae, may remain viable for a few years if kept cool and dry, but most start to deteriorate after a year, especially if they are stored in damp, warm conditions. Seeds in sealed foil packets last for several years; however, once the packets are opened, the seeds deteriorate.

F1 hybrid seeds are available for many annuals and some biennials; these produce plants that are vigorous and true to type with even growth and flower characteristics. These seeds are ideal for the gardener who is seeking uniformity, but for most ordinary garden purposes the well-produced, open-pollinated seeds are equally satisfactory and provide some variation in the plants.

Pelleted seeds

Seeds may be individually coated with a paste, or pelleted, to form a small, smooth ball. This enables them to be handled separately, so that they can be more easily spaced in containers or the open ground. If pelleted seeds are space-sown at the correct distance they do not need to be thinned, so, although they cost more, fewer are required. The seeds should be watered thoroughly after sowing to ensure that the moisture needed for germination penetrates the seed coat as quickly as possible. Pelleted seeds are normally available only for F1 hybrids.

Seed tapes and gels

Seed tapes are tissuelike, soluble strips with evenly spaced seeds embedded within them. The tapes are laid at the base of a drill, then covered with a thin layer of soil. Gel kits can be purchased for fluid sowing – seeds are added to a paste that suspends and thereby evenly spaces the seeds throughout it. The mixture is then squeezed along a prepared drill. It is important not to allow the mixture to dry out. Both these methods distribute the seeds evenly so that less thinning is required than for hand-sown seeds.

Small seedlings already well established in wedges or plugs of soil mix are also available, ready for potting up individually in small pots or for planting in compartmentalized trays. They should be grown on in an unheated greenhouse or frame, or on a sunny windowsill, until they are at the planting-out stage. They are much cheaper than bedding plants.

Sowing

When and where to sow annuals and biennials depends on when they are required to flower and on the temperature they need for germination.

Hardy annuals

When the soil has warmed up to at least 45°F (7°C) in the spring, sow hardy annuals where they are to flower. If sown in successive batches until midsummer, hardy annuals provide a long summer display.

Some hardy annuals, if sown *in situ* in the fall, germinate to produce small plants that overwinter satisfactorily outdoors and flower in late spring or early summer the following year. Candytufts (*Iberis*), pot marigolds (*Calendula*), and poppies (*Papaver*) are some examples.

Seeds of hardy annuals can also be sown in pots or seed trays and either planted out in their final positions in late fall or overwintered in a cold frame to be planted out in spring. This technique is particularly useful in gardens with clay soil that is slow to warm up in spring.

Hardy biennials

Most hardy biennials can be sown outdoors from late spring until midsummer. The optimum time varies according to what is being grown:

Growing perennials as annuals

Many tender and half-hardy perennials can be difficult to overwinter and often do not flower as well in subsequent years.

To be grown as true perennials they need to be overwintered under glass, but it is often easier to propagate the plants from cuttings each year or to grow them afresh from seed. Tender perennials grown in this way often produce a much better display, particularly in cold areas.

Those that are best propagated by tip cuttings include *Acalypha*, *Alternanthera*, marguerites (*Argyranthemum frutescens*), *Iresine*, *Justicia*, *Lantana*, *Pachystachys*, and *Tibouchina*. Take the cuttings in late summer or early fall (see PERENNIALS, "Stem tip cuttings," p.164) and then overwinter them in a frost-free place such as a greenhouse, sun porch, or heated cold frame, or indoors under fluorescent lights. By late spring, after the last frosts, the young plants can be planted out.

Tender perennials usually propagated from seed (see "Sowing," right) include snapdragons (*Antirrhinum*), wax begonias (*Begonia semperflorens*), gazanias, *Gerbera*, flowering tobacco (*Nicotiana*), castor bean (*Ricinus*), petunias, and scarlet sage (*Salvia splendens*).

Some plants can be raised either from cuttings or seed; they include *Browallia*, *Catharanthus roseus* (syn. *Vinca rosea*), *Coleus*, *Felicia*, heliotrope (*Heliotropum*), *Hypoestes*, *Impatiens*, *Nierembergia*, bedding geraniums (*Pelargonium hortorum* cultivars), and *Pentas*.

ANNUALS THAT ARE BEST SOWN IN SITU

Agrostemma
Anchusa capensis
Borago officinalis
Centaurea cyanus, C. moschata
Clarkia
Collinsia bicolor
Consolida ambigua
Cynoglossum amabile
Eschscholzia californica

Eschscholzia californica

Gilia capitata
Gypsophila elegans
Limnanthes douglasii
Linaria maroccana
Linum grandiflorum
Malcolmia maritima
Malope trifida
Mentzelia lindleyi
Papaver rhoeas, P. somniferum
Phacelia campanularia
Scabiosa atropurpurea
Silene coeli-rosa

forget-me-nots (*Myosotis*) grow rapidly so should not be sown until midsummer, while Canterbury bells (*Campanula medium*) need longer to develop and should be sown in late spring or early summer.

The young plants may be transplanted to their final flowering position in fall or, if they are not crowded, the following spring. Premature flowering before winter reduces the spring display, so pinch out any flower buds that form during the first season.

Half-hardy annuals and biennials

In cold regions, sow seed of half-hardy annuals in containers during spring, at a temperature of 55–70°F (13–21°C), according to the particular genus. Half-hardy biennials may be sown in containers under cover in midsummer. In warmer climates, sow half-hardy annuals and biennials directly outside once the soil temperature reaches the optimum for germination.

Tender perennials such as *Impatiens* cultivars and gazanias can be raised from seed in the same way as half-hardy annuals. Other tender perennials, such as marguerites (*Argyranthemum frutescens*) and *Osteospermum*, and annuals that do not produce seeds, such as some double nasturtiums (*Tropaeolum*), can be treated as half-hardy biennials. Propagate by taking cuttings in fall, overwinter them in frost-free conditions, then plant them out in late spring (see PERENNIALS, "Stem tip cuttings," p.164).

Sowing in open ground

There are two main methods of sowing outdoors *in situ*: broadcast and in drills. For both, a seedbed should be prepared first. Dig over the soil to one spade's depth, then rake over the area and firm. Do not sow in soil that is too rich, since this encourages leaf growth at the expense of flower production. In soils lacking nutrients, however, a dressing of 2oz/sq yd (70g/sq m) of a balanced fertilizer should be forked in prior to sowing (see "Soil nutrients and fertilizers," p.532–3).

Prepare a plan showing the position of each cultivar, using any areas likely to be shaded to grow shade-tolerant plants. Before sowing the seed, mark the outline of the area for each cultivar with grit, sand, or a stake so that it is easy to check the balance of colors, heights, and habits of each of the different plants to be used.

BROADCAST SOWING

1 *Prepare the soil by raking to produce a fine tilth. Scatter the seeds thinly over the prepared area by hand or from the packet.*

2 *Rake over the area lightly at right angles to cover the seeds so that they are disturbed as little as possible.*

MARKING OUT ANNUAL BORDERS

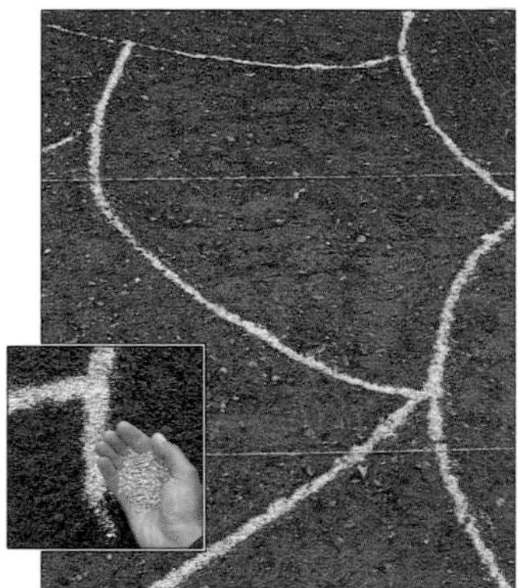

1 *Sprinkle grit or sand on the soil, or score the soil with a stick, to mark out interlocking areas for sowing seeds.*

2 *The seedlings may appear too sparse at first, but they will blend together as they grow.*

Broadcast sowing

This method is particularly suitable for annuals that produce deep taproots, such as *Clarkia*, *Gypsophila*, and poppies (*Papaver*). They are best sown where they are to flower since they do not transplant readily. Sprinkle seeds thinly and evenly on the surface of the prepared seedbed and rake them in lightly. Label, then water the area gently but thoroughly with a fine spray.

Sowing in drills

Seeds sown in drills produce seedlings growing in straight rows at regular intervals, so they are readily distinguished from weed seedlings, which are randomly distributed. The seedlings initially look regimented but, once thinned, will form a dense and informal planting.

Using either a trowel tip or the corner of a hoe, mark out shallow drills 3–6in (8–15cm) apart, depending on

SOWING IN DRILLS

1 *Using a line of string as a guide, make a furrow about 1in (2.5cm) deep with a hoe.*

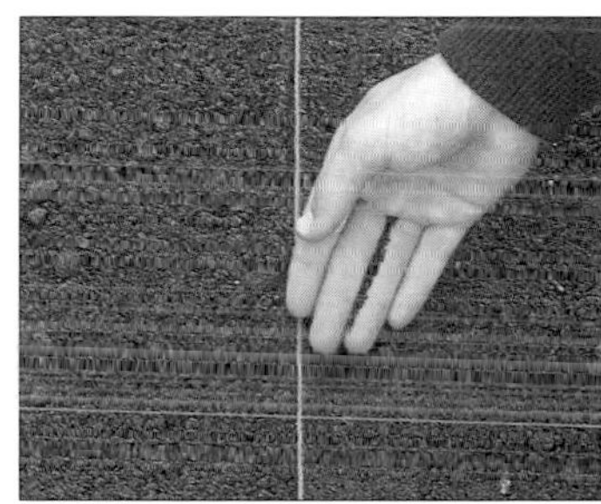

2 *Carefully dribble the seeds from your hand to ensure that they are scattered evenly along the drill.*

ALTERNATIVE STEP

If the seeds are pelleted, place them individually in the base of the drill.

3 *Rake the soil back over the drill without dislodging the seeds. After labeling the row, water the soil using a fine spray.*

Self-seeding Annuals and Biennials

Annuals and biennials that self-seed either true to type or with minor variations

Agrostemma
Angelica archangelica
Antirrhinum majus
Borago officinalis
Calendula officinalis
Centaurea cyanus
Chrysanthemum segetum
Clarkia amoena
Collinsia bicolor
Digitalis purpurea
Eschscholzia californica
Hesperis matronalis
Limnanthes douglasii
Linaria maroccana
Lobularia maritima
Lunaria annua
Malcolmia
Myosotis
Nigella damascena
Oenothera biennis
Omphalodes linifolia
Onopordum acanthium, O. arabicum
Papaver rhoeas, P. somniferum
Platystemon californicus
Silene armeria
Silybum marianum

Tanacetum parthenium

Tanacetum parthenium
Tropaeolum majus
Vaccaria hispanica
Verbascum
Viola (many spp.)

Thinning Seedlings

Individual Seedlings
Press on either side of the seedling to be retained (here larkspur, Consolida ambigua) *while pulling out the unwanted ones around it. Refirm and water.*

Seedling Groups
Gently lift groups of seedlings (here sweet William, Dianthus barbatus) *with plenty of soil around the roots if they are to be replanted. Firm in the remaining seedlings.*

the ultimate size of the plants. Sow seeds thinly and evenly by sprinkling or placing them along each drill at the appropriate depth for the annuals being sown, then carefully draw back the displaced soil with a rake or hoe to cover them. Label each row, and water gently but thoroughly with a fine spray.

Thinning

To prevent overcrowding, the seedlings usually need to be thinned. Do this when the soil is moist and the weather mild, taking care to retain the sturdier seedlings where possible and to achieve even spacing. To minimize disturbance to a seedling being retained, press the soil around it with your fingers as the surplus seedlings are extracted.

If seedlings are very dense, dig them up in clumps, retaining plenty of soil around the roots; do not disturb the other seedlings in the area more than is necessary. Some biennials such as forget-me-nots (*Myosotis*) and honesty (*Lunaria*) germinate readily, and if sown where they are to flower should be thinned appropriately – forget-me-nots to 6in (15cm) and honesty to 12in (30cm), for example.

The thinnings may be used to fill sparse areas caused by uneven sowing or irregular germination, or they may be transplanted for use elsewhere. Select the strongest and healthiest of the thinned seedlings for transplanting, then replant them where needed at the appropriate spacings and water them lightly to settle their roots.

Many annuals and biennials scatter their seeds freely, often producing dense clumps of seedlings. These need to be thinned to the appropriate distances to enable the young plants to develop without competition.

Sowing in pots or trays

Half-hardy annuals are usually sown in containers so that they can develop under cover and then be planted out as young plants when conditions are favorable. Hardy annuals may also be sown in containers left outside. Transplant the seedlings to their flowering positions when there is sufficient room.

Pots, seed pans, seed trays, and packs are all suitable containers, depending on the number of seeds to be sown and the space they require. Peat pots are also useful for seedlings that do not transplant well since the whole pot may be planted out without disturbing the roots.

Sowing the seeds

Fill the chosen container to its rim with standard seed soil mix and press in lightly around the edges with the fingertips to make sure that there are no air pockets. To settle the soil mix, tap the container against a hard surface, then gently firm it so that the top of the soil mix is slightly below the rim of the container. Water with a fine spray and leave for an hour or so to drain.

Sow the seeds thinly on the surface of the soil mix, tapping them from the seed packet or from a fold of paper to achieve an even spread. Large or pelleted seeds can be sown individually in compartmentalized packs or spaced out in trays or pans. Very small seeds are easier to sow if they are mixed first with a small amount of fine sand; this produces a more even distribution.

Cover the seeds to about their own depth with sieved soil mix, then water lightly, to avoid disturbing the seeds or the surface of the soil mix. Dustlike seeds, such as those of begonia, should be left uncovered and watered from below: place each container up to its rim in water until the surface of the soil mix is moist. Do not leave them soaking for too long since waterlogging may cause the seeds to rot before germination or encourage seedling diseases (see "Damping off," p.566).

To maintain even humidity, place a piece of glass or clear plastic sheeting over the container; do not let it touch the soil mix surface

Supporting and protecting seedlings

Support is required for slender-stemmed or tall annuals. Carefully insert peasticks or thin twigs into the soil around young plants; the supports should be slightly shorter than the ultimate height of the plants so that they will be concealed when the plants reach their mature size. These supports will also help protect the seedlings from possible rodent and bird damage.

Alternatively, stretch wire netting, with a mesh no greater than 1in (2.5cm), over the seedbed, bending it down at the edges so it does not touch the seedlings. Secure it firmly in the soil, using a stick or wire pin. The plants grow up through the mesh and cover the netting when fully grown.

Supporting with Twigs
Peasticks or thin twigs may be pushed into the soil among the seedlings. Tall annuals (here larkspur, Consolida ambigua) *grow to hide the support.*

Wire Protection and Support
Protect seedlings (here Eschscholzia) *with mesh wire netting bent to form a cage. The netting will support the seedlings as they grow through it.*

SOWING IN A TRAY

1 Fill the seed tray with a standard seed soil mix, then level with a presser board to 1/2in (1cm) below the rim.

2 Sprinkle the seeds thinly over the surface of the soil mix to achieve an even distribution.

3 Cover the seeds with a layer of sieved, moist soil mix to about the same thickness as the seeds themselves. Water the seeds in lightly.

4 Place a piece of glass or clear plastic sheeting over the tray to maintain even humidity.

5 Shade the tray with netting if the tray is in direct sunlight. Remove both glass and netting as soon as germination starts.

SOWING IN DEGRADABLE POTS

Fill a 2in (5cm) degradable pot with seed soil mix to within 1/2in (1cm) of the rim. Sow three seeds on the surface; cover them thinly with soil mix and water them. These may be thinned to two once they have germinated. The whole pot is planted out when the young plants are well developed.

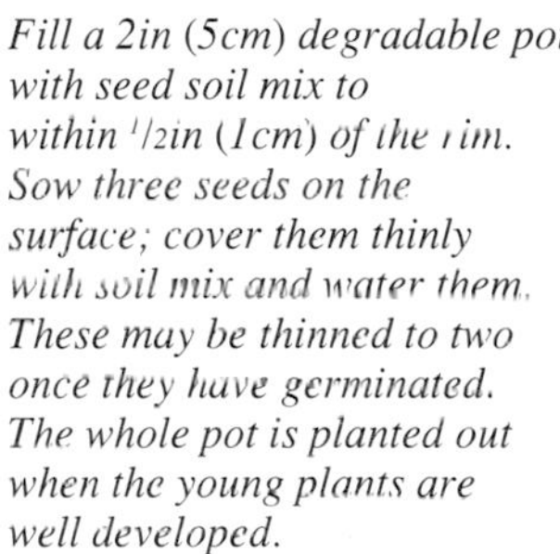

because this may disturb the seeds. Place the container on a windowsill or a greenhouse bench, and shade it with fine netting or newspaper if it receives direct sunlight. As soon as the first seedlings germinate, the cover should be removed. Grow them in good light and keep the soil mix moist until they are sufficiently large to prick out.

Pricking out

Seedlings raised in trays or pans need to be transplanted into larger containers before they become overcrowded, because they may quickly become weak and spindly if deprived of sufficient space or light. This process is known as pricking out or pricking off. It enables the seedlings to continue to develop properly until they are ready for planting out in the garden.

Fill the new containers with a soil-based mix and firm gently to eliminate any air pockets. Small pots, no more than 3in (6cm) in diameter, or compartmentalized plastic packs are ideal for individual seedlings; larger pots, pans, or trays can be used for several plants.

To prick out, first knock the container of seedlings against a tabletop or bench to loosen the soil mix slightly and remove it intact from the container. Then hold each plant gently by the small seed leaves to avoid bruising the foliage, stems, or growing tips, and loosen it with a widger or other small implement. Take care not to damage the roots. Carefully lift each plant from the soil, retaining some of the moist soil mix around the roots to ensure that there will be little check to growth when the seedlings are replanted.

Use a dibber to make holes in the soil mix 1 1/2–2in (4–5cm) apart, and insert a seedling into each hole. Make sure that all the roots are covered with soil mix, then gently firm in each seedling using fingers or a dibber, and level the soil mix. As

Seeds with special requirements

A few seeds need special conditions in order to germinate successfully. Begonia, *Impatiens*, and *Coleus* seeds require light and prefer a constant temperature of 70°F (21°C). Primroses prefer light, but need temperatures of no more than 68°F (20°C). *Phacelia*, pansies (*Viola* x *wittrockiana*), and other *Viola* should be germinated in the dark. Seeds of *Thunbergia alata* and pelargoniums require 70–75°F (21–4°C) to germinate. Scarify (break down by scratching) pelargonium seed before sowing (see "Scarifying and soaking," p.160); prescarified seeds are now available. Seeds of bells-of Ireland (*Moluccella laevis*) are difficult to germinate unless they have been stratified: set the seed pan in a refrigerator for a couple of weeks before bringing it into a temperature of 65–70°F (18–21°C) for a further two or three weeks.

PRICKING OUT INTO A PACK

1 When the seedlings (here marigolds) are large enough to handle, tap the tray on a hard surface to loosen the soil mix.

2 Carefully separate the seedlings, handling them by their seed leaves. Keep plenty of soil mix around the roots.

3 Transplant each seedling into a separate section of a pack. Firm the soil around each one with fingers or a dibber, and water.

Annuals in pots

Many annuals make excellent pot plants. Prick out young seedlings into divided trays or individual pots and, when the roots have just filled the container, transfer each seedling to a larger pot prepared with soil-based potting mix. The pot size will vary according to the species or cultivar and time of sowing. Shift plants sown in late summer into 3½in (9cm) pots over the winter when growth is slow, and transfer them later to their final pots – either 5in (13cm) or 7in (19cm), or much larger pots for groups of three or five plants per container. Transplant spring-sown annuals directly into their final pots or containers.

Many annuals (here Schizanthus) *are very useful for providing an early, colorful display in a cool greenhouse in spring.*

each container is filled, water with a fine spray to settle the soil mix. Increase the humidity around the seedlings by covering the containers with clear plastic for a few days while the seedlings reestablish themselves. Make sure that the plastic does not touch the leaves, because this may encourage rot. Return the seedlings to their previous growing conditions to develop further.

If seedlings are ready for planting out, but this is delayed because of a late frost, pot them on into a larger container. This ensures that growth is not checked, so the long-term success of the plants is not jeopardized.

Seeds that have been sown singly in packs or space-sown will not need pricking out but must be hardened off before planting out.

Hardening off

All half-hardy annuals that have been raised either under glass or in any other controlled environment need to be acclimatized gradually to the outdoor conditions before being planted out. The aim of this is to harden the plants, reducing their dependence on artificial heat and protection without exposing them to sudden environmental changes that might cause damage.

When raising bedding plants in an unheated greenhouse, it may be sufficient to leave the ventilation open for progressively longer periods until, just before planting out, the vents are permanently open. If a cold frame is available, move the plants out into it in sequence, starting with the most frost-resistant, such as snapdragons and gazanias, to give more growing space. In the North, provide heating cables to warm the frame and in most of the country, lay old blankets over the cold frames at night if necessary to supply additional insulation. Acclimatize the plants in the frame by leaving the sashes open for increasingly longer periods once the danger of hard frost has passed.

When cold weather is forecast, the frames or greenhouse must be shut earlier than on a night when the minimum expected temperature is not close to freezing.

If a cold frame is not available, a few trays can be started on a sunny windowsill and moved outdoors when the weather permits. Take the trays outside during warm days for increasing lengths of time, and move them back indoors at night before the temperature drops to or below freezing. When nighttime temperatures are expected to be only a degree or so above freezing, move the plants against the house wall and cover them with an old blanket. Eventually they may be left out overnight unprotected, against a house wall at first, but finally out in the open. They are then ready to plant out.

Plants purchased from a garden center are likely not to be hardened off. Buy them early, while the selection is good, but harden them off as above before planting them out.

Planting out

Plant out half-hardy seedlings once all danger of frost has passed. This is particularly important in the case of more tender plants such as begonias and *Salvia splendens*. Provided that they have been hardened off, some half-hardy annuals will tolerate cool, but not frosty, conditions for short periods.

Before you plant out seedlings, first prepare the bed (see "Sowing in open ground," p.177), water the young plants thoroughly, and then allow them to drain for an hour or so. To remove a plant from its pot, invert it, supporting the stem with a finger on either side. Then tap the rim against a hard surface to loosen the root ball from the pot. Break apart cell packs or divided trays to remove each seedling individually with its root ball undisturbed.

If plants are in trays without divisions, hold the tray firmly with both hands, and tap one side sharply on the ground to loosen the soil mix. Gently slide out the contents in one piece. Separate plants carefully with your fingers, keeping as much soil as possible around the roots. Alternatively, remove each plant gently using a widger or other small tool.

Make a hole sufficiently large to accommodate the root ball readily. Space the plants so that the leaves will just touch when the plants are fully developed. Normal planting

HARDENING OFF

POLYTUNNEL
Place half-hardy annuals (here Tagetes) *in a polytunnel. Lift the sides for ventilation, as required.*

COLD FRAME
Seedlings may also be placed in a cold frame left open for progressively longer intervals.

FIRST-YEAR GROWTH

Biennials such as Canterbury bells make only vegetative (leafy) growth in their first year. Flowers develop the following summer.

PLANTING OUT INTO OPEN GROUND

1 *Break the pack apart and carefully remove each seedling (here* Tagetes) *with its root ball intact.*

2 *Place each plant in a hole large enough to take its root ball, ensuring that the plant is slightly lower in the soil than it was in its container.*

3 *Gently firm the soil in the well around the plant so that there are no air pockets. Water the area.*

HOW TO BUY ANNUALS

BEDDING PLANTS

GOOD EXAMPLE
Compact, vigorous growth
POOR EXAMPLE
Healthy, green foliage
PETUNIAS
Leggy, bare stems
SALVIAS
Dead leaves

POTGROWN ANNUALS

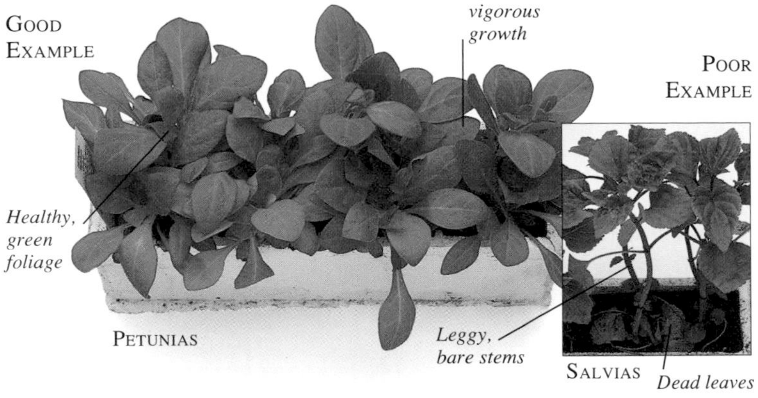

GOOD EXAMPLE
POOR EXAMPLE
Bushy, sturdy growth
Healthy buds developing
Moist soil mix
IMPATIENS CULTIVAR
Yellowing, discolored leaves

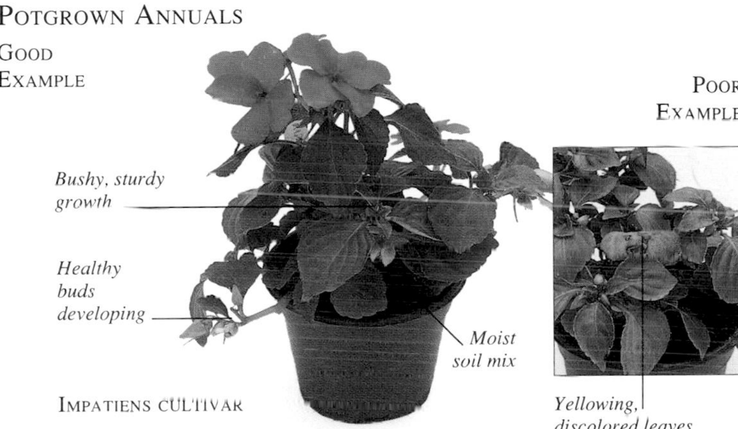

distances range from 6 to 18in (15 to 45cm), depending on the habit of the species or cultivar being grown.

Check that the plants are at the same depth as in the container, then firm the soil around the base of the stem, without compacting the soil too much. After planting, gently break up the soil surface between the plants with a hand fork. To settle them in, water the plants thoroughly using a high-phosphorus soluble fertilizer (such as 10-52-10) to stimulate root production.

Pinching out

As young annuals develop, some, such as snapdragons (*Antirrhinum*), may need to be pinched out to encourage the plants to produce side shoots and to develop a bushy habit. Do not pinch out plants such as *Celosia* or stocks (*Matthiola*) that have strong terminal shoots, because these develop the main flower spikes and also produce lateral growths during the summer.

Pinching is done by nipping the growing tip off a young plant. This may be necessary even with annuals that branch naturally, especially when a few plants in a bed produce stronger shoots than others. If a uniform growth habit is required, pinch tall plants at five or six joints by removing the tip of each long shoot back to the required height.

Pinching delays flower production, so it should not be carried out if an early display is preferred.

Bedding plants

Buying more mature annuals and biennials to plant out directly into containers, beds, or borders can save time and may be necessary if no space is available to grow half-hardy annuals from seed. However, most growers routinely offer only varieties that have been proven to grow well in their area. When planning to grow something unusual, you may need to start the plants yourself.

Judging the quality of bedding plants

Sturdy young plants with evenly balanced, short-noded shoots and healthy foliage are most likely to establish themselves well and give the best results. The plants should have well-developed root systems but must not be potbound. Do not buy plants with yellowing or discolored foliage or those in dry soil mix since, although they usually grow on, they often do not develop well, and produce fewer flowers.

Planting in containers

For an immediate display in ornamental containers, use annuals or biennials that are potgrown. They will flower throughout the season without outgrowing the container. Plan the positions of the plants carefully, arranging trailing types at the sides or front of the container and taller plants toward the back or center.

Place crocks in the base of the container to cover the drainage holes and fill loosely with a soil-based potting mix. Water the plants well before planting. Remove each from its pot, tease out the roots gently, then place it in position in the container. Firm the soil mix around each plant, then water thoroughly.

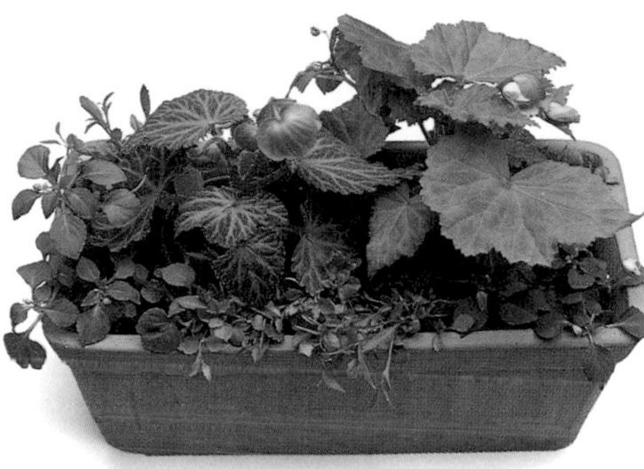

1 *Water the chosen plants thoroughly and decide how they are to be arranged before beginning to plant up the container. Begonias,* Lobelia, *and* Impatiens *cultivars are used in this arrangement.*

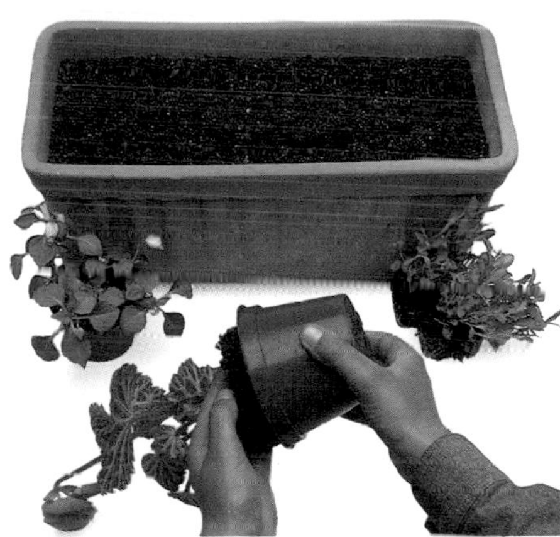

2 *Fill the trough half or three-quarters full with moist soil mix. Invert each pot and support the plant as the root ball slides out. Gently tease out the plant roots.*

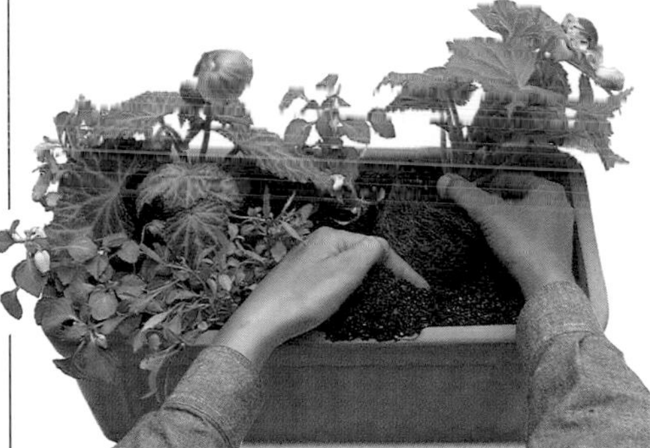

3 *Scoop back the soil mix and place the plant in position so that the neck of the plant will be 1/2in (1cm) below the rim of the windowbox.*

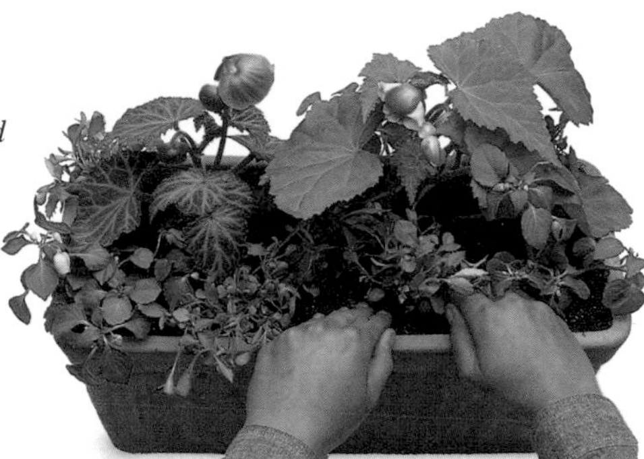

4 *Plant up the remaining plants, then firm gently around them, especially at the sides and corners, so that there are no air pockets remaining. Add more moist soil mix if necessary, and level the surface before watering thoroughly.*

Half-hardy bedding plants are sold at various stages from seedling to flowering plant, often well ahead of when it is safe to plant them outdoors. Make sure that you have appropriate conditions under cover to grow them on properly if necessary. Check also that they have been hardened off if they are for immediate planting outside. Acclimatize seedlings slowly until all danger of frost is past; sudden exposure to frost or cold wind may kill plants produced in heated greenhouses. They may then be planted outdoors.

Planting and supporting annual climbers

Plant climbing annuals where they can climb naturally through a shrub or small tree or be trained against a wall or other support. If a twining annual is to be grown through a shrub, position the plant at the perimeter of the shrub, on the side where it will receive the most sunlight, with a stake leading the shoots into the host plant if necessary.

If the climber will be grown up a wall or fence, provide a support to suit its habit of growth (see CLIMBING PLANTS, "Types of support," p.98). Plant it 12in (30cm) from the base of the wall or fence to enable the roots to obtain sufficient moisture.

Twining climbers may also be grown up a wigwam of several stakes tied securely near the top. Push the stakes well into the soil first and plant just outside the wigwam, then tie in the young seedlings to the stakes.

PLANTING OUT CLIMBING ANNUALS

PLANTING BESIDE A HOST
Twining annuals such as morning glories (Ipomoea) *should be planted about 9in (22cm) from the host's stem.*

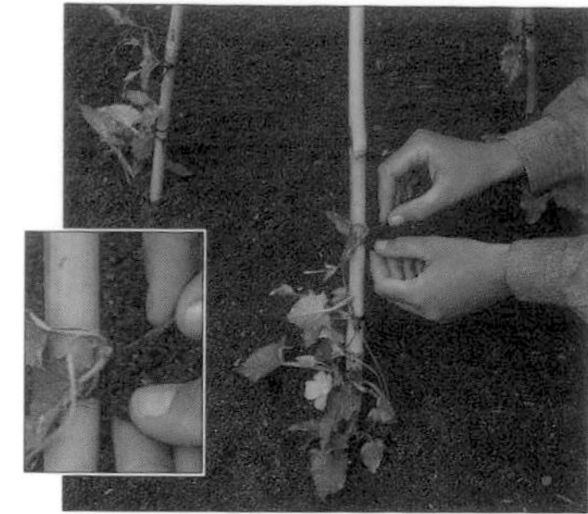

SUPPORTING WITH STAKES
A tripod provides support for twining annuals (here Thunbergia alata). *Tie a seedling loosely to each of the stakes.*

Planting annuals to a design

Before starting to plant up a bed or border, assemble all the bedding plants to be used and check them off against the plan. Place the plants, still in their containers, roughly in position on the prepared soil to make sure that the bed will be neither too crowded nor too sparsely planted. Now is the time to make any final adjustments to plant positioning – it will be too late once they are in the ground. Keep a few plants in reserve to replace any that may die.

1 *Mark out the design of the whole bed before starting to plant. Work from the center outward, or from the back of the bed to the front. Use a board or kneeler for kneeling on so that the soil does not become compacted, making it difficult to work and inhibiting drainage.*

2 *Plant the seedlings carefully, handling the plants as little as possible. Firm the soil around each. Complete one section of planting before moving on to the next.*

3 *As each section of planting is completed, trim off any damaged, uneven, or straggly shoots to make the patches of plants more compact.*

4 *Water thoroughly section by section so that the seedlings planted first do not dry out while the others are being planted.*

5 *Keep the bed well watered while the seedlings are becoming established. Remove any discolored or damaged foliage that might spoil the display. Should any plants die, replace them to fill the gaps.*

Routine care

ANNUALS generally require little maintenance since they have a relatively short life. They do need to be watered regularly during drought, however, especially if they are grown in containers, and should be deadheaded to prolong flowering. Tall annuals may require staking during or soon after planting to prevent them from blowing over or toppling under their own weight. When the foliage starts to die down after flowering or at the end of the season, the plants should be cleared away.

SUPPORTING CLIMBING ANNUALS

When planting climbers (here Eccremocarpus scaber) *near a wall or fence, support them on wire or a trellis. Tie the stems to the support while still supple.*

SUPPORTING TALL ANNUALS

Support tall annuals such as Salpiglossis *by pushing stakes into the soil around the pot and twining string around the stakes. As the plants develop they hide the stakes.*

Watering, feeding, and weeding

Young annuals and biennials that are planted in open ground should be watered regularly with a sprinkler or hose, soaking the bed thoroughly. Once the plants have become established, water only during prolonged dry weather.

Annuals rarely need extra feeding if the soil has been well prepared. A liquid fertilizer may be applied on very poor soils as flower buds develop. Biennials may benefit from a little fertilizer, but only those grown for show purposes need regular feeding. Overly rich conditions produce vigorous vegetative growth at the expense of flowers.

Keep annuals and biennials free from weeds since these compete for light, water, and soil nutrients. Pull out any weeds by hand while they are still small, and remove self-sown seedlings in the same way if they are not required or are too numerous.

Providing supports

Many annuals and biennials have rather slender stems, which benefit from some support. Use small, bushy branches (peasticks) for plants with a mature height of up to 3ft (1m). When the plants are an inch or so high, insert the sticks in the soil around them so that they can grow up through the sticks, which will quickly be covered and hidden.

Tall annuals in containers may be supported by inserting a few stakes around the edge of the pot and tying soft string around the stakes – the supports are hidden by the plants as they develop. Very tall plants, such as hollyhocks (*Alcea*) or sunflowers (*Helianthus*), may need to be individually staked. Push the stake into the soil where it will be least visible and, as the plant develops, tie in the stem at intervals as required.

Some scrambling annuals that do not twine or have tendrils will need to be tied in to their support. Attach the leading shoots with soft string and continue to tie occasionally as needed to maintain the shape of the plant. Twining annuals and those that have tendrils may need occasional guidance.

Annuals as dried or cut flowers

Dried or fresh flowers of many annuals and biennials are decorative indoors. Harvest everlasting flowers such as *Xeranthemum*, *Helipterum*, and *Limonium* when they are about half open, then hang them upside down in a warm, well-ventilated area. Cut *Helichrysum* flowerheads before they show color to help keep their shape when dried. Cut fresh flowers as the buds show color. Dip the ends of Iceland poppies (*Papaver nudicaule*) into boiling water to seal them and avoid air locks that prevent water uptake.

1 *Cut flowers for drying (here statice,* Limonium sinuatum) *as the heads start to open. Use a slightly angled cut as near as possible to the base of the stem.*

2 *Many everlasting flowers may be dried upside down in bunches fastened with soft string or raffia. Once they have dried, any excess stem may be cut off to suit the flower arrangement.*

Maintaining annuals in containers

Plants in windowboxes, hanging baskets, or other containers need little maintenance apart from liberal watering and regular deadheading to maintain the display. Check daily during both wet and dry weather to make sure that the soil mix remains moist, and feed with half-strength 20-20-20 soluble fertilizer every two weeks.

When a plant has finished flowering, remove it from its container, disturbing the other plants as little as possible, and replace it with a later-maturing plant. Hardy biennials can be overwintered outside. But if the plants are likely to be damaged by frost, place the container under cover.

1 *Continue to deadhead flowers in order to keep the display attractive. When plants have finished flowering remove them, taking care not to damage the roots of remaining plants.*

2 *Add fresh, moist soil mix and fill the gaps with new plants to continue the display. Firm gently and water thoroughly to help the plants establish themselves quickly.*

Deadheading

To prolong the flowering period, remove flowerheads as they fade, cutting near the base of the stalk. The plants (here violas) will produce new blooms for some time.

Deadheading

In many cases, the flowering season of plants may be extended and their appearance improved by promptly removing any flowerheads that are fading or dead. This prevents a plant from setting seed, and its energy is used to produce additional flowers. Snap off any faded flowers between the fingers and thumb, breaking the stems cleanly. Use a pair of sharp scissors or pruners for tougher stems or where there is a danger of disturbing the plant as the dead flowerheads are removed.

Do not deadhead if the seeds or fruits form part of the ornamental characteristic of the annual or biennial, as they do with honesty (*Lunaria*), *Hibiscus trionum*, and ornamental corn (*Zea mays*), for example. Nor should plants be completely deadheaded if their seeds are required for growing the plant during the following season.

A few annuals and biennials, such as poppies (*Papaver*), do not produce more flowers after deadheading.

Saving seeds

Seeds can easily be collected from many annuals for sowing the following year. However, the seeds saved from most garden-grown cultivars will not produce plants that possess flowers or habit characteristics similar to those of their parents. It is often worth saving seeds only from those annuals and biennials that stay true to type, such as *Nigella* or honesty (*Lunaria*).

Deadhead those plants that have poor flowers so that no seeds are formed and later collected for sowing the following season. Such seeds are unlikely to produce plants with good-quality flowers.

Self-sown seedlings are likely to vary to some extent in character and quality but may nevertheless produce quite acceptable plants. Distinct cultivars of *Eschscholzia*, Excelsior Series foxgloves (*Digitalis*), sweet alyssum (*Lobularia maritima*), pot marigolds (*Calendula*), forget-me-nots (*Myosotis*), and many other annuals and biennials usually vary in flower color and other characteristics from the original plant.

When seed capsules turn brown and begin to split, cut them off and spread them on paper-lined trays in a warm, sunny place until they are fully dry. Extract the seeds and clean away any debris. Packet, label, and store them in dry, cool conditions until they are required for sowing.

Clearing the bed

In fall, once the flower display is over, lift and compost all dead and dying plants after any seeds required have been gathered. Discard any diseased plants that might spread infection. Perennials grown as annuals or biennials, such as pansies (*Viola* x *wittrockiana*) and primroses, can be lifted and replanted elsewhere, where they may grow and flower satisfactorily for several years. Others, for example wallflowers (*Cheiranthus*), where winter hardy, and snapdragons (*Antirrhinum*), seldom grow as well after their first year, so they are usually not worth retaining.

Tender perennials such as begonias and *Impatiens* cultivars can be lifted and potted up in late summer to continue flowering in the house, conservatory, or greenhouse. Short-lived perennials, such as hollyhocks (*Alcea*), should be cut down in fall and retained since they sometimes survive for several seasons, although the quality and vigor of the plants will deteriorate. It is not worth keeping plants of the new F1 strains of pelargonium since they are quite easy to raise from seed, and you eliminate the risk of overwintering diseases. Where hardy, *Eccremocarpus scaber* will survive for years in protected positions outside.

Fall Cleanup

When annuals have finished flowering, carefully loosen the soil around their roots with a fork and then rake up and compost or discard the old plants.

Pests and diseases

The pests most likely to affect annuals and biennials, both when they are seedlings and when they are more mature, are slugs and snails (p.550), cutworms (p.561), fungus gnats (p.572), caterpillars (p.551), and aphids (p.552); plants may also be attacked by gray mold/*Botrytis* (p.552) and other fungal problems (see "Fungal leaf spots," p.554). Fungicides may prevent or check these diseases, but often little can be done beyond pulling out and discarding badly infected plants. Any young seedlings under cover may suffer from damping off (p.570), a group of soilborne diseases, which cause the plants to rot and collapse.

Saving Seeds

1 *Seeds may be collected when the capsules or seedheads (here* Nigella*) have been dried on blotting paper or newspaper and release their seeds.*

2 *Once the seedhead has dried, shake the seeds out and separate them from any other debris. Store them in a labeled envelope in a dry place at a cool temperature.*

Cutting Down Short-lived Perennials

1 *Not all seedheads ripen at the same time. To prevent self-seeding, remove flowered stems before any seedheads ripen fully.*

2 *Short-lived perennials such as hollyhocks may flower for several seasons if cut down immediately after flowering.*

3 *Carefully cut each stem at its base, ensuring that the new growth that has been produced during the growing season is not damaged in the process.*

8

The Rock Garden

Some of the *loveliest garden plants come from mountain ranges around the world, where they have evolved and adapted to survive in a surprising diversity of specialized habitats. These range from rock face niches to aprons of loose scree, and from the short, sparse turf of alpine pasture to the richer meadow grasses of lower altitudes. With alpines and rock garden plants, you can furnish a garden with a wealth of beautiful species that retain the charm of wildflowers unembellished by the hybridizer's art. They often display disproportionately large or prolific flowers in an unequaled range of clear, jewel-like colors. Because some alpine and rock plants are adapted to specific environments, which may be difficult to reproduce in a garden, they present a challenge to even the most experienced gardeners. Happily, many more are amenable and undemanding plants that will grow readily in a suitably prepared site in the open garden. They will richly reward a little extra time and attention paid to their requirements.*

Designing a rock garden

Alpines are plants that grow at high altitudes, above the tree line, although the term is often loosely used to include a vast range of low-growing rock garden plants, including many bulbs, that may be grown at relatively low altitudes. Their diminutive form and graceful habit make them well suited for grouping together in fascinating, brilliantly colored collections.

True alpines

Alpines may be deciduous or evergreen woody plants, or they may be herbaceous, or grow from bulbs, corms, or tubers – there are very few annual alpines. They are characteristically hardy, adapted to survive in extremes of climate, and compact, with few over 6in (15cm) tall. In their native mountain habitat, the dwarf or creeping habit of alpines reduces their wind resistance and helps them to withstand the heavy weight of snow in winter.

In alpine regions, plants experience brilliant sunshine and fresh, constantly moving air during the growing season. Their cushion- or mat-forming habit and their small, fleshy, hairy, or leathery leaves protect them from water loss in high winds and hot sun. Edelweiss (*Leontopodium alpinum*), for example, has its entire surface covered in woolly hairs that help to conserve moisture, while the leaves of houseleeks (*Sempervivum*) have fleshy, water-retaining tissue.

Although most alpines are adapted to extremes of temperature, few withstand constant wetness at the roots in winter or warm, humid, summer conditions. In their native habitats, they often grow in thin, poor soil that lacks nutrients and has a low organic content but which allows rapid drainage. Most develop extensive, spreading root systems to seek out nutrients and moisture.

A Well-furnished Rock Garden
This gently sloping rock garden is studded with a diverse range of alpine plants, including herbaceous plants, shrubs, and conifers. Seen here in late spring, it will continue to provide color and interest well into fall.

Rock garden plants

Rock plants are simply those slow-growing plants of relatively small stature that are suitable in scale for growing in rock gardens. They include dwarf trees and shrubs, which are particularly useful for framework, or background, plantings, and many other plants that do not necessarily come from alpine regions. Some, such as *Armeria maritima*, originate in coastal habitats, while many miniature bulbs are native to sunny, Mediterranean hillsides. In common with true alpines, they share the need for a free-draining soil and are therefore suitable for planting among alpines.

Since many true alpines bloom in the spring and early summer, rock garden plants are especially valuable if they are late blooming, since they may be used to extend the season of interest.

Alpines and rock plants in the garden

The usually restricted size of alpines and rock garden plants fits particularly well into the confines of the small, modern garden. Few other types of plant are so characteristically neat and compact, allowing a substantial collection of species and hybrids to be grown in a relatively small space.

Garden-tolerant plants

Many alpine species, and their more showy cultivars, are undemanding in their cultural requirements and may be grown easily in the open garden. They present a wealth of habit and form, ranging from tiny, cushion-forming plants to spreading mound- and mat-formers. Some of the easier alpines bloom well into summer and almost invariably produce a profusion of flowers. The low-growing cultivars of *Aubrieta*, phlox, and *Veronica* form dense mats of clear, bright color when in bloom, and can be used to edge beds; their informal, spreading habit gently softens straight lines.

Specialist alpines

Other alpine genera, such as some *Androsace* and the tight cushion-forming saxifrages, have special requirements, in particular a need for extremely free-draining soil and protection from excessive winter moisture. Most also require plenty of sun, but their roots need to be cool. Lower-altitude, woodland species often prefer dappled shade and may need moist, acid soil.

The rich and varied colors and diverse forms of many specialist plants may still be enjoyed in the garden, however, as long as well-drained conditions and a suitable exposure are provided. The best way to fulfill these requirements is to raise the plants in some way from the underlying garden soil. Plant them in specially constructed or carefully controlled environments and use prepared, gritty, free-draining soil or soil mixes.

Some alpine plants need a cool root run and shelter. Rock gardens and pockets within stone or brick walls are an ideal way to grow such plants and to display them to their best advantage in natural-looking surroundings. In more formal garden settings or where space is limited, raised beds or troughs and sinks are attractive alternatives, especially when they are constructed from materials that complement any existing hard landscape features. Free-standing troughs and sinks also allow color to be introduced at a variety of heights and on hard surfaces such as patios and paths.

PLANTING IN THE OPEN GARDEN
Daphne x burkwoodii 'Somerset' *has a profusion of pale pink flowers that spill over the edge of a mixed border and drift into the plants on either side.*

The rock garden

A sunny south- or southwest-facing slope makes an ideal site for the stony outcrops of a rock garden. Well-constructed rock gardens emulate natural rock formations and make strikingly beautiful features. They replicate, as nearly as possible, the natural habitat of alpine plants, re-creating the conditions in which they thrive – the soil beneath the rocks provides the cool, moist, but freely draining root run that they particularly enjoy.

Planning a rock garden

For the greatest visual impact, a rock garden should be constructed on as generous a scale as the site allows. Where possible, choose a naturally sloping, open site that will provide good drainage. A series of rocky outcrops with gullies running in between is highly attractive, especially if streams and pools are also included in the design.

A sunny exposure will suit most rock plants, although those that require shade may be grown in cooler, shady pockets on the north side of large rocks. Thoughtful placing of the rocks during construction (see p.195) will provide a wide range of planting areas and niches to meet the needs of many alpine plants.

Choosing plants

Several alpine species, such as *Gentiana verna* with its flowers of intense blue in spring, do best in deep pockets of well-drained, gritty soil, while the mat-forming *Polygonum affine* 'Donald Lowndes', for example, thrives in broader terraces between rock strata. Both *Lewisia* Cotyledon Hybrids and *Saxifraga* 'Tumbling Waters', which has cascades of white flowers over rosettes of lime-encrusted foliage, are most at home in the narrow crevices between vertical stone faces.

Plan the planting design to include as much seasonal variation as possible. Alpine bulbs such as *Crocus laevigatus* 'Fontenayi' and *Iris histrioides* 'Major' help to bring

A BLAZE OF SUMMER COLOR
The brilliant red flowers of Sedum spurium *and* Helianthemum *cascading down the rocky outcrop make a pleasing contrast with the gray-green stems and leaves of the* Dianthus *and* Hebe pinguifolia 'Pagei' *just behind them. The fresh green foliage of the surrounding plants provides a bright but cool counterpoint.*

A TIERED ROCK GARDEN

In late spring, a collection of alpines and rock plants provides abundant color and variety of form. Some evergreen dwarf shrubs and early flowering bulbs interplanted among the rocks will extend the season of interest.

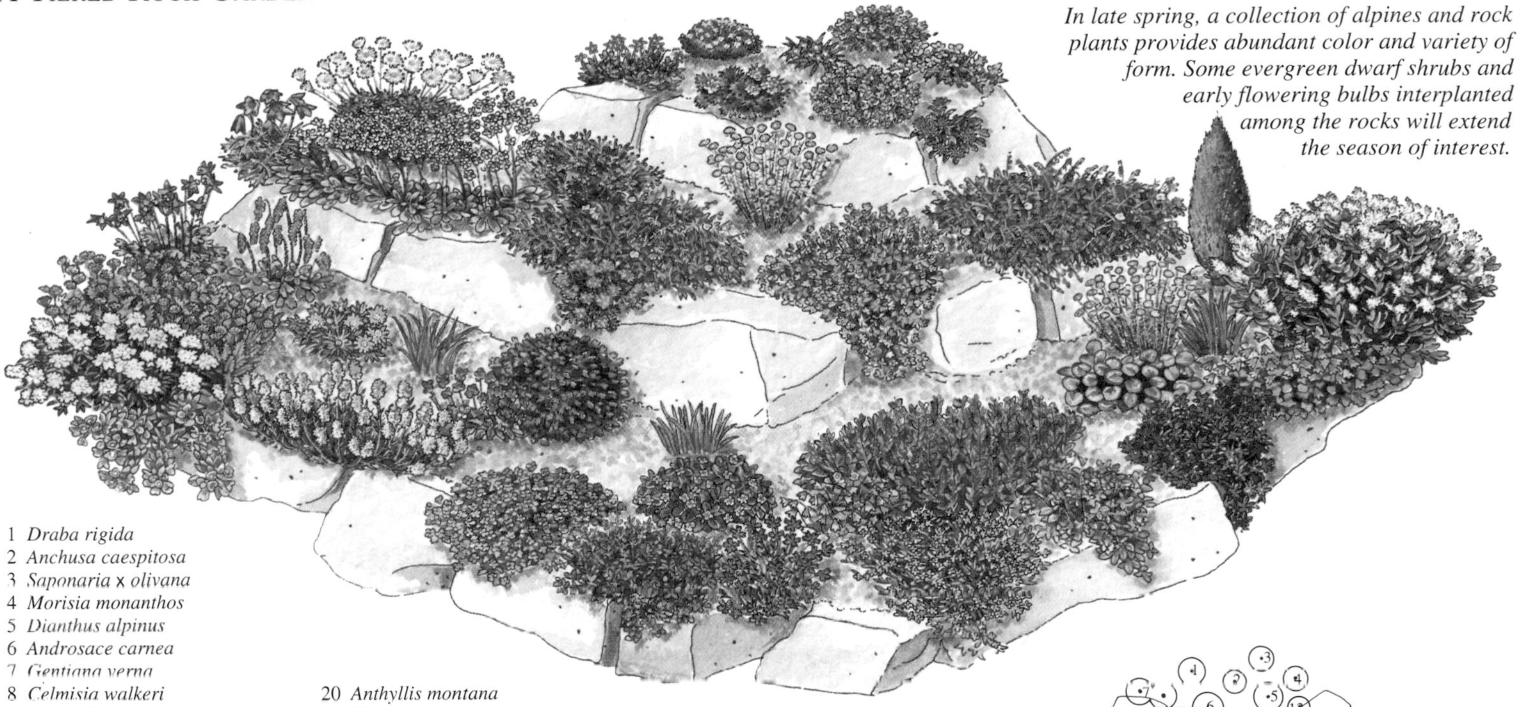

1 *Draba rigida*
2 *Anchusa caespitosa*
3 *Saponaria* x *olivana*
4 *Morisia monanthos*
5 *Dianthus alpinus*
6 *Androsace carnea*
7 *Gentiana verna*
8 *Celmisia walkeri*
9 *Pulsatilla vulgaris*
10 *Saxifraga* 'Southside Seedling'
11 *Berberis* x *stenophylla* 'Corallina Compacta'
12 *Linum perenne*
13 *Physoplexis comosa*
14 *Helianthemum* 'Wisley Primrose'
15 *Parahebe catarractae*
16 *Helianthemum* 'Wisley Pink'
17 *Armeria juniperifolia*
18 *Chiastophyllum oppositifolium*
19 *Aquilegia alpina*
20 *Anthyllis montana*
21 *Crocus* 'Cream Beauty'
22 *Euryops acraeus*
23 *Iris* 'Joyce'
24 *Viola* 'Haslemere'
25 *Picea mariana* 'Nana'
26 *Narcissus minor*
27 *Diascia rigescens*
28 *Cyclamen coum* subsp. *coum* and *coum* 'Album'
29 *Galanthus nivalis* 'Scharlockii'
30 *Narcissus* 'Tête-à-tête'
31 *Juniperus communis* 'Compressa'
32 *Hebe canterburiensis*
33 *Campanula cochleariifolia*
34 *Phlox douglasii* 'Crackerjack'
35 *Origanum* 'Kent Beauty'
36 *Daphne cneorum*
37 *Phlox* 'Camla'
38 *Androsace lanuginosa*
39 *Gypsophila cerastioides*
40 *Crocus dalmaticus*
41 *Aubrieta* 'Joy'
42 *Aethionema grandiflorum*
43 *Euphorbia myrsinites*
44 *Iberis sempervirens*

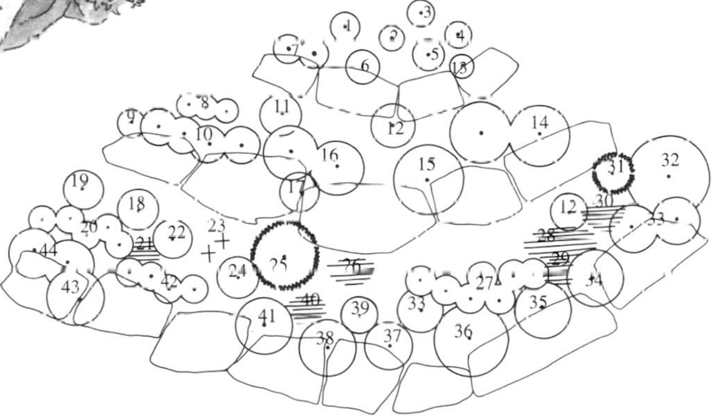

the garden to life in late winter or early spring, and *Cyclamen hederifolium* and *Sternbergia lutea* add interest in fall. For year-round color, include evergreens, such as the dwarf *Chamaecyparis obtusa* 'Nana Pyramidalis' and *Juniperus communis* 'Compressa', and dwarf shrubs such as *Genista lydia*.

Add texture and structure to the planting by using species with unusual leaves or stems and variation in height and form. Contrasting leaf textures can be particularly striking: bold, fleshy, rosette-forming plants may be used to offset the delicate, feathery leaves and flowers of *Pulsatilla* species, for instance. A combination of spreading, cushion-forming, and trailing alpines with several dwarf shrubs or trees, provides great visual interest. The sword-shaped silver leaves of *Celmisia coriacea* contrast well with mat-forming plants such as *Polygala calcarea* 'Bulley's Variety', with deep blue flowers in late spring and early summer, and *Campanula cochleariifolia*, with clusters of pale blue or white bells in summer.

A TAPESTRY OF COLOR
In this vivid display, the rich colors and varied forms of the alpines blend with the evergreen shrubs and dwarf conifers, which will give year-round interest when the flowers have faded.

A Peat Bed

Alpines that thrive in acid soil and damp, woodland conditions are best grown in a specially constructed peat bed. Site the bed in a partly shaded area of the garden perhaps next to, but not beneath, a light-foliaged tree so that the plants receive dappled sunlight for part of the day.

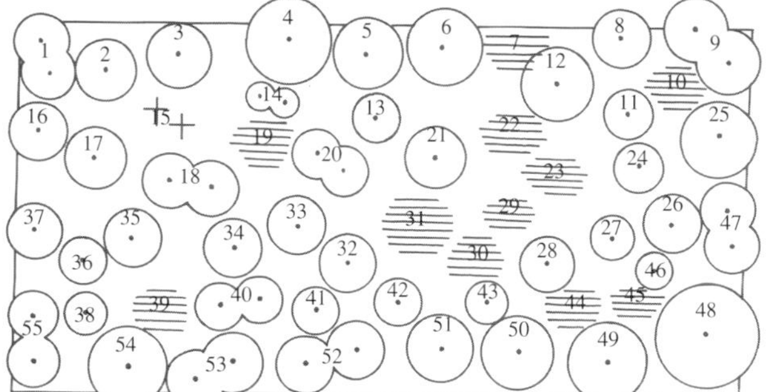

1 *Cyathodes colensoi*
2 *Hacquetia epipactis*
3 *Arctostaphylos uva-ursi* 'Point Reyes'
4 *Rhododendron* 'Curlew'
5 *Anemone nemorosa* 'Robinsoniana'
6 *Trillium grandiflorum*
7 *Erythronium* 'Pagoda'
8 *Betula nana*
9 *Dryas octopetala*
10 *Narcissus bulbocodium* subsp. *bulbocodium*
11 *Jeffersonia dubia*
12 *Phlox* 'Chatahoochee'
13 *Dodecatheon* 'Red Wings'
14 *Dicentra cucullaria*
15 *Celmisia coriacea*
16 *Phlox divaricata* subsp. *laphamii*
17 *Trillium erectum*
18 *Gentiana septemfida*
19 *Erythronium hendersonii*
20 *Phyllodoce empetriformis*
21 *Daphne arbuscula*
22 *Lilium mackliniae*
23 *Erythronium oregonum*
24 *Gentiana acaulis*
25 *Salix reticulata*
26 *Salix* x *boydii*
27 *Polygala chamaebuxus*
28 *Phyllodoce caerulea*
29 *Galanthus nivalis* 'Lutescens'
30 *Nomocharis pardanthina*
31 *Erythronium* 'White Beauty'
32 *Anemonella thalictroides*
33 *Cassiope* 'Edinburgh'
34 *Rhodohypoxis* 'Douglas'
35 *Anemone* x *lipsiensis*
36 *Hepatica nobilis* var. *japonica*
37 *Cassiope lycopodioides*
38 *Trillium rivale*
39 *Scilla siberica* 'Atrocaerulea'
40 *Polygonatum hookeri*
41 *Corydalis solida* 'George Baker'
42 *Rhodothamnus chamaecistus*
43 *Rhodohypoxis* 'Margaret Rose'
44 *Narcissus cyclamineus*
45 *Cyclamen purpurascens*
46 *Calceolaria* 'Walter Shrimpton'
47 *Saxifraga oppositifolia*
48 *Linnaea borealis*
49 *Gentiana sino-ornata*
50 *Vaccinium vitis-idaea* 'Minus'
51 *Andromeda polifolia* 'Compacta'
52 *Gaultheria cuneata*
53 *Polygala chamaebuxus* var. *grandiflora*
54 *Phlox stolonifera* 'Ariane'
55 *Lithodora diffusa* 'Heavenly Blue'

Scree formations

On mountain slopes, the natural weathering of rock outcrops produces a mass of small, broken rocks and stones. These loose, stony slopes, known as screes, are home to many plants that need plenty of moisture at their roots during the growing season, but grow best through an apparently dry 6in (15cm) surface layer of stones. Scree dwellers are among the most beautiful and jewel-like of alpine plants and well worth the extra care needed to grow them.

The scree bed

The scree bed attempts to re-create the highly specialized habitat of natural scree dwellers. A scree is a deep, preferably gently sloping bed of loose rock fragments of varying size, into which is mixed a suitable soil mix (see p.196). Screes may also be constructed on flat sites, raised from ground level to assist drainage, becoming, in effect, a specialized form of raised bed (see opposite).

Scree dwellers usually form low mats or cushions of dense foliage; many bear their small, brilliantly colored blooms in such profusion that the flowers almost completely obscure the leaves. The neutral background of small stones offers an ideal foil for the rich textures and colors of this type of planting.

Specialist plants, for example *Vitaliana primuliflora*, *Anchusa caespitosa*, and *Myosotis alpestris*, thrive in screes. Other rock garden plants that are easier to grow also appreciate the conditions created in a scree bed. Some species, such as *Achillea clavennae* and *Artemisia glacialis*, are grown primarily for their silver foliage, which provides a cool contrast for stronger colors. A number of species, including *Androsace carnea* subsp. *laggeri*, which bears a mass of pink blooms in early summer, naturally self-seed. The tiny, blue, bell-shaped flowers of *Campanula cochleariifolia* also spring up around the garden but may become a nuisance if the plants compete with less robust species.

Integrating the scree bed

Where space is available, one or more scree beds may be integrated with a rock garden to form a bold, unified design and provide a broad range of habitats. A backdrop of large rocks skirted by scree beds is particularly effective.

Alternatively, pockets of scree mixture can be included in a rock garden to accommodate specialized scree dwellers that need particularly good drainage around their necks. *Dianthus haematocalyx*, for example, is a tightly tufted pink whose deep rose petals have an unusual buff underside; it benefits from a soil surface of loose, dry stones.

The visual impact of a scree bed is enhanced by incorporating just a few carefully positioned, larger rocks. Plants can then be allowed to skirt their base or to grow over them to soften their outlines.

Peat beds

Alpine plants that require an acid soil or a woodland environment are not always easily accommodated in a rock garden. Acid-loving plants such as *Arctostaphylos*, *Cassiope*, gentians, and most *Vaccinium* species will thrive only in soil with a low pH; woodland plants do best in moist, shady conditions and leafy, humus-rich soil. Specially constructed peat beds are an excellent way of providing a moist, acidic growing medium and, when sited in dappled shade, closely imitate woodland conditions, extending the range of species that may be grown.

Site and materials

Peat beds may be constructed either as individual garden features or as extensions to a rock garden. The shady, north-facing side of a rock garden provides ideal conditions. Do not place a peat bed beneath trees, since water dripping from the leaves after rain may rot the plants. For best results, the site should be in sun for part of the day.

Traditionally, the acidic medium of the peat bed is based on sphagnum moss, which has a naturally low pH, good aeration, and excellent water retention. Depending on the source of the moss, the pH may vary considerably; it may even be alkaline. Before purchasing large quantities, determine the pH of a single bale to be sure it is acidic enough.

Raised beds

In small gardens, raised beds make highly economical use of limited space. In larger gardens, narrow raised beds can make a useful and attractive boundary feature. The formal appearance of raised beds blends in well with the design and layout of many modern gardens. In areas where suitable rock is not easily available or is prohibitively expensive, a raised bed provides a good substitute for a rock garden.

Since drainage in raised beds is entirely independent of the underlying soil, these structures are especially useful in gardens with poorly drained soils (such as wet, heavy clay) that are otherwise unsuitable for the cultivation of alpines. In addition, the dimensions of a raised bed may be planned so that the bed will accommodate a cold frame sash to allow cultivation of choice species that require protection from too much winter moisture, without restricting airflow around the plants.

Various materials may be used for the construction of a suitable raised bed, including traditional bricks or dry stones, pressure-treated lumber, and railroad ties. For further information, see Structures and Surfaces, "Raised beds," p.507.

Planting in raised beds

Large raised beds can be divided into separate areas or compartments, and different soil mixes used in each to suit the specific requirements of different plant groups. Rocks can be introduced to the surface of the soil mix and bedded in to provide textural contrast as well as vertical niches and crevices for those plants that demand them.

Rectangular raised beds present several exposures so that plants with different requirements may be planted in niches on their sunny or shady side, if required. In addition to growing plants in the bed itself, the walls of the bed may be designed to incorporate planting niches, in the same way as walls that are used for trailing species.

Choose plants that will flower in succession as the seasons progress. The dense, evergreen rosettes of *Haberlea rhodopensis* send up sprays of funnel-shaped flowers in spring, and may be succeeded in summer by *Aquilegia flabellata* 'Nana', a clump-forming alpine that produces bell-shaped, soft blue flowers, each with fluted petals and a short spur. Both of these plants thrive in semishade and are small enough to be planted in a raised bed without overcrowding it.

For a sunnier exposure, choose compact species of *Dianthus*, such as *D. alpinus* and *D.* 'Bombadier', with *Erinus alpinus* 'Dr. Haenele' trailing from the retaining wall.

Walls

Garden walls may be modified, if required, to provide appropriate sites for alpines and rock garden plants. The walls of raised beds and those used to retain banks of soil on a terraced slope can be modified in the same way. If possible, however, leave spaces, crevices, or cracks between the stones or brickwork during the construction of such walls so that these may be planted up when building is complete.

Choosing plants

The most suitable plants to choose are cushion- or mat-forming plants such as *Acantholimon glumaceum*, which forms evergreen cushions that are clothed in pink flowers during summer, or *Dianthus deltoides* and other alpine pinks. Plants that are

A Low Raised Bed
Here, a raised alpine bed flanks one side of a narrow stone path. The plants draw the eye along the path and entice the visitor to the open lawn beyond.

A Dry-stone Wall
Crevices in a dry-stone wall provide ideal conditions for a variety of trailing and spreading plants, since drainage between the stones is good. The plants also enjoy the benefit of a cool root run.

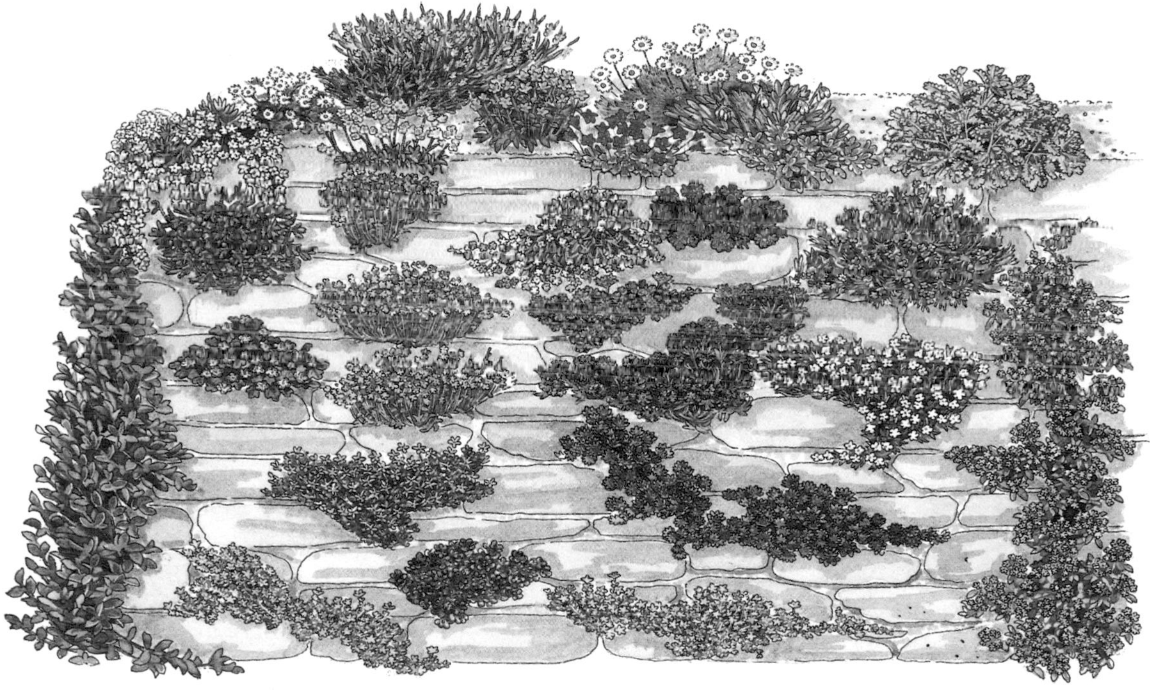

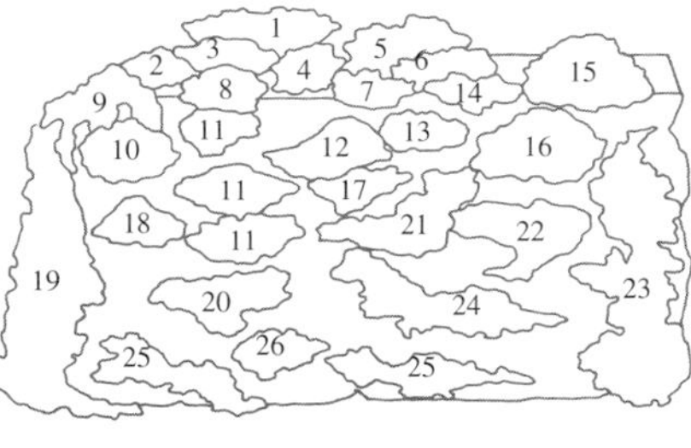

1 *Genista sagittalis*
2 *Anacyclus depressus*
3 *Helichrysum selago*
4 *Linum flavum*
5 *Chrysanthemum hosmariense*
6 *Onosma albo-roseum*
7 *Campanula* 'Birch Hybrid'
8 *Achillea* x *kellereri*
9 *Saxifraga* 'Tumbling Waters'
10 *Penstemon newberryi* f. *humilior*
11 *Erinus alpinus*
12 *Gypsophila repens* 'Dorothy Teacher'
13 *Armeria juniperifolia*
14 *Sedum kamtschaticum* 'Variegatum'
15 *Tanacetum argenteum*
16 *Acantholimon glumaceum*
17 *Sedum spathulifolium* 'Cape Blanco'
18 *Erodium corsicum*
19 *Polygonum vacciniifolium*
20 *Arenaria purpurascens*
21 *Tropaeolum polyphyllum*
22 *Arenaria montana*
23 *Saponaria ocymoides*
24 *Jovibarba hirta*
25 *Sedum acre*
26 *Sedum obtusatum*

prone to rotting at the collar, such as *Lewisia* and *Ramonda* species, are well suited to being grown in walls, since the roots enjoy the cool conditions and extra drainage provided by the crevices. The trailing, semi-evergreen *Asarina procumbens*, with its creamy white, snapdragon-like flowers, and the shrubby *Penstemon newberryi* f. *humilior*, bearing a profusion of flowers on gently arching branches, are also ideal for walls.

Dry-stone walls

These provide ample room for the root systems of many rock garden plants to penetrate, and also allow sharp drainage. Free-standing, single or double dry-stone walls may be used to form boundaries or dividers in the garden and, with careful choice of suitable plants, make extremely attractive features.

The well-drained tops of dry-stone walls provide an ideal home for mat-forming plants such as *Gypsophila repens* or *Saponaria ocymoides*, both of which cascade attractively over the edge of the wall. The neat, spreading rosettes of lime-encrusted saxifrages and houseleeks (*Sempervivum*) can be dotted at intervals across the surface. Using both vertical faces of a wall will allow both sun- and shade-loving plants to be grown.

Troughs and sinks

Old stone sinks and troughs for feeding and watering animals make handsome containers for rock plants; unfortunately, they are both scarce and expensive. However, troughs made of reconstituted stone or hypertufa, and glazed sinks coated with this material (see p.198) are ideal, inexpensive alternatives. Troughs and sinks may be used as features in patios and courtyards, or on terraces and graveled areas in larger gardens.

Planting in troughs

By carefully selecting dwarf and slow-growing species you can create a miniature rock garden in a trough. The smallest alpine plants are often the most intricate and beautiful. Use *Antennaria dioica* 'Minima' and other compact alpines and rock plants for trough planting.

Introduce a few small conifers, such as *Chamaecyparis obtusa* 'Nana Pyramidalis' or *Juniperus communis* 'Compressa', and dwarf trees such as *Ulmus parvifolia* 'Geisha' as framework plants. For the middle and foreground of the trough, showy flowering plants such as *Campanula zoysii*, *Dianthus alpinus*, or *Bolax gummifera* may be used. Miniature shrubs may be added to provide contrasting form and color throughout the year.

An Alpine Trough Collection
A collection of troughs makes an appealing feature. Large troughs accommodate dwarf trees and shrubs as well as smaller alpine plants.

Growing plants in other containers

Where containers are selected to complement other hard landscape features of the garden, such as walls and paths, they bring a cohesive element to the overall design of the garden. Containers provide an opportunity to grow alpines in a small garden, and may also be used to flank pathways or steps.

Choosing plants

Containers are especially suitable for cultivating miniature species, and they allow plants such as the tiny *Primula scotica*, with its golden-eyed purple flowers, to be appreciated and grown in a situation where they will not be swamped by larger and more vigorous neighbors. Grouping several containers together provides a good opportunity to build up collections devoted to plants of one genus that flourish under similar environmental conditions.

A long season of interest can be achieved by underplanting low-growing, mat-forming plants such as *Raoulia australis* and *Globularia cordifolia* with late-winter flowering dwarf bulbs, for example *Narcissus watieri* or *Iris reticulata* and its many cultivars.

Choosing a container

The range of decorative containers suitable for alpines and rock garden plants is enormous. Make sure that the container has adequate drainage. If an appropriate soil mix is then used and the plants are regularly watered and well maintained, almost any container may be used to good effect.

Large flower pots and terracotta tubs are suitable for small collections of the tiniest alpines, and particularly for those that trail over the edges of the pot, such as *Silene schafta*. Small containers are ideal for compact, slow-growing alpines such as *Androsace chamaejasme* and *Sempervivum arachnoideum*, which will provide a display over several years before they start to outgrow their situation.

Where winters are cold, move unglazed terracotta pots and tubs, such as those sold as strawberry jars, indoors to stop them from flaking and disintegrating.

An Unusual Container
Many different types of container can be used for rock plants and alpine species. Here, part of a hollowed-out tree trunk has been planted with Sedum spathulifolium 'Cape Blanco', *valued for its small clusters of tiny yellow flowers above the rosettes of silvery green leaves.*

The alpine house

In the wild, many alpines spend their winter dormancy insulated by a deep snow blanket that shields them from excess water, cold drying winds, and severe cold. Temperatures under the snow hover at, or just below, the freezing point. In gardens at lower altitudes, where conditions are very different, the more exacting alpines need protection.

A simple, open cloche may be sufficient protection for some plants. However, a specially designed greenhouse, or alpine house, (see Greenhouses and Frames, "Alpine house," p.477) greatly extends the range that may be grown, and allows the enthusiastic gardener to grow some of the most challenging plants.

Using an alpine house

An alpine house will accommodate a huge range of the choicest alpines in carefully controlled conditions. The season of interest in the alpine house can be maintained throughout the early winter months, when color in the open garden is scarce. Interest increases rapidly in early spring, when the majority of true alpines flower. Where dwarf shrubs, bulbs, conifers, and ferns are also included in the collection, there will be something to attract attention throughout the year.

Alpine houses are generally used for plants unsuited to growing in the open. But many less demanding alpines, and even robust plants that are strong enough to withstand early spring frosts and rain, may be grown to perfection in an alpine house (see also Alpine Houses and Frames, pp.210–12).

Planter's guide to rock plants

Exposed Sites

Rock plants that tolerate exposed or windy sites

Antennaria dioica
Campanula portenschlagiana
Carlina acaulis
Chiastophyllum oppositifolium
Crepis incana
Dryas octopetala
Erigeron karvinskianus
Eryngium, some ❄, ⛰
Euphorbia myrsinites
Hebe, some ❄, ⛰
Helianthemum
Limonium bellidifolium
Pterocephalus perennis
Sedum, some ❄, ⛰
Sempervivum
Silene vulgaris subsp. *maritima*
Veronica spicata

Air Pollution

Rock plants that tolerate polluted air

Aubrieta
Aurinia saxatilis
Campanula garganica, *C. poscharskyana*
Erinus alpinus
Euphorbia, some ❄, ⛰
Sedum, some ❄, ⛰
Sempervivum

Dry Shade

Rock plants that tolerate dry shade

Ajuga pyramidalis, *A. reptans*
Dianthus carthusianorum, *D. deltoides*
Diascia cordata, *D.* 'Ruby Field'
Erodium guttatum
Genista sagittalis
Gypsophila dubia, *G. repens*
Helleborus, some ❄
Lamium maculatum
Saponaria ocymoides
Waldsteinia ternata

Waldsteinia ternata

Moist Shade

Rock plants that do best in moist shade

Adonis amurensis
Cassiope
Cyclamen hederifolium, *C. purpurascens*
Daphne blagayana
Galax aphylla
Hepatica nobilis, *H. transsilvanica*
Hylomecon japonicum
Iris cristata
Meconopsis cambrica
Primula, some ❄ (many spp. and cvs)
Sanguinaria canadensis
Shortia uniflora
Stylophorum diphyllum
Trillium

Scree Gardens

Acantholimon glumaceum
Aethionema pulchellum, *A.* 'Warley Rose'
Alyssum montanum

Androsace lanuginosa

Androsace lanuginosa, *A. sarmentosa*, *A. sempervivoides*
Dianthus alpinus, *D. anatolicus*, *D. echinacea*
Erinus alpinus
Gypsophila aretioides
Hutchinsia alpina
Linaria alpina
Papaver burseri, *P. miyabeanum*, *P. rhaeticum*
Sempervivum
Silene acaulis
Viola cornuta 'Minor', *V. jooi*

Crevices and Paving

Aubrieta deltoidea (many cvs)
Aurinia saxatilis
Campanula cochleariifolia, *C. portenschlagiana*
Erinus alpinus
Erodium chamaedryoides
Geranium sanguineum var. *striatum*
Globularia cordifolia
Mentha requienii
Onosma albo-roseum, *O. echioides*
Pratia pedunculata
Scabiosa graminifolia
Thymus, some ❄

Wall Crevices

Antirrhinum glutinosum, *A. molle*
Aurinia saxatilis 'Citrina'
Campanula portenschlagiana
Erinus alpinus
Globularia cordifolia
Haberlea rhodopensis (shade)
Lewisia, Cotyledon Hybrids, *L. tweedyi*
Onosma taurica
Polemonium pulcherrimum
Ramonda myconi (shade)
Saxifraga callosa, *S. cochlearis*, *S. longifolia*, *S. paniculata*
Silene vulgaris subsp. *maritima* 'Flore Pleno'

Planting in Troughs

Anchusa caespitosa
Androsace (small spp. and cvs)
Antennaria dioica 'Minima'
Arenaria purpurascens
Asperula suberosa
Dianthus alpinus, *D. freynii*, *D. glacialis*
Dryas octopetala 'Minor'
Edraianthus pumilio
Gentiana saxosa, *G. verna* var. *angulosa*
Helianthemum oelandicum
Linum suffruticosum subsp. *salsoloides* 'Nanum'
Myosotis rupicola
Omphalodes luciliae ❄
Oxalis enneaphylla
Paraquilegia anemonoides
Petrophytum hendersonii
Phlox subulata
Primula farinosa, *P. marginata*

Saxifraga sancta

Saxifraga, some ❄ (many spp. and cvs)
Sedum cauticola
Soldanella alpina, *S. montana*
Thymus serpyllum 'Minus'
Vitaliana primuliflora

Planting in Tufa

Androsace (small spp. and cvs)
Campanula piperi, *C. zoysii*
Draba mollissima, *D. polytricha*
Edraianthus pumilio
Paraquilegia anemonoides
Physoplexis comosa
Potentilla nitida
Saxifraga, some ❄ (many types, especially the Kabschias)
Viola cazorlensis, *V. delphinantha*

Raised Beds

Aethionema 'Warley Rose'
Androsace
Antirrhinum molle, *A. sempervirens*
Aquilegia discolor, *A. flabellata*
Armeria juniperifolia
Bolax gummifera
Callianthemum anemonoides
Campanula raineri, *C. zoysii*
Daphne arbuscula, *D. cneorum*, *D. petraea* 'Grandiflora'
Dianthus, some ❄
Draba bryoides, *D. polytricha*
Edraianthus dinaricus, *E. graminifolius*
Erinacea anthyllis
Gentiana acaulis, *G. verna* var. *angulosa*
Globularia meridionalis, *G. repens*
Haberlea rhodopensis
Leontopodium alpinum, *L. nivale*
Lewisia (some spp. and hybrids)
Origanum (some spp. and hybrids)
Oxalis adenophylla, *O. enneaphylla*, *O.* 'Ione Hecker'
Papaver burseri, *P. miyabeanum*
Paraquilegia anemonoides
Primula auricula, *P. marginata*
Ramonda myconi
Saxifraga cotyledon, *S. longifolia*, *S. paniculata*, *S.* 'Tumbling Waters'
Sempervivum
Silene acaulis
Verbascum 'Letitia'

Dwarf Shrubs

Berberis x *stenophylla* 'Corallina Compacta'
Betula nana
Chamaecyparis obtusa 'Intermedia'
Cryptomeria japonica 'Vilmoriniana'
Daphne cneorum, *D. retusa*, *D. sericea*
Dorycnium hirsutum
Erinacea anthyllis
Euryops acraeus
Genista delphinensis
Hebe buchananii 'Minor'
Helichrysum coralloides

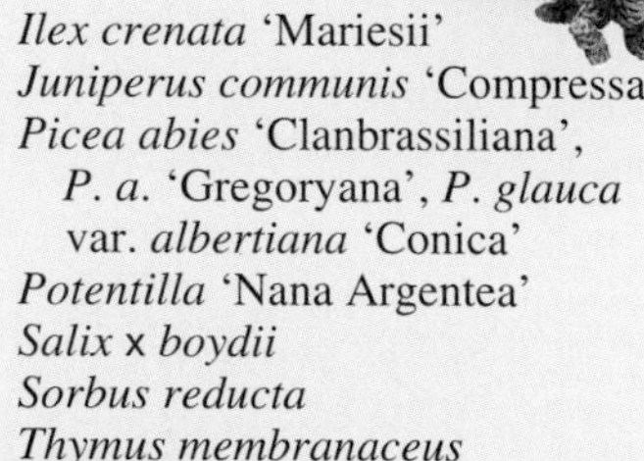

Helichrysum coralloides

Ilex crenata 'Mariesii'
Juniperus communis 'Compressa'
Picea abies 'Clanbrassiliana', *P. a.* 'Gregoryana', *P. glauca* var. *albertiana* 'Conica'
Potentilla 'Nana Argentea'
Salix x *boydii*
Sorbus reducta
Thymus membranaceus

Key

❄ *Not frost hardy*
⛰ *Rock garden species only*

Construction, soil preparation, and planting

VARIOUS methods may be used to grow alpine plants in gardens. Planting them in a rock garden is perhaps the best-known method, although this can take up a great deal of space. For a smaller display, screes, raised and peat beds, and the crevices of walls can make very attractive features. Where space is more limited, troughs, sinks, and other containers can also be used for a fine alpine display.

ROCK PLANTS THAT REQUIRE ACID SOIL

Arctostaphylos alpina
Cassiope
Corydalis cashmeriana, *C. flexuosa*
Cyananthus
Epigaea gaultherioides, *E. repens*
Galax urceolata
Gentiana sino-ornata
Glaucidium palmatum
Haberlea rhodopensis
Kalmia angustifolia, *K. polifolia* 'Microphylla'
Leiophyllum buxifolium
Leucopogon fraseri
Leucothöe keiskei
Linnaea borealis
Lithodora diffusa
Menziesia ciliicalyx
Mitchella repens
Ourisia caespitosa, *O. coccinea*, *O.* 'Loch Ewe'
Paris polyphylla
Pernettya

Phyllodoce caerulea

Phyllodoce caerulea, *P. glanduliflora*, *P. nipponica*
Pieris nana
Polygala chamaebuxus, *P. vayredae*
Primula boothii, *P. edgeworthii*, *P. gracilipes*, *P. sonchifolia*
Pyrola rotundifolia
Rhododendron (dwarf spp. and cvs)
Shortia soldanelloides
Soldanella villosa
Tanakaea radicans
Vaccinium delavayi, *V. myrtillus*, *V. uliginosum*

Buying plants

The rock garden should be regarded as a feature that, with careful choice of plants, will provide much interest throughout the year.

Before buying any plants, refer to standard texts to find out the likely range of plants that is suitable for a particular type of locality in terms of climate, soil, and general situation. Visit established rock gardens in parks and botanic gardens, as well as specialist nurseries, to assess the relative merits of various plants for your own requirements. The shape, form, and color of foliage, fruits, stems, and the overall growth habit are often as important as flowers.

Where to buy plants

Plants are available from a wide range of sources, including garden centers and specialist nurseries. Nonspecialist outlets often sell a limited range of colorful cultivars and easily grown species; these may form large, spreading clumps that quickly overwhelm more delicate plants in the rock garden.

The experienced nurseryman is able to advise on the most suitable choice of plants for a particular situation, and often has display beds of mature plants. These give a good indication of the ultimate size, spread, and habit of different plants, and are invaluable at the planning stage. Such specialist outlets can also be consulted for information on soil mixes and suppliers of rock.

A much wider range of plants will be offered by the specialist grower, who is also able to provide detailed advice on cultivation – this is particularly useful for the beginner. Demand for rare or unfamiliar plants sometimes means that general suppliers may carry stocks of plants that are best left to the specialist, since they are often unsuitable for the average rock garden. Such plants may be attractive but are often expensive and may be difficult to cultivate. They offer a rewarding challenge, but purchase them only after obtaining advice on growing them.

Selecting alpine plants

Choose plants that have healthy, compact foliage, and no sign of pests and diseases or water deprivation. Do not buy plants with yellowing or weak growth, since this indicates that they have been kept in poor light. Labels should bear the name of the plant as well as details of flowering times and brief cultivation requirements. Plants should not be potbound, and the roots should be barely visible, if at all, through the hole in the base of the pot. Do not purchase any plants that have rooted into the material on the surface of the display area, since these are almost certain to be potbound.

The top-growth of a plant may remain healthy for some time after the root system has been damaged or has actually died, so check that the plant has a healthy root system by sliding it out of its pot and inspecting the root ball carefully.

Large specimens are sometimes available, but unless they are grown on correctly, with careful attention to watering, they may take much longer to become established than smaller, vigorous ones.

Select plants that are as weed-free as possible. Before planting, gently scrape off the grit or surface soil mix so that any weed seeds are removed. Introducing weeds such as pearlwort (*Sagina procumbens*) and creeping oxalis (*Oxalis corniculata*) causes problems because, once established, they are difficult to eradicate.

A number of plants that are sold for growing in the rock garden, such as some of the ornamental onions (*Allium*), are overprolific seeders. Choose carefully to avoid introducing such problem plants.

HOW TO SELECT ALPINE PLANTS

GOOD EXAMPLE

SAXIFRAGA

POOR EXAMPLE

Unbalanced, weak growth

Weeds in soil mix

Roots curled around inside of pot

Siting a rock garden or scree bed

Good siting is critical for a rock garden or scree bed because alpine plants require good light and well-drained conditions to thrive. The rock garden or scree should also blend in with the rest of the garden. Before starting construction, draw a rough plan on paper showing the rock garden or scree bed in relation to other garden features. A scree may be integrated into a rock garden or built as a separate feature.

SITING A ROCK GARDEN

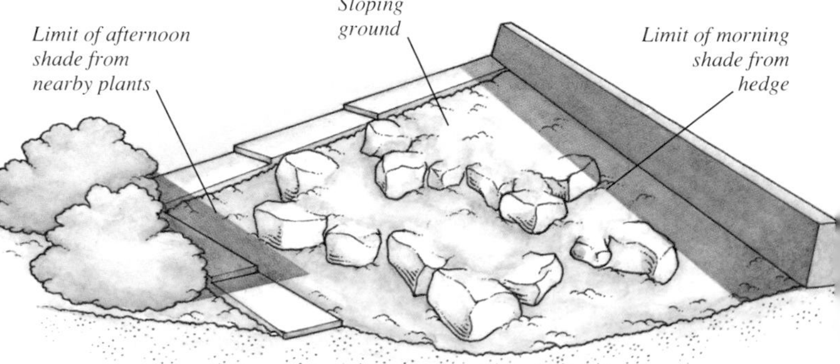

Build a rock garden on sloping ground, if possible, to ensure sharp drainage. Choose an open site that receives full sun, away from the roots and overhanging branches of trees and large shrubs.

Choosing the site

Choose an open, sunny site away from the shade of overhanging trees. Trees drip water onto the plants beneath and shed their leaves in fall, which could smother plants or create a damp atmosphere leading to rot. Their roots may also compete with the plants for moisture and nutrients. Do not site a rock garden or scree in a frost pocket or on a site exposed to cold, drying winds.

A sloping site is ideal for a rock garden: it will have good drainage, and the artificial outcrops of rock can be made to look more natural, providing different pockets and exposures to suit a variety of plants. Level sites present more problems than sloping ones; scree beds (see p.188) or raised beds (see p.189) are usually better for such sites.

It is best to preserve a feeling of space by siting the rock garden or scree so that a distant view is visible beyond it. In small, enclosed gardens, boundary fences or walls that rise behind the rock garden can be concealed with suitable climbers. Plan any water features, such as a pond or stream, into the design at an early stage. In large rock gardens, paths or stepping-stones are essential to provide access and to facilitate garden maintenance.

Making a natural-looking feature

A rock garden or scree is best sited where it will blend into an informally planted area of the garden, such as on a slope, by a terrace, or as a natural-looking outcrop from an area of shrubs. If the rock garden or scree is to be next to a lawn, position it so that it does not interfere with cutting and edging the lawn. It is unlikely to look natural if placed next to such features as herbaceous borders, bedding displays, or any other formally planted areas such as the vegetable or fruit garden. If the main garden is rather formal, it may be better to grow alpines in a rectangular raised bed (see p.200) rather than trying to integrate the informality of a rock garden into the otherwise formal design.

Natural strata

Sedimentary rock, such as limestone, occurs naturally in distinct layers, or stratum lines, that are clearly visible to the eye. Rocks of this type can easily be split along the stratum lines for use in rock gardens.

Sedimentary rocks that occur in nature always have stratum lines following the same direction; it is important to place the stones in a rock garden to simulate their natural orientation, otherwise they will look too obviously artificial.

NATURAL STRATUM LINES

Choosing stone

Use locally available stone for rock garden construction, wherever possible, to harmonize with the local landscape and to reduce transportation costs. However, this may not be possible in regions where supplies of natural rock are limited or where the local stone is unsuitable.

Do not use soft, quick-weathering rock, such as shale, or hard, featureless, igneous rocks without strata, such as granite and basalt. Hard stone with no clear strata may be inexpensive, but it is difficult to use, takes several years to acquire a weathered appearance, and seldom looks natural. Other materials, such as slate, are also used, but they are sometimes difficult to blend in.

Buying stone

If possible, visit local quarries to inspect the rock and choose suitable pieces, ensuring that the rocks are not too large to handle after being delivered. Choose stone in a range of different sizes, since this makes it easier to construct a natural-looking outcrop. Garden centers may offer a range of stone, although there is sometimes a limited choice of size and shape.

Sandstone

The most suitable rocks are the various sandstones, in which the natural strata or layers are clearly visible. One great advantage of using rocks with stratum lines is that they may be split easily, making it relatively easy to create planting pockets and natural-looking fissures in the rock.

Limestone

Be sure to obtain permission before harvesting any limestone.Where it occurs locally, try to get weathered rock from fields or woods. These will be slightly rounded and will have a patina of moss or lichens. New rock, for example from building sites or road cuts, takes several years to mellow.

Tufa

Tufa is a porous, limy rock that is formed as deposits around mineral springs. It is filled with numerous air pockets and its light weight makes it easy to transport and handle. Cavities for plants may be dug or drilled out of its relatively soft surface. It provides ideal conditions for many plants that require free drainage, but it is scarce and expensive.

Types of stone

Tufa is an excellent choice for the rock garden because its soft, porous nature means that plants may be grown in cavities on the surface as well as in crevices between the stones. Natural-looking, weather-worn sandstone is also a good choice, as is limestone (if available secondhand).

TUFA

SANDSTONE

LIMESTONE

ROCK PLANTS THAT PREFER SANDY SOIL

Acaena caesiiglauca, *A. microphylla*
Achillea x *kellereri*
Aethionema 'Warley Rose'
Arabis ferdinandi-coburgi 'Variegata'
Arenaria montana
Armeria juniperifolia
Artemisia schmidtiana 'Nana'
Ballota pseudodictamnus
Cytisus x *beanii*
Dianthus carthusianorum, *D. deltoides*
Erodium guttatum
Gypsophila repens
Helianthemum
Iberis saxatilis

Lewisia, Cotyledon Hybrids

Lewisia, Cotyledon Hybrids
Linum suffruticosum
Onosma echioides, *O. taurica*
Phlox bifida
Saponaria ocymoides
Sedum, some ❄
Sempervivum

ROCK PLANTS THAT TOLERATE VERY ALKALINE SOIL

Aethionema
Alyssum
Anemone magellanica
Aubrieta
Campanula, some ❄
Chrysanthemum hosmariense
Dianthus, some ❄
Draba
Erysimum helveticum
Geranium farreri
Gypsophila repens
Helianthemum
Leontopodium alpinum

Origanum 'Kent Beauty'

Origanum
Papaver burseri, *P. miyabeanum*
Pulsatilla
Saponaria ocymoides
Saxifraga, some ❄
Sedum, some ❄
Sempervivum
Silene schafta
Thymus caespititius

KEY
❄ *Not frost hardy*

How to Prepare the Site and Place the Stone

1 Place a 6in (15cm) layer of coarse rubble, such as broken bricks, on the proposed site to form a mound and improve drainage in the rock garden.

2 Cover the mound with inverted sod to prevent soil from being washed down to the layer of rubble at the base.

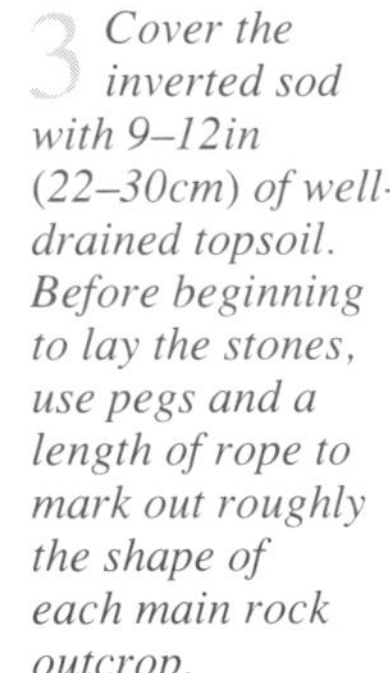

3 Cover the inverted sod with 9–12in (22–30cm) of well-drained topsoil. Before beginning to lay the stones, use pegs and a length of rope to mark out roughly the shape of each main rock outcrop.

4 Using a spade, dig out a hollow for each large piece of stone to make it more stable when placed in position.

5 Use a crowbar to maneuver large stones into their final positions. Ensure that the stones are well supported by wedging smaller stones or bricks underneath.

6 Fill in underneath and in between the stones with garden soil, making sure that each stone is firmly in place.

7 Build each outcrop of the rock garden in the same way. Tread down the soil gently around the stones (see inset) to eliminate air pockets and to make sure that each stone is firmly seated.

8 When all the stones are in place, fill in around them with more garden soil so they are buried by one-third of their depth to ensure complete stability. Loosen the soil between the rocks so that it is not compacted.

9 Add a layer of specially prepared soil mix to the top 2–3in (5–7cm) of the rock garden and around the stones. Use a mix of equal parts soil, compost or leaf mold, and sharp sand or grit.

10 The rock garden, once completed, should look as natural as possible. It should also provide a range of exposures and planting pockets to create environments that suit different types of plant.

Preparing the site for a rock garden

Never attempt to construct rock gardens when the soil is wet, since heavy rocks may compact the soil and severely damage its structure; this interferes with drainage and causes problems with the establishment and growth of the plants. If the site is grassed, cut the sod carefully and remove it for later use when constructing the rock garden.

Clearing weeds

Remove all perennial weeds from the site and, if siting the rock garden near trees or shrubs, remove any suckers that these may have produced. Perennial weeds are very difficult to eradicate from an established rock garden, so it is essential to dig them out or kill them with a weedkiller at this stage. Spray the whole area with a systemic weedkiller several weeks before construction begins, to kill the deep roots of perennial weeds and clear the site of vegetation.

Drainage

Make sure that the site, particularly if level, is well drained. If necessary, install a soakaway or other drainage system (see SOILS AND FERTILIZERS, "Improving drainage," p.531). This is important on heavy clay soils. Do not simply dig deep holes – these act as sumps in which the water remains, unless they are connected to a drainage ditch. Raising the rock garden above the level of the surrounding ground helps to improve drainage. On naturally sloping sites drainage is not usually a problem, although a drainage ditch or soakaway may be needed at the lowest point.

If the underlying drainage is good, just dig the soil over and remove any perennial weeds. Then settle the soil by treading it gently to avoid subsequent sinking. Fork over the surface of the soil to maintain a good soil structure.

Constructing a rock garden

To visualize the finished rock garden, make a miniature rough scale model, using plastic foam bits or small stones to simulate rock outcrops. Use different sizes of stone and place them at various levels, linking them, if required, by groups of outlying rocks and small scree areas. On large sites, construct several outcrops, linked by gullies or scree beds, and incorporate water features, if desired. Outlining the proposed shape on site with a hose may help. Aim for a natural look, with miniature cliffs and valleys, along natural stratum lines. Plan the planting, bearing in mind the relative vigor and ultimate spread of the plants. Once the design is satisfactory, construction of the rock garden may begin.

Building the base

Put down a 6in (15cm) layer of coarse rock, broken bricks, stones, or pea gravel. Spread over this a layer of inverted pieces of sod, if they are available; these prevent the rock garden soil mix from clogging the free-draining layer at the base, without inhibiting normal drainage. If sod is not available, use landscape fabric or a few layers of burlap.

Purchase topsoil or bring in good soil from elsewhere in the garden, ensuring that it is as weed-free as possible. Use this for the top layer of the rock garden. Specially prepared, well-drained soil mix (see "Special mix," p.196) should be used for filling in between rocks where plants are to be grown.

Placing the stone

Rock is heavy and rough on the hands, so wear gloves and protective footwear. Use rollers to move large rocks, and arrange for the load to be delivered as close to the site of the rock garden as possible. To maneuver large rocks into their final positions, it may be necessary to use a block and tackle, with a steel crowbar as a lever for final adjustments. Mark the approximate positions of larger rocks first, to avoid unnecessary labor.

Select first the large stones that will act as keystones – the dominant rocks from which each outcrop is developed. Place the largest of the keystones first, and position the remaining ones so that the strata flow naturally from them to form the outcrops in the required directions.

Further large stones acting as subsidiary keystones may then be used to extend the outcrops. Use enough rock to make the outcrops realistic, while leaving sufficient room for planting. Check progress visually as construction proceeds. If the rocks being used have stratum lines, ensure that these all run in the same direction and at the same angle.

The rocks should be placed to provide the widest range of opportunities for planting. For example, butting rocks together serves to create the narrow crevices in which a variety of plants may thrive. Where space allows, a carefully planned, tiered rock garden may produce a number of useful, broad planting pockets between the rocks.

Bury the rocks to a third of their volume and tip them backward slightly. This ensures stability and allows water to run back off the rock into the bed rather than onto the plants beneath. Stand on the rocks to make sure that they are stable.

As rocks are positioned, fill in planting spaces with prepared soil mix and firm it in. Any obvious unconformities in the rocks may then be masked by careful planting.

How to plant during construction

To provide a cool, well-drained cavity for growing alpines and rock plants, plant them between two layers of stone as the rock garden is constructed. Position the plants in the soil close to a stone that has already been firmed in and add a little soil mix around the roots, firming gently. Use wooden boards to protect the plants as the next stone is placed in position against the first to form a planting pocket or cavity. The boards may then be removed and the second stone firmed in place. Add more soil mix around the plants and fill in with soil between the stones before top-dressing.

1 *Position the plants against a firmed stone. The crowns should face outward and the roots lie against the rock face. Add soil mix, and firm to eliminate air pockets.*

2 *Place wooden boards on top of the stone between the plants so that the second stone may be placed in position without crushing the plants.*

3 *When the second stone is in position, remove the wooden boards. Ensure that the stone is stable by firming it well down into the soil.*

4 *Fill in around the stones with topsoil, burying them to a third of their depth. Add prepared soil mix around the roots of the plants and firm in gently.*

5 *Add a 1in (2.5cm) layer of stone chips, gravel, or grit as a top-dressing to improve surface drainage and to create an attractive and natural finish.*

Soils for rock gardens and scree beds

In nature, many alpines and rock garden plants grow in soil that is largely made up of rock fragments and gravel, usually with some accumulations of humus-rich detritus, which retains moisture. Such a growing medium is extremely well drained, and it is important to simulate this as closely as possible in a rock garden or scree bed.

Ordinary garden soils may be adapted, to some extent, for cultivating most rock garden plants and alpines by adding peat, compost, and/or grit. Large quantities of grit are required to provide the rapid drainage that is needed for the more moisture-sensitive species, such as those grown in scree beds.

Standard mix

A mix of 1 part clean garden soil, 1 part peat or compost, and 1 part sharp sand or coarse grit is suitable for most rock garden plants. The humus-rich materials ensure moisture retention, while the sand or grit maintains good drainage.

Scree mixture

Scree plants require an extremely free-draining soil mix. Make up a mixture using the same ingredients as for the standard mix, but in different proportions: 3 parts coarse grit or stone chips (not sand) instead of 1 part. In order to produce a more freely draining soil mix, increase the proportion of stony material included in the mix. In dry areas, this proportion may have to be reduced to 2 parts. Alternatively, use a more retentive mix of 2 parts soil, 2 parts leaf mold or peat, 1 part sharp sand, and 4 parts stone chips.

Special mix

Some choice alpines, such as the tiny, cushion-forming *Androsace* species and saxifrages, need very free-draining soil mix. These plants usually come from high altitudes where soil nutrient levels are low. Use a mix of 2 or 3 parts stone chips or gravel to 1 part soil, leaf mold, peat, or compost.

Acid-loving plants

For acid-lovers use a mix of 4 parts lime-free leaf mold, peat, composted bark, or compost with 1 part coarse sand. On a naturally alkaline soil, however, growing plants in pockets of acid mixture is only practical in the short term, due to the inevitable percolation of lime into the soil, which soon kills them. A better solution is to grow these plants in peat beds (see p.202).

HOW TO PLANT A ROCK GARDEN

1 Before starting to plant, water all the plants and allow them to drain. To check the planting arrangement, set out the pots on the surface of the bed, taking account of the eventual height and spread of the plants.

2 Carefully remove each plant from its pot and loosen the root ball a little to encourage the roots to spread. Remove any moss and weeds before planting.

3 Using a trowel, dig a hole large enough to accommodate the root ball. Ease the plant into the hole, and label.

4 Fill in around the plant with soil mix and firm gently, making sure that there are no air pockets between the root ball and the soil mix.

5 Top-dress the soil mix with a layer of grit or gravel, easing a little around the collars of the plants.

6 Continue to plant in the same way until the rock garden is complete. Check that the whole area is properly top-dressed, and water in the plants well.

THE FINISHED ROCK GARDEN *The plants will soon grow to produce an attractive and natural-looking rock garden.*

Planting a rock garden

Alpines and rock garden plants are almost always purchased as pot plants and may be planted at any time of the year. However, it is better not to plant them when the ground is either wet or frozen, or during very warm or dry periods.

Water all the plants thoroughly before planting and allow them to drain. Set the plants out in the planned positions while still in their pots to give an idea of the finished design. Make any rearrangements at this stage and adjust planting distances, allowing for the vigorous and rapid growth of some types. Slide each plant carefully out of its pot and remove any weeds from the soil mix. Inspect the roots and top-growth for pests and diseases and treat, as necessary, before planting (see PLANT PROBLEMS, pp.547–79).

Make a planting hole with a trowel or hand fork, ensuring that the hole is big enough to accommodate the roots. Loosen the root ball, position the plant in the hole, and firm in the soil mix. The plant should sit with the collar slightly above the surface of the soil mix to leave room for a top-dressing of gravel or chips.

When all the plants are in place, water them in thoroughly. Keep them moist until they are established and

PLANTING IN A SCREE BED

Plants that require excellent drainage do best in scree beds. When planting, remove the bulk of the soil mix from around the roots and spread out the roots in the scree mixture. This will encourage the roots to spread quickly. Keep well watered until new growth appears.

starting to make new growth. If planting is followed by a dry period, water the plants at approximately weekly intervals until the roots have penetrated the surrounding soil mix. Thereafter, there should be no need to water except during a drought.

Planting in crevices

Alpines and rock garden plants may be difficult to establish in crevices and need extra care when planting. It is preferable to plant them at the construction stage, although this is not always possible. If planting in the crevices of an established rock garden, use a small tool such as a widger to make a planting hole.

Use young, rooted cuttings with vigorous root systems. If only pot-grown plants are available, trim the root balls and top-growth to the appropriate size before planting. Put a small stone in the crevice and place a little soil mix on top, then ease in the roots with a widger so that the plant faces outward. Add more soil mix around the plant and firm in. Place a small stone on top of the root ball for extra support.

Aftercare

Use netting or other deterrents to protect newly planted alpines from birds. Periodically refirm any plants that may have worked loose, adding new soil mix if necessary. Label the plants or maintain a planting plan to record their names at the time of planting; update planting plans and labeling as plants are added, replaced, or relocated.

Constructing a scree bed

Prepare the site in a similar way to a rock garden, installing artificial drainage, if necessary (see SOILS AND FERTILIZERS, "Improving drainage," p.531). Sloping sites have naturally good drainage, but on flat ground screes are best raised slightly above the ground to assist drainage, and retained within low walls, logs, or old railroad ties in the same way as raised beds (see p.200).

Scree beds should be 12–16in (30–40cm) deep. About half of the depth should be composed of coarse stones, as for rock gardens, and the upper layer of scree mixture (see opposite). Mark out the site with a rope or hose, and remove the sod from grassed areas. Lay the stone foundation and line the entire planting area with thinly cut, inverted pieces of sod or landscape fabric cut roughly to shape.

Finish off the bed with a 6–8in (15–20cm) layer of scree mixture, and firm by gently treading over the whole area. Water the bed and allow it to settle, then top up with scree mixture any areas that may have sunk before loosening the surface with a hand fork.

Planting in a scree bed

It may be more difficult to establish plants in a scree bed than in a rock garden, since the freely draining soil mix tends to dry out before the plants are established. Proper care during planting and conscientious watering are the keys to success.

The well-developed root systems of potgrown alpines do not readily penetrate the gritty scree soil mix, so gently shake off most of the soil mix (especially if peat based) from the roots. Keep the bare roots moist. Place the plant in a planting hole with its roots spread out, and fill in carefully with scree mixture. Top-dress with stone chips and water immediately and thoroughly.

Scree mixes are fast-draining, so water young plants regularly until they are established. In their natural habitats, scree dwellers have deep and extensive root systems to seek out water and nutrients, so when established they will survive for long periods without watering.

Top-dressing rock gardens and screes

After planting is completed, the rock garden or scree bed may then be top-dressed with stone chips, grit, or gravel. This material should match as closely as possible the rock used at the construction stage.

Top-dressing has a number of advantages: it provides an attractive and natural setting for the plants and blends in better with the rocks than bare soil, creates especially good drainage around the collars of the plants, inhibits weed growth, conserves moisture, and protects the soil surface from compaction during heavy rain or watering.

The layer of top-dressing on a rock garden should be at least 1in (2.5cm) deep, while on a scree bed it may be 3/4–6in (2–15cm) deep, depending on the plants grown; for most screes, a 3/4–1 1/4in (2–3cm) layer is sufficient.

HOW TO PLANT IN A VERTICAL CREVICE

1 *Prepare the crevice for planting by removing the old soil mix and any debris with a widger or teaspoon. Put a small stone at the base of the crevice.*

2 *Add a 1in (2.5cm) layer of equal parts good soil, coarse grit, and leaf mold. Ease in the roots of the plant (here* Campanula*).*

3 *Cover the roots with another 1in (2.5cm) layer of soil mix. To keep the plant in place, top the soil mix with a small stone that slopes down into the rock face.*

4 *Add more plants, spacing them at least 4in (10cm) apart. Cover the roots of the last plant with soil mix, then water the crevice to settle the soil.*

Troughs, sinks, and other containers

Alpines and rock garden plants look particularly attractive when grown in troughs and sinks, although most containers are suitable, provided that they allow good drainage and are frostproof. Choose the correct site at the outset since, once filled, they are heavy and difficult to move. Rocks may be placed in the containers, if desired, to create the look of a miniature rock garden; this should be done before planting up the container. Select a soil mix to suit the plants to be grown and choose plants that have similar growth rates.

Types of container

Old stone sinks and animal-troughs have traditionally been used to grow alpines and rock garden plants, but they are now scarce and expensive. Glazed sinks coated in hypertufa, or troughs made entirely of hypertufa or of reconstituted stone, are now often used, as are large terracotta pots and tubs. All should have drainage holes to ensure that there is a free flow of water through the soil mix. If extra drainage holes are needed, they should be at least 1in (2.5cm) in diameter. If the base of the container is not flat, make the drainage holes at the lowest point.

Covering glazed sinks

Deep, glazed, flat-bottomed sinks can easily be made to resemble stone containers by coating them with hypertufa. Ensure that the sink is clean and dry before coating it, then score the surface with a tile- or glass-cutter to form a rough surface to help the hypertufa adhere to the sink. To aid adhesion further, paint the surface with a bonding agent before applying the hypertufa.

Make hypertufa from 1–2 parts sifted peat, 1 part coarse sand or fine grit, and 1 part cement. Add sufficient water to form a thick but still workable paste. Apply this to the outside of the sink and also inside, down to well below the final level of the soil mix. Put the hypertufa on by hand (wear gloves); it should be ½–¾in (1–2cm) thick. Roughen the surface so that it resembles stone. When the hypertufa is fully dry, after about a week, scrub the surface with a wire brush and coat with liquid manure, buttermilk, or mossy soil to encourage the growth of mosses and lichens for a more natural look.

COVERING A GLAZED SINK WITH HYPERTUFA

Glazed sinks covered with hypertufa make fine containers for alpines.

Hypertufa troughs

Troughs may be made entirely from hypertufa, if required. The mixture should be prepared as for covering glazed sinks, but the proportion of sand and grit increased to 3 parts to make a stiffer mix.

Use two wooden boxes that fit inside one another, with a cavity of 2–3in (5–7cm) between them. Stand the larger box on blocks so that it may be lifted once finished. Pour a thin layer of the hypertufa mix into the base. Cover the mix and the box sides with strong wire netting and pour in another layer of hypertufa mix. Press thick dowels or pegs through the hypertufa to make drainage holes. Fit the smaller box inside the larger, and fill the space with the mix, tamping it down to remove air pockets.

When the cavity is full, cover the trough with a sheet of plastic for at least a week while the mix sets and protect the trough from frost, if necessary. When the mix has set hard, remove the boxes and dowels. If the boxes do not slide off easily, ease them off carefully with a fine chisel and a small hammer. Roughen the surface of the trough with a wire brush and paint on a coat of liquid manure to encourage algal growth.

HOW TO MAKE A HYPERTUFA TROUGH

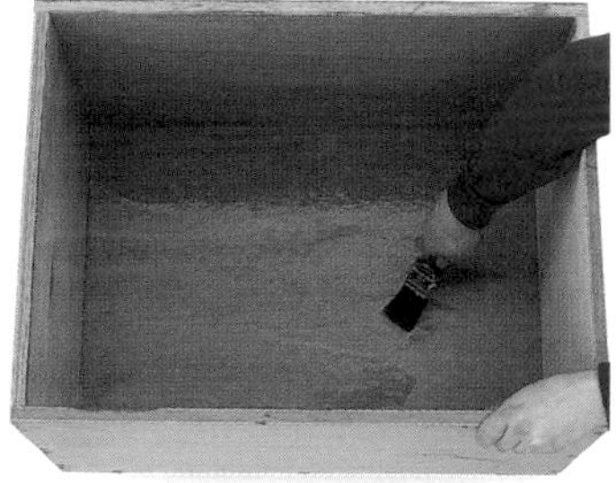

1 You will need two boxes to make the trough, one slightly larger than the other. Coat the boxes with oil to prevent the hypertufa from sticking.

2 Place a 1in (2.5cm) layer of hypertufa mix in the base of the larger box. Put wire netting on top of this layer and around the sides to reinforce the trough. Then add another layer of hypertufa.

3 Press several thick wooden dowels into the wire and hypertufa base to make the drainage holes for the bottom of the trough.

4 Put the smaller box centrally on top of the hypertufa base, making sure the vertical netting is between the two boxes. Fill the cavity with the hypertufa mix, tamping down well as you fill.

5 Cover the top of the hypertufa with a plastic sheet until the mix has set (which usually takes about a week). Secure the sheet in place with a weight, and protect the trough from frost.

6 When the hypertufa has set, remove the wooden form from the outside of the trough. If the hypertufa has stuck to the box, carefully dismantle the box with a hammer and chisel.

7 The surface of the hypertufa will be smooth and straight. For a more natural-looking appearance, scrub the outside of the trough with a wire brush or coarse-grained sandpaper to roughen the surface.

8 Remove the smaller box and the dowels, using a hammer and chisel if necessary. To encourage moss growth, paint the outside of the trough with liquid manure.

Siting containers

An open position, with sun for at least part of the day, is ideal for most plants. Do not place containers in windy sites, unless tough plants are being grown, or on lawns, since it is difficult to maintain the surrounding grass. Avoid slopes, which cause instability, and put containers as close as possible to a tap or hose.

Raise troughs and sinks off the ground, up to a height of about 18in (45cm); the plants may then be viewed comfortably and water will drain away readily. Stone or brick pillars at the corners of a container provide sturdy, stable supports. These must bear the weight of the container without danger of tipping, and should not block the holes. Tilt any sink containing just one hole so that excess water can drain.

Placing rocks and tufa

Virtually any type of rock may be used in troughs and sinks. Rocks give height, and allow a greater depth of soil mix. A few large rocks are better than many small ones. Niches and crevices in the rocks can also be used to support plants, especially if hard tufa is used. Tufa's light weight and the ease with which planting holes can be excavated in it make it ideal. Roots spread into the porous rock, which is well aerated but also retains water.

Whatever type of rock is used, bury it from one-third to one-half of its depth in the soil mix to ensure that it is firmly seated.

Filling the container

Most rock garden plants thrive in standard potting soil mix, preferably with some additional drainage material. Add about one-third by volume of $^1/_4$–$^3/_8$in (6–9mm) stone chips, and mix in some slow-release fertilizer. Acid-loving plants need a lime-free soil mix, with added granite or sandstone chips.

Cover the drainage holes with broken crocks or squares of plastic-coated window screen. Fill the bottom of the container one-quarter to one-third deep with coarse stone, gravel, or stone chips. Add a layer of fibrous peat or inverted, thinly cut sod. Fill up with slightly moist soil mix, and firm it gently.

Position pieces of rock or tufa on the soil mix, and bed them in as the container is filled. Place rocks to form crevices and niches, providing both shaded and sunny faces to suit different plants, and add randomly placed smaller pieces of stone to simulate a small-scale rock garden. Water thoroughly and allow to drain completely before planting.

Planting

Choose compact, slow-growing plants that will not swamp their neighbors and quickly exhaust the available nutrients. Do not overplant the container, and replant as soon as it becomes overcrowded (see p.204).

Position container-grown plants, still in their pots, on the soil mix or make a plan on paper of the planting design. Make planting holes, carefully slide the plants out of their pots, and loosen the root balls. Place the plants in the holes, fill in with soil mix, and firm. When complete, water thoroughly. Then add a layer of top-dressing to help ensure surface drainage, using chips or gravel that complement any rocks included.

Planting in tufa

If plants are to be grown in tufa rock, use a drill or a hammer and chisel to make holes at least 4in (10cm) apart. They should be about 1in (2.5cm) in diameter and 2–3in (5–7cm) deep, angled at 30–45° on vertical or sloping surfaces, or straight down on horizontal planes. Soak the tufa, then put a little sharp sand in each hole, and add some soil mix. Use young, rooted cuttings or small plants, since they establish easily. Wash the roots before planting. Ease the plants into the holes with a small dibber or a pencil and sprinkle in soil mix until the hole is full. Ensure that the neck of the plant is not standing above the hole. Firm the soil mix and wedge small pieces of tufa around the plants to hold them in place. Water thoroughly and keep the tufa moist until the plants are established. In hot, dry weather, soak the tufa regularly.

How to Plant Up an Alpine Trough

1 *If planting in tufa, first drill holes about 1in (2.5cm) wide, 2–3in (5–7cm) deep, and no less than 4in (10cm) apart. Immerse the tufa in water overnight.*

2 *Lay fine-mesh netting over the trough base, cover the holes with crocks, and add 3–4in (7–10cm) of coarse grit.*

3 *Partly fill the trough with a gritty, moist soil mix, firming it in stages. Set the tufa in place so that $^1/_3$–$^1/_2$ of it is buried to keep it stable.*

4 *Continue to fill with soil mix and firm well to allow about 2in (5cm) for top-dressing and watering. Insert a little soil mix into the tufa holes for planting.*

5 *Wash the roots of the plants to go in the tufa, and ease them into the planting holes. Dribble soil mix into the holes, firm, and put small rock pieces around the plants.*

6 *Set the plants, still in their pots, on the soil mix to check that the arrangement and spacing are satisfactory, then plant and firm them in.*

7 *Water the soil mix thoroughly, then top-dress the trough with a 1–2in (2.5–5cm) deep layer of coarse gravel or stone chips.*

The Finished Trough

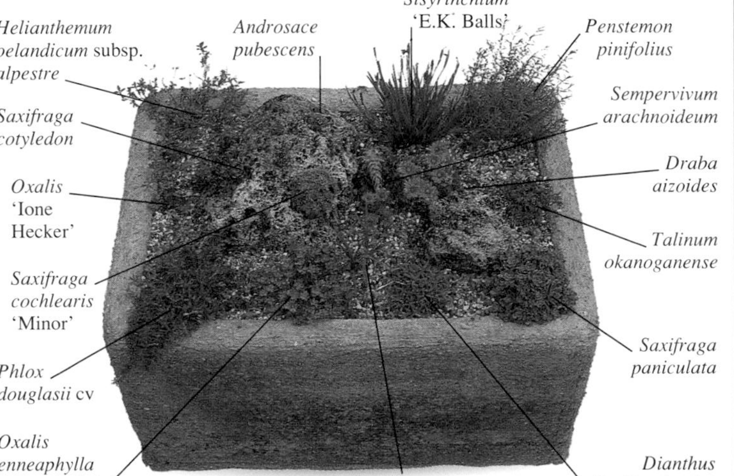

Walls

Alpines and rock garden plants may be grown in the crevices of dry-stone walls, including the retaining walls of raised beds and sloping banks. Trailing plants are especially effective when grown in this way. For details on constructing a wall, see "Dry-stone walls," p.506.

If possible, plan for any planting in walls before construction work starts. The most practical approach is to leave planting niches at intervals in the wall and plant them up when the building work is finished.

It is also possible to position the plants as construction proceeds. This produces excellent results, since the plants can be placed at the desired level, and ensures good contact between the roots of the plants and any soil behind the wall. Planting during construction also makes it easier to eliminate air pockets in the soil mix and to firm soil around the roots.

Planting in existing walls is another option, but some of the soil may need to be removed first with a widger or teaspoon before planting. Replace the original soil mix, or use a fresh mix, to fill the crevices.

How to Build a Dry-stone Retaining Wall

MAKING THE FOOTINGS
Dig a trench 15in (38cm) deep. Fill with 10in (25cm) of crushed stone. Place a large stone on top.

PLACING THE STONES
Slope the stones backward and downward for stability and so that water is carried into the soil mix.

FILLING BETWEEN STONES
As you build, fill crevices between the stones with a mixture of soil, leaf mold, and sand or grit.

Filling with soil mix

To fill the planting crevices in walls, use 3 parts clean garden soil, 2 parts coarse fibrous peat or compost, and 1–2 parts sharp sand or grit.

Use extra grit, sand, or stone chips for plants that are to be grown in the lower planting areas of the wall, since this will help to ensure good drainage. Make sure the drainage materials have the appropriate pH.

Planting

Choose plants that grow well in the exposure and conditions available in the wall. Use seedlings or small rooted cuttings, which are easily inserted into the wall crevices. Carefully remove old soil mix from the roots and ease them into the hole, using a small dibber or a pencil. Do not try to cram roots into too small a space since this damages the plants.

Trickle in fresh, moist soil mix and firm it to remove air pockets. It may be helpful to wedge small stones around the collars of the plants to hold them in place and prevent the soil mix from being dislodged.

Water thoroughly from the top of the wall and spray the plants regularly until established. After several days, top up any sunken areas with more soil mix. Periodically check the plants and firm any that have worked loose.

How to Plant in a Dry-stone Wall

1 *If planting in an existing wall, check that there is an adequate amount of soil mix in the crevices to support the plants.*

2 *Use seedlings or small rooted cuttings. Place them on the flat of a stone and, using a widger, ease the roots into the crevices. The plant shown here is a* Sempervivum.

3 *Bed the plants down into soil mix and pack more soil mix into the crevices to hold the plants in position. Firm the plants in with your fingers.*

4 *For larger plants, scoop out some soil mix from the crevices. Ease the roots into the holes and add more soil mix while holding plants in position.*

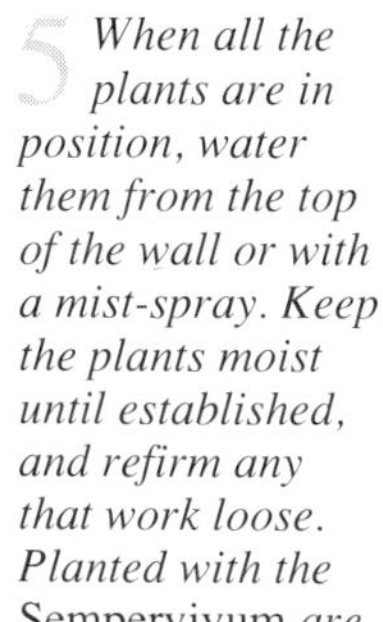

5 *When all the plants are in position, water them from the top of the wall or with a mist-spray. Keep the plants moist until established, and refirm any that work loose. Planted with the* Sempervivum *are two saxifrages.*

Raised beds

A wide range of alpine plants can be grown in raised beds, both in the beds themselves and in crevices in the supporting walls. The bed's design should harmonize with the house and garden. Depending on the needs of the chosen plants, a raised bed may be positioned in either sun or shade. Fill the bed with well-drained soil mix to suit the plants (see p.196). If necessary, plants may be protected in winter with glass or plastic covers placed over the bed.

Siting

For most alpines and rock garden plants, raised beds should be sited in an open, sunny position away from the shade cast by overhanging trees or nearby buildings and fences. Place a raised bed in shade only if woodland or other plants requiring cooler, shadier conditions are to be grown.

To aid mowing, a raised bed that is positioned on a lawn should have a border of paving slabs or bricks set just below the level of the grass. Raised beds that are constructed for elderly or impaired gardeners should have wheelchair access, and the beds should be of a height and width to allow the plants to be tended and viewed easily.

On sites where the construction of a ground-based scree bed is not possible because of poor drainage, a scree may be placed on the surface of a raised bed instead (see p.197).

Materials and design

Raised beds can be made from old wooden railroad ties, pressure-treated lumber, stone, brick, or other suitable material. Stone is the costliest; new or secondhand bricks and ties are cheaper and easier to use.

The bed may be almost any shape, but it should harmonize with the general design of the garden. Rectangular beds are the most common. The ideal height for a raised bed is 24–30in (60–75cm), although a tiered bed is also attractive and may be more appropriate where space is limited. The width should be no more than 5ft (1.5m) to allow comfortable access – the center of the bed should be within arm's reach to allow weeding from all sides.

Large beds may need an irrigation system; install water pipes and outlets before filling the beds with soil mix.

Construction

Retaining brick walls for raised beds should be vertical; the thickness of one brick is usually adequate. They are built in the same way as a conventional wall and may be mortared, but small gaps should be left between bricks at intervals for plants to be inserted. There should also be gaps at the base for drainage. For further information, see STRUCTURES AND SURFACES, "Raised beds," p.507.

Raised beds may also have stone retaining walls. If they are built without mortar, they need a slight inward slope for stability (see "Dry-stone walls," p.506). Dry-stone walls are time-consuming to build, since each stone needs to be chosen and positioned carefully. Either small or large crevices can be left between the stones to be planted with alpines. If railroad ties are used, crevice planting is not possible.

Soil for raised beds

Use a mix of 3 parts clean garden soil, 2 parts coarse fibrous peat, acidic leaf mold, or compost, and 1–2 parts grit or sharp sand, pea gravel, or crushed stone. For plants that need acid conditions, use lime-free soil, organic matter, and grit. To grow plants that need different soil types in a large bed, divide it into sections with plastic sheeting to keep the sections apart, and fill each with an appropriate soil mix.

Preparing the raised bed

Fill the bottom third of the bed with coarse gravel or stones, then place a layer of inverted sod or fibrous peat over the top to prevent the drainage material from becoming clogged. Fill the bed with prepared soil mix, which should be well worked into all the corners and firmed as filling proceeds. Incorporate a balanced organic or slow-release fertilizer. Some settling always occurs, so water the bed thoroughly and leave it for two or three weeks. Top up any sunken areas with more soil mix before planting.

Adding rocks gives the look of a rock garden in miniature and enhances the appearance of raised beds. Set pieces of rock of varying sizes into the soil mix to provide suitable sites for a range of different plants. Several large pieces of rock arranged together as outcrops are more visually pleasing than scattered rocks.

Planting and top-dressing

Make a planting plan or set out the plants on the surface of the bed to see how they will look. Dwarf conifers and small shrubs, tufted and cushion-forming alpines, trailing alpines (at the edges of the bed), and some of the smaller bulbs are ideal. Select plants for year-round interest. Plant as for rock gardens (see p.196), with trailing plants near the edges; any crevices in the retaining walls may also be planted up as for dry-stone walls (see opposite).

After planting, top-dress the bed with stone chips or coarse grit, to match any rocks. Work a ½in (1cm) deep layer of the top-dressing carefully around the plants and beneath their collars. This looks attractive, suppresses weeds, and reduces evaporation. Water the bed regularly until the plants are established.

Winter protection

Many alpines dislike excessive winter moisture, even in the well-drained conditions of a raised bed. Where winter snow is unreliable, protect alpines with cloches or sheets of glass or plastic. Use bricks or a wire frame to support the sheets, and fasten down the covering.

Such protection should be put in place in late fall and removed the following spring. If the whole bed needs covering, build a wooden framework for a glass or plastic roof. Plenty of air must circulate around the plants so that they remain as dry as possible, so do not cover the sides of the protective frame.

A RAISED ALPINE BED

A wide range of alpine plants can be grown in a raised bed, both in the bed itself and in crevices in the retaining walls. If rocks are included, these will provide sunny and shady exposures to suit the needs of different plants.

1 *Androsace lanuginosa*
2 *Saponaria* x *olivana*
3 *Origanum* 'Kent Beauty'
4 *Cytisus ardoinii*
5 *Daphne petraea* 'Grandiflora'
6 *Anchusa caespitosa*
7 *Globularia meridionalis*
8 *Penstemon pinifolius*
9 *Dianthus alpinus*
10 *Androsace carnea* subsp. *laggeri*
11 *Edraianthus serpyllifolius*
12 *Saxifraga scardica*
13 *Helichrysum selago*
14 *Morisia monanthos*
15 *Anacyclus depressus*
16 *Erinacea pungens*
17 *Saxifraga* 'Southside Seedling'
18 *Saxifraga burseriana*
19 *Phlox* 'Camla'
20 *Androsace pyrenaica*
21 *Saxifraga grisebachii* 'Wisley Variety'
22 *Parnassia palustris*
23 *Draba rigida*
24 *Euryops acraeus*
25 *Dianthus* 'La Bourboule'
26 *Androsace carnea*
27 *Daphne arbuscula*
28 *Bolax gummifera*
29 *Penstemon newberryi* f. *humilior*
30 *Dianthus pavonius*
31 *Gentiana verna*
32 *Sagina boydii*
33 *Saxifraga* 'Jenkinsiae'
34 *Saxifraga oppositifolia*
35 *Corydalis solida* 'George Baker'
36 *Cyananthus microphyllus*
37 *Phlox stolonifera* 'Ariane'
38 *Soldanella alpina*
39 *Ranunculus alpestris*
40 *Calceolaria* 'Walter Shrimpton'
41 *Gentiana saxosa*
42 *Edraianthus pumilio*
43 *Vitaliana primuliflora*
44 *Daphne cneorum*
45 *Lewisia*, Cotyledon Hybrids
46 *Raoulia australis*
47 *Phlox bifida*
48 *Androsace villosa*
49 *Lewisia* 'George Henley'
50 *Ramonda myconi*
51 *Arenaria balearica*

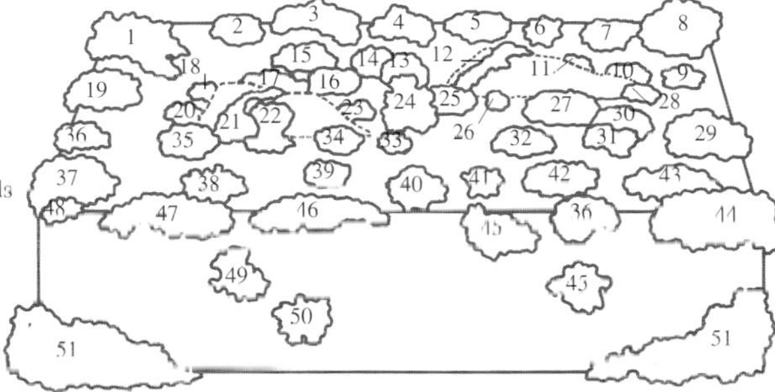

How to Construct a Peat Bed

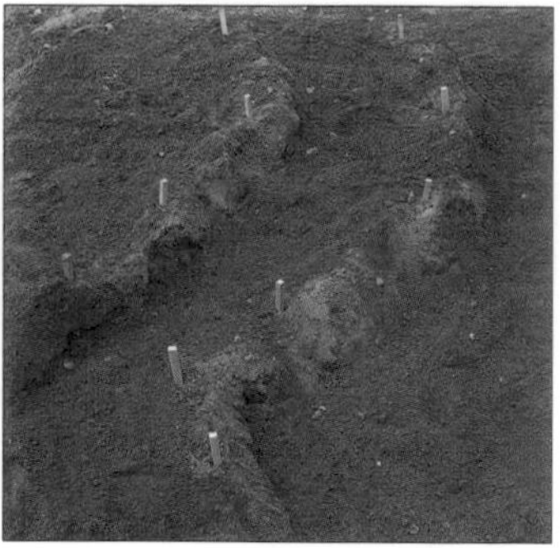

1 Use a site that is clear of perennial weeds, and remove annual weeds. Mark contours with sticks, and terrace the slope with 30in (75cm) wide steps.

2 Soak the peat blocks before use. Make a shallow trench at the base of the lowest step and lay a wall of vertical peat blocks, sloping them inward. Butt them together and firm.

3 Fill the terraces to the top of the blocks with 2 parts peat, 2 parts acid soil (with slow-release fertilizer), and 1 part lime-free sharp sand or grit.

Alternative Method

Lay the peat blocks horizontally. Push stakes down through the blocks to hold them in place.

4 When all the terraces are filled, allow the peat bed to settle for several days. Water the bed regularly during this period to keep the peat moist and top up with further soil mix, if necessary, before planting.

THE FINISHED BED
Plant up the bed with acid-loving rock garden plants and compact, slow-growing shrubs for a fine display. Water often to keep the peat blocks and soil mix moist, especially in the first year. Top-dress the bed with bark chips to conserve moisture and suppress weeds.

Peat beds

Peat beds provide ideal conditions for a wide range of acid-loving and woodland plants. In gardens with alkaline soils, peat beds should always be isolated from the ground with a plastic or butyl rubber liner so that lime cannot enter the soil.

Consider the needs of the plants when deciding where to place a peat bed, and construct the bed so that it blends in well with the rest of the garden. It is not necessary to use pure peat if acidic peat substitutes are locally available. Plants may be grown on the surface of the bed and in wall crevices to produce an attractive arrangement.

Siting

Choose a site that receives sun and dappled shade, ideally facing away from direct sun. An area next to a rock garden, on a slope, or by the side of a building is appropriate. Peat beds on exposed sites in full sun lose moisture rapidly and need frequent watering. Dense tree shade is unsuitable, and the tree roots nearby soon exhaust the moisture and nutrients. Waterlogged sites and frost pockets are also not suitable.

Materials and design

Peat blocks can be used to build the walls of the bed, although these are difficult to obtain unless you live in an area where peat is harvested. Other suitable materials include logs and railroad ties.

On a slope, the materials may be arranged in steps to create terraces. The steps can be either straight or curved, but it is important to make the finished structure look fairly natural. On flat sites, peat beds may be constructed with retaining walls in a similar way to raised beds.

Constructing the bed

Mark out the shape of the bed with a length of rope or hose. On soils where lime is present, lay a sheet of heavy-duty plastic or butyl rubber to isolate the bed from the underlying soil and prevent any seepage of lime into the soil mix. Mound the ground under the sheet so that excess moisture drains off, with a layer of sand on top to prevent stones from damaging the sheet. Tuck its edges into a surrounding trench.

If peat blocks are used, they should be soaked thoroughly with water and then allowed to drain before building the walls or terraces of the bed. To make terraces on a sloping site, place peat blocks or logs in an upright position in a stepped formation. Seat them well into the ground to ensure stability, and backfill with an acidic soil mix.

If building a peat bed with retaining walls, set the first layer of blocks, ties, or logs in a shallow trench about 3in (7cm) deep around the perimeter. Angle the blocks so that the inside edges are a little lower than the outer ones. This gives the wall a slight slope and strengthens the structure. Lay subsequent rows of blocks (to a maximum of three layers) on top of the first, so that the joint between each pair of blocks falls in the middle of the block immediately below.

Butt the blocks tightly together and push sharpened stakes vertically down through the blocks at frequent intervals to hold them firmly in place. If desired, leave several gaps between the blocks as niches for planting suitable species.

Filling peat beds

A suitable soil mix for peat beds consists of 2 parts fibrous peat moss, 2 parts fibrous soil (with a low pH), and 1 part lime-free sand or grit. If available, you could also use coconut fiber, well-rotted, sieved compost, and leaf mold, if they are water-retentive. Check the pH of all of the materials intended for the soil mix and do not use any with a pH close to or above 7, since this indicates alkalinity. Add a slow-release, acid-based fertilizer.

Fill the bed with soil mix, treading it down lightly. Water the bed thoroughly and leave it for several days to allow the soil mix to settle. Before planting, top up sunken areas of the bed with additional soil mix.

Planting and top-dressing

Draw up a detailed planting plan on paper or set out the pots on the surface of the bed. Position trailing plants in crevices in the walls, and place small shrubs in the bed itself to provide focal points. Use prostrate shrubs and trailing species to mask the joints between the blocks.

Plant as for rock gardens (see p.196), and insert plants into any crevices as for walls (see p.200). Firm in the plants and water thoroughly. Add extra soil mix after settling, if necessary. Top-dress with bark chips and water regularly during the first season after planting.

Routine care

EVEN when alpines and rock plants are established in the garden, it is essential to care for them regularly. Beds, troughs, and sinks must be kept clean and free of weeds. Although the plants do not usually need nutrient-rich soil, they should be fed at intervals and watered whenever the soil becomes dry. Top-dressings, which improve drainage around the collars of the plants, suppress weed growth, and reduce evaporation of water from the soil, should be replenished occasionally.

Alpines and rock garden plants benefit from periodic removal of dead wood, leaves, and flowers, and should be kept trimmed. Troughs, sinks, and other containers should be replanted as soon as they become overcrowded. Check plants routinely for signs of pest infestation and disease, and treat them as necessary. In cold or wet weather, some plants may need winter protection.

Weeding

The use of clean soil mix when planting should minimize problems with weeds, at least for the first few years. Try to remove all weeds as soon as they appear, certainly before they flower and set seed. If perennial weeds do become established and are difficult to remove, paint the foliage carefully with a systemic weedkiller, which is transmitted to the roots and kills them. For further information, see PLANT PROBLEMS, "Controlling weeds," p.577.

When weeding, use a hand cultivator or weeder to loosen and aerate compacted soil around young plants, if necessary.

Feeding

Newly planted areas should not normally need feeding for some years if the original soil mix has been correctly prepared and includes slow-release fertilizer. After some time, however, the growth of the plants may begin to slow down and flowering become sparser. This can be remedied by gently scratching in around the plants a dressing of bone meal each spring, combined with a slow-release fertilizer.

Alternatively, carefully remove the top-dressing and a layer of about ½in (1cm) of soil mix from the surface of the bed and replace it with fresh soil mix and a further top-dressing of grit.

Top-dressing

The type of top-dressing used for alpines and rock garden plants depends on the plants that are grown, although it should match any of the rocks and stones that feature in beds and rock gardens as closely as possible. Any top-dressings used in troughs, sinks, or raised beds should also harmonize well with the container or retaining walls.

Coarse grit or stone chips are suitable for most situations, but limestone chips should not be used around lime-hating plants. For plants grown in peat beds, a top-dressing of bark chips will complement the plantings and conserve moisture.

Renewing top-dressings

Top-dressings may need to be renewed from time to time, since grit or stone chips gradually wash away, especially on slopes, and bark tends to decompose and mix in with the underlying soil mix. Watch for bare patches throughout the season and top up as necessary. Pay close attention to top-dressings in the fall, to ensure good soil coverage in winter and to avoid compaction by heavy rain. Check again in early spring and top up as necessary. A slow-release fertilizer may be applied at the same time.

Watering

Established plants growing in rock gardens and screes root deeply into the soil and do not usually need more water than is supplied by rainfall. In droughts, however, the area should be thoroughly soaked. Do not water in very cold conditions or during the heat of the day; early mornings or late evenings are the best times. Soak occasionally rather than giving small amounts of water frequently. If the soil mix is dry at a depth of 1¼–2in (3–5cm), water thoroughly until the water has penetrated to the full depth of the roots. During an average summer this may be needed only two or three times, but in very dry summers it may be required more frequently.

WEEDING

Weed around young plants with a Cape Cod weeder or similar tool, which also loosens and aerates the soil. Remove any top-dressing first and replace it after weeding.

RENEWING TOP-DRESSING

1 *Remove the old top-dressing and some soil mix (see inset) Fill in around the plants with fresh soil mix (see p.196).*

2 *Top-dress the bed with a fresh layer of coarse grit or gravel, adding some around and beneath the collars of the plants.*

Watering in containers, raised beds, and under cover

Alpines and rock garden plants that are grown in raised beds, sinks and troughs, under frames, and in the alpine house will need more regular watering, since the soil dries out more quickly than in rock gardens and scree beds.

It is preferable to hand-water troughs and sinks if specialist collections of plants are being grown, so that each plant may be provided with the correct amount of water. This is time-consuming, however, particularly where there are several containers to be watered.

Plants grown in pots in alpine houses and frames should be watered individually. If the pots are plunged in gravel or stone chips, water both the pots and the surrounding material. Some alpine plants have water-sensitive foliage and therefore dislike overhead watering; if this is the case, regularly soaking only the plunge material should provide sufficient moisture for these plants.

Trimming and pruning

Alpines and rock garden plants need to be cut back periodically to maintain a natural, compact shape and healthy growth, and to restrict them within their allotted space.

Pruning woody plants

To keep rock garden shrubs and woody perennials healthy, remove any dead, diseased, or damaged wood. Check the plants regularly and prune them cleanly, using pruners or sharp scissors.

Severe pruning is unnecessary because most dwarf shrubs are slow-growing and do not outgrow their positions for many years. When

REMOVING DEAD GROWTH

In spring, after all danger of frost has passed, cut out any dieback from plants, trimming stems back carefully to healthy growth with sharp scissors or pruners.

Removing Dead Rosettes

1 *To remove dead rosettes from plants such as saxifrages, cut out the rosettes with a sharp knife without disturbing the rest of the plant.*

2 *Top-dress the exposed soil to prevent weeds growing through the gaps until the plant produces fresh growth.*

Cutting Back after Flowering

1 *After flowering, cut back stems (here* Helianthemum*) to half their length to encourage healthy, new growth.*

2 *The plants will remain compact and produce a good crop of flowers the following year.*

Renovating an Alpine Bed

1 *Plants that spread rapidly (here* Paronychia kapela *subsp.* chionaea*) may eventually smother less vigorous plants nearby. Cut them back in spring.*

2 *Dig up or pull out clumps of encroaching plants. Straggly plants should be cut back severely. Make sure that plants nearby have plenty of room to grow.*

3 *Add a dressing of balanced fertilizer to the bed, before placing a fresh layer of top-dressing on the surface of the soil mix around the plants.*

pruning, aim to maintain the natural shape of the plant, especially in the case of dwarf conifers.

Removing dead flowers and foliage

Regularly remove all dead flowers and leaves, and any unwanted or unsightly seedheads, with a sharp knife, pruners, or scissors.

Pick over small alpine plants by hand, using tweezers, if necessary, to remove dead leaves and flowers. Carefully cut out dead rosettes from plants such as saxifrages; do not pull them off by hand, however, because this may loosen healthy rosettes.

Helianthemum species and cultivars, in particular, need clipping annually after flowering, cutting back the stems by about half their length to encourage growth for flowering the following year. Genera such as *Arabis*, *Aubrieta*, and *Aurinia* also benefit from a hard annual pruning after flowering, which helps to keep them compact and free-flowering. Some plants may produce a second flush of flowers if cut back before they set seed.

Encroaching plants

Overvigorous plants and old, straggly ones that start to encroach on their neighbors should be cut back in early spring. Mat-forming plants may simply be pulled out by hand; others may need to be lifted with a hand fork. Support nearby plants and refirm any that are accidentally lifted. Remove or cut back plants to allow a clear area of bed around all the remaining plants so that they can grow unimpeded. Hard-pruned plants should be top-dressed with a balanced fertilizer in order to promote strong, new growth.

Replanting an alpine trough

Plants in containers eventually need replanting when nutrients in the soil mix are exhausted. Water thoroughly before carefully removing the plants. Discard the soil mix and replace it with a fresh, suitable mix (see p.196), containing a slow-release fertilizer. Trim roots and top-growth before returning plants to the container, allowing for their eventual spread. Top-dress with gravel.

Winter protection

Plants in troughs, sinks, or raised beds, and some alpine bulbs, may need protection from winter moisture. Use a single, propped pane of glass, an open cloche, or, for large areas, a cold frame sash, which will give overhead protection without inhibiting air circulation. Ensure that covers are firmly secured or weighted down. Snow retention can be increased by placing a layer of evergreen branches or pine boughs loosely over the plants.

Controlling pests and diseases

Few serious problems affect alpines and rock garden plants, but some of the more common pests and diseases may need to be controlled. Regular, basic garden hygiene is often sufficient to control most problems encountered. Aphids (p.552) are likely to be troublesome if alpines are grown in too rich a soil, which induces soft, lank growth.

Coarse top-dressings around plants tend to deter slugs and snails (p.550) but some control is still necessary, particularly for choice alpines, such as *Campanula zoysii*, which are susceptible to attack from these pests. Control insects such as ants (p.572), which will excavate under cushion-forming plants. Prevent birds from disturbing newly planted specimens by covering the plants with netting.

Fungal diseases may quickly become established in alpine houses and frames (see "Hygiene," p.212).

Propagation

MANY alpines and rock garden plants may be propagated from seed, although some plants are sterile and do not produce seeds. In addition, cultivars seldom come true from seed and must be increased in other ways. Alternative methods include cuttings and division.

Seed

Propagation from seed is the best way to produce large numbers of plants. Since many alpines flower in early spring, ripe seed is often available from midsummer, and may be sown immediately. Germination will usually occur rapidly and strong seedlings will be produced before winter. Fall-sown seeds can remain dormant until spring; if germination occurs, overwinter the seedlings in frames. It may sometimes be better to store seeds over winter and sow in early spring, although short-lived seeds should be sown as soon as they are ripe.

Seed collection and storage

Collect seeds as the seedheads become ripe. Remove them while still attached to the stems and place them in paper (not plastic) bags to dry out. Enclose in envelopes any that might split open on drying. Store seeds in a cool, dry, well-ventilated place. Most alpines have seed capsules from which the seeds can be extracted by rubbing between the fingers. Fleshy fruits may need to be squashed and left on paper to dry.

Separate the seeds from the debris by sieving or hand-picking when dry. Put in envelopes, label, and seal, and place these in an airtight container in a cool place.

Presowing treatment

Seeds with hard coats need special treatment to allow them to absorb water. Scarify by chipping the seed coat with a sharp knife or rubbing with a file or fine abrasive paper. In some cases, soaking the seeds for 12–24 hours will accelerate the take-up of water.

Hard-cased seeds of woody rock garden plants do not respond to scarification alone; they also need exposure to cold (stratification). Store the seeds in boxes of moist sand outdoors for two or three months during winter, and sow in spring; alternatively, sow the seed in pots of seed soil mix and keep these in the freezer or refrigerator, sealed in plastic bags, for several weeks before plunging the pots in the ground outside until the seeds germinate. Some seeds, such as *Trillium* and peonies (*Paeonia*), need alternating periods of cold and warmth to germinate successfully.

Sowing the seed

Use clean clay or plastic pots, and place broken crocks over the drainage holes. A soil mix of equal parts sieved peat and perlite is suitable, or use soil-based seed soil mix, mixed with an equal amount of perlite or sharp sand. Fill the pots and firm the soil mix. Tap out small seeds thinly and evenly and space large seeds by hand, covering them to their depth with soil mix. Mix fine seeds with fine, dry sand before sowing, but do not cover with more soil mix.

After sowing, cover all but fine seeds with a 1/4–1/2in (5–10mm) layer of 1/4in (5mm) diameter grit or pea gravel, to deter mosses and liverworts and to protect the seeds from heavy rain or watering. Label the pots and stand them in water to half their depth, removing them when the soil mix surface becomes moist. Keep the soil mix moist.

Germination

Speed of germination depends on the type and age of the seeds, and when they are sown. Some seeds take months or years to germinate.

A cool, sheltered site outdoors is ideal for the seeds of most alpines. Plunge pots in moist sand to maintain an even temperature and reduce the need for watering. When seedlings appear, move the pots to a cold frame. Germination can be speeded up by placing the pots in gentle heat in early spring, but do not expose the seeds to high temperatures.

Pricking out and potting up

Prick out seedlings when they are 1/4–1/2in (5–10mm) tall and when two true leaves have formed. Knock out the soil mix and separate the seedlings. Handle only by the leaves or cotyledons to avoid damage to stems and roots. Pot up seedlings individually in small clay pots or plastic pots, or in cell packs using low-fertility soil-based potting mix combined with an equal amount of grit. Fill the container, settle the soil mix, and make a hole for the roots. Put the seedling in the hole, fill with soil mix, and firm lightly.

Top-dress seedlings in individual pots with a 1/4–1/2in (5–10mm) layer of grit. Water thoroughly with a fine spray, and place the containers in a lightly shaded position until the seedlings are established. Water them as required. When the roots are visible through the drainage holes, pot them on.

Seeds that are slow to germinate often do so erratically, and if only a few seedlings appear, prick them out as soon as they are large enough to handle. Disturb the rest of the soil mix as little as possible, and cover it with fresh top-dressing. Put the pot back into the frame in case more seeds germinate, and pot up the seedlings as they emerge.

Rock Plant Seed to be Sown Fresh

Anemone
Celmisia
Codonopsis
Corydalis
Cyclamen (alpine spp.)
Dodecatheon
Hepatica
Meconopsis
Primula (alpine spp.)
Pulsatilla
Ranunculus (alpine spp.)

Sowing Seed

1 *Prepare a pot by filling it with equal parts of seed soil mix and horticultural sand. Firm the soil mix gently to level the surface and to eliminate air pockets.*

2 *Small seeds (here Lewisia) should be tapped out evenly over the surface of the soil mix. Space larger seeds by hand.*

3 *Cover the seeds with a fine layer of soil mix, then top-dress with grit to protect the seeds and prevent the growth of mosses. Water in and label.*

4 *Prick out seedlings when they have 2 true leaves (see inset). Lift the seedlings carefully, handling them by the leaves only.*

5 *Fill pots with equal parts of soil-based potting mix and grit. Pot up the seedlings singly, firming with a dibber.*

6 *Top-dress with grit, water, and place the seedlings in light shade. Pot on the seedlings when the roots fill the pot.*

Rock Plants that may be Propagated by Cuttings

Softwood
Adenophora
Anchusa caespitosa
Anthemis
Asyneuma
Aubrieta
Campanula, some ❄

Aubrieta deltoidea 'Argenteo-variegata'

Cassiope
Daphne jasminea
Dianthus, some ❄
Dionysia
Draba
Eriogonum ovalifolium
Eriophyllum lanatum
Gypsophila aretioides, *G. repens*
Penstemon, some ❄
Phlox, some ❄
Polygala, some ❄
Primula (alpine spp.)
Silene acaulis
Viola, some ❄

Viola 'Jackanapes'

Greenwood
Aubrieta
Aurinia
Cassiope
Erodium, some ❄
Geranium, some ❄

Semiripe
Cassiope
Claytonia
Clematis alpina, *C.* x *cartmanii* 'Joe'
Convolvulus boissieri, *C. sabatius*
Daphne
Diascia
Erica, some ❄
Erinacea anthyllis
Hebe, some ❄
Helianthemum

Helianthemum 'Fire Dragon'

Key
❄ *Not frost hardy*

Softwood and greenwood cuttings

Softwood cuttings are taken from the nonflowering, leafy shoots of a plant during periods of active growth, usually in spring.

Greenwood cuttings are taken in early summer when growth has slowed down; although slightly riper than softwood cuttings, they require the same treatment.

Taking the cuttings

Take the cuttings early in the morning, when the shoots are fully turgid. For softwood cuttings select strong, young shoots that are soft and pliable, with no trace of woodiness or hardening. In contrast, greenwood cuttings may be just beginning to harden at the base. Take cuttings about 1–3in (2.5–7cm) in length, using a sharp knife. Place them immediately in a plastic bag to conserve moisture and to prevent them from wilting.

Inserting the cuttings

Trim the base of each cutting cleanly with a sharp knife just below a node (leaf joint) and remove the lower leaves. Pinch off any shoot tips that are soft, particularly if these are showing signs of wilting.

Fill pots with standard cuttings soil mix and make holes for the cuttings with a small dibber. Insert each cutting into the soil mix by up to half its length so that the lowest leaf is just above the surface.

Label the cuttings and water with a fungicide solution, then place them in a closed propagator with gentle bottom heat, or in a mist propagation unit. Alternatively, seal the pots in plastic bags. Keep the cuttings in good light but out of direct sun, because otherwise the air and soil temperature may become too hot and the cuttings will wilt.

Remove dead and diseased cuttings with tweezers, since these may infect their healthy neighbors. Watering is seldom required until after rooting. Look for signs of new growth, and check for rooting by gently pulling at the cuttings. Once they are well rooted, pot them up.

Potting up

Water the rooted cuttings well, and gently slide them out of the pot. Carefully separate them before potting them up individually, using equal parts of soil mix and grit.

Top-dress with a 1/2in (1cm) layer of sharp grit. Water the cuttings thoroughly and return them to the propagator, keeping them out of direct sun. Keep the cuttings well watered. Once fresh growth appears, place the cuttings in a cold frame and harden them off carefully before planting them out.

Semiripe and ripewood cuttings

Semiripe cuttings are taken in mid- to late summer from nonflowering shoots of the current season's growth. The shoots offer distinct resistance to pressure when bent gently and should be beginning to harden at the base. Ripewood cuttings are taken from evergreen plants during late summer and fall when the wood has fully ripened.

Taking the cuttings

The cuttings will vary in length with the plant concerned from 1/2 to 1 1/2in (1 to 4cm) or more. Cut them from the parent plant using a sharp knife or pruners. Make a clean cut below a node and remove soft tissue at the tips. Remove the lower leaves and dip the ends into hormone rooting powder. Alternatively, take cuttings with a heel and trim the heel with a sharp knife to remove any snags.

Potting up

The following spring, when the cuttings have rooted, repot or pot up those in frames in equal parts soil mix and grit, or plant out in a nursery bed, but only after danger of frost is passed. Water well.

Keep the rooted cuttings moist and sheltered from direct sun. Give them a liquid feed in the growing season. Transplant them into their permanent positions in fall.

Small cuttings root best in pots of cuttings soil mix, topped with a 1/2in (1cm) layer of fine sand. Make holes in the sand and insert the cuttings by one-third to one-half of their length. Label, water with a fungicide, and place in a propagator in a cool greenhouse. Check regularly for disease. Water sparingly and, as growth begins, apply a dilute liquid feed.

If large numbers of cuttings are taken, they can be inserted into a cold frame with drainage at the base. Fork over the soil in the frame and then add a mixture of 1 part peat or compost and 1 part grit; top with a 1in (2.5cm) layer of sand. After inserting the cuttings, water them and close the frame. Open the frame in mild weather. If there is a danger of frost, insulate the frame.

Softwood Cuttings

1 *In spring, choose young, nonflowering shoots (here, from* Gypsophila repens) *and take cuttings 1–3in (2.5–7cm) long. Put the cuttings in a plastic bag.*

2 *Trim off the base of the cuttings, and the lower leaves and soft tips (see inset). Fill a pot with moist soil mix, inserting the cuttings by up to half their length.*

3 *Water and label the cuttings. Place the pot in a sealed plastic bag, keeping it in good light but out of direct sun.*

4 *When rooted, pot up the cuttings singly, holding them by the leaves only. Top-dress the pots, water well, and label.*

Leaf cuttings

This method is suitable for plants with fleshy leaves, such as *Haberlea*, *Ramonda*, and *Sedum*.

Using a sharp knife, cut healthy, strong, and relatively young leaves from the stem at their base. Prepare pots with a mixture of equal parts of standard cuttings soil mix and sand. Insert each cutting at a 45° angle, so that it is just held in place by the soil mix. Enclose each pot in a plastic bag and, when the plantlets appear, pot them up individually.

Basal cuttings

Some plants, such as *Primula marginata* and its cultivars, may be propagated from basal cuttings. These are taken from young shoots at the base of the plant at, or just above, soil level. Basal cuttings are usually taken in spring, but may also be taken in summer or fall.

Use a well-drained, commercial cuttings soil mix, or a mix of equal parts of soil and peat or compost with 2 parts grit. Fill pots with soil mix, and firm.

Trim the base of each cutting cleanly just below a node. Make sure that the cutting is not hollow at the base. Remove the lower leaves and dip the base in hormone powder.

Insert one-third to one-half of each stem into the soil mix, keeping the leaves clear of the soil. Water well and place the pots in a shaded, closed propagator or cold frame. Rooting takes three to six weeks, after which the cuttings can be potted up individually or lined out in nursery beds or a cold frame to grow on.

BASAL CUTTINGS

In spring, take cuttings 2–3in (5–7cm) long with new leaves and a short stem. Trim the base and remove the lower leaves, inserting the cuttings to the depth indicated.

Selecting cutting material

For all types of cutting, always choose strong, healthy stems or leaves that show no sign of pests or diseases. Nonflowering shoots that are in active growth should be used. Except for basal cuttings, do not take the cuttings from the base of any plant, because this part may be weaker than elsewhere. Do not take all the cuttings from the same area on the parent plant since this may make it look lopsided.

After taking the cuttings, immediately place them in a clean plastic bag to prevent any moisture loss. Many cuttings will root readily if they are inserted into pots of cuttings soil mix with added grit. Alternatively, simply use washed river sand. Insert the cuttings at the depths indicated.

SEMIRIPE (Phlox) *In mid- to late summer, select shoots that are just hardening but not woody. Remove $1^1/_4$in (3cm) lengths, trimming to about $^1/_2$in (1cm).*

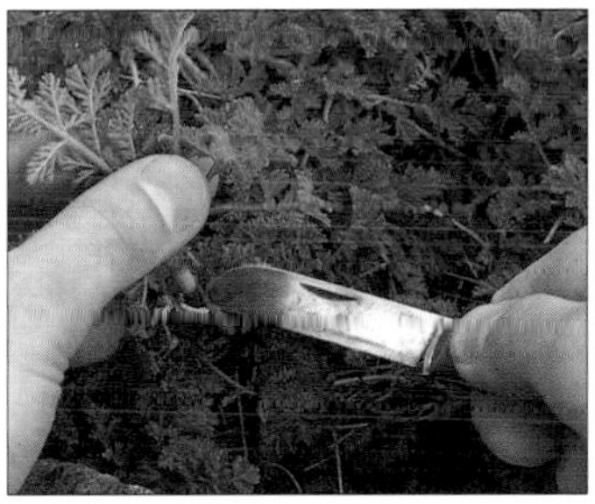

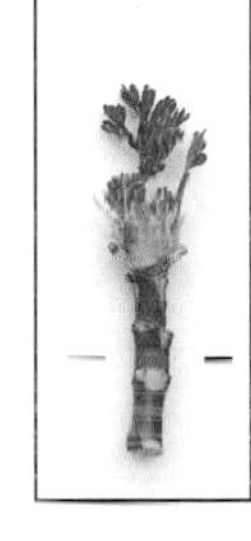

GREENWOOD (Erodium) *Take cuttings from the soft tips of new shoots in early summer. Remove 1–3in (2.5–7cm) lengths and trim them to about $^1/_2$in (1cm).*

ROSETTE (Saxifraga) *In early to mid-summer, select new rosettes. Cut the rosettes about $^1/_2$in (1cm) below the leaves. Trim each cleanly across the base.*

RIPEWOOD (Dryas) *In late summer and fall, select new shoots and take cuttings that are about 1in (2.5cm) long. Trim them to about $^1/_2$in (1cm) below the base of the leaves.*

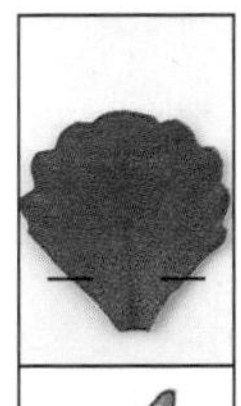

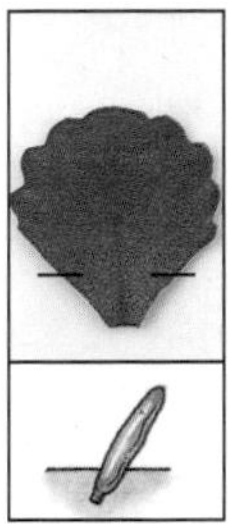

LEAF (Sedum) *Throughout the growing season, select mature leaves that are undamaged, cutting off selected leaves. Trim each cleanly across the base.*

ROCK PLANTS THAT MAY BE PROPAGATED BY CUTTINGS (CONT.)

Semiripe (cont.)
Helichrysum selago
Lepidium nanum
Lewisia
Linum arboreum

Polygala chamaebuxus

Lithodora diffusa
Origanum amanum, *O. rotundifolium*
Parahebe catarractae
Phlox 'Chatahoochee', *P. subulata*
Polygala
Rhododendron
Veronica

Dryas octopetala

Ripewood
Dryas
Eriogonum
Juniperus communis 'Compressa'
Rosa
Salix

Rosette
Androsace
Armeria juniperifolia
Azorella trifurcata
Bolax gummifera
Draba
Helichrysum milfordiae
Jovibarba
Saxifraga, some ❄
Sempervivum

Sempervivum tectorum

Leaf
Haberlea
Jancaea, syn. *Jankaea*
Lewisia
Primula gracilipes
Ramonda
Sedum, some ❄
Sempervivum

KEY
❄ *Not frost hardy*

Division

Many alpines and rock garden plants can be successfully propagated by division. In some cases, division is the only possible method of increasing the stock if seed is rarely produced or the plant is sterile.

Plants that are particularly suitable for division include mat-forming species, which produce a mass of fibrous roots, and clump-forming plants that produce clusters of shoots that are readily separated.

Rock Plants that may be Propagated by Irishman's Cuttings

Achillea ageratifolia
Arenaria montana
Aurinia
Gentiana acaulis, G. verna
Phlox subulata
Primula auricula,
P. marginata
Silene
Veronica peduncularis

Rock Plants that may be Divided

Achillea ageratifolia
Alchemilla alpina,
A. ellenbeckii
Allium sikkimense
Antennaria dioica
Arenaria montana
Artemisia schmidtiana 'Nana'
Campanula carpatica,
C. cochleariifolia
Chiastophyllum oppositifolium
Gentiana acaulis,
G. sino-ornata

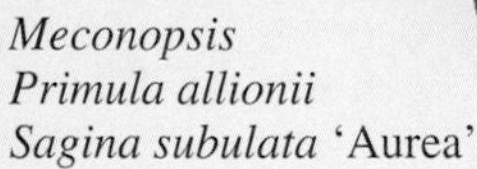

Gentiana sino-ornata

Meconopsis
Primula allionii
Sagina subulata 'Aurea'

Rock Plants that may be Propagated by Root Cuttings

Anacyclus depressus
Carduncellus rhaponticoides
Centaurea pindicola
Gentiana lutea
Geranium, some ❄
Meconopsis delavayi
Morisia monanthos
Papaver lateritium
Phlox mesoleuca
Primula denticulata
Pulsatilla
Roscoea cautleoides

Key
❄ *Not frost hardy*

A number of clump-forming plants have a tendency to die out at the center. These may be divided to rejuvenate them by replanting only the youngest, most vigorous pieces.

When to divide

Most plants are best divided in early spring, when new growth is just beginning. Do not divide plants in cold and frosty weather, or when the ground is frozen or waterlogged.

Plants can also be divided in early fall, which allows new roots to be made while the soil is still warm. Where hard winters are expected, spring division may be safer, since this allows a full growing season for establishment. Some plants, for example *Primula* and *Meconopsis*, should be divided immediately after flowering, when they enter a period of strong vegetative growth. They must be well watered after replanting until they are fully reestablished.

How to divide

Lift plants and shake off the soil. For large clumps, insert the tines of two garden forks back-to-back into the center of the clump; lever the plant into two halves. Tease these smaller clumps apart by hand or cut them with a sharp knife to produce a number of small pieces with healthy roots and growth buds. The older, woody, central part of the plant should be discarded.

If not replanting or potting up the divisions immediately, wrap them in plastic bags or moist burlap and store them out of direct sun. Divisions of most hardy plants can be replanted immediately into their permanent positions. If, however, plants are particularly precious, or the divisions are quite small, it may be safer to pot them up and place them in a cold frame until they are established before planting them out. Use 1 part low-fertility soil-based potting mix and 1 part grit or a lime-free mix for acid-lovers. If replanting in the open ground, make holes large enough to allow the roots to be spread out fully. Firm in and water well. Keep the soil moist until the plants are established.

Irishman's Cuttings

1 *Lift the rooted shoots close to the base of the plant (here* Veronica*) and remove them with a sharp knife. Trim off side shoots and straggly roots (see inset).*

2 *Pot up the cuttings individually. Place a little gritty soil mix in a pot, insert the cutting, then add more soil mix. Firm gently, water, and top-dress.*

How to Propagate by Division

1 *Plants with fibrous roots (here* Gentiana acaulis*) may be divided and replanted to provide new plants. Lift a clump of the parent plant and shake off the soil.*

2 *Using hand forks back-to-back, loosen the root mass and divide the clump into pieces. If necessary, cut away sections from the clump with a knife.*

3 *The plants should have a good root system. Replant them outdoors into their permanent positions, firming around the roots. Add top-dressing around the plants and water thoroughly with a fine spray.*

Irishman's cuttings

These are essentially side shoots that have already rooted. Thymes and other creeping rock plants produce this sort of cutting. The technique is particularly useful for plants with woody rootstocks that are not easily divided, or for those that naturally produce offsets or runners.

Before taking the cuttings, brush away surface soil from the base of the parent plant. Cut rooted pieces from the plant with a sharp knife and pot them up in equal parts of low-fertility soil-based potting mix and grit. Alternatively, plant them out in a cool, sheltered spot in the garden until well established.

Root cuttings

A limited number of alpines and rock garden plants, for example *Geranium sanguineum* and *Primula denticulata*, may be propagated from root cuttings. Take root cuttings from the healthiest-looking roots in either late fall or early winter, when the plants are dormant.

Selecting material
Choose a strong, healthy plant and lift it from the soil. Select young, vigorous roots and cut them from the parent plant. The cuttings should be about 2in (5cm) long. Cut the roots straight across at the top end (nearest the plant's stem) and use sloping cuts at the lower end (nearest the root tips). Wash the cuttings in tepid water and replant the parent stock immediately or, if old and straggly and no longer required, discard it.

Inserting the cuttings
Use pots at least 4in (10cm) deep. Put broken crocks over the drainage holes and place over these a 1in (2.5cm) layer of low-fertility soil-based potting mix. Fill the pots with washed sand, then firm. Make several planting holes in each pot around the edges.

Insert the cuttings into the holes, with the straight ends uppermost and the tops level with the surface of the sand. Cuttings of plants with thin, wiry roots can be laid flat on the surface of the soil mix. Top-dress with fine grit. Label the pots, water thoroughly, and place them in a cold frame on a layer of grit or gravel or in a propagator. Close the frames in cold weather; otherwise, they should be ventilated freely.

Water the pots when new growth appears. When the new shoots are growing strongly, check that the cuttings have made new roots before potting them up: gently knock them out of their pots to inspect them.

Potting up rooted cuttings
Slide the cuttings out of their pots and separate them carefully. Pot them up singly, using low-fertility soil-based potting mix combined with an equal amount of sand. Instead of sand, a mix of peat or compost and sand can be used. Top-dress the pots with 1/2in (1cm) of sharp sand or grit. Water and then place outside, out of direct sun. Leave until the new plants are established, watering as required.

HOW TO PROPAGATE BY ROOT CUTTINGS

1 *In late fall or early winter, using a hand fork, carefully lift a healthy plant (here* Primula denticulata) *with a well-developed root system.*

2 *Wash the roots clean of soil, then select thick, healthy roots for the cuttings. Using a sharp knife, cut off selected roots close to the crown of the plant.*

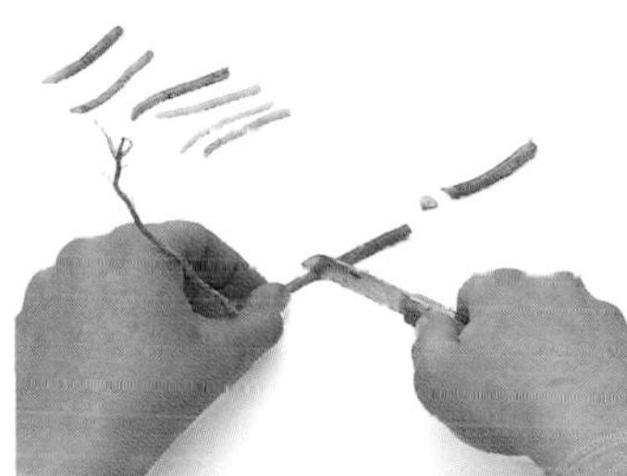

3 *Prepare 2in (5cm) lengths of root, cutting each one straight at the thicker end (closest to the parent plant) and angled at the lower end.*

4 *Place a layer of soil mix in the base of a pot, then fill almost to the brim with sharp sand. Insert the cuttings so that straight ends are just level with the sand surface.*

5 *Cover the sand with a 1/2in (1cm) layer of grit. Water and label the cuttings, then place the pot in a propagator or on the greenhouse bench.*

Scooping rosettes

Plants that grow quickly or form rosettes, for example *Primula denticulata*, may be propagated *in situ* in early spring from root cuttings by scooping out the rosettes with a sharp knife to expose the top of the rootstock. Select strong-growing rosettes and brush the tops of the roots with fungicidal powder to prevent gray mold/*Botrytis* (see p.559); cover them with a thin layer of horticultural sharp sand.

Shoots should soon appear on each root apex. When the shoots are about 1–2in (2.5–5cm) tall, lift the clump carefully with a hand fork. Separate the clump into individual small plants that have healthy-looking, vigorous shoots and roots, pulling them apart by hand or dividing them with a sharp knife.

Pot up the young plants to grow on, using equal parts of potting mix and horticultural sand. Water thoroughly, and place outside in a shady site. Keep moist and plant out the young plants when their roots have filled the pots.

HOW TO SCOOP ROSETTES

1 *Scoop out the live crowns of rosette-forming plants (here* Primula denticulata) *with a sharp knife, so that the tops of the roots are visible (see inset).*

2 *Dust the exposed roots with fungicidal powder (see inset) to protect them from molds and fungi. Lightly cover with sharp horticultural sand.*

3 *When new shoots appear from the roots, lift the whole clump, using a hand fork or trowel. Take care not to damage the new roots.*

4 *Divide the clump into individual plants, each with one shoot and well-developed roots. Pot them up using equal parts potting mix and sand.*

Alpine houses and frames

SOME high-altitude alpines grow well in the open garden in temperate climates, provided that their specific requirements of situation and soil are satisfied. Most, however, will perform considerably better if they are grown under cover. Many alpines bloom in late winter and very early spring when, if left in the open, their delicate flowers may be damaged by inclement weather, eaten by slugs or snails, or pecked by birds.

In an alpine house, plants are protected from winter moisture, cold, drying winds, and sudden, sharp cold, as well as from most pests. This enables a far wider range of alpines and rock plants to be grown, either in pots or in ground-level or raised beds, to provide an eye-catching and lasting display.

USING AN ALPINE HOUSE
Part of the house may be used to grow young plants (foreground) in beds supported by brick pillars.

Using an alpine house

An alpine house is a cold or cool/frost-free greenhouse (see p.481) designed for growing and displaying alpines and rock plants under controlled conditions. Often, half of the house is used for growing the plants, and the other half for displaying them. Alternatively, the plants can be grown in cold frames and brought temporarily into the house for display. Alpine houses are not practical in areas with very cold winters or long, hot summers.

Displaying the plants

Alpines can be displayed in pots simply placed on the staging or, more commonly, plunged up to their rims in a layer of sand. Plunging keeps roots cool and moist and reduces temperature fluctuations, while allowing easy irrigation of plants that dislike overhead watering. Specially built display beds are an attractive option. Create miniature rock gardens in the alpine house, either waist-high where staging is strong enough to support the weight, or at ground level. These may have some permanent planting as well as areas of sand or sandy soil mix into which different plants can be plunged, according to season. Lightweight tufa rocks may be incorporated and planted up to enhance this type of display.

Siting the alpine house

Choose a firm, level site away from the shade of trees, fences, walls, and tall buildings if possible. Siting the alpine house on a north–south axis is ideal but any open, sunny position is acceptable. Always avoid hollows where cold air forms frost pockets, and do not site it in exposed, windy situations. Try to position the alpine house where it will harmonize with other garden features, perhaps even using it as a focal point. For further information on greenhouses, ventilation, shading, and staging, see GREENHOUSES AND FRAMES, pp.483, 484, and 487.

AN ALPINE HOUSE DISPLAY
A wide range of rock plants may be grown in pots and attractively displayed in raised sand beds in an alpine house.

Using frames

Frames should be sited near the alpine house, where they may be used to protect a range of choice plants from climatic extremes, as an overflow area, or for storage when plants are not in flower. They are very useful for bulbs that need to be kept dry when dormant, or for plants that will not tolerate the very hot conditions that may arise in summer. Frames incorporate a top sash that must be opened as required to provide good ventilation; a standard sash frame is suitable but other types are available. The sashes can be removed in summer, but they should be kept on if the frame contains dormant bulbs. Those plants that do not tolerate direct summer sun can be protected by covering the frame with mesh shading (see GREENHOUSES AND FRAMES, "Meshes and fabrics," p.484). Pots in a frame are usually plunged in a material such as washed builder's sand over a layer of stones to give them good drainage and hold them upright.

CARE OF ALPINES AND DWARF BULBS AFTER FLOWERING

ALPINES INDOORS
After flowering, pots of alpines needing careful watering (here Dionysia *spp.) should be plunged in sand under cover.*

ALPINES OUTDOORS
Alpines that tolerate variable summer weather conditions, such as saxifrages, may be plunged in open cold frames after flowering.

BULBS INDOORS
Pots of dwarf bulbs that have finished flowering may be kept dry by plunging in sand or gravel under benches.

PROTECTING FLOWERING ALPINES
Alpines coming into flower may be grown in outdoor frames before bringing them into the alpine house for display.

Alpines in pots

Growing alpines in pots ensures that special watering, soil mix, or feeding requirements can be provided for individual plants.

Plastic and clay pots

Although plastic pots are suitable for growing alpines and retain moisture well, clay pots are more traditional – important if the plants are to be exhibited. The soil mix in plastic pots dries out more slowly than in clay pots, so take care not to overwater the plants. Clean and sterilize all pots before use: sterilants based on dilute solutions of household bleach are suitable, mixing 9 parts water to 1 part bleach.

Soil mixes

All alpines need a freely draining soil mix and benefit from a layer of broken crocks in the bottom of clay pots, or grit in plastic pots. Even moisture-loving plants will not tolerate stagnant conditions.

Most species grow well in soil-based potting mix combined with an equal amount of grit. Those from high alpine habitats of scree and rock-face crevices, such as some *Androsace* species and other cushion-forming plants, need a less fertile and more freely draining mix if they are to retain their neat, natural habit. In rich soil mixes, they quickly become soft and lush and are then more prone to attack by pests and diseases. For these plants use a mix of up to 3 parts grit to 1 part soil-based mix. Introduce plants to these lean mixes when they are young, since they may not adapt easily if they have been potted on from a more fertile medium.

A number of species, usually ones from woodland habitats, or those that occur in humus-rich pockets in rocky habitats, such as *Haberlea* and *Ramonda*, require well-drained soil mixes that are rich in organic matter. For these, a mix of 1 part each of soil-based potting mix and grit, with 2 parts leaf mold, compost, or peat will be suitable. Take care to check on the individual needs of each plant in order to select an appropriate soil mix, and ensure that all ingredients for lime-hating plants are lime-free.

Top-dressings

After planting up the pots (see right), top-dress them with a layer of grit or stone chips to enhance the plant's appearance, to keep the area around the neck of the plant well drained, and to prevent the growth of mosses and liverworts. Use a top-dressing that is appropriate to the pH requirements of the plant; for example, limestone chips may be used for lime-loving species, or granite grit for lime-hating plants.

Some small, cushion-forming alpines are very sensitive to the presence of water around their necks so, as well as top-dressing with grit, prop small wedges of rock beneath their cushions in order to keep them clear of the surface.

Repotting

When a plant has outgrown its pot, transfer it carefully into a slightly larger pot, disturbing the root ball as little as possible. Pot on herbaceous and shrubby plants in spring and summer, when they are growing strongly; bulbs should be potted on when they are dormant. Plant to the same level as in the previous pot, firm in fresh soil mix, and then add a new layer of top-dressing.

Water well after potting by standing the pot in at least 1–2in (2.5–5cm) of water until the top of the soil mix becomes moist. Then remove the pot to avoid the risk of root rot.

Planting in beds

The beds may be at ground level or raised 3ft (1m) high. Raised beds allow plants to be tended and viewed

Repotting a Saxifrage

1 *The roots of this saxifrage can be seen growing through the drainage hole at the bottom of the pot. The plant is potbound and should be repotted.*

2 *Choose a pot that is one size bigger than the one that the plant is growing in. Use crocks and gravel to provide drainage at the base of the pot.*

3 *Arrange the crocks over the drainage hole. The crocks should then be covered with a layer of gravel.*

4 *Remove the plant from its pot by tapping sharply on the base to loosen the root ball; tease out the roots a little to encourage them to penetrate the new soil mix.*

5 *Cover the crocks in the larger pot with a little soil mix; position the plant so that the neck is at the same level as in the original pot, and fill in with soil mix.*

6 *Spread the gravel top-dressing over the surface of the soil mix, taking care to tuck it under the collar of the plant to keep it sharply drained.*

7 *Place the pot in a bowl of water and leave it until the soil mix and gravel top-dressing appear damp.*

8 *Then remove the pot and place it on a layer of sand in a cold frame, where any excess moisture can easily drain off. This will prevent any risk of root rot.*

9 *The repotted plant can then be plunged in sand in a cold frame or bed to grow on.*

REMOVING DEAD LEAVES

Tweezers should be used regularly to remove any brown or withered leaves from alpine plants such as this Campanula pilosa.

more easily and are especially useful for physically impaired gardeners. The staging must drain well and be solidly constructed to bear the weight of the bed (see also GREENHOUSES AND FRAMES, "Raised beds," p.486).

Use a soil mix of 3 parts good sterilized garden soil, 2 parts coarse fibrous peat or compost, and 2 parts sharp sand or grit. Add rocks to the bed to create a miniature rock garden. Tufa is particularly useful because it is lightweight and very moisture-retentive, and because plants can be grown directly in it. Plant out alpines in the bed, avoiding species that are invasive and free-seeding, but leave some gaps for plunging a succession of seasonal, potgrown specimens. Ferns and other shade-loving species may be grown under a raised bed.

Routine maintenance

Alpines have specialized growing requirements and need considerable attention throughout the growing season. Plants that are regularly repotted rarely need additional feeding, but when fertilizers are used, be sure that they are low in nitrogen – high nitrogen levels will lead to soft, lush growth that is uncharacteristic of alpines and more prone to pests and diseases.

Ventilation

Ventilating surfaces must occupy at least 25 percent of the glass area, since the aim is to provide the maximum possible air circulation at all times. In spring and summer, the vents and the greenhouse door can remain open permanently, unless there is strong wind or heavy rain. Use a screen of small-diameter mesh over vents and doors to keep out cats and birds. During heavy rain and windy weather, close the vents on the receiving side to avoid drip on the foliage and to reduce strong drafts that may damage foliage and flowers. In severe winds, it is safest to close all vents and doors.

In winter, open the vents fully (unless it is freezing, windy, raining, or snowing) but close them before nightfall to retain any residual warmth. In very cold weather, allow temperatures in the alpine house to rise gradually before ventilating; on bright, sunny days, however, open the vents as soon as possible to prevent the temperature from rising too rapidly. In damp, foggy weather, especially in areas with high levels of atmospheric pollution, close down the house completely to keep out cold, damp air, and use a small fan to maintain air circulation.

Temperature

Shading will be necessary during sunny weather, from late spring to fall, to avoid scorching tender, new growth, and to help reduce temperatures. Do not use heavy shading since this might cause etiolation or lopsided leaning of plants toward the available light source. In very hot weather, damp down the house floor to reduce temperatures and maintain atmospheric humidity; plants may be lightly misted with cool water in the evenings.

Heating should be used to stop the pots from freezing in severe weather. A method of heating that does not produce excessive fumes or moisture is best (see GREENHOUSES AND FRAMES, "Heating," p.482).

Hygiene

Remove dead foliage and faded flowers regularly to reduce the risk of fungal attack. Check the plants for pests and diseases, and treat any outbreaks promptly (see PLANT PROBLEMS, pp.547–79). Always keep the floor of the house clean to minimize the risk of diseases, and make sure that the glass is clean so that plants receive maximum light.

Watering

Water regularly throughout the season, especially on sunny spring and summer days, when water loss is rapid. If plants are allowed to dry out between waterings, growth may be severely checked and flower buds may shrivel. For pots standing on staging, water from above but avoid splashing the foliage. Plunged clay pots derive moisture from the surrounding material but may need additional watering in warm periods. For plants that are sensitive to moisture on their foliage, water the plunge medium around the pots.

As fall approaches, reduce watering as plants prepare for dormancy. During winter, alpines need to be kept dry but not dust dry (for plunged pots, the plunge medium should be just damp to the touch).

Winter maintenance

A spell of clear, dry weather during late summer is a good time to store the plants in a frame and clean the alpine house (see GREENHOUSES AND FRAMES, "Routine maintenance," p.491). Clean and top up the sand or grit on beds and renew labels. Then transfer pots back from the frame.

Exhibiting

Alpines for showing should be in the best possible condition on exhibition day. No matter how perfect the plant, it will lose marks if poorly presented in a less than scrupulously clean pot, or if top-dressings are thin or show evidence of algal growth. Remove all evidence of weeds, pests, and diseases. Check plants for dead, discolored, or misshapen leaves and faded flowers, and remove these carefully with tweezers.

Clay pots should be scrubbed clean with a wire brush or scourer. Alternatively, they may be double-potted: insert the specimen in its pot into a larger, new pot, filling any space between the pots and covering the inner rim with top-dressing. Renew all top-dressings with materials appropriate to the plant's natural habitat, then relabel. Support tall, fragile plants during travel with tripods of split stakes. Water plants thoroughly the day before the show and allow them to drain before packing them for transportation. Carry extra top-dressing to renew any lost in transit.

TRANSPORTING PLANTS

When transporting fragile plants (here Fritillaria uva-vulpis)*, make a tripod from split stakes bound at the top with twine, and tie in stems.*

PREPARING PLANTS FOR EXHIBITION

1 *Use fine sand together with a wire brush or scouring pad to clean the outside of clay pots. This will remove any algae or fertilizer salts.*

2 *Replenish the top-dressing. For this* Dionysia aretioides *the medium is coarse gravel, but stone chips, grit, or pine needles may be used, depending on the plant.*

3 *Add new, clearly written labels. Pack the pots carefully in a tray using newspaper to hold them steady, and carry extra top-dressing for last-minute renewal.*

9

Bulbous Plants

*F*ROM THE CHEERFUL *golden daffodil trumpeting the arrival of spring to the* Colchicum, *herald of fall, bulbous plants ring in the changes of the seasons throughout the year with glorious flower displays. Some possess handsome foliage and others are valued for their fragrance, but it is their blooms that make bulbs essential in a well-planned garden. They offer a wide variety of form and color, from the tall grandeur of the gladiolus spike to the tiny cups of the smallest crocus, from bright primary shades to delicate pastel hues. Whether they form bold patterns in a formal bed, fill in the detail of a mixed border, provide a splash of color in a container, or create sweeping highlights beneath trees or in grass, bulbs bring vitality to the more permanent plantings of the garden.*

Designing with bulbs

GROWING bulbs is an easy way to brighten up the garden with decorative, often flamboyant, and sometimes fragrant displays. The bulbs that are grown in the garden are dominated by hardy favorites, for example crocuses, irises, daffodils, hyacinths, and tulips, of which there is an immense variety of both species and cultivars. Many tender bulbs also deserve a place in the garden, including dahlias, begonias, fragrant *Crinum*, gladioli with their colorful spikes, fiery *Tigridia*, and stately *Galtonia*.

The key characteristic of bulbs is that they generally provide visual interest for only one season, remaining dormant and unnoticed for the remainder of the year. This can be an asset with careful planning, making bulbs invaluable as border plants as well as ideal for naturalizing in grass or for growing in containers.

In many gardens, bulbs may be left to increase naturally from year to year while their dying foliage is hidden by the developing growth of herbaceous plants or shrubs that provide a succession of interest. Many bulbs, including the popular crocuses, daffodils, and snowdrops (*Galanthus*), increase very rapidly in most sites. Bulbs may also be lifted after flowering and replanted each year to create room for other seasonal plants, making them especially convenient for small gardens or restricted areas.

USING BULBS IN A MIXED BORDER
The dusky, purple-pink globes of Allium sphaerocephalon *pick up the color theme of this mixed border, providing a strong accent of color and form amid herbaceous perennials in various shades of pink.*

Seasons of interest

The main bulb season is from early spring to early summer, but many other bulbs flower outdoors or under cover at other times of the year. For color in late winter when most of the garden is dormant, early bulbs such as pink *Cyclamen coum*, deep blue *Iris histrioides* 'Major', and white snowdrops may be grown outdoors, and other bulbs forced indoors. Bulbs that flower in summer or fall are often larger, and of more exotic shapes and hues than spring bulbs.

Where to grow bulbs

If given the well-drained soil that they need to grow and flower well, bulbs are among the easiest of all garden plants to cultivate. There are numerous cultivars and species now available that thrive in all exposures except deep, constant shade.

Many bulbs in cultivation come from areas with a Mediterranean climate, so they need to be grown in sunny sites and prefer hot, dry summers – although a huge range of bulbs flourishes in the open garden in regions with summer rainfall.

Bulbs that would normally grow in woodland thrive in moist, light shade. Many others, including some described as sun-loving, do best in the light shade cast by nearby shrubs, walls, or trellises. Even dry shade is tolerated by most hardy cyclamen. Bulbs with white or pale flowers appear almost luminous in dusky light, and look ethereal when planted in a shaded site.

Whatever the setting, bulbs usually look best planted in groups of the same species or cultivar, whether jostling shoulders with other plants or forming a single, swaying sea of color in a formal bed or in grass.

The different types of bulbous plant

BULB (*Hyacinthoides hispanica*)

CORM (*Gladiolus* 'Perky')

In this book, the term "bulb" refers to all bulbous plants, including corms, tubers, and rhizomes as well as true bulbs. The terms "corm," "tuber," and "rhizome" are used only in their specific sense throughout. With all bulbous plants, a portion of the plant is swollen into a food storage organ that enables the plant to survive when dormant or when conditions are unsuitable for growth.

Bulbs

True bulbs are formed from fleshy leaves or leaf bases, and frequently consist of concentric rings of scales attached to a basal plate. The outer scales often form a dry, protective skin or tunic, as found in daffodils, Reticulata irises, and tulips. With some lilies (*Lilium*) and *Fritillaria* species, the scales are separate and no tunic is formed. Juno irises are unusual in having swollen storage roots beneath the bulbs.

Corms

Corms are formed from the swollen bases of stems and are replaced by new corms every year. They are common in the family Iridaceae, which includes crocuses, gladioli, *Romulea*, and *Watsonia*; usually they have a tunic that has been formed from the previous year's leaf bases. In the Liliaceae and related families, they are found in such genera as *Brodiaea* and *Colchicum*.

TUBER (*Dahlia* 'Monk Marc')

RHIZOME (*Iris* 'White City')

Tubers

"Tuberous" is a term applied to many plants with swollen, often irregularly shaped stems or roots used for food storage. It is often misapplied, for example to the tuberlike roots (actually rhizomes) of *Anemone blanda* and the long, thin rhizomes of *A. nemorosa* (for convenience, both are included here as bulbous plants). True tubers of various kinds are found in *Corydalis*, in some orchids such as *Dactylorrhiza*, in cyclamen species (although these are often called corms), and in plants such as *Ranunculus asiaticus* where they are lobed or clustered together.

Rhizomes

Rhizomes are swollen, usually more or less horizontal, underground stems, found in the Iridaceae, notably in irises, and in Liliaceae.

Formal beds

Bulbs make a valuable contribution to formal bedding displays. Spring-flowering bulbs are excellent for planting *en masse* in a bed to be occupied by bedding annuals later in summer, since they may be lifted and stored during their dormant season. Hyacinths and tulips are classic bedding bulbs because of their strong, sculptural forms; in general, the larger, showy flowers of hybrids best suit a formal position in the garden. Plant in blocks of color, each of one type of bulb, or in mixed groups that flower at different times to provide a long display of color during the spring. Bulbs may completely fill the bed or be combined with companion plants having flowers in complementary or contrasting colors, such as deep blue forget-me-nots (*Myosotis*) and fiery wallflowers (*Cheiranthus*).

There is also scope for formal planting with summer- or fall-flowering bulbs: *Galtonia*, with its elegant white or green spikes, or the more compact cultivars of gladioli (especially the Primulinus and Butterfly groups) look impressive when planted in large blocks bordered by purple or white sweet alyssum (*Lobularia maritima*) or any similar, low-growing ground cover. *Agapanthus* Headbourne Hybrids, with their large, rounded flowerheads of blue or white, combine well with the graceful pink blooms of *Nerine bowdenii*.

A PAGEANT OF COLOR *Ranks of tulips parade along these formal beds in bold, bright blocks of contrasting color, creating an energetic counterpoint to the quiet orderliness of the formal garden. White tulips are interspersed among those of stronger hue to prevent the color combinations from appearing too strident.*

Mixed herbaceous and shrub borders

Bulbs fill in the permanent planting of a border with a lively variety of seasonal color. Loose drifts may blend in with the general design or draw the eye with splashes of bright color. Architectural bulbs, such as *Crinum* x *powellii* with its huge pink or white trumpets, punctuate borders with an arresting contrast of height and form. Grow some bulbs through low ground cover plants so that their blooms appear to float above the mat of foliage. For a more informal cottage border, consider using species bulbs since fancy hybrids may look out of place.

Mixed plantings for spring flowering

Planting bulbs in a mixed border extends the flowering season and provides an array of fresh, bright color from late winter to early summer. Before the herbaceous perennials and deciduous shrubs in the border begin to grow and spread, bring the front to life with the smaller daffodil species, pale or dark blue Reticulata irises, snowdrops, (*Galanthus*), and the golden cups of winter aconites (*Eranthis hyemalis*).

Plant starry carpets of pink and blue *Anemone blanda*, *Chionodoxa*, and *Scilla bifolia* beneath such early-flowering shrubs as *Corylopsis*, *Forsythia*, and witch hazel (*Hamamelis*) to complement their display, or grow pale yellow drifts of the more freely increasing dwarf daffodil species and hybrids.

For later in spring, a much wider range of bulbs is available. Larger plants, such as the tall daffodils, *Fritillaria* species (for example the

USING BULBS IN A MIXED BORDER

In this border, a variety of bulbs has been planted among shrubs and herbaceous perennials to create a bed that changes in mood with the seasons.

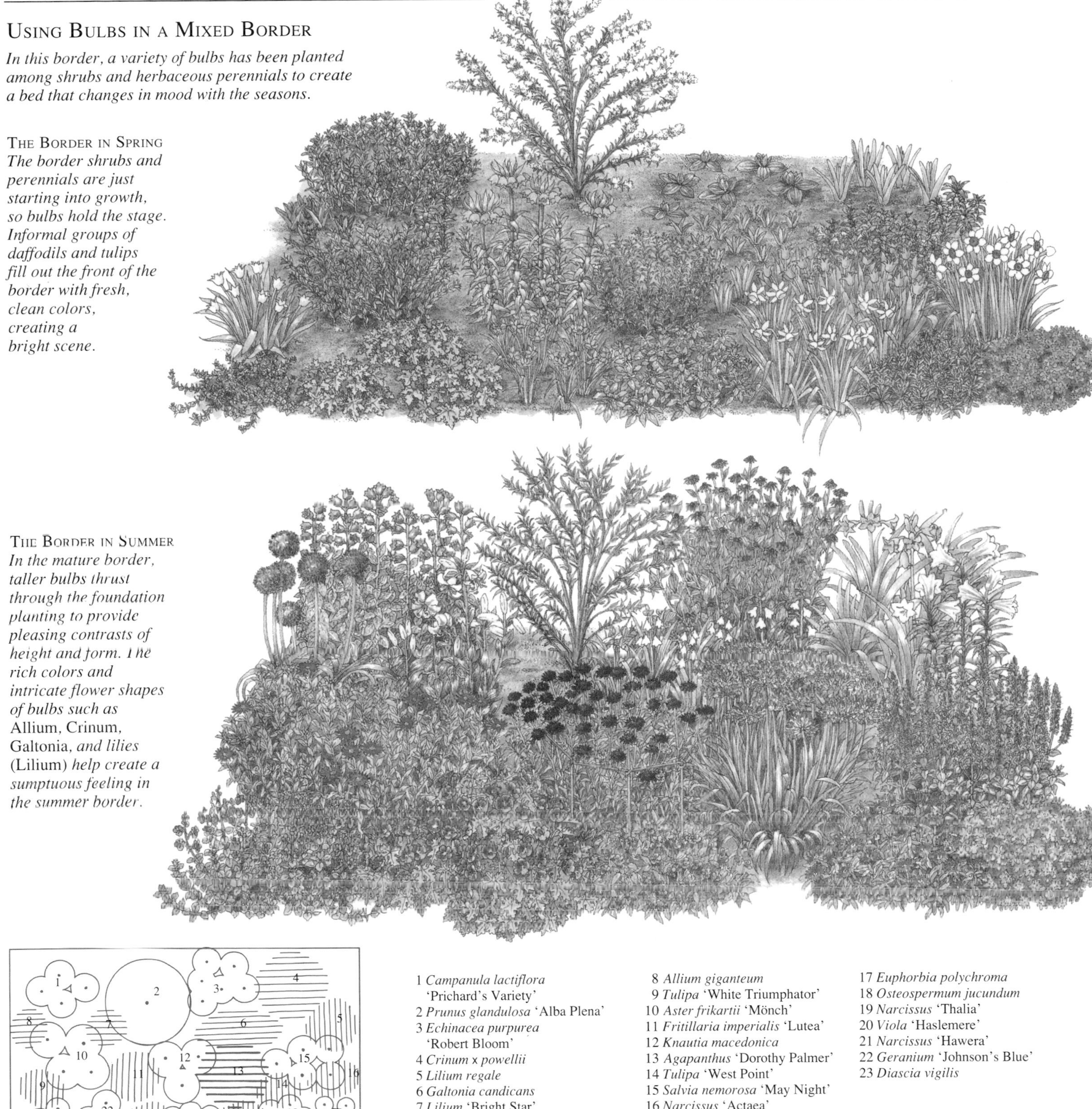

THE BORDER IN SPRING
The border shrubs and perennials are just starting into growth, so bulbs hold the stage. Informal groups of daffodils and tulips fill out the front of the border with fresh, clean colors, creating a bright scene.

THE BORDER IN SUMMER
In the mature border, taller bulbs thrust through the foundation planting to provide pleasing contrasts of height and form. The rich colors and intricate flower shapes of bulbs such as Allium, Crinum, Galtonia, *and lilies* (Lilium) *help create a sumptuous feeling in the summer border.*

1 *Campanula lactiflora* 'Prichard's Variety'
2 *Prunus glandulosa* 'Alba Plena'
3 *Echinacea purpurea* 'Robert Bloom'
4 *Crinum* x *powellii*
5 *Lilium regale*
6 *Galtonia candicans*
7 *Lilium* 'Bright Star'
8 *Allium giganteum*
9 *Tulipa* 'White Triumphator'
10 *Aster frikartii* 'Mönch'
11 *Fritillaria imperialis* 'Lutea'
12 *Knautia macedonica*
13 *Agapanthus* 'Dorothy Palmer'
14 *Tulipa* 'West Point'
15 *Salvia nemorosa* 'May Night'
16 *Narcissus* 'Actaea'
17 *Euphorbia polychroma*
18 *Osteospermum jucundum*
19 *Narcissus* 'Thalia'
20 *Viola* 'Haslemere'
21 *Narcissus* 'Hawera'
22 *Geranium* 'Johnson's Blue'
23 *Diascia vigilis*

purple-black *F. persica* and the regal *F. imperialis*), or tulips may be used in casual groups to give height among the shrubs and perennials.

Mixed plantings for summer and fall flowering

A number of bulbs add greatly to the beauty of the garden in summer. Although often regarded as only of secondary importance, in fact many summer- and fall-flowering bulbs are quite tall and robust enough to hold their own among the surrounding flowering perennials, and they offer a dazzling range of colors and flower forms.

Early in the season, try *Camassia leichtlinii* 'Alba' with its creamy white flower plumes; the large, purple globes of *Allium aflatunense*; *Triteleia laxa* (syn. *Brodiaea laxa*) for its loose, purple-blue clusters of bloom; and the bold scarlet goblets of *Tulipa sprengeri*.

Follow them with vivid or pastel gladioli, sun-loving lilies (*Lilium*) in a huge range of colors and forms, arching sprays of blazing red or yellow *Crocosmia*, and, later, the slim pink, red, or white spires of *Schizostylis*. The tender greenish white *Eucomis* with its pineapple-like flowerheads brings an exotic touch to the border planting.

In fall, continue the display with fragrant, pink trumpets of *Amaryllis belladonna*, brilliant yellow funnels of *Sternbergia lutea*, and blue to white forms of fall-flowering crocuses.

Naturalizing bulbs

When left undisturbed, many bulbs readily increase to form flowing drifts of color. Allowing them to naturalize in this way gives interest to areas of the garden that otherwise might not be given over to flowering plants. Species, which are more delicate in hue and form than most cultivars, create a natural appearance when planted in large, informal groups.

Planting with specimen trees

Bulbs make perfect partners for specimen trees with deep roots and light, deciduous canopies. Use bulbs that flower mostly in spring and fall to form a decorative ground cover when the tree has few leaves to deepen the shade. In spring the soil beneath the tree is moist and sunlit, ideal for anemones, crocuses, daffodils, or *Scilla*. Hardy fall-flowering cyclamen, with mottled, silvery foliage and softly folded petals, tolerate the dry summer conditions and enjoy partial shade.

Plant bulbs whose flowers complement a tree's habit. White-flowered bulbs, for example, mirror the white blossoms of ornamental cherries (*Prunus*); the goblet-shaped flowers of crocuses echo the chalice form of magnolia blooms; and bulbs with pendent flowers imitate the habit of a weeping tree.

Use dwarf cultivars to naturalize the area around a newly planted tree or shrub, since rapidly increasing bulbs such as large daffodils can greatly reduce the available food.

Woodland settings

Bulbs are invaluable grown as large, informal pools of color to enhance the beauty of deciduous woodland.

Bulbs for Bright Highlights
Loose drifts of slender tulips bring brilliant color to this mixed border and contrast with the soft, mounded foliage of the perennials.

Many do best in woodland conditions, blending well with other woodland plants such as ferns, hellebores (*Helleborus*), primroses (*Primula*), and foamflower (*Tiarella*).

The succession of bloom and contrast of form and height among bulbs can create the subtle variations and tranquil mood of a woodland. White snowdrops (*Galanthus*) and cyclamen species in pinks and purples make a striking combination, while drifts of *Scilla* and *Chionodoxa* add shades of blue.

Spanish bluebells (*Hyacinthoides hispanica*, syn. *Scilla campanulata*) or many of the more rampant grape hyacinths (*Muscari*), together with the delicate white sprays of lily-of-the-valley (*Convallaria majalis*), provide swaths of blue and white. These can all colonize considerable areas once established. English bluebells (*Hyacinthoides non-scripta*) should be planted on their own since they rapidly invade other plantings.

Planting in grass

Bulbs can transform grass, whether a bank, a section of a lawn, or an entire meadow, into a bright carpet of spring or fall color that spreads more thickly each year. The bulbs must be robust species that can withstand competition from grass roots. Many of the larger bulbs look best in tall grass where, after flowering, their fading foliage is less obtrusive.

Plant early-flowering bulbs in grass that is mown from spring onward: their leaves will have time to die down before the grass is cut. Later-flowering bulbs, such as *Camassia* and species lilies, may be grown with grass and wildflowers in meadows that are not cut until late summer. Bulbs that bloom in fall start into growth and flower before the end of the usual mowing season, so the grass must be left unmown after late summer. Alternatively, plant bulbs in irregular but defined areas so that it is possible to mow around them.

Daffodils are the classic choice for grass, and a remarkable range – especially the more robust species and hybrids – can be grown in this way. Many crocuses grow well in grass where they are protected to some extent from mice and squirrels. A more delicate feeling may be achieved with the pendent bells of the summer snowflake (*Leucojum aestivum*) and the snake's-head fritillary (*Fritillaria meleagris*), which shiver softly in the breeze.

Some of the dwarfer bulbs do well where the grass is less vigorous, particularly in partly shaded areas. *Chionodoxa* species, the purple *Crocus tommasinianus*, *Scilla* species,

Woodland Charm
Hardy Cyclamen coum *and crocuses in deep and pale shades of pink, lilac, and violet colonize a woodland, clustering prettily around the base of the trees to provide a show of color when the trees are bare.*

A Natural Planting
Naturally spreading clumps of fall-flowering Colchicum byzantinum *spring up through a mat of greenery to display their starry blooms. The dark green, velvety moss on the base of the tree provides an attractive foil for the shining, purple-pink flowers.*

SPRING SPECTACLE
Naturalized crocuses cover this lawn with vivid purple, magenta, and yellow. The bulbs are planted in great swaths of a single hue that merge with each other to create a sea of color. Snowdrops (Galanthus) *planted among the crocuses provide highlights of white.*

some daffodil species (e.g. *Narcissus cyclamineus*), and snowdrops all do well in these conditions.

Bulbs planted on the grassy outskirts of a formal garden soften the rigidity of formal beds, but the informal frame also provides a contrast that strengthens the focus on the formal plantings (see "Naturalizing in grass," p.226).

Bulbs with alpines

Using bulbs with alpines in the rock garden, trough, or peat bed can prolong the season because most alpines flower only in late spring. The erect habit, upright flowers, and spearlike leaves of bulbs contrast well with the low, mounded, or spreading habit of most alpine plants. Choose dwarf bulbs with dainty blooms to complement the character of the alpines, and plant some bulbs to grow through and brighten the alpine planting. Avoid mat-forming alpines that exhaust the soil around the bulbs, thus depriving them of food.

AN ALPINE SETTING
The unusual beauty of the bell-like flowers of Fritillaria acmopetala *is best shown off in the small-scale planting of an alpine garden.*

In the rock garden

Many smaller bulbs, especially the more exacting species for which sharp drainage is essential, thrive in sunny or partially shaded rock gardens. Dwarf bulbs look attractive when planted in pockets of rock or offset against the grit top-dressing of the bed, which also stops their delicate flowers from being muddied during wet weather. If planting very small alpines in the bed, do not use the taller bulb species, which would appear out of proportion to their neighbors.

In troughs

Old stone troughs make an attractive setting for a collection of dwarf bulbs and smaller alpine plants, since their tiny charms may be appreciated at close hand. The bulbs benefit from the gritty, well-drained soil, and may easily be given the careful watering that they need.

To keep the display in proportion, grow the smallest species and their less robust hybrids; rapidly increasing bulbs may swamp neighboring alpines. Many of the smaller species offer intriguing flowers, such as purplish brown and yellow *Fritillaria michailovskyi* and several *Narcissus* species in white and yellow.

Rhodohypoxis are excellent for troughs, producing pink, red, or white starry flowers through most of the summer. Keep the bulbs moist during the growing season, and give them an occasional liquid feed. The genus *Cyclamen* includes species that are suitable for troughs in spring and fall, ranging in hue from pure white to deepest purple-pink.

In a peat bed

A peat garden, with its terraced beds, peat-block walls, and a soil mix consisting mainly of leaf mold and peat or compost, provides perfect conditions for the dwarfer woodland bulbs, whether planted on their own or with ericaceous shrubs or alpines. Try *Corydalis solida*, with purplish gray flowers, or the lady's slipper (*Cypripedium calceolus* var. *pubescens*), yellow with chocolate-maroon wings, among many others. The plant choice is determined to an extent by the degree of shade.

Bulbs to associate with water gardens

A few bulbs do well in damp, poorly drained conditions and provide some of the most striking flowering plants to grow around water. Their strong shapes and colors create pleasing reflections; plant them in clumps to contrast with the flat, open surface of the water. Several handsome rhizomatous irises and the arum lily (*Zantedeschia aethiopica*), with large, white spathes above broad, arrow-shaped leaves, thrive in pond margins. Both the snake's-head fritillary and summer snowflake (*Leucojum aestivum*) grow naturally in wet meadows and thrive in moist sites or damp beds around ponds.

Other bulbs that enhance water gardens are the magnificent purple-red *Iris ensata* (syn. *I. kaempferi*), and *Dierama pendulum* with its wandlike flower sprays. Both of these require a soil that is well drained as well as moist.

Bulbs in containers

Growing bulbs in ornamental pots, windowboxes, and other containers provides a varied and spectacular display throughout the season. Careful choice of bulbs may extend the season to include late winter as well as spring and summer. Plant a single species or cultivar in each container to provide a uniform display, and then group the containers together for a mass of color.

Place pots of bulbs with fragrant flowers (e.g. hyacinths or Tazetta daffodils) near the house entrance where they may be fully appreciated. Pots used for spring bulbs may be used for summer-flowering plants later: when the bulbs die down, lift and replant them in the garden (or store them) and replace them with annuals or tender perennials.

BULBS IN POTS
Larger bulbs are naturals for use in containers. Here, Lilium regale *provides the focus of interest in this grouping of pots, which have been arranged on different levels and in gradations of size to draw the eye upward. The huge, white lily trumpets combine with white pelargoniums and terracotta tones to form an attractive composition that is in harmony with the natural stone wall and greenery behind it.*

Some larger bulbs are sufficiently commanding to be planted on their own in containers. Tall lilies (*Lilium*) or *Crinum* x *powellii*, in pink or white forms, are particularly suitable. Any *Agapanthus* species or hybrid provides a long season of showy flowers. Alternatively, group several bulbs of varying heights and colors in a large container such as a half barrel to provide a feature on a patio.

Windowboxes

When planting in windowboxes, choose smaller bulbs that are in proportion to the size of the container. They are excellent for planting in layers below other plants to make best use of limited space; the bulbs thrust through the surface planting to create a pleasing contrast of height and form. Blending the plants with early-flowering pansies (*Viola* x *wittrockiana*) and ivy (*Hedera*), followed by trailing tender perennials and annuals, gives a prolonged display of color.

Bulbs under cover

Growing bulbs under cover extends the range that may be cultivated to include many rare species that need particular care. In temperate or cold regions, tender bulbs may be grown that would not survive unprotected in the garden. In regions with summer rainfall, it is the most practical way of growing many of the species bulbs currently in cultivation that need a dry, summer resting period. Bulbs may be planted in pots or in a greenhouse bed or bulb frame. This allows easier control of the local environment to accommodate the individual needs of a wide range of bulbs, be it a summer drying-off period or protection from excessive winter moisture, cold, or frost.

Bulbs in pots

Growing bulbs in pots allows each plant to be grown in conditions that best suit its individual requirements, especially when cultivating small stocks of uncommon bulbs. The pots are easily transferred from outdoors to the shelter of frames or greenhouses when required, or from the greenhouse to the conservatory to enjoy them when in full flower.

Pot cultivation in a cool greenhouse enables many bulb species that are otherwise of borderline hardiness in temperate climates to be grown. Many are South African and South American bulbs with a variety of richly colored blooms, such as *Watsonia* with its dense spikes of deep pink and red. The shelter of a cool greenhouse is needed for tender bulbs such as *Gloriosa* and winter-flowering *Veltheimia*. Tender species or cultivars of such genera as begonias, *Canna*, or *Crinum* should also be overwintered in a cool greenhouse, and brought out when in bloom to enhance the summer display in the open garden.

If desired, bulbs may be grown in shade and the soil mix adjusted accordingly to grow small woodland bulbs. These include *Trillium rivale*, which has finely spotted petals in pink or white, and tender terrestrial orchids such as the free-flowering *Calanthe* species.

Gardeners with an alpine house may add a little height and splashes of color to the display by interspersing the plants with pots of dwarf spring bulbs. The alpine house environment is especially suitable for rare or tender bulbs (e.g. ice-white *Narcissus cantabricus* or bright blue *Tecophilaea cyanocrocus*).

Greenhouse beds

Tender bulbs may be planted directly in prepared greenhouse beds, rather than in pots, for a more natural and vigorous display. The bulbs may be combined in a mixed bed with other plants that flower in summer when the bulbs are dormant. Choose companion plants that tolerate a dry period coinciding with that needed by the bulbs, or that can be plunged in plastic pots and watered without the moisture reaching the bulbs around them.

Spreading, heat-loving plants such as *Osteospermum*, gazanias, and many silver-foliaged plants could be used in this way, and then removed or cut back hard at the end of summer when the bulbs start into growth. Late-flowering *Brodiaea*, *Calochortus*, and *Triteleia* prolong the flowering season still further: group them together but water them separately. Summer-growing bulbs such as the tender *Nerine* species, *Eucomis*, and some *Gladiolus* species do not need interplanting.

Bulb frames and raised beds

The term "bulb frame" usually refers to a raised bed devoted solely to bulbs; it is covered with a cold frame or sashes during the natural resting period of the bulbs in summer, and also in winter to protect them from excessive rainfall, which could cause them to rot. Alternatively, a frame may simply cover bulbs in pots plunged in a sand bed. Such frames may be made more attractive by using stone for the sides. Bulb frames

Bulbs for cut flowers

Many bulbs have flowers that can be cut for the house since their shapely, often solitary, flowers on long stems make them especially suitable for floral arrangement. A few have powerful scents that can fill a room, and most are long-lasting if picked before the blooms reach maturity. Some, such as daffodils, are so vigorous and prolific that they may be cut without leaving a gap in the garden display. Alternatively, set aside a separate area to grow bulbs especially for cutting.

Gladioli make fine cut flowers and are often used in this way, since the taller cultivars are difficult to place satisfactorily in an open border.

Wonderfully fragrant freesias are tender or half-hardy bulbs commonly grown under cover to provide cut flowers. They have a long flowering season during the winter but make somewhat straggly pot plants that need staking, so they are best cut for display indoors where they will last well. They also grow outside in milder areas.

***Schizostylis coccinea* 'Sunrise'**

***Crocosmia* 'Lucifer'**

***Narcissus* 'Cheerfulness'**

***Dahlia* 'Early Bird'**

***Freesia* 'Everett'**

***Gladiolus* 'Tesoro'**

***Zantedeschia aethiopica* 'Crowborough'**

Nerine bowdenii

***Alstroemeria* Ligtu Hybrids**

***Tulipa* 'Clara Butt'**

Allium giganteum

***Lilium* 'Enchantment'**

are the best alternative to the alpine house as a place to grow tender or exacting bulb species without the root restriction of pots, and are used mainly by enthusiasts or collectors. This method of cultivation suits most bulbs, other than those accustomed to some summer rainfall (such as woodland and high mountain species). Some of the crocus, daffodil, *Fritillaria*, and tulip species, Juno and Reticulata irises, and the more difficult *Brodiaea* and *Zigadenus* species tend to be less successful in temperate climates as open garden plants. These bulbs may not survive excess moisture unless they are protected in bulb frames or seasonally covered raised beds during the dormant season.

Forcing bulbs

A good way of bringing color and fragrance indoors during the winter and early spring is to force bulbs in pots. The bulbs are kept in a cool to cold, dark place for a few months before bringing them into the light to encourage them to flower earlier than they do naturally. Hyacinths, tulips, amaryllis (*Hippeastrum*), daffodils, and irises are all suitable. Some hardy bulbs such as crocuses may abort their flowers if forced too quickly. A gentler method is to grow bulbs under cover in pots, bringing them indoors a week or two before they would normally bloom in the open garden, so that the warmth stimulates them into bloom.

Planter's guide to bulbous plants

EXPOSED SITES

Bulbs that tolerate exposed or windy sites

Anemone
Chionodoxa
Colchicum
Crocus
Cyclamen, some ❄
Fritillaria (dwarf spp.)
Galanthus
Ipheion
Iris reticulata
Muscari, some ❄
Narcissus (dwarf spp. and cvs)
Ornithogalum, some ❄
Oxalis, some ❄

Oxalis depressa

Scilla, some ❄
Sternbergia lutea
Triteleia
Tulipa (dwarf spp.)

WALL PROTECTION

Bulbs that benefit from the protection of a wall

Agapanthus, some ❄ (most spp.)
Alstroemeria
Amaryllis belladonna
Anomatheca laxa
Bloomeria crocea
Eucomis ❄
Fritillaria persica
Gladiolus, some ❄ (tender spp.)
Gynandriris sisyrinchium
Habranthus, some ❄ (some spp.)
Hippeastrum advenum ❄
Hymenocallis
Ixia ❄
Moraea spathulata
Nerine bowdenii
Schizostylis coccinea
Scilla peruviana
Sparaxis ❄
Sternbergia lutea, *S. sicula*
Tigridia ❄
Tulbaghia, some ❄
Watsonia ❄
Zephyranthes candida

DRY SHADE

Bulbs that tolerate dry shade

Anemone nemorosa
Arum italicum 'Pictum'
Cyclamen coum, *C. hederifolium*, *C. repandum*
Galanthus nivalis (forms)
Hyacinthoides non-scripta
Ranunculus ficaria

MOIST SHADE

Bulbs that do best in moist shade

Anemone apennina, *A. blanda*, *A. ranunculoides*
Arisaema, some ❄ (most spp.)
Arum italicum
Cardiocrinum
Corydalis (some spp.)
Eranthis
Erythronium
Fritillaria camschatcensis, *F. cirrhosa*, *F. roylei*
Galanthus
Ipheion uniflorum
Leucojum aestivum, *L. vernum*
Lilium (some spp.)

Lilium hansonii

Narcissus cyclamineus, *N. triandrus*
Nomocharis
Notholirion
Scilla bifolia
Trillium
Tulipa sylvestris

FLOWERS FOR CUTTING

Agapanthus, some ❄
Allium (some spp.)
Alstroemeria (taller spp. and cvs)
Amaryllis belladonna
Anemone, De Caen Series, *A.*, St. Brigid Series
Camassia
Clivia ❄
Crinum, some ❄
Crocosmia
Dahlia ❄
Dierama, some ❄
Freesia ❄
Galtonia
Gladiolus, some ❄
Gloriosa ❄
Iris, Dutch Hybrids
Ixia ❄
Lilium
Narcissus, some ❄
Nerine, some ❄
Ornithogalum, some ❄ (tall spp.)
Polianthes ❄
Ranunculus asiaticus ❄ (forms)
Schizostylis coccinea
Sparaxis ❄
Tulipa
Watsonia ❄
Zantedeschia, some ❄

ARCHITECTURAL PLANTS

Allium christophii, *A. giganteum*
Canna ❄
Cardiocrinum giganteum
Crinum x *powellii*
Eucomis ❄
Fritillaria imperialis
Lilium (most spp. and cvs)
Veltheimia ❄

ROCK GARDENS

Bulbs suitable for planting in rock gardens

Albuca humilis ❄
Allium (dwarf spp.)
Anemone (some spp.)
Bellevalia (some spp.)
Brodiaea (smallest spp.)
Bulbocodium vernum
Colchicum (small spp.)
Corydalis (some spp.)
Crocus
Cyclamen (hardy spp.)
Fritillaria (many spp.)
Galanthus
Ipheion
Iris (dwarf spp.)
Leucojum (some spp.)
Muscari, some ❄ (noninvasive spp.)
Narcissus (dwarf spp. and hybrids)
Ornithogalum, some ❄ (dwarf spp.)
Oxalis, some ❄ (some spp.)
Puschkinia
Rhodohypoxis
Romulea, some ❄ (some spp.)
Scilla, some ❄
Sternbergia lutea, *S. sicula*
Tulipa (dwarf spp.)
Zephyranthes candida

BULBS FOR ALPINE HOUSES

Albuca ❄
Anemone (some spp.)
Anomatheca
Arum, some ❄ (some spp.)
Babiana ❄
Bellevalia
Bongardia chrysogonum
Bulbocodium vernum
Calochortus
Colchicum (small spp.)
Crocus
Cyclamen, some ❄
Fritillaria (most spp.)
Gagea, some ❄
Galanthus
Habranthus, some ❄
Hippeastrum, some ❄ (dwarf spp.)

Moraea huttonii

Iris (dwarf spp.)
Leontice
Leucocoryne ❄
Leucojum (some spp.)
Merendera
Moraea, some ❄ (some spp.)
Muscari, some ❄ (some spp.)
Narcissus (dwarf spp.)
Ornithogalum, some ❄ (dwarf spp.)
Oxalis, some ❄ (some spp.)
Pancratium, some ❄
Pinellia
Rhodohypoxis
Romulea, some ❄
Scilla, some ❄
Sternbergia
Tecophilaea
Tulipa (dwarf spp.)
Zephyranthes, some ❄
Zigadenus

KEY
❄ *Not frost hardy*

Tulips and daffodils

Tulips and daffodils are highly valued for the bold splashes of color they bring to the garden in spring. Grow them together to extend the flowering season in a mixed border: some daffodils bloom quite early in the year, while many tulips last well into late spring. Tulips are excellent for beds or borders, and many daffodils are especially suitable for naturalizing in grass. Dwarf forms are ideal for rock gardens, alpine houses, or containers, where they may be seen at close range.

Tulips

This diverse, versatile genus is horticulturally classified in 15 divisions based on flower form, but may conveniently be grouped by flowering season and garden use.

Early tulips

Single early tulips have classic, goblet-shaped blooms, some with striped, flushed, or margined petals. Early doubles have long-lasting, open bowl-shaped flowers, often flecked or margined in contrasting colors. Traditionally used for cutting, in formal bedding, or as border edgings, many may also be grown in pots indoors. In informal designs their elegant outlines contrast well with spreading or prostrate plants.

Tulips in a Spring Border
The strong, vertical stems and distinctive flowercups of tulips provide height, structure, and vivid color in an informal spring border.

Midseason tulips

This grouping includes Triumph tulips, with their simple, conical blooms, and the Darwin hybrids, with rich and intensely colored flowers, often with a satiny, basal blotch and dark, velvety anthers. Both types are sturdy, robust, and noted for their weather resistance.

Late tulips

Some of the most vibrant colors and intricate forms are seen in late-flowering tulips. They include the graceful lily-flowered types, vivid and extravagant Parrot tulips, green-tinged Viridifloras, and exuberantly striped and feathered Rembrandts. Peony-flowered forms are suited to informal cottage gardens. All are attractive used informally with dark green or gray ground covers or in formal bedding designs.

Dwarf species and hybrids

Compact Kaufmanniana hybrids produce brightly colored blooms early in the spring, while the taller Fosteriana and Greigii tulips usually flower a little later. Many have very attractively marked foliage. The dwarf species are ideal for containers, raised beds, or rock gardens. *Tulipa sprengeri* and *T. sylvestris* tolerate light shade and will naturalize in thin grass.

Cultivation and propagation

Most tulips thrive in fertile, well-drained, humus-rich soils, in sun and with shelter. In ideal conditions, some robust cultivars persist from year to year. Many, however, are best regarded as short-lived perennials, to be lifted after a few years and discarded. Where soils warm up rapidly, unless planted deeply at 10–12in (25–30cm), the

Growing in Containers
The lily-flowered tulips 'West Point' *here display their pointed blooms.*

Types of tulip

Tulips include an impressive range of flower forms, from the simple, upright goblets of single-flowered tulips to the frilled and twisted petals of Parrot tulips and the open, double blooms of peony-flowered forms. They are available in most colors except true blue, from the purest white to the deepest purple, with many glorious shades of yellow, red, and crimson in between. Many of the dwarf tulips also have attractively marked leaves.

Single

***Tulipa* 'Dawnglow'**
Darwin hybrid

***T.* 'Queen of Night'**
Single late

***T.* 'Spring Green'**
Viridiflora

***T.* 'Greuze'**
Single late

Double and Parrot

***T.* 'Peach Blossom'**
Double early

***T.* 'Estella Rijnveld'**
Parrot

Dwarf Species and Hybrids

T. tarda
Dwarf species

***T.* 'Dreamboat'**
Greigii hybrid

***T.* 'Giuseppe Verdi'**
Kaufmanniana hybrid

Extending the Flowering Season
Growing tulips and daffodils together provides a continuous display of color for many weeks throughout spring.

bulbs usually divide into several smaller ones, which after a few years are too small to produce flowers.

Dwarf tulips generally require open, gritty soils in full sun; lift and replant only when overcrowded. Propagate by offsets (see p.233) or, for species, by seed (see p.234). Tulips are prone to tulip fire/blight (see p.555) and other problems (see p.232).

Daffodils

Daffodils (*Narcissus*) are among the easiest and most rewarding bulbs to grow. They are horticulturally divided into 12 groups, based on the form of the flowers and on the species originally used in breeding them.

Daffodils in containers

Most daffodils can be grown in pots, if they are deep enough to allow at least 2in (5cm) of rooting medium beneath the bottom of the bulbs. Tazettas, with clusters of up to 12 scented blooms, are often grown under glass or as pot plants to bloom from late fall to spring. The richly fragrant jonquil hybrids are also useful for house decoration. Small species such as *N. cantabricus* and *N. romieuxii* produce blooms early in the year in the alpine house; they may also then be brought indoors.

Daffodils in the garden

Valuable for formal spring bedding and to give early color in the mixed border, daffodils are among the most reliable of bulbs for naturalizing: they rarely need lifting in borders or grass. Even tiny species such as *N. cyclamineus* and *N. minor* will thrive in thin grass. Dwarf daffodils are ideal for rock gardens and raised beds; some, such as *N. asturiensis*, *N.* 'Tête-à-tête', and *N.* 'Little Gem', flower early in the year.

Cultivation and propagation

Daffodils will grow in almost any soil type, but prefer well-drained, moist, slightly alkaline conditions.

Naturalizing Daffodils in Grass
In an informal or wild garden, daffodils may be grown in grass, bringing welcome color to a shady corner or the ground beneath a tree.

They thrive in sun or light, dappled shade. Plant the bulbs two to three times their depth in late summer or early fall. When bulbs are naturalized in grass, do not cut the old foliage until at least six weeks after flowering. Bulbs in containers must be grown in cool conditions, with plenty of fresh air. Temperatures above 45°F (7°C) while rooting is taking place may cause flowers to abort. Place the pots in a cold place such as a cold frame after planting, and bring them into a cool room about 12–16 weeks later. Once flower buds appear, blooming can be advanced by raising the temperature gently although not exceeding 63°F (17°C).

Propagate by offsets (see p.233) or by chipping (see p.237); plants may also be raised from seed (see p.234). Daffodils may be infested by narcissus basal rot (p.569), narcissus nematodes (p.569), and bulb flies (p.569).

Types of daffodil

Daffodils provide a wide variety of shapes and forms, from the tiny, exquisite Cyclamineus hybrids with their swept-back petals, to the tall trumpet daffodils and the more showy double forms. Modern developments include the split corona and collarette types. In addition to the characteristic bright golden flowers, cultivars display a wide range of shades of white, yellow, pink, and orange, some with touches of red and green and often in combination.

Dwarf Species and Hybrids

Narcissus triandrus
Dwarf species

N. romieuxii
Dwarf species

N. 'Jumblie'
Cyclamineus hybrid

N. 'Pride of Cornwall'
Tazetta

Single

N. 'Passionale'
Large-cupped

N. 'Fortune'
Large-cupped

N. 'Ambergate'
Large-cupped

Double

N. 'Irene Copeland'
Double

N. 'Tahiti'
Double

Dahlias

Dahlias flower from the middle of summer to the first frosts in fall, providing bright color in the garden for several months. All are frost tender. They are excellent border plants and can be grown in various soil types, providing that the soil is fertile and well drained.

If grown for exhibition or for cut flowers, dahlias are best planted in rows in specially prepared beds. The dwarf bedding dahlias, usually grown annually from seed (see Annuals and Biennials, "Sowing in pots or trays," p.178), are suitable for planting in containers. Dahlia flowerheads have a diversity of petal forms in a wide color range, from white to rich yellow through pinks and reds to purples.

Dahlias are classified according to the size and form of their flowerheads. The decorative and cactus types are subdivided by the size of their blooms: miniature under $4\frac{1}{2}$in (115mm); small $4\frac{1}{2}$–7in (115–70mm); medium 7–9in (170–220mm); large 9–$10\frac{1}{2}$in (220–60mm); and giant over $10\frac{1}{2}$in (260mm).

Dahlia Flower Types

Single
D. 'Yellow Hammer'
Flowerheads with 8–10 broad florets that surround an open, central disk.

Anemone
D. 'Comet'
Fully double flowerheads with one or more rings of flattened ray florets surrounding a group of shorter, tubular florets.

Collarette
D. 'Easter Sunday'
A yellow disk in the center, with a collar of small florets lying between the disk and the larger florets.

Water Lily
D. 'Vicky Crutchfield'
As their name implies, these flowerheads look like water lilies, and have broad, flat florets.

Decorative
D. 'Frank Hornsey'
Fully double. Florets have broad petals rounded at the ends, usually curling gently inward along their length, flat, and slightly twisted.

Ball
D. 'Wootton Cupid'
Rounded flowerheads with spirally arranged florets. The petals are rolled for over half their length.

Pompon
D. 'Small World'
Similar to ball dahlias but much smaller, to a maximum diameter of 2in (52mm), and more globular; the petals are rolled for the whole of their length.

Cactus
D. 'Majestic Kerkrade'
Fully double, with narrow, pointed petals curled backward or quilled, which are either straight or incurving.

Semicactus
D. 'So Dainty'
Fully double. The ray florets have pointed, straight or incurving, broad-based petals that curve backward.

Cultivation

Dahlias thrive in well-drained, fertile soils of pH 6–7. They are heavy feeders, so dig in plenty of manure or compost in spring, then add bone meal at 4oz/sq yd (125g/sq m), allowing the soil to settle a few weeks before planting. Alternatively, prepare the bed in fall, leaving it roughly dug so that frost action can break up the soil.

When and where to plant
Dahlias may be planted as potgrown plants, as dormant or just-sprouting tubers or clumps, or as rooted cuttings from tubers. Plants in leaf may be preferable to tubers, because they are often more vigorous. Tubers and clumps may be planted directly, about three weeks before the last frosts, whereas plants in leaf should not be planted until all danger of frost has passed.

Choose an open, sheltered site that is not overshadowed. Immediately before planting, top-dress with a balanced fertilizer at 4oz/sq yd (125g/sq m) worked well into the soil. Tie young plants into their stakes to support them as they develop.

Planting potgrown dahlias
When planting potgrown dahlias, stakes should be positioned at the appropriate spacings. Plants that will grow 4–5ft (120–50cm) tall are best planted 2–3ft (60–90cm) apart, and those that will grow 3–4ft (90–120cm) tall, 2ft (60cm) apart. Water the plants in their pots and allow to drain. Plant with care to avoid disturbing the root ball, and firm gently, leaving a slight depression at the base of the stem. Water thoroughly. The plants will make a clump by late fall; this may be lifted and stored for replanting in spring.

Selecting Plants

When planting out a potgrown dahlia or rooted cutting, select young plants with a vigorous root system and disease-free foliage.

Planting a Clump

Insert a 3ft (1m) stake in a planting hole. Place soil around the clump so that the base of the new shoots is 1–2in (2.5–5cm) below soil level.

Planting tubers and clumps
Plant out tubers and clumps about three weeks before the last frost date, preparing the ground as for potgrown plants. Prepare a planting hole at least 9in (22cm) across and about 6in (15cm) deep, place the tuber or clump in the hole, and cover. Mark the position of the plant with a stake placed just to the side; this will indicate the plant's exact position when inserting its sturdier support stake.

Planting rooted cuttings
Tubers may be grown on in the cold frame or greenhouse to provide cuttings (see opposite). Plant out the rooted cuttings after all danger of frost has passed.

As growth develops, water the plants moderately; to retain moisture, mulch with well-rotted compost or manure when the plants are 12–15in (30–38cm) high. Do not place the mulch directly against the base of the plants since this may encourage stem rot.

Pinching and disbudding
When the dahlias have grown to about 15in (38cm), remove the growing points to encourage side shoots. Insert two more stakes to make a triangular support and tie the shoots in, with about 6in (15cm) between ties.

PINCHING

1 *When the plant is about 15in (38cm) high, pinch out the central shoot to encourage the development of side shoots.*

2 *When the plant has 6–8 side shoots, pinch out the top pair of buds. Tie in the stems to stakes.*

The number of shoots allowed to develop should depend on the size of the blooms required. For giant or large blooms, restrict each plant to 4–6 shoots; for medium and small blooms, allow 7–10 shoots. To produce high-quality blooms, remove (disbud) pairs of buds developing below the terminal bud. Disbud at least two pairs of these side (wing) buds; for giant blooms, take out three pairs. Remove them carefully before they grow large; if removed too late, ugly scars will appear.

DISBUDDING

Pinch out the side (wing) buds growing below the terminal bud on each young plant, so that the bud that remains will develop into a larger bloom.

Summer feeding

Six weeks after planting, feed with a high nitrogen and potassium fertilizer, either in granular form, or by weekly applications of liquid fertilizer to the roots or leaves. As flower buds develop, extra potassium in the liquid fertilizer gives strong stems and good flower color, especially for pink shades; this is important when growing for exhibition.

The tuber's development during late summer and early fall is stimulated by the shortening daylength. During this period, apply a split application of muriate of potash and superphosphate at the manufacturer's recommended rate. Avoid contact with leaves or stems since this may cause scorch.

Pests and diseases

Dahlias are attacked particularly by aphids (p.552), thrips (p.553), spider mites (p.552), and earwigs (p.563). These may be controlled by spraying regularly. Discard any plants infected with viruses (p.555).

Lifting and storing clumps

When the foliage has been blackened by the first frosts in fall, trim back the stems to about 6in (15cm). Lift and clean the clumps of soil, trim off any fine roots, and treat the clumps with fungicide. Place them upside down for a few weeks in a frost-free place to dry out.

Label the clumps and pack them in boxes in vermiculite, perlite, fine turface, peat, or a similar medium. Store in a cool, frostproof place. Inspect the clumps regularly in winter: if any mildew or rot develops, scrape it out and dust the wound with sulfur. Mist-spray if needed to prevent shriveling.

LIFTING AND STORING

1 *Cut the stems to about 6in (15cm) above ground level. Loosen the soil and ease the clumps out. Remove excess soil.*

2 *Store the clumps upside down for about 3 weeks in a frost-free place so that the stems dry out thoroughly.*

3 *When the stems have dried out, place the clumps in a cool, frost-free place and cover them with a layer of peat or vermiculite. Keep them dry until spring.*

Propagation

Divide established clumps in spring. First bring them into growth in a cold frame or greenhouse. Place the clumps gently into a tray of soil mix, spray with water, and keep them warm and damp, but not waterlogged. As soon as shoots develop, divide the clump into sections with a sharp knife, ensuring that each piece has at least one growing shoot. Pot up each section separately using a general-purpose soil mix.

Alternatively, in late winter, force clumps at 60–65°F (15–18°C). When shoots are 3in (7.5cm) long, take basal cuttings, trim at a node, and root in a propagating case with bottom heat. Grow on under glass and harden off before planting out.

Showing dahlias

Cut blooms in the morning or evening, making sure that the length of the stem is in proportion to the bloom. When exhibiting, blooms should be well developed with undamaged florets. Read the schedule and present the correct number of stems staged in the container, with the blooms facing the front.

HOW TO PROPAGATE BY BASAL CUTTINGS

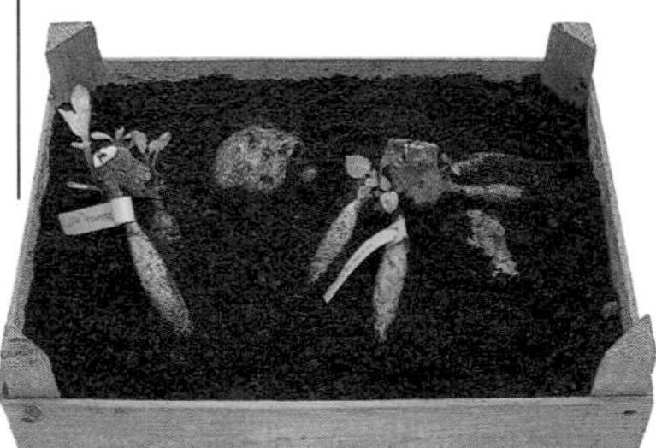

1 *In late winter, force the clumps in the greenhouse. Take cuttings when the young shoots each have 2 or 3 pairs of leaves.*

2 *With a knife, remove each shoot, with a thin segment, or heel, from the parent clump. Trim the basal leaves from each cutting.*

3 *Insert the cuttings in a pot of moist soil mix. Place in a propagator or plastic bag to root. Then pot up singly to grow on.*

Soil preparation and planting

MOST bulbous plants have long dormant periods underground after flowering and need relatively little attention for much of the year. However, the initial stages of selecting good stock, preparing the soil, and planting bulbs correctly do contribute significantly to long-term success in cultivating bulbs.

HOW TO SELECT BULBS

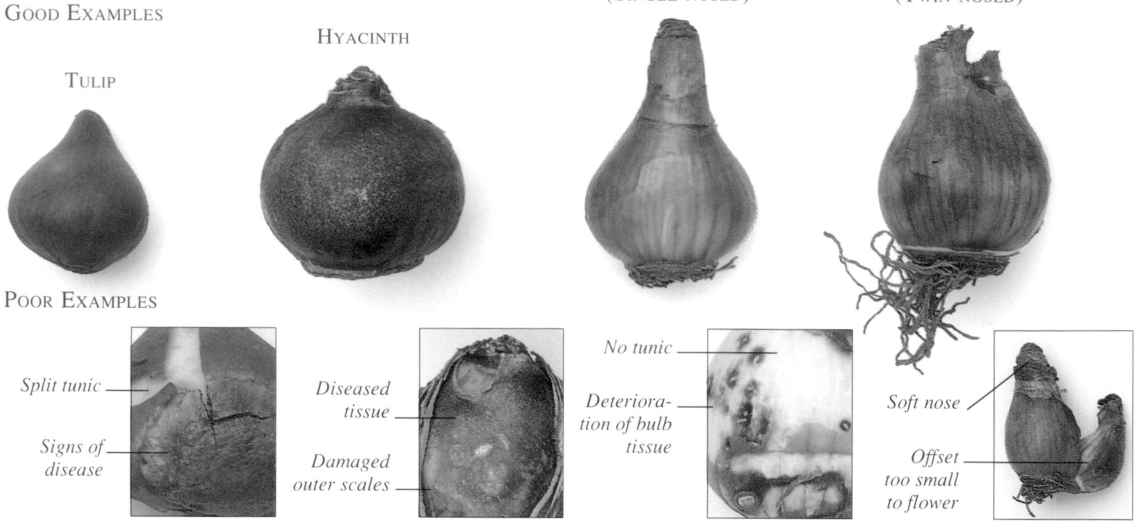

GOOD EXAMPLES

TULIP

HYACINTH

DAFFODIL (SINGLE-NOSED)

DAFFODIL (TWIN-NOSED)

POOR EXAMPLES

Split tunic

Signs of disease

Diseased tissue

Damaged outer scales

No tunic

Deterioration of bulb tissue

Soft nose

Offset too small to flower

Buying bulbs

There is considerable variation in the quality and size of bulbs available commercially, so examine any bulbs carefully before buying them. Different types of bulb are sold at various times of the year; always buy them when they are as fresh as possible. Select bulbs that are appropriate to the planting site: most need sun, some require shade, and others will naturalize in grass.

Conservation

Conserving bulbs in the wild is of the utmost importance, and strict rules govern their importation. Before purchasing bulbs, check (wherever possible) that the stocks on sale at nurseries and garden centers have been obtained from sources of cultivated bulbs, rather than from stocks that have been collected in the wild.

Dry bulbs

Most bulbs are sold in a dry state during their dormant period. Buy these as early as possible before they start into growth; most daffodils, for example, normally start producing roots in late summer, and most other spring-flowering bulbs will begin to grow by early fall. Fall-flowering crocuses and *Colchicum* species and hybrids especially benefit from early planting: specialist nurseries sell them in midsummer.

All fall-flowering bulbs are best bought and planted by late summer. Bulbs tend to deteriorate if kept dry too long; they have a shorter growing period and take some time to recover and flower satisfactorily, so buy and plant them as soon as they are available. Many bulbs, usually those that have a summer growing season, including *Galtonia*, gladioli, and *Tigridia*, are available for purchase in spring.

When buying bulbs, make sure that they are healthy and firm with strong growing points. Avoid those with soft or diseased areas or insect damage. Bulbs that are much smaller than average for their type, and bulb offsets, will not produce flowers in their first season.

Juno irises are unusual in having permanent storage roots beneath the bulb; if these have broken off, do not buy the bulb since it will not develop satisfactorily. Tulips should have intact skins or tunics, otherwise they may be vulnerable to disease.

CHOOSING CORMS, TUBERS, AND OTHER BULBOUS PLANTS

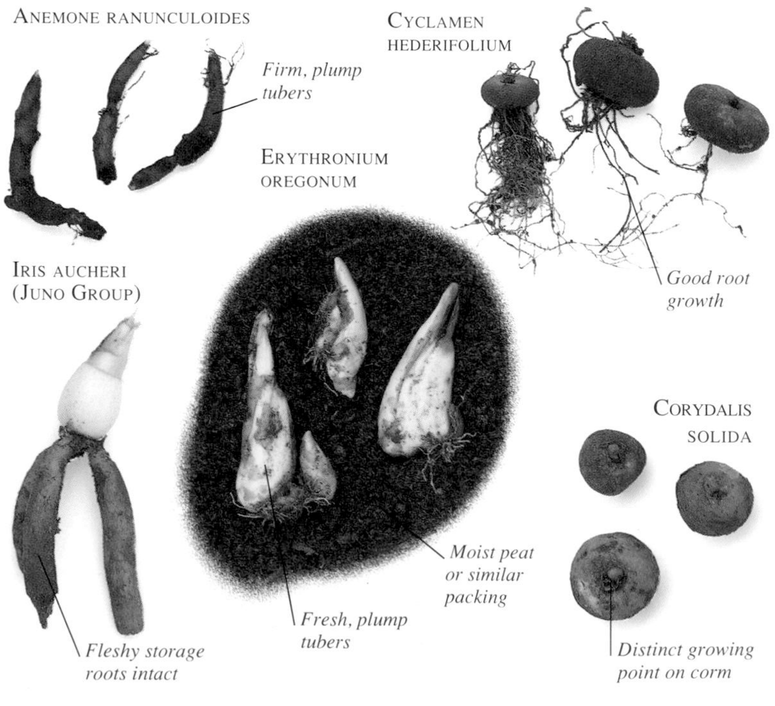

Snowdrops in the green

If possible, obtain snowdrops in the green (i.e. still in leaf) after flowering, preferably just as the leaves begin to yellow at the tips. Fall-planted dry bulbs, although much cheaper, often fail to establish well. Although rarely obtainable, a few specialist nurseries do supply snowdrops in the green.

Moist bulbs

Although most bulbs may be stored dry, a few are better kept in slightly moist bark, peat, shredded wood, or some similar material. This particularly applies to some of the shade-loving bulb species such as *Erythronium*, *Anemone nemorosa*, and *Trillium* that are normally found growing in damp woodland.

When buying cyclamen tubers, look for those with fibrous roots that are stored in moist bark or that are in root growth in pots. Cyclamen with healthy roots establish much more successfully than dry tubers and so, although more expensive, are a much better buy.

Potgrown bulbs

Pots of bulbs in active growth, and frequently in flower, are often sold in nurseries and garden centers. These are usually bulbs that were not sold when dormant and have been potted up. They grow satisfactorily and may be planted at once without disturbing the roots. Alternatively, they may be kept in pots until they have flowered and planted as dry bulbs after they have died down. They are more expensive, however, than dry bulbs.

The influence of different soil types

Bulbs grow in a range of soil types, habitats, and climates throughout the world; the conditions in which they occur naturally indicate their needs in cultivation. Most hardy bulbs are from Mediterranean-type climates and thrive in a warm, sunny site, in freely draining soils that warm up quickly in spring and become dry in summer. Some bulbs tolerate heavy soils that are moist during the growing season, as long as they are baked dry in summer. If the soil is moderately fertile and humus-rich, many bulbs increase steadily from year to year by seed or vegetative means. Most do best in a near-neutral or slightly alkaline soil.

Good drainage is vital; most bulbs are prone to rot while dormant if the soil is wet and poorly aerated. A few occur in the wild in riverside or swampland habitats. These thrive in moist (or even permanently wet) soils that do not dry out in summer.

Light soils

Sandy or light soils usually warm up rapidly in spring and provide the good drainage that most bulbs need, although they are often deficient in humus and nutrients. Dig in plenty of well-rotted compost or manure before planting and, in early spring, top-dress with a balanced fertilizer applied at the manufacturer's recommended rate. Always incorporate manure below the level at which the bulbs are planted to avoid the risk of disease or chemical damage. If using fresh manure, dig it in at least three months before planting. More fertile, sandy, and loamy soils benefit from extra organic matter, although fertilizer dressing is unnecessary in the first year. In rock gardens, dig in coarse grit to make up at least one-third of the top 12in (30cm) of soil for the extra drainage that most dwarf bulbs need.

Heavy soils

Heavy clay soils often need a lot of work to improve their drainage; on very poorly drained soils, a drainage system must first be installed to grow bulbs successfully. Coarse sand or grit at a rate of at least 1 1/2–2 buckets/sq yd (sq m) dug into the whole planting area will be required to make a significant difference. Heavy applications of well-rotted organic matter also improve the soil structure and therefore the drainage. For further information, see "Soil structure and water content," p.528.

Shady areas

Shade-loving bulbs most often occur naturally in woodland habitats, but grow well in any shady situation, as long as the soil is properly prepared: it should be rich in nutrients and humus and also retain moisture. Incorporate plenty of leaf mold or some other organic matter, such as well-rotted manure or compost, before planting. Acid-loving woodland bulbs thrive in the peat garden where at least half the soil is leaf mold, peat, or compost.

CORRECT PLANTING DEPTHS

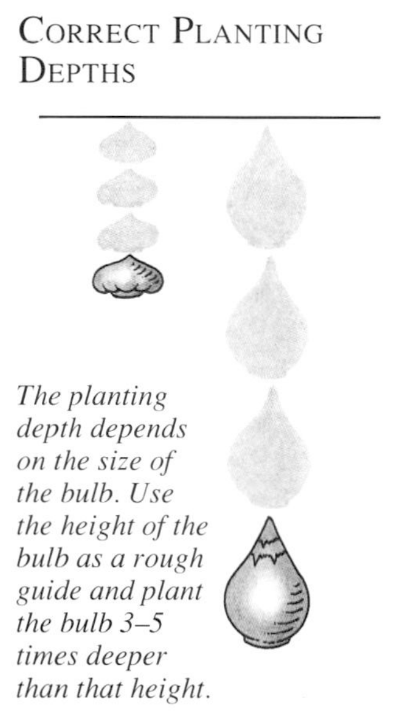

The planting depth depends on the size of the bulb. Use the height of the bulb as a rough guide and plant the bulb 3–5 times deeper than that height.

Planting time

Dry bulbs should be planted as soon as possible after purchase. If the bulbs have been stored over winter (see "Lifting, drying, and storing," p.231), plant them at the end of their dormant period before they start growing. Potgrown bulbs may be planted after purchase throughout the season, or kept in their pots until after they die down and treated as dry bulbs. Plant summer-flowering bulbs, including those that bloom in late summer under cover, and bulbs in the green, in early to midspring.

Planting in the open

Bulbs are usually best planted several to a large hole dug out with a spade, but also may be planted singly. Do not make the outline of the planting area or the spacing of the bulbs symmetrical since this looks unnatural, and if one or two bulbs fail they leave unsightly gaps.

Bulbs may also be planted together in layers for a succession of bloom (see right).

Planting depths and spacing

Plant bulbs with three to five times their own depth of soil above them (deeper in light than in heavy soils) and two to three bulb widths apart. Remove soil to the correct depth, fork some bone meal into the bottom of the hole, and insert the bulbs.

It may be difficult to identify the top of a bulb, especially with rootless cyclamen tubers. The upper surface is usually flatter than the lower, or sometimes concave. *Corydalis* tubers can be almost globular, but usually have some sign of shoot growth on the top. If it is impossible to be sure, plant the bulb on its side.

Replace the soil, breaking down any clods. Firm gently so that there are no air spaces around the bulbs. Give fall-planted bulbs an occasional deep watering until winter sets in. Lightly mulch areas of spring-planted bulbs to conserve moisture.

PLANTING BULBS IN THE OPEN

1 Dig out a large hole in well-prepared ground. Plant the bulbs (here tulips), at least 3 times their own depth, and 2–3 widths, apart.

2 For a natural effect, space the bulbs randomly. Once they are in position, gently draw the soil over them with your hand to avoid displacing or damaging them.

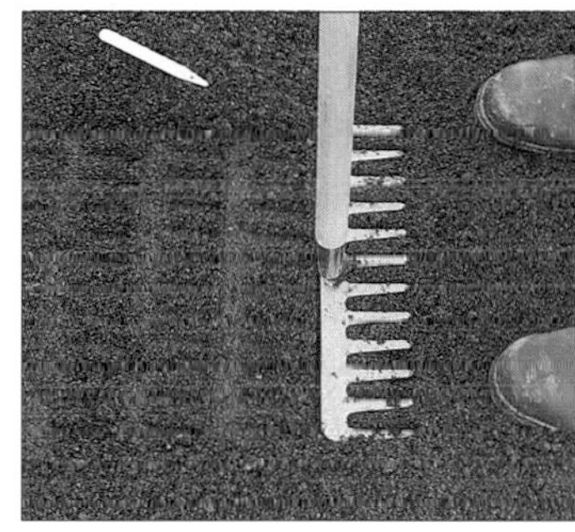

3 Tamp down the soil over the planted area with the back of a rake. Avoid treading on the soil surface, because this might damage the growing points.

PLANTING BULBS SINGLY

Plant each bulb in a separate hole at the appropriate depth. Draw back the prepared soil with a trowel and firm it down gently afterward.

Potgrown bulbs

Bulbs that have been purchased as potgrown plants may be planted in the open ground once the tops have died down. Keep watering them until the foliage turns yellow; this allows the bulbs to gather strength for flowering the next year. When planting the bulbs outdoors, make a hole large enough to accommodate the whole pot, so that the contents may be planted without disturbance.

PLANTING BULBS IN LAYERS

Two or more kinds of bulb may be planted in the same space. Plant each kind at its correct depth, carefully covering each layer before planting the next type of bulb.

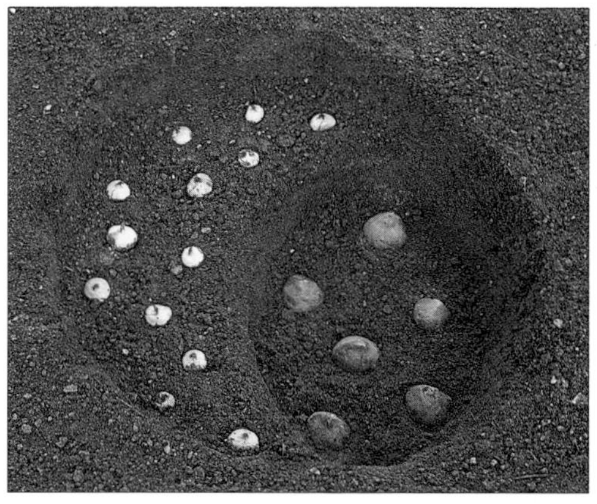

HOW TO PLANT CYCLAMEN IN ROOT GROWTH

1 Select a planting site where the soil is rich in leaf mold or humus, or prepare the soil as necessary, working in organic matter well below the depth of the planting hole to encourage the roots to grow into the soil after planting. Allow it to settle for a day or two, then make a hole that is deep enough to plant the tuber with its roots spread out below it.

2 Plant the tuber so that it will lie with its upper surface just visible at soil level. Fill in around the roots with soil, taking care not to damage the roots.

3 Gently firm the soil around the tuber with your fingers, leaving the growing point just exposed. Lightly cover it with a loose mulch.

If the bulbs are potbound, gently tease out the roots at the base before planting to encourage them to grow out into the soil. If they are growing in a peat-based soil mix, keep the bulbs under cover in winter, otherwise the peat acts as a sponge and the dormant bulbs rot in the waterlogged soil mix.

Planting tubers and corms in root growth

A number of woodland species, such as cyclamen, are best planted when they are in root growth, rather than as dry bulbs, since they will become established more quickly. They are also more likely to flower in their first season after planting; dry corms or tubers are much less reliable in this respect. Planting in root growth also eliminates any problems in distinguishing between the bottoms and tops of tubers or corms. Work plenty of leaf mold or well-rotted organic matter into the soil before planting to create the moist, humus-rich conditions that woodland bulbs require, otherwise the bulbs will not thrive.

Planting depth and spacing

Calculate the spacing and planting depth for corms and tubers in the same way as for dry bulbs (see "Planting in the open" and *Correct Planting Depths*, p.225), but allow extra space for the roots.

Cyclamen are unusual in that they grow near the soil surface in the wild, so do not plant the tubers too deeply or they may not flower. Make sure that their tops are at about the same level as the surrounding soil. They may be planted more closely than other bulbs, but they should be spaced at least their own width apart.

Planting

Plant the corms or tubers singly or as a group. It is important for the planting hole to be sufficiently deep and wide to properly accommodate the roots. Spread them out in the hole to help the plants establish more quickly. Fill in the hole and firm well to remove any air spaces.

The tops of cyclamen tubers may be left exposed or, if preferred, lightly covered with a loose mulch. Use leaf mold or, if the bed already has a top-dressing, coarse grit.

Naturalizing in grass

When planting bulbs that are to be naturalized in grass, first cut the grass as short as possible. Random rather than regimented planting achieves a more natural effect; scatter the bulbs gently by hand over the area and plant them where they

PLANTING LARGE BULBS IN GRASS

1 Clean the bulbs (here daffodils), removing any loose outer coatings and old roots. Scatter the bulbs randomly over the planting area, then make sure that they are at least their own width apart.

2 Make an individual hole for each bulb, using a bulb planter to remove a circle of sod and a core of soil to a depth of about 4–6in (10–15cm).

3 Place a pinch of bone meal, mixed with a little of the soil from the core, into each hole and put in a bulb, making sure that the growing point is uppermost.

4 Break up the underside of the core over the bulb, so that it is completely covered with loose soil. Then replace the remains of the core on top of it.

5 Replace the lid of sod, and firm it in gently, taking care not to damage the growing point of the bulb. Fill in any gaps in the grass with more soil.

Planting Small Bulbs in Grass

1 *Using a half-moon edger (or spade), cut an H shape in the sod. Cut to the full depth of the half-moon blade to make sure that it penetrates the soil below.*

2 *Undercut the sod and fold back the flaps to expose the area of bare soil beneath. Take care not to crack or tear the sod unduly.*

3 *Using a hand fork, loosen the soil beneath to a depth of at least 3in (7cm), mixing in a little bone meal at a rate of about ½oz/sq yd (15g/sq m).*

4 *Press the bulbs (here crocuses) gently but firmly into the soil, taking care not to damage the growing points. Space the bulbs randomly at least 1in (2.5cm) apart.*

5 *Score the underneath of the sod with a hand fork to loosen the soil, so that the bulbs will be able to grow up through the sod easily.*

6 *Roll the sod flaps back into position, taking care not to dislodge the bulbs or to damage the sod. Firm down the sod, particularly along the seams.*

Using a Fork to Plant Small Bulbs

1 *Push a garden fork into the grass to the appropriate depth and rock it back and forth. Repeat at random over the rest of the planting area.*

2 *Thoroughly mix a little bone meal with some garden soil. Trickle a small amount of this mix into the bottom of each hole, using a widger or a small spoon.*

3 *Place a single bulb in each hole, growing point uppermost, ensuring that it is buried at twice its own depth. Then cover all the planted bulbs with soil.*

Naturalizing in Grass

Allium moly
Anemone apennina,
A. blanda (and cvs),
A. pavonina
Camassia
Chionodoxa
Colchicum autumnale,
C. speciosum

Crocus pulchellus

Crocus biflorus,
C. chrysanthus,
C., Dutch Hybrids,
C. flavus, *C. nudiflorus*,
C. ochroleucus,
C. pulchellus, *C. speciosus*,
C. tommasinianus
Dactylorrhiza fuchsii,
D. maculata
Eranthis hyemalis
Erythronium dens-canis,
E. revolutum,
E. 'White Beauty'
Fritillaria meleagris,
F. pyrenaica
Galanthus caucasicus,
G. elwesii, *G. nivalis*
Gladiolus communis subsp. *byzantinus*
Hyacinthoides hispanica
Leucojum aestivum,
L. vernum
Muscari, some ❄

Narcissus 'Fortune'

Narcissus (some dwarf and most large spp.),
N. bulbocodium,
N. cyclamineus, *N. nanus*,
N. obvallaris, *N. poeticus*,
N. pseudonarcissus,
N. pumilus, *N. triandrus*
Ornithogalum nutans
Puschkinia scilloides
Scilla bifolia, *S. siberica*
Tulipa sprengeri, *T. tarda*

Key
❄ *Not frost hardy*

have fallen, making sure that they are at least one bulb's width apart. Dig holes with a trowel or use a bulb planter, which cuts out plugs of sod and soil to a depth of about 4–6in (10–15cm); dig deeper if necessary for larger bulbs.

Check that all the holes are at the correct depth and that the bulbs are the right way up, before inserting them and replacing the sod.

Planting large groups of small bulbs in grass

It is easier and less time-consuming to plant large numbers of very small bulbs, such as crocuses, by lifting a section of sod and planting a whole group of bulbs in the soil beneath, rather than planting each bulb individually. Loosen the soil beneath the sod since it may be compacted; fork in a little balanced fertilizer or some bone meal. Position the bulbs randomly, at least their own width apart. Replace the sod over the bulbs, and firm it by hand or tamp it down gently with the back of a rake.

Alternatively, in lighter soils, use a broad-tined garden fork to make a series of holes in the sod, and rock the fork back and forth in the ground to enlarge the holes slightly so that they easily accommodate the bulbs. The tines should be inserted to three times the depth of the bulb, for example 3in (7cm) for crocuses. Repeat this at random for the entire planting area, so that the final arrangement of holes is in straight but crisscrossing lines. Mix a little bone meal with soil and place some in each hole before planting the bulbs singly, then top-dress the whole area with more prepared soil.

HARDY BULBS FOR FORCING

Allium neapolitanum, *A. oreophilum*
Arisaema
Camassia
Chionodoxa

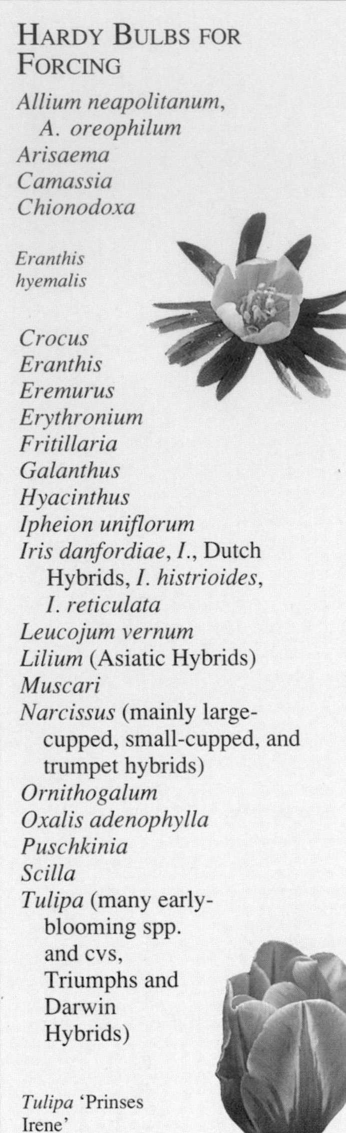

Eranthis hyemalis

Crocus
Eranthis
Eremurus
Erythronium
Fritillaria
Galanthus
Hyacinthus
Ipheion uniflorum
Iris danfordiae, *I.*, Dutch Hybrids, *I. histrioides*, *I. reticulata*
Leucojum vernum
Lilium (Asiatic Hybrids)
Muscari
Narcissus (mainly large-cupped, small-cupped, and trumpet hybrids)
Ornithogalum
Oxalis adenophylla
Puschkinia
Scilla
Tulipa (many early-blooming spp. and cvs, Triumphs and Darwin Hybrids)

Tulipa 'Prinses Irene'

HOW TO PLANT BULBS IN POTS

1 *Plant the bulbs (here daffodils) at twice their own depth, and one bulb's width apart.*

2 *Cover the bulbs with soil mix to ½in (1cm) below the rim. Top-dress with grit (see inset), and label.*

PREPARING CLAY POTS

Before planting bulbs in a clay pot, place a single crock – or several, according to the drainage requirements of the plant – over the drainage hole in the base before adding soil mix.

Planting in ornamental containers

Bulbs may be planted in troughs, tubs, patio pots, or any ornamental container that is clean and has sufficient drainage holes in the base to allow water to drain away quickly. Place a layer of crocks or another drainage material at least 1in (2.5cm) deep in the bottom of the container. Raise the pot off the ground with bricks or pot feet to stop water from gathering in the base and, if the pot is made of ceramic or terracotta, help guard it against cold damage.

Vary the soil mix, whether it be soil-based, rich in leaf mold, or very gritty, to suit the requirements of different types of bulb. The soil mix must be free draining or it may become waterlogged and the bulbs may rot. Insert them at the same depths and spacing as for standard pots (see *How to Plant Bulbs in Pots*, above).

Soil mixes for pots, beds, and frames

A good general soil mix, containing the required humus content and drainage may be prepared as follows: mix together 2 parts peat, 3 parts coarse grit, and 4 parts soil; then add a base fertilizer or some bone meal at a rate of 1oz/1 gallon (25g/5 liters) and (except for lime-hating plants) garden lime at a rate of 1oz/4 gallons (25g/18 liters).

For bulb beds make up sufficient soil mix for a layer that is at least 12in (30cm) in depth, with a layer about 2in (5cm) deep, of well-rotted compost or manure beneath it.

A similar mix is suitable for most bulbs, in pots or other containers both indoors and outside. If using a commercial potting mix, add some grit or coarse sand – at least one-third by bulk – because these soil mixes are often not sufficiently well drained for use with most bulbs.

Woodland bulbs grown in pots or containers require a well-drained mix with additional organic matter that is rich in nutrients, for example a mixture of 3 parts leaf mold or compost, 2 parts good garden soil, and 1 part sharp sand or grit.

Forcing hardy bulbs

Forcing is the process of bringing a plant into flower out of season. It is easy to force most bulbs in containers both indoors and outdoors because the growing conditions can be tailored to the particular needs of the plant. Suitable soil mixes may be used for different types of bulb, and plants can be given the correct seasonal care, from planting in fall, encouraging roots to form in winter, and bringing into bloom in early spring.

Similar control is possible when cultivating bulbs that are planted directly into a greenhouse bed or bulb frame; the planting method is the same under cover as for bulbs grown in the open (see "Planting in the open," p.225).

Choosing clay or plastic pots

Bulbs may be planted in either clay or plastic pots. Clay pots are not as readily available, but they are more suitable for bulbs that are unable to tolerate excessive moisture, because the soil mix dries out more quickly after watering than in plastic pots. Plastic pots are now extensively used and are perfectly satisfactory as long as they are filled with a freely draining soil mix; water the soil mix less frequently than with clay pots. For plants that need moist conditions, such as woodland bulbs, the greater water retentiveness available in plastic pots is particularly valuable.

If using clay pots, place one or more crocks over the drainage hole; no crocking is necessary for plastic pots as long as the soil mix itself is well drained. A piece of screening placed over drainage holes prevents worms from entering the pot.

Planting in pots

Ideally, bulbs should be planted in pots at the same depths as bulbs grown outdoors (see "Planting depths and spacing," p.225). However, this is often not possible with larger bulbs, in which case make sure the pot is deep enough to allow at least 1in (2.5cm) of moist soil mix beneath the bulb. When filling the pot with soil mix, allow ½in (1cm) of space below the rim of the pot. A standard 6in (15cm) pot provides room for these requirements for many bulbs and will take at least three daffodils or five to six tulips.

Select similar-sized bulbs of the same variety for forcing, otherwise flowering may be irregular. For crocuses and other small bulbs, a 6in (15cm) pan holds ten to 12 bulbs.

Place a layer of soil mix at least 1in (2.5cm) deep in the pot and space the bulbs evenly on this. Do not press the bulbs into the soil mix too firmly since this may compress the soil just beneath the roots of the bulbs and impede their growth. Leave about one finger-width between each bulb. Position tulip bulbs with the flat side facing out: the first leaf will then grow over the edge of

BULBS IN A PLUNGE BED

Plunge the labeled pots up to their rims in a sand bed or cold frame. Check the pots regularly to ensure that the soil mix does not dry out.

the pot. Work more soil mix down between the bulbs and firm gently. Small bulbs should be covered completely, but tulips and daffodils may be left with the tip of the bulbs showing. Top-dress the pot with a generous layer of horticultural grit, which helps to retain moisture and improves the appearance of the pot. Label with the plant name, the date of planting, and source. Do not allow the soil mix to dry out completely. Check regularly; as bulbs begin to root and grow, more frequent watering will be necessary.

Cold storage of pots

After planting, keep the pots in a cold frame or cold greenhouse. Bulbs in pots are particularly susceptible to cold damage; in severe winters, pots in a cold frame or unheated greenhouse may freeze solid. Protect them by sinking the pots in a plunge bed of coarse sand, perlite, or grit, mixed with enough peat to stop the insulating material from collapsing into the hole when the pots are taken out. Alternatively, the pots may be plunged in a straw-lined trench in the garden and covered with an insulating layer of straw, loosely packed leaves, or perlite. The lining and covering should be thick enough to prevent the pots from freezing in midwinter.

If only a few pots are being forced, they may be placed in a refrigerator, a root cellar, or a cool corner of a basement. The temperature should remain between 35–40°F (2–4°C). Do not store the pots with apples, which produce ethylene gas that can cause flowers to abort.

Check periodically in winter for watering needs. After about ten weeks, begin checking for pots ready to bring into gentle warmth. Early-flowering varieties need less cold treatment than later-flowering ones, which may need up to 16 weeks. When ready, new shoots are visible and roots show at the base of the container. Move the containers into a cool room or greenhouse, between 50–55°F (10–12°C), and keep them out of direct sunlight initially. Once the shoots turn green and elongate, move them into more light and warmer conditions, and keep moist but not wet. In the home, flowers will last longer if the pots are moved into a cool room at night. (For care after flowering, see "Bulbs in containers outdoors," p.231).

Bulbs that have been forced into bloom should be planted in the garden once spring arrives or allowed to go dormant in their pots and then planted out in fall. They will not force well for a second year.

Bulbs in a Straw-lined Trench

After planting in pots, give hardy bulbs their necessary cold period by storing outdoors. Cover thickly with straw to prevent the soil mix from freezing solid. Water if necessary during warm spells.

Popular bulbs for forcing indoors

Some bulbs can be planted in pots and bowls and kept indoors in the dark to induce them to flower early. The bulbs are best grown and displayed in a 60°F (16°C) room. In hotter conditions, the flower stems grow very quickly and look out of character, and the flowers do not last as long as in cool conditions.

Hyacinths

A popular bulb for indoor forcing is the fragrant hyacinth. Specially prepared bulbs are available; if they are given suitable treatment, they will come into flower by midwinter.

Buy the hyacinth bulbs in early fall and plant them in bowls filled with bulb fiber or moistened soil mix. Plant the bulbs close together, so they are not quite touching one another, with their growing tips protruding just above the top of the fiber or soil mix. Put the newly planted bulbs in a cool, dark place: a closed cupboard in a cool room is suitable. This encourages the flowering stems to develop before the leaves and allows the root systems to become well established. Keep the fiber or mix just moist by carefully watering between the bulbs.

Leave the bowls in the dark for about eight weeks, or until the pale new shoots are about 1½–2in (4–5cm) high and the flower buds are just visible. Once they have reached this stage, bring the bulbs into the daylight, but do not expose them to bright sunlight. Do not remove the bowls of bulbs from the dark earlier than this, because the leaves will grow very rapidly and obscure the flowers. Once exposed to the light, the leaves will gradually acquire their natural green color.

Tender daffodils

Some tender daffodils, including *Narcissus* 'Paper White' and 'Soleil d'Or', may be grown in bulb fiber in the same way as hyacinths. They do require more light, however, and should be placed on a sunny windowsill as soon as the shoots appear above the bulb fiber. If the light is inadequate, daffodils may become both pale and excessively tall, and they will require staking for support.

Amaryllis

The large-flowered *Hippeastrum* hybrids, commonly known as amaryllis (true *Amaryllis* are not forced), are popular as indoor plants. Garden centers and stores supply them complete with a suitable soil mix, ready to be planted in pots and grown to flowering in a warm, light room.

After flowering, remove the dead flowers, but do not cut down the stalk until it shrivels. Keep the plants in a well-lit room and water regularly. Feed once a month with a flowering house plant fertilizer. When danger of frost is past, plunge the pot outside in light shade. Reduce watering in late summer to induce dormancy. When the leaves turn yellow, store the pot in a cool location, but remember to bring it indoors before frost. After about three months, the bulb may start to grow, so check regularly. If growth does not start naturally, watering begun six weeks before Christmas should produce flowers for Christmas.

Forcing Hyacinths in a Container Indoors

1 *Place some moist bulb fiber or soil mix in the bottom of a container. Position the bulbs and fill with fiber, leaving the bulb crowns just visible at the surface. Leave them in a cool, dark place.*

2 *When the flower spikes are visible between the pale leaves, bring the container into bright, indirect light.*

Growing hyacinths in water

Hyacinth bulbs may be forced in water, in special glasses designed to hold one bulb with its base just at water level. Place a bulb in its glass in a cool room away from sunlight and keep the water level topped up to just below the base of the bulb. It rapidly produces roots which grow down into the water.

Wait until the flower buds begin to show color before moving the rooted hyacinth into a warm, brightly lit room. The flowering shoots then develop and produce blooms. After flowering, discard the exhausted bulb since it is unlikely to provide a good display the following year.

Fill the glass with water up to the neck and place the bulb in the top so it sits just above the water. Leave in a cool place. As the roots grow, keep the water topped up.

Routine care

Bulbs do not require a great deal of maintenance if the correct environment is provided. If they flower poorly, the most likely cause is overcrowding: this is easily remedied by dividing them and replanting in a fresh site. Bulbs are not prone to pests or diseases, but any present must be controlled promptly.

Bulbs in grass

Bulbs left to naturalize in grass do not need as much attention as those planted in other sites in the garden, but correct timing in mowing is very important. Deadhead regularly and feed occasionally; this will help the bulbs stay healthy and able to multiply steadily over the years.

Fertilizing

Bulbs in grass should not be fed with fertilizers high in nitrogen, since these increase the vigor of the surrounding grass at the bulbs' expense. If a feed is needed (e.g. for daffodils that fail to flower freely), use a high-potassium fertilizer to encourage the production of blooms.

Deadheading

Prompt removal of faded blooms improves vigor in bulbs by preventing them from wasting energy on unwanted seed production. After flowering, pinch through the stems below the seedpods. If the seed capsules will be harvested later or left to seed naturally, leave some to ripen on the plant, then cut the stems to the ground after harvesting the seed.

Cutting Down Bulbs in Grass after Flowering

Leave clumps of bulbs (here daffodils) planted in grass until the leaves start to turn yellow. Then cut them down to ground level with shears before mowing the grass.

When to mow

If cultivating early-flowering bulbs such as daffodils, do not cut the grass until at least six weeks after they have flowered, or until the foliage is turning yellow. If growing bulbs that increase by self-seeding, do not mow the grass until the seed capsules have been able to shed all their seed – usually about three weeks after the leaves begin to die down.

Fall-flowering bulbs such as *Colchicum* start into growth before the end of the lawn-mowing season. When the first leaves or tips of the flowering shoots appear, mow with the blades set high enough to avoid them; stop mowing when the shoots are too tall to escape the blades.

In a wildflower meadow that includes late-flowering spring bulbs, delay mowing until mid- to late summer, when all the foliage has died down completely.

Staking

A few tall bulbs with slender stems need staking. Stake these plants as soon as they are tall enough for a tie to be put around them; tie in the stems again when the plants are near their full height and are about to flower. Where the bulbs are planted in groups, place bamboo stakes on the inward-facing side of the stems so that they are concealed by the growing plants. Insert the stakes well away from the base of the stems so that the bulbs are not damaged.

1 *Support a tall, single-stemmed plant such as a gladiolus with a bamboo stake when the plant is 6in (15cm) tall. Attach the stem to the stake with string or raffia.*

2 *When the flower buds are forming, tie in the stem to the stake just below the buds to prevent the stem from breaking when the buds open.*

Staking Bulbs in Groups

For plants such as lilies that grow in clumps, place one or more stakes in the center of the clump. Tie in surrounding stems to each stake with a figure-eight loop so that the stems do not rub against the stakes.

Deadheading

Unless the seeds are to be used for propagation, cut down all dead flower stems of bulbs in the border (here Allium*) with pruners to ground level.*

Bulbs in borders and woodland

The level of maintenance required for bulbs in herbaceous or mixed borders, or in woodland, depends on whether they are intended to be temporary or permanent fillers. Permanent bulb plantings need little maintenance until the bulbs become overcrowded, when they should be lifted and divided (see opposite).

If the ground is well prepared, no feeding is necessary during the first year. An application once or twice in a season of a low-nitrogen, high-potassium fertilizer, which promotes flowering rather than leafy growth (see Soils and Fertilizers, "Types of fertilizer," p.532), will encourage a fine display in subsequent years.

Bulbs need adequate moisture during the growing season, especially in woodland, and it may be necessary to water them if there is a prolonged early drought. Deadhead them at regular intervals in the same way as for bulbs in grass.

Care of temporary plantings is the same as for the first-year care of bulbs that are permanently planted. Lift the bulbs for storing at the end of the growing season (see opposite).

Removing dead leaves

After the bulbs in the border have finished flowering, allow the leaves to die down completely before removing them. Do not tidy the leaves by tying them together while still green because this reduces their capacity to photosynthesize and store energy in the bulb in readiness for the next growing season, and therefore the bulb loses vigor. It also makes them die down prematurely.

When to Harvest Seeds

If seeds are required, do not deadhead until the seed capsule (here Fritillaria*) is brown and begins to split. The ripe seeds are then ready to harvest for sowing or storing.*

Lifting and dividing overcrowded bulbs

If mature bulbs flower less freely than in previous years, the deterioration is usually due to overcrowding. This may not be obvious unless the bulbs are visible near the soil surface, as is often the case with *Nerine*.

Lift crowded clumps during the dormant season, before the root growth starts. Separate the clumps into individual bulbs and replant them in irregular groups. Insert separately at three to five times their own depth and two to three bulb widths apart. Plant small offsets or bulblets between bulbs of flowering size. Alternatively, grow them in pots, in a nursery bed, in a frame, or in the garden in the same way as for two-year-old seedlings (see "Care of seedlings," p.234).

If, on lifting, the bulbs are found not to be overcrowded, but are deteriorating or no longer thriving, inspect them for pests and diseases (see p.232). If there is no obvious explanation for their failure, replant them in a different site that is well drained and has sufficient light and nutrients. Alternatively, grow the bulbs in pots in a cold frame or greenhouse until they recover.

Lifting, drying, and storing

Bulbs planted temporarily in beds or borders should be left *in situ* until the foliage has begun to yellow. Then lift and clean them, lay them out on a tray to dry, and store them in paper (not plastic) bags in a dry place until the next planting season. If there is any sign of fungal disease, dust them with fungicide. Alternatively, lift them in full growth soon after flowering or as the foliage dies down and replant them immediately in another part of the garden so that they may die down naturally.

Dwarf bulbs in the rock garden or raised bed

The principles of routine care of bulbs in borders also apply to dwarf species in raised beds or in the rock garden. Many of the rarer bulbs are slow to increase, however, and do not become overcrowded for several years. Keep them reasonably moist during the growing season, particularly in drought conditions, and feed them regularly with a high-potassium, low-nitrogen fertilizer.

If seed is required, harvest the seed capsules when ripe; then clear away the dead leaves to improve the appearance of the bed and reduce the likelihood of disease.

How to Divide an Overcrowded Clump

1 *When bulbs planted in the open become overcrowded, use a garden fork to lift the whole clump as the leaves die down. Take care not to damage them.*

2 *Divide the clump of bulbs (here* Nerine*) by hand, separating it first into smaller clumps and then into individual bulbs. Remove any dead or diseased material.*

3 *Discard any unhealthy bulbs. Clean the good bulbs with care, removing the loose tunics, in preparation for replanting them singly in freshly prepared soil.*

Bulbs in containers outdoors

Bulbs in containers should not be allowed to dry out when in growth and should be fed regularly with a high-potassium fertilizer to boost flower production. Wait until the foliage of spring-flowering bulbs has died back naturally, then lift and clean them, and store them in a cool, dry place during summer. Replant the bulbs in a container of fresh soil mix in early fall for a display in the following spring. Alternatively, if the container is needed for a summer display, transfer the bulbs while still in the green to a spare bed, and allow them to die back before lifting, cleaning, and drying them in the normal way.

Spring-flowering species such as crocuses, daffodils, and hyacinths may be transplanted directly into the garden for naturalizing. Store summer-flowering bulbs in a cool, dry place over winter and replant them in spring.

Some bulbs, such as lilies (*Lilium*), do not grow well if allowed to dry out completely after flowering. Keep them moist by plunging them in their pots in a shaded place or in a cold frame to rest. Repot the lilies every year in the spring.

Bulbs in frames and covered raised beds

Bulbs that are grown in frames or under cover need similar treatment after planting to those in borders (see opposite), but they require special care with watering and feeding.

Remove the covers of the raised beds or frames during the growing season, but replace them temporarily during excessively cold or wet weather. Keep the bulbs watered in dry periods. When most of the bulbs are beginning to die down, replace the covers until the beginning of the next growing season.

How to Lift, Dry, and Store Bulbs

1 *When the leaves are turning yellow, about a month after flowering, gently lift the bulbs (here tulips) with a fork. Put them in labeled containers to avoid confusing different bulbs.*

2 *Clean the soil off the bulbs and rub off any loose, flaking tunic tissue. Cut or carefully pull off the dying foliage. Discard any bulbs that show signs of damage or disease.*

3 *Place the bulbs on a wire tray, spaced so that they do not touch, and leave them to dry overnight. Then dust them with fungicide and store them in clean, clearly labeled paper bags.*

Improve the vigor of the bulbs by feeding them once the nutrients in the original soil mix are exhausted. Use a granular fertilizer sprinkled on the soil mix surface as the bulbs come into growth, or apply a liquid feed every two or three weeks. In the latter part of the season, use a high-potassium, low-nitrogen feed to produce a good display of blooms.

Bulbs in pots under cover

In coastal regions where winters are mild and summers rainy, bulbs that need a warm, dry summer and a winter and spring growing period grow well in an unheated or cool greenhouse. Keep such bulbs dry from the time their leaves die down until their natural growing period begins again either in late summer or early fall.

During the growing season, give the pots a good soaking when they are nearly dry, but take care not to overwater them, especially in winter. Give them extra water in the growing season up to flowering time, after which gradually reduce watering until the leaves die down. Do not allow some hardy bulbs, such as crocuses from mountainous areas and woodland bulbs, to dry out completely; keep the soil mix slightly moist during the summer.

Bulbs such as *Galtonia* from areas with summer rainfall, such as parts of South Africa and South America, must be watered regularly so that they keep growing during the summer; they should then be allowed to dry out during their natural dormancy in winter.

Renewing soil mix

Changing the top layer of soil mix in a pot of bulbs supplies them with enough nutrients for a further year. Before they start to grow, gently scrape away the old soil mix to expose the tops of the bulbs. If they are healthy and not overcrowded, cover them with fresh, moist soil mix of the same type that is in the pot. Separate and repot overcrowded bulbs or, if hardy, plant them out.

Repotting

Bulbs may sometimes be kept in the same pot for several years, but they eventually become overcrowded and need repotting – usually indicated by a failure to flower well and by undersized or unhealthy foliage. At the end of dormancy, repot the bulbs to encourage them to start into growth. Pot up larger bulbs singly, as for the initial potting up and in a similar soil mix (see "Planting in pots," p.228). Plant small bulbs or bulblets between the adult ones or pot them up separately (see "Care of seedlings," p.234).

In early spring, repot tender bulbs that are dormant in winter when the new growth is about to begin.

Fertilizing

If the bulbs are kept in the same pot for several years, feed them regularly throughout the growing season at alternate waterings with a liquid feed containing a high-potassium, low-nitrogen fertilizer. Extra feeding is unnecessary if the bulbs are repotted or the top layer of soil mix in the pot is replaced each year.

Care of forced bulbs

When they are ready to be brought into the light, place forced bulbs, according to their needs, on a shady windowsill or in a cool, bright room (see "Cold storage of pots," p.229). The bulbs tolerate slightly warmer conditions when their flower buds are well formed. Rotate the bowl periodically and keep the soil mix moist. Forced bulbs are generally in a poor condition after flowering. Discard them or plant them out in the garden where they will eventually, perhaps after two years or more, flower again in their normal season.

Amaryllis (*Hippeastrum*) may be kept in good condition from year to year by renewing the top layer of soil mix with a fairly rich, well-drained mix before growth resumes. Do not water them for at least two months during dormancy, and repot them if they are overcrowded.

Bulb problems

Bulbs occasionally fail to flower and are known as blind bulbs. In a long-established clump this problem is often due to overcrowding, so the bulbs should be lifted and replanted separately in fresh soil (see "Lifting and dividing overcrowded bulbs," p.231). Shortage of water during the growing season is another possible cause.

Newly planted bulbs that are blind may not have been stored correctly, or they may not yet be fully mature. *Iris danfordiae*, *Fritillaria* species such as *F. recurva* and *F. thunbergii*, and some other bulbs do not flower regularly even in nature, and so are described as shy-flowering. Do not dig up such bulbs unless they look unhealthy or seem crowded, since they may eventually flower if left undisturbed. It may be helpful to plant the bulbs especially deeply, because this discourages them from dividing into bulblets.

Pests and diseases

During the growing season, keep a careful watch for the symptoms of diseases and pests, and control any problems as soon as they arise. When planting, repotting, or propagating dormant bulbs, inspect them and destroy any badly damaged bulbs.

Bulbs may suffer from rot or fungal diseases, including ink spot (p.569), which infects bulbous irises, and iris soft rot (p.569), which damages all irises. Iris borers (p.566) primarily affect rhizomatous irises. Aphids (p.552) can cause the spread of viruses (p.555). Spider mites (p.552) occasionally affect bulbs grown under cover.

Repotting Overcrowded Bulbs

1 *Remove some soil mix from the pot to inspect the bulbs (here daffodils). If they have become overcrowded in the pot, they should be repotted.*

2 *Carefully tip out the contents of the pot, and remove the bulbs from the soil mix. Discard any dead material or any bulbs that show signs of pests or disease.*

3 *Separate any pairs or clumps of bulbs with large offsets into individual bulbs by gently pulling them apart.*

4 *Select only healthy bulbs and clean them, rubbing with finger and thumb to remove any loose, outer tunics. Dust the bulbs with fungicidal powder.*

5 *Replant the bulbs in a pot of fresh, moist, bulb soil mix. Insert them at twice their own depth, and space them at least their own width apart.*

Propagation

MANY bulbs increase naturally by forming offsets or bulblets around the bulb, and may be propagated by separating these from the parent bulbs. Those that do not divide freely may be increased by cutting them into sections and treating these as new bulbs. Some are propagated by other vegetative means such as scaling or scooping. Seed propagation yields larger stocks, but bulbs may take several years to flower.

How to Propagate Bulbs from Offsets

1 *In the spring, before active growth begins, lift a clump of bulbs (here* Crinum) *with a garden fork. Shake excess soil from the roots and pull the clump apart.*

2 *Select a large bulb with several well-developed offsets. Clean off the soil from the offsets and pull them away from the parent bulb, taking care to preserve any roots.*

3 *Prepare 6in (15cm) pots with a moist, sandy soil mix. Insert a single offset into each pot, and cover it with about 1in (2.5cm) of soil mix. Label and water.*

Dividing bulbs

During the growing season, many bulbs increase by forming offsets from the parent bulb, usually within the bulb tunic. Separate them every year or two, and plant them out or pot them up individually. If left, they may become seriously overcrowded and take longer to develop to flowering size. The offsets may be small and numerous, as with some *Allium* species, or larger and fewer, as with daffodils and tulips.

Other bulbs may form bulbils in the leaf axils, as with lilies (*Lilium*) and some *Calochortus* species, or bulblets around the base of the bulb; both may be used for propagation. (Some lilies, such as some American species and hybrids, produce small rhizomes. Pot these up, placing them horizontally, to grow on for one or two years before planting out in the open garden.)

Propagation from offsets

Some bulbs, for example *Crinum*, may be increased by lifting and dividing a clump. Pull the offsets gently from the parent plant, or cut the basal plate at the point at which they are attached to the larger bulb. Clean off any loose material or soil, and dust cut surfaces with fungicide.

Replant the larger bulbs in the garden in a well-spaced group. Pot up smaller offsets separately, or insert several in a larger pot or deep tray. Keep them for one or two seasons in a cool greenhouse to grow on; then plant out in the open.

Propagation from bulblets and bulbils

Bulbs raised from bulblets will generally flower a year or two earlier than those grown from seed. When repotting bulbs, remove the bulblets from around the base of the parent bulb, and insert them in rows in trays. Use well-drained soil mix with a little slow-release fertilizer added. Space the bulblets in the tray as when sowing seed (see "Sowing the seeds," p.234) and cover them with a 1in (2.5cm) layer of soil mix. Label, and grow them on in a shaded part of the garden. Keep the soil mix moist; if using clay pots, plunge them in beds to keep them damp. Treat the bulblets thereafter as for seed (see p.234). Bulbils may be removed and treated similarly (see LILIES, *Propagating from Stem Bulbils*, p.239).

Gladiolus cormels

Gladioli often form small cormels at the base of the corm. Remove these from the parent and treat them as bulblets (see left). Alternatively, plant them in rows at three to five times their own depth in fertile, well-drained soil, either in a bulb frame or in a nursery bed. They may be left in place to flower two to three years later. In cold regions, they must be lifted and stored for winter.

How to Propagate Gladiolus by Cormels

1 *When the plant has finished flowering and the foliage is dying back, use a hand fork to lift the corm. Cormels should have developed all around the basal plate of the corm. Store all the corms over winter in a cool, dry place.*

2 *In late winter or early spring, pull off cormels; they should readily come away from the parent corm. The cormels may vary in size, but all may be used.*

3 *Half fill a tray with moist, gritty soil mix. Insert cormels, growing points upward, in rows 1in (2.5cm) apart. Fill the tray with more soil mix; level, firm, and label.*

Bulbous Plants that may be Divided

Offsets
Allium (some spp.)
Alstroemeria
Arum, some ❄
Crinum, some ❄
Crocus
Galanthus
Iris, Juno group,
I., Reticulata group (some spp.)
Leucojum
Lilium
Muscari, some ❄ (some spp.)
Narcissus, some ❄
Nerine, some ❄
Ornithogalum, some ❄
Tulipa

Gladiolus 'Deliverance'

Bulblets
Allium (some spp.)
Fritillaria acmopetala, *F. crassifolia*, *F. pudica*, *F. recurva*, *F. thunbergii*
Iris, Reticulata group (some spp.)
Muscari, some ❄ (some spp.)

Cormels
Gladiolus, some ❄

KEY
❄ *Not frost hardy*

Bulbs from seed

This method of propagation produces a large number of bulbs that initially are free from any viruses (except those specifically transmitted by seed), unlike division, which passes on any disease present in the parent bulb to the young plants.

Most bulbs take from three to five years to reach mature flowering size from seed. A few bulbs, such as *Cardiocrinum*, die after flowering, but their seeds may be collected and sown regularly every year to ensure a steady succession of healthy plants that will mature and provide flowers in each growing season.

Collecting seeds

The seed capsules of bulbs are carried on the old flowering stems, but some plants, mainly crocuses and Reticulata irises, have capsules formed at or just above ground level which are difficult to see.

Watch the ripening capsules carefully for signs of splitting, because the seeds may be shed quickly. Remove the capsules as they begin to turn brown and start to split. Extract the seeds as soon as possible. A few bulbs, such as *Corydalis*, shed seeds when the capsules are still green; cut off and store the capsules in paper bags until the seeds are shed. Let the seeds dry without extra heat, and store them until sown in labeled paper packets in a cool, dry, and airy place. Do not use plastic bags since they seal in the moisture and the seeds may rot.

How to Propagate Bulbs from Seed

1 *Prepare the pot: fill it to within 1/2in (1cm) of the brim with commercial seed soil mix mixed with a quarter part coarse sand. Firm it well with a tamper.*

2 *Sow the seeds evenly over the soil mix by tapping the open packet, holding it near the surface so that the seeds (here* Fritillaria meleagris*) do not bounce out.*

3 *Use a sieve to scatter a thin layer of fine soil mix evenly over the seeds. There should be just sufficient soil mix to conceal the seeds.*

4 *Top-dress the pot with at least 1/2in (1cm) of coarse grit, adding it carefully to avoid disturbing the soil mix or seeds.*

5 *Label the pot. Place it in a shady situation in the open. Plunge the pot in damp sand and water, as required, to keep the soil mix moist.*

When to sow seeds

The following method is suitable for most spring-flowering, hardy bulbs such as *Fritillaria*, daffodils, and tulips. The best time to sow is early fall, but if seed is available earlier, sow immediately. Germination should follow in early spring.

Seed soil mix for bulbs

Use a commercial soil-based seed mix, with one-quarter part coarse sand added if the mixture does not have a sandy appearance. A suitable soil-based mix may be made from 2 parts sterile soil, 1 part peat or compost, and 1 1/2 parts very coarse sand or seed-grade perlite with superphosphate and lime each added at a rate of 1oz/4 gallons (25g/18 liters). Some commercial soil mixes containing only peat may also be used, but they contain only enough nutrients for a few months.

Sowing the seeds

Clay or plastic pots may be used, but it is easier to maintain adequate moisture levels in plastic pots. If using a clay pot, place some crocks at the bottom for drainage. Fill the pot with soil mix and firm it before sowing the seeds thinly on the surface. Space large, flat seeds of bulbs such as *Fritillaria* or tulips one seed's width apart, and smaller, rounded seeds about 1/4in (5mm) apart. Sieve a light covering of the soil mix over the seeds so that they are no longer visible, and then cover with a generous layer of grit or aquarium gravel. Label the pots with the plant name, source, and date. Stand them in a shady place in the open garden, or plunge them in a sand frame, and keep them moist.

Care of seedlings

When the seedlings have germinated, bring the pots into full light in a cold frame or greenhouse. Keep them moist until they show definite signs of dying down, and then stop watering them. Seedlings of bulbs that are not naturally dry in summer even in their dormant period, such as certain *Crocus* species from mountainous areas, should be kept slightly moist. Start watering again in early fall, or as soon as there is new growth, and keep the pots watered until the growth dies down.

Leave most bulbs for two growing seasons before repotting, unless they grow very vigorously. It is not essential to feed seedlings in the first growing season, but larger bulbs form if they are fed regularly in the second. Use a commercial liquid feed as used for tomatoes, but at half the manufacturer's recommended strength.

One-year-old Bulb Seedlings

At the end of the growing season, one-year-old bulb seedlings (here Fritillaria meleagris*) are often not vigorous enough to pot on. Let the foliage die back, and cease watering.*

Removing seedlings from pots

After the seedling bulbs have completed two seasons of growth, or one in the case of very vigorous bulbs, pot them up into the soil mix recommended for use with mature bulbs (see "Soil mixes for pots, beds, and frames," p.228). After the foliage has completely died back (toward the end of the dormant period), empty out the pot. Separate out the young bulbs, clean, and repot them in fresh, moist soil mix to start them into growth. It is better to grow them in pots for two or three years until they are large enough to establish successfully outdoors.

Keeping seedlings in pots

Seedling bulbs may be grown on in pots and planted out together with the soil mix to avoid handling the bulbs and disturbing their root growth. Pot on a complete potful of one-year-old seedlings into a slightly larger pot, and feed them regularly while they are in growth in the second year. If they are large enough by the end of the season, plant the entire potful of young bulbs in the open garden when they are dormant or just starting into growth. Give them an extra feed after planting to avoid any delay in flowering. If they are too small, keep them in the pot, and feed them regularly for another year.

Woodland species

Many shade-loving bulbs grow best in a soil mix that contains some leaf mold. For seed sowing, use a soil mix of 1 part sterilized leaf mold, 1 part peat or compost, and 1 part

POTTING UP SEEDLINGS

1 *Carefully knock out the entire pot contents; some of the bulbs (here* Fritillaria raddeana) *will be visible among the soil mix. Remove all the bulbs carefully.*

2 *Replant the young bulbs in a pot of fresh, gritty bulb soil mix, placing them at twice their own depth and spaced their own width apart.*

sterilized soil, with a further 1 1/2 parts of coarse horticultural sand or seed-grade perlite.

The growth of many of these bulbs, for example *Erythronium* and *Trillium*, is slow. Planting the whole panful of seedlings after two or three years' growth into a well-prepared peat bed is better than regular repotting over several years, which repeatedly disturbs the roots.

TWO-YEAR-OLD BULB SEEDLINGS

After 2 years, seedling bulbs (here Calochortus tolmiei) *may vary noticeably in size, but all should develop satisfactorily.*

Cyclamen

Seeds of hardy cyclamen germinate most readily if sown as soon as they are ripe, usually in midsummer. If using dry seeds, soak for about 24 hours before sowing to aid germination. Sow as described opposite.

The seedlings generally grow well in their first year, and the young tubers may then be repotted in seed soil mix (see opposite), preferably while they are still in growth. Add 1 part leaf mold to 3 parts of the soil mix to encourage vigorous growth. The tubers usually develop well if planted several to a pan, rather than singly. Insert them with their roots spaced out and cover the tops with grit or sharp sand.

Place the pans in a shaded cold frame to grow on for a second year. In spring of the third year, repot the tubers singly using the same soil mix and leave them until they are approaching flowering size. Plant them out in the garden in late summer.

Growing lilies from seed

Sow the seeds in pots about 4in (10cm) deep filled with peat, compost, or seed soil mix based on soil or peat, preferably as soon as they are ripe (in late summer or early fall). Sow the seeds thinly to avoid the need for pricking out, cover them with fine grit, and place the pots in a cold frame or cold greenhouse.

In some lilies, the seedlings germinate two to six weeks after sowing. Others may take several months to germinate. Lily seeds differ in the way they germinate. With hypogeal lilies, root formation occurs initially; a cold period is then needed to stimulate leaf production. Seeds of epigeal lilies usually (but not always) germinate fairly rapidly with both root and shoot development occurring almost together (see also PRINCIPLES OF PROPAGATION, *How a Seed Germinates*, p.538).

EXTRACTING CYCLAMEN SEEDS

Harvest the seed capsules in early summer when they are beginning to split. Shake out the seeds and soak them in a bowl of tepid water overnight to assist germination.

PLANTING OUT WOODLAND BULBS

1 *Plant out woodland species without separating the young bulbs. Invert a pot of 2-year-old bulbs (here* Erythronium). *Slide out the mass of bulbs and soil mix.*

2 *Plant the entire potful of soil mix and bulbs, so that the top of the bulb mass is at least 1in (2.5cm) below the surface. Firm, label, and water lightly.*

Overwinter the pots in a cold frame or sheltered place outdoors, then bring the pots into a cold greenhouse in spring. Do not discard the containers even if no seedlings appear after the first year; germination can take two or occasionally more years, depending on the species.

Leave the germinated seedlings in their pots for their first growing season and liquid feed them regularly. Alternatively, prick them out when they have two true leaves into a soil-based potting mix. Repot them regularly or transfer them to nursery beds until they are large enough to plant out in the garden. This process takes from one to three years, depending on the species.

Tender bulbs

Sow the seeds of tender bulbs as described above, but keep the pots at a temperature above freezing during the winter, plunged in bulb frames or beds under cover. Seeds of many tender species, for example amaryllis (*Hippeastrum*), germinate more quickly if bottom heat is used (this is usually supplied by heating cables; see GREENHOUSES AND FRAMES, p.488) and a minimum temperature of 70°F (21°C) is maintained.

If the germination characteristics of a particular plant are uncertain and there is plenty of seed available, sow half with bottom heat and half in normal greenhouse temperatures. If germination has not taken place within six to eight weeks in heat, move the pots to a cooler place. Some genera, notably *Alstroemeria*, germinate rapidly when a warm period is followed by a cool period.

Sow fleshy seeds of bulbs such as *Clivia* fresh, directly from the seed capsule while it is still green. If left in the capsule, the seeds may germinate *in situ*, and they should then be removed and sown in the normal way. Grow on the seedlings (see "Care of seedlings," opposite). Seedlings of some genera, such as *Hippeastrum*, remain in active growth for more than one season; if so, keep the soil mix moist, and the plants may grow until they flower without going dormant.

Seeds with erratic germination

Seeds of certain bulbs, for example Juno irises, germinate very erratically, sometimes over several years. If, after two seasons, only a few seedlings have appeared, repot the entire potful without disturbing the soil mix; late-germinating seedlings often appear a year or so later.

Germination in plastic bags

Seeds of some genera may be germinated in plastic bags rather than pots; this is most frequently done with lilies (*Lilium*), but is applicable to most bulbs with large seeds, for example *Fritillaria*, tulips, and tender genera such as *Hippeastrum*.

Mix the seeds with three or four times their bulk of moist peat, vermiculite, or perlite. The medium used should not exude water when squeezed. Add a little fungicide, place the mixture in small plastic bags, then seal and label them.

For seeds that benefit from an initial warm period, such as those of the smaller *Hippeastrum* species, keep the bags at approximately 70°F (21°C), for example on top of a refrigerator. When the seeds have germinated, prick out the seedlings into pots or trays of well-drained cuttings soil mix and keep them in cooler conditions. If the seeds have not germinated after six to eight weeks, transfer the bags to a cold frame or cool greenhouse until germination occurs, and grow on.

How to Scale Lilies

1 Clean the lily bulb; remove and discard any damaged, outer scales. Gently snap off about 6 good scales, as close as possible to the base of the bulb.

2 Place some fungicidal powder in a plastic bag and add the scales. Shake the bag gently so that all the scales are thoroughly coated with the fungicide.

3 Remove any surplus fungicide from the bag. Place the coated scales into a second bag containing a 50:50 mix of peat and perlite, or peat and vermiculite.

4 Inflate the bag, then seal and label it. Store at about 70°F (21°C) in a warm, dark place.

5 When small bulblets have developed on the scales, remove the scales if they are soft. If they are fleshy and firm, leave them attached to the bulblets.

6 Plant the groups of bulblets either singly in small pots or several in a pan. Top-dress the pots with grit, label them, and leave them in a warm, light place.

7 The following spring, harden off the young bulbs by placing the pots in a cold frame.

8 In the fall, when the bulbs have grown on, remove them from the pots and separate them. Pot them up individually or plant them in their permanent positions.

Scaling

Scaling is an important method of propagating lilies (*Lilium*), but it may also be used for other genera that have bulbs consisting of scales, for example some species of *Fritillaria*. The bulbs of most lilies are composed of concentric rings of scales attached at their lower ends to a basal plate. If these scales are detached from the parent bulb close to the base, so that they retain a small piece of basal tissue, they may develop bulblets, normally near the base of the scale. Portions of scales that lack this tissue seldom form bulblets.

Remove lily scales for propagation in late summer or early fall before root growth starts. Lift the dormant bulbs, then remove a few of the scales. Usually only a few are needed, and the parent bulb may be replanted to flower the following season. If many new plants are required, scale the whole bulb. Alternatively, without lifting the parent bulbs, remove the soil from around them and snap off a few scales.

Select only disease-free, plump, unblemished scales. If using only a few scales for propagation, coat them with fungicide, then mix them together with some damp peat and perlite or peat and vermiculite in a plastic bag. Seal the bag and place it in a warm, dark place at about 70°F (21°C) for approximately three months. Then place the bag in a cold place, such as a refrigerator (but not a freezer), for six to eight weeks to encourage bulblets to develop. When these form, fill some pots with a free-draining soil mix. Insert one or more scales, with their small bulblets attached, so that the tops of the scales are just below the surface of the soil mix.

Keep the pots in a shaded cold frame or cool greenhouse in hot weather. During the summer, plunge the pots of hardy bulbs in a frame or sheltered position in the open garden. At the end of the first growing season, separate the bulblets and repot them individually in a freely draining soil mix suitable for mature bulbs (see "Soil mixes for pots, beds, and frames," p.228). Grow them on in a cold frame or a cool greenhouse until the following spring when they

How to Propagate Bulbs by Twin-scaling

1 Remove the brown outer scales of a bulb (here a daffodil). With a sharp knife, trim off the roots without damaging the basal plate, and slice off the nose.

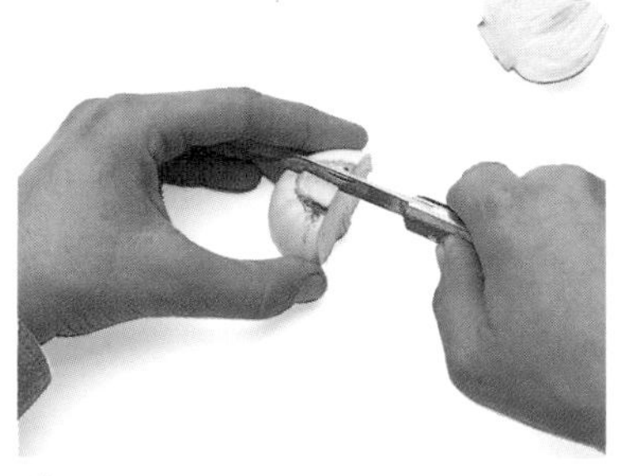

2 Place the bulb upside down on its cut end. Cut downward through the basal plate to divide it into small sections, each piece having a section of basal plate.

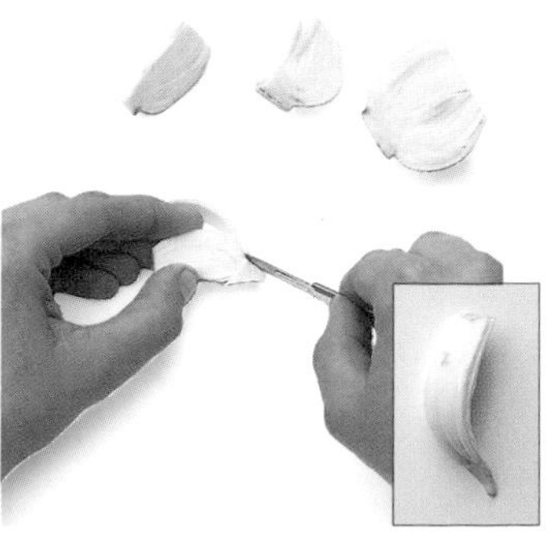

3 Divide the sections into pairs of scales by peeling back the layers. Use a scalpel to cut each pair away with a piece of the basal plate attached (see inset).

may be repotted into a container or planted in their flowering position in the garden.

Alternatively, after dusting with fungicide, insert the scales in trays filled with 2 parts damp vermiculite, perlite, or peat mixed with 1 part coarse sand. Keep them moist and shaded, preferably in a warm greenhouse at about 70°F (21°C), for two months. In spring, move them to a cool place to promote good leaf growth; the bulblets may then be repotted singly and grown on for a year before being planted out.

Twin-scaling

This is used to build up stocks of genera such as daffodils, hyacinths, and snowdrops (*Galanthus*). Cut up the bulbs into pairs of scales, with each pair retaining a small section of the bulb's basal plate. Be sure to keep your hands, the knife, and the cutting surface scrupulously clean so that no disease has the opportunity to infect the cut scales. After dusting the twin-scales with fungicide, treat them in the same way as single scales (see opposite).

HOW TO PROPAGATE BULBS BY CHIPPING

1 *When the foliage has died down, lift the dormant bulbs and select a healthy, undamaged specimen (here* Hippeastrum*). Trim off the growing tip and the roots, taking care not to cut into the basal plate.*

2 *Place the bulb on a clean cutting surface, with its basal plate uppermost. With a clean, sharp knife, carefully cut down into the bulb, dividing it into halves.*

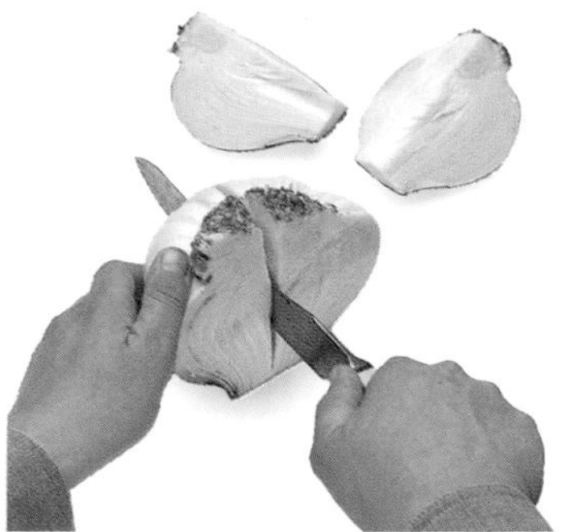

3 *Cut each half of the bulb again in the same way, making sure that the basal plate is divided equally between the individual segments.*

4 *Repeat until the bulb has been cut into about 16 chips. Soak them in fungicide for 10–15 minutes, occasionally agitating the container. Drain off any excess moisture.*

5 *Half fill some plastic bags with 11 parts vermiculite, moistened with 1 part water. Put several chips in each bag. Seal the bags with rubber bands or plastic twist-ties. Store in a warm, dark, airy place.*

6 *When bulblets appear around the basal plate of the chips, plant the chips individually into 3in (6cm) pots filled with a well-drained soil mix. Place in a sheltered position to grow on.*

Cutting bulbs into sections

Sectioning bulbs is not widely used by amateur growers, but it is useful for plants that do not divide freely or set seed. Bulbs may be sectioned near the end of the dormant period: parts of the basal plate may be cut through, or the entire bulb may be cut into pieces.

Chipping

Many bulbs may be propagated at the end of the dormant period, for example in the early fall, by cutting them into several segments (chips). Chipping allows more rapid propagation of bulbs that do not increase rapidly by offsets; it also serves to build up stocks of new cultivars. Large bulbs, such as daffodils or amaryllis, may be cut into as many as 16 chips; smaller daffodils and others, for example snowdrops (*Galanthus*), are usually chipped into four or eight segments.

Good hygiene is essential to avoid disease infecting the chips through their exposed cut surfaces. Wear gloves for cleanliness and protection since some people are allergic to the sap the bulbs release when cut. Clean and sterilize the bulbs with rubbing alcohol to help prevent rot. Use a knife or scalpel that has been sterilized in rubbing alcohol to cut the bulbs on a clean, disinfected surface. Soak the chips in a suitable fungicide after cutting. Alternatively, dust the cut surfaces with flowers of sulfur.

Store the chips in the dark for 12 weeks in plastic bags of vermiculite that contain plenty of air. A temperature of 68–77°F (20–25°C) gives good results for most genera. Separate the young bulblets that develop on the chips, and pot them on into pans of freely draining soil mix. They generally reach flowering size in two or three years.

Cutting up bulbs that have growing points

Some cyclamen species, particularly *C. hederifolium* and *C. rohlfsianum*, form multiple growing points on the surface of the tubers. The corms of several genera, such as *Crocosmia* and *Gladiolus*, do the same. Such tubers and corms may be propagated by cutting them up, as long as each section has a growing point.

Prepare 2–3in (5–6cm) pots with a few crocks at the bottom for good drainage and almost fill them with well-drained soil mix. Dust the

BULBS THAT MAY BE PROPAGATED BY CHIPPING

Allium
Crinum, some ❄
Galanthus
Hippeastrum, some ❄
Hyacinthus
Iris
Muscari, some ❄
Narcissus, some ❄
Scilla, some ❄
Sternbergia

Hippeastrum 'Striped'

KEY
❄ *Not frost hardy*

CUTTING UP BULBS FOR PROPAGATION

1 *Take a large, healthy bulb (here* Cyclamen hederifolium*) and cut it into pieces with a clean knife. Each piece must have at least one growing point. Dust the cut surfaces with fungicide.*

2 *Leave the pieces (see inset) on a wire tray in a warm, dry place for 48 hours, until the cut surfaces form a callus. Pot them up individually into pots containing sharply drained soil mix.*

pieces with fungicide, insert them singly with their growing points uppermost in the soil mix, and cover the tubers with more soil mix. Top-dress the pots with grit, label, and leave in a cool greenhouse until they begin to grow. Keep the soil mix moist enough to sustain the sections until growth starts.

Grow them on in well-lit conditions in a cold frame, and shade them from the hot summer sun. Water with care; do not let young plants dry out when in growth. Plant them out the next fall.

Simple cutting

Make cuts 1/4in (0.5cm) deep with a sharp knife through a bulb's basal plate; the number of cuts depends on the bulb's size. Dust the cuts with fungicide. Keep the bulb in a plastic bag of damp perlite or vermiculite, and some fungicide, in a warm place.

The damage to the basal plate induces bulblets to form along the cuts. When these have formed, insert the bulb upside down in a gritty soil mix made of 1 part peat to 1 part perlite or coarse sand. The bulblets will develop above the old bulb. A year later, carefully separate the bulblets, and plant them in trays in a cool greenhouse to grow on.

HOW TO PROPAGATE HYACINTHS BY SCOOPING

1 *Use a clean, sharpened teaspoon or a knife to scoop out the inner part of the bulb's basal plate, leaving the outer rim intact. Discard the basal plate.*

2 *Dip the cut surfaces in fungicide, then lay the bulbs, with their scooped areas uppermost, on a tray of sand. Place the tray in a warm place.*

3 *Water the sand lightly as needed to keep it moist. When bulblets form around the edge of the scooped base, separate them from the parent and pot them up.*

Scooping hyacinths

Scooping is a technique used for the commercial propagation of hyacinths. The center of the basal plate of the bulb is scooped out and discarded, the exposed surface dusted with fungicide, and the bulb kept upside down in warm, dark conditions. Numerous small bulblets eventually form on and around the cut surface. They may then be separated from the parent bulb and grown on in the same way as bulblets (see "Propagation from bulblets and bulbils," p.233) in individual pots.

Basal cuttings

The sprouting tubers of a few bulbs may be used in late winter for basal cuttings – young shoots that retain a piece of the parent tuber from which new roots develop. Place the cuttings in a pan of moist soil mix until they root and then pot up. For details of the technique, see DAHLIAS, *How to Propagate by Basal Cuttings*, p.223. Grow on the rooted cuttings in a warm greenhouse until danger of frost is past. Harden them off in a cold frame and plant out in early summer. Propagate tuberous begonias and gloxinias (*Sinningia speciosa*) in this way in spring.

Scoring and scooping *Trillium*

Various cutting techniques may be used to propagate *Trillium* rhizomes in late summer, after the leaves have died down.

One method that avoids lifting the parent plant is to remove sufficient soil to expose the top of a rhizome and to score lightly a shallow cut around the growing point of the rhizome. Dust the cut with a fungicide and cover the rhizome with a top-dressing of peat and coarse sand in equal parts, or cover with soil if it is light and well draining. Small rhizomes should form along the cut, and in time they should become large enough to separate.

Alternatively, lift the rhizomes and scoop out their growing points. Make concave scoops, rather than cutting across the base of the growing points, to ensure that no soft tissue remains that could rot. Dust the cut surfaces with fungicide and replant the rhizomes. Small rhizomes should then form around the excised growing tip.

One year later, expose the rhizomes, remove the young ones, and grow them on in pots as described for young seedlings (see "Care of seedlings," p.234).

HOW TO PROPAGATE TRILLIUMS BY SCORING

1 *Carefully scrape away the topsoil to expose the rhizome. Score a shallow incision around it with a sharp, clean knife, just below the growing point (see inset).*

2 *Use a clean, soft brush to dust the cut surface of the rhizome with fungicidal powder.*

3 *Carefully cover the scored rhizome with a mix of peat and coarse sand in equal parts to the same level as before. Gently firm it with your fingers.*

4 *A year later, remove the topsoil to expose the rhizomes and remove any young ones that have formed. Pot them up individually and grow them on.*

CUTTING OUT GROWING POINTS

1 *Remove the growing point of the rhizome entirely by making a cut in the form of a concave scoop with the tip of a clean, sharp knife.*

2 *Dust the cut surfaces of the parent rhizomes with fungicide. Cover them up again with soil and firm the soil down lightly.*

Lilies

LILIES are among the most graceful of summer-flowering plants. Their tall, slim stems bear flowers with an enormous variety of dazzling colors and exotic shapes. There are a great many to choose from – more than 80 species lilies and thousands of hybrids, which are more tolerant of different conditions and so are often easier to grow.

Lily classification

Lilies are classified according to their origins, parentage, and flowers:
Div.I Hybrids of Asiatic species such as *L. cernuum* and *L. davidii.*
Div.II Hybrids of *L. martagon* and *L. hansonii.*
Div.III Hybrids of *L. candidum* and *L. chalcedonicum.*
Div.IV Hybrids of American species lilies.
Div.V Hybrids of *L. longiflorum* and *L. formosanum.*
Div.VI (Aurelian hybrids): Trumpet lilies and *L. henryi* crosses.
Div.VII (Oriental hybrids): From Japanese species.
Div.VIII All other hybrids.
Div.IX All other species and their cultivars.

Where to grow lilies

Lilies are excellent border and woodland plants and make superb companion plants for shrub roses. A few of the smaller lilies may be used to add summer color to the rock garden when most alpine plants have already finished flowering. Lilies look splendid planted in containers, especially on terraces and patios. Div.V lilies are not fully hardy, but make excellent pot plants for the cold greenhouse and conservatory.

Planting and care

Always buy fresh bulbs and plant them immediately. Do not buy dried or shriveled bulbs. Most lilies grow well in a range of soils. Div.III lilies prefer alkaline soils and full sun; Div.VII hybrids must be grown in lime-free soil or ericaceous soil mix in containers; Div.IV hybrids are best suited to damp, woodland conditions. Plant lilies in fall or spring at two to three times the depth of the bulb in well prepared, free-draining soil; *L. candidum* needs only 1in (2.5cm) of soil above the bulb and should be planted in late summer. The routine care of lilies is similar to that of most bulbs (see pp.230–32). Stake the plants well so that their flowering stems do not snap.

Propagation

Lilies may be propagated easily by stem bulbils, scaling, or seed. Use simple division for *L. pardalinum* and Div.IV hybrids. Always propagate from healthy stock.

Bulbils and bulblets

Species such as *L. lancifolium* (syn. *L. tigrinum*), *L. bulbiferum*, and their hybrids produce stem bulbils in the leaf axils and bulblets at the base of the old flowering stem. Remove these and pot them up to grow on. The following fall, either plant out the whole pan of young bulbs or pot them up individually.

Seed, scaling, and division

Sowing seed produces vigorous, virus-free bulbs (see "Growing lilies from seed," p.235), but is slow; Div.V lilies are easy to propagate in this way. For details of division and scaling, see pp.233 and 236.

LILY FLOWER SHAPES

Lilium martagon (scented, nodding, turkscap flowers)

L. bulbiferum* var. *croceum (chalice-shaped)

L. monadelphum (scented trumpets)

***L.* 'Connecticut King'** (upward-facing, cup-shaped blooms)

L. regale (fragrant, outward-facing trumpets)

L. chalcedonicum (scented turkscaps)

Pests and diseases

Lilies are particularly vulnerable to several viruses (p.555) transmitted by aphids. Visible symptoms are mottled or twisted leaves. *L. lancifolium* and some of its hybrids are carriers but show no symptoms; keep them away from other lilies to minimize infection. Gray mold/*Botrytis* (p.552) may cause problems in damp, windless conditions. The red lily beetle (p.550) destroys leaves and flowers.

PROPAGATING FROM STEM BULBILS

1 *Throughout summer, as soon as the bulbils loosen and are ripe, collect them from the leaf axils of the lily stems by carefully picking them off.*

2 *Insert the bulbils in pans of moist soil-based potting mix, pressing them gently into the surface. Cover with grit, and label (see inset). Place in a cold frame until young bulbs develop.*

RAISING LILIES FROM BULBLETS

1 *After flowering, lift the bulb and dead stem, pick off the bulblets, and replant the main bulb. Alternatively, leave the bulb in the ground, cutting the stem above it to remove the bulblets.*

2 *Plant the bulblets at twice their depth, in pots of soil-based potting mix, and place in a protected spot until spring. You may also plant them in a line in the garden to grow on.*

10

The Water Garden

A WATER FEATURE *is an irresistible attraction in any garden. There is a style to suit every setting, whether it is a formal pool graced by water lilies and the bright gleam of goldfish, a trickling stream bordered by ferns, or a simple pond reflecting the sculptural silhouette of a clump of irises. Even the smallest and quietest patio garden can be brought to life by the murmur of running water and the dancing patterns of light. Creating a water garden provides habitats for a specific range of plants as well as attracting a host of wildlife, including newts, frogs, toads, dragonflies, and songbirds, and perhaps even water birds. Water may be either restful or exciting: still water is valued for its properties of reflection and tranquility, while moving water – whether in the form of a classical fountain or a rushing waterfall – adds a delightful sound and a dynamic vitality to the garden.*

Designing a water garden

UNLIKE any other element in the garden, water brings an ever-changing pattern of reflections, sounds, and movement that is particularly appealing. Even when frozen, its surface creates contrasts of color and texture. A pond is a popular form of water feature but there are others: a waterfall, fountain, or watercourse, for instance.

A water feature allows you to grow plants that do not thrive in other conditions, from the floating frogbit (*Hydrocharis morsus-ranae*) and water hyacinth (*Eichhornia crassipes*) to the bog garden candelabra primroses (*Primula* spp.).

When deciding which type of water feature to create, bear in mind the size and style of the garden. If large and informal, a meandering watercourse may be suitable, while in an enclosed town garden, a raised formal pool might be appropriate. Water may even be included in a garden for children in the form of an attractive bubble fountain, in which the water splashes over stones and is recirculated without forming an area of any great depth.

A NATURALISTIC WATER GARDEN
In an informal or semiwild garden, a gently meandering stream provides a lush, cool area by which to sit and relax. Clouds of pink rhododendrons add both height and color to the design, while marginal plantings of bright yellow Iris pseudacorus, *ferns, and rushes form a transition between the stream and the garden.*

Siting a pond

Exploit the reflective quality of water by siting a pond where it mirrors an eye-catching feature – a specimen plant or statue, perhaps. It may help to lay a reflective sheet in the proposed site to give an idea of reflections to be seen during the day and evening; check it from major viewpoints such as the house and patio. An open, sunny position, away from buildings and overhanging trees, provides the best conditions in which to grow most water plants.

If planning to create a pond on land prone to flooding, check that there is no danger of fertilizer or pesticide residues leaching into the water from an adjacent vegetable garden or farmland. These substances invariably affect pond life adversely. Direct potential overflows to a suitable drainage system. Land with a high water table may cause problems because, in very wet periods, water pressure from below may push a pond liner out of shape.

Do not site a pond in a frost pocket or in a very exposed position, since this restricts the range of plants that may be grown and protection may have to be provided in winter.

Informal ponds

In an informal garden, a natural sunken pond may look most appropriate. Usually, this is in an irregular, curved shape, bordered with natural materials such as sod or stones to link it with the garden. The water surface is, however, only part of the total design: the inclusion of marginal and moisture-loving plants

A FORMAL POOL
Water lilies (Nymphaea) *bring elegance and color to a rectangular pond. A sundial links the informality of the plants to the pool's formal margins.*

around the pond, to soften or hide its outline completely, helps to create a lush and refreshing feature.

As when planting in a border or bed, consider how the plants will combine to create complementary and contrasting associations of color, texture, and form.

Formal ponds

In contrast to the natural feeling of an informal pond, a formal pool makes a much bolder statement. It may be raised or sunken and is usually of a regular, geometric design. As a rule, less space is devoted to planting than in an informal pond, although plants with floating leaves and flowers (e.g. water lilies) are often included. Sculptural plants such as certain ferns, grown next to the pool, provide attractive reflections. A fountain or waterspout to complement the style of the pond can be an ornamental addition.

Far from being disguised, the edge of the pond may form an important feature, perhaps made of attractive paving. If the pool is raised, a wide edge can form a seat that is particularly suitable for elderly or impaired people.

In many cases formal ponds are sited so that they form a striking focal point in the garden: for example, at the main axis of paths, or where they may be conveniently viewed and enjoyed from the windows or terrace of the house.

Fountains

The style and size of a fountain should be considered in the context of the surrounding pool and the overall design of the garden. Often used in a formal garden as a focal point, a fountain is also invaluable for adding height to a design, and for its dynamic contributions of sound, movement, and light. A fountain is particularly dramatic if lit at night.

A cobblestone or bubble fountain, in which water bubbles over stones into a small underground reservoir, looks more informal than a standard fountain and is ideal in a garden where children play.

As well as being ornamental, fountains also provide a practical function: the splashing action oxygenates the water, and this is beneficial to fish. Most water plants do not flourish in disturbed water, however, so they should not be grown close to a fountain.

Waterspouts

While a fountain or waterfall might be too large in an average garden, a waterspout can provide the pleasure of running water in the smallest garden or even in a conservatory. There are many styles, from the classical lion's head or gargoyle above a pool to a simple bamboo pipe trickling water over stones.

A waterspout is usually fixed to a wall, with a pump and pipe similar to those used for a watercourse. The pump circulates water from a pool or reservoir to the rear of the spout and out through the mouth.

Streams, watercourses, and waterfalls

Few gardens have a natural stream or waterfall, but it is possible to create a circulating watercourse spilling out into a pool or underground reservoir. Making a watercourse or waterfall is an attractive way of exploiting a change of level in the garden. It may be used to link parts of the garden as well as providing points of interest between levels.

In an informal garden, a watercourse may be made to look more natural by edging it with rocks or stones and moisture-loving plants such as ferns and irises. Ornamentals that have large leaves, for example *Rheum palmatum*, are particularly valuable for watercourses made from liners or preformed units since they help to disguise the edges.

Bog and wildlife areas

In an informal or naturalistic design, a bog garden makes an attractive feature. Most appropriate next to ponds, bog gardens provide a gradual and natural transition from aquatic to moisture-loving plants and ideal conditions for wildlife.

TRADITIONAL WATERSPOUT
A waterspout is attractive even in a tiny garden. Here, mellow stone complements this traditional spout.

Bog gardens

Creating a bog garden is a better way of using waterlogged land than struggling against nature by trying to drain it. While the ground next to a manmade pool is unlikely to be wet enough to provide suitable conditions for growing bog plants, using a liner under the soil will retain sufficient moisture.

Bog gardens bring freshness in late summer when many other plants are showing stress from drought. However, most bog plants die back naturally after frost, so they do not provide great interest in winter.

Wildlife ponds

A water feature increases diversity in a wildlife garden, providing a habitat for waterfowl, frogs, newts,

AN INFORMAL WATERCOURSE
A terrace of dams formed from thick slabs of stone creates cascades of water that spill into a shallow, cobblestone-lined pool. Overhanging plants such as ivies (Hedera), *Japanese maple* (Acer palmatum), *and primroses* (Primula) *help to break up the rigid line of the stone. The meandering path of the watercourse also helps to give the design an appealing informality and charm.*

LINKING THE POOL WITH THE GARDEN
Rugged pieces of stone form a practical yet pleasing edging to this semiformal pool. Rock plants provide a colorful link with the garden beyond.

and an enormous range of insects. Limiting the planting to only native species may attract more wildlife, although many native plants can prove invasive. The inclusion of some exotic ornamentals can make the pond a decorative feature as well. Informal ponds with muddy bottoms and shallowly sloping edges interspersed with large, flat stones are particularly suitable, providing ideal conditions for amphibians.

Container water gardens

In a small garden or patio, or where major construction work is impractical, it is still possible to have a pool by using an appropriate ornamental container, such as a sealed and lined half barrel. A container is suitable for growing only a few selected plants, however, and remember that fish probably will not be able to survive in it outdoors over winter. If using a metal container, it should be sealed with a waterproof paint or liner; otherwise, it may be harmful to both plants and fish.

CONTAINER POOL
A decorative, sealed metal cauldron provides the perfect place to cultivate one or two miniature water lilies, for example Nymphaea pygmaea 'Helvola'.

Plants for the water garden

In any water garden, plants are vital to the design. Lush foliage and flowers enhance the pool and link it with the rest of the garden, while certain plants help to maintain clear water and, in the case of oxygenators, provide good conditions for fish.

Plants suitable for a water garden range from those that thrive in deep water to those requiring moist soil only around their root tips. They are usually grouped into six categories: oxygenators, deep-water plants, surface floaters, marginals, bog plants, and moisture-loving plants.

Oxygenators

Lagarosiphon major (syn. *Elodea crispa*) and *Myriophyllum* species are examples of oxygenators – submerged, fast-growing plants that will help to clean and oxygenate the water. In sunny weather, submerged algae may turn a new pond green within a week or two of installation. Oxygenating plants, however, compete for the dissolved mineral salts on which algae thrive and starve them out so that the water eventually becomes clear once more. Such oxygenators are essential if you are planning to keep fish in the pool.

Deep-water plants

These flourish in a depth range of 12–36in (30–90cm). This category includes plants such as *Aponogeton* and *Hydrocleys*, with water lilies (*Nymphaea*) forming the largest group (see pp.244–5). Apart from their ornamental value, their floating leaves also help to reduce algae by cutting down the amount of light allowed to reach the water.

Surface floaters

Floating plants, such as *Trapa natans* and *Azolla caroliniana*, perform a similar function to the deep-water plants, especially during the establishment phase. It is vital not to let them cover too much of the water surface, however, since oxygenators and aquatic animals may suffer if there is not enough light.

Marginals

Marginal plants are grown at the edges of pools in shallow water usually about 3–6in (7–15cm) deep, but occasionally up to 12in (30cm). Many of these plants are extremely attractive, such as *Iris laevigata* 'Variegata' with fans of green- and cream-striped leaves and lavender-blue flowers. They are valuable in an informal pond for breaking up the outline. In a pool installed to attract wildlife, marginals provide cover for wildfowl and various small creatures. Some species such as *Mentha aquatica* and *Veronica beccabunga* also help to oxygenate the water.

Bog plants

Bog-loving plants such as *Lysichiton* or some *Caltha* species thrive in waterlogged soil and can withstand occasional flooding. Under a bog-plant heading, nursery catalogs may include plants that grow in moist or even wet soil but do not tolerate a soil that is constantly waterlogged. When ordering, check with the nursery to ensure that any chosen plants can tolerate high water levels around the roots.

Moisture-loving plants

These thrive in soils that contain extra moisture without being waterlogged. Moisture-lovers include many herbaceous perennials, such as *Astilbe*, *Ligularia*, and *Primula florindae*. They all associate well with marginal plants in the areas surrounding natural, informal pools, where the growing conditions are ideal for them.

Planting associations

Create a varied and attractive display by mixing plants with different heights and growth habits around the pool. Similar design principles should be applied as for planting in the rest of the garden to develop a successful design with a diversity of shapes and forms (see also "Principles of planting," pp.21–6). Site *Gunnera manicata*, for example, so that its immense, platterlike leaves tower over the jutting swords of *Acorus calamus*. Use plants at the edge of the pond to act as a foil for floating plants or deep marginals – for instance, an island of water lilies such as *Nymphaea alba* with its pure white blooms would be beautifully offset by a drift of ostrich ferns (*Matteuccia struthiopteris*).

Plants with contrasting colors and textures also provide the potential for some spectacular combinations. For example, the upright, scarlet flower spikes of *Lobelia cardinalis* would form a fine contrast with the heart-shaped, blue-gray leaves of *Hosta sieboldiana*.

Plan the planting to supply interest throughout the seasons. Including evergreen foliage plants such as

BOG GARDEN
The boggy ground next to a pond is ideal for plants such as Primula bulleyana *and* Iris laevigata. Phormium tenax *gives the design its focus.*

Bergenia at the pool edges provides continuity of form and color, while other types of plant – ranging from the golden flowers of the marsh marigold (*Caltha palustris*) in spring to the summer-long display of the water forget-me-not (*Myosotis scorpioides*) with its delicate blue flowers – may be used for creating a changing seasonal display.

Fish

While most ornamental fish live in harmony with aquatic plant life, the inclusion of larger specimen fish necessitates certain precautions in pond design and planting. Oxygenating plants provide oxygen only in daylight, and fish may suffer from stress during warm, sultry nights unless additional oxygen is provided – for example, from the water agitation created by the splashing of a fountain.

If planning to keep large koi carp, remember that they may disturb the roots of water lilies and other deep-water plants, so anchor the soil over the roots with large stones. Pools for these fish should be at least 3ft (1m) deep and have vertical sides projecting above the surface so that the carp cannot leap out. Goldfish and orfe are easier to manage; orfe are ideal decorative fish that enjoy shallow water and feed on any insect larvae present. In the wildlife garden, native species such as sunfish may be suitable and less damaging to tadpole populations.

Planter's guide to water plants

Shallow Marginals
(6in/15cm depth of water)

Acorus gramineus,
A. g. 'Variegatus'
Alisma parviflora
Calla palustris

Calla palustris

Caltha leptosepala,
C. palustris, *C. p.* 'Alba',
C. p. 'Flore Plena'
Carex elata 'Aurea',
C. pendula, *C. riparia*
Colocasia esculenta ✽
Cotula coronopifolia
Cyperus 'Haspan',
C. involucratus ✽, *C. longus*
Damasonium alisma
Decodon verticillatus
Eriophorum angustifolium,
E. latifolium
Houttuynia cordata,
H. c. 'Chamaeleon', syn. *H. c.* 'Variegata', *H. c.* 'Plena'
Hydrocleys nymphoides ✽
Iris laevigata, *I. versicolor*

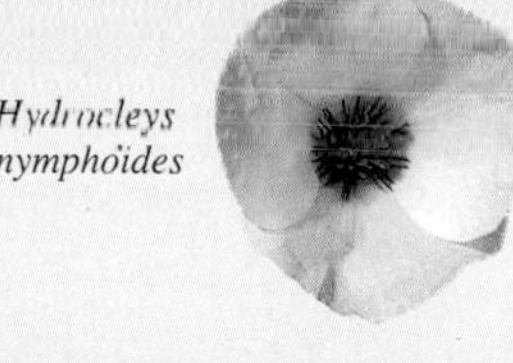
Hydrocleys nymphoides

Juncus effusus, *J. e.* f. *spiralis*,
J. e. 'Vittatus', *J. ensifolius*
Lobelia paludosa
Lysichiton americanus,
L. camtschatcensis
Mentha aquatica
Mimulus cardinalis,
M. cupreus, *M. guttatus*,
M. ringens
Myosotis scorpioides,
M. s. 'Mermaid'
Peltandra alba
Polygonum amphibium
Sagittaria latifolia, *S. sagittifolia*,
S. s. 'Flore Pleno'
Sparganium minimum
Typha minima
Zizania aquatica ✽

Deep Marginals
(12in/30cm depth of water)

Acorus calamus,
A. c. 'Variegatus'
Alisma lanceolatum,
A. plantago-aquatica
Butomus umbellatus
Cyperus papyrus ✽
Glyceria maxima 'Variegata'
Hottonia palustris
Iris pseudacorus
Nelumbo lutea ✽, *N. nucifera* 'Alba Grandiflora' ✽, *N. n.* 'Alba Striata' ✽, *N. n.* 'Rosa Plena' ✽
Phragmites australis,
P. a. 'Variegata'
Pontederia cordata, *P. lanceolata*
Ranunculus lingua 'Grandiflora'
Saururus cernuus
Scirpus lacustris,
S. l. subsp. *tabernaemontani* 'Albescens', *S. l.* subsp. *t.* 'Zebrinus'
Sparganium erectum,
syn. *S. ramosum*
Thalia dealbata ✽, *T. geniculata* ✽
Typha angustifolia, *T. latifolia* 'Variegata', *T. stenophylla*,
syn. *T. laxmannii*
Zantedeschia aethiopica 'Crowborough'

Deep-water Plants

Aponogeton distachyos
Euryale ferox ✽
Nuphar advena, *N. lutea*
Nymphaea, some ✽ (most spp.)
Nymphoides indica, *N. peltata*
Orontium aquaticum
Victoria amazonica ✽, *V. regia* ✽

Submerged Oxygenators

Callitriche hermaphroditica,
syn. *C. autumnalis*
Ceratophyllum demersum
Ceratopteris thalictroides ✽
Elodea canadensis
Fontinalis antipyretica
Hydrocleys parviflora ✽
Lagarosiphon major,
syn. *Elodea crispa*
Myriophyllum aquaticum,
syn. *M. proserpinacoides* ✽
Potamogeton crispus
Preslia cervina
Tillaea recurva

Surface Floaters

Azolla caroliniana ✽, *A. filiculoides*
Ceratopteris pteroides ✽
Eichhornia azurea, *E. crassipes* ✽
Hydrocharis morsus-ranae
Lemna trisulca
Limnobium spongia,
L. stoloniferum
Nymphoides aquatica
Phyllanthus fluitans
Pistia stratiotes ✽

Pistia stratiotes

Riccia fluitans
Salvinia auriculata ✽, *S. natans* ✽
Stratiotes aloides
Trapa natans
Utricularia minor, *U. vulgaris*
Wolffia arrhiza ✽

Bog and Moisture-loving Plants

Alnus glutinosa, *A. incana*
Anemone rivularis
Aruncus dioicus 'Kneiffii'
Arundo donax 'Variegata'
Astilbe x *arendsii*, *A. chinensis*,
A. simplicifolia
Astilboides tabularis
Cardamine pratensis
Cephalanthus occidentalis
Cimicifuga americana,
C. racemosa
Cornus alba
Eupatorium purpureum
Euphorbia palustris
Filipendula rubra, *F. ulmaria*
Gunnera chilensis, *G. manicata*
Hosta (most spp.)
Iris ensata, *I. sibirica*
Leucojum aestivum
Ligularia clivorum, *L. przewalskii*
Lobelia cardinalis, *L. fulgens* ✽
Magnolia virginiana
Osmunda regalis
Parnassia palustris
Peltiphyllum peltatum
Phalaris arundinacea
Phragmites communis
Polygonum amplexicaule,
P. bistorta, *P. campanulatum*
Primula alpicola, *P. denticulata*,
P. florindae, *P. helodoxa*,
P. japonica, *P. pulverulenta*,
P. rosea, *P. secundiflora*,
P. sikkimensis
Rheum alexandrae, *R. palmatum*,
R. p. 'Atrosanguineum'
Rodgersia aesculifolia, *R. pinnata*,
R. podophylla
Salix alba, *S. babylonica*,
S. daphnoides, *S. matsudana* 'Tortuosa'
Scrophularia auriculata 'Variegata'
Senecio smithii
Taxodium distichum
Trollius x *cultorum*,
T. europaeus,
T. ledebourii

Trollius europaeus

Recommended Plants for Aquariums

Alternanthera philoxeroides ✽
Anubias barteri ✽
Aponogeton crispus ✽,
A. madagascariensis ✽
Bacopa monnieri
Cabomba caroliniana ✽
Cryptocoryne ciliata ✽
Echinodorus bleheri ✽, *E. maior* ✽
Hygrophila polysperma ✽
Ludwigia arcuata ✽
Luronium natans
Myriophyllum hippuroides ✽
Nymphoides humboldtiana ✽
Potamogeton crispus
Salvinia natans ✽
Utricularia exoleta ✽, *U. vulgaris*
Vallisneria gigantea ✽

Key
✽ *Not frost hardy*

Water lilies

THE elegant floating cups and lush foliage of water lilies (*Nymphaea*) are a graceful addition to any water garden, whether it is in an informal rural setting or a formal city courtyard. The flower forms vary from open and starlike to goblet-shaped, peony-like blooms, with colors ranging from the simple purity of white or cream to striking shades of red, yellow, or even blue. Some are offset by dark purplish green leaves, while others have foliage that is attractively mottled. Certain species have richly perfumed flowers; these are best grown in a raised pool where their scent may be more easily enjoyed.

While most water lilies bloom in the daytime, some tropical cultivars such as 'Missouri' and 'Red Flare' open at dusk – these are best enhanced by complementary lighting to create a bold display after dark. Native to tropical and subtropical zones, these lilies may be grown in temperate regions in a conservatory pool or outdoors in hot weather.

For best results, water lilies need several hours of full sun each day and should be grown in an open, sunny part of the pool, otherwise they develop a mass of leaves but few blooms. They also prefer calm water: grow the lilies well away from a fountain or waterfall so that they are not disturbed by the movement. Tropical species usually grow more quickly than hardy ones and require high light intensity, ample fertilizer, and warm water at a minimum of 68°F (20°C).

In addition to being decorative, water lilies help to keep the water clear because their large, spreading leaves create shade, thereby helping to control algal growth.

Hardy and Tropical Water Lilies

***Nymphaea* 'Attraction'**

***N. pygmaea* 'Helvola'**

***N.* 'Fire Crest'**

***N. marliacea* 'Chromatella'**

***N.* 'American Star'**

***N.* 'Blue Beauty'**

***N.* 'Escarboucle'**

***N.* 'Virginalis'**

***N. marliacea* 'Carnea'**

Care and cultivation

Most water lilies have thick tubers that grow roughly vertically, with fibrous roots beneath; cultivars of *N. odorata* and *N. tuberosa* have longer, fleshy rhizomes that grow horizontally near the soil surface.

Planting

Hardy water lilies should be planted from late spring to late summer so that they will be well established before winter; do not plant out tropicals until the risk of frost has passed.

For planting, use containers that are 12–14in (30–35cm) across and 6–7½in (15–19cm) deep, depending on the size and vigor of the cultivar. Alternatively, plant in submerged beds 12–18in (30–45cm) deep and 18–24in (45–60cm) square.

Prepare the plant by trimming back long roots and cutting off old or damaged leaves and flower buds. The older leaves make the plant too buoyant to anchor itself under water, and produce little food for the plant. New leaves will quickly replace them. When planting tropical water lilies, insert a tablet of slow-release fertilizer in the soil.

If the planted container is not too heavy, water well before placing in the pond so that any soil shrinkage can be corrected. Lower the basket into place with strings as for planting deep-water plants (see p.253).

In a new pool, the containers may be positioned on the bottom before the pool is filled. Cover them with only 3–6in (8–15cm) of water initially; raise the containers on blocks if necessary so that they have the correct depth of water above them. As the plants grow, gradually lower the containers in stages until they finally rest at the correct depth. Tropical water lilies may be planted at their permanent depth immediately, however, since they grow quickly and prefer shallower water than most hardy cultivars.

Feeding

Water lilies usually benefit from limited additional feeding; insert a tablet of slow-release fertilizer into the soil or soil mix approximately every six weeks during the growing season. This gradually releases small quantities of plant food without discoloring the water or encouraging the growth of algae.

Planting a Tuberous Water Lily

1 *Using pruners or a sharp knife, trim back to within 2in (5cm) of the tuber any roots that are damaged or excessively long.*

2 *Cut off any dead or damaged leaves, or those with broken stalks. Retain new, young leaves and flower buds.*

3 *Line the basket and partly fill it with dampened soil. Position the tuber so that the crown is within 1½in (4cm) of the rim.*

4 *Pack soil firmly around the tuber, ensuring that the crown remains 1½in (4cm) above the level of the soil.*

A FLOATING GARDEN
The strong, straight lines of a wooden deck bridge offset the platelike leaves and colorful blooms of an island of water lilies.

PROPAGATION BY BUD CUTTINGS

1 *Remove the plant from its container and wash it. Using a sharp knife, remove strong-growing buds from the root by cutting flush with the tuber.*

2 *Fill 4in (10cm) pots with soil or aquatic soil mix, firm, and press a single cutting into the surface. Top-dress with grit.*

3 *Immerse the pots in water and keep them in a greenhouse or heated frame, partially shaded; plant out the following spring.*

Division
To maintain healthy growth, divide water lilies when the foliage is crowding the water surface, or when roots have outgrown the container. In spring, cut off pieces from the crown, each with a young, strong shoot and about 6in (15cm) of attached tuber, and replant in fresh soil. The old crown may be discarded.

Propagation

Most tuberous water lilies may be propagated by means of bud cuttings; rhizomatous types may have their rootstocks divided (see p.256). Some water lilies may be raised from seed, or from separated plantlets.

Bud cuttings
Some tuberous water lilies produce side shoots ("eyes") that may be used to propagate new plants. In spring, cut the eyes from the roots and dust them with charcoal or sulfur. Press into a prepared pot, top-dress, and immerse in water; leave the pots in a greenhouse or cold frame at 59–64°F (15–18°C). As the plants develop, pot them on and gradually increase the water depth until fall. Overwinter in a cool place and plant out the following spring.

Seed
With the exception of *N. odorata* and *N tetragona*, hardy water lilies do not readily set seed; tender or tropical water lilies set large quantities. Before collecting seed, enclose ripening capsules in muslin bags to prevent the seeds from floating away. Sow hardy seed at once before it dries out. Tropical water lily seed should be washed and allowed to dry, then stored in bags at room temperature. Tropical water lily seed is best sown in spring.

Sow the seeds evenly, still attached to their jellylike bladders, in pans of seed soil mix. Sprinkle with soil mix, water, and then place the pans in a container and cover with 1–2in (2.5–5cm) of water. Hardy water lily seed requires a minimum temperature of 55°F (13°C) to germinate, tropical seed 73–81°F (23–7°C)

When the seedlings are large enough to handle, carefully lift, rinse, and plant them in pans submerged in 2–3in (5–7.5cm) of water. Pot on later into 3in (6cm) pots in 3–4in (8–10cm) of water.

After overwintering, the tubers produce young plants that may be detached and potted on.

Plantlets
Certain day-blooming tropical water lilies produce plantlets that may form and bloom while still attached to the parent leaf. Alternatively, they may be transplanted into shallow pans in water and then grown on at a temperature of 59–64°F (15–18°C); gradually increase the water level, then pot them up into aquatic containers.

Aquariums

Small, submerged tropical plants may be easily grown in the controlled environment of an aquarium. As well as being attractive, these plants provide shelter for fish. Choose small, gregarious fish, avoiding any that eat or disturb plants. Landscaping with suitable rocks and wood will also help to increase the interest.

As in a garden pool, a good water chemistry balance is maintained by achieving the correct levels of light, temperature, fish, and organic matter. Aquariums should not be placed too near a sunny window, since the high light intensity encourages algal growth. Use lime-free, washed sand or gravel to cover the aquarium base, in a layer 3in (8cm) deep at the front, rising to 4–5in (10–12cm) at the back.

Heating the water to 73–9°F (23–6°C) by means of thermostatically controlled cables in the sand enables a wide range of plants to be grown. Provide artificial lighting for approximately 12 hours each day; wide-spectrum fluorescent tubes emit the necessary ultraviolet light. For pristine water clarity, circulate the water through a decanting filter with a small electric pump.

FRESHWATER AQUARIUM
This tank provides a fine setting for plants such as Baldellia ranunculoides *with upright, oval leaves and the feathery* Hygrophila difformis, *while tropical fish add color and movement.*

Constructing ponds and watercourses

For many years, manmade ponds were mostly constructed from heavy materials such as stone, concrete, or brick. Since the advent of plastics and fiberglass, however, it has become easier to install your own pond and also to create a more naturalistic design, if desired.

The best shape, size, and material for the pond depends to a large extent on the size and style of your garden, the preferred method of construction, and cost. Flexible liners allow you maximum freedom of shape and size. They are ideal where a natural look is required since the edge may be easily concealed and the lining material itself is relatively unobtrusive; also, they are the best choice for large ponds. Rigid, preformed pools are easier to install, but there is only a limited range of shapes and sizes. While they are excellent for small ponds, larger units are difficult to maneuver, and very large sizes are not available. Hard materials such as concrete provide the strongest and most long-lasting pools, but they are also the most difficult and slowest to construct.

There are several methods of constructing watercourses. Flexible liners are versatile and particularly suitable for naturalistic designs. Where strength and durability are more important, or where the design incorporates a series of shallow cascades, preformed rigid units may be more appropriate. Liners and rigid units may be used in combination.

Flexible liners

Most new garden pools are constructed using a flexible lining sheet of synthetic rubber or plastic, which provides a waterproof barrier between the soil and the water. These flexible liners are available in a wide range of sizes and can be cut to fit any shape of pool. Before buying a liner, decide on the site and size of the pond: marking out the desired shape with string and pegs makes it easier to check the placement.

Butyl rubber is arguably the best pond-lining material. It is much stronger than either polyethylene or PVC, with a life expectancy of about 40–50 years, but it is also more expensive. Butyl is very pliable and is tough enough to resist tearing or deterioration caused by ultraviolet light, bacterial growth, and temperature extremes. To line an informal pool, particularly if part of the material may be exposed to sunlight, it is best to use a top-quality butyl liner that is 1/4in (7mm) thick.

PVC liners are reasonably strong and tear-resistant, and some come guaranteed for ten years. They are resistant to both cold and fungal attack, but after several years of exposure to sunlight they may harden and crack. These liners are usually blue or black in color, or black on one side and beige on the other. It is usual to place them with the dark side on top since darker colors absorb light and heat and look more natural than lighter colors.

Polyethylene is the cheapest of all the lining materials; it is easily torn and cracks after constant exposure to sunlight. Where it can be protected from light or from accidental damage, it is an economical material to use. It is particularly suitable as a lining for bog gardens, where it is covered by a layer of soil.

Measuring the liner

To calculate the size of liner required, first determine the maximum length, width, and depth of the pool. The liner should measure the maximum width of the pool plus twice its depth, by the maximum length plus twice its depth. Add 1ft (30cm) to both width and length to allow for a 6in (15cm) flap at each edge to prevent leakage. A pool measuring 6 x 8ft (2 x 2.5m) and 2ft (60cm) deep would require a liner 11 x 13ft (3.5 x 4m).

Installation

First spread out the liner away from the site, in the sun if possible: the warmth will make it more flexible and easier to handle. Mark the required shape of the pond on the site with string and pegs, a hose, or a length of rope, then mark the soil just inside this line. Dig to a depth of approximately 9in (23cm), making the pool sides slope inward at an angle of 20° from the vertical. The slope prevents the sides from caving in, makes it easier to install the liner, and ensures that if the pool freezes in winter the ice can expand upward without causing damage.

If planning to grow marginal plants, cut a shelf about 9in (23cm) wide to provide adequate planting positions, and then continue digging at a slight angle until the desired depth – normally 20–24in (50–60cm) – is reached. Check that the rim of the pool is level all around by using a straight board and spirit level across both the length and the width of the hole. This is extremely important, since if the pool is not level water

Installing a Flexible Liner

1 *Mark out the proposed shape of the pond using string and wooden pegs or a hose, and then start to excavate the hole. Form marginal planting shelves where required about 9in (23cm) broad and 9in (23cm) deep.*

2 *Use a board and spirit level to check that the hole is level. Remove from the hole all tree roots and sharp stones that might otherwise pierce the liner when it is installed.*

3 *Spread fiberglass insulation or heavy-duty landscape cloth over the base and sides to act as a cushion for the flexible liner. Trim the material level with the top of the hole.*

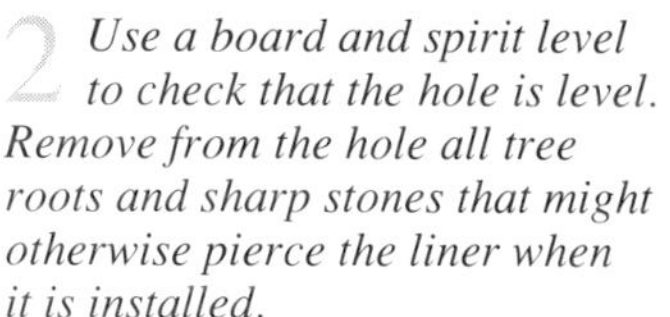

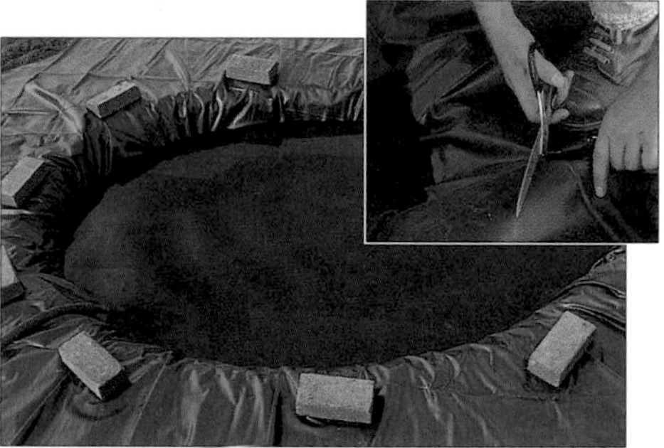

4 *Drape the liner evenly across the hole and weight all edges. Slowly fill the pool with water, tugging at the liner edges to eliminate creases. Trim off any excess liner, leaving an overlap of about 6in (15cm).*

5 *Provide an edging around the rim of the pond with paving slabs or stones, bedded on mortar, or with sod. Check that the edging stones or slabs are level and then tamp them into place.*

6 *The edging stones should overhang the pool by about 2in (5cm) so that the liner cannot be seen. Do not drop mortar into the water or the pond will have to be emptied and refilled.*

may spill over the edge. If including edging stones, remove 2in (5cm) of soil to a width of 12in (30cm) all around the pool, so that the stones can be firmly bedded in later.

Once the hole is excavated, remove any roots and sharp stones that could puncture the liner, and tamp the soil firmly. To protect and cushion the liner, spread an undersheet of fiberglass insulation or heavy-duty landscape cloth, or a 1in (2.5cm) layer of damp sand in the hole. Undersheets are preferable since they are both stable and durable; sand may eventually shift, leaving part of the liner exposed to damage from stones that may have been missed.

Drape the liner over the hole, so that the center touches the base, leaving an overlap on all sides. Anchor it all the way around before starting to fill the pool slowly with water. Weighed down by the water, the liner will stretch and sink to mold itself into the contours of the pool. As more liner is required, remove some anchoring stones, tug the edges of the liner to ensure that it is straight, and form neat folds at the sides if it starts to crease.

When the pool is filled, remove the remaining stone weights and check again that the rim is level all around; add or take away soil if necessary until it is level. Cut off any excess liner, leaving a 6in (15cm) flap all around the edge; this surplus may be hidden beneath rocks, sod, or paving stones bedded on mortar. The stones should protrude slightly over the pool edge to hide the liner. Take care not to let any mortar slip into the water; if this happens you should empty the pond and refill it.

Making planting beds

If including vigorous water plants in a large pool, it may be better to plant them in permanent beds or containers such as concrete pipes or trash barrels rather than in planting baskets. These larger beds allow a greater root run, and tall plants are less likely to be displaced by wind. Beds may be sited on the marginal shelves or on the pond base for growing deep-water aquatics.

To build retaining walls on the shelves of a pond liner, first install the pool and fill it with water to stretch the liner into its ultimate shape, then lower the water level to expose the shelves. Protect the surrounding liner with a cushion of surplus liner scraps, then build the walls. The bed should be a minimum of 9in (23cm) deep and wide. Apply pond sealant to the bed before planting.

PREFORMED MOLDS

Preformed fiberglass or plastic pools are available in a wide range of sizes and shapes. Most designs include planting shelves for marginal plants.

Preformed pools

The simplest pools to install are those preformed from fiberglass or plastic. These are available in a variety of shapes and are often contoured to provide ledges on which to grow marginal plants. Fiberglass ponds are more expensive than those made of plastic, but they are tough and weather resistant, with a life expectancy of at least ten years.

Installation

Level the site as much as possible and clear away any debris. If the mold is symmetrical in shape, invert it and mark out its outline using pegs and string. For asymmetrical shapes, stand the mold the right way up, supporting it on bricks if necessary to keep it stable and level; mark out the contours with long stakes, pushed vertically into the ground, and string or rope.

To dig a hole that matches the mold, first remove soil down to the level of the marginal shelf. The topsoil may be reserved for use in the garden, while the subsoil should be set aside for backfilling around the pond later. Place the pool in the prepared hole, and press it down firmly onto the soil to leave a clear impression of the shape of the base. Lift out the mold, then dig out the central, deeper area that has been marked out by the pool base, allowing approximately 2in (5cm) extra depth all over the entire hole for the cushioning material.

Clear the hole of any sharp stones, tree roots, or debris, tamp the soil firmly, and line it with a 2in (5cm) layer of damp sand, heavy-duty landscape cloth, or fiberglass insulating material. Put the mold in place and check that it is level, otherwise the water will run to one end when the pool is filled.

Ensure that the pool sits firmly on the bedding layer, then add about 4in (10cm) of water. With sand or sifted soil, backfill around the sides to the same depth as the water, ramming the soil firmly under the shelf; ensure that there are no gaps and that the pool remains absolutely level. Continue the process of adding water, backfilling, and checking the level until the pool is full. Finally, firm the soil around the pool and mask the edges with paving stones bedded on mortar or sod.

INSTALLING A PREFORMED POND

1 Firmly support the fiberglass or plastic mold with bricks to keep the pond level and upright, and then mark out its shape by pushing a series of stakes into the ground all around the edges. Lay a length of rope around the stakes to mark out the precise outline that will need to be excavated.

2 Excavate the hole 2in (5cm) deeper than the mold, following its profile of shelves and base as accurately as possible.

3 Use a board, laid across the width of the pond, and a tape measure to check that the depth of the hole is correct, and use a spirit level to check that the base is flat. Adjust as necessary.

4 Remove any tree roots and sharp stones, and then line the hole with a 2in (5cm) layer of sand. Lower the mold into place and check with a spirit level and board that the mold is set level.

5 Fill with water (here pond water) to a depth of 4in (10cm). Backfill around it to the same depth with sifted soil or sand. Tamp firmly. Continue to add water, backfill, and tamp.

Concrete ponds

Often used for formal ponds where its rigidity is an advantage, concrete is durable and is suitable for ponds of almost any size. Construction does, however, require more skill and expertise than is needed for installing a liner or preformed pool.

In areas prone to long periods of severe cold, concrete ponds should be constructed with walls that slope outward at an angle of 30–45°; this minimizes the risk of cracking since the ice can expand upward and outward as it freezes. Ponds of the same size that have vertical walls provide a larger area of deep water, which may be important if you plan to keep fish. Construction is more laborious than for a pond with sloping sides since the wet concrete has to be supported with a wooden form until it hardens (see below).

Construction

When digging the hole for a concrete pond, add an extra 6in (15cm) to all dimensions to allow for the volume occupied by the concrete; if there is to be a shelf for marginal plants, see "Flexible liners: Installation," p.246. Line the hole with 500 gauge plastic sheeting, then spread 2in (5cm) of concrete over the base. For added strength, place a sheet of galvanized wire reinforcing mesh over this and cover with a second 2in (5cm) layer of concrete. When the concrete has slightly hardened, roughen the surface around the edge to a width of 6in (15cm) to form a firm grip for the side walls.

After about 48 hours, or when the base is dry, install a vertical wooden form 4in (10cm) in from the sides, bracing it at the corners. Thoroughly soak the form with water, slide a piece of galvanized wire mesh between the form and the sides of the hole, then pour in the concrete. If a walled, marginal shelf is required, this form will need to be higher (see below). Leave the form for about two days to allow the concrete to set completely. For a marginal shelf, repeat the procedure with another two stages as for the main body of the pool. Remove a band of soil around the pool edge to a depth of 3in (8cm); lay crushed stone in this area as a base for the edging stones.

A few days later, apply a sealant that prevents lime in the concrete from leaching out into the water and harming the plants and fish. Finally, fill the pool and check the alkalinity of the water with a pH test kit. If close to neutral (pH7) it is safe to introduce plants, and, after a further two weeks, fish. If alkaline, this may be due to hard tapwater or ineffective sealant. In either case, delay planting water lilies and marginals for a few weeks as the pH will gradually become more neutral. Oxygenators and surface-floaters generally tolerate alkaline water, and may therefore be included sooner.

Raised pools

The walls of raised pools must be strong enough to resist the pressure of the water; if necessary, seek professional help. Raised pools are more vulnerable to cold damage than sunken pools, and a minimum depth of 24in (60cm) is needed for fish.

Construction

The best way to construct a raised pool is with double walls, built in the same way as a house cavity wall. The exterior wall can be made from walling stones or bricks. The interior wall, which will be hidden, can be constructed with a cheaper brick or walling stone. The walls need to be close enough together to be linked with commercial wire wall ties. A flexible liner is used inside the interior wall.

Mark out the required shape with string and pegs, then construct concrete footings (see *How to Make a Concrete Footing*, p.504) 4–6in (10–15cm) deep and 15in (38cm) wide for the walls. Rake over the base, remove any sharp stones, and cover with a layer of fine sand or heavy-duty landscape cloth. Then construct the double side walls, incorporating the wire ties at intervals to link the two walls.

RAISED POOL
Wide slabs have been used for this contemporary raised pool so that the edge also forms a seat. The adjacent patio is also made from the same slabs in order to create a harmonious design.

Lining a raised pool

The liner may be fitted so that an attractive stone or brick surface is exposed above the water on the inner wall: before laying the top two courses, fit the liner in the pool then over the inner wall and into the cavity of the double wall. The top two courses should then be mortared in place, securing the liner; the surplus liner is tucked underneath the coping. This prevents the appearance of conspicuous white "tide lines" on black liners when the water level drops in summer due to evaporation; it also ensures that no leakage occurs through the stone. Finally, mortar the coping stones on top of the double wall and cut off any surplus liner to create a neat edge to be covered by the coping.

Using a liner to make a watercourse

Watercourses may be constructed to meander over small changes in level, or to be faster moving over a steeper gradient with several falls and a pool at the bottom. The proposed route of the watercourse should be marked out and the position and depth of the height changes noted. Use flexible liners for a natural appearance.

If the water movement is powered by a pump, the outlet for the proposed watercourse, usually a header pool, must contain enough water not to show major variations in level when the pump is turned on and off. One unobtrusive way of creating an outlet is with an underground header pool fitted with a flexible liner.

CONSTRUCTING A CONCRETE POND WITH VERTICAL WALLS

MAKING THE POND
Line the pond area with plastic sheeting. Build the pond in stages, allowing the concrete to set at each stage. Lay the base first, using reinforcing wire mesh between 2 layers of concrete. Once set, install a vertical form, braced at the corners, insert mesh between the pond wall and form, and pour in concrete. Repeat the process for a marginal shelf.

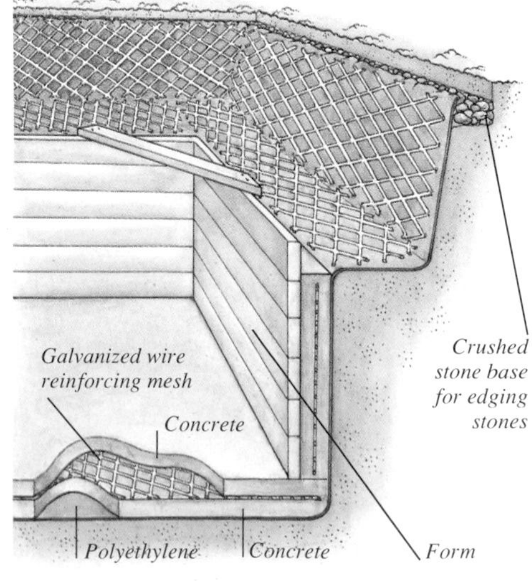

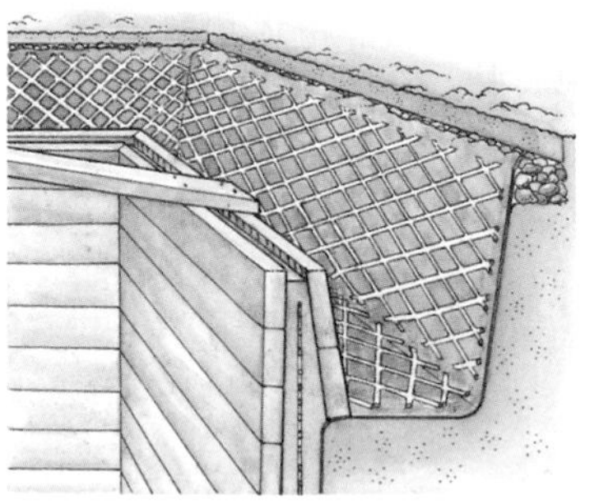

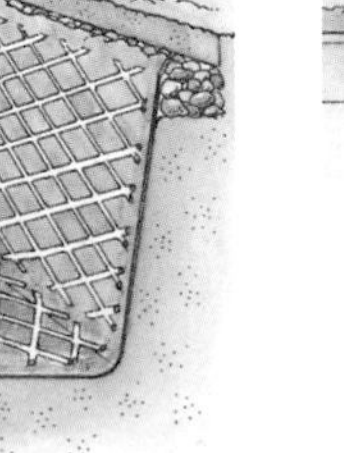

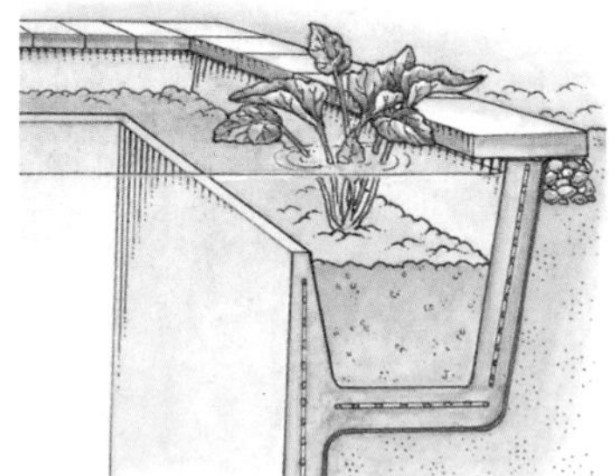

MAKING A WALLED MARGINAL SHELF
A walled marginal shelf allows direct planting. Proceed as before, making the vertical form higher to retain at least 9in (23cm) of soil (left). Once set, concrete the base of the shelf as before and then the outer shelf wall. After the concrete has set, lay the edging stones so that they will overlap the water by about 2in (5cm). Apply sealant and fill the marginal shelf with soil. Plant up and then fill the pool with water (right).

Cover the pool with a sturdy mesh and place a layer of rocks and stones on top; the water pours out between the rocks into the watercourse.

As well as the flexible liner, non-porous rock is needed to mask the watercourse edges and to create the waterfalls, while small pebbles or stones are attractive on the bottom of the watercourse.

Amount of liner required for the watercourse

The route, dimensions, and changes of level in the watercourse are the factors that determine how much lining material will be required.

If the route is fairly straight, one piece of liner may be used. This should be the maximum width plus twice the depth by the length of the watercourse, allowing for any changes in height between the top and bottom, plus about 6in (15cm) at either end of the course so that it can overlap into the header and base pools. A twisting watercourse is best made from a succession of liner pieces, each overlapping the next by 6in (15cm) to avoid unwieldy folds and excessive wastage. Allow for these overlaps when calculating the amount of liner needed.

Construction

Make a bank of soil slightly larger than the dimensions of the watercourse, with the highest point where the header pool or water source will be and the lowest point adjacent to the base pool. Then mark the outline on the soil. Starting from the lowest point, cut steps into the bank to form the falls and cascades; the flatter sections – the treads of the steps – should be made with a slight fall in the opposite direction to the water flow so that they are covered by water even when the water supply is turned off. For the header pool, dig a hole at the uppermost point at least 24in (60cm) square and 16in (40cm) deep. Rake the bottom, remove any sharp stones, then compact the soil with the back of a spade. Spread heavy-duty polyester matting or similar material over the course. The flexible liner may then be fitted into the channel, allowing approximately 12in (30cm) of liner on either side, which will later form the vertical side walls. If using more than one piece of liner to form the length of the watercourse, overlap them by 6in (15cm). Place the higher piece so that it overlaps the lower one where there is a fall or downward slope so that water flows away from the seam. Dig a channel next to the watercourse for the pipe that will circulate water from the base pool to the header pool (see *Recirculating Water in a Watercourse*, p.250).

Set rocks in place to form the steps and sides of the watercourse, arranging them until the grouping is satisfactory. Lift the liner at the sides behind the rocks and pack soil in to just above the waterline. If plants at the edge are to be included, plant them at this stage in the soil behind the rocks. To provide increased stability, mortar the rocks into position using a waterproof cement.

Using rigid units to make a watercourse

Preformed modular units may be combined in various ways and installed to incorporate falls of different heights. Strong, interlocking units are unlikely to move should any future subsidence of the underlying soil or sand occur. Installation by two people is recommended, since final adjustments in levels may require lifting one side of a unit while sand is backfilled underneath.

Mark out the proposed area with string and dig out the watercourse to accommodate the units. Allow extra depth for a level layer of sand beneath them. Work from the bottom up, positioning the lowest unit so that the lip overlaps the base pool

Making a Watercourse with a Flexible Liner

1 *Build a soil bank to the required height and mark the shape of the watercourse. Working from the bottom, shape the steps and header pool.*

2 *When complete, compact the soil with the back of a spade. Remove sharp stones and line the course with a cushioning layer of polyester matting, cutting it to fit.*

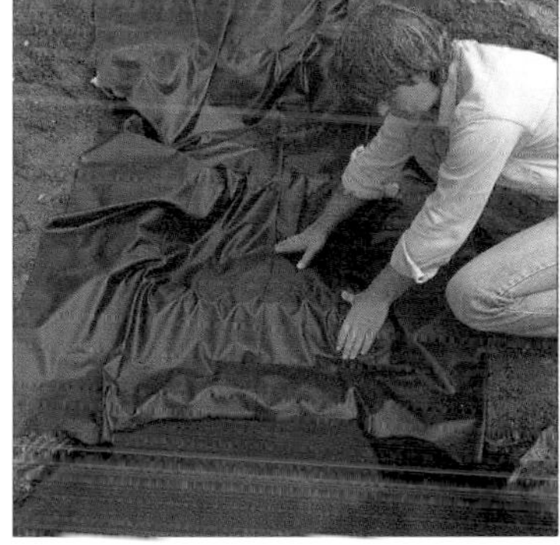

3 *Lay the liner in place with the bottom edge overlapping the pool. Cut to fit, leaving 12in (30cm) on each side. Smooth the liner into the contours of the channel.*

4 *Starting at the base, set rocks in place to form the steps. To prevent water from escaping, tuck in the liner edges behind the rocks. Backfill firmly with soil.*

5 *Continue working upward, arranging rocks and pebbles to form the falls and sides of the watercourse. Ensure that the sides are sufficiently steep to prevent water from escaping.*

6 *Position plants in the crevices between rocks to soften the edges of the watercourse. Bury the water pipe alongside so that it overhangs the header pool.*

7 *Disguise the end of the pipe with strategically placed pebbles. Finish off the construction with a 1in (2.5cm) layer of decorative gravel around the edges of the watercourse to create an attractive, natural setting. Check that the water flows at the correct rate and with the desired effect. Adjust the position of the rocks if necessary before finally cementing them in.*

and ensuring that it is level. Remove it and bolt on a vertical plate that determines the height of the waterfall. To ensure watertight seams, use a silicon sealant around each bolt. Install the linked units, making any final adjustments by backfilling or removing excess sand so that they are level. Once the first unit is level, a small amount of water may be added to increase stability.

The following units, and the final header pool, are then bolted on in the same way. Once each is attached and the levels checked, partially fill the watercourse with water and backfill with sand around the outside edges as before. Conceal the edges with rocks and plants.

Circulating the water

To circulate water from the base pool to the header pool in a watercourse, link the two pools with a flexible pipe attached to a pump. The pipe may be pushed well down into the header pool to hide it; in this case, a one-way valve should be fitted. Alternatively, keep the end of the pipe above the water surface and disguise it at the pool edge with an overlapping stone or slab. Sink the pipe in a trench alongside the stream and cover it with thin pieces of stone to protect it from being pierced.

Pumps and filtration

Two types of pump are available for garden use: surface-mounted and submersible models. For most small installations involving a fountain or watercourse, a submersible pump is quite adequate. Larger installations may require a surface-mounted pump that is housed in a separate, ventilated chamber.

If using a submersible pump, place it in the base pool, raised on bricks or blocks to help prevent debris from being sucked into the inlet strainer.

RECIRCULATING WATER IN A WATERCOURSE

Raise a submersible pump on blocks on the pond base. Attach a flexible pipe; bring it out to one side and bury it in a trench 10in (25cm) deep and 3in (7cm) wide, next to the pool. Push the other end into the header pool.

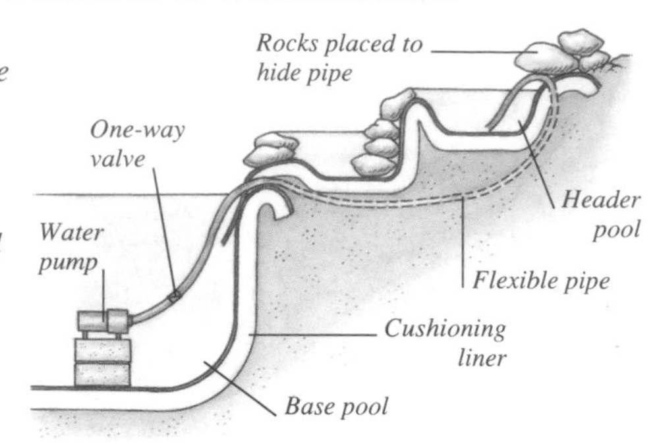

If circulating water through a watercourse, connect a pipe to the pump to carry water up to the header pool (see diagram). Use only approved waterproof connectors with pumps and other electrical fittings. Protect outdoor wiring with armored sleeving and always include a ground fault circuit interrupter for safety.

Usually there should be no need for filtration. If there are large numbers of fish or if it is difficult to maintain submerged plants, physical or biological filtration may be needed. Filter kits that fit onto the suction inlet of submersible pumps are available, but larger installations may need a biological filter.

MAKING A WATERCOURSE WITH RIGID UNITS

1 Mark out the watercourse perimeter, prepare the base pool, then remove soil to the dimensions of the units, allowing extra depth for a level base of sand beneath.

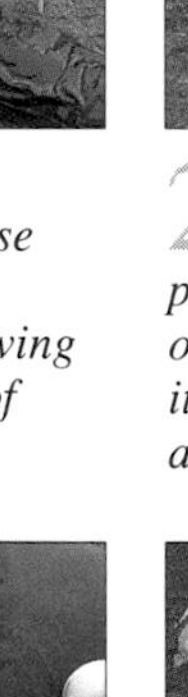

2 Spread a ½in (1cm) layer of sharp sand over the base, then put the first unit in place so that it overlaps the main pool. Check that it is level and backfill with sand around it to provide a firm base.

3 Remove the unit and bolt it to a plate that forms the fall. Seal the seams, then install the unit, adding or removing sand as necessary so that it is level. Backfill behind the base of the plate.

4 Prepare the base for the header pool, covering it with sand. Bolt the base to the upper part of the plate and seal the joins. Backfill the base with sand so that it is firm and level.

5 Install a submersible pump in the base pool, connect a flexible pipe, and lay it in a trench alongside the watercourse. Push the other end down into the header pool.

6 Fill in the trench with soil. Snap into place the precast facing. Place stones around the pool edge and watercourse, hiding the pipe where it leaves the base pool and enters the header pool.

7 If desired, place stones under the lip of the lowest unit to mask the pool edge. Add plants around the watercourse to enhance it and soften its rigidity. Some units include integral shelves to accommodate marginal plants. Fill the header pool with water, then turn on the pump.

Planting and stocking

While most plants are grown for their ornamental features, some also help to maintain the quality and appearance of water by keeping down algae (see "Plants for the water garden," p.242). There is a wide range of planting containers available, allowing flexibility when planting and making routine maintenance relatively simple.

Selecting water plants

When selecting plants, look for clean, fresh-looking, and vigorous specimens, growing in tanks that are free from algae and duckweed (*Wolffia*). Check that the undersides of the leaves are free from jellylike deposits of snail eggs, and that there are no strands of blanketweed in the foliage. Mail-order plants should appear plump and green; if they look weak and limp they are unlikely to grow well.

If buying plants by mail order, use a specialist supplier. It is worth paying a slightly higher price since the plants are more likely to be clean and disease free and to have been propagated in the nursery. Reputable suppliers should also pack the plants with care, and ship them on the same day that they are lifted.

When buying oxygenators for a new pool, allow at least five bunches for every square yard or meter of water surface. They are generally sold as bunches of unrooted cuttings about 9in (23cm) long. They should be weighted at the bottom with a piece of lead to keep the plants anchored, in case they become loosened after planting.

Since oxygenators are extremely susceptible to drying out, they should be kept moistened in a plastic bag or submerged in water until they are ready for planting in the pond.

Selecting Plants for the Water Garden

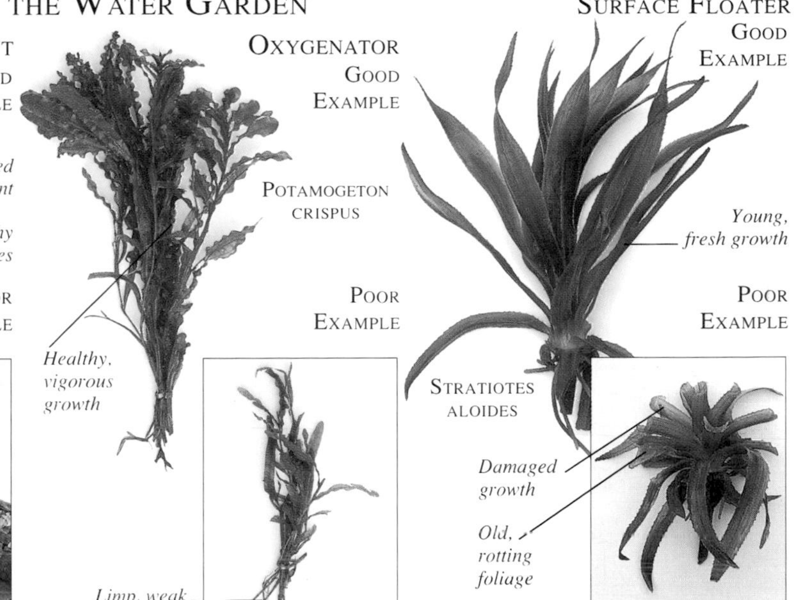

Containers and planting beds

The most convenient way of growing aquatics is in specially made baskets. This makes it easy to lift and divide or replace the plants when necessary, and it is also a relatively simple matter to alter the planting arrangement when desired.

Planting baskets

Planting baskets have wide, flat bases to provide stability in the water, which is important for tall marginals on narrow shelves. They also have open lattice walls, allowing water and gases to circulate through the soil. Most should be lined with burlap or landscape fabric to prevent the soil from seeping out, although containers with a very fine mesh, which eliminates the need for a liner, are available from some suppliers.

Planting baskets range from 11in (28cm) in diameter with a 2¼gallon (10 liter) capacity for medium-sized water lilies, down to 1½in (4cm) in diameter with a 2fl oz (50ml) capacity, for use in aquarium planting. Larger, circular tubs without lattice walls, which are preferable for vigorous water lilies, are also available.

Planting directly in soil beds

In wildlife ponds, aquatics may be planted directly into a layer of soil on the bottom of the pool and on marginal shelves. In most pools, however, this is inadvisable since the vigorous species spread rapidly, swamping their slower-growing neighbors. In addition, subsequent removal or thinning out of plants can be extremely difficult.

Permanent beds

A good compromise is to build permanent planting pockets or beds on the base of the pool and around the edges during construction, which are easily planted up before the pool is filled (see also "Making planting beds," p.247). This makes it possible to maintain a natural appearance while controlling the plants' spread.

Planting Baskets

Planting baskets are available in various sizes to suit different plants. All except those with a very closely woven mesh should be lined.

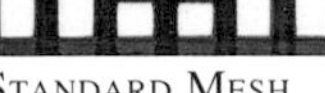

STANDARD MESH

CLOSELY WOVEN MESH

Planting

The pool should be filled with water a few days before planting to allow the water temperature to reach that of the surrounding air, and to mature. During this period, the water in the pool may become populated with microorganisms that disperse impurities in the water and create an environment most beneficial to plants, fish, and other pond life.

Unlike the majority of terrestrial plants, aquatics should be planted while in active growth, preferably between late spring and midsummer, when water temperatures are warm and there is plenty of sunlight. If planted in late summer and early fall, the plants have little time to become established before they die down. Water lilies must have time to build up food reserves before winter if they are to survive and grow satisfactorily the following season.

The planting medium

Aquatic plants grow quite well in good garden soil, preferably a heavy soil; if possible, use soil that has not been fertilized or manured recently. Sieve out any loose organic matter since this will rot or float when the planting basket is submerged.

Commercial soil mixes made for terrestrial plants should not be used for aquatics: besides containing peat, which tends to float, they contain added fertilizers that will encourage algal growth (see p.254). A handful of coarse bone meal mixed into the soil in a large planting basket is all the fertilizer required. If the suitability of the garden soil is in any doubt, use a prepared aquatic soil mix from a specialist supplier.

Planting depths

The ideal planting depth varies, depending on the type of plant, and can differ even within a given group of plants. Planting depths should be measured from the top of the soil in the basket or planting pocket to the water surface (see right).

It is important not to plant too deeply: without adequate sunlight for photosynthesis, plants will die. When planting young specimens, it may be necessary to stand the containers on bricks or blocks at first so that the plants are not completely submerged. As the plants grow, gradually lower the baskets until they reach the appropriate depth.

Bog and moisture-loving plants

The area bordering a natural pool is ideal for bog and moisture-loving plants, but correct growing conditions can be supplied next to a man-made pond by creating special beds.

Mark out the planting beds, then dig out at least 18in (45cm) depth of soil, removing any roots of perennial weeds such as quackgrass. Form sloping sides at the edges. Drape a flexible liner (thick-gauge plastic sheeting is suitable for this purpose) into the hole, ensuring that the top edge of the liner finishes just below the existing soil level.

Although a number of vigorous, moisture-loving plants tolerate saturated soil, most will grow better if the liner is pierced to allow slow seepage of water from the bed. The slight movement of water through the soil also helps to prevent stagnant conditions. Cover drainage holes with gravel so they do not become clogged up with soil.

Keep the soil moist according to the requirements of your plants. Alternatively, simplify watering by sinking a perforated, rigid pipe into the bed. Block the pipe at the far end and cover it with a layer of gravel or stones to prevent the holes from becoming blocked. Fit the pipe to a hose connector, which should remain above the soil surface.

Refill the bed with soil, and then mulch with a deep layer of coarsely sieved organic matter to help prevent moisture loss. Do not incorporate bulky additives throughout the whole bed since sufficient moisture is retained by the liner.

Planting, which is best done in spring, is carried out in the same way as in ordinary soil, although the whole bed should be thoroughly soaked afterward. Plants that enjoy these moist conditions will grow vigorously, so very invasive species are best confined to sunken containers to prevent them from crowding out neighboring plants.

PLANTING A BOG PLANT

1 *In the prepared bed, dig a hole sufficiently wide and deep to accommodate the root ball of the plant.*

2 *While supporting the plant (here* Caltha palustris*) with one hand, gently ease the root ball out of the container, taking care not to damage the roots.*

3 *Place the plant in the hole so that it is at the correct depth; the soil should always reach the same level as it did in the container.*

4 *Using your hands, thoroughly firm the soil all around the crown of the plant. Soak the whole area with water.*

PLANTING DEPTHS

Place plants at the appropriate depth for the species, measured from the top of the soil to the water's surface. When planting young water lilies (Nymphaea)*, raise the baskets on bricks. Lower baskets as the plants grow.*

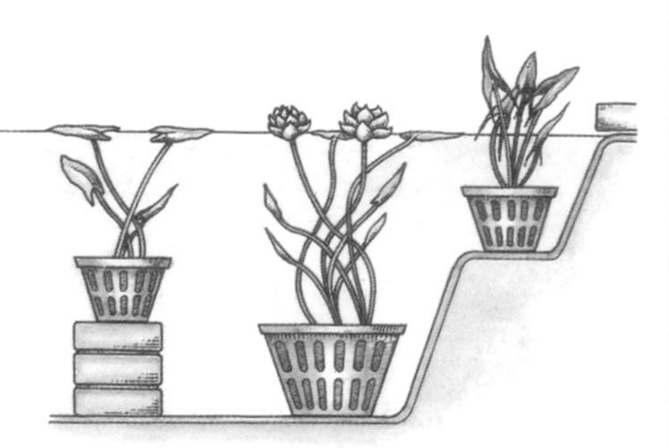

Marginal plants

Primarily included for their ornamental flowers or foliage, marginal plants are grown at the pool edges with their roots in shallow water. Ornamental pools usually include a shelf to accommodate marginal plants, which may be grown either in baskets or in pockets built directly onto the shelf (see also "Making planting beds," p.247).

Most marginals require approximately 3–6in (8–15cm) of water above their crowns; it may be necessary to raise the planting baskets to ensure that the plants are at the correct depth until they are established. The more vigorous species, known as deep marginals, should be planted in 12in (30cm) or more of water, either on a deeper shelf or on the bottom, away from the margin.

When planting marginals, take into account their height, spread, and vigor. Plant rampant growers singly in containers to stop them from smothering slower-growing plants. If using containers, always make sure that there is sufficient room for root development; for most marginals, a container at least 9in (23cm) in diameter is necessary. Plant marginals in prepared containers or planting beds of soil and top-dress with pea gravel; if using containers, place them on the marginal shelf or the bottom of the pond, as appropriate, so that the plants are at the correct depth.

Deep-water plants

As for marginals, these plants are usually grown in aquatic containers or planting beds. Most of them are best planted fairly shallowly at first so that their leaves are able to float on the surface of the water and photosynthesize in the sun.

Whether planting in beds or freestanding containers, settle the plants firmly in the soil because they are very buoyant and may be dislodged. Always plant in moist soil, and soak containers well before immersing them in the pool. A top-dressing of coarse grit or pea gravel to a depth of 1in (2.5cm) prevents soil from floating out and clouding the water and discourages fish from disturbing the plant roots.

When submerging the containers in deep water, thread string through

Surface floaters

With a new planting, include some surface-floating plants to discourage the growth of algae. When the ornamental plants become more established, some of the floaters should be removed. In a large pond, a line may be drawn across the pond from both ends to bring plants within reach. Duckweeds in particular are very persistent, so choose less vigorous species.

Surface-floating plants have no anchorage since their roots obtain nutrients directly from the water. Their initial positioning is unimportant since the groups are moved around on the surface by wind.

Surface-floating plants (here Stratiotes aloides*) may be placed on the water's surface; in warm weather they multiply rapidly, giving valuable surface shade.*

Planting oxygenators

Incorporating oxygenating plants is one of the first priorities when planting in a new pool. This is because their cleaning and oxygenating properties are vital to the oxygen content of the water and to the health of the fish population.

Keep the plants wet after purchasing them and until they are ready to plant. Even during the planting process, they should not be left exposed to the air longer than is absolutely necessary.

Species vary in the effectiveness with which they oxygenate the water, depending on the time of year and the pH of the water, so plant a selection of four or five species to ensure that enough plants thrive to maintain correct oxygen levels throughout the year. Keep only one species in each container to prevent stronger-growing plants from crowding out less vigorous species.

Prepare a planting basket and make planting holes in the soil, then insert a bunch of cuttings into each hole and firm them in. Cover the soil with grit or pea gravel, water thoroughly, and place the basket on the bottom of the prepared pond at a depth of 18–24in (45–60cm).

1 *Line a basket and almost fill with damp soil mix, then firm. Make planting holes and insert bunches of cuttings (here* Lagarosiphon major).

2 *Firm in the plants. Trim off excess liner, top-dress with ½–1in (1–2.5cm) pea gravel, and lower the basket into the pond.*

the sides to form handles; this makes it much easier to position the basket, which can then be gradually lowered onto the bottom.

Stocking with fish

Like water plants, fish are best introduced to the pool during the warmer months. In cooler temperatures, fish become semidormant and are more prone to stress when moved. Allow at least two weeks after planting before stocking with fish to allow plant roots to establish.

Unless there is supplementary filtration, overstocking with fish may encourage algae, which feed on excess waste. Calculate a maximum of 20in (50cm) of fish body length (when fully grown) per square yard or meter of water surface or 2in (5cm) per 1sq ft (1,000sq cm). It is advisable to stock the pool in two stages, introducing half the fish eight to ten weeks before the rest. This allows the bacteria that feed on the fish waste products to multiply to a sufficient level to deal with the waste. If too many are introduced at once, the water may become polluted and the fish starved of oxygen. Leaving a waterfall or fountain on overnight to agitate the water will provide temporary relief.

Fish are usually supplied in a large, clear plastic bag containing a small amount of water and inflated with oxygen. On arrival, do not release the fish straight into the pond: they are very sensitive to sudden changes in temperature, and the water in the pond is likely to be colder than that in the bag. Float the unopened bag on the water until the water temperature in the bag is the same as in the pool. In hot, sunny weather, shade the bag with newspaper. A small amount of pool water may be gradually introduced into the bag before the fish are released. Do not lift the bag to examine the fish closely; this causes them extreme stress.

Other water creatures

As well as fish, a number of other aquatic life forms may be introduced to the pond as useful scavengers. Trapdoor snails (*Viviparus maniatus*) are often sold specifically for this purpose. Ordinary pond snails are likely to be a nuisance because they eat water lily leaves. Mussels and freshwater clams are excellent scavengers, cleaning up where fish have been overfed, as well as filtering out algae. Mussels require a pan of coarse sand 2–3in (5–8cm) deep in which to burrow.

Planting Deep-water and Marginal Plants

1 *Choose a planting basket to accommodate the plant roots, and line it with burlap or closely woven polypropylene.*

2 *Fill the basket with heavy, moist soil to a depth of at least 2in (5cm). Center the plant (here* Aponogeton distachyos).

3 *Fill with more soil to within ½in (1cm) of the rim of the basket, firming the plant in well to give it good anchorage.*

4 *Top-dress the container with washed grit or pea gravel to a depth of 1in (2.5cm).*

5 *Trim away any surplus liner with scissors. Tie string handles to the rim of the basket on opposite sides.*

6 *Hold the basket by the string handles and gently lower it onto blocks or the marginal shelf. Release the handles.*

Adding Fish to a Pond

Float the unopened bag until the water temperature in the bag matches that of the pond. Slowly introduce some pond water to the bag before gently releasing the fish.

Routine care

GOOD construction and siting, and ensuring the right balance of water, plants, and fish should help to keep a pond relatively trouble-free. However, occasionally structural repairs may be necessary, for example, if the pool is damaged or leaks. Algae and weeds must also be kept in check, while many plants will benefit from periodic division.

Structural repairs

Any sudden or persistent loss of water is likely to indicate a leak. If a pool is leaking, it will be necessary to drain and inspect it. Accommodate the fish and plants in a suitable container, such as a wading pool.

Most ponds may be drained either with an electric pump or by siphoning off the water. First check visually that the pond's edges are level; water may be overflowing at the lowest point. With a watercourse, switch off the pump and check the level in the base pool: if constant, the leak is in the watercourse.

REPAIRING A FLEXIBLE POND LINER

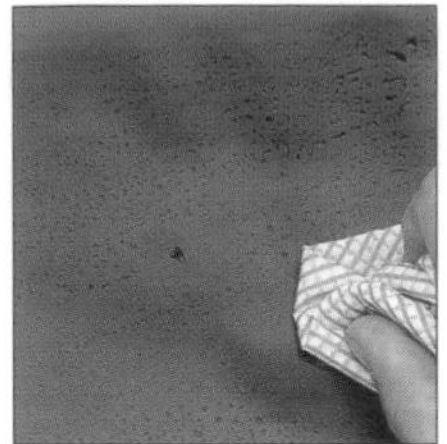

1 *Thoroughly dry the area of damaged liner and then clean it carefully with rubbing alcohol and a soft cloth.*

2 *Apply special double-sided adhesive sealing tape over the tear and wait for it to become tacky.*

3 *Cut out a patch from spare liner and press it firmly onto the adhesive, ensuring that the edges are stuck down flat.*

Flexible liners

If the water level in a lined pool drops or the flow of water in a watercourse decreases, check that no part of the edge of the liner has slipped below water level. Leaks may also be caused by punctures. The simplest way to repair a butyl liner is with double-sided adhesive tape, which is obtainable from water garden suppliers. This is used to secure a patch of butyl liner over the hole. The pool may be refilled after one hour.

REPAIRING A CRACK IN A CONCRETE POND

1 *If a crack is very fine, use a club hammer and chisel to widen it slightly.*

2 *Clean off any algae and debris from the surrounding area with a wire brush.*

3 *With a trowel, fill the crack with mortar or a commercial sealing compound. Allow it to dry.*

4 *Brush with a pool sealing compound to prevent toxins from leaching out into the water.*

Preformed pools and units

If a pool or watercourse unit is inadequately supported or the ground underneath it is not properly compacted, it may eventually crack under the weight of the water. Repair cracks with a fiberglass repair kit. Allow the compound to harden thoroughly because it may be toxic when fluid. Before refilling the pool with water, ensure that the base is firmly bedded down and that soil is compacted around the sides to support the water pressure adequately.

With rigid, interlocking units, check the sealant around the bolts and reseal if necessary.

Concrete pools

The most common cause of leaking is through cracks created by cold damage or subsidence. Inspect the pool carefully since water can escape through even a hairline crack. If the crack is very fine it is usually necessary to widen it slightly and brush clean any debris before sealing it with mortar. Allow the mortar to dry, then paint with sealant.

Water quality

Once a balance of plants and animal life is established, the water should remain clear without needing further attention. If there are marked changes in the numbers of fish or plants, or if there is a sudden introduction of tap or flood water, however, the water balance may be upset and a surge of harmless, but unsightly, algal growth may result.

Algae

Algae depend on sunlight, carbon dioxide, and dissolved mineral salts for their survival. Reduce the amount of light that they receive by growing sufficient plants (water lilies, deep-water aquatics, and floaters) so that their floating leaves cover between 50 and 70 percent of the water surface. The introduction of oxygenating plants, which are efficient at absorbing minerals and carbon dioxide, helps starve out the algae. In addition, take care to keep down the amount of organic matter in the pool by regularly removing dead and decaying leaves and flowers.

Green water due to algal growth may occur in a newly planted pool, or one that has recently been cleaned out. Normally this problem clears itself within a short time.

If the water is persistently cloudy, even with adequate populations of surface and submerged leaves, it may be necessary to use an algicide or, in very acid water, to alter the pH. Change the acidity level gradually, adding small quantities of ground limestone weekly until the water is neutral. For a small pond with a surface area of 40sq ft (4sq m) or less, introduce no more than 4oz (110g) of ground limestone at any one application.

Blanketweed

A filamentous form of algae called blanketweed (*Spirogyra*) is sometimes found in pools with otherwise clear water; if left unchecked, it chokes the plants and restricts the free movement of fish. Remove it periodically by winding it onto a stick or lifting it out with a garden rake; in severe cases use an algicide.

REMOVING BLANKETWEED

Insert a stick into the mass of blanketweed (Spirogyra) *and twist it. The weed wraps around the stick and may then be pulled free.*

THINNING OUT AN OVERGROWN OXYGENATOR

1 In spring or fall, thin out overgrown submerged plants, either by combing them off the water's surface with a rake, or by lifting out the basket and trimming back with a sharp knife.

2 Thinning out oxygenating plants prevents them from becoming congested. Do not remove too much growth, however, since this may leave the pond's surface area too exposed to sunlight, and allow algae to proliferate. Oxygenators are best thinned little and often.

FLOATING LOG

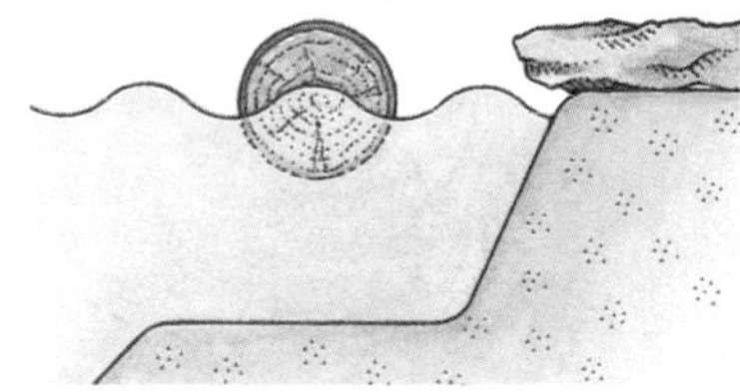

In freezing conditions, floating a log on the water will absorb the pressure of the ice and help to prevent cracks in pool walls. Break up the ice occasionally to oxygenate the water.

Clear out the dead material quickly, since decaying matter will reduce the water's oxygen content.

Pond cleaning

If the water is kept clear of fallen leaves and the plants are regularly trimmed, it should be necessary to clean the pond only every few years to remove decaying organic matter from the base. After cleaning, the water chemistry must again be carefully balanced.

Plant care and control

Water plants do not require much attention, but periodic division and repotting helps to keep them healthy and attractive. Their overall vigor normally makes it necessary for them to be kept in check rather than encouraged, although certain water lily cultivars will require some feeding (see p.244).

Thinning out and division

In late spring or early fall, thin out or divide overgrown plants or any that are crowding their neighbors. Lift container-grown plants and check whether they have become root-bound. If so, remove the plants from their containers and divide them with back-to-back forks or by hand. Tight and thick roots may need to be split with a spade or a knife. Replant the divided clumps singly.

After the first growing season, submerged oxygenating plants may become overgrown and entangled with weeds. In small pools, the oxygenators are easily thinned by pulling out a few handfuls; in larger ponds, use a garden rake to comb out excess growth. Alternatively, lift the container from the pool and cut back the plants by one-third to a half. Do not thin out all the plants drastically at any one time since this causes a sudden change in the water balance and encourages algal growth.

Fall maintenance

The most important task in fall is to keep the water free from decaying vegetation. When the marginal plants begin to die down, remove dead and dying foliage regularly and prune back the excess growth of submerged plants. If there are deciduous trees and shrubs nearby, cover the surface of the pool with a fine-mesh plastic net to catch fallen leaves, and keep it in place until the trees are bare of foliage.

In cold areas, protect tender plants by removing them from the pool and placing them in a bucket of water to overwinter in temperatures that remain above freezing. Cut off the ripe seedpods of invasive plants to prevent them from setting seed. Feed the fish before they hibernate.

If a pump is fitted, remove it from the pool and clean it thoroughly. Replace any parts that may be worn, and store it in a dry place until spring.

Winter care

In winter, ice may form, trapping methane gas released by submerged, decaying vegetation, with potentially lethal effects on the fish. Ice also exerts pressure on the sides of concrete pools as it expands and may cause them to crack. Ensuring that a small area of the pool remains ice-free prevents this and allows methane to escape into the air. Float a log on the surface or, alternatively, use a floating electric pool heater. This gives out just enough heat to maintain a small area of open water.

REPOTTING A MARGINAL

1 Plants that are growing in containers will eventually become root-bound and need thinning out. Roots protruding through the container wall indicate that a plant should be divided and repotted. The plant shown here is Iris pseudacorus.

2 Remove the plant from its container and divide it into smaller clumps, teasing the roots out by hand. Very tightly packed roots may be pulled apart with hand forks used back-to-back.

3 Repot each clump in a separate container filled with damp soil. Water well and top-dress with grit or pea gravel before placing in the pool. Trim off surplus burlap with scissors.

Pests and diseases

Pests are less of a problem in a pool stocked with fish, since the fish eat the insect larvae. Any infestations can be cleared by hand or washed off plants with a hose; insecticide sprays are unsuitable for water gardens and are highly toxic to fish. In summer, aphids (p.552) often attack the aerial parts of water lilies and other aquatics, causing discoloration and decay. Dislodge them with a jet of water or submerge the leaves for 24 hours, weighting down infested parts with burlap.

Diseases attacking aquatic plants are relatively few, and mostly concern water lilies. Fungal disease is indicated by the premature yellowing or spotting of the leaves. If the symptoms persist, treat the plant with copper fungicide in a separate tank.

Propagation

Most water plants, especially marginals, may be propagated by division. Other methods are also used, depending on the type of plant: many submerged oxygenators and some creeping marginals, for example, are propagated by cuttings, while a number of floating plants naturally produce runners, plantlets, or turions, which grow into new plants. Moisture-loving species that grow around the pool edge, as well as some aquatics, may be raised from seed or increased by division.

Cuttings are best taken and plants divided in spring or early summer, when high temperatures and long daylight hours provide excellent conditions for new plant growth.

Water Plants that may be Propagated by Softwood Cuttings

Bacopa monnieri
Cabomba caroliniana ❁
Callitriche hermaphroditica
Ceratophyllum demersum ❁
Decodon verticillatus
Egeria densa ❁
Elodea canadensis
Hydrocleys parviflora ❁
Hygrophila polysperma ❁
Lagarosiphon major
Limnophila heterophylla
Ludwigia arcuata ❁
Myriophyllum, some ❁
Potamogeton crispus
Tillaea recurva
Trapa natans

Water Plants that may be Divided

Tubers
Aponogeton distachyos
Colocasia esculenta ❁
Nelumbo nucifera ❁
Zantedeschia, some ❁

Rootstock
Acorus calamus
Butomus umbellatus
Calla palustris
Caltha palustris
Cryptocoryne ciliata ❁
Damasonium alisma
Decodon verticillatus
Eriophorum angustifolium

Caltha palustris 'Flore Pleno'

Key
❁ *Not frost hardy*

Division

A large number of marginal plants may be readily propagated by division. The exact technique that should be used depends on both the plant's root system and its pattern of growth. For further information, see "Dividing perennials," p.162.

Plants with fibrous or creeping roots

Plants that have extensive fibrous or creeping roots, such as *Typha latifolia*, may be divided by levering apart the rootstocks. Simply pull the rootstocks apart with your hands; if the roots are tightly compacted, use two garden forks positioned back-to-back and lever apart.

Each divided portion should include a growing point (a horizontally placed, terminal shoot). Cut off the old, brown roots and remove any dead leaves. Trim the new roots before replanting the divided portions in individual containers. Level the soil with the base of the shoots. Firm them in, then top-dress lightly with a layer of gravel. Cover the container with approximately 2–3in (5–8cm) of water.

Butomus umbellatus may be divided but may also be propagated from bulbils that form in the axils of the leaves. These are separated and then grown on individually (see Lilies, *Propagating from Stem Bulbils*, p.239).

Rhizomatous plants

For plants with strong, rhizomatous roots, such as irises, pull apart the root mass and divide it into sections with a sharp knife, each containing at least one bud and preferably some young roots. Cut off any long roots and trim back the foliage, if needed. Do not trim the foliage back to below the water line since the newly cut surface tissue may begin to rot.

Plant the division in a suitable container, firming the soil around the roots and just covering the rhizome. Cover the soil with a layer of gravel and immerse the basket in the pool so that the roots are covered by about 2–3in (5–8cm) of water. Rhizomatous plants with creeping surface stems, such as *Calla palustris*, may be lifted and divided into sections, each containing a bud. The sections should be replanted individually in the same way as other rhizomatous plants.

Propagating by Softwood Cuttings

1 *In spring and summer, cut off healthy young shoots (here of* Myriophyllum). *Tie with wire into small bunches of 3 to 6 cuttings 4–6in (10–15cm) long.*

2 *Using a dibber, make holes in damp soil in a prepared planting basket lined with burlap. Insert the bunches of cuttings to a depth of about 2in (5cm).*

Dividing Fibrous Rootstocks

Remove the plant from the container or lift it from the soil with a fork. Insert two forks, placed back-to-back, into the root mass and lever them apart, dividing the plant. Repeat to divide further, then trim and replant the divisions. The plant shown here is Acorus calamus.

Dividing Rhizomatous Plants

1 *Lift the plant (here* Acorus calamus). *Split the root mass into sections with your hands. Each part should have a good root system and several healthy shoots.*

2 *Use a sharp knife to trim back long roots and foliage by approximately one-third to a half of their original length.*

3 *Line a container with burlap and partially fill with damp soil. Plant each division so that the rhizome is just covered with a thin layer of soil.*

Cuttings

Most submerged oxygenating plants may be quite easily propagated by softwood cuttings taken in spring or summer; this also helps to keep plants in check. Fast-growing oxygenators, such as *Elodea canadensis* and *Potamogeton crispus*, should be regularly replaced by young stock.

Prepare the cuttings by pinching or cutting off healthy, young shoots, inserting them into pots or trays of soil, and submerging them. The cuttings may be inserted individually or tied into small bunches of six. Cuttings of some creeping marginal plants, for example *Mentha aquatica* and water forget-me-nots (*Myosotis scorpioides*), should be inserted singly rather than in bunches. The cuttings establish quickly and may be potted up and planted in position after two to three weeks.

Some tuberous water lilies may also be propagated by cuttings, although a different method is used (see "Bud cuttings," p.245).

Runners and plantlets

Many of the floating plants that are invasive in tropical lakes and rivers propagate themselves by means of runners or plantlets produced on long, adventitious shoots. The water hyacinth (*Eichhornia crassipes*) and *Pistia stratiotes* can populate vast areas of warm water in this way. In shallow water, the young plantlets quickly root into the rich mud at the bottom, drawing up fresh nutrients and sending out yet more runners. The plantlets may simply be snapped off and replaced on the water surface to grow separately. In warm areas the water hyacinth can become invasive.

A dwarf form of the papyrus, *Cyperus papyrus* 'Nanus' (syn. *C. p.* var. *viviparus*), forms young plantlets in the flowerhead. If the head is bent over and immersed in a container of soil and water, the plantlets root and develop; these can be divided and potted up separately.

PROPAGATION OF RUNNERS OR PLANTLETS

1 *Some floating plants (here water hyacinths,* Eichhornia crassipes*) form plantlets. In spring, remove a plantlet by snapping the connecting stem.*

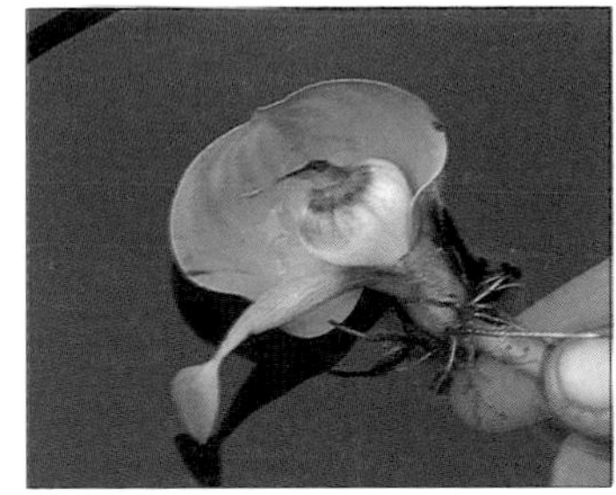

2 *Place the plantlet directly on the water surface, supporting it gently with your hand until it floats upright.*

Turions

Some water plants, such as *Hydrocharis morsus-ranae*, produce swollen buds known as turions that become detached from the parent and survive the winter at the bottom of the pool. In spring these turions rise to the surface and develop into new plants.

The turions of *Hottonia palustris* develop from the mud in spring without floating to the surface. Since these are difficult to collect, wait for them to develop into young plants before lifting and replanting them in their new positions.

The turions may also be collected in fall and stored in soil in a submerged seed tray covered with 6in (15cm) of water throughout the winter. In spring, when the emerging buds float to the surface, they may be collected and potted up into prepared containers of soil.

Seed

Most moisture-loving plants and some aquatics including *Aponogeton distachyos*, *Euryale ferox*, *Orontium aquaticum*, *Trapa natans*, and tropical water lilies (see *Hardy and Tropical Water Lilies*, p.244) may be grown from ripe seed collected in summer or fall.

Keep the seeds cool and moist until ready to sow. If using dried seeds, germination will be delayed or the seeds may have lost viability. Aquatic plant seeds should be grown in submerged or partially submerged conditions, similar to their natural habitat. When sowing seed, first prepare containers such as seed trays or pans by filling them with an appropriate aquatic soil mix or garden soil passed through a 1/4in (7mm) sieve. The growing medium should not contain any fertilizers, since they encourage algae, which could smother germinating seedlings.

Sow the seeds on the surface of the growing medium, and then cover them with a shallow layer of fine grit before placing the tray in a large watertight container, such as a plastic bowl or an aquarium. Fill the container with water until the tray is just covered, and leave it on a greenhouse bench in partial shade, or on a well-lit windowsill, at a minimum temperature of 64°F (18°C). The following spring, the seeds should start to germinate.

When the first two true leaves appear, carefully prick out the seedlings into individual pots and leave them immersed in water in the greenhouse for another year. Transfer the plants to the pool when the water warms up in spring.

WATER PLANTS THAT MAY BE DIVIDED (CONT.)

Rootstock (cont.)
Lysichiton
Mentha aquatica
Menyanthes trifoliata
Myosotis scorpioides
Nuphar lutea
Peltiphyllum peltatum
Pontederia cordata
Ranunculus lingua
Sagittaria sagittifolia
Saururus cernuus
Thalia dealbata ❄
Typha latifolia

Lysichiton camtschatcensis

Offsets
Eichhornia crassipes ❄
Hydrocharis morsus-ranae
Limnobium stoloniferum
Marsilea quadrifolia
Nymphoides aquatica
Pistia stratiotes ❄
Sagittaria graminea, *S. sagittifolia* 'Flore Pleno'
Salvinia auriculata ❄, *S. natans* ❄
Stratiotes aloides

Salvinia auriculata

Plantlets
Aponogeton undulatus ❄
Azolla caroliniana ❄
Baldellia ranunculoides
Ceratopteris cornuta ❄
Eichhornia crassipes ❄
Hottonia palustris
Nuphar advena
Nymphaea, some ❄
Utricularia exoleta ❄
Wolffia arrhiza ❄

KEY
❄ *Not frost hardy*

SOWING SEED

1 *Sow the seeds evenly by tapping them from paper onto a pan of firmed aquatic soil mix or sieved garden soil.*

2 *Cover the seeds with a shallow layer of fine grit. Then place the pan in a large plastic bowl.*

3 *Gradually add water to the bowl so that the pan is just covered. Place in a well-lit position at about 64°F (18°C) until germinated.*

11

Cacti and Other Succulents

Cacti and other *succulents display a unique variety of size, shape, color, and texture. Some have plump, smooth surfaces, while others have curved or straight, sometimes colorful spines or a covering of silky hair. Their forms range from the symmetrical rosettes of* Echeveria *to the squat, globular* Echinocactus *and the fluted columns and candelabra of some desert cacti. Many bloom only briefly and bear large, brightly colored flowers, while others flower for longer periods, producing a mass of exquisite blooms. In cool-temperate climates, most cacti and other succulents are grown in the greenhouse or as house plants, but the hardier species also make beautiful garden displays. In warmer climates, there is scope to create an outdoor desert garden. Whether grown as single specimens or grouped for contrast of form, color, and texture, the great diversity of cacti and other succulents, combined with their remarkable tolerance of dry conditions, make them ideal for containers, both indoors and out.*

Designing with cacti and other succulents

Many cacti are native to the desert regions of the southern US and Mexico, where rainfall is low and intermittent and there are great extremes of temperature. In contrast, some of the most floriferous cacti originate in the warm, humid rain forests of Central and South America. These plants are usually epiphytic, which means that they grow on other plants, either weaving through host trees or lodging in niches in their branches.

Other succulent plants occur in a far greater range of habitats than cacti, and, since they are found in over 20 different plant families, show a wide diversity of characteristics. Their natural habitats include the semiarid regions of Central America, Africa, and Australasia, as well as the more temperate and cold climates of Asia, and northern parts of Europe and North America.

Characteristics of succulents

Cacti and other succulents show a number of adaptations, such as reduced leaf size and loss of leaves in very dry weather, that are designed to conserve water by reducing transpiration. The distinguishing feature that is common to all, however, is the presence of water-storing, fleshy tissue in the stems, leaves, or roots. It is this tissue that allows succulent plants to withstand long periods of drought.

Cacti are easily distinguished from other succulents by structures called areoles, the cushionlike growths on their stems from which the spines, hairs, flowers, and shoots develop.

Succulent plants can be loosely divided into three groups, depending on which part of the plant contains the moisture-retaining tissue. (Some genera, for example *Euphorbia*, may be represented in more than one group.) Most cacti are stem succulents, as are some succulent plants from the Asclepiadaceae and Euphorbiaceae families. Others, including *Aloe*, *Echeveria*, *Lithops*, and *Sedum*, are leafy succulents. Plants in the third group are known as caudiciform succulents and have the water-storing tissue in a swollen rootstock (the caudex), although this often extends into the stem, as in *Adenium obesum*. Plants that belong to this group are mostly found in the families Apocynaceae, Cucurbitaceae, and Convolvulaceae.

Form and habit

The diverse forms and growth characteristics of cacti and other succulent plants may be used to create a range of compositions. The

A Natural Grouping
Collections of succulent plants make an impressive display. Here Euphorbia canariensis *towers above* Agave americana 'Variegata' *and* A. attenuata.

VARIETY OF FORM
The strong, architectural leaves of Agave americana *(center) make a sharp contrast with the orange flower spikes of the* Aloe *species (left) and the spiky, blue-gray leaves of a* Senecio *cultivar in the foreground.*

tall columns of *Cleistocactus strausii*, for example, make strong, vertical lines that contrast well with foreground plantings of smaller, spherical forms such as *Echinocactus grusonii* and *Rebutia* species, or the characteristically flattened segments of some *Opuntia* species.

Several species have a creeping habit that adds a horizontal element to a design. *Carpobrotus edulis*, for instance, as well as *Lampranthus* and *Ruschia* species, makes dense carpets of growth that provide excellent ground cover.

Trailing succulent plants, for example *Ceropegia woodii* as well as *Schlumbergera* and *Rhipsalis* species, produce cascades of slender stems or leaves that are often displayed in hanging baskets. A number are scrambling climbers: *Aloe ciliaris* and *Selenicereus* species add height to mixed plantings if given the support of a trellis or the branch of a tree. In warm, frost-free climates, the jointed and climbing stems of *Hylocereus* species are most attractive when sprawling over walls.

Flowering cacti and other succulents

Cacti and other succulents often produce exquisite blooms and will flower regularly once they reach maturity, although this may take between one and 40 years. Most are day-blooming, with individual blossoms sometimes lasting for several days. Some epiphytic cacti are winter-flowering and have blooms that are carried in succession over long periods.

However, others bloom only briefly, the flowers sometimes appearing soon after sunset and fading as evening advances. Many of the large, columnar cacti produce buds that gradually unfold during the evening and then fade in the early morning hours.

The flowers, often of delicate appearance and silken texture, are usually exceptionally large in comparison with the size of the plant, and their color range is mainly at the warm end of the spectrum with a profusion of rich yellows, hot scarlets, and vivid carmines. A number of genera, often those of the family Mesembryanthemaceae, and some of the epiphytes, have sweetly scented blooms. Some species, especially members of the family Agavaceae, are monocarpic (they die after flowering and setting seed). A number of small, nonflowering offsets are often formed around the flowering rosette, however, and these flower in subsequent years.

Outdoor display

With careful selection and skillful arrangement, attractive collections of cacti and other succulents can be grown outdoors even in relatively cool conditions. Few succulents, however, tolerate excess moisture; even the hardy species require good drainage. These grow well in raised beds where water drains away freely. Among the hardiest are *Opuntia humifusa*, *Sedum*, houseleeks (*Sempervivum*), *Crassula sarcocaulis*, and *Maihuenia poeppigii*.

A number of desert cacti, particularly some *Lampranthus* and *Opuntia* species, tolerate sharp drainage and high temperatures in summer and surprisingly low temperatures in winter, although not the combination of cold and wet.

In mild areas that have few frosts, the range of plants is extended to include the spectacular rosettes of *Agave americana* and its cultivars, *A. filifera*, and *Beschorneria yuccoides*. Half-hardy species need a freely draining site with the shelter of a warm, sunny wall for additional protection. Where temperatures are unlikely to fall far below 45–50°F (7–10°C), such as in the southern and southwestern US and the more southerly parts of Europe, there are few restrictions when choosing succulents for outdoors.

Mixed plantings

When growing nonsucculent and succulent plants together, it is important to choose plants that have similar needs for light, soil type, and watering schedules. In frost-free gardens, compatible nonsucculents include *Salvia*, *Nerium*, *Mirabilis*, and *Catharanthus* species, all of which provide additional color and variety. Bulbs and rhizomes such as

FLOWERING SUCCULENTS

Ferocactus setispinus

Oroya neoperuviana

Parodia chrysacanthion

Strombocactus disciformis

Lithops pseudotruncatella* var. *pulmonuncula

Rebutia muscula

HARDY AND HALF-HARDY SUCCULENTS

Beschorneria yuccoides (half hardy)

Maihuenia poeppigii (hardy)

***Sedum spectabile* 'Brilliant'** (hardy)

Agave filifera (half hardy)

Opuntia humifusa (hardy)

Sempervivum montanum (hardy)

Clivia, *Cyrtanthus*, and *Sprekelia* species are also good choices in mixed plantings.

In cooler regions, annual species and plants that are grown as annuals, such as *Portulaca grandiflora* and *Lampranthus* species, are suitable for planting outdoors among groups of perennial cacti and succulents.

Desert gardens

In arid climates where temperatures seldom fall below 50°F (10°C), the complete range of cacti and other succulents may be grown in a desert garden to create a fine landscape feature. Where the subsoil is particularly heavy, collections of plants can be grown in raised beds to ensure the excellent drainage that these plants require.

Use smaller species at the front of the bed, so that their delicate beauty is not obscured by taller plants. Allow clump-forming plants, such as many *Echeveria*, *Haworthia*, and *Mammillaria* species, sufficient space to develop fully. These low-growing, cluster-forming species flower at different periods from spring to fall, to give color during the warmer months.

Tall, erect, columnar cacti and other succulents are ideal for background planting. Choose plants such as the tall, single-stemmed *Cephalocereus senilis*, the branching *Cleistocactus strausii*, or the towering, treelike *Euphorbia candelabrum*.

A DESERT GARDEN
The branching arms of Euphorbia candelabrum *balance the surrounding globular and columnar cacti to complete this striking collection.*

Containers outdoors

Most cacti and other succulents have shallow roots and respond well to being grown in containers. Select containers that enhance the shape and form of the plants – a wide, shallow bowl, for example, is the natural choice for displaying low-growing and creeping species, whereas those with stronger form, such as *Agave attenuata*, are much better suited to large pots or urns.

Troughs are particularly useful for creating imaginative combinations of plants of quite different sizes and habits. Hanging baskets are suitable for displaying a variety of trailing and pendent species.

Choosing and siting the plants

In cool regions, but where temperatures seldom fall below freezing, many species will thrive outdoors in troughs and pots, provided that these are raised above the ground to allow water to drain away freely. A warm, sheltered position such as a corner of a covered patio or balcony, where the plants can more easily be protected from rain, will provide the ideal environment.

The foliage shapes of *Sedum* and neat rosettes of *Sempervivum* may be used to form a contrast with the leafy forms and brilliant blooms of *Lewisia* species and cultivars, or with the green-flowered *Echinocereus viridiflorus* and the scarlet, early summer blooms of *Echinopsis chamaecereus*. Other species, such as *Agave parryi*, which has symmetrical rosettes of plump, gray-green leaves, or *Opuntia polyacantha*, with its brilliant display of yellow flowers, make striking focal points if they are planted on their own in large bowls.

In warmer climates, there is much greater scope for growing cacti and other succulents outdoors in containers. In large pots, group plants that flower at different periods and have striking foliage forms: the purple-leaved *Aeonium arboreum* 'Schwarzkopf'; *Aloe barbadensis*, which has yellow flowers; and the red-flowered *Crassula falcata*. These provide structural interest all year and give a succession of attractive blooms throughout the warmer months.

Where temperatures do not consistently fall below 55°F (13°C), many dwarf cacti, such as species and cultivars of *Gymnocalycium*, *Mammillaria*, and *Rebutia*, survive well in outdoor bowls and troughs in the garden. These dwarf, cluster-forming species have fascinating forms and textures and put out flowers with vibrant color that will last for many weeks.

Indoor display

The protected environment of the greenhouse or conservatory, which allows practically complete control of light, temperature, humidity, and water, provides ideal conditions for an extensive range of cacti and other succulents. Most of the plants recommended for outdoor cultivation in warm climates will thrive under cover in cooler regions.

The adaptations of cacti and other succulents that help them to survive

MIXED PLANTING
The neat rosettes and delicate, nodding flowerheads of Echeveria *provide a dainty contrast with the straplike leaves of* Agave filifera *(center), the focal point of this attractive combination.*

AN OUTDOOR CONTAINER
This varied collection of tall, spreading, and pendent cacti and other succulents creates a highly decorative and unusual feature on a balcony outdoors.

An Indoor Bed
The bright foliage of Agave americana 'Medio-picta', *offset by the rosettes of* Orostachys chanetii, *is a bold centerpiece in this greenhouse bed.*

in harsh, arid environments in the wild also make them well suited to the warm, dry conditions of the centrally heated home, where many other plants may fail to thrive. Since different species are adapted to a variety of environmental conditions, they may be selected to suit a number of situations in the home.

The variation in their shape and habit, and their beautiful flowers, ensure that these plants provide interest throughout the year.

Providing the right conditions

The great majority of cacti and other succulents need high light levels, warmth, and good ventilation to thrive, although some, the leafy succulents in particular, may need protection from direct sun in summer to avoid leaf scorch.

There is an important group, however, that requires shady conditions, or at least filtered light: the epiphytes that come from the humid, shaded rain forests of Central and South America.

Epiphytic plants are among the most floriferous of cacti and other succulents, and they can be used to add bold splashes of color and interest to shady corners of the home or garden. The best known of this group are the Christmas cactus (*Schlumbergera bridgesii*), *Rhipsalidopsis gaertneri*, and *R. rosea*. Some of the loveliest are the magnificent hybrids created by crossing *Epiphyllum* species with those of *Echinopsis*, *Heliocereus*, *Hylocereus*, and *Nopalxochia*. The resulting hybrids produce extraordinarily beautiful and sometimes fragrant flowers in spring and summer, ranging in color from pure white, through cream, yellow, and orange to red and deepest purple.

Plants for the greenhouse and conservatory

Plants in a greenhouse or conservatory can be grown in pots or open beds, either at floor level or raised on benches. Planting in open beds offers potential for growing larger species and even for creating a miniature desert garden.

When in growth, many species from warm habitats need bright light, a fairly dry atmosphere, and a temperature of 64°F (18°C) if they are to develop to their full potential and bear flowers. These conditions are more easily provided under glass than in the home, and many cacti grow and flower most successfully in the greenhouse.

Some, notably *Rhipsalis* species, require fairly high levels of humidity (80 percent) to thrive, and nearly always perform best in the humid atmosphere of a conservatory. Other groups that are well suited to the conservatory and greenhouse are those that need space to grow and flower well. These include the clambering *Selenicereus* (the most outstanding species is queen-of-the-night, *S. grandiflorus*) and several *Hylocereus* species, all of which do best in filtered light.

When drawing up planting plans for a greenhouse or conservatory, combine groups of cacti and other succulents that have similar cultural needs, to make maintenance easier.

Container-growing indoors

Many cacti and other succulents will thrive in indoor containers if provided with warm, bright, and draft-free conditions. Use small pots for displaying individual plants, or large bowls for planting a variety of compatible species together.

Wear gloves when handling spiny plants such as *Agave*, *Mammillaria*, and *Opuntia*, because their sharp spines may easily become embedded in your fingers if you brush against them, causing a painful injury.

Bowl gardens

If planted with different species that have the same cultural requirements, bowl gardens are particularly suitable for growing succulent plants indoors. One or two plants with an erect habit, for example young specimens of *Cephalocereus*, *Cleistocactus*, or other columnar genera, could provide the focal point of the bowl. Alternatively, use a leafy succulent such as *Crassula ovata* as the main plant. Fill the rest of the bowl with smaller plants such as *Echeveria* and *Lithops*. Free-flowering cacti such as *Mammillaria*, *Notocactus*, and other globular cacti are also good choices for planting in a bowl garden indoors.

A Hanging Basket
The graceful stems and flowers of Kalanchoe manginii *cascade like a waterfall against the house wall.*

Hanging baskets

Succulents in hanging baskets make colorful displays in the home or conservatory. Pendent cacti, such as *Aporocactus flagelliformis*, and trailing succulent plants such as *Kalanchoe*, *Rhipsalidopsis gaertneri*, and *Schlumbergera* species and cultivars, are the most suitable plants to choose, since they will trail attractively over the edge of the basket. *Sedum morganianum* and other semitrailing species are also attractive in hanging baskets.

Plant hanging baskets with just one specimen, or use several species for a harmonious but varied arrangement of shape and texture. In general, nonepiphytic plantings require bright light, but epiphytes need either partly shaded conditions or bright but filtered light, so position the baskets accordingly.

Greenhouse Display
The rich color and diverse forms of Crassula, Echeveria, Echinocactus, *and* Mammillaria *species, among others, provide a sumptuous collection of plants for the greenhouse bench.*

Planter's guide to cacti and other succulents

Damp Conditions

Succulents that tolerate damp conditions

Crithmum maritimum
Salicornia europaea
Suaeda fruticosa, S. maritima
Umbilicus intermedius, U. rupestris

Shade

Succulents that tolerate shade

Lewisia, Cotyledon Hybrids,
L. leeana
Orostachys chanetii ❄, *O. spinosus* ❄
Rhodiola crassipes
Sedum dasyphyllum, S. montanum,
S. rosulatum, S. sediforme,
S. spectabile, S. ternatum,
S. villosum
Sempervivum arachnoideum,
S. ruthenicum

Bowls and Troughs

Sun

Adenium obesum ❄
Aeonium arboreum ❄,
A. nobile ❄
Agave filifera ❄, *A. stricta* ❄,
A. victoriae-reginae ❄
Aloe humilis ❄, *A. longistyla* ❄,
A. rauhii ❄
Astrophytum myriostigma ❄,
A. ornatum ❄
Cephalocereus senilis ❄
Cereus forbesii ❄, *C. peruvianus* ❄
Cleistocactus strausii ❄
Cotyledon teretifolia ❄,
C. undulata ❄
Crassula falcata ❄, *C. ovata* ❄,
C. rupestris ❄, *C. socialis* ❄
Echeveria agavoides ❄,
E. derenbergii ❄, *E. pilosa* ❄
Echinocactus grusonii ❄
Echinocereus blanckii ❄,
E. pentalophus ❄

Echinocereus pentalophus

Echinopsis chamaecereus ❄,
E. eyriesii ❄,
E. multiplex ❄, *E. oxygona* ❄
Espostoa lanata ❄
Euphorbia flanaganii, E. milii ❄,
E. obesa ❄
Faucaria felina ❄
Ferocactus acanthodes ❄,
F. latispinus ❄
Gasteria batesiana ❄,
G. liliputana ❄
Glottiphyllum linguiforme ❄
Gymnocalycium baldianum ❄,
G. gibbosum ❄, *G. mihanovichii* ❄
Haworthia cooperi ❄,
H. limifolia ❄, *H. reinwardtii* ❄
Jatropha podagrica
Kalanchoe blossfeldiana ❄
Lithops bella ❄, *L. dorotheae* ❄
Lobivia densispina ❄,
L. jajoiana ❄, *L. pentlandii* ❄,
Mammillaria bocasana ❄,
M. compressa ❄, *M. gracilis* ❄,
M. hahniana ❄, *M. mystax* ❄,
M. rhodantha ❄,
M. spinosissima ❄,
M. zeilmanniana ❄
Opuntia microdasys ❄
Orbea variegata
Pachypodium geayi ❄, *P. lameri* ❄
Parodia leninghausii ❄,
P. mutabilis ❄
Rebutia albiflora ❄, *R. aureiflora* ❄,
R. heliosa ❄, *R. marsoneri* ❄,
R. minuscula ❄, *R. senilis* ❄
Sansevieria trifasciata 'Hahnii' ❄,
S. t. 'Laurentii' ❄
Sulcorebutia glomeriseta ❄,
S. steinbachii ❄
Thelocactus bicolor ❄,
T. nidulans ❄

Thelocactus bicolor

Trichocereus pachanoi ❄,
T. pasacana ❄, *T. spachianus* ❄

Partial shade

Epiphyllum oxypetalum ❄
(and hybrids)
Hoya australis ❄, *H. carnosa* ❄
Rhipsalidopsis gaertneri ❄,
R. rosea ❄
Schlumbergera bridgesii ❄,
S. truncata ❄ (and hybrids)

Hanging Baskets

Aporocactus flagelliformis ❄
Ceropegia haygarthii ❄, *C. woodii* ❄
Epiphyllum oxypetalum ❄
(and hybrids)
Hatiora salicornioides ❄
Hoya bella ❄, *H. linearis* ❄,
H. polyneura ❄
Kalanchoe jongsmanii ❄,
K. manginii ❄, *K. pumila* ❄
Rhipsalidopsis gaertneri ❄,
R. rosea ❄
Rhipsalis cereuscula ❄,
R. mesembryanthemoides ❄,
R. pachyptera ❄
Schlumbergera bridgesii ❄,
S. truncata ❄ (and hybrids)
Sedum morganianum ❄

Succulents that Tolerate Temperatures Down to 32°F (0°C)

Agave americana ❄, *A. lophantha* ❄,
A. parryi ❄, *A. utahensis* ❄
Echinocereus viridiflorus ❄
Echinopsis chamaecereus ❄
Opuntia humifusa, O. hystricina ❄
Sedum anglicum ❄, *S. cyaneum* ❄,
S. dasyphyllum, S. formosanum ❄,
S. hispanicum ❄, *S. lanceolatum* ❄,
S. rupestre ❄, *S. spectabile*
Sempervivum (most spp.)
Umbilicus, some ❄ (spp. only)

Succulents that Tolerate Temperatures Down to 45°F (7°C)

Agave attenuata ❄, *A. parviflora* ❄
Aloe arborescens ❄, *A. aristata* ❄,
A. barbadensis ❄, *A. brevifolia* ❄,
A. distans ❄, *A. spinosissima* ❄,
A. variegata ❄
Beschorneria yuccoides ❄
Bulbine frutescens ❄, *B. latifolia* ❄,
B. mesembryanthemoides ❄
Caralluma europaea ❄
Carpobrotus acinaciformis ❄,
C. edulis ❄
Cereus chalybaeus ❄, *C. jamacaru* ❄
(and other columnar spp.)
Crassula sarcocaulis ❄,
C. sarmentosa ❄
Echeveria cuspidata ❄, *E. elegans* ❄,
E. gibbiflora ❄, *E. pubescens* ❄
Echinocereus chloranthus ❄,
E. enneacanthus ❄,
E. pentalophus ❄
Echinopsis chamaecereus ❄
Gasteria angulata ❄, *G. distichia* ❄,
G. verrucosa ❄

Kalanchoe tubiflora

Kalanchoe marmorata ❄,
K. tubiflora ❄
Lampranthus falcatus ❄,
L. multiradiatus ❄
Lewisia, Cotyledon Hybrids
Opuntia exaltata ❄, *O. fragilis* ❄,
O. polyacantha ❄, *O. rastera* ❄,
O. robusta ❄, *O. subulata* ❄
Orostachys chanetii ❄, *O. spinosus* ❄
Oroya neoperuviana ❄
Pelargonium acetosum ❄,
P. echinatum ❄, *P. tetragonum* ❄
Rosularia modesta ❄
Senecio haworthii ❄,
S. macroglossus ❄

Flowering Cacti

Day-flowering

Aporocactus flagelliformis ❄
Astrophytum myriostigma ❄

Astrophytum myriostigma

Echinocereus engelmannii ❄,
E. triglochidiatus ❄, *E. viereckii* ❄
Echinopsis aurea ❄,
E. chamaecereus ❄,
E. kermesina ❄, *E. multiplex* ❄
Epicactus ❄
Gymnocalycium bruchii ❄
Hatiora salicornioides ❄
Helioceréus speciosus
var. *superbus* ❄
Lobivia famatimensis ❄,
Mammillaria blossfeldiana ❄,
M. bocasana ❄, *M. hahniana* ❄,
M. microcarpa ❄, *M. nana* ❄,
M. spinosissima ❄,
M. zeilmanniana ❄
Matucana aureiflora ❄
Nopalxochia phyllanthoides ❄
Opuntia lanceolata ❄,
O. paraguayensis ❄
Parodia brevihamata ❄,
P. graessneri ❄, *P. haselbergii* ❄,
P. leninghausii ❄,
P. mammulosa ❄, *P. mutabilis* ❄
Rebutia aureiflora ❄,
R. marsoneri ❄, *R. senilis* ❄
Rhipsalidopsis gaertneri ❄,
R. rosea ❄
Schlumbergera x *buckleyi* ❄,
S. truncata ❄, *S. t.* var. *delicata* ❄
Strombocactus disciformis ❄
Sulcorebutia glomeriseta ❄
Thelocactus bicolor ❄

Night-flowering

Cephalocereus senilis ❄
Cryptocereus anthonyanus ❄
Echinopsis eyriesii ❄
Epiphyllum cartagense ❄
Eriocereus bonplandii ❄
Espostoa lanata ❄, *E. melanostele* ❄
Haageocereus acranthus ❄,
H. setosus ❄, *H. versicolor* ❄
Harrisia gracilis ❄
Hylocereus ocamponis ❄
Pachycereus pringlei ❄
Selenicereus grandiflorus ❄,
S. macdonaldiae ❄
Setiechinopsis mirabilis ❄
Trichocereus fulvilanus ❄,
T. spachianus ❄, *T. terscheckii* ❄

Key

❄ *Not frost hardy*

Soil preparation and planting

MANY cacti and other succulents grow naturally only in desert or rain forest conditions, but they also make striking displays out of doors in cooler climates. Whether grown indoors or outside, specially prepared, well-drained soil or soil mix is essential. A sunny site with adequate protection from cold is also required for most species.

Buying cacti and other succulents

When buying cacti and other succulents, choose healthy, unblemished plants that show new growth or have flower buds forming. Do not buy damaged or slightly shriveled specimens, or any with dull, dry, or limp segments. Also reject plants that have outgrown their pots.

Planting in a raised bed or desert garden

Cacti and other succulents require well-drained conditions, so they benefit from being planted in a bed

RAISED BED CONSTRUCTION

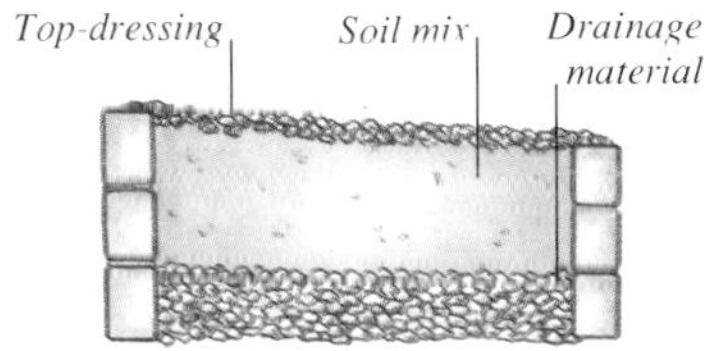

A raised bed has a deep gravel base and free-draining soil mix.

SELECTING CACTI AND OTHER SUCCULENTS

GOOD EXAMPLE

REBUTIA SPECIES

GOOD EXAMPLE

Plump, fleshy leaves

Healthy, new growth

POOR EXAMPLE

CRASSULA OVATA

Shriveled leaves

that is raised at least 10in (25cm) above ground level. To ensure good drainage, make the bed slightly sloping and provide a thick base of gravel or crocks that is at least one-third of the total height of the bed.

Never construct the bed on a concrete or other impermeable base since this impedes drainage. Choose a bright, sunny site with a minimum temperature of 41°F (5°C). In cooler areas, provide adequate protection for tender species (see COLD AND WIND PROTECTION, pp.520–21).

Preparing the soil mix

Cacti and other succulents do not usually thrive in ordinary garden soil, because it is not sufficiently well drained. It needs to be replaced by or supplemented with a carefully prepared growing medium. Good garden soil that has a pH level of 6–6.5 may be used as the basis of a homemade soil mix. It must be sterilized first, however, to kill pests or weed seeds that might be present and to eliminate diseases.

To prepare the soil mix, combine 2 parts sterilized garden soil with 1 part peat or fine shredded sphagnum moss or compost, 1 part sharp sand or washed grit, and a little slow-release balanced fertilizer.

If the garden soil is alkaline, use a commercial soil-based mix combined with sharp sand or grit in a ratio of 1 part sand or grit to 3 parts soil mix. Commercial mixes can be used straight out of the bag.

Handling cacti

Most cacti have sharp spines. When moving or planting them, either wear gloves or take other protective measures.

When handling spiny cacti, such as this Ferocactus, *wrap a loop of folded paper around the plant.*

Placing the plant in the bed

Water the plant, then carefully remove it from its pot. Check the root ball for disease or pest infestation (see also p.265), and treat any infections before planting.

Dig a hole of appropriate size and place the plant so that its base is at the same level in the soil as it was in its container. Fill in around the roots with soil mix, and firm, making sure that the stems and leaves are above soil level. Top-dress with grit to protect the plants from excess moisture and reduce soil water evaporation. Allow the plants to settle, then water lightly at first, gradually increasing the amount until the plants are well established and producing new growth.

PLANTING IN A BED OUTDOORS

1 *To plant a succulent (here* Espostoa lanata), *moisten the soil mix in the pot, then dig a hole large enough to accommodate the root ball in a prepared, well-drained bed. Allow space for the development of the plant and those around it.*

2 *Remove the cactus from the pot and place it in the hole at the same depth as it was in the pot. Firm the soil mix around the root ball.*

3 *Top-dress with a 1/4in (5mm) layer of clean 1/8in (3mm) grit. Water after 2–3 days, when the plant has settled.*

Succulents in containers

A collection of cacti and other succulents grown in pots, bowls, or troughs provides an attractive focal point on a patio or windowsill.

Preparing the soil mix

The soil mix used should be well drained and preferably slightly acid with a pH of 6–6.5. Use 1 part sand or grit to either 3 parts soil-based potting mix or 2 parts soilless mix.

A more acid soil mix may be required for epiphytic succulents (such as certain *Hoya* species) and cacti (*Rhipsalis* and *Schlumbergera* in particular) native to forest areas. Mix 1 part organic matter (such as sphagnum moss, compost, or leaf mold) with 2 parts standard potting mix; add sand or grit to ensure adequate drainage.

Choosing the pot or container

Both clay and plastic containers are suitable for growing cacti and other succulents. Soil mix in plastic pots retains moisture longer than that in clay pots, which means that the plants need less frequent watering, but clay pots provide better aeration around the roots. Choose containers that have one or more drainage holes in the base to ensure that water drains away quickly. The size of pot or container should always be proportionate to the size of the plant but never less than 4in (10cm) deep; tuberous-rooted species such as *Wilcoxia* species do best in a pot with a depth of at least 6in (15cm).

Planting in containers

Always thoroughly wash all containers before use to remove possible sources of infection. Place a layer of drainage material (washed gravel or broken crocks) in the base, to approximately one-third of the depth of the container. Large troughs as well as deep bell- or urn-shaped pots need at least a 3in (8cm) base of gravel or crocks to ensure sufficiently sharp drainage. Fill the container with soil mix to within 1/2in (1cm) of the rim.

Carefully remove the plant from its pot, discarding any top-dressing, and insert it into the new container so that the top of the root ball is at the same level in the soil mix as it was in the original pot. Firm the plant into the soil mix, and then top-dress with coarse gravel or grit.

When planting several cacti or other succulents in one container, space the plants so that there is room for them to develop. To create a more natural display, decorative pieces of rock or pebbles may be added to the composition.

Allow the plants to settle for a few days before watering. Water routinely (see opposite) only when the plants are well established.

Hanging baskets

To create an attractive and slightly unusual feature, plant trailing succulent species in a hanging basket. Make sure that the basket is completely clean. Wire baskets should be lined with a commercial liner or a layer of sphagnum moss. Do not line the basket with plastic sheeting, since this restricts drainage. If using a plastic basket that has a fixed drainage tray, place a layer of small pebbles or gravel in the base instead of sphagnum moss.

Fill the basket with an appropriate potting mix, without disturbing the moss or pebbles, then insert the plants in the same way as for other containers. Do not overcrowd the basket, since most suitable species have a naturally spreading or pendent habit; one plant is often sufficient to fill an average-sized basket. Top-dress with gravel or grit if extra drainage is required, then allow to settle for a few days before watering. Once the plant is established and showing new growth, routine watering can be started (see opposite).

PLANTING IN A BOWL

Crassula ovata
Cereus peruvianus
Mammillaria muehlenpfordtii
Aloe 'Black Gem'
Mammillaria polythelle

1 *Select a group of plants that have similar cultivation requirements, and moisten the soil mix in the pots. Plan the group by positioning the pots in the container, placing the taller plants at the back.*

2 *Prepare the container, placing a 2in (5cm) layer of drainage material – gravel or crocks – in the base and covering this with a layer of soil mix (1 part sharp sand, 3 parts soil-based potting mix).*

3 *Remove the plants from their pots, place them in the container, and fill in with soil mix.*

4 *Top-dress the planted container with a 1/4in (5mm) layer of 1/8in (3mm) gravel.*

PLANTING IN A HANGING BASKET

1 *Line a wire hanging basket with a layer of moist sphagnum moss. The layer should be 1 1/4in (3cm) thick when compressed.*

2 *Fill the basket almost to the brim with a mix of 1 part sharp sand to 3 parts soil-based potting mix. Prepare a hole for the plant in the center of the basket.*

3 *Insert the plant (here a* Schlumbergera*), spreading out the roots. Fill in with soil mix so that there are no air pockets around the roots.*

4 *Wait for 2–3 days after planting before watering the finished basket.*

Routine care

Cacti and other succulents need little maintenance in order to thrive, but they must have adequate light, warmth, and ventilation. Feed and water as appropriate for the particular species, and check regularly for signs of diseases or pests. Repot plants in containers as soon as they outgrow them, to prevent them from becoming potbound.

The right environment

Place cacti and other succulents in a position appropriate to their individual cultural needs. Most species need full sun, although some prefer dappled or continuous shade. The ideal maximum daytime temperature in spring and summer is 86°F (30°C), and the nighttime temperature, 66°F (19°C). During the dormant season, most plants should be kept at a temperature of at least 45°F (7°C), although species from the tropics and equatorial regions generally require a warmer environment, with a minimum temperature of 55°F (13°C).

Ventilation

Good ventilation is essential, although cacti and other succulents should not be exposed to drafts. For plants grown in a greenhouse it may become necessary to use blinds or apply commercial shading to the outside of the glass, if ventilation is insufficient to keep the temperature below 81°F (27°C) (see "Shading," p.484). In exceptionally hot weather, watering the greenhouse floor will help to reduce the temperature. Occasionally, plants grown in the open may need some shade to protect them in extreme heat.

Watering and feeding

Cacti and other succulents require more water when they are growing actively (which is usually in spring and summer), and less when they are resting. Take care not to overwater them, especially during cool periods, but be sure to water them enough to prevent complete dehydration. Succulents from forested areas often bloom between late fall and early spring, so they require more water at this time.

Watering

During the growing season, moisten the soil or mix thoroughly with tepid water, allowing it to dry out almost completely before watering again. Provided that the plants are grown in free-draining soil, surplus moisture drains away quickly.

Water early in the day or in the late evening, because the plants may scorch if they are covered in water droplets in bright sunshine. Alternatively, potgrown plants may be watered by placing the container in a shallow pan of water, so that the water permeates the soil mix but does not touch the stems or leaves. Remove the container from the water to drain as soon as the surface of the soil mix appears moist; the plants will rot if left standing in water.

Epiphytic plants and those that need shaded conditions should be kept moist but not wet. An occasional, light mist-spray maintains a reasonable level of humidity.

Feeding

During the growing season, feed cacti and other succulents to help maintain healthy, vigorous growth and to encourage flowering. Several commercial fertilizers are available but a standard, well-balanced liquid fertilizer containing all the major nutrients is satisfactory. Apply in accordance with the manufacturer's instructions at monthly intervals. Never apply fertilizer when a plant is dormant or the soil is dry since this may damage the stems and foliage.

Hygiene

Cacti and other succulents may need occasional cleaning, since dust sometimes accumulates on the leaves or between the spines. During the growing season, house plants may be sprayed lightly with water; succulents in the greenhouse or garden may be hosed down carefully, provided that they are not in direct sun.

Pests and diseases

Check cacti and other succulents routinely for pests and diseases. The most prevalent pests are mealybugs (p.552), scale insects (p.554), spider mites (p.552), root mealybugs (see "Mealybugs," p.552), and fungus gnats (p.572).

Diseases of cacti and other succulents are rare, although poor cultural conditions or excess nitrogen in the soil may encourage the development of black rot, which principally afflicts epiphytic cacti and *Stapelia* species. The plants become disfigured and may die. There is no treatment, so, if it appears that a plant is likely to die as a result of infection, take healthy shoots or sections as cuttings and grow them on to replace the diseased plant.

Repotting

Cacti and other succulents should be repotted as soon as the roots begin to show through the drainage holes – usually every two to three years for fast-growing species. Repot slow-growing plants every three to four years. Always water a plant before repotting so the roots do not dry out while being potted.

Carefully remove the plant from its current pot. Inspect the roots, looking for signs of pests or disease, and treat if necessary. Cut out any dehydrated or dead roots, and dust the cuts with fungicide. Choose a new container at least one size larger than the current one and repot, ensuring the planting depth is the same.

REPOTTING SUCCULENTS

1 *When a succulent (here* Aloe arborescens) *has outgrown its container, repot it, selecting a container that is at least one size larger than the current one. Moisten the soil mix before sliding the plant out of its pot.*

2 *Gently tease out any roots that have become coiled or compressed.*

3 *Place some crocks and a little soil mix in the new pot. Position the plant at the same depth as it was in the previous container.*

4 *Carefully fill in around the root ball with more soil mix, firming in stages to eliminate any air pockets between the roots. Do not water until the plant is settled in the new pot, usually after several days.*

Propagation

Cacti and other succulents may be propagated from seed, from leaf or stem cuttings, by division, or by grafting. Division and cuttings are the easiest methods. Raising plants from seed is slower and more difficult but provides the opportunity to obtain selected variants from within species, and to raise new hybrids by hand pollination. Grafting is useful for rare species and hybrids, and for those slow-growing succulents that are difficult to propagate by other methods.

PROPAGATION FROM SEED

1 *Cover the base of the pot with crocks, then add at least 1/2in (1cm) of coarse gravel mixed with a little charcoal.*

2 *Fill the pot to within 1/2in (1cm) of the brim with moist seed soil mix, and firm. Sprinkle fine seeds evenly over the surface.*

3 *Apply a fine, light mist-spray to the surface of the soil mix. Take care not to overwater.*

4 *Cover the seeds with a top-dressing of sterilized, gritty sand – only a very thin layer is required.*

5 *Label and place the pot in a plastic bag. Keep in partial shade, at a minimum temperature of 70°F (21°C).*

SOWING LARGE SEED

Press each seed into the soil mix, sowing at twice the seed's own depth. Space seeds about 1/2in (1cm) apart so that they have room to develop.

Propagating plants from seed

Seeds of cacti and other succulents vary widely in shape and size, and some of them have special requirements. Some fine seeds are slow to germinate, while some larger ones have a thick coating (such as those of several *Opuntia* species) and seldom germinate unless they have been stratified. These should be placed in a refrigerator for 48 hours.

Sowing

Sow seed under cover between late winter and late spring. Place a layer of coarse gravel, combined with a sprinkling of charcoal chips, in the base of a seed tray or pot. Fill almost to the top with seed soil mix, then smooth over and firm lightly.

Sprinkle fine seeds evenly over the surface, water lightly, and barely cover with sterilized, sharp sand or a sand and grit mix. Larger seeds should be pressed into the soil mix, allowing ample space between them, then covered with coarse sand or grit. Stand pots or trays of larger seeds in tepid water and leave them until the upper surface of the soil is moist, then remove the containers and let the surplus moisture drain.

Place the containers in a propagator, maintaining a temperature of 70°F (21°C). Alternatively, seeds in pots can be sealed in a clear plastic bag. Keep the seeds in partial shade until they have germinated.

Care of seedlings

When the seedlings appear, remove the pots from the plastic bags or the propagator and provide additional ventilation. Spray the seedlings with fungicide to discourage damping off. Maintain a temperature of 70°F (21°C), giving further light and air as the seedlings develop.

Pricking out

After six to 12 months (depending on the species), when the seedlings are large enough to be handled without damaging them, prick them out singly into 3in (6cm) pots. Prepare the pots with a layer of crocks and fill almost to the brim with moist soil mix, then firm gently.

PRICKING OUT SEEDLINGS

1 *When the seedlings are large enough to handle, lift a clump from the pot, taking care not to damage the roots.*

2 *Divide the clump into individual small plants, retaining as much soil mix as possible around the roots (see inset).*

3 *Insert each seedling into a pot containing 3 parts cactus soil mix to 1 part gritty sand. Keep the top-growth clear of the soil mix.*

4 *Top-dress with a 1/4in (5mm) layer of 1/8in (3mm) gravel, and label. Do not water the seedlings for 3 or 4 days.*

Remove a group of seedlings and separate them out carefully. Plant out the seedlings singly, top-dress them with a thin layer of gravel, and then label each pot. Keep the young plants at a minimum temperature of 59°F (15°C). After a few days, water them sparingly, then gradually increase the amount until, usually after three or four weeks, the normal watering routine can be followed (see p. 265).

Leaf cuttings

Some succulent plants, for example many species of *Crassula* and *Echeveria*, may be propagated from leaf cuttings. These should be taken from the parent plant in spring or early summer when there is plenty of new growth.

Choose firm, fleshy leaves and remove them carefully from the parent plant. Sever them with a sharp knife or pull them gently downward, ensuring that a small piece of stem remains attached to the base of each. Put the severed cuttings on a clean piece of paper, and place them in partial shade at a temperature of 50°F (10°C). Leave them for a day or two until each one has formed a noticeable callus.

PROPAGATION FROM LEAF CUTTINGS

1 *Remove a healthy leaf by carefully pulling it away from the parent plant. It should break off at the base, with a small piece of stem attached.*

2 *Allow 24–48 hours for the wound to callus (see inset). Fill a pot with equal parts fine peat or compost and sand. Insert the cutting so that the base is gently but securely held in the soil mix.*

3 *Top-dress with gravel or grit, and label. When new growth has been developing for about 2 weeks (see inset), the rooted cutting is ready to pot up into soil-based potting mix.*

Fill pots almost to the brim with equal parts of peat or screened compost and sharp grit or sand. Each cutting should be inserted in an upright position in a pot so that the stem of the leaf is just held in place in the top of the soil mix. Firm the soil mix around the cuttings with your fingers.

Cover the surface with a light top-dressing of gravel or grit to help keep the cuttings in position. Label the pot and place it in dappled shade, making sure that you maintain a regular temperature of 70°F (21°C). Keep the young cuttings moist by watering them every day with tepid water. Use a fine mist-spray to cause least disturbance to the cuttings.

Rooting does not take long, normally occurring within a few days. Approximately two weeks after new growth appears, pot up the rooted cuttings into suitably sized pots of standard, soil-based potting mix. Replace the top-dressing.

SUCCULENTS THAT MAY BE PROPAGATED BY LEAF CUTTINGS

Adromischus cooperi ❄, *A. festivus* ❄
Aeonium arboreum ❄
Begonia incana ❄, *B. venosa* ❄
Cotyledon ladismithiensis ❄, *C. undulata* ❄
Crassula ovata ❄, *C. perfoliata* ❄
Dudleya ingens ❄, *D. rigida* ❄
Echeveria agavoides ❄, *E. elegans* ❄
Fenestraria aurantiaca ❄
Gasteria batesiana ❄
Glottiphyllum linguiforme ❄
Graptopetalum amethystinum ❄
Haworthia attenuata ❄, *H. planifolia* ❄
Hoya australis ❄, *H. carnosa* ❄
Kalanchoe beharensis ❄, *K. tomentosa* ❄
Lenophyllum pusillum ❄, *L. texanum* ❄
Orostachys chanetii ❄

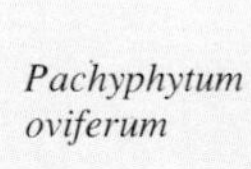

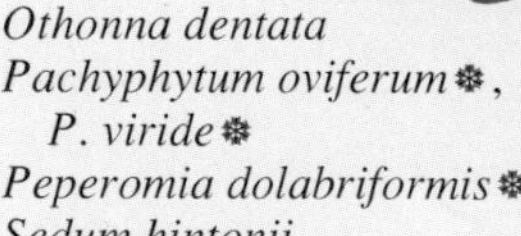

Pachyphytum oviferum

Othonna dentata
Pachyphytum oviferum ❄, *P. viride* ❄
Peperomia dolabriformis ❄
Sedum hintonii, *S. sempervivoides* ❄
Senecio fulgens ❄, *S. jacobsenii* ❄
Streptocarpus saxorum ❄
Thompsonella platyphylla ❄
Umbilicus chloranthus ❄
Xerosicyos danguyi ❄

KEY
❄ *Not frost hardy*

Producing hybrids

When growing cacti and other succulents in a mixed collection, cross-pollination may occur, ie pollen from the flowers of one species or variety pollinates those of another to produce hybrid offspring. Sometimes these hybrids are improvements on other types raised and may be worth propagating. More frequently, however, they are not worth keeping.

To be sure of raising plants with the desired characteristics, it is necessary to control the pollination process. Controlled pollination can be used to produce plants of the same species (which retain the parental characteristics) or purposely to produce hybrid offspring from different species (which combine the characteristics of the parent plants).

To produce a new hybrid, choose the parent plants, usually species of the same genus, in an attempt to combine the best characteristics (such as leaf shape or flower color) of both parents. To prevent unwanted pollination by insects, just before the stigma appears receptive or the anthers are ready to dehisce, tie a small paper bag loosely over the flowers that are to be used. Transfer the pollen from the anthers of one parent flower to the stigma of the second parent by hand, using a soft, fine brush. Then re-cover the hand-pollinated flower with a paper bag.

Many cacti and other succulents are not self-fertile, and it is essential to cross-pollinate in order to obtain seed. If a species is self-fertile, however, cover the flowers with a bag, as above, to prevent cross-pollination by insects. A gentle tap on the bag is usually sufficient to spread pollen onto the stigmas within the flower to achieve self-pollination.

As the fruits ripen from green to red they become soft and fleshy and may release seed. If not, slice the fruits open and leave them for two or three days in a partially shaded but warm position so that the pulp dries out. Then wash the seed to remove the pulp and dry it on blotting paper before sowing.

To produce a batch of hybrid seed (here from a Schlumbergera*), dust pollen from the anthers of one of the selected parent flowers onto the stigmas of the other parent, using a fine-haired brush.*

SUCCULENTS THAT MAY BE PROPAGATED BY STEM CUTTINGS OR SECTIONS

Adromischus ❄
Aeonium ❄
Aporocactus ❄
Bergerocactus ❄
Caralluma ❄
Cephalocereus ❄
Cereus ❄
Ceropegia ❄
Cleistocactus ❄
Cotyledon ❄
Crassula ❄
Echeveria ❄
Epiphyllum ❄
Euphorbia, some ❄
Greenovia ❄
Heliocereus ❄
Huernia ❄
Kalanchoe ❄

Kalanchoe 'Wendy'

Nopalxochia ❄
Opuntia, some ❄
Oreocereus ❄
Oscularia ❄
Pachycereus ❄
Pachyphytum ❄
Pedilanthus ❄
Pelargonium ❄
Pereskia ❄
Rhipsalis ❄
Ruschia ❄
Sarcocaulon ❄
Schlumbergera ❄
Sedum, some ❄ (some spp.)
Selenicereus ❄
Senecio, some ❄
Stapelia ❄

KEY
❄ *Not frost hardy*

Stem cuttings and stem sections

Stem cuttings may be used to propagate many species of succulent, including *Euphorbia*, *Stapelia*, and most columnar cacti.

Take stem cuttings or sections in early to mid-spring. The amount and type of stem material that is removed depends on the plant. Some cacti such as *Opuntia* consist of a series of rounded pads or sections that can be severed with a sharp knife at the joint or base for propagation. For plants that have flattened, leaflike stems, for example *Epiphyllum*, make a cut across a stem to remove a short length. To avoid disfiguring the plant, remove a complete "leaf" at the point where it joins the main stem, and treat this as the cutting or cut it into several sections (see below). Most columnar cacti, and some species of *Euphorbia*, may have sections of stem removed to provide cuttings (see below).

All *Euphorbia* and some Asclepiads produce a milky latex when cut. To stop the flow, dip the cutting into tepid water for a few seconds. Seal the cut on the parent plant by holding a damp cloth against the wound. Avoid getting the sap on your skin, since it can cause irritation.

Leave stem cuttings in a warm, dry place for approximately 48 hours to allow a callus to form, before potting them up in suitable soil mix.

STEM CUTTINGS

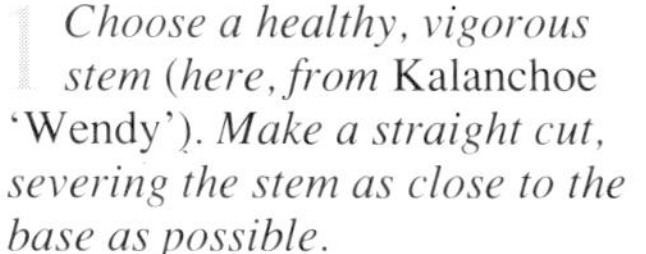

1 *Choose a healthy, vigorous stem (here, from* Kalanchoe 'Wendy'*). Make a straight cut, severing the stem as close to the base as possible.*

2 *Trim the stem (see inset) just below a node. Remove lower leaves, if necessary, to give* ½*in (1cm) of clear stem.*

3 *Insert each cutting into a soil mix of equal parts fine peat or compost and sharp grit or sand. The leaves should be just clear of the soil mix surface.*

Inserting the cuttings

Insert one stem cutting centrally into a prepared pot, or place several small ones around the edge of the container. The cuttings should be inserted just deeply enough to stay upright but not too deeply, as otherwise the base of the cuttings may rot before they have rooted. Stem cuttings from succulents that bear true leaves, such as *Pereskia* species, need to have the lower leaves removed before they are inserted, in the same way as nonsucculent plants. Apply a mist-spray of tepid water occasionally, but do not overwater, because this may cause the cuttings to rot. Rooting normally takes place after approximately two weeks, although cuttings from some genera such as *Selenicereus* may take a month or more.

PROPAGATION FROM PAD SECTIONS

1 *Sever a pad, making a straight cut across the joint. Leave the section in a warm, dry place for about 48 hours to allow the wound to callus (see inset).*

2 *Insert the cutting into a pot containing equal parts fine peat or compost and sharp grit or sand, and label. Once rooted (approximately 2–4 weeks), pot on into standard potting mix.*

Propagation from stem sections

Many cacti and other succulents may be propagated from a small section of stem rather than from a complete one. Use lengths of about 2–4in (5–10cm), depending on the species. For columnar cacti, remove a section of stem (below), cutting it off at the appropriate point. For cacti with flattened, leaflike stems, cut the stem laterally into pieces (right). Then treat each section as a stem cutting.

COLUMNAR STEM SECTION
Sections of stem taken from some columnar cacti may be treated as cuttings.

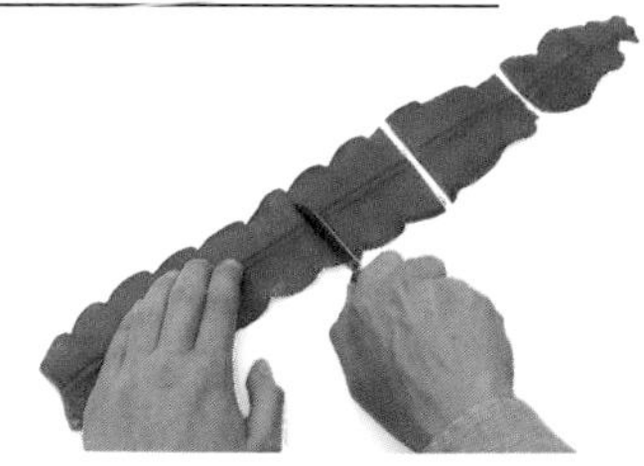

LEAFLIKE STEM SECTION
Remove a stem (here Epiphyllum*) and cut it into sections.*

INSERTING A STEM SECTION

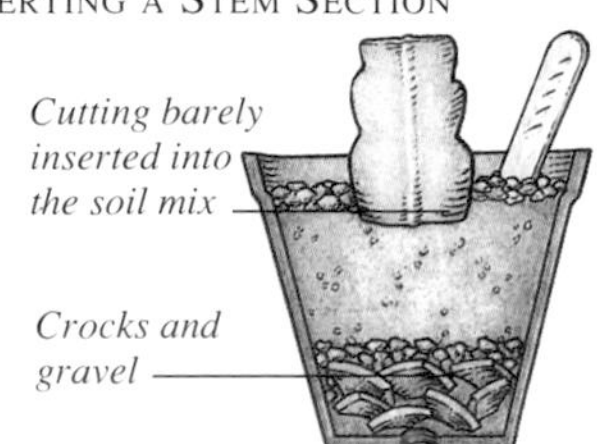

Division of offsets

A large number of clump-forming cacti and other succulents, such as *Conophytum*, *Mammillaria*, and *Sedum*, may be propagated from offsets early in the growing season.

Clump-forming offsets

Scrape away the top layer of soil from around the parent plant to reveal the base of the offsets, and carefully detach one or more from the parent plant, as required, with a sharp knife. Treat any wounds on the offsets with fungicide, leaving them to dry for two to three days to allow a callus to form. Pot up rooted offsets immediately.

Rootless offsets should be inserted into soil mix made up of equal parts fine peat or compost and sand. If the offsets have already developed roots, use a standard potting mix. Use appropriately sized containers with a layer of crocks at the bottom for drainage. Pot up the offsets separately and water them in lightly.

Keep the potted offsets in semishade for about two weeks at a minimum temperature of 59°F (15°C), and water them again after the first week. Once new growth appears, the plants should be potted on into a standard potting mix and the normal watering routine followed (see p.265).

Division of Clump-forming Offsets

1 *Gently scrape away the top surface of the soil mix around an offset. Cut straight across the joint and allow the wound to callus (see inset).*

2 *Using a soil mix of equal parts coarse sand and peat or compost, insert the offset just below the surface of the soil mix.*

3 *Top-dress with ¼in (5mm) of grit, label, and place in semishade. Water after 3–4 days.*

4 *When new growth appears, pot on into a standard potting mix, top-dressing as before.*

Offset tubers

Some tuberous-rooted succulents such as *Ceropegia* produce small offset tubers around the main tuber of the parent plant. These can be treated as divisions and grown on to produce new plants. During the dormant season, remove some of the soil mix to reveal the offsets and separate them from the parent plant using a clean, sharp knife. Treat the cut surfaces of rootless offsets with fungicide and allow a callus to form. Insert each offset tuber in a clean pot that contains a mix of equal parts peat or compost and coarse sand.

If the offsets have roots, place them directly into a standard potting mix. Top-dress with a thin layer of washed, sharp grit, and label. Place the pots in semishade and maintain a temperature of 64°F (18°C). Allow the tubers to settle for three or four days and then water them regularly with a fine mist-spray. As soon as growth starts and some young shoots begin to appear, follow the normal watering routine (see p.265). Pot on into a standard potting mix as soon as the young plants have grown several shoots and have become well established.

Division of Offset Tubers

1 *Scrape away some soil mix from around the main tuber and carefully detach offset tubers. Lift them without damaging the roots, if present (see inset).*

2 *Treat wounds with fungicide, and allow to callus. If roots are present, insert into potting mix, otherwise use equal parts of fine peat or compost and sand.*

3 *Top-dress with a ¼in (5mm) layer of ⅛in (3mm) sharp grit. Label the pot but do not water for several days.*

Succulents that may be Propagated by Division of Offsets

Agave, some ❄
Aloe ❄
Aloinopsis ❄
Caralluma ❄
Carruanthus ❄
Conophytum ❄
Copiapoa ❄
Coryphantha ❄
Crassula ❄
Dactylopsis ❄
Delosperma ❄
Dinteranthus ❄
Dracophilus ❄
Duvalia ❄
Ebracteola ❄
Echidnopsis ❄
Echinocereus ❄
Echinopsis ❄
Epithelantha ❄
Erepsia ❄
Escobaria ❄
Faucaria ❄
Gasteria ❄
Glottiphyllum ❄
Greenovia ❄
Gymnocalycium ❄
Haworthia ❄
Huernia ❄
Juttadinteria ❄

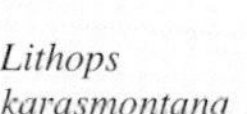

Lithops karasmontana

Lithops ❄
Lobivia ❄
Mammillaria ❄
Meyerophytum ❄
Mitrophyllum ❄
Orbea, some ❄
Orostachys ❄
Parodia ❄
Pleiospilos ❄
Pterocactus ❄
Pygmaeocereus ❄
Rebutia ❄
Rhombophyllum ❄
Sarcozona ❄
Sedum, some ❄
Semnanthe ❄
Sempervivum
Stapelia ❄
Stomatium ❄
Sulcorebutia ❄
Tephrocactus ❄
Thelocactus ❄ (a few spp.)
Weingartia ❄
Wigginsia ❄

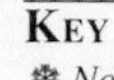

Wigginsia vorwerkiana

KEY
❄ *Not frost hardy*

SUCCULENTS THAT MAY BE PROPAGATED BY DIVISION OF ROOTSTOCK

Agave, some ❄
Aloe ❄
Argyroderma ❄
Caralluma ❄
Carpobrotus ❄

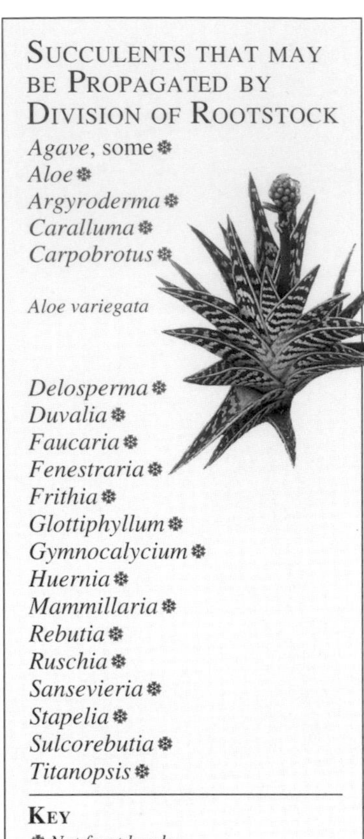

Aloe variegata

Delosperma ❄
Duvalia ❄
Faucaria ❄
Fenestraria ❄
Frithia ❄
Glottiphyllum ❄
Gymnocalycium ❄
Huernia ❄
Mammillaria ❄
Rebutia ❄
Ruschia ❄
Sansevieria ❄
Stapelia ❄
Sulcorebutia ❄
Titanopsis ❄

KEY
❄ *Not frost hardy*

Division of rootstock

Many genera of the Aizoaceae such as *Delosperma* and *Frithia*, some clump-forming cacti, and genera such as *Aloe*, are readily propagated by division. For some cultivars of *Sansevieria*, division is the only reliable method of retaining variegation, since leaf cuttings may produce plants that revert to plain green. Divide clump-forming cacti and other succulents early in the growing season.

Lift the whole plant from its pot, and carefully pull apart or cut the rootstock into a number of smaller pieces, each with a healthy bud or shoot and well-formed roots. Treat all cut areas with fungicide and pot up each section separately into standard potting mix. Label, water, and place in a semishaded position until well established.

Alternatively, cut away a piece of the rootstock without lifting the parent plant, and ease a section out of the soil with a hand fork. Dust the cut surfaces with fungicide and pot up as for offset tubers (see p.269). Fill any gaps that are left around the parent plant, using a standard soil mix, and water lightly.

DIVISION OF ROOTSTOCK

1 *Lift the plant (here* Sansevieria trifasciata). *Divide it into sections by cutting straight through the rootstock.*

2 *Discard old, woody material and any soft or damaged roots before replanting each new section.*

Grafting

Some cacti and other succulents, notably certain members of the Asclepiadaceae, such as *Edithcolea* and *Pseudolithos*, are slow to mature and flower when grown on their own roots. By grafting them onto established specimens of related species that are quicker to mature, they can be induced to flower in a comparatively short length of time. During the growing season the topgrowth, or scion, of the required

APICAL-WEDGE GRAFTING

1 *Prepare the rootstock by trimming off the tip, making a straight cut through the stem with a clean, sharp knife.*

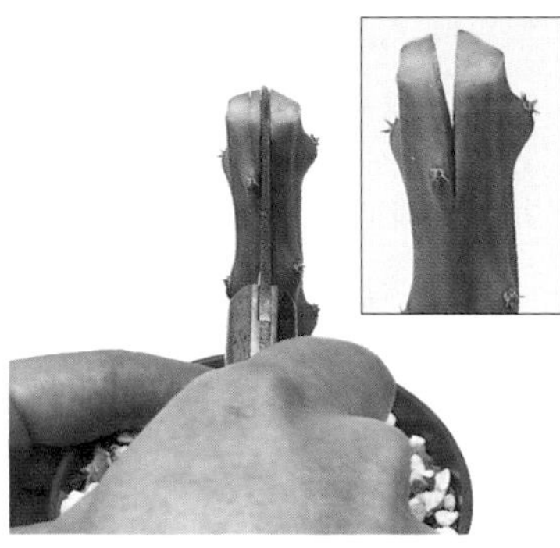

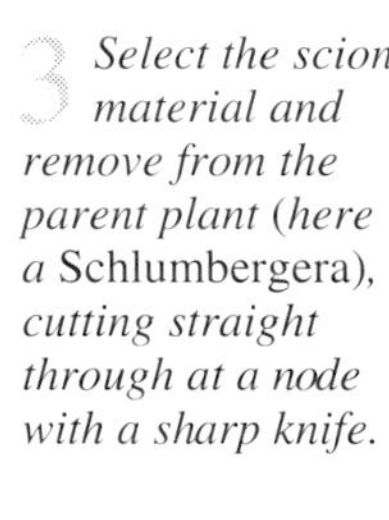

2 *Make a slender V-shaped cleft (see inset) in the stock, to a depth of about ¾in (2cm).*

3 *Select the scion material and remove from the parent plant (here a* Schlumbergera), *cutting straight through at a node with a sharp knife.*

4 *Trim the lower end of the scion to a narrow wedge shape to match the V-shaped cleft in the stock plant.*

5 *Insert the scion wedge into the cleft in the stock plant (see inset), making sure that they are in close contact.*

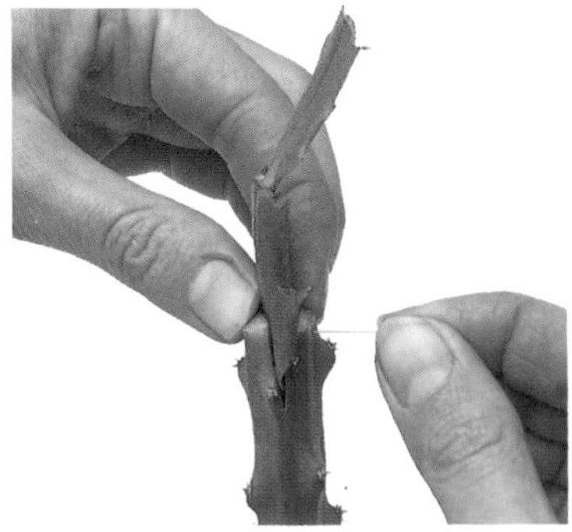

6 *To secure the scion in place in the clefted stock, insert a cactus spine through the grafted area.*

Dab of glue on outside of graft union

ALTERNATIVE METHOD
Bind the graft firmly with a dab of superglue.

plant is grafted onto the rootstock of one of the more vigorous species. Three methods of grafting may be used: apical-wedge grafting, flat grafting, and side grafting.

Apical-wedge grafting

Epiphytic cacti are often propagated by apical-wedge grafting in order to create an erect standard or treelike plant. Use *Pereskiopsis* or *Selenicereus*, which are sturdy but of slender growth, as the rootstock.

To produce the rootstock, take a stem cutting (see p.268) of the selected plant. When this has rooted and shows evidence of new growth, it is ready to be used for grafting. Slice off the tip and then make two slanted, downward cuts into the top of the rootstock stem to produce a narrow, vertical, V-shaped slit approximately 3/4in (2cm) long.

Select a healthy shoot from the scion plant and prepare it by trimming the lower end into a wedge shape to match the cleft in the stock. Insert the prepared scion wedge into the cleft so that the cut surfaces match as closely as possible. Secure the stock and scion firmly in position by either pushing a cactus spine horizontally through the graft or using a dab of superglue.

Place the grafted plant in partial shade at a temperature of 70°F (21°C). The stock and scion should unite within a few weeks. Once this has happened, remove the spine (if used), dusting with fungicide any holes made by the spine. When fresh growth appears, water and feed as for established plants (see p.265).

Flat grafting

This method may be used to propagate crested variants (succulents with atypical, often contorted growth), certain other succulents with tufts of hair, and *Gymnocalycium mihanovichii* and *Lobivia silvestrii*, whose seedlings may lack chlorophyll. Genera for use as rootstocks include *Echinopsis*, *Harrisia*, *Hylocereus*, and *Trichocereus*.

Make a straight, horizontal cut through the stem of the rootstock at the required height. Then remove the rib margins with a sharp knife to form a beveled edge, and trim off any spines near the cut.

Prepare the scion in a similar way, and position its base on the cut surface of the stock plant. Place rubber bands over the top of the scion and under the base of the pot to keep the scion securely in place. Make sure that the bands are not too tight.

Leave the grafted plant in a well-lit position, but not in full sun. Keep the soil mix barely moist until the scion and the stock have united (normally in one to two weeks), when the rubber bands can be removed. Thereafter, water and feed as for established plants.

When grafting asclepiads, use either the fleshy tubers of *Ceropegia* or the robust stems of *Stapelia* as rootstocks. *Ceropegia*, in particular, make excellent stock plants for some of the Madagascan and Arabian asclepiads, which may otherwise be difficult to propagate.

Side grafting

This method is useful if the scion is too slender to be grafted onto the top of the stock. It is very similar to side-veneer grafting, used for woody plants. Prepare the stock by slicing off the top at an oblique angle, then trim the base of the scion to match the stock as closely as possible. Secure them together with a spine or superglue; treat as for flat grafting.

FLAT GRAFTING

1 *Slice off the top of the rootstock with a sharp knife to produce a flat surface.*

2 *Trim the cut surface to produce a slightly beveled edge. Hold the stem without touching the wounded area.*

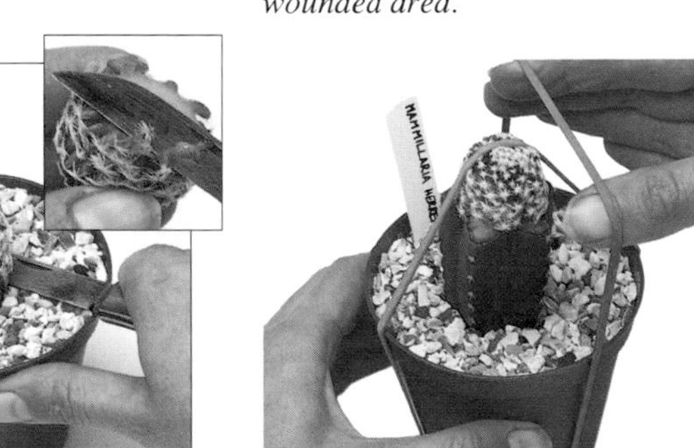

3 *Cut the scion material, slicing through at the base. Bevel the edge of the scion (inset) so that it will fit closely onto the stock.*

4 *Place the scion on the stock and secure firmly, but not tightly, with rubber bands. Label with the name of the scion plant.*

5 *Place the pot in good light at a minimum temperature of 61°F (16°C). Remove the rubber bands when new growth appears.*

SIDE GRAFTING

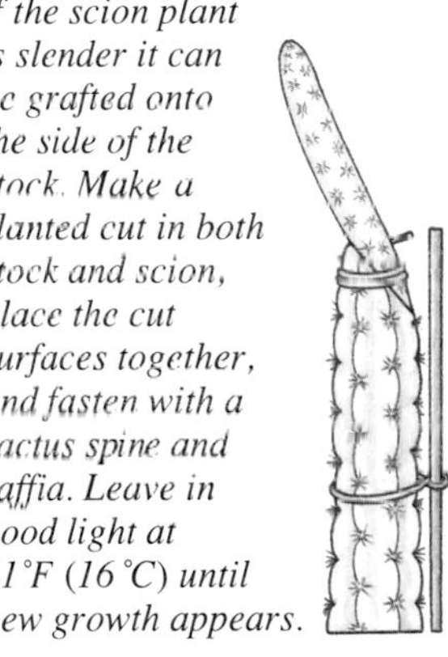

If the scion plant is slender it can be grafted onto the side of the stock. Make a slanted cut in both stock and scion, place the cut surfaces together, and fasten with a cactus spine and raffia. Leave in good light at 61°F (16°C) until new growth appears.

SUCCULENTS THAT MAY BE GRAFTED

Flat grafting
Alluaudiopsis ❄
Astrophytum ❄
Austrocactus ❄
Aztekium ❄
Blossfeldia ❄
Buiningia ❄
Discocactus ❄
Duvalia ❄
Echinopsis chamaecereus ❄
Edithcolea ❄
Epithelantha ❄
Frailea ❄
Gymnocalycium mihanovichii (and cvs) ❄

Gymnocalycium mihanovichii 'Red Head'

Hoodia ❄
Lophophora ❄
Luckhoffia ❄
Maihuenia
Mammillaria ❄
Mila ❄
Nopalxochia ❄
Notocactus ❄
Orbea, some ❄
Parodia ❄
Pediocactus ❄
Pelecyphora ❄
Pseudolithos ❄
Pygmaeocereus ❄
Sulcorebutia ❄
Tavaresia ❄
Trichocaulon ❄
Turbinicarpus ❄
Uebelmannia ❄

Aporocactus flagelliformis

Side grafting
Aporocactus flagelliformis ❄
Cryptocereus ❄
Disocactus ❄
Lepismium ❄ (flat-stemmed spp.)
Rhipsalidopsis ❄
Rhipsalis ❄ (spp. with rounded or angled stems)
Weberocereus ❄ (spp. with rounded stems)
Wilcoxia ❄

Schlumbergera 'Gold Charm'

Apical-wedge grafting
Hatiora ❄
Rhipsalidopsis ❄
Schlumbergera ❄
Strophocactus ❄
Wittiocereus ❄

KEY
❄ *Not frost hardy*

12

The Lawn

From the striped, velvety green carpet in traditional formal gardens to the closely mown turf of a sports field or the rough grassland under a grove of trees, there are many different types of lawn. Whether it is viewed as a showpiece in its own right, a foil for colorful beds and borders, a playing surface for children, or simply a relaxing haven, the lawn can be both a functional and attractive part of the garden. For centuries, grass has been chosen to create lawns because it is visually appealing, pleasant to walk on, tolerates wear, and may be cut low without being damaged. A few other species such as chamomile and Dichondra *may also be used for lawns, but they are generally much less hard-wearing than grass. Frequently undervalued as merely a flat surface underfoot, the lawn may make a much more important contribution to the garden – it may be used to complement plantings, soften hard surfaces, separate and define distinctive features, and unify the garden as a whole.*

Creating lawns

A healthy, well-maintained lawn is an attractive feature that also provides a clear area in which to walk, play, and relax. For some gardeners, the lawn is primarily ornamental, while for others its function is paramount and wearability is the most important consideration. In addition to formal and utility lawns, grass may be used for sports such as croquet and badminton, in orchards and wild gardens, for wide paths and gently sloping banks.

Some broad-leaved plants, for example chamomile (*Chamaemelum nobile*), may also be used to form lawns. They should, however, be considered primarily ornamental, to be admired rather than extensively used, because they are less tolerant of wear than grass (see "Nongrass lawns," p.275).

When deciding on the type and shape of the lawn as well as where to site it, consider how it will link to the rest of the garden – to other plants, features, and the overall layout – so that it forms a compatible, unifying part of the design.

Grass

Grass is the plant most commonly chosen for a lawn because it is hard-wearing and attractive. It may also be repeatedly cut low without damage because the growing point is at the base of the plant.

A Formal Lawn
Here, the close-clipped, pristine expanse of a high-quality formal lawn provides a uniform, fine-textured foil for an elegant planting of white Agapanthus, *silver-gray* Senecio, *and other complementary plants, plus a platform to offset an ornamental garden seat and pots of marguerites* (Argyranthemum frutescens).

Mown lawns

Mown areas of grass include high-quality lawns, utility lawns, and sports fields. A primarily ornamental, high-quality lawn is suitable where a perfect, uniform appearance is paramount; it tolerates some wear but requires a considerable amount of maintenance to keep it in pristine condition. If the grass is likely to be subject to heavier wear – by being used as a play area, for example – opt for a utility lawn; this should also be attractive, but it may contain minor imperfections and requires less maintenance.

Sports areas, such as those used for touch football or volleyball, demand a hard-wearing surface that can be cut low. To stop unnecessary additional wear, they are best sited separately from the main lawn.

Long grass and meadows

As part of a wild garden or orchard, unmown grass and a flower-filled meadow are very attractive, but not very practical for a utility lawn since the grass is relatively long. Meadows need very little maintenance, however, and therefore may be suitable for an area such as a slope or a stream bank where mowing is difficult. Meadows often thrive on impoverished soils, so this may be a good way of using a part of the garden where little else grows.

In informal or semiwild gardens, bulbous plants such as daffodils look pretty when they are naturalized in a grassy area. The bulbs are best planted in an established area of

CONTRASTING TEXTURES
Altering the height of cut creates low-relief geometric patterns and provides definition or interesting textures in an area of lawn.

medium or long grass that does not need frequent mowing, such as on a bank (see also BULBOUS PLANTS, "Planting in grass," p.216).

Mixing long and short grass

Using different grasses in various parts of the garden, or varying the height of cut, helps to define separate areas and adds textural contrast. For example, a closely mown path running through a tall, flower-rich meadow provides an eye-catching shift in height, color, and texture, and also encourages people to walk only on the path.

In large gardens, consider having a small, low-cut, high-quality lawn sited near the house where its fine appearance may be easily enjoyed; a path or steps could then lead to a utility lawn farther away, while an area of long grass and wildflowers

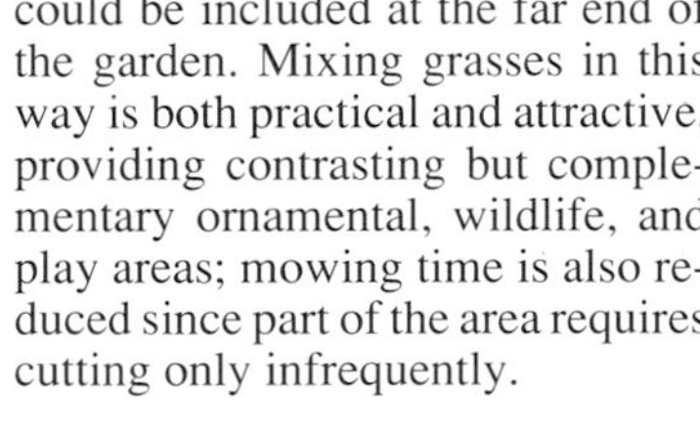

could be included at the far end of the garden. Mixing grasses in this way is both practical and attractive, providing contrasting but complementary ornamental, wildlife, and play areas; mowing time is also reduced since part of the area requires cutting only infrequently.

Form and position

The lawn may well be the largest single area in the garden, so it is important to plan its shape and position carefully within the context of the overall design. Take into account both practical and esthetic considerations so that the lawn will be pleasant to use, convenient to maintain, and an enhancing, integral part of the garden plan.

Shape

The shape of the lawn may harmonize with the garden style or be used to dictate it. A symmetrical layout of geometrically shaped lawns bordered by paths would be elegant and appropriate in a highly stylized formal garden. In a small garden, a simple shape such as a circle could be visually striking and might be echoed imaginatively by the introduction of a circular pool or patio and containers packed with ornamental plants.

A curved, irregular design lends the garden an appealing fluidity, linking the different elements with a sweeping plane of uniform color. Broad, flowing curves can be created to set off the planting in a border and to lead the eye to a focal point, such as an architectural plant or a fountain. Steer clear of fussy scalloped edges or awkward angles, however, because they may detract from the impact of any planting and generally make mowing difficult.

INFORMAL LAWN
The bold, curving sweep of an informal lawn is echoed by a winding gravel path beyond and a ribbon of gold-leaved plants in an adjacent border.

Space permitting, it may be more pleasing to have more than one lawn: for example, two or more of similar or complementary shapes could be linked by paths or archways. The farther lawn could be partially screened so that it provides an intriguing, half-glimpsed reflection of the nearer one.

Design functions

As well as being attractive in its own right, the lawn may fulfill different design criteria for both plants and hard features. Uniform areas of grass create a natural bond between otherwise disparate elements, leading the eye from one part of the garden to another. A statue or specimen tree sited in a lawn has maximum impact, since the surrounding sea of plain color separates it from other more distracting elements. In a large lawn, one or two flowerbeds or trees may be extremely effective if they are positioned so that they break up the green expanse. But resist the temptation to dot the entire lawn surface with eye-catching features: besides making maintenance more time-consuming, the overall picture may be cluttered and disjointed.

The uniform texture and color of grass form a neutral background that enhances other planting particularly well. The level surface acts as a foil for more sculptural plants – the strong silhouette of a columnar tree, the jutting spread of a prostrate shrub – as well as for the variety of shapes, colors, and textures found in a mixed or herbaceous border.

Paths and access

Narrow areas of grass are usually subject to concentrated wear and are difficult to mow; for these reasons, paths narrower than about 3ft (1m) may be impractical. For a frequently used route across a lawn, such as from the house to the garden shed, consider laying stepping-stones or a hard path to prevent uneven wear.

If possible, leave at least one side of the lawn open for access; if there are only one or two narrow openings, the grass may become damaged at these points.

Edging

Edging the lawn with a band of paving stones or bricks helps to define its shape and that of the borders, and also has practical advantages. It makes it easier to cut the lawn right to its edge while avoiding the risk of damaging other plants. Sprawling or trailing plants may be allowed to overhang the edge, breaking up any awkward rigidity, but without depriving the grass beneath of light. In

GRASS PATHS
Including a closely mown grass path through the garden allows a clear view of adjacent plants. Here, a broad, straight path contrasts with the informal planting of daffodils and shrubs and clearly indicates where people are expected to walk.

addition, ornamental containers may be set on the hard edging as focal points or to provide an interesting change of level. Alternatively, a narrow mowing strip of bare soil may be created at the edge of a lawn. This is particularly useful if the lawn is adjacent to a wall or fence since the grass may be more easily mown up to the edge.

HIGH-QUALITY OR UTILITY?

Grass varies in appearance, growth rate, and wear resistance: high-quality grass (right) has a fine texture; utility grass (far right) is better for a family lawn.

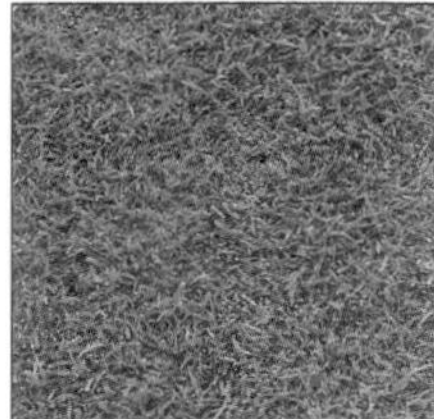

HIGH-QUALITY

UTILITY

Climatic considerations

Turf grasses are commonly divided into two main groups, depending on their temperature tolerance. Those that grow mainly in a temperate climate, preferring temperatures of 59–75°F (15–24°C), are known as cool-season grasses, while those that grow best in subtropical or tropical climates, thriving in temperatures of 79–95°F (26–35°C), are known as warm-season grasses. Seek local horticultural advice in transitional areas between cool- and warm-season grass regions.

Warm-season grasses are not normally used for lawns in temperate regions because they turn brown during winter as they become dormant. Nevertheless, some species can be grown satisfactorily.

Cool-season grasses

Temperate or cool-season grasses are widely used for lawns throughout North America, the UK, northern Europe, and other regions with similar climates (see "Climate zones," p.514). The grasses that are most commonly found in cool-season lawns are bents (*Agrostis*), fescues (*Festuca*), bluegrasses (also known as meadow grasses, *Poa*), and perennial ryegrass (*Lolium perenne*).

Bents are low-growing and, of all grasses, are the most tolerant of close mowing. Fescues are fine-leaved and may be cut low; they are quite hard-wearing, and some species grow in poor soils. Meadow grasses are more resistant to wear but cannot be mown very low, and some have quite coarse leaves. Ryegrass is extremely hard-wearing and tolerates most soils, including heavy clay, but is coarse-textured and does not like to be closely mown. Annual bluegrass (*Poa annua*) is also found in many lawns, but is often considered a weed by gardeners since it quickly runs to seed, forming coarse patches among fine-leaved grasses.

Cool-season grasses are usually sown as mixtures of more than one species, although in some areas of temperate North America, Kentucky bluegrass, which is also known as smooth-stalked meadow grass (*Poa pratensis*), is grown on its own. If sowing a single-species lawn, however, it is common to mix several cultivars together because this improves the lawn's disease resistance and overall color (see "Choosing the right cultivars," opposite).

Warm-season grasses

These grasses occur naturally in tropical and subtropical regions, including South America, Africa, and Asia, especially southern China. They are therefore adapted to grow successfully in a wide range of warm climatic zones.

The major warm-season grasses that are planted in lawns and other areas of intensive use are the various species and cultivars of Bermuda grass (*Cynodon*), St. Augustine grass (*Stenotaphrum secundatum*), and zoysia grasses (*Zoysia*).

The Bermuda grasses include common Bermuda grass (*Cynodon dactylon*), African Bermuda grass (*C. transvaalensis*), Bradley Bermuda grass (*C. incompletus* var. *hirsutus*), and Magennis Bermuda grass (*C.* x *magennisii*).

Three species of zoysia grass are appropriate for use as lawns: Japanese lawn grass (*Zoysia japonica*), Manila grass or Japanese carpet grass (*Z. matrella*), and Mascarene grass (*Z. tenuifolia*). Zoysia grasses grow particularly well in regions that have very warm summers combined with cool winters.

Warm-season grasses are usually grown as a single species turf because they have a strong, creeping habit and do not mix well together. If other grasses are included, they tend to form distinct, unsightly patches of differing color and texture. Warm-season species become dormant and lose their color at temperatures below 50°F (10°C), which can cause problems where climatic conditions are ideal only during summer. In these areas, cool-season grasses such as ryegrasses and fescues may be oversown in fall to improve the color of the lawn in winter.

Selecting the right grass

Before selecting seed or sod, assess the relative importance of the lawn's appearance, wearability, and maintenance needs. Of the many grass mixtures available, some are best for areas of heavy use, while others give attractive color and texture. The grass seed should also be suited to the growing conditions such as soil type, drainage, and degree of shade.

High-quality lawns

To create formal, high-quality lawns, where a perfect appearance is the prime consideration and very heavy wear is not anticipated, select grass species that create an attractive, uniform texture and color.

Cool season For the highest-quality lawns, a mixture of Kentucky bluegrass (*Poa pratensis*), perennial ryegrass (*Lolium perenne*), and red fescue (*Festuca rubra* var. *rubra*) is the best choice for most soils and regions. On the West Coast, or for special areas such as home putting greens, bents may be used.

Warm season Cultivars of the common Bermuda grass (*Cynodon dactylon*) are excellent for high-quality lawns. There are several improved cultivars that tolerate heat, drought, and heavy wear. Zoysia grasses (*Zoysia*) also form a high-quality, slow-growing turf.

Utility lawns

Lawns that are primarily functional, perhaps providing a play area for children or a space for outdoor entertaining, need to be relatively hard-wearing, but they must still provide an attractive, even surface. Grasses for this purpose do not usually create the perfect texture and color of a high-quality lawn, since this is inevitably of secondary importance.

Cool season For hard-wearing lawns, the major grass is perennial ryegrass; it is usually mixed with red fescue, Kentucky bluegrass, and chewings fescue (*Festuca rubra* var. *commutata*). New varieties of tall fescue (*Festuca arundinacea*) are very hard-wearing and hardy to at least -20°F (-30°C).

Warm season The Bermuda grasses (see "Warm-season grasses," left) are tough enough for most utility lawns but may need frequent mowing. St. Augustine grass (*Stenotaphrum secundatum*) has a coarser texture but is also suitable, particularly for shady areas. For a low-maintenance lawn, choose a grass such as bahia grass (*Paspalum notatum*), carpet grass (*Axonopus*), or centipede grass (*Eremochloa ophiuroides*). These require less frequent mowing, but since they have coarse-textured leaves, they do not provide a very fine finish.

Games and sports areas

Areas of grass used for playing ball games or sports require particularly wear-tolerant species and selected cultivars. In addition, some sports fields must be able to tolerate a very low cut and have a fine finish to

PLAY AREAS
If the lawn is to include an area for games or play, as in this garden, use a particularly hard-wearing grass mixture in order to prevent the lawn from becoming patchy.

minimize the effect of the grass on the run of the ball.

Cool season A mixture of bents and fescues as for high-quality lawns (see opposite) tolerates some wear and is suitable for areas such as croquet lawns, bowling greens, and golf putting greens; very heavy use, however, soon damages the grasses. If a more hard-wearing surface is needed, such as for playing football, it is better to opt for a mixture containing perennial ryegrass or tall fescue (see "Utility lawns," opposite).

Warm season Bermuda (see "Warm-season grasses," opposite) and St. Augustine grasses should provide a reasonably hard-wearing and attractive surface. Some cultivars are more tolerant of wear than others, so take care to select those recommended as suitable for sports areas.

Meadows

For meadows, whenever possible use grass species that are native to the area: as well as being more likely to flourish, they do not look incongruous or artificial (see also WILDFLOWER AND MEADOW GARDENING, p.167). Usually a meadow seed mixture consists of slow-growing grasses and various native, broad-leaved flowering species. In addition to climate, factors such as soil type, soil moisture, and exposure may influence the choice of species sown; some prefer extremely dry, well-drained conditions, whereas others grow well on marshy ground.

Cool season Bents and fescues are usually included, while a short-lived grass such as Italian ryegrass (*Lolium multiflorum*) may be added to provide initial, fast ground cover. If mown, the Italian ryegrass will die out within two years, leaving behind the fine-leaved grasses and broad-leaved flowering plants. Some species need an overwintering or cold period before they will germinate, and so may not appear in the first year after sowing.

Warm season In areas where warm-season grasses are grown, meadows are not usually cultivated, although many roadsides in Texas feature low-maintenance but spectacular meadows, thanks to the beautification efforts of the 1960s.

Problem areas

For lawns in difficult sites, such as shady, wet, or dry areas, choose a grass mixture that is specially designed for such conditions. If the problem is extreme, it may be better to grow ground cover plants instead (see GROUND COVERS, pp.150–51).

Cool season In wet, shady areas, grass does not readily grow into a dense, vigorous turf. There are some species, however, that are more tolerant than others: rough-stalked bluegrass (*Poa trivialis*) with Kentucky bluegrass, redtop (*Agrostis gigantea*), and red fescue will form a lawn that will stand up to both wear and close mowing. In dry shade, use mostly red fescue, with some redtop and Kentucky bluegrass added for a better appearance.

In very dry regions, use grasses native to such areas, such as western wheatgrass (*Agropyron smithii*) or buffalo grass (*Buchloe dactyloides*), both of which grow naturally on the great plains of North America, or fairway crested wheatgrass (*A. cristatum*), native to the dry, cold plains of Russia and Siberia. The wheat-grasses generally produce medium- to low-quality lawns; cut to a height of 1in (2.5cm) or less to prevent weed encroachment.

Warm season For shady areas, St. Augustine grass is a good choice; it is also salt-tolerant and so is valuable for coastal gardens. It is coarser than the various forms of either Bermuda or zoysia grasses, however, so is generally used only where finer species do not thrive.

Choosing the right cultivars

Many modern grass cultivars have been specially bred to provide qualities that are particularly valued in lawns, such as uniform color, disease resistance, wear-tolerance, and compact growth. When selecting grass seed, therefore, make sure that the mixture includes not only the correct species (such as *Festuca rubra* var. *commutata*) but also a modern cultivar of that species, for example 'Koket', 'Jamestown', or 'Menuet'. New cultivars are introduced periodically, so check with the retailer which cultivars are the best available for your particular lawn requirements. The grass mixture should not contain agricultural cultivars; these are bred to produce vigorous vertical leaf growth for grazing and need frequent mowing. They also tend to spread less, and so do not always produce a dense, uniform cover.

Nongrass lawns

Although lawns are usually established with grasses, other evergreen species are sometimes used. These include chamomile (*Chamaemelum nobile*), *Cotula* species, *Dichondra micrantha*, and even various species of moss. Unlike grasses, these ground cover plants do not stand up to heavy, continual wear, so they are rarely the best choice for the main lawn; they may, however, be used for primarily ornamental areas. Grow them in a patio or courtyard garden to provide a welcome patch of green; as a living edge for the base of a fountain, raised pond, pedestal urn, or statue; or next to a patio or path to creep over edges and relieve the rigidity of the hard surface.

Chamomile leaves release a sweet, applelike fragrance when crushed underfoot, but they do not tolerate heavy wear; the nonflowering clone 'Treneague' is naturally low-growing and especially suitable for lawns. *Cotula*, which has fernlike leaves, is considerably more hard-wearing because it forms a thick carpet of creeping stems; it also flourishes in moist conditions.

Dichondra, a ground-hugging plant, has small, round leaves that look like water-lily pads. Prepare soil as for a lawn, or plant from plugs (see "Vegetative propagation," p.279). In shade, plants may grow up to 6in (15cm) tall and will need regular mowing; in sun, they remain low. *Dichondra* grows most successfully in warm areas and does not survive temperatures lower than 25°F (-4°C).

Another option is to create a tapestry lawn with a patchwork quality by growing a number of low, mat-forming plants together. It is best to use plants that grow at a similar rate, such as the various creeping thymes (*Thymus praecox* var. *arcticus* 'Coccineus', *T. p.* var. *a.* 'Doone Valley', *T. caespititius*, etc.), otherwise one species may gradually predominate and so upset the balance of the original design. As for other nongrass lawns, tapestry lawns should not be heavily used.

FLOWERS IN GRASS
The grass in this informal orchard is dotted with bright yellow buttercups (Ranunculus) *and the vivid red, white, and purple cups of naturalized tulips.*

MOSS LAWN
Where grass may be difficult to grow, such as in the dappled shade of deciduous trees, a moss lawn provides an adaptable alternative. Unlike a grass lawn, however, it should be walked upon only in order to maintain it.

Soil and site preparation

Thorough site preparation is the key to establishing a successful new lawn. Although the treatment may be time-consuming and expensive, in the long run it is easier and cheaper to prepare the site properly at the outset than to try to alleviate problems at a later stage. The general principles of preparation apply to all sites, but decisions on drainage, soil improvement, and irrigation should depend on the individual site and the climate.

Clearing the site

It is important to clear the site completely, removing any large stones and rubble and all plant growth, including any tree stumps or roots. If the site is already partially grassed but in too poor a condition to be worth renovating, then remove all the turf (see also "Renovating a neglected lawn," p.285).

Eradicating weeds

Eliminate any perennial weeds with underground rhizomes or deep taproots, such as couch grass or quackgrass (*Elymus repens*), dandelion (*Taraxacum officinale*), bindweed (*Convolvulus arvensis*), and Canada thistle (*Cirsium arvense*), because they regenerate rapidly from small pieces of root or rhizome. It is difficult to dig these out entirely, so before cultivating the soil, spray with a systemic weedkiller and allow the weeds to die back completely before raking them away.

Once the lawn grass is established, broad-leaved weeds may still be controlled using selective weedkillers, but weed grasses will be more difficult to eliminate, so it is sensible to use a weedkiller to clear the ground initially.

Annual weeds such as lamb's-quarters (*Chenopodium album*) and shepherd's purse (*Capsella bursa-pastoris*) may be controlled by mowing after the grass has germinated. However, it is preferable to remove annual weeds before sowing.

Preparing the soil

The ideal topsoil for a lawn is a well-drained, sandy loam at least 8in (20cm) and preferably 12in (30cm) in depth, overlying a well-structured and free-draining subsoil. In these conditions the grass becomes deep-rooted and obtains ample water and nutrients from the soil.

Other soils may also be suitable, but if the soil does not drain freely and the lawn is likely to be heavily used, even in wet conditions, then the drainage should be improved. If the topsoil is very shallow or poor, it may be necessary to add new topsoil; this may be moved from other parts of the garden or bought, although for large areas the latter is very expensive.

If the soil has a naturally high sand content, and is therefore too free-draining, incorporate some well-rotted organic matter to help retain nutrients and water (see "Soil structure and water content," p.528). Be careful, however, not to add too much; organic matter quickly rots down, and this may result in soil sinkage and an uneven lawn surface in later years.

After clearing the site, plow, rototill, or dig over the whole area, removing any large stones that are brought to the surface, then rake the ground to produce a fine tilth. Breaking up the soil in this way makes subsequent leveling easier, as well as relieving compaction and improving the soil structure. On heavy clay soils, however, rototilling or plowing may create a compacted layer (hardpan) below the soil surface, which could impede drainage: if necessary, break it up using a subsoiling machine or by double digging. For further information, see "Soil cultivation," pp.526–9.

Drainage

Lawns on free-draining soils, and those in regions with low rainfall, are unlikely to require draining. In heavy clay soils, drainage may be improved by digging washed and sieved river sand into the soil. Up to 6in (15cm) can be added, but this is expensive and laborious. In any soil that is not free-draining, installing a drainage system during the preparation stage will avoid continual and expensive attempts to alleviate the problem after the lawn is established.

The best type of drain for lawns consists of a row of pipes laid in a trench that is backfilled with gravel. The ideal depth of the drain and the distance between drains will vary from site to site depending on the type of soil and the rainfall. For most loamy soils receiving moderate rainfall, one drain every 15–25ft (5–8m) is needed. Heavier clay soils or sites in areas with a high rainfall will need drains laid at closer intervals (see also Soils and Fertilizers, "Improving drainage," p.531).

Adjusting the soil pH

For new lawns, the pH is unlikely to need adjusting, unless previous use has left the site in poor condition. Most grasses grow well at pH levels of 5.5–7. Fine fescues and bents grow best at pH 5.5–6.5, while perennial ryegrass (*Lolium perenne*), Kentucky bluegrass (*Poa pratensis*), and many warm-season grasses grow better at pH 6–7. Soil-testing kits for measuring pH are available from garden centers.

If the soil is very acidic (below pH 5), dig or rototill lime into the soil; the exact amount depends on the degree of acidity (see "Liming," p.533). Then leave the site for about a week before applying fertilizer. Lime may be added once the lawn is established, but since large amounts spread on grass may encourage certain diseases, use only a small quantity and repeat the following year if necessary. If uncertain about what to do, seek advice from an agricultural or horticultural college, or an agricultural extension agent.

Leveling the site

In gardens that have only minor undulations and deep topsoil, the site may be roughly leveled by raking soil from the high spots to fill the hollows, firming at intervals to settle the soil. Although it is not essential for the ground to be precisely level, awkward bumps and hollows

How to Level the Ground

1 *Firm the site well, especially at the edges, by tamping with the back of a rake or by treading. Mark some pegs at the same point on each peg. Insert a row of pegs at the site edge. If next to paving, the marks should be level with its surface.*

2 *Add a second, parallel row of pegs about 3ft (1m) from the first row. Place a level on top of these to check that they are level with the previous row. Adjust the pegs as necessary.*

3 *Repeat the process to create a grid of pegs all at the same level. Rake up the soil to the top of the marks on the pegs, adding topsoil to fill any hollows. Once the ground is level, the pegs may be removed.*

ACCURATE LEVELING

To level the ground, first create a grid of premarked pegs and knock them into the soil at the same depth. Add or remove soil until it is level with the marks on the pegs.

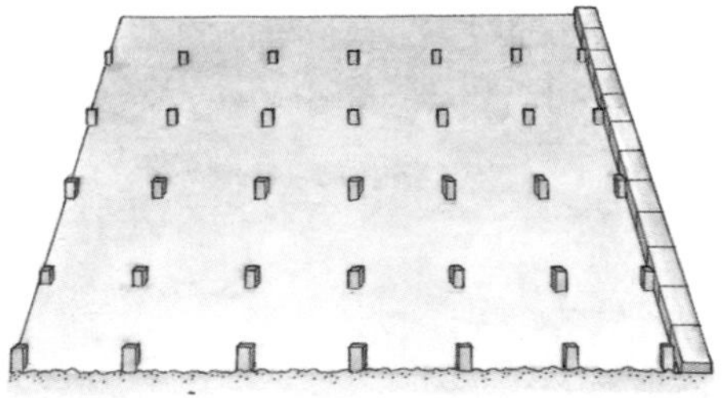

may cause problems when mowing. In some instances – for example, for an orchard or an area of rough sports grass – leveling by eye should be sufficient. But if a perfectly level surface is required, such as for a formal lawn, a more accurate method should be used.

Achieving an accurate level

After leveling the ground roughly, an exact level may be achieved by knocking pegs into the ground all at the same depth to form a grid.

Start from a straight edge such as a path or patio, or create a taut line with string. Then take a number of identical pegs and make a mark on each one at the same distance from the top. Starting from the straight edge, knock the pegs into the ground at equal intervals so that the marks are at the required level of the lawn, or approximately ³/₄in (2cm) below this if sodding. Add a second row of pegs and then further rows until the site is covered by a grid of pegs.

Use a level – placed on a straight wooden board if necessary to span across the rows – to check that the pegs within the rows are all at the same height. Then adjust the level of the soil so that it is aligned with the mark on each peg.

Substantial leveling

If the site needs more substantial leveling or the topsoil is very shallow, the subsoil must be leveled first. To do this, remove the topsoil, rototill or dig over the subsoil, then rake, level, and firm it roughly before replacing the topsoil in an even layer at least 8–12in (20–30cm) deep. To prevent the filled areas from sinking later, firm them thoroughly at intervals, adding more topsoil if necessary, and allow the site to settle before preparing the surface.

Creating a slope

Making the lawn slope gently away from the house or patio improves drainage and ensures that water does not drain into the foundation. A method similar to leveling is used, but each successive row of pegs is marked farther up or down to form a sloping grid. For example, to create a gradient of 1:100, make the marks on each row of pegs successively lower by ¹/₁₀₀ of the distance between the rows. If sloping the lawn down toward the house, install a drain or soakaway (see "Drainage systems and soakaways," p.531) to prevent water from reaching the house.

CREATING A SLOPE

Decide how many rows of pegs will be used, and then mark the pegs for each row at different heights in order to achieve the desired gradient (see left). Using a level, create a grid of pegs as for leveling, and rake soil up to the marks.

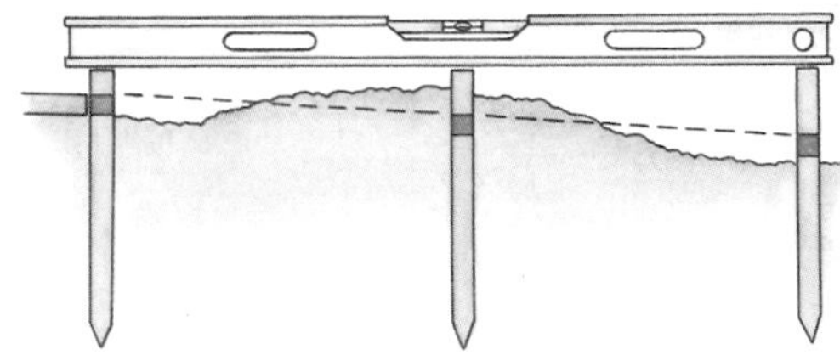

INSTALLING A DRAIN

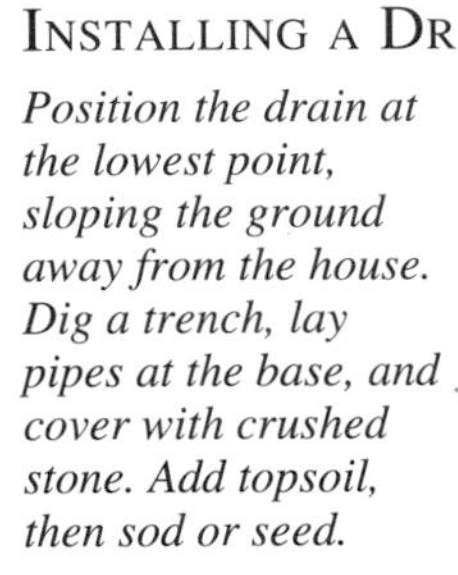

Position the drain at the lowest point, sloping the ground away from the house. Dig a trench, lay pipes at the base, and cover with crushed stone. Add topsoil, then sod or seed.

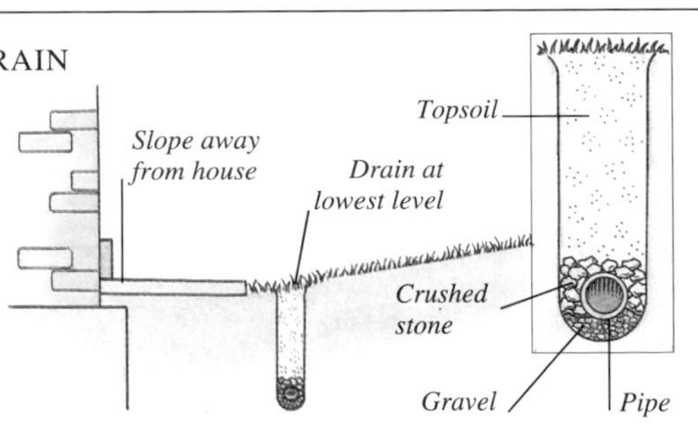

Final site preparations

Once the soil has been drained and leveled, the final surface may be prepared so that the site is ready for establishing a lawn.

Firming and raking

Tread the soil evenly all over to firm it and to ensure there are no soft spots that might later sink, making the lawn vulnerable to scalping during mowing. It may be necessary to tread the area about three times before the soil is sufficiently settled, but take care not to compress the soil too much, and do not firm wet soil because it will become compacted. Even so, the soil may settle further over the course of the next year or two, leaving small hollows. These should be leveled when they occur by applying a sieved sandy top-dressing (see p.284).

After firming, thoroughly rake the surface to produce a fine tilth. The soil should be level, without humps or hollows, and with a fine crumb texture. If sowing seed, remove any stones larger than about ¹/₂in (1cm) across during raking; if sodding, it is only necessary to remove stones over 1in (2.5cm).

Leave the prepared site for about three to four weeks to allow any weed seeds to germinate; any weeds should then be either hoed off or treated with a contact weedkiller. Gently rake them off several days later, once they have died, taking care not to disrupt the leveled soil.

Fertilizing

A few days before establishing the lawn, and once the surface has been prepared, apply fertilizer to the site. This should contain the three major nutrients to ensure good growth: nitrogen (N), phosphorus (P), and potassium (K). Sites that have not been fertilized for many years may be deficient in all three. Phosphorus is especially important during the early stages of growth. Use either a simple fertilizer such as superphosphate or, preferably, a balanced granular fertilizer that contains all three nutrients, such as 7–21–7; apply all fertilizers according to the manufacturer's instructions.

PREPARING THE SOIL SURFACE

1 *Firm the surface by treading it evenly, or by tamping it with the back of a rake. Repeat, if necessary, until the entire site is well firmed.*

2 *Rake the soil to a fine tilth, and leave it to allow any weeds to germinate. Apply a weedkiller and, after about 2–3 days, rake off the weeds, making sure that no roots remain.*

3 *Apply a base dressing of a balanced granular fertilizer, and lightly rake it into the surface of the soil. Leave the site for a few days before sodding or seeding.*

Establishing a lawn

THERE are various methods of establishing a lawn. For cool-season grasses in temperate areas, the gardener may choose between seeding and sodding; for warm-season grasses in subtropical and tropical regions, vegetative propagation methods may also be used.

Seeding a lawn is usually the cheapest method, but it takes up to a year before the lawn can be subjected to heavy wear. Establishing a lawn by vegetative means takes longer and is more costly than seeding. Sodding, although more expensive, gives an immediate visual effect, and the lawn may be used within two to three months; it is advisable to use sod if you have pets that may disturb grass seedlings before they are established.

Sodding

There is a wide range of sod types available, including specially and commercially grown sod, meadow and treated meadow sod, and fine-grass sod; the type chosen depends on considerations of site and expense. Always buy sod from a reputable garden center or sod farm.

If possible, inspect the sod before buying it to make sure that it is in good condition, of the right quality (see "Selecting the right grass," p.274), and that the soil is a free-draining loam rather than a heavy clay. Check that there are no weeds, pests, or diseases, nor an excessive amount of thatch (the organic matter consisting of decaying grass, stolons, and rhizomes that accumulates on the soil surface); there should, however, be enough organic matter to hold the sod together.

Commercially grown sod

Commercially grown sod is widely available and contains different grasses for various uses. It is raised from the newest grass cultivars and treated to make it free from weeds and disease. Sod that is guaranteed free of annual meadow grass (*Poa annua*) is also available from the top producers, although at a high price. If you need a very large quantity of special sod, and are prepared to wait 18 months for it to be grown and harvested, it may also be grown to order, but this is expensive.

Meadow sod

This is usually grown for agricultural purposes and therefore is less fine in texture; it may have been either sown recently or grown in a long-established field. It is usually the cheapest sod, since it may contain coarse, vigorous agricultural grasses and broad-leaved weeds such as daisies (*Bellis perennis*). The quality varies greatly, however, so it is especially important to buy meadow sod from a reputable supplier to ensure that it is of reasonable quality. If the weeds are eliminated by the use of selective weedkillers, the improved sod is described as treated meadow sod. Lawns established with meadow sod may be coarse and need more frequent mowing, but are perfectly adequate for utility or family use.

Fine-grass sod

Considered by many to be the best sod available, fine-grass sod contains fine fescues (*Festuca*) and bents (*Agrostis*). It is used mainly for lawn bowling greens and golf putting greens and requires high maintenance. In the home garden, it should be mown at least every second day or the lawn will turn brown upon mowing. Commercially grown sod, with new cultivars, is sold at larger sod farms.

Sizes of sod

Sod is available in a range of sizes and shapes. High-quality sod is often sold in 1ft (30cm) squares and lower quality sod in lengths of 3 x 1ft (90 x 30cm). Major producers usually supply sod of all qualities in units of 1sq yd (1sq m).

Storing sod

Sod is best lifted and relaid in its new position within the same day. If there is an unavoidable delay, lay the sod flat on paving or plastic sheeting, preferably in a slightly shaded area, and keep it watered; in hot weather, it may dry out very quickly, so check it regularly. If the sod is left rolled up, it will not receive enough light, so the grass will turn yellow and eventually die.

Laying sod

Sod may be laid at almost any time of the year except during prolonged spells of extreme temperatures. If possible, choose a time when rain is expected in the next day or two. Sod should be laid on moist, but not wet, soil to encourage rapid rooting.

Starting at the edge of the site, lay the first row of sod pieces in a straight line. Standing on boards placed on the sod, rake over the soil on which the next row is to be laid. Lay this next row so that the pieces form an alternate bond, like bricks in a wall.

Do not finish a row with a small segment of sod beside the edge, because it will be vulnerable to damage and drying out. If necessary, lay the last complete piece of sod at the edge, and fill the gap behind with the trimmed segment. Lay further rows until the site is covered.

Shaping the edge

When all the sod has been laid, cut the edges to fit the final shape of the lawn. For a curved edge, lay a hose or rope along the curve, and cut just inside it. For a straight edge, use a string between pegs to mark the lawn edge. Align a board with this guideline and cut along it using a half-moon or power edger. Repeat the procedure until the entire edge has been cut.

HOW TO ESTABLISH A LAWN USING SOD

1 *Lay the first row of sod alongside a straight edge such as a patio or path. Place each new piece exactly flush with its neighbor.*

2 *While kneeling on a board placed on the first row of sod, lay the next row with the sod joints staggered. Proceed in the same way for the rest of the lawn.*

3 *Tamp down each piece with the back of a rake to make sure that there are no air pockets. Alternatively, roll the lawn with a light roller.*

4 *If no rain is forecast, water the sod well. Keep the pieces moist until they have rooted into the topsoil or they may shrink and gaps will appear.*

STORING SOD

Lay the sod as soon as possible; if it is essential to store it, spread the pieces out flat – grass side up – so that they receive enough light, and keep them watered.

Aftercare

Either tamp down the sod with the back of a rake or roll the lawn with a light roller to ensure that there are no air pockets between the sod and the soil. In wet conditions, however, do not roll until the sod has rooted and knitted together. Brush a light top-dressing (see p.284) between the pieces of sod to encourage the roots to spread.

Do not allow the sod to dry out before the grass has rooted through. It is essential to water the sod thoroughly so that it reaches the soil below, otherwise the pieces of sod may shrink in dry or hot weather, leaving large gaps between them.

Moving sod

Sometimes it may be necessary to lift and re-lay sod. Cut and lift it in uniformly sized pieces so that they fit together when they are re-laid.

Cutting

First, divide the sod to be lifted into lengths 12in (30cm) wide by cutting along the edge of a board with a half-moon edger. Move the board 12in (30cm) in from the previous cut to form each new length. Then cut each length at right angles to form pieces about 18in (45cm) long. Alternatively, a mechanical sod lifter may be rented; this cuts the sod to the size and depth required and also lifts the newly cut pieces.

Lifting

Once cut, lift the pieces of sod with a flat spade, carefully severing each piece from the underlying soil and roots. As work begins, remove a wedge of sod next to the first piece to be lifted, then insert the spade under the sod without damaging the edge of the piece. Undercut each piece of sod to a depth of at least 1–1¼in (2.5–3cm). Stack the lifted pieces of sod grass to grass, soil to soil, on a hard surface such as paving. (For further information, see "Storing sod," opposite.)

Trimming

After the sod has been lifted, trim it all to the same depth using a specially constructed shallow box the same size as the cut sod. Leave one of the shorter sides open and, if possible, cover the remaining top edges with a smooth metal strip. Place each piece of sod upside down in the box and, using a sharp blade, remove the excess soil by slicing along the top of the box.

LIFTING SOD FOR RE-LAYING

1 *Cut into strips the sod to be lifted: insert 2 short stakes a little way apart, 12in (30cm) in from the sod edge, and lay a board flush against them. Stand on the board and cut along its edge.*

2 *Cut each strip into pieces about 45cm (18in) long, then undercut the sod to a depth of at least 2.5cm (1in). To stack them, lay grass to grass, soil to soil, on a path or piece of plastic sheeting.*

TRIMMING THE LAWN EDGE

CURVED EDGE
Lay a hose or rope to the required shape and secure with wire hoops. Standing on a board, cut just inside the hose.

STRAIGHT EDGE
Stretch a taut string along the required line and align a board with this. Then, standing on the board, cut along its edge.

Vegetative propagation

Lawns grown from warm season grasses or the cool-season creeping bentgrass (*Agrostis stolonifera*), which produces vigorous stolons and rhizomes, may also be established by vegetative means such as stolonizing, sprigging, or plugging. The best time of year for creating a lawn by one of these methods is late spring or early summer, on a site prepared as for sowing grass seed. It will take about two months for the material to root and spread over the soil. As for grass seedlings, regular irrigation is essential.

To establish a lawn by stolonizing, spread stolons evenly over the soil at the supplier's recommended rate, top-dress with a light, sandy soil, roll, and water. Alternatively, for sprigging, stolons and rhizomes are planted in holes or furrows 2–3in (5–7cm) deep and 3–6in (7–15cm) apart, then firmed in and watered. For plugging, small pieces of sod, or plugs, are planted at intervals of 6–12in (15–30cm).

Sprigging and plugging are gradually falling out of use with the greater availability of warm-season grasses in the form of sod, and as seed that germinates readily and consistently is developed.

Seeding

Grass seed is best sown in warm, moist conditions so that it will germinate and establish quickly: early fall is usually best. Spring-sown grass is also successful but the soil is colder than in fall and there is more competition from weeds. Seed may be sown in summer if irrigation is available, but in hot conditions young grass seedlings suffer heat stress and may wilt or even die.

Sowing rates

Grass sowing rates vary, depending on the mixture or species (see *Sowing Rates*, p.280). Although there is some leeway to allow for factors such as depletion caused by birds eating the

ESTABLISHING A LAWN BY SPRIGGING OR PLUGGING

SPRIGGING
Lay sprigs into furrows 2–3in (5–7cm) deep and 3–6in (7–15cm) apart. Cover with topsoil, firm in, and water. Alternatively, sprigs can be broadcast over a prepared bed and top-dressed.

1 PLUGGING
Use small pieces of sod with a ball of soil around the root system. Space them on 6–12in (15–30cm) centers evenly throughout prepared soil, tamp lightly around each plug, and water.

2 *Regular watering and fertilizing will help plugs root in and spread to form a uniform lawn. Avoid heavy wear on a sprigged or plugged lawn until it is well established.*

seeds, it is important not to sow seed in much greater or smaller quantities than the recommended rate. Sowing too little seed may allow weed seedlings space to compete with the grass, and the lawn will take slightly longer to establish. Sowing too much seed may cause other problems by producing humid conditions among the seedlings. This encourages damping off (p.570), which can damage the young lawn in a very short time, particularly in warm, humid weather (see also "Lawn problems," pp.573–4).

Sowing seed

Seed may be sown either by hand or, faster and more evenly, by a machine. First calculate the amount of seed needed by multiplying the size of the area to be sown (in square yards or meters) by the recommended sowing rate (the amount of seed per square yard or meter). Before sowing the seed, shake the container to mix the seeds thoroughly and ensure that small seeds do not settle to the bottom, thus giving an uneven distribution of grass types.

Sowing by machine

This is the best way to sow seed over a large area. Measure out the correct amount of seed for the lawn and divide it in half. For even coverage, sow half of the seed in one direction and half at right angles to this. A well-defined lawn edge may be achieved by laying plastic sheeting or burlap at the site edge and running the machine just over it; this also prevents the uneven distribution that may occur when stopping the machine at the end of a strip. Excess seed may be gathered and reused.

Sowing by hand

If sowing by hand, first divide the area into small, equal-sized sections, using string and stakes or pegs; this makes it easier to sow the seed evenly. Then measure out the correct amount of seed for one section and accurately divide the batch of seed in half. Transfer one half-batch into a measure, such as a small cup, to make it easier and faster to measure out each subsequent amount. Work on one section at a time, scattering half the seed of a batch in one direction, then sow the other half at right angles to this before moving on to the next section.

Aftercare

After sowing, lightly rake over the surface. Unless rain is forecast, water the site with a sprinkler. Germination will occur in one to two weeks, depending on grass species, soil and air temperature, and moisture. Protect the site from birds by covering it with netting or brushwood until the seedlings have established.

Water the site regularly in dry weather since young grasses are very susceptible to drought. Once the seedlings have emerged, the surface may be gently firmed with a lightweight roller (see p.466).

Cutting

When the grass has reached approximately 2in (5cm), cut it to a height of 1in (2.5cm). (For the first two or three cuts, use a rotary mower: a reel mower with a roller may tear young leaves.) Then rake up and remove all excess clippings. If the lawn was sown in late summer or early fall, mow when necessary through late fall in order to maintain the grass at about 1in (2.5cm) high. During the following spring, gradually adjust the height of the cut until the desired height is reached, depending on the type of grass used (see also "Frequency and height of cut," opposite). Young grasses are vulnerable to damage by wear, so try to use the lawn as little as possible during its first growing season.

ESTABLISHING A LAWN BY SOWING SEED

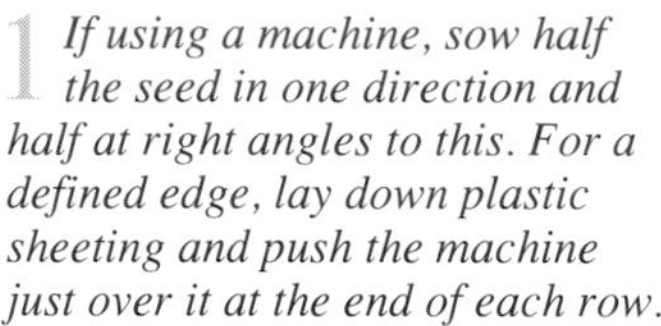

1 *If using a machine, sow half the seed in one direction and half at right angles to this. For a defined edge, lay down plastic sheeting and push the machine just over it at the end of each row.*

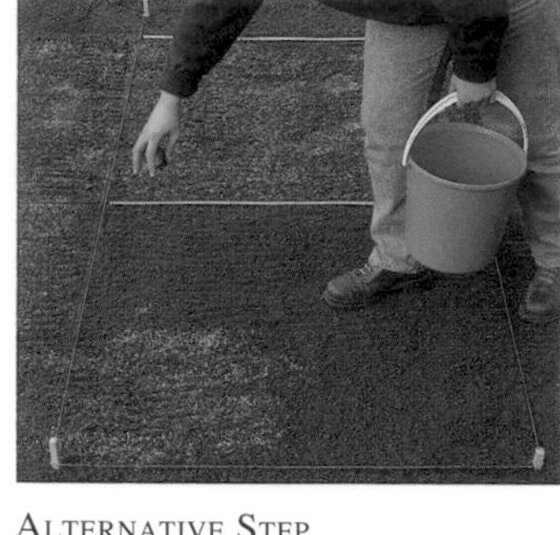

ALTERNATIVE STEP
If sowing by hand, mark the site into equal areas. Weigh enough seed for a single area, then scatter it evenly, half in one direction and half at right angles to this.

2 *After sowing, lightly rake over the surface. In dry conditions, water the site regularly to encourage the seeds to germinate.*

3 *The grass seedlings should take 7–14 days to emerge. Once the grass is about 2in (5cm) high, cut it to a height of 1in (2.5cm) with a rotary mower.*

SOWING RATES

MIXTURES	oz/sq yd	g/sq m
Fescues and bents	3/4–7/8	25–30
Perennial ryegrass and other species	1–1 1/8	35–40
Flower-rich mixtures (depending on mixture)	1/16–1/8	2.5–5
SINGLE SPECIES		
Bents (*Agrostis*)	1/4–5/16	8–10
Carpet grass (*Axonopus*)	1/4–3/8	8–12
Common Bermuda grass (*Cynodon dactylon*)	1/8–1/4	5–8
Centipede grass (*Eremochloa ophiuroides*)	1/24–1/16	1.5–2.5
Red fescue (*Festuca rubra* var. *rubra*)	1/2–3/4	15–25
Perennial ryegrass (*Lolium perenne*)	5/8–1 1/8	20–40
Bahia grass (*Paspalum notatum*)	7/8–1 1/8	30–40
Kentucky bluegrass (*Poa pratensis*)/Smooth-stalked meadow grass	5/16–1/2	10–15

Hydromulching

Hydromulching may be considered for establishing very large utility lawns. In hydromulching, grass seed or sprigs are mixed with water, fertilizer, and fiber mulch, and the slurry is sprayed directly onto the prepared seedbed. The mixture holds the seeds in place and helps retain moisture until roots are firmly established.

Because of the equipment involved, hydromulching is usually done by lawn-care companies. Consult with a specialist to determine the mixture of grasses suitable for your lawn; common Bermuda grass (*Cynodon dactylon*) and its hybrids are used most frequently in the South and Kentucky bluegrass (*Poa pratensis*) in the North.

Moss lawns

Although it is generally regarded as a lawn problem, moss can be used to create entire lawns.

Usually associated with dampness and shade, mosses grow either in sun or shade in a variety of soils, from moist to dry, acidic to alkaline, light to heavy. Drier conditions favor gray mosses, while green mosses thrive on wet soils.

Moss lawns may be introduced in any season. Work compost into the soil, water, then lay down cushions or mats of moss, including some of the earthy matter in which it was growing – pine needles, forest litter, rotting wood – and press firmly. (Obtain moss from woods, farms, or neighbors who are anxious to get rid of it. It transplants well.)

Mist the transplanted material and new growth daily; do not walk on the moss until established. Use a broom to sweep leaves and debris away. Moss lawns need periodic weeding and no mowing. They can be walked on occasionally, to perform maintenance tasks, but are never suitable for games.

Routine care

Once the lawn is well established, regular maintenance is needed to ensure its health and attractive appearance. The amount required depends on the lawn's size and type as well as the site and climate. In general, the most frequent tasks are mowing and watering, but annual maintenance may also include such things as fertilizing, top-dressing, aerating, and, where necessary, controlling moss, weeds, pests, and diseases. For large lawns, using mechanical or power tools, which may be rented, often makes maintenance tasks faster and easier (see "Lawn-care tools," pp.466–7).

Mowing

In addition to making the lawn a pleasure to walk on, regularly cutting the grass helps to create a dense, healthy turf with an even, attractive finish. Mowing is needed most frequently in the warm, moist conditions of late spring and late summer. However, during drought conditions, it is best either not to mow at all or to set the mower to a higher cut. Delay mowing during very wet or cold weather: wet grass can clog the mower or the mower may slip, and mowing in frost damages the grass. When using a power mower, always wear sturdy or steel-toe shoes with nonslip soles and heels, especially if mowing on a slope. Wear goggles if mowing in stony ground or near graveled areas.

Mowers

For most lawns, either a reel or a rotary mower will provide a suitable finish. A reel mower that incorporates a roller provides the finest finish for a high-quality lawn, but a rotary mower gives a perfectly acceptable surface for a utility lawn.

For most North American lawns, rotary mowers are the best all-around choice; they are widely available, fast, and efficient, and they provide good results. For large properties, riding mowers let the operator cut the grass with a commanding view of the lawn and comparatively little physical effort. Riding mowers are inappropriate for small, uneven, or stony lawns.

However, nonmotorized reel mowers are becoming an increasingly popular choice, especially among the ecologically aware. Reel mowers, also called push mowers, do not use gasoline, so they do not put out harmful fumes. They also tend not to be as hazardous to use as rotary mowers. The owner of a reel mower is likely to get a workout, since the energy needed to get a smooth cut comes from the operator rather than a gasoline engine. For more information, see "Lawn mowers," p. 465.

Frequency and height of cut

The frequency of mowing and the height of cut depend on a number of factors, including the type of grasses grown, how the lawn is used, and the time of year, but little and often is a good general rule to follow. Try to remove no more than half the leaf growth at any one time. If the grass is cut sporadically and drastically, it will struggle to recover after each mowing, which will result in a noticeable decline in the lawn's quality. Frequent mowing is necessary during the spring flush of growth. This tapers off with the arrival of summer, and it may not be necessary to mow at all for part of the summer. Growth begins again with cooler weather. In mild areas, an occasional mowing may be required in winter.

High-quality lawns may be cut even as low as 1/4in (0.5cm) but they need to be mown frequently – every two or three days in active growth – to maintain their appearance. Utility lawns should be left to grow longer than this, because the grasses do not tolerate such a low cut; this also helps to protect the surface against drying out.

It is not necessary to mow all areas to the same height. Try two or three heights of cut for different grass areas to add texture and interest to the garden. For practical reasons, cut the main area to be used for walking or playing to a height of about 2 1/2–3in (6–8cm). Keeping the grass at this length protects the surface against drying. Mow the areas under trees less frequently – every two or three weeks in summer – to a height of 4–6in (10–15cm). Leave any areas of meadow at 6in (15cm) or more; they will need no more than three cuts per year and should not be cut until the flowering species have shed their seed in midsummer (see WILDFLOWER AND MEADOW GARDENING, p.167). Since they are mown infrequently, these areas produce much more growth and debris, which should be raked up and removed after each mowing.

MOWING STRIPS

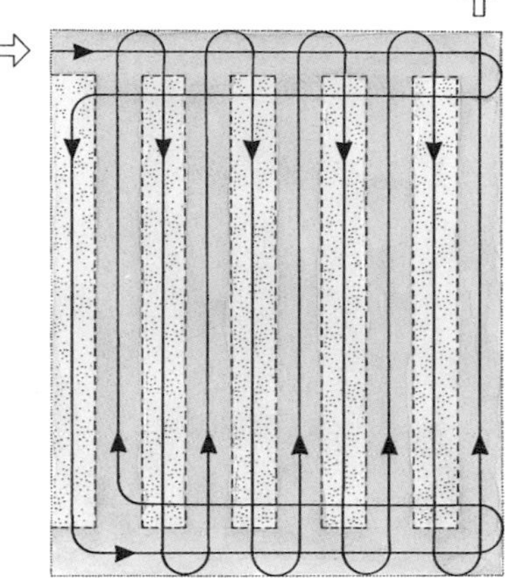

REGULAR SHAPE
First mow a wide strip at each end of the lawn for turning space, then mow up and down the lawn in slightly overlapping runs.

IRREGULAR SHAPE
Mow a strip around the lawn edge, then mow a straight strip up the center. Mow up and down one-half of the lawn, then the other half.

Mowing efficiently

Efficient mowing, especially with a riding mower, can save a lot of time. If the lawn is square or rectangular, first mow a wide strip at either end of the lawn to provide turning space. Then mow up and down in straight strips, slightly overlapping the previous run to make sure that all the grass is mown.

If the lawn is of an irregular shape, first mow all around its edge. Then, starting at the center of one end, mow a straight line down the middle by picking out an object or tree beyond the end of the lawn and then pointing the mower directly toward it. Mow straight strips up and down one-half of the lawn, then return to the center and mow the other half in a similar fashion.

Mowing sports fields

On areas to be used for ball games such as croquet or putting, vary the direction each time you mow to prevent a grain from developing. Grain is produced by grass growing in one direction and influences the run of the ball.

Grass clippings

On fine lawns where a high-quality finish is required, use a mower that collects grass clippings as it cuts or rake them up afterward, then add them in layers to the compost heap. On most utility lawns, using a modern mulching mower, which cuts the clippings into small pieces and drops them in the wake of the mower, will eliminate many thatch problems and will help feed the lawn.

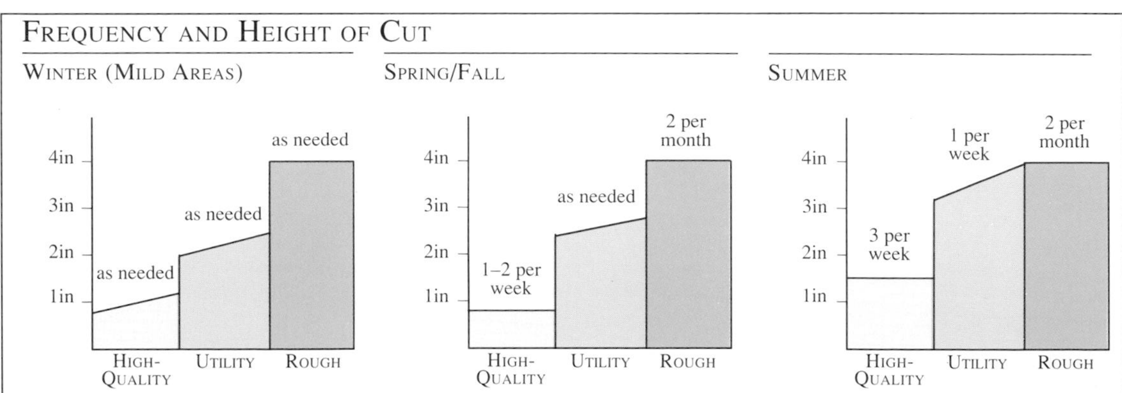

Utility lawns containing earthworms will benefit from clippings left on the lawn; the clippings will be recycled by the earthworms and the plant nutrients returned to the soil. Another related way to recycle nutrients is by composting. Even leaving fine clippings on the lawn to break down slowly is preferable to relegating them to landfills, where their components will be unavailable to the ecosystem for years to come.

Removing fallen leaves

In fall and winter, clear away any fallen leaves from the lawn by brushing or raking them up and removing them; a layer of leaves left on the lawn reduces evaporation, and the resulting humidity can encourage lawn diseases.

Trimming edges

After mowing, create a neat finish by trimming the lawn edges with long-handled edging shears, a mechanical edging machine, or a nylon-line trimmer with an adjustable head for edging (see "Lawn-care tools," pp.466–7). If the lawn edges become irregular, recut them once or twice a year with a half-moon edger, cutting against a board for a straight line; for very large lawns, it is faster and less laborious to use a power edger for this task.

CLEARING LEAVES

Remove any fallen leaves and debris by brushing the lawn briskly with a spring-tined rake. For large lawns, use a leaf sweeper or blower to speed up the task.

Watering

Grass generally resists drought well once established, but growth slows down and the lawn turns brown in prolonged dry spells. To maintain growth and color, it is essential to water the lawn thoroughly in very dry periods. Water either in the early morning or in the late afternoon to minimize evaporation.

Start to water as soon as you notice that the grass does not spring back up after the lawn has been walked on – this is known as footprinting. It is vital to give the lawn enough water; after watering, the soil should be moist to a depth of 4–6 in (10–15cm). Shallow watering encourages plant roots to remain near the surface, making the lawn more susceptible to drought. Dig a small hole to check that the soil is damp to the required depth; make a note of the time that it took to water the lawn sufficiently to guide you in future. Alternatively, an electric moisture meter may be used for evaluation. Push the sensor into the soil to register the moisture level.

On heavy soils, where the drainage is restricted, it is important not to apply too much water since this restricts oxygen and mineral intake by the roots. If pools of water remain on the lawn for some time after heavy rain or watering, the lawn may need additional drainage (see "Improving drainage," p.531).

Areas of grass that need regular watering are best served by a built-in, pop-up sprinkler system installed underground. When the water is turned on, the pressure lifts the sprinkler heads from below ground level and water is released. When the water is turned off, the heads return underground and out of sight. Such systems may also be set to operate automatically but, of course, are much more expensive than a sprinkler or hose, which is perfectly satisfactory for most lawns. For information, see "Watering aids," pp. 468–9.

CUTTING THE EDGE OF THE LAWN

EDGING BY MACHINE
Periodically recut the lawn edge to retain the lawn's shape and create a well-defined finish. For large lawns, use a power edger: align the cutting blade along the required new edge and guide the machine forward.

TRIMMING THE EDGE
After mowing, trim the grass overhanging the lawn edge with long-handled edging shears, or use a nylon-line trimmer adapted to work vertically.

EDGING BY HAND
If recutting the edge manually, use a sharp half-moon edger, cutting along the line of a board for a straight edge.

Fertilizing

As with all plants, grasses require nutrients to grow, and regular applications of fertilizer help ensure a vigorous, healthy lawn. Most of the nutrients essential for growth are plentiful within the soil, but three – nitrogen (N), phosphorus (P), and potassium (K) – are often applied as a supplement. Nitrogen is the most commonly added nutrient: it is removed in grass clippings and is essential for the production of new growth stimulated by mowing. Nitrogen-deficient grass is generally yellow-green in appearance and lacking in resilience and vigor.

Fertilizers are the easiest and most usual way to apply nutrients to lawns; both organic and inorganic products are available (see also "Soil nutrients and fertilizers," pp.532–3). The exact amount of fertilizer that is required depends on how quickly water drains from the soil, how much rainfall or irrigation is received by the lawn, whether or not the grass clippings are removed, and on the type of grasses grown. On heavy clay soils that are rich in nutrients, and where rainfall or irrigation rates are low, only light fertilizing is necessary. However, light, sandy soils that are well watered and that lose nutrients quickly by leaching need greater amounts to produce healthy lawns.

Types and constituents of fertilizer

For most lawns, three applications of fertilizer a year are sufficient (see chart, opposite). Apply a spring fertilizer as soon as the grass begins to green up and again at the beginning of summer, and a fall/winter one after routine maintenance in early fall. All seasonal fertilizers contain nitrogen, phosphorus, and potassium, but in differing proportions, because nitrogen, applied too late in the year, may stimulate soft, lush growth and encourage diseases such as snow mold (p.573). Select a fertilizer that contains a mixture of both slow- and fast-release nitrogen; this helps the lawn to green up within two to three days and stay green for several weeks.

Weed-and-feed compounds help to control moss and broad-leaved weeds and to fertilize the lawn all in one operation. Do not assume, however, that a weed-and-feed fertilizer will eliminate all of your lawn weeds. As with pesticides, the herbicide's effectiveness depends on applying it properly to the weeds it can control at the correct time. Always read the package carefully before buying any herbicides.

How to apply fertilizer

It is essential to apply fertilizer evenly to avoid variations in growth and the risk of damaging or even

WATER PENETRATION

Shallow watering may make the lawn vulnerable to drought (right); apply enough water to moisten the soil to a depth of about 4–6in (10–15cm) (far right).

How to Apply Fertilizer

Measure the correct amount of fertilizer for the area and divide it in half. Apply the first half in one direction, working up and down the lawn in adjoining but not overlapping runs. Apply the second half at right angles to this. Close off the supply when you turn the machine at the end of each run.

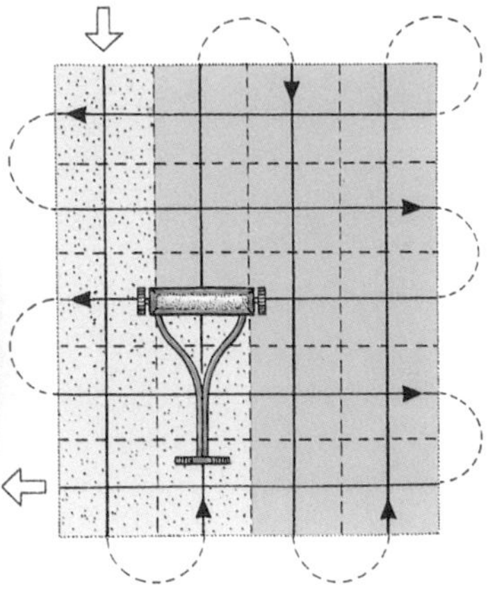

killing the grass. Any variation in the rate of application will generally be more than obvious within a week, and excessive doses may leave a dead patch behind. Although fertilizer may be spread manually, it is both easier and more accurate to apply it by machine.

Probably the simplest method is to use a drop-type spreader. This machine is pushed up and down the lawn, as if mowing, but so that each pass abuts the previous one without overlapping it. To ensure even coverage over the lawn, it is best to divide the fertilizer into two batches and apply half in one direction and the rest at right angles to it.

Alternatively, a cyclone or broadcast spreader may be used to apply the fertilizer over a larger area; however, the spread may be uneven. To reduce the risk of fertilizer being distributed unevenly, set the machine to half the application rate and make adjacent runs at half the distance apart of the machine's spread. For example, if the extent of the spread is 6ft (2m), make the runs 3ft (1m) apart. After using either type of machine, be certain to wash it out thoroughly, because fertilizers are corrosive and may, therefore, damage any metal parts.

Uneven Distribution

Take care to apply fertilizer evenly because uneven distribution may make the lawn patchy; it could damage or kill areas of grass.

Before applying fertilizer, calibrate the spreader to obtain the correct distribution rate. To calibrate a spreader, first find a dry, flat area of concrete or asphalt, and chalk out a measured area of 4sq yd (4sq m), for example. Set the spreader to medium and fill it a quarter full. Using the machine, spread the fertilizer as evenly as possible over the marked area, as if over the lawn, then brush up all the fertilizer within the area and weigh it. Divide this weight by the area, in this case 4sq yd (4sq m), to give the application rate in ounces per square yard (grams per square meter). Adjust the machine setting accordingly, and then check the application rate again over the same measured area. Continue this process until the rate is correct.

Annual maintenance

In addition to routine tasks such as mowing and watering, regular maintenance is required to keep a lawn healthy and to reduce the risk of serious pest or disease problems (see chart, below). A maintenance program should involve aeration (including thatch removal or scarifying), fertilizing, and the control of weeds, moss, pests, and diseases (see "Lawn weeds," p.286, and "Pests and diseases," p.286).

It is also important for the continued good health of the lawn to top-dress the grass as well as to rake or brush it regularly to clear away leaves and other debris (see "Removing fallen leaves," opposite).

Tasks that may be necessary at least once a year include recutting any edges that have become uneven or jagged, and repairing any damaged or worn patches of grass by resodding or reseeding (see "Repairing lawn damage," p.285). Winter is the most convenient time to check all equipment carefully since the lawn does not need regular attention. Sharpen all cutting edges, oil tools where necessary, and send the mower for servicing, so that it will be in peak condition for the first cut of the new season.

Dethatching

It is important to reduce excessive thatch, the organic matter consisting of decaying blades of grass, rhizomes, and stolons that accumulates on the soil surface. A certain amount of thatch – up to about ½in (1cm) deep – is beneficial since it reduces evaporation and helps to protect the lawn from wear. In excess, however, it prevents water from reaching the soil beneath and may itself become saturated, interfering with drainage. The removal of thatch also encourages new grass growth and so promotes healthy, vigorous turf.

Aerating the lawn

Aeration is vital since it allows deep root growth and so helps the lawn to become established, as well as reducing soil compaction.

There are several ways of aerating the soil. These include scarifying, slitting, hollow tining (also known as coring), and spiking. It is preferable not to undertake these tasks in dry conditions, however, since they make the lawn more vulnerable to drought. Early spring is the best time, since the grass is growing

Annual Maintenance Program

Maintenance Procedure	Early/Mid Spring	Mid/Late Spring	Early/Mid Summer	Mid/Late Summer	Early/Mid Fall	Mid/Late Fall	Winter
Mowing	Roll before mowing if sod is lifted by frost	Mow weekly Adjust mower to summer cut height	Mow 1–3 times a week as required	Mow 1–3 times a week (set mower higher in dry periods)	Adjust height of cut as growth rate slows	Set mower to winter cut height	Lightly mow if there is new growth
Watering		May be needed in dry regions	Water as necessary	Water well in dry periods	Occasionally water if dry		
Fertilizing		Apply spring fertilizer	Summer fertilizer		Apply fall/winter fertilizer		
Aerating and scarifying	Dethatch if necessary when dry enough	Lightly scarify			Spike or slit areas subject to heavy wear	Aerate lawn if not done in early fall	
Weed and moss control			Apply weedkiller		Apply contact weedkiller if not applied in early summer		
Pest and disease control	Check for snow mold. Rake lawn if present		Look for chinch bug and treat if found	Look for white grubs and diseases			
Other procedures	Recut edges if required. Carry out any restoration work				Top-dress after fall renovation	Remove fallen leaves	Remove leaves. Service tools

SCARIFYING

BY MACHINE
For large areas of lawn, use a mechanical or power scarifier. Work the machine back and forth across the lawn as if mowing.

BY HAND
Pull a spring-tined rake vigorously across the lawn to remove thatch and dead moss. Ensure that the tines of the rake reach well down into the soil surface.

rapidly and will recover quickly from these renovation procedures. First mow the lawn to its normal height. After maintenance work, apply a low-nitrogen fertilizer, and avoid using the lawn for one to two weeks to encourage recovery.

Scarifying

This technique helps to remove thatch and permits air to enter the surface of the lawn. These processes are important since the soil organisms that naturally break down thatch require air to live. For small areas, scarifying may be done manually by vigorously raking the lawn with a spring-tined rake. This is hard work, however, so it may be worth renting a mechanical or power scarifier instead. To remove the maximum amount of thatch, scarify the lawn in two directions, one at 90° to the other. Any moss should be killed prior to scarifying so that it will not spread to other parts of the lawn (see "Moss," p.286).

Slitting or verticutting

For slitting, a special machine penetrates the soil with a flat, sharp blade to 3–4in (8–10cm) deep. The blades cut through the thatch, allowing air into the soil and thereby encouraging a dense, healthy turf.

Hollow tining or coring

This removes some thatch, aerates the soil, and relieves soil compaction, all in one operation. A mechanical or hand tiner removes a core of grass, thatch, and soil, making a series of holes across the lawn, about 4in (10cm) apart. Allow the cores to remain on the lawn surface. Once they have dried, they can be crushed by being raked or by walking on them, and become a top-dressing. Hollow tining may take longer to do than spiking and slitting because soil is removed rather than simply being pushed sideways.

Spiking

This allows air into the soil, thereby encouraging root growth; it can also relieve soil compaction. Use a mechanical or hand spiker, or, for small areas, a garden fork. Angle the spikes back slightly to raise the turf gently without breaking it up. This encourages deep root growth by creating fissures in the soil.

AERATING

AERATING BY MACHINE
For large lawns, use a mechanical or power aerator; work the machine in slightly overlapping runs.

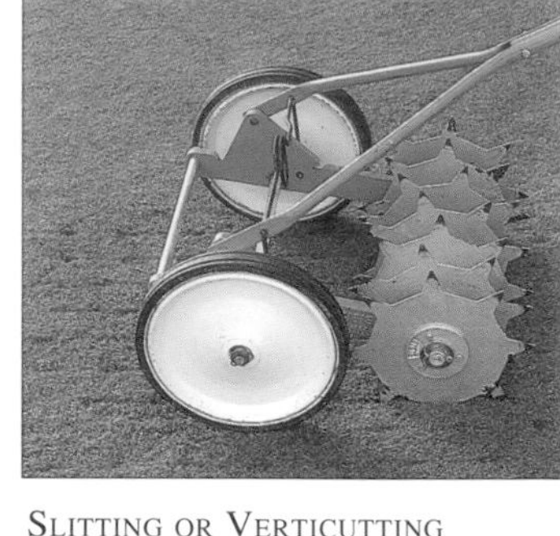

SLITTING OR VERTICUTTING
Slitting, which must be done with a special machine, allows air into the soil; push the machine back and forth across the lawn.

HOLLOW TINING
Use a specifically designed tool, working methodically across the lawn to lift out cores of grass and soil 1/4–3/4in (0.5–2cm) wide.

SPIKING
For small lawns, spiking using a garden fork is adequate; insert the fork straight in, then lean it back slightly to let in more air.

Top-dressing

Where soils are shallow and the lawn is poor, it will be beneficial to top-dress the lawn. Top-dressing also helps break down thatch by keeping the lawn open and aerated, fills core holes, and helps to level the surface. For most lawns, a sandy mixture of 6 parts medium-fine sand, 3 parts sieved soil, and 1 part peat, compost, or leaf mold is suitable; alternatively, a sandy topsoil may be used. Apply the top-dressing with a drop-type fertilizer spreader or a shovel; do not apply a layer any deeper than 1/4in (6mm) at any one time. Spread the selected top-dressing across the lawn with a rake or flat board to achieve uniform distribution. Using a flat board also helps level any slight irregularities in the surface of the lawn.

TOP-DRESSING

1 *Prepare the top-dressing by mixing medium-fine sand with topsoil and peat or leaf mold. Pass the mixture through a 1/4in (5mm) mesh sieve.*

2 *Weigh out the correct amount of top-dressing for the lawn area and apply it on a dry day. For a large lawn, it is best to use a spreader.*

ALTERNATIVE STEP
For small areas, the top-dressing may be applied by hand; spread it evenly over the lawn with a shovel or spade.

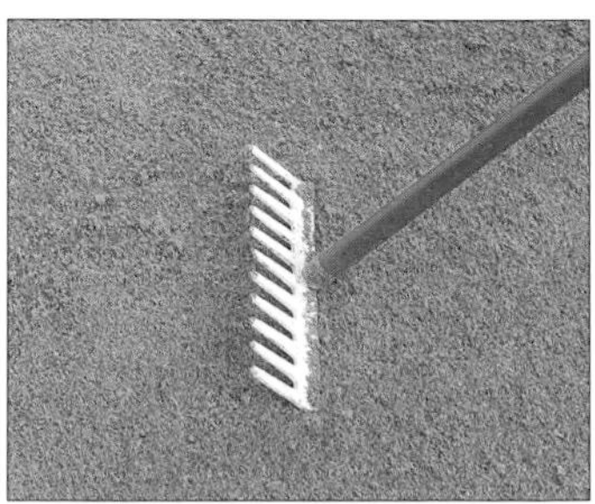

3 *Use the back of a rake to work in the dressing, keeping a steady pressure to distribute the dressing evenly. Then water the lawn thoroughly.*

Rolling
Rolling is not essential, but if done in spring it may help to resettle the surface after any maintenance work carried out the previous fall or after any possible upheaval caused by frost. A roller should not be filled more than about a quarter full with water, and should not be used at all on clay soils. The traditional practice of rolling lawns frequently is unnecessary and could cause the problems associated with compaction, particularly on heavy soils.

Renovating a neglected lawn

In some cases, a neglected, patchy lawn may be improved by renovation; if, however, it is dominated by weeds and moss, it may be preferable to remove the old turf and establish a new lawn instead. The best time to start renovation work is in either early spring or late summer. Avoid midsummer, when the lawn is under heat stress.

A renovation program involves a series of procedures that restore the lawn to a good condition. First, in early spring, cut the grass to about 2in (5cm) using a rotary mower, and remove any clippings. Feed with a high-nitrogen fertilizer such as 10–6–4 at about a quarter of the recommended rate. Repeat this feeding every three to four weeks except when the lawn is experiencing heat stress. Water thoroughly during periods of drought. Once the daytime temperature is above 70°F (21°C), apply a selective weedkiller. Reseed any remaining bare patches in early fall, at least eight weeks before freeze-up. At the beginning of fall, aerate the lawn, and apply a fall/winter fertilizer. A regular maintenance program should then be followed so that the lawn is kept in optimum condition (see *Annual Maintenance Program*, p.283).

Repairing lawn damage

If an area of the lawn becomes damaged or patchy, perhaps because of uneven wear, it may usually be repaired by removing the unwanted part, then sodding or seeding. Using sod or seed that is the same type as the rest of the lawn is important; if the lawn type is unknown, use a piece of sod from a less prominent part of the lawn to replace the damaged area. If the problem of lawn damage occurs repeatedly, it may be necessary to consider introducing a completely different and more hard-wearing surface such as gravel or paving (see STRUCTURES AND SURFACES, pp.492–513).

Repairing a damaged edge
Edges that have been damaged in only one or two small areas may be repaired quite simply. Using a half-moon edger and a straightedge, such as a short wooden board, mark out a small section of sod containing the damaged part. Slice under the section of sod with a spade, and push it toward the lawn edge until the poor area is outside the lawn. Then trim off the damaged part to align the sod with the existing lawn edge. This leaves a gap within the lawn, which should be gently forked over and a granular or liquid fertilizer added. Then resod or add a little soil and reseed the newly exposed area with an appropriate grass mixture. Ensure that the repair will grow to be flush with the rest of the lawn.

Alternatively, lift the sod, then turn it around and replace it so that the damaged area is within the lawn. Repair the damage by sodding or seeding, taking care to ensure that any new sod is laid level with the surrounding lawn.

Repairing a damaged patch
If there is a damaged patch within the lawn, first cut out and lift a piece of sod containing the damaged area. Fork over the soil, then fertilize it, if required, and lightly firm the soil.

HOW TO REPAIR A DAMAGED EDGE

1 *Using stakes and string, mark out a small, straight-sided section of sod containing the damaged part; cut out the area with a half-moon edger.*

2 *Carefully undercut the sod with a spade, then slide it forward until the damaged part is beyond the lawn edge.*

3 *Align a board with the lawn edge, then cut along it to trim off the damaged section so that the sod is level with the rest of the lawn edge.*

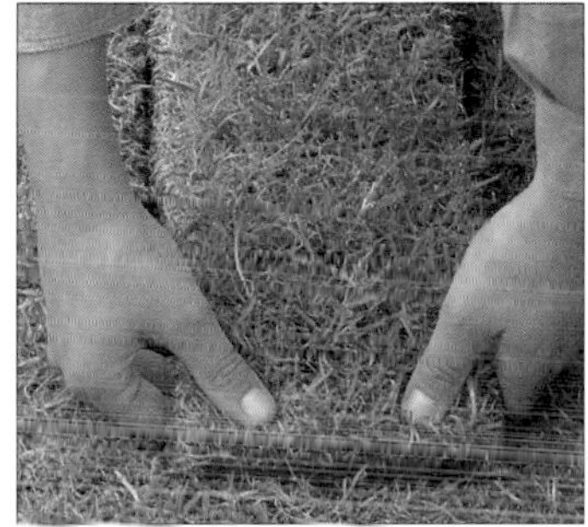

4 *Cut a new piece of sod to fit the resulting gap and ease it into the hole; if it is too large, trim it so that it forms an exact fit.*

5 *Adjust the soil level beneath the new sod, if necessary, by adding or removing soil until the new piece sits level with the rest of the lawn.*

6 *Once the level is correct, tamp the new piece firmly into place by standing on a board and shifting your weight.*

7 *Sprinkle some sandy top-dressing over the repaired area, particularly into the seams, and water thoroughly.*

ALTERNATIVE METHOD

1 *Cut out a section containing the damaged part. Turn it so that the damaged piece faces the lawn, and firm it into place.*

2 *Add a little sandy soil, if necessary, so that the damaged part is level with the rest of the lawn, then sow grass seed over the damaged section, and water well.*

HOW TO REPAIR A DAMAGED PATCH

1 *Using a half-moon edger and the edge of a board, cut around the damaged area, then undercut the sod with a spade and remove it.*

2 *Lightly fork or rake over the area of exposed soil to loosen it, and then apply a liquid or granular fertilizer if required.*

3 *Carefully tread over the soil to settle it and firm the surface before resodding.*

4 *Place a new piece of sod in the hole, cutting it to fit with a half-moon edger.*

5 *Check that the new sod is level with the rest of the lawn; if necessary, adjust the soil level beneath the sod. Then firm in the sod and water well.*

Lay a new piece of sod to fit the exposed space, raising or lowering the soil level beneath, if necessary, so that the new sod is level with the rest of the lawn, and tamp it down in position with the back of a rake or your hands. Top-dress and water the repaired surface well.

Leveling a hump or hollow
Small humps or hollows within the lawn may be leveled easily. First cut a cross through the sod on the problem area and peel back the cut sod. To level a hollow, fork over the soil beneath and fill in with topsoil, then lightly firm the ground. For a hump, remove the excess soil until the ground is level, and firm. Fold back the cut sod and tamp it down with the back of a rake before top-dressing and watering.

On larger areas, it may be necessary to remove complete sections of sod entirely, level the soil beneath (see "Leveling the site," p.276), and then carefully re-lay the sod over the original area.

Lawn weeds

Although some weeds such as slender speedwell (*Veronica filiformis*) and white clover (*Trifolium repens*) may look attractive in utility lawns, they are considered undesirable in high-quality, closely mown lawns. Many broad-leaved weeds can survive in grass that is mowed, but excessive numbers may make the grass suffer so, even in a utility lawn, control may be needed. Unless lawn clippings are collected, mowing may spread weeds that can root from small pieces of stem. On small lawns, dandelions (*Taraxacum officinale*) and plantains (*Plantago*) may be cut out by hand, but for a large lawn, it is easiest to use a selective weedkiller when the weeds are growing actively. This may be in granular or liquid form and can be part of the lawn fertilizing program.

Moss
Almost always undesirable, moss may be found in lawns for many reasons, including soil compaction, poor drainage, low fertility, insufficient light, mowing too closely, and extremes of soil pH; it can be a problem even in the best-kept lawns. Treat moss with a chemical moss killer, then remove it by scarifying (see p.284). If the problem continually recurs, identify and correct the possible causes; these may involve improving soil aeration, drainage, and fertility and, on light soils, top-dressing to assist water retention. Adopting an annual maintenance program should help to control the problem. For further details see PLANT PROBLEMS, "Lawn weeds," pp.578–9.

Pests and diseases

There are several species of insect that live in the soil and feed on grass roots. These include white grubs of June beetles and Japanese bettles, chinch bugs, and sod webworms. Moles and ants can also cause problems by excavating soil and forming hills.

Several lawn diseases, including brown patch (see "Drought," p.570), dollar spot, fairy rings, snow mold, and red thread, attack lawns, particularly in hot, humid areas; snow mold is a problem in cold regions too and may occur under snow. Preventive sprays may be necessary, but in cooler temperate and maritime climates it is usual to spray only in serious cases. For treatment of pests and diseases, see "Lawn problems," pp.573–4.

LEVELING A HOLLOW OR HUMP

1 *Cut a cross right through the hump or hollow in the sod, using a half-moon edger; the cross should reach just beyond the problem area.*

2 *Fold back the cut sections of sod, taking care not to pull them too roughly to avoid cracking.*

3 *For a hollow, fill in the ground beneath with a good sandy topsoil; for a hump, remove some of the soil until the entire surface is level.*

4 *Replace the folded-back sod and lightly firm to check that the level is correct. Adjust the soil level beneath (if necessary), firm, top-dress, and water well.*

13

THE HERB GARDEN

*W*HETHER GROWN ON *their own as an ornamental feature, with other plants in a border, or among the ordered ranks of a vegetable plot, herbs are an invaluable addition to any garden. They have always been prized for their culinary, cosmetic, or curative uses, but they also make highly decorative garden plants. Although few have spectacular or showy flowers, many are graced by attractive foliage and almost all are worth growing for their scent alone – ranging from the fresh, citrus tang of lemon balm to the aniseed aroma of fennel and the sweet apple perfume of chamomile. Their heady fragrance is hard to resist and their nectar-filled flowers tempt bees and butterflies, adding the drowsy hum of insects to complete the restfulness of an herb garden.*

Designing with herbs

HERB growing combines the delights of the flower garden with the productivity of the vegetable plot. The results are decorative, excellent in aroma and flavor, and inexpensive to produce. By definition, an herb is any plant that has culinary or curative uses, so the range is surprisingly wide. Herbs include trees and shrubs, not just herbaceous perennials and annuals.

Historically, herbs have been used for flavoring and preserving food, and, in addition, for making medicines and toiletries. Their aesthetic appeal has always been important too, and their ornamental qualities, as well as their practical uses, are of equal value today.

STRUCTURED INFORMALITY
Growing a rich profusion of herbs brings a wealth of fine scents and contrasting textures to the garden. In this herb garden, clipped dwarf hedges add structure while bold blocks of herbs such as golden marjoram contrast with casual plantings of feathery fennel and low alpine strawberries.

Herbs in the home

Although fresh and dried herbs are widely available, they rarely have as fine an aroma or flavor as those harvested from your own garden. Enjoy their scents indoors as well as outside by using them fresh in flower arrangements or dried to make potpourri or to fill herb pillows.

For the adventurous, herbs may also be used to make richly colored dyes: tansy flowers (*Tanacetum vulgare*) produce yellow dye, and sorrel roots (*Rumex acetosa*) yield a soft pink color. Exotic paper may be embedded with herb flowers and leaves. Furniture wax can be made with marjoram (*Origanum vulgare*).

Culinary uses

Freshly harvested herbs are an important ingredient in many classic combinations, such as tomato and basil salad, potato mayonnaise with chives, and May wine with sweet woodruff. Some flowers can be used as an edible decoration: borage, chives, elder, and pot marigold are all simple to grow and produce attractive flowers. Stalks, such as angelica for crystallizing or branches of rosemary for barbecues, are also easily grown but are rarely available otherwise. Aromatic seeds and spices are easier to obtain but again are simple, and mostly cheap, to produce.

Certain herbs, such as lemon balm and peppermint, may be infused in boiling water to make herb teas. They are a good alternative to ordinary tea and coffee because they do not contain tannin or caffeine. Most are made from dried leaves, flowers, or seeds, although they may also be made from fresh herbs.

Medicinal herbs

In many parts of the world, herbal medicine is commonplace and the herb garden is a source of homegrown treatments for all sorts of ailment. Mint, for example, is a mild local anesthetic, a powerful antiseptic, and a remedy for digestive problems. Herbs are also grown for processing into drugs by the pharmaceutical industry. In general, it is inadvisable to use herbs for medicinal purposes without specialist knowledge or advice.

Cosmetic and scented preparations

A number of herbs have beneficial effects on the condition of skin or hair, and are included in beauty products. Rosemary, chamomile, and mint are used in shampoos and conditioners, thyme as an antiseptic for mouthwashes, and pot marigold and elderflower in skin lotions.

Aromatic herbs may be enjoyed all year if they are made into scented household articles such as linen sachets and pomanders. Commercially, they are also used in perfumery; extracting oils and essences is, however, usually too complex to undertake at home.

Herbs in the garden

The majority of herbs grown today are still the wild species, but many cultivars are also now available, differing in habit or in the color of their foliage or flowers. This diversity makes them even more valuable as decorative garden plants, while their scent and other properties are usually similar, if not identical, to the species.

The appeal of herbs lies largely in their fragrance, which, in contrast to that of other plants, usually derives from the foliage rather than the flowers. Essential oils are released when the leaves are warmed or crushed; on a sunny day, the scent from an herb garden fills the air.

A few herbs have brightly colored flowers, which may be used to great advantage: the orange of pot marigolds (*Calendula officinalis*) offset by bronze fennel (*Foeniculum vulgare* 'Purpureum'), or the blue of borage (*Borago officinalis*) with silver-gray wormwood (*Artemisia absinthium*), for example.

Certain herbs are reputed to benefit other plants: some pungent plants such as southernwood (*Artemisia abrotanum*) are said to repel insects if crushed or infused. Growing chamomile (*Chamaemelum nobile*) in the garden is supposed to increase the health and vigor of nearby plants.

Where to grow herbs

Herbs, like other plants, should be grown in conditions that are similar to their natural habitat to ensure that they are healthy and vigorous. Many herbs are Mediterranean in origin, and these usually prefer plenty of sunshine and a free-draining soil.

Several herbs tolerate a damp, partially shaded site, provided that they are not waterlogged or in dense or permanent shade. Most variegated and golden cultivars thrive in light shade. As a rule, gray-foliaged herbs do not tolerate high humidity. Pineapple mint (*Mentha suaveolens* 'Variegata') and golden forms of lemon balm (*Melissa officinalis*) and feverfew (*Tanacetum parthenium*, syn. *Chrysanthemum parthenium*) retain their color best when lit by either morning or evening sun but shaded at midday.

Herbs may be grown in a variety of situations. A separate herb garden in an attractive design provides an appealing feature and need not take up much space. It may be preferable to have a culinary herb patch, or herbs in containers, within easy reach of the kitchen. Some herbs are decorative enough to be grown with other plants in a bed or border, while others may be better sited in the vegetable garden. Culinary herbs should always be sited away from possible contamination by pets or roadside pollution.

Herbs that Tolerate Moist Shade

- Angelica (*Angelica archangelica*)
- Chervil (*Anthriscus cerefolium*)
- Chives (*Allium schoenoprasum*)
- Elder (*Sambucus nigra*, *S. n.* 'Aurea', *S. n.* 'Marginata')
- Feverfew (*Tanacetum parthenium*, *T. p.* 'Aureum')
- Lemon balm (*Melissa officinalis*, *M. o.* 'All Gold', *M. o.*'Aurea', *M. o.* 'Variegata')
- Lovage (*Levisticum officinale*)
- Mints (*Mentha*)
- Parsley (*Petroselinum crispum*)
- Sorrel (*Rumex acetosa*)
- Sweet cicely (*Myrrhis odorata*)
- Tansy (*Tanacetum vulgare*)
- Woodruff (*Asperula odorata*)

Herb gardens

If there is space, it is worth creating a separate herb garden to grow many different herbs together for a strong impact and to reap the benefit of their combined scents in one place. Making a special feature of the plants allows plenty of opportunity to create an interesting pattern or design using blocks of complementary or contrasting colors. As well as being a highly ornamental way of displaying the herbs, it makes harvesting easier. Herb gardens are traditionally bordered by low, clipped hedges of boxwood (*Buxus sempervirens*), but a less formal edging of hyssop (*Hyssopus officinalis*) or lavender (*Lavandula*) would also be suitable.

Beds and borders

Herbs may also be grown with other ornamental garden plants. This is useful where there is no space for a separate herb garden, or for herbs that are border plants in their own right, such as bee balm (*Monarda didyma*) and rue (*Ruta graveolens*). Gray-leaved species are especially fine in a silver border or as a contrast to plants with blue, pink, or purple coloring such as purple sage (*Salvia officinalis* 'Purpurascens').

Stately architectural plants are valuable as focal points on their own or at the back of a border. Fill gaps in borders with colorful annuals such as poppies (*Papaver*), blue borage (*Borago officinalis*), and dark-leaved basil (*Ocimum basilicum* 'Purpurascens').

Planting aromatic herbs next to doorways, paths, and seats makes it easy to enjoy their scents to the fullest. Low, spreading herbs such as wild thyme (*Thymus serpyllum*), lawn chamomile (*Chamaemelum nobile* 'Treneague'), and creeping savory (*Satureja spicigera*) are suitable for rock gardens or en masse to form a fragrant carpet. These and other, more upright, herbs such as chives (*Allium schoenoprasum*) make an unusual and attractive edging to a border or path.

Herbs in the vegetable garden

For culinary herbs that are used in large quantities, such as parsley (*Petroselinum crispum*), the vegetable plot may be the best site. This may also be the most convenient place for fast-growing herbs such as chervil (*Anthriscus cerefolium*) and dill (*Anethum graveolens*) that are sown in succession and do not transplant successfully. The herbs may be grown in straight rows among the vegetables or as an ornamental border around the edge of the vegetable garden.

Growing herbs in containers

Many herbs grow well in containers. From a hanging basket to a plastic pail, almost any container is suitable, provided that it has drainage holes and that a layer of porous material is added before planting in it.

In small gardens or on balconies, the entire herb garden may consist of containers, imaginatively positioned on walls, steps, shelves, and windowsills, as well as at ground level. If space is at a premium, using a strawberry jar (a pot with planting pockets) offers an attractive and functional way of growing a number of different plants together. Even if you have a separate area for herbs or grow them with other ornamentals or vegetables, it is often convenient to have one or two pots of commonly used herbs near the door.

Some of the best herbs for containers are chervil, parsley, chives, compact marjoram (*Origanum vulgare* 'Compactum'), rock hyssop (*Hyssopus officinalis* subsp. *aristatus*), and thymes (*Thymus*). Large plants such as rosemary (*Rosmarinus officinalis*) and bay (*Laurus nobilis*) often look good grown as single specimens in pots or tubs. Growing slightly tender herbs such as myrtle (*Myrtus communis*), lemon verbena (*Aloysia triphylla*), and rose-scented geranium (*Pelargonium graveolens*) in containers is convenient because they may be brought inside during winter. They also make good conservatory plants.

CARTWHEEL BED
A cartwheel design provides a decorative and practical way of growing a small range of herbs.

CONTAINER GARDENING
Even in the smallest garden, there is room to grow a variety of aromatic herbs in a group of pots.

Paving and patios

Planting herbs in the gaps between paving stones is an attractive option for herbs that prefer well-drained conditions, such as thymes and creeping savory. Allow the plants to spread so that an occasional light tread releases their fragrance.

Patios are often ideal for displaying a variety of tender or Mediterranean herbs that enjoy warmth and shelter, while an exotic touch may be added by including plants such as lemon trees (*Citrus limon*), cardamom (*Elettaria cardamomum*), or ginger (*Zingiber officinale*) grown in ornamental containers.

Raised beds

Growing herbs in raised beds makes it easier to enjoy their fragrance at close quarters as well as being practical for the physically impaired, providing good access for planting, maintenance, and harvesting. Raised beds must have strong retaining walls and should be no more than approximately 30in (75cm) wide and at a comfortable height for working (see also STRUCTURES AND SURFACES, "Raised beds," p.507).

Raised beds are also a good option on paved areas against a wall (but not above the level of the basement walls) and in any site where the soil is not free-draining. Choose small, compact herbs for raised beds, and control their spread by regular pruning and dividing.

FORMAL HERB GARDEN
This well-planned layout is divided by brick paths, which provide a formal framework for a number of geometric herb beds.

Designing an herb garden

Whether informal or formal, an herb garden should be designed so that it is compatible with the style of the rest of the garden and the house. Take into account maintenance resources when planning: in general, informal herb gardens need less initial structural work than formal ones, and routine care may be less time-consuming, depending on the plants used and the size and complexity of the design. It is also possible to combine elements of both formal and informal designs; for example, a well-defined, symmetrical pattern of paths could form a framework for a free planting of herbs of different heights, habits, and colors.

Informal designs

An informal design largely depends for its success upon the complementary habits and colors of the herbs. Many variegated and colored-leaved forms such as golden marjoram (*Origanum vulgare* 'Aureum') and purple sage are especially dramatic in such a design. Try green- and gold-leaved plants together, for example, or those with purple and silver foliage.

There is greater freedom to use plants of different heights and habits than in a formal design: tall ones may be used strikingly without upsetting the balance and impact of the design, and the overall impression of colorful harmony and rich abundance allows greater flexibility for experimenting with bold, innovative, or even daring combinations. Consider including a few simple pots or rustic containers as well.

Formal designs

These designs are usually based on geometric patterns and framed by low hedges or paths. Each small bed created by the pattern is then planted with one kind of herb, giving bold blocks of color and texture. At its simplest, the design may take the form of a cartwheel bedded into the soil with a different herb planted in each segment. These designs often look particularly impressive when viewed from above, so consider siting the herb garden where it may be overlooked from an upper window or a slope. When choosing plants, do not include tall, invasive, or sprawling herbs that may spoil the rest of the design when fully grown.

A formal garden with paths is labor-intensive initially but soon looks mature and needs little structural maintenance. One that includes a framework of dwarf hedges that require regular clipping may be considerably more demanding. The hedging may outline the design or take on the complex shapes of a knot garden (see "Knot gardens," p.31). Suitable plants for dwarf hedges include boxwood, hyssop, lavenders, shrubby germander (*Teucrium fruticans*), and winter savory (*Satureja montana*) planted about 9–12in (22–30cm) apart.

Making a plan

To draw up a plan, first measure the site and surrounding features accurately, taking account of any changes in grade. Also note where shadows fall at different seasons as well as at different times of day.

Whether the garden is to be formal or informal in style, remember that herbs should be within arm's reach for convenient care and harvesting. For beds or borders in open ground, access by paths or stepping-stones will greatly help to reduce harmful soil compaction.

Transfer the measurements to graph paper, working to scale. In order to compare a number of different designs, draw each design on a sheet of tracing paper laid over the master plan.

Finally, decide on which herbs to grow and mark them on the plan. Take into account their cultivation requirements, habit, color, eventual height and spread, and the amounts that will be required for harvesting. Herbs in containers may also be included in the garden design to provide focal points.

HERBS IN A PATIO GARDEN
Enliven a patio or courtyard, and soften the effect of the hard elements, by planting herbs directly into the gaps between paving or in gravel.

PLANNING A FORMAL HERB GARDEN

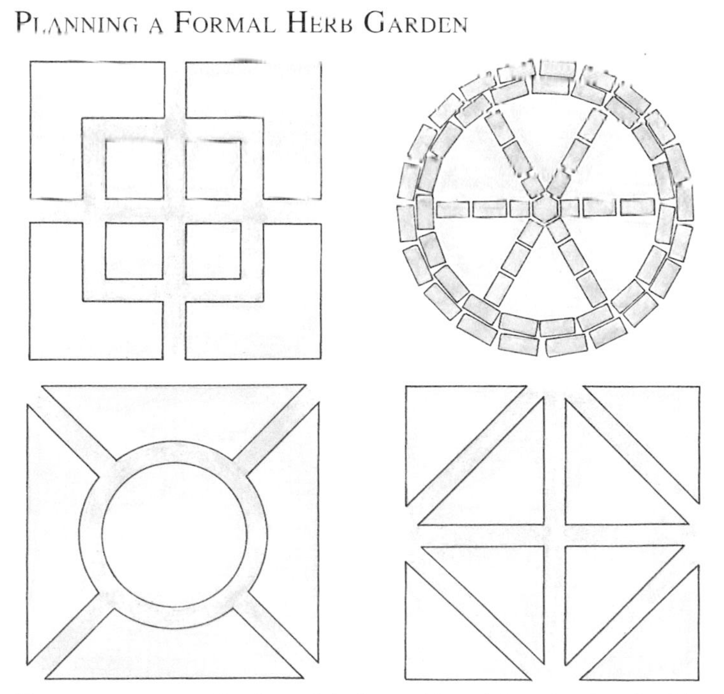

There are many possible formal designs, although imagination should be restrained by considerations of balance and proportion. Cartwheel and chessboard layouts are popular, but unusual geometric patterns also provide plenty of opportunity to create an eye-catching feature.

Directory of common herbs

Chives
(*Allium schoenoprasum*)

Hardy, herbaceous, clump-forming perennial with hollow, grasslike leaves and mauve flowers. Good as a low edging for borders. May be forced for winter use (see p.294). Use the leaves, which have a mild onion flavor, as a garnish and flavoring in salads, dips, soft cheeses, and soups; the edible flowers make a decorative addition to salads.
Harvesting and storing Cut leaves and flowers as available to use fresh. For freezing and drying, cut leaves before flowering and chop finely.
Propagation By seed sown in spring (see p.160) or by division in fall (p.162).
Related species and variants Variations in height, flower color, and flavor are available. Chinese, or garlic, chives (*A. tuberosum*) have a mild garlic flavor and white flowers.

Lemon verbena
(*Aloysia triphylla*)

Half-hardy, upright, deciduous shrub with pointed, oval leaves. Plants will be cut back by frost but grow again from the base in mild areas. The leaves have a strong lemon scent and are used in herb teas, desserts, potpourri, and teas.
Harvesting and storing Pick leaves during the growing season for using fresh or for drying.
Propagation By softwood cuttings (see p.81).

Dill
(*Anethum graveolens*)

Hardy, upright annual with flat heads of greenish yellow flowers and feathery, blue-green leaves. Do not plant dill near fennel since this may result in cross-pollination and the loss of its distinctive flavor. Runs to seed quickly. Use the leaves or, for a stronger flavor, the aromatic seeds in soups, sauces, potato salad, pickles, and fish dishes.
Harvesting and storing Pick leaves in spring and summer before flowering. Cut seedheads as they ripen in summer.
Propagation By seed sown in spring and early summer (see p.176); may not transplant well.

Angelica
(*Angelica archangelica*)

Hardy biennial with large, divided leaves and large flowerheads. A bold, architectural plant. Unless seeds are required, remove seedheads before ripening to prevent unwanted seedlings. The young stalks may be candied; the leaves are used in cooking, especially in fruit desserts and fish dishes.
Harvesting and storing Gather fresh leaves in spring and summer. Cut the young stalks for crystallizing in spring or early summer. Cut seedheads as they ripen in summer.
Propagation By seed sown in fall (see p.176); seeds lose viability within three months of ripening.

Chervil
(*Anthriscus cerefolium*)

Hardy annual with bright green, fernlike leaves. Runs to seed quickly in hot, dry conditions. The leaves have a fine, subtle flavor, reminiscent of parsley and anise. Use the leaves in egg dishes, salads, soups, and sauces.
Harvesting and storing Gather leaves before flowering. Freeze or dry them gently to preserve their delicate flavor.
Propagation By seed sown at monthly intervals from spring to early fall (see p.176); do not transplant. May also be sown in trays under glass in early fall for winter use.

Horseradish
(*Armoracia rusticana*)

Hardy perennial with large, coarse leaves. Plants are persistent and difficult to eradicate. The stout, white-fleshed roots have a pungent flavor and are grated into coleslaw, dips, and sauces, especially horseradish sauce. Young leaves are used in salads or sandwiches.
Harvesting and storing Pick the young leaves in spring. Harvest the roots in fall when the flavor is at its peak, or as required.
Propagation By division (see p.162), 6in (15cm) root cuttings (p.165), or by seed (p.160).

Southernwood
(*Artemisia abrotanum*)

Hardy, semievergreen subshrub with finely divided, gray-green foliage. May be used to form a low hedge, trimmed in summer; it is also attractive in mixed borders. Flowers are rarely produced in cool climates. Use the aromatic leaves in potpourri and as an insect repellant.
Harvesting and storing In summer, pick leaves as required for using fresh or for drying.
Propagation By softwood cuttings in summer, semiripe heel cuttings in late summer, or hardwood cuttings in fall (see pp.81–4).

Wormwood
(*Artemisia absinthium*)

Hardy, deciduous subshrub with deeply divided, grayish green leaves. Good as a border plant or informal hedge. Prune to within 6in (15cm) of the ground in spring. The aromatic leaves are intensely bitter; they were formerly used to flavor alcoholic drinks but are now regarded as toxic. The foliage is attractive in herbal decorations and posies.
Harvesting and storing Pick foliage in summer for use fresh or dried in arrangements.
Propagation By softwood cuttings in summer (see p.81) or by semiripe heel cuttings in late summer (p.83).
Variants 'Lambrook Silver' is a cultivar with silver-gray foliage.

French tarragon
(*Artemisia dracunculus*)

Hardy perennial with upright stems and glossy, narrow leaves. In very cold areas, it may need winter protection, but it can be forced for winter use. The leaves are commonly used in béarnaise sauce, *fines herbes*, tartar sauce, and egg and chicken dishes, as well as to flavor vinegar.
Harvesting and storing Cut sprigs of foliage throughout the growing season, leaving two-thirds of the stem to regrow. The leaves are best frozen but may also be dried.
Propagation By division of rhizomes in spring (see p.163) or by stem tip cuttings in summer (p.164). Seed is not available: that sold as tarragon is the Russian species.
Related species Russian tarragon (*A. dracunculoides*) is a hardier species, but it unfortunately has an inferior flavor.

Woodruff
(*Asperula odorata*, syn. *Galium odoratum*)

Hardy, creeping perennial with star-shaped white flowers that appear above the whorls of narrow leaves in spring and early summer. An excellent ground cover in damp shade. The dried leaves are used in potpourri and herb tea.
Harvesting and storing Gather the leaves for drying just before the flowers open in spring.
Propagation By division in fall or spring (see p.162) or by seed sown in early fall (p.160), but germination may be slow.

Borage
(*Borago officinalis*)

Hardy, upright annual with hairy foliage and intense blue flowers. Add the cucumber-flavored leaves and the flowers to cold drinks and salads. Crystallize the flowers for use in cake decoration or as a garnish.
Harvesting and storing Pick young leaves and use fresh. Gather the flowers (without calyces) in summer to use fresh, freeze in ice cubes, or crystallize.
Propagation Sow seed from spring to early fall (see p.176). Self-sows in light soils.
Variants There is also a form with white flowers, *B. o.* f. *alba*.

Pot marigold
(*Calendula officinalis*)

Bushy, hardy annual with bright orange flowers. A colorful plant for borders and containers. Deadhead to prolong flowering. Use the petals to flavor and color rice, cream cheese, and soups, and to garnish salads. Chop the young leaves into salads. Dried petals may be used to add color to potpourri.
Harvesting and storing Pick open flowers in summer and remove petals for drying. Gather leaves when young.
Propagation By seed sown in fall or spring (see p.176). Self-sows freely.
Variants Double-flowered forms in shades of cream, orange, and bronze are widely available.

Caraway
(*Carum carvi*)

Hardy biennial with feathery leaves and, in the second year, flat heads of tiny white flowers. Aromatic seeds are used in baking, confectionery, cheeses, and meat stews such as goulash. Add the leaves to soups and salads.
Harvesting and storing Gather leaves when young. Collect the ripe seedheads in summer.
Propagation By seed in fall (see p.176).

Chamomile
(*Chamaemelum nobile*)

Hardy, creeping, vigorous perennial, forming a dense mat of finely cut, feathery leaves. Good at the edge of paths and borders, or between paving stones. May be planted as an ornamental lawn (see p.275). Use the apple-scented leaves in potpourri; the aromatic flowers are used in potpourri and herb teas.
Harvesting and storing Pick leaves at any time as required. Gather flowers when fully open in summer and dry whole.
Propagation By division in spring or fall (see p.162), or by stem tip cuttings of side shoots in summer (p.164).
Variants 'Treneague' is a dwarf, nonflowering form that is particularly suitable for lawns and gaps in paving. *C. n.* var. *flore-pleno* has attractive double flowers.

Coriander
(*Coriandrum sativum*)

Hardy annual with divided foliage and small, white or pale mauve flowers. The plants have a distinctive odor and are not commonly grown indoors. The lobed lower leaves (known as cilantro) are used in curries, chutneys, sauces, and salads. The seeds, which have a sweet, spicy flavor, are used in baking, chutneys, and sausages.
Harvesting and storing Pick young leaves for using fresh or for freezing. Gather seedheads as they ripen.
Propagation By seed in fall or spring (see p.176).

Cumin
(*Cuminum cyminum*)

Tender annual with delicate leaves and white or pale pink flowers. Requires heat for the seeds to ripen. The aromatic seeds are used in curries, pickles, yogurt, and Middle Eastern dishes.
Harvesting and storing Gather seedheads as they ripen.
Propagation By seed sown in late spring in a warm site or under cover (see p.177).

Fennel
(*Foeniculum vulgare*)

Hardy perennial with fine filigree leaves and clusters of yellow flowers. A tall, graceful plant for borders. Use the leaves and leaf sheaths for their aniseed flavor in salads and meat and fish dishes. Seeds are used in baking, fish dishes, and herb teas.
Harvesting and storing Cut leaves and leaf sheaths when still young. Gather seedheads as they ripen.
Propagation By seed sown in spring (see p.160) or by division in fall (p.162).
Variants 'Purpureum' is an attractive bronze cultivar; Florence fennel (*F. v.* var. *dulce*) is grown as an annual for use as a vegetable (see p.346).

Hyssop
(*Hyssopus officinalis*)

Hardy, semievergreen subshrub with spikes of small, dark purple-blue flowers. Suitable for growing as a low hedge. The aromatic leaves are used sparingly in soups, bean dishes, stews, game, and pâté.

Harvesting and storing Gather leaves any time for fresh use; pick young leaves in early summer to dry.
Propagation By seed (see p.84), division (p.88), or by softwood cuttings in spring (p.81).
Variants Pink- and white-flowered varieties are available. Rock hyssop (*H. o.* subsp. *aristatus*) is a dwarf form especially suitable for containers.

Orris
(*Iris* 'Florentina', syn. *I. florentina*)

Hardy perennial with off-white flowers and sword-shaped leaves. Plant so that the rhizomes are exposed to full sun. The thick rhizome is bitter when fresh but develops a violet scent after drying and prolonged storage. It is ground for using as a perfume fixative in potpourri and linen sachets.
Harvesting and storing In fall, dig up rhizomes at least three years old. Peel, split, and dry, leaving them for up to two years before grinding.
Propagation By division of rhizomes in late spring or early fall (see p.163).
Related species *I. pallida* is also grown as orris in the same way.

Bay
(*Laurus nobilis*)

Small evergreen tree or large shrub with dark, leathery, pointed leaves. Makes an excellent container plant. May be clipped for topiary or pruned hard to restrict size. In cold areas, it must be grown indoors over winter. Use the leaves in *bouquet garni* and for flavoring stock, marinades, sauces, custards, and meat and fish dishes.
Harvesting and storing Pick leaves any time for using fresh. Dry mature leaves in summer.
Propagation By semiripe heel cuttings of side shoots in late summer (see p.53) or by layering in summer (p.55).
Variants 'Aurea' has yellow-flushed leaves.

Lavender
(*Lavandula angustifolia*)

Evergreen, bushy shrub with narrow, gray-green leaves and upright, mauve flower spikes. Hardy to about -10°F (-23°C). The flowers are used in potpourri, linen sachets, herb pillows, and tea. They may also be crystallized or used to flavor oil or vinegar.
Harvesting and storing Gather flowering stems in summer, and air-dry.
Propagation By cuttings of semiripe, nonflowering shoots in summer (see p.82).
Related species Several other species and

cultivars exist, varying in habit, foliage, flowering time, and flower color. They include dwarf cultivars, such as 'Hidcote', and white-flowered forms, for example 'Nana Alba'. French lavender (*L. stoechas*), which is half hardy, has purple flowers crowned by purple bracts.

Lovage

(*Levisticum officinale*, syn. *Ligusticum levisticum*)

Hardy perennial with divided leaves and clusters of pale green flowers; a tall plant, suitable for the back of a border. The leaves have a strong flavor, resembling celery and yeast, and are used in soups, stocks, and stews; add the raw young leaves to salads. The aromatic seeds are used in baking and vegetable dishes, and the young stalks may be crystallized. Blanch plants under pots in spring for use as a vegetable.
Harvesting and storing Pick young leaves in spring and freeze or dry. Gather young spring stalks for crystallizing. Cut blanched stalks in spring, after they have been under pots for two to three weeks, leaving central shoots to grow.
Propagation By seed sown as soon as ripe in late summer (see p.160) or by division in spring or fall (p.162).

Lemon balm

(*Melissa officinalis*)

Hardy, clump-forming perennial with oval, toothed leaves. Add the lemon-scented leaves to cold drinks and to sweet and savory dishes, or infuse them to make a refreshing herb tea.
Harvesting and storing Pick leaves before flowering for using fresh or for drying.
Propagation By seed sown in spring (see p.160) or division in spring or fall (p.162).
Variants Yellow-variegated cultivars, such as 'Aurea', are available; grow them in partial shade to avoid leaf scorch.

Mint

(*Mentha spicata*)

Hardy, herbaceous perennial with tiny mauve flowers in summer. May be invasive (see p.294). Use the leaves to make mint sauce, in salads and drinks, and with potatoes or peas.
Harvesting and storing Pick leaves before flowering and dry or freeze, or chop and infuse in vinegar.
Propagation By stem tip cuttings rooted in spring or summer (see p.164), or by division in spring or fall (p.162).
Related species The numerous species and cultivars have slightly differing foliage and scents. Some, such as pineapple mint (*M. suaveolens* 'Variegata'), have variegated leaves. Peppermint (*M.* x *piperita*) has purplish green leaves used in peppermint tea and in syrups, candy, and desserts, while eau-de-cologne mint (*M.* x *piperita* 'Citrata') has purple-flushed foliage and a perfume. Bowles' mint (*M.* x *villosa* 'Alopecuroides') has rounded leaves with a fresh spearmint aroma and purplish pink flowers.

Bee balm

(*Monarda didyma*)

Hardy, herbaceous perennial with heads of red claw-shaped flowers in summer. An excellent border plant for moist soil. Infuse the aromatic leaves in tea for an "Earl Grey" flavor, and add them to summer drinks, salads, pork dishes, or potpourri. Use the flowers to add color to salads and potpourri.
Harvesting and storing Pick leaves in spring or just before flowering in summer for using fresh or for drying. Gather flowers in summer.
Propagation By seed in spring (see p.160), stem cuttings in summer (p.164), or division in early spring (p.162).
Related species and variants Cultivars with red, pink, white, or purple flowers are available. *M. fistulosa* has lavender flowers.

Sweet cicely

(*Myrrhis odorata*)

Hardy, herbaceous perennial with flat heads of tiny white flowers in summer. The fernlike leaves, which have an aniseed flavor, are used mainly in fruit dishes to reduce acidity but may also be added to salads. The thick taproot can be eaten raw or cooked as a vegetable. The large seeds are added to fruit dishes.
Harvesting and storing Pick leaves in spring and early summer for drying. Collect unripe seeds in summer and dry or pickle them. Dig up roots in fall for using fresh.
Propagation By seed sown outdoors in fall (see p.161). Self-sows readily.

Basil

(*Ocimum basilicum*)

Annual with toothed, pointed-oval leaves. In cold regions, basil must be grown under cover or in a warm position. Grows well in pots on a sunny windowsill. The highly aromatic leaves are used in salads, vinegars, pesto, and pasta dishes.
Harvesting and storing Pick leaves when young in summer and freeze, dry, or use to flavor herb oil or vinegar. Pack leaves in jars of oil to preserve them.
Propagation By seed sown in warmth in late spring (see p.177).
Related species and variants 'Purpurascens' is an attractive, purple-leaved cultivar with pink flowers. The compact bush basil (*O. b.* var. *minimum*) is hardier but has less flavor.

Marjoram

(*Origanum vulgare*)

Hardy, herbaceous perennial with tiny white or mauve flowers in summer. Needs warmth and full sun for its flavor to develop. The aromatic leaves are used widely in cooking, especially in pizzas and pasta sauces.
Harvesting and storing Pick leaves for immediate use or for drying or freezing, just before flowers open.
Propagation By seed sown in spring (see p.160), division in spring or fall (p.162), or by basal stem or root cuttings of nonflowering shoots in summer (pp.164–5).
Variants The various species and hybrids differ in hardiness, flavor, and flower and foliage color. Golden marjoram (*O. v.* 'Aureum') is one well-known cultivar. The low-growing 'Compactum' is ideal for containers and edging.

Parsley

(*Petroselinum crispum*)

Hardy biennial with bright green, crinkled leaves and, in its second summer, flat heads of tiny, greenish yellow flowers. Good for growing in pots. Use the leaves whole or chopped as a garnish and in *bouquet garni*, sauces, and egg and fish dishes.
Harvesting and storing Pick leaves of plants in their first year and use fresh or freeze.
Propagation By seed sown at intervals from early spring to late summer (see p.176).
Variants *P. c.* 'Neapolitanum' is a flat-leaved parsley with a stronger flavor.

Aniseed

(*Pimpinella anisum*)

Half-hardy annual with deeply divided leaves and, in late summer, heads of tiny white flowers. In cold regions, it must have a sunny, sheltered position for the seed to ripen. Add the leaves to fruit salads. The aromatic seeds are used in baking, confectionery, and sweet and savory dishes.
Harvesting and storing Pick lower leaves in spring for immediate use. Collect seedheads as they ripen in fall.
Propagation By seed sown in late spring in its final position because it is difficult to transplant successfully (see p.177).

Rosemary

(*Rosmarinus officinalis*)

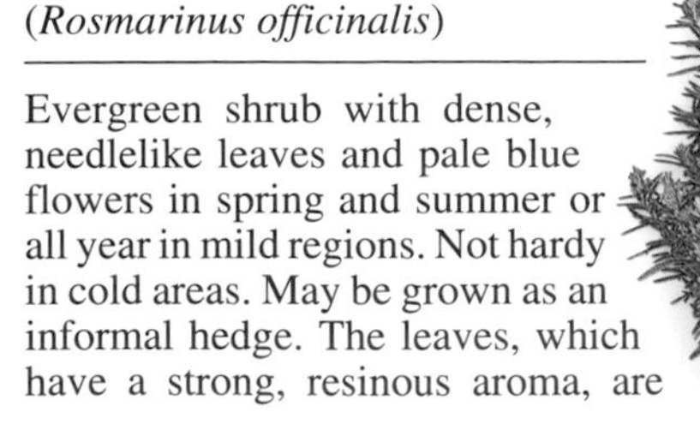

Evergreen shrub with dense, needlelike leaves and pale blue flowers in spring and summer or all year in mild regions. Not hardy in cold areas. May be grown as an informal hedge. The leaves, which have a strong, resinous aroma, are

used in meat dishes, especially with lamb, and to make potpourri and hair rinses. The flowers may be added to salads.
Harvesting and storing Pick leaves and flowers as required for immediate use. Gather sprigs during the growing season for drying.
Propagation By seed sown in warmth in spring (see p.84), semiripe cuttings in late summer (p.82), or layering in fall (p.86).
Variants Cultivars with flowers in shades of blue, pink, and white are available. The erect cultivar 'Miss Jessopp's Upright' is suitable for hedging. 'Severn Sea' has bright blue flowers and a dwarf, arching habit ideal for containers. 'Arp' is hardiest and has paler leaves.

Sorrel
(*Rumex acetosa*)

Hardy, upright perennial with docklike leaves. Remove the flower spikes to prolong leaf production. Protect with cloches for a winter supply. The young, tender leaves, which have a sour taste, are used in salads, soups, and sauces.
Harvesting and storing Pick young leaves before flowering for using fresh or freezing. Frozen leaves can be used in cooked dishes.
Propagation By division in either spring or fall (see p.162), or by seed sown in spring (p.160).
Related species The low-growing species, French, shield, or buckler-leaf sorrel (*R. scutatus*), has small, fine-flavored leaves.

Rue
(*Ruta graveolens*)

Evergreen subshrub with divided, gray-green foliage and greenish yellow flowers in summer. Hardy to about 0°F (-18°C). Handling rue on sunny days may cause a skin rash. Use the pungent leaves with a light hand in salads and sauces, and to flavor cream cheese.
Harvesting and storing Pick leaves as required for immediate use, protecting hands with rubber gloves on sunny days.
Propagation By seed sown in spring (see p.84), or cuttings of semiripe side shoots in late summer (p.82).
Variants There are cultivars that have cream-variegated and blue leaves, for example 'Variegata' and the compact 'Jackman's Blue'.

Sage
(*Salvia officinalis*)

Evergreen subshrub with gray-green foliage and purplish blue flowers. Hardy to -15°F (-27°C). An excellent plant for shrub borders and rose gardens. The aromatic leaves are used in poultry stuffings, rich meat dishes, and herb teas, and to flavor cheese.
Harvesting and storing Pick leaves as needed to use fresh. Gather leaves before the flowers open for drying.
Propagation By seed sown in spring (see p.84), softwood cuttings in summer (p.81), or semiripe heel cuttings in early fall (p.83).
Variants Cultivars include purple sage (*S. o.* 'Purpurascens') with purple leaves, 'Tricolor' with white-streaked, pink-flushed leaves, and 'Albiflora' with white flowers.

Lavender cotton
(*Santolina chamaecyparissus*)

Evergreen subshrub with narrow, divided, silver-gray leaves on upright stems. In summer, it bears masses of yellow button flowerheads. Hardy to 0°F (-18°C). It is good as a low hedge, especially to provide a contrasting color in knot gardens (see p.31). Add the aromatic leaves to potpourri and dry flowers for decoration.
Harvesting and storing Pick leaves for drying in spring and summer. In summer, gather flowers as they open for drying.
Propagation By cuttings of semiripe side shoots in late summer (see p.82).
Variants 'Lemon Queen' has bright green foliage and cream flowers; 'Nana' is a dwarf form, only 6in (15cm) tall, *S. virens* has green leaves.

Winter savory
(*Satureja montana*)

Hardy, evergreen subshrub with tiny, white to pink flowers in summer, and small, narrow, aromatic leaves. Use the leaves in bean and cheese dishes.
Harvesting and storing Pick any time for using fresh. When flower buds appear, gather leaves to dry or freeze.
Propagation By seed sown in spring (see p.84), division in spring or fall (p.88), or by softwood cuttings taken between late spring and early summer (p.81).
Related species Creeping savory (*S. spicigera*) is a low species ideal for containers, edging, and rock gardens. Summer savory (*S. hortensis*) has lilac flowers and a fine flavor.

Bible leaf
(*Tanacetum balsamita*)

Hardy perennial with small, daisylike flowers in late summer and oval gray-green leaves. The leaves have a citrus-mint fragrance; use them sparingly in cooking and also in potpourri.
Harvesting and storing Gather leaves in spring and summer for using fresh or for drying.
Propagation By division (see p.162).

Feverfew
(*Tanacetum parthenium*, syn. *Chrysanthemum parthenium*)

Hardy, semievergreen perennial with light green, chrysanthemum-like leaves; in summer and fall it is covered with long-lasting, daisylike flowers. An easy-to-grow, attractive plant for borders and containers. Use the pungent leaves in sachets to deter clothes moths. The aromatic flowers are added to potpourri.
Harvesting and storing Pick leaves and flowers in summer for drying.
Propagation By seed sown in spring or fall (see p.160), division in fall (p.162), or basal stem cuttings in summer (p.164). Self-sows freely.
Variants Cultivars vary in height and foliage, with single or double flowers. The golden-leaved 'Aureum' is highly recommended.

Thyme
(*Thymus vulgaris*)

Hardy, evergreen, low-growing subshrub with tiny leaves and, in summer, pale lilac flowers. May be grown as an edging for borders, between paving stones, and in containers. Add the aromatic leaves to *bouquet garni*, stuffings, sauces, soups, stocks, and meat dishes.
Harvesting and storing Pick leaves at any time to use fresh. Gather flowering tops for drying, stripping leaves and flowers from the stalks when quite dry. Fresh sprigs may also be infused in oil or vinegar.
Propagation By seed (see p.84) or division in spring (p.88), layering in spring or fall (p.86), or by semiripe heel cuttings in late spring or early summer (p.83).
Related species and variants The many species and cultivars vary in height, foliage, and flower color. Wild thyme (*T. serpyllum*) is a low, mat-forming plant with mauve flowers. *T. praecox* var. *arcticus* 'Coccineus' and 'Snowdrift' have, respectively, magenta and white flowers, and 'Doone Valley' has scented foliage with gold markings. *T.* x *citriodorus* has lemon-scented leaves and lilac flowers. *T. vulgaris* 'Silver Posie' has silver-margined leaves.

Ginger
(*Zingiber officinale*)

Tender, deciduous perennial with tall, canelike stems and lance-shaped leaves. The thick, tuberous rhizome is highly aromatic and is used in baking, preserves, confectionery, chutneys, sauces, and many oriental dishes.
Harvesting and storing Dig up young rhizomes and peel them for using fresh or preserving in syrup. For drying, dig up the rhizomes as the leaves turn yellow.
Propagation By division of rhizomes as they start to sprout (see p.163).

Soil preparation and planting

THE ideal site for an herb garden is sunny and open but sheltered, with neutral to alkaline soil, and good drainage. These growing conditions suit the majority of common herbs such as lavender (*Lavandula angustifolia*), winter savory (*Satureja montana*), sage (*Salvia officinalis*), marjoram (*Origanum vulgare*), rosemary (*Rosmarinus officinalis*), and thyme (*Thymus vulgaris*), most of which are Mediterranean in origin.

Preparing the site

If possible, prepare the ground well in advance, preferably in fall. First, remove all weeds, taking care to eliminate any persistent perennial weeds such as quackgrass (*Elymus repens*), using a weedkiller if necessary. Then dig over the soil, leaving it in a rough state over the winter to be broken down by frost.

In early spring, remove any weeds that have appeared, fork in well-rotted organic matter (such as garden or mushroom compost), and rake the soil to a fine, level tilth. The objective is to provide a free-draining and reasonably fertile soil. Feeding with manure or inorganic fertilizers is not recommended, especially for Mediterranean herbs, since it produces soft growth that has little aroma or resistance to cold.

On heavy clay soil, it may be necessary to improve the drainage (see SOILS AND FERTILIZERS, "Improving drainage," p.531); alternatively, the herbs may be grown in raised beds or containers. Most herbs tolerate a slightly acid soil; if the pH is below 6.5, however, add a dressing of lime when preparing the soil (see SOILS AND FERTILIZERS, "Liming," p.533).

Planting invasive herbs

If planting invasive herbs such as mints (*Mentha*), tansy (*Tanacetum vulgare*), or woodruff (*Asperula odorata*, syn. *Galium odoratum*) in open ground, restrict their spread by growing them in sunken containers. Old buckets, large pots, or even heavy-duty plastic bags are suitable, although it is usually necessary to make drainage holes. For best results, lift and divide the plants each spring and replant young, vigorous pieces in the containers using fresh soil mix; if not replenished, nutrients are quickly depleted and the herbs may deteriorate and become more prone to disease, such as rusts (see p.554).

1 *Dig a hole large enough to accommodate a large pot or old bucket. Make drainage holes in the pot, then place it in the hole and fill with a soil and compost mixture.*

2 *Plant the herb (here mint), firming in well; add enough soil mix to conceal the pot's rim, and water thoroughly. Each spring, replant and replace the soil mix in the pot.*

Herbs in winter

Although herbs are harvested mainly in spring and summer, the availability of many can be extended almost all year.

Sown in late summer or early fall, a number of herbs such as chervil (*Anthriscus cerefolium*), coriander (*Coriandrum sativum*), and parsley (*Petroselinum crispum*) continue to grow throughout the winter if they are protected from severe cold by cloches or a cold frame. They also grow well in pots placed on a sunny windowsill.

Herbaceous perennials that die down in winter, such as chives (*Allium schoenoprasum*), French tarragon (*Artemisia dracunculus*), and mints (*Mentha*), may be forced for winter use. In early fall, dig up mature plants, divide them, and replant in containers of soil-based potting mix. If kept in a bright place that is free from frost and drafts, they produce fresh shoots throughout the winter that may be harvested regularly. Discard forced plants in spring or plant them out; if planted out, do not pick their leaves for at least a season to allow them time to recover vigor.

Evergreen herbs, such as winter savory, thyme, and rosemary, may be gathered throughout the year, but limit winter harvesting to reduce stress to the plants.

Planting container-grown herbs

Container-grown herbs may be planted throughout the year, but the best time is in spring when they establish rapidly. If they have been kept in a heated greenhouse during the winter, gradually harden them off in a cold frame before planting them out.

Water well before planting, because dry root balls are difficult to wet once below ground. To avoid trampling and compacting the soil in a bed, it is best to stand on a board in order to reach the planting positions. Set out the herbs (still in their pots) according to your planting plan and check that each has sufficient room to develop, depending on its growth rate and spread.

Whatever the weather, water thoroughly after planting in order to settle the soil around the plants and provide even moisture for new root growth. After planting, pinch out the tips of clump-forming herbs and trim back shrubby herbs to encourage new side shoots and to develop a bushy habit.

HOW TO GROW HERBS FOR FRESH WINTER USE

1 *Choose a dry, preferably overcast, day in early fall to lift a clump of herbs (here chives) from the garden using a fork.*

2 *Divide the clump into smaller pieces with your hands or a hand fork. Shake loose as much of the soil as possible from the roots.*

3 *Plant up the divided pieces into pots or trays of soil mix. Water well and cut back the top-growth.*

4 *Place the plants in a bright, frost-free place. Once they are about 4in (10cm) high, harvest the leaves regularly to maintain a supply of new growth.*

Planting an herb garden to a design

Whether creating an intricate, formal design or a simple, informal one, plan carefully, both on paper and on site, to ensure success. Make plans well in advance: start in the winter for planting in the spring, or as early as the preceding summer if you are raising the plants yourself.

As for all planting, thoroughly prepare the ground, clearing any weeds and raking the surface of the soil to a fine tilth (see "Preparing the site," opposite).

Once you have determined the design and the planting plan on paper, mark the basic outline of the herb garden, including any paths, on the prepared site. Make any adjustments to the layout at this stage if required. Container-grown herbs are convenient because they can easily be set out according to the plan and the arrangement checked before actual planting begins.

If using sod or heavy materials such as paving, bricks, or stone, lay them before planting. Paths made of lighter, loose materials, such as grit, gravel, or shredded bark, may be laid before or after planting. When making paths of grit or gravel, provide retaining boards or edging tiles to prevent the paving material from spreading onto the plants in the beds.

1 *On ground prepared for planting, mark out the herb garden according to the planned design, including any paths or paved areas. Use stakes and string, or grit. Remove the string after planting.*

2 *Lay out the plants, still in their pots, to check the overall look and spacing. If using grit or gravel for the paths, sink boards at the edges to keep the material in place.*

3 *Once the design is completed, plant and water the herbs. Planting them densely achieves the desired result more quickly.*

4 *Lay the paths, adding grit or gravel evenly in between the boards; level the surface.*

5 *Keep the herb garden watered and weeded. Pinch out growing tips to promote bushy growth and prune as necessary.*

DESIGN FOR AN HERB GARDEN

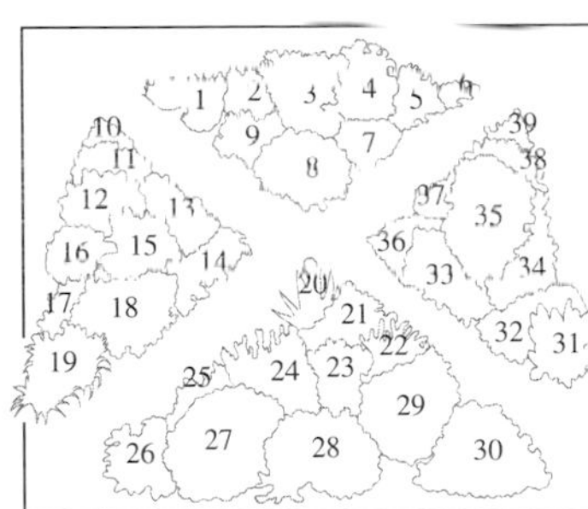

1 Chives (*Allium schoenoprasum*)
2 Compact marjoram (*Origanum vulgare* 'Compactum')
3 Bee balm (*Monarda didyma*)
4 Wormwood (*Artemisia absinthium*)
5 Hyssop (*Hyssopus officinalis*)
6 Wild thyme (*Thymus serpyllum*)
7 Silver-variegated thyme (*Thymus vulgaris* 'Silver Posie')
8 Marjoram (*Origanum vulgare*)
9 Pineapple mint (*Mentha suaveolens* 'Variegata')
10 Chamomile (*Chamaemelum nobile*)
11 French sorrel (*Rumex scutatus*)
12 French tarragon (*Artemisia dracunculus*)
13 Yellow-variegated sage (*Salvia officinalis* 'Icterina')
14 Parsley (*Petroselinum crispum*)
15 Sweet cicely (*Myrrhis odorata*)
16 Lavender cotton (*Santolina chamaecyparissus*)
17 Creeping savory (*Satureja spicigera*)
18 Golden lemon balm (*Melissa officinalis* 'Aurea')
19 Chinese chives (*Allium tuberosum*)
20 Orris (*Iris* 'Florentina')
21 Borage (*Borago officinalis*)
22 Pink hyssop (*Hyssopus officinalis* 'Rosea')
23 Purple sage (*Salvia officinalis* 'Purpurascens')
24 Pink lavender (*Lavandula angustifolia* 'Rosea')
25 Thyme (*Thymus vulgaris*)
26 Dark-leaved basil (*Ocimum basilicum* 'Purpurascens')
27 Rosemary (*Rosmarinus officinalis*)
28 Summer savory (*Satureja hortensis*)
29 Southernwood (*Artemisia abrotanum*)
30 Sweet marjoram (*Origanum majorana*)
31 Bible leaf (*Tanacetum balsamita*)
32 Golden feverfew (*Tanacetum parthenium* 'Aureum')
33 Chervil (*Anthriscus cerefolium*)
34 Pot marigold (*Calendula officinalis*)
35 Bronze fennel (*Foeniculum vulgare* 'Purpureum')
36 Woodruff (*Asperula odorata*)
37 Lavender cotton (*Santolina chamaecyparissus* 'Lemon Queen')
38 Sorrel (*Rumex acetosa*)
39 Lemon thyme (*Thymus* x *citriodorus*)

This small garden includes a wide range of aromatic and culinary herbs; they have been grouped in beds of restricted color and divided by symmetrical paths for a traditional, formal design, softened by the informal plant groupings within the beds.

Routine care

Most herbs flourish and require little attention once established. Maintenance largely consists of cutting back plants in spring and summer to encourage healthy growth, and tidying up dormant plants in winter. Herbs in containers usually need routine watering and feeding during the growing season, while periodic repotting or top-dressing is also necessary. Growing herbs in the right conditions should minimize any pest or disease problems; take action as necessary (see PLANT PROBLEMS, pp. 547–79) but then wait one or two weeks after treatment before using the herbs.

Cutting back

Herbs that are valued for their fresh, young foliage may be cut back to produce a regular supply of leaves. Remove flowering stems of sorrel (*Rumex acetosa*) as they appear. Chives (*Allium schoenoprasum*) and marjoram (*Origanum vulgare*) may be left until after flowering because the flowers are attractive and useful as flavorings. Variegated forms of marjoram, mint (*Mentha*), and lemon balm (*Melissa officinalis*) fade, but they produce bright new foliage if the plant is cut back hard shortly before flowering.

The growth of invasive herbs should be checked regularly. Even when planted in sunken containers, they produce surface runners which must be removed before they spread too far. Remove any reverted, plain shoots from variegated herbs as soon as they appear.

Pruning Lavender

1 *In late summer or early fall, cut off all the dry flower stalks with pruning shears and lightly clip the shrubs to maintain a neat, tighter finish.*

2 *Early the following spring, cut back shoots by 1in (2.5cm) or more of the previous year's growth, making sure that some green growth remains.*

Deadheading and pruning

Unless planning to save the seed, remove the dead flowerheads from most herbs so that energy is channeled into growth. Deadheading annuals such as borage (*Borago officinalis*) lengthens the flowering season. Certain herbs such as angelica (*Angelica archangelica*) self-sow prolifically; these may become a nuisance if they are left to set seed.

Deadhead and prune shrubby herbs such as lavender (*Lavandula*) and thyme (*Thymus*) by trimming lightly with shears after flowering. Hard pruning in spring encourages side shoots and new growth from the base; thyme, however, is best pruned lightly but often during the growing season.

Mulching

Mulch only established herbs that thrive in moist soil, such as mint and bee balm (*Monarda didyma*). In summer, mulch after rain to retain moisture and to enrich the soil as it breaks down into humus. Use an inorganic mulch such as grit around Mediterranean or gray-leaved plants in heavy soil to reduce the risk of rotting.

Fall cleanup

The extent to which herbs are cut back in fall partly depends on personal preference. In cold areas, leaving the dead foliage of herbaceous perennials until spring helps to protect them against cold and wind. Remove any dead leaves that have fallen on thyme and other low-growing, evergreen herbs because they may encourage fungal attack.

Winter protection

In cold weather, tender herbs should either be brought under cover or otherwise protected (see COLD AND WIND PROTECTION, pp.520–21). In spring, cut them back and plant them out again, or propagate new plants from cuttings. The hardiness of a number of herbs such as sage (*Salvia officinalis*) and lavender varies according to the species or cultivar; check this when buying.

Replanting a Strawberry Jar

1 *Each spring, replace or divide and replant the herbs in a strawberry jar if they have outgrown the pot or need rejuvenating.*

2 *First lift the plants from the top, then dig out the soil mix, carefully removing the plants from the pockets. Tip out any remaining soil mix. Replace the drainage material.*

3 *Add fresh soil mix up to the level of the lowest pockets. Divide or replace the old plants. Place each plant at the inside of a pocket, then gently pull the foliage through the hole.*

4 *Pack soil mix around the roots and up to the next level, firming well after each addition. Water thoroughly.*

Herbs in containers

Most herbs are easy to grow in containers and require little maintenance. They are, however, more prone to drying out than plants in the open ground, so in hot weather, check soil moisture daily and water thoroughly when dry. During the growing season, feed the herbs every two weeks with a liquid fertilizer.

During cold periods, bring herbs in containers under cover in good light. Frostproof pots may be left outdoors, but insulate them by burying them to their rims in the ground.

Repotting

Inspect herbs periodically to check that they are not becoming potbound. Look out for such signs as roots protruding through the base of the pot, rapid drying out, pale foliage, and weak new growth. Repot during the growing season to encourage new root growth.

If repotting is impractical, renew the top 1–2in (2.5–5cm) of soil mix, incorporating well-rotted organic matter or a slow-release fertilizer. It will then be unnecessary to feed the herbs for about a month.

Propagation

HERBS may be propagated by a wide variety of methods, depending on the type of plant and the quantity of new plants required. Sowing seed is a simple, inexpensive way to raise a large number of plants and is necessary for annuals and biennials, although it may also be used for other plant groups. Cuttings are used to propagate various perennials as well as shrubs and trees, while division is suitable for a number of perennials, and layering is a good method for some shrubby herbs. For further information on propagating individual species and cultivars, see "Directory of common herbs," pp.290–93.

Raising new plants from seed

Most herbs are easy to grow from seed; they may be sown in containers or, where large quantities are required, in drills in the open ground. Seed may also be sown directly into the cracks between paving stones where it would be difficult to insert plants. Prepare a finely raked seedbed for any seedlings that you intend to transplant outside from containers. Spring is generally the best time for sowing seed, although some annual herbs may also be sown in early fall.

Annuals and biennials

Hardy annuals such as pot marigolds (*Calendula officinalis*) and borage (*Borago officinalis*) may be sown in the spring or – to provide flowers late in the next spring – in fall. Sow biennials such as caraway (*Carum carvi*) and angelica (*Angelica archangelica*) outdoors in late summer or early fall for flowering the following summer. Thin out the seedlings twice: once after germination so that two or three remain at each position, and again after a few weeks so that only the strongest is left in place.

Short-lived herbs that are used regularly in large quantities, such as parsley (*Petroselinum crispum*), coriander (*Coriandrum sativum*), and chervil (*Anthriscus cerefolium*), may be sown at intervals of three to four weeks from early spring to early fall. This provides a succession of foliage for harvesting throughout the year, although in some areas it may be necessary to provide protection from cold with cloches. Annual herbs of the carrot family (Umbelliferae) – chervil and dill (*Anethum graveolens*), for example – are difficult to transplant successfully and are best sown directly in their final positions.

Basil (*Ocimum basilicum*) is one of the more difficult herbs to grow from seed unless kept warm and moist. In cold areas, sow basil seed very thinly indoors in pots or trays in late spring, and keep it at a minimum temperature of 70°F (21°C). Prick out the seedlings once they are large enough to handle, and keep them in a sunny, well-ventilated place. In cold, damp conditions, basil seedlings are prone to damping off (p.570) and gray mold/*Botrytis* (p.559). Plant them out once all danger of frost is past or grow them in containers under cover. In warm climates, basil may be sown directly outdoors (see ANNUALS AND BIENNIALS, "Sowing in open ground," p.177).

Perennials

If raising perennial herbs from seed, sow the seed in warmth in spring and grow on the seedlings in pots until they are large enough to be hardened off and planted out. Plant and care for them as for container-grown herbs (see p.294).

Most cultivars of perennial herbs do not come true from seed, however, and must be propagated by either cuttings or layering. An exception to this is variegated rue (*Ruta graveolens* 'Variegata'). Nonflowering forms, such as lawn chamomile (*Chamaemelum nobile* 'Treneague'), cannot be raised from seed; new plants should be propagated by cuttings or division.

SOWING BASIL SEED IN CONTAINERS

1 *Tap seeds from a fold of paper onto firmed soil mix. Lightly cover with sieved soil mix and keep moist at a minimum temperature of 70°F (21°C).*

2 *Once the seedlings are large enough to handle, carefully lift them with a widger, holding them by the leaves, not by the stems, to prevent damage.*

3 *Prick out seedlings singly into cell packs of firmed soil mix, then keep moist in a sunny, well-ventilated place. Plant them out after frost danger or grow them in containers under cover.*

Mound layering

This method is particularly suitable for propagating shrubs such as sage (*Salvia officinalis*), rosemary (*Rosmarinus officinalis*), lavender (*Lavandula*), and thyme (*Thymus*) that tend to become woody at the base or center with little or no new growth. In spring, mound free-draining soil over the base of the plant, leaving just the top exposed. This stimulates new shoots to develop roots in a manner similar to stooling (see ORNAMENTAL SHRUBS, p.87). Leave the soil in place, replenishing it if it is washed away by heavy rain, until new roots have been established in late summer or fall. Then cut off the shoots from the parent plant and pot them up or plant them out.

MOUND LAYERING SHRUBBY HERBS

1 *To stimulate rooting, mound 3–5in (7–12cm) of sandy soil over the crown of the plant (here thyme) so that just the tips of the shoots are visible.*

2 *Once the layered stems have established new roots, remove them with a knife or pruning shears. Pot up the rooted layers individually or plant them out.*

HERBS THAT MAY BE PROPAGATED BY MOUND LAYERING

Hyssop (*Hyssopus officinalis*)
Lavender (*Lavandula angustifolia, L. stoechas*)
Lavender cotton (*Santolina chamaecyparissus, S.virens, S.rosmarinifolia*)
Rosemary (*Rosmarinus officinalis*)
Sage (*Salvia lavandulifolia, S. officinalis*)
Salvia officinalis
Southernwood (*Artemisia abrotanum*)
Thyme (*Thymus cilicicus, T.* x *citriodorus* and cvs, *T. vulgaris* and woody cvs)
Winter savory (*Satureja montana*)
Wormwood (*Artemisia absinthium*)

Harvesting and preserving

THE flavor of herbs varies according to the growing conditions, the season, and the time of day. Because the level of essential oils fluctuates with light and temperature, it is important to harvest herbs at the right time to ensure that they are at their peak. There are various methods of preserving herbs so that their scents and flavors may be enjoyed all year. For advice on specific herbs, see the "Directory of common herbs," pp.290–93.

Harvesting

Herbs should be harvested on a warm, dry day after the dew has dried but before the plants are exposed to hot sunshine, which evaporates the essential oils. Always try to harvest herbs in a way that helps to maintain the plant's shape and vigor: choose straggly or invasive shoots, and with clump-forming herbs such as chives (*Allium schoenoprasum*) and parsley (*Petroselinum crispum*) pick the outer leaves to encourage new growth in the center. Use only foliage free from damage and insects.

Leaves and shoots may be picked at any time during the growing season but are at their best before flowering. Evergreen herbs may be harvested in winter but this should be limited. Handle aromatic leaves gently: bruising releases the essential oils. Use or preserve herbs as soon as possible after harvesting.

Collecting flowers, seed, and roots

When harvesting flowers, pick them on a warm, dry day, when they are fully opened. Collect seed in summer or early fall by cutting off whole seedheads as they turn brown but before they are completely ripe and starting to shed. Roots may be lifted at any time of year, but the flavor is best in fall.

PRESERVING HERBS BY AIR-DRYING

1 *Pick healthy, unblemished shoots or leaves (here sage) on a dry morning, before the heat of the day releases the herb's essential oils.*

2 *Tie the shoots into bundles, then hang them upside down in a warm place. Once dry, strip the leaves from the stalks and store them in dark glass jars.*

Preserving

The main methods of preserving herbs are drying and freezing. In addition, a number of herbs are suitable for flavoring vinegars, oils, or jellies, and a few may be crystallized (candied) for decorating cakes and desserts. Store dried herbs in dark glass or ceramic containers, because exposure to light speeds the deterioration of their aromas.

Air-drying

Do not wash herbs because this may encourage molds to develop. Dry herbs by hanging them upside down in a warm, dry place away from direct light. Alternatively, place leaves, flowerheads, or petals in a single layer on a rack covered with muslin, netting, or paper towels. Leave them in a warm, dark, well-ventilated place until crisp.

Microwave drying

For microwave drying, wash the herbs, pat them dry, then place in a single layer on paper towels. Microwave them for two to three minutes, checking every 30 seconds and rearranging if necessary to ensure even drying. Cool, then crumble and store as for air-dried herbs.

Drying seedheads

Cut seedheads in summer or early fall as they turn brown, then place them in a paper bag or hang them upside down and cover them with muslin to hold the seeds as they fall. Keep them in a warm, dry place to ripen; remove the seeds when dry and store them in jars or bags. Seed to be used for sowing should be kept in a cool, dry, frost-free place.

FREEZING HERBS IN ICE CUBES

Freeze borage flowers and mint leaves singly in ice-cube trays for adding to drinks. Chop fresh herbs such as parsley or chives and place in ice-cube trays, adding about 1tbsp of water to each 1tbsp of herb.

Drying roots

Most roots are best used fresh, but some may be dried and ground. First wash the roots thoroughly, then peel, chop, or slice them, before spreading them out on absorbent paper. Dry them in either a cool oven or at 122–40°F (50–60°C) in a dehydrator until brittle, then crush or grind them before storing.

Freezing

Many soft-leaved herbs such as parsley and basil retain their color and flavor better when frozen than when dried. Pack whole sprigs into labeled plastic bags and freeze them; they crumble easily for use once frozen. For long-term storage, blanch them before freezing by dipping them first in boiling water, then in ice water. Pat dry and freeze.

DRYING SEEDHEADS

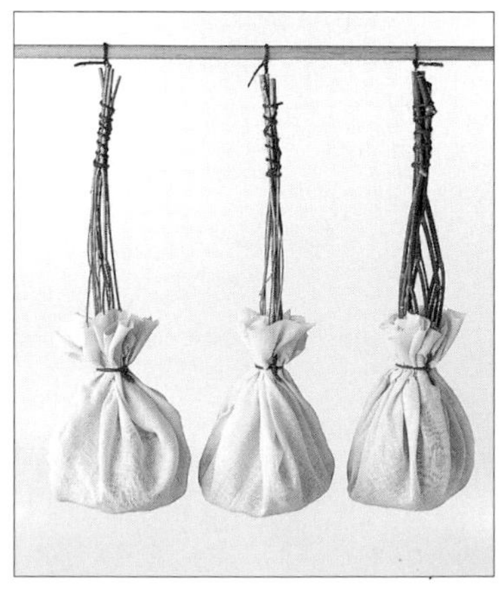

Cover the seedheads with muslin or a paper bag, secured in place with string or a rubber band, then hang them upside down in a warm place until dry.

Freezing in ice

Herbs may be frozen in water to form ice cubes. This is a good way of preserving borage flowers and mint leaves to use as a decorative addition to drinks, and the ice also protects the herbs from damage during storage. Herbs for cooking should be chopped before freezing because this is difficult to do once they have thawed. Place the ice cubes in a sieve and drain the water before use.

Making herb oils and vinegars

Many herbs, such as French tarragon, thyme, oregano, and lavender, may have their flavors preserved by being steeped in oil or vinegar.

To make flavored oil, loosely fill a clear glass jar with the fresh herb, add a flavorless oil such as safflower, and seal. For a sweet oil such as lavender, use almond oil as the base instead. Leave the jar in a sunny spot for two weeks, shaking or stirring daily. (For a stronger flavor, replace the herbs and repeat the process.) Strain and bottle, adding a fresh sprig of the herb for identification. Basil leaves may be preserved by being packed in oil; the leaves themselves may be used in pasta sauces and other cooked dishes and the oil in salad dressings.

Herb vinegars are made in a similar way, using wine or cider vinegar, but the herbs should be lightly crushed before steeping. Warm the vinegar, pour it over the herbs, and proceed as above.

14

The Vegetable Garden

More and more people are discovering the deep satisfaction of growing their own vegetables. They do so for many reasons: for some gardeners it is the joy of a freshness and flavor rarely to be found in store-bought produce, while for others it is a chance to grow exotic crops or some of the more unusual varieties that they cannot otherwise obtain. Another motive, for those who favor organic methods, is the knowledge that their produce is untainted with potentially harmful chemicals. Then again, there are gardeners who find a well-tended vegetable patch, with its variety of leaf color and texture, just as beautiful as a herbaceous border. Modern science and methods of cultivation, coupled with the outstanding vigor and resistance to disease of many of today's cultivars, enable even newcomers to vegetable growing to experience the considerable pleasure and satisfaction of bringing to the table fine vegetables that they have sown, tended, and harvested in their own gardens.

Designing a vegetable garden

A healthy, productive area for growing vegetables may be created in a garden of any size, from a large, sunny patch to the smallest townhouse garden. The vegetables may be grown in a separate plot or integrated with flowerbeds.

Good growing conditions are essential if vegetables of quality are to be produced. Virtually any site can, however, be made suitable, perhaps by erecting windbreaks if it is exposed, or taking the necessary steps to improve soil fertility and drainage. This cannot be done overnight, but within a year or two very satisfactory results may be obtained.

Choosing the site

Most vegetables lead short but pampered lives, so the ideal situation for a vegetable garden provides warmth, sunlight, shelter, and fertile, well-drained, loamy soil with an adequate water supply. The chosen site should be open but not exposed, and not overshadowed: trees cast shade, drip on plants, and remove nutrients and moisture from the soil, and buildings may create shade and tunnel damaging winds across the plot.

Shelter from wind

Providing shelter from wind is one of the most important factors in vegetable growing. Wherever possible,

A Well-designed Garden
This thriving vegetable garden is both well designed and properly maintained, with an open, but not exposed, site. The beds all contain different crops, and a network of paths allows easy access to each bed.

THE IDEAL VEGETABLE GARDEN

This vegetable garden is shown in midsummer. The east and west boundaries are marked by sturdy screens of windbreak netting to shelter the garden. To the north is a brick wall with a warm, south-facing border at its base. This is used for sun-loving crops such as tomatoes and zucchini. The south is marked by rows of Jerusalem artichokes, which act as a hedge or windbreak during the summer and fall.

The four main beds are laid out on the narrow bed system; they are 4ft (1.2m) wide so that the center of each bed is easily reached from the surrounding paths. Each is planted with vegetables from one of the four main rotation groups. From mature spring cabbages to arugula seedlings, the beds are planned to provide a succession of crops. At the southern end of the garden, the beds are permanently planted with perennial vegetables such as rhubarb and asparagus.

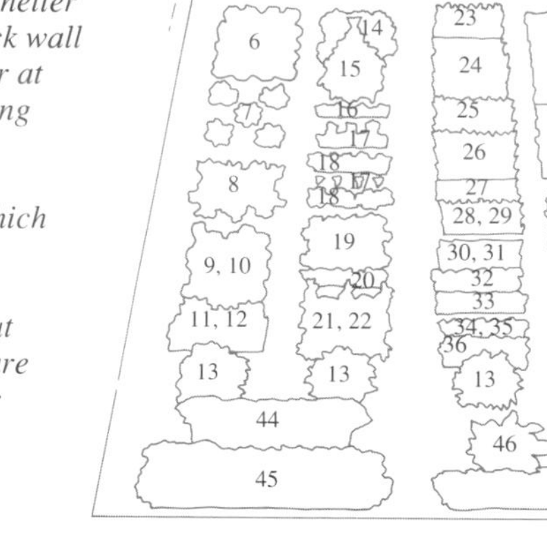

1 Zucchini
2 Cucumbers
3 Staked tomatoes
4 Bush tomatoes
5 Sweet peppers
6 Spring cabbages
7 Summer cauliflowers
8 Broccoli
9 Brussels sprouts
10 Lettuces (as a main crop)
11 Sprouting broccoli
12 Corn salad
13 Globe artichokes
14 Broad beans
15 Scarlet runner beans
16 Dwarf scarlet runner beans
17 Swiss chard
18 Peas
19 Dwarf snap beans
20 Beets
21 Sweet corn
22 Mizuna greens
23 Garlic
24 Bulb onions (fall-planted)
25 Shallots
26 Bulb onions (spring-planted)
27 Scallions
28 Leeks (for fall harvesting)
29 Summer purslane
30 Leeks (for winter harvesting)
31 Miner's lettuce
32 Endive (curly type)
33 Arugula (salad rocket)
34 Bok choi
35 Salad Bowl lettuces
36 Spinach
37 Potatoes (early)
38 Potatoes (maincrop)
39 Parsnips
40 Radishes
41 Carrots
42 Self-blanching celery
43 Celeriac
44 Asparagus
45 Jerusalem artichokes
46 Rhubarb

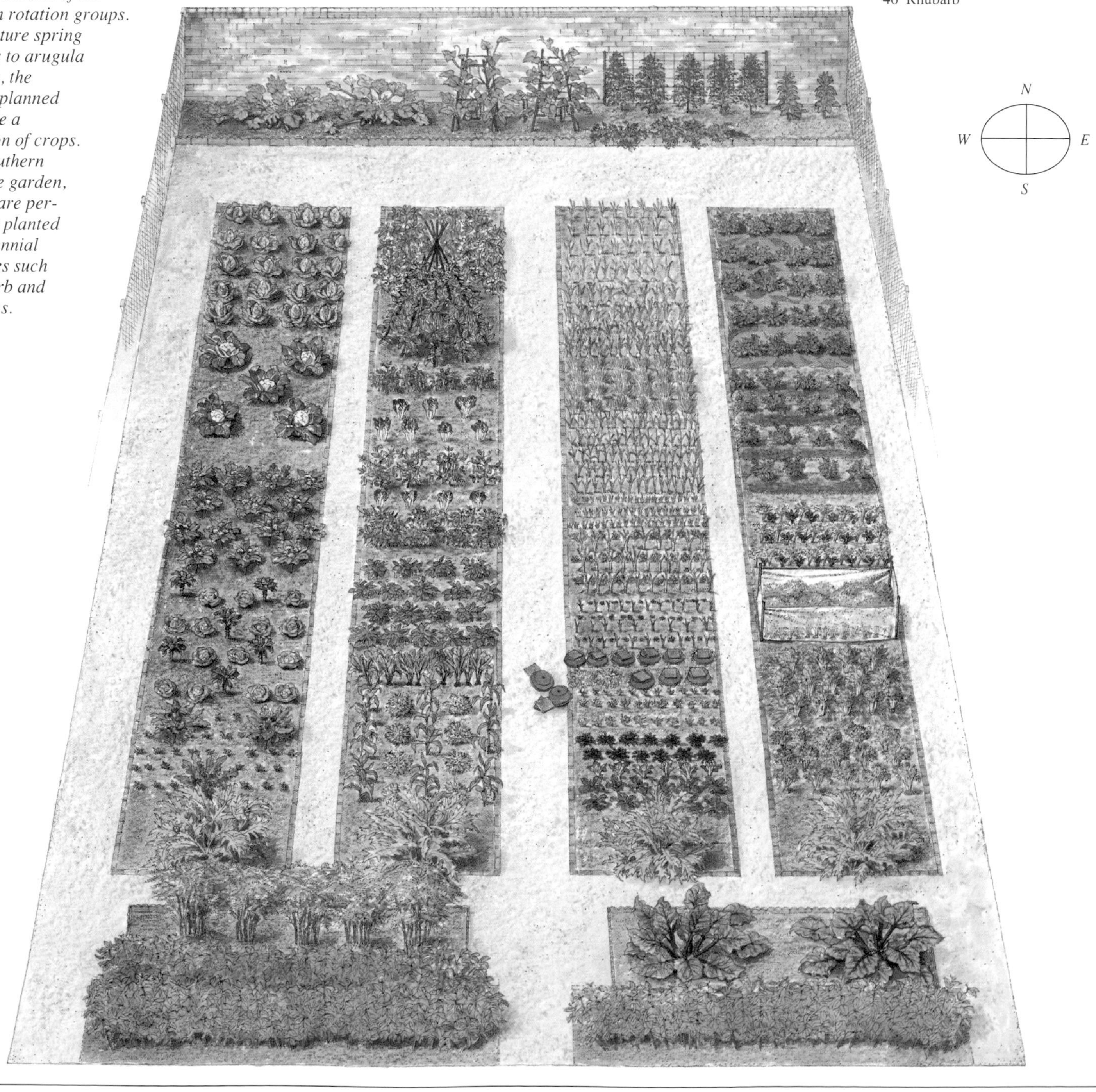

N
W
E
S

avoid windy sites: even light winds may decrease vegetable yields by 20–30 percent, and strong winds are often devastating. Vegetables in coastal gardens may be damaged by desiccating, windborne salt spray.

Windbreaks

In gardens exposed to wind, windbreaks should be erected. They should be about 50 percent permeable, allowing the wind to filter through, rather than being solid structures that force the wind over them and create an area of turbulence on the other side (see also COLD AND WIND PROTECTION, pp.520–21, and CLIMATE AND THE GARDEN, "Wind," p.518).

Effective windbreaks may be either a living barrier, such as a hedge, or a structure, such as a fence or a screen of windbreak netting. Hedges are attractive but take time to become established, require maintenance, take up considerable space, and compete for soil, water, and plant nutrients; they are therefore only appropriate in quite large gardens. For further information, see HEDGES AND SCREENS, pp.58–60. A windbreak of trees should be considered only in a very large garden. In smaller gardens, fences, lattice, or windbreak netting fastened to posts or stakes is more practical.

A windbreak gives shelter for a distance roughly five times its height. A very exposed garden may need a windbreak approximately 6ft (2m) high. In this case, nets and posts must be strong, since they will be subjected to great strain in high winds. Lower, short-term windbreaks can be erected between rows of plants or beds; netting windbreaks no more than 18in (45cm) high and 10–13ft (3–4m) apart, attached to stakes, are very useful.

If gaps in buildings or trees create a wind tunnel across the garden, erect a barrier extending 3ft (1m) beyond the gap in each direction. Deciduous shrubs or a hedge may be planted in the gap, with an artificial windbreak to shelter the plants until they are established.

Slopes

A sloping site is less easy to work than a flat one. Soil erosion after heavy rain may be a problem on steep slopes; setting the beds across the slope may help. A site on a south-facing slope is an advantage in cool-temperate climates because it warms up rapidly in spring. In hot climates, site beds on a north-facing slope because here they will have relief from intense sun.

Positioning

The orientation of vegetable beds often makes little difference to open-ground crops, although greenhouses and frames must be oriented correctly to maximize their efficiency. Position tall crops, such as climbing beans, carefully: in temperate climates, place them where they will not shield dwarf-sized plants from the sun, and in hotter climates use them to provide some shade.

Sites below garden walls

In temperate and northern climates, the ground at the foot of a south-facing garden wall is a warm, sheltered place that is useful for growing early spring and late fall crops and, in summer, tender, sun-loving crops such as tomatoes and eggplants. Keep these beds fertile and well watered so that the soil does not dry out. North-facing walls may be used to provide some shade for plants such as lettuces and peas that suffer in high temperatures.

ALLOCATING SPACE
Each element in this garden has been sited to produce optimum growing conditions for the crops. The greenhouse and frame are positioned to receive maximum light, the hedge filters the prevailing wind, and tall plants, such as the scarlet runner beans, do not overshadow the smaller vegetables.

Maintaining soil fertility

A friable loam is ideal for growing vegetables: it is rich in plant nutrients and supports a population of earthworms and microorganisms to break down organic matter. It has a good structure, and remains workable even in adverse conditions: it does not become sticky during wet weather or dusty in dry periods, but always retains a crumbly texture, so that the soil is well aerated. This is important for both the organisms living in the soil and the roots of the vegetables themselves. An ideal soil is both well drained and moisture-retentive, and should be slightly acid (pH 6–6.5). In such a soil, most vegetables grow well and need little extra feeding.

Soil types

Vegetables may be grown successfully on a range of different soil types. At one extreme are the porous, sandy soils, which warm up quickly in spring and are ideal for early crops. Nutrients are washed out rapidly from these soils, however, and crops that are planted in them often need extra feeding.

At the other extreme are heavy clays. Naturally sticky and cold (and sometimes waterlogged), clay soils warm up slowly in spring but are rich in nutrients, and, once their structure has been improved by incorporating organic matter (and if necessary, drainage), they are fertile and retain moisture well. Heavy feeders such as the cabbage family grow well on clay soils. For further information, see "Soil and its structure," pp.524–5.

In practice, most soils are a mixture of different types, and although few of us start with perfect soil, it can usually be improved by working in organic matter regularly.

Using organic matter

Crops continuously remove nutrients from the soil and from naturally

ALTERNATING ROWS
Provided that the fertility of the soil is maintained, rows of vegetables may be arranged to maximize yields by alternating rows of fast- and slow-growing crops (here different types of lettuce and a range of brassicas). The fast-growing lettuces will have been harvested by the time the brassicas have reached maturity.

decomposing organic matter. In almost all soils, fertility must be maintained by replenishing the supplies of organic matter. The main forms available to gardeners are animal manures (preferably with a high straw content but little sawdust or wood shavings), spent mushroom compost, seaweed, or compost.

A layer of organic matter 3–4in (8–10cm) deep, applied over most of the ground each year, should maintain structure and fertility. It may be spread on the surface or dug into the soil. If organic matter is spread on the soil surface in the fall, it may be left for the worms to work in. This is particularly beneficial on light soils where heavy winter rainfall can cause nutrients to be washed out. Any organic matter remaining on the surface in spring should be forked in. Well-rotted organic matter is a useful mulch and can be used at any point in the growing season.

In the fall, dig organic matter into heavy soils and into light soils that freeze solid in the winter, spreading it evenly throughout the soil as deeply as possible (see also "Mulching," p.308).

VEGETABLES IN ROUND BEDS
In addition to providing easy access to the vegetables grown, round beds may be used as part of the design of a garden or as a link between ornamentals and vegetables. Here, rhubarb is surrounded by chicory, which may be substituted by other annual crops in subsequent plantings.

Green manuring

This is the practice of growing crops specifically to dig into the soil to improve its fertility. In the vegetable garden a green manure may be grown and dug in between crops, or over the winter to augment plant nutrients and avoid leaving the soil bare (see SOILS AND FERTILIZERS, "Green manures," p.533).

Drainage

Good drainage is essential; where there is a serious problem, it may be necessary to lay tile drains (see SOILS AND FERTILIZERS, "Improving drainage," p.531). In most cases, working in organic matter improves drainage markedly, since this will encourage earthworms, which improve the soil structure by forming a network of drainage channels.

A PATCHWORK OF CROPS
Square beds with soil paths between them provide a neat framework for manageable rows of vegetables. A plot laid out like this allows a variety of crops to be grown, and is designed for a simple method of crop rotation.

Preserving soil structure

Good soil structure is easily destroyed by physically damaging the soil, for example by walking on it or cultivating it when it is either very wet or very dry, or from heavy rain beating down on the surface. Laying out the garden in narrow beds (see "The bed system," right) to minimize the need to tread on the soil, and keeping the surface continuously mulched (see "Mulching," p.308) will help to preserve the soil structure.

Planning the vegetable garden

The layout of a vegetable garden is determined by the size, shape, and nature of the garden and the demands of the household. The quantity and choice of vegetables to be cultivated depends on the aims of the gardener. These may be to attain self-sufficiency; to produce gourmet vegetables and well-flavored, unusual cultivars that are unavailable locally; to grow produce for the freezer; or to save money.

The following are a few guidelines that give an indication of the main factors to be considered.

A place for perennials

Most vegetables are grown as annuals on a different piece of ground each year. The few perennial vegetables, such as rhubarb, asparagus, and globe artichokes, should be grouped in a permanent bed at one side or end of the garden, separated from the annual vegetables. If there is space, they may be intercropped with fast-growing vegetables.

Vegetables in containers

Gardeners who are limited to terraces, concrete yards, patios, roofs, or balconies often grow vegetables in containers to provide an attractive and productive display. Although vegetables are more difficult than flowers to grow successfully in containers, they are still worth the effort involved. Place containers on paths and low walls to make the best use of the space available, and plant them up with dwarf and decorative cultivars. Suitable containers include terracotta pots and tubs, as well as commercial brands of grow bag filled with soil mix.

Growing vegetables in rows

A traditional vegetable garden consists of a number of rectangular plots each several yards wide, in which vegetables are grown in widely spaced rows. This method allows easy access between individual rows.

The bed system

Although the traditional layout of vegetable plots is still used, the modern trend is to grow vegetables in smaller, narrower beds, with the plants evenly spaced in all directions. This is known as the bed system. In practice, the beds may be of any shape or size: square, round, or even crescent-shaped, as long as the center of the bed is reached easily from the path, so that all sowing, planting, routine care, and harvesting can be done without walking on the soil. The paths between the beds may be of soil, grass, concrete, bark, stones, brick, sawdust, or any other suitable material.

The main benefit of growing vegetables in narrow beds is that the soil structure is preserved by using the access paths between the beds rather than walking on them. Also, organic matter and manure are concentrated on areas where the crops grow, rather than being wasted on pathways and working areas where they are not used by the plants.

High yields may be obtained from narrow beds by growing plants in patches at equidistant spacing, which makes the best use of available space and minimizes competition between plants. Uniform spacing also helps to suppress weed germination by allowing fully grown broad-leaved vegetables to make a canopy over the soil.

A place for herbs

For practical purposes, it is best to grow herbs as near the kitchen as possible, and within easy access of paths. Compact herbs such as chives, marjoram, and parsley make neat, attractive edgings to vegetable beds; the larger perennials such as mint, sage, and rosemary are often best grown in a separate bed. For further information, see The Herb Garden, "Where to grow herbs," p.288.

Vegetables in flowerbeds

Because many gardens are no longer spacious enough to allow a complete area to be devoted to vegetables, there has been a move toward integrating vegetables into flowerbeds or, alternatively, planting them in groups of beds designed in an attractive pattern. Wherever possible, vegetable cultivars are selected for their decorative qualities, and then grouped to display them attractively.

This approach is known as "edible landscaping" in North America and "potager gardening" in Europe. There is enormous scope for gardeners to develop their own ideas. The only requirement for growing vegetables in flowerbeds is ensuring that the soil fertility is maintained at the level necessary for the chosen vegetables.

Climatic factors

Most vegetables grow only when the average daytime temperature rises above about 43°F (6°C) between spring and fall. The number of growing days with suitable daytime temperatures that occur between these seasons is governed by factors such as latitude, altitude, and degree of exposure, and largely determines what may be grown outdoors in any locality.

Temperature requirements

Vegetables are sometimes classified as warm- or cool-season crops, depending on their physiological needs, particularly those relating to temperature. Most brassicas and several bulb and stem vegetables cannot withstand intense heat, whereas more tender vegetables such as tomatoes are damaged or killed by freezing temperatures. Cultivars of some vegetables have been bred to resist cold, and the growing season of many vegetables may be extended by growing them under cover (see p.311). See individual vegetables for specific requirements.

A Productive Display
This example of edible landscaping groups a squash climbing a supporting arch with a profusion of yellow and red nasturtiums beneath. All thrive in warm, sunny conditions.

Combining Vegetables and Herbs
This informal garden has vegetables intermingled with herbs. Scarlet runner beans climb up an arch, parsley and chives ring red and green Salad Bowl lettuces in the center bed, and sweet corn develops among feathery dill.

Daylength

The number of daylight hours, or daylength, differs according to the latitude and season, and vegetable cultivars have a varying response to daylength at different stages of growth. Short-day plants grow and seed only if the daylength is less than 12 hours; long-day plants only if it is more than 12 hours.

This affects the sowing time, particularly of crops that are grown for their seeds, such as beans; others must be harvested before flowering. Onions, for example, are naturally long-day plants: when the daylength is 16 hours or more, onions stop making leafy growth and start to develop a bulb. The more leafy growth that has been made up to this point, the larger the bulb that forms. Onion seeds should therefore be sown early in the year so that the plant will develop as much leafy growth as possible before the daylength increases.

Cultivars are available that have been adapted to long or short days or that are daylength neutral. Examples are mentioned under individual vegetables later in the chapter; the safest course is to choose cultivars recommended for your area.

Rotation

Rotation is a system by which vegetable crops are grown on different areas of the plot in succession in consecutive years.

Advantages of rotation

The principal reason for rotating crops is to prevent a buildup of soil-borne pests and diseases specific to one group of crops. If the same type

Vegetables in a Windowbox
Vegetables can thrive in small containers such as this windowbox. Here shallow-rooted lettuces, young cabbages, tomatoes, and strawberries have been chosen not only for their culinary uses, but also for their decorative qualities.

of host crop is grown every year in the same soil, its pests and diseases increase rapidly in number and often become a serious problem, whereas in the absence of their host they gradually die out. Various types of potato and tomato nematode, clubroot (which attacks almost all brassicas) and onion white rot are some of the common garden problems that may be alleviated by rotating crops.

Other benefits stem from rotating vegetables. Some crops, for example potatoes, blanket the soil so well that they smother most weeds, so it is useful to follow them with crops that are difficult to weed, such as onions. Most vegetables in the legume family, including peas and beans, fix nitrogen in the soil by means of nodules on their roots and make it available for the next crop. Therefore nitrogen-hungry crops such as leafy brassicas, potatoes, or spinach should follow legumes.

Several vegetables, including perennial types and many salad plants, do not fall into a principal rotation group. Salad plants stay in the ground for a short time and are therefore useful for intercropping or to fill temporary gaps in vegetable beds. As with the other vegetables, they should not be grown in the same patch of ground year after year. Perennial vegetables are best grown in a permanent bed of their own and so are not rotated. For the most important vegetable groups, see *Rotation of Vegetable Crops*, right.

Drawbacks of rotation

A weak point in the rotation theory is that, to be completely effective, rotation should take place over a longer time scale than the usual three or four years: clubroot and white rot infections can stay in the soil for up to 20 years. Rotations on that scale are out of the question in small gardens. Another shortcoming is that, in practice, the distance between beds is often so small that soilborne pests and diseases can easily spread from one to the next.

Planning for rotation

Despite the disadvantages, rotation is a sensible practice, and gardeners should try to build it into their garden plans, taking care at least to follow a crop of one vegetable type with a vegetable from another group.

Draw up a list of the main vegetables that you want to grow, with a rough indication of the quantities required. Growing vegetables that are climatically unsuited to the area is usually unsatisfactory, particularly in small gardens. List the various beds in the vegetable garden. Group the selected vegetables in their rotation groups (e.g. all legumes and pod crops, or all brassicas), with a miscellaneous category for vegetables not in the main groups (see *Rotation of Vegetable Crops*, right).

Month-by-month planning

Make a chart with a column for each month of the year, and for every vegetable on your list fill in the months during which it will be in the ground. Remember that this period may be shortened by raising plants in containers (see "Sowing indoors," p.307) for transplanting later, and lengthened by the use of some form of cover early and late in the season (see "Growing under cover," p.311). Some crops, such as parsnips and cabbages, are sown once a year; but with others, such as lettuces and radishes, repeat sowings may provide a continuous supply during the growing season.

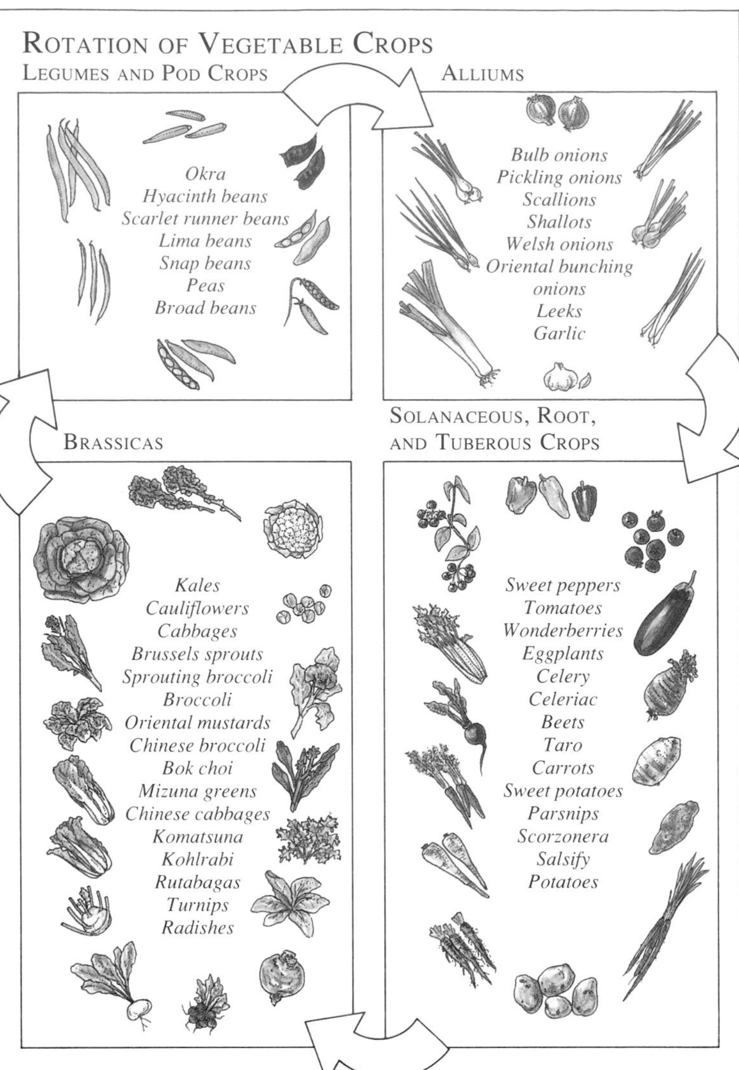

Vegetables are divided into four groups. Sweet corn and summer and winter squash, however, do not fit into the major vegetable groups, but still need rotating. If you are growing only a small amount of these, it may be possible to include them in one of the groups (e.g. Alliums). Otherwise, treat them as a separate group and rotate them on a five-year basis.

Planning a layout

Allocate each bed (or several beds if needed) to a different rotation group of vegetables, and write in the most important crop that each bed will grow. Refer to your month-by-month chart, and indicate a suitable crop to precede or follow it. For example, if Brussels sprouts are cleared in mid-spring, they may be followed by carrots, lettuces, or peas. Except where winters are harsh, assume that most pieces of ground will bear two crops a year. Use this basic plan to rotate crops in subsequent years.

Consider the overall plan as a rough guide only. Many factors, in particular the weather, have a direct bearing on the success and failure of crops. The key to success lies as much in flexibility as in strict adherence to the plan. Keeping detailed records of your planting is an invaluable guide to improving performance in future seasons.

INTERCROPPING
Lettuces and sweet corn planted together mature at varying rates. The fast-growing lettuces are ready to harvest before the sweet corn is fully grown.

Intercropping

For maximum yield over a given area, crops of vegetables may be combined in a single bed. A fast-growing crop, such as radishes, is planted at the same time as a slow-growing crop, such as parsnips. A checkerboard pattern gives maximum efficiency, but alternate rows also work well. Fast growers make almost immediate use of the available space, but they reach maturity before the slow-growing crops need the room. Make sure that the short-term crop is not shaded by more slowly maturing vegetables.

Sowing and planting

THE most common method of raising vegetables is from seed. There are several methods for sowing outdoors or under cover; use the most suitable for the chosen cultivar and the space available. Care in the early stages ensures healthier, more productive crops. Thin or transplant seedlings to their final position in the garden, greenhouse, or container before they become overcrowded.

Choosing seed

In the past, seed was sold only as ordinary, "naked" seed, but it is now also available prepared in a variety of ways to make sowing and germination easier.

Purchasing seed

Always buy good-quality seed, preferably vacuum-packed to preserve viability. Many of the best cultivars are F1 hybrids, bred by crossing two selected parents. Although expensive, they are very vigorous and productive. Vegetable seeds differ widely in their viability: to be safe, buy seed dated for the current year, or test a sample before sowing (see "Pregerminating seed," below).

Prepared seed

Pelleted seeds are individually coated with clay to form tiny balls that are easier to sow evenly than naked seed. This is useful for handling particularly fine seeds such as those of carrots. Pelleted seeds should be carefully placed in a drill one by one, which saves transplanting later. They are sown in the normal way, but the clay coating must be kept moist until after germination.

Seed is also available embedded, evenly spaced, in paper sheets or tapes, which disintegrate in the soil after sowing. The tapes are laid in a drill and covered with soil as for ordinary seed. The backing gives protection in the early stages of germination and reduces thinning.

Pregerminating seed

To start ordinary seed early, it may be pregerminated indoors. This is useful for seed that germinates slowly in cold soil and may rot before germination. Space seeds on damp paper towels and put them in a warm place. Keep them moist until germination, then sow them carefully in containers or in open ground. This method may also be used to test a sample of old seed for viability before sowing.

Storing seed

Packets often contain more seed than is required for the current season. If stored incorrectly, seed will lose its viability quite quickly. To save seed with the least loss of viability, fold over the packet and seal it with tape. Put all the packets in a food-storage container with a tight-fitting lid. Before sealing the container, add a stay-dry package (such as those that come with electronic equipment) to absorb moisture. Store the container in the coldest part of the refrigerator. Most vegetable seeds can be frozen without any harm.

Sowing outdoors

Vegetables are sown either *in situ*, where they grow to maturity, or in a seedbed from which they are transplanted to their permanent position. *In situ* sowing is used for crops that are harvested young, such as scallions and radishes, or vegetables that do not transplant well, such as carrots and parsnips. Most other vegetables may be sown in a seedbed, in rows up to 6in (15cm) apart.

Successful sowing outdoors requires warm, well-prepared soil. Germination occurs for most vegetables once temperatures are over 45°F (7°C), so do not sow seed in cold soil. In several cases, lettuces for example, germination is poor at high temperatures. Particular temperature requirements for germination are given under individual vegetables. Soil temperature may be measured with a soil thermometer, but most gardeners use their own knowledge of the soil to assess if it is warm enough for germination to occur.

Preparing the ground

Before sowing, dig the soil, then rake the surface until it has a fine texture or tilth, removing stones and large clods. Rake when it is neither very wet and heavy nor very dry. If soil sticks to your shoes, delay until it has dried out a little, but not so much that it is dusty.

If sowing in wet soil, standing on a board prevents damaging the structure of adjacent soil. This is not necessary with the bed system (see p.302) since the seed may be sown from the surrounding path.

Guidelines for sowing

Seeds are sown at different depths according to their size. Unless otherwise directed, sow small seed such as onions about 1/2in (1cm) deep, brassicas 3/4in (2cm) deep, peas and sweet corn about 1in (2.5cm) deep, and beans up to 2in (5cm) deep. The most important requirement is to sow thinly so that seedlings are not crowded in the early stages. Various methods of sowing are described below; whichever is used, it is vital to preserve surface moisture. In dry weather, cover the soil after sowing with plastic sheeting or newspaper. Remove any covering when the first seedlings appear.

Sowing in a drill

This is the most common method of sowing vegetables. Mark a row with a string line and make a small, even channel (a drill) in the soil to the required depth. Take pinches of seed to scatter along the drill. Either space the seeds evenly, or station sow at intervals in groups of three or four seeds to be thinned later to one seedling per station. If the seed is sown *in situ*, space the stations half the required distance between the mature plants to allow for losses; stations may be closer if seedlings are to be transplanted. Consider station sowing fast-growing crops such as radishes between slow-growing crops such as parsnips: the radishes are pulled up before the intervening space is needed by the parsnips. After sowing, cover the seed with soil, drawing it back lightly with a hoe or rake, firm the area gently, and water with a fine spray from a hose or watering can.

If sowing in unavoidably wet conditions, line the drill before sowing with dry, light material such as sand or vermiculite. If conditions are very dry, water the drill before sowing, lightly press each seed into the soil,

SOWING IN A DRILL

1 *Mark out the drill using pegs and string. Use the corner of a hoe or a trowel to make the drill, ensuring that it is the depth required for the seed.*

2 *Sprinkle the seeds thinly and evenly along the drill. Stand on a board placed parallel to the drill to prevent compaction of adjacent soil. Cover the seeds without dislodging them.*

ALTERNATIVE METHODS

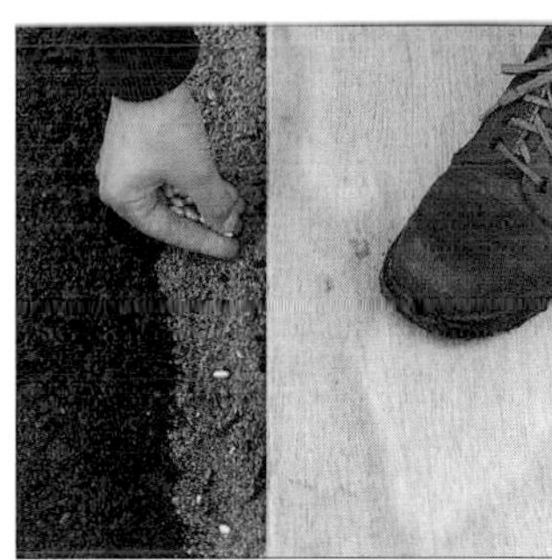

WET CONDITIONS
If the soil drains slowly or is very heavy, sprinkle a layer of sand at the base of the drill, sow the seed, then cover it.

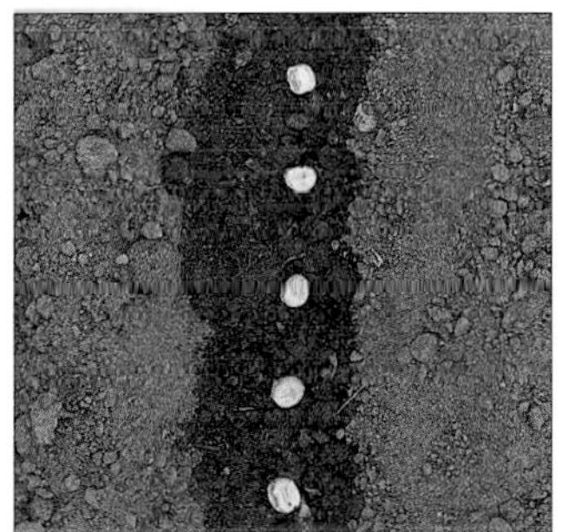

DRY CONDITIONS
When the soil is very dry, water the base of the drill, then sow the seeds and lightly press them in before covering with dry soil.

SOWING IN A WIDE DRILL

1 *Use a draw hoe to mark out parallel drills 6–9in (15–23cm) wide and flat at the base.*

2 *Sow seeds the required distance apart in the drill.*

3 *Cover the seeds with soil using the hoe. Take care not to dislodge them.*

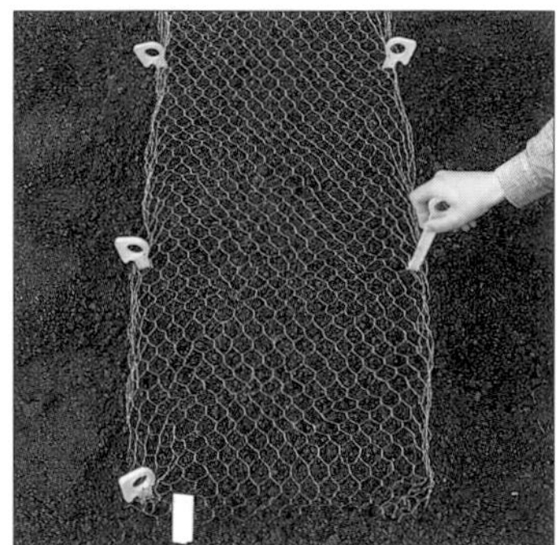

4 *Protect seeds from birds or animals by pegging wire netting over the drill.*

then cover them with dry soil. This slows down the rate of evaporation and helps the seeds to stay moist until they germinate.

Wide drills
Use wide, flat drills for plants that are grown closely together, such as peas, early carrots, and seedling crops. Make each drill up to 9in (23cm) wide and to the required depth. Space the seeds evenly in the drill, and cover carefully.

Large seed
The seed of beans and squash may be sown individually by placing a seed in a hole made by a small dibber or a finger. Make sure that each seed is at the base of the hole and in contact with the soil. Sowings of tender plants such as melons may be covered with glass jars or cut-off plastic bottles, which are removed once the seedlings emerge.

Broadcasting seed
In this method, the soil is first raked to produce a fine tilth; the seed is then scattered as evenly as possible, either by hand or from a packet. Rake the soil lightly again afterward to cover the seed.

Cut-and-come-again seedling crops
Many leafy or salad vegetables may be sown for harvesting at the seedling stage when they are at their most nutritious. Once cut, they often resprout to produce a second and third crop. This method is a very productive way to make use of a small area, and such crops are ideal for sowing under or between slower-maturing vegetables.

To obtain seedling crops, sow seed either broadcast or in wide drills or rows about 3in (8cm) apart; seedlings do not need thinning and are often ready for their first cut in a few weeks.

Successional crops
Vegetables that grow fast but rapidly pass their prime or run to seed (lettuces, for example) should be sown little and often. To avoid both gluts or gaps in cropping, wait until one sowing has emerged before making the next.

Thinning

Young seedlings need to be thinned to prevent overcrowding. Thin to the final spacing in stages, rather than immediately, to allow for any loss from pests and diseases; at each stage, aim to leave a seedling just clear of its neighbors. If the seeds have been sown *in situ*, continue to thin until they are at the spacing required for mature plants. Very small seedlings should be thinned by nipping them off just above ground level to avoid disturbing the roots of adjacent plants. Clear thinnings away since their scent may attract pests. Seedlings of plants such as lettuces, cabbages, and onions may be lifted for transplanting, and the soil gently refirmed around the remaining seedlings.

Planting

Plant or transplant vegetables when they are as young as possible so that they can grow without further check. Exceptions to this are plants raised in cell packs or containers (see opposite). Do not transplant root vegetables once the taproot has started to form since this may distort it.

BROADCASTING

1 *Prepare the area to be sown by raking carefully in one direction to produce a fine tilth. Sprinkle the seed thinly and evenly over the surface.*

2 *Rake lightly at right angles to the original direction to cover the seed, then water thoroughly with a fine spray from a hose or can.*

THINNING SEEDLINGS

To thin small seedlings, nip them out at ground level so that the roots of the remaining seedlings are not disturbed.

Before taking plants from a seedbed, water around their roots; if the ground into which they are being planted is dry, water it lightly. Pick up a plant by a leaf rather than the stem or roots, which are easily damaged. Make a hole slightly bigger than the roots and position the plant in the hole, replacing the soil so that the lower leaves are just above soil level. Firm around the stem to anchor the plant. In hot weather, water seedlings,

TRANSPLANTING SEEDLINGS

Lift seedlings gently, keeping as much soil around the roots as possible. While moving them, place the seedlings in a clear plastic bag to retain moisture.

PLANTING DEPTH

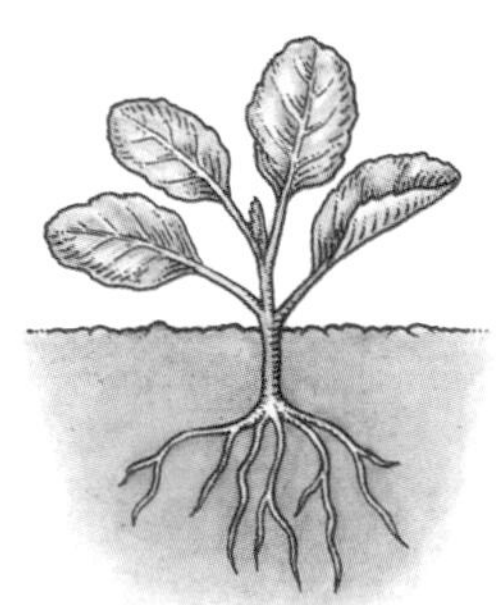

Plant vegetable seedlings so that their lowest leaves are just above soil level. Planting too high exposes the stalk, which may not support the weight of the mature vegetable.

and then shade them with fine-mesh netting or newspaper cones until they are established. Keep the soil moist for a few days after planting (see "Critical watering periods," p.308).

Spacing
Different vegetables have individual spacing requirements, which sometimes determine their final size. Traditionally, vegetables are grown in rows with a recommended spacing between the plants, as well as between the rows.

They may alternatively be grown with equidistant spacing between the plants – the average of the recommended spacing between plants and rows; so plants 6in (15cm) apart, in rows 12in (30cm) apart, may alternatively be grown 9in (23cm) apart each way. This method probably gives the best results: plants have an equal share of light, air, moisture, and soil nutrients, and as they mature they form a canopy over the soil, which suppresses weeds (see also "The bed system," p.302). Vegetables may also be grown close together within widely spaced rows.

Sowing indoors

Vegetable seed may be sown indoors, in a cool greenhouse, or on a windowsill. This is helpful in climates with cool or short summers, for tender vegetables, and for those that need a long growing season. It is also a way of producing healthy seedlings and overcoming problems with germination, since the temperature is more easily controlled.

After germination, keep most seedlings at a lower temperature in a spacious, light, protected environment until they are planted out. Where this is not possible, it may be practical to buy more mature plants.

Seed trays
Sow seed in a small pan or seed tray, in standard seed soil mix (for details see Annuals and Biennials, "Sowing in pots or trays," p.178). When the seedlings have two or three small leaves, prick them out into a seed tray of potting mix, spaced 1–2in (2.5–5cm) apart. Seedlings usually need to be kept slightly warm. Put them in a well-lit, draft-free place to grow quickly and evenly. Transfer larger plants to individual pots before planting them out.

Cell packs and small containers
Cell packs are individual units in which seeds are sown and plants grown for planting out directly. This produces plants of high quality that grow on well: seedlings have no competition and so develop a healthy root ball, which is hardly disturbed when planted out in their final position. They do, however, need more space and soil mix in the early stages than those that are planted in trays.

Many sizes of cell are available, all designed to fit into a standard tray. Small containers include clay or plastic pots, degradable pots, and soil blocks made of compressed soil mix. The soil mix may be enclosed in netting, which roots can easily penetrate as they grow.

Sow two or three seeds per unit; then thin the seedlings to leave the strongest. In some cases, such as onions and leeks, several seeds are sown and grown together, planted out as a unit at a wider spacing than usual, and grown on to maturity.

Hardening off
Plants raised indoors must be acclimatized to lower temperatures and wind before being planted in the open. Harden off by placing seedlings outdoors for increasing lengths of time. Eventually leave them out overnight against a wall, and then plant out.

Sowing and Transplanting

1 Fill the cell pack with seed soil mix and make a hole 1/4in (5mm) deep in each section. Sow 1 or 2 seeds per section. Cover with soil mix, then water.

2 Remove each plant from the cell pack. Make a hole to take its root ball. Place the plant in the hole with its lower leaves just above the surface; firm and water.

Vegetative propagation

A few vegetables are usually raised vegetatively from offsets, tubers, corms, bulbs, or cuttings. This may be because they rarely set seed or, if raised from seed, are variable, or because vegetative propagation is faster. Details are given under individual vegetables (pp.313–54).

Growing vegetables in containers

Containers are useful for growing vegetables where space is limited, or to extend the vegetable garden into a paved area. They are used in the greenhouse, especially if the soil is infected with soilborne diseases and it is impractical to sterilize or replace it. Vegetables need richer growing medium and more consistent and thorough watering than flowers and so are hard to grow well in containers unless they are carefully maintained.

Choosing the vegetables
The best vegetables for containers are compact, quick-maturing plants, such as lettuces, radishes, and beets, or robust, undemanding, leafy vegetables, such as Swiss chard; fruiting vegetables, such as peppers, eggplants, and tomatoes, also flourish. Fast-maturing seedling crops also grow well. Dwarf cultivars are excellent since they do not need support. Do not use vegetables that are deep-rooting, slow to mature, or very tall or large, such as brassicas, parsnips, or celery. Raise plants for containers in cell packs; sow cut-and-come-again seedling crops in the container.

Preparing the container
The larger the container, and the greater its volume of soil or soilless mix, the better. Large vegetables that are gross feeders, such as potatoes and tomatoes, generally need a container at least 10in (25cm) deep and wide. For large or top-heavy vegetables, the container must be strong and stable.

Good drainage is essential. If there are no drainage holes, make several of at least 1/2in (1cm) diameter in the base; cover them with crocks to prevent blockage. For grow bags, follow the maker's instructions; drainage holes are not usually made since they would allow infection to enter when laid on diseased soil.

The soil or soilless mix must be light and well aerated, since frequent watering will compact it. Lighten garden soil with well-rotted compost mixed with coarse sand and sphagnum moss.

In hot and windy weather, containers dry out rapidly by evaporation through the top and, if not made of plastic, the sides. To minimize this, do not put them in exposed sites or at the foot of a hot wall. Line nonplastic containers with plastic sheeting perforated with drainage holes.

Dwarf broad beans

Fast-maturing, compact lettuces

Stable plastic container to retain moisture

Peas supported by peasticks (bushy twigs)

Routine cultivation

THE best vegetables are produced when the plants are maintained in the optimum conditions for growth. Keep them free from weeds, and water them thoroughly as required. Mulches may be used to retain moisture and to suppress weeds. The level of nutrients needs to be maintained as the crop grows.

Watering

Most vegetables need reasonably moist soil; they vary, however, in the amount of water they require as well as when they most need it (see "Critical watering periods," below). Overwatering may lead to loss of flavor in tomatoes and carrots, and, in root crops, to the development of leaves at the expense of root.

How to water

It is more efficient to water heavily and occasionally rather than frequently and lightly; very young plants, however, should be watered lightly and frequently so that they never dry out. Light watering evaporates rapidly without reaching the plants' roots, and encourages shallow surface rooting rather than the deep rooting that enables plants to withstand drought. Direct the water at the base of each plant. Water in the evening when less moisture will evaporate, and allow time for the plants to dry before nightfall.

Watering equipment

Water young plants with a fine spray from a can. For general watering in small gardens, a can may be adequate; in larger gardens, use a handheld hose, regulating the flow with a nozzle attached to the end.

A practical choice in vegetable gardens is either a soaker hose or a porous hose laid among the plants (see also TOOLS AND EQUIPMENT, "Soaker hoses," p.469). These allow water to flow through fine holes, usually watering a strip about 12in (30cm) wide. The tubing can be easily moved from crop to crop, and some types of porous hose may be buried shallowly in the soil.

Critical watering periods

There are periods in the growing cycle of vegetables when water is particularly beneficial; these vary according to the individual vegetable. In prolonged dry weather, confine watering to these periods.

Germinating seeds, seedlings, and newly transplanted plants should never be allowed to dry out, so water frequently and lightly.

Leafy and salad vegetables, such as spinach, chard, most brassicas, and lettuces, require frequent watering to help them crop heavily. The most critical period is between ten days and three weeks before maturity; during this period, but only in very dry conditions, apply a single heavy watering of 5 gallons/sq yd (23 liters/sq m). Outside this period, give half this amount weekly during dry weather.

The critical point for fruiting crops such as tomatoes, peppers, beans, zucchini, cucumbers, and peas is when the flowers are forming and fruits or pods are developing. If conditions are dry during this time, water weekly at the rate for leafy crops (above). Do not water heavily before the critical period since this produces leafy growth at the expense of fruit.

Root crops, such as carrots, radishes, and beets, need moderate watering during the growing period. In the early stages, water at a rate of 1 gallon/sq yd (5 liters/sq m) if the soil is dry. Increase this rate fourfold when the roots start to swell, watering every two weeks if dry conditions persist.

Minimizing the need to water

To conserve soil moisture, particularly in dry areas, dig the soil deeply, working in plenty of organic matter to improve soil structure and moisture retention and to encourage deep rooting. Keep the soil surface mulched (see "Mulching," right) and keep down weeds, which compete for moisture. Do not hoe in dry weather since this encourages moisture to evaporate from the soil. Erect windbreaks to protect from desiccating winds (see "Shelter from wind," p.299). In areas prone to drought, adopt slightly wider spacing so that the roots can spread farther to take moisture from a larger area.

WATERING VEGETABLES WITH A SOAKER HOSE

A soaker hose laid between rows of vegetables ensures that the water will reach the roots of the plants and penetrate deeply into the soil.

Controlling weeds

A vegetable garden should be free of weeds. They compete for water, nutrients, and light, may physically suffocate plants, and may harbor pests and diseases (see PLANT PROBLEMS, "Weeds," pp.575–9).

Perennial weeds

Wherever possible, clear a vegetable garden of perennial weeds before starting to grow crops. Dig out deeply rooted and spreading perennials, taking care not to leave in the soil small pieces of root that will sprout again. Where a weed problem is very serious, either use appropriate weedkillers or smother the weeds with a lightproof mulch, such as old carpet or heavy black plastic. Most weeds (except very persistent ones) will die if covered for six to 12 months. While crops are growing, take care to prevent or control perennial weeds.

Annual weeds

These germinate and grow very rapidly and become a nuisance if they are allowed to seed freely in the vegetable garden. Pay particular attention to weeding in the first three weeks after crops germinate, when they are most affected by competition. Pull up weeds by hand or hoe shallowly to avoid bringing deeper weed seeds to the surface. Remove the weeds to prevent rerooting.

Minimizing weed growth

During the growing season, weed growth may be greatly reduced by mulching crops (see below) and also by growing vegetables at equidistant spacing (see "Spacing," p.307). Once they have reached a reasonable size, most form a canopy over the ground, which suppresses weeds.

Stale seedbeds

Spring sowings or plantings are the most vulnerable to annual weeds. Where the soil has not been cultivated recently and may be full of weed seeds, prepare the soil in advance; allow the first flush of weeds to germinate, and hoe them off before sowing or planting (see also SOILS AND FERTILIZERS, "The stale seedbed technique," p.528).

Mulching

A mulch is a layer of organic or inorganic material laid on the soil around plants. Where the surface is kept mulched, the need to cultivate is lessened or even eliminated.

Organic mulches

Bulky organic mulches add nutrients to the soil and improve the soil structure. They may be in the form of compost, spent mushroom compost, dried lawn clippings, seaweed or well-rotted, straw-rich, animal manures. Do not use any materials derived from wood, such as sawdust

CONSERVING SOIL MOISTURE

Many vegetables such as beans drop their flowers if the soil around their roots dries out. Water the crops well, then apply a mulch by carefully forking it onto the border. A mulch prevents soil-moisture evaporation, and also insulates the soil, suppresses weeds, and protects the surface from heavy rain and erosion.

and pulverized or shredded bark, unless they are at least two years old, because their decomposition uses up soil nitrogen.

Organic mulches are best applied to growing crops in spring and early summer when the soil is moist. They maintain the temperature and moisture levels of the soil once they are applied so, if possible, mulch after the soil has warmed up in spring but before it starts to dry out. Never mulch cold, wet, or very dry soil. In areas with high rainfall and on heavy soil, however, an organic mulch is best spread on the ground in fall to allow the worms to work it in.

In practice, it is often easiest to apply organic mulches when planting, watering plants first if necessary. Alternatively, mulch young seedlings that are already planted and growing strongly and are at least 2in (5cm) high. A mulch may be 1–3in (2.5–7cm) deep or more; aim for a deep mulch if the purpose is to keep down weeds.

PLANTING THROUGH A BLACK-AND-WHITE PLASTIC MULCH

1 *Dig a trench around the area to be planted, lay down the mulch with the white side upward, and secure its edges firmly into the soil.*

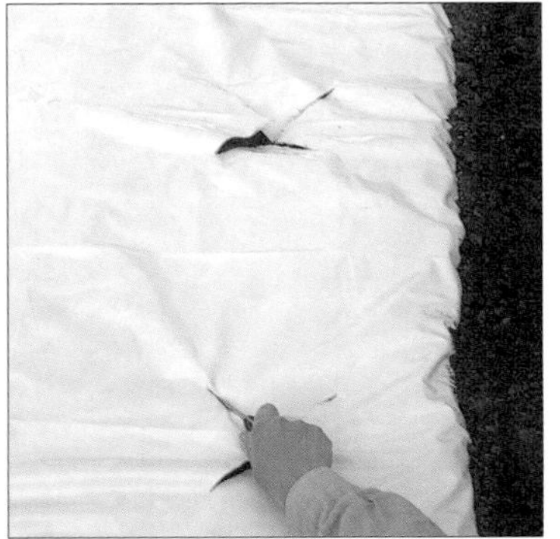

2 *Make cross-shaped slits in the plastic the required distance apart, and dig a hole in the soil large enough to take the plant's root ball.*

3 *Remove the plant (here a tomato) from its pot, and place it in the hole. Firm the soil around the root ball and water. Stake if necessary.*

Plastic film mulches

These are sheets of plastic that may be black, white, or transparent. Depending on which kind is used, they raise soil temperatures to bring on crops early, suppress weeds, reflect heat up to ripening fruit, and keep fruiting vegetables clean and free from soil splash. Shiny film mulches help deter flying pests.

Black films are mainly used to suppress weeds, although they also raise the soil temperature. Early potatoes may be grown under black films instead of being hilled up (see "Potatoes," p.354).

White films are used mainly to reflect light and warmth onto ripening fruit such as tomatoes and melons. Some films are made with the lower side black to suppress weeds, and the upper side white to reflect light. These films raise soil temperatures about 12°F (7°C) more than black films. Transparent films are used mainly to warm up the soil in spring, or to prevent soil splash.

It is simpler to lay films before planting or sowing crops. If desired, lay soaker or porous hoses in position first, then lay the film on the ground or over the bed to be covered. Make slits 3–4in (7–10cm) deep in the soil around the bed, and anchor mulch by tucking the edges into the soil, carefully using a spade or a shovel. This is simpler on slightly mounded beds. To plant, cut cross-shaped slits in the film with a knife, make a hole in the soil beneath, then carefully ease the plants through into the soil and firm. Sow large seeds such as sweet corn by making holes in the plastic and pushing the seeds through. When seedlings appear, guide them through the holes so that they are not trapped.

When necessary, water carefully through the planting holes. Slugs may be attracted to films: lift the film edges carefully and remove them or use a commercial slug killer.

Feeding

In fertile garden soils, into which plenty of organic matter is regularly worked, most vegetables will grow satisfactorily without the use of additional fertilizers. However, because it takes a few years to build up soil fertility, supplementary feeding will be necessary on poor soils or to correct deficiencies and, in some cases, to obtain higher yields.

Soil nutrients

Plants need a range of nutrients; the three most important for vegetables, and those most commonly in short supply, are nitrogen (N), phosphorus (P), and potassium or potash (K). For further information, see "Soil nutrients and fertilizers," pp.532–3.

Maintain adequate levels of phosphorus and potassium with an annual application of compost at 5–11lb/sq yd (2–5kg/sq m) or manure at 12lb/sq yd (5.5kg/sq m). Alternatively, use inorganic fertilizers such as superphosphate (for P) and potassium sulfate (for K) at levels that are recommended by the manufacturer, or apply them in complete fertilizers that contain N, P, and K.

Potassium is washed out of soil slowly, so reserves last into the following season. Phosphorus is not lost through leaching, but may be "locked up" in insoluble forms and not available to plants; reserves may need replenishing if soil analysis indicates that they are low. Nitrogen is constantly leached out and reserves need to be replenished continually, by adding either organic matter (which releases nitrogen as it breaks down) or inorganic fertilizers.

Vegetables vary in their need for nitrogen. For further information, see *Nitrogen Requirements*, p.310, which indicates the broad requirements of different groups using a fertilizer with 21 percent N content. Rates therefore vary according to which fertilizer is used; nitrogenous fertilizers include ammonium nitrate and potassium nitrate.

Applying fertilizers

Fertilizers are sold in dry forms (dusts, granules, and pellets) and as concentrated liquids (see "Types of fertilizer," p.532). They can be applied either as a base-dressing before sowing or planting, or as a top-dressing to give a boost during growth (see "Applying fertilizers," p.533).

Apply nitrogenous fertilizers in spring, a month before sowing or planting; additional applications may be made later in the growing season. Never apply nitrogen in the fall or the nutrient will be washed out of the soil before most vegetables are planted. Phosphorus and potassium fertilizers are applied at any time, often in the fall or, where complete fertilizers are used, at the same time as nitrogen, in spring.

Feeding in organic systems

If extra feeding is necessary, use slower-acting organic fertilizers. Manure "tea" is useful in many cases. Soak a burlap bag of dried manure, preferably from sheep, in a barrel of water until the resulting liquid is the color of weak tea. Use this to feed plants with little risk of overfeeding.

Various commercial and general-purpose liquid feeds are available, some based on animal manures and others on seaweed extracts. The latter appear to be particularly beneficial to growth, even though their nutrient levels are not very high. They are either watered in or applied as a foliar feed.

Container-grown vegetables

The soil mix in containers can dry out very rapidly in hot weather. To conserve moisture, keep the upper surface mulched with up to 2in (5cm) of organic material, stones, or a sheet mulch. Be prepared to water thoroughly twice a day.

Occasional feeding may be necessary; use an organic or inorganic fertilizer at diluted strengths, according to the manufacturer's instructions. Top-dress the soil mix in the container in spring, and change the soil mix completely every two or three years when it becomes compacted and less productive.

Pests and diseases

Healthy plants can resist most pest and disease attacks. Therefore good care of plants will keep problems caused by pests and diseases to a minimum. Learn to recognize the most common pests and diseases in your garden, and take the appropriate preventive measures wherever feasible. Avoid using chemicals in the vegetable garden as far as possible. Apart from inherent dangers and the risk of residues in the soil as well as on the plants, they may kill the natural enemies of many pests and diseases. If using chemical controls seems unavoidable, try to use organically approved products at least. In a few cases, biological control – the introduction of a pest's natural enemy – may be used. For general information and details about specific pests and diseases, see PLANT PROBLEMS, pp.547–79.

Healthy practices

To reduce problems with pests and diseases, keep the soil fertile and well drained, work in plenty of organic matter, and rotate crops regularly (see p.303). Grow suitable crops for the climate, choosing (wherever possible) cultivars with pest and disease resistance or tolerance (see the lists of recommended cultivars for individual vegetables, pp.313–54). Always purchase disease-free plants. Raise plants in cell packs wherever feasible and harden off plants raised indoors. If growing plants under cover, always use clean seed trays and pots and sterilized potting mix.

Common pests

Animals and birds that may attack vegetables include deer, rabbits, mice, moles, and pigeons. In cases of persistent attack, erect wire fences or nets around the garden or over crops, use humane animal traps, and deter large birds with humming wire and small ones with strands of black thread. In damp climates slugs and snails may be the most serious of all pests. They are primarily night-feeders – collect them after dark by flashlight and discard them. Where chemical controls are used, they must be handled carefully.

Soil pests, such as slugs and cutworms, commonly attack young plants, sometimes biting through the stems of plants at ground level. They tend to be worse in newly cultivated ground. Thorough digging exposes them to the birds. Many soil pests are night-feeders and may be easily caught by flashlight .

Microscopic soil pests known as nematodes or eelworms attack certain groups of plants, including potatoes. Rotate crops to prevent the pests from becoming established, and grow resistant cultivars where they are available.

Sucking insects, including many species of aphid, as well as carrot rust flies, cabbage root maggots, and thrips, damage a range of plants by sucking the sap; they may spread virus diseases in the process. Knowledge of the pests' habits may help to prevent attacks – by making earlier or later sowings, for example. Use sticky yellow traps to catch aphids, collars (see *Collaring Seedlings*, p.313) to deter pests such as cutworms, and netting barriers against carrot rust flies (see p.350). Chemical or organic sprays may control outbreaks.

Various caterpillars attack a wide range of plants. (Newly planted brassicas, in particular, are prone to attack by cutworms. A collar of aluminum foil will protect young plants.) Pick caterpillars off by hand or use the biological control *Bacillus thuringiensis*, or organic or chemical sprays. Fine nets placed over vegetables prevent butterflies or moths from laying eggs on the plants. Small beetles such as flea beetles nibble seedling leaves of brassicas; control them with sprays, and protect plants with fleecy film. Large beetles such as Colorado potato beetles pose serious problems.

Pests may multiply very rapidly in high temperatures. The most serious are whiteflies and spider mites, both of which attack a wide range of crops. They have become very resistant to most standard chemical sprays. As soon as these pests are noticed, introduce some form of biological control to restrict their numbers (see p.548).

Common diseases

Diseases are caused mainly by fungi, bacteria, and viruses. Infected plants develop a range of symptoms that in some cases merely disfigure plants, but in others will kill them. Damping-off diseases, for example, infect and usually kill young seedlings; dig up and put affected plants in the garbage.

Diseases spread very rapidly in conditions that are favorable to their development, and once established are difficult to control. Preventive measures and good garden hygiene are vitally important to prevent diseases from spreading and becoming established. A few sprays may be used in anticipation of an attack. Choose disease-resistant cultivars.

Clubroot, a soil infection, is one of the most serious problems affecting members of the cabbage family. Raising the soil pH by applying lime (see "Liming," p.533), and raising plants in sterile soil in packs so that they are vigorous, may help to control this infection.

Physiological disorders

Some problems experienced with growing vegetables are due to incorrect cultural conditions. The most common problem is premature bolting (flowering and setting seed), caused by sudden low or high temperatures, drought, or sowing at the wrong time. Fruits may fail to set due to lack of pollination, erratic watering, or drought. If there are mineral deficiencies in the soil, cauliflower curds may fail to grow. Further details are given under individual vegetables (see pp.313–54), with advice on how to create healthy growing conditions.

CREATING HEALTHY GROWING CONDITIONS

Keep vegetable beds (here of ornamental cabbages and carrots) and paths free of weeds and debris; remove diseased plant material. Water and feed carefully – excess can be as damaging as too little. Thin seedlings early to avoid stunting, and remove the thinnings. Encourage rapid germination of home-grown plants by sowing indoors if conditions are adverse outside.

NITROGEN REQUIREMENTS (using fertilizer with 21 percent N content)

VERY LOW ½oz/sq yd (12g/sq m)	LOW 1–1⅓oz/sq yd (25–35g/sq m)	MEDIUM 1½–2oz/sq yd (45–55g/sq m)	HIGH 2½–3½oz/sq yd (70–100g/sq m)	VERY HIGH 4oz/sq yd (110g/sq m)
Carrots	Asparagus	Amaranths	Beets	Bok choi
Garlic	Beans (all)	Broccoli	Brussels sprouts	Cabbages (spring, summer, winter)
Radishes	Celeriac	Broccoli raab	Celery	Chinese broccoli
	Chicory (all)	Cabbages (for storage)	Leeks	Chinese cabbages
	Cucumbers	Cauliflowers	Malabar spinach	Komatsuna
	Endive	Eggplants	Melons	Mizuna greens
	Florence fennel	Hot peppers	Potatoes (maincrop)	Oriental mustards
	Gherkins	Jerusalem artichokes	Spinach beet	Rhubarb (cutting years)
	Globe artichokes	Kales	Swiss chard	
	Kohlrabi	Lettuces		
	New Zealand spinach	Potatoes (early)		
	Okra	Rhubarb (young)		
	Onions (all)	Spinach		
	Parsnips	Sprouting broccoli		
	Peanuts	Sweet corn		
	Rutabagas	Sweet/chili peppers		
	Salsify	Sweet potatoes		
	Scorzonera	Taro		
	Summer squash	Watermelons		
(Peas do not require any extra nitrogen)	Tomatoes	Winter squash		
	Turnips (and turnip tops)	Wonderberries		
	Zucchini			

Growing under cover

THE productivity of a vegetable garden may be increased greatly in climates with a short growing season by growing plants under cover in a protected environment for some or all of their life cycle. The shorter the growing season, the more useful cover will be.

Under cover, air and soil temperatures are increased, and crops are sheltered from chill winds. This lengthens the growing season by up to two months. The quality and yields of many crops are improved by higher temperatures and shelter.

Cover may be used to start crops early in spring for planting outside when temperatures rise. Half-hardy summer vegetables that would not mature outdoors during the growing season may ripen under cover; in cool climates, okra and eggplants, for example, ripen fully only under cover. The winter cropping period of many vegetables may be extended; lettuces, peas, oriental brassicas (see p.319) and spinach, for example, all stop growing in the open but continue under cover.

Make the most of cover by ensuring that the soil underneath is fertile and weed-free. Vegetables require extra watering under cover – mulch them where practical to cut down on watering. Plants started under cover may be set back if abruptly exposed to the elements. Harden them off gradually where appropriate.

Greenhouses and frames

Cover may be provided by anything from a greenhouse to a cold frame or a plastic polytunnel. For full details, see GREENHOUSES AND FRAMES, pp.474–91.

Greenhouses

A permanent, glazed greenhouse provides an excellent growing environment. It is easily ventilated and retains heat at night better than plastic film. Diseases may build up in soil if crops such as tomatoes are grown for several consecutive years. The soil must then be changed or sterilized, or crops grown in containers. Supports may be required for tender climbing vegetables.

Walk-in polytunnels

These are made of heavy-duty, clear plastic sheeting on metal supports. They are cheaper and easier to erect than greenhouses, and may be moved to a different site if required. Ventilation is hard to control, however, increasing the risk of pests and diseases if temperatures rise rapidly; holes may be cut in the film in summer and taped over in winter. The film needs to be replaced every two or three years.

Low polytunnels

These are cheap, mobile, and flexible; the lightweight plastic film may be rolled back for ventilation and watering. They provide shelter from wind and are useful in most gardens, especially for the final stages of hardening off seedlings and protecting vegetables in unsettled spring and fall weather. Low polytunnels are limited by their height and flimsiness, however, and give little protection from low temperatures. They also need to be well anchored in windy situations.

Garden frames

Being relatively small, frames are most beneficial in gardens lacking space for a greenhouse or polytunnel. Some types are portable. They are easily ventilated, and may be heated by electric soil-heating cables. They are useful for raising and hardening off seedlings. Their low height limits the range of crops that may be grown, although the lids may be removed to allow semihardy crops to mature. Garden frames may be blacked out for forcing crops such as Belgian endive and endive.

Cloches

Although individual cloches cover only a small area, when placed end to end they can be used to cover an entire row. To make maximum use of cloches, move them from one crop to another during a season; for example, protect overwintering salad greens, then start early potatoes or dwarf beans in spring, then ripen early melons in midsummer.

LOW POLYTUNNEL

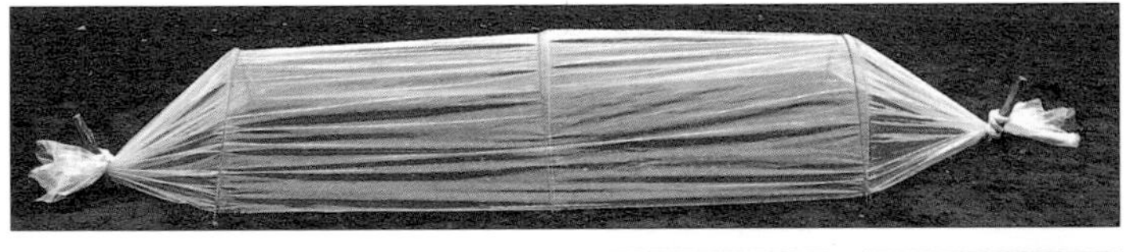

Use wire hoops pushed into the ground 3ft (90cm) apart to support plastic film, which is tied at each end to a stake. Tie strings over the plastic and secure them at the base of each hoop.

Floating row covers

These are various types of film, including perforated plastic film, fine netting film, and nonwoven fleecy film. All may be laid over low polytunnel hoops or directly over crops after sowing or planting, and anchored shallowly in the soil or weighted down. The covers are lifted by the crops as they grow.

Floating row covers promote earlier crops and higher yields by raising air and soil temperatures and protecting plants from wind and (in some cases) insect pests. All give better ventilation than unperforated plastic films. Weed beds carefully before laying floating covers, since they are awkward to lift for weeding later.

Perforated plastic films

These are perforated with tiny slits or holes. They are generally used in the early stages of growth. Disadvantages include overheating in hot weather, minimal frost protection, and the risk of plants being chafed. To "wean" plants, slit plastic films down the center a few days before removing them completely.

Netting films

Fine netting films are strong and last for several seasons. They are well ventilated so may usually be kept on until plants mature. They have little effect on temperature, but protect against wind. Provided that they are well anchored at the edges, they protect against many insect pests.

Fleecy or fibrous films

These light, soft, nonwoven films usually last one season. Depending on the films' weight, they may protect against frost and flying insect pests; the films are more permeable to light and air than plastics. Many vegetables may be grown under fleecy film until they are nearly mature.

USING FLOATING ROW COVERS

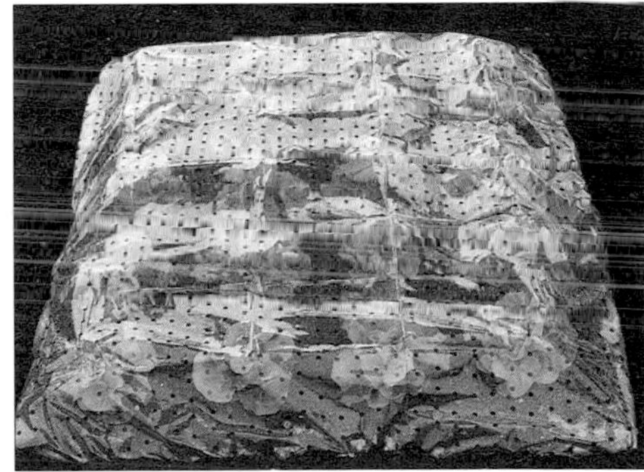

PERFORATED PLASTIC FILM
Floating row covers are spread over a bed of seedlings and hilled up at the edges so that they are loose enough to allow for growth. Perforated plastic film protects the seedlings but allows ventilation.

NETTING FILM
This protects plants against insect pests and wind damage.

FLEECY FILM
This is effective against light frost and deters insect pests.

Harvesting and storing

How and when vegetables are harvested, and whether they are used fresh, stored, or both, depends on the nature of the vegetable and the climate. The shorter the growing season and the more severe the winter, the greater the incentive to store vegetables, either naturally or by freezing. For details, see individual vegetables (pp.313–54) and *Vegetables that Freeze Well*, below.

Harvesting

Follow the guidelines under individual vegetables for how to harvest. Most vegetables are harvested at maturity, but some, notably leafy plants and brassicas, may be cut at various stages, and will often resprout for a second and third crop.

Cut-and-come-again harvesting

This method of harvesting is suited to vegetables that resprout after an initial cut has been made, enabling them to be used fresh over a fairly long period. Crops may be harvested at the seedling stage, or later when they are semimature or mature.

Harvest seedling crops when they are 2–4in (5–10cm) high, cutting about 3/4in (2cm) above soil level. Some, for example arugula and cress, may be cut and left to resprout several times in succession. See also "Cut-and-come-again seedling crops," p.306.

Some semimature or mature crops, if harvested by cutting 1–2in (2.5–5cm) above soil level, will resprout, producing more leaves and, in some cases, edible flowering shoots (see "Harvesting and storing oriental brassicas," p.319).

The technique is suited to certain types of lettuce, endive, sugar loaf chicory, oriental greens, and Swiss chard. It is useful in cool climates in fall and early winter because plants treated this way survive lower temperatures than they would otherwise and may be very productive, especially under cover.

VEGETABLES THAT FREEZE WELL

Asparagus 1
Beets 1 3
Broad beans 1
Broccoli 1
Broccoli raab 1
Brussels sprouts 1
Carrots 1 3
Cauliflowers 1 2
Celery 2
Chinese broccoli 1
Chinese cabbages 1 2
Eggplants 1 2
Hot peppers 1 2
Hyacinth beans 1
Kales 1
Kohlrabi 1 2
Lima beans 1
New Zealand spinach 1
Okra 1
Parsnips 1 3
Peas 1
Pole beans 1
Potatoes (small and new potatoes only) 1
Rhubarb 2
Rutabagas 1 2
Scallions 2
Scarlet runner beans 1
Snap beans 1
Spinach 1
Spinach beet 1
Sprouting broccoli 1
Summer squash 1 2
Sweet corn 1
Sweet peppers
Swiss chard 1
Tomatoes 1
Turnips 1 2 3
Winter squash 2
Wonderberries 1
Zucchini 1

KEY
1 Blanch
2 Dice, slice, purée, or shred
3 Freeze only when young

Storing

The length of time that vegetables may be stored depends on the storage conditions and on the vegetable or cultivar. For details, see individual vegetables. The main cause of deterioration after harvesting is water loss, so aim to keep this to a minimum. Do not store damaged or diseased specimens: they may rot.

Vegetables often freeze well; almost all need to be blanched either in steam or boiling water and cooled quickly before freezing. The only exception to this is sweet peppers, which may be frozen without any initial preparation.

Leafy vegetables and brassicas

Leafy vegetables and various types of brassica, such as broccoli and cauliflowers, have such a high water content that few of them store well. An exception is the winter-storage cabbage, which may be stored either hanging in nets or on a bed of straw, in a frost-free shed or cold frame. Several brassicas freeze well; some cultivars are bred for the purpose. Freeze only top-quality produce.

STORING STRINGS OF ONIONS
Braid together the dried onion leaves to form strings of bulbs. These may be hung outside in warm weather to dry further, and then brought indoors to be stored in frost-free conditions.

Fruiting vegetables

Vegetables such as tomatoes, eggplants, and cucumbers usually have an optimum time for harvesting, although fruits may also be harvested immature. If they are to be stored for winter use, they are best made into preserves or deep frozen.

Sweet peppers keep in good condition for many months if whole plants are pulled up and hung in a dry, frost-free place. Certain cultivars of winter squash may be stored for several months. Leave the fruit on the plant until it is mature, then pick and cure it in the sun to harden the skin so that it forms an effective barrier to water loss, and store it in a dry, frost-free environment (see also "Winter squash," p.331).

Bulbs

Certain cultivars of onion, shallot, and garlic will keep for many months. Lift the crop when mature or nearing maturity, and dry it in the sun (or under cover in wet climates), until the outer skins are papery. Handle the bulbs carefully to avoid bruising. Hang them as braided strings, in nets, or spaced out on trays, in well-ventilated, frost-free conditions (see also *Storing Onions in a Box*, p.341).

Root vegetables

Some root vegetables, such as carrots and potatoes, may be either harvested young and eaten immature or left to mature and lifted and stored at the end of the season. A few, such as parsnips, are extremely hardy and, except in severe winters, may be left in the ground until required.

Prepare vegetables carefully for storing, removing any foliage since this will rot. Store only healthy, unbruised specimens. Potatoes are susceptible to frost; store them packed in lightproof sacks in a frost-free place.

Root vegetables such as beets and carrots easily lose moisture, so store them in layers in boxes of moist sand or peat in a cool shed or cellar (see *Storing Carrots*, p.350). They may also be stored in outdoor clamps: pile them on straw and cover with more straw, and, in moderately cold areas, a layer of soil to give protection against frost (see *Making a Rutabaga Clamp*, p.349).

STORING RED CABBAGES

Lay the cabbages on slats covered with straw in a cool, well-ventilated, frost-free place. Leave gaps between them to allow free air circulation and discourage rotting.

Western brassicas

Winter cabbage

Broccoli

Cauliflower

Curly kale

Savoy cabbage

Brussels sprouts

WESTERN brassicas include kales, cauliflowers, cabbages, Brussels sprouts, sprouting broccoli, broccoli, turnip tops, broccoli raab, kohlrabi, rutabagas, and turnips. They are usually cooked, but some are used raw. For kohlrabi, rutabagas, and turnips, see pp.346, 348, and 349 respectively.

COLLARING SEEDLINGS

Newly planted brassicas are especially prone to attack by cutworms. Protect the plant by pushing a collar of aluminum foil or half a frozen-juice can into the soil around the plant.

Western brassicas are naturally biennial but are cultivated as annuals for their leaves and roots, and as biennials for flowerheads and shoots. Each type displays considerable variation, and there is often a range of cultivars for different seasons. Western brassicas are cool-season crops with varying degrees of frost tolerance; most perform poorly at high temperatures, so in warm climates grow them in winter. In temperate climates, they may provide crops for much of the year.

Siting Western brassicas

An open situation with fertile, well-drained, moisture-retentive soil is required. Rotate brassicas (see p.303) to avoid a buildup of clubroot. If this is a problem, lime the soil (see p.533) to bring the pH to 6.5–7. Most Western brassicas need medium levels of nitrogen (see p.310), but they should not be planted on freshly manured ground since this causes overlush growth that is prone to pests. A base-dressing may be applied to the area before planting (see "Applying fertilizers," p.309).

Sowing and planting Western brassicas

Western brassicas prefer firm soil; they may be planted after a previous vegetable crop without forking the soil. Sow *in situ*, in a seedbed, or indoors in trays or cell packs for transplanting. If the soil is infected with clubroot, sow in cell packs, transferring to pots before planting out. Tall, top-heavy brassicas such as Brussels sprouts should be planted 4in (10cm) deep. Hill up the stem as it grows by building a small mound of soil around it to a depth of about 4in (10cm); in windy sites, support the stem with a stake 3ft (1m) high. Plant brassicas firmly, with the lower leaves just above soil level. In some cases, spacing may be varied to determine the size of the brassica.

Cultivating Western brassicas

Mulch Western brassicas after planting to suppress weeds. In dry weather, water as for leafy vegetables (see "Critical watering periods," p.308). Apply a nitrogenous fertilizer during growth.

Flea beetles (p.550), slugs and snails (p.550), damping off (p.570), cabbage root maggots (p.566), whiptail (p.558), and cutworms (p.566) all affect young plants. Caterpillars (p.551), cabbage whiteflies (p.552), mealy aphids (see "Aphids," p.552), and clubroot (p.555) attack plants at all stages of growth.

Kales (*Brassica oleracea* Acephala Group)

Grown as annuals or biennials depending on the type, dwarf kales are 12–16in (30–40cm) tall, with a 12in (30cm) spread; tall types grow to 3ft (90cm) and spread up to 24in (60cm). Some American kales are known as collards. Plain (such as the tall 'Champion') and curly-leaved types (such as the medium-sized 'Blue Surf') and curly-broad hybrids (such as the tall 'Westland Winter') usually produce leaves from a central stem. The leaves of all kales, and the spring-flowering shoots and young leaves of broad-leaved types, are used cooked or raw. Kales are the hardiest brassicas, some surviving at 5°F (-15°C); many also tolerate heat. All prefer fertile, well-drained soils and need medium nitrogen levels (see p.310).

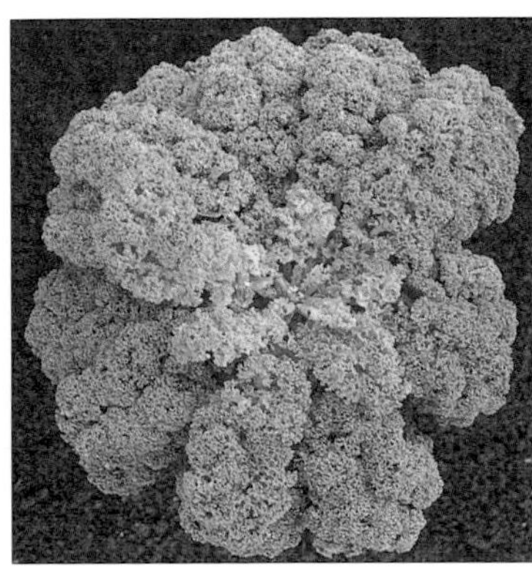

CURLY KALE

Sowing, planting, and routine cultivation

Sow seed in early spring for summer crops, and in late spring for fall and winter crops. Sow *in situ* or in seedbeds, cell packs, or seed trays for transplanting; dwarf forms should be spaced 12–18in (30–45cm) apart, tall forms 30in (75cm) apart.

Give overwintering types a nitrogenous top-dressing in spring to encourage growth. In severe winters, grow dwarf cultivars under cloches or low polytunnels. Kales are usually unaffected by pests and diseases.

Growing under cover

For very early, tender kales, sow seed in early spring in rows 6in (15cm) apart, or in wide drills. Either harvest them as large seedlings, or thin the seedlings to 3in (7cm) apart and cut when they form plants 6in (15cm) tall, leaving the stumps to resprout for a second harvest.

Harvesting and storing

Some cultivars mature seven weeks after sowing, but plants can stand a long time in the ground. Snap off the leaves as required in fall and winter to encourage new growth. Pick the shoots in spring when they are about 4in (10cm) long, before the flowers open. Kales freeze well.

ORNAMENTAL KALES

Ornamental kales are grown mainly for winter decoration in the garden or for garnishing salads. Leaves are variegated green, red, white, or purple.

Cauliflowers (*Brassica oleracea* Botrytis Group)

Grown as annuals or biennials, cauliflowers form an average head (or curd) of about 8in (20cm) in diameter; the plants are 18–24in (45–60cm) tall, with a spread of up to 3ft (90cm). They are classified by the main season of use, usually winter (with a distinction between those for frost-prone and frost-free areas), early summer, and summer/fall, although these groups overlap (see *Cauliflower Types*, below). Most types of cauliflower have creamy or white curds, but there are attractive, distinctively flavored types with green or purple curds. The curds, and in some cases the young leaves surrounding them, are cooked or used raw in salads. Smaller curds, or mini-cauliflowers, about 2in (5cm) in diameter, may be specially grown from early summer cultivars.

Cauliflowers are a cool-season crop and do not usually grow well in areas with high summer temperatures. Several cultivars are frost hardy, but cauliflowers may only be harvested all year in areas with frost-free winters. For soil and site, see "Siting Western brassicas," p.313; overwintering cauliflowers need a sheltered situation outside, and are not usually grown to maturity under cover. All cauliflowers need a moisture-retentive soil, with medium nitrogen levels (see p.310) and a pH of 6.5–7.5.

Sowing and planting

Success with cauliflowers depends on sowing the correct cultivar at the appropriate time, and allowing plants to develop with as few checks to growth (from transplanting or dry soil, for example) as possible. Where drought is likely in summer, grow fast-maturing mini-cauliflowers or spring-heading types, which will benefit from fall rains.

The main sowing times and spacings are given in the chart below. Cauliflowers are usually sown in seed trays, cell packs, or a seedbed for transplanting, but may be sown *in situ* and thinned to the correct spacing. Generally, the later the planting, the larger the cauliflower will grow and the wider the spacing required. Seed germinates best at a temperature of about 70°F (21°C).

For a very early summer supply, sow seed in fall, in seed trays or cell packs, then pot up seedlings in small pots. Put the pots into a well-ventilated frame or under cloches for the winter. Alternatively, sow *in situ* in frames or under cloches, thinning to 2in (5cm) apart. Harden off seedlings before planting them out in spring. For a later crop, sow indoors in gentle heat in early spring, and prick out into small pots.

RECOMMENDED CAULIFLOWERS

Winter
'Glacier'

Early summer
'Andes'
'Cashmere'
'Early Snow Ball'
'Snow Crown'
'Snow King'
'Taipan'
'White Summer'

Summer/fall
'Imperial'
'Siria'
'Snow Pak'
'White Fox'
'White Rock'
'White Sails'

'White Sails'

Green cultivars
'Alverde'
'Chartreuse'
'Romanesco'

Purple cultivars
'Purple Head'
'Royal Purple King'
'Violet Queen'

MINI-CAULIFLOWERS

PROTECTING CAULIFLOWER CURDS

1 *In winter and early spring, mature curds of overwintering types may need protection from severe frost.*

2 *Wrap the leaves up around the central curd, securing them with soft string.*

For summer/fall and winter groups, sow the first batch indoors in seed trays or cell packs, or *in situ* in frames or under cloches. Successive sowings may be made either in a seedbed outdoors, or in cell packs for transplanting later on.

To obtain mini-cauliflowers, select an early summer cultivar to be sown in spring or early summer; sow several seeds per station, 6in (15cm) apart, thinning to one seedling after germination. Alternatively, raise plants in packs and plant them out 6in (15cm) apart. For a continuous supply, make successive sowings.

Routine cultivation

Cauliflowers need regular water throughout the growing period. In dry conditions, water at a rate of 5 gallons/sq yd (23 liters/sq m) every two weeks. Overwintering cauliflowers require low nitrogen levels when planted or they will be too soft to survive the colder conditions. A nitrogenous fertilizer or organic liquid feed may be applied in spring.

To prevent white curds from discoloring in sunny weather, tie the leaves over the curds. This may also be done in winter and spring to protect curds of overwintering types from the elements; most modern cultivars, however, have leaves that naturally tend to cover the curds.

Pests and diseases

For cauliflower pests and diseases, see "Cultivating Western brassicas," p.313. Cauliflowers are also attacked by pollen beetles (p.563).

Harvesting and storing

The time from sowing to maturity varies from approximately 16 weeks for summer/fall cauliflowers to about 40 weeks for winter ones. Cut the curds while they are still firm and tight. Mini-cauliflowers mature about 15 weeks after sowing and should be picked immediately since they deteriorate quickly. All cauliflowers, and in particular the mini-cauliflowers, freeze well.

PURPLE-HEADED CAULIFLOWER

CAULIFLOWER TYPES

GROUP	WHEN TO SOW	WHEN TO PLANT	SPACING	WHEN TO HARVEST
Winter (frost-free areas)	Late spring	Summer	28in (70cm)	Winter/very early spring
Winter	Late spring	Summer	25in (63cm)	Early spring
Early summer	Fall/early spring (sow under glass)	Spring	21in (52cm)	Early to midsummer
Summer/fall	Mid- to late spring	Early summer	22–5in (55–63cm)	Late summer to late fall

Cabbages (*Brassica oleracea* Capitata Group)

Most cabbages are grown as annuals. Plants are generally 8–10in (20–25cm) tall, with a spread of up to 28in (70cm). The average head is about 6in (15cm) in diameter.

They are grouped according to their season of maturity, although there is some overlap between the groups. Leaves are dark or light green, blue-green, white, or red, and smooth or crinkled (savoy). Cabbage heads are pointed or round, and vary in their density. Spring greens are either loose-leaved cultivars or standard spring cabbages harvested before the head forms. Cabbage leaves are eaten either cooked or raw and sliced in salads. They may also be pickled. Stems and stalks may be sliced finely and cooked if they are tender enough. Some types of winter cabbage may be stored.

Cabbages grow best at 59–68°F (15–20°C). Do not plant in temperatures over 77°F (25°C). The hardiest cultivars may survive temperatures as low as 14°F (-10°C) for short periods. Cabbages are not usually grown under cover.

To grow well, cabbages need soil that is fertile, moisture-retentive, and humus-rich with a pH level above 6. Spring, summer, and fresh winter cabbages require very high nitrogen levels, and winter-storage cabbages medium nitrogen (see p.310). Do not give spring cabbages a nitrogenous base-dressing at planting, since the nitrogen will probably be washed from the soil over the winter; top-dress in spring instead.

Mature Spring Cabbages

Sowing and planting

Sow the chosen cultivars at the correct time for their group (see *Cabbage Types*, below). Sow seeds in seedbeds or cell packs and transplant seedlings to their final position on average five weeks later. Appropriate spacing varies according to type (see chart below) and it may be modified to vary the size of the head; adopt closer spacing for smaller heads, and wide spacing to produce larger heads. A collar may be placed around each seedling stem when transplanting to protect against cutworms (see *Collaring Seedlings*, p.313). Ensure that young seedlings have sufficient moisture until they are well established.

For spring greens either grow a greens cultivar, spacing the plants about 10in (25cm) apart, or use a heading spring cultivar and space plants 4–6in (10–15cm) apart. Cut

Fall Cabbage

Red Summer Cabbage

Savoy Cabbage

Cabbage Types

Group (Time of Maturity)	Description	Main Sowing Period	Average Spacing
Spring	Small, pointed or round heads	End of summer	12in (30cm)
	Loose-leaf greens	End of summer	10in (25cm)
Early summer	Large, mainly round heads	Very early spring (sow under glass)	14in (35cm)
Summer	Large, round heads	Early spring	14in (35cm)
Fall	Large, round heads	Late spring	20in (50cm)
Winter (for storage)	Smooth, white-leaved, winter white types	Spring	20in (50cm)
Winter (to use fresh)	Blue, green, and savoy leaf types	Late spring	20in (50cm)

Recommended Cabbages

Spring
'Durham Early'
'Earliana'
'Emerald Cross'
'Fast Track'
'Golden Cross'
'Greensleeves' (greens only)
'K-K Cross'
'Primax'
'Stonehead'

'Golden Cross'

Early summer
'Cheers'
'Early Curly'
'Golden Acre'
'Hispi' F1
'Pacifica'
'Spivoy' F1

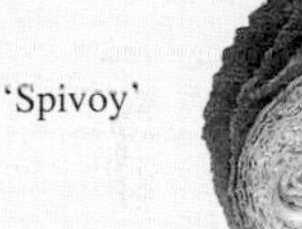
'Spivoy'

Summer
'Gourmet'
'Minicole' F1
'Red Rookie'
'Ruby Ball' F1 (red)
'Royal Vantage'
'Savoy King'
'Savoy Queen'

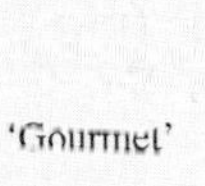
'Gourmet'

Fall
'Apex' F1
'Autoro' F1
'Perfect Ball' F1
'Rapier' F1

Winter (for storage)
'Jupiter'
'Multikeeper'
'Stonar'
'Survivor'

Winter (to use fresh)
'Aquarius'
'Celtic' F1
'Ice Queen' F1 (savoy)

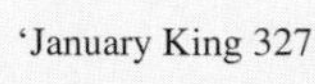

'January King 327'

'January King 327'
'Julius' F1 (savoy)

Harvesting Spring Greens

Plant spring cabbages 6in (15cm) apart. When they have grown on, but before they start to form a compact heart, harvest alternate plants, cutting them at the base. Use these as spring greens.

How to Obtain a Second Crop

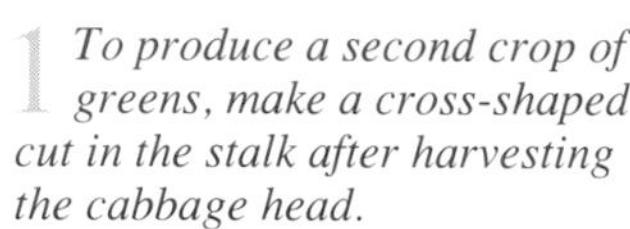

1 To produce a second crop of greens, make a cross-shaped cut in the stalk after harvesting the cabbage head.

2 A few weeks later, several miniature heads should have sprouted, ready for a second harvest.

them young as loose greens; every second or third plant may be left to heart up if a heading cultivar is used.

Routine cultivation

To increase their stability, hill up winter cabbages as they grow. Protect spring cabbages under cloches or floating row covers, and apply a liquid feed or a nitrogenous top-dressing in spring; feed others in the growing season. Keep cabbages moist throughout growth (see "Critical watering periods," p.308).

Pests and diseases

For pests and diseases that may affect cabbages, see "Cultivating Western brassicas," p.313. Southern blight (p.560) may also occur.

Harvesting and storing

Spring and summer cultivars vary in their ability to stand in good condition once the head has matured; modern cultivars often stand longer than traditional ones. Normally the plant is dug up once the head has been cut, but spring and early summer cultivars may produce a second crop if the head is cut to leave a 4in (10cm) stalk in the ground. Using a sharp knife, make a shallow cross in the top of the stem to encourage new growth. Provided that the soil is kept fertile and moist, three or four more small heads may develop together on the stalk.

Storage cabbages (winter white cultivars and appropriate red cabbages) should be lifted before heavy frost. Dig them up and carefully remove any loose outer leaves. Place them on slatted supports or straw on the floor of a shed, or suspend them in nets. Store the heads at just above freezing point, with relatively high humidity. They may also be stored in a cold frame, provided that it is ventilated on warm days to discourage rotting (see also *Storing Red Cabbages*, p.312). Cabbages may keep for four or five months.

Preparing Cabbages for Storing

Before storing cabbages, carefully remove any loose or discolored outer leaves without damaging the head (see inset). Inspect the cabbages regularly while they are in storage and remove leaves that are rotting.

Brussels sprouts (*Brassica oleracea* Gemmifera Group)

These are biennials grown as annuals, and vary in height from about 14in (35cm) for the dwarf forms to 30in (75cm) for the tall forms, with a spread of up to 20in (50cm) in both cases. Brussels sprouts are loosely divided by their time of maturity into early, midseason, and late groups. The earlier types tend to be dwarfer and less hardy. The modern F1 cultivars are an improvement over the older, open-pollinated ones; they perform better on fertile soils, are less prone to lean (since they have a stronger root system), and have more compact, even sprouts. The tight sprouts that develop on the stem are cooked or shredded raw into salads. The mature leaves at the top of the plants may also be eaten. There is a well-flavored, but less productive, red cultivar, 'Rubine'.

Dwarf Brussels Sprout Plant

Brussels sprouts are typical cool-season brassicas; the hardiest cultivars survive temperatures of 14°F (-10°C). If sown in succession where winters are mild, Brussels sprouts provide a constant crop from early fall to late spring. Apply a high-nitrogen fertilizer shortly before planting (see p.310). Avoid using freshly manured ground since this encourages blown and loose, rather than firm, sprouts. For soil and site requirements, see "Siting Western brassicas," p.313.

Hilling Up Brussels Sprouts

About a month after planting out, hill up Brussels sprouts by drawing the soil around the base of the stem to increase stability. At this stage they may also be staked if they are in an exposed site.

Sowing and planting

Starting with the early-maturing cultivars, sow in succession from mid- to late spring as the soil begins to warm up. For a very early crop, sow in gentle heat under cover in early spring. Sow in seed trays or in a seedbed for transplanting, or *in situ* in firm ground; most Brussels sprouts do not grow well in cell packs.

Thin out or transplant to the required spacing in early summer, generally four to five weeks after sowing. Plant dwarf cultivars about

18in (45cm) apart, and tall cultivars about 2ft (60cm) apart. Use closer spacing to produce smaller sprouts of a more uniform size, and wider spacing for large sprouts that mature in succession and so may be picked over a longer period. Wide spacing also encourages good air circulation, which keeps plants healthy and disease-free. Plant tall cultivars deeply and hill up the stems as they grow to provide extra stability. Keep young plants moist until they are well established.

Removing Leaves

Snap off any yellowing or diseased leaves that develop because these may carry fungal diseases that could spread to the whole crop. This also improves air circulation.

Brussels sprouts, with their slow rate of growth, may be intercropped in the first few months with fast-maturing vegetables.

Routine cultivation

Keep beds weed-free. Since plants are widely spaced, extra watering is required only in very dry conditions, when they should be watered at the rate for leafy crops (see "Critical watering periods," p.308). A top-dressing of a nitrogenous fertilizer or an organic liquid feed may be applied in late summer if the plants are not growing vigorously. Remove any withered or diseased leaves from the stems as they appear.

If sprouts are wanted for freezing, grow an early cultivar that matures in fall, and nip off the sprout top or growing point in late summer, when the lower sprouts are roughly ½in (1cm) in diameter. All the sprouts will then mature for picking together, rather than in succession.

Pests and diseases

The most common problems are mealybugs (p.552), which can colonize the individual sprouts, and downy mildew (p.552). For other diseases likely to affect Brussels sprouts, see "Cultivating Western brassicas," p.313.

Harvesting and storing

Brussels sprouts are ready to harvest about 20 weeks after sowing. Their flavor is improved after they have been exposed to some frost. Pick the lowest sprouts first by snapping them off at the base; the upper sprouts will continue to develop. If the sprouts are intended for freezing, pick them before the outer leaves become damaged by winter weather; freeze only top-quality sprouts. Sprout tops may be harvested by cutting them off at the end of the season.

After harvesting, dig up the plants and break up the stems with a hammer. This deters the buildup and spread of brassica diseases, and enables the stems to rot down more quickly when composted.

Where winters are very severe, uproot the whole plants before the ground freezes and hang them in a cool, frost-free place; the sprouts will remain fresh for several weeks.

F1 and Open-pollinated Sprouts

Modern F1 hybrids produce sprouts that are compact, evenly spaced, and of uniform size. Traditional open-pollinated cultivars are more likely to produce blown sprouts widely varying in size.

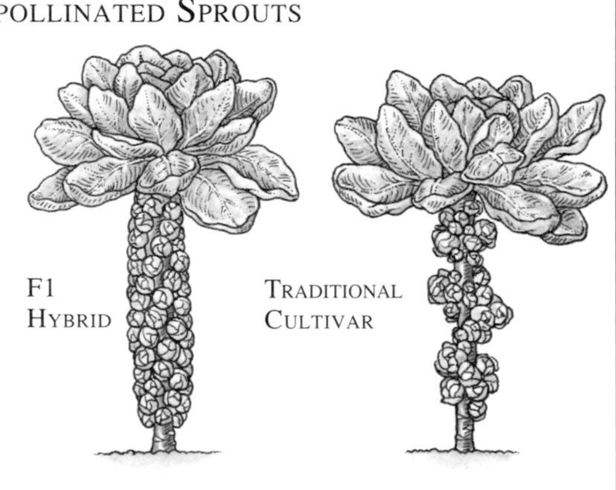

Recommended Brussels Sprouts

Early
'Green Comet'
'Jade Cross E'
'Oliver' F1

Midseason
'Achilles' F1
'Citation'
'Valiant'

Late
'Citadel' F1
'Odette' F1

'Jade Cross E'

Sprouting broccoli (*Brassica oleracea* Italica Group)

These large, biennial plants may reach a height of 2–3ft (60–90cm) and a spread of 2ft (60cm). There are purple and white forms; the purple is more prolific and hardier. The flowering shoots that develop in spring are eaten cooked.

Purple Sprouting Broccoli

Sprouting broccoli is considered one of the hardiest winter vegetables, surviving temperatures of about 10°F (-12°C). Because it is a slow maturing vegetable that occupies the ground for up to a year, it requires a fertile soil and medium nitrogen levels (see p.310). Avoid shallow and sandy soils and sites exposed to strong winter winds.

Sowing, planting, and routine cultivation

Sow in spring, either in a seedbed or in cell packs. Transplant from early to midsummer, spacing plants at least 2ft (60cm) apart, and planting them deeply for stability.

Plants may need staking in the fall in areas where they will overwinter. If birds peck at the leaves, cover the plants with netting to protect them for the winter. For further cultivation requirements, see "Cultivating Western brassicas," p.313.

Pests and diseases

Sprouting broccoli is, in theory, affected by common brassica pests, but in practice is fairly trouble-free. Pollen beetles (p.563) attacking the flowering shoots are an increasing problem in some areas.

Recommended Sprouting Broccoli

'Italian Sprouting'
'Nine Star Perennial'
'Purple Sprouting'
'White Sprouting'

'Purple Sprouting'

Harvesting and storing

Pick shoots as they mature. Snap them off when they are about 6in (15cm) long, while the flowers are in bud. Pick regularly to encourage the production of more shoots; plants may crop for up to two months. Sprouting broccoli freezes well.

Broccoli (*Brassica oleracea* Italica Group)

Regular (nonsprouting) broccoli is grown as an annual or biennial, and produces compact plants about 18in (45cm) tall, with a spread rarely over 15in (38cm). Cultivars are classified as early, midseason, and late, with the earliest maturing the fastest. F1 hybrids are more productive than the original cultivars. The compact terminal head and the young side shoots are best eaten lightly cooked; they are also eaten raw.

Broccoli is a cool-season crop and should not be grown in areas where the average mean temperature is above 59°F (15°C). Young plants tolerate some frost, but it may damage embryonic and young heads once they start to develop. Broccoli needs an open site in moisture-retentive, fairly fertile soil with medium nitrogen levels (see p.310).

Harvesting Broccoli

1 *Just before the flower buds open, harvest the first central head by cutting through the stalk.*

2 *This encourages side shoots to develop; these can also be harvested and more side shoots will be produced.*

Recommended Broccoli

Early
'Emperor' F1

'Emperor'

'Green Comet' F1
'Leprechaun' F1
'Packman' F1

Midseason
'Green Valiant' F1
'Premium Crop' F1

Late
'Corvet' F1
'Legend' F1

Sowing and planting

Sow in succession from spring to early summer for a crop during summer and fall. Broccoli seedlings do not transplant well, so either sow two or three seeds per station *in situ*, or sow in cell packs and transplant seedlings to moist ground, disturbing the roots as little as possible. For an early crop, make the first sowings indoors; these plants are, however, especially prone to bolting when transplanted.

Broccoli plants grow well at various spacings. For the highest overall yield, space plants 9in (22cm) apart each way, or 6in (15cm) apart in rows spaced at 12in (30cm). Closer spacing produces smaller terminal shoots, which mature together and are suitable for freezing.

Routine cultivation

Keep the bed weed-free. Broccoli plants need plenty of water to crop well – 2 gallons/sq yd (11 liters/sq m) every two weeks. In very dry conditions, water as for leafy crops (see "Critical watering periods," p.308). A nitrogenous top-dressing or an organic liquid feed may be applied once the terminal heads have been cut in order to encourage additional side shoots to develop.

Pests and diseases

For pests and diseases that may affect broccoli, see "Cultivating Western brassicas," p.313. Problems may also be caused by pollen beetles (p.563) and downy mildew (p.552).

Harvesting and storing

Broccoli is a fast-maturing brassica, ready 11–14 weeks after sowing. The main head should be cut when it is 3–4in (7–10cm) in diameter, while still firm and before the flower buds open. Side shoots will subsequently develop; cut these when they are about 4in (10cm) long. Broccoli freezes well.

Turnip tops and broccoli raab (*Brassica rapa*)

Over the centuries different brassicas have been grown for cutting in the immature stages for use as quick-maturing greens. The two types commonly used for this purpose today are turnip tops (*Brassica rapa* Rapifera Group) and broccoli raab (*Brassica rapa* Utilis Group), which is also known as turnip rape and by a number of Italian names such as *cime di rapa*, *rapini*, and *broccoletti*.

They are grown as annuals or biennials, generally with single stems that reach a maximum height of about 12in (30cm). The leaves, young stems, and sweetly flavored young flowerheads are eaten cooked as spring greens, or raw in salads.

Turnip tops and broccoli raab are cool-season brassicas. Grow them in spring and fall in hot climates, or all year where summers are cool. All turnip cultivars are suitable; broccoli raab has no named cultivars. Both grow best in fertile, moisture-retentive soil and require low to medium nitrogen levels (see p.310).

Broccoli Raab

Sowing, planting, and routine cultivation

Sow thinly broadcast or in rows 4in (10cm) apart. For larger plants, thin to 6in (15cm). For an early crop in cold areas, make the first sowing indoors in early spring. Plants need little attention subsequently.

Harvesting and storing

Harvest plants within seven to eight weeks of sowing. Make the first cut when they are leafy and 4in (10cm) tall, or wait until the immature flowering shoots appear and the plant is 8–10in (20–25cm) tall. Cut about 1in (2.5cm) above ground level. In cool weather, the plants resprout to give two or three further cuttings over a period of four or five weeks. Cut as long as the stems are tender. Use turnip tops and broccoli raab fresh since they do not store well.

Turnip Tops

Oriental brassicas

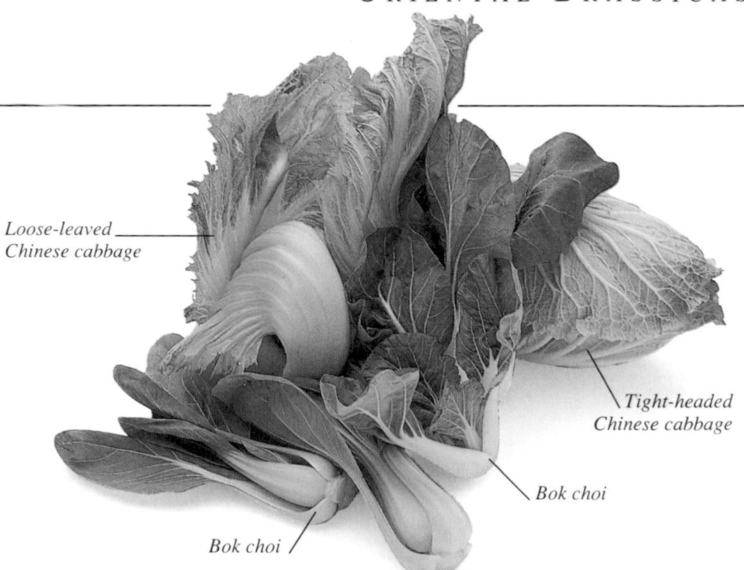

SEVERAL oriental brassicas are now being introduced to the West. They have many features in common with Western brassicas but tend to be faster growing and have a wider range of uses than Western brassicas. If they are given the right conditions they are highly productive. They are grown as annuals or biennials.

Oriental brassicas are cultivated mainly for their leaves and leafy stems, but also for their young, sweetly flavored flowering shoots. Leaf shape and color vary from the glossy, white-ribbed leaves of some bok choi cultivars, and the feathery green leaves of mizuna greens, to the purplish green of oriental mustards. Oriental brassicas are nutritious, succulent, and crisp, and are mild to peppery in flavor. Cook them, preferably by stir-frying or steaming, or use young leaves and shoots raw in salads.

Oriental brassicas are best suited to climates with cool summers and mild winters, although many cultivars are available that are adapted for hotter climates. Most will withstand light frost, especially if harvested when they are semimature as a cut-and-come-again crop (see p.312). A few oriental brassicas, such as komatsuna and some of the mustards, are extremely hardy.

In temperate climates, oriental brassicas grow best in late summer and fall. Where winter temperatures fall only a few degrees below freezing, they may be grown as a winter crop under cover in unheated structures; if planted late in the summer they may crop from fall to spring, although they will stop growing at low temperatures.

Oriental brassicas require similar conditions to Western brassicas (see "Siting Western brassicas," p.313) but, being fast-growing, hungry, and thirsty plants, the soil must be rich in organic matter, moisture-retentive, and fertile. They never develop well in poor, dry soil. Most of them have very high nitrogen requirements (see p.310).

Sowing and planting oriental brassicas

All standard methods of sowing may be used; where there is a risk of plants going to seed prematurely (bolting), sow seed in cell packs or *in situ*. Many have a tendency to bolt when days are lengthening, particularly when this is combined with low spring temperatures. In these cases, in northern latitudes, delay sowing until midsummer, unless plants are started off in heat or cultivars with bolting resistance are used. If bolting continues to be a problem, grow oriental brassicas as seedling crops, and harvest the leaves before the plants start to bolt.

Their rapid rate of growth makes oriental brassicas ideal for intercropping among slower-maturing vegetables, especially for cutting as a cut-and-come-again seedling crop, when their flavor is superb.

Cultivating oriental brassicas

Oriental brassicas are generally shallow rooting and so need regular watering. In very dry conditions, water at the rate for leafy crops (see "Critical watering periods," p.308). They should also be kept mulched.

Oriental brassicas and Western brassicas are susceptible to the same pests and diseases (see "Cultivating Western brassicas," p.313). Those with tender leaves are very prone to slugs and snails (p.550), caterpillars (p.551), and flea beetles (p.550). They may be grown under fine nets to provide some protection.

Harvesting and storing oriental brassicas

Most oriental brassicas mature within two to three months after being sown. They may be harvested at four different stages from seedling to mature plant.

They may be harvested at the seedling stage using cut-and-come-again techniques (see "Cut-and-come-again harvesting," p.312), or left a few weeks longer and cut as semimature plants. When the plants are fully mature they may be either harvested all at once or alternatively cut about 1in (2.5cm) above ground level so that they sprout again for a second crop. The flowering shoots that develop naturally from mature plants may also be harvested before the flowers open.

In the West, oriental brassicas are mainly used fresh, although most will keep for a few days if refrigerated. In the Orient, leaves are pickled or dried, and Chinese cabbages are stored for off-season supplies.

Oriental mustards *(Brassica juncea)*

The mustards are a varied group of annuals and biennials, forming large, often coarse-leaved plants. Leaf texture may be smooth, blistered, or deeply curled; some cultivars have purple leaves. The mustards are naturally very robust and less prone to pests and diseases than most oriental brassicas. Several, including the purplish green 'Miike Giant', 'Osaka Purple', and 'Xue Li Hong' survive at least 14°F (-10°C). The distinctive flavor may be piquant, becoming stronger as they run to seed. The leaves are used cooked but may also be eaten raw in salads when young or if sliced.

Sow from mid- to late summer in temperate climates for harvesting from fall to spring, and in late spring in cold regions for harvesting in summer. The seed is small and is sown in shallow soil *in situ* or in cell packs. Thin or plant out seedlings 6in (15cm) apart for harvesting young, and 14in (35cm) apart for growing to larger plants. If they are planted under cover in fall, plants are more tender, but will run to seed earlier the following spring.

Oriental mustards mature in six to 13 weeks, depending on the cultivar. Cut single leaves as required.

PURPLE-LEAVED ORIENTAL MUSTARD

Chinese broccoli
(Brassica rapa var. alboglabra)

These annuals, also known as Chinese kale, form stout plants with thick, blue-green leaves, growing up to 18in (45cm) tall. The succulent, flavorful, chunky flower stems, which may be ³/₄in (2cm) thick, are generally cooked.

Chinese broccoli tolerates higher summer temperatures than many other brassicas, and withstands light frost. In warm and temperate climates, sow from late spring to late summer. For a very early crop, make a first sowing under cover in spring to transplant outside. For a protected early winter crop, plant under cover in fall. In cool climates, delay sowing until midsummer since sowings made earlier than this may bolt.

Sow seed *in situ* or in cell packs. For small plants, to be harvested whole as soon as the flowering shoots appear, grow plants 5in (12cm) apart with 4in (10cm) between rows. For large plants, to be cropped over a longer period, space plants 12in (30cm) apart each way. Cut the main shoot first, as for broccoli (see opposite); further side shoots will continue to develop for harvesting later. Large plants take nine to ten weeks to mature.

CHINESE BROCCOLI

Bok choi

(*Brassica rapa* var. *chinensis*)

Bok choi is a biennial usually grown as an annual, forming a loose head of fairly stiff leaves with wide midribs that broaden out markedly and overlap at the base. There are many types, the most common being white-ribbed and green-ribbed, available as F1 cultivars 'Joi Choi' (white) and 'Mei Qing Choi' (green). They vary in size from squat forms about 4in (10cm) tall to large plants 18in (45cm) tall. Bok choi is succulent and mild in flavor, and may be eaten either cooked or raw.

Bok choi grows best at cool temperatures of 59–68°F (15–20°C). Most cultivars will tolerate some frost in the open but survive lower temperatures under cover grown as winter cut-and-come-again crops. A few are suited to hotter climates.

In temperate climates, sow seed throughout the growing season. There is some risk of premature bolting with spring sowings, so confine these to cut-and-come-again seedling crops. Sow seed *in situ* or in cell packs. Spacing depends on cultivar and size of plant required, ranging from 4in (10cm) apart for small cultivars to about 18in (45cm) apart for the largest cultivars. In late summer, transplant bok choi under cover for a fall crop.

Bok choi may be harvested at any stage from seedlings to the young flower shoots of mature plants.

BOK CHOI

HARVESTING SEEDLINGS

Bok choi may be harvested at the seedling stage. If they are cut about 1in (2.5cm) from the ground, new leaves will sprout.

Seedling leaves will be ready for harvesting in three weeks. They may be cut 1in (2.5cm) above ground level and will resprout. Mature plants may be cut higher and will also resprout for a second harvest.

Mizuna greens (*Brassica rapa* var. *nipposinica*)

Mizuna greens are annuals or biennials, depending on climatic conditions. They have dark green, glossy, deeply serrated, almost feathery leaves and slender, white, juicy stems forming a rosette up to 18in (45cm) in diameter and about 9in (23cm) tall. They are highly decorative, especially when grown as an edging or in blocks. Mizuna greens are eaten cooked, or raw when leaves are harvested young and tender.

MIZUNA GREENS

They are very adaptable, capable of tolerating both high summer temperatures (provided that they are in moisture-retentive soil) and winter temperatures down to 14°F (-10°C).

They may be sown throughout the growing season. Resistance to bolting is good and seed may therefore be sown in seed trays or cell packs, in a seedbed for transplanting, or *in situ*. For a tender winter crop, sow in late summer to transplant under cover. Space plants 4in (10cm) apart for small plants harvested young, and up to 18in (45cm) apart to obtain large plants. Mizuna greens are useful for intercropping if cut at the seedling stage.

Mizuna greens mature eight to ten weeks after sowing and may be harvested at all stages; seedling leaves may be ready within two or three weeks (see "Harvesting and storing oriental brassicas," p.319). The plants are vigorous, and are capable of resprouting several times after they have been cut initially.

Chinese cabbages (*Brassica rapa* var. *pekinensis*)

These are annuals or biennials usually grown as annuals. Chinese cabbages have dense, upright heads. The leaves are marked by prominent white veins, the broadened midribs overlapping at the base rather like bok choi. The barrel type forms a stout head about 10in (25cm) high, the cylindrical type a longer, less compact head up to 18in (45cm) high. Leaf color ranges from dark green to almost creamy white, especially in the center. There are also some very attractive loose-headed types. Mild-flavored with a crisp texture, Chinese cabbages are excellent in salads and lightly cooked.

For preferred climatic conditions see "Bok choi" (left). Most headed types are likely to bolt if they are sown in spring, unless a temperature of 68–77°F (20–25°C) is maintained during the first three weeks of growth. It is best to delay sowing until early summer. Some loose-headed types may be sown in spring. If they start to bolt, treat them as cut-and-come-again crops, although the leaves of some cultivars may be rough-textured and hairy when young. Sow seed in cell packs or *in situ*; thin or transplant seedlings to 12in (30cm) apart. Plenty of moisture throughout growth is vital. Chinese cabbages have soft leaves that are susceptible to pests (see "Cultivating oriental brassicas," p.319).

Chinese cabbages mature eight to ten weeks after sowing, and can be harvested at any stage since they respond well to cut-and-come-again treatment both after the main heads have been cut, and during growth, as semimature plants.

RECOMMENDED CHINESE CABBAGES

'China Pride' (barrel)
'Jade Pagoda' F1 (cylindrical)
'Kasumi' (barrel)

'Jade Pagoda'

HARVESTING CHINESE CABBAGES

1 *Harvest Chinese cabbage (here a loose-leaved cultivar) by cutting about 1in (2.5cm) above soil level.*

2 *After a few weeks, new leaves will have formed and may be cut. Stumps may resprout several times.*

Komatsuna (*Brassica rapa* var. *perviridis*)

The komatsuna group, also known as mustard spinach, is extremely diverse; its members form large, productive, robust, healthy plants, often with glossy leaves that may be up to 12in (30cm) long and 7in (18cm) wide. The flavor of the leaves resembles cabbage, with a touch of spinach, and they are eaten cooked, or raw, finely sliced in salads.

Komatsuna plants tolerate a wide range of temperatures and will survive 10°F (-12°C). Some cultivars are suitable for tropical climates.

Plants are less likely to bolt from early spring sowings than most oriental brassicas, and they are more drought-tolerant. For sowing and spacing, see "Mizuna greens" (left). Komatsuna makes a satisfactory winter crop under cover.

KOMATSUNA

Leaves may be harvested at all stages (see "Harvesting and storing oriental brassicas," p.319). Mature plants are usually ready to be harvested eight weeks after sowing.

Leafy and salad vegetables

THIS group of vegetables is grown for the great variety of leaves that it produces, which may be eaten raw in salads, or cooked. The freshly picked leaves are both delicious and highly nutritious. The range of leaf color also gives them decorative value. Careful choice of cultivar and the right growing conditions ensure a year-round supply. If seeds are sown in succession, gluts of crops maturing together may be avoided. Due to the high moisture content of the leaves, many store for only two or three days; however, a few are suitable for freezing.

Amaranths (*Amaranthus* spp.)

These rapidly growing annuals reach a height of about 24in (60cm) and a spread of 12–15in (30–38cm). *Amaranthus cruentus*, the most commonly grown as an edible crop, has oval, light green leaves; amaranth cultivars are mostly local – they include 'Fotete', 'Green Spinach', and 'Stubby'. *A. tricolor*, or Chinese spinach, has red, yellow, or green leaves and greenish white flowers; cultivars include 'Lal Sag Rouge', 'Tampala', 'Banerjee's Giant', and 'Crystal'. *A. caudatus* has pale green leaves and is often grown as an ornamental plant for its vivid red, tassel-like flowers. Amaranth species are also known as African or Indian spinach. The leaves of the plants and immature flower buds are cooked and eaten in the same way as spinach.

Amaranths are tropical and subtropical plants that require temperatures of 72–86°F (22–30°C) with a humidity of above 70 percent to crop well. They may also be grown in temperate climates in greenhouses or outdoors in a sunny, sheltered site. Moderately deep, well-drained, fertile soil with a pH of 5.5–7 and medium to high nitrogen levels are required (see p.310).

AMARANTHUS CRUENTUS

Sowing and planting

Sow outdoors in spring, once the temperature is high enough, in rows 8–12in (20–30cm) apart. Thin seedlings to 4–6in (10–15cm) apart when they are about 2–3in (5–7cm) high. Protect with plastic covers or under cloches until the young plants have become established.

In cool areas, or for an earlier crop, seed may be sown in trays in a greenhouse; prick out seedlings into 3 or 3½in (6 or 9cm) pots when they are large enough to handle. Transplant them outdoors when they are 3–3½in (7–9cm) tall, spacing them 4–6in (10–15cm) apart.

Routine cultivation

Keep amaranth beds weed-free, and water regularly. Apply a balanced fertilizer or organic liquid feed every two to three weeks. Give additional dressings of nitrogen and potassium every three weeks on less fertile soils. Apply an organic mulch around the base of the plants to retain moisture and warmth. When the plants are 8in (20cm) tall, pinch out the growing point to encourage lateral shoots and to produce a heavier crop.

Pests and diseases

Downy mildew (p.552), powdery mildew (p.552), caterpillars (p.551), and aphids (p.552) may affect amaranths outside, and thrips (p.553) and damping off (p.566) under cover.

Growing under cover

When seedlings are 3in (7cm) tall, transplant them to 8in (21cm) pots, grow bags, or beds, spacing them 15–20in (38–50cm) apart each way. Keep them at a minimum temperature of 72°F (22°C). Water, and maintain 70 percent humidity by damping down in hot weather.

Harvesting and storing

Amaranths are ready to harvest eight to ten weeks after sowing. Using a sharp knife, cut young shoots up to 4in (10cm) long when the plants are about 10in (25cm) tall; they will produce further shoots over several months. Continue picking them as required. Amaranths are best eaten fresh; alternatively, they may be stored for up to one week at 32°F (0°C) and 95 percent humidity.

AMARANTHUS TRICOLOR

Malabar spinach (*Basella alba*)

Also known as Ceylon, Indian, or vine spinach, these short-lived, twining perennials may grow to 12ft (4m) tall if supported. Var. *alba* has dark green leaves; var. *rubra* has red stems and leaves. The oval or round leaves are eaten cooked; the purple berries are not normally eaten.

Malabar spinach is a tropical and subtropical plant that requires a temperature of 77–86°F (25–30°C). Lower temperatures reduce the growth rate, resulting in smaller leaves. Larger leaves are, however, produced in light shade. Well-drained and highly fertile soil with a pH of 6–7.5 and high nitrogen levels (see p.310) are required for good growth.

Sowing and planting

Sow in seed trays or 3 or 3½in (6 or 9cm) pots, maintaining the required temperature range. When the seedlings are 4–6in (10–15cm) tall, transplant them to well-prepared beds, spacing the plants 16–20in (40–50cm) apart each way.

Routine cultivation

Support plants by staking or by tying in the stems to a vertical or horizontal trellis. Keep plants weed-free and water as necessary. Mulch with organic material. Apply a balanced fertilizer or liquid feed every two to three weeks during the growing period. When the seedlings reach a

SUPPORTING MALABAR SPINACH

Malabar spinach may be supported on a trellis parallel to the ground, raised about 12in (30cm) above soil level. The stems should be evenly spaced on the trellis so that they do not become overcrowded.

height of about 18in (45cm), remove the growing point to encourage branching. Remove flowering shoots to encourage leaf production.

Propagate plants by taking cuttings 4–6in (10–15cm) long; insert them in small pots until rooted and then transplant as described for seedlings.

Pests and diseases

Malabar spinach is generally free of pests and diseases. Root-knot nematodes (p.566) may, however, affect plants, and aphids (p.552), leafhoppers (p.553), whiteflies (p.552), and spider mites (p.552) may also be troublesome.

Growing under cover

Transplant seedlings to grow bags or to 8–10in (21–25cm) pots. Remove the growing tips when the seedlings are about 12in (30cm) tall to encourage branching, and damp down regularly to maintain high humidity. Tie in developing shoots.

Harvesting and storing

Harvest ten to 12 weeks after transplanting by cutting young terminal shoots about 6–8in (15–20cm) long; this encourages further shoots to develop over several months. Eat leaves within two days of picking, or refrigerate them for a few days.

Swiss chard and spinach beet (*Beta vulgaris* Cicla Group)

These spinachlike biennials belong to the beet family. Swiss chard, also known as seakale beet, forms large, glossy-leaved plants. The individual leaves may be up to 18in (45cm) long and 6in (15cm) wide. The midribs widen into broad leaf stalks up to 2in (5cm) in diameter that may be white, red, creamy yellow, or pink. Leaf color varies according to cultivar, from deep green ('Fordhook Giant') to greenish yellow ('Lucullus') and reddish green ('Rhubarb Chard'). Leaves and midribs are normally cooked; the latter require longer cooking and are often treated as a separate vegetable. Spinach beet, or perpetual spinach, forms smaller-leaved plants, with narrow green leaf stalks. It is eaten lightly cooked or raw.

WHITE-STEMMED SWISS CHARD

Although chard and spinach beet are essentially cool-season crops, growing best at 61–4°F (16–18°C), they tolerate higher summer temperatures than spinach (see p.325) without bolting, and survive winter temperatures of 7°F (-14°C). They may be grown in a wide range of soils other than acid ones, provided the soil is moisture-retentive and fertile, containing plenty of organic matter. Plants may remain in the ground for up to 12 months, requiring high nitrogen levels (see p.310).

Sowing and planting

For a continuous supply, sow seed in spring (plants may crop until late spring the following year), and again in mid- to late summer (for plants cropping until the following summer). Sow *in situ* in rows 15in (38cm) apart for spinach beet or, for Swiss chard, 18in (45cm) apart; thin seedlings early to 12in (30cm) apart. Plants may be grown closer together in more widely spaced rows, but avoid overcrowding, since this may encourage downy mildew.

RED-STEMMED SWISS CHARD

Alternatively, seed may be sown in seed trays or cell packs for transplanting. Germination is usually rapid. Spinach beet may be sown closely for use as a cut-and-come-again seedling crop (see p.306).

Routine cultivation

Chard and spinach beet are naturally healthy and vigorous and usually require little attention. Give an organic mulch to keep down weeds and preserve moisture; apply a nitrogenous fertilizer or organic liquid feed during the growing season if plants are not developing well.

Pests and diseases

Earwigs (p.550) may attack seedlings. Bacterial or fungal leaf spots (p.554) and downy mildew (p.552) may also be problems.

Growing under cover

In mild climates, chard and spinach beet are excellent winter crops under cover. Sow in cell packs in late summer and transplant under cover in early fall, or broadcast spinach beet for cut-and-come-again seedling crops (see p.306). They often crop through winter and spring.

Harvesting and storing

Leaves are ready to be harvested eight to 12 weeks after sowing. Cut the outer leaves first and continue picking as required; alternatively, harvest the whole plant by cutting the leaves about 1in (2.5cm) above ground level. Further leaves are then produced from the base over many months. Both Swiss chard and spinach beet may be frozen.

Endive (*Cichorium endivia*)

RECOMMENDED ENDIVE

Curled (early and summer)
'Frisan'

Green curled
'Tosca'

Escarole (all sowings)
'Full Heart Batavian' **Ow**
'Nuvol'

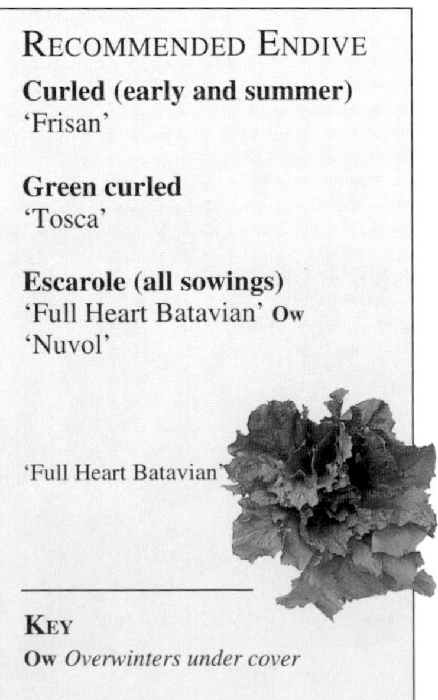

'Full Heart Batavian'

KEY
Ow *Overwinters under cover*

Endive is an annual or biennial plant that forms a flat or semiupright leaf rosette 8–15in (20–38cm) in diameter. The most distinct types of endive are serrated- or curled-leaved endive, green curled endive, and broad-leaved escarole; there are also intermediate types. Outer leaves are dark to light green and the more tender, inner leaves creamy yellow. Endive is slightly bitter and is blanched to make it sweeter. Used mainly in salads, it is shredded to reduce bitterness or may be cooked.

Endive is a cool-season crop that grows best at 50–68°F (10–20°C), but withstands light frost in the open; the hardier cultivars survive 15°F (-9°C). Bitterness generally increases at high temperatures. Some curled types are quite heat-tolerant, while escarole types tend to withstand greater cold. There is a risk of premature bolting from spring sowings if temperatures fall below 41°F (5°C) for an extended period. Endive performs much better than lettuce in the low light levels of northern winters and therefore makes a useful winter greenhouse crop.

For soil and site requirements, see "Lettuces," p.324. Summer crops may be grown in light shade; always grow fall crops on well-drained soil to avoid the risk of rotting. Endive has a low nitrogen requirement (see p.310).

Sowing and planting

Choose appropriate cultivars for each season. Sow in late spring for a summer crop or in summer for a fall crop, either *in situ* or in cell packs or seed trays. Thin or plant out the seedlings 10–15in (25–38cm) apart, using the widest spacing for spreading cultivars. Curled types may be sown as cut-and-come-again seedling crops (see p.306), most usefully in late spring and late summer.

Routine cultivation

To blanch leaves, choose nearly mature plants with dry leaves and blanch a few at a time since they deteriorate rapidly after blanching.

For complete blanching *in situ*, cover each plant with a bucket. For partial blanching, lay a large plate or piece of cardboard over the center. With escarole types, bunch up the leaves and tie them together. Protect the plants against slugs until they are ready for harvesting, which is after about ten days. In fall, plants for blanching should be lifted before

BLANCHING ENDIVE

1 Ensure that the endive is dry, then lay a plate over the center to blanch the leaves partially.

2 The center should have turned white and be ready for harvesting after about 10 days.

severe weather disfigures them; transplant them into a darkened frame or dark area under greenhouse staging, then blanch as for Belgian endive (see below).

Pests and diseases
Slugs (p.550) and aphids (p.552) are the most common problems. For other pests and diseases that affect endive, see "Lettuces," p.324.

Growing under cover
Protecting plants under cover provides a year-round supply. For use in winter and early spring, transplant seedlings in early fall from seed trays or cell packs under cover. Sow as a cut-and-come-again seedling crop (see p.306) under cover in spring for harvesting early, and in early fall for a late crop.

Harvesting and storing
Harvest endive between seven and 13 weeks after sowing, depending on the cultivar and season. Pick leaves as needed, or cut across the crown, allowing the plant to resprout. Mature plants respond well to cut-and-come-again treatment (see "Cut-and-come-again harvesting," p.312). Endive leaves do not store well, so should be eaten fresh.

Chicory (*Cichorium intybus*)

There are many types of chicory, all with a distinctive, slightly bitter taste. Nearly all are very hardy and are useful crops for growing in cooler months. Their diverse colors make them attractive in salads, and some types may also be cooked. All types have low nitrogen requirements (see p.310).

Belgian endive

Similar in appearance to dandelions (*Taraxacum officinale*), this biennial has pointed leaves about 8in (20cm) long, with a spread of about 6in (15cm). Its chicons (the whitened, compact, leafy shoots obtained from lifting the roots and forcing and blanching them to make them sweeter) may be eaten raw or cooked. The green leaves may also be used, but taste more bitter.

RECOMMENDED CHICORY

Belgian endive
'Flash'
'Turbo' F1
'Witloof Zoom' F1

Radicchio
'Adria'
'Alto'
'Augusto'
'Cesare' (early)
'Marina'
'Medusa'

'Cesare'

'Red Treviso'
'Red Verona'

Sugar loaf chicory
'Pan di Zucchero'
'Poncho'

Belgian endive grows best at 59–66°F (15–19°C). It is generally forced for winter use. Grow the plants in an open site in reasonably fertile – but not freshly manured – soil.

The plants require a fairly long growing season. Sow seed outdoors *in situ* in spring or early summer, in rows 12in (30cm) apart. Thin the seedlings to about 8in (20cm) apart. Keep plants weed-free. Water them to prevent the soil from drying out.

Belgian endive may be forced *in situ* in light soils and areas with mild winters. In early winter, cut the green leaves about 1in (2.5cm) above ground level. Cover the stumps with soil, making a ridge about 6in (15cm) high; the chicons will grow and force their way through.

Force indoors if the garden soil is heavy or winters are severe, or if an earlier crop is required. Dig up the plants in late fall or early winter. Cut the leaves to 1in (2.5cm) and trim roots to about 8in (20cm); reject any that are very thin. The roots may be forced immediately or stored for forcing a few at a time in succession during the winter and early spring. To store the roots, lay them flat in boxes with moist sand between each of the layers and keep them in a frost-free shed or cellar until they are required.

To force indoors, plant several of the prepared roots in a large pot or box filled with soil mix or garden soil, and cover with an inverted pot or box of the same size. Block any drainage holes to keep out light. Keep the soil moist, and maintain a temperature of 50–64°F (10–18°C). Roots may also be planted under greenhouse staging or in a garden frame. Make a lightproof area by stretching black plastic over wire hoops or attaching it to a wooden support. Do not use plastic in spring if temperatures soar, since aphid damage and rotting may occur. Belgian endive is normally free of pests and diseases.

Harvest chicons forced outside after eight to 12 weeks when about 4in (10cm) high by moving the soil and cutting the heads 1in (2.5cm) above the neck. Plants forced indoors should be ready after three to four weeks. Stumps may resprout to give a second crop of smaller chicons. Keep chicons wrapped or refrigerated after cutting since they become green and bitter on exposure to light.

FORCING AND BLANCHING BELGIAN ENDIVE

1 In late fall or early winter, lift the mature plant carefully. The central leaves may be tender enough to eat.

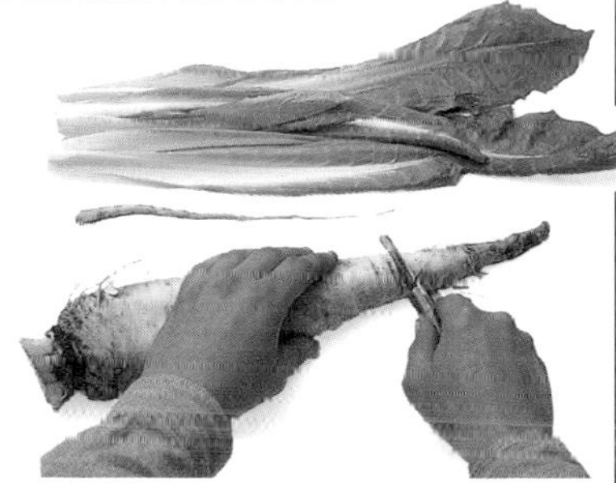

2 Using a sharp knife, trim the leaves to 1in (2.5cm) from the crown, and slice off the base of the root and any side roots, leaving the root 8–9in (20–22cm) long.

3 Put a layer of moist potting soil mix or garden soil into a 9in (24cm) pot. Place 3 trimmed roots in the mixture and firm so that they stand upright, then fill the pot to within 1in (2.5cm) of the rim and firm, leaving the crowns exposed.

4 Line another pot with aluminum foil or black plastic to cover the drainage holes, and place it over the roots to block the light. Keep at 50–64°F (10–18°C). Harvest the chicons 3–4 weeks later by cutting just above soil level.

Radicchio

This is a varied group of perennials usually grown as annuals. The typical radicchio, also known as red chicory, is a low-growing plant with bitter, reddish green outer leaves and a compact heart. It is eaten raw in salads, shredded to reduce bitterness, or may be cooked.

Radicchio tolerates a wide range of temperatures and soil conditions, but is mainly grown for use in the cooler months. Cultivars vary in their frost tolerance. 'Red Treviso' is exceptionally hardy; it may be forced in the same way as Belgian endive (see p.323). The new F1 hybrids produce more solid heads than traditional cultivars. Sow in early and midsummer, *in situ* or in seed trays for transplanting. Plant 10–14in (25–35cm) apart, depending on the cultivar. Transplant summer-sown crops under cover in fall.

Eight to ten weeks after sowing, pick single leaves or harvest the whole head. Radicchio stands a long time after maturing; in temperate climates, protect with low tunnels in late fall so that the plants develop more solid heads.

Sugar loaf chicory

Sugar loaf chicory is green-leaved, forming a conical head not unlike Romaine lettuce in both shape and size. Its inner leaves are naturally blanched and slightly sweet. For use, and for climate, soil, and cultivation requirements, see "Radicchio" (left).

Sugar loaf chicory may be sown in spring as a cut-and-come-again seedling crop (see p.306); harvest the seedlings before temperatures rise, causing leaves to coarsen. For mature plants, thin seedlings to 10in (25cm) apart, and harvest in late summer to fall. The plants tolerate some cold and provide winter crops if grown under cover.

Harvest leaves as needed, or cut the mature heads. The heads keep for a few weeks in cool, dry, frost-free conditions. They may also be piled up, turned inward, and covered with straw to form clamps (see *Making a Rutabaga Clamp*, p.349).

SUGAR LOAF CHICORY

Lettuces (*Lactuca sativa*)

Lettuces are annual, low-growing plants; they usually have green leaves, although some cultivars have red or reddish green leaves.

There are several distinct types. Romaine (cos) lettuces have long, substantial, well-flavored leaves with loose hearts; semicos types are shorter with very sweet, crunchy leaves. Butterhead, or Boston, lettuces have smooth, soft leaves, which form a rounded, compact heart; crispheads (known as icebergs when marketed with the outer leaves removed) have crispy leaves forming a heart. Loose-leaf lettuces, typified by the Salad Bowl types, do not form hearts so are slow to bolt and may be cut over a long period; their leaves are often indented and are very decorative. They are the most nutritious form of lettuce and may also be used for cut-and-come-again seedling crops (see p.306).

Lettuces vary from 4in (10cm) to over 12in (30cm) in spread. The Romaine types are about 10in (25cm) tall, others about 6in (15cm) high. Lettuces are primarily used as salad vegetables, but outer and older leaves may also be cooked or used in soups.

Lettuces are cool-season crops, growing best at 50–68°F (10–20°C). Cool nights are essential for good results. Some cultivars are tolerant of heat or cold. Germination is poor above 77°F (25°C); at these temperatures, plants tend to bolt rapidly and may become bitter, although loose-leaf lettuces are slower to bolt than other types.

Grow in an open site, or in light shade in very hot weather. Lettuces need fertile, moisture-retentive soil and, although they fall into none of the rotation groups, should not be grown in one patch of soil for two years in a row to prevent the build-up of fungus disease. They require medium nitrogen levels (see p.310).

LOOSE-LEAF LETTUCES ('LOLLO ROSSA')

Sowing and planting

Cultivars appropriate for the season must be sown. For a year-round supply in cool climates, sow from early spring to late summer at two- to three-week intervals. At the end of summer or in early fall, sow hardy cultivars that overwinter outdoors or under cover to produce a spring crop. In warm climates, only heat-tolerant cultivars should be sown during the summer.

In cool climates, sow seed *in situ*, in a seedbed, or in trays or cell packs for transplanting. Sowings in summer are best made *in situ*, since seedlings may wilt when transplanted unless they have been raised in cell packs. Seed may become dormant in high temperatures; this is most likely to occur several hours after sowing and may be overcome by watering after sowing to cool the soil, by putting seed trays or cell packs in a cool place to germinate, or by sowing seed in the afternoon so that the critical period occurs at night when temperatures are lower.

HARVESTING LOOSE-LEAF LETTUCES

Loose-leaf lettuces may be harvested by cutting across the leaves 1in (2.5cm) above ground level. Leave the stump to resprout.

RECOMMENDED LETTUCES

Romaine
'Paris Island Cos'
'Red Majestic'
'Rosalita'

'Paris Island Cos'

Semicos
'Winter Density' **Ow**

Butterhead
'Burpee Bibb'
'Buttercrunch'
'Pirat'
'Sangria' (bicolor)
'Tom Thumb'

Loose-leaf
'Black-seeded Simpson'
'Grand Rapids'
'Green Ice'
'Lollo Rossa'
'Oakleaf'
'Salad Bowl'

'Salad Bowl'

Crisphead
'Green Lake'
'Iceberg'
'Ithaca'
'Minetto'
'Warpath'

'Green Lake'

KEY
Ow *Overwinters under cover*

Transplant lettuces in moist conditions when they have five or six leaves, with the base of the leaves positioned just above soil level. In hot weather, shade young plants until they are established. Space small cultivars 6in (15cm) apart, and larger ones about 12in (30cm) apart.

Sow hardy cultivars for overwintering outdoors *in situ* or under cloches or in frames; thin to about 3in (7cm) apart in fall and to the full distance apart in spring. Floating row covers or cloches put over the plants in spring improve their quality and help them to mature earlier.

Most types of lettuce may be grown as cut-and-come-again seedling crops, especially loose-leaf types, including the traditional European "cutting" cultivars, and some Romaine types (see "Cut-and-come-again seedling crops," p.306).

Routine cultivation

Keep lettuce beds weed-free. Apply a nitrogenous fertilizer or organic liquid feed if growth is slow. In dry conditions, water the plants at a rate of 5 gallons/sq yd (23 liters/sq m) per week. The most critical watering period is about seven to ten days before maturity (see also p.308). In late fall or early winter, protect lettuces with cloches to improve the quality of the crop.

Pests and diseases

Problems include greenfly and root aphids (see "Aphids," p.552), cutworms (p.561), slugs (p.550), mosaic virus (see "Viruses," p.555), downy mildew (p.552), boron deficiency (p.560), and gray mold/*Botrytis* (p.559); birds may attack seedlings. Some cultivars show aphid resistance and others have some tolerance to mosaic virus and downy mildew.

Protecting Seedlings

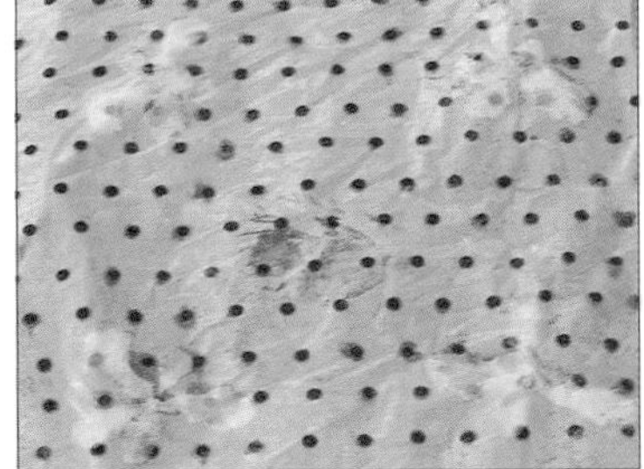

Protecting seedlings with perforated film helps them mature more quickly early in the season.

Growing under cover

In cool climates, earlier lettuce crops may be obtained by sowing or planting in early spring in an unheated greenhouse, beneath cloches or floating row covers, or in cold frames. Some cultivars may also be grown under cover in winter for early spring cropping; for midwinter crops, gentle heat is usually required.

Harvesting and storing

Loose-leaf lettuces should be ready about seven weeks after sowing, butterheads after ten or 11 weeks, and Romaine and crispheads after 11 or 12 weeks. Cut Romaine, butterhead, and crisphead types soon after maturing to prevent bolting. They may be stored for a few days in a refrigerator. Pick the leaves of loose-leaf types a few at a time, as required, since they do not store well, or cut across the plants 1in (2.5cm) above soil level, leaving the stumps to resprout.

Spinach (*Spinacia oleracea*)

This fast-growing annual reaches a height of 6–8in (15–20cm), with a spread of about 6in (15cm). The highly nutritious leaves are smooth or crinkled, and round or pointed, depending on the cultivar. They are eaten lightly cooked or, when young, raw in salads.

Spinach is a cool-season crop, growing best at 61–4°F (16–18°C), although it will grow well at lower temperatures. Small plants and seedlings may survive 15°F (-9°C). Grow cultivars recommended for the area; many are prone to bolt in long days (see "Daylength," p.303), especially after a cold period or in hot, dry conditions. Recommended cultivars that may be used as seedling crops or mature plants include 'Melody', 'Space', and 'Tyee'.

Spinach tolerates light shade in summer, and needs a soil with medium nitrogen levels (see p.310). For other soil requirements, see "Swiss chard and spinach beet," p.322.

Sowing and planting

Sow in cool seasons as spinach will not germinate in temperatures above 86°F (30°C). Sow *in situ*, placing individual seeds about 1in (2.5cm) apart in rows spaced about 12in (30cm) apart. For a continuous crop, sow in succession, after seedlings of the previous sowings have appeared. Thin early as for Swiss chard (see p.322), to about 3in (7cm) for young plants, or to 6in (15cm) apart for large plants.

Spinach may also be grown as a cut-and-come-again seedling crop (see p.306) for use in salads. For this, sow in early spring and early fall under cover, and also in late summer to overwinter where winters are not too harsh. For routine cultivation, pests and diseases, and growing under cover, see "Swiss chard and spinach beet," p.322.

Harvesting and storing

Cut leaves between five and ten weeks after sowing at any stage once the plants are about 2in (5cm) tall. Either cut individual leaves, or cut the heads about 1in (2.5cm) above the ground and leave them to resprout; alternatively, pull up whole plants. In warm areas, harvest plants young, before they start to run to seed. Use the leaves fresh soon after picking, or store by freezing.

Spinach

New Zealand spinach (*Tetragonia tetragonioides*, syn. *T. expansa*)

A half-hardy, creeping perennial, New Zealand spinach is also grown as an annual. The plants have thick, triangular leaves about 2in (5cm) long with a spread of 3–4ft (90–120cm). The leaves are used in the same way as spinach (see above).

New Zealand spinach tolerates drought and high, even tropical, temperatures, but cannot withstand frost. It grows best in an open site on reasonably fertile and moisture-retentive soil, and needs low nitrogen (see p.310). It is generally less prone to bolting than spinach.

Seeds may be slow to germinate, so to aid germination soak them in water for 24 hours before sowing. In cool climates, sow seed indoors and plant out at 18in (45cm) each way after all risk of frost has passed. Otherwise sow seed *in situ* outdoors after the last frost, thinning in stages to the final spacing. Keep the seedlings weed-free (mature plants cover the soil, suppressing weeds). Pest or disease problems are rare.

Start picking the young leaves and the tips of the stems six or seven weeks after sowing. Pick frequently to encourage further young growth for three or four months. New Zealand spinach should be used fresh immediately after picking, or frozen.

Picking New Zealand Spinach

Pick the young leaves and tips of stems of New Zealand spinach before seedheads start to form. Plants will continue to make new growth that may be harvested until the first frosts.

Minor salad vegetables

THERE are many lesser-known vegetables worth cultivating to use raw in salads, either on their own or mixed with other vegetables. They are suitable for growing in small gardens and containers. The leaves are distinctly flavored and nutritious, especially if used young. Apart from summer purslane and iceplants, all tolerate a few degrees below freezing, or even lower temperatures on well-drained soil with wind protection. In cool climates, most may be grown under cover in winter for higher yields. Most are fast-maturing but make lusher growth in nitrogen-rich soil. Many are best sown as cut-and-come-again seedling crops (see p.306). They are usually free of pests and diseases.

Upland cress (*Barbarea verna*)

This biennial, low-growing plant has a spread of 6–8in (15–20cm); upland cress is also known as American land cress. The glossy, deep green leaves have a strong flavor similar to watercress, and are used as a watercress substitute, either raw or cooked. Upland cress is very hardy, remaining green in winter. It grows best in the shade; it runs to seed rapidly in heat, becoming coarse and very hot-tasting. It may be intercropped between taller vegetables or used as a bed edging.

Grow upland cress in fertile and moisture-retentive soils. Sow seed in spring for an early summer crop, or in late summer for a fall and overwintering crop. It may be grown in unheated greenhouses in winter. Sow *in situ*, thinning to 6in (15cm) apart, or in seed trays to transplant. Pick leaves seven weeks after sowing when they are 3–4in (7–10cm) long. If a few plants are left to run to seed in spring they seed freely, and the seedlings may be transplanted where they are needed. Flea beetles (p.550) may attack young plants.

UPLAND CRESS

Mustard (*Brassica hirta*)

Mustard is similar to cress in its habit and is often partnered with it. It is grown for the sharply flavored seedling leaves which may be used raw in salads. It is a cool-season crop that runs to seed very rapidly in hot weather. Its leaves tend to become coarse if it is grown in areas with heavy rainfall.

In temperate climates, outdoor sowings are most successful in spring and fall *in situ*, using any of the methods suggested for cut-and-come-again seedlings (see p.306).

Mustard, like cress, is a useful crop for growing under cover from fall to spring. It may be sown without soil either on moist paper towels in a saucer placed on a windowsill, or in a sprouter; alternatively, it may be sown in a seed tray of potting mix or soil. These methods may be used all year. Mustard germinates faster than cress, so if the two are required together, the mustard should be sown two or three days later than the cress. A sowing every seven to ten days ensures a continuous supply of this vegetable.

Harvest mustard by cutting as required when the seedlings are about $1^1/_2$–2in (3.5–5cm) tall. It runs to seed much more rapidly than cress, and will normally provide no more than two or three cuts.

MUSTARD

Salad rape (*Brassica napus*)

This annual plant has light green, mild-flavored leaves and is often used as a substitute for mustard in salads. It is fast-growing but slower to run to seed than either mustard or cress. The leaves are used raw as seedlings, while larger leaves may be cooked as greens.

Salad rape survives temperatures of 14°F (-10°C), and tolerates moderate heat. The plants grow in a wide range of soils. In temperate climates, sow under cover in early spring and late fall; sow in succession outdoors until early fall. Indoors, grow on a windowsill as for mustard (left). Outdoors, sow broadcast, or in rows or wide drills. Make the first cut after ten days; when plants reach 24in (60cm), harvest small leaves over several months.

HARVESTING SALAD RAPE

Cut leaves of salad rape at any stage from seedling to 3in (7cm) long. In good conditions, three cuts of seedling leaves may be possible.

Arugula (*Eruca vesicaria*)

This hardy, spicy Mediterranean plant is used in salads; older plants may be cooked. Arugula is also known as rucola, salad rocket, Mediterranean rocket, or roquette. It grows best in moisture-retentive soil in cool weather; in cool climates, it is good under cover in winter, and as a cut-and-come-again seedling crop. Sow broadcast or in rows to cut as seedlings, or thin to 6in (15cm) to cut when larger. Seedlings are ready in three weeks. Flea beetles (p.550) may attack arugula.

ARUGULA

Cress (*Lepidium sativum*)

This fast-growing plant is grown for its seedling leaves, which are used raw. Cress is also known as garden cress, curly cress, or peppercress. There is a fine-leaved and a broad-leaved form. It is a moderately hardy, cool-season crop, running to seed rapidly in hot weather unless sown in light shade. In cool climates, cress grows well under cover in the winter months. It may stop growing at very low temperatures, but starts again when temperatures rise. It is useful for inter- and undercropping.

Except in very cool areas, cress is best sown in spring and late summer or early fall; avoid sowing in hot weather. Either sow on moist paper towels in a saucer and place on a windowsill or sow in a sprouter; this will give one cut. To obtain several consecutive cuts, sow in a seed tray of light soil, or broadcast in the ground in single rows, or in wide drills. Cut ten days after sowing when seedlings are up to 2in (5cm) high. If sown in the ground, up to four successive cuts may be made.

BROAD-LEAVED CRESS

Iceplants (*Mesembryanthemum crystallinum*)

Grown as perennials in warm climates and as tender annuals elsewhere, iceplants have a sprawling habit, succulent stems, and thick, fleshy leaves, covered with sparkling bladders. The leaves and young stems taste refreshing and slightly salty. They are used raw in salads or cooked like spinach.

Iceplants need a sunny position in light, well-drained soil. In warm climates, sow *in situ* outdoors; in cool climates, sow indoors in the spring, transplanting to 12in (30cm) apart after all risk of frost has passed. Slugs (p.550) may attack seedlings. Plants may be propagated by means of cuttings (see Perennials, "Stem tip cuttings," p.164). The first picking of the young leaves and tender pieces of stem may be made about four weeks after planting. Harvest plants regularly to encourage further growth, and remove any flowers that appear. Leaves and stems keep fresh for several days.

Iceplants

Miner's lettuce (*Montia perfoliata*)

This is a hardy annual with heart-shaped leaves and dainty flowering shoots. The mildly flavored, slightly succulent leaves, stems, and flowering shoots are used raw in salads. Also known as winter purslane or claytonia, it thrives in cool weather. It prefers well-drained conditions but grows well even in poor, light soil. Once established, it self-seeds rapidly; the shallow-rooted, invasive seedlings are easily pulled up.

Make the main sowing in late summer for a fall to early winter crop outdoors. Sow in spring for a summer crop. Grow either broadcast as a cut-and-come-again seedling crop (see p.306), or in rows, or 4in (10cm) wide drills; seed may be sown *in situ* or in seed trays. Thin seedlings to 6–9in (15–23cm) apart. Start cutting 12 weeks after sowing, allowing plants to resprout.

Miner's Lettuce

Summer purslane (*Portulaca oleracea*)

This half-hardy, low-growing plant has slightly succulent leaves and stems that are used raw or cooked. There are green- and yellow-leaved forms; the green type has thinner leaves, is more vigorous and possibly better flavored, but the yellow or golden form is attractive in salads. The plants need a warm, sheltered site with light, well-drained soil.

Grow summer purslane either as a cut-and-come-again seedling crop (see p.306) or as single plants. In cool climates, sow in a seed tray in late spring, planting out 6in (15cm) apart, after all risk of frost. Make early and late summer sowings under cover as a cut-and-come-again seedling crop. In warm climates, sow *in situ* throughout summer. Cut the seedlings, or young shoots of single plants, from four to eight weeks after sowing. Cut regularly, always leaving two basal leaves, and remove any flowers that develop. Slugs (p.550) may attack plants.

Golden Summer Purslane

Watercress (*Rorippa nasturtium-aquaticum*)

A hardy aquatic perennial, watercress (also known as *Nasturtium officinale*) has nutritious, sharply flavored leaves that are used in salads and soups. Its natural habitat is fresh running streams, with slightly alkaline water at about 50°F (10°C).

Root cuttings by placing stems in fresh water; they will soon root and may be planted at the edge of a stream in spring, spaced 6in (15cm) apart. Watercress may be grown in moist garden soil, but it is easier to grow in 6–8in (15–21cm) pots. Put a layer of gravel or moss in each pot, fill with rich soil, and stand it in a dish of cool, clean water. Plant three or four rooted cuttings per pot, and stand it in a sheltered position in good light. Change the water at least daily in hot weather. Cut leaves as needed.

Watercress Grown in a Pot

Dandelions (*Taraxacum officinale*)

Hardy perennial weeds, dandelions spread up to 12in (30cm). Wild and cultivated forms are grown for the young leaves, which are used raw. The cultivated forms are larger and slower to run to seed. Dandelion leaves are slightly bitter, but blanching sweetens them. The flowers and roots are also edible. Dandelions tolerate a range of well-drained soils.

Sow in spring in seed trays for transplanting, or *in situ*, spacing 14in (35cm) apart. Blanch in succession from late summer, covering dry plants with a large, lightproof bucket. Harvest the leaves when they are elongated and creamy yellow. Dandelions die back in winter, but reappear in spring; the plants will continue to grow for several years.

Blanching Dandelion

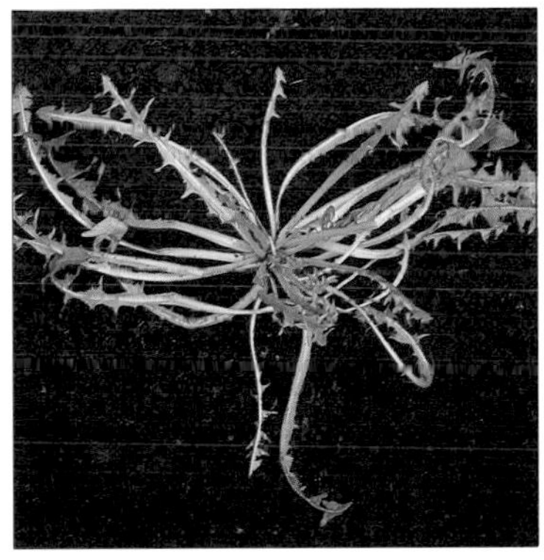

When the plant has several leaves, cover it with a bucket 12in (30cm) tall. Harvest the creamy yellow, elongated leaves after a few weeks.

Corn salad (*Valerianella locusta*)

Grown for fall and winter salads in cool climates, this hardy annual forms small, mild-flavored plants. Corn salad is also known as lamb's lettuce or mache. There are two types: the floppy, large-leaved type, and the smaller, upright type with darker green leaves, which is reputedly the hardier. It tolerates a wide range of soils. In cold climates, grow it under cover in winter to obtain more prolific and tender-leaved plants. Corn salad is a useful crop for inter- or undercropping vegetables such as winter brassicas.

Corn salad may be grown as a cut-and-come-again seedling crop (see p.306) or as individual plants. Sow from midsummer onward *in situ*, broadcast, in rows, or in wide drills. Keep the seeds moist until germination. Thin seedlings to 4in (10cm) apart. Corn salad is slow-growing and may take 12 weeks to mature. Harvest leaves individually or cut across the plants, leaving them to resprout for a second cut.

Large-leaved Corn Salad

Fruiting and flowering vegetables

SOME of the most exotic and succulent vegetables fall into the fruiting and flowering group of vegetables. Many – tomatoes, peppers, eggplants, and melons, for example – are tropical or subtropical in origin; in cooler areas these may need to be grown under cover or in a warm situation. In cool climates, others such as squash, sweet corn, and pumpkins need to be germinated indoors but may be planted outdoors to grow to maturity. All need a warm, sheltered situation to ripen their fruits and for pollination to be successful.

Sweet peppers (*Capsicum annuum* Grossum Group)

Also called bell peppers, these annuals have a bushy habit and may grow up to 30in (75cm) tall with a spread of 18–24in (45–60cm). The fruits are usually oblong, range in size from 1¼–6in (3–15cm) long and 1¼–3in (3–7cm) in diameter, and may be green, cream, yellow, orange, red, or dark purple. The mature fruits are eaten cooked or raw, whole and stuffed, or sliced.

Sweet peppers are tropical and subtropical plants needing a minimum temperature of 70°F (21°C) with a humidity of 70–75 percent. Temperatures over 86°F (30°C) may reduce fruit set and cause buds and flowers to drop. In temperate climates, plants may be grown under cover or outside in a sunny, sheltered site. Moderately deep, fertile, well-drained soil with medium nitrogen levels (see p.310) is required.

SWEET PEPPERS

Sowing and planting

Sow seed in spring indoors in trays of soil mix with a pH of 5.5–7. Prick out the seedlings into 3–3½in (6–9cm) pots and plant out ten to 12 weeks after sowing, spacing them 18–20in (45–50cm) apart each way. In cooler regions, pot on seedlings and do not plant out until all risk of frost has passed and nights are warm, or flowers will drop.

RECOMMENDED SWEET PEPPERS

- 'Ace' F1
- 'Bell Boy' F1
- 'Californian Wonder'
- 'Canape' F1
- 'Cherry Sweet'
- 'Early Prolific'
- 'Gypsy' F1
- 'Hungarian Wax'
- 'Lipstick'
- 'Orovelle'
- 'Purple Beauty'
- 'Ultra Gold' F1
- 'Yolo Wonder'

Routine cultivation

Pinch out the terminal growing point of established plants to encourage a bushy habit, and stake cultivars over 24in (60cm) tall. Water regularly to prevent leaf and bud drop, and mulch with organic material. Apply a balanced fertilizer every two weeks. Protect plants outdoors with plastic covers, if necessary.

Pests and diseases

Plants may be attacked by aphids (p.552); they may also be affected by spider mites (p.552), whiteflies (p.552), caterpillars (p.551), blossom end rot (see "Calcium deficiency," p.564), and thrips (p.553).

Growing under cover

Sow as above in early spring. When the seedlings are 3–4in (8–10cm) tall, pot them into 8in (21cm) pots or transplant into grow bags or well-prepared greenhouse beds. Space plants at least 20in (50cm) apart and stake taller cultivars. Maintain the recommended temperature and a humidity of 70–75 percent by regularly damping down.

RIPENING SWEET PEPPERS

As they ripen, the fruits change from green to red, yellow, orange, or dark purple, and the flavor becomes sweeter.

Harvesting and storing

Harvest the peppers 12–14 weeks after transplanting and before the first frost if the plants are growing outside. Some cultivars are best used when the fruits are green, but others may be left on the plants for two to three weeks until they change color to red or creamy yellow. Cut off individual peppers; they may be stored in cool, humid conditions for up to 14 days at 54–9°F (12–15°C). Entire plants may also be stored if pulled before first frost (see "Fruiting vegetables," p.312).

HARVESTING SWEET PEPPERS

Some peppers are best harvested when green; others may be left to turn red or yellow. Cut the stalk about 1in (2.5cm) from the fruit.

Chili peppers (*Capsicum annuum* Longum Group)

This form of *Capsicum annuum* has pointed fruits up to 3½in (9cm) long. Popular cultivars include 'Jalapeño', 'Anaheim Chili', 'Poblano', and 'Serrano'.

The plants are cultivated in the same way as sweet peppers (see left); chili peppers are slightly more tolerant of high temperature levels, however. They may be picked for use at any stage when the color is green to red. If they are growing outside, they should be harvested before the first frost is expected.

The hot flavor, which increases with the maturity of the chili fruit, comes from the white pith and seeds inside. If the flavor is too hot, the pith and seeds may be removed and discarded.

RIPENING CHILI PEPPERS

RED CHILI PEPPERS

Hot peppers (*Capsicum frutescens*)

These plants, also known as cayenne peppers, are branching perennials that grow to 5ft (1.5m) tall and bear small, narrow, orange, yellow, or red fruits that may hang from the branches or be carried upright, depending on the cultivar. They are highly pungent and are used in sauces and as a general flavoring.

Hot peppers are tropical and subtropical plants and therefore cannot tolerate frost. Space plants 24in (60cm) apart in each direction, and cultivate in the same way as sweet peppers (see opposite), although they generally require more water. Staking is not normally necessary.

Hot peppers need a long growing period, and the first fruits are usually produced about 15–18 weeks after planting. They should be allowed to ripen fully before being picked. They may be frozen or dried and stored for several months.

HOT PEPPERS

RECOMMENDED HOT PEPPERS

'Cayenne Large Red Thick'
'Cayenne Long Slim'
'Hungarian Yellow Wax Hot'
'Red Cherry Small'
'Super Cayenne' F1

'Super Cayenne'

Watermelons (*Citrullus lanatus*)

Watermelons are annual, tropical or subtropical plants with spreading stems that grow to 10–12ft (3–4m). Their fruits are rounded or oblong, green or cream, striped or mottled, and may grow to 24in (60cm) in length; they are eaten raw. Plants need a temperature of 77–86°F (25–30°C) and are grown outdoors where the growing season is long; they need at least 70 frost-free days. Well-drained, sandy soils with medium nitrogen levels (see p.310) and a pH of 5.5–7 are needed. Incorporate a general-purpose fertilizer and well-rotted manure into the soil before planting.

WATERMELON

Sowing and planting

Sow in early spring under cover, in trays or 3–3½in (6–9cm) pots, at a temperature of 72–77°F (22–25°C). When the seedlings are 4–6in (10–15cm) tall, harden them off. Plant them out after all risk of frost has passed, spaced at least 3ft (1m) apart. Protect from wind and cold weather with plastic screens.

Routine cultivation

Mulch to retain moisture, and apply a balanced fertilizer or liquid feed every two weeks until the fruits begin to develop. Pinch out the growing points of the main shoots when they are 6ft (2m) long and train side shoots between other plants in the row. To assist formation of fruits, hand-pollinate the flowers (see "Summer squash and zucchini," p.332). Reduce sublateral growths from the side shoots to two or three leaves after fruits start to develop, and place a pad of dried grass or a block of wood beneath each fruit to protect it from soilborne pests and diseases.

Pests and diseases

Humidity levels over 75 percent encourage leaf diseases, particularly powdery mildew (p.552) and mosaic virus (see "Viruses," p.555). Likely pests include aphids (p.552), root-knot nematodes (p.566), and fruit flies (p.565).

Growing under cover

Watermelons are extremely vigorous and are not normally grown in a greenhouse. They may be grown under plastic covers, spaced 3ft (1m) apart; remove covers at flowering time to reduce humidity and encourage insect-pollination.

Harvesting and storing

Harvest ten to 14 weeks after sowing; mature fruits give a hollow sound when tapped. They may be stored 14–20 days at 50–54°F (10–12°C).

RECOMMENDED WATERMELONS

'Black Sugar Baby' F1
'Charleston Gray'
'Dixie Queen' F1
'Nova' F1
'Sunshine' F1
'Sweet Favorite' F1
'Yellow Baby'

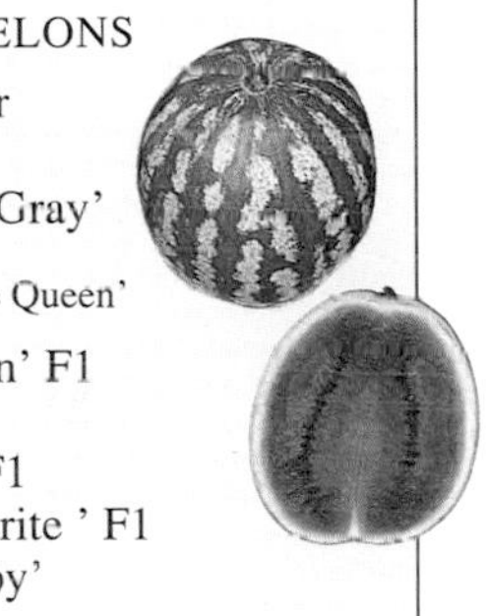

'Dixie Queen'

Melons (*Cucumis melo*)

These annuals grow on long, spreading vines or as compact bushes. The three major types are cantaloupe, winter or casaba, and muskmelons (including honeydew). Cantaloupes have gray-green, thick, rough skins with deep grooves and orange flesh. Winter melons have smooth yellow or yellow and green striped skin, and yellow or green flesh. Muskmelons vary in size but are usually smaller than cantaloupes and winter melons and often have fine reticulated markings on smooth skins; they have orange flesh. Honeydews have smooth skins and green flesh. Winter melons and some cantaloupes are suitable for greenhouse culture.

MUSKMELON

Melons are tropical plants requiring a minimum temperature of 64°F (18°C) for germination, rising to 77°F (25°C) during the growing period. In very sunny, sheltered sites, growing in the open is possible but in temperate climates plants are grown in cold frames or in a greenhouse. They need a well-drained, fertile soil with a pH of 6.5–7, a high humus content, and high nitrogen levels (see p.310). Add a general-purpose fertilizer and well-rotted compost or manure.

Sowing and planting

Sow seed under cover in early spring in trays or in 3–3½in (6–9cm) pots (two seeds per pot), removing the weaker seedling if both germinate. After about six weeks, and when all risk of frost is past, the seedlings should be hardened off and planted out, spaced 3ft (1m) apart with 3–5ft (1–1.5m) between rows. Plant each seedling on a slight mound and protect young plants until they are established from wind and cold weather with cloches or plastic tunnels.

RECOMMENDED MELONS

Cantaloupes
'Ambrosia' F1
'Burpee Hybrid'

Muskmelons
'Classic' F1
'Sweet Dream'

Honeydews
'Earlidew'
'Sweetheart' F1

Winter melons
'Crenshaw'
'Santa Claus'

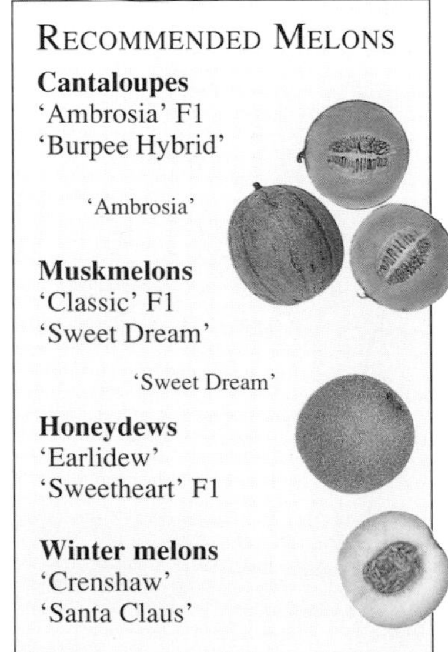

'Ambrosia'

'Sweet Dream'

Pinching Melons

Allow 1 flower per lateral to set, and then pinch or cut out the growing tip of each lateral at 2–3 leaves beyond the developing fruit.

Routine cultivation

After five leaves have developed, pinch out each growing point to encourage further shoots. When these are well developed, reduce them to about four of the most vigorous shoots. Train two shoots on either side, between adjacent plants in the row. Remove any protective covering when the plants begin to flower to encourage insect-pollination. Hand-pollinate them if required (see "Summer squash and zucchini," p.332).

Thin to one fruit per shoot when the fruits are 2.5cm (1in) in diameter, and pinch all sublaterals at two to three leaves beyond the developing fruits. Pinch out the main shoots when they are 3–4ft (1–1.2m) long and remove any further sublaterals that form. Place a pad of dried grass, a tile, or a piece of wood beneath each developing fruit to protect it from soilborne diseases.

Water regularly and feed every ten to 14 days with a liquid feed as the fruits begin to develop; reduce watering and feeding as fruits ripen.

Pests and diseases

Aphids (p.552), powdery mildew (p.552), spider mites (p.552), whiteflies (p.552), *Verticillium* wilt (p.559), spotted cucumber beetles (p.563), and striped cucumber beetles (p.571) may cause problems.

Growing under cover

To raise melons in a cold frame, plant seedlings singly in the center. After pinching, train four laterals to grow toward the corners. As the plants develop, increase ventilation and gradually reduce humidity. Once the fruits start forming, remove the sashes, replacing them at night in cold weather. In hot weather, shade lightly.

Melons may be grown in a greenhouse if the distance from the base of the side walls to the ridge is at least 6ft (2m). Plant seedlings onto well-prepared mounds (see "Cucumbers and gherkins," below). Grow as single or double cordons, training on stakes tied to horizontal wires up to the ridge. Space plants 15in (38cm) apart for single cordons, 2ft (60cm) for double cordons. They may also be grown in grow bags or 24–5cm (9–10in) pots placed on greenhouse staging.

For a single cordon, pinch out the growing point when the main shoot is 6ft (2m) long to encourage lateral growth. Pinch laterals at five leaves and sublaterals at two leaves beyond the flowers. For a double cordon, pinch out the main shoot and let two shoots develop vertically; train as above. Support developing fruits in 2in (5cm) mesh slings attached to the ridge. To aid pollination do not damp down during flowering. Maintain a temperature of 75°F (24°C) at night and 86°F (30°C) in the day.

Harvesting and storing

Harvest 12–20 weeks after sowing. Cantaloupe and muskmelons are sweet-smelling when mature, and the fruit stalks crack. Separate the fruits gently from the stalks. Store for 14–50 days at 50–59°F (10–15°C), depending on the cultivar.

Cucumbers and gherkins *(Cucumis sativus)*

Most are annual trailing vines that grow to 3–10ft (1–3m); there are a few compact bush cultivars. The immature fruits are eaten raw, pickled, or served in soup.

Cucumbers are characteristically rough-skinned, spiny, and 4–6in (10–15cm) long. Modern cultivars, many of Japanese origin, are smoother and up to 12in (30cm) long, with improved cold tolerance and disease resistance. They are mainly grown outdoors and are insect-pollinated. Gherkins are cucumbers with short, often stumpy fruits up to 3in (7cm) long, harvested young, and used mainly for pickling. Apple and lemon cucumbers are round, yellow-skinned ridged cucumbers that grow up to 2½in (6cm) in diameter. English and greenhouse fruits are smooth and over 12in (30cm) long. They do not require pollination to set fruit and, if pollinated, may produce bitter, swollen fruits; use the modern all-female cultivars to remove the risk of accidental pollination.

Cucumbers are warm-season vegetables, growing best between temperatures of 64–86°F (18–30°C). They have no frost tolerance and most are damaged at temperatures below 50°F (10°C). In northern latitudes, outdoor types may produce male flowers alone early in the season; female flowers, then fruits, occur later. Grow cucumbers in a sheltered site in fertile, humus-rich soil that is well drained but moisture-retentive: the roots must not dry out. Lime very acid soils. The plants need low nitrogen levels (see p.310).

Greenhouse types must be grown with minimum night temperatures of 68°F (20°C) and in high humidity. Never grow outdoor types in the same greenhouse with all-female cultivars since undesirable cross-pollination will occur.

Gherkin

Sowing and Planting Out

1 *Fill a small pot with seed soil mix to within 1in (2.5cm) of the rim. Place 2 or 3 seeds on their sides in the soil mix, then cover them to a depth of about ¾in (2cm). Water well and label. Save the strongest plant.*

2 *Prepare a hole 12in (30cm) wide and 12in (30cm) deep, and fill with well-rotted compost. Pile the soil on top to make a mound about 6in (15cm) high. Plant the cucumber on top of this mound. Firm in and water.*

Sowing and planting

Cucumbers transplant badly, so seed for outdoor varieties should be sown *in situ* after all risk of frost has passed or alternatively in small pots or cell packs. If sowing outside, prepare holes at least 12in (30cm) wide and deep, working in plenty of well-rotted compost or manure as you backfill. Cover with about 6in (15cm) of manured soil made into a small mound to ensure sharp drainage. Place seeds on their side about ¾in (2cm) deep, sowing two to three per pot or site.

Seed germinates at a minimum soil temperature of 68°F (20°C). Thin to one seedling after germination. Seed sown in pots needs a minimum temperature at night of 60°F (16°C) until the seedlings are planted out, about four weeks after sowing. Space climbing types 18in (45cm) apart; bush types, and climbing types if trailing over the ground, should be spaced about 30in (75cm) apart. In cool climates, protect plants from strong winds after planting.

Routine cultivation

Grow trailing types up supporting fences, nets, or stakes, or allow them to twine up strings. Nip out the growing point after five or six leaves have appeared, and train the resulting stronger growths up the support, tying them in if necessary. When these shoots reach the top of the support, nip them out two leaves beyond a flower; laterals will develop on which more fruits will form. As fruiting continues, feed plants every two weeks with a high-potassium

Bush Cucumbers

fertilizer or equivalent organic liquid feed. Regular watering is essential during the growing period, particularly after transplanting, so that plants establish quickly, and during flowering and fruiting to ensure healthy fruit formation (see "Critical watering periods," p.308).

Pests and diseases
Snails (p.550), aphids (p.552), powdery mildew (p.552), cutworms (p.561), spider mites (p.552), whiteflies (p.552), squash vine borers (p.553), cucumber mosaic virus (see "Viruses," p.555), spotted cucumber beetles (p.563), and striped cucumber beetles (p.571) may cause problems.

Growing under cover
Grow as in the open using appropriate cultivars – the all-female selections are recommended. Pinch the main shoot of each plant at the top of the supports and nip off side shoots beyond the first leaf. Damp down greenhouses to control pests.

Harvesting and storing
Harvest cucumbers regularly from about 12 weeks after sowing, when the sides of the fruits are parallel and they are about 6–8in (15–20cm) long. Harvest gherkins when they are 1–3in (2.5–7cm) long.

Climbing Cucumbers

Recommended Cucumbers and Gherkins

Ridged cucumbers
'Burpless Tasty Green' F1
'Bush Champion' F1

'Bush Champion'

Smooth cucumbers
'Burpee Hybrid II'
'Sweet Slice'
'Sweet Success'

Japanese cucumbers
'Kyoto'
'Suyo Long'

Gherkins
'Calypso'
'Cross Country'
'Lemon'

'Cross Country'

Winter squash (*Cucurbita maxima, C. moschata, C. pepo*)

This is a very diverse group of annuals, with fruits ranging from 1lb (450g) to well over 66lb (30kg). They include pumpkins and the inedible ornamental gourds. The skin may be smooth, warted, or ridged, and green, cream, blue-green, yellow, orange, red, or striped, the color often changing with maturity. Their shapes range from round, long, squat, or onion-shaped to a two-layered turban shape. Most form very large trailing plants with huge leaves; some are compact and bushy. Both young and mature fruits may be eaten cooked, either fresh or after storage. Shoots and young leaves may be cooked and flowers eaten raw or cooked. Some cultivars have edible seeds.

Winter Squash on a Tripod

For climate, site, and soil preparation requirements, see "Cucumbers and gherkins," opposite. Winter squash require medium to high nitrogen levels (see p.310).

Sowing and planting
Seed may be soaked overnight before sowing to hasten germination. Sow as for cucumbers (see opposite). Space plants 6–10ft (2–3m) apart, depending on the cultivar. For large cultivars, prepare holes up to 18in (45cm) deep and 24in (60cm) wide. Insert a marker stake when planting so that the center of the plant can be found if watering is necessary. Protect and mulch after planting.

Routine cultivation
A top-dressing of a general fertilizer may be applied soon after planting. Shoots may be trained in circles on the ground using bent wire to hold down the stems, or grown on supports, such as tripods. Where only a few large fruits are needed, remove all but two or three of the other fruits while still young.

Winter squash are deep-rooting, so watering should be needed only in very dry weather.

Pests and diseases
Slugs (p.550) may attack in early stages; later, squash vine borers (p.553), cucumber mosaic virus (p.555), spotted cucumber beetles (p.563), and striped cucumber beetles (p.571) may cause problems.

Harvesting and storing
Cut away any foliage shading the fruits to encourage them to ripen. Harvest winter squash 12–20 weeks after planting. Leave fruits for storing on the plant to mature as long as possible: the stem starts to crack and the skin hardens when the fruit is ripe. Pick before the first frost, cutting each fruit with a long stalk.

After harvesting, most storage types must be exposed to the sun for ten days to cure (further harden) the skin so that it forms a barrier, slowing the rate of water loss. Cover the fruits at night if frost threatens, or cure indoors at 81–90°F (27–32°C) for four days. Acorn types may be stored without first being cured. Store winter squash at about 50°F (10°C) in a well-ventilated place. They may be kept from four to six months, and, in some cases, even longer, depending on the conditions and the cultivar grown.

Recommended Winter Squash

'Blue Hubbard'
'Buttercup'
'Butternut' F1
'Golden Hubbard'
'Honey Delight'

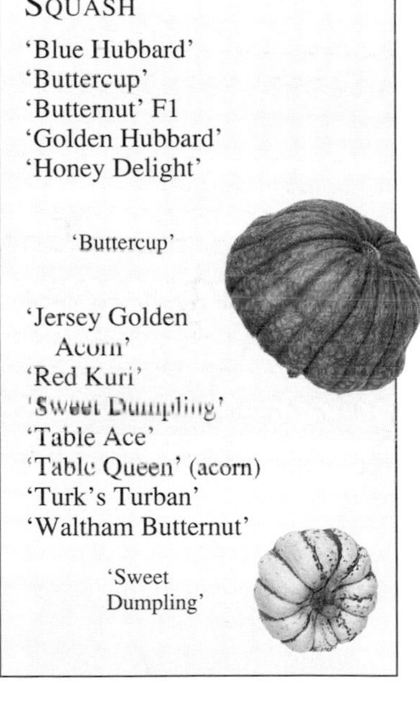
'Buttercup'

'Jersey Golden Acorn'
'Red Kuri'
'Sweet Dumpling'
'Table Ace'
'Table Queen' (acorn)
'Turk's Turban'
'Waltham Butternut'

'Sweet Dumpling'

Curing Winter Squash

When it is ripe, cut the squash off the plant with as long a stalk as possible. Leave the squash in the sun for about 10 days so that the skin hardens.

Summer squash and zucchini (*Cucurbita pepo*)

Summer squash and zucchini are annual plants that trail for several feet or form compact plants of 3ft (90cm) spread. They most commonly have cylindrical fruits about 12in (30cm) long and 5in (13cm) in diameter. Zucchini are normally harvested young, as are other squash whose fruits are tender-skinned when young. Summer squash may be trailing or bushy with green, yellow, white, or striped skin. Custard squash have flattish, fluted-edged fruits; crookneck squash have swollen fruits with a bent neck. There are also round-fruited cultivars. Spaghetti squash are squashlike in shape, but with hard skins; cooked, the flesh resembles spaghetti. All the fruits are generally cooked. Young leaves and shoot tips may also be cooked, and flowers eaten raw or cooked.

Summer squash are warm-season crops, needing temperatures of 64–81°F (18–27°C). Frost intolerance, soil, and soil preparation are as for cucumbers (see p.330). They need low nitrogen levels (see p.310).

Hand-pollinating

Summer squash and zucchini are generally insect-pollinated but in cold seasons, if fruits are not setting, it may be necessary to hand-pollinate. The female flower has a tiny bump (the embryonic fruit) behind the petals which the male flower lacks (see below); this makes it easy to distinguish between them.

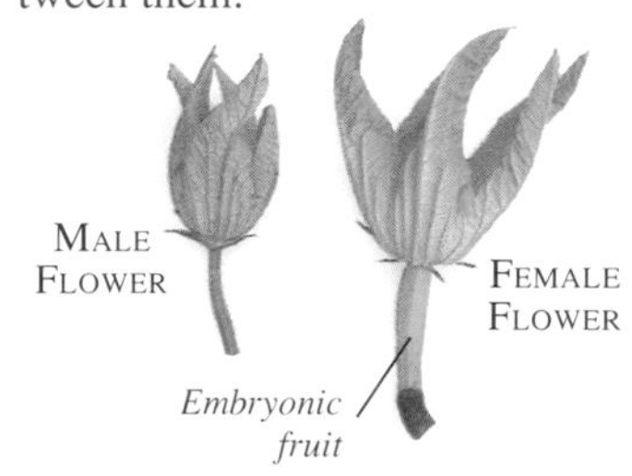

To hand-pollinate, take a male flower, remove all the petals and press it against the female flower. Alternatively, use a fine paintbrush to transfer the pollen from the stamens of the male flower to the stigma of the female.

Sowing and planting

Sow as for cucumbers (see p.330) when the soil temperature is at least 59°F (15°C). Place each seed about 1in (2.5cm) deep. Sow *in situ* after all risk of frost has passed, or germinate indoors. Space bush types 3ft (90cm) apart, and trailing types 4–6ft (1.2–2m) apart. In cool areas, protect young plants with cloches or floating row covers. In hot areas, floating row covers will protect young plants against insects. Mulch after planting.

BUSH SQUASH

Routine cultivation

Trailing types may be grown up strong supports. The shoots may also be trained in circles, using bent wire to peg down the stems. Toward the end of the season, nip off the ends of the shoots. Feed and water as for cucumbers (see p.330).

Pests and diseases

Slugs (p.550) may attack in early stages; squash vine borers (p.553), cucumber mosaic virus (see "Viruses," p.555), spotted cucumber beetles (p.563), and striped cucumber beetles (p.571) may cause problems.

Growing under cover

This is appropriate only in cool climates when a very early crop is required. Use bush cultivars.

Harvesting and storing

Harvest squash seven to eight weeks after planting. Some types may be stored for a few weeks if they are kept well ventilated at about 50°F (10°C) with high humidity. Spaghetti squash may be stored for several months.Pick zucchini when they are about 4in (10cm) long, preferably with the flower attached since this indicates freshness. Harvest shoots from the top 6in (15cm) of stem; new growth is soon made. If harvesting flowers, pick male ones after the females have set.

HARVESTING ZUCCHINI

Cut zucchini when they are 4in (10cm) long, with a short stalk. Handle the fruits carefully to avoid bruising them. Regular harvesting will encourage more fruits.

RECOMMENDED SUMMER SQUASH

'Butterstick'
'Early White Bush'
'Golden Girl'
'Gold Slice'
'Peter Pan'
'Scallopini' F1

'Early White Bush'

'Seneca Prolific'
'Sunburst'
'Sundrops'

'Vegetable Spaghetti'

Spaghetti squash
'Orangetti' F1
'Tivoli' (bush-type spaghetti squash)
'Vegetable Spaghetti'

Zucchini
'Ambassador' F1
'Black Jack'
'Burpee Hybrid'
'Cocozelle'
'Elite' F1
'Gold Rush' F1
'Roly Poly'
'Sundance'

Globe artichokes (*Cynara scolymus*)

These perennial plants have blue-gray leaves and thistlelike flowers. Globe artichokes may grow up to 4–5ft (1.2–1.5m) tall with a 3ft (90cm) spread. They are grown for the green and purple flower buds, which have edible, fleshy pads (the hearts) at the base of the outer scales and the top of the flower stem; the hearts are cooked or pickled. A reliable cultivar is 'Green Globe'.

Globe artichokes grow best in cool climates at 55–64°F (13–18°C) and tolerate light to medium frosts. They need an open but not exposed site, with fertile, well-drained soil into which plenty of compost or well-rotted manure has been dug, and low levels of nitrogen (see p.310).

Sowing and planting

Globe artichokes are normally increased by division. Using a sharp knife, two hand forks, or a spade, divide healthy, established plants in the spring; each division should have at least two shoots with a tuft of leaves and a good root system. Plant these divisions 24–30in (60–75cm) apart and trim the tips of the leaves to 5in (13cm). Globe artichokes may be raised from seed either indoors or

DIVIDING GLOBE ARTICHOKES

In spring, lift an established plant and divide it using two hand forks, a spade, or a knife. Each division should have at least two shoots and strong roots.

outdoors in spring, but the results are variable; thin or plant out seedlings at the correct spacing. In future years, divide the most productive plants to build up a good stock. Named cultivars can be raised only from divided offsets. Plants should be replaced every three years to maintain vigor and cropping levels.

Routine cultivation

Keep the planting area free of weeds and well mulched to conserve soil moisture. Do not allow the roots of globe artichokes to dry out in summer or become waterlogged in winter. If severe cold is expected, hill up the base of each plant, covering with a thick layer of straw; remove the covering in spring.

Pests and diseases

Lettuce root aphids (see "Aphids," p.552) may cause problems.

Harvesting and storing

In favorable conditions, some heads may be cut in the late summer of the first season. More flowering stems will be produced in the second season. Pick before the scales open, when the buds feel plump. Remove the hairy choke and stalk before freezing; the hearts may be pickled.

GLOBE ARTICHOKE

Tomatoes (*Lycopersicon esculentum*)

These are annual plants in temperate areas and short-lived perennials in the tropics. The main trailing stem of the staking (indeterminate) types grows to over 8ft (2.5m) long in warm climates, with vigorous side shoots. The shorter semideterminate types and the bush (determinate) types stop growing earlier than the staking types, and the stems end in a fruit cluster. Compact dwarf types may grow up to 9in (23cm) across and as tall.

Ripe tomato fruits are red, yellow, orange, pink, or white, and round, flat, plum- or pear-shaped. The tiny currant tomatoes (*Lycopersicon pimpinellifolium*) are 1/2in (1cm) in diameter; cherry types, 1in (2.5cm); and giant beefsteak types, up to 4in (10cm). All are eaten raw or cooked.

Tomatoes grow best at 70–75°F (21–4°C) or higher temperatures, but do not grow well below 61°F (16°C) and do not tolerate frost. They need high light intensity. In cool climates, grow them in a sheltered site outdoors or under cover; they are often grown in containers. Tomatoes tolerate a wide range of fertile and well-drained soils, with a pH of 5.5–7; lime very acid soils (see "Liming," p.533). Crops need to be rotated (see p.303).

Prepare the ground by working in plenty of well-rotted manure or compost at least 12in (30cm) deep, since tomatoes are deep-rooted gross feeders. Apply a general fertilizer before planting; tomatoes need high levels of phosphorus (see "Soil nutrients," p.309) but low levels of nitrogen (see p.310).

Sowing and planting

In warm climates, sow seed *in situ* in spring and thin seedlings to the correct spacing. In cool climates, six to eight weeks before the last frost is

BUSH TOMATOES

expected, sow seed 1/4in (6mm) deep, at about 80°F (27°C), in seed trays or cell packs. Transplant into 2–3in (5–6cm) pots at the two- or three-leaf stage; give the seedlings ample ventilation, space, and light. They can stand short periods of low temperatures if day temperatures rise to compensate. Harden off before planting out when night temperatures are over 45°F (7°C) or soil temperatures at least 50°F (10°C) and the risk of frost is over. Plant out when all danger of frost is past.

For extra-early crops, warm the soil by putting water-filled crop protectors into position about eight weeks before the last frost date. Tomato transplants can be put out two to four weeks later. In windy locations, shield new transplants with plastic or paper sleeves held away from the plants.

Staking types Plant indeterminate and semideterminate types on stakes with 15–18in (38–45cm) between plants in single rows 18in (45cm) apart, or in double rows with 3ft (90cm) between the pairs of rows.

Alternatively, plant in homemade or commercial tomato cages, which provide support without the need to tie in. Make sure that the mesh is large enough to get your hand through for picking.

Indeterminate cherry tomatoes such as 'Sweet 100' can grow 12ft (4m) tall or more. The plants may be trained up heavy strings.

Bush and dwarf types Bush types sprawl on the ground; space them 12–36in (30–90cm) apart, depending on the cultivar. Dwarf types may be more closely spaced than this. Cover with cloches or floating row covers in the early stages. Bush types grow well when mulched with black plastic (see "Mulching," p.308).

Routine cultivation

All types of tomato should be watered and mulched heavily once the soil is warm. In dry conditions, water tomatoes weekly at a rate of 2 gallons (11 liters) per plant. Plants in containers need more frequent watering and supplementary feeding with a tomato fertilizer. Take care not to overwater or overfeed.

Staking types Tie in plants to the support stakes or wires as they grow, and remove all suckers (side shoots) when they are about 1in (2.5cm) long. In late summer, remove the terminal shoot two leaves above a flower cluster to allow the remaining fruits to develop and ripen before the first frost. In cool climates, remove supports at the end of the season, bend the plants over *in situ* on straw, and cover them with cloches to encourage the crop to ripen.

GROWING IN A WIRE CAGE

Tomatoes may be grown in wire cages as an alternative to staking. Firmly push the cages into the soil around newly set plants.

RECOMMENDED TOMATOES

Staking (indeterminate)
'Beefmaster'
'Better Boy'
'First Lady'
'Golden Boy'
'Roma'

'Sun Gold'
'Supersteak'
'Sweet 100'

Semideterminate
'Celebrity'
'Ultra Girl'

Bush (determinate)
'Husky Gold'

'Patio Hybrid'
'Pixie'
'Rutgers'
'Viva Italia'

TRAINING STAKING TOMATOES

1 On staking tomatoes, regularly pinch out suckers (side shoots) as they develop.

2 In late summer, nip out the tip of the main shoot 2 leaves above the top flower cluster.

Pests and diseases
Tomato plants are affected by damping off in seedlings (p.566), leafhoppers (p.553), potato cyst nematodes (p.572), and tomato late blight (p.564). They are also affected by whiteflies (p.552), several mosaic viruses (see "Viruses," p.555), gray mold/*Botrytis* (p.564), magnesium deficiency (p.557), boron deficiency (p.560), Southern blight (p.560), foot and root rots (p.567), and blossom end rot (see "Calcium deficiency," p.564). Use disease- and nematode-resistant cultivars, indicated in catalogs by V, F, and N after the cultivar name. Interplanting with French marigolds may deter whiteflies.

Growing under cover
In cool climates, tomatoes may be grown in greenhouses or polytunnels. Polytunnels, which can be moved to a fresh site, are better than greenhouses, where soilborne diseases may develop unless the soil is replaced every three years. Alternatively, crops may be grown in containers or by ring culture (plants are grown in "rings" or bottomless pots filled with soil mix, resting on pea gravel). Cultivars may also be grafted onto disease-resistant rootstocks. After the first cluster has set, feed weekly with a high-potassium fertilizer or an organic liquid feed.

Harvesting and storing
Pick fruits as they ripen. Harvest the earliest bush types seven to eight weeks after planting. Before frost, pull the plants up by the roots and hang them upside down indoors to ripen. Harvest staking types after ten to 12 weeks. Tomatoes freeze well.

GROW BAGS

Tomatoes may be planted in grow bags outdoors or in greenhouses. Growing tomatoes in bags prevents the plants from being infected by soilborne diseases.

Wonderberries (*Solanum* x *burbankii*)

These annual plants grow to about 30in–3ft (75cm–1m) tall with a spread of 24in (60cm). Several cultivated forms of the wonderberry, or sunberry, are grown; all have oval, light green leaves as well as round purple berries up to ½in (1cm) in diameter. The leaves and young shoots are used like spinach. The unripe fruits contain a poisonous alkaloid, so pick only ripe berries and cook them thoroughly.

Wonderberries are tropical and subtropical plants requiring temperatures of 64–77°F (18–25°C) with a humidity of at least 70 percent. They may be grown in the open in sunny, sheltered sites, but in cooler areas, greenhouse cultivation is recommended. A fertile, well-drained soil with a pH of 5.5–7 is preferable; medium nitrogen levels are required (see p.310).

Sowing and planting
Sow seed in spring in trays in the greenhouse. Prick out the seedlings when they are large enough to handle, into 3–3½in (6–9cm) pots. When they are 3–4in (8–10cm) tall, harden them off and transplant; space plants about 16–20in (40–50cm) apart, with approximately 24in (60cm) between rows.

Routine cultivation
Wonderberries need high levels of soil moisture; mulch well and water regularly. Apply an all-purpose fertilizer or an organic liquid feed every ten to 14 days during the growing period. Pinch out the growing point when plants are 12in (30cm) tall to encourage lateral branching, and stake plants that grow higher than 24in (60cm). Keep the ground around plants free from weeds.

Pests and diseases
Aphids (p.552) are the major pest. Spider mites (p.552) and thrips (p.553) may also attack plants.

Growing under cover
When the seedlings are about 4–6in (10–15cm) tall, transplant them into 8in (21cm) pots or grow bags, leaving at least 20in (50cm) between the plants, or transplant them into well-prepared greenhouse beds, spacing the plants 20–24in (50–60cm) apart each way. Reduce the level of humidity during flowering to promote pollination.

WONDERBERRIES

Harvesting and storing
Harvest shoots nine to 11 weeks after transplanting; continue removing shoots 4–6in (10–15cm) long to encourage lateral growths. To produce berries, do not remove shoots but allow plants to become bushy and to flower. Harvest the fruit about 14–17 weeks after sowing, removing bunches with a sharp knife. Ripe berries may be stored for ten to 14 days at 50–59°F (10–15°C).

Eggplants (*Solanum melongena*)

Short-lived perennials normally cultivated as annuals, eggplants form small bushes about 24–8in (60–70cm) tall with a spread of about 24in (60cm). Also known as aubergines, cultivars differ mainly in the shape, size, and color of the fruits, which may be oval, pear-shaped, or round, dark purple, yellowish green, or white, and weigh 7–18oz (200–500g). The fruits are generally sliced and cooked.

Eggplants are tropical and subtropical plants requiring temperatures of 77–86°F (25–30°C), with a minimum humidity of 75 percent. Below 68°F (20°C), growth may be checked. Grow in full sun and protect newly planted plants from cold winds and low temperatures, which may stunt growth and cause bud drop.

Eggplants require a deep, fertile, well-drained soil and medium nitrogen levels (see p.310).

Sowing and planting
In spring, sow seed under cover in trays using a light, slightly acid (pH 6–6.5) soil mix: soak the seed in warm water for 24 hours first to encourage germination. Prick out into 3–3½in (6–9cm) pots. In warm climates, plant out the seedlings into well-prepared beds when they are 3–4in (8–10cm) tall, spacing them about 24–30in (60–75cm) apart each way. Pinch out the terminal

RECOMMENDED EGGPLANTS

'Black Beauty'
'Burpee Hybrid'
'Easter Egg'
'Ichiban'
'Little Fingers'

'Easter Egg'

Eggplants

growing points of the plants to promote a bushy habit. In temperate climates, pot them up singly into 6in (15cm) pots; plant out after all danger of frost has passed.

Routine cultivation

Stake cultivars over 24in (60cm) tall. Keep plants well watered, otherwise leaves and buds are liable to drop, and mulch to preserve moisture. Apply a balanced fertilizer or liquid feed every two weeks during the growing season. Prune back mature plants to stimulate growth. To produce large fruits, restrict the number per plant to five or six.

Pests and diseases

Eggplants may be attacked by aphids (p.552). Spider mites (p.552), mealybugs (p.552), caterpillars (p.551), thrips (p.553), and powdery and downy mildew (p.552) may also be troublesome.

Growing under cover

Sow seed in early spring at 68–86°F (20–30°C). When the seedlings are 3–4in (8–10cm) tall, transfer them to 8in (21cm) pots or grow bags, and pinch out the tips. Maintain the temperature above the minimum required during the growing period. Damp down greenhouses to help discourage spider mites.

Harvesting and storing

Harvest 16–24 weeks after sowing, when fruits reach full color and are unwrinkled. Cut the fruit stalks close to the stem. Eggplants may be stored for up to two weeks in humid conditions at 54–9°F (12–15°C).

Harvesting Eggplants

Cut eggplants while their skin is still purple and shiny; once it loses its shine, the flesh will taste bitter. Cut the stalk at least 1in (2.5cm) from the fruit.

Sweet corn (*Zea mays*)

Sweet corn is an annual that grows to at least 30in–5½ft (75cm–1.7m) and has an average spread of 18in (45cm). Male tassels and female ears (cobs) are borne on the same plant. The ears are golden, white, or bicolored white and yellow, and cooked or eaten raw when young. New "supersweet" (sugar-enhanced) cultivars are available.

Sweet corn needs a long growing season of 70–110 frost-free days after planting. It requires temperatures of 61–95°F (16–35°C), but pollination is poor in hot, dry conditions; in warm climates, grow in an open site. In cool climates, grow early-maturing cultivars in a frost-free, sheltered site. Sweet corn is shallow-rooting and grows on a wide range of fertile, well drained soils with medium nitrogen (see p.310).

Sweet Corn Planted in a Block

Male and female flowers are carried on the same plant. The male flowers (inset, top), which release pollen, are produced in tassels up to 40cm (16in) in length at the tip of the plant. The female flowers (inset, bottom) are silky strands under which each ear forms. The strands are sticky to collect pollen. The female flowers are wind-pollinated, so plant in a block rather than a row to ensure good pollination.

Recommended Sweet corn

Early
'Earlivee'
'Seneca Star' F1
'Sunrise' F1

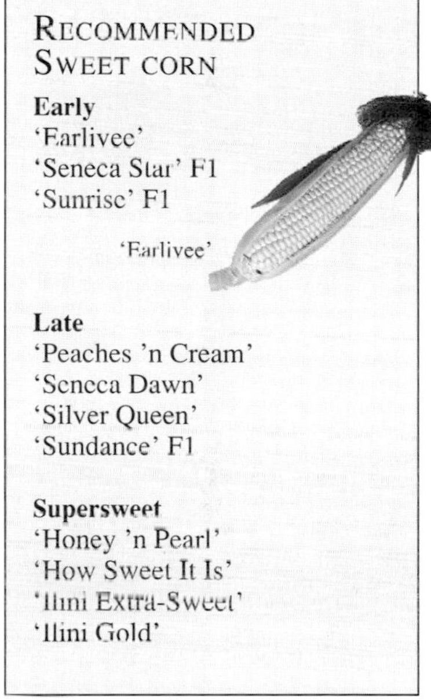

'Earlivee'

Late
'Peaches 'n Cream'
'Seneca Dawn'
'Silver Queen'
'Sundance' F1

Supersweet
'Honey 'n Pearl'
'How Sweet It Is'
'Illini Extra-Sweet'
'Illini Gold'

Sowing and planting

Seed does not germinate at soil temperatures below 50°F (10°C). In warm climates, sow seed in spring *in situ*, 1in (2.5cm) deep and 3in (7cm) apart, thinning to the correct spacing after germination. Seed may be sown through plastic mulches. In cool climates, sow indoors in cell packs and plant out seedlings when the soil temperature reaches 55°F (13°C), or sow *in situ* after all risk of frost has passed. In wet soils, use treated seed that will not rot.

To ensure good pollination and full ears, plant corn in blocks of at least four plants each way. The average spacing is 12in (30cm) apart; short cultivars may be closer, tall ones farther apart. In cool climates, cover with floating row covers or cloches after sowing or planting, removing them at the five-leaf stage. The supersweet types need higher temperatures to germinate and grow and should not be planted with other types because the sweetness will be lost if they are cross-pollinated. Baby-corn is obtained by planting early cultivars about 6in (15cm) apart and harvesting ears when they are about 3in (7cm) long.

Routine cultivation

Hoe shallowly when weeding to avoid damaging the roots. In exposed areas, hill up the stems to 5in (13cm) to increase stability. Watering is not necessary, except in very dry conditions, until flowering starts and when the kernels are swelling. Water at a rate of 5 gallons/sq yd (23 liters/sq m). Mulching with several thin layers of grass clippings helps reduce evaporation.

Pests and diseases

Spotted cucumber beetle larvae (p.566), asparagus beetles (p.550), cutworms (p.561), smuts (p.565), corn rootworms (p.566), armyworms (p.572), and raccoons (see "Small animals," p.572) may attack.

Harvesting and storing

Pick just before required, since the sweetness deteriorates within hours; supersweet types retain their sweetness for two or three days. Sweet corn freezes well, especially if removed from ears before freezing.

Testing Sweet Corn for Ripeness

Once the silks have turned brown, peel back the husks and press into a kernel with a fingernail. If the liquid that appears is milky, the ear is ripe; if watery, it is underripe; and if doughy, overripe.

Podded vegetables

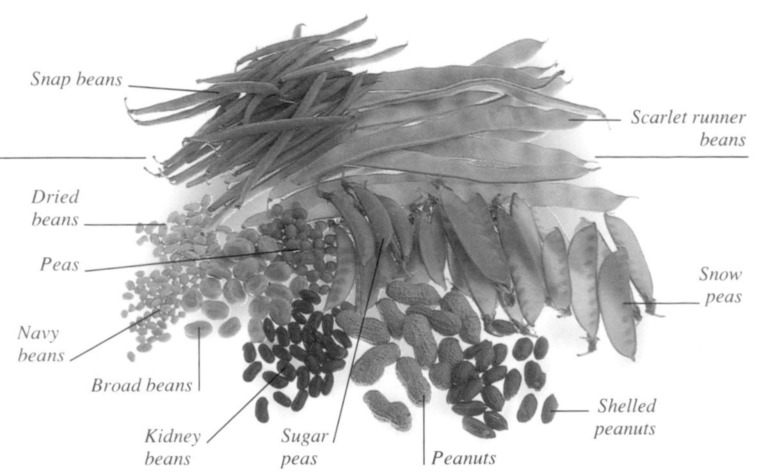

VEGETABLES in this group all produce seedpods. Some are grown for these pods, which may be cooked and eaten whole, while others are grown for the seeds, which are extracted and cooked or eaten raw. The seeds of some may be dried; most may be frozen. Several of the plants are decorative as well as functional and may be used for screening or trained over arches. Podded vegetables often need sheltered conditions at specific temperatures for pollination; they usually require a rich soil to which organic matter has been added before planting.

Okra (*Abelmoschus esculentus*)

These tender annual plants are also known as lady's fingers. The fast-maturing cultivars may grow to 3ft (1m) with a spread of 12–16in (30–40cm); the slow-maturing ones (mainly grown in the South) are up to 6ft (2m) tall. The pods are 4–10in (10–25cm) long and white, green, or red. Recommended cultivars include 'Clemson Spineless', 'Green Velvet', and 'Burgundy'. Immature pods are eaten as a cooked vegetable; mature pods may also be dried and powdered for use as a thickener.

OKRA

In warm-temperate and subtropical areas, plants may be grown in the open in favorable, sunny conditions. Seeds germinate only at soil temperatures of at least 61°F (16°C); after germination a stable temperature in the range 68–86°F (20–30°C) is needed for optimum growth. Most modern cultivars are daylength neutral (see "Daylength," p.303). Plant in well-drained soil, adding plenty of organic material during preparation. Okra plants need low to medium nitrogen levels (see p.310).

Sowing and planting

Soak seed for 24 hours before sowing to aid germination. When soil temperatures reach 61–4°F (16–18°C), sow seed *in situ* in rows 24–8in (60–70cm) apart, leaving 8–12in (20–30cm) between plants. In warm-temperate areas, sow in spring under cover at 68°F (20°C) or above, in trays or 3–3½in (6–9cm) pots. When seedlings are 4–6in (10–15cm) tall, harden off and transplant to well-prepared beds, spacing as above.

Routine cultivation

Stake tall plants and protect from strong winds with screens or plastic covers, if necessary. Remove all weeds, water regularly, and apply an organic mulch to retain soil moisture. Pinch out the growing points when seedlings are about 24in (60cm) tall to promote branching. Apply a general-purpose fertilizer or liquid feed at two-week intervals to encourage rapid growth. Do not overfeed with nitrogen since this delays flowering.

Pests and diseases

Plants are most likely to be damaged by aphids (p.552), caterpillars (p.551), and powdery mildew (p.552). Whiteflies (p.552), spider mites (p.552), thrips (p.553), and fungal leaf spots (p.554) may also be troublesome.

Growing under cover

Seedlings may be transplanted into well-prepared beds in the greenhouse or in grow bags, spacing the young plants at least 16in (40cm) apart. Maintain a temperature above 68°F (20°C) and a humidity of over 70 percent. Spray the plants as necessary to control pests and diseases, and apply an organic liquid feed or a general-purpose fertilizer.

Harvesting and storing

Each plant may produce up to a few dozen pods. The pods may be harvested approximately eight to 11 weeks after sowing, depending on the cultivar. Sever the pods from the plant with a sharp knife when they are still small and tender; overmature pods may become fibrous. Pods may be stored in perforated bags at 45–50°F (7–10°C) for up to ten days.

Peanuts (*Arachis hypogaea*)

These tender annual plants, also known as groundnuts and monkey-nuts, originated in South America. Plants grow to a height of 24in (60cm) with a spread of 12in (30cm) for the more upright Spanish-Valencia types, or up to 3ft (1m) for the less common, prostrate, Virginia types. The Spanish-Valencia types are often divided into Spanish, with two seeds per pod and light brown seed coats, and Valencia, with up to four seeds per pod and dark red seed coats. The stems of the Valencia types are usually thicker than those of the Spanish. The Virginia forms have two seeds per pod, with dark brown seed coats.

The fertilized flowers produce shootlike structures that penetrate the soil where the immature fruits develop into peanuts. Removed from their pods, the nuts are eaten fresh or roasted, or used in cooking.

Peanuts are tropical plants that need average temperatures of about 68–86°F (20–30°C) and a relative humidity of 80 percent, although some forms grow well in the warmer subtropics. A frost-free site is essential. Rainfall at flowering time may adversely affect pollination.

Peanut cultivars are generally daylength-neutral (see "Daylength," p.303). Sandy, well-drained loams with a pH of 5.5–6.5 containing extra calcium, potassium, and phosphorus are preferable. The plants also need low nitrogen levels (see p.310).

Sowing and planting

Sow seeds *in situ*, removed from their shells, in spring or when soil temperatures exceed 61°F (16°C). In cooler climates, sow under cover in trays or 3½in (9cm) pots, keeping temperatures over 68°F (20°C).

When the seedlings are 4–6in (10–15cm) tall, harden them off and transplant them to well-prepared beds. Whether directly sown or transplanted, the plants should be spaced 6–12in (15–30cm) apart about 24–8in (60–70cm) between the rows. Protect them with cloches or polytunnels where necessary.

Routine cultivation

Hill up around the roots when the plants are 6in (15cm) tall, and hoe regularly to encourage the fertilized flowers to penetrate the soil. Remove all weeds, and water well in dry periods. Do not water plants during the flowering period since this may lead to poor pollination.

SPANISH-VALENCIA PEANUT PLANT

Pests and diseases

Plants may be affected by aphids (p.552), thrips (p.553), and caterpillars (p.551); spider mites (p.552), and whiteflies (p.552) may also cause problems. Fungal leaf spots (p.554), root and stem rot (see "Southern blight," p.560), and rosette virus (see "Viruses," p.555) may also be troublesome.

Growing under cover

Sow seed as described above. Transplant the seedlings when they are 4–6in (10–15cm) tall into grow bags, or well-prepared greenhouse beds. Maintain a temperature over 68°F (20°C), reducing humidity at flowering time to aid pollination.

Harvesting and storing

Harvest the pods 16–20 weeks after sowing for the upright types, and three to four weeks after this for the prostrate types. Virginia types, which produce two seeds per pod, may require up to 25 weeks from sowing to harvesting. Assess the stage of maturity by uprooting one or two pods. Dry the pods in the sun, then remove the peanuts for storing in cool, dry conditions. They keep for several months.

Hyacinth beans (*Lablab purpureus*)

These dwarf or climbing, short-lived tender perennials are also known as dolichos beans and lablab beans. Both long- and short-podded cultivars occur. Climbing forms may grow to 12–20ft (4–6m), while dwarf forms reach 3ft (1m) with a spread of about 2ft (60cm). The pods range in color from green to purple. Young pods and mature seeds are eaten cooked; the latter should be cooked thoroughly. Young seedlings, raised in the dark, may be used as bean sprouts, either raw or cooked.

Hyacinth beans may be grown in subtropical and warm-temperate regions in sunny sites. The plants require a temperature of 64–86°F (18–30°C) with a minimum humidity of 70 percent; cool weather may adversely affect pollination since it discourages pollinating insects. Daylength-neutral cultivars are available (see "Daylength," p.303).

Most soils are suitable for hyacinth beans, particularly those high in organic matter; good drainage is essential. Some cultivars respond well to applications of superphosphate. Hyacinth beans need low nitrogen levels (see p.310).

HYACINTH BEANS

Sowing and planting

Sow *in situ*, in spring or at other times of the year if temperatures are high enough. In temperate areas, sow seeds under cover, in trays, or in 3–3½in (6–9cm) pots at a depth of 1in (2.5cm). When the seedlings are 4–6in (10–15cm) tall, harden them off and transplant into well-prepared beds. Space climbing cultivars 12–18in (30–45cm) apart, allowing 30–36in (75–100cm) between rows; space the dwarf cultivars 12–16in (30–40cm) apart with a distance of 18–24in (45–60cm) between rows.

Routine cultivation

Climbing cultivars should be supported by individual stakes at least 6ft (2m) high or as for scarlet runner beans (see below). Water the plants regularly, and mulch to conserve moisture. Protect young plants as necessary and remove all weeds. Apply a general-purpose fertilizer or a liquid feed every ten to 14 days until flowering. Pinch out the growing points of dwarf cultivars to encourage a bushy habit; the shoots of climbing cultivars should be trained or tied in to the stakes.

Pests and diseases

Aphids (p.552), thrips (p.553), caterpillars (p.551), root-knot nematodes (p.566), powdery mildew (p.552), fungal leaf spots (p.554), and some viruses (p.555) may be troublesome; whiteflies (p.552) and spider mites (p.552) may also affect plants.

Growing under cover

Transplant seedlings to grow bags or well-prepared beds in the greenhouse, spacing the plants at least 20–24in (50–60cm) apart. Alternatively, seedlings may be grown on in 8–10in (21–5cm) pots (two plants may be grown in the larger pots). Maintain a temperature of at least 68°F (20°C) and reduce humidity by providing adequate ventilation at flowering time to improve pollination. Hyacinth beans may also be propagated from softwood cuttings (see PRINCIPLES OF PROPAGATION, "Stem cuttings," p.540), taken early in the growing season, which root readily in high humidity.

Harvesting and storing

Harvest the young pods six to nine weeks after sowing, when they are fully grown but before the seeds develop; the mature pods containing seeds may be harvested after ten to 14 weeks, before they become fibrous. If the plants remain healthy after the first crop, cut back the main stems to about half their length to encourage a second crop. Hyacinth beans freeze well.

Scarlet runner beans (*Phaseolus coccineus*)

SCARLET RUNNER BEANS

These perennial climbers are grown as annuals in temperate and cool climates. Plants grow to over 10ft (3m) tall, with a spread of about 12in (30cm); some naturally dwarf cultivars form bushes about 15in (38cm) tall. They have pink, red, white, or bicolored flowers.

The flat pods, over 10in (25cm) long and up to ¾in (2cm) wide, are eaten cooked; immature seeds and dried mature seeds may also be cooked. With some cultivars, it may be necessary to remove the strings along the pods.

Scarlet runner beans are a temperate or cool-season crop that does not withstand frost. Plants need a growing season of about 100 frost-free days, and they grow best at 57–84°F (14–29°C). At higher temperatures, especially if combined with high humidity, the pods may not set unless the plants are in light shade. In cool climates, choose a sheltered situation to encourage pollinating insects. Plants are deep-rooting and need fertile, moisture-retentive soil. Prepare the soil by digging a trench one spade deep and 60cm (24in) wide, working in well-rotted straw or compost. Runner bean crops should be rotated (see p.303) and need low nitrogen levels (see p.310).

Sowing and planting

Before planting climbing types, erect a strong support system of poles or stakes over 8ft (2.5m) long, tied to a horizontal pole or to each other to form a wigwam. Commercial supports or towers are available. Plants

RECOMMENDED SCARLET RUNNER BEANS

Standard
'Enorma'
'Goliath'
'Painted Lady'
'Prize Winner'

'Prize Winner'

'Scarlet Runner'

Dwarf
'Hammond's Dwarf Scarlet'

Stringless
'Desiree'
'Red Knight'
'White Dutch Runner'
'White Knight'

may also be twisted up nylon netting, strings, or wires pegged to the ground; do not use plastic-coated netting since the plants do not cling to it. Sow seed *in situ* 2in (5cm) deep, after all risk of frost has passed, bearing in mind that a minimum soil temperature of 59°F (15°C) is needed for germination. In cool areas, sow seed indoors in seed trays and harden off seedlings before transplanting outside. Grow climbers in double rows 2ft (60cm) apart or in circular wigwams, spacing the plants 6in (15cm) apart. Bush forms may be grown in groups at the same spacing. Mulch well to retain moisture after germination or planting out.

BEAN SUPPORTS

There are various ways to support climbing beans, depending on the space available. Mature plants will obscure the support structure beneath.

CROSSED STAKE ROW

Two rows of 8ft (2.5m) stakes, crossed and secured to a horizontal bar

WIGWAM

8ft (2.5m) stakes tied near the top

NETTING SUPPORT

4in (10cm) square nylon net fixed to a pole frame

TRAINED ON A WIGWAM

Routine cultivation

Protect seedlings with cloches or floating row covers. To convert climbing forms into bushes, nip out the growing shoots when plants are 9in (23cm) high. Such plants crop earlier but have lower yields.

Watering is especially important when the flower buds appear and pods are setting (see "Critical watering periods," p.308). At these times water at a rate of 1–2 gallons/sq yd (5–11 liters/sq m) twice a week.

Pests and diseases

Slugs (p.550) in the early stages, pollen beetles (p.563), fungal leaf spots (p.554), foot and root rots (p.560), halo blight (see "Bacterial leaf spots and blotches," p.554), Southern blight (p.560), and viruses (p.555) may be troublesome in scarlet runner beans.

Harvesting and storing

Harvest after 13–17 weeks. Pick pods when they are at least 7in (17cm) long and tender; picking prolongs the cropping period. Scarlet runner beans freeze well.

Lima beans (*Phaseolus lunatus*)

DWARF LIMA BEANS

Also known as butter beans, lima beans are tender annuals and short-lived perennials. Some forms of lima bean climb, while others are dwarf and branching. Climbing cultivars may grow to a height of 9–12ft (3–4m), dwarf cultivars to 3ft (90cm), spreading to 16–18in (40–45cm). The young pods and mature seeds are eaten cooked; the seeds may also be dried or germinated in the dark for use as bean sprouts.

The lima bean is a tropical plant requiring a minimum temperature of 64°F (18°C) for germination. Temperatures above 86°F (30°C) may adversely affect pollen formation. In subtropical and warm-temperate areas, growing in the open is possible only in full sun, using plastic screens or covers for protection until the plants are fully established.

Small-seeded cultivars flower only in short daylengths of about 12 hours but the large-seeded cultivars are normally daylength neutral (see "Daylength," p.303).

Most cultivars thrive in a wide range of soil types, but a sandy, well-drained loam with a pH of 6–7 is preferable. Lima beans require low to medium nitrogen levels (see p.310). The procedures for sowing, planting, routine cultivation, and growing undercover are as described for hyacinth beans (see p.337).

Pests and diseases

Aphids (p.552), thrips (p.553), caterpillars (p.551), whiteflies (p.552) and spider mites (p.552) may cause problems. Diseases include powdery mildew (p.552), fungal leaf spots (p.554), and viruses (p.555).

RECOMMENDED LIMA BEANS

Climbing
'Florida Butter'
'King of the Garden'
'Prizetaker'

Dwarf
'Fordhook 242'
'Henderson'

'Fordhook 242'

Harvesting and storing

Harvest whole pods young, mature seeds about 12–16 weeks after sowing. Store both above 39°F (4°C) at 90 percent humidity for up to two weeks. Lima beans may be frozen.

Snap beans (*Phaseolus vulgaris*)

These tender annuals have pole (climbing), bush, and intermediate forms. They are also known as French, green, or string beans. Height and spread are as for scarlet runner beans (see p.337). The pods are 3–8in (7–20cm) long. They may be round, flat, or curved in shape; diameter ranges from pencil thickness (for the filet types) to about ¾in (2cm); they may be green, yellow, purple, red, or green flecked with purple. The yellow waxpod types have a waxy texture and excellent flavor. Types vary in the stringiness of the pods; stringless cultivars are widely available. Snap beans may be eaten raw in salads or lightly steamed.

Some related beans are grown specifically for drying the seeds. These include kidney, pinto, navy, and white beans; all are grown as for snap beans. Dried seeds are used in stews.

Snap beans grow in similar conditions to scarlet runner beans (see p.337) but the seeds need a minimum temperature of 54°F (12°C) to germinate. The optimum growing temperature is 61–86°F (16–30°C); seedlings do not tolerate temperatures below 50°F (10°C). The plants are self-pollinated and grow best in rich, light soil. Good drainage is essential to prevent root rot. Work plenty of well-rotted compost or manure into the soil before planting, and always rotate crops (see p.303). Seed may be dressed with the appropriate bacterial inoculant, or rhizobium granules may be applied to the soil at planting; this treatment increases current and subsequent yields by encouraging the formation of nitrogen-fixing root nodules. Snap beans usually need low nitrogen levels (see p.310).

PREGERMINATING SNAP BEANS

1 *Spread the beans out on moist tissue paper in a tray without drainage holes. Keep damp, at a minimum of 54°F (12°C).*

2 *When the delicate shoots begin to appear and before they turn green, carefully pot up the beans or sow them directly in their final position outside.*

Sowing and planting

Seed may be pregerminated before sowing. Sow seed or pregerminated seed 1½in (4cm) deep *in situ* or indoors as for scarlet runner beans (see p.337), and make successive sowings throughout the summer. If necessary, warm the soil beforehand with cloches. Space pole forms as for scarlet runner beans. Bush types may be grown at an equidistant spacing of 9in (22cm) in staggered rows for the highest yields. In cold climates, protect after planting with cloches or floating row covers.

Routine cultivation

Support pole types as for scarlet runner beans; use twigs to support intermediate types. Stems may also be hilled up to keep plants upright. Mulch and do not allow plants to dry out completely; extra watering at a rate of 5 gallons/sq yd (23 liters/sq m) may be necessary in dry conditions at flowering time.

Pests and diseases

Slugs (p.550), root aphids and black bean aphids (see "Aphids," p.552), fungal leaf spots (p.554), foot and root rots (p.560), halo blight (see "Bacterial leaf spots and blotches," p.554), and viruses (p.555) may affect snap beans. Under cover, spider mites (p.552) may be a problem.

Growing under cover

In cool climates, bush snap beans may be grown to maturity in a greenhouse or polytunnel, or under cloches. Space plants as in the open.

HILLING UP

Plant out the beans 6in (15cm) apart, and once they have formed several pairs of leaves, hill them up to support them.

Harvesting and storing

Harvest after seven to 13 weeks. Pick young beans regularly to use fresh or freeze. For shelled beans, see below; store in an airtight jar.

DRYING BEANS

In damp climates, pull up plants and hang them by the roots in a dry, frost-free place. Once dried, remove the pods and extract the beans.

RECOMMENDED BEANS

Pole
'Blue Lake'
'Kentucky Blue'
'Northeaster'

Bush
'Bush Blue Lake'
'Contender'
'Derby'
'Dorabel' (wax)
'Goldcrop' (wax)
'Improved Tendergreen'
'Provider'
'Royal Burgundy' (purple podded)
'Tenderlake'

'Royal Burgundy'

Beans for drying
'Jacob's Cattle'
'Maine Yellow Eye'
'Vermont Cranberry'

Peas (*Pisum sativum*)

Peas are annuals that grow from 18in (45cm) to over 6ft (2m) tall and have an average spread of 9in (23cm). Plants cling to supports with tendrils; modern semileafless types are almost self-supporting. Peas are grouped according to the time taken to mature. The early groups are dwarfer and lower yielding. Pods are usually green, but there are purple-podded cultivars.

Shelling-pea types are grown for the fresh peas in the pods; some may be dried. Petits pois are small, fine-flavored peas. Wrinkle-seeded cultivars are usually sweeter but less hardy than smooth-seeded types. Edible-podded types (snow peas and sugar peas) may be eaten before the peas mature. Snow peas have flat pods and are eaten young; round-podded sugar types are used when semimature. Peas and pods are often cooked, but may be eaten raw.

SEMILEAFLESS PEAS

Peas are a cool-season crop, growing best at 55–64°F (13–18°C). The flowers and pods cannot withstand frost. Grow peas in an open site, in reasonably fertile, moisture-retentive, well-drained soil; they will not tolerate cold, wet soil, or drought. Work plenty of well-rotted compost or manure into the soil before planting. Peas should be rotated (see p.303). The plants have nitrogen-fixing nodules on their roots, and do not require any extra nitrogen during growth.

Sowing and planting

Make the first outdoor sowings as soon as the soil is about 50°F (10°C). Germination is much slower at lower temperatures. The first sowings may be made under cloches or floating row covers using dwarf cultivars. For successive crops, either sow seeds at 14-day intervals or sow cultivars from different groups at the same time so that they mature in succession. Avoid midsummer sowings in warm areas, since high temperatures also impede germination. If sowing an early type late, allow about ten weeks before frost is expected for the pods to ripen. Where winters are mild, sow hardy, early-maturing cultivars in late fall to overwinter.

Sow the seed 1¼in (3cm) deep in patches so that plants can support each other, spacing individual seeds 2–3in (5–7cm) apart. Alternatively, make a flat-bottomed drill up to 9in (23cm) wide, spacing seeds 2in (5cm) apart each way (see "Wide drills," p.306). The drills should be 24–36in (60–90cm) apart, the wider spacing for tall cultivars. Seed may also be sown in double rows 9in (23cm) apart, spacing seeds ½in (1cm) apart.

Routine cultivation

Protect seedlings against birds with horizontal netting as pea guards. Once the tendrils have developed, remove the pea guards and erect supports: use wire netting, pea nets, or brushwood on either side of a drill.

Semileafless and dwarf types need less support. When the peas have several leaves, mulch them to keep the roots cool.

Once plants are flowering and forming pods, water every week (unless rainfall is high) at a rate of 5 gallons/sq yd (23 liters/sq m).

Pests and diseases

Aphids (p.552) and pea moths (p.565) are the most common pests; mice (p.568) may also be troublesome since they eat seeds. Damping off (p.566), foot and root rots (p.560), Southern blight (p.560), and *Fusarium* wilt (p.560) are occasional problems.

Growing under cover

Early spring and late fall sowings may be made under cover; grow dwarf peas to maturity under cloches for early or overwintering crops.

Harvesting and storing

Harvest early types 11–12 weeks after sowing, and maincrop peas after 13–14 weeks. Pick snow pea types when the immature peas are just forming inside the pods, or leave them to mature and then shell them normally. Pick shelling peas and sugar types when the pods have swollen. All may be frozen. For how to store pods on plants, see *Drying Beans*, p.339.

SUPPORTING PEAS

When seedlings have developed tendrils, push peasticks into the ground, as upright as possible, all around the outside of the patch (above). As the peas grow, the tendrils wrap around the peasticks and the peas grow up them (right).

RECOMMENDED PEAS

Early
'Burpeeana'
'Knight'
'Laxton's Progress'
'Little Marvel'

Maincrop
'Alderman'
'Green Arrow'
'Lincoln'
'Olympia'

Sugar peas
'Mammoth Melting Sugar'
'Oregon Sugar Pod'
'Snappy'
'Sugar Anne'
'Sugar Bon'

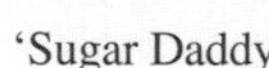

'Sugar Bon'

'Sugar Daddy'
'Sugar Snap'

Broad beans (*Vicia faba*)

These annual plants are also known as fava beans. They range in height from 12in (30cm) for dwarf cultivars to about 5ft (1.5m), with an average spread of 18in (45cm). Broad beans are grouped according to the time they take to mature. The broad pods are up to 1in (2.5cm) wide and 3-6in (7–15cm) long, with green, white, or pinkish red seeds ¾–1in (2–2.5cm) long. The immature bean seeds, as well as the young pods and leafy shoot tips, may be cooked. The shelled beans freeze well.

Broad beans are a cool-season crop, growing satisfactorily only at temperatures below about 59°F (15°C). Some cultivars are very hardy, the immature plants surviving 14°F (-10°C) on well-drained soil. Some that are adapted to higher temperatures have recently been bred. Grow spring and early summer sowings in an open site, and fall sowings for overwintering in a sheltered site in reasonably fertile, well-manured soil. Rotate broad bean crops (see p.303). The plants need low nitrogen levels (see p.310) because their root nodules fix atmospheric nitrogen.

DWARF BROAD BEANS

Sowing and planting

Sow seed *in situ* in spring and early summer as soon as the ground is workable. Seed germinates at fairly low temperatures. For an early crop, sow seed in late fall to early winter of the previous year – the plants need only be 1in (2.5cm) high before winter. In very cold areas, seed may be sown indoors in winter and transplanted outside in spring after the risk of frost has passed.

Sow seed about 1½in (4cm) deep, spaced about 9in (23cm) apart each way. Grow either in double rows, with 3ft (90cm) between the pairs of rows, or evenly spaced in blocks across a bed. The taller cultivars may be supported with strands of wire attached to strong stakes or poles placed around the rows or blocks of plants. If necessary, dwarf cultivars may be supported with twigs to keep their pods clear of the ground. Overwintering crops and those sown in early spring may be protected with cloches or floating row covers in the early stages of growth.

Routine cultivation

Do not allow the plants to dry out; water as for snap beans (see p.338). Once flowering starts, pinch out the growing tips to encourage pods to form and to combat aphids. Hill up overwintering plants to protect them against the elements.

Pests and diseases

Tropical root rots (p.567), aphids (p.552), chocolate spot (p.555), and foot and root rots (p.560) may affect broad beans, causing problems at all stages of growth.

PINCHING OUT

When the beans are in full flower, pinch out the growing tip of each plant. This will remove any black aphids and concentrate the plant's energy into producing beans.

Harvesting and storing

Harvest broad beans that were sown in spring after 12–16 weeks, and those sown in fall after 28–35 weeks. Pick them while the pods are fresh and plump with the swelling beans and before they become old and leathery.

The beans may be frozen, or dried at the end of the growing season for use during the winter months as for snap beans (see p.338).

RECOMMENDED BROAD BEANS

Dwarf
'Sutton'

Early
'Albinette'
'Aquadulce Claudia' (fall sowing)
'Aquadulce Loreta' (fall or early spring sowing)
'Broad Windsor Long Pod'
'Express'
'Witkiem Major'

Late
'Ipro'
'Statissa'

'Statissa'

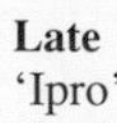

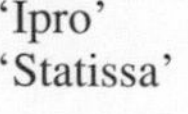

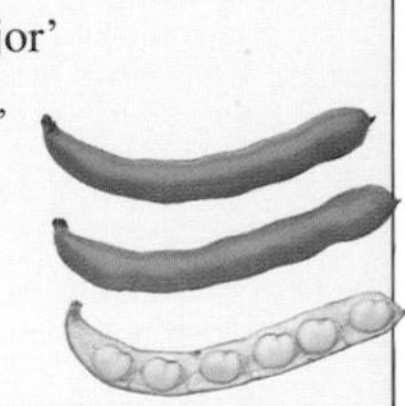

'Witkiem Major'

Bulb and stem vegetables

VEGETABLES grown for their bulbs or stems include members of the onion family as well as a varied group of other plants that, with the exception of Florence fennel, are mostly hardy and slow-maturing. Celeriac, kohlrabi, and Florence fennel form swollen stems just above ground level, rather than true bulbs. The onion family should be rotated as one group; for rotation groups for the other vegetables, see p.303. Both asparagus and rhubarb are perennial vegetables that should be planted in permanent beds that have been specially prepared for them.

Garlic
Leeks
Scallions
Bulb onions
Celery
Florence fennel
Red bulb onions
Asparagus
Shallots

Bulb onions (*Allium cepa*)

These are grown as annuals. The bulbs may be rounded or flattened, or have a long torpedo shape. They normally have brown or yellow skins with white flesh, although some have red skin and pinkish white flesh; the leaves grow 6–18in (15–45cm) long. Immature and mature bulbs are eaten either raw or cooked. Some cultivars are suitable for storage. The green-leaved thinnings may be used as scallions (see p.342).

Bulb onions are a cool-season, cold-tolerant crop, growing best at 55–75°F (13–24°C). Cool temperatures are required in the early stages of growth. Cultivars need different daylengths in order for the bulbs to swell; long-day types should be chosen for northerly latitudes, and short-day types for southerly latitudes (see also "Daylength," p.303).

Grow them in an open site, on fertile, medium to light soil that is well drained. Prepare the soil by digging in a good deal of well-rotted manure, preferably the fall before planting. Do not plant on newly manured ground. An all-purpose feed may be worked into the seedbed before sowing. They have low nitrogen requirements (see p.310).

Sowing and planting

Onions may be raised from seed or sets (small bulbs specially grown and harvested immature the year before). Seed is cheaper but slower to develop; sets are easier to grow but usually available for only a few cultivars. Bulb onions require a long growing season, particularly if large bulbs are required or if they are to be stored.

Sow in spring when the soil is workable, on a firm seedbed, sowing seed very thinly ½in (1cm) deep, in rows 9–12in (23–30cm) apart. Thin out the seedlings in stages. For the highest yield of medium-sized onions, space 1½in (4cm) apart; for larger onions, thin seedlings to 2–4in (5–10cm) apart.

To extend the growing season in northern latitudes, start under cover in seed trays or cell packs at 50–59°F (10–15°C) from late winter to early spring. Harden off seedlings at the two-leaf stage and plant out at the appropriate spacing. Cell packs may also be multisown with five seeds per section and each section planted out as a unit, with 10in (25cm) between units (see also *Transplanting Leeks*, p.343).

Certain cultivars may be sown in summer or fall to overwinter for earlier crops the following year. This is inadvisable where winters are very severe or very wet since seeds may rot before germination. Traditional summer-sown cultivars are reasonably hardy and may be sown *in situ* in late summer, thinning to 1in (2.5cm) apart in fall and in stages to the final spacing in spring. Japanese overwintering onions are also suitable for sowing at this time; they are hardier than other bulb onions, but are unsuitable for storage. The precise sowing date for these is critical. Sow during the summer at the recommended date for the area, spacing and thinning as above.

Most sets are planted in the early spring. If using heat-treated sets, consult the suppliers for planting times. Plant at the above spacing in shallow furrows so that the tips protrude just above the soil. Recently introduced sets for planting during fall may be available.

Routine cultivation

Keep the site weed-free, especially when the onions are young and susceptible to competition from weeds. Onions are fairly shallow-rooted and need little water once established, except in very dry conditions. Overwintering onions may be given a nitrogenous fertilizer or organic liquid feed if necessary in spring.

Pests and diseases

Onion maggots (p.569), onion white rot (p.569), downy mildew (p.552), and, in storage, onion neck rot (p.569) are common problems that affect onions.

Harvesting and storing

Spring-sown bulb onions will take 12–18 weeks to mature, summer-sown onions up to 42 weeks. Pull or lift them as needed to use fresh.

For storage, wait until the leaves have died back naturally (do not bend them over by hand), and then carefully uproot all the onions. In sunny conditions, leave them in the sun to dry for about ten days, either hung in nets or supported off the ground on an upturned seed tray to allow maximum ventilation. In wet conditions, hang them indoors in a cool place. The outer skins and leaves must all be thoroughly dry before the bulbs are put into storage.

Handle the bulbs gently since any bruises will encourage storage rots. Do not store onions that are bull-necked; these should always be used first. Store onions either hanging in nets or braids (see *Storing Strings of Onions*, p.312) or packed carefully in layers in boxes. They must be kept at 32–45°F (0–7°C) and in low humidity (i.e. below 40 percent). Average storage life is three to six months, depending on the cultivar.

STORING ONIONS IN A BOX

Prepare onions carefully for storing. Bull-necked onions (those with thick necks above the bulbs, see far right) should be rejected. Be careful not to damage any onions for storing since this encourages rot. Place them in layers in a box and store them in a place that is well ventilated and frost-free.

RECOMMENDED BULB ONIONS

Onions for fall harvesting
'Albion' F1
'Carmen' F1 (pink)
'Norstar'
'Tarmagon'
'Turbo'

Red onions (use fresh or store)
'Benny's Red'
'California Wonder Red'
'Creole C-5'
'Creole C-5'
'Lucifer'

Traditional and Japanese overwintering onions
'Beltsville Bunching'
'Hardy White Bunching'
'Ishikuro'
'Keep Well' F1
'Kincho'
'Riverside Sweet Spanish'
'Walla Walla Sweet'
'White Evergreen'

Scallions

Traditional European scallions, or bunching onions, are cultivars of bulb onions suitable for using young. Pull them when the green leaves are 6in (15cm) tall, with a whitened shank and tiny bulb. A widely grown cultivar is 'White Lisbon'. For climate, soil requirements, and pests and diseases see "Bulb onions," p.341. Lime acid soil (see p.533).

In spring, sow thinly *in situ*, in rows 4in (10cm) apart, or bands 3in (7cm) wide and 6in (15cm) apart. For continuous crops, sow every three weeks in summer. Overwintering cultivars (e.g. 'White Lisbon Winter Hardy') may be sown in late summer for an early spring crop; protect them in winter with cloches. Water the onions in dry conditions. Scallions are ready for pulling after two months.

THINNING SCALLIONS

If densely sown, harvest seedling scallions to leave the others spaced 1in (2.5cm) apart. Those remaining will continue to grow and may be harvested when required.

Pickling onions

These bulb onion cultivars produce small white bulbs (also known as cocktail onions) in northerly latitudes, and larger bulbs in southerly latitudes. They may be used when they reach about thumbnail size, either fresh or for pickling. Cultivars include 'Silver Queen' and 'Snow Baby'. They prefer fertile soil, but tolerate fairly poor soil. For climate, cultivation, and pests and diseases, see "Bulb onions," p.341.

In spring sow seed *in situ*, either broadcast or in bands about 4in (10cm) wide, spacing seeds 1/2in (1cm) apart. Thin only if larger onions are required. Harvest onions after about eight weeks when the foliage has died back; use fresh, or dry and store as for bulb onions (see p.341) until required for pickling.

PICKLING ONIONS

Shallots (*Allium cepa* Aggregatum Group)

These distinctively flavored, onion-shaped bulbs form clumps of about a dozen bulbs. There are yellow- and red-skinned forms; all may be used fresh or after storing, and are eaten raw or cooked. The green leaves of young shallots may be used fresh as scallions.

Climate and soil requirements, routine cultivation, and pests and diseases are as for bulb onions (see p.341). Shallots are very hardy. Buy virus-free sets that are ideally about 3/4in (2cm) in diameter. Plant in early spring, or during winter in mild areas. Plant as for bulb onion sets (see p.341), spacing the sets about 7in (18cm) apart each way. Each set will develop into a clump, maturing in early summer. For an early crop of green leaves, plant small sets in fall, spacing them in the ground, or in seed trays under cover, about 1in (2.5cm) apart.

Harvest green leaves as needed. For good-sized bulbs, do not pick the leaves; lift the bulbs once the foliage has died down. To store, dry as for bulb onions (see p.341); good stocks store for up to a year.

PLANTING SHALLOTS

Make a drill 1/2in (1cm) deep. Push the sets into the drill about 7in (18cm) apart so that the tips show above the soil.

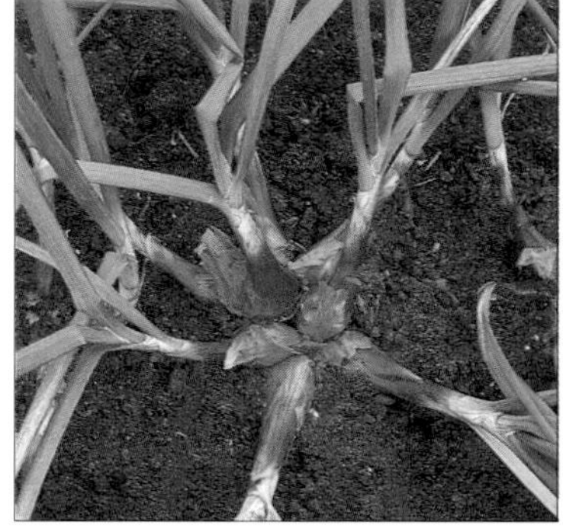

SHALLOTS

Welsh onions (*Allium fistulosum*)

These onions are very hardy perennials. They have hollow leaves up to 18in (45cm) tall and 1/2in (1cm) in diameter, growing in clumps of 9in (23cm) diameter on average; the bases of the leaves are thickened at and below ground level. The leaves remain green all year, even at temperatures as low as 14°F (-10°C), so they are a useful winter vegetable. The leaves and tiny bulbs may be eaten either raw or cooked.

Climate and soil requirements, cultivation, and pests and diseases are as for bulb onions (see p.341). Sow seed *in situ* in spring or summer in rows about 12in (30cm) apart. Thin the seedlings in stages until they are about 9in (23cm) apart, or propagate by dividing established clumps and carefully replanting the younger outer sections of the clumps to the above spacing. Leaves may be harvested from 24 weeks after sowing; cut individual leaves as required, or pull up part or all of the clump. Established clumps can become very thick and should be divided every two or three years. Welsh onions do not store well.

WELSH ONIONS

Oriental bunching onions

These have been developed from Welsh onions. They are perennials usually grown as annuals or biennials for harvesting at any stage from seedlings to large plants. Mature plants have thickened white shafts 1in (2.5cm) in diameter and 6in (15cm) high. All parts are edible. There are cultivars for planting and harvesting year-round, and for a wide range of climatic conditions.

For soil requirements, see "Bulb onions" (p.341). Sow seed *in situ* in spring and summer, in rows 12in (30cm) apart. Thin out in stages up to 6in (15cm) apart, depending on the size required. Seed may also be sown in trays and planted out. Sow the hardiest cultivars, such as 'White Evergreen' or 'Ishikuro', in fall and overwinter to use in early spring. Some cultivars, such as 'Ishikuro', may be hilled up several times during growth to obtain long, white shafts. Young leaves may be picked four weeks after sowing.

ORIENTAL BUNCHING ONIONS

Leeks (*Allium porrum*)

These are biennials, grown as annuals, reaching 18in (45cm) tall and 6in (15cm) across. The edible part is the sweetly flavored, thick white shank that forms below long blue-green leaves. This may be blanched by hilling it up or by deep planting. Leeks with short, thick shanks are called pot leeks. All types are used cooked, as a vegetable or in soups.

Leeks are a cool-season crop and grow best below 75°F (24°C), but will tolerate higher temperatures if kept moist. Cultivars range from early and moderately hardy to late and very hardy. Grow in open sites on fertile, moisture-retentive soil, working in plenty of manure or compost and a nitrogenous fertilizer if the soil is low in nitrogen (high levels are needed; see p.310). Do not plant on compacted soils. Leeks must be rotated (see p.303).

Sowing and planting

Leeks need a long growing season; start them as early in the year as possible, sowing in succession. Sow ½in (1cm) deep in an outdoor seedbed for transplanting when 8in (20cm) tall. Alternatively sow *in situ* in rows 12in (30cm) apart. Thin or transplant the seedlings at the three-leaf stage to 6in (15cm) apart. Use closer spacing if smaller leeks are preferred. For well-blanched stems, make holes 6–8in (15–20cm) deep with a dibber and drop a seedling in each; make sure that the roots reach the soil at the base. Water gently, then allow soil to fall in around the plants as they grow. Leeks may also be planted on the flat and blanched by hoeing up soil around the stems, 2in (5cm) at a time, as they grow.

To extend the growing season, sow under cover as for bulb onions (see p.341). Leeks respond well to being multisown in cell packs with up to four seeds per cell. Plant out the groups of seedlings at an even spacing of 9in (23cm).

Leek Plants

Sowing in a Cell Pack

Fill a cell pack with seed soil mix to within ½in (1cm) of the top. Sow 4 leek seeds in each cell pack on the surface of the soil mix. Cover with a thin layer of soil mix, and water.

Routine cultivation

Water thoroughly until the leeks are well established, and thereafter only in exceptionally dry conditions. Keep beds weed-free. Mulch to retain soil moisture if necessary.

Pests and diseases

Stem and bulb nematodes (p.558), onion maggots (p.569), rusts (p.554), and onion white rot (p.569) may all be troublesome.

Transplanting Leeks

Each section of a cell pack may be planted out as a whole; plant the clumps 9in (23cm) apart.

Single Seedlings

Leeks sown outdoors may be transplanted to their final position in holes 6–8in (15–20cm) deep and 4–6in (10–15cm) apart.

Harvesting and storing

Leeks may be harvested 16–20 weeks after sowing but can stand for many months. Lift them as required from summer onward; the hardy cultivars may be lifted throughout winter into spring, except in very severe climates. Leeks do not store well out of the ground. If the site they occupy is required for another crop, dig up the plants and heel them in elsewhere.

Heeling In Leeks

To store outdoors, lift the leeks and lean them against one side of a V-shaped trench. Cover the roots and white stems with soil and firm lightly. Lift and use as required.

Recommended Leeks

'Blauwgroene Winter – Alaska' l
'Carina' l
'Gabilan' m, l
'Giant Musselburgh' e
'King Richard' e
'Large American Flag' l
'Longina' l
'Otina' e
'Pancho' e, m
'Splendid' m
'Strata' l
'Swiss Giant – Pancho' e
'Varna' (all season)

Key
e early
m midseason
l late

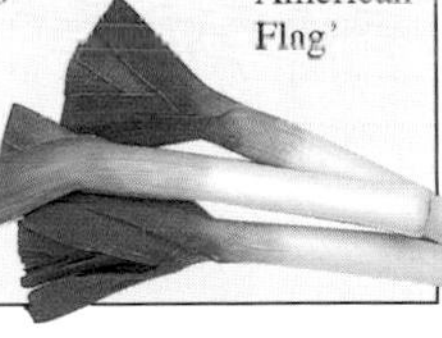

'Large American Flag'

Garlic (*Allium sativum*)

Biennials grown as annuals, garlic plants grow up to 2ft (60cm) tall with a spread of about 6in (15cm). Each produces an underground bulb up to 2in (5cm) in diameter. There are pink- and white-skinned forms, and many selections are available that are adapted to different climatic zones. Garlic is grown mainly for the strong-flavored cloves that form the bulb and may be stored for a year-round supply. The cloves are used either fresh or after storing for seasoning, and may be eaten both cooked and raw.

Garlic tolerates a wide range of climates, but needs a period of one to two months at about 32–50°F (0–10°C) in winter. Some variants are extremely hardy; use those recommended for your area. Garlic grows best in an open, sunny position on light soil that does not have to be very fertile, so do not grow it on freshly manured ground. Good drainage is vital. Garlic needs very low levels of nitrogen (see p.310).

Sowing and planting

For planting, split off individual cloves at least ½in (1cm) in diameter from a mature bulb. Always use healthy, virus-free stock. To produce large bulbs, garlic needs a long growing season, so wherever possible plant cloves in the fall. In very cold areas and on heavy soils, delay planting until the early spring, or plant the cloves in cell packs in winter, one per section. Then place the cell packs in a sheltered position outdoors to provide them with the necessary cold period. Plant them out in the ground after they have started to sprout in spring.

Plant the cloves upright with the flat base plates downward, at about twice their own depth. Space them

Planting Garlic Cloves in Cell Packs

Plant one clove 1in (2.5cm) deep in each section of a cell pack. Cover the cloves with more soil mix.

about 7in (18cm) apart each way or 4in (10cm) apart in rows 12in (30cm) apart. The bulbs tend to push themselves upward as they grow.

Routine cultivation

Little attention is required during growth other than keeping the beds free of weeds. For pests and diseases that may affect garlic, see "Bulb onions," p.341.

Harvesting and storing

Garlic takes between 16 and 36 weeks to mature, depending on the variant and time of planting. Uproot the plants as soon as the leaves have started to die back so that the bulbs do not resprout; if they are allowed to resprout, they are more likely to rot when stored.

Dry them thoroughly after lifting as for bulb onions (see p.341). Handle the bulbs very carefully when preparing them for storage to avoid bruising. Store the bulbs hanging in bunches or braids made with the dry leaves, or place them loose on trays kept in dry conditions at 41–50°F (5–10°C). Garlic may be stored for up to ten months, depending on the variant and storage conditions.

Storing Garlic

After harvesting garlic, tie the leaves loosely together with raffia or braid them. Then hang each bunch in a cool, dry place.

Celery (*Apium graveolens*)

A biennial plant, celery grows to 12–24in (30–60cm) tall, with a spread of 12in (30cm). Traditional trench celery has white, pink, or red stems that are blanched before use. Self-blanching types have creamy yellow stems that may be partially blanched. American green types have green stems. Intermediates are also available. Celery stalks are eaten raw or cooked and the leaves used as a seasoning or garnish.

As a temperate-climate crop, celery grows best at 59–70°F (15–21°C). Depending on the cultivar and conditions, it tolerates light or moderate frost; trench cultivars with red stems are hardiest. Some have improved resistance to bolting. Grow celery in an open site in fertile, moisture-retentive, but well-drained soil; lime acid soil (see p.533). Rotate celery (see p.303), but do not plant it near parsnips since both are susceptible to celery flies. Dig plenty of well-rotted organic matter into the soil before planting. For trench celery, prepare a trench 15in (38cm) wide and 12in (30cm) deep in fall before planting; work in manure or soil mix, and replace the soil to ground level. Celery needs a high level of nitrogen (see p.310).

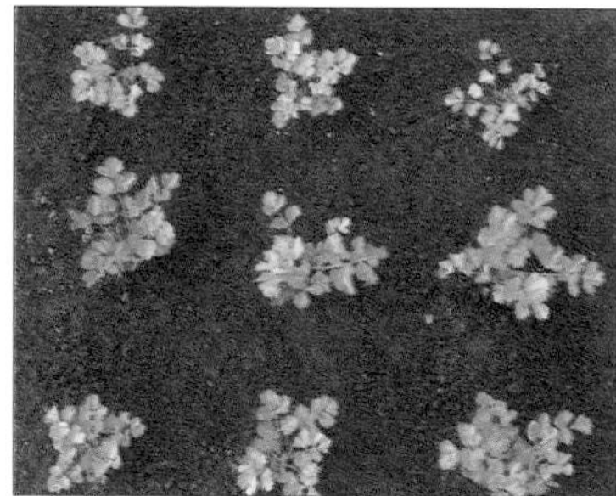

Celery Seedlings in a Block

Sowing and planting

Sow in spring *in situ* after all risk of frost is past, or indoors in seed trays or cell packs at 59°F (15°C) no more than ten weeks before the last expected frost. Use seed treated with a fungicide to avoid celery leaf spot. Sprinkle seed onto the soil mix or cover it shallowly: light is needed for germination. Do not sow too early; plants may bolt if the temperature falls below 50°F (10°C).

Thin out seedlings with four to six true leaves; plant out indoor-sown seedlings after all risk of frost is past. Reject any with blistered leaves. Plant self-blanching types 9in (23cm) apart in blocks to increase natural blanching. Young plants may be covered with cloches or floating row covers that should be removed after a month. Plant trench celery seedlings 15in (38cm) apart in single rows. They may be planted in trenches, or on the flat.

Routine cultivation

Celery requires steady growth, with no checks from water shortage or sudden drops in temperature. Apply a nitrogenous fertilizer or organic liquid feed about a month after planting. Once the plants are established, water them weekly at a rate of 5 gallons/sq yd (23 liters/sq m).

To sweeten self-blanching types, tuck a thick layer of loose straw around the plants when they are 8in (20cm) tall. To blanch celery in a trench, tie stems loosely together with soft string and fill in the trench gradually, hilling up the stems as they grow. If planted on the flat, wrap specially made collars or 9in (23cm) strips of heavy, lightproof paper around the stems when the plants are 12in (30cm) tall. To extend the blanched area, add a second collar three weeks later. In winter, cover trench celery with straw to protect against frost.

Pests and diseases

Slugs (p.550), celery flies (see "Leaf miners," p.553), cabbage root maggots (p.566), boron deficiency (p.560), and fungal leaf spots (p.554) are the most common pests and diseases of celery.

Harvesting and storing

Harvest self-blanching and green celery 11–16 weeks after planting and trench celery in late fall. Cut the stalks before they become pithy. Before frost threatens, lift and store the remaining plants in high humidity in a cool, frost-free place. They will keep for several weeks.

Blanching Celery

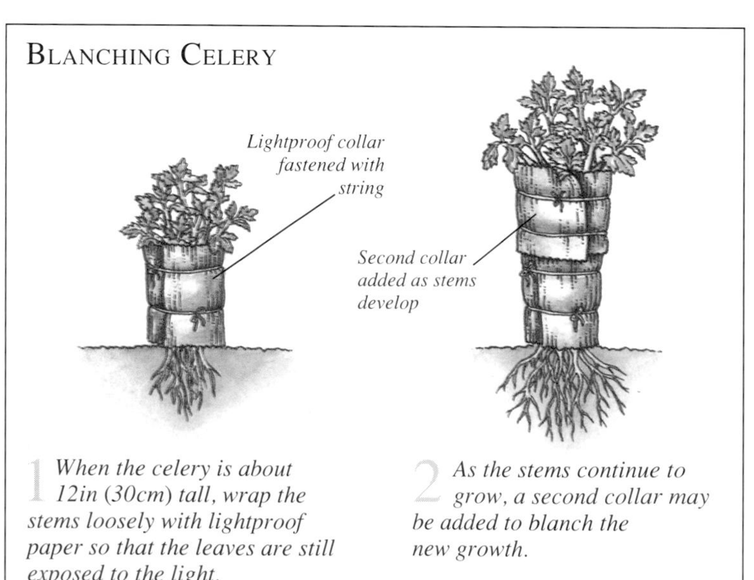

1 *When the celery is about 12in (30cm) tall, wrap the stems loosely with lightproof paper so that the leaves are still exposed to the light.*

2 *As the stems continue to grow, a second collar may be added to blanch the new growth.*

Recommended Celery

Self-blanching
'Celebrity'
'Golden Self Blanching'

Trench
'Fordhook Giant'
'Giant Pascal'
'Tendercrisp'
'Ventura'

American green
'Par-Cel'
'Tall Utah'

'Tall Utah'

Lifting Celery

Lift self-blanching celery plants before the first frosts. Clear the straw from around the stem and use a fork to uproot the whole plant.

Celeriac (*Apium graveolens* var. *rapaceum*)

This is a biennial plant that grows 12in (30cm) high with a spread of 15in (38cm). The swollen "bulb" at the stem base is cooked and also grated raw in salads. The leaves are used for seasoning and garnishing.

Celeriac is a cool-temperate crop, withstanding 14°F (-10°C) if the crowns are protected with straw. Plants tolerate light shade if the soil is moist. For soil requirements, see "Celery,"opposite; celeriac needs low nitrogen levels (see p.310).

PLANTING OUT CELERIAC FROM A CELL PACK

Plant out celeriac from a cell pack when it is 3–4in (8–10cm) high with 6 or 7 leaves. Space the young plants 12–15in (30–38cm) apart; take care not to bury the crowns.

Sowing and planting

Celeriac needs a six-month growing season for the bulb to develop. Germination may be erratic. Sow seed indoors in early spring, preferably in cell packs. If using trays, prick out seedlings to 2–3in (5–7cm) apart or pot them singly into small pots or cell packs. Harden off the young plants before planting out when they are about 3in (7cm) tall. Space them 12–15in (30–38cm) apart with their crowns at soil level, not buried.

Routine cultivation

Mulch after planting and water well, especially in dry conditions. Plants may be fed during the growing season (see "Celery," opposite). Toward the end of the summer, remove some of the coarse outer leaves to expose the crowns, encouraging the bulbs to develop. To protect from frost, tuck a loose layer of straw 4–6in (10–15cm) thick around the crowns.

Pests and diseases

Celeriac may be affected by the same pests and diseases as celery (see opposite), but is normally healthy.

CULTIVATING AND PROTECTING CELERIAC

1 *Toward the end of the summer, as the swollen stem bases develop, remove a few of the outer leaves to expose the crowns.*

2 *Before the first frosts, mulch around the base of the plants with a 6in (15cm) layer of straw to protect the crowns.*

Harvesting and storing

Celeriac may be harvested from late summer until the following spring. The bulbs are ready for use when they are 3–5in (7–13cm) in diameter.

The flavor is best and the bulbs will keep longer if the roots are left in the ground over winter. Where winters are very severe, dig up the plants in early winter without damaging the bulbs; trim off the outer leaves, leaving a central tuft, and store the plants in boxes of damp soil in a cool, frost-free place.

RECOMMENDED CELERIAC

'Alabaster'
'Brilliant'
'Dolvi'
'Prague'
'Zwindra'

'Brilliant'

Asparagus (*Asparagus officinalis*)

Asparagus is perennial and may be productive for up to 20 years. Its light, fernlike foliage grows over 3ft (90cm) tall, with a spread of about 18in (45cm). It is cultivated for the delicious young shoots or spears that push through the ground in spring. Male and female plants are available; the females produce berries. Male plants are higher yielding; very productive, all-male, F1 hybrid cultivars are now also available. Asparagus is normally eaten cooked.

Asparagus is a cool-season crop, growing best at 61–75°F (16–24°C) in regions with cool winters that provide the necessary dormant period. Choose an open site, avoiding exposed situations and frost pockets. Asparagus tolerates a very wide range of moderately fertile soils, although acid soils should be limed (see p.333). Good drainage is essential. Do not make a new asparagus bed where asparagus has been grown before, since soilborne diseases may persist. Remove all perennial weeds from the site and prepare the ground by digging it over and working in manure or soil mix. Asparagus may also be grown in raised beds to improve drainage. It has low nitrogen requirements (see p.310).

PLANTING ASPARAGUS CROWNS

Dig a trench about 12in (30cm) wide and 8in (20cm) deep with a central, mounded ridge that is 4in (10cm) high. Place the asparagus crowns on the ridge about 15in (38cm) apart. Spread the roots out evenly and cover them with about 2in (5cm) of soil to the level of the crowns.

Sowing and planting

Asparagus is traditionally grown by planting one-year-old purchased plants, or crowns, in spring. The crowns are fleshy and must never be allowed to dry out before planting.

Grow them about 15in (38cm) apart, either in single or double rows, with the rows spaced 12in (30cm) apart. Plant the crowns about 4in (10cm) deep by first making a small trench with a central, mounded ridge along the flat base. Spread out the roots evenly over the ridge and cover them with soil to the level of the crowns. Fill in the rest of the trench with soil gradually as the stems grow, leaving 3–4in (8–10cm) of the stems exposed.

Raising asparagus from seed is cheaper, but the results are more variable. Sow seed 1in (2.5cm) deep *in situ* in spring, and thin out to about 3in (7cm) apart. Plant out the largest the following spring, or, if

RECOMMENDED ASPARAGUS

Traditional
'Martha Washington'
'Mary Washington'
'Viking'

All-male cultivars
'Centennial'
'Jersey Giant' (syn. '4-56')
'Jersey Knight'
'Supermale'
'UC-157'

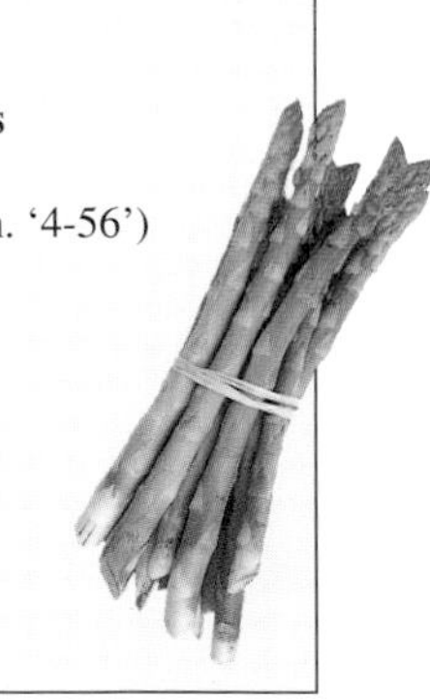

'Jersey Giant'

CUTTING BACK ASPARAGUS STEMS

Using pruners, cut back the stems in fall to within about 1in (2.5cm) of ground level.

preferred, sow seed indoors in cell packs in early spring at 55–61°F (13–16°C). The seedlings grow rapidly and may be planted out in permanent positions in early summer.

Routine cultivation
Asparagus requires little attention other than keeping the beds weed-free. Hoe shallowly in order to avoid damaging the roots. When the foliage turns yellow in fall, cut the stems back to approximately 1in (2.5cm) above the soil.

Pests and diseases
Slugs (p.550) at an early stage and asparagus beetles (p.550) on more mature plants are the most serious pests. The soilborne fungal disease crown rot (p.571) may destroy plants in long-established beds.

Harvesting and storing
Asparagus must be allowed to build into a strong plant before it is harvested in midspring. Good modern cultivars may be cut lightly in the second season. The following year, limit cutting to a six-week period; subsequently, cutting may continue over eight weeks if the plants are growing well. Harvest the spears when they are about 6in (15cm) high and fairly thick. Cut at an angle, taking care not to damage nearby spears. Remaining spears will continue to grow. Asparagus freezes well.

HARVESTING ASPARAGUS

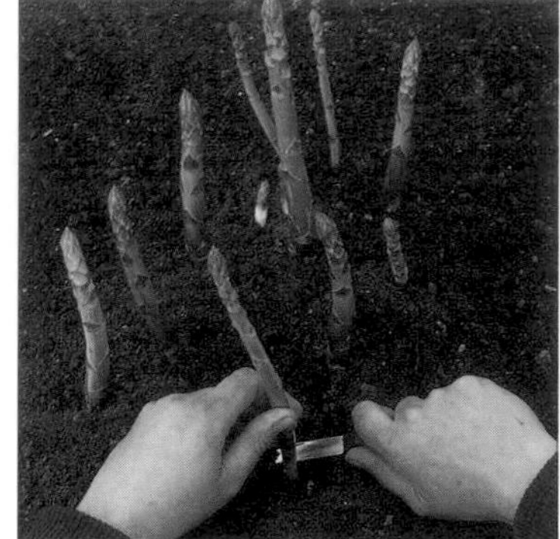

When the spears are 5–6in (12–15cm) high, cut each stalk 1–2in (2.5–5cm) below soil level.

Kohlrabi (*Brassica oleracea* Gongylodes Group)

These annual plants from the brassica family are grown for the white-fleshed, turniplike, swollen stem or "bulb" that forms just above ground. Kohlrabi reaches 12in (30cm) high and has an average spread of 12in (30cm). The outer skin is pale green (sometimes described as white) or purple. The bulbs are nutritious, flavorful, and used cooked or raw.

Kohlrabi is a cool-season crop, growing best at 64–77°F (18–25°C). Young plants tend to bolt prematurely in temperatures below about 50°F (10°C). For soil requirements, see "Siting Western brassicas," p.313. Kohlrabi grows well in light soils and withstands drought better than most brassicas. It has low nitrogen requirements (see p.310).

Sowing and planting
In mild climates, sow seed outdoors in succession from spring through to late summer, using the hardier purple forms for late sowings. In hot climates, sow in spring and fall. Sow *in situ* either in rows about 12in (30cm) apart, thinning seedlings to about 7in (18cm) apart, or space the seeds about 10in (25cm) apart in each direction. Under cover, sow earlier in gentle heat in trays or cell packs. Plant out seedlings when they are no more than 2in (5cm) high. Protect early outdoor crops with cloches or floating row covers.

GREEN KOHLRABI

Routine cultivation
Kohlrabi is fast-maturing; little attention is required during growth other than keeping beds weed-free.

Pests and diseases
Clubroot (p.567), cabbage root maggots (p.566), and flea beetles (p.550) may affect plants. See also "Cultivating Western brassicas," p.313.

Harvesting and storing
Depending on the cultivar and season, kohlrabi may be ready for cutting between five and nine weeks after sowing. Traditional cultivars should be eaten when they are no larger than tennis balls or they will become woody; improved modern cultivars are still tender at a diameter of about 4in (10cm).

Leave later crops in the soil until heavy frost threatens, since the flavor deteriorates once lifted. In cold areas, lift in fall. Leave a central tuft of leaves on each bulb to help keep them fresh; store them for up to two months in boxes of moist sand.

RECOMMENDED KOHLRABI

Traditional
'Purple Vienna'
'White Vienna'

'Purple Vienna'

Modern
'Blaro' (purple)
'Grand Duke'

Florence fennel (*Foeniculum vulgare* var. *dulce*)

Grown as an annual, Florence, or sweet, fennel is distinct from the perennial herb fennel. The plants grow up to about 2ft (60cm) high and have a spread of about 18in (45cm). The anise-flavored, flattened "bulb" of overlapping scales that develops at the base of the leaf stalks is eaten cooked or raw. The decorative fernlike foliage may be used as a flavoring or garnish.

Florence fennel tolerates a wide range of climates, from temperate to subtropical. It thrives at a warm, even temperature, but mature plants can withstand a light frost. Grow it in an open situation, in very fertile, moisture-retentive, but well-drained soil into which plenty of humus has been worked. Florence fennel grows well in light soils but must not be allowed to dry out. It has low nitrogen requirements (see p.310).

Sowing and planting
In cool northern latitudes, sow seed from early to midsummer; traditional cultivars are likely to bolt if sown in spring, so use modern, bolt-resistant cultivars for earlier sowings. In warmer climates, sow in spring for a summer crop and again in late summer for a fall crop. Florence fennel does not transplant well and may bolt prematurely if checked, so sow seed either *in situ* or in cell packs for transplanting when the seedlings have no more than four leaves. Space the young seedlings about 12in (30cm) apart each way. Both early and late crops may be protected from frost by covering with cloches or floating row covers.

Routine cultivation
Little attention is required; keep beds weed-free. Florence fennel needs to be kept moist, so water thoroughly and mulch. When bulbs start to swell, hill them up to half their height to make them whiter and sweeter.

FLORENCE FENNEL

Harvesting Florence Fennel

1 *Cut the fennel bulb about 1in (2.5cm) above soil level. Leave the base in position.*

2 *Feathery leaves will usually sprout from the base of the stem within a few weeks.*

Pests and diseases
Florence fennel rarely suffers from any pests or diseases. Most problems stem from lack of water, fluctuating temperatures, or transplanting, all of which may cause bolting.

Harvesting and storing
Harvest the bulbs when they are well rounded, about 15 weeks after sowing or from two to three weeks after hilling up. Pull them up whole, or cut across the bulbs about 1in (2.5cm) above ground level. The stump will usually resprout to produce small sprigs of ferny foliage that may be used for flavoring or as a garnish. Florence fennel does not store well; eat it as fresh as possible.

Recommended Florence Fennel

'Fennel Fino'
'Neopolitan'
'Romy'
'Supewadremen'
'Sweet Florence'
'Zefa Fino' **Br**

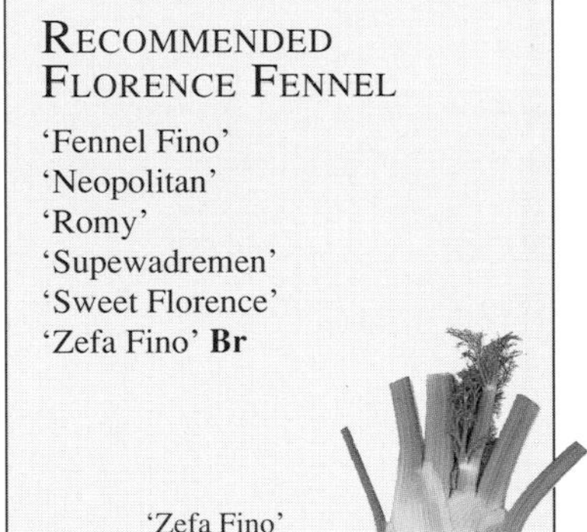

'Zefa Fino'

Key
Br *Bolt resistant*

Rhubarb (*Rheum* x *cultorum*)

This perennial lasts over 20 years in good conditions. Rhubarb grows about 24in (60cm) or more high and up to 6ft (2m) across. The leaves may be 18in (45cm) wide. The pale green or pinkish red leaf stalks, which may be 2ft (60cm) long, are harvested young and used cooked.

Rhubarb is a temperate-climate crop and does not thrive at high temperatures; the roots survive lows down to -20 °F (-30°C). Recommended cultivars include 'Valentine', 'Cherry Red', and 'Victoria'. It grows on a wide range of soils, as long as they are rich and well drained. Before planting, dig in plenty of manure or soil mix. Rhubarb needs medium nitrogen levels when young and very high nitrogen once it is mature (see p.310).

Sowing and planting
Rhubarb is normally propagated by planting "sets," each consisting of a fleshy rootstock with at least one bud. Sets are about 4in (10cm) in diameter. Plant them in the dormant season from fall to spring, preferably in fall. Either buy virus-free sets, or separate a set from a healthy two- or three-year-old plant, once its leaves have died back, by lifting the plant and slicing through the crown; replant the parent. On light soils, plant the set so that 1in (2.5cm) of soil covers the buds; on heavy or wet soils, plant with the buds just above ground level. Space the plants 3ft (90cm) apart.

Rhubarb may also be raised from seed, although the results are variable. Sow seed in spring, 1in (2.5cm) deep in rows 12in (30cm) apart, in a seedbed outdoors. Thin the seedlings to 6in (15cm) apart, and plant out the strongest-looking ones in their permanent positions in fall, or in spring the following year.

Routine cultivation
Mulch the plants heavily, and water them in dry weather. Apply a heavy dressing of manure or compost every fall or spring and a nitrogenous dressing or organic liquid feed in spring. Remove flowering stems.

Rhubarb may be forced in the dark to obtain very tender stems. Cover the dormant crowns in late winter with a 4in (10cm) layer of straw or leaves, then a forcing pot, or a large bucket, at least 18in (45cm) high; leave this on for about four weeks until stems are large enough.

Pests and diseases
Crown rot (p.571) and viruses (p.555) may attack established plants.

Harvesting and storing
Harvest in spring and early summer. With plants raised from sets, start pulling lightly the first year after planting; with plants grown from seed, wait until the second year. In subsequent years, pull heavily until the quality starts to deteriorate in summer. Forced stems are ready to harvest about three weeks earlier than unforced ones.

Dividing Rhubarb

1 *Lift or expose the crown. Cut through it carefully using a spade, ensuring there is at least 1 main bud on each section. Prepare the soil by digging in manure.*

2 *Replant the sections (sets) $2^{1}/_{2}$–3ft (75–90cm) apart. Fill in around each root so that the bud is just above the surface. Firm, and rake around the bud.*

Forcing Rhubarb

For an earlier, tender crop, cover the dormant buds (see upper inset) in winter with straw or leaves inside a forcing pot or any large container that excludes light. The plant will produce tender pink stems a few weeks later (see lower inset).

Harvesting Rhubarb

When the rhubarb stems are ready, they may be harvested by gripping each stem at the base and twisting it while pulling it upward and outward.

Root and tuberous vegetables

ROOT vegetables are the mainstay of the kitchen garden. As the name suggests, most are grown for their swollen roots or tubers. A few, such as turnips, beets, and taro, are also used for their young leaves; some radish cultivars also produce edible seedpods. A variety of root vegetables may be grown and harvested in succession for a steady supply; many store quite easily, sometimes still in the ground, for use throughout winter. Salsify and scorzonera may be overwintered in milder areas for their flowering shoots produced in spring.

Beets (*Beta vulgaris* subsp. *vulgaris*)

Beets are biennial plants grown as annuals. They grow to about 12in (30cm) tall and about 10in (24cm) across. The swollen root forms at ground level and may be round, flat, or cylindrical. It is on average 4in (10cm) in diameter, and about 8in (20cm) or more deep in the long forms. The flesh is normally red but may be yellow, white, or even have concentric pink and white rings. The skin is similarly red, yellow, or off-white. The sweetly flavored roots are mainly used cooked, either fresh or stored, but may also be pickled. The fresh young leaves (tops) may be used as greens.

Beets grow best and develop the deepest colors in cool, even temperatures, ideally of 61°F (16°C). Grow in an open site on rich, light soil with high nitrogen levels (see p.310). Apply half the nitrogen before sowing. Lime very acid soils.

THINNING SEEDLINGS

When the beet seedlings have produced 3 or 4 leaves, thin clumps growing close together to the required spacing by nipping off the top green leaves at soil level without disturbing the remaining seedlings.

Sowing and planting

Beet "seeds" each contain a cluster of two or three seeds, the seedlings of which must be thinned out early. Some cultivars, such as 'Mobile' and 'Monopoly', have been bred to produce single, or mono-germ, seed, which needs little or no thinning.

To overcome slow germination, soak seed in warm water for 30 minutes before sowing. Some cultivars may bolt if sown early or in unfavorable conditions, so choose bolt-resistant cultivars for sowings early in the season.

In spring, sow seed *in situ* outdoors when the soil is workable and has warmed up to at least 45°F (7°C). Sow seed 1/2–3/4in (1–2cm) deep, with the spacing determined by the type of beet and the size required. Grow maincrop beets in rows 12in (30cm) apart, thinning to 3–4in (7–10cm) apart. For pickling beets about 1in (2.5cm) in diameter, space rows 3in (7cm) apart, thinning seedlings to 2 1/2in (6cm).

For earlier crops, sow in early spring under cloches, in frames, or indoors in seed trays or cell packs, transplanting outside when the seedlings are 2in (5cm) tall. Sow three mono-germ or ordinary seeds per cell pack (see "Cell packs and small containers," p.307); thin as necessary. Early beets need plenty of space, so plant indoor-sown seedlings in rows 9in (23cm) apart, then thin them to 3 1/2in (9cm) apart. For continuous supplies of young beets and beet tops, sow seed at intervals of two to three weeks until hot summer weather arrives. Sow cultivars for storage in late summer, a minimum of ten weeks before the first heavy frost is expected.

HARVESTING BEETS

Carefully grip the leaf stems and pull the beet from the soil; it should lift easily since it is shallow-rooted. Avoid damaging the roots as far as possible, since they will bleed if they are cut.

Routine cultivation

Water only to prevent the soil from drying out, at a rate of 2 gallons/sq yd (11 liters/sq m) every two weeks. Apply the remaining nitrogenous fertilizer during active growth.

Pests and diseases

Beets may be affected by cutworms (p.561), aphids (p.552), damping off (p.566), fungal leaf spots (p.554), and boron deficiency (p.568).

RECOMMENDED BEETS

'Boltardy' **Br**
'Burpee's Golden' (stores well) **Br**

'Burpee's Golden'

'Chioggia Striped' **Br**
'Detroit Dark Red'
'Early Wonder'
'Formanova'
'Little Ball'
'Lutz Green Leaf'
'Sweetheart'
'Warrior'

KEY
Br *Bolt resistant*

Harvesting and storing

Harvest beets at any stage from small, immature roots 1in (2.5cm) in diameter to fully mature roots; this will be from seven to 13 weeks after sowing, depending on the cultivar, the season, and the size required. In mild areas, beets may be left in well-drained soil in winter, protected with a layer of straw up to 6in (15cm) deep, but they eventually become rather woody. Otherwise lift them before severe frost. Twist off the leaves (cutting causes bleeding) and store the roots in moist sand in a frost-free place. Beets normally keep until midspring.

Rutabagas (*Brassica napus* Napobrassica Group)

Biennials from the brassica family, rutabagas are grown as annuals and reach a height of 15in (38cm) with a spread of 15in (38cm). The root flesh is usually yellow, but sometimes white, and the skin is generally purple, buff, or a combination of both. The large, often irregularly shaped, underground roots, which may be 8in (20cm) in diameter and as long, are sweetly flavored and used cooked. This hardy, cool-season crop grows best on light, fertile soil with low nitrogen levels (see p.310). For climate and soil requirements, see "Siting Western brassicas," p.313.

Sowing and planting

Rutabagas need a growing season of up to 26 weeks to mature fully. Sow seed from early to late spring *in situ*, 3/4in (2cm) deep in rows 15in (38cm) apart, thinning early and in stages until the seedlings are about 9in (23cm) apart.

RECOMMENDED RUTABAGAS

'Altasweet'
'Laurentian'
'Purple Top Yellow'

'Altasweet'

Routine cultivation
Keep beds weed-free, and if conditions are very dry, water at a rate of 2 gallons/sq yd (11 liters/sq m).

Pests and diseases
Downy mildew (p.552), powdery mildew (p.552), boron deficiency (p.568), and flea beetles (p.550) may affect rutabagas. Some cultivars are resistant to mildew. For other pests and diseases, see "Cultivating Western brassicas," p.313.

Harvesting and storing
Rutabagas generally mature in fall and, being hardy, may be left in the soil until the end of the year, when they should be lifted carefully to prevent them from becoming woody. Except in very cold climates, covering with a thick layer of straw provides sufficient protection until the rutabagas are lifted. Store rutabagas in clamps outdoors or in crates under cover (see *Storing Carrots*, p.350) for up to four months.

MAKING A RUTABAGA CLAMP

Choose a sheltered, well-drained site and stack the roots on an 8in (20cm) layer of straw in a pyramid, with their necks facing outward. Cover with a layer of longer straw. In very cold climates, protect further with a 12in (10cm) layer of soil.

Turnips (*Brassica rapa* Rapifera Group)

These are biennials from the brassica family grown as annuals. The plants are about 9in (23cm) high with a spread of about 10in (25cm). The underground roots swell to 1–3in (2.5–7cm) in diameter and are round, fairly flat, or long. The flesh may be either white or yellow and the skin white, pink, red, or yellow. The young leaves, known as turnip tops, may be eaten as greens (see "Turnip tops and broccoli raab," p.318). Turnip roots are used either fresh or stored, usually cooked.

Turnips are a temperate-climate crop, growing best at about 68°F (20°C). They are reasonably hardy, tolerating light frost. For general climate and soil requirements, see "Siting Western brassicas," p.313. Grow turnips in moist soil, since they bolt prematurely in dry conditions. Early types, many small and white, grow fast and are excellent for early spring and summer crops; the hardier types are used fresh during summer and winter and for storage. They require low to medium nitrogen levels (see p.310).

Sowing and planting
Start sowing seed of early turnips in spring as soon as the ground is workable, or sow under cover. Make successive sowings at three-week intervals until early summer. Sow maincrop types in late summer *in situ*, ¾in (2cm) deep. Space early types in rows that are 9in (23cm) apart, thinning seedlings to 4in (10cm); space maincrop types in rows 12in (30cm) apart, thinning to 6in (15cm).

HARVESTING TURNIPS

Harvest turnips by pulling them from the soil by their leaves. Do not leave them in the ground too long or they may become woody.

Routine cultivation
Keep beds weed-free. In dry weather water at a rate of 2 gallons/sq yd (11 liters/sq m).

Pests and diseases
Flea beetles (p.550) may affect seedlings; other problems include boron deficiency (p.568), powdery mildew (p.552), and downy mildew (p.552). Turnip gall weevils cause hollow swellings on the roots that may be mistaken for clubroot but are rarely serious; discard affected plants. For other pests and diseases, see "Cultivating Western brassicas," p.313.

Harvesting and storing
Harvest early turnips after about five weeks, maincrop types after six to ten weeks. Pull them before they become woody. Lift turnips for storage before the first frost, then store for up to three or four months in outdoor clamps covered with straw.

RECOMMENDED TURNIPS

'Golden Ball'
'Just Right'
'Purple Top Milan'
'Purple Top White Globe'
'Snowball'
'Tokyo Cross' F1
'Tokyo Market'

'Golden Ball'

Taro (*Colocasia esculenta*)

This herbaceous, frost-tender perennial grows to about 3ft (1m) tall, with a spread of 24–8in (60–70cm). The plants have large, long-stalked leaves, which may be green or greenish purple. Taro, sometimes known as cocoyam, is grown for its large, swollen tuber, which is eaten cooked. The young leaves and shoots are also edible, and may be cooked and used as greens.

TARO PLANT

Taro is a tropical and subtropical plant that requires temperatures of 70–81°F (21–7°C), with humidity levels over 75 percent. In temperate areas it needs a very sheltered, sunny site, or it may be grown under cover. Taro is adapted to short daylengths of about 12 hours (see "Daylength," p.303); it rarely produces flowers. Some forms are tolerant of light shade. Moisture-retentive soil is essential for success because many forms of taro are sensitive to dry soil conditions. Fertile soil that has a high organic content and a slightly acid pH level of 5.5–6.5 is recommended; prepare soil before planting. Taro requires medium to high levels of nitrogen (see p.310).

Sowing and planting
Seeds are rarely available, so propagation is usually from existing tubers. Plant mature tubers or portions of tubers with dormant buds *in situ* in well-prepared beds. Space the tubers about 18in (45cm) apart with 3ft (90cm) between rows.

Taro may also be propagated by cuttings. Sever the tops of tubers with a horizontal cut; each cutting should consist of several leaves 4–5in (10–12cm) long, a central growing point, and a small portion of the tuber. Plant the cuttings in their final positions at the above spacing; if the temperature is below the optimum 70°F (21°C), plant them in 8–10in (21–5cm) pots of standard soil mix to grow on under cover until the temperature is high enough for transplanting outside.

Routine cultivation
Taro needs a constant supply of water for the highest yields, so water regularly. Apply an organic mulch to conserve moisture, and feed with a general-purpose fertilizer at two- to three-week intervals. Keep beds free of weeds. The plants should be hilled up around the stems once they are established to encourage the tubers to develop.

Pests and diseases
These are rarely serious for taro grown in the open, but aphids (p.552), thrips (p.553), spider mites (p.552), and fungal leaf spots (p.554) may reduce tuber yields. Under cover, taro is vulnerable to the same pests and diseases as for those grown outside; whiteflies (p.552) may also be troublesome.

Growing under cover

Propagate from tubers (see p.349). When these have rooted, transfer them to well-prepared greenhouse beds, 8–12in (21–30cm) pots, or grow bags, ensuring that the roots are disturbed as little as possible.

Water and feed the plants regularly, maintaining a temperature of 70–81°F (21–7°C) and humidity of more than 75 percent by damping down. Tubers that are cultivated under cover tend to be smaller than those grown outdoors.

Harvesting and storing

Taro is slow to develop and reach maturity. Harvest the tubers 16–24 weeks after planting, when the leaves start to turn yellow and plants die down. Lift taro grown in the open carefully using a fork; plants under cover may be lifted gently out of their pots or grow bags. Try not to damage the tubers since this encourages rotting.

Healthy tubers may be stored for about eight to 12 weeks at a temperature of 52–5°F (11–13°C), with humidity of 85–90 percent.

TARO TUBER

Carrots *(Daucus carota)*

These are biennials grown as annuals. Their swollen orange taproots may be up to 3in (8cm) in diameter at the neck and up to about 12in (30cm) in length. The feathery, green foliage grows to about 24in (60cm), with a 12in (30cm) spread. Carrots are normally long and tapered but may be rounded. There are many types: early ones are usually small and slender and used young; maincrop types are larger and are used fresh or stored. Carrots are eaten either cooked or raw.

Carrots are a cool-season crop, tolerating the same temperatures as beets (see p.348). Grow in an open site on light and fertile soil. Deep-rooted types require reasonably deep, stone-free soil. Work in plenty of organic matter, preferably in the fall before sowing. The fertile, loose soil of established raised beds is particularly suitable for growing carrots. Rake the soil into a fine tilth before sowing. Carrots should be rotated (see p.303). They need very low nitrogen levels (see p.310).

RECOMMENDED CARROTS

Early
'Baby Orange – Amstel'

'Earlibird Nantes'

'Earlibird Nantes' F1
'Gold Pak'
'Little Finger'

'Thumbelina'

'Nanco' F1
'Nantes Half Long'
'Orbit' (baby)
'Short 'n' Sweet'
'Spartan Premium 80'
'Thumbelina'
'Toudo'

Maincrop
'Bolero'
'Imperator'

'Danver's Half Long'

'Danver's Half Long'
'Danver's 126'
'Red Cored Chantenay'
'Royal Chantenay'
'Scarlet Wonder'
'Seminole'

PROTECTION AGAINST CARROT RUST FLY

Surround the patch of young carrots with a protective barrier 2–3ft (60–90cm) high. The barrier may be made either of fine mesh netting or stiff, clear plastic, both of which also help to warm the soil inside.

Sowing and planting

Sow early types in spring *in situ* as soon as the soil is workable and has warmed up to 45°F (7°C). Earlier sowings may be made under cloches, in frames, or under floating row covers; remove these after a few weeks. Sow maincrop types from late spring until early summer. A second sowing of early types may be made in late summer and protected with cloches.

Sow seed sparingly about 1/2–3/4in (1–2cm) deep, either broadcast or in rows 6in (15cm) apart. Thin early carrots to 3in (7cm) apart; maincrop carrots should be thinned to 1 1/2in (4cm) to obtain medium-sized carrots or farther apart if large carrots are needed. Carrots do not transplant well unless sown in cell packs: sow seed of deep-rooted cultivars singly, those of round-rooted ones, several together. The latter, if sown in cell packs, do not need thinning and should be planted out as a group at slightly wider spacing than for maincrop carrots.

Routine cultivation

Remove weeds regularly once the carrots have germinated and until the foliage hinders further weed growth. Water at a rate of 3–5 gallons/sq yd (16–23 liters/sq m) every two or three weeks.

Pests and diseases

Carrot rust flies (p.566) may be a serious problem. The egg-laying adult flies are attracted by the smell of carrot foliage; thin in the evening, nipping off the seedlings at ground level and removing the tops from the site. Root and leaf aphids (see "Aphids," p.552), carrot motley dwarf virus (see "Viruses," p.555), and boron deficiency (p.568) may be troublesome.

Harvesting and storing

Harvest early cultivars about seven to nine weeks after sowing, maincrop cultivars after ten to 11 weeks. Pull them by hand or fork them out. On well-drained soils in areas with mild winters, carrots may be left in the soil in winter (see *Protecting Parsnips*, p.352). Otherwise lift them before heavy frost, cut or twist off foliage, and store in boxes in a cool, dry place for up to five months.

THIN SOWING

Sow carrot seeds about 1in (2.5cm) apart so that the seedlings will need little thinning later. The seed should be 1/2–3/4in (1–2cm) deep.

HARVESTING YOUNG

Early cultivars may be harvested when they are very young. Pull them up in a bunch when they are 3–4in (8–10cm) long.

STORING CARROTS

Twist the foliage off the carrots; place roots on a layer of sand in a box. Cover them with more sand and continue in layers.

Jerusalem artichokes *(Helianthus tuberosus)*

These are perennial plants, also known as sunchokes or girasoles. The distinctively flavored tubers are 2–4in (5–10cm) long, about $1^1/_2$in (4cm) in diameter and, in most cultivars, very bumpy. 'Fuseau', however, produces smooth tubers. The plants may grow up to 10ft (3m) tall. The tubers are normally cooked but may be eaten raw. Jerusalem artichokes grow best in temperate climates and are very hardy. They tolerate a wide range of soils and require medium nitrogen levels (see p.310). They may be planted as a windbreak screen.

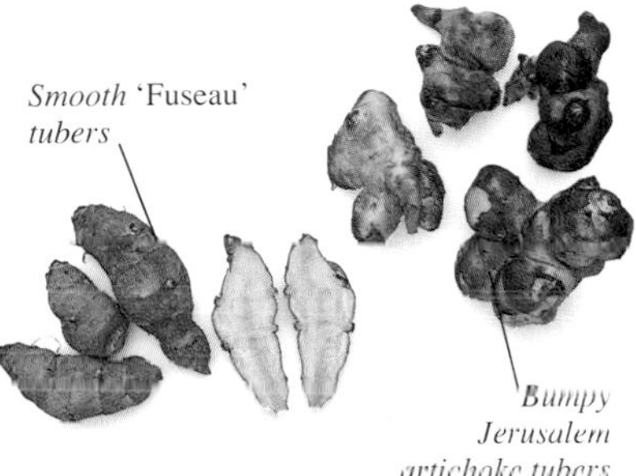

Smooth 'Fuseau' *tubers*

Bumpy Jerusalem artichoke tubers

Sowing and planting

Plant tubers as soon as the ground is workable in spring. Those the size of a hen's egg may be planted whole; cut large ones into pieces, each with several buds. Make a drill, planting about 5in (12.5cm) deep and 12in (30cm) apart. Cover with soil.

Routine cultivation

When the plants are about 12in (30cm) tall, hill up the stems to half their height for stability. In late summer, cut the stems back to 5ft (1.5m), removing any flowerheads at the same time. In very exposed sites, stake or support the stems. Water in very dry conditions. When the leaves start to yellow, cut the stems back to just above ground level.

Planting

Make a drill 4–6in (10–15cm) deep. Place the tubers in the drill 12in (30cm) apart with the main bud facing upward. Cover carefully so the tubers are not dislodged.

Cutting Down

Toward the end of the summer, cut down the stems to about 5ft (1.5m), so that the plants will not suffer wind damage. The tubers will continue to develop unchecked.

Harvesting and storing

Harvest the tubers 16–20 weeks after planting. Lift them only when required, since they keep best in the ground, and take care not to damage the roots. Save a few tubers to replant or leave some in the soil for the following year. Otherwise, remove even small tubers since they rapidly become invasive. In severe climates or on heavy ground, lift in early winter and store in a cellar or in clamps outdoors (see *Making a Rutabaga Clamp*, p.349) for up to five months.

Sweet potatoes *(Ipomoea batatas)*

These tender perennials are grown as annuals. They have trailing stems that grow to 10ft (3m) or more if unpruned. Cultivars vary considerably in leaf shape and tuber size, shape, and color. Tubers are eaten cooked; the leaves may be used in the same way as spinach (see p.325).

Sweet potatoes are tropical and subtropical, requiring a temperature of 75–9°F (24–6°C). In warm climates, they need a sunny site; in temperate climates, they should be grown under cover, but tuber yields are smaller. Most cultivars are short-day plants (see "Daylength," p.303).

Highly fertile, well-drained, sandy loams with a pH of 5.5–6.5 and medium to high nitrogen levels (see p.310) are required.

Sowing and planting

In the tropics and subtropics, plant sweet potatoes at the start of the rainy season. In warm and temperate climates, plant in spring. Make raised ridges about 30in (75cm) apart, then plant the tubers 2–3in (5–7cm) deep in the ridge, spacing them 10–12in (25–30cm) apart. Alternatively, take 8–10in (20–25cm) stem cuttings from mature plants and insert them to half their length just below the apex of the ridge.

Cultivars raised from seed will provide reasonable crops. Sow indoors in trays or 8–10in (21–5cm) pots at a temperature of at least 75°F (24°C). When seedlings are 4–6in (10–15cm) high, harden them off and transplant outside.

Routine cultivation

Water and weed regularly, and mulch to conserve moisture. Train shoots to spread around the plant. Apply a general purpose fertilizer at two- to three week intervals until the tubers have formed. Protect from winds.

Pests and diseases

Aphids (p.552), caterpillars (p.551), root-knot nematodes (p.566), fungal leaf spots (p.554), *Fusarium* wilt (p.567), Southern blight (p.560), and various viruses (p.555) affect sweet potatoes growing outdoors. Under cover, whiteflies (p.552), thrips (p.553), and spider mites (p.552) may be troublesome.

Growing under cover

Sow seed, as described above, transplanting seedlings to grow bags or prepared beds. Alternatively, take cuttings and insert three or four into 6in (15cm) pots. Maintain a minimum temperature of 77°F (25°C) and a humidity of over 70 percent by damping down regularly. When roots develop, transfer plants to greenhouse beds or grow bags. Water regularly and remove the growing points of shoots longer than 2ft (60cm) to encourage development of lateral shoots. Keep the temperature below 82°F (28°C), and the growing area well ventilated.

Harvesting and storing

Harvest 12–16 weeks after planting, when the stems and leaves turn yellow. Crops from seed are ready three or four weeks later. Lift the tubers, using a fork, without damaging them. In order to store sweet potatoes they must first be cured for four to seven days at temperatures of 82–6°F (28–30°C) and humidity of 85–90 percent (see "Winter squash," p.331). They may be stored in shallow trays for several months at 50–59°F (10–15°C).

Sweet Potato Plant

Stem Cuttings for Growing under Cover

1 *Select healthy, vigorous shoots and cut them off the parent plant with pruners.*

2 *Remove the lower leaves and trim each shoot below a node to 8–10in (20–25cm). Insert in pots and grow on under cover.*

Recommended Sweet Potatoes

- 'Centennial' (orange-fleshed)
- 'Excel' (orange-fleshed)*
- 'Georgia Jet' (orange-fleshed)
- 'Jewel' (white-fleshed)
- 'Sumor' (white-fleshed)*
- 'Vardaman' (orange-fleshed)

Key

* *Resistant to root-knot nematodes*

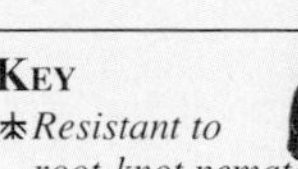

Parsnips (*Pastinaca sativa*)

Parsnips are biennials grown as annuals. The taproot grows to 2in (5cm) across at the neck and about 4in (10cm) long in short forms and up to 9in (23cm) in long types. The leaves are about 15in (38cm) long and 12in (30cm) wide. The roots are eaten cooked.

Parsnips are a hardy, cool-season crop, and prefer light, deeply cultivated, stone-free soils. On shallow soils, grow the shorter forms. Lime very acid soils and rotate crops (see p.303). Parsnips have low nitrogen requirements (see p.310).

Recommended Parsnips

'Avonresister' (short)
'Cobham Improved Marrow' (medium)
'Gladiator' F1 (long)
'Harris Model' (long)
'Lancer' (long)
'Tender and True' (long)

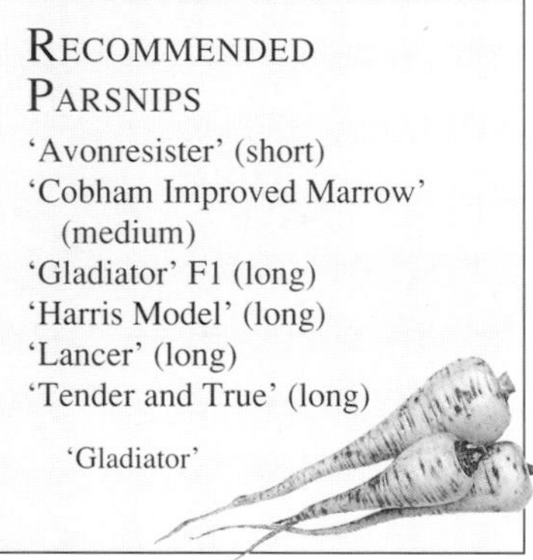
'Gladiator'

Sowing and planting

Always sow fresh seed. Parsnips need a long growing season and so should be sown as soon as the soil is workable in spring, but not in cold or wet soil. Sow seed *in situ* $^{3}/_{4}$in (2cm) deep in rows 12in (30cm) apart. Thin the seedlings to 4in (10cm) apart to produce large roots, or 3in (7cm) for smaller roots. A faster-germinating crop such as radishes may be intersown; to allow for this, station sow several parsnip seeds at intervals of 4in (10cm), and thin to one seedling per station. To start parsnips earlier, sow seed in cell packs with gentle heat under cover and transplant seedlings before taproots develop.

Routine cultivation

Always keep beds free of weeds. In very dry conditions water the plants as for carrots (see p.350).

Pests and diseases

Parsnips may be attacked by celery flies (see "Leaf miners," p.553), lettuce root aphids (see "Aphids," p.552), and carrot rust flies (p.566). Use cultivars resistant to parsnip canker (p.567) where possible; of those recommended, all but 'Tender and True' are resistant. Boron deficiency (p.568) may occasionally be troublesome.

Harvesting and storing

Parsnips mature in about 16 weeks. Their flavor is improved by frost and, except in very severe climates, they may be left in the soil during winter and lifted as required. The leaves die back in winter, so mark the ends of the rows with stakes so that the plants are easily found to harvest. Where winters are very severe, cover the rows with 6in (15cm) of straw to keep the soil from freezing and to make lifting easier. Young parsnips may be lifted and frozen.

Intersowing

In a prepared drill, sow 3 parsnip seeds every 4in (10cm) and then sow radish seeds between them, about 1in (2.5cm) apart.

Protecting Parsnips

In severe climates, cover the plants with layers of straw to a depth of 6in (15cm). Hold in place with wire hoops and mark each row.

Radishes (*Raphanus sativus* and *Raphanus sativus* Longipinnatus Group)

There are several types of radish, some biennial and others annual; all are grown for the swollen roots. Small, round types have roots up to 1in (2.5cm) in diameter; small, long types up to 3in (7cm) long. The leaves of both may grow to about 5in (13cm) high. Large forms include oriental radishes (Longipinnatus Group), known as daikon or mooli, and the large, overwintering, winter radishes. Roots of large, round cultivars may be over 9in (23cm) in diameter, those of large, long cultivars up to 24in (60cm) long, while the plants grow 24in (60cm) tall with a spread of 18in (45cm).

Radish skin color is red, pink, white, purple, black, yellow, or green; the flesh is normally white. Small roots are used raw when fresh, and large roots are used raw or cooked, fresh or stored. Immature seedpods from cultivars such as 'Münchner Bier' and young seedling leaves from most cultivars are edible raw.

Radishes are mainly a cool-season crop, but there are cultivars suited to a wide range of growing conditions. Some daikon and all overwintering types are frost-tolerant. Grow radishes in an open site, although midsummer crops tolerate light shade. Radishes prefer light, rich, well-drained soil, preferably manured for the previous crop, and very low nitrogen levels (see p.310). Radishes should be rotated (see p.303).

Sowing and planting

Sow standard, small types outdoors throughout the growing season, starting when the soil is workable. Sow at 15-day intervals for a continuous crop. Very early and late sowings may be made under cover, using small-leaved cultivars bred for growing under cover. Delay sowing most oriental daikon until summer to prevent bolting. Some bolt-resistant cultivars may be sown earlier. Sow overwintering radishes in summer.

Radishes are normally sown *in situ*. Small types grow very fast and may be used for intercropping (see "Parsnips," above). Broadcast seed very thinly, or sow $^{1}/_{2}$in (1cm) deep in drills 6in (15cm) apart. Thin the seedlings to at least 1in (2.5cm) apart, never allowing them to become overcrowded. Alternatively, seeds may be spaced 1in (2.5cm) apart so that no thinning is needed. Sow large types about $^{3}/_{4}$in (2cm) deep, in rows about 9in (23cm) apart, thinning to 6–9in (15–23cm), depending on the cultivar. Small types may be used for cut-and-come-again seedling radish leaves (see "Cut-and-come-again seedling crops," p.306).

Routine cultivation

Radishes should never be allowed to dry out. In periods of dry weather, water the crop every week at a rate

Harvesting

Radishes are ready to harvest 3–4 weeks after sowing. If the radishes are being used for intercropping, pull them up carefully without disturbing the roots of the other seedlings in the row.

Recommended Radishes

Small
'Cherry Belle'
'Easter Egg'

'French Breakfast'

'French Breakfast'
'Long White Icicle'
'Münchner Bier'
'Red Pak'
'Red Prince' (syn. 'Prinz Rotin')
'Snow Belle'
'Sparkler'
'Valentine'

Daikon
'April Cross' F1 (slow bolting)
'Mino Early'
'Miyashige'

Overwintering
'Black Spanish Round'
'China Rose'
'China White'

'Black Spanish Round'

of 2 gallons/sq yd (11 liters/sq m). Overwatering, however, encourages leaf rather than root development.

Pests and diseases

Radishes may be attacked by flea beetles (p.550), cabbage root maggots (p.566), and slugs (p.550).

Harvesting and storing

Small radishes mature three to four weeks after sowing, most large types after eight to ten weeks. Pull small types soon after they mature, since most will become woody if they remain in the ground for long. Large types, however, may be left in the ground for several weeks with no risk of deterioration. Overwintering radishes may be left in the soil for lifting when required, except in severe winter weather or if they have been grown in heavy soil. In these cases, lift the roots and store them in boxes of moist sand in a frost-free place, or outside in clamps for three or four months (see *Making a Rutabaga Clamp*, p.349). Where radish seed is required for propagation, leave a few plants to produce seed. Harvest the pods while they are still young and green, then dry them and collect the seeds.

Scorzonera (*Scorzonera hispanica*)

This hardy perennial is normally grown as an annual. Plants grow to about 3ft (90cm) tall and have yellow flowerheads. The black-skinned, white-fleshed roots are 8in (20cm) or more long, and about 1½in (4cm) across at the neck. They have an unusual flavor and are eaten cooked. Both the young leaves and shoots (chards) of overwintered plants are edible, and the young flower buds and their flower stalks are also delicious cooked. For soil, climate, and manuring requirements, see "Carrots," p.350. A fertile, deep, light soil is essential for good roots to develop. Scorzonera has low nitrogen requirements (see p.310).

Scorzonera Plants

Sowing and planting

Sow fresh seed *in situ* in spring about ½in (1cm) deep, in rows about 8in (20cm) apart, thinning out seedlings to 4in (10cm). Water at a rate of 3–5 gallons/sq yd (16–23 liters/sq m) in dry spells. For routine cultivation, see "Carrots," p.350. Pests and diseases rarely affect scorzonera.

Harvesting and storing

The roots need at least four months to develop. They may be left in the soil throughout the winter (see *Protecting Parsnips*, opposite), or lifted and stored in boxes in cool conditions. Start lifting the roots for use in the fall and continue into spring. If they are only pencil-thin, leave the remaining plant roots to thicken for harvesting the following fall.

For chards, cover the plants with about 5in (13cm) of straw or leaves in early spring. The young, blanched leaves will push through this layer. Cut them when about 4in (10cm) tall. For flower buds, leave a few roots in the soil during winter with no covering; these will flower the following spring or early summer. Pick the unopened buds with about 3in (8cm) of stem.

Scorzonera Roots

Salsify (*Tragopogon porrifolius*)

A hardy biennial with purple flowers, salsify is known as vegetable oyster or oyster plant, due to its taste. It is similar to scorzonera in appearance and use, and has the same climate, soil, cultivation, harvesting, and storage requirements. Salsify roots need to be eaten in their first winter.

Salsify Roots

If the roots are overwintered, the flower buds may be eaten the following spring. Pick the buds with short stalks, preferably in the morning before they open.

Potatoes (*Solanum tuberosum*)

Potatoes are tender perennials that grow to an average height of 2ft (60cm), with a similar spread. There are numerous potato cultivars, displaying enormous variation in their underground tubers.

A typical mature tuber is about 3in (7cm) long and 1½in (4cm) wide with white or pinkish red skin and white flesh, but there are yellow- and blue-fleshed cultivars, often used in salads. Potatoes are eaten cooked, fresh or after storing.

Potatoes are a cool-season crop, growing best at 61–4°F (16–18°C). Neither plants nor tubers tolerate frost. Depending on the cultivar, they require a growing season of 90–140 frost-free days. They are divided into early, second early, and maincrop groups, depending on the number of days required to mature. The earlies grow fastest but are generally lower yielding. Potatoes need at least 20in (500mm) of rainfall or irrigation during the season.

Grow potatoes in an open, frost-free site; they need well-drained, fertile soil at least 2ft (60cm) deep that is rich in organic matter. Although tolerant of a wide range of soils, acid soils (pH 5–6) are preferred.

Potatoes are subject to several soilborne pests and diseases, and so crops must always be rotated (see p.303). Prepare the ground well by digging in plenty of organic matter. A complete fertilizer may be worked in just before planting. Early potatoes need medium nitrogen; high nitrogen is required for maincrop potatoes (see p.310).

Planting

Grow cultivars recommended for the area. Plant small tubers (known as seed potatoes) that have been specially raised and are certified disease-free. In northern latitudes with a short growing season, potatoes (especially the earlies) are sprouted indoors to start them into growth about six weeks before planting. Place the tubers in a shallow tray, with the eyes or buds uppermost, in even light in a cool but frost-free room. Planting is easiest when the sprouts are about ¾in (2cm) long, but they may be planted with sprouts of any length. For large early potatoes, leave only three sprouts per plant, rubbing off the others. Otherwise, the more sprouts per tuber, the higher the yield.

Sprouting Seed Potatoes for Planting

To sprout seed potatoes, place them in a box or tray in a single layer with the end of the potato containing the most eyes uppermost. Store in a light, frost-free, but well-ventilated place until the sprouts have grown to about ¾in (2cm) in length.

Plant outside when there is no longer risk of heavy frost and once the soil temperature has reached 45°F (7°C). Make drills 3–6in (7–15cm) deep or make individual holes, and place tubers upright with the eyes or sprouts at the top, covering them with at least a 1in (2.5cm) layer of soil. Plant early potatoes 14in (35cm) apart in rows 17in (43cm) apart, second early and maincrop potatoes 15in (38cm) apart in rows 27in (68cm) and 30in (75cm) apart respectively.

In cool areas, cover early potatoes with cloches, clear plastic sheeting, or floating row covers (see p.311). When shoots emerge, cut holes in the covers and ease the foliage through. Remove floating covers about a month later, cutting them down the center first to acclimatize the potatoes to cooler conditions for a few days. Early potatoes may also be planted under black plastic, which excludes light and makes hilling up unnecessary; this is not recommended for maincrop potatoes since watering is difficult. Lay the plastic on the ground, anchor the edges in the soil, and plant the potatoes through cross-shaped slits in the plastic. Alternatively, plant the potatoes, cover them with plastic, make slits, and pull the stems through when the plants start to push up the plastic.

Potatoes are sometimes grown from seedlings, plantlets, or eyes. These are planted in seed trays and transferred outside, after hardening off, once all risk of frost has passed.

Routine cultivation

If frost threatens after the leaves have appeared, cover them at night with a light layer of straw or newspaper. Plants normally recover from light frost damage. Unless grown under black plastic, potatoes need to be hilled up to prevent tubers near the surface from becoming green and unpalatable and sometimes toxic. When the plants are about 9in (23cm) tall, hoe up soil around the stems to a depth of about 5in (13cm). This may be done in stages.

In dry conditions, water early potatoes every 12 days at a rate of 3 gallons/sq yd (16 liters/sq m). Delay watering maincrop potatoes until the young potatoes are the size of marbles – check the size of the tubers by scraping back the soil beneath one plant – then give one watering of at least 5 gallons/sq yd (23 liters/sq m). Potatoes may be given an organic liquid feed or a nitrogenous top-dressing during growth.

Pests and diseases

Cutworms (p.566), snails (p.550), Colorado potato beetles (p.551), potato cyst nematodes (p.572), millipedes (p.550), and blackleg on potatoes (p.570) may be troublesome. For details of potato late blight (including resistant cultivars) and other problems affecting potatoes, see "Potato tuber problems," p.568.

Harvesting and storing

Harvest early potatoes when, or just before, the flowers open. Potatoes under black plastic may be harvested by lifting the sheeting – they should be on the surface. Leave healthy maincrop potatoes in the soil for as long as possible; in fall, cut the haulm (the stems) of each plant to about 2in (5cm) above ground level, and leave the potatoes for another two weeks, to harden the skins, before lifting. In areas with warm, wet summers where potato blight is prevalent, cut the haulm in late summer and discard the foliage; lift the potatoes two weeks later.

Lift potatoes for storage on a dry, sunny day and leave them in the sun for two hours, then store them in the dark in paper sacks in a cool, frost-proof place. Give extra protection if frost threatens. Potatoes may also be stored for up to six months outdoors in well-insulated clamps (see p.349) or in a cellar. Young, or new, potatoes may be frozen. For new potatoes to be eaten during winter, plant a few tubers in the middle of summer and cover with cloches in fall.

Recommended Potatoes

Early
'Caribe'
'Jemseg'
'Norgold Russet'
'Onaway'
'Warba'
'Yukon Gold'

'Warba'

Second early
'Acacia Russet'
'Brigus'
'Purple Chief'
'Red Gold'
'Red Lasoda'
'Viking'

Maincrop
'Blue Mac'
'Blue Victor'
'Butte'
'Carola'
'Cherokee'
'Chieftain'
'Maris Piper'
'Pink Pearl'
'Shepody'

'Rose Finn Apple'

For salads
'Asparagus'
'German Yellow'
'Lady Fingers'
'Rose Finn Apple'
'Ruby Crescent'
'Russian Banana'

Planting Potatoes

1 *When planting maincrop potatoes, make a drill 3–6in (7–15cm) deep, using a draw hoe. Place them in the drill 15in (38cm) apart with the sprouts upward. Cover carefully once planted.*

2 *Draw up the soil around the stems when the foliage is about 9in (23cm) high. Hilling up prevents tubers that form near the surface from turning green and being unfit to eat.*

Alternative Method

1 *To plant under black plastic, unroll the plastic and anchor it by burying the edges. Make a cross-shaped cut where each potato is to be planted. Place each potato 4–5in (10–12cm) deep in the soil under each cut.*

2 *Once the haulm has been cut, the plastic can be pulled back and the crop of potatoes will be lying on the soil surface, ready to harvest. Yields may be lower than when growing by hilling up.*

Harvesting Potatoes

In fall, cut the haulm (stems) cleanly with a knife to about 2in (5cm) above ground level. Leave the potatoes in the ground for another 2 weeks before lifting.

Salsify (*Tragopogon porrifolius*), see Scorzonera, p.353

15
The Fruit Garden

The satisfaction of growing, harvesting, and tasting your own fresh fruits is one of the great pleasures of gardening. A fruit garden may be highly decorative as well as productive: some plants have attractive, fragrant blossoms or fine foliage while, in many cases, the fruits themselves are as ornamental as they are edible, from the bright gleam of cherries to the blushing tones of peaches. A wide range of fruits can be grown in most areas; in cool regions, growing under cover makes it possible to cultivate an extensive variety. In a large garden, there may be room to devote an area exclusively to fruit – whether in a formal layout with neat rows of trees, bushes, and canes, bordered by trained fans or cordons, or in an informal orchard. If space is limited, incorporate fruits into the rest of the garden by edging a bed with alpine strawberries or by growing a grapevine over a pergola; even in a small patio garden, there should be space for one or two citrus trees in pots or wall-trained apples or pears.

Planning the fruit garden

Fruits have traditionally held a prominent place in the garden, and today, with a wide range of cultivars and many dwarf fruit trees available ideal for the average garden, fruit growing is increasing in popularity. There are always some fruits that will thrive in the given climatic and growing conditions, although the majority prefer a good soil and a sunny situation. In warm climates, a wide range of fruits may be cultivated outdoors; however, some fruits that require periods of cold dormancy before flowering will not usually be successful.

Where only a few fruit plants are required, the gardener may prefer to grow them within the ornamental garden rather than in a specialized fruit garden; many fruit trees are suitable for growing as specimens in a lawn. Alternatively, if space is very limited, most fruits may be cultivated in containers, either free-standing or trained against a support.

If planning to grow plants in large numbers, however, it is best to create a separate fruit area within the garden; this makes it possible to grow fruits with similar requirements together, and to protect them against pests and cold damage. This is possible even in a small garden, as long as suitable rootstocks are chosen and trees are carefully trained. If grown as espaliers, fans, or cordons around the borders of a garden, fruit trees may be both ornamental and a source of fresh crops. Thoughtful planning as well as careful selection of cultivars and methods of training make it possible to provide fresh fruit supplies over several months, and if there is some storage and freezing space available, the produce from a fruit garden may be enjoyed all year.

In cool areas, the range of fruits that may be grown is even wider if some protection under cover is available. Reliable crops of peaches, nectarines, figs, grapes, or more tender fruits may be obtained by growing plants in a greenhouse, although ample room is needed for even a single tree. Protection and shelter are required by many of these fruits if they are grown outdoors.

The range of fruits

The different groups of fruit plants may be categorized according to their stature, their growth and fruiting habit, and their hardiness.

Tree fruits (top fruits) include apples, peaches, and figs. The term embraces both pome fruits (those having a core with small seeds, such as apples and pears) and stone fruits (those containing stones, such as cherries, peaches, and plums), as well as a few other fruits, including mulberries and persimmons.

Fan-trained Peach Tree
A fan-trained peach tree grown against a wall provides a dramatic accent as well as a high yield of fruit from a limited space. Growing fruit in this way also provides some protection in cooler areas.

The word "vine" is used to describe woody, fruiting climbers such as kiwi fruits and grapes; in some countries, the term is usually applied only to *Vitis vinifera*, the grapevine.

The category soft fruits includes bush fruits, cane fruits, and strawberries, which are herbaceous. Bush fruits are naturally shrubby, forming a compact, bush shape, although they may also be trained into other forms. Blackcurrants, redcurrants, whitecurrants, and gooseberries are the most commonly grown bush fruits. Plants described as cane fruits produce canelike shoots that bear the fruits; raspberries, blackberries, and hybrid berries, such as loganberries, are in this group. Most develop their canes in one season, and bear fruit on these the next, while producing new canes that will fruit the following year.

Certain fruit-bearing plants cannot withstand frost and need warm, subtropical temperatures to develop and ripen fully; these may be categorized as tender fruits. Tender fruits include citrus, pomegranates, pineapples, tree tomatoes, and prickly pears. Some are also tree fruits, but have been grouped here with tender fruits because of their need for consistently warm temperatures.

Nuts include all plants that produce fruits with a hard outer shell around an edible kernel, for example hazelnuts, almonds, and pecans.

FRUIT FOR FROST-FREE AREAS
Oranges grow well outdoors only in warm, virtually frost-free regions such as Florida, California, Mediterranean countries, and South Africa. They often produce 2 crops a year and may bear flowers at the same time as an earlier orange crop is maturing. In colder climates, oranges can be grown in a greenhouse, provided that it is warm and large enough.

TREE FORMS

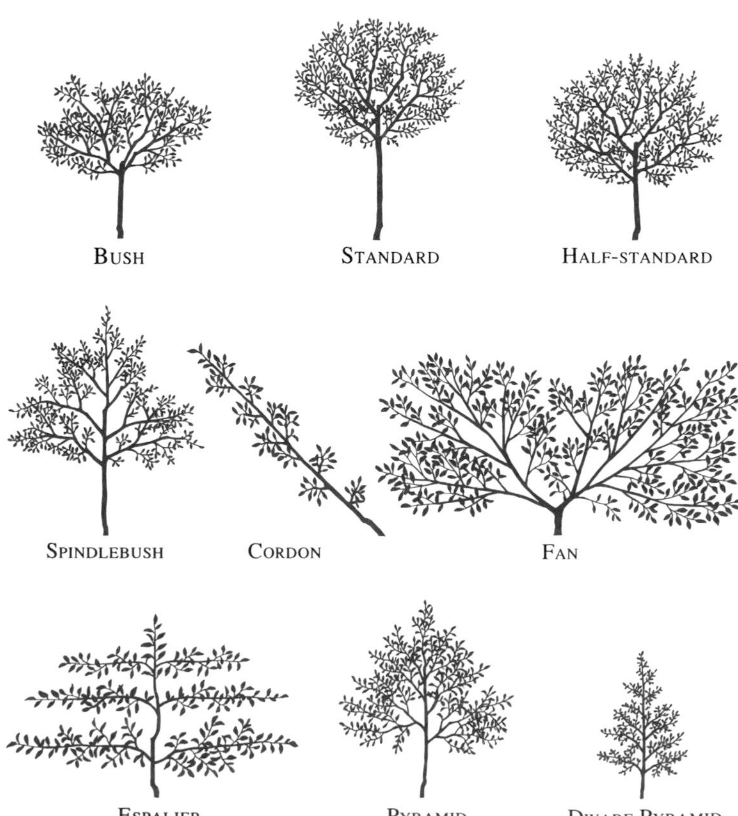

Unrestricted and trained forms

Many fruits, particularly tree fruits, and to a lesser extent vines and some soft fruits, may be trained into a variety of forms. When deciding which forms to grow, bear in mind the space available, the relative ease of harvesting, and the degree of pruning and training needed to produce a plant that crops well. The choice of rootstock for fruit trees also determines their ultimate size (see "Rootstocks and tree size," p.359).

With the correct technique, tree and bush fruits may be trained almost as desired. The principle is to train young shoots into the required shape while they are still pliable; the branches then retain this form with regular, basic pruning.

Unrestricted tree forms

These forms develop, with limited pruning, in much the same way as a natural tree; they include the bush tree, standard, half-standard, and spindlebush. The bush and spindlebush are more compact than the standard and half-standard, and are suitable for small gardens.

A bush tree has a trunk up to 3ft (90cm) tall, with branches radiating out from the top third. It has an open center, thus allowing the branches maximum light and space. Bush trees are small to medium sized, that is, 5–12ft (1.5–4m).

The half-standard is similar to the bush, but the trunk measures 3–5ft (1–1.5m) with an overall height of 12–15ft (4–5m). The standard is similar in form but with a trunk measuring 5–7ft (1.5–2.2m) and an overall height of 15ft (5m) or more.

The spindlebush is a small tree growing up to 7ft (2.2m) tall with branches that are trained to radiate out from the central leader at a wide angle. It has fewer branches than other lightly pruned forms, but each branch is pruned to be as productive as possible. The lowest branch is usually about 18in (45cm) from ground level.

Trained forms

Some fruit trees and bushes are suitable for growing in trained (or restricted) forms. These forms include cordons, fans, and espaliers. They need careful training initially and are then maintained by regular summer pruning, to restrict vegetative growth, with a minimum of winter pruning. Most require support wires, secured either to free-standing posts or against a wall or fence. Wall-trained forms are often favored in temperate climates for fruits such as peaches because the fruits receive maximum sun and also benefit from the reflected heat of the wall. All the trained tree forms are ideal for small gardens, since they make it possible to cultivate a variety of fruits in a restricted space. Maiden plants that have been grafted onto dwarfing rootstocks are usually used for training restricted forms.

A cordon is restricted to a single stem 5–6ft (1.5–2m) long, clothed with fruiting spurs to produce a high yield in a small area. It is usually planted at an angle of about 45° but may also be grown vertically or horizontally. Most commonly used for apples and pears, it is also useful with red- and whitecurrants and gooseberries. Double (sometimes known as U), triple, or multiple cordons may be formed by pruning a maiden plant so that it forms two or more parallel stems. Cordons that have more than a single stem are usually trained vertically.

A fan is trained with the main branches radiating in a fan shape from a short, 10in (25cm) trunk and is suitable for tree fruits that are grown against walls and fences.

TRAINED CORDONS
Apple cordons make good use of a fence, while alpine strawberries provide an edging for the border.

An espalier is trained with matching pairs of horizontal branches extending at regular intervals from a central stem. Each branch is clothed in short, fruiting spurs. The number of pairs of branches is variable depending on space and tree vigor. This method is particularly suitable for apples and pears grown against walls or fences.

Unlike the other trained forms, the pyramid is free-standing; its branches radiate from a central trunk, with an overall pyramidal form that is maintained by regular summer pruning to produce trees of small to medium size. Dwarf pyramids are similar but are grown on a more dwarfing rootstock.

Integrating fruits into the garden plan

Fruits may be grown either in a separate area on their own or intermingled with other plants. The choice depends on space, personal preference, and the range of fruits to be included. In either case, assess the impact that the fully grown fruit plants will have on the adjacent or surrounding plants. Planning and siting are particularly important because most fruits are long-term plants that require consistently good conditions to flourish and crop well over many years. In addition, with the exception of a few fruits such as strawberries, it is seldom practical or worthwhile to transplant them to other positions as they grow larger.

The planned fruit garden

Where a range of different fruits is desired, it is well worth growing the plants together in a single area. When planning a fruit garden, take into account the preferred growing conditions of each type of plant and recommended planting distances; for example, site tall fruit trees where they will cast the least shade on smaller bushes nearby. Also make sure that the space allocated for each plant is sufficient for it to develop naturally to its mature size.

Plants that have similar cultivation requirements may be grouped together to simplify practical operations such as applying fertilizer: for example, redcurrants and gooseberries need more potassium than other fruits. Grouping plants also makes it easier to protect them from birds (with a fruit cage) or wind damage (with a windbreak).

ORNAMENTAL DIVIDER
Apple espaliers form an attractive screen providing a fine display of spring blossoms followed by handsome fruits in fall.

For an ornamental border, edge the fruit garden with a row of trained trees; cordons or dwarf pyramids are especially suitable because they need a minimum of support and occupy comparatively little space.

In planning the position of fruit trees (particularly apples, pears, sweet cherries, and some plums), remember that a self-sterile cultivar should be sited near a cultivar with

PLAN FOR A LARGE FRUIT GARDEN

A large plot, 35 x 54ft (11 x 17m), provides space for a range of fruit. Here, the chosen apple and pear cultivars will crop over a long period, and the soft fruit has been grouped for easier maintenance. The more tender peaches and grapes thrive in a lean-to greenhouse.

1 Apple 'Discovery' (on 'M26'/'Ottawa 3')
2 Apple 'Lodi' (on 'M26'/'Ottawa 3')
3 Apple 'Red Delicious' (on 'M26'/'Ottawa 3')
4 Apple 'Sunset' (on 'M26'/'Ottawa 3')
5 Apple 'Cox's Orange Pippin' (on 'M26'/'Ottawa 3')
6 Apple 'Golden Delicious' (on 'M26'/'Ottawa 3')
7 Plum 'Redcoat' (on 'Pixy')
8 Plum 'Victoria' (on 'Pixy')
9 Damson 'Prune' (on 'Pixy')
10 Pear 'Rescue' (on 'Quince A')
11 Pear 'Bartlett' (on 'Quince A')
12 Pear 'Doyenné du Comice' (on 'Quince A')
13 Pear 'Golden Spice' (on 'Quince A')
14 Blackcurrant 'Boskoop Giant'
15 Blackcurrant 'Ben Lomond'
16 Blackcurrant 'Ben Sarek'
17 Redcurrant 'Red Lake'
18 Gooseberry 'Careless'
19 Gooseberry 'Leveller'
20 Raspberry 'Autumn Bliss'
21 Sour cherry 'Meteor'
22 Raspberry 'Royalty'
23 Loganberry (thornless)
24 Tayberry
25 Blackberry 'Lucretia'
26 Grape 'Black Hamburgh'
27 Peach 'Harbrite' (on 'St. Julien A')
28 Strawberry 'Kent'
29 Sweet cherry 'Stella' (on 'Colt')
30 Fig 'Brown Turkey'

which it will cross-pollinate (see "Pollination requirements," p.360), or it will produce few if any fruits.

For many fruits there is a wide choice of cultivars that ripen at different times; this makes it possible to plan for a succession of fruits that may be regularly harvested, rather than a single glut. Some fruits, late-ripening apples and pears for example, may be stored for long periods, so if a steady supply is required, more space should be devoted to these than to earlier-ripening cultivars.

Fruit in the small garden

There are various ways to make the most of a limited area for fruit growing so that it provides a high yield and is an attractive feature. Whenever possible, choose trees grafted on dwarfing rootstocks (see "Rootstocks and tree size," opposite) and use training methods that make the best use of the available space. Train trees and soft fruits such as redcurrants and gooseberries into cordons against the house or garden wall, rather than as bushes, since cordons need less room for a comparable fruit yield than fans or espaliers. Grow grapevines over a sturdy pergola or ornamental arch. Cane fruits may also be trained in a variety of ways, depending on space. Strawberries may be grown in vertical grow bags attached to a stake, fence, or other structure.

If there is room for only a single tree, then it is essential to choose a self-fertile cultivar (see "Pollination requirements," p.360). It is also worth selecting plants with a prolonged cropping season, unless there is ample storage and freezer space.

Mixed planting

In a primarily ornamental garden or one where there is insufficient space for a dedicated fruit garden, fruits may be planted among other plants. One or more fruit trees may make attractive specimens in the lawn or grown in containers on a sunny terrace or patio. Fruit cordons or dwarf pyramids can be framed as an ornamental divider, providing an unusual and productive screen, with attractive blossoms in spring and ripening fruits in late summer to fall. Trained forms of bushes or trees may be grown on almost any type of garden structure, such as a pergola, fence, or shed, provided that the exposure is suitable.

When fruits are planted with ornamentals, make sure that all the plants' needs are compatible. For example, if the fruits need nets for protection from squirrels, this may impede the growth of surrounding plants and look out of place. Particular care is also needed to ensure that fruit-tree sprays do not adversely affect any nearby ornamental plants.

Strawberries are often grown among other plants either in a vegetable garden or – a popular use of alpine strawberries – along the edge of a border or raised bed.

SMALL FRUIT GARDEN

This small fenced area supports no fewer than 17 fruit cultivars, providing abundant crops from early summer through to fall. The plot measures only 12 x 28ft (4 x 9m) with a 6ft (2m) fence surrounding it. Careful choice of cultivars and rootstocks coupled with correct training of the trees allows a wide range of fruits to be accommodated. The apple and pear cordons provide especially good yields from a limited space.

1 Sweet cherry 'Stella' (on 'Colt')
2 Pear 'Earlibrite' (on 'Quince C')
3 Pear 'Bartlett' (on 'Quince C')
4 Pear 'Doyenné du Comice' (on 'Quince C')
5 Raspberry 'Marcy' (summer-fruiting)
6 Plum 'Victoria' (on 'Pixy')
7 Raspberry 'Autumn Bliss' (fall-fruiting)
8 Peach 'Redhaven' (on 'St. Julien A')
9 Gooseberry 'Careless'
10 Gooseberry 'Leveller'
11 Whitecurrant 'White Grape'
12 Redcurrant 'Red Lake'
13 Apple 'Lodi' (on 'M9')
14 Apple 'McIntosh' (on 'M9')
15 Apple 'Sunset' (on 'M9')
16 Blackcurrant 'Ben Sarek'
17 Sour cherry 'Meteor' (on 'Colt')

FRUIT IN A BORDER
The compact, rounded shape of a lemon tree laden with fruit punctuates an informal planting, providing a charming contrast to the colorful display of roses and English daisies. Gardeners in warmer climates may enjoy this sort of planting.

Choosing a site

A sunny, sheltered position, where the plants will produce fruits of good quality and flavor, is ideal. Sites with some light shade are also acceptable but provide fewer ripening hours, so are best used for soft fruits or early-ripening cultivars of apples, pears, and plums. Plants on a south-facing slope may produce crops earlier than elsewhere, but since they also flower earlier, they are more likely to suffer frost damage.

Growing against supports

Walls, fences, pergolas, and arches all provide an ideal site for growing trained trees, especially if they are exposed to maximum sun. These structures make good use of space and allow the fruits to develop and ripen well; fruits trained on supports are also easier to protect from pests and frost than fruits in the open garden. The wall or fence must be high enough to accommodate the chosen fruits: 4ft (1.2m) would be enough for soft fruits, or for apples or pears trained as cordons or espaliers, but a height and spread of 6ft (2m) or more are required for a fan-trained apple, pear, cherry, plum, or peach. Pergolas and arches are likely to provide sufficient height, but ensure that there is space for the plants to grow as they mature. The structure must be able to support heavy crops, even in strong winds.

Frost and wind

Avoid planting in frost-prone sites, because flowers, unopened buds, and fruitlets are all susceptible to damage. The coldest air collects where the ground is lowest, and a frost pocket will form in a valley floor or at the foot of a sloping garden. Shaded areas remain frost-covered longer than sunny ones – the duration of the frost is often as critical as its severity.

Exposure to wind discourages pollinating insects and therefore greatly reduces the regularity of cropping. Strong winds also cause considerable crop damage. Drafty sites, such as between two buildings, should be avoided, but a well-placed windbreak may be very effective in diverting or filtering wind to improve the conditions. Trees or large shrubs are preferable to solid barriers because they filter wind that would otherwise swirl over the barrier and damage plants on the other side (see CLIMATE AND THE GARDEN, "How a windbreak works," p.519).

A CORDON ARCH
Fruit trees trained as vertical cordons over a series of arches provide an attractive architectural feature as well as abundant crops of fruit. The structure must be sufficiently strong to support the weight of trees heavily laden with fruit in fall.

Growing fruits under cover

Crops native to warm climates, such as peaches, nectarines, and grapes, are ideal for greenhouse cultivation in cooler climates, but skill and attention to detail are required to maintain them in good condition and obtain satisfactory crops. If fruits are to be grown with other plants in the same greenhouse, ensure that their temperature, humidity, and ventilation requirements are compatible. It is important that the greenhouse have the maximum possible number of side and top vents to provide a free flow of air. As for planting in open ground, the soil needs to be fertile and well drained for the plants to thrive.

A number of tender fruits such as tree tomatoes and pomegranates may be grown successfully under cover. In mild climates, they are often grown as ornamental plants, since they seldom crop heavily, even under glass.

Trained fruits

Tree and soft fruits that are suitable for training may also be treated in this way when grown in a greenhouse. Check that there is enough space for the chosen cultivar to develop and grow to its mature size, and ensure that suitable fittings for training the plant in the chosen form are in place before planting.

Fruits in pots

Strawberry plants that are grown in individual pots in a greenhouse or under a cloche will produce ripe fruits earlier than those in the open, thereby prolonging the fruiting season if both cultivation methods are used. Tender fruit trees such as citrus may be grown in pots that are placed outdoors during summer and returned under cover for winter.

Growing fruits in containers

Container growing is useful for cultivating fruits where space is limited. The pots should be placed in sunny, sheltered sites and may be used on paved areas such as patios to provide ornamental features as well as crops of fruits. It is also a way of controlling the root growth, and therefore the vigor, of plants such as figs that (particularly in temperate climates) may make excessive vegetative growth at the expense of the crop.

Most fruits may be grown successfully in a large pot, half barrel, or similar container with a diameter of at least 12in (30cm). Strawberries may be grown either singly in 4in (10cm) pots or in strawberry jars (containers with side planting pockets). Fruits need more regular care in containers than when in the open ground, particularly with watering and feeding, because the root systems are confined and easily dry out.

Deciding which plants to grow

Whether planning an entire fruit garden or choosing just two or three trees, it is vital to select plants that will thrive in the given soil and climatic conditions without growing too large for their allotted space.

Check the compatibility of different cultivars for pollination purposes before deciding which to grow (see "Pollination requirements," p.360). The final choice should also depend on the size of the crop required and the harvesting time.

Rootstocks and tree size

Tree size is determined largely by the rootstock onto which the tree has been grafted. Choose rootstocks that are of appropriate vigor for the planting area or training space available. Apple trees grown on dwarfing rootstocks such as 'M26' or 'M9', for example, are likely to suit most gardens; their relatively small size makes picking, pruning, and spraying easier. If a large tree is required, select one that is grown on a more vigorous rootstock. For further details, see pp.360 and 371.

Pollination compatibility

Most cultivars of apples, pears, sweet cherries, and some plums are not satisfactorily self-fertile. They therefore need to be planted close to one or more suitable cultivars of the same fruit that are in flower at about the same time so that insects are able to cross-pollinate all the trees. For example, the apple cultivars 'State Fair', 'Delicious', and 'Wolf River' need to be planted together for all to be cross-pollinated successfully. When planning a fruit garden, take into account the minimum number of trees required for pollination to occur, and position compatible cultivars adjacent to each other to help ensure satisfactory fertilization and cropping.

Crop size and timing

Within the limits of space available, the amount of fruits that are required will determine the number of plants that should be obtained, bearing in mind that crop levels inevitably vary from year to year. The amount of storage or freezer space available may govern the size of crop that can be handled. Try to balance the numbers of early-, mid-, and late-ripening cultivars of each fruit grown in order to provide a consistent supply over a long period rather than a brief glut.

Early-ripening apples and pears do not keep well for more than a day or two, so do not grow more than can be consumed quickly: one or two cordons yielding 5–11lb (2–5kg) per tree should suffice. If you have plenty of storage space, plant a high proportion of late-ripening cultivars, the fruits of which can be stored for several months. Plums are also liable to produce gluts, and the fruits must be used quickly unless they are frozen or otherwise preserved.

When deciding whether to plant early- or late-ripening cultivars, remember to take climatic factors into account. For example, late-ripening apples or pears are not a good choice for a region with a short summer or if the proposed site is shady, because there will not be enough time or sun for the fruit to ripen fully.

GRAPE CANOPY
A grapevine thrives in the warm but well-ventilated atmosphere of a conservatory or greenhouse. Care must be taken to prevent the ripening bunches from becoming scorched by the sun.

Site, soil preparation, and planting

FRUIT-BEARING plants require soil that is well structured, adequately drained, and fertile. Before planting fruits, therefore, choose and prepare a suitable site so that it provides the necessary conditions.

Preparing the site

Prepare the site at least two months before planting. Remove all weeds, especially perennial ones, before preparing the soil (see PLANT PROBLEMS, "Weeds," pp.575–9).

Soil types

A loam is ideal and produces high yields of good-quality fruits. Clay soils may produce very good crops if drainage is good, but they are slow to warm up in spring; growth and therefore cropping may be later. On sandy soils, plants come into growth earlier, since the soil warms up quickly in spring. Heat is lost equally rapidly, however, which creates a greater risk from frost; sandy soil is also prone to drought. Sandy soils are usually less fertile than others, so the quality and flavor of fruits grown on these may be inferior to those of fruits that are produced on more fertile soil.

On alkaline soils, lime-induced chlorosis caused by manganese and iron deficiencies (see p.557) may be severe, causing leaves to turn yellow and adversely affecting the quality and yield of fruit. In extreme cases, it will prove impossible to grow certain fruits satisfactorily; pears and raspberries, in particular, suffer badly. The use of chelated iron alleviates the problem, but regular treatment may be necessary and is expensive. Annual mulches of farmyard manure and compost help by providing some of the trace elements required.

Improving the soil

For soft fruits, dig in generous amounts of well-rotted manure or garden compost and fertilizer to improve water retention and fertility. In preparation for planting tree fruits, fertilizers should not be used unless the soil is very poor, since this may encourage excessive soft growth rather than fruiting wood.

Drainage problems

Although poor drainage is more likely on heavy clay soils, it may occur in many types of soil. Improve the soil structure where possible (see "Soil structure and water content," p.528), and install a drainage system if necessary (see SOILS AND FERTILIZERS, "Installing drains," p.531). Where drains cannot be installed, plant fruits in raised beds (see STRUCTURES AND SURFACES, "Raised beds," p.507).

Adjusting the pH level

Soil with a pH level of 6–6.5 is ideal for all fruits except blueberries, which need an acid soil of pH 4–5.5. Soils below about pH 5.8 will need liming (see p.533). If planting in soil with a pH level over 7, top-dress regularly with ammonium sulfate and mulch with acid compost to lower the pH in the short term.

Preparing the support for a trained fruit tree or bush

If a fruit tree or bush is to be trained against a solid support such as a wall or fence, fix horizontal parallel wires to the support with vine eyes and a straining bolt to keep the wires taut as the fruits develop. The eyes should hold the wires 4–6in (10–15cm) from the support to allow air to circulate around the branches and leaves of the plant. The spacing of the wires will vary, depending on the type of fruits grown. If using a free-standing post-and-wire support, secure the wires firmly to the posts. Just before planting, attach bamboo stakes to the wires at the appropriate angles, and tie in the young plants to begin the training process.

Buying plants

Always choose fruits that will thrive in the conditions in your garden. Check that the ultimate size of the plant or tree will fit the available space and that there is room to train it into the desired form. Pollination needs also must be considered before deciding which cultivars to buy.

Specialist fruit nurseries are often the best and most reliable source of supply. They offer a wide range of old and new cultivars and will also advise about suitable rootstocks. Wherever possible, buy plants that are certified free from disease.

It is best to buy young plants, since these become established quickly and may be shaped and trained to your own requirements. Plants are available bare-root or in containers. Container-grown plants are available throughout the year, but bare-root plants only in late fall and in spring when the plants are dormant and may safely be lifted.

BUYING FRUIT TREES

BARE-ROOT TREE

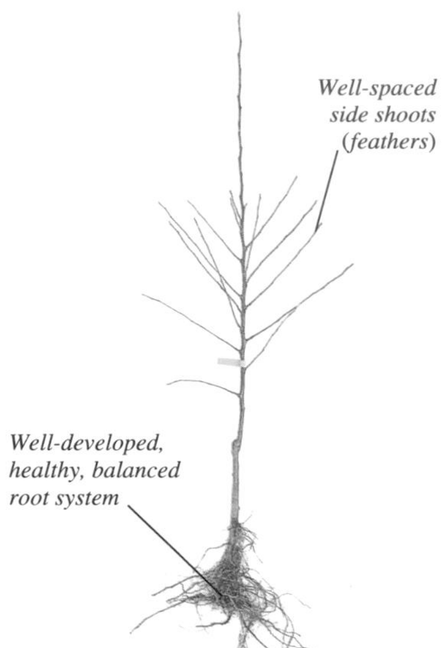

CONTAINER-GROWN TREE

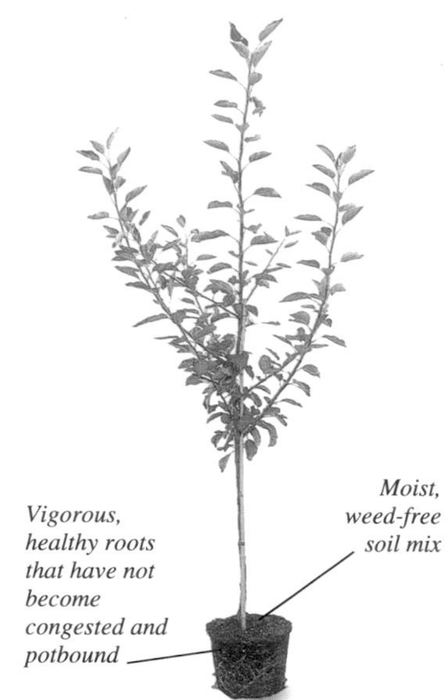

Reject plants with a potbound root system, since these seldom develop well. When buying bare-root plants, make sure that the roots have not dried out, and select plants with balanced main and fibrous roots.

Choose fruit trees that are healthy, with sturdy growth and, if two or three years old, with well-spaced laterals. Inspect plants carefully, and do not buy any with signs of pest infestation, damage, or disease, or those that are lacking in vigor.

Pollination requirements

Most soft fruits and some tree fruits are self-fertile: they produce a crop without needing a pollinating cultivar nearby, and may therefore be grown singly. Apples, pears, nearly all sweet cherries, and some plums are not reliably self-fertile, however. To produce a successful crop, self-sterile cultivars need to be cross-pollinated by another cultivar of the same fruit. Usually, one pollinating cultivar is sufficient, but some apples and pears must be grown close to two other cultivars for all trees to produce good crops.

For cross-pollination to occur, the flowering periods must overlap. This is not a problem in most of North America, where blooming seasons are so short that all flowering periods overlap. In areas with longer seasons, cultivars are sometimes divided into several flowering groups, from early to late. Cultivars for cross-pollination should be in the same, preceding, or following group. Nurseries and catalogs generally provide this information.

Certain cultivars of some fruits, however, will not cross-pollinate. For sweet cherries and pears, these are classified in incompatibility groups, which are indicated in the plant lists. Seek advice if in doubt. A few sweet cherry cultivars will pollinate all other cultivars in flower at the same time; these are known as universal pollinators.

ROOTSTOCK

A graft union between rootstock and scion is identifiable by a noticeable kink in the stem 4–12in (10–30cm) above the soil mark, especially on young fruit trees that have only recently been propagated. When planting, make sure that the graft union is not below soil level.

Selecting rootstocks

Many tree fruit cultivars offered for sale will have been grafted onto a compatible rootstock, since cultivars do not breed true from seed and cannot be raised consistently from cuttings. The rootstock controls the growth rate and size of the mature tree, while the scion determines the cultivar of fruits produced. Some rootstocks have a dwarfing effect (useful for a small garden) and induce early fruiting. A few rootstocks are resistant to certain diseases.

Selecting fruit trees
Young fruit trees may be purchased at several stages of growth – choose the one most appropriate for the form that the tree is to take. Maiden whip trees (with side shoots) take at least one year longer than other forms to train and fruit. One-year-old feathered maidens are popular with experienced growers because their side shoots enable the earliest possible training. Two-year-old trees fruit more quickly, and good specimens are easily trained. Three-year-old, trained trees are more expensive and can be harder to reestablish.

Planting in open ground

Container-grown plants may be planted at any time of year except when the ground is frozen or waterlogged, or during drought. Plant bare root plants in late fall or early spring while they are dormant; soak the roots well before planting. In frosty periods, heel them in temporarily in moist, frost-free soil until conditions are suitable for planting.

Planting fruit trees
If planting a number of trees, measure the site and mark out the planting positions with stakes. Dig a hole for each tree at least one-third wider than the tree's root system; firm the base of the hole and slightly mound it.

Insert a stake into the hole 3in (8cm) away from the center to allow for the tree's growth in girth as it matures. The stake height depends on the form into which the tree is to be trained (for details, see under individual fruits). Trees on dwarfing rootstocks need permanent staking; remove the stake of those on other rootstocks after three years.

Place the tree in the hole, making sure that the soil mark on the stem is at ground level, and spread out the roots. Do not cover the union between rootstock and scion, otherwise the scion may root and the rootstock's influence would be lost.

Backfill in stages with soil, while another person holds the tree upright, shaking it gently from time to time so that the soil settles in between the roots. Firm the soil; when the hole is nearly full, break up the soil around the edges to obtain a uniform soil firmness over a greater area. Firm and level the area, and attach the tree to the stake using a soft, pliable tie with a firm cushion between tree and stake to prevent chafing. Protect the tree from rabbits and other animals with chicken wire.

Fruit trees to be planted against a wall or fence should be positioned 6–9in (15–22cm) away from the support, with the branches sloping gently inward. This ensures that the roots are in good soil and allows for future expansion of the trunk.

Planting soft fruits and vines
Bush and cane fruits are planted as for fruit trees, but no staking is needed. Plant only up to the soil mark: planting too deeply inhibits a plant's growth. For vines, make the planting holes or trench wide enough for the roots to be fully extended, and train the vines against a support.

Planting in containers

Water the young plant thoroughly before planting. Use a moist, soil-based potting mix, leaving 1in (2.5cm) between the soil mix surface and the rim of the pot for watering. Water again after planting, and keep the soil mix moist until growth begins, then water regularly.

PLANTING CORDONS

IN THE OPEN GROUND
Space trees 2½ft (75cm) apart (top). Attach a stake at an angle of 45° to horizontal wires (bottom left) stretched between sturdy posts. Tie each tree securely to a stake (bottom right).

AGAINST A FENCE
Fix wires 4–6in (10–15cm) away from the fence to allow for the growth of the trees and give good air circulation. Plant the trees 6–9in (15–22cm) from the fence.

PLANTING A FRUIT BUSH

1 *Dig a hole large enough to accommodate the roots of the bush when spread out. Place a stake across the hole to check that the level of the surrounding soil is the same as the soil mark on the main stem.*

2 *Backfill the hole with soil; tread on the soil gently to ensure that no air pockets remain between the roots. Rake over the soil lightly to level the surface.*

PLANTING A FRUIT TREE

1 *Dig a hole one-third wider than the tree's root system. Drive in a stake to a depth of 18in (45cm) about 3in (8cm) from the center of the hole.*

2 *Slightly mound the soil at the base of the hole and place the tree in the center. Use a stake to check that the soil mark on the stem is level with the soil surface.*

3 *Spread out the tree's roots, then gradually fill the hole with soil. Firm to ensure that the tree is well anchored and that there are no air pockets between the roots.*

4 *Attach a buckle-and-spacer to the top of the stake and then to the tree so that the cushion is between the stem and the stake (see inset). Adjust as necessary.*

Routine care

Most fruit plants need regular maintenance to ensure that they are healthy and produce high-quality crops. Routine operations vary, depending on the type of fruit, growing conditions, and season.

Fruit thinning

Fruit thinning is necessary for a number of tree fruits, particularly apples, pears, and plums, to provide good-sized, high-quality fruits. It also prevents branch breakages by ensuring balanced crop distribution. In addition, thinning helps to prevent biennial bearing (to which some fruit cultivars are prone), that is, bearing heavy crops one year and little or no fruit the next.

Thin initially by hand or with scissors to remove disfigured fruits; later, thin again to leave the fruits room to develop fully and to receive enough sun and air to ripen. Details of how and when to thin are given under each fruit.

How to Thin Fruit

1 *Thinning of some fruits is required to obtain fruit of a good size and quality. If it is left unthinned, the fruit is usually small and of poor flavor.*

2 *Remove unhealthy or disfigured fruits first, then reduce the remainder to at least 2–3in (5–8cm) apart, depending on the type of fruit.*

Fertilizing, mulching, and watering

Apply manures and fertilizers when needed, observing crop performance and checking for any leaf discoloration that may denote nutrient deficiencies. In hot, dry summers, watering will usually be necessary; a trickle watering system (see p.469) uses water most efficiently.

Care of tree fruits

In early spring, mulch newly planted trees and any that are not thriving with manure or compost. First check that any problem is not caused by a pest or disease; if it is, treat as recommended in Plant Problems, pp.547–79. Once the trees reach flowering size, apply a balanced fertilizer at a rate of 3–4oz/sq yd (105–40g/sq m) in early spring. Do not overfeed, particularly with nitrogen, since this may produce soft, disease-prone growth.

If a particular nutrient is needed, use specific fertilizers: potassium sulfate to correct potassium deficiency; ammonium nitrate to supply nitrogen; superphosphate to provide phosphorus. Apply these in spring at a rate of 1oz/sq yd (35g/sq m), except superphosphate, which is normally applied at three times this rate every three or four years. Correct magnesium deficiency (p.557) by spraying the foliage, after flowering, with a solution of Epsom salts. In severe cases, repeat the treatment after three weeks. Other deficiencies, especially of manganese and iron (p.557), may also arise. If, more rarely, deficiencies of zinc, copper, or other elements are suspected, seek the advice of a specialist.

Apply fertilizers evenly over the entire branch spread (see below). Where trees are grown in grass, mow regularly and leave the mowings *in situ*; they rot down and return nutrients to the soil, helping particularly to avert potassium deficiency.

Care of soft fruits

Mulch soft fruits regularly in spring with rotted farmyard manure. Use fertilizers as indicated for tree fruits; nitrogen and potassium are the most essential nutrients. Apply fertilizer over the whole area; in the case of raspberries, spread the dressing at least 2ft (60cm) on either side of the row. With strawberries, dig in manure before planting.

Fruit in containers

Although soil-based potting mixes contain nutrients, plants should be fed in the growing season in order to replace the nutrients as they are used; nitrogen and potassium in particular are often needed. Fruit plants in containers require watering more frequently than those planted in open ground. Check the soil mix regularly – at least once a day in hot, dry weather – and keep it moist.

Each winter, fruit trees and bushes in pots should be top-dressed or repotted. To top-dress, remove the top 1in (2.5cm) of soil mix with a hand fork and replace with fresh soil mix. In alternate winters, where possible, repot the plant. Remove the plant from its container, and gently comb away some of the old soil mix from the root ball, using a hand fork or wooden stick. Cut out any coarse roots, taking care not to damage the fibrous roots, and repot into a larger, clean container (see also "Planting in containers," p.361).

Stakes and ties

The stakes and ties of all fruit trees should be checked regularly. When the cushioning or ties are weak or worn out, the tree may rub against the stake, and *Nectria* canker (p.570) on apples or bacterial canker (p.571) on apples and stone fruits may develop. Check the base of the stake: this may rot and then the tree may topple in high winds, particularly just before a heavy crop is to be gathered. On trained trees, ensure that branches are not tied too tightly to stakes or wires, since this will restrict growth and damage the tree. Loosen any ties if necessary.

Supporting branches

Tree fruits grown in unrestricted forms may need to have their branches supported when the tree is heavily laden with fruit, even if the

Fertilizing Fruit Trees

Using string and a peg, mark a circular area around the tree, slightly beyond the spread of the branches. This indicates where fertilizer should be applied – over the whole span of the tree's root system.

Supporting Laden Branches

Tie several pieces of nylon string to a centrally placed pole attached to the main trunk. Use a nail to stop the string from slipping down the pole. Tie at least one string to each heavily laden branch (away from the fruits) to support it.

fruits have been correctly thinned. If only one or two branches are affected, support them on forked stakes or rope them in to stronger branches. If several branches are overloaded, secure a sturdy stake either to the trunk or to the main stake and tie a rope to each branch and to the top of the stake; this technique is known as "maypoling."

Protecting plants

Fruit trees and bushes may need to be protected from bad weather or cold with windbreaks or insulation. Protection against birds and animals may also be necessary.

Wind protection

Maintain windbreaks (see p.519) properly so that they remain effective, and prune natural barriers such as trees or shrubs if they become thin to encourage bushier growth. Check that posts supporting windbreak netting or fences are secure and repair them as necessary.

Cold protection

Most cold damage is caused by spring frosts that kill or injure buds, flowers, or fruitlets overnight. Severe winter cold may cause bark splitting and dieback, so in areas where low temperatures are common, select cultivars that are bred to withstand the conditions. In subtropical regions, there should be few problems; if necessary, cover small trees and bushes with polyester fabric or spun polypropylene sheets.

Very slight cold seldom causes any serious damage: 28°F (-2°C) is frequently the danger point. The duration of the cold is usually more important than the temperature alone: 27°F (-3°C) for a quarter of an hour would cause little or no damage, whereas sustained over three hours, it could cause substantial losses.

If frost is forecast, protect strawberries, bushes, and even small trees by using old curtains, burlap, or layers of newspaper to cover the plants completely and trap warm air around them. Remove the covers each day once the temperature has risen above the freezing point. For further information, see COLD AND WIND PROTECTION, pp.520–21.

Protection from animals

In winter, squirrels occasionally damage fruit buds by feeding on the nutritious center of the buds and discarding the outer bud scales. This damage is much more serious than the loss of ripe fruit, because it denudes whole branches permanently, making it necessary to prune them back to obtain new young shoots, which will not fruit for two or more seasons. The best protection is to place nets over the trees or bushes. If snow is forecast, support the net or remove it temporarily, since the weight of the snow on the net may damage branches underneath.

Ripening fruit should also be protected against birds. Small areas may be temporarily covered with netting, but for large areas it is preferable to erect a fruit cage instead. It is impractical to protect large fruit trees, although those trained against supports may be enclosed by attaching netting to the support. The mesh of any net used must be small enough to exclude tiny birds. Protect strawberries in a patch with a low, temporary cage.

Pest, disease, and weed control

It is advisable to check plants once a week for signs of pest and disease problems; they may then be treated at an early stage before extensive damage has been caused (see PLANT PROBLEMS, pp.547–79). If viral diseases (pp.555 and 565) are suspected, seek professional advice to confirm that this is the problem; strawberries, raspberries, loganberries, blackberries, and blackcurrants are especially vulnerable. The only practical solution is to dig up infected specimens with their roots and discard them, otherwise the virus may spread to adjacent plants.

Weed control is also essential. Remove seedling weeds and mulch to inhibit germination of weed seeds. Perennial weeds should be dug out or spot-treated as soon as they are noticed. For further details, see "Weeds," pp.575–9.

Plants under cover

In cool-temperate climates, some fruits may need to be grown under cover. These include all the tender fruits, as well as a number of other fruits that either have flowers that are vulnerable to damage by spring frosts or require a long ripening period, for example peaches and many late-ripening grapes.

In subtropical climates, fruit trees are rarely grown under cover, since the only climatic problems encountered are exceptionally cool periods and heavy rainfall, which most are able to tolerate.

Plants that need to be under cover all year are best grown in greenhouses; walk-in polytunnels are of limited use because temperature levels and adequate ventilation are hard to maintain (see also GREENHOUSES AND FRAMES, "Choosing a greenhouse," pp.476–9).

Particular care is needed to maintain free air circulation around plants grown in greenhouses to discourage diseases that may be caused by the increased heat and humidity. Support wires for trained fruits should be secured at least 12in (30cm) away from the glass or plastic of the greenhouse. Control any pests and diseases and apply fertilizer as recommended under individual tree fruit entries. For details of pruning fruits grown in a greenhouse, see "Pruning under cover," p.366.

Growing tender fruits (for example citrus, guava, pomegranate, and olive) in containers makes it possible to bring them under cover when necessary. In cool areas, place tender plants grown in pots outside in a sunny position in spring and bring them under cover again in fall. Overwinter the plants in the greenhouse at a temperature of at least 50°F (10°C).

PROTECTING AGAINST BIRD AND ANIMAL DAMAGE

BUD STRIPPING
Animals stripping buds from branches over winter cause permanent damage, leading to unproductive, bare wood.

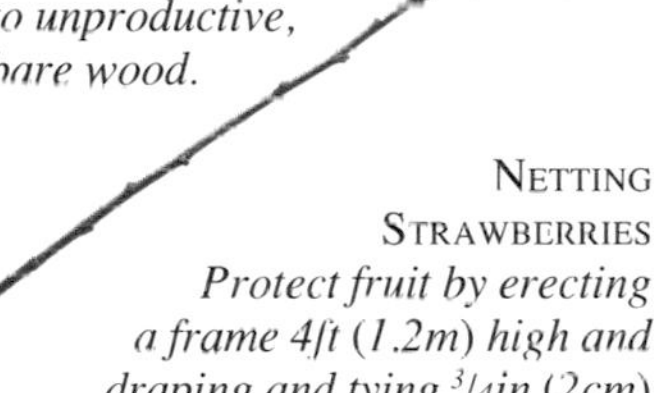

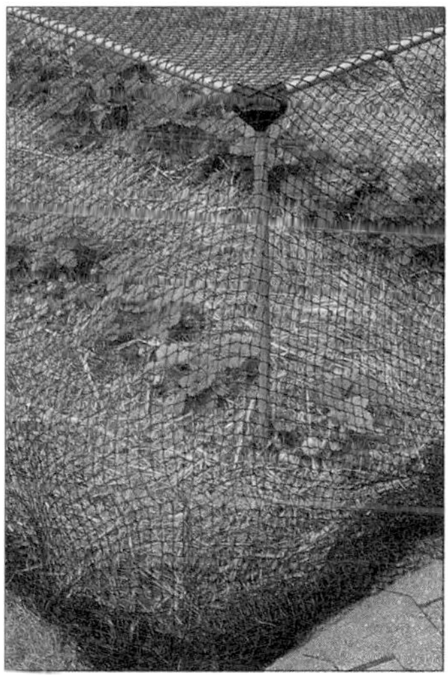

NETTING STRAWBERRIES
Protect fruit by erecting a frame 4ft (1.2m) high and draping and tying ¾in (2cm) mesh netting over it. Secure the base so that birds and squirrels cannot get underneath.

FRUIT CAGE
Fruit bushes or small fruit trees may be protected by a cage constructed from metal supports covered with wire or plastic netting.

PROTECTING TRAINED TREES
Fruit trees trained against supporting wires may be protected with a ¾in (2cm) mesh net fixed at the top and secured firmly to the support.

Pruning and training

FRUIT trees and bushes need correct, regular pruning and (in many cases) training to yield a good crop. The degree and method required depend on the desired shape and the fruiting time and habit as well as on the individual type of fruit. Relatively limited pruning is needed to produce an open-center bush tree, for example, whereas extensive formative pruning and training are required for a fan or espalier to produce a symmetrical network of well-trained branches.

Aims of pruning and training

Initially, young trees and bushes should receive formative pruning and training to produce the desired shape (such as a cordon) and to develop a strong, balanced framework. With established plants, the aim of subsequent pruning is to maintain the health and shape of the plant and ensure a good yield of fruit.

Pruning

This is the cutting out of unwanted shoots and branches, either because they spoil the plant's framework or because they are unproductive. Correct pruning maintains an open, uncrowded structure to allow the maximum amount of sun to reach the ripening fruits and to simplify spraying and harvesting. It also includes the removal of dead, diseased, damaged, or old, unfruitful wood.

On young plants, pruning may be combined with training to form a particular shape. Unwanted shoots are removed completely; those retained may be cut back to stimulate the growth of side shoots. The established, cropping tree, bush, or plant is pruned to encourage optimum growth and fruit production.

Training

The selection and, in many cases, the tying in of shoots to create a specific shape is known as training. Forms close to the natural shape, such as the bush, require much less training than, for example, a fan, which is produced by precise selection, spacing, and tying in of individual shoots onto a supporting framework of stakes and wires.

Over- and underpruning

Take care not to over- or underprune, because both of these restrict fruitfulness and may encourage disease. Repeated severe pruning results in increased, vigorous, vegetative growth and little or no fruit, since few fruit buds are able to develop. This is especially damaging on a plant that is already vigorous. Underpruning leads to overcrowded branches that will receive less sun, which is essential to ripen the fruit; the branches may also rub together, exposing the tree to the risk of diseases such as *Nectria* canker (p.570). Pruning a young tree too lightly may also cause early overcropping that could stunt the tree and even break branches by overloading them.

When to prune

The time of pruning depends both on the specific treatment and on the kind of fruit. In the pruning procedures described here and under the individual fruits, "year one" refers to the first 12 months after planting, "year two" to the following 12 months, and so on.

Winter pruning is standard practice on untrained apple, pear, quince, and medlar trees; on vines; and on black-, red-, and whitecurrants, gooseberries, and blueberries. Water shoots, which take much energy from the tree and spoil its shape, should be cut flush to the branch from which they arise. Any diseased wood and borer-infested branches (see "Stem borers," p.559) should also be removed. Summer pruning is essential on trained forms of tree fruits, grapevines, currants, and gooseberries. This reduces their vigor and contains them within the limited space they occupy; it also concentrates the plants' energies on fruit production. Many tender fruits are pruned directly after fruiting.

How to prune

When deciding on the extent of pruning, always take into account the vigor both of the individual shoot and of the whole tree. Vigorous growth should be pruned lightly; this usually involves thinning out a percentage of shoots completely and leaving the remainder unpruned. Prune weak growth more severely, but check first that no disease, such as canker, is causing the weakness.

Where to cut

It is important always to prune to just above a healthy bud and to make a clean cut; cutting midway between buds or leaving a ragged end may cause dieback and increase the shoot's vulnerability to disease. If removing a shoot or branch completely, cut it back to the point of origin but leave the bark ridge and branch collar intact rather than cutting flush with the parent stem.

INCORRECT PRUNING

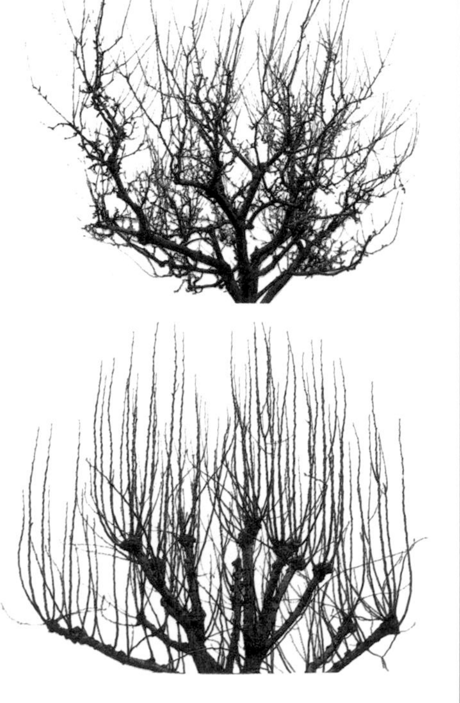

UNDERPRUNING
A tree that is pruned very lightly or irregularly will develop overcrowded shoots that will not receive sufficient light to ripen the fruits. The branches may also rub together, increasing the risk of certain diseases.

OVERPRUNING
If a fruit tree is pruned excessively, this will stimulate a mass of vigorous vegetative shoots. These shoots will produce few, if any, fruit buds, so the crop will be poor.

WHERE TO MAKE A PRUNING CUT

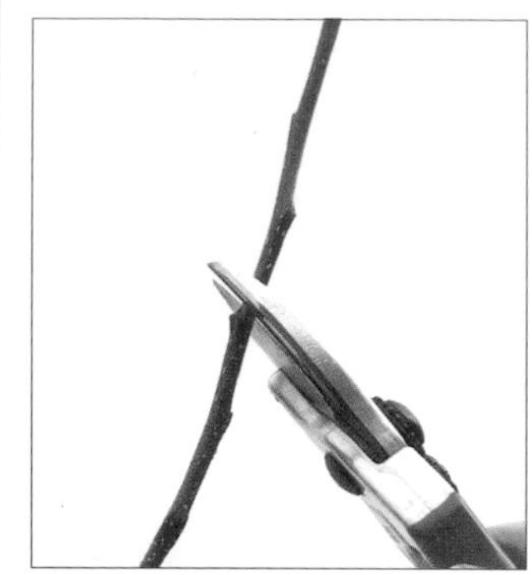

CUTTING TO A BUD
Cut just above a bud at a 45° angle, sloping the cut away from the bud. Do not cut too close (or the bud may be damaged), nor too far away (or the stem may die back).

CUTTING TO A REPLACEMENT SHOOT
As when cutting to a bud, make an angled cut sloping away from the replacement shoot.

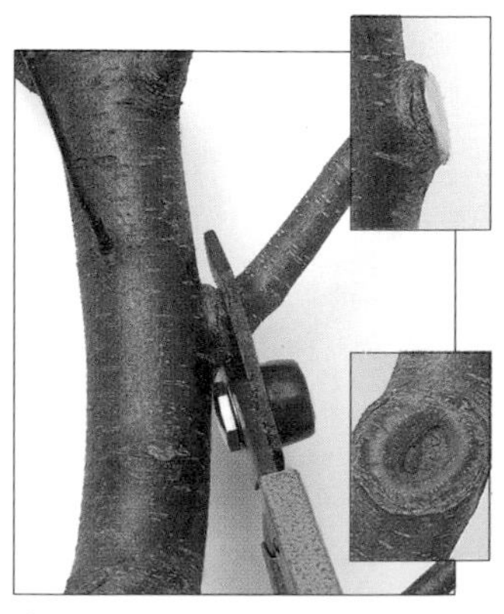

CUTTING BACK TO A MAIN BRANCH
Make a clean cut, leaving the branch collar intact (inset, top). The tree is then less susceptible to disease, and the wound heals faster (inset, bottom).

REMOVING A BRANCH

1 *Using a pruning saw, make the first cut approximately 12in (30cm) away from the trunk. Saw at right angles to the branch from underneath, to about a quarter of the way through.*

2 *Start the second cut at the top of the branch, slightly farther out than the first cut. Saw right through the branch; if it breaks away, the bark will tear only as far as the first cut.*

3 *When making the final cut, take care not to damage the bark ridge at the top of the branch or the collar at the base. If necessary, start the cut from below and cut down from above to meet it.*

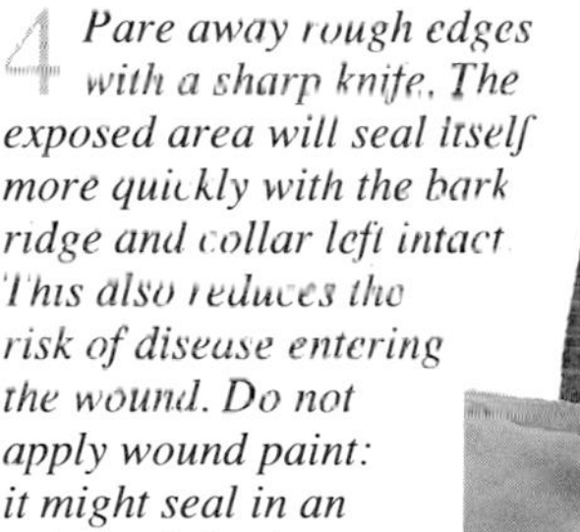

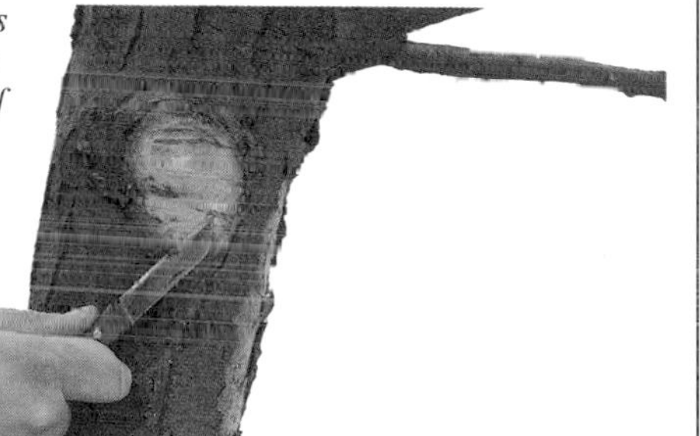

4 *Pare away rough edges with a sharp knife. The exposed area will seal itself more quickly with the bark ridge and collar left intact. This also reduces the risk of disease entering the wound. Do not apply wound paint: it might seal in an existing infection.*

To prevent the branch or bark from tearing before cutting is completed, undercut first before finishing the cut from above. Cut back to the point of origin or to a well-placed, healthy branch as a suitable replacement. Do not leave a stub, or the cut end will die instead of healing. Pare away any rough edges with a sharp knife.

Fruiting habits

How a plant is pruned depends on its fruiting habit. For example, sweet cherries form fruit mainly on spurs on two-year and older wood, so many of the older shoots must be retained. Sour cherries, however, fruit on one-year-old shoots; when pruning, leave most of the young shoots but remove some of the old, unproductive wood.

Training for shape

A young tree is usually bought as a "feathered maiden" (a one-year-old tree with side shoots). Initial pruning consists of selecting shoots to be retained, shortening them as required, and removing unwanted shoots. If a young tree is bought as a maiden whip (a one-year-old tree without side shoots), it should be cut down to a bud after planting, the height depending on how the tree is to be trained. This encourages the growth of side shoots. When these develop, the tree, now two years old, is equivalent to a feathered maiden. Formative pruning continues for the first two or three years until the desired shape has been obtained.

Training for fruitfulness

The vigor and fruitfulness of shoots may be adjusted by raising or lowering selected laterals or, with oblique cordons, the whole tree. Horizontal growths are more fruitful than vertical ones, so tying a lateral closer to the horizontal makes it produce more fruit. If one lateral is less vigorous than another and more side shoots are needed, raising it will stimulate vegetative growth. For an established, cropping tree or bush, pruning is more important than training; even on an untrained tree, less fruitful or unbalanced shoots may be tied down in summer to increase their yield.

PRUNING A MAIDEN WHIP TO FORM A FEATHERED TREE

WINTER, YEAR 1
To produce vigorous "feathers" (side shoots) on a maiden whip tree, cut it back with an angled cut just above a bud at the required height.

WINTER, YEAR 2
By the following winter, a number of new side shoots should have been produced below the pruning cut.

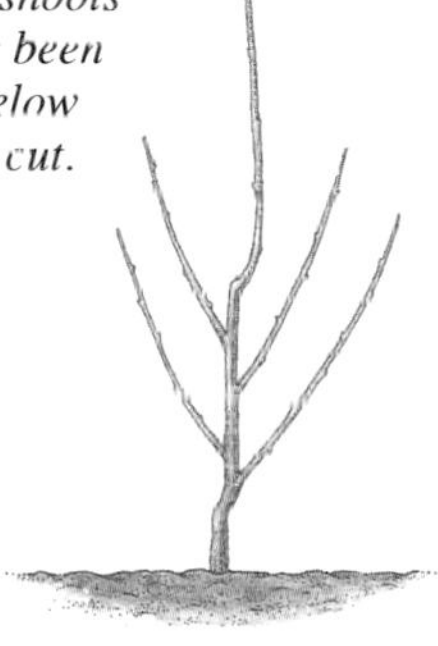

TRAINING ON STAKES

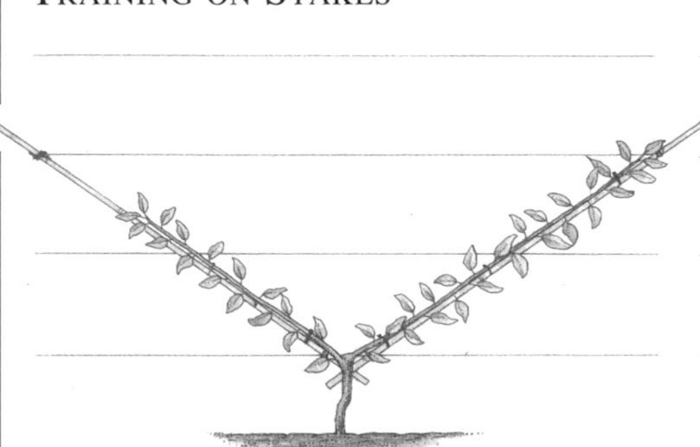

1 *The vigor of laterals of trained trees may be altered by adjusting the angle at which they are trained. This technique corrects uneven growth on either side of the same tree.*

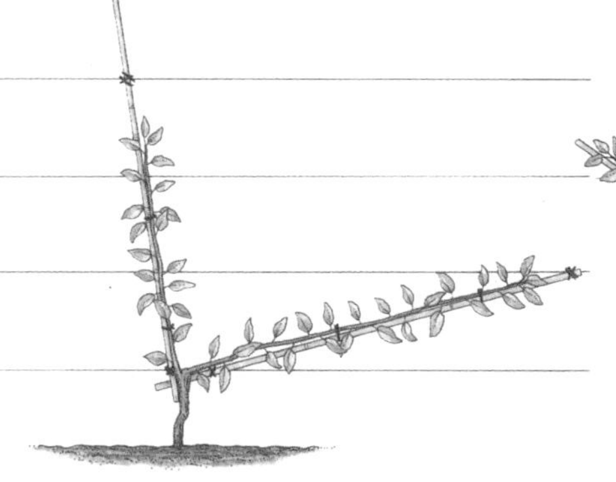

2 *Lower a young, strong-growing lateral, with its stake, at the start of or during the summer to reduce its vigor; raise a lateral to encourage it to grow more quickly. Retie the stakes to the wires.*

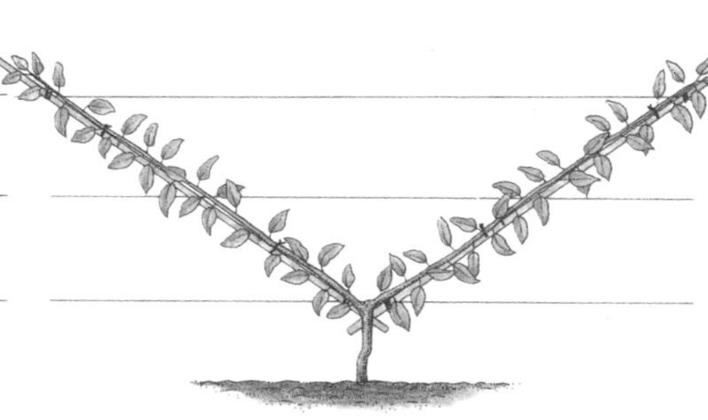

3 *By the end of the summer, the branches may be returned to their original positions; they should be more even in length.*

Curbing excessive vigor

Extremely vigorous trees that produce rapid vegetative growth at the expense of cropping may benefit from root pruning. On apples and pears only, bark-ringing (see p.373) may also be used as a last resort to curb vigor; it should not be used on stone fruits because it may kill them. Both methods will induce the formation of fruit buds, so the beneficial effects will be seen in increased blossoms and fruiting one or possibly two years later.

Root pruning

Trees may be root pruned at any age, but only when they are dormant. When pruning the roots of a young tree, first lift it by digging around it, then remove soil carefully from around the fibrous roots, taking care not to damage them. Cut back a few of the thick roots in the process. Then replant the tree firmly and stake it.

Larger trees need to be root pruned *in situ*, with the root system on one side of the tree pruned one winter, and the other side a year or two later. To do this effectively, make a trench 18in–4ft (45cm–1.2m) wide, depending on the size of the tree, to expose the main roots. These should be severed and a section of each root removed. Then fill in the trench, firm, and mulch; in some cases, staking may be required to provide support until the tree is fully stable.

Root Pruning to Improve Fruiting

1 Mark out the position for a trench around the tree using string and a peg. The trench should form an even semicircle just below the outermost spread of the branches. Prune the root system on only one side of the tree one winter; prune the other side a year later.

2 Dig out a trench around the tree at the marked line; it should be at least 18in (45cm) wide and approximately 24in (60cm) deep.

3 At the base of the trench, use a fork to remove soil from around the thick roots without damaging the fibrous roots.

4 Sever each woody root on either side of the trench with a pruning saw, discarding the central section. Leave the fibrous roots unpruned.

5 Backfill the trench with soil, firm well, then cover the area with an organic mulch to retain moisture and help the tree reestablish. Stake if necessary.

Pruning under cover

Prune back branches and shoots of plants grown in a greenhouse so that they do not touch the glass or plastic surfaces, because otherwise they may suffer sun scorch and growth will be constricted or damaged. Regular pruning also allows more light to reach the developing fruits and helps them to ripen.

Renovation

If a tree is too old to crop well, and has rotten or severely diseased branches or trunk, it should be grubbed out. If the trunk and the main branches are sound, however, and the tree is merely overcrowded, it can be rejuvenated by means of renovative pruning followed by correct routine care.

Renovative work should be carried out in spring or summer on stone fruits and in winter on apples, pears, and other pome fruits. Cut out any branches that are dead, damaged, or diseased, or so low that they may trail on the ground when laden with fruit. Also remove crowded or crossing branches, because these will shade the developing fruits, and, if they rub together, may become prone to diseases such as canker. On a vigorous tree, it is advisable to stagger this pruning over more than one year; pruning too severely on a single occasion may only induce more vigorous, vegetative growth.

Once this initial thinning has been achieved, more precise pruning, such as spur thinning, may be carried out (as described for routine pruning under individual fruit entries). Chemical inhibitors are available to curb the regrowth of water shoots around the cuts, but wound paints are not recommended because they may seal in any infection.

Renovating a Neglected Tree

1 Remove overcrowded, rubbing, or crossing branches to let in light and air by cutting them back to their point of origin, or to a vigorous sublateral facing in the required direction.

2 Any branches that are damaged or affected by a disease such as canker (shown above) should be removed completely, or cut back to a healthy shoot.

Harvesting and storing

MANY home-grown fruits may be enjoyed long after their normal harvesting time if correctly harvested and stored. While most are at their best eaten fresh, a number keep their flavor well even after prolonged storage. For details on harvesting and storing specific fruits, see the individual fruit entries.

Harvesting

Most fruits are best picked when fully ripe for using fresh. Fruits for storing are usually harvested slightly earlier, however, when they are mature but not yet completely ripe and still firm. Since not all the fruits on a single plant ripen at the same time, it is usually necessary to harvest over a period; this provides a succession of fresh supplies.

For tree fruits such as apples and pears, test for ripeness by holding a fruit in the palm of the hand, then gently lift and twist. If ripe, the fruit will come away easily complete with its stalk; if unripe, it should be left for a day or two.

When harvesting, use any damaged, diseased, or bruised fruits immediately, since they will rot quickly; rot then spreads rapidly to adjacent fruits in storage.

Soft fruits must be picked completely dry, otherwise many may be affected by rot unless the fruits are used immediately. Regular picking, at least every other day, is advisable for strawberries, raspberries, blackberries, and hybrid berries.

Always take care not to damage the plant when harvesting – by pulling fruit off sharply, for example. Some types of fruit, such as cherries, grapes, and mangos, should be cut off the plant to avoid the risk of accidental damage.

Storing

There are various ways of keeping fruits for later use, including cool storage, freezing, and preserving; the most suitable method depends on the type of fruit. Some fruits, especially those that have a high acid and sugar content, such as apples, apricots, and figs, may also be oven-dried at 120–40°F (49–60°C). Drying ovens for home use are available.

When preparing fruits for storage, handle them carefully to avoid bruising. Always store different cultivars in separate containers that are free from any residues or aromas that may taint the fruits.

Cool storage

Apples and pears in particular may be kept for several weeks, or even months, in the right conditions – consistently cool, dark, and slightly damp. Various other tree fruits, such as lemons, may also be stored this way, although they do not usually keep for such a long period. Most nuts keep well for up to a few months. Soft fruits cannot be stored in this way. The required temperature and degree of humidity vary for different fruits, but most should be stored in slatted trays and boxes to allow free air circulation. Some apple and pear cultivars, however, tend to shrivel and are better kept in clear plastic bags. Check unwrapped fruits regularly and remove any that show signs of disease or rotting.

Freezing

This is ideal for most soft fruits, except strawberries, and for a number of tree fruits. Small fruits such as raspberries are usually frozen whole, while large fruits such as apples are best chopped or sliced to ensure even and thorough freezing. Remove any stalks (and fruit stems of currants), then open-freeze whole fruits spread out on trays. Once they are frozen – after two to four hours – transfer the fruits to plastic boxes or bags, excluding as much air as possible, and keep them frozen until needed. Strawberries and some soft-fleshed tree fruits such as plums are often puréed before being frozen.

Preserving and bottling

All soft fruits and a number of tree fruits such as apricots and damsons may be made into preserves. In most cases, the entire fruit is used, while some such as grapes and blackberries are better strained, with only the juice used to make jelly.

Citrus fruits, pineapples, and most stone fruits, such as cherries, may be bottled in sugar syrup with alcohol (such as rum, brandy, or cognac) if desired to preserve them. Citrus peel may also be candied or dried for use in baking.

FREEZING SOFT FRUITS

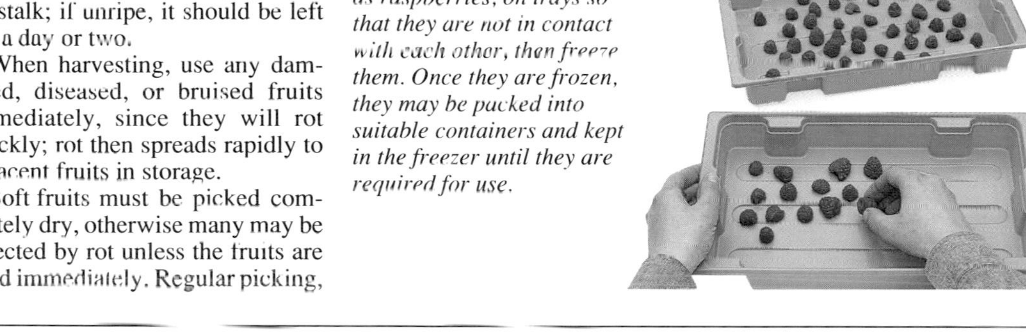

Spread out soft fruits, such as raspberries, on trays so that they are not in contact with each other, then freeze them. Once they are frozen, they may be packed into suitable containers and kept in the freezer until they are required for use.

STORING APPLES

1 *Wrap each fruit individually in tissue paper to prevent rot and keep it in good condition.*

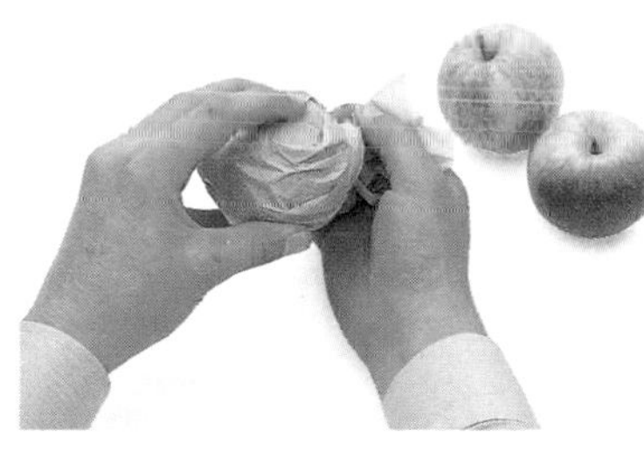

2 *Carefully fold the tissue paper around the fruit, holding the fruit lightly to avoid bruising it.*

3 *Place each wrapped fruit on its folded end in a wooden slatted box or other well-ventilated container, and store in a cool place.*

ALTERNATIVE METHOD

Store fruits of cultivars that tend to shrivel quickly in a plastic bag. Make several holes in the bag before filling it with no more than 6lb 8oz (3kg) of fruit. Seal the bag loosely.

FRUITS THAT FREEZE WELL

- Apples **Sl**
- Apricots **Sl**
- Blackberries and all hybrid berries **Sk**
- Blackcurrants **Sk**
- Blueberries **Sk**
- Cherries (sour) **Sk**
- Cherries (sweet) **Sk**
- Damsons **Sk** (with or without stones)
- Gages **Sk**
- Gooseberries **Sk**
- Grapes **Sk**
- Nectarines **Sl**
- Peaches **Sl**
- Plums **Sk**, **Sl**
- Raspberries **Sk**
- Redcurrants **Sk**
- Whitecurrants **Sk**

KEY

Sk *Remove stalks (and stones where applicable)*

Sl *Remove cores or stones and slice and peel if required*

Propagation

TREE fruits (except figs) are usually propagated by grafting; figs, grapes, and many soft fruits by cuttings, although if *Phylloxera* (see p.397) is a problem, grapevines should be grafted. Some fruits produce runners, layers, or suckers; all produce new plants. Several tender fruits and some nuts may be grown from seed, but hardy fruits seldom grow true to type from seed.

Bud-grafting

Both chip-budding and T-budding are used to increase the stock of fruit trees. They are economical methods of propagation, since a new tree is produced from a single bud. Grafting should be carried out in midsummer, using as the rootstock an established plant with a stem that is at least 1/2in (1cm) thick. A bud from the scion plant is cut from a ripe shoot (the budstick) of the current season's growth and grafted onto an incision in the rootstock.

Propagating by chip-budding
Select a healthy budstick and carefully remove a bud (the budchip), taking care not to damage the cambium layer. Remove a sliver of rind from the rootstock and place the budchip onto the exposed wood of the rootstock so that the cambium layers are in close contact. Bind the budchip tightly onto the rootstock to hold it in place. When the bud and rootstock have united, the bud will start to swell and the binding may be removed. The following winter, trim the rootstock just above the grafted bud to encourage a strong shoot to develop from the graft in spring.

CHIP-BUDDING

1 *Choose a vigorous shoot of the current season's ripened wood as the budstick. The shoot should be approximately pencil thick and have well-developed buds.*

2 *Hold the budstick firmly and, using a clean, sharp knife, slice off the soft tip and remove all the leaves to produce a clear length of stem.*

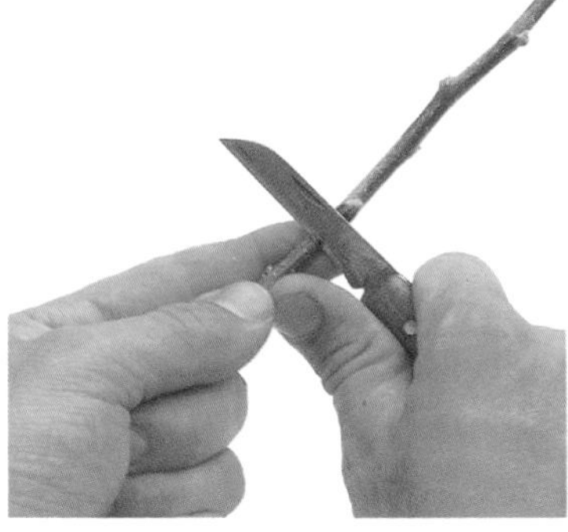

3 *To remove a budchip, first slice into the budstick about 3/4in (2cm) below a bud. Cut down to a depth of about 1/4in (5mm), slanting the blade at an angle of 45°.*

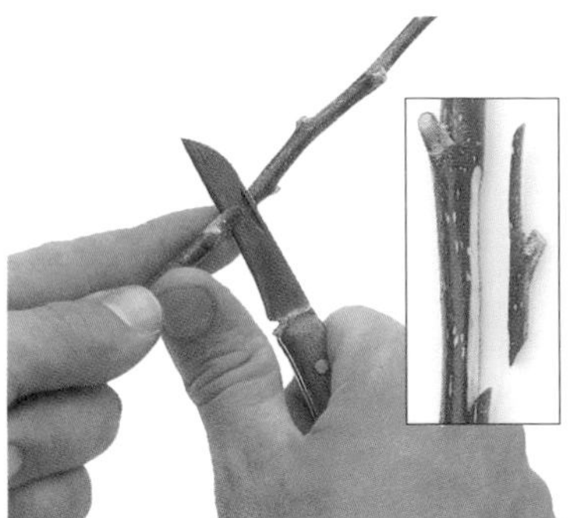

4 *Make another incision about 1 1/2in (4cm) above the first. Slice downward behind the bud toward the first incision, taking care not to damage the bud.*

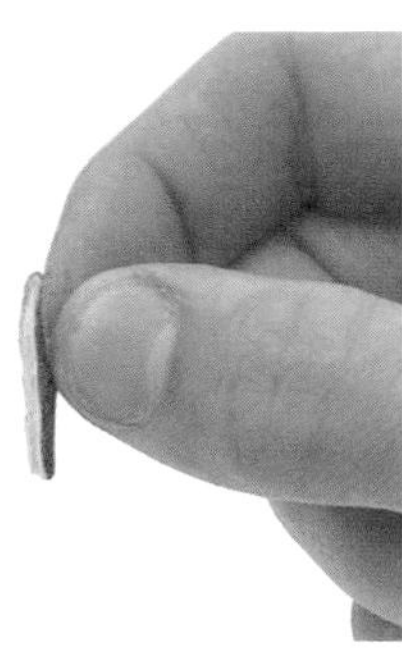

5 *Remove the budchip, holding it by the bud to keep the cambium layer clean. Place the budchip in a plastic bag to prevent it from drying out.*

6 *To prepare the rootstock, stand astride the plant and, using a sharp knife, remove all the shoots and leaves from the bottom 12in (30cm) of stem.*

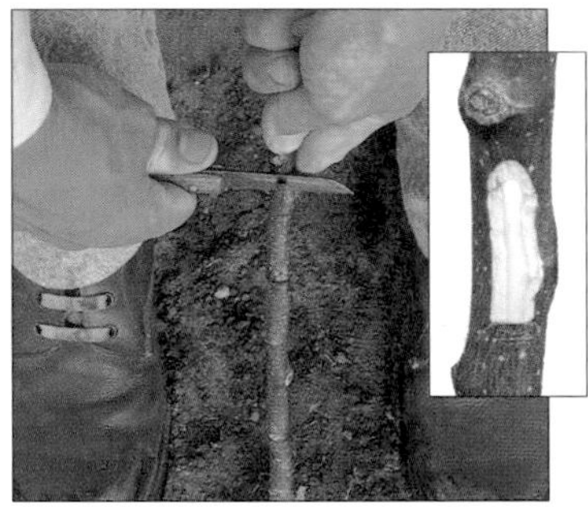

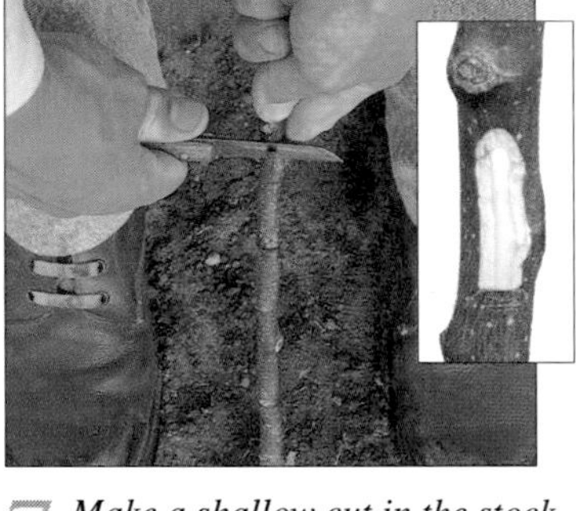

7 *Make a shallow cut in the stock. Remove a sliver of rind to reveal the cambium layer (see inset), leaving a "lip" at the base. Do not touch the exposed wood.*

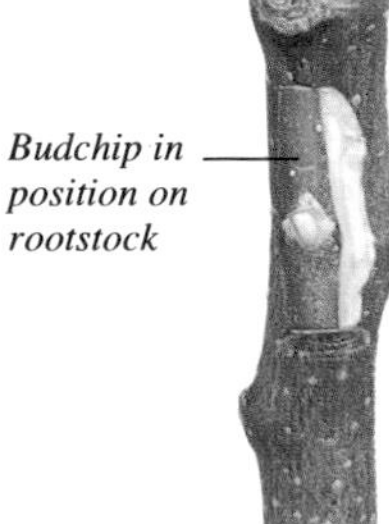

8 *Place the budchip onto the prepared lip of rind, offset if necessary, so that the exposed cambium layers of budchip and rootstock match and touch.*

9 *Bind the budchip to the rootstock with plastic tape. Carefully remove the tape after a few weeks when the budchip has united with the rootstock.*

10 *Late the following winter, remove the top of the rootstock. Cut cleanly with pruners just above the grafted bud, using an angled cut.*

11 *During the summer, a shoot from the grafted bud will develop. The new tree is then at the maiden whip stage (see "Selecting fruit trees," p.361).*

Propagating by T-budding
In this technique the preparation of the rootstock and scion bud is similar to chip-budding, except that two slits are made in the rootstock, to form the shape of a T. This allows the bark of the rootstock to be lifted slightly so that the scion bud may be tucked behind it. Removing the scion bud with a leaf stalk attached makes it easier to handle; the stalk is removed before the bud is bound to the rootstock. The rootstock should be cut back the next winter.

For this technique to be successful, the bark of the rootstock must lift smoothly: in dry weather, rootstocks need to be watered for up to two weeks before T-budding takes place.

Whip-and-tongue grafting

This is a common method of grafting for tree fruits. It may be used as an alternative to budding, but it is usually more successful with pome than with stone fruits. Use well-established rootstocks that have been planted either the previous winter or, preferably, two winters before grafting takes place.

The scion material should have at least three buds and should be taken in midwinter from a healthy shoot of the previous season's growth. Heel it in until ready for grafting. In late winter or early spring, prepare the stock by cutting off the top of the stem and removing any side shoots. Using a sloping cut, slice off a small piece of bark from the top of the remaining stem; make a shallow incision in the exposed cambium layer, to create a tongue.

Trim the scion to a length of three or four buds, then, using a sloping cut, slice off a small piece of bark close to a bud but on the opposite side to it. Make a further shallow incision, to match that in the stock, and hook the resulting tongue onto the one on the rootstock. Make sure that the two cambium layers are in

T-BUDDING

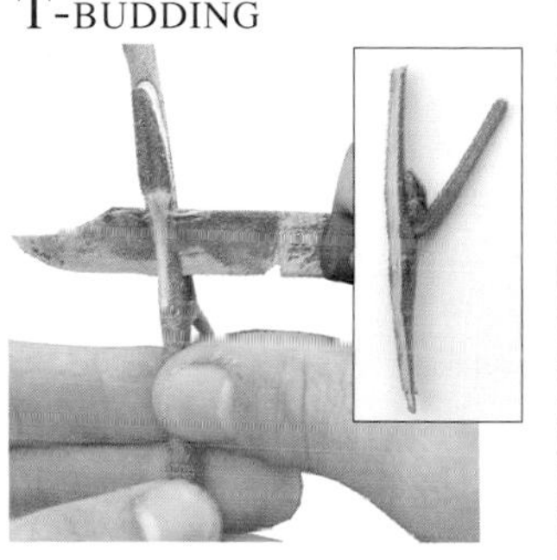

1 *From the current season's growth, select a ripened shoot as the scion, and remove the leaves. Remove a bud by slicing underneath it (see inset).*

2 *Make a T-shaped cut in the stock about 9in (22cm) above ground level, and open the flaps of bark.*

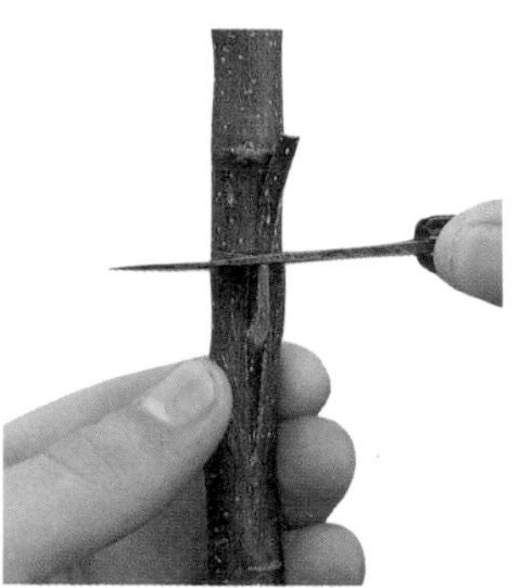

3 *Place the bud behind the flaps of bark, trimming the top level with the horizontal cut on the stock. Bind the bud as for chip-budding.*

WHIP-AND-TONGUE GRAFTING

1 *In midwinter, remove healthy, vigorous hardwood shoots from the scion tree. Cut lengths of about 9in (22cm), cutting obliquely just above a bud.*

2 *Make bundles of 5 or 6 scions. Choose a well-drained, sheltered site and heel them in to keep them moist but dormant, leaving 2–3in (5–8cm) above the soil surface.*

3 *In late winter or early spring, prepare the rootstocks just before bud break. Cut off the top of each rootstock about 8–10in (20–25cm) from ground level.*

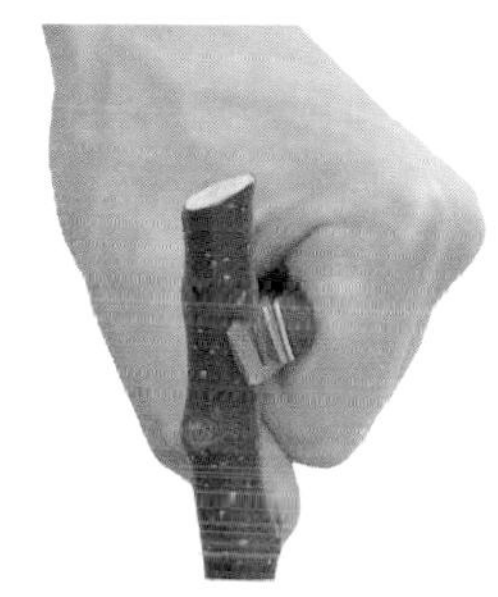

4 *Trim off any shoots from the rootstock with a sharp knife, then make a 1½in (3.5cm) upward-sloping cut on one side to receive the scion.*

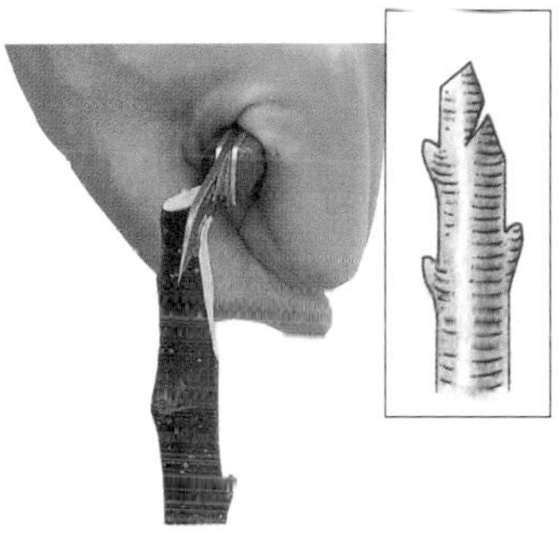

5 *Make a slit ½in (1cm) deep about one-third of the way down the exposed cambium layer, to form a tongue into which the scion may be inserted (see inset).*

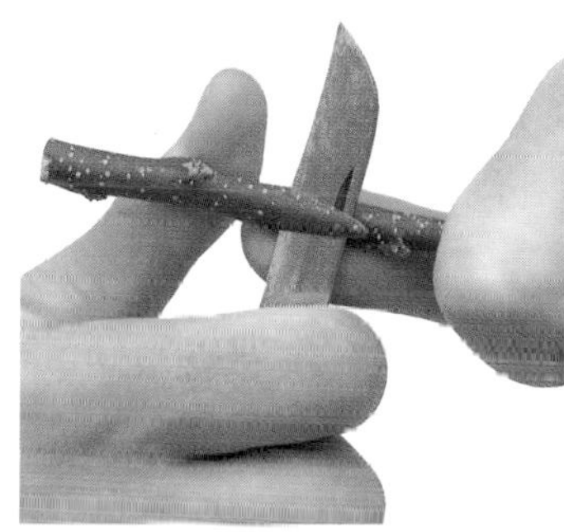

6 *Lift the scions, cut off any soft growth at the tips, and trim to 3 or 4 buds. For each, cut off a piece of bark behind a bud that is about 2in (5cm) from the base.*

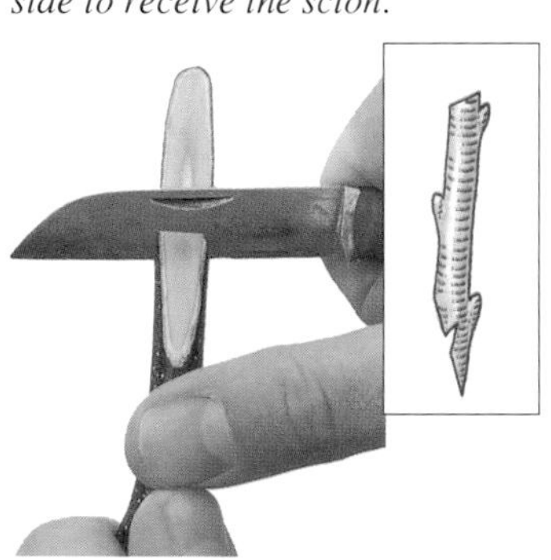

7 *Without touching the cut surface with your hand, cut the cambium layer (see inset) to match the tongue in the rootstock.*

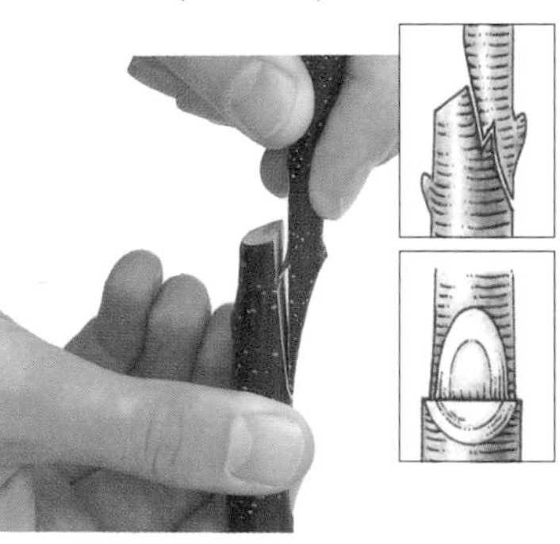

8 *Place the scion into the tongue on the stock (inset, top). Use the arches of the cambium layers as a guide (inset, bottom) to ensure the exposed surfaces fit together well.*

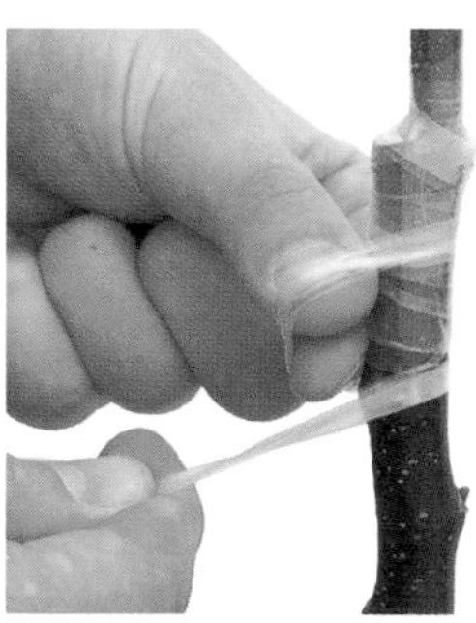

9 *Bind together stock and scion with clear plastic tape. When the cut surfaces start to callus, remove the tape by carefully scoring it downward.*

close contact, then bind the graft firmly. Remove the binding carefully when a callus has formed around the graft union. By spring, buds on the scion will have started to grow. Select the best shoot that develops (keeping others pinched back) to form a maiden whip tree (see "Selecting fruit trees," p.361).

Cuttings

Hardwood, softwood, and leaf-bud cuttings may be used to propagate certain fruits. Always select cutting material from a healthy parent plant that crops regularly.

Hardwood cuttings

Figs, grapes, currants (white, red, and black), and gooseberries may be propagated from hardwood cuttings, usually taken in fall.

Select a well-ripened shoot of the current season's growth and trim off the leaves and soft tip. Remove some or most of the buds, depending on the fruit being propagated, and trim off the top and base. The exact preparation and length of the cuttings vary slightly; details are given under individual fruit entries.

If the soil is well cultivated, the cuttings may be inserted into a narrow trench in the open ground. If the soil is heavy, sprinkle sand into the bottom of the trench to improve drainage, or place the cuttings in a pot of moist, sandy soil mix. Transplant the cuttings one or two years later.

Softwood cuttings

Guavas, pomegranates, tree tomatoes, and blueberries are propagated from softwood cuttings (where the climate is warm enough for the wood to ripen sufficiently, blueberries may also be propagated from hardwood cuttings). Take the cuttings in midsummer and place them in pots of cuttings soil mix (see p.536). Harden off the young plants before transplanting to their permanent positions.

Leaf-bud cuttings

Stocks of blackberries and hybrid berries may be increased quickly by leaf-bud cuttings (see p.408). Take the cuttings in late summer: remove short lengths of stem, each with a bud and leaf attached; insert them in soil mix with the buds just above the surface. Once rooted, the cuttings may be potted up or planted out.

Runners, layers, and suckers

Some fruits send out runners, layers, or suckers, which root naturally at stem nodes while still attached to the parent plant. This process may be exploited to increase fruit stocks.

Runners

Strawberries (but not all alpine strawberries) produce creeping horizontal stems, or runners, which root where they come into contact with the ground and may be used for propagation. As the runners are produced, spread them out evenly. Allow them to root, and then lift and sever them (see p.406).

Layers

Blackberries and hybrid berries may be propagated by layering, although some hybrids are slow to root. The tip of a shoot is induced to root by carefully pegging it down in the soil or in a pot of moist soil mix (see *Tip Layering*, p.407). A year later, when the tip has rooted and produced new growth, it may be severed from the parent plant and transplanted to its permanent position.

Suckers

Established cane fruits such as raspberries naturally produce suckers that are usually hoed off. If retained, rooted suckers may be lifted and severed in fall, when the plants are dormant but the soil is still warm. Transplant the rooted suckers directly to their permanent positions (see *Propagating by Suckers*, p.410). Figs, hazelnuts, and filberts also produce suckers: if the suckers have good root systems, sever them with a spade and replant in the same way.

Seed

Propagation from seed is the usual method of increasing stock of many tender fruits, including avocado (see p.422), guava, and papaya.

The alpine strawberry is one of the few hardy fruits that may be raised successfully from seed (see p.406). Hazelnuts, walnuts, and chestnuts may also be raised from seed with a reasonable chance of success, although cultivars selected for the quality of their fruit need to be propagated vegetatively. For details, see ORNAMENTAL TREES, "Raising trees from seed," p.54.

HARDWOOD CUTTINGS

1 *Dig a narrow trench 6in (15cm) deep. If the soil has a high clay content, sprinkle a little sand into the bottom of the trench to improve drainage.*

2 *Choose a ripened stem from the current season's growth (here, from a fig tree). Remove lengths of at least 12in (30cm), cutting flush with the main stem.*

3 *Cut off all the leaves and the soft growth at the tip of each cutting, then trim to about 9in (22cm). Make an angled cut above the top bud and a straight cut at the base.*

4 *Place the cuttings in the prepared trench, spacing them 4–6in (10–15cm) apart and burying two-thirds of the stems. Firm the soil, and label.*

5 *The cuttings will take several months to root. Toward the end of the following growing season, they should have developed sturdy new growth.*

6 *After leaf drop in fall, carefully lift the rooted cuttings, wrapping the roots in plastic to keep them from drying out. Transplant the cuttings to their permanent positions to grow on.*

Tree fruits

THE fruits in this group, known also as top fruits, are the largest-growing forms in the fruit garden. They may be divided into two main categories: pome fruits, such as apples and pears, have a seed-containing core; stone fruits, such as cherries and apricots, have a hard central stone. There are also certain other fruits within this group that fit into neither of the above categories, such as figs, mulberries, and persimmons.

Cultivating tree fruits is a long-term undertaking that requires careful planning. The size and shape or form of the trees are important considerations. Left to grow naturally, many tree fruits would become much too large for the average-sized garden. However, smaller forms grown on dwarfing rootstocks have been developed. Fruit trees may also be trained and pruned as fans, espaliers, or cordons and grown flat against walls or fences, making it feasible to grow them in even the smallest of spaces.

Another factor to consider is the number of trees required. Many fruit trees are self-sterile and, to produce fruit, need at least one other tree of the same type to act as a pollinator. Even self-fertile trees crop more heavily if pollinators are present.

Some tree fruits, such as figs, prefer a long, hot growing season and are difficult to cultivate in cooler climates. Growing them under cover provides protection and improves fruit and crop size, as well as flavor.

Once a tree fruit has been selected and planted, it is important to follow the correct pruning methods. Good pruning not only builds a strong framework of branches but also encourages and maintains maximum cropping for many years.

Apples (*Malus sylvestris* var. *domestica*)

Apples are one of the most widely grown hardy fruits, and both dessert and culinary cultivars offer a great variety of flavors and textures.

Tree size may be considerably reduced now that dwarfing rootstocks are more widely available. This allows a number of different apples to be grown in small gardens where only one large tree could have been accommodated before. Apple trees may readily be trained into almost any shape. Cordon-, espalier-, and fan-shaped forms are particularly useful for growing trees against walls and fences.

The extensive choice of cultivars covers a period of ripening from midsummer to late winter, and fruit may be stored until midspring, given suitable conditions. There are cultivars and rootstocks suitable for most climates, including those with severe winters. For flowering to occur, the trees must be subjected to at least 900 hours below 45°F (7°C) to meet the chilling requirement. Apples are not grown successfully in tropical or subtropical regions, since they do not receive adequate chilling.

Site and planting

When planting, make sure that each tree has sufficient space to develop to its full size. Select the most appropriate size of tree (largely determined by the rootstock) for your garden. In most cases, more than one apple tree will be required for pollination.

Site

A sunny, sheltered site is essential for consistently good crops. Walls for trained fruit should not be shaded and should preferably be in full sun. For shaded gardens or those in a region with short summers and cool temperatures, choose cultivars that ripen early. Where late frosts occur, select late flowering cultivars so that the blossoms will not be damaged.

Apples will grow in most well-drained soils (see "Preparing the site," p.360). The more dwarfing the rootstock, however, the more fertile the soil should be.

Rootstocks

Choice of rootstock depends on the tree size required and the soil type. Many apple rootstocks are prefixed by M or MM, which stand for Malling and Malling Merton respectively, the research stations in the UK where the rootstocks were developed. The 'Ottawa' range of rootstocks was developed at the Central Experimental Farm, Ottawa, Ontario. A wide range of rootstocks is available, from 'M27', which is very dwarfing, to the vigorous 'M25'. For normal garden purposes, 'M9' is recommended for dwarf trees, 'M26' for larger ones, and 'Ottawa 3' for medium-sized trees (see *Planting Distances*, p.372). Cultivars on 'M27' bear fruit within three years of being grafted but require good growing conditions. Where the soil is poor, use a more vigorous rootstock: for example, where a dwarf tree is required use 'Ottawa 3'. The vigor of the cultivar also determines the size of the mature tree. Triploid cultivars grow larger than diploids (see below); use a more dwarfing rootstock for a triploid than for a diploid to attain a tree of similar size.

Pollination

No apples are reliably and consistently self-fertile: diploids must be planted near a second, compatible cultivar; triploid apples, which will not pollinate other cultivars, require two compatible cultivars nearby to pollinate them. Cultivars are divided into groups according to their time of flowering; a cultivar from one group may be cross-pollinated by another from the same group or one in the group before or after it if flowering times overlap. However, short North American blooming seasons make flowering group designations less meaningful. Some cultivars are incompatible: of those listed on pp.372 and 373, 'Cox's Orange Pippin' will not pollinate 'Kidd's Orange Red' or 'Suntan' and vice versa. If in doubt about compatibility, ask a fruit nursery for advice.

ROOTSTOCKS

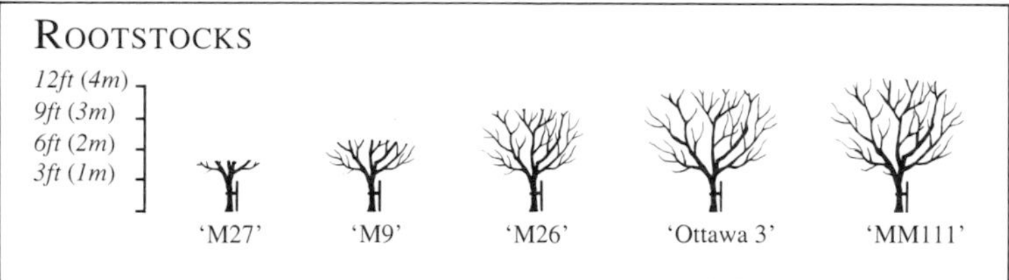

Planting

Bare-root trees are best planted when dormant, preferably in fall because the soil is still warm; they may be planted until late winter (except when it is frosty), but keep them moist in spring so that they establish well. Container-grown trees may be planted at any time, unless the ground is frozen or very wet; water before planting so that the roots are moist. Using the soil mark as a guide, plant each tree at its original planting depth (see *Planting a Fruit Tree*, p.361).

If the tree is to be trained, fit the supports and wires securely in place before planting (see under individual tree forms for details). For all untrained trees, staking when planting is essential and should be permanent for those on dwarfing rootstocks.

Planting distances (see p.372) depend on how the trees are to be trained, as well as on the vigor of the chosen rootstocks and cultivars.

RECOMMENDED DESSERT APPLES

'George Cave'

Early
'Akane' ☆
'Anna'
'Brookland'
'Carroll'
'Discovery'
'Early McIntosh' **B**
'George Cave'
'Lodi' **B**
'Transparent'
'Vista Bella' **Vg**

Midseason
'Cortland'
'Cox's Orange Pippin' ☆
'Delicious'
'Ellison's Orange'
'Empire'
'Fameuse'
'Freedom'
'Golden Delicious'
'Greensleeves'
'King of the Pippins'
'Liberty'
'Macoun' **B**
'McIntosh' **T**
'Ribston Pippin' **T**, ☆
'St. Edmund's Pippin' ☆
'Spartan' ☆
'Spigold' **T, B**

'Worcester Pearmain'

'State Fair'
'Sunset' ☆
'Wealthy'
'Wolf River'
'Worcester Pearmain'

Late
'Ashmead's Kernel' ☆
'Cornish Gillyflower' ☆
'D'Arcy Spice' ☆
'Duke of Devonshire'
'Gala'
'Idared'
'Jonagold' **T, Vg**
'Jupiter' **T, Vg**
'Kidd's Orange Red' ☆
'Laxton's Superb' **B**
'Newtown Pippin'
'Orleans Reinette' ☆
'Rome Beauty'
'Rosemary Russet'
'Sturmer Pippin'
'Suntan' **T, Vg**, ☆
'Tydeman's Late Orange' ☆
'Winston'

KEY
T *Triploid (unsuitable as pollinator)*
B *Biennial bearing*
Vg *Vigorous growth*
☆ *Excellent flavor*

Routine care

Establish a regular maintenance program to ensure that trees stay healthy and crop well. Feed and mulch periodically as required. Blossom and fruit thinning are annual tasks required to ensure satisfactory cropping. Check trees regularly for signs of pests and diseases, and damage from rubbing stakes and ties.

Blossom thinning and biennial bearing

Certain cultivars, such as 'Northern Spy', tend to produce heavy crops in alternate years, with little or no blossoms or fruit in intervening years. This is known as biennial bearing.

Blossom thinning can largely correct this; it involves removing nine of every ten blossom clusters by pinching them out, leaving the rosette of young leaves around each intact. The tree then produces a moderate, rather than heavy, crop and its resources are channeled into producing fruit buds for the following year, which would otherwise have been fruitless. On large trees, where it would be impractical to thin blossoms over the entire tree, biennial bearing can be corrected by blossom thinning a few branches.

If trees that normally crop regularly start to crop biennally, this may be due to the loss of blossoms from frost and the resulting loss of crop; this may then induce a tree to overcrop the following year. The tree may not have sufficient resources to develop adequate fruit buds for the third year, so a biennial tendency is set in motion. Disease or pest infestation causing a setback in one year may have a similar effect.

Fruit thinning

Thinning is essential where heavy crops have set, to improve fruit size, quality, and flavor and to help prevent branches from breaking. On young trees, overheavy cropping strains the tree's resources and slows the growth of new buds. Some thinning is possible on the young fruitlets, but it is simpler to carry out the whole task in early summer, after the "June drop," when the tree naturally sheds imperfect and infertile fruits.

Use pruners to remove the center (or "king") fruit of each cluster, which is sometimes abnormally shaped; then cut out any fruits that are damaged. In about midsummer, thin the clusters again so that there is one good fruit per cluster. Fruit of dessert cultivars should be spaced 4–6in (10–15cm) apart, and that of culinary cultivars 6–9in (15–22cm) apart. These distances may vary according to the individual cultivar and the size of fruit required.

PLANTING DISTANCES

TREE FORM	ROOTSTOCK	DISTANCE BETWEEN TREES	DISTANCE BETWEEN ROWS
Bush	'M27'	4–6ft (1.2–2m)	6ft (2m)
	'M9'	8–10ft (2.5–3m)	10ft (3m)
	'M26'	10–14ft (3–4.75m)	15ft (5m)
	'Ottawa 3'	11–18ft (3.5–5.5m)	18ft (5.5m)
Half-standard	'MM111'	24–8ft (7.5–9m)	24–8ft (7.5–9m)
Standard	'MM111', 'M25' (or Seedling crab)	24–32ft (7.5–10.5m)	24–32ft (7.5–10.5m)
Spindlebush	'M9' or 'M26' (and triploids on 'M27')	6–7ft (2–2.2m)	8–10ft (2.5–3m)
	'Ottawa 3'	6–7ft (2–2.2m)	11ft (3.5m)
Cordon	As bush	30in (75cm)	6ft (2m)
Fan/espalier	'M9'	10ft (3m)	
	'Ottawa 3'	14ft (4.75m)	
	'MM111'	18ft (5.5m)	
Dwarf pyramid	'M27'	4ft (1.2m)	6ft (2m)
	'M9' or 'M26'	5ft (1.5m)	6–7ft (2–2.2m)
	'Ottawa 3'	6ft (2m)	7ft (2.2m)

Fertilizing, watering, and mulching

Water trees in spells of hot, dry weather, apply fertilizer annually, and mulch as necessary (see "Care of tree fruits," p.362). If growth is poor, apply ammonium sulfate in spring at a rate of 1oz/sq yd (35g/sq m) of area under the canopy.

Stakes and ties

Inspect stakes and ties regularly to check that they are not rubbing against the bark of trees and that ties are not too loose; adjust them as necessary. Trees grown on dwarfing rootstocks such as 'M9' and 'M26' produce few taproots and need permanent staking to provide support.

Pests and diseases

Common pests that may be troublesome include tent caterpillars (p.553), wasps (p.565), codling moths (p.565), European apple sawflies (p.565), apple maggots (p.565), apple psyllids (p.562), and spider mites (p.552). Diseases include scab (p.564), brown rot (p.564), powdery mildew (p.564), bitter pit (see "Calcium deficiency," p.564), and *Nectria* canker (p.570).

APPLE THINNING

1 *Thinning is essential if the apple tree is carrying a heavy crop. After the "June drop," which is a normal occurrence, the remaining fruits will require further thinning if the crop is still heavy.*

2 *Remove enough fruitlets (especially any that are malformed) to leave about 4–6in (10–15cm) between dessert apples and 6–9in (15–22cm) between culinary apples and only 1 fruitlet per cluster.*

Pruning and training techniques

Apple trees produce flowers and fruit mainly on two-year-old and older shoots and on short spurs produced on the older wood. Two-year-old shoots carry both large fruit buds and smaller, pointed growth buds. Fruit buds produce flower clusters and then fruit, while growth buds form into fruit buds for the following year or into side shoots or fruiting spurs. One-year-old shoots may also carry fruit buds, but these flower later than those on older wood. Tip-bearing cultivars produce markedly fewer spurs (see right).

Once their branch framework is established, trained trees need to be pruned (mainly in summer) to maintain shape, curb vegetative growth, and stimulate the production of fruit buds. Untrained trees require moderate pruning in winter to stimulate growth for the next season's fruit and to maintain an open, well-balanced structure so that they crop well and the fruit is of good quality.

FRUIT BUDS AND GROWTH BUDS

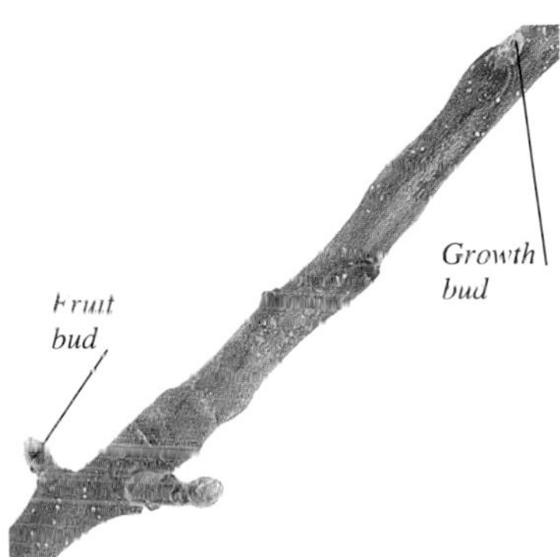

Large fruit buds develop on 2-year-old and older wood. The smaller buds are growth buds and are found mainly on 1-year-old wood.

NICKING AND NOTCHING

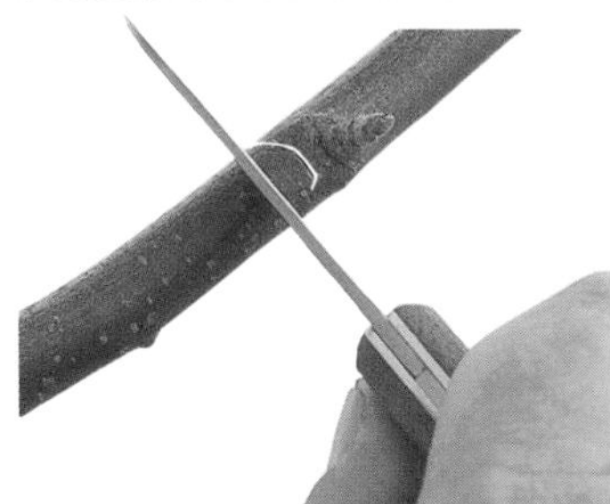

NICKING
To weaken bud growth, make a nick in the bark just below the bud and into the cambium layer.

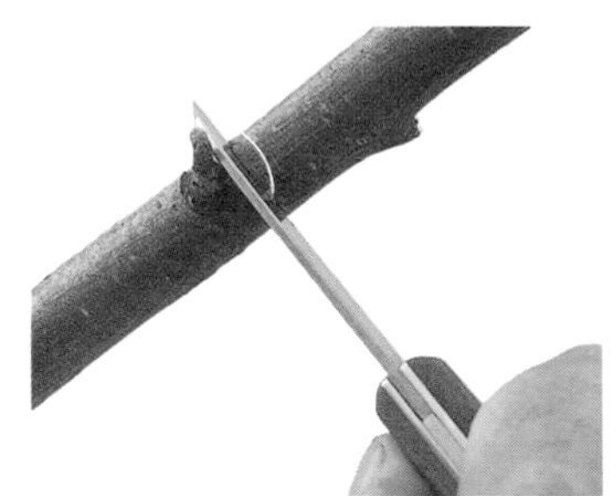

NOTCHING
To stimulate bud growth, make a notch through the bark into the cambium layer just above the bud.

Tip bearers and spur bearers

Cultivars differ in the way they bear their fruit. Tip bearers carry much of the crop at, or near, the shoot tips; spur bearers carry it along the whole shoot on short jointed spurs.

Some well known cultivar names such as 'Delicious' encompass many different varieties. When buying new trees, determine whether they are spur or tip bearers. Spur bearers, easily trained as cordons, espaliers, and fans, are preferable for small gardens. Tip bearers are best grown as standard, half-standard, or bush forms; once established, they need renewal pruning only (see p.374).

Nicking and notching

Sometimes it may be necessary to correct the balance of the branch framework of a trained tree. This may be achieved by nicking, which weakens the growth of a particular bud, or notching, which strengthens it. Notching may also be used to stimulate the production of side shoots on bare lengths of stem.

Nicking and notching are most effective in spring when the sap is rising. Make a nick or a small incision with a sharp knife just below a growth bud to inhibit it; make a notch just above it to increase its vigor and stimulate new growth.

Bark-ringing

On excessively vigorous apple and pear trees (but not on stone fruits) that produce unsatisfactory crops, bark-ringing may be used as a last resort to curb vegetative growth and induce a greater fruit set. In late spring, remove a narrow band of bark from around the trunk through to the cambium layer at a height of about 3ft (1m). This reduces the flow of nutrients and hormones back to the roots, so that they are concentrated in the upper part of the tree.

Bark-ringing must be carried out carefully or the tree may die. First measure out the width of the band, which must be only 1/8in (3mm) on a small tree, graduating to no more than 1/2in (1cm) on a very large tree, then score the band with a knife. Cut through the bark and the cambium layer and remove the bark within the band down to the hardwood all the way around. Seal the wound at once with several layers of waterproof adhesive tape – it must cover the wound without touching the cambium layer.

BARK-RINGING

1 *Stick tape around the trunk as a guide for 2 parallel cuts. The ring may be 1/8–1/2in (3mm–1cm) wide, depending on the age and size of the tree.*

2 *The parallel cuts should be made through both the bark and the cambium layer. Carefully remove the ring of bark with the blunt side of the knife blade.*

3 *Wind waterproof tape around the ring so that it covers the wound without touching the cambium layer. Remove the tape when the wound has healed.*

RECOMMENDED CULINARY APPLES

Early
'Battleford' **De**
'Duchess'
'Early Victoria', syn. 'Emneth Early' **B**
'George Neal' **Sb,** ☆
'Grenadier' **Sb**
'Parkland' **De**

Midseason
'Arthur Turner'
'Bismarck'
'Blenheim Orange' **T, Vg,** ☆
'Collet' **De**
'Cortland' **De**
'Golden Noble' ☆
'Gravenstein' **T, B**

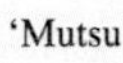

'Mutsu'

'Mutsu' **De, T, B, Vg**
'Norland' **De**
'Peasgood Nonsuch' ☆
'Red Baron' **De**
'Royal Jubilee'
'Sweet Sixteen' **De**

Late
'Bramley's Seedling' **T, Vg**
'Crawley Beauty'
'Edward VII'
'Golden Russet' **De**
'Granny Smith' **De**
'Haralson' **De**

'Edward VII'

'Howgate Wonder' **Vg**
'Melrose' **De**
'Monarch' **B, Vg,** ☆
'Northern Spy' **De, B**
'Novaspy' **De**
'Rhode Island Greening' **T, B**
'Wealthy' **De, B**
'Winesap' **De, T**
'Yellow Bellflower' **De**

KEY
De *Dessert use also*
T *Triploid (unsuitable as pollinator)*
B *Biennial bearing*
Vg *Vigorous growth*
☆ *Excellent flavor*

The wound should heal over by the fall, when the waterproof tape may be removed. The following year, the tree should produce many more blossoms and, if conditions favor it, a much heavier crop of fruit because the reaction of any wounded plant is to reproduce.

Winter pruning
There are three main techniques for winter pruning, all of which stimulate new growth. Spur pruning and thinning should be done only on cultivars that produce plenty of spurs, not on tip bearers. Renewal pruning is appropriate for spindlebushes and all tip bearers, as well as for vigorous cultivars that would be overstimulated by hard pruning. Regulated pruning is suited to cultivars that are naturally very vigorous, particularly triploids such as 'Gravenstein', 'Mutsu', 'Spigold', 'Winesap', and 'Jonagold'.

It may be necessary to vary the degree and type of pruning from year to year depending on the extent of growth, the quantity of fruit produced, and the age of the tree.

Spur pruning involves cutting back branch leaders and young laterals to stimulate the growth of sublaterals and fruiting spurs. The extent of pruning required depends on the tree's vigor–the greater the vigor, the lighter the pruning, since pruning stimulates growth.

Shorten branch leaders on vigorous trees by only a few buds (but on weaker ones by up to one-third) to stimulate new sublaterals to form. Shorten young laterals to three to six buds where growth is good but to three or four buds on weaker trees so that spurs form. On a stronger tree, shoots up to 6in (15cm) long may be left unpruned.

Spur thinning is necessary as a tree ages to prevent fruits from becoming overcrowded. If left unthinned, the spurs become entangled and carry inferior fruit. When spur systems become congested, remove the older wood in favor of the younger. In time, it may be necessary to saw off whole spur systems to allow room for new ones to develop.

Renewal pruning involves the annual cutting back of a proportion of older, fruited shoots to their base to stimulate the growth of new, young wood. Keep the center of a bush tree open by pruning out any vigorous growth that is crossing or shading other laterals so that all the branches are well spaced. Remove only a little of the tip from branch leaders and none at all on vigorous trees.

Regulated pruning consists of removing shoots and sometimes long sections of large branches that are crowded or crossing, particularly in the center of the tree, to keep the branch framework open. Remove old wood to make room for new shoots. Do not tip prune the branch leaders.

Summer pruning
This is carried out to keep trained trees within their allotted space. It involves removing a large proportion of the new growth each summer to slow down vegetative growth.

The Modified Lorette System is the standard method of summer pruning in temperate climates with cool, unpredictable summers. It is carried out once the young shoots have become woody at the base. Maiden (new) laterals more than 9in (22cm) long that grow directly from the main stem or a main branch should be reduced to three leaves above the basal cluster. Prune back side shoots arising from spurs and existing laterals to one leaf above the basal cluster. Continue to prune in this way as shoots mature.

WINTER PRUNING

SPUR PRUNING

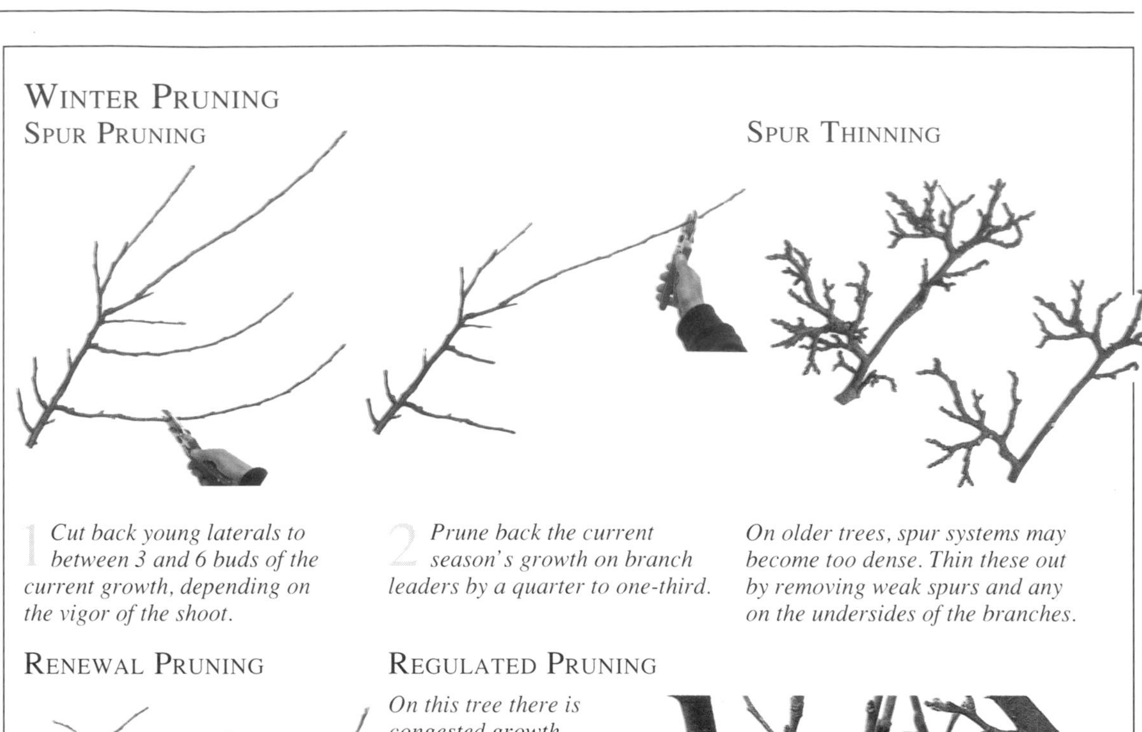

1 Cut back young laterals to between 3 and 6 buds of the current growth, depending on the vigor of the shoot.

2 Prune back the current season's growth on branch leaders by a quarter to one-third.

SPUR THINNING

On older trees, spur systems may become too dense. Thin these out by removing weak spurs and any on the undersides of the branches.

RENEWAL PRUNING

Prune out a good proportion of the older shoots that have already borne fruit (left). This will encourage new shoots to develop (right).

REGULATED PRUNING

On this tree there is congested growth. Correct this by removing any branches that are crossing or touching each other, and thin out any sublaterals or laterals that are overcrowded.

SUMMER PRUNING (MODIFIED LORETTE SYSTEM)

Prune trees when the lowest third of all new growth has become woody.

Cut back laterals on the main stems to 3 leaves above the basal cluster.

Basal cluster

BEFORE PRUNING

Trim any side shoots to 1 leaf.

AFTER PRUNING

To help prevent side shoots, or secondary growths, from developing behind the pruning cut, leave a small number of the longer shoots unpruned; tie these shoots securely to other branches so that they are roughly horizontal and draw the sap down. Do not shorten any of them until after fruiting. Then, in midfall, cut back any secondary growth shoots to one bud.

The Full Lorette System should be used in warmer climates. Prune back new laterals to about 2in (5cm), repeating at intervals through the summer. Shorten the laterals to $^3/_4$in (2cm) once they are woody at the base. Prune any secondary growths in late summer in the same way.

APPLE BUSH

YEAR 1, WINTER PRUNING

Prune back the leader to a selected lateral, leaving 2 or 3 strong laterals below it.

Cut back each of these laterals by two-thirds to an upward-facing bud. Remove all other laterals.

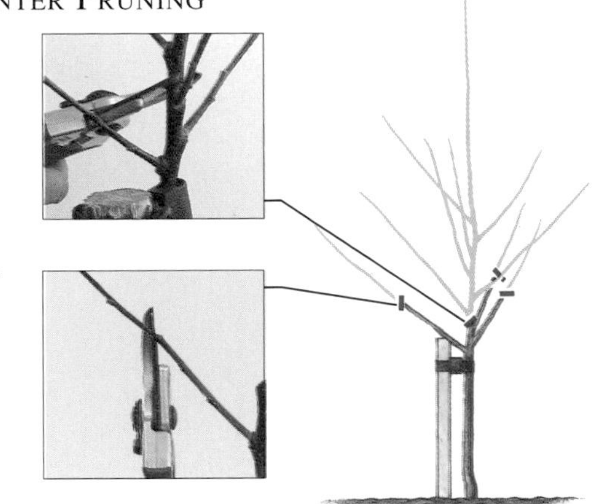

YEAR 2, WINTER PRUNING

Sublaterals that are not needed for secondary branches should be pruned back to 4 or 5 buds.

Prune back branch leaders and well-placed sublaterals by half to outward-facing buds.

Bush

The open-center or goblet-shaped bush is comparatively simple to maintain; it is ideal for larger gardens where there is plenty of space.

ESTABLISHED BUSH, SPUR PRUNING IN WINTER

Prune vigorous branch leaders, leaving two-thirds of the previous season's growth. Weaker branch leaders should be cut back by two-thirds.

Cut back to 5 or 6 buds any young side shoots growing from permanent branches to form spurs.

Formative pruning

Start with a well-feathered maiden tree; the laterals will form the first branches. After planting, while the tree is dormant, cut back the leader to a strong lateral 24–30in (60–75cm) above ground level, leaving at least two or three well-spaced laterals below it radiating out like the spokes of a wheel. These form the basis of the branch system; shorten them by two-thirds, cutting to an upward-pointing bud. Remove all other laterals.

If a maiden whip is used, or a feathered maiden tree that has few or no suitable laterals, cut back the leader in winter to a strong bud 24–30in (60–75cm) from the base, then make a small nick under the top two buds; this depresses their growth and encourages shoots from the lower buds to grow. Remove any unwanted laterals completely.

By the end of the following summer, three or four strong, healthy laterals should have developed to produce a plant equivalent to a pruned, feathered maiden.

Strong growth should develop the following summer. If one lateral grows faster than the others, tie it down nearly horizontally to slow its growth. Remove any inward- or downward-growing and weak shoots.

In the second winter, select several well-spaced shoots arising from the original laterals to build up the branch framework, and shorten them by half, cutting to outward-facing buds. If any are not needed for the framework, shorten them to four or five buds, and remove completely any shoots crossing the open center. As growth continues in the second summer, remove any vigorous, upright shoots that unbalance the shape of the tree. By the third winter, the final branch formation should be established, with eight to ten main branches as well as several subsidiary ones.

Routine pruning

Only winter pruning (see opposite) is necessary for bushes once the framework is established; the pruning required will depend on the amount of growth made by the tree and on whether it is a tip or spur bearer. A tip bearer requires renewal pruning. Spur bearers require spur pruning and thinning.

ESTABLISHED BUSH, RENEWAL PRUNING IN WINTER

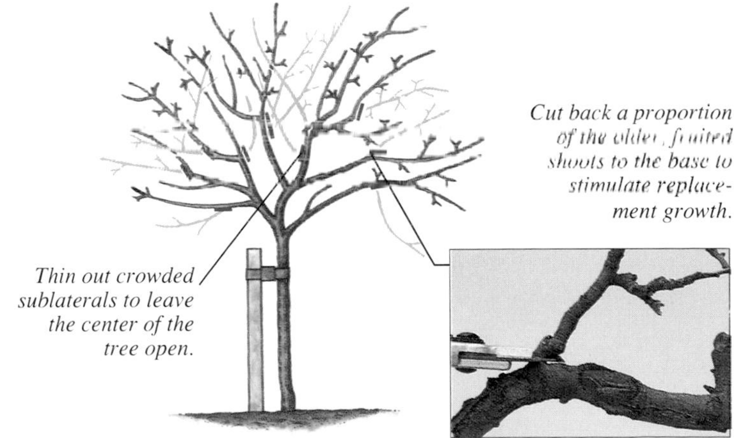

Cut back a proportion of the older, fruited shoots to the base to stimulate replacement growth.

Thin out crowded sublaterals to leave the center of the tree open.

Standard and half-standard

Few gardens are large enough to accommodate a standard or half-standard tree, but these make fine specimen trees where there is space.

Two or three years' training and pruning is needed to produce a clear stem of 4–4$^1/_2$ft (1.2–1.35m) for a half-standard, or 6–6$^1/_2$ft (2–2.1m) for a standard. After planting a feathered maiden or maiden whip, tie in the leading shoot to a stake and cut any laterals back hard to 1in (2.5cm) in winter. In spring and summer, periodically pinch or cut back any feathers to a few leaves; this helps to thicken the main stem. Repeat this procedure in the second year.

In the following winter, remove most of the laterals and cut back the leader to the desired height for either a half-standard or a standard; if the tree is not of the required height, grow it on for a third year. Several laterals should then develop below the cut; select and retain three or four well-spaced laterals to form the basic branch framework. Then train as for an open-center bush (above).

Subsequent pruning of the tree is also as for a bush, but growth will be much stronger because the tree is grafted on a vigorous or a very vigorous rootstock. Carry out regulated pruning on the established tree; it is necessary to prune hard only if the tree is not growing satisfactorily.

Spindlebush

A spindlebush is trained into the shape of a pyramid or cone, to a height of 7ft (2.2m); once established, only renewal pruning and pruning to keep the shape are required.

Numerous variations of the spindlebush have been developed, but the basic aim is to keep the three or four lowest branches dominant by removing shoots that would otherwise develop in the center of the tree. Any shoots that do develop higher in the tree are allowed to fruit and are then pruned back hard, to be replaced by fresh growth.

Formative pruning

Plant a strong feathered maiden, supporting it with a 6ft (2m) stake. Cut back the leader in the winter to about 3ft (1m), or to just above the topmost lateral if this is higher. Select three or four vigorous and evenly spaced laterals that are about 2–3ft (60–90cm) from the base. Prune back each lateral by half to a downward-pointing, healthy bud and remove all other laterals.

If growth is strong, tie down any upright laterals toward the end of the first summer, in order to suppress growth and encourage the tree to fruit. If growth is weak, the upright laterals do not need to be tied down until the next summer.

Tie down the laterals with strong string secured to wooden or hooked metal pegs driven into the ground at an angle around the tree. If using wooden pegs, hammer a large U staple into the top of each one so that a string may be secured to it. Tie each string loosely to the branch so that it pulls down the branch to a 30° angle. Long branches may need to be tied in two places.

Remove any excessively vigorous shoots growing upward from the main stem or laterals; do not attempt to tie them down, since they may break. Train the central stem vertically by tying it to the stake.

The second winter after planting, shorten the central leader by one-third of the new growth, cutting to a bud on the opposite side of the pruning cut made the previous winter. This helps to maintain a straight stem. Make sure that the strings are not constricting the tied-down shoots; once the growths have hardened and will remain in a more or less horizontal position, remove the strings. The following summer, tie down some of the vertical shoots and remove completely any that are exceptionally vigorous or too close to the main stem, or that unbalance the branch framework.

By the third winter, laterals higher in the tree should have developed and been tied down to form further tiers of branches. They should be nearly horizontal, since this encourages early fruiting, and should not overshadow the lower framework branches if this can be avoided.

In the third summer, when the tree should produce fruit for the first time, tie down selected new side shoots in late summer and remove any excessively strong shoots.

Routine pruning

From the fourth or fifth year onward, renewal pruning (see p.374) is necessary in winter: shorten some of the old, fruited wood. Some of the shoots, particularly those that are higher in the tree, should be pruned back hard close to the trunk to encourage the development of replacement growths.

If the central leader is too vigorous, it may be cut back a little to a weaker lateral that will replace it. This concentrates vigor in the lower branches and helps to retain the pyramid shape, allowing maximum light to reach the fruits. In summer, continue cutting out completely any excessively vigorous and strongly upright-growing shoots.

Cordon

A feathered maiden may be trained as an oblique cordon on wires secured to posts or to a wall. Space three horizontal wires 24in (60cm) apart; the lowest should be 30in (75cm) from the ground. Fix the wires 4–6in (10–15cm) clear of the support to allow free air circulation. Attach a stake to the wires at an angle of 45°, then plant a feathered maiden by it (see "Training for shape," p.365) and tie in the main stem to the stake.

Formative pruning

In the winter immediately after planting, shorten all lateral shoots that are over 4in (10cm) in length to

APPLE SPINDLEBUSH

YEAR 1, WINTER PRUNING

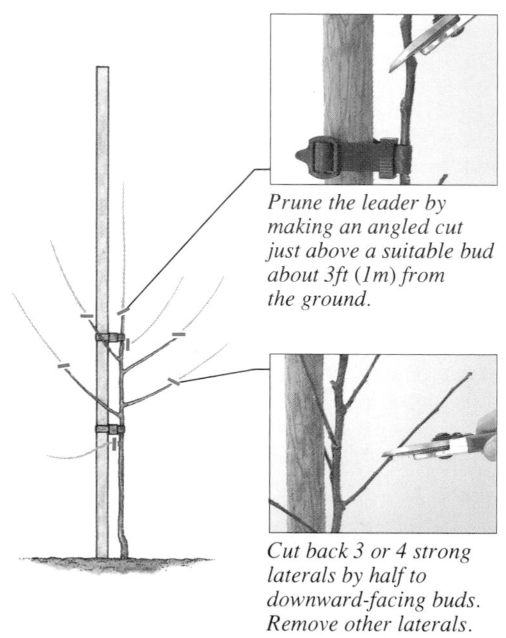

Prune the leader by making an angled cut just above a suitable bud about 3ft (1m) from the ground.

Cut back 3 or 4 strong laterals by half to downward-facing buds. Remove other laterals.

YEAR 1, SUMMER PRUNING

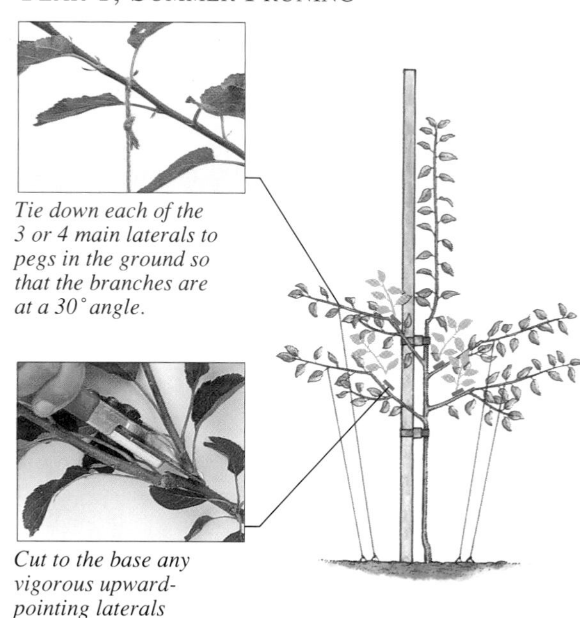

Tie down each of the 3 or 4 main laterals to pegs in the ground so that the branches are at a 30° angle.

Cut to the base any vigorous upward-pointing laterals or sublaterals.

YEAR 2, SUMMER PRUNING

Repeat summer pruning as for Year 1, concentrating on removing any upright growths.

ESTABLISHED SPINDLEBUSH, WINTER PRUNING

Cut back to 1 bud any large, old, upper branches with loppers or pruners.

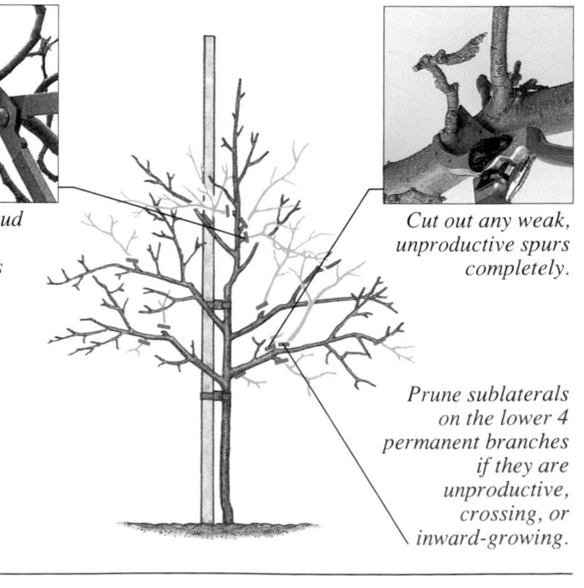

Cut out any weak, unproductive spurs completely.

Prune sublaterals on the lower 4 permanent branches if they are unproductive, crossing, or inward-growing.

three or four buds. For tip-bearing cultivars, shorten the leader by about one-third; do not attempt to prune the cordon further.

From the first summer onward, prune the new shoots in mid- to late summer, once they have become woody at the base. Not all shoots ripen together, so pruning should continue over several weeks. Use the Modified or Full Lorette System (see "Summer pruning," p.374). The time of pruning depends on climate and on which system is used.

Routine pruning

Winter pruning is essential to prevent congestion: reduce overgrown spur systems and completely remove those that are overcrowded. If the cordon is not producing enough well-spaced laterals, shorten the leader by about a quarter of its length to encourage strong growth.

Once a cordon has extended beyond the top wire, lower its angle of growth slightly to provide space for the leader to extend. When it reaches the top wire, trim it back to one leaf of new growth in late spring. Alternatively, if the leader is vigorous, cut it back in late spring to a side shoot near the top wire to curb its growth.

Continue on the Modified or Full Lorette System; on an established cordon, this largely involves cutting side shoots to one leaf.

Double cordon

A double cordon is usually grown vertically but may be grown at an angle if desired. Feathered maidens and maiden whips may be trained as double cordons. The process is similar in each case, except that maiden whips must form side shoots before training can begin (see "Forming a double cordon," right).

If using a feathered maiden, prune the leader to two side shoots of equal vigor, one on either side, about 10in (25cm) above soil level. Do this during the winter immediately after planting. Tie the side shoots to stakes at an angle of 35°. Train the new growth upward in summer while it is still supple, with at least 18in (45cm) between the vertical arms of the U; each arm is subsequently treated as a single cordon.

Fan

A wall or fence is an ideal support against which to grow a fan-trained apple tree; select a cultivar on a dwarfing rootstock so that it may be comfortably accommodated in the available space. Fix horizontal support wires about 6in (15cm) apart,

APPLE CORDON

YEAR 1, WINTER PRUNING

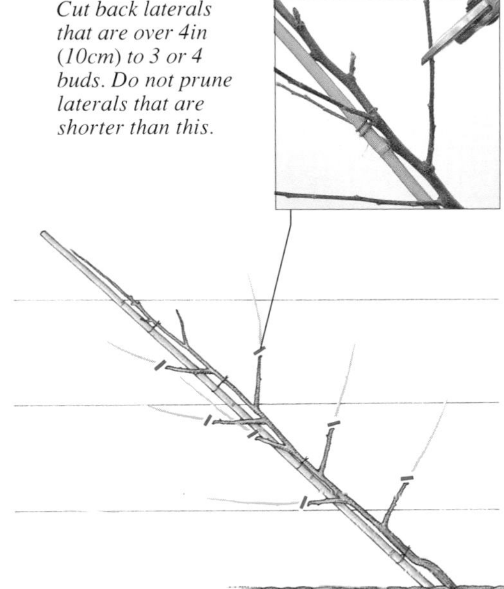

YEAR 1, SUMMER PRUNING

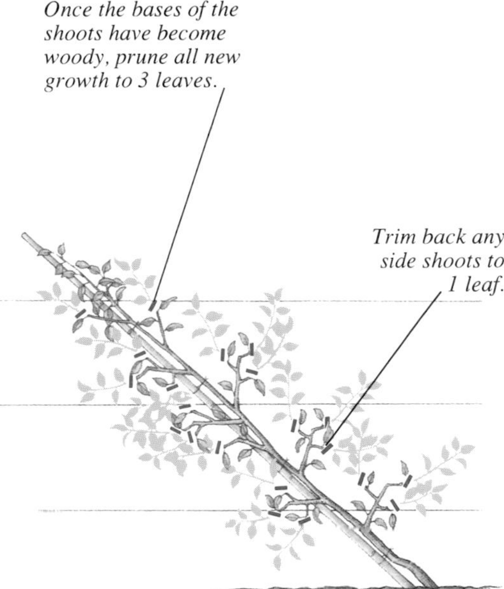

ESTABLISHED CORDON, WINTER PRUNING

ESTABLISHED CORDON, SUMMER PRUNING

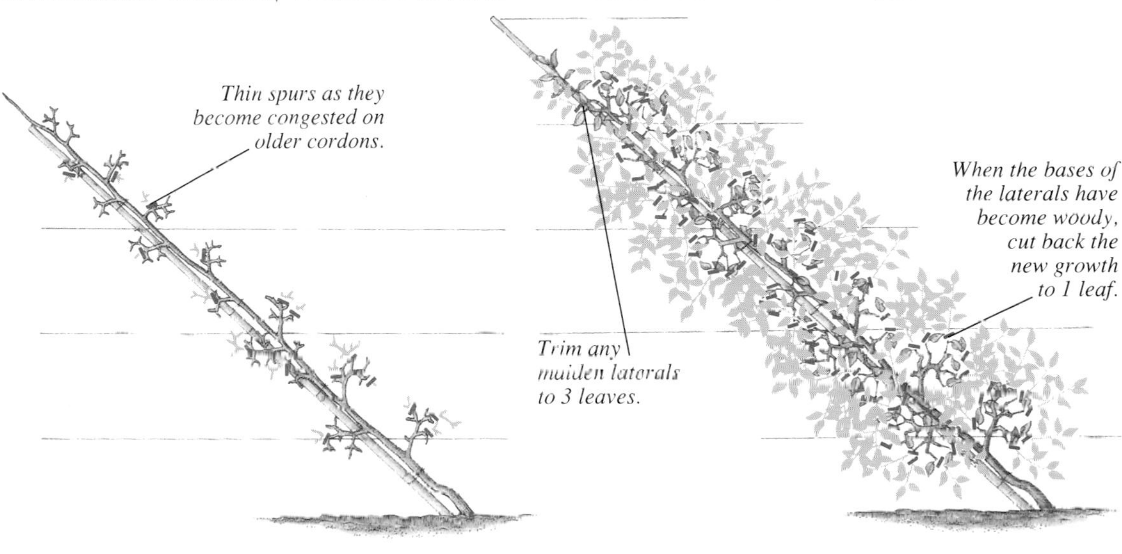

Forming a double cordon

To train a maiden whip as a double cordon, cut back the newly planted tree to about 10in (25cm) from soil level during the first winter, leaving a strong bud on either side below the cut. The following summer, when new shoots have been produced, tie the two uppermost shoots to stakes at an angle of 45°, lowering them to 30° later in the season. When the shoot tips are more than 18in (45cm) apart, train them upward by tying them to vertical stakes.

Once the basic U shape of the double cordon has been formed, the two vertical arms should each be pruned in the same way as a single cordon.

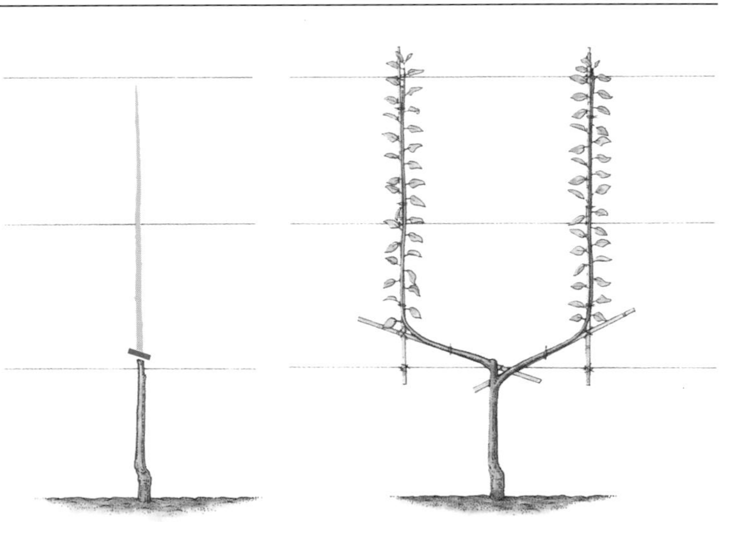

starting at 15in (38cm) from soil level. The initial development of the framework is as for peaches (see p.389); once established, it should be pruned on the Modified Lorette System (see p.374), with each arm being treated like a single cordon. This encourages fruiting spurs to develop along the arms.

Espalier

For this tree form, one or more pairs of opposite shoots are trained at right angles to the main stem onto support wires 15in (38cm) apart. An espalier usually has two or three tiers, but more are possible with trees of sufficient vigor and where there is room to accommodate them. If a maiden whip is used, the first tier of branches may then be trained more readily at the required height.

Formative pruning

After planting a maiden whip, prune back the leader to a bud just above the lowest wire. The following summer, train the uppermost shoot vertically to form a new leader; as the two strongest laterals below this develop, tie each to a stake at an angle of 45° to form the first branch tier. Cut or pinch back all other, lower shoots to two or three leaves. Tie down the laterals of the first tier into their horizontal position toward the end of the first growing season. If the two main arms develop unevenly, lower the more vigorous shoot to check growth and raise the weaker shoot to induce vigor. Once the two are balanced, tie them into their horizontal positions (see also *Training on Stakes*, p.365).

The following winter, remove completely any laterals that have developed other than the main arms. To create the second tier, first look for two strong buds about 15in (38cm) above the first tier, then cut back the central leader to the bud above these. Shorten each first-tier arm by one-third to a downward-facing bud; where growth is very vigorous, leave the arm unpruned.

The bud to which each arm is cut back will produce a shoot that should be trained horizontally during the second summer after planting. Cut back other sublaterals according to the Modified Lorette System (see p.374). The second pair of arms will form, and these should be trained in the same way as the first pair. Repeat this process as necessary to obtain the required number of tiers.

Routine pruning

Once the arms of the topmost tier are well established, prune back the

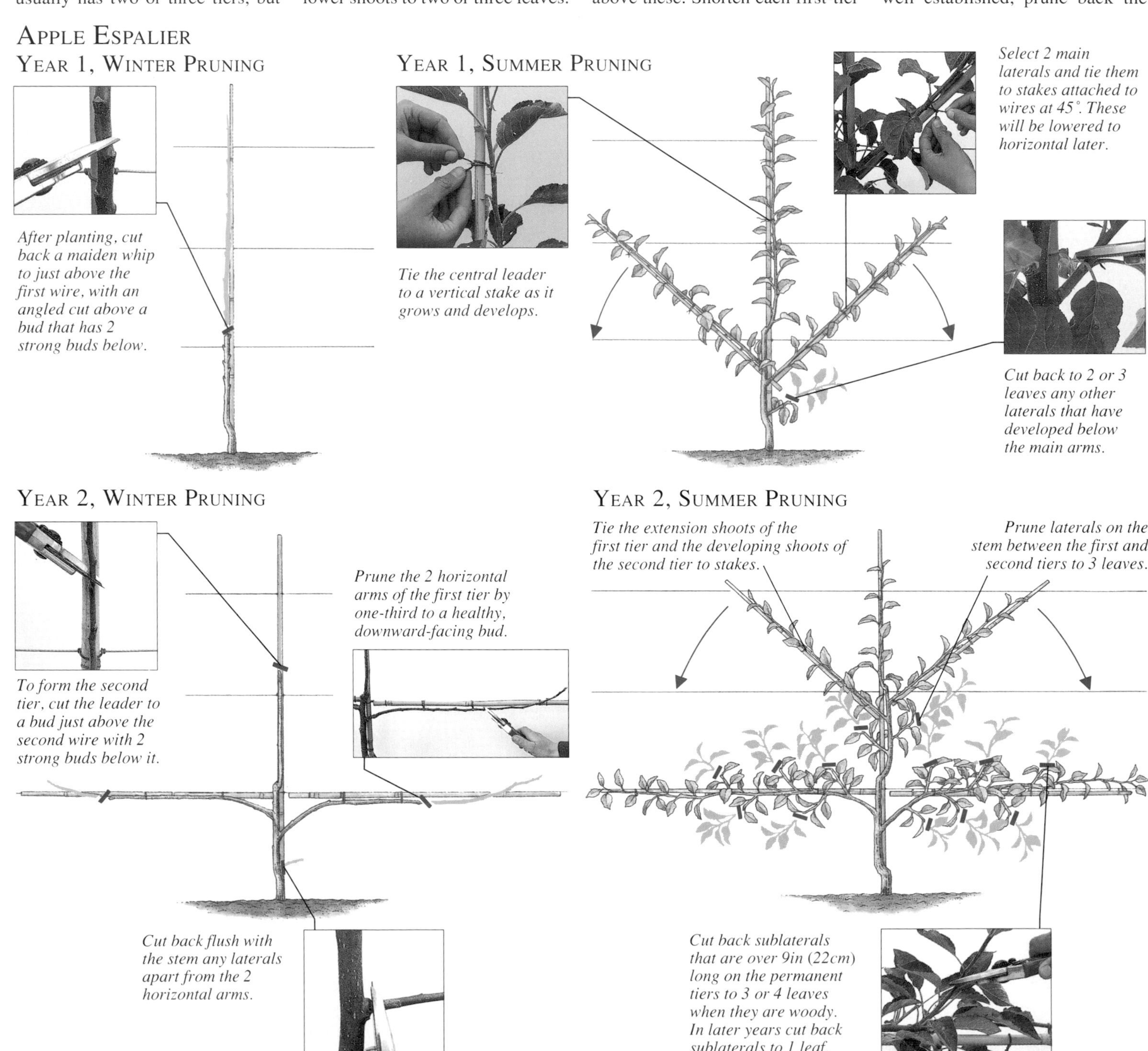

PICKING

Support the apple in the palm of your hand and twist it slightly. If the apple comes away easily from the spur, it is ready for picking.

central leader in winter to just above this tier. The espalier should thereafter be pruned in summer following the Full or Modified Lorette System (see p.374).

Dwarf pyramid

The dwarf pyramid is a compact tree form suitable for a small garden or for a container. It needs permanent staking if grown on an 'M27' or 'M9' rootstock; cultivars on other rootstocks need staking for four to five years. For pruning details, see "Pears: Dwarf pyramid," p.381.

Secondary growth often develops after summer pruning. These unwanted shoots inhibit the formation of fruit buds, so prune two to three weeks later than usual to help retard their growth if this is a problem. If secondary growth continues to appear, leave one or two shoots unpruned to act as sap-drawers (see "Summer pruning," p.374).

Harvesting and storing

Early-ripening apples should be gathered just before they are fully ripe or they soon become mealy. Late-maturing cultivars must not be picked too soon, however, or the fruits will shrivel in storage.

Wrap sound, undamaged fruits individually in tissue paper and, keeping different cultivars separate, store them in slatted boxes or crates in a cool place (see p.367). Fruits from young or overvigorous trees store less well than those from more mature trees and should therefore be used first. For further information on harvesting and storing, see p.367.

Propagation

Apple trees may be propagated by chip-budding or T-budding in summer (see pp.368 and 369) or by whip-and-tongue grafting in early spring (see p.369). If possible, use certified scions and rootstocks.

Grafting over

Grafting over is a technique used to grow a selected cultivar on an established apple or pear tree to replace part of the original cultivar. This is done to introduce a new pollinator for adjacent trees or to try a new cultivar; because the roots and main branch system are already established, the new cultivar bears fruit quickly. There are two methods: top working and frame-working.

Top-working

Initially, this entails heading (cutting) back most of the main branches to within 24–30in (60–75cm) of the main branch fork in spring. Leave one or two smaller branches unpruned to act as sap-drawers to reduce the number of new shoots that form around pruning cuts. Trim the cuts where branches have been sawn off. Two or three scions are used per branch, but only the most vigorous one is grown on; the presence of the others may initially help keep canker from developing in the cut surface. Scions may be either rind- or cleft-grafted (the latter is rarely used by amateurs and is not described here).

For rind grafting, take dormant scions from the previous season's growth of the desired cultivar and prepare them with angled top cuts and tapering basal cuts. Cut away a sliver of bark on the other side of the tapering cut to prevent the bark from being damaged when inserted into the branch. When rind grafting branches of about 1in (2.5cm) in diameter, place two scions opposite each other. Larger branches can accommodate three evenly spaced scions. Make a vertical cut for each scion in the bark of the prepared branch. Carefully lift the bark and slide the scion into position underneath. Bind the graft firmly into position and seal the cut surfaces with grafting wax. Scion growth is rapid and ties must be released.

Retain the most vigorous scion and remove the others. Frequently, more than one shoot will develop from the selected scion; allow the best one to grow unchecked as the basis for the new branch. Shorten any others if they are less vigorous than the retained shoot, but remove them completely if they are of equal vigor. After three or four years the new cultivar should start to crop regularly. Subsequently, prune the new branch according to the individual tree form.

Frame-working

In this method, most of the branch framework is retained and many scions are grafted onto different parts of the tree. Frame-working is preferred by commercial growers since trees crop more quickly than if top-worked.

HOW TO RIND GRAFT

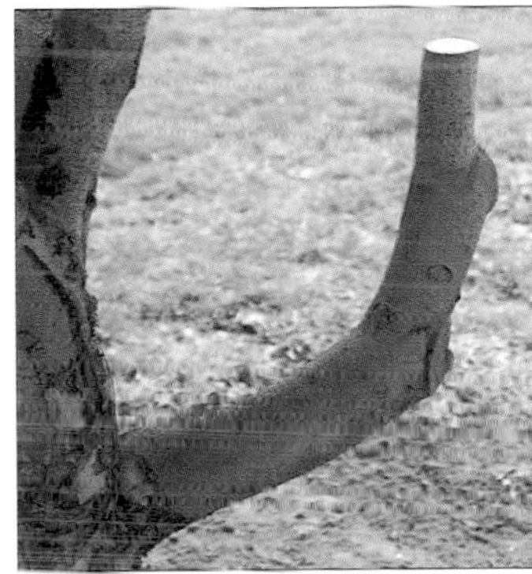

1 *In early spring, cut off most of the main branches to within 24–30in (60–75cm) of the trunk. Leave 1 or 2 branches uncut to draw the sap.*

2 *Make a vertical cut 1in (2.5cm) long through the bark of 1 of the trimmed branches. If it is 1in (2.5cm) in diameter, make 2 evenly spaced cuts; if larger, make 3 cuts.*

3 *Use the blunt side of the knife blade to ease the bark away from the cambium layer.*

4 *Prepare scions 3 buds long, each with an angled cut at the top and a 1in (2.5cm) tapering cut at the base. Insert them with the tapering cut facing inward.*

5 *When 2 or 3 scions have been inserted into the branch, bind the grafts tightly with strong string, winding it around the whole branch to hold the scions in place.*

6 *Apply grafting wax to the exposed areas. When the scions have united with the branch, retain only the most vigorous one and remove the others.*

Pears (*Pyrus communis* var. *sativa*)

Pears need more consistently warm conditions than apples to crop reliably. Late-ripening cultivars require dry and warm conditions throughout late summer and early fall. They have a winter chilling requirement of 600–900 hours below 45°F (7°C).

Pears may be trained much like apples; bush, dwarf pyramid, cordon, and espalier forms are the most suitable for small gardens. Pears are usually grown on quince, rather than pear, rootstocks because this produces smaller trees. Some new rootstocks are in development.

RECOMMENDED DESSERT PEARS

'Doyenné du Comice'

Early
'Ayres'
'Clapp's Favorite' ☆
'Dr. Jules Guyot'
'Earlibrite'
'Gifford'
'Harrow Delight'
'Hudar'
'Marguerite Marillat'
'Moonglow'
'Rosée de Juliette'
'Summercrisp'
'Ubileen'

Midseason
'Abbé Fetel' **B**
'Aurora'
'Bartlett' **Ig**
'Beurré Hardy'
'Beurré Superfin' ☆
'Bosc'
'Bristol Cross'
'Conference'
'Devoe'
'Douglas'
'Doyenné du Comice' ☆
'Fondante d'Automne' **Ig**
'John'
'Lincoln'

'Conference'

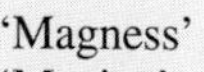

'Magness'
'Maxine'
'Max-Red Bartlett'
'Merton Pride' **T**
'Nova'
'Packham's Triumph'
'Parker'
'Pineapple'
'Rescue'
'Santa Claus'
'Spartlett'

KEY
Ig *Incompatibility group (pears in this group will not pollinate each other)*
T *Triploid (unsuitable as pollinator)*
B *Biennial bearing*
☆ *Excellent flavor*

Site and planting

Pears flower earlier than apples, in mid- to late spring, and may be damaged by frosts. Pears are not fully self-fertile; cross-pollination is needed for a good crop.

Site

Pears require a warm, sheltered, and sunny site. The soil should retain moisture but must be well drained, particularly for trees on quince rootstocks (see below). Pears tolerate wetter conditions than apples. Trees on poor or sandy soils produce fruits of inferior flavor, while those on shallow alkaline soils may suffer from lime-induced chlorosis, a nutritional problem caused by deficiencies of manganese and iron (see p.557). Such sites may be improved by mulching regularly with large amounts of organic matter and occasionally applying chelated iron and manganese.

Rootstocks

As well as producing relatively small trees, growing pears on quince rootstocks induces early fruiting. 'Quince A' is moderately dwarfing (similar to 'M26' in apple); 'Quince C' is more dwarfing (similar to 'M9' in apple). A few cultivars, however, do not make a good union with quince rootstocks and may need double-working (see p.382).

Pollination

Provision for cross-pollination should always be made by planting two compatible cultivars. Some cultivars are triploid, and a very few are male sterile: these require two pollinators near them. Incompatible cultivars are indicated in *Recommended Dessert Pears*, left and opposite, and *Recommended Culinary Pears*, opposite.

Planting

Plant pears in fall when the soil is still warm or by early winter at the latest. This allows trees to establish before coming into growth, which may occur very early in a mild spring. Planting distances (see below) depend on the choice of rootstock and the form in which the trees are grown (see "Pruning and training," right).

ROOTSTOCKS

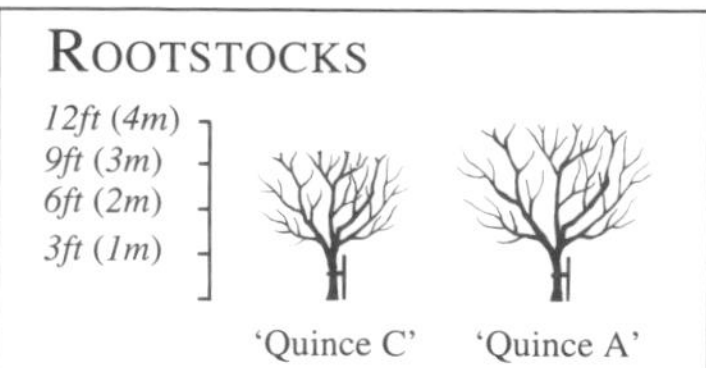

Routine care

Regular maintenance, including fruit thinning, feeding and watering, and checking for pest and disease problems, is similar to that required for apples (see p.372). For general information, see pp.362–3.

Fruit thinning

After the natural shedding of fruitlets at or soon after midsummer, thin out to leave one fruit per cluster if the crop is heavy, but two per cluster if cropping is lighter.

Feeding, watering, and mulching

Water and fertilize trees as needed (see p.362). It is particularly important to give pears adequate nitrogen: in spring, apply light dressings of up to 1oz/sq yd (35g/sq m) of ammonium sulfate to maintain levels during the growing season. Mulch around newly planted trees in spring.

Pests and diseases

Pears may be affected by rabbits (see "Small animals," p.572), wasps (p.565), aphids (p.552), caterpillars (p.551), fire blight (p.555), pear thrips (p.565), scab (p.555), and brown rot (p.564). Pear leaf blister mites produce pustules in the leaves. Destroy affected leaves in summer. Some pear cultivars, especially 'Conference', may develop parthenocarpic fruits. These are cylindrical and may be produced when partial fertilization has occurred; the fruit continues to grow misshapen. Provide a suitable pollinator and give shelter to encourage more pollinating insects.

PLANTING DISTANCES

TREE FORM	ROOTSTOCK	DISTANCE BETWEEN TREES	DISTANCE BETWEEN ROWS
Bush	'Quince C'	11ft (3.5m)	18ft (5.5m)
	'Quince A'	14ft (4.75m)	18ft (5.5m)
Cordon	'Quince A' or 'C'	30in (75cm)	6ft (2m)
Espalier	'Quince C'	11ft (3.5m)	
	'Quince A'	14ft (4.75m)	
Fan	As espalier	As espalier	
Dwarf pyramid	'Quince C'	4ft (1.2m)	6ft (2m)
	'Quince A'	5ft (1.5m)	6ft (2m)

Pruning and training

Pruning requirements and techniques are similar to those for apples, but pears tolerate harder pruning once they have started to crop. Fruiting occurs predominantly on two-year-old and older wood. On pears, spur production is usually more prolific than on apples, and spurs should be thinned regularly on established trees. Very few pear cultivars are tip bearers.

Training and pruning to develop a cordon or an espalier are as for apples. Both are pruned by the Modified Lorette System in temperate areas or, in warmer climates, by the Full Lorette System (see "Apples: Summer pruning," p.374). A fan is formed in the same way as for peaches (see p.389), but, once established, prune as for an apple fan (see p.377). Pears are normally pruned two or three weeks earlier than apples, soon after midsummer.

Where excessive vigor occurs at the expense of cropping, root pruning (see p.366) where possible or, as a last resort, bark-ringing (see p.373) may be carried out.

Bush

Initial training and pruning of a bush are as for apples (see p.375). Several pear cultivars (for example 'Doyenné du Comice') have an upright growth habit; when pruning branch leaders of these cultivars, cut to an outward-pointing bud. Shoots that are upright should be tied down at the base before they ripen fully, as part of the initial training process, to encourage a wider angle of growth. Pruning on very vigorous bushes is normally much lighter after the second year. Where vigor is lacking, shorten new laterals to five or six buds or fewer, adjusting this recommendation if the tree's vigor improves.

The few tip-bearers (for example 'Merton Pride') need to be renewal pruned as described for tip-bearing apples (see p.374). Established spur-bearing trees need considerable spur shortening and thinning, and occasional branch thinning, in winter.

Dwarf pyramid
Prune back the leading shoot of a feathered maiden after planting to 20–30in (50–75cm) from the ground, and reduce any laterals to 6in (15cm); remove weak or low laterals. In the first summer, prune extension growth on the laterals, and any new laterals, to five or six leaves to downward-facing buds. This encourages horizontal growth and induces early fruiting. Cut back sublaterals to three leaves. The following winter, prune the leading shoot to leave 10in (25cm) of the new growth, cutting to a bud on the opposite side to that of the previous year's pruning. In each subsequent year, prune the leader to buds on alternate sides. When the leader reaches the required height, prune back in late spring to leave one bud of the new growth.

Once the initial framework has been formed, nearly all pruning is carried out in mid- to late summer, depending on season and location. It is important that shoots have become

PEAR, DWARF PYRAMID

YEAR 1, WINTER PRUNING

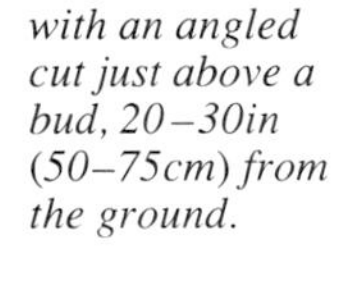

Cut back the leader with an angled cut just above a bud, 20–30in (50–75cm) from the ground.

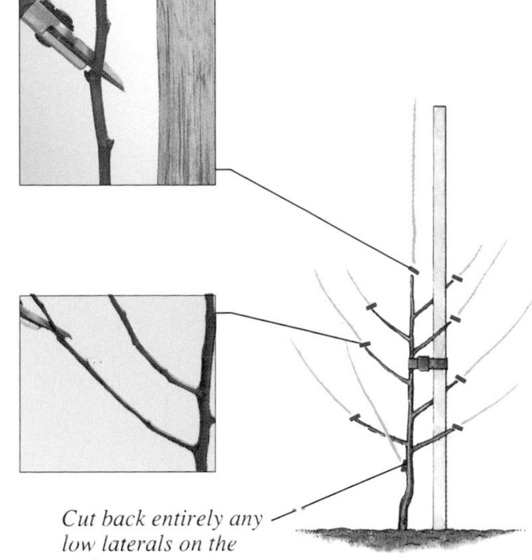

Prune back each lateral to a downward-facing bud about 6in (15cm) from the main stem.

Cut back entirely any low laterals on the main stem.

YEAR 1, SUMMER PRUNING

Cut back new growth at the tips of the main laterals to 5 or 6 leaves on the extension growth.

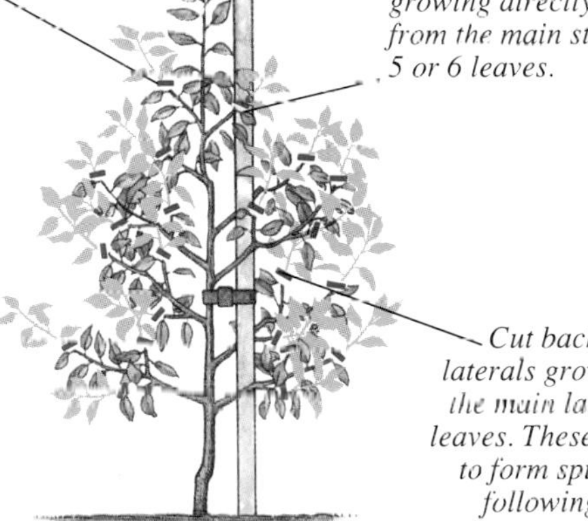

Prune new laterals growing directly from the main stem to 5 or 6 leaves.

Cut back any sublaterals growing from the main laterals to 3 leaves. These will start to form spurs for the following summer.

YEAR 2, WINTER PRUNING

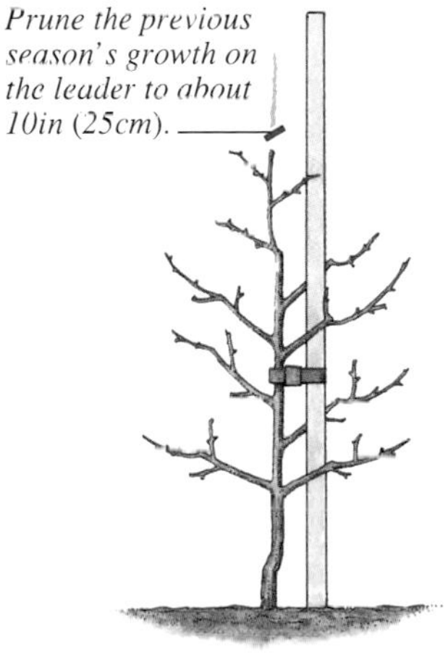

Prune the previous season's growth on the leader to about 10in (25cm).

RECOMMENDED DESSERT PEARS (CONT.)

Midseason (cont.)
'Twentieth Century'
'Ure'

Late
'Beurré d'Anjou'
'Comice'
'Duchess'
'Dumont'
'Golden Spice'
'Gorham'
'Highland'
'Joséphine de Malines'
'Kieffer'
'Luscious'
'Orcas'

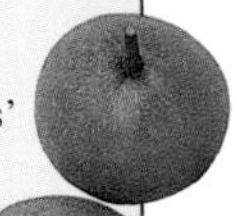

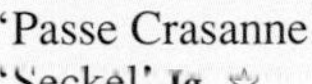

'Joséphine de Malines'

'Passe Crasanne'
'Seckel' **Ig,** ☆
'Warren'
'Winter Nelis' ☆

RECOMMENDED CULINARY PEARS

Midseason
'Beurré Clairgeau'

Late
'Catillac' **T**
'Vicar of Winkfield' **T**

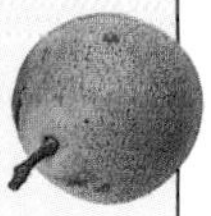

'Catillac'

KEY
Ig *Incompatibility group (pears in this group will not pollinate each other)*
T *Triploid (unsuitable as pollinator)*
☆ *Excellent flavor*

YEAR 2 AND ROUTINE SUMMER PRUNING

Trim sublaterals from existing laterals or spurs to 1 leaf beyond the basal cluster.

Cut back new growth at the ends of the permanent branches to 5 or 6 leaves.

Cut back laterals growing from the main branches to 3 leaves.

ESTABLISHED DWARF PYRAMID, WINTER PRUNING

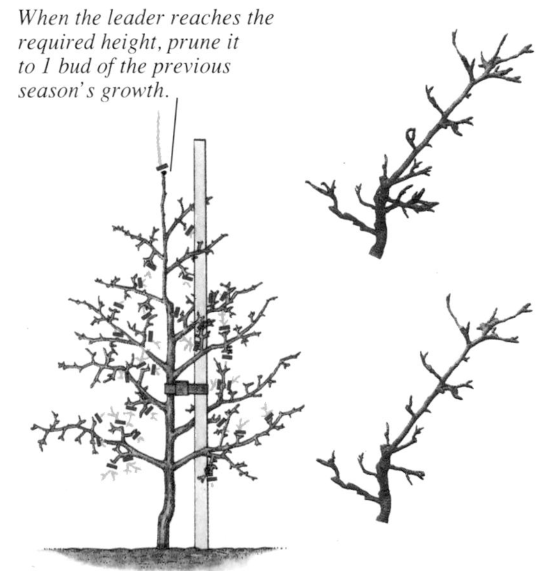

When the leader reaches the required height, prune it to 1 bud of the previous season's growth.

BEFORE
The spurs on the darker wood at the base of this shoot are congested and require thinning.

AFTER
Thin by removing any unproductive or overlapping spurs. Trim out excess fruit buds to leave 2 or 3 evenly spaced buds per spur.

woody at their base before they are pruned; the operation is therefore spread over three or four weeks, and a few shoots may not be ready to prune until early fall. Do not shorten shoots that are 6in (15cm) or less in length. Cut back branch leaders to six leaves of new growth and prune any sublaterals to one leaf above the basal cluster. Any shoots arising directly from the main branches should be shortened to three leaves. If any secondary growth develops, leave a few of the shoots unpruned as for apples (see "Summer pruning," p.374) to draw the sap.

The only major operation for winter pruning is the shortening of the central leader already described plus, in later years, some spur thinning and shortening. If the spur systems are allowed to become congested, the tree loses vigor and small, overcrowded fruits are produced.

Harvesting and storing

Time of picking is most important, especially for cultivars that ripen in late summer and early fall. If left on the tree too long, the fruits will have turned "sleepy" and brown at the center. Gather them at the first sign of a change of ground color on the skin from dark to slightly lighter green. If in doubt, gently lift and twist a fruit: if it comes away easily, it is almost ripe and will be at peak flavor in a few days. If the stalk breaks, wait for a few days longer. Several harvests need to be made because all fruits do not ripen simultaneously. Fruits of late-ripening cultivars and those grown in cool climates must be left on the tree until mature to develop their full flavor.

Store pears in cool conditions, laying them in slatted boxes. Do not wrap them since this makes the flesh discolor. The fruits of later-ripening cultivars should be conditioned before eating: keep them at room temperature for a day or two and eat when the flesh gives under gentle pressure by the thumb near the stalk. The flavor is then at its fullest.

Propagation

For most pear cultivars, chip- or T-budding or whip-and-tongue grafting (see "Propagation," p.368) onto a 'Quince A' or 'Quince C' rootstock is usually successful. Grafting over may also be used to change the cultivar of an existing tree to another, preferable cultivar (see p.379).

Double-working pear cultivars

The few pear cultivars that are incompatible with quince rootstocks need to be double-worked: a cultivar that is compatible with both the quince rootstock and the selected scion cultivar is used as an interstock between the two. The cultivar 'Beurré Hardy' is the most widely used interstock; 'Vicar of Winkfield' may also be used for all pear cultivars that require double-working. These include 'Dr. Jules Guyot', 'Marguerite Marillat', and 'Packham's Triumph'. Two methods of double-working may be used: double chip-budding and double grafting.

Double chip-budding entails carrying out chip-budding for two years in succession: in the first year, a scion of the interstock is budded onto a suitable quince rootstock; in the second year, a scion of the selected cultivar is budded onto the interstock on the opposite side. The method is as for chip-budding (see p.368).

For double grafting the same principle should be followed. Graft the interstock onto the quince rootstock in early spring using the whip-and-tongue method (see p.369). In late winter or early spring, cut back the grafted interstock and graft the incompatible cultivar scion onto the interstock. Alternatively, the incompatible cultivar scion may be budded onto the interstock in summer, following the grafting of the interstock in spring. Remove all shoots from the interstock as they arise, but retain those from the cultivar scion for strong growth in future years.

Double Budding
Insert the budchip 2in (5cm) above the first graft and on the opposite side, so that the resulting stem will grow out straighter when the bud develops. Cut off the interstock above the new bud once the scion shoot has developed. Remove any shoots on the interstock.

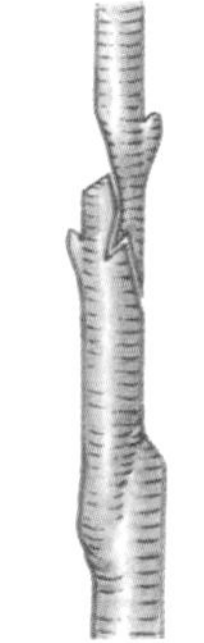

Double Grafting
This follows the same principle as double budding: cut back the interstock a year after it is grafted, once the sap starts to rise, and graft on the required scion. Leave 2in (5cm) between grafts; position the scion graft on the opposite side from the previous one.

Quinces (*Cydonia oblonga*)

Quinces are fruits grown mainly in temperate regions. As bushes, they reach 10–15ft (3.4–5m); they may also be trained as fans. The fruits are apple- or pear-shaped and are covered with grayish white down. The most widely grown cultivars are 'Champion', 'Orange', 'Portugal', and 'Smyrna'. Quince trees have a chilling requirement of 100–450 hours below 45°F (7°C) to flower.

Site and planting

Quinces require a reasonably sunny site. The protection provided by a nearby wall may be beneficial in cold areas. Moisture-retentive, slightly acid soils are preferred; marked alkalinity usually causes lime-induced chlorosis.

'Quince A' is normally used as a rootstock. Where trees are grown on their own roots, suckering may be difficult to control. Quinces are generally self-fertile, but the provision of pollinators is claimed to improve cropping levels. Plant quinces in spring if bare-root, or throughout the year if container-grown, spacing them approximately 12–15ft (4–5m) apart.

Routine care

Cultivation requirements are as described under "Care of tree fruits," p.362. Once established, quinces need little attention. Occasional feeding at the standard rate may be necessary, particularly on poor soils, while watering and mulching may also be required. Quinces are comparatively easy to grow, but fungal leaf spots (p.554) may be troublesome.

Pruning and training

Quinces fruit on spurs and on the tips of the previous summer's growth. Bushes may be left to grow into multistemmed trees or pruned in the early stages as for apples (see p.375), with an open-centered, well-spaced branch framework.

Pruning of established trees is minimal, with occasional thinning in winter of old, overcrowded growth. Not every lateral should be pruned, however, since this removes too many fruit buds.

Harvesting and storing

Pick the fruits when the skins have turned from green to gold, usually in late fall. Store fruits in boxes in a cool, well-ventilated, dark place. Do not wrap the fruits: quinces stored in plastic bags will discolor internally.

Because quinces have a strong aroma, they should be stored separately, so that they do not contaminate the flavor of other fruits. Quinces are often used in preserves.

Propagation

Quince trees may be propagated either by chip-budding onto 'Quince A' rootstocks in summer (see p.368) or by taking hardwood cuttings in fall (see p.370).

Quince Tree
Leave a generous grass-free area around young quinces, so that all the nutrients are absorbed by the trees and not shared with the grass.

Medlars (*Mespilus germanica*)

Medlars are decorative, spreading trees with golden fall color and large white or pinkish white flowers in mid- to late spring. Medlar trees are most commonly grown as bushes, or as half-standards where larger specimens are required. They are self-fertile and have a chilling requirement of 100–450 hours below 45°F (7°C). The fruits are apple-shaped and somewhat flattened with prominent, horny calyces. Their flavor is an acquired taste; the fruits are used to make preserves.

RIPENING MEDLARS
The small, brown fruits ripen in fall and measure 1–2in (2.5–5cm) across.

Site and planting
A sunny, sheltered site is preferable, although medlars tolerate partial shade. They may be grown in a wide range of soils, with the exception of those that are highly alkaline or poorly drained. Adequate moisture is essential to obtain strong growth and a good crop of fruits.

Trees grown for the quality of their fruits are usually grafted on 'Quince A' rootstocks, although half-standards are sometimes available on seedling pear rootstocks. Medlar trees are best planted in late fall to winter. Half-standards should be spaced at a distance of 25ft (8m), and bushes at 14ft (4.75m).

Routine care
Cultivation requirements are generally as for apples (see p.372). Medlars may sometimes be affected by leaf-eating caterpillars (p.551) and fungal leaf spots (p.554).

Pruning and training
Train a bush tree as for apples (see p.375). For half-standards, pruning is initially as for apples. Once the main framework is established, occasionally thin branches in winter to maintain an open framework, removing overcrowded, diseased, or dead growth.

Harvesting and storing
Leave fruits on the tree for as long as possible so that they develop their full flavor. Pick them in late fall when the stalk parts easily from the tree, preferably in dry weather. The fruits are unpalatable immediately after picking and must be stored before use. Dip the stalks in a strong salt solution to prevent rotting, then store the fruits, calyces downward, on slatted trays, so that the fruits do not touch. Use when the flesh has become soft and brown.

MEDLARS

Propagation
Propagate by chip- or T-budding (see pp.368 and 369) or whip-and-tongue grafting (see p.369).

Plums, gages, damsons, and bullaces (*Prunus* spp.)

Among the many kinds of plum are European plums (selections of *Prunus domestica*); gages (*P. domestica* and *P. insititia*); damsons, Mirabelles, and bullaces (*P. insititia*); cherry plums (*P. besseyi* hybrids); and the Japanese plums (*P. salicina*, syn. *P. triflora*). Crosses of Japanese plums with native American plums (such as *P. americana*) have produced hybrids that combine the size and sweetness of the Japanese plums with the hardiness of American plums.

Regions with cool-temperate climates are ideal for European plums, damsons, and bullaces; in warmer areas with earlier springs, Japanese plums and Mirabelles are more widely grown. All types of plum prefer areas that have plenty of sun and relatively low rainfall. Myrobalan plums are rarely grown for their fruit but are often used as vigorous rootstocks.

There is a wide range of cultivars adapted to different climates, and with more dwarfing rootstocks now available, plums are ideal for even small gardens. Damsons usually make smaller trees than plums. The compact pyramid tree and dwarf bush forms are particularly suitable for small gardens. For the choicest fruit in cool climates, grow fan-trained trees on warm, sunny walls. European plums and damsons have a chilling requirement of 700–1,000 hours below 45°F (7°C), and the Japanese plum one of 500–900 hours.

Site and planting

Plums need a warm, sheltered site to ensure that the flowers are pollinated successfully. Pollination requirements are complex – some cultivars are self-fertile, whereas others require suitable pollinators nearby.

Site
All plums flower early in spring, Japanese plums markedly so and cherry plums earlier still, so that spring frosts are always a hazard. They are, therefore, best planted in a relatively frost-free site. Plums need to be sheltered from wind to avoid damage to the trees and also to encourage pollinating insects.

Most soils are suitable, but avoid those that are highly alkaline or poorly drained. Plums on poor, sandy soils need extra feeding and watering (see "Feeding, watering, and mulching," p.384).

Rootstocks
'Pixy' (dwarfing) and 'St. Julien A' (moderately vigorous) are best for small to medium-sized trees, 7–12ft (2.2–4m). For trees up to 13ft (4.5m), choose 'Myrobalan B' (incompatible with some cultivars) or 'Brompton' (universally compatible). 'Marianna' is excellent for Japanese plums but is incompatible with some European plums. Plum trees tend to produce suckers, but this is less common with modern rootstocks.

ROOTSTOCKS

12ft (4m)
9ft (3m)
6ft (2m)
3ft (1m)

'Pixy' 'St. Julien A' 'Brompton' 'Myrobalan B'

Pollination
European plums and damsons may be self-fertile, partially self-fertile, or self-sterile. Fortunately, some very popular cultivars, such as 'Stanley', are self-fertile, but planting suitable pollinators nearby will ensure more consistent cropping. Cultivars that are not self-fertile must always be planted with compatible pollinators nearby. Some Japanese plums are self-fertile, but most give better results when planted near a suitable pollinator. Plum cultivars that will not pollinate certain others are indicated in the lists of recommended cultivars on pp.384 and 385, which also give details of flowering times. Seek advice about pollination of individual trees when buying.

Planting
This should be completed as early as possible in late fall or early winter because growth starts early in spring. In cold areas, plant in spring only.

PLANTING DISTANCES

TREE FORM	ROOTSTOCK	DISTANCE BETWEEN TREES	DISTANCE BETWEEN ROWS
Bush	'St. Julien A'	12–15ft (4–5m)	18ft (5.5m)
Half-standard	'Brompton' or 'Myrobalan B'	18–22ft (5.5–7m)	22ft (7m) minimum
Fan	'St. Julien A'	15–18ft (5–5.5m)	
Pyramid	'St. Julien A' or 'Pixy'	8–12ft (2.5–4m)	12–20ft (4–6m)

RECOMMENDED DESSERT PLUMS AND GAGES

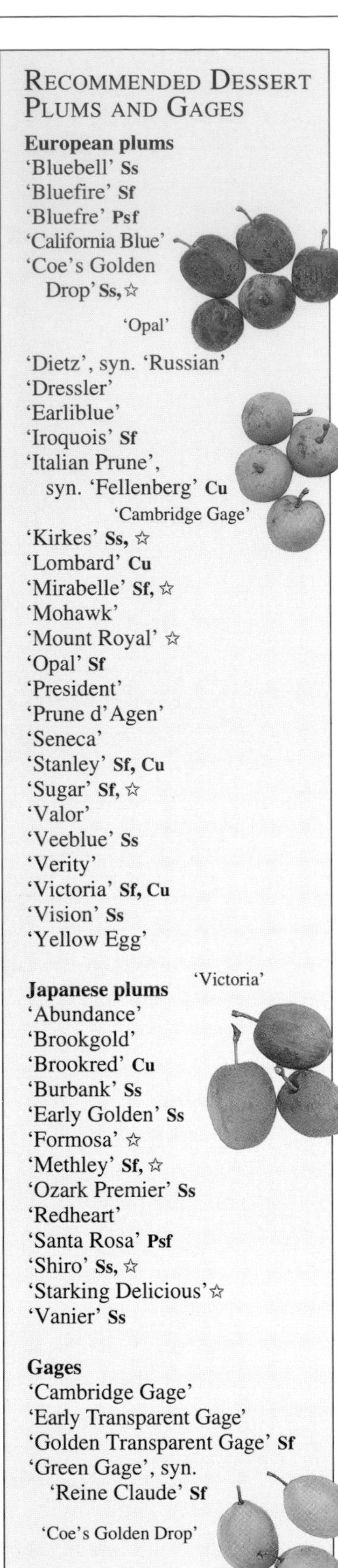

European plums
'Bluebell' **Ss**
'Bluefire' **Sf**
'Bluefre' **Psf**
'California Blue'
'Coe's Golden Drop' **Ss,** ☆

'Opal'

'Dietz', syn. 'Russian'
'Dressler'
'Earliblue'
'Iroquois' **Sf**
'Italian Prune', syn. 'Fellenberg' **Cu**

'Cambridge Gage'

'Kirkes' **Ss,** ☆
'Lombard' **Cu**
'Mirabelle' **Sf,** ☆
'Mohawk'
'Mount Royal' ☆
'Opal' **Sf**
'President'
'Prune d'Agen'
'Seneca'
'Stanley' **Sf, Cu**
'Sugar' **Sf,** ☆
'Valor'
'Veeblue' **Ss**
'Verity'
'Victoria' **Sf, Cu**
'Vision' **Ss**
'Yellow Egg'

'Victoria'

Japanese plums
'Abundance'
'Brookgold'
'Brookred' **Cu**
'Burbank' **Ss**
'Early Golden' **Ss**
'Formosa' ☆
'Methley' **Sf,** ☆
'Ozark Premier' **Ss**
'Redheart'
'Santa Rosa' **Psf**
'Shiro' **Ss,** ☆
'Starking Delicious' ☆
'Vanier' **Ss**

Gages
'Cambridge Gage'
'Early Transparent Gage'
'Golden Transparent Gage' **Sf**
'Green Gage', syn. 'Reine Claude' **Sf**

'Coe's Golden Drop'

'Laxton's Gage'
'Old Greengage'
'Oullins Gage'
'Reine Claude de Bavay' **Sf,** ☆

KEY
Sf *Self-fertile*
Psf *Partly self-fertile*
Ss *Self-sterile*
Cu *Also for culinary use*
☆ *Excellent flavor*

All trees are best staked for two years; stake those on 'Pixy' rootstocks permanently. Planting distances (see p.383) are determined by the chosen tree form and by the vigor of the rootstock.

Routine care

Feed and water trees regularly, and check for pests and diseases. Fruit thinning should be carried out as necessary. If spring frosts are likely, protect wall-trained trees in bloom with a burlap cover (see COLD AND WIND PROTECTION, pp.520–21).

Fruit thinning

This is an important procedure both to give larger, better-flavored fruits and to reduce the risk of branches breaking from the heavy weight of too many fruits. Fruitlets may be thinned early if the set is heavy. After the stones have formed and natural fruit drop has occurred, thin the remaining fruit to about 2–3in (5–8cm) apart for small fruits and 3–4in (8–10cm) for larger cultivars (such as 'Victoria'). Scissors are best for this job since they are quicker to use than pruners.

Feeding, watering, and mulching

Plums require plenty of nitrogen; apply a spring dressing at the rate recommended under "Care of tree fruits," p.362. Mulch annually with well-rotted manure or compost, and water as required, particularly in prolonged spells of hot weather. Plums planted against fences or walls will need more regular watering than those grown in the open.

Pests and diseases

Plums may be attacked by rabbits (see "Small animals," p.572), wasps (p.565), aphids (p.552), and plum curculio (p.564). Diseases that may affect plums include black knot gall (p.561), bacterial canker (p.571), and brown rot (p.564). Any trees that are badly infected with black knot, bacterial canker, or (less commonly) viruses (p.555) should be dug up and discarded without delay.

All stone fruit trees may be affected by the physiological disorder known as gummosis. Trees that have this problem exude a translucent, amber-colored, gumlike substance from the trunk and branches, while plums may also form gum around the stone within the fruit. The gum is produced by the trees as a result of stress caused by disease, adverse soil conditions, or physical damage caused by, for example, strong winds or a heavy crop. If gummosis is noticed, try to identify the cause and alleviate the problem if possible.

Birds may also be troublesome; if they attack the fruit buds, it may be necessary to place fine mesh nets over the trees during the winter to prevent damage (see also p.565).

PLUM BUSH

YEAR 1, EARLY SPRING PRUNING

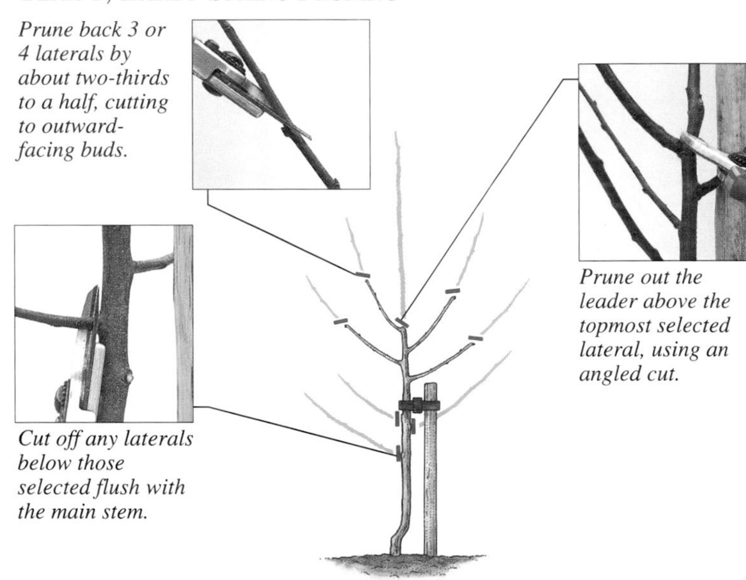

Prune back 3 or 4 laterals by about two-thirds to a half, cutting to outward-facing buds.

Prune out the leader above the topmost selected lateral, using an angled cut.

Cut off any laterals below those selected flush with the main stem.

Pruning and training

Plum trees produce fruit at the base of one-year-old shoots, as well as on two-year-old wood and spurs. Once trained, they require less pruning on unrestricted forms than apples or pears. In cool-temperate climates it is essential to prune in summer (after training) to minimize the risk of black knot (p.561). Trained trees require routine summer pruning to maintain their restricted shape. Remove any damaged or diseased branches immediately, cutting back to healthy wood.

Bush

In early spring when the buds are breaking, start training a newly planted feathered maiden. Select three or four strong, evenly spaced laterals, the highest at about 3ft (90cm) from ground level, and prune them by about two-thirds or a half to healthy, outward-facing buds. These laterals will form the

YEAR 2, EARLY SPRING PRUNING

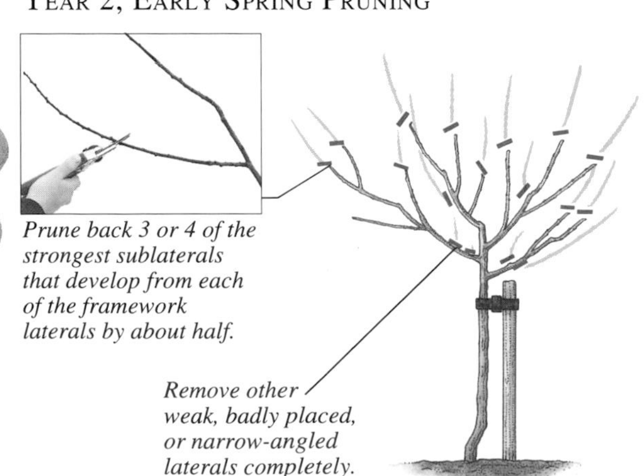

Prune back 3 or 4 of the strongest sublaterals that develop from each of the framework laterals by about half.

Remove other weak, badly placed, or narrow-angled laterals completely.

PRUNING A MATURE BUSH

If sublaterals are unproductive, damaged, or dead (as here), cut them back in summer to the point of origin or to a suitable replacement shoot.

basic framework of branches. Then prune out the leader, making an angled cut above the highest of the selected laterals. Cut back to the main stem unwanted laterals below those selected.

The following early spring, choose three or four of the strongest sublaterals that have developed on each of the pruned laterals and shorten them by half. To achieve a balanced framework, trim off weak or badly placed laterals and pinch out any shoots growing from the main stem. Subsequently, restrict pruning of young trees to the removal in summer of excessively vigorous or awkwardly placed growths. With older trees, thin some branches in summer to avoid overcrowding.

If using a maiden whip, prune it to about 3ft (90cm). The following spring, laterals should have developed, and it may then be trained as a feathered maiden.

Half-standard

Choose three or four well-spaced laterals on a feathered maiden; cut back the leader just above the uppermost lateral at 4½ft (1.35m), then prune each of the chosen laterals by one-third to a half. Remove any lower laterals. Subsequent pruning of the sublaterals and training to form an open-center head is the same as for a bush. Half-standard trees are less easy to manage than pyramid or bush plums when mature because of their greater size.

Spindlebush

Similar in shape to a plum pyramid (see p.386), the spindlebush requires a little more space but does not need the same annual summer pruning. Pruning and training are as for apple spindlebushes (see p.376), but prune in early spring when the buds break.

Tie down upright shoots and keep the top of the tree in check by removing the more vigorous shoots and retaining the less vigorous ones to produce fruit. In this way the conical shape is maintained.

Fan

Train a plum fan initially as for a peach fan (see p.389) to produce main branches or ribs to train against horizontal support wires. When

RECOMMENDED JAPANESE–AMERICAN HYBRID PLUMS

'Alderman'
'AU Producer'
'AU Roadside'
'Early Golden'
'Elite'
'Gracious'
'Kahinta' ☆
'La Crescent' ☆
'Pembina'
'Perfection' ☆
'Purple Heart'
'South Dakota'
'Superior' ☆
'Tecumseh' ☆
'Toka' ☆
'Underwood'
'Waneta'

'Waneta'

RECOMMENDED CHERRY PLUMS

'Compass'
'Red Diamond'
'Sapalta'

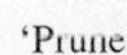
'Prune'

RECOMMENDED DAMSONS

'Blue Damson'
'Farleigh' **Psf**
'French Damson'
'Prune', syn. 'Shropshire' **Sf**, ☆

KEY
Sf *Self-fertile*
Psf *Partly self-fertile*
☆ *Excellent flavor*

ESTABLISHED PLUM FAN

SPRING PRUNING

Thin new side shoots to about 4in (10cm) apart.

Cut out any side shoots that are growing toward the center of the fan or are badly placed.

SUMMER PRUNING

Tie in any laterals needed to extend the framework or to replace older wood.

Cut back side shoots that are not needed for the permanent branch framework to 5 or 6 leaves.

Cut back wrong-pointing or awkward shoots to those facing in the required direction or flush with the stem.

AFTER FRUITING

In the fall, after the fruit has been harvested, prune back to 3 leaves all the side shoots that were shortened to 5 or 6 leaves earlier in the summer.

training the young fan, retain some side shoots to fill in gaps and pinch back others to one bud. Remove any very vigorous side shoots or those growing at an awkward angle.

On an established fan, remove side shoots growing inward toward the wall, fence, or center of the fan in spring or as soon as they appear. Thin the remainder to 4in (10cm) apart and pinch or cut them back to six leaves during the summer unless they are required to fill spaces in the fan framework. After the crop has been picked, shorten these shoots to three leaves.

Pyramid

Plant a feathered maiden against a strong stake and, in early spring, cut back the central leader to a healthy bud at a height of about 5ft (1.5m). Remove any laterals growing below 18in (45cm) from the ground. Shorten the remaining laterals over 9in (22cm) long by half their length. When the bases of the young shoots are turning woody later in the summer, cut back extension growth on the main branches and new (maiden) laterals to about 8in (20cm); at the same time, reduce sublaterals to about 6in (15cm). To start forming the pyramid shape, cut main branches and sublaterals back to downward-facing buds so that growth is more or less horizontal. Remove any laterals that are very vigorous or upward-pointing. Tie in the central leader to the stake, but do not prune it until the following spring, then shorten it by two-thirds of its new growth. Once the tree has reached a height of about 6ft (2m) on 'Pixy' or 8ft (2.5m) on 'St. Julien A', cut back the central leader. This should be delayed until late spring, however, because this reduces its subsequent growth; cut it back to a bud about 1in (2.5cm) from the old wood. Continue annual summer pruning as previously described, cutting branch leaders to downward-pointing buds and removing any excessively vigorous, upright shoots, especially those growing in the upper parts of the tree, to maintain the pyramid shape.

On mature pyramids, overcrowding will develop; in summer, trim off any badly placed, old wood as necessary. Maintain the pyramid shape by keeping any vigorous or dominant upper branches in check.

Harvesting and storing

For the best flavor, allow fruits to ripen fully; for freezing or preserving, pick them when ripe but still firm. In wet weather, gather the ripening crop before brown rot or wasps spoil it. Split skins may occur with some cultivars in moist conditions. Keep the fresh fruits in a cool, dark place and use within a few days.

Propagation

Chip- or T-budding is most usual (see pp.368 and 369); whip-and-tongue grafting (see p.369) is less reliable for plums than for apples and pears.

PLUM PYRAMID

YEAR 1, EARLY SPRING PRUNING

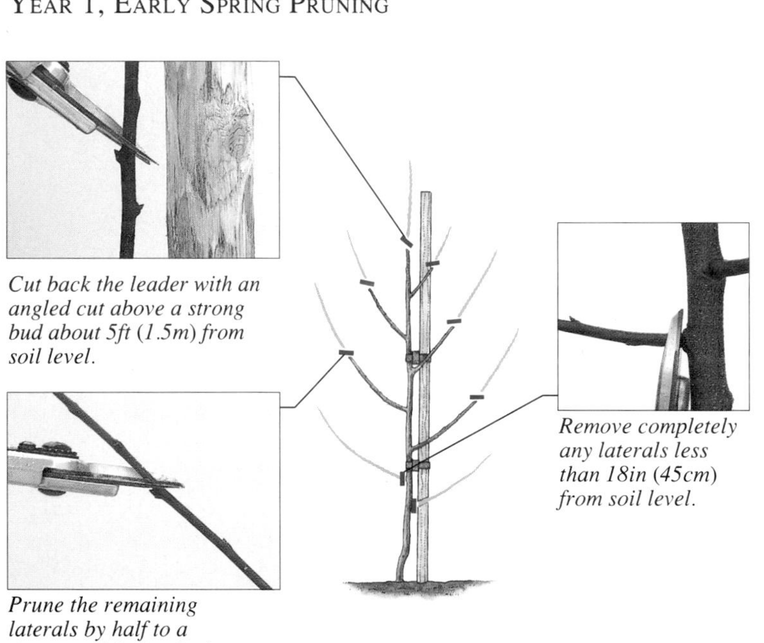

Cut back the leader with an angled cut above a strong bud about 5ft (1.5m) from soil level.

Prune the remaining laterals by half to a downward-facing bud.

Remove completely any laterals less than 18in (45cm) from soil level.

YEAR 1, SUMMER PRUNING

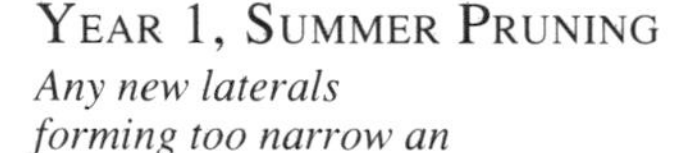

Any new laterals forming too narrow an angle with the main stem should be removed. Do not prune the central leader.

Cut back any sublaterals to 6in (15cm) with an angled cut just above a leaf.

Cut back new growth at the tips of the main branches to about 8in (20cm).

YEAR 2, EARLY SPRING PRUNING

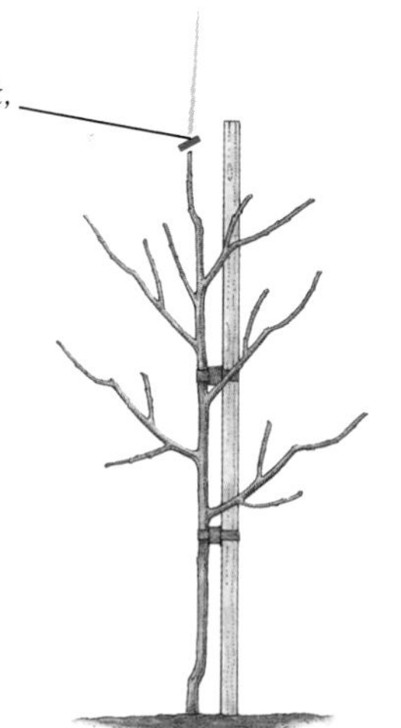

Just before bud break, shorten the central leader by two-thirds of its new growth.

ESTABLISHED PYRAMID, SUMMER PRUNING

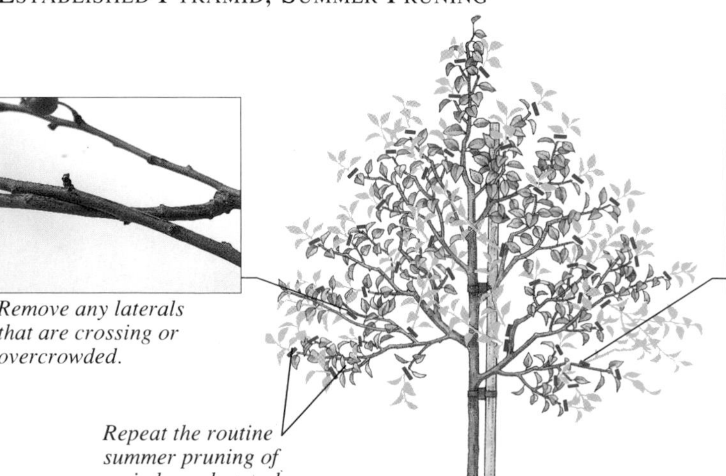

Remove any laterals that are crossing or overcrowded.

Repeat the routine summer pruning of main branches and sublaterals.

Cut back any dead or unproductive wood to a healthy shoot or to the point of origin.

Peaches and nectarines (*Prunus persica* and *P. p.* var. *nectarina*)

Peaches and nectarines are grown in many temperate regions. They have a chilling requirement of 600–900 hours below 45°F (7°C). Sunny, reasonably dry summers are essential to produce good crops; in cooler climates, peaches may be grown under cover. A range of cultivars is available for different climates (see *Recommended Peaches*, right, and *Recommended Nectarines*, p.388); they are yellow-, pink-, or white-fleshed. On cling peaches the flesh tends to cling to the stone; other peaches are known as freestone. The nectarine is a smooth-skinned form of the peach and requires very similar treatment, although it prefers warmer growing conditions.

Peaches and nectarines are usually grown in bush form, but fans are popular in temperate climates since they allow the fruits to receive maximum sunlight for ripening. Some naturally compact (genetic dwarf) cultivars are ideal for growing in pots.

Site and planting

Peaches flower early in the year and so should be protected from frost; a south-facing wall is an ideal site.

Site

Maximum sun is necessary, in a sheltered site that is not susceptible to spring frosts. In cooler climates, a sunny wall or a greenhouse is needed. Peach trees in areas with high rainfall may be badly affected by peach leaf curl (p.557) unless given some protection (see "Routine care," right).

Deep, fertile, slightly acid soils (pH 6.5–7) are ideal for growing peaches. If grown on sandy soils they need extra feeding and watering; shallow, alkaline soils often give rise to lime-induced chlorosis.

Rootstocks

The plum rootstock 'St. Julien A' is used to provide a moderately vigorous tree; 'Brompton' is used if more vigor is required. In some areas, seedling peach rootstocks are preferred, using vigorous selections resistant to root-knot nematodes.

HAND-POLLINATION

Peaches may be hand-pollinated once the blossoms are fully out. On a warm, dry day, use a small, soft brush to transfer the pollen from the anthers of one flower to the stigmas of another.

Pollination

Nearly all cultivars are self-fertile. An exception is 'J. H. Hale', which requires a nearby pollinator that flowers at the same time (seek advice when buying). In areas with wet or uncertain weather, pollination may be erratic or poor, but this can be improved by hand-pollination.

Planting

Plant peach trees by midwinter if possible, because growth starts very early. Stake bush trees for the first two years. Planting distances vary depending on the tree form and rootstock (see chart, below).

Routine care

For details of maintenance and cultivation requirements, see "Care of tree fruits," p.362. Lime-induced chlorosis may lead to manganese/iron deficiency (p.557), which must be treated as soon as possible. Protect the developing foliage of fan-trained peaches against peach leaf curl, and frost to some extent, with a plastic lean-to in winter and early spring.

PROTECTING PEACH FANS

In the fall, at leaf drop, cover the tree with a plastic shelter open at both ends for ventilation. This keeps the leaf buds dry and inhibits peach leaf curl spores from germinating.

Fruit thinning

To produce large fruits, thinning will be needed. When the fruitlets are about the size of hazelnuts, thin them to one fruit per cluster. Later, when they are walnut sized and some fruitlets have been shed naturally, thin the peaches to a spacing of 6–9in (15–22cm); in warm climates closer spacing may be used.

Feeding, watering, and mulching

In dry areas, watering is necessary to support both growth and fruiting.

RECOMMENDED PEACHES

Early
'Candor' **W, S, Y**
'Desert Gold' **W, S, Y**
'Earliglo' **Y**
'Early Redhaven' **Y**
'Flavorcrest' **W, Y**
'Floridahome' **W, Wh**
'Harbelle' **Y, S**
'Harbinger' **C, Y, ☆**
'Harrow Diamond' **Y**
'J.H. Hale' **Y**
'Maycrest' **W, Y**
'Saturn' **P**
'Springtime' **W, S, Wh**
'Suncrest' **W, Y**

'Earliglo'

Midseason
'Bonanza' **Gd, Y**
'Glohaven' **W, Y**
'Harbrite' **Y**
'Harken' **Y, ☆**
'La Feliciana' **W, Y**
'Peregrine' **Wh, ☆**
'Redhaven' **Y, S**
'Reliance' **Y**
'Rochester' **Y**
'Vivid' **P**

'Peregrine'

Late
'Babygold No. 5' **Gd, Y**
'Canadian Harmony' **Y**
'Cresthaven' **W, Y, ☆**
'Fayette' **W, Y**
'Loring' **Y**
'Zachary Taylor' **C, Y, ☆**

KEY
W *Warm climate needed*
Gd *Genetic dwarf (good for pot culture)*
C *Cling*
Y *Yellow flesh*
Wh *White flesh*
P *Pink flesh*
S *Semifreestone*
☆ *Excellent flavor*

ROOTSTOCKS

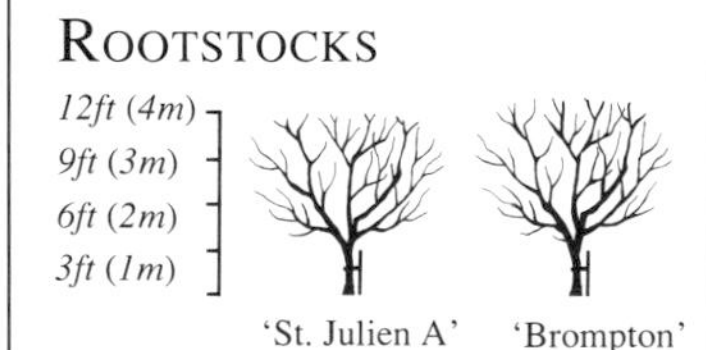

PLANTING DISTANCES

TREE FORM	ROOTSTOCK	DISTANCE BETWEEN TREES	DISTANCE BETWEEN ROWS
Bush	'St. Julien A'	15–18ft (5–5.5m)	18ft (5.5m)
	'Brompton' or seedling peach	18–24ft (5.5–7.5m)	24ft (7.5m)
Fan	'St. Julien A'	11–15ft (3.5–5m)	

THINNING

1 *As they form, thin peaches to 1 fruit per cluster, removing first any fruits growing toward the wall or fence.*

2 *These remaining fruits will need thinning again later, in order to leave 1 fruit every 6–9in (15–22cm).*

RECOMMENDED NECTARINES

Early
'Independence' W, ☆
'Nectared No. 1'
'Nectar Zee' ☆
'Pocahontas'
'Sun Red' W, ☆

Midseason
'Flavortop' W, ☆
'Hardired'
'Heavenly White' ☆
'Independence' W, ☆
'Nectared No. 4'

Late
'Red Gold' ☆

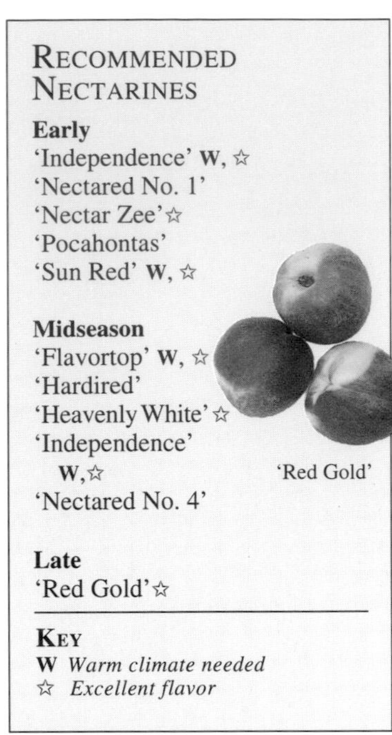
'Red Gold'

KEY
W *Warm climate needed*
☆ *Excellent flavor*

Mulching in spring once the soil has warmed up helps the soil retain its moisture. Adequate nitrogen is essential to promote new growth for cropping, and potassium is needed to enhance hardiness and fruit quality.

Pests and diseases
Peaches may be attacked by aphids (p.552), spider mites (p.552), earwigs (p.550), and root-knot nematodes (p.566); diseases include peach leaf curl (p.557), bacterial canker (p.571), gray mold/*Botrytis* (p.552), and gummosis (see "Plums: Pests and diseases," p.384).

Growing under cover

Peach trees under cover are best fan-trained so that the fruits receive maximum sun. The greenhouse must be able to accommodate a minimum span of 9ft (2.75m). Fertile, moisture-retentive soil is essential. A trained tree should be grown against suitable support wires spaced at 6in (15cm) intervals, starting at 15in (38cm) from the ground.Secure the wires so that they are held about 9in (22cm) away from the glass. Full ventilation is essential in winter to allow adequate chilling.

In early spring, but not too early if no heat is available, reduce ventilation to start the tree into growth. Keep the temperature at 40–50°F (8–10°C) for up to two weeks and then raise it to 68°F (20°C).

Trees under cover grow rapidly; always feed and water them well. Occasional copious watering is preferable to frequent light applications. Spray the foliage with a mist of tepid water, and damp down the greenhouse floor on hot days.

Pollinate the trees by hand when in bloom (see *Hand-pollination*, p.387). Do not spray or damp down during the flowering season, since this may prevent pollination. Start again once the flowers have dropped, to help control spider mites; stop spraying and damping down when the fruits begin to ripen.

Fruit thinning is essential to ensure that the fruits develop to their full size (see p.387).

Pruning and training

Peach and nectarine trees bear fruit only on shoots produced the previous year. The first fruits usually develop the third year after planting. Pruning is aimed at encouraging new growth and replacement shoots to maintain a well-balanced, open branch framework. There are three different kinds of bud: plump fruit buds; small, pointed growth buds; and triple buds that have a plump, central fruit bud with growth buds

PEACH BUSH

YEAR 1, EARLY SPRING PRUNING

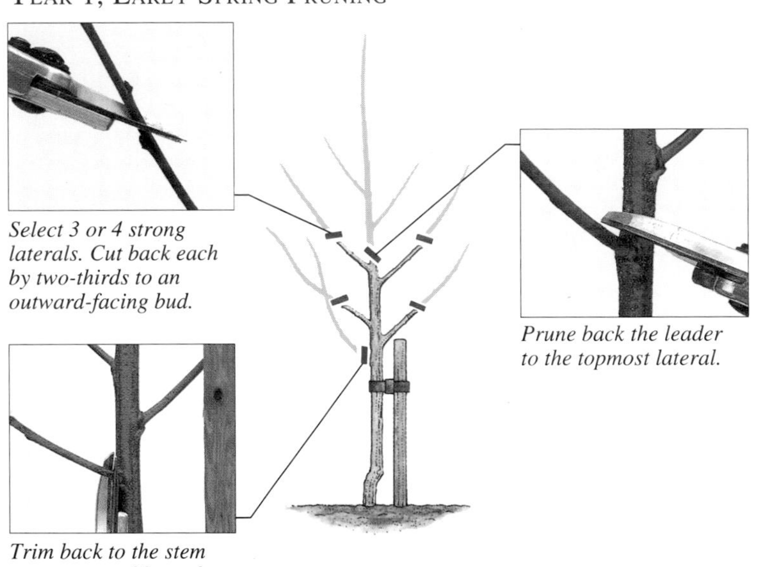
Select 3 or 4 strong laterals. Cut back each by two-thirds to an outward-facing bud.

Prune back the leader to the topmost lateral.

Trim back to the stem any unwanted laterals.

YEAR 1, SUMMER PRUNING

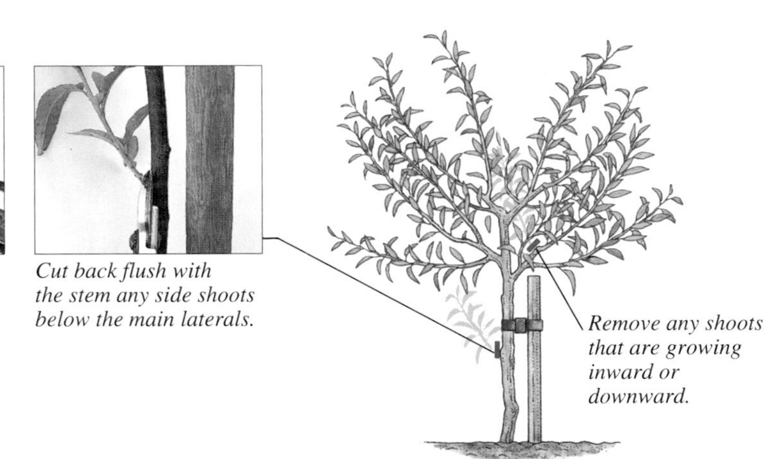
Cut back flush with the stem any side shoots below the main laterals.

Remove any shoots that are growing inward or downward.

YEAR 2, EARLY SPRING PRUNING

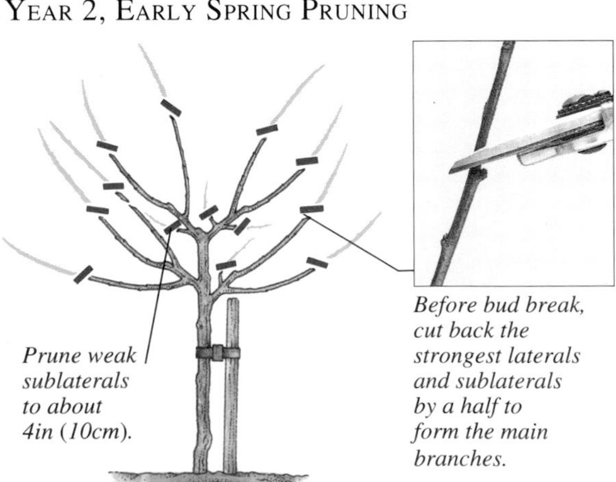
Prune weak sublaterals to about 4in (10cm).

Before bud break, cut back the strongest laterals and sublaterals by a half to form the main branches.

ESTABLISHED BUSH, EARLY SUMMER PRUNING

Cut back to a replacement bud or shoot up to a quarter of shoots that have fruited.

Remove old, unproductive wood, as well as any crowded or crossing branches.

on either side. On branches where extension growth is required, prune back to a growth bud, or, if there is no growth bud, to a triple bud.

Bush

Plant a feathered maiden between late fall and late winter. In early spring select three or four strong, well-spaced laterals with the topmost one about 2½–3ft (75–90cm) from the ground; prune back the leader to just above the top lateral. Prune back each of the selected laterals by two-thirds and remove all other unwanted laterals. During summer, remove any badly placed or low shoots that have developed.

The following early spring, before bud break, select strong laterals and sublaterals to form the basic framework. Cut these back by about half to a bud; prune any other sublaterals to about 4in (10cm).

Once the tree is well established, keep the center open by removing some of the older, fruited shoots each summer; occasionally, unproductive branches may need to be cut out.

Fan

Partially trained fans are sometimes available; if buying one of these, make sure that it has been correctly trained (as shown below). A fan should be developed from two branches trained out approximately 12in (30cm) above the ground at 40°. The central leader immediately above them should have been removed to channel vigor equally to both sides of the tree. A fan that retains its long, central leader and has side branches radiating out at an angle along its length will produce excessive growth at the top of the fan, leaving the base bare.

Formative pruning

Set up support wires as for an apple fan (see p.377). After planting a feathered maiden, choose two laterals about 12in (30cm) above the ground and remove the leader above them. Prune the selected laterals to about 15in (38cm) to form the first two "arms" and tie them to stakes at 40°. Prune back all other laterals to one bud as a reserve until the two main shoots have developed.

In summer, tie in the leader and selected side shoots to stakes as they develop, to start forming the framework "ribs." Select and train in two equally spaced shoots on the upper side of each branch and one underneath. Pinch back any other shoots on the stem to one leaf, and remove any shoots on the ribs that are badly placed. Before bud break in the second spring, cut back the extension growth on the two main arms by one-third to a strong bud to promote growth and the fan's development.

In early summer, continue tying in the selected developing shoots. Pinch back weak shoots and remove any that are very vigorous or pointing in the wrong direction.

The following early spring, shorten these new ribs by a quarter. During the third summer, select further shoots to complete the main ribs or branches of the fan. Any space in the center of the tree will soon be filled in by side shoots. Thin side shoots produced from the main branches early in the season to 4–6in (10–15cm) apart. Retain those lying naturally along the plane of the fan, but remove any that are awkwardly placed or growing straight outward or inward toward the wall or fence. Tie in the retained shoots; they should produce fruit the following year. Pinch back overlapping shoots to four to six leaves.

Routine pruning

The aim of pruning in spring is to ensure a constant supply of well-placed young shoots each year. At the base of each flowered shoot that will carry fruit in the forthcoming summer, there are usually two buds or young shoots; pinch out (disbud) one of these to prevent growth from becoming congested. The remaining one will carry fruit the following year. A second bud about halfway up the shoot may also be retained as a reserve in case the other one becomes damaged. After harvesting, remove the fruited wood, and tie in a replacement shoot at the base of each shoot that is cut out.

Continue this process annually; retain two replacement shoots if there is space in the framework. Without rigorous pruning, a peach tree soon becomes congested with old wood that bears no fruit.

PEACH FAN

YEAR 1, EARLY SPRING PRUNING

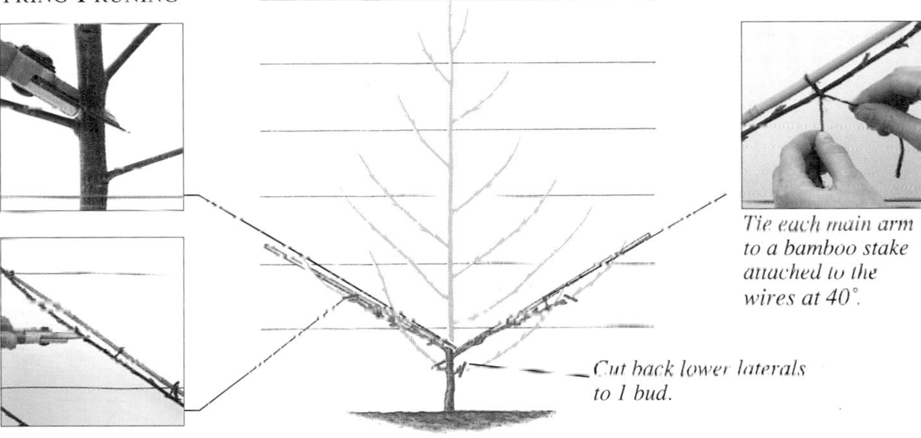

Choose 2 laterals, 1 on either side, 12in (30cm) from the ground, to form the main arms. Cut out the leader just above the higher lateral.

Prune back each arm to about 15in (38cm) to a strong bud to encourage side shoots or "ribs" to form.

Tie each main arm to a bamboo stake attached to the wires at 40°.

Cut back lower laterals to 1 bud.

YEAR 1, SUMMER PRUNING

Choose 2 side shoots on the top of each arm and 1 underneath and tie them to well spaced stakes attached to the wires. Pinch back other shoots to 1 leaf.

YEAR 2, EARLY SPRING PRUNING

In early spring, cut back the extension growth on the 2 main arms by one-third to strong buds facing in the required direction.

YEAR 2, EARLY SUMMER PRUNING

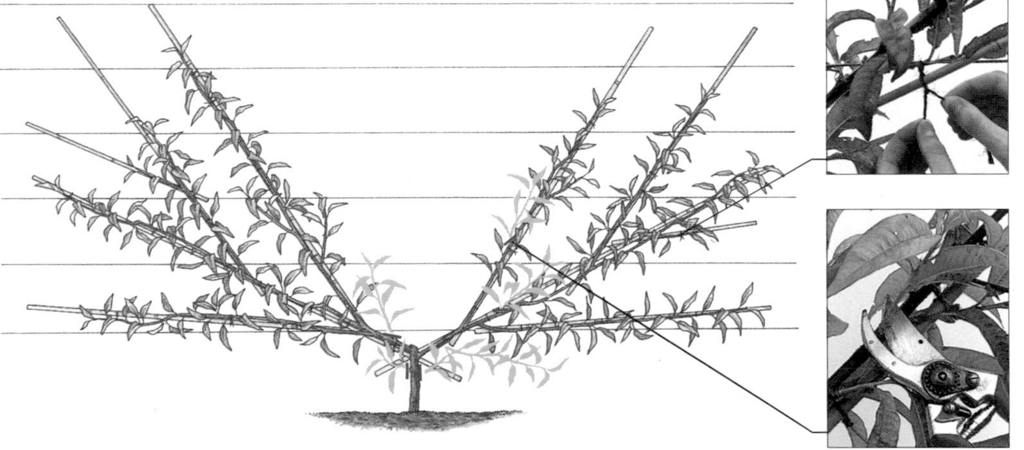

Train in developing side shoots by tying them to stakes to extend the permanent framework.

Cut back any wrong-pointing side shoots to the point of origin, and remove any shoots emerging below the 2 main arms.

YEAR 3, EARLY SPRING PRUNING

Cut back each of the main ribs by a quarter to stimulate further growth and extend the framework.

YEAR 3, EARLY SUMMER PRUNING

Thin young side shoots to 4–6in (10–15cm) apart by pinching out unwanted shoots. Pinch out any shoots that are growing toward the wall or fence or in the wrong direction.

YEAR 3, SUMMER PRUNING

Pinch back any shoots that overlap the ribs to 4–6 leaves as they develop.

As the remaining side shoots develop, tie them to stakes to fill in the framework. These shoots should fruit the following year.

ESTABLISHED FAN, PRUNING AFTER FRUITING

Cut back each fruited shoot to a suitable replacement near its base.

Tie in the replacement shoot to fill the gap. These shoots should be evenly distributed over the whole fan.

Harvesting and storing

Harvest the fruits when they are fully ripe. Rest them in the palm of your hand and apply gentle pressure with your thumb on the part of the fruit nearest the stalk. If the flesh gives slightly, the fruit is ready for picking. For the finest flavor, peaches and nectarines are best eaten as soon as possible after picking. If necessary, they can be stored for a few days by placing the fruits in a container lined with soft material and keeping it in a cool place.

Propagation

Peaches and nectarines are usually propagated by chip- or T-budding (see pp.368 and 369) in summer. Seedling peaches are variable in quality but are often vigorous and may produce excellent crops.

Apricots (*Prunus armeniaca*)

Apricots are more difficult to grow than many other fruits. Not all cultivars thrive in certain areas, so always seek advice when selecting trees. The chilling requirement for apricots is 350–900 hours below 45°F (7°C), most cultivars being at the lower end of this range. They flower extremely early in the year.

Although dry, sunny summers are needed for successful cropping, drought conditions may cause serious bud drop late in the season. In cool climates, apricots may be grown under cover or fan-trained against a warm wall. In warm areas, the bush form is popular.

Site and planting

Apricot trees should be planted in a sunny, sheltered, and frost-free site in order to produce good crops of fruit. In cool areas, it is essential to grow them against a sunny wall or in a greenhouse to protect the flowers from low temperatures and frost in late winter and early spring.

A deep, slightly alkaline loam is the most suitable soil. Apricots are least likely to thrive on sandy and alkaline soils. It is also best to avoid planting them on heavy soils, particularly in areas that have cool, wet winters, since this may make them prone to dieback.

For rootstocks, both seedling apricots and peaches are widely used. A seedling peach rootstock tolerates wetter conditions than a seedling apricot rootstock and produces a smaller tree. The plum rootstock 'St. Julien A' is also often used; this is moderately vigorous.

Apricots are self-fertile; in cool areas, however, flowers should be pollinated by hand.

Plant in late fall or very early winter (see *Planting Distances*, opposite) before bud break. Stake bush trees securely for the first two years.

PLANTING DISTANCES

TREE FORM	ROOTSTOCK	DISTANCE BETWEEN TREES	DISTANCE BETWEEN ROWS
Bush	'St. Julien A'	15–18ft (4.5–5.5m)	18ft (5.5m)
	Seedling peach or apricot	18–22ft (5.5–7m)	22ft (7m)
Fan	'St. Julien A'	15–18ft (4.5–5.5m)	

Routine care

In general, maintenance and cultivation requirements are as for other tree fruits (see "Care of tree fruits," p.362).

In warm regions where heavy cropping is common, blossoms may need thinning to counteract biennial bearing (see p.372). Remove badly placed fruitlets, and carry out the main thinning after any fruits have dropped naturally and the stones have started forming. Thin so that there is a single fruit on each truss; leave about 3in (7cm) between fruits.

In cool areas, branch dieback occurs frequently; cut back affected branches to clean wood as soon as possible. Earwigs (p.550), bacterial canker (p.571), brown rot (p.564), and gummosis (see "Plums: Pests and diseases," p.384) cause problems. Use peach rootstocks where nematodes are prevalent.

Pruning and training

Fruits are borne both on one-year-old shoots and on older spurs. Pruning is aimed at maintaining the shape of the tree and removing any old, unproductive wood. If young trees are too vigorous, they may be root pruned (see p.366). Prune and train an apricot bush as for plums (see p.384).

Initial fan training of apricots is as for peaches (see p.389). On an established fan, thin young shoots to 4–6in (10–15cm) apart as they develop in the spring, and remove any shoots that are pointing downward, toward the center of the fan, or inward to the wall. Pinch back the sublaterals to six leaves if they are not required to fill gaps, and reduce any side shoots to one leaf later in the season. After fruiting, prune sublaterals to three leaves.

Harvesting

Pick the fruit when it is fully ripe and comes away easily from its stalk. Use immediately, because fresh apricots do not store well; alternatively, they may be frozen, used in preserves, or dried (see "Storing," p.367).

Propagation

Apricots may be propagated by chip- or T-budding (see pp.368 and 369), using seedling peach or 'St Julien A' rootstocks.

RECOMMENDED APRICOTS

Early
'Early Moorpark'
'Goldrich'
'Harcot' **W**
'Hemskerk' ☆
'Jerseycot'
'Skaha' **W**
'Sundrop' **W**
'Veecot'
'Velvaglow' **W**

'Hemskerk'

Midseason
'Alfred'
'Brookcot'
'Farmingdale'
'Goldcot' **W**
'Harglow'
'Hargrand' **W**, ☆
'Puget Gold' **W**
'Scout'
'Sunrise'
'Westcot'

Late
'Harlayne' **W**, ☆
'Harogem' **W**, ☆
'Harval' **W**
'Moorpark'
'Shipley's', syn. 'Blenheim'
'Vivagold' **W**

KEY
W *Warm climate needed*
☆ *Excellent flavor*

ESTABLISHED APRICOT FAN, EARLY SUMMER PRUNING

To fill gaps in the framework, tie in young side shoots once they have hardened at the base.

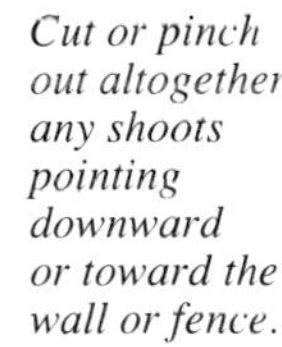

Cut or pinch out altogether any shoots pointing downward or toward the wall or fence.

Cut or pinch back to 5 or 6 leaves any sublaterals not needed as replacement shoots.

THINNING

Thin out the young shoots to leave them 4–6in (10–15cm) apart. Tie them in to the wires as they develop.

AFTER FRUITING

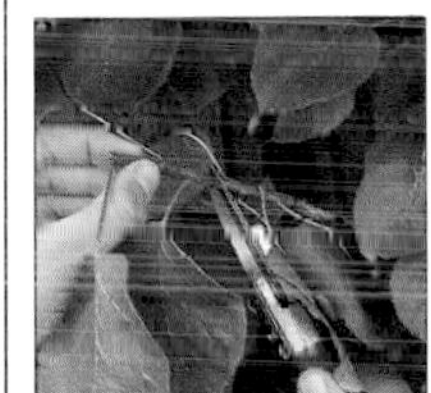

Using pruners, cut back to 3 leaves the shoots that were reduced to 6 leaves earlier in the summer.

Sweet cherries (*Prunus avium*)

Sweet cherry trees may grow to a height and spread of 25ft (7.5m) or more and, since most cultivars are self-sterile, two trees are often necessary to produce a crop. There are as yet no reliable dwarfing rootstocks (see p.392), so sweet cherries are best suited to an orchard or large garden. For an average garden, choose a self-fertile cultivar. Ideally, the tree should be fan-trained on a wall or fence: this restricts growth and makes it easier to protect the tree from birds and from rain just before picking, which may cause the fruits to split. Sweet cherries have a chilling requirement of 800–1,200 hours below 45°F (7°C).

Duke cherries are thought to be hybrids between the sweet cherry and the sour cherry. They are not very widely grown but, where chosen, require treatment and spacing similar to sweet cherries. Some Duke cherry cultivars are self-fertile, and combinations of sour cherries and Duke cherries are compatible.

Site and planting

Sweet cherries need a warm, sheltered site to produce a good crop. It is important to choose cultivars carefully to make sure that they will pollinate each other; this should be checked before buying trees (see "Pollination requirements," p.360).

ROOTSTOCKS

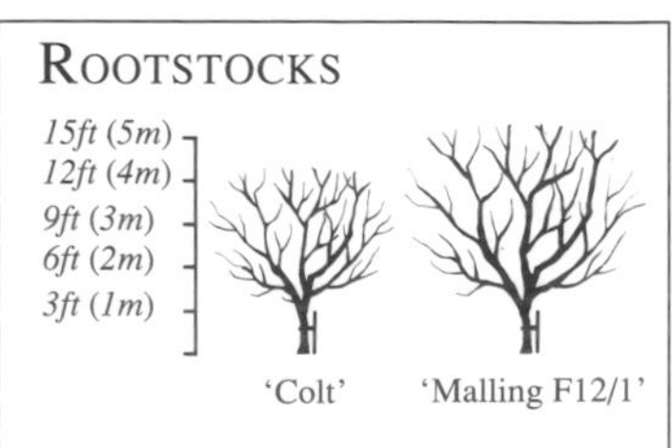

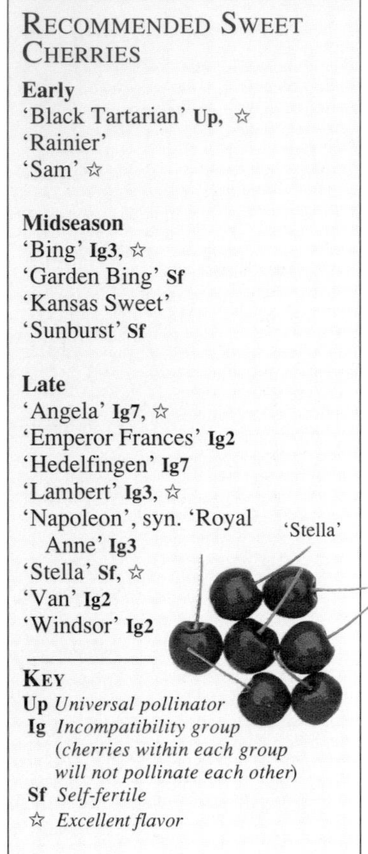

RECOMMENDED SWEET CHERRIES

Early
'Black Tartarian' **Up**, ☆
'Rainier'
'Sam' ☆

Midseason
'Bing' **Ig3**, ☆
'Garden Bing' **Sf**
'Kansas Sweet'
'Sunburst' **Sf**

Late
'Angela' **Ig7**, ☆
'Emperor Frances' **Ig2**
'Hedelfingen' **Ig7**
'Lambert' **Ig3**, ☆
'Napoleon', syn. 'Royal Anne' **Ig3**
'Stella' **Sf**, ☆
'Van' **Ig2**
'Windsor' **Ig2**

KEY
Up *Universal pollinator*
Ig *Incompatibility group (cherries within each group will not pollinate each other)*
Sf *Self-fertile*
☆ *Excellent flavor*

Site

Choose an open, sunny, and sheltered site. If the cherry is to be grown as a fan, the support must be at least 8ft (2.5m) high and 15ft (5m) wide, with a reasonably sunny exposure; a tree grown on a cold wall will produce fruit of poor quality and flavor. A good, deep, well-drained soil is essential, because trees grown on shallow, poor soils produce small fruits and are less long-lived.

Rootstocks

'Colt', a semidwarfing rootstock, is suitable for bush or fan-trained trees in small gardens. 'Malling F12/1', which is very vigorous, is used where there is space. Two new dwarfing rootstocks, 'Inmil' and 'Camil', are under trial; their longevity and cropping potential are as yet unproven.

Pollination

The pollination requirements of sweet cherries are complex. The majority are self-sterile, and they fall into distinct groups within which any combination is incompatible. Unless a self-fertile cultivar is obtained, it is important to choose a pair of trees that are from different groups and that flower at the same time. A few sweet cherries are universal pollinators; that is, they will pollinate any cherries that flower at about the same time (see *Recommended Sweet Cherries*, left).

Planting

Sweet cherries should be planted in late fall or winter if bare-root, or at any time if container-grown. Construct the necessary supports and wires before planting fan-trained plants. Allow 15–18ft (5–5.5m) between trees that are to be fan-trained and between half-standards.

Routine care

Fruit thinning is unnecessary. Little or no feeding should be needed, apart from mulching (see "Care of tree fruits," p.362.) If growth is poor, apply ammonium sulfate at the rate of 1oz/sq yd (35g/sq m) of area under the canopy. Sweet cherries need thorough watering in dry conditions, but sudden watering on dry soils may cause the fruits to split.

As the fruits begin to color, protect them from birds by draping netting over fan-trained trees. Bush and half-standard trees are difficult to net, however, so pick fruits as soon as they ripen.

The most likely pests and diseases to afflict sweet cherries are cherry aphids (see "Aphids," p.552), tent caterpillars (p.553), brown rot (p.564), black knot (p.561), and bacterial canker (p.571); cut out any branches with signs of black knot or bacterial canker as soon as they are noticed.

Pruning and training

Sweet cherries fruit on spurs on two-year-old and older wood. Mature trees should be pruned in summer to restrict vegetative growth and induce the formation of fruit buds. Train and prune half-standards and bushes as for plums (see p.384).

Fan

Sweet cherry fans are established as for peaches (see p.389). If there are conveniently placed laterals on a feathered maiden, however, it may be possible to select four rather than two laterals to speed up the development of the fan. Tie these laterals to stakes (attached to wires), which radiate out at 35–45° from the stem. In the spring following planting, prune back the selected shoots to 18–24in (45–60cm) and remove all other laterals that have developed.

During the summer, select two or three well-placed shoots from each branch and tie them in to fill the available space; remove the remainder. All branches or ribs on the young tree may be tip pruned at bud break (but never earlier) to reduce the risk of black knot and bacterial canker.

On older fans, spurs may be thinned or shortened in spring (see "Winter pruning," p.374) and branch leaders pruned to shorter replacement laterals to reduce height. In summer, pinch back all shoots not needed for the framework to six leaves, then to three after fruiting. Upright or very vigorous growths should be removed or tied horizontally to prevent the fan from becoming unbalanced.

Harvesting and storing

Pick fruits when fully ripe, complete with stalks, and eat or cook them immediately. If the fruits are to be frozen (see p.367), pick when firm.

Propagation

Chip- and T-budding are the usual ways to propagate (see pp.368 and 369). 'Colt' rootstocks are compatible with all cultivars, as is the more vigorous 'Malling F12/1' rootstock.

ESTABLISHED SWEET CHERRY FAN, SUMMER PRUNING

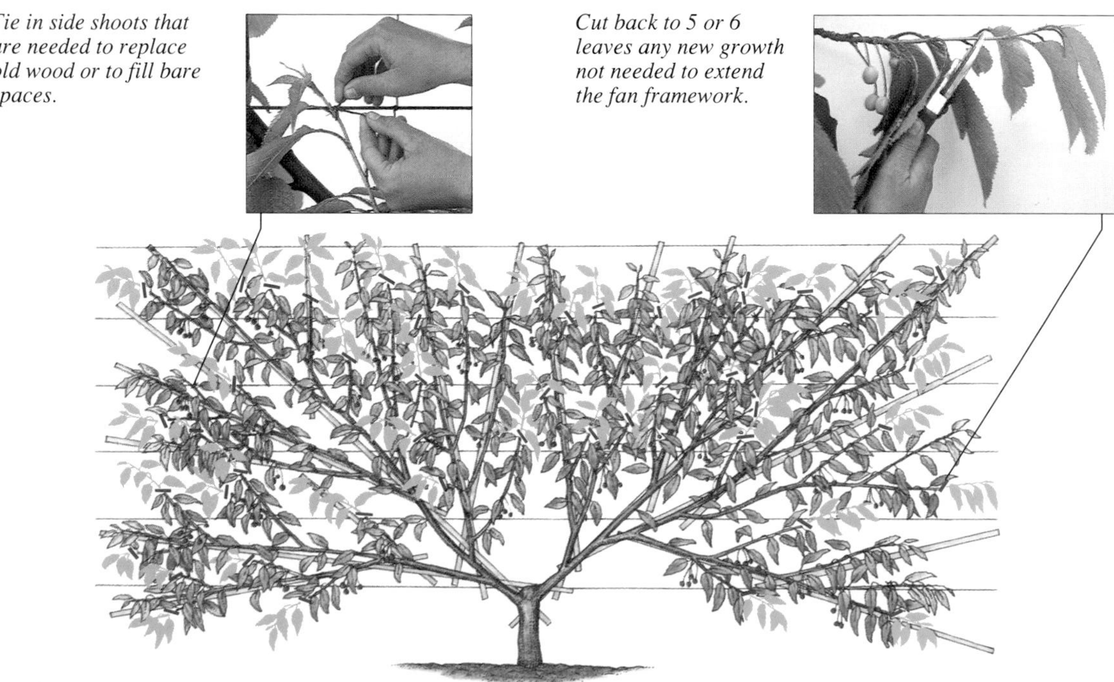

Tie in side shoots that are needed to replace old wood or to fill bare spaces.

Cut back to 5 or 6 leaves any new growth not needed to extend the fan framework.

AFTER FRUITING

After the crop has been harvested, cut back all the laterals that were pruned to 6 leaves in early summer to 3 leaves.

Sour cherries *(Prunus cerasus)*

Sour or acid cherry trees are much smaller than sweet cherries, and all cultivars are self-fertile, so they are more suitable for the average garden. The fruiting habit also differs in that the crop is borne mostly on one-year-old shoots produced the previous summer. The fruit is not usually eaten raw but is prized for preserves and other culinary uses. Sour cherries have a chilling requirement of 800–1,200 hours below 45°F (7°C).

Site and planting

Site and soil requirements are generally as for sweet cherries (see p.391), but sour cherries are hardier and may also be grown against a north- or east-facing wall or fence.

The recommended rootstock, as for sweet and Duke cherries, is 'Colt'. It is best to obtain cultivars such as 'Meteor' (the most popular) from a specialist fruit supplier since inferior, less fertile selections exist.

ROOTSTOCK

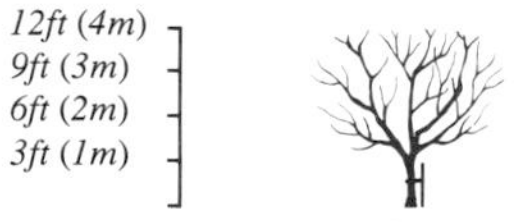

12ft (4m)
9ft (3m)
6ft (2m)
3ft (1m)

'Colt'

Plant trees to be trained as bushes and fans 12–15ft (4–5m) apart, and for fans provide a minimum support height of 7ft (2.2m).

Routine care

Sour cherries have the same cultivation requirements as sweet cherries (see p.391). Greater attention to feeding, particularly with nitrogen, may be necessary to encourage young replacement shoots, but do not overfeed. Irrigation is important in dry areas. Netting is essential to protect the fruits from birds (see p.363). Since sour cherries may be trained into small tree forms, such as the bush or dwarf pyramid, they may be grown in a fruit cage. Sour cherries are affected by the same pests and diseases as sweet cherries (see "Routine care," opposite).

Pruning and training

Sour cherries are pruned on a renewal system to produce a constant supply of one-year-old wood on which fruit is produced. A proportion of the older wood should be removed each year. Prune trees in spring and summer, since this reduces the risk of leaf diseases.

Fan

This is trained as for a peach fan (see p.389). Renewal pruning to encourage young growth once cropping starts is important because of the restricted space. In spring, on an established fan, pinch out badly placed or overcrowded new shoots and thin the rest to leave them 4in (10cm) apart. Tie these into support wires as they develop. Retain one or, where space permits, two developing shoots low down on each fruiting shoot. Tie in one of these to replace each fruiting shoot that is cut out after harvesting. The second shoot may be used as a reserve in case the first is damaged, or to fill a gap in the fan. To rejuvenate older fans, prune back to young shoots on older wood in spring and fall.

RECOMMENDED SOUR CHERRIES

Early
'Early Richmond' **Sf**

Midseason
'Montmorency' **Sf**

Late
'Meteor' **Sf**

KEY
Sf *Self-fertile*

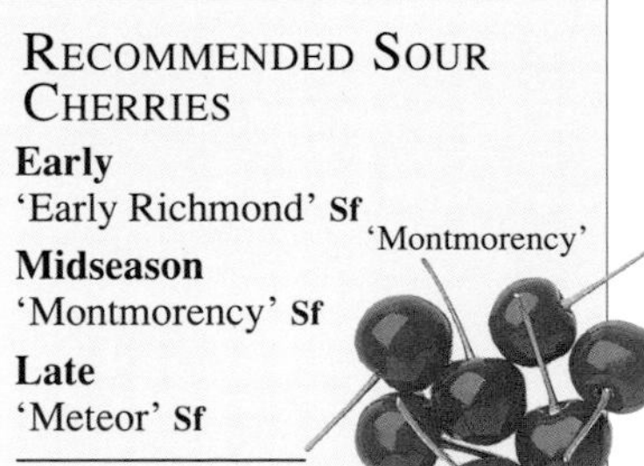

'Montmorency'

ESTABLISHED SOUR CHERRY FAN

SPRING PRUNING

Remove any wrong-pointing young shoots, cutting them back flush with the stem.

Thin the young, developing shoots to about 4in (10cm) apart, if necessary.

SUMMER PRUNING, AFTER FRUITING

Cut back each fruited shoot to a suitable replacement near its base.

Tie in the replacement shoots to maintain even spacing. These should fruit the following year.

Remove any wrong-pointing shoots that have developed and were not removed in the spring, cutting them back flush with the stem.

ESTABLISHED SOUR CHERRY BUSH, PRUNING AFTER FRUITING

Cut back a quarter of the fruited shoots to replacement shoots near the base of each.

Each year, cut back a few older, crossing, or unproductive laterals to replacement shoots.

Bush
The bush is built up as for a peach bush (see p.389). After the third or fourth year, once the bush is established, renewal pruning is essential. In early fall, after fruiting, cut back a quarter of the fruited shoots, preferably to replacement shoots, to maintain even spacing and leave room for the young growth that will carry the next year's crop. Remove old wood at the same time. If pruning is neglected, fruiting will decrease and be restricted to the tree's outer edge.

Harvesting

Hand-picking may injure the shoots and encourage infection, so cut stalks with scissors. Cook, freeze, or preserve soon after picking (see "Harvesting and storing," p.367).

Propagation

The usual methods are chip- and T-budding (see pp. 368 and 369). All cultivars are compatible with 'Colt' and 'Malling F12/1' rootstocks.

HARVESTING SOUR CHERRIES

Harvest by cutting each stalk close to the lateral, not by pulling, which may damage the bark and increase the risk of bacterial canker (see p.571).

Persimmons (*Diospyros kaki* and *D. virginiana*)

Asian persimmons (*Diospyros kaki*) are deciduous, slow-growing trees that will eventually reach a height of 30–50ft (10–15m) and a spread of about 30ft (10m). The fruits are globular, and they may be yellow, orange, or red when ripe. The hardier American persimmon (*D. virginiana*) attains similar dimensions; the fruits are typically smaller than those of Asians.

Outdoor cultivation of Asian persimmons in areas with a minimum temperature of 50°F (10°C) is possible, but a range of 61–72°F (16–22°C) during fall is preferable. Most Asian cultivars have a low chilling requirement of 100–200 hours below 45°F (7°C). During the growing season they need at least 1,400 hours of sunshine to fruit. American persimmons are hardier, with a greater chilling requirement.

Site and planting
A sheltered and sunny site is preferable. A well-drained and fertile soil is essential, with a pH of 6–7.

ASIAN PERSIMMON

Mature trees are relatively drought-resistant, but they require irrigation if there is inadequate rain in the growing season.

Vigorous seedlings of *Diospyros kaki* are suitable as rootstocks, but *D. virginiana* is most frequently used for this purpose.

Although some persimmon cultivars have both male and female flowers on the same tree, a number have only one or the other. The most widely grown cultivars have only female flowers; these will produce fruit without pollination, but the fruits are small and astringent. A pollinator cultivar, with male flowers, must therefore be grown nearby. A ratio of one pollinator plant to eight or ten female-flowering plants is usually adequate. Trees should be spaced at about 15ft (5m).

Prepare planting holes in well-manured ground; add organic material and general-purpose fertilizer.

Routine care
Apply fertilizer around the trees every three to four months, using a general-purpose mixture with medium nitrogen levels. Conserve moisture in the soil by mulching with organic matter, and water regularly in the dry season. Keep the ground around the trees weed-free.

The major pests that affect persimmons grown in the open are thrips (p.553), mealybugs (p.552), scale insects (p.554), and fruit flies (p.565). Common diseases that may cause problems include crown gall (p.561) and anthracnose and other fungal leaf spots (p.554).

Growing under cover
If growing persimmons in a greenhouse, plant them in prepared beds or in large containers with a minimum diameter of 14in (35cm); use a very fertile soil mix incorporating a general-purpose fertilizer with medium nitrogen levels. Maintain a temperature of at least 61°F (16°C) and a humidity of 60–70 percent. Water regularly during the growing season and apply a general-purpose fertilizer every three to four weeks.

It is necessary to pollinate the flowers by hand for a successful fruit set (see *Hand-pollination*, p.387). During the summer, move plants in containers into the open; leave them outside in the fall until their chilling requirement has been met.

Pruning and training
Cultivars vary greatly in vigor. Dwarf and semidwarf cultivars are trained in a similar way to an apple spindlebush (see p.376). Prune young trees for the first three years during the dormant season to form a framework. Restrict all subsequent pruning to the removal of crowded or unproductive branches, and to cutting back branch leaders annually by about one-third of their new growth.

Harvesting and storing
Pick fruits when they are fully ripe. Cut fruits from the tree, leaving the calyx and a short fruit stalk attached. Seal the fruits in clear plastic bags and store them at 32°F (0°C); they should remain in good condition for up to two months.

RECOMMENDED PERSIMMONS

American
'Early Golden'
'Meader'
'Ruby'

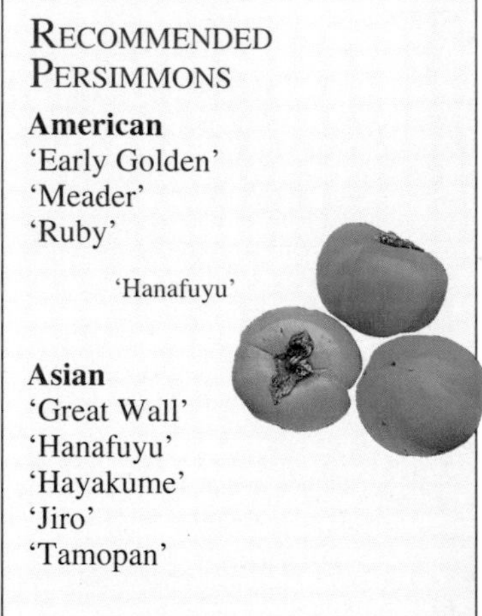

'Hanafuyu'

Asian
'Great Wall'
'Hanafuyu'
'Hayakume'
'Jiro'
'Tamopan'

Propagation
Persimmon trees may be propagated by seed, by grafting, from cuttings, or from rooted suckers.

Sow seed taken from mature fruits immediately in containers; kept at 82°F (28°C), it usually germinates in two to three weeks. In 12 months, the seedlings provide stocks suitable for grafting. Handle seedlings carefully when transplanting.

Cultivars may be propagated by chip- or T-budding (see pp.368 and 369) or by whip-and-tongue grafting (see p.369). Softwood cuttings (see p.53) taken in summer and treated with hormone rooting powder should root in a mist unit with basal heat.

Rooted suckers may be detached from the base of the parent tree (provided that it has not been budded or grafted). Establish them in containers before planting them out in their final positions.

Figs (*Ficus carica*)

Figs are among the oldest fruits in cultivation and belong to the family Moraceae. They have a low chilling requirement of 100–300 hours below 45°F (7°C) and thrive in regions with a long, hot growing season.

Site and planting

Figs require a sunny position and in cool areas need a wall for more warmth and protection from severe cold; this should be at least 10–11ft (3–3.5m) wide by 7ft (2.2m) high.

Figs prefer slightly alkaline, deep, rich, moisture-retentive soils and a warm, dry climate. Cooler, wetter conditions induce too much growth, with poorer crops. When the pH is less than 6, lime the soil (see p.533).

Where space is limited, a concrete or brick pit, or box, may be built below soil level to restrict the root system and produce a smaller tree. The pit should be 2ft (60cm) square and have a base that is not solid but filled with broken bricks or stones to a depth of 10–12in (25–30cm); this will provide drainage and restrict root growth downward.

In cool climates, figs may also be grown in pots placed in a sunny, sheltered site and transferred to cold but frost-free conditions in winter. Use a container 12–15in (30–38cm) in diameter, with several large drainage holes, and filled with a soil-based potting mix.

No specific rootstocks have yet been introduced, and trees are grown on their own roots. Modern cultivars are self-fertile.

Select two-year-old, potgrown specimens and plant these in spring, teasing the roots gently loose from the soil ball before planting. Space unrestricted trees 20–26ft (6–8m) apart; those planted in a pit need only half this spacing.

Routine care

To overwinter branches carrying the embryo figs, tie a dense layer of straw around them (see also COLD AND WIND PROTECTION, *Burlap and Straw Cover*, p.520). At the same time, remove any unripe figs from the previous summer. It may be necessary to protect the ripening fruits against birds and wasps.

FRUIT PLACEMENT

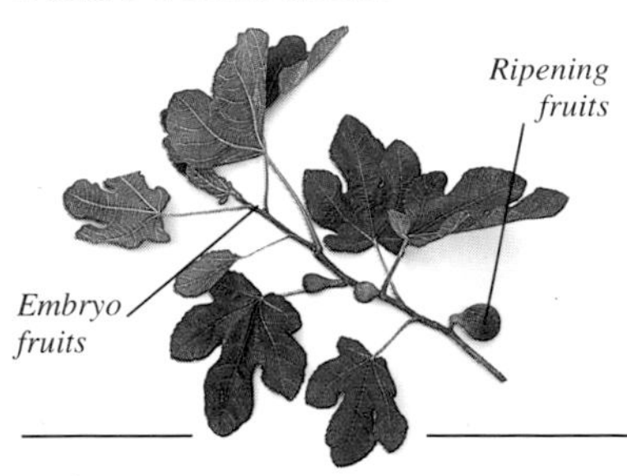

Feeding, watering, and mulching

A spring mulch of well-rotted manure is all that is normally required, but trees with restricted roots need extra nutrients. This may be in the form of a balanced fertilizer applied at a rate of 2oz/sq yd (70g/sq m) of root area, and supplemented during the summer with occasional liquid feeds. Avoid overfeeding.

Watering is essential in hot, dry weather, especially where the roots are restricted. Potgrown figs need regular watering throughout the growing season. Repot them and prune the roots every two years.

Pests and diseases

Figs in the open are usually problem free, but wasps (p.565) and birds (p.565) may attack fruits. When growing fig trees under cover, spider mites (p.552), mealybugs (p.552), whiteflies (p.552), wasps (p.565), mice (p.568), and *Nectria* canker (p.570) may be troublesome.

Growing under cover

In cool areas, fan-trained figs may be grown under cover and will crop more regularly than in the open. The roots must be contained to restrict growth. Once growth starts, water regularly, but reduce watering as the fruits ripen, to prevent the skins from splitting. Prune as for figs grown outdoors, but leave a more open tree to allow as much light as possible to reach the leaves and fruit.

Pruning and training

In warm climates, figs need only light pruning and are usually grown in bush form. Two crops per season are normally produced, an early one from embryo figs (about the size of small peas) formed late in the previous season, followed by the main crop, which is both formed and ripened during the same summer. Meanwhile, further embryo fruits develop to repeat the process.

In cool climates, figs are trained either as open bushes or as fans. Only the first crop from embryo figs will have time to ripen. Remove those that do not ripen to concentrate the tree's energies into producing new embryo fruits.

ESTABLISHED FIG BUSH

SPRING PRUNING

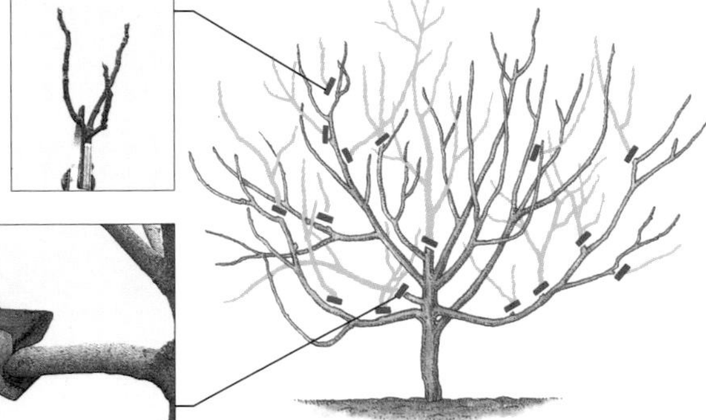

Cut back cold-damaged shoots to healthy wood and thin out wrong-pointing shoots and any that are overcrowded.

Cut out a proportion of the remaining shoots or, on older trees, branches to 1 bud to promote new growth.

SUMMER PRUNING

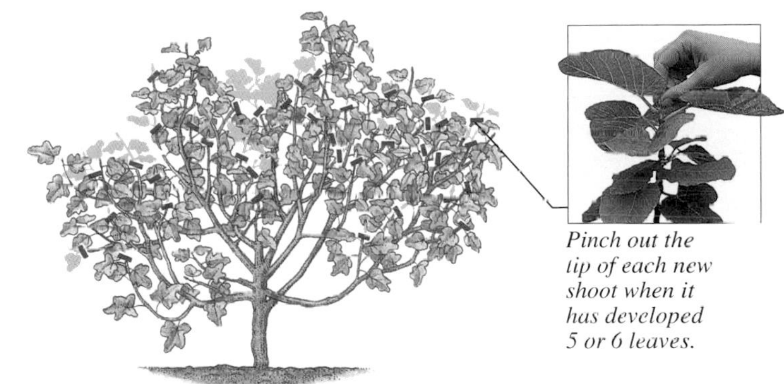

Pinch out the tip of each new shoot when it has developed 5 or 6 leaves.

Bush

Purchase a tree with three or four branches rising about 2ft (60cm) above ground. Prune these back by half their length in the first winter to encourage further branches to form and establish a basic framework. Potgrown trees should branch at 15in (38cm) from the base so that they are compact and not top-heavy.

Pruning of established trees differs with the climate. In warm climates in spring, shorten spreading branches to more vertical shoots and leave some growth in the tree's center to protect the bark from sun scorch. In cooler climates, remove all crowded, crossing, or frost-damaged branches; keep the center open by taking out all upright shoots and pruning to buds on the lower sides of branches.

Lengths of bare wood should be cut back to one bud to promote new growth. In the summer, pinch out new shoots or side shoots to five or six leaves to encourage fruit to form.

Fan

Plant a two-year-old tree with two or three strong shoots. Tie down the two best-placed as for peach fans (see p.389) and tip prune lightly. Prune back trees without suitable side shoots to about 15in (38cm) to encourage lateral growth. The fan is then developed as for peaches but with greater space between branches to allow for the fig's larger foliage.

Prune the established fan in early spring to remove old, fruited wood and any that is cold-damaged or badly placed; leave the younger wood. Also prune back a proportion of younger shoots to one bud to induce fresh growths close to the main branches. Wherever possible, tie in the unpruned shoots to fill any

RECOMMENDED FIGS

Early
'Celeste' ☆
'Osborne Prolific'
'White Marseilles' ☆

Midseason
'Alma'
'Brown Turkey' ☆
'Brunswick'

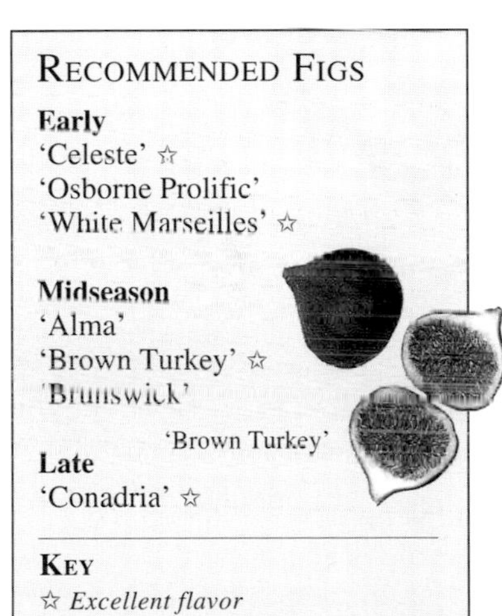

'Brown Turkey'

Late
'Conadria' ☆

KEY
☆ *Excellent flavor*

spaces and remove all others. Pinch out the tips of new growths to five leaves in midsummer. The resulting new shoots should then develop embryo fruits for overwintering.

Harvesting and storing

Pick the fruits when fully ripe. Ripe fruits tend to hang down, are very soft to the touch, and may have slight splits in the skin. Figs are best eaten fresh but may also be dried.

Propagation

Seed-raised plants vary in fruit quality. Hardwood cuttings of one-year-old wood from selected cultivars should be used. Take cuttings (see p.370) 12in (30cm) long and insert them in well-prepared, well-drained ground. Protect them with cloches. Figs may also be propagated by rooted suckers, severed from the parent tree and transplanted.

ESTABLISHED FIG FAN

SPRING PRUNING

Once all risk of frost has passed, cut all cold-damaged shoots back to their point of origin.

Cut back a proportion of young shoots to 1 bud to encourage replacement growth that will produce embryo fruits.

Tie in the shoots so that they are evenly spaced over the fan.

Cut off wrong-pointing shoots to the point of origin or to a well-placed sublateral.

Cut back a proportion of old, bare wood to 1 bud or node to promote new growth.

SUMMER PRUNING

Pinch back new shoots to 5 leaves to encourage embryo fruits to form in the leaf axils.

Mulberries (*Morus nigra*)

Mulberries belong to the Moraceae family. Black mulberries reach a height of 20–30ft (6–10m) and are grown for their fruit. White mulberries (*M. alba*) are not usually grown for their fruit.They grow up to 10ft (3m) tall. The chilling requirement is high, and the trees begin growth late in the season.

Site and planting
Moist, slightly acid soils are preferable. Mulberries are usually grown on their own roots and are self-fertile. Plant in late fall, spacing trees 25–30ft (8–10m) apart; in cold areas, plant in spring.

Routine care
Cultivation is similar to that of apples (see p.372). Mulch and water in dry weather. Mulberries are generally pest- and disease-free.

Pruning and training
Mulberries are grown as either half-standards or standards. Prune only to establish a strong framework of four to five branches, and thereafter remove branches only if they are badly placed or crowded. The trees should be pruned when fully dormant in winter since shoots and roots bleed profusely if cut or damaged between early spring and fall. If bleeding does occur, cauterize the wounds as quickly as possible with a hot poker or other iron implement.

Harvesting and storing
Pick the fruit when fully ripe in late summer, or allow it to drop onto a suitable temporary surface (such as a sheet of plastic) to keep it clean. Eat mulberries fresh, or freeze them.

Propagation
Mulberries may be propagated by simple or air layering (see p.86) or by hardwood cuttings about 7in (18cm) long, taken with a heel (see p.83), known as "truncheons."

BLACK MULBERRY

Vines

VINES require warm, sheltered positions for successful fertilization and to ripen their fruits. Grapes, kiwi fruits, and passion fruits all belong to this group. In cool areas, they should be given a sheltered environment, or they may be grown under glass. Vines fruit on long, flexible stems of one-year-old wood and need to be pruned after fruiting each year to encourage them to produce a supply of new shoots; these grow rapidly and need to be carefully trained into their supports so that they receive the maximum amount of light and air.

Red table grapes

White table grapes

Kiwi fruits

Grapes (*Vitis vinifera*)

Through the ages grapes have traditionally been one of the choicest fruits for eating or for making wine. The European grape (*Vitis vinifera*) and its cultivars are generally considered to be of the highest quality. American grapes (*V. labrusca*, *V. riparia*, *V. rupestris*) have been hybridized with *V. vinifera* to widen the choice of cultivars for table and wine grapes in cooler climates and to improve disease resistance. In the warm, humid Gulf Coast region of the US, *Muscadina rotundifolia* (formerly *Vitis rotundifolia*) is grown.

The fruits need a hot, dry summer to ripen. Warm-temperate regions suit a wide range of cultivars; many cultivars may be grown successfully in cooler climates, however, in protected sites or in greenhouses. Decorative pergolas, arches, or other structures may support them. Pruning methods vary: cultivars grown for table grapes are pruned to produce fewer, higher-quality fruits; those grown for wine grapes are pruned to obtain the greatest quantity of fruits. Grapes are usually self-fertile and wind-pollinated.

Table grapes

It is comparatively easy to produce high-quality table grapes in warm areas. In cooler climates, they may be grown against a sunny, warm wall or, preferably, in a greenhouse. For details of greenhouse cultivation of table grapes, see "Growing under cover," right.

Site

A warm, sheltered, sunny site free from frost at flowering time is ideal. Grapes need a reasonably fertile, well-drained soil, with a pH of 6–7.5. Avoid planting them on very rich soil, since this encourages excess growth at the expense of fruits. Sharp drainage is essential for success because grapes will not tolerate wet soils; improve the soil or install a drainage system if necessary (for details, see SOILS AND FERTILIZERS, "Improving drainage," p.531).

In cool climates, grapes grown on a warm, sunny wall give reasonably good results but will not match the quality of grapes grown under cover. Early-ripening cultivars should be used for wall cultivation to obtain table fruits by late summer. Support vines with horizontal wires, held in place by vine eyes, 1–2in (2.5–5cm) from the wall.

Grapes are usually grown on their own roots, except in areas where *Phylloxera* is a hazard (see "Pests and diseases," right); in this case, seek local advice on which rootstock to use. The use of a rootstock may have other advantages, too, such as greater tolerance of a high pH or wet soil conditions, and control of overvigorous growth.

Planting

Cultivate the soil thoroughly before planting. In poor or sandy soils, add well-rotted manure or compost, then firm the area and water well. The soil by a wall is often dry, so thorough preparation, with the addition of ample organic matter, is usually required to improve water retention. Plant bare-root vines in early spring; specimens in containers may be planted at any season. Space single cordons at least 4ft (1.2m) apart, double or U cordons at twice that spacing; the arms of multiple cordons should be 24in (60cm) apart.

Routine care

Water thoroughly during the growing season whenever conditions are dry, reducing watering gradually as the fruit ripens. Particular care is needed with grapes grown on a wall, since they may be in a rain shadow. Mulch to retain moisture. Once vigorous young shoots develop, feed with a high-potassium fertilizer every two to three weeks; if growth is poor, give high levels of nitrogen instead. Stop feeding as soon as the fruits start to ripen.

If using the cordon system, retain no more than one bunch per 12in (30cm) of vertical stem, or rod, for best-quality grapes; remove intermediate bunches at an early stage. Thin the fruits to obtain both well-shaped bunches and large, evenly sized grapes (and to discourage mildew). Use grape-thinning scissors and a small forked stick to expose portions of the bunch so that small fruits in the center may be removed. Some cultivars need a second thinning as the fruits develop further.

Pests and diseases

Grapes are affected by many problems including scale insects (p.554), black vine weevils (p.551), spider mites (p.552), whiteflies (p.552), wasps (p.565), downy mildew (p.552), gray mold/*Botrytis* (p.564), shanking of grapes (p.564), and root-knot nematodes (p.566). Under cover, mealybugs (p.552) and powdery mildew (p.564) may also be troublesome.

Grape *Phylloxera* is a serious pest in warmer climates, where this aphid-like insect attacks the roots of European grapes; galls may also form on the leaves. The attack causes severe stunting and is often fatal. However, the use of resistant rootstocks and resistant hybrids of American cultivars has greatly reduced its incidence. In the Gulf Coast region, Muscadine cultivars and related hybrids resistant to Pierce's disease (PD) must be planted.

Growing under cover

In cool climates, grow grapes in a greenhouse, preferably with heating. Other crops with compatible temperature and humidity requirements may also be grown in the greenhouse. In a lean-to greenhouse, the warmth from the back wall is particularly beneficial, especially if there is little or no direct heating. Greenhouses with both top and side ventilation give the best results.

The soil must be fairly fertile, weed-free, and well drained, with a pH of 6–7.5. Drainage must be $2^1/_2$ft (75cm) deep: grapes are deep-rooted. Plant as for grapes grown outdoors. Hand-pollinate by tapping the stems or supports around midday or by drawing the hand gently down the flower cluster. This will release pollen onto flowers below.

Either train vines directly onto the back wall or plant them at the foot of the glass wall, training them on support wires that are 9in (22cm) or

THINNING GRAPES

1 *Once the bunches have been thinned to 12in (30cm) apart, the fruits will need thinning as they swell, to increase the size of the grapes and to allow air circulation between them.*

2 *With a forked stick and grape scissors, expose portions of the bunch and snip off unwanted grapes. The bunch should then be wide at the top, tapering toward the base.*

Recommended Table Grapes

Early
'Beta' **Bl**
'Buffalo' **Bl**
'Edelweiss' **Wh**
'Ontario' **Bl**
'Schuyler' **Bl**
'Seneca' **Wh**
'Swenson Red' **R**
'Van Buren' **Bl**
'Vanessa' **R**

'Edelweiss'

Midseason
'Alwood' **Bl**
'Canadice' **R, S**
'Fredonia' **Bl**
'Himrod' **R, S**
'New York Muscat' **Bf**
'Olden' **Bf**
'Remaily' **G, S**
'Saturn' **R, S**
'Steuben' **Bl**
'Valiant' **R, S**
'Venus' **Bl, S**
'Vinered' **R**

Late
Late-ripening cultivars ripen outside only in areas with reliably warm summers.
'Blackrose' **Bl**
'Cardinal' **R**
'Daytona' **P**
'Fry' **Br, M**
'Golden Muscat' **G**
'Jumbo' **Bf, M**
'Nesbitt' **Bf, M**
'Orlando Seedless' **Wh, S**

'Nesbitt'

'Perlette' **G, S**
'Ribier', syn. 'Alphonse Lavalee' **Bf**
'Sultanina', syn. 'Thompson Seedless' **G, S**

'Orlando Seedless'

Key
Bf *Black fruit*
Bl *Blue fruit*
Br *Bronze fruit*
G *Gold fruit*
R *Red fruit*
Wh *White fruit*
M *Muscadine fruit*
S *Seedless available*

more from the glass. Plant vines at one end of free-standing houses, then train up and along the roof on wires. For details of cultivation, see "Routine care," p.397. A soil auger may be used to gauge levels of moisture in the soil; use tepid water for the first waterings of the season.

Control ventilation carefully; keep it at a maximum in winter to ensure adequate winter chilling of the vines. Reduce to a minimum in late winter to induce growth. Vary the amount according to the weather to maintain even temperatures. Slight ventilation is advisable, and adequate warmth is needed at flowering to aid pollination. After fruit set, good air circulation is needed to control gray mold/*Botrytis* and mildew.

Damping down and mist-spraying help control spider mites. Do not damp down on dull days, or during flowering or ripening periods.

Fork over the bed carefully in late winter, avoiding the root area; remove ½in (1cm) of soil from the surface and replace it with soil-based mix. After the first watering, mulch with well-rotted manure or compost around the base of the vines.

Once the fruits ripen, they need a "finishing period" during which they remain on the vine to attain maximum color and flavor: allow two to three weeks for early cultivars, and longer for late-ripening ones. Provide good ventilation, netting ventilators to exclude birds if these are a problem.

Pruning and training

The usual method for table grapes is to develop single or double (U) cordons or rods on which permanent fruiting spurs are formed. These produce high-quality fruits.

Grapes fruit on the current season's growth. Spring and summer pruning, therefore, is aimed at restricting new growth from the rods so that one bunch of grapes develops from each spur. It also restricts the growth of foliage enough to expose the developing fruit to sun, particularly in cool climates. In hot climates, take care that sun scorch does not occur. Carry out winter pruning before midwinter to restrict bleeding.

Single cordon After planting, while the vine is dormant, shorten the stem to a strong bud a few inches above the ground. In summer, train one leading shoot onto a vertical bamboo stake and pinch or cut back any laterals to five or six leaves. Shorten all the sublaterals (shoots

Grape, Single Cordon

Year 1, Winter Pruning

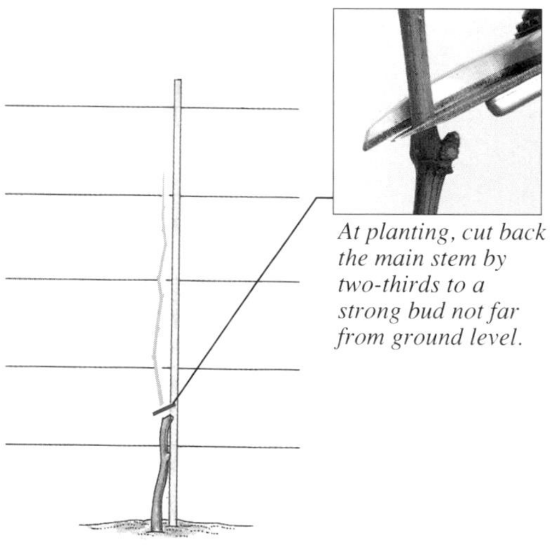

At planting, cut back the main stem by two-thirds to a strong bud not far from ground level.

Year 1, Summer Pruning

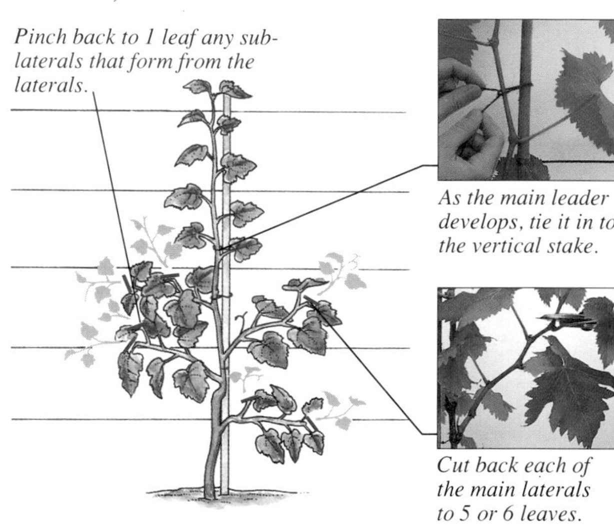

Pinch back to 1 leaf any sublaterals that form from the laterals.

As the main leader develops, tie it in to the vertical stake.

Cut back each of the main laterals to 5 or 6 leaves.

Year 2, Winter Pruning

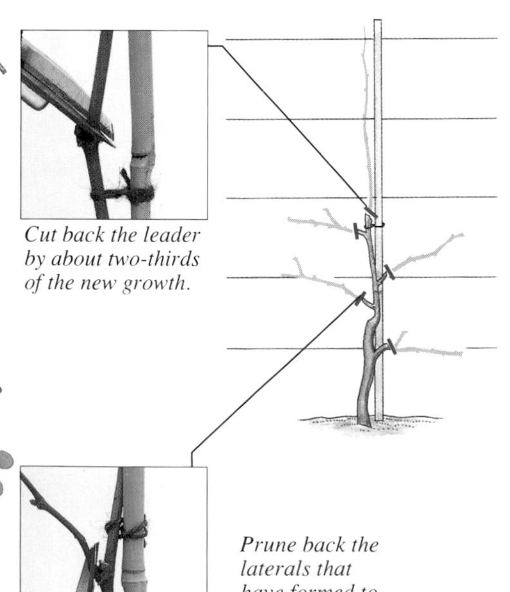

Cut back the leader by about two-thirds of the new growth.

Prune back the laterals that have formed to 1 strong bud.

Year 2, Summer Pruning

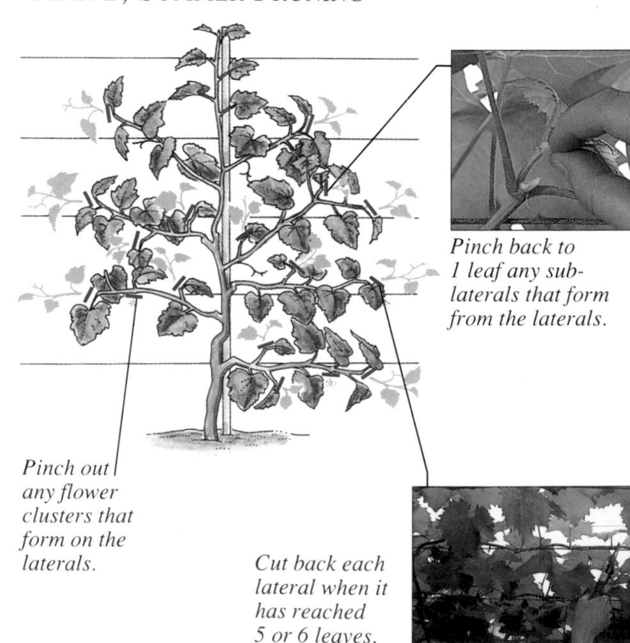

Pinch back to 1 leaf any sublaterals that form from the laterals.

Pinch out any flower clusters that form on the laterals.

Cut back each lateral when it has reached 5 or 6 leaves.

that are growing from the laterals) to one leaf. Remove any shoots that develop from the base.

During the second winter, reduce the leader by two-thirds of the new growth to well-ripened wood and laterals back to one bud. In the second summer, tie in the leading shoot as it extends. Pinch or cut the side shoots to five or six leaves and sublaterals to one leaf. Remove any flower clusters; do not allow the vine to fruit until the third year.

In the third winter, shorten the leading shoot by two-thirds of its new growth, and cut back all the laterals to one strong bud to create spurs that will bear fruiting shoots.

Routine pruning Carry out routine pruning from the third year onward. In spring, let two shoots grow at each spur and pinch out others. Retain the stronger of the two for fruiting, and pinch back the weaker to two leaves, keeping it as a replacement in case the fruiting shoot breaks. In summer, as flower clusters develop, retain the best, pruning out the others to leave one per lateral. Stop laterals at two leaves beyond the chosen flower clusters. Pinch out laterals not carrying flowers at about five leaves and any sublaterals at one leaf.

Each winter continue to remove two-thirds of the new growth from the leader, but when it has reached the top of its support, cut it back annually to two buds. Cut laterals to one strong bud. If spur systems become congested in later years, either remove part of the system with a pruning saw or, if there are too many spurs on the rod, remove some of them completely. The spurs should be 9–12in (22–30cm) apart. The rod should be untied from its wires to about halfway down its length and bent over until nearly horizontal for a few weeks during winter to encourage the even development of shoots the following spring; afterward, retie the rod vertically.

Double cordon This may be formed by training in two shoots horizontally in the first summer. Prune each back to 2ft (60cm) the following winter. The next year, train the extension growths vertically. These form two vertical arms; prune each arm as a single cordon.

Multiple cordon Train in two shoots in the first summer and in winter prune each back to 2ft (60cm). Train the extension growths horizontally, and choose a strong shoot every 2ft (60cm) to train vertically in order to

Harvesting Table Grapes

Avoid touching the fruits and spoiling the bloom. Cut each bunch complete with a handle consisting of 2in (5cm) of woody stem from either side of the bunch.

Year 3, Winter Pruning

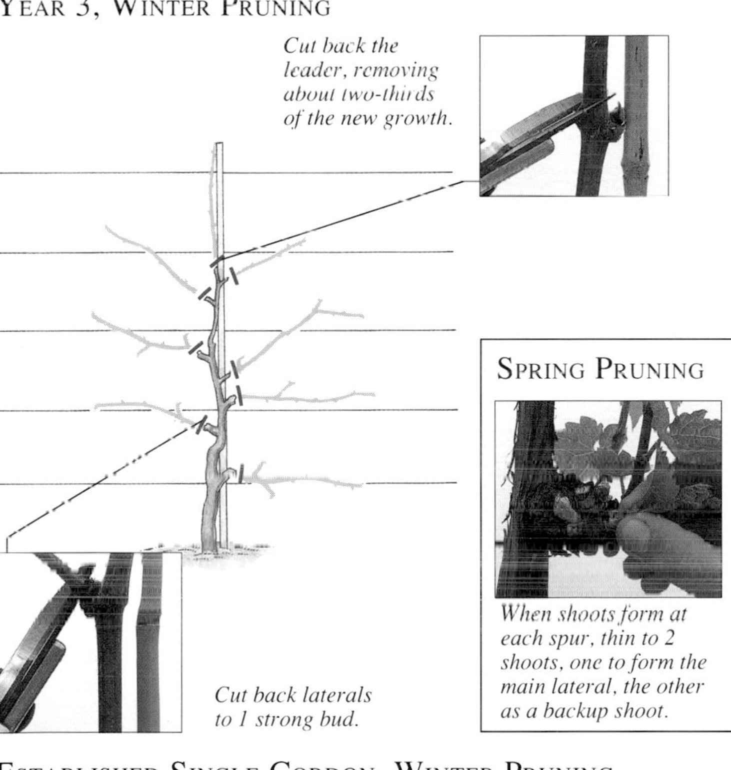

Established Single Cordon, Summer Pruning

Established Single Cordon, Winter Pruning

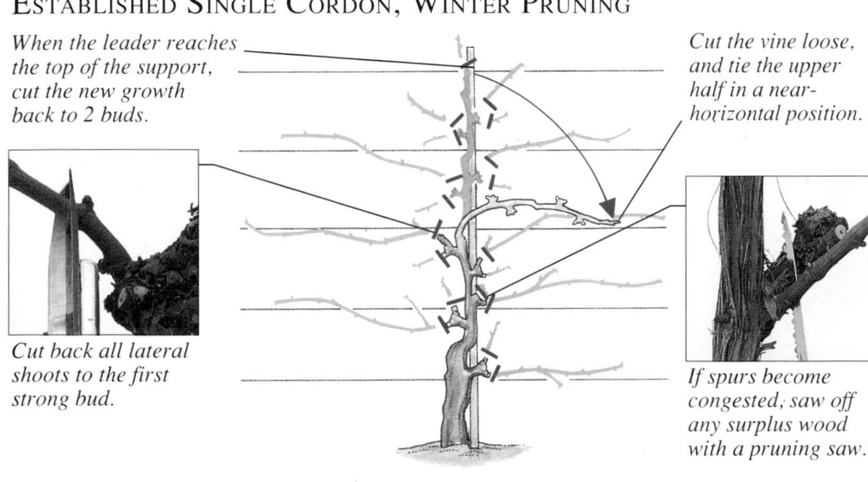

Multiple Cordon

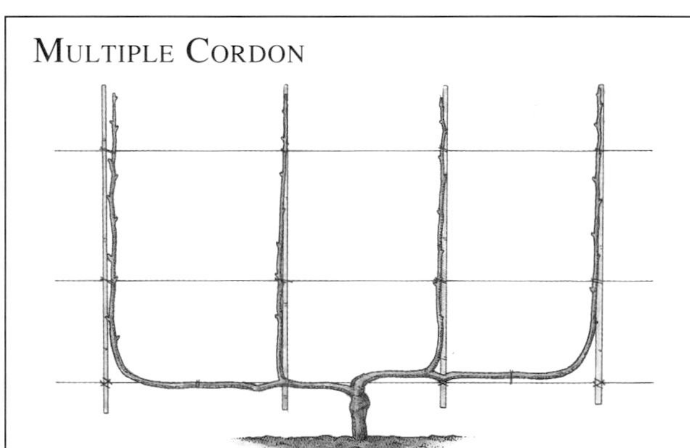

A multiple cordon may be trained with as many vertical rods as space allows. Once established, each arm is pruned in the same way as a single cordon.

RECOMMENDED WINE GRAPES

Early
'Aurora' **Wh**
'Kay Gray' **Wh**
'Muscat Ottanel' **G**
'St. Croix' **Wh**

Midseason
'Baco Noir' **Bf**
'Cayuga White' **Wh**
'Chardonnay', syn. 'Pinot Chardonnay' **Wh**
'Dechaunoc', syn. 'Seibel 9549' **Bl**

'Muscat Ottanel'

'Delaware' **R, Tu**
'Duchess' **Wh**
'Gamay' **R**
'Geneva White 5' **Wh**
'Marechal Foch' **Bl**
'Niagara' **Wh, Tu**
'Pinot Noir', syn. 'Spatburgunder' **Bl**

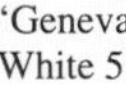

'Geneva White 5'

'Sovereign Rose' **P**
'Sovereign Tiara' **G**
'Ventura' **Wh**
'Villard Blanc' **Wh**
'Vivant' **Wh**
'Zinfandel' **R**

Late
Late-ripening cultivars ripen outside only in areas with reliably warm summers.
'Blanc du Bois' **Wh**
'Catawba' **R**
'Chenin Blanc' **Wh**
'Doreen' **Br, M**
'Golden Isles' **Br, M**
'Hunt' **Bf, M**

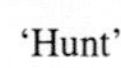

'Hunt'

'Noble' **Bf, M**
'Pinot Gris' **R**
'Sauvignon Blanc' **Wh**
'Scuppernong' **Br, M**
'Seyval Blanc', syn. 'Seyve Villard 5276' **Wh**
'Vincent' **Bl**
'White Riesling' **Wh**

KEY
Bf *Black fruit*
Bl *Blue fruit*
Br *Bronze fruit*
G *Gold fruit*
P *Pink fruit*
R *Red fruit*
Wh *White fruit*
M *Muscadine fruit*
Tu *Table use also*

form the number of arms required. Once established, prune each arm as a single cordon.

Alternative pruning methods Some cultivars will not produce adequate fruit-bearing shoots from the basal buds left by spur pruning. In such cases, longer lengths of ripened wood, or canes, are retained when winter pruning the buds from which fruit-bearing shoots will be produced. Other canes are cut back to three or four buds to produce strong new growths to replace the old fruiting canes the following winter. This process is repeated annually. Many other renewal systems may also be used to train table grapes (for details on the double Guyot system, see "Pruning and training: Guyot system," opposite).

Harvesting and storing
Tie back or remove some of the foliage to allow more sun to reach the ripening fruits. Cut ripe bunches from the vine with a short piece of woody stem – the handle – and place in a container with soft lining so that the fruits are not damaged and their bloom is not spoiled.

Bunches may be stored for a week or two at room temperature by cutting a longer handle and placing this in a narrow-necked container of water, with the fruit hanging down on the outside of the container.

Propagation
Grapes may be propagated by hardwood cuttings or grafting (for details, see "Wine grapes: Propagation," p.402, and "Bud-grafting," p.368).

Wine grapes

Grapes may be grown for wine in areas with long, dry, sunny summers and adequate soil moisture. In cooler climates, early and midseason cultivars grown on warm walls or under cover give good results.

Site and planting
Most well-drained soils with a pH of 6–7.5 are suitable. Clear weeds before planting. Rootstocks are as for table grapes (see "Table grapes: Site," p.397). The flowers are usually self-fertile, and are pollinated by the wind. Before planting, erect a row of support posts. Fix a single wire 15in (38cm) above the ground and double wires at 30in and 4ft (75cm and 1.2m). Loop both double

GRAPE, DOUBLE GUYOT

YEAR 1, WINTER PRUNING

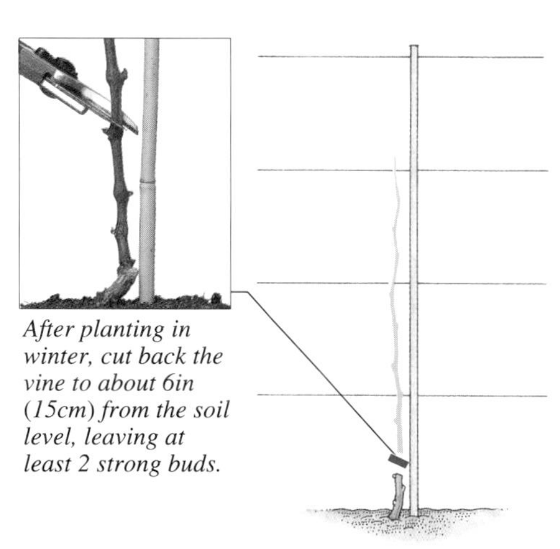

After planting in winter, cut back the vine to about 6in (15cm) from the soil level, leaving at least 2 strong buds.

YEAR 1, SUMMER PRUNING

As it develops, tie in the leader to a vertical stake with twine in a loose figure-eight knot.

Prune any laterals that develop back to 5 leaves.

Remove any competing shoots developing below the main leader.

YEAR 2, WINTER PRUNING

YEAR 2, SUMMER PRUNING

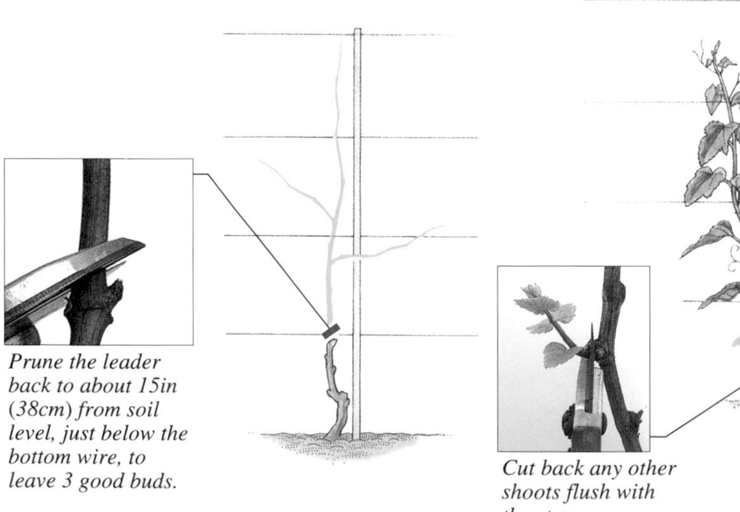

Prune the leader back to about 15in (38cm) from soil level, just below the bottom wire, to leave 3 good buds.

Cut back any other shoots flush with the stem.

Allow 3 main shoots to develop; tie them loosely to a central stake by looping string around all 3 shoots and the stake.

wires around the posts to form a figure eight. Plant one- or two-year-old vines in winter, 5–6ft (1.5–2m) apart, in rows 6ft (2m) apart.

Routine care

Remove any weeds, and water to establish young vines in dry conditions; water cropping vines only in drought conditions, since too much water reduces grape quality. Give a light, annual, early spring application of a balanced fertilizer, and apply potassium sulfate in alternate years. Use a foliar spray of magnesium sulfate to correct magnesium deficiencies (see p.557). Mulch every other year with plenty of well-rotted compost, or annually if the soil quality is poor. Fruit size is not important for wine quality, so thinning is necessary only in cold areas to improve sugar levels.

Pruning and training

Some cultivars need spur pruning (see "Table grapes: Pruning and training," p.398); many, however, require annual replacement of old canes to fruit regularly.

Guyot system This is widely used for wine grapes, since it produces a prolific crop in a limited space. It involves annual training of horizontal rods from which fruiting shoots are trained vertically. In the double

YEAR 3, WINTER PRUNING

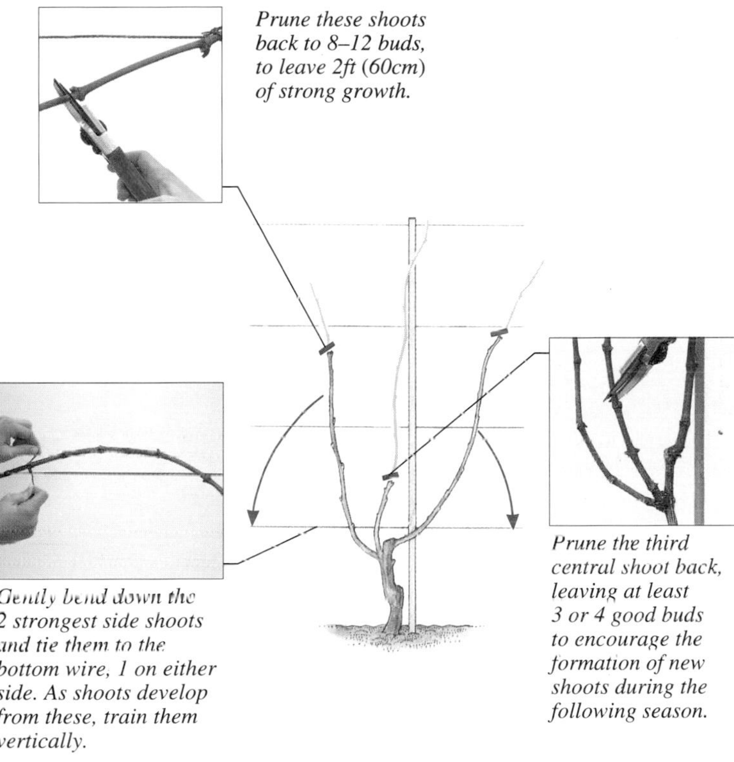

YEAR 3, SUMMER PRUNING

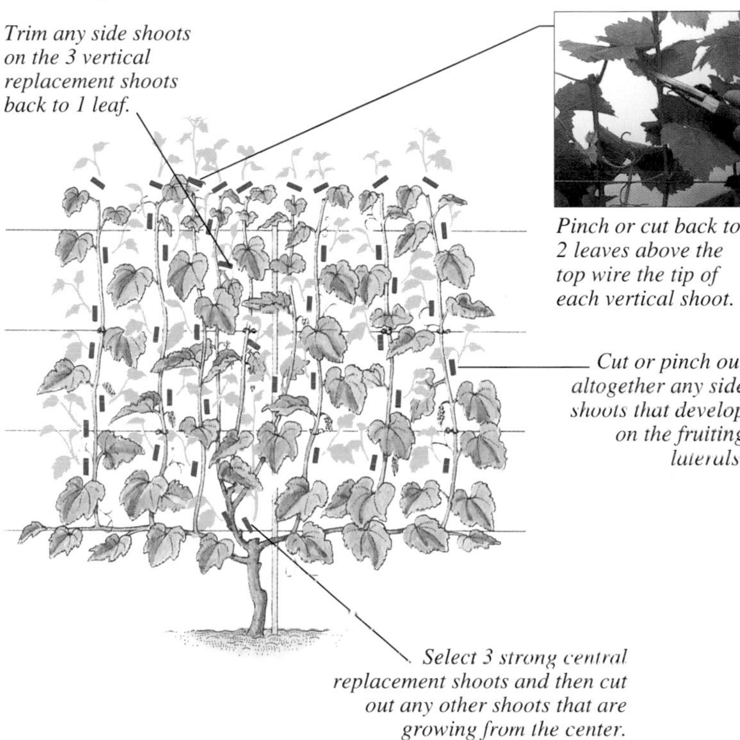

ESTABLISHED DOUBLE GUYOT, WINTER PRUNING

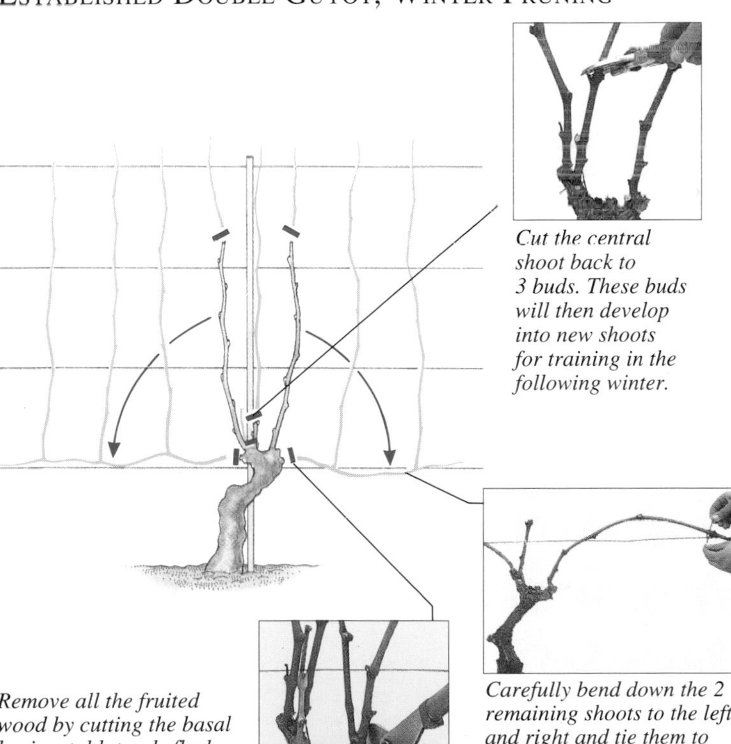

ESTABLISHED DOUBLE GUYOT, SUMMER PRUNING

Guyot, two rods on each plant are trained in this way; in the single Guyot system, only one.

To train a vine by the double Guyot system, cut it back during the first winter to two strong buds above ground level. In the first summer, let one shoot develop and tie it to a vertical stake or wires. Remove other low shoots and cut any laterals to five leaves. In the second winter, cut back to just under the lowest wire, making sure that there are at least three strong buds remaining.

The next summer, let three strong shoots develop and tie them in vertically. Remove low shoots. In the third winter, tie down two of the shoots to the bottom wire, one on either side. Tip prune these to eight to 12 buds; they will produce fruiting shoots the following summer. Cut the third shoot back to three or four buds to produce replacement shoots, so that the whole process may be repeated. (For the single Guyot system, allow two shoots to develop; tie down one and cut back the other.)

During the third summer, select three of the best central shoots growing from the rod and tie loosely to a central post or stake; cut out other, weaker, central shoots. Pinch back to one leaf any side shoots that form on the three replacements. Train the shoots from the two arms vertically through the parallel wires. If growth is strong, allow a few bunches of grapes to develop on them. Pinch or cut out shoot tips at two leaves above the top wire; remove any side shoots on the fruiting shoots.

Routine pruning For winter pruning, cut out all old, fruited wood, leaving three replacement shoots. Tie two of these down, one on either side, and tip prune as for the third winter. Prune the third shoot to three strong buds. Routine summer pruning and training of replacement shoots is as for the third summer. Cut out any overcrowded shoots obscuring the fruits. Remove any leaves shading the grapes six weeks before they are expected to ripen.

REMOVING FOLIAGE

When the grapes are developing, cut off any leaves that shade the ripening fruit directly. Do not remove too many, because this may cause scorch from excess sunlight.

HARVESTING WINE GRAPES

Bunches of wine grapes may be harvested simply by cutting the stalk with pruners.

Harvesting

Cut the bunches from the vines with pruners; the grapes should be fully ripe and completely dry.

Propagation

Propagate from hardwood cuttings prepared in winter when pruning, using wood from the hardened base of one-year-old shoots. To plant in the open, take sections about 8in (20cm) long, trimming above and below a bud, and insert the cuttings 6in (15cm) deep in sandy soil.

Under cover it is possible to use shorter one- or two-bud cuttings. Grow these singly in 3½in (9cm) pots or insert five cuttings in an 8in (21cm) pot. Place the pots in a cold frame. Pot on each young rooted plant the following summer.

HARDWOOD CUTTINGS

Trim the stems into lengths of about 8in (20cm), making an angled cut above a bud at the top and a flat cut below a bud at the base. Insert each cutting to two-thirds its length into a trench in sandy soil.

TWO-BUD CUTTINGS

1 *While pruning at leaf drop, trim off a long section of ripened wood from the current season's growth. Then remove any remaining leaves or tendrils.*

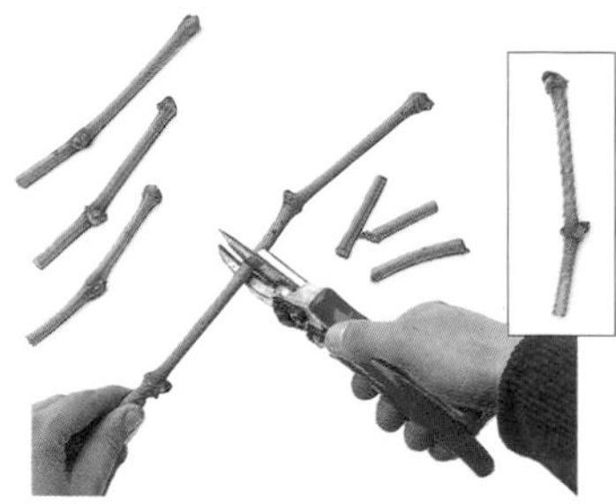

2 *Divide the stem into cuttings with 2 buds, with an angled cut above the top bud and a horizontal cut between 2 nodes below the lower bud. Remove a ½in (1cm) length of rind above the lower cut.*

3 *Insert cuttings in a soil mix of 2 parts peat, 1 part soil, and 1 part sand, the lower bud just below the surface. Label, water, and place in a protected spot.*

4 *When the cuttings have rooted, they should be potted on individually into 4in (10cm) pots to grow on.*

Kiwi fruits (*Actinidia deliciosa*)

Deciduous trailing climbers, kiwi fruits were originally known as Chinese gooseberries. The vines will grow up to 28ft (9m) in length. The berries have hairy brown skin and green pulp, with small black seeds.

Warm, moist conditions are preferable during the growing season, the optimum temperature range being 41–78°F (5–25°C). Dormant plants will, however, tolerate several degrees below freezing and require chilling for a period of at least 400 hours below 42°F (7°C) to encourage good flower production.

Site and planting

Kiwi fruits can be grown only in the open in sunny, sheltered areas, since plants in growth are sensitive to adverse weather conditions. The soil should be well aerated, deep, and rich in organic matter, with a pH of 6–7. Incorporate a general-purpose fertilizer into the site at a rate of 2–4oz (50–110g) per plant.

Kiwi fruits are dioecious, with plants bearing either male or female flowers. One male is needed for every eight or nine female plants to ensure adequate fertilization.

Erect a post and wire support, with wires at 12in (30cm) intervals. Plant either rooted cuttings or grafted plants 12–15ft (4–5m) apart in rows 12–18ft (4–6m) apart, staking the vines until they are tall enough to reach the supporting wires.

Routine care

Mulch the plants heavily and apply a general-purpose fertilizer rich in phosphorus and potassium. Water regularly, particularly in prolonged dry periods. Keep rows weed-free. Fruit thinning is rarely necessary.

RECOMMENDED KIWI FRUITS

'Abbot' **F**
'Blake' **F**
'Bruno' **F**
'Chico No. 3' **M**
'Hayward' **F**
'Matua' **M**
'Monty' **F**
'Saanichton' **F**

'Bruno'

KEY
F *Female*
M *Male*

How to Support Kiwi Fruit

A common method is to train the plants as espaliers on horizontal wires with 2 main laterals per plant arising from the main stem, with fruiting laterals (see inset) at intervals of about 20in (50cm).

Plants grown in the open may be liable to root rot (see *Phytophthora* root rots, p.567). Under cover they may be infested with thrips (p.553), scale insects (p.554), and root-knot nematodes (p.566). Fruit rot may also occur as a result of infection of the petals. Infection spreads to the fruits, which then drop early. The spread of the disease is promoted by high humidity. Spraying flowers at petal fall with thiram or a similar fungicide gives reasonable control.

Growing under cover

This is rarely practical due to the long, trailing growth of the plants, in exposed conditions, however, plants grown in the open may be protected from excessive wind and hail by a light plastic screening material.

Kiwi fruits may be grown in walk-in polytunnels if the appropriate environmental conditions can be provided. Soil preparation and cultivation details are the same as for plants grown in the open.

Pruning and training

Commercial crops are often grown on a T bar or overhead pergola structure. Another commonly used system is to train plants as espaliers on horizontal wires: each plant then has two main laterals arising from the main stem, and fruiting branches at intervals of 20in (50cm). For details, see "Apple: Espalier," p.378.

The fruits are produced on one-year-old wood, so all fruited side shoots should be cut back to two to four buds in the dormant season.

Harvesting and storing

Kiwi fruits start to bear fruit three to four years after planting. Harvest them as they soften. Snap or cut them from the branch, with the calyx attached; keep them cool. If wrapped in plastic film, fruits store for several months at 32°F (0°C).

Propagation

Both soft- and hardwood cuttings may be rooted successfully. Softwood cuttings should be taken in spring; trim to 4–6in (10–15cm) and insert in cuttings soil mix (see p.370). Hardwood cuttings are taken in late summer; these should be 8–12in (20–30cm) long and inserted in sandy soil mix (see p.370).

Selected cultivars may also be grafted onto vigorous seedling stocks; the most common methods are T-budding and whip-and-tongue grafting (see p.369).

Passion fruits (*Passiflora* spp.)

Passion fruits are climbing plants, with individual stems reaching many feet in length. The globular fruits are either purple or yellow when ripe, and may be up to 3in (7cm) in diameter. The two species most commonly grown for their fruits are the yellow-fruited *P. edulis* f. *flavicarpa* and the purple *P. edulis*.

The optimum temperature range for the purple passion fruit is about 68–82°F (20–28°C). The yellow passion fruit prefers temperatures over 75°F (24°C) and does not tolerate frost; purple types may withstand frost for short periods. Moderate to high humidity is required for satisfactory growth.

Site and planting

Select a sunny site, protected by windbreaks if necessary. Soils may vary in type but must be well drained, with a pH of about 6.

Cross-pollination by insects, normally bees, is usual, but hand-pollination may be necessary in wet weather; hand-pollination has been found to increase the yield of plants that are grown in the open.

Passion fruits require support, in the form of a wire trellis. Before planting, insert stout uprights, 10ft (3m) long, at intervals of 12ft (4m) each way. Link adjoining uprights in rows by tying with one or two strands of wire.

Take care to prepare the planting holes thoroughly, adding both organic material and a general-purpose fertilizer with medium to high levels of nitrogen. Establish the plants at about 10–12ft (3–4m) apart each way, or less if only a few plants are grown. The yellow form is usually planted 3m (10ft) apart each way.

Routine care

Apply a general-purpose fertilizer that has a medium to high nitrogen content at a rate of 1–2lb (0.5–1kg) per plant per year, preferably in equal dressings at intervals of three to four months. Apply an organic mulch in spring, and weed and water regularly during the dry season.

Pests affecting plants in the open as well as under cover include fruit flies (p.565), aphids (p.552), spider mites (p.552), and various scale insects (p.554). Root-knot nematodes (p.566) and *Fusarium* wilt (p.560) may also be serious in some subtropical areas. "Woodiness" is caused by cucumber mosaic virus (see "Viruses," p.565), which is transmitted by aphids. Because passion fruit vines are susceptible to nematodes and various wilt diseases, replace the plants every five or six years with healthy seedlings, rooted cuttings, or grafted plants.

Growing under cover

This is possible in temperate areas, but fruits may not be produced unless the optimum temperatures and conditions are provided; hand-pollination is generally necessary. Provide wire supports as for outdoor plants. Grow plants either in prepared beds or in large containers at least 14in (35cm) in diameter. Use a well-drained, fertile soil mix with a high organic content, and incorporate a general-purpose fertilizer into the soil mix before planting. Maintain a minimum temperature of 68°F (20°C) and humidity of 60–70 percent. Apply a liquid feed or a general-purpose fertilizer once a month, and water regularly.

PASSION FRUITS

Pruning and training

Train two main growing stems along the wires to form a permanent framework. If these have not produced laterals by the time they are 2–3ft (60–90cm) long, pinch out their tips. Allow the lateral shoots, on which the fruits will be produced, to hang down as they develop each spring. Prune these laterals so that they are never less than 6in (15cm) from the soil. Once the plant is established, each winter cut back the current season's fruited shoots, since these will not bear fruit again.

Harvesting and storing

Pick fruits when they begin to change color, from green to either purple or yellow. The fruits should be ripe eight to 12 weeks after fruit set, depending on the cultivar. Fruits may be stored for up to 21 days if maintained at an even temperature of at least 43°F (6°C) and at a constant humidity level of 85–90 percent.

Propagation

This is usually by sowing seed or raising cuttings; passion fruits may also be propagated by bud-grafting.

Seed may be extracted from the fully ripe fruits, and should be fermented for three to four days, then washed and dried. Sow the seed under cover in trays or 3–3½in (6–9cm) pots of seed soil mix, and keep at a temperature of at least 68°F (20°C). When the germinated seedlings are 8–14in (20–35cm) tall, transplant them to open ground, after hardening off, or grow them on under cover.

Cuttings 6–8in (15–20cm) long should be prepared and inserted into a tray or pot filled with cuttings soil mix. Apply bottom heat and mist-spray to encourage rooting.

For details of bud-grafting, see p.368. Healthy bud-grafted plants should be transplanted into their permanent positions to grow on when approximately 6in (15cm) tall.

If nematodes or wilt diseases are a serious problem, the purple cultivars may be grafted onto resistant rootstocks. Vigorous seedlings of the yellow-fruited type are normally used for this purpose.

Soft fruits

All the usually cultivated soft fruits are bush or cane fruits, except for strawberries, which are herbaceous perennials. Bush fruits include blueberries, gooseberries, and black-, red-, and whitecurrants. Cane fruits include blackberries, hybrid berries, and raspberries. All produce succulent fruits that are eaten fresh, or preserved, canned, or frozen. Most soft fruits grow best in cool climates. They prefer a well-drained, moisture-retentive, and fertile soil. A sunny site is best and gives fine-quality fruit, but in most cases a little shade is tolerated. Almost all cultivars are self-fertile. Pruning methods depend on whether fruit is produced on one-year-old wood, on older wood and spurs, or on both.

Strawberries (*Fragaria* x *ananassa*)

Strawberries are low-growing, herbaceous plants that may be grown in most gardens, either in the open ground or in containers. There are three distinct types of strawberry plant: summer-fruiting, everbearing, and alpine.

Summer-fruiting strawberries produce nearly all their fruit in an intensive two- to three-week period in midsummer. Some cultivars also give a smaller fall crop.

Everbearing (perpetual-fruiting) strawberries crop briefly in summer, cease for about two months, and then produce a succession of fruits in fall. They grow best in regions that have mild, frost-free fall weather.

Alpine strawberries produce small, delicately flavored fruits from midsummer to fall.

Variations in daylength (see The Vegetable Garden, p.303) affect the formation of flowers in some cultivars. It is therefore important to choose those appropriate for the latitude of the particular garden: nearer the tropics, for example, the cooler temperatures that are essential for growth and cropping may be found only at high altitudes.

Site and planting

Strawberries are best grown where new plantings may be made regularly on fresh ground, since cropping, fruit size, and plant health deteriorate if the same ground and plants are used after the third year. If you have room, grow one-, two-, and three-year-old plants in succession, discarding the oldest plants and planting new runners in fresh ground each year.

Site

Sunny, warm sites give the best-flavored fruit. Sandy soils produce the earliest crops, loams and well-drained clays the heaviest and most flavorful; alkaline soils do not produce good results. Slightly acid conditions with a pH of 6–6.5 are ideal. Good drainage is vital to avoid soilborne diseases. Planting strawberries after potatoes can be risky, since the ground may be infected with *Verticillium* wilt (p.559).

To prolong the fruiting season, plantings may be split. Choose a warm, sheltered position for the earliest crops; sunny, open ground for the main crop; and a less sunny site for late-ripening fruits.

Pollination

Most strawberry cultivars are self-fertile. Some cultivars, however, fruit only if several plants of a different cultivar that flowers at the same time grow nearby.

Planting

The planting time for strawberries depends on geographical location. Seek expert advice if in doubt. In cool-temperate regions, late summer to early fall planting is best and ensures the heaviest crops the following summer. For later plantings, remove flowers in spring to allow plants to become well established before they begin to bear fruit.

Use plants of certified stock, if possible, and plant in fresh ground, where strawberries have not been grown for at least three years. Replace plants every two or three years and grub out and discard any old plants nearby to prevent the spread of viral diseases. Clear all weeds and apply generous amounts of well-rotted farmyard manure, unless plenty remains in the soil from the preceding crop. On hungrier sandy or gravelly soils, rake in a dressing of a balanced fertilizer as well, at a rate of 3oz/sq yd (105g/sq m), just before planting. Space strawberries at 18in (45cm) intervals in slightly raised rows, 2½ft (75cm) apart, so that rainwater runs off. Plant with the base of the central crown at soil level, firm in the plants, and water well. On wet sites, plant in raised beds (see Structures and Surfaces, "Raised beds," p.507).

Strawberries may also be planted through sheets of black plastic, which smother weeds, retain soil moisture, and encourage early cropping by

Buying Healthy Strawberry Plants

Planting Strawberries under Black Plastic

1 *In moist soil, mark out a 3ft (90cm) wide bed with string. Mound the soil in the center, and cover the bed with a length of black plastic 4ft (1.2m) wide.*

2 *Dig a narrow trench on either side of the bed and, using a spade, anchor the edges of the plastic sheet firmly in the trenches to keep it from blowing away.*

3 *Make cross-shaped cuts in the plastic (see inset) at 18in (45cm) intervals. Plant the strawberries through the slits and firm the soil around their crowns.*

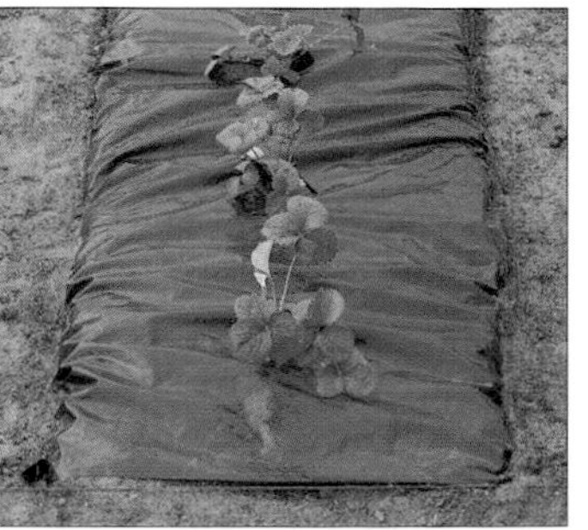

4 *Tuck in the cut plastic around the crowns of the plants. The finished row of strawberries should be slightly raised so that rain drains away from the plants.*

warming the soil. Anchor the plastic firmly, then make planting slits at the required intervals.

Routine care

Strawberries need regular watering. Ripening fruits should be netted against pests, and kept off the soil to keep them clean. Remove surplus runners, weed, and regularly check for pests and diseases. Flowers may need protection from cold in spring: double-thickness sheets of newspaper are very effective.

Protecting the fruits

Before the fruit clusters develop fully, lay clean, dry straw or commercial mats beneath them to prevent soil splash on the fruits; this is unnecessary for plants grown through plastic. Protect the fruits from birds before they redden, using posts to support fruit nets (see p.363). Nets also help discourage raccoons.

How to Keep Strawberries Clean

When the strawberries are in flower or the fruits are forming, put a thick layer of straw underneath and between the plants to prevent the ripening fruits from touching the soil.

Alternative Method

Alternatively, strawberry mats may be laid carefully around the crowns to protect the developing fruits.

Removing Runners

Remove excess runners as they develop. Pinch them out close to the parent plant, taking care not to damage any other foliage.

Controlling runners

Pinch out runners as they appear, unless they are needed to help form matted rows (see "Growing under cover," below).

Watering and weeding

Water strawberries when newly planted, then regularly during the growing season, especially after flowering to promote the development of quality fruits. Water plants under plastic only in very dry weather, watering through the planting slits. Keep beds free of weeds.

Pests and diseases

Strawberries may be eaten by small animals (see p.572), squirrels (p.565), millipedes (p.550), and slugs (p.550), and are vulnerable to aphids (p.552), viruses (p.565), gray mold/*Botrytis* (p.564), fungal leaf spots (p.554), and spider mites (p.552). Discard diseased or stunted plants. Red core and strawberry beetles are not widespread, but are serious where they occur. Red core is a soilborne disease, more prevalent in heavy soils, causing the foliage to collapse and die. The only remedy is to change the site. Strawberry beetles take seeds from the outside of the fruits, encouraging rotting. They feed on weed seeds, so weed beds well; control the beetles with slug pellets.

Growing under cover

Strawberries grown in a heated greenhouse fruit up to one month earlier than those grown outdoors, but have less flavor. Establish runners in 3in (6cm) pots of seed soil mix as early as possible (see p.406). Before the roots fill the pots, transplant into 6in (15cm) pots of potting mix. Keep the plants outside until midwinter, protected from heavy rain, then move them into the greenhouse in a position of maximum light. When new leaves form, maintain minimum temperatures of 45°F (7°C) at night and 50°F (10°C) during the day.

Adjust the ventilation to maintain these temperatures. Water and damp down frequently to keep a moist atmosphere and reduce the risk of spider mite infestation. Increase the temperature by about 5°F (3°C) when flower clusters start to develop; during flowering, raise the temperature again by the same amount and stop damping down. Pollinate flowers by hand with a soft brush; do this around midday on a bright day. Remove late-forming flowers to improve the size of the ripening fruits. To enhance flavor, lower the temperature as fruits begin to ripen.

For plants grown in the open, cloches placed over plants in late winter advance ripening by about three weeks, and polytunnels by one to two weeks (see p.490). Both should be well ventilated on warm days. Under cloches or plastic tunnels, strawberries may be grown in matted rows, in which the planting distance is halved to give maximum yield. Runners may be retained to increase the density of the planting. Revert to the usual spacing after the first year by removing every other plant, otherwise fruit quality deteriorates and routine care becomes increasingly difficult.

Picking Fruits

Pick dessert strawberries by the stalk to avoid bruising the fruit. Strawberries for jam may be picked without the stalk.

Harvesting and storing

Harvest dessert strawberries when fully ripe, complete with stalks, and use them at once for the best flavor. Pick strawberries for jam when ripe but still firm. Pick the fruit every other day and remove diseased or damaged fruit. Strawberries may also

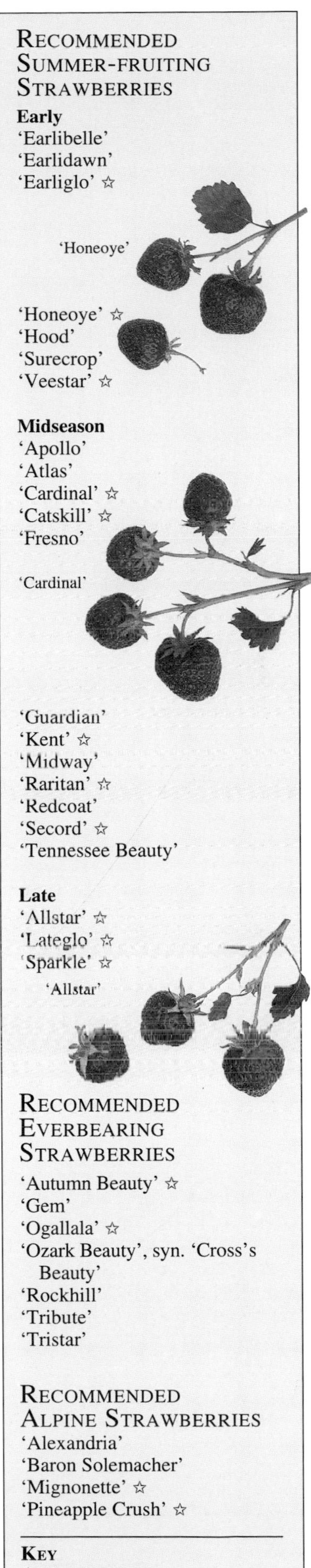

Recommended Summer-fruiting Strawberries

Early
'Earlibelle'
'Earlidawn'
'Earliglo' ☆
'Honeoye' ☆
'Hood'
'Surecrop'
'Veestar' ☆

Midseason
'Apollo'
'Atlas'
'Cardinal' ☆
'Catskill' ☆
'Fresno'
'Guardian'
'Kent' ☆
'Midway'
'Raritan' ☆
'Redcoat'
'Secord' ☆
'Tennessee Beauty'

Late
'Allstar' ☆
'Lateglo' ☆
'Sparkle' ☆

Recommended Everbearing Strawberries

'Autumn Beauty' ☆
'Gem'
'Ogallala' ☆
'Ozark Beauty', syn. 'Cross's Beauty'
'Rockhill'
'Tribute'
'Tristar'

Recommended Alpine Strawberries

'Alexandria'
'Baron Solemacher'
'Mignonette' ☆
'Pineapple Crush' ☆

Key
☆ *Excellent flavor*

be canned or preserved. If frozen, the fruits, except those of the cultivar 'Veestar', lose their firmness.

After harvesting, clear surplus runners, weeds, and straw from the site. Cut off the old foliage from plants, taking care not to damage the young leaves. Apply a balanced fertilizer and water it in if the soil is dry. Where plants are growing through a plastic mulch, make a fresh planting unless they are thriving.

Propagation

Each year plant one or two certified virus-free young plants well away from established fruiting beds. Control aphids and remove all flowers. The plants will produce a healthy supply of runners for up to two years; then start afresh with new, certified stock. Some everbearing cultivars produce few runners.

Clearing the Foliage after Harvesting

As soon as the crop has been picked, remove the old foliage to leave 4in (10cm) of stem above the young leaves and crown. Discard straw, foliage, and other debris from around the plants to minimize the risk of pests and diseases.

How to Propagate by Runners

1 *Plant certified virus-free plants especially to produce runners. As runners form, spread them out evenly around the parent plant.*

2 *Once a runner has rooted and is making vigorous new growth, lift it carefully, using a hand fork, without damaging the roots.*

3 *Sever the rooted runner from the parent plant. Transplant it to well-prepared soil or pot it up singly for planting out later.*

Alpine strawberries

Alpine strawberries (*Fragaria vesca* Semperflorens Group) have small, fragrant, sweetly flavored fruits and make a neat and attractive edging for flower borders or vegetable plots. They tolerate cooler conditions than most other strawberries and prefer partial shade in the summer in warm areas. Their fruiting season lasts from midsummer to late fall.

Plants deteriorate after about two years, so should be propagated regularly from either runners or seed. To separate seed from the fruits, leave the strawberries to dry, then squash them between finger and thumb. Sow the seed in pots of standard seed soil mix and maintain them at 64–75°F (18–24°C). Prick out seedlings when they have two true leaves. Plant out young strawberries in early summer.

Alpine Strawberry

How to Propagate from Seed

1 *Use dried fruits, squashing them gently between finger and thumb so that the seeds fall off. Hold the fruits over a clean container to collect the seeds.*

2 *Fill a 3in (6cm) pot with seed soil mix. Sprinkle the seeds thinly on the surface, then cover them with a thin layer of soil mix and a layer of fine grit.*

Blackberries and hybrid berries (*Rubus fruticosus* and *Rubus* hybrids)

The fruits of cultivated blackberries and hybrid berries such as loganberries and boysenberries are borne on canes in late summer. The hybrids have arisen from crosses between different *Rubus* species or cultivars.

Site

Before planting, the ground should be well prepared and fertilized, as for raspberries (see p.408). Buy blackberries and hybrid berries from specialist nurseries and, if possible, choose plants that are included in a certification program to ensure healthy, virus-free stock. Thornless cultivars are usually less vigorous than prickly ones. Blackberries and hybrid berries are all self-fertile and consequently may be grown singly.

Blackberries and hybrid berries need a sunny or partially shaded position. Do not plant them in exposed sites.

Provide support for the canes: walls and fences, with horizontal wires set up at 12in (30cm) intervals, are ideal.

A post 10ft (3m) long sunk 2ft (60cm) into the ground may also be used as a basic support, but for vigorous cultivars erect a post-and-wire fence. Position the posts at 12–15ft (4–5m) intervals with four horizontal wires running between them, the lowest at 3ft (90cm) from the ground, the highest at 6ft (2m). On light, sandy soils, provide extra support for the end posts by bracing them with diagonal wooden props. This will help to prevent the wires from sagging under the weight of the canes.

Planting

Plant during late fall; if the weather is severe, delay until late winter or early spring. Some hybrids may be killed in very cold areas, so seek local advice. Plant shallowly, spreading out the roots well and firming the soil at the base of the plants. Space vigorous cultivars 12–15ft (4–5m) apart, less vigorous ones 8–10ft (2.5–3m) apart. After planting, shorten the canes to 9in (22cm).

Buying Healthy Blackberry Plants

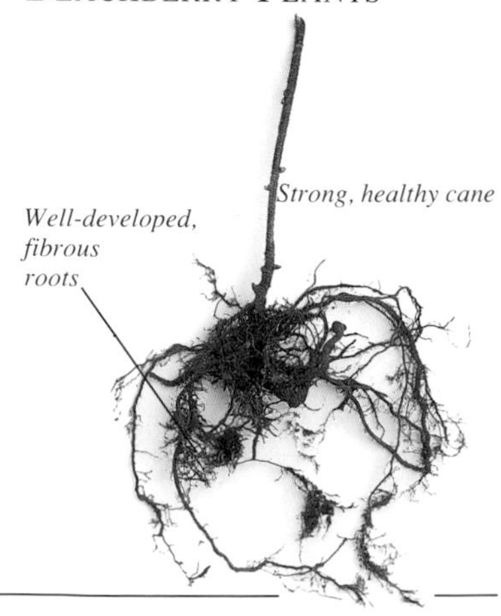

METHODS OF TRAINING

ALTERNATE BAY
Train new canes to one side of the plant, while the older ones fruit on the other side.

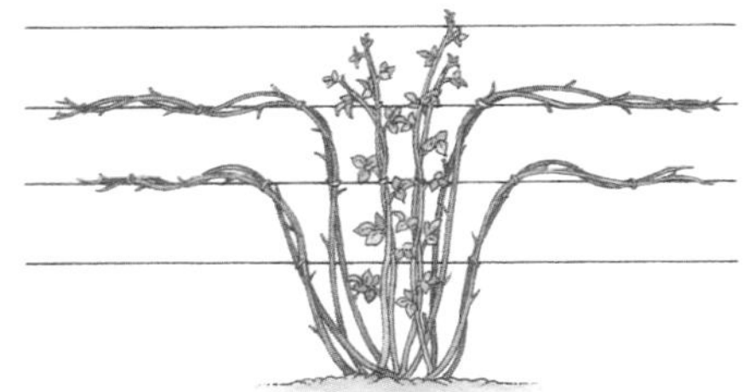

ROPE
Train fruiting canes in groups along wires, leaving new canes to grow centrally.

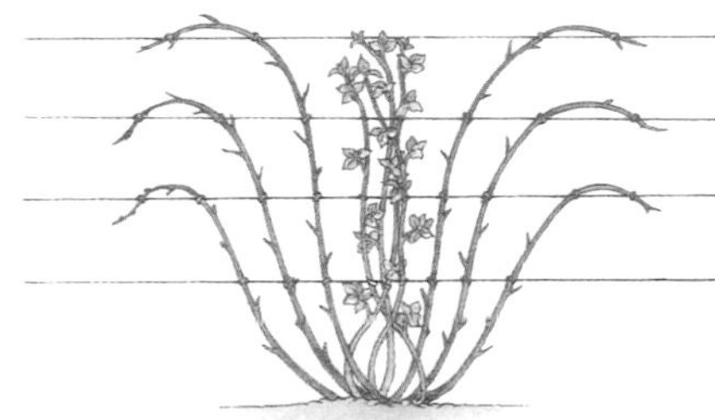

FAN
Fan-train fruiting canes individually to the left and right, and train new canes centrally.

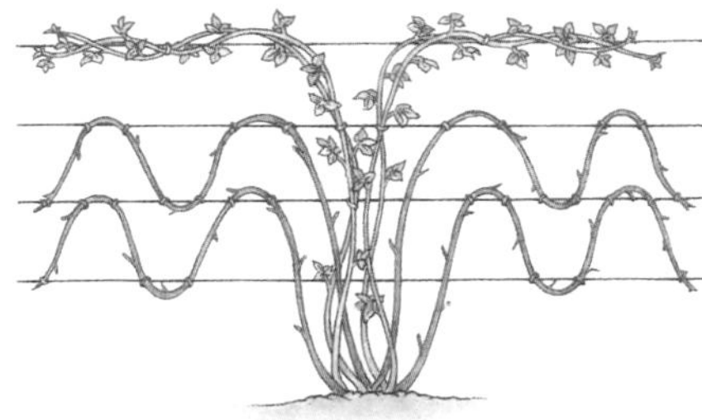

WEAVING
Weave fruiting canes through the lower wires. Train new canes centrally and along the top wire.

RECOMMENDED BLACKBERRIES

Early
'Brazos'
'Cherokee'
'Comanche'
'Lucretia'

'Comanche'

Late
'Black Satin'
'Darrow' **Rg**
'Hull'
'Smoothstem'
'Thornfree'

RECOMMENDED HYBRID BERRIES

Boysenberry
Loganberry
Marionberry
Sunberry **Rg**
Sylvanberry
Tayberry **Rg**
Youngberry

Tayberry

KEY
Rg *Rampant growth*

PRUNING ESTABLISHED BLACKBERRIES AFTER FRUITING

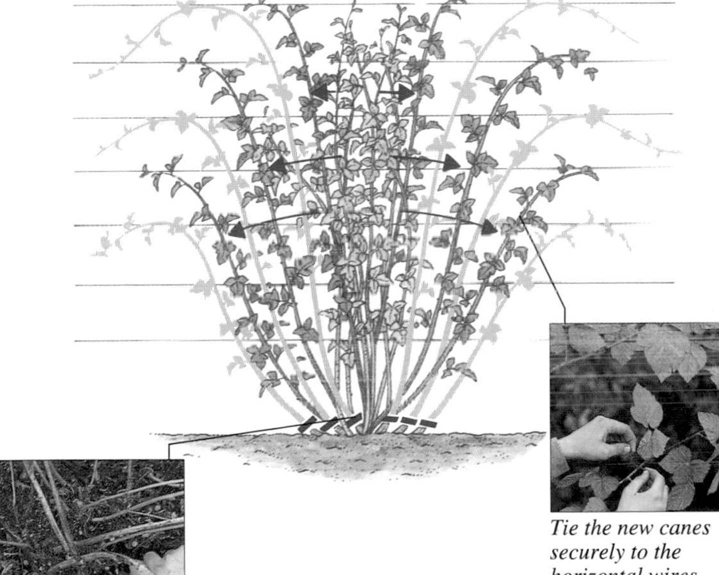

Cut down all the fruited canes to ground level near the base of the stem.

Tie the new canes securely to the horizontal wires according to the training system used.

Routine care

Maintenance requirements are as for raspberries (see p.409).

Pests and diseases

Problems may be caused by raspberry borers (p.559), fruit worms (p.564), gray mold/*Botrytis* (p.564), and viruses (p.565), although resistance varies between hybrids.

Pruning and training

The plants fruit on one-year-old wood, so training needs to separate fruiting canes from newly developing ones. For small gardens, the rope and fan methods (see above) are best. The alternate bay and weaving systems use much more space, but weaving is the best method for vigorous plants. After cropping, cut out the fruiting canes at ground level. Retain and tie in those canes that have grown during the current season, but remove any that are weak or damaged. In early spring, cut back the tip of each cane if it shows any signs of dieback resulting from cold.

Harvesting and storing

Pick the fruits regularly; unlike raspberries, the central plug stays within the picked fruit. For exhibiting, pick fruits complete with their stalks. Blackberries may be stored by canning, preserving, or freezing.

Propagation

To provide a few new plants, use tip layering (see below). In summer,

TIP PRUNING COLD-DAMAGED STEMS

Inspect the canes for signs of cold damage in early spring and, if necessary, cut back the tips of affected canes to healthy wood.

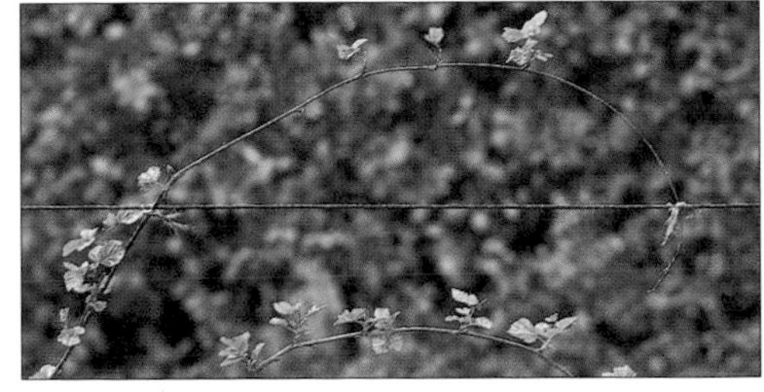

TIP LAYERING

1 *Bend over the tip of a healthy, vigorous shoot and place it in a hole 4in (10cm) deep. Fill the hole with soil and firm down well.*

2 *Once the tip has rooted in late fall, cut the old stem close to the young, rooted plant to sever it from the parent. Pot up the new plant, if required, or transplant in spring.*

bend a shoot to ground level and place the tip in a hole dug in the soil. Cover it with soil and firm. Once the tip has rooted in late fall, sever it from the parent plant. Transfer the young plant to its final growing position in spring.

To produce a larger number of young plants, remove shoots, 12in (30cm) long, of the current season's growth in late summer; take leaf-bud cuttings from them, with a leaf and a piece of stem. Place several cuttings in one 5 1/2in (14cm) pot in a moist atmosphere or cold frame; they should root in six to eight weeks. Harden them off and plant them out in late fall or, where winters are harsh, in early spring. Transplant the young canes to their final positions a year later.

HOW TO PROPAGATE BY LEAF-BUD CUTTINGS

1 *Select a strong, healthy shoot from the current season's growth, taking at least 12in (30cm) of stem with plenty of well-developed leaf buds.*

2 *Make a cut 1/2in (1cm) above a bud: slice downward to remove the bud and a portion of stem about 1in (2.5cm) long, with a leaf attached.*

3 *Place 3 cuttings in a 5 1/2in (14cm) pot, with the stem portions at an angle and growth buds just above the soil. Water, label, and place in a cold frame.*

Raspberries (*Rubus idaeus*)

A number of raspberry cultivars have been produced by crossing the European wild red raspberry (*Rubus idaeus*) with the American raspberry (*R. idaeus* var. *strigosus*) and the North American black raspberry (*R. occidentalis*).

Raspberries are a cool-season crop, growing best where there is plenty of moisture. Fruits vary in color from dark red to yellow. There are two main types of raspberry: summer-fruiting, which has a short season of heavy cropping in midsummer, and fall-fruiting, which has an extended cropping period beginning in late summer and continuing until the start of severe frost.

Site and planting

The site needs thorough preparation before planting, since raspberries do not crop well on poor soils, particularly if in competition with weeds. Raspberries are self-fertile.

Site

Raspberries should be planted in a sheltered, sunny position. They tolerate partial shade, and in hotter regions some shade may be a positive advantage.

The soil should be rich in humus and moisture-retentive but also well drained, because raspberries do not tolerate poor drainage. Sandy, alkaline, and poor, stony soils need an annual, heavy dressing with humus-rich material, and regular watering. In addition, if raspberries are grown on lime-rich soil, they may suffer from chlorosis (see "Manganese/iron deficiency," p.557).

Preparation

Clear all perennial weeds before planting, since they are extremely difficult to deal with later. Prepare an area at least 3ft (90cm) wide, and dig in plenty of well-rotted manure.

Construct permanent supports. For a post-and-wire support, set a single row of stout posts 10ft (3m) apart. Run three lengths of wire or nylon string between the posts, setting them at heights of 30in (75cm), 3 1/2ft (1.1m), and 5ft (1.5m). Keep the wires or strings taut and tie in the canes with twine by continuous lacing (weaving between the canes and wires) to prevent the canes from being blown along the row.

The parallel wires method requires two rows of posts, with posts at the above spacing and rows 30in (75cm) apart. Run two pairs of parallel wires along the posts, one pair at 30in (75cm), the other at 5ft (1.5m), then crisscross between them with wire or strong string. The canes are supported by the crosswires and do not need to be tied in.

For the Scandinavian system, erect two rows of posts, as above, but with 3ft (90cm) between rows, then run a single wire along each row at a height of 3ft (90cm). Twist fruiting canes along the wires, allowing new canes to grow in the open, central space.

Obtain certified virus-free canes; otherwise use suckers taken from established plants of known good health and cropping performance.

Planting

Plant dormant canes in well-manured ground at 15–18in (38–45cm) intervals, in rows 6ft (2m) apart. Plant in fall or early winter, since this

SUPPORTING AND TRAINING METHODS

The post-and-wire method is useful if space is limited. The parallel wires method gives the canes more room, but is not suitable in windy conditions. The Scandinavian system bends young canes around each other and the wire; the canes are not tied in or tip pruned. This method needs more space than the others.

SCANDINAVIAN SYSTEM

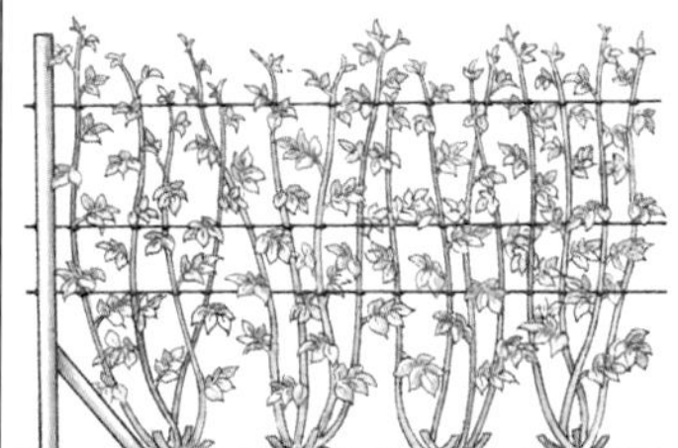

POST AND WIRES

PARALLEL WIRES

HOW TO PLANT RASPBERRIES

1 *Prepare a trench 2–3in (5–8cm) deep in well-manured ground. Plant the canes 15–18in (38–45cm) apart. Spread out the roots carefully and backfill the trench with soil.*

2 *Firm the soil around the bases of the canes, ensuring that they remain vertical. Prune canes back to a bud about 10in (25cm) from the ground. Rake over the soil lightly.*

encourages the canes to establish quickly. Spread out the roots evenly at a depth of 2–3in (5–8cm), and gently firm them in. Prune the canes to 10in (25cm) from the ground.

Routine care

In spring, mulch with well-rotted manure. Apply this on either side of the row, taking care not to bury the canes. If manure is unavailable, apply regular dressings of a balanced fertilizer (see "Care of soft fruits," p.362) and mulch with compost or leaf mold to conserve moisture.

Flowers usually appear too late to be damaged by cold and so do not need protection. Remove weeds and water the plants regularly and thoroughly. Remove any suckers more than 9in (22cm) from the main row.

Pests and diseases

Raspberry fruit worms (p.564) and borers (p.559) are the main pests. Gray mold/*Botrytis* (p.564), spur blight/cane blight (p.559), and viruses (p.565) may also be a problem.

Pruning and training

As soon as new canes are established, by about midsummer, cut out the canes that were shortened at planting time.

Summer-fruiting raspberries should have all fruited canes removed at ground level after cropping. Tie in the new canes (see *Supporting and Training Methods*, opposite), spacing them 3–4in (8–10cm) apart. Cut out damaged and weak canes so that those remaining receive as much light and air as possible. Loop over and tie in tall canes to prevent wind damage.

Fall-fruiting raspberries (see p.410) should have all canes cut to ground level in late winter. The new canes grow, then fruit in the fall.

The following spring, trim canes to 6in (15cm) above the topmost wire, cutting back any tips with cold damage. Remove dead, diseased, or crowded canes or any growing more than 9in (22cm) from the row.

Harvesting and storing

Pick the fruit when it is firm to ripe for preserves and freezing, and when it is fully ripe for eating fresh, harvesting every other day if possible.

How to Remove Unwanted Suckers

If suckers become overcrowded or are growing too far outside the row, as here, lift them and sever from the parent plant.

Recommended Summer-fruiting Raspberries

Early
'Baba Berry' **R**, ☆
'Boyne' **R**
'Chief' **R**
'Gatineau' **R**
'Killarney' **R**
'Madawaska' **R**
'Southland' **R**

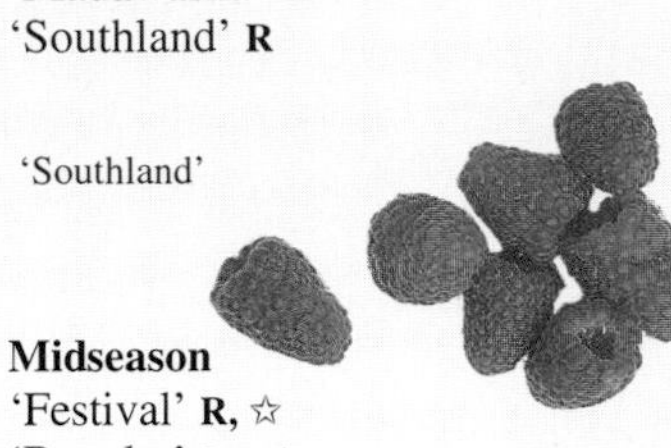

'Southland'

Midseason
'Festival' **R**, ☆
'Royalty' **Pu**, ☆
'Willamette' **R**

Late
'Cumberland' **Bf**
'Dormanred' **R**, ☆
'Marey' **R**
'Newburgh' **R**

Recommended Fall-fruiting Raspberries

'Autumn Bliss' **R**
'Fall Gold' **Y**, ☆

'Autumn Bliss'

'Heritage' **R**, ☆
'Latham' **R**

Key
Bf *Black fruit*
R *Red fruit*
Pu *Purple fruit*
Y *Yellow fruit*
☆ *Excellent flavor*

Pruning at the End of the First Season

1 *By about midsummer, cut down to ground level the old canes that were shortened when planting was carried out.*

2 *Tie the current season's strongest canes to the support wires (see inset) when they reach about 3ft (90cm). Remove weak shoots and those growing more than 9in (22cm) from the row.*

Established Raspberries, Pruning after Fruiting

1 *When all the fruit has been picked, cut back all the fruited canes to ground level.*

2 *Tie the current season's strongest canes to the support wires when about 3ft (90cm) tall, spacing them 4in (10cm) apart. Here the continuous lacing method is used.*

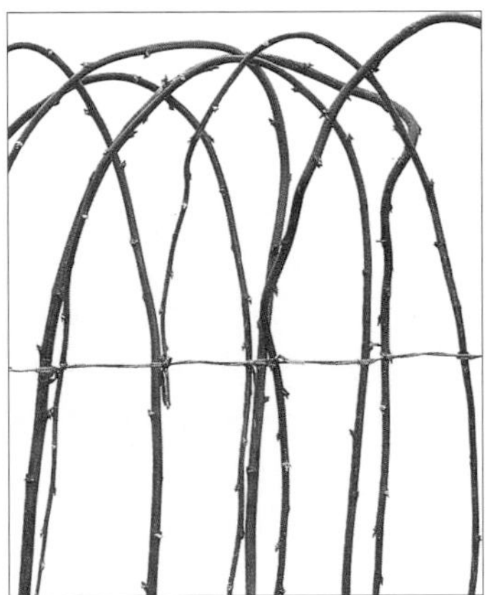

3 *At the end of the growing season, loop any tall canes over the top wire and tie them in.*

Spring Pruning

Before the growing season begins, tip prune all the canes to a healthy bud. Wherever possible, the cut should be made about 6in (15cm) above the top supporting wire.

Detach the fruit from the central plug and the stalk; fruits for exhibiting should be picked complete with stalk, however. Remove and discard diseased or damaged fruits promptly to prevent the spread of infection to healthy fruits.

Propagation

In late fall, select strong suckers that are growing away from the main fruiting row, and lift and replant them while they are dormant. Ensure that they are from plants that are known to be healthy and free-cropping; where doubt exists, use certified virus-free canes from fruit nurseries instead.

PROPAGATING BY SUCKERS

Lift suckers carefully in fall and sever them from the parent plant. Remove any remaining foliage. Ensure that the suckers are healthy and replant where new stock is required. Water in thoroughly.

Fall-fruiting raspberries

These should be sited in a sunny, sheltered position where the plants will quickly become established and the fruits should ripen in as short a time as possible. The fruits are borne freely on the upper part of the current season's canes. Planting and cultivation requirements are as for summer-fruiting raspberries.

Pruning of fall-fruiting raspberries is carried out in late winter before growth starts; the fruited canes are all cut down to the ground to stimulate new canes, which will fruit in the fall.

LATE-WINTER PRUNING
Before new growth starts, cut down all the canes to ground level. Fruit will be produced in fall on the new season's canes.

Blackcurrants *(Ribes nigrum)*

Blackcurrants thrive only in cool-temperate regions. The bushes flower early and so are prone to cold damage on exposed sites. They fruit in midsummer. (In parts of the US their cultivation is prohibited because they are hosts for a rust disease on white pine.) Jostaberries, a hybrid between blackcurrants and gooseberries, are cultivated in the same way.

Site and planting

The ground should be well prepared before planting to provide the best conditions for the continual production of new fruiting shoots. Remove all weeds from the site before planting, and dig in plenty of manure or garden compost.

Site

Choose a sunny site, sheltered from cold winds; some shade is tolerated. Protect blackcurrants from spring frosts if necessary (see COLD AND WIND PROTECTION, pp.520–21). Blackcurrants grow in a range of soils, but deep, moisture-retentive soil is most suitable. Avoid wet, poorly drained ground. A pH of 6.5–7 is preferable; lime very acid soils (see p.533). Blackcurrants are self-fertile.

Planting

Plant disease-free bushes from certified stock. Bushes sold under certification programs are normally two years old, but one-year-old plants from disease-free stock are also ideal. Planting in late fall is preferable; blackcurrants may be planted throughout the winter in mild areas. Always handle plants carefully to avoid damaging the basal buds. Space the bushes 4–5ft (1.2–1.5m) apart, with the same distance between rows. After planting, cut down all the shoots to one bud to encourage strong, new growth.

Routine care

In spring, apply a mulch of well-rotted manure as well as nitrogen and potassium fertilizers at a rate of 1oz/sq yd (35g/sq m). If manure is not available, increase the amount of fertilizer (see "Care of soft fruits," p.362) and mulch around the base of bushes with compost or leaf mold to conserve soil moisture.

Water in dry weather, but not as the fruits ripen, since this may cause the skins to split. Net bushes to protect ripening fruits from birds.

Pests and diseases

Sawfly larvae (p.551), aphids (p.552), and gall mites (p.558) may affect blackcurrants. Gray mold/*Botrytis* (p.564), powdery mildew (p.564), and fungal leaf spots (p.554) may also be troublesome.

Pruning and training

Regular pruning is essential to maintain high yields. Most of the fruits are borne on shoots produced the previous season. Pruning, together with adequate feeding, encourages strong, new shoots to develop.

Cut all stems to one bud above ground level after planting. The following year, remove downward-pointing or weak shoots. Thereafter, prune established bushes before late winter by cutting to the base a quarter to one-third of two-year-old wood, and any older, weak wood. No tip pruning is required. New shoots are pale tan, two-year-old wood is gray, and older wood black.

If a bush needs rejuvenating, cut out a greater proportion of the old wood, retaining only those branches from which strong, young shoots have developed. If few shoots develop yet the bush is healthy, cut down the whole plant to just above ground level in winter. Most bushes then rejuvenate well if fed and mulched, but one year's crop is sacrificed. The new shoots may need thinning, with the strongest retained. After ten years or so it is better to replace a bush than to try to rejuvenate it.

NEW AND FRUITED SHOOTS

BLACKCURRANT BUSH
YEAR 1, WINTER PRUNING

Immediately after planting, cut back all stems to 1 bud above soil level.

YEAR 2, WINTER PRUNING

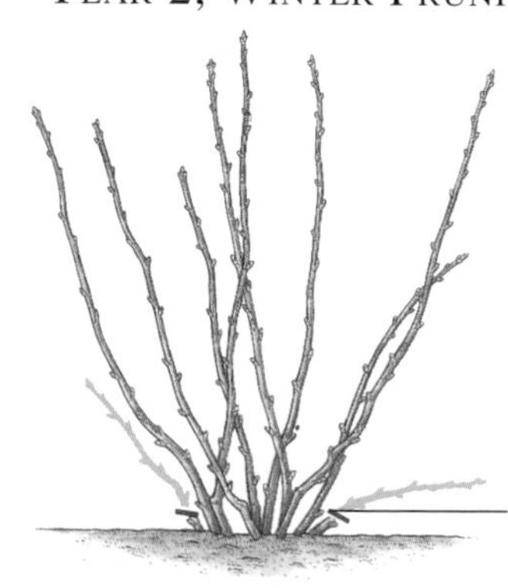

The bush should develop 7 or 8 strong, new shoots. Cut back any weak or low-growing shoots to about 1in (2.5cm) above soil level to encourage new growth from the base.

ESTABLISHED BUSH, PRUNING AFTER FRUITING

Cut out the old wood and a quarter to one-third of 2-year-old stems to stimulate new growth.

Remove any weak, damaged, or low-growing shoots, cutting close to the main stem.

Harvesting and storing

Blackcurrants are borne on fruit stems in bunches. Harvest the fruits when dry and ripe but still firm. Remove the whole bunch, not the individual fruits, which may otherwise be damaged. Early-ripening cultivars soon shed their fruits, but late-ripening cultivars retain their fruits much longer. Fruits may be either eaten fresh or stored by canning, preserving, or freezing.

Propagation

Blackcurrants are propagated from hardwood cuttings (see p.370) taken from healthy bushes in fall. Retain all buds on the cuttings to encourage basal shoots to grow.

HARDWOOD CUTTINGS

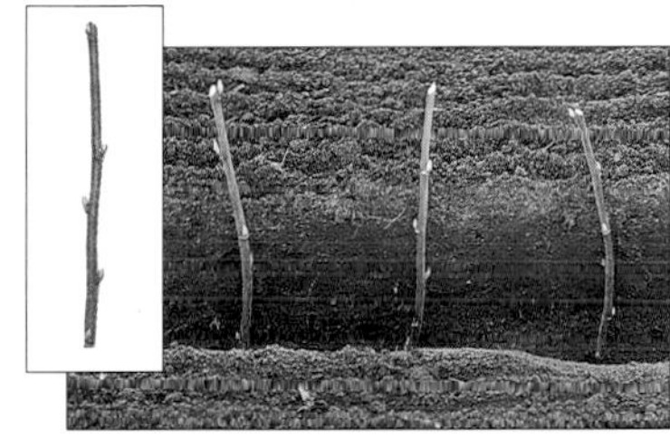

Insert 8–10in (20–25cm) cuttings in a trench, leaving 2 buds exposed.

RECOMMENDED BLACKCURRANTS

Early
'Amos Black'
'Boskoop Giant'
'Magnus'

Midseason
'Ben Lomond'

'Ben Lomond'

'Ben More'
'Ben Nevis'
'Blackdown'
'Climax'
'Consort'
'Wellington XXX'

Late
'Ben Sarek'
'Black September'
'Raven'
'Tinker'

'Ben Sarek'

Very late
'Champion'

Redcurrants and whitecurrants (*Ribes sativum*)

These fruits require a cool climate. Whitecurrants are a color variant of redcurrants. As with blackcurrants (opposite) cultivation is prohibited in parts of the US.

Site and planting

Redcurrants and whitecurrants need a sunny site but tolerate some shade; in hot climates, some shade may be necessary. Protect plants from winds to prevent stems from breaking, and in high temperatures to prevent scorch (see p.556).

Prepare the soil well before planting, as for blackcurrants (opposite). Heavier, moisture-retentive, but well-drained soils are preferable. Potassium deficiency may occur on very sandy soil. All cultivars are self-fertile.

When buying young bushes, make sure that the plants are from healthy stock that crops well. Plant in fall or winter: space bushes 4–5ft (1.2–1.5m) apart, cordons at 12in (30cm), and fans at 6ft (2m).

Routine care

For details of care, see blackcurrants (opposite). Maintain high potassium levels by applying potassium sulfate if necessary (muriate of potash may scorch the foliage).

Pests and diseases
Net the plants throughout the winter to prevent birds from damaging the buds. If the buds are damaged, delay winter pruning until just before bud break, and then prune to healthy buds. Aphids (p.552), sawfly larvae (p.551), gray mold/*Botrytis* (p.564), and spider mites (p.552) may affect plants.

Pruning and training

Redcurrants and whitecurrants are normally grown as open-center bushes but may be trained on wires as cordons, double cordons, or fans. Fruits develop on spurs produced by pruning back the side shoots.

Bush
A one-year-old bush should have two or three strong, young shoots; shorten these by half in late winter. Remove any that are less than 4in (10cm) from the ground to produce a short leg.

The following winter, shorten new growth by half to form the main branches, pruning to an outward-pointing bud. Prune side shoots

REDCURRANT BUSH
YEAR 1, WINTER PRUNING

Remove any side shoots growing within 4in (10cm) of soil level by cutting flush with the stem. This will form a short leg at the base.

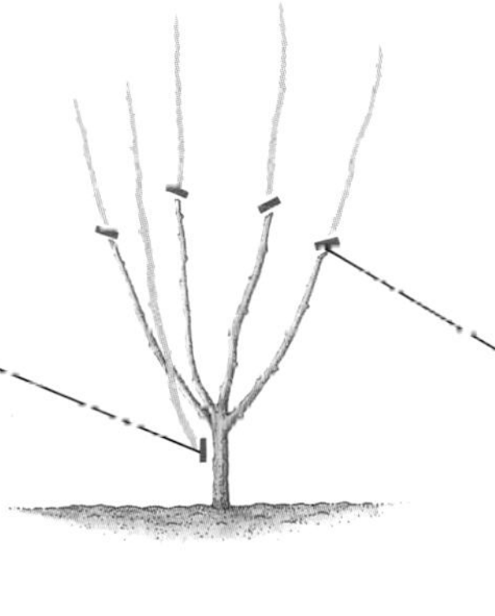

Prune each stem to an outward-facing bud (or to an upright shoot) about halfway along its length.

YEAR 2, WINTER PRUNING

To form the permanent branches, shorten leaders and side shoots by half of the new growth, cutting to outward-facing buds.

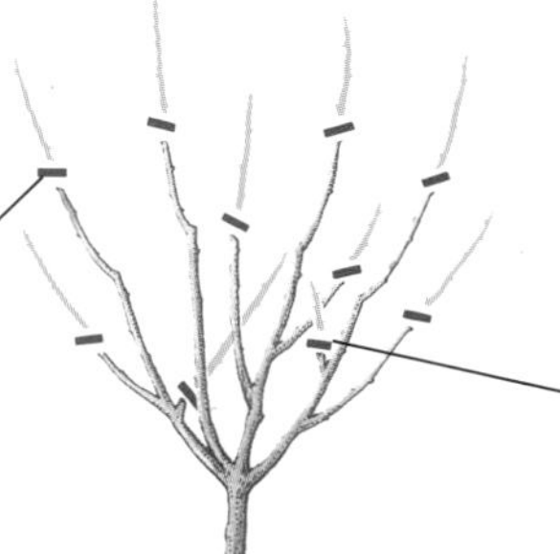

Cut back to 1 bud any side shoots crowding the center or growing downward.

ESTABLISHED BUSH, WINTER PRUNING

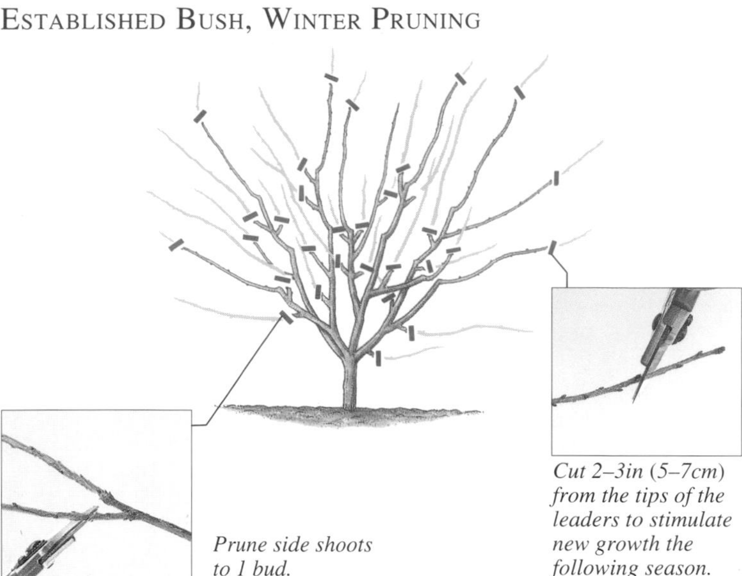

Prune side shoots to 1 bud.

Cut 2–3in (5–7cm) from the tips of the leaders to stimulate new growth the following season.

growing inward or downward to one bud. Prune established bushes by cutting back side shoots to one bud and tip pruning main branches.

Cordon

Single cordons are usually trained vertically. Set up wires at 24in (60cm) and 4ft (1.2m) from the ground. Select a main shoot on a one-year-old plant and train it against a stake; prune back the shoot by half, then cut back all other shoots to one bud.

In summer, prune side shoots to five leaves of new growth. Shorten these side shoots to one or two buds in winter, and prune the leader by a quarter of the new growth. When the leader reaches the top of its support, trim it to one bud. A double cordon is developed by training two shoots at about 30° to the ground as for apples (see "Forming a double cordon," p.377); they are subsequently trained vertically when 12in (30cm) apart. Each branch is then pruned as for a single cordon.

Fan

Fan-trained redcurrants and whitecurrants are established as for a peach fan (see p.389). Each branch should then be pruned as for a cordon.

Harvesting and storing

Harvest redcurrants and whitecurrants as for blackcurrants. The plants tend to retain ripe fruits a little longer than most blackcurrants. Fruits may be canned, preserved, or frozen.

Propagation

Take hardwood cuttings in early fall. Use young shoots 12–15in (30–38cm) long, and remove all but the top three or four buds, to produce a plant with a short stem.

Insert the cuttings in moist, fertile soil, burying them by about half their length, and firm well. Once rooted, transplant the young plants to their final positions.

RECOMMENDED REDCURRANTS AND WHITECURRANTS

Early
'Cascade' (red)
'Jonkheer van Tets' (red)

Midseason
'Diploma' (red)
'Red Lake' (red)
'Stephens No. 9' (red)
'White Grape' (white)
'White Imperial' (white)

Late
'Cherry' (red)

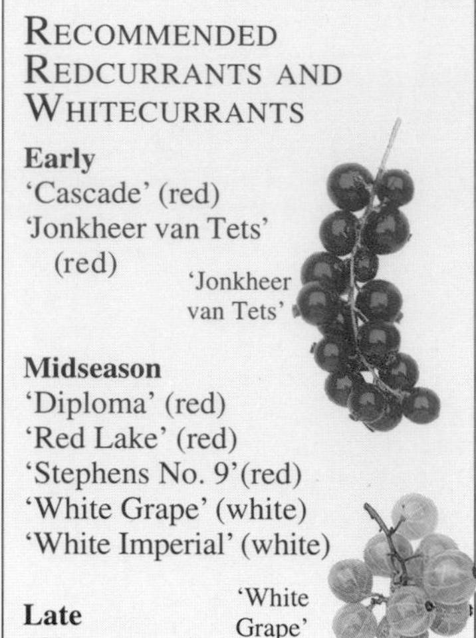

'Jonkheer van Tets'

'White Grape'

HARDWOOD CUTTINGS

Cuttings should be 12in (30cm) long. Retain only the top few buds.

REDCURRANT CORDON

YEAR 1, WINTER PRUNING

YEAR 1, SUMMER PRUNING

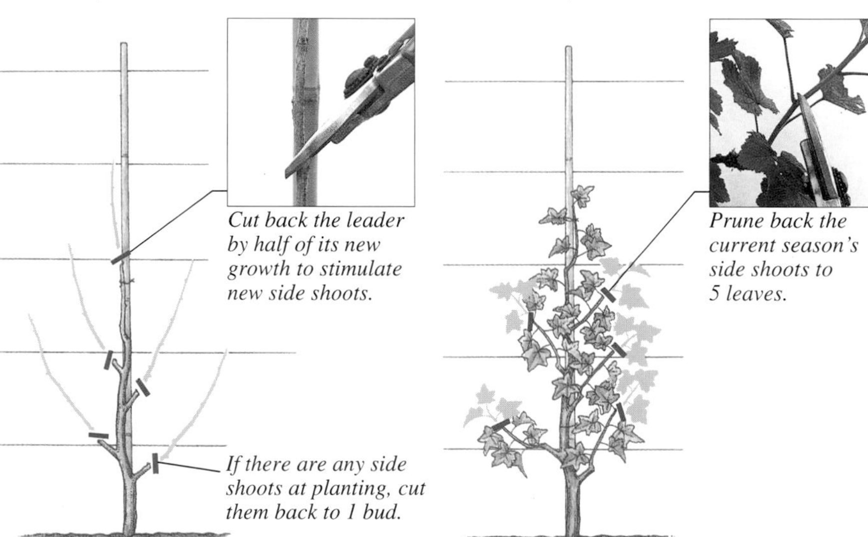

Cut back the leader by half of its new growth to stimulate new side shoots.

If there are any side shoots at planting, cut them back to 1 bud.

Prune back the current season's side shoots to 5 leaves.

ESTABLISHED CORDON, WINTER PRUNING

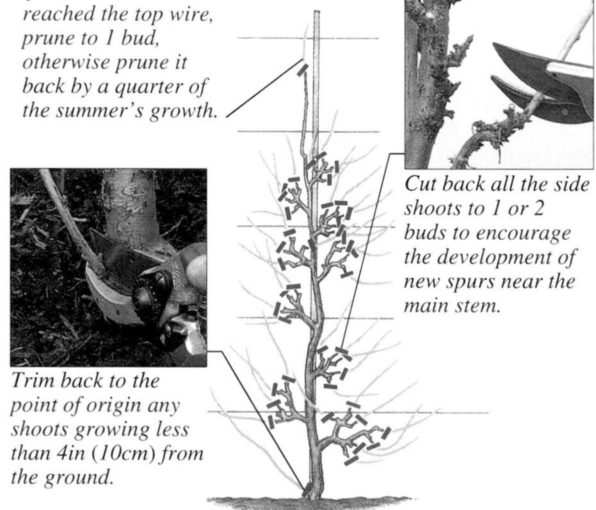

If the leader has reached the top wire, prune to 1 bud, otherwise prune it back by a quarter of the summer's growth.

Cut back all the side shoots to 1 or 2 buds to encourage the development of new spurs near the main stem.

Trim back to the point of origin any shoots growing less than 4in (10cm) from the ground.

Gooseberries (*Ribes uva-crispa*)

Gooseberries are easy to grow but, like currants (also *Ribes*), need cool conditions and, if summer temperatures are high, adequate shade. Fruits ripen yellow, red, white, or green, depending on the cultivar. Methods of cultivation, pruning, and training are similar to those used for redcurrants.

Site and planting

Growing conditions and planting distances are as for redcurrants (see p.411). All cultivars are self-fertile. As with blackcurrants (p.410), cultivation is restricted in parts of the US, since the plants host a rust disease that affects white pine.

Routine care

General maintenance is largely as for blackcurrants (see p.410). Gooseberries require high potassium levels and regular mulching, ideally with well-rotted manure. New shoots on young bushes are vulnerable to breakage and need protection from strong winds. If the crop is heavy, thin the fruits in late spring.

Pests and diseases

Deer (p.572) may cause severe bud loss, so protect plants where feasible. If the buds have been attacked, delay winter pruning until bud break, then prune to live buds. Plants may be affected by powdery mildew (p.564), which attacks the tips of shoots; sawfly larvae (p.551); and bacterial or fungal leaf spots (p.554).

Pruning and training
Young plants may be trained as bushes, cordons, or fans as for redcurrants. A number of gooseberry cultivars, such as 'Leveller', have a natural drooping habit, however. To prevent stems from trailing to the ground, prune to upward-pointing buds, particularly when training young bushes.

Bush For initial pruning, see redcurrants (p.411); aim to create an open-center bush on a stem 4–6in (10–15cm) long. Established bushes may be pruned by regulated or spur pruning in winter.

Regulated pruning is the simpler method: remove low, crowded, and crossing shoots to maintain well-spaced growth at the center of the bush. Also remove any old, unproductive branches and select new, young shoots to replace them.

Spur pruning is more labor intensive: all the side shoots are shortened to a suitable bud 3in (8cm) from the main branches. The branch leaders also need to be tip pruned.

GOOSEBERRY BUSH

YEAR 1, WINTER PRUNING

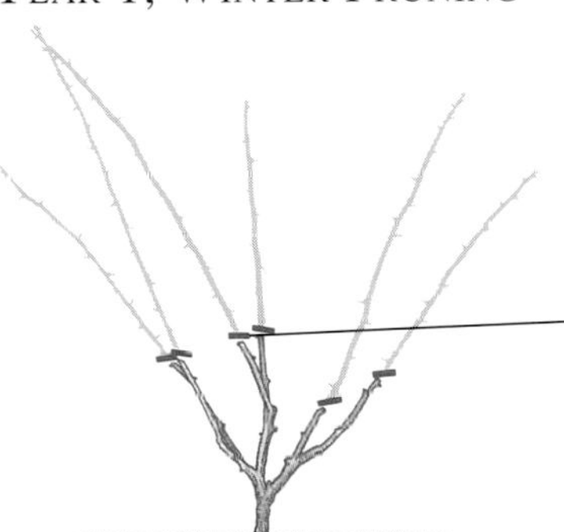

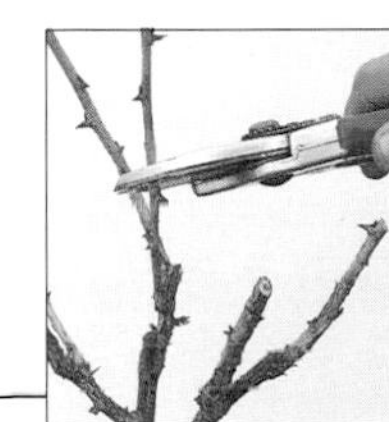

Prune back all the shoots by a half to three-quarters to an outward-facing bud.

ESTABLISHED BUSH, REGULATED PRUNING, WINTER

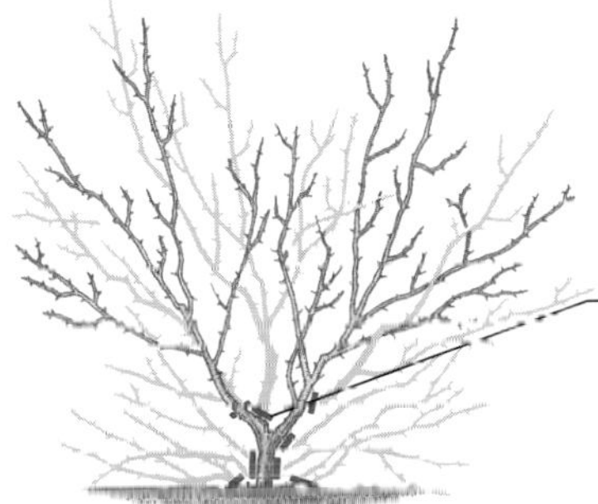

Cut out older branches to prevent overcrowding and to maintain an open center.

The bush should have mainly young shoots, evenly spaced, pointing up- or outward.

ESTABLISHED BUSH, SPUR PRUNING, WINTER

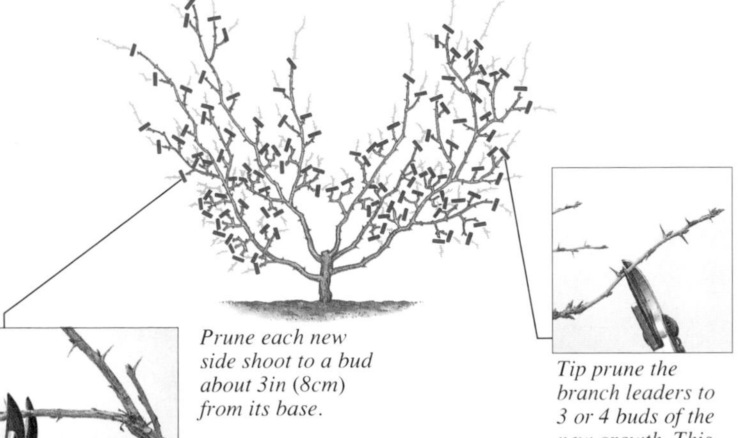

Prune each new side shoot to a bud about 3in (8cm) from its base.

Tip prune the branch leaders to 3 or 4 buds of the new growth. This encourages the formation of spurs.

GOOSEBERRY STANDARD

Standard Cultivars to be trained as standards are grafted onto *Ribes odoratum* or *R. divaricatum* stock. Select one shoot of the rootstock and train it vertically, keeping any side shoots short. It will take about three years to grow to a suitable height. When the stem has thickened and reached about 3½–4ft (1.1–1.2m), trim off the side shoots and graft on the selected cultivar using whip-and-tongue grafting (see p.369). Use a strong stake to support the stem. The scion will develop and branch naturally the following summer. The next winter, establish the framework as for a bush, and then prune and train in the same way.

Cordon and fan These are trained as for redcurrants (see opposite). Once established, prune in summer, reducing new side shoots to five leaves. In winter, shorten shoots to 3in (8cm) and tip prune leaders.

Harvesting and storing
Fruits should ripen by midsummer. Gooseberries for cooking may be picked green as part of thinning, but allow dessert-quality cultivars to ripen fully for the best flavor, ensuring that they are protected from birds. Yellow-, white-, and red-berried cultivars should be left to ripen to their full color before they are picked. All freeze well.

Propagation
Layering is the easiest method. American gooseberries are easy to root from hardwood cuttings; the European varieties may take two years. When the rooted cutting is lifted, rub off all low buds and side shoots, otherwise troublesome suckers will develop.

RECOMMENDED GOOSEBERRIES

Early
'Abundance' (red) **A**
'Catherine' (yellow) **A**
'Early Sulphur' (yellow) **A**

'Downing'

Midseason
'Achilles' (dark red) **A**
'Clark' (red) **Rm, E**
'Downing' (green) **A**
'Hinnomaeki Red' (red) **A**
'Leveller' (yellow) **E**
'Oregon Champion' (green) **A**
'Pixwell' (red-purple) **Th, A**
'Poorman' (red) **Rm, A**
'Whinham's Industry' (red) **E**

'Whinham's Industry'

Late
'Captivator' (red) **Th, A**
'Lancashire Lad' (red) **Rm, E**
'Ross' (red) **A**
'Silvia' (red) **A**
'White Lion' (white) **E**

KEY
Rm *Some resistance to mildew*
Th *Nearly thornless*
A *American cultivar*
E *European cultivar*

HARDWOOD CUTTINGS

1 *In early fall, take cuttings of well-ripened young shoots. Trim to 12–15in (30–38cm) with an angled cut above a bud at the top and a straight cut at the base. Insert in a trench to half their length.*

2 *The following fall, carefully lift the rooted cuttings. Remove basal buds or shoots less than 4in (10cm) from the base (see inset) before transplanting the young plants.*

Blueberries (*Vaccinium corymbosum* and *V. ashei*)

Highbush blueberries (*Vaccinium corymbosum*) are derived from the American wild blueberry. They produce clusters of dark purplish blue fruit with a gray bloom. Blueberries require a cool, moist climate and 700–1,200 hours below 45°F (7°C), except for cultivars adapted to very warm areas ('O'Neal' and 'Sharpblue'). All need very acid soil. Highbush blueberries grow to a height of 4½–6ft (1.3–2m) and are deciduous, with striking fall color.

Rabbit-eye blueberries (*Vaccinium ashei*) are grown in the same way as the highbush group but tolerate less acid soils and drier conditions. They are cultivated mainly in the US and Australia. The fruits are smaller and grittier than highbush blueberries.

Cropping, in mid- to late summer, is light at first, but yields of 5lb (2.25kg) of fruit per bush may be obtained after five or six years, and on older bushes considerably more. Although blueberries are self-fertile, the plants produce larger crops when two or more cultivars are planted close together.

HIGHBUSH BLUEBERRY BUSH

Site and planting

Blueberries need a sunny location, although they tolerate some shade. The soil must be well drained. Clear all perennial weeds from the site before planting, and if the soil is alkaline, correct this by mixing a 6in (15cm) layer of acidic compost with the existing soil to a depth of at least 2ft (60cm). Alternatively, apply flowers of sulfur at a rate of 2–4oz/sq yd (50–120g/sq m).

Blueberries may also be grown in large pots or tubs with a diameter of 12–15in (30–38cm), filled with ericaceous soil mix.

Plant in late fall or early spring, spacing bushes 5ft (1.5m) apart. Cover the roots with 1–2in (2.5–5cm) of soil, and mulch with acid compost or leaf mold. Growing a mixture of cultivars results in better fertilization and heavier crops.

Routine care

To promote growth and cropping and to maintain acidity, apply a dressing each spring of ammonium sulfate at 1oz/sq yd (35g/sq m), potassium sulfate at 1oz/sq yd (35g/sq m), and bone meal at 3oz/sq yd (105g/sq m). Keep plants mulched with acid compost, and water with rainwater. Avoid root disturbance when weeding.

Pests and diseases

The fruits may be eaten by birds, so provide protection by netting the bushes (see "Protection from animals," p.363). Other pests and diseases rarely cause trouble.

ESTABLISHED BLUEBERRY BUSH, WINTER PRUNING

Cut weak or unproductive shoots back to where a strong new shoot can take over.

Cut older, nonfruiting branches to ground level to stimulate new basal shoots.

Cut back any low or downward-pointing branches to their point of origin or to a branch growing in the required direction.

Pruning and training

Blueberries fruit on two- or three-year-old wood. New bushes need little pruning for two or three years, but cut out weak shoots to provide a strong basic framework.

Thereafter, prune to ensure regular production of new shoots from the base, as for blackcurrants (see p.410), by cutting out some of the oldest wood each year.

Harvesting and storing

The fruits ripen over a period of several weeks. Pick over the bushes carefully, harvesting only the ripe fruits, which part easily from the cluster. Blueberries may be successfully stored for later use by preserving, canning, or freezing.

Propagation

Take 4–6in (10–15cm) softwood cuttings in midsummer, dip them in hormone rooting powder, and then insert them in an acidic, peat/sand rooting medium. Place the cuttings in a propagator until rooted, then transplant to a larger pot. Harden off before planting out.

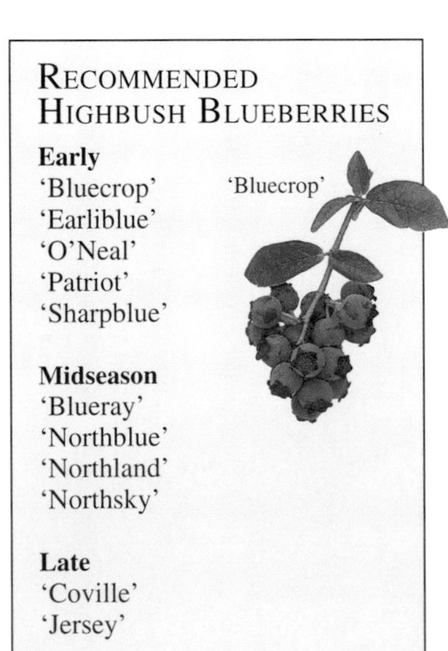

RECOMMENDED HIGHBUSH BLUEBERRIES

Early
'Bluecrop'
'Earliblue'
'O'Neal'
'Patriot'
'Sharpblue'

Midseason
'Blueray'
'Northblue'
'Northland'
'Northsky'

Late
'Coville'
'Jersey'

'Bluecrop'

BLUEBERRY SOFTWOOD CUTTINGS

1 *Select suitable softwood material and take cuttings at least 4in (10cm) long. Cut just above a leaf joint.*

2 *Trim the base of each cutting just below a node with a sharp knife, and remove the leaves from the lower third of the cuttings. Dip the ends of the cuttings in hormone rooting powder.*

3 *Prepare a pot of acid cuttings soil mix. Make holes with a dibber and insert each cutting so that the basal leaves are just above the soil mix. Water, label, and place the pot in a propagator.*

Tender fruits

Most tender fruits originate from tropical and subtropical regions, where they thrive in the warm, dry conditions. Apart from olives, which need to be treated to remove their bitterness, many may be eaten straight from the tree, or stored for a short period of time in suitable conditions. Members of the citrus family that are too acid for eating, such as lemons and limes, are grown either for their juice or for use in preserves and marmalades. Since tender fruits are generally grown in hot climates, where the soil may be lacking in nutrients, it is important to prepare the site adequately when planting: an extra 4–6oz (110–80g) of slow-release fertilizer forked into the bottom of the planting hole will help the plants to establish quickly.

In cool-temperate climates, some tender fruits may still be grown, in containers or under cover, as long as the correct temperature and humidity levels are provided. Although many do not consistently ripen their fruits under cover, they nevertheless make attractive ornamentals.

Pineapples (*Ananas comosus*)

Pineapples are tropical perennials that produce terminal fruits, each composed of up to 200 seedless fruitlets. For best results they need full sun and temperatures of 64–80°F (18–30°C) with humidity of 70–80 percent. Cultivar groups include the Cayenne Group, the Queen Group, and the Spanish Group; the Spanish has the sweetest flavor.

Site and planting

Select a sunny site that is sheltered from strong winds. Pineapples tolerate a wide range of soils but prefer a sandy, medium loam with a pH of 5–6.5. Plant suckers about 12in (30cm) apart, with 24in (60cm) between rows, or at a spacing of 20in (50cm) each way.

Routine care

Use a general-purpose fertilizer with medium potassium and high nitrogen levels at intervals of two to three months, at a rate of 2oz (50g) per plant. Correct any iron and zinc deficiencies by spraying with a 2 percent solution of ferrous or zinc sulfate. Water pineapples regularly in dry weather, and apply an organic mulch to conserve soil moisture.

Pests and diseases

Pests that may affect pineapples include mealybugs (p.552), root-knot nematodes (p.566), scale insects (p.554), spider mites (p.552), and thrips (p.553).

The most serious disease affecting pineapple plants in the open is heart-rot, caused by *Phytophthora cinnamoni* and *P. parasitica*, fungi that often affect pineapples grown in wet conditions. Since this is difficult to treat, it is advisable to guard against infection by planting resistant cultivars where these are available. All suckers that are required for propagation should be dipped in a fungicide, since the fungus enters through wounds.

Growing under cover

Plant rooted pineapple cuttings in well-prepared beds with good drainage, or use pots at least 12in (30cm) in diameter. Use a soil mix with a high organic content, and apply a liquid feed every three to four weeks. Maintain a temperature of at least 68°F (20°C) and humidity of about 70 percent. Water regularly and thoroughly, particularly while young plants are establishing.

Harvesting and storing

Harvest the fruits when they begin to turn yellow by cutting the stem 1–2in (2.5–5cm) below each fruit. Pineapples may be stored for up to three weeks at 46°F (8°C) and at 90 percent humidity.

Propagation

The terminal crown shoot may be used as a cutting; remove it with about ½in (1cm) of the fruit attached. Pineapples may also be propagated by suckers that arise from the leaf axils, the base of the stem, or below the fruit; these may be detached with a sharp knife. Dip the cut surfaces of shoots in a fungicide, then leave them to dry for several days. Remove the lower leaves and insert the cuttings in pots of sandy cuttings soil mix. Pot them on into 6in (15cm) pots when rooted.

Propagating Pineapples from Suckers

Sever basal shoots or suckers and leave to dry before inserting in a sandy cuttings soil mix (see inset).

Pineapple

Propagating Pineapples from the Crown Shoot

1 *Scoop out the crown shoot of a ripe pineapple with a sharp knife, ensuring that you do not cut through the base of the shoot. Dip the wound in fungicide and leave for several days to dry.*

2 *Insert the prepared cutting into a pot of sandy cuttings soil mix and maintain at a temperature of at least 64°F (18°C). The cutting should be rooted and ready to pot on within a few weeks.*

Recommended Pineapples

Cayenne Group
'Hilo'
'Smooth Cayenne'
'Sugar Baby'

Queen Group
'Natal Queen'
'Ripley Queen'

Spanish Group
'Red Spanish'
'Singapore Spanish'

Papayas (*Carica papaya*)

Papayas are slender, generally single-stemmed, tropical trees, growing up to 12–15ft (4–5m) with a spread of 3–6ft (1–2m) at the crown. The fruits may be up to 8in (20cm) long when mature. Temperatures of 72–82°F (22–8°C) with humidity of 60–70 percent are normally required for fruiting; some cultivars will withstand temperatures as low as 59°F (15°C), although flowering and fruiting may then be poor.

Site and planting

Choose a warm, sunny site with protection from strong winds. Papayas require fertile, well-drained soil, with a pH of 6–7; good drainage is essential, since the trees are sensitive to waterlogging.

Many cultivars of papaya are dioecious, with male and female flowers produced on separate plants, but monoecious cultivars are sometimes available. One male tree is usually sufficient to pollinate five or six female trees. Pollination is normally by insects and wind. Plant at a spacing of 8–10ft (2.5–3m).

RECOMMENDED PAPAYAS

'Fairchild' **D**
'Higgins' **Mo**
'Kapoho' **Mo**
'Solo' **Mo**
'Sunrise' **Mo**

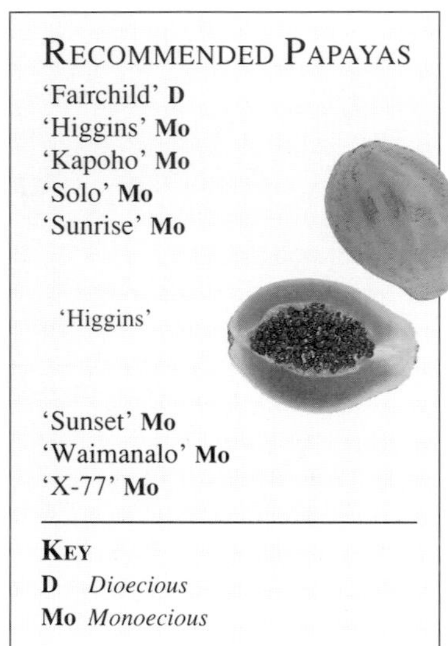

'Higgins'

'Sunset' **Mo**
'Waimanalo' **Mo**
'X-77' **Mo**

KEY
D *Dioecious*
Mo *Monoecious*

Routine care

Apply a general-purpose, balanced fertilizer, 2lb 3oz–3lb 6oz (1–1.5kg) per tree per year, in two or three separate dressings during the growing season. Water regularly in dry conditions, and conserve moisture with an organic mulch. Papayas may be affected by viruses and nematodes after three or four years; if this happens, replace diseased papayas with seedlings or young plants of named cultivars.

Pests and diseases

Common pests in the open are root-knot nematodes (p.566); papaya diseases include anthracnose (see "Fungal leaf spots," p.554), bunchy top virus (see "Viruses," p.555), and damping off of seedlings (p.570). Papaya trees grown under cover may also be attacked by aphids (p.552), thrips (p.553), whiteflies (p.552), and mealybugs (p.552).

Growing under cover

In temperate areas, papayas may be grown successfully under cover, if adequate light and temperature levels are provided. Raise seedlings or cuttings as described under "Propagation," below. Transplant them when they are 8–10in (20–25cm) tall into prepared beds, or pots with a minimum diameter of 14in (35cm). Use a fertile soil mix, to which a slow-release fertilizer has been added. Maintain a temperature of at least 72°F (22°C) and humidity of 60–70 percent. Apply a liquid feed or light dressings of fertilizer with medium to high nitrogen content every three to four weeks. The plants should be watered regularly.

PAPAYA TREE

Pruning and training

Remove any lateral branches, since these are unproductive. After fruiting, prune to 12in (30cm) from the ground; of the new shoots that arise, select the strongest as the new leader and cut back the others.

Harvesting and storing

Harvest the fruits when they are orange to red. They may be stored at 50–55°F (10–13°C) with 70 percent humidity for up to 14 days.

Propagation

Seed is the usual method of propagation. Sow the seed under cover in trays or, preferably, in bottomless pots 2½–3½in (6–9cm) in diameter. Handle the seedlings carefully, since papayas are sensitive to root disturbance. Harden them off, then plant them out when they are 12–18in (30–45cm) tall. To obtain adequate numbers of female plants when dioecious cultivars are used, plant seedlings in clumps of three or four, thinning to one female plant after flowering begins. Monoecious seedlings may be planted singly.

Cuttings are usually obtained by pruning mature trees to 12–16in (30–40cm) from the ground and using the new shoots as cuttings. Dip their bases in hormone rooting powder and grow on under cover.

Citrus (*Citrus* spp.)

The genus *Citrus* includes oranges, lemons, and a number of other edible species (see opposite). Citrus form small, widely branching trees on trunks of 20–24in (50–60cm) in circumference. The trees will reach a height of 10–30ft (3–10m) and a spread of 15–25ft (5–8m). Limes are the most compact, grapefruits among the largest and most vigorous. Lemon trees have a more upright habit than the other species. Also discussed here is the kumquat, formerly included within the genus *Citrus* but now classified as *Fortunella*. Its cultivation requirements are similar to those of *Citrus*.

Citrus is a subtropical genus. All species and hybrids are evergreen and have aromatic leaves. For optimum growth, they require a temperature of 58–86°F (15–30°C), although most species will survive short periods at 32°F (0°C). They thrive at altitudes of 320ft (100m) or above, with humidity levels of 60–70 percent, unless otherwise stated. Flowering is not seasonal but occurs during warm periods with regular rainfall; flowers and fruits may coincide. Many species of citrus make excellent plants for growing in containers under cover in temperate areas.

Site and planting

Citrus prefer a sunny exposure and should be protected by windbreaks in exposed areas. They tolerate a wide range of soils but do best in fertile, well-drained, slightly acid soils (pH 6–6.5). Young citrus respond well to highly fertile soil.

Rootstocks

Sweet orange may be used, since it is compatible with all widely grown citrus species and cultivars. Rough lemon rootstocks produce early-bearing, vigorous trees resistant to tristeza (quick decline) viruses, but their fruits may have thick rinds and a low acid and sugar content. Sour orange is also a good universal rootstock, but it is susceptible to tristeza viruses.

Trifoliate orange is a dwarfing rootstock that is suitable for cooler areas. It has some resistance to nematodes but is not compatible with certain cultivars of lemon. Cleopatra mandarin and Rangpur lime are also used as rootstocks. Seedling rootstocks may also be raised – for details, see "Propagation," opposite.

Pollination

Most citrus, including sweet orange, are self-fertile, so a pollinator is not normally required; many, for instance the 'Washington' sweet orange, also produce seedless fruits.

Planting

Planting distances vary between 15ft (5m) and 30ft (10m) each way, depending on the vigor of the species or cultivar chosen, so seek specialist advice from the nursery when

SWEET ORANGE TREE

purchasing a tree. Citrus are sensitive to waterlogging, so on a site where the soil is not sufficiently well drained, plant each tree on a slight mound, 2–3in (5–7cm) high, to allow excess water to run off.

Routine care

During the first few years, feed citrus trees with a balanced fertilizer that has a high nitrogen and medium potassium level at a rate of 2lb 3oz (1kg) per tree per year. The fertilizer should be given in two or three doses, applied at regular intervals around the base of each tree, when the trees are in active growth. Double the quantity of fertilizer after five years. A mulch helps retain moisture.

Remove all weeds around the bases of the trees, and water thoroughly in dry weather, particularly when the flowers or fruits are developing. The nonseasonal habit of fruiting makes fruit thinning unnecessary. Remove any suckers.

Pests and diseases
Various mealybugs (p.552), scale insects (p.554), thrips (p.553), spider mites (p.552), aphids (p.552), root and crown rots (see "*Phytophthora* root rots," p.560), fungal leaf spots (p.554), and scab (p.564) may affect citrus grown in the open and under cover. Root-knot nematodes (p.566) may be serious pests on some soils. In the tropics and subtropics, fruit flies may be a problem (p.565).

Many citrus species and cultivars may be infected with tristeza virus, which is spread by aphids and causes stem pitting on grapefruits, limes, and citrons. Infected trees will lose vigor and produce small fruits. The virus is most likely to affect cultivars that are budded onto sour orange rootstocks. Spray against aphids, or use alternative rootstocks.

Growing under cover

In temperate areas, several cultivars of sweet orange, tangerine, lemon, and lime, as well as the Seville orange and kumquat, may be grown as ornamentals under cover, although they may not be relied on to bear fruit. Before planting, prepare the beds well, or use large containers, at least 2ft (60cm) in diameter, filled with a nutrient-rich soil mix. Maintain a minimum temperature of 68°F (20°C) with at least 75 percent humidity, and water the citrus plants regularly. Apply a liquid fertilizer each month once the young trees are well established.

Pruning and training

Shorten the main branches of newly planted trees by one-third in the first year. This encourages lateral growth and produces a rounded shape. After fruiting, prune only to remove dead, diseased, or crossing branches and any that touch the soil. Citrus may also be trained as standards or half-standards (see p.375), particularly if grown as ornamentals.

Harvesting and storing

Citrus fruits may take from six to eight months, or even longer, from fruit set to ripen, depending on the climate (the lower the temperature, the longer the period required). In areas of low sunshine, mature citrus fruits may remain green.

Harvest the fruits when they have ripened by cutting them at the fruit stalk with pruners or a sharp knife, or by pulling the fruit stalk from the tree with a slight twist. Undamaged fruits may be stored for several weeks at 38–42°F (4–6°C).

Propagation

Some citrus may be raised from seed. Most citrus seeds are polyembryonic and therefore clonal, reproducing characteristics of the parent tree. The quality of fruits from non-polyembryonic cultivars is variable. For named cultivars the usual means of propagation is by budding.

To raise citrus trees from seed, use fresh seed, sowing it in trays or pots of seed soil mix at a depth of $1^1/_4$–2in (3–5cm). Water the seeds frequently and maintain a temperature of 77–90°F (25–32°C). When the seedlings are large enough to handle, prick them out into 4 or $4^1/_2$in (10 or 12cm) pots. When they are 8–12in (20–30cm) high, transplant them into 8–12in (20–30cm) pots, or plant them out, after hardening them off. Alternatively, repot seedlings into 10–15in (25–38cm) pots and plant in the open when they are 2–3ft (60–90cm) tall.

T-budding (see p.369) is the usual method of propagating citrus vegetatively. Use seedling citrus stocks with stems $^1/_2$in (1cm) in diameter. After three to four weeks, remove the budding tape and cut the stock growth above the budded area halfway across. When the bud shoot is 1in (2.5cm) long, the stock growth above the budded shoot may be removed entirely.

Ripe Sweet Oranges

Species of citrus

Limes (*Citrus aurantiifolia*)
Limes fall into three groups. Key limes, also known as West Indian or Mexican limes, have small, thin-skinned fruits with seeds; fruits are used when the skin is yellow. 'Tahiti'-type limes (actually *C. latifolia*) are larger and seedless. The third group includes 'Bearss' and other tart limes.

Most limes are grown as seedlings but may also be reproduced by bud-grafting onto lemon rootstock.

Sour, Seville, or bitter oranges (*Citrus aurantium*)
The sour, or bitter, orange is used mainly as a rootstock. The fruits, which are used for making marmalade, are about 3in (7cm) in diameter, rounded, with thick peel. They are fairly acidic, but some forms of the species bear fruits of lower citric acid content.

Lemons (*Citrus limon*)
Most lemon cultivars produce seeded fruits that may remain green, rather than turning yellow, even when fully mature. To grow successfully in the open, they require an altitude of 960–1,600ft (300–500m), with little variation in temperature, and need a minimum temperature of 68°F (20°C).

An interesting hybrid between lemon and lime is the "lemonime"; this may be grown in the open in subtropical areas or as an ornamental under cover in temperate areas.

Citrons (*Citrus medica*)
The fruits of the citron are ovoid and yellow, with a thick rind and a rough surface, and may be up to 6in (15cm) long; the pulp is acid with little juice.

No specific citron cultivars have been recorded. Citrons are grown mainly for their peel, which is usually candied for use in the confectionery

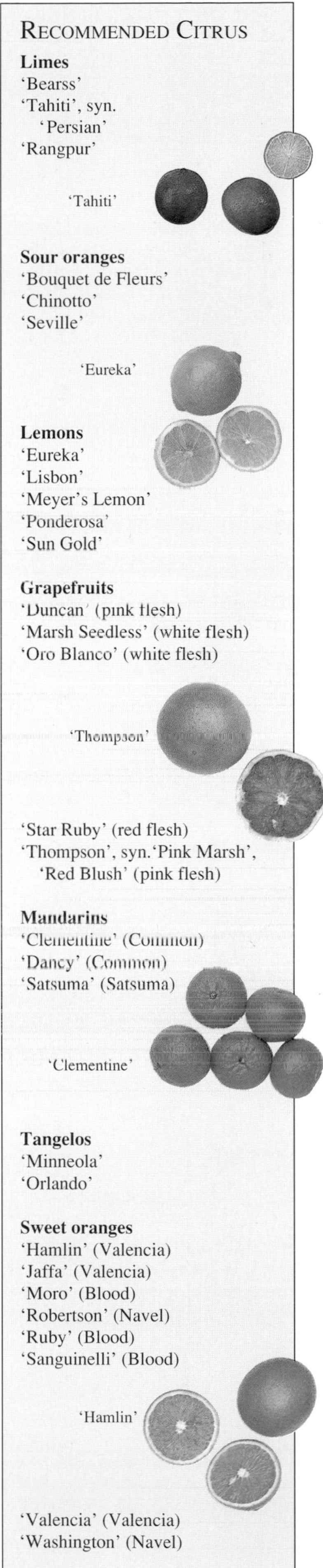

Recommended Citrus

Limes
'Bearss'
'Tahiti', syn. 'Persian'
'Rangpur'

Sour oranges
'Bouquet de Fleurs'
'Chinotto'
'Seville'

Lemons
'Eureka'
'Lisbon'
'Meyer's Lemon'
'Ponderosa'
'Sun Gold'

Grapefruits
'Duncan' (pink flesh)
'Marsh Seedless' (white flesh)
'Oro Blanco' (white flesh)
'Star Ruby' (red flesh)
'Thompson', syn. 'Pink Marsh', 'Red Blush' (pink flesh)

Mandarins
'Clementine' (Common)
'Dancy' (Common)
'Satsuma' (Satsuma)

Tangelos
'Minneola'
'Orlando'

Sweet oranges
'Hamlin' (Valencia)
'Jaffa' (Valencia)
'Moro' (Blood)
'Robertson' (Navel)
'Ruby' (Blood)
'Sanguinelli' (Blood)
'Valencia' (Valencia)
'Washington' (Navel)

trade. Citrons make attractive ornamentals, however; in temperate areas they may be grown under cover (see p.417).

Grapefruits (*Citrus paradisi*)
The fruits of the grapefruit are large, rounded, up to 4–6in (10–15cm) in diameter, and yellow. Most cultivars are well adapted to growing at or just above sea level, provided the temperature exceeds 77°F (25°C). There are two principal groups of grapefruit in cultivation, one with white pulp, the other with pink flesh, ranging in color to deep red. Seeded and seedless cultivars are available in both groups.

Mandarins or tangerines (*Citrus reticulata*)
Mandarins, or tangerines, generally require temperatures above 64°F (18°C), but very high temperatures may result in loss of fruit quality. Cross-pollination between trees frequently occurs; this gives rise to fruits with many seeds. Some varieties have a particularly loose skin that makes the fruits easy to peel.

The Satsuma Group is the one most frequently cultivated. The fruits of cultivars in this group are mainly slightly flattened and seedless, with a well-developed orange color and sweet flavor. Some cultivars have a "navel," a miniature fruit that develops at the end of the fruit. The other three groups are the Cleopatra Group, which is widely used as a rootstock but has unpalatable fruits itself; the King Group; and the Common Mandarin Group (which includes the cultivar 'Clementine').

Tangelos and ugli fruits (*Citrus reticulata* x *C. paradisi*)
These hybrids between the grapefruit and the mandarin inherit characteristics from their parents: the fruits are larger than those of the mandarin but have easily peeled skin. They may be grown under cover in temperate areas, where they occasionally bear fruit.

Sweet oranges (*Citrus sinensis*)
Most sweet oranges, including the widely grown 'Jaffa' orange, belong to the Valencia (or Common) Group. The fruits are medium to large and spherical to ovoid, with few or no seeds. Oranges in this group may be slightly acidic but they have an excellent flavor.

Sweet oranges are usually grown from seed, but a few cultivars are propagated vegetatively by budding. Seedlings are also used as rootstocks for grafting with other species. Sweet orange cultivars are classified into three groups: Navel oranges, Blood oranges, and Valencia oranges.

Navel oranges have a small secondary fruit at the main fruit apex and are usually seedless. They have an excellent flavor and grow well in slightly cooler climates; California is noted for its Navels. Blood oranges are similar, but their pulp, flesh, and juice are red (except when grown at high temperatures).

Two sweet orange crops at different stages of development may be borne on a tree at the same time.

Kumquats (*Fortunella japonica*, *F. margarita*)
Originating in China, kumquats are fairly hardy: they can withstand temperatures down to 23°F (-5°C) for short periods. The fruits, which are eaten unpeeled, are small and yellow. Those of *Fortunella japonica* are rounded in shape, while those of *F. margarita* are ovoid.

The Calamondin (x *Citrofortunella microcarpa*) is a mandarin-kumquat hybrid; it is grown as an ornamental in temperate regions.

Tree tomatoes (*Cyphomandra betacea*)

Also known as tamarillos, tree tomatoes are subtropical trees growing to 10–15ft (3–5m), with a spread of 5–8ft (1.5–2.5m). They are most productive at 68–82°F (20–28°C) with 70 percent humidity. The red, orange, or yellow fruits are ovoid and may be 3in (7.5cm) long.

RIPE TREE TOMATOES

Site and planting
Tree tomatoes require a sunny situation and need protection from the wind in exposed sites. Fertile loam soils produce the best results. Allow a planting distance of about 10ft (3m) each way.

Routine care
A general-purpose fertilizer with medium to high nitrogen should be applied every two to three months at a rate of 4oz (110g) for each tree. Water well during dry periods, and use an organic mulch around the base of the plants to prevent loss of moisture from the soil.

Pests and diseases
Tree tomatoes in the open may be affected by aphids (p.552). They are susceptible to cucumber mosaic virus and potato virus Y (see "Viruses," pp.555 and 565); *Phytophthora palmivora* and *P. infestans* (see "Tomato/potato late blight," p.555) may also cause problems. Under cover, plants may be attacked by thrips (p.553), whiteflies (p.552), and spider mites (p.552).

Growing under cover
Tree tomatoes may be grown in containers with a diameter of at least 14in (35cm) or in well-prepared beds. Use fertile soil mix, to which a general-purpose fertilizer has been added. Maintain the correct temperatures and humidity, water regularly, and apply a liquid feed every three to four weeks.

Pruning and training
When plants reach a height of 3ft (1m), remove the growing point to encourage branching. Little pruning is needed apart from removing crowded and crossing branches and diseased or dead wood.

Harvesting and storing
Tree tomatoes usually fruit one to two years after planting. Detach the fruits using a sharp knife when they start to change color. They may be stored for up to two weeks at a temperature of 39–43°F (4–6°C).

TREE TOMATOES

Propagation
Sow seed under cover; pot the seedlings individually into 4in (10cm) pots when they are 1¼–2in (3–5cm) tall. When they reach 6–10in (15–25cm), harden off and plant out in the open. Propagation is also easy from softwood cuttings: select shoots 4–6in (10–15cm) long and use a sandy (but not acid) soil mix. Follow the procedure as for blueberries (see p.414).

Loquats (*Eriobotrya japonica*)

A member of the family Rosaceae, the loquat is an attractive evergreen tree growing to 22ft (7m) or more tall, with a spread of about 15ft (5m). Loquats are best suited to a subtropical environment and need a minimum temperature of 59°F (15°C) to flower and fruit regularly. They are grown commercially in both California and Florida. In cooler climates loquats may be successfully grown under cover, since they are able to withstand relatively low temperatures for short periods. Some cultivars have a low chilling requirement.

Loquats bear clusters of fragrant cream-colored flowers, followed by bunches of round yellow fruits 1¼–3in (3–8cm) long with tough skins. The pulp is soft and sweet.

Rootstocks for loquats include quince (*Cydonia oblonga*), hawthorns (*Crataegus* spp.), and vigorous seedlings. Most loquat cultivars are self-pollinated, but cross-pollination by insects may occur.

Site and planting
Select a warm, sunny situation. Windbreaks should be erected to reduce wind damage and moisture evaporation. Loquats tolerate a wide range of soils, but a well-drained, fertile loam is most suitable. The trees should be planted at a distance of 12–15ft (4–5m) each way.

Routine care

Apply a top-dressing of general-purpose fertilizer at a rate of about 16oz (450g) per tree every three to four months. Loquats must be regularly watered to keep the roots moist during dry periods; regular applications of organic mulch help to reduce water loss. Keep the surrounding area free of weeds.

To ensure the production of large fruits, thin the bunches at an early stage of their development. Remove any that are weak or damaged, leaving healthy, evenly spaced fruitlets.

Pests and diseases

Plants in the open have few problems. Under cover, however, loquats may be attacked by thrips (p.553), mealybugs (p.552), spider mites (p.552), and whiteflies (p.552).

Growing under cover

Young seed-raised plants may be grown in containers or planted out in well-prepared beds when they are about 18in (45cm) tall. Use a soil-based mix, with a slow-release fertilizer incorporated, and maintain a temperature of at least 64°F (18°C) during the summer. Water them regularly, and apply a liquid feed every month.

Pruning and training

Minimal pruning is required for loquats other than tip pruning all overvigorous shoots and removing wayward branches; any crossing, damaged, dead, or diseased branches should also be removed.

Harvesting and storing

Harvest when the fruits soften and begin to turn rich yellow or orange. Short-term storage is possible at temperatures of 41–50°F (5–10°C).

Propagation

Loquats may be propagated by seed, sown $^3/_4$–1$^1/_4$in (2–3cm) deep in containers filled with a sandy seed soil mix, and maintained at not less than 64°F (18°C). Transplant the seedlings to their final positions when they are 3–4in (7–10cm) high. Other techniques that may be used for propagating loquat cultivars include T-budding (see p.369), side-veneer grafting (see *Propagating Trees by Side-veneer Grafting*, p.56), and air layering (see The Indoor Garden, p.456).

Ripe Loquats

Loquat Tree

Mangos (*Mangifera indica*)

Mangos are tropical evergreen trees that often reach 100ft (30m) when grown from vigorous seedlings. If dwarfing rootstocks and compact-growing clones are used, the trees' height may be restricted to 22–30ft (7–10m). The spread is about 25ft (8m) for dwarf types.

Mango fruits vary from 2 to 12in (5 to 30cm) in length and may weigh from 3$^1/_2$oz (100g) up to about 4lb 6oz (2kg). They have a leathery skin and may be orange, yellow, green, or red, depending on the cultivar. The single seed may constitute 25 percent of the total volume of the fruit. Cultivars are available that are adapted to growing in subtropical areas with a temperature range of 70–77°F (21–5°C) and humidity above 60 percent; the higher temperature is regarded as the optimum for most cultivars. For successful flowering and good fruit set, mangos require a high light intensity and a dry period.

Mango Tree

Site and planting

Select a warm, sunny exposure. If necessary, provide protection from strong winds, since high moisture loss may seriously affect the growth of the trees, very low humidity may worsen the situation, and lead to leaf scorch, seed abortion, and fruit drop.

Soil type is less important for mangos than it is for most other tree crops, and both sandy loams and medium clays are suitable, provided they are well drained. Mangos need a pH of between 5.5 and 7.5.

Dwarfing rootstocks are rapidly becoming available; these are often more suitable, particularly for small gardens, than nonselected local cultivars. If dwarfing rootstocks are not available, polyembryonic seedlings produced from parent trees selected for their high quality of fruit and yield are to be preferred.

Pollination is successful only in relatively dry weather, since high humidity and heavy rainfall limit fertilization (flowering usually begins after a period of cool or dry weather). A solution of potassium nitrate, applied as a spray, may promote flowering. Pollination is mainly by insects, although some mango cultivars are self-fertile.

Space compact and dwarf cultivars 25ft (8m) apart each way; more vigorous cultivars require a spacing of 30–40ft (10–12m).

Routine care

Feed with a general-purpose fertilizer with medium potassium and high nitrogen levels, at a rate of 2lb 3oz–3lb 5oz (1–1.5kg) per tree per year. This should be applied in three or four doses during the growing season; after the fourth year of growth, double the amount.

Water mangos well during dry periods, particularly in the first three years of growth, since plenty of moisture is essential for root development. An organic mulch retains moisture and suppresses weeds. Fruit thinning is rarely necessary.

Pests and diseases

In the tropics, mangos are liable to attack by fruit flies (p.565) and mealybugs (p.552); various types of scale insect (p.554) may also be a problem. Diseases that may affect trees in the open include fungal leaf spots (p.554) and powdery mildew (p.552).

Mangos grown under cover may also be subject to damage by aphids (p.552), whiteflies (p.552), thrips (p.553), spider mites (p.552), and certain forms of powdery and downy mildews (p.552).

Mangos

Growing under cover

Mangos grown from seed are likely to be too vigorous for growing under cover unless they have been grafted onto a dwarfing rootstock, when they will form attractive, ornamental trees. They may be grown in large containers or well-prepared beds. In temperate regions, flowering will generally occur under cover only toward the end of the growing season, and only if the optimum growing conditions have been provided. Fruiting cannot be guaranteed, however, and is dependent on successful pollination.

Transplant young plants when they are about 3ft (1m) tall. They will require a soil mix containing a slow-release fertilizer with a medium potassium and high nitrogen content. Ensure that a minimum temperature of 70°F (21°C) and humidity of about 75 percent are maintained. Mangos grown under

RECOMMENDED MANGOS

'Aloha'
'Cooper'
'Edgehill'
'Haden'
'Kent'
'Tommy Atkins'
'Villasenor'

'Tommy Atkins'

cover should be watered regularly and given a liquid feed every month. Supplement this with sprays of a nitrogenous fertilizer if the leaves turn yellow due to lack of nitrogen.

Pruning and training
Restrict pruning to tip pruning the leading shoot when it is about 3ft (1m) long to encourage lateral branching. Remove overcrowded or very vigorous growth during the early years to ensure an evenly spaced, rounded tree canopy. Once the tree is established, pruning is limited to the removal of diseased, dead, or crossing branches, or those that are congested.

Harvesting and storing
Mangos fruit three to four years after planting. The fruits should be picked when they begin to change color. Handle them carefully to avoid any damage by bruising.

Any mangos that are slightly immature may be stored at 48°F (10°C) for two to four weeks, maintaining humidity of 90–95 percent; they should ripen during this time.

Propagation
Propagation from seed is possible for polyembryonic cultivars, or various methods of grafting may be used instead. For seed propagation, remove the pulp of ripe fruits. To hasten germination, soak the seed in water for 48 hours and carefully remove the seed coat. Sow immediately in beds or containers, using well-prepared soil mix, and with the convex side of the seeds uppermost. Lightly cover them with soil mix, and water them.

The resulting seedlings may be polyembryonic and similar to the parent tree, but they are also likely to be very vigorous and take five to eight years to bear fruits that may prove variable in quality. A mango seed usually produces at least one such vigorous seedling resulting from self- or cross-pollination; any such seedlings should be discarded. The remaining seedlings are ready for transplanting to containers at least 6in (15cm) in diameter within six to eight weeks and may be used for rootstocks. Alternatively, they may be grown on as fruiting trees.

Mangos may also be propagated vegetatively, although stem cuttings often fail to root successfully. Approach-grafting is a good alternative. Take a container-grown rootstock that is about one year old. Place the container near the scion branch still growing on the parent tree. Using a sharp knife, take a shallow, vertical slice 2–2½in (5–6cm) long from the side of the rootstock and scion, thus exposing the cambium layers. Place the matching cut surfaces together and bind them firmly. After two to three months the two should have united. Cut the top off the rootstock and sever the scion from the parent plant.

Other successful methods of propagating mangos are by T-budding (see p.369) and air layering (see THE INDOOR GARDEN, p.456).

Olives (*Olea europaea*)

Olives are evergreen trees, growing 28–40ft (9–12m) tall, with a spread of 22–8ft (7–9m). The fruits may be gathered while they are still green, or when they are fully ripe and have turned black. They may measure up to 1½in (4cm) long.

Olives grow well in subtropical areas with an optimum temperature range of 41–77°F (5–25°C). They need long, hot summers for the fruits to ripen fully, followed by winter temperatures that are low enough to meet the chilling requirement of the specific cultivar. Seek specialist advice on which cultivars grow best in your area. Winter temperatures below the optimum will result in cold damage. Hot, dry winds and cool, wet weather during the flowering period reduce fruit set. In temperate areas olives are occasionally grown as ornamental trees in warm gardens, but seldom flower or fruit. Given suitable growing conditions, an olive tree may attain a great age.

RECOMMENDED OLIVES

European cultivars
'Ascolano'
'Barouni'
'Leccino'
'Manzanillo'
'Mission'
'Picual'
'Salonenque'
'San Fernando'
'Santa Caterina'
'Sevillano'

Black table olives

Site and planting
A wide range of soils is suitable, although low to medium fertility is preferable, since soils that are very fertile are likely to result in excessive vegetative growth. The site must be well drained. Olives grow well on alkaline soils, including those with a high level of salts, provided that the pH level does not exceed 8.5. Windbreaks should be used in exposed areas.

Most cultivars are self-fertile, but pollinators may be necessary to increase fruit yield in cooler climates. Olives are pollinated by insects and also by wind; high humidity levels inhibit pollination.

The usual planting distance varies from 22ft (7m) to 40ft (12m) each way, depending on the habit of the cultivar. All olives should be staked to avoid wind damage. Closely planted trees may be thinned by removing alternate trees when the canopies begin to overlap.

Routine care
Top-dress with a general-purpose fertilizer with medium to high levels of nitrogen at a yearly rate of about 1–2lb (0.5–1kg) per tree, applied in two or three doses when the trees are in active growth. Applications of potassium and, possibly, boron supplements may be necessary on some soils. Water olives regularly during dry periods, particularly for the first two to three years after planting. Mulching with organic material is also beneficial. Keep the planting area free of weeds.

OLIVE TREE

OLIVES

Fruit thinning may be necessary if the trees show signs of biennial bearing (see "Apples: Blossom thinning and biennial bearing," p.372). Thinning is generally done by hand, but applications of a spray containing alpha naphthalene acetic acid four to 18 days after flowering may also be effective.

Pests and diseases
Olives grown in the open may be affected by various types of scale insect (p.554) and root-knot nematodes (p.566). Olive diseases include *Verticillium* wilt (p.559). Trees grown under cover may be affected by whiteflies (p.552), thrips (p.553), and spider mites (p.552).

Growing under cover
Rooted cuttings or budded plants should be grown either in prepared beds, or in containers no smaller than 12–14in (30–35cm) in diameter; use a fertile soil mix that incorporates a slow-release fertilizer with medium levels of potassium and nitrogen. Apply a liquid feed every three to four weeks, and water the trees regularly.

Maintain a high temperature – above 70°F (21°C) – in summer and as low a temperature as possible in winter. Olives grown in containers may be placed in the open during the summer months.

Pruning and training
Prune newly planted olives by removing the leading shoot when it is about 5ft (1.5m) tall; select three or four strong laterals to provide the basic framework. Subsequent pruning consists of removing older branches to encourage the growth of new shoots, since fruits are produced on one-year-old wood mostly at the edges of the tree canopy.

Harvesting and storing
Olive trees grown in the open are likely to flower and fruit in three to four years from planting; yields

generally increase until the tree is 15 years old, after which they remain fairly constant.

Olives are processed to remove their bitterness. Fruits used for fermenting should be harvested when they are fully ripe but still green. Olives for eating without being processed may be harvested when black and firm, then packed in dry salt. When thoroughly dehydrated, the olives are stored in oil.

Fruits that are required for oil production should be left on the tree until they are fully ripe. They are harvested by shaking the tree so that the olives fall onto a cloth or fine netting placed on the ground below the tree canopy.

Propagation

Olives are usually propagated by stem cuttings, but selected cultivars may also be increased by bud-grafting. Cuttings may be either hardwood (from one- or two-year-old wood) or leafy, semiripe cuttings from the current season's growth.

Hardwood cuttings, which are taken during the winter, should be about 12in (30cm) in length. Remove the leaves from the lower half of each cutting, and soak its base for 24 hours in hormone rooting solution. Insert the cuttings to half their length in cuttings soil mix, leaving them for about 30 days to root while maintaining a temperature of 55–70°F (13–21°C). Transplant the cuttings singly into pots, and raise them in greenhouse conditions.

Alternatively, take semiripe cuttings 4–6in (10–15cm) long (see ORNAMENTAL TREES, p.53). Named olive cultivars may be propagated by T-budding (see p.369), always budding onto vigorous, olive seedling rootstocks.

Prickly pears (*Opuntia ficus-indica*)

This member of the cactus family is grown mainly in the subtropics. Although many of its forms are relatively low-growing and spreading in habit, some may eventually attain a height of 6ft (2m).

Most prickly pears will tolerate semiarid conditions, with an optimum temperature range of 64–77°F (18–25°C); they will survive at lower temperatures, with a minimum of 50°F (10°C). Full sunlight is essential for satisfactory growth.

The stems of prickly pears consist of flattened, elliptic sections, 12–20in (30–50cm) long, which are almost spineless in many of the cultivated forms but very spiny on wild and naturalized plants.

PRICKLY PEAR

Prickly pear fruits, which are produced from the upper part of the sections, are purple or red when ripe, and about 2–4in (5–10cm) long. They contain a soft, juicy pulp with many seeds. Prickly pears are pollinated by insects.

Site and planting

Prickly pears thrive in subtropical regions, where they are able to tolerate lengthy periods of drought. They are sensitive to poor drainage and saline conditions, however, and prefer sandy, well-aerated soils, with an ideal pH of 5.5–7.

Rooted sections are usually established 6–7½ft (2–2.4m) apart, with a spacing of 6–10ft (2–3m) between each row.

Routine care

Fertilizers are not normally required, unless the soil is particularly poor. Keep the planting site weed-free. Pests are rarely a problem. Some species of *Pythium* (see "Damping off," p.566), however, may affect prickly pears in humid conditions.

Growing under cover

Use a sandy soil mix to which a slow-release fertilizer has been added. Maintain the temperature at 64–77°F (18–25°C), with humidity of 60 percent or below. Little watering is required once the plants have become established.

Harvesting and storing

Prickly pears produce fruits three to four years after planting. Detach the fruits carefully from the stem sections using a sharp knife. They are best eaten within a few days after they have been harvested but may be stored for short periods in cool conditions if necessary.

Propagation

Detach whole stem sections from the parent plant; if these are very large, cut them horizontally into two or three pieces. Allow them to callus in a sunny, sheltered place for several days before inserting them into a sandy soil mix. The sections should take two to three months to root; they may then be potted on into 6–8in (15–21cm) pots, or transplanted to their final positions. Water the new plants regularly until they are established.

PROPAGATING PRICKLY PEARS FROM STEM SECTIONS

1 *Using a sharp knife, cut a whole section away from the parent plant. It is advisable to wear gloves, since the spines irritate the skin.*

2 *After allowing the section to dry out for a few days, place it in a sandy soil mix and firm it in. The section should be well rooted in 2–3 months.*

Avocados (*Persea americana*)

The avocado is a subtropical evergreen tree that may grow to a height of 30–45ft (10–15m), with a similar spread. Its fruits are pear-shaped, with a large, central, rounded seed. Fruit size and skin texture vary with the cultivar, and colors range from green to russet: The main types of avocado are Guatemalan, Mexican, and a hybrid of the two.

The optimum temperature range for growth and fruit development is 68–82°F (20–28°C), with humidity of over 60 percent; some Mexican and Guatemalan cultivars are able to withstand temperatures as low as 48–58°F (10–15°C), but they do not usually produce flowers at such low temperatures.

Site and planting

Avocado trees may be grown in the open in subtropical areas, provided the temperature is within the range given above. Their branches are brittle, so it is necessary to provide windbreaks in exposed areas to prevent them from being seriously damaged by the wind.

Select a site with maximum exposure to sun if possible. Avocados need a well-drained soil, since their roots are extremely sensitive to waterlogging. Medium loam soils with a pH of 5.5–6.5 are preferable, but a sandy or clay loam may be

RECOMMENDED AVOCADOS

- 'Bacon' (Mexican)
- 'Duke' (Mexican)
- 'Fuerte' (Mexican x Guat.)
- 'Green Gold' (Mexican x Guat.)
- 'Hass' (Guat.)
- 'Reed' (Guat.)
- 'Rincon' (Guat.)
- 'Zutano' (Mexican)

'Rincon'

Avocado Tree

suitable, provided it has been improved and the drainage is good (see also "Preparing the site," p.360).

If grafted plants are to be used, those on rootstocks that are known to be both vigorous and resistant to avocado root rot (*Phytophthora cinnamoni*) are preferable. Avocados may be self-pollinated, but the best crops are produced if at least two cultivars are planted near each other. Choose cultivars whose flowering periods coincide or overlap. When planting, allow 20ft (6m) each way between the trees.

Routine care

Apply a general-purpose fertilizer with a medium potassium and nitrogen content when the trees are in active growth. The recommended rate is 3lb 4oz–4lb 6oz (1.5–2kg) per tree every year, preferably in two or three doses. Use an organic mulch around the base of each tree, leaving 10in (25cm) clear around the stems.

Water avocado trees during dry periods, particularly during the first three years when they are becoming established. Keep the area around the base of the trees free from all weeds. It is not normally necessary to thin the fruits on avocado trees.

Pests and diseases

Avocados may be affected by avocado root rot (see "*Phytophthora* root rots," p.560) and *Cercospora* spot or blotch (see "Fungal leaf spots," p.554). They may be attacked by such pests as whiteflies (p.552), thrips (p.553), spider mites (p.552), and mealybugs (p.552).

Growing under cover

Establish young plants either in well-prepared beds or in containers with a minimum diameter of 8in (21cm). Maintain temperatures of 68–82°F (20–28°C) and humidity of 70 percent. For container-grown plants, pot on into containers at least 12in (30cm) in diameter, taking care not to disturb the plants' root systems.

Water containerized avocados regularly, and apply either a general-purpose fertilizer with a medium level of both potassium and nitrogen at intervals of two to three weeks, or a liquid feed. In temperate climates, flowering and fruiting are rare under cover, due to the trees' daylength and light intensity demands.

Pruning and training

Avocado trees need little pruning beyond shaping the tree during its early growth to ensure that an evenly spaced, rounded canopy develops. Once the tree is established, remove any diseased, damaged, or crossing branches after fruiting.

Harvesting and storing

Seed-raised trees start to bear fruit when they are between five and seven years old; budded or grafted plants are productive at three to five years after planting. The fruits may remain on the tree for up to 18 months without maturing, but they usually ripen rapidly after harvesting.

Cut the fruits from the tree using pruners. Handle them carefully to avoid bruising. Store them at temperatures above 48°F (10°C) and at 60 percent humidity. Any damaged fruits should be discarded.

Propagation

Avocado trees are easily grown from seed and reproduce virtually true to type. Select healthy, undamaged seeds and soak them in hot water at 106–30°F (40–52°C) for 30 minutes to inhibit infection from avocado root

Ripe Avocados

rot. Cut a thin slice from the pointed end, then dip the wound in a fungicide. Sow the seed in sandy seed soil mix with the cut end slightly above the soil surface; germination takes about four weeks. The seedlings may be grown on in containers until they are about 12–16in (30–40cm) tall. They should then be ready for transferring to their final positions.

To propagate named cultivars onto disease-resistant rootstocks, side-wedge grafting (see Principles of Propagation, p.544) or saddle grafting (see Ornamental Shrubs, p.88) may be used.

Growing Avocados from Seed

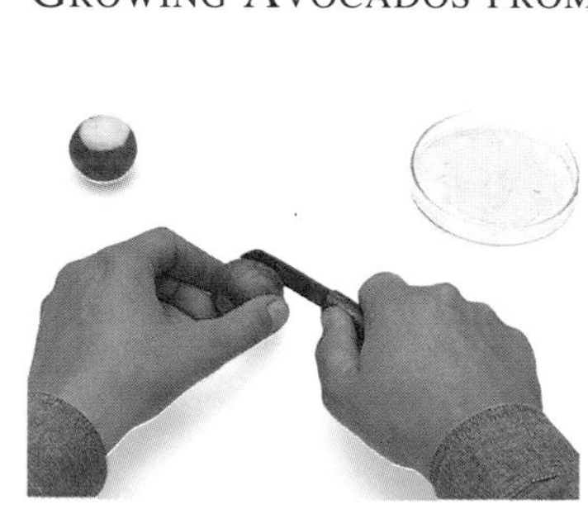

1 *Soak the seed in hot water, and then prepare it by cutting about 1/2in (1cm) off the pointed end with a sharp knife. Dip the wound in fungicide.*

2 *Place the seed in a 6in (15cm) pot of moist sandy seed soil mix so that the cut top of the seed is just above the soil surface.*

3 *Several weeks later the seed will germinate to produce a shoot and roots.*

Guavas (*Psidium guajava*)

Guava trees grow to a height of up to about 25ft (8m) and have a spread of 22ft (7m). They are widely grown in both tropical and subtropical regions and thrive in temperatures ranging from 72–82°F (22–8°C). The preferred humidity level is 70 percent or less: a higher level may reduce the quality of the fruits produced.

Guava fruits are 2–4in (5–10cm) in diameter, with either white or pink flesh. The flowers are normally pollinated by insects.

Site and planting

A sheltered site is preferable, protected by windbreaks if necessary. Guavas tolerate a wide range of soils, but a well-drained loam is ideal. The pH may range from 4.8 to 8, but a pH of approximately 6 is most desirable.

When planting, allow a spacing of 15ft (5m) in each direction between the trees. The young trees should be securely staked in areas that are exposed to strong winds.

Routine care

Guavas respond well to applications of a general-purpose fertilizer with a medium potassium and nitrogen content. Use this at a rate of 2lb 3oz–4lb 6oz (1–2kg) of fertilizer for each tree per year, divided into two or three top-dressings during the growing season. Weed the area around the bases of the trees, keep them well watered, and apply a mulch of organic matter, which helps to retain soil moisture.

Guavas

GUAVA TREE

Pests and diseases
Pests are rarely a serious problem, but in the open, aphids (p.552), fruit flies (p.565), and scale insects (p.554) may require control. Plants under cover may also be infested by whiteflies (p.552) and thrips (p.553). Guava seedlings are sensitive to damping off (p.566).

Growing under cover
Guavas may be grown in either well-prepared beds or large containers at least 12–14in (30–35cm) in diameter, using a fairly rich, commercial soil mix to which a slow-release fertilizer has been added. Maintain a minimum temperature of 72°F (22°C), with humidity of 70 percent. Water plants regularly, and apply a liquid feed every three to four weeks. To improve the chances of fruiting, cross-pollination by hand may be necessary. A relatively dry atmosphere should be maintained during the flowering period.

Pruning and training
When the young trees are about 3ft (1m) tall, cut back the leading shoot by about two-thirds to encourage branching. Subsequent pruning can be limited to the removal of any dead, crossing, or diseased branches, and any low branches that droop down and touch the soil.

Harvesting and storing
Guavas cultivated in the open generally fruit after one to three years, depending on cultivar and environmental conditions. The fruits ripen about five months after fertilization and may be picked when they begin to turn yellow. Handle them carefully, since they bruise easily. They may be stored for up to three to four weeks at a temperature of 45–50°F (7–10°C), with relative humidity of 75 percent.

Propagation
Guavas are usually propagated from seed. For the increase of specific cultivars, air layering, cuttings, or bud-grafting may be used.

Sow seed in a fertile, sterile soil mix in trays or 3in (6cm) containers; germination normally occurs in two to three weeks. The seedlings may vary in quality: pot the strongest ones on into 6in (15cm) pots when they are 8in (20cm) tall. Harden the young plants off and transplant them when they are 12in (30cm) tall.

Selected guava cultivars may be chip-budded (see p.368) onto vigorous seedling guava rootstocks, the stems of which should have a diameter of at least 1/4in (5mm). No specific rootstocks are recommended; select only strong, healthy plants, preferably self-pollinated, as parents for rootstock seeds.

Guavas may also be increased by softwood cuttings 5–6in (12–16cm) long (see p.540). Plants produced by these buddings or cuttings may be planted out when they are about 12in (30cm) tall. In the open, guavas may be increased by simple layering (see ORNAMENTAL TREES, p.55) or by air layering (see THE INDOOR GARDEN, p.456). With the latter, hormone rooting powder applied to the girdled sections increases the success rate.

RECOMMENDED GUAVAS
'Beaumont' (pink flesh)
'Malherbe' (pink flesh)
'Mexican Cream' (white flesh)
'Miami White' (white flesh)

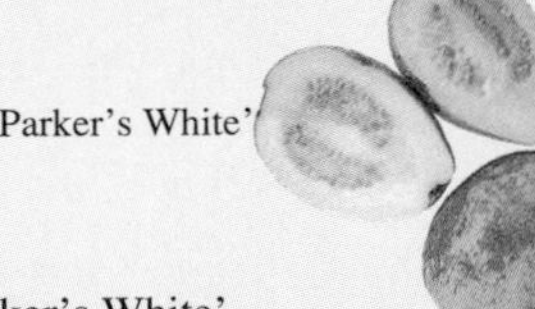

'Parker's White'

'Parker's White' (white flesh)
'Patillo' (pink flesh)
'Patnagola' (white flesh)
'Red Indian' (pink flesh)
'Ruby' (pink flesh)
'Supreme' (white flesh)

Pomegranates (*Punica granatum*)

Pomegranates form small ornamental trees or bushes 6–10ft (2–3m) tall with a spread of 3–5ft (1–1.5m). They are evergreen in the subtropics but deciduous in cooler climates. The globular fruits are up to 4in (10cm) in diameter, with leathery yellow or red skins. The optimum temperature range is 64–77°F (18–25°C), but temperatures just below freezing are tolerated for short periods. Dry weather and a high temperature, ideally 96°F (35°C), are required for fruiting. In temperate climates, therefore, pomegranates are usually grown for their orange-red summer flowers and fall color; a dwarf cultivar of the species, *Punica granatum* 'Nana', fruits freely under cover in temperate areas.

POMEGRANATE FLOWER AND FRUIT

Site and planting
Select a sunny exposure, sheltered by windbreaks in exposed conditions. Heavy loam soils with a pH level of about 7 are generally suitable, if they are well drained. Most cultivars are self-fertile. Plant seedlings, rooted cuttings, or suckers 12–20ft (4–6m) apart each way.

Routine care
Once plants are established, apply a general-purpose fertilizer every two to three months at a rate of 4oz (110g) for each tree per year. Mulch the site and keep it free of weeds; water the trees regularly during dry weather. Cut out all suckers.

Pests and diseases
Pomegranates grown in the open are generally trouble-free; under cover, they may be affected by whiteflies (p.552), aphids (p.552), spider mites (p.552), and thrips (p.553).

Growing under cover
Plant pomegranates in well-prepared beds or containers with a minimum diameter of 14in (35cm), using a fertile soil mix with slow-release fertilizer added. Maintain a temperature range of 64–77°F (18–25°C) and humidity of 60–70 percent. Apply a liquid fertilizer every three to four weeks, and water the plants regularly. Plants in containers may be moved into the open in summer.

Pruning and training
Select three or four main branches to form a framework, and remove any crowded, crossing, or diseased branches. Cut out any suckers not required for propagation.

Harvesting and storing
Fruiting should start about two to three years after planting. Harvest the pomegranates when they turn yellow or red; they may then be stored for several weeks at 39–43°F (4–6°C).

Propagation
Pomegranates are usually propagated from cuttings or root suckers. Insert hardwood cuttings (see p.370) in sandy soil mix, and give bottom heat until they have rooted. Softwood cuttings (see *Blueberry Softwood Cuttings*, p.414) require bottom heat and mist (use a soil mix with a neutral pH). Pot on both types into 4–6in (10–15cm) pots when they have rooted. Root suckers may be carefully separated from the parent plant and replanted. Alternatively, dry off the seed; sow it in pots or trays of seed soil mix, maintaining a temperature of 72°F (22°C).

POMEGRANATE TREE

POMEGRANATES

Nuts

SEVERAL nut-bearing trees and bushes are suitable for gardens; they prefer a sunny, open situation. Some, such as sweet chestnuts, walnuts, and pecans, eventually form large trees and make handsome specimens. In small gardens, an almond tree may make a fine feature, although it may produce nuts only in warm climates. Hazelnuts and filberts may be pruned as compact bushes in a fruit garden or planted in informal groups in a wild garden. Most nuts (but not almonds) are monoecious, having separate male and female flowers on the same plant.

Pecans (*Carya illinoensis*)

Pecans are deciduous trees that may grow to 100ft (30m) high with a spread of 50–70ft (15–20m), so they are suitable only for large gardens. They grow best in warm-temperate climates: temperatures over 100°F (38°C) may lead to bark damage and the production of low-quality nuts; flowers may be damaged if the temperature drops below 34°F (1°C). Pecans have a chilling requirement of 150–250 hours below 45°F (7°C) in order for flowering to occur. The nuts are ovoid, ¾–1in (2–2.5cm) long, and most cultivars have a relatively thin shell.

Pecans are monoecious, but the male flowers are often open before the females on the same tree, so it is best to grow two or more cultivars near each other to ensure that fertilization takes place. Since pecans are wind-pollinated, heavy rainfall when the trees are flowering adversely affects pollination; after such conditions, crops may be poor.

Site and planting

Choose selected cultivars that have been grafted onto pecan seedling stock, since trees raised from seed may not produce fruit of good quality. Pecans quickly develop a long taproot, so plant young trees: older, potgrown plants with congested roots are seldom successful. Pecans need a site that is sheltered from strong winds and thrive on deep, fertile soils with a pH of 6–6.5.

Plant the trees when they are dormant (see *Planting a Fruit Tree*, p.361), spacing them 25ft (8m) apart.

RECOMMENDED PECANS

'Chariton'
'Desirable'
'Early Best'
'Hastings'
'Gloria Grande'
'Lucas'
'Mohawk'
'NC-4'
'Snags'

PECANS

Routine care

Apply a top-dressing of a balanced fertilizer at a rate of 2–4oz/sq yd (70–140g/sq m) under the canopy annually. Keep the planting site free of weeds, and water the trees during dry periods until they are established. Pecans are moderately resistant to drought but require plenty of water during the summer months.

Pecan trees are seldom affected by pests and diseases; *Phytophthora* root rots (p.567) and aphids (p.552) may sometimes be a problem.

Pruning and training

Train pecans with a central leader initially (see "Central-leader standard trees," p.48). Once the trees are established, pruning is restricted to removing crossing and congested branches and any dead wood.

Harvesting and storing

The first crop may be produced after five years; full production is reached after 15–20 years. The nuts are usually harvested by hand. They may be stored in cool, dry, airy conditions for several months.

Propagation

Whip-and-tongue grafting of selected cultivars onto vigorous pecan seedling rootstocks is the most usual method of propagation (see p.369). The seedlings to be used as stock plants should be raised in deep pots or plastic sleeves, since their long taproots are sensitive to damage during transplanting.

Chestnuts (*Castanea* spp.)

A fungal disease has made the native American chestnut (*Castanea dentata*) all but extinct. Better results come from the Chinese chestnut (*C. molissima*) and Spanish chestnut (*C. sativa*). These trees produce excellent fruit, but their malodorous flowers are liabilities. Choose modern Chinese–American hybrids or hybrids of Chinese, Japanese, and European chestnuts, such as 'Colossal'. Chestnuts are monoecious and wind-pollinated.

CHESTNUTS

Site, planting, and routine care

A fertile, moisture-retentive soil with a pH of 6 is preferred; allow 30–40ft (10–12m) between trees (see *Planting a Fruit Tree*, p.361). Water young trees. Fertilizing is unnecessary on prepared sites. Trees may be affected by *Armillaria* root rots (p.567).

Pruning and training

Train as central-leader standards (see p.48). On established trees, remove congested, crossing, or dead branches.

Harvesting and storing

Nuts are borne after about four years. Harvest in fall. Cook nuts fresh, or hull the nuts, soak them for 48 hours, discarding any that darken, then dry and store in a cool, airy place.

Propagation

Propagate from selected cultivars by bud-grafting or whip-and-tongue grafting onto seedling stock of chestnut (see pp.368 and 369).

Hazelnuts and filberts (*Corylus avellana* and *C. maxima*)

Hazelnuts and filberts are valued for their winter catkins and their nuts. Unpruned, they reach a height and spread of 12–15ft (4–5m). They are deciduous and monoecious, and crop best in cool, moist summers. The chilling requirement is 800–1,200 hours below 45°F (7°C). Winter temperatures below 13°F (-10°C) may damage the male flowers (catkins), although the female flowers are usually less vulnerable. The outer husk or calyx of the hazelnut does not completely envelop the nut. The filbert has a husk that is longer than the nut and often completely encloses it; a subgroup of filberts has frilled husks and is known as frizzled filberts. Hazelnuts and filberts are wind-pollinated; many are self-fertile. Recommended cultivars include 'Barcelona', 'Daviana', 'Du

HAZELNUTS

FILBERTS

Chilly', 'Ennis', 'Royale', 'Rush', and 'Winkler'; 'Rush' and 'Winkler' are the hardiest. The nuts of hazelnuts and filberts are brown and irregularly egg-shaped.

Site and planting

A partially shaded, sheltered position is preferable. A soil pH of 6 is best; very rich soil may cause excessive soft growth at the expense of cropping. Adequate moisture with good drainage is important. Plant in fall or early winter, 15ft (5m) apart (see *Planting a Fruit Tree*, p.361).

Routine care

Weed and mulch regularly; water in dry spells. On poor soils apply a balanced fertilizer in spring at a rate of 3oz/sq yd (105g/sq m) under the canopy. Trees are usually trouble-free, but they may be attacked by nut weevils unless sprayed in late spring and again in early summer.

Pruning and training

Hazelnuts and filberts are usually grown as open-center bushes, each with an 18in (45cm) stem and eight to 12 main branches. On young plants, prune the leaders in winter to 22in (55cm); good laterals should then develop. Remove any shoots growing down low on the main stem and all but the best-placed, strongest shoots needed to develop the framework. Shorten these by a third in winter. The following winter remove any excessively strong, upright growth and, if necessary, tip prune side shoots to form a framework.

Established bushes bear heavier crops if pruned in late summer using

BRUTTING HAZELNUTS

In late summer, strong shoots of the current season's growth that are about 12in (30cm) long are broken and left hanging. This helps the formation of flower buds.

a technique known as "brutting." Break the longer side shoots halfway along their length, and let them hang. This opens up the bush and encourages more female flowers to form. In winter, when the catkins release pollen, shorten the brutted shoots to three or four buds; remove old or overcrowded shoots.

Harvesting and storing

Nuts are borne after three to four years. Gather them when the husks begin to yellow. Dry, then store.

Propagation

Suckers produced from roots may be used for propagation. In winter, remove them, each with a root ball, and grow on in a nursery bed or plant directly in their final positions. Trees may also be propagated by simple layering (see p.86) in fall.

Walnuts (*Juglans regia*)

English walnuts (strictly speaking, Persian) are deciduous trees that may reach a height of 60ft (18m) with a similar spread; they are suitable only for large gardens. Named cultivars should always be planted for fruit, since seedlings may produce poor-quality nuts. Walnuts are monoecious and wind-pollinated. Most are self-fertile, but some cultivars produce male catkins and pollen before the female flowers are receptive. To overcome this problem, plant nearby a reliable pollinator such as the old French cultivar 'Franquette'. Walnuts have a chilling requirement of 500–1,000 hours below 45°F (7°C). The gnarled nuts develop within a pitted shell.

Site, planting, and routine care

A well-drained, moisture-retentive soil is best. Walnuts prefer a pH of 6.5–7 but tolerate some alkalinity. Since flowers and young shoots are susceptible to frost damage, avoid cold sites. Walnuts have a long taproot, so select young plants rather than older, potgrown ones whose roots may be congested. Plant in late fall or winter (see *Planting a Fruit Tree*, p.361), with 40–60ft (12–18m) between trees.

RECOMMENDED WALNUTS

All cultivars listed are self-fertile.
'Broadview'
'Colby'
'Hansen'
'Lake'
'Metcalfe'
'Somers'
'Young's B1'

Walnuts may be slow to establish, but after two to three years, once the root system is well developed, stronger growth occurs. Bacterial leaf blotch and blight may be a problem (see "Bacterial leaf spots and blotches," p.554).

Pruning and training

Walnuts should be trained as central-leader standards (see p.48). Prune in midwinter since the trees do not bleed when they are dormant. Remove any strong shoots that make a narrow angle with the stem, to leave a well-balanced framework of evenly spaced branches. Thereafter, little pruning is required apart from cutting out overcrowded, crossing, or congested branches in winter and removing dead wood as required.

Harvesting and storing

Walnut trees may need many years before they start bearing. Walnuts for pickling should be picked in summer before the hulls and shells harden. In early fall, the hull or casing cracks to release the nut, still in its shell.

WALNUTS

Gather the crop before the shells become discolored. Clean, then gently dry the nuts. Store them in cool, airy, slightly humid conditions.

Propagation

The usual methods are whip-and-tongue grafting (see p.369) or chip-budding (see p.368) cultivars onto seedlings of the American black walnut (*Juglans nigra*). In cool climates, keep a grafted tree under glass until the graft has taken, then move the container to a protected site in the open. Plant young trees in their final positions in fall or winter.

Almonds (*Prunus dulcis*)

Left unpruned, sweet almonds grow about 15–20ft (5–6m) tall, with a similar spread. They crop regularly only in areas with warm, dry summers and frost-free winters. The chilling requirement is 300–500 hours below 45°F (7°C). In cool areas they are often grown as ornamentals. Almonds are insect-pollinated. Most cultivars are partly self-fertile, but crops will be better if a pollinator is planted nearby. The nuts are flattened and pointed, with a pitted shell.

Site, planting, and routine care

Almonds require a sheltered, frost-free site and a well-drained soil, preferably with a pH of 6.5. Plant them 20–22ft (6–7m) apart (see *Planting a Fruit Tree*, p.361).

Cultivation of almonds is as for peaches (see p.387). Peach leaf curl (p.557) and bacterial canker (p.571) may affect almond trees.

Pruning and training

Almonds are usually pruned and trained as bushes, as for peaches (see p.388). Nuts are borne on one-year-old wood. In summer, on established trees, remove a quarter of the old shoots that have cropped in previous seasons to encourage fresh growth.

Harvesting and storing

The nuts are borne after three to four years. Gather them as their hulls

ALMONDS

start to crack. Clean and dry the almonds before storing them.

Propagation

Almonds are usually propagated by chip-budding (see p.368). Rootstocks vary according to soil type: almond seedlings are often used for dry regions, while peach seedlings are more suitable for heavier soils.

RECOMMENDED ALMONDS

'Ayles' **Sf**
'Ferraduel' **Psf**
'Ferragnes' **Psf**
'Guara' **Sf**
'Steliette' **Sf**

KEY
Sf *Self-fertile*
Psf *Partly self-fertile*

16
The Indoor Garden

The garden may be enjoyed in comfort despite the vagaries of the seasons by bringing it indoors or under cover – into the house, a garden room, or a greenhouse. Flowering pot plants may be grouped together in a wicker basket for an ornamental tabletop display, a sunny windowsill may become a garden in miniature, and a lush, small-scale jungle may be created in a conservatory. The palette of leaf and flower colors, forms, and textures is as rich as that of outdoor plants. Equally, the approach may vary, from using plants as interior design accessories that are bought at the height of their perfection, displayed, enjoyed, and then discarded, to growing collections of rare plants that demand long-term enthusiasm and attention to detail. In regions subject to frost, the evergreen foliage and exotic blooms of tropical or subtropical plants that would not survive in the open garden thrive in their protected environment, to brighten even the dullest of days with an ever-changing, living decor of foliage and flower.

Displaying plants indoors

The range of plants that may be grown in the home and the greenhouse offers a wealth of form, color, and texture. Plants may be chosen for their handsome foliage or the beauty of their blooms, from the exuberant hues of *Bougainvillea* to the cool elegance of calla lilies (*Zantedeschia*). Others, such as Jerusalem cherry (*Solanum pseudocapsicum*), are selected for their brightly colored fruits.

The choice depends on whether the display is to be permanent, when plants with interesting form and foliage are the best choice, or temporary, when the seasonal interest of plants such as hybrid *Cyclamen* may be used to give spots of color.

Plants can reinforce or contrast with the style of the indoor setting, whether it is a farmhouse kitchen or a formal and sophisticated urban living room. The plants may dominate the scene and give a room its essential character, create pockets of interest, or simply add to the detail. Whatever result is desired, select plants that will both thrive in and enhance their intended position.

Foliage and form

Plants that have attractive foliage are invaluable for long-term indoor display. They may have huge leaves, as does Japanese aralia (*Fatsia japonica*), or a mass of dainty ones, such as those of baby's tears (*Soleirolia soleirolii*). Leaves may have subtle or striking patterns and colors, as do *Calathea* species, or interesting shapes, for example the Swiss-cheese plant (*Monstera deliciosa*).

Foliage also has different textures, ranging from the high gloss of the rubber plant (*Ficus elastica*) to the corrugated surfaces of friendship plant (*Pilea involucrata*) and the soft texture of velvet plant (*Gynura aurantiaca*). Some plants are chosen for their strong forms, whether they are spiky bromeliads, graceful palms and ferns, or pebblelike living stones (*Lithops*).

Grouping plants

When planning an arrangement, carefully choose plants so that those with strongly colored flowers or patterned leaves do not detract from each other. Experiment with contrasts by placing plants together before making a purchase.

Architectural plants such as palms make very fine specimen plants or striking focal points. Smaller plants have impact when arranged together on a tiered stand, but they may be used singly as a dainty finishing touch. A mass of identical plants, such as a bowl of hyacinths, makes a strong yet simple statement.

A Garden Room
Yellow Abutilon, *blue* Agapanthus, *purple and white* Streptocarpus, *and lush foliage create a gardenlike setting in which to relax.*

A Contrast of Strong Shapes
Ivy (Hedera), Dieffenbachia, *Japanese aralia* (Fatsia japonica), *and* Platycerium bifurcatum *complement the pale blue* Plumbago.

The indoor environment

The specific temperature and light requirements of plants are the most important factors in deciding where to position them indoors (see "Planter's guide to indoor plants," p.431). If the conditions do not fulfill the plants' needs, they will soon become stressed and unhealthy. Newly purchased plants that have just come from controlled conditions are especially vulnerable.

Temperature

Although most modern houses are kept warm during the day in winter, the temperature is often allowed to drop markedly at night – a problem for many house plants of tropical origin. Place these plants where they are protected from drafts and are not subject to wide fluctuations in temperature. Do not leave tender plants on windowsills at night, especially if the drawn curtains close off residual warmth from the room, or place plants directly above radiators or heaters that are in use. To flower, indoor plants need warmth, but if the temperature is too high for the individual species the blooms quickly fade and die.

Light

Most plants thrive in bright, filtered sunlight or in a well-lit position that is not in direct sun. Plants that have variegated leaves need more light than those with plain green leaves, but sunlight that is too strong will damage the foliage. Flowering plants such as amaryllis (*Hippeastrum*) need good light to flower well, but excessive light can shorten the life of the blooms. Indeed, few indoor plants tolerate direct sunlight.

Insufficient light results in plants with pale, stunted new leaves, and drawn-out (etiolated) growth with long, thin, weak stems. Some variegated plants may begin to produce plain leaves. In time, the mature leaves will turn yellow and fall. A plant thus weakened is especially vulnerable to pests and diseases.

The amount of natural light in a room depends on the number, size, height, and orientation of the windows. Light levels fall quickly as the distance from the window increases. There is far less natural light in winter than in summer; some plants may need to be moved in response to the seasonal light variation – a plant trolley is ideal for this purpose.

If plants start to grow lopsidedly toward a source of light, turn them slightly when watering them. If light levels are too low for healthy growth (most plants need 12–14 hours of daylight per day), supplementary grow lamps are effective.

Positioning the plants

With a little forethought and planning, it is possible to find a handsome house plant that flourishes in almost every site indoors, from a brilliantly lit room to a dim passage or alcove.

The indoor setting

Consider the impact of plants in the room. Are they in proportion to the room? A tiny pot plant is lost in a large space. Is the background suitable? Plain, pale walls show flowering plants to advantage. Does the plant color blend with the decor?

Hanging baskets and shelves suit trailing plants, while positions at eye level are best for plants with delicate flowers or foliage. Train climbers, such as kangaroo vine (*Cissus antarctica*) and heartleaf philodendron (*Philodendron scandens*), on a trellis to create a screen.

Use plants to enliven empty corners or areas, such as an unused fireplace that provides an instant frame for a display. Large plants or groups may play an architectural role as room dividers or as a link between the house and the garden.

Plants for various light levels

Bright, sunny conditions suit succulent plants as well as plants with woolly, waxy, or gray leaves. Wax plant (*Hoya carnosa*), pelargoniums, and variegated pineapple (*Ananas comosus* 'Variegatus') also grow best in direct sunlight. Tender bonsai, kept indoors all year, may be grown under lights (see Bonsai, pp. 434–5). In indirect or filtered light, grow foliage begonias such as *Begonia rex*, epiphytic orchids such as *Phalaenopsis*, and *Spathiphyllum* with their striking white spathes.

For corners that are far from a window, choose ferns and tough-leaved plants such as parlor palm (*Chamaedorea*), Japanese aralia (*Fatsia japonica*), and ivy (*Hedera*). Expose the plants to brighter light occasionally, if only for a few days.

Kitchens and bathrooms

Temperature and humidity can fluctuate in kitchens and bathrooms, especially small ones, so choose plants that can tolerate extremes. Smooth, hard surfaces contrast well with the soft, feathery forms of ferns. Bathrooms often have low levels of light, ideal for *Episcia*, Boston fern (*Nephrolepis*), or aluminum plant (*Pilea cadierei*). Trailing plants such as heartleaf philodendron make an elegant display on high bathroom shelves. In brightly lit positions, grow herbs such as chives and parsley, or dwarf tomato cultivars such as 'Patio Hybrids' or 'Pixie'.

Tolerant plants

Attractive foliage plants that are tolerant of a wide range of conditions include cast-iron plant (*Aspidistra*), spider plant (*Chlorophytum*), kangaroo vine, and mother-in-law's tongue (*Sansevieria*). Flowering plants are more exacting, but potted chrysanthemums (see p.154) or forced bulbs (see p.219) may give short-term floral color.

Containers

Choose a container whose material, color, and shape blends with the decor and shows the individual plant

Hazards of a Windowsill

Too much sunlight, excessive heat from radiators, and drafts through the frame can seriously weaken or kill house plants that are placed on a windowsill.

Variation of Light Levels within a Room

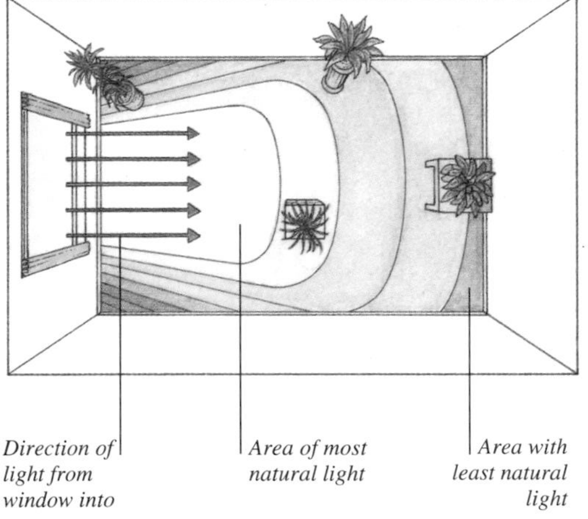

The farther away from a window a plant is sited, the less natural light it will receive. If the plant is 6ft (2m) away, the light level may be as little as 20 percent of that by the window. Plants that are placed close to a window but to one side of it derive little benefit from the position, especially if the windowsills are very deep.

A Hanging Garden
This temporary planting creates an instantly attractive, high-level feature.

or group to its best advantage. The choice is vast, both in style and materials, allowing a range of effects from rustic to ultramodern. Some plastic containers are available with an integral reservoir, which reduces the need for watering. Other types are specially manufactured for hydroculture (see *Cross Section of a Hydroculture Pot*, p.447). The most unlikely household objects, such as birdcages, cooking utensils, and kettles, can make unusual and striking plant holders.

Hanging baskets

Hanging baskets are a popular feature on porches, balconies, patios, and terraces, but may also be an attractive way of growing indoor plants. Hang them in stairwells, from rafters, by windows, or from freestanding supports for an economical and colorful use of space. A group of baskets suspended at varying heights makes a fine display.

Arching fern fronds, the rosettes of epiphytes, and the cascading habit of many foliage plants lend themselves perfectly to hanging baskets. Vary the planting during the year to take advantage of seasonal displays. In a winter arrangement, Christmas cactus (*Schlumbergera bridgesii*) provides a mass of bright color, as do fuchsias in summer. Temporary arrangements may be created by planting a basket with pot plants, but they will need replanting each year. Permanently planted baskets are easier to manage, especially if devoted to a single large plant.

Choosing a hanging container

Hanging baskets are available in various materials and designs. When choosing and positioning them, take into account the fact that most plants require frequent watering. Plastic-coated wire hanging baskets are practical indoors only in rooms that have water-resistant floors; some rigid plastic baskets have drip saucers, which are a practical solution. Also available are attractive, although heavy, pottery and terracotta hanging pots, and wooden, wrought iron, or wicker baskets.

A planted basket is heavy, especially when just watered, so it must be supported by strong rope or chain from a hook or bracket fixed securely to a ceiling joist or a solid wall.

Terrariums and bottle gardens

Terrariums are enclosed glass containers, often decorative in their own right, used to display small plants in the home. They were popular in the 19th century as a way of providing a suitable microclimate for ferns, but all slow-growing ornamental plants that need a humid atmosphere thrive in a terrarium. A selection of plants with contrasting leaf textures and colors is the most effective. Use flowering plants carefully because the dead blooms rot in the moist conditions. Terrariums may be built permanently into a window to house a lush arrangement of larger plants.

Bottles can also be used to create a diminutive landscape of foliage plants. As long as the neck is sufficiently wide to allow the insertion of the plants and routine aftercare, any shape or color of bottle may be used, but bear in mind that tinted glass cuts out some of the light.

Indoor lighting

A display may be enhanced by ordinary floodlights or spotlights, or given dramatic contrasts of light and shade with uplighting or downlighting. Do not place plants too close to the light source since the heat may damage them. Ordinary incandescent bulbs do not significantly improve either food production (photosynthesis) or growth.

Plants for the office

Introducing plants into an office not only brightens it visually, but may help to muffle noise, refresh the air, and create a less stressful ambience. In a modern, open-plan office that is air-conditioned and fully glazed, temperatures are constant, air pollution is minimized, and space and light are plentiful – almost ideal growing conditions. Older buildings with smaller windows and little climatic control present more challenging conditions.

Use self-watering containers, especially if the plants are sited near electrical equipment, or plunge several plants into a large container. Unless maintenance contractors are employed, ensure that responsibility for care is clearly assigned.

Suitable plants

Evergreen, shiny-leaved plants are as tough and tolerant in an office as they are in the home. The popular genus *Ficus* includes plants of every shape and size, from the lustrous, huge fiddle-leaf fig (*F. lyrata*) to the small-leaved, leathery mistletoe fig (*F. deltoidea*).

Another large and impressive genus with handsome leaves is *Philodendron*, which includes climbers and trailers. The tenacious, long-lived Swiss-cheese plant (*Monstera deliciosa*) climbs slowly but eventually reaches several feet in height and spread.

Garden rooms and conservatories

The garden may be brought indoors, either into a garden room, which is a living space furnished with container plants, or into a conservatory, which is devoted principally to planting. In temperate climates, both can be used to give winter shelter to container-grown plants that spend the summer months outdoors. A conservatory can also provide the warm, humid environment needed by tropical and subtropical plants.

The high light levels usually found in conservatories encourage colored leaves to assume intense hues, and plants to flower well. Scented flowering plants, for example *Jasminum polyanthum*, are especially welcome in a confined space, where fragrance lingers in the air.

Select plants that suit the conservatory's orientation and temperature, bearing in mind that glass structures can be costly to heat in winter and very hot in summer.

Create a lush profusion of planting by taking full advantage of all the available space: grow plants at different levels in raised and ground-level soil beds, in pots on the floor, on windowsills and shelves, and in

Seasonal Color
In this room, a white poinsettia (Euphorbia pulcherrima), *carmine azalea* (Rhododendron), *and Calamondin orange* (x Citrofortunella microcarpa) *add winter interest to a permanent framework of evergreen foliage plants.*

Cool Conservatory

The foliage and flowering plants shown here are among the many that thrive in the cool, but frost-free, conditions of a lean-to conservatory to create a fine display.

1 *Plumbago auriculata* (syn. *P. capensis*)
2 *Chlorophytum comosum* (syn. *C. capense* of gardens)
3 *Campanula isophylla*
4 *Saxifraga stolonifera* 'Tricolor' (syn. *S. sarmentosa*)
5 *Pelargonium* 'Mini Cascade'
6 *Camellia japonica*
7 *Sedum morganianum*
8 *Streptocarpus* 'Heidi'
9 *Ceropegia woodii*
10 *Callistemon citrinus* 'Splendens'
11 *Correa pulchella*
12 *Calceolaria* 'Sunshine'
13 *Nierembergia hippomanica* var. *violacea* 'Purple Robe'
14 *Prostanthera rotundifolia*
15 *Polygala myrtifolia* 'Grandiflora'
16 *Rehmannia elata*
17 x *Citrofortunella microcarpa* (syn. *Citrus mitis*)

Multilevel Display
Staging, shelves, and floor space are used to maximum advantage in this cool greenhouse. Impatiens *cultivars,* Plumbago, *and* Streptocarpus *flowers are complemented by a variety of foliage plants, including ivy* (Hedera), *scented-leaved pelargoniums, polka-dot plant* (Hypoestes), *button fern* (Pellaea), *and piggyback plant* (Tolmiea).

hanging baskets. Large tropical or subtropical plants and climbers that are free-standing are useful for training on a trellis or wires fixed to the walls; grapes will grow over and clothe the wall and roof. Use plants in the conservatory that complement those in the open garden; this will create a visual link between the two as well as a sense of space.

Indoor water features

A sunken or raised pool or a half barrel can accommodate tropical water lilies or other tender aquatic and marginal plants. A simple and elegant waterspout will provide the restful murmur of falling water and help to maintain humidity (see also The Water Garden, pp.240–57).

Growing plants in a greenhouse

The control of light, temperature, and humidity in a greenhouse will allow a much wider range of plants to be grown than in a garden that is subject to frost. It also extends the season of display and cropping from early spring until late fall, or even throughout the year if desired.

Uses of a greenhouse

A greenhouse is very useful in cool-temperate climates, where there is frost, strong wind, or excessive rain. It can be used for propagation; raising and growing tender plants or flowers for cutting; or for crops such as salads, early vegetables, and even fruit. Many plants grow faster under cover and fruit or flower more profusely than they would outdoors. Half-hardy plants can be grown in containers outdoors and transferred to temporary shelter in the greenhouse when needed.

The greenhouse may hold a specialized collection of plants such as alpines (see pp.210–12), cacti (see pp.258–71), ferns (see pp.158–9), and orchids (see pp.440–43). Alternatively, a mixed collection of foliage and flowering plants that enjoy similar conditions may provide a display throughout the year.

The greenhouse layout

The traditional, free-standing greenhouse interior consists of a central path with waist-high staging at the sides and far end. Wide greenhouses may also have staging in the center. Staging (see also p.487) is essential; even if removed in summer for border crops, it may be used at other times of the year for raising seedlings, propagating cuttings, and displaying pot plants. Slatted or meshed staging is used for pot plants to prevent pools of water and to ensure that air circulates freely, particularly in winter.

For extra display space, use tiered staging, bench beds, or soil borders. If the glass begins at ground level, ferns and other shade-loving plants (and dormant plants) may be grown (or rested) under the staging. Raised beds are useful for displaying small plants, such as alpines and cacti, that are planted directly in the beds or in pots plunged into gravel or sand.

The ornamental greenhouse

Although a greenhouse is often more practical in use than a conservatory, part or all of it can be devoted to ornamental displays. Groups are usually more attractive than widely spaced plants. Feature a single genus or assemble a variety of plants, displaying them in a random pattern or as a landscape in miniature. Try to include contrasts of leaf form, size, and texture; control the use of color, whether from flowers or foliage, to create a harmonious arrangement.

A lean-to greenhouse against a house wall can double as a conservatory. Make the most of the back wall by growing climbers, which need only a 12in (30cm) wide bed or pot. Paint the wall white to help to reflect light and provide a contrasting background for the plants.

The greenhouse environment

Essential requirements for success are adequate ventilation and heat, as well as shading in summer; water and electricity are also important.

The temperature range of a greenhouse depends on its purpose, but there are four basic types of greenhouse: cold (unheated), cool or frost-free, temperate, and warm. For

AN INTERIOR GARDEN
Where space allows, a naturalistic landscape can be created within a greenhouse. Here, foliage plants including Cordyline, Eucomis, Justicia, *and* Phormium *provide a lush framework that is offset by the colorful blooms of flowering plants such as blue* Agapanthus, *pink fuchsias, and white and salmon pelargoniums.*

further information, see GREENHOUSES AND FRAMES, "Creating the right environment," pp.481–5; see also "Planter's guide to indoor plants," opposite.

The cold greenhouse

An unheated greenhouse protects against any extremes of wind and rain and is significantly warmer, even in summer, than outdoors. It extends the growing season by providing the plants with an artificially early spring and late fall.

Depending on the severity of winter, many hardy annuals, biennials, and shrubs can be overwintered in an unheated greenhouse. Half-hardy annuals and bulbous plants can be started early to plant out when the garden soil has warmed up and danger of frost is past. A cold greenhouse is also useful for raising seedlings and getting an early start with vegetables. As an alpine house it can be used to provide the conditions needed for growing alpines and rock plants (see ALPINE HOUSES AND FRAMES, pp.210–12).

An unheated greenhouse does not exclude frost for more than an hour or two, so it is not suitable for overwintering plants that are not frost hardy. Sunlight, or even bright light, raises the temperature during the day, but night temperatures can drop almost as low as those in the open garden. In temperate climates, most greenhouses built against a warm house wall give conditions similar to those in a cool greenhouse (see below), but this will not prevent tender plants from being killed by a few days of really sharp frosts.

The cool greenhouse

Freedom from frost increases the range of plants that may be grown. A frost-free greenhouse is also easier to manage, since protective measures become unnecessary. Daytime temperatures of 41–50°F (5–10°C) and a minimum at night of 36°F (2°C) allow ornamentals to be enjoyed throughout the year.

In a cool greenhouse, hardy bulbous plants, particularly those with delicate blooms that are not noticed in an open garden, flower earlier, providing color in late winter and early spring. Here tender patio plants may be raised and overwintered; house plants may be revived and propagated in warmer months; and winter-flowering plants such as fragrant Parma violets (*Viola*) may be grown in bench beds or in pots. Grown under cover, chrysanthemums and perpetual-flowering carnations (*Dianthus*) provide a good supply of cut flowers; while hardy annuals raised from seed sown in late summer sowings give early flowers. The cool greenhouse must have a heating system capable of excluding frost and maintaining a minimum temperature in all weather conditions (see GREENHOUSES AND FRAMES, "Heating," p.482). Even if the greenhouse is not heated throughout, an electrically heated propagator, or a propagating bench, will enable the gardener to make an early start on raising new plants in the spring.

AN ORNAMENTAL COLLECTION
A warm greenhouse may be devoted to displaying a collection of plants from a particular group such as orchids or cacti. Tropical plants such as these forest cacti thrive in the heat and high humidity provided by the greenhouse. A luxuriant show is produced by the richly hued flowers and cool, fleshy foliage of Epiphyllum, Heliocereus, Pfeiffera, *and other forest cacti at the height of their summer glory.*

The temperate greenhouse

Raising the temperature to 50–55°F (10–13°C), with a nighttime minimum of 45°F (7°C), widens the scope still further. If kept in a temperate greenhouse, plants associated with the essentially frost-free climates of California, the Mediterranean, South Africa, and parts of Australia and South America may be enjoyed in harsher climates than they could normally bear. These include yesterday, today, and tomorrow (*Brunfelsia*), bird of paradise (*Strelitzia*), and *Cymbidium* orchids. If zonal pelargoniums are kept at 48°F (9°C) they will flower all year.

The warm greenhouse

A minimum temperature of 55°F (13°C) to 64°F (18°C) in a warm greenhouse allows cultivation of subtropical and tropical plants, as well as facilitating year-round propagation or flowering displays. Tender plants, for example a number of orchids (see pp.440–43) and many bromeliads (see pp.432–3), are at their best when grown in a warm greenhouse.

The warm greenhouse needs controllable heating throughout the year, even in summer in cooler climates. This incurs considerable heating costs in temperate zones. Equipment such as thermostats, double glazing, fans, automatic ventilation, an automated watering and damping-down system, cooling pads, and shading helps to control conditions and facilitates routine care. A warm section in a cool greenhouse is a useful, cheaper option; a warm conservatory, or plant room, is another possibility.

Planter's guide to indoor plants

WARM GREENHOUSE

(Minimum 55–64°F/13–18°C)

Flowering plants
Aeschynanthus ❄ ◎
Anthurium ❄
Aphelandra ❄ ◎
Brunfelsia ❄ ◎
Columnea ❄ ◎
Euphorbia fulgens ❄,
E. pulcherrima ❄
Hibiscus rosa-sinensis ❄
Hoya bella ❄
Justicia ❄
Kohleria ❄ ◎
Medinilla ❄ ◎
Pachystachys ❄
Ruellia ❄ ◎
Saintpaulia ❄ ◎

Sinningia 'Red Flicker'

Sinningia ❄ ◎
Smithiantha ❄ ◎
Spathiphyllum ❄ ◎

Foliage plants
Aechmea ❄ ◎ (and most bromeliads)
Aglaonema ❄ ◎
Begonia rex ❄ ◎ (and other spp.)
Calathea ❄ ◎
Chamaedorea ❄ ◎ (and most palms)
Codiaeum ❄ ◎
Dieffenbachia ❄ ◎
Dracaena ❄ ◎
Ficus, some ❄
Fittonia ❄ ◎
Maranta ❄ ◎
Peperomia ❄ ◎
Philodendron ❄ ◎
Tradescantia, some ❄, ◎

TEMPERATE GREENHOUSE

(Daytime 50–55°F/10–13°C; night minimum 45°F/7°C)

Flowering plants
Achimenes ❄
Begonia ❄ ◎
Catharanthus ❄
Cyclamen, some ❄, ◎
Exacum ❄ ◎
Haemanthus ❄
Impatiens, some ❄, ◎

Impatiens, *Novette Series* 'Red Star'

Schlumbergera ❄ ◎
Strelitzia ❄
Streptocarpus ❄ ◎

Foliage plants
Asparagus, some ❄
Coleus ❄ ◎
Jacaranda ❄

COOL GREENHOUSE

(Daytime 41–50°F/5–10°C; night minimum 36°F/2°C)

Flowering plants
Abutilon, some ❄
Bougainvillea ❄
Browallia ❄
Calceolaria, some ❄, ◎
Callistemon, some ❄
Cestrum, some ❄
Chrysanthemum, some ❄, ◎
x *Citrofortunella* ❄
Cuphea ❄
Datura, some ❄
Freesia ❄
Fuchsia, some ❄
Gerbera ❄
Hippeastrum, some ❄
Hoya ❄
Jasminum, some ❄
Lachenalia ❄
Lantana ❄
Lapageria ❄
Nerium ❄
Passiflora ❄
Pelargonium ❄
Plumbago, some ❄
Primula, some ❄
Schizanthus ❄
Senecio, some ❄

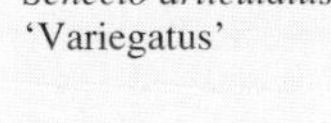

Senecio articulatus 'Variegatus'

Sprekelia ❄
Streptosolen ❄
Tibouchina ❄ ◎
Veltheimia ❄
Zantedeschia, some ❄
Zephyranthes, some ❄

Foliage plants
Aspidistra ❄
Chlorophytum ❄
Cissus rhombifolia ❄
Rhoicissus ❄
Ricinus ❄

COLD GREENHOUSE

Flowering plants
Agapanthus (hardy spp.)
Anemone
Antirrhinum (hardy spp.)
Camellia (hardy spp.)
Cheiranthus (hardy spp.)
Crocus
Cyclamen (hardy miniature spp.)
Dicentra
Erica
Hyacinthus
Jasminum (hardy spp.)
Narcissus
Rhododendron (hardy azaleas in shady greenhouse)

Foliage plants
Adiantum ◎ (hardy spp.)
Euonymus
Fatsia ◎
Hedera ◎ (hardy spp.)
Laurus nobilis ❄
Phormium ❄
Tolmiea ❄

PLANTS THAT PREFER DIRECT LIGHT INDOORS

Warm room (64°F/18°C and over)
Ananas ❄ ◎
Bougainvillea ❄
Euphorbia pulcherrima ❄
Ficus, some ❄
Hibiscus rosa-sinensis ❄
Hippeastrum, some ❄
Justicia ❄
Opuntia, some ❄
Solanum pseudocapsicum ❄ ◎

Cool room (40–64°F/5–18°C)
Billbergia ❄
Browallia ❄
Campanula isophylla ❄ ◎
Capsicum ❄ ◎
Chlorophytum ❄
Clivia ❄
Coleus ❄ ◎
Crassula, some ❄
Cyclamen, some ❄, ◎
Cyrtanthus ❄
Echeveria ❄
Gerbera ❄
Hyacinthus
Jasminum, some ❄
Kalanchoe ❄
Nerine, some ❄

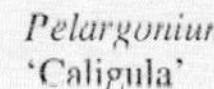

Pelargonium 'Caligula'

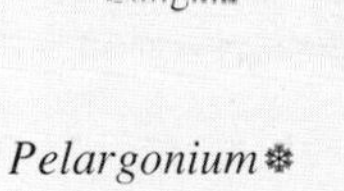

Pelargonium ❄
Streptocarpus ❄ ◎
Veltheimia ❄

PLANTS THAT PREFER INDIRECT LIGHT INDOORS

Warm room – medium light (64°F/18°C and over)
Adiantum, some ❄, ◎
Aechmea ❄ ◎ (and all bromeliads)
Caladium ❄
Codiaeum ❄ ◎
Cryptanthus ❄ ◎
Dieffenbachia ❄ ◎
Howea ❄
Hypoestes ❄
Kohleria ❄ ◎
Mandevilla ❄ ◎
Maranta ❄ ◎
Neoregelia ❄ ◎
Peperomia ❄ ◎
Pilea ❄ ◎
Saintpaulia ❄ ◎
Sansevieria ❄
Schefflera ❄
Sinningia ❄ ◎
Spathiphyllum ❄ ◎
Streptocarpus ❄ ◎
Syngonium ❄ ◎
Thunbergia ❄
Tradescantia, some ❄, ◎

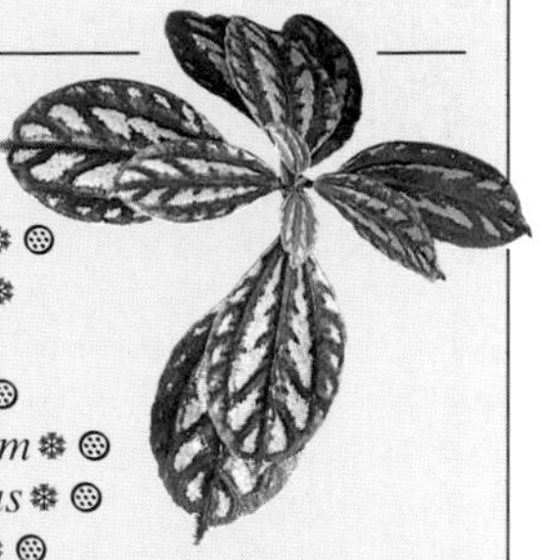

Pilea cadierei

Warm room – poor light (64°F/18°C and over)
Asplenium, some ❄
Calathea ❄ ◎
Chamaedorea ❄ ◎
Cissus ❄
Dracaena ❄ ◎
Episcia ❄ ◎
Fittonia ❄ ◎
Hedera, some ❄, ◎
Philodendron ❄ ◎

Cool room – medium light (40–64°F/5–18°C)
Epiphyllum ❄ ◎
Epipremnum ❄
Fatsia ◎
Grevillea ❄ ◎
Monstera ❄
Platycerium ❄ ◎
Primula malacoides ❄ ◎,
P. obconica ❄ ◎
Schefflera ❄
Sparmannia ❄ ◎

Cool room – poor light (40–64°F/5–18°C)
Aspidistra ❄
x *Fatshedera* ◎
Hedera, some ❄, ◎
Pteris ❄ ◎
Rhoicissus ❄

HYDROCULTURE

Anthurium ❄
Chamaedorea ❄ ◎
Cissus ❄
Codiaeum ❄ ◎
Dieffenbachia ❄ ◎
Dracaena ❄ ◎
Euphorbia milii ❄
Ficus benjamina ❄
Hedera, some ❄, ◎
Monstera ❄
Nephrolepis ❄ ◎
Saintpaulia ❄ ◎
Schefflera ❄
Spathiphyllum ❄ ◎
Streptocarpus ❄ ◎
Yucca, some ❄

KEY
❄ *Not frost hardy*
◎ *Requires high humidity*

Bromeliads

BROMELIADS, the 2,000 or so members of one of the most diverse and exotic families, the Bromeliaceae, are a fascinating group of plants that can make curiously beautiful specimens for the home, the warm greenhouse, or conservatory. Most are tropical epiphytes growing naturally on tree branches and rock faces, clinging by means of anchorage roots. These plants obtain moisture and nutrients via their leaves directly from the atmosphere, often from mists and low, moisture-laden clouds. Others are terrestrial, growing in the earth.

Almost all bromeliads are rosette-forming, frequently with strikingly colored or variegated foliage, and many produce flamboyant blooms. Their forms range from the long and graceful, silvery strands of Spanish moss (*Tillandsia usneoides*) to the imposing *Puya alpestris*, which holds its massive spike of tubular, metallic blue flowers above a rosette of arching, spiny foliage.

METHODS OF DISPLAY

BINDING WITH MOSS *Wrap moistened sphagnum moss around the roots of large plants (here a cultivar of* Tillandsia latifolia) *and attach to the mount by binding with wire, nylon line, or raffia. The moss must be kept moist at all times.*

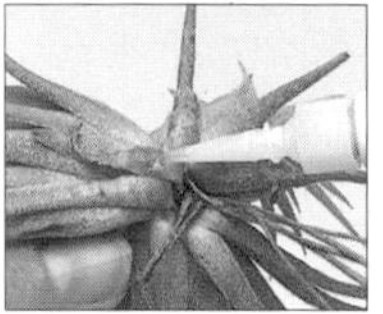

USING ADHESIVE *Place adhesive onto the mount and plant roots (see inset), then gently press the plants (here* Tillandsia tectorum, *above, and* T. ionantha) *into position.*

Displaying epiphytes

Most epiphytes are displayed to their best advantage if attached to a tree or branch, simulating the way that they grow in nature; this also helps the epiphytes avoid basal rot, which may occur if plants are grown in soil mix. Old, branched sections of trees cut to size are ideal.

Bromeliad trees

If using an upright branch, secure it firmly in a deep container with concrete or, if small, a strong adhesive. Alternatively, an artificial tree or branch may be constructed from a metal or wire framework covered in bark. There is a wide range of epiphytes suitable for displaying in this way, including many species from the genera *Aechmea*, *Catopsis*, *Guzmania*, *Neoregelia*, *Nidularium*, *Tillandsia*, and *Vriesea*. Use young plants if possible since they are easier to mount and tend to become established more quickly.

Prepare the plants by gently removing any loose soil mix from around the roots, then wrap the roots in moistened sphagnum moss and bind them to the support. Soon the plants will root onto their support and the binding may be removed. Some small plants may be lodged securely in crevices without being bound, or attached with adhesive, as described for *Tillandsia*, below.

Displaying *Tillandsia*

Tillandsia species may be mounted individually or in groups on pieces of driftwood or cork bark, on rocks, or even on natural crystal. Position each plant with a small amount of adhesive. Make sure that the base of the rosette is free from adhesive so that new root growth is not inhibited. Press the plant onto the mount and secure it with a rubber band, twine, or wire, until the glue has set.

Epiphytes as pot plants

A number of naturally epiphytic genera, particularly those with colored foliage, and the usually epiphytic species and cultivars of *Aechmea*, *Billbergia*, *Neoregelia*, *Nidularium*, and *Vriesea* may also

BROMELIADS SUITABLE FOR GROWING INDOORS

***Ananas bracteatus* 'Tricolor'**

Tillandsia stricta

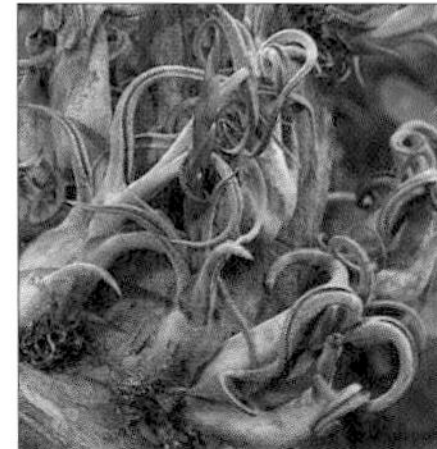

Tillandsia caput-medusae

Neoregelia carolinae* f. *tricolor

Bromelia balansae

Aechmea fasciata

Cryptanthus bivittatus

Guzmania lingulata

Guzmania lingulata* var. *minor

Vriesea splendens

be grown as pot plants, provided that an appropriate soil mix is used. It must be an extremely open, porous mixture, high in humus and almost lime-free. For this, use half coarse sand or perlite, and half peat or leaf mold. To ensure that any extra moisture drains away swiftly, add pieces of partly composted tree bark to the potting medium.

Growing terrestrials

There are several hundred terrestrial bromeliads belonging to the genera *Abromeitiella*, *Ananas*, *Dyckia*, *Hechtia*, *Portea*, and *Puya*. In regions where temperatures never fall below 45–50°F (7–10°C), a wide variety of terrestrials may be grown outdoors. *Fascicularia bicolor* may even be grown without protection in temperatures as low as 32°F (0°C).

Terrestrial bromeliads often have stiff, spiny leaves and a spreading habit. While they may be grown in pots as house plants, they perform much better if given more space in a greenhouse or conservatory border or, where conditions permit, out of doors. With their eye-catching foliage and strong outlines, they make a distinctive addition to the garden, particularly if combined in designs either with cacti and other succulents or with subtropical plants.

Routine care

Because most bromeliads originate from tropical rain forests, they need warm, humid conditions in order to thrive; most need a minimum temperature of 50°F (10°C). In the right conditions they require little maintenance but, indoors, special attention is needed in order to maintain the necessary humidity.

Watering

Since epiphytes draw moisture from the air, they should be mist-sprayed once every day rather than watered conventionally at their roots; use soft water or rainwater when possible, particularly for genera that do not tolerate lime, such as *Aechmea*, *Neoregelia*, *Nidularium*, *Tillandsia*, and *Vriesea*. In spring and summer, add a dilute (quarter-strength) liquid orchid fertilizer to the spray every four to five weeks to keep the plants healthy and vigorous (see ORCHIDS, "Feeding," p.442).

Where plants are growing with sphagnum moss around their roots, keep the moss moist by regularly spraying it with tepid water and also mist-spray the foliage occasionally.

DIVIDING ROOTSTOCKS

Gently tease or cut the offset away from the parent plant (here Billbergia nutans) *so that the root system remains undamaged.*

Bromeliads whose rosettes form a natural well or urn in the center should be kept filled with water, particularly in hot, dry conditions. Change the water and apply a dilute foliar feed to the leaves occasionally.

Propagation

Bromeliads may be propagated by vegetative methods or by seed. Most epiphytic plants produce offsets that may be removed and grown on separately, while stoloniferous terrestrial kinds may be divided at the start of the growing season.

Offsets of epiphytes

Many epiphytic bromeliads are monocarpic, meaning that the rosettes flower only once and then die. Before they flower, however, they form offsets around the base of the mature rosette. The offsets should be left in place until they are about one-third the size of the parent plant. In many cases, the offsets may be removed by hand, but some will have to be cut off with a sharp knife, as close to the parent plant as possible. Replant the parent plant.

Once removed, the offsets should be transferred immediately into prepared containers of free-draining soil mix, with their bases just held firm in the soil mix (see "Epiphytes as pot plants," opposite). Keep the young plants slightly shaded at about 70°F (21°C), and lightly mist-spray them with tepid water daily.

Offsets of the nonmonocarpic species may be detached from the parent plant and attached to mounts in the same way as for adult plants. The offsets may have no roots, but these will soon develop if the plants are regularly mist-sprayed and if a few strands of moist sphagnum moss are fixed at the base of the rosettes to retain moisture.

Offsets of terrestrials

Some terrestrial bromeliads, for example some *Ananas* and *Hechtia*, have stoloniferous rootstocks that also produce offsets. At the start of the growing season, lift the parent plant from the ground, or remove it from its container, so that the offsets may be cut off without injuring the parent plant. Then replant the parent and pot up the offsets in a soil mix of 1 part shredded peat, 1 part leaf mold, and 1 part coarse sand or grit.

Raising plants from seed

Most bromeliad seeds are sown like other seeds, although it is important to sow them when they are fresh because, with a few exceptions, they do not remain viable for long.

A less conventional method is used for *Tillandsia* seeds. These are sown on bundles of conifer twigs, such as *Thuja*, that are packed with well-moistened sphagnum moss and then bound together. Hang the bundles in a slightly shaded position, mist-spray them regularly, and ensure that there is free air circulation but no drafts. If kept in a temperature of about 81°F (27°C), seeds will germinate in around three to four weeks. Young plants may then be transferred to branches or other types of support and grown on.

HOW TO PROPAGATE TILLANDSIA BY SEED

1 *Make a bundle of* Thuja *twigs interspersed with moist sphagnum moss, binding it with string, raffia, or wire.*

2 *Sprinkle the seeds evenly over the prepared bundle; they will adhere readily to the moist moss.*

3 *Water the seeds with a light mist-spray and then hang up the bundle in position (see inset). Continue to mist-spray on a regular basis.*

HOW TO PROPAGATE BY DIVISION OF OFFSETS

1 *When the offsets are about one-third of the size of the parent (here* Aechmea*), sever them at the base with a knife. Retain any roots they may have.*

2 *Pot each offset into a mix of equal parts shredded peat, leaf mold, and sharp, gritty sand, inserting it so that the base stays on the surface.*

Bonsai

BONSAI is the art of producing miniature trees and shrubs, mainly through specialized pruning techniques. Several styles of bonsai have been developed, all of which aim to produce a graceful plant resembling a full-sized tree or natural feature such as a waterfall or mountain. Bonsai are grown in shallow containers, indoors or outdoors, depending on the species.

Bonsai styles

There are five basic styles with many variations. All are based on the ways trees grow naturally, and are defined by the angle of the trunk, so choose the right style for your plant.

Formal upright This has a tapered trunk, well-placed branches, and grows straight upward, indicative of an open growing area.

Informal upright This shape is often seen in nature, curving or bending to adapt to its growing conditions.

Slanting This bonsai has a trunk leaning by up to 45° as if to reach the light; its roots often become more substantial to anchor the tree.

Semicascade This grows up out of its pot, then dips down so that the tip ends above the bottom of the pot.

Full cascade This grows at an upward slant and dips into a sinuous fall, with its tip level with or below the bottom of the pot. This form is grown in a tall container for balance.

Many other styles are recognized; over-rock or clinging-to-rock styles and group plantings, known as forests, are particularly popular.

Bonsai choices

The basic bonsai shape is created by pruning a young plant while also pruning its roots and restricting them in a container. Pruning requirements vary according to the species; the information below is intended only as a general outline.

Choosing the plant

There are two basic groups: hardy bonsai, which must be summered outdoors and protected in winter, and tender bonsai, which may be kept indoors all year and even grown under lights.

Many small-leaved, woody plants are suitable for training as bonsai. Popular hardy evergreen choices include *Pinus thunbergii* and *Juniperus procumbens* 'Nana', which provide year-round foliage. Many pyracantha and cotoneaster have the bonus of colorful berries.

Among hardy deciduous species, honeysuckles (*Lonicera*) and hawthorns (*Crataegus*) have small leaves, whereas maple (*Acer*) species have striking foliage that changes color throughout spring, summer, and fall. Azaleas (*Rhododendron*) and *Wisteria* have spectacular blossoms, whereas *Betula pendula* and *Euonymus alatus* feature attractive bark. Easy-to-grow tender bonsai include weeping fig (*Ficus benjamina*), with interesting aerial roots, and dwarf pomegranate (*Punica granatum* 'Nana'), which bears small leaves and fruit. *Serissa foetida* is available in single- and double-flowered forms. *Schefflera actinophylla* has large leaves that reduce over time; *Cuphea hyssopifolia* has small, very narrow leaves and pinkish purple flowers.

Buy a healthy, potgrown plant with balanced branches and a sturdy trunk. Alternatively, bonsai may be raised from seed, cuttings, or seedlings, and the plants shaped from the outset. Container plants may be planted out for several years before training to thicken the trunk.

Selecting a container

It is essential, in the art of creating a bonsai, to choose the right container. Choose one that is in scale with the tree and, if for a slanting tree, deep enough to balance the top-growth. Ceramics (with unglazed interiors), wood, plastic, or stone may be used. The container needs drainage holes and a base rim or small feet to elevate the pot: this increases drainage and aeration, and discourages pests. Hardy bonsai need a frostproof pot.

Creating a bonsai

To create the chosen style, prune the roots and top-growth when planting the new bonsai. Then plant the tree and wire the trunk and branches to produce the desired form.

BASIC BONSAI TOOLS

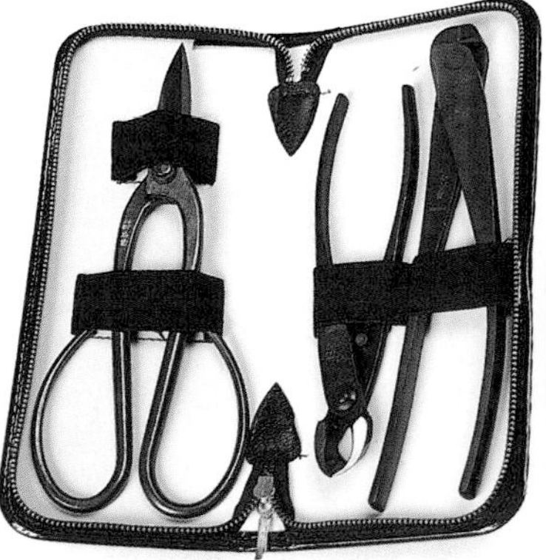

Bonsai tools can be bought singly or in sets. This basic set includes trimming shears (left) for use on branches, leaves, and roots; a concave branch cutter (center) for pruning; and a wire cutter (right) for trimming and removing wire.

Initial root and top pruning

Remove the bonsai from its original container. Trim the roots, as sparingly as possible, to make a shallow root system that will fit the selected container. Shorten or completely remove shoots and branches to emphasize the basic framework of the chosen style and to stimulate shoots and buds to form near the branches.

Planting

Prepare the container by placing nylon mesh over the drainage holes. To secure the root ball, thread an anchorage wire through two drainage holes; pull the ends of the wire up and over the sides of the container.

Spread a soil-based mix in the base of the pot and position the bonsai so that it faces in the best direction for viewing. Pull the anchor wire across or through the root ball, twist the ends together, and bend them down. Work dry soil mix between the roots, then backfill. Top-dress with moist moss or gravel.

Wiring

Most bonsai need to be trained with wire to produce the desired shape. Wrap wire, usually copper, aluminum, or copper-coated aluminum in various gauges, evenly around trunk and branches. Between late fall and early spring is generally the best time to wire; to make the tree more flexible, stop watering three days before wiring. For deciduous trees and most tender bonsai, wiring can be left in place for three to six months; for evergreens, six months to a year. Check and renew wiring often to prevent the wire from cutting into the branches.

How to Create a Bonsai

1 *Gently loosen, then remove the soil from the root ball. Comb the roots, carefully pulling them outward and downward.*

2 *Prune long and downward-growing roots. Rotate the plant (here* Cotoneaster horizontalis*) to determine the best angle for viewing.*

3 *Using trimming shears, remove all growth that is not appropriate to the chosen style. Shorten branches and thin them out to reveal the trunk.*

4 *Prepare the container, anchor the plant, then fill with soil mix. Here a large root remains above the surface as an extra feature. Top-dress with moss and stones, firming them into place.*

5 *New leaves will grow to fill out the bonsai, which is an informal upright shape. The alternating branches form a balanced plant, and the foliage is well distributed with the greatest mass at the base and the smallest at the apex.*

Routine care

Bonsai need detailed attention to maintain their shape. Protect outdoor plants from cold and wind. Treat pests and diseases as soon as they are noticed (see pp. 547–79).

Watering and feeding

Water regularly – a few times a day in hot or windy conditions. For moisture-loving species, insert wicking (such as nylon yarn) in the soil, and place the wick tip in water.

Feed bonsai with a balanced fertilizer during the growing season. In fall, apply a food high in phosphorus and potassium. Never fertilize newly root-pruned or repotted bonsai.

Pruning top-growth

Top-growth needs pruning to remove unwanted branches and leaves and encourage more, smaller branches and leaves. Species grown as bonsai are usually pruned at the same time as full-sized plants. For bushy, short-noded growth, cut back regularly any long, straggly shoots. Different species have specific needs; seek advice from a specialist.

Root pruning and repotting

Root pruning encourages stronger, more fibrous roots; it is usually done in the spring when repotting. Root prune and repot every year for new bonsai and every two to three years for mature plants. Trim roots by one-third, cutting them at an angle so that they heal quickly; replant with fresh soil mix in a clean pot.

Wiring Techniques

Wire branches while they are supple, when young or in late fall or early spring. Leave room for branches to thicken. Start the wire in the soil, and wind it up the trunk and around the lowest branch. Wire together higher branches for support. Use fine gauge wire at the apex.

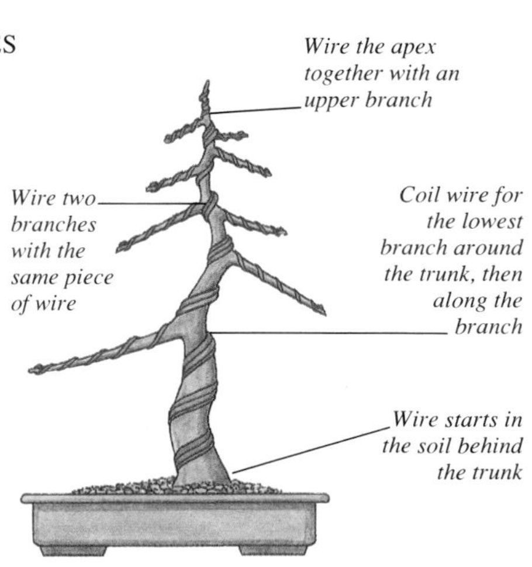

Soil preparation and planting

STRONG, healthy plants, suited to an indoor environment, are vital for success. Since pot plants grow in a limited amount of soil, it is important to use appropriate soil mixes and to maintain the level of nutrients in the soil mix with correct feeding.

Choosing plants

If possible, buy plants that have been grown locally or have been acclimated if brought in from distant growing areas. Each plant should be labeled with its full name and cultivation details.

Look for sturdy plants with strong stems, healthy foliage, and vigorous growing points; reject any that have weak growth, dieback, or discolored, wilting, or brown-edged leaves. Choose younger plants, which should adapt more easily than larger specimens to new conditions. Do not buy potbound plants or those with dry, weedy, or moss-covered soil mix – they have been starved of nutrients and seldom recover fully. Make sure that the growing tips and leaves are free of pests and diseases.

Flowering plants should have plenty of buds that are just starting to color. Climbing plants should be correctly pruned and trained. Do not buy tropical plants in winter, since sudden fluctuations in temperature may have damaged them. If transporting plants in cold weather, wrap them in newspaper for insulation.

Selecting a House Plant

Positioning a plant

Place each plant in a room that provides the levels of temperature, humidity, and light that it requires. Flowering house plants that are of subtropical or tropical origin flower poorly or not at all if kept too cool or in poor light, whereas many foliage plants tolerate cool and shady areas. Cacti and other dry atmosphere plants need light, airy, and dry conditions; plants such as *Begonia rex* require more humidity. If conditions in your home are not ideal for a particular plant, a different cultivar of the same genus may be more suitable.

Potting mixtures

Always use good-quality, prepared potting soil mixes for indoor plants. Soil-based mixes are generally most suitable, because they contain and retain more nutrients, dry out less quickly, and are easier to rewet than peat-based mixes. They are also heavier, providing stability for big pot plants.

Peat-based soil mixes are used for most commercially available house plants. They have little inherent fertility compared with soil-based mixes, and plants grown in them require careful, regular feeding. These soil mixes tend to lose their structure in time, causing poor aeration and watering difficulties.

Lime-haters such as camellias need lime-free or ericaceous soil mixes. Other groups of plants such as orchids (see pp.440–43) need specialized soil mixes. For further information, see SOILS AND FERTILIZERS, "Soil mixes," p.535 .

Grouping plants

For ease of management, plants with similar needs for water, humidity, temperature, and light should be grouped together. If planting into

Plant supports

Various supports are available for house plants. Choose one that is suitable for the growth habit of the plant, taking into account its speed of growth and eventual size.

Plants with aerial roots grow well up a moss pillar. Tie in the shoots until the roots penetrate it; keep the pillar damp by misting. Trailing or climbing plants with several stems may be trained onto wire hoops. Use a single hoop or several, depending on the plant's vigor. A balloon shape of up to eight wires is attractive, allowing good air circulation and access to light for plants with many stems.

Many climbers support themselves by means of twining stems, leaf stalks, or tendrils, and grow readily up bamboo tripods; they may need tying in at first. Single-stemmed plants need only a stake for support; insert the stake before planting to avoid damaging the roots. For details of support aids, see TOOLS AND EQUIPMENT, "Ties and supports," p.472.

MOSS PILLAR
Twine stems with aerial roots around a pillar, tying them in so that they are in contact with the moss.

WIRE HOOP
Train trailing plants around wire hoops inserted into the potting mix. Tie them in regularly as they grow, adding extra hoops if necessary.

STAKE
Insert a stake into the soil mix before planting. Tie in the stem of the young plant.

BAMBOO TRIPOD
Encourage stems or tendrils of climbing plants to twine around the stakes by tying them in.

the same container, ensure that the potting mix suits all the plants. In permanent arrangements, use plants with similar growth rates, otherwise vigorous specimens may swamp their more delicate neighbors.

To increase the humidity level in a dry, centrally heated building, group individually potted plants on wet gravel in shallow bowls or trays. Alternatively, place plants on upturned pots in a tray of water, with their roots above water level.

Plunging pot plants

Plants arranged in large containers may be plunged in their individual pots into water-retentive material, such as turface, to reduce water loss and improve the local humidity. (Turface can absorb up to 40 percent of its own weight in water, so a watertight outer container should be used.) Any plant that is past its prime or too big can then be readily removed. Alternatively, divide (see "Propagation by division," p.451) and replant it.

Bark and peat are useful as plunge materials, but plants may root into the medium, making them difficult to remove. Overwatering peat may result in waterlogging, which can rot the roots. Moisture meters are useful to help determine when the plants need water.

Planting a hanging basket

For the balcony, conservatory, or greenhouse, use slatted or plastic-coated wire baskets with a 2in (5cm) mesh. Insert plants through the sides to form a ball of flowers and foliage. Indoors, where dripping water would cause damage, use solid baskets, with attached drip trays or an outer container that has no drainage holes. Water such hanging baskets with care to avoid waterlogging.

While planting the basket, sit it on a bucket or large pot to keep it stable and clear of the ground. Wire baskets tend to dry out very quickly, but a lining of plastic sheeting reduces moisture loss. The plastic-lined basket is unattractive initially, but is soon obscured by the growing plants. Alternatively, line the basket with long-strand sphagnum moss; a plant saucer placed between the moss and the soil mix forms a small reservoir of moisture. Multipurpose soil mixes based on peat or soil are suitable, although soil-based mixes are easier to rewet.

Plant the basket in stages from the base. If necessary, cut the plastic to insert plants through the sides; a roll of paper around their top-growth protects them during this process.

Sinking Plants into a Large Container

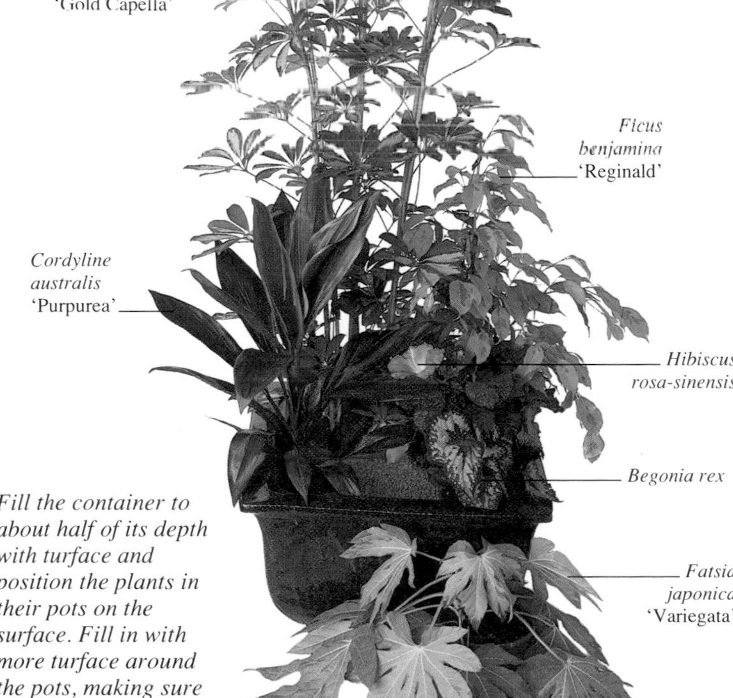

Fill the container to about half of its depth with turface and position the plants in their pots on the surface. Fill in with more turface around the pots, making sure that each pot is sunk up to its rim.

How to Plant a Hanging Basket

1 *Line the bottom of the basket with a layer of moist sphagnum moss, packed tightly to a thickness of at least $1^{1}/_{4}$in (3cm). Add moist, soil-based potting mix to a depth of approximately 2in (5cm). Firm the soil mix.*

2 *Insert the trailing plants by carefully guiding their root balls through the sides of the basket from the outside, so that the root balls are level with the soil mix. Add more soil mix around the roots and firm them in.*

3 *Keep adding moss and soil mix, while inserting more plants at various levels around the sides of the basket to produce a balanced display. Firm the soil mix as you add the plants. Continue until the soil mix is within 1–2in (2.5–5cm) of the rim.*

4 *Edge the top with moss. Insert plants of a more upright habit in the top of the basket. Fill in with soil mix. Firm it around the plants so that the surface slopes down slightly toward the center for efficient watering.*

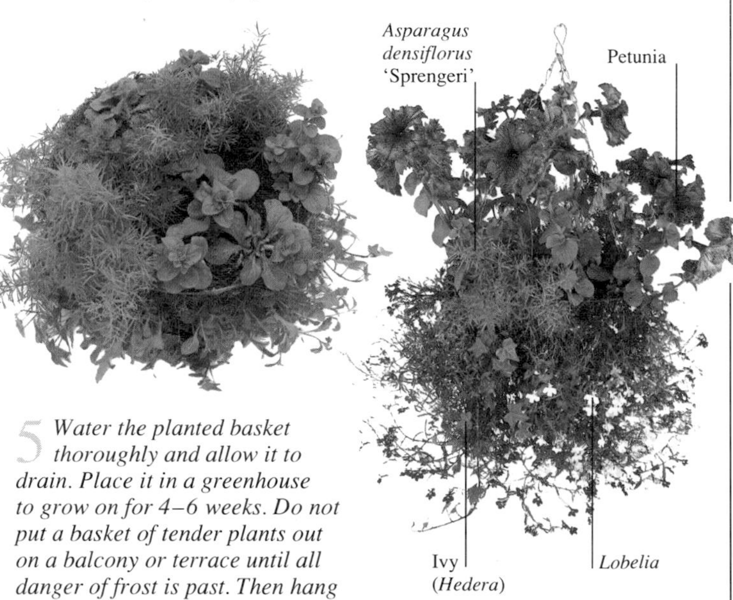

5 *Water the planted basket thoroughly and allow it to drain. Place it in a greenhouse to grow on for 4–6 weeks. Do not put a basket of tender plants out on a balcony or terrace until all danger of frost is past. Then hang it from a suitable, sturdy support.*

RECOMMENDED PLANTS FOR TERRARIUMS

Acorus gramineus 'Pusillus'
Adiantum raddianum ❄
Asparagus densiflorus 'Sprengeri' ❄
Begonia 'Tiger Paws' ❄
Callisia ❄
Chamaedorea elegans ❄
Cissus discolor ❄
Codiaeum ❄
Dizygotheca elegantissima (seedlings) ❄
Dracaena sanderiana ❄
Episcia ❄
Ficus pumila ❄
Fittonia verschaffeltii ❄
Hedera (miniatures)
Hypoestes phyllostachya ❄
Ludisia discolor
Maranta leuconeura ❄
Nertera granadensis
Pellaea rotundifolia ❄
Pellionia daveauana ❄
Peperomia caperata ❄
Pilea cadierei ❄, *P. spruceana* ❄
Plectranthus oertendahlii ❄
Pteris cretica ❄
Saintpaulia (miniatures) ❄
Selaginella ❄
Sinningia pusilla ❄
Soleirolia soleirolii
Sonerila margaritacea
Syngonium hoffmannii ❄
Tradescantia cerinthoides ❄, *T. fluminensis* ❄, *T. spathacea* ❄

Fittonia verschaffeltii

KEY
❄ *Not frost hardy*

Planted baskets are heavy, so make sure that supporting chains and hooks are sound. A universal hook allows the basket to be rotated to receive an even amount of light.

Planting in a terrarium

Before planting, clean the terrarium thoroughly to avoid contamination with algae and fungal diseases, which thrive in enclosed and humid environments. Choose a mixture of tall, upright plants and smaller, creeping ones and decide how to arrange them before starting to plant.

Since a terrarium is self-contained, it must have a layer of drainage material, such as turface, gravel, or pebbles, as well as some horticultural charcoal, which absorbs any gaseous by-products and helps keep the soil mix fresh. A lightweight, free-draining, but moisture-retentive potting mix is the most suitable planting medium. Extra peat or perlite can be added to keep the soil loose and well aerated.

Use young plants with root systems that are sufficiently small to establish easily in shallow soil mix. Soak them thoroughly before planting, and remove dead foliage that might encourage rot. Insert the plants into the soil mix, allowing space for them to spread. If the terrarium is too small to accommodate a hand easily, attach a spoon to a stick to assist planting, and a cork or thread spool to another stick to make a firming implement. Cover bare areas with moss or pebbles to stop the soil mix from drying out, and water lightly before replacing the lid.

Once established, terrariums require very little or no watering (see "Maintaining terrariums and bottle gardens," p.445). If excess condensation appears on the glass, ventilate it a little until there is only a slight misting of the glass in the morning.

PLANTING A TERRARIUM

1 *Plan the arrangement with taller plants either at the back (as here) or in the center, depending on whether the terrarium will be viewed from the front only or from all sides. The plants used here are:*

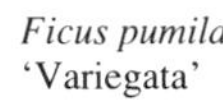

2 *Cover the terrarium base with a 1–2in (2.5–5cm) deep layer of pebbles and a few pieces of horticultural charcoal. Add 1in (2.5cm) of moist potting mix.*

3 *Remove each plant from its pot and shake off any loose soil mix. Gently tease out the roots, reducing the size of the root ball, to help the plant establish.*

4 *Use a widger or other small implement to make hollows for the plants, and insert them carefully, allowing space between them for further growth.*

5 *Fill in around the plants with more moist soil mix and firm the surface. A cork fixed to the end of a thin stake provides a tamper of suitable size.*

6 *Using tweezers, place a layer of moss (or pebbles) over any bare areas of soil mix between the plants. This will prevent the soil mix from drying out.*

7 *Spray the plants and the moss lightly with a fine mist of water and replace the lid. The terrarium is now ready for display.*

Growing Plants in a Soil Bench

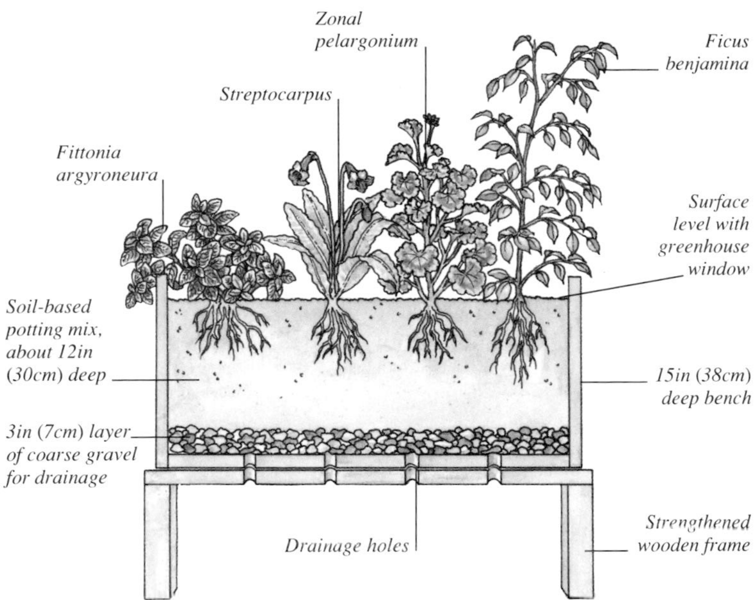

Prepare the soil bench for planting by placing a layer of drainage material in the bottom and then filling the bench with soil-based potting mix. Plant a selection of ornamentals for a fine display in the greenhouse.

Planting a bottle garden

Bottle gardens provide an attractive way of growing very small, slow-growing plants in an enclosed microclimate. Many of the smaller plants grown in terrariums are suitable (see *Recommended Plants for Terrariums*, opposite).

Use any clean, plain or slightly colored glass bottle, as long as the neck is wide enough to allow plants to be inserted easily. If the neck is too narrow to take a hand, make special tools from thin stakes, loops of wire, and common household utensils, such as a dessert fork and teaspoon, to help with planting and routine care.

With the aid of a wide funnel or cardboard tube, pour turface into the bottle to provide a 1 1/4in (3cm) layer of drainage material and add a handful of horticultural charcoal to keep the soil mix sweet. Cover it with a 2–3in (5–7cm) layer of dampened, peat-based potting mix. If the bottle is to be viewed from the front, use a widger to bank up the soil mix at the back. Level the soil mix if the bottle is to be viewed from all sides.

Begin planting at the sides of the bottle and work in toward the center. Remove the plants from their pots, and shake off any excess soil mix. Carefully lower each plant into a planting hole, using tweezers, tongs, or a length of wire twisted into a noose. Space the plants at least 1 1/4in (3cm) apart to allow room for growth. Cover the roots with soil mix, and use a cork tamper to firm it gently.

Trickle a cupful of water down the sides of the bottle to dampen the soil mix, and cover bare areas with sphagnum moss to keep it moist. Clean the inside of the glass with a sponge fixed to a length of stake or stiff wire. If the bottle garden is not sealed after planting, water occasionally, but do not allow water to stand.

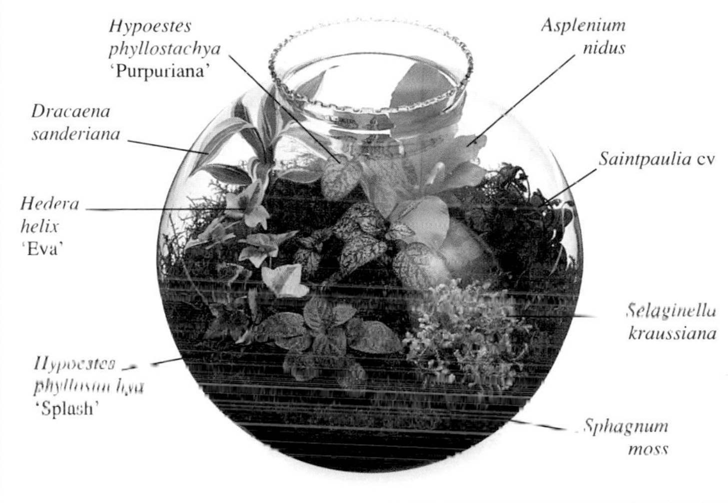

Soil preparation and planting under cover

Conservatories and greenhouses allow control of the environment and extend the range of plants that can be grown in temperate or cool climates.

Soil beds and bed benches

Although conservatory and greenhouse ornamentals may be grown in pots, a large number, particularly climbers and woody shrubs, can be planted permanently in soil borders. For a new conservatory, consider at the planning stage if soil borders are needed. Raised and well-drained soil beds provide a good method of display. Prepare soil beds well since ornamentals may be in place for some years. Make the beds four weeks before planting to allow the soil to settle, and at least 12in (30cm) deep, with 3–6in (7–15cm) of drainage material at the base.

A bench bed is useful for propagating and raising different plants, and for growing specialized plant collections. Bench beds are shallow raised beds, usually at waist height, on supporting frames or pillars. They are ideal for small plants and for use with soil-heating cables (see p.488), mist units (see p.488), and automated watering systems (see p.485). Site the bench to make maximum use of available light.

Bench beds are usually built from aluminum or wood, lined with wire mesh or perforated plastic. They should be at least 6in (15cm) deep and no more than 3ft (1m) wide for easy access. A 3in (7cm) layer of drainage material is sufficient.

Soil mixes under cover

For soil beds, use a well-drained, soil-based mix enriched with organic matter at a rate of about 2.2 gallons/10sq ft (10 liters/sq m). Do not use unsterilized garden soil since it can harbor pests, diseases, and weeds. No safe chemical soil sterilization methods are available to amateurs; heat-sterilizing units, although effective, are expensive and hard to find

In general, use soil-based mixes under cover because they contain nutrients and trace elements that do not leach out as readily as in less rich peat-based mixes; soil-based mixes are also easier to rewet.

It is important to select the appropriate soil mix for specific purposes and for groups of plants with special needs. Most container-grown plants require a good-quality, soil-based mix that is free-draining and of approximately neutral pH. Tropical plants prefer more humus-rich, leafy soils, so incorporate additional leaf mold in the soil mix before filling containers or soil beds. Most ferns, heathers, and many lilies (*Lilium*) need an ericaceous soil mix, as do hydrangeas, in order to produce blue flowers rather than pink ones.

Ornamental plants grown in borders need a dressing every year of 2–3oz/sq yd (50–85g/sq m) of a balanced fertilizer with a mulch of well-rotted compost in spring for strong growth. If the planting needs renewal after several years, remove and dispose of the plants, having propagated them first. Then dig in some well-rotted compost or manure and add a slow-release granular fertilizer before replanting.

In beds of ornamental plants, there is seldom such a buildup of pests and diseases that it is necessary to change or sterilize the soil. With crop plants grown in borders where pests and diseases can increase rapidly, the soil usually has to be replaced annually or sterilized if a suitable method is available. Crop plants are better cultivated in grow bags or containers, where the soil mix can be disposed of if problems occur. Always ensure that the bases of containers with drainage holes do not come into contact with the border soil. This avoids cross-contamination by pests and diseases.

Planting

Always select plants that grow well in the range of temperatures provided (see "Planter's guide to indoor plants," p.431). Make sure that ornamentals or crop plants are planted at spacings that allow free air circulation and so inhibit the spread of pests and diseases. Position the plants to receive optimum light and ventilation for their growing requirements. Make full use of temperature, light intensity, humidity, and air-circulation controls that are provided in a well-built and fitted-out greenhouse.

Orchids

INCLUDED in the orchid family are some 750 genera, nearly 20,000 species, and many thousands more hybrids. Their exotic blooms and intriguing habit make them very desirable ornamental plants, mostly for indoor display, although there are a significant number of beautiful terrestrial species that are hardy. When choosing which to grow from the vast range of types available, consider the conditions and care that you are able to provide. Some orchids have fairly rigorous demands for growing conditions, but many hybrids are specially bred for ease of cultivation and can be successfully grown and propagated in the home.

Terrestrial orchids

As the name suggests, these orchids grow in the ground, in widely varying habitats. Most of those that inhabit temperate to cold regions die down after flowering and exist in a resting state as tubers or similar underground storage organs during the winter. These hardy and near-hardy terrestrials often have flowers that, although individually small, bloom in dense spikes. Many are attractive plants for the rock garden or alpine house (see pp.210–12).

Some terrestrials, such as the slipper orchids belonging to the genus *Paphiopedilum*, come from warmer regions, where they inhabit sheltered sites such as the forest floor. Never having to face harsh weather conditions, these remain evergreen throughout the year, but – because they are not hardy – they need to be cultivated in a greenhouse.

Epiphytic orchids

Epiphytic orchids, which form a very large proportion of those grown by enthusiasts, are fundamentally different in their structure and habit of growth. As implied by their name (derived from the Greek *epi*, upon, and *phyton*, plant), they make their homes in the branches of trees.

They are not parasites (because they do not feed off the tree) but lodgers: they take their nourishment from substances dissolved in rainwater and from debris accumulated around their roots. A few orchids known as lithophytes live in a similar manner on rocks. In temperate climates, epiphytes need to be grown under glass.

Sympodial and monopodial

Epiphytes have two methods of growth: sympodial and monopodial. Sympodial orchids, such as *Cattleya* and *Odontoglossum* species and hybrids, have creeping rhizomes. Each season new growths arise from growing points on the rhizomes and develop into swollen stem structures known as pseudobulbs. Flowers of the different sympodial species vary greatly, and may appear from the top, base, or side of the pseudobulbs.

Monopodial orchids grow in what is called an indeterminate manner. The stem continues to elongate indefinitely, growing taller and taller as new leaves and stem are produced at the apex. Monopodials include many of the most spectacular orchid genera, such as *Phalaenopsis* and *Vanda*. These are native to the warmer regions of the world, climbing their way upward toward the light through dense jungle foliage. Most monopodials bear their flowers in branched, often gracefully arching, flowerheads from axillary points along their stems; aerial roots are also often produced from these points to give new growth.

Choosing plants

If you are a beginner, it is best to obtain plants from a specialist orchid nursery, where they will have enjoyed an ideal environment and not suffered any setbacks. Specialists are also a valuable source of advice on suitable species for the conditions you have at home. Hybrid orchids are generally the easiest to grow, being themselves bred partly for vigor and ease of care. The species thrive best in environments similar to those in which they grow naturally, and these conditions are not always easy to re-create.

Owing to commercial techniques of mass production, many orchids are no longer prohibitively expensive. For a modest price, plants that are attractive but have not yet won a special award may be bought when you visit specialist nurseries and see them in flower. Least expensive of all are unflowered seedlings that may take several years to come into bloom; the result is uncertain, but there is always the exciting possibility that one of the seedlings may be a future award-winner.

RECOMMENDED ORCHIDS

Dendrobium nobile

***Cymbidium* Strath Kanaid**

***Vanda* Rothschildiana**

Paphiopedilum callosum

Cattleya bowringiana

Miltonia candida* var. *grandiflora

POTTING MIX FOR EPIPHYTIC ORCHIDS

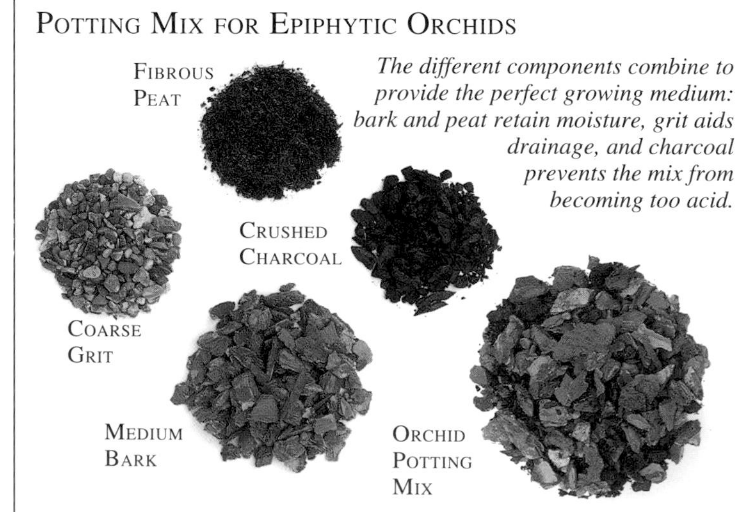

The different components combine to provide the perfect growing medium: bark and peat retain moisture, grit aids drainage, and charcoal prevents the mix from becoming too acid.

Cultivation

The unusual structure and growth habit of epiphytic orchids gives them a reputation for being very delicate, and therefore difficult to grow. With knowledge of a few guidelines and careful preparation, however, most of the difficulties can be avoided.

Potting mix

Although most epiphytes can be grown in pots, their roots are specially adapted to open conditions on trees (or rocks in the case of lithophytes), so they cannot endure the close-textured soil mixes suitable for most other plants. Orchid potting mixes must drain very freely after watering; if they remain wet for long, the roots are likely to rot.

Chopped pine or fir bark makes an excellent potting medium, with some additions to keep the mixture open and prevent it from becoming sour. A suitable mix is as follows: 3 parts medium-grade bark (dust-free), 1 part coarse grit or perlite, 1 part charcoal pieces, and 1 part broken dry leaves or shredded coconut fiber or peat. A wide range of specialized mixes can usually be obtained from orchid nurseries.

Terrestrial orchids also require a much more free-draining potting mixture than most plants. A suitable potting mix can be made up of 3 parts fibrous peat, 3 parts coarse grit, and 1 part perlite, with the addition of 1 part charcoal.

Potting

When a plant has filled its container, it should be transferred to a new pot a size or two larger to provide space for further growth. Choose a pot that will accommodate the roots and allow for one or two years' growth but no more; a pot that is too large for the root system is likely to lead to stagnant conditions in the potting mix. To assist drainage, many growers fill the bottom quarter of the pot with broken crocks, pieces of plastic foam, or large grit. Crocks add extra weight to plastic pots, making them less likely to be knocked over.

Hold the plant with one hand so that the crown is just below the rim of the pot and place the potting mix around the roots, tapping the pot sharply to settle the mix. Use relatively dry mix, which should be thoroughly watered after repotting. The plant, especially the roots, should be disturbed as little as possible, and kept out of strong light.

Some epiphytes do well in containers that allow more air to reach the roots, such as hanging baskets made of wire or wooden slats. Such containers are essential for species of *Stanhopea* because their flowers grow down through the potting mix to emerge on the underside.

When potting on sympodials, old pseudobulbs of two to three seasons' growth that have lost their leaves (usually called back bulbs) may be removed and used for propagating (see p.443). Place the rear of the plant against one side of the pot, leaving space on the opposite side for the new growth to develop.

Support

Many orchids are sturdy enough not to need support. Others, however, require careful staking to look their best, particularly those with long flowering stems that carry many heavy blooms. Use upright stakes or stout wires, to which the stems may be tied as unobtrusively as possible. Do this as the stems are growing and before the flower buds open. Avoid changing the position of the plants or the display will be spoiled because the flowers will face in different directions.

Growing on bark

Some orchids that do not grow successfully in containers will thrive if mounted on pieces of either bark or tree fern with moss at their roots, although they then require a constantly humid atmosphere. Initially they must be tied firmly to the slab; nylon thread is ideal for this purpose. New roots should soon appear; these will adhere firmly to the slab and thus secure the plant.

Routine care

For successful cultivation, it is vital to provide orchids with their particular care requirements; these vary according to the species.

Temperature

While the hardy terrestrials (notably *Cypripedium* species) do well in the rock garden or alpine house, others (usually described as half hardy) may also be grown in these unheated conditions in mild areas. They include the cool-growing genera *Pleione* and *Bletilla*, which need only enough heat to ensure frost-free conditions.

A cool greenhouse, with a minimum night temperature in winter of 50°F (10°C), is suitable for a large number of different orchids, including some *Brassia*, *Coelogyne*, *Cymbidium*, *Dendrobium*, *Laelia*, *Odontoglossum*, *Oncidium*, and *Paphiopedilum* species and hybrids.

The intermediate house, with a minimum winter night temperature of 55–60°F (13–15°C) will greatly extend the range of possibilities to include species and hybrids of *Cattleya* and its relatives, and a wider selection of the *Odontoglossum* group and of *Paphiopedilum* species and hybrids, as well as many other attractive and beautiful orchids.

The warm house, with a minimum night temperature of at least 65°F (18°C), provides the necessary conditions for species and hybrids of *Phalaenopsis* and *Vanda* and their many relatives, as well as the heat-loving species and hybrids of *Dendrobium*, and many orchids from the hot and humid lowlands of the tropics and subtropics.

Watering and humidity

These are perhaps the most important factors in orchid cultivation. Watering should be frequent enough to avoid drying, but not so frequent that the potting mix becomes soggy – once or twice a week for most of the year is usually sufficient. In the summer months plants may need watering every day, and during the period of shorter winter days only once every two or three weeks.

Rainwater is usually recommended, but drinkable tapwater is safe. Water plants in the early morning. Do not let water remain too long

How to Display Epiphytic Orchids

Most epiphytes may be grown in pots, although they may also be successfully cultivated in a hanging basket or on bark. Keep the plants in a constantly humid atmosphere until established.

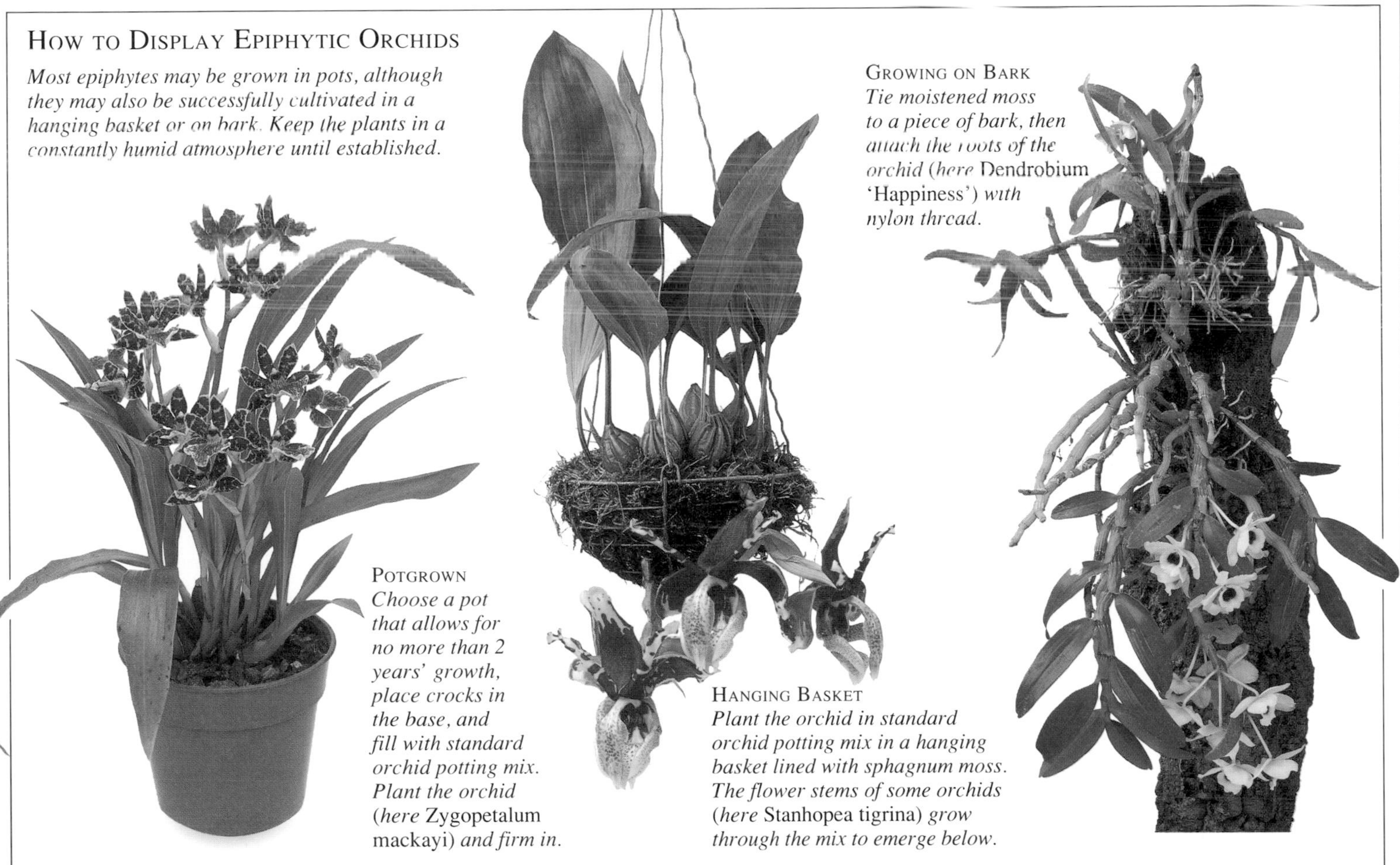

GROWING ON BARK
Tie moistened moss to a piece of bark, then attach the roots of the orchid (here Dendrobium 'Happiness'*) with nylon thread.*

POTGROWN
Choose a pot that allows for no more than 2 years' growth, place crocks in the base, and fill with standard orchid potting mix. Plant the orchid (here Zygopetalum mackayi*) and firm in.*

HANGING BASKET
Plant the orchid in standard orchid potting mix in a hanging basket lined with sphagnum moss. The flower stems of some orchids (here Stanhopea tigrina*) grow through the mix to emerge below.*

on the foliage, or it may cause leaf spotting if the plants are exposed to hot sun. Overwatering must be avoided, but water thoroughly, so that the potting mix is evenly moist. Allow the mix to become nearly – but not quite – dry before watering again; if in doubt, delay watering.

During the growing season, orchids need a high level of humidity. This may be achieved by damping down the orchid house by spraying water over the paths and soil and on the staging between plants. Do this early in the morning; as the day progresses, the water will be drawn up as vapor. This daily damping down may be discontinued when the natural conditions are cold and damp. Be careful, however, because in extremely cold weather the heating system may make the air very dry, and the greenhouse may need to be damped down more often.

Orchids grown in the home as windowsill plants must be chosen from those that do not demand very high humidity. Even these may benefit from additional local humidity by standing them on a layer of moist gravel or expanded clay aggregate in a tray or deep saucer.

Feeding

Since modern orchid potting mixes contain little nourishment, orchids will need feeding during their growing period. Liquid fertilizers are the most convenient and these can be added during watering. Any commercial, general-purpose brands sold for pot plants may be used. Orchids are not heavy feeders, so it will be necessary to dilute the fertilizer to half the strength recommended for other pot plants. Feed the orchids once every three weeks from spring to fall, and only every six weeks (if at all) during the winter.

Ventilation

Most orchids, especially the popular cool-greenhouse kinds, require free-moving air conditions. They dislike cold drafts, however, which can cause flower buds to drop and slow down growth. Ventilators should be only partially opened in spring, when sunny days may be accompanied by chill winds, and closed well before the temperature starts to drop in the late afternoon. As days become warm, ventilators may be opened wider and for a longer time. Remember, however, that water vapor is quickly lost through open ventilators and humidity is reduced, so that extra damping down is needed. A small electric fan, inexpensive both to buy and run, will keep the air moving without letting out humidity or letting in drafts.

Shading

Although different orchids may have different light requirements, from the shade-loving *Paphiopedilum* orchids to the sun-loving *Laelia* species and hybrids, some form of shading is needed to protect new growth from being scorched by the sun and to prevent the greenhouse from overheating. The cheapest method is to use a greenhouse shading compound. White is more efficient than green in reflecting back the sun's rays, and it becomes almost transparent in rain, letting in more light on dull days. More effective, but more expensive, are manual or automatic roller blinds, made either of wood slats or plastic mesh.

Dormancy

An important and integral part of an orchid's life cycle is the dormant period, when growth is halted. During this time, which in the case of some orchids may last only a few weeks and in others several months, they need very little water, if any, in order to survive.

Although plants' requirements vary, the general rule is that those orchids that lose their leaves when dormant should not be watered until new growth begins. Water sparingly at first, then normally (taking care not to overwater). Plants that keep their leaves will need to be given only a little water during the dormant period to avoid dehydration.

How to Propagate by Keikis

1 *When a new plantlet with aerial roots (a "keiki") has formed from a node, cut it away carefully from the parent plant with a sharp knife.*

2 *The selected cutting should have healthy leaves and an evenly developed root system.*

3 *Holding the plantlet by its stem at planting level, pot up the young plant in a 3in (6cm) pot with the roots just below the potting mix surface.*

Propagation

Vegetative propagation methods are the easiest for the amateur to learn. They also have the advantage of

How to Propagate by Stem Cuttings

1 *Using a sharp knife, cut off a section of stem at least 10in (25cm) long, just above a leaf node or at the base of the plant.*

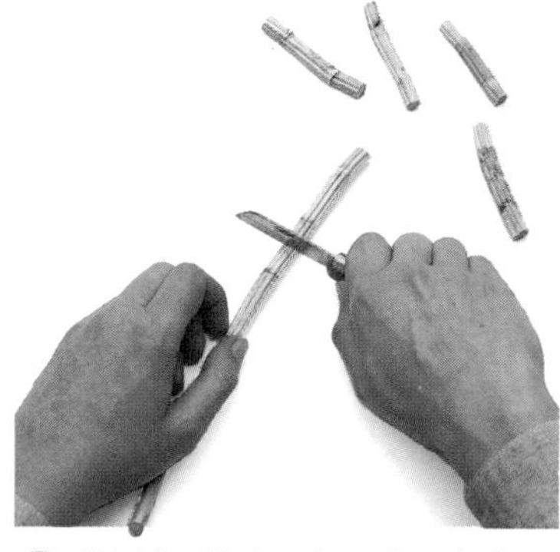

2 *Divide this into lengths of about 3in (7cm), cutting midway between leaf nodes. Each cutting should have at least one node.*

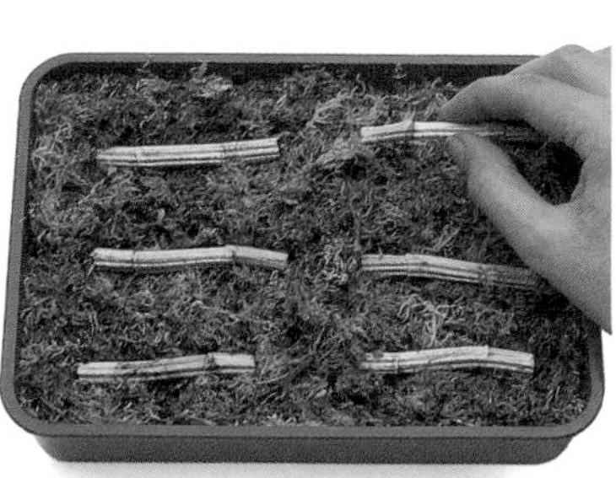

3 *Lay the cuttings in a tray on a layer of moist sphagnum moss and store in a humid place out of direct sunlight.*

4 *After several weeks, the dormant buds will have developed into plantlets, which will then be ready to pot up.*

producing offspring which are identical to the parent plant, so that the results are predictable.

Keikis
The simplest cuttings, which are commonly known to orchid growers as keikis, are small plantlets that appear adventitiously (that is, atypically) from the nodes on stems of monopodial orchids, such as *Dendrobium*. As soon as these plantlets have developed a few vigorous roots, they should be carefully severed from the parent plant with a sharp knife, and then potted into a standard orchid potting mix. Water them sparingly at first, but remember to spray the leaves with a fine mist until the roots have become established and the plants have had a chance to become accustomed to their new environment.

Stem cuttings
Cuttings may also be made from the stems (often called canes) of many *Dendrobium* and *Epidendrum* orchids. With a sharp knife, cut off sections up to 12in (30cm) in length. Divide these into cuttings 3–4in (7.5–10cm) long, each with at least one dormant bud. Lay the cuttings on damp sphagnum moss or a similar moist material, and keep them in a humid, shaded place. When the buds have produced plantlets, detach these and pot them up separately.

Division
The usual method of propagating sympodial orchids such as *Cattleya*, *Cymbidium*, and *Odontoglossum* is by division. Simply cut through the rhizome between pseudobulbs and pot up the pieces separately. Each piece should have at least three healthy pseudobulbs and a healthy dormant bud to produce new growth.

Back bulbs offer another way of propagating sympodials such as *Cymbidium*. Remove a back bulb, preferably one with roots, by cutting the rhizome just beyond it. Insert the back bulb in grit, sharp sand, or standard orchid potting mix, with the cut side of the bulb nearest the edge to allow space in the center for new growth. Place in a cool, shady place, and keep moist. Shoots should appear in two or three months. When the bulbs have developed roots, pot them on.

Commercial techniques
Growing orchids from seed is a difficult technique and requires specialized knowledge and skills. Orchids raised commercially from seed are germinated in flasks of nutrient jelly in a laboratory environment. They may also be propagated by meristem culture: microscopic pieces of plant tissue are grown on under laboratory conditions to mass-produce replicas of the original plant. As a result, first-class cultivars may now be purchased at a reasonable price. However, both techniques are highly specialized. They are seldom practiced by amateurs.

How to Propagate by Division

1 When the orchid has grown too large for its pot and has several leafless bulbs, it may be divided. The plant shown here is a Cymbidium.

2 Remove the orchid from its pot, then divide the plant by separating or cutting it into 2 sections; each section should have at least 3 healthy pseudobulbs.

3 When dividing the orchid, any leafless back bulbs may be pulled away. Discard shriveled ones, and retain those that are firm for potting up separately.

4 Trim each section of the divided plant by removing surplus potting mix and cutting off any dead roots with pruners.

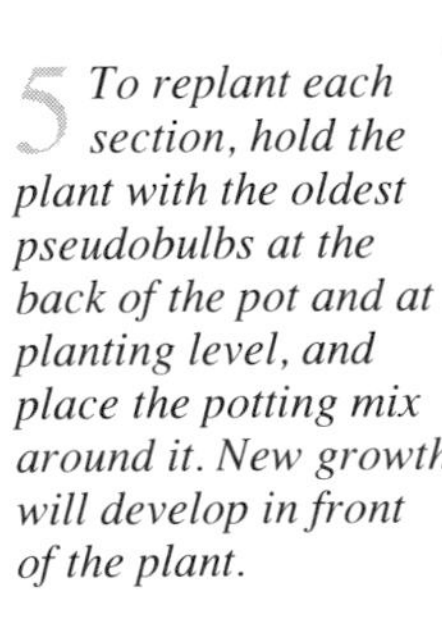

5 To replant each section, hold the plant with the oldest pseudobulbs at the back of the pot and at planting level, and place the potting mix around it. New growth will develop in front of the plant.

Propagation by Back Bulbs

1 Plant back bulbs singly at one side of a 3in (6cm) pot. Place the cut side of the bulb nearest the edge.

2 Within 2 or 3 months a new shoot will grow toward the center of the pot.

Propagation in Flasks

Meristem culture takes place under sterile conditions. Microscopic pieces of plant tissue are placed in a flask on a special nutrient medium such as agar jelly; they then develop into young orchid plants.

Routine care

Unlike plants grown outdoors, indoor plants are not subject to the extremes of the seasonal cycle so need relatively little attention. They require only watering and fertilizing, and generally an annual potting on, to perform at their best.

Watering and humidity

A common problem with indoor plants is overwatering. In general, water when the surface of the soil mix is nearly dry or the pot feels light. Some plants, such as African violets (*Saintpaulia*) and their relatives, do best in an evenly moist soil.

Water plants frequently while they are in active growth, less in winter when they are dormant – twice a month or even less may be enough. Wet the soil mix thoroughly, but do not leave the pot standing in water. Some plants, such as cyclamen, are susceptible to root rot; to water them, let the pots stand in a little water until the soil mix is dark and damp. If tapwater is hard, use distilled water or rainwater for lime-hating plants.

Buildings are often poorly ventilated and the atmosphere too dry for many indoor plants. Maintain the necessary humidity by grouping pot plants on wet gravel in trays or in containers (see "Grouping plants," p.436), or on capillary matting (see "Care of indoor plants before going away," p.446).

Cool- and warm-vapor electric humidifiers are available. Bowls of water placed in a room so that the water evaporates are also effective. Plants that need high humidity benefit from being mist-sprayed with soft water. Use sprays sparingly on plants with hairy leaves, and avoid sunlight since spots of water on the leaves can cause scorch.

Cleanliness

Always remove dead leaves and flowers promptly since they may harbor diseases or pests. Do not allow dust or grime to build up and block the light; dust the foliage with a soft brush. Thoroughly spray the plants occasionally to keep them clean and fresh, but do not spray cacti or plants with hairy leaves unless the weather is warm enough for any excess moisture to evaporate rapidly, or the leaves may rot. Use leaf shine only on glossy-leaved plants; check first that it is compatible with individual species.

Fertilizing

Pot plants grow in relatively small volumes of soil mix and soon use up the available nutrients. Frequent watering also leaches out nutrients, so the plants could starve if they do not have regular feeding throughout the growing season.

Balanced fertilizers are available in various forms: water-soluble or liquid (most convenient for indoor plants), granular, and solid. Always be careful to follow the manufacturers' instructions, and never apply fertilizer to dry soil mix because it will not soak through evenly and may damage the roots.

Pinching out

The appearance of many pot plants, especially trailing plants, can be improved by pinching out growing tips on young plants to encourage more side shoots. This keeps the foliage bushy and increases the number of flower buds. Only pinch plants that are in active growth.

Preserving Humidity around Pot Plants

Create suitably humid conditions for indoor plants by providing them with their own microclimate. Loosely pack a shallow tray with turface or gravel and fill it with water. Group several pot plants on the tray. Keep the water topped up so that the gravel or turface remains wet.

Maintaining Plant Hygiene

Cleaning Smooth-leaved Plants
Gently wipe each leaf (here variegated Ficus elastica*) with a clean, moist, soft, and lint-free cloth.*

Removing Dead Leaves
Pinch out dead leaves and stems at the base of the plant (here Nephrolepis exaltata*) or cut them out.*

Neglected plants

With the exception of orchids and palms, most plants that have weak, leggy, or damaged growth, or sparsely spaced leaves, produce new, vigorous growth if cut back hard to a healthy bud or joint in early spring. Cut back a neglected fern to the crown; keep it moist and in medium light to induce new growth.

Plants that root readily are best renewed from cuttings, while some plants are rejuvenated by air layering (see p.456). Revive exhausted plants by repotting or with a rest in a shaded greenhouse. To rescue an overwatered plant, remove all the sodden soil mix from the root ball, trim off rotting foliage and roots, and repot it in fresh soil mix. Refresh an underwatered plant by immersing the pot in water until the bubbles stop rising, then let the pot drain.

Potting on and top-dressing

Indoor plants also need periodic potting on to accommodate their growth and to replenish the soil mix. A potbound plant has retarded growth and water runs straight through the soil mix. Pot on before this so that the plant develops well. A few plants, such as amaryllis (*Hippeastrum*), enjoy confined roots, so pot them on less often and top-dress occasionally.

The best time to pot on is at the start of the growing season, although fast-growing plants may need potting on several times in one season. The process may delay flowering because the plant initially concentrates its energy on new root growth. Avoid potting on a dormant plant.

Potting on
Ensure that the root ball is completely moist so that it comes easily out of its pot without damaging the roots. Turn the pot upside down and slide the plant out into your hand. If the pot is too big to lift easily, run a knife around the inside, then lay the pot on its side. Support the plant

How to Renew Top-dressing

Hippeastrum

1 *Use a widger to remove the top 1–2in ($2^1/_2$–5cm) of the old soil mix, taking care not to damage the plant's roots.*

2 *Replace it with fresh, moist soil mix to which a small amount of fertilizer has been added. Firm the soil mix well around the crown and water.*

with one hand and roll the pot, gently tapping the sides with a wood block to loosen the soil mix fully before removing the plant.

Put fresh potting mix in the new pot until the plant is positioned at the same depth as before, with space allowed for watering. Make sure that the roots are spread out and the plant centered. Fill in with more soil mix, and firm gently. Water, but do not feed the plant for four to six weeks so that it will send out new roots into the soil mix in search of food. Keep the plant out of direct sun for a few days to recover.

Repotting
If a plant is in the largest available container, has grown to its full size, or is very slow-growing, repot it into the same size pot to renew the soil mix. Take the plant out of its pot, removing as much of the old soil mix as possible. Prune out damaged or diseased roots before repotting the plant in fresh soil mix.

Top-dressing
Do not routinely repot plants that react badly to root disturbance, or enjoy confined roots. At the start of each growing season replace the old, surface soil mix with fresh soil mix enriched with balanced fertilizer. Repot only when necessary.

Hanging baskets

Hanging baskets need regular care. Never allow the soil mix in a basket to dry out. Water it thoroughly; in very warm weather, this will need to be done both morning and evening. If the plants wilt, soak the basket in a bowl filled with water.

Feed plants in a basket regularly with a balanced liquid fertilizer, and control any pests. Deadhead flowering plants, clip back trailing plants that are too long, and thin out any untidy or tangled growth. Remove and replace any dead plants.

Maintaining terrariums and bottle gardens

A closed container rarely needs water, but if required, use a long-necked watering can to trickle water against the glass; this avoids disturbing the soil mix. Use just enough water to clean the glass and moisten the surface. If the glass is continuously obscured by mist, the soil mix is too wet – remove the cover or cork until it clears. To get rid of condensation or algae inside the glass, use a small

How to Pot On an Indoor Plant

1 *Before potting on a plant (here* Dracaena deremensis 'Souvenir de Schriever'), *make sure that its root ball is moist by watering it thoroughly an hour beforehand. Select a pot that is one or two sizes larger than the old one. Make sure the pot is clean (whether washed, disinfected, or new) to avoid spreading diseases. The fresh potting mix should be of the same type as that in the old pot.*

2 *Remove the plant by inverting the pot and sharply tapping the rim on a hard surface to loosen the root ball. Support the plant as it slides out of the pot.*

3 *Gently tease out the root ball with a small fork or fingers. Put some moist potting mix in the base of the new pot.*

4 *Insert the plant so that its soil mark is level with the rim base. Fill in with soil mix to within ½in (1.5cm) of the rim, firm, water, and place in position (right).*

Keeping plants from year to year

To renew flowering plants grown for winter color indoors, plunge them in their pots into outdoor beds when all danger of frost is past. Choose a relatively cool spot, with indirect light, and keep them watered with soft (lime-free) water. At the end of summer, repot or top-dress them, bring them back indoors, and feed them regularly once flower buds appear. To keep a cyclamen successfully after it has flowered, do not water it until new growth starts, then remove old roots, and repot in soil-based potting mix so that the corm is level with the surface. Put it in a cool, well-lit place, and water regularly.

WINTER-FLOWERING POT PLANTS
In late spring, transfer the plants, here azaleas (Rhododendron), *to a plunge bed in semishade outdoors. Sink each pot up to its rim in weed-free soil or another suitable plunge material, allowing space for the plants to grow. Bring them in before frost threatens, and keep them cool until the buds open.*

CYCLAMEN
Let the leaves die down after flowering. Place the pot on its side under a shrub or a greenhouse bench or in a cold frame.

Replanting a Terrarium

1 *When a terrarium becomes overgrown, carefully remove any plants that have grown too large. Divide them or select new, small plants. Try to leave the surrounding soil mix undisturbed.*

2 *If needed, trim the remaining plants with scissors. Thin out the surface moss where necessary by removing some with tweezers, keeping adjacent plants firmly in place with a cork-and-stake tamper.*

3 *Divide low-growing plants that have outgrown their allotted space. Use a widger to replant the divisions and the new plants (see inset). Firm with a little fresh soil mix, using the tamper.*

4 *Trickle water down the inside of the glass until the soil mix is just damp. Then replace the lid.*

sponge attached to a stake. Keep the container out of direct sunlight and move it occasionally, especially if it is in a shaded place in winter. Remove dead leaves and control pests and diseases.

Trim the plants from time to time so that each has enough light and space. A razor blade inserted into the end of a stake is useful for pruning plants in small-necked bottle gardens. If any plants encroach upon others, either replace them with smaller plants, or replant the entire container (see above).

Plants in greenhouses

These need regular, sometimes daily, attention, even if the greenhouse is equipped with automatic systems. Watering, ventilation, misting, and feeding are especially important in summer, as is heating in winter, and proper hygiene at all times. Routine care of pot plants, including feeding and potting (see pp.444–5), is similar to that of indoor plants.

Watering

In the enclosed greenhouse environment, correct watering is crucial. The amount needed varies with the season and the weather. In summer, water more on sunny than on cloudy days. Use a hose in a big greenhouse, with a low water pressure to avoid washing surface soil mix away from the roots. A watering can is best in a small or mixed greenhouse, where plants have differing water needs: some pot plants may need watering several times on a hot day. Stand the can in the greenhouse until the water temperature is the same as that of the plants. Do not overwater, especially in winter, since wet soil leads to rotting. For full instructions on watering (e.g. by capillary matting, drip feeds, or trickle systems), see p.485. Self-watering pots are also useful; an outer pot holds water that is borne by capillary action along a wick to the soil mix in an inner pot.

Humidity

Plants need moist, but not stagnant, air. In hot, sunny weather, damp down by splashing the floor, particularly hard surfaces, with water each morning and evening, or more often in very hot weather. This keeps the greenhouse humid and temporarily cools the air. (Soil floors hold the most moisture, while tiled or concrete floors dry most quickly.) If the air is too humid, plants cannot transpire water vapor from the leaves to keep cool, and may overheat and wilt, so ventilate the greenhouse to dry out the air. In very hot climates, or for plants with particular needs, automated cooling systems and special humidifiers may be necessary (see Greenhouses and Frames, "Humidity," p.484).

Dank, cold air encourages fungal diseases to attack plants. In winter, keep the air dry by ventilating the greenhouse when weather permits, or install a fan or a dehumidifier.

Care of indoor plants before going away

When going away, it is possible to ensure that indoor plants do not dry out. To keep water loss to a minimum, move plants into the shade and use one of the following watering methods. Group pot plants on a capillary mat on an upturned tray, draining board, or shelf. Let the mat trail into another tray, a sink, or bath that is filled with water to supply the plants. Holes in plastic pots allow the water through, and clay pots are as good if saturated beforehand. Stand large or single pots on wick waterers, which draw water into the soil mix from a reservoir by means of a wick. Alternatively, water the plant thoroughly, allow it to drain, and place it in a sealed plastic bag to avoid moisture loss. Check for and control any pests or diseases before going away.

Capillary Matting
Place pot plants on one end of a piece of wet matting. Leave the other end submerged in a water reservoir. The plants must be above the water so that they can draw it up as they need it.

Plastic Bag
Hold a clear plastic bag away from the foliage with split stakes. Seal with a plastic twist-tie or fold the neck of the bag under the pot.

Temperature regulation
Use ventilation to control temperatures in the greenhouse and avoid severe fluctuations that can harm plants. Too much ventilation slows growth; too little leads to high temperatures. On windy days, ventilate the greenhouse on the leeward side to avoid harmful drafts. For further information, see GREENHOUSES AND FRAMES, "Ventilation" (p.483) and "Shading" (p.484).

Hygiene
Keep the greenhouse clear of all debris that may harbor pests, and remove dead leaves and flowers before they rot. Wash or renew the gravel on benches if it is infested with tiny snails or clogged with soil. Each fall, take the plants outside and clean the greenhouse. Choose a still, warm day when the change in their environment is least likely to harm the plants. A thorough scrubdown is preferable, otherwise give the greenhouse a sweeping and hosing down (see GREENHOUSES AND FRAMES, "Routine maintenance," p.491).

Cold protection
In unheated greenhouses, where winters are not harsh, prevent plant roots from freezing by keeping them nearly dry. Cover plants with a layer of plastic sheeting or newspaper, and cover beds with straw. Insulate the base of shrubs and climbers with straw or similar material, secured with netting or twine. Plunge small pots in sand.

Pests and diseases

Regularly check buds, growing points, and the backs of leaves, and take early remedial action. Destroy badly infested plants, and isolate less affected specimens until they are clear of trouble. Isolate newly purchased plants for two weeks and control pests and diseases before placing them with other plants. Particular problems may be caused by black vine weevil larvae (p.566) and spider mites (p.552), especially in dry, centrally heated air.

In warm, moist greenhouse conditions, pests and diseases such as gray mold/*Botrytis* (p.559) and powdery mildew (p.552), aphids (p.552) and hence viruses (p.555), and whiteflies (p.552) can spread rapidly. During the annual cleanup, (see "Routine maintenance," p.491) remove plants likely to be harmed by chemicals; spray the greenhouse to control any pests or diseases before replacing the plants. See also PLANT PROBLEMS (pp.547–79).

Hydroculture

This system has developed from hydroponics, which is a technique for growing plants in water to which all necessary nutrients are added. In hydroculture, "water roots" (which are slightly different from plant roots growing in soil) are supported in an open-mesh pot of inert growing medium and nutrients are added to water in an outer, watertight container. A calibrated, floating marker in a clear plastic indicator measures "maximum," "optimum/best," or "minimum" water levels.

Hydroculture has several advantages: it is easy to provide the plants with a precise and appropriate amount of air, water, and nutrients; the growing medium is clean, well drained, odorless, free from overacidity and clogging, which discourages weeds, pests, and diseases; and growth is often faster and stronger than in soil. Bulbs, cacti, orchids, and many plants that are commonly grown in offices flourish under hydroculture; see also "Planter's guide to indoor plants," p.431.

CROSS SECTION OF A HYDROCULTURE POT

The inner culture pot holds the plant and the growing medium (here turface), which may be placed in any suitable watertight container.

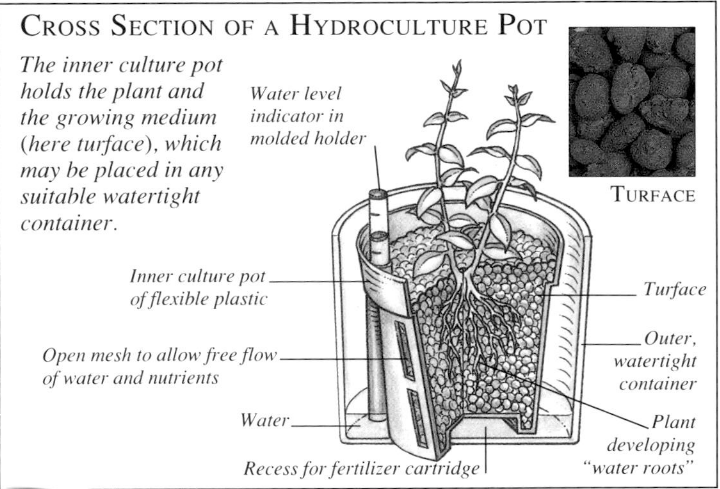

Preparing plants
Plants are best obtained from specialist nurseries or raised from cuttings, although some will transfer from soil. Between early spring and early fall, choose a young, healthy plant and remove it carefully from its pot. Soak the root ball in water at room temperature for half an hour until the soil comes away from the roots, and gently rinse the roots clean.

Planting
If using a fertilizer cartridge, clip it firmly into the culture pot base before planting. Wash and soak some turface, then half fill a culture pot with it. Place the plant in the pot, then spread out its roots and carefully fill the pot to its rim with turface. Insert the water level indicator. Place planted culture pots either singly or in groups in watertight containers; clear glass is unsuitable because it lets light reach the roots. Water to the "optimum/best" mark on the indicator. Keep the plants at 64–77°F (18–25°C). If they have previously been grown in soil, cover them with clear plastic bags to prevent them from drying out while water roots develop.

WASHING PLANT ROOTS

Wash off soil traces under slowly running, cool water while holding the plant (here a Dieffenbachia).

A TABLETOP DISPLAY

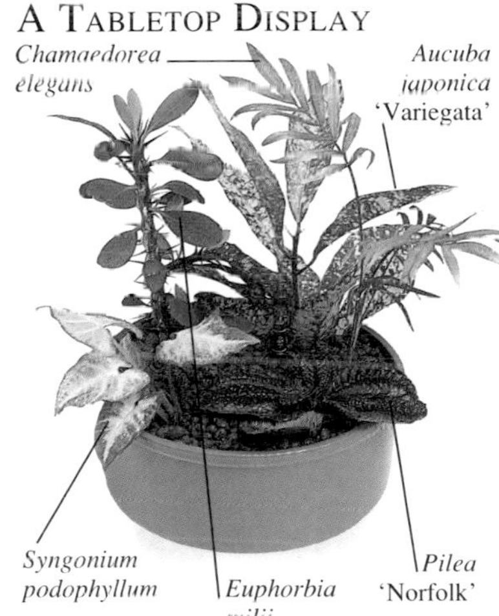

Group several plants in inner culture pots in a larger bowl.

Watering
The roots, kept moist by the capillary action of the porous growing medium, dislike being in water for long periods, so let the level drop to "minimum" before watering. Occasionally keeping to "minimum" level for 2–3 days encourages new root formation. Never keep to "optimum" for more than two weeks. Before going away, top up the containers to "maximum" level or stand the culture pots in a tray. Add water and nutrients until the level rises to about 1¼in (3cm).

Feeding
Various soluble fertilizers are available; follow the supplier's instructions. Minerals in the tapwater react with the fertilizers to release nutrients, which are then absorbed as needed by the plant.

Propagation from cuttings
Prepare cuttings in the normal way (see p.453), then root them in a jar of water or plant directly in small culture pots. Insert the cuttings 1–1½in (3–4cm) deep in 1/16 – 1/8in (2–4mm) turface. Cover them with a plastic bag or place in a propagator to reduce evaporation, and keep them in bright, indirect light for two weeks. As soon as new growth appears, remove the cover. Start normal watering and feeding two weeks after planting.

TYPES OF FERTILIZER

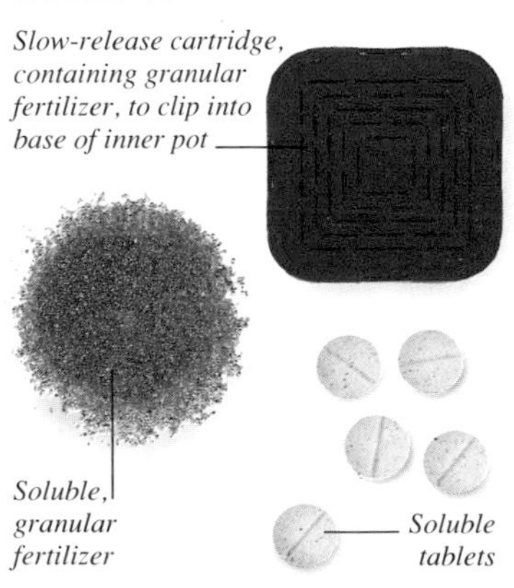

Fertilizers for use with hydroculture pots are formulated to suit tapwater of various hardnesses.

Fuchsias

FUCHSIAS are extremely adaptable plants, cultivated for their attractive, pendent flowers, which range from modest, slender tubes to double, bicolored blooms with distinctive, swept-back sepals. Fuchsias of upright habit may be trained as standards, while lax or trailing cultivars look very attractive when planted in hanging baskets and windowboxes. All species and cultivars may be used in summer bedding or grown in containers; in mild areas, many may be used in permanent plantings. Breeders have produced a vast range of tender, half-hardy, and hardy hybrids.

Most fuchsias cannot tolerate intense sun or warm greenhouse conditions. In cold areas, even those considered half hardy should be wintered indoors, preferably in a cool greenhouse or sunporch.

Propagation

Fuchsias grow easily from cuttings, and plants propagated in this way are usually superior to those raised from seed. Cuttings may be taken whenever plants have suitable, nonflowering shoots. If taken in early spring, they can make exhibition plants by late summer; if taken in late summer, cuttings can be overwintered in a greenhouse for late spring flowering. The tips removed when pinching out will also root.

Growing new plants from root cuttings is a slow process, only of use when the crown of a plant has been killed by frost (for further details, see "Root cuttings," p.84).

Cuttings

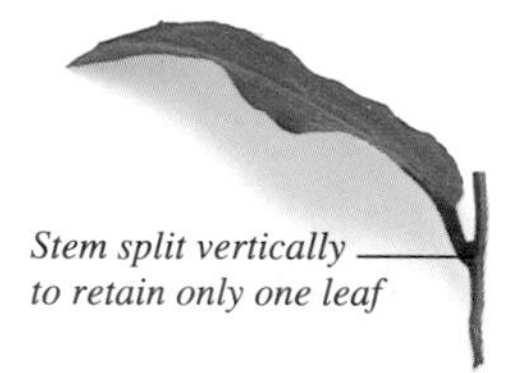

Cuttings may be taken at any time of the year from growing tips, when pinching the plant, or from leaves.

Half-hardy and Tender Fuchsias

***F.* 'Celia Smedley'**
Upright habit. Suitable for training as a standard. Half hardy.

***F.* 'Lady Thumb'**
Lax habit. Suitable for training as a miniature standard. Half hardy.

***F.* 'Thalia'**
Upright habit. Suitable for training as a standard. Frost tender.

***F.* 'Estelle Marie'**
Upright habit. Suitable for training as a standard. Half hardy.

***F.* 'White Ann'**
Upright habit. Suitable for training as a standard. Half hardy.

F. fulgens
Upright habit. Edible but acidic fruits. Frost tender.

Softwood cuttings

Cut the stem below a node, with the tip and three sets of leaves. Remove the lowest two sets and proceed as for other shrubs (see p.81).

To produce several cuttings, cut a young shoot into sections, each with a group of leaves and about ½in (1cm) of stem above and below the leaves. These may be split to form single-leaf cuttings, provided that the bud in the leaf axil is undamaged. Provide bottom heat to accelerate rooting, especially early in the year. Maintain a moist atmosphere, but allow air to circulate freely so that the cuttings do not damp off.

Once rooted, transplant them into 3in (6cm) pots of potting mix, and feed weekly with a high-nitrogen liquid fertilizer. In the early stages, do not use feeds that are high in phosphorus and potassium.

Pot on into 5in (13cm) pots when the roots reach the outside of the soil ball. Use peat-based soil mix with good drainage. Plant out or set outside after the last frost.

Training

Fuchsias are most commonly trained into bushes or standards. Espaliers and fans may be created in the same way as fruit trees (see p.378, and "Peaches: Fan," p.389).

Bush fuchsias

Begin training bushes as soon as the young plants have developed three sets of leaves. To form a bush, pinch out the growing tip to stimulate two to four side shoots to grow. When

How to Train a Bush Fuchsia

1 *When the fuchsia cutting has developed 3 sets of leaves, pinch out the growing point. This will stimulate the production of side shoots lower down the stem.*

2 *A few weeks later, when several side shoots have developed, pinch out the top set of leaves from each side shoot to encourage further branching.*

3 *Continue to pinch out the growing points of new side shoots as they develop.*

4 *Stop pinching out side shoots when the plant has a symmetrical shape with evenly spaced shoots. Lax plants may need staking.*

HOW TO TRAIN A STANDARD FUCHSIA

1 When the cutting is about 6in (15cm) high, pinch out any side shoots as they appear in the leaf axils.

2 Continue to do this to produce a long, straight stem. Tie the plant to a stake.

3 When the standard reaches the required height, allow it to produce 3 more sets of leaves, then pinch out the growing tip.

4 Pinch out the tips of the side shoots that form at the top of the stem so that they will branch further.

5 Once the head has filled out, the leaves on the stem will usually drop off naturally, or they may be carefully removed.

these have each developed two sets of leaves, pinch the shoots until the plant is as bushy as needed.

Each pinching increases the potential number of flowers but delays flowering. To time flowering for exhibition purposes, pinch for the last time 60 days before the show for single cultivars, 70 days for semi-doubles, and 80 days for doubles.

Standard fuchsias

To train a standard, allow the tip of the young plant to grow and wait until side shoots appear. Then pinch out all the side shoots, but do not remove the leaves on the main stem. Tie the stem at intervals to a stake to provide support for the plant.

Continue until the required length of bare stem has been reached. Conventional stem lengths for a standard are: miniature standard, less than 10in (25cm); quarter standard, 10–18in (25–45cm); half standard, 18–30in (45–75cm); and full standard, reaching 30–42in (75–107cm). Allow a further three sets of leaves to develop, then pinch out the tip. After this, training involves the same pinching procedures as for a bush.

It will take 18 months to achieve a full standard and about six months for a quarter or miniature standard.

Growing fuchsias in containers

Fuchsias grow well in containers both indoors and outdoors, and, if well cared for, flower from soon after planting until late fall and sometimes through winter. Position them where they are shaded during the hottest part of the day. Choose one cultivar per container, since cultivars grow at different rates. Mixtures of fuchsias and other plants also make a successful display.

Planting

Use three good plants for a 9in (24cm) diameter basket or half basket, a minimum of four for a 12in (30cm) basket, and more for a larger one. For hanging baskets, select young, bushy plants that have been stopped several times.

Use either homemade or commercial soil mix, both of which should incorporate slow-release fertilizers to reduce the need for regular additional feeding.

HANGING BASKET

Line a basket with sphagnum moss and fill it with soil mix. Place a small pot of gravel, half the depth of the basket, in the center with its rim at soil level; this will distribute water evenly around the roots. Plant small fuchsias around the edge, facing outward at 45°.

Routine care

Water sufficiently to keep the soil moist but not waterlogged – at least once a day for hanging baskets, every few days for plastic pots. Never leave pots standing in saucers of water.

Fuchsias in hanging baskets benefit from a balanced liquid feed in late summer. Hardy garden fuchsias need a dressing of general fertilizer or bone meal after pruning in spring and again during summer. Mature plants do not need regular feeding, but give a high-potassium liquid feed when flowering begins.

Black vine weevils (p.551), aphids (p.552), whiteflies (p.552), spider mites (p.552), and gray mold/*Botrytis* (p.559) can be troublesome. At the first signs of rusts (p.554) remove infected leaves and spray with a systemic fungicide.

Overwintering

Fuchsias are hardier than is thought; bedded-out plants can often be left *in situ*, although it is a good idea to take cuttings in early fall as insurance against frost damage. Standards should always be brought under cover in winter.

Hardy fuchsias

In areas where minimum temperatures are not lower than 20°F (-6°C), mulch with straw over the crowns. Even if the plants are cut back by frost, they will shoot from the crown like a herbaceous plant. Do not prune until new growth starts in spring, then cut back to ground level.

Nonhardy fuchsias

Before frost, move frost-tender fuchsias summered outdoors into a greenhouse. If a minimum temperature of 46°F (8°C) is maintained, they may continue flowering through the winter.

Alternatively, overwinter tender bedding fuchsias in a frost-free area such as a minimally heated cold frame or sunporch. Lift and pot up plants, remove the green tips and leaves, and keep the plants dormant through the winter – not quite dry and as cool as possible.

In spring, shake the roots clear of soil, repot the plants into slightly smaller pots, and prune back hard. Water them and encourage fresh growth by lightly spraying the wood.

OVERWINTERING A HARDY FUCHSIA

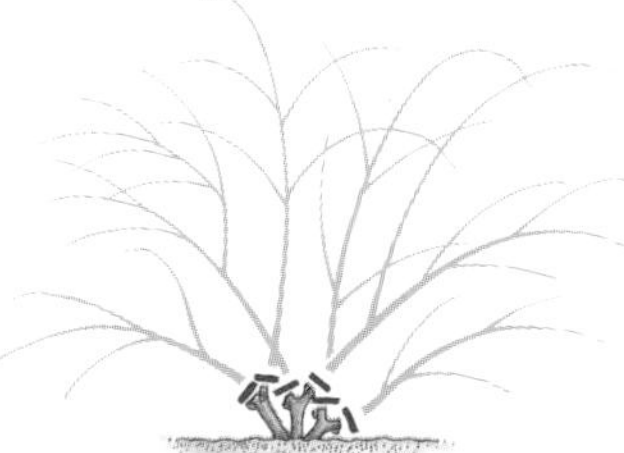

Hardy fuchsias may be left in situ *over the winter. Cover the base with straw or loose, dry leaves; the bare branches will also provide some cold protection. In the spring, prune them to strong new buds near ground level.*

Training and pruning plants grown under cover

THE basic principles of training and pruning under cover are much the same as for outdoors, although it may be necessary to adapt them to accommodate extended flowering periods and limited space. Climbing plants that are too tender to be grown in the open may be readily cultivated under cover. If properly trained and pruned, they make efficient use of confined space and provide shade for other plants.

ESTABLISHING THE SUPPORT FRAMEWORK

Stretch wires tightly between vine eyes (see inset). Tie in the stronger shoots and prune them to downward-growing buds to encourage horizontal growth.

Plant supports

Plants that need support when grown under cover include ornamental climbers, some shrubs, annuals, fruiting vegetables, fruit trees, and grapes (*Vitis*). True climbers find their own way up supports (see "Climbing methods and supports," p.92), while shrubs, grown as climbers against a wall, need tying in.

Some grapes require a permanent, rigid support securely attached to the framework of a wooden greenhouse or to the glazing bars of an alloy-framed one. Wires, stretched horizontally along the walls of the greenhouse, are useful for training all climbers. In lean-to greenhouses, stretch the wires between vine eyes attached to the rear wall to avoid cutting out light. Alternatively, attach the wire to drilled and bolted vertical wall supports. Keep the wires taut by using a straining bolt at the end of each wire. Space the wires at equal intervals: grapes require a 10in (25cm) spacing; fruit trees 15–18in (38–45cm). Tie in the stems of climbers with soft string to horizontal or vertical support wires.

Netting may be attached to the framework of the greenhouse and used to support plants. Plastic netting deteriorates and needs replacing after one or two seasons, so it is not suitable for perennials. Instead, use plastic-coated wire netting.

There are also some useful specially made, wire-mesh frameworks and various forms of wooden trellis available: fix them securely to supports attached to the greenhouse wall. Train the plants gently along netting or mesh as they grow, and tie them in with soft string.

Annual ornamental climbers, or fruiting vegetables such as tomatoes, may be tied with soft string to bamboo stakes placed vertically at 6–12in (15–30cm) intervals. Alternatively, drop lengths of strong string from secure hooks in the roof to the base of the plants. Tie the string loosely below the plant's first true leaf, then wind it around the stems and run it back to the frame. Never let the string become too tight around the stem of the plant. For details of the treatment needed for particular plants, see the pruning and training sections in the relevant chapters.

CLIMBING PLANTS FOR GROWING UNDER COVER

Prune after flowering

Allamanda cathartica 'Hendersonii' ❋ ◎
Bougainvillea ❋
Clerodendrum thomsoniae ❋ ◎
Distictis buccinatoria ❋
Jasminum, some ❋
Kennedia rubicunda ❋
Mandevilla splendens ❋ ◎
Pandorea jasminoides ❋
Passiflora, most ❋
Senecio, some ❋
Solanum wendlandii ❋ ◎
Stephanotis floribunda ❋ ◎
Thunbergia ❋

Mandevilla splendens

Prune as required

Agapetes macrantha ❋
Asarina erubescens ❋
Cissus ❋
Cobaea scandens ❋
Gynura aurantiaca ❋ ◎
Hoya ❋
Ipomoea horsfalliae ❋

KEY
❋ *Not frost hardy*
◎ *Requires high humidity*

Pruning plants grown indoors

Like plants that are grown outdoors, many indoor plants require regular pruning to maintain their vigor and encourage flowering. Others simply become too big for the space available, or need cutting back in order to maintain an attractive and balanced framework. Most plants may be trained and shaped by pruning, cutting back, or pinching out. Drastic pruning is required only to remove old, weakened sections or to renovate a neglected plant.

Always use tools with well-sharpened blades to avoid damaging the remaining stems, and make a downward, sloping cut above a bud to stimulate the growth of new shoots. A sharp knife is ideal for working on soft stems; use a pair of pruners for woody ones.

When and what to prune

The best time for pruning depends on the flowering season of the plant and on the age of wood on which plants bloom. Some plants flower only on the new season's growth, and on these the old growth may be safely cut back in the spring without harming the production of the next season's flowers. Others flower on older wood, so should be cut back after flowering. See guidelines given on pruning ornamental shrubs (pp.73–80), climbers (pp.102–5), and on pruning to produce fruit on grapes (pp.398–402) and tree fruits (pp.371–96).

CUTTING BACK AFTER FLOWERING

Cut back the flowered shoots to leave two or three buds. This encourages the production of next season's flowering shoots, which should be tied horizontally into the wires.

Pruning to restrict growth

Under glass, space for shrubs and climbers is always limited. Although major problems can be avoided by choosing the most suitable plant for the size of the greenhouse, it may be necessary to restrict growth to stop plants from blocking the light. Climbers that grow in the ground have to be rigorously controlled after they have filled their allotted space since they may overwhelm other plants.

Few shrubs and ornamental climbers grown under glass flower on old wood (but do check first), so pruning back fairly hard after flowering is generally advisable and safe. The time of flowering varies not only from species to species but also according to temperature and location. Cut back overlong stems in fall; remove stray shoots whenever they appear, regardless of whether it is time to prune or not.

Some plants flower for much of the year under glass, yet must be pruned to control them. In early spring, cut out the previous season's growth on mature *Abutilon* hybrids, and cut back *Coronilla* and *Hibiscus*. *Hoya* species and cultivars continue to flower on old stems, so do not remove them. *Agapetes* flowers on old wood, but may need cutting back to induce bushiness.

Pinching out

To improve the shape and increase the number of flowering shoots on young, climbing, or trained shrubs, pinch out the tips of new shoots throughout the growing season.

Shrubs that respond well to this treatment include fuchsias, *Abutilon*, *Brunfelsia*, *Centradenia*, *Hibiscus*, *Reinwardtia*, and *Tibouchina*.

FALL PRUNING TO RESTRICT GROWTH

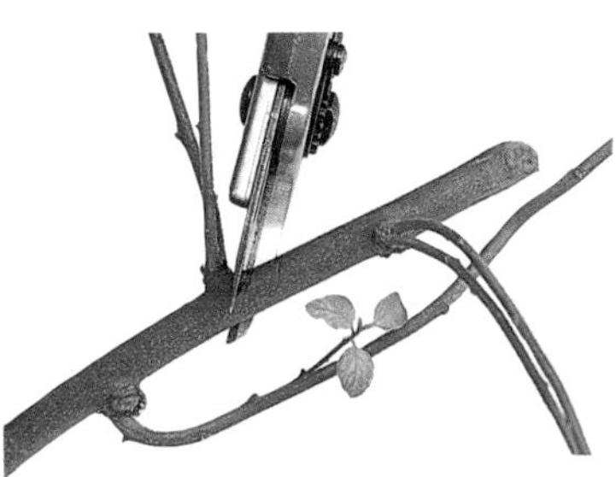

In the fall, cut out the weaker shoots and reduce dense growth. This allows plenty of light to penetrate the foliage and encourages the development of strong shoots to form a sturdy framework.

Propagation

PROPAGATING indoor plants is an economical way to increase your stock and to replace old plants with younger, more vigorous specimens. Successful propagation requires clean conditions, warmth, light, and sufficient humidity.

The easiest method of propagation is by division, which produces only a few plants at one time. The majority of new plants for growing indoors or under cover are grown from seed or cuttings, however, since these methods usually yield a greater number of new plants. Some plants may be increased by layering.

Propagation by division

Division is a quick way to propagate plants. Many plants produce plantlets, runners, offsets, or bulbils, which root themselves and may be severed from the parent and potted up.

Dividing the rootstock

Before dividing a pot plant, water the root ball thoroughly and allow it to drain. Herbaceous and clump-forming plants may be gently pulled apart or cut into separate pieces, each with its own root system, and repotted. Use a sharp knife to separate the fleshy roots of rhizomatous plants; retain vigorous sections with young growth and fibrous, feeding roots. Prune any long, thick roots, and any that are damaged. Dust the wounds with fungicide. Replant each division in a clean pot using a similar soil mix to that used for the parent plant. Water the plants appropriately and keep them in good light, but out of direct sun, until they are established. See also "Potting on and top-dressing," p.444.

Dividing plantlets

Plantlets are small versions of the parent plant that grow on its leaves, stolons, stems, or inflorescences. Once they are large enough to handle, detach them with about $1^{1}/_{4}$in (3cm) of the leaf stalk or stolon, where appropriate. Insert the plantlet stalk in a pot of peat-based potting mix so that the plantlet rests on the surface. Water the pot and cover it with a clear plastic bag to preserve the humidity. Roots should form in about three weeks. After this, the plantlet may take several more weeks to resume growth, at which point it is ready to pot on.

Dividing rooting runners

Some plants, such as *Saxifraga stolonifera* (syn. *S. sarmentosa*) and *Episcia*, spread by runners. If these are rooted individually in pots of soil mix, they may then be severed from the parent to make new plants.

Dividing offsets and bulbils

Offsets are small plants that develop around the base of plants. Choose a well-developed one with some roots. Cut or break it off cleanly from the main stem and insert it in a pot of

INDOOR PLANTS THAT MAY BE DIVIDED

Plantlets/runners
Chlorophytum ❄
Episcia ❄, some ◎
Haworthia ❄
Saxifraga stolonifera ❄ ◎

Maranta leuconeura var. *kerchoviana*

Rootstock
Adiantum, some ❄, ◎
Anthurium ❄
Aspidistra ❄
Calathea ❄ ◎
Cyperus ❄
Maranta leuconeura ❄ ◎
Phlebodium aureum ❄ ◎
Phyllitis ❄ ◎
Pteris cretica ❄ ◎
Stromanthe ❄ ◎

KEY
❄ *Not frost hardy*
◎ *Requires high humidity*

HOW TO PROPAGATE POT PLANTS BY DIVISION

1 *Thoroughly water the plant (here* Calathea*) an hour before dividing it. Support the plant, then invert the pot and tap its rim on a hard surface. Slide out the plant.*

2 *Remove surplus soil mix, either by gently shaking the plant or by teasing some of the soil mix away with your fingers, so that the roots are accessible.*

3 *Use hands or a hand fork to separate the root ball into sections, each with a portion of roots. Take care not to damage the stems or fibrous roots.*

4 *Using a clean, sharp knife, trim back any thick roots so that the divisions will fit into their new pots, but take care to leave the delicate fibrous roots intact.*

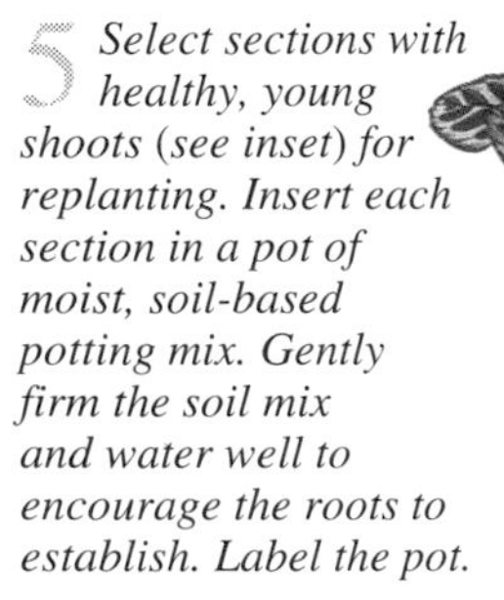

5 *Select sections with healthy, young shoots (see inset) for replanting. Insert each section in a pot of moist, soil-based potting mix. Gently firm the soil mix and water well to encourage the roots to establish. Label the pot.*

PROPAGATION BY ROOTING RUNNERS

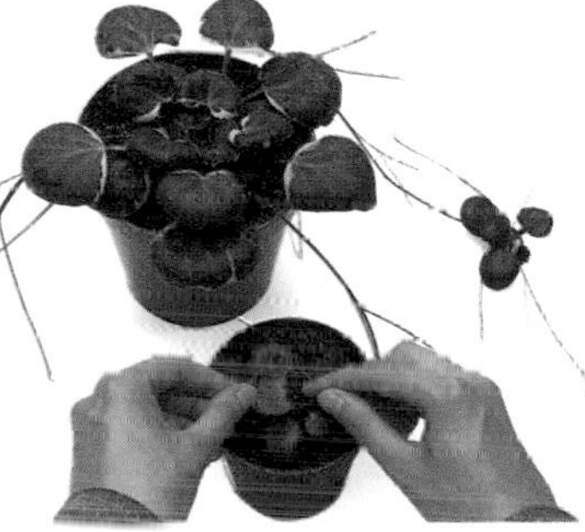

1 *Peg down runners (here* Saxifraga stolonifera*) in individual 3in (6cm) pots of moist, standard cuttings soil mix. Keep them well watered.*

2 *After a few weeks, separate each rooted plantlet, still in its pot, from the parent by cutting the runner close to the young plant. Label the pot.*

moist potting mix. Cover the pot with a clear plastic bag until new growth is produced.

Some plants produce bulbils on the fronds or in the leaf axils. Detach these and root them in moist, soil-based potting mix. For further information, see LILIES, *Propagating from Stem Bulbils*, p.239.

Growing indoor plants from seed

The seed of pure species breeds true, but that of many hybrid indoor plants does not. Uniform results may be obtained, however, from selections, or first generation (F1) hybrids of biennials, annuals, and a few perennials, such as cyclamen and pelargoniums.

Seed soil mixes and containers

Use a soil mix prepared specifically for seed (see SOILS AND FERTILIZERS, "Propagation soil mixes," p.536). It should be a free-draining and open-textured mix, which holds moisture without becoming sodden or forming a hard crust on the top.

A variety of containers can be used, such as half pots, pans, and half or quarter seed trays. Always use a size of container that is appropriate to the number of plants required. Special cell packs that allow each seed to grow in its own individual plug of soil are also readily available.

When to sow

Most seeds are spring-sown, but seeds of early spring-flowering species are usually sown in fall. Annuals may be sown in several batches from spring to early summer for a succession of blooms. Seeds of many exotic species are spring-sown but often germinate freely if sown as soon as they are ripe. It may be difficult, however, to keep the young seedlings alive in winter.

Preparing the seed

Some seeds need special treatment to help them germinate. Seeds with hard coats often need presowing treatment, such as soaking in warm water. The time required varies from about ten minutes for *Cordyline australis* to about 72 hours for banana seed. Other hard-coated seeds, such as *Caesalpinia pulcherrima*, will not germinate if the seed coat is not chipped with a knife or file. If the seed is too small to handle, gently abrade it between two sheets of fine sandpaper. Follow the supplier's instructions on the seed packet to ensure success.

Sowing the seed

Overfill the container with standard seed soil mix and tap it on the bench; scrape off the surplus so that the soil mix is level with the container rim. Firm the soil mix to within ½in (1cm) of the rim.

Water the soil mix before sowing the seed, and allow the container to drain well. (Watering with a watering can after sowing may bunch the seed or wash it together, leading to problems with overcrowding and damping off later.)

Sow all seed thinly and evenly. Tiny seed is easier to sow if it is first mixed with horticultural sand. Place large seeds far enough apart to allow seedlings to grow without being thinned later on. Alternatively, sow the seeds singly into small pots, cell packs, or soil blocks.

As a general rule, cover seeds with soil mix to the depth of their smallest diameter. Very tiny seeds, however, or seeds that require light to germinate, should be left uncovered on the surface of the soil mix. Cover the container with a sheet of glass, a plastic bag, or a propagator lid to stop the soil mix from drying out and maintain humidity. Place the container in the correct temperature, in bright but not direct light, and allow the seed to germinate.

Germination temperatures

Seeds usually germinate at 10°F (5°C) higher than the minimum needed by the same plant in growth. As a general rule, a temperature of 59–64°F (15–18°C) is suitable. The correct temperature varies for different seed, so follow the instructions given on the seed packets. Plants that are raised under cover for growing outside germinate at 50°F (10°C) or less. Many tropical or subtropical plants need 75–9°F (24–6°C) to germinate. If it is hard to maintain such temperatures indoors, consider using a heated propagating case. Although there are many different types and sizes, most have thermostats that allow a specific temperature to be maintained.

Aftercare of sown seed

Wipe off any condensation on covers to discourage fungal diseases. After seven to ten days, check the containers daily for signs of germination and remove the covers as soon as the seedlings appear. Germination times vary greatly, however, so some larger seeds may take several months to germinate. Keep the soil mix moist; use either a watering can or, for very delicate seedlings, a mist-sprayer.

Feeding should not be necessary if seed was sown in soil mix containing a small amount of nutrient. However, seedlings that are to stay in their container for some time may benefit from a liquid feed as they grow. If the seedlings start to bend toward light, turn them daily and shade with cardboard or shade netting if there is danger of sun scorch.

Pricking out the seedlings

When the seedlings are ½in (1cm) high, they may be pricked out into larger pots or packs. Water them first, allow them to drain for an hour, then loosen them by tapping the side of the container. Lift the seedlings out of the container using a small, flat implement. If the seedlings are clumped together, use a dibber or pencil to tease them apart. Handle the seedlings carefully by the leaves since the stems are easily damaged.

Use a dibber to make holes in some fresh soil mix in a container. Lower each seedling into place so that it is at the same depth as before. Place more soil mix around the roots and lightly firm in each seedling. Small seedlings should be set about 1in (2.5cm)

INDOOR FLOWERING PLANTS THAT MAY BE RAISED FROM SEED

Alonsoa ❄
Begonia ❄ ◎
Browallia ❄
Caesalpinia pulcherrima ❄
Campanula ❄ ◎
Clitoria ❄
Cobaea ❄
Cordyline australis
Cuphea ❄
Cyclamen, some ❄, ◎
Exacum affine ❄ ◎
Impatiens ❄ ◎
Jacaranda mimosifolia ❄
Pelargonium (modern zonal hybrids) ❄
Primula x *kewensis* ❄ ◎,
P. malacoides ❄ ◎,
P. obconica ❄ ◎,
P. sinensis ❄ ◎

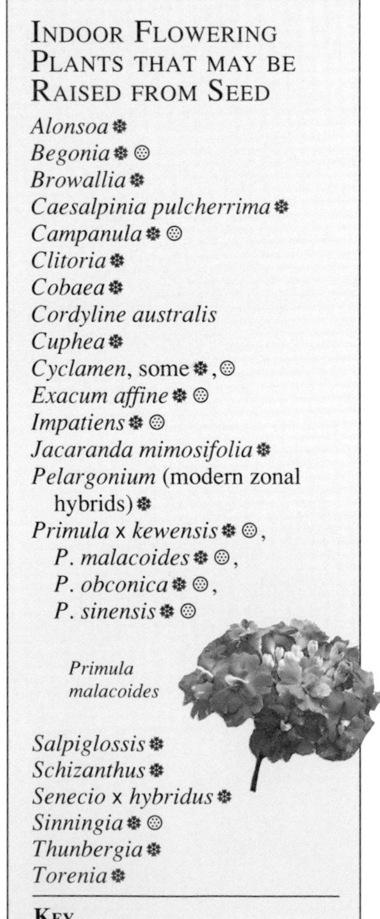

Primula malacoides

Salpiglossis ❄
Schizanthus ❄
Senecio x *hybridus* ❄
Sinningia ❄ ◎
Thunbergia ❄
Torenia ❄

KEY
❄ *Not frost hardy*
◎ *Requires high humidity*

RAISING INDOOR PLANTS FROM SEED

1 *Mix very fine, dustlike seed (here* Campanula) *with dry, fine sand in a bag; this makes it possible to sow the seed more evenly. Sow larger seed by hand.*

2 *Sow the mixture thinly onto a pot of moist seed soil mix, using a small fold of paper held close to the soil mix surface. Label and place in a propagator.*

3 *When the seedlings are large enough to handle by their leaves, use a dibber to prick them out into a container of moist potting mix.*

4 *Once the seedlings have become established, pot them on singly into individual pots or cell packs to grow on. Water and label each pot.*

apart, and larger ones about 2in (5cm). Water the seedlings with a fine spray. For seedlings that are sown individually in a cell pack, lift the seedling with its plug of soil mix, and pot it up.

Potting on

Once the roots of plants have filled the containers, they need potting on (see p.444). The new pot should be large enough to allow for a 1in (2.5cm) gap all around the root ball. Insert the plant so that the base of its stem is level with the surface of the soil mix. Settle the soil mix by tapping the pot on a bench, firm it lightly, and water with a fine spray.

Once potted on in normal soil mix, the new plants can be treated as mature specimens. Ensure that the correct conditions are maintained; different indoor plants have widely varying requirements.

Propagation from cuttings

Most tender indoor plants may be readily propagated from softwood (tip) cuttings (rooted in soil mix or in water), leaf-bud, or leaf cuttings. Semiripe or woody cuttings may be taken from indoor shrubs. The important factors for success with cuttings are timing, hygiene, warmth, and humidity.

Semiripe cuttings

Take cuttings of semiripe wood from the current season's growth, in summer after the main flush of fast, spring growth but before the wood is fully ripe. Suitable material is firm, but flexible, and offers some resistance if bent. Plants grown under cover may reach maturity before midsummer, so check new shoots carefully from early summer onward. For details of the technique, see ORNAMENTAL SHRUBS, "Semiripe cuttings," p.82.

Leaf-bud cuttings

Genera such as *Ficus* and *Hoya* may be increased by leaf-bud cuttings, a type of semiripe cutting. Cut stems into 1–2in (2.5–5cm) lengths, each with a single leaf and leaf axil bud. Then insert them into pots of cuttings soil mix and place the pots in a propagator at a temperature of 59–64°F (15–18°C). For further details, see ORNAMENTAL SHRUBS, "Leaf-bud cuttings," p.83.

Softwood cuttings

These are taken in early spring. Select new, short-noded side shoots and remove them with a clean, sharp knife. When preparing the cuttings, make precise cuts so that no snags are left on the stems. Dip the base of each stem in hormone rooting powder and, using a dibber or a pencil, insert several cuttings into each pot of standard cuttings soil mix. The cuttings may be placed close together or arranged around the edges of a pot, making sure that their leaves do not touch.

Place the pot in a propagator or cover it with a plastic bag to reduce water loss – make sure that the bag does not touch the cuttings, however. Leave the pot in a warm, bright position but out of direct sunlight. Check the cuttings each day or two and, if necessary, clear any condensation by opening the propagator or bag for a while.

It should take about four to six weeks for new roots to form. At this stage, when young growth can be seen, transfer the cuttings to individual pots of peat or soil-based mix to grow on. Keep the young plants in a warm, lightly shaded place until they are well established.

INDOOR PLANTS THAT MAY BE PROPAGATED BY SOFTWOOD CUTTINGS

Abutilon, some ❁
Acalypha ❁ ◎
Aeschynanthus ❁ ◎
Alloplectus ❁ ◎
Bougainvillea ❁

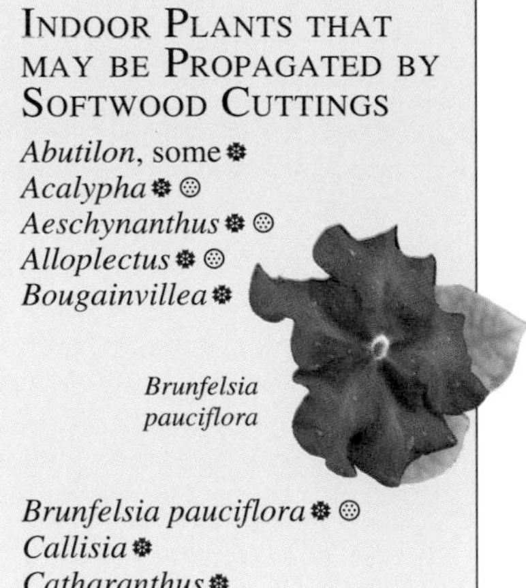
Brunfelsia pauciflora

Brunfelsia pauciflora ❁ ◎
Callisia ❁
Catharanthus ❁
Cissus ❁
Codiaeum ❁ ◎
Coleus blumei ❁ ◎
Columnea ❁ ◎
Crassula, some ❁, ◎
Crossandra ❁ ◎
Epiphyllum ❁ ◎
Epipremnum ❁
Euphorbia pulcherrima ❁
Ficus benjamina ❁
Fittonia ❁ ◎
Gardenia ❁ ◎
Gynura ❁ ◎
Hibiscus, some ❁

Hibiscus rosa-sinensis 'The President'

Hoya ❁
Impatiens repens ❁ ◎
Iresine ❁ ◎
Ixora coccinea ❁ ◎
Jasminum mesnyi ❁
Justicia ❁
Kalanchoe ❁
Mandevilla splendens ❁ ◎
Pachystachys ❁
Passiflora ❁
Pelargonium ❁
Pellionia ❁
Pentas lanceolata ❁
Peperomia ❁ ◎
Pilea ❁ ◎
Plumbago auriculata ❁
Polyscias ❁ ◎
Rhipsalidopsis gaertneri ❁, *R. rosea* ❁
Rhipsalis ❁ ◎
Rhoicissus capensis ❁
Ruellia ❁ ◎
Schlumbergera ❁ ◎
Sonerila ❁ ◎
Sparmannia ❁ ◎
Stephanotis ❁ ◎
Streptosolen ❁
Syngonium ❁ ◎
Tibouchina ❁ ◎
Tradescantia, some ❁, ◎

KEY
❁ *Not frost hardy*
◎ *Requires high humidity*

PROPAGATING FROM SOFTWOOD CUTTINGS

1 *Fill a 5in (13cm) pot with moist cuttings soil mix and tamp it down until it is level.*

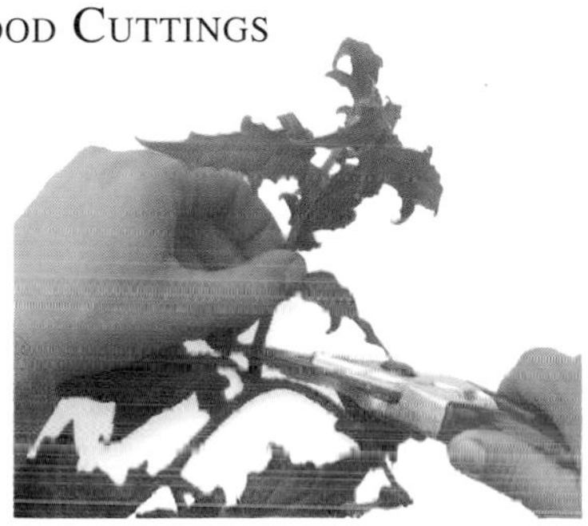

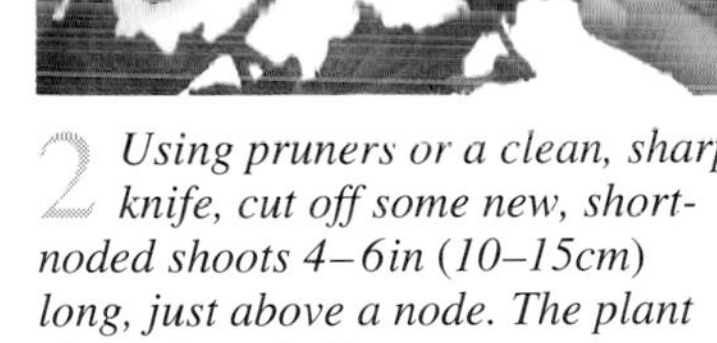

2 *Using pruners or a clean, sharp knife, cut off some new, short-noded shoots 4–6in (10–15cm) long, just above a node. The plant shown here is* Gynura aurantiaca.

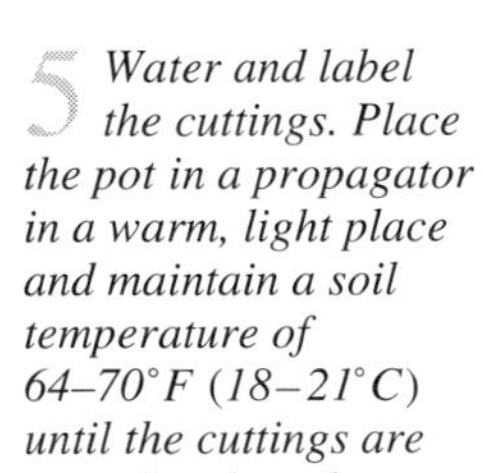

3 *Trim each cutting just below a node, removing the lower leaves to create a length of clean stem at the base (see inset). Do not leave snags, which might rot.*

4 *Dust the cuttings with hormone rooting powder and insert them in the pot so that the leaves are just above the soil mix.*

5 *Water and label the cuttings. Place the pot in a propagator in a warm, light place and maintain a soil temperature of 64–70°F (18–21°C) until the cuttings are rooted and ready to pot on.*

Rooting softwood cuttings in water

The simplest method of rooting softwood cuttings is to place them in a glass or jar of water in a bright, warm position. Prepare each cutting as for a normal softwood cutting, ensuring that the lower leaves are cleanly removed. Support the cutting on netting placed over the glass so that the stem is suspended in the water. When the roots develop and there is fresh growth, pot up the cuttings. Prepare pots with drainage material and 1in (2.5cm) of soil mix. Hold each cutting in a pot with its roots spread and fill in with soil mix until the roots are covered. Firm and water the cuttings thoroughly.

PROPAGATING SOFTWOOD CUTTINGS IN WATER

1 *Using a sharp, clean knife, remove healthy, short-noded cuttings 4–6in (10–15cm) long from a healthy, vigorous plant (here* Coleus). *Cut each just above a node.*

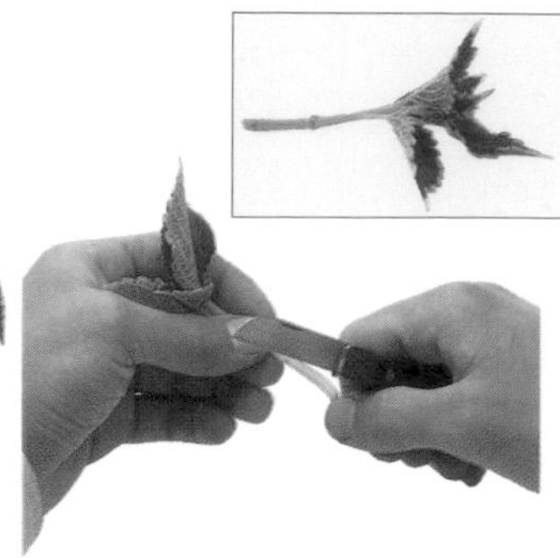

2 *Trim each cutting below a node and remove the lower leaves to create a length of clean stem at the base (see inset).*

3 *Insert the stems through a piece of chicken wire over the top of a jar of water. Ensure that the stems are in the water.*

4 *Keep the water topped up so that the lower end of each cutting is always below the surface. A network of roots should develop.*

5 *When the cuttings are well rooted, carefully plant each one into a 3in (6cm) pot of sandy potting mix.*

Propagating from leaves

Some plants may be propagated easily from whole leaves or leaf sections. In some cases, the leaves are inserted in soil mix (or water), while in others they are scored or cut up before being inserted or secured flat onto the soil mix. Each leaf should produce a number of small plantlets where the leaf veins have been cut.

Whole leaves

Certain plants, often those with fleshy leaves growing in rosettes such as African violets (*Saintpaulia*) and gloxinias (*Sinningia speciosa*), as well as Rex and rhizomatous begonias and some succulents (see p.267), may be increased from leaf cuttings.

For the cuttings, choose healthy, undamaged, fully grown leaves and cut them off close to the base of the leaf stalks. Trim each stalk with a straight cut 1¼in (3cm) below the leaf blade. Insert the cuttings individually into prepared pots of cuttings soil mix (1 part sand and 1 part peat), label, and water. Place the pots in a propagator or cover each one with a clear plastic bag or improvised cloche (see below). As soon as each leaf cutting produces plantlets, remove its cover. Grow on until plantlets are large enough to be teased apart and potted on individually.

Alternatively, leaves with long stalks (especially African violets) may be rooted in water, although rooting tends to take longer than in soil mix.

Scored or cut leaves

The leaves of plants with prominent veins, such as Rex begonias and various members of the family

HALF-LEAF SECTIONS

1 *Divide the leaf (here* Streptocarpus) *by cutting out the midrib and exposing the veins.*

2 *Insert the sections, cut edges down, in shallow trenches. Gently firm them in.*

PROPAGATING INDOOR PLANTS FROM LEAF CUTTINGS

1 *Cut healthy leaves from the parent plant (here* Saintpaulia). *Insert each stalk in a small pot of cuttings soil mix so that the leaf blade touches the soil mix.*

2 *Water, label, and cover the pots. Small cloches made from the bases of plastic beverage bottles are suitable. Leave them in a warm, light place out of direct sunlight.*

3 *Each leaf should produce several plantlets. When these develop, remove the covers and grow them on until they are large enough to pot up individually.*

Gesneriaceae, for example *Streptocarpus*, will produce small plantlets if they are scored or cut up and the cut veins are then kept in contact with moist soil mix. The leaves may be divided either in half (cut lengthwise through the midrib) or into small sections, or they may be scored through.

Whichever method is used, keep the container in a propagator or in a clear plastic bag in a bright place but out of direct sunlight. Inflate the bag so that it does not touch the leaf sections, and seal it. The leaves being propagated should be kept at 64–75°F (18–24°C).

When clumps of plantlets develop from the cut veins, carefully lift and separate them, retaining a little soil mix around the roots of each one, and pot them up individually into 3in (6cm) pots of cuttings soil mix.

Some succulent plants, including *Sansevieria* and those that have flattened, leaflike stems such as *Epiphyllum*, may also be propagated from "leaf" sections, although these are treated slightly differently. For details, see CACTI AND OTHER SUCCULENTS, "Propagation from stem sections," p.268.

PROPAGATION FROM CUT LEAVES

1 *Select a young, healthy leaf (here* Begonia rex) *and make a ½in (1cm) long incision with a sharp knife straight across each of the strongest veins on the underside of the leaf (see inset).*

2 *Place the leaf, cut side downward, on a tray of cuttings soil mix. Pin its veins to the soil mix. Label and place the tray in a propagator or a plastic bag.*

3 *Leave the tray in a warm place out of direct sunlight. When the plantlets have developed, carefully separate them from the leaf (see inset) and pot them on singly.*

LEAF SQUARES

1 *Cut 4 or 5 square sections the size of a postage stamp from a healthy leaf. Each piece should include a strong vein.*

2 *Place the sections, veins downward, on moist soil mix. Pin with wire hoops, then treat as other leaf sections.*

Propagation of tuberous begonias

When begonia tubers die back naturally in fall, store them in their pots at 41–50°F (5–10°C) in a dry place over winter. Alternatively, lift and clean the tubers, dust their crowns with fungicide, and store them in boxes of dry sand, vermiculite, or peat.

At the beginning of the growing season, place the tubers in a tray of moist, sandy soil mix (1 part sharp sand, 1 part peat-based soil mix). Place them in a temperature of 55–61°F (13–16°C). When new buds are clearly visible, cut the tubers into sections, making sure that each has at least one bud and some roots. Dust the sections with fungicide and allow them to dry for a few hours in a warm place. When the cut surfaces have formed calluses, pot up the sections in soil-based potting mix. Do not firm the mix heavily or water it, since this encourages fungal attack.

Alternatively, allow new shoots to develop on the tubers, and use these as basal cuttings. Take the cuttings so that each retains an eye. Dip the base of each cutting in hormone rooting powder and insert them, ¾in (2cm) deep, around the edge of a pot or pan of soil-based potting mix.

1 *In fall, lift the dormant tubers and clean them. Dust the crowns with fungicide and overwinter them in a dry place.*

2 *In spring, place the tubers, concave side upward, 2in (5cm) apart and 1in (2.5cm) deep, in a tray of moist, sandy soil mix.*

3 *When shoots appear, cut the tubers into sections, each with a bud and some roots. Dust cut surfaces with fungicide and allow to dry.*

4 *Pot up the sections singly in 5in (13cm) pots, with the top of each level with the soil mix surface. Water a little, and label.*

5 *Keep the pots in a propagator in a warm, frost-free place until the sections are established, then pot them on singly.*

BASAL CUTTINGS

Remove 2in (5cm) shoots from the tuber, each with an eye of tuber at the base. Pot them up and treat as divided tubers.

Propagation by layering

Layering involves wounding the stem of a plant, inducing it to produce roots, and then separating the rooted stem. This method has a high success rate since the layered stem receives nutrients from the parent plant while it is developing.

Some indoor plants may be propagated by layering – either in air or in the soil. Air layering produces a fairly large, new plant from an older specimen but it may take some considerable time. Simple layering in soil provides new stock quite quickly.

Air layering

This is an excellent method for replacing old or damaged house plants, for example the rubber plant (*Ficus elastica*) and its relatives. The top of the plant, or tip of a branch, may be encouraged to form new roots, and is then severed from the parent.

Choose a section of stem of new growth that is straight, about 4in (10cm) long, and at least as thick as a pencil. Cut the bottom off a clear plastic bag to create a transparent sleeve and slip it over the stem or, if the leaves are too large to do this, fold a clear plastic sheet around the stem and tape up the seam. Secure the sleeve below the selected area of the stem.

Using a sharp knife, make a shallow, upward-slanting cut in the side of the stem, then wedge this tongue open with moist sphagnum moss. Alternatively, on woody plants, score two rings 1/2–3/4in (1–2cm) apart below a healthy leaf joint on the selected area of the stem; the scores should be just deep enough to penetrate the bark without harming the wood. Carefully peel off the bark between the rings, leaving the cambium undisturbed.

In both cases, dust the cut area with rooting powder. Pack the sleeve with damp sphagnum moss and seal it to prevent the moss from drying out. If the stem of the plant is heavy, provide sturdy support.

It may be many months before the roots show. If the sphagnum moss begins to dry out, open up the plastic sleeve, add a little water, and reseal. When roots begin to grow, sever the layered stem from the parent and pot it up into a soil-based potting mix. Water the young plant sparingly until it is established.

Simple layering

Climbing or trailing shoots may be layered into soil while they are still attached to the parent plant.

Choose a long, vigorous shoot and peg it down into a small pot of moist cuttings soil mix. After three to four weeks, roots should start to grow into the soil mix and new shoots begin to form. The rooted layer may then be detached from the parent plant. Several shoots may be layered at the same time, each in its own pot.

When severing the new plants, always take care not to spoil the shape of the parent plant. For further information, see CLIMBING PLANTS, p.113.

SIMPLE LAYERING

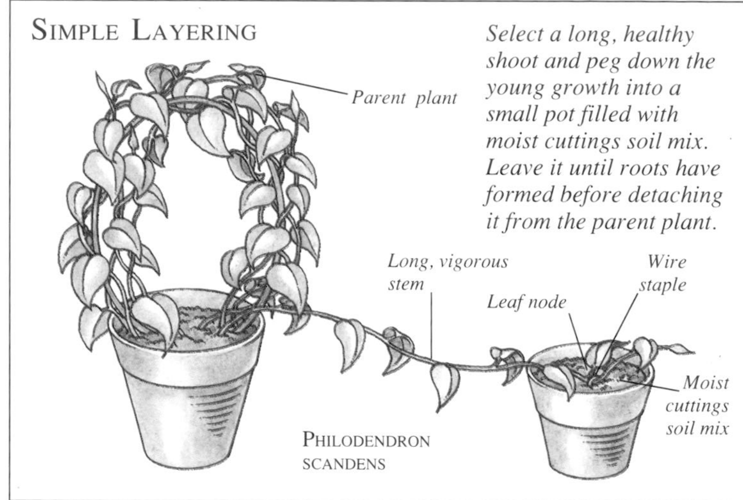

Select a long, healthy shoot and peg down the young growth into a small pot filled with moist cuttings soil mix. Leave it until roots have formed before detaching it from the parent plant.

HOW TO PROPAGATE BY AIR LAYERING

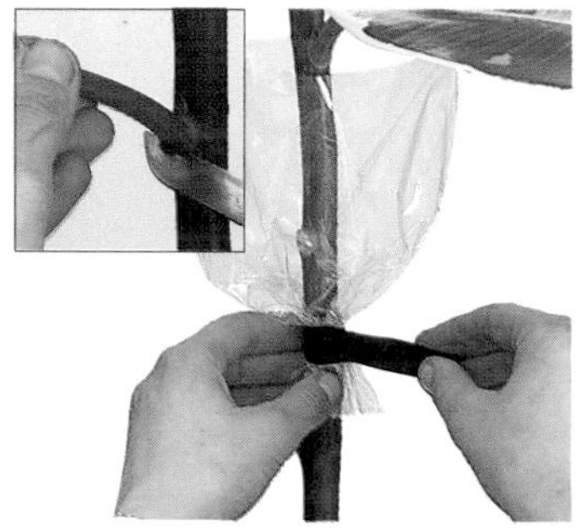

1 *Trim the leaves (here* Ficus elastica 'Tricolor'*) from a straight length of stem (see inset). Slide a plastic sleeve over the stem and seal the lower end with tape.*

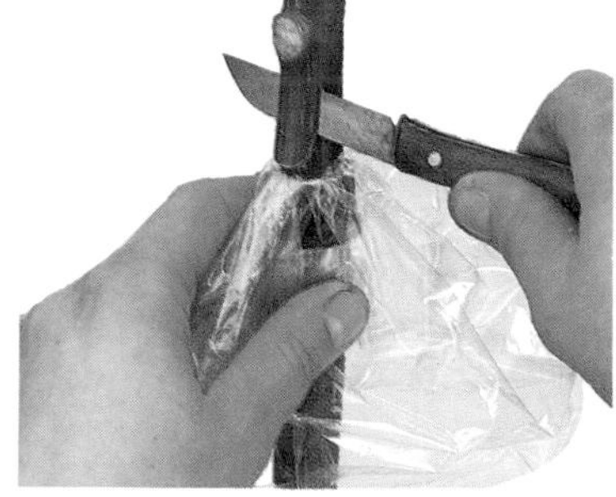

2 *Fold down the sleeve. Hold the stem firmly and cut a "tongue" in it, making a slanted, upward incision 1/4in (5mm) deep and 1in (2.5cm) long.*

3 *Apply hormone rooting powder to the wound and push moist sphagnum moss into the incision, using a split stake or the back of a knife blade.*

4 *Roll the sleeve back into position around the packed incision. Fill the sleeve with more moist sphagnum moss.*

5 *When the sleeve is tightly packed with sphagnum moss, secure the upper end to the stem with tape.*

6 *When the new roots are visible through the sleeve, cut through the stem just below the root ball with pruners. Remove the plastic sleeve.*

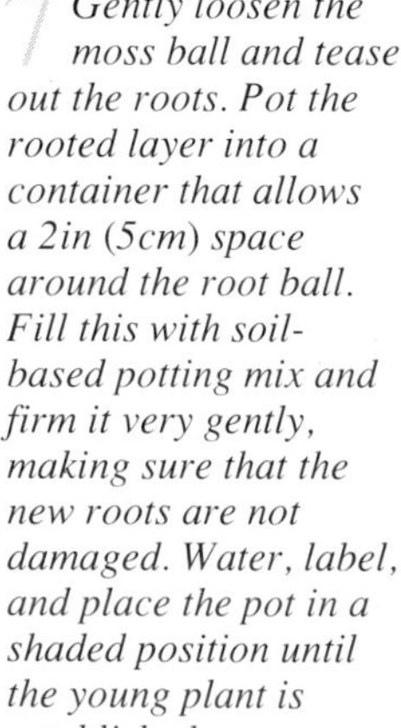

7 *Gently loosen the moss ball and tease out the roots. Pot the rooted layer into a container that allows a 2in (5cm) space around the root ball. Fill this with soil-based potting mix and firm it very gently, making sure that the new roots are not damaged. Water, label, and place the pot in a shaded position until the young plant is established.*

Part Two

Maintaining the Garden

How to choose tools and greenhouse equipment; style your garden with structures and surfaces; manage the effects of climate and soil; and control pests, diseases, and weeds

1

Tools and Equipment

Keeping a garden *looking its best throughout the year involves a certain amount of maintenance, from routine tasks such as mowing the lawn and raking to occasional procedures such as hedge-trimming and rototilling. While it is unnecessary and expensive to invest in an entire catalog's worth of garden equipment, having the correct tool for the job undoubtedly makes the work easier and faster, and produces a more professional result. Besides basic tools, for example a spade or a fork, which will be in almost constant use, there will be other items that you cannot do without. Depending on individual requirements, these might include a sprinkler for watering, a wheelbarrow for moving garden materials and refuse, or a supply of plastic seed trays. Assessing the type and amount of work you do in the garden makes it easier to decide which tools and equipment you need; choosing them with care ensures that they will be durable and comfortable to use, as well as practical and economical.*

Buying and using tools

Most modern gardening tools are based on traditional designs, although some may be improvements or variations on old concepts. A few completely new tools, however, have been successfully introduced. For example, until the 1980s, shredders and nylon-line trimmers were hardly known; yet they are now firmly established because they fulfill a demand not met by traditional tools.

Before buying a tool, the most important point to bear in mind is its function – it must perform correctly the task it is meant to do. Consider exactly what you need a particular tool for and how frequently you will use it. A simple, inexpensive pair of pruners, for example, will be adequate if wanted only for pruning a few rosebushes once a year. However, if they are needed for intensive use, it is better to invest in a high-quality, more heavy-duty pair. Before purchasing a tool, wherever possible always try to check that it is:

- the best type of tool for the task;
- the right size and model to suit your needs;
- comfortable to use.

In large gardens, or for laborious or time-consuming tasks, consider using power tools; however, because they are expensive and need careful handling, be sure that they are really needed before going ahead.

To ensure that tools perform well and last a long time, it is important that they are properly maintained. Immediately after use, clean off any soil, grass clippings, or other plant material and wipe metal parts with an oily rag; all pruning and cutting tools will also need regular sharpening. Tools that are not needed over the winter months should be especially well oiled and then stored in a dry place.

In addition, factors such as expense and storage space must be taken into account: if a tool is needed only infrequently, renting may be a more sensible option, especially for relatively expensive, bulky tools.

Safe use of tools

If you are not sure how to use a tool, ask for advice when buying or renting, or contact the manufacturer. Correct use gives good results and helps prevent accidents. Make sure that the weight and length are suitable: a tool that is too heavy will be difficult to handle; one that is too short may cause back strain. Keep power tools in good repair and follow safety recommendations. Avoid the risk of shock: plug electrical tools only into receptacles protected with ground fault circuit interrupters (GFCIs). The GFCI cuts the power in microseconds when a shock-producing ground fault occurs (see also "Electrical safety," p.464).

Digging Correctly
Keeping your back straight, not curved, when digging, hoeing, or raking helps to prevent backache.

Using Power Tools
Take particular care when using power tools, and always wear appropriate protective clothing.

Renting tools

If you decide to rent, book equipment in advance, especially tools likely to be in seasonal demand, such as power aerators and cultivators. Check whether the rental firm will deliver and pick up.

The condition of rented tools varies considerably. Some, especially power tools, may even be potentially dangerous to operate. Always:

- Check for missing or loose parts. These may not be obvious, but if in doubt do not accept the tool.
- Look for loose bolts and fittings on tools such as power cultivators that are subject to vibration.
- Ask for power tools to be started, and check carefully for excessive vibration and noise.
- On electrical tools, look for frayed, cut, or exposed wires. Do not assume that the wiring is satisfactory just because the tool works adequately.
- For two-cycle engines, determine the gas/oil ratio and keep an adequate supply on hand. Check and refill periodically.
- On four-cycle engines, check the oil in the engine and transmission.
- Ask for a demonstration or instructions if you have never operated the tool before. This is particularly important with tools such as chain saws, which can be dangerous to use.
- Buy or rent any recommended protective clothing such as goggles, gloves, and ear protectors.
- Before signing the delivery note, comment on the contract or delivery note if you have noticed any faults.

Cultivation tools

The type of cultivation tools required depends on the nature of your garden. If you grow mainly vegetables or are cultivating a new garden, tools for digging will be a priority. If, however, the garden is well established with lawns and perennial borders, surface cultivation tools such as hoes will be more important.

Spades

A spade is an essential tool, excellent for general cultivation, lifting soil, and digging holes for planting. There are two major types: standard digging spades, and the smaller and lighter border (also called ladies') spades. Some manufacturers also produce an intermediate-sized or medium spade that is suitable for general digging but is lighter than a standard spade.

Some spades have a tread, which makes it easier to push the blade into the soil and less likely to damage footwear; these spades are, however, heavier and more expensive. For extensive digging, a larger spade (known as a "heavy"), which has a 8 x 12in (20 x 30cm) blade, may prove quicker to use.

If you find digging difficult or if the soil is very heavy, it may be worth buying an automatic spade to make the task less of a strain.

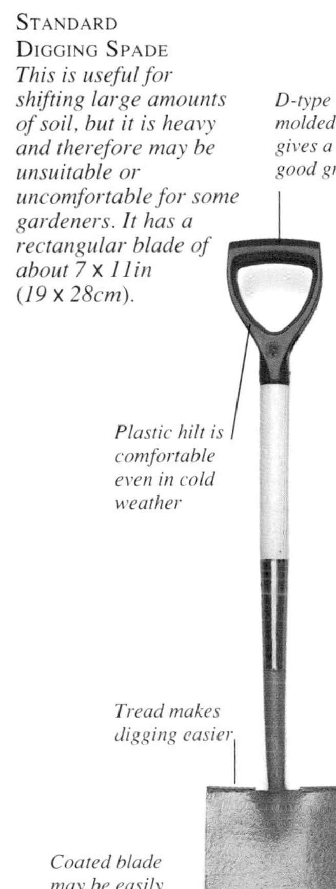

STANDARD DIGGING SPADE *This is useful for shifting large amounts of soil, but it is heavy and therefore may be unsuitable or uncomfortable for some gardeners. It has a rectangular blade of about 7 x 11in (19 x 28cm).*

STAINLESS STEEL BLADE *This is useful for a spade since it makes lighter work of digging and never rusts.*

AUTOMATIC SPADE *Operating on a spring-and-lever system, the spade throws the soil forward without the need to bend. It is expensive, but may be worthwhile for the impaired or for those with back trouble.*

BORDER SPADE *With a blade only 5 x 9in (13 x 23cm), this is designed for digging in confined spaces, for example a planting hole in a border, but it is also good for any general light work.*

Forks

Garden forks are used for general cultivation, lifting root crops (which are more likely to be damaged with a spade), and shifting bulky material such as manure and garden compost. Most garden forks have four heavy metal prongs, and are generally available in two sizes: standard and border (or ladies'). Less common are medium, or youth, forks, an intermediate size between standard and border forks.

Other variations are also sometimes found. For example, a potato fork has broad, flat prongs and, generally, a larger head than a standard fork; it may be easier to use than a spade when digging heavy ground.

The head and neck of a fork should be forged in a single piece, with no welds or rough surfaces; the shaft should fit into a long socket in the neck. Some forks have shorter necks, the head held in place by two long metal plates riveted to the front and back of the wooden shaft. These are usually weaker and are uncommon.

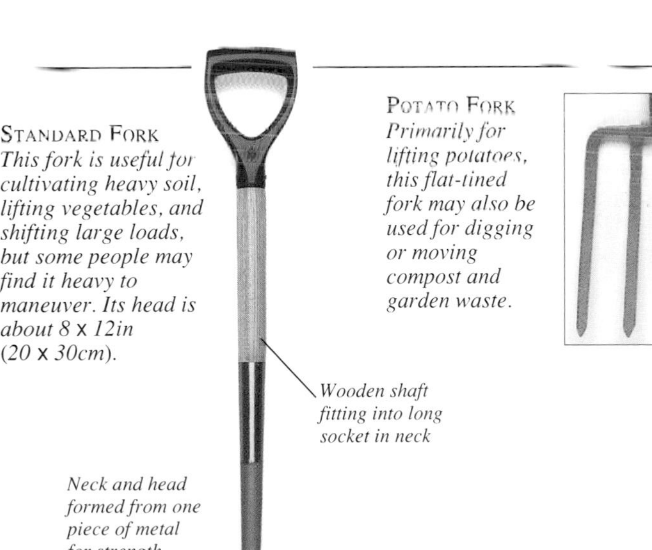

STANDARD FORK *This fork is useful for cultivating heavy soil, lifting vegetables, and shifting large loads, but some people may find it heavy to maneuver. Its head is about 8 x 12in (20 x 30cm).*

POTATO FORK *Primarily for lifting potatoes, this flat-tined fork may also be used for digging or moving compost and garden waste.*

BORDER FORK *This is best for light work in borders and similar restricted areas. The size of the head – 5½ x 9in (14 x 23cm) – makes it suitable for anyone needing a small, lightweight fork.*

Which metal?

Carbon steel is used for most garden tools. If it is routinely cleaned and oiled after use, this metal should not rust. Although stainless steel is more expensive, it does make digging easier because soil falls away from the blade more readily, and it has the additional advantage of being rustproof. Tools that have a nonstick coating may make clearing and working the soil easier, but the coating may wear off after long use.

Handles and hilts

A spade or fork shaft should be the correct length for the user's height to minimize back strain. The standard shaft length is 28–29in (70–73cm); a longer shaft, available up to 39in (98cm) long, will almost certainly be more comfortable for people over 5ft 6in (1.7m) tall.

Shafts are made from wood or metal, the latter sometimes covered with plastic or nylon. Both are generally strong, but even metal shafts may break if put under too much stress and, unlike wooden ones, they cannot be replaced. Metal shafts, even plastic-coated, are colder than wood to hold in winter. Try out the tool, as if using it, to assess which type feels best.

D-TYPE HILTS *These are the most common type, but they may be uncomfortable for those with large hands, particularly when wearing gloves.*

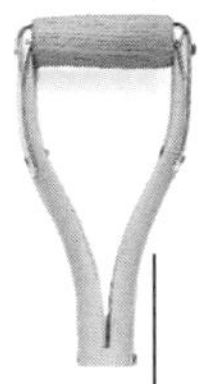

Y-TYPE HILTS *Similar to D-type hilts, but they may be weaker since they are formed by splitting the shaft wood.*

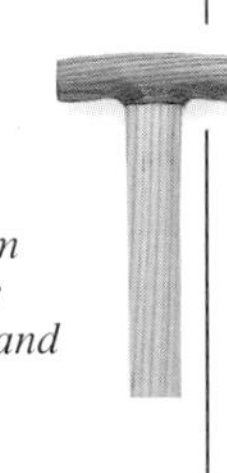

T-TYPE HILTS *These have a crosspiece joined to the shaft end. Some gardeners find them comfortable, but they are not commonly available and may have to be ordered.*

Hoes

Hoes are excellent for weeding and aerating soil; some types may be used to form seed drills. The Dutch hoe is probably the most versatile and is ideal for weeding between rows of plants and for creating drills. Apart from draw, digging, and onion hoes, there are other hoes available for specific uses.

Using a Dutch Hoe
Hold the hoe so that the blade is parallel to the soil surface.

Dutch Hoe
This traditional hoe, also called a scuffle hoe, is good for weeding around plants. It removes surface weeds without damaging plant roots.

Combination Hoe
This is suitable for chopping off weeds, drawing drills, and hilling up. Use the prongs to break up soil and draw seed drills.

Triangular Hoe
Use the point for drawing a V-shaped drill; the flat side is for weeding narrow spaces in between plants.

Digging Hoe
This has one or two chisel-like blades. It is used with a swinging motion to break up small areas of hard ground.

Short-handled hoe for use in confined areas

Onion Hoe
This small hoe (above), also called a hand, or rock garden, hoe, is for weeding between onions and other closely grown plants where a standard hoe might cause damage. It is like a short-handled version of a draw hoe, and is used while squatting or kneeling.

Molded handle ensures a secure grip

Draw Hoe
This hoe (right) is good for chopping weeds, drawing up soil around plants, making flat-bottomed drills, and, with the blade corner, making V-shaped drills.

Curved neck makes the hoe easier to use in between plants without damaging them

Rakes

Rakes are excellent for leveling and breaking up the soil surface before planting and for gathering garden debris. There are two main types: general garden rakes and lawn rakes (see "Rakes and aerators," p.467).

A flathead rake is stronger than a bowhead rake, and the more teeth a rake has, the faster an area is covered: 12 teeth are adequate, but 16 or more are preferable for large areas. A 3ft (1m) wide wooden rake is useful in a large garden.

Heads and shafts

Most rake and hoe heads are made from solid carbon steel; stainless steel ones are more expensive and do not work any better, although they are easier to clean and do not rust. Some rakes have a nonstick coating.

Shafts may be made from wood, aluminum, or plastic-covered metal. Shaft length is important: you should be able to stand upright while hoeing or raking to reduce strain on the back. Most people find a 5ft (1.5m) shaft comfortable, but a longer handle may be preferred.

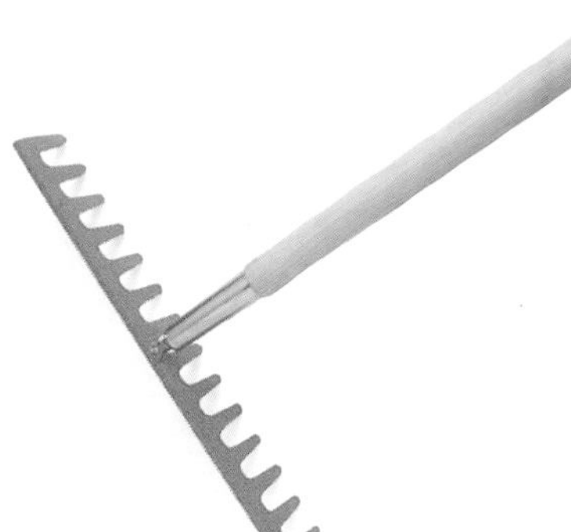

Flathead Rake
This has short, wide, rounded teeth and is valuable for leveling soil, clearing the ground, and general garden cleanup.

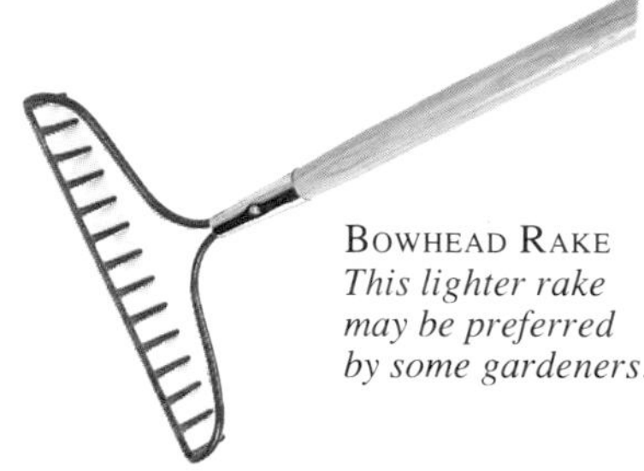

Bowhead Rake
This lighter rake may be preferred by some gardeners.

Trowels and hand forks

A trowel is useful for digging holes for small plants and bulbs, and for working in containers and raised beds. A hand, or weed, fork may be used for weeding, lifting small plants, and planting.

Most trowel blades and hand fork prongs are made from stainless steel, coated steel (e.g. chrome-plated), or ordinary carbon steel. Unlike carbon steel, stainless steel does not rust and is easy to keep clean but it is expensive. Coatings gradually tend to wear off in time. Some trowels have extra-long handles – up to 12in (30cm) – for more leverage. Hand forks with handles 4ft (1.2m) long reduce the need to bend when weeding the back of a border. Wooden, plastic, and plastic-coated handles are all generally comfortable to hold; metal ones tend to be cold.

Hand Fork
Often used for lifting small plants or loosening the soil when weeding. Unlike a trowel, it does not compact the soil, so it may be preferable to use when planting in heavy soil.

Narrow-bladed Trowel
Sometimes known as a rock garden or transplanting trowel, this is ideal for working in very confined areas such as rock gardens as well as for general transplanting tasks.

Wide-bladed Trowel
This is useful for planting bulbs and bedding or other small plants, especially in confined areas such as containers and windowboxes.

Hand-weeding tools

For weeding between paving, bricks, or rocks, a Cape Cod weeder with its narrow, hooked blade, is ideal. An asparagus knife has a pronged blade suitable for levering up lawn weeds.

SPECIALIZED WEEDERS
A Cape Cod weeder (right) can be used in narrow crevices. An asparagus knife (far right) may be used to lift lawn weeds without damaging the sod.

Manual cultivators

A hand, or pronged, cultivator is used to break up the surface of compacted soil or to loosen weeds. It has a three- or five-pronged metal head on a long shaft and is pulled through the soil, generally from a standing position. Some adjustable models have removable, central prongs.

Specialized hand cultivators may be useful for certain tasks. A star-wheeled cultivator, or miller, for example, forms a fine tilth when pushed back and forth through the soil, so is good when preparing a seedbed or surface from sod.

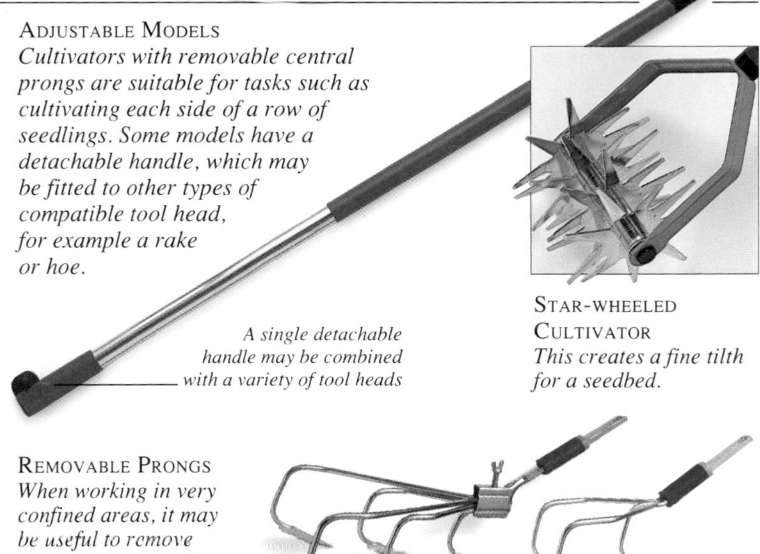

ADJUSTABLE MODELS
Cultivators with removable central prongs are suitable for tasks such as cultivating each side of a row of seedlings. Some models have a detachable handle, which may be fitted to other types of compatible tool head, for example a rake or hoe.

A single detachable handle may be combined with a variety of tool heads

STAR-WHEELED CULTIVATOR
This creates a fine tilth for a seedbed.

REMOVABLE PRONGS
When working in very confined areas, it may be useful to remove some prongs to make the head smaller.

Rototillers

A rototiller, or power cultivator, is used for tackling laborious tasks like turning over the soil in neglected ground. It breaks up compacted soil and reduces it to a tilth fine enough for planting. It is impractical for use in densely planted areas, however, and does not eliminate the need for hand digging. Gas-powered cultivators are powerful and generally have a wide range of attachments but need more routine maintenance than electric ones. Electric cultivators are excellent for small jobs, being easier to maneuver, less noisy, and cheaper than gas-powered types. Trailing cords may be a problem.

On most cultivators the handle height is adjustable. Some also have handles that pivot and lock sideways; this allows you to walk alongside the machine rather than behind it, preventing you from trampling the ground already cultivated.

Cultivators come in three main types: front-, mid-, and rear-engined. **Front-engined cultivators** have tines behind the driving wheels. They are easy to steer but, because of the way the weight is distributed, are suitable only for shallow cultivation. **Mid-engined cultivators** are propelled by tines rather than wheels. This may make control difficult, but the engine weight over the rotors makes deep cultivation easier than with a front-engined type. **Rear-engined cultivators** are best for maneuvering in difficult places and for forming deep holes. The tines, on a boom at the front, are swept from side to side as the cultivator is propelled along. The machines may be tiring to control.

MINI-ROTOTILLER
Useful in small or confined areas, a mini-rototiller is much easier to maneuver than a standard rototiller. A special attachment allows rear wheels to be fit for easier transporting to and from the work site.

Overlapping tines leave no areas of unturned soil

ROTOTILLER
This front-engined gas model is stable and easy to control. It is expensive, but makes an excellent job of straightforward cultivation over a large area.

Bumper bar
Engine
Battery
PTO engagement lever
Throttle control (accelerator)
Dead man's handle cuts the power if the grip is relaxed
Forward/reverse lever
High/low gear lever
Lever adjusts depth of cultivation
Rear tines produce a fine finish for a seedbed

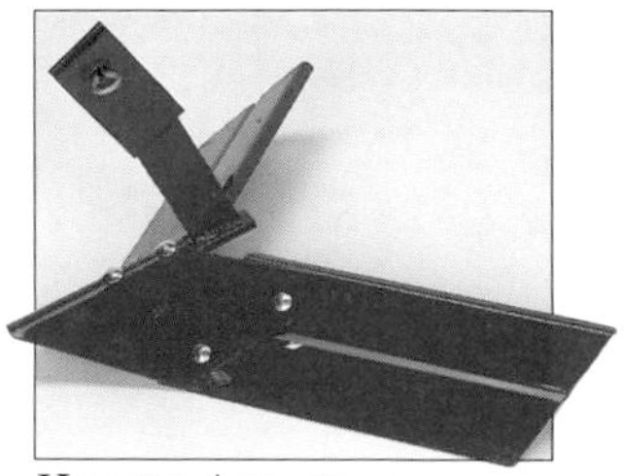

HILLING ATTACHMENT
Used in place of the tines, this tool throws soil on either side of the row, and is useful for hilling up row crops.

Pruning and cutting tools

When pruning, it is important to use the appropriate tool for the task and to make sure that it is sharp so that it cuts cleanly, easily, and safely. Using a blunt blade can leave a plant with a ragged wound that is prone to infection or that can cause dieback. Take particular care when working with power tools such as hedge trimmers or brushwood cutters (see "Electrical safety," p.464).

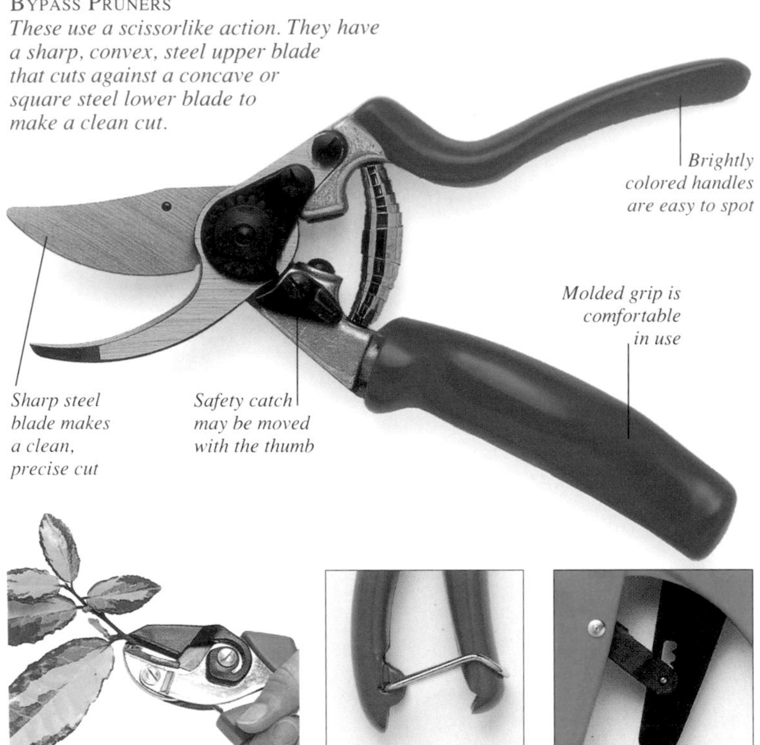

BYPASS PRUNERS
These use a scissorlike action. They have a sharp, convex, steel upper blade that cuts against a concave or square steel lower blade to make a clean cut.

FLOWER GATHERERS
These are designed to grip the stem after cutting.

SAFETY CATCH
This catch clips the handles together.

RATCHET SYSTEM
This makes cutting tough stems easier.

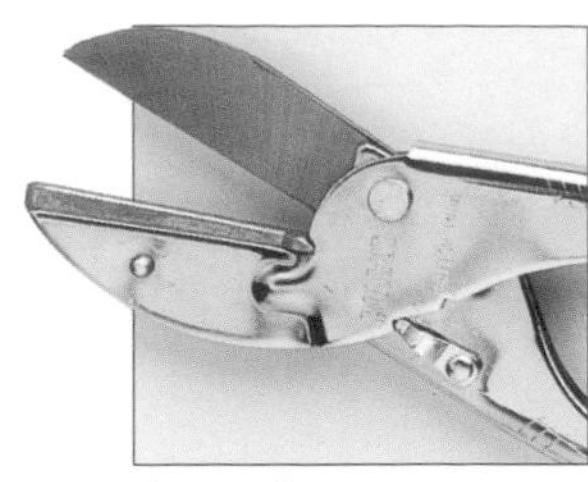

ANVIL PRUNERS
These must be kept sharp, otherwise the blade crushes the stem against the anvil instead of cutting it.

PARROT-BEAK PRUNERS
These give a clean cut, but may be damaged if used to cut wood more than 1/2in (1cm) thick.

Pruners

Pruners are used for pruning woody stems up to about 1/2in (1cm) thick and soft shoots of any thickness; they may also be used for taking cuttings for propagation. They can be used single-handed and are more controllable and easier to handle safely than a knife, particularly by inexperienced gardeners.

There are three main types of pruner: bypass, curved, or side anvil; parrot-beak; and anvil. Bypass and parrot-beak pruners have a scissorlike action; anvil pruners have a sharp, straight-edged upper blade that cuts against a square-edged lower anvil. In some designs (swing-anvils), the blade is pivoted in such a way that it remains parallel to the anvil as it cuts, preventing the stem from sliding out.

For cutting soft-stemmed plants, a light, comparatively cheap pair is adequate. For pruning fruit trees and shrubs with woody shoots up to 1/2in (1cm) thick, a pair of heavy-duty pruners is preferable.

If possible, try out the pruners to check that they are comfortable and easy to operate. The handle material and shape, how wide they open, and the pressure of the spring keeping them open all vary considerably. Metal handles may be very cold to hold, but most handles are now plastic or plastic-covered metal. All pruners are fitted with a safety catch that locks the blades in the shut position. Check that it is easy to operate with one hand and that it cannot be flicked off accidentally.

Pruner blades may be made from stainless steel, carbon steel, or coated steel. Coated blades are easy to wipe clean, but are unlikely to last as long as high-quality stainless or carbon steel blades, which keep their sharpness and cut cleanly and easily. When buying high-quality pruners, ensure that they can be dismantled for sharpening without special tools and that new blades are available.

Some models have a ratchet system for cutting through a shoot in stages. These require less effort and so are suitable for those who find conventional models a strain, but they are slower to use.

Flower gatherers, or flower pickers, hold the flower stem after cutting. They are invaluable if cutting flowers often, otherwise pruners or scissors will suffice.

Maintenance

Clean the blades of cutting tools after each use with an oily rag or steel wool to remove any sap that has dried on, then lightly oil them. Periodically tighten the blade tension of garden shears; this makes them cut more efficiently and produces a better finish.

Most pruning tools are easy to sharpen. Remove blades that are badly blunted or damaged, and regrind or replace them.

Long-handled pruners or loppers

A pair of long-handled pruners, or loppers, is useful for removing woody stems 1/2–1in (1–2.5cm) thick, where pruners might be damaged, and for thinner branches that are difficult to reach.

The long handles give additional leverage, making it easier to cut through thick stems. They are usually wood or plastic-covered tubular steel or aluminum. Blades are made of stainless steel, carbon steel, or coated steel, as for pruners.

The weight and balance of long-handled pruners are important because you may have to hold them at full stretch or above your head. Make sure that you will be able to operate them easily and without strain.

Most long-handled pruners have a bypass blade motion, others an anvil action. Both are satisfactory designs, and the choice is a matter of personal preference. Designs with a ratchet are sometimes available and are particularly useful for cutting through thick or tough branches and to reduce the strength needed for cutting.

All long-handled pruners require regular maintenance to keep them in peak working condition.

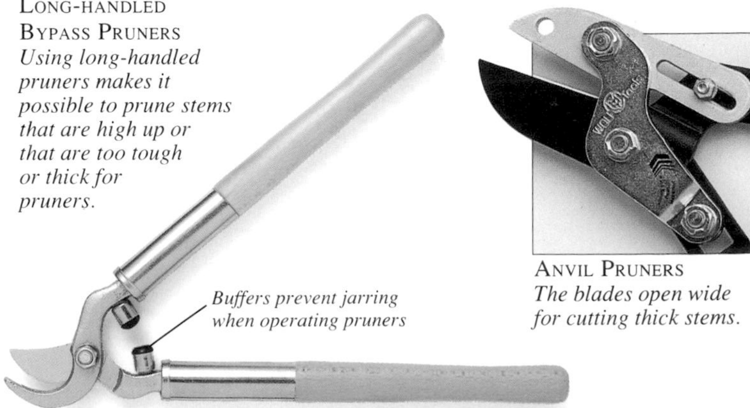

LONG-HANDLED BYPASS PRUNERS
Using long-handled pruners makes it possible to prune stems that are high up or that are too tough or thick for pruners.

ANVIL PRUNERS
The blades open wide for cutting thick stems.

Tree pruners

A tree pruner is suitable for cutting branches up to 1in (2.5cm) thick that would otherwise be out of reach. The cutting device is positioned at the end of a pole that is usually 6–10ft (2–3m) long, although some extend to 15ft (5m). The carbon steel blade is operated by a lever system or a cord; both are efficient, although the lever system is more popular. Some cord models have telescopic poles so that the length may be adjusted; they are also more convenient to store. Tree pruners may have saw or fruit-picker attachments.

TREE PRUNER

Hooked end is lowered over the branch to be cut

Pruning saws

Use a pruning saw for severing branches more than about 1in (2.5cm) thick. Because sawing in a confined space between other branches (often at an awkward angle) may be difficult, various types of pruning saw have been developed. Those that are most commonly available are general-purpose pruning, Grecian or rigid-handle curved, double-edged or two-edged, folding, and bow saws. If pruning is a major task in the garden, it may be necessary to have more than one saw for different types of work. A Grecian saw is one of the most useful pruning saws for an amateur.

All pruning saws should have hardpoint, heat-treated teeth, which are harder and stay sharper longer than ordinary teeth. They must be professionally sharpened. Saw handles are plastic or wood; choose whichever feels more comfortable and has a secure grip. Be sure to score a groove in the branch and then insert the saw blade to reduce the risk of its slipping during use.

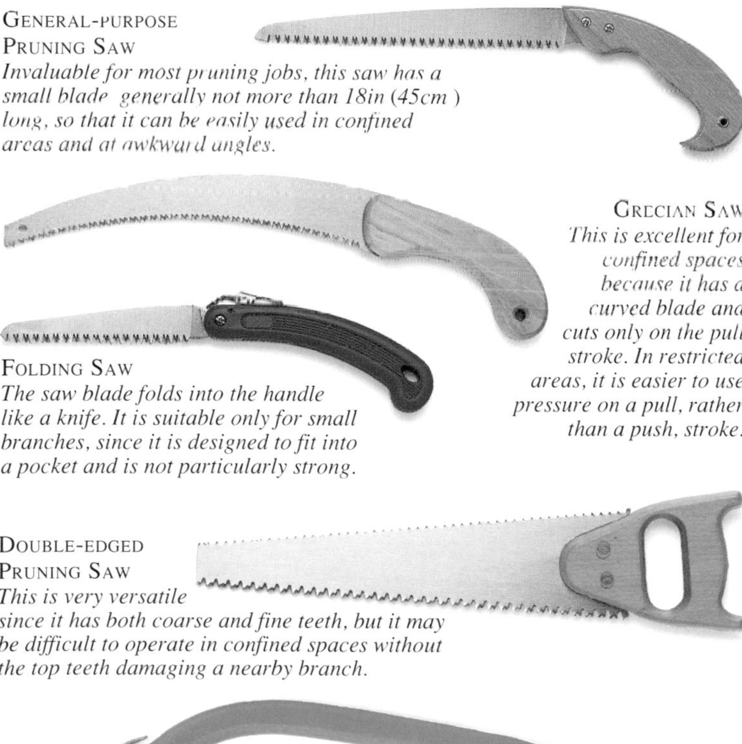

GENERAL-PURPOSE PRUNING SAW
Invaluable for most pruning jobs, this saw has a small blade generally not more than 18in (45cm) long, so that it can be easily used in confined areas and at awkward angles.

GRECIAN SAW
This is excellent for confined spaces because it has a curved blade and cuts only on the pull stroke. In restricted areas, it is easier to use pressure on a pull, rather than a push, stroke.

FOLDING SAW
The saw blade folds into the handle like a knife. It is suitable only for small branches, since it is designed to fit into a pocket and is not particularly strong.

DOUBLE-EDGED PRUNING SAW
This is very versatile since it has both coarse and fine teeth, but it may be difficult to operate in confined spaces without the top teeth damaging a nearby branch.

BOW SAW
This is used to cut through thick branches quickly, but is too large to operate in a confined area.

Garden knives

A garden knife may be used for light pruning tasks instead of pruners, and is more versatile. It is also convenient for taking cuttings, preparing material for grafting, harvesting certain vegetables, and cutting string.

There are various types of garden knife available, including general-purpose, grafting, budding, and pruning or peach pruners. Most knives have a carbon steel blade that is either fixed or folds into the handle. If choosing the folding type, check that it is easy to open, and that the spring holding the blade in position is neither too strong nor too slack. Always dry knife blades after use, and wipe them with an oily rag. Sharpen knives regularly to the same angle as when new.

Most gardeners prefer a knife with a plastic or wooden handle rather than a metal one, which may feel cold and uncomfortable.

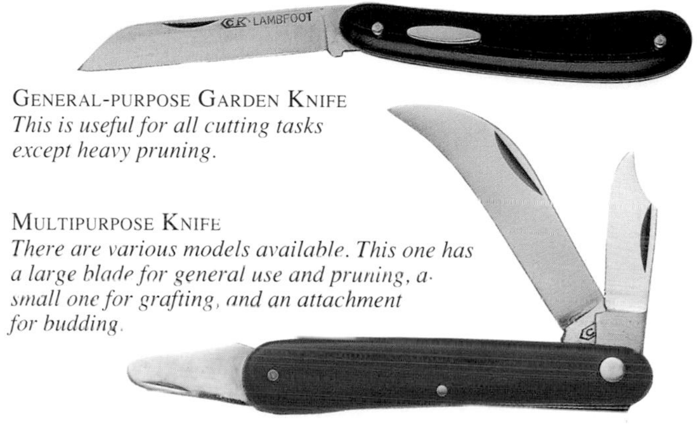

GENERAL-PURPOSE GARDEN KNIFE
This is useful for all cutting tasks except heavy pruning.

MULTIPURPOSE KNIFE
There are various models available. This one has a large blade for general use and pruning, a small one for grafting, and an attachment for budding.

GRAFTING
This straight-bladed knife is suitable for general tasks, and for making accurate cuts when grafting.

BUDDING
The blade projection is used for pushing open the rootstock incision when propagating by bud-grafting.

PRUNING
The large blade curves downward for a controlled cut when pruning.

Garden shears

Shears are used mainly for trimming hedges, but are also invaluable for cutting small or awkward areas of long grass (see also "Lawn-care tools," pp.466–7), clipping topiary, and cutting back herbaceous plants.

For soft-stemmed hedges, a light pair is adequate. For large hedges with tough, woody stems, a heavy-duty pair will be needed.

Weight and balance are important; before buying, check that the shears are centrally balanced and the blades are not too heavy, or they will then be tiring to operate.

Most shears have straight blades although a few have wavy-edged blades: these cut through mature wood easily and help to trap the shoots so that they are not pushed out with the scissor action of the blades. They are difficult to sharpen (see also "Maintenance," opposite).

STANDARD SHEARS
Shears usually have one notched blade to hold a thick shoot during cutting.

SINGLE-HANDED SHEARS
These have a spring mechanism similar to pruners that allows them to be operated with one hand. Some types have blades that swivel – useful for cutting at an angle or vertically (as for edging a lawn). They are suitable only for cutting grass or very soft stems.

Hedge trimmers

For gardeners with large hedges to cut, a power hedge trimmer may be worthwhile because it takes much less time and effort to use than ordinary, manually operated shears.

The longer the blade, the faster the hedge can be cut and the easier it is to reach a tall hedge or across the top of a wide one. Hedge trimmers with very long blades are heavy and often poorly balanced, however. A 16in (40cm) blade is adequate for normal garden use, but if cutting extensive hedges a 24in (60cm) blade saves considerable time. Blades may be either single- or double-sided; the latter speed up the cutting time but are not as easy to control as single-sided blades, so hedge shaping may be more difficult.

The ease of handling is also influenced by the blade action. Models with reciprocating- or double-action blades, which move against each other, are generally preferred by most gardeners. Single-action models, in which one moving blade cuts against a second, stationary blade, cause vibration and can therefore be tiring to operate.

The finish of the cut is largely controlled by the spacing of the teeth along the blade. Teeth that are narrowly spaced produce a smooth, even finish on a hedge that is regularly trimmed, while more widely spaced teeth usually cope better with thicker twigs but leave a rougher cut.

PROTECTIVE CLOTHING
When operating power tools, wear protective clothing such as goggles, ear protectors, and thick gardening gloves (see also p.471).

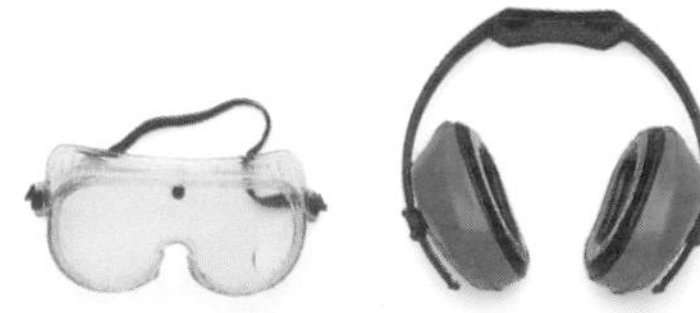

POWER HEDGE TRIMMER
This makes hedge trimming faster and easier than it is when using garden shears. Electric models are light and easy to maneuver, while gas versions are powerful and unhampered by trailing cords.

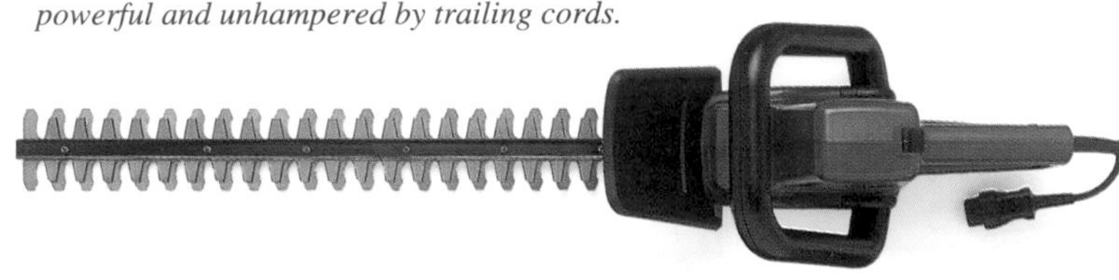

Gas, electricity, or batteries?
Hedge trimmers may be powered by gas, electricity, or batteries. Gas hedge trimmers may be operated anywhere and are generally powerful and relatively free from vibration. They are, however, noisier, heavier, and more expensive than electric or battery-powered ones and usually require more maintenance.

Electric hedge trimmers are more commonly used by amateurs and are better for small jobs. Being lighter, they are easier to handle than gas trimmers; they are also cleaner to use and cheaper to buy.

Electric hedge trimmers are the most convenient for hedges within 100ft (30m) of a power supply. As with other electric tools, the trailing cord can be inconvenient and even hazardous; the machine must not be used in wet conditions. Safety features are very important when handling such a potentially dangerous tool: for example, they should always be operated with a residual current device, commonly called a ground fault circuit interrupter (see also "Electrical safety," below).

Battery-powered hedge trimmers are good for hedges in a distant part of a large garden or where there is no convenient power supply. They are usually run from a spare car battery. When fully charged, they are reasonably powerful, but maintaining a charged battery and moving it around can be time-consuming and laborious. They are more expensive than electric models.

Rechargeable hedge trimmers

Hedge trimmers powered by a rechargeable battery are cordless, easy to maneuver, and comparatively cheap. They are excellent for small, regularly trimmed hedges, but they lack the power to cut thick shoots and long hedges satisfactorily. Since there are no trailing cords, rechargeable machines present fewer safety hazards than other types of electric trimmer. They can be recharged using the unit provided with the tool.

Brushwood cutters

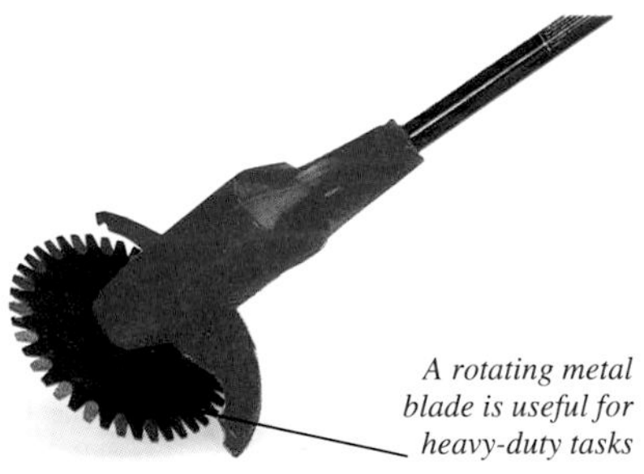

A rotating metal blade is useful for heavy-duty tasks

A brushwood cutter is excellent for slashing through tough weeds, undergrowth, and very long grass. The rotating head has a metal fine-toothed blade or slasher. This makes it suitable for far heavier tasks than those that can be tackled with a nylon-line trimmer (see "Lawn-care tools," p.466), but it is more tiring to operate. Some models take plastic blades, but these are not as tough or durable. In addition to their cutting blade, some may be fitted with a nylon line for trimming grass.

Since they need powerful engines to work effectively, most brushwood cutters are gas-driven. Electric models are usually lighter, less noisy, and require less maintenance, but are less efficient for heavy work.

Chain saws

Chain saws are suitable for sawing logs or large branches and for extensive tree surgery and felling. Because they cut with a powered, toothed chain revolving at high speed, they can be dangerous and should be handled with great care; it is advisable to be trained in their safe use.

Electric chain saws are useful for small jobs and are cheaper than gas types, but strict safety precautions are essential (see right).

Gas-driven chain saws are more powerful and therefore suitable for very large gardens or woodlands, but they are noisy, heavy, often difficult to start, and create fumes.

ELECTRIC CHAIN SAW
An electric chain saw is suitable for most sawing tasks; it is lighter and easier to handle than a gas-powered version and generally requires less maintenance.

Revolving, toothed chain

Electrical safety

- Keep cords only just as long as is necessary. Trailing cords are inconvenient and potentially hazardous, because they may be cut by moving blades.
- Have outside sockets installed by a qualified electrician at suitable points in the garden to keep cords short and safe.
- If extension cords are needed, ensure that they have the same number of wires as the tool: if the tool is grounded, the extension cord should be too.
- Double-insulated tools do not require a grounded (3-prong) socket or extension. All other electric tools do.
- Do not use an electric tool during or just after rain since this may cause electrical shorts.
- Always disconnect the power supply before adjusting, inspecting, or cleaning a tool.
- Never touch a severed or damaged cord before disconnecting it from the socket.
- Tools should be fitted with a ground fault circuit interrupter.

Lawn mowers

When choosing a lawn mower, take into account the size of your lawn and the type of cut required. If only a small area needs mowing, a manual lawn mower should suffice, but for a larger lawn, buy a power mower. There are reel and rotary mowers available: reel models usually provide the finest cut, while rotary types are better for longer, tougher, or overgrown grass.

Grass should be mown more closely during periods of rapid growth and left longer when less growth occurs, such as late fall, or when hot and dry in summer, so check that the height of cut is easily adjustable (see also The Lawn, "Frequency and height of cut," p.281). For a fine finish without loose grass, choose a mulching mower or a model with a grass catcher (see also "Grass clippings," p.281).

Manual lawn mowers

Manual mowers are relatively cheap, quiet, have no awkward cords, and require very little maintenance.

There are two types of manual lawn mower: those driven by wheels at the side and those operated by a chain drive from a heavy rear roller. A side-wheel mower is easy to push but may be difficult to use at the edge of a lawn – if its side wheels are not in contact with the grass, they do not turn the reel blades. Since there is no rear roller, it does not produce a strip pattern on the turf. Mowers with a rear roller make it easy to mow over an edge.

Power lawn mowers

There are two basic types of power lawn mower: reel and rotary. They run on gas or electricity. Power mowers are potentially dangerous on steep slopes because they are designed for flat surfaces.

Reel mowers

These mowers either are entirely self-propelled or have a power blade; the latter type may be heavy and tiring to operate. Most reel mowers have a rear roller, which is essential if you want a lawn with a strip pattern; the heavier the roller, the more pronounced the strip.

Gas-driven reel mowers often have broader cutting widths than electric ones. This reduces the cutting time but makes them more difficult to maneuver.

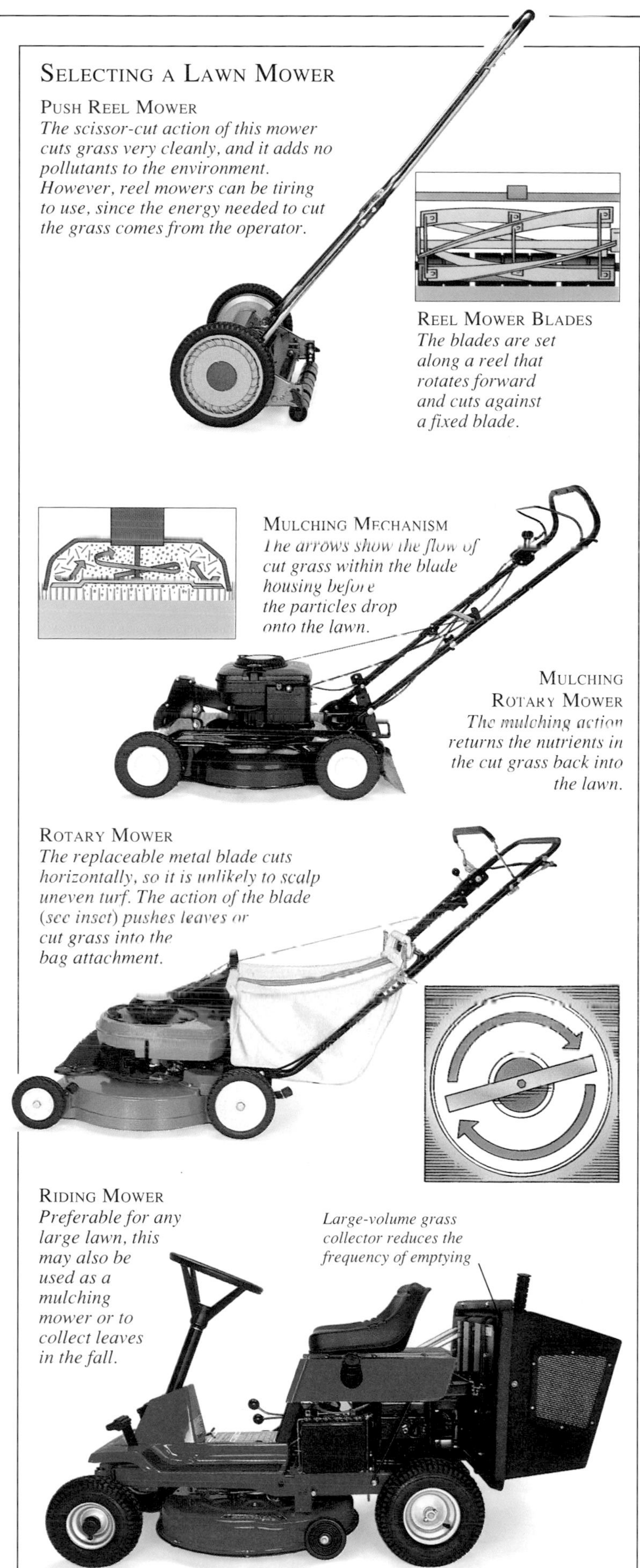

Selecting a Lawn Mower

Push Reel Mower
The scissor-cut action of this mower cuts grass very cleanly, and it adds no pollutants to the environment. However, reel mowers can be tiring to use, since the energy needed to cut the grass comes from the operator.

Reel Mower Blades
The blades are set along a reel that rotates forward and cuts against a fixed blade.

Mulching Mechanism
The arrows show the flow of cut grass within the blade housing before the particles drop onto the lawn.

Mulching Rotary Mower
The mulching action returns the nutrients in the cut grass back into the lawn.

Rotary Mower
The replaceable metal blade cuts horizontally, so it is unlikely to scalp uneven turf. The action of the blade (see inset) pushes leaves or cut grass into the bag attachment.

Riding Mower
Preferable for any large lawn, this may also be used as a mulching mower or to collect leaves in the fall.

Large-volume grass collector reduces the frequency of emptying

Rotary mowers

These have replaceable metal or plastic blades that cut grass with a scythelike motion as they rotate horizontally. Rotary mowers have wheels; only a few rotary mowers are fitted with rollers. They work better than reel mowers for sites that are slightly uneven or have long grass, but most models cannot cut very low. Riding mowers, convenient for large lawns, are almost always rotary models.

Which power source?

Electricity is more convenient and cleaner than gas, but is not suitable for powerful engines. If used for very long grass or extensive areas, an electric mower may overheat. Convenience and safety should also be considered. Access to a power supply is essential, although the trailing cord may be a hazard. Do not use electric mowers on wet grass.

Gas lawn mowers are not hampered by cords but are more expensive to purchase and maintain. They may not start readily unless they are fitted with an electric ignition.

Safety

- Blades must be well protected so that they do not come into contact with the operator's feet. However safe the mower appears, the operator should always wear strong, protective shoes.
- The blade brake must stop the blades rotating within five seconds of being turned off.
- The mower should have a lock-off switch, which requires two operations to turn on an engine. This reduces the risk of a child accidentally switching it on.
- A dead-man's handle should be fitted. Held in when mowing, this turns off the engine when released.

Maintenance

A few simple precautions keep a mower working efficiently.

- After use, disconnect power, then clean engine and blades.
- Replace blunt blades promptly.
- Oil and lubricate regularly.
- Service the mower yearly.
- Periodically check that spark plugs are clean and adjusted.
- Clean filters and air intakes of gas mowers regularly.
- Periodically check the oil level on four-cycle engines.
- Drain the tank before you store a gas-powered model.

Lawn-care tools

In addition to lawn mowers, a number of other tools are useful for maintaining a healthy and attractive lawn. Manual tools are usually adequate for smaller lawns but, for large areas, power tools are faster and less tiring to operate.

Edging tools

A neat, well-defined edge provides the perfect finishing touch to a well-mown lawn and emphasizes the lawn's shape and outline (see also *Cutting the Edge of the Lawn*, p.282). There are two main lawn edging tools: half-moon edgers and long-handled shears, although power edging machines and certain nylon-line trimmers may be used.

Shafts for long-handled shears are wood, steel, or plastic-coated steel; all are strong and the choice is really a matter of personal preference.

LONG-HANDLED EDGING SHEARS
These are useful for trimming overhanging grass around a lawn edge. The handles should be sufficiently long so that there is no need to stoop. If either too short or too heavy, the shears may be tiring to operate.

HALF-MOON EDGER
Also known as an edging iron or lawn edger, this is used with a rocking motion to cut away worn or uneven lawn edges and to remove small pieces of sod for repair. It has a sharp, curved metal blade attached to a long wooden or metal handle.

Lawn edging materials

To prevent a lawn from gradually decreasing in size when turf is removed with tools such as a half-moon edger, outline the lawn with bricks, paving slabs, terracotta edging tiles, or metal or plastic edging strips. This helps to ensure an even edge and inhibits grass from spreading onto paths and borders. A brick or paving-slab edge also enables side-wheel mowers to be driven right to the lawn edge. Plastic strips, which are usually green, are less likely than metal edging strips to damage mower blades, and are cheaper. However, plastic strips may deteriorate quickly.

Nylon-line trimmers

A nylon-line trimmer is useful for trimming grass in awkward areas that cannot easily be reached by a mower. It may also be used for slashing ground cover plants or soft-stemmed weeds, although a more powerful brushwood cutter may be needed for tough undergrowth (see p.464). The nylon cutting line is flexible and easily replaced, so it is possible to work right up to a wall, mature tree, or paving without damaging the tool. It is also safer than a fixed blade or cutter if there is an accident. Always wear goggles, since flying stones are hazardous.

As for most other power tools, nylon-line trimmers may be driven by electricity or gas, and similar considerations of safety, convenience, and weight apply. Electric models are more common and are suitable for gardens where they are needed for small areas only. They are light and easy to operate, but their area of use is restricted by the cord length. For safety, they should have a dead-man's handle and be plugged into a receptacle with a ground fault circuit interrupter. Never use them on wet grass (see also "Electrical safety," p.464).

A gas-driven nylon-line trimmer is ideal for larger gardens and for areas where there is no power supply. It is more expensive and needs more maintenance than an electric trimmer. It is also heavier and therefore may be more tiring to maneuver. For safety, it should have a quick, easy way to stop the engine.

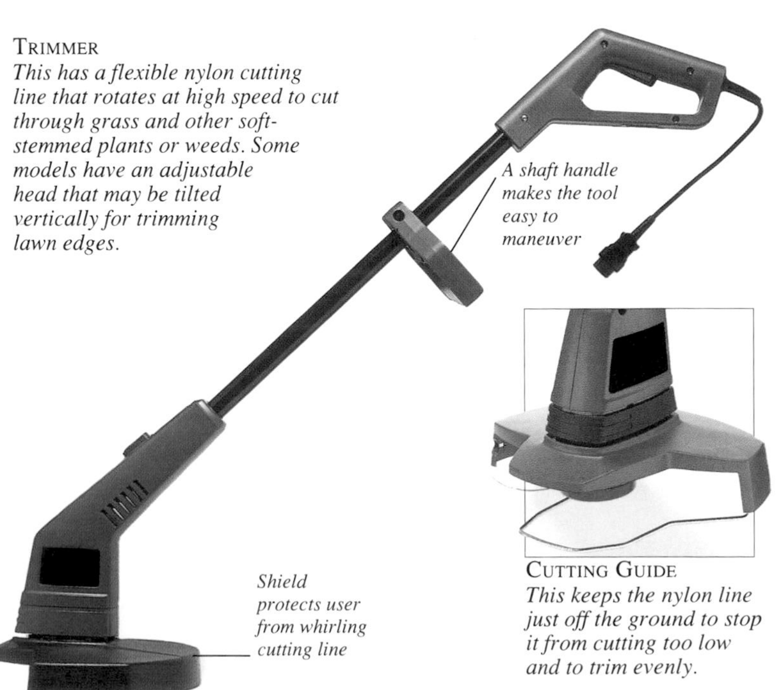

TRIMMER
This has a flexible nylon cutting line that rotates at high speed to cut through grass and other soft-stemmed plants or weeds. Some models have an adjustable head that may be tilted vertically for trimming lawn edges.

CUTTING GUIDE
This keeps the nylon line just off the ground to stop it from cutting too low and to trim evenly.

Garden rollers

A garden roller, which may be made of metal or water-filled hollow plastic, is used to level the surface during initial ground preparation before sowing grass seed or laying sod. It also settles the soil around young grass seedlings. Rolling established lawns regularly is no longer recommended, however; on heavy soils particularly, it tends to compact the turf and therefore impede drainage, which may lead to problems such as moss and poor grass growth.

Long-handled lawn shears

Long-handled lawn shears are helpful for trimming grass in awkward places, such as beneath overhanging plants or around trees, paving, or walls, and for tidying any stalks missed during mowing. The blades, set at right angles to the handles, are positioned parallel to the ground, not vertically as in edging shears. While lawn shears are useful for very small areas, they have largely been superseded by power nylon-line trimmers, which are faster and more versatile. However, trimmers are heavier to hold and maneuver than shears and are more expensive since they are power tools.

LONG-HANDLED LAWN SHEARS
These may be useful for cutting grass in small areas that would be difficult to cut with a mower.

Rakes and aerators

Tools for clearing up fallen leaves and garden debris, and for reducing thatch (a layer of decaying organic matter) and soil compaction, help to keep a lawn in good condition.

Lawn rakes are primarily used to gather up fallen leaves. Some types may be helpful in removing thatch and dead moss. There are three types of lawn rake: spring-tined, flat-tined, and scarifying, or aerator, rakes (see also "Rakes," p.460). In addition, power lawn rakes, which are suitable for large lawns, are available.

Aerating, whether by spiking, scarifying, slitting, or hollow-tining, helps to reduce thatch – which should not exceed a layer ½in (1cm) in depth – and lets air into the soil. The result of proper dethatching and aerating is to encourage healthy, vigorous turf with deep root growth (see also The Lawn, "Annual maintenance," p.283).

On small areas, aerating may be done by spiking the turf with a garden fork, but for most lawns a more powerful tool, for example a hollow-tined aerator also known as a plugger, or star-wheeled slitter attachment (see right), will be needed. Although a slitter aerates the soil faster than a hollow-tined aerator, its tines may not penetrate the turf deeply enough to be effective.

Spring-tined Lawn Rake
This is used for clearing out dead grass and moss, removing small stones and debris, and lightly aerating a lawn. Its light head has long, flexible, rounded wire tines.

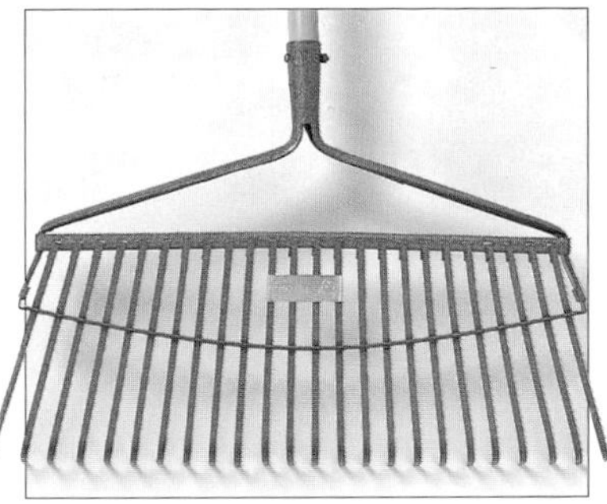

Flat-tined Lawn Rake
Excellent for gathering up leaves and loose material, this has long, flexible, flat tines of plastic or metal, and a light head to minimize damage to new growth.

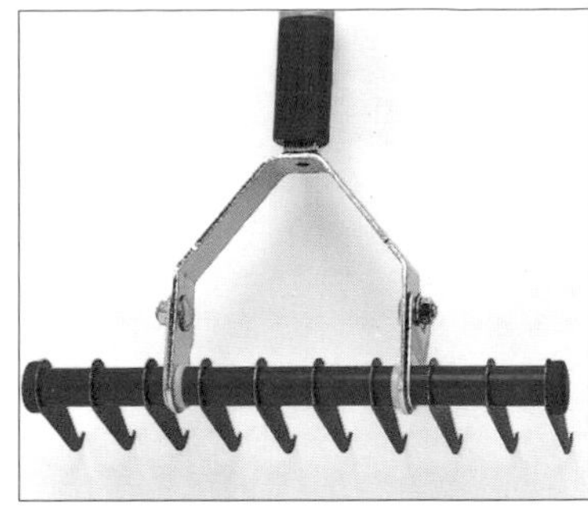

Scarifying Rake
This cuts deeply into thatch and even into the sod itself. Its rigid metal tines are usually flat, with sharp points. Because it may be heavy and tiring to use, a model with wheels either side of the rake head may be preferable.

Hollow-tined Aerator (Plugger)
This hollow-tined power aerator penetrates deeply through the sod into the soil. The tines remove cores of sod and soil, opening up compacted sod.

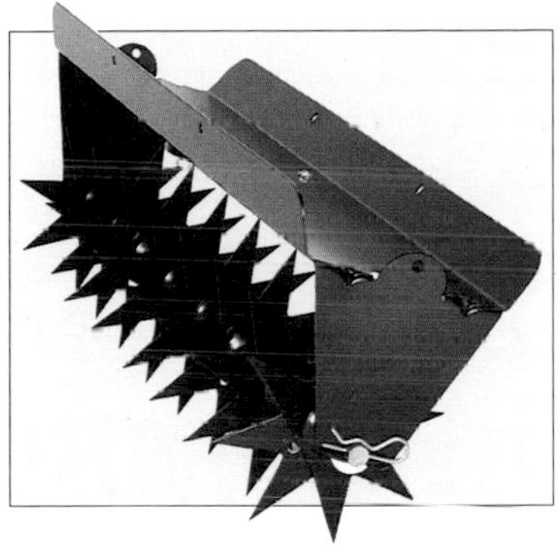

Star-wheeled Slitter Attachment
This attachment for riding mowers (see p.465) aerates the soil faster than a hollow-tined aerator.

Sweepers and blowers

At its simplest, a leaf sweeper may be an ordinary stiff broom or besom brush used to sweep away small debris; this kind of basic sweeper is ideal for clearing pathways and small areas of the garden.

For large lawns, however, using a power leaf blower saves both labor and time. The leaves are quickly and easily blown into rows or piles, which may then be raked up and discarded or added to a compost pile.

Some power models have flexible attachments designed for use in flowerbeds, borders, and other areas of the garden that are particularly hard to reach. Larger models of power blower, especially push models, may prove worthwhile in large gardens, but they are expensive to buy and they may be noisy to operate. Smaller models may be cheaper and quieter in addition to being lighter.

Besom
This is an inexpensive brush suitable for sweeping up leaves and light debris.

Push Leaf Blower
This cleans up garden leaves by blowing, rather than sweeping, them into a pile for collection. It is very useful for large, paved surfaces.

Backpack Blower
This blower is carried on the operator's back and is very useful for small, tight, and irregularly shaped areas.

Handheld Blower
This is useful for small jobs.

Fertilizer spreaders

A fertilizer spreader is suitable for the accurate distribution of fertilizer, grass seed, and granular weedkillers. It consists of a hopper on wheels with a long handle. Check that the application rate is adjustable and that the flow may be switched off when turning at the lawn edge. After setting the application rate, always check that it is correct by fertilizing a test area first (see "Applying fertilizers," p.533). A hose attachment for applying a fertilizer with water is useful for feeding a lawn (see *Hose-end Attachments*, p.468).

Fertilizer Spreader
A spreader applies fertilizer evenly, thus avoiding scorching the grass.

Watering aids

Irrigation makes it possible to grow plants that require more water than is provided by rainfall, and to grow plants both indoors and in the greenhouse. Equipment such as hoses and sprinklers helps make routine watering easier and faster.

GARDEN WATERING CANS
These should have a generous capacity to reduce the need for repeated refilling. For general-purpose use, a 2 gallon (9 liter) can, which holds 18lb (8kg) of water, is a convenient size.

Watering cans

A watering can is practical in the house, greenhouse, or for small areas outside. Choose a lightweight can that will not be too heavy to carry when full. The opening of the watering can should be wide enough to make filling easy, and the can itself should feel comfortable and well balanced. A can that has a strainer at the base of the spout helps to prevent the rose from becoming clogged by debris in the water.

PLASTIC OR METAL?
Most watering cans are now made from plastic, but traditional galvanized metal ones, which are heavier and more expensive, are still available; both types are sturdy and durable.

GREENHOUSE WATERING CAN
This has a long spout, so that it is easy to reach plants at the back of a bench, and an interchangeable rose for both fine and coarse sprays for watering seedlings and mature plants.

Water barrels

A water barrel collects and stores rainwater from the house or greenhouse roof, invaluable during dry periods and for acid-loving plants. The barrel should have a tap, and a lid to keep out insects and debris, which pollute the water and might block the tap. If necessary, raise the barrel on blocks to allow room for a watering can beneath the tap. Some water barrels divert water back to a drain when the barrel is full.

INDOOR WATERING CAN
This should have a long spout to reach into plant pots and windowboxes, and to help control the flow.

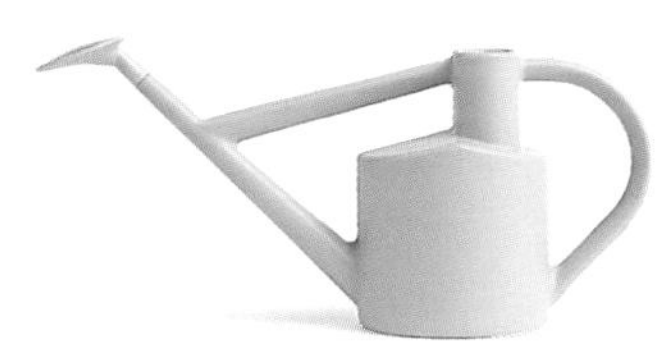

Caution with weedkiller

Do not use the same watering can for watering the garden and for dispensing liquid weedkillers. Keep a special can with a dribble bar, clearly marked, for applying chemicals.

Which rose?

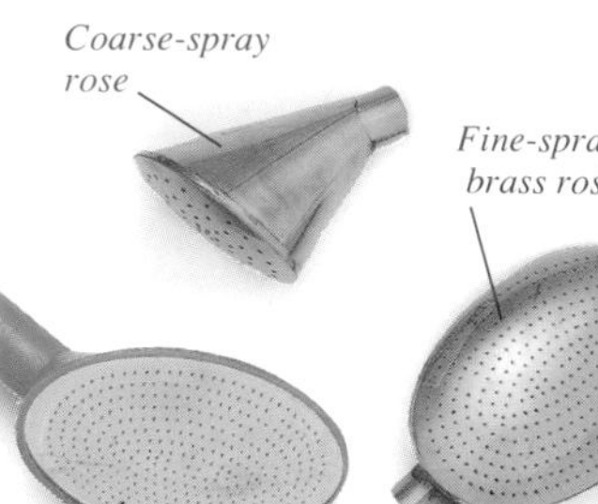

A fine rose is best for seeds and seedlings because the resulting spray does not damage them or wash the soil mix or soil away from them. For more established plants, a coarse-spray rose, which delivers the water faster, is preferable.

Roses are manufactured in a choice of materials: brass, brass-faced plastic, and all-plastic. Plastic is less durable and cheaper than brass but is still satisfactory for most uses. In general, metal roses give a finer spray.

Using a dribble bar, which is attached to a watering can, makes it more accurate than a rose for applying weedkiller. It also reduces spray drift, which can be a problem with a rose.

Hoses

A hose is invaluable for irrigating distant parts of the garden and for areas that require copious watering. Most hoses are made from PVC; they vary in the way they are finished or reinforced, which affects their flexibility and their resistance to kinking. Any kinks interrupt water flow and eventually weaken the hose wall. Double-walled and reinforced hoses are resistant to kinking but relatively expensive. Whichever type of hose you choose, make sure that it is long enough to reach all parts of the garden; some types may be lengthened with an extension.

A flat hose is mounted on its own reel and cannot be used unless the entire hose is unreeled. Flat hoses are made in fixed lengths with connectors and nozzles prefitted. Some kink readily unless laid in a straight line; they may also be difficult to wind up because all the water must be drained out first.

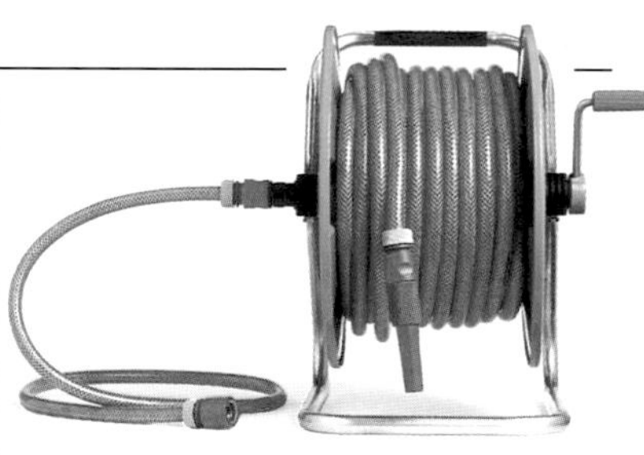

HOSE REEL
A reel with a handle or wheels is easy to move around the garden. Some reels allow water to flow through the hose even when partially wound.

FLAT HOSE
A flat hose winds neatly onto its own reel and is easy to store.

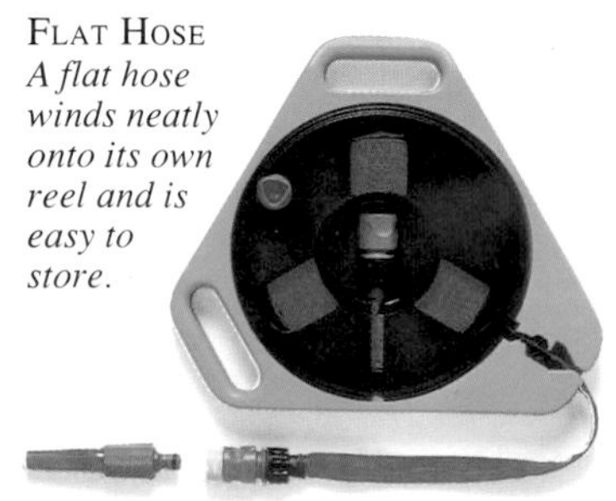

Sprayers

Use sprayers, either portable devices or attachments fitted to the end of a hose, to apply pesticides, weedkillers, and fertilizers, and to water or mist-spray plants. Compression types, pumped up before use, are most suitable for general use; small trigger-pump sprayers are for misting house plants or applying pesticides to a few plants. For a large area, use a knapsack sprayer.

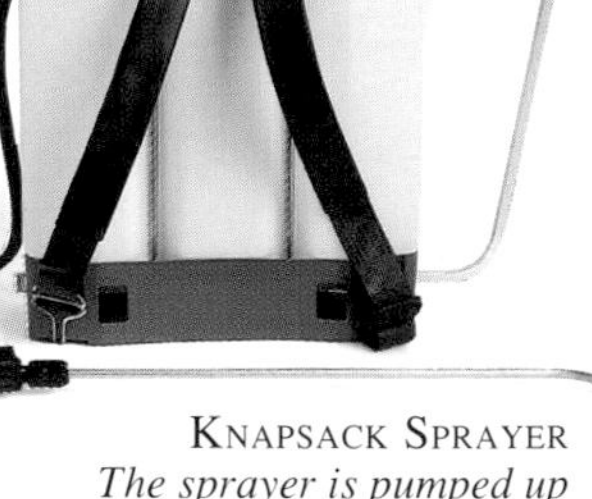

KNAPSACK SPRAYER
The sprayer is pumped up by the lever and is suitable for large areas.

TRIGGER-ACTION HOSE ATTACHMENT

Nozzle allows spray to be adjusted to jet or mist

Trigger

FERTILIZER PULSE HOSE ATTACHMENT

Central chamber for fertilizer

HOSE-END ATTACHMENTS
These may be connected to a hose to spray large numbers of plants simultaneously. Some have a trigger-action nozzle; most have an adjustable spray. Special attachments (left) are available for applying fertilizer and water together.

Garden sprinklers

A garden sprinkler automatically delivers a fine spray of water over a specific area. Because it works while unattended, it saves time and effort. It also distributes the water economically, since the spray, when applied over a long period, penetrates the soil better than water delivered from a watering can or hand-held hose. A sprinkler is generally attached to a garden hose.

There are various types of sprinkler to suit a range of needs: some are best for a lawn, for example, while others are preferable for irrigating a flowerbed or vegetable patch. The simplest is a standing sprinkler, which usually waters a limited, circular area. It is suitable for lawns, but is liable to form puddles, so must be moved around to achieve an even distribution. In a flowerbed the spray is often obstructed by foliage, giving unsatisfactory results, although some models have a long spike to raise the head above the surrounding plants.

Other forms of sprinkler in which water pressure is used to rotate the sprinkler heads give better, more even coverage. Rotating sprinklers and pulse-jet sprinklers swing around to deliver water in a wide circle. Oscillating sprinklers deliver water over a rectangular area through a series of holes in a bar that rocks back and forth.

A traveling sprinkler (also called a walking sprinkler) is useful for large, level areas such as a big lawn; it is convenient but expensive. The sprinkler delivers spray over a rectangular area while being propelled along a straight track (usually a hose) by the force of the water. The rate of travel and size of area covered on either side of the track depend on the water pressure.

TYPES OF SPRINKLER

STANDING SPRINKLER
Standing sprinklers are intended primarily for use on lawns, most being mounted on a spike to push into the ground. They usually deliver water in a circle, but a few water in a semicircular, rectangular, or fan shape.

ROTATING SPRINKLER
Good for lawns, beds, and borders, this type of sprinkler covers a large circular area and applies the water evenly. The spray is delivered through nozzles on the arms, which are attached to a spinning pivot, driven by the force of the water. Those that are fitted with long stems are the best type for watering beds and borders.

PULSE-JET SPRINKLER
This type of sprinkler is invaluable for covering large, circular areas of lawn, beds, or borders. It has a single jet on a central pivot, which rotates in a series of pulses, ejecting spurts of water. Except on lawns, the delivery head is generally set on a tall stem for increased coverage.

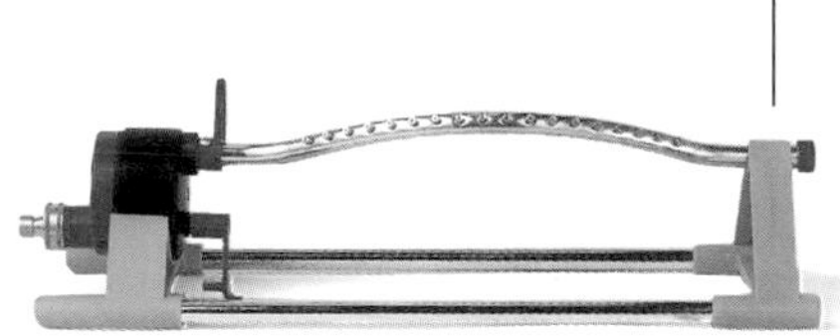

OSCILLATING SPRINKLER
This is best used at ground level; it is not suitable for positions where surrounding foliage will interfere with the range of the spray. Water is sprayed through the brass jets in the oscillating arm. This sprinkler delivers water fairly evenly over a rectangular area, the size of which may be easily adjusted.

Underground sprinkler systems
These are permanent systems, ideal for irrigating lawns and rock gardens. They are unobtrusive and simple to operate, and are best installed when the area needing irrigation is first constructed, preferably by a professional. PVC pipes and connecting joints are laid in the form of a grid so that they supply various watering heads, to which hoses or sprinklers are attached. The sprinkler from each head delivers an even supply of water to a given area.

Always continue watering until the ground is thoroughly wet, because this helps to even out the distribution to any overlapping areas. This type of watering system is usually the most expensive: it requires antisiphon valves to meet water authority standards, and possibly a water meter and other fittings.

Soaker hoses

Soaker hoses are useful for irrigating lawns or rows of plants. They are hoses with small perforations along their length. With the holes facing upward, a soaker hose produces a fine spray over a rectangular area and can be used to water lawns. With the holes placed toward the ground, water is directed to the base of plants – an excellent way to irrigate vegetables and other plants grown in rows. Choose a soaker hose carefully because some cannot be used as sprinklers, since their holes are so small that the water just trickles out even when the holes are facing upward.

Porous hoses are a variation on soaker hoses. A network of porous hoses enables water to seep slowly into the soil. They are particularly suitable for newly planted beds and borders. The connections may be varied and the system moved around as required on the soil surface, or the hoses may be buried 4–6in (10–15cm) below the surface as a permanent irrigation system.

Hose timers

Hose timers may be used with ordinary garden sprinklers or more elaborate watering systems. They fit between a tap and the hose or irrigation pipe. Most hose timers turn off the water after a predetermined time. The more sophisticated ones also turn on the water. Some may be linked to a soil-moisture detector that overrides the program if the ground is already sufficiently wet.

COMPUTERIZED TIMER
This allows you to program watering times and duration in advance, to irrigate plants while you are busy or away.

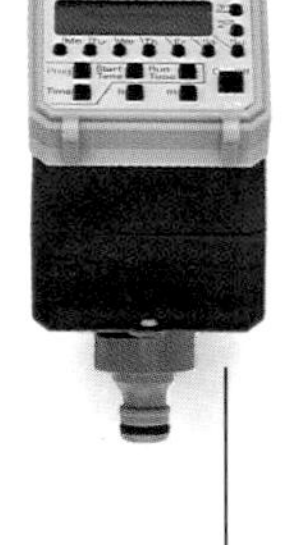

WATER TIMER
This can be set to turn off the water after a preset period, from about 5 minutes to 2 hours.

Trickle, or drip-feed, systems

These are used for plants that benefit from individual watering. The water drips gently beside the plant, minimizing soil disturbance around the roots. A trickle system works well in a shrub border, along a hedge, or for vegetables. It can also be used for plants in containers, grow bags, and windowboxes. Ideal in arid regions where water is in short supply or very costly, a trickle system does not give plants more water than they need. However, unless fitted with a hose timer, it can waste water, and needs regular cleaning to prevent the tubes and drip heads from becoming blocked with algae and debris.

TRICKLE WATERING SYSTEM
The delivery hose is connected to a unit that filters the water and reduces the pressure. The water then flows along a network of tubes supported by spikes stuck into the ground. Systems of this kind can be extended by buying additional drip heads and lengths of tube.

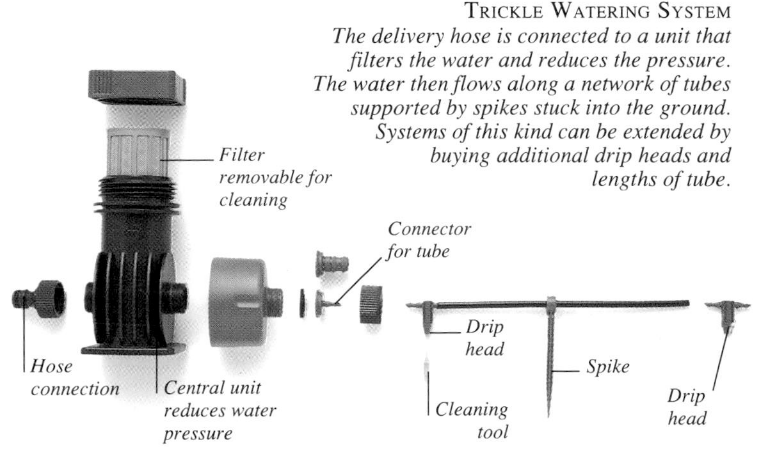

General garden equipment

In addition to tools for cultivating and maintaining the garden, a wide range of other accessories such as carrying equipment and planting aids may be useful, depending on your own individual requirements.

Wheelbarrows

Wheelbarrows are useful for transporting plants, soil, and materials such as soil mix and garden debris. They may be made of metal or plastic, the former being more durable. Painted metal soon rusts if the paint is chipped; even galvanized metal trays rust eventually. Plastic trays, although lighter, may split.

Most traditional wheelbarrows have an inflatable tire to cushion the load. Check regularly and inflate the tire as needed; an underinflated tire makes pushing the wheelbarrow very difficult, especially if the tray is heavily loaded. Garden carts, as barrows with two wheels and a single handle are usually called, are stable and easy to load and unload, but are less maneuverable than standard barrows on uneven ground.

Sheets and bags

A carrying sheet or bag is suitable for transporting light but bulky garden waste such as hedge clippings; when not in use, it takes up very little space. It should be lightweight, with strong handles, and made of a tough, tearproof material, such as woven plastic. Carrying bags have a larger capacity than sheets. Trugs and baskets are good for light tasks such as carrying flowers or fruit.

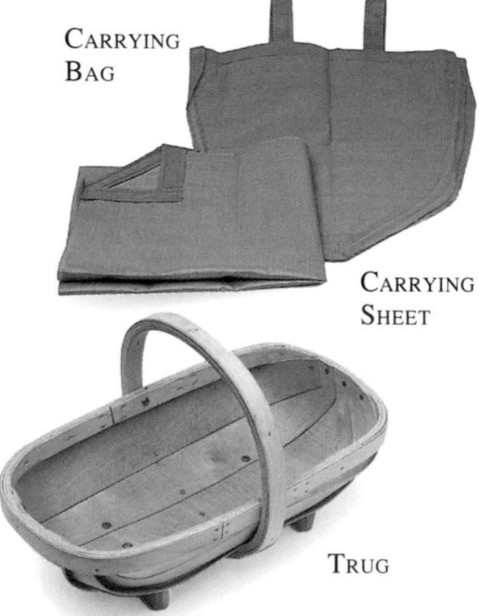

CARRYING BAG

CARRYING SHEET

TRUG

TYPES OF WHEELBARROW

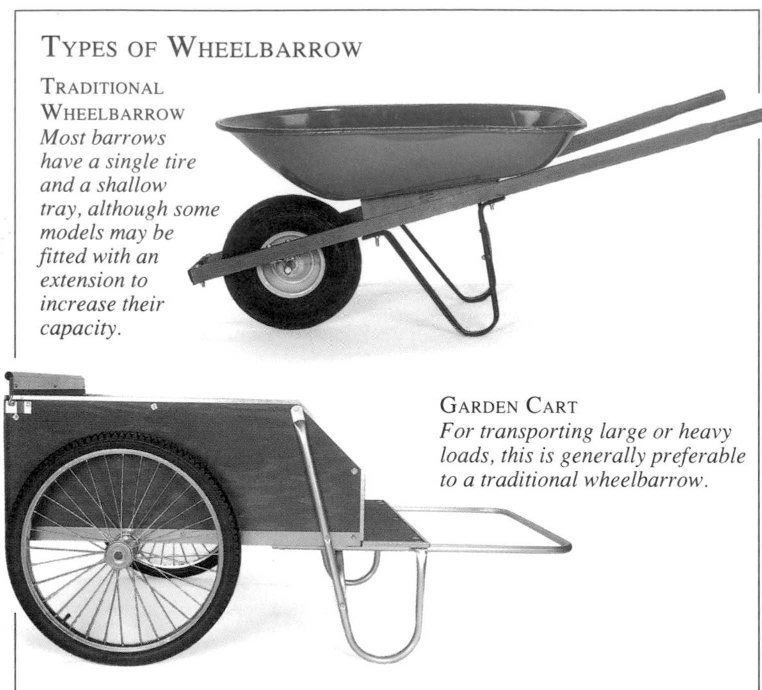

TRADITIONAL WHEELBARROW *Most barrows have a single tire and a shallow tray, although some models may be fitted with an extension to increase their capacity.*

GARDEN CART *For transporting large or heavy loads, this is generally preferable to a traditional wheelbarrow.*

Plastic bags

Clear plastic bags are excellent for a number of purposes: preventing cuttings material from drying out after collecting them, for example, and for covering cuttings in pots to raise humidity around them. Most food and freezer bags are suitable provided that they are not too thin, since they are then less effective at retaining moisture.

Kneelers and knee pads

A kneeler or knee pads, cushioned and covered with a waterproof material, make kneeling more comfortable, particularly when weeding or planting. Knee pads are simply strapped to the knees; they are often sold in only one size, so check that they fit before buying. Kneeling stools support the knees on a slightly raised platform and have hand rests to give support when kneeling down and standing up. They may also be turned upside down for use as a small stool for working at raised beds or greenhouse benches.

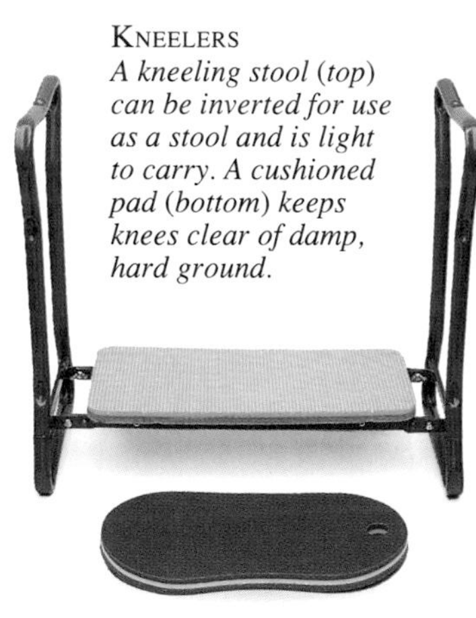

KNEELERS *A kneeling stool (top) can be inverted for use as a stool and is light to carry. A cushioned pad (bottom) keeps knees clear of damp, hard ground.*

Compost bins

A compost bin should have a lid to keep warmth in, easy access to the compost by slats or panels, and a capacity of at least 10cu ft (0.28cu m) to generate sufficient heat to accelerate the rotting process. Avoid wire mesh bins or those with large gaps between the slats, because they allow the heat generated to escape.

Traditional, wooden compost bins are available precut for easy self-assembly. Plastic compost bins are generally more efficient than metal or wooden ones because they conserve moisture and reduce the need to water. There are plastic bins available that may be rotated to turn the compost, but this does not necessarily make good compost more quickly than a well-designed, traditional bin (see SOILS AND FERTILIZERS, *Making a Compost Bin*, p.535).

Incinerators

Open-mesh incinerators, some of which may be folded up after use, are good for burning dry material such as twigs and leaves. Galvanized steel, drum-type incinerators are suitable for slowly burning damp, woody material. However, open burning, once a standard gardening practice, is now illegal in many areas; seek advice before you begin. Many gardeners prefer to recycle garden waste by shredding and composting it.

Shredders

A compost shredder chops woody or tough garden waste, such as old corn stems, hedge trimmings, and prunings, until it is fine enough to break down quickly on a compost heap. Shredders are usually electrically powered and should not be left outdoors when not in use. They are heavy to move around, so choose one with wheels, unless there is space to use and store it in one place.

For safety, make sure that the power is automatically disconnected when the hopper is removed (see "Electrical safety," p.464). The funnel should be easy to use, but you must not be able to touch the blades.

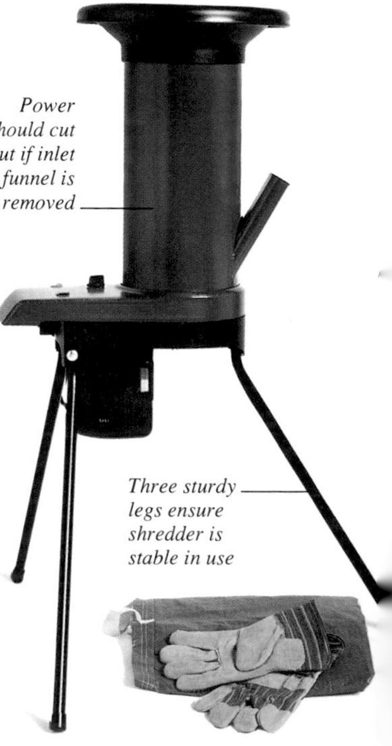

USING A SHREDDER *The inlet funnel should not allow direct access to the blades. Wear goggles and gloves to shield against flying debris and thorny stems.*

Planting and sowing aids

General garden tools or household items are often used for planting and sowing; for example a stick or pencil, instead of a dibber, will make a planting hole. Specialized tools, however, do make some tedious and repetitive jobs simpler and quicker.

Seed sowers and planters
These facilitate accurate and even sowing of seed. There are four main types: shakers, plungers, wheeled sowers, and seed-tray sowers.
Shakers are hand-held devices that may be used for sowing seed in prepared drills. Skill is required to ensure even seed distribution.
Plungers insert each seed individually to a predetermined depth.
Wheeled seed sowers are good for distributing seeds evenly in an outdoor drill. With a long handle, they can be worked from a standing position, making sowing less tiring.
Seed-tray sowers are thin, plastic or wooden boards with molded protrusions on one side. When pressed onto the seed soil mix they firm the surface and make evenly spaced holes for sowing seed.

Bulb planters
A bulb planter is useful if planting a number of bulbs individually; for planting groups of small bulbs, a trowel or hand fork is better. A bulb planter removes a plug of soil or sod, which is then replaced on top of the bulb after planting; models with a clawlike action release the plug by pressure on the handle.

Gardening gloves

There is a range of gardening gloves for various purposes: some keep hands clean when working with soil or soil mix; others also provide protection against thorns.

Leather and fabric gloves are useful for tasks such as pruning roses to guard against thorns. When buying leather ones, check that the leather extends far enough to protect all of the palm. All-leather or suede gloves give very good protection, but may be uncomfortably hot in warm weather. Gauntlet types cover the wrists and lower forearms.

Many gloves are made of fabric and vinyl. Some are impregnated with vinyl, others just have a vinyl grip on the palms. They are good for most jobs and keep hands cleaner than fabric alone. Vinyl-coated gloves are useful for messy jobs, such as mixing concrete, but are too thick for jobs needing a sensitive touch.

FABRIC WITH VINYL GRIP
SUEDE GAUNTLETS
SUEDE AND FABRIC
COTTON FABRIC

Dibbers and widgers

A dibber is a pencil shaped tool used for making planting holes. Use a small dibber to transplant seedlings or insert cuttings, and a large one for transplanting vegetables such as leeks that require a wide hole to allow space for growth, and for planting through a sheet mulch. A widger, which is like a narrow spatula, is good for lifting seedlings and rooted cuttings with the minimum of root disturbance.

Garden lines

A garden line is used mainly in vegetable plots as a guide for forming straight rows, but is also invaluable for other tasks, such as marking out areas when planning or designing, or forming a straight edge when planting a hedge or constructing a wall or patio.

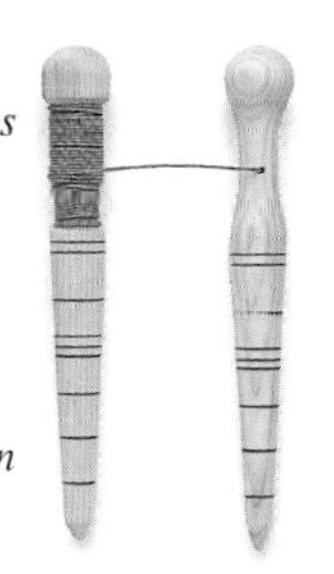
GARDEN LINE
Most garden lines have a pointed stake at either end for inserting into the ground. Grooves allow you to stretch a level line between the stakes.

Sieves

Garden sieves generally have a mesh of ¹/₈–¹/₂in (3–12mm) and are used to separate out coarse material from soil or soil mix. Choose a sieve with a large mesh to remove twigs and stones from soil before sowing, potting up, or planting; use one with a smaller mesh when covering fine seeds after sowing. Those with a wire mesh tend to be more effective and durable than plastic ones.

WIRE-MESH SIEVE
SIEVE WITH FINE PLASTIC MESH

Thermometers

A greenhouse thermometer measures the current air temperature. A minimum-maximum thermometer records both the lowest and highest temperatures; it is the best type for both garden and greenhouse use since it also helps determine the warmest and coldest parts of the garden. A soil thermometer registers soil temperature and is helpful in deciding when to sow seed.

MINIMUM-MAXIMUM THERMOMETER
GREENHOUSE THERMOMETER

Rain gauges

A rain gauge is used for measuring amounts of rainfall or irrigation; it is helpful for identifying areas of the garden that are affected by rain shadow. It should have clear markings and a smooth inside surface for easy cleaning. Many gauges have a short spike for inserting into the ground.

Measurements are clear so that water level is easy to read
Spike for stability
PLASTIC RAIN GAUGE

PLANTING AND SOWING TOOLS

SMALL DIBBER
WOODEN GARDEN DIBBER FOR OUTDOOR USE
BULB PLANTER
WIDGER
WHEELED SEED SOWER
METAL GARDEN DIBBER

Ties and supports

Ties are used for various purposes in the garden, but in particular to secure a climbing, scrambling, or fragile plant. Ties must be secure without constricting the stem. Use a light material such as twine or raffia on soft-stemmed plants, which are damaged easily. Supports are needed to protect some plants from wind or rain.

General ties

Garden string or twine in 3-ply is adequate for most tying jobs. Raffia, which is good for binding joins after grafting and as a lightweight tie, and soft strings, such as green twine, may disintegrate after a year or so. Clear plastic tape and special rubber ties are excellent for use in grafting. Tar-impregnated string or polypropylene twine is a reliable, weather-resistant tie but, if used to secure plants to a support, may have to be loosened and retied annually.

Plastic-coated tying wire is strong and, since it lasts for several years, needs adjusting as the plant grows. It is good for fixing labels to training wires or as a trellis and joining stakes. It may come on a reel with a convenient built-in cutter.

Plant rings

These are split rings of wire; plastic-covered rings are also available. Plant rings are designed to be opened and closed easily around a plant stem and its support. They are suitable for light jobs such as attaching a house plant to a stake.

Tree ties

Rubber tree ties are strong, durable, and useful for securing a young tree to a stake. They should be easily adjustable so that an expanding stem is not constricted. Select one with a buffer so that the stake does not chafe the stem, or use a padded tie in a figure-eight form (see also "Tree ties," p.41). Nail ties to the stakes.

Wall fixings

Specially designed plant stickers may be used for tasks such as securing the stem of a climber directly to a wall or any other support. Lead-headed nails are stronger; and they have the additional advantage of a soft spur that may be bent over to attach stems and small branches to a wall.

Vine eyes hold stretched wires to which wall plants are then secured. On wall masonry, use flat vine eyes; for timber and wall plugs, screw in eyelet vine eyes.

Stakes

Bamboo stakes are excellent for supporting single-stemmed plants, but they eventually split and rot. More permanent and expensive are PVC stakes and plastic-covered steel rods. Support clumps of border plants with metal link or ring stakes (see PERENNIALS, "Staking," p.156). Trees and standard roses should be supported with sturdy wooden stakes.

Labels and markers

Labels for garden use should be durable, weather resistant, and large enough to contain all the information you want to note. Plastic labels are cheap and may be reused; if written on with pencil, they should remain legible for a season. Most plastic labels discolor gradually with age and become brittle, but they are ideal for labeling trays of seeds and cuttings. Looped labels and those with ties may be secured around the stem of a plant and are useful if labels at eye level are required.

For more permanent, water-resistant markers, use those coated with a black material; these are written on by scratching through to the white plastic beneath, but they cannot be marked with a new name. Aluminum labels, which are more expensive, will last almost indefinitely, but the lettering may have to be renewed every few years.

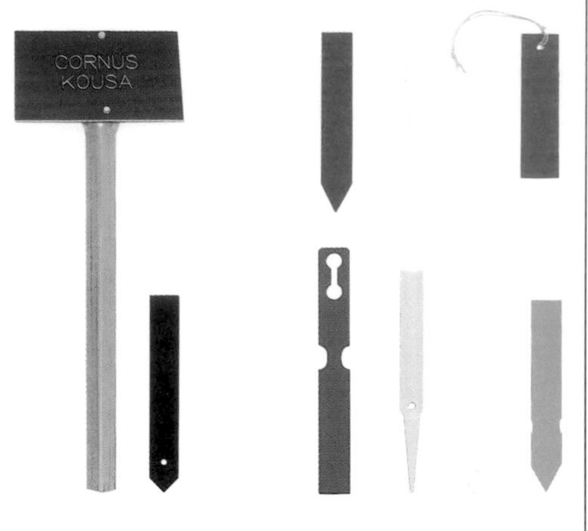

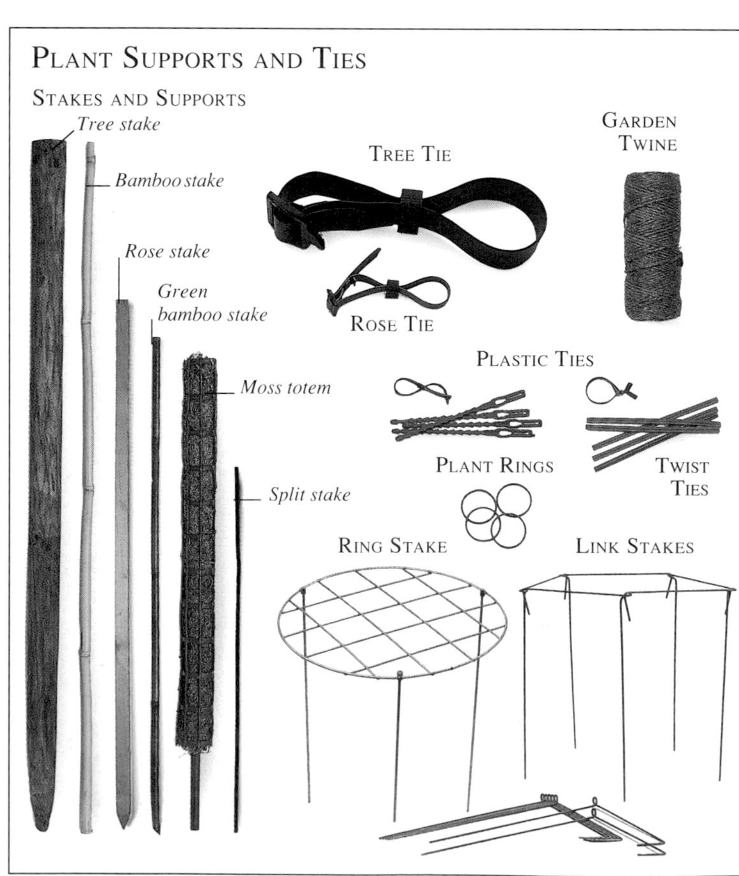

Netting

Netting is available in various materials and mesh sizes for a range of uses, such as supporting plants, protecting fruit from birds, and shading greenhouse plants (see "Shading," p.484). For plant support, choose a mesh of 2in (5cm) or more; it may be hard to disentangle plants from a smaller mesh. For many annual climbers and some clematis, thin, flexible plastic netting is adequate; heavier plants need semirigid plastic nets. For fruit protection, use commercial plastic netting with a mesh of ½–¾in (1–2cm). Protect seedlings and winter vegetables from birds with 1in (2.5cm) mesh netting.

Wire netting may be placed around plants to provide protection from animals such as rabbits. It is also useful for reinforcing concrete when constructing a pond or trough.

Use a plastic snow fence to protect plants in exposed sites (see *Windbreaks*, p.521). Knitted plastic netting may deteriorate in about four years, whereas molded plastic should last at least twice as long. Windbreak webbing is even more long-lasting but very obtrusive. Durability is less important if a temporary windbreak is needed.

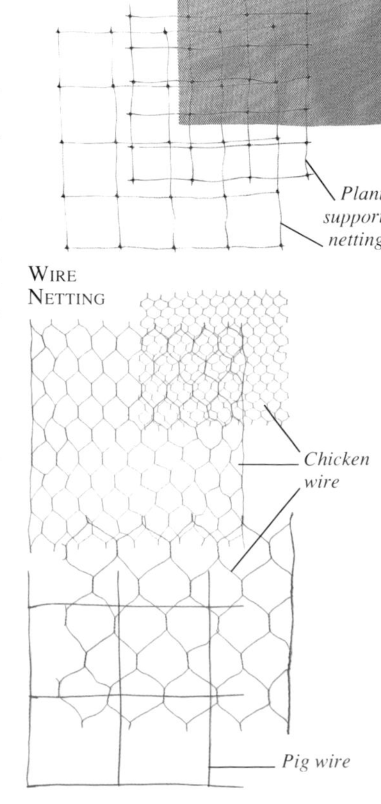

Pots and trays

Pots are available in a wide range of sizes, but there are two basic shapes: round and square. Although round pots are more traditional, square pots hold more soil mix for the same width and pack neatly together, thereby saving space. Round pots are classified by the inside diameter at the rim; square ones by the length of the rim along one side. Most pots have slightly sloping sides so that a plant and its root ball may be easily removed intact for repotting or planting out.

Most pots are made of clay (terracotta) or plastic. Clay is traditional, heavier, and expensive; plastic, however, is more common, lighter, and cheaper. Most plastic pots are manufactured from polypropylene, which deteriorates in cold weather. Pots made of a polypropylene/polyethylene mix do not become brittle in cold weather and are preferable for raising plants outdoors. Pots made of polyethylene only are cheapest and least durable.

Standard pots are at least as deep as they are wide; they are the most common type of pot. Bulb or seed pans are one-half as tall as they are wide at the top; they are useful for germinating seeds. Azalea pots are three-fourths as tall as they are wide at the top; they are often used commercially for plants with relatively small rootballs, such as evergreen azaleas. Use sweet pea tubes for very deep-rooted seedlings. For plants that will remain in the pot for some time, long Toms are preferred.

Other special use pots include lattice pots (which have mesh sides), hydroculture pots (a form of double pot), and forcing pots, which are placed over plants to exclude light. Tarpaper ring pots, sometimes used for greenhouse tomato culture, are bottomless and hold soil mix on top of a growing aggregate.

Pots and Pans

Pots as well as other containers, such as troughs and urns, are used for cultivating and displaying plants both indoors and outside. The smaller pots, pans, and azalea pots are suitable for propagating and growing on young plants.

Degradable pots and pellets

These are good for plants that resent root disturbance, since they can be planted out into the bed. A plant's roots grow through the sides and base of the pots into the surrounding ground. They are generally made from compressed peat and various other fibers (often sphagnum moss and wood fiber, sometimes impregnated with plant food).

Peat pellets are good for seeds and rooting cuttings and must be expanded with water before being used. Many gardeners create their own degradable pots from cones made from double thickness newspaper.

Pot saucers

These are particularly useful for indoor use, when watering plants from beneath and to catch surplus water, which should then always be emptied to prevent waterlogging the growing medium. Saucers are available to match clay or plastic pots.

Seed trays

Traditional wooden seed trays have largely been replaced by plastic ones, which are easier to clean but often more fragile. Very thin plastic trays are cheap and flexible but are unlikely to last more than a year or two. Strong plastics are more rigid and expensive; they may become brittle and split with age but, if stored away from sunlight and extreme cold when not in use, they should last for several years.

Which material?

Plastic pots are:

- lightweight and ideal where less weight is important (on indoor shelves or balconies);
- inexpensive;
- easy to clean;
- durable, although they may eventually split or crack;
- more or less impermeable, so soil mix dries out more slowly than in clay pots;
- good for use with capillary watering systems (see p.485);
- available in various colors.

Clay pots are:

- heavy and stable, so are good for large plants that might be top-heavy in a plastic pot;
- expensive but attractive, so they are often preferable for displaying plants;
- difficult to clean;
- breakable and, unless frost-proof, may crack or flake;
- porous, so the soil mix is less likely to become waterlogged, although plants may need more frequent watering;
- excellent for alpines because they provide extra drainage;
- fair for capillary watering systems (see p.485).

Cell packs

With cell packs or modular systems, plant roots are not damaged when separating each unit, whereas seedlings grown in seed trays suffer some initial root damage when transplanted. Expanded plastic foam trays with individual planting cells insulate the soil mix, encouraging growth. They are useful for seeds or pricked-out seedlings, and are as expensive as good-quality polypropylene seed trays but do not last as long.

Trays and Cell Packs

These are used for sowing seeds, inserting cuttings, or growing on young plants. Use a rigid, outer tray to hold flimsy, single-use inserts containing plastic cells. Cell packs are useful for pricking out seedlings and sowing seeds singly.

Long Tom

This pot suits deep-rooted plants that would be restricted by a standard pot.

Tarpaper Ring Pot

This specialized bottomless pot holds soil mix over a growing aggregate.

Sweet Pea Tubes

These are for growing seedlings that develop long or brittle taproot systems.

Hydroculture Pot

The outer pot holds the water supply; the inner one contains the growing medium.

Biodegradable Pots

Use for propagating plants that resent root disturbance when transplanted.

Lattice Pot

This pot for aquatics lets in water, but should be lined with burlap to retain soil.

2

Greenhouses and Frames

MANY PEOPLE RESIST *the idea of installing a greenhouse in the mistaken belief that it is expensive or that it requires detailed gardening knowledge to maintain and use it properly. This is not the case. As well as being the perfect all-weather space for tasks that occur throughout the year, a greenhouse can be an extremely cost-effective investment, allowing you to propagate and grow plants that can later be transferred outside to the garden itself at relatively little cost. Cold frames, like greenhouses, are a boon to gardening, and can easily be integrated into the smallest of spaces. On a large site, greenhouses and frames can be screened from the rest of the garden by shrubs, climbing plants, or trees. In a smaller site, a greenhouse may need more careful integration to ensure that it does not detract from the overall garden picture. Gardening under cover more than compensates for the initial cost and effort, and it opens up a new world of year-round gardening pleasures.*

Gardening under cover

Greenhouses, cold frames, and cloches are useful additions to any style of garden and are available in a range of sizes to fit whatever space is available. Each type of structure has a distinctive function, but they are usually used in conjunction with each other. The most productive gardens use all three.

Unheated structures

Unheated greenhouses are used primarily to advance or extend the growing season of hardy and half-hardy plants. Cold frames fulfill a similar function, although they are also often used for hardening off plants that have been propagated in the greenhouse and for storing dormant plants. Cloches are used *in situ* over plants in the garden itself.

Heated structures

A heated greenhouse is far more versatile than either an unheated greenhouse or a cold frame, and allows a much greater range of plants to be grown. These include many frost-tender species that do not grow satisfactorily in temperate or cold climates without protection. In addition, a heated greenhouse provides a suitable environment in which to propagate plants.

GREENHOUSE STYLE *This traditional-style greenhouse is an integral part of the garden, which extends right up to the sides of the greenhouse. The hedges and trees provide shelter but are not close enough to reduce light penetration significantly. The wooden framework will need to be treated every year or so with wood preservative to give weather resistance, but otherwise only minimal maintenance is required.*

ELEGANT DESIGN
Greenhouses with plastic-covered frames can be extremely attractive, as well as functional. This one is a decorative garden feature in its own right.

POSITIONING THE GREENHOUSE

If the greenhouse is used mostly in the summer, its longest axis should run north to south. If good light in spring is a priority, however – when the sun is lower in the sky – orient the greenhouse east to west to make the best use of available light.

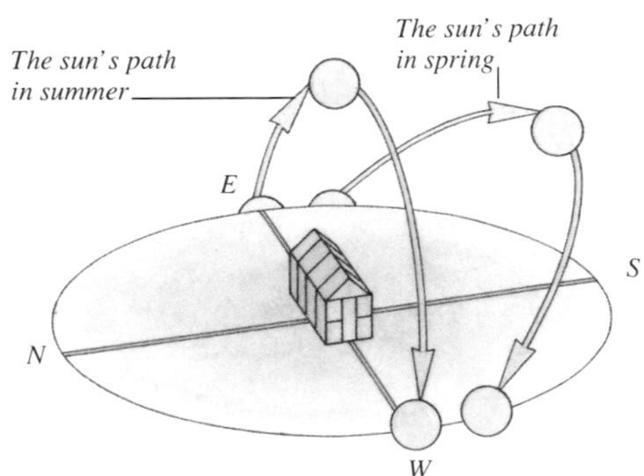

Siting the greenhouse

A greenhouse is best positioned so that it blends in with the overall garden design. It should be positioned in a sheltered site where enough light is available for the plants to grow and thrive. Too much shade will limit the range of plants that may otherwise be grown easily, whereas an exposed site will make the greenhouse expensive to heat or may mean that the plants are not adequately protected on cold nights.

Early planning

It is always worth spending the time to make sure you have chosen the right spot before buying a greenhouse. If possible, make detailed notes in winter or spring of where shadows are cast in the garden by houses and any neighboring garages, trees, or other large, nearby features. Do not site a greenhouse where it will be in shade for more than a few hours each day. Orienting the greenhouse north–south by its longest axis makes the best use of light in summer. For raising annuals and vegetables in spring, or overwintering tender specimens, an east–west orientation provides good light for much of the day.

If there is a possibility that you will want to extend the greenhouse in the future, or build a second smaller one, allow enough space on the site to meet your needs.

Free-standing greenhouse

The best place to site a free-standing greenhouse is in a sheltered, light area away from buildings and large trees. If the site is high or exposed, choose a position that is sheltered by a hedge that acts as a windbreak, or build a fence or other screen. Windbreaks should not cast too much shade onto the greenhouse itself, however. They need not be tall; an 8ft (2.5m) hedge provides shelter for a distance of 40ft (12m) or more.

Do not position a free-standing greenhouse near or between buildings, since this could create a wind tunnel that may damage the greenhouse and the plants inside. Locations at the bottom of a slope or near walls, hedges, or fences on the side of a slope should not be used to site a greenhouse because cold air may become trapped there (see CLIMATE AND THE GARDEN, "Frost pockets and frost damage," p. 515).

Lean-to greenhouse

Place a lean-to greenhouse against a wall that receives a mixture of sun and shade. Do not site it where there is sun for most of the day, otherwise the greenhouse may overheat in summer, even with shading and a good ventilation system.

Access

Bear in mind the need for easy access. A site that is reasonably close to the house is preferable to one at a distance. Also make sure that there is a clear area in front of the greenhouse door for loading and unloading. Any paths leading to the greenhouse should be level. They should preferably have a hard, resilient surface and be wide enough to accommodate a wheelbarrow.

Utilities

Choose a greenhouse site that will be accessible to water and electricity connections, if these services are needed. Consider including both hot and cold water for convenience, especially in winter. Although electricity is not essential for heating, it is necessary for lighting as well as for some thermostatic controls, timing switches, heating cables and mats, and other items.

CHOOSING THE SITE

An open but sheltered site is best for a greenhouse – it should not be positioned in the path of a wind tunnel. If there is no natural protection from the wind, construct a windbreak.

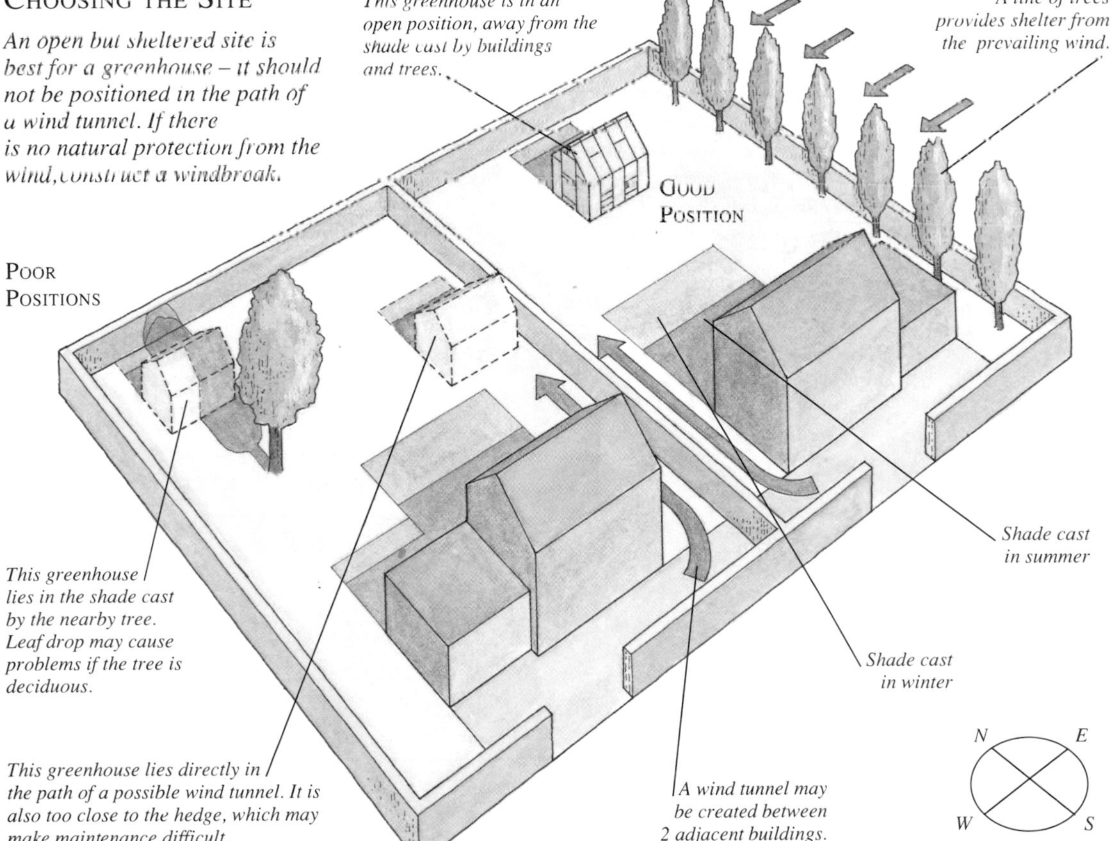

Choosing a greenhouse

Before buying a greenhouse, carefully consider how it will be used in order to select the most suitable style, size, and materials. For example, a greenhouse that is used as a garden room will differ significantly from one that is purely functional. If growing tropical and subtropical plants, an attractively shaped greenhouse, perhaps with room for staging in the center, might enhance the floral display.

Many different styles of greenhouse are available. Some make best use of space or provide optimum ventilation; others conserve heat well or allow better light penetration. When priorities have been decided, the final choice of style will depend on personal preference.

TRADITIONAL SPAN

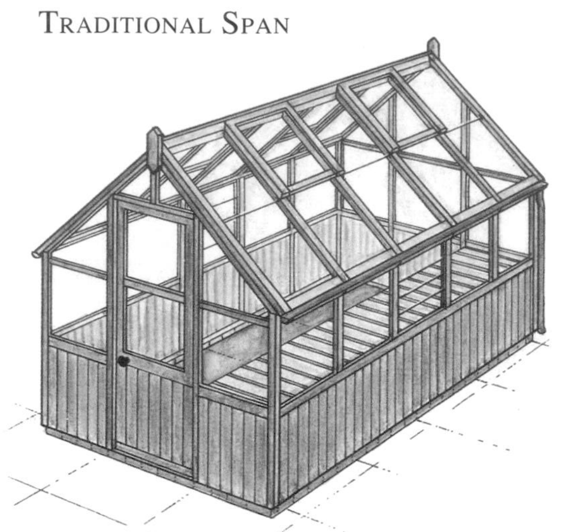

DUTCH LIGHT

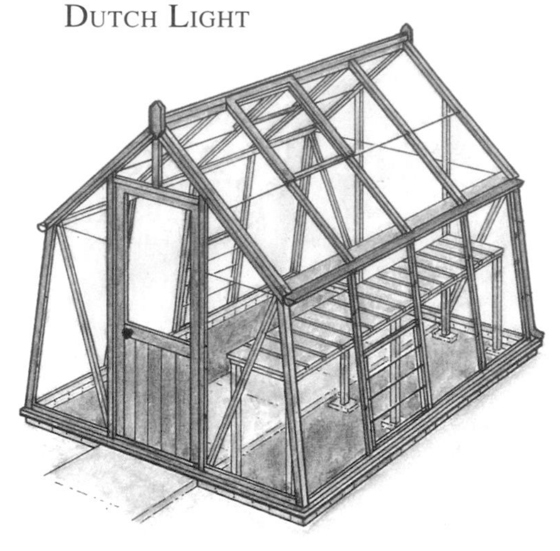

Conventional greenhouses

The more conventional types of greenhouse are suitable for a very wide range of plants. They include traditional span, Dutch light, three-quarter span, lean-to, and Mansard (or curvilinear) greenhouses. All of these may have an aluminum or wooden framework, and either all-glass or part-solid walls (except Dutch light greenhouses). Conventional greenhouses also have a wide range of compatible accessories, including staging and shelves.

Traditional span

The vertical sides and even-span roof of a traditional span greenhouse are extremely practical in terms of growing space and headroom. For raising seedlings and growing border crops, a traditional span greenhouse is likely to provide the best use of space for the least cost.

Dutch light

The sloping sides of Dutch light greenhouses are designed to allow in maximum light, so these greenhouses are suitable for border crops, especially low-growing ones such as lettuces. The large panes of glass (lights) are expensive to replace because of the size – the traditional dimensions are $30^3/_4$ x 59in (77 x 145cm). The glass panes slide into the frame and are secured using cleats fixed with galvanized nails.

The panes of glass on the roof overlap slightly to keep out rain and increase rigidity of the panes. This may cause loss of heat, if the panes overlap too loosely.

THREE-QUARTER SPAN

LEAN-TO

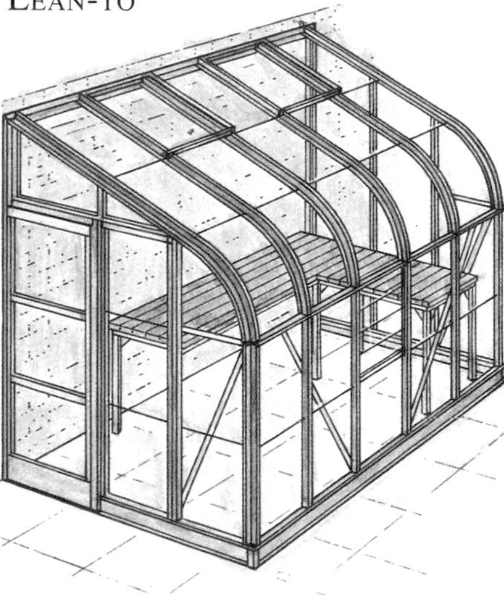

MANSARD

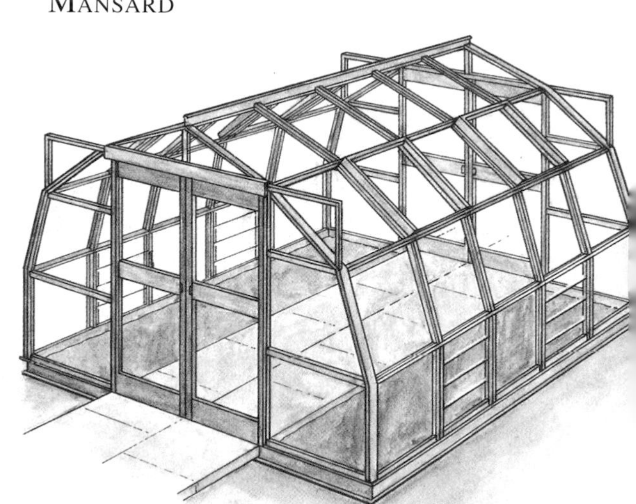

Three-quarter span

A three-quarter span greenhouse is positioned with one of its sides against a wall. Light is a little more restricted than in a free-standing model, so this type of greenhouse is best positioned beside a sunny wall, although this may mean that additional shading is required in summer. The wall provides extra warmth and insulation in the greenhouse, especially if it is a house wall (see also "Lean-to," right).

Lean-to

Where there is insufficient space for a free-standing structure, a lean-to greenhouse is an invaluable choice, particularly if a mainly decorative showhouse is favored.

Many are similar in appearance to conservatories and may be used as garden rooms. Installing electricity, natural gas, or a water supply in a lean-to that is adjacent to a house wall is cheaper and generally involves less work than laying wires or pipes to a greenhouse that is some distance from the house. In addition, the warmth of the house wall may reduce the level of heating required. The wall stores heat, from both the sun (especially if the wall is south-facing) and the domestic heating system, which is then released into the greenhouse.

The wall also provides good insulation, so that less heat escapes from a lean-to than from many other types of greenhouse.

Mansard

The Mansard (curvilinear) greenhouse has slanting sides and roof panels that are designed to allow maximum entry of available light. The full benefit is gained only in an open position with no shade from surrounding buildings or trees. A Mansard greenhouse is suitable for plants that need maximum light during the winter, when daylight hours are short and light levels are also correspondingly low.

DOME-SHAPED

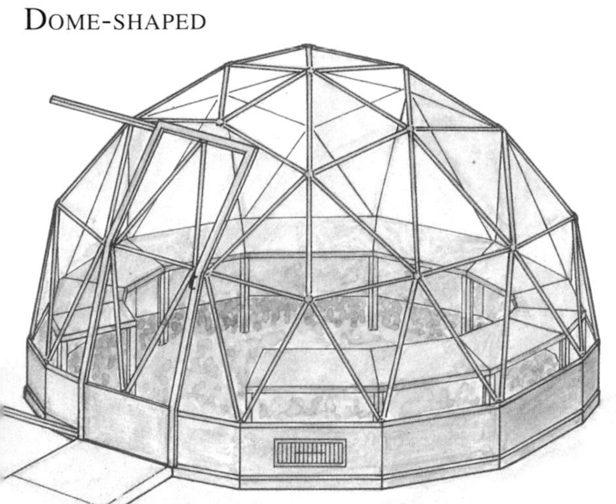

POLYGONAL

ALPINE HOUSE

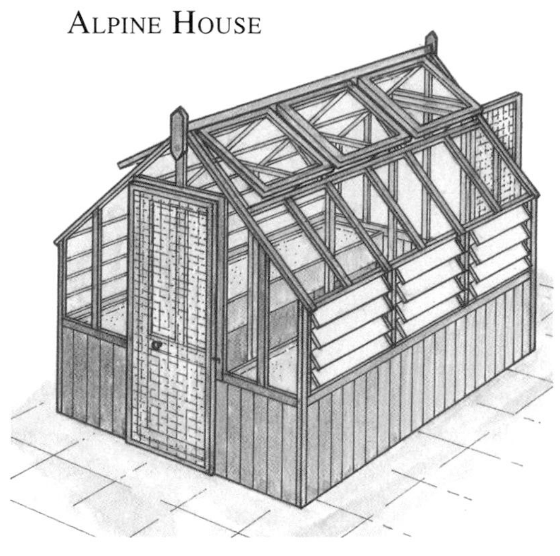

Specialist greenhouses

There are many specialist types of greenhouse, including dome-shaped, polygonal, alpine house, conservation, mini, and polytunnel, all of which differ markedly in appearance from the more conventional types. Some are designed as highly decorative garden features in their own right, while others may offer particularly good value or be suited to specific types of plant.

Dome-shaped
This is an elegant design that is particularly useful in exposed positions since it is stable and offers less wind resistance than traditional greenhouses. Light transmission is excellent because the multiangled glass panes and aluminum frame allow in maximum light. Dome-shaped structures may have limited headroom around the edge, and plants may also be difficult to reach. Extensions are not generally available, and fittings may be limited to those produced by the manufacturer.

Polygonal
Octagonal and other polygonal greenhouses are frequently chosen where appearance is important, and they may provide a focal point within the garden. They are generally more expensive than traditional greenhouses of similar size and, because they are not very common, there may be a limited choice of accessories. The irregular shape may also restrict growing space. Fitting replacement panes of glass in a polygonal greenhouse is more difficult than in a conventional structure.

Alpine house
This type of greenhouse is traditionally wooden-framed with louver vents extending all along the sides for the most effective ventilation. Usually, alpine houses are not heated and are closed only in the coldest winter weather, so insulation is not required. Unsuitable for tender plants, they are used for plants that thrive in bright, well-ventilated conditions, yet which require some overhead protection from dampness and rain. Their shape is similar to that of a traditional span greenhouse.

CONSERVATION

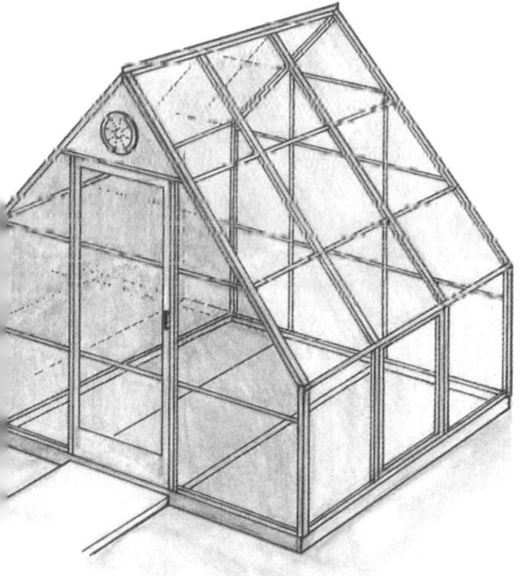

MINI

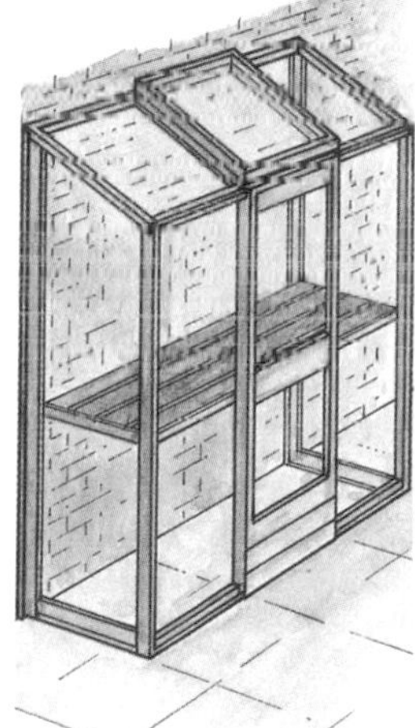

POLYTUNNEL

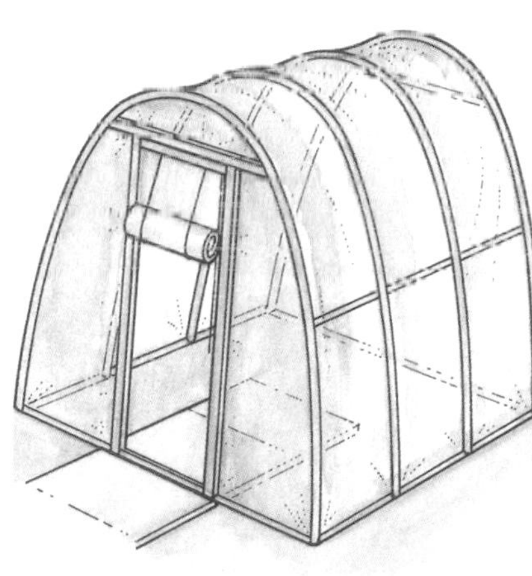

Conservation greenhouse
This type of greenhouse has many special features that are designed to save as much energy as possible. The roof panels are angled to allow optimum light penetration in winter yet reduce hot summer sun, and mirrored surfaces are also used to reflect light within the greenhouse itself. Solar collectors may be used to store heat in winter. Double glazing and insulation are fitted as standard features.

Mini-greenhouse
This provides a useful, low-cost introduction to greenhouse gardening. Mini-greenhouses are usually aluminum and placed against a wall or fence. They should preferably face southeast or southwest so that maximum light penetrates. It is the best choice if only a small number of plants is to be grown, since space is limited. However, there is often useful space beneath the staging for overwintering plants or for storage.

Access may be a problem – all work has to be done from the outside. Ventilation may be inadequate, and rapid temperature changes often occur. This type of house is normally used only during the spring peak growing season.

Plastic polytunnel greenhouse
Where visual appearance is not important and low-cost protection is required – such as in the vegetable plot – a polytunnel greenhouse has many benefits. It consists of a large, tunnel-shaped frame covered with heavy-duty transparent plastic sheets. It is widely used for crops that require some protection but not the warm conditions of a traditional greenhouse. Polytunnels keep out some of the winter cold and provide useful wind protection throughout the year. Since they are light and relatively easy to move, they are often used in plots where crop rotation is carried out.

For a large growing area, commercial polytunnels are a cost-effective investment, but for a small garden a more traditional shape may be a better choice. Some polytunnels include staging, although most are intended primarily for growing crops at ground level, directly in the soil, in pots, or in grow bags.

Ventilation may be a problem. The door offers a reasonably efficient method of ventilation, especially in large tunnels with openings at each end. Some have sides that roll up. The plastic sheeting should be routinely checked and replaced every year or two, since it gradually becomes brittle and likely to rip, as well as opaque, thereby restricting light penetration.

Choosing the size

The greenhouse will almost inevitably seem too small once it is filled with plants so, if possible, buy one that can be extended. Although a large greenhouse costs more to heat than a small one, it is possible to partition off a section in winter, and leave the remainder unheated (see "Thermal screens," p.482).

Space considerations

A greenhouse that is used primarily for ornamentals should have plenty of room inside for staging, which may be tiered, and possibly a central or end display. To provide space for propagation and growing on, it may be necessary to divide up the space with a partition. Alternatively, use a cold frame for propagation.

Length, width, and height

A length of 8ft (2.5m) and a width of 6ft (2m) are the minimum, practical dimensions for a general-purpose, traditional greenhouse. A smaller greenhouse than this limits the range of plants that may be grown, and may make it difficult to control the environment. Drafts and rapid heat buildup in summer tend to be more of a problem in small greenhouses, and may lead to sudden fluctuations in temperature. In greenhouses that are more than 6ft (2m) wide, it may also be difficult to reach pots and ventilation toward the back of the staging. Erecting staging to a width of 2ft (60cm) on either side allows a path of the same width to run down the middle.

If border crops are to be grown, choose a greenhouse that is 8ft (2.5m) wide with borders to a width of 3ft (1m). A width of 8ft (2.5m) is also suitable if a wider path is required for a wheelchair or to enable a wheelbarrow to be used easily.

Many small greenhouses have low eaves and comparatively low ridges, which make it tiring to work over the border or staging for long periods. To gain more height, build the greenhouse on a brick base or dig out a sunken path.

Choosing the materials

Greenhouses are made in a range of materials. The most important considerations when choosing both the framework and glazing for the greenhouse are practicality, expense, and the amount of maintenance required. The appearance of the materials may also be important.

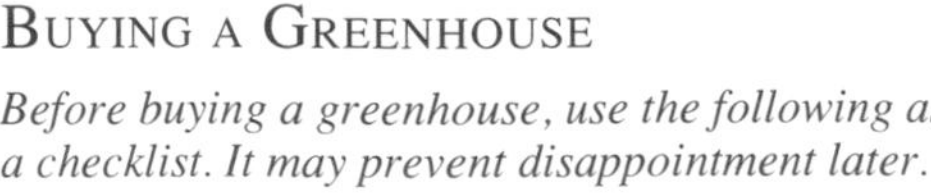

BUYING A GREENHOUSE

Before buying a greenhouse, use the following as a checklist. It may prevent disappointment later.

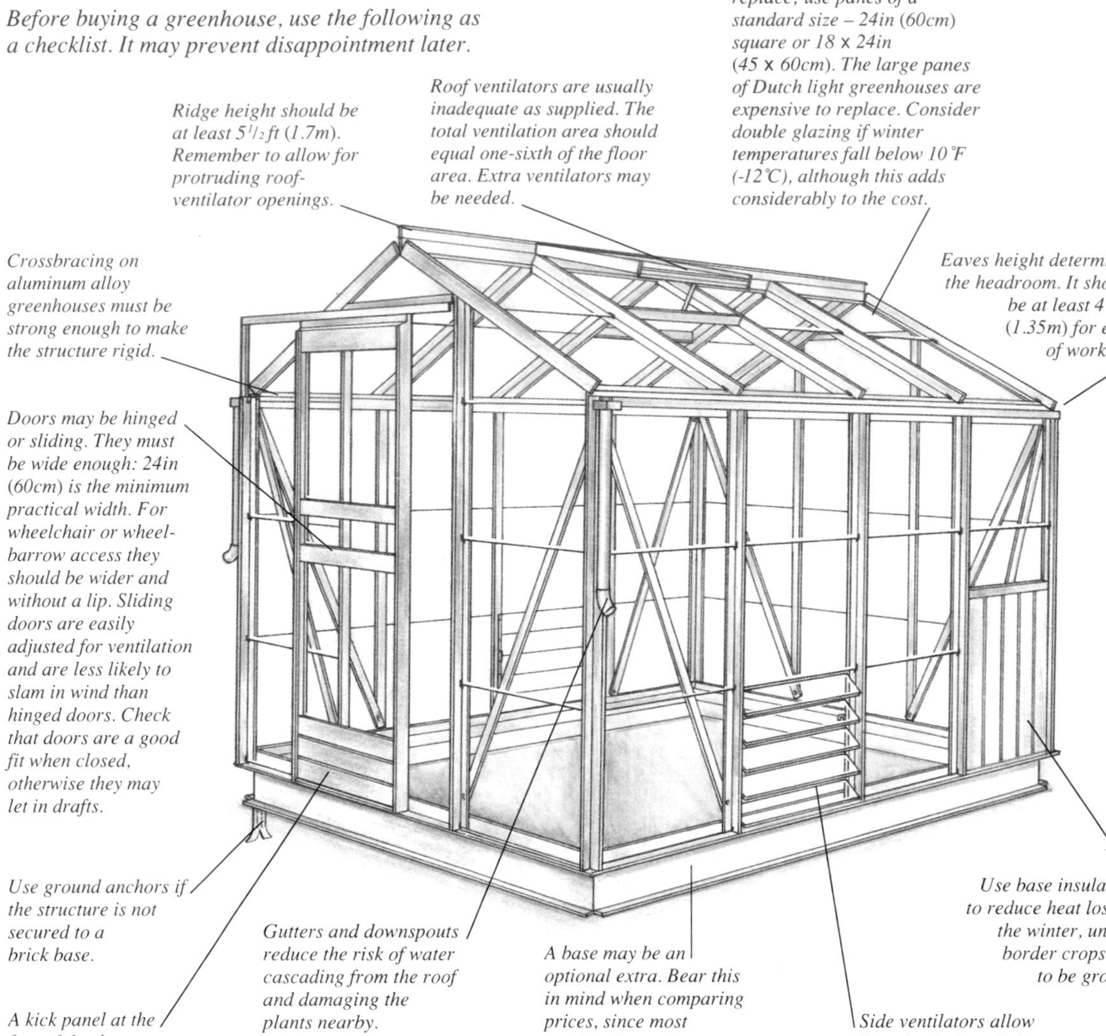

The framework

Wooden frameworks have been the traditional choice and are generally considered to be the most attractive. They may be expensive, however, and are also heavy to construct. If possible, choose a durable hardwood. Cedar, cypress, and redwood are excellent choices. They are rot-resistant, do not warp easily, and, if treated every year or two with a quality wood preservative, retain their color well.

Some woods are regionally abundant or are the traditional choice. Check with a local contractor or building supply store to determine which wood is best for your needs and budget (see also "Wooden framework," p.491).

Greenhouses with aluminum alloy frames are almost completely maintenance-free. They do not retain heat quite as well as wooden

CONSTRUCTION MATERIALS

WOOD
A wooden frame is the traditional choice for garden greenhouses. Hardwoods are low maintenance.

ALUMINUM
Aluminum alloy frames are light but extremely sturdy and need only minimum maintenance.

STEEL
Plastic-coated steel frames are very strong but must be treated regularly to prevent rust.

frames but the difference is minimal and should not be considered a serious disadvantage.

Galvanized steel is also often used for greenhouse frames. Steel frames are light and easy to construct but extremely strong. They are cheaper than wooden or aluminum frames but must be painted regularly (see "Metal framework," p.491). Aluminum and steel frames are narrower than wooden ones and allow larger panes of glass to be used, resulting in better light penetration.

Glass panes
Regular glass is the most satisfactory glazing material for a greenhouse. It allows excellent light penetration, far better than modern high-tech substitutes. It is easy to clean, does not discolor, and retains considerably more heat than plastic glazing materials. Glass is not as robust as plastic glazing, however, so breakages and cracks may be a problem, since damaged panes must be replaced quickly.

Plastic glazing
Plastics are generally more expensive and less durable than glass. They discolor more readily and also tend to become scratched over time, which is both unsightly and, more important, may cut down on the amount of light that is transmitted if the discoloring is severe.

Acrylic sheets are used to glaze the curved eaves of many greenhouses because the acrylic may be shaped easily to give an elegant outline to the structure. Condensation occurs more readily on its surface than on a conventional glass pane. Rigid polycarbonate sheets are also often used to glaze greenhouses. They are easy to handle, lightweight, virtually unbreakable, and have good insulating properties. They are relatively easily scratched, however, and tend to discolor.

Twin-walled polycarbonate has particularly good insulating qualities, but its opacity may be a major problem in the greenhouse.

Sizing
Most local glass merchants will cut glass panes to size for little cost. However, it is important to make sure that any measurements you give are accurate. Calculate them carefully, ensuring that there will be sufficient clearance for the glass to engage with the mounting system that is to be used. If plastic glazing material is used, it will be supplied in sheets and is not usually difficult to cut to size at home using a sharp craft knife and straightedge.

GLAZING MATERIAL

Rigid plastic glazing material is light and easy to fit. This is twin-walled polycarbonate, which provides good insulation.

Erecting the greenhouse

A greenhouse requires far less maintenance and lasts much longer if it is properly erected in the first place. The information listed below is necessarily of a general nature because it applies to many different greenhouse types and designs. Always follow the manufacturer's instructions for particular advice. If in doubt on any point, check the details with either the supplier or the greenhouse manufacturer.

Before beginning to construct a greenhouse, look into the applicable local building codes. Greenhouses often require a building permit, and building inspectors will be involved throughout the process.

Preparing the site

Always erect a greenhouse on firm, level ground, otherwise the frame may warp and become twisted and cause the glass to crack. The site must first be cleared of weeds, since persistent weeds are very difficult to eradicate when the greenhouse is erected in position. If the site selected for the greenhouse has been recently dug over, allow the soil to settle for a few weeks, and then compact it with a heavy roller.

Foundations
Aluminum greenhouses that are smaller than 6ft wide and 8ft long (2 x 2.5m) do not usually require a thick concrete base. Simply dig a hole at each corner approximately 10–18in (25–45cm) deep, then wedge in the ground anchors (see p.480) with stone chips and pour in a concrete mix to fix them securely. If a more substantial foundation is required, dig a trench approximately 10in (25cm) deep, filling it with 6in (15cm) of compacted stone chips. Fix the anchoring bolts in place and finish off with poured concrete or paving slabs, making sure that the ground is level.

Brick bases
A brick base must be constructed to the precise measurements provided by the manufacturer, on solid concrete footings deep enough to withstand your winter conditions. Check with local contractors for the footing depths recommended for your area. For further instructions, see *How to Make a Concrete Footing*, p.504.

Wooden greenhouses

The sections of a wooden greenhouse are usually supplied complete and only need to be bolted together and then fixed to the base.

Base
Either use interlocking concrete blocks for the base, or build a solid concrete foundation or brick base (see "Foundations" and "Brick bases," left and above).

Sides, gable ends, and roof
Before the greenhouse is delivered, check what kind of bolts or fixings are required and whether they will be supplied. First bolt the sides and gable ends together to form the main framework. Follow the supplier's advice for the exact method of fixing this to the base or foundations, since designs vary. The foot of the frame may contain integral anchorage points for securely bolting it down. Bolt any internal partitions to the frame, then add the roof sections and bolt them in place.

Some wooden greenhouses are supplied as sections with unglazed frames, with the glass or plastic glazing supplied separately. Others have preglazed frames, but these are heavy to move – two or more people may be required to support them.

If the wood has not been treated and is not rot-resistant, it is important to paint all the woodwork with a preservative at this stage, before the greenhouse is glazed.

Glazing
If putty is to be used for glazing, it is usually supplied with the greenhouse. Apply it to the glazing bars, and seat the glass carefully. The glass panes are usually secured in place with galvanized steel or brass sprigs. If these are not supplied by the manufacturer, they may be purchased from any hardware shop.

If a dry glazing system (that is, one that does not require putty) is to be used, simply follow the supplier's instructions.

Whichever method is used, glaze the sides and gable ends first, overlapping the panes by ½in (1cm). Use soft metal overlap clips to hold the glass panes firmly together.

BUILDING A BRICK BASE

If using a brick base for the greenhouse, lay proper foundations first. Check with the greenhouse manufacturer before building the base to make sure that the dimensions are correct.

CONCRETE FOUNDATIONS

For solid greenhouse foundations, dig a trench to match the dimensions of the greenhouse, filling it with stone chips and a layer of concrete.

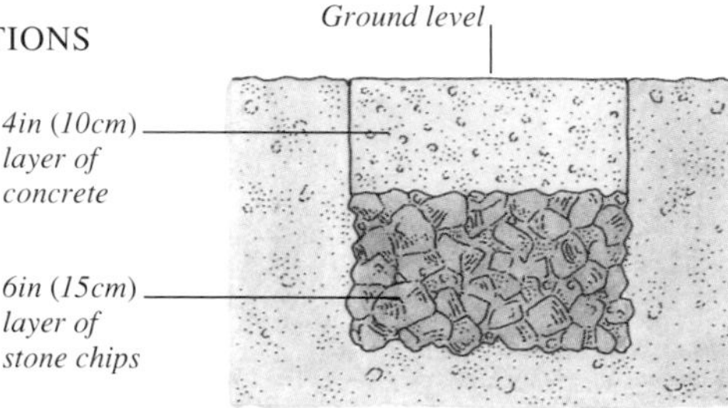

GLAZING BARS AND CLIPS FOR METAL GREENHOUSES

GLAZING BARS
These form the framework of the greenhouse.

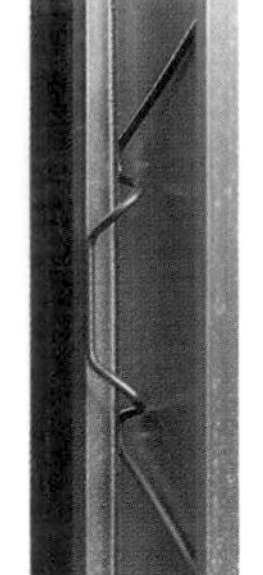

W-SHAPED WIRE CLIP
Use this type of clip to hold glass and plastic panes firmly in place.

SPRUNG BAND CLIPS
An alternative to wire clips, these fix onto the frame.

Ventilators and door

Ventilators are supplied as an integral part of the preassembled sections, so the number you ordered should be in place. Screw on hinged doors and simply insert sliding doors into the runners.

Metal greenhouses

Greenhouses with metal frames are delivered in home-assembly kit form, and the frame is supplied in sections – the base, sides, gable ends, and roof. The sections are in turn divided into separate component pieces that need to be bolted together.

Base

Assemble the base first, ensuring that it is perfectly level and square to prevent any warping and twisting of the frame. Measure from each corner to the one diagonally opposite – the measurements must be the same. The base must be securely anchored; this is particularly important in windy or exposed areas.

If fixing ground anchors to a concrete foundation, use the anchoring bolts provided, otherwise simply set the ground anchors in rubble and concrete at each corner of the base.

A GROUND ANCHOR

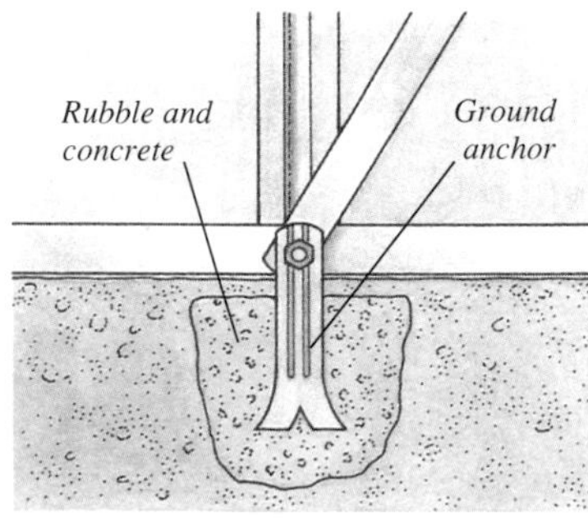

Small greenhouses may be secured using ground anchors. Wedge them in place with stone chips before pouring in a concrete mix.

Sides, gable ends, and roof

Assemble the sides, gable ends, and roof sections in the sequence recommended by the manufacturer in the instruction sheet. The sides are usually put together first.

First make sure that everything has been included. Then, before assembling, lay out on the ground all the pieces for each section, in their correct relative positions. Bolt the pieces for each section (sides and gable ends) together. Decide at this point where the vents are to be positioned and leave suitable gaps for them, as necessary. Do not tighten the nuts until all the sections are fully assembled and have been loosely put together.

Bolt the sections together one to another, and then to the base, then bolt on the roof bars and ridge bar.

Ventilators

Ventilator frames are assembled separately, then bolted onto the roof and sides as required, before glazing. This gives greater flexibility than with wooden greenhouses when choosing both the number and position of ventilators. The hinges of roof ventilators usually slide in a groove in the molding.

Glazing

Glazing strips are usually used for metal greenhouses. Cut the strips to the appropriate length, and then press them into the grooves in the glazing bars – shaped pieces of metal that form the framework to hold the glass securely in position.

Glaze the sides of the greenhouse first, placing the glass squarely between the glazing bars, leaving about 1/8in (3mm) clearance on each side of the glass panes for the glazing clips to be attached. The upper panes of glass should overlap the lower ones by about 1/2in (1cm). Secure them with overlap glazing clips – pieces of metal bent into S shapes that hook over the lower pane and hold the upper one firmly in place.

Once each pane is in position, use glazing clips, pressing them into place between the glazing bars and panes to hold the glass. A little pressure will be required to overcome the natural spring in the metal.

Glaze the gable ends of the greenhouse and then the roof, using the same technique.

Fitting the door

Metal greenhouses usually have sliding doors. These should be bolted together and slid into the runners provided in the end frame. A stop is supplied for bolting on afterward to prevent the door from coming off the runners if it is opened too quickly. The door should be glazed when it has been fixed in position.

Fitting the staging

The staging supplied by the manufacturer is designed to be bolted or screwed to the framework. This is best done at the same time as the greenhouse is erected, especially for octagonal and dome-shaped greenhouses, which have staging specially designed to fit. If solid staging is used, leave a gap of several inches between the inside of the greenhouse and the staging to allow free air circulation.

Installing electricity, natural gas, and water

Installing an outdoor power supply is not a job for the amateur. The installation of electricity in a greenhouse must be properly carried out by a qualified electrician, although considerable savings may be made by excavating the trench for the cord yourself and then refilling it later when the job is completed. Alternatively, the cord may be run overhead if your greenhouse is close to the house and it will not be unsightly. Your electrician will be able to advise you whether or not this is a practical option. Armored cords and waterproof fittings should always be used for safety.

Electricity has many practical uses in the greenhouse: it provides power for heating, lighting, propagators, timers, heating cables, and electrically powered garden tools of various types.

Natural gas is useful for heating the greenhouse. If the greenhouse is sited close to the house, it may be possible to extend the system; otherwise, use an outside tank. Consult your local utility to discuss the feasibility and cost of installing lines for natural gas. You might save money by offering to do the digging yourself.

If you already have an outdoor faucet, you may be able to add a branch to its pipe and run it to the greenhouse. In regions with cold winters, either the system must be buried below the frost line or, if the greenhouse will not be used during the winter, provisions must be made to drain all the lines before the onset of severe cold.

FITTING A PANE IN A METAL GREENHOUSE

Attach overlap glazing clips to the base of the pane. Wearing gloves, lift the pane into place, gently pressing the top edge into position before hooking the bottom edge onto the lower pane. Secure the pane with glazing clips (see inset), pressing them gently until they slot into position.

Creating the right environment

Creating the right balance of conditions in a greenhouse to suit the plants grown in it is the essence of successful greenhouse gardening.

For tender plants, the temperature maintained is vital. In a heated greenhouse, choose an efficient, reliable, and economical heater. In any greenhouse, good insulation to retain heat and keep out drafts must be balanced with the need for thorough ventilation. Shading is essential in most greenhouses during warm and hot months to help prevent the plants from overheating; see PRINCIPLES OF PROPAGATION, *Shading Greenhouses (Temperate climates)*, p.544.

Atmospheric humidity should be kept at a level that suits the plants being grown. Automatic methods of watering tend to increase humidity so, for most plants, special humidifiers may not be essential. Special lighting is often useful to increase the growth potential of plants.

Greenhouse temperature

The choice of plants to be grown in a greenhouse is determined largely by the temperature at which it is maintained (see "The greenhouse environment," p.429). There are four categories of greenhouse: cold, cool, temperate, and warm. The environment is controlled slightly differently in each type.

Cold

A cold greenhouse is not heated at all. Insulation (see p.482) is needed to keep out the worst of the winter cold, and some form of shading (see p.484) is needed in summer. Thorough ventilation (see p.483) is important throughout the year.

A cold greenhouse can be used to grow summer crops, to overwinter slightly tender plants where winters are mild, or to propagate cuttings (although a propagator will increase the success rate; see p.488). An unheated greenhouse may also permit an early display of spring bulbs.

An unheated greenhouse is suitable for alpines – some types are specifically designed to provide maximum ventilation for these plants (see "Alpine house," p.477), although any greenhouse with louver ventilators along the sides is adequate.

Cool/frost-free

A cool greenhouse is one that is heated just enough to keep out frost. This means that a minimum daytime temperature range between 41°F (5°C) and 50°F (10°C), and a nighttime temperature of no less than 35°F (2°C), is needed.

To ensure that these temperatures are maintained, a heater capable of a large temperature lift is a necessity in winter, in case the outside temperature falls many degrees below freezing. An electric heater with a thermostat (see p.482) is most likely to do this efficiently. Insulation, thorough ventilation, and shading control are necessary, as with cold greenhouses.

A frost-free greenhouse may be used to grow all the types of plant mentioned for cold greenhouses. In addition, frost-tender plants can be overwintered, and summer crops or flowering pot plants grown. A propagator will be needed for germinating seeds. Young seedlings will benefit from the extra light provided by a grow lamp (see p.485).

Temperate

A slightly warmer greenhouse with a minimum daytime temperature range between 50°F (10°C) and 55°F (13°C), and with a minimum nighttime temperature of 45°F (7°C), is suitable for growing a good selection of hardy, half-hardy, and tender pot plants, as well as vegetables.

Additional warmth is necessary in spring for propagation, supplied by a propagator or by boosting the ordinary heating for the required period. Supplementary lighting from a grow lamp is useful. Shading and good ventilation are required, especially in warm and hot months.

Warm

A warm greenhouse has a daytime temperature range between 55°F (13°C) and 64°F (18°C), with a minimum nighttime temperature of 55°F (13°C). Such high temperatures enable the amateur gardener to grow a large range of plants, including tropical and subtropical ornamentals, fruits, and vegetables. Use a warm greenhouse for propagating plants and raising seedlings without propagation equipment, although a grow lamp will be useful.

Very good ventilation (preferably automatic), cooling pads, an efficient method of shading, and high humidity (see p.484) in hot weather are essential.

THE GREENHOUSE EFFECT

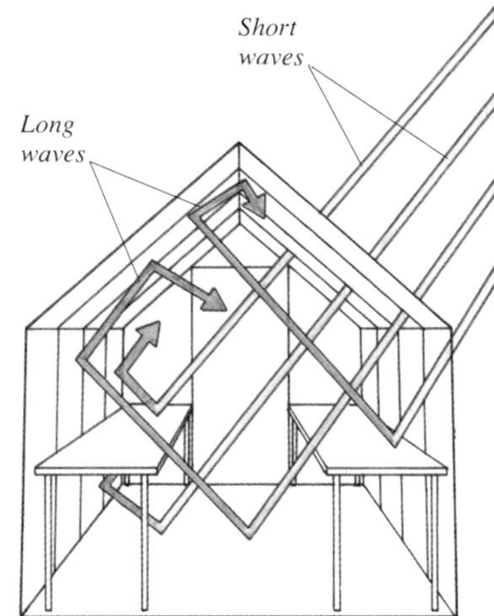

Light passes through glass as short-wave radiation, warming everything inside, including floor, staging, soil, and plants. Heat then reradiates from the warmed objects as long waves, which cannot pass through the glass, and so increases heat inside the greenhouse.

HOW TO BALANCE THE ENVIRONMENT OF A GREENHOUSE

	HEATING (see p.482)	INSULATION (see p.482)	VENTILATION (see p.483)	SHADING (see p.484)	HUMIDITY (see p.484)	WATERING (see p.485)	LIGHTING (see p.485)
COLD No minimum temperature	None.	Insulate against severely cold drafts and damp, foggy weather in winter.	Thorough ventilation is essential to prevent damp, stagnant conditions in winter.	Shade vulnerable plants in summer with a shading wash, blinds, meshes or fabric, or rigid sheets.	Unlikely to be a problem in summer. Maintain a "dry" atmosphere in winter by ventilating.	Water by hand in winter. Use a capillary system, soaker hose, or trickle system in summer.	Grow lamps are unlikely to be needed for the type of plants grown.
COOL Minimum temperature 35°F (2°C)	A thermostatically controlled electric heater is preferable, but gas or kerosene heaters may also be used. A cold alarm is useful if tender plants are grown.	In winter, as for a cold greenhouse. In spring, good insulation is extremely important if frost-tender plants are grown.	Ventilate freely, especially if a gas or kerosene heater is used, to disperse water vapor and toxic fumes.	Shade to control the temperature in summer – shading washes or blinds do this most efficiently. Fit automatic blinds, if possible.	Damping down is beneficial to increase humidity in summer.	As for a cold greenhouse, except that an overhead system may also be used in summer.	Grow lamps may be useful, especially in spring when natural light is poor, for plants at an early stage of development.
TEMPERATE Minimum temperature 45°F (7°C)	A heater (preferably electric) fitted with a thermostat is required. A cold alarm is also essential.	As for cold and cool greenhouses. Thermal screens are useful in spring for propagation.	As for a cool greenhouse. Automatic vent openers are extremely useful in summer.	As for a cool greenhouse.	Maintain high humidity in spring and summer, especially around cuttings and seedlings.	An automatic watering system is useful throughout the year.	Grow lamps are useful in winter and spring for extending daylength.
WARM Minimum temperature 55°F (13°C)	As for a temperate greenhouse.	Good insulation is essential throughout the year to minimize heating costs.	Automatic vent openers fitted to several vents simplify temperature control enormously.	Automatic blinds are desirable in summer.	High humidity is required throughout the year.	As for a temperate greenhouse.	As for a temperate greenhouse.

Heating

It is important to maintain the correct temperature in the greenhouse for the range of plants you have chosen to grow. Select a heater that is powerful enough to maintain the required minimum temperature efficiently. Other factors to consider when choosing a greenhouse heater include convenience, the cost of installation, and running costs.

Electric heaters

These are generally the most reliable, efficient, and convenient to use in the greenhouse, although an electricity supply will be needed to run them (see "Installing electricity, natural gas, and water," p.480). They are usually thermostatically controlled, which means that no heat is wasted, and they do not require regular refueling or maintenance. In addition, electric heaters do not produce fumes or water vapor.

A number of different types of electric heater is available. These include fan heaters and waterproof tubular heaters, both of which heat the greenhouse effectively. Convector heaters are also used but these do not distribute heat as efficiently. Tubular heaters need to be fitted to the sides of the greenhouse, just above floor level. Other heaters may be moved around as desired.

Electric fan heaters are particularly useful because they promote good air circulation, which helps to maintain an even temperature and minimizes the spread of disease. They may also be used to cool the greenhouse in warm weather if the heating element is switched off.

Natural gas heaters

Natural gas heating systems can be run off your house lines (see "Installing electricity, natural gas, and water," p.480) or from an outside tank. They are not as convenient to use as electric heaters: although they may have thermostats, these are not usually calibrated in degrees, so you will need to experiment.

If an outside tank is used, most suppliers will routinely check it to keep it filled, depending on the temperature. Consider having two bottles connected by an automatic switch-over valve in case one runs out. Propane gas releases fumes and water vapor as it burns, so ventilation is important.

Kerosene heaters

These are not as efficient as electric or natural gas heaters in their use of fuel because they are not controlled by a thermostat. Kerosene heaters may therefore be expensive to run if a high temperature needs to be maintained, since some energy may be wasted. However, they are inexpensive to buy in the first place and there is no installation cost.

When using kerosene heaters, thorough ventilation is required because some plant-toxic fumes and water vapor are produced as a by-product of combustion; a humid, stagnant atmosphere may encourage disease if ventilation is poor. Other drawbacks include the need to transport and store fuel, and to check the fuel level and wick every day (to ensure that it is burning cleanly).

Circulated hot water

Solid fuel (that is, coal, coke, and wood) hot water systems are now rarely used in greenhouses. Oil- and gas-fired circulated hot water systems are sometimes used, but seldom in small greenhouses.

Although the distribution of heat through hot water pipes provides good heat transfer, often only about 50 percent of the energy released is used. Greenhouses attached to a house may be heated by connecting them to the home heating system. Check with local contractors and utilities for details.

Thermometer and cold alarm

If the heater in a greenhouse is not thermostatically controlled, use a maximum/minimum thermometer to check that the correct overnight temperatures are being maintained for the plants being grown.

In regions where the temperature can be severe, a cold alarm is a useful safeguard if the greenhouse contains tender plants. If the air temperature unexpectedly drops to near freezing, for example through a power failure or heater breakdown, an alarm bell will sound remotely (this will usually be somewhere in the home), allowing you time to protect the plants.

A Cold Alarm

Install a cold alarm if growing tender plants that may be damaged or killed if the temperature falls.

Insulation Material

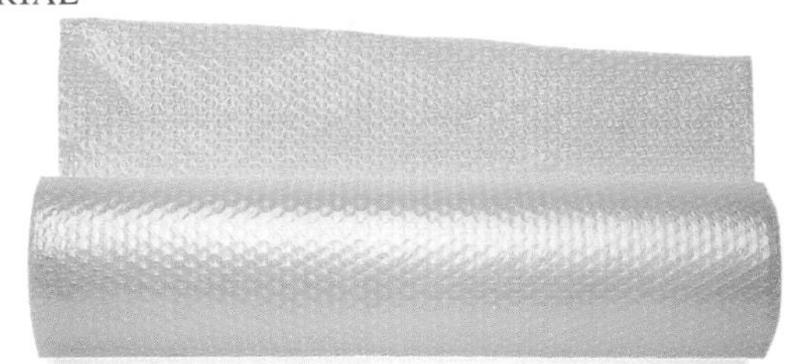

Bubble plastic is useful for insulating a greenhouse and reduces heat loss considerably. Cut it to size and attach it securely to the framework.

Insulation

Insulation in the greenhouse may reduce heating costs considerably. If a minimum temperature of 45°F (7°C) is required, for example, the cost of insulation may be recovered within just a few seasons – in a single winter in particularly cold areas. The higher the temperature to be maintained, and the colder the region, the more cost-effective insulation is likely to be. Care in choosing the right material is required, however, since some insulation materials may reduce the amount of light reaching the plants.

Double glazing

The most efficient method of insulating the entire greenhouse is to fit double glazing. This is best done at the time of construction, if possible. Double glazing is expensive, but the long-term money and energy savings can be great.

Flexible plastic insulation

Bubble plastic, which consists of double or triple skins of transparent plastic with air cells in between, is a very efficient method of insulation. A single layer of plastic sheeting is not as efficient as bubble plastic at reducing heat loss, but it is less expensive and does not cut out so much light. Plastic sheets can be used in winter as a form of double glazing. To attach the insulation material, use suction-pad fasteners or clips that fit into the greenhouse frame.

Thermal screens

These consist of sheets of clear plastic or translucent material, such as a cross-laminated fabric, that are attached to wires between the eaves and drawn horizontally across the greenhouse in the evening. They are useful for conserving heat at night because they restrict the amount of heat that rises above the eaves, trapping the warmth lower down around the plants.

Vertical screens may also be used to partition off a heated section at one end of the greenhouse with plastic sheeting, leaving the remainder of the area unheated. Plants can be overwintered and early seedlings raised in the heated section.

Special kits for making thermal screens are available, or plastic sheeting and the necessary fixings may be obtained separately.

Base insulation

Base insulation on the floor of glass-to-ground greenhouses reduces heat loss significantly. In winter, place plastic foam panels along the foot of the glass panes to provide extra insulation, removing them before summer border crops are planted.

Thermal Screens

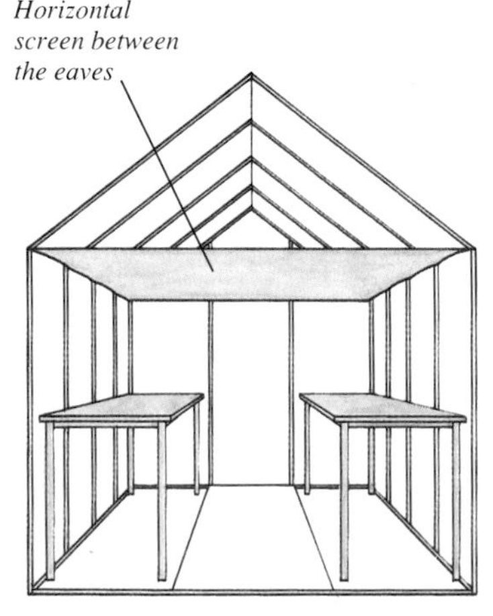

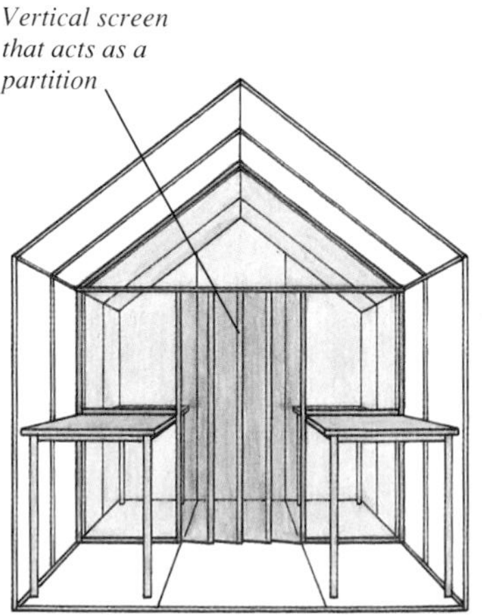

Thermal screens can be drawn horizontally between the eaves. They can also be drawn vertically to partition off a section of the greenhouse that needs to be heated to a higher temperature.

Ventilation

Good ventilation is essential in a greenhouse, even in winter, to avoid a buildup of stuffy or damp, stale air, and to control temperature. In warm areas, air circulation is very important in summer to prevent serious disease problems. It is important that the area covered by ventilators should be equal to at least one-sixth of the floor area.

Extra ventilation

Few greenhouses are supplied with enough ventilators as standard, so order additional air vents or extractor fans when buying a greenhouse. This is an especially important consideration with wooden greenhouses, since it is usually difficult to add them later.

Extra ventilation is particularly important if kerosene or natural gas heating systems are used, to prevent water vapor and fumes from building up to an unacceptable level.

Wind ventilation system

Air exchange in a greenhouse occurs when external air movements, caused by gusts of wind, replace interior warm, humid air with fresh air. If ventilators are placed on the sides and roof of the greenhouse, and are also staggered, this will ensure that air circulates throughout the entire area – if vents are placed directly opposite one another, air will simply blow straight through the greenhouse.

Doors may also be kept open in summer to increase ventilation. Consider adding a screen door to keep out birds and pets.

Chimney ventilation system

Chimney-effect ventilation depends on warm, humid air rising out of roof vents and being replaced by fresh air that is drawn in as a result through lower ventilators. For greatest efficiency, position them along the lower sides of the greenhouse either above or below the staging.

Fan ventilation system

Fan ventilation is a mechanically driven system that works by extracting air from the greenhouse at head height, or slightly higher, and drawing in fresh air through vents lower down and usually at the opposite end of the greenhouse.

Hinged ventilators

These may be fitted to the sides or roof of the greenhouse and should open wide, to an angle of about 45°. This will allow maximum airflow while at the same time preventing direct gusts of wind from entering the greenhouse and possibly causing damage to the plants or even to the structure itself.

THE PRINCIPLES OF GREENHOUSE VENTILATION

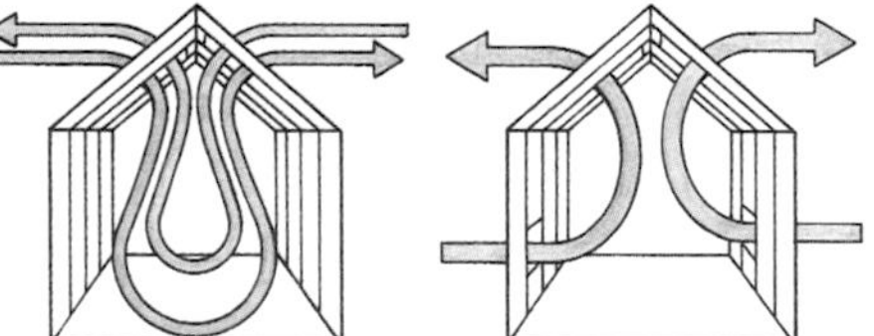

WIND EFFECT
Fresh air blows into the greenhouse, circulates, and then escapes through an open vent on the opposite side.

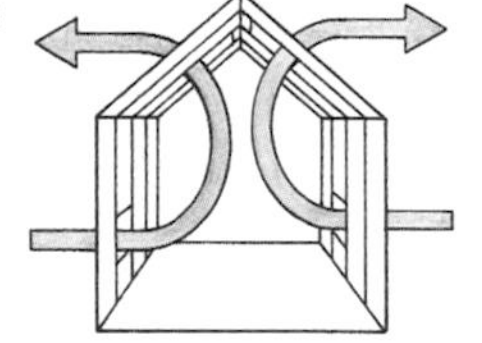

CHIMNEY EFFECT
Warm air rises and escapes through open vents in the roof, drawing fresh, cooler air in lower down.

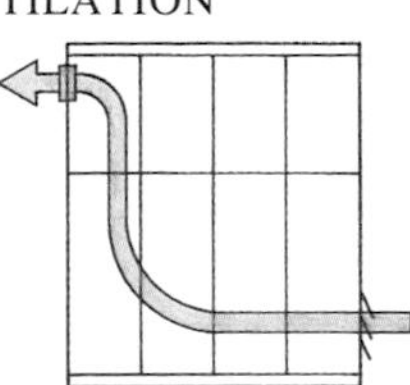

FAN VENTILATION
Air is drawn out by a fan at the top of the greenhouse and drawn in through open vents lower down.

Louver ventilators

Usually positioned below the height of the staging, louver window ventilators are particularly useful for controlling the flow of air throughout the greenhouse in winter, when roof ventilators may allow too much heat to escape. The louver vents must close tightly, however, so that they exclude all drafts.

Automatic vent openers

Autovent openers simplify temperature control significantly, since they are designed to open automatically whenever the temperature rises above a predetermined level. These devices are essential if a heating system that has no thermostat has been installed in the greenhouse.

With any type of greenhouse, automatic vent openers should be fitted to at least some of the hinged or louver ventilators. This is easily done by closely following the manufacturer's instructions.

They may be set to open at a range of temperatures, but make sure that the automatic system you choose will function within the temperature range required. Set this to operate at a temperature that is just below the optimum for the plants in order for the vents to open before the temperature inside rises to an unsuitable level.

Many autovent designs are available. Some work by the expansion and contraction of a wax plug contained in a metal or plastic cylinder; the movement of the wax works a piston that opens and closes the ventilator. Other models make use of metal rods that alter their shape as the temperature rises and falls.

LOUVER VENTS

These are fitted on the side of the greenhouse above ground level to improve the flow of air through the interior. The opening mechanism has a lever and is simple to operate (see insets).

Evaporative coolers

In hot, dry climates, evaporative coolers are useful. They are relatively inexpensive to buy and run.

Extractor fans

The type of extractor fan that is designed primarily for use in kitchens and bathrooms is also ideally suited for use in the greenhouse. An additional bonus with using these extractor fans is that most are fitted with a thermostatic control, an essential requirement for greenhouses.

Choose a fan that is powerful enough for the size of your greenhouse. The extraction rate is usually quoted in cubic feet or cubic meters per hour. As a general guide, a 6 x 8ft (2 x 2.5m) greenhouse requires a fan capacity of 10,000cu ft (300cu m) per hour, but a smaller one may be perfectly adequate if other types of ventilation are also used.

A louver window – positioned at the opposite end of the greenhouse from the extractor fan and set lower down – is essential to provide a flow of fresh air to replace the stale air that is drawn out by the fan.

Buy a fan that is fitted with louver flaps that close when the fan is not actually working so that drafts are excluded. To extend the working life of the fan, the motor should not be set to run constantly at maximum capacity. It is much better to choose a model that is slightly more powerful than is strictly necessary for the greenhouse.

HINGED VENTS

Vents that open by a hinge mechanism are normally fitted to the roof of the greenhouse. Make sure that they open wide and that they are securely fixed when open.

AUTOVENT OPENER

This autovent works by the expansion and contraction of wax in a cylinder as the greenhouse temperature rises and falls.

Shading

This will help to control the temperature of the greenhouse if the ventilation system is insufficient. It also protects vulnerable plants from too much direct sunlight, reducing the risk of leaf scorch and preventing flower colors from fading in strong sunlight. Shading applied primarily to control heat should be on the outside of the greenhouse; internal shading is unlikely to reduce the temperature significantly.

The amount of shade required in a greenhouse depends on the season and the plants being grown. In the months of strongest sunlight, shading that reduces the light by 40–50 percent is suitable for a typical mixed greenhouse. Ferns generally prefer approximately 75 percent filtered light, while most cacti and other succulents require very little or no shading at all.

Shading washes

These are often the most efficient method of reducing heat from the sun, while still allowing enough light to penetrate for good plant growth. Paint or spray the wash onto the outside of the glass at the beginning of the sunny season. Reapply if heavy rains prematurely remove the shading before late summer.

Shading washes are inexpensive, but they may be messy to apply and their appearance is sometimes unattractive in a small garden where the greenhouse is a major feature. Some washes become more transparent when wet, so that on rainy days or in dull weather they allow more light to penetrate.

Blinds

These are used mainly on the outside of the greenhouse to control temperature. They are more versatile than shading washes, since they may be rolled up or down, depending on the intensity of light required. They can also be used where only a section of the greenhouse needs to be shaded. However, manually operated blinds need constant attention. Automatic blinds, which come into operation as soon as the temperature rises to a predetermined level, are more convenient to use, but are relatively expensive.

Meshes and fabrics

Flexible mesh shading materials are suitable for either interior or exterior use. They are less adaptable than blinds because they are generally fixed in position for the entire season. They are used more commonly to provide shading for plants that do not require high light levels than to reduce temperatures.

Woven and knitted fabrics are also suitable for both interior and exterior greenhouse use. The amount of light reduction varies considerably, depending on the type of fabric fitted. The quality of light allowed through to the plants is usually perfectly adequate for good growth, although the temperature is not significantly reduced.

FLEXIBLE MESH

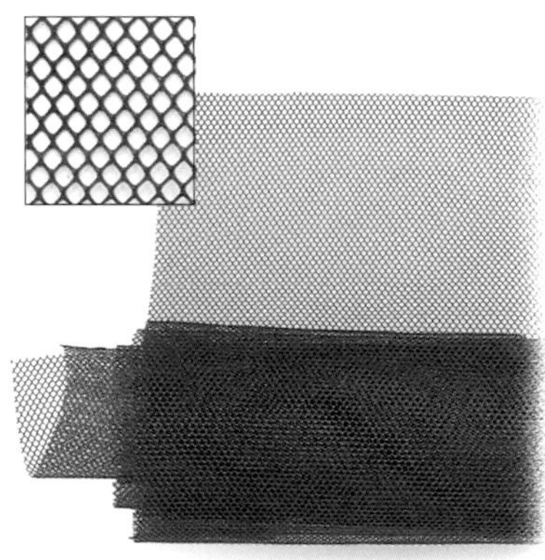

Plastic mesh netting can be cut to length and used either internally or externally for shading plants in a greenhouse.

SHADING THE GREENHOUSE

Shading washes are applied to the outside of a greenhouse to prevent the temperature inside from rising too high, without greatly reducing light. The washes may be left on throughout the season.

ROLLER BLINDS

Blinds are a versatile method of shading the greenhouse. They should be durable, since they will be in place for long periods.

Cross-laminated fabric and some plastic meshes are recommended for internal shading only.

Tinted bubble plastic can also be used for shading. It cuts down the light by almost 50 percent, but it reduces temperature only slightly.

Rigid sheets

Rigid polycarbonate sheets (usually tinted) are sometimes used for shading in greenhouses. The sheets may be fixed either inside or outside, as recommended by the greenhouse manufacturer. They cut down the light considerably and, unless they are white, the quality of light transmitted may not be sufficient for good plant growth.

Humidity

Humidity is a measure of the quantity of water vapor in the air. The humidity of the air influences the rate at which plants transpire; this is their mechanism for drawing water (along with nutrients) from roots to leaves, where the water then evaporates from leaf pores. As water evaporates, the plant is cooled down.

Establish the preferred humidity levels of the plants in your greenhouse, then control the amount of moisture in the atmosphere to suit them. Humidity can be increased using various techniques (see "Increasing humidity," right) and reduced by ventilation (see p.483).

Plant requirements

Many tropical plants from humid climates require high levels of humidity for healthy growth and will not survive in a dry atmosphere. However, a very humid atmosphere reduces the rate of transpiration and evaporation to a level that may be harmful to some plants. They may suffer damage from overheating unless cooler, drier air is brought in by ventilation.

If the air is dry and the humidity level low, plants transpire more rapidly, often losing a great deal of moisture. Plants that are not adapted to cope with low humidity will wilt as a result, unless additional water is supplied at the roots. Dry-climate plants often have specific anatomical features that reduce the rate of transpiration in drought conditions (see CLIMATE AND THE GARDEN, "Drought," p.517). However, it is very expensive to reduce humidity below the ambient level, which in summer can be 95 percent.

Measuring humidity

The level of humidity in a greenhouse depends to an extent on the temperature of the air. Warm air is capable of holding more moisture than cold air before it becomes saturated. Relative humidity is a measure of the amount of water vapor in the air expressed as a percentage of saturation point at the same temperature. A humid atmosphere is defined as having a relative humidity of about 75 percent; a dry atmosphere has a relative humidity of about 35 percent.

Wet and dry bulb thermometers, used in conjunction with hygrometric tables, may be used to measure the relative humidity of the atmosphere. Hygrometers, which have a dial that gives readings for both the temperature and the humidity, are also available. As a general guide, a relative humidity below 75 percent, but above 40 percent, is beneficial for most greenhouse plants during the growing season. At levels above 80 percent, diseases such as gray mold/*Botrytis* and mildew may become a problem.

In winter, humidity should be maintained at a lower level, but the exact level required will depend on the types of plant grown and the temperature of the greenhouse.

Increasing humidity

Greenhouses can be damped down during warm and hot months by splashing water – predominantly on the floor and on any staging – from a watering can or hose. This has the result of increasing the level of atmospheric humidity. An automatic spray system simplifies humidity control, especially for plants that require very high humidity. In a small greenhouse, mist-spraying by hand or providing a tray filled with water that slowly evaporates into the air is usually adequate.

Watering

A traditional watering can is still the most efficient, if perhaps the most time-consuming, method of watering a mixed collection of plants in a small greenhouse. Since you can easily monitor the flow, all of the plants are watered according to their individual requirements.

An automatic watering system is a useful addition to the greenhouse in summer. If the greenhouse is left unattended on a regular basis, however, an automatic system becomes essential, since some pot plants may need to be watered several times a day if the weather is very hot.

Capillary systems

Watering systems that rely on capillary action to draw up water are often used in a greenhouse.

Plant pots may be placed on a 3/4–2in (2–5cm) layer of clean sand (which retains moisture well) that is spread on the greenhouse staging and kept permanently wet. Moist sand adds considerable weight to the staging, however, so make sure that it is sturdy enough to take the extra load. In addition, protect wooden staging from the wet sand by lining it with sheets of plastic or aluminum foil, otherwise it will rot. Alternatively, place the sand in aluminum trays.

Add a length of plastic gutter to the edge of the bench and keep it filled with water. This can be done by hand or automatically from an overhead tank connected to the water supply, in which case the system should be controlled by a float valve.

Capillary matting, which is widely available in rolls and is simply cut to the required size, is far lighter, easier to keep clean, and just as acceptable as sand. To keep the capillary matting continuously moist, trail the edge into a water trough or other reservoir of water. The water may be topped up by hand or supplied automatically, as above.

For a capillary system to be effective, there must be sufficient contact between the soil mix in the pots and the source of moisture so that water is continuously supplied to the plants' root systems. Plastic plant pots usually allow good contact between the soil mix and the moist sand or matting. Clay pots, however, may each require a wick. This is cut out of a piece of spare capillary matting or nylon yarn and placed in the drainage hole to bridge any gaps between the soil mix and the mat.

During the winter months, do not use capillary watering systems in the greenhouse, since most plants are dormant, or are growing only slowly, and therefore require a reduced intake of water. The perpetually damp mat or sand may also increase humidity in the greenhouse to unsatisfactory levels for the plants (see "Humidity," opposite).

Overhead systems

A system of overhead pipes, with nozzles from which water is sprayed onto the plants below, is widely used in commercial greenhouses. This is an ideal system for watering a large number of plants that are all at a similar stage of growth. However, it is not suitable for the small amateur greenhouse that contains a wide variety of plants. Overhead watering systems are also expensive to install and create too humid an atmosphere if used in the winter.

Soaker hoses

These are widely used in the garden, and can also be used inside the greenhouse to water border crops or to keep capillary matting moist. In very hot weather, however, soaker hoses may not supply a sufficient flow of water to the plants.

Trickle irrigation systems

This type of irrigation system consists of a series of small-bore tubes, each with an adjustable nozzle. The tubes are placed in the individual pots or grow bags, or near plants growing in the greenhouse border.

Most trickle irrigation systems are fed with water from a reservoir that is filled in turn from a hose connected to the water supply. It is possible, however, to use water directly from the supply.

The rate of water delivery must always be monitored very carefully and adjusted according to the needs of the plants. These needs vary depending on the time of year and the vagaries of the weather.

Lighting

If a power supply is already installed in the greenhouse (see "Installing electricity, natural gas, and water," p.480), lighting units are not expensive to add at any time, and running costs are also low. In addition, the lights produce a little extra heat for the plants. Ordinary fluorescent lamps provide enough illumination to work by comfortably.

WATERING SYSTEMS

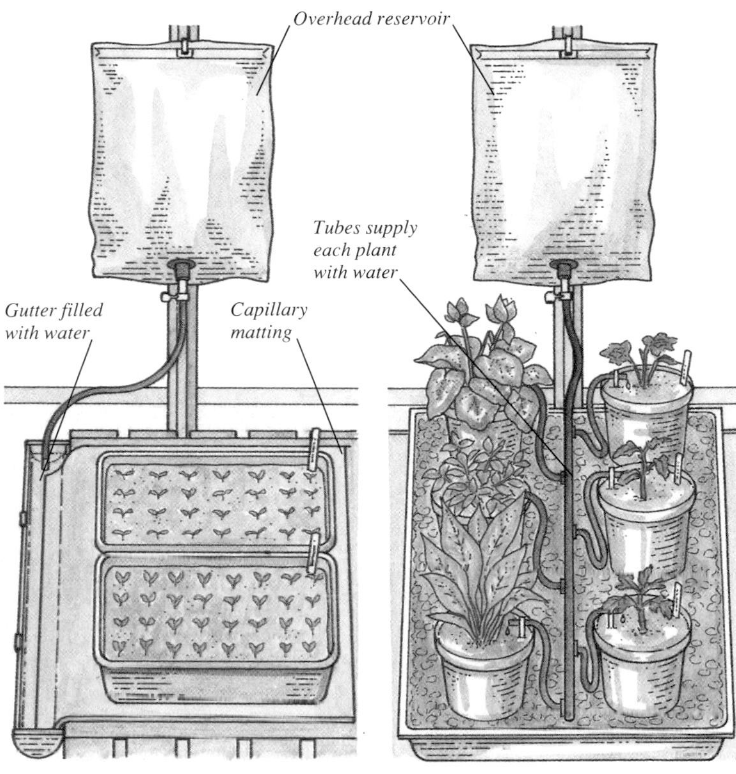

CAPILLARY WATERING
An overhead reservoir feeds water to a gutter fixed to the staging. The matting soaks up water, which is absorbed by soil mix in the trays.

TRICKLE IRRIGATION
Trickle systems supply water directly to each pot by means of tubes, which could be from an overhead reservoir.

Grow lamps

The special quality of lighting produced by grow lamps is required to increase daylength (see THE VEGETABLE GARDEN, "Daylength," p.303) for specific purposes during the fall and winter months, when light levels are consistently low.

Fluorescent tubes that produce good light to improve plant growth can be obtained from specialist aquarium suppliers and garden centers. They do not produce much heat, and so can be placed close to the plants. The lights are fitted with reflectors that cast the light downward, where it will do the most good. For best effect, the tubes should be mounted 10–12in (25–30cm) above the foliage. Mercury fluorescent lamps and mercury vapor lamps also provide a suitable quality of light to encourage good plant growth.

Metal halide lamps are the best, if most expensive, form of grow lamp, emitting light that is close to the spectrum of natural light. They illuminate a large area but cast their light in a circular pattern, which may be inconvenient in a small greenhouse, since the corners may not be adequately lit.

Most grow lamps suitable for use in the greenhouse need special fittings because of the moist, humid atmosphere. If in doubt, ask the advice of a qualified electrician.

Light meters

Where lighting is important, light meters are useful since they measure light levels much more accurately than can be judged by eye. Some meters are supplied with information about the light levels preferred by a wide range of commonly cultivated plants.

A GROW LAMP

This provides additional light to improve plant growth. Secure it directly above the plants, if possible.

Using the space

To make the best use of the limited space in a greenhouse, plan the layout carefully. Cultivation in raised beds, borders, grow bags, or containers placed on the ground, staging, or shelves are all suitable methods; often, a combination is best.

Raised beds

These are used mainly in alpine houses, where sharp drainage is required. Raised beds may be expensive to construct using new bricks, but old bricks are satisfactory. Leave a large gap between a raised bed and the wall of a greenhouse so that air can circulate and moisture from the soil mix does not penetrate the wall. For details see STRUCTURES AND SURFACES, "Raised beds," p.507.

Beds that are raised to normal bench height are suitable only for lean-to greenhouses or for those with a tall brick base. For small plants that do not require a great depth of soil, a stone trough placed on brick pillars or legs may be used. Alternatively, construct a raised container by fixing rigid metal sheets or paving slabs on top of brick pillars, making the walls by laying several brick courses around the top. Line the bed with a sheet of heavy plastic, pierced frequently to ensure that the bed will be adequately drained. A layer of coarse gravel at the bottom also improves drainage.

Raised beds for taller plants need not be so high and so do not need to stand on brick pillars. They are usually built up from ground level with basal seep holes for drainage and simply filled with soil mix.

Borders and grow bags

A glass-to-ground greenhouse is required to grow plants directly in a border, to ensure that plants receive enough light. Borders with a width of 3ft (1m) are acceptable in a greenhouse that is 8ft (2.5m) wide. Make the beds wider if staging is placed over the borders, so that the staging does not interfere with the in-ground plants. Plants in containers may also be placed on top of the border.

The soil in greenhouse borders may become infected with disease if the same plants are grown repeatedly over many years. If this is the case, or if the greenhouse floor is concreted over, grow bags may be used. Grow bags provide a convenient method of cultivation, since they retain moisture well and remove the need to dig and fertilize the soil

INSIDE THE GREENHOUSE

Organize the elements within the greenhouse sensibly to make the best possible use of the limited space. Here is a well-planned layout for a lean-to greenhouse.

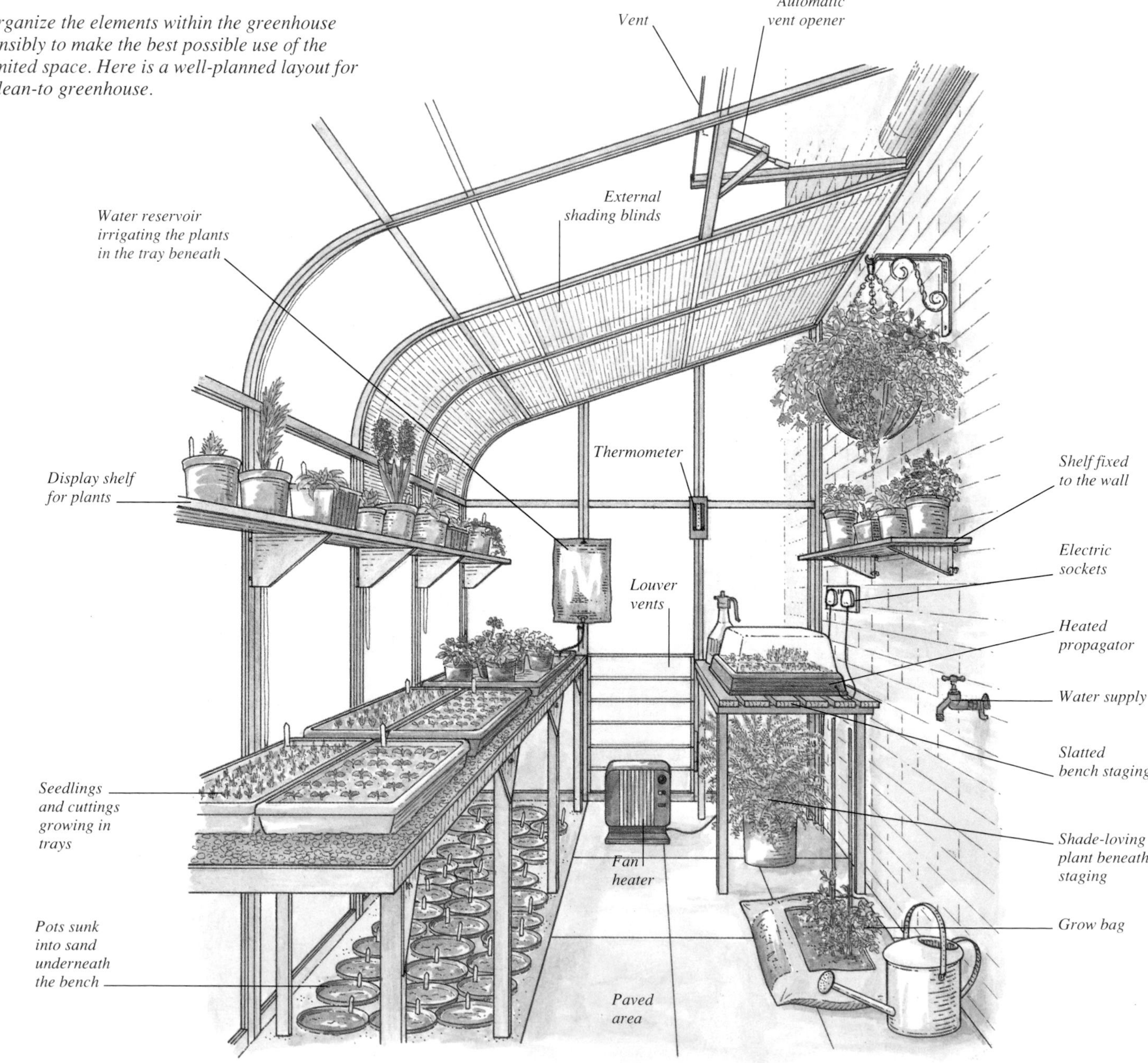

DISPLAYING THE PLANTS

Plants in the greenhouse should be arranged to make attractive displays. If the greenhouse is heated, a wide variety of plants may be grown throughout the year to maintain the display of flowers and foliage. Place dormant plants beneath the staging to make more room for other plants in season.

before planting. Most of the nutrients in the soil mix contained in the grow bags are used up during the season, so fresh grow bags should be used each year.

Staging

Staging is important for any ornamental or mixed greenhouse, since bringing plants closer to the light encourages healthier growth. Even if removed for summer border crops, staging is necessary for propagating and growing on young plants.

Positioning the staging

The most satisfactory arrangement for a small or mixed greenhouse is to have a central path with staging along the sides, and possibly across one end. Remove half of it for border crops when necessary, and retain the permanent staging to display ornamentals. The permanent staging should be positioned on the side where it will cast the least shade on the border crops.

Central staging

Larger ornamental greenhouses that are designed primarily as showhouses may have staging placed in the center, with a path around the edge. Two staging benches can be placed back-to-back, preferably with tiered staging in the center to enhance the display of plants.

The right size and height

For convenience, make the benches 18–24in (45–60cm) wide. Wider benches are useful in a large greenhouse but they may be difficult to reach across. All staging needs to be of sturdy construction to support the weight of plants, containers, and soil mix. Always leave a generous gap between the back of any staging and the sides of the greenhouse to allow air to circulate.

Most amateur greenhouses also have to serve as a potting shed. A convenient height for staging that is also used as a work surface is approximately 30–36in (75–90cm); it should be lower if a seated working position is required.

Free-standing staging

It is sometimes useful to have staging that can be dismantled and stored away, bringing it into the green house for short periods, for instance when raising seedlings in spring. Free-standing staging may not fit the greenhouse quite as well as staging that is built in, and may not look as attractive, but is more flexible in use. It must be easy to assemble and sturdy since it will be in use for many years. If border crops are grown for most of the year, open-mesh staging, which folds back neatly against the side of the greenhouse when it is not needed, is convenient for short periods.

Free-standing modular staging systems can be built up into tiers and provide an attractive way of displaying plants. Slatted, mesh, or solid modular systems are available.

FREE-STANDING STAGING

Movable benches allow great flexibility, since they can be moved around to accommodate the plants, or removed altogether.

FIXED STAGING

Most greenhouse manufacturers supply permanent staging that is made from the same materials as the greenhouse. It is best fitted at the same time as the greenhouse is constructed.

Permanent staging

Built-in staging and shelves may put a strain on the framework of a greenhouse, especially light, aluminum alloy structures. Gravel or sand, if used, adds extra weight to the staging, particularly when it is wet. Buy staging that is specially built, if possible. If in doubt, check with the greenhouse manufacturer before fitting any permanent staging.

Slatted and mesh staging

If you are growing alpines or cacti and succulents in pots, it is preferable to use slatted or mesh benches, which allow a freer flow of air than solid staging. However, slatted and mesh staging are not suitable for use with capillary watering systems.

For a wooden greenhouse, use wooden slatted benches; for an aluminum alloy or galvanized steel greenhouse, metal or plastic-mesh benches are more appropriate.

Solid surface staging

Solid staging allows more pots to be accommodated than slatted staging (it is difficult to keep pots upright between the slats), but may require more ventilation.

If using a capillary watering system, choose solid aluminum staging that has a level surface for the matting or sand. Some types of staging have reversible sections that produce raised flat surfaces for mats if placed one way, and dishlike sections for sand or gravel if reversed.

Shelves

Shelves in the greenhouse can be used for both storage and display. Permanent shelves often cast shade on the plants below, so it is preferable to install fold-away shelves, which may be used in spring when space is short and then put away for the rest of the year.

In a small greenhouse, where there is not enough headroom for hanging baskets, shelves can be used to display trailing plants.

SLATTED STAGING

Wooden-slatted staging is an attractive choice. The slats allow better air circulation around the plants than solid-surface staging does, but slats are not suitable for a capillary watering system, unless pots are placed in trays on the bench.

Propagation aids

The propagation of many plants requires higher temperatures than can realistically be maintained in the greenhouse. Therefore, to save on fuel bills, propagation aids are often used to provide the extra heat required. They may also increase the success rate when sowing seed or taking rooting cuttings. For the greenhouse, choose a propagator that is large enough to hold at least three standard seed trays.

An electric power supply in the greenhouse is essential if heated propagators, mist units, or heating cables are to be used. Mist units also require a constant water supply as well as a power supply.

Unheated propagators are of limited use in the greenhouse, but they usually provide sufficient humidity for rooting cuttings in summer.

Heated propagators

A heated propagator should have a heating element that is capable of providing a minimum soil mix temperature of 59°F (15°C) in winter and early spring, when temperatures outside may fall below freezing.

If tropical plants are to be propagated, the unit must have a more powerful heating element that can maintain a temperature of 75°F (24°C). The propagator should preferably be fitted with an adjustable thermostat, which allows greater flexibility of temperature.

Use rigid plastic lids, since these are more likely to retain the heat than thin plastic covers. Adjustable ventilators are useful, because they allow moisture to escape and prevent the atmosphere inside the propagator from becoming too humid.

Domestic propagators

Some small heated propagators are designed for windowsill use. Usually holding just two seed trays, they are generally too small to be of practical use in the greenhouse, and they often do not have a thermostat. They may not generate enough heat in a cold or cool greenhouse, since the heating element is intended to operate in a room indoors.

Heating mats

These are designed to be used with unheated propagators or ordinary seed trays, either of which may be placed on the heating mats. A plastic hood must be placed over seed trays to maintain warmth and humidity. Heating mats do not raise the temperature as efficiently as heated tray propagators (see below) and are only suitable for one or two trays.

Heated tray propagators

These have a self-contained heating element in the base, and are more useful than heating mats (see above), especially if they are fitted with an adjustable thermostat.

Mist units

Cuttings may often be rooted more rapidly and in greater numbers in a mist unit than by using other more traditional means. Mist units are convenient, since they remove the need to water cuttings frequently.

The easiest and most convenient mist units to use are self-contained, enclosed units that include a heating element, thermostat, transparent cover, and a misting head. The constantly humid atmosphere created by the misting head provides a suitable environment in which to root cuttings quickly, by maintaining a constant film of water on the propagating material. Heat loss by evaporation is also reduced. There is also less risk of the cuttings being affected by fungal diseases because, when the misting head is in operation, most disease spores are washed out of the air and from the leaves before they can infect plant tissues. On a small scale, a similar environment is created by enclosing a pot of cuttings in a clear plastic bag.

For large numbers of plants, a mist propagation unit is more practical. Some units are designed for use without a cover on an open greenhouse propagating bench. They are used in conjunction with heating cables and require a specially constructed greenhouse bench. If sited in a greenhouse where a mixed collection of plants is grown, however, the high humidity created by an open mist unit may prove unsuitable for some types of plant. In this situation, it would be preferable to install a closed mist unit.

A Mist Propagation Unit

A soil thermostat controls the temperature of the soil mix, which is heated by cables. The misting head is controlled by a sensor (connected to a solenoid) located near the cuttings. When the atmosphere becomes too dry, the misting head is activated.

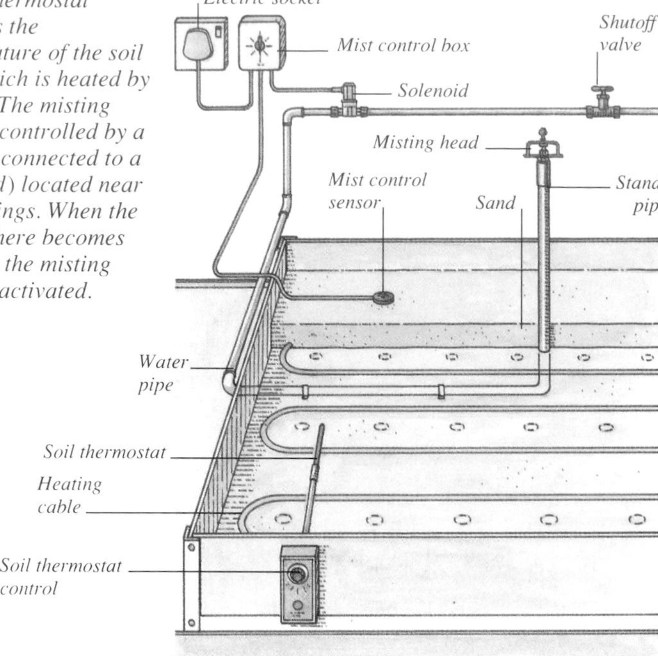

Heating cables

Intended primarily for heating the soil mix in a conventional propagator or on a mist bench in the greenhouse, heating cables may also be used to heat the air in an enclosed space, such as a cold frame or homemade propagator. The safest system to use is a cable with a wired-in thermostat that is connected to an insulated, fused socket.

Cover any heating cable with wire mesh to protect it from being accidentally cut.

Heating cables are sold in lengths that are designed to heat a given area. A 75-watt cable, for example, measures 20ft (6m) and provides enough heat for a bench area of 7sq ft (0.7sq m) in a greenhouse that has some form of heating. A cable with a higher wattage would of course be needed for practical use in a similar area in an unheated greenhouse or in a cold frame that is outside the greenhouse.

The cable should be laid at a depth of 2–3in (5–8cm) in a series of S bends (ensuring that the loops do not touch) in a bed of moist sand.

Using Heating Cables

In this propagating case, cables are used to heat both soil and air. Each set of cables has a thermostat, which ensures that the temperature never falls below a preset level.

Cables warming the air
Air thermostat
Control box
Soil thermostat
Heating cable
Drainage holes
Sand

A Windowsill Propagator

Propagators designed for windowsills are best used in a greenhouse only during summer, when temperatures are high.

Cold frames and cloches

Cold frames and cloches relieve pressure on greenhouse space, but they are also extremely useful in their own right. They are likely to be used most intensively in spring to harden off plants raised in a greenhouse, but they may also be used throughout the year to grow a wide range of crops. They are most useful where winters are mild because they are unheated, but even in areas with severe winters they can be used to add several weeks at either end of the season.

Cold frames

The most popular type of cold frame has glass (or clear plastic) sides as well as glass sashes (frame tops that contain the panes of glass), although sometimes wood and bricks are used for the construction. Glass-to-ground models usually have a metal framework for extra strength.

Frame sashes

Choose a frame that has removable or sliding sashes for easy access. Some also have sliding front panels, which may be useful to supply extra ventilation. Hinged sashes that are wedged open still provide protection from heavy rain but sliding sashes are often removed entirely during the day, leaving the plants very vulnerable to heavy rain. Lightweight aluminum frames with their sashes wedged open may be at risk in strong winds, however, so choose a model that has a hinged top and adjustable casement stays to secure the sashes safely.

Wooden frames

Traditional wooden frames are now difficult to obtain and are usually expensive, but can be made cheaply at home from secondhand timber. The wooden sides retain heat well. It is not very difficult to attach heating cables (see opposite) to the inside of the frame to provide extra warmth. Paint or stain the wood to preserve it.

Aluminum alloy frames

These are available from horticultural specialists and are relatively inexpensive. They vary considerably, usually sold packed flat for easy transportation and assembled on site. Aluminum alloy frames let in more light than either wooden or brick frames, but they do not have such good insulating qualities and may not be as strong. It may be necessary to use ground anchors for lightweight frames.

HOW TO USE COLD FRAMES

PLANTING IN THE FRAME
Plants may be grown directly in the cold frame, if required. Always prepare the base with a thick layer of drainage material, such as broken crocks or coarse gravel, before adding a 6in (15cm) layer of good garden soil or soil mix.

PROTECTING CROPS
Here, the cold frame has been placed directly onto the soil in the vegetable plot. Vegetables are growing through slits in a plastic sheet (see The No-till System, *p.536) laid on the surface of the soil.*

VENTILATION METHODS OF COLD FRAMES

HINGED SASHES
Hinged tops can be wedged open on warm days to prevent the plants from overheating.

SLIDING SASHES
Sliding tops are less vulnerable to gusts of wind, but they do not protect plants from heavy rain.

Brick frames

These are rarely used nowadays, but they may still be built at home if a cheap supply of old bricks is available and if the sashes can be made. Brick frames are generally warm and draftproof.

Suitable sizes

The minimum practical size for a cold frame is 2 x 4ft (60cm x 1.2m). Often, however, the frame has to fit into whatever space is available (as near the greenhouse as possible), so choose the largest affordable frame that fits the space.

Height is important if the frame is to be used for plants in pots or for tall vegetable crops. In order to increase the height of a frame temporarily, raise it on loose bricks.

Insulation

The range of plants that can be successfully overwintered in a frame is increased if the frame is well insulated. The frame needs to be draftproof; there should be no gaps around the glass or framework, and the top and any sliding front panels must fit well.

Glass-to-ground and plastic-sided frames may need insulating in cold weather with sheets of plastic foam. Cut the sheets to size, and place them against the inside of the frame to reduce drafts and heat loss.

On cold nights, particularly when a deep freeze is predicted, frames may require additional outer protection: use layers of burlap or old carpet to cover the tops, tied down firmly or held in position with pieces of heavy wood. This protective covering should always be removed during the day, otherwise plants may suffer from lack of light. Alternatively, use several layers of thick, clear plastic sheeting for extra protection. This can be left in place during the day since it does not reduce the light to the same degree.

Ventilation

Good ventilation is essential in warm weather. Most frames have sashes that can be wedged open to allow fresh air inside. Often, the sashes also slide along to allow more ventilation, and are eventually removed completely when young plants need to be hardened off.

Light

Aluminum frames (but not brick or wooden frames) may be moved around the garden to take advantage of the best light at various times of the year. If a frame is permanently sited, it should be positioned where it will receive the maximum amount of light in winter and spring, provided that the site is not too exposed.

Frames need shading in summer but, for year-round use, one that lets in as much light as possible is best.

Glazing materials

Glass is the best glazing material for cold frames; it transmits light well, allows the frame to warm up quickly, and retains heat better than most plastic materials. Broken or cracked panes should be replaced as soon as possible, so a frame that allows the individual panes to be replaced easily should be chosen. Some are glazed using glazing clips or glass panels that slide into the framework, making glass replacement relatively quick and simple.

Where glass may be a potential danger for children or animals, or where the cost of the frame is the main consideration, use plastic glazing material.

Cloches

A range of cloche designs and materials is available, so choose a cloche that suits the types of plant to be grown. Cloches tend to be used mainly in the vegetable garden, but they are equally useful for protecting ornamental plants and seedlings that need a little extra warmth early in the season.

Materials

Glass is the best choice if cloches are to be used extensively for most of the year and moved from crop to crop. It has good light transmission and allows the frame to warm up quickly in sunlight. Clear plastic material (of various thicknesses) is an alternative. Plastic cloches are generally less expensive than those made of glass but do not allow such good light penetration, nor do they retain as much heat.

Single-thickness plastic is the least satisfactory material for retaining heat, but it is cheap and useful where high temperatures are not necessary. Plastic cloches last longer if they have been treated with an ultraviolet inhibitor and are stored out of direct sunlight when not in use.

The minimum thickness that is suitable for cloches is 150 gauge, but 300, 600, or 800 gauge provides much greater protection. PVC is thicker and more rigid, and has similar qualities to polypropylene (see below). Molded PVC and PVC sheeting should last for at least five years or more if treated with an ultraviolet inhibitor.

Cloches made from twin-walled polycarbonate offer good insulation and should last for ten years or more. Polypropylene is used in some injection-molded cloches and in corrugated sheets; it retains heat better than plastic, but not as well as glass or twin-walled polycarbonate. It lasts for five years or more if treated with an ultraviolet inhibitor.

TENT CLOCHE

BARN CLOCHE

End pieces

These are an important part of most cloches – without them a cloche may become a wind tunnel, damaging the plants inside. The end pieces should fit well to preclude drafts, but they should be easy to remove to provide additional ventilation when required.

Tent cloche

A tent cloche is inexpensive and simple to construct from two sheets of glass to form a tent shape. It is suitable for germinating seeds, protecting young seedlings in spring, and covering low-growing plants.

Tunnel cloche

A tunnel cloche may be made from either rigid or flexible plastic. Generally, flexible-plastic, continuous-tunnel cloches are used for crops such as strawberries and early carrots. The plastic must be supported by wire hoops (positioned over the row of plants) and tensioned with wires. Heavy-duty plastic that has been treated with an ultraviolet inhibitor should be used.

Rigid models are generally more attractive but more expensive than tunnel cloches that are made of flexible plastic. They are also easier to move around, since they do not need to be dismantled first.

Some tunnel cloches have self-watering features (see right).

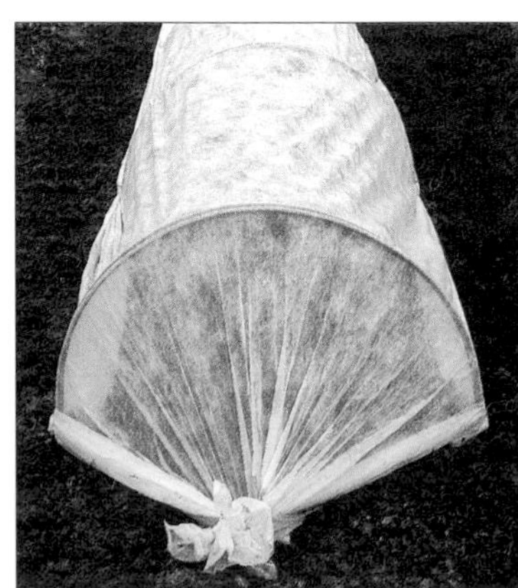

TUNNEL CLOCHE

Barn cloche

This has almost vertical sides supporting a sloping, tent-shaped top. Its extra height makes it useful for relatively tall plants, but extra materials and complicated fittings make it more expensive than a tent cloche.

Some glass and rigid plastic barn cloches have lifting or removable tops to provide ventilation in warm weather, while still offering wind protection. This makes weeding, watering, and harvesting easier.

Flexible PVC is sometimes used for barn cloches, but these tend to be lower and therefore less versatile than those using other types of material, unless the top is removable or can be wedged open.

Dome-shaped cloche

Made from rigid plastic, dome-shaped cloches are easy to move around but are more expensive than tent or tunnel cloches. They have more space at the edges than tent and tunnel cloches, although the overall height may be no greater.

Self-watering cloche

Watering plants beneath cloches is difficult and time-consuming if the cloches have to be lifted or moved.

A self-watering cloche is designed to allow rainwater to trickle through gradually to the plants below. Alternatively, it may have a tubular system that is connected to a hose.

SELF-WATERING CLOCHE

Floating row cover

A floating row cover (also known as a floating mulch) consists of a sheet of perforated plastic sheeting or a light garden blanket, which is placed over the ground where crops have been recently sown.

Floating row covers are permeable, allowing rainwater to penetrate to the soil below. This is a great advantage, since it reduces the need to water. The perforations in plastic floating row covers enable the sheet to stretch a little as the crop grows beneath it. Garden blankets are sufficiently lightweight to rise with the growing crop. Both perforated plastic and blanket floating row covers allow air to pass freely through the material and also have useful insulating properties. Garden blankets also protect plants from light frosts. For further information, see THE VEGETABLE GARDEN, p.311.

The sheets or blankets should be anchored firmly into the soil at the edges of the beds with soil, stones, or pegs. Whole beds may be covered with a floating row cover, if desired, or pieces can be cut to fit smaller areas or even individual plants.

Individual cloche

These are usually used to protect individual plants in the early stages of growth. They may also be placed over any small, vulnerable plants during severe winter weather, such as hard frost, deep snow, heavy rain, and high winds.

Homemade individual cloches, such as waxed paper protectors and cut-off plastic bottles, are easy to make and are much less expensive than store-bought models but may not be as attractive.

INDIVIDUAL CLOCHE

Wall-of-water cloche

This unusual design is useful for single plants and consists of a circle of hollow, clear plastic tubes, into which water is poured. The tubes form the wall of the cloche, which alters in shape depending on the water level. If the tubes are half filled, they cave in at the top, protecting the plant from above as well as from the sides.

WALL-OF-WATER CLOCHE

Routine maintenance

Regular maintenance is necessary to preserve greenhouses and to keep frames and cloches clean. Fall is usually a convenient time to attend to the maintenance work: cleaning and disinfecting the greenhouse structure and equipment at this time of year minimizes problems from overwintering pests and diseases.

It is important to do this work on a mild day before the very cold weather begins. Tender plants can then be put outside while the preparations for winter are carried out.

CLEANING BETWEEN PANES

To remove dirt from between overlapping panes in the greenhouse, use a thin, rigid strip of plastic to loosen any deposits before spraying or hosing down with water.

Exterior maintenance

Choose a dry, still day for routine work on the outside of the greenhouse. Before making a start, gather together all necessary materials for cleaning, repairing, and repainting.

Cleaning glass and plastic glazing

Glass should be cleaned with water only, using a hose and long-handled brush, but if it has become very dirty, better results are achieved by brushing with a solution of lime remover. Protect skin and eyes by wearing gloves and goggles, and rinse off the solution thoroughly with running water.

A commercial window cleaning solution may also be used but it will not remove ingrained dirt. Dirt also tends to become trapped between overlapping panes. Push a thin plastic label between panes to loosen dirt and algae, then use the water jet from a hose to remove it. Shading washes are best removed by rubbing them off with a cloth.

Repairing glass

Panes of glass and plastic panes that are slightly cracked may be temporarily repaired with transparent glazing tape. Broken and badly cracked panes, however, should be replaced completely and as soon as possible after the damage is noticed, to prevent harm to plants.

To replace a pane in an aluminum alloy greenhouse, remove the spring glazing clips and the adjoining pane, if necessary, and reglaze using the old clips (see p.480).

If the panes are bedded on linseed putty (as in many older wooden greenhouses), remove the glazing tacks and the panes of glass carefully. Chip away the putty with a small chisel to leave a smooth surface. Clean the glazing bars with sandpaper before reglazing.

Apply a priming paint to any unpainted or untreated wood on the glazing bars. Pay particular attention to knots in the wood, which may be potential entry points for moisture. When the paint is fully dry, replace the panes by setting them on a bed of putty or glazing mastic, using glazing tacks to hold them.

Gutters and downspouts

Check that gutters and downspouts are in good repair. Use a hose to clear any blockages. Small leaks in gutters can be sealed with mastic or other sealant, but badly leaking sections of gutter will need to be replaced completely.

Metal framework

Aluminum greenhouses require only minimal structural attention. Although they lose their bright color, the grayish patina that forms protects the metal from the weather.

Steel frames and fittings should be checked for rust and, if necessary, treated with rust remover. Repaint every few years.

Wooden framework

Cut out any rotting wood and replace it, applying wood preservative and replacing rusty hinges as necessary. Softwood greenhouses need regular painting: strip off flaking paint, wash down, then apply primer and good-quality exterior paint. Hardwood greenhouses are more rot-resistant, requiring only a coat of wood stain every year or two, which also restores the color.

Ventilators

Windows and ventilator fans should be checked for ease of operation, working parts oiled if necessary, and glass or plastic cleaned. Also ensure that any fan-blade guards are securely in place.

MAINTAINING THE GREENHOUSE

An annual check in fall should be enough to keep your greenhouse in good working order.

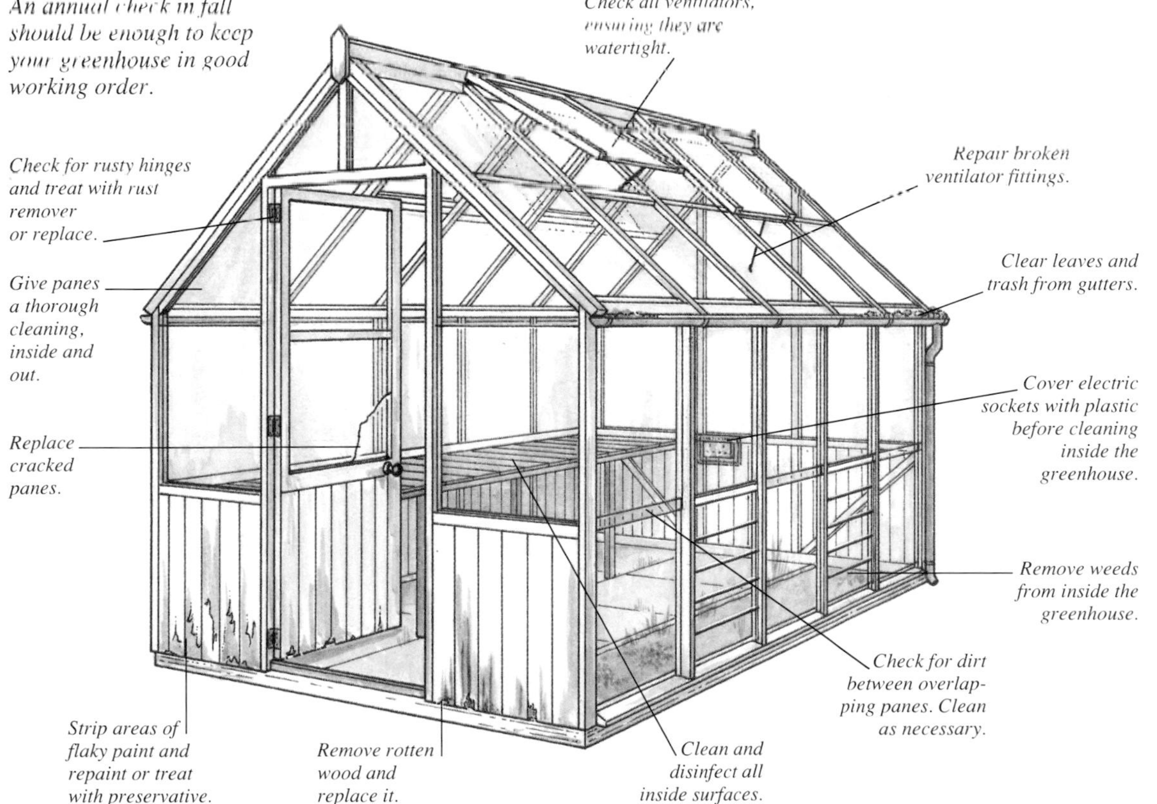

Inside the greenhouse

Before cleaning and disinfecting the inside of a greenhouse or frame, turn off any electric power supply at the source, cover electric sockets and fittings with plastic, and remove all plants to a safe place.

Cleaning and disinfecting

Glass and plastic glazing materials should be cleaned as described under "Exterior maintenance," above. Clean the glazing bars by scrubbing with a disinfectant solution. Fine steel wool can be used, but not on anodized (colored) aluminum.

Scrub brickwork and paths with a garden disinfectant and rinse with clean water. The disinfectant can be used, diluted according to the manufacturer's instructions, to sterilize the staging and other surfaces. Apply it with a paintbrush or as a coarse spray, wearing protective gloves, a face mask, and goggles.

Sanitation

Before returning plants to the greenhouse, check them for pests and diseases and treat as required. For details on which pests and diseases are likely to affect the plants you grow, consult the "Routine care" sections of the appropriate chapters.

3

STRUCTURES AND SURFACES

THE STRUCTURES AND *hard surfaces of a garden act as the framework around which plants can grow and mature over the seasons. If thoughtfully designed, pergolas, fences, or trellises can add welcome height to any planting design, as well as providing privacy and shelter. Paths can lead visitors along planned routes, revealing piecemeal the garden's splendors; a deck attached to the house makes a perfect setting for a meal; while a shaded patio, perhaps at the rear of the garden, might be an ideal place for relaxation. As well as being practical, structures and surfaces are often attractive features in their own right, providing year-round architectural and textural interest. They may be designed so that they contrast or blend with the planting: the bold shape of a circular patio would make a striking contrast with the gentler lines of sprawling plants, whereas a rustic pergola is an appropriate support for cottage-garden climbers such as scarlet runner beans, rambling roses, and clematis.*

Designing with structures and surfaces

Hard landscape elements are vital in helping to form the framework of a garden design and may be as ornamental as they are functional. In a new garden, features such as a terrace or a pergola are valuable for providing interest while the plants are growing and becoming established. In a more mature garden, sympathetically designed structures complement softer elements such as a lawn or the planting in a border, and give the garden solidity and substance all year round.

When planning and designing structures, consider them in the context of their setting and in relation to each other. Materials, style, size, and shape should all be compatible, both with the house and the overall design of the garden. A terrace or wall adjacent to the house often looks most attractive if built of the same materials, forming a cohesive link between house and garden. Local materials are often preferable because they tend to look appropriate in the setting. The degree of formality is another important consideration; in a formal garden, for example, a mellow brick wall boundary would be ideal, while in an informal cottage garden a picket fence or rustic wooden pole fence would be more suitable.

Structures may be used to link, define, or separate different elements or parts of the garden. A gently curving path leads the eye along the garden, providing a unifying line, while a wide, straight path separates the features on either side. Steps create an interesting change of level and demarcate separate areas as well as joining them visually and providing access from one part to another. If the steps adjoin a patio, they may look best if constructed from the same materials and in a similar style – curved steps appropriately linked to a circular patio, for example.

DESIGNING WITH HARD LANDSCAPE
Hard materials have been used here to form the main framework of the design, creating interest while the planting is becoming established and providing a foil for the softer shapes of the plants. The curving path adds a sense of movement, while the innovative use of mixed materials provides satisfying textural contrasts.

The order in which you undertake construction work largely depends on your individual priorities and the requirements of the site. It might be necessary to erect a flanking wall first because it will help to retain the soil of a raised bed. In another garden, laying a path might be the first priority to allow easy access with wheelbarrows to the rear of a site where work is in progress.

This chapter covers most straightforward structural projects that may be undertaken by an amateur, from hard surfaces such as patios, terraces, and paths, to boundaries and divisions (for example walls or fences) as well as other structures such as raised beds and pergolas. In addition, certain hard elements are covered in full in other chapters: see THE WATER GARDEN, pp.246–50, for details on constructing ponds and watercourses; see THE ROCK GARDEN, pp.192–202, for rock gardens, alpine troughs, and peat beds.

Patios and terraces

A patio is an ornamental feature as well as a functional one, providing an area for meals and relaxation, with plants in beds or containers, and perhaps a raised pool. An open paved area, with a balustrade or low wall, is more accurately described as a terrace. Patios and terraces are usually paved, although wooden decking (see pp.499–500) is popular as an alternative in some areas.

Choosing a site

Patios and terraces are usually sited close to the house, often with glass doors allowing direct access. This is convenient for providing power sources for lights and other equipment, but if the site is not warm and sheltered, it may be better to choose an alternative position. Designing the patio at an angle of 45° to the house, perhaps at a corner, may ensure that it receives sun for most of the day. A patio may also be built away from the house to make use of a fine view across the property.

Two or more small patios may be more useful than one large one. One may be sited in an open, sunny spot, the other in a cooler position to provide a welcome, shady retreat on a summer's day.

Shelter and privacy

A warm, sheltered patio can be enjoyed both earlier and later in the season than one that is subject to strong winds. If the site is exposed to winds, provide both shelter and seclusion with screens, such as a trellis, covered with climbing plants. A pergola (see pp.511–12) roofed with lattice will screen the patio from above and provide shade. Avoid siting a patio under large trees, however: these will cast too much shade, they drip long after rain has stopped, their roots may dislodge and heave the paving, insects could be troublesome, and falling leaves may become a nuisance.

Preparing the Subbase for Patios and Paths

1 *Mark out the area with pegs and string, setting the string at the ultimate level of the path or patio. Use a builder's square to check that the corners are set at right angles.*

2 *Dig down to firm subsoil and tamp down with a plate compactor. Allow for a 4in (10cm) depth of crushed stone, a 2in (5cm) layer of sand, if needed, plus the thickness of the surface layer.*

3 *Drive in a grid of leveling pegs every 6ft (2m). For a patio, incorporate a slight slope so surface water drains away. Use a level and board to ensure that pegs are level with strings.*

4 *Spread a 4in (10cm) layer of crushed stone over the entire site, and then compact it so that it is level, using the pegs as a guide. Add sand, if necessary, and compact the area again.*

Drainage Slope

Mark pegs at the same distance from the top of each, then pound them in, in rows 6ft (2m) apart – the first at the top of the slope. Put a 1in (2.5cm) scrap of wood on a peg in the second row. Make the two rows level, remove the scrap, and repeat.

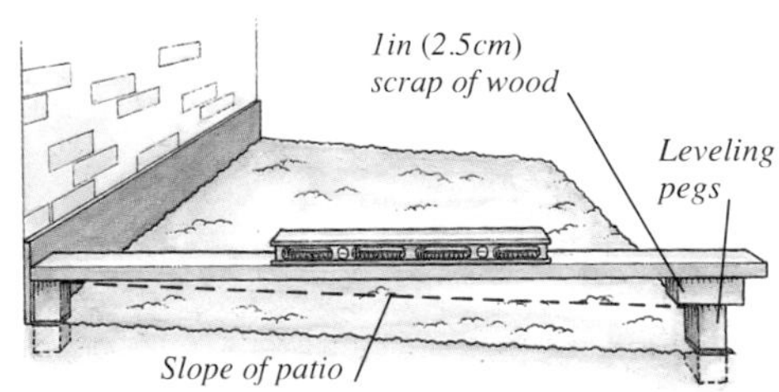

A suitable size

Size is less important for a terrace that is simply a link between house and garden than for a patio that is to serve as an outdoor room. It should be in proportion to the garden: if too small it may look trivial, if too large it may overpower a small garden. Allow about 4sq yd (3.3sq m) for each person likely to use it. For a family of four, a patio about 16sq yd (13sq m) is a practical size.

Choosing a surface

Simplicity is the key to good design. If the patio is to accommodate furniture, climbers, and container plants, paving should be unobtrusive. Bear in mind that colored paving may look fussy and often weathers to dreary shades. Variety is best achieved by mixing textures: small areas of brick or gravel among paving slabs, railroad ties intersecting bricks or clay pavers, or cobblestones with stone slabs.

Also decide if, for example, a hard-wearing surface is needed, or one that is not slippery when wet: choose from such materials as concrete (p.494), paving slabs (p.495), natural stone (p.496), tiles (p.496), bricks and pavers (p.497), or granite setts and cobblestones (p.499).

Foundations

Patios, paths, and driveways (see p.501) need firm foundations to ensure that the paved surface remains stable once in use. The load-bearing requirements must also be taken into account: few patios will be required to support very heavy loads, but driveways need more substantial foundations because they may be used by heavy vehicles as well as cars. Climate is another factor: in areas with long cold and dry periods, for example, concrete foundations may crack if not sufficiently deep; seek local advice as necessary.

Before undertaking any excavation work, check the location of all the service pipes and cables on your property with the local utility company to avoid damaging them.

Water runoff

To drain off water, the surface of a patio should slope slightly; a fall of about 1in/6ft (2.5cm/2m) is usually sufficient. Calculate the combined depth of the subbase and surface material and mark this as a line at the same distance from the top of each of a number of leveling pegs. Insert one row at the top of the slope so that the mark is at soil level, the top of the peg indicating the desired level of the finished paving. Insert a second row of pegs 6ft (2m) down the slope. On each peg in this row in turn, place a small, 1in (2.5cm) thick scrap of wood (a shim) and lay a level on a board between this peg and one in the first row. Adjust the height of the lower peg until the top of the shim and the upper peg are level. Remove the shim and repeat the process, working down the slope. Then rake the soil so that it is level with the mark on each of the pegs. The tops of the subbase and the surface material of the finished construction should be level.

Basic procedure

Remove any plant growth from the area, including tree roots, then dig out loose topsoil to reach firm subsoil. Consolidate this using a plate compactor. For most patios and paths, but not those that might bear heavy loads (see "Load-bearing surfaces," p.494), firm subsoil and, if needed, a 4in (10cm) layer of crushed stone covered with 2in (5cm) sand, is a serviceable foundation. Use more crushed stone if necessary to bring the surface of the subbase up to the required level.

On unstable soils, such as muck or heavy clay, or where frost penetrates deeply into the soil, footings should run deeper than normal, as far down as 10in (25cm). Check the footing

How to Lay Concrete

1 *After marking out the site, dig it out to a depth of 8in (20cm). Drive leveling pegs into the ground 3ft (1m) apart along the string lines. Set them horizontal using a board and a level.*

2 *Remove the string lines and nail wooden boards to the inner faces of the pegs, butted end-to-face at the corners. This form holds the concrete in place until it sets hard.*

3 *Divide large sites into sections no more than 12ft (4m) long using forms. Spread crushed stone 4in (10cm) deep and tamp it down with a roller.*

4 *Starting with the first section, tip in the concrete and spread it level so that it is slightly higher than the form. Work the concrete well into the edges.*

5 *Using a wooden beam that spans the width of the form, compact the concrete with a downward chopping motion. Then slide the beam from side to side to level the surface.*

6 *Fill any hollows that appear after leveling using fresh concrete, and level it again.*

7 *Lay a protective waterproof covering such as a plastic tarp over the concrete until it dries. Remove the form when the concrete has set hard.*

depths specified by your local building codes before proceeding with any further construction.

Load-bearing surfaces
For areas such as driveways that need to support heavy weight, lay a subbase of at least 4in (10cm) of compacted crushed stone or rubble, with a further 4in (10cm) of concrete on top. This concrete may be used as the top surface or as a base for another material such as asphalt or pavers bedded in mortar. On clay or unstable soils, or if the surface is to be used by heavy vehicles, lay 6in (15cm) of concrete on top of the base. If mixing your own concrete for the foundations, see below. In large areas of concrete, it is essential to leave expansion gaps (see "Expansion joints," p.502).

Concrete

Concrete is relatively quick and easy to lay and makes a hard-wearing and durable surface. It may be made more attractive by adding a textured finish (see p.502).

Ordering concrete
If you intend to lay a large area of concrete and there is access for large vehicles, having ready-mixed concrete delivered will make the job easier and quicker. Give the supplier the site measurements and information about the intended use of the surface to ensure that the correct amount and mix is delivered, or use a supplier who will mix it for you on site. This saves time and effort, but requires advance preparation and usually some helpers, since you have to tackle the job immediately.

Concrete and mortar mixes
The following proportions for concrete and mortar mixes are suitable for most projects. For an explanation of terms, see p.499.
Wall footings, drive foundations, and bases for precast paving
1 part cement
$2^1/_2$ parts sharp sand
$3^1/_2$ parts $^3/_4$in (20mm) aggregate
(or 5 parts combined aggregate to 1 part cement, omitting the sand)
***In situ* (poured) concrete paving**
1 part cement
$1^1/_2$ parts sharp sand
$2^1/_2$ parts $^3/_4$in (20mm) aggregate
(or $3^1/_2$ parts combined aggregate to 1 part cement, omitting the sand)
Bedding mortar (for bedding paving, and jointing paving bricks)
1 part cement
5 parts sharp sand
Masonry mortar (for garden brickwork)
1 part masonry cement
3 parts fine sand
All these proportions are measured by volume and not by weight. The consistency of the mix required for different jobs varies considerably. When mixing either concrete or mortar, start by adding only about half a part of water to one part of cement. This will provide a very stiff mix. Continue to add water gradually until you reach the consistency you need.

In hot climates, setting retardants may sometimes be necessary in mortar and concrete mixes, while in cold climates, antifreeze products may have to be incorporated. Seek local advice, if necessary. It is best to avoid laying concrete and mortar when the weather is close to freezing or above 90°F (32°C).

Laying concrete

First mark out with string the area to be concreted, and excavate as deeply as needed for local conditions. Drive a number of wooden leveling pegs into the ground at intervals of 3ft (1m) around the edge, using the string as a guide. Nail boards to the inside faces of the leveling pegs to make a form at least 8in (20cm) deep, which confines the concrete until it sets.

Divide up large sites into small sections no more than 12ft (4m) long using more boards. On top of the subsoil, spread at least 4in (10cm) of compacted crushed stone. Taking one section at a time, pour the freshly mixed concrete inside the form to a depth of 4in (10cm) and work it well into the edges. Use a wooden beam spanning the width of the form to

Utility meters

Utility meters must always be unobstructed to allow easy access for readers. Most meters may be hidden behind a fence or surrounded by shrubs (which should not be thorny, however).

When constructing or planting nearby, be aware that the utility company may at some time have to destroy plantings or structures in order to service or replace the meter.

Call the utility company before digging. Pay particular attention to meters when using heavy equipment, since even an accidental hit from a shovel may do serious damage.

compact the mix, then level the concrete by drawing the beam back and forth in long, smooth strokes. Use a trowel or wood float in corners.

Paving slabs

Concrete paving slabs are popular for patios, paths, and driveways. They are available from many garden centers and building supply stores in a range of sizes, textures, and colors, and are easy to lay once the base has been prepared. Some designs may be available only in one area. Large suppliers usually produce catalogs and deliver direct.

Sizes and shapes

Most slabs are sold either 24 x 24in (600 x 600mm) or 24 x 36in (600 x 900mm), with smaller slabs made to integrate with them. Not all slabs have a shaped edge designed to butt join; a half slab may be slightly less than half the size of a full one, to allow for mortar between the joints.

Circular slabs are suitable only for stepping-stones and small areas of paving with an infill of a loose material, such as gravel. Hexagonal slabs are useful if you prefer a pattern without regular, parallel lines; half slabs are available for a straight edge. Some slabs are available with a "bite" out of one corner, so that when four slabs are laid together a planting hole is created at the center.

Quantities

If laying a pattern with slabs of different sizes or colors, draw a plan on graph paper to calculate the number of each required, and allow up to 5 percent extra for breakages (especially if many have to be cut; see "Cutting paving slabs," p.496). Try to work to dimensions that minimize the need to cut slabs.

Laying paving slabs

If laying a patio, establish a line that you can use as a straight edge and ensure that there is a slight slope for drainage; the patio should always slope away from a building. A house wall is a practical base line to work from, but you may want to leave a small gap between the wall and paving for planting. In that case, start from a level line that is parallel to the wall of the house. With pegs and string, mark out the area to be paved, making it a size and shape that requires the fewest possible slabs to be cut. If the slabs are not to be butted, allow about 1/4–1/2in (0.5–1cm) for the mortar joints. Seek advice from the supplier if in doubt.

Preparing the site

Clear the site and prepare a subbase with crushed stone (see p.493). If you intend to cement the stones in place, you will need wooden spacers about 1/2in (1cm) thick to place between the paving slabs to allow room for filling with mortar.

Positioning the slabs

Work from one corner, placing a row of slabs in each direction with spacers between to make sure that the dimensions are correct. Adjustments are easy to make at this stage. Using a bricklayer's trowel, lay a strip of bedding mortar along each edge where the slab is to be laid, to form an area slightly smaller than the slab. If the slab is 18in (45cm) across or more, lay a cross of mortar within the box. The mortar ridges should be about 1 1/4–2in (3–5cm) high. This "box and cross" method combines strength with easy adjustment. Lay the slab in position and tamp it down with the handle of a club hammer or mallet. Use a level to check that it is firm and straight.

PAVING SLAB STYLES

TEXTURE
Surface textures range from smooth to stippled, scored, or roughly pebbled.

HEXAGONAL PAVERS
These are an attractive alternative to rectangles or squares. Half blocks are used for straight edges.

WEATHERED PAVERS
If a more natural look is desired, a range of weathered stone pavers is available.

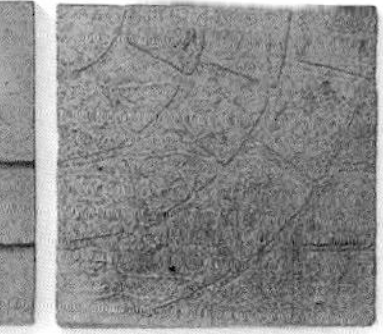

POINTED SLABS
Some slabs are pointed to give special patterns or effects. Those with a "bite" taken out may be fitted together for a planting hole.

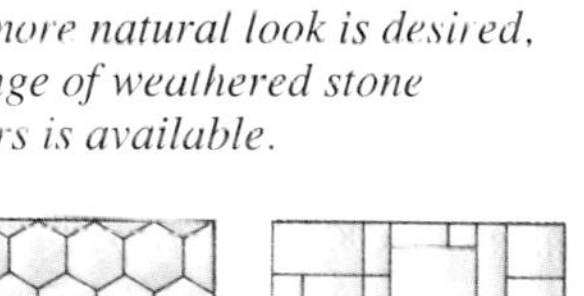

PAVING PATTERNS
A variety of pleasing patterns may be created with different shapes and sizes of paver.

CAST AND PRESSED SLABS
Cast slabs (sloping edges) are for light/medium use. Pressed slabs (straight) are lighter but stronger.

HOW TO LAY PAVING SLABS

1 *Mark out the area and prepare the subbase (see p.493). Lay strips of mortar to form a square just smaller than the slab. Include a cross strip for large slabs.*

2 *Position the slab and tamp down. Use a level to check that it is even. Repeat, using spacers for 1/2in (1cm) mortar gaps between the slabs.*

3 *Remove the spacers before the mortar sets. Fill the joints with a stiff mortar. Tamp down. Joints should be recessed about 1/16in (2mm). Brush mortar from the slabs.*

USING A JIGGER
This device has a central slit. After aligning the slit and joint, the gap can be filled without spilling mortar on the slabs.

Repeat with successive slabs, using spacers between each one. Check the levels in each direction after every three or four slabs. Remove the spacers while you can still reach them without walking on the paving, and before the mortar sets. If you have to walk on the paving before the mortar has dried, stand on boards to distribute your weight more evenly over the area.

How to Cut Slabs

1 Place the slab on a firm, flat surface and, using the corner of a bolster and a straight edge, score a groove on both faces and edges to mark the cutting line.

2 Using a bolster and club hammer, carefully work along the scored line to deepen the groove on the faces and edges of the paving slab.

3 Raise the slab onto a length of wood. Align the groove with the edge of the wood and tap the slab sharply with a hammer handle until it splits.

Finishing off

After a couple of days, fill the joints with a very stiff mortar mix (it should almost be crumbly to avoid staining the surface of the paving). Rub a dowel or a rounded piece of wood over the pointing for a crisp finish, leaving it about 1/16in (2mm) below the paving surface. Alternatively, brush a dry mortar consisting of 1 part cement to 3 parts sand into the joints.

Brush surplus mortar off the surface. Spray the joints with a fine mist from a hose-end sprayer or a watering can fitted with a fine rose. Sponge mortar from the surface immediately, before it stains the slabs.

Cutting paving slabs

If you have many slabs to cut, it is best to rent a power masonry saw. For only a few, use a bolster (a broad-edged cold chisel) and club hammer. Always wear goggles when cutting paving blocks. With a corner of the bolster, score the line where you need to cut all around the slab, then chisel a groove about 1/8in (3mm) deep along this line; you may have to work around the slab several times, using the bolster to define and deepen the groove. If the slab has to fit into a tight space, cut it about 1/4in (6mm) smaller than needed to allow room for any rough edges that may be left when the slab splits.

Place the slab on a firm surface and raise the smaller part of the slab to be cut on a length of wood. Tap it sharply with the handle of a club hammer until a split forms along the line of the groove. Trim any protrusions carefully with the bolster to make a smooth edge.

Random paving

Random paving has an informal appearance. It can be laid on sand, which will allow plants to be grown between the joints, or on mortar for a firmer finish; if using the latter, fill in the joints with bedding mortar.

Defining the edges

Use string lines to mark out the area to be paved and prepare a subbase for the paving (see p.493). Allow a slight slope for drainage (see "Water runoff," p.493) if necessary. Define the edges by laying a few yards (meters) of edging material first, working from one corner if laying a patio, or the two edges if laying a path. This may simply be large pieces of random paving, with at least one straight edge, which can be laid to form the sides of the patio or path, or it could be wood, brick, or concrete. If using paving slabs, mortar these into position, even if bedding the remaining slabs on sand.

Laying the random paving

Rough-lay an area about 3ft (1m) square without mortar, fitting the pieces together like a jigsaw puzzle. Keep the gaps small. It may be necessary to trim some pieces to size. Introduce a large piece occasionally, and fill in with smaller ones.

Bed the pieces on sand or mortar, using a level on a straight edge to ensure that they are even. Use a mallet or block of wood and a hammer to bed each piece firmly in position. Lift pieces and add or remove sand or mortar as necessary until all paving stones are level.

Filling the joints

If bedding random paving on sand, finish off by brushing dry sand into the joints. If using mortar, mix a stiff, crumbly, almost-dry mortar, and use a pointing trowel to fill the joints (see "Finishing off," left). If using a dark-colored stone, such as slate, use a concrete dye (a powder that you mix with the sand and cement) to make the joints less conspicuous. The color will look different when dry, so test the dye on a small area and allow it to dry before deciding on the amount of color to add.

Natural stone

Natural stone looks good, but is expensive and difficult to lay. Some types, such as sandstone, may be available cut into regular sizes and with an even edge. "Dressed" stone looks more natural; it is trimmed to a regular shape and has an attractive, uneven finish. Lay sawed or dressed stone in the same way as paving slabs, adding or removing mortar to produce a level surface.

Fieldstone is irregular, and has no straight edges. This stone is suitable for laying as random paving, and it looks much more appealing than broken concrete slabs, but it can form an uneven walkway. Upper and lower faces may differ; try to match them.

Tile surfaces

Quarry tiles, which are made of clay fired to a very high temperature, are useful for linking outdoor and indoor areas – perhaps where the paving inside a conservatory links with that outside. Glazed ceramic tiles may be more ornamental, giving an enclosed patio the impression of a

How to Lay Random Paving

1 Using string lines and pegs to mark the height of the edges, prepare a subbase (see p.493). Lay the edging pieces first, placing their straight edges facing outward.

2 Lay large slabs in the center, filling in with smaller ones. Check that central slabs are level with the edging pieces and bed them on sand or mortar. Use a piece of wood and a club hammer.

3 Fill the joints with almost-dry mortar, or brush in sand. With a mortar finish, use a trowel to bevel the mortar so that any surface water will always drain away from the slabs.

Mediterranean courtyard for example, but many are not frostproof. When selecting tiles, always check that they are suitable for using outdoors in your area. Tiles are difficult to cut, especially if they are not rectangular, so where possible design the area to make use of full tiles.

Laying tiles

Since tiles are thin and sometimes brittle, they need to be laid on a concrete subbase (see "Load-bearing surfaces," p.494). Quarry tiles may be laid on bedding mortar (see p.494). Soak the tiles in water for a couple of hours before use so that they do not absorb too much moisture from the mortar.

Glazed ceramic tiles are best glued to a level concrete base using outdoor tile adhesive (obtainable from a building supply store). Spread this on the back of the tiles, following the manufacturer's instructions, then press the tiles into position on the prepared concrete base.

Finish off an area of glazed tiles with a grout (available from building supply stores) to fill the gaps, perhaps colored to match or contrast with the tiles.

HOW TO LAY BRICK PAVING

1 *First, prepare the subbase (see p.493), allowing space for the edging bricks. Use string lines and pegs to set the edging bricks at the desired height.*

2 *Mortar in the edging bricks, and bed the others in the required pattern, tamping them level. At intervals, check levels in all directions.*

3 *Spread a thin layer of dry mortar over the surface and brush it between the joints. Sprinkle with water to set the mortar, and clean the surface.*

Bricks and pavers

Bricks and clay or concrete pavers (also called interlock) are most effective when laid in small areas. A large expanse may be divided up with other materials, such as gravel or railroad ties. Alternatively, lay bricks in two or more complementary patterns or colors.

For a patio situated next to a house built of brick, using bricks or pavers is an excellent way of visually linking the house and garden.

Choosing bricks

The range of bricks available is quite wide; it is possible to find a type that suits virtually any patio or terrace.

For a large volume of bricks, contact a brick company to see if they will deliver. Building supply stores sell bricks in any quantities. Be sure to choose bricks that are appropriate for outdoor paving and resistant to wetting and freezing.

Choosing pavers

Clay pavers are as attractive as bricks and are usually produced in shades of red. They have a thinner profile than concrete pavers or bricks. Concrete pavers may lack the warm colors of bricks, but they will make a practical surface. They are generally found in gray, blue-gray, or buff shades and are produced in a range of shapes.

Laying bricks

First make a suitable subbase (see p.493). Bricks should ideally be bedded on mortar. First lay the edging strips (or edging bricks), bedded on a concrete footing and then fixed with mortar between the joints. Prepare the bedding mortar (see p.494) and lay it to a depth of 1in (2.5cm). Bed the bricks onto this, spacing them evenly to leave joints for mortar; use thin strips of hardboard or wood as spacers between bricks if desired. Once an area is complete, brush a dry mortar over the bricks. To remove air pockets, press this into the gaps with a narrow piece of wood. In damp weather, moisture from the ground and air will set the pointing; in dry weather, speed up setting by spraying with water.

Types of brick

Bricks are available in a wide variety of styles, textures, and colors, providing an attractive and practical building material. Take care to choose the most appropriate type. They should be suitable for the proposed purpose and coordinate well with the house, patio, or other hard landscape features.

ENGINEERING BRICKS
Engineering bricks are very hard-wearing. If used for paving, make sure they have good wet-weather grip. They may cost more than ordinary bricks.

CORED BRICKS
Cored bricks have holes. They may be used on edge for paving with a narrower profile, but are not economical for large areas.

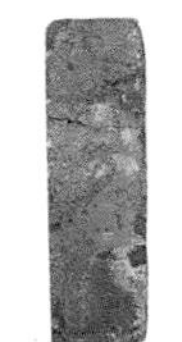

FACING OR STOCK BRICKS
These are used to face buildings, providing an attractive finish. They are available in a variety of colors, and may be rough or smooth in texture. They may be unsuitable for paving since they may not be able to withstand severe weather conditions.

BRICKS WITH "FROGS"
A frog is an indentation in one face of a brick. Frogged bricks may be used for paving if they are laid on edge or the frogs face downward.

Patterns in brick

Bricks can be laid in several different ways to create attractive patterns. Three examples are shown below.

BASKET WEAVE

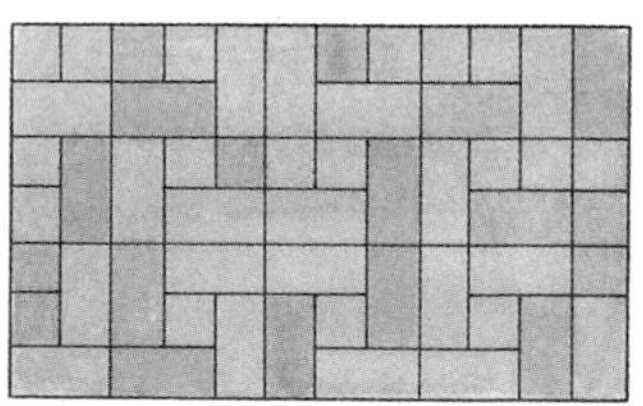

INTERLOCKING BOXES

HERRINGBONE

Cutting bricks and pavers

Bricks and thick pavers may be difficult to cut. If cutting is necessary, it can be done by the company that supplied the material or by using a rented masonry saw. Using these options, it is possible to cut bricks accurately, neatly, and quickly. Alternatively, they may be cut to the desired shape with a bolster and club hammer (see "Cutting paving slabs," p.496), although the cuts made by these tools may not be as clean.

Laying pavers

Pavers are bedded onto sand using a plate compactor; they nest together with small gaps between. Since the pavers can be lifted and relaid, this type of paving is sometimes called flexible paving. Blocks $2^1/_2$–$2^3/_4$in (6–6.5cm) thick are adequate for garden projects.

Preparing the site and laying edge restraints

First, prepare a subbase suitable for local conditions (see "Foundations," p.493). Where there are no existing firm edges (such as walls), lay permanent edging strips. The simplest way to do this is to use specially made edge restraints or edging pieces, which are available from paving manufacturers. These must be set into position in concrete. Alternatively, $1^1/_2$ x 4in (38 x 100mm) pressure-treated lumber held in place with strong pegs at least 2in (50mm) square may be used.

Large areas should be broken up into manageable sizes, such as 3ft (1m) squares, using temporary wooden rails. Spread a layer of sharp

Pavers, tiles, setts, and cobblestones

Pavers (also called interlock) vary greatly in size, color, and thickness. They are also finished in many different ways, so that their texture and final shape (either formal and geometric or more informal and natural) contribute greatly to the style of the garden. Considerably more distinctive results may be achieved using terracotta tiles, granite setts, Belgian blocks, or cobblestones.

Clay Pavers
These red pavers may be laid either as stretchers, that is longitudinally, or as headers, placed end on.

Wire-cut Clay Pavers
Wire-cut clay pavers have a dragged finish and a roughened surface on all sides, which serves to provide extra grip in the finished paving.

Interlocking Pavers
These clay or concrete pavers can be used to create unusual patterns. Pressed pavers in blocks (far right) are produced in a range of colors.

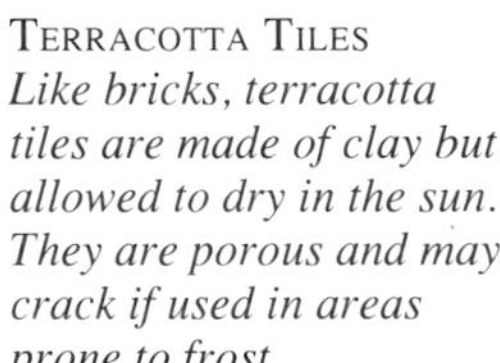

Terracotta Tiles
Like bricks, terracotta tiles are made of clay but allowed to dry in the sun. They are porous and may crack if used in areas prone to frost.

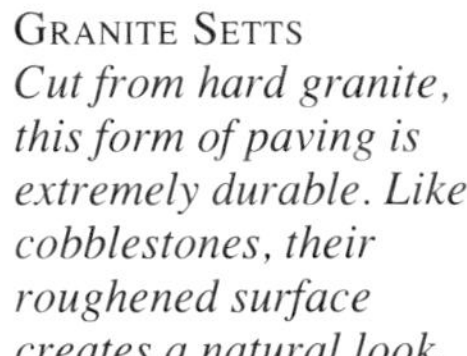

Granite Setts
Cut from hard granite, this form of paving is extremely durable. Like cobblestones, their roughened surface creates a natural look.

Belgian Blocks

Cobblestones
Cobblestones (below) are large, rounded stones formed by the action of the sea or glaciers. They can be set in mortar to form an interestingly textured finish, but are uncomfortable to walk on and should be used only in small areas or in combination with other paving materials. When laying cobblestones, form firm edges with bricks or lengths of concrete edging, set in concrete.

Imitation Granite Setts
These reconstituted stone pavers are lighter and cheaper than granite. Belgian blocks have a more weathered look.

How to Lay Flexible Paving

1 *After preparing the subbase (see p.493), set edging strips of concrete or wood in position around the edges of the site. Use a level and a club hammer to tap the edges level.*

2 *Divide large areas into bays 3ft (1m) square with boards. Add 2in (5cm) of sand. Level the sand to the tops of the boards with a length of wood. Remove the boards and fill the vacated spaces with sand.*

3 *Lay the pavers to the required pattern, working from one corner of the site. Lay only whole blocks at this stage, leaving until last any cut ones required to fill the gaps in the design.*

4 *Vibrate the pavers into the sand or tamp down with a club hammer and length of wood. Brush dry sand over the surface and make 2 or 3 passes with a plate compactor.*

sand evenly to a depth of about 2in (5cm). The top surface of the sand should be just high enough that about one-third of the paving block will protrude above the surrounding wooden rails. Adjust the amount of sand as work proceeds.

Positioning and bedding the pavers

Do not walk on the sand while laying the pavers, and keep it dry. Work from one corner of the site to lay the pavers. When some are laid, place a kneeling board over the pavers to continue working. Lay as many whole blocks as possible, then fill in with cut pavers around any obstacles as necessary (see "Cutting paving slabs," p.496).

When about 6sq yd (5sq m) of paving has been laid, bed the pavers into the sand. The easiest way to do this is with a plate compactor, but do not go too near the incompleted edge. If only laying a small area of paving, the blocks can be tamped down with a heavy club hammer over a block of wood that is large enough to span several pavers at once. Continue to lay pavers and bed or tamp them down.

When the whole area is finished, brush dry sand into the joints and settle in position with the plate compactor. Create a mowing edge of bricks, pavers, or concrete slabs where it is difficult to mow right to the lawn edge. Bed the paving material on mortar, with the top just below the grass level, so that the mower is not damaged.

A COMBINATION OF PAVING EFFECTS
A mixture of different paving materials, including square stone slabs, random paving, and brick edging, blends well with informal planting.

Setts and cobblestones

Bed granite or imitation setts on 2in (5cm) of bedding mortar (see p.494) and brush stiff mortar into the joints (see "Finishing off," p.496). Spray the surface with water to clean it and set the mortar mix.

Cobblestones may also be set in mortar. They are uncomfortable to walk on, so use for small areas or with other materials. When laying, form firm edges with bricks or lengths of concrete edging. Lay 1½in (3.5cm) of bedding mortar on 3in (7.5cm) of compacted crushed stone.

Terms explained

Aggregate is crushed stone or gravel used to make concrete. Fine aggregate contains particles up to ¼in (½cm), coarse aggregate from ¼in to 3in (½cm to 7cm). Combined aggregate contains sand and stone.
Bedding mortar is used for laying paving stones. It is made with sharp sand instead of soft (builder's) sand.
Cement is a gray powder containing limestone, the setting agent of concrete and mortar.
Concrete is a hard-setting building material made of a mixture of cement, aggregate, sand, and water.
Crushed stone has angular particles that are graded by size, the finest grade being stone dust.
Dry mortar is a stiff mix often used to fill the joints in paving.
Masonry cement has additives that make it unsuitable for concrete. Use only for mortars.
Mortar is a mixture of cement, sand, and water used principally for bricklaying.
Portland cement is a type of cement. Use ordinary Portland cement for most concreting jobs. It can also be used for mortars.
Sand is graded by particle size. Sharp sand is gritty, clean, and contains no salt. Avoid or wash ocean-beach sand, since salt stops cement from hardening.

Decks

Wooden decking is popular as a hard surface in warm, dry climates. Decks may be used anywhere, however, provided that pressure-treated lumber is used.

It is best to build the deck on a level or gently sloping site. For a raised deck on a steeply sloping site, it is advisable to seek specialist assistance, since it would need to be well designed and constructed.

In some areas there are building regulations that state that all exterior areas of decking must be able to support a stipulated minimum weight. It may also be necessary to obtain a building permit in some areas and have the work inspected. If in any doubt concerning the regulations, check your local building ordinances. Simple parquet decking (see p.500), which is laid on gravel and sand, should not require a building permit.

WOODEN DECKING
A wooden patio or veranda overlooking the garden makes a very imposing feature, especially when crowned with a pergola to provide summer shade. However, wooden decking needs to be very well constructed, and it is usually best to have the job done by experts. Features such as rails, steps, and wooden supports require regular maintenance (see p.500).

Wood for decking

Western red cedar is a good choice because of its natural rot resistance, although regularly treating it with a preservative ensures a longer life. Other wood is suitable but must be pressure-treated with a preservative. When using pressure-treated lumber, always paint cut ends with a wood preservative. Short lengths of lumber can be made up into decking panels to produce a wide variety of practical, attractive patterns.

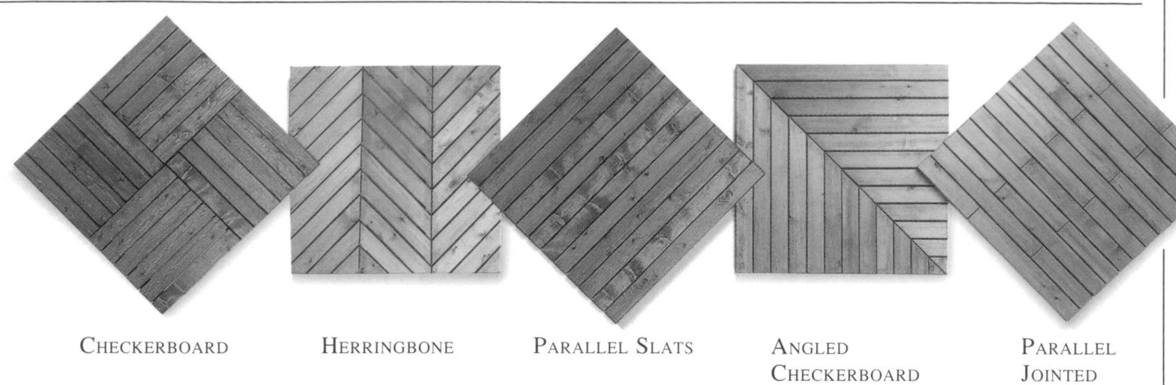

CHECKERBOARD HERRINGBONE PARALLEL SLATS ANGLED CHECKERBOARD PARALLEL JOINTED

Slatted decking

This type of decking is suitable for level or gently sloping ground. It is simple to construct and requires few special fittings.

For an area beside a house, construct a concrete foundation (see *How to Lay Concrete*, p.494) with a gentle fall away from the house for water drainage. Onto the concrete base, mortar a row of bricks spaced about one brick apart at right angles to the intended direction of the decking. Add further rows of bricks at intervals of 16in (40cm). Check constantly that all the bricks are level, because they will support the joists.

Lay joists 2 x 3in (50 x 75mm) over the bricks, inserting a sheet of plastic between the bricks and the joists. If joining lengths of wood, make sure there is a brick beneath the point where the joists abut, and screw a plain bracket across the join. Always check that joists are even, using a level and a straightedge to ensure accuracy.

Lay 1 x 10in (25 x 250mm) boards at right angles to the joists. Allow ½in (10mm) gaps for free drainage and a little movement in the wood. Ensure that joins in the decking are staggered from row to row and that the boards are butt-joined over a supporting joist. Secure the boards with brass or other rustproof screws, countersunk beneath the surface. Fill the holes with a wood filler that matches the color of the wood.

Finish the deck neatly with a low brick or block edging, cutting the decking so that it overlaps the edging by 2in (5cm). Alternatively, a length of facing wood can be screwed or nailed along the cut edges.

Parquet decking

It is possible to buy parquetlike wooden squares intended primarily for paths, which can also be used for decking. Alternatively they can be easily made. About 3ft (1m) square is a practical size. Buy 2 x 4in (50 x 100mm) treated wood, cut into 3ft (1m) lengths, and sand the ends smooth. Two lengths form the supports at opposite sides of the square, while the others are laid across them as slats. Use spacers to ensure that these slats fill the area evenly, and fix with two nails at either end. Prepare a base on firmed ground or subsoil with 3in (7.5cm) of compacted gravel topped with 3in (7.5cm) of sand. Level and tamp before laying the squares in alternate directions. Nail them together if necessary to ensure their stability, driving the nails in at an angle.

DECKING STEPPING-STONES
Decking can be used to create an unusual "stepping-stone" path across a pond. When positioned and angled for esthetic impact, the squares add a stylish, geometric element to informal planting and the soft play of light on the pond surface. Here, parallel slats are laid in alternate directions to add a dynamic sense of movement to the overall design.

Applying stains

Western red cedar turns a very obvious red color when wet. It may, however, be stained any color to suit the surroundings. It is best to use stains that allow any moisture in the wood to escape; if trapped beneath an impermeable layer, it would eventually cause the surface color to lift. Wooden surfaces to be stained should be dry and free from dirt. Follow instructions regarding stirring or thinning, and apply the stain with a good-quality paint brush, brushing in the direction of the grain. Do not overload the brush, which leads to uneven coverage, but work the stain well into the wood. Several applications will be needed, but wait until each coat is completely dry before applying more.

Maintenance

All wooden surfaces need regular maintenance. Once a year, check for splits or cracks. Damaged boards will need to be replaced. Check that no bolts, screws, brackets, or nails have rusted. If galvanized fittings are scratched, their protective coating may be damaged and rust will appear. Brass fittings, which do not rust, are preferable in wooden decking. If the stain wears thin in areas of heavy foot traffic, clean the surface and reapply the stain (see above). Fungal growths may appear at some stage. Fungicides are available, but it is better to remove growths by brushing with a stiff broom. In some regions, termites can cause problems in decking; if in doubt, consult a pest control firm.

SUPPORT FOR WOODEN DECKING

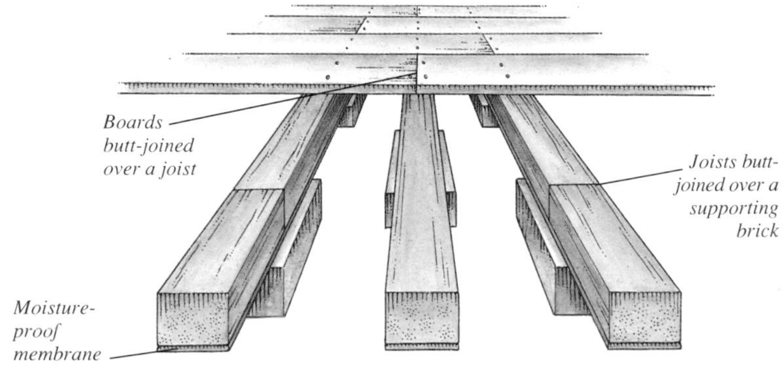

When joining two lengths of wood to form a joist, make sure that the join lies over one of the supporting bricks. Lay the boards at right angles to the joists, positioning all butt joins directly over a supporting joist.

Paths and steps

Paths and steps play a major role in good garden design. They help form the framework of the garden, link its various elements, and may lead the eye to a focal point. Consider setting a path at an angle, off-center, or following an indirect route. Steps provide interesting changes of level and create very different effects, depending on whether they are straight or curved, wide or narrow, and shallow or steep.

Practical considerations

Paths to the garden shed or the greenhouse need to be wide enough to take a wheelbarrow and should also provide a dry and solid surface. Paths to the front door or for strolling through the garden should be sufficiently wide for two to walk abreast: about 3–4ft (1–1.2m).

Materials and design

The choice of materials and the laying pattern may be used to set or enhance the garden style. Combining materials, such as paving stones with cobblestones, bricks with gravel, or concrete paving slabs with bricks or clay pavers, often makes an appealing design for a path.

Stepping-stone paths may be laid in many parts of the garden. They are a good choice, for example, when you do not want to spoil the line of a lawn, but they can become muddy in wet weather. Before you start, place the paving stones on the surface to check the spacing; they should be spaced at a natural pace. On lawns, set them into the grass so that their surface is safely below mowing level.

Where winters are relatively dry, paths may be made of wood, either in the form of log sections used as stepping-stones or to make a series of square, slatted units as described in "Parquet decking," opposite.

On sloping sites, steps may be an essential part of a path. They may also be valuable as a design feature even on a relatively flat site. Steps should harmonize with their setting: in a woodland garden, for example, shallow log risers and gravel treads would be suitable while, in a modern setting, brick risers and concrete slab treads might be more appropriate.

Driveways

A driveway can have a considerable impact on a design, especially in a small garden. There may be little choice in where to position a driveway, unless a new garage is to be built at the same time. It is possible to make a driveway look attractive by choosing a suitable surface and positioning ornamental plants nearby.

SUBTLETY WITH STONE
Here, the mottled texture of the embedded stones is complemented by Alchemilla mollis *and defined by seams of moss.*

LOG SECTIONS
Logs sawn into sections make a harmonious series of stepping-stones through an area of woodland, blending perfectly with the setting.

Asphalt

Asphalt is best used for driveways and paths that need not be attractive – the path to the shed, for example. It can also be used to cover a damaged concrete path. Add texture by rolling stone chips into the surface. If asphalt is not locally available in small quantities, use cold patch. Asphalt is best laid in warm weather. Unless it is well laid, asphalt may break up after a few years; for heavily used areas such as a main driveway hire a qualified contractor to lay the asphalt.

Preparations

Asphalt can be laid on any firm surface such as concrete or gravel. Never lay it on bare earth or crushed stone since it will be difficult to obtain a firm and level surface that will last. If necessary, make a stable base by spreading a mixture of gravel and sand 2–3in (5–8cm) thick over firm ground or compacted crushed stone. If an old path or driveway is the base, first paint inside any holes or cracks with driveway sealer and leave for about 20 minutes before filling them with asphalt. To ensure good water drainage, lay a driveway on a slight slope.

The edges of an asphalt path often weaken and crumble, so use concrete edging blocks (obtained from building supply stores), bricks, or lengths of pressure-treated lumber to provide a firm edging.

BRICK PATHWAYS
A brick path can become a design feature in its own right, adding texture and color to a garden entrance. Here, the soft pink of the brick harmonizes with the surrounding plants and leads the eye to the rose-covered arch and the less formal grass area beyond.

Application

Apply a layer of driveway sealer to bind the surface. Stir it first, then pour it from the container and spread with a stiff brush. Apply the asphalt and rake to an even depth of about ¾in (2cm).

Firm the surface by tamping it with the back of a rake to remove large air pockets, then make several passes with a heavy garden roller. Keep the surface of the roller damp to prevent the asphalt from sticking to it. Top up any visible depressions, and roll the surface again. If using stone chips, sprinkle evenly and roll again to bed them in.

Bricks and pavers

The sympathetic coloring of bricks and clay pavers makes them excellent materials for paths within the garden. Because the individual units are small, it is relatively easy to adjust to changes of level and even to lay a path to a curve. A variety of effects can be created depending on the laying pattern used (see "Patterns in brick," p.497)

Construction

Mark out the proposed line of the path with pegs and string, calculating where cut bricks or pavers may be needed to create a sharp curve. If the path will be subjected to heavy wear, prepare a deep foundation (see "Load-bearing surfaces," p.494). For one that will receive lighter use, a 3in (8cm) subbase of crushed stone firmed and leveled with stone dust should be sufficient.

First lay a suitable edging (see "Edging paths," p.502) along one side of the path, then lay the path itself in sections about 3ft (1m) long. Pavers should be bedded in a 2in (5cm) layer of dry sand (see "Laying pavers," p.498), while bricks require a 1in (2.5cm) bed of mortar (see "Laying bricks," p.497). As you complete each section, tamp the bricks or pavers into place, checking that they are level with a straightedge and level. Then lay the edging on the other side of the path to complete this section. Repeat the process for each section until the path has been laid.

To finish off a path made of pavers, brush dry sand into the joints. For a brick path, brush a dry mortar mix in between the joints (see "Finishing off," p.496), making sure that there are no large air pockets. If necessary, compact the mortar using a piece of wood slightly thinner than the width of the joints. Finally, sprinkle with a fine spray of water from a watering can or wash down gently with a hose-end sprayer to moisten the mortar and clean the bricks.

Concrete

Concrete poured *in situ* is a practical and hard-wearing surface material that is especially suitable for wide paths and driveways. Its appearance can be made more attractive by adding texture (see below). Concrete can also be colored using special dyes added to the mix. Since the color often looks different once the concrete has dried, use dyes with caution. Color a small test piece first and let it dry rather than judge the final apearance by the wet mix.

Divide a wide concrete path with rows of bricks or lengths of broad wood that will become part of the finished design. These will avoid the need for laying expansion joints during construction.

Preparing a base

Prepare a suitable foundation (see "Basic procedure," p.493). Next, make the form to hold the concrete in place until it sets. Use lengths of wood 1in (2.5cm) thick, and at least the depth of the concrete. Use 2 x 2in (5 x 5cm) pegs, not more than 3ft (1m) apart to hold the form in place. Lengths of wood may be joined by nailing a block of wood to the outside of the two pieces to bridge them together.

Making curves

To make gentle curves, mark out the shape that you want to create, and hammer pegs into the ground set closely together. Soak lengths of softwood in water to make them pliable, and then bend and nail them to the pegs. Sharp curves can be made in a similar way, with the addition of a series of saw cuts on the inside of the curve. The saw cuts should reach about halfway through the wood to increase its flexibility. Alternatively, use several thicknesses of thin hardboard, which is easy to bend and shape.

Expansion joints

Concrete will crack if not laid with breaks to allow for expansion and a degree of movement. Divide the area into sections no more than 12ft (4m) long, using fixed pieces of wood as temporary divisions. If using ready-mixed concrete, where the load has to be used all at once, use hardboard cut into sections, and leave these in position until the concrete has set.

Adding texture

A concrete path poured *in situ* can be made more attractive by adding texture. Use these techniques on a few sections only, or alternate patterns between sections, to create an interesting overall result.

Exposed aggregate gives a pleasant, nonslip finish. Spread gravel or crushed stone evenly over the concrete before it sets, then tamp it gently into the surface. When the concrete is nearly hard, brush the surface to expose more of the aggregate, then spray it with water to wash away fine particles. Different textures and colors can be created by using aggregates with particles of various sizes and colors.

Brushed finishes are easy to create. After tamping the concrete gently, push the bristles of a soft broom over the surface to produce a fairly smooth finish; for a ridged effect, use a stiff broom once the concrete has begun to set. You can also brush in a series of swirls, or straight or wavy lines.

Stamped patterns can be made with special tools or with inventive objects such as pastry cutters and seashells. This technique is best kept to very small areas. To create leaf impressions, use large leaves such as sycamore, pressing them into the surface with a trowel and then brushing them out once the concrete has hardened.

Coarse texture

Medium-coarse texture

Fine texture

HOW TO LAY A GRAVEL PATH

1 *Dig out the base of the path to a depth of 7in (18cm) and set the edges. Compact the base. Drive in pegs at 3ft (1m) intervals to anchor the edge restraints.*

2 *If the path borders a lawn, excavate an extra 1in (2.5cm) so that the path is below grass level (inset). Put down layers of crushed stone, sand and coarse gravel, and pea gravel. Rake level.*

Laying concrete

Mix the concrete (see p.494) and pour it into the form. If mixing in small batches, fill alternate bays, then remove the dividers once the concrete has set and pour concrete into the remaining bays. Use a length of wood to tamp the concrete level, working from the center toward the joints. If the path or driveway is wide, using a tamping board with another person will make the job easier. Tamping leaves a slightly ridged surface. If a smooth finish is required , use a wood float in gentle, sweeping motions. A steel float will produce an even smoother surface.

Concrete paving slabs

Paving slabs are available in a wide range of colors, shapes, and finishes. They are easier to lay than concrete poured *in situ*, but more difficult to lay to a curve than bricks or pavers. They combine well with other materials, for instance with cobblestones set along the edge or with small strips of gravel between each slab. This is a useful technique for creating curved paths since it makes the uneven joints less obtrusive. For details on laying paving slabs, see p.495.

Grass

Grass paths are useful for linking a series of lawns, or for broad walks between beds. They should be as wide as possible: this helps them stand up to concentrated wear. They also need less water than narrow sod. Put down sod for a grass path in the same way as for a lawn (see THE LAWN, "Laying sod," p.278).

Gravel

Gravel is easy to lay, presents no problems when creating curves, and is not expensive. There are drawbacks, however: unless well bedded and used with retaining edges, loose gravel can get onto adjoining surfaces, it can be uncomfortable and noisy to walk on, and it is not an easy surface on which to push a wheelbarrow or a stroller.

Construct a firm base by excavating the ground to take about 4in (10cm) of compacted crushed stone, 2in (5cm) of a sand and coarse gravel mix, and 1in (2.5cm) of gravel. For a fine finish, use pea gravel.

In a formal setting with mainly straight edges, concrete edging strips can be used; in other settings bricks or treated lumber may be more appropriate. If using wood, anchor it with pegs about 3ft (1m) apart. Apply the gravel in several stages, raking and rolling it to produce a slight camber for drainage. To help compaction and create a solid path, water the gravel occasionally with a fine spray while rolling.

Edging paths

Plastic edge restraints sold as lawn edging are easily cut to size and hold a path of bricks or pavers in place invisibly. Lengths of treated lumber may also be used, held in place with wooden pegs. It is possible to use boards temporarily while building the path, then remove them and fill in the gaps with concrete. For a brick edging, lay matching or contrasting bricks on edge. Secure them with mortar; this also helps to stop weeds from growing.

Building steps

To calculate the number of steps you need to build, divide the height of the slope by the height of one riser (including the depth of the paving slab and mortar). It may be necessary to adjust the height of the steps to fit the slope. Mark the position of the risers with wooden pegs and then excavate the soil to form a series of soil steps.

Make a concrete footing (see p.504) for the base riser, and allow it to set. Then construct the riser using bricks or blocks set in masonry mortar (see p.494). Check that they are even using a straightedge and level, and backfill behind the riser with compacted crushed stone or sand and gravel.

Prepare a bed of mortar on top of the riser and lay the first tread; it should slope forward slightly to shed water, and overlap the riser at the front by 1–2in (2.5–5cm). Mark the position of the next riser on the tread, and mortar it into position.

Tread to riser ratio

For ease of use, it is important that the width of the tread and the height of the riser are in the correct proportion to each other. As a general rule, the width of the tread and double the height of the riser should total about 26in (65cm). First, choose the height of the riser, double it and deduct it from 26in (65cm) to give the width of the tread. You may wish to add 1–2in (2.5–5cm) for an overhang.

For the steps to be safe, the treads should measure at least 12in (30cm) from front to back. The height of the risers is normally between 4in (10cm) and 7in (18cm).

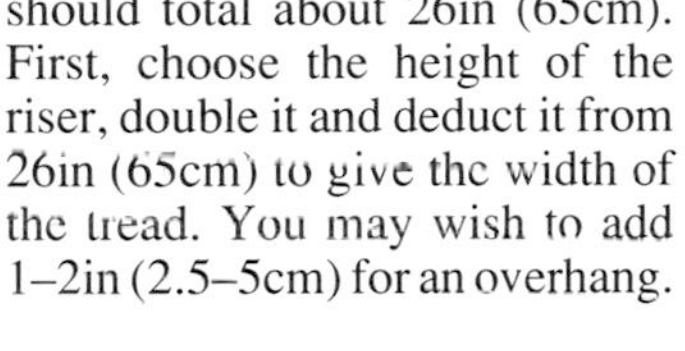
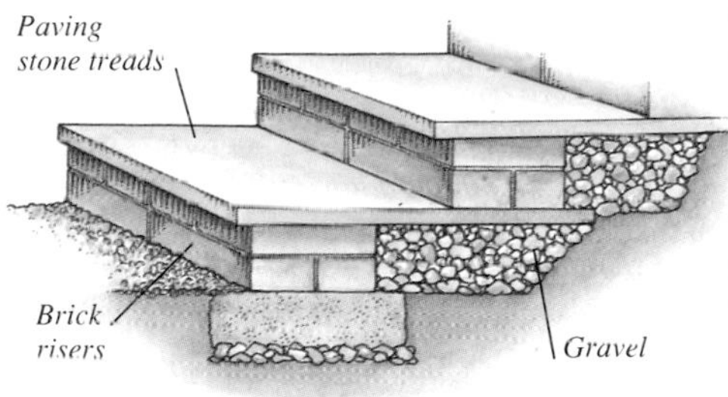

WOOD AND GRAVEL STEPS
Here railroad ties are filled in with gravel to create a curving flight of gently rising steps, with flanking plants softening the edges.

HOW TO BUILD STEPS INTO A BANK

1 *Measure the height of the bank to work out how many steps are needed (see left). To do this, drive a peg into the top of the slope and a post at the bottom. Tie string horizontally between the two, then measure the distance between ground level and the string.*

2 *Use string and pegs to mark the sides, then run strings to mark the fronts of the treads. Dig out the steps and compact the earth at each tread position.*

3 *Construct a footing for the riser, 6in (15cm) deep and twice the width of the bricks. Fill with concrete over a 3in (7cm) crushed stone base.*

4 *When the concrete has set, lay the first riser on the footing. Use a string line stretched between pegs to ensure bricks are straight and level.*

5 *Backfill with crushed stone to the height of the bricks and tamp down. Set the paving slabs on ½in (1cm) of mortar, with a small gap between them.*

6 *The slabs should have an overhang of 1–2in (2.5–5cm) at the front and a slight, forward slope for drainage. Mark the position of the second riser on the slabs and mortar the bricks in place. Fill in and set the treads as before. Continue for the remaining steps. Finally, mortar the joints between the slabs.*

Walls

Boundary walls have been a feature of gardens since the early days of enclosures, and in the last century walled gardens were a common feature on large estates. Nowadays, however, large boundary walls are uncommon, having given way to cheaper fences or hedges.

Garden walls are often decorative as well as practical. If they have a planting cavity, low walls can be particularly attractive and, because they require less substantial foundations and supporting piers, they are also easy and cheap to construct.

Materials

Boundary walls may be constructed from various materials, including brick, and for low walls precast concrete walling blocks. Screen block walls (opposite) are a practical and decorative alternative to solid walls and are also suitable for dividing off parts of the garden. These blocks are made specifically for outdoor use. When buying bricks, however, always check with the supplier that they are suitable for garden walls: bricks should be frostproof and able to withstand moisture penetration from both sides.

Walls may also be constructed from a combination of materials, for example brick with facing panels of local stone such as flint. Large, plain walls may be painted with a masonry paint (usually white or a pale color) on the garden side. This reflects the light and contrasts well with wall shrubs or other plants.

How high to build?

There may be restrictions placed on the height of walls in local building codes, so check this before building. A low block wall is a straightforward job that anyone handy with materials and tools should be able to tackle. Brick and concrete block walls higher than about 3ft (1m) require advice from an expert and should have a strengthening pier every 8ft (2.5m).

COMBINED MATERIALS
Brick and flint are juxtaposed here to create a striking garden divider. The mixture of straight and curved lines reinforces the blend of styles. When combined in this way, diverse materials enhance each other.

Concrete footings for walls

The width of the footing for all walls should be two to three times the width of the wall. For walls lower than 3ft (1m), deep and substantial foundations are not necessary.

For a half-brick wall (i.e. the width of a single brick), dig a trench the length of the wall and 15in (38cm) deep. Place 5in (13cm) of crushed stone in the bottom and tamp it down. Then pour in 4in (10cm) of concrete, allowing it to harden completely for a few days before laying the bricks or concrete blocks. For a

Walling materials

Bricks are the most popular choice of walling material, although concrete blocks manufactured to imitate natural clay bricks may also be used. If you want to build a wall to match the brickwork of existing buildings, used bricks are available in many colors and styles.

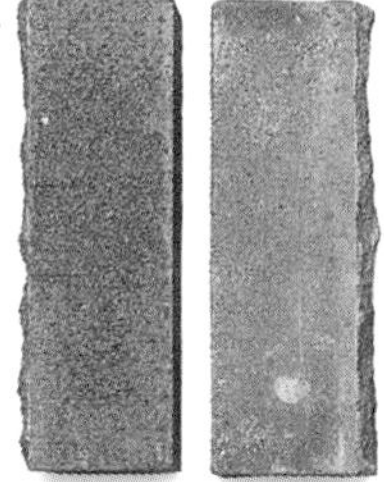
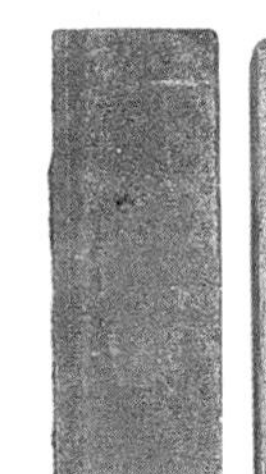
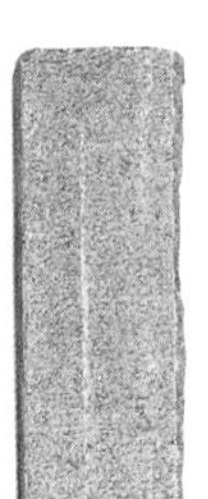

SMOOTH-TEXTURED BRICKS
These are most suitable for facing the front of a wall. They come in a range of colors.

MOTTLED ENGINEERING BRICKS
These contribute a rough-hewn appearance; they are also the hardest of all the bricks.

PRECAST CONCRETE BLOCKS
These contain medium-textured gravel.

ROCK-FACED CONCRETE BLOCKS
The brick-red color imitates the look of clay bricks. They are also available colored to look like sandstone.

SMOOTH BLOCKS
These concrete blocks suit a modern design.

HOW TO MAKE A CONCRETE FOOTING

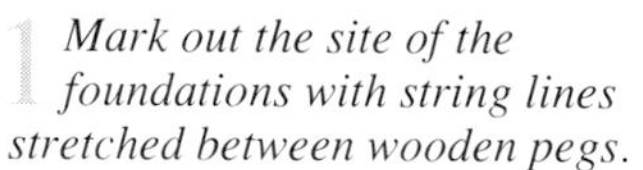

1 *Mark out the site of the foundations with string lines stretched between wooden pegs.*

2 *Dig a trench of the required depth. Check that the base is level and the sides vertical. Drive in pegs to the level for the concrete. Align with a level and a length of wood spanning the pegs.*

3 *Soak the trench with water and allow it to drain. Then add 5in (13cm) of crushed stone and tamp it down. Pour in concrete, slicing into the mix with a spade to dispel air bubbles.*

4 *Compact the concrete by tamping it down firmly with a length of wood. Level it to the tops of the pegs. Leave the surface rough as a key for the mortar for the first course of bricks.*

How to Build a Screen Wall

1 Place a course of blocks and pilasters alongside a prepared footing to position the supporting rebars. Before the footing sets, knock in the rebars, leaving enough exposed to reach the middle of the highest pilaster.

2 Lay a ½in (1cm) bed of mortar around the rebar. Lower the pilaster onto the mortar and align it with a level. Then fill the inside of the pilaster with concrete for reinforcement.

3 Mortar the footing and the first screen block. Repeat at the other end of the section.

4 Position one block at either end of the first section. To align the intervening blocks, push pegs into the ground and stretch a string between them, passing it over the pilasters and the blocks.

5 Position the next block, and knock it gently into place with the handle of a trowel. Repeat this procedure along the row of blocks, regularly checking the alignment with a level. Remove the string.

6 Start the second row by placing the pilasters and filling them with concrete as before. Then lay the second row of blocks using chicken wire bedded in the mortar to strengthen the bonding.

7 Finish the second row. Mortar the pilaster caps and coping stones into position. Check levels, tidy up the pointing, and square off the mortar at the base of the wall with a trowel.

full-brick wall, which is two bricks wide, or for a double wall with a space for planting cavities, dig the trench 2in (5cm) deeper and add 2in (5cm) extra concrete. For a brick or concrete block wall, the top of the footing need only be 6in (15cm) below ground level. For a concrete screen, the top of the footing may be just below ground level, provided reinforcing rebars are used. On heavy clay or in cold areas, increase the depth of the footing so that it is below the frost line. For higher walls, seek the advice of a specialist.

Block patterns

Many different geometric and free-form patterns of screen wall blocks are available for easy-construction garden walls.

LEAF

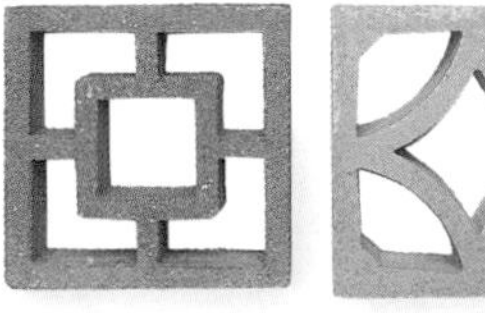

SQUARE CURVED DIAMOND

Bricklaying

To ensure that the first course is straight, stretch two parallel strings along the footing, the space between them equal to the width of the wall. Lay a ⅜in (10mm) bed of masonry mortar (p.494) along the footing. The first brick of a course is laid unmortared, then the second is "buttered" on one end and laid up against it. As you lay, check frequently with a level that the bricks are even and horizontal. If too high, tap them down gently with the trowel handle. Insert more mortar under any that are too low. Check also that the mortar joints are all ⅜in (10mm) thick.

Repeat the process for subsequent courses. For walls with planting cavities, leave weep holes (unmortared gaps between bricks) for drainage in the first course that is completely above ground level.

Before the mortar dries, use a pointing trowel to give the joints a neat, beveled finish. Vertical joints should all be beveled in the same direction; horizontal ones should slope slightly downward to aid water runoff.

Brick bonding

There are many brick bonding patterns. If you are a beginner at bricklaying, keep to one that is easy to lay and does not require many cut bricks. The simplest of all is a running, or stretcher, bond, in which all the bricks are laid lengthways.

Screen walling

In parts of the garden where a brick wall would form too solid a barrier, a screen wall of specifically made, pierced concrete blocks (see left and above) may be more appropriate. Walls of this kind are supported at each end and at 8–10ft (2.5–3m) intervals by piers built of hollow pilaster blocks. These are normally reinforced with rebars set in the footing and filled with mortar or concrete. Even so, screen walls are not strong, so for walls higher than 6ft (2m) seek professional advice.

Some popular bonds

Running bond is used for walls one brick thick; Flemish and English bonds use both stretchers and headers (bricks laid respectively lengthwise and widthwise) in a full-brick wall.

RUNNING BOND

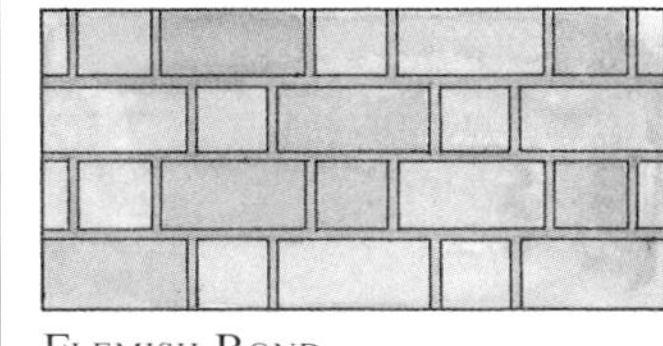

FLEMISH BOND

ENGLISH BOND

TYPES OF COPING

A DECORATIVE FINISH
Upright stones have been set in mortar as a coping for a dry limestone wall.

A FULL-BRICK WALL
This Flemish-bonded wall is topped by a course of headers – bricks laid across the full width of the wall.

STONE COPING
Large stone slabs form a solid coping that complements a wall of flints mortared in courses.

SOFTENING THE WALL
The hard line of the wall's edge is softened by a display of trailing flowering plants to create a colorful curtain. The crevices between the dry stones provide ideal spaces for shallow-rooting rock garden plants.

Coping

Coping, which forms the top course of a wall, prevents frost damage by shedding rainwater so that it does not seep into the joints. It also gives the wall a finished appearance.

Specially made, curved coping bricks are available, but these are often only the width of the wall and are strictly cappings, since they do not throw the drips clear of the wall. Wider concrete slabs are used for copings on brick as well as concrete block walls. Coping is especially important for precast concrete block walls because it helps to bond the blocks. Suppliers often call coping for concrete blocks "cap blocks."

Dry-stone walls

Dry-stone walls may be laid on concrete footings (see p.504) or a foundation of crushed stone. They may be planted with alpines (see p.200), and look attractive if a cavity is left in the top for trailing plants.

Dig a trench and make a firm base of compacted crushed stone or gravel. The base of the wall should be one or two courses below ground level. Use a taut line to maintain a level construction, and build up the wall with broad tie-stones and smaller random stones to bond the wall together. The wall should be wider at the bottom than at the top. To achieve a consistent slope or "batter," make a batter board, a wooden frame in the shape of the desired cross section of the wall. An inward slope of about 1in for every 24in (2.5cm for every 60cm) is usually sufficient. Use a level to keep the batter board perpendicular. Finish off with large, flat stones or a row of vertical stones laid on edge (and mortared if desired) as a decorative coping.

Retaining walls

Retaining walls may be used to terrace a garden or contain the soil in a raised bed (see opposite). Dry stones, special concrete blocks, or bricks may be used. Seek professional advice for any retaining wall more than 2½ft (75cm) high or one on a steep slope, because it may be necessary to reinforce it to withstand the pressure of soil and water. Rather than building one large retaining wall, terracing the garden in a series of shallow steps may be better. In some regions, permission is required to build a high retaining wall, and regulations may demand that contractors be hired to construct it from poured concrete.

Insert a drain (see "Installing drains," p.531) running horizontally along the back of the wall, and backfill the lower half of the wall with crushed stone. If using concrete blocks or bricks, build the wall on a concrete footing (see p.504) set below the lower soil level, and leave weep holes for drainage between every second or third brick in the lower courses of the wall.

Dry-stone walling is a good choice for a low retaining wall, since alpines can be grown in the exposed face. Place large stones on a firm foundation of concrete or compacted crushed stone, and lay subsequent courses of stone with an inward slope (a batter) of 1–2in for every 12in (2.5–5cm for every 30cm) of height. The wall should be perpendicular on the retaining side (see THE ROCK GARDEN, *How to Build a Dry-stone Retaining Wall*, p.200). If it is not to be planted with crevice plants, the wall may be mortared to make it stronger (see "Bricklaying," p.505); otherwise, pack garden soil between the stones for additional stability.

Constructing retaining walls

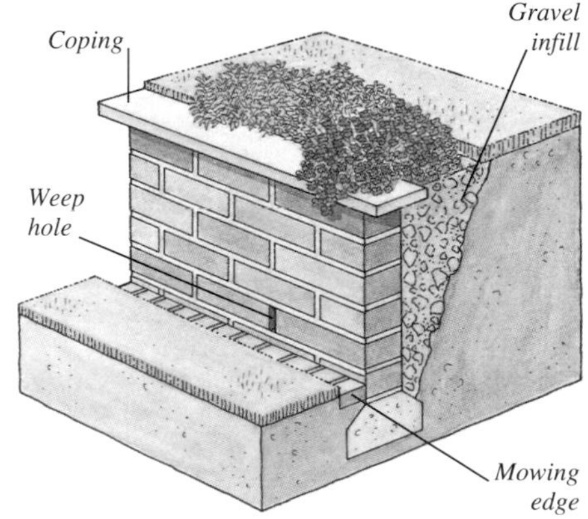

CONSTRUCTION
On the left is a section of a brick wall with a vertical, unmortared joint acting as a weep hole. On the right is a wall built of hollow concrete blocks. Hollows may be filled with wet concrete, or with soil for plants.

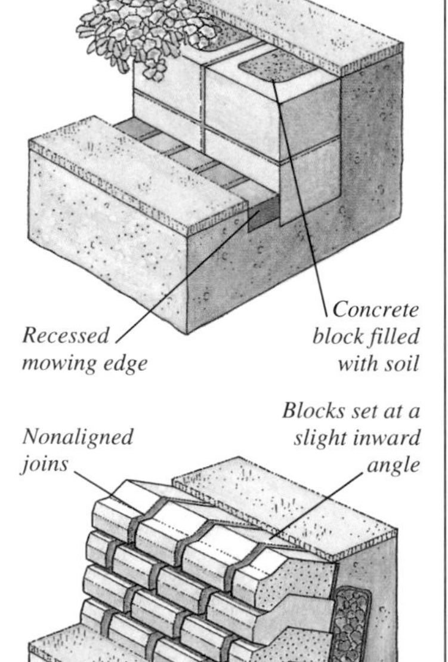

PREFORMED BLOCKS
There are several shapes of commercial preformed concrete blocks especially made for retaining walls. They can be laid with butt or open joins and can be positioned to form shallow curves without being cut.

Any retaining wall used to hold back soil on a slope must be extremely strong. Bear in mind that the higher the wall, the stronger it will need to be. Remember, too, that wet soil is heavier than dry soil, and water must be allowed to drain out through weep holes left at the base of the wall. If the units of construction are large, the retaining wall will be even stronger than if small bricks or blocks are used.

Raised beds

Raised beds provide a strong design element in a garden, perhaps surrounding a sunken garden or providing changes of level. Small groups of raised beds, or a series of linked beds, are ideal for an area that is mainly paved, while a single, distinctive raised bed makes a good foil for an attractive specimen plant.

Where the soil in a garden is poor, or unsuitable for growing certain plants, raised beds can be extremely useful: they enable acid conditions to be created in a garden with alkaline soil, for instance. Moreover, plants in raised beds have more room to develop and need less attention than those in tubs or other containers, in which the soil dries out fast.

Raised beds have the great advantage that they can be reached from a sitting position. A well-planned series of raised beds makes gardening possible for physically impaired gardeners. The height of the beds will need to be tailored to the requirements of the individual gardener and the width must be narrow enough for the whole bed to be within easy reach. The beds should be linked by easily negotiated, wide garden paths (see pp.501–2). In areas with cold winters, raised beds will freeze more deeply than the open ground. This may limit to some extent the range of plants that can be grown.

Materials

Raised beds may be built from a wide range of materials: mortared bricks (see "Types of brick," p.497), concrete walling blocks (see "Walling materials," p.504), unmortared natural stone (see "Dry-stone walls," opposite), railroad ties, or sawed logs. Brick or concrete block walls may be topped with a coping (see opposite) wide enough to sit on.

Brick beds

A large rectangular brick bed is easy to construct, but may appear rather unimaginative. A number of smaller linked beds at different heights will create a more visually stimulating feature, as will a circular raised bed. Always choose frostproof bricks; ordinary house bricks may be unsuitable – check with the supplier. A half-brick wall is usually strong enough for this purpose.

Rectangular beds

Prepare a footing (see *How to Make a Concrete Footing*, p.504) at a depth that allows the first course of bricks to lie below ground level. When the footing has set, use a masonry mortar mix (see p.494) to lay the courses of bricks (see "Bricklaying," p.505). Lay whole bricks at right angles to form the corners.

Circular beds

For a circular bed, the bricks should ideally be cut to give a smooth curve, but full bricks may be used. First lay the bricks loosely to a radius of about the right size that does not create wide gaps at the edge. Prepare the footing and, when this has set, lay the bricks so that they almost touch on the inside edge of the wall. Use wedges of mortar to fill the gaps on the outer face. Stagger the courses as with a conventional bond and use half bricks all the way around the final course to give it a smooth curve.

Ericaceous plants

If plants that require acid soil are to be grown in the raised bed, line the inside of the walls, when completed, with a butyl rubber liner or several coats of a waterproof paint. This stops lime in the mortar from leaching into the bed.

Concrete block beds

Concrete walling blocks are a good choice for raised beds if matching materials have been used for other garden structures and surfaces. The blocks may be too large for circular beds, but are ideal for rectangular ones. The beds are constructed in a similar way to brick beds.

Natural stone

Raised beds may be built using natural stone laid dry. Use the technique for dry-stone retaining walls (see "Dry-stone walls" and "Retaining walls," opposite), but keep the beds low and small.

For a bed higher than about 24in (60cm), it is best to mortar the stones securely in place. Even with a low bed, it may be necessary to use a certain amount of mortar at the corners for stability.

Railroad ties

Railroad ties, which blend unobtrusively with most plants and garden surfaces, are ideal for large, low, raised beds, but they are heavy and difficult to handle: do not make the walls more than three ties high. They may be purchased in full or half lengths; try to build walls in multiples of these to eliminate the need for sawing. If it is necessary to cut special lengths, you will need to use a chain saw.

It is not necessary to provide a footing, since the length and weight of the ties make them inherently stable. Create a level surface to lay them on, using rammed gravel, then bond the ties like bricks. If more than two courses high, drill vertical holes in the ends of each tie, then insert rods or pipes long enough to sink 1ft (30cm) into the soil.

MATERIALS FOR RAISED BEDS

Half-brick wall using a running bond

Soil level

Crushed stone base

1in (2.5cm) concrete footing

BRICK BED

Ideally, brick beds should be built with frostproof bricks. After preparing the concrete footing (see p.504), lay the first course of bricks below soil level. Stagger the courses to strengthen the walls.

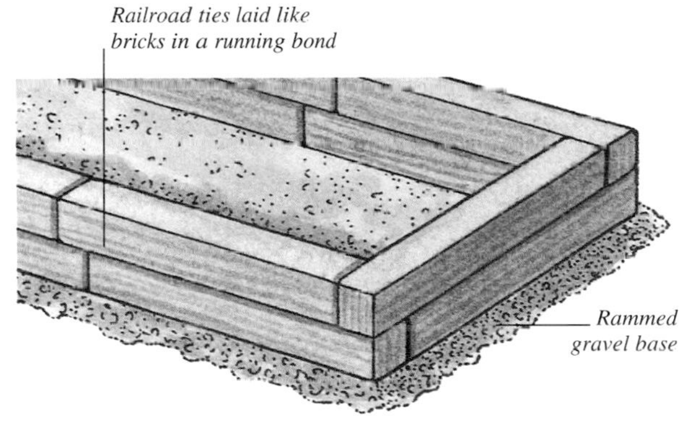

TIES

Railroad ties are particularly good for low raised beds. No footing is needed because the ties are themselves very stable. Ensure that they have not been treated with a preservative that is toxic to plants.

Sawed logs

Logs make attractive edgings for woodland-style beds, and for very low informal beds in a natural setting. For higher raised beds, logs of a uniform size and thickness should be used. Ideal logs may not be readily available, however, and the corner joints are difficult to construct. If this type of raised bed is to be built, it may be better to buy the sawed logs in easily assembled kit form, available from home centers and garden-supply stores.

Watering

The growing medium in a raised bed will drain more rapidly than the soil of in-ground garden borders, so it is important to water plants more frequently. In particular, the soil in immediate contact with the retaining walls tends to dry out and shrink. In extreme conditions, this could expose the fibrous feeding roots of plants growing around the edges. The frequency with which this happens is in direct proportion to the amount of clay that was used in the fill soil: the more clay in the mix, the more shrinkage takes place; the more humus, the less it happens (see SOILS AND FERTILIZERS, "Using soil additives," p.529).

Fences

Fences are commonly used as property boundary markers, but they may also act as windbreaks or as decorative features within the garden. They may be erected more quickly and cheaply than brick- or block-built walls, and many have the additional advantage of affording almost instant privacy. In general they do, however, require more maintenance than a wall. To make a fence into a decorative element, it may be clothed with climbers or have trellis paneling fixed to the top.

The first step before erecting any fence is to mark out the line of fencing with a string line. If it is to be on a boundary between two properties, all the fencing and fence posts must be on your side of the boundary. For other legal requirements regarding fences, see "Laws on fences," p.510.

Basic elements

Fences are made from three basic elements: posts, rails, and siding.
Posts are the heavy vertical members that have one end inserted into the ground. They are usually made of lumber but can be made of manufactured metal (see also *Erecting a Fence using Metal Post Supports*, opposite).
Rails are medium-weight horizontal members attached between the posts; they often act as support for the siding (see right). On wooden fences, these rails are usually made of 2 x 4in (5 x 10cm) lumber. The number of rails on a wooden fence depends on the height of the fence: usually two for fences up to 5ft (1.5m) tall, and three on taller fences.

Bottom and center rails can be inset into posts for a smooth finish. (Top rails are usually positioned across the top of the fence.) The inset cuts made in the posts, into which the rails are fitted, are called dado cuts. To avoid weakening posts, do not cut dados into opposite sides of the post at the same level.

Horizontal board fences, which are made up of boards nailed directly to the posts, do not need rails, although a top rail is often used.
Siding is a collective term, often used to describe the thinner dimension lumber that runs vertically from the top to the bottom rails or horizontally across the rails.

Siding comes in many forms, from the pickets on a picket fence to the alternate overlapping boards on a wavy-edged fence that gives complete privacy. Many fence designs call for vertical siding boards to be nailed to the rails at different spacings, depending on the privacy, sunlight, and air circulation desired. The panels of a panel fence (see p.509) are another form of siding. Used loosely, "siding" includes chain link mesh and other nonwood materials.

Fence types

Basketweave fencing is usually sold as prefabricated panels, generally in a range of heights. Thin interwoven slats of pine or fir are fixed to a light softwood frame. It provides good privacy, but is not very strong.

Closeboard fencing consists of overlapping vertical feather-edged boards, usually of softwood, as siding nailed to a pair of horizontal rails. The thick edges of the boards are nailed over the thin edges. It may be constructed *in situ*, but is also available (as shown here) in the form of panels. Closeboard is one of the strongest forms of fencing, and it also offers good security and privacy.

Wavy-edged fencing has siding of overlapping, irregularly edged boards, and is a common form of panel fencing (see also p.513). It provides an adequate level of security.

Shingle fences consist of overlapping cedar shingles (wooden "tiles") that are nailed to a wooden framework to produce a strong, solid fence. They offer good security and privacy, depending on their height.

Picket fences have vertical wooden "pales" spaced about 2in (5cm) apart, fixed to horizontal rails, and are more decorative than functional. Plastic picket fences are available that require far less maintenance than traditional wooden ones. Neither kind offers much security or privacy.

Ranch-style fencing uses as siding thin planed boards attached horizontally to stout posts. The wood is either painted or simply treated with preservative. There are plastic versions of this style of fencing available, which need less maintenance, but neither is secure.

Splitwood fencing consists of split vertical stakes about 3in (7.5cm) apart, linked by strands of galvanized wire. It is suitable only as a temporary fence.

Post-and-rail fences have two or more horizontal poles or rough-sawed wooden rails fixed between adjacent posts. They form an inexpensive boundary marker.

Interference fencing has horizontal boards fixed on both sides of the posts, the boards on one side facing the gaps on the other. It makes a better windbreak than a solid fence, and it provides acceptable if not total privacy.

Wattle hurdles are flimsy panels of interwoven woody stems. Two examples are shown here. They may be made *in situ* or bought as ready-made panels. They are held in place by stout stakes and are particularly useful when a new hedge is becoming established in a garden, offering interim privacy as well as good protection against both small and large animals. Within a relatively short period of time, however, they can begin to look ragged and unattractive, and they are also troublesome to maintain and repair.

Lattice fences are made from sawed lumber or rustic wood. They resemble large partitions of a diamond-shaped trellis. They are useful for an informal boundary marker, but offer little privacy.

Chain link consists of a wire mesh, which is usually attached to concrete, wooden, or iron posts. Galvanized wire mesh lasts for about ten years, plastic-coated wire mesh longer. It is a good choice where an animal-proof boundary is required. It is also the first choice where maximum security is needed because it can be topped with barbed wire, and you can see through it. Since chain link fences are generally less expensive than fences with wood siding, they are often used where a large barrier of 6ft (2m) or higher is needed.

Welded wire consists of an open wire mesh stapled to wooden posts and rails. It is used primarily to fence off larger animals where appearance is unimportant.

Post-and-chain fences may have chains of metal or plastic, attached to wooden, concrete, or plastic posts. They are used to mark boundaries where more substantial fences are not required.

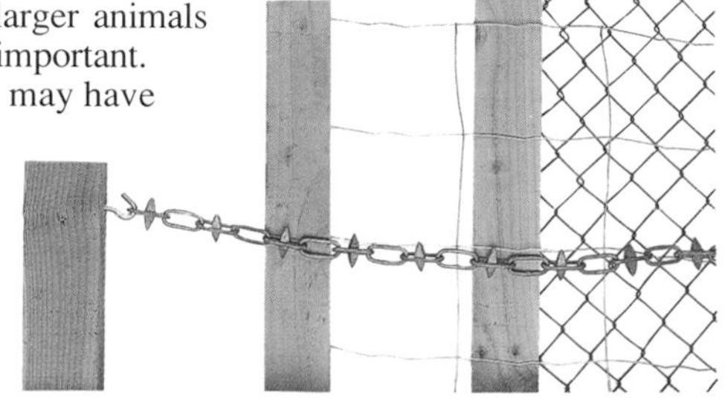

Posthole diggers

If a number of holes are needed for fence posts, buy, rent, or borrow a manual posthole digger or a posthole digger attachment for a garden tractor outfitted with a hydraulic system. (There are several types of manual digger; each has its merits, so consult a specialist before buying.) Using a manually operated posthole digger may be strenuous, depending on the site, type of soil, and amount of moisture in the soil. Power diggers are much easier to use and save time and effort.

How to Erect a Panel Fence

1 *Dig a hole 30in (75cm) deep and pack a 6in (15cm) layer of crushed stone in the base. Insert the first post and check the above-ground height of the post against the fence panel.*

2 *Pack crushed stone around the post and pour in concrete. Tamp it down. Add more concrete and tamp again. Keep checking that the post is vertical.*

3 *Lay a fence panel on the ground to position the next hole accurately. Use a string line as a guide, then dig the next hole.*

4 *Fit a gravel board between the post holes. Level the ground until the board lies horizontally. Check with a level.*

Concrete Spurs

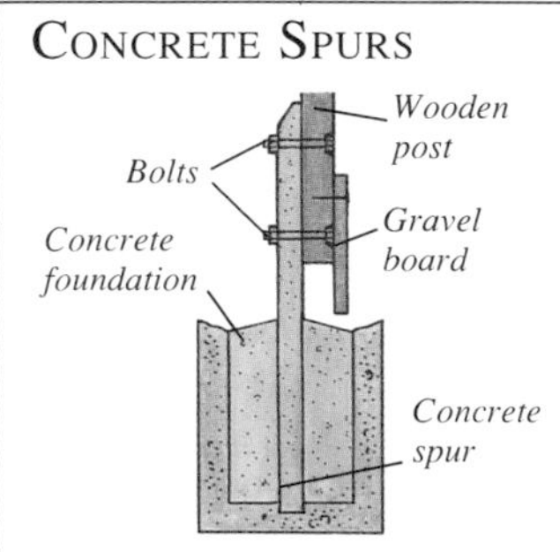

To avoid damage through contact with damp soil, bolt wooden fence posts to a concrete spur set in a concrete foundation.

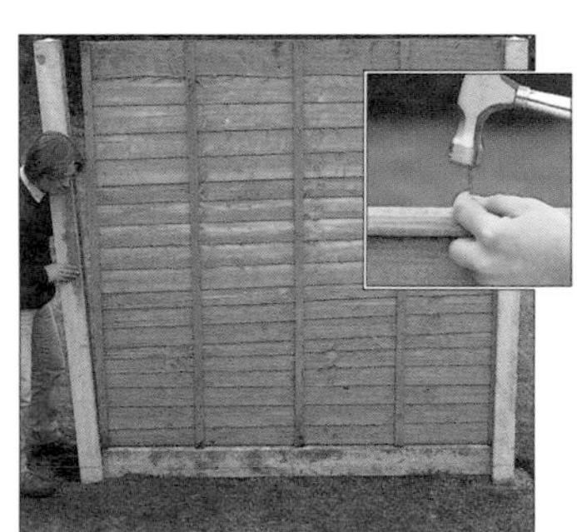

5 *Slot the panel into the groove in the first post. Insert the next post and pack into position with crushed stone. Secure molded wooden coping to the panel top.*

Panel fences

One of the simplest forms of fencing is a panel fence. It may be constructed using wooden or concrete posts. With concrete posts, the panels are simply slotted into grooves on either side of the post. For details, see *How to Erect a Panel Fence*, left. Another advantage of concrete is that it does not rot.

If you prefer wooden posts, the panels have to be screwed or nailed into position. Protect the bases of wooden fence posts by using either metal post supports or concrete spurs (see below). The latter are short posts that are embedded in a firm concrete foundation. They are bought ready-made with two holes through which the wooden posts are bolted to the spur just above ground level.

To build a fence with wooden posts dig a hole for the first post, then stretch a line along the run of the fence to ensure that it is straight. For a panel 6ft (2m) high, you will need $8^1/_2$ft (2.75m) lengths of wood for the posts and the post holes should be 30in (75cm) deep. Fill the bottom with a 6in (15cm) base of crushed stone, then stand the post in the hole and pack it with more crushed stone to hold it in position. Check that it is upright with a level. Using the panel as a width guide, dig a hole for the second post, making sure that it is aligned with the string line. Level the ground between the post and the hole and lay a gravel board – a length of wood (or concrete) fixed between fence posts at ground level to prevent panels from coming into contact with the soil and rotting. A wooden gravel board should be secured to the first post with galvanized nails. Attach a fence panel to the post using 3in (75mm) galvanized nails driven through predrilled holes, or screw them together with metal fixing brackets. Place the second post into its hole, ensuring that it is vertical and fits closely against the fence panel; fix the gravel board and panel as before. Repeat with the remaining posts, gravel boards, and panels.

Erecting a Fence using Metal Post Supports

1 *Place a scrap of wood and the fixing accessory in the socket of the post support. Use a sledgehammer to drive the support directly into the ground.*

2 *Keep checking that the support is being driven in vertically. Hold the level against all 4 sides in turn.*

3 *Insert the fence post into the socket at the top of the support and secure it by nailing through the slatted holes. Some sockets are fitted with clamping bolts.*

4 *Using a string guide, hammer in further post supports. Nail the fencing (here a panel of picket fence supported on bricks to keep the rails horizontal) to the posts.*

INSET RAILS

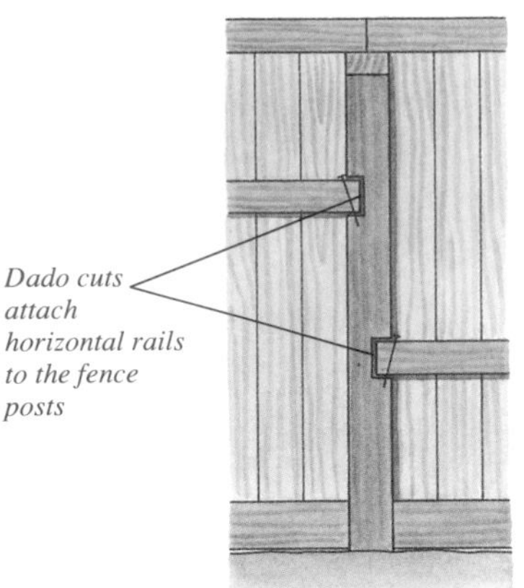

For a smooth finish, set rails into posts using dado cuts. Alternate the cuts to avoid weakening the post.

Saw the tops of the posts to an equal height above the panels if necessary. Treat any sawed surfaces with wood preservative, and finish each post with an overhanging wooden cap that deflects rainwater.

Lodge the posts firmly in position with wedges of scrap lumber and crushed stone, and use a level to check that they are vertical. Pack a stiff concrete mix (see p.494) around the base of each post, and use a trowel to create a slope away from each side as a runoff for water.

Metal post supports

Metal post supports may be sunk into the ground and wooden posts inserted into them (see *Erecting a Fence using Metal Post Supports*, p.509). This technique reduces the length of the boards needed for fence posts and keeps them out of the soil, which prolongs the life of the wood. Use 24in (60cm) metal post supports for fences that are up to 4ft (1.2m) high and 30in (75cm) supports for fences up to 6ft (2m).

Before driving the support into the ground, fit a scrap of wood from a post into the socket. This protects the support. Most manufacturers provide an attachment that fits over the scrap while the support is hammered into place.

Make sure that the spike is entering the ground at an exact right angle. To do this, hold a level against each of the four sides of the socket in turn. Secure the post by tightening the clamping bolts in the socket, or if these are not provided, fix the post with screws or nails through the slatted holes. For added strength and durability, metal post supports may also be set in a foundation of crushed stone and concrete.

Sloping ground

There are two ways to erect a fence on sloping ground: the fence may be constructed as a series of stepped horizontal sections or may slope with the ground. The method you should employ is largely dictated by the type of fencing you want to use.

A stepped fence

Panel fences, which cannot be satisfactorily cut, should be stepped. The upright posts need to be longer than they would be on level ground, the extra height depending on the width of the fence panels and the gradient. The triangular gap beneath each panel may be filled by building a low brick wall, stepped so that the panels sit on it. Alternatively, cut angled boards and fix them in the gaps.

A sloped fence

To build a fence that slopes with the ground, set a temporary post at the top of the slope and stretch a line between this and the bottom post. Use a fencing system that consists of individual boards nailed to rails (such as a picket fence). Instead of running horizontally between the posts, the rails should run parallel to the slope. Cut the base of each board at an angle to match the slope. Fix the boards to the rails vertically, resting them on another board.

SLOPING GROUND

STEPPED FENCE
Horizontal fence panels are erected as they would be on level ground, and stepped down a brick wall built onto the slope.

SLOPED FENCE
The line of the fence runs parallel to the slope; the posts and the boards are set at the same height as they would be on level ground.

Wood and wood preservatives

Native conifer lumber (arborvitae in the East, red cedar and redwood in the West) is an excellent fencing material. The lumber is easy to work with and is exceptionally resistant to the elements. It also weathers attractively. Other durable hardwoods, including cedar, may also be suitable, but tend to be more expensive.

If possible, buy lumber that has been pressure-treated, and be sure to treat any surfaces that you cut. Unless fences are made of naturally rot-resisting wood such as redwood or cypress, treat them regularly with a wood preservative. Reapply creosote or water-based preservatives every four years, the solvent-based products every two or three years.

Creosote is a widely used treatment for preserving fencing. It has a very powerful smell, however. Wear protective clothing when applying this substance, since it is poisonous if swallowed, inhaled, or absorbed through the skin. Creosote is not recommended for fences used to support plants. Solvent-based preservatives may also be effective. These come in a range of colors.

Water-based preservatives are less unpleasant to use and less toxic to plants. They prevent the growth of surface molds, and improve the appearance of the wood (they may alter the wood's color slightly). However, they are generally less effective at controlling rot.

Preservative should be applied to dry wood only. When erecting a fence, any cut ends should be soaked in preservative for 24 hours before use. Keep all preservatives away from plants, and always wear gloves.

Maintenance

Broken wooden support posts are one of the most common maintenance problems. If the damage to the support post is at soil level, the most effective method of repair is to use a concrete spur (see p.509). This is a short post sunk into the ground alongside the existing wooden one and bolted to it to give extra support.

Dig a hole 18–24in (45–60cm) deep around the damaged post and saw off the rotten part. Paint the cut end of the wooden post with a wood preservative. Place the concrete spur in the hole, resting it against the post, and pack crushed stone around the base to support it. Push bolts through the holes in the spur and tap them with a hammer hard enough to leave an impression on the wooden post. Remove the bolts and spur, then drill holes through the post for the bolts. Bolt the concrete spur onto the post, tightening the nuts from the spur side so that the wooden post is not damaged.

Make sure that the post and spur are vertical, if necessary bracing them in position temporarily with stakes driven into the ground. Then fill the hole with a fairly stiff concrete mix (see "Concrete and mortar mixes," p.494), ramming it down firmly as you work to remove any air pockets. After about a week, once the concrete has set, remove the supporting stakes and saw off any surplus length from the protruding bolts, taking care not to leave rough ends that could cause injuries.

Broken rails are easily repaired with special metal brackets. Some of these brackets are designed to brace a broken rail in the middle, while others will support a rail that has rotted where the end fits into the post. Both types are simply screwed into place.

Laws on fences

As soon as you decide to put up a fence, check your local ordinances to determine what laws relate to fences in your area. They may govern such things as height, materials, and location. Unless you are certain of where your boundaries lie, have your property surveyed. If you build a fence on your neighbor's land, it becomes the property of your neighbor. You may be able to build on the property line with your neighbor's agreement, otherwise the fence will have to be on your own land.

It is advisable to obtain a neighbor's agreement on property line, fence design, materials, height, and perhaps on working out a cost-sharing agreement. Your neighbor may also be prepared to share the cost of repairing the fence.

Trellises

Trellises, which are usually made of wood, are both a practical and a decorative feature in a garden. They may be secured to the tops of fences or walls or fixed against them. Alternatively they may be used on their own as partitions or screens. Curved and more intricately designed trellis panels are available for creating garden arbors. Panels come in a range of shapes and patterns, most consisting of standard diamonds or squares; herringbone trellises are particularly suitable for screening.

Trellises are most frequently used to support climbing plants. For a free-standing screen, a heavy duty trellis is essential, particularly if it is to support vigorous climbers; the wooden frame should be at least 1in (2.5cm) in depth. If the trellis is to be used to extend the height of a wall or a fence, a lighter weight may be acceptable. When buying a trellis, make sure it has been pressure-treated, and treat any sawed ends with a wood preservative (see opposite). Trellises primarily intended for supporting climbers are also available in wire and plastic.

Erecting a trellis

For a free-standing trellis, panels may be fixed to fence posts in the same way as ordinary fence panels (see "Panel fences," p.509). To attach panels to a fence with wooden posts, use metal post extenders. Remove the post cap and slide the metal extender over the top of the post. Insert the required length of extension post and replace the original cap on top of the extension. To fix a lightweight trellis above a masonry wall, attach lumber pieces 3/4 x 2in (2 x 5cm) to the sides of the trellis and screw them to the wall. If the trellis is to be fixed against a wall, allow at least 4in (10cm) between the wall and the trellis for good air circulation. Hinged fixings allow access for maintenance (see CLIMBING PLANTS, "Fixing a trellis panel to a wall," p.98).

TRELLISES

Trellises can complement the architectural detailing of the structure to which they are attached as well as provide support for climbing plants. They are available in a wide variety of shapes and woods. A jointed trellis is much sturdier than a concertina-style trellis held together by small staples.

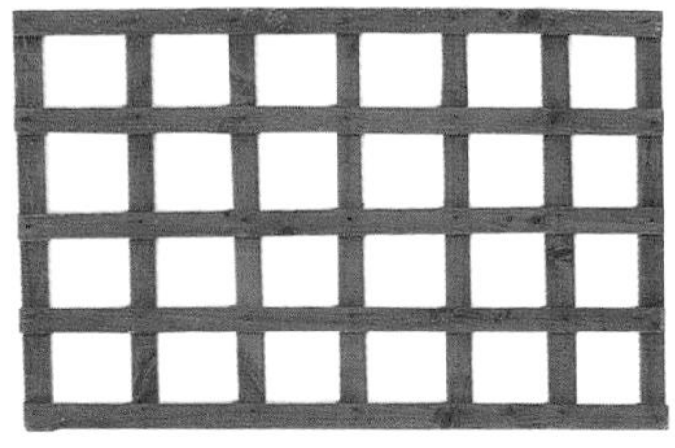

LATTICE PANEL

DIAMOND-SHAPED LATTICE PANEL

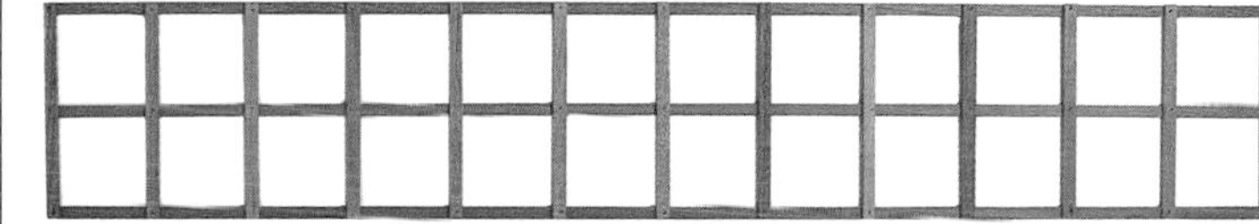

LARGE-SQUARED TRELLIS

Pergolas and rustic work

The word "pergola" originally meant a covered walkway formed by plants grown up a trellis. Today the term describes any structure consisting of uprights supporting horizontal beams, over which plants are grown.

Traditionally, pergolas were made of rustic poles, but sawed lumber is often a better choice, especially where the pergola is combined with wooden decking or where the house forms one of the supports. Sawed lumber may be used in combination with brick columns or with painted scaffold poles serving as uprights. Hardwoods such as oak are often used for sawed lumber pergolas, but softwoods are perfectly adequate, provided they have been pressure-treated with a preservative.

Pergola construction

Draw your design on graph paper to work out the quantities of materials required, but buy a little more than you think you will need, because you may wish to modify the design slightly during construction. The height of the pergola should be at least 8ft (2.5m) if plants are to be grown over it, to allow room to walk beneath. If the pergola spans a path, the uprights should be positioned far enough apart to allow for the growth of plants on either side.

Supports

Set wooden support posts in gravel and concrete in holes at least 2ft (60cm) deep (see "Panel fences," p.509), or use metal post supports (see p.509). If you are building a pergola over a patio, special metal shoes designed to be fixed in a concrete base are available. To avoid breaking up an existing concrete or paved surface, build a brick shoe and fit the post into it (see *Joints and Supports*, p.512).

Sawed lumber support posts should be 4 x 4in (10 x 10cm) in cross section. Scaffold poles may be used instead of wooden uprights but must be set in concrete because of their greater weight. Alternatively, if the weight that is to be carried is substantial, build brick or concrete block columns on substantial footings (see "Bricklaying," p.505).

Crossbeams

For crossbeams (roof beams), use either the same lumber as for the uprights or boards 2 x 6in (5 x 15cm) in section. These are sometimes sold ready-shaped and notched to fit

WOODEN PERGOLA ON A BRICK PATIO
The materials used to construct this pergola are few and simple, yet the design is most effective. A large square trellis has been fixed behind the square brick pillars that support the crossbeams.

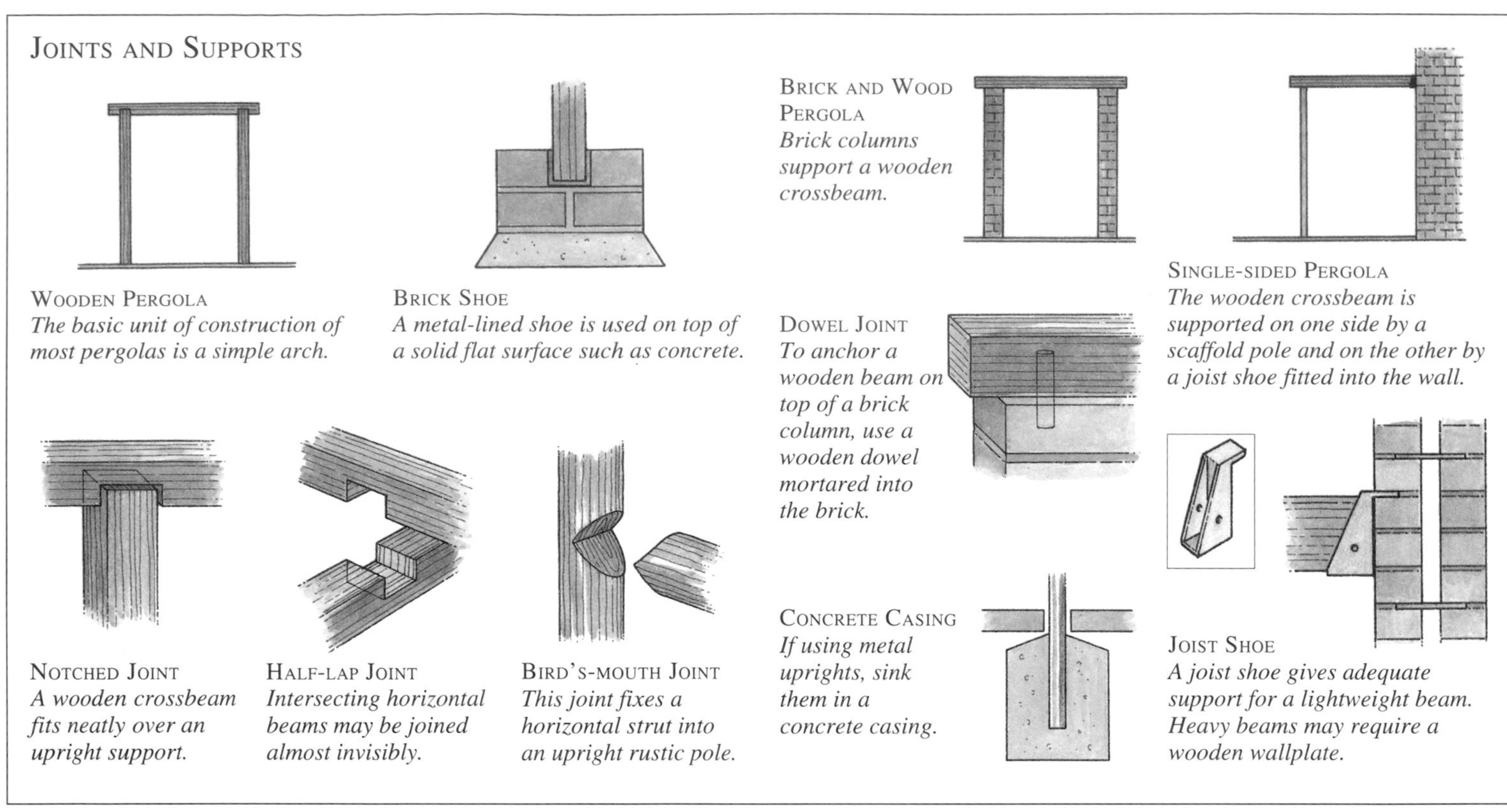

JOINTS AND SUPPORTS

WOODEN PERGOLA
The basic unit of construction of most pergolas is a simple arch.

BRICK SHOE
A metal-lined shoe is used on top of a solid flat surface such as concrete.

BRICK AND WOOD PERGOLA
Brick columns support a wooden crossbeam.

SINGLE-SIDED PERGOLA
The wooden crossbeam is supported on one side by a scaffold pole and on the other by a joist shoe fitted into the wall.

DOWEL JOINT
To anchor a wooden beam on top of a brick column, use a wooden dowel mortared into the brick.

NOTCHED JOINT
A wooden crossbeam fits neatly over an upright support.

HALF-LAP JOINT
Intersecting horizontal beams may be joined almost invisibly.

BIRD'S-MOUTH JOINT
This joint fixes a horizontal strut into an upright rustic pole.

CONCRETE CASING
If using metal uprights, sink them in a concrete casing.

JOIST SHOE
A joist shoe gives adequate support for a lightweight beam. Heavy beams may require a wooden wallplate.

over the tops of the uprights. Lighter lumber may be used for decorative rafters laid between the crossbeams.

Joints for beams and uprights

It is possible to assemble all the overhead woodwork by means of galvanized brackets and screws, but the structure will be stronger, and more attractive, if you use carpentry joints (see above). To fix an overhead beam to an upright, use a simple notched joint. This kind of joint is especially useful if the crossbeams are to project beyond the uprights – to serve as supports for hanging containers, for example.

Treat the cut surfaces of the joint with wood preservative (see p.510) before nailing them together. Avoid driving the nails in at right angles; skew-nailed joints hold together better when the structure flexes in the wind. If extra strength is needed, screw a T bracket where the upright meets the horizontal.

If you are using scaffold poles to support wooden crossbeams, effective joints may be created by drilling circular holes of the same diameter as the scaffold into the beams. The depth of the holes should be half the thickness of the wood.

Wooden pergolas are often supported by a wall of the house. To attach a wooden crossbeam to the wall you will need to use a metal joist shoe mortared into the brickwork. When the supports are brick columns, the wooden horizontals are fixed with dowels, which are mortared into the brick (see above).

You may wish to roof over the pergola with a network of intersecting rafters. Where two beams of equal thickness meet, a half-lap joint gives a strong, neat finish.

Many designs also incorporate corner braces between the uprights and the crossbeams to give the pergola greater rigidity. The wood for the braces should measure about 2 x 2in (5 x 5cm) and should fit as closely as possible into notches cut in the beams.

Cut the braces to the required length, then hold them up to the framework to mark the position and shape of the notches. Use a drill and chisel to cut the notches. When all the necessary adjustments have been made, treat all the cut surfaces with preservative before nailing the braces into the notches.

Rustic work

Rustic work consists of all kinds of garden structures made from poles (usually of cedar or fir), rather than sawed lumber. A popular material for arches and screens as well as pergolas, the poles may either be dressed (with the bark stripped off) or be left with the bark on as an attractive finish. If you use poles with bark, bear in mind that the bark is likely to become a refuge for various garden pests.

The vertical poles that support the structure should be about 4in (10cm) in diameter. They may be bedded in concrete (see "Panel fences," p.509) or set in the open ground. In the latter case, sink them to 18–24in (45–60cm) of their length to ensure stability. If the bark is to be left on, strip it from the bases of the poles up to a point that extends 1in (2.5cm) above soil level when they are in position. Whether the bark is left on the poles or stripped off, soak the ends in wood preservative overnight. Set the uprights in their positions. The crossbeams and corner braces needed to complete the structure may be fixed later, once the concrete around the vertical members (if concrete is used) has set.

The poles used for the main crossbeams and corner braces should have a diameter of about 3in (7cm), but thinner poles may be used for the decorative latticework.

It is possible to preassemble some sections of the structure by laying them out on the ground according to the design, then cutting some poles to length and making the necessary joints. Saw all the crosspieces only as you need them to ensure that they fit exactly.

There are many joints that may be used in the construction of a rustic pergola or arch. Half-lap joints (see above), similar to those used for sawed lumber, are useful where the poles intersect. To attach a horizontal crossbeam to an upright, use a bird's-mouth joint (see above). All cut ends should be painted with a wood preservative before you assemble the structure.

As with sawed lumber, it is always best to nail the joints together at an angle to give them extra rigidity.

Other plant supports

It is possible to provide permanent support for climbing plants without erecting a trellis or a pergola. Striking results can be achieved with relatively simple structures.

Tripods

Rustic tripods are an excellent way of integrating climbers into a mixed or herbaceous border. Dressed rustic poles are better than those with bark for this purpose, since they are less likely to attract potential pests. For large plants, use poles with a diameter of about 6in (15cm). If the tripod is in a bed, sink the poles in holes filled with gravel.

Pillars

For a more formal look along the back of a border or to flank a path, erect a row of single pillars made of brick or reconstituted stone. The bases of the pillars should be set firmly in concrete. To help climbers grow up the pillars, use plastic-covered large-mesh netting. Secure the net around the pillars by tying it together with plastic-covered wire.

Garden sheds

Sheds are valuable outbuildings for storing garden tools and equipment. A simple toolshed will keep hand tools dry and clean, but a larger shed with space to set up a workbench along one wall is a better investment.

Designs

A variety of different shed designs is available. There are three basic roof styles to select from: gable (an inverted V shape), gambrel (the shape commonly associated with barn roofs), and lean-to (a sloping half-roof – one side of the shed may be against a wall). Medium to large walk-in sheds usually have gable or gambrel roofs. Lean-to roofs are normally used only on small sheds, sometimes called garden lockers.

Prefabricated garden sheds are packaged as kits, complete with assembly instructions. Putting the directions on a videotape is a new and helpful innovation.

Typically, medium to large sheds have sliding windows on one or more walls to admit light and air. Many sheds also offer an anchor kit, to protect the building from strong winds, or a just-add-concrete foundation kit, which must be assembled before erecting the structure.

Materials

Garden sheds may be constructed from a variety of materials – wood, steel, aluminum, or vinyl. The choice of material depends on the intended uses of the shed as well as on expense and maintenance needs.

Wood

The single best material for a garden shed is wood; it blends in sympathetically with plants, especially after the new wood has weathered with age. Durable woods such as cedar are preferable, since they are naturally resistant to rot.

Most sheds, however, are made of softwood, which is much cheaper than cedar. Try to find a shed made of pressure-treated lumber rather than of wood that has simply been dipped or painted. Treat with a preservative when new, and maintain regularly. Wooden sheds should be lined with waterproof building paper (which can be obtained from a building supply store) to reduce the risk of moisture penetration and to protect tools from rusting.

When shopping for wooden sheds, in addition to the ten points shown and described below, check how the joints are held together. In terms of strength and longevity, bolts and wooden screws are best, followed by galvanized nails, with staples being the poorest choice.

Metal

Garden sheds made of steel cost less per square foot than wooden ones. The price varies according to the quality of galvanized steel used and how thoroughly it is coated with plastic. The higher the cost of a metal shed, the longer it should resist rust. The plastic-coated-steel sheds come in a range of colors; many of the sheds have small windows.

Sheds made of interlocking sheets of aluminum are readily available. Most have a sliding door, and some an acrylic sheet window. Often small, these sheds are intended primarily for tool storage and are virtually maintenance-free.

All vinyl

Sheds made of vinyl resin panels are easy to assemble, and require no elaborate maintenance. When necessary, simply wash them off with a garden hose and allow to air-dry.

Choosing a Wooden Shed

The life of a wooden shed depends on the quality of the construction and of the wood. Whenever possible, compare erected sheds – most major suppliers will have a good selection to choose from. Pay close attention to the features indicated below.

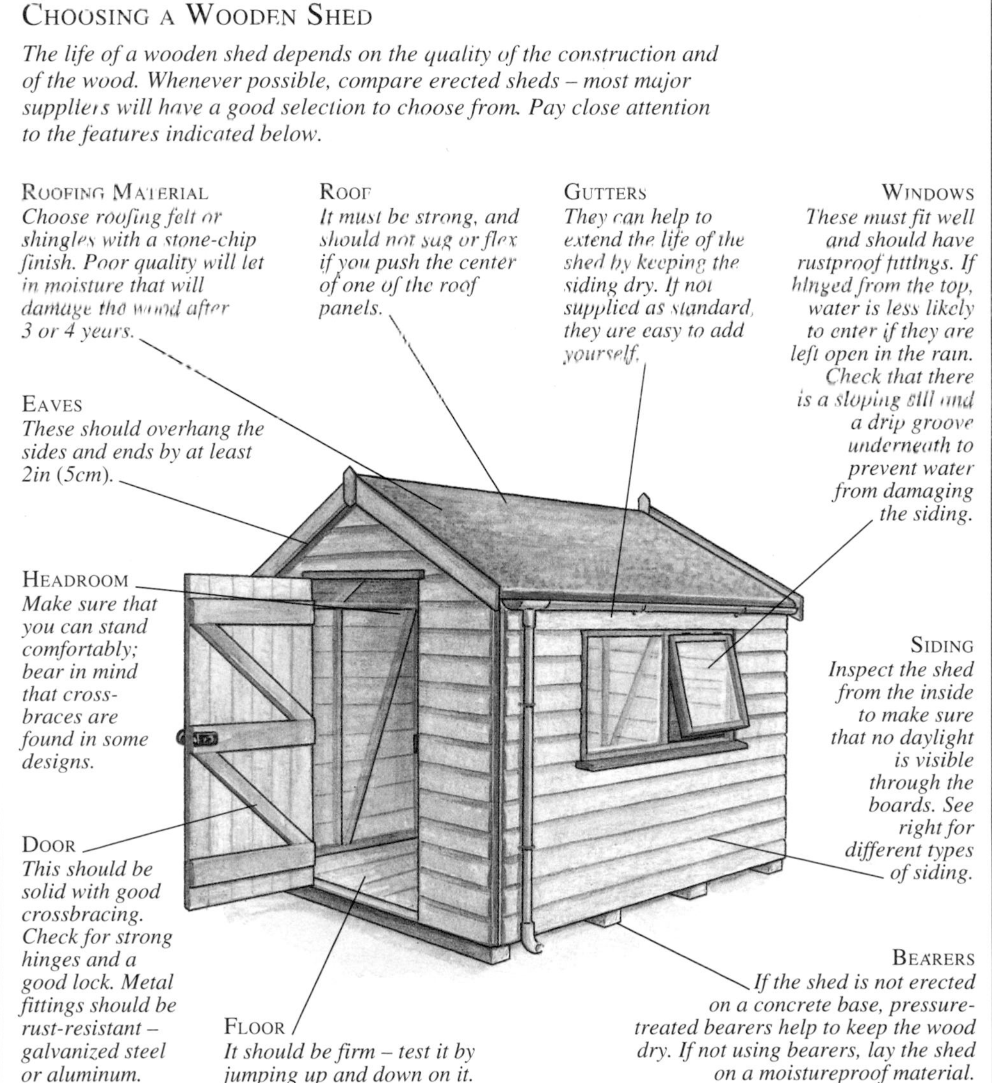

Types of Siding

Tongue-and-Groove
This siding usually offers good weather protection.

Feather-Edged, Overlapping Weatherboard
This may warp or buckle unless it is thick.

Rebated Weatherboard
This gives a closer fit than feather-edged weatherboard.

Rebate Shiplap
As well as being durable, this has an attractive finish.

Wavy-Edged Weatherboard
This rough-edged board, which is also called rustic siding, may not be weatherproof.

4

Climate and the Garden

CLIMATE HAS A *considerable influence on plant growth and, perhaps more important, on garden practice. Much of the satisfaction in gardening lies in meeting the challenges of the weather, often by exploiting its effects to the gardener's advantage. Choosing plants that thrive in the prevailing climate is fundamental to success, but although some plants will perform well only in their natural habitat, many are more adaptable and may be grown elsewhere, as long as suitable conditions are provided. The effects of climate on plants are complex, and made more so because the weather is constantly changing, often with interaction between two or more elements. A plant's responses to weather conditions are also shaped by its location within the garden, stage of maturity, and the length and intensity of the plant's exposure to inclement weather conditions. Through an understanding of the weather and an awareness of its impact, a gardener will be better able to grow healthy, productive, and attractive plants.*

Climate zones

World climate may be divided into four broad but clearly defined zones: these are tropical, desert, temperate, and polar.

Tropical climates are characterized by high temperatures and heavy, sometimes seasonal, rainfall, and support luxuriant evergreen vegetation. Deserts have average daytime temperatures in excess of 100°F (38°C) but often very cold nights, with annual rainfall of less than 10in (25cm); only adapted plants, such as cacti, survive in these conditions. Temperate regions have changeable daily patterns, but rainfall is generally evenly spread throughout the year and temperatures are less extreme than in the tropics or deserts; deciduous plants are more common here than evergreens, since they are better adapted to these conditions. Polar regions experience extreme cold, strong winds, and low rainfall, so little plant growth is possible.

In addition to these four broad zones, intermediate zones such as subtropical and Mediterranean are also recognized.

Regional climate

Conditions within climate zones are determined by geographical factors such as latitude, altitude, and proximity to the sea, which increases rainfall and moderates temperature.

The North American climate
North America has a great deal of regional variation. The continent can be roughly divided into several areas based on climate, but topographical variation and proximity to large bodies of water create significant differences within regions. In both the US and Canada, coastal climates are influenced by warm air and water currents, and by rain from the surrounding oceans.

For general purposes, areas are defined (see "Gardening in different regions," pp.522–3) with respect to temperature range, number of frost-free days, precipitation, humidity, sun, wind, and the plants that may be grown in each one.

The great extremes of summer and winter temperatures in central parts of North America are influenced by both latitude and the continental land mass. The Atlantic and Pacific oceans and the Gulf of Mexico are too far away to have any moderating effect on temperatures. During winter, the cold land mass of Canada has more impact.

Within Canada, growing seasons range from the very short Arctic season, with high light intensity, to longer, milder seasons in British Columbia, with lower light intensity. Areas with deep, reliable snow cover can grow a wider range of perennial plants than warmer parts with midwinter thaws.

SPRING FROST
The play of light on the frost-tinged foliage and flowers of hardy plants brings an ethereal quality to the garden. Working with the weather rather than against it will ensure satisfying results throughout the year.

Elements of climate

The elements of climate that directly affect plants and the techniques used to grow them are temperature, frost, snow, rain, humidity, sun, and wind. Of these, temperature is usually regarded by gardeners as the most important: it determines the choice of plants to be grown as well as the length of the growing season.

Temperature

Plant processes such as photosynthesis, transpiration, respiration, and growth are vitally dependent on temperature. Each plant species has a minimum and a maximum temperature beyond which these vital processes fail to take place. The maximum temperature is around 96°F (35°C) for most plants, while the minimum is highly variable. Where very low temperatures occur, plant tissue may be destroyed (see "Freezing and thawing," right).

Air and soil temperatures are the most important climatic factors influencing the onset and breaking of dormancy in plants. Dormancy, in turn, chiefly determines the length of a plant's growing season.

Air temperature

Sunshine produces radiant energy that raises the ambient or air temperature significantly. In temperate and cooler climates, a sheltered site that benefits from the warming effect of full sun may be used to grow plants from warmer regions that might not otherwise thrive.

An important relationship exists between altitude and air temperature: given the same latitude, highland sites are cooler than lowland ones – for every 1,000ft (300m) increase in altitude, the temperature drops by 1°F (0.5°C). High-altitude sites thus have a shorter growing season, which together with the cooler temperatures dictates the range of plants that may be grown.

Soil temperature

The temperature of the soil is important for good, healthy root growth and directly relates to the rate at which plants are able to absorb water and nutrients from the soil. The successful germination of seeds and development of shoots also depend on suitable soil temperatures (see PRINCIPLES OF PROPAGATION, "Requirements for germination," p.538).

The speed at which soil warms up and the temperature maintained during the year depend on soil type and the orientation of the site. Sandy soils warm up more quickly than clay, and well-drained, fertile soils stay warm longer than those that are compacted or infertile (see also "Soil types," p.524).

Sites with a natural, gentle incline toward the south warm up quickly in spring because they gain more benefit from the sun than level or north-facing ground. They are therefore ideal for early vegetable crops. North-facing slopes, on the other hand, stay relatively cool and may be used to grow plants that thrive in cooler conditions.

Dormancy

Plants become dormant to limit their exposure to adverse weather; most have at least a short period of full dormancy. Many woody plants shed their leaves in fall to avoid excessive transpiration, while most herbaceous and bulbous plants die down completely in winter and remain dormant below the ground.

The temperature of the soil and air are the most important factors involved in the onset and breaking of dormancy. It is possible to exploit this knowledge by, for example, keeping plants in a dormant state through cold storage. Dormant scions for grafting may be stored until sap begins to rise in the rootstock, and shrubs may be stored in the same way, if necessary, until the soil is warm enough for planting.

On the other hand, bulbs grown in pots and winter-flowering azaleas, for example, may be awakened from dormancy and brought into early flowering by bringing them into a bright, warm place.

Frost

Frost is a great hazard in gardening and is considered to be more crucial than the average minimum temperature for the area. Even hardy plants may be vulnerable to unusually low temperatures, particularly after they have produced new growth in spring, and an unexpected severe frost has serious implications.

Frost (frozen atmospheric moisture) forms on objects when their surface temperature drops below 32°F (0°C). It takes several forms: in a hoarfrost, crystals of ice are formed from water that has condensed from a humid atmosphere; black frost is more likely in a drier atmosphere, and blackens the leaves and stems of plants. Ground frost results when the temperature of the soil falls below freezing; the depth of penetration of the ground frost depends on its intensity and duration.

Frost is most likely to occur on cold, still nights when the cold air collects at a level just above the ground. Most at risk are woody plants whose tissue has not ripened (hardened) well, usually due to a lack of sun and warmth during fall.

The risk of spring frost in any area determines the date after which it is safe to sow or plant out tender plants such as tomatoes, dahlias, and half-hardy bedding plants. The onset of the fall frost determines the end of their growing season. If tender plants are kept from year to year, they should be taken indoors or given adequate protection (see COLD AND WIND PROTECTION, pp.520–21).

FROST POCKETS

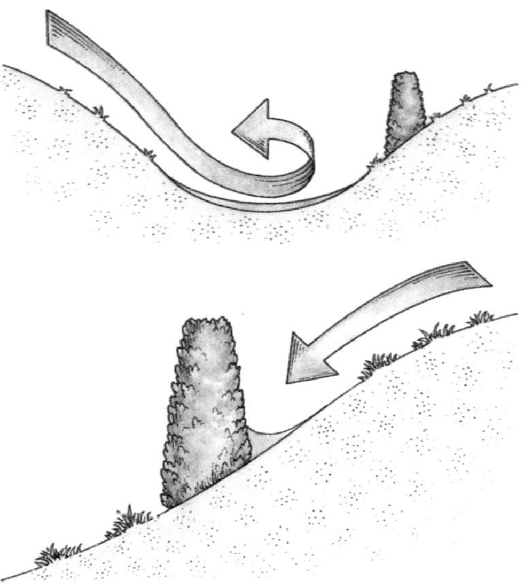

Since cold air sinks, it will always collect at the lowest point it can reach, forming a frost pocket. Valleys and ground hollows are therefore most susceptible to frost pockets, and any plants in the vicinity will suffer as a result. Cold air also collects in front of closely planted hedges and other solid obstructions such as walls and fences, with the same effect.

Frost pockets and frost damage

Dense, cold air flowing down a slope eventually becomes trapped; any valley or hollow is therefore a potential frost pocket. The cold air accumulates in the depression and backs up the sloping sides of the valley, increasing the area of potential damage.

Thick barriers formed by established trees or hedges along hillsides may obstruct the passage of cold air down a slope, and frost pockets will form in front of them. The problem may be avoided by thinning or removing the trees or hedges to allow cold air to flow through.

When the ground is frozen, water is no longer available to plant roots. Deep-rooted deciduous trees and shrubs are not affected even by deep frost, because many of their roots penetrate well below the frost line, but plants with shallower roots, such as small evergreen shrubs, may not be able to replace the moisture lost by continued transpiration. Severe ground frost can also cause newly planted, young, or shallowly rooted plants to rise, or heave, out of the soil; they should be carefully refirmed as soon as the thaw begins.

The risk of frost damage to plants kept outside permanently can be reduced by various protective measures (see COLD AND WIND PROTECTION, pp.520–21).

Freezing and thawing

Frost itself does not always cause great damage to plants, but alternate freezing and thawing does. Frozen cell sap expands on thawing, which destroys plant cell walls, often killing tender plants. The thaw may damage the flowers, shoots, buds, and leaves of hardier plants and sometimes even the roots. In extreme cold, the bark of some woody plants may split.

Repeated hard freezes followed by rapid thaws and subsequent waterlogging of the soil causes the greatest damage to roots. Late frosts in spring are particularly damaging to new top-growth, causing blackening of the leaves and injury to new buds and flowers.

Duration of frosts

The duration of the frost is also relevant to the amount of damage caused to the plant. For example, a temperature that drops to 27°F (-3°C) for a quarter of an hour may cause no damage, whereas the same temperature sustained over three hours could result in substantial losses.

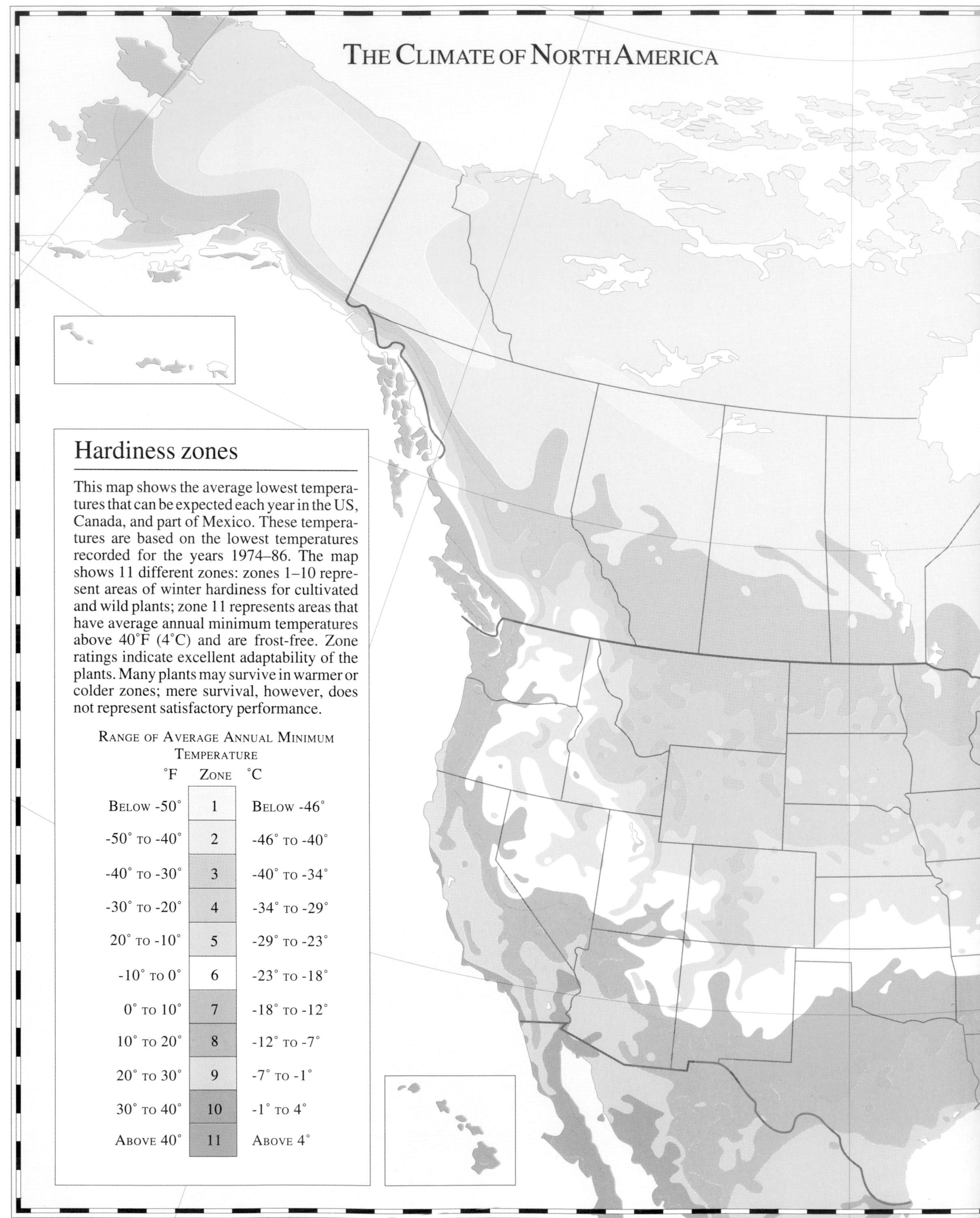
THE CLIMATE OF NORTH AMERICA
Hardiness zones
This map shows the average lowest temperatures that can be expected each year in the US, Canada, and part of Mexico. These temperatures are based on the lowest temperatures recorded for the years 1974–86. The map shows 11 different zones: zones 1–10 represent areas of winter hardiness for cultivated and wild plants; zone 11 represents areas that have average annual minimum temperatures above 40°F (4°C) and are frost-free. Zone ratings indicate excellent adaptability of the plants. Many plants may survive in warmer or colder zones; mere survival, however, does not represent satisfactory performance.
RANGE OF AVERAGE ANNUAL MINIMUM TEMPERATURE
°F ZONE °C
BELOW -50° 1 BELOW -46°
-50° TO -40° 2 -46° TO -40°
-40° TO -30° 3 -40° TO -34°
-30° TO -20° 4 -34° TO -29°
20° TO -10° 5 -29° TO -23°
-10° TO 0° 6 -23° TO -18°
0° TO 10° 7 -18° TO -12°
10° TO 20° 8 -12° TO -7°
20° TO 30° 9 -7° TO -1°
30° TO 40° 10 -1° TO 4°
ABOVE 40° 11 ABOVE 4°

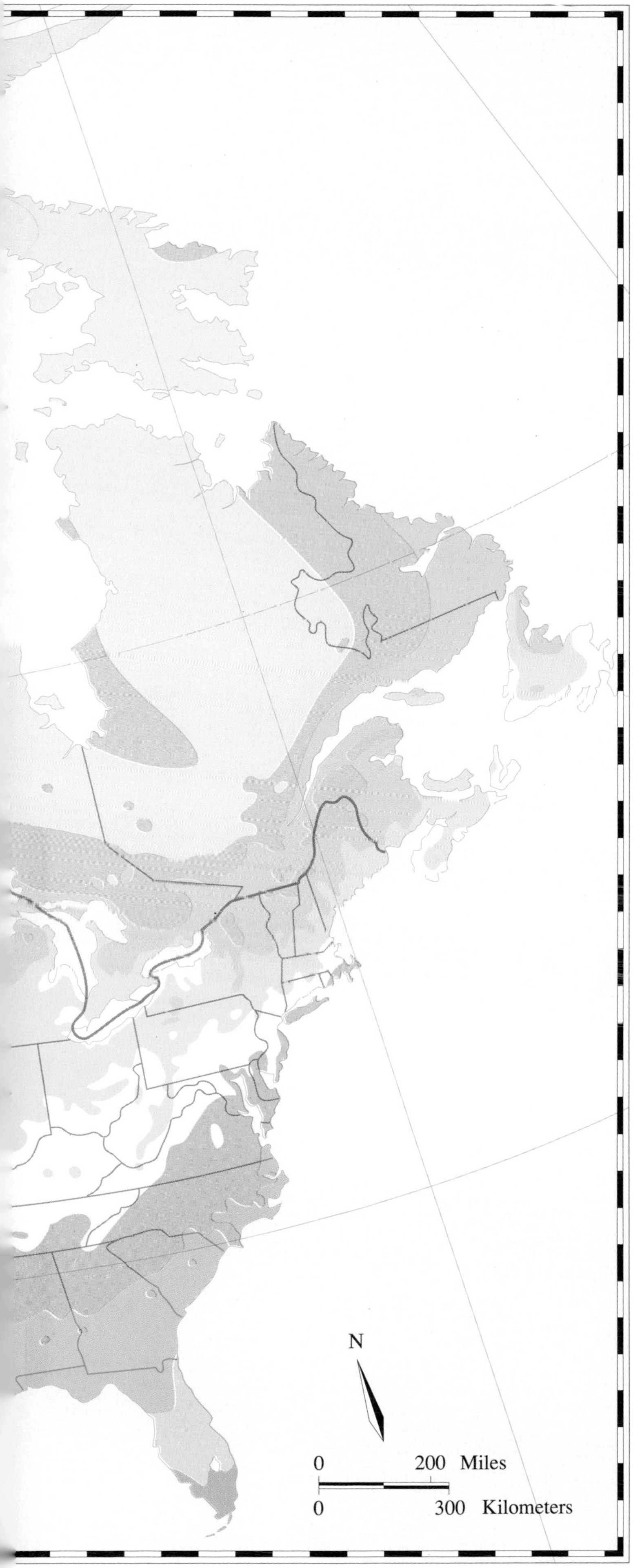

N

0 200 Miles

0 300 Kilometers

THE EFFECTS OF SNOW

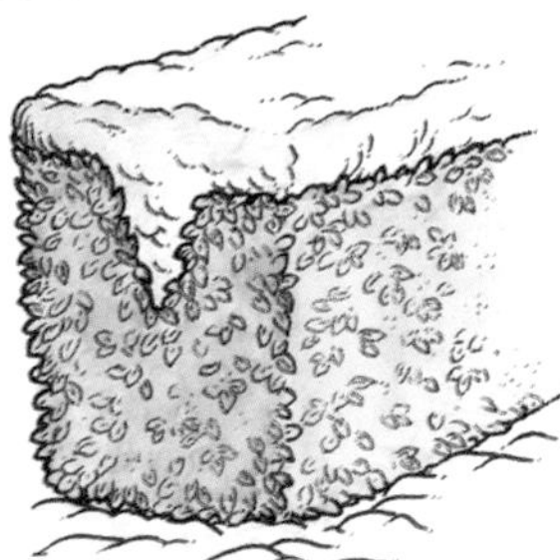

SNOW DAMAGE
The considerable weight of heavy snow may force apart hedges or evergreen shrubs and trees if it is allowed to settle for too long. Always clear snow from such plants as soon as possible.

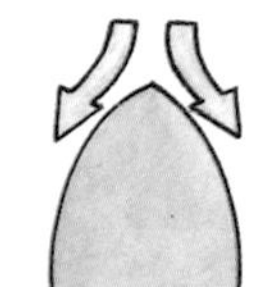

ARCHED HEDGE
Shape hedges to avoid snow accumulation.

Frost as an aid to cultivation
Despite the danger to plants, frost may sometimes be helpful in cultivation. For example, soil water expands when it freezes, shattering soil clods into much smaller soil particles; this is particularly useful on clay soils that may otherwise be unworkable. Low soil temperatures also reduce the numbers of some soil-inhabiting pests.

Snow

When atmospheric temperature falls close to (but not below) freezing, water droplets freeze in clouds or rain and may fall as snow.

Snowfall produces a useful supply of water upon thawing and often provides valuable insulation for plants. A blanket of snow insulates the soil beneath and can keep it much warmer than the minimum air temperature; it also helps to reduce frost heaving. Heavy snow followed by severe cold, however, may damage branches and twigs. Wherever possible, remove thick layers of snow from vulnerable plants.

Rainfall

Water is the main constituent of cell sap and is vital for photosynthesis, the complex means by which carbon dioxide and water are converted into living plant tissue. Photosynthesis is also fundamental to transpiration, whereby a plant is kept from wilting and nutrients are transported through it. Respiration, germination of seeds, and the subsequent development of roots, shoots, leaves, flowers, and fruit are also dependent upon good water supplies.

Rainfall is the principal source of water for plants grown in the open. Much rainfall is lost through evaporation and runoff, but most of the moisture that soaks into the soil is absorbed by soil particles or held as a thin film around them. Water and essential nutrients, which are absorbed in solution, are then extracted from the soil by plant root hairs.

SNOW PROTECTION
A snow blanket protects high-altitude plants from freezing temperatures.

For optimum growth, plants need a steady supply of water. In reality, however, rainfall is variable in both frequency and quantity.

Waterlogging
In badly drained soil, a buildup of water leads to waterlogging. Most plants are well equipped to survive an occasional heavy downpour, but where waterlogging is prolonged, roots may die through lack of oxygen, except in the case of specially adapted plants such as marginal aquatics, bald cypress (*Taxodium distichum*), and willows (*Salix*). Most plants fail to establish on permanently waterlogged sites; in such locations, drainage must be improved (see p.531).

Drought
Plant development is more often restricted by too little available water rather than by too much. Drought during the summer, when temperature and sunlight are at or near maximum levels, is a common problem. Wilting is the first outward sign of drought; plant functions are slowed down until more water is available, and water loss by transpiration is reduced by partial closure of the stomata on leaf surfaces.

Many plants that originate in arid regions have special adaptations such as hairy, sticky, glossy, spiny, narrow, or fleshy leaves that help to reduce water loss through transpiration. Cacti and other succulents, which have water-storing tissue in their leaves, stems, or roots, can survive long periods of drought.

The soil
In areas of low rainfall, various techniques may be used to increase the amount of water available to

RAIN SHADOW

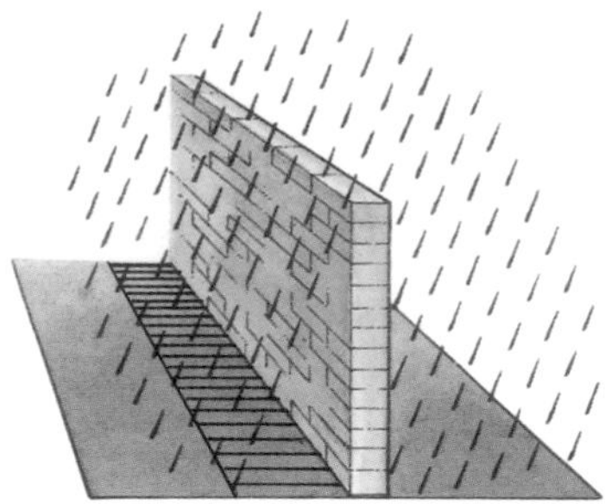

Ground in the lee of a wall or solid fence (see shaded area above) receives less rainfall than ground on the windward side, since the wall or fence creates an area of rain shadow.

WIND TURBULENCE

Exposed areas on rising ground may suffer severe wind damage. Gusts of air meeting resistance from the land are diverted around the sides and over the top of hills, gathering in intensity at the same time.

WIND TUNNELING

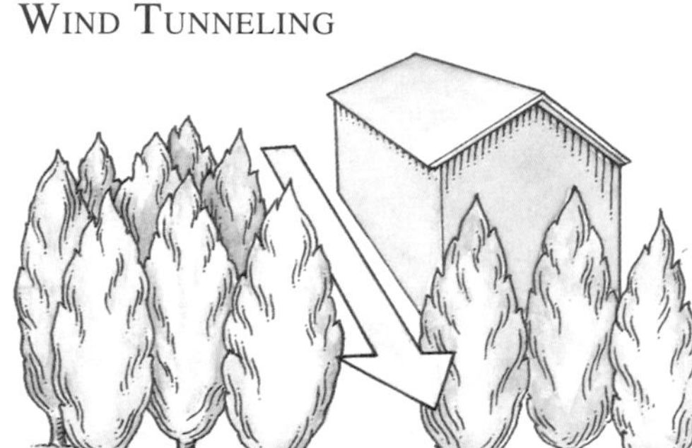

A wind tunnel created between buildings and trees may cause a great deal of damage to plants in its path, since air is forced through the narrow channel at great speed. If gardening in such an area is unavoidable, construct a windbreak to protect your plants.

plants from the soil, such as removing weeds (see pp.575–9), mulching, and increasing humus content by digging in organic matter (see SOILS AND FERTILIZERS, "Mulches," p.534, and "Using soil additives," p.529). In addition, plants derive more benefit from rainfall if grown in an open position away from buildings, fences, and trees, which often produce areas of rain shadow.

Torrential rain may damage soil structure, but the worst effects may be avoided by gardening on well-drained sites. Where this is not possible, drainage may be improved by deep digging or by installing artificial drainage aids (see SOILS AND FERTILIZERS, "Double digging," p.528, and "Installing drains," p.531).

Humidity

Humidity levels are determined by the quantity or proportion of water vapor in the atmosphere and the moisture content of the soil.

The point at which the air becomes saturated varies according to sunlight, temperature, and wind. Atmospheric humidity is usually referred to as relative humidity, which is the amount of water vapor present in the air expressed as a percentage of saturation point.

The effects of humidity

In areas of heavy rainfall, atmospheric humidity is high. Certain plants thrive in conditions of exceptional humidity – ferns and mosses, for example. If necessary, humidity may be increased by damping down around plants (see GREENHOUSES AND FRAMES, "Increasing humidity," p.484). This is also of great value when propagating plants to reduce loss of water by transpiration.

High relative humidity may have unfavorable effects, however: fungal diseases, for example gray mold/*Botrytis*, flourish in the moist conditions created by high humidity.

Sunlight

Sunlight provides radiant energy to raise the temperature and humidity of soil and air, and plays a major role in stimulating plant growth.

For most plants, sunlight and the consequent high temperatures encourage maximum new growth, flowering, and fruiting. A sunny summer also results in greatly enhanced food storage in plants and helps to firm protective tissue, which means that better propagating material is produced.

Daylength

The duration of daylight in a given 24-hour period (daylength) is determined by latitude and season, and it affects flowering and fruiting in some plants, such as strawberries, *Kalanchoe*, and chrysanthemums. "Short" days have less than 12 hours of daylight, while "long" days have more than 12 hours. By using artificial lighting or blacking out the natural light, the flowering times of plants that are daylength-sensitive may, if required, be manipulated for exhibitions or flower shows. Germination of seeds and seedling development are advanced by the same method (see GREENHOUSES AND FRAMES, "Grow lamps," p.485).

SUNSHINE AND SHADE

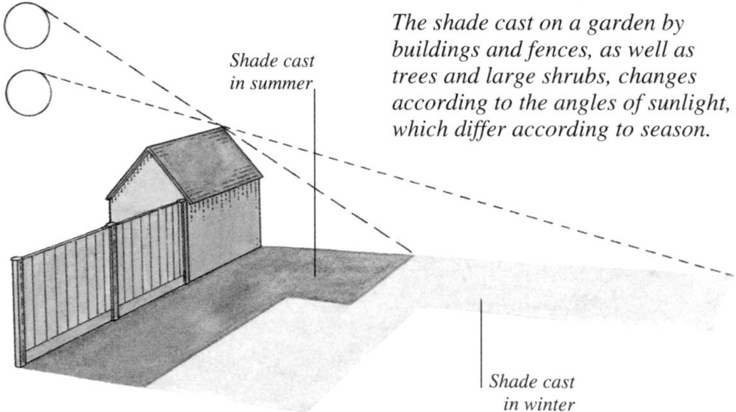

The shade cast on a garden by buildings and fences, as well as trees and large shrubs, changes according to the angles of sunlight, which differ according to season.

How plants respond to sunlight

Plants always grow toward the direction of sunlight: a shrub that is positioned close to a wall, for example, will develop more shoots and foliage on the side away from the wall. In the same way, plants that are subjected to a poor or localized light source become drawn or etiolated as they try to reach more light. The intensity of sunlight dictates flower opening in some plants: for example, *Ornithogalum umbellatum* opens its flowers only in good light conditions.

Sun or shade

Most leafy plants require the maximum amount of light to achieve optimum growth. Some garden plants thrive in direct, strong sunshine, while others will not tolerate it. Half-hardy plants, most fruits and vegetables, roses, and plants of Mediterranean origin all thrive best in full sun. On the other hand, many rhododendrons prefer to have some shade, whereas ivies (*Hedera*) and periwinkles (*Vinca*) tend to do best in heavily shaded areas.

Excessive sunshine

Strong sunlight may scorch the flowers and leaves of plants, especially of house plants when they are first put out for the summer. It may also split fruits or the bark of shrubs and trees. To prevent these problems, always choose an appropriate site when planting, and for vulnerable plants provide shade in summer, especially in greenhouses and frames (see GREENHOUSES AND FRAMES, "Shading," p.484).

Wind

Wind often damages plants and their environment, but it also has some benefits: it plays an important part in pollen and seed dispersal, and it may also be useful in cooling plants down, provided that they have enough water to prevent desiccation. In addition, gentle winds prevent the development of a stagnant atmosphere and deter plant diseases that might otherwise thrive.

On the other hand, wind may discourage beneficial insects and make it difficult to control pests, diseases, and weeds: spraying is dangerous in windy conditions because the spray drifts onto other plants. Many more serious problems are caused by the wind, however, although there are various ways of protecting plants.

Wind damage

If woody plants are exposed to strong winds continually, their top-growth becomes unbalanced, giving the plants a one-sided appearance. The exposed shoot tips are also likely to be damaged or scorched. Trees that grow on hilltops and on exposed coastal sites are examples.

Strong winds and storms

The greater the velocity of wind, the more damage it causes. In high winds, shoots and stems of plants may be broken and, in gale force conditions, trees may be uprooted or their root systems seriously weakened. Strong winds may also cause damage to fences, greenhouses, and other structures in the garden. On sandy or peaty soil, the wind may cause soil erosion.

Scorching and cold damage

Strong winds in high temperatures increase the rate at which water is lost from plants, leading to desiccation of leaves and shoots. Even moderate winds have a detrimental effect, and may prevent plants from reaching full growth. Where temperatures are low and there is continual wind, plants will suffer cold damage (see "Frost," p.515).

Effects of topography

The severity of the wind depends to a large extent on topography. Coastal sites often have no natural protection from salt-laden wind coming in off the sea. Hilltop sites may be equally exposed, because the wind gusts around and over the hill, causing additional turbulence.

Wind tunnels are created by the channeling of air between hillsides and along valleys, through corridors of established trees, or between adjacent buildings. This has the result of considerably intensifying wind speed and strength, so avoid planting in these areas. Windbreaks are a very useful means of providing shelter from wind. They may be either constructed, such as fences or screens, or natural, for example tree or shrub hedges.

How a windbreak works

Whichever type of windbreak is used, it should be approximately 50 percent permeable. Solid barriers deflect the wind upward, producing an area of low pressure directly behind them, which draws air downward to fill the vacuum, causing further turbulence.

Fences or screens need to be up to 12ft (4m) high for maximum protection as a garden boundary, but may be as low as 18in (45cm) for low-growing plants such as vegetables and strawberries. To achieve the greatest benefit across a large area, windbreaks should be placed at regular intervals roughly equal to ten times their height.

WINDBREAKS

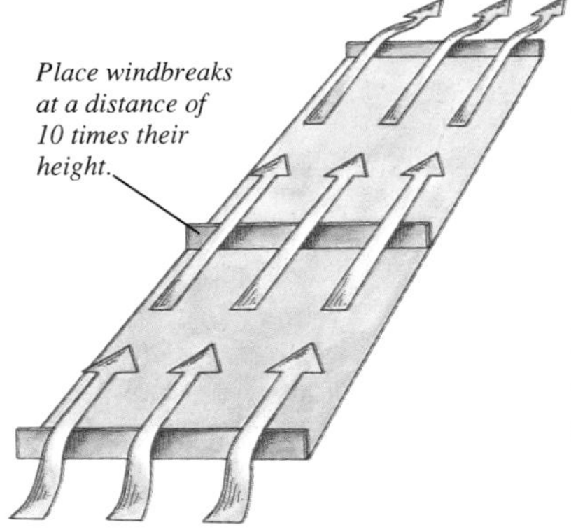

A SERIES OF WINDBREAKS
Across a large area of flat ground, construct several semipermeable fences or screens to break the force of the wind.

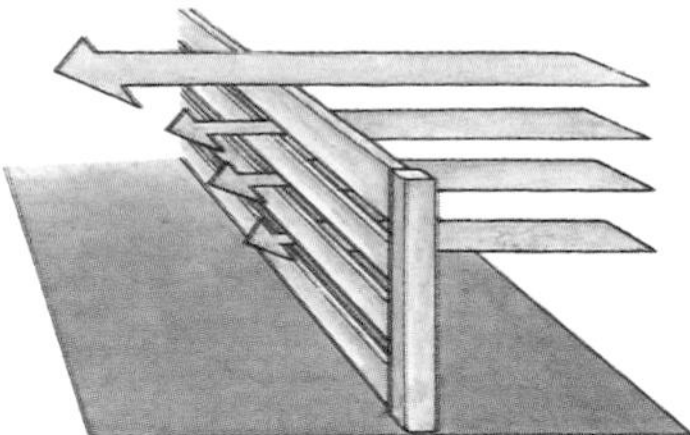

REDUCING WIND SPEED
A windbreak should be semi-permeable. Gusts of air still pass through, but at reduced speed.

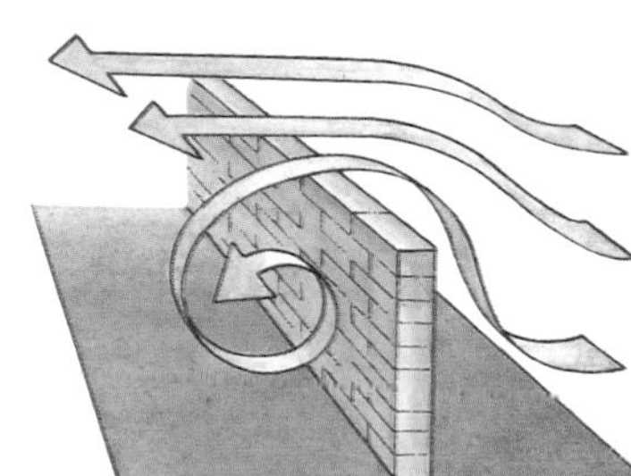

NONPERMEABLE WINDBREAK
A solid windbreak is ineffective. Air is forced upward, then pulled down to create a downdraft.

Microclimate

Differences in topography often mean that local climate varies considerably from the norm within a climate region. A site in a natural dip or hollow may be relatively warm if it is protected from the wind; on the other hand, if the hollow is shaded from sunshine it will be quite cool. Rainfall may be significantly less in gardens in the lee of high ground than in others in the same locality but on the windward side.

The garden and its plants further adapt the local climate and introduce features that give rise to a microclimate specific to the garden; this may differ markedly from that of the surrounding area.

Exploiting a microclimate

To alter the microclimate of a garden, the gardener can easily adapt certain features to provide specific conditions. For example, the soil in raised or sloping beds that face the sun will warm up quickly in spring, producing ideal conditions for early crops or flowers. If the soil is free-draining, the same area may be used for plants that prefer dry conditions. South-facing fences and walls are excellent places to grow tender climbers, wall shrubs, and trained fruit trees, since they are in sun for much of the day. The structures also absorb a great deal of heat that is then released to the plants, which improves flowering and fruiting.

Wind shelter

A row of trees or a fence provides a sheltered area for plants that might otherwise suffer wind damage. The growing conditions on each side of such a windbreak will be different: the ground close to a hedge or fence on the leeward side will rarely receive rain and may also be sheltered from the warming effect of the sun.

Shaded areas

Areas of shade in the garden beneath tree canopies, hedges, or large shrubs receive the same sort of light as in natural woodland and may be suitable for plants that enjoy such an environment. If a greater degree of shade is required, plants may be grown against north-facing walls, although these sites may be colder.

A bog garden

The edges of a pond or stream, or a low-lying part of the garden, may be used to create the bog-like conditions in which moisture-loving plants thrive.

Greenhouses and frames

Using greenhouses, frames, and cloches gives greater control over the elements, enabling the gardener to create a variety of microclimates in a small space (see GREENHOUSES AND FRAMES, pp.474–91).

THE MICROCLIMATE OF A GARDEN

The potential for several different growing environments exists in even the smallest gardens. Naturally occurring features create their own areas of microclimate. Garden features may be either exploited or manipulated to provide the conditions that plants from many different regions require.

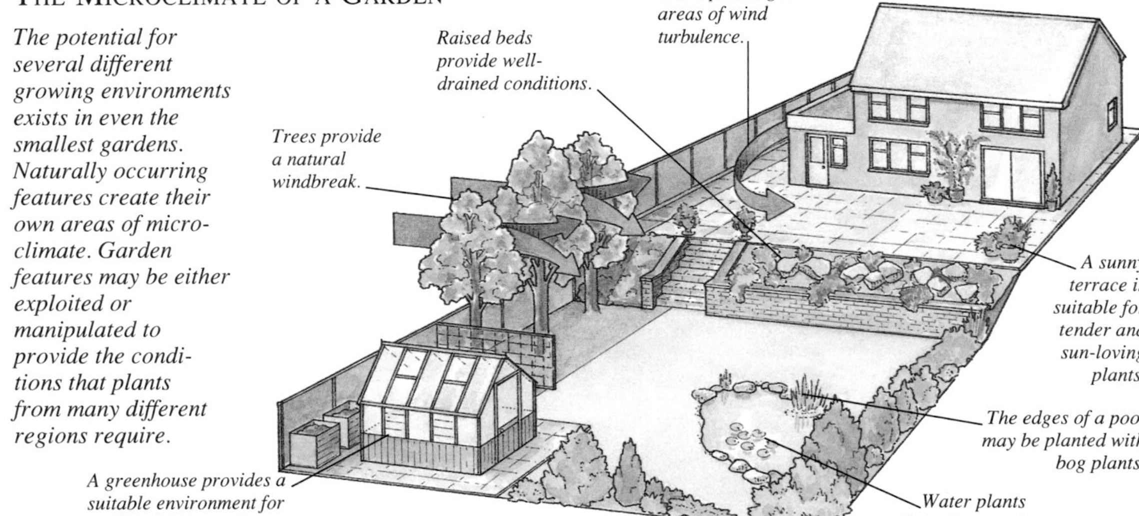

Cold and wind protection

SELECT plants that will thrive in a given climate zone rather than attempting to alter the growing conditions. Trying to grow very tender plants in a cold climate will almost certainly end in disappointment. For species that normally do well in a site but may suffer in harsh winters, providing protection against cold and wind is a sensible precaution. Efficient wind protection enables the gardener to grow a wide range of plants and is particularly useful for large plants, for those in open ground that cannot easily be brought under cover, and for early-flowering shrubs and trees that are more susceptible to cold than later-flowering species. Protection is also needed from strong winds, which can break the stems of woody plants and damage fragile ones; winds may also carry salt spray from nearby roads or the sea, causing browning of the foliage.

Preventive measures

Gardeners can take precautions to avoid cold damage: for susceptible plants, choose sheltered sites (such as in front of a warm wall or on a sunny bank) and do not plant in frost pockets. Tender climbers, for

PROTECTING SMALL TREES AND SHRUBS

STRAW INSULATION
Tie in the branches, then surround the tree with wire netting secured to 3 stakes in a partial circle 12in (30cm) from the tree. Pack straw into the gap, then secure the netting to a fourth stake. Cover the top with more straw. Attach a sheet of plastic to the netting.

STRAW BARRIER
Pack a thick layer of straw between 2 layers of wire netting. Surround the plant, filling any gaps with extra straw, and tie in place.

BURLAP STRIPS
Tie in the branches or leaves, then wrap the tree (here a palm) in strips of burlap, winding it around and tying it in place at intervals with string or twine. Protect the base of the trunk with straw.

BURLAP AND STRAW COVER
Pack straw around the shrub's branches, working from the bottom up. Loosely wrap burlap around it, and tie with string.

NETTING OVER A FRAMEWORK
When wall-trained fruit trees blossom, protect them from frost at night with woven nylon netting, rolled down to cover the tree but held away from the blossoms by stakes.

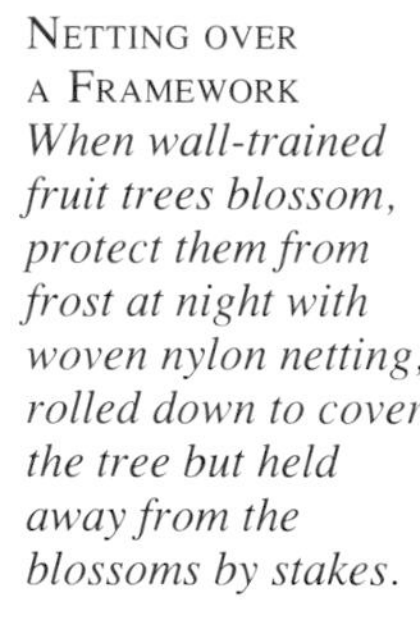

STRAW AND NETTING FOR WALL-TRAINED PLANTS
Protect a tree or shrub against a fence or wall by packing straw behind the branches. Fix netting at the top and bottom of the fence. Pack more straw between the netting and plant until it is covered.

MOUNDING UP SOIL
Protect the graft union of bush roses from extreme cold by mounding up soil around the crown, to a depth of 5in (12cm).

TRENCHING ROSES

1 *Loosen the root ball, then dig a trench long enough to take the height of the bush when laid on its side and about 12in (30cm) deeper than the width of the bush.*

2 *Line the trench with a 4in (10cm) layer of straw, and lay the bush down. Pack straw around and above the shoots.*

3 *Insert stakes and tie strings between them to hold the bush down. Fill in with soil, mounding it up to cover the bush to a depth of 12in (30cm).*

example, may be grown against a house wall (which will be warmer than a garden wall) or in containers that can easily be moved to a sheltered position. Seedlings, summer bulbs, and tubers should be planted out only when all danger of spring frost has passed, and roses and other shrubs should not be fed late in the season, since this encourages new soft growth that may then be damaged by fall frost. Allowing healthy, deadheaded herbaceous plants to die down naturally means that the foliage and stems will protect the crowns in winter, while a deep mulch of slowly decomposing organic matter provides protection for the roots of all plants. Check plants regularly in winter, firming any that have been heaved out of the ground.

Cold protection

The aim of cold protection is to insulate the plants from the extremes of freeze and thaw conditions by maintaining a constant temperature.

Insulation

In milder regions, wrapping plants in burlap, carpet, or several thicknesses of newspaper is effective in protecting the top-growth from damage. These materials also help moderate soil temperature fluctuations in colder areas, lessening damage to roots. Burlap helps to slow the warming process caused by a thaw and keeps plants dormant through any midwinter mild spells. Straw packed around the plant beneath the burlap provides additional insulation and is suitable for wall-trained trees and shrubs, climbers, root crops, strawberries, and small fruit trees and bushes. Once temperatures rise above freezing, this cover can be removed. Wall-trained plants need to be detached from their support, if possible, and the stems gathered together before wrapping.

Small shrubs and trees growing in areas colder than their usual winter hardiness zone can be protected by building a loose wire-netting cage around them and then packing this with dry leaves or straw. Plastic sheeting tied or stapled over the top of the cage will keep the insulating layer dry. Alternatively, pack straw in between and behind the stems before covering over.

Mounding with mulches or soil

For perennial plants that die down to a dormant crown, place a mulch or a few forkfuls of leaves over the crown and keep it in place with straw or prunings from evergreens. Roses and other woody plants can be protected by mounding soil around the base or laying them in a trench. In very cold regions, the soil mound should be covered with a layer of straw. Root vegetables can be protected from cold damage in the same way and can then be harvested even during rather severe cold spells.

Cloches

If only a few individual plants need protection, the best solution is to use a cloche, which acts like a miniature greenhouse, warming the soil and maintaining an even temperature. Emerging shoots of frost-sensitive plants, such as asparagus, can be protected with almost any household container: an old bucket, a large plant pot, or a sturdy cardboard box will all do the job quite adequately. Specially designed plastic foam and clear plastic cloches are available. More permanent cloche protection can be provided by glass cloches, polytunnels, or cold frames. For further information, see GREENHOUSES AND FRAMES, pp.474–91.

WINDBREAKS

DOUBLE NETTING
Protect fragile-stemmed plants from wind, using flexible double netting.

SNOW FENCE
Lengths of plastic snow fence, attached to stakes, protect plants from drifting snow and prevailing winds.

WOVEN HURDLES
Place woven hurdles at intervals between the plants, setting them at an angle into the prevailing wind, to deflect any strong gusts.

Wind protection

Wind protection aims to reduce the wind speed before it reaches any plants, thereby reducing physical damage to branches and stems and preventing further water loss. Many tender plants have greatly improved chances of survival if they are planted in the lee of a good hedge. A 5ft (1.5m) hedge will reduce the wind speed by 50 percent for plants within 23ft (7.5m) of the hedge (see HEDGES AND SCREENS, pp.58–60).

Tree and shrub species vary widely in their ability to withstand wind. The most tolerant species are those with small, thick, spiny, or waxy leaves, such as x *Cupressocyparis leylandii*, arborvitae (*Thuja*), and hollies (*Ilex*). Of deciduous trees, alders (*Alnus*), alpine currant (*Ribes alpinum*), willows (*Salix*), and hawthorn (*Crataegus*) are particularly wind hardy. Windbreaks made from stakes and netting, or commercial windbreaks, can be used while the hedge grows.

COVERS FOR FROST AND SNOW PROTECTION

CLOCHE
Use a cloche to protect roses and other young shrubs, seedlings, and tender herbaceous plants. An empty water bottle makes an excellent, low-cost cloche.

LOW POLYTUNNEL
Protect low-growing plants such as strawberries with a polytunnel stretched over wire hoops. The plastic may be raised at either side for ventilation during the day.

NEWSPAPER
Protect the new growth of potatoes and other tender crops against frost at night by covering them with sheets of newspaper, mounded up on either side to keep them in place.

SNOW FRAME
Use plywood panels, cross-braced with a wooden strut, to protect some evergreen shrubs from heavy snowfall.

Gardening in different regions

Within a country as vast as the United States there is wide variation in climate, soil, and planting traditions. Differences are significant even within the five generally accepted regions of the contiguous states of America: the Northeast; the Southeast; the Midwest, High Plains, and Western Mountains; the Southwest; and the Pacific Northwest. The following accounts of these five regions each describe their climate and soil type and provide general planting recommendations. The climate zone in which you live is one of the most important factors in determining what will grow in your garden. The US Department of Agriculture map on pp.516–17 defines these zones and gives the average annual minimum temperatures within each region. In seed and nursery catalogs a hardiness zone next to the name of a plant indicates its hardiness to cold. A plant's tolerance of heat and for what duration are also vitally important in its successful cultivation, as are such cofactors as average rainfall, prevailing winds, light intensity, daylength, and the number of frost-free growing days in your area. Other relevant influences on gardening are the type of soil in your garden and its relative fertility, as well as which plants will grow best and why. Within the United States gardening traditions differ not only in the range of ornamental plants cultivated but also in the amount of ground dedicated, for example, to fruit, vegetables, and the lawn.

Northeast region

Bounded to the north by Canada, to the east by the Atlantic Ocean, to the south by Zone 6, and to the west by Lake Michigan and southward.

Gardening in the Northeast region is defined by altitude and proximity to the Atlantic Ocean. Weather can, on occasion, be extremely cold or hot but is generally considered excellent for all gardening pursuits. The wide range of soils suits an extensive selection of plants.

Climate

The region has a temperate climate, but summers may be tropical during a wet season or like the Mediterranean in a dry one. In a year's cycle, inland temperatures can span from -30°F (-35°C) to near 100°F (38°C). There are 90 –180 frost-free days each year. Coastal gardens are cooler in the summer, warmer in fall and winter, but slightly cooler in the spring as compared to those inland. They are also subject to hurricane damage, primarily in late summer and early fall.

Each year the region receives some 30–40in (750–1,000mm) of rainfall, fairly evenly distributed. Springs are typically wet and cool, falls sunny and dry. Summers are variable from hot and very humid to hot and dry, and winters cold and moist. Snow cover varies from year to year and cannot be counted on except in more northerly and westerly parts of the region. Wet snows that lie in one place can be disastrous, especially if they occur late, after plants have started to grow. Ice storms, which are potentially damaging to woody plants, are more likely in late fall or winter.

The area is blessed with sunshine. In fact, dull, winter days notwithstanding, one main problem is sunscorch and windburning among needle and broad-leaved evergreens, when there is strong sun and wind during cold weather.

Soils

Gardeners in the Northeast experience a variety of soils, from thin and rocky in New England to deep, rich, and often acidic (pH 5.5–6.5) in Ohio. Some soils are quite limey, such as in parts of northwestern Connecticut, and others sandy, such as on Cape Cod and in parts of New Hampshire. Amending the soil with well-rotted compost or other organic material is always sound practice, as is watering slowly and deeply in dry spells and mulching to conserve moisture.

Planting traditions

In fall, sharp variations between warm days and cool nights help paint the Northeast in brilliant leaf colors found in both native and Asiatic trees and shrubs – sugar, red, and Japanese maples (*Acer*), oaks (*Quercus*), *Sassafras albidum*, *Oxydendrum arboreum*, *Amelanchier*, *Vaccinium corymbosum*, *Nyssa*, and *Euonymus alata*.

Some shade and flowering trees popular in the region include *Tilia cordata*, European and American beeches, and *Gleditsia triacanthos* 'Moraine'. Crabapples (*Malus*) are a big success, hardy in the coldest regions; *Cornus kousa* makes a superb flowering tree, appearing a little later than the overall burst of bloom that accompanies spring in the Northeast. Also successful in the region are hawthorns (*Crataegus*), *Halesia*, and *Laburnum*. Shrubs including roses can be readily orchestrated to provide flowers and colorful berries throughout the year.

Among the most dependable large evergreens are the native pines (*Pinus*) – white, red, and pitch. *Pinus thunbergiana* withstands salt spray and hurricane winds along the coast. Perhaps best of the shrubby evergreens are *Taxus cuspidata* and *T.* x *media*. There are also numerous other evergreens – needle and broad-leaved – such as *Juniperus chinensis* 'Pfitzerana' and other low junipers, *Pinus mugo*, and *Pieris floribunda* and *P. japonica*.

All kinds of bulb are grown throughout the region, the most popular being fall-planted, spring-blooming tulips, hyacinths, daffodils, and crocuses. Gladioli, *Canna*, and *Caladium* also thrive.

Vegetables may be grown up to nine months of the year and root crops harvested for twelve. Gourmet-quality vegetables and herbs have become popular throughout the Northeast, and local market gardeners respond with fresh produce that is varied and tasty.

Orchards may contain a good range of fruits. Large numbers of apples are produced as well as blueberries and cranberries. Brambles and strawberries are also popular; grapes for both eating and making wine; figs are commn throughout Zone 7, often needing some protection against winter deep freezes.

Most lawns are of bluegrass (*Poa*) and fine-leaved fescues (*Festuca*). A local trend is to reduce the size of the lawn.

Southeast region

Bounded to the north by Zone 6, to the east by the Atlantic Ocean, to the south by the Gulf of Mexico, and to the west by eastern Oklahoma and eastern Texas.

Altitude and latitude help define gardening in the Southeast. This generally warm region supports a wide range of plants ranging from tropicals through subtropicals to those of the temperate world. Most soils need amendment.

Climate

As defined here, this region enjoys relatively warm winters hardly ever colder than 0°F (-18°C), except in the higher elevations where cold can be bitter, to -35°F (-37°C). Frost-free days range from 365 to 140 or fewer each year.

Average rainfall is generous, 30–70in (750–1,750mm), and favorably distributed through the year. Humidity is high and sunshine plentiful.

Snow occurs at the higher altitudes. Hurricane winds are always a possibility along the coastlines.

Soils

Soils tend to be acidic clays, although sand dominates the coastal plains and a few locations have excellent loams. The high temperatures found in this region when accompanied by high humidity rapidly burn humus, so gardens in such areas benefit from generous and regular applications of well-rotted compost or other organic matter.

In most of the Southeast, high soil temperatures in spring and summer favor crabgrass (*Digitaria sanguinalis*) as a weed, which may necessitate the use of a preemergent herbicide before the seeds sprout or a postemergent herbicide in early summer.

Planting traditions

Through Zones 7–9, azaleas (*Rhododendron*) and camellias are among the region's most-loved flowering shrubs. They give blooms in all seasons except possibly mid- and late summer. In the warmer zones, Zones 9–10, gardeners can enjoy such exotic shrubs or small flowering trees as *Hibiscus rosa-sinensis*, *Ixora*, oleander (*Nerium oleander*), *Gardenia*, and *Osmanthus fragrans*. Inland, both north- and westward, where freezing occurs in winter, flowering dogwoods (*Cornus florida*) and *Cercis canadensis* are found everywhere. Boxwoods (*Buxus*), although troubled increasingly by nematodes, are favored for hedging, and roses grow exceptionally well. Also worthwhile for the garden are magnolias, native and Asiatic hollies (*Ilex*), *Lagerstroemia indica*, and oaks (*Quercus*).

In the mildest zones of the region, vegetables and other food crops such as citrus and papaya are grown year-round. Florida is noted for its oranges and grapefruit. Warm parts of the Southeast are also renowned for peaches while apples, pears, and grapes gain favor at higher altitudes. Strawberries are the most popular small fruit. Highbush blueberries succeed exceptionally well in gardens of the interior that are likely to be extremely hot all summer. Vidalia onions are a popular specialty crop. In most of Zones 7–8, pecans – the Southeast's favorite true nut – thrive, while colder areas within these zones are better suited to growing black walnuts and Chinese chestnuts. Peanuts are virtually synonymous with southern Georgia.

Suitable grasses for lawns in Zones 8 and southward include St. Augustine (*Stenotaphrum secundatum*), Bermuda (*Cynodon*), centipede (*Eremochloa ophiuroides*) especially for poor soils, and Manila or Japanese carpet (*Zoysia matrella*). In cooler areas, cool-season grasses such as Kentucky bluegrass (*Poa pratensis*) and fine-leaved fescues (*Festuca*) are the rule. The Meyer strains of *Zoysia* are another possibility here. In borderline warm–cool climates, Bermuda and zoysia lawns are frequently overseeded with annual ryegrass (*Lolium perenne*) in the late fall, to provide a lawn that is green all winter.

Midwest, High Plains, and Western Mountain region

Bounded to the north by Canada, to the east by Lake Michigan and southward, to the south by the northern boundary of Zone 6 through to Oklahoma and Nevada, westward to eastern Oregon, and eastern Washington in the west.

Although this region is vast, its gardeners have much in common, most notably four distinct seasons every year and extreme and sudden changes in cold and heat, moisture and drought. To conserve moisture, soils need regular mulching. The comparatively limited range of native plants is gradually being extended by new cultivars and species.

Climate

Winter and summer can be violent and wet or dry. Spring and fall tend to favor gardening. Temperatures can fall as much as 40°F (22°C) in an hour or less. Frost-free days range from 100 in the north to 200 and more in the south. When the temperature plummets to subzero, the survival of shrubs and herbaceous perennials often depends on a protective snow cover. Particularly in areas inclined to high winds – western Oklahoma and Kansas, eastern Colorado, and northward through the High Plains – blizzards typically pile snow over parts of the garden while inches away the ground may be swept clean.

Rainfall can be scarce toward the south and west of the region, sometimes hardly more than 15in (380mm), while it can be twice this amount elsewhere. Drip irrigation systems are exceptionally effective in drier locations.

Humidity in the High Plains is low whereas that in the Midwest is quite high. Winds are a constant in the drier areas, no matter what season.

Soils

Soils are variable, from peaty toward the northeast of the region to sandy, clayey, or gravelly elsewhere. Especially in parts of Ohio, Indiana, Illinois, and Iowa, the soils are notably rich, loamy, and of adequate depth. In other areas, generous applications of compost or other organic humus are an annual ritual, ideally in late fall or early winter. The freezing and thawing action can then condition such materials so that they are more useful to plants in the ensuing season.

Planting traditions

Favorite deciduous trees are maples (*Acer*), ash (*Fraxinus*), *Gleditsia*, *Celtis*, *Sorbus*, and *Tilia americana*. *Elaeagnus angustifolia*, while not native to this region, is well adapted to the climate and soils. Also favored are narrow-leaved evergreens such as native pines (*Pinus*), spruces (*Picea*), and junipers (*Juniperus*).

Commonly planted native shrubs include roses (*Rosa*), honeysuckle (*Lonicera*), red-, yellow-, and gray-twig dogwoods (*Cornus*), *Physocarpus*, and *Viburnum*. Some successfully introduced ornamentals include lilacs (*Syringa*), *Euonymus*, and *Spiraea*.

Annual and perennial flowers thrive in gardens throughout the region. Among the most popular are chrysanthemums, daylilies (*Hemerocallis*), and lilies.

Vegetables and fruits are grown successfully throughout the region by selecting those kinds adapted to the length of the growing season. Fruits generally benefit from the cold but also flower late enough to escape most spring frosts. Most cool- and warm-weather vegetables are possible, from lettuces and radishes in spring to cucumbers, zucchini, and tomatoes in summer. Apples, pears, sour cherries, strawberries, brambles, and grapes are among the fruits cultivated in the region.

Cool-season lawns are the rule: bluegrass (*Poa*) and fine fescues (*Festuca*) in areas with good rainfall; buffalo grass (*Buchloe dactyloides*) may be used in drier, colder climates.

Southwest region

Bounded to the north by southern Oregon and the northern boundary of Zone 6 through Texas, New Mexico, Arizona, Utah, Nevada, and California, to the east by western Oklahoma and west Texas, to the south by Mexico, and to the west by the Pacific Ocean.

Almost regardless of altitude, latitude, and the annual highs and lows of temperature, this region is defined by the availability of water. A visit to the desert or drier parts of any state a day or two after it has rained will underline the all-you-add-is-water reality that makes gardening here both challenging and potentially rewarding. The urgent need for water conservation has inspired some gardeners to experiment with dry, warm-climate natives from the Mediterranean and southern hemisphere, particularly Australia. All gardeners, however, need to add well-rotted compost or other organic matter to their soils.

Climate

Frost occurs throughout higher elevations of the region. Frost-free days range from 365 to 150 or fewer at higher elevations. Blizzard snow happens at high elevations and is not a reliable source of garden water. The region has very sunny weather and humidity is low. Winds are usually strong and constant.

Because annual rainfall is generally low throughout the region, environmentalistic gardeners are increasingly using native plants and vigorously applying the precepts of xeriscaping, the overriding rule of thumb being not to set in motion any garden that will require undue irrigation during normal periods of dry weather.

Soils

Soils are typically alkaline so large quantities of organic matter are needed to make it suitable for nonnative crops. Iron may also be required to reduce the pH to 6.5 or whatever is desired. Adding organic matter to the soil is essential. It makes alkaline or sandy soils more hospitable to cultivated flowers and food crops as well as increasing moisture absorption and retention.

Planting traditions

Coastal gardens of California are a gardener's paradise, where water for irrigation is available and almost any plant will grow. Elsewhere in the region, native trees, shrubs, ground covers, and perennials are increasingly being favored for their ability to succeed without undue coddling.

Annuals are a chief source of garden color. Bulbs such as *Agapanthus* and *Clivia* grow all year in the region's warmest parts while elsewhere any of the usual spring-flowering bulbs can be grown successfully in properly prepared soil and a modicum of irrigation. Summer bulbs are also popular throughout the region. Dahlias are very well suited to the higher altitudes.

When irrigated, vegetables and fruit thrive throughout the Southwest region, even commercially in the warmer parts. Pears, apples, and sour cherries can be cultivated at colder, higher altitudes while toward the warmer parts different cultivars of these fruits can be grown as well as apricots, peaches, and nectarines.

Lawns in the northeast of this region are often Bermuda grass (*Cynodon*), with some zoysia and buffalo grasses (*Buchloe dactyloides*). The last is often favored because it needs less mowing than other types and no irrigation. St. Augustine grass (*Stenotaphrum secundatum*) is favored in the areas south and east of the Dallas–Fort Worth area, whereas westward lawns are more likely to be buffalo grass or Bermuda grass.

Pacific Northwest region

Bounded to the north by Canada, to the east by the eastern borders of Washington State and Oregon, to the south by northern California, and to the west by the Pacific Ocean.

The lives of gardeners in this region are tremendously influenced by the Japanese ocean current. This current greatly modifies the weather because it carries a mildness in temperature unknown elsewhere at such latitude. Excepting certain tropicals and subtropicals, almost any plant can be grown successfully in the region. Most soils need amending with well-rotted compost.

Climate

Coastal gardens are most affected by the Japanese ocean current, but its mildness does penetrate into the interior, bringing with it climatic surprises. In the Puget Sound of Washington and the Willamette Valley of Oregon, the climate is generally moist, with mild winters and hot summers, some 70–80°F (21–7°C). Coastal gardens are normally cooler in summer, around 60°F (16°C), and, in winter, accosted by water-laden winds. Coastal northern California tends to be milder in winter with less rain than gardens farther north. Gardens east of the region's formidable mountain ranges experience severe frost, freezing winters, and hot summer days.

Frost-free days vary: 90–120 at higher elevations, 365 along the coast. Snow is heaviest at higher elevations along the Cascade and Sierra Nevada Mountains. Eastern parts of the region are driest; those west of the mountain range the wettest. Humidity can be high in the wetter parts of the region, sometimes dictating the need for fungicidal treatments against foliar diseases. Eastern parts are sunny while those westward, on the ocean side of the mountains, are more likely to be cloudy, foggy, misty, and to have heavy rainfalls.

Soils

Most coastal soils in the Northwest are acidic, with a pH of 5.5 or below, while the others are slightly higher, to around pH 7.0 in eastern localities. To thrive in coastal soils, most plants need extra phosphorus and potassium. Soils in wetter areas tend to be humus-rich, yet they may also be sandy.

Planting traditions

While gardeners in less auspicious climates may envy the choice of plants available in this region, even in the Pacific Northwest gardening is more successful if plants are chosen according to their appropriateness to the local soils and moisture conditions. Trees and shrubs that are native to the region include *Pseudotsuga menziesii*, oaks (*Quercus*), pines (*Pinus*), willows (*Salix*), various maples (*Acer*), *Cornus nuttallii*, *Sambucus caerulea*, *S. pubens*, *Mahonia aquifolium*, *Rhododendron macrophyllum*, *R. occidentale*, and mock oranges (*Philadelphus*). Some favorite native perennials and bulbs are lupines (*Lupinus*), *Xerophyllum tenax*, *Zauschneria*, and *Camassia*.

Fruit and vegetables such as corn, tomatoes, okra, and eggplants are, however, more likely to thrive in the warm interiors of the Pacific Northwest. Much of the nation's commercial lawn grass is produced in this region.

5

Soils and Fertilizers

Soils are highly complex and dynamic materials that are made up of minute particles of weathered rock of different types, accumulated organic matter, and plant and animal life right down to the microscopic level. Healthy soil is essential to successful plant growth: it physically supports plants and supplies them with water, air, and a variety of mineral nutrients. If the soil in your garden does not at first appear to be ideal, there is a range of possible solutions; virtually any soil may be improved with a little time and effort. It is possible, for example, to drain the soil if it is waterlogged or to improve its structure and water-holding capacity by the addition of organic matter such as compost or well-rotted manure. Extra nutrients are easily added to the soil with fertilizers, and lime may be added to make acidic soils more alkaline. Mulches and top-dressings improve plant growth because they prevent weed seeds from germinating and reduce water loss from the soil, and some also have an ornamental function. For container-grown plants, there is a wide range of potting soil mixes available to suit every purpose.

Soil and its structure

Most soil is classified according to its clay, silt, and sand content. The size and proportion of these mineral particles help determine the chemical and physical behavior of the soil. Clay particles are less than $^1/_{16,000}$in (0.0016mm) in diameter; silt particles are up to 25 times larger than the largest clay particles; and sand particles may be 1,000 times larger – up to $^1/_{16}$in (1.6mm) in diameter.

Soil types

Loam soils have the ideal balance of mineral particle sizes, with between 8 and 25 percent clay, which results in good drainage and water retention, combined with high fertility.

Clay soils are heavy, slow draining, and slow to warm up in spring, but are often highly fertile. They are easily compacted, however, and may bake hard in summer.

Both sandy and silt soils have a low proportion of clay particles, making them much less water-retentive than clay. Sandy soils are particularly light and drain freely; they need frequent irrigation and feeding. However, they warm up quickly in spring and are easily improved with organic matter. Silts are more retentive and fertile than sandy soils but tend to compact more easily.

Soil characteristics

Clay soils have more than 25 percent clay particles and are characteristically wet and sticky. Soils containing less than 8 percent clay are classified as either silt or sandy soil, depending on whether silt or sand particles predominate. Muck is formed where wet, acid conditions prevent full decomposition of organic matter, which therefore remains on or near the soil surface. Alkaline soil, however, normally drains freely, and organic matter incorporated into it decomposes rapidly.

Sandy Soil
A dry, light, free-draining soil, easy to work but relatively infertile.

Muck
Rich in organic matter, muck is dark and moisture-retentive.

Clay
A heavy, slow-draining soil, usually with a high nutrient value.

Alkaline Soil
Pale, shallow, and stony, this is free-draining and moderately fertile,

Silt
Silt is reasonably moisture retentive and fertile but compacts easily.

Organic or muck soils are generally wet and acidic; however, they support excellent plant growth, if drained, fertilized, and limed, if required. Alkaline soils are shallow and moderately fertile, and they drain freely.

The profile of the soil

Soils may be divided into three layers, or horizons: topsoil, subsoil, and a layer derived from the parent rock. Topsoil contains most soil organisms and many of the nutrients. It is generally dark, because it contains organic matter that is added artificially or naturally by leaf drop. Subsoil is usually lighter in color; if it is white, the parent rock is probably limestone. If there is little or no color change between topsoil and subsoil, the topsoil may be deficient in organic matter.

Weeds and wild plants help to indicate the type of soil in a garden and any characteristics it may have, although their presence is only a guide. Birch (*Betula*), blueberries (*Vaccinium*), bluebells (*Mertensia*), and hemlock (*Tsuga*) are all signs of acid soil, as are many garden plants such as rhododendrons. Beech (*Fagus*) and ash (*Fraxinus*) indicate that the soil is likely to be alkaline. Wild plants may also indicate the chemical profile of the soil: nettle and dock, for example, suggest a rich, fertile soil that is high in phosphorus, while clover indicates a soil that is low in nitrogen.

Identifying your soil

Rub a small amount of moist soil between your fingers. A sandy soil feels quite gritty and will not stick together or form a ball, although a sandy loam is slightly more cohesive. A silt soil feels silky or soapy to the touch. A silty loam may show imprints when pressed with a finger. A loamy clay soil holds together well and may be rolled into a cylindrical shape. Heavy clay soil may be rolled even more thinly, and develops a shiny streak when smoothed. All clay soils feel sticky and slightly heavy.

SANDY SOIL
Sandy soil feels gritty when rubbed between finger and thumb. The grains do not stick together.

CLAY SOIL
Clay soil feels sticky when wet and may be rolled into a ball that changes shape when pressed.

SOIL PROFILES

Soil is usually made up of layers of topsoil and subsoil, and a lower layer derived from underlying rock. The depth of each layer may vary.

Acidity and alkalinity

Soil pH is a measurement of acidity or alkalinity – the scale ranges from 1–14. A pH below 7 indicates an acid soil, while a pH higher than 7 indicates an alkaline soil. Neutral soil has a pH of 7.

The pH of soil is usually controlled by its calcium level. Calcium is an alkaline element that almost all soils tend to lose through leaching (meaning that it is washed through the soil by water). Soils over limestone, which are rich in calcium, are more or less unaffected; other soils, especially sands and sandy loams, gradually turn more acidic.

Alkalinity may be increased, if necessary, by liming (see p.533) or introducing lime-rich material such as mushroom compost.

Electronic pH meters and soil test kits may be used to measure pH. Make several tests across the garden, since pH may vary; readings are very unreliable after liming.

The effect of pH

Above all, pH affects the solubility of soil minerals and hence their availability to plants. Acid soils tend to be deficient in phosphorus and sometimes contain excess manganese and aluminum. Alkaline soils tend to lack manganese, boron, and phosphorus.

Soil pH also affects the number and type of beneficial soil organisms, as well as pests and diseases. For example, earthworms dislike acid soils, but clubroot and wireworms are common in acid conditions. On alkaline soils, potato scab occurs more frequently.

Optimum pH

The pH range for good plant growth is between 5.5 and 7.5. A pH of 6.5 usually is optimum, depending on the plants to be grown. Muck soils have an optimum pH of 5.8, however. The highest vegetable yields are generally obtained from neutral soils, but most ornamentals tolerate a wide pH range. Some are more sensitive; calcicoles (lime lovers) and calcifuges (lime haters) are adapted to extreme pH ranges and their growth suffers if they are planted in soil with the wrong pH level.

TESTING pH LEVEL

Soil test kits use a chemical solution that changes color when mixed with soil in a small test tube. The color is then matched against a chart that indicates the pH level of the soil sample.

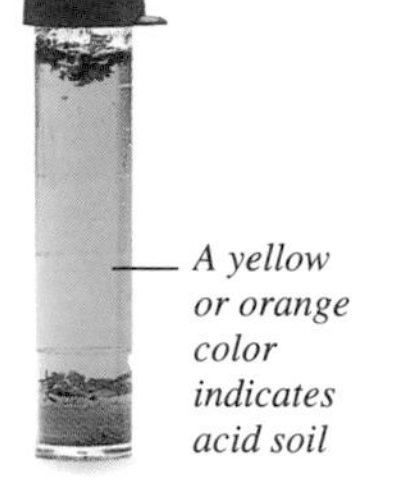

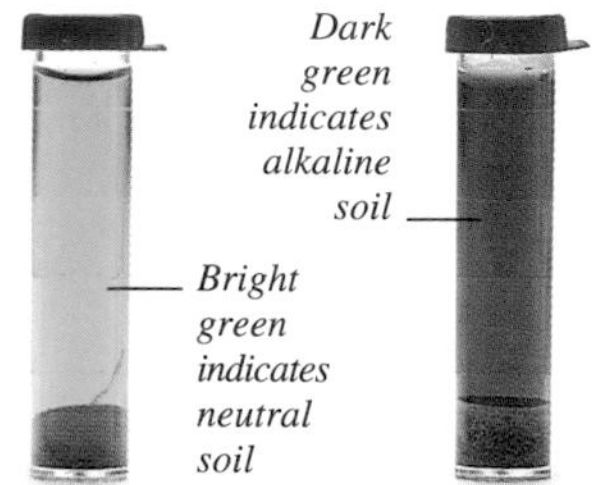

Soil organisms

Certain soil organisms are essential to maintain soil fertility. Beneficial bacteria and fungi prefer well-aerated soil and generally tolerate a wide pH, although most fungi prefer acidic conditions. One group of fungi (mycorrhizae) live in association with plant roots, and improve the take-up of nutrients from the soil.

Small soil animals, such as mites, play a vital part in the breakdown of organic matter. Microscopic worms and nematodes (eelworms) help to control pests, although some are themselves pests.

Larger soil animals, particularly earthworms, improve soil structure when feeding and burrowing; the passage of soil through an earthworm's body binds soil particles into crumbs, increasing aeration and improving drainage.

BENEFICIAL ORGANISMS

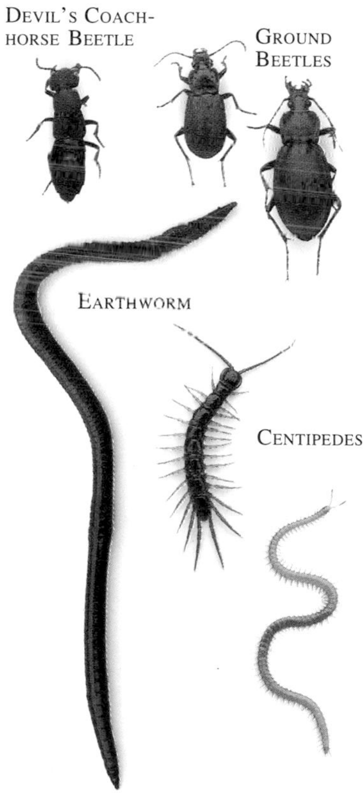

Healthy soil contains a teeming community of earthworms and other organisms, which help to aerate the soil and break down organic matter.

Soil cultivation

Correct methods of soil cultivation, including weeding, digging, and adding soil improvers, are vital to successful long-term plant growth.

Weeds compete with cultivated plants for space, light, nutrients, and water – in fact, all the essentials. They may also harbor diseases of many types, which makes their eradication or control vital.

Several digging techniques are used to cultivate the soil in different ways, depending on the condition of the soil and the plants that are to be grown. If the condition of the soil is poor, it may be improved by the addition of organic material, usually at the same time as digging.

Clearing an overgrown garden

Badly neglected, overgrown plots may be cleared using either tools or chemicals, so use whichever method is appropriate for the site (see also Plant Problems, "Controlling weeds," p.577).

Mechanical clearance

Slash as much top-growth as possible using a nylon-line trimmer, brushwood cutter, or scythe, and clear it away from the area. Then, with a rotary mower, cut any remaining growth as low as possible before digging out and removing all the vegetation that is left on the site.

Alternatively, use a rototiller to churn up the soil and chop up the weeds. Make several passes with the rototiller to break up the matted vegetation, then rake it up and remove it from the surface. The chopping action of the tines, however, will cut the roots or rhizomes of perennial weeds into pieces that regenerate rapidly. After rototilling, therefore, it is essential to rake over the plot and remove by hand all remaining weeds.

Chemical clearance

Following the manufacturer's instructions carefully, spray with a systemic weedkiller, allow it to be absorbed, and then clear away the dead top-growth. If necessary, respray any vegetation that escaped the first application of weedkiller.

Remove the dead vegetation or incorporate it into the soil. Most gardeners prefer to prepare the whole site for planting, but trees, shrubs, and other vigorous ornamentals may be planted directly into holes prepared in the dead vegetation.

On sandy soil, many weedkillers are rapidly leached out, so use only contact weedkillers, which break down when in contact with soil. In organic gardens, where it is not desirable to use chemicals, or if the layout of a garden makes it difficult to apply weedkiller evenly, use mechanical or other methods of weed control, for example mulches (see p.534) and organic practices such as the deep-bed system (see p.536).

Clearing a Site of Weeds

Using Weedkiller
A neglected or weed-infested site must be thoroughly cleared before planting takes place. Treat tough weeds with a chemical weedkiller.

Forking out Weeds
Fork up the roots of large weeds and pull them out, holding the main stem close to the soil so that the whole root system is removed.

Weed control

In practically all gardens the soil is full of weed seeds and fragments of perennial weed roots. Weed seeds are brought into the garden from neighboring land by the wind and in the soil or soil mix around bought plants. Cultivation, by its very nature, disturbs the soil, and often brings weed seeds to the surface, where they are able to germinate (see "The stale seedbed technique," p.528). Soil cultivation also allows small pieces of perennial weed roots to regenerate and start a new growth cycle over again.

It is virtually impossible to clean a soil completely of weeds, but regular weeding, rather than sporadic attempts that are then followed by periods of neglect, is the best method of control. Although tedious, hand-weeding with a hand fork is one of the most efficient methods of controlling weeds, since you can ensure that the whole plant is removed from the bed. It also causes the least disturbance to existing plants.

Hoeing

Hoes are used to remove annual weeds and also help to aerate the soil (see also p.460). Unless used carefully, however, they may damage the surface roots and top-growth of nearby cultivated plants. Hoeing mainly works only in the surface soil and seldom goes deep enough to destroy the roots of perennial weeds; pull these out by hand or destroy them with a systemic weedkiller (see Plant Problems, "Foliage-acting weedkillers," p.577).

Sterilizing the soil

Some soil pests and diseases, such as bacterial soft rot of irises and nematodes, are so aggressive and persistent that soil sterilization may be the only effective treatment to eliminate them.

Soil sterilants should only be used as a last resort, since they are indiscriminate and kill all organisms, beneficial as well as harmful. This may lead to long-term problems in the garden, because harmful pests

Rototilling the Soil

1 *For cultivating large areas of soil, it is worth renting a rototiller. Adjust the machine's handlebars to a comfortable position, then press down on the handlebars so that the tiller blades penetrate the soil to their full depth.*

2 *After rototilling, rake up and remove any pieces of perennial weeds from the surface of the soil, otherwise they will reestablish and grow again.*

Soil Sterilization

Soil sterilization may be the only method of eradicating some pests or diseases. Cover the sterilized soil with weighted-down plastic (any soil used for this should be discarded).

are likely to reinvade and thrive unhindered, since there will be no natural predators to control them.

Chemical soil sterilants are highly poisonous and can be applied only by a licensed operator. The sterilant is applied as a drench that percolates and vaporizes through the pores of the soil. The soil surface is then covered with plastic to prevent the gases from escaping. After a soil sterilant has been applied, it will be several weeks before it is safe to plant in the treated soil.

Digging and forking

Cultivating the soil by digging and forking helps to provide suitable conditions for good plant growth by aerating the soil and breaking up any surface crust (cap). Organic matter and fertilizers may be incorporated at the same time, if required. On heavily compacted ground, digging helps to improve both soil structure and drainage.

The most common method of cultivation is digging with a spade; single and double digging are in general the most effective and labor-efficient digging methods. Some garden beds, however, may not be suited to such a methodical approach to soil cultivation, especially where there are already many established plants. In these circumstances, forking and simple digging may be useful alternatives.

Disadvantages of digging

There are some disadvantages associated with digging. It increases the rate of breakdown of organic matter, particularly in sandy soils, which in the long term reduces soil fertility. In addition, while soil structure is temporarily improved by cultivation, after a while the soil settles down and may become compacted, resulting in poor aeration and drainage unless the soil is dug again.

When to dig

It is preferable to dig in fall, if possible. The soil is then exposed to winter cold and snow, which help break down large clods of soil and improve soil structure.

From midwinter until early spring, the ground is frequently wet or frozen and impossible to work. Heavy soil must never be dug when it is wet, since this may cause severe and permanent structural damage.

Using a fork

Much digging work involves lifting and turning the soil. Forks, which are shaped to penetrate the soil easily, are excellent for opening up and loosening soil – but not for lifting it. Forking is less harmful to the soil structure than using a spade, because it tends to break the clods along existing, natural fracture lines rather than along artificially sliced ones.

Forking is suitable for rough digging and for turning the soil but not for creating fine tilths (see "Forming a tilth," p.528). It is also useful for clearing weeds from the soil, particularly perennial weeds such as quackgrass (*Elymus*), but take care not to leave behind small pieces of plant that will regenerate.

Simple digging

When digging, some gardeners prefer simply to lift out a spadeful of soil, invert it, drop it back in its original position, and chop it up. This method is known as simple digging. It is a quick and relatively easy form of cultivation and is suitable for cleaning the soil surface of any debris and nonpersistent weeds, incorporating small amounts of manure and fertilizers, or creating a surface tilth. Simple digging is often the best option when working in irregularly shaped beds or around existing plants.

Single digging

Single digging is the term applied to a methodical and labor-efficient approach to cultivation that ensures an area has been completely dug to a uniform standard, and to the depth of a spade (known as a spit).

Mark out with lines the area to be cultivated. Then, beginning at one end of the plot, dig out trenches to a spade's depth and about 12in (30cm) wide. Place the soil from the first trench in a pile on the ground in front. Work backward along the plot, turning the soil from each subsequent trench into the one in front.

FORKING

Fork over the soil when it is moist but not waterlogged. Work methodically, inserting the fork then turning it over (see inset) to break up the soil and aerate it.

SIMPLE DIGGING

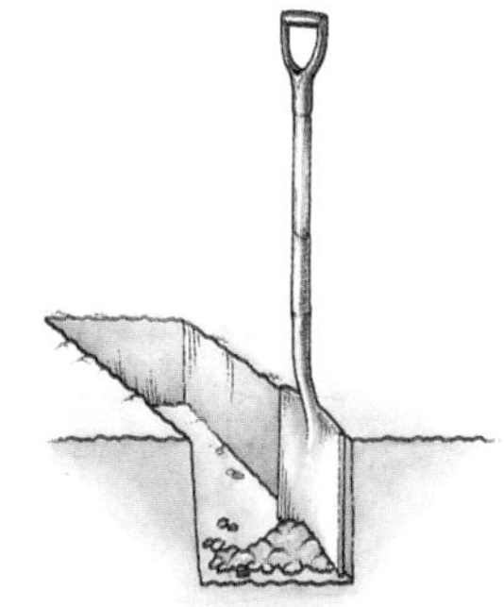

Most spades have a blade 10in (25cm) long. This is the depth of trench required when digging 1 spit deep.

1 *Drive the spade into the soil to its full depth, keeping the blade upright. Press down firmly on the blade with the ball of your foot.*

2 *Pull back on the handle and lever soil onto the blade. Bend knees and elbows to lift the spade; do not try to lift too much, especially where the soil is heavy.*

3 *Twist the spade to turn the soil over. This introduces air into the soil and encourages the breakdown of organic matter.*

SINGLE DIGGING

Mark out the bed, then dig a series of trenches, working backward so that you do not compact the soil. Turn the soil from each trench into the one in front, using soil from the first trench to fill the last.

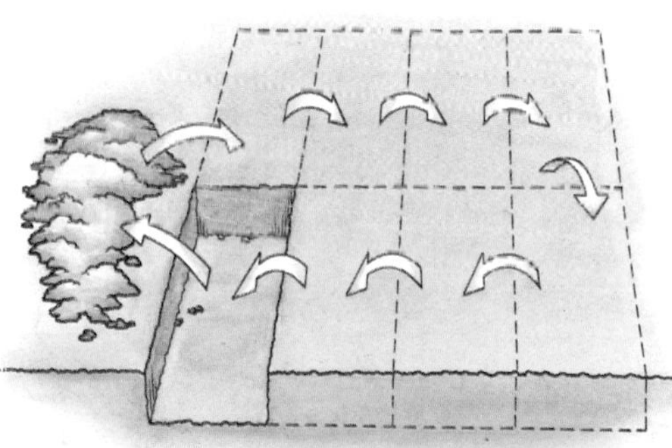

1 *Dig out a trench 1 spit deep and about 12in (30cm) wide. Insert the spade vertically and lift the soil onto the ground in front.*

2 *Dig a second trench, turning the soil into the trench in front. Invert the soil to bury annual weeds and weed seeds.*

Adopt this method on regularly shaped plots and where soil uniformity is important – in vegetable gardens and formal beds, for example. Single digging is also useful where large quantities of organic matter need to be dug in, or where double digging is impractical.

Take the opportunity to incorporate lime (if needed) and fertilizers, such as bone meal, into the bottom of each trench before replacing the soil. Weeds, especially deep-rooting perennial ones, should be removed as a matter of course.

Double digging

Double or trench digging, in which the soil is worked to a depth of two spits rather than one, should be carried out if the ground has not been previously cultivated or if drainage needs to be improved.

In grassed areas, the sod may be stripped off the top, thrown into the trench bottom, and chopped up with a spade before backfilling the soil. Lime and fertilizers should also be incorporated, if required, and perennial weeds removed, as in single digging.

When double digging, it is essential that subsoil is not mixed with topsoil. On sites where the topsoil is less than two spits deep, standard double digging should be used, since this method ensures that the soil from the upper and lower spits are kept separate. The lower spit does not need to be brought to the surface – it may be forked or dug over *in situ*, although if more thorough cultivation is required it is also turned.

Mark out the area with lines, as for single digging, then remove the soil from the upper and lower spits of the first trench and from the upper spit of the second, laying it aside on the ground in three separate, clearly marked, piles. Soil may then be transferred from the lower spit of the second trench to the base of the first trench, and from the upper spit of the third trench to the top of the first. In this way, topsoil and subsoil remain completely separate. Continue digging further trenches in the same way and, at the end of the bed, use soil that was saved from the first two trenches to fill the appropriate spits of the final two.

If the topsoil is more than two spits deep, there is no need to keep soil from the upper and lower spits separate, and all the soil from one trench may simply be transferred to the trench in front (see above).

DOUBLE DIGGING

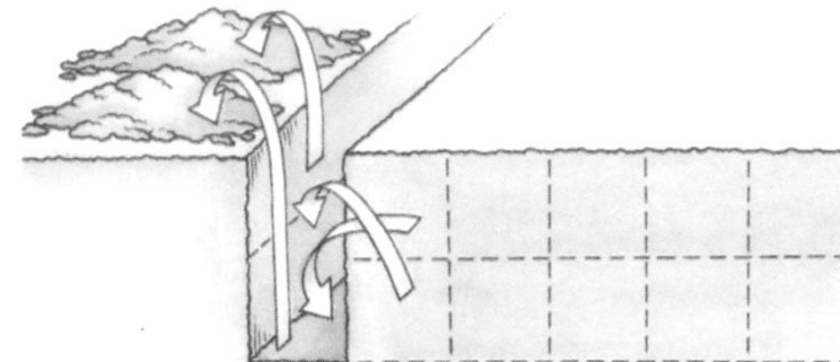

STANDARD DOUBLE DIGGING *Dig out trenches 2 spits deep and turn soil from each trench into the ones in front; do not mix soil from the upper and lower spits.*

DOUBLE DIGGING FOR DEEP TOPSOILS *Where the topsoil is at least 2 spits deep, soil from the upper and lower spits may be mixed or transferred. Dig out 2 spits from the first trench, setting the soil aside to fill the final trench, then transfer soil from the upper spit of the second trench to the bottom of the first. Soil from the lower spit of the second trench should be transferred to the top of the first, and so on.*

IMPROVING STRUCTURE

To improve soil structure, dig in organic material such as well-rotted manure or compost, according to the needs of the soil.

Forming a tilth

A tilth is a fine surface soil that is suitable for seed germination. It consists mostly of small soil particles, and is moisture-retentive and level. Surface tilth ensures good contact between seed and soil, so that moisture is absorbed easily. If possible, prepare seedbeds a month before sowing by digging the soil and allowing it to weather. Just before sowing, break up clods with a rake, level the ground by treading gently, and then rake to provide the fine tilth required for seeds.

SURFACE TILTH

A crumbly, even-textured soil with fine particles provides a good tilth for seed germination. It is water-retentive yet also provides free drainage.

Soil structure and water content

For plants to grow and flourish over a period of many years, the soil needs to have a good inherent structure. On medium and heavy soils, in particular, plant growth depends on good soil structure.

In a well-structured soil, the particles form crumbs that exist as part of an interconnecting network of pores, through which water, nutrients, and air circulate. The structure of the soil therefore determines its ability to hold water, the rate at which it drains, and its fertility. A poorly structured soil may become too freely drained or waterlogged, and nutrients will be lost by leaching.

The stale seedbed technique

This method of cultivation involves disturbing the soil by shallow digging to bring weed seeds to the surface. Existing weeds are also removed at the same time. The weed seeds are then allowed to germinate and grow, and the seedlings killed with a contact weedkiller or by shallow hoeing – this time disturbing the soil as little as possible. Seed may then be safely sown in the weed-free ground, as required. Further weed seeds inevitably germinate during the season, but since the main weed flush has been destroyed, subsequent weed control will be relatively simple.

1 *As an experiment, the soil on the right of this plot has been dug over, while the soil on the left has been left undisturbed.*

2 *After a few weeks, weed seeds have germinated on the cultivated ground. The undisturbed soil has relatively few weeds.*

Poorly structured soil

A poorly structured soil tends to be too wet in winter and too dry in summer. Water frequently runs off the surface rather than percolating deep down, yet once the soil is wet it drains slowly. A soil such as this is difficult to work, and in summer it may become hard and concretelike. As a result, plant roots have great difficulty penetrating the soil and plant growth is impeded.

Cultivating heavy soil during wet weather may make it compacted. When soil particles are compressed, the amount of air in the soil is reduced and so drainage is hindered.

Walking on the soil in wet conditions damages the structure of the surface layer – the soil crumbs break down and fine particles at the surface form a crust, which then prevents air and oxygen from reaching the plants' roots and also prevents seeds from germinating. This is known as capping and may occur on some soils (particularly silts) following heavy rain or if the soil is watered too heavily.

Improving soil structure

To improve poor structure, cultivate the soil to as great a depth as possible by double digging (without mixing subsoil with topsoil), incorporating organic or inorganic additives to help bind the soil particles into crumbs. This will do much to improve both aeration and water retention. On severely waterlogged sites, a suitable drainage system may need to be installed (see p.531).

Using soil additives

The choice of additives to use is dependent on the type of soil. Most may be either applied to the surface or incorporated into the soil. Organic material such as animal manure and compost improves the structure of any type of soil and also provides valuable nutrients. In addition, animal manure encourages earthworms, which will further benefit soil content and structure (see "Soil organisms," p.525).

A light, sandy soil may be improved by forking in a top-dressing of a heavy, clay-rich topsoil. The addition of grit or sharp sand will lighten clay soils.

On compacted soil and clay soil, add manure, compost, and/or lime (but not for acid-loving plants) to improve its structure by encouraging crumb formation.

On silt, add small amounts of clay to improve soil structure, and incorporate manure, compost, peat, and other organic materials to encourage crumb formation.

The amount of additive required depends on the condition of the soil, but a good rule of thumb is to apply about a 2–4in (5–10cm) layer of bulky additives. Some materials, particularly inorganic compounds and water-retaining gels, should be added in much smaller quantities, so it is important to follow the manufacturer's instructions.

Soil Additives

Adding compost, well-rotted manure, or peat improves the soil structure and helps to hold moisture in the soil. Mushroom compost is alkaline by reaction and therefore should not be used with plants requiring acid conditions. Lime binds clay soil particles together into crumbs by a process known as flocculation.

Subsidiary benefits of soil additives

Additives also maintain a good balance of air and water in soil. Sand, gravel, and coarse organic matter may be used to improve drainage in silty, compacted, and heavy clay soils. Sand or gravel is often used along channels in the soil, keeping a path open for water, rather than being worked in. Some additives, such as compost, peat, well-rotted manure, and water-holding gels (which hold many times their weight in water) act as sponges and may be used to improve water retention in free-draining, sandy soil. On compacted soil, water-holding gels are useful for improving water retention without reducing aeration.

Additions of clay will improve the fertility of impoverished soil. Clay, peat, compost, and, to some extent, bark and leaves help to retain nutrients that might otherwise be lost by leaching.

Problems with additives

Some additives should not be used in certain soil conditions. Fine sand, for example, added in small amounts to heavy soil may make poor drainage worse by blocking the soil pores. Use a more open material, such as gravel or coarse sand, instead.

Fresh manure gives off ammonia and sometimes other substances that may be toxic to plants. If it is not possible to compost the manure or to mature it until it is well rotted, apply it to the soil surface in the fall and leave the soil uncultivated over winter. The manure will gradually rot down and be incorporated into the soil by earthworms.

Fresh straw, leaves, and bark use up nitrogen during their decomposition process, contributing to a possible nitrogen deficiency in the soil unless additional nitrogen fertilizer is applied to the soil at the same time.

When making compost (see p.535), never use plant remains that are infected with viruses or any material that contains perennial weeds – both are difficult to control. This material should be discarded.

Comparing Soils

Good Soil
A well-structured soil has a crumbly, moist texture, with a network of pores that holds both air and water. The soil crumbs bind together but do not form a hard cap.

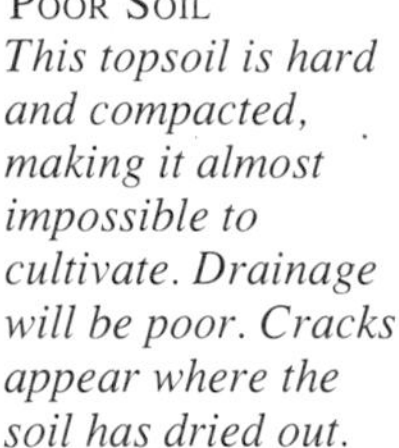

Poor Soil
This topsoil is hard and compacted, making it almost impossible to cultivate. Drainage will be poor. Cracks appear where the soil has dried out.

Soil Problems

Compaction
In compacted soil, the pores between the soil particles have been badly compressed. This results in slow drainage and poor aeration.

Blue Mottling
Blue mottling on the soil surface indicates stagnant, waterlogged soil that needs to be drained. The soil may also have an unpleasant smell.

Hardpan
This is an almost impermeable layer of severely compacted soil. Water will not drain through until the hardpan is broken up. Drains may need to be installed.

Capping
A crust or cap forms on the soil when soil crumbs on the surface are damaged by heavy rain or watering, or by walking on the soil when it is wet.

Water

Adequate water is crucial for good plant growth; the amount available depends to some extent on the plant itself but also on soil type and structure, and the method of watering. Water is often in short supply and should not be wasted, so it is important to use good watering and water-conserving techniques. It is also useful to know which plants are susceptible to drought (and when) and which are drought-resistant.

An excess of water in the soil (waterlogging) can be as damaging to plants as a lack of soil water. Cultivating the soil and adding organic matter and grit will do much to improve drainage in saturated soil, but on severely waterlogged sites an appropriate drainage system should be installed.

METHODS OF WATERING

BASIN-WATERING
Scoop out soil from around the base of the plant, and fill the resulting basin with water.

POT-WATERING
Bury a large pot that has a drainage hole close to the plant and fill the pot slowly with water.

Soil water

In a well-structured soil, water is held in fine capillary pores, which are usually less than 1/160in (0.16mm) in diameter, with air in the larger pores; it is therefore possible for soil to be described as both moist and well drained.

Water is most readily available to plants from pores of the largest diameter. As the pores become smaller, it becomes increasingly difficult for the plants to extract moisture, which means that some soil water always remains unavailable.

Clay soils

Clay soils hold the greatest amount of water but they have a high percentage of fine capillary pores, so plants are not always able to extract enough water for their needs.

HOW NOT TO WATER

Do not water plants at a rate that causes puddling on the soil surface, since this leads to runoff and can erode the soil very quickly.

Sandy soils

Sandy soils contain coarse pores, and so the water held within them is more readily available than in clay. Sandy soils, however, have a high drainage rate, and there is relatively little capillary movement of water sideways and upward.

Loams

Loams usually contain a balanced mix of coarse and relatively fine pores – the coarse pores allow rapid drainage while the finer ones retain water, much of which may be extracted by plants in dry conditions.

The water table

Moisture rises to the soil surface by capillary action from the water table below. Heavy clay soils may be saturated to 6ft (2m) above the water table, with some moisture available to plant roots as much as 11ft (3.5m) above it. Silt and most clay soils are saturated to 5ft (1.5m), with moisture available to roots 8ft (2.5m) above the water table. The figures for fine sand are 5ft (1.5m) and 7 1/2ft (2.4m) respectively, and for coarser sand 1ft (30cm) and 3ft (1m). On gravel, there is no water rise at all.

Watering techniques

The aim of watering is to recharge the soil so that reserves will be sufficient to last until the next watering or rainfall.

Always water thoroughly so that water is available deep in the soil. Frequently applying a little water is of limited value, because much of it simply evaporates off the soil surface before it has a chance to penetrate down to the roots of plants.

Moisture take-up

The water supply to a plant is limited by the size of its root system. By improving drainage (see p.531) and rectifying compaction by double digging (see p.528), if necessary, plants are able to develop deeper root systems, with a comparative increase in growth.

The main limitation when watering, however, is the rate at which the soil takes up the moisture. On average, soil absorbs only about 3/8in (8mm) depth of water per hour. Water applied to the soil faster than it is absorbed (for example, by a hand-held hose or watering can with a rose) collects in a pool on the surface until the area covered is capable of taking it all in. After watering in dry conditions, it is worth examining the soil with an auger – it may be surprising just how little the water has penetrated. If the soil around the roots of the plants is still dry, give the area several further, longer applications once the first application has soaked in.

To reduce water runoff, the ground may be modified by terracing or dishing to create a hollow basin around each plant (see above), which ensures that water reaches the roots. Pot-watering (see above), garden sprinklers (see p.469), and trickle or drip-feed systems (see p.469) are efficient methods of watering, since water is supplied to the roots over several hours.

Water-conserving techniques

Mulching the surface of the soil (see p.534) improves rain penetration and minimizes evaporation. By controlling weeds effectively (see p.577), you will ensure that no soil water is wasted on unwanted plants.

Water deficiency

Once a plant begins to wilt, its growth rate has already begun to slow down. In many areas, water use will exceed water supply during summer, so the soil suffers a net loss of moisture. Digging additives such as manure into the soil improves structure (see "Using soil additives," p.529) and water retention, which helps to prevent a water deficit from occurring, but unless an existing deficit is made up by irrigation, the soil becomes progressively drier. Regular watering is therefore essential.

The local meteorological office will have figures for the typical monthly water loss from the soil and through leaves by transpiration (known as potential evapotranspiration), and also for the average monthly rainfall. These figures are useful when calculating how often to water but, for greater accuracy, it is better to take your own rainfall measurements each month.

Seasonal needs

The point at which a water deficit begins to hinder plant growth depends on the plants themselves. High-yield plants usually need plenty of water, so the soil should be kept moist. Some plants have critical periods of growth, during which time water supplies are vital: the first half of summer, for example, is much more important than the second for young ornamental trees. Fruit trees need ample water as the fruits swell, as do potato tubers. Newly planted trees are likely to require watering throughout their first season since their top-growth is frequently out of proportion to their root system.

Watering is especially important for newly planted or transplanted plants, and those in shallow soils and in containers. Seedlings, too, have low drought resistance, and a reliable water supply is essential.

Xeriscaping

In areas of normally low rainfall, interest is increasing in xeriscaping, which promotes growing naturally drought-adapted plants under a program of water-saving methods.

Purists use only native North American plants, limiting their selections to species growing within a given radius of their gardens, or they may include any suitable North American species or cultivar. Other gardeners combine native and nonnative plants.

Drip emitters and other irrigation techniques may supplement natural rainfall. Organic mulches may be used to conserve moisture; in very arid regions, however, where organic mulches may be difficult to obtain, rocks and gravel are much cheaper and are ecologically correct.

Waterlogged soil

Waterlogging occurs when the amount of water entering the soil exceeds the amount that drains out. Particularly vulnerable are those areas where the water table is high (see opposite) or where the soil is compacted and thus poorly structured.

Roots (except those of bog plants) are unable to function properly in waterlogged soil and may eventually die if drainage is not improved. Wet soil is often low in certain nutrients (notably nitrogen) and, as a result, mineral deficiencies may prove a problem. Since wet soil tends to be cold, plant growth may be slow in spring. Diseases such as clubroot also flourish in waterlogged soil.

Rushes, sedges, and mosses growing on the ground suggest that the soil may be waterlogged. A sharp dividing line between peaty topsoil and subsoil also indicates poor drainage. On waterlogged clay, the soil may have a stagnant smell and a yellow or blue-gray color.

Poor drainage may be confirmed by pouring water into a hole that is 12–24in (30–60cm) deep. If the water remains for hours or even days, the soil needs draining. If digging deeper or trying to push a sturdy metal rod into the soil meets with resistance, this indicates a layer of hardpan (see *Soil Problems*, p.529).

Improving drainage

Where waterlogging is not severe and there is excess surface water only, this may be diverted from the site by shaping garden surfaces so that the water flows into drainage ditches. To improve drainage on sites where there is a high water table, install an underground drainage system, preferably using a specialist contractor to carry out the work. If drains already exist on the site, check for blockages in the drainage ditches, or for damaged drainage pipes.

Drainage ditches and French drains

A system of open ditches is the best method of carrying away any excess water. These should be 3–4ft (1–1.2m) deep, with sloping sides. Just as efficient but less obtrusive are French drains, which are gravel-filled drainage ditches topped with upturned sod and topsoil.

Drainage systems and soakaways

A soakaway is a gravel-filled pit into which excess water runs via underground drains or drainage ditches (see below). This method of drainage is recommended for sites where there is surface compaction, since it breaks through any hardpan layer. To construct a soakaway, dig a trench approximately 5ft (1.5m) wide and up to 6ft (2m) deep. Fill it with crushed stone, topped with a layer of coarse sand or gravel, and lay sod or a grate over the top. Install drains about 24in (60cm) below ground level to lead from the surrounding land to the soakaway.

Water storage areas

Alternatively, create a water storage area where water can collect in a pond or large container, or can gradually soak away. A pond is beneficial to wildlife, but its success depends on the degree of sediment in the drainage water – too much will make a pond rich in nutrients, therefore becoming prone to silting up and excessive algal growth.

Water that is collected in containers may be recycled for use in the garden. Collecting water that is allowed gradually to soak away helps to replenish groundwater reserves and reduces silt pollution of rivers.

HOW TO LAY DRAINAGE PIPES ON A FLAT SITE

This cross section of a drainage trench shows a tile drain in place on a layer of gravel or crushed stone, with another layer on top, followed by coarse sand and inverted sod.

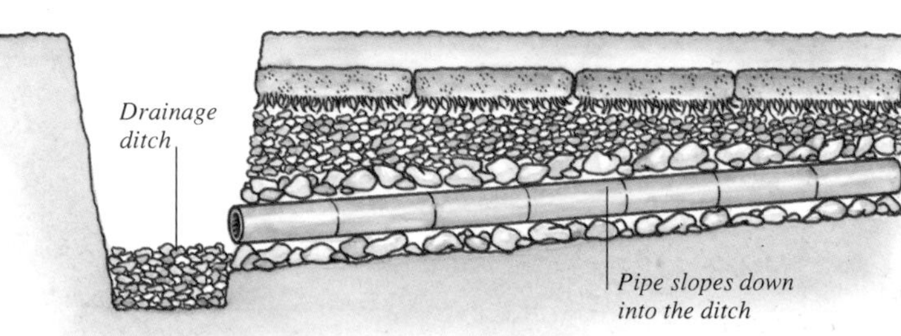

On a flat site, the plastic pipes or tile drains should be sloping. This will allow the water collecting in them to flow into a connecting ditch or a soakaway in another part of the site.

Installing drains

A system of perforated plastic pipes or tile drains laid in a herringbone pattern underground provides an efficient method of drainage. Lay the pipes or tile drains in trenches on a bed of gravel, then cover them with further layers of gravel and sand, before refilling the trench with topsoil. Water from the surrounding site can seep through the gravel and into the pipes, which then carry it to a drainage ditch or soakaway. On level ground, slope the pipes to encourage water to drain away quickly. Where the ground slopes, simply lay pipes parallel to the ground. Install drains before plants are in place, if possible, since the work causes considerable upheaval.

A DRAINAGE SYSTEM ON A SLOPING SITE

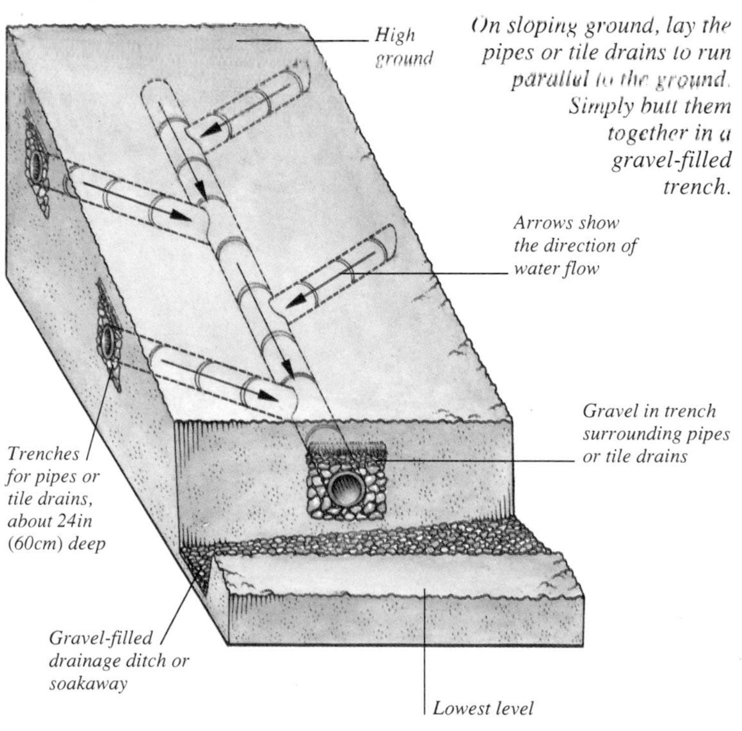

On sloping ground, lay the pipes or tile drains to run parallel to the ground. Simply butt them together in a gravel-filled trench.

Soil nutrients and fertilizers

The nutrients needed by plants are composed of mineral ions, which are absorbed in solution from the soil through the roots and used with carbon dioxide and water to make food. Macronutrients include nitrogen (N), phosphorus (P), potassium (K), magnesium (Mg), calcium (Ca), and sulfur (S); these are required in relatively large amounts by plants.

Micronutrients, or trace elements, are equally important but required only in small amounts; they include iron (Fe), manganese (Mn), copper (Cu), zinc (Zn), boron (B), molybdenum (Mb), and chlorine (Cl).

To ensure healthy plant growth, fertilizers containing nutrients may be added to the soil, but this is only necessary when the soil is unable to provide adequate amounts of the nutrients required. On the majority of soils, only nitrogen, which promotes vigorous growth, phosphorus (phosphates), for assisting strong root growth, and potassium (potash), which improves flowering and fruiting, need to be added regularly. This is because the most common nutrient deficiency problems for plants are caused by a lack of these nutrients. Nitrogen deficiency (see p.556) causes reduced growth, and potassium deficiency (see p.556) causes leaf discoloration. Phosphorus deficiency (see p.556) is less common. Manganese/iron deficiency (see p.557) causes leaves to brown, and may be a problem if acid-loving plants are grown in alkaline soil or watered with hard water.

Types of fertilizer

Deciding the amount and which type of fertilizer to apply can be complex. Understanding how each type works will make gardening more productive and even perhaps more environmentally friendly.

Bulky organic fertilizers

Weight for weight, bulky organic fertilizers supply fewer nutrients than inorganic fertilizers. For example, 0.98 tons (1 tonne) of manure typically contains 13.2lb (6kg) of nitrogen, 2.2lb (1kg) of phosphorus, and 8.8lb (4kg) of potassium; the equivalent amount of nutrients in a chemical form is provided by only 66lb (30kg) of inorganic fertilizer.

Manures are, however, integral to organic growing because the fibrous organic matter that makes them so bulky provides greater benefits than a simple nutrient analysis would suggest. Manures normally contain high levels of micronutrients, and are a long-term source of nitrogen. However, they may vary in quality, some batches having a poor nutrient content. Manures also provide the conditions in which worms thrive. Additions of manure improve the structure and water content of most soils (see p.528); since this encourages root growth, it increases the uptake of nutrients by plants.

Concentrated fertilizers

Commercial mixtures of blood, bone and other meals are good examples of concentrated organic fertilizers. They are easy to handle and contain fairly consistent proportions of nutrients but are relatively expensive for each unit of nutrient. Their slow release of nutrients is partly dependent on breakdown by soil organisms, so they may not be useful when these organisms are inactive, as in cold weather.

Soluble fertilizers

Soluble inorganic fertilizers contain high percentages of a given nutrient, weight for weight, and most are easy to carry, handle, and apply, although a few are unpleasant to handle. They are usually the cheapest source per unit of nutrient. They give a quick boost to plants deficient in nutrients, and they permit precise control over the timing of nutrient release. However, a large proportion of soluble fertilizer may be wasted on sandy soils because of leaching.

When using soluble inorganic fertilizers, be selective about which mineral ions are applied to the soil, since some may be damaging to particular plants. Redcurrants, for example, are sensitive to chloride salts, such as potassium chloride, so sulfates should be used instead. Large applications of some inorganic salts make the soil more saline and may harm beneficial soil organisms. Apply soluble inorganic fertilizers in split applications, sparingly but fairly frequently, rather than in a single, large dose.

NUTRIENT CONTENT OF FERTILIZERS

	% NITROGEN (N)	% PHOSPHORUS (P_2O_5)	% POTASSIUM (K_2O)
ORGANIC			
Animal manure	0.6	0.1	0.5
Compost	0.5	0.3	0.8
Bone meal	2	14	–
Tankage	7	10	–
Hoof and horn	14	2	–
Seaweed meal	2.8	0.2	2.5
Blood meal	12	–	–
Mushroom compost	0.7	0.3	0.3
Rock phosphate	–	26	12
Wood ash	0.1	0.3	1
Cocoa shells	3	1	3.2
INORGANIC			
Balanced fertilizers	available in various proportions		
Ammonium nitrate	35	–	–
Superphosphate	–	20	–
Muriate of potash	–	–	60
Potassium sulfate	–	–	49

Slow-release fertilizers

These are complex fertilizer formulations that are designed to release nutrients gradually. Some slowly degrade in the soil, while others absorb water until they swell and burst open. Many have membranes that gradually release nutrients from an internal store. By varying the thicknesses of these membranes, a mix is produced that will supply nutrients to plants over many months or even years in some cases.

Slow-release inorganic fertilizers are expensive, but they overcome many of the drawbacks of soluble fertilizers, such as the need for split applications and the loss of nutrients from the fertilizer by leaching. They make feeding container-grown plants much less time-consuming,

COMPARING FERTILIZERS

COMPOST

MUSHROOM COMPOST

COCOA SHELLS

BONE MEAL

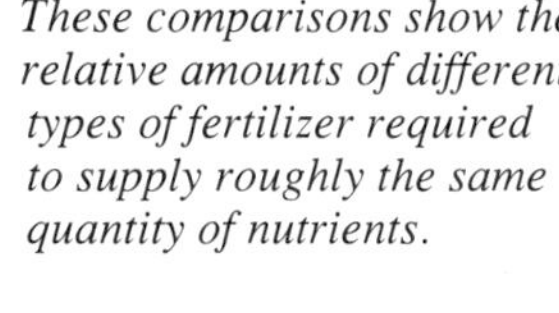

These comparisons show the relative amounts of different types of fertilizer required to supply roughly the same quantity of nutrients.

SOLUBLE INORGANIC FERTILIZER

SLOW-RELEASE FERTILIZERS

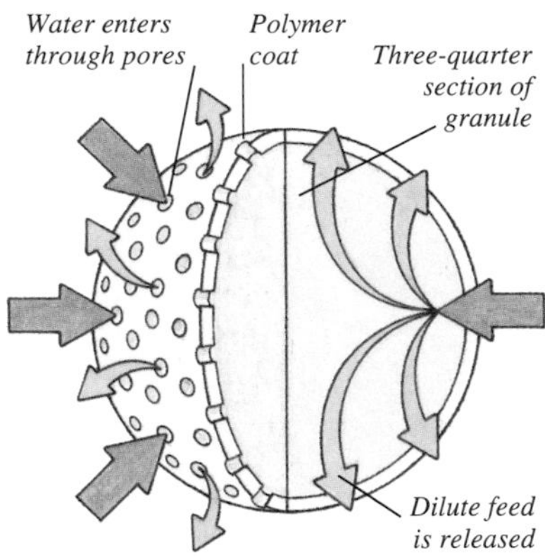

Water enters the fertilizer granules through pores in the polymer coat, which builds up pressure inside, splitting the granules open.

since they remove the need to add fertilizer each time the plants are watered during the growing season. The nutrient release pattern of slow-release fertilizers may be difficult to predict, however, especially with long-term formulas, since the breakdown depends on the pH level of soil, as well as on the moisture content and temperature of the soil.

Green manures

These are plants that are grown purely to be dug back into the soil to improve fertility and add to the organic content. They are used on land that would otherwise be left fallow and can help to prevent nutrients from being washed away, since fallow land is more prone to leaching. Do not use invasive plants as green manures, however.

Buckwheat, ryegrass, and oats are excellent green manures. Mixtures of fast-germinating annuals are also used. Plants such as peas, clovers, and alfalfa have nitrogen-fixing bacteria in root nodules that enable them to obtain nitrogen from air in the soil. The organic matter these plants provide may contribute as much nitrogen as would be added in a standard fertilizing schedule; it has a low carbon:nitrogen ratio and so breaks down rapidly, providing easily available nitrogen.

Applying fertilizers

Fertilizers may be scattered over the surface of the soil or placed around individual plants. Some fertilizers are also available in liquid form for application to the soil surface or as foliar feeds directly onto leaves.

When applying fertilizers, always use gloves and do not breathe in any of the dust or vapor arising from them. Use only the recommended quantities, since too much fertilizer could damage the plants.

Broadcast fertilization

Scattering fertilizer over the whole soil surface benefits the greatest area of soil and minimizes the risk of plant injury from overfeeding. In dry weather, however, the uptake of some nutrients may be poor, particularly of immobile nutrients such as phosphorus, so, whenever possible, dig phosphates into the soil.

When broadcast fertilizing, do not allow any of the material to touch the leaves or stems of plants, since scorching may result.

Fertilizer placement

Fertilizing around the base of a plant (but not so that it touches the stem) is an economical and efficient feeding method, because healthy plant roots should quickly spread through the fertilized area.

Liquid fertilizers

Dissolving fertilizer in water before application is a particularly efficient method of applying nutrients, especially if the soil is dry. Do not use liquid feeds when rain is forecast, since the liquid may be washed away, and apply the feeds early in the day to avoid possible sun scorch.

Foliar fertilizers

Liquid fertilizers sprayed onto leaf surfaces are known as foliar feeds; they may be used to correct mineral deficiencies that are caused by certain soil conditions, such as high pH. For deep-rooted plants, such as fruit trees, foliar feeds may also be used to correct deficiencies of nutrients that are relatively insoluble.

Liming

Liming or adding lime-rich material such as mushroom compost increases the alkalinity of the soil. This is sometimes desirable to improve yields on the vegetable plot but is seldom worthwhile for ornamental plants. It is usually preferable to choose ornamentals that are adapted to the existing conditions.

Types of lime

Ordinary lime (calcium carbonate) is usually the best choice because, although bulky, it is easy to handle and relatively safe to use. Quicklime (calcium oxide) is more efficient at raising pH but since it is caustic it may scorch plant material; there is also a risk of overliming with quicklime. Slaked, or hydrated, lime (calcium hydroxide) is made by treating quicklime with water; it is slightly less efficient than quicklime but it is less caustic and easier to handle.

Applying lime

Lime may be spread on the soil at any time of year, but it should be applied as far in advance of planting as possible and preferably be well dug in. Choose a windless day and always wear protective goggles. Do not lime the soil every year, because overliming may contribute to nutrient deficiencies. Always take pH readings in several different parts of the plot first, since any uneven rates of breakdown may cause temporary, localized problems. The following table indicates the average amount of lime required (per oz/sq yd) for a particular type of soil of a given pH to achieve a pH level of 6.5 (see also "Optimum pH," p.525).

LIMING

Using a spade, spread the lime over the surface of the soil, then distribute it evenly with a rake (see inset). Do not plant or sow for about a month.

STARTING pH	SAND (oz/sq yd)	LOAM (oz/sq yd)	CLAY (oz/sq yd)
4.5	6.7oz	10oz	14oz
5.0	5.5oz	8.3oz	11.6oz
5.5	4.6oz	6.7oz	9.2oz
6.0	4.2oz	5.5oz	7.6oz

To raise soil pH quickly, add lime during digging or other cultivation methods. If required for established plantings, lime may be applied as a top-dressing and watered in.

Do not apply lime at the same time as manure because lime reacts with the nitrogen-rich manure, releasing nitrogen in the form of ammonia. This may damage plants and wastes nitrogen. If required, apply lime and manure in alternate years.

GREEN MANURING

Sow seed for green manures on fallow ground. Cut the plants to the ground when about 8in (20cm) tall, digging them in after a day or two.

HOW TO APPLY FERTILIZER

BROADCASTING
To apply fertilizer in accurate amounts over large areas, mark out the plot into square yards or meters, using string or stakes. Fill a pot or bowl with the recommended quantity of fertilizer and sprinkle it evenly over each section of the plot.

PLACEMENT
Sprinkle the fertilizer around the base of the plant, making sure that none touches the leaves or stems.

Top-dressings and mulches

Top-dressings and mulches are materials that are applied to the surface of the soil. They are used to improve plant growth in some way, either by reducing weed competition, by increasing the organic or nutrient content, or by reducing water loss from the soil. They may also be used decoratively.

Top-dressings

The term top-dressing is used in two ways. First, it describes surface applications of soluble fertilizers around plants. Second, it refers to additives that are applied to the soil surface or to lawns. For example, a lawn may be top-dressed with sand or fine organic material, which will eventually be washed in by rain.

Gravel or grit is sometimes used as a top-dressing for plants in beds and containers to provide quick drainage away from the collars of plants that are sensitive to excess moisture. They also act as a mulch and discourage growth of mosses or lichens on the soil surface.

Plants may also be top-dressed with gravel or stone chips simply to achieve a decorative result.

MATERIALS USED AS TOP-DRESSINGS

TOP-DRESSINGS AS ADDITIVES
Some top-dressings, such as bark and well-rotted compost, are added to the soil around plants to provide humus and a steady supply of nutrients. Sand, mixed with soil and peat, is used as a top-dressing on lawns to improve aeration.

SAND

DECORATIVE TOP-DRESSINGS
Materials such as gravel and grit are added to the soil mix surface in containers or to the soil surface in a border or bed, particularly around low-growing plants such as alpines. These materials improve surface drainage as well as setting off the plants.

GRAVEL

BARK

COMPOST

COARSE GRIT

CRUSHED STONE

Mulches

Mulches are available in organic and inorganic forms and improve plant growth in several ways: they regulate soil temperature, insulating plant roots from temperature extremes; they reduce water loss from the soil surface; and they help stop weed seeds from germinating by preventing light from reaching them.

Always remove all perennial weeds before mulching, otherwise they benefit from the mulch to the detriment of your plants. A winter mulch, used to prevent plants from heaving during midwinter thaws, is best applied after the soil has cooled down or even frozen. It must be removed in the spring as soon as it thaws or it will keep the cold in the soil. After the soil has warmed up in the spring, apply a summer mulch, or the soil will remain too cool.

Organic mulches

To be effective, an organic mulch should be long-lasting and not easily dislodged by rain. It should also have a loose structure that allows water to pass through it quickly.

Coarse bark is one of the most useful organic mulches because it prevents weed seeds in the soil beneath from germinating, and weeds that do appear are easily removed.

Compost and peat are not quite as satisfactory because they provide an ideal medium for the germination of weed seeds and are quickly mixed into the soil by worms, although this process does improve the texture of the soil as a result.

Inorganic mulches

Landscape fabrics are thin, woven materials that are widely available and easy to use. They prevent the growth of both weed seeds and perennial weed pieces. At the same time they allow rain and nutrients to pass through. Anchor them over the soil surface and cover with soil or mulch to retard breakdown. Make X-shaped slits for planting. Plastic sheet mulches raise the soil temperature slightly and are particularly useful when growing crops such as melons. A disadvantage of sheet mulches is that, once they are in place, organic matter cannot be incorporated into the soil; it also decays more slowly underneath a sheet mulch. If required, extra nutrients may be added through holes punched in the plastic sheeting, and then watered in. Unless sheet mulches are perforated, almost no water evaporates from the soil, and rain cannot penetrate it. Therefore do not place a sheet mulch on dry soil or on soil that tends to be waterlogged or slow draining.

Floating row covers are sheets of light plastic or loosely woven fiber fleece that are used like cloches – as the crop grows, the cover is raised by the plants. Floating covers are often perforated or permeable to allow rain and air through to the soil. Their main purpose is to increase soil temperature; they may also act as a barrier against pests and frost.

LOOSE MULCHES

APPLYING THE MULCH
A loose mulch regulates soil temperature, retains moisture, and discourages weeds. It should preferably be about 4–6in (10–15cm) deep.

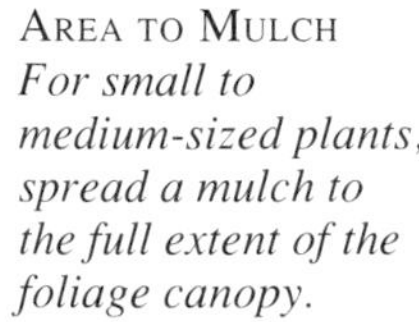

AREA TO MULCH
For small to medium-sized plants, spread a mulch to the full extent of the foliage canopy.

LANDSCAPE FABRIC

Landscape fabric controls weeds over a large area and should remain in good condition for several years. Anchor with pins and cover with soil or mulch.

Compost and soil mixes

Compost is decayed organic matter and is a valuable additive prized for its soil-improving properties. There are many kinds of soil mix, each made from precise combinations of (mainly) organic materials; they are used for growing plants in containers and for propagation.

Compost

The contribution of compost to the productivity of the garden can be enormous. It should be added to the soil when the rate of breakdown of the organic matter has leveled off; by this stage, it should be dark, crumbly, and sweet-smelling.

Making compost

To make a compost heap, build up a mixture of nitrogen-rich material (such as grass clippings) and carbon-rich material (such as bark and shredded paper), preferably in a proportion of 1:2. Almost any vegetable waste may be composted, but meat and cooked foods should not be used, since these attract vermin. Do not use thick layers of grass clippings: they inhibit air movement. Pruning clippings may be used, although any woody stems must be shredded first. Use only young weeds; those with seed, or about to set seed, should be discarded, as should all noxious, perennial weeds.

Compost additives

Many materials compost satisfactorily, but additional nitrogen will speed up the process. The nitrogen may be provided as artificial fertilizer, commercial starter compost, or, preferably, as manure, which has the advantage of containing high levels of soil organisms. Add this, as necessary, to the compost heap so that there are alternate layers of organic material and manure.

If the material in the compost heap is acidic, microorganisms will not work efficiently – adding lime will make it more alkaline.

The composting process

The process of making compost generates a high temperature, which encourages the natural breakdown of organic matter to operate quickly and also helps to kill weed seeds and some pests and diseases. To heat up sufficiently, a compost heap should be at least 1 cubic yard (1 cubic meter) in size, but 2 cubic yards is preferable. Compost reaches its maximum temperature in two or three weeks and matures in about three months. Turning the heap speeds up the process and ensures complete breakdown. An ammonia odor indicates that the compost is too rich in nitrogen; a smell of rotten eggs means that the heap lacks air.

Slow composting

Composting may be undertaken in an unintensive way. Heaps of moist leaves, for example, eventually rot down, even if they are not in a bin. No starter material is added, and the heap is not turned. There will, however, be some material that does not break down fully, and this will need to be composted again.

Soil mixes

Pot plants need a growing medium that is both well aerated and water-retentive, with a resilient structure that can withstand heavy watering. For best results, always use the most suitable type for the purpose.

The essential difference between the two most common mixes is that soil-based mixes contain real soil; soilless mixes, which are usually peat-based, do not. Although soilless mixes did not become popular until the 1960s, they are preferred today because they are cheaper, lighter, and more readily available.

Soil-based potting mixes

These should contain high-quality soil that is rich in organic matter. The soil is usually obtained by stacking sod for six months or more, and should be sterilized, either chemically or by heating the soil to a high temperature, to kill pests and weed seeds and eliminate diseases.

Soil-based mixes provide better conditions than soilless ones for long-term growth. They contain a steady supply of nutrients, and are free-draining, with good aeration and structure. They do not dry out as rapidly as peat-based soil mixes and are less prone to waterlogging. Plants also grow on more readily when transplanted to garden soil.

Traditionally, gardeners have grown potted plants in a variety of soil-based potting mixes. The basic recipe is 1 part garden soil (a good loam, preferably sterilized and free of stones, sticks, and other foreign matter is ideal), 1 part sphagnum moss, and 1 part perlite, vermiculite, or clean, sharp sand. If the mix needs extra organic matter for a leafy tropical plant from the rain forest, such as many indoor foliage plants, add an extra part of well-rotted compost, leaf mold, or sphagnum moss. If the mix needs extra drainage, perhaps for a cactus or other succulent, add an extra part of sand or perlite.

Soilless potting mixes

Widely used in commercial horticulture, soilless potting mixes are lightweight and clean to use. Many products that were previously available only to professionals may now

---

Making a Compost Bin

1 *To make the first side, lay 2 4x4s (the uprights) on the ground at least 3ft (1m) apart. Nail boards across them, butting the joints together. Leave a 3in (8cm) gap as an air chimney at top and bottom.*

2 *Make the second side; nail scraps of wood across the top to hold the sides in place temporarily. Nail on the back boards.*

3 *Nail a 2x4 inside the front 4x4s (inset) for the front boards to slide between. Fix a piece of wood at the base as a stop.*

4 *Nail boards across the top and bottom of the front panel, to stabilize the bin when the front boards are removed*

5 *Check that the front boards slide easily between the uprights. If necessary, saw a little off the ends.*

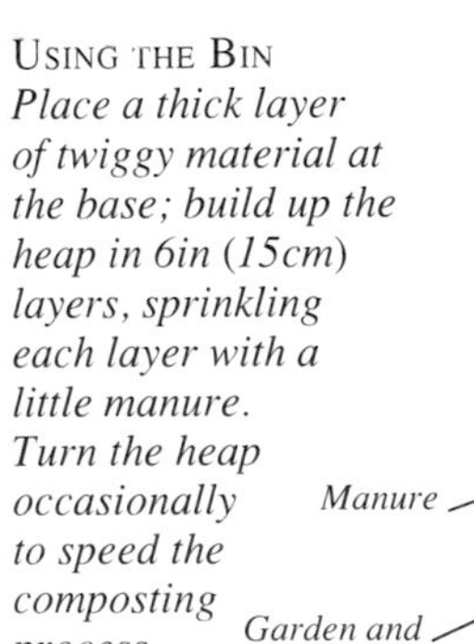

Using the Bin
Place a thick layer of twiggy material at the base; build up the heap in 6in (15cm) layers, sprinkling each layer with a little manure. Turn the heap occasionally to speed the composting process.

be purchased by amateur gardeners, and are very convenient to use.

Many soilless mixes are based on peat, which combines moisture retentiveness with good aeration and is relatively stable and long-lasting. Soilless peatlite (sphagnum moss, perlite, and vermiculite) may also be used. Soilless mixes are low in nutrients and do not hold them well compared with soil, so plants grown in these mixes need to be fed more often than with soil-based mixes. Apply a balanced inorganic fertilizer since many organic fertilizers are not suited to soilless culture. Soilless mixes dry out rapidly and are hard to rewet, and overwatering results in waterlogging, which leads to root rot and other problems.

Plants grown in soilless potting mixes may adapt poorly when transplanted to garden soil. Teasing out the roots and shaking some of the soil mix from the root ball often stimulates the roots to grow into the soil. Most soilless potting mixes break down rapidly, so that the volume of soil mix shrinks and the remaining material loses much of its structure. Repot when the mix shrinks away from the pot, which allows water to run uselessly between the rootball and the pot, or when the surface of the mix becomes slimy or difficult to wet.

One of the most common soilless mixes is Cornell Peatlite Mix A. To make 1 bushel (0.36cu m) measure 4 gallons (18 liters) no.2 or no.3 grade horticultural vermiculite; 4 gallons (18 liters) shredded sphagnum moss; 2 tablespoons dolomitic limestone; and 2 tablespoons potassium nitrate or calcium nitrate.

Add 1 pint (600ml) of warm water to the sphagnum moss to moisten it. Put all ingredients into a large plastic bag, then shake to mix well.

Peat substitutes

The use of peat-based potting mixes poses environmental problems in countries where bogs are an endangered habitat. Alternative potting mixes, such as those based on coconut fiber and bark, are available in some areas, but trials on their usefulness are not yet complete.

Special soil mixes

These soil mixes are used for plants that have specialized growing requirements. Orchid potting mixes are very free-draining and often contain charcoal and fine bark. Alpine soil mix is very free-draining and sometimes poor in nutrients, to suit the plants. Ericaceous soil mixes have a low pH and are suitable for growing lime-haters, such as rhododendrons.

Bulb fiber

This is made from undecomposed sphagnum moss, which has an open structure, and is used to grow bulbs in containers that do not have drainage holes, when poor aeration may be a problem. It gives physical support and retains moisture reasonably well. Its lack of nutrients is unimportant, since bulbs have internal food reserves.

Propagation soil mixes

When sowing seed (particularly fine seed) and rooting cuttings, a higher success rate is achieved if propagation soil mixes are used.

Standard seed soil mix

Fine seed needs to have good contact with the soil mix in order to germinate, and should be sown in specially prepared seed soil mix, which is fine-textured, moisture-retentive, and low in nutrients, since salts may damage seedlings.

Standard seed soil mix is made using 2 parts (by volume) sterilized soil, 1 part peat, and 1 part sand. To each cubic yard is added 2lb superphosphate of lime and 1lb ground limestone (1.2kg and 594g respectively for a cubic meter).

Standard cuttings soil mix

Soil mixes for rooting cuttings are free-draining and intended for use in high-humidity environments. They may be based on bark, perlite, or coarse sand. Cuttings soil mixes are low in nutrients, so cuttings need feeding once rooted.

A standard cuttings soil mix typically contains equal parts of sand and peat. To each cubic yard (meter) is added 7½lb (4.4kg) dolomitic lime; 2½lb (1.5kg) each of bone meal or dried blood, superphosphate of lime, and calcium carbonate; and 4oz (148g) each of potassium nitrate and potassium sulfate. An absence of soil may mean that a specific micronutrient fertilizer should be added.

Organic practices

Organic growing methods often aim to minimize the need for cultivation of the soil to preserve natural fertility and reduce weeds. Materials such as manure and other organic fertilizers (see p.532) are integral to organic growing practices, since they help to maintain a good soil structure.

The no-till system

Cultivating the soil paradoxically creates the conditions in which weeds flourish and sometimes causes the natural soil structure to deteriorate. The no-till system is a method of soil cultivation that, in order to preserve the soil structure and prevent loss of nutrients, uses minimal digging, favoring the use of a trowel whenever possible. The no-till system also makes use of mulches for suppressing weeds and conserving moisture. At its extreme, potatoes, for example, need not be buried in the soil but may, instead, be planted on the soil surface below a thick covering of mulch.

THE NO-TILL SYSTEM

1 *To grow potatoes, lay the tubers on the soil surface, then cover with a 6–8in (15–20cm) layer of mulch.*

2 *Cover the potatoes with black plastic, fixing it down securely. Make slits for the shoots to grow through.*

The deep-bed system

Using the deep-bed system, the soil structure is improved to the required depth with one thorough cultivation (see "Double digging," p.528). Large amounts of organic matter are incorporated at the same time, after which further digging is avoided. If compaction is prevented, by not walking on the beds, further cultivation becomes unnecessary. A natural soil structure develops, encouraged by the organic matter and the high worm population. Further organic matter is added only as mulches and top-dressings.

Because the only disturbance to the surface occurs when planting, any weed seeds below germination level remain dormant and only weed seedlings from windblown seeds need to be removed.

THE DEEP-BED SYSTEM

1 *Cultivate the ground deeply and dig in organic matter. To make the bed, mound the surface, using topsoil from the surrounding area, so that the bed is raised slightly.*

2 *The bed should be no more than 5ft (1.5m) wide to allow easy access. Because the soil condition is so much improved, it is possible to plant 4 times as densely as in a conventional bed.*

6

Principles of Propagation

Propagating plants is *often instinctively undertaken by gardeners, for example when they divide an overcrowded clump of perennials or bulbs, and is a natural extension of plantsmanship. Plant propagation is not difficult once the underlying principles are understood, and it is the best, most satisfactory, and cheapest way to extend the number of plants in the garden. In addition, it provides many opportunities for exchanging plant material with other gardeners, and thereby further increases the range of plants available in cultivation. More advanced techniques include hybridizing in order to create plants with new characteristics such as a different growth habit or flower color. To many people, the transition from a seed into a healthy plant, the development of a seemingly lifeless hardwood cutting into a vigorous new tree or shrub, or the formation of a young plant on a piece of leaf is a fascinating process. An understanding of the techniques that are outlined in this chapter should bring the multiple rewards to be gained from successful plant propagation within the reach of every gardener.*

Seeds

Seed is by far the most common way by which flowering plants reproduce in nature. It is a sexual method and, as such, always presents the possibility of a variety of genetic combinations, so that the resulting seedlings are variable. Such variation provides the basis by which plants adapt to their environment, and enables the breeding and selection of cultivars with new combinations of desirable characteristics. Seeds may more or less breed true but frequently vary considerably within a species. In horticulture, variation is disadvantageous if the plants raised are to retain particular characteristics, but advantageous when new, improved characteristics are being sought.

Reproductive Parts of a Rose Flower

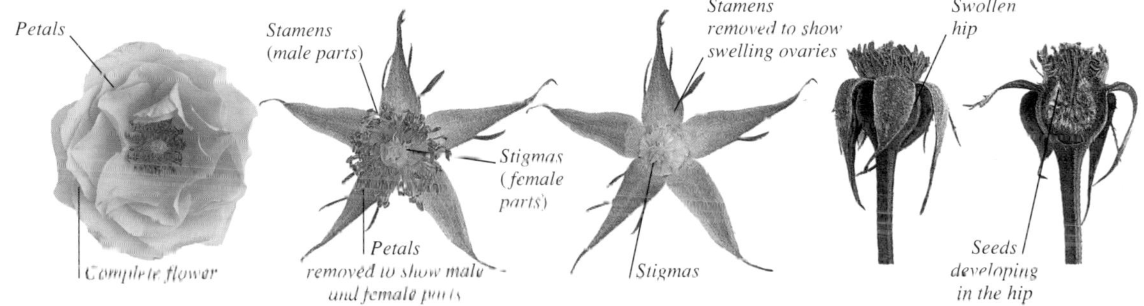

The parts of a flower needed for reproduction are the stamens (the male part, which bears the pollen) and the pistils (the female part, which consists of one or more stigmas, styles, and ovaries). The petals attract pollinators.

How the seed develops

Most plants are hermaphrodites – that is, each flower bears male and female parts. As the flower matures, pollen is transferred onto one or more stigmas of the same flower (self-pollination) or of a flower on another plant of the same species (cross-pollination) by insects, birds, water, or wind. The pollen grains then produce pollen tubes, which grow down the style toward the eggs in the ovary, and fertilization occurs when the male and female nuclei fuse. From these develop the embryos, which, nourished by adjacent storage tissue within a seed, are capable of forming complete new plants.

Collecting and storing seed

In general, seed should be collected from a plant as soon as it is ripe and then stored in a dry, dark, airy place at 34–41°F (1–5°C) until it is used. Certain seeds, however, have special requirements. Some are viable for only short periods and should be sown as soon as possible. Others may be stored for very long periods at low temperatures without losing viability. Fleshy fruits should be soaked and softened in water, the seeds removed from the flesh, and then air-dried at 50–68°F (10–20°C). Before they are dry, however, seeds of most stone fruits (e.g. cherry) and that of some berried shrubs (e.g. *Berberis* and cotoneaster) need warm or cold stratification (see p.538).

Keep a close watch on fruits that split to release their seeds. As soon as a seed capsule splits, harvest it together with other capsules that are nearing maturity, even though they have not yet opened. Dry them in clean paper bags before separating out the seeds. When a few wind-distributed seeds blow away, collect the mature seed by covering the seed-bearing branches with fine muslin or paper bags, or cut one or two seed-bearing branches and place them in water indoors to mature.

How to overcome dormancy

The seeds of some plants have built-in mechanisms to assist in controlling the time of germination; for example, many seeds do not germinate in late fall, when conditions are unfavorable for seedling growth, but remain dormant until the temperature and other factors are more suitable. This dormancy is achieved by a variety of means including the presence of chemical inhibitors in the seed, by hardened seed coats that must rot or be breached before the seed can germinate, or by the need for the seed to experience alternating cold and warm periods. Several horticultural methods have been developed to overcome this natural dormancy so the seeds will germinate more quickly and are therefore less likely to fail.

Scarification

The aim is to break down the hardened seed coat and allow water to enter, thereby speeding up germination.

SCARIFICATION

Before planting, carefully nick the hard coat on seeds such as Paeonia lutea *with a clean, sharp knife so that the seed can absorb moisture.*

Large, hard-coated seeds, such as those of the legume family, may be nicked with a knife. Smaller seeds may be shaken in a jar lined with sandpaper or one containing sharp gravel.

Warm stratification

This is used for hard-coated seeds of many woody species (see *Tree Seed Requiring Stratification*, p.55, and *Shrub Seed that Requires Special Treatment*, p.85). Place the seeds in a plastic bag in either an equal volume of sand and leaf mold, or an equal volume of slightly moist peat and sand, and store for four to 12 weeks at 68–77°F (20–25°C). This is usually followed by a period of cold stratification prior to the seeds being sown.

Cold stratification

Soak the seeds for a period of up to 24 hours, then add them to a mix of moist peat and sand in a plastic bag or place them in an open dish with moist filter paper. Refrigerate the seeds at 34–41°F (1–5°C) for four to 12 weeks until germination starts. Alternatively, place the seeds in a perforated can containing 1 part seed to 3 parts moist sand and bury the can outdoors, at a depth of 2ft (60cm), for one or two winters. Periodically, dig up the can and check for germination. Once this occurs, sow the seeds immediately.

SOAKING BEFORE COLD STRATIFICATION

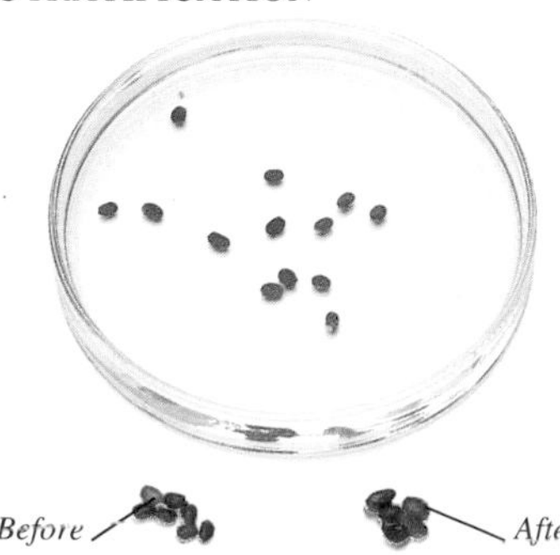

Lupine seeds, soaked in water for 24 hours before cold stratification, will swell slightly.

Requirements for germination

In order to germinate, a seed needs water, air, warmth, and, for some species, light. The growing medium needs to be a fine soil mix capable of drawing water up to seeds placed near its surface. To aid this capillary rise, the soil mix is firmed lightly using a presser board. Without this firming, air pockets occur, and the water columns essential for capillary rise are broken. The soil mix, however, must not be compacted or so damp that air cannot penetrate; seeds will almost certainly fail in such anaerobic soil mix because they cannot obtain the oxygen vital for growth. Seed soil mixes have only about a quarter of the fertilizer content of potting soil mixes and often contain a fungicide to prevent damping-off diseases (p.570).

For the most successful results, the temperature for germination of most seeds should be 68–86°F (20–30°C). A steady temperature may be maintained by using a heated propagator (see p.488).

Light requirements vary during germination: some seeds need light (e.g. *Alyssum*, begonia, *Calceolaria*, and *Genista*), but others are inhibited by it (e.g. *Allium*, delphinium, *Nigella*, and phlox). There is no way of distinguishing seeds requiring dark conditions from those needing light by physical examination; if the dark/light requirement is unknown, initially keep the sown seed in the dark; if it fails to germinate after a period of some weeks, place it in the light.

Sowing and aftercare

After sowing the seed in containers or in open ground, do not allow the soil mix to dry out or become too waterlogged; cover the containers with glass or plastic and set in an appropriate place (see "The propagation environment," p.544). The first sign of germination is the emergence of the radicle (primary root) followed, in epigeal germination, by the cotyledons (seed leaves), which provide the initial food reserves. The true foliage leaves appear later and generally differ from the cotyledons.

When the seedlings are large enough to handle, they should be pricked out (see ANNUALS AND BIENNIALS, "Pricking out," p.179). Failure to do so results in weak growth, because the crowded seedlings compete for light and nutrients and readily succumb to fungal infection. Once transplanted, return the seedlings to the warm germination environment to reestablish; then gradually harden them off by placing the containers in cooler conditions (see "Hardening off," p.545). A cold frame, closed at first, then opened in stages, provides a suitable environment for hardening off seedlings.

HOW A SEED GERMINATES

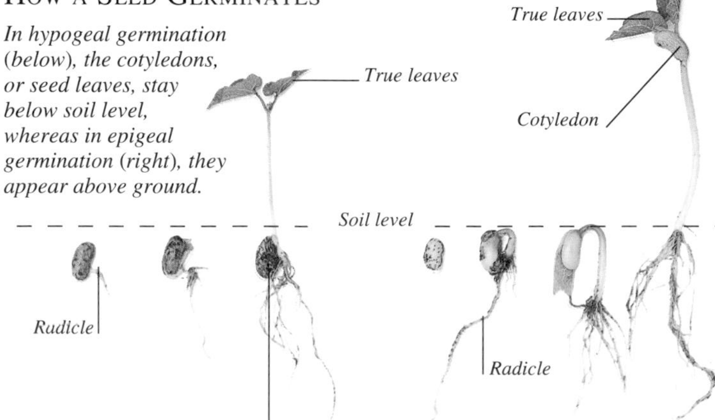

In hypogeal germination (below), the cotyledons, or seed leaves, stay below soil level, whereas in epigeal germination (right), they appear above ground.

SEEDLING GROWTH

HEALTHY SEEDLINGS
Sturdy, well-spaced nasturtium (Tropaeolum) *seedlings flourishing under glass are ready to be pricked out.*

Long, thin stems

UNHEALTHY SEEDLINGS
If not pricked out early enough, the seedlings will become pale, crowded, and etiolated – and may die.

TRUE LEAVES

As the cotyledons, or seed leaves, wither, the true leaves gradually take over the process of photosynthesis.

Producing hybrid plants

When hybridizing plants, it is important to prevent self-pollination. For controlled cross-pollination, petals, sepals, and stamens are removed from the flowers on the proposed female parent and the denuded flowers protected from insects by paper or plastic bags until the stigmas on the female plant are sticky and receptive. Pollen, previously collected from air-dried stamens, is then transferred to the stigmas and the flowers are protected from insects once again until fertilization has occurred. Hybrid seed will develop in the ovaries and should be collected when ripe and according to its requirements (see also THE ROSE GARDEN, "Hybridizing," p.132).

F1 and F2 hybrids

For the gardener seeking uniformity and near-perfection, F1 and F2 hybrid seed is available for a limited range of plants, mostly annuals. Such seed needs complex plant breeding techniques and is therefore more expensive.

The first generation derived from crossing two carefully maintained, genetically inbred plants of the same species is termed a "first filial generation," or F1, hybrid. This process combines the benefits of greater uniformity that can result from inbreeding with the vigor that can flow from crossbreeding. F1 hybrids are usually more vigorous than their parents and give uniformity in flower characteristics such as color and form that seldom occurs with open-pollinated seed. Sometimes two controlled crosses from four selected lines are used to produce a "second filial generation," or F2, hybrid – retaining some of the vigor and uniformity of the F1 parents but often with other favored characteristics less evident in the F1s.

Layering

Layering is a natural form of propagation: roots are induced to develop by covering a stem with soil while it is still attached to the parent plant. The rooted portion of stem is then separated from the parent plant and grown on.

The stem to be layered is often cut, bark-ringed, or twisted. This partially interrupts the flow of hormones and carbohydrates, which, as they accumulate there, help to promote root growth. The tissues beyond the constriction are slightly water-stressed, and this, too, favors root formation. Another important root stimulus is the exclusion of light from the stem: light-starved cells then become thin-walled and roots form more readily. In order to further stimulate rooting, use a rooting hormone at the point of layering.

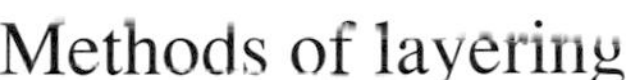

Methods of layering

Layering methods are classified in three groups: those in which a stem is brought down to the soil (simple, serpentine, natural, and tip layering); those in which soil is mounded over a stem (mound layering, trench layering, and French layering); and air, or Chinese, layering, where the "soil" is brought up to the plant stem. The word "soil" is used loosely here to mean any growing medium such as peat, sand, sawdust, or sphagnum moss.

Simple layering

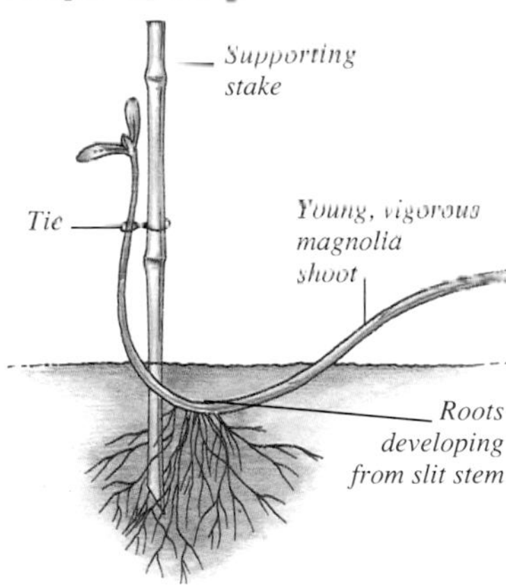

This method is best carried out between fall and spring. The parent plant should be young and pruned the previous season to produce vigorous, flexible stems, which can be brought down to soil level and will root readily. A slanting cut is made on the underside of the stem to be layered, which is firmly pegged or secured at this point into the soil. The shoot tip is tied to a vertical stake inserted in the soil. The following fall, if the layer is well rooted, it can be cut from the parent plant (see also ORNAMENTAL SHRUBS, "Simple layering," p.86, and CLIMBING PLANTS, "Simple layering," p.113).

SERPENTINE LAYERING

Serpentine layering

This modified form of simple layering is used for plants with pliable stems, such as clematis. Long, young stems are mounded with soil, leaving buds exposed to produce aerial shoots (see also CLIMBING PLANTS, "Propagation by serpentine layering," p.113).

Natural layering

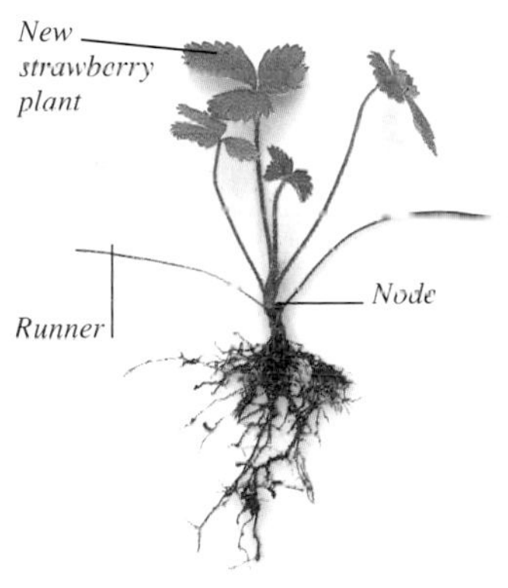

Some plants such as strawberries reproduce naturally by sending out a series of runners. These then root at a node, forming a new plant. Once the new plant is fully established, sever it from the parent and grow on (see also "Strawberries: Propagation," p.406).

Tip layering

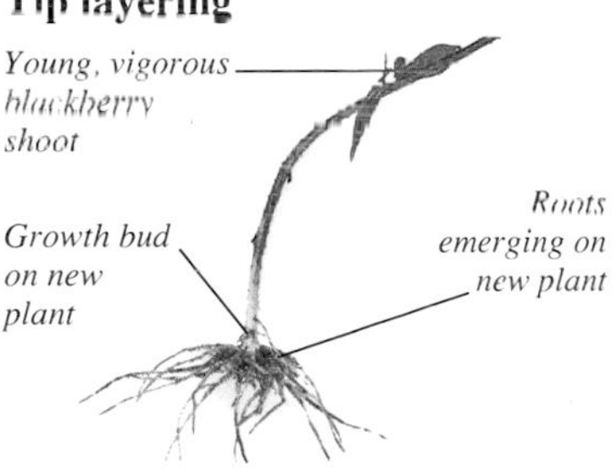

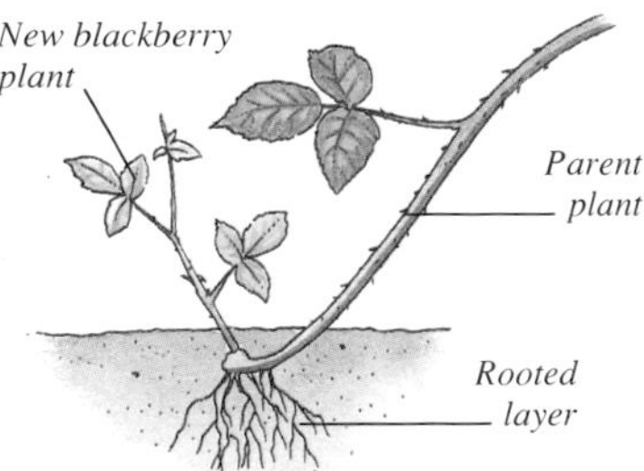

This method is for shrubs and climbers that produce roots from their shoot tips; one of the most common examples in nature is the blackberry. In summer, a young, vigorous shoot tip is buried in soil in a hole 3–4in (7–10cm) deep. A new shoot, having developed from the tip, appears a few weeks later; the young plant may then be separated from its parent. Grow on the rooted layer *in situ*; transplant it the following spring, if required (see also "Blackberries: *Tip Layering*," p.407).

Mound layering

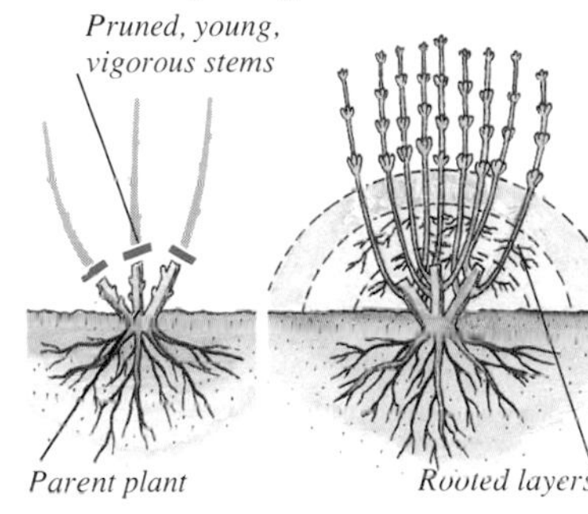

Although important for the commercial production of rootstocks, mound layering, or stooling, is used by amateurs only for a few woody plants. The stems of a young parent plant are cut back in late winter or early spring to within 3in (8cm) of the ground. When the new shoots are about 6–8in (15–20cm) long, mound soil up over their bases, and again twice more until summer. With plants that root easily, such as thyme and sage, there is no need to cut the stems back before mounding. By fall the stems will have rooted; they are then separated from the parent plant and transplanted (see also THE HERB GARDEN, "Mound layering," p.297).

Trench layering

Trench, or etiolation, layering is primarily for fruit rootstocks, especially those that are hard to root. The parent plant is planted at an angle, to make it easier for its shoots to be pegged down in shallow trenches and covered with soil. The rooted shoots can be detached from the parent to form new plants.

TRENCH LAYERING

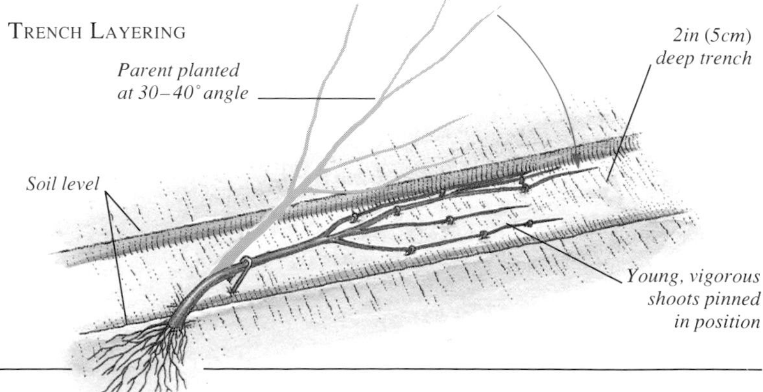

French layering

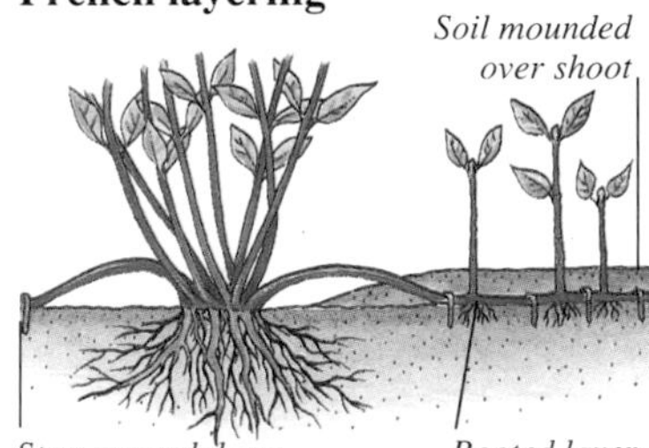

French, or continuous, layering is a modified form of mound layering. In late winter, peg young shoots from the parent stem to the ground. Any new growths are gradually hilled up to a depth of 6in (15cm). These new shoots should have rooted by fall and after leaf drop may be separated and grown on (see also ORNAMENTAL SHRUBS, "French layering," p.87).

Air layering

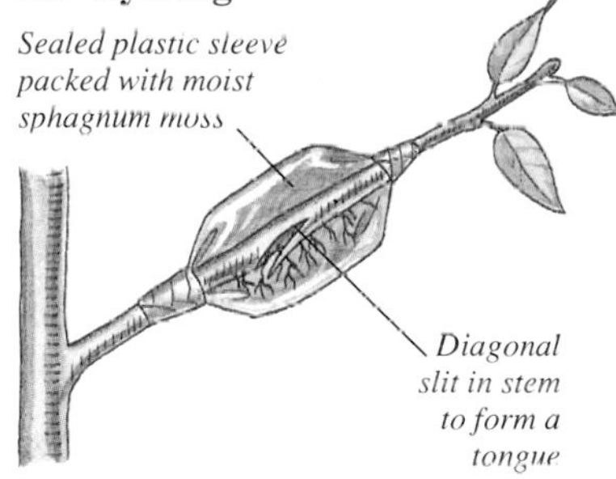

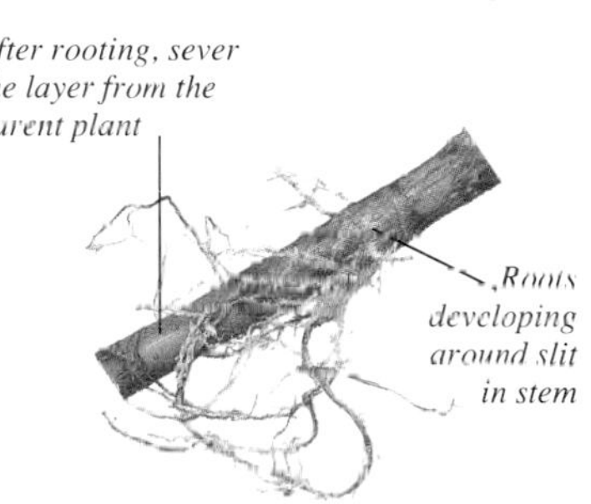

Use air, or Chinese, layering – also known as marcottage – on some trees, shrubs, and house plants. In spring or summer, slit an aerial shoot and pack the tongue with sphagnum moss; cover with plastic until roots develop (see *Air Layering a Shrub*, p.87, and THE INDOOR GARDEN, "Air layering," p.456). Rooting may take up to two years.

Cuttings

Propagation from cuttings is the most common vegetative method. There are three main types: stem, leaf, and root. Stem cuttings produce roots directly from the stem itself or from the mass of thin-walled, wound-healing tissue (callus) that develops at its base. These roots are called adventitious, which literally means added. Some large leaves can be used as cutting material and will develop adventitious roots from near their veins. Vigorous, young roots may also be used for cuttings – propagation by root cuttings is a simple and economical method neglected by most gardeners. Suitable species will produce both adventitious stem buds and roots on the root cutting.

How roots form

Adventitious roots most often develop from young cells produced by the cambium – a layer of cells that generates tissues involved in the thickening of stems. They are usually located close to food- and water-conducting tissues, which provide nourishment as they develop.

Adventitious root growth is also helped by natural hormones called auxins, which accumulate in the base of a cutting. Natural auxins can be supplemented by synthetic auxins, which are available as talc-based powders or as solutions. These aid rooting when applied to the base of a cutting and are recommended for all plants except those that root very easily. Use only a little hormone, however, because too much could harm immature tissue.

Rooting hormones can be bought with low concentrations of active ingredient for soft cuttings and higher concentrations for hardwood material; some contain a fungicide, which helps to prevent infections entering the cuttings through the wounded tissues.

CALLUS PADS

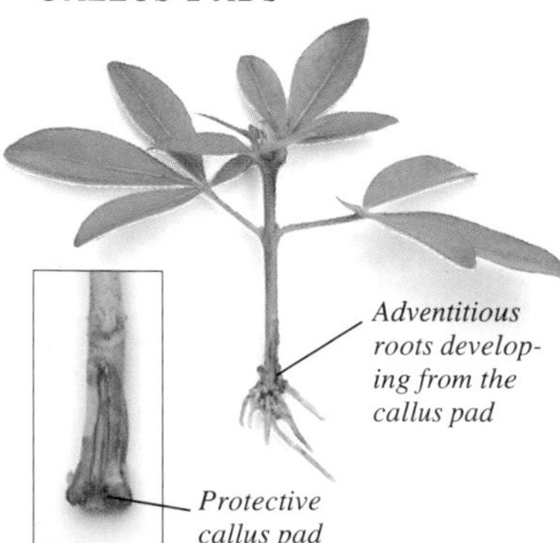

Plants that are difficult to root (here Choisya ternata) *form a callus pad of wound-healing tissue at the base of a stem cutting, where they have been severed from the parent plant.*

SOFTWOOD CUTTINGS

The soft, green stem on a softwood cutting (here Hydrangea macrophylla) *usually turns brown as it matures and develops its root system.*

Stem cuttings

Stem cuttings are often classified by the maturity of the stem tissue into softwood, greenwood, semiripe, and hardwood (or ripewood). The distinction is useful, though imprecise, because tissues develop continuously throughout the growing season.

Softwood cuttings
These are taken in spring, when the new shoots of the parent plant are almost fully developed and just beginning to harden. Such cuttings are generally made from the shoot tips (tip cuttings), but new, young basal shoots (basal cuttings) of herbaceous perennials are also used (see PERENNIALS, "Basal stem cuttings," p.164). Since young material roots most readily, softwood cuttings often provide the best chance of rooting species that are hard to propagate. However, they need a supportive environment since they lose water and wilt quickly (see "The propagation environment," p.544).

Greenwood cuttings
These are taken from early to midsummer, from slightly more mature wood, when growth begins to slow. They root slightly less readily but survive better than softwood cuttings, although they still require a supportive environment in which to develop into new plants before being hardened off.

Semiripe cuttings
Taken in late summer, semiripe cuttings are less prone to wilting since the stem tissues are firmer and woody (see ORNAMENTAL SHRUBS, "Semiripe cuttings," p.82). Some genera with large leaves, for example *Ficus* and camellia, may be propagated more economically by taking a short section from a semiripe stem just above and below a leaf bud, retaining a single leaf (see ORNAMENTAL SHRUBS, "Leaf-bud cuttings," p.83).

Hardwood cuttings
Fully mature, hardwood (or ripewood) cuttings are taken at the end of the growing season from fall through spring, when the tissues are fully ripened. They are the easiest to maintain in a healthy condition but are often slow to root. Hardwood cuttings fall into two categories: leafless deciduous and broad-leaved evergreen cuttings. Growth of many glossy-leaved evergreens, such as holly (*Ilex*) and rhododendron, wilts readily when young early in the season since their protective leaf waxes develop slowly; they are therefore best propagated by semiripe or hardwood cuttings (see also ORNAMENTAL TREES, "Hardwood cuttings," p.52; CLIMBING PLANTS, "Propagation from hardwood cuttings," p.111; and THE ROSE GARDEN, "Hardwood cuttings," p.129).

SEMIRIPE CUTTINGS

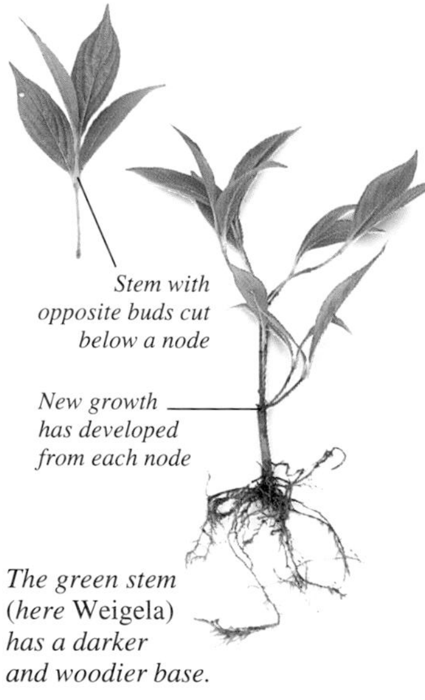

The green stem (here Weigela) *has a darker and woodier base.*

LEAF-BUD CUTTINGS

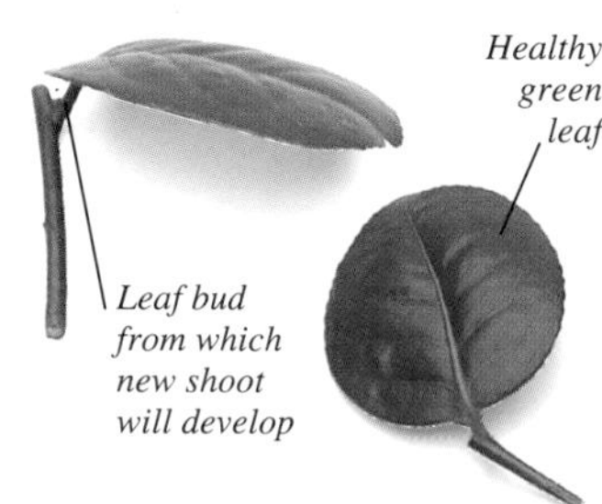

A short piece of semiripe stem (here camellia) provides sufficient food reserves for a leaf-bud cutting, since it produces some food through its leaf.

HARDWOOD CUTTINGS

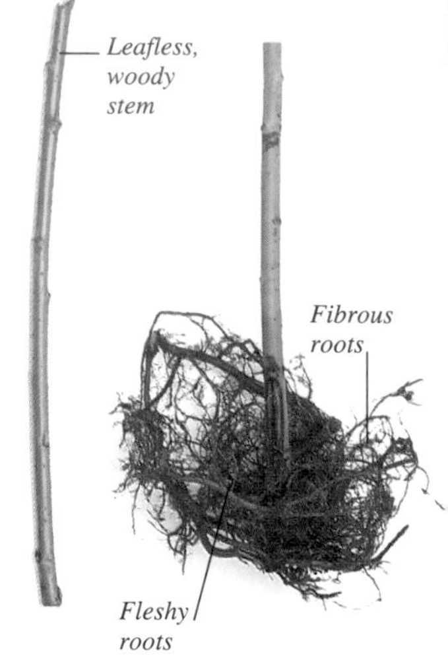

Hardwood cuttings (here Salix alba) *are the longest type of stem cutting since they need large food reserves while their roots slowly develop.*

When to take stem cuttings

There are no hard and fast rules about when to take stem cuttings of a particular species, so if cuttings taken in spring fail to root, further cuttings can be taken later in the season and treated according to the relative maturity of the shoots.

Plants that are difficult to root are best propagated early so that the new plants have time to mature before winter. Because the action of root-producing hormones is suppressed by flower-initiating ones, use cuttings without flower buds wherever possible; if cuttings with flower buds must be used, remove these buds.

Preparing stem cuttings
Stem cuttings are normally prepared by trimming just below a node, or leaf joint, where the cambium (the layer of cells involved in stem thickening) is most active. A few easy-rooting

NODAL CUTTING

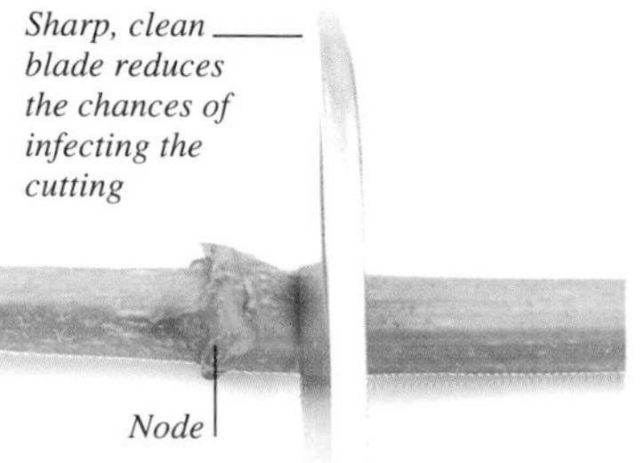

Most cuttings (here Hydrangea paniculata) *root most satisfactorily at their nodes and so should be trimmed just below a node.*

INTERNODAL CUTTINGS

Internodal cuttings (here Clematis montana) *utilize scarce propagating material in an economical way.*

PREPARING CUTTINGS

To reduce stress from water loss on leafy cuttings (here rhododendron), remove some leaves, halve others.

cuttings, for example willows (*Salix*), have preformed roots at the nodes, and these start to develop when the stem is cut from the parent plant. For these and for cuttings with densely crowded leaves on each stem, cut between nodes (internodal cutting).

The length of the cutting will depend on the species but is commonly 2–5in (5–12cm), or includes five or six nodes. The lower leaves are stripped to give a clean stem for insertion. To assist the cuttings in rooting, semiripe and hardwood cuttings are often wounded by removing a sliver of bark from the lowest 1in (2.5cm) of the cutting. This exposes a greater area of cambium and thereby stimulates roots to form. Some cuttings, especially semiripe ones, may be taken by pulling a side shoot away from the main shoot with a small heel of bark still attached (see ORNAMENTAL SHRUBS, "Heel cuttings," p.83). A heel may provide added protection for a cutting until it has produced roots, although there is no satisfactory scientific explanation for this response.

With the exception of leafless, hardwood stem cuttings, which contain food reserves from the previous growing season, few cuttings are able to produce roots and shoots without supplementing their food reserves through photosynthesis. However, active leaves lose water through their pores, which is not easily replaced, and excessive water loss will cause failure. To achieve a balance between retaining photosynthetic tissue and reducing water loss, trim away all but a few full-sized leaves, leaving any immature leaves. If the remaining leaves are large, as on many broad-leaved trees and large shrubs, reduce each by half to minimize water loss.

WOUNDING

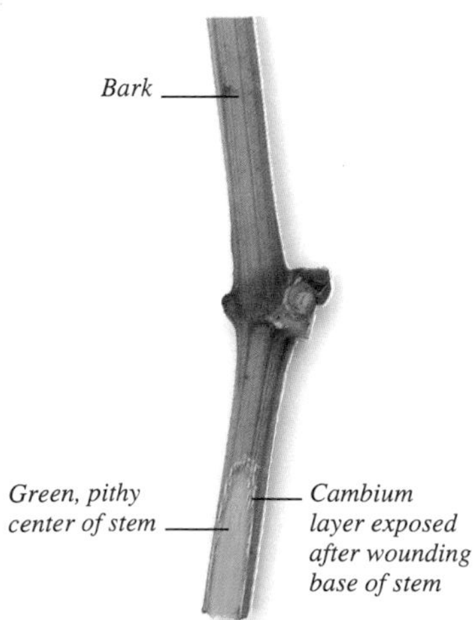

Use a very sharp, clean knife to make a shallow, angled, downward cut at the base of semiripe and hardwood cuttings such as grape (Vitis).

Leaf cuttings

For some plants, whole leaves (with or without leaf stalks) or sections of leaves may be taken as cuttings and inserted or secured onto the soil mix. With whole leaves laid flat, the veins should be nicked at intervals since new plantlets form at the cut surfaces of large leaf veins. Propagate plants such as *Sinningia* and *Streptocarpus* from cut sections of fully expanded, undamaged leaves. African violets (*Saintpaulia*) and *Peperomia* may also be propagated from entire leaves with their stalks (see also THE INDOOR GARDEN, "Propagating from leaves," p.454).

LARGE LEAVES

Large leaves of plants such as begonia may be divided into small pieces, each of which will form callus at a nicked vein and then adventitious roots.

Root cuttings

Root cuttings are taken in the dormant season from young, vigorous roots of about pencil thickness for most trees and shrubs, but the roots may be somewhat thinner for some herbaceous plants such as phlox.

The length of the cutting

This is dependent on the environment in which the root cutting is to develop: the warmer the environment, the faster new shoots will appear and, therefore, shorter cuttings with smaller food reserves may be used successfully, although these should be at least 1in (2.5cm) in length. Root cuttings that are 1–2in (2.5–5cm) long are best grown on in a greenhouse, and those over 2in (5cm) long in a cold frame. For sumac (*Rhus*) and lilac (*Syringa*), which can be propagated in open ground, 4–6in (10–15cm) long root cuttings should be used.

Inserting root cuttings

It is important to insert root cuttings the correct way up since the new roots always form at the distal end (that is, the end that was farthest from the crown of the parent plant). Cuttings should be inserted vertically so that their other (proximal) ends are flush with the soil surface; herbaceous root cuttings, however, are frequently inserted horizontally (see also PERENNIALS, "Root cuttings," p.165).

The rooting medium

Cuttings need air (to obtain oxygen) and water in their rooting medium, but if the medium is too wet, the cuttings rot. Standard cuttings soil mix must, therefore, have a more open structure than soil-based potting mix. The rooting medium should also be warm in order to speed up development of the roots: 64–77°F (18–25°C) is ideal for cool-temperate species, and up to 90°F (32°C) for those from warm climates. If necessary, use bottom heat (see p.544).

SMALL LEAVES

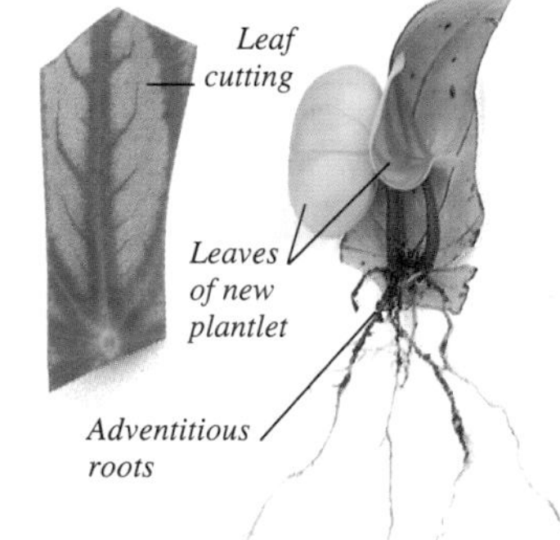

To encourage callus to form, and rooting to occur, small leaves such as Peperomia *may be trimmed at the edges.*

ROOT CUTTINGS

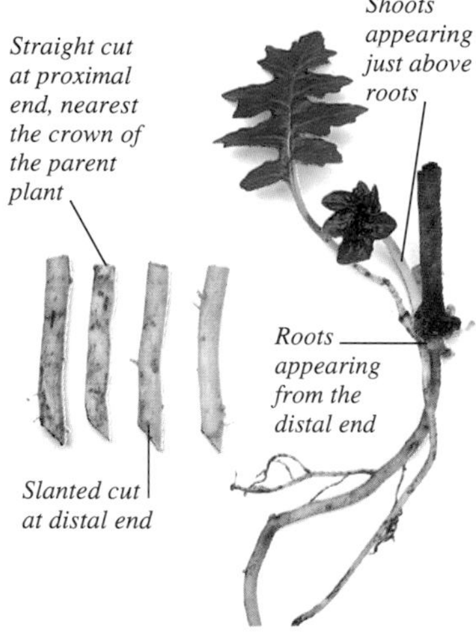

To help distinguish the two ends when taking root cuttings (here Acanthus mollis), *make differently angled cuts.*

PROTECTIVE ENVIRONMENT

Leafy cuttings grow best in a humid environment, such as within a plastic bag secured over a container; keep the plastic away from the leaf surfaces.

Caring for the cuttings

After insertion, keep leafy cuttings turgid in the humid atmosphere of a closed case, mist unit, propagator, or other similar environment. Leafless cuttings that have been planted outdoors, either directly into the soil or in a container, as appropriate, should be protected by either a clear plastic tunnel or a cold frame.

Every ten days, water the rooting medium lightly if required, and spray with a fungicide to help prevent disease; at the same time, lift the sashes or remove the plastic over the enclosed cuttings, to enable air to circulate, for a 5–10 minute period.

Once rooted, cuttings should be potted up individually and those growing under cover gradually hardened off (see p.545).

Storage organs

Storage organs have diverse structures, including bulbs, corms, rhizomes, root and stem tubers, and turions. Most plants with storage organs will increase naturally by producing offsets, which should be lifted and divided to prevent overcrowding. Offsets will flower more quickly than seed-raised plants and will be identical with the parent, whereas seed-raised plants may be variable in character.

The main propagation methods apart from division are to cut the storage organs into sections and to stimulate them to produce offsets by wounding; these offsets or sections will soon form complete plants if provided with a warm, dark place in which to develop. The cut surfaces should always be dusted with a fungicide since they easily succumb to fungal attack.

Bulbs

NONSCALY, OR TUNICATE, BULB

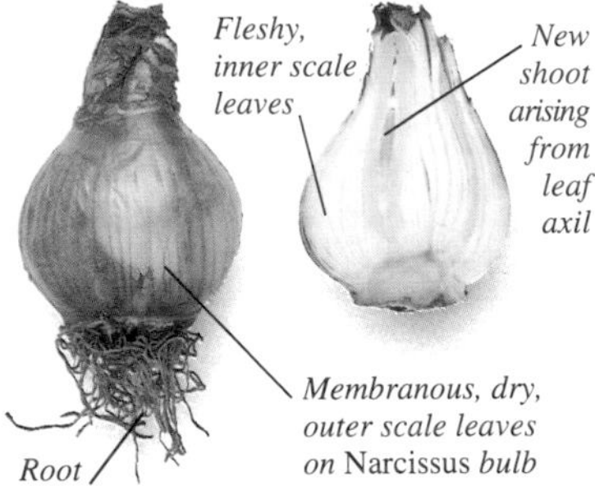

SCALY BULB

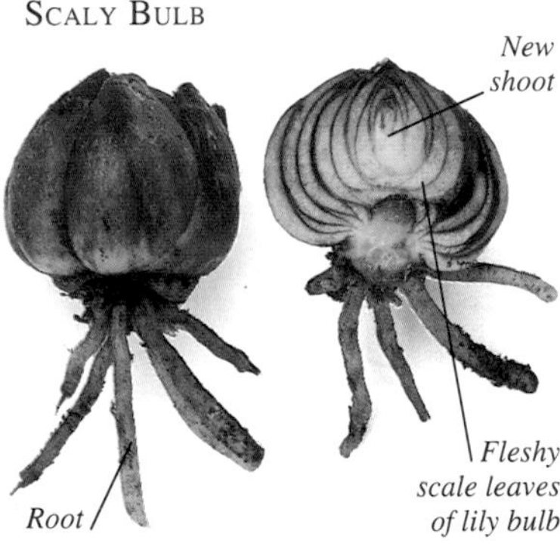

Bulbs may be propagated by chipping; division of offsets, bulbils, or bulblets; scaling or twin-scaling; and scooping or scoring. The gardener can tell only from experience which is best for which bulb, but for lists of plants appropriate to each method, see BULBOUS PLANTS, "Propagation," pp.233–8.

Chipping

Nonscaly, or tunicate, bulbs such as snowdrops (*Galanthus*), that do not naturally increase quickly, may be multiplied rapidly by chipping. This method involves cutting each bulb into up to 20 pieces, depending on its size. Each piece, which generally consists of three or more scale leaves and a

CHIPPING

Bulblets develop between the scale leaves on a chipped bulb such as snowdrop (Galanthus) *in air temperatures that do not exceed 77°F (25°C).*

section of basal plate, is then soaked in or dusted with a fungicide. The chips may be incubated (see "Chipping," p.237) or placed in a 1:1 mix of peat and sand or peat and perlite in a container in a cool place and left undisturbed for up to two years. Then separate the bulblets and repot or replant as required.

Division of offsets

Bulbs have wide, fleshy scale leaves that act as food storage organs. At their base are axillary buds, which may enlarge naturally to form offsets. When the bulbs are lifted at the end of the growing season, these may be separated and planted out individually (see "Dividing bulbs," p.233).

DIVISION OF OFFSETS

Carefully remove each offset from a bulb (here Narcissus*) by cutting or pulling.*

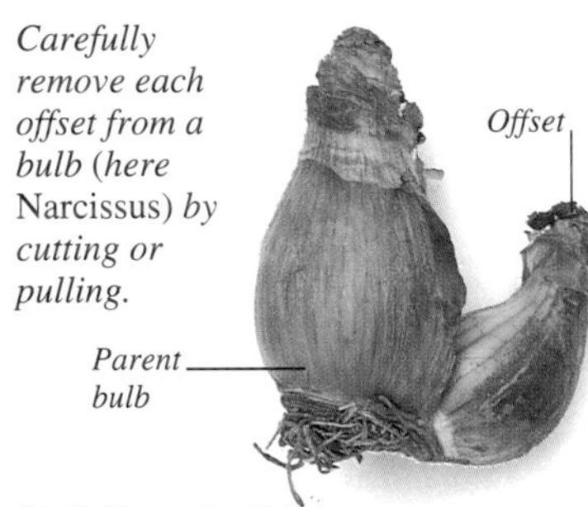

Bulbils or bulblets

Bulbils are produced on flowerheads or stems; bulblets develop on the bulb itself or on stem roots. Both may be detached and planted up to develop into new bulbs (see also LILIES, "Bulbils and bulblets," p.239).

Scaling

Scaling involves the removal of bulb scales, which are then induced to form bulblets. It is used for bulbs such as fritillaries (*Fritillaria*) and lilies

SCALING

Bulblets appear at the base of individual scale leaves of loose-scaled bulbs, here lily (Lilium).

Scale leaf
New top-growth
Rooted bulblet

TWIN-SCALING

Two bud scales and a section of basal plate are used for nonscaly bulbs (here Narcissus*).*

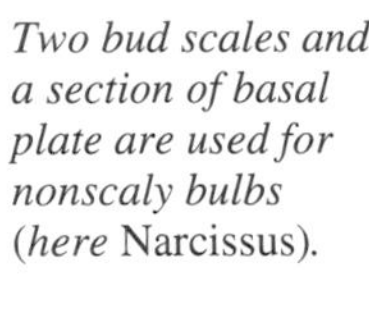

(*Lilium*) that are made up of fairly loose scales. Individual scale leaves are pulled away from the basal plate of a mature bulb and then left in a plastic bag containing moist vermiculite or a peat and grit mix, in a warm, dark place. Bulblets appear at the scale bases, usually after two months. Grow on the scales in a container until the bulblets are large enough to be separated (see also "Scaling," p.236).

Twin-scaling

Nonscaly, or tunicate, bulbs such as daffodils and snowdrops may be twin-scaled. In this, the bulb is cut vertically into eight to ten sections and each of these is divided into pairs of bud scales with a small section of basal plate. These are incubated and grown on in the same way as in scaling, above. (See also "Twin-scaling," p.237.)

Scooping and scoring

Some bulbs, such as hyacinths, can be propagated by either scooping or scoring the bulb. This causes callus tissue to develop, which encourages bulblets to form. For scooping, the basal plate of a mature bulb is scooped out at the center, leaving just the outer

SCORING

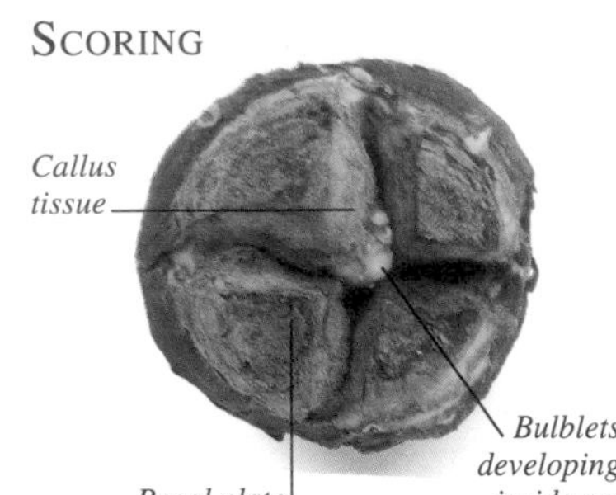

Shallowly cutting the basal plate of some bulbs (here hyacinth) stimulates the growth of bulblets.

edge of the basal plate intact; for scoring, two shallow cuts at right angles are made into the basal plate. The bulb is then stored in a warm, dark place until bulblets have formed; these are then detached and grown on separately (see also "Simple cutting," p.238; "Scooping hyacinths," p.238; and "Scoring and scooping *Trillium*," p.238).

BULBILS AND BULBLETS

Some lilies (Lilium), *for example* L. lancifolium, *produce small, bulblike structures known as bulbils on their stems above the ground. Others, for example* L. longiflorum, *may develop similar bulblets on bulbs or stem roots in the soil.*

Corms

GLADIOLUS CORM

Corms are reduced, compact, underground stems with a solid internal structure. Most corms produce several buds near the apex; each bud naturally forms a new corm. Miniature corms, or cormels, are produced as offsets

RAISING CORMELS

In fall, separate the new corm and cormels from the parent and grow on.

DEVELOPMENT OF A CORMEL

Cormels may take up to 3 years to reach flowering size. This sequence shows their development in the first year.

between the old and new corms in the growing season (see also BULBOUS PLANTS, "Gladiolus cormels," p.233).

Larger corms may be increased artificially by cutting them into pieces, each with a growing bud, just before the growing season. When planted in a pot or the open ground and lightly covered with soil, these cut sections will develop into new corms.

Rhizomes

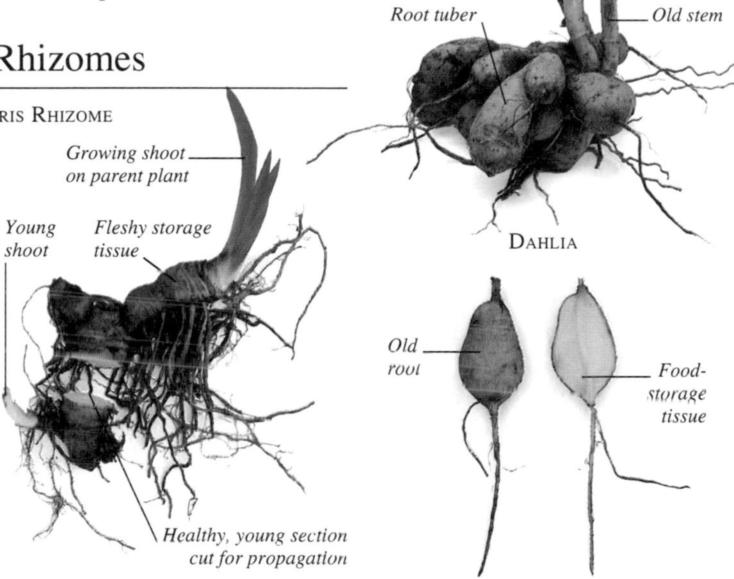

These consist of a horizontally growing shoot, usually beneath but sometimes on the soil surface. They are propagated by cutting the rhizome into young, healthy sections, each with one or more growth buds, which are planted up individually (see also PERENNIALS, "Division of rhizomatous plants," p.163; BULBOUS PLANTS, "Scoring and scooping *Trillium*," p.238; and ORCHIDS, "Division," p.443).

Root tubers

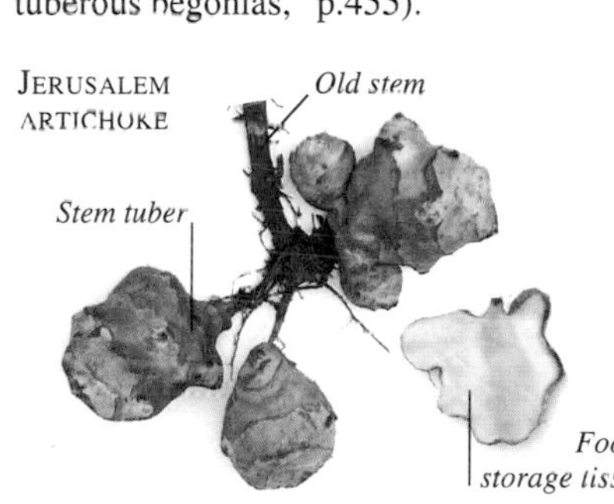

A root tuber is a portion of root at the stem base that swells during summer and is modified into a storage organ, or tuber, as in dahlias. Such plants may be propagated in spring by dividing a cluster of tubers into healthy pieces, each with a developing shoot (see also *Cutting Up Bulbs for Propagation*, p.237). Root tubers may also be propagated by basal cuttings of the young, emerging shoots in spring (see DAHLIAS, *How to Propagate by Basal Cuttings*, p.223).

Stem tubers

The stems of some plants (e.g. potatoes and Jerusalem artichokes) are modified to produce tubers that act as storage organs. Tuberous begonias, for example, form perennial tubers at the bases of their stems, which enlarge each year. In spring, these can be cut into pieces, each with a growth bud. Each piece will produce basal shoots, which can be used as basal cuttings (see DAHLIAS, *How to Propagate by Basal Cuttings*, p.223) or grown on to form a new tuber (see "Propagation of tuberous begonias," p.455).

JERUSALEM ARTICHOKE

Old stem

Stem tuber

Food-storage tissue

Other types of storage organ

Plants such as *Saxifraga granulata* and some *Kalanchoe* and *Asparagus* species develop round, bulblike buds at their shoot axils. These buds can be separated and grown on individually in the same way as bulblets or cormels (see opposite).

In some water plants, such as *Hydrocharis* and *Myriophyllum*, these relatively large bud structures are known as turions. When mature, they drop off the parent plant naturally, sink to the bottom of the water, and develop into new plants.

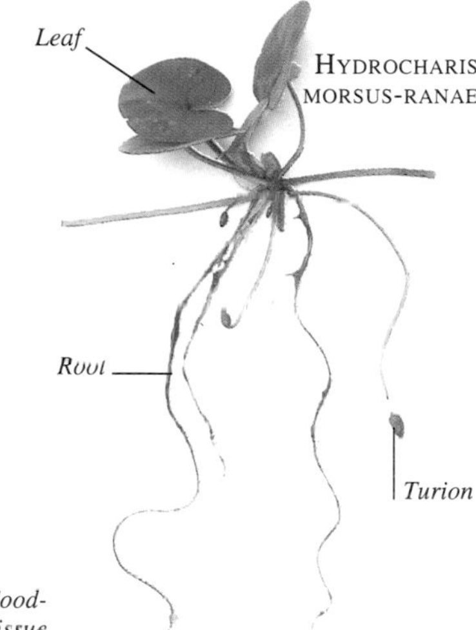

Grafting and budding

In a wide range of woody plants and a few herbaceous ones, a budded stem, or scion, is grafted onto a rootstock, or stock, of another species or cultivar, to achieve a composite plant with more desirable characteristics. Most apple, pear, and stone fruit trees are propagated in this way. The stock may be more resistant than the scion to root disease or more suited to a particular environment. Often (especially with fruit trees), the stock is selected because it controls the growth of the scion to produce a dwarfed or a particularly vigorous plant. Sometimes, a scion cultivar that is difficult to increase from cuttings is grafted onto easily rooted stock. The rootstock also influences the age at which the tree bears fruit and its size and skin quality – dwarfing rootstocks generally conferring earlier fruit-bearing. Conversely, the rootstock's growing cycle may be affected by the scion cultivar, which in turn influences cold hardiness. Reactions to soil acidity can also be affected by interactions between rootstock and scion cultivars.

The scion may take the form of a single bud on a short portion of stem (usually known as budding) or it may be a multibudded length of stem.

When to graft

Most grafting is normally undertaken in late winter to early spring, when the cambium is particularly active; these warm conditions also favor the growth of callus cells. Hot weather later in the season may dry out the thin-walled cambial cells.

T-budding, on the other hand, is most often done in mid- to late summer, when well-developed scion buds are available and young stock material is of suitable diameter. For success, the stock plant needs to be growing actively, so that the bark can be lifted from the wood to allow the bud to be inserted – an action known as bark slipping. Chip-budding, however, may be undertaken over an extended season because the chip is positioned beside the stock rather than slipped under its bark.

How to graft

Because grafting cuts inevitably damage plant cells, and the thin-walled cells at the graft union are vulnerable to fungi and bacteria, it is essential that knives are sterile and sharp, so that a single cut is sufficient. The propagation environment, prepared plant material, and ties must also be scrupulously clean.

Once stock and scion material have been selected and cut to shape, according to the type of graft, position the two pieces carefully so that there is maximum cambial contact. If the grafting materials are of different widths, ensure that cambium on at least one side of the graft is in contact. Central to the grafting process is the activity of the cambium – a continuous, narrow band of thin-walled cells between the bark and the wood – which produces new cells that are responsible for stem thickening. Within days of grafting, the region between the stock and scion should fill with thin-walled callus cells. The cambial cells on the stock and scion next to the young callus then influence neighboring cells, so that a complete cambial bridge forms between the two parts. Further divisions of this new cambium produce water- and food-conducting tissue, which functionally joins the scion and stock.

CAMBIUM LAYER

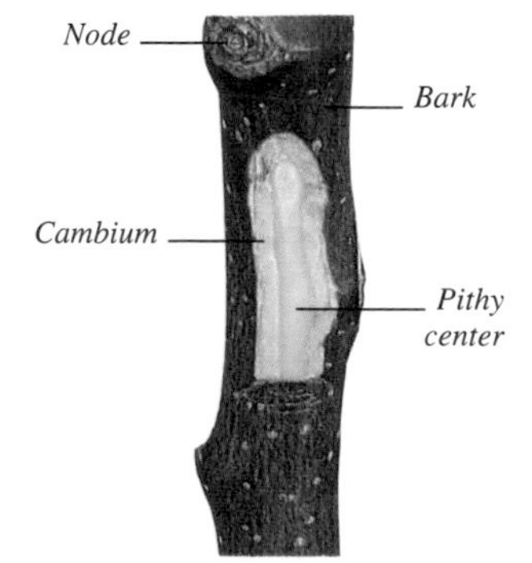

For successful grafting, the scion cambium must be matched as closely as possible to that of the stock.

Traditionally, grafts were bound with raffia, and then coated with wax to prevent drying. However, waxing is used less often now that raffia has mainly been superseded by clear plastic tape, which seals the join better. Once grafted, potgrown stocks should be kept in a suitable protective environment (see "Greenhouses," p.544, and "Cold frames," p.545).

Regularly examine the graft, and remove the tape once the graft appears to have taken. The following growing season, cut back the stock plant just above the new shoot that has developed from the grafted scion.

Chip-budding

A chip of ripe wood is removed from the rootstock and replaced with a matching chip of similar size from the scion, or budstick, containing a bud (see The Fruit Garden, *Chip-budding*, p.368).

T-budding

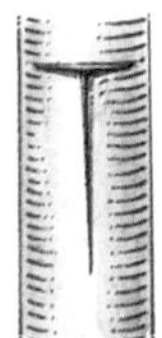

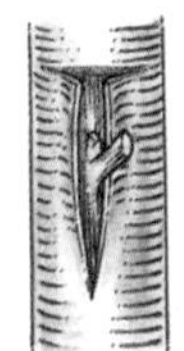

In this technique, just the scion bud is grafted onto the rootstock by cutting a T in the stock bark and inserting the bud beneath (see The Rose Garden, "Bud-grafting," p.130).

Side-veneer grafting

A short, downward cut through the cambium layer of the stock is followed by a sloping cut down toward the base of the first cut. The chip is removed and replaced by the scion, which is shaped to match the stock (see Ornamental Trees, "Side-veneer grafting," p.56, and Ornamental Shrubs, "Side-veneer grafting," p.88).

Side-wedge grafting

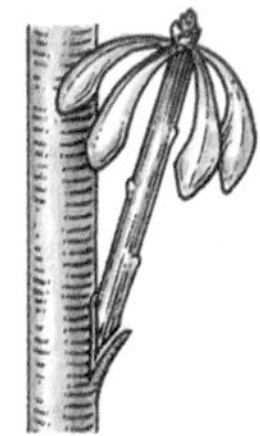

A downward, slightly inward cut is made into the side of the stock. The scion is then prepared by making two oblique cuts at the base. The scion's wedge-shaped base is inserted into the rootstock cut so that the cambium aligns and is bound in position.

Apical-wedge grafting

The stock is cut flat and a wedge-shaped chip is removed from the center, into which the scion is then inserted (see Ornamental Shrubs, "Apical-wedge grafting," p.89).

Saddle grafting

The top of the stock is saddle-shaped, with upward-sloping sides. The scion is shaped so that it fits closely over the top of the rootstock (see Ornamental Shrubs, "Saddle grafting," p.88).

Basal-whip grafting

Cut back the stock at an oblique angle to 2–3in (5–8cm). Then prepare the scion to match. If the scion is thinner than the stock, first cut the stock horizontally, then obliquely to match.

Flat grafting

Both the stock top and scion base are cut horizontally (see Cacti and other Succulents, "Flat grafting," p.271).

Whip-and-tongue grafting

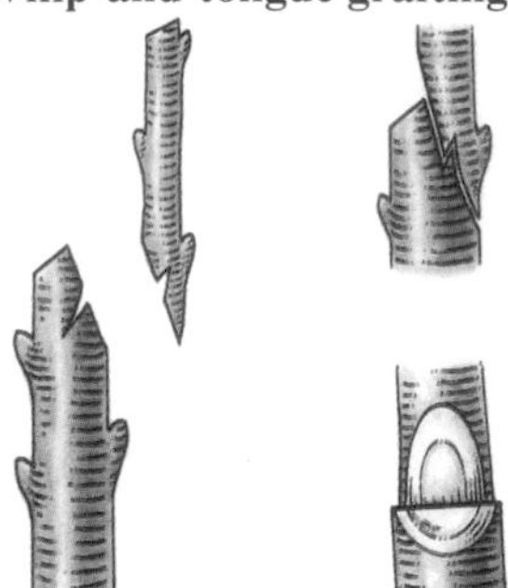

Make matching sloping cuts on the rootstock and scion, then cut shallow tongues along the sloping cuts, so that the scion interlocks securely with the stock (see The Fruit Garden, "Whip-and-tongue grafting," p.369).

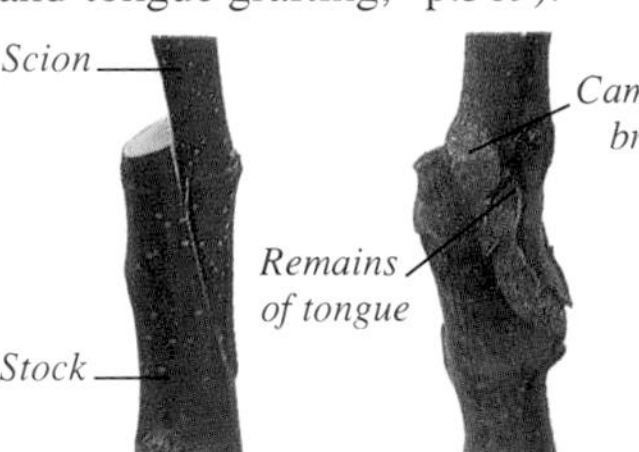

Whip-and-tongue Graft
The rootstock and scion gradually unite to function as one plant.

The propagation environment

During propagation, plants are at their most vulnerable and their environment is, therefore, vitally important. The choice of environment depends on which propagation method is chosen and on the relative maturity of the plant material itself. Propagation from leafy cuttings, for example, requires a more closely regulated environment than for leafless cuttings.

Greenhouses

It is essential that the greenhouse has adequate ventilation and, in the growing season, appropriate shading (see "Creating the right environment," p.481). For two months on either side of midsummer, a shading wash on the outside of the glass will ensure that propagated plants are not stressed unnecessarily by extreme weather conditions (see "Shading washes," p.484). Additional protective shading can be provided by mounting some shade cloth on wire runners across or along the length of the bench or greenhouse. The curtain can be opened during dull weather.

Protecting leafy cuttings

Because leafy cuttings initially have no roots and cannot easily take up water to replace that lost from the leaves, they must have further protection within the greenhouse.

Clear plastic sheeting or a plastic bag placed over a tray of cuttings and tucked underneath is perfectly satisfactory if appropriate shading is provided. Water vapor condensing on the inside of the plastic helps to protect the cuttings against desiccation. Soft cuttings may succumb to disease if the plastic touches them; insert a framework of split stakes or wire in the soil mix to keep the plastic off the cuttings. In such closed systems, however, excessive air temperatures may build up in very hot conditions and the containers of cuttings should be kept in a shaded place out of direct sunlight.

Shading Greenhouses (Temperate climates)

To prevent the greenhouse from overheating when propagating, add one or more layers of shading, depending on the weather conditions and season. Greenhouses in open, sunny sites are particularly vulnerable to overheating.

		Spring	Summer	Fall	Winter
Dull Days	Whitewash		▬	▬	
Bright Days	Layer of shade cloth	▬	▬	▬	▬
	Additional shade cloth	▬	▬	▬	
	Whitewash		▬	▬	

Rigid-topped Propagator

Because most of the moisture in a rigid-topped propagator is retained within the unit, cuttings remain turgid and so are more likely to root quickly and healthily.

Rigid plastic propagators need shading similar to that needed by plastic sheeting, and generally provide a drier environment, because water vapor may leak through their ventilation openings: these should be kept closed until the cuttings have rooted and are ready to be hardened off.

A mist unit provides the best system for summer propagation, but for winter and early- and late-season propagation it should be combined with bottom heat. Ideally, the mist unit should maintain a constant water film on the leaf surfaces; some water will still be lost from the leaves by transpiration but this is amply replaced by water applied from the misting process. Since the mist is applied in bursts, however, the greenhouse humidity fluctuates and so, inevitably, each leaf's water film is imperfect and some water loss occurs. Complete mist systems consist of supply pipes, water filter, nozzles, and a solenoid and sensor to regulate the misting frequency (see "Mist units," p.488).

For softwood cuttings, which wilt readily, the best system is to arrange a low, clear plastic tent just above the misting nozzles. This ensures a higher ambient humidity between mist bursts than does open mist. It is important to shade such a closed mist system in bright weather.

Bottom heat

Most biological processes are speeded up when temperatures are higher, and therefore raising the temperature of the soil mix usually increases the rapidity with which seeds germinate and cuttings root.

Cables or heating mats are most convenient for small greenhouses (see "Propagation aids," p.488). The temperature is controlled by a rod thermostat or electronic controller. If they are used in closed mist systems, excessive

EFFECTS OF BOTTOM HEAT

CUTTING GROWN WITH HEAT

CUTTING GROWN WITHOUT HEAT

Poor, short roots

Long, strong, healthy roots

air temperatures may build up in bright conditions, during which the heating must be switched off.

Heated propagator units

These self-contained units are useful for extending the propagation season in minimally heated greenhouses (see "Heated propagators," p.488). Propagator units have heat loads that are well in excess of the 15 watts/sq ft (160 watts/sq m) recommended for mist systems, so they must be fitted with effective thermostats, otherwise damagingly high temperatures may occur in sunny weather.

Cold frames

Cold frames provide a valuable increase in soil and air temperatures while maintaining high humidity and providing light for plants to grow successfully. They can be used to raise seedlings early in the season, protect grafts, and propagate leafless and leafy cuttings. They may also be fitted with bottom heat (see opposite).

Because such low structures have no great volume, they easily overheat in sunny conditions unless ventilated and shaded well (see "Cold frames," p.489). Conversely, when temperatures fall below 23°F (-5°C), frames must be insulated with thick layers of burlap, straw, or salt hay to avoid cold damage to the plant material.

CIRCULATING AIR IN A COLD FRAME

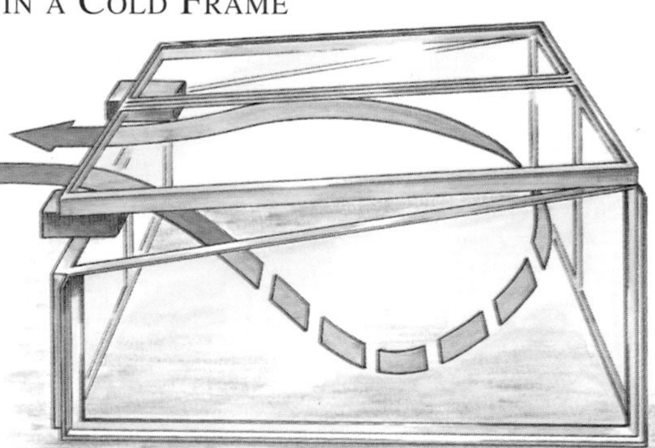

Since cold air expands and rises as it heats up, the lid of a cold frame must be propped open in warm weather to allow some air to escape and the temperature to remain reasonably cool.

Cloches and polytunnels outdoors

Glass and clear plastic cloches and tunnels are most often used to give seedlings an early start in the season in the vegetable garden. A wide range of easily rooted cuttings also do well in such an environment (see "Cloches," p.490). Additional shading, such as shade netting, is required in bright, sunny weather.

Growing the propagated plant

To propagate plants well, the gardener needs not only to prepare the material properly but also to care for and grow on the young plants in a suitable environment until they have developed sufficiently to survive in the garden. At key stages during propagation, practical inexperience or carelessness may kill well-rooted plants.

Caring for plants being propagated

Since most forms of propagation involve cutting various parts of the plants being increased, plant tissues are exposed to possible infection; it is therefore important to maintain hygienic conditions in the propagating area. Tools and benches should be regularly and thoroughly cleaned (using a mild disinfectant if necessary), and dead and damaged plant material removed. Potting soil mixes must always be fresh and sterile. Fungicidal solutions may also be applied to give protection to seedlings (such as captan) and leafy cuttings (such as captan or thiram), following the manufacturer's instructions.

When preparing pots or trays of soil mix for sowing seed, lightly firm the soil mix using a presser board, especially around the edges of the container. Water is drawn up through the soil mix by capillary action and, without this firming, air pockets occur and the water columns essential for capillary rise are broken. However, do not overfirm soil-based mixes: a medium filled with roots must be well aerated and have an open structure for optimum plant growth.

FIRMING THE SOIL MIX

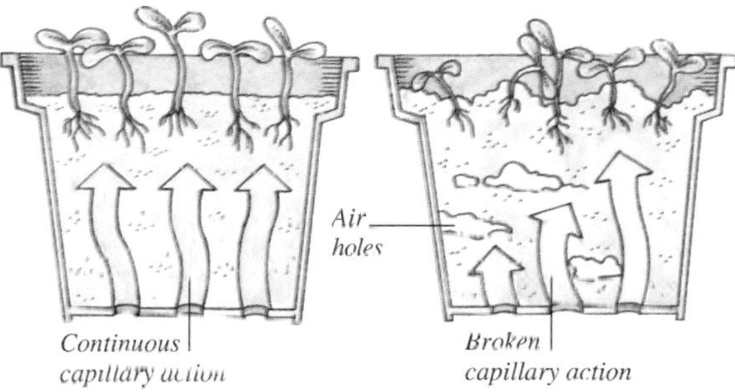

Ensure that seeds are germinated in evenly pressed, level soil mix so that capillary action and therefore seedling growth are not hindered by air pockets in the soil mix.

The soil mixes in which propagated plants are growing should be moist, but not wet, at all times. Too wet a medium will reduce the oxygen available, and the roots may die or succumb to disease. It is also important to maintain the correct environment until the young plants are sturdy enough to be hardened off (see "The propagation environment," opposite). Prick out seedlings to avoid overcrowding, since unless air is allowed to circulate freely around young plants, stagnant conditions may arise and cause damping off (p.566). Remove fallen leaves and dead matter immediately.

Most organic potting mixes are acid (with a pH value of less than 7), and the ideal range for an organic mix is pH 5–5.5. Test kits are available to measure the pH. A very alkaline soil or soil mix reduces the amount of phosphorus, iron, boron, and manganese available to the plant, whereas too acid a soil reduces the available calcium and magnesium. For feeding the plants, a commercial liquid fertilizer should be applied strictly in accordance with the manufacturer's instructions.

DAMPING OFF

Seedlings are more likely to damp off if they are overcrowded, especially if grown in damp, poorly ventilated conditions, or if they are allowed to suffer cold damage.

Hardening off

Hardening off, or acclimatizing the propagated plants to the outside conditions, must not be rushed since, over a period of days, the natural waxes coating the leaves undergo changes in form and thickness to reduce the rate of water loss. The stomatal pores on the leaf also need to adapt to a less supportive environment.

Turn off the heat, if appropriate, in the propagator or mist unit. Then, in the daytime, raise the covers for increasingly long periods. Finally, the covers may be removed for both day and night. This process also applies to plants grown under plastic bags. If the plant has been in the protective environment of a greenhouse and eventually needs to be planted outdoors, move it next into a cold frame. This, too, should be closed at first, then opened in stages. The hardening-off process may take two to three weeks.

Outdoor nursery beds

If propagating plants in any quantity, an outdoor nursery bed can provide the best conditions in which to grow on recently propagated plants and young seedlings in pots and other containers, once they have been hardened off. The nursery bed may be of any suitable size. First prepare a level site and then enclose it with 3in (8cm) high, wooden edging boards. There are two types of outdoor bed: water-permeable fabric beds and sand beds.

WATER-PERMEABLE FABRIC BED

Use edging boards to enclose the nursery bed and line with water-permeable fabric placed directly onto the soil.

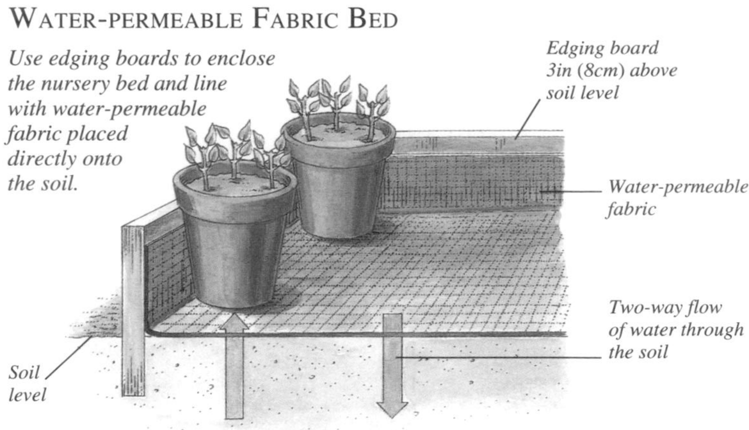

SAND BED

With this type of nursery bed, the containers are set directly onto the coarse sand topping.

Edging board 3in (8cm) above soil level

Sand

Plastic sheeting cut 1in (2.5cm) below the top of the edging boards

Two-way flow of water through the sand

Soil level

Leveled soil

Water-permeable fabric beds
In this, the simpler option, black polypropylene, woven fabric, or landscape fabric is laid over the prepared soil surface within the wooden edge boards. The fabric suppresses weeds and helps to isolate plants set on its surface from soilborne diseases. Water-permeable fabric beds also enable containers to drain freely, yet give the plants access to soil water through capillary action. If the soil is not well drained and sandy, or if the surface is uneven, level it with sand before laying the fabric.

Sand beds
A sand bed has the advantage over a water-permeable fabric bed of reducing the amount of watering necessary. Lay an oversize plastic sheet that is folded double over the prepared soil and up over the edging boards. Cover the plastic with coarse, lime-free sand to within 1in (2.5cm) of the top of the edging boards. Then trim the plastic sheeting to the sand level. Fill in to the top of the edging boards with more sand and level off by drawing another board across the top. Place containers directly on the sand. The sand enclosed within the plastic liner provides a water reservoir, which reduces the frequency of watering needed and prevents potting soil mixes from drying out. Excess water drains away between the boards and the plastic sheeting. More complex sand bed designs incorporate drainage pipes and automatic watering systems.

Advanced techniques

Since the mid-20th century, many new propagation methods have been introduced commercially. These are, as yet, generally confined to nurseries using advanced technologies, but the results of their developments are affecting several branches of commercial and amateur horticulture.

Micropropagation

Micropropagation uses explants, or tiny pieces of young plant material. Each explant is grown on in a glass or plastic container in a medium containing organic nutrients, mineral salts, hormones, and other elements needed for growth, and is placed in a closely controlled, sterile environment. The explant multiplies to form numerous shoots or complete plantlets, which are then rooted as microcuttings or, if they have already rooted, weaned to greenhouse conditions. Sterile conditions are vital throughout, and transfer of the plant material from the culture to a greenhouse is especially difficult.

Micropropagation is used mainly for valuable plants, for example for the rapid introduction of new cultivars, for plants difficult to propagate by other means, and to produce disease-free stock. Technical improvements and automation should eventually reduce costs substantially.

MICROPROPAGATION

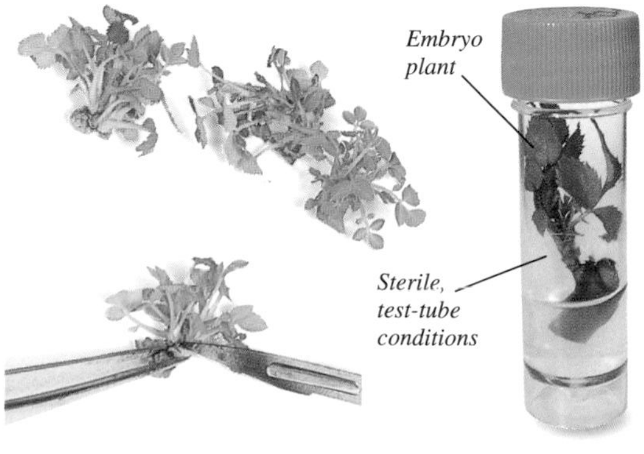

A microscopic portion of plant tissue is extracted from a plant under sterile conditions. This portion, or explant, is then divided (right) and grown on in test-tube conditions (far right). Once sufficiently large, these embryo plants may be further divided or grown on to form plantlets.

Genetic engineering

It is now possible to identify and even extract particular genes from a plant's cells and to introduce these into another cell, not necessarily of the same species. Using such methods, resistance to certain fungi, viruses, and pests has been introduced into otherwise susceptible species. For example, some lettuce, tomato, and pepper cultivars that are susceptible to cucumber mosaic virus can be given a gene that minimizes its effect. Petunias and tobacco plants can now also be made resistant to certain herbicides.

The potential for genetic engineering is vast, especially for the development of agricultural crops such as rice and other vegetables. Examples include special potatoes that do not suffer from low-temperature sweetening for chip manufacture; canola seed that has been altered so that it yields more oil for food processing; and tomatoes into which a gene has been inserted to allow them to be harvested commercially while red and ripe (rather than while green and unripe), so that they are tastier but firmer and less prone to damage during transportation to market.

Advances in seed propagation

New methods have been developed to improve the speed and uniformity of seed germination for the gardener. Seeds are soaked in solutions of salts, such as sodium chloride or potassium nitrate, or in polyethylene glycol solutions. They are thus primed for germination but are dried before the radicle emerges and are then packaged ready for sale. The seeds can be sown conventionally as required.

Fluid drilling and pelleted seed have been developed to make uniform sowing easier. In fluid drilling, seed primed for germination is contained within a gel base, for example in a fungicide-free wallpaper paste, which can then be squeezed along the seed drill. In pelleted seed, primed seed is coated in an inert material that may contain fungicides, nutrients, and/or a fluorescent dye. The seeds can then be handled individually and sown more evenly. Pelleted seed is made for bedding plants with small seeds and some vegetable crops.

Artificially produced seeds

Some flower tissues, when introduced into a special liquid culture medium, develop numerous embryos – each similar to the embryo within a seed. Artificial seed is produced by separating the embryos from the medium and giving them a synthetic coating. This process is known as somatic embryogenesis and may eventually lead to the manufacture of vast numbers of genetically uniform, so-called, seeds.

Hydroculture

Instead of soil mix, seeds and cuttings are propagated in a culture solution or an inert supporting medium, such as sand, gravel, clay granules, or rock wool, and bathed in nutrient solution (see THE INDOOR GARDEN, "Hydroculture," p.447). This technique is used in regions where a suitable soil mix is not easily obtainable.

7

PLANT PROBLEMS

EVEN THE MOST carefully tended gardens may suffer problems caused by plant diseases and disorders, the ravages of pests, and the choking of plants by weeds. By following all the principles of good cultivation outlined in this book, it should be possible to keep these problems to a minimum. When a problem does arise, it is essential that you diagnose it, and then decide upon the appropriate course of action to remedy the situation. The choice of treatments available to amateurs now includes a variety of organic and biological methods, as well as the use of chemicals. Good garden management depends upon learning how to prevent plant problems from occurring and, if this fails, to recognize them at an early stage when they can be treated more easily.

Pests, diseases, and physiological disorders

Most plant problem symptoms are easy to see. A tree, shrub, or plant may wilt or become discolored, or it may fail to come into leaf or to bloom at all. Insects, which may be the cause of the plant's poor health, may be seen on part or all of the plant. Sometimes an infestation or disease in the roots may be noticed first through symptoms in the leaves. This chapter gives detailed information on how to prevent and control the pests, diseases, and physiological disorders that can cause such problems.

What is a pest?

Pests are animals that cause damage to cultivated plants. Some, such as slugs, snails, and rabbits, are well known; most, however, are small invertebrates such as mites, nematodes, sowbugs, and millipedes, which are less evidently plant pests. The largest group by far in this category are the insects. Pests may damage or destroy any part of a plant or, in some cases, even the whole plant. They feed in various ways – by sap sucking, leaf mining, defoliating, or tunneling through stems, roots, or fruits. Sometimes they cause abnormal growths known as galls. Some pests also indirectly damage plants by spreading viral or fungal diseases, while others coat plants with a sugary excrement (honeydew) that encourages the growth of sooty molds.

What is a disease?

A plant disease is any pathological condition caused by other organisms, such as bacteria, fungi, or viruses. Fungal diseases are the most common, bacterial diseases less common. The symptoms that these organisms produce vary considerably in appearance and severity, but the growth or health of the plant is almost always affected and, in severe attacks, the plant may even be killed. The rate of infection is affected by factors such as weather and growing conditions. In some cases, the disease-causing organism (pathogen) is spread by a carrier, such as an aphid. The pathogen is sometimes visible as a discoloration on the plant, as with rusts. Symptoms such as discoloration, distortion, or wilting are typical signs of infection.

HOW TO DIAGNOSE PLANT SYMPTOMS

In a case where it is obvious that the leaves have been eaten away by some kind of pest, turn to the section on "Eaten leaves" to identify the cause.

When a plant shows several symptoms, look either in the section on the whole plant or in the part that deals with the worst aspect, here discolored leaves.

What is a disorder?

Plant disorders usually result from nutritional deficiencies or from unsuitable growing or storage conditions. An inappropriate temperature range, inadequate or erratic water or food supply, poor light, or unsatisfactory atmospheric conditions may all lead to physiological plant disorders. Problems may also be caused by deficiencies of the mineral salts that are essential for healthy plant growth.

Weather, cultural, or soil conditions may lead to a range of plants being affected. The problems become apparent through symptoms such as discolored leaves or stem wilt. A plant that lacks water, food, or the appropriate environmental conditions not only will appear unhealthy but will also be far less able to resist attack from either insect pests or diseases caused by fungi, viruses, or bacteria. Unless problems are correctly diagnosed and treated, affected plants may die.

How to use this chapter

This part of the book enables the gardener to diagnose and treat plant problems. It is organized according to the site of the symptoms (such as distorted flowers or discolored leaves) in sections covering leaves, stems, flowers, fruit, roots and tubers, bulbs, whole plant, and lawns. Within the main sections the problems are grouped by the type of symptom; for example, all yellow leaf spots will be found together.

To identify a problem, look in the appropriate section. If you cannot find it there, turn to the cross-references at the end of that section. Each entry lists the plants affected, the symptoms, the cause of the problem, and how to control it. On p.574 is a list of the controls mentioned, together with the names of treatments currently available.

Prevention of problems

Always buy strong, vigorous plants that look healthy. Do not purchase plants that are showing dieback or discolored stems, that have leaves that are an abnormal color for the time of year, or that are wilted or distorted. Do not buy plants showing significant pest infestations or disease. Check the root ball of container-grown trees and shrubs: do not buy them if they are either potbound or showing poor root development.

Check that the plant is suitable for its intended position, taking into account the type, texture, and pH of the soil, the exposure of the site, and whether the plant is hardy in your area. Plant carefully, making sure that the ground is well prepared and that the roots are properly spread out. Each type of plant has different requirements for watering, feeding, and, where appropriate, pruning. If a plant is badly diseased or infested by pests, it may be impossible to revive it; such plants should be removed, especially if there is a risk that the trouble might spread to healthy plants nearby. If the plant does not thrive, try to discover the underlying cause and treat as necessary to overcome the problem.

Organic control

Organic control uses natural methods to help plants both resist and recover from attack by pests and diseases. Such methods have long played their part in gardening, but in recent years they have attracted an increasing level of interest.

Organic treatments and traps

A few chemical preparations originate from natural sources; pyrethrum, for example, is derived from the pyrethrum daisy. Other organic treatments are rotenone dust and sulfur dust. These may be obtained as ready-made powders or liquid sprays; they are safe to use and spray damage is not a problem. They have short persistence, however, and act only on contact with the pest or disease, which necessitates regular and thorough applications. Organic traps may easily be constructed. Earwigs may be trapped in inverted flower pots, and wireworms in old potatoes or carrots spitted on a stick and buried. In greenhouses, whiteflies (which are attracted to the color yellow) may be caught on a piece of yellow cardboard smeared with grease. Inspect these traps regularly and dispose of the pests.

COMPANION PLANTING
Dwarf marigolds (Tagetes patula) *attract hoverflies, which feed on aphids that may attack nearby plants.*

ORGANIC EARWIG TRAP

An inverted flower pot filled with dried grass and placed over a stake attracts earwigs (see p.550). Remove the pot and burn the grass every other day.

Companion planting

Certain companion plants grown in association with a crop can help to reduce pest and disease attack. For example, some strong-smelling herbs such as mint and garlic may repel pests that are attracted to plants by smell, thereby keeping them away from nearby plants. Deliberate planting of host plants may deflect pests away from other plants or attract predators to feed on the pests: because nasturtiums (*Tropaeolum*) are susceptible to aphids, plant dwarf marigolds (*Tagetes patula*) nearby since these attract hoverflies, which feed on the aphids.

Resistant plants

Some plants are resistant to attack by pests or diseases. Plant breeders have been able to profit from this, and have produced cultivars with a higher-than-average resistance to some pests or diseases. Cultivated plants resistant to pests include some butterhead lettuces, which are seldom attacked by the lettuce root aphid. Plants resistant to disease include some tomato cultivars, which resist tomato leaf mold, and several modern shrub roses, which show some resistance to diseases such as powdery mildew, rust, and blackspot.

In some cases, the resistance appears to be total, but even a resistant plant may succumb to a given disease if its growing conditions are poor or if other factors, such as adverse weather, weaken the plant. Before buying plants, check if there are disease- or pest-resistant cultivars readily available from local suppliers or via mail order. The availability of resistant plants varies from year to year, so check catalogs annually for this type of information.

Garden hygiene

Maintaining a tidy and well-managed garden is one of the most important ways to keep pests and diseases under control. Select vigorous plants and ensure that they have the optimum growing conditions for successful growth. Examine plants to identify any new problem as soon as possible, since a well-established infection or infestation is always far more difficult to deal with than one that is identified and treated early.

The regular removal and disposal of diseased parts of plants, and some pests such as cabbage white caterpillars, will certainly help to control infections. Any debris from infested or diseased plants (or any material suspected of being infested or diseased) should be discarded, otherwise the pest or pathogen may survive, overwinter, and reinfect the plant in spring. Garden debris should be discarded or, where appropriate, composted.

Crop rotation

Rotating vegetable crops, usually on a three- or four-year basis, helps prevent soilborne pests and diseases from building up to a damaging level. For further details on planning a crop rotation system, see THE VEGETABLE GARDEN, "Rotation," p.303. Although a strict rotation plan is generally used for vegetables, it is also worth rotating annuals and bulbs where feasible, since this reduces the buildup of diseases like aster yellows and tulip fire/blight.

Growing a particular kind of plant in the same ground for a number of years may also lead to problems (for example "Rose-sick soil," p.120). If a disease such as aster yellows becomes evident, remove all the plants and grow other, botanically unrelated plants that are not susceptible on the site.

Biological control

This term describes the limiting of pest damage by the deliberate introduction of natural enemies such as predators, parasites, and diseases. In the greenhouse, where pests may have developed immunity to chemicals, it is often the only effective way of controlling them.

Use of biological controls is less practical in the relatively uncontrolled conditions of the open garden, especially where pesticides are used, since they may kill the controls as well as the pests. Not all pests and diseases can be countered by appropriate biological controls; other controls may be introduced as more work is done on insect and disease ecology.

Greenhouse controls

Biological controls for use in the greenhouse may be obtained from specialist suppliers. Some examples are listed below.

PEST	BIOLOGICAL CONTROL
Spider mites	Predatory mites (*Metaseiulus occidentalis*)
Whiteflies	The parasitic wasp *Encarsia formosa*
Mealybugs	Ladybugs (*Cryptolaemus montrouzieri*)
Soft scale insects	The parasitic wasp *Metaphycus helvolus*
Aphids	Fly larva predators (*Aphidoletes aphidimyza*)
Thrips	Predatory mites (*Amblyseius* spp.)
Black vine weevil larvae	Nematode predators (*Heterorhabditis* spp.)
Caterpillars	The bacterial disease *Bacillus thuringiensis*

Introduce the control before plants are heavily infested, because it may be a number of weeks before it becomes effective.

Most predators and parasites require daytime temperatures of at least 70°F (21°C) and good light intensity in order to breed faster than the pests. Restrict the use of pesticides, since most are harmful to biological controls; the exceptions are pirimicarb against aphids, and insecticidal soaps,

which control a wide range of small insects and mites. Some of the most troublesome pests, especially spider mites, whiteflies, and black vine weevil larvae, have now developed such a high degree of immunity to the pesticides that were employed against them that biological control is usually the only effective treatment now available.

Beneficial garden animals

Insects and other creatures found in gardens are by no means all destructive. Many are not only useful to the plant but actually essential for its survival; for example, a large number of fruits, vegetables, and flowers rely on pollinating insects, such as honeybees, to carry pollen from one flower to another to enable fertilization to take place. In other cases, some species of natural predator can help to control certain types of pest and should therefore be encouraged to visit the garden.

Raccoons, skunks, frogs, and toads feed on many ground-dwelling plant pests. Birds may be the cause of some damage in the garden, but this disadvantage is usually far outweighed by the enormous quantities of insect pests that they devour. Some invertebrates, for example centipedes, prey on a range of soil-dwelling pests. It is possible to distinguish centipedes from the somewhat similar millipedes (which are often harmful) by the number of legs that are carried on each segment of their bodies: centipedes have only one pair per body segment, whereas millipedes have two pairs.

Spiders are also useful allies because their webs trap countless insects. Certain insects, however, are invaluable in the garden. Ladybugs, for example, are beneficial since both the larvae and the adult beetles feed on destructive pests such as aphids. Ants and wasps, whose activities might damage some plants, may still help the gardener by preying on other insect pests.

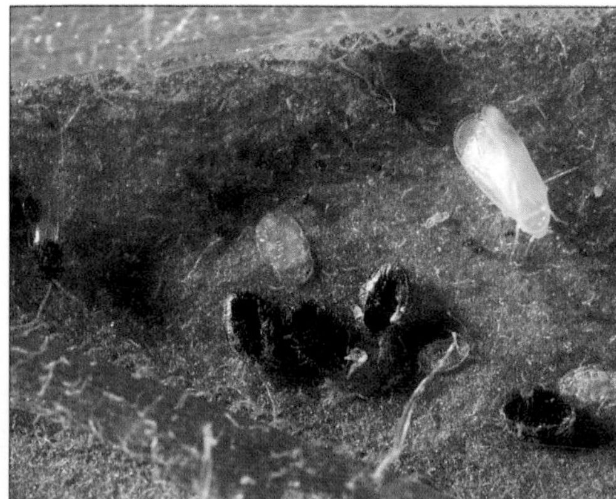

BIOLOGICAL CONTROL
Encarsia formosa *wasps parasitize whitefly larvae, causing them to blacken and eventually die.*

Chemical control

Chemical control is the term used to describe the action of destroying plant pests and diseases by applying synthetic compounds to plants or soil. Although the emphasis on organic control is presently becoming stronger, the responsible and sparing use of chemicals still has a valuable role to play in pest and disease control. A sensible combination of the most suitable aspects of both methods may often provide the best solution to these difficult and often recurrent problems.

Pesticides and fungicides

Most pesticides (which are used to kill insects, mites, and other pests) and fungicides (which are used to control diseases caused by fungi) work either by being brought into contact with the pest or disease organisms, or they are systemic.

Contact pesticides kill pests when they crawl over a treated surface or when they are directly hit by the chemical (when sprayed, for example). Contact fungicides may kill germinating fungal spores and prevent further infection, but they have little effect on established fungal growths.

Systemic chemicals are absorbed into the plant tissues and are then transported by the sap stream throughout the entire plant. Fungicides of this type, for example triforine, kill fungi in the plant tissues. Systemic pesticides, such as dimethoate and oxydemeton-methyl, are predominantly used against sap-sucking pests and are less useful (unless they are mixed with a contact compound) against pests that have chewing mouthparts, such as caterpillars, beetles, and earwigs.

Thorough spraying of affected plants, especially on the undersides of leaves, is essential with all pesticides. Pesticide-resistant strains may sometimes occur, particularly with persistent greenhouse pests such as whiteflies and spider mites.

Fungi that are frequently treated with systemic fungicides may also develop resistant strains. This problem can sometimes be overcome by using a different type of compound, but with greenhouse pests the use of biological control (where possible) is often a better alternative (see opposite).

Formulation of chemical preparations

The active ingredient of a chemical preparation kills the organism, and the way in which a preparation has been formulated determines its efficacy and use. Pesticides and fungicides are available as concentrated liquids, dusts, powders (with which a wetting agent may be incorporated to ensure penetration of the active ingredient), smokes, baits, and ready-to-use diluted liquids. Many of these preparations are now formulated for maximum effectiveness and safety (read labels carefully), for gardeners and for the environment, although in the past many environmentally harmful chemicals were available.

Using chemicals safely

The federal Environmental Protection Agency (EPA) classifies pesticides into three groups: *banned, restricted* (for use by licensed applicators only), and *general.* Home gardeners may use products in the general category only. Check with state and county authorities to learn which pesticides you can use. Recommendations in this book are intended for general guidance only. They were current at the time of the book's production. Some products are not approved for use in Canada.

Pesticide labeling is dictated by law. **Usage must be consistent with labeling.** For instance, if a product is labeled for use only on fruit trees, it is illegal to use it on leafy vegetables. Also, if a pesticide is labeled for use only as a wettable powder for spraying, for example, it cannot be applied dry directly to the soil. Penalties for misuse are severe. If you have any questions about pesticides, discontinue use and confirm that the application will be in accordance with law. Always take precautions:

- think before you spray: is it really necessary?
- choose the chemical carefully – make sure it is the right one for the job;
- apply the preparation at the rate and frequency stated on the label;
- never combine chemicals unless the manufacturer recommends this;
- always observe any suggested precautions;
- do not spray in the wind, to avoid damaging adjacent plants;
- do not spray during the middle part of the day (or at any time of the day on hot days) because hot, sunny weather increases the risk of scorching plants;
- avoid contact with skin and eyes;
- do not inhale dusts, smokes, or sprays;
- make sure that the chemical does not drift into other people's gardens;
- keep pets and children away during use;
- never eat, drink, or smoke when applying;
- dispose of any excess carefully and wash out any apparatus thoroughly;
- use apparatus for chemicals alone;
- store chemicals out of reach of children and animals;
- store chemicals in their original containers, with their original labels, and keep any explanatory leaflets with them;
- wash hands thoroughly after use.

Phytotoxicity

Some plants are likely to suffer adverse reactions to fungicides and insecticides. This is known as phytotoxicity. The manufacturer's instructions often list those species that should not be treated. Such lists cannot, however, be complete, since the reaction of many ornamental plants to certain chemicals is as yet unknown. Test on small areas first.

Various other factors, including the stage of growth and the environmental conditions surrounding the plant, can also increase the likelihood of a plant being damaged by chemical treatments. For example, young seedlings, cuttings, and flower petals are much more sensitive than mature foliage to variations in the growing conditions, and may be adversely affected by the application of some chemical treatments. Similarly, plants under stress should never be treated with chemicals.

Leaf problems

Eaten leaves

Slugs and snails

Plants affected All seedlings, climbing plants, herbaceous perennials, hostas, small annuals, bulbous plants, vegetables, including potatoes (see also "Slugs," p.568), and strawberries.
Symptoms Holes appear in the foliage and stems may be stripped; silvery slime trails may be left on the leaves or the soil surface. Small holes are visible on the outside of bulbs and the underground part of their stems, leading to large cavities inside.

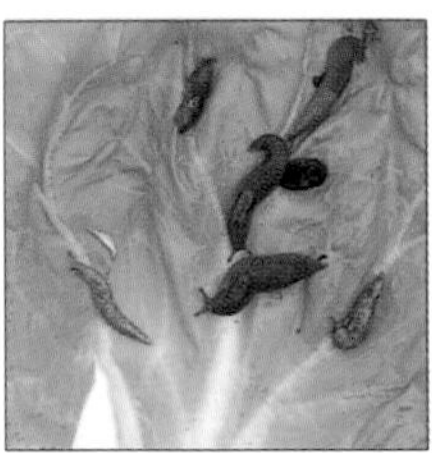

Slugs under leaves

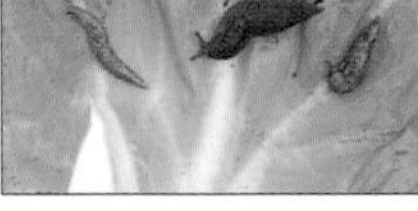

Holes in leaves

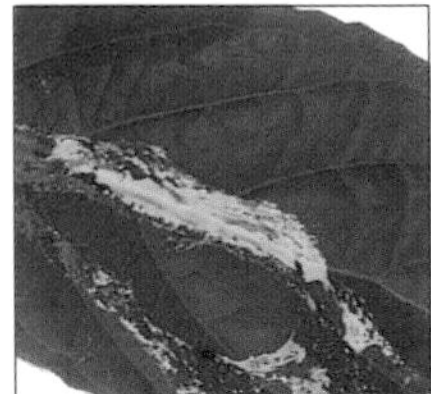

Silvery slime trails

Stems stripped

Cause Slugs (e.g. *Milax*, *Limax*, and *Deroceras* spp.) and snails (e.g. *Helix aspersa*), slimy-bodied mollusks that feed mainly at night or after rain.
Control Cultivate regularly to expose eggs, and avoid the use of organic fertilizers and mulches. Scatter methiocarb or metaldehyde slug pellets among plants, or spray with liquid metaldehyde or silicon dioxide.

Earwigs

Plants affected Shrubs, perennials, and annuals, commonly dahlias, chrysanthemums, and clematis. Also apricots and peaches.
Symptoms Young leaves are eaten in summer. See p.563 for other symptoms.
Cause The earwig (*Forficula auricularia*), which is a yellowish brown insect ³/₄in (2cm) long with a pair of curved pincers. Earwigs hide during the day and feed at night.
Control Loosely stuff pots with hay or straw, and invert pots on stakes among susceptible plants (see p.548); earwigs use these traps as daytime shelters. Remove and destroy pests. Alternatively, spray at dusk with permethrin, diazinon, carbaryl, or rotenone.

Adult earwigs

Leaves eaten away

Sowbugs

Plants affected Seedlings and other soft growth, including strawberry fruits.
Symptoms Holes may appear in seedlings and in leaves near shoot tips, but sowbugs are not generally pests; they mainly eat decaying plant material and are often found on plants that have already been damaged by other pests and diseases.
Cause Sowbugs (e.g. *Oniscus*, *Porcellio*, and *Armadillidium* spp.), also known as pill bugs and roly-polys. They are gray or brownish gray, sometimes with white or yellow markings, and up to ¹/₂in (1cm) long with hard, segmented bodies. They feed at night and hide during the day in dark shelters or under rocks or tree stumps.
Control Always clear away plant debris and keep greenhouses tidy to reduce shelter. Protect seedlings with carbaryl dust, or scatter methiocarb pellets.

Millipedes

Plants affected Seedlings and other soft growth, strawberry fruits, and potato tubers.
Symptoms Seedlings and soft growth are eaten; slug damage on potato tubers and bulbs is enlarged (see p.568). Roots and stems may be eaten in dry periods. Damage is rarely serious.

Common millipedes

Cause Millipedes (e.g. *Blaniulus*, *Orthomorpha*, and *Spirobolus* spp.), black, gray, brown, or creamy white animals that feed below or at soil level. They have hard, segmented bodies with two pairs of legs per segment (centipedes, which are beneficial predators, have only one pair per segment). The spotted snake millipede (*Blaniulus guttulatus*) is the most damaging species. Its slender, creamy white body is up to ³/₄in (2cm) long with a row of red dots along each side. Millipedes are encouraged by soils with a high organic content.
Control Cultivate the soil thoroughly and maintain good hygiene. Use inorganic rather than organic fertilizers in problem areas, especially where potatoes are being grown. Millipedes, once present, are difficult to control, but carbaryl dust or methiocarb pellets may have some effect.

Flea beetles

Plants affected The seedlings of brassicas, leafy vegetables, radishes, wallflowers (*Cheiranthus*), and stocks (*Matthiola*).
Symptoms Holes and pits appear on upper surface of leaves; plants may die if attack is severe.

Cause Small black or metallic blue beetles (e.g. *Phyllotreta* spp.), sometimes with a yellow stripe running down each wing case. They are usually ¹/₁₆in (2mm) long, with enlarged hind legs that enable them to leap off from plant surfaces when disturbed. They overwinter in plant debris.
Control Clear away plant debris, particularly in fall. Sow seed in warm soil and water seedlings regularly to help rapid growth through the vulnerable stages. Apply diazinon granules before sowing, or dust emerged seedlings with rotenone, pyrethrum, or carbaryl, or spray with diazinon.

Asparagus beetles

Plants affected Asparagus.
Symptoms Leaves are eaten; the epidermis is removed from stems, causing the upper growth to dry and turn brown. Damage occurs between late spring and early fall.
Cause Both the adult and larval asparagus beetle (*Crioceris asparagi*). The adult beetles are ¹/₄in (6mm) long, with yellow and black wing cases and a reddish thorax. The larvae are grayish yellow.

Adults *Larvae*

Control Pick off light infestations by hand. If serious, spray with pyrethrum, rotenone, or permethrin; if plants are in flower, spray at dusk to protect bees.

European viburnum beetles

Plants affected *Viburnum*.
Symptoms Holes are eaten in the leaves; this occurs first in early summer, when the foliage may be reduced to just veins, and then again in late summer.
Cause The European viburnum beetle (*Pyrrhalta viburni*). The initial period of damage in early summer is caused by the creamy white larvae, which are up to ¹/₄in (6mm) in length and have black markings. The second phase of damage, occurring in late summer, is caused by the adult beetles, which are grayish brown in color.
Control Spray with permethrin, pyrethrum, malathion, diazinon, or insecticidal soap when the larvae first appear.

Red lily beetles

Plants affected Bulbous plants, especially lilies (*Lilium*) and fritillaries (*Fritillaria*), and occasionally *Polygonatum*.
Symptoms Leaves and flowers are eaten from early spring to midfall.
Cause The adult and

larval red lily beetle (*Lilioceris lilii*). Adults are 3/8in (9mm) long and bright red. Larvae are reddish brown with black heads, and covered in black excrement.
Control A long egg-laying and emergence period (midspring to midsummer) makes control difficult. Pick off by hand; otherwise spray with permethrin, insecticidal soap, or diazinon.

Black vine weevils

Adult weevil

Plants affected Yews (*Taxus*) and shrubs, mainly rhododendrons, hydrangeas, *Euonymus*, and camellias; also grapes, strawberries, other herbaceous plants, and fuchsias.
Symptoms Notches appear in leaf margins, often near the ground, from midspring to midfall.
Cause The adult black vine weevil (*Otiorhynchus sulcatus*), a grayish black beetle 3/8in (9mm) long, with a short snout and elbowed antennae; it emerges at night to feed.

Irregular holes in leaf margins

Control Damage occurs over a long period, and control is difficult, although good hygiene and the removal of plant debris reduce the number of hiding places. Established plants can tolerate damage, but, if the problem is serious, spray at dusk with permethrin, which will give slight control.
See also "Black vine weevil larvae," p.572.

Plant bugs

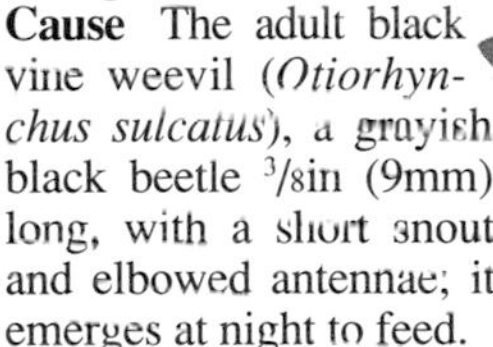

Plants affected Shrubs and perennials (especially chrysanthemums, asters, gladioli, zinnias, and dahlias), annuals, vegetables (rarely), and fruits.
Symptoms The leaves at shoot tips are distorted with small holes. Damage occurs in summer. See p.563 for other symptoms.
Cause Tarnished plant bugs (*Lygus lineolaris*), brown insects 1/4in (6mm) long. Four-lined plant bugs (*Poecilocapsus lineatus*) are greenish with four black wing stripes. Their toxic saliva kills plant tissues, causing leaves and flowers to wilt and die.
Control In winter, clear up plant debris. Spray at first sign of damage, with dimethoate, carbaryl, methoxychlor, pyrethrum, or permethrin.

Leaf-cutting bees

Plants affected Roses mainly but also trees and other shrubs.
Symptoms Lozenge-shaped or circular pieces of uniform size are removed from the margins of the leaf.
Cause Leaf-cutting bees (*Megachile* spp.), which use the leaf pieces to build their nests. They are up to 1/2in (1cm) long and have ginger hairs on the underside of their abdomen.
Control Leaf-cutting bees are of some benefit in the garden as pollinating insects and, unless plants are heavily damaged, control is not necessary. If they are a persistent nuisance, swat the bees as they return to the leaf to feed.

Sawfly larvae

Sawfly larvae eating

Plants affected Trees, shrubs, perennials, bulbous plants, and fruits. Particularly affected are conifers, willows (*Salix*), *Aruncus dioicus*, *Geum*, *Aquilegia*, Solomon's seal (*Polygonatum*), roses, gooseberries, and currants.
Symptoms Plants are defoliated.
Cause The larvae of various sawfly species (e.g. *Nematus*, *Pristiphora*, and *Diprion* spp.); caterpillar-like larvae that are up to 1 1/4in (3cm) long and generally green, sometimes with black spots. Bristly rose slug (*Cladius isomeris*), a serious pest in the East, is greenish white with stout spines. Most larvae grip the leaf edge and wave their bodies in an S shape when they are disturbed, but this does not occur with larvae that attack on *Geum* or Solomon's seal.

Leaves eaten away

Control Where possible, remove by hand. Spray serious infestations with pyrethrum, permethrin, insecticidal soap, or malathion.

Colorado potato beetles

Plants affected Potatoes, tomatoes, eggplants, peppers, flowering tobacco (*Nicotiana*).
Symptoms Leaves are eaten, leaving only the main vein. Crop yield is greatly reduced. Plants may be killed.
Cause Larvae of the Colorado potato beetle (*Leptinotarsa decemlineata*), orange-red grubs up to 1/2in (1cm). More visible are the bright yellow and black striped adults, and the orange egg masses on the underside of the leaves.
Control Hand-pick adults and remove egg masses. Rotate crops. Spray larvae with San Diego strain of *Bacillus thuringiensis*. Spray large grubs and adults with insecticidal soap, carbaryl, or methoxychlor.

Cabbage caterpillars

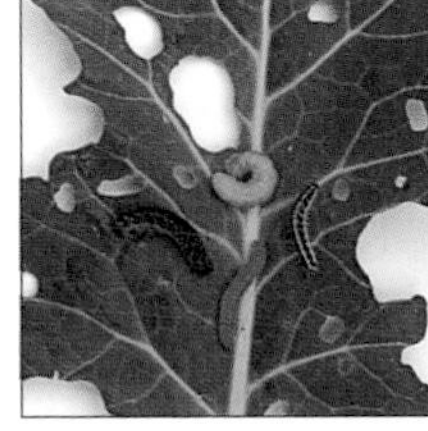

Plants affected Mainly brassicas, including cabbages, cauliflowers, and Brussels sprouts. Some perennial and annual ornamentals, e.g. nasturtiums (*Tropaeolum*).
Symptoms Holes appear in the foliage between late spring and early fall, and caterpillars may be found in the hearts of brassicas and on leaves.
Cause Caterpillars of the small cabbage white butterfly (*Pieris rapae*), pale green with velvety hairs.
Control Pick off the young caterpillars by hand. For serious infestations, use the bacterial control *Bacillus thuringiensis*, or apply rotenone, pyrethrum, permethrin, or carbaryl.

Gypsy moths

Plants affected Many deciduous trees and shrubs, especially apples (*Malus*), hawthorns (*Crataegus*), oaks (*Quercus*), and lindens (*Tilia*).
Symptoms Leaves are eaten and plants may be defoliated. Repeated attacks will kill plants.
Cause Larvae of the gypsy moth (*Lymantria dispar*), which hatch from overwintering egg masses laid on the bark. While young, the larvae spin silken threads that act as parachutes and carry them from tree to tree. The larvae are black with two white lines down the back separating rows of spots, blue at the front and red at the rear. The caterpillars are covered with tufts of long hair. They grow to 2in (5cm) when mature and are voracious feeders that can defoliate an entire tree in 2–3 days.
Control Spray with *Bacillus thuringiensis* as soon as noticed. Watch for overwintering egg masses and scrape off or spray with mineral oil.

Caterpillars

Plants affected Many garden plants.
Symptoms Leaves, and occasionally also flowers, are eaten away.
Cause Caterpillars of various species of butterfly and moth, which feed on plant material. The most common in gardens are cabbage caterpillars (see left), tent caterpillars (see p.553), and leaf tiers and rollers (see p.554).
Control Pick off caterpillars by hand, if possible. For serious infestations, spray with *Bacillus thuringiensis*, carbaryl, or insecticidal soap.

Small animals

Plants affected Low-growing plants, young trees.
Symptoms Low-growing leaves are eaten, and the bark of young trees is gnawed away, especially during spells of cold weather.
Cause and control See p.572 for details.

Deer

Plants affected Most garden plants, especially trees, shrubs (including roses), and herbaceous plants.
Symptoms Shoots and leaves are eaten; tree bark is rubbed and frayed, and stripped in winter.
Cause and control See p.572 for details.

See also "Tent caterpillars," p.553; "Leaf tiers and rollers," p.554; "Bacterial leaf spots and blotches," p.554; "Shothole," p.554; "Cutworms," p.561; "Japanese beetles," p.563; and "Iris borers," p.566.

Discolored and wilted leaves

Aphids

Plants affected Trees, shrubs, climbing plants, roses, perennials, annuals, bulbous plants, vegetables, fruits, and indoor plants.
Symptoms Leaves are often sticky with honeydew (aphid excrement), blistered, or blackened by sooty molds; stems and buds may also be covered. See also p.557.

Black aphid on stem

Blistered leaf

Cause Aphids (including those known as greenfly or plant lice) that cluster on stems and the undersides of leaves, sucking the sap; some attack roots. They are up to ¼in (6mm) long, either wingless or winged, and green, yellow, brown, pink, gray, or black; some, e.g. the woolly apple aphid, are covered in a fluffy white wax. Aphids may transmit viruses (see pp.555, 562, and 565).
Control Aphids can be controlled by fly larva predators, such as *Aphidoletes aphidimyza*. Apply mineral oil in winter against aphid eggs on deciduous fruit trees and bushes. Spray other plants, before heavy infestations develop, with strong limewater, malathion, acephate, insecticidal soaps, pyrethrum, or rotenone, or use a systemic insecticide, such as dimethoate, oxydemeton-methyl, or pirimicarb.

Whiteflies

Plants affected Both indoor and outdoor flowering plants, also some vegetables and fruits.
Symptoms Leaves are covered with sticky honeydew (whitefly excrement) and a form of sooty mold. Small white insects fly off the plants when they are disturbed.

Adult whiteflies

Cause Whiteflies, active, white-winged insects 1/16in (1.6mm) long that rest beneath young leaves; the immature, scalelike nymphs, which are immobile, whitish green (or black if dead), flat, and oval, are also found here. Several species occur, the most widespread of which is the greenhouse whitefly (*Trialeurodes vaporariorum*). In the open, several plants are attacked by greenhouse whitefly and by *Aleyrodes* spp.

Whitefly nymphs

Control The parasitic wasp *Encarsia formosa* provides effective biological control in greenhouses from midspring to midfall, if introduced early. Both greenhouse and garden whiteflies may be sprayed with permethrin, pyrethrum, acephate, or insecticidal soaps on three or four occasions at five-day intervals; pesticide-resistant strains of greenhouse whitefly do, however, occur.

Mealybugs

Plants affected Indoor and greenhouse plants, succulents, vegetables, grapes, some tender fruits, and *Citrus*.
Symptoms A fluffy white substance appears in leaf and stem axils. Plants may be sticky with honeydew (excrement) and blackened with sooty molds. Roots may also be affected.
Cause Various mealybugs (e.g. *Pseudococcus* and *Phenacoccus*); soft-bodied, grayish white, wingless insects up to ¼in (6mm) long, often with white, waxy filaments trailing from their bodies. Root damage is caused by root mealybugs.
Control Outside, ladybugs (*Cryptolaemus montrouzieri*) give biological control. If this fails, spray with malathion, acephate, or an insecticidal soap at intervals of two weeks. Indoors, wipe with a swab dipped in a 50 percent rubbing alcohol solution.

Lace bugs

Plants affected Rhododendrons, evergreen azaleas, *Andromeda*, *Kalmia*, *Platanus*.
Symptoms Pale green to yellow mottling on the upper leaf surface, with sticky spots on the undersurface where feeding takes place.

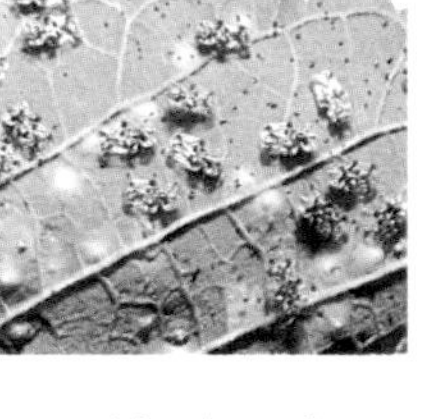

Cause Nymphs of *Stephanitis pyroides* (mostly on azalea) and *S. rhododendri*. Eggs are laid on the underside of the leaf or on twigs in fall and hatch in spring. There may be several generations each year.
Control Spray with carbaryl or insecticidal soaps in spring as overwintering eggs hatch, and repeat as needed during the summer.

Powdery mildew

Plants affected Trees, shrubs, roses, perennials, annuals, bulbous plants, vegetables, fruits, and many indoor plants.
Symptoms A fungal growth, usually white and powdery, appears on the leaves; on rhododendrons it is buff-colored and felty. Usually found on the upper surface, it may appear on the lower side only or on both sides. A purple discoloration may develop. Leaves yellow and fall early. Flowers and fruits are also affected (see p.564).

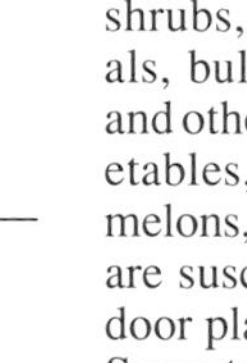

Cause Various fungi, including species of *Sphaerotheca*, *Oidium*, and *Uncinula*, which thrive on plants in dry soil. Some have restricted host ranges; others attack widely. Spores are spread by wind and rain splash; fungus may overwinter on host plants.
Control Avoid growing susceptible plants on dry sites; water and mulch as necessary. Remove and discard affected areas promptly. If the problem persists, use a suitable fungicide, for example dinocap, sulfur, or captan.

Downy mildew

Plants affected Perennials, annuals, stocks (*Matthiola*), bulbous plants, vegetables, including brassicas, some fruits, lettuces, and many seedlings.
Symptoms A fluffy or mealy white fungal growth develops on the lower surface of the foliage, while the upper surface is blotched either yellow or brown; the older leaves are usually the most seriously affected. Growth is stunted and the plant is prone to secondary infections such as gray mold/*Botrytis* (see below).
Cause Species of *Peronospora* and *Bremia* fungi, which are encouraged by humid conditions.
Control Sow seeds thinly and do not overcrowd plants. Improve ventilation, air circulation, and drainage; avoid overhead watering. Remove affected leaves and spray plants with zineb.

Gray mold/*Botrytis*

Plants affected Trees, shrubs, perennials, annuals, bulbous plants, vegetables, fruits, and most indoor plants. Soft-leaved plants are particularly vulnerable to this condition.
Symptoms A fuzzy, gray fungal growth appears on the foliage, causing it to discolor and rapidly deteriorate; the infection may then spread into the main body of the plant. See pp.559, 562, and 564 for other symptoms.
Cause and control See pp.559 and 562 for details.

Spider mites

Plants affected Trees, shrubs, perennials, annuals, bulbous plants, cacti and other succulents, vegetables, and fruits. Beans, melons, apples, and plums are susceptible, as are indoor plants.

Symptoms The leaves become dull and increasingly yellowed as a fine, pale mottling develops on their upper surface. They fall prematurely, and a fine silk webbing may cover the plant.
Cause Spider mites, eight-legged animals less than 1/16in (1.6mm) long. They are yellowish green, red, orange, or almost colorless. There are several species; the most common is the two-spotted, or greenhouse, spider mite (*Tetranychus urticae*); this affects both garden and indoor plants in summer. Some species are beneficial predators (see p.548).
Control The rapid reproduction of the mites and the existence of pesticide-resistant strains make control difficult. Discourage those in greenhouses by spraying water underneath leaves and maintaining high humidity; the predatory mite *Metaseiulus occidentalis* provides an effective biological control of *T. urticae* if introduced before heavy infestations develop. Nonresistant spider mites may be controlled with sprays of malathion, dimethoate, or insecticidal soaps on three or four occasions at five-day intervals.

Thrips

Plants affected A wide range of shrubs, perennials, annuals, bulbous plants, vegetables, fruits, and indoor and greenhouse plants. Gladioli, rhododendrons, dahlias, daylilies, peonies, ferns, *Citrus*, pears, peas, and onions are commonly attacked.
Symptoms A silver-white discoloration with tiny black dots appears on the upper leaf surface. See p.562 for other symptoms.
Cause Various species of thrips or thunderfly (e.g. *Thrips simplex*, *T. tabaci*, *Frankliniella occidentalis*, and *Heliothrips haemorrhoidalis*), brownish black insects with narrow bodies up to 1/16in (1.6mm) long, sometimes crossed with pale bands. Immature nymphs are a pale yellow-orange but otherwise resemble the adults. Both adults and nymphs feed on the upper surface of the leaf. They thrive in hot, dry conditions.
Control Water plants regularly. Reduce the temperature in greenhouses with shading and ventilation. Spray with acephate, chlorpyrifos, permethrin, pyrethrum, diazinon, malathion, or dimethoate as soon as damage is seen. Predatory mites (*Amblyseius* spp.) are also an effective control.

Tent caterpillars

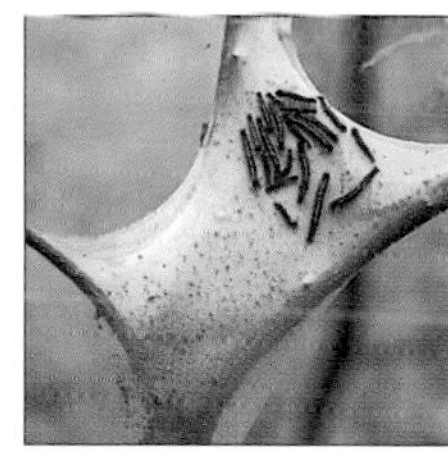

Plants affected Many deciduous trees, especially *Prunus* and *Malus*.
Symptoms Large white nests are spun in the forks of branches. The larvae move out by day to feed on leaves, returning at night.
Cause Tent caterpillars that are black and hairy with a white line down the back and blue spots, of the eastern tent moth (*Malacosoma americanum*), or reddish brown with a blue line on either side of the Californian tent moth (*M. californicum*).
Control Apply mineral oil spray in late winter to kill eggs. Look for shiny bands of eggs on small branches and prune out. Remove nests while young if reachable, or break open with a stick and spray with *Bacillus thuringiensis*, carbaryl, permethrin, or methoxychlor. Alternatively, remove tents and caterpillars and, if legal in your area, burn in a bonfire well away from trees and houses. A species of fly (*Sarcophaga aldrichi*) may serve as a natural control; the fly lays its young in the caterpillar and eventually kills the host. Many birds feed on tent caterpillars.

Leafhoppers

Spots on leaves

Adult leafhoppers

Plants affected Trees, shrubs, perennials, annuals, vegetables, and fruits. Rhododendrons, roses, pelargoniums, primroses (*Primula*), and tomatoes are most vulnerable.
Symptoms A coarse, pale spotting appears on the upper leaf surface.
Cause Leafhoppers, such as the rose leafhopper (*Edwardsiana rosae*) and the six-spotted leafhopper (*Macrosteles fascifrons*), green or yellow insects 1/16–1/8in (1.6–3.2mm) long that leap from the plant when disturbed. Their bodies are widest just behind the head. The rhododendron leafhopper (*Graphocephala coccinea*) is pale blue and orange-red, and 1/4in (6mm) in length. The creamy white, immature nymphs are less active.
Control Spray beneath the leaves with malathion, carbaryl, dimethoate, permethrin, or pyrethrum when leafhopper activity is seen. Controlling leafhoppers will reduce the spread of aster yellows (see p.571), since leafhoppers are the carriers.

Pear and cherry slugworms

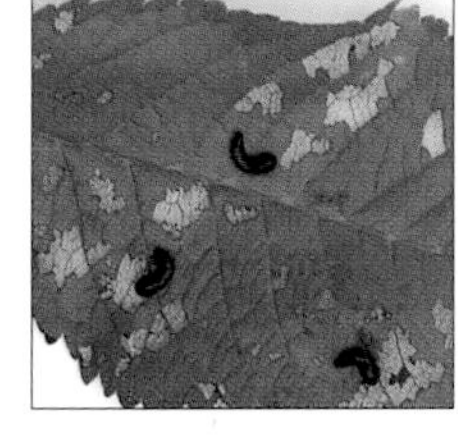

Plants affected Pear and plum trees; also fruiting and ornamental cherries (*Prunus*), *Chaenomeles*, hawthorns (*Crataegus*).
Symptoms The leaves develop whitish brown patches where the larvae graze away the surface.
Cause The pear and cherry slugworm (*Caliroa cerasi*), the larval stage of a small black-bodied sawfly. The larvae are up to 1/2in (1cm) long and are broadest at the head end. They are covered by a black slimy substance and consequently resemble slugs. They feed mainly on the upper leaf surface. Two or three generations occur between early summer and early fall.
Control Spray upper and lower leaf surfaces thoroughly with pyrethrum, rotenone, permethrin, or malathion as soon as the larvae are first seen.

Psyllids

Plants affected Bay (*Laurus nobilis*), boxwood (*Buxus*), and pears.
Symptoms The leaf margins of bay are yellowed, thickened, and curled; boxwood leaves are stunted; pear leaves are sticky with honeydew (excrement) and blackened with sooty mold. Damage occurs throughout the spring and summer. See p.557 for other symptoms.
Cause Psyllids (e.g. the bay, *Trioza alacris*, the box, *Psylla buxi*, and the pear, *Psylla pyricola*), the flattened and immature nymphs of small, aphidlike, winged insects. The nymphs are 1/16in (1.6mm) long and usually gray or green.
Control Prune out and discard or burn affected shoots. Spray the plant thoroughly with dimethoate, rotenone, pyrenone, or carbaryl, either in spring or when the damage is first seen.

Leaf and bud nematodes

Dark patches

Plants affected Annuals and most herbaceous perennials. Most commonly attacked are begonias, chrysanthemums, and *Anemone* x *hybrida*.
Symptoms Brownish black patches appear on leaves as islands or wedges between the larger veins.
Cause Microscopic nematodes (*Aphelenchoides*) that feed in large numbers inside infested leaves.
Control Discard all affected leaves or destroy the whole plant as soon as the infestation is noticed. For chrysanthemums, dip the dormant stools in clean, nematode-free water held at a constant temperature of 115°F (46°C) for at least five minutes to obtain clean cuttings. There is no chemical control available to the amateur gardener.

Wedges between veins

Leaf miners

Linear blotching

Plants affected Trees, shrubs, perennials, and vegetables, especially birch (*Betula*), hollies (*Ilex*), apples, chrysanthemums, and *Aquilegia*.
Symptoms White or brown areas appear within the leaf, often of characteristic shape for the particular leaf miner, e.g. linear, circular, or irregular.
Cause Larvae of various flies, e.g. the columbine leaf miner (*Phytomyza aquilegivora*) and the chrysanthemum leaf miner (*Phytomyza syngenesiae*); moths, for example the arborvitae leaf miner (*Argyresthia thuiella*); beetles, such as the willow leaf mining weevil (*Rhynchaenus rufipes*); and sawflies, such as the birch leaf mining sawfly (*Fenusa pusilla*).
Control Remove and destroy affected leaves if the plant is lightly infested. Spray seriously infested plants with dimethoate, chlorpyrifos, or malathion when damage is first noticed.

Irregular discoloration

Squash vine borers

Plants affected Summer and winter squashes, cucumbers, melons.
Symptoms Sudden wilting of leaves and stems and excrement around entry hole. Larvae may be visible nesting in stems.
Cause and control See p.559 for details.

Potato viruses

Plants affected Potatoes.
Symptoms Various, the most common being crinkling and mottling of foliage (potato rugose virus); leaves becoming thick, leathery, and rolled, sometimes discolored on the underside (potato leaf roll virus); plants grow erect, with small, dark leaves, and lack vigor (potato spindle tuber virus); upper leaves are rolled with red or yellow margins (potato witches' broom).
Cause A number of viruses which are spread by aphids (see opposite) and leafhoppers (see left).
Control Plant only certified seed potatoes, and diligently control outbreaks of aphids (see opposite) and leafhoppers (see left).

Leaf tiers and rollers

Plants affected Trees (ornamental and fruit), shrubs, perennials, annuals, and bulbous plants.
Symptoms Two leaves may be bound together with fine silk threads, or one leaf may be either similarly attached to a fruit or folded over on itself. Brown, dry, skeletal patches appear on the leaves.
Cause The caterpillars of moths such as *Archips argyrospila*, which feeds on apples, oaks, quinces, and roses, and *Pandemis limitata*, which attacks many trees and shrubs. They graze away the inner surfaces of leaves. They are up to 3/4in (2cm) long, and are generally dark green or yellow with brown heads. The caterpillars wriggle backward rapidly when they are disturbed.
Control Wearing gardening gloves or using paper towels, squeeze bound-up leaves to crush the caterpillars or pupae that are inside. If the problem is serious, spray the affected plants very thoroughly with permethrin or carbaryl.

Scale insects

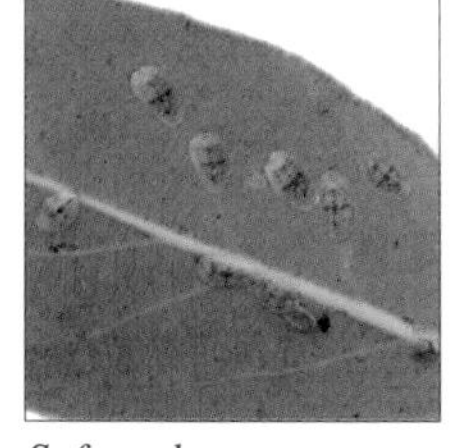

Soft scale

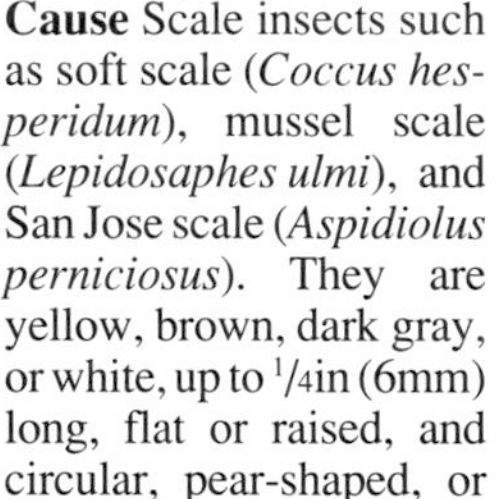

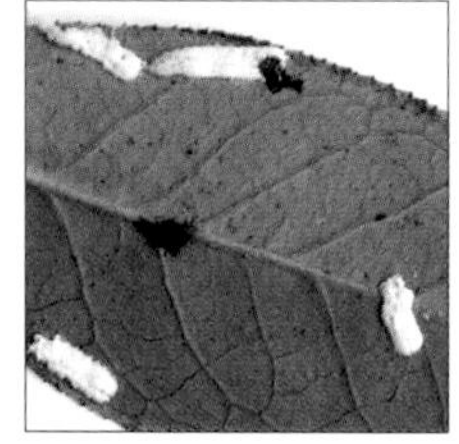

Egg deposits

Plants affected Trees, shrubs, cacti and other succulents, fruits, and indoor and greenhouse plants.
Symptoms The foliage is sticky with honeydew (excrement) and blackened with sooty molds. Plant growth may be slow. White, egg-containing deposits may also appear. See also p.559.
Cause Scale insects such as soft scale (*Coccus hesperidum*), mussel scale (*Lepidosaphes ulmi*), and San Jose scale (*Aspidiolus perniciosus*). They are yellow, brown, dark gray, or white, up to 1/4in (6mm) long, flat or raised, and circular, pear-shaped, or oval. They are found on lower leaf surfaces and stems.
Control Spray deciduous trees with dormant oil in winter, and other plants with malathion, acephate, chlorpyrifos, diazinon, bendiocarb, or carbaryl (most effective when the newly hatched scale nymphs are present – all year on greenhouse plants, early to midsummer outside). *Metaphycus helvolus* is an effective biological control for soft scale insects.

Bacterial leaf spots and blotches

Spots Yellowing

Plants affected Trees, shrubs, roses, perennials, annuals, bulbous plants, vegetables, fruits, and indoor plants.
Symptoms Various spots or patches develop. They may appear water-soaked, and are often angular with a yellow edge or halo ("halo blight"). As spots merge, the leaf is killed. Black tarlike spots appear on delphinium leaves.
Cause *Pseudomonas* bacteria, spread by insects, rain splash, or windborne seeds.
Control Avoid wetting the foliage. Remove all affected leaves. Practice good sanitation in fall and spray woody plants with sulfur in winter.

Rusts

Small brown spores

Pale discoloration

Rust on bluebell leaf

Plants affected Trees, shrubs, perennials, annuals, bulbous plants, vegetables, fruits, and indoor plants; mints (*Mentha*), roses, raspberries, and blackberries are commonly attacked.
Symptoms Small bright orange or brown patches of spores develop on the lower leaf surface, each corresponding to a yellow discoloration on the upper surface. Spores may appear in concentric rings or pustules. Winter spores, dark brown or black, are sometimes also produced, and the leaves may fall early. Pustules may also develop either on, or apparently bursting from within, the stem. Some plants, e.g. junipers, develop gelatinous growths. In severe cases stems become extensively distorted and ruptured. Dieback may follow.
Cause Fungi, most often species of *Puccinia* and *Melampsora*. The spores are spread by rain splash and air currents and may overwinter on plant debris. A few rusts are systemic.
Control Most rusts have two generations per season, the first on apples, for example, the second on junipers. Troublesome rusts in North America alternate between apples or hawthorns and junipers or arborvitae, or between currants and pines. The removal of one host will give control. For other plants, spray with a ferbam and sulfur mixture.

Corky scab

Plants affected Cacti and other succulents, especially *Opuntia* and *Epiphyllum*.
Symptoms Corky or brown, irregularly shaped spots appear on the plant. These areas later become sunken.
Cause Either high humidity or levels of light that are excessively high.
Control Take measures to improve the growing conditions of the plant. In extreme cases, however, the plant must be discarded, after having been used for propagation purposes, if desired.

Shothole

Plants affected Edible and ornamental cherries (*Prunus*), peaches, nectarines, plums, gages, and *Prunus laurocerasus*; also other trees, shrubs, and woody perennials.
Symptoms Discolored (usually brown) spots develop on the foliage; the dead leaf tissue then falls away, leaving holes and giving the plant an untidy, ragged appearance. In severe cases, large areas of leaf are lost.
Cause Several fungi, including *Coccomyces hiemalis*, are usually responsible for this condition, but occasionally bacteria are involved. Plants that are lacking in vigor are most likely to show symptoms of shothole.
Control Try to improve the general growing conditions and the overall health of the affected plant. If the problem persists, spraying the plant thoroughly with a copper-based fungicide may help.

Fungal leaf spots

Plants affected Trees, shrubs, roses, perennials, annuals, bulbous plants, vegetables, fruits, and many indoor plants.
Symptoms Discrete, concentrically zoned spots appear on the leaves; close inspection may reveal pinprick-sized, fungal, fruiting bodies. Spots may be a range of colors but are frequently brown or slate-gray. In severe cases they merge, sometimes obscuring most of the leaf surface. Early leaf fall may occur, but in some instances there is little damage or effect on the overall vigor of the plant. Blackspot on roses is a fungal leaf spot.
Cause A wide range of fungi.
Control Remove all affected parts, and rake up and discard or burn any leaves that have already fallen. Spray with triforine.

Sooty mold

Plants affected Many plants, both outdoors and under cover, but especially birches (*Betula*), lindens (*Tilia*), oaks (*Quercus*), roses, *Citrus*, and plums.
Symptoms Black, sooty deposits cover the upper surface of leaves. Mold may cover the leaves, blocking light to the point that the plant is unable to photosynthesize. Leaves fall prematurely.
Cause Fungi from genera such as *Aethaoderma*, *Morfea*, *Phragmocapnias*, and *Scorias*, which grow on the honeydew secreted by aphids (see p.552), mealybugs (p.552), and some leafhoppers (p.553).
Control Prevent buildup of pest colonies by spraying with water as soon as noticed. On small plants, wash leaves with a soft sponge and water. On trees, use a hose-end sprayer to wash off mold.

Chocolate spot

Plants affected Broad beans.
Symptoms Chocolate-colored spots or streaks appear on both leaves and stems, sometimes merging to cover a whole leaf. In extreme cases the entire plant is killed.
Cause *Botrytis fabae*, a fungus that thrives in wet spring weather. Plants growing in very acid soils are susceptible, as are those with soft, lush growth. Winter-sown crops are most severely affected by this condition.
Control Sow seed thinly, first dressing the soil with potassium sulfate, and avoid excessive use of nitrogen fertilizers. Remove and discard affected plants at the end of the harvest.

Scab

Brown patches

Plants affected *Malus*, including both ornamental and fruiting species, pyracanthas, pears, *Citrus*, and loquats.
Symptoms Dark and greenish brown patches, scabby and sometimes blistered, develop on the foliage; any affected leaves may fall early. See p.564 for other symptoms.
Cause The fungi *Venturia inaequalis*, *V. pirina*, *Spilocaea pyracanthae*, and *S. pomi*, which thrive in warm, damp weather. They may overwinter on infected leaves or shoots; pear scab is especially likely to overwinter.

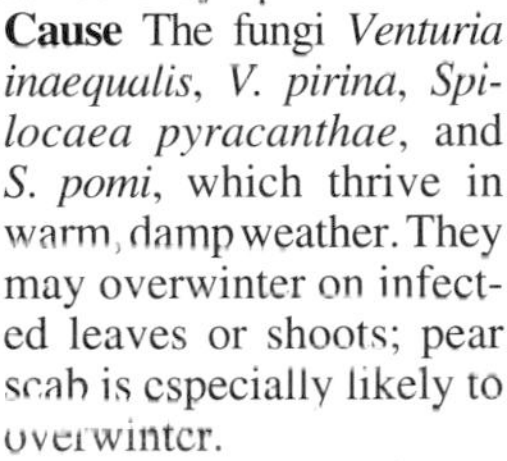

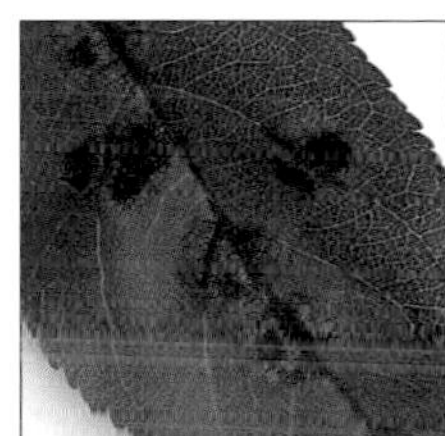

Dark blotches

Control Plant resistant varieties. Keep the plant open-centered by pruning, remove any scabby shoots and fruits, and rake up and discard all fallen leaves. Spray plants with a suitable fungicide, such as thiram. Do not store any affected fruits.

Lily gray mold

Plants affected Lilies (*Lilium*), especially *L. candidum* and *L.* x *testaceum*.
Symptoms Dark green, water-soaked blotches develop on the leaves, later turning a pale brown; the foliage then withers but remains on the stem. Where the pathogen enters a leaf axil the stem may rot. Black sclerotia (fungal resting bodies) may form on dead tissues.
Cause The fungus *Botrytis elliptica*, which is encouraged by wet weather. Spores produced on the leaf lesions (or, in spring, from the sclerotia) are spread by rain splash and wind.
Control Grow on a well-drained site; clear away affected debris. Spray with Bordeaux mixture at the start of the season.

Viruses

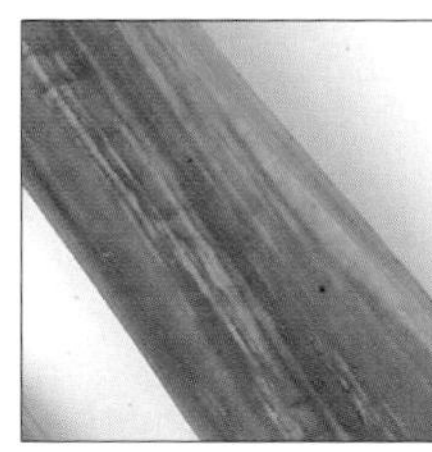

Yellowish streaks

Ringspots

Plants affected All plants.
Symptoms Leaves are undersized, distorted, or grouped in rosettes. Patterns of yellow discoloration (mosaics, ringspots, mottles) are common. See pp.562 and 565 for other symptoms.
Cause A large number of viruses, some with very wide host ranges. Submicroscopic virus particles in the sap of infected plants may be transmitted to healthy tissues by sap-feeding pests such as aphids (p.552), by nematodes or other soilborne pests, through handling, or on pruning or propagating tools; some are seedborne.
Control Buy certified (virus-free) plants where possible. Keep potential carriers, e.g. aphids (see p.552), under control, and make sure that the site is free of weeds since these may harbor viruses. Remove and discard affected plants as soon as possible; always handle suspect plants after those that appear healthy, and do not propagate from them. Use a new site for any replacement plants.

Tulip fire/blight

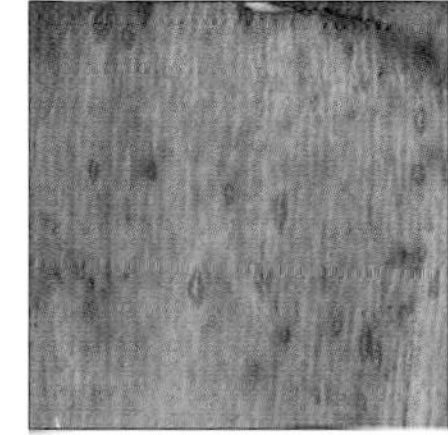

Plants affected Tulips.
Symptoms The leaves are covered with pale brown, spore-producing blotches. Both leaves and shoots are deformed and stunted, and later become covered in dense, gray, spore-bearing, fungal growths and black sclerotia (fungal resting bodies). The bulbs develop sunken brown lesions and small black sclerotia. See p.562 for other symptoms.
Cause The fungus *Botrytis tulipae*, which flourishes particularly in wet seasons; the spores are spread by wind and rain. The sclerotia persist in the soil, later germinating when tulips are planted again in the same area.
Control Remove affected leaves and shoots (or preferably the whole plant) immediately. If blight infestation symptoms are noticed, lift and dry bulbs at the end of the season, discarding any with sclerotia, and dip the remaining bulbs in a suitable fungicide solution, e.g. captan. Wait at least two years before replanting the site with tulips; alternatively, change the soil in the flower bed.

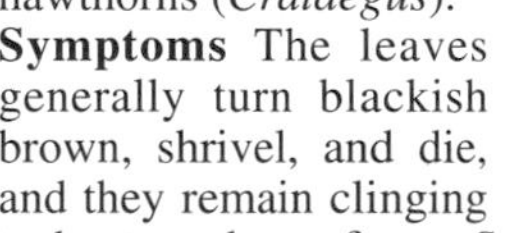

Clubroot

Plants affected The family Cruciferae, especially brassicas (e.g. cabbages, Brussels sprouts, rutabagas), and radishes. Also some ornamentals, such as stocks (*Matthiola*), candytufts (*Iberis*), and wallflowers (*Cheiranthus*).
Symptoms Plants are stunted and discolored; foliage wilts in hot weather. See also p.567.
Cause The slime mold *Plasmodiophora brassicae*, which thrives in poorly drained, acid soils, and is also found on manure and plant debris. It is easily spread on boots and tools, and the spores are very resilient, remaining viable for 20 years or more, even in the absence of a host plant. Weeds that are susceptible to the disease (e.g. shepherd's purse and wild mustard) may be a source of infection.
Control Remove and burn affected plants. Keep the area free of weeds, lime the soil, and improve drainage where feasible. Raise new plants in pots of soil-based potting mix so that their roots are well developed when planted out. Commercial chemical dips may be used at the planting stage.

Tomato/potato late blight

Plants affected Tomatoes (in the open and occasionally under cover), potatoes.
Symptoms Patches of brown discoloration develop on the leaf tips and edges; in damp conditions these may often be ringed with a white fungal growth. The leaf tissue is killed, and where the patches merge the whole of the affected leaflet may eventually die. See also "Tomato late blight," p.564, and "Potato late blight," p.568.
Cause The fungus *Phytophthora infestans*, which thrives in warm, moist conditions. Spores produced on the foliage of tomato and potato plants, and on potato haulms, are carried from plant to plant by wind and rain, and these may be washed down into the soil to infect potato tubers.
Control Avoid overhead watering. Hill up potatoes deeply to provide a barrier that will help protect the tubers against falling spores, and choose resistant cultivars, for example 'Cherokee', 'Kennebec', 'Plymouth', and 'Essex'. Protect both tomatoes and potatoes by spraying thoroughly with a copper-based fungicide. Spray plants before they blossom (this is especially important in wet seasons), spray tomatoes as soon as they have been pinched.

Fire blight

Plants affected Members of the family Rosaceae that bear pome fruits, mainly pears, apples, some *Sorbus*, cotoneasters, and hawthorns (*Crataegus*).
Symptoms The leaves generally turn blackish brown, shrivel, and die, and they remain clinging to the stem; those of some *Sorbus* and hawthorns may turn yellow and fall. Oozing cankers appear on the branches, and the whole tree may eventually die. See p.571 for other symptoms.
Cause The bacterium *Erwinia amylovora*, which is produced from the cankers, attacks via blossoms. It is carried from plant to plant by wind, rain splash, insects, and pollen grains.
Control Remove the affected plants or prune out affected areas to at least 24in (60cm) past the damaged area; dip the saw in disinfectant between cuts and before using it on another tree. Inspect inner wood to ensure that no staining remains.

Fertilizer burn

Plants affected Ornamental plants growing in containers and hanging baskets, house plants, and lawns.
Symptoms Foliage develops discolored areas along the veins or around the leaf edges, often followed by severe wilting. Plants may die rapidly afterward. On lawns, dead areas may be in stripes or patches.
Cause Soluble fertilizer incorrectly dissolved so that solids are watered into the container or basket; or dry fertilizer applied at wrong rate. Manure that is applied too fresh may burn plants. Lawns may be burnt if fertilizer is applied in overlapping stripes, or if a drop-type spreader is shut off incorrectly.
Control Take care when mixing and applying fertilizer. Grow tomato seedlings on manure (tomatoes react quickly to fertilizer overdose or toxic chemicals). In the case of accidental overdose, water repeatedly to dilute the fertilizer to safe levels.

Transplant shock

Plants affected Potentially all plants
Symptoms Soon after transplant, leaves droop and yellow, and plant wilts. Plants may die.
Cause Plant is stressed from improper handling during transplant or incorrect conditions.
Control Avoid shock by transplanting with care and providing appropriate cultural requirements.

Insecticide/fungicide damage

Plants affected Some indoor and garden plants.
Symptoms Discrete spots or patches, often bleached or scorched, appear on leaves, which may fall; the plant usually survives.
Cause Commonly, chemicals used at the wrong rate or interval, or applied during hot, sunny weather. Some plants are damaged by fungicides or insecticides applied correctly, and susceptible species should be noted on the packaging; check carefully before using.

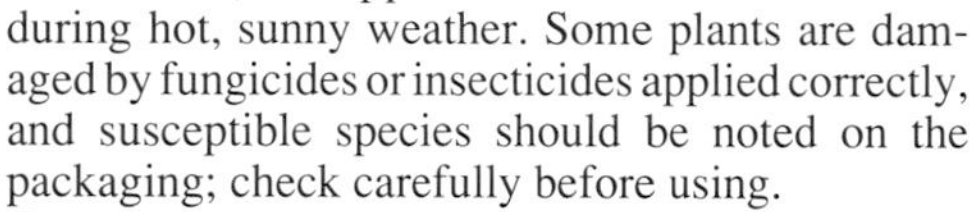

Control Use commercial chemicals only and always follow the manufacturer's instructions.

Contact weedkiller damage

Plants affected All plants.
Symptoms Pale, bleached spots appear on the contaminated foliage, sometimes turning brown, and small bumps may appear on stems. Bulbs exposed to contact weedkillers before their foliage has died down show a very pale, almost white, leaf color the following season. In severe cases, vigor may be reduced and the plant may even die. Usually plants grow out of the symptoms.

Cause Spray drift during windy conditions, or from careless application. Poorly cleaned sprayers and watering cans may also lead to contamination.
Control Follow the manufacturer's instructions. Use a dribble bar applicator or watering can in preference to a sprayer, and keep separate equipment for use with weedkillers.

Drought

Plants affected All plants, especially those that are young and container-grown, or in light, sandy soils.
Symptoms Fall color develops early and defoliation may occur, sometimes followed by dieback. Plants wilt and growth is stunted. See pp.563, 570, and 573 for other symptoms.
Cause Prolonged or repeated water shortage due to dry soil, excessive water loss from leaves of plants on exposed sites, injured or restricted roots, or soil compaction. Plants in small containers are vulnerable in hot weather, since peat-based mixes allowed to dehydrate are hard to rewet.
Control Water plants regularly; check those growing in hot or sunny positions. Mulch, where appropriate, to improve moisture retention. It is easier to prevent drought than to treat it: plants exposed to prolonged water shortage are less likely to recover once adequate water is supplied or temperatures lowered than those suffering a sudden shortage.

High temperatures and scorch

Plants affected In particular, plants with fleshy leaves or flowers, those near glass, and seedlings; also trees, shrubs, perennials, annuals, bulbous plants, vegetables, fruits, and indoor plants.
Symptoms The leaves wilt, turn yellow or brown, become dry and crisp, and may die; the tips and margins are often affected first. In extreme cases the stems die back. Scorching produces brown patches on the upper or exposed parts of the plant; foliage close to glass is very susceptible. Affected leaves may shrivel completely. Scorched petals turn brown and become dry and crisp. Roses may show "balling" (as the outer petals dry up they enclose the bud). Fruits are also affected (see p.564).

Cause Very high or fluctuating temperatures in a closed environment (e.g. a greenhouse); scorching is caused by bright, but not necessarily hot, sunlight. Scorch problems are increased by moisture on the leaves and fruit, and by faults in the glass near plants, both of which magnify the sun's rays. Shade-loving plants (e.g. some *Impatiens*) scorch badly if planted in bright sunlight.
Control Where possible, shade greenhouses, provide adequate ventilation to keep temperatures down, and move plants away from any faults there may be in the glass. Avoid overhead watering and spraying in sunny weather. Locate shade-loving plants in a site with at least dappled shade.

Low temperatures

Plants affected Trees, shrubs, perennials, annuals, bulbous plants, vegetables, fruits, indoor plants; seedlings and young plants are most vulnerable.
Symptoms Leaves, especially those of seedlings, are sometimes bleached, and brown, dry patches develop; evergreen foliage may turn completely brown. Cold injury results in puckered, withered, or discolored (often blackened) leaves, and a lifting of the lower leaf surface, which gives the foliage a silvered appearance. Rotten patches, brown and dry or dark and soft, develop on the petals, especially on exposed flowerheads. Frost injury may leave petals withered or discolored and the whole flower may be killed. See pp.559 and 570 for other symptoms.

Cause Low temperatures or occasionally great fluctuations in temperature. Plants in exposed positions or frost pockets are likely to be affected.
Control Provide winter protection for young or tender plants, and those grown in exposed positions.

Nitrogen deficiency

Plants affected Trees, shrubs, perennials, annuals, bulbous plants, vegetables, fruits, and indoor plants.
Symptoms Pale green leaves are produced, and these sometimes develop either yellow or pink tints. Overall growth is reduced and the whole plant may eventually become slightly spindly.
Cause Growing plants either in poor, light soils or in restricted surroundings such as hanging baskets, windowboxes, or other types of container.
Control Use green manures on affected areas, or apply a high-nitrogen fertilizer, e.g. nitrate of ammonia, dried blood, or soluble commercial fertilizer.

Potassium deficiency

Plants affected Edible and ornamental fruiting plants, mainly currants, apples, and pears.
Symptoms The foliage turns blue, yellow, or purple, with a brown discoloration either in blotches or on the leaf tips or margins. Some leaves may roll inward; they are fairly soft and therefore prone to attack by pathogens. Flowering, fruiting, and general growth of the whole plant may be reduced.
Cause Growing plants in soils either with a light texture or with a high lime or peat content.
Control Improve the soil texture. Dress with muriate of potash or a high-potassium fertilizer.

Phosphate deficiency

Plants affected Potentially all plants may suffer, but this particular deficiency is unlikely to occur in most gardens.
Symptoms Plant growth is slow, and the young foliage may appear dull or yellowed.

Cause The leaching out of phosphates in acid soils and areas of high rainfall. Plants growing in heavy clay soils, in deep peat soils, or in soils with a high iron content are the most likely to be at risk from this condition.
Control Apply bone meal or superphosphate.

Manganese/iron deficiency

Plants affected Trees, shrubs, perennials, annuals, bulbous plants, vegetables, fruits, and indoor plants. Acid-loving plants growing in alkaline soils are often affected.
Symptoms A yellowing or browning starts at the leaf margins and extends between the veins. The overall leaf color may also be rather yellow.
Cause The cultivation of plants in unsuitable soils or mixes; acid-loving plants, in particular, are unable to absorb adequate trace elements from alkaline soils. Regular watering with very hard water, buried debris (e.g. builders' rubble), and rain runoff from mortar in walls are all possible causes of a locally raised soil pH.
Control Choose plants that are compatible with the soil type and clear the area of any builders' debris. Use rainwater, not tapwater, for susceptible plants. Acidify the soil before or after planting, and apply acid mulches. Apply a chelated or fritted form of trace elements and chelated iron.

Magnesium deficiency

Plants affected A wide range of both outdoor and indoor plants; common in container-grown nursery stock. Tomatoes, roses, and chrysanthemums are most often affected.
Symptoms Distinct areas of discoloration, usually yellow but occasionally red or brown, develop between the leaf veins (interveinal chlorosis), and the affected leaves may fall early.
Cause Acid soils; heavy watering or rainfall, both of which leach out magnesium; or high potassium levels, which make it unavailable. Plants fed on high-potassium fertilizers to encourage flowering or fruiting (e.g. tomatoes) are susceptible.
Control Treat plants and/or soil with Epsom salts in fall; add dry to the soil at a rate of 1oz/10sq ft (25g/sq m), or apply a foliar spray of $7\frac{1}{2}$oz Epsom salts in $2\frac{1}{4}$ gallons of water (210g in 10 liters), adding a non-detergent dishwashing liquid.

Waterlogging

Plants affected Potentially all plants.
Symptoms Leaves turn yellow and the plants wilt.
Cause Too much water in the growing medium, owing to poor structure or drainage, or overwatering.
Control Improve soil structure and drainage.
See also pp.566 and 570.

See also "Irregular water supply," "Edema," "Peach leaf curl," "Hormone weedkiller damage," "Mycoplasmas," all below; "Azalea galls," p.558; "*Verticillium* wilt," p.559; "*Cytospora* canker," p.560; "*Fusarium* wilt," p.560; "*Phytophthora* root rots," p.560; "Foot and root rots," p.560; "Etiolation," p.561; "Blossom wilt," p.562; "Smuts," p.565; "Iris borers," p.566; "Carrot rust flies," p.566; "Narcissus nematodes," p.569; "Iris soft rot," p.569; "Onion maggots," p.569; "Blackleg on potatoes," p.570; "*Coryneum* canker," p.570; "Oak wilt," p.571; "Aster yellows," p.571; "Clematis wilt," p.571; and "Anthracnose," p.572.

Distorted leaves

Irregular water supply

Plants affected All garden plants, especially container-grown ones.
Symptoms Leaves and flowers are distorted. Stems may split. See p.565 for other symptoms.
Cause An irregular supply of water leads to irregular growth. Sudden availability of water after a drought brings rapid swelling, rupturing stems and distorting the upper parts of the plant.
Control Provide a regular and adequate supply of water for plants, especially in hot or windy weather. Do not suddenly overwater plants after drought conditions. Apply a regular mulch around the plants, where appropriate, since this will help conserve the moisture in the soil.

Edema

Plants affected Potentially all plants, but particularly pelargoniums, camellias, eucalyptus, *Peperomia*, and succulents.
Symptoms Raised, warty patches appear on the foliage; they may extend across the whole leaf. The patches are of a color similar to that of the rest of the leaf, but later turn brown.
Cause Excessively high moisture levels in either the air or the growing medium, which give the plant cells an unusually high water content. As a result of this, small groups of cells swell, forming the outgrowths, and later burst, leaving brown patches on the leaves.
Control Improve air circulation around the plants by increasing ventilation, and by ensuring correct plant spacing. Decrease the amount of watering and try to improve drainage wherever possible. Although the damaged leaves will not recover, do not pick them off: new leaf growth will be normal.

Peach leaf curl

Plants affected Peaches, nectarines, almonds, and related ornamental *Prunus* species in the open.
Symptoms Leaves become distorted, blistered, and sometimes swollen, later turning a deep red; a white fungal growth then develops on the leaf surfaces. The foliage falls, but a second flush of healthy leaves will be produced afterward.
Cause The fungus *Taphrina deformans*, which is encouraged by cool, wet conditions. Spores are carried by wind or rain to shoots, bud scales, and cracks in the bark, where they overwinter.
Control Pick off affected leaves before they turn white. To prevent infection, spray leaves with a copper-based fungicide in mid- to late winter, and again 14 days later, or spray with ferbam after leaf drop and again in spring before the leaves unfurl.

Hormone weedkiller damage

Plants affected Broad-leaved plants, mainly roses, tomatoes, grapes, and conifers.
Symptoms Leaves are small, narrow, often thickened, and with prominent veins. They may be cup-shaped and extremely distorted. The petioles become twisted. Small bumps may appear on stems. See p.565 for other symptoms.
Cause Contamination by a growth regulator or hormone-type weedkiller, often originally used a considerable distance away; minute quantities may cause extensive damage. Common sources of trouble are spray drift and the use of sprayers or watering cans that have previously been used for applying weedkillers.

Distorted leaves

Stunted leaf buds

Control Always apply weedkillers according to manufacturer's instructions, placing protective barriers around adjacent garden plants to prevent spray drift. Keep one sprayer or watering can for use with weedkillers only. Store weedkillers in their original containers, away from soil mixes, fertilizers, and plants. Affected plants usually outgrow the symptoms if damage is not extensive.

Aphids

Plants affected Trees, shrubs, climbing plants, roses, perennials, annuals, bulbous plants, vegetables, fruits, and indoor plants.
Symptoms Leaves are stunted and distorted.
Cause and control See p.552 for details.

Psyllids

Plants affected Bay (*Laurus nobilis*), boxwood (*Buxus*), and pears.
Symptoms The leaf margins of bay are yellowed, thickened, and curled; boxwood has stunted stems and cupped, slightly distorted leaves. Damage occurs to boxwood in spring, and to bay throughout the summer. See p.553 for symptoms on pears.
Cause and control See p.553 for details.

Mycoplasmas

Plants affected Trees, shrubs, perennials, annuals, bulbous plants, vegetables, fruits (especially strawberries), and indoor plants.
Symptoms Leaves may be undersized, distorted, and covered with patterns of discoloration. This condition on strawberry plants, which is known as green petal, produces young leaves that are small, irregularly shaped, and yellowed; in addition, the older foliage turns a distinctly red color when flowering has ceased. See p.562 for other symptoms.
Cause Mycoplasmas, which are believed to be

related to bacteria. Mycoplasmas are spread from plant to plant by aphids (see p.552). Strawberry green petal is commonly transmitted by leafhoppers, which pick up the infection from clover plants suffering from phyllody disease. Mycoplasmas give rise to different symptoms in the different hosts.
Control Discard all affected plants, buy only certified fruit stock, and control aphids (see p.552) and leafhoppers (p.553). Remove weeds from neighboring areas, because they may harbor the disease.

Gall mites

Plants affected Trees and shrubs, including plums, pears, walnuts, grapes (*Vitis*), maples (*Acer*), lindens (*Tilia*), elms (*Ulmus*), hawthorns (*Crataegus*), mountain ashes (*Sorbus aucuparia*), broom (*Cytisus/Genista*), beeches (*Fagus*), and blackcurrants.

Pale leaf blotches

Symptoms These vary according to the species of mite, and include: whitish green or red pimples or spikes on foliage (maples, elms, lindens, and plums); creamy white or pink hairs on lower leaf surfaces (maples, lindens, and beeches); raised, blistered areas on upper leaf surfaces, with pale hairs underneath (walnuts and grapes); thick, curling leaf margins (beeches and hawthorns); pale leaf blotches, later turning brownish black (mountain ashes and pears); and stunted leaves (broom). Plant vigor and overall appearance are not affected.

Stunted leaves

Cause Microscopic gall mites, or eriophyid mites, secreting chemicals that induce abnormal growth.
Control Remove affected leaves and shoots if desired. There is no effective chemical control.

Gall midges

Plants affected Many garden plants, especially violets (*Viola*), *Gleditsia*, and roses.
Symptoms Violet leaves thicken and fail to unfurl. *Gleditsia* leaflets swell and fold over to form podlike galls. Young shoots on roses become deformed and die, and flower buds fail to open.
Cause Whitish orange maggots up to 1/16in (1.6mm) long that feed within the galled tissues; three or four generations may occur in a summer. These are the larvae of three types of midge: the gleditsia gall midge (*Dasineura gleditchiae*), the rose gall midge (*D. rhodophaga*), and the violet gall midge (*Phytophaga violicola*). The adults are tiny, grayish brown flies.
Control Remove and destroy affected leaves. The larvae are well protected inside the galls, but spraying with dimethoate in late spring, when the galling first occurs, may provide some control.

Gall wasps/cynipid wasps

Plants affected Oaks (*Quercus*) and roses.
Symptoms Symptoms on oaks include: flat disks on the lower surface of leaves in fall; benign, spherical, woody growths (marble galls) or pithy oak apples on shoots in spring; yellowish green or red bunches of currant galls on the catkins; and yellowish green, sticky "knopper" galls on acorns. Species rose stems and hybrid rose suckers develop swellings covered in yellowish pink, mosslike leaves (mossy rose galls or "Robin's pincushions") in late summer. Damage to the plant is minimal.
Cause The larvae of gall wasps, or cynipid wasps; they secrete chemicals as they feed.
Control No treatment is necessary.

Azalea galls

Plants affected Rhododendrons and azaleas, especially *Rhododendron simsii* grown as an indoor plant.
Symptoms Fleshy, pale green swellings (galls) that develop on the foliage or flowers, later turning white.
Cause The fungus *Exobasidium vaccinii*, which is encouraged by high humidity. The spores are insect- or airborne.
Control Remove and destroy the galls before they turn white. If the disease persists, spray the plants with ferbam, zineb, or Bordeaux mixture.

Whiptail (molybdenum deficiency)

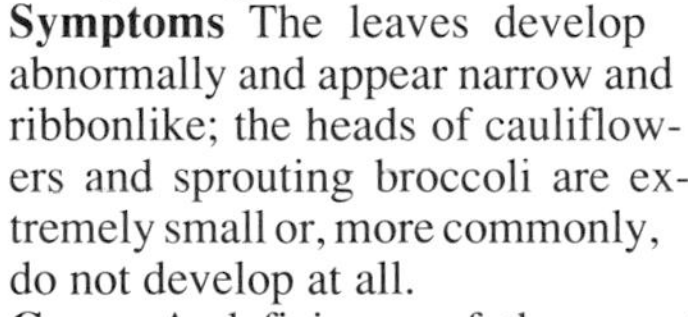

Plants affected All brassicas, most particularly cauliflowers and sprouting broccoli.
Symptoms The leaves develop abnormally and appear narrow and ribbonlike; the heads of cauliflowers and sprouting broccoli are extremely small or, more commonly, do not develop at all.
Cause A deficiency of the trace element molybdenum, most often occurring in acid soils.
Control Increase the alkalinity of the soil with lime. Treat the soil with molybdenum before sowing or planting out susceptible crops.

Bulb scale mites

Plants affected *Hippeastrum*, especially those grown indoors, and daffodils.
Symptoms Growth is stunted, the leaves become curved, and saw-toothed scarring starts to appear along the leaf margins and flower stems.
Cause The microscopic, white bulb scale mite (*Steneotarsonemus laticeps*), which feeds in the neck region of the bulb.
Control Discard infested bulbs. Buy only those of good quality from reputable suppliers. There is no chemical control available to amateur gardeners.

Honeysuckle witches' brooms

Plants affected Several species of honeysuckle (*Lonicera*), but especially cultivars of *L. tatarica*.
Symptoms New growth of leaves and shoots is stunted and has a tassel-like appearance. Some twiggy branches die later or are easily blown off by strong winds. Flowering and fruiting are much reduced and may be absent.
Cause A reaction by the plant to toxins in the saliva of an aphid, *Hyadaphis tatarica*, which overwinters as eggs and, on hatching, feeds on the new shoots, causing them to become distorted.
Control Spray with mineral oil in winter to kill overwintering aphid eggs (see p.552). In spring, as new growth begins, spray at seven to 10 day intervals with insecticidal soap, carbaryl, or malathion.

Chestnut leaf blight

Plants affected All varieties of chestnut and buckeye, including *Aesculus glabra*, *A. octandra*, *A. pavia*, *A. hippocastanum*, and *A.* x *carnea*.
Symptoms Water-soaked areas that rapidly turn brown appear on the leaves. The leaves often curl, become distorted, and drop early.
Cause The fungus *Guignardia aesculi*, which overwinters on fallen leaves. Spores are released in spring as the new leaves unfurl.
Control Good sanitation, picking up the leaves as they fall. Give susceptible trees a winter spray of lime sulfur, then spray with zineb at bud break and repeat twice more at ten-day intervals.

Nematodes

Plants affected Phlox and *Allium*, including onions.
Symptoms Leaves may be spotted with small, rough yellow patches known as spickels. Phlox are stunted, with narrow shoot-tip leaves and swollen stems; onion leaves and stems are swollen and soft. Plants may be killed by a heavy attack.
Cause Microscopic nematodes (*Ditylenchus dipsaci*) feeding in the plant tissues.
Control Destroy affected plants. Where infested onions have been growing, plant nonsusceptible vegetables for the next two years. Obtain nematode-free phlox from root cuttings.

See also "Powdery mildew," p.552; "Leaf and bud nematodes," p.553; "Potato viruses," p.553; "Scab," p.555; "Viruses," p.555; "Leafy gall," p.561; "Smuts," p.565; "Ink spot," p.569; and "Anthracnose," p.572.

Stem, branch, and leaf-bud problems

Stems discolored or with pests visible

Low temperatures

Plants affected All plants. Soft-stemmed and young plants are most vulnerable.
Symptoms Brown, dry patches develop on the stems – especially those of *Acer*. Stems may blacken, wither, or split, giving access to organisms that cause dieback. The splits become enlarged if moisture freezes; the plant may die. See pp.556 and 570 for other symptoms.
Cause Low temperatures or occasionally great fluctuations in temperature. Plants growing in exposed positions are most likely to be affected.
Control Provide winter protection for young or tender plants, and those growing in exposed positions.

Verticillium wilt

Plants affected Many garden and greenhouse plants.
Symptoms Stained vascular system of stems and roots, creating longitudinal brown stripes. Woody plants deteriorate over several years, and may die.
Cause Several species of the fungus *Verticillium* present in the soil, plant remains, or new stock.
Control Remove any affected plants and soil near the roots. Clean pruning tools thoroughly after use on diseased or suspect plants. Keep weeds under strict control and do not grow susceptible plants in the affected area.

Slime flux/wet wood

Plants affected Trees, shrubs, and woody perennials, especially clematis.
Symptoms The stem dies back and a pink, yellow, or off-white slime oozes from its base (often thick and pungent).
Cause Stem injury (often through cold or wounding) when sap pressure is high, just before the leaves break. The sap released from the wound has a high sugar content and is colonized by various microorganisms (in particular yeasts, bacteria, and fungi), which cause the thickening and discoloration.
Control Avoid injury to stems of susceptible plants. Remove affected stems, cutting back to healthy growth, below ground level if necessary. Given adequate food and moisture, the plant should produce more shoots.

Spur blight/cane blight

Plants affected Raspberries. Spur blight may also attack loganberries.
Symptoms With spur blight, purple areas develop around the nodes in late summer; these increase in size and turn a silvery gray. Numerous tiny, black sclerotia (fungal resting bodies) develop in the center of each blotch. Buds may die, or may produce shoots that die. With cane blight, deterioration starts just above soil level as the fungus enters through points of injury and causes the base of the cane to develop dark discoloration and to become brittle. The foliage withers. Weakened plants are more prone to this problem than strong specimens.
Cause The fungi *Didymella applanata* (spur blight) and *Leptosphaeria coniothyrium* (cane blight).
Control Maintain plants well. At the first sign of disease, cut out affected canes, going to below soil level for cane blight.

Scale insects

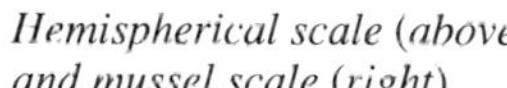

Hemispherical scale (above) and mussel scale (right)

Plants affected Indoor and greenhouse plants, trees, shrubs, fruits, and cacti and other succulents.
Symptoms The stems are sticky with honeydew (excrement), and they appear blackened with sooty molds. Heavily infested plants may also show slow growth. White, waxy deposits containing eggs also occasionally appear on the stems.
Cause and control See p.554 for details.

Squash vine borers

Plants affected Summer and winter squashes, cucumbers, melons.
Symptoms Sudden wilting of stems and leaves; excrement around entry hole. Larvae nesting in stems.
Cause Larvae of *Melittia satyriniformis*, a red and black clearwing moth. The white larvae, which grow up to 1in (2.5cm) in length, feed inside the stem, causing foliage to wilt and eventually die.
Control Slit stem above entry point to find larvae and remove them. Heap soil over damaged part to aid in root formation. Dust with rotenone at weekly intervals while plants are small.

Stem borers

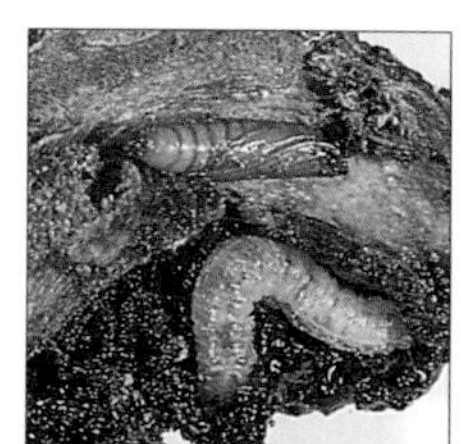

Plants affected Many trees and shrubs, including birches, pines, poplars, locusts, willows, lilacs, and peaches.
Symptoms Larvae, pupae, and a black gummy substance are found in holes in the trunk. Frass (chewed wood) may be seen at the base of the tree, in bark crevices, or at entry hole. Branches or the crown may die back. Branches become brittle.
Cause Larvae of various beetles and moths tunneling into the plant, particularly on trees under stress.
Control Inject malathion or methoxychlor into holes. Spray dimethoate in spring or midsummer.

Raspberry borers

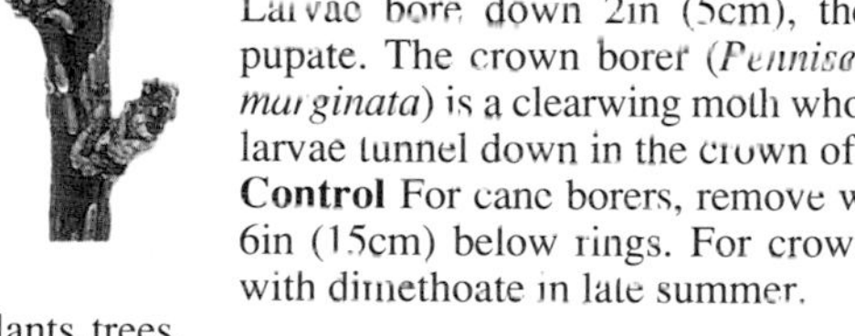

Plants affected Raspberries and blackberries.
Symptoms The tip of the shoot wilts (cane borer) or the entire fruiting cane wilts (crown borer). Beetles may be seen on new shoots.
Cause The beetle *Oberea bimaculata* lays its eggs near the shoot tip between two puncture rings. Larvae bore down 2in (5cm), then pupate. The crown borer (*Pennisetia marginata*) is a clearwing moth whose larvae tunnel down in the crown of the plant.
Control For cane borers, remove wilted shoot tips 6in (15cm) below rings. For crown borers, spray with dimethoate in late summer.

Gray mold/*Botrytis*

Plants affected Trees, shrubs, perennials, annuals, bulbous plants, vegetables, fruits, and indoor plants. Soft-leaved plants are vulnerable.
Symptoms Dead and discolored patches develop on the stems and leaves. Rapid deterioration may occur, causing the upper parts of the stem to die. Fungal spores develop on decaying plant material. See pp.552, 562, and 564 for other symptoms.
Cause The fungi *Botrytis cinerea* and, on snowdrops (*Galanthus*), *B. galanthina*, which thrive in damp conditions and where air circulation is poor. Fungal spores are spread on air currents or by rain splash. Fruits may also become infected by contact with those already diseased. Hard, black, resilient sclerotia (fungal resting bodies), produced on plant remains, fall to the ground and may cause later infections.
Control Avoid injury to plants, clear up dead and dying plant material, and provide good air circulation. Remove affected areas. Spray with a fungicide that contains captan or ferbam.

Dutch elm disease

Crook-shaped twigs

Plants affected Elms (*Ulmus*) and *Zelkova*.
Symptoms Notching appears in twig crotches, and young twigs may be crook-shaped. Longitudinal, dark brown streaks develop under the bark. Leaves in the crown wilt, yellow, and die. The tree

may die within two years.
Cause *Ophiostoma ulmi*, a fungus often spread by elm bark beetles as they tunnel under the bark. Infected trees may pass the disease to healthy ones via common root systems.
Control Cut down and remove affected trees.

Longitudinal streaks

Woolly aphids

Plants affected Apples, cotoneasters, pyracanthas.
Symptoms A fluffy, white, moldlike substance appears on the bark in spring. Starting on the larger branches around old pruning cuts and in bark cracks, it later spreads to the new shoots where soft swellings may develop. Aphids may be visible.

Cause The woolly aphid (*Eriosoma lanigerum*), which is a small, black insect that sucks sap from the bark and secretes white, waxy threads.
Control Spray plants with dimethoate, diazinon, or pirimicarb when the pest is seen.

Spittlebugs

Plants affected Trees, shrubs, perennials, annuals.
Symptoms Globules of white froth containing a small insect appear on stems and leaves in early summer. Where the pest feeds on shoot tips, growth may be distorted but damage is minimal.

Cause Spittlebugs, or froghopper nymphs (e.g. *Philaenus spumarius*), cream-colored sap-suckers that secrete a protective froth over themselves. The adults are darker in color, up to 1/8in (3mm) long, and live openly on the plant.
Control If treatment is necessary, remove nymphs by hand or spray with dimethoate or permethrin.

Adelgids

Plants affected Conifers, particularly *Abies*, pines (*Pinus*), spruces (*Picea*), Douglas firs (*Pseudotsuga menziesii*), hemlocks (*Tsuga*), and *Larix*.
Symptoms A fluffy, white, moldlike substance appears on the leaves and stems. Knobby swellings develop on *Abies*, swollen tips on young spruce shoots. A cottony infection develops on Douglas firs, but no galls.

Cause Small grayish adelgids, or conifer woolly aphids (e.g. *Adelges abietis*). Nymphs of *A. cooleyi* feed on spruces, causing the growth of a gall in which they live and pupate. Winged females migrate to Douglas firs to lay eggs.
Control Hand-pick galls. Keep spruces and Douglas firs separate. Spray small trees with carbaryl, malathion, dormant oil, or insecticidal soap in early spring.

Cytospora canker

Plants affected Spruces (*Picea*), pines (*Pinus*), *Abies balsamea*, Douglas firs (*Pseudotsuga menziesii*), hemlocks (*Tsuga*).
Symptoms Small cankers form. Needles turn brown; branches die. Resin drips from the cankers, crystallizing into white deposits.

Cause The fungus *Cytospora kunzei* on spruces, *C. k.* var. *superficialis* on pines, and *C. k.* var. *kunzei* on the other species. Disease is spread by rain splashes, but enters the tree via a wound.
Control Avoid damaging the lower trunk. Sterilize pruning tools. Spray with Bordeaux mixture.

Fusarium wilt

Plants affected Perennials, annuals, vegetables, and fruits; most commonly affected are China asters (*Callistephus*), carnations (*Dianthus*), sweet peas (*Lathyrus odoratus*), beans, and peas.
Symptoms Black patches develop on the stems and the foliage; they are sometimes covered with a white or pale pink fungal growth. Roots turn black and die.
Cause Various species of the microscopic fungus *Fusarium*, which are present in the soil or on plant debris, or are sometimes seedborne; they may also be introduced on new stock. They will build up in the soil when the same type of plant is grown in the same site year after year.
Control There is no cure for affected plants. Remove them and the soil in their vicinity, and destroy the plants. Avoid growing susceptible plants in the area. Propagate only from healthy stock; if possible, grow resistant cultivars.

Phytophthora root rots

Plants affected Trees, shrubs, and woody perennials; maples (*Acer*), Lawson cypresses (*Chamaecyparis lawsoniana*), yews (*Taxus*), apples, rhododendrons, raspberries, and heathers are most commonly attacked.
Symptoms Patches of dead tissue may appear on the stem or the trunk with bluish black stains in the tissue beneath; the foliage is sparse and chlorotic. Dieback may follow, and plants may even be killed. See p.567 for other symptoms.

Cause Various species of the fungus *Phytophthora*, which is frequently found in wet or waterlogged soil. Roots are attacked by swimming spores that build up in the soil and in infected plant remains.
Control Always avoid heavy watering, and wherever possible improve soil drainage in the area. Do not overwater peat-based soil mixes. Dig up and burn all affected plants. Buy only good-quality plants from reputable sources, and choose those that are tolerant or resistant to *Phytophthora*, such as *Tsuga heterophylla* and x *Cupressocyparis leylandii*.

Foot and root rots

Plants affected A wide range, especially petunias and other bedding plants, tomatoes, cucumbers, peas, beans, and young, container-grown plants.
Symptoms The stem bases discolor and shrink inward. This causes the upper parts of the plant to wilt and die off; the lower leaves will usually show the symptoms first. The roots turn black and break or rot (see p.567).
Cause A range of soil- and waterborne fungi that flourish where growing conditions are not adequately hygienic. The fungi may be introduced through use of unsterilized soil mix and contaminated water, and build up in the soil, especially if susceptible plants are repeatedly grown on the same site.
Control Rotate susceptible plants. Maintain strict hygiene and only use fresh, sterilized soil mix and fresh water. Remove affected plants and the soil in the vicinity of their roots.

Southern blight

Plants affected Many vegetable crops grown in warm climates, including many perennials, annuals, and bulbs, beans, sweet potatoes, and tomatoes.
Symptoms Seedlings show symptoms of damping off (see p.566). The collar or stem of older plants rots at soil level, and shoots may turn yellow, wilt, and eventually die.
Cause Invasion via the base of the plant by the fungus *Sclerotium rolfsii* (syn. *Corticium rolfsii*); nematode and insect wounds promote infection. Plants in light, sandy soils, well supplied with moisture, are most at risk.
Control Maintain crops well, remove diseased plants and debris, and avoid growing plants in contaminated areas; remove infected residues or bury them deeply. Seed may be treated with thiram.

Boron deficiency

Plants affected Carnations (*Dianthus*), lettuces, celery, root crops, tomatoes, all fruits. The condition is fairly rare.
Symptoms Growing tips die; plants become stunted and bushy. Celery stems develop transverse cracks and the exposed tissues turn brown; lettuces fail to heart up. Pears become distorted and dimpled with brown, flecked flesh (very similar symptoms to those of the virus disease called stoney pit). Plums are misshapen and may show gumming (see "Pests and diseases," p.384). Strawberries are small and poorly colored. See p.568 for other symptoms.

Cause and control See p.568 for details.

See also "Mealybugs," p.552; "Powdery mildew," p.552; "Rusts," p.554; "Chocolate spot," p.555; "Lily gray mold," p.555; "Contact weedkiller damage," p.556; "Irregular water supply," p.557; "Etiolation," p.561; "Fungal brackets," p.561; "Lightning," p.561; "Smuts," p.565; "Damping off," p.566; "*Armillaria* root rots," p.567; "Blackleg on cuttings," p.570; "Blackleg on potatoes," p.570; "Oak wilt," p.571; "Crown rot," p.571; "Clematis wilt," p.571, "Rose dieback," p.571; "Fire blight," p.571; "Peony wilt," p.571; "Anthracnose," p.572; "Black vine weevil larvae," p.572; and "Armyworms," p.572.

Stem distortion and abnormal growth

Etiolation

Plants affected Seedlings of all garden plants, and soft-stemmed plants.
Symptoms Stems are elongated and often pale, and the plant may grow toward the available light source, developing a lopsided habit. The leaves are chlorotic, and flowering is often reduced.
Cause Insufficient light, often owing to poor siting of the plant or shading from adjacent plants, buildings, and similar structures. Overcrowded plants are susceptible to the condition.
Control Choose and site plants carefully. Ensure that adequate light is provided for seedlings as soon as germination has occurred. Plants only slightly affected should recover if conditions are improved.

Cutworms

Plants affected Low-growing perennials, annuals, root vegetables, and lettuces.
Symptoms Stem bases and leaves of low-growing plants are visibly gnawed and roots may also be affected. Plants grow slowly, wilt, and may ultimately die.
Cause Caterpillars of various moths (e.g. *Peridroma* and *Agrotis* spp.), usually creamy brown in color and 1¾in (4.5cm) long. At night they feed above soil level.
Control Where damage is seen, search for and destroy the cutworms. Protect young plants with an aluminum foil collar pushed into the soil; treat the soil with chlorpyrifos + diazinon; water vulnerable plants with piperonyl butoxide.

Hormone weedkiller damage

Plants affected Broad-leaved plants (mainly roses, tomatoes, and grapes), and conifers.
Symptoms Small bumps may appear on stems. Leaves are distorted and petioles twisted or spiraled. See pp.557 and 565 for other symptoms.
Cause Contamination by a growth regulator or hormone-type weedkiller, often from a great distance; even minute quantities may cause extensive damage. Sources of trouble are spray drift and the use of contaminated sprayers or watering cans.
Control Apply weedkillers according to the manufacturer's instructions, placing protective barriers around adjacent plants. Keep one sprayer or watering can for use with weedkillers only, or preferably use dribble bars. Store weedkillers away from soil mix, fertilizers, and plants. Plants that have been affected usually grow out of the symptoms.

Leafy gall

Plants affected Shrubs, perennials, and annuals, in particular dahlias, chrysanthemums, and pelargoniums.
Symptoms Tiny, distorted shoots and leaves develop on the stem at or near ground level.
Cause *Rhodococcus fascians*, a soilborne bacterium that enters through small wounds. It is easily spread on tools or through propagating from infected plants.
Control Destroy affected plants and remove the soil in their immediate vicinity, and wash after handling them. Do not propagate from infected plants. Maintain strict hygiene, sterilizing tools, containers, and the greenhouse regularly.

Crown gall

Plants affected Trees, shrubs (most commonly cane fruits and roses), and woody perennials.
Symptoms Irregular, rounded, often woody swellings occur on or burst from the stem; plant vigor is not seriously affected. See also p.567.
Cause *Agrobacterium tumefaciens* bacteria, that are prevalent in wet soils, enter the plants via surface wounds and cause the cells to proliferate.
Control Avoid plant damage and improve soil drainage. Cut out and destroy all the affected stems.

Forsythia gall

Plants affected Forsythias.
Symptoms Rough, woody, rounded galls form on the stems. They persist from year to year but rarely have adverse effects.
Cause Unknown; possibly bacterial infection.
Control No action is strictly necessary, but the unsightly galled stems may be removed and the plant sprayed with a copper-based fungicide.

Black knot gall

Plants affected Plums, cherries, apricots; many other species; cultivars of *Prunus*.
Symptoms Large galls, generally sausage-shaped, develop on shoots or branches. They may spread inward toward the crown. Initially brown, they turn black later on, as fruiting bodies develop.
Cause The fungus *Apiosporina morbosa*, which attacks and eventually kills young shoots.
Control Inspect susceptible trees and shrubs each fall for new galls, and prune off. This prevents the formation of fruiting bodies. If fruiting galls are present, spray with ferbam while they are dormant. Repeat as soon as the flower buds show color, at full flower, and again after three weeks.

Fungal brackets

Plants affected Trees, shrubs, woody perennials.
Symptoms Fungal fruiting bodies, often bracket-shaped, appear on the trunk, crown, or near branch stubs or other wounds. Short-lived or perennial, they vary in appearance, often according to weather conditions. General growth is slow, and the tree may develop an excess of dead wood and a thin crown. See p.567 for other symptoms.
Cause and control See p.567 for details.

Witches' brooms

Plants affected Trees, mainly hornbeams (*Carpinus*) and birches (*Betula*); shrubs; woody perennials.
Symptoms Dense clusters of small shoots appear on otherwise normal branches. Leaves discolor early and remain small but vigor is not affected.
Cause Fungi (especially *Taphrina*) and mites (for example *Eriophyes*), which cause the mutations.
Control Cut branches back below the affected area.

Lightning

Plants affected Tall trees, especially those in isolation.
Symptoms Bark may be stripped, and a deep furrow may appear down one side, often following the spiral grain. The heartwood may be shattered, weakening the tree and leaving it susceptible to disease. Dead wood increases in the crown, and the upper crown may be killed.
Cause Lightning.
Control Lightning rods may be attached to valuable tall trees, but this is unlikely to be feasible.

Mechanical wounding

Plants affected Potentially all plants.
Symptoms A neat-edged wound is visible on the stem or bark. Sap from the injured area may ferment into a slime flux (see "Slime flux/wet wood," p.559), and pathogens entering the wound cause dieback or even death. A healed wound may leave a raised area.
Cause Careless use of garden machinery and tools.
Control Remove severely damaged shoots or stems. Wounds on woody plants should be left alone.

Mice

Plants affected Shrubs and young trees.
Symptoms Bark is gnawed from stems and roots.
Cause Mice.
Control Traps are the most effective solution.
See also "Mice, rats, and voles," p.568.

See also "Asparagus beetles," p.550; "Black vine weevils," p.551; "Tent caterpillars," p.553; "Rusts," p.554; "Irregular water supply," p.557; "Nematodes," p.558; "Fasciation," p.563; "Squirrels," p.565; "Spotted cucumber beetle larvae," p.566; "Corn rootworms," p.566; "*Nectria* canker," p.570; "*Coryneum* canker," p.570; "Aster yellows," p.571; "Anthracnose," p.572; "Small animals," p.572; and "Deer," p.572.

Flower problems

Discolored flowers

Gray mold/*Botrytis*

Fungal patches

Plants affected Trees, shrubs, perennials, annuals, bulbous plants, vegetables, fruits, and indoor plants.
Symptoms A fuzzy, gray, fungal growth appears on the flowers in patches, leading to total deterioration. This may later spread to the stems and body of the plant. See also pp.552, 559, and 564.
Cause The fungi *Botrytis cinerea* and *B. galanthina*.
Control Do not plant annuals too closely at first. Avoid injury to plants, clear up dead material, and provide good ventilation. Remove affected areas. Spray with a fungicide containing captan or ferbam.

Total deterioration

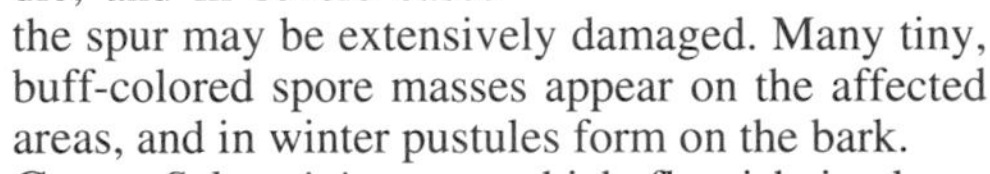

Viruses

Plants affected Most flowering plants, mainly bulbous plants, tomatoes, and strawberries.
Symptoms Flowers are small and distorted, patterned with streaking or color-breaking. See also pp.555 and 565.
Cause A large number of viruses. Submicroscopic virus particles in the sap of infected plants may be transmitted to healthy tissues by aphids, nematodes, and certain other pests, through handling, or on garden tools; some are seedborne.
Control Buy certified (virus-free) plants. Control potential carriers, for example aphids, and keep down weeds. Remove and burn affected plants; handle suspect plants after healthy ones, and do not propagate from them. Use a new site for any replacement plants. There is no chemical control.

Thrips

Plants affected Perennials, often *Achimenes*, *Primula obconica*, *Sinningia*, *Streptocarpus*, African violets (*Saintpaulia*), chrysanthemums, roses, daylilies, peonies, cyclamens, pelargoniums, and gladioli.
Symptoms White flecks appear on the petals; loss of pigmentation can be severe. Heavy attacks stop buds from opening. Leaves discolor to silver-white.
Cause Various species of thrips, e.g. gladiolus thrips (*Thrips simplex*) and flower thrips (*Frankliniella tritici*) in gardens, and western flower thrips (*Frankliniella occidentalis*) in greenhouses. They are sap-suckers. Adults are narrow-bodied, up to 1/16in (1.6mm) long, and brown or black; immature nymphs are creamy yellow. They thrive in hot, dry conditions.
Control Water plants regularly and, in greenhouses, maintain a cool, humid atmosphere. Spray with malathion, diazinon, permethrin, acephate, chlorpyrifos, pyrethrum, or dimethoate. Predatory mites (*Amblyseius* spp.) are an effective control.

Blossom wilt

Plants affected Apples, pears, cherries (*Prunus*), and quinces.
Symptoms The flowers turn brown and wither, but remain tightly clinging to the stem. The adjacent leaves then turn brown and die, and in severe cases the spur may be extensively damaged. Many tiny, buff-colored spore masses appear on the affected areas, and in winter pustules form on the bark.
Cause *Sclerotinia* spp., which flourish in damp conditions. The spores are carried on air currents and infect the plant via the flowers.
Control Remove and burn or discard all infected areas in summer, and spray plants with a copper-based fungicide.

Tulip fire/blight

Plants affected Tulips.
Symptoms Bleached, and often elongated, spots appear on flower petals; severely affected flowers may wither completely. Some of the buds remain tightly closed and become covered in a dense, gray, fungal growth. See p.555 for other symptoms.
Cause The fungus *Botrytis tulipae*, which flourishes in wet seasons, because the spores are spread by wind and rain. The sclerotia (fungal resting bodies) persist in the soil, and will germinate when tulips are planted in the area again.
Control Remove affected leaves and shoots immediately. Lift and dry off bulbs at the end of the season, discarding any with sclerotia, and dip them in a suitable fungicide solution, e.g. captan. Wait two years before replanting the site with tulips, or, if possible, change the soil.

Mycoplasmas

Plants affected Trees, shrubs, clematis, perennials, annuals, bulbous plants, vegetables, fruits (especially strawberries), and indoor plants.
Symptoms Flowers are green, undersized, and sometimes distorted. They do not revert to their usual color and subsequent flushes are also green. Symptoms on clematis are similar to those caused by frost injury, but "frost-damaged" flowers will be replaced by normal-colored blooms later in the season. On strawberries, the condition is called green petal. See also p.557.
Cause Mycoplasmas, which are believed to be related to bacteria. They are spread by aphids (see p.552); but strawberry green petal is more commonly transmitted by leafhoppers (p.553), which often pick up the infection from clover plants suffering from phyllody disease.
Control Discard affected plants, buy certified fruit stock, and control both pests (potential vectors) and weeds (which may harbor the disease).

Rhododendron bud blast

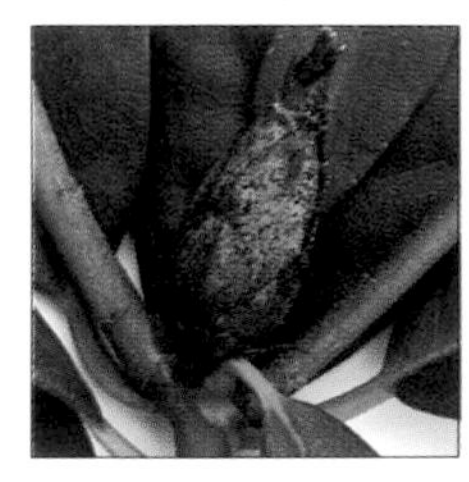

Plants affected Rhododendrons and azaleas.
Symptoms The buds form but do not open. They turn brown and dry, sometimes developing a silver-gray sheen, and during spring become covered in black fungal bristles. The affected buds are not shed.
Cause The fungus *Pycnostysanus azaleae*, which is passed from plant to plant by the rhododendron leafhopper (*Graphocephala fennahi*).
Control If possible, remove and destroy all the affected buds before midsummer, when the leafhoppers become prevalent; also spray against the leafhoppers (see p.553).

Potassium deficiency

Plants affected Both edible and ornamental fruiting plants, but mainly currants, apples, and pears.
Symptoms Flowering, subsequent fruiting, and general growth may be reduced. See p.556 for details of other symptoms.
Cause Growing plants in soils with either a light texture or a high lime or peat content.
Control Improve the soil texture. Dress with muriate of potash or a high-potassium fertilizer.

Apple psyllids

Plants affected Apples.
Symptoms The blossom browns as though it is frost-damaged; small green insects appear on the flower stalks.
Cause Apple psyllid (*Psylla mali*) nymphs, which are flattened, pale green insects up to 1/12in (2mm) in length that suck sap. Heavy attacks will both kill the blossoms and prevent fruit set.
Control Apply dormant oil in winter. Alternatively, spray with dimethoate, or permethrin at the green cluster stage of bud development, before the petals show color.

See also "Powdery mildew," p.552; "High temperatures and scorch," p.556; "Low temperatures," p.556; "Azalea galls," p.558; "Iris borers," p.566; "Aster yellows," p.571; and "Fire blight," p.571.

Distorted and eaten flowers

Drought

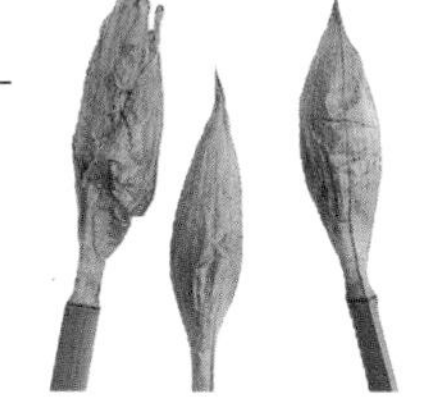

Plants affected All plants, especially those in light, sandy soils or in containers.
Symptoms The buds fail to develop fully, and the flowers are small and sparse. See also pp.556, 570, and 573.
Cause Prolonged or repeated water shortage. Plants in small containers are particularly vulnerable during hot weather, and peat-based soil mixes that are allowed to dry out too much are extremely difficult to rewet. Dry, brown buds on certain plants, e.g. camellias and rhododendrons, are the result of a water shortage the previous year during the period of bud initiation.
Control Water plants regularly, and frequently check those in hot or sunny positions. Mulch, where appropriate, to improve moisture retention. Try to prevent drought rather than treat it: plants exposed to a chronic water shortage are far less likely to recover than those suffering a sudden shortage.

Fasciation

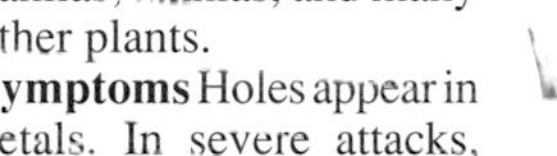

Plants affected All plants, most commonly delphiniums, forsythias, *Daphne*, and *Prunus subhirtella* 'Autumnalis'.
Symptoms Peculiar, broad, flattened flower stems develop. The main stems are also broad and flattened.
Cause In many instances, early damage to the growing point caused by insect, slug, or frost attack, or handling; it may also be due to bacterial infection or genetic malfunction.
Control Fasciation does no harm; affected areas may be either left on the plant or pruned out.

Proliferation

Plants affected Mainly roses, especially the older varieties, but occasionally other ornamentals and fruiting plants.
Symptoms The flower stem grows through the center of the existing flower, and a new flower may form above the first. In some cases several flower buds develop together, surrounded by one set of flower petals.
Cause Early damage to the growing point of the bud, often through frost or insect attack. Where the problem recurs, a virus (see opposite) may be the cause.
Control Severely and repeatedly affected plants, which may be virus infected, should be destroyed. In all other cases, treatment is unnecessary.

Earwigs

Plants affected Shrubs, perennials, and annuals, commonly chrysanthemums, dahlias, and clematis. Also apricot and peach trees.
Symptoms Petals are eaten in summer. See p.550 for other symptoms.
Cause The earwig (*Forficula auricularia*), which is a yellowish brown insect 3/4in (2cm) long.
Control To make a simple earwig trap, loosely stuff small pots with hay or straw. Invert pots on stakes among plants. Earwigs hide in pots; remove and destroy contents daily. Alternatively, spray at dusk with permethrin, diazinon, carbaryl, or rotenone.

Spotted cucumber beetles

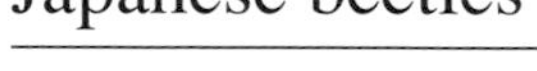

Plants affected Many late-summer flowers, including *Calendula*, *Coreopsis*, *Cosmos*, *Impatiens*, sweet peas (*Lathyrus odoratus*), dahlias, zinnias, and many other plants.
Symptoms Holes appear in petals. In severe attacks, flower buds are damaged. Beetles may be seen.
Cause Spotted cucumber beetles (*Diabrotica undecimpunctata howardi*), 1/4in (6mm) in length. West of the Rockies, the related species *D. u. undecimpunctata* feeds on almost everthing except conifers.
Control Spray with diazinon, carbaryl, rotenone, or insecticidal soaps. See also "Spotted cucumber beetle larvae," p.566.

Rose chafers

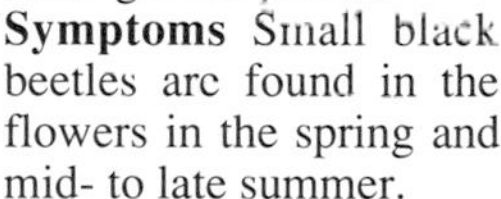

Plants affected Species and hybrid roses. Cultivars of *Rosa rugosa* seem especially vulnerable. Peonies and hollyhocks are occasionally affected.
Symptoms Clusters of beetles are seen on flowers. Holes in petals appear; petals are eaten away; flower buds are eaten and may fail to open.
Cause Rose chafer beetles (*Macrodactylus subspinosus*). This grayish beetle, 1/2in (1cm) long, feeds for four weeks in midsummer. Larvae feed on grass roots and may be mistaken for white grubs of Japanese, June, and Asiatic garden beetles (see p.573).
Control Spray with carbaryl or methoxychlor when when symptoms are first noticed; repeat as needed. Control larvae in lawns (see "White grubs," p.573).

Grasshoppers and crickets

Plants affected Many garden plants but mostly flowers on beans, squashes, and other cucurbits.
Symptoms Flowers have holes in petals; entire flowers may be missing.
Cause Daytime feeding of grasshoppers (e.g. *Melanoplus bivittatus*) and nocturnal feeding of crickets (e.g. *Acheta assimilis*).
Control Bait formulated for cutworms and earwigs generally keeps grasshopper and cricket damage to a minimum. Alternatively, pick grasshoppers and crickets off plants by hand.

Japanese beetles

Plants affected Many trees and shrubs, but especially roses and daylilies.
Symptoms Flowers are eaten by beetles, often working as a group. Unopened buds are rarely attacked. See also "White grubs," p.566.
Cause Metallic green beetles (*Popillia japonica*). Beetles measure about 1/2in (1cm) long, with coppery brown wings and six patches of white hair under the edges of the wings. They feed in daylight. The larvae are a serious pest of lawns (see "White grubs," p.573).
Control Hand-pick beetles off plants and drown them in soapy water, if the numbers are few. Spray with methoxychlor or insecticidal soaps if the attack is heavy. Traps baited with an attractant are available, but these tend to bring in heavier infestations.

Plant bugs

Plants affected Shrubs and perennials (especially phlox, *Caryopteris*, fuchsias, hydrangeas, dahlias, and chrysanthemums).
Symptoms Flowers develop unevenly with undersized ray petals. Fuchsia flowers abort completely. Phlox blossoms may be deformed.
Cause In phlox, phlox plant bugs, orange bugs 1/4in (6mm) long with red nymphs. See also p.551.
Control See p.551.

Pollen beetles

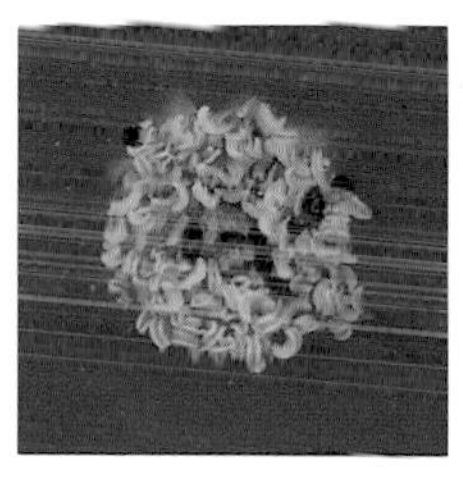

Plants affected Roses, sweet peas (*Lathyrus odoratus*), daffodils, cauliflowers, sprouting broccoli, squashes, turnips, and other garden plants.
Symptoms Small black beetles are found in the flowers in the spring and mid- to late summer.
Cause Pollen beetles (*Meligethes* spp.), which are 1/16in (1.6mm) long and black. The beetles eat some pollen and may remain on cut flowers but otherwise cause little direct damage to the blooms.
Control Pollen beetles cannot be controlled, because vast numbers fly into gardens from canola oil fields, where they breed. It is not advisable to use insecticides – they can cause damage to the petals and harm useful pollinators, e.g. bees. Cut flowers can be freed of the beetles by placing the flowers in a shed or garage with one source of light (e.g. a lamp). The beetles will fly toward the light.

See also "Caterpillars," p.551; "Low temperatures," p.556; "Irregular water supply," p.557; "Azalea galls," p.558; "Honeysuckle witches' brooms," p.558; "Etiolation," p.561; "Viruses," p.562; "Thrips," p.562; "Mycoplasmas," p.562; "Birds," p.565; and "Small animals," p.572.

Fruit, berry, and seed problems

High temperatures and scorch

Plants affected Soft fruits, tree fruits, grapes, tomatoes, and apples, especially green-skinned cultivars.
Symptoms Discolored patches develop on the skin, particularly on the uppermost surfaces of fruits, or on the ones that are more highly exposed.
Cause and control See p.556 for details.

Gray mold/*Botrytis*

Plants affected Fruiting trees, shrubs, perennials, annuals, and indoor plants. Soft, thin-skinned fruits, e.g. strawberries, raspberries, grapes, and tomatoes, are vulnerable.

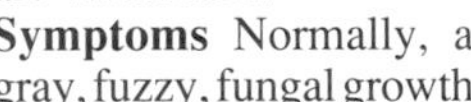

Symptoms Normally, a gray, fuzzy, fungal growth develops on a soft, brown rot. The damage spreads rapidly and the whole fruit may collapse. Unripe tomatoes may develop "ghost spot," where a pale green ring appears on the skin but the rest of the fruit colors normally and does not rot (the unaffected parts may be eaten). See also pp.552, 559, and 562.
Cause and control See pp.559 and 562 for details.

Powdery mildew

Plants affected Most fruits, commonly grapes, peaches, and gooseberries.
Symptoms Whitish gray fungal patches appear on the skin, often turning brown as they mature. Grapes become hard and cracked, and may fail to swell fully; secondary fungi may invade the fruits. Cracking of gooseberries is uncommon and fungal growth can be rubbed off.
Cause and control Hop mildew (*Sphaerotheca macularis*) attacks fruits; grape mildew (*Uncinula necator*) attacks all parts of the plant. See p.552 for details.

Brown rot

Plants affected Cultivated fruits, especially apples, plums, peaches, nectarines, and pears.
Symptoms Soft brown areas develop on the skin and penetrate throughout the flesh. Concentric rings of creamy white pustules then start to appear on the surface. Affected fruits either fall or may become dry and wizened and remain on the tree.
Cause The fungus *Sclerotinia* (*S. fructicola* and *S. laxa*). The pustules produce spores, and these are then carried by wind or insects to other fruits; infection occurs through wounds or blemishes on the surface of the fruit.
Control Prevent injury to fruits (e.g. that caused by pests), and pick off and burn those affected.

Tomato late blight

Plants affected Tomatoes, mainly in the open but also in greenhouses.
Symptoms The fruits first develop a brown discoloration and then start to shrink and rot. Even fruits that may have appeared to be healthy when picked may begin to deteriorate rapidly within a few days.
Cause and control See p.555 for details.

Raspberry fruitworms

Plants affected Mainly raspberries, but also blackberries and hybrid cane fruits.
Symptoms Ripe fruits are dried up and brown at the stalk end; an insect larva may be found inside the fruit.
Cause The raspberry fruitworm (*Byturus rubi*). The females lay eggs on the flowers in early to midsummer. Brownish white larvae up to 1/4in (6mm) long hatch two weeks later. They feed initially at the stalk end of the fruit but then move to the inner plug.
Control Only chemical sprays provide an effective control. Apply malathion, permethrin, or rotenone to raspberries when the first pink fruit appears; to loganberries when 80 percent of the petals have fallen; to blackberries when the first flower opens. A second application may be required for raspberries and loganberries two weeks after the first. Spray at dusk to avoid harming bees.

Scab

Plants affected Pears, pyracanthas, *Citrus*, *Malus*, and loquats.
Symptoms Blackish brown, scabby patches develop on the skin; a severe attack will leave fruits small and distorted. In some cases cracks may develop, which will make the fruit vulnerable to secondary infections.
Cause and control See p.555 for details.

Calcium deficiency

Bitter pit

Plants affected Apples (the condition is known as bitter pit), and tomatoes, eggplants, and sweet peppers (blossom end rot).
Symptoms The flesh of apples is brown-flecked and tastes bitter; the skin is sometimes pitted. Bitter pit may affect fruits on the tree or in storage. Tomato, eggplant, and pepper fruits develop a sunken, brown discoloration at the flower end.

Blossom end rot

Cause A lack of calcium, possibly combined with other nutritional imbalances, resulting from an irregular or poor supply of moisture to the plant's roots, preventing adequate calcium uptake. Groups of cells that are deprived of calcium collapse and become discolored.
Control Avoid very acid growing media. Water regularly and, where feasible, mulch plants. Tomatoes may be sprayed with calcium chloride every ten days from early summer until harvesting.

Plum curculio

Plants affected All stone fruits; apples, pears, and quinces.
Symptoms Beetles are seen on fruit, leaves, or petals. Small crescent-like scars appear on the fruit where the egg was laid. Gray larvae with black heads may be visible within the fruit.
Cause Plum curculio (*Conotrachelus nenuphar*), a dark beetle 1/4in (6mm) long, with four bumps on its wings and a down-curved snout. Adults feed on fruit, leaves, and petals, leaving them open to attack by brown rot (see left).
Control Collect fruit as it drops. Spray at petal drop with insecticidal soap, carbaryl, or diazinon.

Shanking of grapes

Plants affected Grapes.
Symptoms Berry stalks wither. Berries have a watery or sour taste; black varieties turn red, and white ones remain translucent. They may remain on the bunch but shrivel up and are vulnerable to disease, e.g. gray mold/*Botrytis* (see left).
Cause Heavy cropping, either over- or underwatering, or stagnant soil conditions.
Control Cut out withered berries and regularly apply a foliar feed. Decrease the crop for a few years and try to improve general soil conditions.

Blue mold on citrus

Plants affected All *Citrus*, especially oranges.
Symptoms Circular patches of mold, usually with a central depression, appear on the rind. They extend rapidly and develop a distinct blue coloration.
Cause The fungus *Penicillium italicum*, which enters fruits through bruised, wounded, or insect-damaged areas. It typically occurs on stored fruits.
Control Wash fruits with a suitable fungicide.

Irregular water supply

Plants affected Potentially all fruiting plants.
Symptoms Fruits are misshapen and undersized, and a sudden availability of water after a drought may cause their skin and flesh to crack, leaving them vulnerable to diseases that cause rotting. See p.557 for other symptoms.
Cause and control See p.557 for details.

Viruses

Plants affected Pears, cucumbers, melons, squashes, tomatoes, strawberries, and raspberries.
Symptoms Fruits may be undersized, distorted, discolored, or grouped in rosettes. Cucumber mosaic virus produces warty, distorted cucumber, melon, and squash fruits that are blotched dark green and yellow; pear stony pit virus produces distorted and pitted pear fruits with patches of dead, stony cells. See also pp.555 and 562.
Cause and control See p.555 for details.

Hormone weedkiller damage

Plants affected All fruits, but commonly only tomatoes.
Symptoms Plum-shaped tomatoes form. Although they ripen normally and are safe to eat, they may taste unpleasant and be hollow. Fruits that have formed before contamination occurs are not usually affected. See p.557 for other symptoms.
Cause and control See p.557 for details.

Fruit flies

Plants affected Tropical and subtropical fruits.
Symptoms Holes are bored in fruits. Secondary fungal and bacterial infection may occur.
Cause Larvae of fruit flies (*Dacus* and *Ceratitis* spp.), including the Mediterranean fruit fly (*C. capitata*).
Control Lay a bait of malathion and sugar solution.

Wasps

Plants affected Grapes, plums, pears, apples, and figs.
Symptoms Large cavities are eaten in ripe fruits in late summer; wasps may be seen feeding.
Cause Wasps, which are attracted to fruits initially damaged by birds.
Control Protect fruits by placing bags made of muslin or pantyhose over the clusters well before damage is likely to begin. Locate and destroy wasp nests with a commercial wasp spray.

Birds

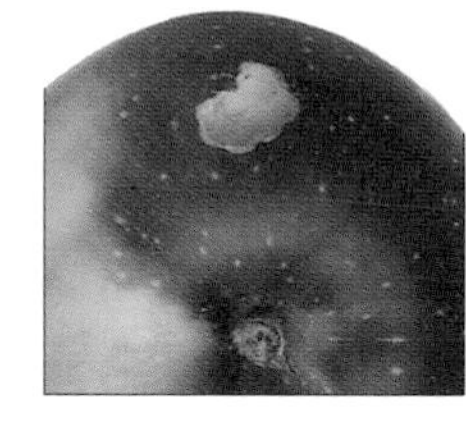

Plants affected Fruits, vegetables, and flowers.
Symptoms Peck marks leave ripe fruits susceptible to infection from brown rot (see p.564); soft fruits are eaten. Vegetables, seedlings, flowers, and buds may be pecked.
Cause Blackbirds, starlings, and other birds.
Control Either net the plants at fruiting time or grow them in a permanent birdproof cage.

Codling moths

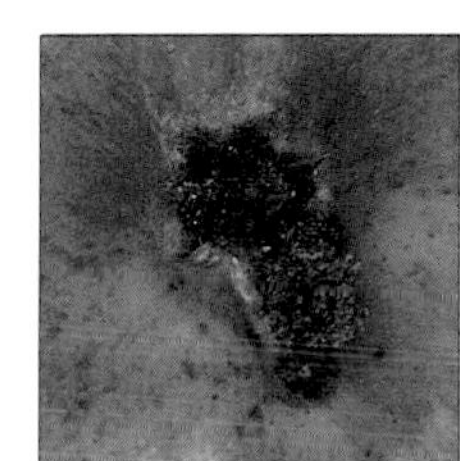

Plants affected Apples, pears, apricots, peaches, walnuts (*Juglans*).
Symptoms Holes are tunneled in ripe fruits.
Cause The caterpillars of the codling moth (*Cydia pomonella*), which feed in the core of the fruit; when mature, each caterpillar makes a frass-filled tunnel to the outside of the fruit.
Control Hang pheromone traps in the trees from late spring to midsummer to catch the male moths, thus reducing egg fertilization. Traps will also indicate when the males are flying, so that sprays may be timed to control the caterpillars as they hatch. If necessary, spray with permethrin or carbaryl in early summer and again three weeks later.

Apple maggots

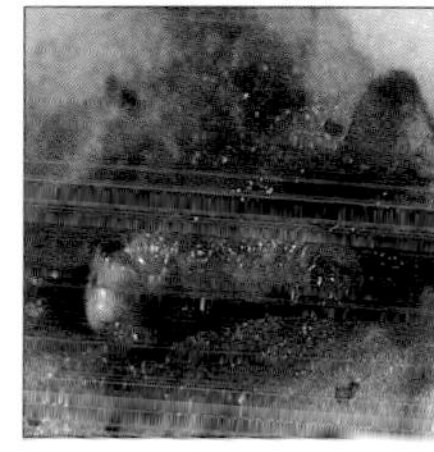

Plants affected Apples, plums, cherries, and blueberries.
Symptoms Brown tunnels wind through the fruit. The entire center of the fruit may become a soft brown pulp. Larvae may be seen in or on fruit. The surface of the fruit is distorted and pitted. The fruit may fall early.
Cause Larvae of the apple maggot (*Rhagoletis pomonella*), a black fly 1/4in (6mm) long, with zigzag black bands on its wings. The larvae emerge from the fallen fruit and pupate in the soil over winter, emerging as adults early the following summer.
Control Pick up and dispose of fallen fruit as soon as it is seen on the ground. Spray young fruit with diazinon or methoxychlor at 7–10 day intervals from early to midsummer.

European apple sawflies

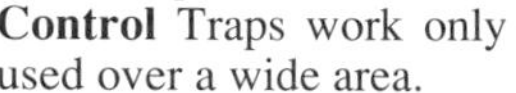

Plants affected Apples.
Symptoms Fruitlets are tunneled and drop off during early to midsummer. The damaged fruits sometimes remain on the tree and become mature, but they are misshapen and have a long, ribbonlike scar on the skin.
Cause The larvae of the apple sawfly (*Hoplocampa testudinea*), white caterpillar-like insects up to 1/2in (1cm) long with brown heads. They are less widespread than codling moths (see left).
Control Spray with rotenone, permethrin, or methoxychlor within seven days of petal fall; spray at dusk to avoid harming bees.

Pear thrips

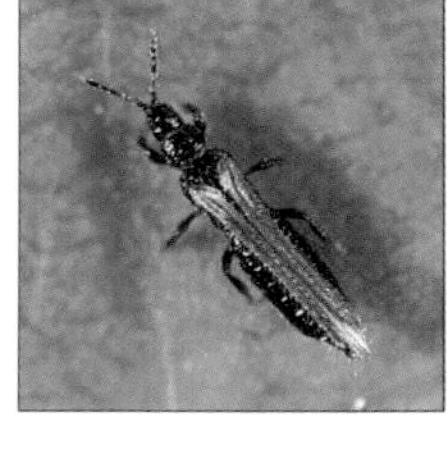

Plants affected Pears, apples, apricots, and plums; maples; other trees.
Symptoms Fruit are distorted and scarred. Small insects may be visible on leaves and young fruit.
Cause Pear thrips (*Teaniothrips inconsequens*) measuring about 1/20in (1.5mm) long, slender, and brown. Nymphs are small and white. Adults scrape plant tissue with their mouthparts and suck juices.
Control No chemical control is available.

Pea moths

Plants affected Peas.
Symptoms Peas in pods are eaten by caterpillars.
Cause The pea moth (*Cydia nigricana*), which lays eggs on pea plants in flower in early to midsummer. The caterpillars are creamy white with brown heads, and are up to 1/2in (1cm) long.
Control Use pheromone traps to catch the male pea moths, reducing the chances of the females mating successfully. Alternatively, spray the young plants with permethrin, 7–10 days after flowering begins. Early- or late-sown peas should not need spraying.

Smuts

Plants affected Sweet corn, *Anemone*, *Trollius*, violets (*Viola*), and also winter aconites (*Eranthis hyemalis*).
Symptoms Round or elliptical pale swellings devlop on the plant and rupture, releasing powdery black masses of fungal spores.
Cause Various fungi, e.g. *Urocystis* and *Ustilago*.
Control Burn affected plants; infection may recur.

Squirrels

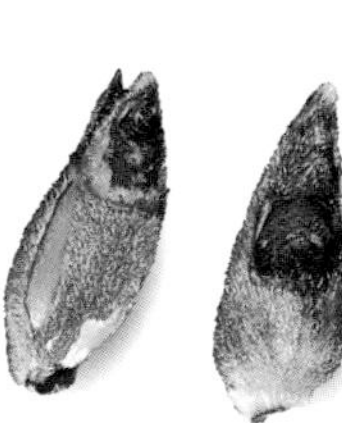

Plants affected Young trees.
Symptoms Bark, buds, ripening fruits, and nuts are eaten.
Cause Squirrels.
Control Traps work only if used over a wide area.

See also "Sowbugs," p.550; "Millipedes," p.550; "Leaf tiers and rollers," p.554; "Potassium deficiency," p.556; "Honeysuckle witches' brooms," p.558; "Japanese beetles," p.563; "Corn rootworms," p.566; "Boron deficiency," p.568; "Drought," p.570; and "Small animals," p.572.

Root and tuber problems

Waterlogging

Plants affected Potentially all plants.
Symptoms Some roots may rot off completely. Those remaining are frequently blackened with a peeling outer surface. The first visible symptom is usually wilting leaves. See also pp. 557 and 570.
Cause Excessive water levels in the growing medium, owing to factors such as poor soil structure, compaction, impeded drainage, or overwatering.
Control Where feasible, improve the structure and drainage of the soil and, if necessary, choose plants that are likely to survive in wet conditions. Check that drainage holes for container-grown plants are adequate and that flow through them is not impeded. Regular use of a foliar feed during the growing season may help to stimulate growth, replacing waterlogged roots.

Damping off

Plants affected The seedlings of all plants.
Symptoms Affected roots darken and rot off, causing the seedling to collapse and die. The disease often starts at one end of the seed tray, spreading rapidly to the other. A fluffy fungal growth may appear on the soil mix as well as on dead seedlings. See p.570 for other symptoms.
Cause Various fungi, such as *Pythium ultimum* and some *Phytophthora*, that are soil- or waterborne and attack seedlings via the roots or the base of the stem. They flourish in moist and unhygienic conditions.
Control There is no effective control once the disease is established, so it must be prevented. Sow seed thinly, improve ventilation, maintain strict hygiene, and avoid overwatering. Use only sterilized soil mix and clean trays and pots. Water occasionally with captan, thiram, or zineb.

Root-knot nematodes

Plants affected Many garden plants, including fruit trees, vegetables, and ornamentals. Plants growing in greenhouses are also susceptible.
Symptoms Galls or swellings appear on the roots or tubers. Overall growth is stunted, and the plant may wilt, yellow, and sometimes even be killed.
Cause Root-knot nematodes (*Meloidogyne* spp.), which are thin, transparent, and only 1/32in (0.5mm) long. The larvae penetrate the roots.
Control Destroy all affected plants. Rotate vegetable crops; choose resistant plants. There is no chemical control available to amateur gardeners.

Black vine weevil larvae

Plants affected Shrubs, perennials, annuals, bulbous plants, and indoor plants; most commonly, begonias, cyclamens, fuchsias, *Impatiens*, primroses (*Primula*, including the Polyanthus Group), *Sedum*, and strawberries. Yews (*Taxus*), rhododendrons, and container-grown plants are particularly vulnerable.
Symptoms The outer tissues of woody seedlings and cuttings are gnawed from the stem bases and roots below ground level. Plants grow slowly, have a tendency to wilt, and finally collapse and die.
Cause and control See p.572 for details.
See also p.572; and p.551 for information on damage caused to leaves by adult black vine weevils.

White grubs

Plants affected Spring- and summer-flowering bulbs; young transplants.
Symptoms Bulbs fail to grow or shrivel and die; transplants wilt and die. Grubs are visible in soil and roots.
Cause White grubs of June beetles (*Phyllophaga* spp.), Japanese beetles (*Popillia japonica*), and chafer bugs (*Macrodactylus subspinosus*), about 1/4in (6mm) long, feeding on the roots; generally found only on reclaimed lawn areas. See also p.573.
Control Drench soil with diazinon, or fork in diazinon crystals. This is usually only a temporary problem; action is seldom necessary a second year.
See also p.573 for problems on lawns.

Cutworms

Plants affected Low-growing perennials, annuals, root vegetables, and lettuces.
Symptoms Cavities appear in root crops, and taproots may be severed, causing plants to wilt and die. See p.561 for other symptoms.
Cause The caterpillars of various moths (e.g. *Peridroma* and *Agrotis*), usually creamy brown in color and up to 1 3/4in (4.5cm) in length. They eat roots and the outer tissues of stem bases.
Control Search for and destroy the cutworms. Water vulnerable plants with piperonyl butoxide, or treat the soil with chlorpyrifos + diazinon.

Iris borers

Plants affected Irises, particularly rhizomatous types such as tall bearded and *Iris tectorum*, but also *I. sibirica* cultivars.
Symptoms Destroyed rhizomes may lead to collapsed plants. Sawtooth edges may appear on the leaves in early summer. As the borers feed in or on the rhizome, foliage gradually yellows. Flowers in bud may turn brown and watery.
Cause Larvae of a small, gray moth (*Macronoctua onusta*), which lays eggs on the old foliage in late summer. The following spring, they hatch and tunnel into the leaves a few inches above the ground. Fully grown borers are about 1 1/4in (3cm) long, white, with a reddish brown head. Their tunneling often introduces iris soft rot (see p.569).
Control Clean up in fall to remove eggs. Spray in spring with rotenone or pyrethrum. Spray plants or drench the soil with dimethoate if tunneling starts.

Carrot rust flies

Plants affected Mainly carrots, parsnips, parsley, celeriac, fennel, dill, and celery.
Symptoms Rusty brown tunnels are bored under the outer skin of mature roots. Small plants develop discolored foliage and may eventually die.
Cause Creamy yellow maggots, larvae of the carrot rust fly (*Psila rosae*), which feed in the surface tissues of the larger roots; in fall they may bore deeper. They are slender, legless, and up to 1/2in (1cm) long.
Control Enclose susceptible plants within a clear plastic fence at least 24in (60cm) high, to exclude the low-flying female flies. Treat seed rows with chlorpyrifos + diazinon or diazinon crystals; growing plants may be protected against the second generation of larvae by watering with a diazinon solution in midsummer. Lift carrots for storage in fall to limit damage.

Cabbage root maggots

Plants affected Radishes and a wide range of brassicas (including broccoli, cabbages, cauliflowers, Brussels sprouts, turnips, and rutabagas).
Symptoms Plants grow slowly and wilt; seedlings and transplants die; tunnels appear in root crops.
Cause Root-feeding larvae of the fly *Delia radicum*, white, legless maggots up to 3/8in (9mm) long. Several generations occur between midspring and midfall, causing damage mainly to young plants.
Control Place collars of aluminum foil or half of a frozen juice can, about 5in (12cm) in diameter, around the base of transplanted brassicas to prevent the female flies from laying eggs in the soil. Alternatively, both transplanted brassicas and seed rows can be protected with chlorpyrifos + diazinon or piperonyl butoxide dust.

Spotted cucumber beetle larvae

Plants affected Corn and beans.
Symptoms Slender, pale yellow larvae 1/2–3/4in (1–1.2cm) long, with brown heads, feeding on the roots. On corn, they eat out the crown of the plant, making it liable to fall over.
Cause Larvae of the spotted cucumber beetle.
Control Rotate crops regularly. See also p.563.
See also "Spotted cucumber beetles," p.563.

Corn rootworms

Plants affected Corn.
Symptoms Poor growth, poor crops (if the attack is bad). Larvae may be visible eating the roots.
Cause The larvae of *Diabrotica longicormis*, threadlike, white, 1/2in (1cm) long worms that burrow through roots and leave brown tunnels. The eggs hatch in late spring, and the larvae feed on corn roots. They pupate in midsummer and emerge as beetles in late summer to feed on corn silks and pollen. After laying eggs in

the soil of cornfields, the beetles die at first frost.
Control Rotate crops regularly to avoid growing corn in contaminated soil. Rotating corn crops with soy beans, alfalfa, or cereal crops may prove particularly effective. Treat soil with diazinon or piperonyl butoxide, and spray ripening cobs with insecticidal soaps as necessary.

Clubroot

Plants affected The family Cruciferae, especially certain brassicas (for example, cabbages, Brussels sprouts, and rutabagas) and radishes, and some ornamentals, including candytufts (*Iberis*), wallflowers (*Cheiranthus*), and stocks (*Matthiola*).
Symptoms Roots are swollen and distorted; plants grow slowly and are often discolored; they wilt in hot weather. See p.555 for other symptoms.

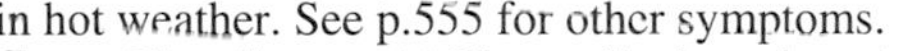

Cause The slime mold *Plasmodiophora brassicae*, which thrives in poorly drained, acid soils, and may also be found on manure and plant debris. It is easily spread on boots and tools, and the spores remain viable for 20 years or more. Weeds susceptible to this disease (e.g. shepherd's purse and wild mustard) may be a source of infection.
Control Remove and burn affected plants. Keep the area free of weeds, improve drainage, and lime the soil. Raise new plants in soil-based mix to encourage root development. Commercial chemical dips may be used when planting.

Phytophthora root rots

Plants affected Trees, shrubs, and woody perennials; commonly maples (*Acer*), yews (*Taxus*), Lawson cypresses (*Chamaecyparis lawsoniana*), apples, rhododendrons, raspberries, and heathers.
Symptoms The larger roots die back from the stem or trunk, although the fine roots may appear perfectly healthy; affected roots usually turn black. See pp.560 and 571 for other symptoms.
Cause Various species of the fungus *Phytophthora*, often found in wet or waterlogged soil. The roots of plants are attacked by swimming spores that build up both in the soil and within infected plant remains.
Control Avoid heavy watering and improve soil drainage. Dig up and burn affected plants. Buy plants from reputable sources and choose those that are tolerant or resistant, e.g. *Tsuga heterophylla* and x *Cupressocyparis leylandii*. There is no chemical control available to amateurs.

Foot and root rots

Plants affected A wide range, especially petunias and other bedding plants, tomatoes, cucumbers, peas, beans, and young, container-grown plants.
Symptoms The roots turn black and break or rot. See p.560 for details of other symptoms.
Cause A range of soil- and water-borne fungi that flourish where growing conditions are unhygienic. The fungi are often introduced in unsterilized soil mix and standing water, and will build up in the soil over several years if susceptible plants are repeatedly grown on the same site.
Control Rotate susceptible plants. Maintain strict hygiene, and use only fresh, sterilized soil mix and clean water. Remove affected plants and the soil in the vicinity of their roots.

Tropical root rots

Plants affected Annual and perennial crops, temperate and tropical, including broad beans, snap beans, cucumbers, melons, pumpkins, and peanuts.
Symptoms Annual plants show a midseason wilting, with rotting of the base of the stem and upper portion of the root; the infected tissues develop lesions and often turn red before decaying. The leaves become chlorotic as their water supply is restricted, and young seedlings may show signs of damping off (see opposite). Peanut shells become blackened and decay rapidly. The infected tissues of perennial crops turn purple and the plants wilt.
Cause Various forms of the soilborne fungus *Fusarium solani*, which often occur as secondary infections. The disease is carried in the soil and infected debris; crops grown in poorly drained, acid soils are particularly at risk. High soil temperatures will encourage the development of pea root rot (*F. solani* f. *pisi*).
Control Rotate crops on a long cycle. Treat seeds with hot water at 131°F (55°C) for 15 minutes. Where possible, improve soil drainage.

Crown gall

Plants affected Trees, shrubs (most commonly cane fruits and roses), and woody perennials.
Symptoms Irregular, rounded, often woody swellings develop on or burst from the roots, and occasionally the whole root system is distorted into a single large swelling. See p.561 for other symptoms.
Cause The bacterium *Agrobacterium tumefaciens*, prevalent in wet soils. The bacteria enter the plant through wounds made on the surface and cause cells to proliferate.
Control Avoid damaging plants and improve soil drainage. Cut out and destroy any affected stems in order to prevent secondary infection.

Armillaria root rots

Plants affected Trees, shrubs, climbers, and some woody perennials; most commonly affected are fruit and nut trees on the West Coast.
Symptoms A creamy-white mycelium develops under the bark at the base of the trunk or stem. Sometimes it also extends upward; tough black rhizomorphs (i.e. fungal strands) appear. In fall, fruiting bodies may develop in clusters on underground roots, at the base of the trunk, and occasionally at some height from the ground; they die back after the first frost. Resin exudes from cracks in the bark of conifers. Prolific flowering or fruiting may occur shortly before death.
Cause The fungus *Armillaria* (principally *A. mellea*) spread either by rhizomorph movement from an infected plant or stump, or through root contact.
Control Destroy affected plants, stumps, and as much of the root system as possible; if necessary, have the stump ground out. Avoid the more susceptible plants, choosing those showing resistance, e.g. yews (*Taxus*), *Cornus*, beeches (*Fagus*), and *Hebe*.

Fungal brackets

Plants affected Mainly trees, and especially mature or overmature specimens, but also shrubs and woody perennials.
Symptoms Fungal fruiting bodies, often bracket-shaped, may appear above ground, following the line of the roots; they are attached to the roots by tiny fungal threads. They vary in appearance, often according to weather conditions. The roots may become hollow and eventually die, making the tree extremely unstable in the ground. Stems are also affected (see p.561).
Cause Various fungi, e.g. *Meripilus* or *Ganoderma*.
Control Seek professional advice, particularly if the tree poses a potential hazard. Removal of fruiting bodies will not prevent further internal decay, but does reduce the chances of spread to other trees.

Parsnip canker

Plants affected Parsnips.
Symptoms The shoulders of affected parsnips rot; the crown, shank, and roots of the plant may also rot, and the foliage may show some spotting. This condition occurs mainly in fall and winter.
Cause Various species of fungus, primarily *Itersonilia pastinaceae*. Some are soil-inhabiting and others produce spores that are washed into the soil from leaf lesions.
Control Grow resistant cultivars. Rotate crops. Prevent injury to parsnip roots, particularly the type of injury caused by carrot rust fly larvae (see p.566). Sow late and closely in order to produce parsnips with small roots, which are less prone to disease, and hill up the rows to provide a barrier against spores washed down from the leaf lesions. Remove all affected plants immediately. Grow parsnips in a deep loam soil with a high pH.

Verticillium wilt

Plants affected A large number of garden and greenhouse plants.
Symptoms The roots deteriorate and die, and if cut longitudinally in the early stages of degeneration they may show a central, vascular column of brown discoloration.
Cause and control See p.559 for details.

Fusarium wilt

Plants affected Perennials, annuals, vegetables, and fruits; most commonly affected are China asters (*Callistephus*), carnations (*Dianthus*), sweet pea (*Lathyrus odoratus*), beans, and peas.
Symptoms Roots turn black and die.
Cause and control See p.560 for details.

Mice, rats, and voles

Plants affected Shrubs, young trees, crocus corms, seedlings of peas and beans, seeds, vegetables, and fruits kept in storage.
Symptoms The outer layer of stems and roots is gnawed. Seeds, seedlings, corms, vegetables, and fruits are eaten.
Cause Mice, rats, and voles.
Control Traps provide the best solution; poisoned baits containing bromadiolone or brodifacoum may also be used to control this problem.

Boron deficiency

Plants affected Roots of carrots, parsnips, rutabagas, turnips, and beets. The condition is fairly rare.
Symptoms The roots are of a poor shape and texture, and are grayish in color. They may split longitudinally and sometimes contain cavities. A brown discoloration known as brown heart may occur in the lowermost sections, often in concentric rings; it is found mainly in turnips and rutabagas, and makes them fibrous, with poor taste. Beets show internal discoloration and may develop cankers. See p.560 for symptoms on stems.
Cause A lack of boron in the soil, or an inability of the plant to take up the trace element owing to unsuitable growing conditions. Most common on very alkaline or heavily limed soils, those that have been very dry, and those where the boron has been leached out. It rarely affects greenhouse plants.
Control Maintain correct soil moisture levels and avoid excessive liming. Before introducing a susceptible plant to a problem site, apply borax at 1oz/20sq yd (35g/20sq m), mixing with horticultural sand for easy and accurate application. Use fritted trace elements.

See also "Aphids," p.552; "Mealybugs," p.552; "Slugs," "Wireworms," below; "Onion maggots," p.569; "Striped cucumber beetles," p.571, and "Fungus gnats or sciarid flies," p.572.

Potato tuber problems

Slugs

Plants affected Potatoes.
Symptoms Circular holes are bored in the outside of potato tubers, and extensive cavities appear in the interior, during late summer.
Cause Slugs.
Control Scatter silicon dioxide or metaldehyde pellets, or spray plants with metaldehyde. Grow less susceptible cultivars; harvest tubers as soon as mature.
See also "Slugs and snails," p.550.

Wireworms

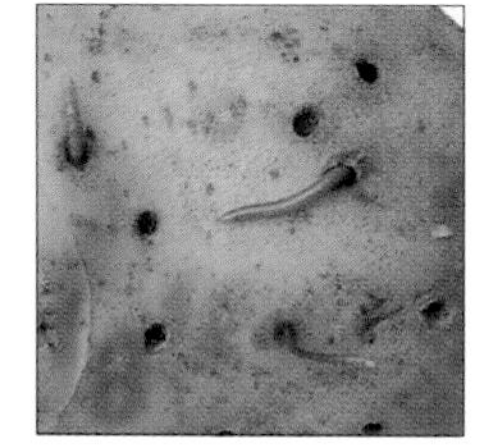

Plants affected Potatoes and other root crops, seedlings, perennials, annuals, and bulbous plants.
Symptoms Tunnels up to 1/8in (3mm) in diameter, superficially similar to those made by slugs, are bored through root crops. Underground parts of other plants are damaged. Small plants wilt and die.
Cause The slender, stiff-bodied, yellowish orange larvae of click beetles (e.g. *Agriotes* spp.), which feed on roots and stem bases. They are up to 1in (2.5cm) long, with three pairs of short legs at the head end and a peglike protuberance beneath the rear end. The problem mainly occurs when grassland is brought into cultivation.
Control Where damage is seen, search for and destroy the wireworms. Lift root crops as soon as they are mature. Water vulnerable plants with diazinon, or treat the soil with chlorpyrifos + diazinon. The pest usually disappears once the ground has been cultivated for about five years.

Potato late blight

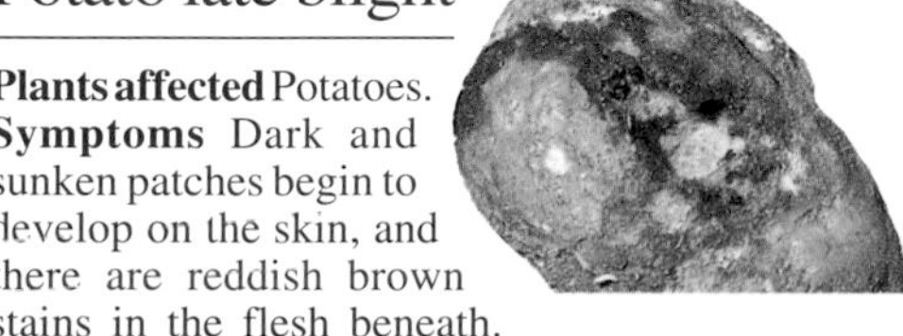

Plants affected Potatoes.
Symptoms Dark and sunken patches begin to develop on the skin, and there are reddish brown stains in the flesh beneath. The tubers develop a dry rot and may also be affected by soft-rotting bacteria. See "Tomato/potato late blight," p.555 for other symptoms.
Cause The fungus *Phytophthora infestans*, which thrives in warm, moist conditions. Spores produced on the foliage and on potato haulms are carried from plant to plant by wind and rain, and may be washed down into the soil to infect potato tubers. The same fungus may also attack tomatoes.
Control Avoid overhead watering. Hill up potatoes deeply to provide a barrier against falling spores, and choose resistant cultivars, e.g. 'Kennebec', 'Essex', 'Pungo', or 'Cherokee'. Spray with a copper-based fungicide; in wet seasons spray before the blight appears.

Common potato scab

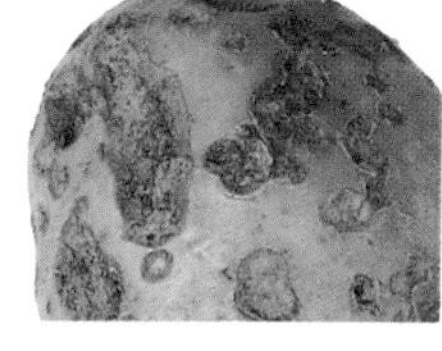

Plants affected Potatoes.
Symptoms Raised, scabby patches develop on the skin, and these sometimes rupture. Damage may be only superficial, but in some instances the tuber becomes extensively cracked and badly disfigured. The flesh of the potato is not generally damaged.
Cause *Streptomyces scabies*, a bacterium-like but mycelium-producing organism, common in soils that are sandy and light with a high lime content, and those only recently cultivated. Disease development is most common during hot, dry summers, and when soil moisture levels are low.
Control Improve soil texture and avoid liming; water regularly. Do not plant potatoes on soil that has recently been used for brassicas. Some varieties show a degree of resistance, such as 'Menominee', 'Ontario', 'Cayuga', and 'Seneca'.

Bacterial rotting

Plants affected Potatoes.
Symptoms The tuber is rapidly reduced to a slimy mass that has a strong smell, while growing or in storage.
Cause Bacteria enter the tuber either through wounds or through damage caused by infections.
Control Maintain good growing conditions, and harvest potatoes carefully in order to avoid injury. Remove all affected tubers immediately.

Internal rust spot

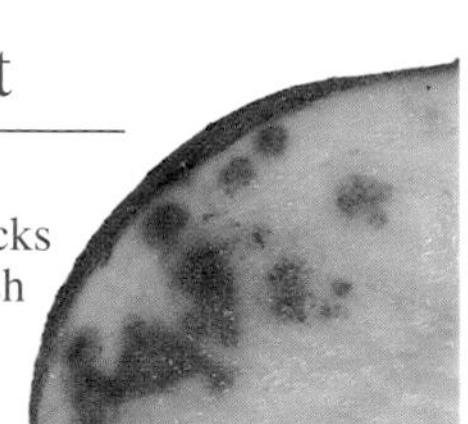

Plants affected Potatoes.
Symptoms Rust-brown flecks develop throughout the flesh of the tubers.
Cause Cultivation either in sandy, acid soils that are low in organic matter, or in soils that are generally low in nutrients – in particular potassium and phosphorus.
Control Incorporate humus into the soil before planting and apply a general fertilizer in spring. Water regularly. Varieties vary in their reaction to poor soils. If the problem occurs, try a different variety the following year.

Potato spraing

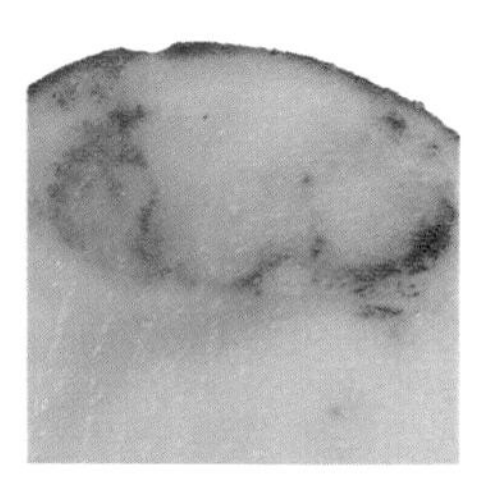

Plants affected Potatoes.
Symptoms A brown, arc-shaped discoloration, often with a corky texture, develops in the often misshapen tuber. Potatoes alone show symptoms, but the viruses (pp.555, 562, 565) can infect *Nicotiana*, China asters (*Callistephus*), gladioli, tulips, hyacinths, and *Capsicum*.
Cause A number of viruses, including tobacco rattle virus, and, less often, potato mop-top virus; these are transmitted by free-living nematodes in the soil.
Control Avoid growing other host plants on the affected site, and grow all potatoes on a fresh site.

Ring rot

Plants affected Potatoes in storage.
Symptoms The vascular tissues of tubers become soft and decay. The disease may eventually reach the tuber surface, producing cracks near the eyes, and secondary rots may develop.
Cause *Clavibacter sependonicum*, a bacterium transmitted by infected tubers used as seed potatoes.
Control Inspect tubers on lifting, do not store any that are suspect, and ensure that all storage containers are clean. Plant only disease-free tubers.

See also "Millipedes," p.550; "Colorado potato beetles," p.551; "Potato viruses," p.553; "Blackleg on potatoes," p.570; and "Potato cyst nematodes," p.572.

Bulb, corm, and rhizome problems

Storage rots

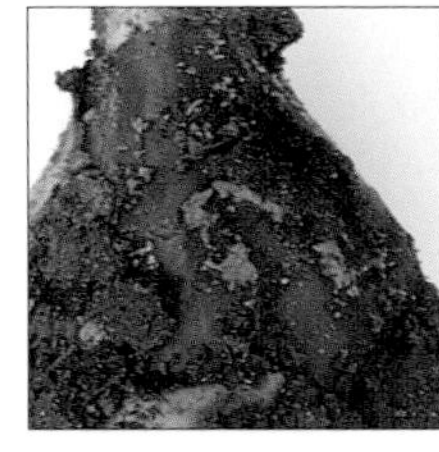

Plants affected Bulbs and corms, especially if damaged or poorly stored.
Symptoms Discolored, sometimes sunken patches develop on the surface of the bulb, or beneath the outer scales or skin. A fungal growth may appear on the patches, spreading through bulb tissues, which become light and dry.
Cause A range of fungi. Infection is often restricted to a very few closely related bulbs or corms, and may affect both those in the ground and those in store. Temperatures that are too low or too high and overdamp conditions encourage the disease.
Control Store and plant only healthy bulbs, and avoid injury to them. Store in suitable conditions, and immediately remove any that show signs of deterioration. Dusting them with a fungicide, such as captan, or sulfur may prevent attack.

Bulb flies

Plants affected Daffodils, *Hippeastrum*, snowdrops (*Galanthus*), English bluebells (*Hyacinthoides non-scripta*), *Cyrtanthus purpureus*, and *Sprekelia*.
Symptoms Bulbs fail to grow or produce only a few grasslike leaves. Maggots, which fill the center of the bulbs with muddy excrement, may be visible.
Cause The narcissus bulb fly (*Merodon equestris*), which attacks sound bulbs, and the lesser bulb fly (*Eumerus* spp.), which attacks damaged bulbs. Narcissus bulb flies lay eggs singly on bulbs in early summer. Adults resemble small bumblebees; larvae are brownish white, up to 3/4in (2cm) long. Lesser bulb fly larvae are similar but never more than 3/8in (9mm) long; there are usually several in a bulb.
Control Avoid planting in warm, sheltered places, which attract adult flies. Discourage egg-laying by firming the soil around the necks of bulbs as they die down, or cover with fine-meshed screens in early summer. There is no effective chemical control.

Ink spot

Plants affected Bulbous irises, *Crocosmia*, *Lachenalia*.
Symptoms Inky stains appear on bulbs, and yellow dots or black craters on fleshy scales. Bulbs may rot away. Black patches or blotches appear on leaves.
Cause The fungus *Bipolaris iridis*, which spreads through the soil to nearby bulbs.
Control Destroy diseased bulbs. Lift bulbs every year, and plant in a new area. Spray with Bordeaux mixture.

Narcissus basal rot

Plants affected Daffodils.
Symptoms After about one month in storage, the basal plate of the bulb becomes soft and brown, and rots. The deterioration spreads to the inner scales, which turn dark brown, and a pale pink, fluffy, fungal growth may then appear between the scales and on the basal plate. The bulb gradually dries out and becomes mummified. Bulbs that become infected in the ground may, if not lifted, rot away in the soil. In some cases, foliage symptoms of yellowing and wilting occur first.
Cause The soilborne fungus *Fusarium oxysporium* f. *narcissi*, which infects bulbs through the basal plate; the fungus is encouraged by high soil temperatures. If the infected bulb is not lifted, it may infect adjacent bulbs. Stored bulbs that are infected but do not show symptoms also act as a source of infection when planted.
Control Lift bulbs early in the season, before soil temperatures rise, and dip them in a solution of thiophanate-methyl. Check bulbs for signs of disease before storing, and discard any that are damaged.

Narcissus nematodes

Plants affected Daffodils, English bluebells (*Hyacinthoides non-scripta*), and snowdrops (*Galanthus*).
Symptoms Bulbs cut transversely reveal brown concentric rings. Plant growth is stunted and distorted, and infested bulbs invariably rot.
Cause The narcissus nematode (*Ditylenchus dipsaci*), which is a microscopic nematode that feeds within bulbs and foliage. Where bulbs have been naturalized, the area of infestation will increase each year as the pest spreads through the soil. Weeds may also harbor narcissus nematodes.
Control Dig up and discard both the infested plants and any others within 1yd (1m) of them. Immersing dormant daffodil bulbs in water at 112°F (44°C) for three hours kills the nematodes without causing bulb damage, but the constant temperature is difficult to maintain without special equipment. Avoid replanting affected areas with susceptible plants for at least two years, and keep weeds under control. No chemical treatment is available.

Iris soft rot

Plants affected Irises.
Symptoms The base of outer leaves decays and the rot then spreads into the rhizome, attacking the youngest parts first. The infected area is reduced to a foul-smelling mass.
Cause The bacterium *Erwinia carotovora* var. *carotovora*, which thrives in waterlogged soil. The bacteria enter the rhizomes through wounds or other damaged areas.
Control Check all rhizomes for any kind of damage before planting, and be extra careful to avoid injuring them. Plant the rhizomes shallowly, and always in good, well-drained soil. Take steps to ensure that iris borers (see p.566), which may be the cause of injury to rhizomes, are kept under control. The prompt removal of any rotting tissue may help to check the problem temporarily, but in the long term the whole rhizome is best discarded.

Onion white rot

Plants affected Onions, shallots, leeks, garlic.
Symptoms The base of the bulb and the roots are covered in a fluffy, white, fungal growth in which hard black sclerotia (fungal resting bodies) become embedded.
Cause The fungus *Sclerotium cepivorum*. Sclerotia in the soil will remain viable for at least seven years and, when stimulated by the presence of new host plant roots, they will germinate, causing infection again.
Control Dig up and discard affected plants as soon as possible. Do not grow susceptible crops on the affected site for at least eight years.

Onion neck rot

Plants affected Onions and shallots.
Symptoms The scales at the neck become soft and discolored; a dense, fuzzy, gray, fungal growth develops on the affected area; and hard black sclerotia (fungal resting bodies) may form. In some severe cases the bulb eventually becomes mummified. The symptoms frequently do not appear until the bulbs are being kept in storage.
Cause The fungus *Botrytis allii*, spread mainly by seedborne fungal spores and the sclerotia present on plant debris.
Control Obtain sets and seed from a reputable source. Encourage the growth of hard, well-ripened onions; do not feed after midsummer, avoid high nitrogen fertilizers, and water regularly. After harvesting, allow the tops of onions to dry off as rapidly as possible. Store under cool, dry conditions with good air circulation, discarding damaged bulbs. Avoid the more susceptible white bulbed onions.

Onion maggots

Plants affected Onions; also shallots, garlic, leeks.
Symptoms Poor growth; the outer leaves turn yellow; maggots found in the bulb.
Cause The root- and bulb-feeding larvae of the onion fly (*Delia antiqua*), white maggots up to 3/8in (9mm) long.
Control Carefully lift and discard infested plants. Treat the soil with chlorpyrifos + diazinon or piperonyl butoxide dust when sowing or planting sets. Seedlings are less tolerant of damage than sets.

See also "Slugs and snails," p.550; "Millipedes," p.550; "Red lily beetles," p.550; "Tulip fire/blight," p.555; "Bulb scale mites," p.558; "Squirrels," p.565; "Mice, rats, and voles," p.568; and "Small animals," p.572.

Whole-plant problems

Drought

Plants affected All plants, especially those that are young, container-grown, or in light, sandy soils.
Symptoms Fall coloration develops early and defoliation, followed by dieback, may occur. Plants wilt and growth is stunted. Flowering and fruit set may decrease markedly. Fruits may be small, sometimes distorted, and of a poor texture. See pp.556, 563, and 573 for other symptoms.
Cause Prolonged or repeated drought due to inadequate or unavailable soil moisture; excessive water loss from the leaves of plants on exposed sites; injured or restricted roots; or soil compaction. Plants in small containers are vulnerable during hot weather, and peat-based soil mixes that dry out too much are extremely difficult to rewet. Dry brown buds on certain plants, such as camellias and rhododendrons, are the result of a water shortage the previous year during the period of bud initiation.
Control Water plants regularly, and frequently check those in hot or sunny positions. Mulch, where appropriate, to improve moisture retention. Drought is more easily prevented than treated; plants exposed to chronic water shortage are less likely to recover once adequate water is supplied or temperatures fall than those suffering acute (sudden) shortage.

Low temperatures

Plants affected Trees, shrubs, perennials, annuals, bulbous plants, vegetables, fruits, indoor plants; seedlings and young plants are especially vulnerable.
Symptoms The leaves are sometimes bleached, and brown, dry patches develop; evergreen foliage may turn brown. Rotted patches develop on petals, especially on exposed flowerheads. Frost injury causes leaves to pucker and petals to wither or discolor. In some cases, whole flowers may be killed. See pp.556 and 559 for other symptoms.
Cause and control See p.556 for details.

Waterlogging

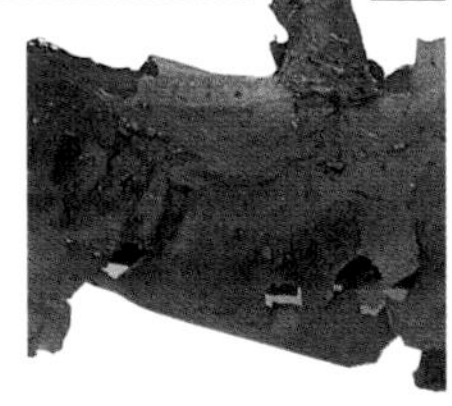

Plants affected Potentially all plants.
Symptoms Leaves may turn yellow, and plants tend to wilt. Bark peels off branches. Roots may rot off completely. Those remaining often begin to blacken and their outer surface peels away easily. See also pp. 557 and 566.
Cause Excessive water levels in the growing medium, owing to poor soil structure, compaction, impeded drainage, or overwatering.
Control Where feasible, improve the structure and drainage of the soil and, if necessary, choose plants that are most likely to survive in wet conditions. Check that container-grown plants have adequate flow through drainage holes. The regular application of a foliar feed during the growing season may help to stimulate growth, replacing waterlogged roots.

Damping off

Plants affected The seedlings of all plants.
Symptoms The seedlings collapse and die as their roots darken and rot off; the disease often attacks seedlings at one end of a seed tray, rapidly spreading to the other. A fluffy fungal growth may appear both on the soil mix and on any dead seedlings. See p.566 for other symptoms.
Cause Various fungi, such as *Pythium ultimum* and some *Phytophthora*, that are soil- or waterborne and attack the seedlings via the roots or stem bases. They flourish in moist and unhygienic conditions.
Control There is no control once the disease is established, so it must be prevented. Sow seed thinly, improve ventilation around seedlings, maintain strict hygiene, and avoid overwatering. Always use sterilized soil mix, clean water, and scrupulously clean seed trays and pots. Water seedlings occasionally with captan, thiram, or zineb.

Blackleg on cuttings

Plants affected Cuttings, most particularly those of pelargoniums.
Symptoms The stems become blackened, shrunken, soft, and rotten, usually at the base; the plant discolors and eventually dies.
Cause A variety of microorganisms, e.g. *Pythium* and *Rhizoctonia*, which are often spread by propagating in unhygienic conditions. Unsterilized soil mix, dirty pots, trays, and tools, and the use of contaminated water are often to blame. The disease is also transmitted by soil moisture.
Control Use clean equipment, sterilized soil mix, and clean water. Dip cuttings in rooting powder containing a fungicide before potting up. Remove affected cuttings immediately.

Blackleg on potatoes

Plants affected Potatoes.
Symptoms The stems collapse, blacken and rot at the base, and the foliage discolors. The disease usually occurs at the start of the season, but any tubers that have formed may also rot. Most of the crop remains healthy; only a few plants show symptoms.
Cause The bacterium *Erwinia caratovora* var. *atroseptica*, which is usually introduced on slightly infected seed tubers that do not show any symptoms at all when they are being planted.
Control Remove affected plants immediately. Inspect tubers on lifting and do not store any that are suspect. Plant only certified stock and allow potato pieces to dry thoroughly before planting; using whole potatoes is preferable. Practice crop rotation.

Bad pruning

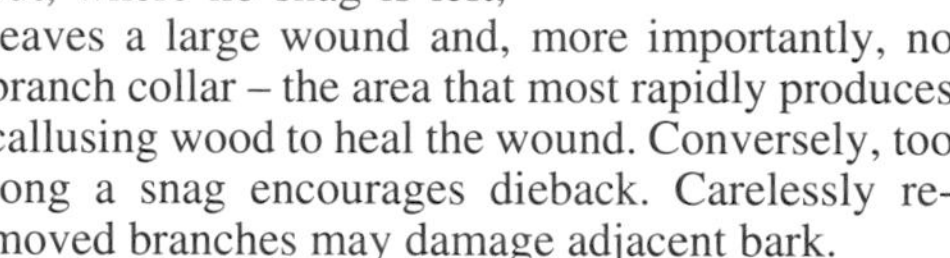

Plants affected Woody perennials, shrubs, and trees.
Symptoms The plant has a poor, unnatural, or uneven shape. Vigor may be reduced and flowering is limited. Snags or whole limbs may die back.
Cause The removal of limbs too close to, or far from, the main limb or trunk. A flush cut, where no snag is left, leaves a large wound and, more importantly, no branch collar – the area that most rapidly produces callusing wood to heal the wound. Conversely, too long a snag encourages dieback. Carelessly removed branches may damage adjacent bark.
Control When pruning a tree or shrub, always be careful to follow the correct method at the appropriate time of year, checking the extent of pruning necessary. Use sharp pruning tools and do not leave any long snags or flush cuts. If necessary, employ a reputable tree surgeon.

Nectria canker

Plants affected Woody perennials, shrubs, trees, especially apples, flowering crabapples (*Malus*), beeches (*Fagus*), poplars (*Populus*), *Sorbus*, mulberries (*Morus*), and hawthorns (*Crataegus*).
Symptoms Small areas of bark, often close to a bud or wound, darken and sink inward; the bark cracks, forming loose, flaky, concentric rings. Enlarged cankers restrict nutrient and water flow, and lead to stem and leaf deterioration. In extreme cases the whole shoot becomes ringed and dies back. White pustules appear in summer, red pustules in winter.
Cause Spores of the fungus *Nectria galligena* and *N. cinnabarina* attack and infect wounds caused by pruning, leaf fall, irregular growth patterns, frost, and woolly aphids (see p.560).
Control Prune affected branches or, on larger limbs, remove the cankered area; treat the resulting wounds with a suitable canker paint. Ensure good tree health by regular watering, fertilizing, and good pest and disease control.

Coryneum canker

Plants affected Conifers, mainly cypresses (*Cupressus*) especially *C. macrocarpa* and *C. sempervirens*, and x *Cupressocyparis leylandii*.
Symptoms Some scattered branches develop dull foliage, which later yellows, dies, turns brown, and is eventually shed. Affected branches develop cankers, which produce copious amounts of resin and are covered with pinhead-sized, black, blisterlike fruiting bodies. When cankers girdle a branch or main stem, it dies.

Cause Airborne spores released from the fruiting bodies of the fungus *Coryneum cardinale* invade trees through the ends of cut branches, fine cracks in the bark, leaf scales, and twig crotches. Infection occurs most readily during the dormant season.
Control Cut out all affected branches or, if severely damaged, remove the whole tree. There is no available chemical control.

Bacterial canker

Plants affected Mainly apples and *Prunus*, in particular cherries and plums.
Symptoms Flat or sunken, elongated cankers develop on the stems; droplets of golden or amber-colored gum ooze from the affected area. The stem starts to deteriorate, and the foliage and flowers may wither and die, or the buds do not break. Foliage may show symptoms of shothole (see p.554).
Cause The bacteria *Pseudomonas syringae* and *P. mors-prunarus*.
Control Remove cankered branches. Spray the foliage with Bordeaux mixture or other copper-based fungicide in late summer and early fall.

Striped cucumber beetles

Plants affected Trees and shrubs; cucumber, melons, winter squashes.
Symptoms Leaf margins and roots are nibbled, holes appear in leaves. Vines wilt, at first only during the day, later permanently. Plants are easily pulled up in later stages since few roots remain.
Cause Slender white larvae, 1/3in (8mm) long, of the striped cucumber beetle (*Acalymma vittata*) feeding on the leaves and roots. Striped adults, 1/4in (6mm) long, feed on pollen and petals of trees and shrubs in spring, and on cucurbits and legumes later in the year. They may transmit bacterial wilt of cucurbits.
Control Cover young plants with mesh-topped boxes pushed into the soil. Dust unprotected plants with rotenone or methoxychlor to control adults.

Oak wilt

Plants affected Most species of oak, but especially those in the red oak group: the black (*Quercus velutina*), red (*Q. rubra*), pink (*Q. palustris*), and scarlet (*Q. coccinea*).
Symptoms Leaves at the top of the tree become dull green and turn brown along the edges. They may also curl and wilt. The discoloration moves rapidly down the crown, and the tree may die in a single summer. Sapwood is usually stained black or brown.
Cause The fungus *Ceratocystis fagacearum*, spread by root grafts, borers, mites, and bark beetles.
Control Grow susceptible trees in isolation so root grafts cannot occur. Prune in late summer only. Sterilize pruning equipment between cuts. Grow oaks from the less-susceptible white oak group.

Phytophthora root rots

Plants affected Trees, shrubs, and woody perennials; maples (*Acer*), Lawson cypress (*Chamaecyparis lawsoniana*), apples, yew (*Taxus*), rhododendrons, raspberries, and heathers.
Symptoms Patches of dead tissue may appear on the stem or the trunk with bluish black stains in the tissue beneath. Foliage is sparse. Dieback may follow, and plants may die. See pp.560 and 567 for other symptoms.
Cause Various species of the fungus *Phytophthora*, which is frequently found in wet soil. Roots are attacked by swimming spores.
Control Avoid heavy watering and improve soil drainage in affected areas. See also p.567.

Crown rot

Plants affected Mainly perennials and indoor plants; also trees, shrubs, annuals, bulbous plants, vegetables, and fruits.
Symptoms The base of the plant rots and may smell unpleasant. Plants may wilt, wither, and die.
Cause Bacterial and fungal organisms entering the stem through surface wounds; overdeep planting also leads to infection.
Control Avoid injury to the stem base and keep the crown free of debris; do not mulch right up to the plant. Ensure that planting depths are correct. Complete removal of the affected area may prevent disease spread, but frequently the whole plant is killed; it should be dug up and destroyed.

Aster yellows

Plants affected China aster (*Callistephus chinensis*) is most affected, but a wide range of plants is attacked.
Symptoms Leaves turn pale yellow, plants become distorted, and flowers change color, often turning green, then brown.

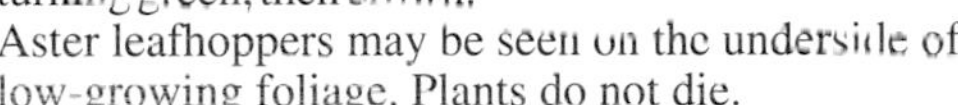

Aster leafhoppers may be seen on the underside of low-growing foliage. Plants do not die.
Cause A mycoplasma-like organism spread by the aster leafhopper (*Macrosteles fascifrons*) from infected plants. Aster leafhoppers, also called six-spotted leafhoppers, are greenish yellow with six black spots, and measure about 1/8in (3mm) long.
Control Pull up and dispose of infected plants as soon as seen. Spray regularly with diazinon or malathion to control leafhoppers.

Rose dieback

Plants affected Roses.
Symptoms The plants die back and may discolor. A fungal growth may develop. Deterioration is extensive in some cases.
Cause Poor planting, poor maintenance, or a poor environment. Severe or repeated attacks of cold, leaf disease, or fungi may also be responsible.
Control Plant roses correctly. Feed and water them regularly. Prune them, and keep diseases and pests under control. Remove dead tissue, then spray or dust cankered roses with a copper-based fungicide.

Fire blight

Plants affected Members of the family Rosaceae that bear pome fruits, mainly pears, apples, cotoneasters, hawthorns (*Crataegus*), and some *Sorbus*.
Symptoms Blossoms wilt and adjacent stem areas discolor. The foliage turns blackish brown, shrivels, and dies, but remains on the stem. Dark greenish brown cankers then form on the branches, producing a bacterial ooze varying in color between yellowish brown and white, depending on the host. The inner surface of the bark and the wood beneath it may be stained brown. Affected limbs die and the tree is killed. See p.555 for other symptoms.
Cause The bacterium *Erwinia amylovora*, which is produced from the cankers and attacks via the blossoms. It is carried by wind, rain splash, insects, and pollen grains.
Control Remove affected plants or prune out affected areas 24in (60cm) past the damage; disinfect the saw between cuts and before using on another tree. Ensure that no staining remains on inner wood.

Clematis wilt

Plants affected Clematis, mainly large-flowered hybrids, e.g. 'Jackmanii', and *C. montana*.
Symptoms The terminal shoots wilt, starting with the youngest foliage, and the petioles begin to darken where they join the leaf blade. Whole sections of the plant may eventually die back.
Cause The fungus *Ascochyta clematidina*, which produces spore-releasing fruiting bodies on the older stems. Other, nonpathogenic causes of wilt (e.g. drought, poor drainage, and graft failure) may be mistaken for this disease.
Control Cut back any affected stems to healthy tissue, below ground level if necessary, and discard cuttings. Spray all the new foliage produced later in the year, and that appearing in the following spring, with Bordeaux mixture.

Peony wilt

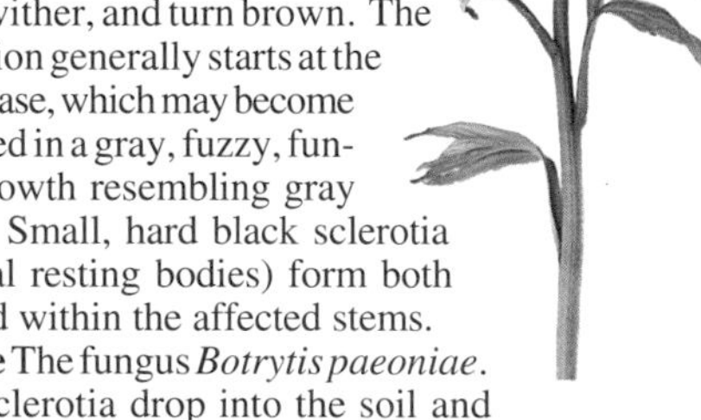

Plants affected Peonies (*Paeonia*).
Symptoms Affected shoots wilt, wither, and turn brown. The infection generally starts at the stem base, which may become covered in a gray, fuzzy, fungal growth resembling gray mold. Small, hard black sclerotia (fungal resting bodies) form both on and within the affected stems.
Cause The fungus *Botrytis paeoniae*. The sclerotia drop into the soil and remain until conditions are favorable (wet years in particular); they then cause new infections.
Control Cut out and destroy the affected shoots of herbaceous peonies to below ground level and spray with Bordeaux mixture; thin out dense plants. Spray the foliage with ferbam.

Anthracnose

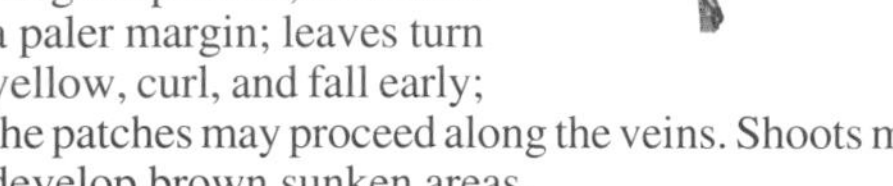

Plants affected Maples (*Acer*), ashes (*Fraxinus*), elms (*Ulmus*), oaks (*Quercus*), sycamores (*Platanus*), walnuts (*Juglans*), and many other trees and shrubs.
Symptoms Small brown spots appear on the leaves enlarging into circular or irregular patches, often with a paler margin; leaves turn yellow, curl, and fall early; the patches may proceed along the veins. Shoots may develop brown sunken areas.
Cause A range of fungi (e.g. *Apiognomonia errabunda*, the maple anthracnose), all of which may be different forms of the same fungus.
Control Remove infected leaves in the fall. Spray plants with ferbam in fall after leaf drop, as buds unfurl in spring, when leaves are half open, and again at full leaf. Fertilize and water the plant well to reduce stress.

Potato cyst nematodes

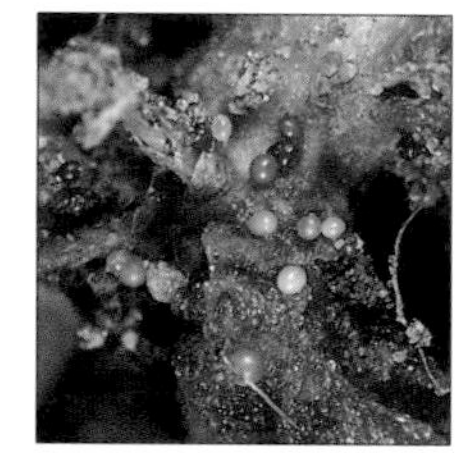

Cysts on roots

Yellowed leaves

Plants affected Potatoes and tomatoes.
Symptoms Plants yellow and die, starting with the lower leaves, and potato tubers remain small. Roots of lifted plants show numerous white, yellow, or brown cysts up to 1/16in (1.6mm) in diameter.
Cause Root-dwelling nematodes that disrupt water and nutrient uptake. Mature females swell and their bodies (known as cysts) burst through the root walls. Cysts contain up to 600 eggs; these remain viable for many years. Cysts of the golden cyst nematode (*Globodera rostochiensis*). This is the most serious nematode that attacks potatoes.
Control Crop rotation discourages the buildup of infestation. Once the soil is infected, the cysts can survive for 17 years and are transported in soil crumbs, potato bags, or pants cuffs. Areas where golden nematodes are known to occur are quarantined and the movement of plants and soil is prohibited. Buy certified nematode-free seed potatoes.

Black vine weevil larvae

Plants affected Shrubs, perennials, annuals, bulbous plants, and indoor plants; fuchsias, begonias, cyclamens, *Impatiens*, primroses (*Primula*, including the Polyanthus Group), *Sedum*, and strawberries are commonly affected. Yews (*Taxus*), rhododendrons, and container-grown plants are particularly vulnerable.
Symptoms Plants grow slowly, wilt, collapse, and die. The outer tissues of seedlings of woody plants and cuttings are gnawed from the stems below ground.
Cause The plump white larvae of the beetle *Otiorhynchus sulcatus*, which are up to 1/2in (1cm) long and slightly curved, with brown heads and no legs. The brown-black adults, 1/3in (8mm) long, lay tiny white eggs in spring and summer, and the damage from the larvae occurs from fall to spring. Damage from adult weevils is minor.
Control Maintain good hygiene to avoid providing shelters for the adults. Treat susceptible plants with diazinon or piperonyl butoxide in midsummer, and again one month later, to kill small larvae. The older larvae are pesticide-tolerant, but biological controls, such as nematode predators (*Heterorhabditis* spp.), are effective. Plan ahead for the emergence of adult black vine weevils in early summer. Set sticky traps around the base of yews and rhododendrons.
See also "Black vine weevils," p.551.

Fungus gnats or sciarid flies

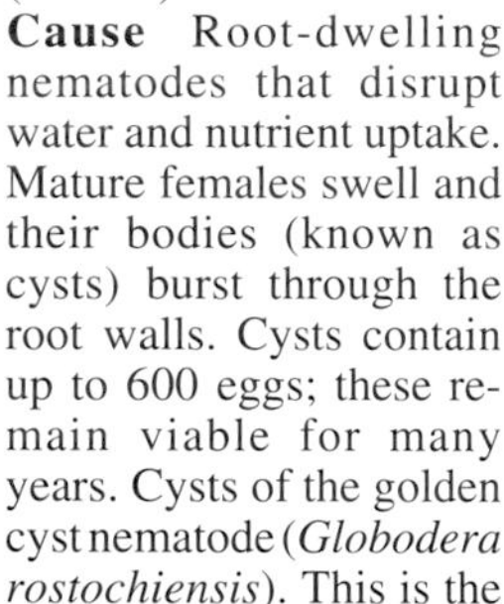

Plants affected Plants grown under cover. Seedlings and cuttings are more susceptible than established plants.
Symptoms Both seedlings and cuttings fail to grow; grayish brown flies run over the soil mix surface or fly among the plants. Larvae may be visible.
Cause The larvae of fungus gnats or sciarid flies (for example *Bradysia* spp.), which feed mainly on dead roots and leaves but may also attack young roots. They are slender, white-bodied maggots up to 1/4in (6mm) long with black heads. The adult flies are of a similar length. They do not cause any problems on healthy, established plants, but are a nuisance in the house.
Control Keep greenhouses tidy, and remove dead leaves and flowers from the soil surface to avoid providing shelters for gnats and flies. Use sticky yellow traps suspended above plants to trap the adult flies. If necessary, water the soil mix with a solution of carbaryl or permethrin to control the larvae.

Armyworms

Plants affected Most vegetables, but especially corn. This is chiefly a pest of farm crops but will eat almost any plant.
Symptoms Leaves and fruits are nibbled. The entire crop may be eaten by an army of caterpillars.
Cause Larvae of armyworm moths (*Pseudaletia unipuncta*), a green caterpillar, turning dark brown with stripes, up to 1 1/2in (4cm) long. The adult is a brownish gray moth.
Control There are many natural predators, including skunks and toads. Spray with *Bacillus thuringiensis* if required.

Ants

Plants affected Most annuals and low-growing perennials.
Symptoms Plants grow slowly and have a tendency to wilt. Heaps of soil may also appear, sometimes even burying some low-growing plants.
Cause Various species of black, yellow, or reddish-brown ants (e.g. *Lasius* and *Formica* spp.), which disturb the roots as they construct their nests. They do not usually feed on the plants, however, and cause relatively little damage.
Control Ants are often abundant and impossible to eliminate; as far as possible their presence should be tolerated. If the problem is severe, water plants with diazinon or set out borax traps.
See also p.574 for problems caused on lawns.

Small animals

Plants affected Many vegetables from seedlings to mature plants; trees and shrubs, bulbs, both dormant and in flower.
Symptoms Rows of seedlings, buds, branchlets are eaten and bark is stripped off, especially during cold weather. Bulbs are dug up and eaten, vegetables and fruit (especially tomatoes) have bites taken out of them, corn is partly stripped and eaten. Other low-growing plants may be grazed down to ground level.
Cause Woodchucks, raccoons, squirrels, rabbits.
Control Erect wire netting at least 3ft (1m) high and sunk another 12in (30cm) below ground level. Do not make it too tight or raccoons can climb over it. Alternatively, protect individual susceptible plants. Cover the base of trees with wire netting or spiral tree-guard collars. Do not feed squirrels in winter.

Deer

Eaten rose shoots

Branch damage

Plants affected Most plants, especially trees, shrubs (including roses), and herbaceous plants.
Symptoms Shoots and leaves are eaten; tree bark is rubbed, frayed, and eaten.
Cause Mainly white-tailed deer, eating shoots, bark, and leaves. Bark is frayed when males mark trees with their scent glands or rub the velvet from their antlers.
Control Erect wire mesh fences at least 6ft (2m) high, or place wire netting around stems and trunks. Repellent sprays or scaring devices, such as hanging tin cans, provide only short-term protection.

See also "Clubroot," p.555; "Irregular water supply," p.557; "*Verticillium* wilt," p.559; "Slime flux/wet wood," p.559; "Spur blight/cane blight," p.559; "Gray mold/*Botrytis*," p.559; "Dutch elm disease," p.559; "*Fusarium* wilt," p.560; "*Phytophthora* root rots," p.560; "Foot and root rots," p.560; "Cutworms," p.561; "Crown gall," p.561; "Fungal brackets," p.561; "Lightning," p.561; "Mechanical wounding," p.561; "Blossom wilt," p.562; "Grasshoppers and crickets," p.563; "Root-knot nematodes," p.566; "White grubs," p.566; "Carrot rust flies," p.566; "Cabbage root maggots," p.566; "Spotted cucumber beetle larvae," p.566; and "Wireworms," p.568.

Lawn problems

Drought

Plants affected Lawns and other grassed areas.
Symptoms Yellowish brown, strawlike patches of variable size develop on the lawn; in extreme cases the whole area may become discolored. Damage usually occurs in summer or early fall.
Cause Dry weather and inadequate watering. Free-draining, sandy soils are most at risk.
Control Water regularly in the early evening, allowing enough water for deep penetration. To improve drought resistance, feed regularly, leave cut grass on the lawn if drought conditions are forecast, and spike and top-dress in the fall. Let the grass grow fairly long before cutting, and avoid mowing too closely.
See also pp.556, 563, and 570 for problems caused to other plants.

Cats and dogs

Plants affected Lawns, seedlings, garden plants.
Symptoms Gardens, especially lawns and other grassed areas, are fouled with droppings; grass and foliage are scorched with urine; and newly planted areas are scratched up.
Cause Cats and dogs. Cats prefer dry soil and newly cultivated areas.
Control Where local dogs are a problem, site plants away from accessible parts of the garden or protect them with netting. Water regularly areas troubled by cats. Repellents based on naphthalene and many other irritating substances are available, but these often give only temporary protection.

Dollar spot

Plants affected Lawns and other grassed areas, particularly those containing fine-leaved bents and creeping fescues.
Symptoms Small, pale, straw-colored patches 1–3in (2.5–7.5cm) in diameter start to develop in early fall, but merge to form larger areas that darken with age.
Cause The fungus *Sclerotinia homeocarpa*, encouraged by compacted or heavy soils and by a high pH; alkaline or limed soils are vulnerable. The disease appears mainly in mild, damp weather.
Control Improve soil aeration and remove thatch. Treat the area with a suitable fungicide, e.g. thiophanate-methyl or thiram.

Brown patch

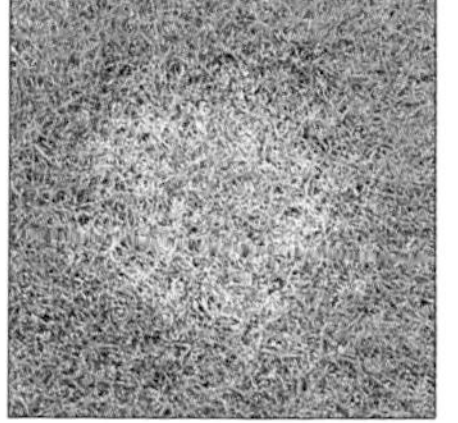

Plants affected Lawns and other grassed areas.
Symptoms Brownish green patches appear on the lawn, resembling chinch bug damage (see right); they may be 20ft (6m) across.
Cause The soilborne fungus *Pellicularia filamentosa*, which attacks grass blades. Excess nitrogen promotes soft growth and leaves plants vulnerable. High temperatures encourage the fungus.
Control Brown patch rarely kills the roots, so plants do recover in time. Spray with ferbam or zineb. Do not apply high-nitrogen fertilizer in late spring. Keep phosphorus and potassium levels high.

Starvation

Plants affected Lawns, sports fields, and other grassed areas.
Symptoms The grass is thin, patchy, and often rather pale; it may be invaded by moss and weeds or attacked by pathogens. Growth is likely to be slow and irregular, occurring in spurts after feeding.
Cause Inadequate feeding or unsuitable fertilizers.
Control Feed the lawn in spring and preferably also in summer and fall, choosing feeds appropriate to the time of year.

Snow mold

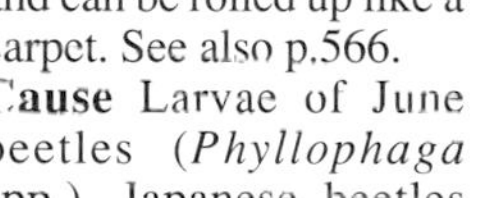

Plants affected Lawns, particularly those that contain a high proportion of annual bluegrass (*Poa annua*).
Symptoms Patches of grass become yellow and die, often merging to form large areas. In damp weather, a white fungal growth appears, causing the grass blades to stick together. It is most prevalent in late winter and early spring, especially on areas of grass that have been walked on while snow covered.
Cause Principally the fungus *Fusarium nivale*, which is encouraged by poor aeration and the overuse of nitrogen fertilizers. Injury makes plants vulnerable.
Control Improve maintenance, regularly aerating and scarifying the lawn. Use grass species that are winter-hardy. Avoid using high-nitrogen fertilizers in late summer to early fall and rake thoroughly after mowing to prevent building up a water-holding mat. Cut grass short in late fall. Treat affected grass with thiophanate-methyl.

Slime molds

Plants affected Common grasses, and occasionally some other plants.
Symptoms Clusters of beige, orange, or white fruiting bodies smother individual blades of grass, and spores are then released, giving the slime mold a gray appearance; the grass looks unsightly but is not harmed. The condition is most common in late spring and early fall.
Cause Slime molds, soil-inhabiting microorganisms that feed on decayed matter. They thrive during periods of heavy rain.
Control Hose down the affected area with a forceful spray. Rake thoroughly to reduce thatch, which holds water and encourages molds.

Red thread

Plants affected Lawns, especially of finer grasses.
Symptoms Tiny, pale pink to red, gelatinous, branching threads of a fungus develop on small patches of grass, which later become bleached. The lawn is only very rarely killed completely.
Cause The fungus *Laetisaria fuciformis*, which is common after heavy rain. It is also troublesome when the soil is nitrogen deficient or poorly aerated.
Control Improve lawn maintenance, aerating, scarifying, and feeding as necessary. Fungicides should not be necessary on a well-kept lawn, but where the problem is severe, thiophanate-methyl may be used to control the problem.

White grubs

Plants affected Lawns and other grassed areas.
Symptoms Brown patches appear and expand rapidly. Dead grass is loose and can be rolled up like a carpet. See also p.566.
Cause Larvae of June beetles (*Phyllophaga* spp.), Japanese beetles (*Popillia japonica*; see p.563), Asiatic garden beetles (*Maladera castanea*), and rose chafers (*Macrodactylus subspinosus*; see p.563). Larvae are plump white grubs up to 1in (2.5cm) long with orange to brown heads. They feed on grass roots.
Control Drench affected areas with diazinon.

Chinch bugs

Plants affected Lawns and other grassed areas.
Symptoms Brown spots, often with a yellowish halo, appear on the lawn and expand slowly. Grass does not pull out. Bugs are visible on leaf blades.
Cause Chinch bugs (*Blissus leucopterus*) and hairy chinch bugs (*B. l. hirtus*), which feed on the crowns and leaf bases. Adults are 1/16in (1.6mm) long, black with red legs. Nymphs are even smaller and are orange to red.
Control Part the grass and watch for movement, or push a bottomless can into the lawn and fill it with warm water; the bugs will float to the surface. Drench affected areas with diazinon or carbaryl. Soy bean plants are said to have a repellent effect.

Melting out

Plants affected Lawns, especially those with a high proportion of Kentucky bluegrass (*Poa pratensis*).
Symptoms Small eye spots, consisting of oval areas with a pale brown center and dark margins, appear on the grass blades. The infection may spread to the

crown, and if it does, the plant will then die. The condition is sometimes mistaken for fertilizer burn, which it resembles. Consider weather conditions.
Cause The fungus *Helminthosporum vagans*, which attacks closely clipped grass in cool, rainy weather, usually in early spring, but sometimes in late fall.
Control The Kentucky bluegrass cultivar 'Merion' is resistant to this disease. Do not mow the grass closer than 1½in (4cm). Apply thiram or zineb to affected areas, or anticipate recurring problems by spraying the lawn in the late fall to discourage the growth of the fungus.
See also "Fertilizer burn," p.556.

Toadstools

Plants affected Lawns and other grassed areas.
Symptoms Fungal fruiting bodies develop, sometimes in distinct circles (fairy rings), and often on buried woody material. Most cause little damage, but fairy rings are both harmful and disfiguring. Two circles of very lush green grass form, one within the other, sometimes several yards in diameter, and the grass in between them dies off; toadstools then emerge on the outer part of this middle zone. A white fungal growth permeates the soil in the area of the ring.
Cause Various fungi, including *Coprinus*, *Mycena*, and the ring-producing *Marasmius oreades*. They all have underground mycelia and are spread to new sites by windborne spores.
Control Brush off *Coprinus* and *Mycena* when they first appear, before their spores are produced. If the fungi are on buried wood, remove them. There is no chemical control available to control fairy rings.

Ants

Plants affected Lawns and other grassed areas.
Symptoms Small heaps of fine soil are deposited on the surface of the lawn, mainly in summer.
Cause Ants (e.g. *Lasius flavus*), usually yellow-brown, which carry soil particles up to the surface as they remove it to extend their underground nests.
Control When deposited soil dries, brush it away. Then water the nest site with carbaryl, permethrin powder or dust, diazinon, or pyrethrum.
See also p.572 for problems caused to other plants.

Skunks

Plants affected Lawns and other grassed areas.
Symptoms Holes are dug in sod, leaving small piles of soil and divots of grass. Skunks may be seen in undergrowth.
Cause Skunks digging for white grubs, although they serve some beneficial purposes, since the grubs they dig for may be harmful. Skunk damage is most severe in fall when the newly hatched grubs are feeding close to the surface.
Control Eliminate white grubs in lawn (see p.573). Turning the soil repeatedly over several days will expose the grubs to predators.

Moles

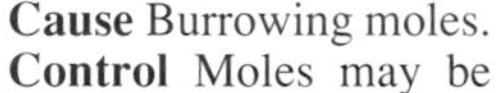

Plants affected Lawns, seedlings, young plants.
Symptoms Heaps of soil (molehills) appear on the lawn and cultivated areas. Roots of young plants and seedlings are disturbed.
Cause Burrowing moles.
Control Moles may be trapped, although they may be deterred by barriers cutting off their tunnels. Push metal sheets about 1ft (30cm) into the ground, through active tunnels.

Controls currently available (with commercial names, where applicable)

In the United States, the federal Environmental Protection Agency (EPA) classifies pesticides into three groups: banned, restricted (for use by licensed applicators only), and general. Home gardeners may use products in the general category only. Check with state and county authorities about which you can use. Recommendations in this book are for general guidance only. They were current at the time of production. Some products are not approved for use in Canada.

Pesticide labeling is dictated by law. **Usage must be consistent with labeling**. For instance, if a product is labeled for use only on fruit trees, it is illegal to use it on leafy vegetables. Also, if a pesticide is labeled for use only on as a wettable powder for spraying, for example, it cannot be applied dry directly to the soil. Penalites for misuse are severe. If you have any questions about pesticides, discontinue use immediately and confirm that the application will be in accordance with the law. The EPA pesticide hotline (1-800-858-PEST) can be a useful resource, or contact your county agricultural extension service agent.

Acephate Orthene

Bacillus thuringiensis Attack BT, Bactospeine, Bactur, Biotrol, Bugtime, Dipel, Foray, M-One, SOK BT, Thuricide

Bendiocarb Ficam, Turcam

Borax Borascu, Pyrobor, Tronabor

Bordeaux mixture Bordocop, Bordo-Mix

Brodifacoum Havoc, Klerat, Matikus, Mouser, PP-581, Pulsar, Rodend, Talon, Volak, Volid

Bromadiolone Actosin-B, Boothill, Bromatrol, Bromone, Brumolin-FF, Brumolin Lanirat, Contrac, Contrax, Eradic, Maki, Musal, Ratimus, Rotox, Super-Caid

Captan Orthocide

Carbaryl Savit, Sevin

Chlorpyrifos Dursban, Lorsban, Pageant

Chlorpyrifos + diazinon

Copper-based fungicide copper sulfate, Cuproxat, K-Cop, Kocide

Diazinon Spectracide

Dimethoate Cygon, DeFend

Dinocap Karathane, Mildex

Dormant oil Cleancrop, Scalecide, Sunspray, Sunspray 6E PLUS, Ultra-Fine, Volck

Ferbam Carbamate, Ferberk, Hexaferb, Knock mate

Insecticidal soap M-Pede, Safer Soap

Iron, chelated (sequestered iron) Iron Chelate DP, Lustre Leaf Micronized Iron

Lime sulfur

Malathion Cythion

Metaldehyde Bug-Geta, Deadline, Slugit, Snarol

Methiocarb Mesrepel, Mesurol, Slug and Snail Bait, Slug-Geta, Slug 'm

Methoxychlor

Naphthalene

Oxydemeton-methyl

Permethrin Ambush, Biomist, Pounce, Ketokil

Pheromone traps Biocattura, Biocontrol, Hercah Luretape, Hercon, Hercon Disrupt, Hercon Lure N Kill Insect Traps, Insectatape with Propexur, Magnet, Phero-Tac, Pherotrapp, Trappit, Traptest

Piperonyl butoxide Butacide

Pirimicarb Pirimor

Pyrenone Pyrenone Crop Spray (composition Pyrethrins, Piperoxyl Butoxide)

Pyrethrum

Rotenone (derris)

Silicon dioxide

Sulfur Brimestone, Consul, Cosan, Cosan-80, Electrosulph, Elosal, Golden Dew, Hexasul, Kolojog, Kolospray, Kumulus, Microflotox, Sofril, Sperlox-S, Spersul, Sulfa-8, Sulfuron, Sulkul, Sulsol, Supercosan, Thiolux, Thion, Thioxit, Tiolene, Zolvis

Thiophanate-methyl Cleary's 3336, Domain, Domain FL, Fungo, Fungo Flo, Systac 1998, Topsin M

Thiram Arasan, TMTD

Triforine Funginex

Wasp spray Shoo-fly

Zineb Dithane Z-78

WEEDKILLERS

Amitrole Aminotriazole weedkiller, Aminotriazole 90, Amitrol T, Amizole, AT, ATA, Chempar Amitrole, Cytrol, Domatol, Ustine X, Weedazole, Vorox, X-A11

Dichlorbenil Casoron, Code 133, Decabane, Dyclomec, H-133, 2,6-DBN

Diquat Actor, Aquacide, Dextrone, Diquatdibmomide, Midstream, Preeglone, Priglone, Reglone, Reglox, Weedkiller Concentrate D, Weedtrine-II

Glyphosate Accord, Arcade, Azinal, Glycel, Hockey, Kleenup, Muster, Ranger, Rodeo, Roundup, Roundup RT, Shackle, Solado, Spasor, Sting

Paraquat Actor Cekuquat, Crisquat, Dextrone, Dextrone X, Dexuron, Esgram, Goldquat 276, Gramanol, Gramoxone, Gramuron, Hebaxon, Herboxone, Paracol Paraquat CI, Pillarquat, Pillarxone, PP148, Sweep

LAWN WEEDKILLERS

Chlorthal dimethyl Dacthal DCPA (WSSA)

Dicamba

MCPA Agrilox, Agroxone, Chiptox, Cornox-M, Dikotex, Hedonal-M, Kilsem, Krezone, Linormone, MCP, Mephanac, Metaxon, Raphone, Rhomenc, Rhomene, Rhonox, Shammox, Shamrox, Trasan, Vacate, Weedar MCPA, Weedone MCPA, Zelan

Mecoprop Ceovotox, CIMPP, Compitox, Cornox-Plus, Hedonal-MCPP, ISO-Cornox, Kilprop, Liranox, MCPP, Mecomec, Mecoper, Mecopex, Mepro, Runcatex, Vi-Par

2, 4-D Citrus Fix, Dacamine, Esteron, Hivol-44, Weedone

Weeds

Weeds are, quite simply, plants that grow where they are not wanted. They have important features in common: they are usually fast-growing and invasive, competing with cultivated plants for food and water; they are able to grow in almost any soil or site; and they often show a marked resistance to control. Weeds may occur in almost any part of the garden.

Cultivated plants may be placed in the weed category in certain circumstances, depending on their habit. If they prove too invasive for their site and overwhelm their neighbors, or if they self-seed freely throughout the garden, they may properly be classified as weeds.

Categorizing weeds

Annual weeds complete their entire life cycle within one year. They set seed that germinates freely; occasionally, as in the case of groundsel (*Senecio vulgaris*), they may even produce several generations in one season. It is important, therefore, to remove annuals at the seedling stage, before they are able to produce seed.

Perennial weeds, by contrast, survive from year to year. Some grow readily from seed, like annuals, but more usually persist by means of various storage organs such as rhizomes, bulbs, bulbils, tubers, and thick taproots. Many perennials are able to proliferate because of poor cultivation techniques that leave small pieces of rhizome or root in the soil when digging over or rototilling.

Controlling weeds

Weeds may be controlled in two main ways: either they may be discouraged from growing by the use of good basic gardening techniques; or they may be removed by manual, mechanical, or chemical means.

The choice of how to remove different weeds depends on various factors: the habit of the plants themselves, the preference of the gardener, and the location of the weeds – whether in borders, lawns, paths, or neglected sites.

CULTIVATED PLANTS AS WEEDS

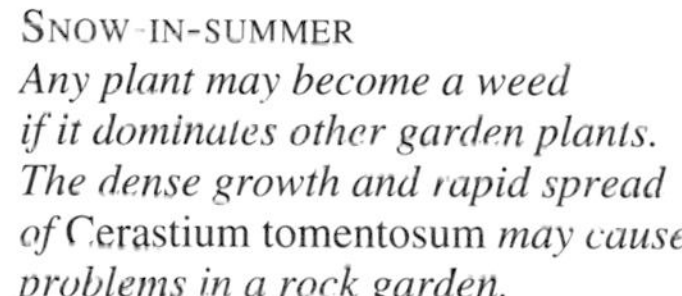

SNOW-IN-SUMMER
Any plant may become a weed if it dominates other garden plants. The dense growth and rapid spread of Cerastium tomentosum *may cause problems in a rock garden.*

RUSSIAN VINE
Although often planted to cover unsightly features rapidly, the Russian vine (Polygonum baldschuanicum) *is an invasive climber that can soon swamp more delicate plants in the vicinity.*

Annual weeds

In common with other annual plants, annual weeds grow, flower, set seed, and die within one year. They occur most frequently in regularly cultivated areas, such as vegetable plots or annual borders, where frequent digging deters perennial kinds. Their rapid growth makes them troublesome among crops raised from seed *in situ* because they smother slower-growing plants and reduce yields of others by competing for moisture, nutrients, and light.

The need for control

It is most important to destroy annual weeds before they produce seeds, since many seeds are small, light, readily windborne, and quick to germinate. Quick-maturing species such as shepherd's purse (*Capsella bursa-pastoris*) may produce several generations in a single season. Common chickweed (*Stellaria media*) smothers nearby plants and is another weed that should be controlled at the seedling stage. Its seeds start to germinate in the fall and continue growing in mild winters to form dense mats.

Many seeds may be buried once they are shed, and lie dormant for many years until they are brought to the surface during site or crop cultivation. The weeds then germinate and grow rapidly. If a site is heavily infested, it should be cultivated regularly when it is crop-free in order to kill germinating seedlings.

Annual weeds may be controlled by hand, mechanical, or chemical means (see "Controlling weeds," p.577).

COMMON ANNUAL WEEDS

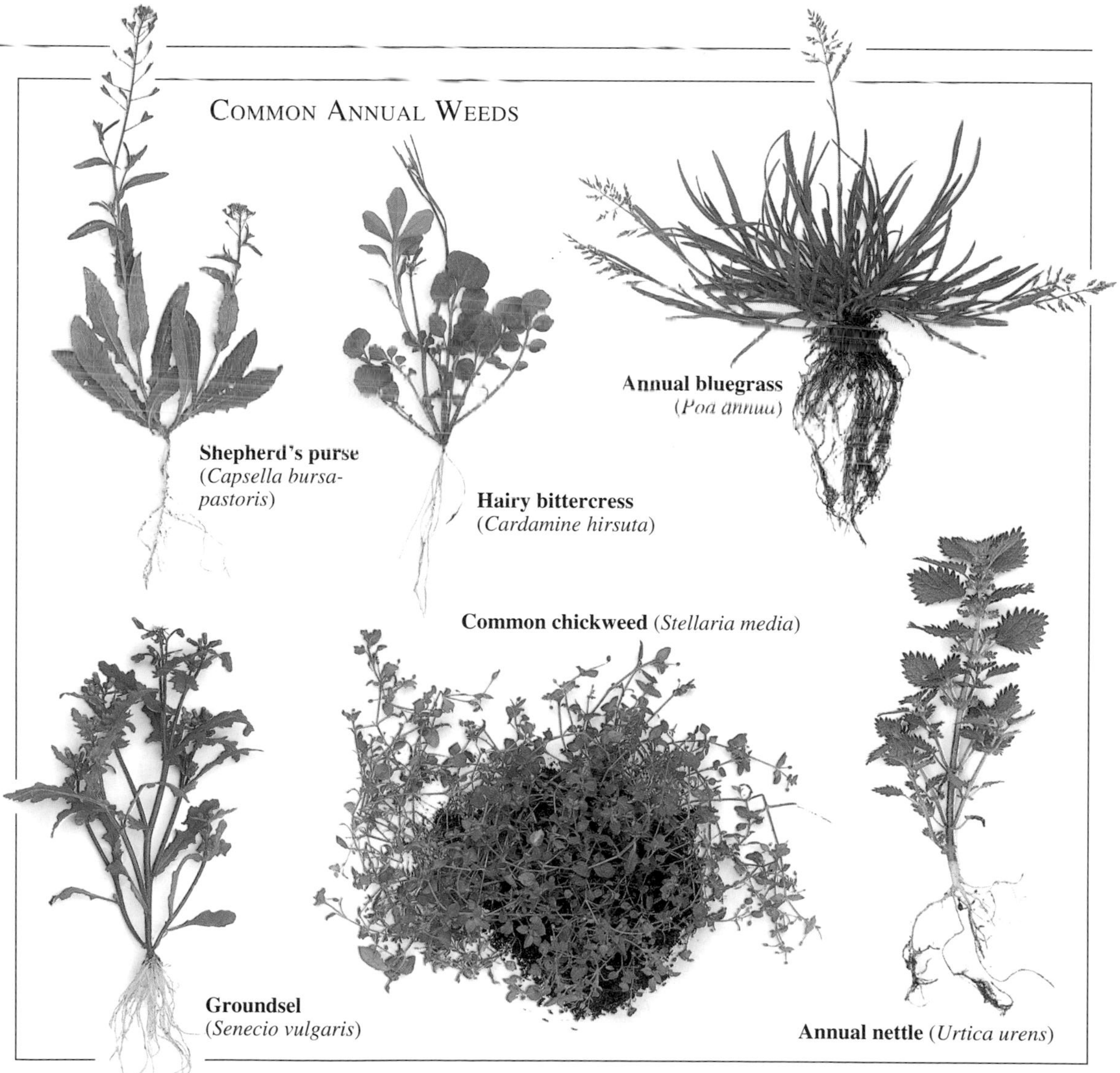

Shepherd's purse (*Capsella bursa-pastoris*)

Hairy bittercress (*Cardamine hirsuta*)

Annual bluegrass (*Poa annua*)

Groundsel (*Senecio vulgaris*)

Common chickweed (*Stellaria media*)

Annual nettle (*Urtica urens*)

Perennial weeds

Perennial weeds persist from year to year, surviving through winter cold and summer heat by storing food reserves in fleshy roots, bulbs, rhizomes, or tubers. They may be divided into two groups: herbaceous kinds and woody-stemmed kinds.

Herbaceous perennials

Most herbaceous perennials die back to the ground in the fall. They survive the winter by storing food in their roots, then reappear in the spring. Examples are Canada thistle (*Cirsium arvense*), broad-leaved dock (*Rumex obtusifolius*), and field bindweed (*Convolvulus arvensis*). Also included in this group are the stemless herbaceous perennials that have leaves arising directly from their roots or rhizomes, for example dandelion (*Taraxacum officinale*) and goutweed (*Aegopodium podagraria*).

Pueraria lobata is one of the most invasive herbaceous vines, particularly in the Southeast. In the West, *Cucurbita foetidissima* spreads rapidly in the area from Nebraska to California and Mexico; the vine develops long-running stems from the central root system and smothers more desirable plants.

Japanese knotweed (*Polygonum japonicum*, syn. *P. cuspidatum* and *Fallopia japonica*) dies back every year, but the tall, shrublike dead stems persist. New growth appears the following year.

Woody perennials

Woody-stemmed perennials survive the winter by storing food in their stems and branches. Some woody plants seed prolifically, with a high germination rate, producing unwanted seedlings throughout the garden. Among trees, *Acer platanoides*, *Ailanthus altissima*, and, especially in the South, *Broussonetia papyrifera* may be particularly troublesome.

Among shrubs, *Berberis thunbergii* and *Euonymus alatus* tend to produce large numbers of seedlings. Among the most invasive shrubs is *Rosa multiflora*, which by some estimates has spread across two-thirds of North America.

Several shrubby honeysuckles (*Lonicera*), including *L. maackii* and *L. tartarica*, may proliferate excessively. Both *L. japonica* and *L. j.* 'Halliana', vines with fragrant yellow and white blossoms, can be useful as ground covers, but they can easily take over entire gardens. Similarly, *Campsis radicans* has attractive trumpet-shaped orange flowers, but it propagates by suckers that spread very rapidly throughout the garden. *Rhus radicans*, *R. diversiloba* in the West, and *R. vernix* spread quickly, and contain a powerful skin irritant.

The need for control

Perennial weeds have underground fleshy roots, rhizomes, and other storage organs that are not easily controlled. Hoeing and digging, along with machine cultivation, break the roots and rhizomes into sections without killing them; many survive and increase the infestation. With most perennial weeds, weedkillers are the most practical and effective control.

Preventing weeds

Both annual and perennial weeds may be prevented from establishing in various ways. These will do much to eliminate tedious weeding later on.

Working the soil

Before planting, clear the site of all weeds, either manually or with chemicals. Weeds are often difficult to eradicate from among established plants, which may need to be lifted and the weeds extracted from the washed root system. Conditioning very acid soils with lime will deter some lawn weeds, such as field woodrush (*Luzula campestris*), that thrive where the soil is acid.

Cultivating healthy plants

Vigorous, healthy plants are able to compete more effectively with weeds than are weak specimens. Plants with spreading foliage, such as *Pachysandra*, provide a dark cover over the soil that discourages weeds.

Some vegetable crops, for example potatoes, compete well with annual weeds and may be grown to help maintain clean ground for a subsequent crop (see THE VEGETABLE GARDEN, "Rotation," p.303).

Ground cover plants

Some plants grow in dense carpets that suppress the germination of weed seeds. They are particularly useful for parts of the garden where, because of shade, or very wet or dry soil, weeds thrive. Choose ground cover plants carefully since some are invasive and may quickly become weeds themselves (for more information, see GROUND COVERS, pp.150–51).

Mulching

In early spring, apply a mulch 1–2in (2.5–5cm) thick of weed-free, organic material such as leaf mold, peat, or processed bark to help prevent weed seeds from germinating and to smother weed seedlings. Do not use compost or insufficiently rotted manure for this purpose, because they almost certainly contain weed seeds.

Established perennial weeds may grow through the mulch but, since they tend to root into the loose material, they are easy to remove.

Black plastic

Laid directly over the soil, black plastic prevents annual weeds from establishing. It can also be effective with perennial weeds: horsetail (*Equisetum arvense*) and field bindweed (*Convolvulus arvensis*) are both less likely to grow if the area is covered for at least two seasons. Cover the plastic with a bark mulch to improve its appearance. Black plastic is particularly useful in fruit and vegetable gardens; make slits in it through which the crops can grow.

Grassing down borders

Some persistent perennial weeds such as horsetail, *Oxalis corniculata*, and *O. stricta* may resist repeated attempts to eradicate them with weedkiller or to dig them out. An alternative approach is to grass down heavily infested borders and maintain them as

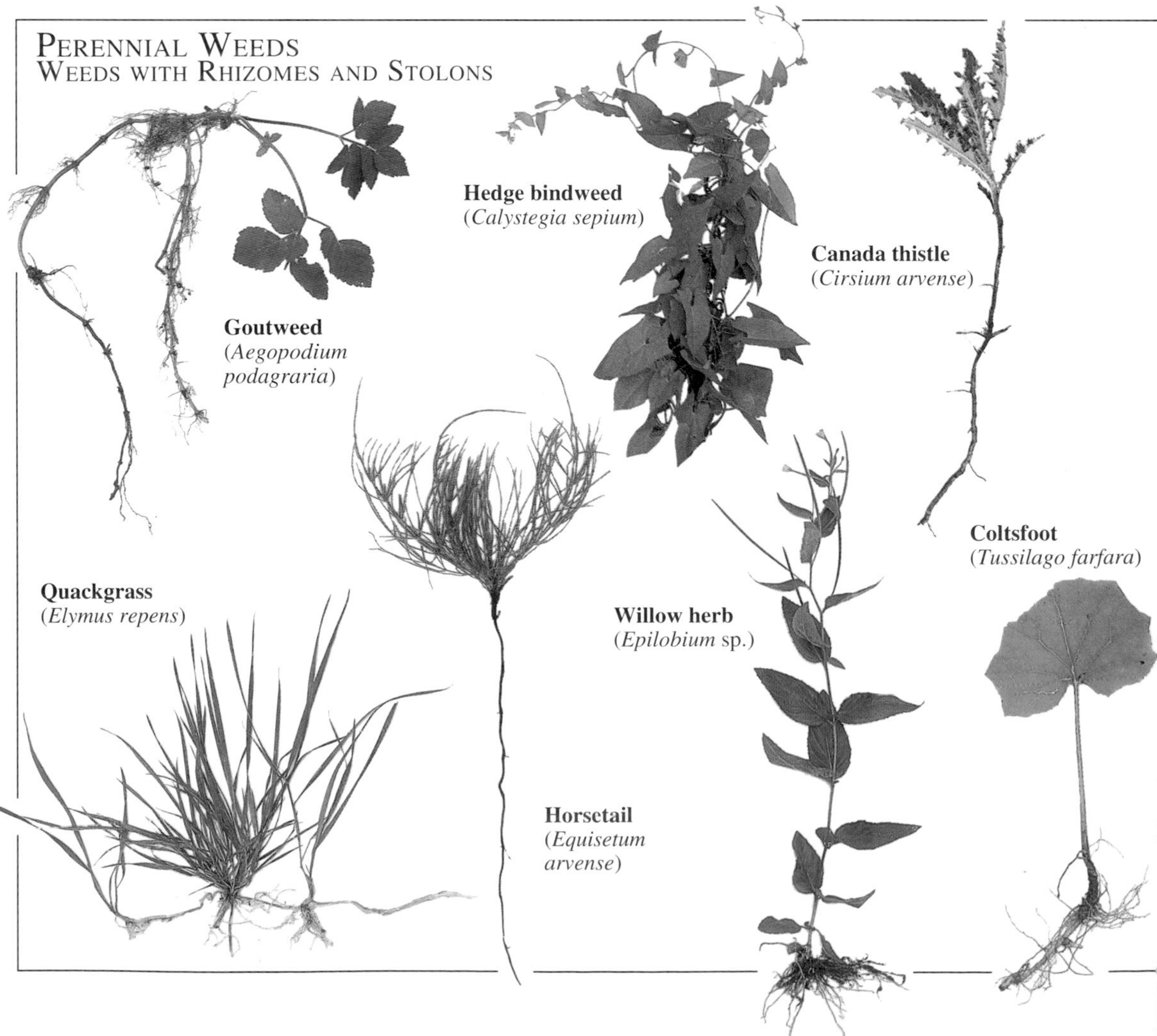

close-mown sod for several years. Given time, this treatment will clear the soil and usually eliminates most of the infestation.

Controlling weeds

Once weeds are present, they may be eradicated in one of three ways: hand-weeding, mechanical control, or chemical control. There are three different types of weedkiller: those that act on the leaves, those that act on the soil (including preemergent weedkillers), and those that act on specific types of plant.

Hand-weeding and hoeing

Hand-weeding, hoeing, and forking are often the only practical ways of removing weeds in flowerbeds, the vegetable garden, and small patches of ground, where weedkillers cannot be used safely without risk of harming nearby garden or crop plants.

Small patches of perennial weeds, such as goutweed and quackgrass, may be forked out, but great care must be taken not to leave in the soil sections of rhizomes, roots, or bulbils that will grow again. Check a month or so later and remove any regrowth.

Hand-weed or hoe in dry weather, if possible, so that the weeds are easily loosened from the soil. In wet weather, remove uprooted weeds from the site to prevent them from rooting back into the soil. Hoe only lightly around cultivated plants to prevent their surface roots from being damaged.

Removing weeds mechanically

Market gardeners often use rotary cultivators (rototillers) with hoeing or cultivating attachments for annual weed control between rows of vegetables, but these machines may be unsuitable for perennials. They simply cut the rhizomes of weeds such as goutweed and quackgrass into many pieces that will continue to grow as new plants. Wherever possible, use weedkillers to kill perennial weeds before digging or cultivating soil.

Foliage-acting weedkillers

Leaf-acting products, or postemergent weedkillers, enter the weeds through leaves or green stems and are applied with a sprayer or watering can and fine rose or dribble bar. There are two different types. The first acts by translocation, moving from the leaves to the roots, and so destroys both annual and perennial weeds. For maximum effect the weeds should be in vigorous growth. The second type works by contact, killing only by direct touch. They destroy annual weeds and the green leaves and stems of perennial weeds, although not the roots of perennials. Some weedkillers act through both leaves and roots.

Soil-acting weedkillers

These are applied to the soil and are absorbed into the roots of growing weeds. From there soil-acting weedkillers move to the parts of the plant above ground level, killing the weeds by interfering with their metabolism. These chemicals kill established annual weeds and may also kill or suppress many established perennial weeds. When planning to use areas that have been treated with soil-acting weedkillers, check the manufacturer's literature for details of residual activity (which may damage desirable plants), and do not sow or plant until the recommended period has elapsed.

Preemergent weedkillers are applied to bare soil or established lawns and kill weed seeds as they germinate. They can be used in shrub borders, between perennials or on annual beds that will receive established transplants, but not where annuals will be grown from seed.

Selective weedkillers

Most selective weedkillers kill broad-leaved weeds and leave narrow-leaved grasses unharmed, provided they are applied at the correct rate.

The range of chemicals

Paraquat (contact action) and **diquat** (contact action) are both quick-acting and will kill annual weeds but only check broad-leaved weeds. They are useful for killing overwintering annual weeds before spring sowing or planting and are inactivated in soil.
Glyphosate (translocated, foliage-acting) is one of the most useful weedkillers for controlling perennial weeds. It is a foliage-acting weedkiller that moves down to the roots, killing or strongly checking even the most difficult weeds. Glyphosate is not selective and should be kept well away from all garden plants. With the majority of weeds, it is most effective when weed growth is well advanced, usually from about midsummer onward, but check the manufacturer's recommendations and follow them. Because glyphosate does not persist in the soil, it is safe to cultivate as soon as weeds are dead.
Dichlobenil (soil-acting, preemergent) is a weedkiller that may be applied, before growth begins, to the soil around well-established fruit trees and bushes and some ornamental shrubs, including roses. It controls or suppresses some perennial weeds such as goutweed, and it controls germinating weed seeds. It is residual and continues to act for several months.
Amitrole (foliage-acting, translocated) is usually combined with contact and soil-acting herbicides to control weeds that have become established in cracks and crevices in paved areas, paths, and drives. The use of amitrole is restricted in both the US and Canada.

WEEDS WITH TUBERS AND FLESHY ROOTS

Field bindweed (*Convolvulus arvensis*)

Lesser celandine (*Ranunculus ficaria*)

WEEDS WITH DEEP ROOTS

Japanese knotweed (*Polygonum japonicum*, syn. *P. cuspidatum* and *Fallopia japonica*)

Brambles (*Rubus* sp.)

Dock (*Rumex* sp.)

Perennial stinging nettle (*Urtica dioica*)

Using weedkillers safely

Care must always be taken when applying weedkillers:

- wear protective clothing, for example rubber gloves and long pants and sleeves, when mixing and applying weedkillers;
- do not apply weedkillers in windy conditions when there is a risk of spray being blown across to nearby plants, which may suffer serious damage;
- use only for appropriate purposes as recommended on the product label; for example, do not use a path weedkiller to keep down weeds in a rosebed;
- always dilute soluble weedkillers according to the manufacturer's instructions;
- always apply weedkillers at the recommended rates on the labels;
- always keep in original containers and make sure that the labels are well secured to the containers so that contents are known and no errors in usage occur;
- never store diluted weedkillers for future use;
- store away out of reach of children and animals, preferably in a securely locked cabinet in a frost-free workshop or shed.

Lawn weeds

Various perennial weeds can be troublesome in lawns. Their common survival factor is their ability to grow and thrive in the adverse conditions of short, regularly mown grass. They usually originate from seeds carried by the wind or by birds. Once lawn weeds have germinated, most are then rapidly spread by the action of mowing, and early treatment is necessary if they are to be eradicated.

Among the most troublesome lawn weeds are: annual bluegrass (*Poa annua*), crabgrass (*Digitaria sanguinalis*), dandelion (*Taraxacum officinale*), creeping Charlie (*Glechoma hederacea*), and plantains (*Plantago* spp.). Some of these persistent weeds do not respond to treatment by lawn weedkillers, and other forms of treatment will be required.

In lawns where the grass is too sparse to offer adequate competition, moss may also become a problem.

Preventing weeds and moss

Good lawn care is an effective preventive measure. The presence of numerous weeds in a lawn usually indicates that the grass is not growing sufficiently vigorously to prevent weeds from establishing. Lack of regular feeding and drought are among the most common reasons for poor growth. Soil compaction and mowing the grass too closely and too regularly may also lead to the spread of moss. For further details on lawn care, see THE LAWN, "Routine care," pp.281–6.

Coarser weed grasses, such as barnyard grass (*Echinochloa crusgalli*), may remain a problem, so clumps may need to be removed, and the patch resodded or reseeded.

Raking to lift creeping stems before mowing may help to check the spread of creeping weeds such as trefoils (*Trifolium* spp.) and creeping Charlie (*Glechoma hederacea*) if the grass is mown immediately afterward.

Removing weeds

If weeds are already present in the lawn, there are two main ways of treating them, depending on the severity of the problem. Either they may be removed by hand if they are not too widespread, or they may be treated with an appropriate weedkiller.

Weeding by hand

Hand-weeding is an effective method of removing a few scattered rosetted weeds such as dandelion (*Taraxacum officinale*) and plantains (*Plantago* spp.). Use an asparagus knife or hand fork to lift the weeds, then firm back displaced sod.

Dealing with moss

Moss may be killed with moss preparations. This is only a short-term solution, however: unless the original conditions that encouraged moss are identified and corrected, the problem usually recurs.

Removing weeds with chemicals

Weedkillers intended specifically for use on lawns work by translocation – moving within the plant from the leaves to the roots – and the weeds begin to distort and shrivel within a few days of application. The chemicals are selective and do not harm lawn grasses at normal dilution rates, but do not use them on seedling grasses within six months of germination.

You should also avoid using lawn weedkillers on newly laid sod, sprigs, or plugs within a six-month period of laying or planting.

LAWN WEEDS

Yarrow (*Achillea millefolium*)

Common mouse-ear chickweed (*Cerastium fontanum*, syn. *C. vulgatum*)

Dandelion (*Taraxacum officinale*)

Nutsedge (*Cyperus esculentus*)

Broad-leaved plantain (*Plantago major*)

Self-heal (*Prunella vulgaris*)

Creeping buttercup (*Ranunculus repens*)

Sheep's sorrel (*Rumex acetosella*)

Creeping Charlie (*Glechoma hederacea*)

Lesser yellow trefoil (*Trifolium dubium*)

Common white clover (*Trifolium repens*)

Slender speedwell (*Veronica filiformis*)

The range of chemicals

Commercial lawn weedkillers normally combine two or more active ingredients in order to control a wider range of weeds.

2,4–D is a selective weedkiller that is particularly effective against broad-leaved, rosetted weeds such as plantains and daisies. This chemical is often combined with mecoprop.

Mecoprop kills various difficult, small-leaved, and creeping weeds such as trefoils (*Trifolium* spp.) and yarrow (*Achillea millefolium*). It is usually combined with 2,4–D.

Chlorthal dimethyl is a preemergent weedkiller used to control crabgrass. It must be applied early in the season (when forsythia is in bloom) and will kill crabgrass as it germinates.

MCPA is a selective herbicide used in both problem-weed mixtures and lawn weedkillers to control weeds that have resistance to other chemicals.

Dicamba is usually combined with 2,4–D and mecoprop or MCPA to control a wider range of weeds.

Lime may be applied on very acid soils as a light winter dressing in the form of ground limestone at 2oz/sq yd (50g/sq m) to deter sorrels. Sorrels can also be controlled by repeat treatment with 2,4–D preparations but, on acid soils, lime is ecologically preferable and is less dangerous to apply.

Buying weedkillers

Lawn weedkillers are usually sold as a concentrated liquid and therefore need to be suitably diluted. They may also be obtained in the form of soluble powder, ready-to-use spray, aerosol, wax bar, or in combination with liquid or granular lawn fertilizers.

Applying weedkillers

Feed the lawn at the start of the growing season. Apply weedkillers when grass and weeds are growing strongly and daytime temperatures reach 70°F (21°C). In the spring, creeping lawn grasses soon colonize any bare patches left as weeds shrivel and die. Great care should be taken when applying weedkillers (see p.577).

Hose-end sprayers can be used for large areas; a watering can with a fine rose or dribble-bar attachment is better for small lawns. Divide the lawn into strips using two garden lines to ensure that the grass has been given complete and uniform coverage.

If possible, wait for two or three days after mowing before applying the weedkiller so that the weeds have time to develop new leaf surfaces to absorb the chemicals. Do not mow the grass for two or three days after spraying to allow time for the weedkiller to work its way down toward the roots.

How often to apply

Some lawn weeds, such as dandelions and plantains, are killed by one or two applications of weedkiller; others, for example the trefoils, may need two or three applications, at four- to six-week intervals. Occasionally a species such as slender speedwell (*Veronica filiformis*) may survive several applications.

Where a weed shows no response to repeated applications of various weedkillers, the only solution is to remove it by hand. This will mean either removing and replacing infested areas of sod or, alternatively, feeding, scarifying, and aerating the sod to strengthen it and weaken the weed.

Neglected sites

Different treatments need to be adopted according to how long the area has been neglected and how great a hold the weeds have obtained. Sites that have been neglected for some time may take a season, or even longer, to clear for vegetable growing.

Short-term neglect

On sites that have been neglected for up to a year, most of the weeds are likely to be annuals. Kill these with one or two applications of the contact weedkillers paraquat or diquat in the spring or summer. This has the added advantage of defoliating and weakening any young perennials that may have appeared; it does not kill them, however. Dig these up two or three weeks after the treatment, when they have sufficiently resprouted and can be identified.

If any weed seedlings appear in the meantime, either dig them in or destroy them with a further application of contact weedkiller.

Winter clearance

If the site is being cleared during the winter, remove any overwintering top-growth of annual weeds with a rotary mower. Then dig out any perennial weeds by hand, if possible, before cultivating the area. Clear neglected vegetable plots progressively, beginning at the warmer, sunnier end, where the earliest sowings of crops are to be made and the seedbeds sited.

Longer-term neglect

After a second year of neglect, perennial weeds will become well established, competing vigorously with annual weeds. If the site remains neglected for a further year, by the end of the third growing season the weed population will usually be largely, or entirely, strong-growing perennial weeds. Badly infested sites are difficult to clear by hand or by use of a rototiller (the latter may do no more than turn the weeds back into the soil again). It is more practical to use translocated or soil-acting weedkillers, allowing a full growing season for treatment to take effect.

Cutting down weeds

If beginning clearance in spring, cut down weeds with woody stems, for example brambles or buckthorn, to within 12–18in (30–45cm) from the ground, then spray the whole weed-infested area with 2,4–D.

Using this weedkiller has a dual purpose: it not only kills woody weeds but is also effective against coarse grasses and broad-leaved perennial weeds. It persists in the soil for about three months, which is a disadvantage; being highly soluble, it spreads easily through the soil and, for this reason, should not be used where there are underlying tree or shrub roots, or where it may leach into cultivated areas.

Any weeds that survive treatment with 2,4–D and regrow in summer can then be treated with glyphosate.

Summer spraying

Another method is to cut the weeds back in spring and then allow them to grow unchecked until midsummer. Then spray the site with glyphosate, which acts more effectively on the vigorous young growth stimulated by the spring cut. Glyphosate is a translocated weedkiller; it usually takes three to four weeks to show any effect. No harmful residues are left in the soil; as soon as weeds are dead, the site can be cultivated. Very persistent weeds such as horsetail and bindweed may need subsequent spot treatment, again with glyphosate, possibly for a further two or three growing seasons, to control them fully. Lightly walking on weeds to damage them slightly before spraying helps increase uptake of the herbicide.

Hand Clearance

To remove perennial weeds from a recently neglected site, dig them out by hand. Be sure to extract all the roots to prevent new growth the following spring. If you are clearing the site in spring or summer, defoliate with weedkiller, then wait a few weeks before digging the weeds out by hand. In winter, dig up the perennials that remain after rototilling.

Uncultivated ground

Where previously cultivated land is to be left uncultivated, and is free from perennial weeds, it can be kept clear by regular light cultivations, at intervals throughout the year, with a hoe or with a mechanical tool, such as a rotary cultivator. Alternatively, at intervals, developing weed seedlings can be killed by application of the contact weedkillers paraquat or diquat, or by using glyphosate.

If there are perennial weeds infesting the site, let them grow until midsummer, then spray with glyphosate.

Weeds in cracks and crevices

Weeds in the cracks in paths and brickwork are hard to remove by hand, so chemical control is usually required.

Path weedkillers

In early spring, apply a commercial path weedkiller. Such weedkillers are mixtures of contact and soil-acting chemicals, the latter usually remaining active in the soil for several months. They may also include a foliage-acting, translocated herbicide such as MCPA to deal with any established perennial weeds that are not usually controlled by the low-strength, soil-acting chemicals in these mixtures.

Spot treatment

Perennial weeds in paths may be spot treated or sprayed with glyphosate when regrowth is vigorous. Dichlorbenil granules carefully sprinkled or brushed into the spaces between paving stones will control weeds but should not be applied if crevice plants are being cultivated.

8

BASIC BOTANY

BOTANY – THE SCIENTIFIC *study of plants – covers a number of disciplines. Familiarity with the basics of botany helps the gardener to understand the principles underlying many horticultural techniques, to maintain plants in good health so that they provide fine ornamental displays and high-quality fruit and vegetables, and to obtain appropriate plant material for propagation. The study of the internal arrangement of plant structures (anatomy) and their external construction (morphology) can, for example, provide an explanation of how to graft successfully, create new hybrids, or make pruning cuts that heal quickly. Physiology is the study of a plant's metabolism. It aids in the understanding of a plant's need for water and light, the role of nutrients in plant growth, and the processes of photosynthesis, transpiration, and respiration. Taxonomy – the identification and classification of plants – can indicate close relationships between genera or species that have similar cultivation needs.*

Plant diversity

There are more than 250,000 species of seed-bearing plant. They include annuals, which flower, seed, and die in a year or less; biennials, which grow from seed in their first year and then flower, seed, and die in the second season; and perennials, which live for several to many years, and include woody plants. The word "perennials" is commonly applied to herbaceous plants, while trees and shrubs are referred to as woody plants. Most garden plants have roots, stems, leaves, and fruits; these may be modified for particular purposes.

Roots

These anchor the plant in the soil and absorb water and mineral salts from which the plant manufactures its food. Fleshy taproots penetrate vertically downward, forming sparse lateral roots that are, in turn, finely branched. Fibrous roots consist of a network of fine, threadlike roots that emerge from the base of the stem or from taproots in some plants. The root tips bear fragile root hairs, which are in intimate contact with soil particles from which water and mineral salts are absorbed. Roots are sometimes modified to form storage organs, as is the case in many terrestrial orchids or swollen taproots such as carrots.

Stems

Plant stems provide the above-ground framework of the plant, supporting the leaves, flowers, and fruits. Some stem cells are specialized to conduct food, water, or nutrients from the leaves to all parts of the plant. Food is carried by phloem cells; water and mineral salts

BASIC PARTS OF A PLANT

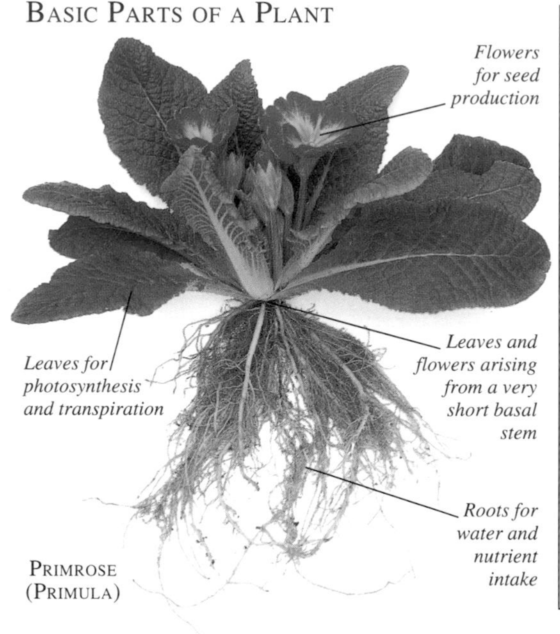

ROOT SYSTEMS

All roots draw up water and minerals and anchor the plant in the soil; some also store food.

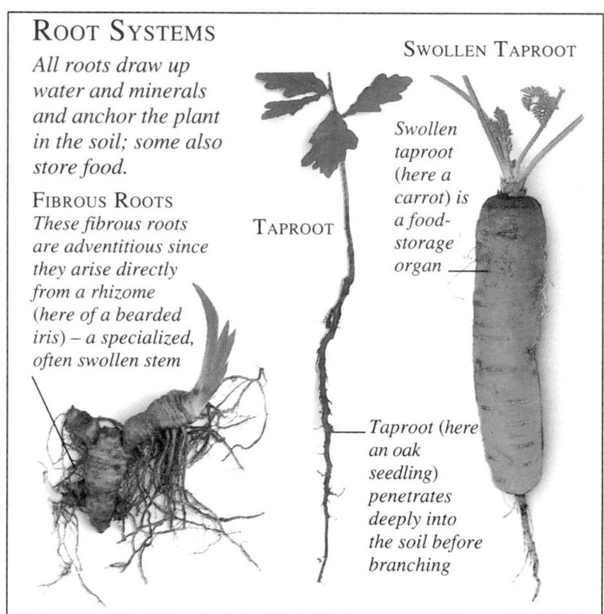

TYPES OF STEM

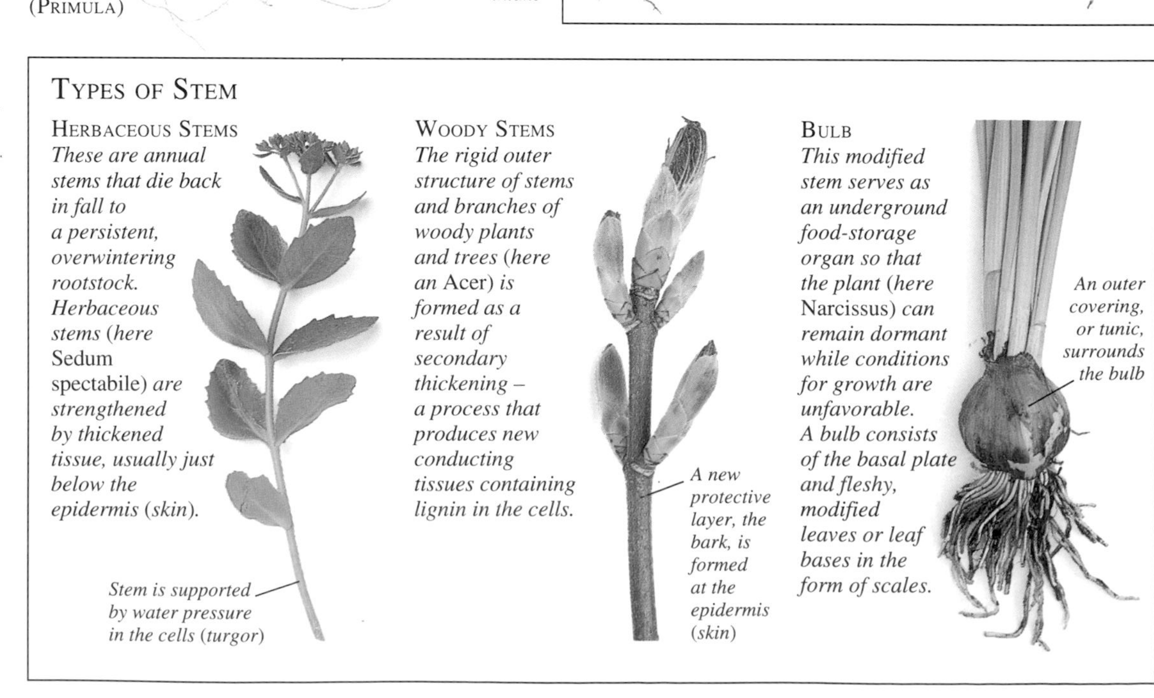

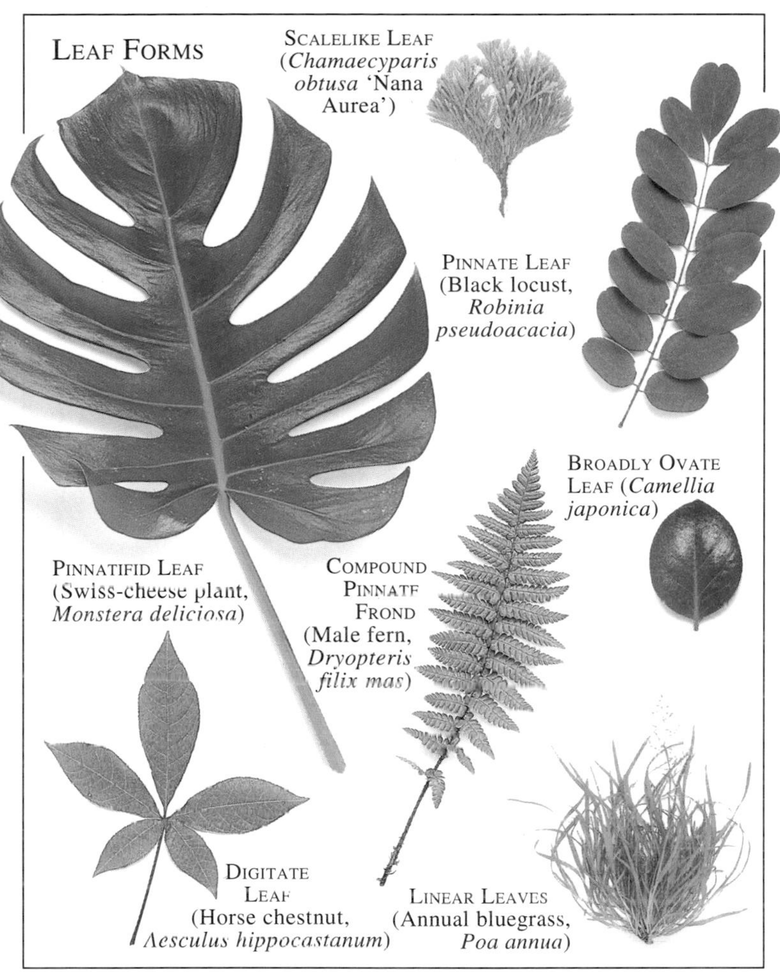

are conducted through xylem cells. Stems are often modified for other functions. Tubers, corms, and rhizomes are swollen stems that are modified for food storage; in cacti, the swollen stems contain water-storage tissue.

Leaves

Leaf form is extremely diverse and may be modified as spines, as in some cacti, or as tendrils, as in the garden pea. Whatever their form, leaves are the manufacturing centers of a plant. They contain the green pigment chlorophyll, which absorbs the energy of sunlight in order to convert carbon dioxide from the air and water from the soil into carbohydrates by the process known as photosynthesis. The by product, oxygen, is essential to most forms of life. The energy required to drive the plant's metabolism is produced through respiration, which breaks down carbohydrates to release energy, carbon dioxide, and water.

Leaves present a relatively large surface so that they maximize absorption of light; they are thin enough for light to penetrate to the cells that contain chlorophyll, and to allow rapid

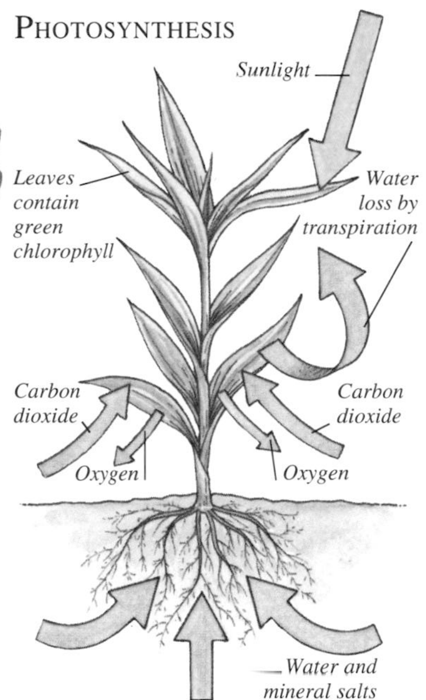

Water and carbon dioxide are converted into carbohydrates and oxygen using the energy of sunlight, which is trapped by the chlorophyll in a plant's leaves.

movement of gases to all cells. Their surfaces contain numerous pores (stomata) through which oxygen and carbon dioxide pass in and out of the leaf. The stomata also control water losses through transpiration. A high evaporation of water vapor from the leaves and a lack of water entering through the plant roots are the cause of plants wilting in dry conditions.

Although only 1 percent of the fresh weight of a plant consists of minerals, they are essential. In solution they are directly concerned with the water balance of the cells, and help regulate the passage of substances between cells. They maintain the correct pH for biochemical reactions and are essential components of chlorophyll and enzymes, the biological catalysts of the plant's internal chemistry.

Fruits and seeds

Seeds are a flowering plant's means of reproduction. Each seed develops from a single fertilized egg, and one or more seeds is contained in a fruit. The many types of fruit disperse their seeds in a variety of ways.

In some fruits, the seeds germinate rapidly with no special treatment; in others, it may be necessary for the seeds to undergo specific treatment in cultivation for them to germinate fairly rapidly. For further information, see PRINCIPLES OF PROPAGATION, "How to overcome dormancy," p.537.

Pods and capsules are dehiscent fruits, splitting along a regular line or lines to release the seed, as in *Aquilegia* and violets (*Viola*). Indehiscent fruits do not split. Good examples are hazelnuts (*Corylus*) and chestnuts (*Castanea*), in which a single seed (kernel) is enclosed in a tough shell. These large seeds have a high moisture and fat content, and deteriorate quickly unless sown fresh or stored in cool, moist conditions. In roses, many small, indehiscent fruits, each containing one seed, are enclosed in a hollow receptacle – the hip. The individual seeds (strictly fruits) need to be extracted before sowing.

Succulent fruits, where the seed is enclosed in flesh, include berries (e.g. bananas, tomatoes, and grapes), which have many seeds; drupes (e.g. plums, cherries, and peaches), which typically have one seed in the form of a stone;

TRANSPIRATION

Plant fluids

Stoma (pore) on lily leaf

Guard cells controlling closing and opening of stomata

Water lost through open stomata (pores)

Water and minerals drawn up from roots

Evaporation of water from the leaf surfaces creates a constant flow of water and nutrients from the roots to the foliage; this is known as the transpiration stream.

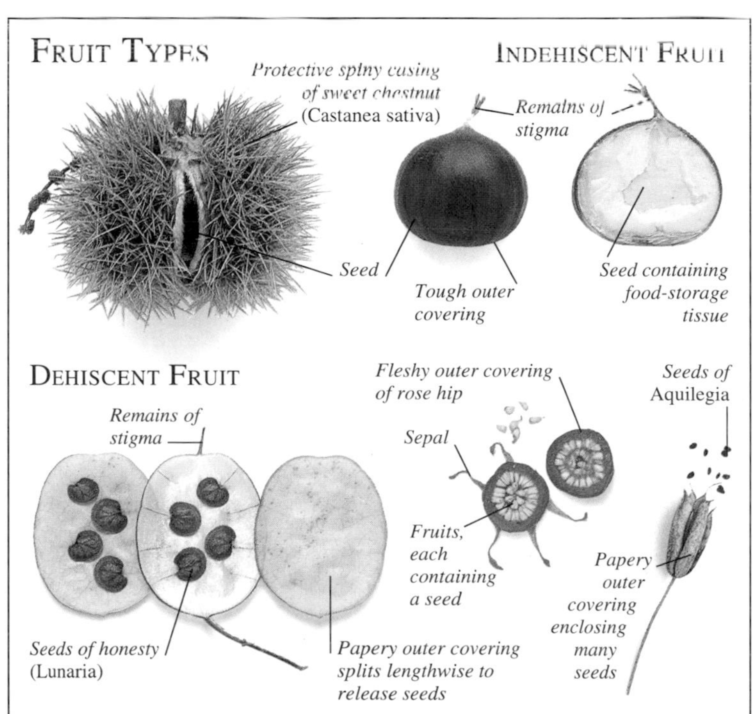

and pomes (e.g. apples, pears, and quinces), which develop from other parts of the flower besides the ovaries. In all these types of fruit, the seed should be removed from the mashed flesh and cleaned before being sown.

Flowers

Flowers are the fifth basic part of a plant, and they show extraordinary diversity in color, scent, and form, with a wide range of adaptations to ensure that they fulfill their reproductive function. They may be borne as showy, individual flowers (*Hibiscus* and tulips) or in many-flowered spikes (*Kniphofia*), racemes (hyacinth), panicles (*Gypsophila*), umbels (*Agapanthus*), or in heads consisting of numerous small florets such as dahlias in the family Compositae.

A flower has four main parts: petals or tepals, sepals, stamens (the male part), and one or more carpels (the female part), which are collectively known as the pistil. Most conspicuous are the petals, carried above a whorl of (usually) green sepals. The male reproductive nuclei are carried in pollen grains, enclosed in an anther attached to a stemlike filament; these vary greatly in number from three in crocuses to 30 or more in buttercups. The carpels enclose the female egg nuclei and have a projecting style, or stylar column, with a stigma at its tip to receive pollen grains. Pollen grains germinate on the stigma, and pollen tubes containing the male nuclei grow through the tissue of the style to fuse with the female nuclei (the process of fertilization), eventually forming seeds.

Many plants bear separate female and male (unisexual) flowers on the same plant, for example birch (*Betula*) and hazelnut (*Corylus*). They are known as monoecious plants. Bisexual, or hermaphroditic, plants have both male and female parts in each flower. A few species bear unisexual and bisexual flowers and are known as polygamous plants. In dioecious plants all the flowers produced are of one sex only; examples are many holly species (*Ilex*), *Aucuba*, and some *Skimmia* variants. Male and female plants must be grown together if they are to set seed; this is especially important where plants are grown for their ornamental berries, as with many hollies and *Pernettya* species and cultivars.

Different but related species do not normally interbreed because they often occur in dissimilar habitats, flower at varying times, or possess minor variations in flower characters that prevent successful interbreeding. In cultivation, such barriers can sometimes be overcome, and hybrids are often created by design (see "Producing hybrid plants," p.538).

Flowering plants of the division Angiospermae produce seeds that are enclosed in an ovary. They differ from the Gymnospermae, which consist of nonflowering plants that bear naked seeds. Angiosperms are divided into monocotyledons and dicotyledons, based on whether there are one or two seed leaves (cotyledons) within the seed itself.

Monocotyledons have leaves with (usually) parallel veins, flower parts in threes or multiples thereof, and often relatively slender, insignificant, nonwoody stems. Dicotyledons have leaves with a branching network of veins; the petals and sepals are in multiples of two, four, or five; and the stems are thickened (and, in trees and shrubs, woody), originating from a special layer of cells within the stem called the cambium. Monocotyledon stems do not possess a cambium layer, so the plants are generally smaller.

Parts of a Flower

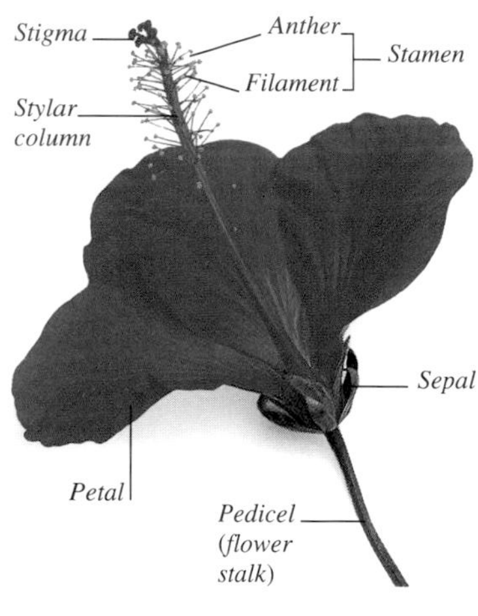

Sexuality in Flowers

Dioecious plants – being either male or female – need a plant of each sex growing close to one another to set seed. Monoecious plants bear separate male and female flowers on the same plant. Bisexual (hermaphroditic) flowers contain both male (stamens) and female (carpels) parts in the same flower.

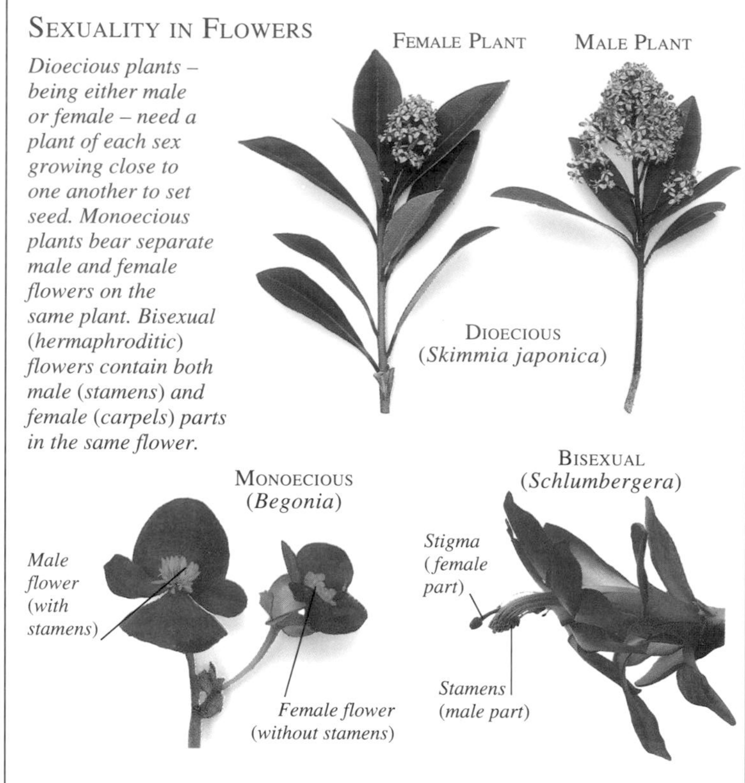

Classes of Flower

Flowering plants are grouped into two classes: monocotyledons and dicotyledons

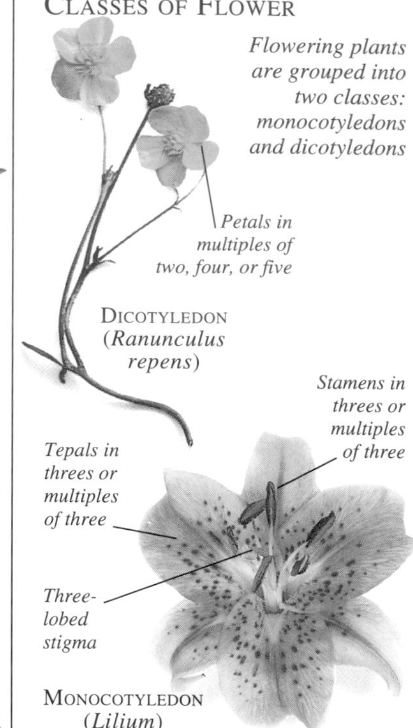

Leaf Veins

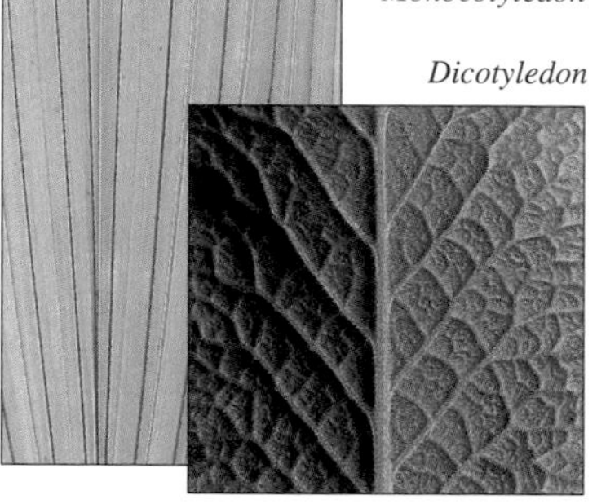

Leaf vein patterns in monocotyledons (here Curculigo recurvata*) are usually parallel; those in dicotyledons (here* Primula*) generally form a network.*

Mutation

A mutation, also known as a sport, is a genetic change in a plant, either natural or induced, that may be exploited horticulturally by propagating the mutated material in order to introduce a new cultivar. Mutations may occur in all parts of the plant, but those of horticultural interest are mainly color mutants or doubled flowers and variegated shoots that occur on a normally green-leaved plant.

Chrysanthemum cultivars often produce mutations, for example one flowerhead in a spray having a different color from the parent plant.

Classification and nomenclature

Plants are referred to scientifically by two names, generally written in italics. The first name, which always has its initial letter capitalized, is that of the genus, the second is the species name, or specific epithet: for example, *Rosa canina*. In nature, species often show minor variations in character; these are given a third name, prefixed by "subsp." (subspecies), "var." (varietas), or "f." (forma): thus *Rhododendron rex* subsp. *fictolacteum*. A cultivar (cultivated variety) is one that has been selected either from the wild or from gardens and grown in cultivation, and whose characteristics are preserved by some means of controlled propagation. The name of such a plant is written in Roman type with an initial capital letter and in single quotation marks: thus *Choisya ternata* 'Sundance'.

Seasonal reminders

THESE notes, distilled from Part One of this book, serve as reminders of important tasks to be done during the gardening year, and of the best times to do them. They should be taken only as a guide – in a cold region, you may have to delay some tasks; in a warm region, you may be able to start them earlier and finish later. Every garden is unique: its position and soil type affect the rate at which the plants grow and therefore the time when various activities are best undertaken. Whatever your conditions, prepare the soil and containers thoroughly before planting; do not plant in frozen, waterlogged, or very dry soil. Water plants well until established. Certain year-round operations are not covered here (such as controlling pests, diseases, and weeds, or potting cuttings). For full details of how to carry out the tasks mentioned, refer to the appropriate specific chapters.

Spring

Soil preparation and planting

Plant hardy plants in beds or containers, including container-grown annual vegetables (under cloches, if necessary) and perennial vegetables. Start planting water garden plants. Sow half-hardy and hardy annuals indoors, and hardy biennials outdoors, in late spring. For a new lawn, sow seed or lay sod. Indoors, prepare greenhouse beds and soil benches; plant ornamentals, terrariums, bottle gardens, and hanging baskets.

Routine care

After flowering, plunge alpines, dwarf bulbs, and winter-flowering indoor plants outside, and re-cover bulb frames. Water established bulbs, cacti, and other succulents. Indoors, increase watering and mist-spray plants as needed. For epiphytes in bloom, keep soil moist.

Feed established plants except annuals; mulch mature trees, shrubs, climbers, perennials, fruits, and, after pruning, roses. In late spring, mulch vegetables. Check stakes and ties; stake climbing and tall plants, if necessary. Erect supports for peas and climbing beans.

For trees and shrubs, cut out suckers and reverted shoots. Remove dead growth of half-hardy perennials; cut back shrubby perennials and overvigorous and straggly rock garden plants. Unless seed is needed, deadhead flowering shrubs, repeat-flowering climbers, bulbs, and indoor plants. Thin dense perennial shoots and pinch young perennials, annuals, biennials, and trailing indoor plants as needed. Top-dress or repot plants in containers (except spring-flowering climbers). If necessary, replenish top-dressing around outdoor rock garden plants. Transplant deciduous shrubs and half-hardy perennials, if necessary. Protect any tender new growth on outdoor plants, and flowers on fruiting plants during late frosts.

In the water garden, clear blanketweed and thin oxygenating plants. Divide and replant or repot overcrowded aquatic and bog plants; overhaul neglected ponds.

Roll lawns before starting mowing if sod has been lifted by frost; repair damaged areas. In mid- to late spring, lightly scarify the lawn and apply fertilizer. Cut grass around bulbs after flowering.

Harvest herb leaves as appropriate. In the vegetable garden, force rhubarb and chicory. Under cover, pollinate peach, nectarine, strawberry, and grape flowers; thin peach and nectarine fruitlets.

Pruning and training

Until midspring, give formative pruning, coppice, and pollard trees and prune deciduous trees that flower in late summer (except those that bleed heavily); renovate evergreen tree hedges. Root prune established trees as needed.

In early spring, prune shrubs that flower on new wood, and all hydrangeas; renovate deciduous shrubs. In midspring, give formative pruning and train shrubs; prune and renovate evergreen shrubs. Coppice and pollard shrubs grown for summer foliage or winter stems. In late spring, prune winter- or spring-flowering shrubs. Start clipping topiary. Root prune vigorous shrubs or those grown in containers.

In early spring, prune deciduous climbers that flower on new wood, evergreens, and, after flowering, those that flower on old wood. Give formative pruning to climbers. Prune Hybrid Teas, Grandifloras, Floribundas, miniatures, standards, Bourbons, Hybrid Perpetuals, and newly planted roses. Give formative pruning to species roses. Cut back roses on pillars.

In the rock garden, prune shrubs and woody perennials. Hard prune shrubby herbs. Pinch out and disbud new grape shoots; disbud and deshoot stone fruit fans under cover. Prune young stone fruit trees, blueberries, hazelnuts, figs, trained trees, and plum pyramids. Bark-ring overvigorous apple and pear trees.

In the indoor garden, cut back weak or damaged growth; prune shrubs and climbers that flower on old wood. In early spring, cut back shrubs and climbers that are in growth all year.

Propagation

Sow seed of hardy plants outside, and of tender plants under cover. Make successive sowings of regularly used annual and biennial herbs. From late spring, sow tender vegetables outdoors. Start sowing annual indoor plants. Collect ripe seed of early-flowering water lilies.

In early spring, divide suckering shrubs, rooted suckers from roses on their own roots, fleshy-rooted perennials, mat- and clump-forming rock garden plants, and dahlias. In late spring, divide marginal plants and collect turions for replanting.

Take softwood cuttings of trees, shrubs, climbers, rock garden plants, oxygenating plants, herbs, and indoor plants. Take basal cuttings of perennials, rock garden plants, dahlias, and tuberous begonias. In late spring, take greenwood cuttings of shrubs. Start taking perennial stem tip cuttings. Take leaf cuttings, in early to midspring, of rock garden and indoor plants, and stem and leaf cuttings or sections of cacti, other succulents, and indoor plants.

Flat-graft and side-graft cacti and other succulents. Graft fruit trees. In early spring, layer trees, shrubs, and climbing plants, and tip layer and stool shrubs. Air layer ornamental trees and, in late spring, mound layer shrubby herbs.

Summer

Soil preparation and planting

Plant container-grown plants, including new strawberry runners and annual vegetables. In late summer, plant containers of shrubs and prepare soil for fall planting of shrubs. Plant winter brassicas, salad and tender vegetables, and, by late summer, fall-flowering bulbs. In the water garden, plant aquatic and marginal plants until midsummer, and deep-water plants until late summer. For lawns, lay sod and sow seed.

Routine care

Water established plants, fruit trees, and lawns as necessary. Regularly water and feed plants in containers and under cover. Mist-spray cacti, succulents, and indoor plants; hose down succulents in the garden or greenhouse. Feed fruit plants as required. After midsummer, apply fertilizer to roses. Mulch vegetables, fruit, and moisture-loving herbs.

Stake and tie tall or climbing plants and vegetables. Remove suckers (and blind shoots) from trees, shrubs, and roses.

Unless seed is needed, deadhead outdoor and indoor plants. In the rock garden, cut out dead rosettes and cut back spring-flowering plants. Continue to pinch perennial shoots, and pinch out growing tips of indoor plants if necessary. Repot cacti and other succulents; pot, repot, or renew top-dressing of indoor plants. Transplant rooted strawberry runners. Lift and heel in early-flowering bulbs. Ventilate, shade, and damp down greenhouses and alpine houses.

In the water garden, clear out any blanketweed from ponds and, in midsummer, feed water lilies.

Mow lawns as appropriate, including grass around fruit trees, but stop mowing in areas with fall-flowering bulbs. Feed the lawn in early or midsummer and aerate lawn areas subject to heavy wear.

Harvest and store herbs, vegetables, and fruits. Hill up potatoes; lift and dry onions in late summer. Stake and tie tomatoes, and pinch them in late summer. In the fruit garden, thin fruitlets as needed; discard rotten fruits. Cut back summer-fruiting strawberries after picking.

Pruning and training

In early summer, prune spring-flowering trees; in midsummer, deciduous trees that bleed heavily and mature pleached trees; and in late summer, young pleached trees and deciduous tree hedges. Remove diseased or dead branches from evergreens. Clip topiary as necessary.

Prune shrubs that flower on old wood after flowering, mature shrub standards, informal shrub hedges, and deciduous shrubs that bleed heavily. For standards, pinch out side shoots on shrubs. After flowering, prune climbers that flower on old wood. Tie in new shoots. Carry out the first pruning stage of *Wisteria*.

Prune ramblers and most old garden roses after flowering. Give renewal pruning to nonremontant shrub, species, and ground cover roses. Peg down Bourbons and Hybrid Perpetuals. Thin Gallica roses and train new shoots of climbing and rambling roses. In the herb garden, cut back herbaceous herbs after flowering, and start cutting back shrubby herbs in late summer.

In the fruit garden, pinch out and train shoots on stone fruit fans; pinch out new fig shoots. Break new side shoots on hazelnuts. Prune sour cherries and fruiting raspberries; train new canes. Prune trained apples, pears, and pyramid plums.

Propagation
Sow seed of all annuals and biennials, including herbs, until midsummer. In late summer, sow hardy annuals and biennials in pots for fall planting. Sow seed of rock garden plants. Make successive sowings of summer vegetables; sow oriental and winter vegetables and herbs for winter and spring crops. Collect and sow seed of perennials and water garden plants (under cover); collect annual, biennial, and bulb seed.

In early summer, divide overcrowded bulb clumps, water lilies, and offsets of clump-forming and some tuberous-rooted cacti and other succulents.

Take softwood cuttings of climbers and, in midsummer, of marginal and oxygenating water garden plants, and of herbs; take basal and greenwood cuttings of rock garden plants. In mid- to late summer, take semiripe cuttings of trees, shrubs, roses, rock garden and indoor plants, and herbs, and ripewood cuttings of rock garden plants. In mid- to late summer, take mallet cuttings of shrubs and leaf-bud cuttings of shrubs, hybrid berries, and blackberries. Take stem-tip cuttings of perennials, stem cuttings of herbs and indoor plants, and leaf and Irishman's cuttings of rock garden plants.

In midsummer, bud-graft ornamental and fruit trees. Graft cacti and other succulents. In late summer, chip-bud shrubs, side-graft deciduous shrubs, bud-graft, layer, and hybridize roses. Tip layer blackberries and hybrid berries. For bulbs, collect bulbils and remove bulblets (and pot them). In late summer, scale and twin-scale lilies and other bulbs.

Fall

Soil preparation and planting
Plant bare-root, balled-and-burlapped, and container-grown hardy plants, including overwintering bulb vegetables; in mild areas, plant out hardy annuals. Plant trees and spring-flowering bulbs in containers. In early fall, sow salad crops and plant winter salad vegetables and oriental brassicas under cover. In midfall, sow hardy, overwintering vegetables and start digging and manuring empty vegetable beds. For the lawn, lay sod and sow seed. In early fall, lift, divide, and pot mature herb plants for winter use indoors; pot up strawberry runners for the greenhouse.

Routine care
Water plants as needed. Start watering bulbs that are dormant, under cover, and forced. Restrict watering of indoor plants, cacti, and other succulents after midfall; allow desert plants to dry out but keep epiphytes moist.

Feed cacti and succulents that start active growth in midfall; reduce feeding of indoor plants. Mulch trees, shrubs, climbers, and perennials. Check and renew stakes and ties as needed. Remove stakes from perennials after flowering.

Deadhead plants unless seed is required. Remove plant debris from around roses and perennials; clear dead annuals and cut out dead rosettes from rock garden plants. Clear fallen leaves from low-growing evergreen herbs. Cut back shrubby herbs in early fall, and tall roses in midfall; except in cold areas, cut down to the ground hardy perennials and those grown as biennials.

Repot or top-dress climbers in containers and winter-flowering indoor plants. Renew top-dressing around rock garden plants. In midfall, transplant established trees, shrubs, and fruit trees if necessary; begin transplanting mature perennials. Lift and store perennials, dahlias, and summer-flowering bulbs; lift and pot perennials grown as annuals.

In late fall, protect tender plants, including container-grown herbs. In cold areas, move shrubs and tender perennials in containers under cover. Protect tender, perennial, and root vegetables in the ground, and frost-tender crowns of water garden plants; move tender floating plants to a frost-free place. Protect plants in an unheated greenhouse from severe cold and raise heat in alpine houses to prevent plants from freezing. Scrub down and fumigate the greenhouse.

In the water garden in early fall, thin oxygenating plants; in mid- to late fall, cut back leaves of marginals and excess growth of submerged plants. Remove dead growth and seedpods of invasive plants; cover ponds with netting. Service and clean the water pump.

Mow lawns as appropriate and feed and water if needed. Control moss, aerate, then top-dress. Clear fallen leaves.

In the vegetable garden, in early fall, stake and hill up winter brassicas in windy areas. From midfall, lift plants for forcing. Harvest and store vegetables and fruits. Bring in winter-flowering indoor plants in early fall.

Pruning and training
Give formative pruning, renovate, and prune deciduous trees (unless they bleed heavily) and tree hedges. In early fall, prune mature pleached trees. In late fall, cut out dead, diseased, and damaged wood from shrubs. Give formative pruning to shrub hedges, and prune evergreen hedges. In windy sites, trim shoots of shrubs after flowering. Prune shrubs and woody perennials in the rock garden.

Prune Floribundas, Hybrid Teas, Grandifloras, climbers, miniatures, standards, and newly planted roses, and train new shoots of climbing roses.

Shorten pinched shoots on plum, apricot, and sweet cherry fans. Remove old canes from blackberries and hybrid berries; train young canes. Prune fan-trained peaches and nectarines after fruiting. In late fall, start to prune apples, pears, and bush fruits. Prune long shoots on indoor-grown shrubs and climbers, unless they bleed heavily.

Propagation
Sow seed of plants that overwinter outdoors, including alpine strawberries, and early-flowering indoor plants (under cover). Collect and sow seed of hardy shrubs, perennials, and roses (in late fall).

Divide shrubs, perennials with fibrous roots, mat- and clump-forming rock garden plants, established clumps of water garden marginals and bog plants (in early fall), and clump-forming and rhizomatous herbs. Chip bulbs.

In early fall, take stem-tip cuttings of perennials, basal cuttings of rock garden plants, and leaf-bud cuttings of shrubs. Take semiripe cuttings of trees (early to midfall), climbing plants, and herbs. Take hardwood cuttings of trees (late fall), shrubs (midfall), climbers, roses, rock garden plants, and herbs; plant hardwood cuttings of gooseberries and currants in open ground. Take root cuttings of rock garden plants.

Prepare rose rootstocks for budding. Layer shrubs and climbers; mound layer shrubby herbs. Divide rooted suckers of raspberries and hazelnuts. Indoors, store begonias before propagating in spring.

Winter

Soil preparation and planting
Plant container-grown, deciduous bare-root, and balled-and-burlapped hardy plants and tree, bush, cane, and vine fruits. In midwinter, check summer-flowering bulbs in storage. In the rock garden, build raised and scree beds when conditions permit. Prepare the site for a new lawn. In the vegetable garden, finish digging and manuring empty beds. Plant vegetables outdoors with protection, and set potatoes to sprout indoors.

Routine care
Water forced bulbs and bulbs under cover, if necessary. As epiphytes come into bud, keep soil moist. Water indoor plants less frequently; keep air around plants fairly dry. Feed fruit plants in late winter. When conditions permit, mulch trees, shrubs, and climbers. Check ties and supports. Remove supports and plant debris from perennials.

In late winter, repot or top-dress plants in containers. Top-dress rock garden plants and fruiting vine borders. Transplant deciduous trees, shrubs, and perennials, if necessary. Throughout the winter, protect nonhardy plants outside from winter damage. In an unheated greenhouse, keep plants nearly dry; if necessary, protect plants from severe cold with plastic sheeting or similar material, or plunge small pots in sand. Protect alpine houses and raised ponds.

Mow established lawns only if necessary; clear fallen leaves. Service all equipment. Force chicory and rhubarb. Harvest and store vegetable crops. In the fruit garden, scrape old bark from grape vines; pollinate peaches under cover.

Pruning and training
Start coppicing and pollarding trees in late winter. Cut out dead, diseased, and damaged wood from trees and shrubs. Give formative pruning and renovate deciduous trees, shrubs, and hedges.

Give formative pruning and train climbing plants in late winter. Prune ornamental vines in early winter, deciduous climbers for shape, and, in late winter, hardy deciduous climbers that flower on new wood. In midwinter, carry out the second stage of pruning *Wisteria*.

Prune roses (in warmer climates) to induce an artificial rest period and give renewal pruning to remontant shrub roses.

Winter prune fruit trees, bushes, fall-fruiting raspberries and young tree roots. Tip-prune summer-fruiting raspberries, blackberries, and hybrid berries.

Propagation
Collect and sow seed of shrubs; sow perennial seed in containers, rose seed produced from hybridizing, seed of hardy rock garden plants, and vegetable seed indoors. In late winter, sow seed of water garden plants under cover.

From late winter, divide shrubs. Start dahlias into growth for division. Scoop rosette-forming rock garden plants.

Take cuttings from sprouting dahlia tubers. Take hardwood cuttings of trees, shrubs, and climbers in early winter. In late winter, plant hardwood cuttings of grapes in well-drained, open ground. Take root cuttings of climbing plants (in early winter), shrubs (in midwinter), perennials, and rock garden plants.

Carry out apical-wedge, side-veneer, and saddle grafting of trees and shrubs. Graft *Gypsophila* cultivars that do not root from cuttings. In late winter, cut back any budded rootstocks from roses.

Prepare trees in late winter for simple layering in spring, and carry out layering of shrubs and climbers. In the fruit garden, divide rooted suckers of raspberries and hazelnuts.

Glossary

The glossary explains horticultural terms that are used in this book. Words in italics within a definition have a separate entry. Fuller explanations and illustrations may be found elsewhere by looking up the term in the index.

Acaricide. A *pesticide* used to control mites. (Cf. *Insecticide*; *Nematicide*.)
Acid (of soil). With a *pH* value of less than 7. (Cf. *Alkaline*; *Neutral*.)
Adventitious. Arising from places where growths do not normally occur; for example, adventitious roots may arise from stems.
Adventitious bud. See *Bud*.
Aerate (of soil). Loosen by mechanical means in order to allow air (oxygen and carbon dioxide) to enter; for example, using a spiked roller to aerate a lawn.
Aerial root. A plant root growing above ground to provide anchorage and, on an *epiphyte*, to absorb atmospheric moisture.
Air layering. See *Layering*.
Alkaline (of soil). With a *pH* value of more than 7. (Cf. *Acid*; *Neutral*.)
Alpine. A plant that grows above the tree line in mountainous regions; loosely applied to rock garden plants that may be grown at relatively low altitudes.
Alpine house. An unheated, well-ventilated greenhouse used for cultivating *alpine* and bulbous plants.
Alternate (of leaves). Occurring successively at different levels on opposite sides of a stem. (Cf. *Opposite*.)
Anemone-centered (of flowers). Flowers or flowerheads in which the central petals or flowers (modified *stamens*) form a cushionlike mound and the outer rim of petals or ray florets are flat and spreading, as in some chrysanthemums.
Annual. A plant that completes its life cycle (*germination* flowering–seeding–dying) in one growing season.
Anther. The part of a *stamen* that produces *pollen*; usually borne on a *filament*.
Apical. See *Terminal*.
Apical bud. See *Bud*.
Apical-wedge grafting. See *Grafting*.
Aquatic. Any plant that grows in water. It may be free-floating, totally submerged, or rooted on the pond bottom with leaves and flowers above the water surface.
Asclepiad. A member of the *family* Asclepiadaceae.
Asexual reproduction. A form of reproduction not involving *fertilization* and, in propagation, often involving mechanical methods (see *Vegetative propagation*).
Auxins. Naturally occurring or artificially synthesized plant growth substances controlling shoot growth, root formation, and other physiological processes in plants.
Awn. A sharp point or bristle, commonly found on a *glume* of a grass *inflorescence*.
Axil. The upper angle between a leaf and a stem, between a main stem and a lateral branch, or between a stem and a bract. (See also *Bud*: *Axillary bud*.)
Axillary bud. See *Bud*.
Back bulb (of orchids). A dormant, old *pseudobulb* without leaves.
Backfill. To fill in a planting hole around a plant's roots with a soil mix.
Ball. See *Root ball*.
Balled. Of a flower that does not open and rots when still in bud.
Balled-and-burlapped. Of plants that have been lifted and had their *root ball* wrapped in burlap or other material to keep it intact during *transplanting*.
Bare-root. Of plants sold with their roots bare of soil.
Bark-ringing. The removal of a ring of bark from the trunk or branches of certain fruit trees, to reduce vigorous growth and to encourage fruit cropping. Also known as "girdling."
Basal plate. A compressed *stem*, part of a *bulb*.
Basal stem cutting. See *Cutting*.
Basal-whip grafting. See *Grafting*.
Base dressing. An application of fertilizer or humus (manure, compost, etc.) applied to or dug into the soil prior to sowing or planting.
Basin irrigation. A form of irrigation whereby soil is scooped out from around the plant or made to form a ridge around it, creating a basin into which water is introduced.
Bastard trenching. See *Double digging*.
Bed system. A method of planting vegetable crops in closely spaced rows, often in blocks or narrow beds for easy access.
Bedding plants. Annuals and biennials (or plants grown as such) raised almost to maturity and then planted out ("bedded out"), often in large blocks for temporary display.
Biennial. A plant that flowers and dies in the second growing season after *germination*.
Biennial bearing. The production of a heavy fruit crop in alternate years, with little or no blossoms or fruit in the intervening years.
Blanch. To exclude light from developing leaves or stems in order to keep the plant tissue soft and palatable.
Bleed. To lose *sap* through a wound.
Blind. Of a plant that fails to produce flowers, or a stem with a growing point that has been damaged.
Bloom. 1) A flower or blossom. 2) A waxy, white or bluish white coating on a stem, leaf, or fruit.
Blown. Of flowers or hearted vegetables (see *Heart up*) that are past full maturity and fading.
Bog plant. A plant whose natural habitat is soil that is permanently damp, or one that thrives in such conditions.
Bole. The *trunk* of a tree from ground level to the first major branch.
Bolt. To produce flowers and seed prematurely.
Bract. A modified, often protective, leaf at the base of a flower or flower cluster. Bracts may resemble normal leaves, or be small and scalelike, or large and brightly colored.
Branch. A shoot arising from the main stem or trunk of a woody plant.
Brassica. A member of the cabbage *family*.
Break. A *shoot* growing from an *axillary bud*.
Broadcasting. Scattering seed or fertilizer evenly over the ground, rather than in furrows or *drills*.
Broad-leaved. Of trees or shrubs that bear broad, flat leaves rather than needlelike foliage.
Bromeliad. A member of the *family* Bromeliaceae.
Bud. A rudimentary or condensed shoot containing an embryonic leaf, leaf cluster, or flower. **Adventitious bud**: one produced abnormally, for example from the stem instead of from a leaf *axil*. **Apical** (or terminal) **bud**: the topmost bud on a stem. **Axillary bud**: one that occurs in an *axil*. **Crown bud**. a flower bud at the shoot tip, surrounded by other, usually smaller, flower buds. **Fruit bud**: one from which leaves and flowers (followed by fruits) develop. **Growth bud**: one from which only leaves or a shoot develop.
Bud union. The point at which the *scion* bud unites with the *rootstock*.
Budding. Bud-grafting, a form of *grafting*.
Budding tape. See *Grafting tape*.
Bud-grafting. See *Grafting*.
Budwood. A shoot cut from a tree to provide a *scion* for *bud-grafting*.
Bulb. A modified *stem* acting as a storage organ and consisting mainly of fleshy, more or less separate or tightly packed, scale leaves (a modified *bud*) on a much reduced stem (*basal plate*).
Bulb fiber. Undecomposed *sphagnum moss*, sometimes with charcoal, in which *bulbs* are grown in containers, often without drainage holes.
Bulbil. A small *bulb*-like organ, often borne in a leaf *axil*, occasionally on a stem or in a *flowerhead*. (Cf. *Bulblet*.)
Bulblet. A small developing *bulb* produced from the *basal plate* of a mature bulb outside the *tunic*. (Cf. *Bulbil* and *Offset*.)
Bush. 1) A small shrub. 2) An open-centered fruit tree with a *trunk* of 3ft (90cm) or less.
Bush fruit. Used of soft fruit bushes such as blackcurrants and gooseberries.
Cactus. A member of the *family* Cactaceae, characterized by fleshy, water-storing tissue in the stems and areoles (specialized groups of cells) from which spines, flowers, and shoots develop.
Calcicole. *Lime*-loving; a plant that thrives in *alkaline* soil.
Calcifuge. *Lime*-hating; a plant that will not grow in *alkaline* soil.
Callus. Protective tissue formed by plants over a wounded surface, particularly in *woody* plants but also at the base of cuttings.
Calyx (pl. **calyces**). The collective name for the *sepals*, the outer *whorl* of segments, usually green, that enclose the flower in bud.
Cambium. A layer of meristematic tissue capable of producing new cells to increase the girth of stems and roots. (See also *Meristem*.)
Capillary matting. Matting made of synthetic fiber that is used to draw water upward by capillary action to irrigate pot plants on capillary beds or benches.
Capping. Formation of a crust that forms on the surface of soil damaged by compaction, heavy rain, or watering. (Cf. *Pan*.)
Capsule. A dry seed case that dehisces (splits open) when ripe to release its seeds.
Carpel. The female part of the flower of flowering plants that contains the *ovules*; several carpels in a flower are collectively known as the *pistil*.
Carpet bedding. The use of groups of closely planted, low-growing, colorful *bedding plants* in various patterns or designs.
Catkin. A racemose (see *Raceme*) flower spike, or a spikelike *inflorescence*, with conspicuous *bracts* and small, often unisexual flowers lacking petals.
Cell pack. Applied to various types of container, particularly those used in multiples for sowing seed and pricking out seedlings.
Central leader. The central, usually upright stem of a *tree*.
Certified stock. Plants certified by the US Department of Agriculture or Agriculture Canada as free from certain pests and diseases.
Chilling requirement. The requirement of plants for a specific period of dormancy below a particular temperature in order for them to initiate flowering.
Chinese layering. An alternative name for air layering; see *Layering*.
Chip-budding. See *Grafting*.
Chlorophyll. The green plant pigment that is mainly responsible for light absorption and hence *photosynthesis* in plants.
Clamp. A method for storing *root crops* outdoors. The crops are heaped up and protected against cold by layers of straw and soil; a hole filled with straw provides ventilation.
Climber. 1) A plant that climbs using other plants or objects as support: **self-clinging climbers** by supporting, *adventitious*, or *aerial roots*, or adhesive tendril tips; **tendril climbers** by coiling their leaf stalks, leaf *tendrils*, or modified *terminal* shoots; **twining climbers** by coiling their *stems*. **Scandent**, **scrambling**, **rambling**, and **trailing climbers** produce long, usually flexuous stems that grow over or through plants or other supports;

they attach themselves only loosely, if at all, to the support. 2) A rose that blooms more than once a year.
Cloche. A small, usually portable, structure made of clear plastic or glass, often in a metal framework; used to protect early crops on open ground and to warm the soil before planting. (See also *Floating row cover.*)
Clone. 1) A group of genetically identical plants produced by *vegetative propagation* or *asexual reproduction.* 2) An individual plant in such a group.
Cold frame. A glazed, boxlike, unheated structure, made from brick, wood, or glass, with a hinged or removable glass or clear plastic *sash*; used to protect plants from excessive cold.
Collar. 1) The part of a plant where the roots meet the stem; also known as the neck. 2) The part of a tree where a main branch meets the *trunk* (or a side branch meets a main branch).
Companion planting. Positioning plants together that are reputed to have a beneficial effect on neighboring plants by discouraging pests and diseases or improving growth.
Compositae. The daisy *family*.
Compost. An organic material, rich in *humus*, formed by decomposed plant remains, and other *organic* matter, used as a soil improver or *mulch*.
Compound. Divided into two or more subsidiary parts, for example a leaf divided into two or more *leaflets*. (Cf. *Simple*.)
Cone. The densely clustered *bracts* and flowers of *conifers* and some flowering plants, often developing into a woody, seed-bearing structure, e.g. a pine cone.
Confused. Of petals, especially in roses, that have an overlapping, irregular arrangement.
Conifer. Gymnosperms, usually evergreen trees and shrubs, that are distinguished from flowering plants (Angiosperms) by the naked *ovules* that are not enclosed in an *ovary* but are often borne in *cones*.
Contact action. The action of a *pesticide* or weedkiller that kills or damages a pest or weed by direct contact.
Coppicing. The annual pruning back of trees or shrubs close to ground level to produce vigorous, usually decorative, *shoots*. (Cf. *Pollarding*.)
Cordon. A trained plant (usually a fruit tree) generally restricted to one main stem by rigorous pruning. A **single cordon** has one main stem, a **double**, or **U, cordon** has two, and a **multiple cordon**, three or more stems.
Corm. A *bulb*-like, underground, swollen *stem* or stem base, often surrounded by a papery *tunic*. A corm is replaced annually by a new corm that develops from a *terminal*, or *lateral*, *bud*.
Cormel. A small *corm* developing around a mature corm, usually outside the main corm *tunic*, as in gladiolus.
Cormlet. A small *corm* arising at the base (and usually within the old *tunic*) of a mature one. (See also *Offset*.)
Corolla. The interior *whorl* of the *perianth* of a flower, consisting of several free or fused *petals*.
Cotyledon. A seed leaf; the first leaf or leaves to emerge from the seed after *germination*, often markedly different from mature leaves. Flowering plants (Angiosperms) are classified into *monocotyledons* (one) and *dicotyledons* (two) depending on how many cotyledons are contained in the mature seed. In conifers (Gymnosperms) they are often produced in *whorls*.
Crest. A ridged outgrowth, often on *perianth segments*, as in orchids and some irises.
Cristate. An exaggerated *crest*, commonly seen in fern fronds and the *inflorescences* of *Celosia* or the stems of cacti.
Crocks. Broken pieces of clay pot, used to cover the drainage holes of pots in order to provide free drainage and air circulation to the root system and to prevent the growing medium from escaping from or blocking the drainage holes.
Crop rotation. A system in which vegetable crops are grown on different sections of a plot on a three- or four-year cycle to minimize the buildup of soilborne pests and diseases in one section.
Cross-fertilization. The *fertilization* of the *ovules* of a flower as a result of *cross-pollination*.
Cross-pollination. The transfer of pollen from the *anther* of a flower on one plant to the *stigma* of a flower on another plant; the term is often loosely applied to *cross-fertilization*. (Cf. *Self-pollination*.)
Crown. 1) The basal part at soil level of a *herbaceous* plant where roots and stems join and from where new shoots are produced. 2) The upper, branched part of a tree above the *bole*.
Crown bud. See *Bud*.
Culm. The usually hollow stem of a grass or bamboo.
Cultivar. A contraction of "cultivated variety" (abbreviated "cv"); a group (or one among such a group) of cultivated plants that has been selected either from the wild or from gardens and grown in cultivation, and whose characteristics are preserved by some means of controlled propagation. (Cf. *Variety*.)
Cupped. Usually of leaves or flowers, shaped like a cup.
Cutting. A portion of a plant (a leaf, shoot, root, or bud) that is cut off to be used for *propagation*. **Basal stem cutting**: one taken from the base of a (usually *herbaceous*) plant as it begins to grow in spring. **Greenwood cutting**: one taken from the soft tips of young growth after the spring growth flush has slowed down; slightly harder and woodier stems than are used for softwood cuttings. **Hardwood cutting**: one taken from mature wood of both deciduous and evergreen plants at the end of the growing season. **Heel cutting**: one taken with a portion of the bark or mature wood at the base. **Internodal cutting**: one in which the basal cut is made between two *nodes* or growth buds. **Leaf cutting**: one taken from a detached leaf or part of a leaf. **Leaf-bud cutting**: one consisting of a short section of stem and a single or double pair of buds or leaves. **Nodal cutting**: one trimmed at the base just below a growth bud or *node*. **Ripewood cutting**: one taken from ripened wood, usually of evergreens, during the growing season. **Root cutting**: one taken from part of a semimature or mature root. **Semiripe cutting**: one taken from half-ripened wood during the growing season. **Softwood cutting**: one taken from young, immature growth during the growing season. **Stem cutting**: one taken from any portion of a plant stem. **Stem tip cutting**: any cutting taken from the tip of a shoot; sometimes applied to softwood and greenwood cuttings.
Cyme. A usually flat-topped, *determinate inflorescence* in which the central or *terminal* flower opens first.
Damping down. Wetting greenhouse floors and staging with water to increase humidity, particularly in very hot weather.
Deadheading. The removal of *spent* flowers or *flowerheads*.
Deciduous. Of plants that shed leaves at the end of the growing season and renew them at the beginning of the next; **semideciduous** plants lose only some of their leaves at the end of the growing season.
Degradable pot. A pot made from degradable material such as compressed peat or paper.
Dehiscence. Term used of *fruits* (usually *capsules*) and *anthers* to describe the process of opening at maturity to release their contents.
Dehiscent. Of a *fruit*, usually a *capsule*, or an *anther* that splits along definite lines to release seeds or pollen.
Determinate. 1) Used of *inflorescences* where the central or terminal flower opens first so that the main axis cannot extend further. (Cf. *Cyme*.) 2) Used of bushy or dwarf tomatoes. (Cf. *Indeterminate*; *Semideterminate*.)
Dibber. A tool used for making holes in soil or potting mix into which seedlings or cuttings are inserted.
Dicotyledon. A flowering plant that usually has two *cotyledons* or seed leaves in the seed; it is also characterized by the (usually) net-veined leaves, the *petals* and *sepals* in multiples of two, four, or five, and by the presence of a *cambium*. (Cf. *Monocotyledon*.)
Dieback. The death of tips of shoots as a result of damage or disease.
Dioecious. Bearing male and female reproductive organs on separate plants. (Cf. *Monoecious*.)
Diploid. Having two basic sets of chromosomes. (Cf. *Triploid*.)
Disbudding. The removal of surplus *buds* to promote the production of high-quality flowers or fruits.
Distal end (of *cuttings*). The end that was originally farthest from the *crown* of the parent plant. (Cf. *Proximal end*.)
Division. A method of increasing plants by dividing them into pieces, each with a root system and one or more shoots (or dormant *buds*).
Dormancy. The state of temporary cessation of growth and slowing down of other activities in whole plants, usually during the winter; **seed dormancy**: non-*germination* of seed (when placed in conditions suitable for germination) due to physical, chemical, or other factors inherent in the seed; **double (seed) dormancy**: nongermination of seeds due to two dormancy factors in the seed.
Double (of a flower). See *Flower*.
Double cordon. See *Cordon*.
Double digging. A cultivation technique in which the soil is worked to a depth of two *spits*. Also known as "trench digging" or "bastard trenching."
Drainage. The passage of excess water through soil; the term is also applied to systems of drainage used to remove excess water.
Drill. A narrow, straight furrow in the soil in which seeds are sown or seedlings planted.
Drupes. See *Stone fruits*.
Emasculation. The removal of the *anthers* before the pollen is shed to prevent *self-pollination* and hence *self-fertilization*.
Epicormic shoots. Shoots that develop from latent or *adventitious* buds on or from the *trunk* of a tree or shrub. (See also *Water shoots*.)
Epigeal. Type of seed *germination* in which the seed is pushed above soil level by elongation of the *hypocotyl*. (Cf. *Hypogeal*.)
Epiphyte. A plant that grows on another plant without being parasitic, and obtains moisture and nutrients from the atmosphere without rooting into the soil.
Ericaceous. 1) Term describing plants of the *family* Ericaceae, usually *lime*-hating and requiring soils of *pH* 6.5 or less (see also *Calcifuge*). 2) Of soil mix, with an appropriate *pH* or acidity for growing ericaceous plants.
Espalier. A plant trained with the main stem vertical and (usually) three or more tiers of branches horizontally placed on either side in a single plane; often applied to fruit trees.
Evergreen. Of plants that retain their foliage for more than one growing season; **semievergreen** plants retain only a small proportion of their leaves for more than one season.
Explant. A tiny portion of a plant prepared and inserted in an aseptic growing medium for *micropropagation* purposes.
Eye. 1) A dormant or latent growth *bud*, such as the eye of a potato or dahlia tuber. 2) The center of a flower, especially if different in color from the petals.
F1 hybrids. First-generation plants obtained from crossing two selected pure-breeding parents to produce uniform, vigorous, and high-yielding offspring. Seed from F1 hybrids does not come *true*.
F2 hybrids. Plants that result from *self-* or *cross-fertilization* of *F1 hybrids*; they are less uniform than their parents.
Falls. The pendent or horizontally placed *tepals* or *petals* of irises and some related plants.
Family. A category in plant

classification, a grouping together of related *genera*, for example the family Rosaceae includes the genera *Rosa*, *Sorbus*, *Rubus*, *Prunus*, and *Pyracantha*; the family Iridaceae includes the genera *Iris*, *Crocus*, *Dierama*, and *Crocosmia*.
Fastigiate. With the branches (usually of trees and shrubs) growing vertically and almost parallel with the main stem.
Feathered. Of *maiden* trees that have several *lateral* branches ("feathers").
Fertile (of plants). Producing viable seed; shoots bearing flowers are also said to be fertile shoots as opposed to nonflowering (sterile) shoots.
Fertilization. The fusion of a *pollen* grain nucleus (male) with an *ovule* (female) to form a fertile seed.
Fibrous. 1) Of roots, fine and often branching and dense. 2) Of soil, containing fiber derived from dead roots.
Filament. The *stalk* of the *stamen* which bears the *anther*.
Fimbriate. Of part of a plant that has a fringed edge. Plant organs with a fringe of hairs are said to be ciliate.
Flat. A shallow tray or container for seeds and cuttings.
Flat grafting. See *Grafting*.
Floating row cover. Lightweight sheet, usually of woven polypropylene (fiber fleece), placed over a crop, which is lifted up by the plants as they grow. It provides some frost protection while allowing water and light penetration.
Floret. A (generally) small flower in a *flowerhead* consisting of many flowers.
Flower. The part of the plant containing the reproductive organs usually surrounded by *sepals* and *petals*. The basic flower forms are: **single**, with one row of usually four to six petals; **semidouble**, with two or three times the normal number of petals usually in two or three rows, **double**, with more than the normal number of petals in several rows with few or no *stamens* produced; **fully double**, flowers usually rounded in shape, with densely packed petals and with the stamens obscured or absent. (Cf. *Flowerhead*.)
Flowerhead. A mass of small *flowers* or *florets* that together appear to form a single flower, as in members of the family *Compositae*.
Flush. A distinct period of bloom.
Force. To induce plant growth, usually of flowers or fruit by control of the environment, normally by increasing the temperature.
Forma (f.). A variant within a *species* usually distinguished only by minor characteristics. *Clematis montana* f. *grandiflora* is a larger-flowered, more vigorous form of *C. montana*; also loosely used for any variant of a species.
Formative pruning. A method of pruning that is carried out on young trees and shrubs to develop the basic branch structure of the desired form or shape.
Foundation planting. The basic, usually permanent, plants complementing a structure and sometimes hiding its base.
Frame. See *Cold frame*.
Framework. The permanent branch structure of a tree or shrub; the main branches that determine its ultimate shape. **Framework plants**: the plants in a garden that form the basis or structure of the design.
Frame-working (of fruit trees). Pruning back all side growths to the main framework and grafting *scions* of a different *cultivar* onto each main framework branch.
French layering. See *Layering*.
Friable (of soil). Of a good, crumbly texture; capable of forming a *tilth* that can be worked easily.
Frond. 1) The *leaf*-like organ of a fern. Some ferns produce both *sterile* and *fertile* fronds, the latter bearing *spores*. 2) Loosely applied to large, usually *compound* leaves such as those of palms.
Frost hardy. See *Hardy*.
Frost pocket. A site, often a hollow, where cold air gathers, subject to severe and often prolonged frosts.
Frost tender. See *Tender*.
Fruit. The fertilized, ripe *ovary* of a plant containing one to many seeds, for example, berries, *hips*, *capsules*, and nuts; the term is also used of edible fruits.
Fruit bud. See *Bud*.
Fruit set. The successful development of fruits after *pollination* and *fertilization*.
Fully double. See *Flower*.
Fully reflexed. See *Reflexed*.
Fungicide. A chemical that kills fungi, especially those responsible for various plant diseases.
Genus (pl. **genera**). A category in plant classification ranked between *family* and *species*. A group of related species linked by a range of common characters; for example, all species of horse chestnut and buckeye are grouped under the genus *Aesculus*. (See also *Cultivar*, *Family*, *Forma*, *Hybrid*, *Species*, *Subspecies*, and *Variety*.)
Germination. The physical and chemical changes that take place as a seed starts to grow and develop into a plant.
Girdling. 1) The removal of bark all around a stem or branch caused by animal or physical damage or by a constricting tie that prevents the flow of water and *nutrients* to the upper part of the plant, eventually causing the death of all the tissue above the girdled trunk or branch. 2) See *Bark-ringing*.
Glaucous. With a blue-green, blue-gray, gray, or white bloom.
Glume. A chafflike, dry *bract* in the *inflorescences* of grasses and sedges.
Graft. To join artificially one or more plant parts to another.
Graft union. The point at which *scion* and *rootstock* are joined.
Grafting. A method of *propagation* by which an artificial union is made between the *scion* of one plant and the *rootstock* of another so that they eventually function as one plant. Methods include apical-wedge grafting; basal-whip (or splice) grafting; bud-grafting (including chip-budding and T-budding); flat grafting; saddle grafting; side grafting (see CACTI AND OTHER SUCCULENTS, "Side grafting," p.271); side-veneer grafting; side-wedge grafting; and whip-and-tongue grafting. (For details see PRINCIPLES OF PROPAGATION, "Grafting and budding,"pp.543–4.)
Grafting tape. Tape used to protect a *graft union* during healing.
Green manure. A quick-maturing, leafy crop such as winter rye that is grown specifically to be dug back into, and thereby enrich, the soil.
Greenwood cutting. See *Cutting*.
Ground color. Main (background) color of petals.
Ground cover. Usually low-growing plants that quickly cover the soil surface and suppress weeds.
Growth bud. See *Bud*.
Half hardy. Used of a plant that will survive some cold but will not overwinter outdoors. The term generally implies an ability to withstand lower temperatures than *tender*.
Half standard. A tree or shrub that has a clear stem of 3–5ft (1–1.5m) between ground level and the lowest branches.
Hardening off. Gradually acclimatizing plants that have been raised under cover to cooler outdoor conditions.
Hardpan. See *Pan*.
Hardwood cutting. See *Cutting*.
Hardy. Able to withstand year-round climatic conditions, including cold, without protection.
Haulm. The top-growth of plants such as potatoes and legumes.
Head. 1) The part of a tree above a clear *trunk*. 2) A dense *inflorescence*.
Head back. To prune back the main branches of trees or shrubs by half or more.
Heading. See *Heart up*.
Heart up. The stage at which vegetables such as lettuces or cabbages begin to produce tight "hearts" or "heads" of inner leaves
Heavy (of soil). Having a high proportion of clay.
Heel. A small piece or strip of bark or wood that is retained at the base of a *cutting* when it is pulled away from a main stem.
Heel cutting. See *Cutting*.
Heeling in. Temporary planting until a plant can be placed in its permanent position.
Herb. 1) A plant grown for its medicinal or flavoring properties or for its scented foliage. 2) Botanically, a *herbaceous* plant.
Herbaceous. A non-*woody* plant in which the upper parts die down to a rootstock at the end of the growing season. The term is chiefly applied to *perennials*, although botanically it also applies to *annuals* and *biennials*.
Herbicide. A chemical used to control or kill weeds.
Hilling up. Drawing up soil around the base of a plant to help prevent *wind-rock*, to *blanch* the *stems*, or to encourage stem rooting.
Hip. The seed-bearing structure of a rose.
Hull. The outer casing of a nut.
Humus. The chemically complex, organic residue of decayed vegetable matter in soil. Also often used to describe partly decayed matter such as *leaf mold* or *compost*.
Hybrid. The offspring of genetically different parents usually of distinct taxa (see *Taxon*). Hybrids between *species* of the same *genus* are known as interspecific hybrids. Those between different but usually closely related *genera* are known as intergeneric hybrids. (See also *F1 hybrids*; *F2 hybrids*.)
Hybrid vigor. An improved growth and yield shown by some hybrids.
Hybridization. The process by which *hybrids* are formed.
Hydroculture. The cultivation of plants in nutrient-rich water, sometimes with sterile aggregates. (See also *Hydroponics*.)
Hydroponics. Growing plants in dilute solutions of nutrients. Applied loosely to any form of soilless culture.
Hypocotyl. The portion of a *seedling* just below the *cotyledons*.
Hypogeal. Type of seed *germination* in which the *cotyledons* remain below the soil surface while the young shoot (plumule) emerges above soil level.
Incurved. Applied to petals of flowers and *florets* that curve inward to form a compact, rounded shape. **Incurving** flowerheads are less compact with more loosely arranged but still incurved florets.
Indehiscent. Of a *fruit* that does not split open to release its seeds. (Cf. *Dehiscent*.)
Indeterminate. 1) Used of an *inflorescence* not terminated by a single flower, in which the primary axis (stem) continues to develop as the lower flowers open (e.g. a *raceme* as in delphiniums). 2) Used of tall or staked tomatoes, which, in a suitable climate, can grow to an indefinite length. (Cf. *Determinate*; *Semideterminate*.)
Inflorescence. A group of flowers borne on a single axis (stem). *Racemes*, *panicles*, and *cymes* are all types of inflorescence.
Informal. Applied to some cultivars of chrysanthemums, dahlias, and other flowers with irregular flower formation.
Inorganic. Of a chemical compound, one that does not contain carbon. Inorganic fertilizers are refined from naturally occurring chemicals or produced artificially. (Cf. *Organic*.)
Insecticide. A *pesticide* used to control or kill insects. (Cf. *Acaricide*; *Nematicide*.)
Insert. To place cuttings in a growing medium.
Intercropping. The growing of quick-maturing vegetable crops between slower-growing crops to make maximum use of the available space.
Intergeneric hybrid. See *Hybrid*.
Intermediate. 1) A term applied to chrysanthemums with flowerheads intermediate in shape between *reflexed* and *incurved*. 2) A hybrid with characters intermediate between its two parents.
Internodal cutting. See *Cutting*.
Internode. The portion of stem between two *nodes*.
Interplanting. 1) The planting of

fast-maturing plants between slower-growing plants to provide a display while they mature. 2) The planting of two or more types of plants together to provide a display of different colors or textures (e.g. tulips among wallflowers). Often used in relation to bedding.
Interspecific hybrid. See *Hybrid.*
Irrigation. 1) General term for watering. 2) The use of a system of basins, channels, or sprinkler systems to provide a controlled supply of water to plants.
Joint. See *Node.*
Knot garden. Beds laid out in a formal, often complex, pattern, formed from dwarf hedges or clipped herbs.
Laced. A term applied to some flowers (e.g. daylilies and irises) that have finely cut petal edges.
Lamina. The blade of a leaf, usually flattened, not including the petiole (leaf stalk).
Lateral. A side growth that arises from a shoot or root.
Layer planting. 1) A form of *interplanting* in which groups of plants planted closely together flower in succession. 2) A planting design such that the groups of plants form layers above each other.
Layering. A method of *propagation* by which a *shoot* is induced to *root* while still attached to the parent plant. The basic form is self-layering, which occurs naturally in some plants. Methods include: air layering (also known as Chinese layering or marcottage), French layering, mound layering (also known as stooling), serpentine layering, simple layering, tip layering, and trench layering. (For details, see PRINCIPLES OF PROPAGATION, "Layering," p.539.)
Leaching. The loss from the top soil of soluble *nutrients* by downward drainage.
Leader. 1) The main, usually central, stem of a plant. 2) The *terminal* shoot of a main branch.
Leaf. A plant organ, variable in shape and color but often flattened and green, borne on the stem, that performs the functions of *photosynthesis*, *respiration*, and *transpiration*.
Leaf cutting. See *Cutting.*
Leaf mold. Fibrous, flaky material derived from decomposed leaves, used as an ingredient in potting media and as a soil improver.
Leaf-bud cutting. See *Cutting.*
Leaflet. One of the subdivisions of a *compound* leaf.
Legume. A one-chambered, *dehiscent fruit* splitting at maturity into two, belonging to the *family* Leguminosae.
Light. Of soil, with a high proportion of sand and little clay.
Lime. Loosely, a number of compounds of calcium; the amount of lime in soil determines whether it is *alkaline*, *acid*, or *neutral*.
Line out. To plant out young plants or insert cuttings in lines in a nursery bed or frame.
Lithophyte. A plant naturally growing on rocks (or in very stony soil) and usually obtaining most of its nutrients and water from the atmosphere.
Loam. A term used for soil of medium texture, often easily worked, that contains more or less equal parts of sand, silt, and clay, and is usually rich in *humus*. If the proportion of one ingredient is high, the term may be qualified as silt-loam, clay-loam, or sandy loam.
Maiden. A *grafted* tree in its first year. (See also *Whip.*)
Maincrop (of vegetables). Those cultivars that produce crops throughout the main growing season, doing so over a longer period than either early or late cultivars.
Marcottage. An alternative name for air layering; see *Layering.*
Marginal water plant. A plant that grows partially submerged in shallow water or in constantly moist soil at the edge of a pond or stream.
Medium. 1) A *soil mix*, potting mixture, or other material in which plants may be propagated or grown. 2) Applied to those soils that are intermediate in character between *heavy* and *light*. (See also *Loam.*)
Mericlone. Genetically identical offspring produced by *meristem* culture.
Meristem. Plant tissue that is able to divide to produce new cells. Shoot or root tips contain meristematic tissue and may be used for *micropropagation.*
Micronutrients. Chemical elements essential to plants but needed only in very small quantities, also known as trace elements. (See also *Nutrients.*)
Micropropagation. Propagation of plants by *tissue culture.*
Midrib. The primary, usually central vein of a leaf or leaflet.
Monocarpic. Flowering and fruiting only once before dying; such plants may take several years to reach flowering size.
Monocotyledon. A flowering plant that has only one *cotyledon* or seed leaf in the seed; it is also characterized by narrow, parallel-veined *leaves*, and parts of the flower in threes or multiples of three.
Monoecious. Bearing separate male and female reproductive organs on the same plant. (Cf. *Dioecious.*)
Monopodial. Growing indefinitely from an apical or *terminal bud* on a stem. (Cf. *Sympodial.*)
Moss peat. See *Peat.*
Mound layering. See *Layering.*
Mulch. A material applied in a layer to the soil surface to suppress weeds, conserve moisture, and maintain a preferably cool, uniform root temperature. In addition to organic materials (such as manure, bark, and compost), plastic, foil, and gravel may also be used. (See also *Floating row cover.*)
Multiple cordon. See *Cordon.*
Mutation. An induced or spontaneous genetic change, often resulting in shoots with variegated foliage or flowers of a different color from the parent plant. A mutation is also known as a sport.
Mycorrhizae. Soil fungi that live in beneficial association with plant roots.
Naturalize. To establish and grow as if in the wild.
Neck. See *Collar.*
Nectar. Sugary liquid secreted from a *nectary*; often attractive to pollinating insects.
Nectary. Glandular tissue usually found in the flower, but sometimes on the leaves or stems, that secretes *nectar.*
Nematicide. A *pesticide* used to control nematodes. (Cf. *Acaricide*; *Insecticide.*)
Neutral (of soil). With a *pH* value of 7, i.e. neither *acid* nor *alkaline.*
Nodal cutting. See *Cutting.*
Node. The point on a stem from which one or more leaves, shoots, branches, or flowers arise. Also called a joint.
Nonremontant. Flowering or fruiting only once in a single *flush*. (Cf. *Remontant.*)
Nursery bed. An area used for germinating seeds or growing on young plants before planting them out in their permanent positions.
Nut. A one-seeded, *indehiscent* fruit with a tough or woody coat, for example an acorn. Less specifically, all fruits and seeds with woody or leathery coats.
Nutrients. Minerals (mineral ions) used to develop proteins and other compounds required for plant growth.
Offset. A young plant that arises by natural, *vegetative* reproduction, usually at the base of the parent plant; in bulbs, offsets are initially formed within the bulb *tunic* but later separate out. Also known as offshoots.
Offshoot. See *Offset.*
Open-pollination. Natural pollination. (See also *Pollination.*)
Opposite. Term describing two leaves, or other plant organs, at the same level on opposite sides of a stem or other axis. (Cf. *Alternate.*)
Organic. 1) Chemically, referring to compounds containing carbon derived from plant or animal organisms. 2) Loosely, applied to mulches, compost, or similar materials derived from plant matter. 3) Also applied to crop production and gardening without the use of synthetic or nonorganic materials.
Ovary. The basal part of the pistil of a flower, containing one or more *ovules*; it may develop into a *fruit* after *fertilization.* (See also *Carpel.*)
Ovule. The part of the *ovary* that develops into the *seed* after *pollination* and *fertilization.*
Oxygenator. Submerged aquatic plant that releases oxygen into the water.
Packs. Compartmented trays in which individual seeds or seedlings are grown.
Pan. 1) A shallow, earthenware or plastic pot that is much wider than it is deep. 2) A layer of soil that is impermeable to water and oxygen and impedes root growth and drainage. Some pans (hardpans) occur naturally on clay or iron-rich soils. Soils capped (see *Capping*) by heavy rain or excess watering, or by continuous use of cultivation machinery, are also known as pans or hardpans.
Panicle. An *indeterminate*, branched *inflorescence* often consisting of several racemose branches (see *Raceme*). The term is also loosely used to describe any type of branching inflorescence.
Parterre. A level area containing ornamental beds, often with low-growing plants and enclosed in dwarf hedges. (Cf. *Knot garden.*)
Parthenocarpic. The production of fruit without *fertilization* having taken place.
Pathogens. Microorganisms that cause disease.
Peasticks. Short, twiggy sticks used to support peas and, more commonly, bushy perennial plants.
Peat. Partially decayed, humus-rich plant matter formed on the surface of waterlogged soils. **Moss** or **sphagnum peat** is largely derived from partially decayed *sphagnum* moss and is used in soil mixes. **Sedge peat** is derived from sedges, mosses, and heathers; it is coarser than moss peat and less suitable for soil mixes.
Peat bed. Beds usually constructed from *peat* blocks and filled with very peaty soil; used to grow acid-loving plants, particularly in areas with soils of high *pH*.
Peat blocks. Blocks of peat cut from natural peat deposits.
Peduncle. The *stalk* of a *flower.*
Peltate (of leaves). A leaf with the stalk usually attached centrally beneath the leaf blade; sometimes the stalk may be off-center within the leaf margin.
Perennial. Strictly, any plant living for at least three seasons; commonly applied to *herbaceous* and *woody* plants (i.e. trees and shrubs).
Perianth. The collective term for the *calyx* and the *corolla*, particularly when they are very similar in form, as in many bulb flowers.
Perianth segment. One portion of a *perianth*, usually resembling a *petal* and sometimes known as a *tepal.*
Perlite. Small granules of expanded volcanic minerals added to growing media to improve aeration.
Perpetual. Of plants that bloom more or less continuously throughout the growing season or over long periods of time.
Pesticide. A chemical substance, usually manufactured, that is used to kill pests including insects (insecticide), mites (acaricide), and nematodes (nematicide).
Petal. A modified leaf, often brightly colored; one part of the *corolla* usually of a *dicotyledonous* flower. (Cf. *Tepal.*)
Petiole. The *stalk* of a *leaf.*
pH. A measure of alkalinity or acidity, used horticulturally to refer to soils. The scale measures from 1 to 14; *pH* 7 is neutral, above 7 is alkaline, and below 7 is acid. (See also *Acid*, *Alkaline*, and *Neutral.*)
Photosynthesis. The production of organic compounds required for growth in plants by a complex process involving *chlorophyll*, light energy, carbon dioxide, and water.
Picotee. A term describing *petals* with a narrow margin of a contrasting color.
Pinching out. The removal of the growing tip of a plant (by finger and thumb) to induce the production of *side shoots* or the formation of flower buds. Also known as "stopping."

Pistil. See *Carpel*.
Pith (of stems). The soft plant tissue in the central part of a stem.
Pleaching. A technique whereby branches from a row of trees are woven together and trained to form a wall or canopy of foliage.
Plumule. See *Hypogeal*.
Plunge. To sink a pot up to its rim in a bed of ashes, peat, sand, or soil to protect the roots of the plant or plants in the pot from extremes of temperature.
Pod. An ill-defined term generally applied to any dry, *dehiscent fruit*; it is particularly used for peas and beans.
Pollarding. The regular pruning back of the main branches of a tree to the main stem or trunk, or to a short branch framework, usually to a height of about 6ft (2m). (Cf. *Coppicing*.)
Pollen. The male cells of a plant, formed in the *anther*.
Pollination. The transfer of *pollen* from *anthers* to *stigmas*. (See also *Cross-pollination, Open-pollination,* and *Self-pollination.*)
Pollinator. 1) The agent or means by which *pollination* is carried out (e.g. insects, wind). 2) Used in fruit growing to describe a *cultivar* required to ensure fruit set on another self- or partially *self-sterile* cultivar.
Polyembryonic. Containing more than one embryo in an *ovule* or *seed*.
Pome. A firm, fleshy *fruit* formed by the fusion of the *ovary* and the hypanthium (the fused base of *calyx* and *corolla*); for example an apple or pear.
Pompon. Usually small, almost globular *flowerheads* made up of numerous *florets*.
Potting mix. A potting medium consisting of a mixture of soil, sand, *peat, leaf mold*, or other ingredients Also called soil mix.
Potting on. Transferring a plant from one pot to a larger one.
Potting up. Transferring seedlings or rooted cuttings into individual pots of soil mix.
Pricking out. The transferring of young seedlings from where they have germinated in beds or pots to positions where they have room to grow on.
Propagation. The increase of plants by *seed* (usually sexual) or *vegetative* (asexual) means.
Propagator. A structure that provides a humid atmosphere for raising seedlings, rooting cuttings, or other plants being propagated.
Proximal end (of *cuttings*). The end that was originally nearest to the *crown* of the parent plant. (Cf. *Distal end*.)
Pseudobulb. The thickened, *bulb*-like *stem* of a *sympodial* orchid arising from a (sometimes very short) *rhizome*.
Quartered rosette. A rosetted flower with the petals arranged in four sections of about the same size.
Raceme. An *indeterminate*, unbranched *inflorescence* with usually many stalked flowers borne on an elongated axis (stem).
Radicle. The embryonic root of a seedling.
Rain shadow. An area of ground next to a wall or fence that is sheltered from prevailing winds and therefore receives less rain than open ground.
Rambler. A trailing climbing rose.
Ray flower (or floret). Small flower with a flattened, elongated *corolla*, as borne in the outermost ring of a *Compositae* flowerhead.
Recurved. Applied to petals of flowers and florets that curve backward.
Reflexed. Applied to petals of flowers and florets that bend sharply backward at an angle of more than 90°. They are sometimes called fully reflexed. Also loosely applied to any flower in which the petals or *perianth segments* are *recurved*.
Remontant. Of a plant that flowers more than once during the growing season (often applied to roses and strawberries). (Cf. *Nonremontant*.)
Renewal pruning. A system in which the *laterals* are constantly cut back to be replaced by young laterals stimulated by pruning.
Respiration. The release of energy from complex *organic* molecules as a result of chemical changes.
Revert. To return to an original state, for example when a variegated plant produces a plain green leaf.
Rhizome. A specialized, usually horizontally creeping, swollen or slender, underground *stem* that acts as a storage organ and produces aerial shoots at its apex and along its length.
Rind. The outer bark of a shrub or tree outside the *cambium* layer.
Ripewood cutting. See *Cutting*.
Root. The part of a plant, normally underground, that anchors it and through which water and *nutrients* are absorbed. (See also *Aerial root*.)
Root ball. The roots and accompanying soil or *soil mix* visible when a plant is removed from a container or lifted from the open ground.
Root crops. Vegetables such as carrots, parsnips, and radishes grown for their edible roots.
Root cutting. See *Cutting*.
Root run. The area of soil into which a plant's roots may extend.
Rooting. The production of roots, usually from cuttings.
Rooting hormone. A chemical compound synthesized in powder or liquid form and used at low concentrations to encourage root production.
Rootstock. A plant used to provide the root system for a *grafted* plant.
Rose (of a watering can). A perforated nozzle that diffuses and regulates the flow of water.
Rosette. 1) A cluster of leaves radiating from approximately the same point, often borne at ground level at the base of a very short stem. 2) A more or less circular arrangement of petals.
Rotation. See *Crop rotation*.
Rounded. Regularly curved, as in a circle.
Row cover. See *Floating row cover*.
Runner. A horizontally spreading, usually slender, stem that runs above ground and roots at the *nodes* to form new plants. Often confused with *stolon*.
Saddle grafting. See *Grafting*.
Sap. The juice of a plant contained in the cells and vascular tissue.
Sapling. A young tree or seedling before the wood hardens.
Sash. The movable, transparent cover of a *cold frame*.
Scandent. Ascending or loosely climbing. (See also *Climber*.)
Scarification. 1) Abrasion or chemical treatment of a seed coat to speed up water intake and induce *germination*. 2) Removing moss and thatch from a lawn using a scarifier or rake.
Scion. A *shoot* or *bud* cut from one plant to *graft* onto a *rootstock* (stock) of another.
Scrambling climber. See *Climber*.
Scree. A slope consisting of rock fragments formed by the weathering of rock faces: simulated in gardens as scree beds, in which high-altitude *alpines* that need excellent *drainage* may be grown.
Sedge peat. See *Peat*.
Seed. The ripened, fertilized *ovule* containing a dormant embryo capable of developing into an adult plant.
Seed dormancy. See *Dormancy*.
Seed leaf. See *Cotyledon*.
Seedhead. A dried cluster of ripe seeds.
Seedling. A young plant that has developed from a seed.
Selection. A plant selected for particular characteristics and usually propagated to retain the same characteristics.
Self-clinging climber. See *Climber*.
Self-fertile. Of a plant that produces viable *seed* when fertilized with its own *pollen*. (See also *Fertilization, Pollination, Self-pollination*, and *Self-sterile*.)
Self-incompatible. See *Self-sterile*.
Self-layering. See *Layering*.
Self-pollination. The transfer of *pollen* from the *anthers* to the *stigma* of the same *flower*, or alternatively to another flower on the same plant. (Cf. *Cross-pollination*.)
Self-seed. To shed fertile seeds that produce *seedlings* around the parent plant.
Self-sterile. A plant unable to produce viable *seed* after self-fertilization, and requiring a different *pollinator* in order for fertilization to occur. Also known as "self-incompatible" – incapable of self-fertilization.
Semideciduous. See *Deciduous*.
Semideterminate. Used of tall or staked tomatoes that will only grow to 3–4ft (1–1.2m) long. (Cf. *Determinate*; *Indeterminate*.)
Semidouble. See *Flower*.
Semievergreen. See *Evergreen*.
Semiripe cutting. See *Cutting*.
Sepal. The outer *whorl* of the *perianth* of a flower, usually small and green, but sometimes colored and *petal*-like.
Serpentine layering. See *Layering*.
Set. 1) A small onion, shallot bulb, or potato *tuber*, selected for planting. 2) A term describing flowers that have been successfully fertilized and have produced small *fruits*.
Sexual reproduction. A form of reproduction involving *fertilization*, giving rise to *seed* or *spores*.
Sheet mulch. A *mulch* using an artificially produced material (e.g. plastic).
Shoot. A branch, stem, or twig.
Shrub. A woody-stemmed plant, usually branched from or near the base, lacking a single *trunk*.
Side grafting. See *Grafting*.
Side shoot. A stem that arises from the side of a main *shoot*.
Side-veneer grafting. See *Grafting*.
Side-wedge grafting. See *Grafting*.
Simple (mainly of leaves). Undivided. (Cf. *Compound*.)
Simple layering. See *Layering*.
Single. See *Flower*.
Single cordon. See *Cordon*.
Single digging. A method of digging in which only the topsoil is turned over to a depth of one *spit*.
Snag. A short stub or frayed end left after incorrect pruning.
Softwood cutting. See *Cutting*.
Soil mark. The usually noticeable point on a plant's stem that shows the original soil level before the plant was lifted.
Soil mix. A potting medium consisting of a mixture of soil, sand, *peat, leaf mold*, or other ingredients. Also called potting mix.
Soilless mix. A potting medium that contains *peat*, usually *perlite* or *vermiculite*, and, sometimes, fertilizer, but no soil. (Cf. *Potting mix*; *Soil mix*.)
Species. A category in plant classification, the lowest principal rank below *genus* containing closely related, similar individuals.
Specimen plant. A striking plant, usually a tree or shrub in prime condition, grown where it can be seen clearly.
Spent (of flowers). Dying or dead.
Sphagnum mosses. Mosses common to bogs; their moisture-retentive nature is valued when used as a component of growing media, for example in orchid cultivation.
Spike. A racemose (see *Raceme*) and hence *indeterminate inflorescence* that bears unstalked flowers along a common axis (stem).
Spikelet. A small spike, forming part of a compound *inflorescence*; often applied to grasses that have a flowerhead consisting of several flowers with basal *bracts*.
Spit. The depth of a spade's blade, usually 10–12in (25–30cm).
Splice grafting. An alternative name for basal-whip grafting (see *Grafting*).
Spoon-type. Applied to the *florets* of chrysanthemums (and some other flowers) in which the quill-like florets expand to form a spoon shape at the tips.
Sporangium. A body that produces *spores* on a fern.
Spore. The minute reproductive structure of flowerless plants, such as ferns, fungi, and mosses.
Sport. See *Mutation*.
Spray. A group of *flowers* or *flowerheads* on a single, branching stem, such as occurs on many chrysanthemums and roses.
Spur. 1) A hollow projection from a petal, often producing *nectar*. 2) A

short branch or branchlet bearing flower buds, as on fruit trees.
Stalk. A general term describing the stem of a leaf or flower (e.g. petiole, peduncle).
Stamen. The male reproductive organ in a plant, consisting of the pollen-producing *anther* and usually its supporting *filament* or *stalk*.
Standard. 1) A tree with at least 6ft (2m) of stem below the first branches (see also *Half standard*). 2) A shrub trained so that it has a clear length of stem below the branches (3–4ft/1–1.2m for roses). 3) One of the three inner and often erect *perianth segments* of the iris flower.
Station sow. To sow seed individually or in small groups at fixed intervals along a row or *drill*.
Stem. The main axis of a plant, usually above ground and supporting leaves, flowers, and fruits.
Stem cutting. See *Cutting*.
Stem tip cutting. See *Cutting*.
Sterile. 1) Not producing flowers or viable seed. (Cf. *Fertile*.) 2) Of flowers without functional *anthers* and pistils (see *Carpel*).
Stigma. The apical portion of a *carpel*, usually borne at the tip of a *style*, which receives *pollen* prior to *fertilization*.
Stock. See *Rootstock*.
Stock plant. A plant used to obtain propagating material, whether seed or vegetative material.
Stolon. A horizontally spreading or arching stem, usually above ground, which roots at its tip to produce a new plant. Often confused with *runner*.
Stone fruits. Fruits, also known as "drupes," with one or more seeds ("stones") surrounded by fleshy, usually edible tissue. They are common in the genus *Prunus* (e.g. apricots, plums, and cherries) and some other plants, such as mangos, that produce *indehiscent*, woody fruits.
Stool. A number of shoots arising, more or less uniformly, from the base of an individual plant, for example some shrubs cut back regularly to produce propagating material and also chrysanthemums.
Stooling. 1) An alternative term for *mound layering*. See *Layering*. 2) The routine pruning back of woody plants by *coppicing*.
Stopping. See *Pinching out*.
Strain. A loose, undefined term sometimes applied to races of seed-raised plants; not a term accepted under the International Code for the Nomenclature of Cultivated Plants because of its imprecise definition.
Stratification. Storage of seed in warm or cold conditions to overcome *dormancy* and aid *germination*.
Stylar column. A column of joined *styles*.
Style. The usually elongated part of a *carpel* between the *ovary* and *stigma*, not always present.
Subfamily. A category in plant classification, a division within the *family*.
Sublateral. A side shoot originating from a *lateral* shoot or branch.
Subshrub. 1) A low-growing plant that is entirely *woody*. 2) A plant that is woody at the base but has soft, usually *herbaceous* growth above.
Subsoil. The layers of soil beneath the *topsoil*; these are usually less fertile and of poorer texture and structure than the topsoil.
Subspecies. A subdivision of a *species*, higher in rank than a *variety* or *forma*.
Succulent (of plants). A plant with thick, fleshy leaves and/or stems adapted to store water. All cacti are succulents.
Sucker. 1) A shoot that arises below ground from a plant's roots or underground stem. 2) On *grafted* plants, a sucker is any shoot that arises below the *graft union*. 3) A side shoot of a tomato plant.
Sympodial. Definite growth of a *shoot* terminating in an *inflorescence* or dying; growth is continued by *lateral* buds. (Cf. *Monopodial*.)
Systemic. Term describing a *pesticide* or *fungicide* that is absorbed and distributed through a plant when applied to the soil or foliage.
Taproot. The primary, downward-growing *root* of a plant (especially a tree); also applied loosely to any strong, downward-growing root.
Taxon (pl. **taxa**). A group of living organisms at any rank; applied to groups of plants or entities that share distinct, defined characters.
T-budding. See *Grafting*.
Tender. Of a plant that is vulnerable to frost damage.
Tendril. A modified leaf, branch, or stem, usually filiform (long and slender) and capable of attaching itself to a support. (See also *Climber*.)
Tepal. A single segment of a perianth that cannot be distinguished either as a sepal or petal, as in *Crocus* or *Lilium*. (See also *Perianth segment*.)
Terminal. At the tip of a stem or branch; usually refers to a bud or flower.
Terminal bud. See *Bud*.
Terrarium. An enclosed container made of glass or plastic in which plants are grown.
Terrestrial. Growing in the soil; a land plant. (Cf. *Aquatic*; *Epiphyte*.)
Thatch. A layer of dead *organic* matter intermingled with living stems that accumulates on the soil surface in lawns.
Thin (of soil). Used loosely of poor soil, prone to *capping* and drought.
Thinning. The removal of seedlings, shoots, flowers, or fruit buds to improve the growth and quality of the remainder.
Tilth. A fine, crumbly, surface layer of soil produced by cultivation.
Tip layering. See *Layering*.
Tip prune. To cut back the growing tip of a shoot to encourage side shoots or to remove damaged growth.
Tissue culture (of plants). The propagation of plants under sterile conditions from very small pieces of plant tissue.
Top-dressing. 1) An application of soluble fertilizers, fresh soil, or *compost* to the soil surface around a plant or to lawns to replenish nutrients. 2) A decorative dressing applied to the soil surface around a plant.
Topiary. The art of clipping and training trees and shrubs into usually intricate, geometric or free shapes.
Topsoil. The uppermost, normally fertile, layer of soil.
Trace element. See *Micronutrients*.
Trailing climber. See *Climber*.
Translocated (of dissolved nutrients or weedkillers). Moving within the vascular system (conducting tissues) of a plant.
Transpiration. The loss of water by evaporation from leaves and stems.
Transplanting. Moving a plant from one position to another.
Tree. A *woody*, perennial plant usually with a well-defined *trunk* or stem with a *head* or *crown* of branches above.
Trench digging. See *Double digging*.
Trench layering. See *Layering*.
Triploid. Having three basic sets of chromosomes. Such plants are normally *sterile*. (Cf. *Diploid*.)
True (True-breeding). Of plants that when self-pollinated (see *Self-pollination*) give rise to offspring similar to their parents.
Trunk. The thickened, woody, main stem of a tree.
Tuber. A swollen, usually underground organ derived from a stem or root, used for food storage.
Tufa. Porous limestone rock that absorbs and retains moisture; used for cultivating alpine plants difficult to grow in garden soil.
Tunic. The fibrous membranes or papery outer skin of *bulbs* or *corms*.
Tunicate. Enclosed in a *tunic*.
Turion. 1) A detached, overwintering, usually fleshy *bud* produced by certain water plants. 2) A term sometimes applied to an *adventitious* shoot or *sucker*.
Twining climber. See *Climber*.
U cordon. A double *cordon*.
Underplanting. Low-growing plants planted beneath larger plants.
Union. See *Graft union*.
Upright. Term describing the habit of a plant with vertical or semivertical main branches. (Cf. *Fastigiate*.)
Urn-shaped (of flowers). Globose to cylindrical in shape with a somewhat constricted mouth; U-shaped.
Variable. Varying in character from the type; particularly of seed-raised plants that vary in character from the parent.
Variegated. Term describing a plant marked with various colors in an irregular pattern; particularly used for leaves patterned with white and yellow markings but not confined to these colors.
Variety. 1) Botanically, a naturally occurring variant (varietas, or var.) of a wild *species*, between the rank of *subspecies* and *forma*. 2) Also commonly but imprecisely used to describe any variant of a plant. (Cf. *Cultivar*.)
Vegetative growth. Nonflowering, usually leafy growth.
Vegetative propagation. The increase of plants by asexual methods normally resulting in genetically identical individuals.
Vermiculite. A lightweight, micalike mineral allowing good water retention and aeration when used in cuttings soil mix and other potting media.
Water shoots. Applied usually to *epicormic* shoots that frequently arise close to pruning wounds on tree trunks or branches.
Whip. A young seedling or grafted tree without *lateral* branches.
Whip-and-tongue grafting. See *Grafting*.
Whorl. The arrangement of three or more organs arising from the same point.
Widger. A spatula-shaped tool used for transplanting or *pricking out* seedlings.
Windbreak. Any structure but often a hedge, fence, or wall that shelters plants and filters strong winds.
Wind-rock. The destabilizing of a plant's roots by strong wind.
Winter wet. Excessive amounts of water that accumulate in the soil during the winter months.
Woody. Ligneous; a term describing stems or trunks that are hard and thickened rather than soft and pliable. (Cf. *Herbaceous*.)
Wound. A cut or broken area in a plant.
Wound paint. A specialized paint that is applied to a cut surface of a plant after pruning.

INDEX

Page numbers given in italics refer to pages on which there are relevant illustrations. In plant entries topics of general information relating to the main entries appear first; subentries for species and cultivars always follow the general subentries.

Aaron's beard, see *Hypericum calycinum*
Abelia
softwood cuttings 81
suggestions for use 66
floribunda, conditions preferred 66
x *grandiflora*, pruning 74
Abeliophyllum distichum, scent 66
Abelmoschus esculentus, see Okra
Abies
pests 560
side-veneer grafting 56
soil type preferred 41
training 49
balsamea, diseases 560
grandis, soil type preferred 42
magnifica, suggestions for use 37
procera, suggestions for use 37
Abromeitiella 433
Abutilon
conditions preferred 66
conditions required 431
in garden room *426*
pinching out 450
pruning 74, 450
softwood cuttings 81, 453
suggestions for use 66
Acacia
seed scarification 54
baileyana, seasonal interest 66
dealbata
pruning 49
scent 34
seasonal interest 37
soil type preferred 42
suggestions for use 37, 66
Acalymma vittata 571
Acaena
tip cuttings 176
caesiiglauca, soil type preferred 193
microphylla, soil type preferred 193
Acalypha, softwood cuttings 453
Acantholimon glumaceum
in dry-stone wall *189*
suggestions for use 189, 191
Acanthus
root cuttings 165, *165*
for seedheads 141
hungaricus, architectural form 141
mollis
architectural form 141
conditions tolerated 141
in mixed island bed *136*
root cuttings *541*
spinosus 23
for drying 141
Acanthus spinosus (*cont.*)
soil type preferred 146
soil type tolerated 147
as specimen plant 140
Acaricide, definition 585
Acephate 552, 553, 554, 562
commercial name 574
Acer
bonsai 434
conditions tolerated 27
for coppicing and pollarding 50
diseases 558, 560, 567, 571, 572
foliage 35
grouping 34
informal arrangement *32*
in layer planting 26
pests 558, 565
physiological disorders 559
pruning 47
seed germination 55
side-veneer grafting 56
stem structure *580*
suggestions for use 27, 28
campestre, soil type tolerated 41
capillipes
bark *35*
seasonal interest 37
suggestions for use 37
cappadocicum, softwood cuttings 53
davidii, seasonal interest 37
griseum
bark *35*
seasonal interest 37
suggestions for use 37
grosseri var. *hersii* seasonal interest 37
japonicum
pruning 74, 75
seasonal interest 25
lobelii, soil type tolerated 41
negundo
seasonal interest 37
soil type preferred 42
soil type tolerated 41
'Variegatum', foliage 34
palmatum
conditions preferred 66
in container 65
pruning 74, 75
seasonal interest 25
seed 85
side-veneer grafting 89
suggestions for use 33, 37
in water garden *241*
'Dissectum Purpureum', in trough *36*
'Senkaki'
seasonal interest 37
suggestions for use 37
pensylvanicum
bark *35*
seasonal interest 37
'Erythrocladum'
suggestions for use 50
platanoides
conditions tolerated 37
soil type tolerated 41, 42
as weed 576
pseudoplatanus
conditions tolerated 37
suggestions for use 37
rubrum
suggestions for use 37
'Columnare' *33*
saccharinum 28
conditions tolerated 37
'Silver Vein'
suggestions for use 37
Acheta assimilis 563
Achillea
division 163
for drying 141
Achillea (*cont.*)
in perennial border *135*
soil type preferred 146
ageratifolia
division 208
Irishman's cuttings 208
clavennae, foliage 188
filipendulina 'Gold Plate', soil type tolerated 147
x *kellereri*
in dry-stone wall *189*
soil type preferred 193
millefolium, see Yarrow
'Moonshine', in mixed island bed *136*
Achimenes
conditions required 431
pests 562
Acid soil
climbers requiring 99
effects on minerals 545
improving 276
liming 524
mineral deficiencies in 525, 556, 557, 558
perennials requiring 147
pH level 585
plants thriving on 15
raised beds to contain 507
rock plants requiring 192
shrubs requiring 62, *62*, 69
trees preferring 41
Acid-loving plants
problems with 532
soil for 196, 529
Aconitum
division 163
seed germination 160
soil type tolerated 147
carmichaelii
conditions tolerated 141
var. *wilsonii*, companion plant for 139
napellus, conditions tolerated 141
Acorus
calamus
division of rootstock *256*
suggestions for use 242
in water garden 243
'Variegatus', in water garden 243
gramineus
in water garden 243
'Pusillus', suggestions for use 438
'Variegatus', in water garden 243
Acrylic sheets, for greenhouse glazing 479
Actinidia
conditions tolerated 97
semiripe cuttings 110
simple layering 113
pruning 103
chinensis 98
deliciosa, as fruit see Kiwi fruits
obtaining seed from 109
kolomikta *111*
foliage 95, *96*
hardwood cuttings 111
soil type tolerated 100
suggestions for use 93
Additives for soil 529, *529*
Adelgids 560, *560*
Adenium obesum 258
suggestions for use 262
Adenophora
division 163
softwood cuttings 206
Adiantum
conditions preferred 431
conditions required 431
division of rootstock 451
watering 158
Adiantum (*cont.*)
capillus-veneris, watering with capillary matting *446*
fritzluthii, propagation *159*
raddianum, suggestions for use 438
Adlumia fungosa, soil type tolerated 99
Adonis
seed germination 160
amurensis
conditions preferred *191*
seed germination 160
Adromischus
stem cuttings 268
cooperi, leaf cuttings 267
festivus, leaf cuttings 267
Adventitious bud 585
Adventitious growth 585
Adventitious roots, see Roots, adventitious
Adventitious stem buds 540
Aechmea
conditions preferred 431
conditions required 431, 433
displaying 432
division of offsets *433*
fasciata *432*
Aegopodium podagraria, see Goutweed
Aeonium
arboreum
cuttings 267, 268
suggestions for use 262
'Schwarzkopf', in containers outdoors 260
nobile, suggestions for use 262
Aeration of soil 585
improving 529
Aerators
hollow-tined 467, *467*
lawn *284*, 467, *467*
scarifying rake 284, *284*, *467*
star-wheeled slitter 467, *467*
Aerial roots, see Roots, aerial
Aeschynanthus
conditions required 431
softwood cuttings 453
Aesculus 22
apical-wedge grafting 56
for avenues 36
conditions tolerated 37
diseases 558
pruning 47
renovating 50
soil type tolerated 41
sowing in containers 54
hippocastanum
conditions tolerated 37
leaf form *581*
suggestions for use 37
indica 'Sydney Pearce' *56*
parviflora
informal shrub grouping *61*
root cuttings 84
seasonal interest 66
Aethaoderma 554
Aethionema
soil type tolerated 193
grandiflorum, in rock garden *187*
pulchellum, suggestions for use 191
'Warley Rose'
soil type preferred 193
suggestions for use 191
African Bermuda grass, see *Cynodon transvaalensis*
African daisy, see *Arctotis stoechadifolia*; *Dimorphotheca*; *Osteospermum*
African marigold, see *Tagetes erecta*
African spinach, see Amaranths (vegetable)
African violet, see *Saintpaulia*
Agapanthus
conditions preferred 219
conditions required 431
conditions tolerated 141
in containers 140
for cutting 219
flowers 582
in garden room *426*
in greenhouse garden *430*
lawn as foil to *272*
suggestions for use 136, 140, 218
'Dorothy Palmer', in mixed border *215*
Headbourne Hybrids, with bulbs in formal bedding 214
Agapetes
conditions tolerated 97
pruning 450
semiripe cuttings 110
soil required 98, 99
macrantha, pruning 450
Agavaceae, dying after flowering 259
Agave
architectural plant 66
handling 261
division of offsets 269
division of rootstock 270
americana
conditions tolerated 262
hardiness 259
in succulent group *259*
'Medio-picta', in indoor bed *261*
'Variegata', in succulent group *258*
attenuata
conditions tolerated 262
containers for 260
in succulent group *258*
filifera *259*
hardiness 259
in succulent group *260*
suggestions for use 262
lophantha, conditions tolerated 262
parryi
conditions tolerated 262
in containers outdoors 260
parviflora, conditions tolerated 262
stricta, suggestions for use 262
utahensis, conditions tolerated 262
victoriae-reginae, suggestions for use 262
Ageratum
for drying 175
position in border 171
suggestions for use 175
'Blue Danube', in annual border *171*
houstonianum, soil type tolerated 176
Aggregate, definition 499
Aglaonema
care during absence *446*
conditions required 431
Agonis flexuosa, soil preferred 42
Agriotes 568
Agrobacterium tumefaciens 561, 567
Agropyron
cristatum, for lawn 275
smithii, for lawn 275
Agrostemma
self-seeding 178
sowing 177
githago 'Milas', for cutting 175
Agrostis
for lawn 274, 275, 280
for meadow garden 167
in sod 278
gigantea, for lawn 275
stolonifera, propagation 279
Agrotis caterpillars 560, 566

Ailanthus
conditions tolerated 37
as weed 576
Air layering 539, *539*
indoor plants 456, *456*
shrubs 86, *87*
trees 55
Air pollution
climbers tolerant of 97
perennials tolerant of 141
rock plants tolerant of 191
shrubs tolerant of 66
trees tolerant of 37
Air temperature 515
Air-drying, herbs 298, *298*
Aizoaceae, division of rootstock 270
Ajuga
division 157
pyramidalis, conditions tolerated 191
reptans
conditions tolerated 191
for ground cover 138
'Atropurpurea', for ground cover 150
Akebia
climbing method *98*
semiripe cuttings 110
simple layering 113, *113*
quinata
conditions tolerated 97
fruit 95
soil type tolerated 100
vigor 98
Albuca
suggestions for use 219
humilis, suggestions for use 219
Alcea
cutting down *184*
pests 563
position in border 171
staking 183
rosea (syn. *Althaea rosea*)
architectural plant 175
suggestions for use 27
Alchemilla
flowering time from seed 160
soil type preferred 146
alpina, division 208
ellenbeckii, division 208
mollis 117
in cool border *138*
for drying 141
foliage 138
softening lines of path *501*
Alder, see *Alnus*
Aleppo pine, see *Pinus halepensis*
Alexandra palm, see *Archontophoenix alexandrae*
Alexandrian laurel, see *Danäe racemosa*
Aleyrodes 552
Alfalfa, as green manure 533
Algae, in pond 531
avoiding introduction of 251
control 242, 254, *254*
discouraging 252
encouraging 253
green water caused by 254
water balance affecting 254
Algerian iris, see *Iris unguicularis*
Alisma
lanceolatum 243
parviflora 243
plantago-aquatica 243
Alkaline soil
acid-loving plants on 557
annuals tolerating 176
biennials tolerating 176
characteristics 524
climbers tolerating 100
deficiencies 525
effects on minerals 545
growing fruit on 360
growing peaches on 387
growing pears on 380
growing plums on 383
perennials tolerating 147
pH level 585
Alkaline soil (*cont.*)
problems 573
rock plants tolerating 193
shrubs tolerating 62, 69
structure of *524*, 525
trees tolerating 41
Allamanda 97
softwood cuttings 110
cathartica
conditions tolerated 97
growth rate 97
pruning 103, 105
'Hendersonii' *110*
pruning 450
Allegheny vine, see *Adlumia fungosa*
Allium
for cutting 219
deadheading *230*
dwarf, suggestions for use 219
edible, in crop rotation 304
in mixed border *215*
propagation
bulblets 233
chipping 237
offsets 233
seasonal interest 25
seed germination 538
in summer border *25*
unsuitability for rock garden 192
aflatunense, in mixed border 215
Aggregatum Group, see Shallots
cepa, see Onions, bulb
christophii, architectural plant 219
fistulosum, see Onions, Welsh
giganteum *218*
architectural plant 219
in mixed border *172*, *215*
moly, suggestions for use 227
neopolitanum, forcing 228
oreophilum, forcing 228
porrium, see Leeks
sativum, see Garlic
schoenoprasum, see Chives
sikkimense, division 208
sphaerocephalon, in mixed border *213*
tuberosum 290
in herb garden *295*
Alloplectus, softwood cuttings 453
Alluaudiopsis, flat grafting 271
Almonds 424, *424*, 425, *425*
cultivation 425
diseases 425, 557
harvesting 425
recommended cultivars 425
storing 425
Alnus
conditions tolerated 17, 521
suggestions for use 27
cordata
conditions tolerated 37
suggestions for use 37
glutinosa
conditions tolerated 37
suggestions for use 243
incana, suggestions for use 243
Aloe
propagation
division of offsets 269
division of rootstock 270
in succulent group *259*
succulent type 258
suggestions for use 259, 262
arborescens
conditions tolerated 262
repotting *265*
aristata, conditions tolerated 262
barbadensis
conditions tolerated 262
in containers outdoors 260
'Black Gem' *264*
brevifolia, conditions tolerated 262
ciliaris 259
distans 262
Aloe (*cont.*)
humilis 262
longistyla 262
rauhii 262
spinosissima 262
variegata *270*
conditions tolerated 262
Aloinopsis, division of offsets 269
Alonsoa, growing from seed 452
Aloysia
pruning 74
softwood cuttings 81
triphylla, see Lemon verbena
Alpha naphthalene acetic acid 420
Alpine columbine, see *Aquilegia alpina*
Alpine currant, see *Ribes alpinum*
Alpine heath, see *Erica carnea*
Alpine house 190, 210–12, 430, 477, *477*, 585
beds in 211–12
bulbs for 218, 219
damping down 212
displaying plants in 210, *210*
heating 212
raised beds in 486
shading 212
siting 210
using 210, *210*
ventilation 212
watering 203
Alpine lady's mantle, see *Alchemilla alpina*
Alpine meadows 167
Alpine poppy, see *Papaver burseri*
Alpine strawberries, see Strawberries, alpine
Alpine toadflax, see *Linaria alpina*
Alpines, see also Alpine house
acid-loving, soil for 196
adapting to conditions 185
bulbs with 217, *217*
care, after flowering *210*
characteristics 185, 585
choosing 192, *192*
conditions required 186
in containers 190, *190*, 198–9
cutting back after flowering 204, *204*
definition 185
diseases 204
exhibiting 212, *212*
feeding 203, 212
filling gaps between 173
greenhouse for 481
growing under cover 210–12
habitats 185
hygiene 212, *212*
pests 204
planting 196–7, *196*
in beds 211–12
in crevices 197, *197*
in dry-stone walls 200, *200*
during rock garden construction 195, *195*
in raised beds 189, 200–201, *201*
in scree beds 197, *197*
in troughs 199, *199*
plunging after flowering 210, *210*
in pots 211
potting up 205
pricking out 205, *205*
propagation 205–9
basal cuttings 207, *207*
division 208, *208*
greenwood cuttings 206
Irishman's cuttings 208, *208*
leaf cuttings 207
ripewood cuttings 206
root cuttings 208–9, *209*
scooping rosettes 209, *209*
from seed 205, *205*
semiripe cuttings 206, 207
softwood cuttings 206, *206*
Alpines (*cont.*)
protecting 201, 204, 210, *210*
pruning 203, *203*
raised beds for, in alpine house 486
removing dead rosettes 204, *204*
repotting 211, *211*
in rock garden *185*
routine care 203–4, 212
in scree beds 188
seed
collecting 205
germination 205
presowing treatment 205
storage 205
shading 212
shrubs and conifers combined with *187*
soil mixes for 196, 201, 211, 212, 536
soil type required 196
suggestions for use 186–90
top-dressing 203, *203*, 211, *534*
trimming 203–4
in troughs 190, *190*
watering 203, 212
weeding 203, *203*
winter care 212
Alstroemeria
conditions preferred 219
for cutting 141, 219
division of offsets 233
germination 235
Ligtu Hybrids *218*
Alternanthera
stem tip cuttings 176
philoxeroides
growing as annual 175
suggestions for use 243
Althaea rosea, see *Alcea rosea*
Altitude, effect on temperature 515
Aluminum
excess of 525
for greenhouses 478, *478*
markers in 472
sheds of 513
Aluminum plant, see *Pilea cadierei*
Alyssum
seed germination 538
soil type tolerated 193
montanum, suggestions for use 191
Alyssum, sweet, see *Lobularia maritima*
Amaranths (vegetable) 321, *321*
cultivation 321
harvesting 321
nitrogen requirement 310, 321
storing 321
Amaranthus, see also Amaranths (vegetable)
for drying 175
position in border 171
caudatus
architectural plant 175
for drying 174
foliage 321
in mixed border 173
cruentus *321*
tricolor *321*
architectural plant 175
foliage 321
cultivars 321
Amaryllis, see *Hippeastrum*
Amaryllis
distinguishing from *Hippeastrum* 229
belladonna
conditions preferred 219
for cutting 219
in mixed border 215
Amblyseius, as biological pest control 548, 553, 562
Amelanchier
bird damage 563
pruning 74
seed germination 85
soil type tolerated 67
stooling 87
Amelanchier (*cont.*)
canadensis, division of suckers 88
lamarckii
seasonal interest 37
suggestions for use 37
American beech, see *Fagus grandifolia*
American bittersweet, see *Celastrus scandens*
American black walnut, see *Juglans nigra*
American land cress, see Upland cress
American lotus, see *Nelumbo lutea*
American spatterdock, see *Nuphar advena*
Amitrole 577
commercial names 574
Ammonia 529, 533
Ammonium nitrate 309, 362
nutrient content 532
Ammonium sulfate 360, 380, 392
adjusting pH level 360
Ampelopsis
growth rate 97
semiripe cuttings 110
serpentine layering 113
brevipedunculata
soil type tolerated 100
suggestions for use 95
var. *maximowiczii*, growing through trees 95
Amphibians, providing conditions for 242
Amsonia tabernaemontana (syn. *A. salicifolia*), in cool border *138*
Amur grape, see *Vitis amurensis*
Amur honeysuckle, see *Lonicera maackii*
Anacyclus depressus
in alpine raised bed *201*
in dry-stone wall *189*
root cuttings 208
Ananas 433
for fruit, see Pineapples
conditions preferred 431
propagation 433
bracteatum 'Tricolor' *432*
comosus 'Variegatus', conditions preferred 427
Anaphalis 116
conditions tolerated 141
for drying 141
margaritacea (syn. *A. yedoensis*), in mixed island bed *136*
yedoensis, see *A. margaritacea*
Anatomy of plants 580
Anchoring bolts 480, *480*
Anchusa
root cuttings 165
soil type tolerated 147
azurea, root cuttings 165
caespitosa
in alpine raised bed *201*
in rock garden *187*
softwood cuttings 206
suggestions for use 188, 191
capensis
soil type preferred 176
sowing 177
Andromeda, see *Pieris*
Andromeda
division of suckers 88
pests 552
semiripe cuttings 83
soil type required 69
polifolia 'Compacta', in peat bed *188*
Andromischus
cooperi, leaf cuttings 267
festivus, leaf cuttings 267
Androsace
conditions required 186, 196
rosette cuttings 207
(*entry cont.*)

Androsace (cont.)
small species, suggestions for use 191
soil mix for 211
carnea
in alpine raised bed *201*
in rock garden *187*
subsp. *laggeri*
in alpine raised bed *201*
self-seeding 188
chamaejasme, suggestions for use 190
lanuginosa 191
in alpine raised bed *201*
in rock garden *187*
suggestions for use 191
pubescens, in trough *199*
pyrenaica, in alpine raised bed *201*
sarmentosa, suggestions for use 191
sempervivoides, suggestions for use 191
villosa, in alpine raised bed *201*
Anemone
conditions tolerated 219
diseases, fungal 565
flowering time from seed 160
greenhouse conditions required 431
sowing 205
suggestions for use 216, 219
apennina
conditions preferred 219
suggestions for use 227
blanda
conditions preferred 219
in mixed border 214
rhizomes 214
suggestions for use 227
De Caen Series, for cutting 219
hupehensis
conditions tolerated 141
division 163
root cuttings 165
soil type tolerated 147
x *hybrida*
conditions tolerated 141
pests, damaging leaves 553
root cuttings 165
soil type tolerated 147
x *lipsiensis*, in peat bed *188*
magellanica, soil type tolerated 193
nemorosa 28
conditions tolerated 219
rhizomes 214
storing 224
suggestions for use 140
in woodland 140
'Robinsoniana', in peat bed *188*
pavonina, suggestions for use 227
ranunculoides
choosing healthy bulbs *224*
conditions preferred 219
rivularis, suggestions for use 243
St. Brigid Series, for cutting 219
Anemonella thalictroides, in peat bed *188*
Anemopaegma 97
semiripe cuttings 110
softwood cuttings 110
Anethum graveolens, see Dill
Angelica (herb), see *Angelica archangelica*
Angelica archangelica 290, *290*
architectural form 141
conditions tolerated 288
culinary uses 287, 290
foliage 290
harvesting 290
from seed 290, 297
self-seeding 178, 296
storing 290
Angiospermae (angiosperms) 586
classes 582
seed production 582
Anigozanthos manglesii 147
soil type required 147
Animal manures, see Manure
Animals
beneficial 549, *549*
protection from 43, *43*, 363, *363*, 472
small, pests 551, 572
Aniseed 292, *292*
cultivation 292
harvesting 292
Anisodontea, stem tip cuttings 164
Annuals 170–84
architectural 173
borders of 170–72, *170*, *171*
color effects 170
form and texture in 170
grouping plants 171
buying 181, *181*
characteristics 580, 585
clearing at end of season 184, *184*
climbing 96, 97
planting 182, *182*
from seed 109
supporting 182, *182*, 183, *183*
in containers 174
care 183, *183*
seasonal display 174
crop rotation, for disease control 548
for cutting 174, 175, 183
deadheading 183, *183*, 184, *184*
definition 170
designing with 170–74
diseases 184, 562
bacterial 554, 561, 571
fungal 552, 554, 560, 562, 564, 567
for drying 174, 175, 183, *183*
effect of temperatures on 556, 570
for exposed sites 175
F1 hybrids 452
feeding 181, 183
as fillers 26, 173, 288
for foliage 171
in formal bedding 172, *172*
as green manure 533
in greenhouse 430
for ground cover 173, *173*
grouping 171
half-hardy
conditions tolerated 180
definition 170
hardening off 180, *180*
planting out 180, *180*
sowing 177, 178–9, *179*
hardening off 180, *180*
hardy
definition 170
sowing 176
herbs 287
from seed 297
mineral deficiency 556–7
in mixed borders 136, 172–3, *172*
perennials grown as 175
pests 184, 560, 561, 566, 572
affecting flowers 563
damaging leaves 550, 551, 552, 553, 554, 557
pinching out 181
planter's guide 175
planting
in containers 181, *181*
to design 182, *182*
planting out 180, *180*
potting up 180, *180*
pricking out 179, *179*
problems affecting stems and leaf buds 559, 560, 561
routine care 183–4, *183–4*
for sandy soil 176
for scent 175
Annuals *(cont.)*
seasonal display 171
from seed 109, 176–81
seed
buying 176
collecting 184, *184*
with special requirements 179
viability 176
seedlings
buying 176
protecting 178, *178*
supporting 178, *178*
self-seeding 173, 178, 184
for short-term effect 16, *16*
in shrub border 63
sowing
in open ground 177–8, *177*
in pots or trays 178–81, *179*
in situ, varieties for 177
for succession 452
staking 178, 182, *182*, 183, *183*
suggestions for use 170–74
for summer color 25
summer-flowering *170*
thinning 178, *178*
tolerating alkaline soil 176
trailing, for containers 175
watering 183
weeding 183
weeds 575, 577
Anomatheca
suggestions for use 219
laxa, conditions preferred 219
Anredera 97
cordifolia
for fragrance 97
growth rate 97
pruning 103, 105
softwood cuttings 110
soil type tolerated 99
Antennaria dioica
conditions tolerated 191
division 208
'Minima', suggestions for use 190, 191
Anthemis
softwood cuttings 206
tinctoria
basal stem cuttings 164
'E.C. Buxton' *164*
Anther *267*, 582, *582*, 585
Anthericum liliago 23
Antheridium 159
Anthracnose 572, *572*
Anthriscus cerefolium, see Chervil
Anthurium
conditions required 431
division of rootstock 451
hydroculture 431
Anthyllis
seed germination 160
soil type tolerated 147
montana, in rock garden *187*
Antigonon
softwood cuttings 110
leptopus
growth rate 97
pruning 103, 105
Antirrhinum
clearing at end of season 184
conditions required 431
for containers 174
for cutting 174, 175
flowering shoots 181
in formal bedding 172
growing as annual 175, 176
hardening off 180
as pot plant *175*
glutinosum, suggestions for use 191
majus
self-seeding 178
soil type tolerated 176
Princess Series *175*
molle, suggestions for use 191
sempervirens, suggestions for use 191
Ants 204, 572, 574
benefits of 549
on lawn 574
Anubias barteri, suggestions for use 243
Apennine anemone, see *Anemone apennina*
Aphelanchoides 553
Aphelandra, conditions required 431
Aphidoletes aphidimyza 552
as biological pest control 548
Aphids 124, 204
black *552*
catching 310
conifer woolly, see Adelgids
control 552
biological 548, 549
by companion planting 548
disease spread by 547, 555, 558
greenfly 552
lettuce root, resistance to 548
predators of *548*
problems caused by 232, 552, *552*, 557
virus disease carried by 239
on water plants 255
woolly 560, *560*
woolly apple 552
Apical-wedge grafting 57, 89, *89*, 544, *544*
cacti *270*, 271
shrubs 89, *89*
trees suitable for 56
Apiognomonia errabunda 572
Apiosporina morbosa 561
Apium
graveolens, see Celery
graveolens var. *rapaceum*, see Celeriac
Apocynaceae 258
Aponogeton
depth of water for 242
value in water garden 242
crispus, suggestions for use 243
distachyos
division of tubers 256
planting *253*
from seed 257
in water garden 243
madagascariensis, suggestions for use 243
undulatus, propagation by plantlets 257
Aporocactus
stem cuttings 268
flagelliformis 271
in hanging baskets 261
side grafting 271
suggestions for use 262
Apple cucumbers, see Cucumbers, apple
Apple maggots 565, *565*
Apple mint, see *Mentha suaveolens*
Apple psyllids 562, *562*
Apple sawfly 565, *565*
Apples 371–9
bare-root, planting 371
bark-ringing 366, 373, *373*
biennial bearing 372, 373
blossom thinning 372
bulbs under 216
bush
planting distances 372
pruning 375, *375*
conditions required 371
container-grown, planting 371
cordons 356, *356*
double, training 377, *377*
planting distances 372
pruning 376–7, *377*
training 376
crop timing 359
cross-pollination 357, 360
culinary
for flavor 373
fruit spacing 372
recommended cultivars 373
curbing vigor 366, 373, *373*
Apples *(cont.)*
dessert
fruit spacing 372
recommended cultivars 372
diploids 371
diseases 362, 372, 555, 562
bacterial 571
fungal 554, 560, 564, 567, 570, 571
virus 567
drying 367
dwarf pyramid
planting distances 372
pruning 379
staking 379
encouraging fruit set 373
espaliers 357
planting distances 372
pruning 378, *378*
as screen *357*
training 378, *378*
fans
planting distances 372
pruning 378
space required 358
training 377–8
feathered maidens
training
as bush 375, *375*
as double cordon 377, *377*
as spindlebush 376, *376*
feeding 372
for flavor 372, 373
flowering, temperature required 371
forms 371
frame working 379
freezing 367
fruit *371*
thinning 372, *372*
type 355, 371, 582
fruit buds 373, *373*
gas given off 229
grafting over 379
growing against supports 358
growth buds 373, *373*
half-standard
planting distances 372
pruning 375–6
harvesting 367, 379, *379*
June drop 372
"King" fruit 372
late-ripening 358
maiden whip, training
as bush 375
as double cordon 377, *377*
as espalier 378, *378*
mineral deficiencies 556, 562, 564
mulching 372
nicking 373, *373*, 375
notching 373, *373*
pests 372, 560, 564, 565
damaging flowers 562
damaging leaves 551, 552, 553, 554
damaging stems 560
physiological disorders 564
planting 371
distances 372
pleaching 36
pollination compatibility 359
pollination groups 371
propagation 379
grafting 379, *379*, 543
pruning 373–9
Full Lorette System 375
Modified Lorette System 374, *374*
regulated 374, *374*
renewal 374, *374*
renovative 366
spur pruning 374, *374*
spur thinning 374, *374*
summer 373, 374–5, *374*
untrained trees 373
winter 364, 374, *374*
rind grafting 379, *379*
rootstocks 359, 371, *371*
routine care 372
(entry cont. overleaf)

Apples (*cont.*)
self-sterile 357, 360
siting 371
as specimen trees 375
spindlebush
planting distances 372
pruning 374, 376, *376*
training 376, *376*
spur-bearers 373
training 373
staking 372
standard
planting distances 372
pruning 375–6
storing 358, 359, 367, *367*, 379
testing for ripeness 367
thinning fruit 362
tip-bearers 373
training 373
top working 379, *379*
training 371, 373–9
triploids 371
pruning 374
recommended cultivars 372, 373
tying 372
watering 372
'Cox's Orange Pippin'
cross-pollination 359
in large fruit garden *357*
'Delicious', cross-pollination 359
'Discovery', in large fruit garden *357*
'Edward VII' *373*
'George Cave' *372*
'Golden Delicious', in large fruit garden *357*
'Gravenstein', pruning 374
'Jonagold', pruning 374
'Lodi'
in large fruit garden *357*
in small fruit garden *358*
'Lord Lambourne', cross-pollination 359
'McIntosh', in small fruit garden *358*
'Mutsu' *373*
pruning 374
'Northern Spy' 372
'Red Delicious', in large fruit garden *357*
'Spigold', pruning 374
'State Fair', cross-pollination 359
'Sunset'
in large fruit garden *357*
in small fruit garden *358*
'Winesap', pruning 374
'Wolf River', cross-pollination 359
'Worcester Pearmain' *372*
Approach-grafting, see Grafting, approach-
Apricots 390–91
cultivation 390–91
diseases 561
fruit type 371
harvesting 391
pests 550, 563, 565
pruning 391, *391*
recommended cultivars 391
storing 367
'Hemskerk' *391*
Aquariums 245, *245*
plants for 243
Aquatics, see Water plants
Aquilegia
for cutting 141
flowering time from seed 160
fruit type 581
pests 551, 553
seeds *581*
self-sown seedlings 147
alpina, in rock garden *187*
'Crimson Star', from seed 160
discolor, suggestions for use 191
flabellata
suggestions for use 191
Aquilegia flabellata (cont.)
'Nana'
conditions preferred 189
flowers 189
vulgaris, conditions tolerated 141
Arabis
pruning 204
ferdinandi-coburgi 'Variegata', soil type preferred 193
Arachis hypogaea, see Peanuts
Aralia, Japanese, see *Fatsia japonica*
Aralia
root cuttings 84
soil type tolerated 67
elata 'Aureo-variegata'
architectural plant 66
side-veneer grafting 89
Araujia 97
semiripe cuttings 110
sericofera 95
Arbors
climbers on 94
roses on 118, *118*
Arborvitae, see *Thuja*
Arborvitae leaf miner 553
Arbutus
fruit 34
seed germination 85
soil type required 69
x *andrachnoides*
seasonal interest 37
suggestions for use 37
menziesii
seasonal interest 37
soil preferred 41
unedo
seasonal interest 66
side-veneer grafting 89
Archegonium 159
Arches
Bougainvillea on *92*
climbers on *92*
for climbers 27
fruit cordons on *359*
in garden design *19*
grapevines on 358
growing fruit on 358
roses on *118*, 128
rustic work 512
of trees over walkway 36, *36*
Archips argyrospila 554
Architectural plants 22, *22*
annuals 173, 175
biennials 173, 175
bulbs 219
herbs 288
indoors 426
perennials 140, 141
shrubs 66
Archontophoenix alexandrae *33*
Arctostaphylos
semiripe cuttings 83
soil type required 69, 188
alpinus, soil type required 192
uva-ursi
conditions tolerated 66
'Point Reyes', in peat bed *188*
Arctotis
stem tip cuttings 164
stoechadifolia
suggestions for use 175
var. *grandis*, in annual border *171*
Ardisia
conditions preferred 66
japonica, seasonal interest 66
Arenaria
balearica, in alpine raised bed *201*
montana
in dry-stone wall *189*
division 208
Irishman's cuttings 208
soil type preferred 193
purpurascens
in dry-stone wall *189*
suggestions for use 191
Areoles 258
Argemone mexicana
growing as annual 175
soil type preferred 176
Argyranthemum
stem tip cuttings 164, 176
frutescens (syn. *Chrysanthemum frutescens*)
in containers *272*
treating as biennials 177
Argyreia 97
Argyresthia thuiella 553
Argyroderma, division of rootstock 270
Arisaema
conditions preferred 219
forcing 228
triphyllum *167*
Aristolochia
pruning 103, 105
semiripe cuttings 110
durior, soil type tolerated 99
elegans
conditions tolerated 97
growth rate 97
Armadillidium 550
Armeria
soil type preferred 146
juniperifolia
in dry-stone wall *189*
in rock garden *187*
rosette cuttings 207
soil type preferred 193
suggestions for use 191
maritima 117, 185
Armillaria
mellea 567, 571
root rots 567
Armoracia rusticana, see Horseradish
Armyworms 572
Arnebia, root cuttings 165
Aromatic plants, see also Herbs
suggestions for use 21
Aronia
division of suckers 88
pruning 74
arbutifolia, soil type tolerated 67
Artemisia
abrotanum *290*
benefit to other plants 288
foliage 290
harvesting 290
in herb garden *295*
propagation
hardwood cuttings 290
mound layering 290
softwood cuttings 290
in scented preparations 290
storing 290
suggestions for use 290
absinthium *290*
companion plants 288
conditions tolerated 141
decorative uses 290
foliage 290
harvesting 290
in herb garden *295*
propagation
mound layering 297
semiripe heel cuttings 290
softwood cuttings 290
pruning 290
storing 290
'Lambrook Silver' 290
in mixed border *20*
dracunculoides, see Tarragon, Russian
dracunculus, see Tarragon, French
frigida 117
glacialis, foliage 188
lactiflora, growth rate 141
'Powis Castle' 117
foliage 138
planting in container *147*
schmidtiana 'Nana'
division 208
soil type preferred 193
Artichokes
globe, see Globe artichokes
Artichokes (*cont.*)
Jerusalem, see Jerusalem artichokes
Arugula *326*
culinary uses 326
cultivation 326
harvesting 312, 326
in vegetable garden *300*
Arum
division 163
offsets 233
seed germination 160
suggestions for use 219
italicum
conditions preferred 219
'Marmoratum', winter interest 141
'Pictum', conditions tolerated 219
Arum lily, see *Zantedeschia aethiopica*
Aruncus
dioicus
for drying 141
pests 551
soil type tolerated 146
'Kneiffii', suggestions for use 243
sylvester, growth rate 141
Arundo donax
'Macrophylla', growth rate 141
'Variegata'
architectural form 141
suggestions for use 243
Asarina
softwood cuttings 110
soil type tolerated 99
antirrhiniflora, soil type tolerated 100
erubescens 97
pruning 450
suggestions for use 97
procumbens
flowers 190
suggestions for use 190
Asclepiadaceae (asclepiads) 258, 585
Arabian, grafting 271
grafting 270, 271
latex produced by 268
Madagascan, grafting 271
Asclepias tuberosa, conditions preferred 167
Ascochyta clematidina 571
Asexual reproduction 585
Ash, see *Fraxinus*
Ash-leaved maple, see *Acer negundo*
Asiatic garden beetles 573
Asparagus (vegetable) 341, *341*, 345–6
diseases 346
harvesting 346, *346*
intercropping 302
nitrogen requirement 310
pests 346, 550
protecting from frost 521
recommended cultivars 345
site 302, 345
storing 312, 346
in vegetable garden *300*
'Jersey Giant' *345*
Asparagus
conditions required 431
cultivation 345–6, *345*
propagation by shoot-axil buds 543
densiflorus 'Sprengeri'
in hanging basket *437*
suggestions for use 438
in terrarium *438*, *446*
officinalis, see Asparagus (vegetable)
Asparagus beetle 550, *550*
Asparagus knife 461, *461*
Aspen, see *Populus tremula*
Asperula
odorata (syn. *Galium odoratum*) 290, *290*
conditions suitable for 290
Asperula odorata (cont.)
conditions tolerated 288
culinary uses 287, 290
division 290
flowers 290
for fragrance 141
harvesting 290
in herb garden *295*
planting, to restrict spread 294
in scented preparations 290
from seed 290
storing 290
suggestions for use 290
suberosa, suggestions for use 191
Asphalt
for driveways and paths 501
edging 501
laying 501
Asphodeline lutea, soil type preferred 146
Aspidiolus perniciosus 554
Aspidistra
conditions preferred 431
conditions required 431
conditions tolerated 427
division of rootstock 451
Asplenium
conditions preferred 431
in winter 158
bulbiferum, propagation *158*, 159
nidus, in bottle garden *439*
Aster
colors to blend with 139
for cutting 141
division 162, 163
flowering time from seed 160
in mixed border *149*
pests 563
pinching 155, *155*
planting depth *146*
staking *156*
thinning 155
albescens, division of suckers 88
ericoides, planting in groups 138
frikartii 'Mönch', in mixed border *215*
novae-angliae
in wildflower garden 167
'Harrington's Pink' *163*
thomsonii 'Nanus', in cool border *138*
tongolensis, division *145*
turbinellus, in cool border *138*
Aster leafhoppers 571
Aster yellows 548, 553, 571, *571*
Asteranthera
propagation
self layering 113
semiripe cuttings 110
ovata 97
conditions tolerated 97
soil type required 99
Astilbe
in border of mixed textures *138*
conditions preferred 242
division 163
for drying 141
soil type tolerated 146
suggestions for use 152
x *arendsii*, suggestions for use 243
chinensis, suggestions for use 243
simplicifolia
conditions preferred 141
suggestions for use 243
Astilboides tabularis, suggestions for use 243
Astrantia
for cutting 141
division 163
flowering time from seed 160
major
conditions preferred 141
var. *involucrata*, in cool border *138*
Astrophytum
flat grafting 271
myriostigma *262*
suggestions for use 262
ornatum, suggestions for use 262
Asyneuma, softwood cuttings 206

Athyrium
in winter 158
niponicum 'Pictum', suggestions for use 152
Atmospheric conditions, problems caused by 547
Atriplex halimus, hardwood cuttings 84
Aubrieta
conditions tolerated 191
greenwood cuttings 206
pruning 204
softwood cuttings 206
soil type tolerated 193
suggestions for use 186
deltoidea
suggestions for use 191
'Argenteo-variegata' *206*
'Joy', in rock garden *187*
Aucuba
conditions for 66
flower sexuality 582
layering 86
pruning 78
semiripe cuttings 82, 83
soil type tolerated 67
japonica
hardwood cuttings 84
soil type tolerated 69
'Variegata', hydroculture *47*
Auger 530
Auricula primrose, see *Primula auricula*
Aurinia
greenwood cuttings 206
Irishman's cuttings 208
pruning 204
saxatilis 191
Austrocactus, flat grafting 271
Austrocedrus, semiripe cuttings 53
Autovent openers 483, *483*
Autumn crocus, see *Colchicum*
Auxins 540, 585
Avena sterilis, for drying 175
Avenues, trees for 36, *36*
Avocados *415*, 421–2, *422*
cultivation 421–2
propagation, from seed 422, *422*
recommended cultivars 421
'Rincon' *421*
Awn, definition 585
Axil, definition 585
Axillary bud, definition 585
Axonopus, for lawn 274
sowing rate 280
Azalea, see *Rhododendron*
Azalea gall 558, *558*
Azalea pots 473, *473*
Azara
semiripe cuttings 83
suggestions for use 66
Azolla
caroliniana 243
propagation by plantlets 257
value in water garden 242
filiculoides 243
Azorella trifurcata, rosette cuttings 207
Aztec marigold, see *Tagetes erecta*
Aztekium, flat grafting 271

B

Babiana, suggestions for use 219
Baboon flower, see *Babiana*
Baby's breath, see *Gypsophila*
Baby's tears, see *Soleirolia soleirolii*
Bachelor's buttons, see *Centaurea*
Bacillus thuringiensis 551, 553, 572
as biological control 310, 548, 551
commercial names 574
San Diego strain 551
Back bulbs (orchid) 585
potting up 441
propagation by 443, *443*
Backfilling 585
around pond or watercourse 247, *247*, *249*, 250, *250*
Background, features suitable for 22, *22*
Bacopa monnieri
softwood cuttings 256
suggestions for use 243
Bacteria
beneficial 525
colonizing plants 559
Bacterial canker 362, 384, 571
Bacterial diseases 547
affecting bulbs 569
affecting leaves 554, 555, 558
affecting roots and tubers 567, 568
affecting stems 561
affecting whole plant 570, 571
as biological pest control 310, 548, 551
Bacterial leaf spots (blotches) 554, *554*
Bacterial rotting of potatoes 568, *568*
Bags
carrying 470, *470*
plastic 470
Bahia grass, see *Paspalum notatum*
Bait 563, 568
Balance, designing for *13*, 18
Balconies
climbing annuals on 173
gardening on 29, *29*
herbs in containers 288
perennials in containers 140
Bald cypress, see *Taxodium distichum*
Baldellia ranunculoides
in aquarium *245*
propagation by plantlets 257
Balled-and-burlapped, definition 585
Balloon flower, see *Platycodon grandiflorus*
Ballota pseudodictamnus, soil type preferred 193
Bamboos 142–3
cutting back 143
dividing rhizomes 143, *143*
as hedge 59
maturity, time required 142
restricting 143
space required 142
suggestions for use 142
transplanting 143
Bambusoideae subfamily 142
Bananas
fruit type 581
seed germination 452
Banks
building steps into *503*
climbers on 93, 95
dwarf conifers for 38
ground cover on 64, 150
incorporating in design 17, *17*
lawn on 272
retaining walls on 506
roses on 116, 119
in shade 17
Banksia
conditions preferred 66
serrata, soil preferred 42
Baptisia
life expectancy 16
seed germination 160
Barbarea verna, see Upland cress
Barberry, see *Berberis*
Bark
for color 24, *25*, 26
trees for *34*, 35, *35*
formation *580*
Bark (*cont.*)
growing orchids on 441, *441*
ornamental
shrubs for 65
winter, trees for 37
on poles, for rustic work 512
for texture 24
Bark (organic material)
chips
as mulch 70, *101*, 123, 151
on plastic 576
coarse, as mulch 534
in cuttings soil mix 536
mulching with 309
as plunge material 437
as protection for plants in store *157*
as soil additive 529
as top-dressing *534*
Bark slipping 543
Bark-ringing 366, 373, *373*, 585
Barn cloches, see Cloches, barn
Barnyard grass 578
Barrel cactus, see *Ferocactus*
Barrels, see Containers
Basal cuttings, see Cuttings, basal
Basal plate 585
Base dressing 309, 585
Basella alba, see Malabar spinach
Basil *292*
conditions required 292
culinary uses 287, 292, 298
foliage 292
freeze-drying 298
as gap filler in border 288
harvesting 292
in herb garden *295*
planting out 297
preserving in oil 298
pricking out 297
related species 292
from seed 292, 297
sowing in containers 297
storing 292
variants 292
Basin irrigation 585
Baskets 470
Basket-weave fencing 508, *508*
Bastard trenching, see Digging, double
Bathrooms, plants for 427
Batter board 506
Batteries, rechargeable 464
Bay, see *Laurus nobilis*
Bay laurel, see *Laurus nobilis*
Bay psyllid 553
Bayberry, see *Myrica*
Beach pine, see *Pinus contorta*
Bead plant, see *Nertera granadensis*
Beams, joints for 512, *512*
Bean sprouts 337, 338
Beans
climbing, positioning 301
damage caused by mice, rats, and voles 568
diseases 560, 567
dried *336*
dwarf, starting under cloches 311
effect of daylength on 303
growth rate 97
mulching *308*
nitrogen requirement 310
pests 552, 566
sowing 305, 306
watering, critical periods 308
Beans, broad *336*, 340, *340*
bird damage 565
in containers *307*
in crop rotation 304
cultivation 340
diseases 340, 555, 567
harvesting 340
pinching out *340*
recommended cultivars 340
storing 312, 340
in vegetable garden *300*
'Statissa' *340*
'Witkiem Major' *340*
Beans, French, see Beans, snap
Beans, hyacinth 337, *337*
as bean sprouts 337
in crop rotation 304
cultivation 337
harvesting 337
from seed 337
softwood cuttings 337
storing 312, 337
Beans, kidney *336*
Beans, Lima 338, *338*
as bean sprouts 338
in crop rotation 304
culinary uses 338
cultivation 338
harvesting 338
recommended cultivars 338
storing 312, 338
'Fordhook 242' *338*
Beans, navy *336*
Beans, runner
on patio screen 29
pests 563
Beans, scarlet runner *336*, 337–8, *337*, *338*
conditions tolerated 93
in crop rotation 304
culinary uses 337
cultivation 337–8
dwarf, in vegetable garden *300*
growing herbs with *303*
harvesting 338
in ornamental garden *27*
recommended cultivars 337
as screen 174
storing 312, 338
supports for *338*
in vegetable garden *300*
'Prize Winner' *337*
positioning *301*
Beans, snap *336*, 338–9
in crop rotation 304
culinary uses 338
cultivation 338–9, *339*
diseases 339, 567
drying *339*
dwarf, in vegetable garden *300*
harvesting 339
pests 339
pregerminating *339*
recommended cultivars 339
seed dressing 339
storing 312, 339
toxins in 338
'Royal Burgundy' *339*
Beans, soy, as organic control 573
Beaumontia 97
propagation
semiripe cuttings 110
simple layering 113
pruning 103
grandiflora
for scent 96, 97
soil type required 99
vigor 98
Bed system, growing vegetables in 302, 585
Bedding
carpet 585
formal 30
uses 31
Bedding mortar 499
mixes for 494
Bedding plants 585
buying 181, *181*
in containers 26
diseases 560, 567
effect of frost on 515
planting, to design 182, *182*
Beds
alpine
outdoors 186, 200–201, *201*
renovating *204*
routine care 203–4
top-dressing 201, 203, *203*
in alpine house 210, 211–12
bench, preparing 439, *439*
bulb, soil mix for 228
cartwheel, herbs in *288*, 289
color schemes 139
in conservatory 439
designing 19, 137
Beds (*cont.*)
formal, bulbs in 214, *214*
in garden design *19*
in greenhouse 439
height of plants 137
herbs in 288
indoor, for cacti 261, *261*
island
herbaceous 136
mixed *136*
positioning plants 137
shrubs in 63
in lawn 273
narrow bed system *300*
peat, for perennials 147
perennials planted in groups 137, *137*
planting 20
plunge *228*, *229*
in pond
constructing 247
planting 251
raised
advantages of 519, *519*
for alpines 186, 200–201, *201*, 211–12
care 203–4
on balcony *29*
brick 507, *507*
for bulbs 218, 231
for cacti and other succulents 260
planting 263, *263*
circular 507
concrete block 507
construction 147, 201, *263*
design 201, 507
in greenhouse 429, 486
herbs in 288
for lime-hating plants 507
linking 507
materials for 201, 507, *507*
natural stone 507
on patios 29
for perennials 136, 147
of railroad ties 507, *507*
rock plants for 189, *189*, 191
of sawed logs 507
shrubs in 64
siting 200
soil in 507
succulents in, planting 263, *263*
uses 507
watering 507
for roses 116, 117
shapes 137
size 137
sloping, advantages of 519
stepped 17
in vegetable garden 300, *300*, *302*
weeding 155
Bee balm, see *Monarda didyma*
Beech, see *Fagus*
Bees
honey, benefits of 549
leaf-cutting 551, *551*
wildflowers for *167*
Beetles
beneficial *525*
control 310, 549
Beets 348, *348*
bolt-resistant cultivars 348
in containers 307
in crop rotation 304
culinary uses 348
cultivation 348
harvesting 348, *348*
mineral deficiencies 568
nitrogen requirement 310, 348
recommended cultivars 348
seed 348
storing 312, 348
in vegetable garden *300*
watering 348
critical periods 308
'Burpee's Golden' *348*
Begonia
buying seedlings 176
conditions required 431
(*entry cont. overleaf*)

Begonia (*cont.*)
- flower sexuality *582*
- in indoor plant group *444*
- lifting after bedding 184
- in mixed border 173
- overwintering 218
- pests 553, 566, 572
- planting in container *181*
- planting out 180
- propagation
  - basal cuttings 238, 455, *455*
  - division of tubers 455, *455*
  - leaf cuttings 267, 454, *541*
  - leaf sections 455, *455*
  - sowing seed 178, 452
- rhizomatous, leaf cuttings 454
- on roof garden *29*
- seed germination 179, 538
- tuberous
  - propagation 455, 543
    - basal cuttings 238, 455, *455*
    - division of tubers 455, *455*
  - storing 455, *455*
- in windowbox *174*
- *incana*, leaf cuttings 267
- 'Non-Stop', suggestions for use 175
- *rex*
  - conditions preferred 427
  - conditions required 431, 436
  - leaf sections *455*
  - plunging in large container *437*
- Rex group, leaf cuttings 454
- *semperflorens*
  - growing as annual 175, 176
  - as pot plants 175
  - suggestions for use 175
- 'Tiger Paws', suggestions for use 438
- *venosa*, leaf cuttings 267

Belgian blocks *498*
Belgian endive, see Endive, Belgian
Bell peppers, see Peppers, sweet
Bellevalia, suggestions for use 219
Bellflower, see *Campanula*
Bellis perennis
- control 579
- flowers 171
- in formal bedding 172
- in mixed border *358*
- in sod *278*

Bells-of-Ireland, see *Moluccella laevis*
Bench beds, preparing 439, *439*
Benches
- cleaning 545
- as focal point *14*

Bendiocarb 554
- commercial names 574

Bent, see *Agrostis*
Berberidopsis 97
- semiripe cuttings 110
- *corallina*
  - conditions tolerated 97
  - soil type required 99

Berberis
- conditions tolerated 66
- mallet cuttings 83
- seed stratification 537
- semiripe heel cuttings 83
- soil type tolerated 67
- *buxifolia*, division of suckers 88
- *darwinii*
  - pruning 78
  - soil type tolerated 69
- *empetrifolia*, soil type preferred 67
- *julianae*, as hedge 59
- x *stenophylla* 'Corallina Compacta' 191
  - in rock garden *187*
- *temolaica*, seasonal interest 66

Berberis (*cont.*)
- *thunbergii*
  - as hedge 58, 59
  - as weed 576
- *verruculosa*, as hedge 59

Berchemia, semiripe cuttings 110
Bergenia
- conditions preferred 141
- cultivars, in container *157*
- division 163
- planting
  - in groups 137
  - through landscape fabric *151*
- soil type tolerated 147
- suggestions for use 140, 243
- winter interest 140
- 'Ballawley' 151
  - architectural form 141
  - in mixed island bed *136*
  - winter interest 141
- *cordifolia*
  - conditions tolerated 141
  - winter interest 141
  - 'Purpurea', in mixed border *172*
- *purpurascens*
  - in containers 140
  - foliage 138
  - suggestions for use 140

Bergerocactus, stem cuttings 268
Berkheya, soil type tolerated 147
Bermuda grass, see *Cynodon*
Berries
- for color 24
- fruits producing 581
- ornamental trees for 34
- problems 564–5
- shrubs for 65

Beschorneria
- conditions preferred 66
- *yuccoides 259*
  - conditions tolerated 262
  - hardiness 259

Besoms 467, *467*
Beta vulgaris
- Cicla Group, see Spinach beets; Swiss chard
- subsp. *vulgaris*, see Beets

Betula
- diseases 554, 561
- flowers, unisexual 582
- in layer planting 26
- life expectancy 16
- perennials with 140
- pruning 47
- renovating 50
- seed germination 55
- side-veneer grafting 56
- softwood cuttings 53
- soil type indicated by 525
- suggestions for use 28, 32, 37
- white 32
- *albo-sinensis*
  - var. *septentrionalis* 37
- *ermanii* 37
- 'Jermyns', seasonal interest 37
- *nana* 191
  - in peat bed *188*
- *papyrifera*
  - in garden design *19*
  - suggestions for use 27
- *pendula*
  - bonsai 434
  - conditions tolerated 37
  - pests 553, 559
  - soil preferred 42
  - suggestions for use 27, 37
  - 'Dalecarlica' 37
- *pubescens*, conditions tolerated 37
- *utilis* var. *jacquemontii*
  - bark and stem interest *34*, 35, *35*
  - seasonal interest 37
  - suggestions for use 37

Bhutan pine, see *Pinus wallichiana*
Bible leaf, see *Tanacetum balsamita*
Biennials 170–84, 585
- architectural 173

Biennials (*cont.*)
- characteristics 580
  - clearing at end of season 184
  - in cold greenhouse 430
  - collecting seed from 184, *184*
  - for cut flowers 175, 183
  - deadheading 184, *184*
  - definition 170
  - designing with 170–74
  - diseases 184
  - for dried flowers 175, 183
  - for exposed sites 175
  - F1 hybrids 452
  - feeding 183
  - as fillers 173
  - first-year growth *180*
  - in formal bedding 172
  - for ground cover 173
  - half-hardy, sowing 177
  - hardy, sowing 176
  - herbs, propagation, from seed 297
  - in mixed borders 136, 172–3, *172*
  - overwintering 183
  - pests 184
  - planter's guide 175
  - planting, in containers 181, *181*
  - propagation
    - from seed 176–80
    - sowing in open ground 177–8
  - routine care 183–4, *183–4*
  - for sandy soil 176
  - for scent 175
  - seed 176
  - seedlings, buying 176
  - self-seeding 173, 178, 184
  - suggestions for use 170–74
  - for summer color 25
  - supporting 183
  - thinning 178
  - trailing, for containers 175
  - weeding 183

Bignonia
- pruning 103
- softwood cuttings 110
- *capreolata*, climbing method 93

Bilberry, see *Vaccinium myrtillus*
Billardiera
- semiripe cuttings 110
- soil type required 99
- *longiflora*
  - fruit 95
  - pruning 103

Billbergia
- conditions preferred 431
- as pot plant 432
- *nutans*, propagation *433*

Bindweed
- field 576
  - control 276, 576, 579
- hedge 576

Bins, compost, see Compost bins
Biological control 310, 548–9, *549*
Bipolaris iridis 569
Birch, see *Betula*
Birch leaf mining sawfly 553
Bird-of-paradise flower, see *Strelitzia*
Birds 204
- benefits of 549
- damage caused 565, *565*
- deterring 310, 565
- habitats for waterfowl 241
- protecting alpines from 197
- protecting fruit from 357, 358, 363, *363*, 384
- protecting vegetables from 310
- protection from, netting for 472

Bird's-eye primrose, see *Primula farinosa*
Bird's-nest fern, see *Asplenium nidus*
Birthwort, see *Aristolochia*
Bisexual plants 582, *582*
Bishop's cap, see *Astrophytum myriostigma*
Bitter pit *564*
- symptoms and control 564

Bittercress, see *Cardamine*
- hairy, see *Cardamine hirsuta*

Bittersweet, see *Celastrus*
Black alder, see *Alnus glutinosa*
Black bamboo, see *Phyllostachys nigra*
Black frost 515
Black gum, see *Nyssa sylvatica*
Black knot gall 384, 392, 561, *561*
Black mulberries, see Mulberries, black
Black pine, see *Pinus nigra*
Black poplar, see *Populus nigra*
Black rot 265
Black spruce, see *Picea mariana*
Black vine weevils 572, *572*
- adults 551, *551*
- immunity to pesticides 549
- larvae 447, 566, *566*, 572, *572*
  - biological control 548

Blackberries *404*, 406–8
- choosing healthy plants 406, *406*
- cultivation 406–8
- diseases 363, 407, 554, 559
- freezing 367
- harvesting 367, 407
- pests 407, 559, 564
- plant type 356, 404
- preserving 367
- propagation
  - layering 370
  - leaf-bud cuttings 370, 408, *408*
  - tip layering *407*, *407*, 539, *539*
- pruning 407, *407*
- rampant growth 407
- recommended cultivars 407
- storing 407
- supporting 406
- thornless, vigor 406
- training 407, *407*
- 'Comanche' *407*
- 'Lucretia', in large fruit garden *357*

Blackbirds, damage caused by 565
Blackcurrants 410–11
- certification schemes 410
- cultivation 410–11
- diseases 363, 410
- freezing 367
- hardwood cuttings 370, *411*
- harvesting 411
- pests 410, 558
- plant type 356, 404
- pruning 364, 410, *410–11*
- recommended cultivars 411
- shoots, new and fruited *410*
- storing 411
- 'Ben Lomond' *411*
  - in large fruit garden *357*
- 'Ben Sarek' *411*
  - in large fruit garden *357*
  - in small fruit garden *358*
- 'Boskoop Giant', in large fruit garden *357*

Black-eyed Susan vine, see *Thunbergia alata*
Blackleg
- on cuttings 570, *570*
- on potatoes 570, *570*

Blackspot 120, 124, 548, 554, *554*
Blackthorn, see *Prunus spinosa*
Bladderwort, see *Utricularia*
Blanching 585
- endives 322, *323*

Blaniulus 550
- *guttatus* 550

Blanket flower, see *Gaillardia*
Blanketweed, control 254, *254*
Blechnum, conditions required 158
Bleeding, definition 585
Bleeding heart, see *Dicentra spectabilis*
Bletilla, temperature required 441

Blight
- potato 555, *555*
- seedling 560
- tomato 555, *555*, 564, *564*

Blind, definition 585
Blind bulbs 232
Blind shoots, on roses 124, *124*
Blinds, for shading greenhouse 484, *484*, *486*
Blissus 573
Blocks
- concrete, raised beds of 507
- precast concrete *504*
- rock-faced concrete *504*
- screen wall
  - building walls of 505, *505*
  - patterns *505*
- smooth *504*

Blood, dried 556
- in cutting soil mix 536

Bloodmeal, nutrient content 532
Bloodroot, see *Sanguinaria canadensis*
Bloom, definition 585
Bloomeria crocea, conditions preferred 219
Blossfeldia, flat grafting 271
Blossom end rot 564, *564*
Blossom wilt 562, *562*
Blowers, leaf 467, *467*
Blue Atlas cedar, see *Cedrus atlantica* f. *glauca*
Blue Chilean crocus, see *Tecophilaea cyanocereus*
Blue Colorado spruce, see *Picea pungens* var. *glauca*
Blue Douglas fir, see *Pseudotsuga menziesii* var. *glauca*
Blue fescue, see *Festuca glauca*
Blue flag, see *Iris versicolor*
Blue gum, see *Eucalyptus globulus*
Blue lace flower, see *Trachymene coerulea*
Blue lily of the Nile, see *Agapanthus*
Blue mold on citrus 564
Blue oat grass, see *Helictotrichon sempervirens*
Blue passionflower, see *Passiflora caerulea*
Blue poppy, see *Meconopsis*
Bluebell, see *Hyacinthoides*; *Mertensia*
- English, see *Hyacinthoides non-scripta*
- Spanish, see *Hyacinthoides hispanica*

Bluebell wood 26
Blueberries *404*, 414, *414*
- cultivation 414
- fall color 414
- freezing 367
- harvesting 414
- highbush 414
  - pruning *414*
  - recommended cultivars 414
- pests 565
- plant type 404
- propagation
  - hardwood cuttings 370
  - softwood cuttings 370, 414, *414*
- pruning 364
- rabbit-eye 414
- soil type indicated by 525
- soil type required 15, 360, 414
- storing 414
- 'Bluecap' *414*

Bluebottle, see *Centaurea cyanus*
Blue-eyed grass, see *Sisyrinchium bellum*
Bluegrass, annual 575, *578*
- diseases 573
- in lawns 274
- leaf form *581*
- sod free of 278

Bluet, see *Houstonia caerulea*
Blushing bromeliad, see *Neoregelia carolinae*

Bog bean, see *Menyanthes trifoliata*
Bog garden 241, *242*, 519, *519*
  creating 252
  irises for 144
  planting 252, *252*
  site 167
  using natural site for 17
  wildflowers for *167*
Bog plants 242, 243, 585
  conditions tolerated 531
  planting 252, *252*
Bog sage, see *Salvia uliginosa*
Bok choi 319, *319*, 320, *320*
  in crop rotation 304
  cultivation 320
  for fall crop 320
  harvesting 320
    seedlings 320, *320*
  nitrogen requirement 310
  types 320
  in vegetable garden *300*
Bolax gummifera
  in alpine raised bed *201*
  cuttings 207
  suggestions for use 190, 191
Bole, definition 585
Bolting, definition 585
Bomarea
  andimarcana, soil type tolerated 99
  caldasii 97
    suggestions for use 97
Bone meal 556
  amount required compared to other fertilizers 532
  nutrient content 532
Bongardia chrysogonum, suggestions for use 219
Bonsai 26, 434–5
  choosing plants 434
  containers for 434
  creating 434–5, *435*
  hardy 434
  indoors 427
  planting 435
  propagation 434
  pruning 434, 435, *435*
  routine care 435
  styles 434, *434*
  tender 434
  tools for *434*
Borage *291*
  companion plants 288
  conditions tolerated 175
  culinary uses 287, 291
  deadheading 296
  flowers 288, 291
  foliage 291
  freezing flowers in ice 298, *298*
  as gap filler in border 288
  harvesting 291
  in herb garden *295*
  propagation
    from seed 291, 297
    self-seeding 178, 291
    sowing 177
  storing 291
  f. *alba* 291, *291*
Borago officinalis, see Borage
Borax 568, 572
  commercial names 574
Bordeaux mixture 555, 558, 560, 569, 571
  commercial names 574
Borders
  annual 170–72, *170*, *171*
    color effects 170
    form and texture 170
    grouping plants 171
    marking out 177, *177*
  bulbs in, care 230
  color schemes 139
  in conservatory, preparing 439
  cool *138*
  designing 19, *19*, 137
  in greenhouse 478, 486
    preparing 439
  height of plants 137
  height and scale 22
Borders (*cont.*)
  herbaceous 135, *135*
    formal *136*
    grasses for 142
  herbs in 288
  hot *139*
  mixed *20*, 63, 136, *137*, *149*, *152*
    annuals in 172–3, *172*
    bulbs in *213*, 214–15, *215*
    fruit in *358*
    seasonal interest 139, *139*
    specimen tree in 34
  perennials planted in groups 137, *137*
  planting 20
  positioning plants 137
  shapes 137
  shrub 62–3, *63*
  size 137
  weeding 155
  wildflower *167*
Boron 545
  deficiency 525, 560, *560*, 568
  plant requirements 532
Boronia
  semiripe cuttings with heel 83
  softwood cuttings 81
Boston fern, see *Nephrolepis*
Boston ivy, see *Parthenocissus tricuspidata*
Botany, basic 580–82
Botrytis *559*, *562*
  causes 518
  conditions encouraging 484
  control 398, 559, 562
  damage caused by 552
  symptoms 559, 562, 564, *564*
  allii 569
  cinerea 559, 562
  elliptica 555
  fabae 555
  galanthina 559, 562
  paeoniae 571
  tulipae 555, 562
Bottle gardens 428
  care 445–6
  condensation 445
  planting 439, *439*
  tools for 439
Bottle gentian, see *Gentiana andrewsii*
Bottlebrush, see *Callistemon*
Bottlebrush buckeye, see *Aesculus parviflora*
Bougainvillea
  on archways *92*
  climbing method 93, 98
  conditions preferred 431
  conditions required 431
  in containers 96
  indoors 426
  propagation
    hardwood cuttings 111
    semiripe cuttings 110
    softwood cuttings 453
  pruning 103, 104, *104*, 450
  suggestions for use 97
  vigor 98
  'Miss Manila' *103*
Boundaries
  evergreen ground cover on 150
  laws regarding 510
  fences 508
  walls 504
Bouvardia, conditions preferred 66
Bow saws, see Saws, bow
Bower vine, see *Pandorea jasminoides*
Bowl gardens, for succulents 261
Bowles' mint, see *Mentha* x *villosa* 'Alopecuroides'
Bowling green 275
Bowls, see Containers
Box elder, see *Acer negundo*
Box psyllid 553
Boxwood, see *Buxus*
Boysenberries *404*, 406, 407
Braces, corner 512
Brachycome iberidifolia
  soil type preferred 176
  suggestions for use 175
Brachyglottis
  conditions preferred 66
  semiripe cuttings 83
Bracts, definition 585
Bradley Bermuda grass, see *Cynodon incompletus* var. *hirsutus*
Bradysia 572
Brambles, see *Rubus*
Branches, definition 585
Brass buttons, see *Cotula coronopifolia*
Brassia, temperature required 441
Brassica
  hirta, see Mustard
  juncea, see Mustard, Oriental
  napus, see Salad rape
  napus, Napobrassica Group, see Rutabagas
  oleracea
    Acephala Group, see Kales
    Botrytis Group, see Cauliflowers
    Capitata Group, see Cabbages
    Gemmifera Group, see Brussels sprouts
    Gongylodes Group, see Kohlrabi
    Italica Group, see Broccoli; Sprouting broccoli
  rapa
    var. *alboglabra*, see Chinese broccoli
    var. *chinensis*, see Bok choi
    var. *nipposinica*, see Mizuna greens
    var. *pekinensis*, see Chinese cabbages
    var. *perviridis*, see Komatsuna
    Rapifera Group, see Turnip tops; Turnips
    Utilis Group, see Broccoli raab
Brassicas 313–20, 585
  alternating crops with lettuces *301*
  in crop rotation 304
  diseases 552, 555, 567
  freezing 312
  mineral deficiencies 558
  Oriental 319–20
    cultivation 319
    harvesting 319
    nitrogen requirement 319
    storing 319
    winter cropping under cover 311
  pests 304, 550, 551
  sowing depth 305
  storing 312
  temperature requirements 303
  watering, critical periods 308
  Western 313–18
    collared seedlings *313*
    cultivation 313
    nitrogen requirement 313
Brazilian firecracker, see *Manettia inflata*
Break, definition 585
Bremia 552
Brewer's spruce, see *Picea breweriana*
Bricklaying 505
Bricks
  bonding patterns 505, *505*
  choosing 497
  cutting 498
  laying 497, *497*
    patterns for *497*
  paths of 501, *501*
    construction 501
  paving, laying 497, *497*
  raised beds of 507, *507*
  retaining walls of, constructing 506, *506*
  types *497*, *504*
  for walls 504, *504*
Brickwork
  attaching beams to 512, *512*
  mortar mix for 494
  weeding 579
Bridal wreath, see *Spiraea* x *arguta*
Bristle-pointed iris, see *Iris setosa*
Bristly rose slug 551
Briza
  maxima, for drying 175
  minor, for drying 175
Broadcasting, definition 585
Broad-leaved dock 576
Broccoletti, see Broccoli raab
Broccoli 313, 318
  Chinese, see Chinese broccoli
  in crop rotation 304
  cultivation 318
  nitrogen requirements 310, 318
  pests 566
  sprouting, see Sprouting broccoli
  storing 312
  in vegetable garden *300*
  'Emperor' *318*
Broccoli raab 318, *318*
  culinary uses 318
  harvesting 318
  nitrogen requirement 310, 318
  storing 312
Brodiaea
  corm 214
  suggestions for use 218, 219
  laxa, see *Triteleia laxa*
Brodifacoum 568
  commercial names 574
Bromadiolone 568
  commercial names 574
Bromelia balansae *432*
Bromeliad trees 432
Bromeliads 432–3, 585
  conditions preferred 431
  conditions required 431
  epiphytic 432, *432*, 433
  forms 426, 432
  in greenhouse 430
  propagation
    dividing rootstocks 433, *433*
    offsets 433, *433*
    from seed 433, *433*
  routine care 433
  seed viability 433
  suitable for indoors *432*
  terrestrial 433
Bronze fennel, see *Foeniculum vulgare* 'Purpureum'
Broom, see *Cytisus*; *Genista*
Broussonetia papyrifera, as weed 576
Browallia
  conditions preferred 431
  conditions required 431
  propagation 176
  from seed 452
  speciosa, growing as annual 175
Brown, Lancelot 'Capability' 34
Brown heart 568
Brown patch 573, *573*
Brown rot 564, *564*
Bruckenthalia, semiripe cuttings 83
Brunfelsia
  in greenhouse 430
    conditions required 431
  pinching out 450
  pauciflora 453
    softwood cuttings 453
Brunnera
  soil type tolerated 147
  macrophylla, conditions preferred 141
Brushwood cutters 462, 464, *464*
Brussels sprouts *313*, 316–17, *316*, *317*
  in crop rotation 304
  culinary uses 316
  cultivation 316–17
  diseases 317, 555, 567
  dwarf plant *316*
  F1 cultivars 316, *317*
  for freezing 317
  harvesting 317
Brussels sprouts (*cont.*)
  hilling up *316*
  nitrogen requirements 310, 316
  open-pollinated cultivars 316, *317*
  pests 317, 551, 566
  recommended cultivars 317
  red 316
  removing leaves *317*
  storing 312, 317
  in vegetable garden *300*
  'Jade Cross E' *317*
Brutting 425, *425*
Buchloe dactyloides, for lawn 275
Buckeye, see *Aesculus*
Buckler-leaf sorrel 293
  in herb garden *295*
Buckthorn, see *Rhamnus*
Bud, types 585
Bud nematodes 553, *553*
Bud union, definition 585
Bud-grafting
  chip-budding 57, *57*, 368, *368*
    fruit trees 368, *368*
    method 544, *544*
    time for 543
    trees suitable for 56
  double budding 382, *382*
  fruit trees 368–9, *368–9*
  roses 120, 130–31, *130*
  T-budding 369, *369*
    method 544, *544*
    time for 543
  tools for 131, *463*
Bud-stripping, protecting fruit from 363, *363*
Budding, see Bud-grafting
Buddleia
  in formal open-plan garden *14*
  hardwood cuttings 84
  softwood cuttings 81
  alternifolia
    pruning 76
    scent 66
    training, as standard 80
  crispa
    suggestions for use 66
    as wall shrub 64
  davidii
    conditions tolerated 66
    pruning 74, 75, *75*
    soil type tolerated 69
    'Black Knight', in mixed border *20*
  globosa, pruning 74
Budsticks, for grafting 368, *368*
Budwood, definition 585
Buffalo gourd, see *Cucurbita foetidissima*
Buffalo grass, see *Buchloe dactyloides*
Bugbane, see *Cimicifuga*
Bugle weed, see *Ajuga*
Builder's square *493*
Buildings
  clematis on 106
  climbers on 93
  trees near 39
Buiningia, flat grafting 271
Bulb fiber 536, 585
Bulb flies 569
Bulb frames 218
Bulb pans 473
Bulb planters *226*, 227, 471, *471*
Bulb scale mites 558, *558*
Bulb vegetables 341–7
  storing 312
  temperature requirements 303
Bulbils 585
  propagation by 256, 542, *542*
    bulbs 233
    ferns *158*, 159
    indoor plants 451
    lilies 239, *239*
Bulbine
  frutescens 262
  latifolia 262
  mesembryanthemoides 262
Bulblets 585
  potting 231, 232
(*entry cont. overleaf*)

Bulblets (*cont.*)
propagation by 233, 239, *239*, 542, *542*
plants suitable for 233
Bulbocodium vernum, suggestions for use 219
Bulbs (bulbous plants) 213–39, 585
in alpine house 190, 219
with alpines 217, *217*
architectural plants 219
blind, causes 232
in borders, care 230
breaking dormancy 515
bulblets, potting 231, 232
characteristics 213, 214
choosing 224, *224*
conditions preferred 219, 224
conditions required 213
conditions tolerated 213, 219, 225
conservation 224
in containers 26
outdoors 217, *217*, 228, 231
for successional interest 229
under cover 218
in cottage garden 214
crop rotation, for disease control 548
for cut flowers 218, *218*, 219
cutting down 230, *230*
deadheading 230, *230*
definition 214
designing with 213–19
diseases 231, 232, 552, 554, 560, 562, 569, 571
dormant, in frames 210
drainage for 225
dry 224
for dry shade 219
drying 231, *231*, 232
dwarf, care 231
early season 213
effect of temperature on 556, 570
for exposed sites 219
for fall color 25
fall-flowering 215, *216*
planting time 224
feeding 230, 231, 232
as fillers 26, 173
forcing 213, 219, 228–9, *229*, 232, 427
planting out after 232
temperature for 229
in formal bedding 30, 214, *214*
in frames, care 231
in grass 230, *230*
in greenhouse 430
group planting 213
growing with succulents 259
hydroculture 447
in layer planting 23, 26
lifting 213, 231, *231*
mineral deficiency 556–7
miniature
alpines with 190
habitats 185
in mixed borders 136, 139, *213*, 214–15, *215*
in mixed island bed *136*
for moist shade 219
naturalizing 216–17, *216*, *217*, 227
in grass 272
ground cover with 150
planting 226–7, *226*, *227*
nonscaly (tunicate) *542*, 590
origins 213, 224
pests 232, 566, 569, 572
damaging leaves 550, 551, 552, 553, 554, 557
photosynthesis 230
planter's guide 219
planting 224–9
depth *225*
in grass 226–7, *226*, *227*
in layers *225*
in open 225, *225*
in pots 228, *228*
time for 225

Bulbs (*cont.*)
pot-grown 224
choosing pots for 228
planting 225, 228, *228*
in plunge bed *228*, *229*
plunging after flowering *210*
renewing soil mix 232
soil mix for 228
under cover 228, 232
problems 232, 559, 569
propagation 233–8, 542, *542*
basal cuttings 238
bulbils 233, 542, *542*
bulblets 233, 542, *542*
chipping 237, *237*, 542, *542*
cutting into sections 237–8, *237*
cutting up, with growing points 237, *237*
division 231, *231*, 233, *233*, *234*
offsets 231, 233, *233*, 542, *542*
scaling 233, 236–7, *236*, 542, *542*
scooping 233, 238, *238*, 542
scoring 238, *238*, 542, *542*
sectioning 236, *236*
from seed 233, 234–5, *234–5*
simple cutting 238
twin-scaling *236*, 237, 542, *542*
in raised beds, under cover 231
removing dead leaves 230
replanting, after division 231
repotting 232, *232*
in rock garden 186, 219
routine care 230–32
scaly *542*
scented 217
seasons of interest 213
seed
collecting 234
germination 235
harvesting 230, *230*
storing 234
seedlings 234, *235*
shy-flowering 232
sites 213
soil mixes for 228, 536
soil preparation 224–5
soil types preferred 224
soil types tolerated 225
spacing 225
with specimen trees 216
spring-flowering 25, 214
staking 230, *230*
storage rots 569, *569*
storing 230, 231, *231*
structure *580*
suggestions for use 140, 213–19
summer-flowering 25, 215
planting out 521
tender, from seed 235
tunicate, see nonscaly
types 214, *214*, *542*
under cover 218–19, 231
underplanting roses 117
for water gardens 217
watering 230, 232
in woodland 140
care 230
planting out *235*
from seed 234
soil for 225
Bull bay, see *Magnolia grandiflora*
Bullaces 383–6
Bunchberry, see *Cornus canadensis*
Buphthalmum, division 163
Bupleurum
semiripe cuttings with heel 83
fruticosum, conditions tolerated 66
Burlap, protecting plants with 363, *520*, 521
Burnet rose, see *Rosa pimpinellifolia*

Bush, definition 585
Bush basil, see *Ocimum basilicum* var. *minimum*
Bush fruits, see Fruit, soft
Butcher's broom, see *Ruscus aculeatus*
Butomus
soil type tolerated 146
umbellatus
propagation
bulbils 256
division of rootstock 256
in water garden 243
Butter beans, see Beans, Lima
Buttercup, see *Ranunculus*
creeping, see *Ranunculus repens*
Butterflies
common blue 150
wildflowers for *167*
Butterfly bush, see *Buddleia davidii*
Butterfly flower, see *Schizanthus*
Butterfly weed, see *Asclepias tuberosa*
Buttermilk, painting hypertufa with 198
Button fern, see *Pellaea*
Butyl rubber
as pond liner 246
repairing 254, *254*
Buxus
with ferns *159*
hardwood cuttings 84
hedge
in parterre *31*
for rosebeds 116
in knots and parterres 172
pests 553, 557
pruning 78
soil type tolerated 69
suggestions for use 31, 289
sempervirens 90
conditions preferred 66
in container 26
dwarf conifers with 38, *38*
as edging 288
as hedge 58
in framed planting *21*
in garden design *19*
propagation, division of suckers 88
suggestions for use 31
for topiary 90
clipping 91
creating design *90*
'Suffruticosa', as hedge 58
Byturus rubi, see Raspberry fruitworms

C

Cabbage caterpillars 548, 551, *551*
Cabbage family, soil for 301
Cabbage root maggots 310, 313, 566
Cabbages 315–16, *315–16*
Chinese, see Chinese cabbages
colors 315
in cottage garden 27
in crop rotation 304
culinary uses 315
cultivation 315–16
diseases 316, 555, 567
fall *315*
harvesting 316, *316*

Cabbages (*cont.*)
nitrogen requirement 310, 315
ornamental *25*, *310*
architectural plant 173
foliage 171
pests 316, 551, 566
recommended cultivars 315
red, storing *312*
red summer *315*
Savoy *313*, *315*
spring 315–16, *315–16*
storing 316, *316*
transplanting seedlings 306
in vegetable garden *300*
in windowbox *303*
winter *313*
winter storing 312
'Cherry Sundae', architectural plant 175
'Golden Cross' *315*
'Gourmet' *315*
'January King 327' *315*
'Spivoy' *315*
Cabomba caroliniana
softwood cuttings 256
suggestions for use 243
Cacti 258–71, 585
adapted to drought 517
characteristics 258
choosing healthy plants 263, *263*
climate suited to 514
conditions required 259, 261, 265, 436, 484
conditions tolerated 258, 259
in containers 260, 262
indoors 261
outdoors 260
planting 264, *264*
cross-pollination 267, *267*
day-flowering 262
in desert gardens 260, *260*
diseases 265
disorders 554
distinguishing from other succulents 258
dwarf, in containers outdoors 260
dying after flowering 259
environment 265
epiphytic 258
conditions required 261
flowers 259
feeding 265
flowering 259, 262
flowers 258
forms 258–9, *258*
in greenhouse display *430*
habit 258–9
habitats 258
half-hardy, conditions required 259
handling 261, *263*
in hanging baskets 261, 262
hybridizing 267, *267*
hydroculture 447
hygiene 265
indoor display 260–61
light requirement 261
night-flowering 262
outdoor display 259–60
pests 265, 552, 554, 559
planting
in desert garden 263
in raised bed 263, *263*
pots for 264
pricking out 266, *266*
propagation 266–71
division 266
of offsets 269, *269*
of rootstock 270, *270*
grafting 266, 270–71, *270–71*
apical-wedge *270*, 271
flat 271, *271*
side 271, *271*
varieties suitable for 271
leaf cuttings 266, 267, *267*
pad sections *268*
from seed 266–7, *266*
stem cuttings 266, 268, *268*
stem sections 268, *268*
purpose of swollen stems 581
repotting 265

Cacti (*cont.*)
routine care 265
seedlings, pricking out 266, *266*
shading 265
shapes 258
soil mixes for 263, 264, 535
spines 581
succulent type 258
suggestions for use 258–61
temperatures for 265
for troughs 262
ventilation 265
water-storage 258
watering 265
Caesalpina pulcherrima, germination 452
Caladium, conditions preferred 431
Calamondin orange, see x *Citrofortunella microcarpa*
Calanthe, suggestions for use 218
Calathea
conditions preferred 431
conditions required 431
division of rootstock 451, *451*
foliage 426
Calceolaria
germination 538
greenhouse conditions required 431
Bikini Series, in hot border *139*
integrifolia, stem tip cuttings 164
pavonii 97
'Sunshine', in conservatory *429*
'Walter Shrimpton'
in alpine raised bed *201*
in peat bed *188*
Calcicoles, see Lime lovers
Calcifuges, see Lime haters
Calcium 545
deficiency 564, *564*
plant requirements 532
in soil 525
Calcium carbonate 533
in cuttings soil mix 536
Calcium chloride 564
Calcium hydroxide 533
Calcium nitrate 536
Calcium oxide 533
Calendula
conditions tolerated 175
in containers *174*
for cutting 175
for drying 175
in formal bedding *172*
in mixed border *172*
pests 563
self-sown 184
sowing 176
suggestions for use 27
officinalis 291
companion plants 288
cosmetic uses 287
culinary uses 287, 291
flowers 288, 291
harvesting 291
in herb garden *295*
in potpourri 291
propagation
from seed 291, 297
self-seeding 178
soil type preferred 176
soil type tolerated 176
storing 291
suggestions for use 291
variants 291
'Orange King', in annual border *171*
Calico flower, see *Aristolochia elegans*
California bluebell, see *Phacelia campanularia*
California sweet shrub, see *Calycanthus occidentalis*
Californian pepper-tree, see *Schinus molle*

- Californian poppy, see *Eschscholzia californica*; *Romneya*
- *Caliroa cerasii* 553
- Calla lily, see *Zantedeschia*
- *Calla palustris* *243*
  - division of rootstock 256
  - in water garden 243
- *Callianthemum anemonoides*, suggestions for use 191
- *Callisia*
  - softwood cuttings 453
  - suggestions for use 438
- *Callistemon*
  - conditions required 431
  - semiripe cuttings with heel 83
  - suggestions for use 66
  - *citrinus* 'Splendens' *429*
- *Callistephus*
  - for cutting 175
  - diseases 560, 567, 568, 571
  - *chinensis*, soil type tolerated 176
- *Callitriche hermaphroditica* (syn. *C. autumnalis*) 243
  - softwood cuttings 256
- *Calluna*
  - clematis growing through 106
  - dwarf conifers with 38
  - as ground cover 64
  - propagation
    - dropping 86
    - softwood cuttings 81
  - pruning 77
  - soil type required 69
  - suggestions for use 64
  - *vulgaris*
    - conditions tolerated 66
    - soil type preferred 67
- Callus, definition 585
- Callus pads *540*
- *Calocedrus*, semiripe cuttings 53
- *Calochone* 97
- *Calochortus*
  - propagation, bulbils 233
  - suggestions for use 218, 219
  - *tolmei*, seedlings *235*
- *Caltha*
  - conditions tolerated 17, 242
  - soil type tolerated 146
  - *leptosepala*, in water garden 243
  - *palustris* *167*
    - choosing healthy plants *251*
    - division of rootstock *256*
    - planting *252*
    - suggestions for use 243
    - in water garden 243
    - 'Alba', in water garden 243
    - 'Flore Pleno' *256*
      - in water garden 243
- *Calycanthus*
  - pruning 76
  - scent 66
  - *occidentalis*, seasonal interest 66
- *Calystegia sepium*, see Bindweed, hedge
- Calyx, definition 585
- *Camassia*
  - for cutting 219
  - forcing 228
  - suggestions for use 216, 227
  - *leichtlinii* 'Alba', in mixed border 215
- Cambium 540, *543*, 582, 585
  - activity of, in grafting 543
  - joining layers in grafting 89, *89*
  - matching layers in chip-budding *57*
  - revealing *111*, *368*, *541*
- *Camellia*
  - conditions required 431
  - in containers 65
  - effect of drought on 563, 570
  - flower forms, anemone-centered 585
  - germination 85
  - overwintering 72
  - pests 551
- *Camellia* (*cont.*)
  - physiological disorders 557
  - propagation
    - leaf-bud cuttings 83, *540*
    - semiripe cuttings 83, 540
  - pruning 78
  - soil mix for 436
  - soil type required 69
  - suggestions for use 66
  - *japonica*
    - conditions preferred 66
    - conditions tolerated 66
    - in conservatory *429*
    - leaf form *581*
    - leaf-bud cuttings *83*
    - 'Mathotiana', as specimen 63
  - *reticulata*, side-veneer grafting 89
  - *sasanqua*
    - scent 66
    - side-veneer grafting 89
  - x *williamsii*
    - 'Donation' *62*
    - 'Wilber Foss' *69*
- *Campanula*
  - in free planting *21*
  - germination 160
  - planting in crevice *197*
  - propagation
    - division 163
    - root cuttings 165
    - from seed *452*
    - softwood cuttings 206
  - with roses *117*
  - soil type tolerated 193
  - 'Birch Hybrid', in dry-stone wall *189*
  - *carpatica*, division 208
  - *cochleariifolia*
    - propagation
      - division 208
      - self-seeding 188
    - in rock garden 187, *187*
    - suggestions for use 191
  - *garganica*, conditions tolerated 191
  - *isophylla*
    - conditions preferred 431
    - in conservatory *429*
  - *lactiflora*
    - growth rate 141
    - soil type tolerated 147
    - 'Prichard's Variety', in mixed border *215*
  - *medium*
    - first-year growth *180*
    - sowing 177
  - *pilosa*, removing dead leaves *212*
  - *piperi*, suggestions for use 191
  - *portenschlagiana*
    - conditions tolerated 191
    - suggestions for use 191
  - *poscharskyana*, conditions tolerated 191
  - *pyramidalis*, as pot plants 175
  - *raineri*, suggestions for use 191
  - *zoysii*
    - pests 204
    - suggestions for use 190, 191
- Campion, see *Silene*
- *Campsis*
  - propagation
    - semiripe cuttings 110
    - serpentine layering 113
    - simple layering 113
  - pruning 103
  - soil type tolerated 99
  - *radicans*
    - conditions tolerated 97
    - flowers 95
    - as weed 576
  - x *tagliabuana*
    - pruning 105
    - 'Mme. Galen', soil type tolerated 100
- Canada thistle *576*
  - control 276
- Canada wild rice, see *Zizania aquatica*
- Canadian poplar, see *Populus* x *canadensis*
- Canary creeper, see *Tropaeolum peregrinum*
- Canary Island date palm, see *Phoenix canariensis*
- Candelabra primrose, see *Primula*, Candelabra Group
- Candle plant, see *Senecio articulatus*
- Candytuft, see *Iberis*
- Cane blight 559
- Cane borer 559
- Cane fruits, see Fruit, soft
- Canker *366*, 555
  - bacterial
    - control 384, 571
    - plants affected by 362
    - symptoms 571
  - causes 366
  - *Coryneum* 570, *570*
  - *Cytospora* 560, *560*
  - *Nectria* 362, 364, 570, *570*
  - parsnip 567
- *Canna*
  - architectural plant 219
  - overwintering 218
  - *indica*, in hot border *139*
- Canoe birch, see *Betula papyrifera*
- Canola seed 563
  - genetic engineering 546
- Cantaloupes, see Melons, cantaloupes
- Canterbury bells, see *Campanula medium*
- *Cantua*, semiripe cuttings with heel 83
- Cap blocks 506
- Capa de oro, see *Solandra maxima*
- Cape Cod weeder *203*, 461, *461*
- Cape grape, see *Rhoicissus capensis*
- Cape hyacinth, see *Galtonia*
- Cape jasmine, see *Gardenia jasminoides*
- Cape leadwort, see *Plumbago auriculata*
- Cape marigold, see *Dimorphotheca*
- Cape pondweed, see *Aponogeton distachyos*
- Capillary action, movement of water in soil by 530
- Capillary matting 446, *446*, 485, *485*, 585
- Capillary pores 530
- Capillary watering 446, *446*, 485, *485*
- Cappadocia n maple, see *Acer cappadocicum*
- Capping 529, *529*, 585
- *Capsella bursa-pastoris*, see Shepherd's purse
- *Capsicum*
  - conditions preferred 431
  - diseases 568
  - ornamental, as pot plants 175
  - *annuum*
    - Grossum Group, see Peppers, sweet
    - Longum Group, see Peppers, chili
  - *frutescens*, see Peppers, hot
- Capsicums, see Peppers, sweet
- Capsules 581, 585
- Captan 545, 552, 555, 559, 562, 566, 569, 570
  - commercial names 574
- *Caragana*
  - apical-wedge grafting 89
  - germination 85
  - pruning 74
  - *arborescens*
    - side-veneer grafting 89
    - 'Walker', apical-wedge grafting 89
- *Caralluma*
  - division of offsets 269
  - division of rootstock 270
  - stem cuttings 268
  - *europaea*, conditions tolerated 262
- Caraway *291*
  - culinary uses 291
  - flowers 291
  - foliage 291
  - harvesting 291
  - propagation, from seed 291, 297
  - storing 291
  - thinning out seedlings 297
- Carbaryl 550, 551, 552, 553, 554, 558, 560, 563, 564, 565, 572, 573, 574
  - commercial names 574
- Carbohydrates 581, *581*
- Carbon dioxide, converting into carbohydrates 581, *581*
- *Cardamine*
  - *hirsuta*, see Hairy bittercress
  - *pratensis*
    - soil type tolerated 146
    - suggestions for use 243
- Cardamon, suggestions for use 288
- Cardinal flower, see *Lobelia cardinalis*
- *Cardiocrinum*
  - conditions preferred 219
  - dying after flowering 234
  - from seed 234
  - *giganteum*, architectural plant 219
- Cardoon, see *Cynara cardunculus*
- *Carduncellus rhaponticoides*, root cuttings 208
- *Carex*
  - suggestions for use 152
  - *acuta*, conditions required 142
  - *elata*
    - 'Aurea'
      - suggestions for use 142
      - in water garden 243
    - 'Bowles' Golden', in cottage garden *140*
  - *oshimensis* 'Evergold', suggestions for use 142
  - *pendula*, in water garden 243
  - *riparia*
    - conditions required 142
    - in water garden 243
- *Carica papaya*, see Papayas
- *Carlina acaulis*, conditions tolerated 191
- *Carmichaelia*, semiripe cuttings with heel 83
- Carolina yellow jessamine, see *Gelsemium sempervirens*
- Carnation, see *Dianthus*
- Carpel 582, 585
- *Carpenteria*
  - layering 86
  - semiripe cuttings with heel 83
  - *californica* *65*
- Carpet bedding, definition 585
- Carpet grass, see *Axonopus*
- Carpeting plants
  - herbs 288
  - in rock garden 22
- *Carpinus*
  - diseases 561
  - as hedge
    - renovation 60
    - shaping *60*
  - pleaching 36, 51
  - side-veneer grafting 56
  - *betulus*
    - conditions tolerated 37
    - as hedge 58, 59
    - soil type tolerated 41
    - 'Fastigiata' *33*
- *Carpobrotus*
  - division of rootstock 270
  - *acinaciformis*, conditions tolerated 262
  - *edulis* 259
    - conditions tolerated 262
- Carrot rust flies 310, 350, 566, *566*
  - larvae 567
  - protection against 350, *350*
- Carrots *310*, *348*, 350, *350*
  - in crop rotation 304
- Carrots (*cont.*)
  - culinary uses 350
  - cultivation 350, *350*
  - diseases 350, 567
  - harvesting 312, 350, *350*
  - mineral deficiencies 568
  - nitrogen requirement 310, 350
  - pests 350, 566
  - protecting from carrot rust flies 350, *350*
  - recommended cultivars 350
  - roots 580, *580*
  - rotation 350
  - sowing 350, *350*
    - in wide drills 306
  - storing 312, 350, *350*
  - in vegetable garden *300*
  - watering 308, 350
  - weeding 350
  - 'Danver's Half Long' *350*
  - 'Earlibird Nantes' *350*
  - 'Thumbelina' *350*
- *Carruanthus*, division of offsets 269
- Carrying bag 470, *470*
- Carrying sheet 470, *470*
- Carts, garden 470, *470*
- Cartwheel bed, herbs in *288*, 289
- *Carum carvi*, see Caraway
- *Carya*
  - conditions tolerated 37
  - seed germination 55
  - *illinoensis*, see Pecans
- *Caryopteris*
  - scent 66
  - softwood cuttings 81
  - x *clandonensis*
    - pruning 74
    - with roses 117
    - 'Arthur Simmonds', in shrub border *63*
- Casaba melons, see Melons, winter
- *Cassinia*
  - semiripe cuttings with heel 83
  - *fulvida*, conditions tolerated 66
- *Cassiope*
  - conditions preferred *191*
  - propagation
    - greenwood cuttings 206
    - layering 86
    - semiripe cuttings 206
    - semiripe cuttings with heel 83
    - softwood cuttings 206
  - soil type required 188, 192
  - 'Edinburgh', in peat bed *188*
  - *hypnoides*, division of suckers 88
  - *lycopodioides*, in peat bed *188*
- *Castanea*, see also Chestnuts
  - fruit type 581, *581*
  - soil preferred 42
- *Castanospermum australe*, soil type tolerated 42
- Castor bean plant, see *Ricinus communis*
- *Catalpa*
  - propagation
    - apical-wedge grafting 56
    - softwood cuttings 53
  - *bignonioides* 35
    - conditions tolerated 37
    - seasonal interest 37
    - 'Aurea', suggestions for use 37
- *Catananche*
  - for drying 141
  - flowering time from seed 160
  - soil type tolerated 147
  - *caerulea*
    - root cuttings 165
    - 'Major' *165*
- Catchfly, see *Silene*
- Caterpillars
  - armyworms 572
  - biological control 548
  - cabbage 548, 551, *551*

(*entry cont. overleaf*)

- Caterpillars (*cont.*)
  - control 310, 549, 551
  - cutworms 566
  - damage done by 551
  - gypsy moth 551, *551*
  - tent 553, *553*
- *Catharanthus*
  - conditions required 431
  - growing with succulents 259
  - softwood cuttings 453
  - *roseus*
    - conditions tolerated 175
    - as ground cover 173
    - propagation 176
- Catkin, definition 585
- Catmint, see *Nepeta*
- *Catopsis*, displaying 432
- Cats
  - control 573
  - damage to lawn *573*
- Cat's claw, see *Macfadyena unguis-cati*
- Cat's ears, see *Antennaria*; *Calochortus*
- Cattail, see *Typha*
- *Cattleya*
  - method of growth 440
  - propagation by division 443
  - temperature required 441
  - *bowringiana 440*
- Caudex 258
- Cauliflowers *313*, 314
  - in crop rotation 304
  - cultivation 314
  - curds failing to grow 310
  - harvesting 314
  - mineral deficiencies 310, 558
  - nitrogen requirement 310, 314
  - pests 314, 551, 563, 566
  - protecting curds 314, *314*
  - recommended cultivars 314
  - storing 312, 314
  - summer, in vegetable garden *300*
  - types 314
  - 'White Sails' *314*
- Cayenne peppers, see Peppers, hot
- *Ceanothus*
  - flowers 65
  - propagation
    - semiripe cuttings with heel 83
    - softwood cuttings 81
  - pruning 75, *79*
  - suggestions for use 66
  - training 78
    - as wall shrub 78
  - 'Autumnal Blue', pruning 74
  - 'Gloire de Versailles', pruning 74
  - *impressus*, soil type tolerated 69
  - *thyrsiflorus*, soil type preferred 67
- Cedar, see *Cedrus*
  - Japanese, see *Cryptomeria japonica*
  - of Lebanon, see *Cedrus libani*
- *Cedrela sinensis*, see *Toona sinensis*
- *Cedrus*
  - extracting seed 54
  - shape 33
  - side-veneer grafting 56
  - suggestions for use 37
  - *atlantica glauca*, seasonal interest 37
  - *libani*, soil type tolerated 41
- Celandine, lesser, see *Ranunculus ficaria*
- *Celastrus*
  - obtaining seed from 109
  - propagation
    - root cuttings 109, 112
    - self layering 113
    - semiripe cuttings 110
    - serpentine layering 113
  - suggestions for use 94, 97
  - for winter interest 94
  - *orbiculatus*
    - fruit 95
    - renovating *105*
- *Celastrus orbiculatus* (*cont.*)
    - root cuttings *112*
  - *scandens*, soil types tolerated 99, 100
- Celeriac 341, 345, *345*
  - in crop rotation 304
  - culinary uses 345
  - cultivation 345, *345*
  - harvesting 345
  - nitrogen requirement 310
  - pests 566
  - recommended cultivars 345
  - storing 345
  - in vegetable garden *300*
  - 'Brilliant' *345*
- Celery *341*, 344, *344*
  - American green 344
  - blanching 344, *344*
  - in crop rotation 304
  - culinary uses 344
  - cultivation 344, *344*
  - diseases 344
  - harvesting 344
  - lifting *344*
  - mineral deficiency 560
  - nitrogen requirement 310, 344
  - pests 344, 566
  - recommended cultivars 344
  - self-blanching 344
    - in vegetable garden *300*
  - storing 312, 344
  - trench 344
  - 'Tall Utah' *344*
- Celery fly 344
- Cell packs 473, *473*, 585
  - sowing vegetables in 307, *307*
  - types 307
- *Celmisia*
  - sowing 205
  - *coriacea*
    - in rock garden 187
    - in peat bed *188*
  - *walkeri*, in rock garden *187*
- *Celosia*
  - for drying 175
  - flowering shoots 181
  - *cristata*, flowers 171
- *Celtis*
  - conditions tolerated 37
  - *australis*, soil preferred 42
  - *occidentalis*, softwood cuttings 53
- Cement, types of 499
- *Centaurea*
  - for cutting 141
  - flowering time from seed 160
  - staking *156*
  - *cyanus*
    - in annual border *171*
    - conditions tolerated 175
    - for cutting 174, 175
    - for drying 175
    - in mixed border *172*
    - self-seeding 178
    - soil type preferred 176
    - sowing 177
  - *dealbata*
    - conditions tolerated 141
    - dividing 163
  - *hypoleuca*, conditions tolerated 141
  - *macrocephala*, growth rate 141
  - *moschata*
    - for fragrance 175
    - as pot plants 175
    - sowing 177
  - *pindicola*, root cuttings 208
- Centipede grass, see *Eremochloa ophiuroides*
- Centipedes *525*
  - benefits of 549
  - distinguishing from millipedes 549, 550
  - types *549*
- *Centradenia*, pinching out 450
- *Centranthus*
  - soil type tolerated 147
  - *ruber*
    - conditions tolerated 141
    - for fragrance 141
    - soil type preferred 146
- Century plant, see *Agave americana*
- *Cephalanthus occidentalis*, suggestions for use 243
- *Cephalaria*
  - for cutting 141
  - *gigantea*, growth rate 141
- *Cephalocereus*
  - in bowl garden 261
  - stem cuttings 268
  - *senilis*
    - in desert garden 260
    - suggestions for use 262
- Ceramic tiles, see Tiles, glazed ceramic
- *Cerastium*
  - *fontanum*, see Common mouse-ear chickweed
  - *tomentosum*, as weed *575*
- *Ceratitis* 565
  - *capitata* 565
- *Ceratocystis*
  - *fagacearum* 571
  - *ulmi* 560
- *Ceratophyllum demersum*
  - softwood cuttings 256
  - in water garden 243
- *Ceratopteris*
  - *cornuta*, propagation by plantlets 257
  - *pteroides* 243
  - *thalictroides* 243
- *Ceratostigma*
  - softwood cuttings 81
  - *plumbaginoides*, division of suckers 88
  - *willmottianum*
    - pruning 74
    - in shrub border *63*
- *Cercidiphyllum*
  - layering 55
  - *japonicum*
    - soil preferred 41
    - suggestions for use 37
- *Cercis*
  - apical-wedge grafting 56
  - suggestions for use 32
  - *canadensis* 'Forest Pansy' 34
  - *siliquastrum* 35
    - soil type preferred 42
    - soil type tolerated 41
    - suggestions for use 37
- *Cereus*
  - stem cuttings 268
  - *chalybaeus*, conditions tolerated 262
  - *forbesii*, suggestions for use 262
  - *jamacaru*, conditions tolerated 262
  - *peruvianus*
    - in bowl *264*
    - suggestions for use 262
- *Ceropegia*
  - propagation
    - offsets 269
    - softwood cuttings 110
    - stem cuttings 268
  - as rootstock 271
  - soil type tolerated 99
  - *haygarthii*, suggestions for use 262
  - *sandersonii*, climbing method 92
  - *woodii*
    - in conservatory *429*
    - form 259
    - propagation, division of offsets *269*
    - suggestions for use 262
- Certified stock, definition 585
- *Cestrum*
  - conditions required 431
  - softwood cuttings 81
  - suggestions for use 66
  - *elegans*
    - repotting *71*
    - training 79
    - as wall shrub 78
- *Ceterach officinarum*, in rock crevice *158*
- Ceylon spinach, see Malabar spinach
- *Chaenomeles*
  - layering 86
  - pests, damaging leaves 553
  - pruning 76
  - suggestions for use 66
  - as wall shrub 64
  - *japonica*, form 61
  - *speciosa*, as hedge 59
  - x *superba*
    - soil type tolerated 67
    - 'Nicoline' *67*
- Chafer bugs *566*
  - symptoms and control 566
- Chain link fences 508, *508*
- Chain saws 464, *464*
  - safety 458
- *Chamaecyparis*
  - semiripe cuttings 53
  - *lawsoniana*
    - diseases 560, 567, 571
    - as hedge 58
    - soil type tolerated 41
    - 'Lanei' 37
    - 'Stewartii' 37
  - *obtusa*
    - 'Intermedia' 191
    - 'Nana Aurea' *38*
      - leaf form *581*
      - semiripe cuttings *53*
    - 'Nana Pyramidalis'
      - in rock garden 187
      - suggestions for use 190
  - *pisifera* 'Filifera Aurea' *25*
- *Chamaedorea*
  - conditions preferred 431
  - conditions required 431
  - conditions tolerated 427
  - hydroculture 431
  - pruning 78
  - suggestions for use 37
  - *elegans*
    - hydroculture *447*
    - suggestions for use 438
- *Chamaemelum nobile*
  - benefit to other plants 288
  - cosmetic uses 287
  - culinary uses 291
  - foliage 291
  - harvesting 291
  - in herb garden *295*
  - for lawn 272, 275
  - in potpourri 291
  - propagation
    - cuttings of sideshoots 291
    - division 291
  - scent 275, 287
  - storing 291
  - suggestions for use 291
  - var. *flore-pleno* 291
  - 'Treneague' 275, 291
    - propagation
      - cuttings of sideshoots 297
      - division 297
    - suggestions for use 288
- *Chamaerops*
  - architectural plant 66
  - soil type tolerated 69
  - *humilis*, in container 65
- Chamomile, see *Chamaemelum nobile*
- Charcoal *266*, 438, *440*
- *Cheiranthus*
  - attracting insects 135
  - with bulbs in formal bedding 214
  - clearing at end of season 184
  - conditions required 431
  - conditions tolerated 175
  - diseases 555, 567
  - as fillers 173
  - pests 550
  - seasonal display 171
  - suggestions for use 27
  - *cheiri*
    - for cutting 175
    - soil type tolerated 176
- *Chelone glabra*, conditions tolerated 167
- Chemical inhibitors, use after pruning 366
- Chemicals
  - adverse reactions to 549
- Chemicals (*cont.*)
  - classification 549
  - clearing overgrown site with 526, *526*
  - for disease control 549
  - formulation of preparations 549
  - fungicide damage 556
  - insecticide damage 556
  - for pest control 549
  - safety in use 549
  - for soil sterilization 527
  - storage 549
  - types available 574
  - weedkillers
    - damage caused 556
    - lawn 579
    - range 577
- *Chenopodium album*, see Lamb's-quarters
- Cherries 391–4, for ornamental varieties, see *Prunus*
  - bird damage 563
  - bottling 367
  - diseases 392, 393, 554, 561, 562, 571
  - Duke 391
    - rootstocks 393
  - fans, space required 358
  - fruit type 355, 371, 581
  - harvesting 367
  - pests 392, 393, 565
  - seed collection 537
  - sour 393–4
    - bush, pruning 394, *394*
    - cultivation 393–4
    - fan, pruning 393, *393*
    - freezing 367
    - fruiting habit 393
    - harvesting 394, *394*
    - propagation 394
    - protecting from birds 393
    - pruning 365, 393, *393*, 394, *394*
    - recommended cultivars 393
    - rootstocks *393*
    - self-fertile cultivars 393
    - training 393
    - 'Meteor'
      - in large fruit garden *357*
      - in small fruit garden *358*
    - 'Montmorency' *393*
  - sweet 391–2
    - cross-pollination 358, 360
    - cultivation 391–2
    - dwarfing 392
    - fan 392, *392*
    - feathered maiden, training as fan 392
    - freezing 367
    - harvesting 392
    - planting 392
    - pollination 392
      - compatibility 359
    - protecting from birds 392
    - pruning 365, 392, *392*
    - recommended cultivars 392
    - rootstocks 392, *392*
    - routine care 392
    - self-sterile 357, 360
    - siting 357, 391–2
    - size of trees 391
    - storing 392
    - 'Stella' *392*
      - in large fruit garden *357*
      - in small fruit garden *358*
  - 'Camil', as rootstock 392
  - 'Colt', as rootstock 392, *392*, 393, *393*
  - 'Inmil', as rootstock 392
  - 'Malling F12/1', as rootstock 392, *392*
- Cherry laurel, see *Prunus laurocerasus*
- Cherry plums, see Plums, cherry
- Cherry slugworm 553, *553*
- Chervil 290, *290*
  - conditions tolerated 288
  - culinary uses 290
  - foliage 290

(*entry cont.*)

Chervil (*cont.*)
  harvesting 290
  in herb garden *295*
  propagation from seed 290, 297
  protecting for winter use 294
  storing 290
  suggestions for use 288
Chestnut leaf blight 558
Chestnut vine, see *Tetrastigma voinierianum*
Chestnuts 424, *424*
  conditions required 424
  cultivation 424
  fruit type 581, *581*
  harvesting *424*
  propagation from seed 370
  storing 424
  tree size 424
Chewing's fescue, see *Festuca rubra* var. *commutata*
Chiastophyllum oppositifolium
  conditions tolerated 191
  division 208
  in rock garden *187*
Chicken wire *472*
Chickweed 575, *575*
  common mouse-ear, see Common mouse-ear chickweed
Chicons 323, *323*
Chicory 323–4
  nitrogen requirement 310, 323
  red, see Radicchio
  sugar loaf *324*
    cultivation 324
    as cut-and-come-again crop 312
    form 324
    harvesting 324
    recommended cultivars 323
    storing 324
  'Cesare' *323*
Children
  safety during chemical use 549
  water in garden for 240, 241
Chilean bellflower, see *Lapageria rosea*
Chilean firebush, see *Embothrium coccineum*
Chilean glory flower, see *Eccremocarpus scaber*
Chili peppers, see Peppers, chili
Chilling requirement, definition 585
Chimney bellflower, see *Campanula pyramidalis*
Chimonanthus, pruning 74
China, garden design 30
China aster, see *Callistephus chinensis*
Chinch bugs 573, *573*
Chinese broccoli 319, *319*
  in crop rotation 304
  cultivation 319
  harvesting 319
  nitrogen requirement 310
Chinese cabbages *319*, 320
  colors 320
  in crop rotation 304
  culinary uses 320
  cultivation 320
  harvesting 320, *320*
  loose-leaved *319*
  nitrogen requirement 310
  recommended cultivars 320
  tight-headed *319*
  'Jade Pagoda' *320*
Chinese chives 290
  in herb garden *295*
Chinese dogwood, see *Cornus kousa*
Chinese elm, see *Ulmus parvifolia*
Chinese evergreen, see *Aglaonema*
Chinese fringe tree, see *Chionanthus retusus*
Chinese gooseberries, see Kiwi fruits
Chinese hat 134, *134*
Chinese juniper, see *Juniperus chinensis*
Chinese kale, see Chinese broccoli
Chinese lanterns, see *Physalis alkekengi*
Chinese layering, see Air layering
Chinese privet, see *Ligustrum lucidum*
Chinese spinach, see *Amaranthus tricolor*
Chinese thuja, see *Thuja orientalis*
Chinese wisteria, see *Wisteria sinensis*
Chinese witch hazel, see *Hamamelis mollis*
Chionanthus
  layering 86
  retusus, layering 55
Chionodoxa 117
  conditions tolerated 219
  forcing 228
  in mixed border 214
  suggestions for use 216, 227
  forbesii, in mixed island bed *136*
Chip-budding 57, *57*
  fruit trees 368, *368*
  method 544, *544*
  time for 543
  trees suitable for 56
Chipping
  bulbs suitable for 237
  propagation by 237, *237*, 542, *542*
Chisels, bolster 496, *496*
Chives *290*
  conditions tolerated 288
  culinary uses 287, 290
  as edging 303, *303*
  flowers 290
    use 296
  forcing 294, *294*
  freezing in ice *298*
  growing indoors 427
  harvesting 290, 298
  in herb garden *295*
  propagation
    division 290
    from seed 290
  related species 290
  storing 290
  suggestions for use 288, 290, 303
  variants 290
  in vegetable garden 303, *303*
Chloride salts, sensitivity to 532
Chlorine, plant requirements 532
Chlorophyll 581, *581*, 585
Chlorophytum
  conditions preferred 431
  conditions required 431
  conditions tolerated 427
  division of plantlets/runners 451
  comosum (syn. *C. capense* of gardens), in conservatory *429*
Chlorosis 360
  causes 380
  interveinal 557
  lime-induced 387, 408
Chlorpyrifos 553, 554, 561, 562, 566, 568, 569
  commercial names 574
Chlorthal dimethyl 579
  commercial names 574
Chocolate cosmos, see *Cosmos atrosanguineus*
Chocolate spot *555*
  symptoms and control 555
Choisya
  semiripe cuttings 82
  'Aztec Pearl', scent 66
  ternata
    callus on stem cutting *540*
    pruning 78
    scent 66
    soil type tolerated 69
Chokeberry, see *Aronia*
Christmas box, see *Sarcococca*
Christmas cactus, see *Schlumbergera bridgesii*
Christmas rose, see *Helleborus*
Chromosomes 132
Chrysanthemum
  classification 154
  conditions required 154
  for cutting 175
  disbudding 154, *154*
  disbuds 154
  diseases 561
  early-flowering 154
  in fall 139
  florets, forms *154*
  flowerhead shapes 154, *154*
    anemone-centered 585
    incurved *154*
    intermediate *154*, 587
    pompon *154*
    reflexed *154*
    single *154*
    spoon *154*
  in greenhouse 430
    conditions required 154, 431
  as house plant 427
  late-flowering 154
  mineral deficiency 557
  mutation *582*
  overwintering 154
  pests 550, 551, 553, 562, 563
  pinching 154, *154*
  potting up 154
  propagation
    basal stem cuttings *154*, 164, *164*
    of plants infected with nematodes 553
  removing excess laterals *154*
  routine care 154
  spray types 154
    creating 154
  'Alison Kirk' *154*
  carinatum
    conditions tolerated 175
    for cutting 175
  coronarium
    conditions tolerated 175
    for cutting 175
  frutescens, see *Argyranthemum frutescens*
  hosmariense
    in dry-stone wall *189*
    soil type tolerated 193
  'Maria' *154*
  'Morning Star' *154*
  morifolium hybrids 154
  nipponicum, see *Nipponanthemum nipponicum*
  parthenium, see *Tanacetum parthenium*
  'Pennine Jewel' *154*
  'Primrose Gem', in annual border *171*
  'Rose Yvonne Arnaud' *154*
  'Rytorch' *154*
  segetum
    conditions tolerated 175
    for cutting 175
    self-seeding 178
    soil preferred 176
  'Skater's Waltz' *154*
Chrysanthemum leaf miner 553
Cichorium
  endivia, see Endive
  intybus, see Chicory
Cider gum, see *Eucalyptus gunnii*
Cime di rapa, see Broccoli raab
Cimicifuga
  americana, suggestions for use 243
  racemosa, suggestions for use 243
Cineraria, see *Senecio*
Cinnamomum
  semiripe cuttings 53
  suggestions for use 37
Cirsium arvense, see Canada thistle
Cissus 97
  conditions preferred 431
  conditions tolerated 97
  hydroculture 431
  propagation
    semiripe cuttings 110
    simple layering 113
    softwood cuttings 453
  pruning 450
  suggestions for use 97
  vigor 98
  antarctica
    conditions tolerated 427
    training indoors 427
  discolor, suggestions for use 438
  rhombifolia, conditions required 431
Cistus
  conditions preferred 62
  conditions tolerated 66
  soil type tolerated 69
  x *cyprius* *67*
    soil type preferred 67
x *Citrofortunella*
  conditions required 431
  microcarpa (syn. *Citrus mitis*) 418
    in conservatory *429*
    in garden room *428*
Citrons
  fruits 417
  peel 417
  stem pitting 417
Citrullus lanatus, see Watermelons
Citrus, for edible varieties, see Citrus fruits; individual fruits by name
  conditions preferred 66
  diseases 555, 564
  fruit 35
  pests 552, 553, 554
  propagation, air layering 87
  pruning 78
  soil type tolerated 67
  aurantiifolia, see Limes
  aurantium, see Oranges, sour (Seville)
  latifolia, see Limes
  limon, see Lemons
  medica, fruit, see Citrons
  'Meyer's Lemon', seasonal interest 66
  mitis, see x *Citrofortunella microcarpa*
  paradisi, see Grapefruits
  reticulata, see Mandarins; Tangerines
  reticulata x *C. paradisi*, see Tangelos; Ugli fruits
  sinensis, see Oranges, sweet
Citrus fruits 416–18, see also individual fruits by name
  bottling 367
  conditions required 356, 416
  in containers 417
    moving under cover 363
  cultivation 416–18
  diseases 417
  flowering 416
  growing under cover 417
  harvesting 417
  on patio 355
  pests 417
  pollination 416
  in pots 359
  preserving peel 367
  propagation
    from seed 417
    T-budding 417
  recommended cultivars 417
  ripening 417
  rootstocks 416
  species 417–18
  storing 417
  uses 415
Cladius isomeris 551
Cladrastis lutea, seasonal interest 37
Clamp 585
  for rutabagas *349*
  storing vegetables in 312
Clams, freshwater, in pond 253
Claret ash, see *Fraxinus oxycarpa* 'Raywood'
Clarkia (syn. *Godetia*)
  conditions tolerated 175
  for drying 175
  in mixed border 173
  sowing 177
  amoena
    self-seeding 178
    soil type preferred 176
Classical gardens 29, *30*
Classification 582
Clavibacter sependonicum 568
Clay, adding to soils 529
Clay pots, see Pots, clay
Clay soil
  building wall footings on 505
  climbers tolerating 99
  drainage, for lawn 276
  effect of frost on 517
  feeding lawn on 282
  foundations for structures on 493
  growing fruit on 360
  identifying 525, *525*
  improving 529
  lime required to alter pH 533
  mineral deficiency in 556
  perennials for 146
  preparing for lawn 276
  shrubs tolerant of 67
  structure 524, *524*
  temperature 515
  water in 530
  water table 530
Claytonia
  as herb, see Miner's lettuce
  semiripe cuttings 206
Cleistocactus
  in bowl garden 261
  stem cuttings 268
  strausii
    in desert garden 260
    form 259
    suggestions for use 262
Clematis 106–8
  as background planting *22*
  climbing method 92, *98*
  combining with other climbers *93*, *95*
  conditions required 107
  conditions suitable for 29
  conditions tolerated 97, 106
  for containers 97, 106
  diseases 107, 562, 571
  diversity of habits 106
  evergreen 106
    conditions required 107
  flowers 92
    color 106
    forms 106
  in garden design *19*
  group 1, early-flowering spp. and cvs 106, 107
    pruning 107, *107*
  group 2, early, large-flowered cvs 106, 108
    pruning 108, *108*
  group 3, late-flowering spp. and cvs 106, 108
    pruning 108, *108*
  groups 106
  growing on host plant 95, 106
    pruning 108
  growing with roses 118
  growing through ground cover, pruning 108
  growth rate 97
  herbaceous
    conditions preferred 107
    dividing 163
  pests 107, 550, 563
  physiological disorders 559
  planting 100, 107, *107*
  propagation 108
    division 163
    internodal cuttings 108, *108*
    layering *539*
    from seed 108, 109, *109*
    semiripe cuttings 108, 111

(entry cont. overleaf)

Clematis, propagation (*cont.*)
  serpentine layering 113
  softwood cuttings 108, 110
 pruning 103, 105, 107–8, *107*, *108*
 routine care 107
 scented 97
 as screen *93*, 94
 seedheads 106
 siting 107
 soil preparation 106
 soil types tolerated 98, 99, 100, 147
 suggestions for use 94, 97, 106
 supports for 106
 training 107–8
 on trees 34
 alpina
  pruning 107
  semiripe cuttings 206
  suggestions for use 97
  'Frances Rivis' *106*
 Alpina group 106
 armandii *107*
  conditions preferred 106
  for fragrance 97
  pruning 107
 'Barbara Jackman', pruning 108
 'Carnaby', pruning 108
 x *cartmanii* 'Joe', semiripe cuttings 206
 cirrhosa
  conditions preferred 106
  pruning 107
  seasons of interest 96
 'Comtesse de Bouchaud', pruning 108
 'Daniel Deronda', pruning 108
 'Duchess of Albany', pruning 108
 'Duchess of Edinburgh', pruning 108
 'Edith', suggestions for use 106
 'Elsa Spath' *97*
  pruning 108
 'Ernest Markham' *106*
  as ground cover 95
  pruning 108
 florida, pruning 108
 'General Sikorski', pruning 108
 'Hagley Hybrid'
  in mixed border *20*
  pruning 108
 'Henryi' *106*
  pruning 108
 heracleifolia
  soil type tolerated 147
  var. *davidiana*, suggestions for use 106
 integrifolia 106
  suggestions for use 106
 'Jackmanii' *106*
  as ground cover 95
  pruning 108
 'Jackmanii' hybrids
  diseases 571
  suggestions for use 106
 'John Huxtable', in mixed border *20*
 x *jouiniana* 106
  suggestions for use 106
 'Lady Betty Balfour', pruning 108
 'Lasurstern', pruning 108
 macropetala
  in container 96
  pruning 107
  seasons of interest 96
  suggestions for use 97
  'Markham's Pink' *106*
 Macropetala group 106
 'Marie Boisselot' (syn. *C.* 'Mme. Le Coultre'), pruning 108
 'Mme. Le Coultre', see *C.* 'Marie Boisselot'
Clematis (*cont.*)
 montana
  diseases 571
  for fragrance 97
  growing through trees 95
  internodal cuttings *541*
  pruning 103, 107
  as screen 94
  seasonal interest 25
  suggestions for use 95
  vigor 98
  var. *grandiflora*, pruning 107
  var. *rubens* *106*
   pruning 107
  'Tetrarose', flowers 95
 Montana group 106
 'Mrs. N. Thompson', pruning 108
 'Nelly Moser' *106*
  pruning 108
 'Niobe', pruning 108
 orientalis
  conditions required 107
  suggestions for use 106
 paniculata, suggestions for use 93
 'Perle d'Azur' *108*
  pruning 108
 'The President' *106*
  pruning 108
 'Proteus', flowers 106
 recta 106
  soil type tolerated 147
 rehderiana, flowers 106
 tangutica
  conditions required 107
  flowers 106
  pruning 108
  suggestions for use 106
 texensis, suggestions for use 106
 'Ville de Lyon', pruning 108
 viticella
  cutting back 98
  flowers 106
  pruning 108
  suggestions for use 95, 106
  'Abundance', as ground cover *95*
  'Etoile Violette'
   flowers 95
   as ground cover *95*
  'Mme. Julia Correvon' *106*
  'Venosa Violacea', growing through juniper *107*
 'Vyvyan Pennell' *108*
  flowers 106
  pruning 108
Clematis wilt *571*
 cause 107, 571
 symptoms and control 571
Clementines, see Mandarins
Cleome
 architectural role 173
 in formal open-plan garden *14*
 hassleriana, architectural plant 175
Clerodendrum
 root cuttings 84
 softwood cuttings 110
 bungei, division of suckers 88
 splendens 97
 thomsoniae 97
  conditions tolerated 97
  pruning 103, 105, 450
Clethra
 pruning 74
 soil type required 69
 alnifolia
  soil type tolerated 67
  'Paniculata', scent 66
Clianthus
 pruning 103
 semiripe cuttings 111
 puniceus, soil type tolerated 99
Click beetles 568
Climate 514–21
 desert 514
 design and 15
Climate (*cont.*)
 elements of 515–19
 geographical influences on 514
 Mediterranean 514
 microclimate 15
 of North America 514, 516–17
 polar 514
 regional variations 514, 522–3
 subtropical 514
 temperate 514
 tropical 514
 zones 514
  selecting plants for 520
Climbers 92–113, 585
 for acid soil 99
 for alkaline soil 100
 annual 96, 97, 173
  planting 182, *182*
  supporting 182, *182*, 183, *183*
 on background walls 22, *22*
 biennial 173
 on buildings 93
 choosing 99, *99*
 for clay soil 99
 climbing methods 92, 98, *98*
 color 95, *95*
 conditions required 98
 conditions tolerated 93, 98
 in containers 26, 96, 97, 101
  repotting *101*
  top-dressing 101, *101*
 cutting back *101*
 deadheading 101
 designing with 92–6
 diseases 101, 567
 evergreen 97
  pruning 104
  as screen 94
 for exposed sites 93
 exposure for 93
 fast-growing 97
 feeding 101
 flowering on current season's growth 103
 flowering on previous season's growth 103
 foliage for effect 95, *96*
 fruiting 95, 356
 as ground cover 95, 97
 growing on host plants 97
 growing under cover
  plants suitable for 450
  pruning 450, *450*
   time for 450
  in soil beds
  support framework for 450, *450*
  training 450
 herbaceous 97
 host plants for 94
 indoors, supports for 436, *436*
 for interest through seasons 95
 in layered planting 23
 in mixed borders 136
 mulching 100
 for north-facing walls 93
 for patios 29
 on pergolas 94
 pests 101, 550, 552, 557
 on pillars 94
 pinching out 450
 planter's guide 97
 planting
  in containers 99, *99*
  distances from supports 99
  method 100, *100*
  outdoors 99
 planting out 109
 positioning indoors 427
 pot-bound *101*
 pricking out 109, *109*
 propagation 109–13
  cuttings, soil mix for 110
  hardwood cuttings 111, *111*
  root cuttings 112, *112*
  from seed 109, *109*
Climbers, propagation (*cont.*)
  self layering 109, 112, *112*, 113
  semiripe cuttings 110–11, *111*
   with heel 111, *111*
  serpentine layering 113, *113*
  simple layering 113, *113*
  softwood cuttings 110, *110*
 protecting 101, 521
 pruning 102–5
  after flowering *450*
  cutting down to ground 105
  formative 102, *102*
  principles 102
  to restrict growth 450, *450*
  spring 102, *102*
  summer 103, *103*
  under cover 450, *450*
  winter 104, *104*
 renovating 105, *105*
 repotting *101*
 routine care 101
 for sandy soil 99
 scented 27, 96, 97
 screening with 93
 seedlings, planting out 109
 self-clinging 92
 for shade 97
 site 93
 siting 99
 soil preparation 98, 100
 on south-facing walls 519
 spring 25
 suggestions for use 92–6
 supports for 92, 98, 100
 tender
  protecting flower buds 93
  protecting roots 93
  site for 93
 tendril climbers 92
 tolerant of air pollution 97
 training 102–5
  formative 102, *102*
  under cover 450
 on trees 34
 twining 92
 tying in 100
 vigorous 98
 watering 100, 101
 for winter interest 94
Clitoria
 from seed 452
 softwood cuttings 110
 ternatea, growth rate 97
Clivia
 conditions preferred 431
 for cutting 219
 growing with succulents 260
 from seed 235
Cloches 490–91, 586
 barn 490, *490*
 dome-shaped 490
 end pieces for 490
 hardening off in 180
 individual 490, *490*
 maintenance 491
 materials for 490
 microclimates in 519
 for propagation 545
 self-watering 490, *490*
 tent 490, *490*
 tunnel 490, *490*
 types 490, *490*
 uses 474
 vegetables under 311
 wall-of-water 490, *490*
 winter protection with 521, *521*
Clone, definition 586
Closeboard fencing 508, *508*
Clothing, protective
 for chemicals 491
 for power tool use 458, *458*, *464*
Clover
 common white *578*
  in lawn 286
 diseases 558
 as green manure 533
 indicating soil type 525
Clubroot 525, 531, *567*
 causes 555
 control 310, 555, 567
 life in soil 304
 preventing 313
 rotating crops to avoid 304
 symptoms 555, 567
Cluster pine, see *Pinus pinaster*
Clytostoma 97
 pruning 103
 semiripe cuttings 111
 callistegioides
  conditions tolerated 97
  growth rate 97
  pruning 105
Coastal sites
 choosing site 39
 perennials tolerant of 141
 salt spray 520
 shrubs tolerant of 62, 66
 trees tolerant of 37
 wind in 519
Cobaea
 from seed 109, 452
 scandens
  in annual border *171*
  growing as annual 175
  growth rate *97*
  pruning 450
  suggestions for use 173
  f. *alba* *97*
Cobblestones *498*, 499
Cobweb houseleek, see *Sempervivum arachnoideum*
Coccomyces hiemalis 554
Coccus hesperidum 554
Cocoa shells
 amount required compared to other fertilizers *532*
 as mulch *101*
 nutrient content 532
Cocos, architectural plant 66
Cocoyam, see Taro
Codiaeum
 conditions preferred 431
 conditions required 431
 hydroculture 431
 softwood cuttings 453
 suggestions for use 438
Codling moths 565, *565*
Codonopsis
 softwood cuttings 110
 sowing 205
 convolvulacea 97
  conditions tolerated 97
  flowers 95
  suggestions for use 97
Coelogyne, temperature required 441
Colchicum 213
 conditions tolerated 219
 corm 214
 in grass, mowing 230
 planting time 224
 suggestions for use 219
 autumnale, suggestions for use 227
 byzantinum, naturalized *216*
 speciosum, suggestions for use 227
Cold
 damage caused by 519, 556, 571
 preventive measures 520–21
 protecting fruit from 363, *520*
 protecting greenhouse plants from 447
 protecting shrubs from 72, 520, *520*
 protecting tender climbers from 93
 protecting trees from 520, *520*
 protection from 520–21, *520–21*
  insulation *520*
  mounding *520*
 wall footings in areas of 505
Cold alarm 482, *482*
Cold areas, wall footing in 505
Cold frames, see Frames

Coleus
  choosing healthy plant *436*
  conditions preferred 431
  conditions required 431
  in containers 174
  foliage 171
  germination 179
  growing as annual 175
  as pot plants 175
  propagation 176
    softwood cuttings *454*
  blumei
    cuttings 453
    in indoor hanging garden *428*
Collar, of plant, definition 586
Collards 313
Collars
  for brassica seedlings *313*, *566*
  protection against cutworms 561
  tree-guard 572
Colletia
  semiripe cuttings with heel 83
  armata 'Rosea', scent 66
Collinsia bicolor
  self-seeding 178
  sowing 177
Colocasia esculenta
  division of tubers 256
  as vegetable, see Taro
  in water garden 243
Colorado potato beetles 310, 551, *551*
Colorado spruce, see *Picea pungens*
Color schemes *12*, 24, *24*
  effect on perspective 18
  foliage colors in 139
  perennial beds and borders 139
  suiting conditions 139
Colors
  effect of light on 95, 139
  mutation 582, *582*
Colquhounia, pruning 74
Coltsfoot *576*
Columbine, see *Aquilegia*
Columbine leaf miner 553
Columnea
  conditions required 431
  softwood cuttings 453
Combretum grandiflorum 97
Common alder, see *Alnus glutinosa*
Common Bermuda grass, see *Cynodon dactylon*
Common box, see *Buxus sempervirens*
Common camellia, see *Camellia japonica*
Common chickweed 575, *575*
Common elder, see *Sambucus nigra*
Common English ivy, see *Hedera helix*
Common gardenia, see *Gardenia jasminoides*
Common hackberry, see *Celtis occidentalis*
Common honeysuckle, see *Lonicera periclymenum*
Common hop, see *Humulus lupulus*
Common hornbeam, see *Carpinus betulus*
Common houseleek, see *Sempervivum tectorum*
Common juniper, see *Juniperus communis*
Common mouse-ear chickweed *578*
Common myrtle, see *Myrtus communis*
Common pear, see *Pyrus communis*
Common potato scab 568, *568*
Common rue, see *Ruta graveolens*
Common snowdrop, see *Galanthus nivalis*
Common staghorn fern, see *Platycerium bifurcatum*
Common thyme, see *Thymus vulgaris*
Common white jasmine, see *Jasminum officinale*
Compact marjoram, see *Origanum vulgare* 'Compactum'
Compaction of soil *529*
Companion planting
  definition 586
  for organic control 548, *548*
Compositae 586
  flowers 582
Compost 586
  adding to soil 529, *529*
  additives 535
  amount required compared to other fertilizers *532*
  composting process 535
  improving soil fertility with 302
  maintaining nutrient levels with 309
  making 535
  materials to avoid in 529
  as mulch 308, 534
  nutrient content 532
  slow composting 535
  as top-dressing *534*
Compost bins 470
  making *535*
  using *535*
Compost heap
  in garden plan *19*
  siting 14
  size 535
Compost shredders 470, *470*
Concrete
  blocks
    constructing retaining walls of 506, *506*
    raised beds of 507
    for walls *504*
  casing for metal uprights *512*
  coloring 502
  definition 499
  dye for 496
  expansion joints 502
  fence posts in 508
  footing of, making *504*
  for greenhouse foundations *479*
  laying 494, *494*
  mixes 494
  paths of 502
  pavers 497, *498*
  paving slabs 495–6
    cutting 496, *496*
    laying 495, *495*
    paths of 502
    quantities 495
  pond made of
    constructing 248, *248*
    repairing 254, *254*
  reinforcing 248
  spurs for fence posts *509*, 510
  surface finish 502
  textured finishes 502, *502*
Coneflower, see *Rudbeckia*
  purple, see *Echinacea purpurea*
Cones 586
  extracting seed from 54
Confederate jasmine, see *Trachelospermum jasminoides*
Conifer woolly aphids, see Adelgids
Conifers 586
  annuals climbing through 173
  for avenues 36
  buying 39, 40
  chemical damage to 557
Conifers (*cont.*)
  contrasting with deciduous trees *34*
  cuttings 53
  diseases 570
  dwarf 25, 38
    in alpine house 190
    alpines with *187*
    associating with other plants 38
    colors 38
    in containers 65
    forms 38
    growth rate 32
    with heathers *38*
    in rock garden 22
    selecting 38
    size 32
    suggestions for use 38
    in troughs 190
  grafting 56
  as hedges 59, 60
  hormone weedkiller damage 561
  pests 551, 560
  in restricted color border *63*
  in rock garden *185*
  structural planting *22*
  winter color 35
Conophytum, division of offsets 269
Conotrachelus nenuphar 564
Conservation
  bulbs in the wild 224
  of energy, greenhouse for 477, *477*
  garden for 28
Conservatories 428–9
  beds and borders, preparing 439
  cacti for 261
  cool, plant arrangement in *429*
  soil mixes 439
  succulents for 261
Consolida
  architectural plant 173
  for cutting 174
  ambigua
    for cutting 175
    for drying 175
    protecting seedlings 178
    sowing 177
    thinning *178*
Construction work 13
  schedule 20
Container-grown plants
  diseases 560
    fungal 560, 567
  feeding 532
  fertilizer burn 556
  pests 566, 572
  water problems 556, 557, 570
Containers, see also Pots
  alpines in 186, 190, *190*, 198–9
    care 203–4
    planting 199, *199*
    siting 199
  annuals in 174
    care 183, *183*
    climbers 173
    planting 181, *181*
  biennials in, planting 181, *181*
  for bonsai 434
  bulbs in 228
    outdoors 217, *217*, 229
      care 231
    under cover 218
  cacti in 262
    indoors 261
    outdoors 260, *260*
    planting 264, *264*
  climbers in 96, 97
    planting 99, *99*
  daffodils in 221
  dwarf conifers for 38
  fruit in 359, 361, 362
  fuchsias in 449
  grouping *26*
Containers (*cont.*)
  hanging baskets, see Hanging baskets
  herbs in 288, *288*, 294, 296
  for indoor plants 427–8
  lightweight, for roof garden 29
  for office plants 428
  on patios 14, 29
  pelargoniums in 168, *168*, *169*
  perennials in 140, *140*, 147, *147*
    care 157, *157*
  planting 20
  for planting aquatics 251, *251*
  preparing 43
  rock plants in 190, *190*, 198–9
    planting 199, *199*
    siting 199
  on roof garden *29*
  roses in 119
    planting *122*
  for seed sowing 178
  self-watering 446
  shrubs in 64, 65
    care 70, 71, *71*
    planting 69, *69*
    root pruning 80
  succulents 262
    indoors 261
    outdoors 260, *260*
    planting 264, *264*
  suggestions for use 26
  trailing plants for, annuals and biennials 175
  trees in 36, *36*, 37
    planting 43, *43*
    sowing seed 54, *54*, *55*
  tulips in *220*
  vegetables in 302, 307, *307*, 309
    soil mix 307, 309
    suitable types *307*
  water garden in 242, *242*
Convallaria majalis
  conditions preferred 141
  for fragrance 141
  suggestions for use 140, 216
Convolvulaceae 258
Convolvulus
  softwood cuttings 110
  arvensis, see Bindweed, field
  boissieri, semiripe cuttings 206
  cneorum, seasonal interest 66
  'Royal Ensign', in annual border *171*
  sabatius, semiripe cuttings 206
  tricolor 97
    suggestions for use 175
Cooking, herbs used in 287
Copiapoa, division of offsets 269
Coping, finishes for walls 506, *506*
Copper
  deficiency 362
  plant requirements 532
Copper-based fungicides 554, 555, 557, 561, 562, 568, 571
  commercial names 574
Coppicing 23, 36, 49, *49*, 50, 586
  shrubs 77, *77*
  trees suited to 50
Coprinus 574
Coprosma
  conditions preferred 66
  semiripe cuttings with heel 83
Coral cactus, see *Rhipsalis cereuscula*
Coral gem, see *Lotus berthelotii*
Coral honeysuckle, see *Lonicera sempervirens*
Coral vine, see *Antigonon leptopus*; *Berberidopsis corallina*
Coralbells, see *Heuchera*
Cordons 586
  on arches *359*
  form 356, *356*
  grapes, pruning 398–9, *398–9*
  planting
    against fence *361*
    in open ground *361*
  soft fruit
    pruning 412, *412*
    training 412, *412*
  training 356
  tree fruit
    pruning 376–7, *377*, 380
    space required 358
    training 376, 380
Cordyline
  architectural plant 66
  conditions tolerated 66
  in greenhouse garden *430*
  hardwood cuttings 53
  pruning 78
  australis
    germination 452
    from seed 452
    'Purpurea', plunging in large container *437*
Coreopsis
  pests 563
  Early Sunrise Series, growing as annual 175
  Series, for cutting 175
  tinctoria, soil type preferred 176
  verticillata
    dividing 163
    'Moonbeam', foliage 138
Coriander *291*
  culinary uses 291
  flowers 291
  foliage 291
  growing from seed 291, 297
  harvesting 291
  protecting for winter use 294
  smell of plant 291
  storing 291
Coriandrum sativum, see Coriander
Corkscrew rush, see *Juncus effusus* f. *spiralis*
Corky scab 554, *554*
Cormels
  definition 586
  propagation by 233, *233*
  raising *542*
Cormlets, definition 586
Corms *542*, 586
  choosing *224*
  definition 214
  division 233, *233*
  planting 226
    depth 226
    in root growth 226
  propagation 542–3, *542*
  purpose 581
  spacing 226
  storage rots 569
Corn, pests 566, 572
Corn cockle, see *Agrostemma*
Corn poppy, see *Papaver rhoeas*
Corn rootworms 566, *566*
Corn salad
  cultivation 327
  harvesting 327
  large-leaved *327*
  suggestions for use 327
  types 327
  in vegetable garden *300*
Corners, ground cover for 150
Cornfields 167
Cornflower, see *Centaurea cyanus*
Cornus
  bark 65
  conditions preferred 62
  disease resistance 567
  in layer planting 26

(*entry cont. overleaf*)

Cornus (*cont.*)
propagation, stooling 87
alba 23, *65*
propagation
division of suckers 88
French layering 87
hardwood cuttings 84
suggestions for use 243
'Aurea', coppicing 77
'Elegantissima', coppicing 77
'Flaviramea', coppicing 77
'Kesselringii', coppicing 77
'Sibirica'
bark 65
coppicing 77
soil type tolerated 67
for winter effect *25*
'Spaethii', coppicing 77
'Variegata', coppicing 77
alternifolia 'Argentea', pruning 74
canadensis *88*
conditions preferred 66
conditions tolerated 66
division of suckers 88
soil type required 69
'Eddie's White Wonder', seasonal interest 66
florida, as specimen tree 33
kousa
seasonal interest 37
suggestions for use 37
var. *chinensis*, seasonal interest 37
mas 'Variegata', seasonal interest 66
nuttallii, soil preferred 41
stolonifera
conditions tolerated 66
coppicing *77*
pollarding 77
propagation
division of suckers 88
French layering 87
hardwood cuttings 84
'Flaviramea'
seasonal interest 62
for winter effect 25
Corokia
pruning 74
semiripe cuttings with heel 83
Corolla, definition 586
Coronilla
germination 85
pruning 450
varia, soil type tolerated 147
Correa pulchella, in conservatory *429*
Cortaderia
suggestions for use 142
selloana
architectural form 141
cutting back 143, *143*
height 135
as lawn specimen *142*
in mixed group *142*
as specimen plant 140
Corticium rolfsii, see *Sclerotium rolfsii*
Corydalis
conditions preferred 219
planting 225
seed, collecting 234
sowing 205
suggestions for use 219
tubers 214
cashmeriana, soil type required 192
flexuosa, soil type required 192
lutea, soil type tolerated 147
solida
choosing healthy bulbs *224*
suggestions for use 217
'George Baker'
in alpine raised bed *201*
in peat bed *188*
Corylopsis
layering 86
Corylopsis (*cont.*)
in mixed border 214
pruning 74, 76
soil type required 69
Corylus
for coppicing 50
flowers, unisexual 582
fruit type 581
propagation, layering 55
avellana
fruit, see Hazelnuts
as hedge 59
'Contorta'
seasonal interest 66
stems 65
suggestions for use 50
colurna, conditions tolerated 37
maxima
fruit, see Filberts
'Purpurea' *77*
coppicing 77
Coryneum canker 570, *570*
Coryneum cardinale 571
Coryphantha, division of offsets 269
Cosmetics, herbs used for 287
Cosmos
colors to blend with 139
for cutting 175
in mixed border *172*, 173
pests 563
soil conditions tolerated 176
atrosanguineus
for fragrance 141
in hot border *139*
Cotinus
in mixed border 140
pruning 74
coggygria
coppicing 77
propagation
French layering 87
softwood cuttings 53
stooling 87
seasonal interest 62
'Flame', seasonal interest 66
'Grace', coppicing 77
Cotoneaster
bonsai 434
conditions tolerated 66
diseases 555, 571
dwarf
conditions tolerated 66
pruning 78
dwarf conifers with 38
germination 85
pests 560
propagation
semiripe cuttings with heel 83
softwood cuttings 81
pruning 76
seed stratification 537
soil type tolerated 67, 69
for topiary 90
'Autumn Fire', in shrub border *63*
conspicuus
as ground cover 151
seasonal interest 66
'Cornubia', seasonal interest 62
dammeri, as ground cover 150
divaricatus, seasonal interest 62
'Firebird' *83*
horizontalis *150*
conditions tolerated 66
as ground cover 150
'Hybridus Pendulus', side-veneer grafting 89
x *watereri*, hardwood cuttings 84
Cottage garden 14, 27, *27*, 136, 172
bulbs in 214
plants for 140, *140*
roses in 119
Cotton thistle, see *Onopordum acanthium*
Cotula
for lawns 275
coronopifolia, in water garden 243
Cotyledon
stem cuttings 268
ladismithiensis, leaf cuttings 267
teretifolia, suggestions for use 262
undulata
leaf cuttings 267
suggestions for use 262
Cotyledons (seed leaves) 538, *538*, 582, 586
Courtyards 29
perennials in containers 140
Crab cactus, see *Schlumbergera truncata*
Crabapples, ornamental, see *Malus*
Crabgrass 578, 579
Crambe cordifolia
architectural form 141
division 163
form 138
growth rate 141
in layer planting *26*
with roses 116
Cranesbill, see *Geranium*
Crape myrtle, see *Lagerstroemia indica*
Crassula
conditions preferred 431
in greenhouse display *261*
propagation
division of offsets 269
leaf cuttings 267
softwood cuttings 453
stem cuttings 268
falcata
in containers outdoors 260
suggestions for use 262
ovata (syn. *C. portulacea*)
in bowl *264*
in bowl garden 261
choosing healthy plant *263*
leaf cuttings 267
suggestions for use 262
perfoliata, leaf cuttings 267
rupestris, suggestions for use 262
sarcocaulis
conditions tolerated 262
hardiness 259
sarmentosa, conditions tolerated 262
socialis, suggestions for use 262
Crataegus 28
bonsai 434
conditions tolerated 37, 521
disadvantages 35
diseases 554, 555, 570, 571
for fall color 35
pests 551, 553, 558
propagation, chip-budding 56
as rootstock for loquats 418
shaping 60
soil type tolerated 41
laevigata
soil type tolerated 42
as specimen tree *33*
'Paul's Scarlet', suggestions for use 37
x *lavallei*
conditions tolerated 37
'Carrierei'
seasonal interest 37
suggestions for use 37
monogyna
conditions tolerated 37
as hedge 58, 59
Creeping bentgrass, see *Agrostis stolonifera*
Creeping Charlie 578, *578*
Creeping deadnettle, see *Lamium maculatum*
Creeping fig, see *Ficus pumila*
Creeping juniper, see *Juniperus horizontalis*
Creeping phlox, see *Phlox stolonifera*
Creeping savory
in herb garden *295*
suggestions for use 288, 293
Creosote, as wood preservative 510
Crepis incana, conditions tolerated 191
Cress 326
broad-leaved 326, *326*
creeping yellow, see *Rorippa sylvestris*
culinary uses 326
cultivation 326
harvesting 312, 326
upland, see Upland cress
Crest, definition 586
Cretan brake, see *Pteris cretica*
Crevices, planting rock plants in 191, 197, *197*, 200, *200*
Crickets 563
Crimson glory vine, see *Vitis coignetiae*
Crinum 213
chipping 237
for cutting 219
division of offsets 233, *233*
in mixed border *215*
overwintering 218
x *powellii*
architectural plant 219
in mixed border 214, *215*
suggestions for use 218
Crioceris asparagi 550
Cristate, definition 586
Crithmum maritimum, conditions tolerated 262
Crocks, definition 586
Crocosmia
for cutting 219
diseases, fungal 569
in mixed border 215
in perennial border *137*
propagation 237
'Lucifer' *218*
as specimen plant 140
Crocus 213
bird damage 563
conditions required 431
conditions tolerated 219
corm 214
damage caused by mice, rats, and voles 568
division of offsets 233
fall-flowering
in mixed border 215
planting time 224
forcing 219, 228
increase 213
naturalized *217*
planting
depth 227
in grass 227, *227*
in pots 231, 232
seasonal interest 25
seed, collecting 234
seedlings 234
stamens 582
suggestions for use 216, 219
in woodland *216*
biflorus, suggestions for use 227
chrysanthus, suggestions for use 227
'Cream Beauty', in rock garden *187*
dalmaticus, in rock garden *187*
Dutch Hybrids, suggestions for use 227
flavus, suggestions for use 227
laevigatus 'Fontenayi', in rock garden 186
nudiflorus, suggestions for use 227
Crocus (*cont.*)
ochroleucus, suggestions for use 227
pulchellus *227*
suggestions for use 227
'Snow Bunting' 150
speciosus, suggestions for use 227
tommasinianus
in mixed island bed *136*
suggestions for use 216, *227*
'Zwanenburg Bronze' 150
Crocus, fall, see *Colchicum autumnale*
Crookneck squash, see Squash, summer, crookneck
Crop rotation, see Rotation of crops
Croquet lawn 275
mowing 281
Cross vine, see *Bignonia capreolata*
Crossandra, softwood cuttings 453
Cross-fertilization, definition 586
Cross-pollination 537, 586
cacti and other succulents 267, *267*
fruit 359, 360, 380, 418
herbs 290
Crown, definition 586
Crown borer 559
Crown gall 561, *561*, 567, *567*
Crown imperial, see *Fritillaria imperialis*
Crown rot 149, 153, 346, 571, *571*
Crown-of-thorns, see *Euphorbia milii*
Cruciferae, diseases 555, 567
Crucifers, see Brassicas
Cruel plant, see *Araujia sericofera*
Cryptanthus
conditions preferred 431
bivittatus *432*
Cryptocereus
side grafting 271
anthonyanus, suggestions for use 262
Cryptocoryne ciliata
division of rootstock 256
suggestions for use 243
Cryptogramma
conditions required 158
in winter 158
Cryptolaemus montrouzieri, as biological pest control 548, 552
Cryptomeria
soil type preferred 41
japonica
winter color 35
'Vilmoriniana' 191
Cryptostegia, softwood cuttings 110
Cuckoo flower, see *Cardamine pratensis*
Cuckoo pint, see *Arum*
Cucumber mosaic virus 403, 546, 565
Cucumber tree, see *Magnolia acuminata*
Cucumbers 330–31, *330–31*
all-female cultivars 330
apple, fruit 330
bush *331*
culinary uses 330
cultivation 330–31
diseases 331, 560, 565, 567
English *328*, 330
germination 330
greenhouse 330
harvesting 312, 330, 331
lemon, fruit 330
nitrogen requirement 310, 330
pests 331, 552, 553, 559, 571
(*entry cont.*)

Cucumbers (*cont.*)
planting out 330, *330*
recommended cultivars 331
storing 312
trailing types 330
in vegetable garden *300*
watering 308, 331
'Bush Champion' *331*
Cucumis
melo, see Melons
sativus, see Cucumbers; Gherkins
Cucurbita
foetidissima, as weed 576
maxima, see Squash, winter
moschata, see Squash, winter
pepo, see Squash, winter; Zucchini
Cucurbitaceae 258
Culm, definition 586
Cultivars
definition 582, 586
names 582
Cultivation, tools for 459–61, *459–61*
Cultivators
manual 461, *461*
power, see Rototillers
removable prongs *461*
star-wheeled 461, *461*
Cumin *291*
conditions required 291
culinary uses 291
flowers 291
foliage 291
harvesting 291
from seed 291
Cuminum cyminum, see Cumin
Cup-and-saucer vine, see *Cobaea scandens*
Cuphea
flowering time from seed 160
greenhouse conditions required 431
propagation
from seed 452
stem tip cuttings 164
hyssopifolia, bonsai 434
x *Cupressocyparis*
semiripe cuttings 53
soil type tolerated 41
leylandii
balled-and-burlapped *39*
conditions tolerated 521
disease resistance 560, 567
diseases 570
as hedge 58, *58*
'Castlewellan Gold', seasonal interest 37
Cupressus
as background hedge 22
semiripe cuttings 53
side-veneer grafting 56
glabra
soil type preferred 42
soil type tolerated 41
as standard *29*
'Pyramidalis', seasonal interest 37
macrocarpa
diseases, fungal 570
'Goldcrest'
seasonal interest 37
suggestions for use 37
sempervirens
diseases 570
suggestions for use 37
for topiary 90
Curculigo recurvata, leaf vein patterns *582*
Curled pondweed, see *Potamogeton crispus*
Curly kale, see Kales, curly
Currant galls 558
Currants, see also Blackcurrants; Redcurrants; Whitecurrants
freezing 367
in garden design *19*
mineral deficiencies 556, 562
pests 551
pruning 364
Cushion plants, in rock garden 22
Custard squash, see Squash, summer, custard
Cut flowers, see Flowers, cut
Cut-and-come-again crops
harvesting 312
lettuce 324, 325
seedlings 306, 322
Cutting tools 462–4, *462–4*
maintenance 462
Cuttings 540–41, 586
alpines 206–7, *206*, *207*, 208–9, *208*, *209*
basal 223, *223*, 540
alpines 207, *207*
begonias 455, *455*
bulbs 238
dahlias 223, *223*
basal stem 164–5, *164*, 586
blackleg on 570, *570*
bud 245, *245*
cacti 266
climbers 109
cut leaves 454–5, *455*
distal end 586
effect of bottom heat on 545
environment for 541, *541*
fruit 368, 370, *370*
fuchsias 448, *448*
greenwood 540, 586
alpines 206
selecting material for 207, *207*
hardwood 151, 586
climbers 109, 111, *111*
fruit 370, *370*
grapes 402, *420*
method 540, *540*
preparing 541, *541*
roses 129, *129*
shrubs propagated by 83–4, *84*
trees propagated by 52–3, *52*
truncheons 396
heel 541, 586
climbers 111, *111*
shrubs 82, 83, *83*
trees 53
internodal 108, *108*, 541, *541*, 586
Irishman's, alpines 208, *208*
keikis *442*, 443
leaf 540, 541, *541*, 586
alpines 207
indoor plants 454–5, *454*
large leaves *541*
selecting material for 207, *207*
small leaves *541*
succulents 267, *267*
leaf sections 455, *455*
leaf-bud 453, 540, *540*, 586
blackberries 408, *408*
fruit 370
shrubs 83, *83*
leafy, protecting 544, *544*
mallet 83, *83*
methods 540–41
nodal *540*, 586
shrubs 82
trees 53
pad sections, cacti and other succulents *268*
pests 572
proximal end 589
ripewood 586, see also hardwood
alpines 206
selecting material for 207, *207*
root 109, 540, 541, *541*, 586
alpines 208–9, *209*
climbers 112, *112*
perennials 165, *165*
perennials propagated by 165
scooping rosettes 209, *209*
shrub 84
rosette, selecting material for 207, *207*
Cuttings (*cont.*)
selecting material for 207, *207*
semiripe 540, *540*, 586
alpines 207
climbers 109, 110, *111*
indoor shrubs 453
overwintering 82
preparing 541, *541*
roses 129
selecting material for 207, *207*
shrubs propagated by 82–3, *82*
trees propagated by 53, *53*
shrubs 81–4, *81–4*
softwood 109, 448, 540, *540*, 586
alpines 206, *206*
aquatics *256*, *257*
climbers 110, *110*
fruit 370
indoor plants 453–4, *453*
in water 454, *454*
indoor plants propagated by 453
protection for 544
shrubs propagated by 81, *81*
soil mix for 110
trees propagated by 53
soil mixes for 536, 541
stem *442*, 443, 586
perennials suitable for 164
preparing 540–41, *541*
succulents 268, *268*
types 541–41, *540–41*
stem sections, cacti and other succulents 268, *268*
stem tip 586
perennials 164, *164*
succulents 266
two-bud, grapes 402, *420*
time to take 540
tip *448*, 540
trees 52–3, *52*, *53*
wounding 541, *541*
Cutworms 310, 561, *561*, *566*
protecting plants from *313*
Cyananthus
soil type required 192
microphyllus, in alpine raised bed *201*
Cyathodes colensoi, in peat bed *188*
Cycas revoluta, architectural plant *66*
Cyclamen
alpine, sowing 205
choosing healthy plants 224
conditions preferred 431
conditions required 431
conditions tolerated 213, 216, 219
diseases 444
hardy, suggestions for use 27, 219
mulching 226
pests 562, 566, 572
planting 225, 226, *226*
propagation from seed 235, 452
resting 445, *445*
seed, harvesting *235*
sowing 205
suggestions for use 216, 217, 219
tubers 214
watering 444
coum
conditions tolerated 219
indoors 426
suggestions for use 213
in woodland *216*
'Album', in rock garden *187*
subsp. *coum*, in rock garden *187*
hederifolium
choosing healthy bulbs *224*
Cyclamen hederifolium (*cont.*)
conditions preferred 191
conditions tolerated 219
propagation, cutting up, with growing points 237, *237*
in rock garden 187
purpurascens
conditions preferred 191
in peat bed *188*
repandum, conditions tolerated 219
rohlfsianum, cutting up, with growing points 237
Cydia
nigricana, see Pea moths
pomonella, see Codling moths
Cydonia oblonga, see Quinces
Cymbidium
in greenhouse 430
propagation by division 443, *443*
temperature required 441
Strath Kanaid *440*
Cyme, definition 586
Cynara
for drying 141
cardunculus *141*
architectural form 141
in cool border *138*
growth rate 141
scolymus
architectural form 141
growth rate 141
as vegetable, see Globe artichokes
Cynipid wasps 558, *558*
Cynodon
for lawns 274, 275
dactylon 274
hydromulching 280
for lawn, sowing rate 280
incompletus var. *hirsutus* 274
x *magennisii* 274
transvaalensis 274
Cynoglossum amabile, sowing 177
Cyperaceae family 142
Cyperus
conditions tolerated 427
division of rootstock 451
esculentus, see Nutsedge
'Haspan', in water garden 243
involucratus, in water garden 243
longus, in water garden 243
papyrus
in water garden 243
'Nanus' (syn. *C. p.* 'Viviparus'), propagation 257
Cyphomandra betacea, see Tree tomatoes
Cypress, see *Cupressus*
bald, see *Taxodium distichum*
Lawson's, see *Chamaecyparis lawsoniana*
Leyland, see x *Cupressocyparis leylandii*
Cypripedium
conditions for 441
reginae, soil type required 147
Cyrtanthus
conditions preferred 431
growing with succulents 260
purpureus, pests 569
Cyrtomium, in winter 158
Cysts 572
Cytisus
conditions preferred 62
flowers 65
germination 85
pests 558
propagation
semiripe cuttings with heel 83
softwood cuttings 81
soil type tolerated 69
ardoinii, in alpine raised bed *201*
Cytisus (*cont.*)
battandieri, scent 66
x *beanii*, soil type preferred 193
scoparius, soil type preferred 67
Cytospora canker 560, *560*

D

Daboecia
propagation
dropping 86
softwood cuttings 81
pruning 77
suggestions for use 38, 64, 106
Dactylopsis, division of offsets 269
Dactylorrhiza
tubers 214
fuchsii, suggestions for use 227
maculata, suggestions for use 227
Dacus 565
Daffodil, see *Narcissus*
Dahlia 222–3
classification 222
conditions required 222
cultivation 222–3
for exhibition 222, 223
for cutting 219
disbudding 223, *223*
diseases 561
exhibiting 223
in fall 139
feeding 222, 223
flowers 582
types *222*
frost, effect on 515
lifting 223, *223*
mulching 222
in parterre *31*
pests 223, 550, 551, 553, 563
pinching 222, *223*
planting *222*, *222*
propagation
basal cuttings 223, *223*
division of tubers 223
selecting *222*
site *222*
soil preparation 222
storing 223, *223*
tubers *543*
planting 222
wing buds 223, *223*
'Comet' *222*
'Early Bird' *218*
'Easter Sunday' *222*
'Frank Hornsey' *222*
'Majestic Kerkrade' *222*
'Monk Marc' *214*
'Small World' *222*
'So Dainty' *222*
'Vicky Crutchfield' *222*
'Wootton Cupid' *222*
'Yellow Hammer' *222*
Daikon
conditions tolerated 352
recommended cultivars 385
sowing 352
Daisies (weed) 579
Daisy, English, see *Bellis perennis*
Michaelmas, see *Aster*
Daisy-bush, see *Olearia*

Damasonium alisma
division of rootstock 256
in water garden 243
Damp sites
bulbs for 217
incorporating in design 17
succulents tolerating 262
wildflowers for *167*
woodland, wildflowers for *167*
Damping down 446, 484, 586
Damping off 184, 538, 545, *545*, 560, 566, *566*, 570, *570*
Damsons 383–6
conditions preferred 383
forms 383
freezing 367
pollination 383
preserving 367
recommended cultivars 385
rootstocks 383
'Prune', in large fruit garden *357, 385*
Danäe racemosa, division of suckers 88
Dandelion
as edible plant
cultivation 327, *327*
harvesting 327
as lawn weed 286, 578, *578*, 579
as weed 576
eradicating 167, 276
Daphne
fasciation 563
pruning 74
for scent 66
semiripe cuttings 83, 206
sowing 85
arbuscula
in alpine raised bed *201*
apical-wedge grafting 89
in peat bed *188*
suggestions for use 191
bholua
in shrub border *63*
side-veneer grafting 89
suggestions for use 66
blagayana
conditions preferred 191
suggestions for use 64
x *burkwoodii*
softwood cuttings 81
'Somerset' *186*
seasonal interest 62
cneorum
in alpine raised bed *201*
in rock garden *187*
suggestions for use 191
jasminea, softwood cuttings 206
laureola
conditions preferred 66
conditions tolerated 66
mezereum 74
in shrub border *63*
petraea
side-veneer grafting 89
'Grandiflora'
in alpine raised bed *201*
suggestions for use 191
retusa 191
sericea 191
semiripe cuttings 82
Darlingtonia, soil type required 147
Dasineura
gleditchiae 558
rhodophaga 558
Datura
conditions preferred 66
conditions required 431
pruning 74
Daucus carota, see Carrots
Davidia, layering 55
Dawn redwood, see *Metasequoia glyptostroboides*
Daylength 303, 518
increasing with grow lamps 485, *485*
manipulating artificially 518
variations in, effects on strawberry flowering 404
Daylength neutral plants 303, 336, 337, 338
Daylily, see *Hemerocallis*
Deadheading 101, 155, 586
annuals 184, *184*
biennials 184, *184*
bulbs 230, *230*
climbers 101
shrubs 70, *70*
Dead-man's handle *461*, 465, *466*
Deadnettle, see *Lamium*
Decaisnea, pruning 74
Deciduous plants 586
climate suited to 514
Decking 499–500
building regulations 499
parquet 499, 500
slatted, construction 500
stepping stones of *500*
wood, support for 500, *500*
wood patterns 500, *500*
Decodon verticillatus
propagation
division of rootstock 256
softwood cuttings 256
in water garden 243
Decumaria
semiripe cuttings 111
sinensis 97
pruning 103
Deep-bed system 536, *536*
Deer 310, 551, 572
Dehiscent fruit 581, *581*, 586
Delia
antiqua 569
radicum, see Cabbage root maggots
Delosperma
division of offsets 269
division of rootstock 270
Delphinium
basal stem cuttings 164
for cutting 141
cutting back 156, *156*
diseases 554
fasciation 563
flowering time from seed 160
form 138
germination 538
life expectancy 16
in mixed border *149*
with roses *117*
staking 156, *156*
suggestions for use 140
thinning 155
'Black Knight', companion plant for 139
Delta maidenhair, see *Adiantum raddianum*
Dendrobium
keikis 443
stem cuttings 443
temperature required 441
'Happiness', growing on bark *441*
nobile 440
Dendromecon rigida, conditions preferred 66
Deroceras 550
Desert climate 514
Desert gardens 260, *260*
planting 263
Desfontainia spinosa, soil type required 69
Design, see Planning and design
Deutzia
pruning 76
semiripe cuttings 83
soil type tolerated 62, 69
x *elegantissima* 'Rosealind'
hardwood cuttings 84
in mixed border *20*
longifolia
in garden design *19*
hardwood cuttings 84
'Veitchii' *84*
x *rosea*, hardwood cuttings 84
scabra, cuttings 84
Devil's coach-horse beetles *525*
Diabrotica
longicornis 566
undecimpunctata 149
Dianthus
breeding 140
carnations
diseases 560, 567
mineral deficiency 560
perpetual-flowering
in greenhouse 430
for cutting 175
flowering time from seed 160
in framed planting 21
in garden design *19*
pinks, suggestions for use 27
propagation
softwood cuttings 206
stem tip cuttings 164
in rock garden *186*
scent 135
soil type preferred 146
soil type tolerated 147, 176, 193
suggestions for use 27, 135, 191
alpinus
in alpine raised bed *201*
in rock garden *187*
suggestions for use 189, 190, 191
anatolicus, suggestions for use 191
barbatus
conditions tolerated 175
for cutting 175
thinning *178*
'Bombadier', suggestions for use 189
'Brympton Red', for fragrance 141
carthusianorum
conditions tolerated 191
soil type preferred 193
Chabaud Series, for scent 175
chinensis
conditions tolerated 175
scent 175
deltoides
conditions tolerated 191
soil type preferred 193
suggestions for use 189
echinacea, suggestions for use 191
freynii, suggestions for use 191
Giant Chabaud Series, for cutting 175
glacialis, suggestions for use 191
haematocalyx 188
Knight Series, for cutting 175
'La Bourboule'
in alpine raised bed *201*
in trough *199*
'Mrs. Sinkins', in mixed border *172*
'Old Clove Red', for fragrance 141
pavonius, in alpine raised bed *201*
Diascia
propagation
semiripe cuttings 206
stem tip cuttings 164
cordata, conditions tolerated 191
rigescens, in rock garden *187*
'Ruby Field', conditions tolerated 191
vigilis, in mixed border *215*
Diazinon 550, 551, 553, 554, 560, 561, 562, 563, 564, 565, 566, 567, 568, 569, 571, 572, 573, 574
commercial names 574
Dibbers 179, *179*, *452*, 471, *471*, 586
Dicamba 579
Dicentra
conditions required 431
Dicentra (*cont.*)
conditions tolerated 141
for cutting 141
suggestions for use 148
cucullaria, in peat bed *188*
eximia, conditions tolerated 141
formosa
conditions tolerated 141
in mixed border *172*
spectabilis f. *alba*, in cool border *138*
Dichlorbenil 577, 579
commercial names 574
Dichondra
conditions required 275
for lawns 272
micrantha, for lawns 275
Dicotyledons 586
flower forms 582, *582*
leaf veins 582, *582*
stems 582
Dictamnus albus, for fragrance 141
Didiscus coeruleus, see *Trachymene coerulea*
Didymella applanata 559
Dieback 124, 548, 560, 586
in alpines, cutting back *203*
causes 363, 364, 390, 556, 559
in evergreens 77, 91
rose *120, 125*, 571, *571*
Dieffenbachia
conditions preferred 431
conditions required 431
hydroculture 431, *447*
indoors *427*
Dierama
for cutting 219
pendulum, suggestions for use 217
Diervilla lonicera, division of suckers 88
Diggers, posthole 509
Digging 527–8, *527*, *528*
correct position *458*
cultivators for 461, *461*
disadvantages 527
double 528, *528*, 529, 586
to improve drainage 276
simple 527, *527*
single 527, *527*, 589
time for 527
tools for 459, *459*, 460, *460*
Digitalis
conditions tolerated 27
in layer planting *26*
in mixed border 173
self-sown seedlings 147
Excelsior Series
architectural plant 173
self-sown 184
grandiflora, conditions tolerated 141
lutea, conditions tolerated 141
purpurea
architectural plant 175
conditions tolerated 175
cultivars, in mixed border *172*
with roses 116
self-seeding 178
f. *alba*, in annual border *171*
Digitaria sanguinalis, see Crabgrass
Dill 290, *290*
cross-pollination with fennel 290
culinary uses 290
flowers 290
foliage 290
growing with vegetables *303*
harvesting 290
pests 566
propagation from seed 290, 297
storing 290
suggestions for use 288
Dimethoate 549, 551, 552, 553, 558, 559, 560, 562, 566
commercial names 574
Dimorphotheca
barbariae, see *Osteospermum jucundum*
Sunshine Hybrids, in annual border *171*
Dinocap 552
commercial names 574
Dinteranthus, division of offsets 269
Dioecious plants 582, *582*, 586
Dionysia
plunging after flowering *210*
softwood cuttings 206
aretioides, preparing for exhibition *212*
Dioscorea
semiripe cuttings 111
discolor 97
conditions tolerated 97
suggestions for use 97
Diospyros
kaki, see Persimmons
virginiana, see Persimmons
Dipelta yunnanensis, seasonal interest 66
Diploids 371, 586
Diprion 551
Dipteronia, layering 55
Diquat 577, 579
commercial names 574
Disanthus, pruning 74
Disbudding 586
Discocactus, flat grafting 271
Diseases
affecting bulbs 569
affecting flowers 562–3
affecting fruit, berries, and seeds 564–5
affecting lawns 573
affecting leaf buds 559–61
affecting leaves 552, 553, 554–6, 557, 558, 559–61
affecting roots and tubers 566–8
affecting stems 559–61
affecting whole plant 570–72
in biological pest control 548
chemical control 549
definition 547
diagnosing problems caused by 547, *547*
effect of pH on 525
identifying, method 547
organic control 548, *548*
plants resistant to 548
spread by insects 547
Dishing 530
Disinfectant 555, 571
Disocactus, side grafting 271
Disorders
affecting flowers 562, 563
affecting fruit, berries, and seeds 564–5
affecting lawns 573
affecting leaves 554, 556–7
affecting roots and tubers 566, 568
affecting stems and leaf buds 559, 560, 561
affecting whole plant 570, 571
causes 547
diagnosing problems caused by 547, *547*
Distictis 97
propagation
semiripe cuttings 111
softwood cuttings 110
pruning 103
soil type tolerated 99
buccinatoria 98, *98*
pruning 105, 450
Distylium racemosum, semiripe cuttings 53
Dittany, see *Origanum*
Ditylenchus dipsaci 558, 569
Dividers, fruit as 358

Division 586
  alpines 208, *208*
  cacti and other succulents 266
  grasses 143, *143*
  indoor plants 451–2, *451*
  of offsets, cacti and other succulents 269, *269*
  perennials 157, 162, *162*, 163
  of rhizomes
    bamboos 143, *143*
    water plants 256, *256*
  of rootstock
    bromeliads 433, *433*
    cacti and other succulents 270, *270*
    pot plants 451, *451*
    water plants 256, *256*, 257
  shrubs 88, *88*
  of tubers 455, *455*
  water plants 255, 256, *256*, 257
Dizygotheca elegantissima, suggestions for use 438
Dock 167, 276, 576, *577*, 579
  broad-leaved, see Broad-leaved dock
  indicating soil type 525
Dodecatheon
  soil type tolerated 146
  sowing 205
  'Red Wings', in peat bed *188*
Dog fennel, see *Anthemis*
Dogs 573
  damage to lawn *573*
Dog's-tooth violet, see *Erythronium dens-canis*
Dogwood, see *Cornus*
Dolichos beans, see Beans, hyacinth
Dollar spot 573, *573*
Dolomitic lime, in soil mixes 536
Donkey-tail, see *Sedum morganianum*
Dormancy 586
  breaking 54, 85, 109, 160, 537–8
  double 160
  factors affecting 515
  high temperature 324
  plant mechanisms for 537
  reasons for 515
Dormant oil 554, 560, 562
  commercial names 574
Doronicum
  for cutting 141
  division 163
  soil type tolerated 147
  in spring *139*
  winter interest 141
Dorycnium hirsutum 191
Double budding 382, *382*
Double cordons, see Cordons
Double digging, see Digging
Double grafting 382, *382*
Double sea campion, see *Silene vulgaris* subsp. *maritima*
Double-working 382, *382*
Douglas fir, see *Pseudotsuga menziesii*
Downy mildew 552, *552*
Draba
  propagation
    rosette cuttings 207
    softwood cuttings 206
  soil type tolerated 193
  aizoides, in trough *199*
  bryoides, suggestions for use 191
  mollissima, suggestions for use 191
  polytricha, suggestions for use 191
  rigida
    in alpine raised bed *201*
    in rock garden *187*
Dracaena
  architectural 66
  conditions preferred 431
  conditions required 431
  hydroculture 431
Dracaena (cont.)
  deremensis 'Souvenir de Schriever', potting on *445*
  reflexa, in terrarium *446*
  sanderiana
    in bottle garden *439*
    suggestions for use 438
Dracocephalum moldavicum, for fragrance 141
Dracophilus, division of offsets 269
Drainage 586
  areas left without 17
  ditches 531, *531*
  in frames *489*
  French drains 531
  improving 524, 529, 531, *531*
  installing *277*, 531, *531*
  for lawn 276
  laying pipes 531, *531*
  for patios 493, *493*
  for perennials 145
  poor, testing for 531
  for retaining walls 506
  rock garden 195
  slopes helping 17
  top-dressings for 534, *534*
Draw hoe 460, *460*
Dribble bars, for watering cans 468
Dried flowers, perennials suitable for 141
Drills 586
  sowing annuals and biennials in 177, *177*
  sowing vegetables in 305, *305*
Drimys
  semiripe cuttings 83
  winteri, semiripe cuttings 53
Drip feed irrigation systems 469, *469*
Driveways
  concrete 494
  foundations 493, 494
    concrete mix for 494
  materials for 501
  paving slabs 495–6
  preparing subbase 493, 494
Dropping, shrubs 86
Drosera, soil type required 147
Drought 563, 570
  damage to plants 556, *556*
  effect on lawn 573
  plants adapted to 517
  plants tolerant of 530
  problems of 517
Drumstick primula, see *Primula denticulata*
Drupes 581, 590
Dry areas, lawns for 275
Dry gardens 30
Dry shade
  annuals tolerant of 175
  biennials tolerant of 175
  bulbous plants tolerant of 219
  perennials tolerant of 141
  rock plants tolerant of 191
  shrubs tolerant of 66
Dry-stone walls, see Walls, dry-stone
Dryas
  ripewood cuttings 207, *207*
  octopetala *207*
    conditions tolerated 191
    in peat bed *188*
    'Minor', suggestions for use 191
Drying
  flowers 183, *183*
  herbs
    air- 298, *298*
    freeze- 298
    microwave 298
  roots 298
  seedheads 298, *298*
Dryopteris
  conditions tolerated 158
  in winter 158
  filix-mas, leaf form *581*
Duck potato, see *Sagittaria latifolia*
Duckweed, see *Wolffia*
Dudleya
  ingens, leaf cuttings 267
  rigida, leaf cuttings 267
Dutch elm disease 559–60, *559*
Dutch hoe 460, *460*
Dutchman's breeches, see *Dicentra cucullaria*
Duvalia
  division of offsets 269
  division of rootstock 270
  flat grafting 271
Dwarf fan palm, see *Chamaerops humilis*
Dyckia 433
Dyes, for concrete 502

E

Ear protectors *464*
Earthworms 525, *525*
  encouraging 529, 532
  improving soil structure *525*, 536
  in lawn 283, 286
  soil rich in 301
  working mulch into soil 309
  working organic matter into soil 302
Earwigs 549, 550, *550*, 563
  damage caused by 153, 550, *550*
  trapping 548, *548*, 563
Easter cactus, see *Rhipsalidopsis gaertneri*
Easter lily, see *Lilium longiflorum*
Eastern redbud, see *Cercis canadensis*
Eastern white cedar, see *Thuja occidentalis*
Eau-de-cologne mint, see *Mentha* x *piperita* 'Citrata'
Ebracteola, division of offsets 269
Eccremocarpus scaber 97
  in annual border *171*
  growing as annual 175
  on host plant 173
  from seed 109
  soil type tolerated 100
  suggestions for use 96
  supporting *183*
  survival 184
Echeveria
  in bowl garden 261
  conditions preferred 431
  form 258
  in greenhouse display *261*
  in mixed succulent planting *260*
  propagation
    leaf cuttings 267
    stem cuttings 268
  in raised bed 260
  succulent type 258
  agavoides
    leaf cuttings 267
    suggestions for use 262
  albicans, leaf cuttings *267*
  cuspidata, conditions tolerated 262
  derenbergii, suggestions for use 262
  elegans
    conditions tolerated 262
    leaf cuttings 267
Echeveria (cont.)
  gibbiflora, conditions tolerated 262
  pilosa, suggestions for use 262
  pubescens, conditions tolerated 262
Echidnopsis, division of offsets 269
Echinacea purpurea (syn. *Rudbeckia purpurea*)
  conditions preferred 167
  in perennial border *135*
  'Robert Bloom', in mixed border *215*
Echinocactus
  form 258
  in greenhouse display *261*
  grusonii
    form 259
    suggestions for use 262
Echinocereus
  division of offsets 269
  blanckii, suggestions for use 262
  chloranthus, conditions tolerated 262
  engelmannii, suggestions for use 262
  enneacanthus, conditions tolerated 266
  pentalophus *262*
    conditions tolerated 262
    suggestions for use 262
  triglochidiatus, suggestions for use 262
  viereckii, suggestions for use 262
  viridiflorus
    conditions tolerated 262
    in containers outdoors 260
Echinochloa crusgalli, see Barnyard grass
Echinodorus
  bleheri, suggestions for use 243
  maior, suggestions for use 243
Echinops
  root cuttings 165
  soil type preferred 146
  bannaticus, for drying 141
  ritro
    for drying 141
    'Veitch's Blue' *146*
Echinopsis
  division of offsets 269
  hybrids, conditions required 261
  as rootstock 271
  suggestions for use 262
  aurea 262
  chamaecereus
    conditions tolerated 262
    in containers outdoors 260
    flat grafting 271
    suggestions for use 262
  eyriesii 262
  kermesina 262
  multiplex 262
  oxygona 262
Echium
  'Blue Bedder', in annual border *171*
  vulgare, conditions tolerated 175
Edelweiss, see *Leontopodium alpinum*
Edema 557, *557*
Edgers, half-moon *282*, 285, *285*, *286*, *466*
Edging
  fruit as 358
  for herb garden 288
  herbs as 288, 303, *303*
  lawn 273
    materials for 466
    repairing 285, *285*
    shaping 278, *279*
    tools for 466, *466*
  materials for 499
  for paths 27, 295
    plants as 501
Edging *(cont.)*
  for paving 496, *496*, 498, *498*
  for random paving, defining 496
  in rose garden 116
Edging boards 545, *546*
Edible landscaping 303, *303*
Edible prickly pears, see Prickly pears
Edithcolea, flat grafting 270, 271
Edraianthus
  dinaricus, suggestions for use 191
  graminifolius, suggestions for use 191
  pumilio
    in alpine raised bed *201*
    suggestions for use 191
  serpillifolius, in alpine raised bed *201*
Edwardsiana rosea 553
Eelworms, see Nematodes
Egeria densa, softwood cuttings 256
Eggplants *328*, 334–5, *335*
  in containers 307
  in crop rotation 304
  cultivation 334–5
  growing below wall 301
  harvesting 312, 335, *335*
  mineral deficiency 564
  nitrogen requirement 310, 334
  origins *328*
  pests 551
  recommended cultivars 334
  ripening under cover 311
  storing 312, 335
  'Easter Egg' *334*
Eichhornia
  azurea 243
  crassipes 243
    conditions required 240
    propagation
      offsets 257, *257*
      plantlets 257
Elaeagnus
  conditions tolerated 66
  deciduous, semiripe cuttings with heel 83
  scent 66
  semiripe cuttings with heel 83
  angustifolius, conditions tolerated 37
  commutata
    conditions tolerated 66
    layering 86
  x *ebbingei* 'Gilt Edge', seasonal interest 66
Elder, see *Sambucus*
Electricity
  compared to gasoline 464, 465, 466
  in greenhouse, installing 480
  for greenhouse heating 482
  safety 458, 464, 488
  supply to greenhouse 475
Elettaria cardamomum, suggestions for use 288
Elm, see *Ulmus*
Elm bark beetles 560
Elodea
  canadensis 243
    softwood cuttings 256, 257
  crispa, see *Lagarosiphon major*
Elymus repens, see Quackgrass
Emasculation, definition 586
Embothrium coccineum, soil preferred 41
Encarsia formosa, as biological pest control 548, *549*, 552
Endive 322–3
  blanching 322, *323*
  cultivation 322–3
  curled
    recommended cultivars 322
    in vegetable garden *300*
  as cut-and-come-again seedling crop 312
  escarole, recommended cultivars 322

(entry cont. overleaf)

Endive (*cont.*)
forcing 311
harvesting 323
nitrogen requirement 310, 322
overwintering 323
cultivars for 322
'Full Heart Batavian' *322*
Endive, Belgian 321, *321*
culinary uses 323
cultivation 323
forcing 311, 323, *323*
form 323
harvesting 323
recommended cultivars 323
storing 323
English bluebell, see *Hyacinthoides non-scripta*
English holly, see *Ilex aquifolium*
English oak, see *Quercus robur*
Enkianthus
pruning 74
softwood cuttings 81
soil type required 69
Enzymes 581
Eomecon, soil type tolerated 146
Epicactus, suggestions for use 262
Epicormic shoots 586, see also Water shoots
Epidendrum, stem cuttings 443
Epidermis *580*
Epigaea
gaultherioides, soil type required 192
repens, soil type required 192
Epigeal germination 538, *538*, 586
Epilobium, see also Willow herb
dividing 163
in wild garden *27*
canum, stem tip cuttings 164
Epimedium
conditions tolerated 141
x *rubrum* 150
x *youngianum* 'Niveum' *150*
Epiphyllum
conditions preferred 431
disorders 554
in greenhouse display *430*
hybrids, conditions required 261
propagation
leaf sections 455
softwood cuttings 453
stem cuttings 268
stem section *268*
cartagense, suggestions for use 262
oxypetalum
conditions tolerated 262
suggestions for use 262
Epiphytes 586
aerial roots 585
bromeliads
displaying 432, *432*
feeding 433
mist-spraying 433
as pot plants 432
propagation by offsets 433, *433*
cacti 258
apical-wedge grafting 271
conditions required 261
flowers 259
watering 265
indoors 428
orchids
conditions preferred 427
cultivation 440
growing without pots 441
habitats 440
methods of growth 440
monopodial 440
potting 441
soil mix 440, *440*
sympodial 440
succulents
conditions required 261
watering 265
Epipremnum 97
conditions preferred 431
conditions tolerated 97
softwood cuttings 453
suggestions for use 97
aureum, growth rate 97
Episcia
conditions preferred 431
conditions tolerated 427
propagation by runners 451
suggestions for use 438
Epithelantha
division of offsets 269
flat grafting 271
Epsom salts 362, 557
Equipment 458–73, see also Tools
general garden 470–72, *470–72*
for watering 468–9, *468–9*
Equisetum, see Horsetail
Eranthis
conditions preferred 219
forcing 228
hyemalis 228
diseases 565
in mixed border 214
suggestions for use 227
Erapsia, division of offsets 269
Ercilla
semiripe cuttings 111
volubilis, soil type tolerated 99
Eremochloa ophiuroides
for lawn 274
sowing rate 280
Eremurus
forcing 228
form 138
seasonal interest 25
soil type tolerated 147
Erica
clematis growing through 106
dwarf conifers with 38
conditions required 431
as ground cover 64
with clematis *95*
propagation
division of suckers 88
dropping 86
layering 86
semiripe cuttings 206
softwood cuttings 81
pruning 77
soil type required 69
suggestions for use 64
arborea var. *alpina*, soil type preferred 67
carnea
conditions tolerated 66
mulching *151*
'December Red' *150*
'Vivellii', in shrub border *63*
cinerea, soil type preferred 67
lusitanica, scent 66
x *williamsii* 'P.D. Williams' *62*
Ericaceous plants 586, see also Lime haters
Erigeron
for cutting 141
karvinskianus, conditions tolerated 191
Erinacea
anthyllis 191
semiripe cuttings 206
suggestions for use 191
pungens, in alpine raised bed *201*
Erinus alpinus
conditions tolerated 191
in dry-stone wall *189*
suggestions for use 191
'Dr. Haenele', suggestions for use 189
Eriobotrya japonica
architectural 66
as fruit, see Loquats
Eriocereus bonplandii, suggestions for use 262
Eriogonum
ripewood cuttings 207
ovalifolium, softwood cuttings 206
Eriophorum
angustifolium
division of rootstock 256
in water garden 243
latifolium, in water garden 243
Eriophyes (eriophyid mites) 558, 561
Eriophyllum lanatum, softwood cuttings 206
Eriosoma lanigerum 560
Erodium
greenwood cuttings 206, *207*
root cuttings 165
chamaedryoides, suggestions for use 191
corsicum, in dry-stone wall *189*
guttatum
conditions tolerated 191
soil type preferred 193
Erosion, on slopes 301
Eruca vesicaria, see Arugula
Erwinia
amylovora 555, 571
caratovora
var. *atroseptica* 570
var. *carotovora* 569
Eryngium
conditions tolerated 191
foliage 138
in free planting *21*
root cuttings 165
for seedheads 141
soil type tolerated 147
x *oliverianum*, in cool border *138*
tripartitum, soil type preferred 146
variifolium, conditions tolerated 141
Erysimum
stem tip cuttings 164
helveticum, soil type tolerated 193
Erythronium
conditions preferred 219
forcing 228
seedlings, planting out 235, *235*
storing 224
americanum 167
dens-canis, suggestions for use 227
hendersonii, in peat bed *188*
oregonum
choosing healthy bulbs *224*
in peat bed *188*
'Pagoda', in peat bed *188*
revolutum, suggestions for use 227
'White Beauty'
in peat bed *188*
suggestions for use 227
Escallonia
conditions tolerated 62, 66
cuttings 83
as hedge 59
pruning 78
'Apple Blossom', in mixed border *20*
'Donard Seedling', pruning 78
'Langleyensis' *58*
Eschscholzia
conditions tolerated 175
as ground cover 173
propagation, self-seeding 184
protecting seedlings *178*
californica 177
in meadow garden 167
in mixed border 173
self-seeding 178
soil type preferred 176
sowing 177
Eschscholzia (*cont.*)
'Monarch Art Shades', in annual border *171*
Escobaria, division of offsets 269
Espalier-trained plants 586
form 356, *356*
pruning 49, 357
fruit 378, *378*, *380*
ornamental 49
as screen 357
spacing 372
training 49, 356, 357, 378, *378*
Espostoa
lanata
planting *263*
suggestions for use 262
melanostele, suggestions for use 262
Essential oils, from herbs 288
Ethylene, given off by apples 229
Etiolation 427, 561
Etiolation layering, see Trench layering
Eucalyptus
bark 32
conditions tolerated 37
coppicing 50
physiological disorders 557
pollarding 50, *77*
scent 34
coccifera, suggestions for use 37
dalrympleana
bark 35, *35*
seasonal interest 37
suggestions for use 37, 50
ficifolia, soil type preferred 42
globulus, suggestions for use 50
gunnii, suggestions for use 50
niphophila, suggestions for use 37
pauciflora
seasonal interest 37
suggestions for use 50
Eucomis
architectural plant 219
conditions preferred 219
in greenhouse garden *430*
in mixed border 215
suggestions for use 218
Eucryphia
layering 55
pruning 74
semiripe cuttings 53
glutinosa, seasonal interest 37
lucida, softwood cuttings 53
milliganii 62
x *nymansensis* 35
'Nymansay' *53*
suggestions for use 37
Eulalaia grass, see *Miscanthus*
Eumerus, see Narcissus bulb flies
Euonymus
conditions required 431
germination 85
pests 551
self-layering 113
semiripe cuttings 111
soil type tolerated 69
suggestions for use 148
for topiary 90
alatus
bonsai 434
in informal shrub grouping *61*
seasonal interest 62
as weed 576
fortunei 65
conditions preferred 66
conditions tolerated 64, 66, 97
propagation
cuttings 151
division of suckers 88
pruning 78
suggestions for use 66
Euonymus fortunei (*cont.*)
'Emerald Gaiety', reverted shoot *70*
'Emerald 'n' Gold', nonvariegated shoot *70*
'Gold Spot' 151
'Silver Queen'
contrasting with climber *94*
foliage 64
in shrub border *63*
soil type tolerated 99
japonicus
conditions preferred 66
conditions tolerated 66
pruning 78
Eupatorium 15
purpureum, suggestions for use 243
Euphorbia
conditions tolerated 191
hydroculture 431
latex produced by 268
in restricted color border *63*
seasonal interest *25*
seed germination 160
stem cuttings 268
succulent groups 258
amygdaloides
conditions tolerated 141
'Purpurea', suggestions for use 140
subsp. *robbiae*
in mixed island bed *136*
winter interest 141
canariensis, in succulent group *258*
candelabrum, in desert garden 260, *260*
characias
conditions tolerated 141
growth rate 141
winter interest 141
subsp. *wulfenii 25*
in mixed border *137*
flanaganii, suggestions for use 262
fulgens, conditions required 431
milii
hydroculture *447*
suggestions for use 262
myrsinites
conditions tolerated 191
in rock garden *187*
obesa, suggestions for use 262
palustris, suggestions for use 243
polychroma, in mixed border *215*
pulcherrima
conditions preferred 431
conditions required 431
in garden room *428*
softwood cuttings 453
Euphorbiaceae 258
European apple sawflies 565, *565*
European ash, see *Fraxinus excelsior*
European beech, see *Fagus sylvatica*
European fan palm, see *Chamaerops humilis*
European larch, see *Larix decidua*
European viburnum beetles 550, *550*
European Welsh onions, see Onions, Welsh
Euryale ferox
from seed 257
in water garden 243
Euryops
stem tip cuttings 164
acraeus 191
in alpine raised bed *201*
in rock garden *187*
seasonal interest 66
pectinatus
conditions preferred 66
in hot border *139*
Evaporative coolers 483

- Evening primrose, see *Oenothera*
- Evergreens 586
  - climate suited to 514
  - climbing 97
    - planting 99
    - pruning 104
    - as screen 94
    - for winter interest 94, 96
  - combining with deciduous trees 35
  - dieback 91
  - feeding, after pruning 77
  - as ground cover 150
  - as hedge 59
    - shaping 60
  - mulching 78
  - for parterres 31
  - planting time 41
  - propagation
    - cuttings, preparing *53*, 541, *541*
    - hardwood cuttings 540
  - protecting in winter 43, *521*
  - pruning 47
    - established 49, *49*
    - formative 48
  - scorch 91
  - shrubs
    - in containers 65
    - pruning 74, 77–8, *78*
    - renovation 80
  - snow damage to *517*
  - for topiary 90
- Everlasting flower, see *Helichrysum bracteatum*
- Everlasting flowers
  - annuals to dry as 174
  - drying 183, *183*
  - harvesting 183, *183*
- Everlasting pea, see *Lathyrus grandiflorus*; *Lathyrus latifolius*
- *Exacum*
  - conditions required 431
  - *affine*
    - for fragrance 175
    - as pot plants 175
    - from seed 452
- Exhibition
  - alpines 212, *212*
  - dahlias 223
  - roses 134, *134*
- *Exobasidium vaccinii* 558
- *Exochorda*, pruning 76
- Explants 546, 586
- Exposed sites
  - annuals and biennials for 175
  - bulbs for 219
  - climbers for 93
  - perennials for 141
  - rock plants for 191
  - shrubs for 66
  - trees for *37*
- Exposure of garden, effect on soil temperature 515
- Extractor fans 483
- Eye 586
- Eyesores
  - camouflaging 106
  - ground cover plants on 119

F

- F1 hybrids 452, 586
  - method of producing 538
  - qualities 176
- F2 hybrids 586
  - method of producing 538
- *Fagus*
  - for avenues 36
- *Fagus* (*cont.*)
  - clumps as focal point 34
  - copper, suggestions for use 32
  - disease resistance 567
  - diseases 570
  - pests 558
  - plants under 26
  - pleaching 36
  - propagation
    - apical-wedge grafting 56
    - seed 55
    - side-veneer grafting 56
  - soil type indicated by 525
  - *grandiflora*, soil type preferred 41
  - *sylvatica*
    - as hedge 58, 59
    - soil type tolerated 41
    - 'Dawyck Gold'
      - seasonal interest 37
      - suggestions for use 37
- Fair-maids-of-France, see *Saxifraga granulata*
- Fairway crested wheatgrass, see *Agropyron cristatum*
- Fairy lantern, see *Calochortus*
- Fairy rings 574
- Fall
  - annuals for 171
  - color in 25, *25*, 96
  - mixed plantings for *215*
  - perennials for 139
  - shrubs for interest in 62, *66*
  - tasks for 584
  - trees for interest in 35
- *Fallopia*, see *Polygonum*
- Falls, definition 586
- False acacia, see *Robinia pseudoacacia*
- False cypress, see *Chamaecyparis*
- Family, definition 586
- Family garden 14
- Fan-training
  - form 356, *356*
  - shrubs 79, *79*
  - trees, pruning 49
- Fanwort, see *Cabomba caroliniana*
- Fasciation 563
- *Fascicularia bicolor*, temperature for 433
- Fast-growing perennials 141
- x *Fatshedera*, conditions preferred indoors 431
- *Fatsia*
  - conditions preferred 431
  - conditions required 431
  - *japonica*
    - conditions preferred 66
    - conditions tolerated 66, 427
    - foliage 61, 64, 126
    - in garden design *19*
    - indoors *427*
    - 'Variegata'
      - as ground cover 151
      - plunging in large container *437*
- *Faucaria*
  - division of offsets 269
  - division of rootstock 270
  - *felina*, suggestions for use 262
- Fava beans, see Beans, broad
- Feathered maidens, see Maidens
- Feathertop, see *Pennisetum villosum*
- *Felicia*
  - from seed 176
  - stem tip cuttings 164, 176
- Felling trees 45, *45*
- Fences 508–12
  - as background 22
  - basic elements 508
  - chain link 508, *508*
  - clematis on 106
  - climbers on 92, *93*
    - positioning 99
- Fences (*cont.*)
  - closeboard 508, *508*
  - conditions on each side 519
  - as framework 21
  - frost pockets beside 515, *515*
  - fruit trees against, positioning *361*
  - growing fruit on 358
  - interference 508, *508*
  - lattice 508, *508*
  - legal requirements 508, 510
  - maintenance 510–11
  - making decorative 508
  - metal post supports *509*, 510
  - panel *508*, 509–10
    - erecting 509–10, *509*
  - picket 508, *508*
  - post-and-chain 508, *508*
  - post-and-rail 508, *508*
  - posts for 508
    - concrete 508
    - repairs 510
    - wooden 508, *509*
  - rails 508
    - inset *510*
  - ranch-style 508, *508*
  - roses for 118
  - shingle 508, *508*
  - siding 508
  - on sloping ground 510, *510*
  - snow *521*
  - south-facing, plants for 519
  - splitwood 508, *508*
  - stepped 510, *510*
  - types 508, *508*
  - uses 492, 508
  - wattle hurdles 508, *508*
  - wavy-edged 508, *508*
  - welded wire 508, *508*
  - as windbreaks 301, 519, *519*
  - wooden, preservatives for 510
- *Fenestraria*
  - division of rootstock 270
  - *aurantiaca*, leaf cuttings 267
- Fennel, see *Foeniculum vulgare*
- Fennel, Florence 291, 341, *341*, 346–7, *346*
  - cultivation 346–7
  - harvesting 347, *347*
  - nitrogen requirement 310, 346
  - recommended cultivars 347
  - 'Zefa Fino' *347*
- Fennel, sweet, see Fennel, Florence
- *Fenusa pusilla* 553
- Ferbam 554, 557, 558, 559, 561, 562, 571, 572, 573
  - commercial names 574
- Ferns 158–9
  - in alpine house 190, 212
  - conditions preferred 518
    - in greenhouse 484
  - conditions required 158
  - conditions tolerated 27, 427
  - cultivation 158
  - hardy 158
    - planting 158
  - indoors 428
  - in layered planting 26
  - neglected, renovating 444
  - pests 553
  - propagation 158–9, *158*, *159*
    - bulbils *158*, 159
    - spores 159, *159*
  - soil mix for 439
  - suggestions for use 140, 216, 241, 427
  - tender tropical 158
    - conditions required 158
    - potting up 158
    - soil mix for 158
    - suggestions for use 158
    - watering 158
  - for texture 25
  - in water garden *240*
  - in woodland garden 140
- *Ferocactus*
  - handling *263*
  - *acanthodes*, suggestions for use 262
- *Ferocactus* (*cont.*)
  - *latispinus*, suggestions for use 262
  - *setispinus* *259*
- Ferrous sulfate 415
- Fertile plants, definition 587
- Fertilization 582, 587
- Fertilizer burn 556, *556*
- Fertilizers 532–3
  - applying 309, 533, *533*
    - broadcast 533, *533*
    - foliar 533
    - liquid 533
    - placement 533, *533*
    - quantities 533
  - bulky organic 532
  - comparing *532*
  - concentrated 532
  - damage caused by 556, *556*
  - foliar 533, 570
    - sprayers for 468, *468*
  - forms available 309
  - for hydroculture 447, *447*
  - inorganic 587
    - applying 532
    - compared to manure 532
    - nutrient content 532
    - soluble 532
      - amount required compared to other fertilizers *532*
  - for lawns 282
    - application 282, *283*
  - liquid 533
  - as mulch 44
  - nutrient content 532
  - organic
    - nutrient content 532
    - in organic growing methods 536
  - slow-release 70, *447*, 532–3
    - advantages 532
    - method of working 532, *533*
  - soluble 532
  - speed of action 70
  - sprayers for 468, *468*
  - spreaders 467, *467*
    - calibrating 283
  - types 532–3
- *Ferula communis*
  - in cool border *138*
  - growth rate 141
- Fescue, see *Festuca*
  - Chewing's, see *F. rubra* var. *commutata*
  - red, see *F. rubra* var. *rubra*
  - tall, see *F. arundinacea*
- *Festuca*
  - for lawn 274, 275
    - seeding rate 280
  - for meadow garden 167
  - in sod 278
  - *arundinacea*, in lawn 274
  - *glauca*
    - conditions tolerated 141
    - in mixed island bed *136*
    - for seedheads 141
    - winter interest 141
  - *rubra*
    - var. *commutata* 275
      - for lawn 274
      - 'Jamestown' 275
      - 'Koket' 275
      - 'Menuet' 275
    - var. *rubra*
      - for lawn 274
        - sowing rate 280
- Feverfew, see *Tanacetum parthenium*
- Fiber fleece, as mulch 534
- Fiberglass insulation, under pond liner *246*, 247
- Fibrous films, see Fleecy films
- *Ficus*
  - conditions preferred 431
  - conditions required 431
  - for office 428
  - propagation
    - air layering 55, 87
    - hardwood cuttings 53
    - leaf-bud cuttings 453
    - semiripe cuttings 540
- *Ficus* (*cont.*)
  - *benjamina*
    - bonsai 434
    - hydroculture 431
    - softwood cuttings 453
    - in soil bench *439*
    - suggestions for use 37
    - 'Reginald', plunging in large container *437*
    - 'Variegata' *37*
      - supporting *436*
  - *carica*, see Figs
  - *deltoidea*, suggestions for use 428
  - *elastica*
    - cleaning foliage *444*
    - foliage 426
    - 'Tricolor', air layering 456, *456*
  - *lyrata*, suggestions for use 428
  - *pumila*
    - self layering 113
    - suggestions for use 438
    - 'Variegata'
      - in terrarium *438*, *446*
      - watering with capillary matting *446*
  - 'Starlight', in indoor hanging garden *428*
- Fiddle-leaf fig, see *Ficus lyrata*
- Field bindweed, see Bindweed, field
- Field woodrush 576
  - control 579
- Fieldstone, for paving 496
- Figs 395–6, *395*, for ornamental varieties, see *Ficus*
  - conditions preferred 371
  - in containers 359, *395*
  - cultivation 395–6
  - drying 367
  - fruit type 355, 371
  - in greenhouse 355
  - harvesting 396
  - pests 395, 565
  - propagation
    - hardwood cuttings 370, *370*, 396
    - suckers 370, 396
  - pruning 395–6, *395*, *396*
  - recommended cultivars 395
  - storing 367, 396
  - 'Brown Turkey' *395*
    - in large fruit garden *357*
- Figwort, see *Scrophularia*
- Filament 582, *582*, 587
- Filberts 424–5, *424*, see also *Corylus maxima*
  - cultivation 424–5
  - frizzled 424
  - harvesting 425
  - propagation, suckers 370
  - recommended cultivars 424
  - storing 425
- *Filipendula*
  - *palmata*, in border of mixed textures *138*
  - *rubra*
    - growth rate 141
    - suggestions for use 243
  - *ulmaria*
    - for fragrance 141
    - suggestions for use 243
    - 'Aurea'
      - foliage 139
      - soil type tolerated 146
- Fimbriate organs, definition 587
- Fir, see *Abies*
  - Douglas, see *Pseudotsuga menziesii*
- Fire blight 555, *555*, 571, *571*
- Fire lily, see *Lilium bulbiferum*
- Firecracker vine, see *Manettia cordifolia*
- Fireplace, plants in 427
- Firethorn, see *Pyracantha*
- Fish
  - affecting water balance 254
  - in aquarium *245*

(*entry cont. overleaf*)

Fish (*cont.*)
conditions required 243
depth of pond for 248
feeding 255
introducing into pond 253, *253*
stocking pond with 253
usefulness in pond 255
in water garden 243
in container 242
in winter, in pond 255
Fittonia
conditions preferred 431
conditions required 431
softwood cuttings 453
argyroneura, in soil bench *439*
verschaffeltii 438
suggestions for use 438
in terrarium *446*
Five-leaf akebia, see *Akebia quinata*
Five-leaved ivy, see *Parthenocissus quinquefolia*
Flame vine, see *Pyrostegia venusta*
Flaming Katy, see *Kalanchoe blossfeldiana*
Flaming-sword, see *Vriesea splendens*
Flannel flower, see *Fremontodendron*
Flat, definition 587
Flax, see *Linum*
Flea beetles 550, *550*
control 310, 550
Fleabane, see *Erigeron*
Fleecy films, as floating row covers 311, *311*
Floating aquatics 240, 242, 243
choosing healthy plants *251*
stocking pond with 252, *252*
Floating row covers 490, 534
types 311, *311*
Floating water plantain, see *Luronium natans*
Flocculation 529
Florence fennel, see Fennel, Florence
Florets 582, 587
shapes, chrysanthemums *154*
Floss flower, see *Ageratum houstonianum*
Flower gatherers 462, *462*
Flowerhead, definition 587
Flowering currant, see *Ribes sanguineum*
Flowering dogwood, see *Cornus florida*
Flowering gum, see *Eucalyptus ficifolia*
Flowering onion, see *Allium*
Flowering quince, see *Chaenomeles*
Flowering rush, see *Butomus umbellatus*
Flowering vegetables 328–35
Flower-of-an-hour, see *Hibiscus trionum*
Flowers 587
anemone-centered, definition 585
balled, definition 585
bisexual 582, *582*
classes 582, *582*
collecting, for preserving 298
cut
annuals for 174, 175, 183
biennials for 175
bulbs for 218, *218*, 219
perennials for 141
removing pollen beetles 563
discoloration, causes and treatments 562
distorted and eaten 563
diversity 582
Flowers (*cont.*)
double, definition 587
as result of mutation 582
drying
annuals 174, 175, 183, *183*
biennials for 175
perennials for 141
fasciation 563
florets 582
forms 582, 587, 589, 590
growing vegetables with 303, *303*
importance of water to 517
individual 582
informal, definition 587
panicles 582
parts 582, *582*
proliferation 563
racemes 582
reproductive parts 537, *537*
sexuality 582, *582*
spikes 582
squirrel damage 565
sunlight affecting opening 518
trees for 34, *34*
types 582
umbels 582
unisexual 582, *582*
wild, see Wildflowers
Flowers of sulfur 237, 414
Fluorescent lamps, as grow lamps 485
Flush, definition 587
Fly larva predators, as biological pest control 548
Foam flower, see *Tiarella*
Focal points
beside pond *144*
containers as 174
dwarf conifers as 38, *38*
framed by climbers *93*
furniture as *14*, *29*
in indoor plant groups 426
leading eye to 273
in patio garden *29*
perennials as 140
perspective 18
pests 566
planning 18
shrubs, in containers 65
specimen plants as 23
specimen roses as 117, *117*
specimen shrubs as 63
specimen trees as 33, *33*
structural plants as 23
trailing annuals as *173*
Foeniculum vulgare 22, *291*
architectural form 141
cross-pollination with dill 290
culinary uses 291
flowers 291
foliage 135, 291
harvesting 291
in herb garden *287*
propagation
division 291
from seed 291
scent 287
var. *dulce*, see Fennel, Florence
'Purpureum' 291
companion plants 288
in herb garden *295*
Fogging chamber 81, *81*
Foliage, see Leaves
Foliar feeds 309, 533
Fontinalis antipyretica 243
Foot rots 560, *560*, 567, *567*
Footprinting 282
Forcing 587
Belgian endive 323, *323*
bulbs 213, 219, 228–9
care 232
planting out after 232
herbs 294
radicchio 324
Forficula auricularia, see Earwigs
Forget-me-not, see *Myosotis*
Forking 527, *527*
for weed control 577
Forks 459, *459*
hilts 459, *459*
shafts 459
size 459
types
border 459, *459*
hand 460, *460*
potato 459, *459*
standard 459, *459*
Form for concrete 248, *248*, 494, *494*, 502
Forma (f.), definition 587
Formal garden 21, *30*
enclosed *14*
as outdoor room 14
pool in 28
styles 29–31
Formica, see Ants
Forsythia
disease 561
fasciation 563
flowers 65
as hedge 59
in mixed border 214
propagation
hardwood cuttings 84
layering 86
semiripe cuttings 83
softwood cuttings 81
pruning 76
soil type tolerated 67, 69
x *intermedia* 'Spectabilis' *58*
as hedge 59
suspensa, as wall shrub 64
Forsythia gall 561, *561*
Fortunella
japonica, see Kumquats
margarita, see Kumquats
Fothergilla
layering 86
pruning 74
soil type required 69
Foundation planting *16*, 32, *32*, 61, 587
Fountain flower, see *Ceropegia sandersonii*
Fountains 241
bubble 240, 241
Foxglove, see *Digitalis*
Foxtail lily, see *Eremurus*
Fragaria
x *ananassa*, see Strawberries
vesca 'Semperflorens', see Strawberries, alpine
Fragrance, see Scent
Frailea, flat grafting 271
Framed planting 21, *21*, 27
Frames 474, 489, 585
alpines in 210
bulbs in 218, 231
circulating air in *545*
drainage *489*
glazing 489
growing vegetables in 311
hardening off in 180, *180*
insulation 489
materials for 489
microclimates in 519
orientation 301
planting in *489*
for propagation 545
protecting crops with *489*
siting 301, *301*, 489
sizes 489
types 489
uses 474, 489, *489*
ventilation 489, *489*
Framework *16*, 32, *32*, 587
Frame-working 379, 587
France, garden design in 29
Frangipani, see *Plumeria*
Frankliniella
occidentalis 553, 562
tritici 562
Frass 559
Fraxinus
buying 40
conditions tolerated 37
diseases 572
Fraxinus (*cont.*)
propagation
side-veneer grafting 56
whip-and-tongue grafting 56
soil type indicated by 525
soil type tolerated 42
americanus, conditions tolerated 37
excelsior
conditions tolerated 37
soil type tolerated 41
'Pendula', formation 49
ornus, soil type tolerated 41
oxycarpa 'Raywood', suggestions for use 37
Freckle-face, see *Hypoestes phyllostachya*
Free planting 21, *21*
Freesia
conditions required 431
for cutting 219
'Everett' *218*
Freeze-drying, herbs 298
Freezing
fruit, method 367
fruit suitable for 367
herbs, in ice 298, *298*
Fremontodendron, suggestions for use 66
French beans, see Beans, snap
French drains 531
French lavender, see *Lavandula stoechas*
French layering 539, *539*
shrubs 87
French marigold, see *Tagetes patula*
French sorrel 293
in herb garden *295*
French tarragon, see Tarragon, French
Friendship plant, see *Pilea involucrata*
Fringecups, see *Tellima grandiflora*
Frithia, division of rootstock 270
Fritillaria
bulb 214
dwarf, conditions tolerated 219
forcing 228
in mixed border 214
pests 550
propagation
scaling 236, 542
from seed 234
seed
germination 235
harvesting *230*
suggestions for use 219
acmopetala
in alpine garden *217*
division of bulblets 233
camschatcensis, conditions preferred 219
cirrhosa, conditions preferred 219
crassifolia, division of bulblets 233
imperialis
architectural plant 219
in mixed border 215
'Lutea', in mixed border *215*
meleagris
propagation, from seed *234*
seedlings *234*
suggestions for use 216, 217, 227
michailovskyi, suggestions for use 217
persica
conditions preferred 219
in mixed border 215
pudica, division of bulblets 233
pyrenaica, suggestions for use 227
raddeana, seedlings, potting up *235*
Fritillaria (*cont.*)
recurva
division of bulblets 233
flowering problems 232
roylei, conditions preferred 219
thunbergii
division of bulblets 233
flowering problems 232
uva-vulpis, transporting for exhibition *212*
Frizzled filberts, see Filberts
Frogbit, see *Hydrocharis morsus-ranae*
Frogs
benefits of 549
habitats for 241
Fronds 587
bulbils on *158*, 159
sporangia on 159, *159*
Frost
as aid to cultivation 517
areas susceptible to 358
damage caused by 515, 570
to flowers 358, 556, 563
to fruit 358
danger of thaw after 515
design in areas of 15
duration 515
effect on soil 294
forms 515
ground 515
occurrence 515
plants lifted by 515, 521
pockets 240, 358, 515, *515*, 520, 587
ponds in areas of 240
protecting fruit from 358, 363
protecting trees from 45
in spring *514*, 515, 521
trees tolerating 39
value to soil 517
Fruit 587, see also Fruit, soft; Fruit, tender; Fruit, tree; individual fruits by name
biennial bearing 362, 585
bird damage 565
in border *358*
botany 581–2
bottling 367
choosing cultivars 360
choosing plants 359
conditions preferred 355, 518
conditions required 360
conditions suitable for 358
in containers 355, 358, 359
routine care 362
under cover 359
crop size 359
crop succession 359
crop timing 359
dehiscent 581, *581*, 586
diseases 363
bacterial 554, 571
fungal 552, 554, 560, 562, 567
drainage problems 360
effect of drought on 530
effect of temperatures on 556, 570
forms, for small garden 358
freezing 367
fruiting habits, pruning depending on 365
growing against supports 358
growing under cover 359
pruning 363
routine care 363
harvesting 367
importance of water to 517
improving soil for 360
indehiscent 581, *581*, 587
integrating into garden plan 357–8
mineral deficiencies 360, 556–7, 560, 562
in mixed planting *358*
mulching 360
ornamental trees for 34
pests 363
damaging leaves 551, 552, 553, 554, 557

(*entry cont.*)

Fruit (*cont.*)
  plant types 355–6
  planting depth *360*, 361, *361*
  pollination compatibility 359
  preserving 367
  problems 564–5
  problems affecting stems and leaf buds 559, 560, 561
  propagation 368–70, *368–70*
    hardwood cuttings 370, *370*
    layering 368, 370, 539
    leaf-bud cuttings 370
    runners 368, 370
    from seed 370
    softwood cuttings 370
    suckers 368, 370
  protection 355
    from birds and animals 357, 358, 363, *363*
    from cold 358, 363
    netting for 472
    from wind 357, 358, 363
  pruning, under glass 363
  rootstocks, for small garden 358
  routine care 362–3
  seed dispersal 581, *581*
  self-fertile 360
  self-sterile 357, 360
  set 587
  site preparation 360
  siting 357, 358
  in small garden 358
  soil pH level 360
  soil types, effect on quality 360
  spacing 357
  spraying, near ornamentals 358
  squirrel damage 565
  storing 367, *367*
    damage caused by mice, rats, and voles 568
  succulent 581
  suggestions for use 355–9
  suitable for freezing 367
  supports for, under cover 363
  for texture 24
  training, for small garden 358
  types 581, *581*
  weed control 363
Fruit, soft 404–14, see also individual fruits by name
  bush
    plant types 356
    planting 361, *361*
    protecting 521
    pruning 364–6
    range of fruits 356, 404
    training 356, 364–6
  cane
    diseases 567
    hybrid, pests 565
    planting 361
    propagation, suckers 370
    range of fruits 356, 404
    suckers 370
    training, for small garden 358
    type of growth 356
  choosing cultivars 360
  conditions tolerated 404
  cuttings 368
  diseases 564
  freezing 367, *367*
  growing against supports 358
  harvesting 367
  improving soil for 360
  mulching 362
  physiological disorders 564
  preserving 367
  pruning 404
  range of fruits 356, 404
  routine care 362
  self-fertile 360
  soil type preferred 404
  storing 367
Fruit, subtropical, pests 565
Fruit, tender 415–23, see also individual fruits by name
  feeding 415
  in greenhouse 355
Fruit, tender (*cont.*)
  growing under cover 359
  origins 415
  as ornamental trees 415
  overwintering 363
  pests 552
  propagation from seed 368, 370
  pruning 364
  range of fruits 356
  routine care 363
  site preparation 415
Fruit, tree 371–96, see also individual fruits by name
  bare-root
    buying 360, *360*
    planting 361
  bark splitting 363
  bush 356, *356*
  buying 360–61, *360*
    age to choose 361
  categories 355, 371
  choosing healthy plants 360, *360*
  container-grown
    buying 360, *360*
    planting 361
  cordon arch *359*
  cordons *356*
    double (U) 356
    multiple 356
    planting 356
      against fence *361*
      in open ground *361*
    space required 358
    suggestions for use 355
    training 356
    triple 356
    types *356*
  cross-pollination 358, 360, 371
  diseases 571
  dwarf, staking 361
  dwarf pyramid *356*, 357
  effect of nitrogen on 362
  espalier *356*
    space required 358
    suggestions for use 355
    training 356, 357
  fan *356*
    space required 358
    suggestions for use 355
    training 356
  feathered maidens 361
    pruning 365
  feeding 362, *362*
    foliar feeds 533
  forms 356, *356*, 371
    trained 356–7, *356*
    unrestricted 356, *356*
  grafted, planting *360*
  in grass 362
  growing against support, positioning 361
    growing under cover 371
      pruning 366
  half-standard 356, *356*
  improving fruiting
    by root pruning 366, *366*
    by training 365–6
  maiden, training 356
  maiden whip 361
    training for shape 365, *365*
  manuring, dangers of 360
  mineral deficiencies 362
  mulching 362
  pests 554, 566
  physiological disorders 564
  planting
    in containers 361
    in open ground 361, *361*
    position of graft union *360*, 361
  preserving 367
  propagation
    bud-grafting 368–9, *368–9*
    chip-budding 368, *368*
    T-budding 369, *369*
    whip-and-tongue grafting 369–70, *369*
  protecting 361, *520*, 521
  pruning 364–6, *364–6*
    aims of 364
    curbing excessive vigor 366
Fruit, tree, pruning (*cont.*)
    formative 364
      method 364–5, *364*
      over-pruning 364, *364*
      removing branch 364, *365*
      renovation 366, *366*
      spur thinning 366
      time for 364
      under-pruning 364, *364*
  pyramid *356*, 357
  range of fruits 355
  renovation 366, *366*
  root pruning 366, *366*
  rootstocks 359
    selecting 360
  seasonal water requirements 530
  self-fertile 360, 371
  self-sterile 357, 360, 371
  siting, for cross-pollination 357
  size 359
  on south-facing walls 519
  spindlebush 356, *356*
  staking 361, *361*, 362
  standard 356, *356*
  supporting branches 362, *362*
  supports for 450
    preparing 360
  tender 356
  thinning fruit 362, *362*
  trained, pruning 364
  training 364–6
    on stakes 365–6, *365*
    for fruitfulness 365, *366*
    for shape 365, *365*
  tying 362
    to stake 361, *361*
  wall-trained 356
  watering 362
Fruit, tropical, see Fruit, tender
Fruit buds, apples 373, *373*
Fruit cage *363*
Fruit flies 565
Fruit garden 355–425
  in garden design *19*
  grouping plants in 357
  large, plan *357*
  planning 355–9
  small, plan *358*
Fruit rot, of kiwi fruits 403
Fruiting vegetables 328–35
  growing in containers 307
  storing 312
  watering, critical periods 308
Fuchsia 448–9
  conditions required 431
  in containers 449
    with trees 36
  cultivation 448–9
  feeding 449
  in greenhouse garden *430*
  in hanging baskets 449, *449*
  hardy
    overwintering 449, *449*
    pruning 74
  in indoor hanging basket 428
  nonhardy, overwintering 449
  overwintering 449, *449*
  pests 449, 551, 563, 566, 572
  pinching out 449, 450
  propagation 448, *448*
    root cuttings 448
    softwood cuttings 81, 448, *448*
  pruning 449
  standard, training 80, 449, *449*
  in summer bedding *170*
  training 61, 448–9, *448*
    bush 448, *448*
  'Celia Smedley' *448*
  'Estelle Marie' *448*
  fulgens 448
  'Lady Thumb' *448*
  magellanica 58, 66
    conditions tolerated 66
    soil type preferred 67
  'Thalia' *448*
  'White Ann' *448*
Fungal brackets 561, *561*, 567, *567*
Fungal diseases
  affecting bulbs 569
  affecting flowers 562
  affecting fruit, berries, and seeds 564
  affecting lawns 573
  affecting leaves 552, 554–6, 557, 558
  affecting roots and tubers 566–8
  affecting stems, branches, and leaf buds 559–60
  affecting whole plant 570–72
  mist propagation and 488
  spread 547
  on water plants 255
Fungal leaf spots 554, *554*
Fungi
  beneficial 525
  breeding resistance to 546
  colonizing plants 559
  fungicide-resistant strains 549
  systemic control 549
  on wood 500
Fungicides 587
  adverse reactions to 549
  damage from 556, *556*
  forms available 549
  types 549
    contact 549
    systemic 549, 590
  use when scooping rosettes *209*
Fungus gnats 572, *572*
Funkia, see *Hosta*
Furrows, for seeds *177*
Fusarium
  nivale 573
  oxysporium f. *narcissi* 569
  solani 567
    f. *pisi* 567
Fusarium wilt 403, 560, 567

G

Gagea, suggestions for use 219
Gages 383–6
  diseases 554
  freezing 367
  recommended cultivars 384
Gaillardia
  colors to blend with 139
  flowers 171
  root cuttings 165
  aristata, conditions preferred 167
  x *grandiflora* cvs, soil type preferred 146
  pulchella, for cutting 175
Galanthus
  buying in the green 224, *224*
  conditions preferred 219
  conditions tolerated 219
  diseases 559
  forcing 228
  increase 213
  in mixed border 214
  naturalized *217*
  pests 569
  propagation
    chipping 237, 542, *542*
    division of offsets 233
    twin-scaling 238, 542
  seasonal interest 25
  suggestions for use 28, 140, 216, 217, 219
  underplanting roses 117
  in woodland 140
Galanthus (*cont.*)
  'Atkinsii', in mixed island bed *136*
  caucasicus, suggestions for use 227
  elwesii, suggestions for use 227
  'Magnet', in mixed island bed *136*
  nivalis
    conditions tolerated 219
    suggestions for use 227
    'Lutescens', in peat bed *188*
    'Scharlockii', in rock garden *187*
Galax
  aphylla, conditions preferred 191
  urceolata, soil type required 192
Galega
  division 163
  seed germination 160
  soil type tolerated 147
  x *hartlandii*, growth rate 141
Gales, damage caused by 519
Galingale, see *Cyperus longus*
Galium odoratum, see *Asperula odorata*
Gall midges 558, *558*
Gall mites 558, *558*
Gall wasps 558, *558*
Galls 547
  azalea 558, *558*
  black knot 561, *561*
  crown 561, *561*, 567, *567*
  forsythia 561, *561*
  leafy 561, *561*
Galtonia 213
  buying 224
  for cutting 219
  in formal bedding 214
  growing in pots 232
  in mixed border *215*
  routine care 232
  candicans, in mixed border *215*
Ganoderma 567
Garden blankets 490
Garden carts 470, *471*
Garden centers, trees from 32
Garden chafers 566, 574
Garden compost, see Compost
Garden lines 471, *471*
Garden rooms *426*, 428–9
Gardener's-garters, see *Phalaris arundinacea* var. *picta*
Gardenia
  softwood cuttings 453
  jasminoides, in indoor hanging garden *428*
Gardens
  backgrounds 22
  creating design for 17–20
  formal 21
    enclosed *14*
  historic, restoring 31
  informal *12*, 21, *21*
  modifying design 13
  new, creating 14
  planning and design 12–31
  redesigning 13
  restoration 13, 31
  setting 16
  site 15
  small, trees for 37
  styles 27–31
  types 14
Garlic *341*, 343–4
  in crop rotation 304
  cultivation 343–4, *344*
  diseases 344, 569
  harvesting 344
  nitrogen requirement 310, 343
  pests 344, 569
  for repelling pests 548
  storing 312, 343, 344, *344*
  in vegetable garden *300*
Garlic chives 290

Garrya
conditions tolerated 66
semiripe cuttings with heel 83
soil type tolerated 67
elliptica
as hedge 59
'James Roof', in shrub border *63*
Gas, natural
in greenhouse, installing 480
for greenhouse heating 482
Gas plant, see *Dictamnus albus*
Gasoline, compared to electricity 464, 465, 466
Gasteria
division of offsets 269
angulata, conditions tolerated 262
batesiana
leaf cuttings 267
suggestions for use 262
distichia, conditions tolerated 262
liliputana, suggestions for use 262
verrucosa, conditions tolerated 262
Gaultheria
division of suckers 88
cuneata, in peat bed *188*
forrestii, layering 86
shallon 62
conditions tolerated 66
division of suckers *88*
Gaura, flowering time from seed 160
Gazania
in containers 174
growing as annual 175, 176
hardening off 180
sowing 177
stem tip cuttings 164
suggestions for use 175, 218
treating as annuals 177
uniflora, in hot border *139*
Gayfeather, see *Liatris*
Gels, water-retaining 529
Gelsemium sempervirens 97
pruning 103
semiripe cuttings 111
Genetic engineering 546
Genista
conditions tolerated 62, 66
flowers 65
heel cuttings 83
layering 86
pests 561
seed germination 538
softwood cuttings 81
soil for 62
delphinensis 191
lydia, in rock garden *187*
sagittalis
conditions tolerated 191
in dry-stone wall *189*
tinctoria, soil type preferred 67
Gentian, see *Gentiana*
Gentiana
division *208*
soil type required 188
sowing 160
acaulis
division 208, *208*
Irishman's cuttings 208
in peat bed *188*
suggestions for use 191
andrewsii, in meadow garden 167
asclepiadea
conditions preferred 141
seed germination 160
lutea, root cuttings 208
saxosa
in alpine raised bed *201*
suggestions for use 191
septemfida, in peat bed *188*
sino-ornata 208
division 208
in peat bed *188*
soil type required 192
Gentiana (*cont.*)
verna
in alpine raised bed *201*
conditions preferred 186
Irishman's cuttings 208
in rock garden *187*
var. *angulosa*, suggestions for use 191
Genus, definition 582, 587
Geranium, as common name for *Pelargonium* 168
Geranium
conditions tolerated 141
as edging 116
for ground cover 138
in mixed border *137*
propagation
division 163
greenwood cuttings 206
root cuttings 165, 208
in summer border *25*
underplanting roses 117
cinereum var. *subcaulescens*, in mixed border *20*
endressii, conditions tolerated 141
farreri, soil type tolerated 193
'Johnson's Blue', in mixed border *215*
pratense, soil type tolerated 147
sanguineum var. *striatum*
planting in container *147*
suggestions for use 191
Gerbera
conditions preferred 431
conditions required 431
growing as annual 176
German ivy, see *Senecio mikanioides*
Germander, see *Teucrium chamaedrys*
Germination 587
Gesneriaceae, leaf sections 455
Geum, pests 551
Gherkins 330–31, *330*
cultivation 330–31
harvesting 331
nitrogen requirement 310
recommended cultivars 331
'Cross Country' *331*
Ghost spots 564
Giant cowslip, see *Primula florindae*
Giant fennel, see *Ferula*
Giant redwood, see *Sequoiadendron giganteum*
Giant reed, see *Arundo donax*
Giant scabious, see *Cephalaria gigantea*
Gilia capitata
for cutting 175
sowing 177
Ginger 293, *293*
culinary uses 293
division of rhizomes 293
foliage 293
habit 293
harvesting 293
storing 293
suggestions for use 288
Ginkgo
side-veneer grafting 56
biloba
conditions tolerated 37
softwood cuttings 53
Girasoles, see Jerusalem artichokes
Girdling 587, see also Bark-ringing
Gladiolus 213
buying 224
corm 214, *542*
for cutting 219
diseases 568
pests 551, 553, 562
propagation
cormels 233, *233*
by cutting up, with growing points 237
staking *230*
Gladiolus (*cont.*)
storing in winter 233
suggestions for use 218
tender, conditions preferred 219
Butterfly group, in formal bedding 214
communis subsp. *byzantinus*, suggestions for use 227
'Deliverance' *233*
'Perky' *214*
Primulinus group, in formal bedding 214
'Tesoro' *218*
Glass, for greenhouses *478*, 479
Glass-fiber sheds 513
Glasshouse red spider mites, see Spider mites
Glasshouses, see Greenhouses
Glaucidium palmatum, soil type required 192
Glaucium flavum
conditions tolerated 175
soil type preferred 176
Glazing bars 480, *480*
Glazing clips 480, *480*
Glechoma hederacea, see Creeping Charlie
Gleditsia
pests 558
propagation
side-veneer grafting 56
whip-and-tongue grafting 56
triacanthos
soil preferred 42
var. *inermis*, conditions tolerated 37
'Sunburst'
foliage 34
suggestions for use 37
Gleditsia gall midge 558
Globe amaranth, see *Gomphrena globosa*
Globe artichokes 332–3, *333*
cultivation 332–3, *333*
harvesting 333
intercropping 302
nitrogen requirement 310, 332
site 302
storing 333
in vegetable garden *300*
Globe thistle, see *Echinops*
Globeflower, see *Trollius*
Globodera rostochiensis 572
Globularia
soil type preferred 146
cordifolia, suggestions for use 190, 191
meridionalis
in alpine raised bed *201*
suggestions for use 191
repens, suggestions for use 191
Gloriosa
for cutting 219
suggestions for use 218
superba, soil type tolerated 99
Glory bower, see *Clerodendrum thomsoniae*
Glory lily, see *Gloriosa superba*
Glory-of-the-snow, see *Chionodoxa*
Glottiphyllum
division of offsets 269
division of rootstock 270
linguiforme
leaf cuttings 267
suggestions for use 262
Gloves 471, *471*
Gloxinia, see *Sinningia speciosa*
Glume, definition 587
Glyceria maxima 'Variegata'
suggestions for use 142
in water garden 243
Glyphosate 577, 579
commercial names 574
Goat willow, see *Salix caprea*
Goat's beard, see *Aruncus dioicus*
Goat's rue, see *Galega*
Godetia, see *Clarkia*
Goggles, safety *464*, 466
Golden barrel cactus, see *Echinocactus grusonii*
Golden chain tree, see *Laburnum*
Golden-club, see *Orontium aquaticum*
Golden cyst eelworm 572
Golden elder, see *Sambucus nigra* 'Aurea'
Golden feverfew, see *Tanacetum parthenium* 'Aureum'
Golden flax, see *Linum flavum*
Golden larch, see *Pseudolarix amabilis*
Golden lemon balm, see *Melissa officinalis* 'Aurea'
Golden marjoram, see *Origanum vulgare* 'Aureum'
Goldenrod, see *Solidago*
Golden trumpet, see *Allamanda cathartica*
Golden trumpet tree, see *Tabebuia chrysotricha*
Golden willow, see *Salix alba* var. *vitellina*
Golden-chalice vine, see *Solandra maxima*
Golden-rain tree, see *Koelreuteria paniculata*
Gomphrena globosa
for cutting 175
for drying 175
growing as annual 175
soil type tolerated 176
Gooseberries 412–13, *413*
Chinese, see Kiwi fruits
cultivation 412–13
disease resistance 413
diseases 413, 564
freezing 367
hardwood cuttings 370, 413, *413*
harvesting 413
pests 412, 551
plant type 356, 404
potassium requirement 357
pruning
summer 364
winter 364, 413, *413*
recommended cultivars 413
storing 413
training, in small garden 358
'Careless'
in large fruit garden *357*
in small fruit garden *358*
'Downing' *413*
'Leveller' 413
in large fruit garden *357*
in small fruit garden *358*
'Whinham's Industry' *413*
Gordonia, semiripe cuttings 83
Gorse, see *Ulex*
Goutweed 576, *576*, 577
Grafting 587
aftercare 57
apical-wedge 57, 89, *89*, 544, *544*
cacti *270*, 271
shrubs 89
trees suitable for 56
approach- 420
basal-whip 544, 585
bud-grafting
fruit trees 368–9, *368–9*
roses 120, 130–31, *130*
cacti and other succulents 266, 270–71, *270*, *271*
chip-budding 57, *57*
fruit trees 368, *368*
method 544, *544*
time for 543
trees suitable for 56
double budding 382, *382*
double grafting 382, *382*
double-working 382, *382*
flat 544
cacti and other succulents 271, *271*
Grafting (*cont.*)
frame-working 379, 587
fruits 368
methods 543–4, *544*
perennials 166, *166*
preparing rootstock *56*, 88, 89, *89*
rind 379, *379*
rootstocks 543
influence 543
saddle 544, *544*
shrubs 88, 89, *89*
scions
in cold storage 515
influence 543
selecting 88, *89*
shrubs 88–9, *89*
side, cacti and other succulents 271, *271*
side-veneer 56, *56*, 88
method 544, *544*
shrubs 88–9
trees suitable for 56
side-wedge 544, *544*
splice, see basal-whip
succulents 266, 270–71, *270*, *271*
T-budding
fruit trees 369, *369*
method 544, *544*
time for 543
time for 543
tools for *463*
top-working
tree fruits 379, *379*
weeping standards 49
whip-and-tongue 544, *544*
fruit trees 369–70, *369*
trees suitable for 56
Grafting over, apples 379
Graminae family 142
Granite setts *498*, 499
imitation *498*, 499
Grape hyacinth, see *Muscari*
Grape ivy, see *Cissus rhombifolia*
Grape mildew 564
Grapefruits 417, *417*, 418
cultivation 417, 418
recommended cultivars 417
'Thompson' *417*
Grapevines 397–402
American 397
on arches 358
chemical damage to 557
climbing method 93
conditions required 397
diseases 564
European 397
freezing 367
fruit type 581
in greenhouse 355, 359, *359*
growth rate 97
harvesting 367
hormone weedkiller damage 561
Muscadine 397
recommended cultivars 398
ornamental, see *Vitis*
on pergolas 355, 358
pests 551, 552, 558, 565
plant type 356
planting 361
preserving 367
propagation
grafting 368
hardwood cuttings 370, 402, *402*
two-bud cuttings 402, *402*
pruning 364
ripening, removing foliage for 400, *402*
shanking 564, *564*
supports 397, 450
table 397–400, *397*
conditions required 397
diseases 397
double cordon, pruning 399
drainage for 397
feeding 397
growing under cover 397–8
harvesting *399*, 400
(*entry cont.*)

- Grapevines, table (*cont.*)
  - mulching 397
  - multiple cordon, pruning 399, *399*
  - muscat, recommended cultivars 398
  - pests 397
  - planting 397
  - pollination 397
  - propagation 400
  - pruning 397, 398–400, *398–400*
    - spur 398–400, *398–9*
  - recommended cultivars 398
  - rootstocks 397
  - routine care 397
  - single cordon, pruning routine 398–9, *398–9*
  - site 397
  - soil preparation 397
  - soil type required 397
  - spacing 397
  - storing 400
  - supporting 397
  - thinning bunches 397
  - thinning fruits 397, *397*
  - training 397, 398–400, *398–400*
  - wall cultivation 397
  - watering 397
  - wine grapes suitable for 400
  - 'Edelweiss' *398*
  - 'Nesbitt' *398*
  - 'Orlando Seedless' *398*
  - wine 400–402
    - harvesting 402, *402*
    - pruning 397, *400–1*, 401–2
    - recommended cultivars 400
    - 'Black Hamburgh', in large fruit garden *357*
    - 'Geneva White 5' *400*
    - 'Hunt' *400*
    - 'Muscat Ottanel' *400*
- *Graphocephala*
  - *coccinea* 553
  - *fennahi* 562
- *Graptopetalum amethystinum*, leaf cuttings 267
- Grass, see also Lawn; for ornamental varieties, see Grasses
  - for lawns 272–3
    - cool-season 274, 275
    - cultivars to choose 275
    - games and sports areas 274, *274*
    - groups 274
    - high-quality 274, *274*
    - pH levels for 276
    - selecting 274–5
    - utility 274, *274*
    - vegetative propagation 278, 279, *279*
    - warm-season 274, 275
  - for meadow garden 167
  - naturalizing bulbs in 216, *221*
- Grasses 142–3
  - care 143
  - conditions preferred 142
  - conditions tolerated 427
  - cutting back 143
  - deadheading 143
  - distinguishing features 142
  - drying 142
    - varieties for 174
  - ornamental, in contrasting foliage group *138*
  - preparing soil 143
  - propagation 143
    - division 143, *143*
    - from seed 143
  - seed, collecting 143, *143*
  - suggestions for use 142
  - top-dressing 143
  - in winter 156
- Grasshoppers 563
- Grassland, see also Meadow gardens
  - flower-rich 167
  - path through 273
  - planting wildflowers in 167
- Grassland (*cont.*)
  - preparing for wildflower planting 167
  - unmown 272
- Gravel
  - in garden design *19*
  - improving drainage with 529
  - as mulch 531
  - for paths 116
  - paths of
    - edging 295
    - laying 502, *502*
  - in rose garden 116, *117*
  - specimen trees in 34
  - steps of wood and *503*
  - as top-dressing 534, *534*
- Gravel boards 509, *509*
- Gravel garden, site for 17
- Gray mold, see *Botrytis*
- Gray-leaved plants
  - conditions suited to 139
  - herbs 288
    - mulching 296
- Greater periwinkle, see *Vinca major*
- Greater pond sedge, see *Carex riparia*
- Greater quaking grass, see *Briza maxima*
- Greater woodrush, see *Luzula sylvatica*
- Grecian saws, see Saws, Grecian
- Greece, ancient, gardens 29
- Green manuring 302, 533, *533*, *556*, 587
- Green petal 557, 562
- Greenfly, see Aphids
- Greenhouse effect *481*
- Greenhouses 474–91, see also Alpine house
  - access 475
  - anchoring *478*, 480, *480*
  - annuals for pot plants in 175
  - base insulation 482
  - base for *478*
    - building 479, *479*
  - beds and borders, preparing 439
  - bench beds, preparing 439, *439*
  - borders 478, 486
    - infected soil in 486
  - bulbs for 218
  - buying, checklist *478*
  - cacti and other succulents for 261
  - care of plants in 446–7
  - choosing 476–9
  - cleaning 447, 491
  - cold
    - balancing environment in 481
    - plants for 430, 431
    - protecting plants in 447
    - temperature in 430
    - temperature range 481
    - uses 481
  - conservation 477, *477*
  - construction, materials for 478–9, *478*
  - conventional designs 476, *476*
  - cool
    - balancing environment in 481
    - multilevel display in *429*
    - plants for 430, 431
    - temperature range 481
    - temperatures in 430
    - uses 481
  - creating microclimates in 519, *519*
  - damping down 446, 484, 586
  - as decorative feature *475*
  - diseases 447
  - disinfecting 491
  - displaying plants in *486*, 487, *487*
  - dome-shaped 477, *477*
  - door *478*
  - downspouts *478*
    - maintenance 491
- Greenhouses (*cont.*)
  - Dutch light 476, *476*
  - electricity in, installing 480
  - environment 429–30
    - balancing 481
    - creating 481–5
  - erecting 479–80, *479–80*
  - existing, design and 17
  - foundations, laying 479, *479*
  - framework, materials for 478, *478*
  - free-standing, siting 475
  - fruit in 359
    - routine care 363
  - garden in *430*
  - glazing *478*, 479, 491
    - cleaning 491
    - double 482
    - repairing 491
  - grapevines in *359*
  - grow bags in 486, *486*
  - gutters *478*
    - maintenance 491
  - headroom *478*
  - heat loss *478*
  - heated, uses 474
  - heating 481
    - types 482
  - humidity 446, 481
    - increasing 484
    - measuring 484
    - plant requirements 484
    - providing 484
    - reducing 484
  - hygiene 447
  - insulation 481, 482, *482*
  - integrated into garden *474*
  - lean-to 476, *476*
    - displaying plants in 429
    - siting 475
  - lighting 481, 485, *485*
  - mains services 475
    - installing 480
  - maintenance 491, *491*
  - mansard 476, *476*
  - materials for 478–9, *478*
  - metal
    - erecting 480, *480*
    - glazing 480, *480*
    - ventilators 480
  - mini 477, *477*
  - natural gas in, installing 480
  - organization 486–7, *486–7*
  - orientation 301, 475, *475*
  - ornamental displays in *429*
  - paths to 501
  - peaches in 388
  - pests 447, 549, 550, 551, 552, 553, 554, 558, 559, 560, 561, 562, 563, 565, 566, 568, 569, 571, 572, 574
    - biological pest control 548
    - trapping 548
  - planting 439
  - plants in 429–30
    - care 446–7
  - plastic-covered frame *475*
  - polygonal 477, *477*
  - polytunnel 477, *477*
    - hardening off in 180, *180*
  - propagation aids for 488, *488*
  - propagation in 544–5
  - raised beds in 429, 486
  - ridge height 478, *478*
  - sanitation 491
  - shading 472, *472*, 481, 484, *484*, 544
  - shelves *486*, 487
  - site preparation 479
  - siting 301, *301*, 475, *475*
  - size 478
  - soil mixes for 439
  - specialist 477, *477*
  - staging 429, *486*, 487, *487*
    - disinfecting 491
    - fitting 480
    - resting plants beneath *486*, *487*
  - succulents for 261
- Greenhouses (*cont.*)
  - temperate
    - balancing environment in 481
    - plants for 430, 431
    - temperature range 481
    - temperatures in 430
    - uses 481
  - temperature 481
  - thermal screens 482, *482*
  - three-quarter span 476, *476*
  - tomatoes in 334
  - traditional span 476, *476*
  - traditional wood *474*
  - types 429, 476–7, *476–7*
  - unheated, uses 474
  - uses 429
  - vegetables in 311
  - ventilation 446, 447, *478*, 481
    - maintenance 491
    - methods 483, *483*
    - principles 483, *483*
  - warm
    - balancing environment in 481
    - display in *430*
    - plants for 430, 431
    - temperature range 481
    - temperatures in 430
    - uses 481
  - water in, installing 480
  - watering plants in 446
  - watering systems 485, *485*
    - automatic 481
  - wheelchair access 478, *478*
  - wooden
    - erecting 479–80
    - glazing 479
- *Greenovia*
  - division of offsets 269
  - stem cuttings 268
- *Grevillea*
  - conditions preferred 431
  - semiripe cuttings 53
    - with heel 83
  - *robusta*, suggestions for use 37
- *Griselinia*
  - conditions tolerated 66
- Grit
  - paths of, edging 295
  - as top-dressing *228*, 229, 534, *534*
- Ground beetles *525*
- Ground color, definition 587
- Ground covers 150–51, 587
  - annuals for 173, *173*
  - benefits of 150
  - biennials for 173
  - with bulbs in formal bedding 214
  - clematis for 106
  - climbers for 92, 95, 97
  - combining plants for 150–51
  - contrasting forms 24
  - cuttings 151
  - dwarf conifers for 38
  - hostas as 152
  - for lawns 275
  - in layered planting 26
  - mulching *151*
  - ornamental plants *150*
  - patchwork effect 150
  - planting 151
    - through landscape fabric 151, *151*
  - plants unsuitable as 150
  - propagation 151
  - pruning 151, *151*
  - roses as 115, 119
  - rushes for 142
  - selecting plants for 150
  - in shady corners 150
  - in shrub border 63
  - shrubs for 64, *64*
  - spacing *150*, 151
  - specimen plants in 34, 140
  - textural *150*
  - under roses 117
  - uses 150
  - weed control with 95, 150, 576
  - for woodland 140
- Ground elder 576, *576*, 577
- Ground fault circuit interrupter (GFCI) 458
- Ground frost 515
- Groundnuts, see Peanuts
- Groundsel 575, *575*
- Group planting 23
- Grow bags
  - growing tomatoes in *334*
  - preparing 307
  - use in greenhouse 486, *486*
- Grow lamps 427, 485, *485*
- Growth buds, apples 373, *373*
- Growth regulators, damage from 561
- Guavas 422–3, *422*, *423*
  - in containers, moving under cover 363
  - harvesting 423
  - propagation 370, 423
  - recommended cultivars 423
  - storing 423
  - 'Parkers White' *423*
- *Guigardia aesculi* 558
- Gum tree, see *Eucalyptus*
- Gumming 384
  - citrus resistant to 416
- Gummosis 384
- *Gunnera*
  - *chilensis*, suggestions for use 243
  - *manicata*
    - architectural form 141
    - in border 137
    - growth rate 141
    - soil type tolerated 146
    - as specimen plant 140
    - suggestions for use 242, 243
- Guy ropes, for trees 40, *40*, *46*
- *Guzmania*
  - displaying 432
  - *lingulata* *432*
    - care during holidays *446*
    - var. *minor* *432*
- *Gymnocalycium*
  - in containers outdoors 260
  - division of offsets 269
  - division of rootstock 270
  - suggestions for use 262
  - *baldianum*, suggestions for use 262
  - *bruchii*, flowers 262
  - *gibbosum*, suggestions for use 262
  - *mihanovichii*
    - flat grafting 271
    - suggestions for use 262
    - 'Red Head' *271*
- Gymnospermae (Gymnosperms)
  - cotyledons 586
  - seed production 582
- *Gynandriris sisyrinchium*, conditions preferred 219
- *Gynura*
  - softwood cuttings 453
  - *aurantiaca*
    - foliage 426
    - pruning 450
    - softwood cuttings *453*
    - suggestions for use 97
- *Gypsophila*
  - for cutting 141, 174
  - flowers 582
  - root cuttings 165
  - sowing 177
  - *aretioides*
    - softwood cuttings 206
    - suggestions for use 191
  - *cerastioides*, in rock garden *187*
  - 'Covent Garden White', in annual border *171*
  - *dubia*, conditions tolerated 191
  - *elegans*
    - for cutting 175
    - sowing 177
  - *paniculata*
    - cultivars, grafting 166

(*entry cont. overleaf*)

Gypsophila paniculata (*cont.*)
form 138
grafting 166, *166*
as rootstock 166
soil type tolerated 147
'Bristol Fairy', grafting 166
'Flamingo', grafting 166
'Rosy Veil', grafting 166
repens
conditions tolerated 191
softwood cuttings 206, *206*
soil type preferred 193
soil type tolerated 193
suggestions for use 190
'Dorothy Teacher', in dry-stone wall *189*
Gypsy moths 551, *551*

H

Haageocereus
suggestions for use *262*
acranthus 262
setosus 262
versicolor 262
Haberlea
compost for 211
leaf cuttings 207
rhodopensis
conditions preferred 189
flowers 189
soil type required 192
suggestions for use 191
Habranthus
conditions preferred 219
suggestions for use 219
Hackberry, see *Celtis*
Hacquetia epipactis, in peat bed *188*
Haemanthus, greenhouse conditions required 431
Hairy bittercress *575*
Hakea
soil type required 69
lissosperma, soil type preferred 67
Hakonechloa macra 'Aureola', in pot *140*
Halesia, propagation
greenwood cuttings 81
layering 55
softwood cuttings 53, 81
Half-hardy plants, definition 587
Halide lamps, as grow lamps 485
Halimodendron halodendron
conditions tolerated 66
soil type preferred 67
Hall's honeysuckle, see *Lonicera japonica* 'Halliana'
Halo blight 554
Hamamelis
in mixed border 214
propagation
air layering 87
side-veneer grafting 88, 89
pruning 74, *74*
soil type required 69
sucker removal *70*
x *intermedia* 'Diane', seasonal interest 62
mollis
in shrub border *63*
'Pallida', scent 66
vernalis, scent 66
virginiana, scent 66
Hammers 496, *496*, 498, *498*
Hand-pollination *387*
Hanging baskets
annuals in 174, *174*
care 183
cacti in 261, 262
fertilizer burn to plants in 556
fuchsias in 449, *449*
indoors 427, 428, *428*
care 445
choosing 428
feeding 445
planting 437, *437*
plants for 428
positioning 428
watering 445
orchids in 441, *441*
succulents in 261, *261*, 262
planting 264, *264*
supports for 428, 438
types for indoors 428
Hardenbergia 97
conditions tolerated 97
seed preparation 109
semiripe cuttings 111
suggestions for use 97
comptoniana, in containers 96
Hardening off 545, 587
cuttings 53
seedlings 180, *180*
vegetables 307
Hardpan *529*, 531
drainage system on 531
Hardwood cuttings, see Cuttings, hardwood
Hardy plants 587
damage of frost and thaw to 515
Harrisia
as rootstock 271
gracilis, suggestions for use 262
Hatiora
apical-wedge grafting 271
salicornioides, suggestions for use 262
Haulm, definition 587
Haworthia
division of offsets 269
division of plantlets/runners 451
in raised bed 260
attenuata, leaf cuttings 267
cooperi, suggestions for use 262
cymbiformis, division of offsets *269*
limifolia, suggestions for use 262
planifolia, leaf cuttings 267
reinwardtii, suggestions for use 262
Hawthorn, see *Crataegus*
Hazel, see *Corylus*
Hazelnuts 424–5, *424*, see also *Corylus avellana*
cultivation 424–5
harvesting 425
husks 424
pollination 424
propagation
from seed 370
suckers 370
pruning 425
brutting 425, *425*
recommended cultivars 424
storing 425
Head, definition 587
Head back, definition 587
Health, buying plants for 548
Heart-of-flame, see *Bromelia balansae*
Heart up, definition 587
Heart vine, see *Ceropegia woodii*
Heartleaf philodendron, see *Philodendron scandens*
Heart-rot, of pineapples 415
Heather gardens, dwarf conifers for 38
Heathers, see also *Calluna*; *Daboecia*; *Erica*
Heathers (*cont.*)
clematis growing through 106
diseases 560, 567
dropping 86
dwarf conifers with *38*
as ground cover 64
pruning 77
soil mix for 439
soil requirement 15
winter-flowering 26
Heating cables 488, *488*
Heating in greenhouse 481, 482
circulated hot water 482
electric 482
kerosene 482
natural gas 482
types 482
Heavy soil, improving 225, 529
Hebe
conditions tolerated 66, 191
disease resistance 567
pruning 78
with roses 117
semiripe cuttings 206
soil type tolerated 69
suggestions for use 64
buchananii 'Minor' 191
in rock garden 187
canterburiensis, in rock garden *187*
pinguifolia 'Pagei', in rock garden *186*
Hechtia 433
propagation 433
Hedera
annuals climbing through 173
climbing method 92, *98*
conditions preferred 431, 518
conditions required, in greenhouse 431
conditions tolerated 66, 97, 427
in containers 96
with trees 36
damage caused 22
foliage 95
in greenhouse display *429*
as ground cover 34
in hanging basket *437*
hydroculture 431
indoors *427*
miniature, suggestions for use 438
propagation
hardwood cuttings 151
self-layering *112*, 113
semiripe cuttings 111
softwood cuttings 110
repotting *101*
as screen 94
soil types tolerated 99, 100
suggestions for use 93, 94, 97
topiary 31, 90
training to shape *90*
variegated 95
on wall 22
in water garden *241*
in windowbox *174*, 218
for winter interest 94, 96
colchica 'Sulphur Heart', cutting back *101*
helix
suggestions for use 97
as weed 576
'Atropurpurea' 113
'Buttercup', winter interest 96
'Eva', in bottle garden *439*
'Goldheart', winter interest 96
'Ivalace' *90*
'Parsley Crested', winter interest 96
'Pedata', winter interest 96
Hedgehog rose, see *Rosa rugosa*
Hedgerows, wildflowers for *167*
Hedges 58–60
as background 22
choosing plants for 59
Hedges (*cont.*)
conditions on each side 519
double planting 59, *59*
dwarf *59*
in herb garden *287*, 289
herbs for 289
enclosing garden *14*
evergreen 22
existing, design and 17
feeding *60*
formal 59
plants for 58
trimming 58, 60
as framework *16*, 21, *21*
framing statue *13*
frost pockets beside 515, *515*
in garden design *19*
hosta as 152
informal
plants for *58*, 59
pruning 60
maturing 16
mosaic 58
mulching *60*
in neglected garden 13
ornamental 58–9
planting 59, *59*
pruning 59–60, *60*
renovating 20, 31, 60, *60*
roses for 118, *119*, 121, *121*
as screens 36
shaping 60, *60*
to prevent snow from collecting *517*
single planting 59, *59*
snow damage to *517*
soil preparation 59
spacing plants 58, 59
tapestry 59
topiary 90
training 59–60, *60*
trimming 60, *60*
tools for
hand 463, *463*
power 464, *464*
uses 58
wind reduction 58
as windbreaks 301, *301*, 521
window effects 21
Hedge trimmers 464, *464*
battery-powered 464
cutting hedge with *60*
gas and electric compared 464
protective clothing for *464*
rechargeable 464
safety 464
Hedychium gardnerianum, in hot border *139*
Heel, definition 587
Heel cuttings, see Cuttings, heel
Heeling in 121, 587
trees 41, *41*
Helenium
for cutting 141
division 163
in free planting *21*
pinching 155
soil type tolerated 147
Helianthemum 204
conditions tolerated 191
in cottage garden *140*
cultivars, suggestions for use 64
cutting back after flowering 204
in rock garden *185*, *186*
semiripe cuttings 206
soil type preferred 67, 193
soil type tolerated 193
'Fire Dragon' *206*
oelandicum
suggestions for use 191
subsp. *alpestre*, in trough *199*
'Wisley Pink', in rock garden *187*
'Wisley Primrose', in rock garden *187*
Helianthus
division *162*, 163
in fall 139
growth rate 141
Helianthus (*cont.*)
in mixed border *172*
position in border 171
staking 183
annuus 175
architectural plant 175
for cutting 175
flowers 171
suggestions for use 27
Color Fashion Series, for cutting 175
tuberosus, see Jerusalem artichokes
Helichrysum
in containers *19*
for drying 174
drying 183
harvesting 183
soil type preferred 67
in windowbox *174*
bracteatum, soil type preferred 176
coralloides 191, *191*
milfordiae, rosette cuttings 207
petiolare, stem tip cuttings 164
selago
in alpine raised bed *201*
in dry-stone wall *189*
semiripe cuttings 207
Helictotrichon sempervirens, suggestions for use 142
Heliocereus
in greenhouse display *430*
hybrids, conditions required 261
propagation, stem cuttings 268
speciosus var. *superbus*, suggestions for use 262
Heliothrips haemorrhoidalis 553
Heliotrope, see *Heliotropium*
Heliotropium
for containers 174
propagation 176
scent 175
suggestions for use 175
arborescens, growing as annual 175
Helipterum
for cutting 175
for drying 175
drying 183
harvesting 183
Helix aspersa 550
Helleborus
conditions tolerated 191
for cutting 141
seed germination 160
soil type tolerated 147
suggestions for use 216
transplanting 156
winter interest 140
argutifolius
architectural form 141
winter interest 141
foetidus, conditions tolerated 141
niger
conditions tolerated 141
seasonal interest 135
winter interest 141
orientalis 163
conditions tolerated 141
division 163
seasonal interest 135
Helmet flower, see *Aconitum napellus*
Helminthosporum vagans 574
Helxine soleirolii, see *Soleirolia soleirolii*
Hemerocallis
conditions preferred 141
conditions tolerated 141
diseases 149
division *162*, 163
flowers 149, *149*
in free planting *21*
in mixed border *149*
modern hybrids 149
pests 149, 553, 562, 563
(*entry cont.*)

Hemerocallis (*cont.*)
propagation
division 149
from seed 149
routine care 149
site 149
soil type tolerated 149
suggestions for use 136, 149
types 149
winter protection 149
'Circle Round' *149*
'Cream Drop' *149*
'Ice Carnival' *149*
'Leebea Orange Crush' *149*
'Louise Mercer' *149*
'Marion Vaughn' *141*
'Milk Chocolate' *149*
'Stella de Oro' *149*
flowers 149
in hot border *139*
Hemigraphis alternata, suggestions for use 243
Hemispherical scale *559*
Hemlock, see *Tsuga*
Hen-and-chickens fern, see *Asplenium bulbiferum*
Hepatica
sowing 205
nobilis
conditions preferred 191
var. *japonica*, in peat bed *188*
transsilvanica, conditions preferred 191
Heracleum
architectural form 141
mantegazzianum 23, *23*
Herald's trumpet, see *Beaumontia grandiflora*
Herb garden 287–98, *287*
attractions of 287
designing 288, 289
edging 288
formal 289, *289*
geometric designs 289, *289*
informal 289
laying paths in 295
plans for, drawing up 289
planting, to design 295, *295*
roses in 119
Herb pillows 287
Herbaceous borders, see Borders
Herbaceous plants 587, see Perennials
Herbicides 587, see also Weedkillers
Herbs 587
air-drying 298, *298*
architectural 288
aromatic, handling 298
in beds 288, *288*
benefits to other plants 288
in borders 288
as carpet 288
colored-leaved, suggestions for use 289
companion planting 288
conditions preferred 288, 294
conditions tolerated 288
in containers 288, *288*, 289, 294, 296
cosmetic uses 287
culinary, siting 288
culinary uses 287
cultivars 287
propagation 297
cutting back 296
deadheading 296
definition 287
designing with 287–90
drying 298
for dwarf hedges 289
for edging 288
evergreen, harvesting in winter 294, 298
fall cleanup 296
feeding 296
flavor, conditions affecting 298
flavoring oil or vinegar with 298
Herbs (*cont.*)
flowers 288
collecting 298
as focal points 288
foliage 288
forcing 294
in formal herb garden *289*
freezing 298, *298*
in garden 287–9
in garden design *19*
gray-leaved 288
growing indoors 427
handling 298
hardening off 294
hardiness 296
harvesting 294, 298
in home 287
invasive
dividing 294
planting 294, *294*
removing runners 296
medicinal uses 287
microwave drying 298
mulching 296
origins 288
on patio 288, *289*
in paving 288, *289*
pinching out, after planting 294
plant types producing 287
planting
container-grown 294
to restrict spread 294, *294*
preserving 298
propagation
cuttings 296
mound layering 297, *297*
from seed 297
protecting 296
in raised beds 288
repotting 296
for rock garden 288
roots
collecting 298
drying 298
routine care 296
scent 287, 288
seed, collecting 298
seedheads, drying 298, *298*
shrubby, trimming, after planting 294
site preparation 294
soil preferred 294
soil preparation 294
soil tolerated 294
storing 298
in strawberry jar, replanting *296*
suggestions for use 21, 31, 287–90, 303, 427
tender 288, 296
tidying up in winter 296
top-dressing 296
underplanting roses 117, *117*
use after chemical treatment 296
uses 287
variegated
removing plain shoots 296
suggestions for use 289
in vegetable garden 288, 303, *303*
watering 294, 296
for winter use 294, *294*
Hermaphrodite plants 537, 582, *582*
Hesperis matronalis
self seeding 178
at streamside *167*
Heterorhabditis 572
as biological pest control 548
Heuchera
conditions tolerated 141
division 163
soil type tolerated 147
cylindrica 'Greenfinch', in mixed island bed *136*
'Palace Purple'
in mixed island bed *136*
planting in container *147*
winter interest 141
Hibbertia
softwood cuttings 110
scandens 97
Hibiscus
flowers 582
pinching out 450
propagation
apical-wedge grafting 89
softwood cuttings 453
pruning 450
soil type tolerated 69
rosa-sinensis
conditions preferred 431
conditions required 431
plunging in large container *437*
pruning 78
semiripe cuttings 83
'The President' *453*
sinosyriacus 'Lilac Queen' *89*
syriacus
as hedge 59
pruning 74
'Red Heart' *58*
trionum, retaining seedheads 184
Hickory, see *Carya*
Highbush blueberry, see *Vaccinium corymbosum*
High-maintenance garden *13*
Hilling up
definition 587
rototiller attachment for *461*
Hill-top sites, wind on 519
Himalayan birch, see *Betula utilis*
Himalayan pine, see *Pinus wallichiana*
Hinoki false cypress, see *Chamaecyparis obtusa*
Hippeastrum
care 232
Christmas flowering 229
conditions preferred 431
conditions required 431
distinguishing from *Amaryllis* 229
dormancy 229
dwarf, suggestions for use 219
feeding 229
forcing 229
light requirements 427
pests 558, 569
propagation
chipping 237, *237*
from seed 235
renewing top-dressing *444*
root restriction 444
seed germination 235
storing 229
suggestions for use 219
advenum, conditions preferred 219
'Striped' *237*
Hippophäe
germination 85
soil type tolerated 67
rhamnoides, conditions tolerated 66
Hips 581
Hoar frost 515
Hoeing
correct position *458*
time for 308
for weed control 526, 577
Hoes 460, *460*
heads 460
shafts 460
types
combination *460*
digging *460*
draw *306*, *460*
Dutch 460, *460*
onion *460*
triangular *460*
Hoheria
deciduous, pruning 74
lyallii, layering 55
Holboellia 97
serpentine layering 113
Hollows, frost pockets in 515, *515*
Holly, see *Ilex*
Hollyhocks, see *Alcea*
Holm oak, see *Quercus ilex*
Holy flax, see *Santolina rosmarinifolia*
Homes, see Houses
Honesty, see *Lunaria*
Honey locust, see *Gleditsia triacanthos*
Honeybush, see *Melianthus major*
Honeydew 547, 552, 553, 554, 559
Honeydew melons, see Melons, honeydew
Honeysuckle, see *Lonicera*
Honeysuckle witches' brooms 558, *558*
Hoodia, flat grafting 271
Hoof and horn, nutrient content 532
Hoop-petticoat daffodil, see *Narcissus bulbocodium* subsp. *bulbocodium*
Hoops, training house plants on 436, *436*
Hop, see *Humulus*
Hop mildew 564
Hoplocampa testudinea, see Apple sawfly
Hordeum jubatum, for drying 175
Hormone rooting products *82*, 111, 540, 589
Hormone weedkillers, damage caused by 557, *557*, 561, 565, *565*
Hornbeam, see *Carpinus*
Horned poppy, see *Glaucium*
Horned violet, see *Viola cornuta*
Horse chestnut, see *Aesculus*
Horseradish 290, *290*
culinary uses 290
cultivation 290
harvesting 290
storing 290
Horsetail 576, *576*, 579
Hoses 468, *468*
double-walled 468
drip feed system 469, *469*
flat 468, *468*
hose-end attachments *468*
porous 469
on reel 468, *468*
reinforced 468
soaker 469, 485
watering vegetables with 308, *308*
spray attachments *468*
timers for 469, *469*
trickle system 469, *469*
Hosta
classification 152
conditions preferred 141, 148
conditions tolerated 141
in container *157*
diseases 153
feeding 153, 155
foliage 135, 152
in layer planting 26
in mixed border *149*
in moist shade *15*
pests 153, 550
planting 153
depth *146*, 153
time for 146
propagation
division 153, 162, *162*, 163
Ross method 153, *153*
from seed 153
routine care 153
for shade 152, *152*
soil types tolerated 146, 153
suggestions for use 152, *152*, 243
for texture 25
by waterside *28*
'August Moon' *152*
'Blue Angel' 152
'Blue Cadet' 152
'Buckshaw Blue' *23*
crispula, foliage 139
decorata f. *decorata* *152*
fortunei 'Aurea Marginata' 150
Hosta (*cont.*)
'Gold Standard' *152*
'Green Piecrust' 152
'Ground Master' 152
'Halcyon' *152*
'Honeybells' 152
'Krossa Regal' 152
lancifolia 152, *152*
montana 'Aurea Marginata' *152*
plantaginea 152, *152*
var. *grandiflora*, for fragrance 141
sieboldiana
in containers 140
suggestions for use 140, 242
var. *elegans* *152*
architectural form 141
foliage 138
'So Sweet' 152
'Sugar and Cream' 152
'Sum and Substance' 152
'Thomas Hogg', in cottage garden *140*
tokudama 'Aureo-nebulosa' 152, *152*
'Tot Tot' 152
ventricosa *152*
'Aureo-maculata' *152*
venusta 152
'Zounds' 152
Hot peppers, see Peppers, hot
Hot sites, perennials for *139*
Hottonia palustris
propagation by plantlets 257
in water garden 243
Houseleek, see *Sempervivum*
House plants, see Indoor plants
Houses
light variations within room 427, *427*
temperature fluctuations 427
Houstonia caerulea 167
Houttuynia
soil type tolerated 146
cordata
in water garden 243
'Chameleon' (syn. *H. c.* 'Variegata') *150*
in water garden 243
'Plena', in water garden 243
'Variegata', see *H. c.* 'Chameleon'
Hoverflies, attracting *548*
Howea
architectural 66
conditions preferred 431
as specimen tree 33
suggestions for use *37*
Hoya 97
conditions required 431
conditions tolerated 97
propagation
leaf-bud cuttings 453
self layering 113
semiripe cuttings 111
softwood cuttings 453
pruning 103, 450
soil mix for 264
australis
conditions tolerated 262
for fragrance 97
leaf cuttings 267
bella
conditions required 431
suggestions for use 262
carnosa
conditions preferred 427
conditions tolerated 262
for fragrance 97
leaf cuttings 267
linearis, suggestions for use 262
polyneura, suggestions for use 262
Huernia, propagation
division of offsets 269
division of rootstock 270
stem cuttings 268
Hulling, definition 587

Humea elegans
  for fragrance 175
  as pot plants 175
  soil type tolerated 176
Humidifiers 81, *81*
Humidity
  effects of 518
  excessive, dangers of 484
  factors determining 518
  in greenhouse 481
    measuring 484
    plant requirements 484
  high
    plants thriving in 518
    problems 518
  increasing 484
  for indoor plants 437
  indoor pond providing 429
  methods of providing 442
  for orchids 441
  for pot plants 444, *444*
  reducing 484
  relative 484, 518
Humulus
  simple layering 113
  lupulus
    climbing method 92
    conditions tolerated 97
    growth rate 97
    suggestions for use 97
    'Aureus'
      combining with other climbers *95*
      foliage 95
      framing statuary *93*
      soil type tolerated 99
Humus 145, 587
Hurdles, as windbreaks *521*
Hutchinsia alpina, suggestions for use 191
Hyacinth, see *Hyacinthus*
  water, see *Eichhornia crassipes*
Hyacinth beans, see Beans, hyacinth; *Lablab purpureus*
Hyacinthoides
  hispanica (syn. *Scilla campanulata*) *214*
    suggestions for use 212, 219, 227
  non-scripta (syn. *Scilla non-scripta*) 27
    conditions tolerated 219
    pests 569
    suggestions for use 34, 216
Hyacinthus 213
  choosing healthy bulbs *224*
  conditions preferred 431
  conditions required 431
  diseases 568
  flowers 582
  forcing
    in soil mix 228, 229, *229*
    in water 229, *229*
  in formal bedding 214
  grouping 426
  interplanting 173
  propagation
    chipping 237
    scooping 238, *238*, 542
    scoring 542, *542*
    twin-scaling 237
  suggestions for use 217, 219
  transplanting from pots 231
Hyadaphis tatarica 558
Hybrid, definition 587
Hybrid berries 406–8, *407*
  choosing healthy plants 406
  cultivation 406–8, *407*
  freezing 366, 367
  harvesting 367, 407
  origins 406
  plant type 356, 404
  propagation
    layering 370
    leaf-bud cuttings 370
    tip layering *407*, 417
  recommended hybrids 407
  storing 407
  thornless, vigor 406
Hybrid vigor, definition 587
Hybridization 582, 587
  method 538
  roses 132–3, *132–3*
Hydrangea
  blue, soil requirement 15
  flower color 439
  pests 551
  propagation
    self layering 113
    softwood cuttings 81, 110
  pruning 74, 75, 103
  soil mix for 437
  anomala subsp. *petiolaris*
    conditions tolerated 99, 100
    suggestions for use 95
    soil types tolerated 97, 98
  arborescens, stooling 87
  aspera, pruning 75
  macrophylla
    pruning 75, *75*
    softwood cuttings *81*, *540*
  paniculata
    propagation
      nodal cuttings 540
      softwood cuttings 81
      stooling 87
    pruning 75
    'Floribunda', coppicing 77
    'Grandiflora', coppicing 77
    'Unique', coppicing 77
  quercifolia 'Snowflake', seasonal interest 66
Hydrated lime 533
Hydrocharis
  propagation, turions 543, *543*
  morsus-ranae 243
    conditions required 240
    propagation
      offsets 257
      turions *543*
Hydrocleys
  depth of water for 242
  value in water garden 242
  nymphoides *243*
    in water garden 243
  parviflora 243
    softwood cuttings 256
Hydroculture 447, 546, 587
  fertilizers for 447, *447*
  planting 447
  plants for 431
  pots for *473*
    cross-section *447*
  preparing plants for 447, *447*
Hydromulching 280
Hydroponics 447, 587
  hyacinths 229, *229*
Hygiene
  greenhouse 447
  pest and disease control 548
Hygrometers 484
Hygrophila
  difformis, in aquarium *245*
  polysperma
    softwood cuttings 256
    suggestions for use 243
Hylocereus
  conditions preferred 261
  hybrids, conditions required 261
  as rootstock 271
  suggestions for use 259
  ocamponis 262
Hylomecon japonicum, conditions preferred 191
Hymenocallis, conditions preferred 219
Hypericum
  pruning 74
  soil type tolerated 62, 69
  calycinum
    cuttings 151
    as ground cover 150
    pruning 151, *151*
  x *moserianum*, hardwood cuttings 84
Hypertufa
  covering sink with 198, *198*
  making trough of 198, 198
Hypocotyl, definition 587
Hypoestes
  conditions preferred 431
Hypoestes (*cont.*)
  in greenhouse display *429*
  propagation 176
  phyllostachya
    suggestions for use 438
    'Purpuriana', in bottle garden *439*
    'Splash' in terrarium *439*, *446*
Hypogeal germination 538, *538*, 587
Hyssop, see *Hyssopus*
Hyssopus
  suggestions for use 289
  officinalis *291*
    culinary uses 291
    as edging 288
    flowers 291
    harvesting 291
    in herb garden *295*
    propagation
      from seed 291
      softwood cuttings 291
    suggestions for use 291
    variants 291
    subsp. *aristatus* 291
      suggestions for use 295

I

Iberis
  conditions preferred 173
  diseases 555, 567
  as ground cover 173
  sowing 176
  suggestions for use 148
  amara, conditions tolerated 175
  saxatilis, soil type preferred 193
  sempervirens
    in rock garden *187*
    'Snowflake', in mixed island bed *136*
  umbellata, conditions tolerated 175
Ice on pond, making hole in 255, *255*
Iceland poppy, see *Papaver nudicaule*
Iceplants 327, *327*
  cultivation 327
  harvesting 327
Ilex
  conditions tolerated 521
  disadvantages 35
  flower sexuality 582
  fruiting 35
  pests 553
  plants under 26
  propagation
    hardwood cuttings 540
    semiripe cuttings 53, 83, 540
  suggestions for use 33, 148
  topiary 90, *90*
  variegated *25*
  x *altaclerensis*
    conditions tolerated 37, 66
    'Golden King'
      seasonal interest 37
      semiripe cuttings *82*
  aquifolium
    conditions preferred 66
    conditions tolerated 66
    as hedge 58, 59
    in informal shrub grouping *61*
    pruning 78
    'Crispa Aurea Picta' *90*
    'Golden Milkboy', transplanting *72*
Ilex aquifolium (*cont.*)
    'Madame Briot' *58*
  x *altaclarensis*, pruning 78
  crenata 'Mariesii' 191
Illicium, layering 86
Immortelle, see *Helichrysum bracteatum*; *Xeranthemum*
Impatiens
  choosing healthy plants, pot-grown *181*
  conditions preferred 171, 173
  conditions required 431
  in containers 174
  cultivars, lifting after bedding 184
  effect of sun on 556
  in greenhouse display *429*
  as ground cover 173, *173*
  pests 563, 566, 572
  planting, in container *181*
  propagation from seed 179, 452
  soil type preferred 176
  suggestions for use 171
  in summer bedding *170*
  treating as annuals 177
  New Guinea cultivars 174
  Novette Series, 'Red Star' *431*
  repens, softwood cuttings 453
  walleriana
    conditions preferred 175
    growing as annual 175
    as pot plants 175
    suggestions for use 175
Incense plant, see *Humea elegans*
Incinerators 470
Indehiscent fruit 581, *581*, 587
India rubber tree, see *Ficus elastica*
Indian blanket, see *Gaillardia aristata*
Indian cress, see *Tropaeolum majus*
Indian spinach, see Malabar spinach
Indigofera, pruning 74
Indoor garden 426–56
  displaying plants 426–30
  environment 427
  foliage plants 426
  grouping plants 426
  light levels 427, *427*
  lighting 428
  positioning plants 427
  range of plants 426
  temperature fluctuations 427
Indoor plants
  cacti 260–61
  care when going away 446, *446*
  choosing 436, *436*
  diseases 447, 552, 554, 557, 562, 564, 571
  effect of temperature on 556, 570
  feeding 444
  fertilizer burn 556
  foliage, cleaning 444, *444*
  grouping 426, 436–7
  humidity for 437, 444, *444*, 446
  hygiene 444, *444*
  light preferred 431
  mineral deficiency 556–7
  mist-spraying 444
  neglected, renovating 444
  pests 447, 552, 553, 554, 557, 559, 566, 572
  pinching out 444
  planter's guide 431
  planting 439
  plunging in large container 437, *437*
  positioning 427, 436
  potting on 444–5, *445*
  pricking out 452, *452*
Indoor plants (*cont.*)
  problems affecting stems and leaf buds 559
  propagation 451–6
    air layering 456, *456*, 539
    bulbils 451
    cuttings 451, 453–4, *453*, *454*, *455*
    division 451–2, *451*
    layering 451, 456, *456*
    leaf cuttings 454, *454*
    leaf sections 454–5, *454*, *455*
    leaf-bud cuttings 453
    offsets 451
    plantlets 451
    runners 451, *451*
    from seed 451, 452–3, *452*
    semiripe cuttings 453
    simple layering 456, *456*
    softwood cuttings 453, *453*
      in water 454, *454*
  resting 445, *445*
  routine care 444–7
  seed germination 452
  soil mixes for 436, 439
  soil preparation 439
  succulents 260–61
  supports for 436, *436*
  top-dressing *444*, 445
  watering 444
    when going away 446, *446*
  winter-flowering, plunging outdoors 445, *445*
Inflorescence 587
  determinate 586
  indeterminate 587
Informal garden *12*, 14
  styles 27–9
Ink spot 232, 569
Inorganic material 587
  adding to soil 529
Insecticides 587, see also Pesticides
Insects
  beneficial 549
  pests 547
  pollination by 549
Insulation
  frames 489
  greenhouse 481, 482, *482*
  for plants in winter *520*, 521
Intercropping 304, *304*, 587
Interference fencing 508, *508*
Interlock, see Pavers
Internal rust spot *568*
  symptoms and control 568
Internodal cutting, definition 586
Internodes, definition 587
Interplanting 587–8
Intersowing 305, 352, *352*
Ipheion
  conditions tolerated 219
  suggestions for use 219
  uniflorum
    conditions preferred 219
    forcing 228
Ipomoea 97
  planting, beside host plant *182*
  pruning 103
  softwood cuttings 110
  soil type tolerated 99
  suggestions for use 173
  batatas, see Sweet potatoes
  hederacea, cutting back 98
  horsfalliae
    pruning 450
    vigor 98
Iresine
  softwood cuttings 453
  stem tip cuttings 176
Iridaceae, corms and rhizomes 214
Iris
  in balanced design *13*
  bearded 144
    rhizomes *580*
  beardless 144
(*entry cont.*)

Iris (*cont.*)
bulbous 144
diseases 232, 569
classification 144
conditions required 144
conditions tolerated 141, 144
diseases 232, 569
dwarf, suggestions for use 219
foliage 135
in garden design *19*
pests 232, 566
in pots, plunging after flowering *210*
propagation 144
chipping 237
division 162, 163, *163*, 256
rhizomatous 144
division 163, *163*, 256
suggestions for use 217
rhizomes 214, *543*
in spring 139
suggestions for use 148, 241
in summer border *25*
water 144
aucheri, choosing healthy bulbs *224*
'Bold Print' *144*
bucharica 144, *144*
'Carnaby' *144*
chrysographes 144
confusa 144
crested 144
cristata 144, *204*
conditions preferred 191
danfordiae
flowering problems 232
forcing 228
Dutch Hybrids 144
for cutting 219
forcing 228
'Early Light', in hot border *139*
English 144
ensata (syn. *I. kaempferi*) 144
suggestions for use 217, 243
Evansia 144
'Florentina' (syn. *I. florentina*), see Orris
foetidissima
conditions tolerated 141
for seedheads 141
'Variegata'
in mixed island bed *136*
winter interest 141
'Geisha Gown' *144*
gracilipes 144
graminea 144
for fragrance 141
histrioides
forcing 228
'Major'
in rock garden 186
suggestions for use 213
innominata 144, *144*
Japanese 144
japonica 144
'Joyce' *144*
in rock garden *187*
Juno group 144
bulb 214
buying 224
division of offsets 233
seed germination 235
suggestions for use 219
kaempferi, see *I. ensata*
laevigata 144
in bog garden *242*
in water garden 243
'Variegata' *23*
in water garden 242
Louisiana 144
magnifica 144
missouriensis 144
Oncocyclus group 144
orientalis 144
Pacific Coast 144
pallida, use as orris 291
prismatica 144
pseudacorus 144

Iris (*cont.*)
by pool *144*
repotting *255*
in water garden *240*, 243
Regelia 144
reticulata
conditions tolerated 219
forcing 228
suggestions for use 190
Reticulata group 144
bulb 214
in mixed border 214
propagation
division of bulblets 233
division of offsets 233
seed collecting 234
suggestions for use 219
setosa 144
Siberian 144
by pool *144*
sibirica *15*, 144
in cool border *138*
pests 566
suggestions for use 243
Spanish 144
spuria 144
Spuria group 144
tectorum, pests 566
tenax 144
unguicularis
seasonal interest 135
winter interest 141
verna 144
versicolor 144
in water garden 243
'White City' *214*
Xiphium group 144
Iris borers 566, *566*, 569
Iris soft rot 232, 569, *569*
Irishman's cuttings 208, *208*
Iron 545
chelated 360, 380, 557
commercial names 574
deficiency 360, 362, 380, 387, 415, 532, 557
plant requirements 532
problems caused by 556
Irrigation 588, see also Watering
Island beds, see Beds, island
Italian alder, see *Alnus cordata*
Italian cypress, see *Cupressus sempervirens*
Italian ryegrass, see *Lolium multiflorum*
Italianate gardens 29
Italy, villa gardens 29
Itea
ilicifolia
semiripe cuttings with heel 83
suggestions for use 66
virginica, division of suckers 88
Itersonilia pastinaceae 567
Ivy, see *Hedera*
Ixia
conditions preferred 219
for cutting 219
Ixora coccinea, softwood cuttings 453

J

Jacaranda
conditions required 431
mimosifolia
from seed 452
suggestions for use 37
Jack-in-the-pulpit, see *Arisaema triphyllum*
Jacquemontia 97
propagation, cuttings 111
Jade plant, see *Crassula ovata*
Jade vine, see *Strongylodon macrobotrys*
Jancaea (syn. *Jankaea*), leaf cuttings 207
Japanese angelica tree, see *Aralia elata*
Japanese apricot, see *Prunus mume*
Japanese aralia, see *Fatsia japonica*
Japanese barberry, see *Berberis thunbergii*
Japanese beetles 149, 563, 566, 573,
Japanese carpet grass, see *Zoysia matrella*
Japanese cedar, see *Cryptomeria japonica*
Japanese flag, see *Iris ensata*
Japanese gardens 30, *30*
Japanese honeysuckle, see *Lonicera japonica*
Japanese hydrangea vine, see *Schizophragma hydrangeoides*
Japanese ivy, see *Parthenocissus tricuspidata*
Japanese knotweed 576, *577*
Japanese lawn grass, see *Zoysia japonica*
Japanese maple, see *Acer japonicum*; *A. palmatum*
Japanese painted fern, see *Athyrium niponicum* 'Pictum'
Japanese plums, see Plums, Japanese
Japanese privet, see *Ligustrum japonicum*
Japanese sago palm, see *Cycas revoluta*
Japanese snowball tree, see *Viburnum plicatum*
Japonica, see *Chaenomeles*
Jasmine, see *Jasminum*
winter, see *Jasminum nudiflorum*
Jasminum
conditions preferred 431
conditions required 431
propagation, semiripe cuttings 111
pruning 103, 450
scent 96, 97
beesianum, pruning *103*
humile, pruning 76
mesnyi
planting *100*
softwood cuttings 453
nudiflorum
climbing method 93
pruning, formative *102*
in shrub border *63*
winter interest 96
officinale
soil type tolerated 100
suggestions for use 94, 97
training on wire hoop *436*
polyanthum
indoors 428
soil type tolerated 100
suggestions for use 97
winter interest 96
Jatropha podagrica, suggestions for use 262
Jeffersonia dubia, in peat bed *188*
Jerusalem artichokes *348*, 351, *351*
bumpy tuber *351*
cultivation 351, *351*
harvesting 351
nitrogen requirement 310, 351

Jerusalem artichokes (*cont.*)
smooth 'Fuseau' tuber *351*
storing 351
tubers 543, *543*
in vegetable garden *300*
as windbreak *300*, 351
Jerusalem cherry, see *Solanum pseudocapsicum*
Jerusalem sage, see *Phlomis fruticosa*
Jigger *495*
Joints
for beams and uprights 512, *512*
bird's mouth 512, *512*
dowel *512*
half-lap 512, *512*
notched 512, *512*
Joist shoe *512*
Jostaberries 410
Jovibarba
rosette cuttings 207
hirta, in dry-stone wall *189*
Jubaea, architectural plant 66
Judas tree, see *Cercis siliquastrum*
Juglans
pruning 47
nigra
as rootstock 425
soil type tolerated 42
regia, see Walnuts
Juncaceae 142
Juncus
leaves 142
effusus
in water garden 243
f. *spiralis*, in water garden 243
'Vittatus', in water garden 243
ensifolius, in water garden 243
June beetles 563, 573
Juneberry, see *Amelanchier*
Juniper, see *Juniperus*
Juniperus
diseases 554
semiripe cuttings 53
soil type preferred 42
soil type tolerated 41
chinensis 'Aurea', seasonal interest 37
communis
'Compressa' 191
ripewood cuttings 207
in rock garden 187, *187*
suggestions for use 38, 190
'Prostrata' 23
horizontalis
as ground cover 38
'Wiltonii', as ground cover 150
x *media* 'Pfitzeriana', as ground cover 38
procumbens 'Nana', bonsai 434
sabina var. *tamariscifolia*, clematis growing through *107*
scopulorum 'Skyrocket', suggestions for use 37
squamata
'Blue Carpet'
form 61
as ground cover 150, *150*
'Blue Star' *38*
Justicia
conditions preferred 431
conditions required 431
in greenhouse *430*
softwood cuttings 453
stem tip cuttings 176
Juttadinteria, division of offsets 269

Kadsura japonica, conditions tolerated 97
Kalanchoe
conditions preferred 431
in hanging baskets 261
propagation
shoot-axil buds 543
softwood cuttings 453
stem cuttings 268
beharensis, leaf cuttings 267
blossfeldiana, suggestions for use 262
jongsmanii, suggestions for use 262
manginii
in hanging basket *261*
suggestions for use 262
marmorata, conditions tolerated 262
pumila, suggestions for use 262
tomentosa, leaf cuttings 267
tubiflora *262*
conditions tolerated 262
'Wendy' *268*
stem cuttings *268*
Kales 313, *313*
Chinese, see Chinese broccoli
in crop rotation 304
cultivation 313
curly 313, *313*
curly-broad hybrids 313
harvesting 313
nitrogen requirements 310, 313
ornamental *313*
storing 312, 313
'Red and White Peacock', architectural plant 175
Kalmia
deadheading 70
pests 552
propagation
layering 86
sowing 85
soil type required 69
angustifolia, soil type required 192
latifolia *86*
air layering 87
soil type tolerated 67
polifolia 'Microphylla', soil type required 192
Kangaroo paw, see *Anigozanthos*
Kangaroo vine, see *Cissus antarctica*
Keikis, propagation by *442*, *443*
Kennedia 97
propagation
semiripe cuttings 111
serpentine layering 113
rubicunda *99*
growth rate 97
pruning 450
soil type tolerated 99
Kentucky bluegrass, see *Poa pratensis*
Kernel 581
Kerosene, for greenhouse heating 482
Kerria
dividing 88
pruning *76*
Kidney beans, see Beans, kidney
Kilmarnock willow, see *Salix caprea* 'Kilmarnock'
King palm, see *Archontophoenix alexandrae*
King's spear, see *Eremurus*
Kirengeshoma palmata, conditions preferred 141
Kitchen garden, see Vegetable garden

Kitchen waste, adding to compost heap 535, *535*
Kitchens, plants for 427
Kiwi fruits *397*, 402–3
  conditions required 397
  cultivation 402–3, *403*
  harvesting 403
  plant type 356
  recommended cultivars 402
  storing 403
  'Bruno' *402*
Knapweed, see *Centaurea*
Knautia macedonica (syn. *Scabiosa rumelica*), in mixed border *215*
Knee pads 470, *470*
Kneelers 470, *470*
Kniphofia
  for cutting 141
  division 163
  in fall 139
  flowers 582
  in perennial border *135*
  planting time 146
  soil type tolerated 147
  transplanting 156
  caulescens
    conditions tolerated 141
    growth rate 141
    in hot border *139*
    planting in groups 138
  uvaria, growth rate 141
Knives
  asparagus 461, *461*
  budding 131, *463*
  types 463, *463*
Knopper galls 558
Knot gardens 21, 26, 31, 588
  annuals in 172
  hedges for 58
  suitable plants for 31
  weeding 31
Knotweed, see *Polygonum*
  Japanese, see Japanese knotweed
Kochia scoparia f. *trichophylla* architectural plant 175
Koelreuteria paniculata, softwood cuttings 53
Kohlrabi 341, 346
  in crop rotation 304
  cultivation 346
  green *346*
  harvesting 346
  nitrogen requirement 310, 346
  recommended cultivars 346
  storing 312, 346
  'Purple Vienna' *346*
Kohleria
  conditions preferred 431
  conditions required 431
Kolkwitzia
  pruning 76
  softwood cuttings 81
Komatsuna 320, *320*
  in crop rotation 304
  cultivation 320
  hardiness 319
  harvesting 320
  nitrogen requirement 310
Kudzu, see *Pueraria lobata*
Kumquats 416, 418

L

Labels 472, *472*
Lablab beans, see Beans, hyacinth
Lablab purpureus 97
Lablab purpureus (*cont.*)
  growing on tree *96*
  as vegetable, see Beans, hyacinth
Laburnum 35
  chip-budding 56
  conditions tolerated 37
  x *watereri* 'Vossii', suggestions for use 37
Lace aloe, see *Aloe aristata*
Lace bugs 552, *552*
Lace-bark pine, see *Pinus bungeana*
Laced petals 588
Lachenalia
  conditions required 431
  diseases 569
Lactuca sativa, see Lettuces
Ladybugs
  benefits of 549
  as biological pest control 548, 552
Lady's eardrops, see *Fuchsia magellenica*
Lady's fingers, see Okra
Lady's smock, see *Cardamine pratensis*
Lady's-mantle, see *Alchemilla mollis*
Laelia, conditions required 441, 442
Laetisaria fuciformis 573
Lagarosiphon major (syn. *Elodea crispa*) 242, 243
  planting *253*
  softwood cuttings 256
Lagarus ovatus, for drying 175
Lagerstroemia
  softwood cuttings 53, 81
  indica, suggestions for use 37
Lamb's ear, see *Stachys byzantina*
Lamb's lettuce, see Corn salad
Lamb's-quarters, control 276
Lamina, definition 588
Lamium
  conditions tolerated 141
  maculatum 27
    conditions tolerated 191
    height 135
    'Beacon Silver' *150*
      suggestions for use 140
    'Chequers', winter interest 141
    'Roseum', in mixed island bed *136*
    'White Nancy'
      in mixed island bed *136*
      suggestions for use 140
Lampranthus
  conditions tolerated 259
  growing with succulents 260
  habit 259
  falcatus, conditions tolerated 262
  multiradiatus, conditions tolerated 262
Landscape, borrowed *16*
  in Oriental gardens 30
Landscape fabric
  as liner for pond or watercourse 247, 248
  as mulch 534, *534*
Lantana
  conditions required 431
  softwood cuttings 81
  stem tip cuttings 176
Lapageria 97
  conditions required 431
  pruning 103
  seed preparation 109
  simple layering 113
  rosea
    conditions tolerated 97
    site for 93
    soil type required 99
    suggestions for use 97
Larch, see *Larix*
Lardizabala 97
  biternata
Lardizabala biternata (*cont.*)
    soil type required 99
    suggestions for use 94
Large-leaved linden, see *Tilia platyphyllos*
Larix
  pests 560
  side-veneer grafting 56
  decidua, soil preferred 42
Larkspur, see *Consolida*
Lasius, see Ants
Lateral, definition 588
Lathyrus
  grandiflorus 97, *100*
    soil type tolerated 100
    supports for 98
  latifolius 97
    conditions tolerated 97
    soil types tolerated 99, 100
    supports for 98
  odoratus 97, 173
    climbing method 93
    in cottage garden *27*
    for cutting 174, 175
    diseases 560, 567
    for fragrance 97
    pests 563
    scent 96, 175
    suggestions for use 25, 93
Lattice fences 508, *508*
Lattice pots 473, *473*
Laurel, see *Laurus*; *Prunus laurocerasus*; *P. lusitanica*
Laurus
  layering 55, 86
  pests 557
  nobilis *90*
    conditions required 431
    culinary uses 291
    foliage 291
    harvesting 291
    pests 553
    propagation
      layering 291
      semiripe heel cuttings 291
    protecting 291
    as specimen plant 288
    storing 291
    suggestions for use 37, 291
    'Aurea' 291
Laurustinus, see *Viburnum tinus*
Lavandula
  conditions preferred 62
  as edging 27, 116, 288
  as ground cover 150
  hardiness 296
  as hedge 58, 59
  in knots and parterres 172
  propagation
    mound layering 297
    semiripe cuttings 83
  pruning 77, 296, *296*
  with roses 117
  soil type preferred 67
  steeping in oil or vinegar 298
  suggestions for use *24*, 289
  angustifolia *291*
    conditions preferred 294
    culinary uses 291
    flowers 291
    foliage 291
    harvesting 291
    propagation
      mound layering 297
      semiripe cuttings 291
    related species 291
    in scented preparations 291
    storing 291
    suggestions for use 291
    'Hidcote' 292
    'Nana Alba' 292
    'Rosea', in herb garden *295*
  stoechas
    flowers 292
    mound layering 297
    seasonal interest 66
Lavatera
  conditions tolerated 66
  propagation
    softwood cuttings 81
    stem tip cuttings 164
Lavatera (*cont.*)
  pruning 74
  assurgentiflora 74
  cachemiriana, growth rate 141
  maritima
    conditions tolerated 141
    growth rate 141
  thuringiaca, conditions tolerated 141
  trimestris
    conditions tolerated 175
    soil type preferred 176
    soil type tolerated 176
    'Mont Blanc', in annual border *171*
    'Silver Cup' *176*
Lavender, see *Lavandula*
Lavender cotton, see *Santolina chamaecyparissus*
Lawn 272–86
  aerating 283–4, *284*, 467, *467*, 573
  annual maintenance program 283
  ants on 574
  base dressing 277, *277*
  clippings 281
  coarse grasses 578
  conditions tolerated 531
  coring, see hollow tining
  creating 272–5
  design functions 273
  diseases 282, 286, 573–4
    annual control program 283
  drainage 276, *277*
  earthworms in 283
  edges
    repairing 285, *285*
    shaping 279, *279*
    trimming 282, *282*
  edging 273
    materials for 466
    tools for 466, *466*
  effects of drought on 573
  establishing 278–80
  existing, design and 17
  feeding 282–3, 573
    annual program 283
    before seeding or sodding 277, *277*
    method 282, *283*
  fertilizer damage 556
  fertilizers for 282
    uneven distribution *283*
  firming ground for 277, *277*
  footprinting 282
  formal 272, *272*
  grass 272–3
    climatic considerations 274
    cultivars to choose 275
    to suit use 274–5, *274*
  hollow tining 283, 284, *284*
  hydromulching 280
  informal *273*
  leaves on, removing 282, *282*
  leveling humps or hollows 286, *286*
  leveling site for 276–7, *276*, *277*
  liming 276, 573
  mole damage 574
  moss in
    causes 286
    control 283, 286, 578
    creating lawn of 275, *275*, 280
    preventing 578
  molds on 573
  mowing 281–2
    after seeding 280
    annual program 283
    clippings 281, 286
    in drought conditions 281
    frequency 281
    height of cut 281
    for renovation 285
    strips 281, *281*
    tools for 465, *465*
  mowing edge 499
  neglected, renovating 285
  nongrass 275, *275*
  ornamental 272, 275
    herbs for 291
Lawn (*cont.*)
  paths across 273
    stepping-stone 501
  pests 286, 573–4
    annual control program 283
  pH levels for 276
  plants for 272
  play areas 274, *274*
  plugging 279, *279*
  position 273
  problem areas 275
  problems 573–4
  raking 282, *282*, 467, *467*, 578
  raking ground for 277, *277*
  renovating 31, 285
  repairing 285–6, *285*, *286*
  rolling 285, 466
  routine care 281–6
  scarifying 284, *284*, 467, *467*, 573, 589
    annual program 283
  seed spreaders 467, *467*
  seeding 278, 279–80, *280*
    rates 279, 280
    sowing methods 280, *280*
  selecting grass for 274–5
  shape 273
  site preparation 276–7, *276*, *277*
  skunk damage 574
  slitting 284, *284*
  sod
    buying 278
    moving 20
  sodding 278–9, *278*
  soil
    preparation 276, *277*
    requirements 276
  specimen plants in 142, *142*
    fruit trees 355, 358
    trees 34
  spiking 284, *284*
  sprigging 279, *279*
  sprinkler systems for 469, *469*
  starvation 573
  stolonizing 280
  sweeping, tools for 467, *467*
  tapestry 275
  textural contrast in 273, *273*
  thatch 278, 281, 283, 467, 573, 590
  toadstools on 574
  tools for 466–7, *466–7*
  top-dressing 278, 284, *284*, *534*, 590
  trimming, tools for 466, *466*
  trimming long grass, tools for 463, *463*
  types 272
  unmown 272
  utility 272, 274, *274*
    mowing 282
  vegetative propagation 278, 279, *279*
  verticutting 284, *284*
  watering 282, 531
    after seeding 280
    after sodding 278
    annual program 283
    sprinkler systems 469, *469*
  weed and feed mixture 282
  weedkillers 578, 579
    commercial names 574
  weeds 286, 578–9, *578*
    control 578
      annual program 283
      tools for 461, *461*
    creeping 578
    in long grass 275
    preventing 578
Lawn chamomile, see *Chamaemelum nobile* 'Treneague'
Lawn mowers 465, *465*
  blades *465*
  choosing 465, *465*
  gasoline and electricity compared 465
  maintenance 465
  manual 465, *465*

(*entry cont.*)

Lawn mowers (*cont.*)
  power 465, *465*
  rollers on 465, *465*
  safety 465
  types 281, 465, *465*
    hover 465, *465*
    mulching rotary *465*
    push reel *465*
    reel 465, *465*
    riding 465, *465*
    rotary *280*, 465, *465*
Lawn mowings, mulching with 308
Laws, on fences 508, 510
Lawson cypress, see *Chamaecyparis lawsoniana*
Layer planting 23, 26, *26*, 27, 588
Layering 539, 588
  air 539, *539*
    indoor plants 456, *456*
    shrubs 86, *87*
    trees 55
  Chinese, see air
  climbers 109, 113, *113*
  continuous, see French
  dropping 86
  etiolation, see trench
  French 87, 539, *539*
  indoor plants 456, *456*
  methods 539, *539*
  mound 539, *539*
    shrubby herbs 297, *297*
  natural, from runners 539, *539*
  propagation of fruit by 370
  roses 131, *131*
  self 109, 112, *112*, 588
  serpentine
    climbers 113, *113*
    method 539, *539*
  shrubs 86–8, *86–7*
  simple 86, *86*, 113, *113*, 456, *456*
    method 539, *539*
  stooling 87, *87*
    method 539, *539*
  tip 86
    blackberries 407, *407*
    hybrid berries 407, *407*
    method 539, *539*
    shrubs 86
  trees 55, *55*
  trench, method 539, *539*
Leaching 525, 532, 533, 588
Leader, definition 588
Leaf blotches, see Leaf spots
Leaf blowers 467, *467*
Leaf buds, problems 559–60
Leaf cuttings 540, 541, *541*
  alpines 207
  indoor plants 454, *454*
  succulents 267, *267*
Leaf nematodes
  control 553
  damage caused by 553, *553*
Leaf miners
  control 553
  damage caused by 553, *553*
Leaf mold
  definition 588
  in soil mixes 535
Leaf rollers 554
Leaf scorch 484
Leaf sections, propagation by 454–5, *454*
Leaf shine 444
Leaf spots
  bacterial 554, *554*
  fungal 554, *554*
Leaf sweeper 467, *467*
Leaf tiers 554
Leaf-bud cuttings 540, *540*
  blackberries 408, *408*
  fruit 370
  hybrid berries 408, *408*
  indoor plants 453
  shrubs 83, *83*
Leaf-cutting bees 551, *551*
Leafhoppers 553, *553*, 571
  disease spread by 558, 562
Leaflets, definition 588
Leafy gall 561, *561*
Leafy vegetables 321–5
  growing in containers 307
  storing 312, 321
  for succession 321
  watering, critical periods 308
Least duckweed, see *Wolffia arrhiza*
Leaves 588
  adapted to drought 517
  alternate 585
  annuals grown for 171
  architectural *14*
  broadly ovate *581*
  browning 532
  colors
    in perennial beds and borders 139
    trees for 34, *34*
  compound 586
  compound pinnate frond *581*
  contrasting forms, in perennials 138, *138*
  digitate *581*
  discolored 532, *547*, 552–7
  distorted 557–8
  eaten *547*, 550–51
  forms 581, *581*
  golden, in winter, trees for 37
  gray, in winter, trees for 37
  importance of water to 517
  impressions in concrete 502
  indoor plants for 426
  as insulating material 521
  linear *581*
  midrib 588
  opposite 588
  ornamental, perennials for 135
  peltate 588
  pinnate *581*
  pinnatifid *581*
  plants for greenhouse 431
  scalelike *581*
  scented, shrubs 66
  seed (cotyledons) 132, 538, *538*, 582
  shrubs 64
  simple 589
  as soil additive, problems 529
  structure 581
  texture 24, *25*
    annuals for 170
    trees for 34, *34*
  variegated, light requirements 427
  wilted 552–7
  wind-tolerant types 521
Leeks *341*, 343, *343*
  in crop rotation 304
  cultivation 343, *343*
  diseases 343, 569
  harvesting 343
  nitrogen requirement 310, 343
  pests 343, 569
  recommended cultivars 343
  sowing 343
    in cell pack 307, 343, *343*
  in vegetable garden *300*
  'Large American Flag' *343*
Leguminosae (legumes) 588
  in crop rotation 304
  nitrogen-fixing 304
  seed scarification 538
  seed viability 176
Leiophyllum buxifolium, soil type required 192
Lemna trisulca 243
Lemon balm, see *Melissa officinalis*
Lemon cucumbers, see Cucumbers, lemon
Lemon thyme, see *Thymus* x *citriodorus*
Lemon verbena 290, *290*
  in containers 288
  cultivation 290
  harvesting 290
  storing 290
Lemonimes 417
Lemons *415*, 416, 417
  in border *358*
  cultivation 417
Lemons (*cont.*)
  hybrid with lime 417
  recommended cultivars 417
  as rootstock 416, 417
  storing 367
  suggestions for use 288
  'Eureka' *417*
Lenophyllum
  pusillum, leaf cuttings 267
  texanum, leaf cuttings 267
Lent lily, see *Narcissus pseudonarcissus*
Lenten rose, see *Helleborus orientalis*
Leontice, suggestions for use 219
Leontopodium
  alpinum
    conserving moisture 185
    soil type tolerated 193
    suggestions for use 191
  nivale, suggestions for use 191
Leopard lily, see *Dieffenbachia*; *Lilium pardalinum*
Leopard's bane, see *Doronicum*
Lepidium nanum, semiripe cuttings 207
Lepidosaphes ulmi 554
Lepidum sativum, see Cress
Lepismium, side grafting 271
Leptinotarsa decemlineata 551
Leptospermum, semiripe cuttings 83
Leptosphaeria coniothyrium 559
Lesser celandine, see *Ranunculus ficaria*
Lettuce root aphid 548
Lettuces 324–5
  alternating with brassicas *301*
  butterhead *321*, 324
    harvesting 325
    pest resistance 548
  in containers *307*
  crisphead 324
    harvesting 325
  cultivation 324–5, *325*
  as cut-and-come-again crop 312, 325
  diseases 552
  genetic engineering 546
  growing below wall 301
  harvesting *324*, 325
  iceberg 324
  as intercrop *304*
  loose-leaf *321*, 324, *324*
  mineral deficiency 560
  nitrogen requirement 310, 324
  pest resistance 548
  pests 325, 561, 566
  recommended cultivars 324
  Romaine *321*, 324
    harvesting 325
  Salad Bowl types 324
    growing with herbs *303*
    harvesting *324*
    in vegetable garden *300*
  seed germination 305
  semicos 324
  storing 325
  successional cropping 306, 324
  transplanting 306, 325
  in vegetable garden *300*
  watering, critical periods 308
  in windowbox *303*
  winter cropping under cover 311
  'Green Lake' *324*
  'Lollo Rossa' *324*
  'Paris Island Cos' *324*
  'Salad Bowl' *324*
Leucanthemum x *superbum*
  conditions tolerated 141
  from seed *161*
  suggestions for use 136
Leucocoryne, suggestions for use 219
Leucojum
  division of offsets 233
  suggestions for use 219
Leucojum (*cont.*)
  aestivum
    conditions preferred 219
    suggestions for use 216, 217, 227, 243
  vernum
    conditions preferred 219
    forcing 228
    suggestions for use 227
Leucopogon fraseri, soil type required 192
Leucothöe
  semiripe cuttings with heel 83
  soil type required 69
  keiskei, soil type required 192
Leveling
  humps and hollows in lawns 286, *286*
  site 276–7, *276*, *277*
Levisticum officinale (syn. *Ligusticum levisticum*), see Lovage
Lewisia
  in containers outdoors 260
  propagation
    leaf cuttings 207
    semiripe cuttings 207
    sowing *205*
  suggestions for use 190, 191
  Cotyledon Hybrids *193*
    in alpine raised bed *201*
    conditions preferred 186
    conditions tolerated 262
    soil type preferred 193
    suggestions for use 191
  'George Henley', in alpine raised bed *201*
  leeana, conditions tolerated 262
  tweedyi, suggestions for use 191
Leycesteria
  conditions tolerated 66
  pruning 74
Leyland cypress, see x *Cupressocyparis leylandii*
Liatris, division 163
Libertia grandiflora
  conditions tolerated 141
  in mixed island bed *136*
Lice, plant, see Aphids
Light
  absorption by leaves 581, *581*
  deprivation, symptoms of 427
  direct, indoor plants preferring 431
  effect on colors 24, *24*
  indirect, indoor plants preferring 431
  manipulating artificially 518
  plants growing toward 518
  requirements for seed germination 538
  variations within room 427, *427*
Light meters 485
Lighting
  in courtyard or patio 29
  in greenhouse 481, 485, *485*
  grow lamps 485, *485*
Lightning, damage caused by 561, *561*
Lignin *580*
Ligularia
  conditions preferred 242
  in perennial border *137*
  clivorum, suggestions for use 243
  dentata
    in contrasting foliage group *138*
    'Othello', architectural form 141
  przewalskii
    conditions preferred 141
    suggestions for use 243
  stenocephala
    in border of mixed textures *138*
    growth rate 141
Ligusticum levisticum, see Lovage
Ligustrum
  conditions tolerated 66
  shaping 60
  soil type tolerated 69
  for topiary 90
  japonicum, pruning 78
  lucidum
    for avenue 36
    semiripe cuttings 53
  ovalifolium 90
    hardwood cuttings 84
    as hedge 58
Lilac, see *Syringa*
Liliaceae, corms and rhizomes 214
Lilioceris lilii 551
Lilium
  architectural plant 219
  bulb 214, *542*
  care 239
  classification 239
  conditions preferred 219
  conditions required 239
  for cutting 219
  diseases 239, 555
  flower form *582*
  flower shapes *239*
  after flowering 231
  germination 235
  hybrids 239
  in mixed border 215
  pests 239, 550
  planting 239
  propagation 239, *239*
    bulblets 239, *239*, *542*
    offsets 233
    rhizomes 233
    scaling 236–7, *236*, 542, *542*
    from seed 235
      feeding 235
    stem bulbils 233, 239, *239*, *542*
  repotting 231
  seed germination 235
  seedlings 235
  sites suitable for 239
  soil mix for 439
  staking *230*
  suggestions for use 216, 218
  American 239
  Asiatic hybrids, forcing 228
  Aurelian hybrids 239
  'Bright Star', in mixed border *215*
  bulbiferum
    propagation 239
    var. *croceum 239*
  candidum 239
    diseases 555
    planting 239
    suggestions for use 27
  cernuum 239
  chalcedonicum 239, *239*
  'Connecticut King' *239*
  davidii 239
  'Enchantment' *218*
  formosanum 239
  hansonii 219, 239
  henryi 239
  lancifolium (syn. *L. tigrinum*)
    disease carrier 239
    propagation 239
      bulbils *542*
  longiflorum 239
    propagation, bulblets *542*
  mackliniae, in peat bed *188*
  martagon 239
  monadelphum 239
  Oriental hybrids 239
  pardalinum, propagation 239
  regale 239
    in mixed border *215*
    in pots *217*
    with roses 116
  x *testaceum*, diseases 555
  tigrinum, see *L. lancifolium*
Lily, see *Lilium*
  arum, see *Zantedeschia aethiopica*
  Madonna, see *Lilium candidum*
Lily beetles 239
  red 550–51, *550*

Lily gray mold 555, *555*
Lily-of-the-valley, see *Convallaria majalis*
Lilyturf, see *Liriope*
Lima beans, see Beans, Lima
"Limax" 550
Lime 588
adding to compost heap 535
amounts required to alter pH levels 533
applying 533, *533*
dolomitic, in soil mixes 536
effect on soil 524, 525
improving soil with 276, 555, 558, 567
as lawn weedkiller 579
reaction with manure 533
as soil additive 529, *529*
types 533
as weed deterrent 576
Lime haters (calcifuges) 585
pH range 525
raised beds for 507
soil mixes for 69, 436, 536
watering 444
Lime lovers (calcicoles) 585
pH range 525
Lime sulfur 558
Limes *415*, 416, 417
cultivation 417
groups 417
hybrid with lemon 417
recommended cultivars 417
Rangpur, as rootstock 416
'Tahiti' *417*
Limestone
ground, in soil mixes 536
for rock garden 193, *193*
Limestone soil, see Alkaline soil
Limewater 552
Liming 360, 533, *533*
Limnanthes
conditions tolerated 175
douglasii
form 171
propagation
self-seeding 178
sowing 177
soil type preferred 176
Limnobium
spongia 243
stoloniferum 243
propagation by offsets 257
Limnophila heterophylla, softwood cuttings 256
Limonium
for drying 141, 174
drying method 183
harvesting 183, *183*
bellidifolium, conditions tolerated 191
latifolium
conditions tolerated 141
root cuttings 165
soil type preferred 146
'Blue Cloud', in mixed island bed *136*
sinuatum
for cutting 175
for drying 175, *183*
soil type preferred 176
soil type tolerated 176
Linaria
flowering time from seed 160
alpina, suggestions for use 191
maroccana
propagation
self-seeding 178
sowing 177
soil type preferred 176
purpurea, soil type tolerated 147
Linden, see *Tilia*
Lindera, pruning 74
Lines, garden 471, *471*
Ling, see *Calluna vulgaris*
Lining out 588
Link stakes 156, *156*, *472*
Linnaea borealis
in peat bed *188*
soil type required 192
Linum
arboreum, semiripe cuttings 207
flavum, in dry-stone wall *189*
grandiflorum
conditions tolerated 175
sowing 177
narbonense, soil type tolerated 147
perenne, in rock garden *187*
suffruticosum
soil type preferred 197
subsp. *salsoloides* 'Nanum', suggestions for use 191
Liquidambar styraciflua
softwood cuttings 53
suggestions for use 37
Liriodendron tulipifera 37
seasonal interest 37
suggestions for use 37
Liriope muscari
in containers 140
seasonal interest 135
suggestions for use 140
'Variegata', winter interest 141
Lithodora diffusa
semiripe cuttings 207
soil type required 192
'Heavenly Blue', in peat bed *188*
Lithophytes 440, 588
Lithops
in bowl garden 261
division of offsets 269
form 426
succulent type 258
bella, suggestions for use 262
dorotheae, suggestions for use 262
karasmontana 269
pseudotruncatella var. *pulmonuncula 259*
Liverwort, on soil around bought plants 145
Living room, outdoor, garden as 14, 21
Living stones, see *Lithops*
Livistona, suggestions for use *37*
Lizard's tail, see *Saururus cernuus*
Loam 588
friable 301
lime required to alter pH 533
in potting mixes 535
qualities of 301
structure 524
water in 530
Lobel maple, see *Acer lobelii*
Lobelia
flowering time from seed 160
in formal bedding 172
in hanging basket *437*
planting, in container *181*
in summer bedding *170*
trailing, in windowbox *174*
cardinalis
dividing 163
planting time 146
soil type tolerated 146
suggestions for use 242, 243
'Crystal Palace', in annual border *171*
erinus
for containers 174
as filler 173
suggestions for use 175
Cascade Series 174
fulgens
division 163
soil type tolerated 146
suggestions for use 243
paludosa, in water garden 243
Lobivia
division of offsets 269
suggestions for use 262
densispina 262
famatimensis 262
jajoiana 262
pentlandii 262
Lobularia maritima
conditions preferred 173
conditions tolerated 175
in container *26*
in formal bedding 172, 214
as ground cover 173
scent 175
self-seeding 178, 184
soil type preferred 176
soil type tolerated 176
'Snow Crystal' *171*
Locust, see *Robinia pseudoacacia*
Loganberries 406, 407
diseases 363, 559
pests 564
plant type 356
thornless, in large fruit garden *357*
Logs
sawed
as edging 507
raised beds of 507
stepping stones of *501*
Lolium
multiflorum, for lawn 275
perenne
as green manure 533
for lawn 274, 275
sowing rate 280
Lombardy poplar, see *Populus nigra* 'Italica'
Lonas, for drying 175
London pride, see *Saxifraga* x *urbium*
Long-day plants 303, 341, 518
Lonicera
bonsai 434
choosing *99*
climbing
pruning 105, *105*
renovating 105, *105*
conditions tolerated 93
for fragrance 97
growing with roses 118
as hedge, renovation 60
propagation
hardwood cuttings 111
semiripe cuttings 111, *111*
simple layering 113
softwood cuttings 110
pruning 103, 105
soil types tolerated 67, 69, 99, 100
suggestions for use 27, 29, 97
as weed 576
witches' brooms 558, *558*
x *americana 113*
conditions tolerated 97
suggestions for use 93
x *brownii*, conditions tolerated 97
fragrantissima, in shrub border *63*
x *heckrottii*, conditions tolerated 97
japonica 576
'Halliana' 576
korolkowii, seasonal interest 66
maackii 576
nitida
as hedge 58, 59
formative pruning *60*
pruning 78
for topiary 90
clipping 91
periclymenum 92
climbing method 92
'Graham Thomas', suggestions for use 94
'Serotina', seasons of interest 96
pileata
conditions preferred 66
conditions tolerated 66
pruning 78
x *purpusii*
'Winter Beauty', scent 66
sempervirens
conditions tolerated 97
as screen 94
Lonicera (*cont.*)
standishii, scent 66
tatarica 576
witches' brooms 558
x *tellmanniana*, conditions tolerated 97
Loosestrife, see *Lysimachia*
Lophophora, flat grafting 271
Loppers *49*, *50*, 75, 462, *462*
maintenance 462
Loquats 418–19, *419*, see also *Eriobotrya japonica*
cultivation 418–19, *419*
diseases 555, 564
harvesting 419
storing 419
Lords and ladies, see *Arum*
Lotus, see *Nelumbo*
Lotus berthelotii, stem tip cuttings 164
Louver vents, see Ventilation, greenhouse, methods
Lovage 292, *292*
conditions tolerated 288
cultivation 292
harvesting 292
Love-in-a-mist, see *Nigella damascena*
Love-lies-bleeding, see *Amaranthus caudatus*
Low maintenance, design for *13*, 14, *16*
Luckhoffia, flat grafting 271
Luculia gratissima, scent 66
Ludisia discolor, suggestions for use 438
Ludwigia arcuata
softwood cuttings 256
suggestions for use 243
Lumber, see Wood
Lunaria
collecting seed 184
conditions tolerated 175
for drying 174
fruit type *581*
retaining seedheads 184
thinning 178
annua
for cutting 175
self-seeding 178
rediviva, for seedheads 141
Lungwort, see *Pulmonaria*
Lupine, see *Lupinus*
Lupinus 27
basal stem cuttings 164
choosing healthy plant *145*
color combinations *24*
companion plant for 139
cutting back 156
seed germination 160
seed stratification *538*
suggestions for use 140
'The Chatelaine' *160*
Luronium natans, suggestions for use 243
Luzula
conditions preferred 142
conditions tolerated 142
leaves 142
suggestions for use 142
campestris, see Field woodrush
sylvatica 'Marginata', conditions tolerated 141
Lychnis
dividing 163
flowering time from seed 160
chalcedonica, soil type tolerated 147
coronaria, foliage 138
Lycopersicon
esculentum, see Tomatoes
pimpinellifolium, see Tomatoes, currant
Lygus lineolaris 551
Lymantria dispar 551
Lysichiton
conditions tolerated 242
division of rootstock 257
soil type tolerated 146
americanus
architectural form 141
Lysichiton americanus (*cont.*)
in water garden 243
camtschatcensis 257
in water garden 243
Lysimachia
propagation, division 163
soil type tolerated 146
in windowbox *174*
nummularia 'Aurea', bulbs with 150
punctata, in wild garden *27*
Lythrum
division 163
soil type tolerated 146
virgatum, in border of mixed textures *138*

M

Macfadyena 97
semiripe cuttings 111
unguis-cati, pruning 105
Mache, see Corn salad
Macleaya cordata, growth rate 141
Macrodactylus subspinosus 563, 566, 573
Macronoctua onusta 566
Macronutrients 532
Macrosteles fascifrons 553, 571
Madagascar jasmine, see *Stephanotis floribunda*
Madeira vine, see *Anredera*
Madonna lily, see *Lilium candidum*
Madroña, see *Arbutus menziesii*
Madroñe, see *Arbutus menziesii*
Magennis Bermuda grass, see *Cynodon* x *magennisii*
Magnesium 545
deficiency 362, 557, *557*
plant requirements 532
Magnolia
bulbs under 216
propagation
air layering 87
chip-budding 56
layering 86, *539*
side-veneer grafting 89
seed pods 35
soil type required 69
suggestions for use 32
acuminata, soil preferred 41
campbellii 41
propagation
air layering 55
layering 55
seasonal interest 37
soil preferred 41
suggestions for use *37*
'Charles Raffill', suggestions for use 37
var. *mollicomata 34*
'Elizabeth', suggestions for use 37
grandiflora
conditions tolerated 37, 39, 66
propagation
air layering 55
layering 55
semiripe cuttings 53
with heel 83
pruning 49
seasonal interest 37
hypoleuca 55
layering 55
x *loebneri* 'Merrill', suggestions for use 37
(*entry cont.*)

Magnolia (*cont.*)
salicifolia, suggestions for use 37
sieboldii, scent 66
x *soulangiana*, pruning 76
stellata
in garden design *19*
pruning 76
x *thompsoniana*, scent 66
virginiana, suggestions for use 243
Mahonia
propagation
leaf-bud cuttings 83
semiripe cuttings 83
aquifolium
conditions preferred 66
conditions tolerated 66
bealei, form 61
japonica
scent 66
seasonal interest 62
x *media* group, soil type tolerated 67
repens
conditions tolerated 64
division of suckers 88
Maiden pink, see *Dianthus deltoides*
Maiden whips, training
apples 375, 377, *377*, 378, *378*
fruit trees 361, 365, *365*
plums 385
Maidenhair fern, see *Adiantum capillus-veneris*
Maidenhair tree, see *Ginkgo biloba*
Maidens 356
apples 375, *375*, 376, *376*, 377, *377*
cherries 392
fruit trees 361, 365
peaches *388*, 389, *389*
pears 381, *381*
plums 384, *384*, 385, 386, 386
Maihuenia
flat grafting 271
poeppigii *259*
hardiness 259
Maintenance, garden design and 16
Maize, ornamental, see *Zea mays*
Malabar spinach 321–2
culinary uses 321
cultivation 321–2
cuttings 322
feeding 321
harvesting 322
nitrogen requirement 310, 321
storing 322
supporting 321, *321*
Malacosoma
americanum 553
californicum 553
Maladera castanea 573
Malathion 550, 551, 552, 553, 554, 558, 559, 560, 562, 564, 565, 571
commercial names 574
Malcolmia
conditions tolerated 175
self-seeding 178
maritima, sowing 177
Male fern, see *Dryopteris filix-mas*
Mallet cuttings 83, *83*
Mallow, see *Malva*
Malope trifida, sowing 177
Maltese-cross, see *Lychnis chalcedonica*
Malus, for *Malus* grown as fruit trees, see Apples
buying 40
chip-budding 56, *57*
conditions tolerated 37
diseases 555, 564, 570
for fall color 35
features 32
grafting 57
pests 563
propagation, from seed 54
Malus (*cont.*)
soil type tolerated 41, 42
suggestions for use 148
'Cowichan' *42*
'Dartmouth', suggestions for use 37
floribunda
as specimen tree 35
suggestions for use 37
'Golden Hornet'
fruit 35
seasonal interest 37
suggestions for use 37
'Magdeburgensis' *33*
'Profusion', in garden design *19*
sylvestris var. *domestica*, see Apples
tschonoskii, suggestions for use 33, 37
Malva
flowering time from seed 160
alcea var. *fastigiata*, growth rate 141
moschata, growth rate 141
sylvestris, growth rate 141
Malvastrum, stem tip cuttings 164
Mammals, see Animals
Mammillaria
in bowl garden 261
in containers outdoors 260
in greenhouse display *261*
handling 261
propagation
division of offsets 269
division of rootstock 270
flat grafting 271
in raised bed 260
suggestions for use 262
blossfeldiana 262
bocasana 262
compressa 262
gracilis 262
hahniana 262
herrerae, flat grafting *271*
microcarpa 262
muehlenpfordtii, in bowl *264*
mystax 262
nana 262
polythelle, in bowl *264*
rhodantha 262
spinosissima 262
zeilmanniana 262
Mandarins
conditions required 418
cross-pollination 418
hybrid with kumquats 418
recommended cultivars 417
'Clementine' *417*
Cleopatra Group 418
as rootstock 416, 418
Satsuma Group, fruits 418
Mandevilla 97
conditions preferred 431
propagation
semiripe cuttings 111
simple layering 113
softwood cuttings 453
pruning 103
vigor 98
amabilis *111*
splendens *450*
cuttings 453
pruning 450
Manettia
semiripe cuttings 111
softwood cuttings 110
cordifolia, pruning 105
inflata, pruning 105
Manganese 545
deficiency 360, 362, 380, 387, 525, 532, 557
excess 525
plant requirements 532
Mangifera indica, see Mangos
Mangos 419–20
cultivation 419–20
dwarf 419
fruit *415*, 419, *419*
harvesting 367, 420
polyembryonic seedlings 419
Mangos (*cont.*)
propagation 420
approach-grafting 420
from seed 420
recommended cultivars 420
rootstocks 419
storing 420
tree *419*
'Tommy Atkins' *420*
Manila grass, see *Zoysia matrella*
Manipur lily, see *Lilium mackliniae*
Manna ash, see *Fraxinus ornus*
Manure
adding to compost heap 535, *535*
advantages 532
content 302
green, see Green manuring
improving soil fertility with 302
improving water retention with 529
liquid, painting hypertufa with 198, *198*
maintaining nutrient levels with 309
as mulch 123, 308
nutrient content 532
in organic growing methods 536
reaction of lime on 533
as soil additive 529, *529*
"tea" of 309
use for bulbs 225
Manzanita, see *Arctostaphylos*
Maple, see *Acer*
red, see *Acer rubrum*
Maple anthracnose 572
Maranta
conditions preferred 431
conditions required 431
leuconeura
division of rootstock 451
suggestions for use 438
in terrarium *138*
var. *kerchoviana* *451*
Marasmius oreades 574
Marble galls 558
Marcottage, see Air layering
Marginal plants 242, 243, 588
adapting to waterlogging 517
choosing healthy plants *251*
cuttings 257
planting 252, *253*
shelves for 246–7, *246–7*, *250*
repotting *255*
in water garden *240*
Marguerite, see *Argyranthemum frutescens*
Marigold, see *Tagetes*
African, see *Tagetes erecta*
French, see *Tagetes patula*
marsh, see *Caltha palustris*
pot, see *Calendula*
Marionberry 407
Mariposa tulip, see *Calochortus*
Maritime pine, see *Pinus pinaster*
Marjoram, see *Origanum vulgare*
Markers 472, *472*
Marsh marigold, see *Caltha palustris*
Marsilea quadrifolia, propagation by offsets 257
Martagon lily, see *Lilium martagon*
Mascarene grass, see *Zoysia tenuifolia*
Masonry, mortar mix for 494
Masonry cement, definition 499
Masterwort, see *Astrantia*
Matteuccia
by stream *158*
struthiopteris
in formal planting *159*
suggestions for use 242
Matthiola
for containers 174
for cutting 174
Matthiola (*cont.*)
diseases 552, 555, 567
flowering shoots 181
pests 550
for scent 175
bicornis
conditions preferred 175
conditions tolerated 175
Brompton Series
in containers 174
for cutting 175
scent 175
soil type tolerated 176
East Lothian Series
in containers 174
for cutting 175
scent 175
incana
for cutting 175
soil type tolerated 176
Ten-Week Series
in containers 174
for cutting 175
scent 175
Matucana aureiflora, suggestions for use 262
Mayflower, see *Epigaea repens*
Maypoling 363
MCPA 579
commercial names 574
Meadow cranesbill, see *Geranium pratense*
Meadow foam, see *Limnanthes douglasii*
Meadow gardens 27, 28, 167, see also Grassland
alpine 167
bulbs for 216
maintenance 167
mowing 167, 230
planting 167
site 167
soil for 167
sowing 167
uses 212
wildflowers for *167*
Meadow grass, see *Poa*
Meadow rue, see *Thalictrum*
Meadow saxifrage, see *Saxifraga granulata*
Meadow sod 278
Meadows, see Meadow gardens
Meadowsweet, see *Filipendula*
Mealybugs 552, *552*
biological control 548
Mechanical wounding 561
Meconopsis
flowering time from seed 160
propagation
division 208
sowing 205
seed
collecting *160*
germination 160
cambrica, conditions preferred 191
delavayi, root cuttings 208
grandis 'Branklyn' *160*
Mecoprop 579
commercial names 574
Medinilla, greenhouse conditions required 431
Mediterranean cypress, see *Cupressus sempervirens*
Mediterranean rocket, see Arugula
Medium, definition 588
Medlars 383, *383*
cultivation 383
fruit *371*, 383, *383*
harvesting 383
pruning 364, 383
ripening *383*
rootstocks 383
storing 383
tree forms 383
Megachile 551
Melampsora 554
Melanoplus bivittatus 563
Melia azedarach
soil preferred 42
suggestions for use 37
Melianthus major, architectural form 141
Meligethes, see Pollen beetles
Melissa officinalis 292, *292*
conditions preferred 288
conditions tolerated 288
culinary uses 292
foliage 292
harvesting 292
propagation 292
scent 287
storing 292
variegated
conditions required 292
cutting back 296
'All Gold', conditions tolerated 288
'Aurea' 292
conditions tolerated 288
in herb garden *295*
'Variegata', conditions tolerated 288
Melittia satyriniformis 559
Meloidogyne, see Root-knot nematodes
Melons 329–30
cantaloupes 329
casaba, see winter
cultivation 329–30
diseases 565, 567
fruits 329
growing through plastic mulch 309
growing under cover 330
harvesting 330
honeydew *328*, 329
muskmelons *328*, 329, *329*
nitrogen requirement 310, 329
origins 328
pests 330, 552, 553, 559, 571
pinching 330, *330*
pollination 330
recommended cultivars 329
ripening under cloches 311
storing 330
types 329
winter (casaba), fruit 329
'Ambrosia' *329*
'Sweet Dream' *329*
Melting out 573
Mentha
conditions tolerated 288
cosmetic uses 287
culinary uses 287
diseases 554
forcing 294
freezing leaves 298, *298*
medicinal uses 287
mulching 296
planting to restrict spread 294, *294*
repelling pests 548
variegated, cutting back 296
in vegetable garden 303
aquatica
in water garden 242, 243
propagation 257
x *piperita*
culinary uses 287, 292
foliage 292
'Citrata', foliage 292
requienii, suggestions for use 191
spicata *292*
culinary uses 292
flowers 292
harvesting 292
propagation 292
related species 292
storing 292
suaveolens 'Variegata'
conditions preferred 288
foliage 292
in herb garden *295*
x *villosa* 'Alopecuroides'
flowers 292
foliage 292
scent 292

Mentzelia lindleyi
soil type preferred 176
sowing 177
Menyanthes trifoliata, division of rootstock 257
Menziesia
soil type required 69
ciliicalyx
division of suckers 88
soil type required 192
Mercury fluorescent lamps 485
Mercury vapor lamps 485
Merendera, suggestions for use 219
Mericlone, definition 588
Meripilus 567
Meristem culture 443, *443*, 588
Merodon equestris, see Narcissus bulb flies
Merremia 97
tuberosa, soil type tolerated 99
Mertensia
root cuttings 165
soil type indicated by 525
Mesembryanthemaceae, flowers 259
Mesembryanthemum crystallinum, see Iceplants
Mesh, for shading greenhouse 484, *484*
Mespilus germanica, see Medlars
Metabolism of plants 580
energy for 581
Metal halide lamps 485
Metal sheds 513
Metaldehyde 550, 568
commercial names 574
Metaphycus helvolus, as biological pest control 548, 554
Metaseiulus occidentalis, as biological pest control 548, 552
Metasequoia
hardwood cuttings 52, *52*
glyptostroboides
propagation
hardwood cuttings 53
softwood cuttings 53
soil type tolerated 42
'Charles Raffill', suggestions for use 37
Methiocarb 550
commercial name 574
Methoxychlor 551, 553, 559, 563, 565, 571
Metrosideros
excelsa, semiripe cuttings 53
robusta, semiripe cuttings 53
umbellata, semiripe cuttings 53
Mexican flame vine, see *Senecio confusus*
Mexican orange bush, see *Choisya ternata*
Meyerophytum, division of offsets 269
Mezereon, see *Daphne mezereum*
Mice 561, 568
protection from 310
Michaelmas daisy, see *Aster*
Michelia
semiripe cuttings 53
soil preferred 41
Microclimate 15
design and 15
exploiting 519
factors producing 519
in garden 519, *519*
Micronutrients 532, 588, see also Nutrients; Trace elements
Microorganisms
colonizing plants 559
soil rich in 301
Micropropagation 546, *546*, 586, 588
Microwave, drying herbs in 298
Midrib 588
Mignonette, see *Reseda*
Mignonette vine, see *Anredera*
Mikania
pruning 103
softwood cuttings 110
scandens 97
Mila, flat grafting 271
Milax 550
Mildew 157
conditions encouraging 484
control 398
downy 552, *552*
powdery 548, 552, *552*, 564, *564*
on roses 119, 124
Mile-a-minute vine, see *Polygonum aubertii*; *P. baldschuanicum*
Miller, see Star-wheeled cultivator
Millipedes 547, *549*, 550, *550*
distinguishing from centipedes 549, 550
Miltonia candida var. *grandiflora 440*
Mimosa, see *Acacia*
Mimulus
aurantiacus
in hot border *139*
stem tip cuttings 164
Calypso Series, conditions preferred 175
cardinalis, in water garden 243
cupreus, in water garden 243
glutinosus, see *M. aurantiacus*
guttatus
in water garden 243
soil type tolerated 146
Malibu Series
conditions preferred 175
growing as annual 175
ringens, in water garden 243
Mineral oil 551, 552, 553, 558
Minerals
deficiencies
causes 531
correcting 533
problems caused 547
importance of 581
Miner's lettuce 327, *327*
culinary uses 327
cultivation 327
harvesting 327
in vegetable garden *300*
Mini-onions, see Onions, pickling
Mint, see *Mentha*
Mintbush, see *Prostanthera*
Mirabelles 383
Mirabilis, growing with succulents 259
Miscanthus 15
cutting down 143
growth rate 141
in mixed group *142*
suggestions for use 142
sinensis
architectural form 141
'Silberfeder' *142*
Missouri flag, see *Iris missouriensis*
Mist box 81, *81*
Mist propagation 544
Mist propagation unit 488, *488*
Mistletoe cactus, see *Rhipsalis*
Mistletoe fig, see *Ficus deltoidea*
Mist-sprayers 468, 484
Mist-spraying
for bromeliads *433*
for grapevines 398
for pot plants 444
Mitchella repens, soil type required 192
Mites 547, 558
importance to soil 525
predatory 548, 552
Mitraria
propagation, self layering 113
soil for 98
suggestions for use 97
coccinea
conditions tolerated 97
soil type required 99
Mitrophyllum, division of offsets 269
Mizuna greens 320, *320*
cultivation 320
in crop rotation 304
culinary uses 320
harvesting 320
leaves 319
nitrogen requirement 310
in vegetable garden *300*
Mock orange, see *Philadelphus*
Modular systems, see Cell packs
Moist shade
annuals and biennials preferring 175
bulbs preferring 219
herbs tolerant of 288
perennials preferring 141
perennials suitable for *138*
plants for *15*
rock plants preferring 191
shrubs tolerant of 66
Moisture-loving plants 242, 243
planting 252
Mold
blue, see Blue mold
gray, see *Botrytis*
Moles 574, *574*
protection from 310
Molinia caerulea subsp. *caerulea* 'Variegata', suggestions for use 142
Moluccella
germination 179
laevis
for cutting 175
for drying 175
flowers 171
Molybdenum
deficiency 558, *558*
plant requirements 532
Monarda
basal stem cuttings 164
for cutting 141
didyma 292
in border 288
conditions preferred 292
culinary uses 292
division 292
flowers 292
harvesting 292
in herb garden *295*
related species 292
stem cuttings 292
storing 292
variants 292
fistulosa 167
flowers 292
Money plant, see *Lunaria annua*
Monkey flower, see *Mimulus*
Monkeynuts, see Peanuts
Monk's hood, see *Aconitum*
Monocarpic plants 259, 588
Monocotyledons 588
flower forms 582, *582*
leaf veins 582, *582*
stems 582
Monocultures 23
Monoecious plants 582, *582*, 588
Monopodial growth 440, 588
Monstera 97
conditions preferred 431
hydroculture 431
simple layering 113
deliciosa
conditions tolerated 97
foliage 426
growth rate 428
leaf form *581*
self layering 113
suggestions for use 97
Montbretia, see *Crocosmia*
Monterey cypress, see *Cupressus macrocarpa*
Monterey pine, see *Pinus radiata*
Montia perfoliata, see Miner's lettuce
Mooli, see Daikon
Mop-top virus 568
Moraceae 395, 396
Moraea
suggestions for use 219
huttonii 219
spathulata, conditions preferred 219
Morfea 554
Morisia
root cuttings 165
monanthos
in alpine raised bed *201*
in rock garden *187*
root cuttings 208
Morning glory, see *Ipomoea*
Morocco broom, see *Cytisus battandieri*
Morphology 580
Mortar
bedding 499
definition 499
dry 499
laying, for paving 495, *495*
mixes 494
repairing pond cracks with 254, *254*
retardants for 494
Morus
diseases 570
hardwood cuttings 53
alba
height 396
'Laciniata' *53*
nigra, see Mulberries, black
Mosaics 555
Moss
conditions preferred 518
as indication of waterlogging 531
in lawn 286
control 578
annual program 283
preventing 578
lawn established with 275, *275*, 280
on soil mix round bought plants 145, *145*
sphagnum 588, 589
in bottle garden 439, *439*
for bromeliads *432*, *433*
lining hanging basket with *264*
for peat bed 188
pH variations 188
in soil mixes 535, 536
watering 433
Moss campion, see *Silene acaulis*
Moss pillar, growing house plants on 436, *436*
Moss totem *472*
Mossy rose galls 558
Mother spleenwort, see *Asplenium bulbiferum*
Mother of thousands, see *Saxifraga stolonifera*; *Soleirolia*
Mother-in-law's tongue, see *Sansevieria trifasciata*
Moths
arborvitae leaf mining 553
armyworm 572
codling 565, *565*
pea 565, *565*
Mottles 555
Mound layering 539, *539*, see also Stooling
herbs 297, *297*
Mounding up
with earth *520*, 521
with mulch 521
Mountain ash, see *Sorbus*
Mountain avens, see *Dryas*
Mountain buckler fern, see *Thelypteris oreopteris*
Mountain fern, see *Thelypteris oreopteris*
Mountain flax, see *Phormium cookianum*
Mountain gum, see *Eucalpytus dalrympleana*
Mountain hemlock, see *Tsuga mertensiana*
Mountain laurel, see *Kalmia latifolia*
Mountain pride, see *Penstemon newberryi*
Mountain tassel, see *Soldanella montana*
Mouse-ear chickweed, common, see Common mouse-ear chickweed
Moutan, see *Paeonia suffruticosa*
Muck *524*
formation 524
foundations for structures on 493
Muck soil
pH level 525
structure 525
Mucuna 97
simple layering 113
Mulberries 396
black *396*
cultivation 396
harvesting 396
planting 396
propagation 396
storing 396
diseases 570
fruit type 355, 371
white, see *Morus alba*
Mulches 588
after planting 100
on alkaline soil 360
applying 534
area to cover *534*
conserving moisture 530, 531, 557
decorative, on plastic *151*, 576
fertilizers as 44
floating, see Floating row covers
ground covers 151, *151*
inorganic 534
loose 534, *534*
organic 302, 308, 534
for perennials 155, *155*
in containers 157
plastic film 309, *309*
protective 69, 521
sheet 534, *534*, 589
for shrubs 70
for trees 44
after planting *42*
uses 524, 534
for vegetables 308–9, *308*
as weed suppressant 576
Mullein, see *Verbascum*
Multiflora rose, see *Rosa multiflora*
Multiple cordons, see Cordons
Muriate of potash 223, 411, 556, 562
nutrient content 532
Muscadina rotundifolia 397
Muscari
conditions tolerated 219
forcing 228
propagation
chipping 237
division of bulblets 233
division of offsets 233
in spring 139
suggestions for use 216, 219, 227
Mushroom compost
amount required compared to other fertilizers *532*
effect on soil 525

(*entry cont.*)

Mushroom compost (*cont.*)
improving soil fertility with 302
mulching with 308
nutrient content 532
as soil additive 529, *529*
Muskmelons, see Melons, muskmelons
Mussaenda 97
Mussel scale 554, *559*
Mussels, in pond 253
Mustard *326*
culinary uses 326
flavor 326
growing under cover 326
growing with cress 326
growing without soil 326
harvesting 326
sowing 326
Oriental 319
in crop rotation 304
culinary uses 319
cultivation 319
harvesting 319
nitrogen requirement 310
purple-leaved *319*
spinach, see Komatsuna
wild, spreading disease 555, 567
Mutation 582, *582*, 588
causes 561
in shrubs 70
Mutisia 97
propagation
semiripe cuttings 111
simple layering 113
soil type required 99
suggestions for use 97
decurrens, pruning 103
oligodon, soil type tolerated 99
Mycena 574
Mycoplasmas 557–8, 562
Mycorrhizae 525, 588
Myosotis
with bulbs in formal bedding 214
propagation
self-seeding 178, 184
sowing 177
seasonal display 171
in spring border *25*
thinning 178
alpestris, suggestions for use 188
rupicola, suggestions for use 191
scorpioides
in water garden 243
propagation
division of rootstock 257
softwood cuttings 257
soil type tolerated 146
suggestions for use 243
'Mermaid', in water garden 243
Myrica
conditions tolerated 66
root cuttings 84
Myriophyllum 242
conditions tolerated 66
softwood cuttings 256, *256*
aquaticum (syn. *M. proserpinacoides*) 243
hippuroides, suggestions for use 243
proserpinacoides, see *M. aquaticum*
Myrobalan, see Plums, cherry
Myrrhis odorata, see Sweet cicely
Myrtle, see *Myrtus*
Myrtus
as wall shrub 64
communis 66
in containers 288
var. *tarentina*, seasonal interest 66
luna, seasonal interest 37

N

Nails, for wall fixings 472, *472*
Nandina, softwood cuttings 81
Nankeen lily, see *Lilium* x *testaceum*
Naphthalene 573
Narcissus 213
bulb 214, *542*, *580*
choosing healthy bulbs *224*
conditions preferred 221
conditions required 431
cultivation 221
for cutting 219
diseases 569
dwarf
conditions tolerated 219
suggestions for use 219, 221
flower forms 221, *221*
forcing 228, 229
in grass
cutting down 230, *230*
feeding 230
groups 221
growing with tulips *221*
increase 213
in informal planting *273*
interplanting 173
in mixed border 214, *215*
naturalizing 221, 227
cutting foliage 221
in grass *221*, 272
pests 221, 558, 563, 569
planting
in grass *226*
in pots *228*
in pots, temperatures for 221
propagation 221
chipping 237
division of offsets 233, *542*
from seed 234
twin-scaling *236*, 237, 542, *542*
repotting *232*
seasonal interest 25
in spring 139
starting growth 224
suggestions for use 34, 216, 219, 220, 221
transplanting, from pots 231
types 221, *221*
underplanting roses 117
'Actaea', in mixed border *215*
'Ambergate' *221*
asturiensis, suggestions for use 221
bulbocodium
suggestions for use 227
subsp. *bulbocodium*, in peat bed *188*
cantabricus, suggestions for use 218, 221
'Cheerfulness' *218*
cyclamineus
conditions preferred 219
naturalizing 221
in peat bed *188*
suggestions for use 217, 227
Cyclamineus hybrids 221, *221*
'February Gold', in mixed island bed *136*
'Fortune' *221*, *227*
'Hawera', in mixed border *215*
'Irene Copeland' *221*
'Jumblie' *221*
'Little Gem' 221
minor
naturalizing 221
in rock garden *187*
nanus, suggestions for use 227
obvallaris, suggestions for use 227
'Paper White', forcing 229
'Passionale' *221*
Narcissus (*cont.*)
poeticus, suggestions for use 227
'Pride of Cornwall' *221*
pseudonarcissus, suggestions for use 227
pumilis, suggestions for use 227
romieuxii 221
suggestions for use 221
'Silver Chimes' 150
'Soleil d'Or', forcing 229
'Tahiti' *221*
Tazetta, suggestions for use 217, 221
'Tête-à-tête' 221
in rock garden *187*
'Thalia' 150
in mixed border *215*
triandrus 221
conditions preferred 219
suggestions for use 227
watieri, suggestions for use 190
Narcissus basal rot 569
Narcissus bulb flies 569
Narcissus flies 569
Narcissus nematodes 569
Nasturtium, see *Tropaeolum*
Nasturtium officinale, see Watercress
Natal ivy, see *Senecio macroglossus*
Naturalizing
bulbs 216–17, *216*, *217*
care 230
deadheading 230
feeding 230
in grass *221*
varieties suitable for 227
definition 588
Nectar 588
Nectarines 387–90
bud types 388
bush
pruning *388*, 389
training *388*, 389
conditions required 387
diseases 388, 554, 557, 564
fan
pruning 389, *389–90*
training 389, *389*
feathered maiden
training
as bush *388*, 389
as fan 389, *389*
for flavor 388, 390
freezing 367
fruiting 388
in greenhouse 355
growing under cover 359
harvesting 390
pests 388
propagation 390
pruning 388–90, *388–90*
recommended cultivars 388
storing 390
training 388–90, *388–90*
'Red Gold' *388*
Nectary 588
Nectria canker 570, *570*
causes 364
plants affected by 362
Neglected garden
clearing 526, *526*
lawn renovation 285
restoration 13
weeding 579
Neglected fruit trees, renovation 366, *366*
Neillia
pruning 76
thibetica 76
seasonal interest 66
Nelumbo
lutea, in water garden 243
nucifera
division of tubers 256
'Alba Grandiflora', in water garden 243
'Alba Striata', in water garden 243
Nelumbo nucifera (*cont.*)
'Rosa Plena', in water garden 243
Nematicide, definition 588
Nematodes 525, 526, 547, 558, *558*
bud 553, *553*
disease spread by 555
leaf 553, *553*
narcissus 569
potato cyst 572, *572*
predatory 548
root-knot 387, 566
rotating crops to avoid 304
taking cuttings of plants infected with 165, 553
in vegetable garden 310
viruses spread by 568
Nematus 551
Neoregelia
conditions preferred 431
conditions required 433
displaying 432
as pot plant 432
carolinae f. *tricolor 432*
Nepenthes, soil type required 147
Nepeta
dividing 163
as edging 116
in mixed border *137*
x *faassenii*, soil type preferred 146
Nephrolepis
conditions tolerated 427
hydroculture 431
watering 158
exaltata, removing dead leaves *444*
Nerine
conditions preferred 431
for cutting 219
planting depth 231
propagation
division of clump *231*
division of offsets 233
suggestions for use 218
bowdenii 218
conditions preferred 219
in formal bedding 214
Nerium
conditions preferred 66
conditions required 431
growing with succulents 259
semiripe cuttings with heel 83
oleander
in container 65, *65*
pruning 78
soil type tolerated 69
suggestions for use *24*, *26*
Nertera granadensis, suggestions for use 438
Netting 472, *472*, 573
plastic 472, *472*
protecting fruit with 363, *363*
protecting plants with *520*, 521
for reinforcing concrete 248, *248*
securing to pillars 512
for shade 472, *472*
as windbreak *300*, 301, *521*
wire 472, *472*, 572
Netting films, as floating row covers 311, *311*
Nettle
annual *575*
indicating soil type 525
Nettle tree, see *Celtis*
New Zealand cabbage palm, see *Cordyline australis*
New Zealand Christmas tree, see *Metrosideros excelsa*
New Zealand flax, see *Phormium*
New Zealand spinach 325
cultivation 325
harvesting 325, *325*
New Zealand spinach (*cont.*)
nitrogen requirement 310, 325
storing 312, 325
Newspaper, protecting plants with 363, *521*
Newts, habitats for 241
Nicking, apple trees 373, *373*, 375
Nicotiana
conditions preferred 171
diseases 568
in formal open-plan garden *14*
genetic engineering 546
growing as annual 176
pests 551
suggestions for use 171
alata
in mixed border 173
scent 175
'Lime Green', in annual border *171*
x *sanderae*, scent 175
Nidularium
conditions required 433
displaying 432
as pot plant 432
Nierembergia
propagation 176
hippomanica var. *violacea* 'Purple Robe', in conservatory *429*
rivularis, growing as annual 175
Nigella
collecting seed 184, *184*
for drying 174, 175
flowers 171
germination 538
damascena
for cutting 175
in mixed border 173
self-seeding 178
'Miss Jekyll', in annual border *171*
Nippon daisy, see *Nipponanthemum nipponicum*
Nipponanthemum nipponicum (syn. *Chrysanthemum nipponicum*), cutting back 156
Nitrate of ammonia 556
Nitrogen 397
adding to compost heap 535
applying 309
content of fertilizers 532
deficiency 282, 362, 529, 531, 532, 556, *556*
effects of 168, 212, 388
encouraging nitrogen-fixing root nodules 339
excess 573
fixing in soil 304
from green manure 533
for lawn 282
mulches using up 309
plant requirements 532
providing 380
release to plants 309
sources 309
value 532
vegetable requirements 309
No-till system *489*, 536, *536*
Noctua caterpillars 566
Nodal cuttings 53, *540*, 586
Nodes *540*, 588
Nomenclature 582
Nomocharis
conditions preferred 219
pardanthina, in peat bed *188*
Nonremontant, definition 588
Nopalxochia
flat grafting 271
hybrids, conditions required 261
stem cuttings 268

(*entry cont. overleaf*)

Nopaxochia (*cont.*)
phyllanthoides, suggestions for use 262
North America
average minimum temperatures *516–17*, 516
climate 514, 516–17
hardiness zones 516
North-facing walls, climbers for 93, 97
Norway maple, see *Acer platanoides*
Norway spruce, see *Picea abies*
Notching, apple trees 373, *373*
Nothofagus
dombeyi, semiripe cuttings 53
obliqua, soil preferred 42
procera, suggestions for use 37
Notholirion, conditions preferred 219
Notocactus
in bowl garden 261
flat grafting 271
schlosseri, pricking out seedlings *266*
Nuphar
advena
propagation by plantlets 257
in water garden 243
lutea
division of rootstock 257
in water garden 243
Nurseries, trees from 32
Nursery beds 588
outdoors 545–6, *546*
sand 546, *546*
water-permeable fabric 546, *546*
Nut weevils 425
Nutrients 532–3, 588
comparative content of fertilizers 532
composition 532
deficiencies 532, 547
plant requirements 532
translocated 590
for vegetables 309
Nuts 424–5, 588
definition 356
diseases 567
propagation
from seed 368
suckers 370
squirrel damage 565
storing 367
suggestions for use 424
suitable for gardens 424
Nutsedge *578*
Nylon-line trimmers, see Trimmers, nylon-line
Nymphaea 244–5
conditions required 244
in container pool *242*
containers for 244
depth of water for 242, 244
feeding 244
flowers 244
foliage 244
in formal pool *241*
in garden design *19*
hardy *244*
pests 255
planting 244, *244*, *252*
time for 251
position in water garden 243
propagation 245, *245*, 257
bud cuttings 245, *245*
division 245
plantlets 245, 257
from seed 245
routine care 244
scent 244
tropical 244, *244*
feeding 244
from seed 257
Nymphaea (*cont.*)
alba, suggestions for use 242
'American Star' *244*
'Attraction' *244*
'Blue Beauty' *244*
'Escarboucle' *244*
'Fire Crest' *244*
marliacea
'Carnea' *244*
'Chromatella' *244*
'Missouri' 244
odorata
rhizomes 244
seed 245
pygmaea 'Helvola' *244*
in container pool *242*
'Red Flare' 244
tetragona, seed 245
tuberosa, rhizomes 244
'Virginalis' *244*
Nymphoides
aquatica 243
offsets 257
humboldtiana, suggestions for use 243
indica, in water garden 243
peltata, in water garden 243
Nyssa sylvatica
conditions tolerated 37
suggestions for use 37

Oak, see *Quercus*
Oak apples 558
Oak wilt 571
Obedient plant, see *Physostegia*
Oberea bimaculata 559
Ocimum
basilicum *292*
conditions required 292
culinary uses 287, 292, 298
foliage 292
freeze-drying 298
harvesting 292
planting out 297
preserving in oil 298
pricking out 297
propagation from seed 292, 297
related species 292
storing 292
variants 292
var. *minimum* 292
'Purpurascens' 292
as gap filler in border 288
Odontoglossum
method of growth 440
propagation by division 443
temperature required 441
Oenothera
biennis
conditions preferred 175
conditions tolerated 175
self-seeding 178
soil type preferred 176
fruticosa, division 163
missouriensis, stem tip cuttings 164
odorata, for fragrance 141
tetragona 'Fireworks', in mixed island bed *136*
Offices, plants for 428
Offsets 588
planting, bulbs 231
propagation by
aquatics *257*
bromeliads 433, *433*
Offsets, propagation by (*cont.*)
bulbs 233, *233*, 542, *542*
cacti 269, *269*
indoor plants 451
succulents 269, *269*
tuberous 269, *269*
Oidium 552
Oil, for greenhouse heating 482
Oils, herb, making 298
Okra 336, *336*
in crop rotation 304
cultivation 336
harvesting 336
nitrogen requirement 310, 336
recommended cultivars 336
ripening under cover 311
storing 312, 336
Old-lady cactus, see *Mammillaria hahniana*
Old-man, see *Artemisia abrotanum*
Old-man cactus, see *Cephalocereus senilis*
Old-witch grass, see *Panicum capillare*
Old-woman cactus, see *Mammillaria hahniana*
Olea europaea, see Olives
Olearia
conditions tolerated 66
semiripe cuttings with heel 83
soil type preferred 67
phlogopappa *83*
Olives 420–21, *420*
in containers, moving under cover 363
cultivation 420–21
eating 415
fruit 420, *420*
black table *420*
harvesting 420
as ornamentals 37, 420
recommended cultivars 420
storing 421
Omphalodes
linifolia, self-seeding 178
luciliae, suggestions for use 191
Oncidium, temperature required 441
Onion family, rotation 341
Onion hoe 460, *460*
Onion maggots 569
Onion neck rot 569, *569*
Onion white rot 569, *569*
rotating crops to avoid 304
Onions
in crop rotation 304
diseases 569
effect of daylength on 303
nitrogen requirement 310
ornamental, see *Allium*
pests 553, 558, 569
sowing depth 305
sowing in cell packs 307
storing 312, *312*
transplanting seedlings 306
Onions, bulb 341, *341*
bulb types 341
bull-necked 341, *341*
in crop rotation 304
cultivation 341
harvesting 341
Japanese overwintering
recommended cultivars 341
sowing 341
recommended cultivars 341
red, recommended cultivars 341
storing 341, *341*
in vegetable garden *300*
'Creole C-5' *341*
Onions, European Welsh, see Onions, Welsh
Onions, Oriental bunching *342*
in crop rotation 304
cultivation 342
harvesting 342
Onions, Oriental bunching (*cont.*)
recommended cultivars 342
Onions, pickling 342, *342*
in crop rotation 304
cultivation 342
harvesting 342
recommended cultivars 342
storing 342
Onions, Welsh 342, *342*
in crop rotation 304
cultivation 342
harvesting 342
Oniscus 550
Onopordum
acanthium
architectural plant 173, 175
in mixed border *20*, *172*
self-seeding 178
arabicum, self-seeding 178
Onosma
albo-roseum
in dry-stone wall *189*
suggestions for use 191
echioides
soil type preferred 193
suggestions for use 191
taurica
soil type preferred 193
suggestions for use 191
Ontario poplar, see *Populus candicans*
Opal basil, see *Ocimum basilicum* 'Purpurascens'
Open-plan garden *14*
Ophiopogon
conditions tolerated 141
dividing 163
planiscapus 'Nigrescens'
bulbs with 139
foliage 139
in mixed island bed *136*
winter interest 141
Ophiostoma ulmi 560
Opium poppy, see *Papaver somniferum*
Opuntia
conditions preferred 431
conditions tolerated 259, 262
disorders 554
form 259
germination 266
handling 261
stem cuttings 268
exaltata 262
ficus-indica, see Prickly pears
fragilis 262
humifusa *259*
conditions tolerated 262
hardiness 259
hystricina 262
lanceolata, suggestions for use 262
leucotricha, propagation from pad sections *268*
microdasys, suggestions for use 262
paraguayensis, suggestions for use 262
polyacantha 262
in containers outdoors 260
rastera 262
robusta 262
subulata 262
Orange lily, see *Lilium bulbiferum*
Oranges *356*
diseases 564
sour (Seville)
fruits 417
ornamental use 417
as rootstock 416, 417
sweet *415*
cultivation 417, 418
recommended cultivars 417
as rootstock 416, 418
tree *416*
trifoliate, as rootstock 416
Blood Group 418
'Hamlin' *417*
Navel Group 418
Valencia (Common) Group 418
Orbea
division of offsets 269
flat grafting 271
variegata, suggestions for use 262
Orchid cactus, see *Epiphyllum*
Orchids 440–43
back bulbs, potting up 441
choosing plants 440
conditions required 441–2
in containers 441, *441*
cultivation 440–41
dormancy 442
epiphytic 427, 440, 441
displaying *441*
potting mix for 440, *440*
feeding 442
in greenhouse 430
humidity required 442
hydroculture 447
monopodial 440
numbers 440
potting 441
propagation 442–3, *442*, *443*
back bulbs 443, *443*
commercial techniques 443, *443*
division 443, *443*
in flasks 443, *443*
keikis *442*, 443
meristem culture 443, *443*
stem cuttings *442*, 443
pseudobulbs 440
potting 441
recommended *440*
resting 442
routine care 441–3
shading 442
soil mix for 436, 440, *440*, 536
staking 441
sympodial 440
back bulbs 441
propagation by 443, *443*
potting 441
temperatures required 441
terrestrial
conditions required 441
habitats 440
roots 580
tuberous 214
ventilation for 442
watering 441
when resting 442
Oregano, see *Origanum*
Oregon grape, see *Mahonia aquifolium*
Oreocereus, stem cuttings 268
Organic control of pests and diseases
companion planting 548
crop rotation 548
hygiene 548
traps 548
treatments 548
Organic matter 588
adding to soil 301
annual application 302
digging in 302
forms of 302
improving drainage with 524
improving soil structure with 529, *529*
in lawn preparation 276
as mulch 302
mulching vegetables with 308
use in deep-bed system 536, *536*
Organic practices 299, 536
Organisms in soil 525
Oriental bittersweet, see *Celastrus orbiculatus*
Oriental brassicas, see Brassicas, Oriental
Oriental bunching onions, see Onions, Oriental bunching
Oriental garden designs 30
Oriental greens, as cut-and-come-again crop 312
Oriental mustards, see Mustard, Oriental
Oriental poppy, see *Papaver orientale*

- *Origanum*
  - soil type tolerated 193
  - suggestions for use 191
  - *amanum*, semiripe cuttings 207
  - 'Kent Beauty' *193*
    - in alpine raised bed *201*
    - in rock garden *187*
  - *majorana*, in herb garden *295*
  - *rotundifolium*, semiripe cuttings 207
  - *vulgare* *292*
    - conditions preferred 294
    - conditions required 292
    - culinary uses 292
    - as edging 303
    - flowers 292
      - use 296
    - harvesting 292
    - in herb garden *295*
    - propagation 292
    - steeping in oil or vinegar 298
    - storing 292
    - suggestions for use 303
    - use in home 287
    - variants 292
    - variegated, cutting back 296
    - in vegetable garden 303
    - 'Aureum' 292
      - in herb garden *287*
      - soil type preferred 146
      - suggestions for use 289
    - 'Compactum' 292
      - in herb garden *295*
      - suggestions for use 288
- Ornamental
  - containers 473
  - grasses, dried 142
  - greenhouse 429
  - hedges 58–9
  - rosehips 115
  - shrubs 61–7, see also Shrubs
  - thorns 115
  - trees 32–57, see also Trees
- *Ornithogalum*
  - conditions tolerated 219
  - for cutting 219
  - dwarf, suggestions for use 219
  - forcing 228
  - propagation, division of offsets 233
  - *narbonense*, in mixed border *172*
  - *nutans*, suggestions for use 227
  - *umbellatum*, light affecting flower opening 518
- *Orontium aquaticum*
  - from seed 257
  - in water garden 243
- *Orostachys*
  - division of offsets 269
  - *chanetii*
    - conditions tolerated 262
    - in indoor bed *261*
    - propagation, leaf cuttings 267
  - *spinosus*, conditions tolerated 262
- *Oroya neoperuviana* *259*
  - conditions tolerated 262
- Orris 291, *291*
  - cultivation 291
  - harvesting 291
  - in herb garden *295*
  - storing 291
- *Orthomorpha* 550
- *Oscularia*, stem cuttings 268
- *Osmanthus*
  - conditions preferred 66
  - layering 86
  - *delavayi*
    - pruning 76
  - *fragrans*, scent 66
- *Osmunda*
  - in winter 158
  - *regalis*, suggestions for use 243
- *Osteospermum*
  - flowering time from seed 160
  - as pot plants 175
  - propagation
    - stem tip cuttings 164
    - treating as biennials 177
  - suggestions for use 218
  - 'Buttermilk' *164*
    - in hot border *139*
  - *jucundum* (syn. *Dimorphotheca barbariae*), in mixed border *215*
  - 'Starshine', suggestions for use 175
- Ostrich fern, see *Matteuccia struthiopteris*
- *Ostrya carpinifolia*, soil type tolerated 41
- *Othonna dentata*, leaf cuttings 267
- *Otiorhynchus sulcatus* 551, 572
- *Ourisia*
  - *caespitosa*, soil type required 192
  - *coccinea*, soil type required 192
  - 'Loch Ewe', soil type required 192
- Ovary, definition 588
- Overgrown garden
  - clearing 526, *526*
  - restoration 13
- Overwatering 444
- Ovule, definition 588
- *Oxalis*
  - conditions tolerated 219
  - control 576
  - suggestions for use 219
  - *adenophylla*
    - forcing 228
    - suggestions for use 191
  - *corniculata* *577*
    - as weed 192
  - *depressa* *219*
  - *enneaphylla*
    - suggestions for use 191
    - 'Minutifolia', in trough *199*
  - 'Ione Hecker'
    - suggestions for use 191
    - in trough *199*
  - *stricta* *577*
- Oxydemeton-methyl 549, 552
- *Oxydendrum arboreum*, soil preferred 41
- Oxygen, as product of photosynthesis 581, *581*
- Oxygenating plants 242, 243, 588
  - choosing healthy plants 251, *251*
  - conditions tolerated 248
  - cuttings 257
  - numbers required 251
  - planting 251, 253, *253*
  - thinning out 255, *255*
- Oyster plant, see Salsify
- *Ozothamnus*
  - soil type preferred 67
  - *ledifolium*, seasonal interest 66

P

- *Pachycereus*
  - stem cuttings 268
  - *pringlei*, suggestions for use 262
- *Pachyphytum*
  - stem cuttings 268
  - *oviferum* *267*
    - leaf cuttings 267
- *Pachyphytum* (*cont.*)
  - *viride*, leaf cuttings 267
- *Pachypodium*
  - *geayi*, suggestions for use 262
  - *lameri*, suggestions for use 262
- *Pachysandra*
  - conditions tolerated 66
  - discouraging weeds 576
  - *terminalis*, in container *157*
- *Pachystachys*
  - conditions required 431
  - softwood cuttings 453
  - stem tip cuttings 176
- Pacific dogwood, see *Cornus nuttallii*
- Packs 588
  - pricking out seedlings into 179, *179*
  - sowing seeds in 178
- Pad sections, propagating cacti and other succulents by *268*
- *Paederia*, semiripe cuttings 111
- *Paeonia*
  - conditions preferred 148
  - conditions tolerated 148
  - cultivation 148
  - for cutting 141
  - disbudding 148, *148*
  - diseases 148, 571
  - germination 85, 160, 205
  - herbaceous 148, *148*
  - life expectancy 16
  - mulching *155*
  - pests 553, 562, 563,
  - propagation
    - apical-wedge grafting 148
    - by division 148, 162, 163, *163*
    - from seed 148, 161
    - semiripe cuttings 148
  - soil type tolerated 147
  - staking 156, *156*
  - suggestions for use 27, 140, 148
  - transplanting 156
  - tree 148, *148*
    - as cut flowers 148
    - pruning 148, *148*
    - soil type preferred 148
  - types 148, *148*
  - 'Auguste Dessert' *148*
  - 'Ballerina', in mixed border *20*
  - 'Bowl of Beauty' *148*
  - 'Coral Supreme' *148*
  - 'Krinkled White' *148*
  - *lactiflora*, for fragrance 141
  - *lutea*, seed scarification *538*
  - *mlokosewitschii* *148*
  - 'Sarah Bernhardt'
    - in mixed border *172*
    - as specimen plant 140
  - 'Souvenir de Maxime Cornu' *148*
  - *suffruticosa*, flowers 65
- Pagoda tree, see *Sophora japonica*
- Palms
  - buying 39, 40
  - conditions required 431
  - in containers 65
  - grouping 34
  - protecting from cold *520*
  - pruning 49, 78
  - as screen *33*
  - as specimen trees 33
  - suggestions for use 33
- Pampas grass, see *Cortaderia selloana*
- *Pancratium*, suggestions for use 219
- *Pandanus*, architectural plant 66
- *Pandemis limitata* 554
- *Pandorea* 97
  - semiripe cuttings 111
  - *jasminoides*, pruning 103, 450
- Panel fences *508*, 509–10
  - erecting 509–10, *509*
- Panicles 582, 588
- *Panicum*
  - *capillare*, for drying 174
  - *violaceum*, for drying 175
- Pans 473, *473*, 588
  - drainage 109
- Pansy, see *Viola* x *wittrockiana*
- Panther lily, see *Lilium pardalinum*
- *Papaver*
  - deadheading 184
  - division 162
  - flowering time from seed 160
  - as gap filler in border 288
  - propagation, form seed 160
  - seasonal interest 25
  - sowing 176, 177
  - *burseri*
    - soil type tolerated 193
    - suggestions for use 191
  - *lateritium*, root cuttings 208
  - *miyabeanum*
    - soil type tolerated 193
    - suggestions for use 191
  - *nudicaule*
    - for cutting 175
    - cutting 183
    - sealing after cutting 183
  - *orientale*
    - in mixed border *149*, *172*
    - root cuttings 165
    - for seedheads 141
    - soil type preferred 146
  - *rhaeticum*, suggestions for use 191
  - *rhoeas*
    - conditions tolerated 175
    - as ground cover 173
    - propagation
      - self-seeding 178
      - sowing 177
    - Shirley Series *176*
      - soil type preferred 176
  - *somniferum*
    - conditions tolerated 175
    - in mixed border *172*
    - self-seeding 178
    - soil type preferred 176
    - sowing 177
  - Summer Breeze Series, for cutting 175
- Papayas 416, *416*
  - cultivation 416
  - fruits 416
  - harvesting 416
  - propagation from seed 370, 416
  - recommended cultivars 416
  - storing 416
  - tree size 416
  - 'Higgins' *416*
- Paper, as mulch 534
- Paper birch, see *Betula papyrifera*
- Paperbark maple, see *Acer griseum*
- *Paphiopedilum*
  - conditions required 442
  - habitat 440
  - temperature required 441
  - *callosum* *440*
- Papyrus, see *Cyperus papyrus*
- Parachute plant, see *Ceropegia sandersonii*
- *Parahebe*
  - stem tip cuttings 164
  - *catarractae*
    - in rock garden *187*
    - semiripe cuttings 207
- Paraquat 577, 579
  - commercial names 574
- *Paraquilegia anemonoides*, suggestions for use 191
- Parasites, in biological control, temperatures required 548
- Parasitic plants 440
- *Paris polyphylla*, soil type required 192
- Parlor palm, see *Chamaedorea*
- *Parnassia palustris*
  - in alpine raised bed *201*
  - suggestions for use 243
- *Parodia*
  - propagation
    - division of offsets 269
    - flat grafting 271
  - *brevihamata* 262
  - *chrysacanthion* *259*
  - *graessneri* 262
  - *haselbergii* 262
  - *leninghausii* 262
  - *mammulosa* 262
  - *mutabilis* 262
- *Paronychia kapela* subsp. *chionaea*, cutting back *204*
- Parquet decking 499, 500
- Parrot's feather, see *Myriophyllum aquaticum*
- Parsley *292*
  - conditions tolerated 288
  - culinary uses 292
  - as edging 303, *303*
  - flowers 292
  - foliage 292
  - freeze-drying 298
  - freezing in ice *298*
  - growing indoors 427
  - harvesting 292, 298
  - in herb garden *295*
  - pests 566
  - pricking out *297*
  - propagation, from seed 292 297
  - protecting for winter use 294
  - storing 292
  - suggestions for use 288, 303
  - variants 292
  - in vegetable garden 303, *303*
  - 'Neapolitanum' 292
- Parsnip canker 567, *567*
- Parsnips *348*, 352
  - in crop rotation 304
  - cultivation 352
  - diseases 352, 567
  - harvesting 352
  - intercropping 304
  - intersowing 305, 352 *352*
  - mineral deficiencies 568
  - nitrogen requirement 310, 352
  - pests 352, 566
  - storing 312, 352
  - in vegetable garden *300*
  - 'Gladiator' *352*
- Parterres 21, 29, 31, *31*, 588
  - annuals in 172
  - hedges for 58
- Parthenocarpic fruits 380, 588
- *Parthenocissus*
  - climbing methods 93
  - conditions tolerated 93, 97
  - as ground cover 95, 97
  - growth rate 92
  - propagation
    - hardwood cuttings 111
    - self-layering 113
    - serpentine layering 113
    - softwood cuttings 110
  - pruning 103
  - soil type tolerated 99
  - *quinquefolia*
    - climbing method 92
    - conditions tolerated 93
    - in indoor hanging garden *428*
    - vigor 98
  - *tricuspidata* *113*
    - conditions tolerated 97
    - fall display 96, *96*
    - soil type tolerated 100
    - vigor 98
    - 'Lowii' *99*
- Partridge berry, see *Mitchella repens*
- *Paspalum notatum*, for lawn 274
  - sowing rate 280
- Pasque flower, see *Pulsatilla vulgaris*
- *Passiflora* 92, for edible varieties, see Passion fruits
  - climbing method 93, *98*
  - conditions required 431
  - growth rate 97

(*entry cont. overleaf*)

Passiflora (*cont.*)
propagation
semiripe cuttings 111
simple layering 113
softwood cuttings 453
pruning 103, 105, 450
soil type tolerated 99
suggestions for use 94
vigor 98
caerulea
site for 93
soil type tolerated 100
x *caponi* 'John Innes' *105*
edulis, see Passion fruits
edulis f. *flavicarpa*, see Passion fruits
Passion fruits 403, *403*
conditions required 397, 403
cultivation 403
harvesting 403
storing 403
woodiness 403
Passionflower, see *Passiflora*
Pastinaca sativa, see Parsnips
Pathogens 547, 588
Paths 501–2
asphalt 501
brick 497, 501, *501*
construction 501
concrete 494, 502
laying 502
making curves 502
preparing base 502
concrete paving slabs 502
in cottage gardens 27
creating perspective with 18, *18*
design 501
edging 27, 501, 502
foundations 493, *493*
as framework 21, *21*
in garden design 17, *19*
grass 273, *273*, 502
gravel, laying 502, *502*
in informal garden *12*
in lawn 273
matching landscape *16*
materials for 501
natural stone 496
in Oriental gardens 30
pavers 501
paving slabs 495–6
preparing subbase 493, *493*
random paving 496
in rose garden 116
stepping-stone 501
stone *501*
uses 492
in vegetable garden *299*
weeding 579
width 501
wood 501
in woodland garden 28
Patios 493–9
annuals for 174
using vertical space 173
brick surfaces 497
cacti on 260
concrete 494
designing 17, 29
drainage slope 493, *493*
enclosed 29, *29*
foundations 493, *493*
fruit on 355
in containers 359
in garden design *19*
herbs on 288, *289*
natural stone 496
paving, choosing 493
paving slabs 495–6
perennials in containers 140
pergola on *511*
preparing subbase 493, *493*
random paving 496
roses on 119
screening 493
site 493
size 493
succulents on 260
surfaces
choosing 493
textures 493
Patios (*cont.*)
tile surfaces 496
trees beside, disadvantages of 493
in urban garden 14, *14*
uses 492
wooden *499*
Pavers
clay 497, *498*
wire-cut *498*
concrete *498*
cutting 498
imitation granite *498*
laying 498, *498*
paths of 501
construction 501
Paving
brick 497
combining materials *499*
concrete mix for 494
concrete slabs 495–6
cutting 496, *496*
laying 495, *495*
pointing *495*, 496
quantities 495
styles *495*
edging 496, *496*, 498, *498*
flexible, laying 498, *498*
grasses for 142
herbs in 288, *289*
sowing 297
laying, in herb garden 295
mortar mix for 494
natural stone 496
planning 16
random paving
defining edges 496
laying 496, *496*
natural stone 496
rock plants for 191
in rose garden 116
types *498*
wooden decking 499–500
Paw-paws, see Papayas
Paxistima, division of suckers 88
Pea gravel, as top-dressing 253, *253*
Pea moths 565, *565*
Pea root rot 567
Peach leaf curl 387, 557, *557*
Peaches 387–90
bud types 388
bush
pruning *388*, 389
training *388*, 389
cling 387
conditions required 387
in containers 387
growing under cover 359, 388
cultivation 387
diseases 388, 554, 557, 564
fan 387
protecting *387*
pruning 389, *389*, *390*
space required 358
training 389, *389*
on wall *355*
feathered maiden, training *388*, 389, *389*
for flavor 387, 390
forms 387
freestone 387
freezing 367
fruit thinning 387, *387*, 388
fruit type 355, 582
fruiting 388
genetic dwarf cultivars 387
in greenhouse 355
harvesting 390
ornamental, see *Prunus persica*
pests 388, 550, 559, 563, 565
planting 387
pollination by hand 387, *387*
propagation 390
protecting 387
pruning 388–90, *388–90*
recommended cultivars 387
as rootstock
for almonds 425
for apricots 390
Peaches (*cont.*)
rootstocks 387, *387*
routine care 387
site 387
soil type preferred 387
staking 387
storing 390
training 388–90, *388–90*
types 387
wall-trained *355*, 356
'Earliglo' *387*
'Harbrite', in large fruit garden *357*
'J. H. Hale', pollination 387
'Kent', in large fruit garden *357*
'Peregrine' *387*
'Redhaven', in small fruit garden *358*
Peanuts 336–7, *336*
cultivation 336
diseases 336, 567
growing undercover 337
harvesting 337
nitrogen requirement 310, 336
pods *337*
growth 336
shelled *336*
storing 337
Spanish-Valencia types 336, *336*
Virginia types 336, *337*
Pear leaf blister mites 380
Pear slugworm 553, *553*
Pear stony pit virus 565
Pear sucker 553
Pearlwort, see *Sagina procumbens*
Pearly everlasting, see *Anaphalis*
Pears 380–82
bark-ringing 366, 373, *373*
bush
pruning 380
training 380
conditioning 382
conditions required 380
conditions tolerated 380
cordons 356
pruning 380
training 380
crop timing 359
cross-pollination 358, 360, 380
culinary 381
cultivation 380
curbing excessive growth, by bark-ringing 373, *373*
curbing vigor 366
dessert
for flavor *381*
recommended cultivars 380, 381
diseases 380, 555, 562, 564, 565, 571
dwarf pyramid
pruning 381–2, *381*
training 381, *381*
espalier 357
pruning 380
training 380
fan
pruning 380
space required 358
training 380
feathered maiden, training as dwarf pyramid 381, *381*
feeding 380
for flavor 380, 381
flowering time 380
forms 380
frame-working 379
fruit *371*
thinning 380
type 355, 371, 582
fruiting 380
grafting over 379, *379*
growing against supports 358
harvesting 367, 382
late-ripening 358
mineral deficiencies 556, 560, 562
mulching 380
parthenocarpic fruits 380
Pears (*cont.*)
pests 380, 553, 557, 558, 564, 565
planting
distances 380
time for 380
pleaching 36
pollination compatibility 359
propagation
double budding 382, *382*
double grafting 382, *382*
grafting 382, 543
incompatible cultivars 382, *382*
rind grafting 379, *379*
pruning 380–82, *381*
renovative 366
spur thinning 382
winter 364
rootstocks 380, *380*
routine care 380
self-sterile 357, 360
siting 357, 380
"sleepy" 382
soil types, effect on fruit 380
soil unsuitable for 360
spur thinning 380
storing 358, 359, 367, 382
testing for ripeness 367,
thinning fruit 362
top-working 379, *379*
training 380
triploids 380, 381
watering 380
'Bartlett'
in large fruit garden *357*
in small fruit garden *358*
'Beurré Hardy', as interstock 382
'Catillac' *381*
'Conference' *380*
parthenocarpic fruits 380
'Doyenné du Comice' *380*
in large fruit garden *357*
pruning 380
in small fruit garden *358*
'Dr. Jules Guyot', as interstock 382
'Earlibrite', in small fruit garden *358*
'Golden Spice', in large fruit garden *357*
'Marguerite Marillat', as interstock 382
'Merton Pride', pruning 381
'Packham's Triumph', as interstock 382
'Rescue', in large fruit garden *357*
'Vicar of Wakefield', as interstock 382
Peas *336*, 339–40
in containers *307*
under cover 340
in crop rotation 304
cultivation 339–40
damage caused by mice, rats, and voles 568
diseases 340, 560, 567
edible-podded, harvesting 340
as green manure 533
groups 339
growing below wall 301
harvesting 340
nitrogen requirement 310, 339
pests 339, 340, 553, 565
petit pois 339
recommended cultivars 340
semileafless *339*
shelled-pea types 339
harvesting 340
show *336*, 339
sowing 339
depth 305
in wide drills 306
storing 312, 340
sugar *336*, 339
harvesting 340
supporting 339, *340*
tendrils 581
types 339
in vegetable garden *300*
Peas (*cont.*)
watering 308, 340
winter cropping under cover 311
wrinkle-seeded cultivars 339
'Sugar Bon' *340*
Peasticks 588
for seedlings 178, *178*
Peat 529, 588
characteristics 188
improving water retention with 529
as mulch 534
overwatering 437
as plunge material 437
pots made of 161, 178, 473
as soil additive 529
in soil mixes 535, 536
storing tubers in 223
as top-dressing *284*
Peat beds 588
alpines in 188, *188*
bulbs in 217
constructing 202, *202*
design 202
for perennials 147
planting 202
siting 202
soil mix for 202
top-dressing 202, *202*
Peat blocks, definition 588
Peat pellets 473
Peat pots, see Pots, peat
Peat soil, mineral deficiency in 556
Peatlite 536
Pecans *424*
cultivation 424
harvesting 424
recommended cultivars 424
rootstocks, growing seedlings for 424
storing 424
tree size 424
Pedicel *582*
Pedicularis groenlandica, conditions tolerated 167
Pedilanthus, stem cuttings 268
Pediocactus, flat grafting 271
Peduncle 588
Pelargonium 168–9
blackleg 570
with bulbs in pots *217*
conditions preferred 427
indoors 431
conditions required 431
in containers *19*, 168, *168*, *169*, 174
diseases 561
distinguishing from *Geranium* 168
dwarf zonal 168, *168*
F1, F2 hybrids 168
overwintering 184
from seed 169
feeding 168
in formal bedding 172, *172*
germination 179
in greenhouse *430*
growing as annual 175
ivy-leaved 168, *168*
in containers *169*, *174*
miniature zonal 168
in mixed border 172, 173
overwintering 168, *169*
pests 553, 562
physiological disorders 557
as pot plants 175
propagation 169, *169*
from seed 169, 452
softwood cuttings 453
stem cuttings 268
stem tip cuttings 164, 169, *169*
regal 168, *168*
cuttings 169
scented-leaved 168, *168*
in containers *168*
cuttings 169
in greenhouse display *429*
storing 168, *169*
(*entry cont.*)

Pelargonium (*cont.*)
in summer bedding *170*
trailing, for hanging baskets and windowboxes *174*
types 168, *168*
watering 168
zonal 168, *168*
in containers *168*
in greenhouse 430
in soil bench *439*
acetosum, conditions tolerated 262
Breakaway Series 174
suggestions for use 175
'Caligula' *431*
'Dolly Varden' *168*
echinatum, conditions tolerated 262
endlicherianum 168
'Frank Headley' *168*
graveolens, in containers 288
hortorum, growing as annual 176
'Lady Plymouth' *168*
'Mini Cascade', in conservatory *429*
'Mrs. Quilter' *168*
Multibloom Series 174
suggestions for use 175
peltatum 'Amethyst' *168*
'Purple Emperor' *168*
'Royal Oak' *168*
Sensation Series 174
suggestions for use 175
'Summer Showers', suggestions for use 175
tetragonum, conditions tolerated 262
'Timothy Clifford' *168*
Pelecyphora, flat grafting 271
Pellaea
in greenhouse display *429*
rotundifolia, suggestions for use 438
Pellets, peat 473
Pellicularia filamentosa 559
Pellionia
softwood cuttings 453
daveauana, suggestions for use 438
Peltandra alba, position in water garden 243
Peltiphyllum peltatum
conditions preferred 141
division of rootstock 257
soil type tolerated 146
suggestions for use 243
Penicillium italicum 564
Pennisetia marginata 559
Pennisetum villosum, for drying 175
Penstemon
propagation
softwood cuttings 206
stem tip cuttings 164, *164*
'Garnet', in hot border *139*
newberryi
size 61
f. *humilior*
in alpine raised bed *201*
in dry-stone wall *189*
flowers 190
suggestions for use 190
pinifolius
in alpine raised bed *201*
in trough *199*
'Rich Ruby', planting in container *147*
Pentas
propagation 176
lanceolata, softwood cuttings 453
Peony, see *Paeonia*
Peony wilt *571*
symptoms and control 571
Peperomia
conditions preferred 431
conditions required 431
physiological disorder 557
propagation
leaf cuttings 541, *541*
softwood cuttings 453
Peperomia (*cont.*)
caperata, suggestions for use 438
dolabriformis, leaf cuttings 267
Peppermint, see *Mentha* x *piperita*
Peppermint tree, see *Agonis flexuosa*
Peppers
genetic engineering 546
growing in containers 307
origins 328
watering, critical periods 308
Peppers, cayenne, see Peppers, hot
Peppers, chili 328, *328*
cultivation 328
flavor 328
harvesting 328
nitrogen requirement 310
popular cultivars 328
Peppers, hot 329, *329*
conditions required 329
culinary uses 329
harvesting 329
nitrogen requirement 310
recommended cultivars 329
storing 312, 329
'Super Cayenne' *329*
Peppers, sweet 328, *328*
in crop rotation 304
cultivation 328
freezing 312
fruit
color 328
changes when ripening 328, *328*
size 328
harvesting 328, *328*
mineral deficiency 564
nitrogen required 310, 328
recommended cultivars 328
storing 312
in vegetable garden *300*
'Canape' *328*
'Ultra Gold' *328*
Père David's maple, see *Acer davidii*
Perennial sweet pea, see *Lathyrus latifolius*
Perennials 135–69, 588
for acid soil 147
alpine, repotting 211
as annuals 175, 176
moving at end of season 184
architectural plants 140, 141
with bulbs in mixed border *213*
characteristics 580
choosing 135, 145, *145*
for clay soil 146
color 139
in containers 140, *140*, 147
care 157, *157*
repotting 157, *157*
in cottage gardens 140
cutting back 156, *156*
deadheading 155
decorative seedheads 141
designing with 135–40
diseases 157
bacterial 554, 561, 571
fungal 552, 554, 560, 562, 564, 567
division 162, *162*
for dry shade 141
effects of temperatures on 556, 570
for exposed sites 141
exposure 145
F1 hybrids 452
fall cleanup 156, *156*
fast-growing 141
feeding 155
fibrous-rooted, division 162, *162*
fleshy-rooted, division 162, *162*
flowers
for cutting 141
for drying 141
for fragrance 141
foliage 135
yellowing 155
in formal bedding 30
forms, contrasting 138, *138*
Perennials (*cont.*)
in framed planting *21*
in garden design *19*
ground cover 140
height range 135
herbaceous
climbers
planting 99
from seed 109
deer damage to 572
diseases 571
pests 550, 551, 552, 553
protecting crown 521
protecting roots of tender climbers 93
as weeds 576
in herbaceous borders 135, *135*, *136*
herbs 287
from seed 297
improving flowering 155–6
in island beds 136, *136*
in layer planting 23
lifting 157
low-growing, pests 561, 572
for meadow garden 167
mineral deficiency 556–7
in mixed borders *20*, 63, 136, *137*
for moist shade 141
moisture-loving 242
mulching 155, *155*
in peat beds 147
pests 157, 560, 561, 566, 572
affecting flowers 562, 563
damaging leaves 553, 554, 557
pinching 155, *155*
planter's guide 141
planting 146, *146*
in containers 147, *147*
depth 146, *146*
in groups 137, *137*
time for 146
pricking out 161, *161*
problems affecting stems and leaf buds 559, 560, 561
propagation 160–66
basal stem cuttings 164–5, *164*
cuttings 164–5, *164–5*
division 157, 162–3, *162*, *163*
of large plants 145, *145*
grafting 166, *166*
root cuttings 165, *165*
from seed 160–61, *161*
sowing for chilling *161*
sowing in containers 160–61, *161*
sowing outside 161
varieties flowering within two years 160
stem tip cuttings 164, *164*, 176
in raised beds 147
rhizomatous, division 163, *163*
in rock garden *185*
roses with *114*, 116, *117*
routine care 155–7
for sandy soil 146
scale and height 22
for seasonal interest 139
seed
collecting 160, *160*
germination 160, 161
storing 160
self-sown seedlings, transplanting 147, *147*
short-lived, cutting down 184, *184*
for short-term effect 16, *16*
in shrub border, temporary planting 63
shrubby
cutting back roots 157
cutting back to improve flowering 156
shrubs with 139
silhouettes 138
site 145
soil preparation 145
specimen planting 140
staking 156, *156*
Perennials (*cont.*)
storing 157, *157*
suggestions for use 135–40
for summer color 25
tender
lifting after bedding 184
treating as annuals or biennials 170
textures, harmonizing 138, *138*
thinning 155, *155*
tolerating air pollution 141
tolerating alkaline soil 147
top-dressing, in containers *157*
transplanting 156–7
during growing season 157
self-sown seedlings 147, *147*
watering 155
weeding 155
weeds 576–7
control 576, 577, 579
types 576
for winter interest 141
winter protection 156
in woodland gardens 140
woody
diseases
bacterial 567
fungal 554, 560, 561, 567, 570
physiological disorders 559
pruning, bad 570
as weeds 576
Pereskia, stem cuttings 268
Pereskiopsis, as rootstock 271
Perforated plastic films, as floating row covers 311, *311*
Perfumery, herbs used in 287
Pergolas 511–12
attaching to brickwork 512, *512*
brick and wood *512*
clematis on 106
climbers on 94, *94*
training 104, *104*
construction 511–12
existing, design and 17
fruit on 358
grapevines on 358
height 511
materials for 511
on patio *511*
planning 16
roses for 118
rustic work 512
screening patio 493
single-sided *512*
training roses on 128
uses 492
wooden *512*
on wooden decking 499
Perianth, definition 588
Peridroma caterpillars 561
Periwinkle, see *Vinca*
Perlite 588
in soil mixes 535, 536
storing tubers in 223
Permethrin 550, 551, 552, 553, 554, 560, 562, 563, 564, 565, 572, 574
commercial names 574
Pernettya
flower sexuality 582
propagation, division of suckers 88
soil type required 69, 192
mucronata
'Seashell', berries 65
'Wintertime' *62*
Peronospora 552
Perovskia
pruning 74, 75
scent 66
softwood cuttings 81
atriplicifolia
with roses 117
'Blue Spire', in shrub border *63*
Perpetual plants, definition 588
Persea americana, see Avocados
Persian ivy, see *Hedera colchica*
Persian ranunculus, see *Ranunculus asiaticus*
Persimmons 394
cultivation 394
fruit type 355, 371
harvesting 394
recommended cultivars 394
rootstocks 394
storing 394
'Hanafuyu' *394*
Perspective 18, *18*
Peruvian mastic tree, see *Schinus molle*
Peruvian old-man cactus, see *Espostoa lanata*
Peruvian pepper-tree, see *Schinus molle*
Pesticides 587, 588
adverse reactions to 549
classification 574
damage from 556, *556*
forms available 549
immunity to 549
labeling 549, 574
sprayers for 468, *468*
spraying 549
types 549
contact 549, 586
systemic 549, 590
types available 574
use with biological control 548
Pests
biological control 548–9, *549*
breeding resistance to 546
chemical control 549
damage caused to 547
bulbs 569
flowers 562–3
fruit, berries, and seeds 564, 565
lawns 573–4
leaves 550–54
roots and tubers 566, 568
stems and leaf buds 559–61
whole plant 572
definition 547
diagnosing problems caused 547, *547*
diseases spread 547
effect of pH on 525
feeding methods 547
method of identifying problem 547
organic control 548, *548*
companion planting 548, *548*
crop rotation 548
hygiene 548
traps 548, *548*
treatments 548
pesticide-resistant strains 549
plants resistant to 548
refuge for, in bark of poles 512
Petals 537, 582, *582*, 588
confused 586
Petasites fragrans, for scent 141
Petiole, definition 588
Petrea
cuttings 111
volubilis
pruning 105
soil type tolerated 99
vigor 98
Petrophytum hendersonii, suggestions for use 191
Petroselinum crispum, see Parsley
Petunia
choosing healthy plants for bedding *181*
color schemes with 171
conditions tolerated 175
in containers, with trees 36
diseases 560, 567
flowers 171
genetic engineering 546
growing as annual 176
in hanging basket *437*
as pot plants 175
suggestions for use 175
in summer bedding *170*
Peyote, see *Lophophora*
Pfeiffera, in greenhouse display *430*

pH levels 588
adjusting 360
assessing from plants 15
for biochemical reactions 581
effect of 525
effect of fertilizers on 70
high, problems caused by 533
for lawn 276
lime required to alter 533
optimum 525
of potting mixes 545
scale 525
testing *525*
of water in pond 248
changing 254
Phacelia
germination 179
campanularia, sowing 177
Phalaenopsis
conditions preferred 427
method of growth 440
temperature required 441
Phalaris arundinacea
suggestions for use 243
var. *picta*, invasiveness 142
Phaseolus
coccineus, see Beans, scarlet runner
lunatus, see Beans, Lima
vulgaris, see Beans, snap
Phenacoccus 552
Pheromone traps 565
commercial names 574
Philadelphus
conditions tolerated 66
flowers 65
propagation
hardwood cuttings 84
semiripe cuttings 83
softwood cuttings 81, *81*
pruning 76
formative *73*
renovation *80*
scent 66
soil type tolerated 62, 67, 69
'Dame Blanche' *69*
Philaenus spumarius 560
Philesia magellanica, soil type required 69
Phillyrea
conditions tolerated 66
pruning 78
latifolia, soil type tolerated 41
Philodendron
conditions preferred 431
conditions required 431
conditions tolerated 97
self-layering 113
softwood cuttings 110
suggestions for use 97, 428
scandens
growth rate 97
simple layering *456*
suggestions for use 427
training indoors 427, *436*
Phlebodium aureum, division of rootstock 451
Phloem 580
Phlomis
conditions preferred 62
soil type preferred 67
chrysophylla, seasonal interest 66
fruticosa, soil type tolerated 69
russeliana
conditions tolerated 141
for drying 141
Phlox
annual, position in garden 171
for cutting 141
cutting back *156*
germination 538
life expectancy 16
nematode-free 558
pests 556, 558, 563
propagation
root cuttings 165, 541
semiripe cuttings *207*
softwood cuttings 206
suggestions for use 136, 186
thinning *155*
Phlox (cont.)
bifida
in alpine raised bed *201*
soil type preferred 193
'Camla'
in alpine raised bed *201*
in rock garden *187*
'Chatahoochee'
in peat bed *188*
semiripe cuttings 207
decussata, root cuttings 165
divaricata subsp. *laphamii*, in peat bed *188*
douglasii
cultivars, in trough *199*
'Crackerjack', in rock garden *187*
mesoleuca, root cuttings 208
paniculata
for fragrance 135, 141
'Eva Cullum', in mixed border *20*
stolonifera 'Ariane'
in alpine raised bed *201*
conditions preferred 141
in peat bed *188*
subulata
Irishman's cuttings 208
root cuttings 165
semiripe cuttings 207
suggestions for use 191
Phoenix
architectural plant 66
foliage 34
as specimen tree 33
suggestions for use 37
canariensis, soil type preferred 42
dactylifera, suggestions for use 37
Phormium
architectural plant 66
conditions required 431
conditions tolerated 66
division 163
in greenhouse *430*
soil type preferred 67
soil type tolerated 146
winter interest 141
cookianum, conditions tolerated 141
tenax
architectural form 141
in bog garden *242*
conditions tolerated 141
growth rate 141
as specimen plant 140
'Sundowner', in mixed island bed *136*
Phosphates, see Phosphorus
Phosphorus 545
applying 309, 533
content of fertilizers 532
deficiency 362, 525, 532, 556, *556*, 568
for lawn 282
maintaining levels 309
plant requirements 532
sources of 309
uses 277
value of 532
Photinia
semiripe cuttings with heel 83
villosa, pruning 76
Photosynthesis 230, 252, 517, *538*, 541, 581, *581*, 588
leaves for *580*
Phragmites
australis
conditions required 142
in water garden 243
'Variegata', in water garden 243
communis, suggestions for use 243
Phragmocapnias 554
Phygelius, stem tip cuttings 164
Phyllanthus fluitans 243
Phyllitis, division of rootstock 451
Phyllodoce
caerulea *192*
in peat bed *188*
soil type required 192
empetriformis, in peat bed *188*
glanduliflora, soil type required 192
nipponica, soil type required 192
Phyllody disease 558, 562
Phyllophaga 566, 573
Phyllostachys nigra, maturity, time required 142
Phyllotreta 550
Phylloxera 368, 397
Physalis alkekengi, for seedheads 141
Physically impaired
access to greenhouse 478, *478*
aids for 507
gardening for 288
Physiological disorders, see Disorders
Physiology 580
Physoplexis comosa
in rock garden *187*
suggestions for use 191
Physostegia
companion plant for 139
dividing 163
Phytomyza
aquilegivora 553
syngenesiae 553
Phytophaga violicola 558
Phytophthora 566, 567, 570
root rots 560, 567, 571
cinnamoni 415
infestans 555, 568
parasitica 415
Phytotoxicity 549
Picea
diseases 560
extracting seed 54
pests 560
side-veneer grafting 56
soil preferred 41
training 49
abies
conditions tolerated 37
'Clanbrassiliana' 191
'Gregoryana' 191
breweriana, suggestions for use 37
glauca var. *albertiana* 'Conica' *38*, 191
as specimen 63
mariana 'Nana' *38*
in rock garden *187*
omorika, suggestions for use 37
pungens
var. *glauca*, conditions tolerated 37
'Montgomery' *38*
sitchensis, conditions tolerated 37
Pickerel weed, see *Pontederia cordata*
Picket fences 508, *508*
Pickling onions, see Onions, pickling
Picotee 588
Pierce's disease (PD) 397
Pieris
foliage 64
heel cuttings 83
soil type required 69
'Forest Flame', seasonal interest 66
nana, soil type required 192
Pieris rapae 551
Pig wire *472*
Pigeons, protection from 310
Piggyback plant, see *Tolmiea*
Pilea
conditions preferred 431
softwood cuttings 453
cadierei *431*
conditions tolerated 427
in indoor plant group *444*
suggestions for use 438
Pilea (cont.)
involucrata, foliage 426
'Norfolk', hydroculture *447*
spruceana, suggestions for use 438
Pileostegia 97
propagation
semiripe cuttings 111
simple layering 113
pruning 103
suggestions for use 97
viburnoides
conditions tolerated 97
pruning 103
Pill bugs, see Sowbugs
Pillars
climbers on 94
training 104, *104*
climbing roses on 118
constructing 512
moss, growing indoor plants on 436, *436*
securing netting to 512
siting 94
training roses on 128
Pimpinella anisum, see Aniseed
Pinching out 588
annuals 181
climbers 450
indoor plants 444
Pincushion cactus, see *Mammillaria*
Pine, see *Pinus*
Scots, see *Pinus sylvestris*
Pineapple flower, see *Eucomis*
Pineapple galls 560
Pineapple lily, see *Eucomis*
Pineapple mint, see *Mentha suaveolens* 'Variegata'
Pineapples 415, *415*
bottling 367
conditions required 356, 415
cultivation 415
fruits 415
harvesting 415
ornamental, see *Ananas*
propagation 415, *415*
storing 415
Cayenne Group 415
Queen Group 415
Spanish Group 415
Pinellia, suggestions for use 219
Pinguicula, soil type required 147
Pink dandelion, see *Crepis incana*
Pink hyssop, see *Hyssopus officinalis* 'Rosea'
Pink lavender, see *Lavandula angustifolia* 'Rosea'
Pinks, see *Dianthus*
Pinus
diseases 560
extracting seed 54
in garden design *19*
pests 559, 560
side-veneer grafting 56
training 49
bungeana, seasonal interest 37
contorta, conditions tolerated 37
halepensis, suggestions for use 37
mugo, bonsai 434
nigra
conditions tolerated 37
soil type tolerated 41
suggestions for use 37
pinaster, soil preferred 42
radiata
soil preferred 42
suggestions for use 37
strobus, as hedge 58
sylvestris 28
conditions tolerated 37
suggestions for use 37
'Gold Coin' *38*
thunbergii, bonsai 434
wallichiana, suggestions for use 37
Piperonyl butoxide 561, 566, 567, 569, 572
commercial names 574
Pirimicarb 548, 552, 560
commercial names 574
use with biological control 548
Pistia stratiotes 243, *243*
offsets 257
Pistil 582, 585
Pisum sativum, see Peas
Pitcher plant, see *Nepenthes*; *Sarracenia*
Pith 589
Pittosporum
germination 85
semiripe cuttings 83
eugenioides 'Variegatum', side-veneer grafting 89
tobira, scent 66
Plane, see *Platanus*
Planning and design 12–31
annuals and biennials 170–74
assessing existing features 17
bedding 182, *182*
budgeting 13
with bulbous plants 213–19
with cacti and succulents 258–61
changing existing garden 13
with climbers 92–6
components *14*
creating a design 17–20
deceiving the eye 18
final plan 19, *19*
fixed features
incorporating 17, *17*
planning 14, *14*
fruit garden 355–9
large *357*
small *358*
herb garden 287–9, *289*
planting to design 295, *295*
high-maintenance *13*
importance of planning 12
indoor garden 426–30
informal style *12*
lawns 272–5
long-term effects 16, *16*
low-maintenance *13*
major considerations 12
open-plan style 14, *14*
with perennials 135–40
perspective 18, *18*
planning work 20
planting plans 20
principles of design 18
principles of planting 21–6
professional help 13
proportion 18
in relation to setting 16
in relation to site 14, 17
rock garden 185–90
with roses 114–19
rough plan 14
scale plan 17, *17*
schedule of work 20
shape, choosing 18, *18*
short-term effects 16, *16*
shrubs 61–5
site appraisal 15
spacing plants 26
structures and surfaces 492
styles 27–31
choosing 18, *18*
with trees 32–6
vegetable garden 299–304
water garden 240–43
Plant associations 22, 586
climbers combined 93, *93*
climbers growing through other plants 94, *94*
layered planting 23, 26
naturalistic 23, *23*
Plant bugs 551, *551*, 563
Plant diversity 580
Plant lice, see Aphids
Plant problems 547–79
diagnosing symptoms 547, *547*
method of identifying 547
prevention 548
Plant rings 472, *472*
Plantago
control 286, 578, 579
as weed 167
major *578*
Plantain lily, see *Hosta*

Plantains, see *Plantago*
Planters
bulb 471, *471*
seed 471
Planting
design 21
fall tasks 584
height and scale relationships 22
layered 23
plans 20
principles of 21–6
rock garden 196–7, *196*
during construction 195, *195*
roses 121, *121*, *122*
spacing 26
spring tasks 583
structural 22, *22*
summer tasks 583
time for 20
to avoid problems 548
tools for 471, *471*
winter tasks 584
Planting traditions, regional differences 522–3
Plantlets, propagation by
indoor plants 451
potatoes 354
water plants 245, 257, *257*
Plants
architectural 22, *22*
basic parts 580–82, *580–82*
bisexual 582, *582*
buying 548
dioecious 582, *582*
height and shape relationships 22
hermaphrodite 582, *582*
monoecious 582, *582*
polygamous 582
shape and form 23, *23*
specimen 23, *23*
Plasmodiophora brassicae 555, 567
Plastic film/sheet
black, as weed suppressant 576
bubble 482, *482*, 484
for cloches 490
as floating row cover 311, *311*, 490
glazing greenhouse with 479, *479*
insulating greenhouse with 482, *482*
as mulch 309, 534, *534*
planting strawberries under 404, *404*
polytunnel of 477, *477*
shading greenhouse with 484
Plastic labels 472
Plastic netting, see Netting, plastic
Plastic pots, see Pots, plastic
Plastic sheet, see Plastic film/sheet
Plastic ties 472, *472*
Platanus
diseases 552
hardwood cuttings 53
pests 552
pleaching 36
x *hispanica*, suggestions for use 37
Plate compactor *493*, *498*
Platycerium
conditions preferred 431
bifurcatum, indoors *427*
Platycodon grandiflorus, in cool border *138*
Platystemon californicus, self-seeding 178
Play areas, lawn for 274, *274*
Pleaching 36, *36*, 51, *51*, 589
Plectranthus oertendahlii, suggestions for use 438
Pleione, temperature required 441
Pleiospilos, division of offsets 269
Plovers' eggs, see *Adromischus festivus*
Plugging, establishing lawn by 279, *279*
Plum curculio 564, *564*
Plumbago
conditions required 431
in greenhouse display *429*
indoors *427*
pruning 103
semiripe cuttings 111
auriculata
in conservatory *429*
growth rate 97
softwood cuttings 453
suggestions for use 97
capensis, see *P. auriculata*
Plume poppy, see *Macleaya*
Plumeria rubra var. *acutifolia*, scent 34
Plums 383–6
cherry
flowering time 383
recommended cultivars 385
'Prune' *385*
conditions preferred 383
conditions required 383
cross-pollination 358, 360
culinary, recommended cultivars 385
cultivation 383–4
dessert, recommended cultivars 384
diseases 384, 554, 561, 564, 571
dwarf bush 383
European 383
recommended cultivars 384
fan 383
space required 358
feeding 384
for flavor 384, 385
flowering time 383
forms 383
freezing 367
fruit thinning 362, 384
fruit type 355, 581
gummosis 384
harvesting 386
Japanese 383, 384
recommended cultivars 384
Japanese–American hybrids 383, 385
mineral deficiency 560
Myrobalan 383
pests 384, 565
damaging leaves 552, 558
physiological disorders 384
planting 383
pollination 383
compatibility 359
propagation 386
protecting
from birds 384
from frost 384
from wind 383
pruning 384–6, *384–6*
bush 384–5, *384*
fan 385, *385*
half-standard 385
maiden whip 385
pyramid 386, *386*
spindlebush 385
pyramid 383
rootstocks 383, *383*
routine care 384
self-fertile 384, 385
self-sterile 357, 360, 384
site 383
siting 357
soil types tolerated 383
split skins 386
staking 384
storing 386
suckers 383
training 384–6, *384–6*
bush 384, *384*
fan 385, *385*
feathered maiden 384–6, *384*, *386*
pyramid 386, *386*
spindlebush 385
watering 384
'Brompton'
as rootstock 383, *383*
for peaches 387, *387*
'Cambridge Gage' *384*
Plums (*cont.*)
'Coe's Golden Drop' *384*
'Marianna', as rootstock 383
'Myrobalan B', as rootstock 383, *383*
'Opal' *384*
'Pixy', as rootstock 383, *383*, 386
'Redcoat', in large fruit garden *357*
'St. Julien A', as rootstock 383, *383*, 386
for apricots 390
for peaches 387, *387*
'Victoria' *384*
in large fruit garden *357*
in small fruit garden *358*
thinning fruit 384
'Waneta' *385*
Plumule, definition 587
Plunge bed, bulbs in *228*, *229*
Plungers 471, *471*
Plunging 589
alpines, after flowering 210, *210*
materials for 437
Poa
for lawns 274
annua, see Bluegrass, annual
pratensis
diseases 573
for lawn 274, 275
hydromulching 280
sowing rate 280
'Merion' 574
trivialis, for lawn 275
Poached-egg flower, see *Limnanthes douglasii*
Podded vegetables 336–40
conditions required 336
in crop rotation 304
storing 336
suggestions for use 336
Podocarpus, semiripe cuttings 53
Podranea 97
propagation
semiripe cuttings 111
simple layering 113
pruning 103
Pods 581, 589
Poecilocapsus lineatus 551
Poet's daffodil, see *Narcissus poeticus*
Poet's narcissus, see *Narcissus poeticus*
Poinsettia, see *Euphorbia pulcherrima*
Polar climate 514
Polemonium
conditions tolerated 141
division 163
flowering time from seed 160
pulcherrimum, suggestions for use 191
Poles, for rustic work 512
Polianthes, for cutting 219
Polka-dot plant, see *Hypoestes*
Pollarding 36, 49, 589
pruning after 50, *50*
shrubs 77, *77*
trees suited to 50
Pollen 589
dispersal by wind 518
in flower 582
Pollen beetles 563, *563*
Pollination 589
cross- 537
cacti and other succulents 267, *267*
fruit 359, 360, 380, 418
herbs 290
hand- *387*
insects needed for 549
methods 537
open- 588
self- 537
Pollution, air
climbers tolerant of 97
perennials tolerant of 141
rock plants tolerant of 191
shrubs tolerant of 66
trees tolerant of 37
Polyanthus, see *Primula*, Polyanthus Group
Polycarbonate
for cloches 490
for greenhouse glazing 479, *479*
for greenhouse shading 484
Polyembryonic seed 417, 589
Polyester fabric, as frost protection 363
Polyester matting, as liner for pond or watercourse 249, *249*
Polyethylene
as pond liner 246
pots made of 473
Polygala
division of suckers 88
semiripe cuttings 207
softwood cuttings 206
calcarea 'Bulley's Variety', in rock garden 187
chamaebuxus *207*
in peat bed *188*
soil type required 192
var. *grandiflora*, in peat bed *188*
myrtifolia 'Grandiflora', in conservatory *429*
vayredae, soil type required 192
Polygamous plants 582
Polygonatum
conditions tolerated 141
pests 550, 551
planting depth 146
suggestions for use 140
hookeri, in peat bed *188*
Polygonum (syn. *Fallopia*)
conditions tolerated 97
growth rate 97
propagation
semiripe cuttings 111
serpentine layering 113
soil type tolerated 146
affine 'Donald Lowndes', conditions preferred 186
amphibium, position in water garden 243
amplexicaule, suggestions for use 243
aubertii
pruning 103, 105
as screen 94
soil type tolerated 100
training 102
vigor 94, 98
baldschuanicum
as screen 94
soil type tolerated 100
training 102
vigor 94
as weed *575*
bistorta
suggestions for use 243
'Superba', conditions preferred 141
campanulatum, suggestions for use 243
cuspidatum, see Japanese knotweed
japonicum, see Japanese knotweed
vacciniifolium, in dry-stone wall *189*
Polypodium, in winter 158
Polypropylene
for cloches 490
for pots 473
sheets as frost protection 363
for ties 472
Polyscias, softwood cuttings 453
Polystichum
bulbils 159
in winter 158
Polytunnels 477, *477*
fruit in 363
hardening off in 180, *180*
low *311*
growing vegetables in *311*
winter protection in *521*
for propagation 545
Polytunnels (*cont.*)
walk-in, growing vegetables in 311
Pome fruits, see Pomes
Pomegranates 423, *423*
conditions required 356, 423
cultivation 423
dwarf form 423
bonsai 434
flowers *423*
fruit 423, *423*
harvesting 423
softwood cuttings 370
storing 423
tree size 423
under cover 359
Pomes 589, see also Fruit, tree; individual fruits by name
definition 355, 371
diseases 555, 571
fruit type 582
pruning, renovative 366
Poncirus, pruning 74
Ponds
algae in 253, 531
control 242, 254, *254*
blanketweed control 254, *254*
building 13
bulbs for margins of 217
chemicals leaching into 240
circulating water 250, *250*
cleaning 255
concrete, construction 248, *248*
construction 246–8, *246–8*
reinforcing 248, *248*
decking stepping stones in *500*
diseases 255
fall maintenance 255
filtration 250
fish in 242, 243
stocking 253, *253*
flexible liner
installing 246–7, *246*
repairing 254, *254*
formal 241, *241*
in garden design *19*
ice on, making hole in 255, *255*
indoors 429
informal 240
irises around edge of *144*
linking with garden *242*
marginal shelves
constructing
in concrete pond 248, *248*
in flexible-liner pond 246, *246*
microclimate in *519*
pests 255
pH level of water 248
changing 254
planting beds in 247
preformed molds
installation 247, *247*
repairing 254
raised
construction 248, *248*
lining 248
repairs, structural 254, *254*
routine care 254–5
scavengers in 253
sediment in 531
siting 27, 240
style 28
water quality 254
as water storage area 531
in wild garden *27*
for wildlife 241
winter care 255
Pontederia
soil type tolerated 146
cordata
division of rootstock 257
in water garden 243
lanceolata, in water garden 243
Pools, see Ponds
Poor man's orchid, see *Schizanthus*
Popillia japonica, see Japanese beetles

Poplar, see *Populus*
Lombardy, see *Populus nigra* 'Italica'
Poppy, see *Papaver*
corn, see *Papaver rhoeas*
Iceland, see *Papaver nudicaule*
opium, see *Papaver somniferum*
Oriental, see *Papaver orientale*
Populus
buying 40
conditions tolerated 37
for coppicing and pollarding 50
diseases 570
foliage 34
growth rate 32
hardwood cuttings 53
pests 559
root suckers 45
roots, damage from 39
soil type tolerated 42
alba, soil type tolerated 41
x *canadensis* 'Serotina Aurea', suggestions for use 50
candicans 'Aurora' *50*
suggestions for use 50
nigra 'Italica'
conditions tolerated 37
as screen 36
tremula, grouping 34
Porcellio 550
Portea 433
Portland cement, definition 499
Portugal laurel, see *Prunus lusitanica*
Portuguese heath, see *Erica lusitanica*
Portulaca
as filler 173
grandiflora
growing with succulents 260
soil type preferred 176
oleracea, see Summer purslane
Post-and-chain fencing 508, *508*
Post-and-rail fencing 508, *508*
Posthole diggers 509
Posts
concrete spurs for 509, 510
fence 508
metal supports for 509, *509*
repair 510
Pot leeks, see Leeks
Pot marigold, see *Calendula*
Pot plants, see also Indoor plants
annuals as 175, 180
biennials as 175
diseases 447
epiphytes as 432
feeding 444
in greenhouse
care 446–7
cold protection 447
watering 446
humidity for 444, *444*
neglected, renovating 444
pests 447
potting on 444–5, *445*
top-dressing *444*, 445
watering 444, 485, *485*
winter-flowering, plunging outdoors 445, *445*
Potager gardening 303, *303*
Potamogeton crispus 243
choosing healthy plant *251*
softwood cuttings 256, 257
suggestions for use 243
Potash, see Potassium
Potassium 230, 397, 556
applying 309
content of fertilizers 532
deficiency 362, 532, 556, *556*, 562, 568
effect on magnesium 557
effects of 168, 231, 388
for lawn 282
life in soil 309
maintaining levels 309
plant requirements 532
sources of 309
Potassium (*cont.*)
uses 223
value of 532
Potassium chloride, sensitivity to 532
Potassium nitrate 309, 419
in cuttings soil mix 536
Potassium sulfate 123, 309, 362, 411, 555, 574
in cuttings soil mix 536
nutrient content 532
Potato fork 459, *459*
Potato late blight 555, *555*, 568, *568*
Potato leaf roll virus 553
Potato mop-top virus 568
Potato nematodes 572, *572*
rotating crops to avoid 304
Potato rugose virus 553
Potato scab 525, 568, *568*
Potato spraing 568, *568*
Potato vine, see *Solanum jasminoides*
Potato witches' broom 553
Potatoes *348*, 353–4
blackleg on 570, *570*
to clean ground 576
cultivation 353–4
disease resistance 555, 568
diseases 353, 354, 553, 555, 568, 570
disorders 568
genetic engineering 546
groups 353
growing in containers 307
harvesting 312, 354, *354*
hilling up 354, *354*, 555, 568
nitrogen requirement 310, 353
pests 353, 354, 550, 551, 568, 572
planting 353–4, *354*
under black plastic 309, 354, *354*
under floating row covers 354
under mulch 536, *536*
protecting 354, *521*
recommended cultivars 354
rotation 304, 353
sprouting seed 353, *353*
starting under cloches 311
storing 312, 354
sweet, see Sweet potatoes
tubers 543
colors 353
problems 568
size 353
in vegetable garden *300*
water requirements 530
for winter harvesting 354
'Rose Finn Apple' *354*
'Warba' *354*
Potential evapotranspiration 530
Potentilla
propagation
layering 86
softwood cuttings 81
shrubby, soil type tolerated 69
'Elizabeth', seasonal interest 62
fruticosa, as hedge 59
'Nana Argentea' 191
nitida, suggestions for use 191
Potpourri 287, 290, 291
Pots, see also Containers
azalea 473, *473*
bulbs in, under cover 228
clay
capillary watering 485
characteristics 473
cleaning 212, *212*
compared to plastic 211, 228, 264
drainage 109
preparing for bulbs 228, *228*
preparing for sowing seed 234
degradable 473, *473*, 586
making 473
sowing seeds in *179*
Pots (*cont.*)
drainage 109
hydroculture pots *447*, 473, *473*
lattice 473, *473*
long Toms 473, *473*
ornamental, see Containers
peat 161, 473
sowing annuals in 178
plastic
adding weight to 441
characteristics 473
compared to clay 211, 264
removing plants from 180
saucers for 473
for seed sowing 178
self-watering 446
shapes 473
sizes 473
standard 473, *473*
sweet pea tubes 473, *473*
tarpaper ring pots 473, *473*
terracotta *473*
in winter 190
types 473, *473*
watering, capillary system 485, *485*
Potting mixes, see Soil mixes, potting
Potting on, definition 589
Potting up, definition 589
Powder-puff cactus, see *Mammillaria bocasana*
Powdery mildew 548, 552, *552*, 564, *564*
Power tools, see Tools, power
Pratia pedunculata, suggestions for use 191
Predators in biological pest control 548
temperatures required 548
Preserving fruit 367
Preslia cervina 243
Presser *161*
Pricking out 545, 589
alpines 205, *205*
annuals 179, *179*
cacti and other succulents 266, *266*
indoor plants 452, *452*
into pack *179*
perennials 161, *161*
shrubs 85, *85*
Prickly pears 421
conditions required 356, 421
cultivation 421
fruits 421, *421*
harvesting 421
stem sections 421, *421*
storing 421
Primrose, see *Primula*
Primrose jasmine, see *Jasminum mesnyi*
Primula
alpine
softwood cuttings 206
sowing 205
basic parts of plant *580*
conditions preferred 191
conditions required 431
conditions tolerated 27
for cutting 141
flowering time from seed 160
germination 179
leaf vein patterns *582*
lifting after bedding 184
pests 553, 566, 572
propagation
division 208
softwood cuttings 206
sowing 205
scent 175
seed germination 160
in spring 139
suggestions for use 34, 140, 216
in water garden *241*
allionii, division 208
alpicola, suggestions for use 243
Primula (*cont.*)
auricula
breeding 140
Irishman's cuttings 208
suggestions for use 191
boothii, soil type required 192
bulleyana *146*
in bog garden *242*
conditions preferred 141
soil type tolerated 146
Candelabra Group
conditions preferred 240
conditions tolerated 17
on waterside *23*
denticulata
root cuttings 165, 208, *209*
scooping rosettes 209, *209*
suggestions for use 243
edgeworthii, soil type required 192
farinosa, suggestions for use 191
florindae
conditions preferred 141, 242
soil type tolerated 146
suggestions for use 243
gracilipes
leaf cuttings 207
soil type required 192
helodoxa, suggestions for use 243
japonica
conditions preferred 141
suggestions for use 243
x *kewensis*, from seed 452
malacoides *452*
conditions preferred 431
as pot plants 175
from seed 452
marginata
basal cuttings 207, *207*
Irishman's cuttings 208
suggestions for use 191
obconica
conditions preferred 431
pests 562
as pot plants 175
from seed 452
x *polyantha*, seasonal group 171
Polyanthus Group, pests 566, 572
pulverulenta
conditions preferred 141
suggestions for use 243
rosea
soil type tolerated 146
suggestions for use 243
scotica, suggestions for use 190
secundiflora, suggestions for use 243
sikkimensis, suggestions for use 243
sinensis
as pot plants 175
from seed 452
sonchifolia, soil type required 192
vulgaris
conditions preferred 175
in containers 174
as fillers 173
seasonal display 171
in woodland 140
Pristiphora 551
Privacy
gardens for 14
structures to provide 492
Privet, see *Ligustrum*
Chinese, see *Ligustrum lucidum*
Problems 547–79
diagnosing symptoms 547, *547*
method of identifying 547
prevention 548
Proliferation 563
Propagating units, see Propagators
Propagation 589, see also individual techniques
advanced techniques 537, 546
Propagation (*cont.*)
bottom heat for 544, *545*
cacti 266–71
care of propagated plant 545–6
climbers 109–13
dahlias 223, *223*
environment for 544–5
fall tasks 584
fruit 368–70, *368–70*
fuchsias 448, *448*
in greenhouse, aids for 488, *488*
hygiene 545
indoor plants 451–6
principles 537–46
roses 129–33, *129–33*
shrubs 81–9
spring tasks 583
succulents 266–71
summer tasks 584
trees 52–7
vegetative 590
water plants 245, *245*, 256–7, *256–7*
winter tasks 584
Propagators 589
bottom heat 544
germinating seed in 452
heated *486*, 488, *488*, 545
mist units 488, *488*, 544
rigid-topped 544, *544*
rooting grafted shrubs in *89*
for windowsill 488, *488*
Propane gas 482
Prostanthera
scent 66
cuneata, choosing healthy plant *67*
rotundifolia, in conservatory *429*
Protection
for alpines 201
for hardening off 180
for leafy cuttings 544, *544*
netting for 472
for shrubs, newly planted 69
Protective clothing, see Clothing, protective
Prothalli 159
Prunella vulgaris, see Self-heal
Pruners *49*, *50*, 458, 462–3, *462–3*
blades 462
maintenance 462
ratchet system *462*
safety catch 462, *462*
types
anvil 462, *462*
bypass 462, *462*
long-handled 462, *462*
parrot-beak 462, *462*
tree 463, *463*
Pruning
aims 73
bad 570, *570*
bonsai 434, 435, *435*
branched-head standards 48, *48*
brutting 425, *425*
central-leader standards 48, *48*
to change form 23
climbers 102–5
formative 102, *102*
principles 102
spring 102, *102*
summer 103, *103*
under cover 450
winter 104, *104*
coppicing 77, *77*, 586
cutting methods 450
double Guyot system *400–401*, 401–402
espaliers 49
fall tasks 584
fan-trained trees 49
feathered trees 48, *48*
formative 48–9, *48*, 587
fruit trees and bushes 364–6, *364–6*
Full Lorette System 375
ground covers 151, *151*
(*entry cont.*)

Pruning (*cont.*)
  Guyot system 401–2
  hard 73
  honeysuckle 105, *105*
  light 73
  Modified Lorette System 374, *374*
  pollarding 77, *77*, 589
  renewal 589
  renovative, fruit trees 366, *366*
  results 73
  root 49
    for bonsai 435, *435*
    fruit trees 366, *366*
    shrubs 80
  roses 125–8, *125–8*
  shrubs 73–80
    after planting *68*
    aims 73
    deciduous 74–6, *74–6*
    formative 73–4, *73*
    minimal *74*, 75
    principles 73, *73*
    results 73
    in spring *74*, 75
    standards 80
    suckering habit 76, *76*
    summer 76, *76*
    wall 78–9, *79*
  spring tasks 583
  summer tasks 583
  tip 590
  tools for 102, 458, 462–4, *462–3*
    maintenance 462
  for topiary 90
  trees 47–51
    established 49, *49*
    formative 48, *48*
    principles 47, *47*
  weeping trees *48*, 49
  winter tasks 584
  Wisteria 103, *103*
Pruning saws 463, *463*
  bow *463*
  double-edged *463*
  folding *463*
  general-purpose *463*
  Grecian 463, *463*
Prunus
  as arch over walkway *36*
  bulbs under 216
  diseases 554, 557, 561, 571
  evergreen, semiripe cuttings with heel 83
  flowers 35
  form 33
  life expectancy 16
  pests 553
  propagation
    chip-budding 56
    side-veneer grafting 56
    softwood cuttings 53
  pruning 47, 48, 50
  renovating 50
  root suckers 45
  for small gardens 37
  as specimen tree 33
  underplanting 36
  americana *33*, 383
  'Amonogawa', suggestions for use 37
  armeniaca, see Apricots
  avium
    edible varieties, see Cherries
    'Plena', soil type tolerated 41
  besseyi hybrids, see Plums, cherry
  cerasifera, see Plums, cherry
  cerasus, see Cherries, sour
  x *domestica*, see Gages; Plums
    subsp. *institia*, see Bullaces; Damsons; Mirabelles
  dulcis, see Almonds
  glandulosa
    side-veneer grafting 89
    stooling 87
    'Alba Plena', in mixed border *215*
  x *hillieri* 'Spire', see *P.* 'Spire'
  institia, see Bullaces; Gages

Prunus (*cont.*)
  'Kanzan', shape 33
  'Kiku-shidare', suggestions for use 37
  laurocerasus
    diseases 554
    as hedge 78
    pruning 78
    'Otto Luyken', as ground cover 151
    'Schipkaensis', heel cuttings *83*
  lusitanica
    pruning 78, *78*
    semiripe cuttings 53
  maackii 'Amber Beauty', seasonal interest 37
  mume
    seasonal interest 37
    'Beni-shi-dare', training *79*
  'Okame'
    seasonal interest 37
    suggestions for use 37
  'Pandora', suggestions for use 37
  persica
    edible, see Peaches
    'Klara Meyer', training 79
    var. *nectarina*, see Nectarines
  salicina (syn. *P. triflora*), see Plums, Japanese
  sargentii *41*
    seasonal interest 37
    soil type tolerated 41
  serotina, suggestions for use 27
  serrula 26
    bark 35, *35*
    seasonal interest 37
  'Shirofugen', in garden design *19*
  spinosa, conditions tolerated 66
  'Spire' (syn. *P.* x *hillieri* 'Spire'), suggestions for use 37
  subhirtella
    suggestions for use 37
    'Autumnalis' 35
      fasciation 563
      seasonal interest 37
  tomentosa, as hedge 59
  triflora (syn. *P. salicina*), see Plums, Japanese
  triloba, pruning 74, 75
  x *yedoensis*, suggestions for use 37
Pseudaletia unipuncta 572
Pseudobulbs 589
  orchids with 440
  potting 441
  propagation by 443, *443*
Pseudococcus 552
Pseudolarix amabilis, soil preferred 41
Pseudolithos
  flat grafting 271
  grafting 270
Pseudomonas 554
  mors-prunarus 571
  syringae 571
Pseudotsuga
  soil preferred 41
  menziesii
    diseases 560
    pests 560
    var. *glauca* *33*
Psidium guajava, see Guavas
Psila rosae, see Carrot rust flies
Psylla
  buxi 553
  mali, nymphs 562
  pyricola 553
Psyllids 553, *553*, 557
  apple 562, *562*
Psylliostachys suworowii
  for cutting 175
  as pot plants 175
Ptelea, pruning 74
Pteris
  conditions preferred 431

Pteris (*cont.*)
  cretica
    division of rootstock 451
    suggestions for use 438
Pterocactus, division of offsets 269
Pterocarya fraxinifolia, soil type tolerated 42
Pterocephalus perennis, conditions tolerated 191
Pterostyrax, pruning 74
Puccinia 554
Puddling *530*
Pueraria lobata 97
  suggestions for use 96
  vigor 98
  as weed 576
Pulmonaria
  conditions tolerated 141
  division 163
  seasonal interest 135
  in spring 139
  winter interest 141
  saccharata, in mixed island bed *136*
Pulsatilla
  in rock garden 187
  root cuttings 208
  soil type tolerated 193
  sowing 205
  vulgaris
    in rock garden *187*
    root cuttings 165
Pumps, for water garden 250, *250*
Punica granatum
  bonsai 434
  fruit, see Pomegranates
  'Nana' 423
    bonsai 434
Purple loosestrife, see *Lythrum*
Purple mountain saxifrage, see *Saxifraga oppositifolia*
Purple sage, see *Salvia officinalis* 'Purpurascens'
Purple toadflax, see *Linaria purpurea*
Purslane
  summer, see Summer purslane
  winter, see Miner's lettuce
Puschkinia
  forcing 228
  suggestions for use 219
  scilloides 227
  tomentosa
Pussy willow, see *Salix caprea*
Pussy-ears, see *Kalanchoe*
Putting greens 275
  mowing 281
Puya 433
  alpestris 432
PVC
  for cloches 490
  as pond liner 246
Pycnostysanus azaleae 562
Pygmaeocereus
  division of offsets 269
  flat grafting 271
Pyracantha
  berries 61, 65
  bonsai 434, *434*
  conditions tolerated 66
  diseases 555, 564
  as hedge 22, 59
  in mixed border 140
  pests 560
  planting beside wall *68*
  propagation, from seed 84
  pruning 78, *79*
  seasonal interest 66
  seed, extracting from berries *84*
  semiripe cuttings 83
  soil type tolerated 67
  suggestions for use 66
  training *79*
  as wall shrub 64, *64*, 78
  coccinea, in shrub border *63*
  'Golden Charmer' *58*
  'Mohave' 62
    in shrub border *63*
  x *watereri*, in mixed border *20*
Pyramidal bugle, see *Ajuga pyramidalis*

Pyrenone 553
  commercial names 574
Pyrethrum 548, 550, 551, 552, 553, 562, 566, 574
Pyrola rotundifolia, soil type required 192
Pyrostegia 97
  semiripe cuttings 111
  venusta
    growth rate 97
    pruning 103, 105
Pyrrhalta viburni 550
Pyrus, for *Pyrus* grown as fruit trees, see Pears
  chip-budding 56
  conditions tolerated 37
  soil type tolerated 41
  calleryana 'Chanticleer' 37, *37*
    in garden design *19*
    soil type tolerated 42
  communis var. *sativa*, see Pears
  salicifolia 'Pendula'
    for small garden 35
    suggestions for use 37
Pythium ultimum 566, 570

Q

Quackgrass *576*, 577
  control 527
  eradicating 276, 294
  removing from pond site 252
Quaking grass, see *Briza*
Quarry tiles, see Tiles, quarry
Quater, see *Vinca major*
Queen-of-the-night, see *Selenicereus grandiflorus*
Queen's tears, see *Billbergia nutans*
Quercus
  clumps as focal point 34
  diseases 571, 572
  galls 558
  life expectancy 16
  pests 551, 554
  propagation, from seed 54
  root system *580*
  seed scarification 54
  suggestions for use 27
  coccinea, diseases 571
  ilex
    semiripe cuttings 53
    soil type preferred 42
  myrsinifolia, semiripe cuttings 53
  palustris
    soil type tolerated 42
    diseases 571
  robur
    conditions tolerated 37
    soil type tolerated 42
  rubra 28
    conditions tolerated 37
    diseases 571
  semecarpifolia, semiripe cuttings 53
  velutina, diseases 571
  virginiana, conditions tolerated 37
Quick decline viruses 416
Quicklime 533
Quinces 382, *382*
  cultivars grown 382, 390
  cultivation 382, *382*
  diseases 562
  fruit *371*
    type 582
  harvesting 382

Quinces (*cont.*)
  pests 554, 564
  as rootstock for loquats 418
  as rootstock for pears 380, *380*
  storing 382
  winter pruning 364
Quisqualis
  semiripe cuttings 111
  indica 97
    climbing method 93
    for fragrance 97
    pruning 105

R

Rabbits 547, 572
  protection from 310, 472
Raccoons 549, *549*, 572
Racemes 582, 589
Radicchio
  culinary uses 324
  cultivation 324
  F1 hybrids 324
  forcing 324
  form 324
  harvesting 324
  recommended cultivars 323
Radicle 538, *538*, 589
Radishes 352–3
  in crop rotation 304
  culinary uses 352
  cultivation 352–3
  diseases 555, 566
  edible parts 348, 352
  growing in containers 307
  harvesting *352*, 353
  as intercrop 304, 305, 352
  nitrogen requirement 310, 352
  Oriental, see Daikon
  pests 353, 550, 566
  recommended cultivars 352
  storing 353
  in vegetable garden *300*
  watering at critical periods 308
  'Black Spanish Round' *352*
  'French Breakfast' *352*
Raffia, for ties 472
Railroad ties
  cutting 507
  raised beds of 507, *507*
  steps of gravel and *503*
Rain gauges 471, *471*
Rain lily, see *Zephyranthes*
Rain shadow 39, 518, *518*, 589
Rainfall 517–18
  design and 15
  measurements of 530
  torrential, damage from 518
  trees' requirements 39
Raised beds, see Beds, raised
Rakes 460, *460*, *467*
  heads 460
  shafts 460
  types
    bowhead *460*
    flathead 460, *460*
    flat-tined lawn *467*
    lawn *284*, 467, *467*
    power lawn 467, *467*
    scarifying *284*, *467*
    spring-tined lawn *284*, *467*
Raking, correct position for *458*
Ramblers 589
Ramets 149

Ramonda
leaf cuttings 207
soil mix for 211
suggestions for use 190
myconi *204*
in alpine raised bed *201*
suggestions for use 191
Ranch-style fencing 508, *508*
Rangoon creeper, see *Quisqualis indica*
Ranunculus
alpine, sowing 205
in grass *275*
sowing 205
alpestris, in alpine raised bed *201*
asiaticus
for cutting 219
tubers 214
ficaria *577*
conditions tolerated 219
soil type tolerated 146
suggestions for use 140
winter interest 141
in woodland 140
flammula, soil type tolerated 146
lingua
division of rootstock 257
'Grandiflora', in water garden 243
repens *578*
flower form *582*
Raoulia australis
in alpine raised bed *201*
suggestions for use 190
Raphanus sativus, see Radishes
Longipinnatus Group, see Daikon
Rapini, see Broccoli raab
Raspberries *404*, 408–10
American 408
cultivation 408–10, *408–10*
diseases 363, 409, 554, 559, 560, 564, 565, 567, 571, *571*
fall-fruiting 408, 409, *410*
recommended cultivars 409
feeding 362
freezing 367, *367*
in garden design *19*
harvesting 367, 409
North American black, crosses with 408
pests 409, 559, 564
plant type 356, 404
propagation by suckers 370, 410, *410*
pruning 409, *409*, *410*
recommended cultivars 409
soil unsuitable for 360
storing 409
suckers, removing 370, 409, *409*
summer-fruiting 408–9, *409*
training 409
Scandinavian system 408, *408*
yellow *404*
'Autumn Bliss' *409*
in large fruit garden *357*
in small fruit garden *358*
'Marcy', in small fruit garden *358*
'Royalty', in large fruit garden *357*
'Southland' *409*
Raspberry borers 559, *559*
Raspberry fruitworms 564, *564*
Rata, see *Metrosideros robusta*
Rats 568
Rattail cactus, see *Aporocactus flagelliformis*
Rebars *505*
Rebutia
choosing healthy plant *263*
in containers outdoors 260
form 259
propagation
division of offsets 269
division of rootstock 270
albiflora 262
aureiflora 262
Rebutia (*cont.*)
heliosa 262
marsoneri 262
minuscula 262
muscula *259*
senilis 262
Red chicory, see Radicchio
Red chokeberry, see *Aronia arbutifolia*
Red core 405
Red fescue, see *Festuca rubra* var. *rubra*
Red lily beetles 550, *550*
Red maple, see *Acer rubrum*
Red oak, see *Quercus rubra*
Red thread 573, *573*
Red valerian, see *Centranthus ruber*
Red-barked dogwood, see *Cornus alba*
Red-berried elder, see *Sambucus racemosa*
Redbud, see *Cercis*
Redcurrants *404*, 411–12
cordons 356, 412, *412*
cultivation 411–12
freezing 367
hardwood cuttings 370, 412, *412*
harvesting 412
mineral sensitivity 532
netting 411
pests 411, 552
plant type 356, 404
potassium requirement 357
protecting from wind 411
pruning
bush 411, *411*
cordon 412, *412*
fan 412
winter 364
recommended cultivars 412
storing 412
training 358, 412, *412*
'Jonkheer van Tets' *412*
'Red Lake'
in large fruit garden *357*
in small fruit garden *358*
Red-hot poker, see *Kniphofia*
Redtop, see *Agrostis gigantea*
Redwood, see *Sequoia*
Reeds, in wild garden *27*
Regal lily, see *Lilium regale*
Regional differences 522–3
Rehmannia elata, in conservatory *429*
Reinwardtia, pinching out 450
Remontant 589
Renovation
alpine beds *204*
climbers 105, *105*
fruit trees 366, *366*
lawns 31, 285
shrubs
drastic 80, *80*
gradual 80, *80*
Renting tools 458
Repotting
alpines 211, *211*
bulbs 232, *232*
cacti 265
marginal aquatics *255*
shrubs 71, *71*
succulents 265, *265*
trees 44, *44*
Reseda odorata, scent 175
Respiration 517, 581, 589
Reversion, of variegated plants 70, *70*, 589
Rex begonia vine, see *Cissus discolor*
Rhagoletis pomonella 565, *565*
Rhamnus
deciduous, pruning 74
as weed 579
alaternus, conditions tolerated 66
Rhaphiolepis, side-veneer grafting 89
Rhapis, suggestions for use 37
Rheum
dividing 162, 163
Rheum (*cont.*)
feeding 155
soil type tolerated 146
alexandrae, suggestions for use 243
x *cultorum*, see Rhubarb
palmatum 241
in contrasting foliage group *138*
suggestions for use 243
'Atrosanguineum'
form 138, 141
growth rate 141
suggestions for use 243
Rhipsalidopsis
propagation
apical-wedge grafting 271
side grafting 271
gaertneri
conditions required 261
conditions tolerated 262
in hanging basket 261
softwood cuttings 453
suggestions for use 262
rosea
conditions required 261
conditions tolerated 262
softwood cuttings 453
suggestions for use 262
Rhipsalis
conditions required 261
habit 259
propagation
side grafting 271
softwood cuttings 453
stem cuttings 268
soil mix for 264
cereuscula 262
mesembryanthemoides 262
pachyptera 262
Rhizobium granules 339
Rhizoctonia 570
Rhizomes 543, *543*, 589
of bamboos, dividing 143, *143*
definition 214
growth habit *580*
problems 569
propagation
division 163, *163*
scooping 238, *238*
scoring 238, *238*
purpose *580*, 581
weeds with *576*
Rhodiola crassipes, conditions tolerated 262
Rhodochiton atrosanguineum, suggestions for use 173
Rhodococcus fascians 561
Rhododendron
avenue of *62*
azaleas
bonsai 434
breaking dormancy 515
conditions required 431
diseases 562
dwarf conifers with 38
in garden room *428*
heel cuttings 83
pests 552
plunging outdoors *445*
pots for 473
suggestions for use 148
color combinations *24*
conditions preferred 518
conditions tolerated 27
in containers 65
deadheading 70, *70*
diseases 552, 560, 562, 567, 571
drought, effect of 563, 570
dwarf, soil type required 192
galls 558
old cultivars 31
pests 551, 552, 553, 566, 572
propagation
air layering 87, *87*
cuttings 540, *541*
dropping 86
saddle grafting 88, 89, *89*
Rhododendron, propagation (*cont.*)
semiripe cuttings 83, 207
simple layering 86
pruning 76, 78
size 61
soil mix for 69, 536
soil type indicated by 525
soil type required 15, 62, 69, 192
sowing 85
suckers 70
suggestions for use 27
top-dressing *71*
in water garden *240*
augustinii, pruning 78
auriculatum, scent 66
'Curlew', in peat bed *188*
edgeworthii, scent 66
'Fragrantissima', scent 66
Ghent Hybrids, scent 66
'Hinodegiri', flowers 65
'Homebush' *62*
indicum 'Harkurei', bonsai 434
Loderi Group, scent 66
luteum *66*
scent 66
maddenii, conditions preferred 66
occidentale, scent 66
'Polar Bear', scent 66
ponticum
conditions tolerated 66
pruning 78
as rootstock 88
Rustica Hybrids, scent 66
simsii, galls 558
subsection Triflora, pruning 78
vireya, conditions preferred 66
viscosum, scent 66
wardii *62*
Rhododendron bud blast 562, *562*
Rhododendron leafhopper 553, 562
Rhodohypoxis
suggestions for use 217, 219
baurii, in trough *199*
'Douglas', in peat bed *188*
'Margaret Rose', in peat bed *188*
Rhodoleia championii, soil preferred 41
Rhodothamnus chamaecistus, in peat bed *188*
Rhoicissus 97
conditions preferred 431
conditions required 431
capensis, softwood cuttings 453
Rhombophyllum, division of offsets 269
Rhubarb 347, *347*
beds for 341
culinary uses 347
cultivation 347, *347*
forcing 347, *347*
harvesting 347, *347*
intercropping 302
nitrogen requirement 310, 347
recommended cultivars 347
site 302
storing 312
in vegetable garden *300*
Rhus
division 88
root cuttings 84, 541
diversiloba, as weed 576
radicans, as weed 576
typhina
form 33
for small garden 35
vernix, as weed 576
Rhynchaenus rufipes 553
Ribes
hardwood cuttings 84
stooling 87
alpinum, conditions tolerated 521
divaricatum, as gooseberry rootstock 413
Ribes (*cont.*)
nigrum, see Blackcurrants
odoratum
as gooseberry rootstock 413
as hedge 59
sanguineum *87*
pruning 76
sativum, see Redcurrants; Whitecurrants
uva-crispa, see Gooseberries
Riccia fluitans 243
Rice-paper plant, see *Tetrapanax papyriferus*
Ricinus
conditions required 431
growing as annual 176
communis
in annual border *171*
architectural plant 173, 175
foliage 171
growing as annual 175
Rind 589
Rind grafting, tree fruits 379, *379*
Ring culture 334
pots for 473, *473*
Ring rot 568
Ring stakes 156, *156*, *472*
Rings, plant 472, *472*
Ringspots 555
Ripewood cutting, definition 586, see also Cuttings, ripewood
Robinia
conditions tolerated 37
seed scarification 54
side-veneer grafting 56
soil type tolerated 41
whip-and-tongue grafting 56
pseudoacacia
leaf form *581*
pests 559
'Frisia' *26*, *35*, *56*
suggestions for use 37
Robin's pincushions 558
Rock cress, see *Aubrieta*
Rock garden 185–212
bulbs in 217, 219, 225, 231
care 203–4
choosing plants for 186, 192
constructing 195
designing 185–90
drainage 195
dwarf conifers for 38
exposure 186
herbs for *288*
miniature, in alpine house 210
planning 186
plant associations 22
planter's guide 191
planting 196–7, *196*
during construction 195, *195*
planting scheme *187*
site 186
site preparation *194*, 195
siting 192–3, *192*
soil for *194*, 196
soil mix for *194*, 196
stone for 193, *193*
placing *194*, 195
top-dressing 197, 203, *203*
using site features for 17
Rock garden hoe, see Hoes, types, onion
Rock hyssop, see *Hyssopus officinalis* subsp. *aristatus*
Rock phosphate, nutrient content 532
Rock plants
acid-loving, soil for 196
for alkaline soil 193
characteristics 185
in containers 190, *190*, 198–9
cutting back after flowering 204, *204*
diseases 204
edging pool *242*
feeding 203
(*entry cont.*)

Rock plants (*cont.*)
  filling gaps between 173
  habitats 185
  in peat beds 202, *202*
  pests 204
  planter's guide 191
  planting 196–7, *196*
    in crevices 197, *197*
    in dry-stone walls 200, *200*
    during rock garden construction 195, *195*
    in raised beds 201
  potting up 205
  pricking out 205, *205*
  propagation 205–9
    cuttings 206–7, 208–9
      basal 207, *207*
      greenwood 206
      Irishman's 208, *208*
      leaf 207
      ripewood 206
      root 208–9, *209*
      scooping rosettes 209, *209*
      selecting material for 207, *207*
      semiripe 206, *207*
      softwood 206, *206*
    division 208, *208*
    from seed 205, *205*
  protecting 204
  pruning 203, *203*
  in raised beds 189, 200–201
  range of plants 185
  removing dead leaves 212, *212*
  requiring acid soil 192
  routine care 203–4
  for sandy soil 193
  seed 205, *205*
  shrubs and conifers with *187*
  soil mixes for 196, 201
  soil requirements 196
  suggestions for use 116, 186–90
  trimming 203–4
  in troughs 190, *190*
  watering 203
  weeding 203, *203*
Rock rose, see *Cistus*; *Helianthemum*
Rocks, see also Stone
  as mulch 531
  natural stratum lines 193, *193*
  sedimentary 193, *193*
Rocky Mountain juniper, see *Juniperus scopulorum*
Rodgersia
  architectural form 141
  for drying 141
  soil type tolerated 146
  by waterside *28*, *158*
  aesculifolia
    conditions preferred 141
    suggestions for use 243
  pinnata
    conditions preferred 141
    suggestions for use 243
  podophylla, suggestions for use 243
Rollers
  garden 466
  on lawnmowers 465
Rome, ancient, gardens 29
Romneya
  root cuttings 165
  coulteri
    growth rate 141
    soil type preferred 146
Romulea
  corm 214
  suggestions for use 219
Roof gardens 29, *29*
  perennials in containers 140
Root ball 589
Root crops, definition 589
Root cuttings 540, 541, *541*
  alpines 208–9, *209*
  climbers 109, 112, *112*
  distinguishing ends of roots 541, *541*
  perennials 165, *165*
Root cuttings (*cont.*)
  scooping rosettes 209, *209*
  shrubs 84
Root feeder 44, *44*
Root hairs 517, 580
Root nodules 533
Root pruning
  bonsai 435, *435*
  fruit trees 366, *366*
  shrubs 80
Root rots 422, 560, *560*, 567, *567*
  Phytophthora 560, *560*, 567
  tropical 567
Root run 589
Root tubers 543, *543*
  propagation 543
Root vegetables 348–54
  in crop rotation 304
  mineral deficiency 560
  mounding 521
  overwatering 308
  pests 561, 566, 568
  protecting 521
  storing 312
  for successional crops 348
  transplanting 306
  watering, critical periods 308
Rooting hormones *82*, 111, 540, 570, 589
Root-knot nematodes 387, 403, 566
Roots 589
  adventitious 540, *540*, *541*, 585
  aerial 92, *98*, 585
  collecting, for preserving 298
  drying 298
  fleshy, weeds with *577*
  frost and thaw damage to 515
  importance of water to 517
  modified to form storage organs 580, *580*
  problems 566–8
  pruning 49
  purpose 580, *580*
  swollen tap roots 580, *580*
  types 580, *580*
    fibrous 39, *39*, 580, *580*, 587
    "hockey-stick" *39*, 40
    tap 580, *580*, 590
    "water" *447*
Rootstocks 543, 589
  for apples 371, *371*
  for apricots 390, 391
  for cacti 271
  for cherries 392, *392*, 393, *393*
  for citrus 416, 417, 418
  division, see Division, of rootstocks
  for fruit trees 358, 359, 360, *360*
  for gooseberries 413
  for peaches 387, *387*
  for pears 380, *380*
  perennials, preparation 166, *166*
  planting level *360*
  for plums 383, *383*
  preparing for grafting trees 56
  for roses 120, 122, 123, 130
  selecting 543
Roquette, see Arugula
Rorippa
  nasturtium-aquaticum, see Watercress
  sylvestris *576*
Rosa 114–34
  Alba 115
    layering 131
    pruning 127, *127*
    temperatures withstood 124
  on arbor *118*
  on arch *118*
  balling 556
  bare-root
    planting 121, *121*
    selecting 120, *120*
  blackspot *120*, 124, 548
  blind shoots 124, *124*
  Bourbon 115
    as climbers 118
Rosa, Bourbon (*cont.*)
    layering 131
    pegging down 127
    pruning 127
    suggestions for use 128
  breeding 115, 132–3, *132*, *133*
  buying 99
  Centifolia (Provence) 115
    hybridizing 133
    layering 131
    pruning 127, *127*
    temperatures withstood 124
  chemical damage to 557, 561
  China 115
    in mixed planting 116
    pruning 126
  choosing 114, 120, *120*, 121
  chromosomes 132
  classification 115
  climbing 115
    buying 99
    climbing method 93
    combined with other climbers 93, *93*
    conditions suitable for 27, 29
    in containers 119
    layering 131
    planting 122, *122*
    pruning 122, 128, *128*
    as screen *93*, 119
    shrubs to grow with 118
    as standards 118
    suggestions for use *19*, 27
    thornless 118
    training 118, 122, *122*, 128, *128*
    on trees 34
  conditions preferred 518
  conditions required 120
  conditions tolerated 114
  container-grown
    planting 121
    selecting 120, *120*
  in containers 119, *119*
    feeding 123
    planting *122*
  cutting back in fall 124, *124*
  damage caused by deer 572
  Damask 115
    layering 131
    in mixed planting 116
    pruning 127, *127*
    shrubs with 117
    temperatures withstood 124
  deadheading 124, *124*
  designing with 114–19
  dieback *120*, *125*, 571
  disbudding 134, *134*
  disease resistance 548
  diseases 119, 124, 552, 554, 561, 567, 571
  exhibiting 134, *134*
  feeding 123, 521
  Floribunda (Cluster-flowered bush) 115
    cutting back in fall 124, *124*
    exhibition blooms *134*
    as hedge 119
    propagation 131
    pruning 126, *126*
    temperatures withstood 124
  flowers 114, 115, *115*
    in dry conditions 123
    feeding for 123
    reproductive parts *537*
  foliage color 115
  formal plantings 116
  Gallica 115
    propagation 131
    pruning 127, *127*
    shrubs with 117
    temperatures withstood 124
  galls 558
  Grandiflora, see Hybrid Tea and Grandiflora
  ground cover 115, 119, *119*
    layering 131
Rosa, ground cover (*cont.*)
    pruning 127, *127*
    suggestions for use 116
  hardiness 124
  hedges 22, 59, 118, *119*
    spacing 121, *121*
  heeling in 121
  hips *118*, 124, *537*, 581, *581*, 587
    ornamental 115
  Hybrid Musk 115
    pruning 126
    as screen 118
    training 128
  Hybrid Perpetual 115
    pegging down 127
    pruning 127
  Hybrid Tea and Grandiflora (Large-flowered bush) 115, 124
    cuttings 129
    deadheading *124*
    exhibition blooms *134*
    propagation 131
    pruning 125, *125*
    temperatures withstood 124
  hybridizing 132–3, *132*, *133*
  hybrids 115, 132–3
  hygiene 123
  informal plantings 116, *117*
  mildew 119
  mineral deficiency 557
  miniature 115
    in containers 119
    cuttings 129
    as edging to rosebeds 116
    pruning 126, *126*
    with rock plants 116
    spacing 121
    in terraced bed 117
  in mixed plantings 116, *117*, 358
  modern 114
    categories 115
    pruning 125
  Moss
    description 115
    pruning 127, *127*
  mounding up *520*, 521
  moving 124
  mulching 123
  Noisette 115
  nutrients required 123
  old *25*, 31, 114, *114*
    categories 115
    pruning 126
    suggestions for use 27
  Patio rose (Dwarf cluster-flowered bush) 115
    in containers 119
    pruning 126
  pegging down 127, *127*
  pests 124, 551, 552, 553, 554, 558, 562, 563
  planting 121, *121*
  Portland 115
    shrubs with 117
  proliferation 563
  propagation 129–33, *129–33*
    bud-grafting 120, 130–31, *130*
    division 131, *131*
    hardwood cuttings 129, *129*
    layering 131, *131*
    ripewood cuttings 207
    from seed 132, *132*
    semiripe cuttings 129
    suckers 131, *131*
  pruning 125–8, *125–8*
    for exhibition 134
    tools 125
  ramblers 115
    cuttings 129
    as ground cover 119
    layering 131
    planting 122
      by tree 122
    pruning 128, *128*
    scent 114
    as screen 119
    with shrubs 117, 118
Rosa, ramblers (*cont.*)
      structures to grow on 118
      training 118, 122
  remontant 115, 118
  rootstocks 120, 130
    planting 130
  routine care 123–4
  Rugosa
    foliage 115
    pruning 126
  scented 66, 114
  as screen 118
  seasonal interest *25*
  seed
    extraction 132, *132*
    germination 132
  shrub 115
    layering 131
    pruning 126
    shrubs with 117
    as specimen plants 118
  site 120
  societies 114
  soil preparation 120
  soil type tolerated 67
  spacing 121, *121*
  species 115
    flowering 118
    as hedge 59
    layering 131
    pruning 127
    from seed 132
    shrubs with 117
  specimen planting 117
  stakes for *472*
  staking 122, *472*
  standard
    bud-grafting *130*, 131
    in formal rose garden *116*
    placing 116
    planting 122, *122*
    pruning 126, *126*
    rootstocks 130
    selecting *120*, 121
    staking 122, *122*
    suckers 122
      removing 123, *123*
    weeping 118
      forming 118
      pruning 126
  suckers 122
    propagation from 131, *131*
    recognizing 123
    removing 123, *123*
  suggestions for use 21, 31, *114*, 116–19
  supports for 472, *472*
  Tea 115
  on terraces 117
  thorns, ornamental 115
  trailing *116*
  transplanting 124
  trenching *520*, 521
  underplanting 116, 117, *117*, 121, 123
  watering 123
  weed control 123, 577
  weeping standard
    forming 118
    pruning 126
    as specimen 118
  winter protection 124, *520*, 521
  'Albertine' 115
  'Amber Queen', in formal rose garden *116*
  'Apricot Nectar' 119
  'Baby Masquerade' 119
  'Bantry Bay', on arch *118*
  blanda, temperatures withstood 124
  'Blue Moon' 114
  'Buff Beauty' 118
  californica, temperatures withstood 124
  canina
    as rootstock 130
    temperatures withstood 124
  'Céleste' *114*
  'Cerise Bouquet' *114*
  'Chinatown' 118
    layering 131

(*entry cont. overleaf*)

Rosa (*cont.*)
'Complicata' 117
'Constance Spry' *114*
'Crimson Glory' 120
'Dr. Huey' (syn. *R.* 'Shafter'), as rootstock 130
'Dr. J.H. Nicholas' *118*
'Elina' 120
preparing for hybridization *133*
'Europeana'
in formal rose garden *116*
propagation 131
filipes 'Kiftsgate'
growing through trees 95
suggestions for use 95
'Frau Dagmar Hartopp' 118
seasonal interest 66
'Fred Loads', pruning 126
'Frühlingsgold' 118
gallica
var. *officinalis* *119*
'Versicolor' (syn. *R. mundi*) 119, *119*
glauca
foliage 115
temperatures withstood 124
'Gold Medal' 120
'Golden Showers' 128
in formal rose garden *116*
'Golden Wings' 121
'Grouse' 119
layering 131
'Hannah Gordon', exhibition blooms *134*
'Joseph's Coat' 128
'Judy Fischer' *119*
'Laxa', as rootstock 130
'Little White Pet' *117*
'Maid of Honor' 120
'Margaret Merril', in formal rose garden *116*
'Max Graf' *119*
'Mme. Alfred Carrière', suggestions for use 94
moyesii 115
in mixed border *137*
'Geranium', seasonal interest 66
multiflora
conditions tolerated 120
as rootstock 130
temperatures withstood 124
as weed 576
mundi, see *R. gallica* 'Versicolor'
'Nevada' 118
as hedge 59
'New Beginning' 119
'New Dawn', as screen 94
nitida, foliage 115
'Nozomi' 119
omeiensis pteracantha, see *R. sericea* subsp. *omeiensis palustris*
palustris, temperatures withstood 124
'Penelope'
in mixed planting *117*
spread 121
'Pheasant' 119
layering 131
pimpinellifolia
propagation 131
soil preferred 67, 120
'Raubritter' 119
'Red Bells' 119
'Roseraie de l'Haÿ' *58*
as hedge 59
'Rosy Cushion' 119
rugosa 115
as hedge 118
hybrids, pruning 127
propagation 131
hardwood cuttings 84
soil type preferred 120
soil type tolerated 69
temperatures withstood 124
'Sally Holmes' 118
'Sea Foam' 117
'Seagull' 118

Rosa (*cont.*)
sericea subsp. *omeiensis* (syn. *R. omeiensis pteracantha*) 116
'Shafter', see *R.* 'Dr. Huey'
'Stardance' 119
'Summer Fashion', in formal rose garden *116*
'Sun Flare', hybridizing 132
'Sunsprite, in formal rose garden *116*
'Surrey' *119*
'Swany', in formal rose garden *116*
'Trier' 118
'Tropicana' 121
'Valerie Margaret', exhibition blooms *134*
virginiana
foliage 115
temperatures withstood 124
wichuraiana
pruning 127
temperatures withstood 124
'Zéphirine Drouhin' 118
Rosaceae, diseases 555, 571
Rosary vine, see *Ceropegia woodii*
Roscoea cautleoides, root cuttings 208
Rose, see *Rosa*
Rose chafers 563, 573
Rose dieback, symptoms and control 571, *571*
Rose gall midge 558
Rose garden 114–34
designing 116
formal 116, *116*
setting 116
Rose leafhopper 553
Rose sickness 120
Rose stakes *472*
Rose ties *472*
Rosebud cherry, see *Prunus subhirtella*
Rosemary, see *Rosmarinus*
as herb, see *Rosmarinus officinalis*
Rose-pincushion, see *Mammillaria zeilmanniana*
Roses for watering cans 468, *468*, 589
Rose-scented geranium, see *Pelargonium graveolens*
Rosettes 589
removing when dead 204, *204*
scooping 209, *209*
Rosmarinus 292–3
harvesting, in winter 294
soil type tolerated 69
in vegetable garden 303
officinalis *292*
conditions preferred 294
cosmetic uses 287, 293
culinary uses 287, 293
flowers 292
foliage 292
harvesting 293
in herb garden *295*
propagation
layering 293
mound layering 297
from seed 293
semiripe cuttings 293
as specimen plant 288
storing 293
suggestions for use 292
variants 293
'Arp' 293
'Miss Jessopp's Upright', suggestions for use 293
'Prostratus', mound layering 297
'Severn Sea' 293
Ross method of propagation 153, *153*
Rosularia modesta, conditions tolerated 262
Rotation of crops 303–4, *304*, 341, 586
advantages 303

Rotation of crops (*cont.*)
drawbacks 304
for pest and disease control 548, 567, 570, 572
planning for 304
Rotenone 548, 550, 551, 552, 553, 559, 563, 564, 565, 566, 571
commercial name 574
Rototillers 461, *461*
hilling attachment *461*
mini *461*
to clear neglected site 526, *526*
for weed control 577, 579
Rots
brown 564, *564*
crown 149, 153, 346, 571, *571*
in fruit 367
root, see Root rots
Roundleaf mintbush, see *Prostanthera rotundifolia*
Rough-stalked bluegrass, see *Poa trivialis*
Rowan, see *Sorbus aucuparia*
Royal fern, see *Osmunda regalis*
Royal palm, see *Roystonea*
Roystonea, suggestions for use 37
Rubber plant, see *Ficus elastica*
Rubble, using in design 17
Rubus
climbing method 93
hybrid berries, see Hybrid berries
propagation
hardwood cuttings 84
simple layering 86
tip layering 86
as weed *577*, 579
biflorus
bark 61, 65
coppicing 77
cockburnianus, coppicing 77
deliciosa, pruning 76
fruticosus, cultivated, see Blackberries
idaeus, see Raspberries
var. *strigosus*, see Raspberries, American
occidentalis, see Raspberries, North American black
thibetanus, coppicing 77
'Tridel', pruning 76
Rucola, see Arugula
Rudbeckia
conditions tolerated 141
for cutting 141
cutting down *156*
division 163
in fall 139
pinching 155
fulgida *15*
hirta *167*, *175*
conditions tolerated 175
for cutting 175
soil type preferred 176
laciniata 'Goldquelle' *141*
growth rate 141
'Marmalade', in annual border *171*
purpurea, see *Echinacea purpurea*
Rue, see *Ruta*
Ruellia
conditions required 431
softwood cuttings 453
Rumex, see also Dock
acetosa, see Sorrel (herb)
acetosella, see Sorrel (weed)
obtusifolius, see Broad-leaved dock
scutatus 293
in herb garden *295*
Runner beans, see Beans, runner
Runners 589
layering, natural 539, *539*
propagation by
fruit 370
indoor plants 451, *451*
strawberries *406*
water plants 257, *257*

Ruschia
habit 259
propagation
division of rootstock 270
stem cuttings 268
Ruscus
dividing 88
aculeatus, division of suckers 88
Rush, see *Juncus*; *Luzula*; *Scirpus lacustris*
Rushes 142–3
care 143
distinguishing features 142
as indication of waterlogging 531
preparing soil 143
suggestions for use 142
in water garden *240*
Russian comfrey, see *Symphytum* x *uplandicum*
Russian olive, see *Elaeagnus angustifolia*
Russian tarragon, see Tarragon, Russian
Rustic work 512
joints for 512, *512*
Rusts 124, 547, 548, *554*
symptoms and control 449, 554, *554*
Rusty-back fern, see *Ceterach officinarum*
Ruta
as herb 293
graveolens *293*
allergy to 293
in border 288
culinary uses 293
foliage 293
harvesting 293
propagation
hardwood cuttings 84
from seed 293
semiripe cuttings of sideshoots 293
suggestions for use 293
variants 293
'Jackman's Blue' 293
'Variegata' 293
propagation from seed 297
Rutabagas 348–9
in crop rotation 304
culinary uses 348
cultivation 348–9, *349*
diseases 349, 555
harvesting 349
mineral deficiencies 568
nitrogen requirement 310, 348
pests 349, 560
recommended cultivars 348
storing 312, 349
'Altasweet' *348*
Ryegrass, see *Lolium*

S

Sabal
architectural plant 66
suggestions for use 37
Sacred lotus, see *Nelumbo nucifera*
Saddle grafting 88, 89, *89*, 544, *544*
Safety
chemical use 549
compost shredders 470, *470*
electricity 458, 464, 488

Safety (*cont.*)
hand tools 458
lawnmowers 465
power tools 458, *458*, 464, *464*
weedkiller use 557, 577
equipment for 468
Sage (herb), see *Salvia officinalis*
Sagina
boydii, in alpine raised bed *201*
procumbens, as weed 192
subulata 'Aurea', division 208
Sagittaria
soil type tolerated 146
graminea, propagation by offsets 257
latifolia, in water garden 243
sagittifolia
division of rootstock 257
in water garden 243
'Flore Pleno'
propagation by offsets 257
in water garden 243
St. Augustine grass, see *Stenotaphrum secundatum*
Saintpaulia
in bottle garden *439*
conditions preferred 431, 444
conditions required 431
hydroculture 431
in indoor plant group *444*
leaf cuttings 454, *454*, 541
miniatures, suggestions for use 438
pests 562
Salad rape
culinary uses 326
cultivation 326
harvesting 312, 326, *326*
Salad rocket, see Arugula
Salad vegetables 321–27
as intercrop 304,
minor 326–7
conditions tolerated 326
growing under cover 326
nitrogen requirement 326
overwintering, under cloches 311
storing 321
for succession 321
watering, critical periods 308
Salicornia europaea, conditions tolerated 262
Salix
adapting to waterlogging 517
conditions preferred 62
conditions tolerated 17, 37, 66, 521
coppicing 23, 36, 50
pests 551, 559
pollarding 36, 50
propagation
hardwood cuttings 52, 53, 84
internodal cuttings 541
ripewood cuttings 207
stooling 87
roots, damage from 39
soil type tolerated 42
suggestions for use 27
acutifolia
pollarding 77
'Blue Streak'
seasonal interest 37
suggestions for use 50
alba
conditions tolerated 37
hardwood cuttings *540*
suggestions for use 243
'Britzensis' (syn. *S. a.* 'Chermesina')
bark 35
coppicing 77
seasonal interest 37
suggestions for use 50
var. *sericea*, suggestions for use 50
(*entry cont.*)

Salix alba (cont.)
var. *vitellina*
bark 35
pollarded, pruning *50*
suggestions for use 50
babylonica, suggestions for use 243
x *boydii* 191
in peat bed *188*
caprea
as hedge 58
soil type tolerated 67
'Kilmarnock' *33*
formation 49
daphnoides
coppicing 77
seasonal interest 37
suggestions for use 243
'Aglaia', suggestions for use 50
x *erythroflexuosa*, stems 65
irrorata
bark 65
coppicing 77
seasonal interest 66
suggestions for use 50
matsudana 'Tortuosa', suggestions for use 33, 243
melanostachys, seasonal interest 62
reticulata, in peat bed *188*
x *sepulcralis*
seasonal interest 37
'Chrysocoma'
as specimen tree 33
suggestions for use 37
'Erythroflexuosa', suggestions for use 50
Salpiglossis
as pot plants 175
from seed 452
supporting *183*
Salsify
in crop rotation 304
culinary uses 353
flower buds *353*
harvesting 353
nitrogen requirement 310
overwintering 348
roots *353*
storage 353
Salt
trees tolerating 37
in wind 520
Salts, inorganic, harmful effects of 532
Salvia
choosing healthy plants *181*
flowering time from seed 160
flowers 171
growing with succulents 259
pruning 74
stem tip cuttings 164
underplanting roses 117
confertiflora, growth rate 141
farinacea
in annual border *171*
growing as annual 175
fulgens, in hot border *139*
horminum
conditions tolerated 175
for cutting 175
for drying 175
soil type tolerated 176
lavandulifolia, mound layering 297
nemorosa
division 163
in mixed border *137*
soil type tolerated 147
'May Night', in mixed border *215*
officinalis *293*, *297*
conditions preferred 294
culinary uses 293
flowers 293
foliage 293
hardiness 296
harvesting 293
Salvia officinalis (cont.)
propagation
mound layering 297, 539
from seed 293
semiripe heel cuttings 293
softwood cuttings 293
storing 293
suggestions for use 293
in vegetable garden 303
'Icterina', in herb garden *295*
'Purpurascens'
in herb garden *295*
suggestions for use 288, 289
pratensis, division 163
sclarea var. *turkestanica*
architectural plant 175
growth rate 141
splendens
in formal bedding 172
growing as annual 175, 176
planting out 180
uliginosa, growth rate 141
Salvinia
auriculata 243, *257*
propagation by offsets 257
natans
propagation by offsets 257
suggestions for use 243
Sambucus
cosmetic uses 287
culinary uses 287
propagation
hardwood cuttings 84
heel cuttings 83
in restricted color border *63*
nigra
conditions tolerated 288
'Aurea', conditions tolerated 288
'Marginata', conditions tolerated 288
racemosa 'Plumosa Aurea'
coppicing 77
pruning 77
San Jose scale 554
Sand
as additive, problems 529
for building work 499
improving drainage with 529
in seed compost 536
in soil mixes 535, 536
as top-dressing *284*, 534, *534*
Sand beds 546, *546*
Sand phlox, see *Phlox bifida*
Sandstone
for paving 496
for rock garden 193, *193*
Sandwort, see *Arenaria*
Sandy soil
adding clay to 529
annuals for 176
biennials for 176
climbers tolerating 99
effect on pears 380
feeding lawn on 282
growing fruit on 360
growing peaches on 387
growing plums on 383
identifying 525, *525*
improving 529
for lawn 276
water retention 529
lime required to alter pH 533
perennials for 146
rock plants preferring 193
shrubs preferring 67
structure 524, *524*
temperature 515
water in 530
water table 530
weedkillers on 526
Sanguinaria canadensis, conditions preferred *167*, 191
Sanitation 491
Sansevieria
conditions preferred 431
conditions tolerated 427
propagation
division of rootstock 270
leaf sections 455
Sansevieria (cont.)
trifasciata
division of rootstock *270*
'Hahnii', suggestions for use 262
'Laurentii', suggestions for use 262
Santolina
as hedge 58
pruning 78, 151, *151*
scent 66
chamaecyparissus *293*
for decoration 293
flowers 293
foliage 293
in garden design *19*
harvesting 293
in herb garden *295*
in potpourri 293
propagation
mound layering 297
semiripe cuttings of sideshoots 293
pruning 77
storing 293
suggestions for use 31, *117*, 293
'Lemon Queen' 293, *295*
'Nana' 293
rosmarinifolia, mound layering 297
virens 293
mound layering 297
Sap, definition 589
Sapling, definition 589
Saponaria
division 163
soil type tolerated 147
ocymoides
conditions tolerated 191
in dry-stone wall *189*
soil type preferred 193
soil type tolerated 193
suggestions for use 190
x *olivana*
in alpine raised bed *201*
in rock garden *187*
Sarcocaulon, stem cuttings 268
Sarcococca
conditions preferred 66
flowers 65
propagation by division 88
pruning 73
scent 66
confusa, in shrub border *63*
hookeriana var. *digyna* *66*
humilis, pruning *78*
Sarcophaga aldrichi, as biological pest control 553
Sarcozona, division of offsets 269
Sarmienta, propagation
semiripe cuttings 111
serpentine layering 113
Sarracenia flava, soil type required 147
Sash, definition 589
Satsumas, see Mandarins, Satsuma Group
Satureja
montana, see Winter savory
spicigera, see Creeping savory
Saucer magnolia, see *Magnolia* x *soulangiana*
Saururus cernuus
division of rootstock 257
in water garden 243
Savory
creeping, see Creeping savory
summer, see Summer savory
winter, see Winter savory
Savoy cabbage, see Cabbages, Savoy
Sawdust, mulching with 308
Sawflies
birch leaf mining 553
European apple 565, *565*
larvae 551, *551*
Saws
bow *463*
Saws *(cont.)*
chain 464, *464*
safety 458
double-edged pruning *463*
folding *463*
general-purpose pruning *463*
Grecian 463, *463*
masonry 498
pruning 463, *463*
Saxifraga
choosing healthy plant *192*
conditions required 186, 196
in dry-stone wall *200*
plunging after flowering *210*
propagation, rosette cuttings 207, *207*
removing dead rosettes 204, *204*
repotting *211*
soil type tolerated 193
suggestions for use 190, 191
burseriana, in alpine raised bed *201*
callosa, suggestions for use 191
cochlearis, suggestions for use 191
'Minor', in trough *199*
cotyledon
suggestions for use 191
in trough *199*
granulata, propagation, shoot-axil buds 543
grisebachii 'Wisley Variety', in alpine raised bed *201*
'Jenkinsiae', in alpine raised bed *201*
Kabschias, suggestions for use 191
longifolia, suggestions for use 191
oppositifolia
in alpine raised bed *201*
in peat bed *188*
paniculata
suggestions for use 191
in trough *199*
sancta *191*
sarmentosa, see *S. stolonifera*
scardica, in alpine raised bed *201*
'Southside Seedling'
in alpine raised bed *201*
in rock garden *187*
stolonifera (syn. *S. sarmentosa*)
division of plantlets/runners 451, *451*
'Tricolor', in conservatory *429*
'Tumbling Waters'
conditions preferred 186
in dry-stone wall *189*
suggestions for use 191
umbrosa, conditions tolerated 141
x *urbium*
conditions tolerated 141
planting in groups 137
Saxifrage, see *Saxifraga*
Scab 555, *555*, 564, *564*
Scabiosa
for cutting 141
flowering time from seed 160
soil type tolerated 147
suggestions for use 136
atropurpurea, sowing 177
caucasica
division 163
planting time 146
'Clive Greaves' *147*
graminifolia, suggestions for use 191
rumelica, see *Knautia macedonica*
Scabious, see *Scabiosa*
Scaffold poles, joints with beams 512, *512*
Scale insects *554*, 554, *559*, 559
Scaling
propagation by 233, 236–7, *236*, 540, *540*
twin- *236*, 237, 542, *542*
Scallions *341*, 342
in crop rotation 304
cultivation 342, *342*
harvesting 342
recommended cultivars 342
storing 312
using bulb onions as 341
in vegetable garden *300*
Scarification 54, 85, 160, 537, *538*, 589
alpines 205
annuals and biennials 179
shrub seed requiring 85
Scarifying rakes, see Rakes, types, scarifying
Scarlet plume, see *Euphorbia fulgens*
Scarlet runner beans, see Beans, scarlet runner
Scarlet turkscap lily, see *Lilium chalcedonicum*
Scent
annuals and biennials for 175
climbers for 96, 97
flowering trees for 34
roses for 114
shrubs for 65, 66
siting plants for *19*
tree foliage for 34
Schefflera
conditions preferred 431
hydroculture 431
actinophylla, bonsai 434
arboricola 'Gold Capella', plunging in large container *437*
Schinus molle, soil type preferred 42
Schisandra
for fragrance 97
propagation
semiripe cuttings 111
serpentine layering 113
softwood cuttings 110
glaucescens, pruning *104*
Schizanthus
conditions required 431
as pot plants 175, *180*
from seed 452
soil type preferred 176
in summer bedding *170*
Schizophragma
conditions tolerated 93
propagation
semiripe cuttings 111
simple layering 113
softwood cuttings 110
pruning 103
hydrangeoides
conditions tolerated 97
growing through trees 95
suggestions for use 93, 95
integrifolium, soil type tolerated 100
Schizostylis
division 163
in mixed border 215
planting time 146
coccinea
conditions preferred 219
for cutting 219
'Sunrise' *218*
Schlumbergera
conditions required 431
flower sexuality *582*
habit 259
in hanging basket 261, *264*
hybridizing *267*
propagation
apical-wedge grafting *270*, 271
softwood cuttings 453
stem cuttings 268
soil mix for 264
bridgesii
conditions required 261
conditions tolerated 262
(entry cont. overleaf)

Schlumbergera bridgesii (*cont.*)
in hanging basket 428
suggestions for use 262
x *buckleyi*, suggestions for use 262
'Gold Charm' *271*
truncata
conditions tolerated 262
suggestions for use 262
var. *delicata*, suggestions for use 262
Sciadopitys verticillata, soil type preferred 41
Sciarid flies 572, *572*
Scilla
chipping 237
conditions tolerated 219
forcing 228
suggestions for use 216, 219
bifolia
conditions preferred 219
in mixed border 214
suggestions for use 227
campanulata, see *Hyacinthoides hispanica*
non-scripta, see *Hyacinthoides non-scripta*
peruviana, conditions preferred 219
siberica
suggestions for use 227
'Atrocaerulea' *136*, *188*
Scion, definition 589
Scindapsus, self layering 113
Scirpus lacustris
in water garden 243
subsp. *tabernaemontani*
'Albescens', in water garden 243
'Zebrinus', in water garden 243
Sclerotia 555, 556, 559, 571
survival in soil 569
Sclerotinia 562
fructicola 564
homoecarpa 573
laxa 564
Sclerotium
cepivorum 569
rolfsii (syn. *Corticium rolfsii*) 560
Scooping, propagation by
bulbs 233, 238, *238*, 542
rhizomes 238, *238*
rosettes 209, *209*
Scorch 91
causes 518, 519, 556
control 556, 564
from fertilizers 223, 533
from sun 398
symptoms 556, *556*, 564, *564*
Scorias 554
Scoring, propagation by 238, *238*, 542, *542*
Scorzonera *353*
chards 353
in crop rotation 304
culinary uses 353
cultivation 353
flower buds 353
flowers 353
harvesting 353
nitrogen requirement 310, 353
overwintering 348
roots 353, *353*
size of plant 353
storing 353
Scorzonera hispanica, see Scorzonera
Scotch broom, see *Cytisus scoparius*
Scotch heather, see *Calluna vulgaris*
Scotch rose, see *Rosa pimpinellifolia*
Scotch thistle, see *Onopordum acanthium*
Scots pine, see *Pinus sylvestris*
Scree beds 188, 589
planting 197, *197*
Scree beds (*cont.*)
rock plants for 191
site 17, 192–3
soil for 196
top-dressing 197
Screen block walls 505, *505*
Screens
annual climbers as 174
apples as *357*
as background 22
climbers as 93, *93*
enclosing patio 29
fruit as 358
hedges as 58–60
indoor plants as 427
palms as *33*
for patio 493
protecting bulbs with 569
protecting shrubs with 69
on roof garden 29
roses as 118
rustic work 512
thermal 482, *482*
trees as 36
for vegetable garden *300*
as windbreaks 519, *519*
window effects 21
Screw-pine, see *Pandanus*
Scrophularia auriculata
soil type tolerated 146
stem tip cuttings 164
'Variegata', suggestions for use 243
Sculptural plants
perennials 140
set off by lawn 273
Scurvy grass, see *Oxalis enneaphylla*
Sea campion, see *Silene vulgaris* subsp. *maritima*
Sea holly, see *Eryngium*
Sea lavender, see *Limonium*
Sea pink, see *Armeria maritima*
Seakale beet, see Swiss chard
Seaside, see Coastal sites
Seats, in alcoves *22*
Seaweed
improving soil fertility with 302
in liquid fertilizer 309
mulching with 308
Seaweed meal, nutrient content 532
Sedge, see *Carex*
Sedge peat, definition 588
Sedges 142–3
care 143
conditions preferred 142
conditions tolerated 142
distinguishing features 142
as indication of waterlogging 531
preparing soil 143
suggestions for use 142
Sedum
conditions preferred 145
conditions tolerated 191
in containers outdoors 260
hardiness 259
pests 566, 572
propagation
division of offsets 269
leaf cuttings 207, *207*
stem cuttings 268
soil type preferred 146, 193
soil type tolerated 193
succulent type 258
suggestions for use 31
acre, in dry-stone wall *189*
anglicum, conditions tolerated 262
cauticola, suggestions for use 191
cyaneum, conditions tolerated 262
dasyphyllum, conditions tolerated 262
formosanum, conditions tolerated 262
hintonii, leaf cuttings 267
hispanicum, conditions tolerated 262
Sedum (*cont.*)
kamtschaticum, 'Variegatum', in dry-stone wall *189*
lanceolatum, conditions tolerated 262
montanum, conditions tolerated 262
morganianum
in conservatory *429*
in hanging basket 261
suggestions for use 262
obtusatum, in dry-stone wall *189*
rosulatum, conditions tolerated 262
rupestre, conditions tolerated 262
sediforme, conditions tolerated 262
sempervivoides, leaf cuttings 267
spathulifolium 'Cape Blanco'
in dry-stone wall *189*
in tree trunk *190*
spectabile
attracting insects 135
conditions tolerated 141, 262
division 163
for drying 141
foliage 138
in formal border *136*
stem structure *580*
in winter 156
winter interest *139*
'Autumn Joy', in mixed border *20*
'Brilliant' *259*
in mixed island bed *136*
spurium, in rock garden *186*
telephium
conditions tolerated 141
for drying 141
ternatum, conditions tolerated 262
villosum, conditions tolerated 262
Seed
artificially produced 546
botany 581–2
bulbs from 234–5
buying 176
cacti from 266–7, *266*
chilling 160, *160*
cleaning 54, *54*, 84
climbers from 109, *109*
collecting 537
from annuals 184, *184*
from bulbs 230, *230*, 234
from perennials 160, *160*
for preserving 298
from shrubs 84, *84*
definition 589
development 537, 581
dispersal by wind 518
dormancy 586
breaking 54, 85, 109, 160, 537–8
double 160, 586
high-temperature 324
plant mechanisms for 537
extracting from hips 132, *132*
fluid drilling 546
formation by fertilization 582
gels 176
germination 109, 517, 537–8, *538*, 581
bulbs 235
epigeal 538, *538*, 586
erratic 235
factors affecting 515
hypogeal 538, *538*, 587
indoor plants 452
in plastic bags 235
requirements for 452, 538
signs of 538, *538*
herbs from 297
lawn
sowing by hand 280, *280*
sowing by machine 280, *280*
naked 305
Seed (*cont.*)
pelleted 176, 546
sowing *177*, 178
of vegetables 305
perennials from 160–61
polyembryonic 417
pregermination 160, 305
prepared, of vegetables 305
primed 176
problems 564–5
propagation from
advances in 546
principles 537–8
purpose 581
rose, sowing 132, *132*
scarification 54, 85, 160, 179, 537, *538*, *589*
alpines 205
shrubs requiring 85
in sheets 305
shrubs from 84–5, *85*
soaking 85, 160, 452
sowing
broadcast 177, *177*, 585
in drills 177, *177*
pots and pans for 473, *473*
in pots and trays 178–9, 452, *452*
preparations for 545, *545*
seed soil mix 536, 538
station 590
storing 85, 537
damage to 568
stratification 54, 85, 132, 179, 537, 590
alpines 205
cold 538, *538*
perennials requiring 160
shrubs requiring 85
warm 538
succulents from 266
tapes 176, 305
treatment to destroy fungus 567
tree 54–5, *54–5*
viability 85, 176, 537
Seed drills 177, *177*
Seed leaf, see Cotyledons
Seed pans 473, *473*
drainage 109
Seed planters 471
Seed pods, ornamental trees for 34
Seed sowers 471, *471*
Seed trays 473, *473*
drainage 109
removing plants from 180
sowers for 471
Seed-bearing plants, number of species 580
Seedbeds
preparing 177
tools for 461, *461*
stale seedbed technique 308, 528, *528*
Seedheads 589
for color 24
decorative, perennials for 141
drying 298, *298*
Seedling crops
cut-and-come-again, sowing 306
growing in containers 307
harvesting 312
sowing in wide drills 306
Seedlings 589
bulb, care *234*
climbers
planting out 109
pricking out 109, *109*
damage caused by cats and dogs 573
damage caused by mice, rats, and voles 568
damage caused by moles 574
damping off 184, 566, *566*
diseases 178, 552
disorders 561
effect of temperature on 556, 570
growth *538*
Seedlings (*cont.*)
hardening off 180, *180*, 311, 453
healthy *538*
netting for 472
pests 550, 572
planting depth, vegetables *306*
planting out 180, *180*, 521
in plugs 176
pricking out 109, *109*, 179, *179*, 452, *452*, 538, 545
alpines 205, *205*
cacti 266, *266*
into pack *179*
shrubs 85
protecting 178, *178*
with netting 472
seasonal water requirements 530
self-sown
annuals 184
biennials 184
transplanting 147, *147*
separating 180
shrub, protecting 85
small, buying 176
supporting 178, *178*
thinning
annuals and biennials 178, *178*
vegetables 306, *306*
transplanting, vegetables 306, *306*
trees 41
pricking out *54*, 55
unhealthy *538*
vegetable, mulching 309
in winter *521*
Seed-tray sowers 471
Seep hoses, see Hoses
Selaginella
suggestions for use 438
kraussiana
in bottle garden *439*
'Aurea', in terrarium *438*, *446*
martensii, in terrarium *438*, *446*
Selection, definition 589
Selenicereus
conditions preferred 261
as rootstock 271
stem cuttings 268
suggestions for use 259
grandiflorus
conditions preferred 261
suggestions for use 262
macdonaldiae, suggestions for use 262
Self-fertile plants, definition 589
Self-heal *578*
Self-layering 588
climbers 109, 112, *112*, 113
Self-pollination 537, 589
Self-seeding, definition 589
Self-sterile plants, definition 589
Semele 97
Semnanthe, division of offsets 269
Sempervivum
conditions tolerated 191, 262
conserving moisture 185
in containers outdoors 260
in dry-stone wall *200*
foliage 185
hardiness 259
propagation
division of offsets 269
leaf cuttings 207
rosette cuttings 207
soil type preferred 146, 193
soil type tolerated 193
suggestions for use 31, 190, 191
arachnoideum
conditions tolerated 262
suggestions for use 190
in trough *199*
montanum *259*
(*entry cont.*)

- *Sempervivum* (*cont.*)
  - *ruthenicum*, conditions tolerated 262
  - *tectorum* *207*
- *Senecio*
  - conditions required 431
  - conditions tolerated 66
  - cultivars, in perennial border *135*
  - lawn as foil to *272*
  - propagation
    - semiripe cuttings 111
    - softwood cuttings 110
    - stem cuttings 268
  - pruning 450
  - in succulent group *259*
  - suggestions for use 97, 175
  - *articulatus* 'Variegatus' *431*
  - *cineraria*, growing as annual 175
  - *confusus* 97
  - *fulgens*, leaf cuttings 267
  - *haworthii*, conditions tolerated 262
  - x *hybridus*
    - as pot plants 175
    - from seed 452
  - *jacobsenii*, leaf cuttings 267
  - *macroglossus* 97
    - 'Variegatus' *110*
      - in containers 96
      - suggestions for use 97
  - *maritima*, foliage 171
  - *microglossus*, conditions tolerated 262
  - *mikanioides* 97
  - *smithii*, suggestions for use 243
  - *tamoides* 97
  - *vulgaris*, see Groundsel
- Sepals 582, *582*, 589
- *Sequoia*, size 32
- *Sequoiadendron giganteum*
  - bonsai *434*
  - suggestions for use 37
- Serbian spruce, see *Picea omorika*
- *Scrissa foetida*, bonsai 434
- Serpentine layering
  - climbers 113, *113*
  - method 539, *539*
- Serviceberry, see *Amelanchier*
- Set, definition 589
- *Setaria glauca*, for drying 175
- *Setiechinopsis mirabilis*, suggestions for use 262
- Seville oranges, see Oranges, sour (Seville)
- Sexual reproduction, definition 589
- Shadbush, see *Amelanchier*
- Shade
  - bulbs tolerant of 213
  - cacti requiring 261
  - climbers providing 94
  - climbers tolerant of 97
  - design and 15
  - dry
    - annuals and biennials tolerant of 175
    - bulbs tolerant of 219
    - perennials tolerant of 141
    - rock plants tolerant of 191
  - ground cover in 173, *173*
  - lawns in 274, 275
  - moist
    - annuals and biennials preferring 175
    - bulbs preferring 219
    - herbs tolerating 288
    - perennials for *138*
    - perennials preferring 141
    - plants for *15*
    - rock plants preferring 191
  - netting to provide 472, *472*
  - on patio 29, 493
  - perennials for 140, 145
  - plants for 17, 519
  - plants preferring 518
  - rushes for 142
  - sedges for 142
  - shrubs tolerant of 62, 64, 66
- Shade (*cont.*)
  - succulents requiring 261
  - succulents tolerant of 262
  - tender bulbs for 218
- Shade cloth, shading greenhouse 544
- Shading
  - blinds for 484, *484*, *486*
  - flexible mesh 484, *484*
  - in greenhouse 481
    - methods 484, *484*
  - greenhouses 544
  - netting for 472, *472*
  - washes for 484, *484*
- Shakers (seed sowers) 471, *471*
- Shallon, see *Gaultheria shallon*
- Shallots *341*, 342, *342*
  - conditions required 342
  - in crop rotation 304
  - culinary uses 342
  - cultivation 342, *342*
  - diseases 342, 569
  - harvesting 342
  - pests 342, 569
  - storing 312, 342
  - in vegetable garden *300*
- Shanking of vines 564, *564*
- Shape
  - contrasting *23*
  - of lawn 273
- Shasta daisy, see *Leucanthemum* x *superbum*
- Shears
  - garden 463, *463*
  - half-moon edger 466, *466*
  - lawn 466, *466*
  - lawn edging 466, *466*
  - long-handled edging 466, *466*
  - long-handled lawn 466, *466*
  - single-handed *463*
  - standard *463*
  - trimming, for bonsai *434*
  - trimming hedge with *60*
- Sheds 513
  - designs 513
  - in garden design *19*
  - materials for 513
  - metal 513
  - paths to 501
  - siding *513*
  - siting 14
  - vinyl 513
  - wood
    - choosing *513*
    - siding *513*
- Sheep laurel, see *Kalmia angustifolia*
- Sheep's sorrel *578*
- Sheet mulches 534, *534*, 589
- Sheets, carrying 470, *470*
- Shelter
  - design and 15
  - hedges as 58
  - trees to provide 36
- Sheltered sites, shrubs preferring 66
- Shelving, for greenhouse *486*, 487
- Shepherd's purse 555, 575, *575*
  - control 276
  - spreading disease 567
- Shield sorrel, see French sorrel
- Shingle fencing 508, *508*
- Shooting star, see *Dodecatheon*
- Shoots 589
  - importance of water to 517
- Shore pine, see *Pinus contorta*
- Short-day plants 303, 338, 341, 349, 351, 518
- *Shortia*
  - *soldanelloides*, soil type required 192
  - *uniflora*, conditions preferred 191
- Showy lady's slipper, see *Cypripedium reginae*
- Shothole 554, *554*
- Shredders 458, 470, *470*
- Shrubby germander, see *Teucrium fruticans*
- Shrubs 61–89
  - for acid soil 62, *62*, 69
  - for alkaline soil 69
  - alpine, repotting 211
  - alpines with *187*
  - antidesiccant spray for 69
  - architectural 66
  - as background 22
  - balled-and-burlapped
    - buying 67, *67*
    - planting 68
  - bare-root
    - buying 67
    - planting 68
  - bark 65
  - berries 65
  - borders of 62–3
    - design for *63*
  - broad-leaved 585
  - choosing 61, 67, *67*
  - for clay soil 67
  - climbers growing through 95, 106
  - clipping, for topiary 91, *91*
  - in cold greenhouse 430
  - in cold storage 515
  - container-grown
    - buying healthy plants 548
    - planting 68, *68*
  - in containers 26, 64, 65
    - buying 67, *67*
    - care 70, 71, *71*
    - feeding 69, 71
    - planting 69, *69*
    - plants suitable 65
    - repotting 71, *71*
    - root pruning 80
    - soil mix for 69
    - top dressing 71, *71*
    - watering 71
  - contrasting forms 24
  - coppicing 77, *77*, 586
  - damage caused by animals
    - deer 572
    - mice, rats, and voles 568
  - deadheading 70, *70*
  - deciduous
    - interest 61
    - pruning 74–6, *74–6*
      - hard, in spring *74*, 75
      - minimal 74, *74*, 75
      - spring 74, *74*, 75
      - summer 76, *76*
    - renovation 80
  - definition 61, 589
  - as design features 61
  - designing with 61–5
  - diseases 72, 562
    - bacterial 554, 561, 567, 571
    - fungal 552, 554, 560, 561, 562, 564, 567, 570, 571
  - distinguishing from trees 32, 61
  - dwarf 64, 191
    - in alpine house 190
    - pruning 203, *203*
    - in rock garden *185*
  - effect of temperature on 556, 570
  - evergreen
    - interest 61
    - pruning 74, 77–8, *78*
    - renovation 80
    - snow damage to *517*
  - existing, in garden design 17
  - exposure 62
  - for fall color 25
  - fan-training 79, *79*
  - fast-growing, in borders 63
  - fastigiate 587
  - feeding 70
  - flowers 65
    - scent 65
  - foliage 64
  - form 61
  - in formal bedding 30
  - as foundation planting 61
  - in framed planting *21*
  - as framework *16*
  - in garden design *19*
- Shrubs (*cont.*)
  - ground cover 64, *64*, 151
    - pruning 151, *151*
  - guarantees on buying 67
  - half-standard 587
  - hardiness 62
  - hardy, for wall-training 78
  - herbs 287
  - indoor
    - cuttings 453
    - pruning 450
    - supports for 450
  - informal planting *61*, *273*
  - in island beds 63
  - in layer planting 23, 26
  - life expectancy 16
  - male and female 65
  - mineral deficiency 556–7
  - miniature, in troughs 190
  - in mixed border *20*, 63, 136, *137*, 139
  - mulching 70
  - neglected, pruning 73
  - in neglected garden 13
  - nonvariegated shoots, removing *70*
  - for parterres 31
  - pests 72, 559, 560, 566, 571, 572
    - affecting flowers 563
    - damaging leaves 550, 551, 552, 553, 554, 557–8
  - physical damage 72
  - pinching out 450
  - planning positions of 19
  - planter's guide 66
  - planting 68–9, *68*
    - in clay soil 68
    - time for 68
  - pollarding 77, *77*
  - pricking out 85, *85*
  - problems 72
    - affecting stems and leaf buds 559–61
  - propagation 81–9
    - air layering 86, *87*, 539
    - cuttings 53, 81–4, *81–4*, 453
      - hardwood 83–4, *84*
      - heel 82, 83, *83*
      - leaf-bud 83, *83*
      - mallet 83, *83*
      - nodal 82
      - root 84
      - semiripe 82–3, *82*
      - softwood 81, *81*
    - division 81, 88, *88*
    - dropping 86
    - grafting 81, 88–9, *89*
      - apical wedge 89, *89*
      - saddle 88, *89*
      - side-veneer 88
    - layering 81, 86–8, *86–7*
      - dropping 86
      - French 87
      - mound 297, *297*
      - simple 86, *86*
      - stooling 87, *87*
      - tip 86, 539
    - from seed 81, 84–5, *85*
      - sowing
        - in containers 85, *85*
        - outdoors 85
    - stooling 87, *87*
    - suckering, division 88, *88*
  - protecting, newly planted 69
  - pruning 73–80, 450
    - after planting *68*
    - bad 570
    - coppicing 77, *77*
    - formative 73–4, *73*
    - minimal *74*, 75
    - of neglected plants 73
    - pollarding 77, *77*
    - principles 73, *73*
    - root 71, 80
    - in spring 74, *74*, 75
    - suckering habit 76, *76*
    - in summer 76, *76*
    - wall 78–9, *79*
- Shrubs (*cont.*)
  - renovation 20, 80, *80*
    - drastic 80, *80*
    - gradual 80, *80*
  - reversion 70, *70*
    - removing shoots *70*
  - in rock garden 22, *185*
  - on roof garden *29*
  - root pruning 80
  - roses with 117
  - routine care 70–72
  - for sandy soil 67
  - scale and height 22
  - scented 65, 66
  - scrambling, training 79
  - seed, requiring special treatment 85
  - seedlings, protecting 85
  - for shade 64, 66
  - size 61
  - small, protecting *520*, 521
  - in soil beds under cover 439
  - soil for 62
  - soil preparation 67, 68
  - on south-facing walls 519
  - specimen 63–4, *64*
    - siting 64
  - staking 69, *69*
  - standard 590
    - staking 69, *69*
    - training and pruning 80
  - stem structure *580*
  - stems 65
  - structural planting *22*
  - successional interest 62
  - suckers, removing 70, *70*
  - suggestions for use 61–5
  - suiting to site 62
  - on supports, training 73, 450
  - tender, training 78
  - testing for live wood 77
  - topiary 90–91
  - training 73–80
    - principles 73
    - for topiary 90, *90*
  - transplanting 72, *72*
  - two or more seasons of interest 66
  - underplanting roses 117
  - variegated, reversion 70, *70*
  - wall 64, *64*, 66
    - effect of sun on 518
    - planting *68*, 69
    - protecting *520*, 521
    - pruning 78–9, *79*
    - with roses 118
    - training 78–9, *79*
  - watering 70
  - weeding 70, 577
  - as weeds 576
  - wind, tolerant of 521
  - for winter color 26
  - winter protection 72
  - for woodland garden 27
  - young, protecting from cold *521*
- Siberian bugloss, see *Brunnera macrophylla*
- Siberian flag, see *Iris sibirica*
- Siberian squill, see *Scilla siberica*
- *Sidalcea*
  - division 163
  - flowering time from seed 160
  - soil type tolerated 147
- Side-veneer grafting, see Grafting, side-veneer
- Siding *513*
- Sieves 471, *471*
- *Silene*
  - flowering time from seed 160
  - Irishman's cuttings 208
  - *acaulis*
    - softwood cuttings 206
    - suggestions for use 191
  - *armeria*, self-seeding 178
  - *coeli-rosa*, sowing 177
  - *schafta*
    - soil type tolerated 193
    - suggestions for use 190

(*entry cont. overleaf*)

Silene (*cont.*)
vulgaris subsp. *maritima*
conditions tolerated 191
'Flore Pleno', suggestions for use 191
Silicon dioxide 550, 568
Silk-tassel bush, see *Garrya elliptica*
Silphium perfoliatum, growth rate 141
Silts
capping 529, *529*
improving texture 529
structure 524, *524*
water table 530
Silver fir, see *Abies*
Silver lace vines, see *Polygonum aubertii*; *P. baldschuanicum*
Silver linden, see *Tilia tomentosa*
Silver maple, see *Acer saccharinum*
Silver wattle, see *Acacia dealbata*
Silver-bell, see *Halesia*
Silver-leaved plants
conditions suited to 139
for greenhouse 218
underplanting roses 117
Silybum marianum
architectural plant 175
self-seeding 178
Sinarundinaria nitida, conditions tolerated 143
Single cordons, see Cordons
Single-seed hawthorn, see *Crataegus monogyna*
Sinks and washtubs
alpines in 186, 198–9
care 203–4
planting 199
covering with hypertufa 198, *198*
miniature roses in 119
rock plants in 198–9
planting 199
Sinningia
conditions preferred 431
conditions required 431
pests 562
propagation
leaf cuttings 541
from seed 452
pusilla, suggestions for use 438
'Red Flicker' *431*
speciosa
basal cuttings 238
leaf cuttings 454
Sissinghurst, Kent 139
Sisyrinchium
soil type preferred 146
bellum, conditions tolerated 167
'E.K. Balls', in trough *199*
striatum
conditions tolerated 141
'Aunt May', planting depth *146*
Site
appraising 15
changes in level 17
clearing 145
design in relation to 14, 17
leveling 13, 276–7, *276*, *277*
marking out 19
measuring 17
natural features, making most of *17*
neglected, weeding 579
overgrown, clearing 526, *526*
uncultivated, clearing 579
weed clearance 526, *526*, 576, 579
Sitka spruce, see *Picea sitchensis*
Skimmia
conditions preferred 66
flower sexuality 582
propagation
layering 86
semiripe cuttings with heel 83
Skimmia (*cont.*)
japonica
flower sexuality *582*
'Fragrans', in shrub border *63*
subsp. *reevesiana*, in shrub border *63*
Skunks 549, *549*, 572
Slaked lime 533
Slender speedwell 578
control 578, 579
in lawn 286
Slime flux 559, *559*, 561
Slime molds 555, 567, 573, *573*
Slitter, star-wheeled 467, *467*
Sloe, see *Prunus spinosa*
Slopes
building steps into 503, *503*
creating 277, *277*
decking for 500
dwarf conifers for 38
erecting fences on 510, *510*
growing vegetables on 301
incorporating in design 17
lawn on 272
peat beds on 202
retaining walls on 506, *506*
treatment of 17
trees for 39
Slug pellets 405
Slugs 204, 547, *568*
control 310, 550, 568
damage caused 153, 550, *550*, 568
under plastic film 309
Slugworm, pear and cherry 553, *553*
Small gardens
fruit in 355, 358, *358*
fruit tree forms for 356, *356*
herbs in 288
trees for 37
Smilacina
dividing 163
racemosa, conditions tolerated 141
Smithiantha, greenhouse conditions required 431
Smoke tree, see *Cotinus coggygria*
Smooth cypress, see *Cupressus glabra*
Smuts 565, *565*
Snag, definition 589
Snails 204, 547
checking aquatics for eggs of 251
control 310, 550
damage caused 153, 550, *550*
in pond 253
trapdoor, in pond 253
Snakebark maple, see *A. davidii*; *A. grosseri* var. *hersii*
Snake's-head fritillary, see *Fritillaria meleagris*
Snap beans, see Beans, snap
Snapdragon, see *Antirrhinum*
Sneezeweed, see *Helenium*
Snow
damage caused by 517, *517*
protecting topiary from 91
protection from 69, *521*
protection provided by 517, *517*
Snow fence *521*
Snow frame *521*
Snow gum, see *Eucalyptus niphophila*
Snow mold 282, 286, 573, *573*
Snowbell, see *Soldanella*
Snowdrop, see *Galanthus*
Snowflake, see *Leucojum*
Snow-in-summer, see *Cerastium tomentosum*
Soakaways 531, *531*
Soap, insecticidal 550, 551, 552, 558, 560, 563, 564, 567
commercial names 574
use with biological control 548
Soapwort, see *Saponaria*
Sod
commercially grown 27
fine grass 278
laying 278–9, *278*
lifting 279, *279*
trimming after 279, *279*
meadow 278
moving 20, 279, *279*
shaping edge 279, *279*
sizes 278
storing 278, *278*
types 278
Soft fruit, see Fruit, soft
Soft scale 554, *554*
biological control 548
Softwood cuttings, see Cuttings, softwood
Soil 524–36
acid, see Acid soil
acidity
altering 120
deficiencies caused by 525
effect of fertilizers on 70
additives 529, *529*
benefits 529
problems with 529
top-dressings as 534, *534*
aeration 585
improving 529
alkaline, see Alkaline soil
alkalinity
deficiencies caused by 525
increasing 525, 533
blue mottling *529*
calcium in 525
capillary pores 530
capping 529, *529*
changing grade around tree 46, *46*
characteristics 524
chemical clearance 526, *526*
clay, see Clay soil
compacted *529*
additives for 529
conditioning 576
crumb formation 529, *529*
cultivation 526–9
deep-bed system 536, *536*
no-till system 536, *536*
schedule 20
damaging physical structure of 302
diseases 525
drainage 145, 524
improving 531, *531*
installing 531, *531*
testing 531
erosion
caused by wind 519
on slopes 301
fertility, organisms important to 525
friable 587
frost, effect of 294, 517
good *529*
in greenhouse borders, becoming infected 486
hardpan *529*
heavy 587
cultivating in wet weather 529
improving 62, 145, 524
for lawn 276
for roses 120
improving drainage 529
improving structure *528*, 529
increasing water available in 517
layers 525, *525*
light 588
liming 533, *533*
maintaining fertility 301–2
medium 588
moisture conservation 308, *308*
moisture take-up 530
neutral 588
nutrients 309, 524, 532–3
organic matter 301
organisms 525
beneficial 525, *525*
pests 310, 525
Soil (*cont.*)
pH level 15, 525, 588
adjusting 360
effect of 525
effect of fertilizers on 70
high, problems caused by 533
for lawn 276
optimum 525
scale 525
testing *525*
poor 529, *529*
pores 530
preparing 20
for lawn 276
preserving structure 302
problems *529*
problems caused by 547
profile 525, *525*
regional differences 522–3
for rock garden 196
rose-sick 120
rototilling
to clear overgrown site 526, *526*
for weed control 577, 579
sandy, see Sandy soil
for scree bed 196
sterilizing 439, 526, *526*
structure 524–5, *524*
improving *528*, 529
water content and 528–9
subsoil 590
in design 17
in soil profile 525, *525*
temperature 305
importance of 515
testing 15, 145
thermometer for 471
thin 590
tilth 528, *528*, 590
topsoil, in soil profile 525, *525*, 590
types 15, 524
identifying 525, *525*
water content 528–9, 530
water retention 529, 530
improving 529
waterlogged 529, *529*, 557
damage to plants 517
indications of 531
perennials tolerant of 146
plants adapted to 517
problems 531
shrubs tolerant of 67
symptoms 566, *566*, 570, *570*
treatment for 530, 531, *531*, 570
vulnerable areas 531
well-structured *529*
Soil bench, see Bench beds
Soil blocks, sowing seed in 307
Soil mark, definition 589
Soil mixes 535–6, 589
for alpines 211, 212, 536
bulb fiber 536
for bulbs in pots 228
for cacti 263, 264, 535
Cornell Peatlite 536
for cuttings 110
ericaceous 536
for ferns 158
for indoor plants 436, 439
loam-based 436, 439
for orchids 440, *440*, 536
for peat beds 202
peat-based 436
potting 535–6, 538, 589
definition 589
peat substitutes 536
pH range 545
soil-based 535
soilless 535, 589
disadvantages 535
feeding plants in 535
types 535
propagation 536
moisture 545
standard cuttings 536
standard seed 536
for rock garden 196
Soil mixes (*cont.*)
for rooted cuttings 541
for scree bed 196
seed 536, 538
for bulbs 234
firming 545, *545*
for shrubs 69
special 536
sterilizing 159
for succulents 263, 264
types 535
universal 536
Solanaceous crops, in crop rotation 304
Solandra 97
semiripe cuttings 111
maxima
for fragrance 97
pruning 103, 105
vigor 98
Solanum
growth rate 97
propagation
root cuttings 112
semiripe cuttings 111
simple layering 113
softwood cuttings 110
pruning 105
x *burbankii*, see Wonderberries
capsicastrum
conditions preferred 431
indoors 426
crispum *103*
pruning 103
spring *102*
softwood cuttings *110*
soil type tolerated 100
'Glasnevin', suggestions for use 66
jasminoides
pruning 103
suggestions for use 66
melongena, see Eggplants
pseudocapsicum
conditions preferred 431
indoors 426
tuberosum, see Potatoes
wendlandii
pruning 450
soil type tolerated 99
vigor 98
Soldanella
alpina
in alpine raised bed *201*
suggestions for use 191
montana, suggestions for use 191
villosa, soil type required 192
Soleirolia soleirolii (syn. *Helxine soleirolii*)
foliage 426
in terrarium *438*
suggestions for use 438
Solid fuel, for greenhouse heating 482
Solidago
for cutting 141
division 163
for drying 141
canadensis, growth rate 141
Sollya, softwood cuttings 110
Solomon's seal, see *Polygonatum*
Somatic embryogenesis 546
Sonerila
softwood cuttings 453
margaritacea, suggestions for use 438
Sooty molds 547, 552, 553, 554
Sophora japonica, conditions tolerated 37
Sorbaria, pruning 74
Sorbus
berries 35
cultivars, conditions tolerated 37
diseases 555, 570, 571
extracting seed 54

(*entry cont.*)

Sorbus (*cont.*)
for fall color 35
pricking out *54*
propagation
chip-budding 56
from seed 54, *54*
side-veneer grafting 56
seed germination 55
aria
for avenues 36
conditions tolerated 37
soil type tolerated 41
suggestions for use 37
'Lutescens', foliage 35
aucuparia 22
conditions tolerated 37
pests 558
suggestions for use 33, 37
cashmiriana, suggestions for use 37
commixta 'Embley', suggestions for use 37
intermedia, conditions tolerated 37
reducta 191
vilmorinii, suggestions for use 438
Sorrel (herb) *293*
conditions tolerated 288
culinary uses 293
dye from 287
foliage 293
harvesting 293
in herb garden *295*
propagation
division 293
from seed 293
protection for winter 293
related species 293
removing flowering stems 296
storing 293
Sorrel (weed) *578*, 579
Sorrel tree, see *Oxydendrum arboreum*
Southern beech, see *Nothofagus*
Southern blight 560
Southern magnolia, see *Magnolia grandiflora*
Southernwood, see *Artemisia abrotanum*
Sowbugs 547, 550, *550*
Sowing, tools for 471, *471*
Spacing, planning 26
Spades 459, *459*
automatic *459*
blades 459, *459*, 527
border 459, *459*
hilts 459, *459*
Spaghetti squash, see Squash, summer
Spanish bluebell, see *Hyacinthoides hispanica*
Spanish broom, see *Spartium junceum*
Spanish chestnuts, see Chestnuts
Spanish-bayonet, see *Yucca aloifolia*
Spanish-dagger, see *Yucca gloriosa*
Sparaxis
conditions preferred 219
for cutting 219
Sparganium
erectum (syn. *S. ramosum*), in water garden 243
minimum, position in water garden 243
ramosum, see *S. erectum*
Sparmannia
conditions preferred indoors 431
softwood cuttings 453
Spartium
conditions tolerated 66
junceum, soil type preferred 67
Spathiphyllum
conditions preferred 427, 431
conditions required 431
hydroculture 431
Spatterdock, see *Nuphar luteum*
Species, definition 582, 589
Specimen plants 23, *23*, 589
apples 375
architectural perennials 141
backdrop to 140
bulbs with 216
dwarf conifers 38, *38*
fruit trees 355, 358
grasses 142
herbs 288
indoors 426
in lawn *142*, 273
perennials 140
roses 117
shrubs 63–4, *64*
in containers 65
trees 37
Speedwell, see *Veronica*
slender, see Slender speedwell
Spent mushroom compost, see Mushroom compost
Spermatozoids 159
Sphaeralcea, stem tip cuttings 164
Sphaerotheca 552
macularis 564
Sphagnum moss, see Moss, sphagnum
Spickels 558
Spider flower, see *Cleome*
Spider mites 232, 447, 552
control 388, 398, 552
biological 548
damage caused by 552
deterring 310
immunity to pesticides 549
Spider plant, see *Chlorophytum comosum*
Spiders
benefits of *549*
garden *549*
Spiderwort, see *Tradescantia*
Spikelet, definition 589
Spikes (flowers) 582, 589
Spilocaea
pomi 555
pyracanthae 555
Spinach *321*, 325, *325*
cultivation 325
as cut-and-come again crop 325
harvesting 325
nitrogen requirement 310, 325
recommended cultivars 325
storing 312, 325
in vegetable garden *300*
watering, critical periods 308
winter cropping under cover 311
African, see *Amaranthus*
Ceylon, see Malabar spinach
Chinese, see *Amaranthus tricolor*
Indian, see Malabar spinach
New Zealand, see New Zealand spinach
vine, see Malabar spinach
Spinach beets 322
culinary uses 322
cultivation 322
harvesting 322
nitrogen requirement 310, 322
storing 312, 322
Spinach mustard, see Komatsuna
Spinacia oleracea, see Spinach
Spines 581
Spiraea
conditions tolerated 66
in mixed border *137*
propagation
hardwood cuttings 84
mallet cuttings 83
semiripe cuttings 83
pruning *74*
x *arguta*, pruning 76
douglasii, pruning 74
japonica
division of suckers 88
Spiraea japonica (*cont.*)
pruning 74
'Goldflame'
in container 65
foliage 64
prunifolia, pruning 76
thunbergii, pruning 76
Spirit level *246*, *276*, 277, *277*, 493, *493*, *494*, 495, *495*
Spirobolus 550
Spirogyra, control 254, *254*
Spit, definition 589
Spittlebugs 560, *560*
Splice grafting, see Grafting, basal-whip
Splitwood fencing 508, *508*
Sporangium 159, 589
Spores 589
fern propagation by 159, *159*
Sports 582, *582*
reverting to type 70
Sports fields 274
mowing 281
Spotted cucumber beetles 149, 563
larvae 566
Spraing 568, *568*
Spray, definition 589–90
Sprayers 468, *468*
compression types 468, *468*
knapsack *468*
trigger-pump *468*
Spraying, chemicals, safety precautions 549
Spreaders, fertilizer 467, *467*
Sprekelia
conditions required 431
growing with succulents 260
pests 569
Sprigging, establishing lawn by 279, *279*
Spring
annuals for 171
in containers 174
climbers for color in 96
color in 25, *25*
mixed plantings for 214, *215*
perennials for 139
shrubs flowering in 62
shrubs for interest in 66
tasks for 583
trees for interest in 35
Spring snowflake, see *Leucojum vernum*
Sprinklers 469, *469*
oscillating 469, *469*
pulse jet 469, *469*
rotating 469, *469*
standing 469, *469*
traveling 469
underground 282, 469
Sprouting broccoli 317
in crop rotation 304
culinary uses 317
cultivation 317
harvesting 317
mineral deficiencies 558
nitrogen requirement 310, 317
pests 563
purple *317*
recommended cultivars 317
storing 312, 317
in vegetable garden *300*
'Purple Sprouting' *317*
Spruce, see *Picea*
Spur, definition 589
Spur blight 559
Spurge, see *Euphorbia*
Spurge-laurel, see *Daphne laureola*
Squash
curing 312
diseases 565
growing flowers with *303*
pests 563
sowing 306
storing 312
Squash, summer *328*, 332, *332*
bush *332*
crookneck, fruit 332
Squash, summer (*cont.*)
in crop rotation 304
culinary uses 332
cultivation 328, 332
custard, fruits 332
flowers
distinguishing female from male 332, *332*
harvesting 332
habit 332
harvesting 332
nitrogen requirement 310, 332
pests 332, 553, 559
pollinating, by hand 332, *332*
recommended cultivars 332
sowing 332
spaghetti 332
storing 312
trailing types, training 332
'Early White Bush' *332*
'Vegetable Spaghetti' *332*
Squash, winter 331, *331*
Acorn types 331
in crop rotation 304
cultivation 331, *331*
curing 312, 328, 331, *331*
fruit 331
habit 331
harvesting 331
nitrogen requirements 310, 331
pests 553, 559, 571
recommended cultivars 331
sowing 306, 331
storing 312, 331
'Buttercup' *331*
'Sweet Dumpling' *331*
Squash vine borers 553, 559
Squill, see *Scilla*
Squirrels 565, *565*, 572
Squirreltail grass, see *Hordeum jubatum*
Stachys
dividing 157
soil type tolerated 147
byzantina (syn. *S. lanata*) 117
conditions tolerated 141
division 163
'Silver Carpet'
suggestions for use 140
winter interest 141
lanata, see *S. byzantina*
Stachyurus, layering 86
Staff tree, see *Celastrus scandens*
Staff vine, see *Celastrus orbiculatus*
Staghorn fern, see *Platycerium*
Staghorn sumac, see *Rhus typhina*
Staging for greenhouse
positioning 487
types *486*, 487, *487*
Stains, applying to wood decking 500
Stakes 472, *472*
bamboo 472, *472*
link 156, *156*, *472*
preserving 122
ring 156, *156*, *472*
single 156, *156*
split *472*
twigs 156
Staking 472, *472*
annuals 182, *182*, 183, *183*
climbers 92, 98
climbing annuals 182, *182*, 183, *183*
framework for climbers under cover 450, *450*
house plants 436, *436*
perennials 156, *156*
shrubs 69, *69*
trees 40, *40*
Stale seedbed technique 167, 308, 528, *528*
Stalks, definition 590
Stamens *537*, 582, *582*, 590
Standard 590
Stanhopea
flowering 441
in hanging basket 441, *441*
Stanhopea (*cont.*)
tigrina, in hanging basket *441*
Stapelia
propagation
division of offsets 269
division of rootstock 270
stem cuttings 268
as rootstock 271
Staples, U- 376
Star jasmine, see *Trachelospermum jasminoides*
Star magnolia, see *Magnolia stellata*
Star-of-Bethlehem, see *Ornithogalum*
Starvation of lawn, symptoms and control 573
Star-wheeled cultivator 461, *461*
Star-wheeled slitter *467*
Statice, see *Psylliostachys*
Station sowing, definition 590
Statues
in alcoves 22
framed by climbers *93*
framed by hedge *13*
in lawn 273
Stauntonia 97
semiripe cuttings 111
Steel
for greenhouses *478*, 479
sheds of 513
for tools 459
Stellaria media, see Common chickweed
Stem borers 559, *559*
Stem cuttings, see Cuttings, stem
Stem sections, propagation of succulents by 268, *268*
Stem tip cuttings, see Cuttings, stem tip
Stem tubers 543, *543*
propagation 543
Stem vegetables 341–7
temperature requirements 303
Stem wilt 547
Stems 590
abnormal growth 561
cell types in 580
for color 24, *25*, 26
discoloration 548
problems causing 559–60
distortion 561
herbaceous
strengthening tissue in *580*
structure *580*
modified 581
as bulb, structure *580*
ornamental, in winter 62
pith 589
purpose 580–81
types *580*
woody *580*
Steneotarsonemus laticeps 558
Stenotaphrum secundatum, for lawns 274, 275
Stephanandra
pruning 76
stooling 87
Stephanitis
pyroides 552
rhododendri 552
Stephanotis 97
propagation
semiripe cuttings 111
softwood cuttings 453
pruning 103
floribunda *97*
for fragrance 97
in indoor hanging garden *428*
pruning 450
suggestions for use 97
Stepping stones
of decking *500*
paths of 501

Steps
  building 503
    into bank *503*
  materials for 501
  tread to riser ratio 503, *503*
  uses 492, 501
Sterile plants, definition 590
Sterilization of soil 526, *526*
Sternbergia
  chipping 237
  suggestions for use 219
  lutea
    conditions preferred 219
    conditions tolerated 219
    in mixed border 215
    in rock garden 187
    suggestions for use 219
  sicula
    conditions preferred 219
    in mixed border 215
    suggestions for use 219
Stewartia
  flowers 35
  soil preferred 41
  pseudocamellia
    seasonal interest 37
    suggestions for use 37
Stigma *267*, *537*, 582, *582*, 590
Stigmaphyllon 97
  semiripe cuttings 111
  ciliatum
    conditions tolerated 97
    growth rate 97
    pruning 105
Stinking hellebore, see *Helleborus foetidus*
Stipa pennata, for drying 175
Stock, see *Matthiola*
Stock plant, definition 590
Stokesia, for cutting 141
Stolonizing, establishing lawn by 279
Stolons 590
  weeds with *576*
Stomata 517, 581, *581*
Stomatium, division of offsets 269
Stone, see also Rocks
  crushed 499
    for foundations 493, *493*, 494, *504*
    as top-dressing 534
  dressed 496
  natural
    for paving 496
    raised beds of 507
  natural strata 193, *193*
  paths of *501*
  for rock garden 193, *193*
Stone chips, as top-dressing 534
Stone fruits, see also Fruit, tree; individual fruits by name
  bottling 367
  danger of bark-ringing 366
  definition 355, 371, 590
  diseases 362
  grafting 543
  pests 564
  renovation 366
  propagation, from seed 537
Stone plant, see *Lithops*
Stonecrop, see *Sedum*
Stool (plant), definition 590
Stooling 297, 590, see also Mound layering
  method 539, *539*
  shrubs 87, *87*
Stools, kneeling 470, *470*
Stopping, see Pinching out
Storage
  bulbs 231, *231*
  chemicals 549
  fruit 367, *367*
  seed, tree 54
  of sod 278, *278*
Storage organs, propagation 542–3
Storage rots 569, *569*
Strain, definition 590
Strap cactus, see *Epiphyllum*
Stratification 54, 85, 132, 537, 581, 590
  alpines 205
  annuals and biennials 179
  cold 538, *538*
  perennials 160
  shrubs 85
  warm 538
Stratiotes aloides 243
  choosing healthy plants *251*
  introducing into pond *252*
  propagation by offsets 257
Straw
  as additive, problems 529
  plunging bulbs in 229, *229*
  as protection from cold *520*, 521
Strawberries 404–6, *404*
  advancing ripening 405
  alpine *356*, 406
    conditions tolerated 406
    cropping 404
    edging bed 355
    flavor 406
    in herb garden *287*
    propagation, from seed 370, 406, *406*
    recommended cultivars 405
    suggestions for use 358, 406
  choosing cultivars 404
  choosing healthy plants *404*
  clearing foliage after harvesting 406, *406*
  in containers 288, 359
  cultivation 404–6
  diseases 363, 405, 557, 562, 564, 565
  drainage 404
  everbearing
    cropping 404
    recommended cultivars 405
  feeding 362, 406
  flavor
    enhancing 405
    of fruit under cover 405
  freezing 367, 405
  growing under cover 359, 405
  harvesting 367, 405, *405*
  mineral deficiency 560
  netting *363*
  perpetual-fruiting, see everbearing
  pests 405, 550, 551, 566, 572
  plant types 356, 404
  propagation 406, *406*
    natural layering 539, *539*
    runners 370, *406*
  protecting 405, *405*, 521, *521*
    from cold 363
  recommended cultivars 405
  routine care 405
  runners
    growing plants from 405
    removing 405, *405*
  storing 405
  suggestions for use 358
  summer-fruiting
    cropping 404
    recommended cultivars 405
  transplanting 357
  windbreaks for 519
  in windowbox *303*
  'Allstar' *405*
  'Cardinal' *405*
  'Honeoye' *405*
  'Kent', in large fruit garden *357*
Strawberry beetles 405
Strawberry green petal 557, 562
Strawberry jars 288, 359
  replanting herbs in *296*
  in winter 190
Strawberry mats 405, *405*
Strawberry tree, see *Arbutus unedo*
Strawflower, see *Helichrysum bracteatum*
Streams 28, 241
  informal *240*
  plantings beside *167*
Strelitzia
  conditions required 431
  in greenhouse 430
Streptocarpus
  conditions preferred 431
  conditions required 431
  in garden room *426*
  in greenhouse *429*
  hydroculture 431
  in indoor plant group *444*
  pests 562
  propagation
    leaf cuttings 541
    leaf sections *454*, 455
  in soil bench *439*
  'Heidi', in conservatory *429*
  saxorum, leaf cuttings 267
Streptomyces scabies 568
Streptosolen
  conditions required 431
  pruning 103
  softwood cuttings 110, 453
  jamesonii
    pruning 103
    soil type tolerated 99
    suggestions for use 97
String, for ties 472
String beans, see Beans, snap
Striped cucumber beetles 571, *571*
Striped squill, see *Puschkinia scilloides*
Stromanthe, division of rootstock 451
Strombocactus disciformis *259*, 262
Strongylodon 97
  propagation
    semiripe cuttings 111
    simple layering 113
  pruning 103
  macrobotrys
    growth rate 97
    pruning 105
Strophocactus, apical-wedge grafting 271
Structural planting 22, *22*
Structures 492–513
  designing with 492
  repairing 20
  selecting materials for 492
  sequence of projects 492
Stylar column *582*, 590
Style, definition 590
Stylophorum diphyllum, conditions preferred 191
Styrax
  japonica, soil type preferred 41
  officinalis, soil type required 69
Suaeda
  fruticosa, conditions tolerated 262
  maritima, conditions tolerated 262
Subfamily, definition 590
Sublaterals, definition 590
Subshrub, definition 590
Subsoil, see Soil
Subspecies, definition 590
Subtropical plants
  flowering, conditions required 436
  foliage, conditions tolerated 436
Successional interest 25
Succulents 258–71
  adapted to drought 517
  buying 263, *263*
  caudiciform 258
  characteristics 258, 590
  choosing 263, *263*
  compatible nonsucculents 259
  conditions preferred 427
  conditions required 259, 265
  conditions tolerated 258, 259
  in containers
    indoors 261
    outdoors 260, *260*
    planting 264, *264*
  cross-pollination 267, *267*
Succulents (*cont.*)
  damp conditions, tolerant of 262
  in desert gardens 260, *260*
  designing with 258–61
  diseases 265
  disorders 554
  distinguishing features of cacti 258
  environment 265
  epiphytic, conditions required 261
  feeding 265
  flowering 259, *259*
  flowers 258
  forms 258–9, *259*
  grafting, varieties suitable for 271
  groups 258
  habit 258–9
  habitats 258
  half-hardy *259*
    conditions required 259
  in hanging baskets 261, *261*, 262
    planting 264, *264*
  hardy *259*
  hybridizing 267, *267*
  hygiene 265
  indoor display 260–61
  leaf succulents 258
  light requirement 261
  low temperatures, tolerant of 262
  offset tubers 269, *269*
  outdoor display 259–60
  pests 265, 552, 554, 559
  physiological disorders 557
  planting 263, *263*
  pots for 264
  propagation 266–71
    division
      of offsets 269, *269*
      of rootstock 270, *270*
    flat grafting 271, *271*
    grafting 270–71, *270–71*
    hybridization 267, *267*
    leaf cuttings 267, *267*
    offsets 269, *269*
    pad sections *268*
    from seed 266–7, *266*
    side grafting 271, *271*
    stem cuttings 268, *268*
    stem sections 268, *268*
  repotting 265, *265*
  routine care 265
  shade, tolerant of 262
  shading 265
  shapes 258
  soil mixes for 263, 264
  stem succulents 258
  suggestions for use 258–61
  temperatures for 265
  trailing 259
  ventilation 265
  watering 265
  water-storage 258
Suckers 590
  propagation by
    fruit 370
    raspberries 410, *410*
    roses 131, *131*
    shrubs 88, *88*
  recognizing *70*
  removing
    raspberries 409, *409*
    shrubs 70, *70*
    trees 45, *45*
  rose 122
    recognizing 123
  tree 50
Sugar loaf chicory, see Chicory, sugar loaf
Sugared almonds, see *Pachyphytum oviferum*
Sulcorebutia
  propagation
    division
      of offsets 269
      of rootstock 270
    flat grafting 271
Sulcorebutia (*cont.*)
  glomeriseta, suggestions for use 262
  steinbachii, suggestions for use 262
Sulfur 548, 552, 554
  commercial names 574
  as fungicide 554, 569
  plant requirements 532
Sumac, see *Rhus*
Summer
  annuals for *170*, 171
    in containers 174
  climbers for color in 96
  color in 25, *25*
  mixed plantings for 215, *215*
  perennials for 139
  shrubs flowering in 62
  shrubs for interest in 66
  tasks for 583–4
  trees for interest in 35
Summer hyacinth, see *Galtonia candicans*
Summer purslane
  culinary uses 327
  cultivation 327
  golden *327*
  harvesting 327
  types 327
  in vegetable garden *300*
Summer savory
  flavor 293
  flowers 293
  in herb garden *295*
Summer snowflake, see *Leucojum aestivum*
Summer squash, see Squash, summer
Summersweet, see *Clethra alnifolia*
Sun, see also Sunshine
  cacti for containers in 262
  ground cover in 173
  house plants for 427
  perennials for *139*, 145
  scorch from 398
  shrubs for 62
  succulents for containers in 262
Sunberries, see Wonderberries
Sunchokes, see Jerusalem artichokes
Sundew, see *Drosera*
Sundial, beside pool *241*
Sunflower, see *Helianthus*
Sunken gardens 31
  for roses 117
    terraced surround for 117
Sunlight
  plants growing toward 518
  value of 518
Sunshine, see also Sun
  design and 15
  excessive, problems of 518
  importance to plants 515
  plants thriving in 518
Superphosphate 223, 309, 362, 556
Superphosphate of lime
  nutrient content 532
  in soil mixes 536
Supports, see also Staking
  arches, constructing 512
  pergolas, constructing 511–12
  pillars, constructing 512
  preparing for fruit trees 360
  trellis, erecting 511
  tripods, constructing 512
Surface floaters, see Floating aquatics
Surfaces 492–503
  concrete 494
  designing with 492
  load-bearing foundations 494
  natural stone 496
  paving slabs 495–6
  random paving 496
  selecting materials for 492
  tile 496

Swamp lily, see *Saururus cernuus*
Swan River daisy, see *Brachycome iberidifolia*
Swedish ivy, see *Plectranthus oertendahlii*
Swedish whitebeam, see *Sorbus intermedia*
Sweepers, lawn 467, *467*
Sweet alyssum, see *Lobularia maritima*
Sweet bay, see *Laurus nobilis*
Sweet box, see *Sarcococca*
Sweet cicely *292*
conditions tolerated 288
culinary uses 292
flavor 292
flowers 292
foliage 292
harvesting 292
in herb garden *295*
propagation from seed 292
self-seeding 292
storing 292
Sweet corn *328*, 335, *335*
baby-corn 335
conditions required 335
in crop rotation 304
cultivation 328, 335
description 335
diseases 565
harvesting 335
intercropping *304*
nitrogen requirement 310, 335
ornamental, see *Zea mays*
herbs with *303*
recommended cultivars *335*
sowing
depth 305
through plastic 309
storing 312, 335
testing for ripeness *335*
vegetable garden *300*
'Earlivee' *335*
Sweet fennel, see Fennel, Florence
Sweet flag, see *Acorus calamus* 'Variegatus'
Sweet gum, see *Liquidambar styraciflua*
Sweet marjoram, see *Origanum majorana*
Sweet melons, see Melons
Sweet pea, see *Lathyrus odoratus*
Sweet pea tubes 473, *473*
Sweet peppers, see Peppers, sweet
Sweet potatoes *348*, 351, *351*
in crop rotation 304
culinary uses 351
cultivation 351, *351*
curing 351
diseases 351, 560
harvesting 351
nitrogen requirement 310, 351
pests 351
recommended cultivars 351
size of plant 351
storing 351
Sweet rocket, see *Hesperis matronalis*
Sweet scabious, see *Scabiosa atropurpurea*
Sweet shrub, see *Calycanthus*
Sweet sultan, see *Centaurea moschata*
Sweet violet, see *Viola odorata*
Swiss chard 322, *322*
in containers 307
culinary uses 322
cultivation 322
as cut-and-come-again crop 312
diseases 322
harvesting 322
leaf color 322
leaf size 322
nitrogen requirements 310, 322
Swiss chard (*cont.*)
pests 322
red-stemmed *322*
storing 312, 322
in vegetable garden *300*
watering, critical periods 308
white-stemmed *322*
Swiss-cheese plant, see *Monstera deliciosa*
Sword fern, see *Nephrolepsis exaltata*
Sycamore, see *Acer platanus*
Sylvanberry 407
Symphoricarpos, hardwood cuttings 84
Symphytum
conditions tolerated 141
division 163
grandiflorum, conditions tolerated 141
x *uplandicum* 'Variegatum' 151
Sympodial growth 440, 590
Syngonium 97
conditions preferred 431
softwood cuttings 453
suggestions for use 97
hoffmannii, suggestions for use 438
podophyllum
conditions tolerated 97
hydroculture *447*
'Albolineatum', care when going away *446*
Syringa
deadheading 70
flowers 65
pests 559
propagation
apical-wedge grafting 89
layering 86
root cuttings 541
stooling 87
pruning 76
renovation *80*
scent 61, 66
size 30
soil type tolerated 69
microphylla 'Superba', seasonal interest 62
yunnanensis, flowers 65

T

T-budding
fruit trees 369, *369*
method 544, *544*
time for 543
Tabebuia chrysotricha *42*
soil preferred 42
Tagetes
flower variety 171
hardening off *180*
planting out *180*
pricking out, into pack *179*
soil type preferred 176
soil type tolerated 176
erecta, flowers 172
'Golden Gem', in annual border *171*
patula
attracting insects 548, *548*
flowers 172
interplanting tomatoes with 334
'Naughty Marietta', in annual border *171*
Tagetes (*cont.*)
signata
conditions tolerated 175
flowers 172
Talinum okanoganense, in trough *199*
Tall fescue, see *Festuca arundinacea*
Tamarillos, see Tree tomatoes
Tamarisk, see *Tamarix*
Tamarix
conditions tolerated 66
hardwood cuttings 84
soil type preferred 67
ramosissima, pruning 74
Tamper *438*, 439
Tanacetum
argenteum, in dry-stone wall *189*
balsamita *293*
division 293
flowers 293
foliage 293
harvesting 293
in herb garden *295*
scent 293
storing 293
coccineum, division 163
densum *150*
parthenium (syn. *Chrysanthemum parthenium*) *178*, *293*
conditions preferred 288
conditions tolerated 288
flowers 171, 293
foliage 293
harvesting 293
propagation
cuttings 293
division 293
from seed 293
self-seeding 178
in scented preparations 293
storing 293
suggestions for use 293
variants 293
'Aureum' 293, *295*
conditions tolerated 288
vulgare
conditions tolerated 288
dye from 287
planting to restrict spread 294
Tanakaea radicans, soil type required 192
Tangelos 418
recommended cultivars 417
Tangerines
conditions required 418
in containers 417
cross-pollination 418
growing under cover 417
Tankage, nutrient content 532
Tansy, see *Tanacetum vulgare*
Taphrina 561
deformans 557
Taraxacum officinale, see Dandelion
Tarnished plant bugs 551
Taro 349–50, *349–50*
in crop rotation 304
culinary uses 349
cultivation 349–50
harvesting 350
nitrogen requirement 310, 349
propagation
tuber cuttings 349
tubers 349
storing 350
Tarragon
French 290, *290*
culinary uses 290
forcing 290, 294
harvesting 290
in herb garden *295*
in oil or vinegar 298
propagation
division of rhizomes 290
softwood cuttings 290
related species 290
storing 290
Russian 290
Tasmanian blue gum, see *Eucalyptus globulus*
Tasmanian snow gum, see *Eucalyptus coccifera*
Tavaresia, flat grafting 271
Taxodium distichum
adapting to waterlogging 517
conditions tolerated 37
soil type tolerated 42
suggestions for use 243
Taxon, definition 590
Taxonomy 580
Taxus
disease resistance 567
diseases 560, 567, 571
hedge 58
as background 22, 23
renovation 60
in rose garden *116*
shaping *60*
pests 566, 572
pruning 78
soil type tolerated 67
suggestions for use 31, 148
for topiary 90
clipping 91, *91*
baccata
conditions tolerated 37
hedge, supporting climber *94*
soil type tolerated 41
'Aurea', as focal point *38*
'Fastigiata' 22
'Standishii', suggestions for use 37
x *media* *90*
conditions tolerated 37
as hedge 58, 59
Tayberries 407, *407*
in large fruit garden *357*
Teaniothrips inconsequens 565
Tecoma, semiripe cuttings 111
Tecomanthe 97
propagation
semiripe cuttings 111
simple layering 113
Tecomaria 97
propagation
self-layering 113
semiripe cuttings 111
suggestions for use 97
Tecophilaea
suggestions for use 219
cyanocrocus, suggestions for use 218
Tellima grandiflora 'Purpurea', conditions tolerated 141
Telopea speciosissima, soil type required 69
Temperatures
air 515
average minimum in North America 516, *516–17*
design and 15
effect of altitude on 515
high
damage from 556, *556*
symptoms and control 564, *564*
importance to plants 515
inappropriate, problems caused by 547
low
damage caused by 556, *556*, 559, *559*
succulents tolerant of 262
symptoms 570
problems for indoor plants 427
range tolerated 515
for seed germination 538
soil 515
Tenby daffodil, see *Narcissus obvallaris*
Tender fruits, see Fruit, tender
Tender plants 590
damage of frost and thaw to 515
protection from frost 515
protection from wind 521
Tendrils 581, 590
climbers supported by 92
as climbing method *98*
Tent cloches, see Cloches, tent
Tepals *582*, 590
Tephrocactus, division of offsets 269
Terminal, definition 590
Terminal bud, definition 585
Terraces 493–9, see also Patios
building 13
definition 493
microclimate on *519*
roses on 117
site 493
size 493
uses 492
using site features for 17
Terrarium 428, 590
care 445–6
condensation on 438, 445
drainage 438, *438*
planting 438, *438*
potting mix for 438
replanting *446*
Tetragonia tetragonioides (syn. *T. expansa*), see New Zealand spinach
Tetranychus urticae 552
Tetrapanax papyriferus, soil type tolerated 67
Tetrastigma voinierianum
suggestions for use 97
vigor 98
Teucrium
chamaedrys 31
fruticans, suggestions for use 289
Textures 24
harmonizing 138, *138*
Thalia
dealbata
division of rootstock 257
in water garden 243
geniculata, in water garden 243
Thalictrum
conditions preferred 141
conditions tolerated 141
division 163
aquilegiifolium, in mixed border *172*
flavum
growth rate 141
in mixed border *137*
Thatch on lawn 278, 281, 283, 467, 573, 590
Thaw, dangers of 515
Thelocactus
division of offsets 269
bicolor *262*
suggestions for use 262
nidulans, suggestions for use 262
Thelypteris oreopteris, soil type required 158
Thermal screens 182, *482*
Thermometers
greenhouse *471*, *486*
maximum/minimum 471, *471*, 482
soil 471
wet and dry bulb 484
Thinning 178, *178*, 306, *306*, 590
Thiophanate-methyl 569, 573
commercial names 574
Thiram 403, 555, 566, 570, 573, 574
commercial names 574
Thistle, see *Carlina*
Canada, see Canada thistle
Scotch, see *Onopordum acanthium*
as weed 167
Thladiantha
propagation, softwood cuttings 110
pruning 103
dubia 97
Thompsonella platyphylla, leaf cuttings 267
Thorn, see *Crataegus*
Thread agave, see *Agave filifera*
Thrift, see *Armeria maritima*

Thrips 149, 310, 548, 553, 562, *562*
pea 565, *565*
Throatwort, see *Trachelium caeruleum*
Thuja
conditions tolerated 521
diseases 554
as hedge 58
semiripe cuttings 53
soil type tolerated 41
occidentalis
soil preferred 42
'Caespitosa' *38*
orientalis 'Aurea Nana' *38*
Thujopsis, semiripe cuttings 53
Thunbergia
conditions preferred 431
propagation
from seed 452
semiripe cuttings 111
simple layering 113
softwood cuttings 110
pruning 105, 450
alata 97
germination 179
as pot plants 175
soil type tolerated 99
suggestions for use 97, 173
supporting *182*
gregorii, pruning 103
Thyme, see *Thymus*
Thymophylla tenuiloba
as filler 173
suggestions for use 175
Thymus
cosmetic uses 287
fall cleanup 296
harvesting, in winter 294
in knots and parterres 172
propagation
cuttings 208
mound layering 297, *297*, 539
pruning 296
steeping in oil or vinegar 298
suggestions for use 191, 288
for tapestry lawn 275
underplanting roses 117
caespititius, soil type tolerated 193
for lawn 275
cilicicus, propagation, mound layering 297
x *citriodorus*
flowers 293
in herb garden *295*
propagation, mound layering 297
scent 293
membranaceus 191
praecox
in wildlife garden 150
var. *arcticus*
flowers 293
foliage 293
'Coccineus' 275, 293
'Doone Valley' 275, 293
'Snowdrift', flowers 293
serpyllum
flowers 293
as ground cover 150
habit 293
in herb garden *295*
suggestions for use 288
'Minus', suggestions for use 191
vulgaris 293
conditions preferred 294
culinary uses 293
flowers 293
foliage 293
harvesting 293
in herb garden *295*
propagation
division 293
layering 293
mound layering 297
from seed 293
semiripe heel cuttings 293
Thymus vulgaris (*cont.*)
related species 293
storing 293
suggestions for use 293
variants 293
woody cultivars, mound layering 297
'Silver Posie'
foliage 293
in herb garden *295*
Tiarella
conditions tolerated 141
suggestions for use 216
cordifolia 150, *150*
in cool border *138*
polyphylla, winter interest 141
Tibetan peony, see *Paeonia lutea*
Tibouchina
conditions required 431
pinching out 450
softwood cuttings 453
stem tip cuttings 176
Tickseed, see *Coreopsis*
Tiered planting, see Layer planting
Ties 41, *41*, 472, *472*
Tiger lily, see *Lilium lancifolium*
Tigridia 213
buying 224
conditions preferred 219
Tiles
glazed ceramic 496
laying 497
for patios and paths 496
quarry 496
terracotta *498*
Tilia
coppicing and pollarding 50
disadvantages 35
diseases 554
pests 551, 558
pleached 51
suggestions for use 32
pleaching 36, *36*
'Euchlora', pleaching 51
'Petiolaris', suggestions for use 37
platyphyllos
pleaching 51
suggestions for use 37, 50
tomentosa, soil type tolerated 41
Tillaea recurva 243
softwood cuttings 256
Tillandsia
conditions required 433
displaying 432, *432*
from seed 433, *433*
caput-medusae 432
ionantha, displaying *432*
latifolia, displaying *432*
stricta 432
tectorum, displaying *432*
usneoides 432
Tilth 590
Timers, hose 469, *469*
Tip layering, see Layering, tip
Tissue culture, definition 590
Titanopsis, division of rootstock 270
Toadflax, see *Linaria*
Toads, as beneficial garden animals 549, 572
Toadstools 574, *574*
on lawn 574
Tobacco rattle virus 568
Toiletries, herbs used for 287
Tolmiea
conditions required 431
in greenhouse display *429*
Tomato late blight 555, *555*, 564, *564*
Tomato leaf mold 548
Tomato nematode, rotating crops to avoid 304
Tomatoes 333–4, *333–4*
beefsteak 333
bush 333, *333*
in vegetable garden *300*
chemical damage to 557
cherry *328*, 333
Tomatoes (*cont.*)
in crop rotation 304
cultivation 333–4
currant 333
determinates 333, 586
disease resistance 548
diseases 311, 334, 555, 560, 562, 564, 565, 567
dwarf, spacing 333
effect of frost on 515
fertilizer burn 556
fruits 333, 581
genetic engineering 546
ghost spots 564
in grow bags *334*
growing below wall 301
growing in containers 307, 333
growing under cover 334
diseases 311
harvesting 312, 334
hormone damage to 561, 565
as house plants 427
indeterminates 333, 587
training as cordons 333
indoor, supporting 450
mineral deficiency 557, 560, 564
nitrogen requirement 310, 333
origins 328
overwatering 308
pests 334, 551, 553, 572
phosphorus requirements 333
physiological disorders 564
planting, through plastic mulch 309, *309*
plum *328*
recommended cultivars 333
semideterminates 333, 589
staking 333
staking types 333
training *334*
in vegetable garden *300*
storing 312, 334
temperature requirements 303
watering 333
critical periods 308
in windowbox *303*
in wire cage 333, *333*
'Patio Hybrids' 427
'Pixie' 427
'Sun Gold' *333*
'Viva Italia' *333*
Tomatoes, tree, see Tree tomatoes
Tools 458–73, see also Equipment
blades 459, *459*
for bonsai *434*
for bottle garden 439
buying 458
cleaning 458, 545
for cultivation 459–61, *459–61*
for cutting 462–4, *462–4*
for lawns 465–7, *465–7*
maintenance 458
metal for 459
for planting 471, *471*
power
gasoline and electricity compared 464, 465, 466
rechargeable 464
renting 458
safety 458, *458*, 464
for pruning 102, 458, 462–4, *462–4*
maintenance 462
renting 458
safety in use 458, *458*
for sowing 471, *471*
storing 458
use 458, *458*
Toona sinensis 'Flamingo' (syn. *Cedrela sinensis* 'Flamingo'), suggestions for use 50
Top fruits, see Fruit, tree
Top-dressings 309, 590
as additives 534, *534*
for alpines 203, *203*
Top-dressings (*cont.*)
for climbers in containers 101, *101*
decorative 534, *534*
for fruit in containers 362
materials used as 534, *534*
for rock plants 197
for shrubs in containers 71, *71*
uses 524, 534
Top-grafting, see Top-working
Topiary 30, *31*, 90–91, 590
care 91
clipping 91
frequency 91
creating complex design *91*
creating shape 90–91, *90*
creating simple design *90*
designing with 90
designs 90, *90*, *91*
dieback 91
feeding 91
Italianate 29
plants for 31, 90, *90*
renovation 91
repairs 91
scorch 91
winter care 91
Topography, effects on wind 519
Topsoil, see Soil
Top-working
apples 379, *379*
weeping standards 49
Torch lily, see *Kniphofia*
Torenia
from seed 452
fournieri, as pot plants 175
Totem, moss *472*
Trace elements 532, 557
Trachelium caeruleum, as pot plants 175
Trachelospermum 97
for fragrance 97
propagation
self-layering 113
semiripe cuttings 111
suggestions for use 97
jasminoides
soil type tolerated 100
supporting *436*
Trachymene coerulea (syn. *Didiscus coeruleus*), as pot plants 175
Tradescantia
conditions preferred 431
conditions required 431
softwood cuttings 453
x *andersoniana*, division 163
cerinthoides, suggestions for use 438
fluminensis, suggestions for use 438
'Osprey', in cool border *138*
spathacea, suggestions for use 438
Tragopogon porrifolius, see Salsify
Trailing arbutus, see *Epigaea repens*
Trailing plants
annuals 173, *173*
biennials 173
for containers, annuals and biennials 175
for hanging baskets, annuals 174, *174*
indoors
pinching out 444
supports for 436, *436*
positioning 427
Training
climbers, under cover 450
fall tasks 584
shrubs 73–80
fan-training 79, *79*
principles 73
standards 80
wall 78–9, *79*
spring tasks 583
Training (*cont.*)
summer tasks 583
winter tasks 584
Transpiration 517, 580, 581, *581*, 590
in dry conditions 484
reducing in drought 517
reducing water loss by 518
water loss by 530
Transpiration stream *581*
Transplant shock 556
Transplanting
definition 590
shrubs 72, *72*
Transplants, trees 41
Trapa natans 243
from seed 257
softwood cuttings 256
value in water garden 242
Trays, seed, see Seed trays
Tree felling, tools for 464, *464*
Tree fruits, see Fruit, tree
Tree germander, see *Teucrium fruticans*
Tree mallow, see *Lavatera*
Tree pruners 463, *463*
Tree purslane, see *Atriplex halimus*
Tree stakes 40, *40*, *472*
Tree surgeons 50
Tree surgery, tools for 464, *464*
Tree ties 41, *41*
Tree tomatoes 418, *418*
conditions required 356, 418
cultivation 418
harvesting 418
propagation 370, 418
storing 418
under cover 359
Tree trunks, rock plants in *190*
Tree-of-heaven, see *Ailanthus altissima*
Trees 590
for acid soil 41
for alkaline soil 41
arching *33*
for avenues 36
balled-and-burlapped
choosing 39, *39*, 40
planting 43, *43*
planting time 41
bare-root
choosing 39, *39*, 40
planting 43
planting time 41
for bark *34*, 35, *35*
bark splitting 363
as boundary 33
branched-head standard
pruning 48, *48*
training 48, *48*
broad-leaved 585
care, after planting 43
central-leader standard
pruning 48, *48*
training 48, *48*
changing grade around 46, *46*
chip-budding 57, *57*
choosing 32, 39, *39*
climbers on 34, 95, 106
clipping, for topiary 91, *91*
columnar *33*
conditions required 41
conditions tolerated 39, 41, 42
conical *33*
conifers, see Conifers
container-grown
buying healthy plants 548
choosing 39, *39*
planting 42, *42*
soil mix for 40
in containers 26, 36, *36*, 37, 44, *44*, 49
contrasting forms 24
coppicing 36, 49, *49*, 50, 586
creating perspective with 18, *18*
cutting down 45, *45*
damage caused by animals 572
(*entry cont.*)

Trees (*cont.*)
  damage caused by lightning 561, *561*
  damage caused by mice, rats, and voles 568
  damage caused by squirrels 565
  damage caused by tree roots 39
  deciduous
    established, pruning 49
    planting time 41
  as design elements 32–3, *32*
  diseases 45, 552, 554, 560, 561, 562, 567, 570, 571
    affecting flowers 562
  distinction between shrubs and 32, 61
  drip line 44
  effect of high temperatures on 556
  effect of low temperatures on 556, 570
  espalier, pruning 49
  evergreen, see Evergreens
  existing, design and 17
  for fall color 25
  fan-trained, pruning 49
  fastigiate 587
  feathered 41
    pruning 48, *48*
    training 48
  felling 45, *45*
  fertilizing 44
  flowering 34
  forms 33
  as framework of design *16*, 32, *32*
  frost pockets beside 515
  fruiting, diseases 564
  in garden design 19, *19*
  grouping 34
  growth rates 32
  guy ropes for 40, *40*, *46*
  half-standard 587
  heeling in 41, *41*
  herbs 287
  lack of vigor 45
  large 41
  in layer planting 23, 26
  life expectancy 16
  maiden 588
  mineral deficiency 556–7
  in mixed borders 136
  mulching 44
    after planting *42*
  neglected, renovating 50, *50*
  in neglected garden 13
  old 20, 31
  ornamental 32–46
    buying 32
    choosing 32
    features 32, 34
    foliage 34, *34*
    in garden design 32–6
  for patio 29
  patio beside, disadvantages of 493
  perennials with 140
  pests 45, 558, 559, 560, 563, 571, 572
    damaging leaves 551, 552, 553, 554, 557–8
  planter's guide 37
  planting 42–3, *42*, *43*
    in containers 43, *43*
    spacing 34
    time for 41
  planting roses by 122
  pleached 36, *36*, 51
    establishing framework 51, *51*
    pruning, summer *51*
    training 51, *51*
  pollarding 36, 49
    plants suitable for 50
    pruning after 50, *50*
  pricking out *54*, 55
  problems 45
  problems affecting stems and leaf buds 559–61
  propagation 52–7
    air layering 55, 539

Trees, propagation (*cont.*)
    cuttings
      aftercare 53
      hardwood 52, *52*
      heel 53
      nodal 53
      planting depth *52*
      semiripe 53, *53*
      softwood 53
      suitable varieties for 53
    grafting 52, 56–7, *56*, *57*
      aftercare 57
      apical-wedge 57
      chip-budding 57, *57*
      side-veneer 56, *56*
    layering 55, *55*
      suitable varieties for 55
    from seed 52, 54–5, *54*, *55*
  protecting
    from animals 43, *43*
    from cold and wind 43, 45, *520*
  pruning 47–51, *47–51*
    bad 570
    established trees 49, *49*
    formative 48, *48*
    "haircut" pruned, renovating 50
    principles 47, *47*
    removing branches 47, *47*
    removing competing leader 49, *49*
    roots 49
    time for 47
  pyramidal *33*
  renovating 20, 31, 50, *50*
  repotting 44, *44*
  for rock garden 185
  root feeding 44, *44*
  root pruning 49
  round-headed *33*
  routine care 44–6
  for sandy soil 42
  scale and size 22
  for screens 36
  seasonal water requirements 530
  seed
    breaking dormancy 54
    extracting 54
    fleshy, cleaning 54, *54*
    scarification 54
    soaking 54, *54*
    storing 54
    stratification 54
  seedlings 41
  shade from 145
  shapes 33, *33*
  as shelter belt 36
  shrubs to grow beneath 64
  silhouettes *34*, 35
  siting 39
  size range 32
  small, protecting *520*, 521
  for small gardens 35, *35*, 37
  in small plot 17
  snow damage to *517*
  soil depth required 41
  soil preparation 39–41
  specimen
    bulbs with 216
    as focal points 33, *33*
    suggestions for use 33
    varieties to use 37
  spreading *33*
  stakes for *472*
  staking 40, *40*, 42, *42*, 43
  standards 41, 590
    pruning 48, *48*
  stem structure *580*
  for stems *34*, 35
  stumps
    removal 20
    treatment 45
  for successional interest 35
  suckers 50
    removing 45, *45*
  suggestions for use *32*, 32–4
  ties for 472, *472*
  top-dressing 44, *44*
  topiary 90–91

Trees (*cont.*)
  training 47–51
    new leader 49, *49*
    roses on 128
    for topiary 90, *90*
  transplanting 46, *46*
  transplants 41
  trunk 590
  for two or more seasons of interest 37
  undercanopy of shrubs 151
  undercutting 41
  underplanting 36
  on walls, protecting *520*, 521
  water shoots 50
    removing 45
  watering 39, 43, 44
  weeding 45
  weeping *33*
    pruning *48*, 49
    training *48*, 49
  weeping standards
    forming 49
    pruning *48*, 49
  whips 41
  wind scorch 518
  as windbreaks 301, 519, *519*
  wind-tolerant 521
  for winter color 26
  for winter interest 37
  for woodland garden 27
Trefoil, lesser yellow 578, 579
Trellis
  attaching to wall 98, *98*
  as background 22
  clematis on 106
  for climbers 98, *183*
  for containers 99
  erecting 511
  on patio 29
  patterns 511, *511*
  on roof garden *29*
  for roses 119
  screening patio 493
  uses 492, *511*
Trench digging, see Digging, double
Trench layering 539, *539*
Trenching *520*, 521
  roses *520*
Trialeurodes vaporariorum 552
Trichocaulon, flat grafting 271
Trichocereus
  as rootstock 271
  suggestions for use 262
  fulvilanus 262
  pachanoi 262
  pasacana 262
  spachianus 262
  terscheckii 262
Trickle irrigation systems 485, *485*
Trifolium
  dubium, see Trefoil, lesser yellow
  pratense, stem tip cuttings 164
  repens, see Clover, common white
Triforine 549, 554
  commercial names 574
Trillium 28
  conditions preferred 191, 219
  germination 160, 205
  propagation
    scooping 238, *238*
    scoring 238, *238*
  seedlings, planting out 235
  soil type required 147
  storing 224
  erectum, in peat bed *188*
  grandiflorum
    conditions preferred 141
    in peat bed *188*
  rivale
    in peat bed *188*
    suggestions for use 218
  sessile, conditions preferred 141
Trimmers, nylon-line *279*, 458, 466, *466*
Trinity flower, see *Trillium*

Trioza alacris 553
Triple superphosphate, nutrient content 532
Triploids 371, 590
Tripods
  bamboo, for indoor plants *436*
  constructing 512
Tripterygium
  self-layering 113
Tristeza viruses 416, 417
Triteleia
  conditions tolerated 219
  suggestions for use 218
  laxa (syn. *Brodiaea laxa*), in mixed border 215
Trochodendron aralioides, semiripe cuttings 53
Trollius
  diseases 565
  division 163
  root cuttings 165
  soil type tolerated 146
  suggestions for use *243*
  x *cultorum*, suggestions for use 243
  europaeus, suggestions for use 243
  ledebourii, suggestions for use 243
Tropaeolum
  climbing method 92
  in containers, with trees 36
  for ground cover 97
  growing as biennial 177
  growing through shrubs 95
  growing with squashes *303*
  as host plant for pests 548
  pests 551
  seedling growth *538*
  softwood cuttings 110
  soil type tolerated 176
  'Hermione Grasshof', as focal point *173*
  majus
    in annual border *171*
    self-seeding 178
    semitrailing, suggestions for use 175
    soil type preferred 176
    suggestions for use 175
    'Empress of India' 175
    Gleam Series 175
    Whirlybird Series 175
  peregrinum 97
    conditions tolerated 93
    from seed 109
    suggestions for use 97, 173
  polyphyllum, in dry-stone wall *189*
  speciosum 97
    conditions tolerated 97
    as ground cover 95
    suggestions for use 95, 97
    on yew *94*
  tricolorum 97
  tuberosum 97
Tropical climate 514
Tropical plants
  flowering, conditions required 436
  foliage, conditions tolerated 436
  propagator for 488
  soil mix for 439
Tropical root rots 567
Tropical trees, pruning 48
Troughs
  alpines in 186, 190, *190*, 198–9
    care 203–4
    planting 199, *199*
    replanting 204, *204*
  bulbs and alpines in 217
  cacti in 260, 262
  hypertufa, making 198, *198*
  rock plants in 190, *190*, 191, 198–9
    planting 199, *199*
  succulents in 260, 262
Trowels 460, *460*
  narrow-bladed *460*

Trowels (*cont.*)
  rock garden *460*
  transplanting *460*
  wide-bladed *460*
True-breeding plants 590
Trugs 470, *470*
Trumpet creeper, see *Campsis radicans*
Trumpet flower, see *Bignonia capreolata*
Truncheons 396
Tsuga
  diseases 560
  pests 560
  semiripe cuttings 53
  soil type indicated by 525
  heterophylla
    disease resistance 560, 567
    soil preferred 41
    suggestions for use 37
  mertensiana f. *argentea*, seasonal interest 37
Tuberous vegetables 348–54, see also Root vegetables
  in crop rotation 304
Tubers
  basal cuttings 223, *223*
  characteristics 214, 590
  choosing *224*
  definition 214
  division, begonias 455, *455*
  planting 226
    depth 226
    in root growth 226
  planting out 521
  problems 566–8
  purpose 581
  root 543, *543*
    propagation 543
  spacing 226
  stem 543, *543*
    propagation 543
  weeds with *577*
Tubs, see Containers
Tufa 590
  placing 199
  planting alpines in 199, *199*, 212
  for rock garden 193, *193*
  rock plants for 191
Tufted sedge, see *Carex elata*
Tulbaghia, conditions preferred 219
Tulip, see *Tulipa*
Tulip fire blight 555, *555*, 562, *562*
  crop rotation to avoid 548
Tulip tree, see *Liriodendron tulipifera*
Tulipa 213
  in border *220*
  bulb 214
  choosing healthy bulbs 224, *224*
  cultivation 220
  for cutting 219
  diseases 221, 555, *555*, 562, 568
  dwarf
    conditions preferred 221
    conditions tolerated 219
    species and hybrids 220, *220*
    suggestions for use 219
  early 220
  flowers 582
    types 220, *220*
  forcing 228
  in formal bedding 214, *214*
  groups 220
  interplanting 173
  late 220
  lifting *231*
  midseason 220
  in mixed border *137*, *215*, *216*
  naturalized, in grass *275*
  planting *225*
  propagation 221
    division of offsets 233
    from seed 234
      spacing 234

(*entry cont. overleaf*)

Tulipa (*cont.*)
seasonal interest 25
seed germination 235
in spring border *25*
suggestions for use 219, 220
'Clara Butt' *218*
Darwin hybrids 220, *220*
forcing 228
'Dawnglow' *220*
'Dreamboat' *220*
'Estella Rijnveld' *220*
Fosteriana hybrids 220
'Giuseppe Verdi' *220*
Greigii hybrids 220, *220*
'Greuze' *220*
Kaufmanniana hybrids 220, *220*
Parrot 220, *220*
'Peach Blossom' *220*
Peony-flowered 220
'Prinses Irene' *228*
'Queen of Night' *220*
Rembrandts 220
sprengeri
conditions tolerated 220
in mixed border 215
suggestions for use 227
'Spring Green' *220*
sylvestris
conditions preferred 219
conditions tolerated 220
tarda *220*
suggestions for use 227
Triumph hybrids 220
forcing 228
turkestanica 117
Viridifloras 220, *220*
'West Point'
in containers *220*
in mixed border *215*
'White Triumphator', in mixed border *215*
Tunic 590
Tunnel cloches, see Cloches, tunnel
Tupelo, see *Nyssa*
Turbinicarpus, flat grafting 271
Turface
in hydroponics *447*
as plunge material 437
starting tubers in 223
Turgor, supporting stem *580*
Turions 590
propagation by 257, 543, *543*
Turnip gall weevils 349
Turnip rape, see Broccoli raab
Turnip tops 318, *318*
cultivation 318
culinary uses 318
harvesting 318
nitrogen requirement 310, 318
Turnips 348, *348*, 349
in crop rotation 304
culinary uses 349
cultivation 349
diseases 349
harvesting 349, *349*
mineral deficiencies 568
nitrogen requirement 310, 349
pests 349, 566
recommended cultivars 349
storage 349
'Golden Ball' *349*
Turtlehead, see *Chelone glabra*
Tussilago farfara, see Coltsfoot
Tweezers *212*
Twin-scaling, propagation by *236*, 237, 542, *542*
Twine
garden 472, *472*
tar-impregnated 472
for ties 472, *472*
Twining, as climbing method 92, *98*
2, 4–D (weedkiller) 579
commercial names 574
Typha
for seedheads 141
angustifolia, in water garden 243
latifolia
division of rootstock 256, 257
'Variegata', in water garden 243
laxmannii, see *T. stenophylla*
minima, in water garden 243
stenophylla (syn. *T. laxmannii*), in water garden 243

U

U cordons, see Cordons
Uebelmannia, flat grafting 271
Ugli fruits 418
Ulex
conditions tolerated 66
europaeus, soil type preferred 67
Ulmus
diseases 559, 572
pests 558
softwood cuttings 53
parvifolia 'Geisha' 190
Ultricularia
minor 243
vulgaris 243
Umbelliferae, herbs, sowing 297
Umbels 582
Umbilicus
conditions tolerated 262
chloranthus, leaf cuttings 267
intermedius 262
rupestris 262
Umbrella plant, see *Peltiphyllum*
Uncinula 552
necator 564
Underplanting 590
Unisexual plants
obtaining seed from 109
sexing 109
United States, regional differences 522–3
Upland cress 326, *326*
cultivation 326
harvesting 326
Upright habit, definition 590
Urban gardens, formal patio style 14, *14*, 29
Urn plant, see *Aechmea fasciata*
Urns
in alcoves 22
in garden design *19*
Urocystis 565
Ursinia anthemoides, soil type tolerated 176
Urtica urens, see Nettle, annual
Ustilago 565
Utility meters, leaving unobstructed 494
Utricularia
exoleta
propagation by plantlets 257
suggestions for use 243
vulgaris, suggestions for use 243
Uvularia, soil type required 147

V

Vaccaria hispanica
conditions tolerated 175
self-seeding 178
Vaccinium
soil type indicated by 525
soil type required 69, 188
ashei, see Blueberries, rabbit-eye
corymbosum
edible, see Blueberries
layering 86
delavayi, soil type required 192
myrtillus, soil type required 192
parvifolium *62*
uliginosum, soil type required 192
vitis-idaea 'Minus', in peat bed *188*
Valerianella locusta, see Corn salad
Valleys, frost pockets in 515, *515*
Vallisneria gigantea, suggestions for use 243
Vanda
method of growth 440
temperature required 441
Rothschildiana *440*
Variegated plants 590
light requirements 427
reversion 70, *70*, 589
Variegation, as result of mutation 582
Variety, definition 590
Vegetable garden 299–354
allocating space in *301*
beds in *299*, *300*, 302
chemical controls in 310
designing 299–304
exposure 299, *299*
in garden design *19*
healthy practices 310, *310*
herbs in 288
ideal *300*
keeping records 304
layout 302–3
planning 304
month-by-month planning 304
narrow bed system *300*
neglected, weed clearance 579
paths in *299*
planning 304
protecting from animals and birds 310
weed suppression 302
well-designed *299*
Vegetable oyster, see Salsify
Vegetables
alternating rows *301*
bed system 302
bolting 310
brassicas
Oriental 319–20
Western 313–18
bulb 341–7
storing 312
temperature requirements 303
in cold frames *489*
in cold greenhouse 430
conditions preferred 299, 518
conditions required 303
conserving moisture 308, *308*
in containers 302, 307, *307*
drainage 307
plants to avoid 307
preparing containers 307
routine cultivation 309
siting 307
soil mix for 307
changing 309
top-dressing 309
Vegetables (*cont.*)
cut-and-come-again crops, sowing 306, 322
daylength requirements 303
diseases 309–10, 562
bacterial 554, 571
fungal 552, 554, 560, 562, 567
preventive measures 310
effect of high temperatures on 556
effect of low temperatures on 556, 570
exposure for 515
feeding 301, 309
in flower beds 303, *303*
flowering 328–35
in frames *489*
freezing 312
fruit set 310
fruiting 328–35
growing in containers 307
storing 312
supports for 450
watering, critical periods 308
genetic engineering 546
germination 305
green manuring between crops 302
in greenhouse 430, 439
growing days required 303
growing in rows 302
growing under cover 303, 311
hardening off 307, 311
mulching 311
watering 311
harvesting 312
herbs with 303, *303*
improving drainage for 302
improving soil for 301
intercropping 304, *304*
leafy 321–5
pests 550
storing 312
watering, critical periods 308
liming soil for 533
maincrop 588
mineral deficiency 556–7
minor salad 326–7, *326–7*
mulching 308–9, *308*, *309*
netting for protection 472
nitrogen requirement 309
perennial *300*
pests 309–10, 550, 551, 552, 553, 557, 565, 566, 572
physiological disorders 310
planting 306–7
depth *306*
through plastic mulch 309, *309*
podded 336–40
conditions required 336
in crop rotation 304
storing 336
suggestions for use 336
positioning 301
problems affecting stems and leaf buds 559, 560, 561
propagation
from seed 305–7
covering soil 305
soil preparation 305
sowing
broadcast 306, *306*
in cell packs 307, *307*
depth 305
in drill 305, *305*
indoors 307, *307*
large seed 306
outdoors 305–7
in seed trays 307
in situ 305
in small containers 307
in wide drill 306, *306*
stale seedbed technique 308
watering 308
vegetative 307
protecting seed *306*
Vegetables (*cont.*)
protection 299, 472
reasons for growing 299
root 348–54
in crop rotation 304
mineral deficiency 560
mounding 521
overwatering 308
pests 561, 566, 568
storing 312
for successional crops 348
transplanting 306
watering, critical periods 308
rotation 303–4, *304*
advantages 303
drawbacks 304
groups *300*
for pest and disease control 548
planning for 304
in round beds *302*
routine cultivation 308–10
seed
buying 305
naked 305
pelleted 305
pregerminating method 305
prepared 305
in tapes or sheets 305
seedling crops
sowing as cut-and-come-again crop 306
sowing in wide drills 306
seedlings, watering 308
site 299–301
soil types preferred 301, 525
spacing 307
in bed system 302
in drought areas 308
equidistant 307, 308
in square beds *302*
stem 341–7
temperature requirements 303
storing 312
damage caused by mice, rats, and voles 568
successional crops 306
suggestions for use in garden 302–3
supporting 311, 450
thinning 306, *306*
transplanting 306, *306*
watering after 308
tuberous 348–54
in crop rotation 304
watering 308
critical periods 308
equipment for 308
methods 308
minimizing need 308
with soaker hose 308, *308*
time for 308
weed control 308, 576
minimizing growth 308
by mulching 308
windbreaks for 519
Vegetative growth 590
Veltheimia
architectural plant 219
conditions preferred 431
conditions required 431
suggestions for use 218
x *Venidio-arctotis* 'Apricot', in hot border *139*
Velvet plant, see *Gynura aurantiaca*
Venetian sumac , see *Cotinus coggygria*
Ventilation
alpine house 212
automatic vent openers 483, *483*
chimney effect 483, *483*
of cold frames 489, *489*
fan 483, *483*
greenhouse 481
maintenance 491
methods 483, *483*
principles 483, *483*
wind 483, *483*

Venturi
  inaequalis 555
  pirina 555
Veranda , wooden *499*
Verbascum
  flowering time from seed 160
  in mixed border *172*, 173
  root cuttings 165
  soil type tolerated 147
  bombyciferum
    architectural plant 175
    soil type preferred 176
  densiflorum, architectural plant 175
  'Letitia', suggestions for use 191
  olympicum, as specimen plant 140
  thapsus, self-seeding 178
Verbena
  in mixed border 173
  stem tip cuttings 164
  x *hybrida*
    for containers 174
    growing as annual 175
    soil type preferred 176
    suggestions for use 175
  peruviana, in hot border *139*
Vermiculite 590
  in soil mixes 535, 536
  storing tubers in 223
Veronica
  for cutting 141
  propagation
    division 163
    Irishman's cuttings *208*
    semiripe cuttings 207
  suggestions for use 186
  beccabunga, value in water garden 242
  'Crater Lake Blue', in cool border *138*
  filiformis, see Slender speedwell
  gentianoides, conditions tolerated 141
  peduncularis, Irishman's cuttings 208
  spicata
    conditions tolerated 141, 191
    in mixed border *20*
    soil type tolerated 147
  virginica f. *alba*, in cool border *138*
Verticillium wilt 559, *559*, 567
Viburnum
  conditions tolerated 66
  germination 85
  pests 550
  planting *68*
  propagation
    hardwood cuttings 84
    semiripe cuttings 83
    softwood cuttings 81
  pruning 74
  scent 66
  x *bodnantense*
    seasonal interest 62
    in shrub border *63*
  dilatatum 'Xanthocarpum', berries 65
  farreri, choosing healthy plant *67*
  opulus
    berries 65
    soil type tolerated 67
  plicatum 'Mariesii', as specimen plant *64*
  tinus
    pruning 78
    renovation 80
    soil type tolerated 69
    'Eve Price', in shrub border *63*
Viburnum beetle 550, *550*
Vicia faba, see Beans, broad
Victoria
  amazonica, in water garden 243
  regia, in water garden 243
Vigna
  self layering 113
  caracalla, pruning 103
Vinca
  conditions preferred 66, 518
  dwarf conifers with *38*
  as ground cover 34
  pruning 151
  winter interest 141
  major 'Variegata' *150*
  minor
    conditions tolerated 141
    'Atropurpurea', bulbs with 150
  rosea, see *Catharanthus roseus*
Vine eyes *98*, 450, 472, *472*
Vine spinach, see Malabar spinach
Vinegars, herb, making 298
Vines, see also Grapevines; *Vitis*
  fruits growing on 397–403
  on patio screen 29
  propagation
    cuttings 368
      hardwood 370
  training 356
  use of term 356
  on wall *171*
Vinyl resin, sheds of 513
Viola
  deadheading 184
  diseases 565
  fruit type 581
  germination 179
  in greenhouse 430
  pests 558
  propagation
    self-seeding 178
    softwood cuttings 206
    stem tip cuttings 164
  suggestions for use 21
  underplanting roses 117
  in wildlife garden 150
  cazorlensis, suggestions for use 191
  cornuta 'Minor', suggestions for use 191
  delphinantha, suggestions for use 191
  'Haslemere'
    in mixed border *215*
    in rock garden *187*
  'Jackanapes' *206*
  jooi, suggestions for use 191
  labradorica
    conditions tolerated 141
    'Purpurea'
      bulbs with 139
      foliage 139
  odorata
    conditions tolerated 141
    'Czar', for fragrance 141
  tricolor
    as filler 173
    in mixed border *172*
  x *wittrockiana*
    breeding 140
    conditions preferred 175
    in containers 175
    as fillers 173
    in formal bedding 172
    germination 179
    lifting after bedding 184
    scent 175
    suggestions for use 27
    in windowbox *174*
    winter-flowering, in containers 174
Violet, see *Viola*
Violet gall midges 558
Virginia creeper, see *Parthenocissus quinquefolia*
Virginian stock, see *Malcolmia maritima*
Virus diseases/viruses *562*
  affecting bulbs 571
  affecting fruit 363
  breeding resistance to 546
  carriers 232
  causes 555
  control 555, 562, 565
Virus diseases/viruses (*cont.*)
  pests spreading 547, 552, 553
  quick decline 416
  symptoms 553, 555, *555*, 565, *565*
Vistas, planning 18
Vitaliana primuliflora
  in alpine raised bed *201*
  suggestions for use 188, 191
Vitex agnus-castus
  soil type tolerated 69
  suggestions for use 37
Vitis
  conditions tolerated 97
  pests 552, 558
  propagation
    hardwood cuttings 109, 111, *541*
    simple layering 113
  pruning 103, 104
  soil type tolerated 100
  supports for 450
  amurensis, simple layering 113
  coignetiae 92
    conditions tolerated 97
    in contrasting grouping *94*
    fall display 96
    propagation
      hardwood cuttings *111*
      simple layering 113
    soil type tolerated 99
    suggestions for use 94, 97
    vigor 98
  labrusca 397
  riparia 397
  rotundifolia 397
  rupestris 397
  vinifera, see Grapevines
    'Purpurea', suggestions for use 94
Viviparus maniatus 253
Voles *568*
Vriesia
  conditions required 433
  displaying 432
  as pot plant 432
  splendens *432*

Wake-robin, see *Trillium*
Waldsteinia ternata *191*
  conditions tolerated 191
Wall fixings 472, *472*
Wallflower, see *Cheiranthus*
Wall-of-water cloches, see Cloches, wall-of-water
Walls 504–6
  alpines in 189–90
  apples on 371
  attaching climber supports to 98
  as background 22, *22*
  boundary 504
  brick types for *497*
  building of screen blocks 505, *505*
  bulbs needing protection of 219
  clematis on 106
  climbers on 93, 95, *95*, 99
  constructing concrete footings for 504–5, *504*
  coping 506, *506*
  dry-stone
    alpines in *189*, 190
      planting 200, *200*
    constructing 506
    rock plants in *189*, 190
Walls (*cont.*)
  dry-stone retaining, building *200*
  existing, design and 17
  fixing support wires on 360
  footings, concrete mix for 494
  as framework 21
  frost pockets beside 515, *515*
  fruit trees against, positioning 361
  fruit trees trained on 356
  growing fruit on 358
  growing plants beside, effect of sun on 518
  height 504
  materials for 504, *504*
    mixing 504, *504*
  north-facing
    climbers for 93, 97
    growing vegetables against 301
  painting 504
  peaches trained on *355*, 356
  planning 16
  plants growing against 22
  protecting plants on 93, *520*, 521
  raised beds against 289
  retaining
    against site features 17
    building 13, 506, *506*
    drainage for 506
  rock plants for crevices in 191
  rock plants in 189–90
    planting 200, *200*
  roses climbing on 118
  roses on top of 119
  shrubs against 64, *64*
    pruning 78–9, *79*
    training 78–9, *79*
    varieties suitable 66
  shrubs beside, planting *68*, 69
  softening with plants *506*
  south-facing
    growing vegetables against 301
    plants for 519
  strengthening piers for 504
  trees near 39
  uses 492
Walnuts *424*, 425, *425*,
  see also *Juglans*
  American black
    as rootstock 425
    soil type tolerated 42
  cultivation 425
  diseases 572
  harvesting 425
  pests 558, 565
  from seed 370
  recommended cultivars 425
  storing 425
  tree size 424, *425*
Waratah, see *Telopea speciosissima*
Washington grass, see *Cabomba caroliniana*
Washingtonia, suggestions for use 37
Washtubs, see Sinks and washtubs
Wasps *565*
  benefits of 549
  control 565
    commercial names for 574
  cynipid 558, *558*
  damage caused 565
  gall 558, *558*
  parasitic, as biological pest control 548, *549*, 552
Water 530–31
  bulbs for margins of 217
  circulating in watercourses 250, *250*
  conserving 530
  conversion during photosynthesis 581, *581*
  deficiency 530–31
  grasses beside 142
  importance of 517, 530
  irises to grow beside 144
  plants' seasonal needs 530
Water (*cont.*)
  recycling 531
  retention in soil 529, 530
  in soil 530
    in relation to structure 528–9
  storage areas 531
Water arum, see *Calla palustris*
Water barrels 468, *468*
Water chestnut, see *Trapa natans*
Water fern, see *Azolla caroliniana*; *Ceratopteris thalictroides*
Water figwort, see *Scrophularia auriculata* 'Variegata'
Water forget-me-not, see *Myosotis scorpioides*
Water garden 28, *28*, 240–57
  bulbs for 217
  buying plants for 251, *251*
  circulation of water 250, *250*
  in containers 242, *242*
  designing 240–43
  fall maintenance 255
  features 240
  filtration 250
  indoors 429
  informal *240*
  plant associations 242
  planting 251–3
  plants for 240, 242–3
  routine care 254–5
Water hawthorn, see *Aponogeton distachyos*
Water hyacinth, see *Eichhornia crassipes*
Water lettuce, see *Pistia stratiotes*
Water lily, see *Nymphaea*
Water moss, see *Fontinalis antipyretica*
Water plantain, see *Alisma plantago-aquatica*
Water plants 585
  for aquariums 243
  associations 242
  baskets for planting 251, *251*
  bog plants 240, 242, 243
    planting 252, *252*
  care 255
  choosing 251, *251*
  deep-water 242, 243
    planting 252, *253*
  diseases 255
  floating 240, 242, 243
    stocking pond with 252, *252*
  marginals *240*, 242, 243, 588
    adapting to waterlogging 517
    cuttings 257
    planting 252, *253*
    repotting 255
  moisture-loving 242, 243
    planting 252
  oxygenators 242, 243, 588
    cuttings 257
    planting 253, *253*
    thinning out 255, *255*
  pests 255
  planter's guide 243
  planting 251–3, *252–3*
    depths 251
  pots for *473*
  propagation 256–7
    cuttings *256*, 257
    division 255, 256, *256*
    runners 257, *257*
    from seed 257, *257*
    turions 257, 543, *543*
  soil mix for 251
  tender, protecting 255
  thinning out 255, *255*
Water poppy, see *Hydrocleys nymphoides*
"Water roots" *447*
Water shoots 590
  on fruit trees, removing 364
  inhibiting growth 366
  trees 50
    removing 45

Water soldier, see *Stratiotes aloides*
Water supply
in greenhouse 475
installing 480
irregular
damage caused by 557
symptoms and control 565
Water table 530
high, installing drainage system for 531, *531*
Water violet, see *Hottonia palustris*
Watercourses 241, *241*
circulating water 250, *250*
construction 246
with liner 248–9, *249*
with rigid units 249–50, *250*
filtration 250
repairing 254
structural repairs 254
using site features for 17
Watercress
conditions required 327
culinary uses 327
cuttings 327
growing in pot 327, *327*
habitat 327
harvesting 327
Waterfalls 241
Watering
basin watering/irrigation (dishing) 530, *530*, 585
capillary systems 446, *446*, 485, *485*
drip-feed system 469, *469*
equipment for 468–9, *468–9*
in greenhouse
automatic 481
systems 485, *485*
indoor plants 444
during holidays 446, *446*
mistakes, rescuing pot plants after 444
moisture take-up 530
overhead systems 485
pot watering 530, *530*
soaker hoses 485
sprinkler systems 282
techniques 530, *530*
bad *530*
trickle system 469, *469*
in greenhouse 485, *485*
Watering cans 468, *468*
dribble bar for 468
garden *468*
greenhouse *468*
indoor *468*
roses for 468, *468*
Waterlogged soil 529, *529*, 557
damage to plants 517
indications of 531
perennials tolerant of 146
plants adapted to 517
problems 531
shrubs tolerant of 67
symptoms 566, *566*, 570, *570*
treatment 530, 531, *531*, 570
vulnerable areas 531
Watermelons 329, *329*
cultivation 329
harvesting 329
nitrogen requirement 310, 329
pollination by hand 329
recommended cultivars 329
storing 329
'Dixie Queen' *329*
Water-permeable fabric beds 546, *546*
Waterspouts 241, *241*
Watsonia
conditions preferred 219
corm 214
for cutting 219
suggestions for use 218
Wattakaka 97
semiripe cuttings 111
Wattle hurdles 508, *508*
Wax flower, see *Stephanotis floribunda*
Wax plant, see *Hoya carnosa*
Wax vine, see *Senecio macroglossus*
Weather
plant responses to 514
problems caused by 547
Webbing, for windbreaks 472
Weberocereus, side grafting 271
Weeders 461, *461*
Cape Cod *203*, 461, *461*
Weeding
to conserve water 530
by hand 526, *526*, 577
lawns 578
in organic practices 536
tools for 460, *460*, 461, *461*
Weedkillers
application 577
clearing overgrown site with 526, *526*
commercial names 574
contact 526, 577, 579, 586
damage from 556, *556*
foliage-acting 577
hormone, damage caused 557, *557*, 561, 565, *565*
lawn 578, 579
for perennial weeds 576, 577
residual 577
safety in use 557, 577
equipment for 468
selective 577
for lawns 578
soil-acting 577, 579
sprayers for 468, *468*
spreaders 467, *467*
systemic 526
translocated 577, 579, 590
Weeds
annual 575, *575*
control 145, 276, 308, 577
in beds and borders, control 155
categorizing 575
clearing from site 195
on compost heap 535
control 526, *526*, 575, 577
ground cover for 95
stale seedbed technique 308, 528, *528*
in vegetable garden 308
in cracks and crevices 579
cultivated plants as *575*
indicating soil type 525
in knot gardens 31
lawn 286, 578–9, *578*
annual control program 283
perennial 575, 576–7
clearing before mulching 534
control 155, 308, 576, 577, 579
eradicating 145, 195, 276
hand clearance *579*
in meadow garden 167
rhizomes and stolons *576*
types 576
preventing 576
spot treatment 579
suppressing germination 302, 534
tubers and fleshy roots *577*
woody, control 577
Weeping fig, see *Ficus benjamina*
Weeping willow, see *Salix babylonica*
Weevils, nut 425
Weigela
propagation
hardwood cuttings 84
semiripe cuttings 83, *540*
pruning 76, *76*
Weingartia, division of offsets 269
Weinmannia, cuttings 53
Welded wire fencing 508, *508*
Weldenia candida, root cuttings 208
Welsh onions, see Onions, Welsh
Welsh poppy, see *Meconopsis cambrica*
Western brassicas, see Brassicas, Western
Western hemlock, see *Tsuga heterophylla*
Western wheatgrass, see *Agropyron smithii*
Wet areas, lawns for 275
Wet wood 559, *559*
Wetlands 167
Wheelbarrows 470, *470*
garden carts 470, *470*
Wheelchairs, access to greenhouse 478, *478*
Whip-and-tongue grafting, see Grafting, whip-and-tongue
Whips 41, 590, see also Maiden whips
Whiptail, 558, *558*
White, color scheme for perennials 139
White ash, see *Fraxinus americana*
White cedar, see *Thuja occidentalis*
White grubs 566, *566*, 574
in lawn 573, *573*
White mulberry, see *Morus alba*
White poplar, see *Populus alba*
White rots, life in soil 304
White spruce, see *Picea glauca*
White torch cactus, see *Trichocereus spachianus*
White willow, see *Salix alba*
Whitebeam, see *Sorbus aria*
Whitecurrants 411–12, see also Redcurrants
cultivation 411–12
'White Grape' *412*
in small fruit garden *358*
Whiteflies 552, *552*
biological control 548, *549*
deterring 310
immunity to pesticides 549
trapping 548
Whitewash, shading greenhouse with 544
Whorl 590
Whortleberry, see *Vaccinium myrtillus*
Widgers *159*, 197, *197*, *200*, 471, *471*, 590
Wigginsia
division of offsets 269
vorwerkiana 269
Wigwams, as support for beans 337, *338*
Wilcoxia
in containers 264
side grafting 271
Wild daffodil, see *Narcissus pseudonarcissus*
Wild garden 27, *27*
grass in 272
Wild iris, see *Iris versicolor*
Wild marjoram, see *Origanum vulgare*
Wild pansy, see *Viola tricolor*
Wild thyme, see *Thymus serpyllum*
Wildflower gardens 167
Wildflower meadows 27, 28
bulbs in 216
burnoff 167
establishing 167
mowing 167, 230
Wildflowers
in cottage gardens 140
planting in grassland 167
suggestions for use 140
Wildlife gardens 23, 27, *27*, 28
ground cover in 150
water in 241
Willow, see *Salix*
Willow gentian, see *Gentiana asclepiadea*
Willow herb *576*
Willow leaf mining weevil 553
Willow myrtle, see *Agonis*
Wilt
clematis 571, *571*
symptoms and control 571
Wilt (*cont.*)
oak 571
stem 547
Wilting 581
caused by drought 517
Wind 518–19
annuals and biennials tolerant of 175
bulbs tolerant of 219
damage done by 518–19, 520
damage to fruit 358
effects of topography on 519
perennials tolerant of 141
protecting fruit from 357, 358, 363
protecting shrubs from 72
protecting trees from 45, *520*
protecting vegetables from 299–301, *300*
protection from 520, *520*, 521, *521*
floating row covers 311, *311*
rock plants tolerant of 191
shelter from 28, 29, 519
shelter provided by hedge 58
shrubs tolerant of 66
trees tolerant of 37
tunneling 301, 475, *518*, 519
turbulence *518*
areas of 519, *519*
value of 518
Wind tunnel 301, *475*, 518, *518*
Windbreaks *521*, 590
conditions on each side 519
conserving soil moisture with 308
effect of 519, *519*
fences as 508
for fruit 363
hedges as 58, *301*
height 519
netting for 472
positioning 519, *519*
protecting from wind tunneling *518*, 519
for roof garden 29
shelter provided by 301
siting *519*
solid, problems caused by 519, *519*
trees as 36, 39
for vegetable garden 299, *300*, 301
webbing for 472
Windflower, see *Anemone*; *Zephyranthes*
Windowboxes
annuals in 174, *174*
care 183
bulbs in 217, 218
trailing annuals for 174
vegetables in *303*
Windowsills
problems for plants on 427, *427*
propagator for use on 488, *488*
Wind-rock, definition 590
Wing buds 223, *223*
Winged euonymus, see *Euonymus alatus*
Winter
climbers for interest in 94, 96
color in *25*, 26
perennials for interest in 141
protecting alpines in 201, 204
shrubs for interest in 62, 66
tasks for 584
trees for interest in 35, 37
weed clearance 579
Winter aconite, see *Eranthis hyemalis*
Winter heliotrope, see *Petasites fragrans*
Winter jasmine, see *Jasminum nudiflorum*
Winter melons, see Melons, winter
Winter savory *293*
conditions preferred 294
culinary uses 293
flowers 293
foliage 293
harvesting 293
in winter 294
propagation
division 293
mound layering 297
from seed 293
softwood cuttings 293
related species 293
storing 293
suggestions for use 289
Winter squash, see Squash, winter
Winter wet, definition 590
Wintergreen, see *Pyrola*
Winter's bark, see *Drimys winteri*
Wire
chicken *472*
for climbers 98
pegging layers down with 113, *113*
pig *472*
plastic-coated, for ties 472
welded, fences of 508, *508*
Wire cutters, for bonsai *434*
Wire netting, see Netting, wire
Wireworms 525, 548, 568, *568*
Wiring, techniques for bonsai 434, 435, *435*
Wishbone flower, see *Torenia fournieri*
Wisteria
bonsai 434
in containers 96
for fragrance 97
planting 100
propagation
grafting 109
simple layering 113
softwood cuttings 110
pruning 103, *103*
soil type tolerated 99
suggestions for use 94, 97, 148
for winter interest 94
sinensis
climbing method 92
soil type tolerated 100
suggestions for use 97
vigor 98
'Alba'
on pergola 94, *94*
suggestions for use 94
Witch hazel, see *Hamamelis*
Witches' brooms 561, *561*
honeysuckle 558, *558*
Wittiocereus, apical-wedge grafting 271
Wolf's bane, see *Aconitum*
Wolffia
types to choose 252
as weed 251
arrhiza 243
propagation by plantlets 257
Wonderberries 334, *334*
in crop rotation 304
culinary uses 334
cultivation 334
harvesting 334
nitrogen requirement 310
poison in 334
storing 312, 334
Wood
decking of 499–500, *499*
patterns 500, *500*
for edging paving 498
fence posts in 508, *509*
fittings for 500
fungus growths on 500
for greenhouses 478, *478*
maintenance 500
paths of 501
for pergola 511
preservatives for 510
rot-resisting 510
for sheds 513
staining 500
steps of gravel and *503*

Wood anemone, see *Anemone nemorosa*
Wood ash, nutrient content 532
Wood preservatives 491, 510
Wood rose, see *Merremia tuberosa*
Wood spurge, see *Euphorbia amygdaloides*
Woodchucks 572
Woodland gardens *17*, 27, *28*
 bulbs in 216, *216*
  care 230
 perennials for 140
 seasonal interest 167
 stepping stones in *501*
 steps in 501
 trees for 34
 wildflowers for *167*
Woodlands 167
Woodruff, see *Asperula odorata*
Woodrush, see *Luzula*
 field, see *Luzula campestris*
Woodwork
 attaching to brickwork 512, *512*
 joints for beams and uprights 512, *512*
Woody plants, types included as 580
Woolly aphids 560, *560*
 apple 552
 conifer, see Adelgids
Worms, see Earthworms
Wormwood, see *Artemisia absinthium*
Wound, definition 590
Wound paint, definition 590
Wounding 541, *541*
 mechanical 561

XYZ

Xanthorhiza simplicissima
 conditions preferred 66
 root cuttings 84
Xeranthemum
 drying 183
 harvesting 183
 annuum
  for cutting 175
  soil type tolerated 176
Xeriscaping 530
Xerosicyos danguyi, leaf cuttings 267
Xylem 581
Yarrow *578*
 control 579
Yeasts, colonizing plants 559
Yellow asphodel, see *Asphodeline lutea*
Yellow cress, creeping, see *Rorippa sylvestris*
Yellow flag, see *Iris pseudacorus*
Yellow flax, see *Linum flavum*
Yellow foxglove, see *Digitalis grandiflora*
Yellow fritillary, see *Fritillaria pudica*
Yellow morning-glory, see *Merremia tuberosa*
Yellow pitcher plant, see *Sarracenia flava*
Yellow pond lily, see *Nuphar advena*; *N. lutea*
Yellow scabious, see *Cephalaria gigantea*
Yellow skunk cabbage, see *Lysichiton americanus*
Yellow-variegated sage, see *Salvia officinalis* 'Icterina'
Yellowwood, see *Cladrastis lutea*
Yesterday, today, and tomorrow, see *Brunfelsia*
Yew, see *Taxus*
Youngberry 407
Yucca
 architectural plant 66
 conditions tolerated 66
 hydroculture 431
 as specimen plant *23*
 aloifolia, soil type tolerated 69
 filamentosa, conditions tolerated 141
 flaccida
  conditions tolerated 141
  'Ivory', in cool border *138*
 gloriosa
  form 61
  as specimen plant *23*
Zantedeschia
 conditions required 431
 for cutting 219
 division of tubers 256
 aethiopica
  indoors 426
  suggestions for use 217
  'Crowborough' *218*
   in water garden 243
Zauschneria, pruning 74
Zea mays, for edible varieties, see Sweet corn
 retaining seedheads 184
 'Gracillima Variegata', architectural plant 175
 'Japonica Multicolor'
  architectural plant 175
  ornamental value 171
Zelkova
 diseases 559
 carpinifolia, suggestions for use 37
Zenobia pulverulenta 62
 soil type required 69
Zephyranthes
 conditions required 431
 suggestions for use 219
 candida
  conditions preferred 219
  suggestions for use 219
Zigadenus, suggestions for use 219
Zinc
 deficiency 362, 415
 plant requirements 532
Zinc sulfate 415
Zineb 552, 558, 566, 570, 573, 574
 commercial names 574
Zingiber officinale, see Ginger
Zinnia
 for cutting 175
 in formal bedding 172
 pests 551, 563
 soil type tolerated 176
Zizania aquatica, in water garden 243
Zoysia
 for lawns 274, 275
 japonica 274
 matrella 274
 tenuifolia 274
Zoysia grass, see *Zoysia*
Zucchini *328*, 332
 cultivation 332
 flowers 332, *332*
 fruits 332
 harvesting 332, *332*
 nitrogen requirements 310, 332
 pollinating, by hand 332, *332*
 recommended cultivars 332
 in vegetable garden *300*
 watering, critical periods 308
Zygopetalum mackayi 441
Zygote 159

Acknowledgments

Photography credits

The position on the page is given from top to bottom and across the page from left to right. The photographs in plant portrait boxes are numbered sequentially from left to right across the rows and from the top row to the bottom row. Where the picture is in a step-by-step sequence it is given the number of its caption.

ADAS Crown ©: 529 bottom 1–6, 566 center left
A. W. Ambler: 578 bottom row first left
Heather Angel: 547 bottom left
Jane Aspden: 63 bottom, 258, 259 top left
A-Z Collection: 420 center left, 424 center left
Harry Baker: 356 bottom, 424 bottom left and right
Dan Barton: 434 top left
B & B Photographs: 558 bottom center above, 567 top left, 568 bottom left
Gillian Beckett: 220 portrait box 1 and 8
Birmingham Botanical Gardens: 418 left
Boys Syndication: 93 top left, 303 bottom left
Ken Brate: 561 center below
Christopher Brickell: 91 top right, 202 top sequence 4
John M. Burnley: 551 top right
W. Atlee Burpee & Co.: 338 bottom right
Nigel Cattlin ©: 578 top row far right
Prof. Chin: 328 bottom right, 329 top left, 336 center left, bottom right, and inset, 415 center right, inset, and bottom left, 422 bottom, 423 top left, center, and bottom left
Jack K. Clark: 565 top right, 571 center left, 572 bottom center
Bruce Coleman: 563 bottom right
Comstock: 573 bottom right
Eric Crichton: 7 top right, 11, 22, 24 bottom left, 25 top left, 30 bottom right, 31 top, 38 top, 59 top, 64 bottom left and right, 65 bottom right, 94 bottom right, 117 bottom right, 122 top and bottom right, 119 bottom, 136, 137 top right, 138 top left, 140 top, 150 bottom right, 159 bottom left, 172 bottom, 185, 190 top, 213, 214 box 3, 216 bottom left, 220 top left and right, 221 top left and right, 222 portrait box 2, 242 top, 273 top right, 274 bottom, 275 top, 287, 303 top, 304, 506 top right
Geoff Dann:190 bottom
Jack Elliott: 186 top, 217 bottom left
R. J. Erwin: 565 center below
Raymond Evison: 95 top, 106 portrait box 7, 107 bottom left
Forestry Commission: 559 bottom left, 561 center right
Michael P. Gadomski: 578 top center second right
Garden Picture Library: 118 bottom left, 170, 172 top left and top right, 173 top, 189 top, 214 box 4, 241 top right and bottom, 260 bottom left, 429 top right
John Glover: 65 bottom left, 93 bottom right, 240, 474, 475 top
Paul Goff: 434 center left, center right, bottom left, bottom center and bottom right, 435 top, center left, top center right, top right, center and center right
Gilbert Grant: 551 center, center below
Jerry Harpur: 2 courtesy of Chris Grey-Wilson, 14 top, 15 top, 16 top left, 21 bottom right, 24 top and bottom right, 28 top, 29 top, 30 top and bottom left, 31 bottom, 33 top left, 36 top and bottom left, 92, 94 top, 117 bottom left, 137 bottom, 140 bottom, 144 bottom, 187 bottom, 272, 299, 301 top, 355, 356 top, 358 bottom, 359 bottom, 426, 501 top
Grant Hellman: 559 bottom center, 564 center right, 566 bottom center
Holt Studios International: 556 center, center left, center right above, center right below and bottom right, 562 bottom right, 564 top left, 566 bottom right, 568 bottom center, 570 top center and bottom center, 571 top right, 572 center left above, 573 bottom center right and bottom left, 575 bottom left, 578 top center left
Horticulture Research International, Kirton: 242 top sequence 3, 556 bottom center, 560 bottom right, 567 bottom left
ICI Agrochemicals: 555 top right
Clive Innes: 260 top
Wayne Lankinen: 549 top center
Andrew Lawson: 13 top left, 21 bottom left, 23 top, 25 top right to bottom right, 26 top right, 29 bottom, 33 top right, 91 top left, 117 top, 119 top left, 135, 137 top left, 149 bottom left, 152 top right, 214 bottom, 217 top left and bottom right, 242 bottom right, 301 bottom, 430 top
George D. Lepp: 563 top center
Robert Maier: 573 center right
Elvin McDonald: 260 bottom right, 337 center left and inset, 344 center right, 394 bottom
MAFF Crown ©: 570 center
S. E. Marshall: 176 bottom right
Silvia Martin: 499 bottom
Tania Midgley: 357 top
Graeme Moore: 273 top left
Patti Murray: 563 top right
J. Nicholas: 546 bottom
Oxford Scientific Films: 94 bottom left, 574 left
Park Seeds: 338 bottom left and right
Stephen P. Parker: 553 center left
Richard Parker: 552 center
Photos Horticultural: 359 top, 566 top left, 571 top center and center right
Harry Rogers: 559 center below
Royal Botanic Gardens, Kew: 419 center
Royal Horticultural Society, Wisley: 302 bottom, 555 bottom left and right, 558 bottom and center, 559 center right, 560 bottom, center, and center left below, 561 bottom left, 562 center and bottom center, 565 center left above, center right, and bottom right, 567 center right, 568 top left and center right above, 569 center, center right, and bottom right, 572 top left, top right, center left bottom, and bottom right
Harry Smith Horticultural Photographic Collection: 36 bottom right, 58 bottom left, 171 top left, 261, 329 center left, 416 top, 419top left, 420 center right, 425 center, 430 bottom, 573 center left
Donald Specker: 559 top right
Lauren Springer: 33 portrait box 1
Prof. H.D. Tindall: 321 center left and bottom right, 349 bottom, 351 center, 403 bottom, 416 bottom, 417 top, 419 top right and bottom, 422 top left and right
Elizabeth Whiting Associates: 28 bottom, 32, 35bottom, 62 top,186 bottom, 241 top left, 248 top, 289 bottom left
Steve Wooster: 12, 15 bottom, 16 bottom left and right, 17 bottom, 25 bottom left, 61 bottom left, 90, 96 bottom left, 114, 119 top right, 138 top right, 158 top, 492, 501 bottom left, 503 bottom left, 514
Tom Wright: 95 bottom, 173 bottom
Additional photography by:
Jane Burton, Peter Chadwick, Trevor Cole, Eric Crichton, Geoff Dann, John Glover, Jerry Harpur, Neil Holmes, Jacqui Hurst, Dave King, Elvin McDonald, Andrew McRobb, Andrew Lawson, Andrew de Lory, Tim Ridley, Karl Shone, and Gerry Young

Dorling Kindersley would like to thank the following for:

Expert advice
Mr. Ted Andrews (sweet peas); Darrell Apps (daylilies); Peter and Fiona Bainbridge (landscape design and construction); Harry Baker (fruit); Kenneth Bauman (nuts); Don Birkholz (peaches, nectarines); John Bunker (plums, gages); Douglas Burns (pears); Richard Campbell (limes); Brenda Cole (vegetables); Marie-Jose de Saint Victor (pest controls); Phillip Dukes (sweet potatoes); Dr. Bob Ellis (vegetable cultivar lists); Mark Freeman (olives); Dennis Gobbee (rose hybridizing); Richard Goetze (pest controls); Patrick Goldsworthy, British Agrochemical Association (chemical controls); Paul Goodspeed (pest controls); Ken Grapes, Royal National Rose Society; Dale Hellegers (pests and diseases); Roy Klehm (peonies); John Kreutziger (grapes); Harbey Lisle (quinces); George Martin (olives); Ed Mashburn (*Ribes*); Jim Matsuka (cherries); Kenny Maxfield (persimmons); Michael McConkey (figs); Peter Orme (rock garden design and construction); Paul M. Otten (brambles); Ken Paddock (potatoes); Michael Pilarski (kiwis); Terence and Judy Read (grape cultivar lists); David Ronninger (potatoes); Prof. S. Sansavini (fruit cultivar lists); Pat Sawyer (rare fruit); Arty Gordon Schronce (vegetables); Ed Seligman (apricots); Steve Sibbert (olives); Bud Slemmer (lilies); Bryan Smith (strawberries); Carol Spiers (roses); Lee Strassburger (vegetables); Gerald Swaley (weeds); Pham van Tha (fruit cultivar lists); John Warren (apples); James Watson (orchids); Joe Williamson (structures and surfaces).

Providing plants or locations for photographs
Joy Bishop; Brickwall House School, Northiam; Brinkman Brothers Ltd, Walton Farm Nurseries, Bosham; Denbies Wine Estate, Dorking; Mrs. Donnithorne; Martin Double; J. W. Elliott & Sons (West End) Limited, Fenns Lane Nursery, Woking; Elsoms Seeds Ltd, Spalding; Mrs. Randi Evans; Adrian Hall Ltd, Putney Garden Centre, London; Mr. & Mrs. R.D. Hendriksen, Hill Park Nurseries, Surbiton; The Herb and Heather Centre, West Haddlesey; Hilliers Nurseries (Winchester) Ltd, Romsey; Holly Gate International Ltd, Ashington; John Humphries, Sutton Place Foundation, Guildford; Iden Croft Herbs, Staplehurst; Mr. de Jager; Nicolette John; David Knuckey, Burncoose Nursery; Mr. & Mrs. John Land; Sarah Martin; Frank P. Matthews Ltd, Tenbury Wells; Mr. & Mrs. Mead; Anthony Noel, Fulham Park Gardens, London; Andrew Norfield; Notcutts Garden Centre, Bagshot; Bridget Quest- Ritson; Royal Botanic Gardens, Kew; Royal Horticultural Society Enterprises; Lynn and Danny Reynolds, Mrs. Rudd, Surrey Water Gardens, West Clandon; Rolawn, Elvington; Miss. Skilton; Carole Starr; Mr. & Mrs. Wagstaff; Mrs. Wye.

Tools for demonstration photographs
Spear and Jackson Products Ltd, Wednesbury, West Midlands; Ed Jenson of Carl's Equipment, Patchogue, NY; Felco pruners supplied by Burton McCall Group, Leicester.

Supplying equipment
Agralan, Ashton Keynes; Bob Andrews Ltd, Bracknell; Black and Decker Europe, Slough; Blagdon Water Garden Products PLC, Highbridge; Bloomingdales Garden Centre, Laleham; Bulldog Tools Ltd, Wigan; Butterley Brick Ltd, London; CEKA Works Ltd, Pwllheli; Challenge Fencing, Cobham; Anthony Cieri; J. B. Corrie & Co Ltd, Petersfield; Dalfords (London) Ltd, Staines; Diplex Ltd, Watford; Direct Wire Ties Ltd, Hull; Robert Dyas (Ltd), Guildford; Fishtique, Sunbury-on-Thames; Fluid Drilling Ltd, Stratford-upon-Avon; Gardena UK Ltd, Letchworth Garden City; Gloucesters Wholesales Ltd, Woking; Harcros, Walton-on-Thames; Haws Elliott Ltd, Warley; Honda UK Ltd, London; Hozelock Ltd, Birmingham; ICI Garden Products, Haslemere; LBS Polythene, Colne; Merck Ltd, Poole; Neal Street East, London; Parkers, Worcester Park; Pinks Hill Landscape Merchants Ltd, Guildford; Qualcast Garden Products, Stowmarket; Rapitest, Corwen; Seymours, Ewell; Shoosmith & Lee Ltd, Cobham; SISIS Equipment Ltd, Macclesfield; Thermoforce Ltd, Maldon. Tracmaster Ltd, Burgess Hill; Two Wests and Elliot, Chesterfield; Wilkinson Sword, Fiskars UK Limited, Bridgend; Wolf Tools Ltd, Ross-on-Wye.

Additional assistance
Diana Craig, Trent Duffy, Eleanor Hoffman, Caroline Macy, Louise McConnell, K. Selody.

Abbreviations

C	centigrade	ml	milliliter(s)
cf	compare	mm	millimeter(s)
cm	centimeter	oz	ounce(s)
cv(s)	cultivar(s)	p(p)	page(s)
f.	forma	pl.	plural
fl oz	fluid ounce(s)	sp.	species
ft	foot, feet	spp.	species(pl)
g	gram(s)	sq	square
in	inch(es)	subsp.	subspecies
kg	kilogram(s)	syn.	synonyms
lb	pound(s)	var.	varietas
m	meter(s)	yd	yard(s)

Note: The generic and species names of plants are abbreviated to their initial letters after their first full mention in a sentence or a list.